IRAQ AND KUWAIT:
THE HOSTILITIES AND THEIR AFTERMATH

Titles published in the Cambridge International Documents Series

I. *The Kuwait Crisis: Basic Documents*
II. *The Kuwait Crisis: Sanctions and their Economic Consequences*
III. *Iraq and Kuwait: The Hostilities and their Aftermath*
IV. *International Efforts to Combat Money Laundering*

This volume may be cited as:

Weller (ed.),
Iraq and Kuwait: The Hostilities and their Aftermath (1993)

RESEARCH CENTRE FOR INTERNATIONAL LAW
UNIVERSITY OF CAMBRIDGE

CAMBRIDGE INTERNATIONAL DOCUMENTS SERIES, VOLUME 3

Consulting editor: E. Lauterpacht CBE, QC

IRAQ AND KUWAIT: THE HOSTILITIES AND THEIR AFTERMATH

edited by
M. Weller
Research Fellow of the Centre,
Assistant Lecturer in International Law in the University of Cambridge
and Senior Research Fellow, St. Catharine's College, Cambridge

CAMBRIDGE
GROTIUS PUBLICATIONS LIMITED
1993

SALES & ADMINISTRATION	GROTIUS PUBLICATIONS LTD. PO BOX 115, CAMBRIDGE CB3 9BP ENGLAND
TEL.	0223 323410 (44 + 223 + 323410)
FAX	0223 311032 (44 + 223 + 311032)

British Library Cataloguing in Publication Data

Iraq and Kuwait: Hostilities and Their
Aftermath. – (Cambridge International
Documents Series; v. 3)
I. Weller, M. II. Lauterpacht, E.
III. Series
956.05

ISBN 0-949009-98-9

Printed by The Burlington Press (Cambridge) Limited, Foxton, Cambridge

FOREWORD

It is now just over two years since the publication of the first volume of the *Cambridge International Documents Series* containing the first major collection of documents relating to the Iraq-Kuwait hostilities generally. It was followed by a more specialized volume, in two substantial parts, edited by Mr Daniel Bethlehem, presenting comprehensively the materials relating to the sanctions adopted against Iraq and the international treatment of the economic pressures suffered by States in consequence of those measures. The warm, indeed enthusiastic, reception accorded to those volumes has encouraged the Research Centre for International Law to continue this particular sub-series.

The Centre is now pleased to publish the present massive continuation volume, most ably edited by Mr Marc Weller. Prior to the developments chronicled here, the experience of post-Second World War international organizations, especially of the UN Security Council and of the International Atomic Energy Agency, had rarely been taxed by such deep, wide and extended involvement in conflict between neighbouring States and had never been so significantly involved in relations between a State and minorities within its territory. Access to the documentary basis of such developments is essential if they are to be properly analysed and assessed; and it is to be hoped that for most practical purposes what is required will be found in this volume and its companions.

As can be seen, the contents of this volume are drawn from a wide variety of sources systematically and rigorously sifted for pertinent materials until the very last possible moment prior to publication. The most recent item in the collection is dated 5 February 1993; and it has been the seemingly unending flow of such material that has led to the publication of the volume being deferred on more than one occasion. However, it is here now and we will all be glad to have at hand so valuable a work of reference.

The ease with which the reader will be able to make use of the work is enhanced by the detailed Table of Contents, the United Nations Document Index and the Subject Index. We are immensely grateful to Mr Weller for bringing to this project so much vision and vigour as well as for dedicating to it a huge amount of time.

It is the intention of the Research Centre to continue the series with a volume relating to the measures of international arms control taken in relation to Kuwait. Thereafter there will appear a collection of documents relating to the tragic aftermath of the disintegration of Yugoslavia. In due course, an additional volume will be devoted to further developments connected with the Iraq-Kuwait situation.

E. LAUTERPACHT

Research Centre for International Law,
University of Cambridge

March 1993

PREFACE

This volume was originally intended to cover the actual hostilities involving Iraq and the initial attempts of the international community to restore peace and security in the Gulf region, following on United Nations Security Council Resolution 687 (1991). However, the implementation of that Resolution has proved difficult, especially in so far as it relates to controls imposed upon Iraqi armaments and strategic materials, goods and technologies, to the payment of compensation by Iraq and to the demarcation of the Iraq-Kuwait boundary. Iraqi violations of human rights have given rise to further complications.

In order to keep pace with these developments, the size of the present volume has continually expanded. Nevertheless, several sections have had to be cut in order to create space for materials reflecting more recent events and the type-size has had to be reduced throughout. Even at this stage, there are a number of further developments relating to the demarcation of the maritime boundary or to the various aspects of Iraqi compliance with Resolution 687 (1991), which are expected but which could not be reflected in the book. It is hoped that this deficiency can be remedied in a subsequent volume in this Series.

It would not have been possible to assemble the documents for this volume without the kind, continuous and generous help of a large number of individuals and institutions. At the United Nations Headquarters, we are particularly indebted to Ms Patricia Farquar. At the Palais des Nations in Geneva we have received kind assistance from the staff of the United Nations Library. Mr M. Sanmuganathan, the Secretary of the Policy-making Organs of the International Atomic Energy Agency, has provided invaluable assistance in making available otherwise inaccessible materials. Special thanks are due to Ms Elizabeth L. Lee, Mr Martin Wattam and Mr Julian de Wette of the United Nations Information Centre in London. Mr Keith J. A. McVeigh of the Squire Law Library and Mr W. A. Noblett of the Cambridge University Library have provided constant support for the project. The United Kingdom Mission to the United Nations as well as the Legal Advisers of the Foreign and Commonwealth Office and Ms Tricia Rant of the UN Documents Section have also been most helpful.

The entire typescript was prepared with unflagging efficiency by Ms Christine Kay. The proofs were read, often under great pressure of time, by Mrs Marie Pepper. Mrs Jane Gilbert assisted in the compilation of the Table of Contents and the Summary Index. Mr Elihu Lauterpacht, CBE, QC, the Director of the Research Centre, has provided encouragement and generous support for this project throughout. The kind advice and materials received from Mr Christopher J. Greenwood and Mr Daniel Bethlehem are also gratefully acknowledged.

Finally, a tremendous amount of gratitude needs to be expressed to Mr S. Robin Pirrie of Grotius Publications Ltd, and to Mr John Sexton of the Burlington Press. They both tackled the considerable difficulties posed by this project and by the Editor's numerous failings with enthusiasm and great patience. Needless to say, any remaining imperfections are solely the responsibility of the Editor.

M.W.

GENERAL AREA MAP

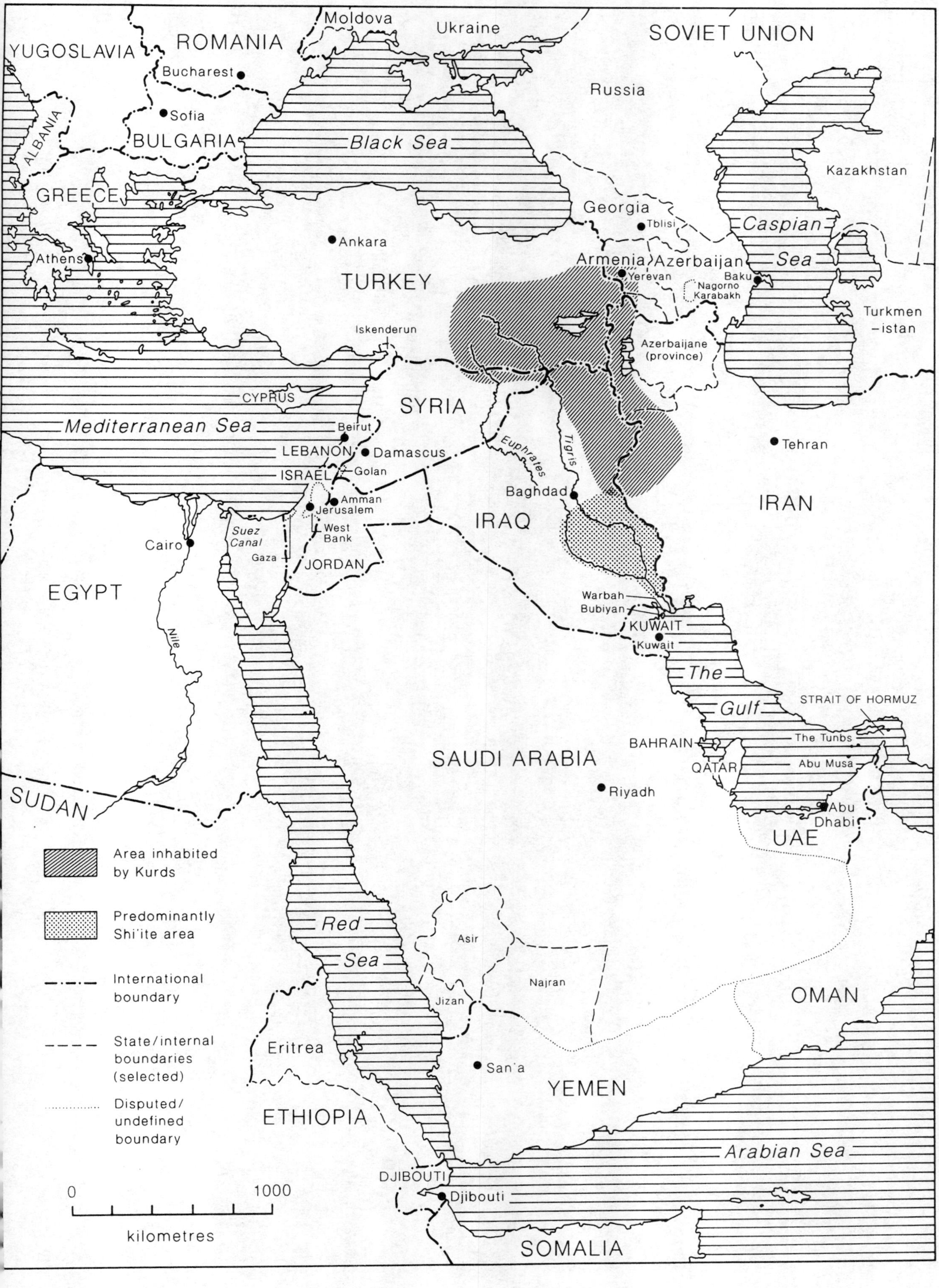

TABLE OF CONTENTS

PART II: THE PRELUDE TO THE HOSTILITIES

PART IV: THE CEASE-FIRE AND ITS IMPLEMENTATION

PART I. GENERAL UN SECURITY COUNCIL MATERIALS

The proceedings of the UN Security Council and the resulting resolutions often touch upon more than one particular issue. It has, therefore, been found convenient to reprint most of these documents in a single section of general materials, rather than to attempt to split them up and reproduce them in the chapters which follow. This way, the flow of events and of the discussions in the Council can be followed chronologically. The treatment of particular issues in the proceedings and resolutions can be readily identified through the summary index. On the other hand, decisions adopted by the Security Council in 1992 concerning specifically the implementation of individual elements of cease-fire Resolution 687 (1991) have been reproduced within the relevant chapters of Part IV of this Volume.

In light of the immense importance of the Council's actions and proceedings concerning the situation between Iraq and Kuwait, it has been considered best to reprint the materials virtually in full, including even the sometimes prolonged procedural debates, as they also tend to have a bearing on matters of wider legal interest. On the other hand, contributions to the debate which are entirely devoid of legal substance, such as words of praise for the Council President, etc., have been omitted.

The United Nations Security Council is composed of 15 members. Five are permanent: China, France, the Soviet Union (now replaced by the Russian Federation), the United Kingdom and the United States. The ten non-permanent members are elected by the General Assembly to serve two-year terms. In 1990, when the first 12 resolutions concerning the situation in Kuwait and Iraq were adopted, the elected members of the Council were: Canada, Colombia, Côte d'Ivoire, Cuba, Ethiopia, Finland, Malaysia, Romania, Yemen and Zaire. On 1 January 1991, Austria, Belgium, Ecuador, India and Zimbabwe replaced Canada, Colombia, Ethiopia, Finland and Malaysia for two-year terms. The non-permanent members for 1992 were Austria, Belgium, Cape Verde, Ecuador, Hungary, India, Japan, Morocco, Venezuela and Zimbabwe.

Decisions of the Security Council on procedural matters are made by an affirmative vote of nine members. Decisions of the Council on all other matters are made by an affirmative vote of nine members including the concurring votes of the permanent members (the veto). The question of whether an issue is a matter of procedure or of substance is treated as a matter of substance. The absence or abstention of a permanent member does not operate as a veto.

1. RESOLUTIONS ADOPTED BY THE UN SECURITY COUNCIL

A. RESOLUTIONS ADOPTED IN 1990

[*EXTRACTS*]

1. Resolution 660 (1990), 2 August 1990

Adopted at the 2932nd meeting by 14 votes in favour, none against, no abstentions, Yemen not participating in the voting.

The Security Council,

Alarmed by the invasion of Kuwait on 2 August 1990 by the military forces of Iraq,

Determining that there exists a breach of international peace and security as regards the Iraqi invasion of Kuwait,

Acting under Articles 39 and 40 of the Charter of the United Nations,

1. *Condemns* the Iraqi invasion of Kuwait;

2. *Demands* that Iraq withdraw immediately and unconditionally all its forces to the positions in which they were located on 1 August 1990;

3. *Calls upon* Iraq and Kuwait to begin immediately intensive negotiations for the resolution of their differences and supports all efforts in this regard, and especially those of the League of Arab States;

4. *Decides* to meet again as necessary to consider further steps to ensure compliance with the present resolution.

2. Resolution 661 (1990), 6 August 1990

Adopted at the 2933rd meeting by 13 votes in favour, none against, Cuba and Yemen abstaining.

The Security Council,

...

Determined to bring the invasion and occupation of Kuwait by Iraq to an end and to restore the sovereignty, independence and territorial integrity of Kuwait,

Noting that the legitimate Government of Kuwait has expressed its readiness to comply with resolution 660 (1990),

Mindful of its responsibilities under the Charter of the United Nations for the maintenance of international peace and security,

Affirming the inherent right of individual or collective self-defence, in response to the armed attack by Iraq against Kuwait, in accordance with Article 51 of the Charter,

Acting under Chapter VII of the Charter of the United Nations,

1. *Determines* that Iraq so far has failed to comply with paragraph 2 of resolution 660 (1990) and has usurped the authority of the legitimate Government of Kuwait;

2. *Decides*, as a consequence, to take the following measures to secure compliance of Iraq with paragraph 2 of resolution 660 (1990) and to restore the authority of the legitimate Government of Kuwait;

3. *Decides* that all States shall prevent:

(a) The import into their territories of all commodities and products originating in Iraq or Kuwait exported therefrom after the date of the present resolution;

(b) Any activities by their nationals or in their territories which would promote or are calculated to promote the export or trans-shipment of any commodities or products from Iraq or Kuwait; and any dealings by their nationals or their flag vessels or in their territories in any commodities or products originating in Iraq or Kuwait and exported therefrom after the date of the present resolution, including in particular any transfer of funds to Iraq or Kuwait for the purposes of such activities or dealings;

(c) The sale or supply by their nationals or from their territories or using their flag vessels of any commodities or products, including weapons or any other military equipment, whether or not originating in their territories but not including supplies intended strictly for medical purposes, and, in humanitarian circumstances, foodstuffs, to any person or body in Iraq or Kuwait or to any person or body for the purposes of any business carried on in or operated from Iraq or Kuwait, and any activities by their nationals or in their territories which promote or are calculated to promote such sale or supply of such commodities or products;

4. *Decides* that all States shall not make available to the Government of Iraq or to any commercial, industrial or public utility undertaking in Iraq or Kuwait, any funds or any other financial or economic resources and shall prevent their nationals and any persons within their territories from removing from their territories or otherwise making available to that Government or to any such undertaking any such funds or resources and from remitting any other funds to persons or bodies within Iraq or Kuwait, except payments exclusively for strictly medical or humanitarian purposes and, in humanitarian circumstances, foodstuffs;

5. *Calls upon* all States, including States non-members of the United Nations, to act strictly in accordance with the provisions of the present resolution notwithstanding any contract entered into or licence granted before the date of the present resolution;

6. *Decides* to establish, in accordance with rule 28 of the provisional rules of procedure of the Security Council, a Committee of the Security Council consisting of all the members of the Council, to undertake the following tasks and to report on its work to the Council with its observations and recommendations:

(a) To examine the reports on the progress of the implementation of the present resolution which will be submitted by the Secretary-General;

(b) To seek from all States further information regarding the action taken by them concerning the effective implementation of the provisions laid down in the present resolution;

7. *Calls upon* all States to co-operate fully with the Committee in the fulfilment of its task, including

supplying such information as may be sought by the Committee in pursuance of the present resolution;

8. *Requests* the Secretary-General to provide all necessary assistance to the Committee and to make the necessary arrangements in the Secretariat for the purpose;

9. *Decides* that, notwithstanding paragraphs 4 through 8 above, nothing in the present resolution shall prohibit assistance to the legitimate Government of Kuwait, and *calls upon* all States:

> (a) To take appropriate measures to protect assets of the legitimate Government of Kuwait and its agencies;
>
> (b) Not to recognize any régime set up by the occupying Power;

10. *Requests* the Secretary-General to report to the Council on the progress of the implementation of the present resolution, the first report to be submitted within thirty days;

11. *Decides* to keep this item on its agenda and to continue its efforts to put an early end to the invasion by Iraq.

3. Resolution 662 (1990), 9 August 1990

Adopted unanimously at the 2934th meeting.

The Security Council,

...

Gravely alarmed by the declaration by Iraq of a "comprehensive and eternal merger" with Kuwait,

...

Determined to bring the occupation of Kuwait by Iraq to an end and to restore the sovereignty, independence and territorial integrity of Kuwait,

Determined also to restore the authority of the legitimate Government of Kuwait,

1. *Decides* that annexation of Kuwait by Iraq under any form and whatever pretext has no legal validity, and is considered null and void;

2. *Calls upon* all States, international organizations and specialized agencies not to recognize that annexation, and to refrain from any action or dealing that might be interpreted as an indirect recognition of the annexation;

3. *Further demands* that Iraq rescind its actions purporting to annex Kuwait;

4. *Decides* to keep this item on its agenda and to continue its efforts to put an early end to the occupation.

4. Resolution 664 (1990), 18 August 1990

Adopted unanimously at the 2937th meeting.

The Security Council,

...

Acting under Chapter VII of the United Nations Charter:

1. *Demands* that Iraq permit and facilitate the immediate departure from Kuwait and Iraq of the nationals of third countries and grant immediate and continuing access of consular officials to such nationals;

2. *Further demands* that Iraq take no action to jeopardize the safety, security or health of such nationals;

3. *Reaffirms* its decision in resolution 662 (1990) that annexation of Kuwait by Iraq is null and void, and therefore demands that the government of Iraq rescind its orders for the closure of diplomatic and consular missions in Kuwait and the withdrawal of the immunity of their personnel, and refrain from any such actions in the future;

4. *Requests* the Secretary-General to report to the Council on compliance with this resolution at the earliest possible time.

5. Resolution 665 (1990), 25 August 1990

Adopted at the 2938th meeting by 13 votes in favour, none against, Cuba and Yemen abstaining.

The Security Council,

...

1. *Calls upon* those Member States co-operating with the Government of Kuwait which are deploying maritime forces to the area to use such measures commensurate to the specific circumstances as may be necessary under the authority of the Security Council to halt all inward and outward maritime shipping in order to inspect and verify their cargoes and destinations and to ensure strict implementation of the provisions related to such shipping laid down in resolution 661 (1990);

2. *Invites* Member States accordingly to co-operate as may be necessary to ensure compliance with the provisions of resolution 661 (1990) with maximum use of political and diplomatic measures, in accordance with paragraph 1 above;

3. *Requests* all States to provide in accordance with the Charter such assistance as may be required by the States referred to in paragraph 1 of this resolution;

4. *Further requests* the States concerned to co-ordinate their actions in pursuit of the above paragraphs of this resolution using as appropriate mechanisms of the Military Staff Committee and after consultation with the Secretary-General to submit reports to the Security Council and its Committee established under resolution 661 (1990) to facilitate the monitoring of the implementation of this resolution;

5. *Decides* to remain actively seized of the matter.

6. Resolution 666 (1990), 13 September 1990

Adopted at the 2939th meeting by 13 votes in favour, Cuba and Yemen against, no abstentions.

The Security Council,

...

Deeply concerned that Iraq has failed to comply with its obligations under Security Council resolution 664 (1990) in respect of the safety and well-being of third State nationals, and reaffirming that Iraq retains full responsibility in this regard under international humanitarian law including, where applicable, the Fourth Geneva Convention,

Acting under Chapter VII of the Charter of the United Nations,

1. *Decides* that in order to make the necessary determination whether or not for the purposes of paragraph 3 (c) and paragraph 4 of resolution 661 (1990) humanitarian circumstances have arisen, the Committee shall keep the situation regarding foodstuffs in Iraq and Kuwait under constant review;

2. *Expects* Iraq to comply with its obligations under Security Council resolution 664 (1990) in respect of third State nationals and reaffirms that Iraq remains fully responsible for their safety and well-being in accordance

with international humanitarian law including, where applicable, the Fourth Geneva Convention;

3. *Requests*, for the purposes of paragraphs 1 and 2 of this resolution, that the Secretary-General seek urgently, and on a continuing basis, information from relevant United Nations and other appropriate humanitarian agencies and all other sources on the availability of food in Iraq and Kuwait, such information to be communicated by the Secretary-General to the Committee regularly;

4. *Requests further* that in seeking and supplying such information particular attention will be paid to such categories of persons who might suffer specially, such as children under 15 years of age, expectant mothers, maternity cases, the sick and the elderly;

5. *Decides* that if the Committee, after receiving the reports from the Secretary-General, determines that circumstances have arisen in which there is an urgent humanitarian need to supply foodstuffs to Iraq or Kuwait in order to relieve human suffering, it will report promptly to the Council its decision as to how such need should be met;

6. *Directs* the Committee that in formulating its decisions it should bear in mind that foodstuffs should be provided through the United Nations in co-operation with the International Committee of the Red Cross or other appropriate humanitarian agencies and distributed by them or under their supervision in order to ensure that they reach the intended beneficiaries;

7. *Requests* the Secretary-General to use his good offices to facilitate the delivery and distribution of foodstuffs to Kuwait and Iraq in accordance with the provisions of this and other relevant resolutions;

8. *Recalls* that resolution 661 (1990) does not apply to supplies intended strictly for medical purposes, but in this connection recommends that medical supplies should be exported under the strict supervision of the Government of the exporting State or by appropriate humanitarian agencies.

7. Resolution 667 (1990), 16 September 1990

Adopted unanimously at the 2940th meeting.

The Security Council,

...

Acting under Chapter VII of the Charter of the United Nations,

1. *Strongly condemns* aggressive acts perpetrated by Iraq against diplomatic premises and personnel in Kuwait, including the abduction of foreign nationals who were present in those premises;

2. *Demands* the immediate release of those foreign nationals as well as all nationals mentioned in resolution 664 (1990);

3. *Further demands* that Iraq immediately and fully comply with its international obligations under resolutions 660 (1990), 662 (1990) and 664 (1990) of the Security Council, the Vienna Conventions on diplomatic and consular relations and international law;

4. *Further demands* that Iraq immediately protect the safety and well-being of diplomatic and consular personnel and premises in Kuwait and in Iraq and take no action to hinder the diplomatic and consular missions in the performance of their functions, including access to their nationals and the protection of their person and interests;

5. *Reminds* all States that they are obliged to observe strictly resolutions 661 (1990), 662 (1990), 664 (1990), 665 (1990) and 666 (1990).

6. *Decides* to consult urgently to take further concrete measures as soon as possible, under Chapter VII of the Charter, in response to Iraq's continued violation of the Charter, of resolutions of the Council and of international law.

8. Resolution 669 (1990), 24 September 1990

Adopted unanimously at the 2942nd meeting.

The Security Council,

...

Conscious of the fact that an increasing number of requests for assistance have been received under the provisions of Article 50 of the Charter of the United Nations,

Entrusts the Committee established under resolution 661 (1990) concerning the situation between Iraq and Kuwait with the task of examining requests for assistance under the provisions of Article 50 of the Charter of the United Nations and making recommendations to the President of the Security Council for appropriate action.

9. Resolution 670 (1990), 25 September 1990

Adopted at the 2943rd meeting by 14 votes in favour, Cuba against, no abstentions.

The Security Council,

...

Acting under Chapter VII of the Charter of the United Nations,

1. *Calls upon* all States to carry out their obligations to ensure strict and complete compliance with resolution 661 (1990) and, in particular, paragraphs 3, 4 and 5 thereof;

2. *Confirms* that resolution 661 (1990) applies to all means of transport, including aircraft;

3. *Decides* that all States, notwithstanding the existence of any rights or obligations conferred or imposed by any international agreement or any contract entered into or any licence or permit granted before the date of the present resolution, shall deny permission to any aircraft to take off from their territory if the aircraft would carry any cargo to or from Iraq or Kuwait other than food in humanitarian circumstances, subject to authorization by the Council or the Committee established by resolution 661 (1990) and in accordance with resolution 666 (1990), or supplies intended strictly for medical purposes or solely for UNIIMOG;

4. *Decides further* that all States shall deny permission to any aircraft destined to land in Iraq or Kuwait, whatever its State of registration, to overfly its territory unless:

> (a) The aircraft lands at an airfield designated by that State outside Iraq or Kuwait in order to permit its inspection to ensure that there is no cargo on board in violation of resolution 661 (1990) or the present resolution, and for this purpose the aircraft may be detained for as long as necessary; or
>
> (b) The particular flight has been approved by the Committee established by resolution 661 (1990); or
>
> (c) The flight is certified by the United Nations as solely for the purposes of UNIIMOG;

5. *Decides* that each State shall take all necessary measures to ensure that any aircraft registered in its

territory or operated by an operator who has his principal place of business or permanent residence in its territory complies with the provisions of resolution 661 (1990) and the present resolution;

6. *Decides further* that all States shall notify in a timely fashion the Committee established by resolution 661 (1990) of any flight between its territory and Iraq or Kuwait to which the requirement to land in paragraph 4 above does not apply, and the purpose for such a flight;

7. *Calls upon* all States to co-operate in taking such measures as may be necessary, consistent with international law, including the Chicago Convention, to ensure the effective implementation of the provisions of resolution 661 (1990) or the present resolution;

8. *Calls upon* all States to detain any ships of Iraqi registry which enter their ports and which are being or have been used in violation of resolution 661 (1990), or to deny such ships entrance to their ports except in circumstances recognized under international law as necessary to safeguard human life;

9. *Reminds* all States of their obligations under resolution 661 (1990) with regard to the freezing of Iraqi assets, and the protection of the assets of the legitimate Government of Kuwait and its agencies, located within their territory and to report to the Committee established under resolution 661 (1990) regarding those assets;

10. *Calls upon* all States to provide to the Committee established by resolution 661 (1990) information regarding the action taken by them to implement the provisions laid down in the present resolution;

11. *Affirms* that the United Nations Organization, the specialized agencies and other international organizations in the United Nations system are required to take such measures as may be necessary to give effect to the terms of resolution 661 (1990) and this resolution;

12. *Decides* to consider, in the event of evasion of the provisions of resolution 661 (1990) or of the present resolution by a State or its nationals or through its territory, measures directed at the State in question to prevent such evasion;

13. *Reaffirms* that the Fourth Geneva Convention applies to Kuwait and that as a High Contracting Party to the Convention Iraq is bound to comply fully with all its terms and, in particular, is liable under the Convention in respect of the grave breaches committed by it, as are individuals who commit or order the commission of grave breaches.

10. Resolution 674 (1990), 29 October 1990

Adopted at the 2951st meeting by 13 votes in favour, none against, Cuba and Yemen abstaining.

The Security Council,

...

Reaffirming that the Fourth Geneva Convention applies to Kuwait and that as a High Contracting Party to the Convention Iraq is bound to comply fully with all its terms and in particular is liable under the Convention in respect of the grave breaches committed by it, as are individuals who commit or order the commission of grave breaches,

...

Deeply concerned at the economic cost and at the loss and suffering caused to individuals in Kuwait and Iraq as a result of the invasion and occupation of Kuwait by Iraq,

Acting under Chapter VII of the Charter of the United Nations,

* * *

Reaffirming the goal of the international community of maintaining international peace and security by seeking to resolve international disputes and conflicts through peaceful means,

Recalling the important role that the United Nations and its Secretary-General have played in the peaceful solution of disputes and conflicts in conformity with the provisions of the Charter,

Alarmed by the dangers of the present crisis caused by the Iraqi invasion and occupation of Kuwait, which directly threaten international peace and security, and seeking to avoid any further worsening of the situation,

Calling upon Iraq to comply with the relevant resolutions of the Security Council, in particular its resolutions 660 (1990), 662 (1990) and 664 (1990),

Reaffirming its determination to ensure compliance by Iraq with the Security Council resolutions by maximum use of political and diplomatic means,

A

1. *Demands* that the Iraqi authorities and occupying forces immediately cease and desist from taking third-State nationals hostage, mistreating and oppressing Kuwaiti and third-State nationals and any other actions, such as those reported to the Security Council and described above, that violate the decisions of this Council, the Charter of the United Nations, the Fourth Geneva Convention, the Vienna Conventions on Diplomatic and Consular Relations and international law;

2. *Invites* States to collate substantiated information in their possession or submitted to them on the grave breaches by Iraq as per paragraph 1 above and to make this information available to the Security Council;

3. *Reaffirms* its demand that Iraq immediately fulfil its obligations to third-State nationals in Kuwait and Iraq, including the personnel of diplomatic and consular missions, under the Charter, the Fourth Geneva Convention, the Vienna Conventions on Diplomatic and Consular Relations, general principles of international law and the relevant resolutions of the Council;

4. *Also reaffirms* its demand that Iraq permit and facilitate the immediate departure from Kuwait and Iraq of those third-State nationals, including diplomatic and consular personnel, who wish to leave;

5. *Demands* that Iraq ensure the immediate access to food, water and basic services necessary to the protection and well-being of Kuwaiti nationals and of nationals of third States in Kuwait and Iraq, including the personnel of diplomatic and consular missions in Kuwait;

6. *Reaffirms* its demand that Iraq immediately protect the safety and well-being of diplomatic and consular personnel and premises in Kuwait and in Iraq, take no action to hinder these diplomatic and consular missions in the performance of their functions, including access to their nationals and the protection of their person and interests and rescind its orders for the closure of diplomatic and consular missions in Kuwait and the withdrawal of the immunity of their personnel;

7. *Requests* the Secretary-General, in the context of the continued exercise of his good offices concerning the safety and well-being of third-State nationals in Iraq and Kuwait, to seek to achieve the objectives of paragraphs 4, 5 and 6 above and in particular the provision of food, water and basic services to Kuwaiti nationals and to the diplomatic and consular missions in Kuwait and the evacuation of third-State nationals;

8. *Reminds* Iraq that under international law it is liable for any loss, damage or injury arising in regard to Kuwait and third States, and their nationals and corporations, as a result of the invasion and illegal occupation of Kuwait by Iraq;

9. *Invites* States to collect relevant information regarding their claims, and those of their nationals and corporations, for restitution or financial compensation by Iraq with a

view to such arrangements as may be established in accordance with international law;

10. *Requires* that Iraq comply with the provisions of the present resolution and its previous resolutions, failing which the Security Council will need to take further measures under the Charter;

11. *Decides* to remain actively and permanently seized of the matter until Kuwait has regained its independence and peace has been restored in conformity with the relevant resolutions of the Security Council.

B

12. *Reposes* its trust in the Secretary-General to make available his good offices and, as he considers appropriate, to pursue them and to undertake diplomatic efforts in order to reach a peaceful solution to the crisis caused by the Iraqi invasion and occupation of Kuwait on the basis of Security Council resolutions 660 (1990), 662 (1990) and 664 (1990), and calls upon all States, both those in the region and others, to pursue on this basis their efforts to this end, in conformity with the Charter, in order to improve the situation and restore peace, security and stability;

13. *Requests* the Secretary-General to report to the Security Council on the results of his good offices and diplomatic efforts.

11. RESOLUTION 677 (1990), 28 November 1990

Adopted unanimously at the 2962nd meeting.

The Security Council,

...

Acting under Chapter VII of the Charter of the United Nations,

1. *Condemns* the attempts by Iraq to alter the demographic composition of the population of Kuwait and to destroy the civil records maintained by the legitimate Government of Kuwait;

2. *Mandates* the Secretary-General to take custody of a copy of the population register of Kuwait, the authenticity of which has been certified by the legitimate Government of Kuwait, which covers the population registration up to 1 August 1990;

3. *Requests* the Secretary-General to establish, in co-operation with the legitimate Government of Kuwait, an Order of Rules and Regulations governing access and use of the said copy of the population register.

12. RESOLUTION 678 (1990), 29 November 1990

Adopted at the 2963rd meeting by 12 votes in favour, Cuba and Yemen against, China abstaining.

The Security Council,

Recalling and reaffirming its resolutions 660 (1990), 661 (1990), 662 (1990), 664 (1990), 665 (1990), 666 (1990), 667 (1990), 669 (1990), 670 (1990), 674 (1990) and 677 (1990),

Noting that, despite all efforts by the United Nations, Iraq refuses to comply with its obligation to implement resolution 660 (1990) and the above subsequent relevant resolutions, in flagrant contempt of the Council,

Mindful of its duties and responsibilities under the Charter of the United Nations for the maintenance and preservation of international peace and security,

Determined to secure full compliance with its decisions,

Acting under Chapter VII of the Charter of the United Nations,

1. *Demands* that Iraq comply fully with resolution 660 (1990) and all subsequent relevant resolutions and decides, while maintaining all its decisions, to allow Iraq one final opportunity, as a pause of goodwill, to do so;

2. *Authorizes* Member States co-operating with the Government of Kuwait, unless Iraq on or before 15 January 1991 fully implements, as set forth in paragraph 1 above, the foregoing resolutions, to use all necessary means to uphold and implement Security Council resolution 660 (1990) and all subsequent relevant resolutions and to restore international peace and security in the area;

3. *Requests* all States to provide appropriate support for the actions undertaken in pursuance of paragraph 2 of this resolution;

4. *Requests* the States concerned to keep the Council regularly informed on the progress of actions undertaken pursuant to paragraphs 2 and 3 of this resolution;

5. *Decides* to remain seized of the matter.

B. RESOLUTIONS ADOPTED IN 1991

1. RESOLUTION 686 (1991), 2 March 1991

Adopted at the 2978th meeting by 11 votes to 1 (Cuba), with 3 abstentions (China, India, Yemen).

The Security Council,

Recalling and reaffirming its resolutions 660 (1990), 661 (1990), 662 (1990), 664 (1990), 665 (1990), 666 (1990), 667 (1990), 669 (1990), 670 (1990), 674 (1990), 677 (1990), and 678 (1990),

Recalling the obligations of Member States under Article 25 of the Charter,

Recalling paragraph 9 of resolution 661 (1990) regarding assistance to the Government of Kuwait and paragraph 3 (c) of that resolution regarding supplies strictly for medical purposes and, in humanitarian circumstances, foodstuffs,

Taking note of the letters of the Foreign Minister of Iraq confirming Iraq's agreement to comply fully with all of the resolutions noted above (S/22275), and stating its intention to release prisoners of war immediately (S/22273),

Taking note of the suspension of offensive combat operations by the forces of Kuwait and the Member States cooperating with Kuwait pursuant to resolution 678 (1990),

Bearing in mind the need to be assured of Iraq's peaceful intentions, and the objective in resolution 678 (1990) of restoring international peace and security in the region,

Underlining the importance of Iraq taking the necessary measures which would permit a definitive end to the hostilities,

Affirming the commitment of all Member States to the independence, sovereignty and territorial integrity of Iraq and Kuwait, and noting the intention expressed by the Member States cooperating under paragraph 2 of Security Council resolution 678 (1990) to bring their military presence in Iraq to an end as soon as possible consistent with achieving the objectives of the resolution,

Acting under Chapter VII of the Charter,

1. *Affirms* that all twelve resolutions noted above continue to have full force and effect;

2. *Demands* that Iraq implement its acceptance of all twelve resolutions noted above and in particular that Iraq:

(a) Rescind immediately its actions purporting to annex Kuwait;

(b) Accept in principle its liability under international law for any loss, damage, or injury arising in regard to Kuwait and third States, and their nationals and corporations, as a result of the invasion and illegal occupation of Kuwait by Iraq;

(c) Immediately release under the auspices of the International Committee of the Red Cross, Red Cross Societies, or Red Crescent Societies, all Kuwaiti and third country nationals detained by Iraq and return the remains of any deceased Kuwaiti and third country nationals so detained; and

(d) Immediately begin to return all Kuwaiti property seized by Iraq, to be completed in the shortest possible period;

3. *Further demands* that Iraq:

(a) Cease hostile or provocative actions by its forces against all Member States, including missile attacks and flights of combat aircraft;

(b) Designate military commanders to meet with counterparts from the forces of Kuwait and the Member States cooperating with Kuwait pursuant to resolution 678 (1990) to arrange for the military aspects of a cessation of hostilities at the earliest possible time;

(c) Arrange for immediate access to and release of all prisoners of war under the auspices of the International Committee of the Red Cross and return the remains of any deceased personnel of the forces of Kuwait and the Member States cooperating with Kuwait pursuant to resolution 678 (1990); and

(d) Provide all information and assistance in identifying Iraqi mines, booby traps and other explosives as well as any chemical and biological weapons and material in Kuwait, in areas of Iraq where forces of Member States cooperating with Kuwait pursuant to resolution 678 (1990) are present temporarily, and in the adjacent waters;

4. *Recognizes* that during the period required for Iraq to comply with paragraphs 2 and 3 above, the provisions of paragraph 2 of resolution 678 (1990) remain valid;

5. *Welcomes* the decision of Kuwait and the Member States cooperating with Kuwait pursuant to resolution 678 (1990) to provide access and to commence immediately the release of Iraqi prisoners of war as required by the terms of the Third Geneva Convention of 1949, under the auspices of the International Committee of the Red Cross;

6. *Requests* all Member States, as well as the United Nations, the specialized agencies and other international organizations in the United Nations system, to take all appropriate action to cooperate with the Government and people of Kuwait in the reconstruction of their country;

7. *Decides* that Iraq shall notify the Secretary-General and the Security Council when it has taken the actions set out above;

8. *Decides* that in order to secure the rapid establishment of a definitive end to the hostilities, the Security Council remains actively seized of the matter.

2. Resolution 687 (1991), 3 April 1991

Adopted at the 2981st meeting by 12 votes in favour, 1 against (Cuba), Yemen and Ecuador abstaining.

The Security Council,

Recalling its resolutions 660 (1990), 661 (1990), 662 (1990), 664 (1990), 665 (1990), 666 (1990), 667 (1990), 669 (1990), 670 (1990), 674 (1990), 677 (1990), 678 (1990) and 686 (1991),

Welcoming the restoration to Kuwait of its sovereignty, independence, and territorial integrity and the return of its legitimate government,

Affirming the commitment of all Member States to the sovereignty, territorial integrity and political independence of Kuwait and Iraq, and noting the intention expressed by the Member States cooperating with Kuwait under paragraph 2 of resolution 678 (1990) to bring their military presence in Iraq to an end as soon as possible consistent with paragraph 8 of resolution 686 (1991),

Reaffirming the need to be assured of Iraq's peaceful intentions in light of its unlawful invasion and occupation of Kuwait,

Taking note of the letter sent by the Foreign Minister of Iraq on 27 February 1991 (S/22275) and those sent pursuant to resolution 686 (1991) (S/22273, S/22276, S/22320, S/22321 and S/22330),

Noting that Iraq and Kuwait, as independent sovereign States, signed at Baghdad on 4 October 1963 "Agreed Minutes Regarding the Restoration of Friendly Relations, Recognition and Related Matters", thereby recognizing formally the boundary between Iraq and Kuwait and the allocation of islands, which were registered with the United Nations in accordance with Article 102 of the Charter and in which Iraq recognized the independence and complete sovereignty of the State of Kuwait within its borders as specified and accepted in the letter of the Prime Minister of Iraq dated 21 July 1932, and as accepted by the Ruler of Kuwait in his letter dated 10 August 1932,

Conscious of the need for demarcation of the said boundary,

Conscious also of the statements by Iraq threatening to use weapons in violation of its obligations under the Geneva Protocol for the Prohibition of the Use in War of Asphyxiating, Poisonous or Other Gases, and of Bacteriological Methods of Warfare, signed at Geneva on 17 June 1925, and of its prior use of chemical weapons and affirming that grave consequences would follow any further use by Iraq of such weapons,

Recalling that Iraq has subscribed to the Declaration adopted by all States participating in the Conference of States Parties to the 1925 Geneva Protocol and Other Interested States, held at Paris from 7 to 11 January 1989, establishing the objective of universal elimination of chemical and biological weapons,

Recalling further that Iraq has signed the Convention on the Prohibition of the Development, Production and Stockpiling of Bacteriological (Biological) and Toxin Weapons and on Their Destruction, of 10 April 1972,

Noting the importance of Iraq ratifying this Convention,

Noting moreover the importance of all States adhering to this Convention and encouraging its forthcoming Review Conference to reinforce the authority, efficiency and universal scope of the convention,

Stressing the importance of an early conclusion by the Conference on Disarmament of its work on a Convention on the Universal Prohibition of Chemical Weapons and of universal adherence thereto,

Aware of the use by Iraq of ballistic missiles in unprovoked attacks and therefore of the need to take specific measures in regard to such missiles located in Iraq,

Concerned by the reports in the hands of Member States that Iraq has attempted to acquire materials for a nuclear-weapons programme contrary to its obligations under the Treaty on the Non-Proliferation of Nuclear Weapons of 1 July 1968,

Recalling the objective of the establishment of a nuclear-weapons-free zone in the region of the Middle East,

Conscious of the threat which all weapons of mass destruction pose to peace and security in the area and of the need to work towards the establishment in the Middle East of a zone free of such weapons,

Conscious also of the objective of achieving balanced and comprehensive control of armaments in the region,

Conscious further of the importance of achieving the objectives noted above using all available means, including a dialogue among the States of the region,

Noting that resolution 686 (1991) marked the lifting of the measures imposed by resolution 661 (1990) in so far as they applied to Kuwait,

Noting that despite the progress being made in fulfilling the obligations of resolution 686 (1991), many Kuwaiti and third country nationals are still not accounted for and property remains unreturned,

Recalling the International Convention against the Taking of Hostages, opened for signature at New York on 18 December 1979, which categorizes all acts of taking hostages as manifestations of international terrorism,

Deploring threats made by Iraq during the recent conflict to make use of terrorism against targets outside Iraq and the taking of hostages by Iraq,

Taking note with grave concern of the reports of the Secretary-General of 20 March 1991 (S/22366) and 28 March 1991 (S/22409), and conscious of the necessity to meet urgently the humanitarian needs in Kuwait and Iraq,

Bearing in mind its objective of restoring international peace and security in the area as set out in recent Council resolutions,

Conscious of the need to take the following measures acting under Chapter VII of the Charter,

1. Affirms all thirteen resolutions noted above, except as expressly changed below to achieve the goals of this resolution, including a formal cease-fire;

A

2. *Demands* that Iraq and Kuwait respect the inviolability of the international boundary and the allocation of islands set out in the "Agreed Minutes Between the State of Kuwait and the Republic of Iraq Regarding the Restoration of Friendly Relations, Recognition and Related Matters", signed by them in the exercise of their sovereignty at Baghdad on 4 October 1963 and registered with the United Nations and published by the United Nations in document 7063, United Nations Treaty Series, 1964;

3. *Calls on* the Secretary-General to lend his assistance to make arrangements with Iraq and Kuwait to demarcate the boundary between Iraq and Kuwait, drawing on appropriate material including the map transmitted by Security Council document S/22412 and to report back to the Security Council within one month;

4. *Decides* to guarantee the inviolability of the above-mentioned international boundary and to take as appropriate all necessary measures to that end in accordance with the Charter;

B

5. *Requests* the Secretary-General, after consulting with Iraq and Kuwait, to submit within three days to the Security Council for its approval a plan for the immediate deployment of a United Nations observer unit to monitor the Khor Abdullah and a demilitarized zone, which is hereby established, extending 10 kilometres into Iraq and 5 kilometres into Kuwait from the boundary referred to in the "Agreed Minutes Between the State of Kuwait and the Republic of Iraq Regarding the Restoration of Friendly Relations, Recognition and Related Matters" of 4 October 1963; to deter violations of the boundary through its presence in and surveillance of the demilitarized zone; to observe any hostile or potentially hostile action mounted from the territory of one State to the other; and for the Secretary-General to report regularly to the Council on the operations of the unit, and immediately if there are serious violations of the zone or potential threats to peace;

6. *Notes* that as soon as the Secretary-General notifies the Council of the completion of the deployment of the United Nations observer unit, the conditions will be established for the Member States cooperating with Kuwait in accordance with resolution 678 (1990) to bring their military presence in Iraq to an end consistent with resolution 686 (1991);

C

7. *Invites* Iraq to reaffirm unconditionally its obligations under the Geneva Protocol for the Prohibition of the Use in War of Asphyxiating, Poisonous or Other Gases, and of Bacteriological Methods of Warfare, signed at Geneva on 17 June 1925, and to ratify the Convention on the Prohibition of the Development, Production and Stockpiling of Bacteriological (Biological) and Toxin Weapons and on Their Destruction, of 10 April 1972;

8. *Decides* that Iraq shall unconditionally accept the destruction, removal, or rendering harmless, under international supervision, of:

(a) all chemical and biological weapons and all stocks of agents and all related subsystems and components and all research, development, support and manufacturing facilities;

(b) all ballistic missiles with a range greater than 150 kilometres and related major parts, and repair and production facilities;

9. *Decides*, for the implementation of paragraph 8 above, the following:

(a) Iraq shall submit to the Secretary-General, within fifteen days of the adoption of this resolution, a declaration of the locations, amounts and types of all items specified in paragraph 8 and agree to urgent, on-site inspection as specified below;
(b) the Secretary-General, in consultation with the appropriate Governments and, where appropriate, with the Director-General of the World Health Organization (WHO), within 45 days of the passage of this resolution, shall develop, and submit to the Council for approval, a plan calling for the completion of the following acts within 45 days of such approval:

(i) the forming of a Special Commission, which shall carry out immediate on-site inspection of Iraq's biological, chemical and missile capabilities, based on Iraq's declarations and the designation of any additional locations by the Special Commission itself;
(ii) the yielding by Iraq of possession to the Special Commission for destruction, removal or rendering harmless, taking into account the requirements of public safety, of all items specified under paragraph 8 (a) above including items at the additional locations designated by the Special Commission under paragraph 9 (b) (i) above and the destruction by Iraq, under supervision of the Special Commission, of all its missile capabilities including launchers as specified under paragraph 8 (b) above;
(iii) the provision by the Special Commission of the assistance and cooperation to the Director-General of the International Atomic Energy Agency (IAEA) required in paragraphs 12 and 13 below;

10. *Decides* that Iraq shall unconditionally undertake not to use, develop, construct or acquire any of the items specified in paragraphs 8 and 9 above and requests the Secretary-General, in consultation with the Special Commission, to develop a plan for the future ongoing monitoring and verification of Iraq's compliance with this paragraph, to be submitted to the Council for approval within 120 days of the passage of this resolution;

11. *Invites* Iraq to reaffirm unconditionally its obligations under the Treaty on the Non-Proliferation of Nuclear Weapons, of 1 July 1968;

12. *Decides* that Iraq shall unconditionally agree not to acquire or develop nuclear weapons or nuclear-weapons-usable material or any subsystems or components or any research, development, support or manufacturing facilities related to the above; to submit to the Secretary-General and the Director-General of the International Atomic Energy Agency (IAEA) within 15 days of the adoption of this resolution a declaration of the locations, amounts, and types of all items specified above; to place all of its nuclear-weapons-usable materials under the exclusive control, for custody and removal, of the IAEA, with the assistance and cooperation of the Special Commission as provided for in the plan of the Secretary-General discussed in paragraph 9 (b) above; to accept, in accordance with the arrangements provided for in paragraph 13 below, urgent on-site inspection and the destruction, removal, or rendering harmless as appropriate of all items specified above; and to accept the plan discussed in paragraph 13 below for the future ongoing monitoring and verification of its compliance with these undertakings;

13. *Requests* the Director-General of the International Atomic Energy Agency (IAEA) through the Secretary-General, with the assistance and cooperation of the Special Commission as provided for in the plan of the Secretary-General in paragraph 9 (b) above, to carry out immediate on-site inspection of Iraq's nuclear capabilities based on Iraq's declarations and the designation of any additional locations by the Special Commission; to develop a plan for submission to the Security Council within 45 days calling for the destruction, removal, or rendering harmless as appropriate of all items listed in paragraph 12 above; to carry out the plan within 45 days following approval by the Security Council; and to develop a plan, taking into account the rights and obligations of Iraq under the Treaty on the Non-Proliferation of Nuclear Weapons, of 1 July 1968, for the future ongoing monitoring and verification of Iraq's compliance with paragraph 12 above, including an inventory of all nuclear material in Iraq subject to the Agency's verification and inspections to confirm that IAEA safeguards cover all relevant nuclear activities in Iraq, to be submitted to the Council for approval within 120 days of the passage of this resolution;

14. *Takes note* that the actions to be taken by Iraq in paragraphs 8, 9, 10, 11, 12 and 13 of this resolution represent steps towards the goal of establishing in the Middle East a zone free from weapons of mass destruction and all missiles for their delivery and the objective of a global ban on chemical weapons;

D

15. *Requests* the Secretary-General to report to the Security Council on the steps taken to facilitate the return of all Kuwaiti property seized by Iraq, including a list of any property which Kuwait claims

has not been returned or which has not been returned intact;

E

16. *Reaffirms* that Iraq, without prejudice to the debts and obligations of Iraq arising prior to 2 August 1990, which will be addressed through the normal mechanisms, is liable under international law for any direct loss, damage, including environmental damage and the depletion of natural resources, or injury to foreign Governments, nationals and corporations, as a result of Iraq's unlawful invasion and occupation of Kuwait;

17. *Decides* that all Iraqi statements made since 2 August 1990, repudiating its foreign debt, are null and void, and demands that Iraq scrupulously adhere to all of its obligations concerning servicing and repayment of its foreign debt;

18. *Decides* to create a Fund to pay compensation for claims that fall within paragraph 16 above and to establish a Commission that will administer the Fund;

19. *Directs* the Secretary-General to develop and present to the Council for decision, no later than 30 days following the adoption of this resolution, recommendations for the Fund to meet the requirement for the payment of claims established in accordance with paragraph 18 above and for a programme to implement the decisions in paragraphs 16, 17, and 18 above, including: administration of the Fund; mechanisms for determining the appropriate level of Iraq's contribution to the Fund based on a percentage of the value of the exports of petroleum and petroleum products from Iraq not to exceed a figure to be suggested to the Council by the Secretary-General, taking into account the requirements of the people of Iraq, Iraq's payment capacity as assessed in conjunction with the international financial institutions taking into consideration external debt service, and the needs of the Iraqi economy; arrangements for ensuring that payments are made to the Fund; the process by which funds will be allocated and claims paid; appropriate procedures for evaluating losses, listing claims and verifying their validity and resolving disputed claims in respect of Iraq's liability as specified in paragraph 16 above; and the composition of the Commission designated above;

F

20. *Decides*, effective immediately, that the prohibitions against the sale or supply to Iraq of commodities or products, other than medicine and health supplies, and prohibitions against financial transactions related thereto, contained in resolution 661 (1990) shall not apply to foodstuffs notified to the Committee established by resolution 661 (1990) or, with the approval of that Committee, under the simplified and accelerated "no-objection" procedure, to materials and supplies for essential civilian needs as identified in the report of the Secretary-General dated 20 March 1991 (S/22366), and in any further findings of humanitarian need by the Committee;

21. *Decides* that the Council shall review the provisions of paragraph 20 above every sixty days in light of the policies and practices of the Government of Iraq, including the implementation of all relevant resolutions of the Security Council, for the purpose of determining whether to reduce or lift the prohibitions referred to therein;

22. *Decides* that upon the approval by the Council of the programme called for in paragraph 19 above and upon Council agreement that Iraq has completed all actions contemplated in paragraphs 8, 9, 10, 11, 12, and 13 above, the prohibitions against the import of commodities and products originating in Iraq and the prohibitions against financial transactions related thereto contained in resolution 661 (1990) shall have no further force or effect;

23. *Decides* that, pending action by the Council under paragraph 22 above, the Committee established by resolution 661 (1990) shall be empowered to approve, when required to assure adequate financial resources on the part of Iraq to carry out the activities under paragraph 20 above, exceptions to the prohibition against the import of commodities and products originating in Iraq;

24. *Decides* that, in accordance with resolution 661 (1990) and subsequent related resolutions and until a further decision is taken by the Council, all States shall continue to prevent the sale or supply, or promotion or facilitation of such sale or supply, to Iraq by their nationals, or from their territories or using their flag vessels or aircraft, of:

(a) arms and related *matériel* of all types, specifically including the sale or transfer through other means of all forms of conventional military equipment, including for paramilitary forces, and spare parts and components and their means of production, for such equipment;

(b) items specified and defined in paragraph 8 and paragraph 12 above not otherwise covered above;

(c) technology under licensing or other transfer arrangements used in the production, utilization or stockpiling of items specified in subparagraphs (a) and (b) above;

(d) personnel or materials for training or technical support services relating to the design, development, manufacture, use, maintenance or support of items specified in subparagraphs (a) and (b) above;

25. *Calls upon* all States and international organizations to act strictly in accordance with paragraph 24 above, notwithstanding the existence

of any contracts, agreements, licences, or any other arrangements;

26. *Requests* the Secretary-General, in consultation with appropriate Governments, to develop within 60 days, for approval of the Council, guidelines to facilitate full international implementation of paragraphs 24 and 25 above and paragraph 27 below, and to make them available to all States and to establish a procedure for updating these guidelines periodically;

27. *Calls upon* all States to maintain such national controls and procedures and to take such other actions consistent with the guidelines to be established by the Security Council under paragraph 26 above as may be necessary to ensure compliance with the terms of paragraph 24 above, and calls upon international organizations to take all appropriate steps to assist in ensuring such full compliance;

28. *Agrees* to review its decisions in paragraphs 22, 23, 24, and 25 above, except for the items specified and defined in paragraphs 8 and 12 above, on a regular basis and in any case 120 days following passage of this resolution, taking into account Iraq's compliance with this resolution and general progress towards the control of armaments in the region;

29. *Decides* that all States, including Iraq, shall take the necessary measures to ensure that no claim shall lie at the instance of the Government of Iraq, or of any person or body in Iraq, or of any person claiming through or for the benefit of any such person or body, in connection with any contract or other transaction where its performance was affected by reason of the measures taken by the Security Council in resolution 661 (1990) and related resolutions;

G

30. *Decides* that, in furtherance of its commitment to facilitate the repatriation of all Kuwaiti and third country nationals, Iraq shall extend all necessary cooperation to the International Committee of the Red Cross, providing lists of such persons, facilitating the access of the International Committee of the Red Cross to all such persons wherever located or detained and facilitating the search by the International Committee of the Red Cross for those Kuwaiti and third country nationals still unaccounted for;

31. *Invites* the International Committee of the Red Cross to keep the Secretary-General apprised as appropriate of all activities undertaken in connection with facilitating the repatriation or return of all Kuwaiti and third country nationals or their remains present in Iraq on or after 2 August 1990;

H

32. *Requires* Iraq to inform the Council that it will not commit or support any act of international terrorism or allow any organization directed towards commission of such acts to operate within its territory and to condemn unequivocally and renounce all acts, methods, and practices of terrorism;

I

33. *Declares* that, upon official notification by Iraq to the Secretary-General and to the Security Council of its acceptance of the provisions above, a formal cease-fire is effective between Iraq and Kuwait and the Member States cooperating with Kuwait in accordance with resolution 678 (1990);

34. *Decides* to remain seized of the matter and to take such further steps as may be required for the implementation of this resolution and to secure peace and security in the area.

3. Resolution 688 (1991), 5 April 1991

Adopted at the 2982nd meeting by 10 votes in favour, 3 voting against (Cuba, Yemen and Zimbabwe), China and India abstaining.

The Security Council,

Mindful of its duties and its responsibilities under the Charter of the United Nations for the maintenance of international peace and security,

Recalling Article 2, paragraph 7, of the Charter of the United Nations,

Gravely concerned by the repression of the Iraqi civilian population in many parts of Iraq, including most recently in Kurdish populated areas which led to a massive flow of refugees towards and across international frontiers and to cross border incursions, which threaten international peace and security in the region,

Deeply disturbed by the magnitude of the human suffering involved,

Taking note of the letters sent by the representatives of Turkey and France to the United Nations dated 2 April 1991 and 4 April 1991, respectively (S/22435 and S/22442),

Taking note also of the letters sent by the Permanent Representative of the Islamic Republic of Iran to the United Nations dated 3 and 4 April 1991, respectively (S/22436 and S/22447),

Reaffirming the commitment of all Member States to the sovereignty, territorial integrity and political independence of Iraq and of all States in the area,

Bearing in mind the Secretary-General's report of 20 March 1991 (S/22366),

1. *Condemns* the repression of the Iraqi civilian population in many parts of Iraq, including most recently in Kurdish populated areas, the consequences of which threaten international peace and security in the region;

2. *Demands* that Iraq, as a contribution to removing the threat to international peace and security in the region, immediately end this repression and expresses the hope in the same context that an open dialogue will take place to ensure that the human and political rights of all Iraqi citizens are respected;

3. *Insists* that Iraq allow immediate access by international humanitarian organizations to all those in need of assistance in all parts of Iraq and to make available all necessary facilities for their operations;

4. *Requests* the Secretary-General to pursue his humanitarian efforts in Iraq and to report forthwith, if appropriate on the basis of a further mission to the region, on the plight of the Iraqi civilian population, and in particular the Kurdish population, suffering from the repression in all its forms inflicted by the Iraqi authorities;

5. *Requests further* the Secretary-General to use all the resources at his disposal, including those of the relevant United Nations agencies, to address urgently the critical needs of the refugees and displaced Iraqi population;

6. *Appeals* to all Member States and to all humanitarian organizations to contribute to these humanitarian relief efforts;

7. *Demands* that Iraq cooperate with the Secretary-General to these ends;

8. *Decides* to remain seized of the matter.

4. Resolution 689 (1991), 9 April 1991

Adopted unanimously by the Security Council at the 2983rd meeting.

The Security Council,

Recalling its resolution 687 (1991),

Acting under Chapter VII of the Charter of the United Nations,

1. *Approves* the report of the Secretary-General on the implementation of paragraph 5 of Security Council resolution 687 (1991) contained in document S/22454 and Add. 1-3 of 5 and 9 April 1991, respectively;

2. *Notes* that the decision to set up the observer unit was taken in paragraph 5 of resolution 687 (1991) and can only be terminated by a decision of the Council; the Council shall therefore review the question of termination or continuation every six months;

3. *Decides* that the modalities for the initial six-month period of the United Nations Iraq-Kuwait Observation Mission shall be in accordance with the above-mentioned report and shall also be reviewed every six months.

5. Resolution 692 (1991), 20 May 1991

Adopted at the 2987th meeting by 14 votes in favour, none against, Cuba abstaining.

The Security Council,

Recalling its resolutions 674 (1990) of 29 October 1990, 686 (1991) of 2 March 1991 and 687 (1991) of 3 April 1991, concerning the liability of Iraq, without prejudice to its debts and obligations arising prior to 2 August 1990, for any direct loss, damage, including environmental damage and the depletion of natural resources, or injury to foreign Governments, nationals and corporations, as a result of Iraq's unlawful invasion and occupation of Kuwait,

Taking note of the Secretary-General's report of 2 May 1991 (S/22559), submitted in accordance with paragraph 19 of resolution 687 (1991),

Acting under Chapter VII of the Charter of the United Nations,

1. *Expresses its appreciation* to the Secretary-General for his report of 2 May 1991; [S/22559.]

2. *Welcomes the fact* that the Secretary-General will now undertake the appropriate consultations requested by paragraph 19 of resolution 687 (1991) so that he will be in a position to recommend to the Security Council for decision as soon as possible the figure which the level of Iraq's contribution to the Fund will not exceed;

3. *Decides* to establish the Fund and the Commission referred to in paragraph 18 of resolution 687 (1991) in accordance with section I of the Secretary-General's report, and that the Governing Council will be located at the United

Nations Office at Geneva and that the Governing Council may decide whether some of the activities of the Commission should be carried out elsewhere;

4. *Requests* the Secretary-General to take the actions necessary to implement paragraphs 2 and 3 above in consultation with the members of the Governing Council;

5. *Directs* the Governing Council to proceed in an expeditious manner to implement the provisions of section E of resolution 687 (1991), taking into account the recommendations in section II of the Secretary-General's report;

6. *Decides* that the requirement for Iraqi contributions will apply in the manner to be prescribed by the Governing Council with respect to all Iraqi petroleum and petroleum products exported from Iraq after 3 April 1991 as well as such petroleum and petroleum products exported earlier but not delivered or paid for as a specific result of the prohibitions contained in Security Council resolution 661 (1990);

7. *Requests* the Governing Council to report as soon as possible on the actions it has taken with regard to the mechanisms for determining the appropriate level of Iraq's contribution to the Fund and the arrangements for ensuring that payments are made to the Fund, so that the Security Council can give its approval in accordance with paragraph 22 of resolution 687 (1991);

8. *Requests* that all States and international organizations cooperate with the decisions of the Governing Council taken pursuant to paragraph 5 of the present resolution, and also requests that the Governing Council keep the Security Council informed on this matter;

9. *Decides* that, if the Governing Council notifies the Security Council that Iraq has failed to carry out decisions of the Governing Council taken pursuant to paragraph 5 of the present resolution, the Security Council intends to retain or to take action to reimpose the prohibition against the import of petroleum and petroleum products originating in Iraq and financial transactions related thereto;

10. *Decides also* to remain seized of this matter and that the Governing Council will submit periodic reports to the Secretary-General and the Security Council.

6. Resolution 699 (1991), 17 June 1991

Adopted unanimously at the 2994th meeting.

The Security Council,

Recalling its resolution 687 (1991),

Taking note of the report of the Secretary-General of 17 May 1991 (S/22614), submitted to it in pursuance of paragraph 9 (b) of resolution 687 (1991),

Also taking note of the Secretary-General's note of 17 May 1991 (S/22615), transmitting to the Council the letter addressed to him under paragraph 13 of the resolution by the Director-General of the International Atomic Energy Agency (IAEA),

Acting under Chapter VII of the Charter,

1. *Approves* the plan contained in the report of the Secretary-General;

2. *Confirms* that the Special Commission and the IAEA have the authority to conduct activities under section C of resolution 687 (1991), for the purpose of the destruction, removal or rendering harmless of the items specified in paragraphs 8 and 12 of that resolution, after the 45-day period following the approval of this plan until such activities have been completed;

3. *Requests* the Secretary-General to submit to the Security Council progress reports on the implementation of the plan referred to in paragraph 1 every six months after the adoption of this resolution;

4. *Decides* to encourage the maximum assistance, in cash and in kind, from all Member States to ensure that activities under section C of resolution 687 (1991) are undertaken effectively and expeditiously; *further decides*, however, that the Government of Iraq shall be liable for the full costs of carrying out the tasks authorized by section C; and requests the Secretary-General to submit to the Council within 30 days for approval recommendations as to the most effective means by which Iraq's obligations in this respect may be fulfilled.

7. Resolution 700 (1991), 17 June 1991

Adopted unanimously at the 2994th meeting.

The Security Council,

Recalling its resolutions 661 (1990) of 6 August 1990, 665 (1990) of 25 August 1990, 670 (1990) of 25 September 1990 and 687 (1991) of 3 April 1991,

Taking note of the Secretary-General's report of 2 June 1991 (S/22660) submitted pursuant to paragraph 26 of resolution 687 (1991),

Acting under Chapter VII of the Charter of the United Nations,

1. *Expresses its appreciation* to the Secretary-General for his report of 2 June 1991 (S/22660);

2. *Approves* the Guidelines to Facilitate Full International Implementation of paragraphs 24, 25 and 27 of Security Council resolution 687 (1991), annexed to the report of the Secretary-General (S/22660);

3. *Reiterates* its call upon all States and international organizations to act in a manner consistent with the Guidelines;

4. *Requests* all States, in accordance with paragraph 8 of the Guidelines, to report to the Secretary-General within 45 days on the measures they have instituted for meeting the obligations set out in paragraph 24 of resolution 687 (1991);

5. *Entrusts* the Committee established under resolution 661 (1990) concerning the situation between Iraq and Kuwait with the responsibility, under the Guidelines, for monitoring the prohibitions against the sale or supply of arms to Iraq and related sanctions established in paragraph 24 of resolution 687 (1991);

6. *Decides* to remain seized of the matter and to review the Guidelines at the same time as it reviews paragraphs 22, 23, 24 and 25 of resolution 687 (1991) as set out in paragraph 28 thereof.

8. RESOLUTION 705 (1991), 15 August 1991

Adopted unanimously the 3004th meeting.

The Security Council,

Having considered the note of 30 May 1991 of the Secretary-General pursuant to paragraph 13 of his report of 2 May 1991 (S/22559) which was annexed to the Secretary-General's letter of 30 May 1991 to the President of the Security Council (S/22661),

Acting under Chapter VII of the Charter,

1. *Expresses* its appreciation to the Secretary-General for his note of 30 May 1991 which was annexed to his letter to the President of the Security Council of the same date (S/22661);

2. *Decides* that in accordance with the suggestion made by the Secretary-General in paragraph 7 of his note of 30 May 1991, compensation to be paid by Iraq (as arising from section E of resolution 687) shall not exceed 30 per cent of the annual value of the exports of petroleum and petroleum products from Iraq;

3. *Decides further*, in accordance with paragraph 8 of the Secretary-General's note of 30 May 1991, to review the figure established in paragraph 2 above from time to time in light of data and assumptions contained in the letter of the Secretary-General (S/22661) and other relevant documents.

9. RESOLUTION 706 (1991), 15 August 1991

Adopted at the 3004th meeting by 13 votes to 1 (Cuba), Yemen abstaining.

The Security Council,

Recalling its previous relevant resolutions and in particular resolutions 661 (1990), 686 (1991), 687 (1991), 688 (1991), 692 (1991), 699 (1991) and 705 (1991),

Taking note of the report (S/22799) dated 15 July 1991 of the inter-agency mission headed by the executive delegate of the Secretary-General for the United Nations inter-agency humanitarian programme for Iraq, Kuwait and the Iraq/Turkey and Iraq/Iran border areas,

Concerned by the serious nutritional and health situation of the Iraqi civilian population as described in this report, and by the risk of a further deterioration of this situation,

Concerned also that the repatriation or return of all Kuwaitis and third country nationals or their remains present in Iraq on or after 2 August 1990, pursuant to paragraph 2 (c) of resolution 686 (1991), and paragraphs 30 and 31 of resolution 687 (1991) has not yet been fully carried out,

Taking note of the conclusions of the above-mentioned report, and in particular of the proposal for oil sales by Iraq to finance the purchase of foodstuffs, medicines and materials and supplies for essential civilian needs for the purpose of providing humanitarian relief,

Taking note also of the letters dated 14 April 1991, 31 May 1991, 6 June 1991, 9 July 1991 and 22 July 1991 from the Minister of Foreign Affairs of Iraq and the Permanent Representative of Iraq to the Chairman of the Committee established by resolution 661 (1990) concerning the export from Iraq of petroleum and petroleum products,

Convinced of the need for equitable distribution of humanitarian relief to all segments of the Iraqi civilian population through effective monitoring and transparency,

Recalling and reaffirming in this regard its resolution 688 (1991) and in particular the importance which the Council attaches to Iraq allowing unhindered access by international humanitarian organizations to all those in need of assistance in all parts of Iraq and making available all necessary facilities for their operation, and in this connection stressing the important and continuing role played by the Memorandum of Understanding between the United Nations and the Government of Iraq of 18 April 1991 (S/22663),

Recalling that, pursuant to resolution 687 (1991), 692 (1991) and 699 (1991), Iraq is required to pay the full costs of the Special Commission and the IAEA in carrying out the tasks authorized by section C of resolution 687 (1991), and that the Secretary-General in his report to the Security Council of 15 July 1991 (S/22792), submitted pursuant to paragraph 4 of resolution 699 (1991), expressed the view that the most obvious way of obtaining financial resources from Iraq to meet the costs of the Special Commission and the IAEA would be to authorize the sale of some Iraqi petroleum and petroleum products; *recalling further* that Iraq is required to pay its contributions to the Compensation Fund and half the costs of the Iraq-Kuwait Boundary Demarcation Commission, and *recalling further* that in its resolutions 686 (1991) and 687 (1991) the Security Council demanded that Iraq return in the shortest possible time all Kuwaiti property seized by it and requested the Secretary-General to take steps to facilitate this,

Acting under Chapter VII of the Charter,

1. *Authorizes* all States, subject to the decision to be taken by the Security Council pursuant to paragraph 5 below and notwithstanding the provisions of paragraphs 3 (a), 3 (b) and 4 of resolution 661 (1990), to permit the import, during a period of 6 months from the date of passage of the resolution pursuant to paragraph 5 below, of petroleum and petroleum products originating in Iraq sufficient to produce a sum to be determined by the Council following receipt of the report of the Secretary-General requested in paragraph 5 of this resolution but not to exceed 1.6 billion United States dollars for the purposes set out in this resolution and subject to the following conditions:

(a) Approval of each purchase of Iraqi petroleum and petroleum products by the Security Council Committee established by resolution 661 (1990) following notification to the Committee by the State concerned;

(b) Payment of the full amount of each purchase of Iraqi petroleum and petroleum products directly by the purchaser in the State concerned into an escrow account to be established by the United Nations and to be administered by the Secretary-General, exclusively to meet the purposes of this resolution;

(c) Approval by the Council, following the report of the Secretary-General requested in paragraph 5 of this resolution, of a scheme for the purchase of foodstuffs, medicines and materials and supplies for essential civilian needs as referred to in paragraph 20 of resolution 687 (1991), in particular health related materials, all of which to be labelled to the extent possible as being supplied under this scheme, and for all feasible and appropriate United Nations monitoring and supervision for the purpose of assuring their equitable distribution to meet humanitarian needs in all regions of Iraq and to all categories of the Iraqi civilian population, as well as all feasible and appropriate management relevant to this purpose, such a United Nations role to be available if desired for humanitarian assistance from other sources;

(d) The sum authorized in this paragraph to be released by successive decisions of the Committee established by resolution 661 (1990) in three equal portions after the Council has taken the decision provided for in paragraph 5 below on the implementation of this resolution, and notwithstanding any other provision of this paragraph, the sum to be subject to review concurrently by the Council on the basis of its ongoing assessment of the needs and requirements;

2. *Decides* that a part of the sum in the account to be established by the Secretary-General shall be made available by him to finance the purchase of foodstuffs, medicines and materials and supplies for essential civilian needs, as referred to in paragraph 20 of resolution 687, and the cost to the United Nations of its roles under this resolution and of other necessary humanitarian activities in Iraq;

3. *Decides further* that a part of the sum in the account to be established by the Secretary-General shall be used by him for appropriate payments to the United Nations Compensation Fund, the full costs of carrying out the tasks authorized by Section C of resolution 687 (1991), the full costs incurred by the United Nations in facilitating the return of all Kuwaiti property seized by Iraq, and half the costs of the Boundary Commission;

4. *Decides* that the percentage of the value of exports of petroleum and petroleum products from Iraq, authorized under this resolution to be paid to the United Nations Compensation Fund, as called for in paragraph 19 of resolution 687 (1991), and as defined in paragraph 6 of resolution 692 (1991), shall be the same as the percentage decided by the Security Council in paragraph 2 of resolution 705 (1991) for payments to the Compensation Fund, until such time as the Governing Council of the Fund decides otherwise;

5. *Requests* the Secretary-General to submit within 20 days of the date of adoption of this resolution a report to the Security Council for decision on measures to be taken in order to implement paragraphs 1 (a), (b) and (c), estimates of the humanitarian requirements of Iraq set out in paragraph 2 above and of the amount of Iraq's financial obligations set out in paragraph 3 above up to the end of the period of the authorization in paragraph 1 above, as well as the method for taking the necessary legal measures to ensure that the purposes of this resolution are carried out and the method for taking account of the costs of transportation of such Iraqi petroleum and petroleum products;

6. *Further requests* the Secretary-General in consultation with the International Committee of the Red Cross to submit within 20 days of the date of adoption of this resolution a report to the Security Council on activities undertaken in accordance with paragraph 31 of resolution 687 (1991) in connection with facilitating the repatriation or return of all Kuwaiti and third country nationals or their remains present in Iraq on or after 2 August 1990;

7. *Requires* the Government of Iraq to provide to the Secretary-General and appropriate international organizations on the first day of the month immediately following the adoption of the present resolution and on the first day of each month thereafter until further notice, a statement of the gold and foreign currency reserves it holds whether in Iraq or elsewhere;

8. *Calls upon* all States to cooperate fully in the implementation of this resolution;

9. *Decides* to remain seized of the matter.

10. RESOLUTION 707 (1991), 15 August 1991

Adopted unanimously at the 3004th meeting.

The Security Council,

Recalling its resolution 687 (1991), and its other resolutions on this matter,

Recalling the letter of 11 April 1991 from the President of the Security Council to the Permanent Representative of Iraq to the United Nations (S/22485) noting that on the basis of Iraq's written agreement (S/22456) to implement fully resolution 687 (1991) the preconditions established in paragraph 33 of that resolution for a cease-fire had been met,

Noting with grave concern the letters dated 26 June 1991 (S/22739), 28 June 1991 (S/22743) and 4 July 1991 (S/22761) from the Secretary-General, conveying information obtained from the Executive Chairman of the Special Commission and the Director-General of the IAEA which establishes Iraq's failure to comply with its obligations under resolution 687 (1991),

Recalling further the statement issued by the President of the Security Council on 28 June 1991 (S/22746) requesting that a high-level mission consisting of the Chairman of the Special Commission, the Director-General of the IAEA, and the Under-Secretary-General for Disarmament Affairs be dispatched to meet with officials at the highest levels of the Government of Iraq at the earliest opportunity to obtain written assurance that Iraq will fully and immediately cooperate in the inspection of the locations identified by the Special Commission and present for immediate inspection any of those items that may have been transported from those locations,

Dismayed by the report of the high-level mission to the Secretary-General (S/22761) on the results of its meetings with the highest levels of the Iraqi Government,

Gravely concerned by the information provided to the Council by the Special Commission and the IAEA on 15 July 1991 (S/22788) and 25 July 1991 (S/22837) regarding the actions of the Government of Iraq in flagrant violation of resolution 687 (1991),

Gravely concerned also by the evidence in the letter of 7 July 1991 from the Minister of Foreign Affairs of Iraq to the Secretary-General and in subsequent statements and findings that Iraq's notifications of 18 and 28 April were incomplete and that it had concealed activities, which both constituted material breaches of its obligations under resolution 687 (1991),

Noting also from the letters dated 26 June 1991 (S/22739), 28 June 1991 (S/22743) and 4 July 1991 (S/22761) from the Secretary-General that Iraq has not fully complied with all of its undertakings relating to the privileges, immunities and facilities to be accorded to the Special Commission and the IAEA inspection teams mandated under resolution 687 (1991),

Affirming that in order for the Special Commission to carry out its mandate under paragraph 9 (b) (i), (ii) and (iii) of resolution 687 (1991) to inspect Iraq's chemical and biological weapons and ballistic missile capabilities and to take possession of them for destruction, removal or rendering harmless, full disclosure on the part of Iraq as required in paragraph 9 (a) of resolution 687 (1991) is essential,

Affirming that in order for the IAEA with the assistance and cooperation of the Special Commission, to determine what nuclear-weapons-usable material or any subsystems or components or any research, development, support or manufacturing facilities related to them need, in accordance with paragraph 13 of resolution 687 (1991), to be destroyed, removed or rendered harmless, Iraq is required to make a declaration of all its nuclear programmes including any which it claims are for purposes not related to nuclear-weapons-usable material,

Affirming that the aforementioned failures of Iraq to act in strict conformity with its obligations under resolution 687 (1991) constitutes a material breach of its acceptance of the relevant provisions or resolution 687 (1991) which established a cease-fire and provided the conditions essential to the restoration of peace and security in the region,

Affirming further that Iraq's failure to comply with its safeguards agreement with the International Atomic Energy Agency, concluded pursuant to the Treaty on the Non-Proliferation of Nuclear Weapons of 1 July 1968, as established by the resolution of the Board of Governors of the IAEA of 18 July 1991 (GOV/2531), constitutes a breach of its international obligations,

Determined to ensure full compliance with resolution 687 (1991) and in particular its section C,

Acting under Chapter VII of the Charter,

1. *Condemns* Iraq's serious violation of a number of its obligations under section C of resolution 687 (1991) and of its undertakings to cooperate with the Special Commission and the IAEA, which constitutes a material breach of the relevant provisions of resolution 687 which established a cease-fire and provided the conditions essential to the restoration of peace and security in the region;

2. *Further condemns* non-compliance by the Government of Iraq with its obligations under its safeguards agreement with the International Atomic Energy Agency, as established by the resolution of the Board of Governors of 18 July, which constitutes a violation of its commitments as a party to the Treaty on the Non-Proliferation of Nuclear Weapons of 1 July 1968;

3. *Demands* that Iraq

(i) provide full, final and complete disclosure, as required by resolution 687 (1991), of all aspects of its programmes to develop weapons of mass destruction and ballistic missiles with a range greater than 150 kilometres, and of all holdings of such weapons, their components and production facilities and locations, as well as all other nuclear programmes, including any which it claims are for purposes not related to nuclear-weapons-usable material, without further delay;

(ii) allow the Special Commission, the IAEA and their Inspection Teams immediate, unconditional and unrestricted access to any and all areas, facilities, equipment, records and means of transportation which they wish to inspect;

(iii) cease immediately any attempt to conceal, or any movement or destruction of any material or equipment relating to its nuclear, chemical or biological weapons or ballistic missile programmes, or material or equipment relating to its other nuclear activities without notification to and prior consent of the Special Commission;

(iv) make available immediately to the Special Commission, the IAEA and their Inspection Teams any items to which they were previously denied access;

(v) allow the Special Commission, the IAEA and their Inspection Teams to conduct both fixed wing and helicopter flights throughout Iraq for all relevant purposes including inspection, surveillance, aerial surveys, transportation and logistics without interference of any kind and upon such terms and conditions as may be determined by the Special Commission, and to make full use of their own aircraft and such airfields in Iraq as they may determine are most appropriate for the work of the Commission;

(vi) halt all nuclear activities of any kind, except for use of isotopes for medical, agricultural or industrial purposes until the Security Council determines that Iraq is in full compliance with this resolution and paragraphs 12 and 13 of resolution 687 (1991), and the IAEA determines that Iraq is in full compliance with its safeguards agreement with that Agency;

(vii) ensure the complete implementation of the privileges, immunities and facilities of the representatives of the Special Commission and the IAEA in accordance with its previous undertakings and their complete safety and freedom of movement;

(viii) immediately provide or facilitate the provision of any transportation, medical or logistical support requested by the Special Commission, the IAEA and their Inspection Teams;

(ix) respond fully, completely and promptly to any questions or requests from the Special Commission, the IAEA and their Inspection Teams;

4. *Determines* that Iraq retains no ownership interest in items to be destroyed, removed or rendered harmless pursuant to paragraph 12 of resolution 687 (1991);

5. *Requires* that the Government of Iraq forthwith comply fully and without delay with all its international obligations, including those set out in

the present resolution, in resolution 687 (1991), in the Treaty on the Non-Proliferation of Nuclear Weapons of 1 July 1968 and its safeguards agreement with the IAEA;

6. *Decides* to remain seized of this matter.

11. Resolution 712 (1991), 19 September 1991

Adopted at the 3008th meeting by 13 votes in favour, Cuba voting against, Yemen abstaining.

The Security Council,

Recalling its previous relevant resolutions and in particular resolutions 661 (1990) of 6 August 1990, 686 (1991) of 2 March 1991, 687 (1991) of 3 April 1991, 688 (1991) of 5 April 1991, 692 (1991) of 20 May 1991, 699 (1991) of 17 June 1991, and 705 (1991) and 706 (1991) of 15 August 1991,

Expressing its appreciation for the report dated 4 September 1991 submitted by the Secretary-General pursuant to paragraph 5 of resolution 706 (1991), [1] [1. S/23006.]

Reaffirming its concern about the nutritional and health situation of the Iraqi civilian population and the risk of a further deterioration of this situation, and underlining the need in this context for fully up-to-date assessments of the situation in all parts of Iraq as a basis for the equitable distribution of humanitarian relief to all segments of the Iraqi civilian population,

Recalling that the activities to be carried out by or on behalf of the Secretary-General to meet the purposes referred to in resolution 706 (1991) and the present resolution enjoy the privileges and immunities of the United Nations,

Acting under Chapter VII of the Charter of the United Nations,

1. *Confirms* the figure mentioned in paragraph 1 of resolution 706 (1991) as the sum authorized for the purpose of that paragraph, and reaffirms its intention to review this sum on the basis of its ongoing assessment of the needs and requirements, in accordance with paragraph 1 (d) of resolution 706 (1991);

2. *Invites* the Security Council Committee established by resolution 661 (1990) to authorise immediately, pursuant to paragraph 1 (d) of resolution 706 (1991), the release by the Secretary-General from the escrow account of the first one-third portion of the sum referred to in paragraph 1 above, such release to take place as required subject to the availability of funds in the account and, in the case of payments, to finance the purchase of foodstuffs, medicines and materials and supplies for essential civilian needs that have been notified or approved in accordance with existing procedures, subject to compliance with the procedures laid down in the report of the Secretary-General as approved in paragraph 3 below;

3. *Approves* the recommendations in the Secretary-General's report as contained in its paragraphs 57 (d) and 58;

4. *Encourages* the Secretary-General and the Security Council Committee established by resolution 661 (1990) to cooperate, in close consultation with the Government of Iraq, on a continuing basis to ensure the most effective implementation of the scheme approved in the present resolution;

5. *Decides* that petroleum and petroleum products subject to resolution 706 (1991) shall while under Iraqi title be immune from legal proceedings and not be subject to any form of attachment, garnishment or execution, and that all States shall take any steps that may be necessary under their respective domestic legal systems to assure this protection, and to ensure that the proceeds of sale are not diverted from the purposes laid down in resolution 706 (1991);

6. *Reaffirms* that the escrow account to be established by the United Nations and administered by the Secretary-General to meet the purposes of resolution 706 (1991) and the present resolution, like the Compensation Fund established by resolution 692 (1991), enjoys the privileges and immunities of the United Nations;

7. *Reaffirms* that the inspectors and other experts on mission for the United Nations, appointed for the purpose of the present resolution, enjoy privileges and immunities in accordance with the Convention on the Privileges and Immunities of the United Nations, and demands that Iraq allow them full freedom of movement and all necessary facilities;

8. *Confirms* that funds contributed from other sources may if desired, in accordance with paragraph 1 (c) of resolution 706 (1991), be deposited into the escrow account as a sub-account and be immediately available to meet Iraq's humanitarian needs as referred to in paragraph 20 of resolution 687 (1991) without any of the obligatory deductions and administrative costs specified in paragraphs 2 and 3 of resolution 706 (1991);

9. *Urges* that any provision to Iraq of foodstuffs, medicines or other items of a humanitarian character, in addition to those purchased with the funds referred to in paragraph 1 of the present resolution, be undertaken through arrangements that assure their equitable distribution to meet humanitarian needs;

10. *Requests* the Secretary-General to take the actions necessary to implement the above decisions, and authorizes him to enter into any arrangements or agreements necessary to accomplish this;

11. *Calls upon* States to cooperate fully in the implementation of resolution 706 (1991) and the present resolution, in particular with respect to any measures regarding the import of petroleum and petroleum products and the export of foodstuffs, medicines and materials and supplies for essential civilian needs as referred to in paragraph 20 of resolution 687 (1991), and also with respect to the privileges and immunities of the United Nations and its personnel implementing the present resolution, and to ensure that there are no diversions from the purposes laid down in these resolutions;

12. *Decides* to remain seized of the matter.

12. RESOLUTION 715 (1991), 11 October 1991

Adopted unanimously at the 3012th meeting,

The Security Council,

Recalling its resolutions 687 (1991) of 3 April 1991 and 707 (1991) of 15 August 1991, and its other resolutions on this matter,

Recalling in particular that under resolution 687 (1991) the Secretary-General and the Director General of the International Atomic Energy Agency were requested to develop plans for future ongoing monitoring and verification, and to submit them to the Security Council for approval,

Taking note of the report and note of the Secretary-General, transmitting the plans submitted by the Secretary-General and the Director General of the International Atomic Energy Agency,

Acting under Chapter VII of the Charter of the United Nations,

1. *Approves*, in accordance with the provisions of resolutions 687 (1991), 707 (1991) and the present resolution, the plans submitted by the Secretary-General and the Director General of the International Atomic Energy Agency [S/22871/Rev.1 and S/22872/Rev.1 and Corr.1.];

2. *Decides* that the Special Commission shall carry out the plan submitted by the Secretary-General, [S/22871/Rev.1.] as well as continuing to discharge its other responsibilities under resolutions 687 (1991), 699 (1991) and 707 (1991) and performing such other functions as are conferred upon it under the present resolution;

3. *Requests* the Director General of the International Atomic Energy Agency to carry out, with the assistance and cooperation of the Special Commission, the plan submitted by him [S/22872/Rev.1 and Corr.1.] and to continue to discharge his other responsibilities under resolutions 687 (1991), 699 (1991) and 707 (1991);

4. *Decides* that the Special Commission, in the exercise of its responsibilities as a subsidiary organ of the Security Council, shall:

(a) Continue to have the responsibility for designating additional locations for inspection and overflights;

(b) Continue to render assistance and cooperation to the Director General of the International Atomic Energy Agency, by providing him by mutual agreement with the necessary special expertise and logistical, informational and other operational support for the carrying out of the plan submitted by him;

(c) Perform such other functions, in cooperation in the nuclear field with the Director General of the International Atomic Energy Agency, as may be necessary to coordinate activities under the plans approved by the present resolution, including making use of commonly available services and information to the fullest extent possible, in order to achieve maximum efficiency and optimum use of resources;

5. *Demands* that Iraq meet unconditionally all its obligations under the plans approved by the present resolution and cooperate fully with the Special Commission and the Director General of the International Atomic Energy Agency in carrying out the plans;

6. *Decides* to encourage the maximum assistance, in cash and in kind, from all Member States to support the Special Commission and the Director General of the International Atomic Energy Agency in carrying out their activities under the plans approved by the present resolution, without prejudice to Iraq's liability for the full costs of such activities;

7. *Requests* the Committee established under resolution 661 (1990), the Special Commission and the Director General of the International Atomic Energy Agency to develop in cooperation a mechanism for monitoring any future sales or supplies by other countries to Iraq of items relevant to the implementation of section C of resolution 687 (1991) and other relevant resolutions, including the present resolution and the plans approved hereunder;

8. *Requests* the Secretary-General and the Director General of the International Atomic Energy Agency to submit to the Security Council reports on the implementation of the plans approved by the present resolution, when requested by the Security Council and in any event at least every six months after the adoption of this resolution;

9. *Decides* to remain seized of the matter.

2. PROCEEDINGS OF THE UN SECURITY COUNCIL

The numbers in square brackets at the beginning of individual speeches refer to the page number of the Provisional Verbatim Record in which that statement can be found.

*The first debate to be reproduced here ostensibly concerns the adoption of a resolution on the United Nations Iran-Iraq Military Observer Group (*see *Volume I, Section 1.10). However, two delegations used the opportunity to air their views on the outbreak of hostilities in the Gulf region.*

A. S/PV.2976, 31 January 1991

ADOPTION OF THE AGENDA

[2] **The PRESIDENT** (interpretation from French):
The provisional agenda for this meeting is before the Council in document S/Agenda/2976. Is there any objection to the adoption of the agenda?

[2] **Mr. ALARCON de QUESADA (Cuba)** (interpretation from Spanish):
We have before us a provisional agenda, the substantive item of which is "The situation between Iran and Iraq", based on the report of the Secretary-General on the United Nations Iran-Iraq Military Observer Group (UNIIMOG), and certain measures have been put forward to the Council. We hope that the Council will be able to adopt them, as it examines the prevailing situation with regard to the important tasks this Group is carrying out.

My delegation believes that it is appropriate for the Council to meet now to renew the mandate of UNIIMOG and to support it fully in the important responsibilities it is discharging.

However, my delegation cannot vote in favour of adopting the provisional agenda without voicing its deep dissatisfaction that the Council has not been able to consider a serious problem that is of concern to the entire world, a matter that is obviously the Council's most basic obligation to take up. Despite the fact that for more than one week a group of members of the Council has been asking for a meeting on an urgent basis and despite the fact that two members of the Council have requested that the Council meet to consider the war situation that currently exists in the region, thus far the Council has not done so, notwithstanding the clear and categorical provisions set forth in the Council's provisional rules of procedure.

In agreeing to consider tonight item 2 on the provisional agenda, my delegation also wishes to express its view that this body has a basic obligation to fulfil in connection with the war situation prevailing in the Gulf, the obligation to consider, to discuss and to hear the ideas and proposals member States wish to put forth -

[2] **The PRESIDENT** (interpretation from French): I call upon the representative of the United States of America on a point of order.

[3] **Mr. PICKERING (United States of America):**
As a point of order, I suggest that, unless the representative of Cuba has a proposal to make with respect to the provisional agenda before us, the debate into which he is entering is completely out of order.

[3] **The PRESIDENT** (interpretation from French):
I agree that we have before us a provisional agenda. If the representative of Cuba wishes to raise a point of order under rule 30 of the provisional rules of procedure - that is, to raise a point of order - the President will be obliged to ask the members of the Security Council to take an immediate decision on his ruling with regard to the adoption of the provisional agenda.

[3] **Mr. ALARCON de QUESADA (Cuba)** (interpretation from Spanish):
I am speaking to item 1 of the provisional agenda, which is entitled "Adoption of the agenda". My delegation has every right to express its disagreement with the manner in which attempts are being made to muzzle the Council, with the activities that have prevailed lately, in violation of our fundamental obligation under the Charter and the provisional rules of procedure. That is the point of order that should be before the members of this Council.

[4-5] **The PRESIDENT** (intrepretation from French):
I should like to remind members of the Council that we are now proceeding pursuant to rule 9 of the provisional rules of procedure, which stipulates that "The first item of the provisional agenda for each meeting of the Security Council shall be the adoption of the agenda." If a member objects to the adoption of the provisional agenda, the President will be obliged to put that challenge to the vote.

[6] **Mr. AL-ASHTAL (Yemen)** (interpretation from Arabic):
You invited us, Mr. President, to comment on the point of order raised by my colleague, the representative of the United States. Despite the fact that rule 9 of the provisional rules of procedure states that "The first item of the provisional agenda for each meeting of the Security Council shall be the adoption of the agenda", there is nothing in that or any other rule to preclude any delegation's asking to make a statement. Therefore -

[6] **The PRESIDENT** (interpretation from French):
I have to interrupt the representative of Yemen, because if he challenges the agenda, and if there is a challenge from our colleague from Cuba, I shall have to ask members of the Council to take a decision on that challenge. Rule 9 is clear:

> "The first item of the provisional agenda for each meeting of the Security Council shall be the adoption of the agenda."

If after the adoption of the agenda members of the Council wish to express their views on the item under consideration - the situation between Iran and Iraq - they may then speak on the item on the agenda, which would previously have been adopted. But if there is a challenge, I shall be obliged to put that challenge to the vote.

[6] **Mr. AL-ASHTAL (Yemen)** (interpretation from Arabic):

In these last few hours of your presidency, Mr. President, I hope you will allow us to comment more widely on the point of order that has been raised. When you interrupted me I was speaking of the point of order raised by the representative of the United States. I said that rule 9 did not preclude a statement by any member of the Security Council before the adoption of the agenda. Therefore, I say that the representative of Cuba has the right to make his statement.

I also wish to inform you, Mr. President, that I, too, should like to make a short statement, lasting about two minutes.

[7] **The PRESIDENT** (interpretation from French):

If members of the Council insist on putting their challenge to the vote, I am obliged to abide by the procedure specified in rule 9 of our provisional rules of procedure. Nowhere in the provisional rules of procedure is it stipulated that statements may be made before the agenda is adopted. We must therefore first adopt the agenda, and then if there is any challenge to this rule I shall request members of the Council to take a decision on that challenge. In other words, some would support that challenge and those who voted against would be those who would take a stand against that challenge and who would be in favour of the strict application of the Council's provisional rules of procedure pursuant to rule 9. The representatives of Cuba and Yemen have challenged the rule that has been proposed.

[7] **Mr. AL-ASHTAL (Yemen)** (interpretation from Arabic):

I did not challenge what you said about rule 9, Mr. President. My delegation considers that we can adopt the provisional agenda, and then I should like to speak on a matter pertaining to the agenda.

[7] **Mr. ALARCON de QUESADA (Cuba)** (interpretation from Spanish):

I had no doubt whatsoever, Mr. President, that I was entirely in order. In any event, the Secretariat might be kind enough to note my country's name, and then after the agenda is adopted we should like to speak in connection with the item on the agenda.

[7] **The PRESIDENT** (interpretation from French):

If there is no objection, I shall take it that the agenda is adopted.

The agenda was adopted.

THE SITUATION BETWEEN IRAN AND IRAQ

REPORT OF THE SECRETARY-GENERAL ON THE UNITED NATIONS IRAN-IRAQ MILITARY OBSERVER GROUP (S/22148)

[8] **The PRESIDENT** (interpretation from French):

I should like to inform the Council that I have received from the representatives of the Islamic Republic of Iran and of Iraq letters in which they request to be invited to participate in the discussion of the item on the Council's agenda. In accordance with the usual practice, I propose, with the consent of the Council, to invite those representatives to participate in the discussion without the right to vote, in conformity with the relevant provisions of the Charter and rule 37 of the Council's provisional rules of procedure.

There being no objection, it is so decided.

At the invitation of the President, Mr. Zarif (Islamic Republic of Iran) took a place at the Council table; Mr. Al-Nima (Iraq) took a place at the Council table.

...

[*The Council then proceeded unanimously to adopt resolution 685 (1991) concerning the United Nations Iran-Iraq Military Observer Group.*]

...

[11] **Mr. AL-ASHTAL (Yemen)** (interpretation from Arabic):

By the resolution just adopted, the Security Council has decided to extend the mandate of the United Nations Iran-Iraq Military Observer Group (UNIIMOG) for a period of one month, until 28 February 1991, in accordance with the Secretary-General's request.

The delegation of Yemen joined in voting in favour of the resolution. After an eight-year war of destruction between Iran and Iraq, a new era of relations between those two countries has begun. We hope that these new relations will help in the establishment of peace and security in the area.

Just as we are closing this chapter of the past, we are witnessing a deterioration of the situation in the region because of the major war operations now taking place in accordance with Security Council resolution 678 (1990).

On 23 January, the countries of the Arab Maghreb called for a Security Council meeting to debate the situation in the region. On 24 January, as representative of Yemen in the Security Council, I put forward a similar request. I find it most regrettable that the Security Council has to date been unable to agree to my request in accordance with rule 2 of the provisional rules of procedure. This is the first time in the history of the Security Council that, regrettably, a request of this kind has not been accepted.

The war in the Gulf may lead to a crisis in the Security Council, which we fear may lead to paralysis of its work. It was incumbent on my delegation to put this problem forward because we believe the Security Council must always stand against war, particularly since these war options have gone beyond our view of resolution 678 (1990). What we are witnessing today is more like an attempt to destroy the military and scientific infrastructure of Iraq than an attempt to liberate Kuwait.

We recognize the need for Iraq to withdraw from Kuwait and for restoration of Kuwait's full sovereignty. We call upon you, Mr. President, and the President for February speedily to consider our request so that the Security Council may, openly in this Chamber, take the appropriate measures.

[12] **Mr. ALARCON de QUESADA (Cuba)** (interpretation from Spanish):

...

My delegation referred to the contradiction facing the Council when we met to consider this agenda item and the situation that has prevailed in the last two weeks. We thought that in this agenda item we had found the right framework for our comments. Nowhere in the provisional rules of procedure have we found any reference to possible constraints on the right of Council members to speak in connection with the adoption of the agenda before its adoption. I do hope that now no one will deny that the subject to which I referred is related - and quite considerably, at that - to the subject of the resolution just adopted.

I would imagine that my colleagues have read the Secretary-General's report (S/22148). Paragraph 19 is the report's longest paragraph, and in it he is obliged to refer to the real war taking place in the region at the present time, which directly affects UNIIMOG's compliance with its mandate. My delegation wishes to draw members' attention to the fact that it does not serve the interests of this body that - as we express our appreciation for the efforts and praiseworthy mission being carried out by the members of UNIIMOG, and as we agree with the Secretary-General's final observations with regard to continuation of the process to consolidate peace and put an end to the most regrettable conflict that has divided Iran and Iraq for so many years - the Council has ironically not yet been able to meet to perform a clear duty spelled out in the provisional rules of procedure, a primarily moral duty: to preserve future generations from the scourge of war, to do whatever can be done for peace. The members of the Council must not be deprived of the right under the Charter to be heard. Above all, the Council must not be placed in a situation in which it could be found to be ignoring the norms governing its activities.

In paragraph 19 of the Secretary-General's report, we read:

> "With the deterioration of the situation in the second week of January 1991 and the requirement to ensure the safety of UNIIMOG personnel, it was decided as a precautionary measure to thin out the staff, both military and civilian, at the headquarters at Baghdad." (*S/22148, para. 19*)

That is appropriate. We agree with that view. We think it only fair to ensure the safety of UNIIMOG personnel, military and civilian. But my delegation is concerned about the thousands of women and children of both sides in this confrontation who are even now losing their lives without the Council's doing anything to prevent this from happening.

[13] The PRESIDENT (interpretation from French):

I think we have now reached the end of our work. However, I wish to reply to a remark made by the representative of Yemen and to say to him that all members of the Council are aware that rule 2 of the provisional rules of procedure was duly applied by the President. He has thus received a mandate from all members of the Council to conduct consultations. It is clearly understood that the members of the Council are unanimous in supporting the principle of convening a formal meeting of the Council. The President has therefore received a mandate to convene to agree on the date of that meeting.

Hence the President for February will continue the consultations that his predecessor, in my person, began, and will prepare for that formal meeting in terms of form, substance and content, as was the case with the 13 other meetings of the Security Council that were the framework for the Council's decisions marked by the adoption of 12 resolutions by its members.

There are no further speakers for this meeting. The Security Council has thus concluded the present stage of its consideration of the item on its agenda.

...

B. S/PV.2977 (Part I), 13 February 1991

[*A meeting of the Council had been formally requested by the delegations of Algeria, the Libyan Arab Jamahiriya, Mauritania, Morocco, Tunisia (on 23 January 1991), by Yemen (on 24 January 1991), and by Cuba (on 28 January)*].

[2] Sir David HANNAY (United Kingdom):

...

I have asked to speak because I wish to propose, in accordance with rule 48 of the provisional rules of procedure, that the Council decide now to meet in private to consider the item on the agenda which we have just adopted. This proposal, as members know, has as its inspiration some thoughts put forward by the representative of Austria in our earlier informal contacts. I wish to take those thoughts up and put them forward as a formal proposal now.

It is clearly right, as the provisional rules of procedure envisage, that as a general rule the Council should meet in public with open attendance and coverage by the media. But the rules of procedure also provide for private meetings in exceptional circumstances. In the view of my delegation, these circumstances are exceptional.

First, the Council has adopted a series of resolutions in response to Iraq's invasion of Kuwait, culminating in resolution 678 (1990), authorizing the use of all necessary means to uphold and implement the earlier resolutions. Military action has been undertaken by a number of Member States cooperating with the Government of Kuwait and has the backing of the Council. It has as its sole purpose the upholding of the Council's decisions.

At the same time, diplomacy is actively under way, as it has been ever since 2 August 1990, to see if there is any way to bring about a peaceful settlement of the conflict on the basis of the Council's resolutions.

The Council therefore has grave and particular responsibilities which it must take into account when deciding how it should act in the context of the present requests for a meeting. We should do nothing which could detract from the Council's unity of purpose or blur the signal that is sent to the outside world. In our view, we cannot afford to send mixed signals when that might only delay the realization that a peaceful solution to this crisis has to begin with Iraqi withdrawal from Kuwait.

This occasion here today calls for serious and careful consideration of all developments away from the glare of immediate publicity. If members or non-members of the Council have proposals to make which they believe could lead to implementation of the Council's resolutions and the liberation of Kuwait, it is right that they should be heard here. But, in our view, members ought to be able to explore carefully with them how those proposals will assist the Council's objectives and, above all, how they have been received by Iraq, which currently constitutes the sole obstacle to peace. All that discussion is better handled in a private meeting.

On past occasions, in the context of Western Sahara in 1975, Council members decided that the format of private meetings would best assist such exploratory discussion designed to clarify ideas and identify possible ways forward. They chose a format which enabled them to enter into a dialogue with those who participated, to ask questions and to receive answers. We believe that that format offers the right model for today's meeting.

In making this proposal, my delegation has no intention of trying to limit participation or restrict knowledge of the proceedings. We recognize that the issues are of universal interest to all Members of the United Nations. It is right that all should be free to attend the debate if they wish to do so and request to do so, and to participate. It is right too that the normal verbatim record should be taken and circulated; I have no intention of limiting and am not proposing to limit that by the use of rule 51. But we do believe that on this occasion the Council will carry out its functions better if the public aspect of the meeting - the presence of the media - does not influence or even distort the course and nature of our debate. That is the reason for the proposal I have made.

...

[4] Mr. AL-ASHTAL (Yemen) (interpretation from Arabic):

...

I have asked to speak in opposition to the proposal put forward by the representative of the United Kingdom. I do so as the Council member who requested the convening of this meeting in the first place; that request was made on 24 January. I oppose the proposal also on behalf of the representatives of the Arab Maghreb States, who, in a letter dated 23 January 1991 addressed to the President of the Security Council, had also requested the convening of a meeting: the representatives of Algeria, the Libyan Arab Jamahiriya, Mauritania, Morocco and Tunisia to the United Nations. That letter was followed by letters from the delegations of Jordan and the Sudan supporting the request for a meeting. On 28 January the delegation of Cuba, a member of the Security Council, made a similar request.

My objection to the proposal that this meeting be held in private is based on the position we adopted in calling for the convening of a meeting in the first place.

Allow me to explain clearly why we oppose the Council's holding a private meeting to consider the deteriorating situation in the Gulf under the agenda item "The situation between Iraq and Kuwait".

The delegation of Yemen, as a member of the Security Council, acts consistently in accordance with the great responsibility it assumed upon becoming a member of the Council. It is in keeping with that sense of responsibility that I shall attempt to explain my delegation's opposition to transforming this meeting into a private one.

The United Nations is a democratic Organization. If there is anything that distinguished the Organization from others, it is its transparency. The Organization has no secrets. Its Charter is clear and its rules and regulations are equally so; all of its proceedings take place in public. This may have resulted from the concern felt by the founding fathers with regard to secret meetings that do not reflect public opinion - meetings in which certain agreements may be hatched in a manner inconsistent with general understanding and, in some cases, even counter to public opinion, to which we must show the deepest respect.

The first words of the Charter are "We the peoples of the United Nations." We are not just the representatives of States. The Security Council does not represent only 15 States: it represents the entire membership of the United Nations and all the peoples of the world. Hence - save in exceptional circumstances to which I shall refer later - everyone expects the Council to meet in public and in a clear and transparent manner.

The exceptions to this established United Nations tradition have been three in number. Members of the Council are familiar with them, as are, I am sure, other representatives here. In 1973 a private meeting was held to consider a draft resolution submitted by States not members of the Council, and during that meeting a statement was heard in explanation of vote, after which the meeting was adjourned. That meeting was attended only by members of the Security Council. A second private meeting was held in 1974 concerning the situation in Cyprus. At that meeting the present Secretary-General of the United Nations, Mr. Javier Perez de Cuellar, was presiding as his country's representative to the United Nations. It was a very short meeting, during which information was submitted by the representative of Turkey; the meeting was then adjourned. In 1975 a third private meeting of the Council was held to hear the representatives of Spain, the Western Sahara and Algeria and to address questions to those representatives on a matter pertaining to the Western Sahara at that time. As I recall, the subject was the so-called Green March. After those questions had been disposed of, the meeting was adjourned.

Today, the representative of the United Kingdom has proposed that this meeting of the Council be transformed into a private one - not for the purpose of putting questions to a delegation on the events in the Gulf or on the situation in the region in general, nor to listen to the parties concerned on any specific question in the Gulf, nor indeed to hear new information from any quarter on the situation in the region, but solely to exclude the media and to begin a series of discussions in which more than 16 Member States have so far inscribed their names to participate. Additional Members may be inscribed on the list of speakers later on. Do we need a private meeting to listen to statements by delegations that represent Members of the United Nations? Do we need a private meeting, particularly since verbatim records of the meeting will be published the following day?

Why do we need a private meeting at all? It has been said that the Council must not appear to be divided and that a public meeting might give the impression that division exists in the Council. No problem is created by difference of opinion. I respect all the members of the Council and the positions taken by their States, and that respect is, I am sure, reciprocated. My delegation voted against one of the resolutions adopted by the Council. What more are we therefore going to do? What is there to conceal, and from whom would we be concealing it?

We are told that a public meeting would serve propaganda purposes: to enable the media to listen to us. I would ask: Why should the media not listen while we discuss a war that is threatening international peace and security? Why can we not express what we want to express before the whole world? Have we not been doing exactly that for six months now? Have we not debated and considered questions pertaining to the Gulf on 12 occasions? Have we not adopted 12 resolutions, the last of which - one of the most important resolutions ever adopted by the Council - was discussed when this Chamber was filled with spectators and in the presence of our foreign ministers?

It is also said that we want a public meeting for domestic consumption in our own countries. Why not? Why can we not speak so that people in our countries can hear what we say?

It is well known that there is great concern in Yemen. It is well known that massive demonstrations are going on in the whole region. As officials and responsible people, we are called upon to express our point of view on this war, to seek by all means possible to contain the war and to do our utmost for the restoration of peace. Why should we not inform public opinion in our countries? Why does public opinion in the West have its value while ours is regarded as having absolutely no value? Maybe public opinion has no value when freedom is not exercised; there are a number of States where we hear of no popular reaction. But for us, when public opinion calls upon the State to do something, while we are members of the Council are we supposed to remain silent, to speak in a private meeting, just among ourselves?

It is enough to look at what is happening in the States of the Arab Maghreb, which have requested that the Council meet, to appreciate the sensitivity of the subject, the seriousness of this request and the position of others. I am speaking now, naturally, on behalf of Yemen, but I am also expressing the feelings of millions of Arabs, millions of Muslims and millions of other people the world over, who every day see on their television screens the tragedies of war and who hope that this war will cease. They hope that the problem will be solved peacefully, in a manner that ensures the independence of Kuwait, the withdrawal of the Iraqi forces from Kuwait and the restoration of Kuwait's sovereignty.

From the very first day we have said that although we are a small country we cannot tolerate the occupation or invasion of another State. We still adhere to that position, because it is in that way that we, all the small countries, defend ourselves. But we also want the crisis to be resolved by peaceful means. We have done a great deal to bring about its solution by peaceful means and in an Arab framework.

A number of questions are being asked, not only by us but by public opinion and the media. There is nothing secret about these questions and inquiries. People ask what are the objectives of the war currently raging on the basis of resolution 678 (1990). That is a legitimate question. When we look at what is happening, when we read of the plans being made, when we see the way in which operations are taking place and when we hear the declarations and statements made by public officials, do we not have the right to ask what the objectives of those military operations are?

The Security Council has authorized the use of all means for the implementation of its resolutions. Do the words "all ... means" exclude peaceful means? Since the phrase was interpreted as meaning the use of force, does not the Council have the right to determine the framework within which force may be used? It is easy to start wars, but it is difficult to control their extent. Sometimes military commanders do not look too intently at the political objectives. The Security Council has one political objective: Iraq's withdrawal from Kuwait, the restoration of Kuwait's sovereignty and the solution of the crisis between Iraq and Kuwait and in the whole region by peaceful means.

When we see on television the military operations taking place in northern Iraq, with civilian areas being targeted, do we not have the right to ask what the objective is? Does not the Council, which adopted the resolution concerned, have the right to ask that in public? Is it not in the interest of the Council and the United Nations that the Council should be constantly scrutinized by the other Members of the United Nations and public opinion?

There are many questions about the way in which the war is being conducted and about the weapons being used. Do we not have the right to ask those questions?

Why are places so remote from Kuwait being bombed? We read in the newspapers of civilian casualties. There was an example of such a report in the *Washington Post* the day before yesterday. It was based on a Kurdish source, not an Iraqi source, because, most regrettably, there seems to be a policy in Iraq not to publicize the civilian casualties. These massive military operations cannot but lead to rampant destruction and widespread innocent civilian casualties. Therefore, I was not surprised to read in the *Washington Post* that Mr. Barazani had said there had been 3,000 casualties - dead and wounded - in certain parts of Sulaymaniyah alone. I was not surprised when he spoke of a bombing raid on a cement factory and a spinning and weaving mill. How does that assist in the liberation of Kuwait?

There are many questions. The event that took place today shakes the conscience of every human being. I do not believe that even the pilots who bombed the shelter, with a reported toll of 500 people, are happy with such results. No human being, on any side of the war, can fail to be disgusted at the use of force in a manner that targets the innocent and the weak and civilian installations.

There is a problem in the Gulf. An error was made by Iraq in its occupation of Kuwait. Are we to allow another error to rectify the first? Are we to allow a third-world country to be destroyed by massive forces? Where is the proportionality in that? There is no proportion in such a reaction, nor in the equipment and the power being used. Is there no other way to solve this crisis?

Do we not have the right to call upon the Security Council to have recourse to all means to arrive at a solution? I agree with Mr. Brzezinski, who in an article published in *The New York Times* said that there seemed to be an insistence on the failure of diplomatic efforts. We now demand that new action be taken through diplomatic means, as is happening currently through Mr. Primakov's visit to Baghdad yesterday. We view with satisfaction that a major Power should be making such an effort in such a situation. We do not feel at all happy when the Council is relaxed, waiting for the results of this war.

I have objected to the convening of a private meeting because nothing beyond what I have just said will be said at such a meeting. We might hear an account from another side, but it will not be any more important or any clearer than what I have just stated. We believe that the Council must not remain remote from the rest of the membership of the United Nations, that no dangerous precedent be set in the history of the United Nations, while we are on the threshold of the so-called new world order, so that this Council is transformed into a secret institution.

This new world order cannot but embrace the entire world, and it cannot be installed except through the United Nations and its Charter, as well as this Council. Short of that, it will only be schemes making use of the United Nations to serve particular purposes.

We are now witnessing the United Nations and this Council giving a blank cheque for the use of force, without attempting to interpret the objectives of the law or without reviewing how the war is conducted or without follow-up on the work for peaceful efforts.

For all the above, we call for this meeting to remain a public meeting. If a private meeting is held, do I then not have the right to wonder why such a private meeting should be held and as to the intention of those who requested it. Those who requested this current meeting do not want a private meeting. What justification is there for a private meeting? Is there a new State member asking for the convening of such a meeting, or do we not need such a meeting and, therefore, perhaps we have to wait until agreement is reached on the convening of a public meeting?

Had it been within our power to participate even in the simplest way possible in putting forward a new idea and making a new effort towards peace through this meeting, we would have done it.

I should like to reaffirm that Yemen is constantly seeking peace in our region. It was with deep sadness that we have witnessed formations, the logic of war, the logic of confrontation, which will lead to nothing but further destruction and deprive our Arab countries of their massive wealth, which is right now being used to attack their children.

...

[17] Mr. ALARCON de QUESADA (Cuba) (interpretation from Spanish:

...

My delegation too wishes to oppose the proposal put forward by the representative of the United Kingdom. I should like at the outset to point out that he referred to certain past situations in which the Council decided to meet in private. But I did not hear anything about the first such precedent, which, I believe, was also a British initiative. In 1956, at the 735th meeting of the Security Council, the Council considered the situation regarding the conflict that had arisen in connection with the Suez Canal as a result of its nationalization, to which the Egyptian Government had proceeded in exercise of its sovereign right, its being a fundamental national resource of that country.

The representative of the United Kingdom at the time spoke in the Council and explained his country's position in connection with the substance of the item that was then under consideration, and he made a similar, but not identical, proposal to the one we have heard today. I shall now quote from the official records of the Council:

> "I have been thinking, during the last day or two, of the best way for us to organize our deliberations with regard to this matter, and perhaps it may be convenient if I indicate my thoughts at this stage to my colleagues.
>
> "It seems to me that, after there has been a chance for those who wish to state their views in public session, it might be a good thing for this Council to move into private session. I would hope that we might reach that point some time on Tuesday, 9 October, perhaps. That would give us an opportunity to consider the next steps in a less formal atmosphere." (*735th meeting, paras. 94 and 95*)

The representative of the United Kingdom put this idea forward on 5 October 1956. During the following four days the Security Council continued to meet and heard all those who wished to speak in public meetings, before the Council proceeded to hold a private meeting.

In that connection, I should like to say, first, that it is regrettable that on this occasion the United Kingdom representative has not pointed to that very valuable precedent. At the very least, that would have served as a kind of courteous apology to a group of non-members of the Council that quite some time ago asked for a meeting of the Council.

It has been said that we should try to avoid giving the impression that we are divided or that there is a lack of cohesiveness in the Council. But how can we avoid giving that impression when we have just adopted an agenda that could not be more revealing? It reads: "The situation between Iraq and Kuwait", and it refers to three letters: the letter of 23 January 1991 from the representatives of the Maghreb States, the letter of 24 January 1991 from the representative of Yemen, and the letter of 28 January 1991 which I addressed to the President of the Security Council.

In any event, what is said at this meeting will inevitably remain in the records of the Security Council. No matter how much anyone may wish to disregard the facts, it will be obvious to all that for the past three weeks the Security Council has been confronted by a situation which, to say the least, is very unusual.

In this respect, I should like to recall at this meeting of the Council the view expressed by the United States Government on 21 April 1966, in regard to a situation that does not even remotely relate to this inexplicable delay in convening the Security Council. The then representative of the United States, Ambassador Arthur Goldberg, deemed it necessary to send an official letter to the President of the Security Council and to ask that it be circulated as an official document of the Council. That is why I have a copy of it before me. I think that, as a colophon to this story about the Council's inability to meet in the midst of a war that is of concern to everyone - at least to everyone except, it would appear, the Security Council, so far - it is important to recall what Ambassador Goldberg said on that occasion, when the Security Council, in the opinion of the United States, was not being convened as quickly as it should have been to consider a question that it should have been considering and that, I repeat, did not even remotely resemble the one before us now. This is what Ambassador Goldberg said in his letter of 21 April 1966:

> "The Security Council is given primary responsibility for the maintenance of international peace and security, according to Article 24 of the United Nations Charter, 'in order to ensure prompt and effective action'. It is required by Article 28 to be 'so organized as to be able to function continuously'. These two Articles established the responsibility of the Council to be available for emergency action to maintain peace and security. The provisional rules of procedure of the Security Council are designed and must be interpreted so as to ensure that the Council can fulfil the responsibilities these Articles place upon it.
>
> "The dominant paragraph of the provisional rules of procedure of the Security Council accordingly is rule 2, which states that 'The President shall call a meeting of the Security Council at the request of any member of the Security Council'. The rule is mandatory and does not give the President the choice of convening or not convening the Council when a member so requests. This has been made clear on numerous occasions. ...
>
> "Even if a majority of Council members are opposed to a meeting, the meeting must be held. Those members opposed to the meeting may express their views on the agenda when the meeting is convened, may seek to adjourn the meeting, or to defeat proposals submitted to it, but the President is bound to convene the Council on a request under rule 2, unless that request is not pressed.
>
> "Subject to rule 2, the President is given, under rule 1, the authority and responsibility to set the time of a meeting. In so doing, the President acts not as a representative of his country but as a servant of the Council, and he does not exercise an arbitrary or unfettered discretion. His decision must be related to the requirements of Articles 24 and 28 of the Charter and of rule 2 of the provisional rules of procedure, and to the urgency of the request and situation. A request for an urgent meeting must be respected and decided upon on an urgent basis, and the timing established responsive to the urgency of the situation." *(S/7261, paras. 1, 2 and 3)*

The letter is of course much longer. I recommend it to anyone wishing to know more about how the major Powers interpreted the Charter and our rules of procedure in other circumstances.

The fact of the matter is that, for reasons I do not need to go into now, on the twenty-eighth day of the war the Council is meeting for the first time - despite the efforts that have been made and the specific requests that have been put forward for some time not only by members of the Security Council but by other Members of the United Nations, on whose behalf it is to be assumed the members of the Council act.

I am sure that, like me, all representatives have received not one, not two, not three but many letters from persons who do not represent Governments, who do not represent States but who are part of the "peoples of the United Nations". Of course I shall not cite all the letters I have received. I shall mention only those from four religious organizations of this country and other countries, as well as international religious organizations, that I have received today. They all remind us of the same thing: that the Security Council has certain obligations *vis-à-vis* world peace; that the Security Council has obligations *vis-à-vis* the children and women, the civilians who are losing their lives now; that the Security Council has an unshirkable responsibility under the Charter to act in order to restore peace, and to do so as a matter of the greatest urgency.

...

Of course, a State has the right to ask that this organ meet as a matter of urgency; it does not have the right to shirk such a request. But this body also has an obligation to show a certain sensitivity to requests that may come from anywhere. And now, finally, thanks above all to your leadership, Mr. President, and to the manner in which you have conducted the proceedings of the Council, which deserves the gratitude and appreciation of all the Members of the United Nations, the Security Council seems to remember that rule 2 exists. But even now, having reached this stage, the principal problem is that this kind of shameful outcome of our unshirkable obligation to meet is taking place without anyone knowing about it, without there being any witnesses, without representatives of other Governments being able to participate, without representatives of the press being present - and they are, after all, those who can convey to ... the many ... writing to us every day, a message of encouragement, such as "Well, at least the Security Council is considering the possibility of restoring peace."

My delegation is categorically opposed to the idea of this meeting's taking place in these circumstances, behind closed doors, simply because the Security Council has for six-and-a-half months been considering the same subject with all the publicity one could possibly imagine. We have met here on 12 occasions to adopt 12 resolutions in front of the television cameras, before live radio microphones, in the presence of dozens of newspapermen, and on every occasion in response to those who had asked for a meeting of the Council.

Before the press, with all the publicity required, the Council adopted resolution 660 (1990), which had the full support of my delegation. It was a resolution that did reflect the unanimous opinion of the members of the Council, and I would say expressed a universally supported view that the independence and sovereignty of Kuwait should be respected and restored, and that the occupation of that territory should cease as soon as possible.

Resolution 661 (1990) was also adopted with full publicity. But let us not be deceived. That resolution did not receive the endorsement of all delegations. Quite clearly it did not. Before the same cameras, which were at that time not considered an obstacle, we put forward our views. At that time we did not believe - and indeed we still hold the same view - that such action was justified. We thought the Council acted over-hastily at a time when the Iraqi authorities were saying they would initiate the withdrawal of their troops from Kuwaiti territory. The representative of Iraq confirmed that here because an important meeting of Heads of Arab States was about to take place. The economic sanctions imposed by resolution 661 (1990) were unparalleled in the history of the United Nations. They were so all-encompassing, so complete, that in effect they represented a double standard from the Security Council. Throughout its history, the Council had never done anything similar, even when there were invasions of small countries by major powerful neighbours or when foreign territories had been occupied through the use of force. Territories occupied by Israel can continue to be occupied without the Council's feeling obliged even to consider Chapter VII. Panama and Grenada can be invaded by a powerful neighbour without the Council's even considering any kind of sanctions. Southern Lebanon can continue to be occupied. Many other such cases might come to anyone's mind.

The Council's inconsistency and its hasty action - we made this point cogently at the time - indicated the will of one particular Power and its determination to use the conflict that had been created with the occupation of Kuwait by Iraq for purposes having nothing to do with the restoration of Kuwaiti independence but rather to create the basis for military intervention in the region.

In the full glare of publicity, two weeks later the Council adopted resolution 665 (1990). Have we forgotten that before its adoption my delegation drew attention to the fact that the Council had not even waited to receive the first report of the Secretary-General on the manner in which the economic sanctions in resolution 661 (1990) were being implemented.

I wondered whether my colleagues had forgotten that in resolution 661 (1990), which Cuba did not vote in favour of, *inter alia*, the Secretary-General had been requested to present his first report on the manner in which the sanctions were being implemented one month after the adoption of resolution 661 (1990). This Council, with all the television cameras running, without any justification, had to adopt a resolution two weeks before the date on which the Secretary-General was to submit his report! My delegation criticized that resolution most harshly because it implied authorization of the use of naval forces already deployed in the region without this Council's having discussed that. But the naval units could not interrupt their exercise in the area and carry out an economic embargo, the strict fulfilment of which had not been questioned by anyone. In respect of the resolution's implementation, we had requested the Secretary-General to submit a report two weeks later. But no one was courteous enough to wait for our Secretary-General's assessment before allowing the use of military units for the alleged implementation of the embargo.

My delegation detected a clear violation of the Charter of our Organization in that resolution. Seeds were sown in that moment that have now borne bitter fruit. Two principles have apparently taken hold in the work of the Council - principles now in vogue in a few countries and which some Governments seem to admire: "deregulation" and "privatization". The Council very quickly forgot that in order to authorize the use of military force in accordance with the Charter, there is a specific procedure that must be followed. The Council must also assume authority when that is done and a certain monitoring must take place. The rules were set aside and certain States were empowered to act on their own initiative. In other words, they were authorized by the United Nations to "privatize" the use of armed force. Finally, in the full glare of publicity, with all the television cameras of the world rolling, the Security Council adopted resolution 678 (1990), which was a culmination of the process of deregulating and privatizing the Council's essential activities.

Resolution 678 (1990) authorized some to use whatever means they felt necessary without the Council taking the steps clearly laid down in the Charter regarding the use of military force. But at least the final paragraph of that resolution states that the Council will remain seized of the matter.

Some day, one of my colleagues who have so eagerly supported these 12 Security Council resolutions should kindly explain to the representatives of public opinion, of the peoples of the United Nations, the strange phenomenon of this body being used on 12 occasions to lay the foundations of so serious a thing as war, as scores of people throughout the world remind us every day - of this war supposedly being conducted pursuant to the Council's resolutions, and of this august body, in a majestic display of its sense of responsibility, remaining aloof ever since the war began.

I believe that mankind requires some sort of explanation of this curious phenomenon.

The Security Council has been used as a kind of glove. When it so suits us, we put it on and use it for certain purposes; when it becomes a bother we simply take it off and throw it away. That will be the unfortunate plight of the Security Council unless it confronts the specific situation that has been created in the Gulf, unless it deals with the war's development in the way only it can do: in the same manner as it discussed and adopted all past resolutions - in public, in the full view of all of those who represent the peoples of the United Nations. Just as in similar public circumstances in the past, we would not all be saying the same thing or taking the same approach, but at least some Members of the Organization would have an opportunity to exercise their right to speak out - to speak to world public opinion and express whatever concerns, anxieties and ideas they might have.

In my delegation's opinion, this meeting is finally beginning, though at a time too far removed from when it was first requested and at the risk of being immediately diverted from the public light, as is preferable to some. Yet my delegation believes that it is our obligation and duty to continue to follow this problem as we have done in the past, especially now that war has broken out in the region. We have every obligation in the world to consider the extent to which events in the military arena truly correspond to the authorization of the United Nations or whether they far exceed it. We must consider - as churches, cultural institutions, individuals and simple citizens of the world request us to do - the tragedy that is being imposed on thousands of civilians, particularly women and children, who are being subjected to the most ferocious and relentless bombing. We must consider, for example, to what extent Security Council resolution 678 (1990) is in line with certain other resolutions, not those of the Security Council but of a body that some may feel lacks a certain importance: the General Assembly of the United Nations.

The General Assembly, on 4 December 1990 - six days after the adoption of Security Council resolution 678 (1990) - adopted a resolution that is very pertinent to our current discussion. The resolution refers to armed attacks that could take place on nuclear facilities. One hundred and forty-one Members of the United Nations voted in favour of that resolution. One Member voted against it - I will let members of the Council check the records to see who it was, though I do not believe it will be difficult for anyone here to guess. Among the 141, there were many States belonging to the so-called coalition that is at present waging war against Iraq, as well as all the States in the Gulf region and a number of members of the Security Council, including some who voted in favour of resolution 678 (1990) and even some who co-sponsored it.

What does General Assembly resolution 45/58 J say? In operative paragraph 1, it says that the General Assembly: (*spoke in English*)

> "*Recognizes* that an armed attack or a threat of armed attack on a safeguarded nuclear facility, operational or under construction, would create a situation in which the Security Council would have to act immediately in accordance with the provisions of the Charter of the United Nations, including measures under Chapter VII" (*General Assembly resolution 45/58 J*).

(*continued in Spanish*)

I infer from that decision that when my colleagues the coalition members of the Council adopted resolution 678 (1990) a week before the adoption of resolution 45/58 J they were voting in favour of the use of all necessary means against Iraq, but ruling out any attack on nuclear facilities, operational or in construction. That must have been their intent or they would not have voted in favour of that resolution, as did the overwhelming majority of Members of the Organization.

Another document, conveyed to the President of the Council by the representative of the United States, contains the transcript of a 23 January press conference given by the United States Secretary of Defense and the Chairman of the United States Joint Chiefs of Staff. At that press conference, General Powell said:

> "We have targeted that nuclear facility they have very carefully. I have looked at the bomb damage assessment myself with trained analysts, and I think I can confirm for you that the two operating reactors they had are both gone, they're down, they're finished." (*S/22168, annex, p. 10*)

It is obvious that a State has informed the Council that it has done something in clear and direct violation of the resolution adopted by the General Assembly subsequent to the Council's adoption of resolution 678 (1990). One can only assume that when the General Assembly resolution was adopted - with affirmative votes of many present around this table who voted also in favour of the Council's resolution - it was because members had decided such things ought not to be done. The International Atomic Energy Agency had clearly enunciated the same position some time earlier.

Is not the Security Council obligated to consider the extent to which there have been violations of those parameters for the use of force authorized in this case by the Council? Is not the Council obligated to meet to consider any measure or idea put forward by any State, even if it does not necessarily pertain to the continuation of the war? It seems to us that "all necessary means" need not be interpreted only as the use of missiles, bombs and bullets. Members may have other views; they may share the opinion we have openly and forthrightly expressed: that the war must stop, that the bombing must stop immediately, and that the Security Council has the obligation to explore other ways and means of resolving the conflict.

We believe the Council must meet in public, in keeping with the requests made by a number of sovereign States Members of the Organization. It must meet in public also because the war is not the property of the 15 representatives seated at this table; it is of legitimate concern and interest to all States Members of the Organization and a source of legitimate concern and anguish for the peoples of the entire world, which have the right to know the views of the Council - which have the right to follow our deliberations and to see that our consideration of this important subject is taking place not in the dark but in the light of day.

[37] The PRESIDENT:

...

The representative of the United Kingdom has proposed that this meeting be held in private, with the understanding that rule 51 of the provisional rules of procedure of the Security Council will not be invoked on this occasion and that the verbatim record of this meeting of the Security Council will be circulated in all the working languages as an unrestricted document in accordance with rule 49, and that attendance and requests for participation will be treated in the usual manner.

We have also heard statements by the representatives of Yemen and Cuba.

The representative of the United Kingdom has proposed that the meeting be held in private. I shall therefore put that proposal to the vote.

I call first on members wishing to make statements before the voting.

[37] Mr. VORONTSOV (Union of Soviet Socialist Republics) (interpretation from Russian):

...

The Soviet delegation supports the proposal that the Security Council meet in private to discuss the situation between Iraq and Kuwait. At the request of a number of States Members of the United Nations, this meeting is taking place at a dramatic moment. The Iraqi leadership persists in its refusal to comply with the resolutions of the Security Council calling for the unconditional and immediate withdrawal of Iraqi troops from Kuwait, despite the hostilities undertaken in accordance with Security Council resolution 678 (1990) to ensure the implementation of the world community's demand.

The Soviet Union is firm in its loyalty to the Council's resolutions and insists on their full and unconditional implementation. That was reaffirmed in the statement made on 9 February by the President of the Soviet Union, Mikhail Sergeiyevich Gorbachev; it is contained in document S/22215, which all members have had an opportunity to see.

The Soviet Union continues to see it as its political and moral duty to do everything it can to ensure the early implementation of Security Council resolutions and an end to the bloodshed. The settlement of the conflict by peaceful means requires that Iraq immediately withdraw its troops from Kuwait. That is precisely the aim of the political efforts of the Soviet Union and a number of other States. Those efforts continue.

Following the personal meeting between Evgeny Primakov and the President of Iraq, held in Baghdad on 12 February, the Iraqi Foreign Minister, Mr. Tariq Aziz, will visit Moscow in a few days' time.

In these circumstances, the present meeting of the Security Council, convened at the request of a number of

States, should promote Iraq's unconditional compliance with the relevant decisions of the Council. It should serve as a lever of joint influence on Baghdad to come to the only correct solution: a statement that it will withdraw from Kuwait.

In our view public debate in the Security Council may be incorrectly interpreted in Baghdad and may thus make more difficult the intensive efforts being made by the Soviet Union and other countries to achieve a peaceful settlement. At the same time we do not exclude the possibility that comprehensive and businesslike discussion of the question of how to arrive at a solution to the Kuwaiti crisis on the basis of the Security Council resolutions in a private meeting of the Council may provide the necessary additional impetus to the diplomatic and political efforts already under way. In tranquil circumstances and free from the public presence, we must attempt to analyse all the questions and ideas in the minds of those who have called for this meeting. We must also raise pertinent questions and have a comprehensive discussion of possible ideas and proposals as to how to begin an intensive search for some peaceful way in which the Council's resolutions can be complied with - that is, Iraq's immediate and unconditional withdrawal from Kuwait - and from that discussion we must then draw the necessary conclusions.

On the basis of the foregoing points, my delegation will vote in favour of the proposal that the Council's further work take place in a businesslike atmosphere in private.

[41] Mr. Pickering (United States of America):

...

We are discussing today an important procedural question about how the Council deals seriously with one of the most important issues it has ever had before it. We have been grappling with the question of what next steps the Council should take regarding the Gulf crisis. A wide variety of concerns have been expressed about the need to maintain the integrity of the Council's decisions, the impact of the war, the failure of Iraq to respond to diplomatic overtures and the need for the Council to remain engaged. We have listened carefully, for my Government shares many of the concerns which have been expressed, even if we do not always agree with all of the conclusions.

After having weighed the pros and cons of a variety of options, we have concluded that the interests of all the members of the Council, and of the Members of the United Nations, can best be served now by a proposal advanced by the Austrian delegation some days ago: the holding of a formal but private meeting of the Security Council. We believe this will enable all who wish to do so to express their views and to exchange ideas in an appropriate setting. At the same time this proposal will enable delegations to get statements on the record if they believe it desirable. But, most of all, I hope that it will offer the opportunity for a serious and constructive discussion, free from the glare of instantaneous publicity and the misinterpretation and misuse to which this meeting might be subject. We have no wish or intent to stifle debate. Indeed, we support this proposal because it will encourage genuine and effective give and take.

We meet at a time of considerable gravity. The Security Council has acted to ensure full Iraqi compliance with its resolutions. It has taken the most difficult of decisions for Member States of the United Nations: to authorize the use of force to confront unprovoked aggression and to achieve a return to international legitimacy and legality. It was compelled to make this decision. A few nations still find it all too easy to turn to violence and aggression to achieve their ends, counting on the acquiescence of others. Unfortunately, Iraq has given the world no reason to believe that it ever intended to comply with the resolutions of the Security Council and the will of the international community.

No one likes the fact that we have been compelled by Saddam Hussein to respond to force with force. There are no greater advocates of peace than those who are called upon to pay the price for defending the principles of international law and conduct contained in the United Nations Charter. Again, we call upon Iraq to withdraw immediately from Kuwait and to comply with the 12 relevant Security Council resolutions. By doing so - and only by doing so - Iraq could end the bloodshed right now, today.

The objectives of the United States and the coalition effort are clear and limited and are set out in the Security Council resolutions. They are: the withdrawal of Iraq from Kuwait, the restoration of Kuwait's legitimate Government and the restoration of international peace and security in the area. Our aims are no broader than to compel Iraq's compliance with the resolutions.

President Bush stated at the outset of coalition activities that we seek neither the destruction of Iraq nor its dismemberment, nor to punish its people for the policy of their leaders. And, despite the propaganda charges to the contrary, never in history have military forces been engaged in battle with so much concern for the limitation of damage to the civilian population. Warfare is indeed a terrible thing. All coalition members are making the maximum effort to avoid civilian casualties. This often means increased risk to our own forces, a cost we are willing to bear. I cannot help but note that this is in stark contrast to Iraq's own policy of deliberately targeting civilian populations for uncertain missile terror attacks. It has also deliberately increased the exposure of its own population by moving military equipment and facilities into civilian areas with the purpose of using innocent Iraqi civilians and their homes as shields against attack.

As President Bush sombrely observed several weeks ago, Americans fight in anger only because we have to fight at all. We did everything we could to avoid this conflict, and we will do our best to bring it to the earliest possible conclusion. Despite the invective to the contrary - some of which we have been subjected to today - this is not a war of hegemony, not a grab for the control of oil reserves and not an attempt to impose an American order on the Arab world. Such foolishness ignores the realities of both Iraqi behaviour and the overwhelming rejection by the Members of the United Nations of that very behaviour. We are in the Gulf, as are the other 30 members of the coalition, to ensure that naked aggression does not succeed. We want to give meaning to the only principles on which a peaceful and prosperous world community can be based. We will stay not one day longer than necessary.

Looking ahead, Secretary Baker outlined on 7 February the expectation of the United States leadership that following hostilities the States of the Gulf themselves and regional organizations such as the Gulf Co-operation Council will take the lead in rebuilding the war-ravaged region and in building a network of new and stronger security ties. No regional State should be excluded from such arrangements.

But what we must discuss today is how the Council will conduct further serious and important discussions on the Gulf crisis. My Government brings one fundamental criterion to this debate: How can we promote the earliest possible withdrawal of Iraq from Kuwait and how can we strengthen the Council's role in achieving this objective? My mathematics may be deficient, but I would like to remind the representative of Cuba that this is something like the 195th day of the war, which began with the Iraqi aggression on 2 August, not the 28th day, as he claims.

All of us in this room, and literally thousands and millions of people throughout the world, in dozens and scores of ministries and institutions, have exerted every effort to avoid this conflict. All want it ended as soon as possible, and all agree on one thing: Iraq must leave Kuwait. Iraq's refusal to accept it and its many deeds in contravention of international law make it in a literal sense an outlaw State.

Iraq continues to reject every proposal from every envoy seeking peace, including, most recently, Iran and Pakistan. It had already spurned the efforts of the United Nations Secretary-General, the Arab League, the Gulf Co-operation Council and the Organization of African Unity and innumerable bilateral initiatives at the highest levels. Iraq's reaction to the latest Soviet envoy regrettably contains nothing new, and it still refuses to consider or countenance withdrawal. Although efforts will continue, Radio Baghdad on 10 February declared that Iraq rejects the idea of a cease-fire and still insists that the independent nation of Kuwait is an integral part of Iraq. With this as prologue, what, then, is the purpose of this meeting?

With only a few exceptions, no member of the Council is suggesting that it back away from resolution 678 (1990). No one is suggesting that there be a cease-fire without concrete evidence that Iraq will withdraw and comply fully with the Council's resolutions. And all of us, I believe, sincerely seek peace. President Bush has made it clear that he welcomes any mediation effort to convince Iraq to comply fully with the Security Council resolutions and to withdraw its forces from Kuwait.

But there are some States, including Iraq, which are trying to call into question the clear, legal obligations the Council has imposed upon it, and the clear, legal authority granted to the coalition military effort, pursuant to resolution 678 (1990). The Council has acted, and the coalition effort has been undertaken, in keeping with the United Nations Charter. The Council continues to monitor the situation. The United States has submitted frequent, full reports to the Council, as required under resolution 678 (1990).

My country holds that the Council should meet when it is in a position to advance its objectives, and to take action. That is what the international community looks to us for. And, given the continuing refusal of Iraq to acknowledge the validity of the Council's demands, that does not now seem to be the case.

We have yet to have defined for us the purpose of a public debate this afternoon. Is it to explore a cease-fire? Iraq has just made it clear that it is not interested in a cease-fire that is accompanied by withdrawal. A cease-fire without withdrawal is not acceptable. We have no intention of offering Saddam Hussein breathing space in which to regroup his military forces. Nor does he have any need of a pause in the fighting to make the decision that he already needs to make.

Is the purpose of this meeting to exchange information on the military effort? Open scrutiny of coalition efforts occurs every day, with thousands of journalists in the Middle East. The exposure to scrutiny of military operations in the Gulf is indeed unprecedented in history.

At the present juncture, when Iraq remains intransigent and it is not clear what additional steps the Council might take to ensure compliance with its resolutions, our concern is that a meeting will be subject either to misinterpretation or to exploitation. Above all else, we must not do anything which will prolong the conflict, and that, most particularly, includes sending signals, which Iraq will misuse or misperceive, that the Council is not firm in its decisions and is not intent on seeing them implemented.

The signal we must send instead, and keep on sending, is that this body and the international community are resolute and united, as they have been since 2 August. We will not tolerate the unprovoked seizure and attempted obliteration of a Member State of the United Nations. We will not tolerate the outrageous behaviour of Iraqi occupying forces in Kuwait, in contravention of international law. We will not accept the obliteration of Kuwait or the terrorizing or torturing of its people. We will not tolerate indiscriminate terror attacks against civilians in Saudi Arabia and Israel. We will not tolerate flagrant violation of the Geneva Conventions relative to the treatment of prisoners of war. And we will not tolerate mindless attacks on the environment. The Council must make it clear that the international community is prepared to do what is necessary to make sure that this aggression, this lawlessness, is not rewarded.

Given the evident and earnest desire on the part of a number of nations for the Council to meet to discuss the Gulf crisis, and notwithstanding our reservations about the genuine usefulness of such a meeting, we shall join with a majority in the Council. We believe that the form of such a meeting should be in keeping with the purpose, which in this case I take to be a serious discussion and exchange of views, commensurate with the importance and sensitivity of the subject. This will also respond to the appeal of a member of the Council that we do nothing now which would endanger its continuing diplomatic efforts to get Iraq to implement the Council's resolutions.

For the reasons I have indicated, we support the Austrian suggestion that we move to a formal private meeting. This will allow non-members of the Council to share their views, while permitting the exchange and circulation of prepared statements that nations may wish to deliver and to make public. It has become clear in recent days that Iraq is fighting a major campaign to discredit this Council, its resolutions, the United Nations and the person and institution of the Secretary-General. Its disregard for the truth is as obvious as its disregard for its neighbours. It is our earnest belief that this formula will meet the concerns which have been expressed in this Chamber, without providing Iraq an opportunity to exploit our debate or to twist the truth.

We again urge Iraq's leadership to turn away from its destructive course and to bring an end to the needless suffering it has inflicted on the people of Kuwait, the people of the international community, and now on its own population. We hope that all States will join us in affirming support for the enforcement of the resolutions of the Security Council, in confirming their support for the Secretary-General and in renewing the call upon Iraq to bring an end to the conflict in the Gulf.

...

[49] Mr. GHAREKHAN (India):

...

Ever since the outbreak of the armed hostilities in the Persian Gulf my delegation has consistently maintained that it is incumbent on the Security Council to remain seized of the matter and continuously to monitor the situation as it develops. That is the Council's generic responsibility, which it specifically assumed under paragraph 5 of resolution 678 (1990).

The war in the Gulf has aroused tremendous concern in the international community. The human and material destruction being suffered by the people of Kuwait and Iraq, the ever-present danger of the war's escalating to higher levels of intensity and engulfing other countries, the ecological disaster that is threatening countries beyond the immediate theatre of operations - all these factors greatly exercise the minds of the Government and people of India.

We are particularly concerned at the possible use of weapons of mass destruction - chemical, biological, nuclear. The use of chemical weapons would be reprehensible and is prohibited by international law; the use of nuclear weapons would threaten the very survival of mankind and has been declared by the General Assembly a violation of the United Nations Charter and a crime against humanity.

My delegation therefore favours the holding of meetings of the Council, on a regular basis, to provide an opportunity for members to review the situation. Indeed, the international community expects no less of the Council. I do not wish to suggest that the Council has been totally inactive during the past four weeks. The Council has tried to keep the matter under review through the instrumentality of informal consultation meetings. This was useful and was in fact first suggested by my delegation. This practice ought to continue. However, the informal meetings cannot be a permanent substitute for official meetings of the Council.

My delegation is deeply concerned that it has not been possible for the Council to meet formally even once on this matter since the expiry of the deadline, on 15 January, set by resolution 678 (1990). This has not reflected well on the prestige of the Council and the United Nations. The Secretary-General also referred to this in his statement to the Council members last week. The perception in which the Council is held by the international community ought to be of concern to the Council; at least, it is of concern to my delegation.

Many delegations - both those of members and those of non-members of the Council - have requested formal, open meetings of the Council to discuss the situation. The Council should welcome this interest on the part of Member States as evidence of the international community's confidence in the Council. In my delegation's view, it would be entirely proper and desirable that the meeting should be public, as is the Council's normal practice. A decision to go against this normal practice should be taken only in very special circumstances, since it could have the unintended effect of arousing avoidable doubts about the Council's functioning. My delegation is not convinced that circumstances today justify such an exception.

At the same time, my delegation is aware that there are some delegations - some of them not representing members of the Council - that would not like the Council to meet at all. On the other hand, there are several members of the Council that feel that, at least as an initial step, it might be useful for the Council to meet in a private session. My delegation is not unmindful of the preoccupation of those delegations. Should the Council decide, by majority, to convert this meeting into a private one, my delegation will of course respect that decision. The Council's provisional rules of procedure provide for it. But this would be the first time that the Council would have taken such an important decision through a vote. I wonder if such a division in the Council is wise or necessary at this stage.

It is my delegation's expectation that at some point in the near future the Council will revert to its traditional method of meeting in official public meetings.

...

[52] Mr. Hohenfellner (Austria):

...

When during our informal consultations, on 24 January, Austria put forward the idea of holding a private formal meeting of the Security Council, we were motivated by the following considerations: to make a compromise suggestion designed to break the deadlock between those who wanted no formal meeting of the Security Council at all as long as relevant Security Council resolutions had not been implemented and those who wanted an immediate public debate; to facilitate the difficult task of the President; to uphold rule 2 of the provisional rules of procedure, since we consider this rule to be of particular importance for the protection of the rights of members of the Security Council who find themselves in a minority; and to accommodate the concerns expressed by members as to the turn a public meeting might take and the wrong signals that it might be perceived to send. In order to give also other States which had already expressed an interest to participate in the debate an opportunity to do so, Austria favoured a liberal use of rule 37. Furthermore, we suggested to waive rule 51, thus allowing the verbatim records of the private meeting to be circulated in the usual fashion.

When we put forward these ideas almost three weeks ago, we were hoping for unanimous agreement by the members of the Council and the speedy convening of such a meeting. Alas, this was not to be. Although our original hopes were not realized, there is still a good case to be made for holding a private meeting. Austria will thus vote in favour. Our position on the substance of the matter will be stated later during the debate.

...

[54-55] Mr. Blanc (France) (interpretation from French):

...

Some States Members of the United Nations, including two members of our Council, have asked for the Council to meet. A meeting must take place when at least one member of the Council has requested it. We also feel that this meeting is strictly in line with resolution 678 (1990), which stipulates that the Council decides to remain seized of the matter. Hence France was in favour of the convening of an official meeting so as to afford everyone an opportunity to state his position.

From that point of view, the formula of a formal private meeting that has been proposed appears to us to be a good compromise between the views of those who would have preferred the Council not to meet and the views of others who would have preferred a public meeting. This formula is particularly welcome because participation in the debate will take place within the framework of accepted practices under our rules, and the verbatim records of the meetings will be published without recourse being made to the rules of the Council that would make it possible to limit the circulation of these records or to make them confidential.

For those reasons, we shall vote in favour of the proposal that has been made.

We feel, however, that at this stage the Security Council cannot take any concrete measures. Indeed, we must note, to our great regret, that Iraq's persistence in refusing to comply with the Security Council resolutions does not, for the time being, offer us any prospects.

...

[56] Mr. Noterdaeme (Belgium) (interpretation from French):

...

I shall confine myself now to the procedural question before us. Later I shall have the opportunity to speak on the substance of the problems under discussion.

Belgium will vote in favour of holding a formal meeting of the Security Council on the situation between Iraq and Kuwait. We believe that, in accordance with the Charter and the Council's provisional rules of procedure and practices, the Council should grant the request of those States that wish such a meeting.

My country, however, shares the concerns of those who, out of respect for the cohesiveness of the Council's work, would like this meeting to take place in private, but open to the participation of all delegations to the Organization that wish to participate in it.

My Government supports all the current diplomatic efforts designed to prevail upon Iraq to withdraw from Kuwait, in accordance with Security Council resolutions. We hope that the Council's meeting today will fall squarely within that context and will make it possible to give consideration to all useful proposals made to that end, particularly those emanating from the countries that have sought this meeting.

My delegation hopes that in that way the Council's meeting will contribute, responsibly and with restraint, to the achievement of a peaceful and rapid solution to a conflict that began on 2 August last year with the invasion and subsequent annexation of Kuwait.

...

[57] **Mr. Ayala Lasso (Ecuador)** (interpretation from Spanish): ...

I shall confine myself to expressing the position of the delegation of Ecuador on the procedural point that has been raised at this meeting of the Security Council. Like other representatives, I shall reserve my delegation's right to speak on substantive issues on a subsequent occasion.

As I stated this morning, in a way that I hoped was clear and unequivocal, my country is very pleased at the convening of this meeting of the Security Council. We have always believed that, in accordance with the applicable rules of procedure - in particular, rule 2 - the Security Council must meet whenever a request for a meeting is made by a Member State. In the present case, the request for a meeting of the Council was made by a considerable number of Arab Maghreb countries. Under resolution 674 (1990), the Council is obliged to

> "remain actively and permanently seized of the matter until Kuwait has regained its independence and peace has been restored in conformity with the relevant resolutions of the Security Council". (*resolution 674 (1990), para. 11*)

Under resolution 678 (1990), the Council must remain seized of the matter.

Consequently, it was obvious to the delegation of Ecuador that the Council has not met formally for a little more than two months now on the situation in the Gulf - a situation that has become more serious, indeed tragic, with every day that passes. Although the Council has dealt with the subject in many informal consultations that have taken place, Ecuador believes that the time has come for the Council to devote itself in a formal meeting to this complex subject, about which all the peoples of the world have expressed their concern and anxiety. It is obvious that on so delicate and important an item not all the views will be the same. That is only natural because this situation is considered from differing political points of view. But we wish to state that the expression of differing views must not be taken as sending a mixed signal to anyone. On the contrary, it is an eloquent, positive demonstration that the United Nations, one of whose organs is the Security Council, was conceived as a forum for discussing and seeking ever-wider agreements in a democratic and constructive spirit.

In proceeding in this way, our Organization is growing stronger, as is the common conviction that there are certain general principles we are all defending, on the basis of which we may well express different views to achieve a common objective: peace among all peoples and nations.

For these reasons, this morning I stated, and I state again now, that Ecuador would prefer a public meeting of the Council. We see no adequate reason for us to opt for a private meeting, which is also a possibility under the applicable rules. Nevertheless, if the majority in the Council should so decide, Ecuador would accept that democratic result and would not stand in the way of a private meeting of the Council.

...

[61] **Mr. Alarcon de Quesada (Cuba)** (interpretation from Spanish):

Clearly, Ambassador Pickering and I studied the same maths, and I know the conflict began 195 days ago. It would, however, be disingenuous indeed on Ambassador Pickering's part for him to assume he could convince anyone - with or without television - that what has been happening since 16 January is not something new and quite different from what was happening before.

From a certain point of view, I also agree with him that the war unleashed on 16 January truly did begin 195 days ago, when the United States began on the one hand to deploy its military forces and on the other to manipulate this organ of the United Nations.

With regard to the objective of those of us who asked for this meeting, let me, for my part, repeat what I said earlier. We have been very frank in our communications to the President of the Council. We requested a meeting of the Council some time ago to discuss, to exchange views and to hear differences of opinion - something that in our opinion is not wrong or condemnable, something that should not cause fear in those who claim they are speaking on behalf of the international community.

To sum up, we propose that this Council, so obedient in facilitating war, now give peace a chance.

[62] **Mr. Bagbeni Adeito Nzengeya (Zaire)** (interpretation from French): ...

The background and circumstances of the Persian Gulf war are of course well known to everybody here. A member of our Organization, Kuwait, was on 2 August occupied and annexed by a militarily powerful neighbour having considerable human and material resources. Article 24 of the Charter states:

> "In order to ensure prompt and effective action by the United Nations, its Members confer on the Security Council primary responsibility for the maintenance of international peace and security, and agree that in carrying out its duties under this responsibility the Security Council acts on their behalf."

Under that Article, the Council considered the situation that had arisen due to the occupation and annexation of a Member of the Organization. It adopted 12 resolutions calling on the occupier, another Member of the Organization, to comply with Article 25 of the Charter, which states:

> "The Members of the United Nations agree to accept and carry out the decisions of the Security Council in accordance with the present Charter."

In so doing, the Council had the support of a very large number of Members of the Organization and of the Secretary-General in its *démarches*, actions and efforts aimed at persuading the occupying Power to order the withdrawal of its forces from Kuwait before 15 January 1991 in order to allow a peaceful and lasting settlement of the situation.

These initiatives and acts of good faith continue and are being stepped up through the good offices of the USSR, the 15 non-aligned countries and other Member States whose major concern remains the liberation of Kuwait, the restoration of the legitimate Government of that country and a lasting peace in the region.

My delegation continues to hope these diplomatic efforts will succeed so that an end can be put to the hostilities in the Persian Gulf.

Until these actions yield the hoped for and desired results, my delegation believes that the Security Council, which is still seized of the item "The situation between Iraq and Kuwait" under paragraph 5 of resolution 678 (1990), should actively follow the development and evolution of the situation in the Persian Gulf in connection with the implementation of the 12 resolutions it has adopted.

How can it discharge its mandate as a decision-making body? It must bear in mind its paramount responsibility to ensure that its resolutions are followed up and implemented.

The Council has several paths open to it. Unless it decides otherwise, it can meet in public under rule 48 of the provisional rules of procedure. But bearing in mind the diplomatic *démarches* of the Special Envoy of the

USSR, Mr. Primakov and the 15 non-aligned countries, and the desire of the members of the Council to consider the situation in the Persian Gulf region in an atmosphere of serenity and resolve to explore and constructively seek new peaceful means of settling the conflict, my delegation feels a formal private meeting of the Council would enable its members to state their views and make their suggestions within the context of a fruitful exchange of views. The goal of course is a halt to the hostilities, to be immediately followed by the liberation of Kuwait and the restoration of peace to the Persian Gulf region.

As has so well been said by the representative of France, as President of the Council for January I worked along these lines with a view to such a compromise, which was almost achieved.

For all of these reasons, my delegation wholeheartedly supports a formal private meeting of the Council as proposed by the representative of the United Kingdom.

[66] The President:

...

I shall now put to the vote the proposal made by the representative of the United Kingdom that this meeting of the Security Council be continued in private.

A vote was taken by show of hands:

In favour:	Austria, Belgium, Côte d'Ivoire, France, Romania, Union of Soviet Socialist Republics, United Kingdom of Great Britain and Northern Ireland, United States of America, Zaire
Against:	Cuba, Yemen
Abstaining:	China, Ecuador, India, Zimbabwe

[66] The President:

The result of the voting is as follows: 9 in favour, 2 against and 4 abstentions. The proposal has therefore been adopted.

Keeping in mind the decision just taken, I propose to suspend the meeting now and resume it tomorrow morning at 11 o'clock. The agenda will be revised to reflect the private character of the meeting.

The meeting was suspended at 7.15 p.m.

C. S/PV.2977 (Part II) (closed), 14 February 1991

[7] Mr. Abulhasan (Kuwait) (interpretation from Arabic):

...

The Security Council is meeting upon a request from some sister Arab States to discuss the recent developments in the Arab Gulf conflict. It may be just and fair to make it clear immediately that in authorizing the multinational forces that are cooperating with my country, Kuwait, to use all possible means to force Iraq's compliance with its relevant resolutions, the Council was merely resorting to the only means left to it by the intransigent Iraqi régime, which has rebuffed all attempts, all efforts and all initiatives to persuade it in a calm and friendly manner to spare Iraq and its people, and indeed the region, the woeful results of the use of force.

...

[16] It was only natural that the Iraqi aggression's effects on the international arena, its effects on the fabric and future of international relations - indeed, on international peace and security - necessitated a decisive move, a move that could brook no delay. It was also obvious that the new world order that was being sought by the international community was an order that could not allow such naked aggression to go unanswered, an order that had no place for a party like the Iraqi régime. Therefore, the international forces began the implementation of the Security Council resolution, and in order to minimize civilian casualties in these military operations they concentrated their bombardment on the Iraqi war machine, wherever they found it. That is the machine that provides the occupier with the means of its aggression, the means to prolong the duration of the occupation.

In these operations, the Kuwaiti armed forces had the honour of firing the first shots in the battle to liberate the blessed land of Kuwait. They succeeded in hitting their targets deep inside Kuwait, supported in that endeavour by aircraft of the Kingdom of Saudi Arabia, Qatar and Bahrain as well as by other forces participating in this honourable and legitimate battle to repulse a vicious, blatant act of aggression and liberate usurped land. All these operations have been, and continue to be, conducted within the context of resolution 678 (1990). The fighting has not been expanded, nor is its target the destruction of Iraq. The only aim is to set Kuwait free from the machine of aggression.

We cannot fail to note here that it was the Iraqi régime that brought this devastation upon itself and upon its people, because of its insistence on aggression, its rejection of the international will, its refusal to comply with the international will, its defiance of the world community's resolutions and the sentiments of world public opinion, its violation of all laws, norms, covenants and principles.

During the very first week of the military occupation, His Highness King Hassan II, of Morocco issued an appeal to Iraq to accept withdrawal and thereby retain its current capabilities. The President of the Soviet Union and Iran issued similar appeals. They fell on deaf ears; they were rejected. There was an insistence on destroying Iraq and its people in order to fulfil personal dreams and ambitions.

Not only did Iraq fail to state its willingness to withdraw and end its aggression against Kuwait and the steadfast, heroic Kuwaiti people: the Iraqi occupation forces have, instead, escalated their acts of brutalization of the Kuwaiti people. We now have firm, reliable information indicating that barbaric acts of execution and rape continue. The official spokesman of the Kuwaiti army in the Kingdom of Saudi Arabia has stated today that the Kuwaiti Resistance has witnessed the liquidation of 200 Kuwaitis in the past few days. These Kuwaitis were brutalized. Among those killed were six women whose breasts were cut off and thrown into the street.

...

[18-20] The Iraqi occupation forces use Kuwaiti houses as sanctuaries and Kuwaiti people as human shields. Information has reached us that Kuwaiti families are being forced to leave their homes and Iraqi soldiers are being installed in their place, with the aim of avoiding new military operations. Anti-aircraft batteries have been placed on the roofs of Kuwaiti houses. That is the way Iraq respects civilian installations. That is an example of Iraqi behaviour towards civilians. There is a concentrated Iraqi military presence in Kuwaiti residences.

The children of Kuwait inside the country have been suffering from shortages in food and medicine for six months now as a result of the steady, continuing pillaging by Iraq of our resources in such supplies. At such a time, the Iraqi invasion forces are storming and assaulting houses of Kuwaitis and other residents and seizing any food supplies they find. The citizens of Kuwait are now being threatened with the spectre of a sweeping famine.

I am sure everyone here knows of the appeals addressed to the Iraqi Government by the Secretary-General of the United Nations and by specialized agencies and humanitarian organizations such as the Red Cross, in which they merely requested permission for food supplies to reach Kuwait and to be distributed under the supervision of those organizations and agencies. The Iraqi Government replied with a resounding "no", even while the Iraqi army inside Kuwait City is stealing the daily bread of our defenceless people.

The people and Government of Kuwait expect the world community in general, and those countries that speak out loudly in defence of the stubborn Iraqi régime in particular, to condemn in the strongest terms these inhuman Iraqi practices perpetrated against the Kuwaiti people - a people whose life, destiny and national resources have been subjected to systematic destruction, to constant plundering, and whose oil and industrial facilities are being held hostage to the crazed dreams of a domineering dictator.

The mining of Kuwaiti ports and oil wells and installations and their being set on fire are vivid examples of this. The Iraqi régime did not stop at attempting to destroy Kuwait's present; indeed, its criminal acts have gone beyond that to the destruction of Kuwait's future and the entire region's economic future through its attempt to ruin our marine environment with the dumping of millions of barrels of oil into the Gulf in a reckless, random manner. It is the biggest environmental crime the world has ever known.

...

[22] Does the Iraqi régime now deserve to be rewarded for its aggression, for its occupation, and for the atrocities it has perpetrated, with a cease-fire?

Should the world community back off from the crucial mission in the service of world peace and security just days after the beginning of the battle of liberation and after the Baghdad régime has rebuffed the overtures of Soviet President Gorbachev, the appeal of Secretary-General Javier Perez de Cuellar and the calls and messages from the Non-Aligned Movement, and all appeals and pleadings?

Should not these countries instead turn first to Iraq to maintain international peace and security, especially since they have found favour with its regime? Should not they direct to that regime their appeals and calls for withdrawal from occupied Kuwaiti lands so that the crisis may be resolved and so that the region may be saved from this destruction? Were not these military operations the only natural outcome of failure in all endeavours for peace in which these very countries were themselves involved more than once? Have they not seen for themselves how the Baghdad regime is unwilling to retreat from its aggression and occupation and to comply with international will?

The only conclusion a sensible mind can draw from all this is that there should be no cessation, no cease-fire whatsoever, before the complete liberation of Kuwait and the restoration of its legitimate Government, because such a move would be counter-productive, a negative message from the Security Council to the Iraqi leadership, which anxiously yearns for controversy, for rift, for disunity to plague the ranks of the Security Council so that it may continue its occupation.

However, the Security Council has been and remains united and coherent in the face of such flagrant violations of all the principles of the Charter and this naked aggression against the sovereignty of a Member State of the United Nations, against a peace-loving nation that has never encroached upon anyone's rights or balked in its obligations to anyone, a country that has never neglected to play its role or to fulfil its commitments towards the general common interests of our international community.

I repeat once against that these countries now calling for a cease-fire ought instead to address the Iraqi régime that initiated the aggression, the régime that persists in the occupation and rejects the peace necessary for it to take the initiative in solving the crisis and take the first basic step to end the military occupations, which is to withdraw from Kuwait and repudiate aggression.

We find it hard to imagine, but these countries which claim that the ongoing military operations have exceeded the scope of liberating Kuwait to target and destroy Iraq, are more concerned about the Iraqi leadership and its dictator than their own peoples. If that claim were true, should not the Iraqi régime preserve the capabilities remaining in its possession, and not throw its people and their destinies into ruin for the sake of greed and personal ambition? It can do that by withdrawing from Kuwait immediately and unconditionally.

Have we not heard the statement of that régime's leader last Sunday, when he declared his complete rejection of a cease-fire, when he declared his insistence on the struggle until the last Iraqi?

By their heroic action, the international forces are for the first time in the history of the United Nations reaffirming collective security and self-defence, which the United Nations Charter intends to be a shield for nations and international stability. They are reaffirming this established reality.

A world order is now dawning. It is being fashioned by the United Nations, and all nations will bask in its sunlight free from force and free from the threat or use of it.

...

[26] **Mr. Pickering (United States of America):**

I will speak only briefly in connection with the statement that we have just heard, on which I would like to congratulate the representative of Kuwait, and with his final words, which sought questions in connection with his presentation and with the events with which he is so familiar in the region, and with respect to which his Government, of course, has been tragically involved.

In that regard, and in full knowledge of and in keeping with our provisional rules of procedure, I would like at this stage to avail myself of the opportunity to address to him a certain number of questions. I do so in keeping with our decision yesterday to try to do everything possible to make fruitful and productive this private meeting of the Security Council and on the basis of past meetings of this character, which have provided opportunities to explore the issues in this fashion and to reply. I hope that the representative of Kuwait will be prepared to respond now or at an appropriate time in the future. I will understand very well if he wishes to have more time in which to provide a response.

I would like to ask him if he would be prepared to describe the status of the efforts of the Government of Kuwait to reach a negotiated settlement of the border and other disputes with Iraq in the period preceding the Iraqi aggression against Kuwait of 2 August 1990.

In addition, I would like to ask whether Kuwait is prepared, in the words of operative paragraph 3 of Security Council resolution 660 (1990), to begin negotiations with Iraq to resolve this dispute once Iraq has complied with the other elements contained in that resolution.

Thirdly, I would like to know if the Government of Kuwait has received from Iraq at any time an indication of any sort that a negotiated settlement consistent with the resolutions of the Security Council is possible.

Finally, does Kuwait believe or have any reason to believe that a cease-fire would help to resolve the problem and to promote the complete withdrawal of Iraqi forces as called for in the Security Council resolutions and particularly in resolution 660 (1990)?

[36] **Mr. Shihabi (Saudi Arabia)** (interpretation from Arabic):

...

For the second time in its history, the United Nations is being tested and has taken a decision of war. For the first time in its history, the international Organization has placed all its strength and prestige in support of a decision to guarantee safety for the peoples of our region, to preserve stability in the world at large and to consolidate its path, notwithstanding the manipulations of the transgressors and the enticements of the irresponsible, both regionally and internationally.

...

[38-40] We would be deceiving ourselves, we would be hypocrites condoning injustice and rejecting reality, if we failed to acknowledge that the Iraqi régime was given every opportunity to return to the path of wisdom, or if we maintained that it would have agreed to leave Kuwait voluntarily if certain sensitivities had only been addressed. That is the discourse of the ignorant. It is to ignore all the attempts at mediation and the fact that after all those attempts Iraq still did not leave Kuwait, even though it was clear that all the world held it to be at fault. In no uncertain terms Iraq was told what would happen if it held onto Kuwait, if it continued to reject Security Council resolutions and refused to heed the warnings of the Security Council and other States.

To Iraq's apologists and those who maintain that we were in duty bound to give Iraq another chance, we say that no usurper in all of history was ever given the opportunity and time that the Iraqi régime was given to desist from its adventures and to evacuate Kuwait.

How many emissaries marched to that régime's leader, advising and guiding him, enlightening and promising, warning and threatening? How many emissaries marched to Baghdad for five and a half months, until the middle of January, explaining the consequences of insisting on oppression and continuing the invasion of Kuwait?

Has the game of the guest hostages been forgotten, the game in which each leader or mediator who arrived in Baghdad was given a number of persons to take back to his country, satisfying the purpose of his visit? We ask those who call today for excuses and apologies for Iraqi aggression, while they know that they are thus sacrificing Kuwait as a State and a people, and putting the whole region under threat:

"What would be your attitude today if your people and country were in the position of Kuwait and its people, invaded by one who does not fear the Creator and does not value the human being? He ransacks it, destroys it, kills its sons and violates its women; he did it yesterday and is doing it today, as he will tomorrow. Or is Kuwaiti blood cheap to you? Are the greedy permitted to shed it?"

Generosity with, and the sacrifice of, the countries of other peoples is a losing exercise which backfires on its perpetrators.

There is an ongoing war at this hour, a war that was started by Iraq on 2 August. There followed a pause of five and a half months, in the hope that the Iraqi régime would desist from its adventures. It is a war in which my country and 27 others are participating today to implement Security Council resolutions and international legitimacy against the Iraqi invasion of Kuwait and against the insistence of the Iraqi régime on continuing its usurpation, ransacking and destruction of the State of Kuwait, at the same time mortgaging the safety and security of the Iraqi people and of the region as a whole. The Iraqi régime bears the whole responsibility, in all its dimensions, for this war, for the price the Iraqi people is paying for it, for what the Kuwaiti people has paid and is paying as a victim of this invasion and for all that the coalition countries are bearing and sacrificing in standing up to aggression. Those who support the Iraqi invasion will share this historic responsibility.

...

[43-45] The question should be addressed to Baghdad: Will the Iraqi régime withdraw from Kuwait, every inch of Kuwait, and implement all Security Council resolutions, or is achieving its dreams and hopes of expansion and aggression still its objective?

We are concerned about the safety of the Iraqi people. But those who claim to care for Baghdad and its people more than its leaders and people do - are hypocrites.

What is required of Iraq for all these operations to stop is its withdrawal from Kuwait and its implementation of Security Council resolutions. As for the deceptive talk of saving a leader's face, being considerate of a President's feelings, or being careful about a leader's sensitivities: in view of the continued slaughter of the people and State of Kuwait and the war in the region, such talk, which is an attempt to deceive peoples, is rejected. We hope that all forums, and above all the Security Council, will reject it.

[46] Mr. Al Ni'mah (Qatar) (interpretation from Arabic):

...

I should like to place before the Council the collective position of the States members of the GCC with regard to current events in the Gulf. The States members of the GCC have adopted a principled position, which has remained unchanged ever since the tragedy that has been visited upon the area, as follows: All Security Council resolutions on the Iraqi aggression against Kuwait should be fully implemented. These States are convinced that the complete withdrawal of Iraqi forces from Kuwait and the restoration of the legitimate Government, headed by Sheikh Al-Sabah, is in keeping with international legitimacy and respect for the provisions of the United Nations Charter. If these resolutions remain unimplemented, the Council will have failed in its responsibility and duty with regard to the maintenance of international peace and security.

The States members of the GCC hold the unanimous view that resort to all necessary means, in accordance with Security Council resolution 678 (1990), is intended to achieve that aim, which has eluded us following upon the failure of economic sanctions and the intransigence of the Iraqi regime, which has rejected all attempts to restore peace by all the parties that have shown a keen understanding for Iraq's interests as well. These attempts are still ongoing; there are parties that have tried to stop the bloodshed and to spare the area further tragedy by convincing the Iraqi leadership to respect international legitimacy and comply with the resolutions of the League of Arab States, the Organization of the Islamic Conference and the Security Council.

However, all these attempts have fallen on deaf ears in Iraq; hence recourse to the other means has been and remains the only way to secure implementation of the resolutions of the Security Council.

The tragedy befalling Iraq and its fraternal people has been brought about by those who have flouted the will of the international community and refuse to take any decision that would put an end to the use of force. Hence Iraq and the people of Iraq have become victims of the aggression launched against Kuwait and the victims of those who obstinately refuse to reverse this aggression against Kuwait. This is a clear and unprecedented violation of the will of the international community.

The members of the Gulf Co-operation Council (GCC) have welcomed the good offices and attempts to bring about peace, wherever they originated. The GCC members expected that such initiatives would bear fruit and that the Iraqi regime would respond positively and fully implement the resolutions of the Security Council. However, our expectations and those of well-meaning and peaceful loving peoples have been swept away by the wind. The efforts on which we had pinned our hopes have come to naught. We had hoped that the Iraqis would regain their senses and respond to the voice of logic and wisdom by accepting the resolutions of the Council, which represents international legitimacy and to which all members of the international community, including Iraq, are committed.

I believe that, while we are witnessing this horrendous event, we cannot but appeal to the Security Council to insist on and remain committed to the resolutions it has adopted and to resort to all means to secure their implementation. We are fully convinced that any slackening in the council would constitute a set-back to international legitimacy and undermine the ability of the United Nations to restore international peace and security and compel compliance from those who fail to respect its decisions. The law of God and the sanctity of humanity should be preserved. These are two pillars of the United Nations and international law.

May I say that the GCC members, given all this suffering, are entitled to seek a new dawn that will bring the full implementation of Security Council resolutions. Should that come about, our region will have its wounds healed and peace will prevail, something which will enable the region once again to follow the path of peace and development.

I would like to refer to the final communiqué of the eleventh session of the Supreme Council of the States members of the Gulf Co-operation Council and to its Doha Declaration.

...

In conclusion, I state again that all attempts to resolve the conflict without resort to all the means necessary to implement the Security Council resolutions should be addressed to fraternal Iraq. After all they have done, after all the disrespect they have shown for the truth, cannot the leaders in Iraq respond positively to the voice of wisdom and reason?

We look to the Security Council in this dark hour. We count on its commitment to and insistence on the implementation of the Security Council resolutions. It can thereby provide us with great help in overcoming the difficulties that have befallen us and avoiding further tragedy for the area. The Council's steadfast attitude will guide the aggressor towards the right path.

The aggressor has flouted the international will and seems to be unable to see the rising sun of the new world order. I appeal to the Security Council to show the aggressor that rising sun. It is extremely difficult to discern the truth in a sea of darkness. But the Security Council's commitment to and insistence on the implementation of the Security Council resolutions will convince the aggressor that it must listen to the voice of reason, thereby enabling mankind to look forward to a better future and setting it on the path towards peace and security and tranquillity. This can be brought about only through the implementation of the resolutions of the Security Council, whose only aim in resorting to the present means has been to liberate Kuwait and restore legitimacy. If this aim is attained, our area's aspirations to peace, security and justice will also be fulfilled.

Through the Security Council, we appeal once again to the leadership in Iraq to listen to the voice of peace, the voice of reason, and to help implement the Security Council resolutions calling for the withdrawal of troops from Kuwait and the restoration of the legitimate Government of Kuwait, without any pre-conditions.

Our hearts are bleeding because of the tragedy that has befallen our people in Kuwait and our people in Iraq. These two homelands, Iraq and Kuwait, are very dear to our hearts. All of us feel such sadness at the suffering of the victims of aggression. Baghdad, like Kuwait City and Riyadh, is very dear to our hears. God knows that we only wish prosperity and peace for Baghdad, a seat of civilization. What can I say at this time when my heart is being broken by what is happening? Blood is being shed for no valid reason.

Tragedies are being inflicted on the city and state of Baghdad. Oh God, how can this be? My face is black with sorrow because those in the leadership are unaware of what is going on. They do not respect good-neighbourliness. They have no respect for a nation that has contributed to the march of human civilization.

Palestine is weeping, Kuwait is weeping, Iraq is weeping because of the aggression that has been committed.

We should be guided by the Holy Koran and the precepts of Islam. God will guide us. Our last word is this: we are grateful to God.

[56] **Mr. Al-Anbari (Iraq)** (interpretation from Arabic):

...

This meeting has been convened more than three weeks after some members of the Security Council, including the five States of the Arab Maghreb, requested a meeting. The delay has been caused by the objection of the United States and its allies intended to mask the crimes their armies are perpetrating against Iraq, again reaffirming that the United States does not want the Council, or the world, to play any positive role since they imposed resolution 678 (1990) and other, previous, resolutions of the Council on the so-called crisis in the Gulf.

The Council's inability to meet in all these weeks - which contradicts its rules of procedure - despite the escalation of the armed aggression against Iraq, again confirms that the Council is no longer an international security council. It has no credibility or legitimacy. It is merely an instrument for the covering up of the worst of international crimes, which is now being perpetrated in the heartland of the Arab nation.

Furthermore the attempt of some members of the Council to stop this being an open public meeting as required by the provisional rules of procedure and to make it a private meeting was aimed at denying some Member States the opportunity to unmask the crimes being perpetrated in the name of this august Council against mankind, against the people of Iraq, and against its rights.

The attempt to justify the holding of such a meeting is an attempt not to give Iraq the impression of hesitation on the part of the Council. But the Security Council has no such impression. It knows that since the so-called crisis in the Gulf began the Council has become an American instrument representing American interests and that the United States will continue its aggression even if the Security Council were to adopt a resolution on a cease-fire or on halting the rain of bombs on the defenceless civilians of Iraq.

This is such a contradiction that the majority of States that requested this meeting are now boycotting it because it has been turned from a public meeting into a private one.

Moments ago we witnessed yet another attempt to open a scenario which would give one or the other State the right to speak for our State through succeeding responses to a number of prepared questions whose only objective is to disseminate propaganda and to deny others the opportunity to speak at an appropriate time.

We are happy that at least this scenario has failed totally.

The nature of the aggression led by the United States against Iraq becomes clear when we consider its background and when we come to know the preparations of the United States for the aggression were started long ago and preceded the so-called crisis in the Gulf and the Council's adoption of resolution 678 (1990) on 29 November 1990. If the United States found in that resolution a fig leaf to cover up the criminal nature of its aggression against Iraq, then that resolution is indeed a document that makes the States members of the Security Council, which adopted it, co-perpetrators of the crime.

It may be recalled that throughout 1990 and up until today the United States and its allies and satellites have waged a hysterical propaganda campaign against Iraq, its leadership and its army. Things escalated until there were allegations that Iraq might have nuclear weapons that threatened international peace and security. That hysterical campaign was aimed at preparing international public opinion, particularly American public opinion, for an aggression against Iraq to eradicate its economic, military and industrial potential.

Following the commencement of the so-called crisis in the Gulf, public-relations companies began making almost sadistic statements; some have even labelled Iraq sadistic and used many other such adjectives. Such words cannot be used to describe Iraq, its people or its army; they are suited, rather, to those now waging aggression against Iraq.

At its forty-fifth session, at a meeting on 4 December 1990, the General Assembly adopted a resolution recognizing that

> "an armed attack or a threat of an armed attack on a safeguarded nuclear facility, operational or under construction, would create a situation in which the Security Council would have to act immediately in accordance with the provisions of the Charter of the United Nations, including measures under Chapter VII". (*General Assembly resolution 45/58 J*)

The only State that voted against that resolution is the very one that conducted attacks against Iraqi nuclear establishments under international supervision on the very first day of the aggression against Iraq. That State is the United States of America, which has the largest arsenal of nuclear, chemical and other weapons of mass destruction.

The fact that the United States was the only Member State of the United Nations to vote against that resolution demonstrates its firm intention to attack the peaceful, safeguarded nuclear facilities in Iraq. If such acts exceeded the framework of Security Council resolution 678 (1990), regardless of its illegitimacy, we believe that they represent at the same time an international crime to which the provisions of Chapter VII of the Charter should be applied against the United States and its collaborators in aggression, in accordance with all the documents of the General Assembly I have just mentioned.

The United States and its collaborators have exploited the so-called crisis in the Gulf to force resolution after resolution; to besiege Iraq by sea, land and air; to prevent food, medicine and spare parts from reaching Iraq in order to starve its people and weaken its economy; to escalate war hysteria; and finally to prepare the political ground for aggression and to wage the war against Iraq that has continued since 16 January.

The second phase of the United States' aggressive policy against Iraq was to try to shoot down any peaceful initiative to solve the crisis, such as that of His Highness King Hussein to hold a mini-summit in Jiddah for the kings and Presidents of Jordan, Egypt, Saudi Arabia, Iraq and Yemen on 5 August 1990. And the United States continues by all means available to abort all Arab and other initiatives.

The third phase of the American plot was the sending of troops and weapons to the sacred Arab peninsula and the Arab Gulf under the pretext of defending against an alleged invasion - an invention of the United States. Following the massing of troops and by a unilateral resolution of 8 November 1990, it declared that its forces in the Gulf had become arrayed offensively against Iraq, even though the Security Council, pushed by the United States, had applied further inhuman economic sanctions against Iraq, again requiring application of the provisions of Chapter VII of the Charter. Any observer of the situation would have noticed the American escalation through propaganda, through the very way statements were made, and through the threats made by American officials and the media.

There was one single goal: to convince American and world public opinion of the inevitability of war and the impossibility of a peaceful solution. America's immediate rejection of President Saddam Hussein's initiative of 12 August 1990 calling for the application of international legitimacy to all States in the area, in accordance with unified rules to be stipulated by the Security Council, to ensure the withdrawal of all forces, taking into consideration the particular aspects of each situation, emphasizes yet again the United States' lack of concern for international legitimacy and peaceful solutions. It is plotting aggression. It is seeking an opportunity to wage aggression under cover of apparent international legitimacy against Iraq and the Arab nation.

However, we all know - all Member States of the United Nations know, the man on the street in the United States and throughout the world knows - that this war is actually an American, North Atlantic, and Zionist immoral war of revenge against Iraq, its people, its army, its leadership and its civilization. It is also a warning to the Arab nation of American and Israeli hegemony.

That fact was reaffirmed by the Israeli newspaper *Ma'ariv* on 12 February, when it said that, in the event of an American victory in the war in the Gulf, such a victory would be that of the white man against the Bedouin and of Christianity and Judaism against Islam. The Voice of America broadcast a quotation from *Ma'ariv* on the 9th of this month. The expressions being used by spokesmen of the American forces in the peninsula demonstrate that racism. They talk of Arab women as "Ninja women" and of Arab Bedouins as "natural inhabitants", as was reported by the *New York Times* on 10 February 1991.

Any talk of an international coalition or claims that the dispute is between Iraq and the world are mere manoeuvres to conceal the provocations and blackmail that have made many Governments cave in to American pressure and collaborate with the United States to hide the truth of American aggression against Iraq. The United States Government is well aware of the ugliness of this war and of its aggression. That is why it has come to describe it as a "just" war, as if it imagined that its terrorism against the States of the world and their people would induce them to believe that raining hundreds of thousands of bombs from high altitudes, burning everything on the ground, and killing Iraqi adults and children alike, could represent a just war.

If America believes that the idea of just war is represented by the Crusades against the Arab and Moslem world, it is only revealing its racist nature. In fact, it is ignoring the American Council of Churches, which in mid-November 1990 condemned the war and called for restoring the legitimate rights of the Palestinians, Lebanese and Cypriots. The United States zeal to avoid human casualties on its side in order to avoid the ire of the American people has made it wage unprecedented technological and chemical warfare through intense high-altitude air-raids, using land-to-land and air-to-air missiles, even though it may lead to the eradication of the Iraqi people and the destruction of the hydroelectrical infrastructure, as well as dams, bridges, roads and trees.

However, the United States claims that it is an honest, civilized country most keen to maintain human rights. The Defense Department, when mentioning the use of chemical weapons when needed in Iraq, adds yet another proof that America, through its aggression, has set aside the Fourth Geneva Convention, which is an attempt to put an end to the "dirty" aspects of war. The use of such gases, in addition to intensive, round-the-clock air-raids that do not discriminate between a mosque and a church, a camp or an old man, makes the United States and its allies outlaws in international illegitimacy.

While we consider here the situation in the Arab Gulf, thousands of bombs are falling on all the cities and villages of Iraq. During the first day of the aggression on 16 January 1990, American aircraft dropped 80,000 tons of explosives, equivalent to one and a half times the force of the nuclear bomb dropped by the United States on Hiroshima.

Since then, the United States and its collaborators in aggression have launched thousands of air sorties each day against Iraq. In the first three weeks there were 45,000 sorties. Eighty-five thousand tons of explosives were dropped on Iraq. In terms of TNT, that is the equivalent of five Hiroshima bombs. The United States Administration and its collaborators - Zionists, Atlantic partners and crusaders alike - are persisting in their aggression against Iraq, caring nothing for the destruction of the air, land and sea environment in Iraq and throughout the Arab Gulf region. During the first two days of the aggression, Iraq's peaceful nuclear and other industrial facilities were destroyed. This has led to the escape of a great deal of radiation and gas, killing many innocent civilians and perhaps causing deformities in future generations.

Such actions show that the United States and its allies will not stop at violating the Charter of the United Nations or at exceeding the objectives and limits of the insulting resolution 678 (1990). They have actually violated the Fourth Geneva Convention on the Protection of Civilian Persons in Time of War; they have violated the Treaty on the Non-Proliferation of Nuclear Weapons, the Universal Declaration of Human Rights, the General Assembly resolution prohibiting attacks on nuclear facilities, both active and under construction, and all religious and moral values.

United States barbarity has not stopped at killing civilians, destroying hospitals, schools and mosques and polluting the environment; it has attacked Iraq's very heritage from Nineveh in the north to Babel in the midlands to Ur in the south. Iraq, the cradle of civilization, contains more than half a million archaeological sites; of these 50,000 are of the highest importance, including between 100 and 200 ancient urban centres that prospered over the ages. This is an attempt to destroy the heritage of human civilization.

His Excellency the Foreign Minister of Iraq has provided comprehensive details of the acts of aggression in his letters dated 24 January 1991 and 1 February 1991 addressed to the Secretary-General. Today, His Excellency sent a third letter on the heinous crime perpetrated by the forces of aggression when they bombed a civilian bomb shelter in a residential quarter of Baghdad. Four hundred innocent civilians, mostly women, children and elderly people, died in that attack - as we saw on television screens the world over. That ugly crime swells the black record of United States-Zionist aggression against our militant people.

We call on the world to condemn that ugly crime and to reveal the truth about the aggression being perpetrated by the traditional forces of colonialism and imperialism under the leadership of the United States. Iraq lays full responsibility in the eyes of history and mankind for those crimes against our people and our country at the door of those parties. To condone such crimes in silence brings shame upon the United Nations. The States which voted in favour of resolution 678 (1990) bear a legal, political and moral responsibility for these crimes, for by bowing the the *[sic]* will of the United States, agreeing to that shameful resolution, they enabled the great criminal, the United States, to perpetrate those crimes. They will continue to bear that responsibility unless they firmly take an honourable position favouring an end to the aggression and the crimes against mankind perpetrated by the United States.

Since the barbaric raids have failed to break the backs of the Iraqi people, those United States raids have grown in intensity. Civilian urban areas have been bombed, along with all kinds of civilian infrastructure such as power stations and sewage facilities. This carries with it the threat of the spread of epidemics among the population, particularly among women and the elderly. We believe the number of women, children and the elderly among the civilian victims has reached tens of thousands.

That brief description of plan prepared long ago by the United States for its aggression against Iraq, and of its implementation through intensive air-raids involving the dropping of tens of thousands of tons of explosives and gases daily from high altitudes - over 30,000 feet - gives the lie to the ridiculous United States claims that it is eager to respect the rules of international humanitarian law and the Geneva Conventions. The way in which the United States attack is being carried out makes the bombardment of civilian facilities and urban areas inevitable: the raids are of great intensity and are being carried out from very high altitudes. We believe that the United States destruction of entire neighbourhoods and other non-military infrastructure is premeditated. The United States knows that such attacks violate all the rules of international humanitarian law, the Fourth Geneva Convention on the Protection of Civilian Persons in Time of War, and other instruments including that recently adopted at the World Summit for Children.

In sum, the United States and its allies have perpetrated, and continue to perpetrate, premeditated international crimes. They are like all the international criminals who came before them; indeed, they make them seem like amateurs.

...

[71] Finally, I must stress that the so-called new world order is nothing but the offspring of a new United States imperialism, an imperialism that disposes of the largest military arsenal in the world but that has no comparable economic or political force. Rather than trying to deal with its economic problems - the deterioration of the United States economy owing to competition in world markets with Japan and Germany - the military establishment decided to rely on military force to gain control of natural resources, and in particular the oil resources of the Arab Gulf. If its hegemony in the Gulf were to be consolidated, the United States would have the upper hand against its competitors in the economic sphere who were under the United States nuclear umbrella until only yesterday and who, according to the present United States plan, must now depend upon a United States military presence in the Gulf to ensure their oil supplies under conditions set by the United States.

It is clear that the United States aggression against Iraq was prepared for with the assistance of pressures brought to bear against members of the Security Council and through attempts made to terrorize the majority of those members. The Council has now lost control over the crisis and, indeed, its credibility in the United Nations and in the world. The United Nations and its credibility as an organization working for peace and international legitimacy are the first victims of United States hegemony in the aftermath of the cold war.

The latest manoeuvres to attempt to delay this meeting of the Security Council and to turn it into a private meeting are merely further evidence of United States hegemony over the United Nations. If the United States continues with its acts of hegemony and aggression, it - God willing - will be the loser. All the States of the Arab Gulf, all the States of the third world, will find themselves kneeling before Zionist-American hegemony, militarily, politically and economically. However, United States aggression and its long-term plans set it on a path of confrontation not merely with Iraq but ultimately with the world as a whole. Force cannot kill off the nationalist uprisings in the world. Force cannot put an end to technological development in Europe and Japan. The United States empire will have an end in Europe and in Asia.

Finally, Iraq has proved to the United States and its collaborators and satellites - and to the world - that aggression against it, however barbaric, will not be just a pleasant stroll for the aggressors. The price will be very high. Iraq is steadfast. Until the aggressors withdraw we shall exercise our right and our duty to resort to legitimate self-defence against the attempts being made by the United States and its co-criminals to kill us off. In the end, God willing, we shall win through our steadfastness, through the strength of our people and our leadership and through the solidarity of the Arab nation and the Islamic peoples of all who love peace in the world.

[72] **Sir David Hannay (United Kingdom)**:
This is the first occasion on which the Security Council has met formally since the expiry on 15 January of the six-week pause of goodwill set up in Security Council resolution 678 (1990) and since my country, along with a considerable number of others, under the authority of that resolution initiated military action designed to bring about the liberation of Kuwait. It is appropriate, therefore, in addition to the submission of the regular reports called for in operative paragraph 4 of Security Council resolution 678 (1990), which we are already providing, to use this occasion to address some of the issues which have been raised in public debate and also by some members of the Council.

Some have suggested that military action being taken by the allies is in some way excessive or disproportionate and thus exceeds the "all necessary means" authorized in resolution 678 (1990) to bring about the liberation of Kuwait. But the nature and scope of the military action is dictated not by some abstract set of criteria but by the military capacity of the aggressor, who has refused all attempts to remove him from Kuwait by peaceful means and has thus necessitated the military action in course. In global terms Iraq has the fourth largest army in the world, after the Soviet Union, China and the United States. It has 1.85 million troops. That army is backed up by a large modern air force; it has more than twice as many battle tanks as Britain and France put together; it is equipped with long-range missiles targeted at and now fired at its neighbours; it is equipped with chemical weapons which it has not hesitated in the past to use against its neighbours and against its own population; it has biological and nuclear weapons programmes whose degree of progress is unknown but whose objective is clear. Iraq's defence expenditure in 1988 was approximately 28 per cent of its gross domestic product. That compares with figures of just over 4 per cent for the United Kingdom, 2.9 per cent for France and 5.6 per cent for the United States.

It is that military machine which seized Kuwait last August; it is that military machine which holds it to this day; and it is that military machine which now has to be removed from Kuwait by force. It is to that aim and in those specific circumstances that the force used must correspond, and it does so.

Now, some have argued that the fighting should be confined to the territory of occupied Kuwait. A moment's thought will show why that self-limitation would not make it possible to achieve the objectives of resolution 678 (1990) - though I may add that coalition attacks are now concentrating more and more on Iraqi ground forces in and around Kuwait. But it requires a massive effort to dislodge this huge Iraqi war machine from Kuwait. Its logistical support and resources extend far beyond the confines of Kuwait. So hostilities cannot possibly be confined to the geographical limits of that country alone.

But that does not mean that the allies have extended their objectives beyond those laid down in successive Security Council resolutions - namely, the withdrawal of Iraq from Kuwait, the return of Kuwait's legitimate Government and the restoration of peace and stability to the region. We have not. We are not seeking to bring about the destruction, occupation or dismemberment of Iraq or to decide who governs that country. We are seeking the liberation of Kuwait, no more and no less. The military action will end as soon as the objectives laid down by the Council have been achieved.

There have, alas, been civilian casualties. That cannot be denied. It is a source of pain and regret. Our quarrel is not with the people of Iraq, but with their rulers. The allied forces have been given the strictest instructions to strive to keep such casualties to the minimum and to avoid damaging sites of religious and cultural significance. That is a sharp contrast to Iraq's performance, which has included the indiscriminate firing of missiles at centres of civilian population and then rejoicing publicly at the anguish and destruction they have caused.

Many reports of objective eyewitnesses have borne testimony to the general accuracy of allied bombing attacks and to the successful avoidance, in the vast majority of the many thousands of sorties flown, of centres of population.

Iraq is a large country, with much uninhabited space. Iraqi military installations and production facilities could easily have been sited far away from centres of civilian population. That they have not been is merely another sign of the Iraqi leadership's disdain for the safety of its own population. There is now increasing evidence that military equipment and installations are actually being moved into civilian areas in order to protect them from attack.

It is rightly asked how this military conflict can be brought to an end. The short answer is by Iraq's committing itself unequivocally and irrevocably to full withdrawal from Kuwait and taking immediate, concrete measures to implement that withdrawal. So far there is no sign of that.

To the contrary, by rejecting the approach made by President Gorbachev after allied military operations began, by its deplorable and unacceptable public attacks on the Secretary-General and by its lack of response to any of the peace initiatives put forward since 15 January, Iraq has made a mockery of the efforts of those who are trying to find a peaceful solution. We have no wish to discourage those efforts, so long as they are firmly based on the 12 Security Council resolutions adopted since the invasion of 2 August. But to be realistic such efforts must begin in Baghdad. That is the door at which they must knock.

The negative response reportedly given by Iraq to the messages from the Iranian authorities gives us no reason at all to be optimistic that Iraq's leaders are ready to take the action that could put an end to the conflict and loss of life.

In these circumstances, the idea of an unconditional pause of any kind makes no sense at all. It would only give Iraq time to regroup its forces and to repair the damage to its military installations, thus ensuring that any resumed hostilities were longer and more costly in human lives that would otherwise be the case.

...

[78] ... It is a confrontation between collective security, as provided for in the Charter of the United Nations, and the law of the jungle. It is a confrontation between a world increasingly committed to international rights and obligations and one where might is right. Since 2 August Iraq has broken any number of its international obligations. It has invaded and annexed its neighbour by force; it has pillaged and tortured Kuwait's population; it has taken hostages; since 15 January it has fired missiles at a country not a party to the dispute; it has defied its obligations towards prisoners-of-war under the Geneva Conventions; and it has resorted to unprecedented environmental terrorism. Now it is threatening further actions against international law.

Once before in this century a system of collective security , the League of Nations, failed to prevail over the law of the jungle, and one of the consequences was the Second World War. My country believes the system of collective security contained in the United Nations Charter is worth fighting for, and we intend to see that it prevails.

I should like to conclude by saying that I was sorry the representative of Iraq so misunderstood the reason why a number of representatives feel that the asking of questions of some of the delegations that appear before the Council was designed to temporize or indeed to make propaganda from those countries that are cooperating with Kuwait over its liberation. In order to make it quite clear that that is not so, I wish now to address to him a few questions that he might be able to answer before the end of the debate. It would certainly help the Council's work if he were able to do so.

First, will Iraq withdraw immediately and unconditionally from Kuwait, as required by the Security Council resolutions?

Secondly, will the representative of Iraq give an undertaking that Iraq will abide by the Geneva Conventions regarding the treatment of prisoners of war?

Thirdly, how are the prisoners of war from the countries of the allies being treated? Why have their names not been given to the International Committee of the Red Cross? Where are they being held, and what conditions?

Fourthly, will the representative of Iraq give an undertaking that Iraq will abide by its international obligations not to use chemical or biological weapons?

I think the answers to those questions could advance the Council's work a very long way if they were helpful. So I hope that the representative of Iraq will reflect very carefully on the possibility of speaking again before our debate is over and giving us some answers to those questions.

Meanwhile, I should like merely to associate myself with the representative of the United States in saying that the questions addressed to the representative of Kuwait are very germane, and I look forward very much to hearing the answers to them before the end of the debate.

The representative of Saudi Arabia might possibly reflect on two questions to which I should like to hear the answers. First, what is the nature of the military threat which Iraq has represented to Saudi Arabia since 2 August and represents today? Secondly, has Saudi Arabia received any indications, directly or indirectly, of Iraq's readiness to comply with Security Council resolutions and withdrawal from Kuwait?

[80] **Mr. Li Daoyu (China)** (interpretation from Chinese):

...

The international community made great efforts to bring about a peaceful settlement of the Gulf crisis. We very much regret that all those efforts failed and war finally broke out.

The war has been going on for nearly a month, inflicting disastrous losses of life and property. Many innocent civilians have been killed and many non-military installations demolished. We express our deep grief and sympathy. We are deeply concerned and worried that there exists a serious danger of the expansion and escalation of the war, and the situation is extremely grave.

From the very start of the Gulf crisis, the Chinese Government has adopted a principled and responsible position. We have opposed Iraqi invasion and annexation of Kuwait and demanded that Iraq withdraw its troops from Kuwait immediately and unconditionally, and restore and respect the independence, sovereignty, territorial integrity and legitimate Government of Kuwait. At the same time, the Chinese Government has consistently held that the Gulf crisis should be settled through peaceful means within the framework of the relevant resolutions of the Security Council. We believe that, while a peaceful solution through negotiations may take longer, the cost will be lower, whereas the use of force will not provide a solution in a short time either, and there exists the possibility of a protracted and expanded war for which all the parties concerned will pay a high price.

Consideration should be given to the fact that war has its own logic, independent of man's will, and that war will lead to many serious consequences, difficult to estimate at present. Modern war is cruel. The longer the war lasts, the more serious the consequences will be. Therefore, we once again call upon the belligerent parties to exercise the greatest restraint and prevent the spread and expansion of the flames of war so that the people of the Middle East and the Gulf region and the countries concerned will be saved from greater disasters, thus creating favourable conditions and providing opportunities for the international community to continue its search for a peaceful solution to the conflict.

The Gulf war has caused universal concern and anxiety in the international community. Some States' leaders have put forward many peace proposals for an early end to the war. We appreciate their efforts. We are of the view that, in order to give peace efforts a chance for progress, there should exist the following elements: first, Iraq should signify that it will withdraw its troops from Kuwait immediately; secondly, the parties concerned agree to seek a peaceful solution; thirdly, the belligerent parties will exercise restraint so as to reduce hostilities and prevent the expansion and escalation of the war; fourthly, the settlement of the Middle East question should be scheduled; fifthly, the arrangements after the Gulf war should be made mainly by the countries in the region and foreign military forces should withdraw from the Gulf region.

The Chinese Government has always supported the positive role played by the Security Council, the Secretary-General and the relevant States Members of the United Nations in seeking a peaceful solution to the Gulf crisis. Together with the international community, we are willing to continue to make our own contributions to achieving an early solution to this crisis and restoring peace and stability in the Gulf region.

[82] **Mr. Munteanu (Romania):**

...

Romania's position on the situation between Iraq and Kuwait has been presented many times before the Council. In fact, from the very first hours after the invasion of Kuwait by Iraq, Romania made known its stand, stating that no reason whatsoever could justify the use of force against a sovereign and independent State. Romania condemned the annexation of Kuwait and demanded the immediate, unconditional and complete withdrawal of the Iraqi forces.

My country is strongly committed to morality and legality in all spheres of domestic and international life. It has made clear in all its statements on the item under consideration that a solution to the Persian Gulf conflict can be based only on the relevant resolutions of the Security Council. It is in this context that we joined in sponsoring and voted in favour of resolution 678 (1990), which authorizes Member States cooperating with the Government of Kuwait to use all necessary means to uphold and implement resolution 660 (1990) and all subsequent relevant resolutions and to restore international peace and security in the area. Because of Iraq's refusal fully to comply with the relevant resolutions of the Security Council, resolution 678 (1990) is in process of being implemented by the use of force. In so doing, the international community made it clear to Iraq that there is no alternative to respecting the United Nations decisions and the principles of international law.

In fact, paragraph 3 of resolution 678 (1990) is addressed to the international community. It is in accordance with that paragraph that my country took recently an important political decision. I had the honour to summarize the content of that decision in a letter addressed to the Secretary-General of the United Nations, subsequently circulated as document S/22206, dated 8 February 1991. With the Council's permission, I should like to recall the main elements of the decision taken by Romania. In accordance with paragraph 3 of Security Council resolution 678 (1990) the Government of Romania has proposed and the Parliament of Romania has approved the sending to Saudi Arabia of a surgical hospital for medical assistance having a capacity of 200 beds and a staff of 360 persons.

Similar approval has been given for the sending to Saudi Arabia of a unit of the Romanian Army at a strength of 180 persons, which can perform tasks of chemical decontamination.

The two units have been formed on a voluntary basis and will be stationed behind the operational area. They will perform a humanitarian mission.

This decision by Romania is based on resolution 678 (1990), which requests all States to provide appropriate support for the actions undertaken to liberate Kuwait and to restore international peace and security in the Gulf area. This decision to send the surgical hospital and the decontamination unit to Saudi Arabia will become effective after the conclusion of the necessary agreements.

It has been rightly pointed out that the failure of attempts to achieve a peaceful solution to the Persian Gulf crisis has created a new situation, in which the destruction and suffering of the people of Iraq, a part of the great Arab nation, are increasing day by day. We deeply regret the human losses and suffering. They are indeed great. But no one should forget who bears the full responsibility for the invasion of Kuwait, for the outbreak of war and for its tragic consequences. It is only through the full implementation of the relevant Security Council resolutions that an end can be put to this tragic situation. That is why Iraq should clearly and unequivocally declare that it will fully comply with the Security Council resolutions.

It should also be stressed that Iraq is not the only country suffering the consequences of the conflict in the Gulf. Above all, we should not forget Kuwait and its plight, its daily suffering and the violation of human rights in that country. Saudi Arabia has lived and is still living under a terrible threat. There is also Israel, subject to an unprovoked attack. On the other hand, all the countries that have invoked Article 50 of the Charter are being confronted with special economic problems arising from the carrying out of measures established by resolution 661 (1990). The Security Council knows very well the price of the implementation of sanctions against Iraq. For Romania, the strict observance of sanctions against Iraq has meant considerable losses, and the hardship is compounded by the already difficult conditions of the Romanian economy. These losses and difficulties come at a moment of decisive importance for the economic reforms in Romania, and they generate additional suffering in the life of our people. Despite these difficulties, Romania is strictly observing and fully applying the Security Council resolutions.

Before concluding, my delegation would like to emphasize again that even at this very critical stage of the Gulf conflict the Security Council, through its formal and informal activities, can contribute to the liberation of Kuwait by ensuring compliance by Iraq with its resolutions, through the maximum use of political and diplomatic means - which should be correctly understood by Iraq.

We strongly reject any suggestion made here yesterday and today of the manipulation or malpractices of this body. This seems, indeed, to be an attack on the dignity of a main body of the United Nations, an avatar of the past, a voice from the dark which sounded so strange in these times of change that I cannot even believe this really happened on these premises. Are we to go back to the ideological division of the world that we so much deplored in the fifties? Would it not be better to address the issue on the basis of international law and the accepted principle of the United Nations that the invasion of foreign lands and the annexation of foreign countries must be condemned? Was it not similar practices that led the founders of the United Nations to conceive of an organization able to stand up to aggression?

My delegation would like also to reiterate its great appreciation of the personal efforts and initiatives of the Secretary-General of the United Nations, who has put his valuable experience at the service of our common endeavours. We commend, too, the proposals and initiatives of other countries that are working for the implementation of the relevant Security Council resolutions on the situation between Iraq and Kuwait and for a dignified course of action leading to the restoration of peace and legal order, in conformity with the Charter of the United Nations.

[88] Mr. Hohenfellner (Austria):

...

Austria, for one, supports a strong role for a strong Security Council. According to Article 24, paragraph 1 of the Charter of the United Nations, however, the Security Council acts on behalf of all the Members of the United Nations. Therefore, the Council's decisions should, as much and as often as possible, be representative of the collective will of the whole international community. Only in that way will it be able to maintain its political and moral legitimacy. We believe that the Council has to be - and has to be allowed to be - just and fair in all the cases brought before it. In our view, the Council has to make every effort to uphold, and if necessary enforce, the rule of law, regardless of where and by whom a breach of law occurs.

Austria is firmly committed to the purposes and the principles of the Charter of the United Nations. It goes without saying that also during our second term as a member of the Council we shall faithfully carry out all our obligations under the Charter and make every effort to contribute to the peaceful resolution of conflicts. In this regard, it is our firm intention to make full use of the specific possibilities of contributing to these endeavours that may be provided by Austria's status as a permanently neutral country.

I should now like to turn to the subject under consideration today, namely the situation between Iraq and Kuwait.

We are meeting here for the first time since the initiation of the use of force by States co-operating with the Government of Kuwait in pursuance of Security Council resolution 678 (1990). It is, however, important to recall that hostilities started as long ago as 2 August, when Iraq invaded Kuwait. In the words of the Federal Chancellor of Austria, Vranitzky, we, who have ourselves once been the victim of military aggression, have good reason to support the action undertaken by the international community against an aggressor. And, as Foreign Minister Mock said in the same debate, held in the Austrian Parliament on 16 January, for Austria the conclusions are clear: solidarity with those whose rights have been violated, and solidarity also with the international community, which is standing up against the violation of rights. Especially, a State the size of Austria has to be interested in international relations, which are determined less by power and more by the rule of law.

Having said that, I should hasten to add that even at this late hour, despite the military action already undertaken, political and diplomatic efforts still have their place and should, indeed, be intensified. The loss of human lives and the material destruction that have already occurred, and the even greater losses in the future in the event that hostilities continue, and especially if they escalate, make the search for ways and means of bringing these hostilities to an early end a moral imperative.

The humanitarian dimension of this conflict is of particular concern to us. Austria, and I myself as Chairman of the Security Council Committee established by resolution 661 (1990), will do the utmost to alleviate the grave situation. When we talk about human suffering, we mean the plight of the people of Kuwait and the civilian population of Iraq. We mean the disastrous consequences for all the people of the region, the hardship imposed on the Jordanian people, the dangers to which the Israeli people are exposed, and the lot of the Palestinians, where aspirations have been neglected. We mean the refugees and migrant workers, and we mean the prisoners of war, and even each and every soldier and their loved ones who do not know how all this will end for them.

What worries me deeply is that nobody can know where all this might end. While it is understandable that attention is being focused on dealing with the immediate situation, we must not lose sight of its long-term implications. It has been said that the Gulf conflict is a defining moment in history. The way in which we deal with, and finally resolve, this conflict will be of paradigmatic importance not only for the future of the region but also for the concept of collective security and the role of the United Nations as a whole. For Austria, the goal is clear. We seek full implementation of all Security Council resolutions beginning with resolution 660 (1990) - no more, no less.

Re-establishing peace and security in the area continues to require, first, a positive reaction by Iraq. It will then, however, also require other steps along the lines given by the Secretary-General in his statement of 15 January, and additional measures. Eventually, only a political solution will provide the necessary framework for a just and lasting settlement of the problems of the region.

I still remember Winston Churchill's words calling for magnanimity in victory and goodwill in peace. We have already seen resolution and defiance. Now we need tangible signs of compliance so that efforts may be resumed to find a political solution. Then we will need magnanimity and goodwill. Austria will not only lend its full support but also attempt to devise its own contribution, which I shall no doubt have the opportunity to present to this Council at a later stage.

[93] **Mr. Ayala-Lasso (Ecuador)** (interpretation from Spanish):

...

On 2 August 1990 the conscience of mankind was shocked by an event as inexplicable as it was illogical. At a time when we were all hailing the unquestionable progress being made along the road of agreement and peaceful dialogue, at a time when the Berlin Wall had fallen, at a time when ideological confrontation seemed to be dissolving and giving way to a common desire to strengthen freedom and democracy internationally, at a time when peoples had assumed full responsibility as the makers of their own destiny, at a time in short when the cold war had come to an end and we could glimpse a new era of respect for international law, all of those expectations were suddenly thwarted with the invasion of a small State, Kuwait, by a powerful neighbour.

The most important principles of the Charter of the United Nations were violated when that invasion took place. Sovereignty, independence and the territorial integrity of a State were violated. When Iraq proclaimed the annexation of Kuwait, it sought to resist another fundamental principle of international law, namely the nullity of territorial conquests through the use of force. In addition, its action was a flagrant rejection of the commitment we have all solemnly undertaken to support peaceful solutions as the sole and exclusive means of resolving disputes.

The international community represented by the Security Council reacted immediately and adopted resolution 660 (1990) condemning the invasion, demanding the immediate and unconditional withdrawal of Iraqi forces and raising an appeal that Iraq and Kuwait initiate negotiations to resolve their differences. Subsequent Iraqi challenges to the community of civilized nations gave rise to the immediate adoption of new Council resolutions. Thus economic sanctions were adopted against the invader. The nullity of the annexation of Kuwaiti territory was declared. It was demanded that Iraq permit and facilitate the departure of third-country nationals, and not endanger their security or health. Violations of diplomatic premises were condemned. It was demanded that the Iraqi authorities and occupation forces immediately cease and desist from taking hostage the nationals of third countries and mistreating and oppressing the nationals of Kuwait and third States and allow them to leave the area immediately. Iraq's attempt to modify the demographic composition of the Kuwaiti population was condemned.

None of the Security Council's demands and appeals were accepted by Iraq. No positive reaction was noted in the process upon which the community of nations embarked to bring about the fulfilment of the goals set forth in Security Council resolution 660 (1990): the immediate and unconditional withdrawal by Iraq from the territory of Kuwait. On 29 November 1990 the Council adopted resolution 678 (1990) authorizing all Member States of the United Nations cooperating with Kuwait to use all necessary means to uphold and implement resolution 660 (1990) and all subsequent relevant resolutions and to restore international peace and security in the region.

After the period granted to Iraq as a "pause of goodwill", the States cooperating with Kuwait, by virtue of the authorization granted under resolution 678 (1990), initiated military operations to bring about the liberation of Kuwait. It is therefore clear that all the Council's resolutions adopted in response to the war initiated by Iraq were geared towards achieving the restoration and application of the principles and rules violated by the invader, leading to the dramatic situation through which we are now living. However, it is equally clear that all resort to force has negative implications that affect and violate the most elementary rights of man and the aspirations of mankind.

Ecuador believes that even when a military action is embarked upon, the goals of which are clearly and unequivocally established and limited in resolutions of the Council, efforts aimed at adopting diplomatic and political measures to resolve the problem should continue and indeed be redoubled. The civilized conscience of mankind and all the peoples of the planet are raising their voices against the war. Diplomacy, in listening to that outcry, must use all its imagination and determination in the search for peaceful solutions.

This is what has occurred. I need not enumerate all of the initiatives that have sought from the very beginning of the invasion of Kuwait, in various regions and various ways, to facilitate a diplomatic and peaceful solution. But I do wish to refer to the recent endeavour of the Non-Aligned Movement and to the Soviet initiative carried out by Mr. Primakov. We wish the greatest possible success to both of those initiatives. These are diplomatic measures that reiterate our universal concern and demonstrate the collective will to take action to bring about the restoration of peace.

I believe it is also desirable to stress that all proposals conducive to laying out the framework of what could be a process of pacification once the military conflict is over have a common denominator: the conviction that we must always leave a door open so that the aggressor may feel encouraged to return to the way of law. The history of human conflict teaches a constant lesson: in order to build authentic peace, we must look not only at present circumstances but also at those which will inevitably follow in the future. Despite the aggressor's obduracy, we must remain persistent in searching for a way out, which, by restoring the rule of law, will make possible a peace that will be more easily accepted and therefore more lasting.

Ecuador supports the Secretary-General in all his efforts to achieve a peaceful solution to this grave problem. We are convinced that his experience and determination and his calm dignity in the face of unjustified attacks will continue motivating him to explore ways and means to facilitate what we all seek: a rapid conclusion to the conflict and the restoration of just and lasting peace.

Latin America has not remained indifferent to events in the Gulf. The Foreign Ministers of the member States of the Rio Group recently met in Caracas to consider the situation. At the end of their deliberations, they published a document from which I shall read the most salient paragraphs. The Foreign Ministers:

> "Agreed in reiterating their support for the resolutions of the United Nations Security Council and in renewing their support for the role that must fall to the Secretary-General of the United Nations in promoting a solution to the conflict that will make possible the restoration of peace in conformity with international law, the initiation of multilateral efforts aimed at a comprehensive, peaceful and definitive settlement of the problems of the region, and the submission of a report on developments in the fulfilment of Security Council resolutions;
>
> "Agreed in condemning the spread of the conflict through attacks upon non-belligerent countries in the area, such as Israel; they agreed on the necessity for strict compliance with the Geneva Conventions on the treatment of prisoners of war, and that the parties to the conflict should abstain from the use of chemical or biological weapons and weapons of mass or indiscriminate destruction;
>
> "Agreed in expressing alarm at the damage to the environment occurring as a result of the conflict;
>
> "Agreed to maintain the question of the Middle East on the agenda for their periodic consultations and to entrusting a committee made up of Colombia, Chile and Ecuador with following up on the Gulf crisis in all its aspects, including consideration of proposals and machinery to enable the Group to make an effective contribution to the advent of a new order of peace in the region based on the participation of all the parties involved and on compliance with United Nations resolutions, including solution of the problem of Palestine".

Ecuador, for its part, has maintained an unequivocal position on this problem. We believe that any solution must be based on strict compliance with the principles of the Charter embodied in the resolutions adopted by the Security Council. To facilitate that, all diplomatic endeavour is welcome and all peaceful initiatives should be explored. The fundamental aim of the Security Council resolutions is the liberation of Kuwait and the restoration of international peace and security in the region. Accordingly, it will be necessary in due course to consider the framework within which to seek implementation of all resolutions of the Council pertaining to the problems of the region, although implementation of the 12 Council resolutions on the Gulf problem is not conditioned upon any consideration extraneous to that specific problem.

It is obvious that permanent peace throughout the region will lead us to examine in a broader perspective respect for and compliance with all relevant resolutions of the Security Council and the establishment of machinery to make them effective. In that context, a conference on peace in the Middle East is of special importance. Once the war is over, the Arab nation will play a prominent role in all aspects of the region's security.

I wish now to discuss humanitarian aspects of the Gulf crisis. Unfortunately, every war has its victims, and that is why war is essentially evil. These losses are irretrievable, for, as Georges Bernanos put it, every human being is immortal and irreplaceable. The peoples of the world, who demand an attempt to find a way to put an end to the hostilities, were grief-stricken by yesterday's news about the results of the air raids. We see quite clearly the different responsibilities borne by those whose violation of international law gave rise to this crisis and by those who are trying to restore the rule of law. None the less, we believe we must strengthen the world Organization's action and its humanitarian image. We believe additional measures can be taken to prevent or alleviate suffering by innocent civilian victims of the conflict. Here too Ecuador fully supports the proposals made by the Secretary-General and by international humanitarian organizations.

Let me conclude by appealing, first, to the Government of Iraq to reflect on and comply with the resolutions of the Security Council, and, secondly, to the members of the coalition supporting Kuwait to strive, without setting aside the just principles they are defending, to promote peace in the region by showing the kind of flexibility that only the defender of justice and reason can show. A great Latin American, born in Mexico, Benito Juarez, said that in relations among nations as in relations among men, peace is respect for the rights of others.

May reason, and thus law, prevail, and may peace be restored throughout the Middle East region. That is the hope of Ecuador, and it is our solemn commitment to work in favour of this cause.

[102] **Mr. Noterdaeme (Belgium)** (interpretation from French:)

For more than six months Iraq has occupied Kuwait; Kuwait's political independence and territorial integrity have been trampled by the Iraqi army. In recent meetings of the Security Council we have had the opportunity to become fully aware of the violations and abuses perpetrated by the occupying troops. For six months Kuwait has been the victim of looting and of the arbitrary will of an illegitimate Power. That intolerable situation has forced hundreds of thousands of inhabitants of Kuwait to flee the country, while Iraqis have been moved into Kuwait to replace them. Most of the country's commercial and economic infrastructure has been pillaged or dismantled; many cultural, medical and social institutions have been devastated.

All this suffering and destruction is rooted in Iraq's refusal to respect the most fundamental provisions of international law, its refusal to recognize the sovereignty of an independent State. If a small peaceful State can today be wiped off the map by a powerful neighbour with no reaction from the international community, few Members of the United Nations will feel safe.

Fifty years ago, similar violations of international law led to a global conflict that rocked the world. It was precisely to put a rapid end to any such threat that our Organization was founded and that it assumed the powers the Security Council has just implemented. For my country - which twice in this century has been invaded, which endured the burden of two lengthy occupations and was twice liberated by an international coalition against totalitarianism and dictatorship - the principle of the defence of Kuwait and of the need to liberate it is crucial and basic.

The invasion and annexation of Kuwait aroused the entire international community to indignation and condemnation. The United Nations gave effective and clear voice to that reaction in an unprecedented mobilization of opinion. That is the context in which the Security Council has condemned Iraq on 12 occasions, first for its aggression, then for its unbending refusal to withdraw from Kuwait.

My Government understands and to a large extent shares the concerns of the countries that called for today's meeting. The daily sight of combat and its aftermath gives rise to a desire to intervene to end the hostilities. Unfortunately, one must immediately remember that the sole cause of the present war in the Gulf was the universally-condemned expansionism of the Iraqi régime and of that country's stubborn refusal to respect the will of the international community.

Since the invasion of Kuwait there have been numerous peace initiatives. They proliferated on the eve of the 15 January deadline and they continue to emerge today. We recall that all those efforts by Western countries and the Soviet Union and by Arab and non-aligned countries - not to mention by the Secretary-General - were met with blunt rejection; President Saddam Hussein obstinately rejected the peace which was, and still is, offered him.

The Security Council has adopted 12 resolutions that clearly outline the objectives and means that must guide us in restoring the full sovereignty of Kuwait.

I would recall that the resolutions aim not only at the liberation of Kuwait and the restoration of its legitimate Government but also at the restoration of international peace and security in the region. The resolutions indicate the legitimate means for liberating Kuwait; never forgetting the path of diplomatic persuasion, they first imposed an embargo against Iraq before legitimizing, as a last resort, the use of force.

It is in the legal framework of those resolutions that the Belgian Government views the action that has been taken and the concerns of the countries who have spoken before the Council. In that connection, Belgium stands by four principles: the objectives set by the Council's resolutions; the means legitimately implemented; the solidarity that must unite the international community; and humanitarian requirements.

In numerous declarations the States that are cooperating with Kuwait within the framework of the Security Council resolutions have reaffirmed their determination to abide by the objectives set forth therein. The military means being used by the coalition forces are clearly impressive. However, that force of arms can only be judged in comparison with the unbelievable apparatus set up by Iraq in its attempt to perpetuate its presence in Kuwait.

For us, respect for the objectives of the Organization in the Gulf conflict implies two fundamental considerations. First of all, only a clear commitment by Iraq to withdraw from Kuwait, followed by concrete actions leading to complete respect for the Council's resolutions, could result in a suspension of hostilities.

It is also essential that we not neglect the second objective set forth in resolution 678 (1990), namely, the conditions that would allow for the effective and lasting restoration of international peace and security in the region. My Government believes that after the liberation of Kuwait the Security Council must play a pivotal role in realizing that goal. Within that context Belgium, which is one of the States members of the European Community, repeats its commitment to work actively to ensure a future of peace, stability and development, with social justice and regional economic solidarity for all the peoples of the region. To that end it will support the setting up of a conference on security and co-operation in the Middle East. The goal of such an undertaking would be the progressive reduction of the misunderstandings and bitterness that continue to prevail in that region by giving pride of place, first, to problems of reconstruction and economic co-operation and then to those of security and respect for human rights. That system would complement the efforts undertaken to promote a solution to the Arab-Israeli conflict. In that connection Belgium renews the commitment it has made to developing a process designed to lead, at an appropriate time and after serious preparation, to a settlement of the Palestinian problem. Here, my Government welcomes the intention of the Secretary-General to appoint in the very near future a new special representative who could begin the preparations for such a process.

To achieve those objectives we should use all the means the resolutions have made available to us. Here, I should like to deal specifically with the proposals put forward by the countries that have requested this meeting. The Belgian Government wishes to make two comments in this regard. First, the use of force, which became inevitable given the attitude of Iraq, should not put a halt to diplomacy. As the Secretary-General emphasized last week, all diplomatic initiatives should be supported that would promote the liberation of Kuwait and, therefore, the end of hostilities.

On the other hand, however, diplomatic efforts unfortunately can no longer exclude at this stage the other means that have been brought into play to ensure respect for international law. A cessation of military operations would be interpreted by the Government of Iraq as a sign of weakness on the part of the international community, and that Government would use it to bolster new arguments to justify its contempt for the Council's resolutions and take it as evidence of an illusory tactical advantage in the field. It is therefore likely that any kind of truce would have an effect contrary to the one hoped for and that it would ultimately serve to prolong hostilities rather than to cut them short.

Only a new element would allow the council usefully to consider the interruption of hostilities. We all know what that element should be: Iraq's unequivocal commitment to withdraw from Kuwait, to be followed immediately by concrete actions providing a convincing illustration of Iraq's intention to abide by all of the Council's resolutions.

We ardently hope to see such a commitment from Iraq that would enable us to put a speedy end to the war and to the sufferings it is causing.

The resolutions adopted by the Security Council are binding on all States. That clear principle of law has two consequences: on the one hand, all States must scrupulously implement the embargo. That is an obligation under Charter VII of the Charter and not the result of a choice allowing for certain differences of interpretation. My Government welcomes the fact that the embargo has effectively been implemented by Members of the Organization. Moreover, Belgium has actively assisted in naval control of the embargo by dispatching four warships to the region. At the present time those ships have engaged in more than 2,500 searches at sea. However, we must note that even the nearly total application of the embargo has not led Iraq to abandon its conquest.

Beyond the embargo, we have all been urged to show solidarity with States co-operating in the liberation of Kuwait. Such co-operation has reflected the means, responsibilities and geopolitical situations of the various States. Indeed, the resolutions leave it up to the States freely to determine the magnitude of their commitment. As for my country, we believe we have contributed to the collective effort through military support and by means of considerable medical assistance.

I should like to conclude with a fourth consideration concerning the humanitarian aspects of the present conflict, to which the Secretary-General referred in a timely matter last week during an informal meeting of the Council. Belgium shares the concerns voiced in this Chamber regarding the suffering of Kuwaiti and Iraqi civilians, a suffering caused by the Baghdad regime's refusal to respect international law.

My Government wishes to emphasize three things in this connection: First we are convinced that the States that are co-operating with Kuwait are doing all in their power to enforce respect for humanitarian law, in particular the Geneva Convention, both concerning the protection of civilians and concerning the treatment of prisoners of war. On the other hand, Iraq's behaviour gives rise to extreme concern. The sufferings inflicted upon Kuwait, the attacks deliberately aimed at civilians in Saudi Arabia and Israel, the fate of prisoners of war, not to mention the treatment meted out to the Kurdish population, the assaults on the environment and appeals to terrorism, are all violations of law and condemned by my country's authorities.

Secondly, my Government will lend its assistance to any efforts designed to provide humanitarian assistance to the civilian population in Iraq and in Kuwait, in particular through the Red Cross and the Red Crescent, organizations to which I should like to pay a tribute for the active roles they are playing. In no case can such assistance be held hostage to the benefit of considerations that are totally foreign to humanitarian aid. In order to avoid that situation my country hopes that, in accordance with resolution 666 (1990), the Committee on Sanctions will be able to meet without delay to make an objective assessment of the essential needs of the civilian populations, particularly of the most vulnerable sectors. That consideration will give us an idea of whether circumstances are likely to justify the inclusion of emergency food assistance to Iraq and Kuwait as part of humanitarian assistance. Such a decision would obviously entail the Iraqi Government's acceptance of effective control to guarantee the destination of supplies sent, as explicitly provided in the Geneva Conventions.

In order to demonstrate its full solidarity in the humanitarian sphere, my country has approved plans for considerable assistance to cope with the needs of thousands of refugees. Our financial assistance is also being addressed to the countries most affected by the economic consequences of the conflict, in particular Turkey, Egypt and Jordan.

Those are the considerations that motivate my Government in dealing with this conflict.

In order to right a flagrant violation of international law the Security Council has had to authorize the use of force, with all the consequences that that entails. Events that have taken place since then have confirmed that that decision was, unfortunately, the only one possible. They have strengthened our feeling that a policy of appeasement would only have provided the international community with a respite and would have forced it to confront later, in an even more dangerous context, the challenge facing it.

That being the case, any diplomatic effort with a serious chance of success deserves to be encouraged. The most important thing remains the evacuation of Kuwait. Only with such a withdrawal can the guns fall silent. It is now up to one single man to decide to do so.

[111] **Mr. VORONTSOV (Union of Soviet Socialist Republics)** (interpretation from Russian):

From the first moment of the outbreak at the beginning of August 1990 of the crisis in the Gulf region, resulting from the Iraqi invasion of Kuwait, the Soviet Union took a strong position of principle, of firm condemnation of the aggression by Iraq against Kuwait and its consequent annexation, as a flagrant violation of the norms of international law, morality and civilized inter-State relations. Together with other members of the international community, the Soviet Union immediately took the side of the victim of aggression and energetically spoke out in favour of the unconditional, immediate and full withdrawal of Iraqi troops from the territory of Kuwait, the restoration of the independence and sovereignty of that State and the restoration of international legality and justice.

At all stages of the conflict the Security Council has done everything in its power to ensure a peaceful solution - I emphasize "peaceful". The Council has adopted 12 resolutions aimed at settling the Kuwait crisis through political and other non-military means.

The President of the Soviet Union, Mikhail Sergeyevich Gorbachev, in his statement of 9 February once again reaffirmed the fundamental fidelity of the Soviet Union to Security Council resolutions, which reflect the will of the international community and the hope of peoples for a new world order excluding aggression and encroachment on the territory and natural resources of others.

Unfortunately, Iraq's rigid intransigence provoked the present tragic course of events. The world found itself faced with a most dangerous armed confrontation, whose alarming reverberations go far beyond the boundaries of the Middle East.

The course of events in the war in the Gulf region is a source of great concern in the Soviet Union. Particularly alarming, and a matter of great regret in our country, are the reports being received of civilian victims.

Military actions have already caused enormous material damage. Entire countries - first Kuwait, Now Iraq and later, perhaps, others as well - are threatened by catastrophic destruction. The dumping of enormous quantities of oil into the Gulf may turn into a drastic ecological disaster.

The Soviet Union has noted the statements made by countries parties to the coalition to the effect that the military operations they are carrying out are limited to the objective laid down in resolutions of the Security Council - namely, the liberation of Kuwait. At the same time, we cannot fail to take into account the fact that a further escalation of the conflict may create a danger exceeding the mandate of the Council's resolutions.

Extremely dangerous developments are seen in the acts of provocation attempting to expand the boundaries of the war to involve Israel and other States and in so doing to give the armed conflict yet another destructive dimension - the Arab-Israeli dimension. There is a growing danger of the use of weapons of mass destruction, above all chemical and bacteriological weapons. The possibility of such a development cannot but be of concern to the Soviet Union, particularly in view of the region's proximity to our southern borders.

As is well known, the Soviet Union has made considerable efforts to prevent the situation in the region from sliding towards armed confrontation. The President of the Soviet Union and the Soviet leadership have on many occasions appealed to the Iraqi leadership, trying to persuade it to show prudence and to carry out the resolutions of the Security Council. We are continuing to engage in contacts with all those who are in a position to promote a settlement of the conflict.

Throughout the entire one-and-a-half-month-long pause of goodwill, and even after the beginning of military operations in accordance with resolution 678 (1990), we appealed to President Saddam Hussein not to make irremediable mistakes, to show a love of peace and to declare the withdrawal of Iraqi troops from Kuwait. Unfortunately, the answers of the Iraqi side to our appeals were unfailingly negative.

In favouring the speedy cessation of hostilities and the start of a search for a political settlement, the Soviet Union is fully aware that without a clearly expressed readiness by the Iraqi leadership to carry out the demands of the international community and to leave Kuwait this cannot be achieved.

The Soviet-American statement of 29 January emphasizes that

> "a cessation of hostilities would be possible if Iraq would make an unequivocal commitment to withdraw from Kuwait. ... such a commitment must be backed by immediate concrete steps leading to full compliance with the Security Council resolutions."

Motivated by a sense of historic responsibility and by humanitarian considerations, and trying to work in all possible ways for a settlement on the basis of the Security Council resolutions, the President of the Soviet Union at this critical time recently publicly appealed once again to the President of Iraq to weigh everything that is at stake for his country and to demonstrate realism, which would make it possible to embark on the path of a reliable and just peaceful settlement.

In this connection, on 9 February President Gorbachev decided to send his personal representative to Baghdad for a meeting with President Hussein. That meeting took place on 12 February. In acting in this way the Soviet Union wishes, together with Arab and other Muslim States, the countries of Europe and Asia, and above all the United States of America and all the other permanent members of the Security Council, not only to assist in bringing about a speedy end to the war, but also to begin preparations for a lasting system of security on an equal footing in a region which is so important to the whole world. That includes, of course, a settlement of the Arab-Israeli conflict and the Palestinian problem, given the decisive role played in this process by those States which are located in the region.

A worthy role in the post-war system must also be played by Iraq, whose people cannot be held responsible for what has happened. We believe that the Security Council must begin that work - preparation for a lasting system of security on an equal footing in the region under discussion - in the very near future.

But the most important thing here today is to extinguish the flames of war in the Gulf as quickly as possible. We believe that the entire international community and all States must actively exert their influence on the Iraqi leadership to force it to change its mind. That is precisely the aim of the continuation of Soviet-Iraqi contacts now taking place in Moscow.

In our view, the present discussion in the Security Council must serve as a clear reaffirmation of the need for the speedy implementation of the resolutions adopted so far by the Security Council, resolutions which have recently been subjected to attacks by Iraq.

Our meeting here is a clear signal to the Iraqi leadership that it must comply with these just and well-founded decisions of the Security Council and in the interests of its people and of peace in the region declare an immediate, full and unconditional withdrawal from Kuwait.

In this connection, I have only one question for the representative of Iraq: When shall we hear such a statement from the Iraqi leadership?

[114] **The President:**

There are a number of names remaining on the list of speakers. With the concurrence of members of the Council, I shall suspend the meeting now until 10.30 tomorrow morning.

The meeting was suspended at 7.50 p.m.

D. S/PV.2977 (Part II) (closed-resumption 1), 15 February 1991

[115] **Mr. Gharekhan (India):**

The Security Council's meeting today comes in the wake of a development that deserves the Council's immediate and careful consideration. I am referring to this morning's communiqué issued by the Revolutionary Command Council of Iraq regarding Security Council resolution 660 (1990) with the aim of reaching an honourable and acceptable political solution, including withdrawal - and I emphasize withdrawal.

Let me stress two cardinal points. Firstly, the origins of the crisis are unmistakable and undeniable, as is the need to reverse the unprovoked aggression and illegal annexation of Kuwait by Iraq. Resolution 660 (1990) addresses precisely this. Secondly, and equally important, the crisis in the Gulf had earlier devastated Kuwait and is now taking a tragic toll in human lives in both Kuwait and Iraq. We have been deeply pained by the hardship suffered by the people of Kuwait for the past several months and, while their sufferings continue and have in fact sharply increased, innocent civilians in Iraq are also undergoing enormous hardship and losses. This devastation must be brought to an end - and the sooner, the better.

The Security Council, mandated to remain seized of the matter, thus has a solemn responsibility on both the counts I have just outlined: implementation of resolution 660 (1990) and restoration of peace in the region.

My delegation believes that we must not close what appears to be a window of opportunity opening out. Diplomacy must be given a chance at this juncture; indeed, it has a duty to exert itself in such circumstances. Too much is at stake in terms of human lives, the safeguarding of international law, the foundations of peaceful ties among sovereign States and the promotion of tranquil and mutually beneficial relations amongst the countries in the Gulf for us to let slip from our grasp any opportunity for peace, no matter how small it might seem at this time.

With all this in mind, my delegation would like to offer some ideas on the way in which the United Nations can continue to address this issue.

Firstly, the Security Council, in taking note of the reported offer from Iraq, should consider ways and means to utilize it towards the full implementation of resolution 660 (1990). In doing so, the Council should engage in discussions on the possibilities available to it to promote a peaceful resolution of the crisis. This, I believe, will strengthen the Council's prestige, credibility and functioning.

Secondly, to underpin our efforts at achieving a peaceful resolution, there should be an immediate cessation, or at the least a suspension, of hostilities in the Gulf. My delegation believes that such a step will provide the necessary environment for the purpose as well as for the commencement of a time-bound process of complete and speedy withdrawal of Iraqi forces from Kuwait.

Thirdly, the role of the Secretary-General in his endeavours to seek peace deserve not only consistent and full support but reinforcement. We would therefore, in the present context, like the Security Council to request the Secretary-General urgently to examine what needs to be done to ensure that a peaceful resolution of the Gulf crisis can be achieved. My delegation would like the Secretary-General to redouble his efforts in this direction. There are other efforts pursued by several countries which can go on in parallel. In particular, I refer to the efforts of the Non-Aligned Movement, which in the very near future will be sending a mission of ministers to Baghdad. I refer also to the efforts of the Soviet Government and of its envoy to Baghdad, and to the forthcoming visit of the Foreign Minister of Iraq to Moscow.

In putting forth those ideas, my delegation's purpose is twofold, as I explained earlier: to ensure implementation of resolution 660 (1990) and to save the Gulf region from further bloodshed and destruction.

India's relations with Iraq and Kuwait go long back into history. Our peoples and Governments have worked together to noteworthy mutual benefit. This legacy of good will animates our wish to see peace returned to the region. We should like to see more secure and durable foundations for peace, stability and cooperation in that vital part of the world, and we believe that the Security Council at this juncture has an inalienable and urgent role to play in promoting this.

[122] **Mr. Blanc (France)** (interpretation from French):

From the very beginning of the crisis launched by Iraq's invasion of Kuwait on 2 August last, France constantly sought - indeed until the very last moment - to promote a peaceful solution.

In that spirit, the President of the French Republic proposed on 24 September last to the General Assembly an approach that postulated as a prerequisite Iraq's adherence to the views of the Security Council. I should like to recall here the fundamental elements of that approach: first of all, affirmation of Iraq's intention to withdraw its troops from Kuwait; then, the international community's guarantee of the withdrawal of military forces as well as the restoration of Kuwait's sovereignty; the substitution, at a later stage, of the dynamics of good-neighbourliness in security and peace for the various elements of confrontation in the Middle East, whether it be the situation in Lebanon or the Arab-Israeli conflict, through an initiative which would avoid an overlapping of conflicts that are different in nature and which would imply direct dialogue between the parties concerned, agreement among neighbouring or adjacent States and international backing - with the idea, at the end of that road, of an international conference; and, finally, a mutually agreed reduction of armaments in the region and the beginning of cooperation from the Middle East to the Atlantic, opening the way to stability and prosperity.

On the basis of those proposals, we unceasingly pursued our attempts to make Iraq abide by our Council's resolutions.

Even quite recently - shortly before the end of the pause of good will decided upon by the Council in its resolution 678 (1990), France undertook an initiative by which the United Nations would address a final appeal to the Iraqi leaders. We hoped that they would immediately declare their intention to withdraw from Kuwait in accordance with a programmed timetable and would immediately begin a massive and speedy withdrawal, on the understanding that the withdrawal would be carried out under United Nations control, with the participation of peace-keeping forces for which Arab countries in particular would be called upon, that a guarantee of non-aggression could be given to Iraq, that negotiations would begin with a view to the achievement of a peaceful settlement, and that once this settlement had been achieved, with respect for the Security Council resolutions, the members of the Council would make an active contribution to the settlement of other problems of the region, in particular the Arab-Israeli conflict and the Palestine problem.

All those proposals presented by France in order to achieve a peaceful solution to the crisis are still valid.

The Iraqi Revolutionary Command Council issued this morning a long declaration, which doubtless contains a new element, distinct from previous categorical declarations. This time the Iraqi authorities envisage withdrawal from Kuwait - but they add on impossible conditions that do not fall under Security Council resolution 660 (1990), which, I recall, provides for immediate and unconditional withdrawal from Kuwait. At the point where we find ourselves, the Iraqi proposal, which does not meet that demand and multiplies conditions, cannot be accepted.

Therefore, we consider that a Security Council initiative aimed at the suspension of hostilities would be pointless. In the present circumstances, it would not hold out any political prospects.

We understand the deep emotion aroused in Arab and Islamic public opinion by the military operation, which affects an Arab and Islamic country and people, as well as the solidarity felt by other countries within the non-aligned group. But it would run counter to the facts to present the action now under way as action pitting the West against the Arab world or the North against the South. This action is the result of resolutions adopted on behalf of the entire international community by the Security Council, and it will be for the Council, moreover, to organize in due time a return to peace, and to play its full role in helping to lay down the conditions for lasting peace and security in the region. It brings together, alongside Western countries, Arab and Islamic countries. Its objective is to make Iraq - which bears the responsibility for a particularly serious violation of international law through its occupation and subsequent annexation of another State, an Arab State, a sovereign State - restore and respect international law.

Still today, we are aware that only Iraq possesses the means to put an end to the present situation by agreeing to abide fully by the Security Council resolutions. We voice the hope that it will do so. Its existence as a sovereign State which, because of its position, its resources and the capabilities of its people, has an important role to play in the region's balance and development is not in question.

[126] **Mr. Alarcon de Quesada (Cuba)** (interpretation from Spanish):

The representative of India has clearly described the specific circumstances in which we are continuing this closed meeting, which the Council began yesterday. I would fully associate my delegation with the comments he has made.

On this occasion my delegation wishes to put before the Council three draft resolutions we have just submitted to the Secretariat for official distribution. They refer to action we believe the Council should envisage as a matter of urgency. They are short, and accordingly I can read them out.

The first reads as follows:

> "The Security Council,
>
> "Deeply concerned by the state of war existing in the Gulf and, above all, by the losses of human life and the destruction of material property caused by the mass bombings suffered by the cities of Iraq,
>
> "Committed to restoring the independence, sovereignty and territorial integrity of Kuwait,
>
> "Considering its primary responsibility for the maintenance of international peace and security, as established in Article 24 of the Charter of the United Nations,
>
> "Convinced that it is its duty to use all peaceful means for the settlement of international conflicts and differences in order to maintain international peace and security and 'save succeeding generations from the scourge of war', as proclaimed in the Preamble to the Charter of the United Nations,
>
> "1. Demands that the bombings of the cities of Iraq be immediately halted and requests that the negotiations for seeking a peaceful resolution of the conflict be immediately intensified without further resort to force;

"2. Decides to remain seized of the matter." (*S/22232*)

Another draft resolution reads as follows:

"The Security Council,

"Reaffirming the need to take steps with a view to reaching a peaceful solution to the present situation in the Gulf,

"Committed to restoring the independence, sovereignty and territorial integrity of Kuwait, and avoiding further losses of life and material property,

"Considering the role which the Secretary-General has played in the elimination and avoidance of situations of conflict and the role he has to play in achieving a peaceful solution to the situation of war prevailing in the Gulf,

"Considering also the efforts which the Secretary-General made to that end before hostilities erupted on 16 January 1991,

"1. Requests the Secretary-General to renew his good offices and mediation efforts without delay, on the basis of his statement to the press of 15 January 1991, and to report back to the Council as soon as possible;

"2. Decides to remain seized of the matter." (*S/22233*)

Another draft resolution would read as follows:

"The Security Council,

"Recalling its resolutions 660 (1990), 661 (1990), 662 (1990), 664 (1990), 665 (1990), 666 (1990), 667 (1990), 669 (1990), 670 (1990), 674 (1990), 677 (1990) and 678 (1990),

"Guided by the purposes and principles of the United Nations, as set out in Chapter I of the Charter of the United Nations,

"Mindful of the provisions of Article 29 of the Charter of the United Nations, which provides that 'the Security Council may establish such subsidiary organs as it deems necessary for the performance of its functions',

"Acting in accordance with rule 28 of the provisional rules of procedure of the Security Council, which states that 'the Security Council may appoint a commission or committee or a rapporteur for a specified question',

"Deeply concerned by the war situation existing in the Gulf region, which endangers international peace and security, and determined to put an end to the hostilities as soon as possible,

"1. Decides to establish an Ad Hoc Committee, composed of all members of the Security Council, to examine the situation currently prevailing in the Gulf region and consider possible formulas for halting armed actions and achieving a peaceful settlement of the conflict on the basis of the above-mentioned resolutions of the Security Council, thus avoiding further loss of life and destruction;

"2. Decides also that the Ad Hoc Committee referred to in paragraph 1 shall begin its work immediately after the adoption of the present resolution;

"3. Decides further that the Ad Hoc Committee shall report back to the Security Council on its findings and on any specific proposals which may have been made not later than 28 February 1991." (*S/22231*)

I should like to add that in submitting these draft resolutions my delegation wishes to associate itself with the sentiments of profound alarm and concern that have been aroused throughout the world by the recent manifestations of the development of the war. It wishes to say it is convinced that so long as the conflict cannot be resolved or redirected through negotiation and dialogue we should at least try to avoid further vast damage being inflicted on the civilian population by the conflict.

We must to the fullest extent possible spare from injury and suffering civilians in Iraq and Kuwait, as well as in Israel, Saudi Arabia and all other nations affected by the conflict. We also believe that, as was mentioned by our colleague from India, the Security Council must now fully assume its responsibilities and try to create a framework in which the different steps being taken - such as the outstanding effort of President Gorbachev or the démarches of the non-aligned countries noted earlier by Ambassador Gharekhan - might enjoy the greatest possible success.

But in addition, the Council itself should consider, evaluate and study any initiative or idea presented by Members of the United Nations in order to help find a solution to this conflict as soon as possible and to try to give dialogue, diplomatic initiative and negotiation a genuine opportunity. We must give peace a chance if we are to save not only the civilian lives that today are threatened by war, but also those of soldiers on either side. I believe that it is the ethical obligation of us all to try to deal with the fate and safety of innocent civilians, first and foremost, but also of the young soldiers - be they from Iraq, the United States, or any other country involved in the conflict - whose lives are threatened by the continuation of the war.

My delegation is, of course, ready and willing to continue the consultations we have begun with some of our colleagues and to consider with all members the draft resolutions we have submitted, which we hope the Council will be able to adopt with all the urgency demanded by the situation.

[132] **Mr. Hatano (Japan):**

...

The Government of Japan has read Iraq's announcement this morning, which includes a new element of its willingness to withdraw from Kuwait. Unfortunately, certain conditions are attached to its acceptance of the relevant Security Council resolutions. My Government, however, is carefully studying this announcement to determine what Iraq's true intentions are.

Ever since Iraq's armed invasion of Kuwait on 2 August 1990, the international community has made every possible effort to achieve a peaceful solution of the crisis. The world community has repeatedly appealed to President Saddam Hussein to comply with the Security Council resolutions. Japan, which had traditionally enjoyed good relations with Iraq, pursued efforts at the highest level of government as well as through diplomatic channels to persuade the Iraqi leadership to withdraw from Kuwait in order to restore justice and peace to the region. In fact, just the day before yesterday, Mr. Nakayama, our Minister for Foreign Affairs, reiterated his appeal to the Iraqi leadership through the Iraqi Ambassador in Tokyo. We intend to continue this effort.

Japan expresses its firm support for the use of force by the United Nations Member States in accordance with Security Council resolution 678 (1990). Japan, for its part, made contributions last fall amounting to $2 billion to multinational forces in the Gulf, in addition to $2 billion in economic assistance to the most severely affected countries in the region. Further, in January, Japan pledged an additional contribution of $9 billion.

My country recalls all too vividly the human suffering and material destruction that resulted from engaging in the Second World War. The entire nation of Japan was then reduced to ashes and its economy utterly destroyed, which made the postwar reconstruction a painstaking and long process. Japan fervently hopes that the hostilities in the Gulf will be brought to an end and that peace and justice will be restored in the region as soon as possible.

The United Nations can play a role at this critical moment and Japan welcomes all peace initiatives, including the efforts of our Secretary-General towards this end. In the event that the withdrawal of Iraq from Kuwait is realized, Japan believes that the United Nations will then play a further constructive role in resolving the problems. However, in order to achieve this goal, we must hear a clearer and unequivocal commitment from the Iraqi leadership. The Japanese Government once again urges President Saddam Hussein to demonstrate his full compliance with the relevant Security Council resolutions.

...

[136] Mr. KIRSCH (Canada):

...

The Security Council is meeting at a momentous time in its history. Having joined together with unprecedented unanimity and authority to deal with an extremely serious threat to international peace and security, the Council wishes now to take stock of the results of its actions.

Of the 12 resolutions adopted by the Security Council in relation to Iraq's invasion of Kuwait, the first resolution, resolution 660 (1990), clearly sets out the requirement that Iraqi troops withdraw immediately and unconditionally from Kuwait. Canada was one of the sponsors of that resolution.

The declaration issued today by the Iraqi leadership is currently under study by the Government of Canada. But we appear to be dealing with a series of conditions of a nature which may well nullify entirely any constructive signal to be drawn from the Iraqi declaration. We urge those who issued that statement to comply fully with the decisions of the Council. Unconditional Iraqi withdrawal from Kuwait would provide the opening we have been looking for, and a route to a settlement of the crisis.

Canada was a member of the Security Council that through the fall of 1990 took decisive action to ensure that the unjustified Iraqi invasion of Kuwait would not be allowed to stand. In 12 resolutions adopted by an overwhelming majority the Security Council clearly expressed the will of the world community to see Iraq quit Kuwait and to see peace and security in the region restored. Comprehensive mandatory sanctions were applied against a United Nations Member State to a degree never seen before. Ultimately, after providing for a significant pause for peace to give diplomacy time to work, the Council authorized the use of all necessary means to ensure that its will would be enforced and peace and security restored.

Force is now being used by a number of United Nations Members to effect Iraq's withdrawal from Kuwait. Force was initiated only after all other reasonable means to secure the enforcement of the Security Council's will had been exhausted, including the valiant intervention of the Secretary-General himself. Indeed, the disappointing and painful recourse to force was the result of reaching the limits of diplomacy, not of the absence of efforts to apply it. The continuing recourse to force is clearly authorized by the legal and moral authority of the Security Council. The conflict that has stemmed from this is both legal and moral; of that there can be no doubt.

The first responsibility of the United Nations is to uphold international peace and security. All too often in its history, aggression of various sorts has not been dealt with decisively by a Security Council divided by ideological and political differences. All too often, regional conflicts and aggression were manipulated by large Powers that could shun the United Nations at will. For Canada and countries like Canada, which have based their diplomacy on the construction of a credible, effective multilateral system, the failure of the United Nations to respond effectively to Iraq's direct challenge to its authority would have once again condemned the United Nations to impotence, rendering it incapable of protecting any country's security, including our own. A discredited United Nations would make the world an even more dangerous and unpredictable place than it already is, as nations around the world, left to their own devices to ensure their security, armed themselves against potentially hostile neighbours.

The international community should be gratified that the United Nations has now proven itself capable of fulfilling the collective security function that its founders intended.

Canada is participating in the coalition of nations using force against Iraq precisely because that force is authorized by and is in support of the United Nations. Canada argued strongly against the unilateral use of force against Iraq because we believed that such force could be justified and sustained successfully only if it had United Nations sanction. Now that the United Nations has demonstrated its capacity to enforce peace and security, we are not sympathetic to those who argue that the United Nations is somehow being used wrongly. The United Nations is properly involved in international action being undertaken to reverse aggression and re-establish peace and security.

We profoundly regret the losses, on all sides, being experienced in this war. Nevertheless, the coalition has no choice but to pursue enforcement measures until the will of the United Nations is enforced. To do any less would call into question the international community's commitment to the United Nations. There is no alternative but to persevere until the goals of the United Nations are realized.

This does not mean that realistic possibilities to end the hostilities should not be pursued. Many countries, which have understandable regard for the welfare of the Iraqi and Kuwaiti peoples, especially the most vulnerable groups, have made a variety of proposals in that regard. We welcome those proposals and share in the humanitarian concerns which underlie them. But all such proposals are predicated, as they must be, on the fulfillment of the basic requirement of Iraqi withdrawal from Kuwait.

Because the rationale of this conflict is not only the liberation of Kuwait but also the protection of the values of the United Nations, its pursuit and aims must also meet the highest international standards. This means, above all, minimizing to the extent possible civilian casualties and otherwise adhering to the laws of war. Despite the intensity of the air attack on Iraq, the coalition forces have taken great care, sometimes at great risk to themselves, to restrict wherever possible their attacks to military targets. Regrettably, the same cannot be said for the Iraqi leadership.

Canada is of the view that coalition war aims must be limited to those agreed to by the United Nations. Those aims do not include the destruction of Iraq; they are rather to enforce Security Council resolutions, to compel Saddam Hussein to quit Kuwait and to restore peace and security to the area - no more and no less.

The United Nations must also ensure that it wins the peace which follows the war. The international community should recognize that this war has unleashed passions and forces that will make a stable and secure peace very difficult. As in past wars, however, planning of successful peace must begin at an early stage. The United Nations itself was created in the aftermath of the last great war. We must ensure that the United Nations emerges from this conflict stronger, more credible and better equipped to contribute to peace in the Middle East and elsewhere.

A number of countries have already advanced useful ideas about the security, political and economic aspects of post-hostilities planning. The Prime Minister and the Secretary of State for External Affairs of Canada have made recent proposals geared to stimulating early consideration of this vital matter. They were discussed with the Secretary-General in Ottawa this past Tuesday.

While clearly it is first and foremost the business of the countries in the region to find together solutions to these problems, we believe that a significant United Nations role is necessary if the negative effects of the war are to be minimized and political reconciliation and economic reconstruction successfully implemented.

In the security field the United Nations could have a vital role in a traditional peace-keeping observer mission, which will be needed to supervise the cease-fire and withdrawal of forces, and possibly in the provision of longer-term peace-keeping forces. There may be other possibilities for direct United Nations involvement even as peace and restoration efforts are under way. The United Nations role as mediator could be important in reintegrating Iraq into the family of nations and in encouraging the use of peaceful dispute-settlement mechanisms in the Gulf region. While longer-term security arrangements are the responsibility of the States in the region, the United Nations could provide the appropriate international guarantees. United Nations support will also be essential in promoting control over the proliferation of conventional arms and weapons of mass destruction, both of which threaten the security of the region and the rest of the world.

We know that other conflicts - notably the Arab-Israeli and the Palestinian issues - contribute to political tension in the region. With the end of the gulf crisis, renewed vigour must be devoted to the successful resolution of those issues. We are hopeful that the United Nations will play a constructive and facilitative role in this process.

The economic consequences of the peace will be daunting. The United Nations has already played an important role in the provision and distribution of humanitarian assistance to the victims of the Gulf crisis. My Government wishes to commend the energetic humanitarian efforts undertaken by United Nations agencies and by the International Committee of the Red Cross to ease the suffering caused by Iraqi adventurism. Immediate post-war reconstruction - including the assessment of environmental damage - and longer-term development in the region can also be influenced positively by the United Nations, and Canada is prepared to play its full part in those efforts.

If there is one thing that the Gulf crisis demonstrates, it is that the United Nations is absolutely essential to a stable and prosperous world. Without the activity of the Security Council the world would not have had an agreed legal framework within which to pursue the current action to reverse the Iraqi occupation of Kuwait. It is essential that the Security Council continue to be resolute until its prescribed goals are achieved. This means, in the first instance, the fulfilment of Security Council resolutions, notably a full and unconditional Iraqi withdrawal from Kuwait. In this vein we urge again that the Iraqi leadership provide the opening for peace that the world has been waiting for by complying fully with resolution 660 (1990) and all other Security Council resolutions.

With Iraqi withdrawal from Kuwait achieved, the prospects for establishing the basis for a stable and durable peace are greater. Canada will work with diligence and determination to make the best use of the best hope there is for peace, namely, the United Nations and its capacity for collective security.

...

[143] **Mr. Traxler (Italy):**

...

As a country that is deeply committed to peace, and in the light of past experience, Italy is firmly convinced that a lasting peace can be built only on the respect for international legality. For that reason, ever since the very beginning of the crisis brought about by the Iraqi invasion of Kuwait Italy has joined the other member countries of the European Community in requesting Iraq to withdraw from Kuwait and restore legality. However, since Iraq obstinately persisted in rejecting that request, the community of nations had no choice but to implement Security Council resolution 678 (1990), with which the Council, acknowledging Iraq's refusal to heed repeated requests for withdrawal, authorized Member States co-operating with the Government of Kuwait to use all necessary means to uphold and implement resolution 660 (1990) and all other relevant resolutions and to restore international peace and security to the area.

Italy, which has always upheld the need to comply with international legality, felt itself in duty bound to join in the effort of the community of States to restore it. Therefore, under the terms agreed upon in association with the coalition of countries co-operating with the Government of Kuwait, Italy has initiated military actions, of which it keeps the Council regularly informed, in compliance with operative paragraph 4 of resolution 678 (1990). Moreover, pursuant to operative paragraph 3 of that resolution, Italy has provided some logistical support to the coalition forces.

My country is thus acting within the framework of, and in strict compliance with, the resolutions of the Security Council. The aims of our action are those defined in resolution 678 (1990), and none other. Certainly, we do not seek any advantage, nor do we pursue any goal, save the restoration of peace and security in the area. Since the scope of that action is so precisely limited, we deplore Iraq's attempts at extending the conflict through its attack against Israel, and we sincerely hope that every effort will be made on all sides to limit civilian casualties to a minimum. At the same time, we urge the Government of Iraq to comply with the provisions of the Geneva Convention concerning the treatment of prisoners of war, and we take note of the responsibilities of the present Iraqi leaders for the violations they are committing.

It is obviously my country's warmest wish that Iraq should finally heed the appeals that are incessantly being made and decide to comply with resolution 660 (1990) and all other subsequent pertinent resolutions, thereby making it possible to restore peace to the region. In fact, in Italy's view, Iraq's withdrawal from Kuwait and the reestablishment of international legality in that country are the necessary prerequisites for the establishment of any new security set-up in the area and for the advancing of any solution to the problems still pending in the Middle East.

We therefore welcomed this morning the announcement by the Iraqi Revolutionary Command Council, and we sincerely hoped that it might turn out to be a harbinger of peace. However, resolution 660 (1990) calls for an immediate and unconditional withdrawal of the Iraqi forces from Kuwait. By the inclusion of a number of conditions, the Iraqi text appears not to be in keeping with the text of resolution 660 (1990), or with any of the other subsequent relevant resolutions of the Security Council. These resolutions represent, and indeed express, the will of the international community, and peace can be restored only in compliance with that will.

Iraq's initiative might represent a move in the right direction, but further steps will be needed to bring Iraqi statements and - even more - Iraqi actions into conformity with the will of the international community. Let us hope that the forthcoming conversations in Moscow will prove fruitful to this end.

...

[146] **Mr. Wilenski (Australia):**

...

I address the Council today as the representative of one of the many United Nations Member States working together, under the auspices of the Council's resolutions, to liberate Kuwait.

Towards that end, as we have already advised the Council, three Royal Australian Navy vessels are at present operating in the Persian Gulf as part of the coalition forces of Member States of the United Nations.

No nation should ever resort to the use of force, however well justified under international law, except with the greatest reluctance. However, the founders of the United Nations recognized that peace enforcement was a necessary, if regrettable, last resort. The system of collective security, enshrined in the United Nations Charter, relies on the ultimate recourse to the joint use of force under international sanction, when other means fail to deter aggression or to compel aggressors to give up their conquests. In sanctioning the use of force to secure Iraq's withdrawal from Kuwait, the Security Council is working within the system carefully constructed by the founders of the United Nations.

The Security Council's handling of Iraq's invasion of Kuwait demonstrates a strengthening of the cooperative spirit in the international community and indicates its desire to make more effective use of the mechanisms of the United Nations in dealing with threats to international peace and security.

As Australia's Prime Minister has observed,

> "If we fail in this first test of the new international order after the cold war, the consequences for our medium- and long-term security and for that of many other countries are deeply disturbing."

Military action in the Persian Gulf is being carried out in accordance with authorization of the Security Council in its resolution 678 (1990) and for the goals it has specifically set in that and preceding resolutions. Those goals are to secure Iraq's unconditional withdrawal from Kuwait and to re-establish Kuwait's sovereignty and independence. There are no other motives for the coalition's action. These two goals are, and will remain, the end point of the multinational forces' action.

We have this morning heard the announcement from Radio Baghdad concerning resolution 660 (1990). Unfortunately, it does not appear that the statement signals Iraq's willingness to comply with the provisions of that resolution and subsequent resolutions.

The Security Council was compelled to authorize the use of military force by the action of the Government of Iraq. Hostilities began not on 16 January, as some seem to suggest, but on 2 August last year, when Iraq invaded Kuwait, later purporting to annex it.

The international community, working through the Security Council, reacted swiftly and decisively to Iraq's aggression. The Council adopted 12 resolutions setting out clearly the means to resolve the crisis in accordance with the principles of the Charter. The message and extent of international support could not have been made clearer to Iraq.

While every effort was made to persuade Iraq to withdraw peacefully from Kuwait, Iraqi troops continued to fortify their positions in Kuwait and to assault and subjugate the Kuwaiti people.

Amnesty International, in a report on 19 December 1990, documented the repeated violations of the human rights of those who remained in Kuwait, including detention, torture, rape and summary executions. The Council also heard first-hand accounts of Iraqi abuses in Kuwait, in a moving session on 27 November 1990, when Kuwaitis who had escaped from Kuwait testified to their experiences.

Every international initiative, every effort at diplomacy, aimed at resolving the crisis by peaceful means was or [*sic*] rejected by Iraq.

The Government of Iraq failed to respond to attempts by other Arab and Islamic countries to bring an early end to the crisis. It failed to respond when other non-aligned countries added their voices to the calls for Iraq's withdrawal. It failed to respond when the Soviet Union and members of the European Community searched for a hint of flexibility. It failed to respond when the United States Government time and again made clear its wish for a peaceful solution. On 12 occasions it failed to respond to the demands of this body, ignoring its obligations under the Charter. Finally, even at the eleventh hour, as the Secretary-General, a man of outstanding diplomatic skill and human compassion, representing all United Nations Members, made a last-minute appeal to President Saddam Hussein, again Iraq failed to respond.

Not once in five months did President Saddam Hussein give any indication of ordering a withdrawal from Kuwait, nor did he show any sign that the damage being done to Iraq's economy and the suffering of its peoples through the stringent implementation of economic sanctions would induce him to comply with the Council's resolutions.

With the passing of the 15 January deadline, and in the face of continued Iraqi intransigence, the members of the international coalition were left with no alternative but to use force, as authorized by the Council's resolution 678 (1990), under Chapter VII of the United Nations Charter, to remove Iraq from Kuwait. As I have previously said, there can be no mistaking whose is the responsibility for the conflict. The Government of Iraq alone must bear that responsibility.

Australia shares the profound concerns expressed by others about the impact on civilians caught up in the conflict and the casualties on both sides. As I recalled a moment ago, the Kuwaiti people have been the victims of brutal and intentional human rights violations for over six months. The plight of the many citizens of third countries deprived of their livelihoods by Iraq's actions has also deeply concerned the international community.

Australia has joined with other countries in providing financial and other assistance to meet these humanitarian needs through both the United Nations and the International Committee of the Red Cross. To date, Australia has pledged $A 5 million to assist international relief efforts.

Civilians will also inevitably be tragically affected by the current phase of hostilities. My Government has publicly expressed its deep regret about the loss of civilian lives. The members of the international coalition have made clear that all efforts will be made to safeguard civilians and civilian sites from the effects of allied attack. In stark contrast, Iraq has compounded its attacks on the civilian population of Kuwait with further attacks aimed at civilian targets in Saudi Arabia and Israel. Furthermore, President Saddam Hussein has threatened to resort to weapons of mass destruction in his efforts to hold on to Kuwait.

Like all members of the international coalition, Australia hopes that our efforts to liberate Kuwait will succeed in as short a time as possible and with the minimum loss of life to combatants as well as civilians from both sides. There can however be no resiling from the goal of liberating Kuwait. Iraq holds the key to the resolution of this conflict. It should reconsider the damage it is inflicting, especially on its own people and immediately and unconditionally withdraw from Kuwait in accordance with the Security Council's resolutions.

When Kuwait is free again, an equally important challenge will then await the international community, namely the restoration of peace and stability in the region.

There is a clear willingness of all those involved in the coalition effort to move on from the Gulf crisis and, strengthened by the principles to emerge from the successful resolution of that crisis, to address all the longstanding problems of the Middle East, including a just resolution of the Palestinian issue and the continuing security of Israel. As others have observed, the successful resolution of the Gulf crisis will provide a springboard to address these issues.

Australia, for its part, stands ready to assist in playing whatever role it can to advance the cause of peace in the Middle East.

There is already considerable discussion of the need to intensify efforts to secure and put in place an appropriate security regime for the region. This will need to cover a range of diverse issues - military, political and economic - including territorial guarantees, arms control agreements, dispute settlement mechanisms and economic reconstruction.

Once the Gulf crisis has been resolved, Australia looks forward to the United Nations and this Council showing the same determination to address these complex issues vital to the peace and stability of the Middle East. Australia will play its part in the international effort that will be needed for this purpose.

...

[152] **Mr. Somavia (Chile)** (interpretation from Spanish):

...

The purpose of my statement is to share with the Council some thoughts of the Government of Chile at a time when nearly 28 weeks have passed since Iraq invaded Kuwait and nearly 4 weeks since the allied forces began military action.

I should like to reiterate that Chile supported and continues to support the 12 resolutions adopted by the Security Council on this tragic situation. In the early hours of 2 August we vigorously condemned the breach of international law and peaceful coexistence as a result of the attack on Kuwait. We quickly implemented the agreed sanctions and since then we have constantly supported the political initiatives to bring about the withdrawal of Iraq from Kuwait and find a peaceful comprehensive solution to the Gulf conflict.

We understand that Iraq's intransigence created the need for the Council to authorize the use of force in order to ensure respect for its resolutions and that many countries considered it necessary to use force to put an end to the conflict which Iraq began on 2 August. Chile is not part of the military coalition, but it has respected the decision which it considers to be legal, in keeping with Security Council resolution 678 (1990).

Chile's position is based on a diplomatic tradition of respect for international law and the inviolability of treaties. We have always considered the defence of principles and law as the basic source of international protection for the smaller countries.

Our position is also based on our belief that, after the cold war, mankind needs to build new forms of international relations based on peace, cooperation and respect for all peoples and countries, whether great Powers or small nations.

We are particularly concerned about the breach of basic rules of international coexistence. The use of force to settle disputes between States endangers peace and stability. Respect for international law and the principles embodied in the United Nations Charter is the essential guarantee of the survival of States.

What is at stake in the Gulf goes beyond the restoration of Kuwait as a sovereign State. What is at stake is the sanctity of the principles of the Charter, the foundation of civilized relations between States, which we want to see respected in all circumstances. Hence, in order to make sure that this fundamental value prevails, it will be necessary in future to react with the same determination in similar situations, should they unfortunately recur. We feel that there must not be a selective application of the principles of the Charter. This is valid for yesterday, for today and for tomorrow.

For all these reasons, we believe that the actions of the United Nations are so very important. If for some reason it were not possible to obtain compliance with the resolutions of the Security Council, the international community would be set back many years in its efforts to create a more peaceful and more just world.

It is from the perspective of these values that Chile wishes to share with the members of the Council some thoughts about the development of the Gulf situation, on the basis of what was agreed to by the Foreign Ministers of the countries members of the Group of Rio at their recent meeting, on 28 January in Caracas, which has been circulated as an official document of the Council.

Above all, we are concerned about the people, the individuals and the untold suffering that so many innocent victims have been experiencing since 2 August. We shall never forget that behind all this there are human beings, be they in the military or civilians, who are suffering and dying; families living in areas of the conflict and not in surroundings of international politics, which we are discussing here, but in tragic uncertainty about their own survival or that of their dear ones.

As the President of Chile, Mr. Patricio Aylwin, has said, we are all saddened when we see human beings killing each other in a distant land.

We are concerned also about the actions that have threatened the environment in the Gulf region, with unforeseeable consequences and ecological effects.

We note also the growing anxiety and concern in the world about the risks of escalation of the confrontation. That is why, like other representatives who have spoken here, we have no doubt that we all clearly feel that the armed conflict should be ended as soon as possible and that Kuwait should again become a free and sovereign State, with its territorial integrity intact.

Until that happens, it will be necessary to act with particular care in regard to everything related to humanitarian law. This includes compliance with the Geneva Conventions in all their aspects, in particular in relation to the treatment of prisoners of war, respect for and protection of civilian persons, and the availability of humanitarian assistance for the victims of the conflict, especially women, children and the elderly. Of particular moral importance for us is the urgent need to avoid recourse to chemical and biological weapons and weapons of mass or indiscriminate destruction, including nuclear devices. We share the concerns of the International Red Cross and support the initiatives undertaken by the United Nations Children's Fund (UNICEF) and the World Health Organization. We echo the appeals made by His Holiness John Paul II in relation to all these questions. They should be the subject of regular consultations by the Security Council in the immediate future.

In this connection, allow me to quote from a statement made yesterday by the Acting Minister for Foreign Affairs of Chile, in which he says that

> "The Government of Chile deeply regrets the shedding of innocent blood and the devastating effects of this war. It draws attention to the need to observe the fundamental provision contained in articles 48 of the Additional Protocols to the 1949 Geneva Conventions, which distinguishes between civilian persons and property, on the one hand, and military combattants and objectives, on the other. In addition, of particular applicability are the provisions of articles 51, paragraph 7, which prohibits the utilization of civilian persons to conceal, favour or obstruct military operations, and article 57, which requires that in military operations that are carried out constant care be taken to protect civilian persons from their effects."

In addition to the foregoing, we think we must make every effort to bring about a peaceful political solution to the conflict, in the context of the United Nations resolutions. However far away or difficult this may seem, we must not stray from this path, for it is the main justification for the existence of the United Nations. We recognize the various efforts made in that direction which are being discussed today in this body. We should consider all initiatives, from wherever they come, that may help to ensure effective compliance with the Council's resolutions.

In this connection, we support the role of the Secretary-General in this task of peace, and we point out that he should have the greatest latitude to act in accordance with his perception of the opportunities and needs that arise, most particularly in humanitarian issues. We categorically reject the obscene language and dubious procedures being used - without success - to cast aspersions on the Secretary-General's excellent record in the service of peace. In the current circumstances, the strengthening of the institution of the secretary-generalship of the United Nations is of the utmost importance. This includes the orderly preparation, here and now, for what should be the important presence of the United Nations in the aftermath of the conflict, once it has been brought to an end. Many tasks will have to be carried out, and it will be necessary to prepare for them so that they can be effectively fulfilled. We wish to repeat here what we have said on other occasions - that Chile is prepared to cooperate to the extent of its limited possibilities in this delicate task.

Accordingly, Chile believes that the Secretary-General's appeal of 15 January remains valid and still constitutes an effective point of departure for the reaching of a comprehensive understanding in the region that takes into account all the interests involved and, following the withdrawal of Iraq from Kuwait, can lead to the advent of a new order of peace in the region, based on the participation of all the parties concerned and compliance with all the United Nations resolutions - to use the words of the Foreign Ministers of the Rio Group.

On the basis of the experience acquired, we must reflect in future on the relationship between the Security Council and the rest of the United Nations. Clearly, the political agreements that have made it possible to take such important decisions would have been impossible during the cold war. This new reality could be an objective step forward that would enable the Council truly to become a "principal organ" of the United Nations, as envisaged in the Charter. At the same time, it represents an enormous challenge to the capability of institutional designs for establishing creative methods of work to ensure that in significant decisions such as those concerning war and peace countries that are not members of the Council are able appropriately to express their views.

When this crisis has ended, it would also be a good idea to reflect on the implications for the work of the United Nations of the machinery activated by Security Council resolution 678 (1990) for the use of force and the maintenance of peace, and on the role that the resolution itself assigns to the Council in deciding "to remain seized of the matter". This must be done in order appropriately to harmonize authorization and implementation in such a delicate matter.

That leads me to the need to begin within the United Nations serious and well-prepared work on the conceptions of security that befit the post-cold-war world and the situation we shall inherit from the Gulf conflict. Every day it becomes clearer that security must be viewed as an integrated notion with strategic and military, but also economic, social, cultural and human, dimensions. At the same time, we must expand the horizons of security to include not only matters relating to the security of states, whether externally or internally, but also a dimension that is as important, if not more important - namely, the security of the individual, of the human being, socially and individually.

All this leads us to the conclusion that the United Nations, including the Security Council, has before it major tasks. Peace requires more imagination and creativity than does war. Vision, courage and determination are needed to promote a world of dialogue and understanding, a world of security for weak and strong alike, a world where the permanent members of the Security Council exercise their responsibilities as a form of public service to mankind as a whole, a world where all the Members of the United Nations feel that they are participants in the building of a planet of greater well-being, equitably shared.

In the final analysis, it is a great challenge for our civilization and for humanistic values shared by the great majority of cultures and religions of the world. There are spiritual demands that, even in times when conflicts seem most insoluble, must not be forgotten. Perhaps giving the deliberations of the United Nations a human face would further enhance the dignity of its lofty and beautiful mission.

I cannot conclude without saying again that the first step on the path to peace in the Gulf is Iraq's withdrawal from Kuwait.

[161] Mr. zu RANTZAU (Germany):

...

The United Nations is at present facing what may be the greatest challenge since its foundation. It is now up to the United Nations to meet this challenge and to live up to its most noble goal enshrined in the Charter: to maintain and restore international peace and security and respect for the basic principles of international law.

The war in the Gulf began on 2 August 1990 with the brutal invasion of Kuwait by Iraq, and not on 16 January 1991 with the armed response from members of the international community.

For more than five months, the international community made constant diplomatic efforts to try to persuade Saddam Hussein to withdraw from Kuwait. The Secretary-General worked actively for a solution of this crisis. The German Government, together with its European partners, joined in these efforts from the very beginning in order to contribute to a peaceful solution of the conflict on the basis of the resolutions of the Security Council. President Saddam Hussein declined. He chose war. Even today, he can still choose to restore peace by implementing fully the resolutions of the Security Council. If he really is finally prepared to do so, he must make an unequivocal and unconditional commitment to withdraw from Kuwait, backed by immediate concrete steps leading to full compliance with the Security Council resolutions.

At stake is the future of all the States of the Middle East region.

At stake is the right to exist of Israel, against which genocide is being perpetrated by a dictator for the second time this century.

At stake is the chance to establish a new peaceful order in which all States, including small ones, can feel safe.

Germany stands firmly behind the Security Council resolutions which express the will of the world community that Iraq must withdraw immediately and unconditionally from Kuwait and that the legitimate authority and the sovereignty, independence and territorial integrity of Kuwait must be restored.

Germany stands by the side of the coalition seeking to enforce the resolutions of the Security Council. We support substantially and in many ways all the countries which, through their armed forces, are carrying the burden of this campaign for the community of nations to restore the rule of law.

We reaffirm our solidarity with Israel. Our historical and moral responsibility has to be proved in this unique situation. We are committed to strengthening the defensive capabilities of Israel in the face of an existential threat.

We stand on the side of the Arab countries which are being attacked by Iraq's dictator or which suffer from other consequences of Saddam Hussein's aggression. The German people are not indifferent to the tragedy and suffering of war. But aggression must never be allowed to stand.

Germany's solidarity with the international coalition in its endeavours to enforce Security Council resolutions, and its determination to support the particularly affected front-line States is not expressed in words alone.

Within existing constitutional constraints on German military participation in United Nations operations, Germany contributes substantially to the military burden-sharing. So far over $9.6 billion has been made available to the coalition States and to Israel. As a member of the Atlantic Alliance, Germany meets its obligation particularly towards its partner Turkey.

Important financial and technical assistance is being made available for the economic stabilization of countries particularly affected in the area.

From the beginning of the crisis the German Government has paid particular attention to emergency humanitarian measures in order to alleviate the suffering of the refugees and the civilian population.

All together, German contributions so far amount to nearly $11.5 billion.

All common efforts to bring President Saddam Hussein to reason must not prevent us from looking beyond this war and restoring peace at the earliest possible moment.

The main priority after the Gulf war is over will be to establish a just and lasting system of peace and stability in the region. For over 40 years the Arab-Israeli conflict and a whole series of other conflicts have been crippling the region, making it waste its resources on armaments and war. This experience must serve as a catalyst for offering the entire region a brighter future. Arrangements for a common system of security have to be developed within the region itself. The nations in the area have the human resources and the capital to transform their region into one of peace, progress and prosperity.

...

[166] **Mr. De Marchant et d'Ansembourg (Netherlands):**

...

Today's meeting is the result of a chain of events that began on 2 August 1990 when Iraq invaded a sovereign State Member of the United Nations. This breach of the peace constituted a grave violation of the basic tenets of the Charter of the United Nations. The Council, acting on the very night of the invasion, in its resolution 660 (1990) condemned the Iraqi invasion and demanded the immediate and unconditional withdrawal of all the Iraqi forces from Kuwait. In its resolution 662 (1990), the Council declared the annexation of Kuwait by Iraq null and void.

However, Iraq has failed to comply with these and subsequent resolutions. Even the economic sanctions imposed by the Council and implemented by virtually all States, in some cases at great cost to their own economies, proved ineffective even after a number of months. When that last chance for a peaceful solution evaporated, while the brutal destruction of Kuwait continued unabated, it became clear that the international community had to resort to other measures.

As the Minister of Foreign Affairs of the Netherlands stated in this context in his address to the General Assembly on 26 September 1990:

> "Sometimes the countering of might with might is unavoidable ... The sad story of the League of Nations has taught the world that we must stand firm and united in the face of aggression". (*A/45/PV.9, p. 53-55*)

Resolution 678 (1990) authorized all necessary means to uphold and implement resolution 660 (1990) and all subsequent relevant resolutions of the Council. However, in order to enable the Government of Iraq to comply with the resolutions before force would be used, resolution 678 (1990) also created a pause of goodwill.

A large number of appeals and efforts at dialogue, including a visit of the Secretary-General to Baghdad and an offer by the 12 States members of the European Community to meet with the Iraqi Foreign Minister, proved in vain. When finally the multinational force started its military action to enforce the Council's decisions, the Twelve expressed their deep regret that use of force had become necessary to oblige Iraq to withdraw from Kuwait and thus re-establish international legality.

In the course of the subsequent armed confrontation, the Iraqi leadership has shown a regrettable disregard for the rules of international law. Furthermore, by his unprovoked missile attacks on Israel, President Saddam Hussein has attempted to draw that country into the Gulf conflict. The present course of action of the leaders of Iraq not only constitutes a threat to the region but will inevitably spell disaster for their own country and its population. It is my Government's fervent wish that this conflict, with its numerous victims, will rapidly come to an end. All that is needed is Iraq's unconditional compliance with the Council's resolutions.

...

[167] **Mr. Razali (Malaysia):**

...

The statement made by the Iraqi Revolutionary Command Council that was broadcast over Radio Baghdad today has introduced an important new element to this debate. I would like to appeal to the Council seriously to weigh every aspect of that statement. Proposals in the past were predicated on the necessity of unconditional Iraqi withdrawal from Kuwait and the reinstatement of Kuwait's Government, and offered, *inter alia*, an end to the military offensive against Iraq, the departure of foreign troops, and the discussion of larger issues, such as Palestine.

Malaysia, together with Yemen, Colombia and Cuba, also worked last year towards such a proposal, which the Council had circulated as document S/21986 of 7 December 1990. Malaysia in turn has supported all the individual and group efforts of the Non-Aligned Movement and the Organization of the Islamic Conference, and has joined the collective appeal to prevail upon Iraq to heed the call of the international community. The leaders of Iraq who have worked so hard to build the country into a modern, proud and successful nation owe it to their people to seek peace now.

Malaysia hopes that the statement made by the Iraqi Revolutionary Command Council indicates a positive step in the right direction on the part of Iraq towards heeding the appeal of the international community. Even if that statement is encumbered by certain conditions, it is the business of the Council to address itself in totality to every aspect of the statement, to seek clarification on the areas that are not clear or have not been spelled out in relation to the pertinent Security Council resolutions.

At this stage, the statement should be seen as an important gesture upon which to develop, certainly not to reject outright. The Council, as the custodian of international peace and security, must respond carefully and constructively in examining all possibilities that may well offer an opening for a breakthrough towards peace. The Council should not make the mistake of allowing doubts to nullify or obstruct the possibility of initiating diplomatic actions. Further, the Council should not allow hardened national positions of Governments to discourage or obstruct possible actions of the Council.

Regrettably, certain countries have come to hasty conclusions. These may have the effect of prematurely killing any prospects for the Council or the United Nations to pursue peace constructively. Malaysia will regard that as highly regrettable. We cannot believe our ears when we hear of reports dismissing the statement as a hoax or a sham, or of appeals to the people of Iraq to take matters into their own hands to make their leader Saddam Hussein step aside.

It is to be reasserted here - and Malaysia has the right to say this, having been one of the then Security Council members that voted in favour of all the resolutions, including resolution 678 (1990) - that the military action against Iraq is a United Nations-authorized international enforcement action under Chapter VII of the Charter, not a result of Article 51 and certainly not a war between any of the allied countries and Iraq *per se*. We have to be very clear about this. No country, however powerful, can arrogate to itself the power to conduct the war entirely on the basis of its own imperatives and interests.

As stated in the 25 January statement by the Government of Malaysia, the massive bombardments and levelling of Iraq indicate clearly an alarming escalation of the military offensive that may well go beyond the original objectives contained in the relevant resolutions. We are also disturbed by statements by some prominent leaders talking about aims of the war effort that are clearly outside the scope of resolution 678 (1990). Further, we do not see at all a clear central role for the United Nations, at least in monitoring and reviewing various aspects of the conflict. The Council has to be reminded that the participating countries are accountable for the actions of their forces to the broader membership of the United Nations.

At this moment it appears that there are no means for, or attempts by, the United Nations or the international community to ensure respect for strictures on the conduct of the war. The Council has been, as it were, sidelined, and the role of the Secretary-General has been placed in abeyance because of the situation. A significant aspect of Malaysia's dissatisfaction with the war is due to that, and to the inability of the Council to do anything about it.

The war has proceeded for 30 days, and it was only two days ago that the Council was in a position to have a general discussion about it. Even now it is being done in closed session, which is indicative of the attempts to prevent the Council from properly addressing the war in all its aspects.

It is no comfort to listen to repeated assurances that civilians are not targets of bombardments when there is an abundance of evidence to show that many houses and other buildings have been flattened by aerial bombardments; there must be hundreds or thousands of civilian casualties. In a collective enforcement action under Chapter VII of the Charter there is even more reason for the allied forces to abide strictly by the humanitarian rules of war and international law, especially with regard to the safety of the millions of civilians, including women and children, caught in the war.

With military actions in their fifth week and with an escalation that presages a bloody, painful and miserable period ahead, it is high time that the Council took stock of the conduct of the war and of developments related to the war. The International Committee of the Red Cross has pointed out its concern about the millions of civilians caught up in the violence without shelter or protection from bombings and occupation. Many people in Malaysia and in other countries, particularly Muslim countries, cannot comprehend the scale and intensity of the offensive against Iraq, the devastation wrought on houses, other buildings, infrastructure and economic potentials and historical and religious sites, or the casualties among innocent civilians. Is all this being done in the name of an international determination to free Kuwait? "All necessary means", those fateful words in resolution 678 (1990): are they being interpreted in their destructive sense as a license?

All this has created serious worries and agony for many countries, particularly Muslim countries and the third world. For Malaysia's part, while as part of the international community we hold consistently to the message directed to Iraq about our determination to evict Iraq from Kuwait and to reinstate Kuwait, to the extent of authorizing force we should also like to transmit another message on behalf of our countries and our peoples about the agonies and sufferings being undergone in the region and elsewhere. That international message is not only for the Iraqi leaders, but also for leaders in the United States, the United Kingdom and other countries which are conducting the military offensive. War, as always, dehumanizes everything. We have to remind ourselves constantly - and this is the responsibility of the Council - that our pursuit of international objectives must not dehumanize us as an institution. When a military action wipes out hundreds of innocent lives, as happened recently, and when one tries to ward off responsibility with transparent devices and to use military doublespeak to blur the impact of one's actions, one is already going down that road of dehumanization. At the same time, while we ask ourselves questions about the scope and conduct of the war we must obviously also ask Iraqi leaders how much more destruction they are prepared to take, with untold misery for their people, before they will accept and undertake a withdrawal from Kuwait, as Iraq certainly must do.

Compared to the situation before 2 August 1990, when the international scene was flushed with confidence in a genuine internationalism and hopes for a new world order, we have gone into reverse. The possibility of an escalated conflict has raised the spectre of general instability and turmoil internationally. Important international structures will be weakened, affecting the role of the United Nations as a vehicle for conflict management and resolution.

Severe ramifications - political and economic and with a bearing on the religious in the Muslim countries - are also very much in evidence. The manner of the military offensive and the ill-considered rhetoric from some countries that are conducting military action have wounded many Muslims. The Council cannot be oblivious to these developments. There are also many in Muslim countries who, rightly or wrongly, are quite convinced that the original objectives of the Security Council resolutions have been forgotten and that there is a coalition of forces to destroy completely an ancient Muslim country, Iraq, historically the confluence of culture and civilization and in contemporary time a source of pride for its modernization and development and a bulwark against Israeli aggression and designs.

Also, we have heard reports about plans being worked out by the major Powers for the future security arrangements for the region in the aftermath of the Gulf war. These seem most insensitive, a throwback to the colonial era when victors distributed among themselves the spoils of war and imposed peace on the defeated and the weak, and certainly unacceptable and incompatible with the notion of a new world order. No Power, however powerful, should play architect or policeman for the region, outright or using surrogates.

As a Muslim nation, Malaysia cannot fail to appeal to Muslim countries, on whichever side they are in this conflict, not to allow this crisis to affect the Palestinian cause, represented by the Palestine Liberation Organization (PLO), even if some are not in full agreement with the position of PLO leaders on the crisis. The Scud missile attacks on Israel have been condemned, but let that not be a reason for the Israeli Government to exploit the situation, turning everything to its advantage. Already the Israelis have bombed parts of southern Lebanon on several occasions in the past few weeks and have committed atrocious violations of the Geneva Convention in the occupied territories without so much as the blink of an eye from the Security Council. The Security Council and partners in the coalition should weigh the recent moves against years and years of repeated arrogant rejection by Israel of Security Council resolutions pertaining to occupied Palestinian and Arab territories and Israel's gross violations of the Geneva Convention.

Above all it must be underlined that thoughts of a partial solution to the Palestinian problem as part of a process of a future security arrangement for the region are unjust and would not ensure long-term peace and stability in the region. Such an idea is tantamount to no more than the so-called Palestine solution of the 1921 Cairo conference.

The question may be asked of the Council whether the use of force as an international weapon for the enforcement of collective security in the name of the United Nations can be regarded as a successful and tenable experiment. If what we are witnessing now is a precursor of what would constitute a future dimension of United Nations action in the post-Cold War era, then Malaysia must conclude that the initial attempt is not salutary and does not bode well for the future.

Finally, Malaysia would like to appeal to the Council to eschew skepticism and negativism, even if the past record of attempts to plead with Iraqi leaders for withdrawal and peace has been disappointing. Malaysia believes that now is the time for the Council to entrust the Secretary-General with reactivating and intensifying all diplomatic efforts. The permanent members of the Council have a special responsibility in this context, especially the Soviet Union, which has maintained a continuing initiative to keep open all chances for peace. The Non-Aligned Movement can also play a role here as well. The Council could well help to co-ordinate all the initiatives at hand and to bring them under a kind of United Nations umbrella.

All of the peoples of the world desire an end to the war. The onus and the responsibility obviously lie with Iraq. But the Council should not be placed in a position where it is so determined and resolute about war that it is unable to respond appropriately to chances for peace. It is my understanding that there are opinions in the Council in favour to reviewing the current military operations in Kuwait and Iraq that involve aerial bombardments of areas with large concentrations of civilians and in city centres. Malaysia would like to support such moves.

...

[176] **Mr. Silovic (Yugoslavia):**

...

In our opinion it is timely and fitting for the Security Council to convene to review the situation in the Gulf. The Gulf crisis and the resulting conflict are dangerous in more ways than one and arouse concern. The concentration of military power, coupled with highly sophisticated technology and the possible use of weapons of mass destruction, adds a particularly dangerous dimension to this conflict and threatens to escalate it horizontally as well as in intensity.

Ever since the outbreak of the Gulf crisis, which was caused by the Iraqi invasion and occupation of Kuwait on 2 August 1990, Yugoslavia has fully supported the resolute stance taken by the Security Council.

At the initiative of Yugoslavia, as current Chairman of the Movement of Non-Aligned Countries, the Movement, as early as the beginning of August, strongly condemned the invasion and annexation of Kuwait and demanded the withdrawal of Iraqi troops and the restoration of Kuwait's territorial integrity and legitimate Government. That position was unequivocally adopted at the Ministerial Meeting of Non-Aligned Countries held at New York on 4 October 1990.

Prior to the 15 January deadline set by the Security Council Yugoslavia had tirelessly endeavoured to contribute to a peaceful solution and to prevent a military showdown. To that end we had meetings and contacts with the Heads of State and foreign ministers of practically all of the countries of the region directly involved and with the permanent and other members of the Security Council, the European Community and the United Nations Secretary-General. The visit of the Foreign Minister of Yugoslavia, His Excellency Mr. Budimir Loncar, to Baghdad and his talks with President Saddam Hussein and Foreign Minister Tariq Aziz were of particular importance. Of course, we have also been constantly in touch with a large number of non-aligned countries.

Following the outbreak of military operations, which started despite all peace-oriented efforts because of Iraq's intransigent refusal to comply with Security Council resolutions, our efforts continued and have been stepped up. We still believe that no efforts should be spared to restore peace as soon as possible. Iraqi compliance with the Security Council resolutions would create conditions for bringing the hostilities to a conclusion and avoiding further losses as well as for peacefully addressing the crisis and the problems of the entire region.

Accordingly, our approach is clearly defined. The action in favour of peace should start with the withdrawal of Iraqi troops from Kuwait. The initial step is, of course, the Iraqi commitment to comply with Security Council resolution 660 (1990). The announcement made earlier this morning in Baghdad understandably caused numerous and different reactions. We are aware of its content but perhaps not of its full meaning. In our opinion, it might signal new possibilities and deserves to be studied further.

The withdrawal of Iraqi troops itself should be accompanied by a cessation of hostilities that should be monitored and guaranteed. In this respect the Secretary-General, in his appeal of 15 January, presented valuable ideas. That would create conditions for the solution of all outstanding problems by peaceful means. Full implementation of the relevant Security Council resolutions would also create conditions for the withdrawal of all foreign troops from the region.

The next step would include the opening of the peace process in the region. The solution of the crisis in the Persian Gulf should contribute to the international community's approaching with equal determination and urgency the Arab-Israel conflict, at the core of which is the problem of Palestine.

All of this is a prerequisite for comprehensive stability, security, peace and progress in the region through appropriate arrangements and with the participation of all the regional States, with adequate guarantees and with the involvement of the Security Council to be worked out.

To achieve those objectives, and as a result of extensive, high-level consultations, Yugoslavia, as Chairman of the Movement of Non-Aligned Countries, convened a consultative informal meeting of a group of foreign ministers of non-aligned countries a few days ago in Belgrade. Our intention was to exchange views on what the non-aligned countries and the Movement itself could do in the present situation to eliminate the cause of the conflict and to address the problem by political means. Following a very fruitful, substantive and concrete discussion, the ministers decided to continue to exert individual and joint efforts in the search for further initiatives towards peace, taking into account ideas and suggestions advanced in that meeting.

On the basis of various proposals and approaches that were suggested, it was agreed that this action should continue, on the one hand towards Iraq and on the other towards the countries of the coalition. To this end, Yugoslavia has already undertaken consultations on the composition of two groups of Ministers of non-aligned countries which would approach and contact all the parties concerned. The future course of these activities will depend on the results of these contacts, primarily those in Baghdad.

The Security Council meets at a grave and dramatic moment and on the eve of the possibility of a new escalation of the war, when ground operations are expected to be launched in all their destructiveness. The prospects are frightening - enormous losses, suffering, ecological degradation and heavy and lasting material and moral damage.

This situation is an overwhelming challenge to the Security Council and the whole of the United Nations. We must continue our endeavours, along the lines of the established priorities, towards a just peace in the Gulf. We must not give up. We must not abandon the fate of millions of people from Iraq, Kuwait and other countries to the winds of war, and we must not abandon our attempts to stop the ongoing tragedy. The deplorable loss of life, the deaths of innocent civilians, mostly women and children, in the bombing of Baghdad two days ago, should be a sobering warning.

Yesterday's statement issued by the Yugoslav Foreign Ministry says:

> "this tragic incident should remind all the parties in this conflict of their commitment, in the spirit of the Geneva Convention, to refrain from all activities that may cause civilian casualties.
>
> "Yugoslavia again calls upon the international community and, in the first place, the parties directly involved to redouble their efforts with a view to finding a peaceful solution by eliminating the root causes of this conflict so as to bring the Gulf war to a speedy conclusion and to avoid its further escalation with unprecedented consequences both for the region and the world at large".

Let me stress once again: the end of the war and stable peace in the Gulf can be achieved only on the basis of the principles of international law and the United Nations Charter, and a political solution to the conflict can only be based on the relevant Security council resolutions. Iraq should be urged again to comply with the will of the international community and thus make it possible to prevent a further tragic chain of events.

Yugoslavia on its own behalf, and as the current Chairman of the Movement of Non-Aligned Countries, stands ready to cooperate fully with the Security Council and the Secretary-General as the embodiment of our Organization in order to contribute to peace in the Gulf, which is vital to the people of that region and the whole of mankind.

...

[182] **Mr. Pickering (United States of America):** I have been heartened by the overwhelming degree of agreement which our discussion over the past several days has revealed. But yesterday's statement by Iraq offered little hope. Its air of unreality and the clear lack of concern over the effect of Iraq's tragic policy on the country itself and on its neighbours can only fill us with unease, even as we confirm our resolve to ensure that international law and the will of the international community are respected.

The reports today from Baghdad are, unfortunately, not much more encouraging. It would seem that at least Iraq has conceded that it will have to withdraw from Kuwait, but it would appear that there is nothing else new here and that it still remains for Iraq to confirm that it will comply with the United Nations resolutions through immediate and concrete actions on the ground - a visible and massive departure from Kuwait.

Iraq has again put forward conditions which it knows are unacceptable, and has added a great number of new ones. There are at least a dozen conditions demanded in one form or another in return for purported Iraqi compliance with resolution 660 (1990). This establishment of linkages and conditions is directly contrary to the words of resolution 660 (1990), which Iraq purports to accept: unconditional withdrawal.

A full study of all these conditions is something that I will not attempt here and now. However, the demand that the Security Council abolish 11 of the 12 resolutions on Iraqi aggression against Kuwait in itself is sufficiently sweeping and outrageous as to deserve mention. Among these resolutions is one declaring the annexation of Kuwait null and void. We can only assume that Iraq wishes to maintain that annexation.

The demand to abolish all those resolutions is something the Council clearly would not accede to in any event, and doing so would require the Council to reward Saddam Hussein for his withdrawal, something we have declared is inconceivable.

Iraq apparently insists that its territorial claims, presumptively to Kuwaiti islands and oil, must also be guaranteed.

Another demand is for the withdrawal of foreign military forces and equipment from the region, including Israel. While absolutely no time-scale is proposed for the purported Iraqi withdrawal from Kuwait, Iraq was quick to fix a one-month time period in its demand for the withdrawal of others. Linkage with the Arab-Israeli issue has been unacceptable to my Government and to many other Governments. Iraq's demands for such linkage would again turn the purported withdrawal from Kuwait into another system of rewards for Iraq, the original aggressor.

Iraq states in effect that it will not agree to the return of the legitimate Government of Kuwait, a major factor in the resolutions which the Council has already passed and which the Council has insisted shall be fully implemented.

Iraq also claims financial support for the repair of damage which it has suffered as a result of its aggression and says that its debts should be cancelled and that it should have a determining voice in dealing with the wealth of the region. Iraq's own commitment to democracy and democratic values stands in stark contrast to its political demands. Iraq's profligate spending over the last decade on military equipment belies its interest in dealing with the plight of the poor in the region and elsewhere.

This obvious attempt to buy time will not help in bringing the conflict to an end. We have been over this ground before. A cease-fire without concrete implementation of complete withdrawal is also not acceptable. Iraq would use the opportunity to regroup and resupply its forces, thus prolonging the war and increasing the risk to coalition members and their forces. This we will not accept.

As President Bush said today:

> "Until a massive withdrawal begins with Iraqi troops visibly leaving Kuwait, the coalition forces acting under resolution 678 will continue their efforts to force compliance with all the resolutions of the United Nations."

I look forward to hearing Iraq's response to the questions posed yesterday by the United Kingdom and Soviet representatives. The United States asks that all United Nations Member States here today join in renewing the call to Iraq to take these necessary steps to end the tragedy which it has caused. An anxious world awaits Iraq's choice for peace. A determined world will not tolerate Iraq's continued aggression and occupation of its small neighbour.

I should like now to say just a few words in reaction to the statement of the representative of Cuba. First let me say how pleased I am that the decision he made in another room not to participate here was not really a decision at all. We are all pleased to see his participation.

The three resolution texts he has presented will of course be studied by all of us. A first response is also in order at this point. It appears to us that two of the draft resolutions are clearly unnecessary and one unacceptable.

Let me be a little more specific about this. One draft resolution proposes a renewal of the Secretary-General's good offices and his role as a mediator, but clearly the Secretary-General needs no further encouragement. He continues to seek all opportunities, I am sure, in order to be of help. His statement of 15 January makes this clear. The role he plays as a result of his position under the Charter was clearly set out by the Council in paragraphs 12 and 13 of resolution 674 (1990). With the Council's permission, I shall quote them. We say that the Security Council:

> "12. Reposes its trust in the Secretary-General to make available his good offices and, as he considers appropriate, to pursue them and to undertake diplomatic efforts in order to reach a peaceful solution to the crisis caused by the Iraqi invasion and occupation of Kuwait on the basis of Security Council resolutions 660 (1990), 662 (1990) and 664 (1990), and calls upon all States, both those in the region and others, to pursue on this basis their efforts to this end, in conformity with the Charter, in order to improve the situation and restore peace, security and stability;
>
> "13. Requests the Secretary-General to report to the Security Council on the results of his good offices and diplomatic efforts."

We can do no better than that.

Another draft resolution sets up a committee of the whole on an *ad hoc* basis. I do not frankly know what such a committee might do that we cannot do right here and now in this Chamber with the full participation of all the Members of this Organization to provide their help and advice. A committee of the whole meeting elsewhere behind closed doors would reverse the process. It is strange that one of the progenitors of an open formal meeting should now, within just a few days, turn to a closed-door restricted session. I leave to him an explanation of this reversal of position. In the meantime, why not continue working here to produce ideas and suggestions? Indeed, I would be pleased now or later to hear any new ideas which he and others may have to offer us.

The third draft resolution is more troubling. It proposes that the bombing of Iraqi cities - if I understand it correctly - should be immediately halted and negotiations begin. Aside from the fact that in Cuba's explanation it indicated a concern not only about Iraqis but Israeli, and possibly Saudis and even Americans, why should his call be limited to one area only?

But there is an even more troubling problem. The draft resolution is in effect a cease-fire with its call for a halt in all further use of force. A limitation on the use of force at this time, precisely when there is no clear indication that it would lead to a withdrawal, would not facilitate the achievement of the objective we all seek. It would be turning the whole process we have followed here in the Council up on its head. We have authorized the use of force to achieve a withdrawal. We have now begun to hear about a vague possibility, hedged around as it is with conditions. It is regrettably not now the time for the Council to set aside its carefully considered decisions and plans and reverse its present course of assuring a withdrawal. Iraq's proposals are not in keeping with resolution 660 (1990) and now is not the time to permit Saddam Hussein to regroup, repair and rebuild his military machine. Military targets in cities are at the centre of the effort to promote and sustain Iraqi aggression against Kuwait and should and must be part of the effort to secure the withdrawal we all seek - an effort which makes all possible efforts to avoid civilian casualties.

[188] Mr. Kharrazi (Islamic Republic of Iran):

...

The Security Council is convened today to discuss one of the most important issues since its inception in 1945 - an issue which deals directly with security and stability at the international level. The grave situation in the Persian Gulf area which resulted from the Iraqi invasion of Kuwait on 2 August 1990 is threatening not only the security of our region but also international peace and security. From the very beginning, the Islamic Republic of Iran called for an immediate and unconditional withdrawal of Iraqi troops from all of Kuwait. We have also opposed the presence of foreign forces in the region. The leadership of the Islamic Republic of Iran made several representations to Iraqi top officials to withdraw from Kuwait and thereby spare the people of Iraq and Kuwait and save the region from the flame of a disastrous war. Unfortunately, the international efforts, including the tireless efforts of the secretary-General of the United Nations and our own efforts, did not bear fruit because of Iraq's continuing occupation of Kuwait, on the one hand, and objectives of foreign military presence which go far beyond the liberation of Kuwait, on the other. We are now faced with another war in this most volatile area whose repercussions will not be limited to the present generation.

More than four weeks have elapsed since the outbreak of the hostilities. The Security Council, which is responsible for the maintenance of international peace and security, has not yet pronounced itself officially on the status of crisis and on the conduct of hostilities. The whole international community genuinely expected the council, which was so very active in adopting resolutions concerning this crisis before 15 January 1991, not to be aloof on the diplomatic front. Unfortunately, some permanent members of the council even attempted to prevent the Security Council from convening in informal consultations to discuss the situation at the early stages of the conflict. The circumstances under which this formal session is convened are quite regrettable and an affront to the democratic process.

Now the world is witnessing the loss of thousands of innocent civilian lives in Iraq and Kuwait and the total destruction of economic resources in Iraq and Kuwait, as well as an ecological disaster. The recent bombing of a public shelter in Baghdad is only one example of casualties inflicted upon defenceless civilians. Where did the Security Council authorize the destruction of the infrastructure of Iraq and Kuwait or the killing of defenceless civilians, who have taken no part in the conflict? Should not the Security Council be prepared to address violations of the rules of international humanitarian law?

The Security Council of the United Nations is being misused again by certain permanent members, as it was misused during the eight years of Iraq's war against Iran and as it has been misused on the question of Palestine for the past 40 years. The misuse of the United Nations machinery as a catalyst for implementation of the foreign policy of certain permanent members of the Security Council is beginning to form an integral part of what is called the "new world order" - a new world order that is being conceived in undeterred use of massive force, a new world order whose final determinant is supremacy of military force.

Speaking quite frankly, we are concerned about the future of our region. We are concerned about the far-reaching objectives of the United States and its allies in the region. There is a great deal of suspicion about the objectives they are pursuing in this war - objectives that go beyond the provisions of the relevant Security Council resolutions. The United States and its allies have yet to convince the people in our region, in terms both of assurances and of deeds, that domination and control of the political, economic and social life of our region is not among the objectives they are pursuing. The Security Council also has a clear responsibility in this regard. It has to give guarantees and assurances that all foreign forces will immediately leave the area following the termination of the hostilities.

The Islamic Republic of Iran has fully respected the resolutions adopted by the Security Council with regard to the Iraqi invasion of Kuwait. We have adopted an active position of non-engagement in the hostilities. However, we are certainly not indifferent to the future of the region or the conduct of the hostilities. We cannot and will not turn a blind eye to the suffering of the civilian population under bombardment and under economic sanctions.

The people of Iraq and Kuwait have suffered almost seven months of economic sanctions. The medicine and foodstuff situation has deteriorated particularly during the past month. For that reason, my country has officially informed the Security Council of this very important humanitarian issue and asked the Sanctions Committee to act promptly on our request to send foodstuffs to Iraq and Kuwait. Unfortunately, our request has not yet been responded to positively. The authorities of the Red Crescent Society of the Islamic Republic of Iran are still waiting for the Sanction Committee's approval to send foodstuffs to Iraq, with the cooperation of the International Committee of the Red Cross. However, several consignments of medicine have already been sent to Iraq by the Iranian Red Crescent Society and the International Committee of the Red Cross.

After hostilities began on 17 January 1991, some countries, including my own, tried to find a peaceful end to this tragic conflict, and they are continuing to do so. Aware of the dangers of the present conflict - namely, its widening and prolongation and the violations of the laws and norms governing the conduct of hostilities - the Islamic Republic of Iran is convinced that, bearing in mind the relevant resolutions of the Security Council, all efforts should be directed towards terminating this conflict as soon as possible through peaceful means.

The Islamic Republic of Iran is convinced that for the achievement of durable peace and lasting security for the area, an endless bloody war is not an option: the real option is the acceleration of efforts to attain a political settlement. Any workable political settlement has to be built upon three major criteria: first, immediately, unconditional and complete withdrawal of Iraqi forces from Kuwait; secondly, rapid withdrawal of all foreign forces from the area; thirdly, a forward-looking scheme of security arrangements to provide for the collective security of the littoral States of the Persian Gulf, with the cooperation of the Secretary-General of the United Nations and without interference by major Powers.

Those criteria have been our guiding principles. Recently, Hujjat-ul-Islam Hashemi Rafsanjani, the President of the Islamic Republic of Iran, sent an oral message to the President of Iraq and presented "some ideas" for peace. A written response has been received from Baghdad which, in our view, leaves the door open for further diplomatic efforts. President Hashemi Rafsanjani intends to dispatch a high-level delegation to Baghdad in a few days to carry a written and detailed response to President Saddam Hussein. The Islamic Republic of Iran considers the announcement by Iraq's Revolutionary Command Council concerning withdrawal from Kuwait as a positive move towards the achievement of a political settlement. This move provides the basis for the Security Council to double its diplomatic efforts to convince Iraq to comply with the relevant Security Council resolutions. My country will leave no stone unturned to that end. We are determined to continue our efforts to avert further destruction and a catastrophe.

In addition to its individual efforts, the Islamic Republic of Iran will continue to take an active part in the collective efforts of some non-aligned countries to find such a political solution.

For some years now the Islamic Republic of Iran has been calling for the establishment of regional security arrangements among the countries in the Persian Gulf. Our position in this regard is clear. Security and tranquillity in our region should be ensured by the countries of the region through their own initiative. We are of the opinion that after the termination of this unfortunate war the littoral States of the Persian Gulf should discuss the ways and means for achieving a security arrangement in this vital region, free from foreign intervention. Any attempt by foreign countries present in our region to consolidate that presence cannot be tolerated by the people of the region. Unfortunately, the way in which the allied forces are conducting the war and their positions regarding the future of the region have given rise to more instability in the Persian Gulf area. We have made it clear time and again that the presence of foreign forces in the region is inherently destabilizing and therefore they must leave the area as soon as the crisis is over. We believe that only the countries of the region, which enjoy a common religion and culture, can, and indeed must, find a proper mechanism for safeguarding peace and security in the Persian Gulf area.

The Security Council has a big responsibility at this crucial juncture. The world is watching these deliberations in the Security Council. It is incumbent upon the Council to monitor the situation closely and to take positions of principle on the prevention of violations of international humanitarian law and of both the prolongation and the widening of the conflict, so as not to undermine the credibility of the United Nations as a whole.

[196] **Mr. Alarcon de Quesada (Cuba)** (interpretation from Spanish):

Frankly, I was surprised to hear the recent comments of the representative of the United States. I had not intended to speak again this afternoon, but out of courtesy to the overwhelming majority of my colleagues in this Chamber who did not have an opportunity to attend what are known as informal consultations, I must speak.

I do not know where Ambassador Pickering got the idea I had ever said I would not speak at this meeting. What we have been talking about a great deal - sometimes in the area between this Chamber and the room next door - is this. All Members of the Organization, including those not members of the Council, should be allowed to speak under whatever conditions they wish, so that the representatives of the press and the general public may hear them. I certainly did not say I would never speak at this meeting of the Council.

As a matter of fact, the reality is quite the opposite of what he has suggested. Everybody knows the Council was prevented from fulfilling its most elementary obligation: to meet. It took a tremendous effort just to get us into this Chamber to do what we have been doing this [*sic*] last few days. That was not exactly because of Cuban opposition. It is a secret to no one that the primary obstacle to this meeting was the position represented by Ambassador Pickering. The Council has become this kind of private meeting - and not because my delegation proposed such a thing, but because of the United States interest in that happening.

He sees a contradiction between our position in favour of an open meeting and our suggestion that a committee of the Security Council be created. We did not suggest that discussion of the war should take place in a small body marked by agoraphobia and night-time meetings, which are perhaps preferred by certain major Powers.

We want normal meetings. The Council has had one related to the situation in the Gulf.

But he omitted a very important detail: that it would be the role of that committee to report to the Council, preferably in public. Preferably it would not have to be a private meeting. Of course, if Ambassador Pickering prefers to have ideas on peace or negotiations discussed in public, there will be no objection from me.

What my delegation is opposed to, and tenaciously, is depriving people of the right to follow the proceedings of the Security Council. My delegation has never been opposed to there being normal negotiating procedures, normal discussions. We know that often peace is not negotiated in public. But that does not contradict the right of individuals to be informed of what is happening in the Security Council.

I regret he was opposed, on the one hand, to the opening of the debate and, on the other, to negotiations moving ahead in that debate. What bothered him the most was that one delegation - not that of the United States - presented a draft resolution and there was an erroneous reference to a cease-fire. That is not what my delegation proposed. I even tried to spell that out in my statement.

We know who decides on shooting. We know who gave the order to shoot. We know who gave the order to approach certain targets. We know who says when one can go from one stage to another in the war. We know who establishes the war's objectives.

Ambassador Pickering did not address that, but on television today everybody saw how the United States interpreted resolution 678 (1990). I do not know in what paragraph of the 12 Security Council resolutions we authorized the commander-in-chief of the forces against Iraq to change that country's Government. Yet that was referred to by the President of the United States.

Ambassador Pickering, who likes to put questions to Ambassadors, might himself be tempted to answer this question: what paragraph did President Bush use in suggesting that there might be [a] coup d'etat in Iraq, that that was one of the alleged objectives of the international community?

My delegation asked the Security Council to do three rather simple things, the first of which was to ask the Secretary-General to continue his good offices. That was one of the most singular aspects of the action taken by the Security Council in connection with the conflict from the very beginning. If that is considered unnecessary, because it has already been covered by a given paragraph in a given resolution, then I would ask what would be the problem - now that there are new developments in the conflict, now that we are welcoming gestures made by a certain Government to resolve the conflict - in the Security Council's asking the Secretary-General to make efforts along these lines? We know he has every right to make such efforts. But the fact is that there is no desire to give support to the Secretary-General along these lines. Let [us] say this openly, quite bluntly.

I would be prepared to say this. We regret television is absent, but from 12 [*sic*] August until the present date there has, among other things, been a concerted effort to keep away from this process any negotiating effort, any alternative along the lines I have just mentioned: that the Security Council may set up a committee to consider alternative formulas to prevent an armed conflict and to bring about peace. Well, that is legitimate. Groups of States can take such actions. But does not the Security Council have responsibilities in respect of international peace and security? What is so strange about the Security Council doing what certain States in the Security Council feel should be done, and what other members of the international community feel should be done?

In connection with this major concern, a cease-fire, I did not ask for that. I am well aware that more than coming to the Security Council would be needed for that: we would have to go to the White House. But I would just say this: let the bombs not fall on civilians. I think that is the position the United States says it has taken. Why should there be any alarm in this connection?

My delegation tried to present its three draft resolutions in the least polemical tone possible and expressed a willingness to discuss any idea that any other member of the Security Council might wish to put forward.

I want to make it clear that when I expressed concern over the plight of civilian populations, I said - and I repeat - that I was referring to those of Iraq, Kuwait, Israel and Saudi Arabia. In fact, I was referring to any other community of innocent human beings who might be affected by this conflict.

If, in our draft resolution, we focus on one aspect of the matter - the problems of civilians in Iraq - it is for a very simple reason: I believe that no matter what rhetorical efforts might be made in private or in public - in a clandestine or open meeting - no one can be unaware of the fact that for a month now an absolutely unprecedented quantity of explosives, bombs and rockets, the fruit of modern technology and human destructive ingenuity, have fallen on the population of a small third-world country. According to some estimates, the fire-power concentrated on Iraq has exceeded the bombardment of Hiroshima or Nagasaki; other estimates put it in excess of all the destructive force of the Second World War.

As to concern over human lives, I added that the Council and the whole world must do their utmost to put a speedy end to this war, in the interests not only of the civilians of the countries affected, but of the soldiers on both sides - above all, the American soldiers, who represent the majority of the coalition forces. I am concerned for them and I believe that we are all morally obligated to be concerned about the lives of these young Americans, who might also be killed in the fighting.

Frankly, I find it difficult to understand how we, a group of diplomats far removed from where the bombs are falling and the guns are firing could be upset by so bold an attempt as to save lives on both sides. Should not the Security Council have been doing whatever it could to pursue the clear objective we have had since the adoption of resolution 660 (1990): restoration of Kuwait's independence, sovereignty, territorial integrity and legitimate authorities without death and destruction?

If I have failed to show sufficient respect for those who are the masters of this great fire-power, it is simply because I cannot agree that they should also be the masters of the Security Council.

[202] Mr. Pickering (United States of America):

I hope the representative of Cuba will carefully read the record of what he has just said. It is still a puzzle to me and I remain impressed by the schizophrenia of that particular statement. Is he for an open meeting or a private meeting? I just do not know, but I think this one is pretty good. We are having a good debate; it is a good exchange. There are 250 people out here who I believe testify to the fact that this is a pretty open forum.

Secondly, President Bush's statement speaks clearly for itself. It needs no explanation.

Thirdly, where was the representative of Cuba and where was all the concern about the killing and the destruction when Kuwait was being raped, tortured and murdered? I have not heard it. I do not know where it was.

Fourthly, read your resolution. It requests that the negotiations for seeking a peaceful resolution of the conflict be immediately intensified without further resort to force. "Without further resort to force" appears to me to mean a cease-fire. Maybe the representative of Cuba has a different explanation.

[202] Sir David Hannay (United Kingdom):

I am prompted to intervene by my wonderment, frankly, at the second presentation by the representative of Cuba, who seems to be otherwise occupied at the moment but whom I will give the opportunity to turn his attention to what I am about to say.

The presentation that he gave bore very little resemblance to reality. He spoke at great length and with great eloquence about the good offices of the Secretary-General. There is only one thing that is stopping the Secretary-General from using his good offices, and that is the flow of insult and calumny coming from Baghdad. How on earth can he use his good offices when he is subjected to letter after letter accusing him quite wrongly of a whole number of nameless crimes? Would not the representative of Cuba perhaps find it more useful if the Cuban embassy in Baghdad could remonstrate with the Government of that country and ask it to stop insulting the Secretary-General? The good offices of the Secretary-General are set out very clearly in the Charter and they are encouraged to be used in Security Council resolution 674 (1990). I have no doubt whatsoever that if there were any opening for the use of those good offices, the Secretary-General would seize it with both hands. But it is rather difficult to advance into a storm of calumny. I think it would be a good thing to get that toned down.

I have completely lost the representative of Cuba on his objective with his committee. By the time he had described that committee to us in great detail, I began at last to recognize the activities that we perform in the consultation room, which he hates going into so much. He perfectly described the nature of the Security Council's meetings in informal consultations of the whole, which he is always telling us are incapable of taking decisions and the wrong place to be discussing matters. So why do not we go in there, if he wishes to, and talk about some of these ideas for finding peace? Why do we have to set up a committee to do so? It seems to me bizarre. Frankly, if the world believes that we are going to bring peace by setting up a committee, they will not give it much credibility.

Concerning the third draft resolution of which the representative of Cuba spoke, like the representative of the United States I would recommend that he look carefully at the text. It appears to give rise to some misunderstanding. It may be that this is partly due to translation faults. I do not know. But it certainly does refer to and go further than the simple bombing, and it is certainly narrower than his own description of the need to cease bombing, because it makes no reference to any bombing except in Iraq.

I believe that it would be a good thing to have a useful discussion at some stage of these draft resolutions, but we shall all need time to study them. I am at your disposition, Mr. President, for having a serious discussion of them. But a serious discussion will not be promoted by the sort of discussion we are having now.

[204] Mr. ALARCON de QUESADA (Cuba) (interpretation from Spanish):

I did not provoke this discussion. The difference between so-called unofficial meetings of the Council and of a committee is that they are so informal that there is no record of agreements or of what is discussed. That makes it possible for some members to distort the proceedings and attribute to others statements that they never made.

As far as where I was when the Security Council studied, discussed and adopted a resolution on the tragic plight of the people of Kuwait, I was here, more or less in the same seat, and I voted in favour of it.

I believe that resolution 677 (1990) was adopted unanimously by the Council last November. It was neither an informal meeting nor a small committee. It was in this room, with spectators. As will be recalled, everyone was present and everyone voted in favour of that resolution.

...

The meeting was suspended at 7.50 p.m.

E. S/PV.2977 (Part II) (closed-resumption 2), 16 February 1991 + Corr.1

[206] Mr. MARKER (Pakistan):

...

Pakistan has from the outset opposed the Iraqi occupation of Kuwait. Pakistan's position and that of the international community of seeking an Iraqi withdrawal from the brotherly Muslim country of Kuwait has been based on upholding fundamental principles of international law and inter-State conduct. International peace and security and the sovereign independence of small and vulnerable States depend on the respect for these principles, which are reflected in the resolutions of the United Nations Security Council, the Organization of the Islamic Conference and the League of Arab States. It is regrettable that in spite of the numerous appeals by world leaders, including the Prime Minister of Pakistan, Iraq could not be persuaded to agree to the withdrawal of its forces from Kuwait.

On its part, the Government of Pakistan made a number of efforts to avert the conflict. In October last year Pakistan joined five other Asian Islamic countries in calling upon President Saddam Hussein to withdraw Iraqi troops from Kuwait in the true Islamic spirit and for the unity and solidarity of the Ummah. The trilateral meeting of the Foreign Ministers of Iran, Pakistan and Turkey held on 3 January 1991 appealed for a peaceful solution to the crisis through the implementation of the relevant resolutions of the Security Council. The meeting also requested the Secretary-General of the Organization of the Islamic Conference to exert all efforts for a peaceful solution, including the possibility of the holding of an emergency meeting of the Conference. Pakistan also endorsed the call by Iran for the holding of an emergency summit meeting of the Conference. The Prime Minister addressed messages to fourteen Heads of State and Government directly involved, impressing upon them the need to find a peaceful solution to the problem. The Prime Minister also sent a direct appeal to President Saddam Hussein to implement the Security Council resolutions and withdraw from Kuwait in order to achieve a peaceful resolution of the crisis and save the Muslim people of the region from a major conflagration.

The Government and the people of Pakistan were therefore deeply shocked and anguished at the outbreak of hostilities between Iraq and the multinational forces. Pakistan has consistently called for a peaceful resolution of the crisis and is profoundly concerned that the efforts for a peaceful solution have failed.

The Prime Minister of Pakistan, Mian Mohammad Nawaz Sharif, accordingly undertook a peace mission to Iran, Turkey, Syria, Jordan, Egypt and Saudi Arabia from 22 to 28 January 1991. He subsequently visited Libya, Tunisia, Algeria and Morocco, and yesterday was in Taif for an exchange of views with the Emir of Kuwait, who is the current Chairman of the Organization of the Islamic Conference. These strenuous efforts which are being undertaken by the Prime Minister of Pakistan reflect the anguish and the sense of urgency which prevail within the Government and amongst the people of Pakistan at the tremendous loss of valuable lives and destruction of property taking place as a result of the hostilities in the Persian Gulf. Pakistan feels that the current situation is perilous for the entire international community, and for the Muslim Ummah in particular. It is our belief that united efforts by the Muslim Ummah are the best method to meet the present crisis - a crisis which, on the one hand, has made Kuwait the subject of illegal occupation and, on the other hand, has resulted in the devastation and destruction that are now taking place, and the death of innocent citizens through heavy bombing. This has caused the deepest anguish and concern throughout Pakistan, and our hearts bleed for these innocent victims of a relentless war.

Pakistan believes that the solution of the Persian Gulf crisis does not lie in the defeat of any one party, and that the only way to obtain a lasting peace is through understanding. Pakistan is therefore continuing its efforts to organize a conference of Foreign Ministers of the Islamic countries. The Prime Minister of Pakistan has proposed a six-point peace formula which incorporates the following.

First, a declaration of cease-fire on the basis of Iraq's clear expression of its commitment to withdraw troops from Kuwait in implementation of the relevant resolutions of the Security Council;

Second, the withdrawal of all foreign forces from the Gulf immediately after the cease-fire, leaving the regional security to be looked after by the countries of the region;

Third, the convening of an emergency session of the Organization of the Islamic Conference to chalk out a unanimous course of action, after taking into consideration all the aspects of the crisis;

Fourth, the deployment of Pan-Islamic forces in the affected area;

Fifth, the implementation of the relevant United Nations resolutions, which should not be limited to Kuwait only but should also include Kashmir and Palestine with the same force and vigour;

Sixth, until a cease-fire is declared, all the holy places in Saudi Arabia and Iraq should be declared peace zones so that there is no risk of their desecration.

My delegation would wish to pay a tribute to the Secretary-General for his untiring efforts during this long and difficult crisis. His deep commitment to the cause of peace has left a profound impression in my country.

My delegation has noted with great interest the announcement made by the Revolutionary Council in Baghdad yesterday, to which the initial reaction of my Government was expressed in a statement today. It reads:

> "Commenting on the statement by the Revolution Command Council of Iraq broadcast by Radio Baghdad, the Foreign Office spokesman stated that while so far the official text of the statement was not available, the Government of Pakistan feels that the offer to accept Security Council resolution 660 was an encouraging opening and a ray of hope for a peaceful solution of the war in the Persian Gulf. The spokesman recalled that Security Council resolution 660 demanded the immediate and unconditional withdrawal of all Iraqi forces from Kuwait.
>
> "The spokesman pointed out that the Prime Minister had just returned from the second leg of his peace mission, during which his discussions with the leaders of the Islamic countries had focused on the need for an urgent and peaceful solution to the Gulf crisis in order to avoid bloodshed and devastation caused by the war in the Gulf."

My delegation also attaches great importance to the initiative taken by President Gorbachev and the talks which are scheduled to take place in Moscow in the immediate future. There are encouraging indications that recourse to diplomacy is still the most effective manner of arriving at a peaceful solution.

It is the sincere prayer and hope of my delegation that the Security Council will continue to exercise its collective wisdom and effort in an endeavour to bring about peace in a troubled region where there has already been so much death and destruction. No words can adequately describe the feelings of anguish and outrage among the people of Pakistan. My delegation will work closely with the Security Council for the purpose of securing a just, honourable and durable peace.

...

[213-215] **Mr. Lagu (Sudan):**

...

The Government of the Republic of the Sudan strongly supports the call for an immediate cease-fire in order to give peace another chance. In this regard the Sudan joins and commends the initiatives of the Arab Maghreb Union, the Hashemite Kingdom of Jordan, the Islamic Republic of Iran and the Islamic Republic of Pakistan, and the recent move taken by the USSR. Sudan commends the persistent endeavours by Yemen and Cuba towards the same goal.

Let me state categorically from the outset that Sudan stands by the independence and sovereignty of the State of Kuwait and that Sudan regrets the occupation of that country and the misery its people now face. However, Sudan equally deplores the presence of the foreign troops in the Gulf. Sudan believes this crisis could have been handled, and can still be handled, within an Arab and Islamic context.

Sudan believes that the prime role of the United Nations, and indeed of the Security Council, is the preservation of peace, security and stability, as stipulated in the Charter. In this context, any actions carried out in the name of the United Nations or on its behalf should be constantly supervised and reviewed by the United Nations, as any deviation from this principle may tempt the parties involved to go beyond the mandate of the United Nations.

Sudan feels that Iraq is currently being subjected to an unfair, excessive campaign, launched under the banner of the United Nations, in operations that seem not to discriminate between military and civilian targets. Consequently, such operations will inevitably lead to the utter destruction of the economic, cultural and scientific infrastructures and the human resources of the country. The tragic incident of the civilian shelter witnessed three days ago is a testimony to this fact. Sudan fears that the purpose of the present campaign goes beyond the liberation of Kuwait. Rather, it aims at crippling the national capabilities of Iraq and at the subjugation of its people under total humiliation.

Sudan appeals for an immediate cessation of hostilities and calls for the commencement of a new diplomatic endeavour to lead to the realization of a peaceful handling of the Gulf crisis. My delegation is thrilled by the ray of hope that appeared yesterday morning from the Iraqi horizon. We request Iraq to raise and beam that ray of hope more visibly. We hope that the other side will reciprocate in good faith and halt the bombing, allowing the dust to settle and the ray of hope to develop and take shape.

In view of the recent commitment by Iraq to abide by resolution 660 (1990), my delegation brings to the attention of this body the elements contained in the joint statement of 29 January, 1991 by United States Secretary of State Mr. James Baker and USSR Foreign Minister Mr. Aleksandr Bessmertnykh, to the effect that any commitment on the part of Iraq to withdraw from Kuwait will lead to the cessation of hostilities and the consideration of a wider peace package in the entire Middle East region. According to *The New York Times* of 31 January, the two Ministers:

> "continue to believe that a cessation of hostilities would be possible if Iraq would make an unequivocal commitment to withdraw from Kuwait".

My delegation therefore appeals to the Security Council to consider this possibility and to interpret the Iraqi signal constructively.

In conclusion, my Government regrets the ongoing war and fervently calls for an immediate halt of the hostilities in order to allow reason to prevail, and for a comprehensive, peaceful approach in considering this particular tragic and unfortunate crisis and all other problems pending in the entire Middle East region.

...

[217] **Mr. MONTAÑO (Mexico)** (interpretation from Spanish):

...

The Government of Mexico has been following with great concern the developments in the Persian Gulf. Together with all the States of the international community, we recognize that this situation does not involve that region alone. Its implications and effects have had, have and will continue to have profound repercussions on all of us, even on those who find themselves geographically distant from the area of conflict. That is why we have decided to participate constructively in the search for a just and peaceful solution.

The same concern was duly expressed last October by the Rio Group at the meeting of Heads of State held in Caracas. The assessment of the situation in the Persian Gulf was more recently discussed during the meeting of Foreign Ministers of the Rio Group also held in Caracas on 28 January, in which our countries reaffirmed their readiness to make an effective contribution to the advent of a new peace order in that region.

For reasons of principle, law and history, Mexico categorically rejects the invasion and claimed annexation of Kuwait by Iraq. This aggression violates the principles of international coexistence. Therefore, we support resolution 660 (1990), adopted by the Security Council on the very day of the invasion. From the outset, we joined in the demand that Iraq withdraw all its forces from the territory of Kuwait.

We profoundly regret that the diplomatic efforts to resolve a dispute between neighbouring countries, with long and profound ties of unity and brotherhood binding them, have failed. The situation is even more regrettable if we consider the harm caused to the people of Kuwait and that now being suffered by the people of Iraq, as well as the negative impact that the war has had on all countries and certainly more severely on developing countries.

Our support for the Security Council resolutions and for the Secretary-General is based on our conviction that therein lies one of the best opportunities to promote a solution to the conflict that would enable the re-establishment of peace in accordance with international law. We are also convinced of the need to undertake multilateral efforts aimed at a comprehensive, peaceful and definitive solution to the problems of that region. The Secretary-General has a fundamental role to play in this process, which my Government recognizes, in order to ensure that the process is fully carried out.

The beginning of hostilities created situations alarming to us all. The extension of the conflict through the condemnable attacks on non-belligerent countries of the area and the potential for regional destabilization add an irrational dynamic to the conflict that should not diminish the determination of those within the United Nations who, like us, are convinced that a peaceful solution should be found as soon as possible. We should not delude ourselves: as the war continues, new sources of conflict will begin to develop from its wounds.

The broad human and material losses caused thus far by the hostilities in the region, which have gravely harmed women and children, compel us all firmly to support the efforts coordinated by the Secretary-General to bring relief to the affected civilian population, and we must ponder other options with the reach of the international community to deal properly with the humanitarian aspects of the situation.

We therefore call upon all parties to the conflict to show the greatest possible restraint while hostilities continue, thus minimizing loss of life and damage to the economic, social and ecological infrastructure of the countries of the area. We join in the Secretary-General's appeal that under no circumstances should chemical weapons or other weapons of mass destruction be used. We also call for continued efforts to find a diplomatic solution to the conflict. No compromise or concession would be more costly than the devastation of war.

We know full well that it is not easy to break the vicious circle of intransigence and inflexibility, but we stress our conviction that it is still possible to find peace through dialogue and negotiation. It is in the interests of all to find the means to safeguard a world order in which potential conflicts can be dealt with through international law.

Another universal concern is that the economic consequences of this action be prevented from severely damaging hopes for the recovery of countries in an unending struggle to overcome the obstacles to our full development. It is our responsibility to prevent the Gulf conflict from becoming a new barrier to the advancement of developing countries to economic and social equity, lest our countries enter again into a cycle with negative effects on our peoples, which we know from experience would only generate new conflicts. The international order to which we all aspire will be a mere illusion unless it is based on meaningful progress in the well-being of the great majority of the world population.

Diplomacy fails only in self-defeat. On 2 August 1990 the United Nations reacted with the efficiency we had all expected of it. In the months that followed, and despite enormous difficulties, the Organization took important steps to ensure that international peace and security should prevail over ruthlessness. No one can doubt that there were numerous efforts at a diplomatic solution to the conflict, and we remain convinced that even now, when pessimism is more in evidence than hope, it will still be possible to find a peaceful settlement of the conflict.

Surely, it is ironic that resolution 678 (1990) both opened the way for diplomacy and legitimized the actions we are now witnessing. My delegation considers that this reality should not exclude conciliatory diplomatic efforts. We consider that continuing to take steps towards a peaceful solution to the conflict which began on 2 August 1990 would not run counter to the provision of resolution 678 (1990), which authorizes States

> "to use all necessary means to uphold and implement resolution 660 (1990) and all subsequent relevant resolutions" (*resolution 678 (1990), para.* 2).

The Security Council should consider a broader debate on the way in which the actions it has authorized are being conducted and should not shirk its primary mandate under the Charter to maintain international peace and security. The benefits of using the international democracy this Organization represents would greatly outweigh a unity based on silence or indifference. We must consider and encourage new proposals. Without losing sight of the main objective of the implementation of the resolutions adopted by the Security Council, let us again give peace a chance to be restored in the near future.

...

[223] **Mr. AKSIN (Turkey):**

...

My delegation has asked to speak in order to record its position at this critical juncture in the post-War history of the Middle East. The present crisis is a direct consequence of the invasion and annexation of Kuwait by Iraq. Turkey has stated clearly that this unprecedented violation of the Charter of the United Nations is totally unacceptable. Iraq's actions have created concern and outrage, and its subsequent intransigence has brought about the tragic war we are all witnessing today. All the diplomatic efforts that were made in the period preceding 16 January, including the final, very commendable, effort of the Secretary-General when he made his trip to Baghdad last month, have been rebuffed by the Iraqi leadership. When a peaceful resolution of the crisis became impossible war became inevitable. There is no way for the Iraqi régime to evade this responsibility. The Iraqi Government is responsible not only for the war that is raging in the Gulf: it is responsible also for the ordeal of the people of Kuwait, who have been brutalized and terrorized by the army of occupation. Iraq also bears full responsibility for the enormous economic damage done to all the countries of the region, and indeed beyond the region. My country is among those that have been seriously affected by the economic consequences of the Gulf crisis.

The loss of life and the massive destruction we are witnessing are a source of profound sadness for us in Turkey. We sympathize deeply with the suffering Iraqi people, who cannot be held responsible for the invasion of Kuwait or the subsequent actions which have inexorably led to armed conflict. The régime in Baghdad has it within its power to end this war. It must do what is morally imperative and act without any further delay.

We are following with close interest the various peace initiatives and diplomatic contacts undertaken in recent days by a number of countries. We have to underline that these peace initiatives cannot succeed without Iraq's agreeing to comply fully and unconditionally with the relevant Security Council resolutions. It is our earnest hope that good sense, wisdom and statesmanship will prevail and that Iraq will pull out of Kuwait so that hostilities can be brought to an early end. If Baghdad is able to show the courage to take this fateful step, it will have contributed to the restoration of international legality, and will have helped bring to an end the suffering of the Kuwaiti as well as the Iraqi peoples.

Such a restoration of international legality can be a first step towards the re-establishment of peace and security throughout the Middle East. That in turn would allow the human and material resources of the region to be devoted to the reconstruction and development of the region.

Turkey is prepared to contribute to the efforts that will be jointly undertaken to bring about a peaceful, stable and secure environment in the region as soon as the present crisis has been overcome. Turkey hopes that the crisis will be rapidly resolved with the least possible suffering and destruction. Turkey also wishes to see Iraq assuming its rightful place as a respected and responsible member of the community of nations, its territorial integrity intact, making its contribution to co-operation and peaceful coexistence in a very sensitive part of the world.

We appeal once again to the Government of Iraq to heed the call of the United Nations and to comply fully and promptly with the Security Council's resolutions.

...

[226] **Mr. ELIASSON (Sweden):**

...

After eight long years of war between Iran and Iraq, a new tragedy is now unfolding in the Persian Gulf region. Its origin is Iraq's invasion of Kuwait. This war started on 2 August last year, when Iraq attacked its smaller neighbour, a loyal member of the United Nations.

It is a tragedy for Kuwait and for the Kuwaiti and Iraqi peoples, but it is also an issue of fundamental importance to all of us. The security and sovereignty of all States are at stake. Solidarity and the vision of collective security are basic pillars of the United Nations.

Sweden's position has been crystal-clear from the start. The invasion and the subsequent annexation of Kuwait are grave violations of the most fundamental principles of international law. Conflicts between States shall be solved by peaceful means, and the acquisition of territory by force can under no circumstances be accepted.

As a Member of the United Nations Sweden supports all Security Council resolutions on the Iraq-Kuwait situation, including resolution 678 (1990). Our support is based on the principle that an ultimate aim for the United Nations is to uphold international peace and security. The fulfilment of this aim may require, as a last resort, in accordance with the Charter the use of force when other measures are inadequate.

We had hoped that the resolutions would help bring about a peaceful settlement of the conflict on the basis of international legality. We regret the situation that developed after 15 January, but by agreeing to withdraw from Kuwait Iraq could have brought an end to the escalating crisis. We are sad to see the failure of diplomacy leading to casualties and to the suffering of a great number of people.

It is now essential that a speedy end to the war be reached on the basis of the United Nations resolutions and international law. We welcome the initiatives undertaken by the Soviet Union, Iran and others.

We understand from the declaration in Baghdad yesterday that Iraq may be ready to comply with resolution 660 (1990) and withdraw from Kuwait. Evidently, that declaration has to be further clarified, but one thing is clear: in accordance with resolution 660 (1990), Iraq has to withdraw unconditionally. If, in unequivocal terms, Iraq would demonstrate its preparedness to comply without conditions with the demands of the Security Council, a cessation of hostilities tied to a complete and rapid withdrawal of Iraqi forces from Kuwait should be considered. Thus, the seriousness of the Iraqi intentions would be put to a test.

In our view the Security Council should continue carefully to monitor developments in the conflict. No openings for a peaceful solution that could lead to the implementation of United Nations resolutions should be overlooked. It should be perfectly clear that resolution 678 (1990) does not authorize the use of military means for purposes that go beyond what the United Nations has determined. It is important, furthermore, to uphold the respect for humanitarian law and for the laws of armed conflict.

How the conflict is going to be brought to an end is of utmost importance for the future of the region and its relations with the rest of the world. This will also affect the role of the United Nations on the world stage and the quality of international cooperation after the cold war.

The United Nations and its Secretary-General have a prominent role to play in preparing for the post-war situation. The Secretariat is, as we understand, already planning for the possibility of a peace-keeping operation after Iraq has withdrawn from Kuwait.

The United Nations will also have to carry the burden with regard to humanitarian needs following the war. That formidable task has to be well prepared. Even as the war is going on, the United Nations system has to face many pressing humanitarian challenges. The forthcoming visit to Iraq by representatives of the World Health Organization (WHO) and the United Nations Children's Fund (UNICEF) could indeed be very valuable.

Sweden will continue to assist the affected population through emergency relief in cooperation with the United Nations, the Red Cross and various Swedish private organizations.

After Iraq has withdrawn from Kuwait, the United Nations, in cooperation with the countries of the region, should also play an active role in the efforts to establish arrangements for regional security and stability in the Persian Gulf area.

Furthermore, the Palestinian problem has to be urgently addressed by the United Nations in the post-war period. Unless we enter a genuine peace process to accommodate the legitimate claims of the Palestinian people the Middle East will continue to be plagued by instability after the end of the Iraq-Kuwait conflict.

In the post-war period the United Nations should also actively contribute to a serious discussion about armaments in the larger Middle East region.

But the basic and most immediate question is: Shall the force of law or the law of force prevail? Iraq has to leave Kuwait. That is a fundamental requirement for international peace and security based on respect for United Nations resolutions and international law.

Let there be no doubt: the key to ending the tragedy taking place in front of us is in the hands of President Saddam Hussein.

...

[231] **Mr. Shihabi (Saudi Arabia):**

I wish merely to make a short intervention in response to the questions addressed to me by the Permanent Representative of the United Kingdom on Thursday.

Sir David asked me:

> "First, what is the nature of the military threat which Iraq has represented to Saudi Arabia since 2 August and represents today? Secondly, has Saudi Arabia received any indications, directly or indirectly, of Iraq's readiness to comply with Security Council resolutions ...?" *(S/PV.2977 (Part II) (closed), p. 79)*

Both are important questions, to which I gladly respond.

The Council knows that before Iraq invaded Kuwait there was an abundance of threats, then military movements and then armies positioned in offensive formations on Kuwait's border. Our surveillance facilities showed the whole picture. Other countries' surveillance facilities also showed the picture.

Our Kuwaiti brethren were worried. We were worried. But we had assurances, specific assurances, from the leadership in Iraq. We had them, our King had them, our Government had them and the President of Egypt personally had them also. The leaders of many countries personally had assurances from the Iraqi leadership that Kuwait would not be invaded.

On 2 August Kuwait, to our shock, was invaded, while negotiations were in progress, six hours after the suspension of a meeting in Jiddah in the negotiating session between the Vice-President of Iraq and the Crown Prince of Kuwait.

A few days later the same formations - 120,000 soldiers strong - were positioned on the borders of Saudi Arabia in the same offensive formation, and our military commanders reported that it was an offensive exercise. We had the same assurances as Kuwait had had, that Saudi Arabia was not threatened, as if the soldiers were only there for the weekend, probably on a pleasure trip.

I think that we should have been very stupid to take those assurances seriously, having already seen what Kuwait had been subjected to, after all the assurances that we had received. Therefore, there was no question in our minds about what that threat meant.

I do not wish to add to that the information we had from other eminent Arab sources about secret designs to which they were privy concerning the intentions of the Iraqi leadership for Saudi Arabia in particular. There was no question in our minds but that Iraq had the same offensive designs as it had had towards Kuwait, and there was no choice but to take the defensive measures that Saudi Arabia took.

I do not think that any responsibility leadership in the world would have undertaken the responsibility of leaving its country without all the necessary measures to defend it under those circumstances. Anybody who claims that Saudi Arabia should have taken a different course is simply not responsible for Saudi Arabia, and simply does not appreciate what should be the responsibility of a leadership towards its people and its country.

We know today the preparations made by the Iraqi forces since the end of the Iran-Iraq war. Iraq simply liquidated all its gains to put an end to that war. Iraq's military preparations, which are clear today, show what kind of designs Iraq had for the area.

I hope that that satisfies Sir David on the first question.

As to the second question, whether we have had any indications, directly or indirectly, that Iraq is ready to comply with Security Council resolutions, we certainly have not had any more indications than members of the Council have had.

The last indication, yesterday, in which the Iraqi Revolutionary Command Council set more conditions for the Security Council to comply with than the Security Council resolutions have demanded of Iraq, unfortunately does not augur well for a peaceful settlement. A pause of five and a half months was given for a peaceful settlement; after the war was initiated on 2 August the Security Council waited until 15 January, with a full pause, for the Iraqi leadership to comply with Security Council resolutions. That is why I am surprised when people ask for a pause now. Was not a pause of five and a half months enough?

Is a statement in which Kuwait is not mentioned any serious indication? Evacuation is mentioned as one of the elements that could be, sort of, discussed. That is no indication to us of peace. In a state of war, a difficult war in which people are suffering so much, many people from more than one country - Iraq and Kuwait, and today Saudi Arabia is also suffering - indications of peace cannot be a passing mention of evacuation.

Such an indication would be the way in which Iraq dealt with Iran when it wanted to settle their problem. In one letter the President of Iraq settled the question with Iran. That is how to settle the matter today, if the Iraqis really mean to stop the war. Otherwise, any indications would be just unfortunate exercises at the expense of people who are exposed, not people who are safe in the bunkers.

I hope I have answered the second question.

...

[236] **Mr. Abulhasan (Kuwait)** (interpretation from Arabic):

The reason I have asked to speak today is to answer the questions put to me by my friend the Permanent Representative of the United States. Before doing so, I should like to read out for the Council the statement issued by my Government following the Iraqi communiqué reported by the media yesterday concerning the so-called Iraqi acceptance of withdrawal from Kuwait, as follows:

> "The media reports on the communiqué issued by the Iraqi regime today, which contains its conditions for withdrawal from Kuwait, adds nothing new to reversing the intransigent Iraqi position. It is to be considered as one link in the chain of the policy of deception, prevarication and procrastination Iraq has followed since its evil invasion of Kuwait. It is a repetition of its attempts and desperate manoeuvres to circumvent the resolutions of the Security Council and to break the isolation imposed on that regime and drive a wedge in the international unanimity against its brutal occupation of Kuwait.
>
> "Kuwait reiterates its clear and firm position: the full and unconditional implementation of all the Security Council resolutions relevant to the question of Kuwait. Kuwait demands that the attention of the world be drawn to the tragedy of the Kuwaiti people, which has stood steadfast on the territory of Kuwait since 2 August last, to the suffering of our children, prisoners of

war and those held in detention camps, and to the plight of those who are exposed to torture and murder at the hands of the forces of the treacherous Iraqi regime.

"Kuwait - while calling upon the international community to continue its firm action to put an end to the bitter situation suffered by the people of Kuwait and intensify its serious efforts to compel the Iraqi regime to comply with all the relevant Security Council resolutions unconditionally and restore legality in a manner conducive to the establishment of security and stability in the region and to strengthening the foundations of the new world order to make the world safe, secure and stable - calls upon the brotherly Iraqi people to stand united against injustice and the tyrant and rid Iraq of its tyrannical leadership whose warped policies have led to many catastrophes the first victims of which were Iraq and Iraqi citizens and to grave consequences that have brought destruction and disunity to the Arab and Islamic Ummah."

With regard to diplomatic efforts that might be undertaken following the issuance of the Iraqi communiqué, my country's position is to welcome and encourage such efforts in order to seek further clarification of the Iraqi position and to bring to bear further pressure on Iraq to cancel the unreasonable and unacceptable conditions contained in its communiqué of yesterday.

At the same time, we do not agree with emerging calls, particularly those from some members of the Security Council, to the effect that a temporary partial or comprehensive cease-fire be declared in order to give ongoing diplomatic endeavours a chance to bear fruit. Diplomatic endeavours have been constant since the initiation of hostilities. Iraqi envoys have travelled abroad and foreign envoys have gone to Baghdad for negotiations, most recently the envoy of the Soviet President. We welcome and encourage these efforts and we wish them to continue in the same manner without any need to introduce another element, that is, a cease-fire, before complete Iraqi compliance with the Security Council resolutions is achieved.

On the contrary, we believe that, while there are some who say that there is some change in the Iraqi position, that change has been brought about by the use of force against the Iraqi leadership. Regrettably, force seems to be the only language understood by the Iraqi regime.

That is our position concerning the current diplomatic endeavours.

I shall now take up the questions posed to me by the representative of the United States. The first is: "What are the efforts that were made by Kuwait to arrive at a negotiated solution on a border demarcation with Iraq before 2 August?" The border agreement between Iraq and Kuwait was signed in 1963 by the former President of Iraq, Mr. Ahmad Hasan al-Bakr, and the late Amir of Kuwait, Sheikh al-Sabah al-Salem al-Sabah.

That agreement was deposited at the time with the United Nations. After that, Kuwait called upon Iraq, through its very-high-level bilateral contacts, through its Ambassador to Baghdad and the Iraqi Ambassador to Kuwait, to establish the technical commissions that had been agreed upon when the agreement was signed for the purpose of the demarcation of the boundaries.

As the Council is well aware, the agreement concluded in 1963 very clearly defined the boundaries between the countries; it is called the League of Arab States line. It was left to the technical commissions to place the boundary markings on the ground, in conformity with the agreement.

Very regrettably, for three years after that Iraq used excuse after excuse to evade the establishment of these commissions - pretexts such as concern over internal questions in Iraq and the developments and changes taking place in Iraq. Sometimes it used the pretext that there were no differences whatsoever on this matter and therefore there was no need to hurry.

In 1966 Iraq agreed to the establishment of the technical commissions. For two years they met sporadically - very sporadically indeed. Iraq did not take the meetings of these commissions seriously at all. Prevarication, procrastination and evasion were the hallmarks of Iraq's conduct.

From 1968 to 1973 the Iraqi Government carried out various acts of aggression across the border and attempts to infiltrate Kuwait's territory.

In 1973 the Foreign Minister of Kuwait, Sheikh Sabah al-Ahmad, travelled to Baghdad in an attempt to put an end to these acts of aggression. He tried to reactivate the work of the technical commissions. Then, His Highness Emir Sheikh al-Jabar al-Ahmad, at that time the Prime Minister, travelled to Iraq and tried to persuade the Iraqi leadership to take these matters seriously. He attempted to lay new, appropriate groundwork for an understanding and to build confidence within the Iraqi Government. Six co-operation agreements were signed between the two countries. Their aim was to strengthen the ties between the two countries so that the boundaries could be demarcated on the basis of political understanding and co-operation.

The visits continued. Kuwaiti laymen became active. Popular institutions in Kuwait joined with the Government in stating that the situation with Iraq could not continue. Many people's delegations travelled to Iraq and met with officials there. In interviews with the current President of the Iraqi régime, the editors of Kuwaiti newspapers always raised the subject, and invariably the answer was: there is no hurry; you do not have to worry about your boundaries; they are wherever you want them to be - within Iraq. As can be seen, this was a clear case of procrastination.

Then the Iraq-Iran war broke out. It lasted for eight years. During that time Iraq unilaterally terminated the border disputes with the Hashemite Kingdom of Jordan and the Kingdom of Saudi Arabia. The Kuwaiti Government did not want to raise this matter with Iraq when it was in such a critical situation. Despite the advice of some friendly States and calls from the people, our response was always that Kuwait, which was providing unlimited support to Iraq in the war with Iran, did not want to blackmail Iraq at a time of such great difficulty for it.

Immediately after the end of the war, the Foreign Minister of Kuwait resumed his correspondence with his Iraqi counterpart. The response he received was that the matter had gone beyond the ministerial level and was now on a higher level.

Immediately thereafter, in 1989, His Highness the Crown Prince and Prime Minister visited Iraq. He raised the whole subject of borders with the Iraqi leadership. There was a flat rejection from the Iraqi Government. It was not open to discussion.

A month later, His Highness the Emir personally went to Iraq. He raised the same question and got the same answer: rejection and prevarication.

But on 15 July 1990 the Iraqi Note was addressed to the League of Arab States. It contained four accusations against Kuwait - all of them baseless. One was that Kuwait did not wish to settle the border question with Iraq.

Two days after the circulation of the Note to the members of the League of Arab States, the Government of Kuwait, for its part, addressed a Note to the League of Arab States in which it called for the establishment of an Arab or international arbitration panel, to be agreed upon between the two parties, to consider the points of disagreement and dispute put forward by the Iraqi Government in its Note. The Arab Presidents actively attempted to avoid escalation of the conflict between Iraq and Kuwait. The Iraqi Government, however, rejected the Kuwaiti proposal for the establishment of an Arab or international arbitration panel. It insisted on bilateral negotiations, between Kuwait and Iraq.

After the intervention by some Heads of Arab States, the Government of Kuwait agreed to a meeting in Jiddah. As members are well aware, that meeting was at a very high level, and was attended by the Vice-President of the Iraqi Revolutionary Command Council and the Crown Prince and Prime Minister of Kuwait.

It was a unique meeting. After his arrival in Jiddah, the Chairman of the Iraqi delegation did not give the impression he was there for a meeting and to discuss points mentioned in a complaint addressed to the League of Arab States. A single meeting was held between His Highness the Crown Prince and the Iraqi side. It was followed by a protocol meeting between the members of the two delegations. The Chairman of the Iraqi delegation said he was indisposed, that he had a headache, and that he wanted to carry out the rituals of Omrah in Holy Mecca, and he evaded the continuation of the meeting.

In order to save what was left of the meetings, Kuwait accepted continuance of them. That happened on the Tuesday and Wednesday. The delegation of Kuwait agreed that the meetings would continue on the Saturday, in Baghdad - that is, two days later, and would be followed by other meetings in Kuwait. That agreement was sponsored by the Kingdom of Saudi Arabia. The two delegations left. Eight hours after that agreement, the Iraqi armed forces marched to swallow Kuwait and attempt to erase it from the map of the world.

Those were our attempts since 1963 concerning the question of the borders.

The second question was this: does the Government of Kuwait accept negotiating with the Government of Iraq after it complies with the elements in paragraph 3 of resolution 660 (1990)? The answer is this. After the adoption of resolution 660 (1990) on 3 August the Government of Kuwait addressed a letter to the Secretary-General, informing him of the State of Kuwait's official acceptance of that resolution. In this Council we declare that after the complete and unconditional withdrawal of the invading Iraqi forces from Kuwait, we are ready to sit with the Iraqi Government to consider all pending matters to solve them by the peaceful means to which Kuwait has always adhered. At the same time we would inform our brothers here that it must be clear in the Iraqi mind that resolution 660 (1990) provides for a complete and unconditional withdrawal. Then, and only then, negotiations would take place to solve the pending problems between two countries by peaceful means.

The third question is this: has Iraq shown readiness to accept any negotiated solution; would it be possible to arrive at a negotiated solution? The answer is that Iraq has occupied Kuwait since 2 August. On 4 August it annexed Kuwait and claimed it was a part of Iraq. The representative of Iraq, who is present here, finds it difficult to say the word "Kuwait". The communiqué which it is claimed indicates Iraq's acceptance of resolution 660 (1990) does not mention the word "Kuwait" at all.

The fourth question is this: do you think a cease-fire would be beneficial in encouraging Iraq to withdraw from Kuwait as provided in the United Nations resolutions? The answer is that I clarified and stated Kuwait's position in my first statement before the Council. We believe a cease-fire, temporary or durable, partial or comprehensive, would be a wrong signal from the Council to the Iraqi Government. It would enable its régime to regroup and again carry out aggression - not only against Kuwait but also against other neighbouring Arab States. That is my answer to the fourth and last question.

The Member States who called for a meeting of the Security Council to consider the situation in the Gulf so as to arrive at a cease-fire in order to convince the Iraqi leadership to accept the Security Council's resolutions will perhaps, after reading the Iraqi communiqué, and having heard the statement of the representative of Iraq a few days ago, realize the futility of their efforts. They may have realized that they are indirectly serving the dreams and illusions of the Iraqi régime. The interventions of the Iraqi régime before the Council and the communiqué issued by the Revolutionary Council of Iraq yesterday have not dealt in any way whatsoever with its crime against Kuwait, and its occupation and destruction of Kuwait. They speak of a war that they claim was imposed upon them for no reason. They speak of everything other than the main reason for this crisis, which those who called for the convening of the Council call the Gulf crisis. The representative of Iraq finds it difficult to mention Kuwait's name because he knows that Iraq's bitter experience in Kuwait is going to turn their régime upside down and rid their people of it. Afterwards, the Iraqi people will be a free people that devotes its energies to building its economy and achieving prosperity. Placing the blame on the Council is a habitual practice engaged in by all those who have lost the causes of their countries. History is against the régime and against the dictator and challenges him to deal with the essence of the subject: the aggression against Kuwait, a peaceful and secure country.

You can turn a blind eye to the truth, but you cannot hide it from the world.

The whole world is going to restore by force the legitimacy destroyed by your regime. Iraq will be compelled to say the word "Kuwait" and to deal with it. The Kuwaiti people will have another score to settle with you. But it will be magnanimous in its dealings and in its attempts to maintain the bonds of good neighbourliness and ties of blood. It will adhere to the genuine principles of the great religion of Islam.

...

[251] **Mr. Al-Anbari (Iraq)** (interpretation from Arabic):

My purpose in attending this meeting was to answer the questions addressed to me by Sir David Hannay, the Permanent Representative of the United Kingdom, and by Mr. Vorontsov, the Permanent Representative of the Soviet Union.

However, what I have heard in this meeting compels me to refer to the reservations I raised on the first day of this meeting concerning its transformation into a private session for liars, dwarfs and hypocrites. Earlier, we heard one respected representative calling for international legitimacy and Iraq's immediate withdrawal from Kuwaiti territory. I do not hesitate to say the name of Kuwait, because the territory of Kuwait is dear to us. But we cannot accept traitors in Kuwait. That representative, whose country has been occupying a third of Cyprus over recent years, is now calling upon us to withdraw.

Another dear colleague made unfounded allegations before the Council that Iraq intended to invade his country. His country never mentioned this alleged intention until after the visit of the United States Secretary of Defense there. God only knows what he told them, but they suddenly claimed that Iraq intended to invade Saudi Arabia.

Before answering the dwarf who sits to my right and who tried to provoke me with sadistic words and even called for a coup against the Iraqi regime, I should like to quote some passages from the statement issued yesterday by the presidency of Algeria.

"This massacre reveals the true nature of the war being waged against the Iraqi people, which today has escalated from an operation designed to systematically destroy Iraq's economic and military potential to an actual war of extermination."

"Algeria resolutely denounces the intentions of certain Powers to try to impose their new order by fire and bloodshed. It also denounces the complicity of certain Arab countries, who are thus lending support to a genocidal campaign against a fraternal people".

... [*deletion in the original*]

"Algeria wishes to recall that the intervention by the coalition forces, perpetrated under the cover of international law is, in reality, a campaign of all-out destruction which, through the massacre of innocents, is assuming the dimensions of a crime against humanity" (*S/22223, p.2*).

I will now be pleased to answer the questions posed by Sir David Hannay on the first day of our meeting. I hope that he will permit me to address some questions to him when I have finished.

As far as I remember, the first question pertained to Iraqi's readiness to withdraw immediately from Kuwaiti territory. I should like to remind Sir David and my colleagues around this table that resolution 660 (1990), which Iraq announced yesterday it is ready to accept, refers to withdrawal from Kuwaiti territory but also refers to immediate and intensive negotiations. Some countries turn a blind eye to that paragraph and concentrate on the former, which proves the correctness of the Iraqi position that all the resolutions of the Security Council should be implemented, and that international legitimacy is indivisible and should not be selectively applied.

Does Iraq respect the Geneva Conventions? Yes. We respect all the Geneva Conventions. However, I should like to remind my colleague Sir David that the Geneva Conventions are not limited to the treatment of prisoners of war. They also address - in the Fourth Convention in particular - the necessity to protect civilians against the consequences and evils of war. That is why I should like to question Sir David's country's commitment and adherence to the Fourth Geneva Convention relative to the Protection of Civilian Persons in Time of War.

Concerning our prisoners of wars, they are being well treated. Their few questions addressed to them on the day they were taken prisoner concerning their names and units are questions approved by the Geneva Conventions on the treatment of prisoners of war. They were shown on Iraqi television only to prove that they were prisoners and that they were alive. However, after some protestations against it, Iraq has since ceased showing prisoners on television.

Where are these prisoners quartered? I do not know. But I can say that their lives are being safeguarded.

Another question of Sir David's concerned whether Iraq was committed not to use chemical weapons. It is. We have said so before. However, even in the original Convention on the prohibition of chemical weapons, Iraq reserved its right to use them in retaliation for their use. I should like to point out that, since the signing of that convention, weapons of mass destruction have been comprehensively developed. That is why we regard chemical weapons as equivalent to nuclear and other weapons of mass destruction.

If any such weapons are used, Iraq will use them too. If the intensive high-altitude aerial bombardment continues, we shall consider it to be tantamount to the use of weapons of mass destruction.

I hope I have answered all the questions asked of me by the representative of the United Kingdom. Now I have some questions to put to him, and I hope he will be able to reply to them either at this meeting or at a later date.

First, to what extent have the United Kingdom and its allies observed the Fourth Geneva Convention on the Protection of Civilian Persons in Time of War, particularly in the light of the indiscriminate nature of the bombing by the United States and the United Kingdom, which continues day and night?

Secondly, why did the United Kingdom prevent the shipment of medical supplies previously contracted for by Iraq with British companies even though these are not covered by Security Council resolutions?

Thirdly, to what extent has the United Kingdom observed the resolution adopted by the General Assembly on 4 December 1990 prohibiting attacks on nuclear facilities, operational or under construction, and noting that the Security Council would have to impose measures under Chapter VII of the Charter on States that carry out such attacks?

Fourthly, did the British Government take the necessary measures to prevent the spread of radiation when it participated in the attacks on those nuclear facilities?

I hope Sir David will answer those questions.

As to the question of my colleague His Excellency Ambassador Vorontsov about Iraq's readiness to withdraw, I think yesterday's Iraqi initiative and the contacts that will take place next Monday between the Iraqi Foreign Minister and the Soviet authorities will provide a final answer to that question.

But let me ask a question of the representative of the Soviet Union: Do the Soviet Union and the United States remain committed to their recent communiqué of 30 January 1991?

In conclusion, I wish to state that the Security Council should not permit any person whatsoever - especially one with no national or even personal identity - in this Chamber to attack a State Member of the United Nations or its representative.

[257] **Sir David HANNAY (United Kingdom):**

I would not usually intervene again in the same debate, but since I spoke on 14 February there have been a number of new developments: a statement by the Iraqi Revolutionary Command Council and the submission of three draft resolutions by the representative of Cuba. I believe it makes sense to comment on these new developments, and also, of course, to address myself to the answers given by the representative of Iraq and to the questions he has put to my Government.

I am glad he answered the questions. I think that has given some sense to the way we are conducting our business here. Although I do not find the answers satisfactory, I am grateful to him for having given them.

The answer he gave me and the representative of the Soviet Union about withdrawal is frankly not really the full answer that is needed if we are to get back on all fours with the Security Council's own resolutions. But I shall come to that, because it is covered in the communiqué of the Revolutionary Command Council. I would just say that it would be so easy to bring a peaceful solution to this crisis if only the representative of Iraq were instructed to reply simply and affirmatively to the question put to him by both myself and the representative of the Soviet Union that, yes, Iraq will withdraw from Kuwait, and will give concrete evidence and take steps to implement that undertaking. All that is needed is a firm commitment to withdraw and the taking of concrete steps implementing it. Unconditional withdrawal from Kuwait is simply not a negotiable item.

I am grateful for the answers he gave to the very serious humanitarian issue I raised about prisoners of war, although I must say that the answers were in most respects inadequate and unsatisfactory. But I note that he stated categorically and without any ambiguity that Iraq applied the Geneva Conventions in respect of prisoners of war. My Government will certainly expect that in future dealings between the International Committee of the Red Cross and the Government of Iraq that undertaking will be validated. If it is not, I am afraid the representative of Iraq will be left looking very foolish indeed. But I express the hope now that it will be validated and not invalidated, and that the Government of Iraq will now fulfil all its obligations, which include the notification of names and giving the International Committee of the Red Cross access to the prisoners, without any further delay and without any attempt to make conditions or to make linkages with other supposed parts of the Geneva Conventions. But I noted that the representative of Iraq did not make such linkages, did not make such conditions, and my Government will now wait to see whether the Government of Iraq does not indeed make such conditions. We will be very glad if that is so.

I am afraid I have to say that I think the explanation given about the presentation of prisoners of war on television by the Iraqi Government was a quite unsatisfactory one and an unconvincing one. There was absolutely no case for showing them on television; that this is permissible is specifically contradicted in the Geneva Conventions. And of course the Geneva Conventions provide for a perfectly good way of ensuring that the next of kin are aware that their relations are prisoners of war, that is to say by communicating their names and details through the International Committee of the Red Cross. So there was no need whatsoever to use television for that purpose, and I find that explanation unconvincing.

I note that the prisoners of war are said to be held in safe places. Again, I think that once the International Committee of the Red Cross has been allowed to see the prisoners they will be the best judges of whether the places are safe or not. That will be very necessary. I do not think it makes any sense to try to make a subjective judgment of this. We noted with horror a statement at an earlier stage by the Government of Iraq that the prisoners of war would be placed in areas where they might be involved in the hostilities, in an attempt to distort or influence the policy of my Government and other Governments which are cooperating with the Government of Kuwait in the military actions. We rejected that fundamentally. If what is meant now by their being in a safe place is that that statement is no longer operative, that is a very good thing, but as I say we will wish to rely on the judgement of the International Committee of the Red Cross as to whether that statement was a correct one or not.

As to the questions the representative of Iraq put to me, I shall give them careful thought, and I shall certainly be willing to reply to them when this debate resumes next week. However, I do not wish to reply to them off the cuff: they are detailed questions, and he can be sure that I shall address them in due course.

Now, if I could just say a word about the communiqué of the Revolutionary Command Council. The least that could be said about it is that it is not the simple and unconditional affirmative on withdrawal from Kuwait that is needed if this conflict is to be ended. It does indeed contain one tiny gleam of light: the word "withdrawal" has at last reentered the vocabulary of the Government of Iraq. Perhaps before too long the word "Kuwait" will reenter it too - I do admit that the representative of Iraq actually used that word this morning, and I welcome that.

However, the gleam of light in this communiqué is promptly obscured behind a huge bank of conditions, conditions that actually contradict any apparent willingness to accept Security Council resolution 660 (1990). That resolution calls for unconditional withdrawal. Acceptance of it is not, therefore, consistent with the posing of conditions. The list of issues that Iraq tries to link to its withdrawal means that the approval of withdrawal is fundamentally contradictory and flawed.

Now, the representative of Cuba has circulated three draft resolutions, and these will need to be discussed in the usual way. But at first sight I would take the view that two of them are unnecessary and one is unacceptable.

The draft resolution setting up an *ad hoc* committee of the Council to look into the Gulf crisis is unnecessary because the Council itself is already seized of the matter. What benefit would converting it into a committee bring? Why does the representative of Cuba, who only two days ago was arguing vigorously for an open meeting of the Council, now try to shift the discussion of this issue into a committee from whose deliberations not only the press but the other Members of the United Nations would be excluded? If his delegation has ideas for achieving a peaceful solution in conformity with the Security Council resolutions, why not put them to the Council at its present closed session? We can always suspend this meeting if he needs more time to put forward suggestions.

Then we have the second draft resolution about the use of the Secretary-General's good offices. Again, this is surely unnecessary. Security Council resolution 674 (1990) gives the Secretary-General every encouragement to use his good offices. That provision remains as valid today as the day it was adopted. I have absolute confidence, as does my Government, that if the Secretary-General sees an opportunity to use his good offices he will seize it with both hands. What is needed for that is, among other things, for the Government of Iraq to cease its public campaign of insults and slurs against the Secretary-General - and perhaps the representative of Cuba's Government in Baghdad could use his influence to that end, and so also could the representative of Iraq who is listening to this debate.

Finally, there is a third draft resolution, about the bombing of Iraq. That bombardment is an integral part of the removal of the Iraqi armed forces from Kuwait. All targets are carefully selected, using precision weapons wherever possible, because they pose a threat to coalition forces or because they support Iraq's illegal occupation of Kuwait. The vast majority of attacks are now taking place in the Kuwait theatre of operations. Where civilian casualties have resulted, this is a source of deep regret, but civilians are not the targets, unlike Iraq's own missile campaign against Saudi Arabia and Israel, which does not achieve a mention in the representative of Cuba's draft resolution.

The way to bring hostilities to an end is for the Iraqi forces to withdraw from Kuwait. Let us hope they do that without more delay.

[263] Mr. Pickering (United States of America):

I want to begin by thanking the representative of Kuwait for his thorough and extremely informative responses to my Government's questions of a few days ago. We are pleased with the responses that he has given.

Our discussions over the past two days have revealed that broad agreement exists among members of the Council, and of the United Nations more generally, on the situation in the Gulf and what remains to be done. We agree that the door to bringing the conflict to an end will open when Iraq begins to comply with the United Nations resolutions.

Friday's statement by Iraq, as we have noted, was discouraging. The announcement yesterday by the Revolutionary Command Council apparently is an acknowledgement of the existence of United Nations resolution 660 (1990), and thus Iraq appears finally to be publicly acknowledging that Kuwait is not its nineteenth province. It is the one, tiny new thing that we have heard - and of course we have just heard from the representatives of Saudi Arabia and Kuwait on the value of Iraqi statements and assurances - and we will be following this closely. However, that statement is frankly discouraging in its recital of old and new conditions.

The task of diplomacy is to separate the encouraging from the discouraging. But it still remains for Iraq to confirm that it will withdraw unconditionally and completely from Kuwait. Its statements regrettably demonstrate that it still maintains the hope - indeed, the delusion - that its aggression will in some way be rewarded.

Iraq's clear, continuing lack of concern for the effects of its disastrous policies on its Arab neighbours and on itself defy reason and fill us with deep unease. The statements in this room have confirmed the resolve of the international community to ensure that the resolutions of the Council, international law and the will of the international community be respected.

Given Iraq's intransigence, the best and only way to bring the conflict to the most rapid conclusion possible is to press ahead on all fronts, military and diplomatic. There is no contradiction between the two. Indeed, the increasing pressure on the battlefield must be complemented by increasing efforts to convince Iraq that it must come to terms with reality. The fighting can be brought to a halt, even today or tomorrow, when Iraq decides to do what it must.

We are all aware that the question here is also the future and the credibility of the United Nations and whether it can succeed in stopping aggression through international collective security. The effort to get Iraq out of Kuwait has had overwhelming international support since 2 August. If the effort were to falter the future consequences for international peace and security would be disastrous, but we cannot and we will not falter. Nor will attempts to obfuscate and delay help in bringing the conflict to an end.

A cease-fire without concrete implementation of withdrawal will not accomplish the objectives of resolution 660 (1990) and will not bring the aggression to a close. We are engaged here in a historic contest between two different views of the world and of the future, between a concept of collective security and international obligations, on the one hand, and continued recourse by nations to warfare and aggression by the strong against the weak, on the other hand. This has been clear since 2 August, when Iraq invaded Kuwait. The international community, the Security Council and the General Assembly universally condemned Iraq's actions. Remembering the terrible lessons of the past, we said, clearly and loudly, "No more."

But Saddam Hussein counted on the fact that he would prevail against a virtually unarmed neighbour; while tough words and even United Nations-imposed sanctions would persist, the world would eventually come to acquiesce. He believed that while his people would suffer he would win in the end. Indeed, some believe that he thinks he will win precisely because he is willing to see or to make his own people suffer. Judging from the words of the Iraqi representatives, this continues, unfortunately, to be the case.

After 2 August many of us engaged in intensive diplomatic efforts with clear and agreed goals in mind, as set out in the Security Council resolutions. Even as Iraq was attempting systematically to remove the State of Kuwait from the map, we made peaceful attempt after peaceful attempt to convince Iraq that its aggression could not stand, that such blatant aggression and disregard for international law would not be tolerated. We tried to make it clear right up to 15 January that the chance of a peaceful solution still existed.

For its part, the United States emphasized that it wanted to avoid conflict. If Iraq chose the road to peace, Iraq would not be attacked, nor would its forces as they withdrew from Kuwait. We assured Baghdad publicly and privately that the United States had no intention of maintaining a permanent ground presence in the area, and that United States forces would not stay one day longer than necessary to deal with the threat. We affirmed our support for the call in resolution 660 (1990) for Iraq and Kuwait to negotiate their differences peacefully. We said we would consult in the Security Council on the future of the sanctions against Iraq once it had demonstrated compliance with the relevant resolutions, and, while emphasizing that Iraqi withdrawal must be unconditional and complete, we made clear the continuing commitment of the United States to peace between Israel and its Arab neighbours and the Palestinians, and made it clear that in the aftermath of the conflict we would renew our efforts to this end.

But every one of us who tried over a period of almost six months got nowhere. The six-month effort produced no movement towards a solution, for Saddam Hussein's strategy in this conflict has nothing to do with resolving Iraq's differences with Kuwait. It has nothing to do with settling the problems of the Middle East nor with improving the plight of the Palestinian people or of the poorer peoples of the Arab world. Indeed, one of the great tragedies of this crisis is that Saddam Hussein has made all of those intractable problems more difficult to deal with by his aggression and his hopes to swallow Kuwait.

When all else failed, the coalition against Iraqi aggression acted, as it continues to act, under the authority given it by the Security Council to implement fully the Council's resolutions. Our goals are not grandiose; they are simple and straightforward: to get Iraq out of Kuwait, to restore the legitimate authority of its Government and to restore peace and stability to the area - period, full stop. Those goals will be achieved, certainly not by the United States alone, but by the United States working together under the authority of the United Nations with the coalition partners, Islamic, European, African, Asian and Latin American. Most especially, it will be achieved in cooperation with the other countries of the Middle East, upon which peace, stability and the future of the area must depend.

In keeping with those goals, and because our dispute is not with the Iraqi people but with its leaders, the coalition has from the very outset carefully planned its operations specifically to do all that it can to minimize civilian casualties. The coalition has focused its efforts exclusively on military targets which support Iraq's tremendous war-making potential and hence its ability to occupy Kuwait and maintain its occupation.

It would be irresponsible in the extreme to deal with the huge Iraqi military establishment in Kuwait, which has had six months to dig in and prepare itself, as if it were an isolated entity. No rational effort to remove Iraq from Kuwait could fail to hit the military targets which support and sustain the Iraqi forces in Kuwait and provide the offensive power to keep them there. Since 16 January no coalition forces have knowingly or deliberately targeted civilians, their homes or civilian facilities. But unfortunately, despite our best efforts, civilians have been killed or injured. We regret this tremendously. War is a terrible thing, and no civilian deaths in Iraq or Kuwait, or in Saudi Arabia or Israel, are in any sense acceptable. This is an unavoidable consequence of war. We will continue to seek to avoid civilian casualties and we will work to bring the aggression and the conflict it has caused to a close as soon as possible.

Iraq has made the situation worse by deliberately placing military materièl in or near schools or medical facilities or places of worship, in violation of the laws of armed conflict, thereby increasing the risk for its own people. Command-and-control centres in Iraq have been placed on top of schools and public buildings. Coalition aircraft have been fired upon by anti-aircraft weapons scattered among the residential neighbourhoods. In Baghdad anti-aircraft sites have been located on roofs. We have all seen the television pictures. The barrages that those weapons have loosed into the air, shells and missiles, also fall back on the cities, causing damage and casualties. Tanks and artillery and other instruments of war have been placed beside homes in small villages, as have combat aircraft. We have seen the MiG 21 fighters parked next to one of the most important ancient archaeological sites in Iraq, the ziggurat at Ur.

Despite this immoral and illegal policy, we in the coalition continue to do our utmost to avoid civilian casualties and damage, even at the cost of increased risks to our own people. We have for the most part been successful, although the Iraqi Government continues to place its civilians in harm's way, and where we have not been successful it has not been for lack of effort or for lack of trying.

This stands in stark contrast with the terror policy of Iraq, which has launched cold-blooded, indiscriminate attacks on the civilian populations of Saudi Arabia and of Israel, which is not even a party to the conflict. It has been the aim and hope of Iraq precisely to create large numbers of civilian casualties in an effort both to widen and change the nature of the conflict. The fact that it has not been able to do so is due in large part to coalition success in defeating the Iraqi air force and destroying Iraqi Scud missiles and their support structures and to the admirable restraint of the people and the Government of Israel.

Furthermore, Iraq has attempted to win sympathy by fueling concern that major sacred Islamic sites in Iraq have been wantonly attacked by coalition forces, but there is no evidence that any of Iraq's four major holy sites - Karbala, An Najaf, Samarra and Kazimiya - have been damaged by coalition bombing, and we are taking every care to avoid doing so. In fact, we have recent very reliable evidence that they are undamaged and now in normal use. We cannot know whether Iraq is using the same care, since Iraq carefully controls those who might be witnesses.

Looking to a future in which a renewed Iraq plays an important role in the region, I can assure the Council that the coalition has no desire whatsoever to destroy the religious and cultural places of Iraq, just as we have no interest in striking other targets not of military value in the effort to liberate Kuwait.

While there is no doubt about the sincerity of concern for Iraqi civilians and culture, we cannot but be struck by the studied silence in some quarters in the face of the atrocities Iraq has committed against the civilian population of Kuwait. Kuwait has suffered severely since 2 August. Since we met in November to review Iraq's record of abuse, the horror continues. The murder of women, children, the sick and the elderly goes on. Torture and executions continue, as does the ruin of the cities and Kuwait's economic and industrial capacity. Yet no journalist or other outside observer has been allowed by Iraq into Kuwait to witness and report for the world the agony of the Kuwaiti people. Unfortunately, very few journalists have even noted the stark contrast between the controlled reporting from Baghdad and the non-access to Kuwait.

Any delay in bringing about Iraqi withdrawal can only add to the tragic suffering of the Kuwaiti people. And from some quarters we continue to hear concern about the effects of combat on Iraq even as Iraq threatens to use chemical weapons not only against coalition forces but also against the civilian populations in Saudi Arabia and Israel, even as it unleashed a horrible environmental disaster by releasing thousands of tons of oil into the Persian Gulf, doing incalculable damage that will take years to undo and exact costs for generations to come to pay, and even as Iraq flouts the basic provisions of the Geneva Convention relative to the Treatment of Prisoners of War, refusing to permit access by the International Committee of the Red Cross and parading prisoners of war on television to make obviously forced statements.

We urge the Government of Iraq to put an end to all this suffering and to put Iraq and Kuwait - indeed the whole region - on the road to recovery instead of continuing down the road of destruction. If Iraq persists, the coalition will win the military conflict. of that, I am certain. But the peace must also be secured, and that is a challenge for all of us, coalition members or not. Every country has a vital stake in seeing to it that the collective effort to restore international legality and peace and security is successful. There must be no reward for Iraq's aggression, if others tempted to brutality and unprovoked attack are to be deterred in the future.

Just as a collective effort is required to defeat the aggressor, so a collective effort will be required to work for justice and security in the future. In such an effort, respect for the sovereignties of the peoples of the Gulf and the Middle East must lie at the heart. It would be absolutely futile for the United States - or indeed any other nation - to think that it can impose its own will or thinking in the Middle East. We join with others in saying that the future of the Gulf region is in the hands of its own people. We look to the States of the Gulf region to take the lead in developing new security arrangements after two major wars in 10 years. No regional State should be excluded, and the United Nations and the rest of the international community have a role in encouraging such arrangements which would prevent further aggression and safeguard the territorial integrity of all States in the area.

We believe that the time has come to deal with arms proliferation and arms control in the region. This includes both conventional weapons and weapons of mass destruction. Right now today, five Middle Eastern nations have more main battle tanks than the United Kingdom or France. At the start of the conflict Iraq had more than both of them together. Iraq has used chemical weapons in war against its own people and is trying to develop biological and nuclear weapons. A destructive pattern of military competition can indeed be changed, and we can and we must work together more effectively to deal with proliferation and to reduce arms flows into the region.

A programme of economic recovery must accompany the effort to improve security. An economic disaster as of yet unknown dimension has occurred in the Gulf, gravely complicated by Iraq's unprecedented environmental terrorism. The people of the Gulf will be paying for a long time the price of Saddam Hussein's policies. Kuwait has been looted and wrecked. Hundreds of thousands of workers have lost their jobs and been dislocated. The Palestinian community in Kuwait alone has been particularly manipulated, victimized and exploited by Iraq. Financial and trade systems have been seriously disrupted. The damage done by the Iraqi invasion is enormous, and the confrontation is taking its own awful toll. After the conflict is over, Iraq itself will have to recover from its second disastrous military adventure in 10 years. The United States will want to consult with a broad range of Governments in the Gulf and elsewhere on how to encourage and support such a reconstruction effort. Any long-term effort to secure the peace must rest on economic stability and growth, and Iraq itself must surely be part of that effort.

No sure security in the Middle East is possible without the search for a just peace and real reconciliation involving Israel, the Arab States and the Palestinians. Long-term security requires genuine respect and tolerance, which will be exceedingly difficult to achieve. The sooner Saddam Hussein's tragic aggression is ended, the sooner efforts to resolve these problems can resume. The war has stirred emotions on all sides which it will be hard to calm. But no one has worked harder than the United States for real conciliation and dialogue between Israel and the Palestinians, and we will continue to do so.

As President Bush made clear in his speech before the General Assembly on 1 October last year, in the aftermath of Iraq's unconditional departure from Kuwait, there may be opportunities to settle the conflict that divides Arabs from Israel.

Before I close, I would like to ask the Council to listen to some frank talk. The debate here has contained its charges and its innuendoes. We have all heard them. This is not a war against Muslims or the Iraqi people. It is a battle to turn back aggression. The Muslim people of Kuwait were aggression's first victims. Now Saddam is sacrificing his own people for his own ends - Muslims and Christians and Kurds and people from other groups. This is not a war to dismember, dismantle or destroy Iraq and its population; it is a use of force authorized by this Council to deal with a breach of international peace and security and its aims are clear and directly related to that purpose. This Organization is of course devoted to the peaceful settlement of disputes. It is pledged also to stop the kind of unprovoked aggression committed by Saddam Hussein against a peaceful Member State. When peaceful settlement has not been able to stop aggression, the Charter provides for the use of force by this Council. We have accepted that awesome responsibility and we are here today because we do accept it. This is not a conflict which began on 16 January 1991; it began on 2 August 1990. We may debate its origins, but we cannot ignore the many steps that were taken over five and a half months to resolve it without the use of force.

We are anxious and indeed eager to turn our focus from war to construction, conciliation and cooperation. It is our fervent hope that out of this tragedy can come new prospects for peace in the Gulf region and new prospects for conciliation and solutions in the Middle East as a whole. it is also our hope that this tragedy will confirm the role of the Security Council as a force for collective security in a world in which the recourse to unprovoked aggression becomes evermore unacceptable.

[274-275] **Mr. Vorontsov (Union of Soviet Socialist Republics)** (interpretation from Russian):

I understood the statement of the representative of Iraq to the effect that the answer to my question will be received by us tomorrow in Moscow from the representative of President Saddam Hussein who will be visiting.

We await that visit with great interest. At that time questions will be asked that have arisen in respect of the statement made by the Revolutionary Command Council of Iraq. Moscow expresses the hope that the upcoming talks to be held in Moscow with the representative of the President of Iraq will enable us to move forward to our constant goal: the fulfilment of all the Security Council resolutions.

As for the question put to me by the representative of Iraq, I should like to assure him that not only the statement of the Minister for Foreign Affairs of the USSR and the Secretary of State of the United States made in Washington but also the statement made in Helsinki by the Presidents of the two countries, the Soviet Union and the United States of America, remain fully valid.

[276] **Mr. Hohenfellner (Austria):**

Since we now are indeed engaged in a debate, in the proper sense, in the Security Council, I too should like to put a question to the representative of Iraq.

There is no doubt that Security Council resolution 660 (1990) has to be implemented completely, which means in all its parts. Operative paragraph 2 of that resolution has been mentioned very often in the Council. It

> "Demands that Iraq withdraw immediately and unconditionally all its forces to the positions in which they were located on 1 August 1990".

Paragraph 3

> "Calls upon Iraq and Kuwait to begin immediately intensive negotiations for the resolution of their differences and supports all efforts in this regard, and especially those of the League of Arab States".

If I understood correctly, the representative of Iraq said earlier today that resolution 660 (1990) calls not only for withdrawal but also for immediate and direct negotiations. My question therefore is: Does the statement by the representative of Iraq mean that Iraq is now prepared also to negotiate with Kuwait?

...

[277] **Mr. Al-Anbari (Iraq)** (interpretation from Arabic):

I had asked to speak in order to comment on what was said by the Ambassador of the United Kingdom, but I shall take the opportunity to comment also on what was said by the representative of the United States, and I may say a word or two about what was said by the representative of Turkey.

As for what was said by Sir David, my aim was to give the best answers to his questions. I should like to emphasize to him that the Iraqi Government did not reject the request by the International Committee of the Red Cross. There are ongoing communications designed to enable the Red Cross to see the prisoners who are now in the hands of the Iraqi authorities.

I should like to refer particularly to one part of Sir David's statement. He used the word "foolish". I protest his use of that word. He is not a third-rate diplomat: he is an excellent, a first-class diplomat. I do not think he really believes that in our statements we should go as low as that. If he repeats the word, I reserve my right to use it against him.

I turn now to what was said by the representative of the United States of America. His country's position *vis-à-vis* the statement of the Revolutionary Command Council yesterday shows that the United States is not interested in peace and does not care for the resolutions of the Security Council, including resolution 660 (1990), which Iraq said it was ready to deal with.

In fact, the United States does not really care about Kuwait. When the Iran-Iraq war had ended and peace had begun to be established between the two countries, the United States saw fit to wage an aggressive campaign against Iraq in order to destroy it, in order to ensure that Iraq would not remain a deterrent force against the Zionist aggression against the Arab States.

As for the crocodile tears the United States representative shed about civilians, and his statement that the United States does not intentionally bomb civilians, my answer is very simple: The way the air raids are carried out - the intensive, continuous, comprehensive air raids from very high altitudes - makes it extremely difficult to distinguish, and the Americans should know in advance they will not be able to distinguish, between civilian and military, between doctors and policemen, between mosques and military installations. American television networks have shown the oldest Chaldean church, in northern Iraq - very close to the oldest archeological centre: Nineveh - which was bombed by B-52 aircraft.

I cannot think of any time when the United States has admitted that it has not respected the Geneva Conventions - despite the fact that it has waged many wars since the Second World War, including those against Panama, Nicaragua and Viet Nam. The United States never admits that any mistakes have been committed by its forces, although we know of the brutal crimes they have engaged in.

Now the United States is presenting us with new terminology. Now it says it has information that Iraq is placing its military facilities among civilians and in the cities, and that this is why they have to bomb them. I should like to ask this: How can any country at war hide tanks or anti-aircraft weapons in a mosque or a church? This is all nonsense.

If Iraq has put some of its air defences in certain civilian buildings, that is legitimate because we are engaged in defence.

They are reminding us of catch-22. They say there are weapons among the civilian population and that is why they have to bomb them. That is the American way. But I should like to emphasize to him that Iraq hopes the United States will be sincere and respond to truly peaceful initiatives and work for the establishment of peace in the entire Middle East region instead of exploiting the so-called Gulf crisis to try and destroy an Arab country that represents the heart of the Arab homeland.

As for what has been said by my colleague from Turkey, I am glad to hear that the Cypriot Muslim people in the land occupied by Turkey live in security and peace. That is what we all want. But the fact remains that the presence of the Turkish forces in Cyprus contravenes resolutions of the Security Council calling on Turkey to withdraw them. For more than 20 years Turkey has not implemented those resolutions. That is a fact he did not address.

As for the questions of my colleague the Ambassador of Austria, who is a man of law, I would be glad to answer them at the first opportunity.

...

[282] Mr. Pickering (United States):

The representative of Iraq has made a number of statements, and I will of course want to study the record of today's proceedings and the previous proceedings. I hope I will have an opportunity to reply as appropriate in due course.

I join with my colleague from the United Kingdom in wanting to assure that the Government of Iraq does everything possible to validate what I take to be at least the first effort on his part to indicate a willingness to abide by the Conventions related to prisoners of war.

Secondly, if he is planning to return to Baghdad in the immediate future I will certainly be glad to provide him with the locations of the places where he can find tanks, artillery and aircraft parked in or near civilian places of activity, including the location of a place I have already named where in recent days aircraft have been parked next to Iraq's most important and most famous archaeological monument.

[282] Mr. Al-Ashtal (Yemen) (interpretation from Arabic):

I do not wish to make a statement or to participate in this debate, though I reserve my right to express the viewpoint of the Republic of Yemen on subjects dealt with at this meeting, in particular in the statement of the representative of the United States, in which he dealt widely with the powers of the Council and the relationship between the current hostilities and the resolutions of the Council and the objectives of these operations, as well as the expected peace and the way a security system would be established in the region on the basis of the principles laid down by the United Nations.

I asked to speak to read out to the Council a statement issued by the Presidential Council in reaction to the proposal made by Iraq, in which it indicated its readiness to deal with resolution 660 (1990), including withdrawal.

The text of the statement is as follows:

> "The Presidential Council of the Republic of Yemen, welcoming the communiqué issued by the Iraqi Revolutionary Command Council, pays high tribute to this historic position taken by the Iraqi leadership on the basis of which it has indicated its readiness to abide by Security Council resolution 660 (1990) in return for a commitment by the coalition forces to an immediate cease-fire and the withdrawal of their forces from the region as well as a commitment by the international community to implement the Security Council resolutions relevant to the question of the Palestinian Arab people and the occupied Arab territories.
>
> "The Presidential Council, while expressing its appreciation for this courageous national resolve, pays tribute to the steadfastness of the brotherly people of Iraq. It calls upon the Security Council urgently to adopt a resolution providing for an immediate cessation of all hostilities. It calls upon all the leaders of Arab and Islamic countries, as well as all peace-loving peoples, to shoulder their historical responsibilities and to take the initiative towards a comprehensive peace in the region, including the withdrawal of Israel from the occupied Arab territories and the restoration of the legitimate national rights of the Arab Palestinian people.
>
> "The Presidential Council also calls on the Arab States cooperating or allied with the foreign forces waging their unjust war against brotherly Iraq to respond to the calls of pan-Arabism and Islam and to their national duty by preventing all the forces mobilized on the front from participating in any military action against Iraqi forces, and by not permitting the allied forces aligned against Iraq to use their territory, airspace or territorial waters for the launching of any attacks against the Iraqi people, their facilities, infrastructure or armed forces.
>
> "The Presidential Council sincerely hopes that all will respond to the call of reason, wisdom and logic to stop the bloodshed and to safeguard the potential of our nation."

A statement was issued by an official source concerning the bombardment of the shelter and the human losses resulting therefrom:

> "The leadership, people and Government of the Republic of Yemen are deeply shocked and saddened at the tragedy that led to the martyrdom of hundreds of women, children and the elderly in brotherly Iraq as a result of the horrible attack against a shelter filled with innocent civilians.
>
> "The Republic of Yemen, while deploring and condemning this carnage and the policy of genocide pursued by the United States of America and its allies in brotherly Iraq, reiterates that the path of peace is the only way to resolve the crisis. The Republic of Yemen reaffirms that the barbaric acts taking place today, including the bombardment of shelters, houses of worship, schools, kindergartens and other civilian facilities by United States and allied forces, not only exceed the resolutions of the Security Council but also run counter to all religions and international conventions.
>
> "The responsibility for the cessation of these inhuman acts falls squarely on the shoulders of the States that have voted for the adoption of Security Council resolution 678 (1990). This was pointed out at that time by the Republic of Yemen, when it spoke of this resolution unleashing the United States and giving it and its allies free reign to destroy the economic, cultural and scientific infrastructure of Iraq".

[287] The President:

I shall now make a statement in my capacity as representative of Zimbabwe.

The month of January was a particularly difficult and trying period for this Council. My predecessor, Ambassador Bagbeni Adeito Nzengeya of Zaire, guided the affairs of the Council with rare skill and effectiveness.

Zimbabwe congratulates him for his sterling efforts, which greatly facilitated the Council's work.

Yesterday, the Revolutionary Command Council of Iraq issued a statement which appears to indicate a change in Iraq's position regarding its withdrawal from Kuwait. Zimbabwe considers the statement to be of significance and importance. The Security Council should take this new development seriously. There are many elements which need to be clarified. Zimbabwe expects this Council to start without delay the process of diplomatic exploration with a view to seizing the opportunity for peace which the new development might offer. The gravity of the situation in the Gulf demands that the Council act sensitively and expeditiously. We cannot afford to let even the slightest opportunity for peace slip through our fingers.

Zimbabwe stands ready to work with all those who may have initiatives that would enable this Council to pursue and take full advantage of this new development.

I now resume my function as President of the Council.

I have a request from a Council member to speak at a later stage. With the concurrence of members of the Council, I shall suspend the meeting now until Tuesday, 19 February, 1991. The time of the meeting will be communicated by the Secretariat.

The meeting was suspended at 2.30 p.m.

F. S/PV.2977 (Part II) (closed-resumption 3), 23 February 1991

[296] **Mr. VORONTSOV (Union of Soviet Socialist Republics)** (interpretation from Russian):

On instructions from the leadership of the Soviet Union, we asked for the resumption of this meeting of the Security Council to report to the Council on our work over the past few days with the special representative of Iraq, Mr. Tariq Aziz, who has visited the soviet Union in response to the plan we proposed on 18 February. In the course of difficult and lengthy talks we succeeded in making more specific the readiness expressed by the Iraqi leadership to withdraw their troops from Kuwait on the basis of the decisions of the Security Council.

Specifically, the matter stands as follows: Iraq agrees to comply with Security Council resolution 660 (1990), that is immediately and unconditionally to withdraw all its troops from Kuwait to the positions they occupied on 1 August 1990. The withdrawal of troops would begin the day after a cease-fire and a halt to all land, sea and air hostilities. The withdrawal of troops would be carried out over 21 days, and troops would be withdrawn from Kuwait City in the course of the first four days. Immediately after the completion of the withdrawal of troops from Kuwait, the reasons for the adoption of other Security Council resolutions would have lapsed, and those resolutions would thus cease to be in force. All military prisoners of war would be released and repatriated in the course of three days following a cease-fire and cessation of hostilities. Confirmation, monitoring and observance of the cease-fire and the withdrawal of troops would be carried out by observers and/or peace-keeping forces to be determined by the Security Council.

It is our belief that in those circumstances it has become possible, for the present, to achieve optimal results. This not only gives us reason to hope for a peaceful settlement of the conflict but also raises real prospects for such an outcome.

Of course, the proposal worked out in Moscow can be further improved, but it represents the best we have been able to achieve thus far.

The Iraqi leadership has accepted that proposal; in that connection we have received an official statement from President Saddam Hussein.

Moreover, in the statement he made in Moscow on 23 February Mr. Tariq Aziz in effect responded positively to the United States statement.

We do not think the results we have achieved so far represent our achievement alone. The possibility that an end could be called to the war today, thereby saving perhaps thousands of lives, stems primarily from the striking unanimity displayed throughout the conflict by the international community and the Security Council. For the first time in the history of international relations since the Second World War, we have been able through our joint efforts to halt aggression and provide a lesson to any future potential aggressor.

Given the current situation, we think it important to continue efforts to achieve a peaceful settlement to the crisis as early as possible. To that end, all relevant Security Council resolutions should be complied with and all existing proposals should be integrated into the settlement.

[297] **Mr. PICKERING (United States of America):**

I too want to provide the Council with an interim report on the approach which the members of the coalition, including, of course, the United States have been taking on the question of a resolution of the issue before the Council. In that regard I want to express our thanks and appreciation for the work the Soviet Union has been doing and for the interim report provided to us by the Soviet representative.

As members of the Council will know, the United States, on behalf of the members of the coalition, presented yesterday a document which outlines our views about how and in what way this issue should move to a rapid settlement. I should like, if I may now, to quote extensively from that document and then, in a few minutes, to provide some commentary on the statement which our Soviet colleague has presented.

Yesterday we said that the Soviet announcement represents a serious and useful effort which is appreciated. But in our view major obstacles remain. The coalition for many months has sought a peaceful resolution of the crisis in keeping with the United Nations resolutions. As President Bush has pointed out to President Gorbachev, the steps the Iraqis are considering would constitute a conditional withdrawal and would also prevent the full implementation of relevant United Nations Security Council resolutions.

Also, there is no indication that Iraq is still prepared to withdraw immediately, in accordance with the terms of Security Council resolution 660 (1990). Full compliance with the Security Council resolutions has been a consistent and necessary demand of the international community, as we all well know here in the Council. The world must make sure that Iraq has in fact renounced its claim to Kuwait and accepted all relevant Security Council resolutions.

Indeed, it is only here in the Security Council that we could agree to lift sanctions against Iraq, and the world needs to be assured in concrete terms of Iraq's peaceful intentions before such action can be taken. In a situation where sanctions have been lifted, Saddam Hussein could simply revert to using his oil resources once again, not to provide for the well-being of his people but instead to rearm, with some intention, perhaps, of repeating his aggression in the future.

So, in a final effort to obtain Iraqi compliance with the will of the international community, the United States, after consulting with the Government of Kuwait and its other coalition partners, declares that a ground campaign will not be initiated against Iraqi forces if, prior to noon, Saturday, 23 February, New York time, Iraq publicly accepts the following terms and authoritatively communicates that acceptance to the United Nations.

First, Iraq must begin large-scale withdrawal from Kuwait by noon, New York time, Saturday, 23 February. Iraq must complete military withdrawal from Kuwait in one week. Given the fact that Iraq invaded and occupied Kuwait in a matter of just hours, anything longer than this from the initiation of withdrawal would not meet with resolution 660's requirement of immediacy. Within the first 48 hours, Iraq must remove all of its forces from Kuwait City and allow for the prompt return of the legitimate Government of Kuwait. It must withdraw from all prepared defenses along the Saudi-Kuwait and Saudi-Iraq borders, from Bubiyan and Warba Islands, and from Kuwait's Rumaila oil-field within the one week specified above.

Iraq must return all its forces to their positions of 1 August in accordance with resolution 660 (1990).

In cooperation with the International Red Cross, Iraq must release all prisoners of war and third-country civilians being held against their will, and return the remains of killed and deceased servicemen. This action must commence immediately with the initiation of the withdrawal and be completed within 48 hours.

Iraq must remove all explosives and booby traps, including those on Kuwaiti oil installations, and designate Iraqi military liaison officers to work with Kuwaiti and other coalition forces on the operational details related to Iraq's withdrawal, to include the provision of all data on the location and nature of any land or sea mines.

Iraq must cease combat-aircraft flights over Iraq and Kuwait, except for transport aircraft carrying troops out of Kuwait, and allow coalition aircraft exclusive control over and use of all Kuwaiti airspace. It must cease all destructive actions against Kuwaiti citizens and property, and release all Kuwaiti detainees.

The United States and its coalition partners reiterate that their forces will not attack retreating Iraqi forces and, further, will exercise restraint so long as withdrawal proceeds in accordance with the above guidelines and there are no attacks on other countries. Any breach of these terms would bring an instant and sharp response from coalition forces, in accordance with Security Council resolution 678 (1990).

In addition, I want to inform the members of the Council that our proposal is there. It remains on the table, on its own conditions, to be accepted at any time. We hope it will be accepted as soon as possible. This position of the coalition therefore stands.

I have heard with interest the report of our colleague from the Soviet Union. I must say that we are pleased with the progress that has been made, even though we feel that the proposal as set forth fails in two important circumstances to meet the tests that are set forth in resolution 660 (1990) itself. One of those circumstances is that of immediacy, the question of timing. The issue of timing, I believe, can best be made clear by careful examination of the proposal which I have just read out, which in our view meets the circumstances of timing as required in the initial resolution.

The second point that I believe is important is the issue which appears in the fourth portion of the Soviet proposal provided to us today in the interim report. That is the question of conditions. It is difficult for us to see how an unconditional proposal - a proposal without conditions - can be so conditioned, particularly in respect of the idea of declaring that Security Council resolutions somehow cease to exist, are null and void or without effect. Obviously, such a step is unacceptable to us on a number of grounds.

First and foremost, there has clearly been no compliance up to this point with Security Council resolution 660 (1990). Thus, without compliance with that resolution - and, for example, the requirement of resolution 662 (1990), that Iraq rescind its purported annexation of Kuwait, which the Council declares to be null and void - it would be most inappropriate and unwise, in our view, to move to declare that such a step by the Council cease to exist and thereby to enshrine the unilateral Iraqi action purporting to carry out that annexation.

Not only has there been no response to Security Council resolutions that speak to Iraq's responsibility for its illegal acts, including breaches of the Geneva Convention of 1949; there have been continuing acts of wanton destruction within the last 24 hours, as we have seen if we all continue to watch the television screens, as I know members do. The enormous fires that are now consuming Kuwaiti oil fields and installations are, in our view, continuing such actions.

In addition, with respect to resolution 660 (1990), it is not clear in the mind of my Government that the proposal which we have heard read out actually involves paragraph 3 of that resolution. Members will recall that paragraph 3, which calls for a beginning of negotiations between Iraq and Kuwait to resolve their differences with the help of others, including members of the Arab League, was put into the resolution by the members of the Council with a clear sense of the importance of that step.

There are, in short, actions called for by these resolutions that remain to be taken. There are legal obligations that flow directly from and by operations of international law which remain to be satisfied. Whether, after all resolutions have been complied with by Iraq, it would make sense to engage the Council in what would become for us the thoroughly novel practice of declaring a resolution as ceasing to be in force, as null and void or without further effect, is a question that we can all examine in due course. It is not a practice, however, in the view of my Government, that should be taken on lightly. Aside from the overtones of rewriting history, there is the question of the effect of any such action taken on the network of legal consequences which flow from and which will continue to flow from the decisions of the Council on the situation created by Iraq's invasion of Kuwait.

The days of the invasion may be numbered. We certainly believe this to be the case. But the consequences would not and could not end so soon. There is, moreover, the important and salient need to restore international peace and security to the region in accord with the strictures of resolution 678 (1990) and with the implications which are clear in the appropriate paragraphs of resolution 674 (1990). We must not dismantle at the stroke of a pen what the Council has built since 2 August until we have reached agreement on how to restore peace and security to the area.

I am delighted to hear at this meeting indications from our Soviet colleague that the Foreign Minister of Iraq either intends to respond or has responded positively to the points I have read out today. I should be delighted to have any clarification of this that can be made.

It is my understanding as well that the President of Iraq plans to speak on television in the new few moments. We shall obviously look forward with hope to hearing what he has to say in response to the proposals we have put forward.

We also continue to hope that Iraq will rapidly come to its senses and will accept the proposals that have been put before it for ending its aggression.

[306] **Mr. Li Daoyu (China)** (interpretation from Chinese):

As announced by the Soviet Union, Iraq has made a positive response to the peaceful initiative of the Soviet Union by indicating its willingness to withdraw from Kuwait unconditionally. This is a major change, in a positive direction, and is a good beginning. We welcome this announcement.

This war which has lasted for more than a month has inflicted huge losses of human life and property on the innocent population of the Gulf region. If the war escalates further, the Gulf region and the people of that region as well as other countries concerned will face even greater suffering. We strongly call on the parties concerned in the conflict to demonstrate their goodwill for a peaceful solution, not to miss this opportunity to end the war and bring about peace at an early date, and to make further efforts to seek a solution that could immediately lead to a peaceful settlement of this crisis.

At such a crucial moment, the Security Council should fulfil its responsibilities by considering and adopting an appropriate plan for the peaceful settlement of the Gulf crisis, thus playing its role in the restoration and preservation of peace and security in that region.

[307] **Mr. GHAREKHAN (India):**

As the Secretary-General said a few days ago, these are testing times for our Organization. The test has perhaps never been as severe or acute as it is today. As my colleague from China, Ambassador Li Daoyu, has just stated, this is the time for the Security Council to discharge its responsibility and to work for peace.

I should like at the outset to thank the representatives of the Soviet Union and the United States for the reports they have presented to us this morning. Of course, my delegation would have been even happier if these reports had been submitted to the Security Council before today. That would have given us more time. But it seems to my delegation that we have not really run out of time. We have time - of course, not to infinity, but enough time to try and see what can be done.

I should like to express my Government's very deep and sincere appreciation for the enormous efforts which President Gorbachev has personally exerted to find a peaceful answer to the crisis in the Gulf region.

At the opening meeting of the Indian Parliament, yesterday, both Houses adopted a unanimous resolution calling upon the Security Council to continue to make all efforts to find a peaceful solution and expressing appreciation to president Gorbachev for his efforts. This meeting of the House of the Indian Parliament took place soon after the first set of proposals were announced in Moscow.

My delegation takes note of three or four points in particular in the statement made by Ambassador Vorontsov. First, after presenting the six points of the proposal, he said that they can be improved, that they are not the final word. I think that Ambassador Pickering referred to them as an interim report. The second point Ambassador Vorontsov made was that it is important for the Security Council to continue to make efforts. His third point was that it is necessary - and I think should be feasible - to prepare an integrated solution on the basis of existing proposals. His fourth point was that Iraq has accepted the Soviet proposals - and Mr. Tariq Aziz seems to have made a statement in Moscow today responding positively to the United States statement of yesterday.

I should like to thank Ambassador Pickering also for officially seizing the Security Council of the United States proposals.

There are, of course, differences between the two sets of proposals, but there are also similarities. Ambassador Pickering mentioned two points with which his country and the members of the alliance have particular difficulty: the question of immediacy, and the fourth point in the Soviet peace plan. Of course it would be naive to minimize the differences. The differences are there; they are real. But there are also similarities; there are also points of agreement. Some differences may be not so difficult to bridge and some differences may be a bit more difficult to bridge.

Under these circumstances it seems to my delegation that what the Ambassador of China just said is important and very relevant. He said that the Security Council should fulfil its responsibility by adopting a plan of action of its own; I understand that to be what my colleague from China was suggesting.

The situation today is so serious, with thousands of lives at stake, that we feel the Security Council must remain in continuous session, if necessary, to try to sort out a plan of action, as proposed by the representative of China.

We not only would urge the Union of Soviet Socialist Republics and the United States to try to work out the differences between their plans of action, but would also like the Council as a whole, and in particular all the non-permanent members, to discharge their responsibility, the mandate entrusted to them - that is, to us, including my country - by the General Assembly as a whole.

If it is not possible, or if it becomes too difficult, for the principal authors of the two plans to resolve their differences, perhaps it is incumbent upon all the 10 non-permanent members at this time to sit together and see what we can do. My delegation would therefore like to suggest to its colleagues, especially the non-permanent members, that we meet, that we sit together and find some way out of what appears to be an impasse. It may not turn out to be an impasse, but if it is, it must not be allowed to remain an impasse. The situation is far too grave for us just to leave everything to others.

I think the representative of the Soviet Union also said that his Government would like the Security Council to consider the different sets of proposals and to produce an integrated plan of action.

[312] **Sir David HANNAY (United Kingdom):**

I should like to begin by thanking the representative of the Soviet Union for the progress report he has just given us on the contacts his Government has had with the Government of Iraq. I should also like to express my Government's thanks for the very great efforts that the Government of the Soviet Union and President Gorbachev personally have made in recent days and to recognize the very considerable changes which they have managed to bring about in the position of the Government of Iraq, which started last week, as we all know, with a position which was a very long way away from the one it has now endorsed.

My Government stands firmly by the offer that was set out on behalf of a number of allies of Kuwait by President Bush yesterday. I would just draw to the attention of the representative of India that that is not simply a United States offer. In any case, we regard it as fair and reasonable, and we stand by it.

I do not want to comment in great detail on the six points referred to us by the representative of the Soviet Union which his Government has worked out with the Iraqi Foreign Minister and which the Iraqi Foreign Minister now apparently - I must say "apparently", because we still do not have what I would call an authoritative endorsement of it by the Government of Iraq at the highest level - accepts.

But I would just make the point that although he stated that Iraq now accepts resolution 660 (1990), and in particular the requirement for an immediate and unconditional withdrawal from Kuwait, the content of some of the other points is in effect a contradiction of that proposition, so there is still, I fear, an inbuilt contradiction in those points.

I will leave aside comments on the time table, which in my Government's view should stand as put forward by the allies of Kuwait in their statement yesterday, and simply concentrate on the fourth point, where I think the Security Council as a whole must look with some care. This fourth point, which relates to the status of the Security Council's own resolutions after an Iraqi withdrawal, seems to us to be fundamentally flawed. It is wrong, I think, in fact to state that the Security Council resolutions will lose their force with an Iraqi withdrawal; purely formally, one must say that only the Security Council itself can make that judgement.

But, more than that, it is, frankly, not the case that the reasons for adopting a number of those provisions will have been removed. It is simply not the case that provisions relating to the damage or the breaches of human rights that have been committed by Iraq will be removed by the removal of Iraqi forces from Kuwait. But whether or not it is factually accurate as a presentation of policy, I am afraid that point is really quite unacceptable. One has only to look at some of the provisions of the Security Council resolutions which would, if this point were accepted, become invalid on an Iraqi withdrawal to understand why that is so and why my Government's view is as it is.

Resolution 661 (1990), for example, is a very firm basis for the establishment of the sovereignty, independence and territorial integrity of Kuwait. It is really an essential part of any withdrawal that Iraq recognize that. It is also the basis on which Kuwait can hope to repossess some of the goods that have been pillaged from it, including all the aircraft belonging to Kuwait Airways.

Resolution 662 (1990) is the basis for the declaration that the annexation of Kuwait is null and void. We all know there is an Iraqi internal law that states that Kuwait is the nineteenth province of Iraq, part of it, of course, being the province of Basrah. Removal of the "null and void" provisions of resolution 662 (1990) would leave the Iraqi law standing, and Iraq could go on arguing this issue for decades. That is not acceptable in circumstances in which Iraq has invaded its neighbour and committed this act of aggression.

Resolution 664 (1990) contains provisions about the holding of nationals against their will. As we all know, there are many thousands of Kuwaiti citizens held in Iraq against their will, and their future must be assured. It cannot just be left to the mercy of the Government of Iraq, which has so grievously maltreated them so far.

Then, resolution 674 (1990) provides for the basis for compensation for damage caused by Iraq - and every day there is more if it - and for the handling of breaches of the Geneva Convention. As I said before, these matters cannot be wiped from the slate by an Iraqi withdrawal.

Finally, in resolution 678 (1990) itself there is a commitment by the Security Council to the peace and security of the region. That must surely be maintained; that is the guideline for all our future action. If you remove that, you merely risk going back in that region to the extremely unstable, extremely insecure situation that prevailed on 1 August. And that cannot be in the interest of any of the countries in that region.

Those are a number of points I wished to make, not in a spirit of criticism or hostility, to the Soviet Union, whose efforts, as I say, have been Herculean in the last 10 days. But it does, I think, demonstrate how we are still a long way from getting the Government of Iraq to accept what it will have to accept if there is to be a peaceful solution.

I had hoped, and I still hope, that the representative of the Government of Iraq at this table will be able to tell us that his Government has accepted the offer that was made by the allies yesterday. That, of course, is the simple and straightforward way to bring this dispute to a peaceful solution at the earliest possible moment.

[316] Mr. HOHENFELLNER (Austria):

I should like first of all to thank the representatives of the USSR and the United States of America for their interim reports submitted to the Council at this meeting. The statements made by a spokesman of President Gorbachev in Moscow on 21 February and, in particular, 22 February, on the results of the talks between the Soviet leadership and the Foreign Minister of Iraq, as confirmed and elaborated today by the representative of the USSR, were a positive signal. They have given reasons for hope that the full implementation of previous Security Council resolutions is now possible and that further military operations may not be necessary.

Also, there are still some uncertainties and open questions as to the modalities of implementation in conformity with those resolutions. These statements and, in particular, that of 22 February, do go a long way indeed. They form the basis for further serious consideration of the remaining questions.

The members of the Security Council should play a major role in this context, bearing in mind that the very objective of our efforts is a political solution based on the full implementation of the relevant Security Council resolutions, in particular the liberation of Kuwait and the restoration of its legitimate Government.

In my statement to the Security Council of 14 February, I declared:

> "... even at this late hour, despite the military action already undertaken, political and diplomatic efforts still have their place and should, indeed, be intensified. The loss of human lives and the material destruction that have already occurred, and the even greater losses in the future in the event that hostilities continue, and especially if they escalate, make the search for ways and means of bringing these hostilities to an early end a moral imperative. ..."

Today more than ever before, we have a historic opportunity for such efforts based on the results of Moscow. I appeal to all to use it.

[317] Mr. ALARCON de QUESADA (Cuba) (interpretation from Spanish):

At the outset my delegation would like to pay tribute to President Gorbachev, who in the last few days, and perhaps even the last few weeks, has devoted time, energy and dedication to trying to find a peaceful solution of this conflict. We also hail the positive outcome of his efforts, which are clearly reflected in the information Ambassador Vorontsov was good enough to give us a few moments ago.

My delegation would like to associate itself with the ideas put forward earlier by other colleagues, particularly the representatives of China and India.

It seems to us that, as a result of the positive outcome of the Soviet efforts, agreements have been reached that, as Ambassador Vorontsov has informed us, have been accepted by the Government of Iraq at the highest level. This implies a fundamental obligation for this Council to get down to work immediately to determine the specific steps and actions it should take to make it possible for this plan for a peaceful settlement of the conflict to be carried out as speedily as possible, and in the most appropriate way.

We believe there should be no doubt whatsoever that the Security Council alone has the responsibility to determine the terms of a peaceful settlement, under which international peace and security must be guaranteed.

At this time I do not wish to dwell on details or specific points on some issues raised by some of our colleagues. I wish only to recall that for more than six months a clear international consensus has been reflected in this Council on the need to ensure full implementation of resolution 660 (1990), which has obviously been the basis of any subsequent action by the Security Council.

The relationship between compliance with that resolution and compliance with other resolutions agreed upon by the Council later could be the subject of an analysis among us, but I am not convinced that this is the time to engage in such a process, when other urgent tasks deserve the Council's immediate attention. I merely wish to draw the attention of my colleagues to the first resolution adopted after resolution 660 (1990) - resolution 661 (1990), in which this Council decided to establish comprehensive economic sanctions against Iraq.

At that time the Security Council decided the following: in paragraph 1 of its resolution 661 (1991), to determine that Iraq had so far failed to comply with paragraph 2 of resolution 660 (1991); and in paragraph 2, to decide, as a consequence, "to take the following measures", which represent the economic sanctions.

The direct cause and effect relationship between economic sanctions as decided upon by the Council and Iraq's failure to comply with the terms of paragraph 2 of resolution 660 (1991) - that is to say, fully to withdraw from Kuwait - is quite obvious and has been stated explicitly by the Council.

In any event, my delegation believes that we could discuss all this, as we must also discuss the definition of what one colleague called a peace plan, or some action to make it possible to facilitate compliance with paragraph 2 of resolution 660 (1991) - a goal sought by the Security Council throughout.

We appreciate the statement made by Ambassador Pickering, containing the proposal made - as indicated in the final paragraph - on behalf of the United States and its partners in the coalition. We take note with appreciation the fact that it has been submitted formally to the Council.

It has been said outside this Chamber that the intent of this proposal was to set a deadline for Iraq and to humiliate that country. I do not know whether that is the precise intention of the sponsors, but the fact that it has been presented to the Council and that 20 minutes have already elapsed after the noon deadline leads me to hope that there is no intention whatsoever to regard it in the same fashion as has been announced outside this Council.

We believe that the Council should act in the manner suggested by our colleague from India. My delegation is fully prepared to work in the manner he has suggested, that is, in continuous session. We also believe that he has made a very useful suggestion with regard to the role that might be played by the non-permanent members. He recalled a very important thing: that we the non-permanent members have been elected by the General Assembly and that we have a special responsibility to try to interpret the anxiety and concerns of all the Members of the United Nations with respect to this problem.

In this spirit, and with this readiness, my delegation trusts that under your wise leadership, Mr. President, the Security Council will make the best possible use of all the time available to it, not because it must take action in the face of some possible threats or deadlines given to the Council, but because we are indeed dealing with a very grave problem involving the lives of thousands of people and because we have the obligation to try to bring about the speediest possible solution to this problem.

[322] **Mr. BLANC (France)** (interpretation from French):

Over the grace period established by the Security Council before 15 January, France spared no effort to promote a peaceful settlement of the crisis. Unfortunately, Iraq refused to comply with the Security Council resolutions.

Recently President Gorbachev took the initiative to make a last attempt to prevail upon Iraq to accept the will of the international community. We commend the praiseworthy efforts of the Union of Soviet Socialist Republics.

Regrettably, the results achieved remain inadequate. As the members of the Security Council know, a last appeal has been made by the members of the coalition setting forth the conditions in keeping with the resolutions of the Security Council that must be accepted by Iraq. We hope that President Saddam Hussein will respond positively to that appeal.

[322] **Mr. NOTERDAEME (Belgium)** (interpretation from French):

First of all I should like to thank our Soviet colleague, Ambassador Vorontsov, for the very important information he has just given to us. My Government had an opportunity yesterday to express its full appreciation for President Gorbachev's extraordinary diplomatic effort.

I also listened with keen interest to the statement of our colleague Ambassador Pickering.

I shall not at this stage comment on the two statements made here - one by the Soviet Union and the other on behalf of the members of the coalition. I merely wish to make one comment. What bothers me the most and makes me a bit perplexed is the fourth point in the Soviet proposal providing for the annulment of all the other Council resolutions once withdrawal had taken place. I really have a great deal of difficulty with this and, if possible, I should like to ask our colleague Ambassador Vorontsov to provide some explanation as to the purpose of this provision.

[323-325] **Mr. AYALA LASSO (Ecuador)** (interpretation from Spanish):

On behalf of Ecuador, may I first express our thanks for the report our colleague Ambassador Vorontsov was good enough to give us at this formal meeting. I believe that his statement not only sheds light on the dynamic efforts the Soviet Union has been making to facilitate the reaching of an agreement that will bring an end to the war in the Gulf as soon as possible but also affords the Security Council an opportunity to become cognizant in a formal meeting of this commendable initiative and to consider it substantively. At least, that is my interpretation of the Soviet Union's request to hold this meeting, since a purely informative exercise - undoubtedly useful in itself - would in the present circumstances be insufficient.

I should also like to express my appreciation to my friend Ambassador Pickering for the information he has given us on the views of the United States of America and the other countries assisting Kuwait with regard to the Soviet plan and on the elements that could bring about an immediate solution to the crisis.

I have noted with great satisfaction the fact that there is a gradually increasing number of significant points of convergence between the two positions, and I am hopeful that that trend might continue. The differences between the two ways of envisaging a solution are both objective and considerable. I believe, however, that the presentation of the two reports has enabled us to see clearly that there is still room for additional progress in diminishing these differences so as to arrive at a plan eventually acceptable to Iraq.

Let me be very clear: my country has stated that the solution to this problem must begin with Iraq's compliance with the resolutions of the Security Council. Ecuador regards that as a fundamental and key point. Along with that, however, there is another point that we regard as essential, and that is that we give peace the greatest possible chance through negotiations. It is at this point in time that we must step up diplomatic efforts and the Council's actions in an attempt to achieve that peace. I agree with the statement of our friend Ambassador Gharekhan, in which he referred not only to the Council's obligation to consider matters dealing with international peace and security but also to our common desire to participate fully in the efforts being made to put an end to the war.

Those are the two issues I wanted to mention at this stage of our work in connection with this item. Obviously, I would be ready and willing to work non-stop, should that prove necessary, and in due course to give my views on all the points of both of the plans we are considering.

[327] **Mr. AL-ASHTAL (Yemen)** (interpretation from Arabic):

The Security Council is meeting today at a very important juncture in the Gulf crisis. It is for that reason that we are participating in the discussion, notwithstanding our objection to the convening of a private meeting. We believe that the Council's meetings should be public. The entire world is focused on the action the Council will take. We hope that the present privacy will be ended as soon as possible.

From the military viewpoint we are on the threshold of a very important development, one that could lead to the expansion of military battles if a large-scale ground war is initiated. A ground war will have incalculable results and its expansion might result in the use of weapons of mass destruction. In any event, the losses in human life and destruction of property will be enormous. All of this must be taken into consideration by the Council at this vital moment.

From the political viewpoint, there has been a very important development: Iraq has at last agreed to implement the resolutions of the Security Council, particularly resolution 660 (1990). Iraq has announced, through its Foreign Minister, that it will withdraw from Kuwait in accordance with the provisions of resolution 660 (1990). In those circumstances matters must return to the Council, and we wonder whether any party, including the members of the coalition, has the right to escalate military action without returning to the Security Council itself. We now have a great opportunity either to achieve peace or to wage war and cause vast destruction. The Security Council must therefore adopt a proper and necessary resolution which in the final analysis will restore peace and security to the region.

Today's meeting, therefore, is of special importance; at it, we must decide how to resolve this problem one way or another. In that connection, I thank the representative of the Soviet Union and the Soviet leadership, who have undertaken a very important effort to find a peaceful solution to the problem.

As members know, this process began on 15 February, when Iraq submitted a proposal for a peaceful solution to the problem. We discussed this question at another informal meeting, at which I said the Security Council had to probe Iraq on its proposals and on its acceptance of the Council's resolutions. I said at that time that the Council had to authorize one party, either the Secretary-General or the President of the Security Council, to represent it and to follow up on the Iraqi proposal.

When the Foreign Minister of Iraq was on his way to the Soviet Union we told the Council that we had to wait; we had to hear from the Soviet delegation about the talks that were to take place in Moscow and about their results. Today I want to thank the representative of the Soviet Union for the clear report he gave the Council on those talks and deliberations.

We now have before us what could be called a six-point peace plan. Iraq has publicly accepted that plan, that includes complete withdrawal in accordance with Security Council resolutions. Therefore, the Security Council must discuss this proposal and adopt the appropriate measures.

We also heard the report of the representative of the United States of America on the steps announced yesterday in Washington on behalf of the coalition forces. We thank Ambassador Pickering for his report on the steps announced yesterday.

At this critical stage the Security Council must discuss the various proposals put forward and reach a final decision. Here I wish to thank the representative of India, who has made a number of proposals relating in particular to what non-permanent members of the Security Council can do. As members know, there are precedents for such action by non-permanent members of the Security Council.

The Security Council must continue its deliberations on this question in a manner the President considers appropriate with a view to finding a solution to this problem that is satisfactory and acceptable to the Council.

[332] **Mr. MUNTEANU (Romania):**

My delegation would like to join delegations that have expressed their appreciation of the efforts made by the Soviet Union to find a peaceful solution to the Persian Gulf conflict.

We have taken note of the fact that the very first element of the Soviet communication conveys to us the agreement by Iraq to implement resolution 660 (1990) without delay and without conditions. At the same time we cannot overlook the fact that major obstacles still remain. Full compliance with all the Security Council resolutions has been a consistent and necessary demand of the international community.

As I have already said before the Council, my country is strongly committed to morality and legality in all spheres of domestic and international life. It has made clear in all its statements on the item under consideration that a solution to the Persian Gulf conflict can be based only on all the relevant resolutions of the Security Council.

In the light of that position of my country, my delegation considers that Iraq should authoritatively communicate to the United Nations its full and unconditional acceptance of all the Security Council's resolutions. It is necessary to have a statement from Iraq that would make it clear that that country has renounced its claim to Kuwait.

On the other hand, we agree with the interpretation given here by other members of the Council that the sanctions against Iraq can be lifted only by the Council itself. The question of declaring null and void a number of resolutions on the situation between Iraq and Kuwait cannot be treated in an easy way. Such a nullification should not in any way be viewed as a precondition; that is unacceptable to my delegation. In fact, it needs very careful and responsible consideration.

What counts is to have solid guarantees that Iraq will not again violate the Charter of the United Nations and the basic principles of international law.

Like other delegations we are ready to pursue our efforts within the Security Council. Such efforts should lead to the strengthening of the solidarity of this body, to the full implementation of all resolutions on the situation between Iraq and Kuwait and to the restoration of peace and security in that area.

[336] **THE SECRETARY-GENERAL:**

I have listened with greatest care to the very important statements made by the representatives of the Soviet Union, the United States, China, India, the United Kingdom, Austria, Yemen, Cuba, France, Belgium, Ecuador and Romania, and would like to express my appreciation for the contributions they have made in the debate today.

The Security Council is meeting at a crucial hour - crucial to an unparalleled degree. I have been informed of the positions taken by all parties in the past 48 hours, and I have watched the progress made in the laudable diplomatic endeavours to bring this destructive conflict to a speedy end in consonance with the resolutions of the Security Council. Openings towards a cessation of the conflict have been clearly revealed in the past two days. It would be tragic in the extreme if the opportunities that have been created were now to be lost. I appeal most earnestly that this not be the case.

The United Nations - and, if I may add, its Secretary-General - are passing through a most trying and, in some respects, painful experience. Since the beginning of the crisis, there has been devastation on a vast scale. The consequences for a vital and strategically most important region of the world are still literally incalculable. We have the obligation to uphold the principles which prompted the Security Council's resolutions, and we have to respond to the supreme moral imperative of preventing further destruction of life. These two objectives should not be irreconcilable.

Our attitudes and decisions at this stage will carry a momentous significance for peace and for the trust of the peoples of the world, across all cultures and continents, in this Organization.

[337] **Mr. Abulhasan (Kuwait)** (interpretation from Arabic):

I should like at the outset to express our gratitude to our friend Mr. Yuli Vorontsov, the Permanent Representative of the Soviet Union, for his preliminary report, which included the outcome of negotiations with the Iraqi régime. In the wake of an appreciated effort made by President Gorbachev in the past few days, I should also like to extend my thanks and gratitude to my friend Mr. Thomas Pickering, Permanent Representative of the United States, for his report. I should like to say that my Government has been cooperating with Arab, Islamic and other friendly countries to compel Iraq to withdraw immediately and unconditionally from Kuwait in accordance with Security Council resolutions, particularly resolution 678 (1990) and has consulted extensively with them.

We agreed to the plan announced yesterday by President Bush and to the detailed programme that followed that communiqué. We believe that President Gorbachev has made significant progress since the first announcement. President Gorbachev's success to date does not, however, deal with all relevant Security Council resolutions. It addresses one paragraph of resolution 660 (1990) concerning the complete and unconditional withdrawal of Iraqi forces to the positions they occupied on 1 August 1990. Regrettably, even that paragraph was not accepted completely by Iraq, which rejected its demand for an immediate withdrawal. Iraq requests the abrogation of all Security Council resolutions on the issue on the basis of its withdrawing troops from territories under its control, as if it were withdrawing them - from Basra, for instance. I mention this because the Iraqi National Assembly unanimously adopted legislation in August - of course, without any debate and by order of the Iraqi President - naming Kuwait as the nineteenth province of Iraq.

We have been informed that Iraq communicated its acceptance of President Gorbachev's proposal to the Soviet Government. Despite our great respect for the Soviet Government, Iraq, as all members of the Council know, has perpetrated an aggression against Kuwait. When Iran was attempting to find a formula for the acceptance of resolution 598 (1987), Iraq insisted that the only acceptable way, which had to be imposed on Iran, was for that country to indicate its acceptance of resolution 598 (1987) through a letter from the Iranian President or Foreign Minister to the Secretary-General of the United Nations. We all know the efforts made by the Iranian representative to find an appropriate formula. However, Iraqi insistence was very clear that this was the only legal manner in which Security Council resolutions are accepted. It took almost a year, during which Iraqi aggression against Iran continued, creating countless victims.

But now we are facing an even more serious and dangerous situation than existed during our debate on Iran's acceptance of resolution 598 (1987). Our acceptance of the statement made yesterday in Moscow by the Iraqi Foreign Minister would freeze the situation for a certain period and create an even more dangerous situation in the future that would claim more lives and more damage to property, which would need to be reconstructed between now and some later aggression launched by Iraq against Kuwait.

In order for Iraq to end this situation, it must do the following:

First, it must inform the Secretary-General of the United Nations, in writing, that it accepts all the Security Council resolutions.

Secondly, it must embark immediately on the implementation of paragraph 2 of Security Council resolution 660 (1990), on withdrawal.

Thirdly, the legitimate authorities must be enabled to return immediately to Kuwait.

Fourthly, Iraq must implement all the other Security Council resolutions by agreeing to an exchange of prisoners of war of all nationalities, including Kuwaitis taken prisoner since 2 August. This must be done immediately after the cease-fire. Arrangements must be made for looking for the missing. We have lists of names and addresses of more than 8,000 prisoners of war and more than 20,000 missing - and this applies only to Kuwaitis. Iraq must also pay full reparations under Security Council resolution 674 (1990), not only to Kuwaitis but also to all third-party nationals.

Fifthly, the legislative authorities in Iraq must abrogate all legislation concerning the annexation of Kuwait and the consideration of Kuwait as the nineteenth province.

I believe that without those elements we should only be freezing the whole question and paving the way for another Iraqi aggression a few years from now. My Government calls upon the Security Council to demand that Iraq immediately cease the present escalation of its inhuman practices against the defenceless Kuwaiti people, to cease committing crimes against the Kuwaiti economy and environment by setting fire to Kuwaiti oil wells and installations, and to cease the destruction of what is left of the Kuwaiti social and economic infrastructure.

Yesterday I sent a letter to the Secretary-General in which I informed him of a serious development that had taken place yesterday. Defenceless Kuwaitis between the ages of 15 and 50 were arrested as they were leaving Friday prayers at a mosque. For absolutely no reason, they were put into buses and transferred to Iraq. The only error committed by these innocent persons is that they are Kuwaitis. Iraq wants to use these innocent persons as a means of pressure in any upcoming negotiations. Iraq fears that these defenceless, innocent Kuwaitis will want to defend the soil of their country and will engage in the liberation of their country.

I have listened to the proposal of my dear friend the Ambassador of India. While I appreciate his interest in bringing about peace and averting any further destruction for Kuwait and Iraq, I say that we should concentrate on persuading Iraq that the only way the region can be free of destruction, the only way that Kuwait and Iraq can be free of destruction, is for all the Security Council resolutions to be accepted and not for certain paragraphs of one resolution to be selectively chosen, for the very-well-known reasons I have set forth clearly in my statement.

...

[342] **Mr. Moussa (Egypt)** (interpretation from Arabic):

...

I extend my thanks and appreciation to President Gorbachev for the efforts he has exerted so far to achieve a peaceful, immediate solution to the present problem, in accordance with the Security Council resolutions. Egypt regards the Soviet initiative as a step in the right direction - the immediate and unconditional withdrawal by the Iraqi forces from Kuwait.

The present contacts between Cairo and Moscow, at the highest level, as well as the contacts between Cairo and Washington, also at the highest level, demonstrate the interest that Egypt takes, because of its responsibilities in the region, in the achievement of an immediate, peaceful solution to the present problem. From the very outset - that is, from 2 August 1990 - we called for a political solution to the problem, and we have continued to do so. Our appeals and political initiatives at the international, regional and Arab levels, have reflected that interest.

In the light of recent developments, the Government of Egypt wishes to make the following comments.

First, we must work quickly to find a peaceful solution to the problem, in order to save lives and the entire region.

Secondly, what is of utmost importance is immediate withdrawal - now, not tomorrow. The Iraqi leadership must understand the dimensions of the entire situation and the serious consequences of any intransigence or delay. The time we have lost so far has been the result of this intransigence and also of Iraq's failure to understand the whole situation.

Thirdly, the withdrawal must take place immediately in accordance with the letter and spirit of the Security Council resolutions, starting with resolution 660 (1990).

Fourthly, Security Council resolution 660 (1990) cannot be accepted only partially, and it cannot be accepted alone, by itself. Negotiations between Iraq and Kuwait, two independent and sovereign countries, must start immediately after the withdrawal, and there must be an official commitment by the Iraqi Government in that respect.

Fifthly, the solution of the problem lies not in immediate withdrawal alone, but in Iraq's rescinding of the annexation of Kuwait. Iraq must do this publicly and officially.

We must also implement all the terms of the 12 resolutions adopted by the Security Council. Therefore, we find totally unacceptable the request to rescind those resolutions or to have them regarded as null and void immediately after withdrawal. The Security Council must implement those resolutions, not rescind them. It has a responsibility to guarantee their implementation. We cannot accept their being rescinded before their full implementation.

Sixthly, acceptance by Iraq must be official and documented and be communicated directly to the Secretary-General of the United Nations.

There are two things I wish to say here. First, I wish to read out the following official statement from the Egyptian Foreign Ministry on the recent developments:

> "In the light of the consultations that have taken place between Egypt, the brotherly Arab countries and the other members of the coalition participating in the liberation of Kuwait, the Ministry of Foreign Affairs of Egypt declares that while we appreciate the good intentions of the Soviet Union in its initiative, that initiative is lacking in certain regards. It does not respond to the main points in the Security Council resolutions concerning the Iraqi invasion of Kuwait, first and foremost of which is the call for the immediate withdrawal of Iraqi forces from Kuwait, without any procrastination or conditions and for the return of legitimacy to Kuwait. Hence we confirm once again our support for the call for the members of the coalition to Iraq to withdraw its forces immediately from Kuwait. Egypt also calls upon the Iraqi leadership to respond quickly to the communiqué by the coalition, and it must end its intransigence. It must measure up to the responsibility and dimensions of the situation facing the Iraqi people, which is causing that people much suffering and much destruction."

Secondly, I wish to comment on the statement by my colleague from India that the 10 non-permanent members of the Council should discuss the situation. While we do not interfere in the request of one member to others, we should like to state very clearly that what should be done now is to call upon Iraq to withdraw its forces immediately and not to make formalistic attempts to procrastinate. Time is of the essence. Any effort now should be concentrated on calling upon Iraq to withdraw its forces and accept the Security Council resolutions without any conditions. There should be a call upon the Iraqi leadership to put aside any other conditions in the light of the serious situation in the region.

Efforts in this regard must be coordinated with the Arab countries concerned. The legitimate interests of the countries of the region should not be disregarded. We must co-ordinate and consult with those countries and we must call upon Iraq to withdraw its forces in accordance with the terms announced yesterday - that is, a withdrawal that must start this very day.

[347] **Mr. Vorontsov (Union of Soviet Socialist Republics)** (interpretation from Russian):

The Soviet delegation wishes to speak again in order to express its profound gratitude to all those who have spoken here of their high appreciation of the efforts of our country and those of President Gorbachev personally to bring about the earliest possible resolution of the Kuwait crisis, the immediate withdrawal of Iraq [*sic*] troops and the total restoration of the sovereignty and independence of the State of Kuwait.

I should like to take this opportunity also to say that we have listened attentively to the detailed points made by the representatives of the United States, the United Kingdom and Kuwait regarding concrete elements of the plan of action worked out in Moscow. In the course of our further work we shall be ready to answer the question raised by the representative of Belgium.

We believe that important work has already begun at this meeting with a view to the further formulation of the plan of action. The Soviet delegation supports the proposals that we should urgently continue work on the plan of action. We think that the main thing now is to produce an integrated solution of the crisis on the basis of the provisions worked out in Moscow and the proposals of the United States and other members of the coalition. We are ready to participate actively in this work, which of course is of the utmost urgency.

[348-350] **Mr. Bagbeni Adeito Nzengaya (Zaire)** (interpretation from French):

My delegation wishes first to express its gratitude to the representative of the Soviet Union, Ambassador Vorontsov, for the tireless efforts of President Gorbachev to bring about a peaceful settlement of the question relating to the occupation of Kuwait by Iraq.

My delegation has followed with interest the statements made by members of the coalition on the Soviet-Iraqi proposals. My delegation believes that at this stage the members of the Council should spare no effort to examine those proposals in depth with a view to identifying elements that it can use to implement fully its 12 resolutions on the question. To that end, the official statements by Ambassador Vorontsov, setting forth the peace plan, and by the Iraqi authorities, accepting the plan, should be made official documents of the Council.

However that may be, my delegation regrets the absence of Kuwait from the consultations in Moscow, since resolution 660 (1990) binds Iraq and Kuwait to carrying out negotiations after the immediate and unconditional withdrawal of Iraqi forces from Kuwait.

As to the proposal made by the representative of India, my delegation also believes that all members of the Council should, regardless, take part in all the Council's formal and informal work with a view to finding the most appropriate way to take the Soviet-Iraqi proposals into account.

[351] **Sir David Hannay (United Kingdom):**

I am speaking again only because I understand the speaker's list has been exhausted.

For the past one hour and twenty minutes I have been hoping to hear a few words spoken by the representative of the Government of Iraq. Since he has not spoken, I have taken the floor again merely to say that I think our debate this morning would be greatly illuminated if we were to hear the views of that Government.

Many references have been made to what the Iraqi Government does or does not accept, whether it is or is not favourable to the views expressed by the countries cooperating with Kuwait, and what it is prepared to do.

I think our further work is going to be extraordinarily difficult without an indication of the views of the

Government of Iraq. This is not a negotiation between the Governments cooperating with Kuwait and the Soviet Union. It is not a negotiation at all. But we do need to know the views of the Government of Iraq.

Now, of course the representative of the Government of Iraq has every right to stay silent. I am not trying to exert any unacceptable pressure. But I do think this opportunity has to be offered before we close our debate.

[351] **Mr. Kadrat (Iraq)** (interpretation from Arabic): Iraq's position is very clear. It has informed the Soviet leadership in Moscow that we have accepted the Soviet peace initiative and agreed to all its points. We have said we can withdraw in conformity with all the provisions of resolution 660 (1990), in accordance with what has been announced by Mr. Tariq Aziz, the Iraqi Foreign Minister, in Moscow. As our friend the Soviet Ambassador made clear a few minutes ago, we find it strange that other conditions and other questions have been put forward at this meeting.

...

The meeting was suspended at 1.25 p.m.

G. S/PV.2977 (Part II) (closed-resumption 4), 26 February 1991

...

[356] **Mr. Vorontsov (Union of Soviet Socialist Republics)** (interpretation from Russian): I have been instructed by the Soviet leadership to report to the Security Council that just a few hours ago a message was received in Moscow from the President of Iraq, Mr. Saddam Hussein, addressed to the President of the USSR, Mikhail S. Gorbachev. The message reads as follows:

> "The Iraqi leadership has decided in accordance with resolution 660 (1990) immediately to withdraw all its troops from Kuwait.
>
> "The order to that effect has already been issued.
>
> "I request you to make urgent efforts for the adoption of a resolution of the United Nations Security Council calling for a cease-fire. The timeframe for the implementation of the troop withdrawal, which has already begun, will be very brief."

I believe that urgent message from the Iraqi President requires no explanation by the Soviet delegation. I should just like to stress that, as the Iraqis have declared, the troop withdrawal has already begun, and accordingly the Security Council can adopt the relevant decision.

[357-360] **Mr. Al-Ashtal (Yemen)** (interpretation from Arabic):

First of all, I wish to thank the Permanent Representative of the Soviet Union, Ambassador Vorontsov, for his initiative in calling for this resumed meeting of the Council and for the message he has just conveyed.

Six and a half months after the outbreak of this crisis, which has now turned into a large-scale war, we are on the threshold of a peaceful diplomatic solution.

If the Security Council is to play a big part in resolving this crisis it must adopt the necessary decision to end the crisis with the implementation of its resolutions, foremost among which is resolution 660 (1990).

We have been informed by the representative of the Soviet Union of the message sent to the President of the Soviet Union by President Saddam Hussein that Iraq has decided to withdraw, that it intends to withdraw within a very short time and that orders to withdraw have been issued. The Security Council must therefore take the necessary decision so that the withdrawal is organized and orderly and so that any further bloodshed in the war may be prevented.

Accordingly, the delegation of Yemen proposes formally that we adopt a resolution affirming in its preamble the resolutions that the Council has adopted, beginning with resolution 660 (1990) and including all the other relevant resolutions. It would then demand a cease-fire, determine the period within which the withdrawal would take place - a short period of time - and organize supervision by the United Nations of the withdrawal process.

We hope that such a resolution will be adopted as soon as possible: so that Kuwait may be liberated, so that its sovereignty may be restored, so that hostilities may cease, and so that we may start building peace in the area.

[361] **Mr. Pickering (United States of America):** I thank my Soviet colleague for having brought us this message this evening.

I want to begin my few remarks tonight by noting that within the past half hour my Government in Washington has reacted to the announcement which we all heard some hours earlier from Baghdad Radio relating to a somewhat similar development. In that regard, I should like to point out that the United States has made it clear that up to this point we continue to prosecute our efforts to remove Iraqi forces from Kuwait, using the military force authorized by the Council.

At this stage we see no reason to change that approach. Our primary concern continues to be, of course, the safety of our own forces and the forces of the coalition. We made it clear that we had heard the Radio Baghdad report, but, first and foremost, we have no way of knowing whether indeed it was a true report. We seem to have heard a slightly different, perhaps somewhat more optimistic, report this evening, but we have seen on the ground - and I am sorry to say this - no evidence of an Iraqi withdrawal.

Iraq, as we all know, has tended to use these statements from time to time as methods of propaganda in a duplicitous fashion and in some cases as ruses of war. We recall the arrival of the Iraqi tanks just some weeks ago at Khafji, when the tanks approached the coalition positions in an attitude of surrender but then immediately turned their gun turrets and did battle.

We are also facing continuing attacks by Scuds, which have today unfortunately taken their highest toll in human life - some 22 American citizens and perhaps, unfortunately, more.

We also noted the fact that we understand that Saddam Hussein has declared that his forces will fight their way out of Kuwait. We have made it very clear that we have no intention of attacking retreating forces. But such forces should certainly lay down their arms and leave. If they are moving as a combat unit with combat equipment, then in our view they are still subject to the rules of war.

We have also made it very clear that we have not rejected anything. We are anxious to have in fact a serious proposal put forward by the Government of Iraq. I sit here tonight and look around this Chamber and notice one startling peculiarity: there is a seat at the end of the table with the nameplate of a country in which we have the most serious interest, and yet - maybe because of the exigencies of the moment, because of the rapidity with which we are meeting, maybe in fact because of the thesis that the actions of the Council have no legitimacy, no legality, in the absence of the Permanent Representative of Iraq; I do not know - whatever the reason may be, we have something here that may speak louder than words, in the absence of a clear position stated before the Council by the Government of Iraq in the person of the Permanent Representative of that country, who is here in this town. I would hope he would come. I would hope he would tell us what his position is, as we have asked. We should like to hear from Saddam Hussein personally and publicly what his position is with respect to this latest step.

As I have said, we have been subjected to many duplicitous statements in the past. I assure you, Mr. President, that I am ready to come back. If the representative of Iraq is ready to attend, I am ready to stay here on call, ready for whatever you might think is the appropriate way to receive the answer. I would hope that the answer is ringingly positive and fully supportive of the resolutions of the Security Council.

We ask no more than that Iraq make clear to us - whenever it is ready but, hopefully, much sooner rather than later - that it is prepared to accept the resolutions of the Security Council and that it is prepared to accept the method of implementation contained in the statement of the coalition partners made on their behalf by President Bush on 22 February.

[363-365] **Mr. Gharekhan (India):**

I should like first to thank Ambassador Vorontsov, the Permanent Representative of the Soviet Union, for bringing to the Council's attention an important communication from his Government. We welcome and deeply appreciate the continued efforts made by President Gorbachev and the Soviet Government to find a peaceful solution to this tragic crisis.

As I said on a previous occasion, my country and my delegation are deeply distressed at the continued loss of life, whether Kuwaiti or Iraqi or American. Loss of life is loss of life: we make no distinction; we feel equally distressed and depressed at this continued loss of life and damage to property.

My delegation can appreciate the point of view of those Governments that would like to have an authoritative representative of the Government of Iraq come here and state its position, whatever it is, to the Security Council. I think this is an understandable and perfectly legitimate point of view.

At the same time, my delegation feels that a communication from the President of the Soviet Union, read out by its representative in the Security Council, cannot be treated lightly. As far as my delegation is concerned, the statement read out by Ambassador Vorontsov carries authentic information. We have no reason to doubt its veracity or the message it is conveying.

The message brought by Ambassador Vorontsov seems to be pretty clear - and here I interrupt myself to note the arrival here within the last few seconds of the representative of Iraq. This is quite welcome not only to my delegation but, I hope, to other delegations also. As I was saying, the message brought by Ambassador Vorontsov is clear: the Government of Iraq is prepared to withdraw without any pre-conditions whatsoever. That is my delegation's understanding of this communication.

We would all recall that the earlier Soviet proposal, which the Soviet delegation presented to us on Saturday, was a six-point plan. Today there seems to be only one point - namely, immediate and unconditional withdrawal from Kuwait. My delegation cannot but welcome this announcement, this initiative, which it would seem is closer than it ever has been to what was contained in the proposal of the coalition.

Therefore, my delegation welcomes and supports this initiative as well as the suggestion made by the representative of the Soviet Union.

...

[367-370] **Mr. Abulhasan (Kuwait)** (interpretation from Arabic):

The Government of Kuwait wishes to express to the friendly Soviet Union and its leadership, including President Gorbachev, its appreciation for their efforts to ensure the establishment of a just peace between Iraq and Kuwait.

The Security Council adopted 12 resolutions on Iraq's aggression against and occupation of Kuwait. These resolutions were communicated to the Government of Iraq by the Secretary-General of the United Nations. Thus, the Government of Iraq should not consider the crushing of its brutal aggression against my country as an acceptance of the *fait accompli*. The Iraqi Government must first communicate to the Secretary-General in writing its acceptance of the 12 resolutions adopted by the Security Council - in the same way as the resolutions were communicated to it by the Secretary-General. Once that has been done, once the Secretary-General receives an official letter from the Iraqi Government, then - and only then - will it be possible to say that Iraq's defeat on the soil of Kuwait has gone beyond the *fait accompli* and has been changed into an acceptance of the 12 resolutions.

Mere withdrawal cannot in any way mean an end to the dispute. This dispute has political, economic and legal consequences. All these consequences have been expressed in resolutions adopted by the Security Council. Thus, acceptance of the resolutions would open the way to dealing with the consequences of the Iraqi aggression against the State of Kuwait. The crushing of the aggression and Iraq's withdrawal from Kuwait would not change anything, in the final analysis.

Those are my comments so far as the form is concerned.

As for the credibility of the Iraqi regime, its record is, regrettably, replete with examples of its lack of credibility.

It is characteristic for this regime to renege on its promises. The members of the Council are all aware that the leader of the Iraqi regime, who aggressed against Iran, tore up the Algiers Agreement he signed with Iran after his aggression against that country, and that after his second aggression, against Kuwait, he resuscitated it. Thus we face a unique phenomenon in international dealings that does not depend on the sincerity of promises and actions.

That is why the situation is too complicated to be considered ended once the forces have been withdrawn. Iraq is responsible to the Council, as are its legislative bodies, to revoke its Parliament's decision to annex Kuwait and to consider it its nineteenth province. It must rescind all resolutions and decisions adopted and issued by the Iraqi Government in this regard.

We are surprised that, at a time when Iraq claims it has begun withdrawing its troops, it has struck at Saudi Arabia and Saudi Arabia's civilians with its missiles. We have seen it burning the oilfields in Kuwait. The number of them burning has now reached more than 500 - half the Kuwaiti production. Not to mention the aggressive actions against defenceless Kuwaitis - the torture, destruction and murder, and the demolition of public buildings by Iraqi tanks using phosphorous bombs - all acts of ferocious revenge.

What the invading Iraqi forces did in Khorramshahr on the eve of Iraq's withdrawal therefrom gives us a clear picture of what the Iraqi forces are doing now in Kuwait City, at a time when they claim to be withdrawing from Kuwait.

We in Kuwait reject anything less than an official letter from the Iraqi regime addressed to the Council or to the Secretary-General, which must include acceptance of all the Security Council resolutions. That is the only thing that can lead to the consideration of any other measures to be taken later.

...

[372] **Mr. Al-Anbari (Iraq)** (interpretation from Arabic):

Before I express the official position of my Government on Security Council resolution 660 (1990), I would recall that the person sitting to my right and several of the members sitting around this table have once or twice protested my not mentioning Kuwait in previous statements. Kuwait has always existed as a geographic fact, but its constitutional position was in question.

Iraq has expressed its determination to withdraw from Kuwaiti territories in implementation of resolution of [*sic*] 660 (1990), in a manner I shall make perfectly clear. It is, however, ironic to hear such insults from this person and his claimed victories and other things he has said. I am reminded of an Arab joke that I shall now tell in English, so that everybody understands:

(*spoke in English*)

> "A mule was asked who his father was. After a while, the mule said 'Well, my uncle is a horse'".

That is the answer to the boasting of this individual about victories and achievements, and to the conditions and preconditions he has just stated before the Council.

(*spoke in Arabic*)

Throughout this day I have been in contact with several of my colleagues, including Your Excellency, Mr. President, and Ambassador Vorontsov of the Soviet Union, and I am aware of what he communicated to the Council. I should like to affirm here that my Government completely supports what the Soviet Ambassador has told the Council. I would add that the Iraqi Government, while accepting resolution 660 (1990), which it seeks to implement fully, has already issued orders to Iraqi troops in Kuwait to withdraw to their positions before 2 August 1990. Iraq is interested in completing its withdrawal as quickly as possible, in a manner that guarantees the safety of our troops in the withdrawal process and ensures that the withdrawal proceeds in an orderly fashion.

Therefore the Foreign Minister of Iraq has informed his Soviet counterpart of a message from President Saddam Hussein to President Gorbachev of the Soviet Union, in which he asks the latter to make efforts to achieve a cease-fire resolution so that the Iraqi troops can withdraw as quickly as possible in a manner that guarantees their safety and prevents their being subjected to aggression.

At this meeting I reiterate my request that the Council immediately adopt a resolution for a cease-fire in which it establishes the necessary machinery to guarantee respect for the cease-fire and the completion of the withdrawal of Iraqi troops as soon as possible.

I do not want to give an opportunity to some who would like to fish in murky waters. I should like to confine myself to what I have already said. But I feel I must say that there are certain parties who have never been interested in the safety of Kuwait, or in international legitimacy, or in the Security Council. They have secret objectives that entail the elimination of Iraq and its military capability, and they have carried out their aggression under the umbrella of the Council and its resolutions.

In response to our request today to implement resolution 660 (1990), on the basis of which all the other resolutions were adopted, those parties will find pretexts to violate that resolution. They will set conditions and preconditions incompatible with the spirit and the letter of resolution 660 (1990). Aware as I am of the objectives of some countries to preclude an orderly withdrawal and achieve continuation of the war in the area to serve their aggressive aims, I wished to mention this in advance.

[376] **Sir David HANNAY (United Kingdom):**

I am glad to be speaking after the representative of Iraq because, as I said at an earlier stage in our discussions this evening, I think it is absolutely essential that we conduct our business on the basis of the clearly defined and announced policy of the Government of Iraq through its own representative, and it is useful indeed to have heard that now. I do not wish by saying so to belittle in any way the communication brought to us by the representative of the Soviet Union. I think it was of great value that he was able to convey that message and that we were able therefore to begin this meeting, but we certainly could not conclude it without hearing direct from the representative of the Government of Iraq the position of his country.

That will remain the case, because this is not just a sort of formalistic problem. It is quite simply that we are trying to restore the rule of international law, and that rule has been broken by the Government of Iraq, and it is the willingness - and the extent of the willingness - of the Government of Iraq to be bound by that rule of law which is the crucial condition for returning to peace from the present, current situation. So it will be the words of the Government of Iraq, spoken through its representative here, which will matter to us.

Now, I must confess that I found the first part of the representative of Iraq's statement pretty worrying, quite apart from the joke in rather poor taste at the expense of my friend from Kuwait. What I found worrying was - if I understood him correctly - and I apologize if the interpretation got it wrong - that he is stating now that his country has no problem with describing Kuwait as a geographical area, but he does not accept it as a constitutional entity. That, I am afraid, is at the heart of all our problems. If he is able to contradict me and to explain what he said after I have spoken, that will no doubt help, but if that is what he is saying then we are not as far forward as I had hoped we were.

Secondly, I note that he mentions only resolution 660 (1990), as if that resolution were somehow different in nature from all the other resolutions that the Council has adopted on the dispute between Iraq and Kuwait. But, frankly, that is not so. Those resolutions are a single corpus of international law adopted under Chapter VII of the Charter of the United Nations, and they are a single whole. They cannot be taken to pieces and dealt with one by one as a process of negotiation. If anybody in this room doubts it, I would recommend that he turn to resolution 678 (1990), which is the basis on which the current action by my country and others cooperating with the Government of Kuwait is being taken, and there he will see that it is stated quite categorically that the Council is determined to secure full compliance with its decisions, all of which are referred to above, that it demands that Iraq comply fully with resolution 660 (1990) and all subsequent relevant resolutions, and that it authorizes the Member States cooperating with the Government of Kuwait to use all necessary means to implement Security Council resolution 660 (1990) and all subsequent resolutions.

So this division between resolution 660 (1990) and the other resolutions does not exist in the jurisprudence of the Council and is not a basis for the taking of decisions by it. So I am afraid that the distinctions that were made this evening are extremely revealing, but they are not a basis on which we are going to move forward very fast. If the representative of Iraq could tell me that this was all a mistake on my part and that his Government intends to comply with and implement all the other resolutions, then nobody will be happier than I.

Finally, I would just say this: the news that has been conveyed to us by the representative of the Soviet Union and now confirmed by the representative of Iraq has come very suddenly. It has now got to be examined very carefully by my Government - that will be done very rapidly too - and we will have to consider how best to move ahead. But my Government, along with other Governments cooperating with the Government of Kuwait, set out very clearly on 22 February the basis on which it would be prepared to consider the withdrawal from Kuwait by Iraqi forces and the military and political provisions that would accompany that.

These matters are set out very carefully in a document that was conveyed to the Government of Iraq. I have not yet heard from any representative of the Government of Iraq - other than in a fairly vituperative way from spokesmen on Baghdad Radio - any response to that document. But a response to that document we will need if we are to move forward, and I hope that the representative of Iraq will be able to get instructions from his capital to respond to that document and the terms that were set out in it, because it remains as germane today as it was the day on which it was uttered, which was last Friday.

As I say, I will now be seeking the instructions of my Government as to the formal response to make to the developments of this evening, but these points I have made will certainly be of great importance to my Government when formulating those instructions.

[379-380] **Mr. Li Daoyu (China)** (interpretation from Chinese):

First of all, I wish to take this opportunity to thank the Permanent Representative of the Soviet Union, Ambassador Vorontsov, for the communication he has conveyed to us.

According to that message, the leadership of Iraq has decided, in accordance with Security Council resolution 660 (1990), immediately to withdraw its troops from Kuwait. In our view this is a positive factor in the evolution of events in the Gulf crisis. We welcome it. We hope that Iraq will immediately take action and implement that decision and complete its withdrawal in the shortest possible time.

The Chinese Government has stood all along for a peaceful solution of the Gulf crisis within the framework of the resolutions of the Security Council. We are deeply concerned and disquieted by the huge loss of life and property as a result of the war. We hope that the parties concerned will take advantage of this opportunity to exercise the utmost restraint and take action immediately so as to create favourable conditions for the earliest possible conclusion of the war and a peaceful settlement of the Gulf crisis.

In view of this new development, we believe that the Security Council should give serious consideration to the role it should play and help to promote Iraq's speedy and complete withdrawal and a comprehensive and peaceful solution of the Gulf crisis.

...

[381] **Mr. Al-Anbari (Iraq)** (interpretation from Arabic):

I did not intend to speak a second time, but I should not like to see the debate being pulled in all directions or to see anyone have the opportunity to avoid a discussion on this very important situation - a discussion which should be based on Iraq's new position which I communicated to the Council a few minutes ago.

I should like to answer Sir David Hannay's question on Kuwait. It is undeniable that Kuwait is a geographic fact. When I mentioned this point earlier, I meant that I had never referred to Kuwait by name in other statements simply because I had found no need to do so. As a geographic fact, Kuwait still stands; it is there.

Now, the situation is different, of course. My country's decision to withdraw from Kuwait in accordance with Security Council resolution 660 (1990) confirms what we have always said: that all should adhere to international law, which should be applied universally and equally. That is the essence of Iraq's initiative of 12 [*sic*] August 1990, which has been criticized and ignored on the pretext that it links one question or issue to the other.

We now hear that all the resolutions adopted by the Council over the past five months must be implemented immediately - although some of them would take years to implement, even if everyone wished to do so. We know what it will take to implement resolution 660 (1990) alone. I should now like to affirm that Iraq will not accept anyone at this meeting to address questions that have nothing to do with that resolution. My Government is interested in seeing - indeed eager to see - the Council adopt a resolution that would guarantee the complete and rapid implementation of resolution 660 (1990), after which the necessary measures should be considered and adopted in order to implement what can or should be implemented in other resolutions.

Without addressing the substance of the other resolutions, I should just like to point out that some have already been implemented, such as that making it possible for foreigners living in Kuwait and Iraq to leave should they so desire. There was no difficulty in implementing that resolution. The difficulty is not a technical one; it simply requires serious study, goodwill and the desire to bring peace and stability to the region. We must find proposals and solutions for every problem we face.

...

[382] **Mr. Abulhasan (Kuwait)** (interpretation from Arabic):

It is no honour for me, either as an individual or as the representative of a State, to lower myself to the position of the representative of the aggressive regime in making what he intended to be a joke. It was a joke in poor taste, reflecting the level of his character and the character of his regime. That is my first point.

My second point - the main point - is this. The statement of the representative of the aggressive regime confirmed what all of us had feared: that the aggressive regime would be selective about the measures recommended by the Council *vis-à-vis* its aggression. After its miserable defeat, every soldier who has surrendered to escape the hell of battle has stated that he was forced to do what he was doing and that he did not believe in it. And more than 25,000 prisoners of war have been taken in just the past 48 hours.

Once the situation had reached this point, the Iraqi Government was forced to select withdrawal; this was imposed on it by virtue of its defeat. The Iraqi regime disregards all other elements. We even heard the representative of the aggressive regime inventing this new legal interpretation: that Kuwait is a geographic fact. But he does not accept it as a constitutional fact. The representative of Iraq has referred to the constitutional fact, but the Security Council speaks of the constitutional fact in its resolution 662 (1990). Iraq's constitutional fact is the one on which it based its annexation of Kuwait to its territory - annexation which the representative of Iraq has stated in the Council is irreversible and final. When Iraq annexed Kuwait illegally, the very representative who is here now said that the legislation annexing Kuwait was final. The verbatim records will bear that out.

How can we agree to a cease-fire, which is tantamount to considering that the aggression did not happen or was inconsequential? How can we turn a blind eye to resolution 662 (1990), which considers the annexation of Kuwait by Iraq null and void? How can the representative of Iraq ask us to forget resolution 667 (1990), which condemns Iraq's closing of the foreign missions in Kuwait?

How can we ignore resolution 674 (1990), which deals with reparations and the applicability of the Fourth Geneva Convention to the situation in Kuwait and Kuwaiti prisoners since 2 August? The number of Kuwaitis who have disappeared exceeds 20,000; they are now suffering in Iraqi prisons.

How can we forget the damages suffered by the citizens of 104 countries who lived in Kuwait until 1 August? However, the representative of the Iraqi regime hastened to say that some of the resolutions have already been implemented. He remembers those resolutions, but he links the resolutions dealing with constitutional requirements - resolutions 662 (1990), 667 (1990) and 674 (1990) - to what he called the 2 August initiative.

Hence we are still in the same position we were on 2 August, that is, the insistence of the Iraqi regime which, in view of very difficult circumstances, accepts only part of resolution 660 (1990) - the part concerning withdrawal.

I should like to put the same question my colleague of Austria put to the representative of Iraq last week: Is the Government of Iraq ready to implement paragraph 3 of resolution 660 (1990) with the legitimate Kuwaiti Government - the very resolution the representative of the Iraqi regime claims to accept?

There is another point, one which Sir David Hannay explained in detail. It relates to the military operations authorized by the Security Council. These operations have been authorized to secure implementation of not only resolution 660 (1990) but also all relevant resolutions. Those who included these resolutions did not seek only withdrawal, and hence the rewarding of the aggressor, for we would be facing a very dangerous situation were we to allow an aggressor like the Iraqi regime to launch aggression in the future against a neighbouring country and later withdraw without punishment, without paying for what it has done. Were we to do this, we would be following the law of the jungle.

That is why resolution 678 (1990) referred to the use of force until Iraq implements all the 12 resolutions of the Security Council. Thus, selectivity in the process of choosing resolutions is unacceptable.

[387] **Mr. Bagbeni Adeito Nzengeya (Zaire)** (interpretation from French):

My delegation had the opportunity to express its view on 23 February, following upon the statement of the representative of the USSR. But, in the light of the new developments, my delegation will continue, along with the other members of the Council, the in-depth discussion on the current stage of the question. Hence it reserves its right to revert to the matter in due course.

But my brief statement - or, rather, my comment - relates to the statement made a few days ago by the representative of a Member State when he referred to pygmies in pejorative terms.

As the representative of Zaire, whose population is nearly 36 million, including approximately 400,000 pygmies enjoying all rights in the country, I should like to say that pygmies are fully fledged human beings and cannot be treated in a discriminatory fashion because of their size, since the size of a human being has never been a criterion for any scale of values.

...

[387] **Mr. Al-Anbari (Iraq):**

I shall speak in English so as to avoid misunderstanding of the kind our colleague from Zaire has just complained about.

As members know, the other day I spoke in Arabic and I used the word "*gizim*", which is the equivalent of the English word "dwarf". When I noted the inaccurate translation, I immediately brought the Secretariat's attention to the meaning of the Arab word I used, and the Secretariat has corrected the record accordingly. So I assure my friend from Zaire that we have full respect for the human dignity of pygmies and other human beings, whether in or outside of Zaire. My intention was solely in the word "*gizim*", which means nothing but "dwarf". So I hope that his fears are now laid to rest.

However, with all due respect to my friend from Zaire, I have to say that I am afraid that there seems to be some attempts on the part of some members attending this meeting to convert it from a serious in-depth discussion of a very critical situation now prevailing in the Gulf to deal with side issues and, I would say, irrelevant issues, for I assume that by now he must have read the correction and be assured that there was no ill-intention or ill-meaning on my part because I was speaking in Arabic and we have no word actually for pygmies except pygmies, and I did use the word for dwarf.

[388-390] **Mr. Alarcon de Quesada (Cuba)** (interpretation from Spanish):

First of all, I should like to thank the representative of the Soviet Union for the information he reported to us and to take this opportunity to repeat our gratitude to the Government of the Soviet Union and President Gorbachev personally for their tireless efforts, which continue in an attempt to put an end as soon as possible to this conflict that has caused such loss of life and material destruction.

I would not like to see this meeting of the Council ending - I believe there are no further speakers - without offering some reflections.

For something more than six months the world has been the anguished witness to a conflict that began on 2 August 1990 with the occupation of Kuwait by Iraqi forces. The Security Council has been devoting sustained attention to this matter.

For something more than six months, at every meeting, all Council members have expressed the wish for full compliance as soon as possible with resolution 660 (1990), the first adopted by the Council on this matter. In many different ways we have repeated to the Iraqi authorities our wish for a withdrawal of their forces from Kuwaiti territory.

Tonight, the representative of Iraq once again, as he had done on Saturday, confirmed his Government's decision to act in that way and, as I heard Ambassador Al-Anbari say, to accept resolution 660 (1990) and its complete implementation.

One might have imagined that this would be a night of rejoicing in this Chamber, and an opportunity for all of us, with the same enthusiasm seen on earlier occasions last year, to proceed rapidly and effectively to create the necessary conditions and circumstances so that the resolution could finally be fully implemented.

The representative of Yemen orally put forward what could be the basic ideas for a draft resolution that would not appear to be excessively complicated were the Security Council ready, in line with what has been stated by all for half a year now, to note that its main objective - the withdrawal of Iraqi troops from Kuwait and the restoration of the sovereignty, independence and territorial integrity of Kuwait - had at last been achieved, and to do so quickly.

But we have witnessed an exercise that has taken place here more than once ever since the Soviet delegation told us of its initiative, an exercise which could put the Council in a position that is absurd to say the least, and one which I as a member do not like to see immortalized in our records.

This meeting, which could be historic not for the decision taken but for those not taken, is being held with the discretion so zealously promoted by some of our colleagues. But at least there will be a verbatim record, and for that record I want to state clearly our profound amazement that we are about to allow ourselves not to react in the only way we logically ought to react.

The meeting began with the danger of an attempt to reduce the important meaning of a message from President Saddam Hussein addressed to President Gorbachev, officially communicated to us by Ambassador Vorontsov, a Permanent Representative deserving of all our respect, and make it out to have been sent merely as a propaganda exercise or ruse of war. Those are the kinds of expressions that will appear when the record of this discreet meeting is distributed to members and non-members of the Council.

Fortunately, Ambassador Al-Anbari subsequently confirmed here that the Government of Iraq has indeed taken the decision earlier communicated to us by Ambassador Vorontsov, who had been informed by

President Gorbachev that he had received such a message from Saddam Hussein.

Yet some members, beyond those armed with the deadly weapon of the veto, are disinclined to stop the war and facilitate compliance with Council resolution 660 (1990).

Someone will ask one day whether it had ever been legitimate concern for the sovereignty, territorial integrity and independence of Kuwait that motivated certain Powers to do what they are doing - and which is now costing thousands of lives and immeasurable material damage for the peoples of the region and for the entire world - or whether in fact the motivation had always been something else and whether it was for that reason that at a time when there should have been joy or satisfaction there was apparently a feeling that someone had caused offense by finally telling us that resolution 660 (1990) was going to be completely implemented.

I heard neither the representative of the Soviet Union nor the representative of Iraq say that in order fully to implement the resolution and thus withdraw Iraqi troops from Kuwait anyone was demanding the nullification or modification, or anything else, of the Council's resolutions.

It has been requested simply that the Council take the basic measures that have always been a part of any process of the withdrawal of military forces in any conflict situation.

No one could seriously think that there can be a withdrawal of military forces under bombardment, under fire, under war conditions.

I invite any of my illustrious colleagues to cite a single such case in history. Many cases - in which the Council has participated actively and diligently - could be cited where in order to effect the withdrawal of military forces from a territory certain basic measures were taken, such as first and foremost a halt to military operations in the region, along with other measures with respect to which the United Nations has long and rich experience in monitoring and verifying that the cessation of hostilities and the withdrawal are taking place properly, so that the withdrawal is orderly and safe and that it has the confidence of both the withdrawing forces and the international community, which thus achieves its main objective.

I wonder whether this is the time for us to get bogged down in an elaborate discourse or mediaeval debate on the texts and their interpretation - for which no one has asked.

I wonder whether this is the moment for us to begin to establish conditions and links which will make one text inseparable from another and will put us in the paradoxical situation - I do not know whether that is the idea of certain colleagues - of our asking Iraq not to withdraw its forces or of the United Nations doing nothing to see that the process takes place in the only way in which it should.

My delegation condemned the war; it was opposed to measures that it considered precipitate, unilateral and arbitrary on the part of the Council. But it voted seriously in favour of resolution 660 (1990), and it seriously requested the Government of Iraq, publicly and privately, to withdraw its forces from Kuwait. When we were officially informed that it had decided to do so, and was beginning the process, we had to hail that decision, because we are consistent in our positions. We have not been indulging in demagoguery, with a false defence of the legitimate rights of Kuwait, which for us are as sacred as those of any other country in the world, great or small.

We are profoundly worried that at a time when the Council should be taking very specific, clear-cut decisions that would permit us finally to achieve implementation of the principal resolution adopted with regard to the crisis - the first resolution, which laid down the basic means for resolving the conflict - the Council will once again be paralysed, will once again fold its arms and allow the war to continue, will go on doing nothing to implement what should be its most cherished resolution.

I do not know how some of my colleagues will explain before history the curious attitude we are witnessing today. If it were just a matter of how to explain tomorrow what is being done today I should not be speaking now, but let us recall that every hour we fail to act, every minute this Council sits with folded arms and again - as the Soviet Government said in its statement (S/22265) last Sunday - lets slip a very real chance of securing a peaceful outcome to the conflict without further casualties and destruction, human beings on both sides are paying with the lives for our disquisitions and diplomatic manoeuvring. Those human beings on both sides deserve our respect, and they oblige us here and now in the Security Council to adopt a resolution like the one our colleague from Yemen has proposed.

If the Council does not do so - and the reasons, the machinery, that might prevent it are no secret - at least I can put on record that my delegation rejects this failure to act and wishes to protest vehemently about a truly scandalous situation.

[397] **Mr. Noterdaeme (Belgium)** (interpretation from French):

I am not accustomed to public debate, and I certainly shall not engage in polemics, because what we have heard this evening is very important. I believe that the communication we received a little while ago from our colleague Ambassador Vorontsov is extremely important. I also believe that what our colleague from Iraq said is extremely important. I believe that we should now put all this to our Governments for consideration, because I hope that it may become the basis of something that is clearly desirable for us all.

Nevertheless, I wish to make just one remark - to our colleague from Iraq. I believe that it would be much easier for the Security Council to arrive at an operational decision on a cease-fire if somewhere in the relevant resolution - either in the preamble or in the operative part - there were a statement that the Security Council notes that the Government of Iraq accepts the application of resolution 660 (1990) and all the other relevant resolutions of the Council. By "relevant resolutions" I simply mean those that put obligations upon Iraq.

That is all I wish to say - and in no polemical spirit - at this stage.

...

The meeting was suspended at 12.35 a.m., Tuesday, 26 February 1991.

H. S/PV.2977 (Part II) (closed-resumption 5), 2 March 1991

[402] **The President:**

...

In accordance with the understanding reached in the course of the Council's prior consultations, I propose to adjourn the private meeting now.

In accordance with the provisions of rule 55 of the provisional rules of procedure of the Security Council, a communiqué must be issued at the close of each private meeting. A draft communiqué has been prepared by the Secretariat along customary lines for the private part of the two thousand, nine hundred and seventy-seventh meeting. At the same time, the verbatim record of this portion of the meeting, as in the case of the preceding parts, will be circulated as an unrestricted document in accordance with rule 49. A draft communiqué has been prepared by the Secretariat and is before members. May I take it that the Council approves the draft communiqué?

It is so decided.

The Security Council has thus concluded its business for this meeting.

I. S/PV.2978, 3 March 1991

...

[2] The PRESIDENT:

The Security Council will now begin its consideration of the item on its agenda. Members of the Council have before them document S/22298, which contains the text of a draft resolution submitted by the United States of America. Belgium, France, Romania, the Union of Soviet Socialist Republics, the United Kingdom of Great Britain and Northern Ireland and Zaire have joined as sponsors of the draft resolution in document S/22298. Members of the Council have before them in documents S/22300 to S/22317: amendments submitted by Cuba to the draft resolution contained in document S/22298.

[3-5] **Mr. PICKERING (United States of America):**

...

It is my pleasure on behalf of the sponsors to present a number of oral revisions to the draft resolution which I understand are generally agreeable to members of the Council.

In operative paragraph 2 (b), first line, after the word "liability", we have decided to add the words "under international law". The paragraph would then read: "Accept in principle its liability under international law for any loss," and so forth.

The second revision is in operative paragraph 3 (a), second line: to delete the words "and other parties".

The third revision is in operative paragraph 3 (d), at the end of the paragraph: to delete the word "Gulf", substituting for it the words "adjacent waters".

The fourth revision, in operative paragraph 5, second line, following the words "to commence", is to add the word "immediately". It would then read: "... to provide access and to commence immediately the release of Iraqi prisoners of war" and so forth.

...

[6] **Mr. ALARCON de QUESADA (Cuba)** (interpretation from Spanish):

...

My delegation would like to submit to the Council a series of proposed amendments (S/22300 to S/22317) to the draft resolution submitted by the United States of America.

I should simply like to say that the amendments are self-explanatory. They seek to ensure that the Council is able to establish a cease-fire and that it will fully assume its responsibility for the way in which that cease-fire is implemented and for the other steps to be taken to restore international peace and security in the region. Other amendments aim simply at adjusting the language of the draft resolution submitted to us in order to ensure that it at least regains a sense of balance and moderation, which at this point a text of this nature should contain.

[7] **The PRESIDENT:**

...

It is my understanding that the Council is ready to proceed to the vote on the draft resolution contained in document S/22298, as orally revised by the United States on behalf of the sponsors, and the proposed amendments contained in documents S/22300 to S/22317. Unless I hear any objection, I shall take it that that is the case.

There being no objection, it is so decided.

Members of the Council have before them amendments submitted by Cuba in documents S/22300 to S/22317. Rule 36 of the Council's provisional rules of procedure states the following:

> "If two or more amendments to a motion or draft resolution are proposed, the President shall rule on the order in which they are to be voted upon. Ordinarily, the Security Council shall first vote on the amendment furthest removed in substance from the original proposal and then on the amendment next furthest removed until all amendments have been put to the vote, but when an amendment adds to or deletes from the text of a motion or draft resolution, that amendment shall be voted on first."

Accordingly, I intend to put the amendments to the vote in the following order: S/22300, S/22301, S/22302, S/22304, S/22310, S/22311, S/22312, S/22317, S/22305, S/22315, S/22306, S/22307, S/22308, S/22309, S/22314, S/22313, S/22303 and S/22316.

I shall first call on those members of the Council who wish to make statements before the voting on the amendments.

[8-10] **Mr. PICKERING (United States of America):**

In the opinion of the sponsors of the draft resolution contained in document S/22298, the profusion of amendments submitted by the delegation of Cuba is not helpful. Both the number and the form of the amendments lead us to believe that the text is not improved by them. Since we regard the text in its current form as effective, balanced and appropriate, it is our intention not to support these amendments.

[11] **The PRESIDENT:**

I shall now put to the vote the amendment contained in document S/22300.

A vote was taken by show of hands.

In favour:	Cuba, Yemen
Against:	Austria
Abstaining:	Belgium, China, Côte d'Ivoire, Ecuador, France, India, Romania, Union of Soviet Socialist Republics, United Kingdom of Great Britain and Northern Ireland, United States of America, Zaire, Zimbabwe

[11] **The PRESIDENT:**

The result of the voting is as follows: 2 votes in favour, 1 against and 12 abstentions. The amendment has not been adopted, it having failed to obtain the required number of votes.

I shall now put to the vote the amendment contained in document S/22301.

A vote was taken by show of hands.

In favour:	Cuba
Against:	None
Abstaining:	Austria, Belgium, China, Côte d'Ivoire, Ecuador, France, India, Romania, Union of Soviet Socialist Republics, United Kingdom of Great Britain and Northern Ireland, United States of America, Yemen, Zaire, Zimbabwe

[11] **The PRESIDENT:**

The result of the voting is as follows: 1 vote in favour, none against and 14 abstentions. The amendment has not been adopted, it having failed to obtain the required number of votes.

I shall now put to the vote the amendment contained in document S/22302.

A vote was taken by show of hands.

In favour:	Cuba, Yemen

Against: None
Abstaining: Austria, Belgium, China, Côte d'Ivoire, Ecuador, France, India, Romania, Union of Soviet Socialist Republics, United Kingdom of Great Britain and Northern Ireland, United States of America, Zaire, Zimbabwe

[12] **The President**:
The result of the voting is as follows: 2 votes in favour, none against and 13 abstentions. The amendment has not been adopted, it having failed to obtain the required number of votes.

I shall now put to the vote the amendment contained in document S/22304.

A vote was taken by show of hands.

In favour: Cuba
Against: None
Abstaining: Austria, Belgium, China, Côte d'Ivoire, Ecuador, France, India, Romania, Union of Soviet Socialist Republics, United Kingdom of Great Britain and Northern Ireland, United States of America, Yemen, Zaire, Zimbabwe

[12] **The President**:
The result of the voting is as follows: 1 vote in favour, none against and 14 abstentions. The amendment has not been adopted, it having failed to obtain the required number of votes.

I shall now put to the vote the amendment contained in document S/22310.

A vote was taken by show of hands.

In favour: Austria, Cuba, Ecuador, India, Yemen, Zimbabwe
Against: None
Abstaining: Belgium, China, Côte d'Ivoire, France, Romania, Union of Soviet Socialist Republics, United Kingdom of Great Britain and Northern Ireland, United States of America, Zaire

[13] **The President**:
The result of the voting is as follows: 6 votes in favour, none against and 9 abstentions. The amendment has not been adopted, it having failed to obtain the required number of votes.

I shall now put to the vote the amendment contained in document S/22311.

A vote was taken by show of hands.

In favour: Cuba, Yemen
Against: None
Abstaining: Austria, Belgium, China, Côte d'Ivoire, Ecuador, France, India, Romania, Union of Soviet Socialist Republics, United Kingdom of Great Britain and Northern Ireland, United States of America, Zaire, Zimbabwe

[13] **The President**:
The result of the voting is as follows: 2 votes in favour, none against and 13 abstentions. The amendment has not been adopted, it having failed to obtain the required number of votes.

I shall now put to the vote the amendment contained in document S/22312.

A vote was taken by show of hands.

In favour: China, Cuba, Yemen
Against: None
Abstaining: Austria, Belgium, Côte d'Ivoire, Ecuador, France, India, Romania, Union of Soviet Socialist Republics, United Kingdom of Great Britain and Northern Ireland, United States of America, Zaire, Zimbabwe

[14-15] **The President**:
The result of the voting is as follows: 3 votes in favour, none against and 12 abstentions. The amendment has not been adopted, it having failed to obtain the required number of votes.

I shall now put to the vote the amendment contained in document S/22317.

A vote was taken by show of hands.

In favour: Cuba, Yemen
Against: None
Abstaining: Austria, Belgium, China, Côte d'Ivoire, Ecuador, France, India, Romania, Union of Soviet Socialist Republics, United Kingdom of Great Britain and Northern Ireland, United States of America, Zaire, Zimbabwe

[14-15] **The President**:
The result of the voting is as follows: 2 votes in favour, none against and 13 abstentions. The amendment has not been adopted, it having failed to obtain the required number of votes.

I shall now put to the vote the amendment contained in document S/22305.

A vote was taken by show of hands.

In favour: Cuba, Yemen
Against: None
Abstaining: Austria, Belgium, China, Côte d'Ivoire, Ecuador, France, India, Romania, Union of Soviet Socialist Republics, United Kingdom of Great Britain and Northern Ireland, United States of America, Zaire, Zimbabwe

[14-15] **The President**:
The result of the voting is as follows: 2 votes in favour, none against and 13 abstentions. The amendment has not been adopted, it having failed to obtain the required number of votes.

I shall now put to the vote the amendment contained in document S/22315.

A vote was taken by show of hands.

In favour: Cuba, Yemen
Against: None
Abstaining: Austria, Belgium, China, Côte d'Ivoire, Ecuador, France, India, Romania, Union of Soviet Socialist Republics, United Kingdom of Great Britain and Northern Ireland, United States of America, Zaire, Zimbabwe

[16] **The President**:
The result of the voting is as follows: 2 votes in favour, none against and 13 abstentions. The amendment has not been adopted, it having failed to obtain the required number of votes.

I shall now put to the vote the amendment contained in document S/22306.

A vote was taken by show of hands.

In favour: Cuba, Yemen

Against:	None
Abstaining:	Austria, Belgium, China, Côte d'Ivoire, Ecuador, France, India, Romania, Union of Soviet Socialist Republics, United Kingdom of Great Britain and Northern Ireland, United States of America, Zaire, Zimbabwe

[16] **The PRESIDENT:**
The result of the voting is as follows: 2 votes in favour, none against and 13 abstentions. The amendment has not been adopted, it having failed to obtain the required number of votes.

[16] **Mr. AL-ASHTAL (Yemen):**
I wonder if we need to vote on the amendment contained in document S/22307, as its language is dependent upon that of the amendment contained in document S/22306. I think the representative of Cuba might wish to withdraw the amendment in document S/22307, since the amendment that would have called for a cease-fire has not been adopted.

[17] **Mr. ALARCON de QUESADA (Cuba)** (interpretation from Spanish):
I am not withdrawing it, but since it is connected with the amendment just rejected, the suggestion made by the representative of Yemen that the Council not vote on it seems logical.

[17] **Sir David HANNAY (United Kingdom):**
May I take it that the representative of Cuba is withdrawing the draft resolution he has put forward for tomorrow, which contains the same phrase?

[17] **The PRESIDENT:**
I shall now put to the vote the amendment contained in document S/22308.
A vote was taken by show of hands.

In favour:	Cuba, Yemen
Against:	None
Abstaining:	Austria, Belgium, China, Côte d'Ivoire, Ecuador, France, India, Romania, Union of Soviet Socialist Republics, United Kingdom of Great Britain and Northern Ireland, United States of America, Zaire, Zimbabwe

[17] **The PRESIDENT:**
The result of the voting is as follows: 2 votes in favour, none against and 13 abstentions. The amendment has not been adopted, it having failed to obtain the required number of votes.
I shall now put to the vote the amendment contained in document S/22309.
A vote was taken by show of hands.

In favour:	Cuba, Yemen
Against:	None
Abstaining:	Austria, Belgium, China, Côte d'Ivoire, Ecuador, France, India, Romania, Union of Soviet Socialist Republics, United Kingdom of Great Britain and Northern Ireland, United States of America, Zaire, Zimbabwe

[18] **The PRESIDENT:**
The result of the voting is as follows: 2 votes in favour, none against and 13 abstentions. The amendment has not been adopted, it having failed to obtain the required number of votes.
I shall now put to the vote the amendment contained in document S/22314.
A vote was taken by show of hands.

In favour:	Cuba, Ecuador, India, Yemen, Zimbabwe
Against:	None
Abstaining:	Austria, Belgium, China, Côte d'Ivoire, France, Romania, Union of Soviet Socialist Republics, United Kingdom of Great Britain and Northern Ireland, United States of America, Zaire,

[18] **The PRESIDENT:**
The result of the voting is as follows: 5 votes in favour, none against and 10 abstentions. The amendment has not been adopted, it having failed to obtain the required number of votes.
I shall now put to the vote the amendment contained in document S/22313.
A vote was taken by show of hands.

In favour:	Cuba, Yemen
Against:	None
Abstaining:	Austria, Belgium, China, Côte d'Ivoire, Ecuador, France, India, Romania, Union of Soviet Socialist Republics, United Kingdom of Great Britain and Northern Ireland, United States of America, Zaire, Zimbabwe

[18] **The PRESIDENT:**
The result of the voting is as follows: 2 votes in favour, none against and 13 abstentions. The amendment has not been adopted, it having failed to obtain the required number of votes.
I shall now put to the vote the amendment contained in document S/22303.
A vote was taken by show of hands.

In favour:	Cuba, Ecuador, India, Yemen
Against:	None
Abstaining:	Austria, Belgium, China, Côte d'Ivoire, France, Romania, Union of Soviet Socialist Republics, United Kingdom of Great Britain and Northern Ireland, United States of America, Zaire, Zimbabwe

[19] **The PRESIDENT:**
The result of the voting is as follows: 4 votes in favour, none against and 11 abstentions. The amendment has not been adopted, it having failed to obtain the required number of votes.
I shall now put to the vote the amendment contained in document S/22316.
A vote was taken by show of hands.

In favour:	Cuba, Ecuador, India, Yemen, Zimbabwe
Against:	None
Abstaining:	Austria, Belgium, China, Côte d'Ivoire, France, Romania, Union of Soviet Socialist Republics, United Kingdom of Great Britain and Northern Ireland, United States of America, Zaire

[19] **The PRESIDENT:**
The result of the voting is as follows: 5 votes in favour, none against and 10 abstentions. The amendment has not been adopted, it having failed to obtain the required number of votes.
Before putting the draft resolution contained in document S/22298, as orally revised, to the vote, I shall

call on those members of the Council who wish to make statements before the voting.

[20] **Mr. Al-Ashtal (Yemen)** (interpretation from Arabic):

...

The Council meets today, fortunately after the suspension of hostilities during the Gulf war. It is meeting after Kuwait restored its sovereignty and independence and resolution 660 (1990) has been observed. There is no doubt that this is a new, clean chapter in the history of the Council which, throughout its resolutions and decisions, has been able to carry out resolution 660 (1990). Since the first day, the delegation of Yemen has called for upholding the basic principles that reject occupation and for the withdrawal of troops and the affirmation of independence and sovereignty of all countries, including the State of Kuwait.

Today we meet after Iraq has committed itself to accepting all the Security Council resolutions, and we hope that all countries will follow suit, especially those that are located in crisis areas of the world, especially in the Middle East - to be frank, Israel.

We begin a new phase in the history of this crisis: it is the beginning of the end of the crisis which has preoccupied the world for seven months and led to such devastation, claiming the lives of tens of thousands - military and civilian, Iraqi and American, Arab and non-Arab.

The draft resolution now before us represents a first step towards ensuring a quick and decisive end to acts of aggression. Therefore, we see in it some positive aspects that cannot be overlooked. First, with regard to humanitarian aspects, concern is expressed for providing care for the prisoners of war on all sides. Naturally, the Council must seek measures to set them free. In this regard, I refer to paragraphs 2 (c) and 3 (c) and paragraph 5. We hope that all prisoners of war and also the detainees will soon be able to enjoy their freedom and return to their families as soon as possible.

There are also paragraphs dealing with military matters, and we think they might be of help in easing the crisis and facilitating a start in establishing peace in the region. In this regard, I refer to paragraph 3 (b), relating to the meeting of military commanders tomorrow, and to paragraph 3 (d), which refers to the removal of mines, thus securing the region for the next steps.

There is also a political aspect, in paragraph 2 (a), pertaining to the rescinding of the actions purporting to annex Kuwait, in keeping with Security Council resolution 662 (1990).

In our view, those positive aspects can contribute to the beginning of a final, peaceful diplomatic solution to this crisis.

On the other hand, we note that the draft resolution is deficient in many respects. It could have tackled other aspects of the crisis, thus expediting a solution to other crisis situations. Among the many deficiencies - which are indeed important - is the fact that the draft resolution does not call for a cease-fire. As we know, there is a suspension of hostilities at the present time but there is no official cease-fire. We had hoped that the draft resolution would call for a cease-fire, especially since there are some arrangements relating to the release of prisoners of war and the removal of mines. Such measures usually accompany a cease-fire. It is strange that the draft resolution does not mention a cease-fire, and this shows the extent of the strictness at this early phase of the last chapter of this crisis.

Secondly, the draft resolution does not mention the end of the embargo against Iraq, particularly as regards food. This is very cruel.

When the Council adopted resolution 661 (1990) and imposed a stringent embargo regime against Iraq and then occupied Kuwait, it was because it was believed that the sanctions would lead to Iraq's withdrawal and implementation of resolution 660 (1990). There has already been war and Iraqi installations have been severely damaged, especially civilian installations such as those for electricity and water and those pertaining to the economic infrastructure that concerns the life of civilians; and tens of thousands have been killed, not to mention the other casualties.

After all this, the people of Iraq, including civilians and military personnel, are enduring enormous sufferings. That is why we find it strange that the draft resolution does not include a reference to the end of the embargo on food. This is a very cruel feature, which cannot be justified on political grounds. It has nothing to do with the regime or with military institutions; it relates strictly to civilians. We listened with admiration to the statement of President Bush in which he expressed the great concern of the United States in regard, particularly, to children and the humanitarian and health aspects of such situations. We believe the draft resolution should have included a paragraph providing for the end of this embargo, to reduce the suffering of children and other vulnerable groups of society.

Thirdly, we would have thought that the draft resolution would attribute a major role - or even a humble role - to the United Nations or its Secretary-General, particularly at this early phase of the ending of the crisis. We had expected the draft resolution to include a reference to the presence of United Nations representatives at the meeting tomorrow, and also to a United Nations presence that could at least be ready for the forthcoming phases in the strengthening of the cease-fire and the maintenance of peace. Unfortunately, however, there was clear opposition to such a reference. I am happy that many delegations here voted in favour of the Cuban amendments that referred to this aspect.

Fourthly, the draft resolution does not refer in any way to the withdrawal of the alliance troops that are now on Iraqi territory. There are a large number of such troops and they now dominate a large number of positions. Yet they are not referred to at all in this important draft resolution. From the very beginning we opposed and rejected the use of force, and we now oppose the continued presence of foreign troops in Iraq against its wishes and without a decision by the Iraqis. We hope that this subject will be dealt with in the first of the draft resolutions to be considered in the future. We hope, too, that those troops will be withdrawn from Iraq as soon as possible.

Fifthly, paragraph 4 of the draft resolution relates to the continued use of force. Although we heard during the informal meeting that such force would be used only for specific purposes, we find it strange that there is still talk about the use of force now that Iraqi troops have been completely withdrawn from Kuwait and the purposes of resolution 660 (1990) have been implemented. We were told that force would be used only for the secondary reasons indicated in the resolution. But how can force be used in connection with a difference about legal questions, or if Iraq does not live up to one of the paragraphs of the resolution? Does this mean that force will be used to compel Iraq to implement such a paragraph? We find this absolutely excessive and against the spirit of the United Nations resolutions. It serves only the objectives of specific countries.

Today we are ending a dark chapter in the history of the Arab nation and also at the international level. We hope that this will mark the beginning of the establishment of a just and stable security system in our region, based on respect, justice and balance. The Security Council has every right to be proud of the almost literal implementation of its resolution. But the Council should start immediately, without any delay, to ensure the implementation of the other resolutions relating to other disputes, particularly the Arab-Israeli conflict. If it does not do that, it could be concluded that the United Nations has been used in one particular case because it has served the interests of some countries. We therefore hope that the Council will continue to work at the same level and at the same pace in adopting the resolutions necessary to implement all the other resolutions still before it.

As for us in Yemen, we shall immediately proceed to pursue the aims we stated at the beginning of the crisis. From the very beginning, we called for a solution of this crisis by peaceful means. We called also for benevolence and co-operation. We called for work within the framework of the League of Arab States, our regional organization. We shall continue to seek the fulfilment of the same aims.

...

[31] **Mr. Alarcon de Quesada (Cuba)** (interpretation from Spanish):

We are now involved in the voting process on the draft resolution in document S/22298. But 24 hours have not elapsed since its first and official presentation to the non-permanent members of this body. My delegation does not claim to abide by this rule of courtesy, behind which our colleagues frequently shield themselves when draft resolutions are involved. I simply wish note to be taken of this fact.

The Council has enabled the representatives of the press and public opinion to be present here to follow our work directly, which we welcome.

The point is not that we are voting on this resolution 24 hours after its presentation; the point is that we could have done so yesterday, had we received the text. But that did not happen, and it was the first attempt by those who have once again convened the Council as a matter of urgency, again remembering what happened last year, and forgetting the calm and modesty that have been evinced on other topics - and with regard to this topic from last November up until just a few hours ago.

My delegation must say we reject attempts to deal with the Security Council as if it were a prisoner. We do not want always to act in an atmosphere of alarm with the discipline and obedience expected of children. If we did not vote on this draft resolution last night, as at one time we were told we would, it was simply because some generals were to meet today. Certainly we must thank those generals and military personnel for having postponed their meeting until tomorrow. Hence, just by chance, there has arisen this opportunity to put it to the vote just 24 hours after its initial appearance.

My delegation will vote against this draft resolution because we deem it to be another step along the path towards conduct we consider would constitute a violation of the United Nations Charter. This draft resolution is a continuation and derivation of resolution 678 (1990), which will remain in the annals of this Organization as a moment of shame when the Security Council abdicated its fundamental obligation. It cannot relinquish that obligation unless we are agreeing that the Council commit suicide. It is the Security Council's obligation to preserve international peace and security. That is an undeniable obligation that cannot be relinquished or ignored. Nor can the Council authorize others to do so without any monitoring, without authority, without supervision of some kind by it.

I do not wish to state the psychological reasons for this, but the text submitted to us thrice reiterates with almost sick emphasis that resolution 678 (1990) remains in effect and the provisions set forth by the Security Council, which relinquish its fundamental obligation, remain in effect. We should not just recall the other resolutions in the first preambular paragraph; we should reaffirm them.

The first operative paragraph says that "all 12 resolutions noted above continue to have full force and effect". Then, as if the reader had still not understood, paragraph 4 states "the provisions of paragraph 2 of resolution 678 (1990) remain valid".

In a previous version of the text, the meaning of the language of paragraph 4 was somewhat less hidden. But in any case, in our view, the consequences are clear enough. Having ended the illegal Iraqi occupation of the territory of Kuwait, and having ensured that it will regain its independence and territorial sovereignty, the Security Council must apparently once again relinquish its obligations and place them on the shoulders of some States in language that can be used for any purpose the generals decide upon.

This resolution does not - as the Security Council is obliged to do - establish a cease-fire. Rather, it establishes conditions that are prerequisites to ensuring that a cease-fire will take place along with a cessation of hostilities in the zone. It does so in a way that may in fact increase tensions and complicate a situation that is already quite complex. It gives the United Nations no functions - nor the Security Council, nor the Secretary-General. One must ask oneself why it has been brought here. So that the trumpets can be sounded? So that it could be adopted last night? Why, unless it was some kind of strategy devised to be used quite far from this Chamber? It is not a naïve effort to reaffirm the responsibility of this Organization for the maintenance of international peace and security.

Moreover, some parts of this text appear to be designed to justify the military occupation of the territory of Iraq. My delegation rejects this.

This draft resolution would support the continuation of military activities perpetrated against that country not because the Council decided to do so, or monitors or supervises such activities. Neither the Council nor the United Nations can get into the theatre of operations; it is just a question of what the generals will decide. It seems they need the adoption of this text tonight very badly.

At a time when the Council relinquishes its privacy and decides to meet publicly, when in many places hopes arise for the cessation of the conflict, it would have been better for the Council to be able to evince magnanimity and a loftiness of spirit in truly moving forward towards a lasting solution of the conflict. Peace can be built neither with a derisory attitude nor with the arrogance of power, nor indeed with the intoxication that some seem to have acquired from the threat or use of force.

My delegation regrets that the Council has on more than one occasion in the past been manipulated into following a course that, unfortunately, almost inevitably has led to military conflict and that it has then been studiously ignored and consigned to oblivion when war broke out in all its fury. This has made it extremely difficult for us to meet to consider any alternative solution to the conflict. Now, once again, we are convened - not to halt hostilities, not to lay down true foundations for peace, not to ensure that the United Nations is in a position to play an active and constructive role in settling the problems of the region, but, rather, to offer us another example of the desire on the part of some to continue to use the Organization for their own purposes, thereby displaying contempt for this institution and humiliating it.

[36] **Mr. Mumbengegwi (Zimbabwe):**

...

The silencing of guns in the Persian Gulf is an important and most welcome event. Zimbabwe joins the Government and people of Kuwait and the peace-loving nations of the world in rejoicing over the liberation of Kuwait and the restoration of the sovereignty and territorial integrity of that country.

We feel that this is an appropriate occasion to pay a tribute to the international community for the unified action it took over the past seven months in upholding the rule of law in relations among States. Zimbabwe also commends the Secretary-General for the unrelenting diplomatic work he carried out in an effort to avert the outbreak of hostilities, as well as for constantly drawing the attention of the international community to the humanitarian situation created by the crisis.

The Security Council is about to take an action on an important draft resolution. Zimbabwe regards this as an important first step in the process of normalizing the situation in the Persian Gulf and in the Middle East region as a whole. The thrust of the draft resolution before us is positive. Zimbabwe welcomes any step towards formalization and towards consolidating what is at present a fragile suspension of hostilities. We would have preferred the Security Council to formalize a cease-fire immediately. However, it is our understanding that the draft resolution now before us constitutes a necessary first step towards such formalization.

Zimbabwe welcomes the intention of the States cooperating with the Government of Kuwait to bring their military presence in Iraq to an early end, as expressed in the last preambular paragraph of the draft resolution before us. We also welcome the provisions that facilitate the rescission of the annexation of Kuwait.

The speedy normalization of the situation in post-war Kuwait and Iraq is set out in operative paragraph 3 of the draft resolution. However, it is Zimbabwe's hope that a situation will not arise in which operative paragraph 4 of the draft resolution will be invoked to resume military operations in the area. Also, Zimbabwe would have preferred to have representatives of the Secretary-General present during the meeting of the military commanders to arrange the military aspects of the cessation of hostilities referred to in operative paragraph 3 (b) of the draft resolution.

There is also an occasion when one cannot avoid thinking of the responsibilities of the Council with respect to other political problems of the region. Zimbabwe was pleased that in dealing with the situation between Iraq and Kuwait the Security Council acted with speed, resolve and single-mindedness and upheld its resolutions and international law. The international community now expects the Council consistently to maintain the same standards as it addressed the other issues in the Middle East, particularly with regard to the Palestinian and other Arab territories occupied by Israel.

History will have on record - and will, indeed, commend - the Council's actions in taking four days to impose economic sanctions and five months to take military measures against Iraq when it occupied Kuwait. But history will not forgive the Council for reneging on its responsibilities in other cases of occupation in the same region. For more than 23 years now Israel has occupied Palestine and other Arab territories in violation of international law and in defiance of numerous Security Council resolutions; yet the Security Council has taken no action against that occupying Power. The credibility and integrity of the Council will be greatly damaged and international law undermined if the Council continues to be perceived as inconsistent and as guilty of applying standards. It is Zimbabwe's view that now is the time for the Council to rectify this unacceptable situation.

[41] The President:

...

I shall now put the draft resolution contained in document S/22298, as orally revised, to the vote.

A vote was taken by show of hands.

In favour:	Austria, Belgium, Côte d'Ivoire, Ecuador, France, Romania, Union of Soviet Socialist Republics, United Kingdom of Great Britain and Northern Ireland, United States of America, Zaire, Zimbabwe
Against:	Cuba
Abstaining:	China, India, Yemen

[41] The President:

The result of the voting is as follows: 11 votes in favour, 1 against and 3 abstentions. The draft resolution has been adopted as resolution 686 (1991).

I shall now call on those members of the Council who wish to make statements following the vote.

[41] Mr. Pickering (United States of America):

Resolution 686 (1991), which the Council has just adopted, signifies a watershed in its affairs. We are entering a new phase in the effort which began on 2 August last year to repel aggression and to restore peace to the Persian Gulf. This resolution turns our attention from a war we never wanted, from the tragedy precipitated by Iraq, to the greatest challenge of all: building lasting peace and security.

From the first hours after Iraq's invasion of Kuwait, the Security Council has been at the centre of the international community's response. The Council made clear that Iraq's aggression would not stand, it established the terms for resolving the crisis, and it imposed sanctions when its efforts at persuasion were rejected by Baghdad. The Security Council demonstrated in November both its resolve to leave open all possibilities for a peaceful solution, and its readiness, after the pause of goodwill, to mandate the expulsion of Iraq by force from Kuwait.

Resolution 678 (1990) set the stage for intensive diplomatic efforts which proved as fruitless as those which preceded it. Almost every Government represented in this room and many outside it in one way or another engaged directly in trying to persuade Baghdad to comply with the Council's resolutions and warned of the calamity ahead if Saddam Hussein remained obdurate. And throughout, the Secretary-General worked with hope and determination, leading the world-wide effort to resolve the crisis peacefully, right up to his far-reaching constructive proposals of 15 January. But Iraq's intransigence led it to compound the catastrophe of the wanton destruction of Kuwait with the catastrophe of war. It is upon the heads of Saddam Hussein and the other leaders of Iraq that the responsibility for this so clearly rests.

Since the end of November and the adoption of resolution 678 (1990), the Council has focussed on its implementation. Now key goals it adopted have been achieved. Aggression has been beaten, firmly and decisively. Those who counted on the use of arms and the ultimate failure of the international community to respond have been beaten, firmly and decisively. They have brought dishonour and ruin to themselves. We are overjoyed that Kuwait is liberated and restored to its rightful place in the international community. We welcome this resolution's paragraphs recalling the appropriate part of resolution 661 (1990) signifying that sanctions are not imposed against Kuwait. We also welcome the immediate re-establishment of normal relations - diplomatic, economic and financial - with Kuwait, its people and its legitimate Government. Today, the Kuwaiti flag and the flags of Kuwait's friends fly again in Kuwait City. Together, today, we pledge ourselves to assist the people of Kuwait in the reconstruction of their ravaged country.

Now the Council turns its attention to the restoration of peace and security in the area, as resolution 678 (1990) recognized would be required. The present resolution points the way. We seek as soon as possible a definitive end to hostilities. This is the first priority. The resolution sets out the measures which Iraq must take and the arrangements which must be put in place to bring this about. Iraq has much to account for, and there is much yet to be done to fulfil the resolutions of the Council and the requirements of international law.

In this resolution, the Council puts forth the immediate requirements: Iraq must make clear that it no longer harbours aggressive intent, and it must take the steps needed immediately to implement the 12 United Nations Security Council resolutions. It must return immediately the prisoners of war. It must return the property it has stolen. It must release immediately all third-country nationals and detained Kuwaiti citizens. It must cease further military action, including any activities related to the missiles Iraq used to attack Saudi Arabia and Israel. It must return immediately the remains of those who died in the war or while held prisoner by Iraq. Iraq must assist the coalition in identifying the location of mines, booby traps, chemical and biological weapons. Until it is clear that Iraq has complied with these requirements, the provisions of resolution 678 (1990) authorizing Kuwait and those cooperating with Kuwait to use all necessary means to ensure Iraqi compliance with the United Nations resolutions clearly will remain in effect.

The United Nations and the Security Council remain at the centre of the effort to fulfill the overarching tasks set by the 12 resolutions adopted thus far: to repel aggression and to build genuine peace and stability. The Council today is providing a broad framework for dealing with this new phase of our task. Tomorrow the military leaders of the coalition meet with Iraq's military leaders to define the details of the arrangements required to put an end to hostilities, with this resolution as the foundation. We hope for early success in those discussions so we can get on with our work.

Even as we are putting this framework into place, the United States, other members of the Council and other States in the region are beginning to consult on the future steps which will be required. Secretary Baker is departing soon for the area to discuss the key questions which need to be addressed in order to ensure that the peace we have secured at such great cost is a lasting one. The nations of the region will clearly take the lead in finding answers to these questions. My country looks forward to working on this in capitals and within the Council. We have a long and difficult road before us, and the Council has a most important role to play.

President Bush said in his address of 27 February, lauding the coalition and the liberation of Kuwait, that this war is now behind us. Ahead of us is the difficult task of securing a potentially historic peace. President Bush has frequently repeated that our quarrel is not with the people of Iraq, but with the leaders of Iraq and their destructive policies. Indeed, the United States will be looking for ways to identify and meet the humanitarian relief needs of the Iraqi people, which has suffered so much under Saddam Hussein. We look forward to the day when Iraq can once again assume full membership in the family of nations. This resolution shows Iraq the way to begin to do so.

International collective security has functioned in the Gulf. All of us now have a responsibility to those who have suffered, to those who have risked their lives and to those of all nations who have perished to see to it that history does not repeat itself. We cannot have paid the price of aggression and its defeat only to allow it to recur. The Council's task now, the one we begin accomplishing today, is to point the way to building a peaceful and secure system which deters the repetition of aggression and suffering we have seen over the past seven months.

[46] **Mr. Vorontsov (Union of Soviet Socialist Republics)** (interpretation from Russian):

The cessation of hostilities in the Persian Gulf is a major international event. The Soviet Union warmly welcomed the liberation of Kuwait, the restoration of its independence, sovereignty and territorial integrity and the return to the country of its legitimate Government.

The culmination of the military conflict in the Persian Gulf is the result of the collective efforts of all the States that took part in the quest for a settlement and joined together to restore the violated rights of an entire people and to prevent the seizure of one country by another. The establishment of this historic precedent involved the participation of many States, including the Soviet Union, the United States and other members of the coalition, including many Arab and Muslim States. For the first time the international community showed its united will in the face of the seizure of one State by another and was able to bring the aggressor to heel. Although this precedent may be imperfect, we should like to believe that it can prevent the emergence in the future of similar situations which are not in keeping with the new era of peaceful policy which, however difficult, is now dawning.

As is well known, from the very outbreak of the conflict the Soviet Union firmly advocated seeking the best possible solution to the problem, above all by peaceful means. That was our policy over the entire period from 2 August last year. The President of the Soviet Union, Mikhail Sergeyevich Gorbachev, consistently pursued our diplomatic policy in that regard through the most active contacts with the leaders of all the major States involved in the crisis. Our country has done a great deal to achieve the cessation of military hostilities and to avoid any further bloodshed.

The Soviet leadership urged the leadership of Iraq to announce without any further delay its acceptance of all 12 Security Council resolutions, and our recommendations ultimately bore fruit. We are convinced that the liberation of the State of Kuwait and the end to Iraqi aggression would have been impossible had those forces involved in the settlement of the conflict not acted in unison throughout all these months.

Now we face some priority tasks. Primarily, we must completely exclude the resumption of any type of military activities. That most urgent task is the purpose of the resolution that has just been adopted, resolution 686 (1991), of which the Soviet Union was a sponsor.

In the near future the Security Council will have to become deeply involved in the final political settlement of the Iraq-Kuwait conflict and the elimination of the consequences of Iraqi aggression. The Soviet Union will continue its active efforts to find a just solution acceptable to all parties.

The international community also faces the urgent task of beginning to work out and agree upon post-crisis arrangements in the region, an important element of which must be the establishment of a security system that not only marks the culmination of recent events but is a safeguard against military conflicts in the future. The Soviet Union has been, and continues to be, in active contact with the leading Arab and Islamic States, the United States and the major European and Asian countries with a view to finding common ground on carrying out that basic task.

The security structure in the Persian Gulf must be based primarily on the interests of the countries of the region, with the understanding that the States of the region themselves must unambiguously and clearly define their own interests. We are convinced that the vitality and reliability of the security system will to a great extent depend upon Iraq's ability to play a positive role in it. It is natural that the establishment of that system should involve a role for the United Nations, including the Security Council and its permanent members.

We believe that in solving the problem of establishing a security system for the Persian Gulf we must actively and productively discuss the question of arms shipments as well.

The events in recent months have put into sharp relief the fact that the international community must make the most determined efforts to convene an international conference on the Middle East. We are convinced that such a conference would allow us to guarantee long-term peace and security for the entire region. Along with all the parties to the conflict, we are determined to deal urgently with a settlement to the Middle East problem and to restore the legitimate rights of the Palestinian people. The protracted nature of the Arab-Israeli crisis is a primary source of instability, lack of trust and the continuing arms race in that region. The time has come for all States to take a fresh approach, remove stereotypes from their thinking and deal more actively with a solution to the problem.

I do not think it would be wrong to state that we have all learned a serious lesson from the conflict and that we shall take that lesson to heart in the future. It would be no exaggeration to say that we are witnessing the beginning of a new era and new relationships. In such new circumstances the Security Council will have to play an active role in discharging the responsibility placed upon it by the Charter.

[49-50] **Mr. LI Daoyu (China)** (interpretation from Chinese):

...

Since the outbreak of the Gulf war, the Chinese Government has repeatedly called for the unconditional withdrawal of Iraqi troops from Kuwait as soon as possible, an early end to the war and the achievement of peace. We are gratified to see that all parties to the conflict have now suspended their military action. We express congratulations on the restoration of Kuwait's independence, sovereignty and territorial integrity and on the resumption by the legitimate Government of Kuwait of the exercise of its rights and powers.

In our view, the Security Council should play a positive role in establishing a formal and stable cease-fire in the Gulf region and in seeking a practical formula for a political solution within the framework of the relevant Security Council resolutions so that the desire of the peoples of the Gulf region and the rest of the world for peace in the Gulf may become a reality.

The resolution which has just been adopted makes reference to securing the establishment of a definitive end to the hostilities. This deserves a positive response, but falls short of stating that the Security Council should have an important role to play with regard to the arrangement and monitoring of the cease-fire. In fact, it extends the time limit during which resolution 678 (1990) remains effective. That goes against the desire of the peoples of all countries for an early end to the war and for the achievement of peace.

It is well known that China has stood all along for settling conflicts through negotiations and abstained in the vote on resolution 678 (1990). We tried to make amendments to the relevant paragraph of the draft resolution on which we voted this evening, but our suggestions were not accepted. In those circumstances, in accordance with China's consistent position in favour of a peaceful solution to the Gulf crisis, the Chinese delegation found it difficult to vote in favour of the draft resolution. It is our hope and belief that through the joint efforts of the international community the sovereignty and territorial integrity of countries in the Gulf region will be respected and lasting peace and security in the Gulf region will be ultimately achieved.

...

[52] **Mr. BLANC (France)** (interpretation from French):

...

France is delighted at the liberation of Kuwait. Since 2 August 1990 the goal of all the efforts of the Security Council has been the restoration of the sovereignty and independence of Kuwait. That goal has been achieved through two essential factors: the unanimous and unequivocal condemnation by the States Members of the United Nations of the aggression against Kuwait; and action by the Security Council, which since August has worked cohesively and with determination.

The long-awaited liberation of Kuwait must not make us forget, in the joy of celebration, the suffering of the Kuwaiti people, its spirit of resistance and the sacrifices it has made. France pays a tribute to its courage. Nor can we remain indifferent to the suffering the Iraqi people has endured as a result of the tragic adventure into which it was led.

We take note of Iraq's acceptance of all the resolutions adopted by the Security Council on behalf of the entire international community. That acceptance is a prerequisite for the re-establishment, on a sound and lasting basis, of stability in the region.

In that connection, resolution 686 (1991), which we have just adopted and of which France was a sponsor, is an indispensable step. That resolution - the first since the liberation of Kuwait - charts the course for a final cessation of hostilities, which we hope can be announced soon. Peace begins when weapons are silenced, but it must then be confirmed and consolidated as quickly as possible.

The United Nations is now faced with a prodigious undertaking. The Organization, first, must consolidate effectively the cessation of hostilities and then, along with the countries of the region and all interested parties, define the conditions for the lasting restoration of peace and security in the region.

Consistent with its mandate, the Security Council in close coordination with the Secretary-General will continue fully to shoulder its responsibilities. The determination the Council has shown for the past seven months, without which the liberation of Kuwait would not have been possible, must be sustained and utilized to settle other conflicts, starting with those of the Near and Middle East.

For its part, France will always strive to ensure that there is one law for all. My delegation therefore stands ready to make an active contribution to the work of the Council in this new phase of its activities.

[53] **Mr. NOTERDAEME (Belgium)** (interpretation from French):

Belgium welcomes the suspension of military operations in the Gulf and Iraq's official announcement of its commitment to comply with the 12 relevant resolutions of the Security Council. That should bring to an end a conflict which has already had too many victims - victims to whom my Government pays its respects.

It is particularly deplorable that the Gulf tragedy occurred at a time when we had every reason to look to the future with confidence. The events in Eastern and Central Europe has given us hope that international relations would henceforth be guided by principles of freedom, democracy and law.

One man did not want that. President Saddam Hussein wanted to divide a world that was asking only to be united.

The international community reacted to that aggressive policy in a patient, firm and united manner.

It was patient: From the first day various means of pressure were employed to make Iraq comply with international law, without ever neglecting diplomatic negotiations. In that vein, the Security Council entrusted to the Secretary-General a mission of good offices, and there were numerous peace initiatives, including those of the non-aligned countries, the Arab world, the Soviet Union and the Western world.

It was firm: When it became clear that Saddam Hussein would stubbornly refuse to seize the opportunities for peace that were offered to him, the international community set in motion the means necessary to ensure respect for the law.

It has been united, since a coalition was formed, of which Belgium is honoured to be a part and which comprises some 30 nations from all continents and representing a broad range of political systems. This is indeed proof that the action undertaken in resolution 678 (1990) was in keeping with the wishes of the international community as a whole.

It is now up to the Security Council to make the necessary arrangements to put an end to the conflict. This is the goal of the resolution we have just adopted. My Government feels that most of its concerns in this regard have been met therein.

Indeed, with regard to the military aspect, the resolution allows for the speedy conclusion of a definitive cease-fire through a number of commitments Iraq must enter into, and these commitments are clearly set forth in paragraphs 2 and 3: the release of all prisoners of war; the release of all Kuwaiti hostages taken to Iraq; the cessation of hostile or provocative actions, including the launching of missiles; and effective cooperation with regard to the clearing of mines - this involves in particular guaranteeing the safety of mine-clearing teams on land and at sea.

With regard to the political aspect, the resolution quite rightly states that Iraq must first and foremost accept by deeds the 12 relevant resolutions of the Security Council. This means that Iraq must on a priority basis rescind any action purporting to annex Kuwait.

Furthermore, my Government also asks that Iraq renounce acts of terrorism and incitement to such acts.

With regard to the humanitarian aspects, we must urgently alleviate the suffering inflicted by Saddam Hussein on the Kuwaiti population and, lest we forget, on his own people. This is why my country attaches great importance to the third preambular paragraph.

Belgium requests the Red Cross and the various national and international humanitarian bodies to redouble their efforts in bringing a maximum of food assistance to the region.

Until our Council establishes a final system of arrangements covering the humanitarian - especially food - needs in Iraq, full use must be made of the opportunities provided by the Committee established under resolution 661 (1990), so that those people who have been sorely tried by the conflict in the Gulf may have the necessary food supplies as soon as possible.

We welcome the report of the mission undertaken jointly by the World Health Organization (WHO) and the United Nations Children's Fund (UNICEF), which should permit the sanctions Committee to be more liberal in granting Iraq food assistance for humanitarian reasons.

I note with satisfaction that the sanctions Committee has already facilitated to the extent possible activities organized by the Red Cross for the particularly vulnerable population groups. My Government has already transmitted to that Committee a request from the Belgian Red Cross to send medical supplies and food to Iraq.

Above and beyond all these immediate steps, the Security Council must in due course focus its attention on more long-term arrangements. The unity in the Council that has enabled us to give back to Kuwait its freedom and independence must now be focused on helping the region recover peace and security.

In this regard, it is clear that, given the complexity of the situation, the countries of the region will have a major role to play. Furthermore, a sense of responsibility on the part of the active members of the coalition will, for obvious reasons, be crucial.

Belgium is convinced that the action of the Security Council aimed at restoring peace and security in the region should be based on four considerations:

First of all, Kuwait's security must be strengthened and guaranteed by insisting on the necessary respect for international borders, an essential element for stability in the region as a whole.

Secondly, we must at all cost avoid a situation in which Iraq might again gain an offensive military potential - including, in particular, missiles - and possess weapons of mass destruction, such as chemical and nuclear weapons. That is why my Government believes that, initially, it will be necessary to maintain a military embargo against Iraq. Then, a more comprehensive solution to the problem of overarmament in the region will be required.

Thirdly, as the 12 countries of the European Community have pointed out, the international community must renew its efforts to arrive at a speedy comprehensive, just and lasting solution of the Israeli-Arab conflict and the Palestinian question. We must actively promote the search for a peaceful solution through dialogue with and among all the parties concerned.

Finally, in recalling the period following the Second World War, Belgium believes, together with its partners in the Twelve, that we must develop a comprehensive approach to the region, one which will deal with security questions, political problems and economic cooperation.

This could be done through a conference on security and cooperation in the Middle East, which would allow us to take up constructively the major problems of the region, first and foremost are of course the Israeli Arab conflict and the Palestinian question, but also the recognition of the State of Israel, the Lebanese problem and the Kurdish question.

In preparing such a conference, it would be useful to appoint a mediator. My Government hopes that such an appointment will be made quickly.

For the reasons I have just given, Belgium joined the sponsors of the resolution we have just adopted.

My Government hopes that in the near future the Security Council will take a stand on the necessary renunciation by Iraq of any form of appeal for and support of terrorism, on the sending of a United Nations observer force and on the lifting of the food embargo.

Finally, the Council should reflect on what I have termed the longer-term arrangements, in order in due course to be in a position to make a substantial contribution also in this sphere.

[59-60] **Mr. Bagbeni Adeito Nzengeya (Zaire)** (interpretation from French):

...

The Council is meeting today in formal and public session on the situation between Iraq and Kuwait, after having held several closed meetings to consider and follow closely developments in the Gulf, in the certainty that the goals it sought, discretely but effectively, have by and large been achieved, given the full implementation of resolution 678 (1990) which has at last allowed for the liberation of Kuwait on 27 February 1991.

That was also the objective that Kuwait, through its Permanent Representative, His Excellency Mr. Abulhasan, had entrusted to the Security Council by stating, on 2 August 1990, that the Council was responsible for the protection of Kuwait as well as for its security, its sovereignty and its territorial integrity, which had just been violated by Iraq. Indeed, he appealed to the Security Council to shoulder its responsibilities and adopt measures to compel Iraq to withdraw its forces immediately and unconditionally and to return to the positions they had occupied on 1 August 1990.

He concluded his request to the Council by recalling that his country, a small country, drew its strength and owed its existence to the legitimacy of the rules of international law incarnated in the Security Council through its role of ensuring respect for the provisions of the Charter by all the States Members of our Organization.

This was, then, a test - or, even more, an occasion for testing the Council's responsibility for the maintenance of international peace and security in the region of the Persian Gulf. To that end, Article 51 of the Charter was invoked. This Article deals with the inherent right of individual or collective self-defence if an armed attack occurs against a Member of the United Nations.

In his reply, on 2 August 1990, the representative of Iraq stated that the Iraqi forces were going to leave Kuwait within only a few days, or at the most a few weeks, because Iraq was not pursuing any goal or objective in Kuwait but wished to maintain cordial and good-neighbourly relations with Kuwait.

Throughout the period of the war, which extended from 2 August 1990 to 28 February 1991, not even a beginning was made on the implementation of this statement about the withdrawal of Iraqi troops. That situation explains the steps the Security Council deemed it necessary to adopt, beginning with resolution 660 (1990) and ending with resolution 678 (1990), with a view to restoring peace and international security to the region as well as Kuwait's independence, sovereignty and territorial integrity.

We should note in this regard that all the first 11 resolutions were peaceful in nature and that even the last resolution, 678 (1990), included a 46-day ultimatum, to enable Iraq to comply with the spirit and the letter of Article 2 of the Charter of the United Nations. During that period many goodwill missions and peace initiatives were undertaken in an attempt to persuade Iraq to withdraw peacefully from Kuwait.

Despite, on the one hand, the initiation of military operations on 16 January 1991 by 28 States Members of our Organization, in accordance with paragraph 2 of resolution 678 (1990) and, on the other hand, the intransigence of the Iraqi authorities, the President of the Soviet Union, His Excellency Mr. Gorbachev, never lost hope and continued his good offices in an attempt to change the Iraqi position.

Thus, at the moment when the coalition forces reached the capital of Kuwait, the Minister for Foreign Affairs of Iraq confirmed, on 28 February 1991, Iraq's agreement to comply fully with all the resolutions adopted by the Security Council on the situation between Iraq and Kuwait.

Is this not an unprecedented example? Twenty-eight nations undertook the task of ensuring the security of small States, thereby demonstrating the determination of our Organization and the international community to institute a new era of peace based on scrupulous respect for the rules of international law and détente that will henceforth characterize the new world order. Is it not, then, imperative for the Security Council to take the steps that will build confidence and peace in the entire region, including the Middle East? For, if the liberation of Kuwait, which honours the Security Council and restores its prestige, has taken only seven months, how can we explain the fact that the Palestinian question, which has existed since the General Assembly adopted resolution 181 B (II) of 29 November 1947, continues to be before the Council, without any peaceful and lasting solutions having been found?

However that may be, my delegation remains convinced that the measures advocated in resolution 686 (1991) does lay down the modalities, in the short term, for putting an end to all the hostilities in the region and imposing strict respect for the rules of international law, in particular all 12 resolutions adopted by the Council on the situation between Iraq and Kuwait. Of course, we hope that in the future relations of friendship, good-neighbourliness and cooperation will prevail among all the States of the region, including Iraq.

It was because of all the aspects stemming from the cessation of hostilities in the Persian Gulf and the overriding necessity to establish a lasting peace in that region that my delegation co-sponsored the draft resolution that has just been adopted by the Security Council as resolution 686 (1991).

...

[64] Mr. Anet (Côte d'Ivoire) (interpretation from French):

...

I wish to tell the Ambassador of Kuwait and, through him, all the people of Kuwait, how pleased my country, Côte d'Ivoire, is to see Kuwait liberated and sovereign. While the Kuwaiti people lost their freedom for approximately seven months, legally they never lost their sovereignty. All just-loving peoples supported Kuwait, as can be seen from resolution 662 (1990), which declared the annexation of Kuwait null and void.

We must now think about the future, about the rebuilding of Kuwait. We can only hope that this will take place in conditions of peace, unity and tolerance.

For my delegation, the liberation of Kuwait symbolizes first and foremost the triumph of justice over brutal force. It marks the dawn of a new era. We hope that this era, whose dawning we greatly welcome, will not stop at the gates of Kuwait. The action of the coalition forces, authorized by the Security Council, will find its true justification in the Council's ability to meet objectively and in a balanced way the many challenges to peace with which it will continue to be confronted. We must begin right now to show by our actions faith and optimism and a deep-seated commitment to the moral and ethical values of peace and justice which constantly imbue the provisions of the United Nations Charter.

In voting in favour of resolution 686 (1991), which sets the standards for a cease-fire that we hope will very soon be monitored by the appropriate United Nations bodies, my delegation wished to contribute to the dawning of an era of peace and justice in the Gulf region in particular and in the entire region.

Need I emphasize that peace is interdependent in time and in space.

As we talk of peace, as we commit ourselves to working for the reign of peace, justice and law, we must remember that our objective requires an effort of will, faith and political courage.

In conclusion, I should like to reiterate Côte d'Ivoire's commitment, along with all those who persistently seek peace, justice and respect for law, to ensure that the new international era that is so deeply desired will be that of true peace unfrustrated, peace that liberates peoples and teaches them tolerance.

...

[66] Mr. Monteanu (Romania):

...

Coming to the item under consideration, my delegation would like to emphasize that, as a sponsor of the resolution just adopted, we find our position adequately reflected in that document. Indeed the Council has to be instrumental in securing the rapid establishment of a definitive end to the hostilities in the Persian Gulf and the restoration of international peace and security in the region in accordance with all the relevant resolutions of the Security Council, including the one adopted this evening.

Over the last seven months my delegation has many times presented the position of Romania on various aspects and stages of the conflict in the Persian Gulf. Our position on the item remains in full harmony and conformity with all the resolutions adopted by the Council concerning the situation between Iraq and Kuwait.

I should now like to summarize the views of my country on the issue under consideration in the light of the recent developments in the Gulf region.

From the very beginning of the conflict Romania has consistently promoted respect for international legality and has firmly supported the efforts of the multinational coalition for the restoration of legal order. After the liberation of Kuwait, the Government of Romania has welcomed with satisfaction the suspension of military operations by the forces of the coalition. My Government also welcomed the acceptance by Iraq of all the resolutions of the Security Council on the crisis in the area.

While reaffirming its determination to pursue the efforts for the full implementation of the Security Council resolutions in cooperation with the international community, Romania considers that the rapid establishment of a definitive end to the hostilities can reopen the way to a peaceful settlement in conformity with the Charter of the United Nations and the fundamental principles of international law.

Romania was particularly happy to witness the liberation of Kuwait. Romania and the Romanian people have been permanently on the side of Kuwait and its people during the ordeal it has experienced through the foreign occupation. Although we have suffered considerable material losses as a result of the conflict in the Gulf, with direct consequences for the economic situation of our country, Romania has strictly observed the sanctions decided on by the Security Council. Now we are ready to make available to friendly Kuwait all the necessary means at our disposal to support the reconstruction of the country and its economic infrastructure.

It is undeniable that the support extended to Kuwait illustrates the clear will of the international community as expressed in the relevant resolutions of the Security Council. It is a victory for the values of international law and legality. These positive events should have a visible impact for the further strengthening of the role and contribution of the United Nations and its institutions in the establishment of a system of collective security and should guarantee the sovereignty, independence and territorial integrity of all States.

Having adopted a new resolution on the item concerning the situation between Iraq and Kuwait, we express the hope that this resolution will determine an adequate response from Iraq. This resolution, as all the resolutions dealing with the situation between Iraq and Kuwait, is not directed against the people of Iraq, which has suffered so much, but is oriented towards a final peaceful solution of the conflict in that area. The Iraqi people should be the natural beneficiary of a peaceful approach, which may enable it to dedicate all efforts and labour to the reconstruction of their country. We are confident that Iraq will soon find its dignified place in the community of nations as a peace-loving country acting for the implementation of the ideals of the United Nations.

We have no doubt that after seven months of defending the basis purposes and principles of the United Nations, the Security Council is giving a bright chance and a testimony to the world organization to fully prove its political and legal potential in the maintenance of international peace and security and in the protection of the supreme values of humankind.

...

[68] Sir David HANNAY (United Kingdom):

...

The debate we are having today and the resolution we have adopted mark the opening of what one could call the third phase of this very serious international crisis.

In the first phase, the Security Council responded with the 12 resolutions we know so well, with a major effort to persuade Iraq to comply with them by peaceful means. That effort lasted many long months and gave rise to an enormous amount of diplomatic activity. Alas, it failed.

The second phase is the one that has just ended, and was characterized by the use of force to give effect to the 12 resolutions we had adopted.

The third phase, which is now beginning, is probably the most difficult, and certainly the most important, of the three, and it is the one that must be dedicated to the restoration of peace and security in the region.

The forces of my country played their full role in the liberation of Kuwait, and we share the sense of pride and relief that the will of the international community and of the Security Council prevailed. It was a triumph for the rule of international law and for collective security.

The United Nations and the international community can now turn to the more difficult task, the task of assisting in the establishment of a durable system of peace and security in the Gulf region, and in the Middle East more widely, and also to the reconstruction of Kuwait and the rehabilitation of its population.

First, however, we have to deal with the immediate aftermath of the hostilities. Some of this task is properly work for the military commanders in the field, and we welcome very much that the meetings will be taking place tomorrow. We hope that those meetings will lead to very rapid progress, but it is right, too, that the Security Council should establish the basic framework within which the conditions can be created for a definitive end to the hostilities, and that is what the present resolution is designed to do. It deals with the immediate future and the next phase, which we hope will be a short one and will lead to the winding down of hostilities.

Much, of course, will depend on the Government of Iraq. We see this resolution as the first of a series that will be needed if we are to establish stability in the region. The requirements it places on the Government of Iraq are not new ones. They flow from the resolutions we have adopted and from the statements previously made on behalf of the Governments assisting and cooperating with the Government of Kuwait. But the requirements must be explicitly accepted by Iraq, and that is essential to permit a definite end to the hostilities.

In recent months the Government of Iraq has, unfortunately, shown how necessary it is to get these clear and formal undertakings - and they must be clear and they must be commitments. We have still, I fear, no access by the International Committee of the Red Cross to the prisoners of war taken from the allied forces. We have still no detailed commitment by Iraq to the timing and modalities of their release. We have still no clear picture about the location of the mines, the explosives and so on in Iraq and in Kuwait. We have no explicit acceptance of the liability for the terrible damage wrought in Kuwait, and we still have much hostility and defiance pouring from the media in Iraq. All this is cause for regret, but we hope that it will be reversed and that the necessary commitments will be made.

It really is essential that Iraq should make its contribution to the climate of confidence and reconciliation by a rapid and formal compliance with the provisions of this resolution. This will then enable us to meet again in the near future and to take the next steps towards the restoration of international peace and stability in the area. That is the wish of my Government and of those with whom we are allied. We will then be able to move on to the broader problems of the Middle East which so urgently need to be resolved.

[72] Mr. GHAREKHAN (India):

...

The Government and people of India have rejoiced in the restoration of the independence, sovereignty and territorial integrity of Kuwait, as well as in the re-establishment of the legitimate Government of the State of Kuwait. The President and Prime Minister of India have already sent warm congratulatory messages to His Highness the Emir of Kuwait. Relations between the Governments and peoples of India and Kuwait have through the years been warm and friendly. Throughout the months of the invasion and the illegal occupation of Kuwait by Iraq our exchanges with the Government of the State of Kuwait continued to be characterized by the traditional warmth. We are taking urgent steps to restore the functional continuity of our Mission in Kuwait, and we are confident that the strengthening and diversification of relations at all levels will be resumed in the near future.

My delegation's approach to this problem is guided by two broad considerations: re-establishment of peace and security in the area as early as possible and the role of the United Nations and the Security Council. The immediate step is to consolidate the cessation of hostilities. My Government welcomed the announcement by the President of the United States, on behalf of Kuwait and the Member States cooperating with Kuwait, of the suspension on 27 February of combat operations in the Gulf. We regard it as a significant step towards the restoration of peace in the area and the re-establishment of durable security and stability.

Obviously, some practical steps have to be taken to ensure that fighting does not resume. Those aspects, we believe, will be discussed by the military commanders of the two sides, perhaps tomorrow. An extremely important requirement is the release of prisoners of war. This must be done in the speediest possible manner because of humanitarian considerations. It goes without saying, of course, that this applies to all prisoners of war on both sides. The same is true for such civilians as might have been illegally detained. They also must be enabled to reunite with their families without delay. This aspect has to be given the highest priority.

Regarding resolution 686 (1991), just adopted, we have had an opportunity to enter into dialogue with its sponsors about the intents and purposes of their proposals. They provided us clarifications and explanations. We appreciate their efforts. As a result, we had a somewhat better understanding of the objectives of the resolution. We can appreciate some of them, but there are points that are not exactly clear to us and there are issues we would have liked to see incorporated in the draft resolution. We feel that with sufficient time to consider the draft resolution, even without taking the weekend and the factor of the time difference into account, and with a more active and prolonged dialogue, we might conceivably have reached a more consensual draft that could have addressed some of the grave and urgent issues in a more positive and purposeful manner and helped in achieving a rapid and durable restoration of peace and security in the area.

Once the pressing humanitarian concerns - such as returns of prisoners of war, return of detainees and the beginning of the return of property - are taken care of, it is imperative for the Council, without any delay, to move to the next step: a permanent or formal cease-fire, as indeed was stated by President Bush in his statement of 27 February.

This important element is missing from the resolution adopted by the Council. Similarly, the procedure to verify compliance by Iraq with whatever it is required to do for a cease-fire is vague. My delegation would have preferred to have the Secretary-General involved in this process, in however indirect a manner. We spent quite some time in the informal consultations on this point, but without resolving it to my delegation's full satisfaction.

A major consideration for my delegation, as I said earlier, is the need to restore peace without delay. As President Bush has said, we must now meet the challenge of securing the peace. The people of this region are extremely anxious for peace - peace with honour and justice. We believe that the time for recrimination should be behind us. It certainly will not be easy for the people to forget the traumatic experiences of the past seven months. This is perfectly understandable. But the Council and the international community should not take any step which will continue to foment mistrust among peoples of the region. Any provision which keeps open the possibility of the resumption of hostilities, as is the case in the present resolution, cannot be accepted by my delegation.

Another point of concern to my delegation is the continuation of the sanctions. The purpose for which the sanctions régime was enacted - and India has implemented that régime at great cost to itself - has been specified in resolution 661 (1990) and would have been fulfilled when one further step, in addition to Kuwait's liberation, had been taken. Resolution 662 (1990), which calls for annulling the purported annexation of Kuwait, is extremely important. It is imperative that Iraq take immediate steps to rescind this measure.

Iraq has already agreed to liability under international law for the loss or damage caused to Kuwait or third countries as a result of Iraq's invasion and illegal annexation. This Iraq has done by agreeing to resolution 674 (1990) along with other mandatory resolutions. My delegation would like the Council to begin an early examination of the question of sanctions. The sanctions are playing havoc, not only with Iraq's economy but also with the economy of my country and indeed the economies of many other countries. They are affecting patterns and flows of world trade. The people of Iraq certainly deserve relief. This important element is also missing from the resolution.

Iraq has officially confirmed its willingness to comply with all relevant Security Council resolutions. Indeed, those resolutions were adopted under Chapter VII of the Charter, and as such are mandatory on all States. Iraq has agreed to take immediate concrete measures in regard to such matters as the return of prisoners of war, in accordance with relevant provisions of international law. These steps should provide enough ground for the Security Council to take appropriate measures to move rapidly towards a durable peace in the area. The Security Council ought also to have an important role, at the appropriate time, along with States of the region and other parties concerned, in expeditiously creating conditions for stable peace and security in the region.

It has been observed time and again by several delegations that the Gulf crisis has demonstrated that the international community cannot tolerate acts of unprovoked invasion and illegal occupation or annexation. The United Nations and the Security Council have rightly led the efforts of the international community in this effort. The 12 resolutions adopted under Chapter VII of the Charter embody the international response. The United Nations and the Council showed the way towards resolving the crisis and they must rightly lead us all in re-establishing peace and security. Such a role of the United Nations and of the Council will only be in accordance with the Charter of the United Nations.

My delegation is of the view that the United Nations has a most important function in re-establishing the conditions of peace in the area by providing its reassuring presence in tangible terms. We believe that even a token United Nations presence will provide renewed hope and assurance to the people in the area.

My delegation is also most concerned about the humanitarian conditions as they now exist in the area, particularly in Iraq and Kuwait. Both the occupation and armed conflict have taken a most severe, often inhumane toll on human life as well as on basic facilities of life, property and economic infrastructure. The recent joint mission of the United Nations Children's Fund and the World Health Organization, the International Committee of the Red Cross, the media and other independent observers have all brought out the stark and distressing conditions in these two countries. This is not the time for retribution or recrimination. We believe that the international community should facilitate provision of foodstuffs and other basic needs of life to the people of the area on a high-priority basis, and that the Security Council must immediately make this possible.

It is for these reasons that my delegation abstained in the vote on the draft resolution.

...

[78] **Mr. Ayala Lasso (Ecuador)** (interpretation from Spanish):

...

On 27 February, the liberation of Kuwait was joyfully announced. We all felt gratified, optimistic and relieved at this news. At the same time, the State that had violated the norms of law finally announced its compliance with the resolutions of the Council that were and continue to be the foundation for an appropriate and permanent solution of this problem. Ecuador and the States members of the Rio Group that analysed the situation took a specific public stand on the matter and recognized that without compliance with said resolutions a solution to the problem was impossible.

Kuwait's sovereignty, independence and territorial integrity were thus restored. The inadmissibility of acquiring territory by force was again confirmed. The rule of law had triumphed over the use of force.

The liberation of Kuwait also made possible the entry into force of a *de facto* cease-fire, and the horrifying loss of human life and the material destruction were thus suspended. The collective action taken by the international Organization had been crowned with success, thus setting a precedent that gives us reason for deep thought. First, we must think about the fact that only through law can international relations be organized in a peaceful way, in accordance with the needs of mankind. Secondly, we must think about the indispensable need constantly and progressively to perfect ways and means to resolve international disputes peacefully, so that as far as possible collective measures do not have to involve the use of force, which, once used, means suffering for the human race. Those are two lessons that I regard as fundamental for the organization of what has come to be called the new international order.

The resolution we have just adopted is a positive and effective step along the path the United Nations must follow in order firmly to establish permanent peace in the area and a security machinery for the region. But it is only a first step. It must be followed - very quickly, it is to be hoped - by others which above all will formalize a permanent cease-fire, rendering unnecessary the use once again of those means which resolution 678 (1990) made available to the member States of the coalition for the purpose of re-establishing law, peace and security in the area. This will require quick and effective compliance in good faith with those obligations that Iraq shoulders in committing itself to abiding by the 12 relevant Security Council resolutions - and now the thirteenth.

It will also be necessary immediately to adopt measures to render null and void domestic legislation with regard to the annexation of Kuwait so as to make perfectly clear the existence of a situation in which Kuwait's sovereignty and territorial integrity are not matters for discussion. There will have to be speedy compliance with the commitment to free prisoners of war and civilian detainees, and there will have to be effective, practical assumption of Iraq's responsibilities under international law for the invasion and the damage caused to Kuwait.

Ecuador voted for the resolution for all those reasons, because the resolution proposes measures to those ends. However, I must say that we should have liked greater clarity as regards the declaration of a cease-fire and the definitive establishment of the cessation of hostilities. We should have liked recognition of the primary, leading role of the international Organization and the Security Council with regard to international peace and security, and we should have liked provision for the possibility of our Secretary-General's submitting to us a report about how to set up and dispatch to the region as soon as possible an observer mission to cooperate in the establishment of lasting peace. Finally, we should have liked the resolution to envisage broad, generous and effective measures to ensure that humanitarian aid is given all those that are suffering, whatever their nationality. We therefore favoured some of the amendments proposed by the delegation of Cuba.

We believe that paragraph 4 of the resolution is in reality a statement of a situation that exists with regard to resolution 678 (1990). I repeat our fervent desire that there shall be no need once again to use force to ensure compliance with Council resolutions.

We must now reflect on how to contribute to the establishment of lasting peace in the region. Here we recognize the prime role the Arab nation, the States of the region, must play. It will be up to them, first, to examine and resolve matters in this regard. The world Organization will, of course, have to give them the greatest cooperation and put itself fully at their service to that end.

Without accepting conditions in the form of linkage to other problems in the region, we have always spoken in favour of the Council's now turning to the solution of other still unresolved problems in the Middle East. We believe that the success the world Organization has enjoyed, by establishing the rule of law and declaring null and void the violations of law that have taken place, must be followed by conduct that will gain it ever greater prestige and allow it clearly to affirm that the approach based on justice, taken in the light of the need for law to prevail, will be applied to all existing situations, or possible future situations, whether in the area or in any other region of the world.

For those reasons I ask the members of the Council to forgive me if I repeat a sentence with which I concluded one of my interventions in our informal consultations: Ecuador, which was not a member of the Council when the war began, is very pleased to be a part of it and to cooperate in the re-establishment of lasting peace in the region.

[86] **The President:**

...

I shall now make a statement in my capacity as the representative of Austria.

Since our last meeting in this Chamber, momentous developments have taken place resulting in a cessation of hostilities. Austria deeply welcomes the liberation of Kuwait and the re-establishment of its independence. Thus the grave violation of basic norms of international law caused by the Iraqi aggression has been rectified. We owe this to the resolve of the international community and in particular of the Member States cooperating with Kuwait in liberating that country pursuant to resolution 678 (1990). Our immediate task now is the consolidation of that de facto situation, which is the aim of the resolution we have just adopted.

We see its main importance in its humanitarian elements, paramount among which are the immediate return of detained Kuwaiti and third-country nationals and the release of all prisoners of war under the auspices of the International Committee of the Red Cross. By the same token, measures will have to be undertaken urgently to safeguard access by the Kuwaiti and Iraqi populations to medical supplies and foodstuffs under the terms of Security Council resolution 666 (1990). We should be aware that urgent measures for further humanitarian relief will be required from the international community.

The next step will be the rapid establishment of a formal cease-fire. The Security Council will therefore remain actively seized of the matter. During this second phase of our work, serious consideration should also be given, in consultation with countries of the region, to a United Nations role in monitoring such a cease-fire. Austria has already declared its readiness to contribute to such a United Nations effort.

Another consideration during this second phase will be a review of the resolutions adopted by the Security Council, including the question of sanctions, as part of the process of re-establishing peace and cooperation in the area.

At the outset I spoke of recent momentous developments. In a third phase we will have to take other important and far-reaching decisions: The Security Council is responsible not only for maintaining security but also for promoting peace. This should be done in cooperation with regional mechanisms. The Security

Council has shown its potential during the Gulf crisis. On the other hand, we all should have learned some lessons. One important lesson is the desirability of strengthening the preventive role of the United Nations and of this Council in particular. Another is that ultimately only political solutions will provide the necessary framework for a just and lasting settlement of this and other problems of the region. Devising such a framework, such an architecture, will be a momentous task indeed. Confidence-building measures, disarmament and the strengthening of non-proliferation arrangements will have to be part of such comprehensive solutions.

Austria has noted with satisfaction the increased - and indeed now almost universal - awareness that dealing with the causes and sources of conflict in the region, including the Arab-Israeli conflict and the Palestinian problem, will be especially important in the aftermath of the Gulf crisis. We are confident that the Security Council can make a substantial contribution to the achievement of a comprehensive settlement in the Middle East.

We owe this, first and foremost, to the peoples of the region. We also owe it, however, to this Council as the organ on which Member States have conferred the primary responsibility for the maintenance of international peace and security.

...

[88] **Mr. ABULHASAN (Kuwait)** (interpretation from Arabic):

...

The Security Council has just adopted a resolution whose complete implementation will, I hope, ring down the curtain on the tragedy written, acted and directed by a régime which was born of aggression and which lived by aggression, a régime whose sole preoccupation was to squander the great wealth of the fraternal people of Iraq with a view to stockpiling weapons, committing aggression, practising expansion, plotting conspiracies and buying off those of weak moral fibre inside and outside Iraq, all while the fraternal people of Iraq grew hungrier and poorer. Despite all this, that people could not say one word to express its hopes or complain of its wounds for fear of the torture, oppression and murder the inhumanity of which we, the sons of Kuwait who have lived for seven months under the yoke of Iraqi occupation, have come to know.

We hope the Iraqi regime will implement resolution 686 (1991) with the utmost promptness and seriousness and that it will remember that the international community, through the forces allied with Kuwait, will accept no stalling tactics. We hope it will remember that under that resolution those forces have the means to impose compliance by force if it is not forthcoming voluntarily. We sincerely hope the Iraqi regime will learn from the bitter experience it has imposed on its people.

Since the beginning of the treacherous Iraqi aggression against my country, Kuwait, your Council, backed by the entire international community, rejected and condemned that aggression, adopting a number of resolutions, including under Chapter VII of the Charter, to put an end to it and reverse it.

Noble international, Islamic and Arab diplomatic endeavours were actively pursued, and Baghdad became the point of convergence for all these efforts at mediation aimed at explaining the gravity of the Iraqi aggression and its effects on international peace and security. Those mediation efforts attempted to spare Iraq, Kuwait and the region the scourges of a devastation whose limits were only known to God. In spite of the 12 resolutions adopted by the Security Council and of the very clear signals of the forces allied with my country, Kuwait, to implement those resolutions - especially resolution 678 (1990) - that military force would be used decisively to deter the aggressor and to put an end to violations of humanitarian laws, the only response of the Iraqi regime was obstinacy born of ignorance, arrogance born of conceit, hollow boasting and rejection.

Then, as members know, on 16 January the military operations began. Thus, Saddam's policy resulted in the destruction of the Iraqi strategic and military infrastructure. Saddam exposed Iraq to a devastation it could have been spared. However, obstinacy, arrogance, ignorance and conceit reigned unabated, in spite of the fact that mediation and diplomatic attempts never ceased, with the aim of averting further destruction of the region and its resources. Foremost among those endeavours were those of President Gorbachev of the Soviet Union and the Secretary-General of the United Nations. In spite of all those noble endeavours, obstinacy and arrogance remained just as they were before the beginning of military operations.

Then and only then - after the entire Iraqi army had been defeated, after its remnants had been crushed and its war machinery destroyed, after the fraternal people of Iraq had begun to lick their wounds and come to discover the horror of their misfortune and the magnitude of their losses - was the process of yielding to and accepting the Council's resolutions set in motion. We may well wonder: why then only? We get the only possible answer: when the imminent danger neared the head of that regime and its henchmen, then and only then did the President of that regime accept to yield to the Security Council resolutions.

It is clear that in the thinking and the conduct of the Iraqi President, it is his personal security and that of his regime that take precedence over the security of the people. For that he has sacrificed the entire Iraqi people and its resources. I wonder before the Council: How many opportunities were missed by that regime to spare Iraq what befell it during and before the military operations? Even after the forced withdrawal of the Iraqi regime and after agreeing to withdraw, he still missed numerous opportunities during which he could have spared innocent bloodshed in the inferno of war. But when the regime accepted, it did so too late: lives were lost, resources squandered, and the victim was the helpless Iraqi people.

Kuwait has been liberated, thanks to the resolutions of your Council and the leadership of those States that cooperated with my country to implement those resolutions. Legitimate authority has returned to Kuwait in the person of His Highness Amir Sheikh Al-Jaber Al-Ahmed Al-Sabah and his Government to exercise its pioneering cultural role in the process of right and amity. The people of Kuwait are now living a new dawn after a very dark night that had settled over its skies for seven horrendous months. The various mass media have begun to bring live pictures of the agony and devastation inflicted by the usurping Iraqi regime on the people of Kuwait and its resources, now that the complete media black-out imposed by that regime on Kuwait for 209 days has been lifted. During the occupation, we brought before the Council, through the Secretary-General, the events of that tragedy and plunder, but the Iraqi regime and its representatives here said that all these were baseless fabrications invented by public relations firms.

The representative of that regime in Washington, when confronted by a question from a female Kuwaiti citizen during a television programme concerning the crimes perpetrated by that regime's henchmen against the unarmed innocent Kuwaiti people, did not hesitate of accusing her of lying. Who is the liar has now become clear to members, since for the past three days they have been witnessing the living pictures of statements by Kuwaitis from inside Kuwait about their suffering at the hands of that regime's executioners.

Now the Council knows, as we also know, that what actually took place was even more horrendous than what we had been conveying. There are more pictures taken and video footage shot by Kuwaiti citizens of the destruction which will be made public.

With the return of freedom, with the restoration of sovereignty and legitimacy, Kuwaitis will now be able to speak about the kind of torture inflicted upon them throughout the period of occupation.

The Prince of Kuwait, the Government of Kuwait and the people of Kuwait will always appreciate the historic role played by the Security Council in guaranteeing and facilitating Kuwait's liberation. We are indebted and grateful to our brothers in the Gulf Cooperation Council and to Egypt and Syria for the sacrifices they made and for the proud and manly position, based on the bonds of Islam and Pan-Arabism, taken by the peoples of those States on the side of right and justice, on the path to a just peace.

We express our great indebtedness and gratitude also to the United States of America, the United Kingdom and France for the outstanding role they played militarily and politically and to the Soviet Union and China for their cooperation with the Security Council in deterring and uprooting aggression.

We also express our great thanks and appreciation to all the States that participated in the coalition against falsehood, to all the States that stood at our side and supported us, to the Non-Aligned Movement and the United Nations.

All those States, proceeding from the resolutions of the Security Council, made history - a history that will be a point of reference for posterity, an impregnable shield that will protect peace based on justice and will deter any aggression contemplated by any aggressor, wherever or whenever it may be. Those States have consolidated the principles that constitute the bases of regional organizations and the United Nations, principles that affirm the inadmissibility of the acquisition of territory by the use of force as well as the independence, territorial sovereignty and international legitimacy of States.

As for those whose approach was not compatible with the principles of the Charter and international legitimacy, they have sent wrong signals to the aggressor, giving him the impression that he would be rewarded through this negative stance and giving him indications that he would reap the fruit of his resort to force. Hence, they bear an abundant part of the responsibility because of their negative position in regard to the aggression.

Liberated Kuwait, its people and its political leadership will always preserve their Islamic and Arab traditions as a pattern of conduct. Kuwait will remain generous in its relations and will pursue its foreign policy in the manner outlined by His Highness Sheikh Jaber Al-Ahmad Al-Jaber Al-Sabah, the Amir of Kuwait, in his statement on 27 September last to the forty-fifth session of the General Assembly. He said:

> "The Kuwait you knew will remain, as always, faithful to its principles, true to its system of values, close to its friends and faithful to its obligations and commitments."

His Highness also said:

> "We shall return to our Kuwait as we knew it, a land of safety and security, an oasis of peace, which embraces all Kuwaitis and foreigners living in our midst as brothers. Together, we shall join hands in concert and harmony to secure our development and progress. This will be a fulfilment of God's promise as rendered in the following verse:
>
> "Oh ye who believe!
> If ye will aid
> (The cause of) Allah,
> He will aid you,
> And plant your feet firmly." (*The Holy Koran, XLVII:7*)
> "And whose word can be truer than Allah's?"
> (*A/45/PV.10, pp. 52 and 53-55*)

The people of Kuwait, a tolerant people, will never forget, because everywhere in Kuwait there is evidence to remind us and remain deep in our minds and hearts. We ask for mercy for our martyrs, the martyrs of freedom, these martyrs from the friendly and fraternal States who fell on the cherished land of Kuwait so that on that land we may once again grow the flowers of freedom, stability and progress.

...

[98] **Mr. Shihabi (Saudi Arabia)** (interpretation from Arabic):

...

Kuwait has been liberated and legitimacy has returned to its rightful place. From the Council table I should like to express my heartfelt congratulations to His Highness Sheikh Jaber Al-Ahmad Al-Jaber Al-Sabah, the Amir of the State of Kuwait, and the Government and people of brother Kuwait on its liberation from the injustice and occupation committed by the regime of a sister Arab country, which should have been a protector of Kuwait and not an aggressor against it.

We salute the State of Kuwait. We salute the Amir of Kuwait and its Government and people for their outstanding steadfastness. They have given us a rare example of solidarity and loyalty, the pillars of a strong nation and State.

I express my appreciation and gratitude also to the custodian of the two Holy Places, King Fahd bin Abdulaziz, who took the historic decision to face up to aggression, treachery and deceit and to defeat the aggressors. I express appreciation, too, to the Saudi Government and people.

The territory of Saudi Arabia has become an extension of Kuwait, and we promise we will not sleep until Kuwait has been liberated. Hence the historic decision by Saudi Arabia to call on brothers and friends to help us defeat the aggression. The Iraqi régime and its President thought that the world was a jungle, and they used slogans to attack that decision out of ignorance. They bear responsibility for this plight.

On behalf of Saudi Arabia I should like to express thanks and deep appreciation to the fraternal and friendly countries that cooperated with us and sent their sons, as we sent ours, to the line of fire to support legitimacy, security and safety in a region that was the cradle of civilization and the birthplace of the Messengers and the Prophets.

I should be remiss if I did not express my deep thanks to this Council for the historic role it has played in formulating a strong international position that has given the United Nations and its Charter the historic place that the founders of the Organization intended them to have. We also wish to express our appreciation to the Secretary-General, Mr. Javier Pérez de Cuéllar, for his untiring efforts and his constructive role, and to express our confidence in him.

I wanted in this intervention to express our thanks at a time when we are at last laying the groundwork for international legitimacy in the Gulf region.

We thank God Almighty that evil has been defeated and that right has been victorious.

We thank all who supported us and stood by us, and those who cooperated with us. We will never forget this.

We call on God Almighty for the right to return to every place in our region, to Palestine and every other part of the world. We hope that the ending of this tragedy and this historic lesson will be the beginning of security, safety and stability for our region and the whole world.

...

J. S/PV.2979, 3 March 1991

...

[2] **The President:**

The Security Council will now resume consideration of the item on its agenda.

Following consultations among members of the Security Council, I have been authorized to make the following statement on behalf of the Council:

> "The Council welcomes the decisions taken to date relating to food and medical needs by the Committee established under resolution 661 (1990), including those just taken to facilitate the provision of humanitarian assistance, including infant formula and water purification material.
>
> "It calls upon the Committee to continue to act promptly on requests submitted to it for humanitarian assistance.
>
> "It urges the Committee to pay particular attention to the findings and recommendations on critical medical/public health and nutritional conditions in Iraq which have been and will continue to be submitted to it by the World Health Organization, UNICEF, the International Committee of the Red Cross and other relevant organizations, consistent with the relevant resolutions, and urges these humanitarian agencies to play an active role in this process and cooperate closely with the Committee in its work.
>
> "The Council welcomes the Secretary-General's announcement that he plans to send urgently a mission led by Under-Secretary-General Martti Ahtisaari comprising representatives of the appropriate United Nations agencies to Iraq and Kuwait to assess the humanitarian needs arising in the immediate post-crisis environment. The Council invites the Secretary-General to keep it informed in the shortest possible time on the progress of his mission, on which it pledges to take immediate action."

The Security Council has completed its business for this meeting. The next meeting of the Security Council to continue consideration of the item on the agenda will be fixed in consultation with the members of the Council.

K. S/PV.2981, 3 April 1991

...

[3-5] **The President** (interpretation from French):

The Security Council will now begin its consideration of the item on its agenda.

Members of the Council have before them document S/22430, which contains the text of a draft resolution submitted by France, Romania, the United Kingdom of Great Britain and Northern Ireland and the United States of America. I should like to draw members' attention to a technical correction in the text of paragraph 19 of the draft resolution: in the tenth line of the English text of that paragraph, the words "and in particular humanitarian needs" should be deleted. This correction will be reflected in the texts of the draft resolution in the other languages.

I wish to inform members of the Council that Belgium has joined the sponsors of the draft resolution in document S/22430.

...

[7] **Mr. Lukabu Khabouji N'Zaji (Zaire)** (interpretation from French):

I should like to inform the Council that my country, Zaire, has joined the sponsors of draft resolution S/22430.

...

[7] **Mr. Abulhasan (Kuwait)** (interpretation from Arabic):

...

The Council's meeting today to vote on the draft resolution before it is indeed another historic event in the context of the present crisis. Its importance is equal to that of the earlier historic meeting at which members of the Council adopted resolution 678 (1990). That resolution, which authorized the countries cooperating with the Government of Kuwait to use all necessary means to compel Iraq to withdraw from Kuwait and to implement all the relevant resolutions of the Security Council.

The draft resolution now before the Council could be regarded as epitomizing all the resolutions concerning Kuwait that the Council earlier adopted in implementing decisively and responsibly the principles of international law and international legitimacy. That effective action represents the Council's keen interest in the present and future of the concept of collective peace and security derived from the United Nations Charter. It also reflects the content and concepts of the new world order that the international family is determined to establish. The international community is also determined to encourage a commitment to that new world order and, if need be, to impose it.

How right the United States Secretary of State was when he spoke in the Council on 29 November 1990, the day on which resolution 678 (1990) was adopted. On that occasion he recalled the failure of the League of Nations to deal with the plight of Ethiopia in 1936, when it was the subject of the invasion, occupation and brutality of an occupier, and he compared that failure with the success of the Security Council in standing firm against the Iraqi aggression against Kuwait and against peace and security in the region.

Mr. Baker pointed out that the appeal made by the late Emperor Haile Selassie of Ethiopia at that time fell on deaf ears in the League of Nations. The efforts of the League of Nations to reverse that aggression and to liberate the people of Ethiopia from the yoke of that occupation and colonization had failed. That failure was followed by a war and disturbances in the international arena.

Undoubtedly, the resounding success of the international community through its solidarity in 1990 to stand up to the Iraqi aggression against Kuwait and to reverse its dangers will remain an example to be followed by succeeding generations.

The international community has learned its lesson. In its unprecedented collective stance it has become certain that to turn a blind eye to the evil of aggression or to condone its crimes means in effect taking part in it.

It was no exaggeration for some to have said recently that history had reached a new starting-point concerning Kuwait when the members of the international family were unanimous in their clear and effective commitment to the United Nations Charter, when they translated their words into deeds and their verbal commitment and moral support into effective action and tangible arrangements.

It was no exaggeration to say that the United Nations Charter, with all its lofty principles, became law when the international community effectively dealt with the brutal Iraqi aggression against Kuwait. It proved that the Organization, with its Security Council, is an effective instrument for collective security and the maintenance of world peace and security, and that all States, large and small, can depend on the security guarantees afforded by the Charter; and it proved that the collective commitment of States to the Charter is the best guarantee for the stability, peace and security of nations.

Let us now ask ourselves whether effective international solidarity will indeed emerge from the rubble and the debris of Kuwait and Iraq, just as the mythical phoenix rose from the ashes. Did the plight of Kuwait and the painful suffering of its people really lay the foundations for the resurgence of the principle of collective security when it lay dormant or was even dying? Can the fact that the international community stood up to the brutal Iraqi aggression and defeated it be considered the dawning of a new age of true international awareness and profound world appreciation of the definite need for all the members of the international community to have the sincere will for collectively dealing with questions affecting their common destiny and standing up to the powers of evil that recognize no boundaries and no conventions?

Yes, the tragedy of Kuwait has spawned all that; it has demonstrated the feasibility and reality of all these vital goals and objectives, as we had always called for repeatedly, even before the crisis. The United Nations and its objectives and successes are but a literal reflection of the conduct of its Members, their commitment to the principles of the Charter and their interest in consolidating these principles.

We are truly witnessing a new dawn in the world that emanates from international legitimacy, and it will become the shield of all States, large and small.

Today, the Council continues this historic, unprecedented march in facing up to criminal aggression by any party, whether in the present or in the future. Therefore, we must remember that the completion of the political aspect of this effort is as important as the military aspect that, by the grace of God Almighty, was carried out by the international forces with great success.

It is inconceivable that an aggressive regime should eliminate a peaceful, secure State, brutalize its population and for eight months before the eyes of the whole world impose on it all manner of oppression and inhuman practices, and then proceed to pollute the marine environment and torch the oil wells, which will continue to burn for a long time to come; it is inconceivable that that regime should be allowed to return to the former situation without being held fully responsible and made to pay all reparations and return all looted property, and without depriving it of the means to carry out aggression and without terminating, under clear international guarantees, all matters left outstanding.

Today, we might not find better proof of the magnitude of the destruction wreaked upon Kuwait than the report of the Secretary-General's representative, Mr. Ahtisaari, which was issued a few days ago after his visit to Kuwait with a technical team. He said:

> "There can be no doubt that a deliberate attempt was made to extinguish Kuwait, its national identity, the pride of its people in their history and achievements. The manner of destruction, with its coordinated vandalism and massive looting, leaves an indelible image. It was a privilege for me and the members of my team to witness the rebirth of a nation, however painful the circumstances." (*S/22409, para. 41*)

I should like to take this opportunity to thank Mr. Ahtisaari and the members of his mission for their sincere efforts in carrying out their mission and for informing the international community of the magnitude of the tragedy visited upon my country by the brutal Baghdad regime.

In speaking of Mr. Ahtisaari's report I am reminded of what he said in a previous report about Iraq's having been set back many years and been subjected to excessive damage. With bitterness and with sadness tugging at our heartstrings, we ask: Who set Iraq back many years? Who was the cause of all this destruction? Who took its people from a state of welfare and progress to this tragic situation, a situation akin to civil war during which the Baghdad regime is now continuing to add to its brutal record of oppressing its own citizens before it began oppressing other peoples?

The cause for this entire state of affairs is that very regime which concluded the Algiers Agreement with Iran in 1975 to establish peace between Iraq and Iran, its neighbour, and then tore the Agreement to pieces before the whole world and trampled it underfoot when it arrogantly and insolently invaded Iran. It is the same regime which arrogantly shirked the duties and obligations of its country under the 1963 Agreement between Kuwait and Iraq. It dealt a blow to the Charter of the Arab League, the Charter of the United Nations and all international laws and norms when it occupied Kuwait hours after official talks between the two countries. That meeting was merely theatrical, a smokescreen behind which that regime could conceal its preparations for invasion and aggression. It is the same regime whose very President in Baghdad in February 1980 made a pledge not to interfere in the internal affairs of Arab States, in which he pointed out the importance of respect for the security and sovereignty of all Arab States, be they large or small. I should like, in this regard, to quote from an interview conducted by the editor of the Egyptian newspaper *Al-Ahram* with President Hosni Mubarak of Egypt, who said:

> "I had previously mentioned what was declared by the Iraqi President before all Heads of State at the Rabat Summit and with the Arab lawyers. The text of his speech is on record everywhere. He said: If Iraq occupies an Arab State, you must stand against Iraq. This is a clear, categorical statement, and if we implement it, can he brand us as traitors and agents? This is truly bizarre."

The Council does not have sufficient time for a detailed account of the record of the Baghdad regime. We need not go into detail since members are well aware of all its actions. Therefore, we call upon the Council to take all necessary measures to guarantee for us and for all the peoples of the region respect by the Iraqi regime for its obligations and duties provided for in all agreements or conventions applicable to it. The Iraqi regime has proven beyond any doubt that it has no credibility, that it disregards all treaties and agreements, that it turns a blind eye to all laws and the most rudimentary principles and norms. For example, despite the fact that Baghdad had declared its acceptance of Security Council resolution 686 (1991), it has yet to return property looted from Kuwait and has not even issued a statement, as is required under that resolution, in which it officially accepts the principle of reparations from a legal standpoint.

The international community must take a decisive and strict stand against this kind of aggressive regime to the very end. We cannot speak of the dawn of a new world order without punishing the outlaws. We cannot allow any State to exploit the problems of borders in order to achieve regional expansion or to carry out aggressive adventures in which armies trample on the innocent and in which bullets and fire take the place of words and dialogue. Therefore, this historic draft resolution of the Security Council must be a shield to protect the region from the evils of the Baghdad regime in the future. It must also be a lesson for any other regime in any other part of the world that might be tempted to carry out such evils, because of tyranny and megalomania. The Council must deal decisively and with full effectiveness with all aspects and all questions. In addition to reparations, guarantees and rights, the question of armaments must be considered. So must the terrifying arsenal of Iraq, on which billions of dollars were spent through many illegal channels, not for the establishment of a national army of defence, but as had become evident, for the achievement of objectives of regional expansion that have become known to all. This arsenal, unfortunately, was created and deployed at the expense of the development of the Iraqi people and, in the final analysis, at the expense of its security and stability and of the lives of its innocent citizens lost in popular uprisings against the regime in the north, the south and other parts of Iraq.

It gives me pleasure to place on record before the Council, from which the battle for the liberation of Kuwait was launched, that Kuwait is free, that its proud people has gone back to the exercise of its rights and duties in the battle of reconstruction and reform, that its legitimate Government has returned to lead its citizens on the road to well-being. The history of any people is but a series of experiences, both painful and happy, that make clear how attached a people is to its constitutional and political regime chosen of its own free will. We are fully confident and convinced that the tragedy of aggression has made our people more loving and proud of its national soil, that it will make our people redouble its efforts to rehabilitate and reconstruct our country. We will carry out this task in the light of our traditions, our values, our constitution and through all our democratic institutions, which have emerged since the independence of Kuwait in 1961.

Kuwait will ensure, as it always has, respect for basic freedoms, human dignity and human rights for all. It will always protect the safety and security of all those residing on its territory, without any discrimination.

Kuwait has distinguished itself as a State whose hospitality is enjoyed by brothers and friends who have come to work together in the service of Kuwait and to earn an honest living. We shall continue to welcome them and to appreciate their work. We shall reject all those who may be ungrateful, all those who might act against Kuwait's interests and against the principles, values and pride of its people. In all our actions towards our residents, whether Kuwaitis or foreign, we are inspired by the teachings of our religion and by the rule of law, and we shall not give way to our emotions.

...

[21] **Mr. Al-Anbari (Iraq)** (interpretation from Arabic):

...

Before the Council voted at its meeting on 29 November 1990 on what became resolution 678 (1990) I had the honour to address the Council, when I spoke of its authorizing, in the second paragraph of the resolution, members of the alliance to use all necessary means to implement resolution 660 (1990) and all subsequent resolutions, including the resolution that was then adopted. That authorization, which included the use of force by the countries of the alliance individually and collectively, went beyond the Security Council's mandate and was in contravention of the Charter.

Our position is based on various considerations. The use of force under a Security Council resolution should be in accordance with Article 42 and all subsequent Articles. It should be confined to the achievement of the objectives specified by the Security Council and should not be intended to achieve the objectives of one country or a group of countries. The Charter provides that should the Council decide to use force to implement its resolutions the international force used should be composed of national forces placed at the disposal of the Security Council, in accordance with bilateral agreements between the Council and the countries concerned, and should be under the direction of the Military Staff Committee and under the United Nations flag. When those conditions are not met, authorization to countries to use force individually or collectively does not guarantee that they will not, individually or collectively, exceed the limits and objectives envisaged by the Council originally. In fact, in the absence of monitoring by the Council it is almost certain that those objectives will be exceeded.

Iraq has accepted resolutions 660 (1990) and 678 (1990) and the rest of the resolutions adopted by the Council under what is called "The situation between Iraq and Kuwait". However, the actions of the alliance under the command of the United States, which started its military operations with an aerial bombardment on the night of 16/17 January this year, operations which continued until after the land military operations had been suspended on 28 February, went beyond the objectives of resolution 678 (1990) in their violence and brutality.

After the United States began its aerial bombardment of Iraq it carried out thousands of raids daily, day and night, from 16/17 January until the declaration of the temporary suspension of offensive operations on 28 February. A total of 88,500 tons of explosives was dropped by aircraft on Iraq. That almost equalled the explosive power of seven atomic bombs of the type the United States dropped on Hiroshima.

The American media portrayed the aerial bombardment as being conducted with the use of the latest military technology, aircraft launching laser-guided bombs or "smart" bombs to hit only strategic and military targets, and not civilian targets. However, the reality was different. The reality was that the offensive forces placed great reliance on the B-52s, which carry only "dumb" bombs launched from an altitude of more than 30,000 feet, thus making it almost impossible to distinguish between civilian and military targets. Bombing civilian targets and killing civilian populations was a deliberate act for which the United States and its partners in the aggression should bear full responsibility.

The American public relations machine used the expression "collateral damage" to describe civilian victims and civilian targets hit by American bombs and the bombs of the other coalition partners. That brings to mind another American expression, "pacification", used by the same American machinery to describe the operations of annihilation and the destruction of villages and forests in Viet Nam, using poisonous chemical material. This is only a new addition to the type of language described by George Orwell in "1984".

The reality exposed by military statistics after the suspension of military operations shows that the majority of the targets hit by American aircraft were not military and that the military targets aimed at were missed. We have only to refer to a report in *The Washington Post* on 16 March 1991, quoting a statement by the Commander of the United States Air Force, General Merrill A. McPeak. The paper said that of the explosives dropped on the cities and villages of Iraq, a total of 88,500 tons, only 7 per cent were in guided bombs.

The report in *The Washington Post* refers to the statement by General McPeak that, of 88,500 tons of bombs dropped on cities and villages of Iraq, barely 7 per cent were guided bombs. If these guided bombs had hit 90 per cent of their targets, then the average hits of the United States bombs totalled only 30 per cent. These weapons missed 70 per cent of the targets, and they hit civilian targets, causing the death of tens of thousands of women and children and the elderly and the destruction of tens of thousands of houses and other civilian installations. That was the statement by the Commander of the United States Air Force reported in *The Washington Post*.

I should like to state here that the actions of the United States and its partners during their military operations against Iraq went far beyond Security Council resolution 678 (1990). Therefore, the United States and its allies should bear the full responsibility for the excesses committed in their operations, which went far beyond the limits and the objectives of resolution 678 (1990). That resolution related only to the withdrawal of Iraqi forces from Kuwait and the restoration of the legitimate authorities.

Here I wish to refer to the report of the mission which was sent to Iraq by the United Nations Secretary-General and which was in Iraq from 10 to 17 March 1991. This mission comprised representatives of most of the organizations and agencies of the United Nations. In its report, dated 20 March 1991, the mission states the following:

> "It should ... be said at once that nothing that we had seen or read had quite prepared us for the particular form of devastation which has now befallen the country. The recent conflict has wrought near-apocalyptic results upon the economic infrastructure of what had been, until January 1991, a rather highly urbanized and mechanized society." (*S/22366, para. 8*).

The mission confined itself to civilian installations and cities; it did not go to military targets. In this report the mission goes on to say:

> "Now, most means of modern life support have been destroyed or rendered tenuous. Iraq has, for some time to come, been relegated to a pre-industrial age, but with all the disabilities of post-industrial dependency on an intensive use of energy and technology." (*ibid.*)

We must ask the United States and its partners to answer the following questions: Was it one of the objectives of resolution 678 (1990) to return Iraqi society and Iraq's economic installations to the age predating the industrial revolution? Or was the comprehensive damage and destruction wreaked upon all the cities and villages of Iraq and all its vital installations merely an involuntary mistake, merely collateral damage?

The draft resolution before the Security Council today refers to the implementation of resolution 661 (1990), which imposed the economic and financial blockade on Iraq and which has been in effect since 6 August 1990, and indeed is still in effect. The draft resolution itself states that the blockade will continue to be in force.

In this connection I must refer again to the report of the United Nations mission which I have already mentioned. The following warning is contained in the final paragraph of that report:

> "It is unmistakable that the Iraqi people may soon face a further imminent catastrophe, which could include epidemic and famine, if massive life-supporting needs are not rapidly met." (*S/22366, para. 37*)

I should like to put another question: Was it necessary to destroy water and sewage facilities in order to achieve the objectives of resolution 678 (1990)? Was the resulting spread of sewage to streets, houses and rivers a secret to forces that take such pride in their technology and their guided laser bombs? Perhaps this too will be described as "collateral damage". Electricity-generating stations were strategic targets, because electric energy was necessary for Iraqi military forces. But these forces, too, need water, air and medicine. Did the poisoning of the water and the air in Iraq and the annihilation of the people of Iraq become a target in order to prevent Iraqi troops from meeting their basic needs? Was it really necessary to annihilate the Iraqi army - in the words used recently by one of the military commanders of the alliance?

What remains of the four Geneva Conventions on the protection of civilian persons in times of armed conflict, the protection of prisoners of war, and other subjects, designed to limit the brutality and inhumanity of war? Are these Conventions to be declared null and void? For the killing of civilians and the destruction of the installations basic to civilian life and safety seem to require, according to United States strategy in its aggression against Iraq, continued bombing, day and night, with no distinction being made between civilian and military targets. The four Geneva Conventions should be respected and observed, not only by small countries but also, and above all, by major Powers, which possess the right of veto and all types of weapons of mass destruction. Foremost among those major Powers are the United States, the United Kingdom and France. Are they immune from sanctions that must be imposed on countries which contravene the provisions of the Geneva Conventions, or the Treaty on the Non-Proliferation of Nuclear Weapons, or the Charter of the United Nations?

The destruction wreaked upon Iraq by the United States and its partners went beyond the limits and the objectives of resolution 678 (1990). This destruction was not only physical destruction: epidemics will spread and basic medical needs will no longer be met. The destruction will have effects for many years among future generations.

In its issue of 18 March 1991, *Time* magazine published a very alarming article, which has been met with very strange silence on the part of the media in the United States. In that article it was stated that Abrams tanks and A-10 Thunderbolt fighter-bombers fired shells made of depleted uranium; this material emits radioactive oxidized uranium; anyone exposed to that particular radiation could be subject to various types of cancer in future years.

If we recall the amounts of explosives that were dropped on civilian and military targets, as well as on the Iraqi countryside - including these bombs that were made of depleted uranium - we must really ask if the United States really observes in its wars any international agreements or moral principles.

Those who would like to justify or find pretexts for these inhuman acts may say that those fears have absolutely no scientific basis or that the United States authorities are unaware of them. However, those fears are based on very substantial scientific facts of which the United States authorities are aware. The magazine referred to the fact that in 1980 the State of New York had to close a plant that used depleted uranium in the wake of the authorities' discovery that the level of radioactivity around the plant was 25 times higher than the acceptable average. If the American authorities knew of that, were they trying - in addition to destroying Iraq economically, annihilating its army, killing tens of thousands of civilians and depriving the rest of the Iraqi people of the basic means of survival for years to come - to weaken the present and future generations of Iraqi society?

In view of this background, I should like briefly to address some of the most important paragraphs of the draft resolution before the Council. Since Iraq announced its commitment to all the resolutions of the Security Council adopted since 2 August 1990 - including the thirteenth, resolution 686 (1991), which states in its last paragraph that the Council would continue to secure the rapid establishment of a definitive end to the hostilities - perhaps the majority of the Council expected that the new United States draft resolution would be confined to lifting the economic blockade imposed on Iraq, freeing its frozen assets and property, announcing a permanent cease-fire and the end of hostilities between Iraq and the countries of the alliance, and establishing peaceful relations in the place of hostilities. However, the new draft resolution raises new questions that previous resolutions never tackled or dealt with in a substantially different way.

My position on the major paragraphs in the draft resolution can be summed up as follows. First, as to the question of boundaries, the Security Council has never before imposed disputed international boundaries on

States Members of the United Nations. Recognized international boundaries represent a basic pillar of the territorial integrity of States. Therefore, the views of all States concerned should be taken into consideration. Iraq views this question and the manner in which it has been addressed in this draft resolution as an infringement upon its sovereignty and territorial integrity. The text contravenes operative paragraph 3 of resolution 660 (1990), which calls upon Iraq and Kuwait to begin negotiations for the resolution of their differences, and among those differences is that of boundaries. Iraq reserves its right to demand its legitimate territorial rights in accordance with international law. Its understanding of the text of the draft resolution is in accordance with the Charter of the United Nations, and the provisions of international law in this respect remain valid.

Secondly, as to the question of reparations, Iraq understands that the text has been arrived at in accordance with international law provisions in resolution 674 (1990) with regard to the principle of reparations. Therefore, Iraq reserves its right to request reparations for all losses that it has incurred through any excess in the use of force as authorized by resolution 678 (1990) for countries to use all necessary means to implement resolution 660 (1990) and all subsequent resolutions. The imposition of reparations on Iraq alone and in the coercive manner of the draft resolution would only lead to the paralysis of Iraq's capacity to rebuild its economy and vital installations, and to keeping the Iraqi people unable, for several generations to come, to achieve a minimum standard of living that would provide for a dignified life.

Thirdly, as to the question of destroying weapons, if the text aims at restoring international peace and security in the region, it is obvious that Iraq's undertaking this alone would not secure that objective. There are countries in the area - foremost among which is Israel, which attacked peaceful Iraqi nuclear installations in 1981 - that possess such weapons. Maintaining their stockpiles would perpetuate the threat that prompted Iraq to arm itself in the first place to defend its national security at the expense of development. Applying the text to Iraq alone and in that manner, which is inconsistent with the declared objective, would be duplicitous and evidence of a double standard in dealing with a question of the same nature. Iraq believes that this text will not achieve the desired objective on a practical level if the Council does not follow it up with a similar and comprehensive integrated programme to disarm the entire region of all weapons of mass destruction. Imposing disarmament on Iraq alone would create a political, military and security vacuum in the area that would tempt more than one country to give vent to its greed at the expense of one or more of its neighbours, rendering the whole area subject to instability, more violence and fighting.

Fourthly, as to the economic blockade, my Government believes that maintaining the land, sea and air blockade and the freeze of assets - in spite of all that was mentioned in the report of the United Nations mission to Iraq and of the fact that Iraq has accepted the implementation of all 13 Security Council resolutions on the issue and removed all the reasons that prompted the Security Council to adopt resolutions 661 (1990), 665 (1990), 669 (1990) and 670 (1990) - would be in contravention of the Charter of the United Nations and could be viewed as economic aggression and a clear violation of the Charter of Economic Rights and Duties of States and human rights covenants, foremost among which are the rights to life, dignity and freedom.

If the Council insists on maintaining the blockade and the economic sanctions, Iraq and the international community in general, particularly the countries of the third world, will discover that the essence of the new world order is the order of United States sovereignty over the entire world and its international Organization, the imposition of the will of the United States on the international community, and the exploitation of the Security Council and the Charter of the United Nations as tools to lend legitimacy to the United States greed for plundering the economic resources of other countries and for imposing its hegemony over the world, thus ushering in a new colonial period more cruel, violent and greedy than the old colonialism, which the world had hoped had ended. Instead, it has returned under the banner of "new world order".

[36] **The PRESIDENT** (interpretation from French):

...

It is my understanding that the Council is ready to proceed to the vote on the draft resolution contained in document S/22430. If I hear no objection, I shall take it that this is the case.

There being no objection, it is so decided.

Before putting the draft resolution to the vote, I shall first call on those members of the Council who wish to make statements before the voting.

[36] **Mr. AL-ASHTAL (Yemen)** (interpretation from Arabic):

...

On 28 February, the President of the United States of America declared the suspension of military operations in the Gulf, and on 2 March, less than 48 hours after the initial declaration, the Security Council adopted resolution 686 (1991). This resolution called on Iraq to implement all 12 Security Council resolutions, including rescinding its actions purporting to annex Kuwait, the release of all prisoners of war, the return of the property seized by Iraq, provision of a map of the locations of all mines and booby-traps and participation in talks to arrange for the cessation of hostilities. The next day, Iraq agreed to implement resolution 686 (1991) and subsequently began to implement all the other resolutions.

About three weeks later, Mr. Ahtisaari, who had gone to Iraq at the head of a mission to assess the humanitarian needs of Iraq, issued his report. The fact is that this report has brought to light the extent of the destruction that has afflicted Iraq and its infrastructure, and has given rise to many comments in the press and other media. In view of the importance of this report, and owing to the fact that it is related to our view of the draft resolution before us, permit me to read out its paragraph 8:

> "I and the members of my mission were fully conversant with media reports regarding the situation in Iraq and, of course, with the recent WHO/UNICEF report on water, sanitary and health conditions in the Greater Baghdad area. It should, however, be said at once that nothing that we had seen or read had quite prepared us for the particular form of devastation which has now befallen the country. The recent conflict has wrought near-apocalyptic results upon the economic infrastructure of what had been, until January 1991, a rather highly urbanized and mechanized society. Now, most means of modern life support have been destroyed or rendered tenuous. Iraq has, for some time to come, been relegated to a pre-industrial age, but with all the disabilities of post-industrial dependency on an intensive use of energy and technology". (*S/22366 para. 8*)

The mission recommended that, in these circumstances of present severe hardship and in view of the bleak prognosis, sanctions in respect of food supplies should be immediately removed, as should those relating to the import of agricultural equipment and supplies. The Security Council approved this recommendation and lifted the embargo that had been imposed on foodstuffs and humanitarian needs.

Today we have before us a long and complicated draft resolution which includes very unjust and very harsh conditions for Iraq and its people in order to achieve an official, formal cease-fire. Among the most important of these conditions are demarcation of the boundaries, guaranteeing the boundaries, destruction of missiles and weapons of mass destruction, payment by Iraq of war reparations and a continuation of the embargo except in respect of food and medicine.

Without going into the details of the draft resolution or speaking about its individual paragraphs and its various parts, I would like to make the following remarks, pinpointing the draft resolution's most important and salient features.

What are its characteristics and features? First, this draft resolution is characterized by the fact that it tends to exceed the United Nations Charter and the Security Council mandate and resolutions.

This can be documented as follows: First, the imposition of the boundaries between Iraq and Kuwait, which is counter to Security Council resolution 660 (1990), which called upon the two parties to begin immediately intensive negotiations for the resolution of their differences. We might mention that the Security Council has never set any boundaries. That task has always been left to negotiations or brought before the International Court of Justice, with the agreement of the parties concerned.

Secondly, there is the guaranteeing of the boundaries set. There is no precedent whatsoever for the Security Council to guarantee the boundaries of any country. Does that not open the door to asking the Security Council to guarantee the boundaries of many other States, an area in which there are many instances of disagreements?

Thirdly, there is the specification of the way in which Iraq should pay reparations resulting from its responsibility for the war. According to international law it is, indeed, a fact that that responsibility should be borne by Iraq. But why should the Secretary-General be involved in a matter that falls within the purview of the International Court of Justice? Article 36 of the Statute of the International Court of Justice clearly stipulates that

> "the Court's jurisdiction comprises all cases which the parties refer to it and all matters specially provided for in the Charter of the United Nations or in treaties and conventions in force."

The Statute continues:

> "The States parties to the present Statute may at any time declare that they recognize as compulsory *ipso facto* and without special agreement in relation to any other state accepting the same obligation, the jurisdiction of the Court in all legal disputes concerning:
> "a. the interpretation of a treaty;
> "b. any question of international law;
> "c. the existence of any fact which, if established, would constitute a breach of an international obligation;
> "d." - and this is the more important provision - "the nature or extent of the reparation to be made for the breach of an international obligation."

With regard to reparations, there is no doubt that there will be many claims made from different quarters. Do we not need a neutral party whose procedures are subject to a set of regulations to decide on such claims?

The draft resolution is also characterized by the narrowness of its outlook, both politically and geographically. It does not address the real needs that must be met if long-term peace and security are to be established, not only in the Gulf area but in the region as a whole - including, of course, the Middle East. This is quite clear from the following: First, we again have the imposition of boundaries instead of a call upon Iraq and Kuwait to negotiate, with the assistance of the United Nations. Is it impossible that in the distant future someone in Iraq or in Kuwait might reopen the file on the boundaries on the basis of the fact that the boundaries were imposed and not agreed upon? Would that help in establishing good-neighbourliness and stability? Or is there perhaps someone who wants to keep the problems between the two countries as they are at present?

Also, there is the question of the destruction of all biological and chemical weapons and other weapons, including ballistic missiles and their related major parts, and repair and production facilities. We would like to emphasize that Yemen supports any action aimed at eradicating weapons of mass destruction in the Middle East region and making that region a nuclear-weapon free zone and an area free from weapons of mass destruction. However, would the destruction of the Iraqi weapons alone help in eradicating similar weapons elsewhere in the region? We do not think so. What would be the consequences of the resulting military imbalance in the area as a result of the destruction of the Iraqi weapons and the creation of a military vacuum? Would that not lead to a race to fill the vacuum between the region's countries, something we are already witnessing? Deals are now being made to purchase billions of dollars of weapons, and everyone is racing to acquire the largest quantity of state-of-the-art weaponry.

On the other hand, the military imbalance in the Middle East would benefit only Israel, which continues to challenge and defy the Security Council and the international community whenever it feels that it has sufficient military power and sources of military power to act without fear of competition from anyone else. Look at the way Israel is behaving today, at a time when the United States and other countries are engaged in attempts to solve the problems of the Middle East.

Israel has begun deporting Palestinians anew, its ministers state that the settlements will continue, and its Prime Minister has said that the Golan will remain as it is. Does this not show that there are great difficulties facing the establishment of peace and security in the region?

Thirdly, this draft resolution is characterized by the application of the same logic as that of resolution 678 (1990), in which the Council gives unlimited authority to an unlimited number of countries to do unspecified things under the banner of the guaranteeing of peace and security in the region. This is quite clear from the following:

First, it is well known that the draft resolution before us aims at the formal declaration of a cease-fire - only a cease-fire. This means that the state of war will continue between Iraq and the forces of the alliance until a definitive end is put to the military operations and hostilities, in accordance with paragraph 8 of resolution 686 (1991). But who will determine this? It will be left to the forces of the alliance. These are the forces that decided to wage the battle, using the authority of the Council, and these are the forces that will decide upon the cessation of the operation. This might take years, because it is related to the guaranteeing of peace and security in the region, let alone the guaranteeing of the boundaries between Iraq and Kuwait. Thus, the foreign forces in the Gulf will get the legitimacy for their presence from the resolutions of the Security Council, under the umbrella of the United Nations.

Secondly, how about the withdrawal of the forces of the alliance, which occupy about 20 per cent of the territory of Iraq? The draft resolution before us refers to this in paragraph 6, when it:

> "Notes that as soon as the Secretary-General notifies the Council of the completion of the deployment of the United Nations observer unit, the conditions will be established for Member States cooperating with Kuwait in accordance with resolution 678 (1990) to bring their military presence in Iraq to an end consistent with resolution 686 (1991);" (*S/22430, para. 6*)

Security Council resolution 686 (1991) speaks about a rapid and definitive end to the hostilities - something which can only be achieved through a peace treaty. In other words, the allied forces will withdraw from Iraq only when certain conditions are met. These conditions will be those accepted by these forces; and, of course, the Security Council did not define those conditions in this draft resolution.

Thirdly, as far as the security arrangements in the area are concerned, the United Nations would not be the party that would establish security in the region, but the Security Council would have to accept or coexist with the security arrangements that would be applied because they would be made using the authority of the United Nations.

Fourthly and lastly, the draft resolution ignores, and is not really sensitive to, the needs and requirements of the Iraqi people. The insistence of the sponsors of the draft resolution that the embargo be continued with regard to the needs of the Iraqi civilians would hurt only the Iraqi people.

Why should the Iraqi people be prevented from importing books, clothes, cooking utensils, construction materials, spare parts for cars and bicycles, refrigerators and air conditioners, toys for children, sporting goods and electrical and other similar equipment? What effect would the importation of these items have on Iraq as far as the military situation is concerned? And why this cruelty to the Iraqi people, who suffered from the aerial bombardment for a whole month, who suffered from the intensified destruction, and who had already suffered the embargo for seven months? Is it not unjust that the Iraqi people - women, children and the elderly - should suffer from both the embargo and the war?

The delegation of Yemen will not support the draft resolution before us for the reasons given. However, we should like to emphasize our consistent position calling for doing the right thing and the solution of the regional disputes between Iraq and Kuwait through peaceful means and mutual agreement, overcoming the past and beginning a new phase in relations based on full respect for sovereignty, non-intervention in the internal affairs of States, and cooperation for the good of the two neighbourly countries and their peoples.

We in Yemen were not - and will not be - a party to the dispute between the brothers and will always work for solidarity within the one Arab family, and tomorrow all these clouds will be dispersed.

...

[51] Mr. Lukabu Khabouji N'Zaji (Zaire) (interpretation from French):

...

The Security Council has before it a draft resolution whose objectives give us a basis to hope that after its adoption the Gulf region, which has been the focal point of the concerns of the entire international community, will finally regain the lasting peace to which it has aspired. The draft, considered quite rightly as the most complex and longest which the Council has taken up, deals with various areas which in some respects have never been examined within this prestigious body of the United Nations.

Zaire believes that the extraordinary nature of the Gulf crisis requires that the Council find extraordinary solutions. This is why my country highly values the intellectual and physical efforts made by the entire Council in order to find solutions designed to establish a lasting peace together with conditions that would ensure stability in the region. In this regard, my delegation believes that the areas covered by this draft resolution - boundaries, troop withdrawal, sanctions, the system of compensating for damages, the elimination of weapons of mass destruction, international terrorism - all of which are to lead to a genuine and permanent cease-fire, are essential unifying elements for the establishment of this peace to which we all earnestly aspire.

With regard to boundaries, Zaire acknowledges that the crisis which broke out in the night of 2 August 1990 between Iraq and Kuwait was primarily caused by border disputes between the two fraternal countries. As a full-fledged member of the Organization of African Unity (OAU), which enshrined the principle of inviolability of borders in its Charter, Zaire believes that strict compliance with this principle would spare us potential conflicts and would ensure stability among neighbouring States. One can easily understand why we value this so highly. Zaire, which shares its borders with nine other countries, could not tolerate a situation whereby this taboo in Africa would be violated elsewhere.

The draft resolution, which acknowledges the importance of negotiations to be undertaken between Iraq and Kuwait regarding the demarcation of the boundary, adds a key element designed to preserve the future: the Council is asked to safeguard the inviolability of that border. And we unreservedly support those provisions.

As to the withdrawal of troops, Zaire, which, at the beginning of this crisis, had stated that it wished to see Iraq comply with its obligations and that it, in turn, as a member of the Council was committed to do its utmost to see to it that the troops were withdrawn from the region, is pleased that the draft resolution advocates the deployment of a United Nations observer unit, which would enable those troops still in the region to withdraw.

Regarding sanctions, my delegation's major concern was to see to it that the civilian population obtained adequate, regular supplies of foodstuffs, medicines and other health products. As these concerns have been met in the decision of the Committee established under resolution 661 (1990), my delegation agrees with the provisions in the draft resolution that is before us.

As to compensation, it is only fair, after a crisis which was not provoked by Kuwait, whose territory was occupied, whose population was displaced and subjected to the cruellest torture and whose economy and environment were destroyed, that Iraq, the aggressor, bear responsibility for its acts and pay for them. This is why we believe that the machinery set up will ensure that the system functions harmoniously and impartially, for it has been placed under the guidance of the Secretary-General.

With regard to weapons of mass destruction, Zaire believes that the countries of the region should work together in order to set up a collective security system. However, bearing in mind the dangers inherent in the weapons of mass destruction accumulated in Iraq and inherent in their abuse, it would be appropriate that steps be taken with a view to their elimination.

As to the cease-fire, Zaire welcomes the fact that the long-awaited stage has finally arrived. Indeed, since the end of the military operations conducted by the countries cooperating with Kuwait, Zaire was waiting for us to reach this decisive cease-fire stage. Today, the draft resolution that we are considering offers us the opportunity of welcoming the establishment of a permanent cease-fire, and we hope that Iraq will comply quickly with its obligations in order to bring this stage closer.

Zaire, whose policy of defending the weak has not changed since 2 August 1990, wishes to reaffirm this policy by stating that in view of all of these elements, which have met with the approval of my country's higher authorities, and in order to show our sympathy for the people and leadership of free Kuwait, Zaire has decided to become a sponsor of the draft resolution that is before us. Therefore, we shall vote in favour of it.

An extraordinary situation requires an extraordinary proposal, and my delegation proposes that the Security Council agree that the draft which in a few moments is to become a resolution - the longest and the most complex the Security Council has ever adopted - be sent by the Secretary-General to the world book of records so as to be recorded in it.

I should like to congratulate and thank the Secretary-General and his two assistants who went to the region and drafted reports whose usefulness has been acknowledged by all.

[56] **Mr. ZENENGA (Zimbabwe):**

...

The Security Council will shortly be taking action on a draft resolution whose major objective is to formalize the cease-fire between Iraq and Kuwait and the Member States cooperating with Kuwait. The draft resolution addresses very complex and extremely delicate issues. It contains decisions which will define some important aspects of the future of the Persian Gulf area and the Middle East region as a whole.

Zimbabwe holds the view that the actions taken by the Council, and indeed by the entire international community, since 2 August regarding the crisis in the Persian Gulf have constituted a justified response to a unique situation created by the invasion and illegal occupation of Kuwait by Iraq. It is in this same light that we interpret the several unprecedented decisions which the Council is about to take in adopting the draft resolution before us.

It is Zimbabwe's understanding that the measures contained in the draft resolution are intended to address some of the major issues that led to the conflict between Iraq and Kuwait. We also understand that some of the provisions in the document, which ordinarily would have caused us enormous discomfort, are designed to ensure that there will be no recurrence of the tragedy that was visited upon Kuwait last August. We have also noted that in the implementation of some of the measures contained in the document the requirements of the people of Iraq, as well as the needs of the Iraqi economy, will be taken into account.

Zimbabwe believes that the objective of establishing in the Middle East a zone free from weapons of mass destruction as well as the objective of a global ban on chemical weapons, which the present draft resolution has addressed, can contribute to durable stability and security in the region. However, we have misgivings regarding whether the approach suggested in the document before us constitutes the best way to achieve those objectives. We would therefore have preferred to have the measures specified in section C of the draft resolution applied within the framework of the whole region.

It was also my delegation's expectation that, in keeping with the commitment it expressed in the presidential statement issued on 3 March regarding the humanitarian aspects of the situation in Iraq, the Council would, through the present draft resolution, proceed beyond the recent decision taken by the Committee established under resolution 661 (1990) and lift all remaining restrictions on the supply of foodstuffs and essential civilian needs to Iraq. Zimbabwe believes this to be the appropriate response to the report of the Secretary-General contained in document S/22366.

Lastly, Zimbabwe's understanding of operative paragraph 32 of the draft resolution is that nothing contained in that paragraphs refers to or applies to the struggles of peoples under occupation who are struggling for self-determination.

...

[58] **Mr. ALARCON de QUESADA (Cuba)** (interpretation from Spanish):

...

The Security Council has before it a draft resolution which will be remembered for more than one reason - perhaps because, as has been suggested, it may be included in a certain book, or because, although the text before us bears a different date, it will be regarded, for several reasons, as the resolution of 1 April.

In dealing with a regrettable conflict, the Council has sometimes shown particular concern to give evidence of its good memory. More than once it has recalled, as it does again in the text before us, all its relevant previous resolutions, one after the other, or has reaffirmed them. The Council has also on more than one occasion shown that it can have a very short memory.

We have said on other occasions that our delegation opposes the use of this body for the ends and purposes of one State, and, furthermore, its use in a way in which the Council quite simply has no right to be used.

The Security Council is a powerful body because the Member States of the Organization agreed to give it particular responsibilities, which were enshrined in the Charter. But the Council totally lacks the legal, political or moral authority to reinterpret the Charter whenever that may suit one of its members in order to recall certain fundamental principles and ignore others when that is found more convenient.

But the Security Council uses its memory in such a peculiar way that it does not remember very well its own texts - although it always starts every discussion of other texts by recalling those previous texts.

In the text now before us, my delegation finds a number of reasons making it absolutely impossible to accept it. On the one hand, it is claimed that this body will assume - so far as I know, for the first time - certain functions with regard to international boundaries, between two Member States. May I say in passing that, in so doing, the Council begins by changing the text of the first of the resolutions which it takes the trouble to recall here. Resolution 660 (1990) obviously established a different approach, an approach much more in keeping with doctrine and international practice than the one the Council now wishes to impose.

My delegation believes that international boundaries should be respected. We believe that the Security Council has the obligation to ensure that those boundaries are not violated. But the Security Council totally lacks the authority to demand respect for certain border lines, or to demarcate them, or to determine in what part of what region of the world those boundaries are violable, boundaries in respect to which it proclaims the determination to shoulder special responsibility.

In the future it will no doubt be recalled that the council is curiously selective. For more than one of us will remember that the conflict we have been discussing for so many months has taken place in a part of the world where there has been and continues to be more than one conflict very closely related to the fact that for some the boundaries do not exist, or are moveable, or are adjustable. And old maps are not always recalled, maps that clearly showed the extent of this entity - which some do not wish to remember - called Palestine. We are not always willing to recall that the Security Council has also shouldered concrete responsibilities with respect to those international boundaries that delimit the area of the State of Israel and of the Republic of Lebanon.

I have mentioned only two examples (as we all know, there are others) of situations in which the Security Council, for the sake of decorum, if nothing else - while affirming, as it does in operative paragraph 4 of the draft resolution which the Council is surely going to adopt, its decision to "guarantee the inviolability" of the boundary mentioned in the text (and this draft resolution, after all, was born on the 1st of April) - at least showed a willingness or a determination to ensure respect for the other international boundaries that also appear in the maps of the region.

The text before us contains other examples of selectivity. One is to be found in the part of the draft resolution dealing in regard to Iraq with the destruction or elimination of weapons of mass destruction.

In the spirit of the 1st of April, the authors of the draft resolution close this chapter of this long draft resolution with a paragraph - paragraph 14 - under which the actions to be taken by Iraq in conformity with paragraphs 8, 9, 10, 11, 12 and 13 are described as "unconditional". This text thought up on the 1st of April thus is intended to indicate that these measures that Iraq is to adopt unconditionally constitute a step towards the goal of establishing in the Middle East a zone free of weapons of mass destruction and all missiles for the delivery of such weapons, and thereby ensuring a comprehensive ban on chemical weapons.

History will show us how much of a joke this is; it will show us what the Security Council is really prepared to do in order to ensure that what, in our view, is a legitimate goal - the prohibition and elimination of this type of weaponry - is not used selectively in order to impose it unilaterally on one State, when everybody knows that in the very same region there is a State without boundaries, or with moveable boundaries, which possesses, manufactures, develops and conducts research on that type of weaponry; and when, furthermore, we know that there is a State that has used force against its neighbours and for many years has been oppressing an entire people: the Palestinian people.

The draft resolution before us still refuses to recognize the reality behind the development of the conflict we have been considering since August. It still does not categorically and explicitly declare what, in my delegation's opinion, the Security Council should have declared quite some time ago - that is, the final cessation of hostilities in the region and the immediate withdrawal of the foreign troops, in particular those which, without any right or justification, continue to occupy a part of Iraqi territory.

We cannot agree to any understanding that there are bad military occupations and good military occupations, that some have the right or the moral authority to send their troops wherever they wish, without having been authorized to do so by anyone; or, furthermore, that those troops can be used as a means of pressure, intimidation and interference in order to achieve other ends.

The Security Council has also for quite some time had the obligation of eliminating all economic sanctions imposed against Iraq, because these sanctions were established on the basis of certain conditions that have ceased to exist.

The Council has persistently ignored the fact that the economic sanctions were established in order to ensure compliance with one paragraph of resolution 660 (1990), which called for the unconditional withdrawal of Iraqi troops from the territory of Kuwait. Now, the Council will disregard another operative paragraph of that resolution which calls for negotiations between Iraq and Kuwait to resolve their differences. I hope that when the first preambular paragraphs of resolutions brought before the Council in future are drafted, the authors will be prudent enough no longer to recall resolution 660 (1990), which for all practical purposes is not realistically accepted in the Council, since we are maintaining the sanctions after one of their objectives has been met and are now reformulating the goal stated in another of its paragraphs. That resolution, which was the basis of the Council's action, will, in actual fact, die at the very moment that the resolution of 1 April comes to life.

But the question of sanctions is one in which we can also see quite clearly the peculiar way in which the Council uses or decides not to use its good memory. The Council tries to ignore the fact that the continuation of those sanctions, imposed rightly or wrongly, is doing great harm to the people of Iraq. The draft resolution ignores something of which the Council is aware - the report of the World Health Organization that was submitted to us by the Secretary-General as a result of the mission carried out by Mr. Martti Ahtisaari. It may be recalled that it was stated in that report that the Council would be called upon to act immediately. And what has the Council done immediately? It has disregarded what that report described in very dramatic terms. This afternoon it will continue and confirm a sanctions regime that is not only unjustified but also the cause of the ongoing problems and suffering of the Iraqi people.

But in addition to that, there is also disregard of the fact that the Security Council bears responsibilities - particularly moral ones - towards those States that are suffering adverse consequences as a result of the ongoing sanctions. It would be very difficult for the Council not to remember that fact, because it has had before it for several days now a communication from representatives of 21 Member States, three of which are members of this Council. The communication reminds us that their countries are facing serious consequences as a result of the maintenance of the economic sanctions, which those States, like all others, are observing. At the end of the communication, sent to us by three colleagues on the Council and 18 non-members, it is said that the Security Council should renew its attention to those problems with a view to arriving at prompt and effective solutions.

They achieved their objective. The Security Council is meeting some 10 days later and saying to the peoples of Iraq and other States that the economic sanctions will continue and that a complex mechanism will come into play. Frankly, I have abandoned trying to understand clearly how that mechanism is going to work - every 30 days, every 60 days, every 120 days or regularly, the Council will continue to look into the operation of the very complex mechanism of various kinds of sanctions that it has deemed advisable to establish.

But we now have a draft resolution that is sufficiently sensitive and responsive not to the claims, suffering and anguish of the people of Iraq or of dozens of States that are suffering the very serious consequences of observing the Council's sanctions, but to the payment of reparations to national Governments and foreign companies. This was clearly seen after the fruitless negotiations carried out by the non-aligned countries with some of the sponsors of this draft resolution. It means that there will be no recognition of an obligation which we consider legitimate - that Kuwait should be fully compensated for its losses resulting from the occupation and violation.

It will go beyond that. There will be benefit. The Governments and corporations are not mentioned, but it is certainly not only the Government, people and corporations of Kuwait who will benefit. If that had been the intention there would have been no rejection of the non-aligned amendment, although we agreed that the process of reparations or compensation should be enforced with respect to a State that was the victim of a violation of international law. My delegation wishes to state, with all due respect for some foreign corporations, that, frankly, it is not terribly motivated to show towards them the generosity and responsiveness that has been totally absent from the Council when dealing with third-world peoples or innocent civilians, such as the Iraqi people.

There is another aspect that we find delicate with respect to compensation. Since the Charter of our Organization, which is supposedly the mandate circumscribing the actions of the Security Council, nowhere grants any powers to this body to decide or determine with respect to claims of this nature, it could be alleged that a body as powerful as this is able to assume rights and responsibilities in areas not defined by the Charter. But I wonder what could possibly be alleged in this case, when the Charter clearly states that the judicial body of this Organization is the International Court of Justice, and clearly grants the Court and not the Council, in Article 36 (d) of the Court's Statute - which is part of the Charter, as we all know - responsibility for dealing with such issues. In the exceptionally long resolution we have before us, members may have noted, and historians in future may note, that no space was found to mention, even once, the International Court of Justice. No doubt, the sponsors know why this was impossible.

The Court, however, is one of the principal organs of this Organization. It has its own powers, the Council has its own powers, the General Assembly has its own powers - and nowhere in the Charter is there any authority whatsoever given to this Council to determine or decide on matters pertaining to compensation or reparations. Moreover, the Charter grants no authority whatsoever to the Council to decide, in the event of disputes or differences, concerning the respective areas of competence of the organs of the Organization. That function was given by the Charter to the General Assembly. Hence if anyone wishes to reinterpret the powers pertaining to each of the various principal organs of the Organization, I believe that in no way can it be inferred, nor can anyone be allowed to think, that by the use or abuse of powers the Council can usurp the place of the General Assembly, the collective body of all the Members of our Organization.

The hour is late; as usual, the Security Council started its meeting with the punctuality which also merits a mention in the book of which our distinguished colleague from Zaire spoke; the reasons for this lack of punctuality are not always either clear or known. Taking into account, though, the fact that it is indeed late, my delegation will not continue commenting on the curious text before us, and will conclude by simply assuring the Council that we will naturally reject it and vote against it.

...

[72] Mr. Gharekhan (India):

...

The draft resolution contained in document S/22430 deals with issues which the Security Council has never before been called upon to consider. The authors of the draft have assured us, bilaterally as well as in the course of informal consultations, that they have put together the various elements of the resolution in the full understanding that the international community is dealing with a unique situation of which there has been no parallel since the establishment of the United Nations; hopefully, there will be none in the future. We have been urged to look at the resolution in the light of this uniqueness of the situation.

Throughout the crisis, India's attitude, as I had occasion to state at the time of the vote on resolution 686 (1991), was governed by two basic considerations: to bring about the speediest possible liberation of Kuwait, and to minimize, to the maximum extent possible, the loss of life and the human suffering in all the countries directly involved in the crisis. The first objective has been accomplished, to the great relief and joy of the Government and the people of India. India's amity with Kuwait and our mutually beneficial exchanges go far back into history. Indian nationals have contributed to and benefited from Kuwait's prosperity and generosity. They also shared Kuwait's burdens and travails.

Liberated Kuwait, though ravaged by Iraqi occupation and war, is now courageously restoring its shattered national structures and institutions. Under-Secretary-General Martti Ahtisaari's report following his visit to Kuwait, document S/22409, speaks of his witnessing "the rebirth of a nation". (*S/22409, para. 41*) We pay a tribute to Kuwait's determination and the results already achieved, as mentioned in Mr. Ahtisaari's report, in laying the foundations, in the space of a few weeks, for its economic recovery and regrowth. We wish Kuwait all success in its gigantic task of rehabilitation and reconstruction.

Regarding the second consideration, minimizing the loss of human life and minimizing human suffering, whether in Iraq or in Kuwait, we do not have all the facts at our disposal. Mr. Ahtisaari's reports on his visits to Iraq and Kuwait, however, seem to have established fairly conclusive evidence to support the view that the loss, suffering and destruction have indeed been extremely widespread and indiscriminate.

Ever since the termination of the armed hostilities, my delegation has been preoccupied with lifting the embargo on the supply of humanitarian needs to the people of both Iraq and Kuwait. As is known to members of the Council, and indeed to others, my delegation had taken the initiative, in which we were joined by our fellow non-aligned members, to prepare a draft resolution whereby the Council would lift sanctions on supplies of foodstuffs and other essential commodities in respect of both countries. It was largely because of the efforts of the non-aligned delegations that the Council took action in devising a much-simplified procedure to meet these humanitarian needs.

Under-Secretary-General Ahtisaari has stated in his report on Kuwait that thanks to its stupendous efforts Kuwait no longer needs humanitarian assistance in the traditional sense. But the people of Iraq, who have been pushed back to the pre-industrial age, to use Mr. Ahtisaari's words, do deserve urgent consideration. I am not referring to military supplies. What I have in mind are provisions which would enable the people of Iraq to get on with their lives and to put behind them the nightmare through which they have lived.

The least that the Council can and should do is formally to lift the sanctions against the supply of all the commodities listed in the Ahtisaari report. It is not necessary, in our view, any longer to insist on even the simplified procedures of notification and no objection. In this respect, although the paragraphs concerned in the draft resolution have been somewhat improved as a result of my delegation's and other delegations' efforts, more could and should have been done. My delegation will in the weeks ahead continue to press on this point.

But, as has been said, the human being does not live by bread alone. In this connection I should like to refer to operative paragraph 19 of the draft resolution. My delegation expects that the Secretary-General, in taking into account the requirements of the people of Iraq, would also bear in mind the requirements of the country to begin the recovery of its shattered economy. This would enable the people of Iraq to work for and look forward to a decent life and to contribute towards Iraq's capacity to meet its future obligations.

My delegation firmly believes that all non-military sanctions against Iraq should also be lifted as soon as Iraq conveys acceptance of the present draft resolution. As regards military sanctions, we are glad that the sponsors have introduced an element of review, which was missing from the earlier version of the draft.

Now that the war is behind us, the Security Council is called upon to lay down a framework and institute measures that, according to the sponsors of the draft, will lead to a durable peace and stability in the Middle East. It goes without saying that India wholeheartedly supports the objective of a comprehensive, just and lasting peace in this much-troubled and conflict-ridden region of the world. My delegation is not convinced that the implementation of the provisions of the draft resolution will, by itself, create the necessary conditions or atmosphere for solving the basic conflicts and contradictions of the region. We believe that there is strength in the conventional wisdom that the region will not enjoy lasting peace and stability until the complex issues dividing the Arabs and the Israelis, the Palestinians and the Israelis, are resolved in a just and mutually satisfactory manner. In my delegation's view the consideration of these issues must not be delayed any longer.

India has consistently held that regional initiatives or arrangements for peace and stability deserve all encouragement, provided they are arrived at by the free and sovereign will of the countries of the region as part of a genuinely cooperative effort. Such arrangements cannot be imposed by external pressure nor can they be lasting if they are of a discriminatory nature taken in the global context. It is also not legitimate to make such arrangements under the mandatory provisions of Chapter VII of the Charter. As already pointed out, such arrangements have to evolve through negotiations based on the exercise of the free and sovereign will of the countries of the region. The international community, acting under the United Nations Charter, can at best encourage, acknowledge and, if requested by the countries concerned, take appropriate action to impart legitimacy to them.

Regarding the provisions in the draft resolution relating to the international boundary, my delegation has studied them with the utmost care and scrutiny. It goes without saying that my delegation will never support any decision whereby the Council would impose arbitrarily a boundary line between two countries. Boundaries are an extremely sensitive issue and must be settled by the countries freely in the exercise of their sovereignty. Any other course would only lay the groundwork for potential trouble in future. In this particular case we find that the boundary between Iraq and Kuwait was agreed upon by the highest authorities of the respective countries as two fully independent and sovereign States. Furthermore, they both took the precaution to register their agreement with the United Nations. Thus, the Council is not engaging itself in establishing any new boundary between Iraq and Kuwait. What it is doing is to recognize that such a boundary, agreed to by the two countries in the exercise of their full sovereignty, exists and to call upon them to respect its inviolability.

As regards operative paragraph 4 of the draft resolution, it is India's understanding that it does not confer authority on any country to take a unilateral action under any of the previous resolutions of the Security Council. Rather, the sponsors have explained to us that in case of any threat or actual violation of the boundary in future the Security Council will meet to take, as appropriate, all necessary measures in accordance with the Charter.

During the past 8 months the Council has adopted numerous resolutions under Chapter VII of the Charter to deal with an emergency of an exceptional nature. Some of the resolutions have been more fundamental than others in terms of their historic and precedent-setting character. Resolutions 678 (1990) and 686 (1991) obviously fall into that category. In addition, resolution 686 (1991), on which my delegation had abstained, suffered from a serious drawback in that it was open-ended regarding the establishment of a permanent cease-fire. My delegation has always advocated that the institution of a formal cease-fire must not be made contingent upon implementation of open-ended conditions indefinite in terms of time-bound implementation. In fact, we have consistently attached great importance to and called for the promulgation of a definitive, formal cease-fire so that the people of Iraq - as, indeed, the international community in general - can get going with normal life and State-to-State relations. We therefore welcome that a formal cease-fire will become effective upon official notification by Iraq to the Secretary-General and to the Security Council of its acceptance of the provisions of the draft resolution. That is a noteworthy improvement on resolution 686 (1991),

From the beginning my delegation has emphasized that the United Nations and the Secretary-General should have a role in the post-crisis situation in the region. We note and welcome the fact that the United Nations, although belatedly, is now being called upon to send an observer unit to monitor the border between Iraq and Kuwait. We would have preferred to have a United Nations contingent also deployed between the Iraqi troops and the forces of countries cooperating with the Government of Kuwait under resolution 678 (1990). However, we note that it is the intention of those countries to withdraw their forces once the United Nations observer unit is deployed along the Iraqi-Kuwait border.

My delegation had extended consultations with the sponsors of the draft resolutions, both bilaterally and along with our non-aligned colleagues. We were able to persuade the sponsors to accept some of our ideas, which have been incorporated in the final text. My delegation's position on the draft resolution will be governed by these considerations.

...

[81] **Mr. Bechio (Côte d'Ivoire)** (interpretation from French):

...

My Government is gratified to see Kuwait recover its rights, its sovereignty and its territorial integrity. Through me, my Government wishes to convey to the people and the Government of Kuwait its very best wishes for prosperity and peace.

Peace for Côte d'Ivoire is virtually a religion. We therefore unreservedly support all initiatives leading to a just and lasting peace in the Gulf region.

Throughout this crisis Côte d'Ivoire would have wished war to be avoided. Unfortunately, we had to wage war. The Council was obliged to ensure that law would prevail. It now remains for the Council to ensure that peace will prevail throughout the region. The draft resolution before us contains positive elements leading, we believe, to the achievement of these objectives.

For all those reasons, my delegation will vote in favour of the draft resolution, which establishes the framework for a final settlement of this crisis.

[82] **The President** (interpretation from French):

...

Since no other member of the Council wishes to speak at this stage, I shall now put to the vote the draft resolution contained in document S/22430, as orally revised.

A vote was taken by show of hands.

In favour:	Austria, Belgium, China, Côte d'Ivoire, France, India, Romania, Union of Soviet Socialist Republics, United Kingdom of Great Britain and Northern Ireland, United States of America, Zaire, Zimbabwe
Against:	Cuba
Abstaining:	Ecuador and Yemen

[82] **The President** (interpretation from French):

The result of the voting is as follows: 12 votes in favour, 1 against and 2 abstentions. The draft resolution has thus been adopted as resolution 687 (1991).

I shall now call on those members of the Council who wish to make statements following the voting.

[82] **Mr. Pickering (United States of America):**

...

The Council has just acted on one of the most important proposals ever placed before it. This resolution is unique and historic. It fulfils the hope of mankind to make the United Nations an instrument of peace and stability. The text before the Council is comprehensive. It has its own internal logic and coherence. It endeavours to get at the core problems which led us into the Gulf crisis, and it shows us what must be done to lead us out. The resolution lays the groundwork for the permanent cease-fire which all parties desire and for the withdrawal of coalition forces from Iraqi territory. It relies heavily on the Secretary-General and the United Nations for its implementation in an unprecedented elaboration of the role of the United Nations in peace-keeping and peace-making, and it establishes clear incentives for rapid implementation and tradeoffs which will in stages produce a return to normalcy and non-belligerency in the Gulf.

As soon as Iraq accepts the provisions of the resolution a formal cease-fire becomes effective, and as Iraq meets the stipulations of the resolution the sanctions regime will be modified, the role of the Secretary-General in overseeing the return to normal relations will be solidified, the coalition forces will be withdrawn, and the mechanisms for implementing the resolution will be put into place.

The involvement of the Secretary-General and the United Nations is central to our approach. We believe this as essential to restoring peace as it was to the defeat of aggression. The Secretary-General and the United Nations are involved in the demarcation of the Iraq-Kuwait border, the deployment of observers, the activation of a special commission to oversee the elimination of weapons of mass destruction, the creation of a compensation regime, the return of Kuwaiti property and the control of arms sales to Iraq.

This is a time of testing for the United Nations and a time of destiny as well. The international community acted through the United Nations to bring an end to aggression and lawlessness. It must now act as well to restore international peace and security.

This resolution is tough, but it is fair. It is fair because it sets out the path by which Iraq can take its place again in the world community. We desire to see that happen with an Iraq which is protected from dismemberment.

Positive steps and attempts to compensate for the damage that has been done will be rewarded and the bitter experience of the past eight months will not be repeated. The unusually long preamble to the resolution outlines the context for Council action and now we begin to put the Gulf war behind us. The resolution focuses on the bases for restoration of peace and security to the region. Foremost among these is respect for the border. The Council notes that Iraq and Kuwait signed Agreed Minutes in 1963 regarding their mutual border. Kuwait registered this Agreement with the United Nations in accordance with Article 102 of the Charter and it was published in the United Nations Treaty Series.

Iraq never protested the Agreement or its registration with the United Nations. But in August 1990 Iraq invaded, occupied and attempted to annex Kuwait. Through the Council, the international community has rejected Iraq's actions. And through the Council, the international community has ejected Iraq from Kuwait. Our task now, consistent with our responsibilities under Chapter VII, is to establish peace in such a way that Iraq never again threatens Kuwait's sovereignty and integrity. For that reason, the resolution demands that Iraq and Kuwait respect their international boundary as it was agreed upon in 1963, asks the Secretary-General to lend his assistance to make arrangements with Kuwait and Iraq to demarcate the boundary and decides to guarantee the inviolability of that boundary.

The circumstances that are before us are unique in the history of the United Nations, and this resolution is tailored exclusively to these circumstances. By this action, the Security Council has only acted to restore international peace in a case where one State violated another's boundary and attempted to destroy that State's very existence by force. Certainly, the United States does not seek, nor will it support, a new role for the Security Council as the body that determines international boundaries. Border disputes are issues to be negotiated directly between States or resolved through other pacific means of settlement available, as set out in Chapter VII of the Charter.

Next, the resolution creates a demilitarized zone and calls for the immediate deployment of an observer force. Its purpose is to deter threats to peace through its very presence astride the Iraq-Kuwait border. And the deployment of observers is one of the necessary conditions if the end of the coalition's presence in Iraq is not to court new dangers.

The next problem is that of weapons of mass destruction - chemical, biological and nuclear - and the missiles with which to deliver them. We have taken extraordinary care in these sections of the resolution to be precise and thorough, as required by the extraordinary circumstances of Iraq's past use of and the threats to use or develop such weapons. The region simply cannot be secure if these weapons remain at the disposal of Iraq. And so, the Council, in this resolution, decides on their elimination in Iraq. We ask the Secretary-General and a Special Commission to plan for and destroy Iraq's chemical and biological weapons and ballistic missiles.

Another section provides for the establishment of coordination between the Secretary-General and the Special Commission and the International Atomic Energy Agency (IAEA) to deal with Iraq's evident clandestine programme to acquire nuclear weapons. The resolution breaks further new ground in requiring Iraq to forswear future efforts to develop such weapons and in establishing a mechanism for international monitoring of Iraq's compliance with these provisions.

Finally, the text makes clear that this attempt by the international community to deal with the unique problem posed by Iraq takes place in a larger, regional context.

The Council is taking other major steps in the area of liability for damage and compensation. The resolution establishes a process of settlement by which all who have suffered direct damage or injury as a result of the illegal Iraqi aggression can claim and receive compensation. It creates a Fund to pay compensation for future claims and a Commission to administer that Fund. The Secretary-General will have a key role in bringing this process into being and will make recommendations to the Council. The Fund will be supported by Iraq's contribution of a certain percentage of its oil revenues, and it is our suggestion that the Fund in turn pay the costs of administering the compensation programme so that it is self-supporting. While no fund will be large enough to handle all the claims against Iraq, this standing mechanism should at least provide the international community a recourse which is financed by Iraq without, as is the Council's clear intent, placing an unbearable burden on Iraq's economy.

Then we come to the question of sanctions. The resolution creates a dynamic and flexible process which links the removal of sanctions to the implementation of the resolution. This is the incentive to implement fully the resolution as soon as possible. Sanctions relating to foodstuffs and supplies for essential civilian needs are lifted at once, subject to certain procedural arrangements. Upon implementation of the provisions dealing with weapons of mass destruction and the compensation regime, the sanctions against Iraq's exports will also be lifted. In the interim, in order to generate financial resources to ensure support of the civilian population, the sanctions Committee is authorized, when necessary, to grant exceptions to the sanctions against Iraqi exports. And the Council will review the sanctions on exports to Iraq every 60 days, in the light of Iraq's policies and implementation of this and preceding resolutions of the Council. Of course, the appropriate committees and States will continue to enforce the sanctions regime as long as any of its parts remains in place. Sales related to chemical, biological and nuclear weapons development and missiles are banned permanently. In the specific case of conventional arms sales to Iraq, a different approach is taken. All aspects of military sales to Iraq will continue to be prohibited, and the Secretary-General will develop implementation guidelines for encouraging implementation. This ban on conventional weapons will be reviewed 120 days after passage and regularly thereafter in the light of Iraq's compliance with this resolution and general progress towards arm control in the region.

In addition to these major innovations, the resolution also provides for the continuation of the return of Kuwaiti property, to which Iraq is committed. It rejects any Iraqi claims for non-performance of contracts due to the crisis that Iraq itself created and reconfirms Iraq's responsibility to repatriate and account for all Kuwait and third country nationals in cooperation with the International Committee of the Red Cross. As a result of Iraq's unprecedented taking of hostages and its open threats to use terrorism in the recent conflict, the resolution requires a commitment from Iraq that it will not in the future commit or support acts of terrorism or terrorist organizations. Upon Iraq's agreement to the terms of the resolution, a formal cease-fire enters into effect, which will make possible the withdrawal of coalition forces from Iraq. Following deployment of the United Nations observers, coalition forces will withdraw from Iraq as rapidly as possible, consistent with operational requirements and logistic considerations. As the processes created by the resolution come into being, we are prepared to work closely with the Secretary-General and other interested parties. In order to facilitate its work, we propose to play an active role in the Special Commission where we and other members of the five permanent members of this body have necessary expertise, which we can make available to it.

We are again today turning a new page in the Council's affairs. This resolution to establish peace and security in the region has no precedent, for the circumstances it addresses are without precedent in the history of the United Nations. Troops have gone into battle before under the United Nations Charter, but the United Nations has never before taken measures to rebuild the peace such as those contained in this historic resolution.

The resolution does not answer every question, but it points the way. Iraq's active participation is essential for this approach to work. It is our hope that the people of Iraq will insist on putting the disaster which their leaders have created behind them and will join with the rest of the international community in building a foundation for lasting peace and security. This means repudiation of the policies of the past and a genuine commitment to the principles of the United Nations Charter, which Saddam Hussein has heretofore acknowledged more through violation than through commitment.

If the people of Iraq will work with us as stability in the Gulf region returns and military tensions recede the international community can turn to assisting with the reconstruction of Iraq as well as of Kuwait, and as the process we are launching today goes forward my Government will exploit whatever opportunities there may be for unblocking progress on the resolution of other problems in the region, including Arab-Israeli issues.

We have opportunities before us now in the Gulf and in the Middle East which my Government is determined not to waste.

...

[92] **Mr. ROCHEREAU de la SABLIERE (France)** (interpretation from French):

...

A month ago France welcomed the adoption of resolution 686 (1991), because it paved the way for a cease-fire. My delegation then favoured the United Nations immediately undertaking the task of consolidating the end of hostilities in a durable manner.

The resolution that we have just adopted, of which we were a sponsor, is designed to attain that objective. Its purpose is to establish a proper cease-fire between Iraq and Kuwait as well as the States Members cooperating with Kuwait in the implementation of resolution 678 (1990). It also sets forth conditions for the withdrawal from Iraqi territory of the forces of the States cooperating with Kuwait.

But, over and above the objective of the cease-fire, which will make it possible for a decisive step to be taken in resolving the Gulf conflict, resolution 687 (1991) also provides important elements which should contribute in the longer term to re-establishing regional security.

In that regard a number of provisions are fundamental: Here I mention first the guarantee of the inviolability of the international boundary between Kuwait and Iraq and the deployment there of a United Nations observer unit. I would also mention the disarmament measures with regard to Iraq, and particularly the reaffirmation of the prohibition of the use of asphyxiating, poisonous or other gases, and of bacteriological methods of warfare, and the need for the destruction of existing stocks.

France has been very insistent that the prohibition on Iraq's possessing biological or chemical weapons and all the arms restriction measures concerning it should be seen in the perspective of regional measures universally approved by the international community. Nevertheless, we agree that under present circumstances their application should be confined in the immediate future to the case of Iraq. Nevertheless, the global and regional scope of our objective is clearly brought out by the resolution, which reflects France's position on this essential point.

The resolution reaffirms Iraq's responsibility under international law for the losses and damages of all kinds resulting from its aggression against Kuwait. In this connection, it provides for setting up machinery for the payment of claims. The principle of reparations was first set out in resolution 674 (1990). In particular, Mr. Ahtisaari's report gave us details about the damage to Kuwait - notably its oil industry. It is only fair that such losses should be properly compensated for by reparations.

The Secretary-General and the United Nations bear heavy responsibilities in the three areas that I have mentioned - the border, disarmament and reparations. The provisions made in this regard respond to our desire to see our Organization play an important role in re-establishing peace in the region.

In the immediate future, the public health and food situation in Iraq demands that everything be done to enable its population, throughout the territory, to return to conditions of normal life. France is gravely concerned about the plight of the civilian population.

A number of United Nations missions, particularly that headed by Mr. Ahtisaari, have revealed the extent of the tragic situation. Unfortunately, the civilian population is not only suffering from the serious material difficulties that the Under-Secretary-General described, but is the victim of unjustifiable violence in both the south and the north, where the inhabitants of Kurdish origin have once again, tragically, been attacked. We believe that the Security Council has a duty to say something about this situation.

The necessary goal of the restoration of lasting peace in the Gulf should not involve measures that are unnecessarily punitive or vindictive against the Iraqi people. It would be unjust if they were held responsible for the actions of their leaders.

That is why the resolution we have just adopted lifts with immediate effect - subject to notification - all the prohibitions set forth in resolution 661 (1990) regarding the sale or supply to Iraq of foodstuffs, as well as related financial transactions. At the same time, it eases the conditions under which Iraq may import essential supplies.

That is also why the resolution provides for Iraq's being able, with the agreement of the Committee on sanctions, to export certain commodities in order to obtain the necessary resources to finance the purchase of essential supplies.

However, our country is well aware that the return to normal living conditions in Iraq is far from being dependent solely on the lifting of sanctions. Therefore, France appeals to the Iraqi authorities to put an end immediately to repression in all its forms and to enter into an unrestricted dialogue about respect for rights, democratization of public life and the realization of the legitimate aspirations of all sections of the Iraqi people. *Inter alia*, it is essential that the just claim of the Kurdish community for respect for its identity within the Iraqi State be fully recognized.

It is now eight months since the Council, in close cooperation with the Secretary-General, fully shouldered its responsibilities with respect to the crisis caused by Iraq's invasion of Kuwait. The momentum should be maintained, as should be our determination to defend the law, a determination that should be applied to setting other conflicts in the Near and Middle East.

...

[95] **Mr. Li Daoyu (China)** (interpretation from Chinese):

...

More than one month has elapsed since the suspension of hostilities in the Gulf region. The international community and especially countries and peoples in that region ardently hope to see the early realization of a formal cease-fire and the withdrawal of foreign military forces so as to create conditions for restoring peace and security in the region, healing the wounds of war in Kuwait and other countries and rebuilding their national economy.

The Chinese delegation, in keeping with its consistent position of opposing the Iraqi invasion and standing for a peaceful settlement of the Gulf crisis, supports the Security Council in its adoption of a resolution on a formal cease-fire. In this regard, China adheres to the following principles:

First, we stand for early realization of a formal cease-fire, the deployment of a United Nations observer unit along the boundary between Kuwait and Iraq and the withdrawal of foreign military forces from the Gulf region, with a view to restoring peace and stability in the region.

Second, on the boundary question, China has always held that the countries concerned should reach agreement and settle the question through negotiations and consultations in accordance with international law. Hence, we respect the agreement on the boundary question reached by Kuwait and Iraq in 1963 through negotiations. In our view, the Agreed Minutes, long ago registered with the United Nations, constitute an effective and legal document.

Third, we are in favour of destroying the Iraqi biological and chemical weapons, and we maintain that the balanced-and-comprehensive principle should be pursued in the control of armament in the Middle East region. We support the goal of establishing a zone free from weapons of mass destruction in the Middle East.

Fourth, the Iraqi invasion has inflicted enormous losses on Kuwait. Victims from Kuwait and other countries are entitled to get compensation from Iraq. However, in actual practice, consideration should be given to the requirements of the people of Iraq and in particular their humanitarian needs, and to Iraq's payment capacity and the needs of Iraqi economic reconstruction.

Fifth, we are in favour of immediate abolition of restrictions on imports into Iraq of foodstuffs and other goods required for the restoration of the people's normal life, and the timely and gradual lifting of other economic sanctions against Iraq in light of the development of the situation.

Sixth, we support Kuwait in its request for immediate release and repatriation of all the Kuwaiti prisoners of war and civilians detained by Iraq.

Since, in the course of consultations on this resolution, a number of amendments proposed by countries concerned, including China, were accepted, and since this resolution will establish a formal cease-fire in the region, we voted in favour of it.

Nevertheless, we cannot but point out that, although the resolution adopted makes it clear that the deployment of a United Nations observer unit will "establish conditions" for the withdrawal of foreign military forces, it fails to provide an explicit timeframe for the withdrawal of foreign military forces. Furthermore, the resolution includes some unnecessary restrictions on the lifting of economic sanctions against Iraq. The Iraqi people are innocent. The Security Council should, in light of the development of the situation, ease and lift economic sanctions as soon as possible, so as to bring the economy of all the countries in the region back to normality at an early date. We also believe that on questions concerning the implementation of the resolution the Security Council should be responsible for handling these matters; and there should be no other interpretation.

China seeks no self-interest in the Gulf region. We are of the view that the general goal for the post-war arrangements in the Gulf region should be to ensure a lasting peace in the region and peaceful coexistence of peoples of all countries there. Based on this point of view, we maintain that the relevant arrangements should be made mainly by the countries in the Gulf region in conformity with the interests of their peoples, while the sovereignty and territorial integrity of all the countries in the region should be respected and there should be no interference in their internal affairs. We hold that the foregoing principles should be taken into full account in the implementation of this resolution.

...

[98] **Mr. Vorontsov (Union of Soviet Socialist Republics)** (interpretation from Russian):

...

It is commendable that in the elaboration of a sound international legal document in a comparatively short time - in the form of the resolution just adopted - the Security Council, on the basis of successful interaction between the Five and all the members of the Security Council as a whole, has been able to draw a line under one of the most serious regional conflicts of recent times and to promote the process of the establishment of lasting peace and stability in the Persian Gulf region, and in the long run in the Middle East as a whole. This is in accordance with the vital interests of the peoples of Kuwait, Iraq and other countries in the region, and also with the task of strengthening peace throughout the world.

The Kuwait crisis and the process of eliminating it were a serious test of the soundness of the new thinking, the new system of international relations. I think we can state with some gratification today that the international community, in the person of the United Nations and its Security Council, has passed that test and demonstrated that a considerable path has been travelled between the cold war and the new system of international relations. The Security Council has proved in practice its ability to implement its obligation under the Charter of the United Nations to maintain and restore international peace and security.

In the resolution adopted today the Security Council has welcomed with satisfaction the restoration of Kuwait's sovereignty, independence and territorial integrity and the return of its legitimate government. It has been possible to achieve this goal because of the unique unanimity demonstrated by the majority of the international community in condemning the aggression, and the resolve to put an end to it within the generally accepted contours of the authority of the United Nations.

The Soviet Union, for its part, did everything in its power to ensure the implementation of the Security Council resolutions by political means. It sought to convince Iraq of the need to heed the will of the international community and not to allow hostilities to escalate to neighbouring countries; and then, when Iraq passed up the opportunity for a peaceful settlement of the conflict, we helped to prevent excessive casualties and destruction. Both during the crisis and in dealing with its aftermath, the Soviet Union has been guided by its fundamental approach, the humanitarian purport of which is that peoples should finally be spared suffering and losses in payment for the crimes and ambitions of their rulers.

The requirements of the resolution adopted are aimed not only at restoring justice but at issuing a serious warning to all those who might be inclined to embark on the path of aggression, occupation and annexation. The international community has finally learned the bitter lesson of the 1930s, when an unchecked aggressor seized one small neighbour after another and plunged the world into general warfare at the cost of tens of millions of human lives. On this occasion, the United Nations proved equal to the situation and acted in accordance with its Charter. However, the peace that has been restored needs to be soundly strengthened.

The crux of the resolution just adopted is to turn the temporary cessation of hostilities into a permanent cease-fire between Iraq and Kuwait and those States cooperating with Kuwait after official notification by Iraq of its acceptance of the resolution. The deployment on the Kuwait-Iraqi boundaries of United Nations observers will create conditions for the withdrawal of the multinational forces from that region. An important element in this process is the demarcation of the boundaries between Iraq and Kuwait in accordance with the agreement to that effect deposited with the United Nations. It is of prime importance to observe the provision that the task of ensuring the inviolability of the boundary between Iraq and Kuwait be borne by the Security Council, which, to that end, may take all necessary steps in accordance with the Charter of the United Nations.

The resolution we have adopted paves the way to forming a post-crisis settlement. In that connection, the most acute issue is that of creating an effective barrier against the use of weapons of mass destruction in that region. From that viewpoint, of great importance are the provisions in the resolution regarding Iraq's destruction of chemical and biological weapons and longer-range missiles, which represent a direct threat to countries in the region, and in the context of Iraq's confirmation of its obligations of the Geneva Protocol of 1925 to bring into play the International Atomic Energy Agency to supervise nuclear sites in Iraq and efforts to create in the Middle East an area free from all such weapons. It is also important that all Middle Eastern countries accede to the non-proliferation Treaty and those international agreements prohibiting chemical and biological weapons. Serious thought should be given to the question of the balanced reduction of supplies of conventional weapons to that region, which is even now overflowing with the most up-to-date varieties of those weapons. The first step along this path is an embargo on supplying arms and military *matériel* to Iraq.

An important function in ensuring the post-crisis settlement in this region belongs to the United Nations, which should play the role of a reliable guarantor of security. This logically derives from the role of the Security Council in organizing the efforts collectively to repulse the Iraqi aggression, and from Security Council resolution 598 (1987).

A key role in determining the parameters of the post-crisis settlement must belong to the States of the region. However, we should not allow the creation of bloc groupings, which would lead to perpetuating old and promoting the emergence of new problems and disagreements. The post-crisis settlement should not be aimed against anyone in particular, but should rather be intended to promote cooperation among all the States of the region concerned, as well as those States that are not directly involved but make an important contribution to the maintenance of peace and stability there. In that context, we should like to state that Iraq, as a sovereign State, must take its rightful place in the political and economic infrastructure of the region. Relations among States in the region should at the same time be based on such fundamental principles of international law as non-intervention in each other's internal affairs, the non-use or threat of use of force, the settlement of disputes by peaceful means, the recognition of the right of all countries of the region to sovereignty and territorial integrity within existing, internationally recognized boundaries.

The adoption of this resolution provides the necessary conditions to restore normal economic relations in the region, the speedy elimination of the consequences of the ecological crisis, and compensation for the damage which has been caused to Kuwait and its people. In particular, those maritime areas that have been polluted by oil will have to be purified, and over 500 burning oil wells will have to be extinguished in Kuwait, which will require considerable effort.

The resolution, we believe, properly reflects the need for a solution to be found to Kuwait's and Iraq's humanitarian problems. Its adoption will make it possible immediately to proceed to supply foodstuffs and medicine, as well as goods and materials intended to meet the fundamental needs of the civilian population. This is of vital importance to the people of Iraq, which is on the brink of starvation and an epidemiological catastrophe.

In summary, I should like to emphasize that, in order to strengthen our success, we must maintain the high degree of interaction already achieved, as well as the cooperation between States Members of the United Nations in the post-crisis period. The steady normalization of the region will have a positive impact on the climate throughout the entire Middle East and will help to resolve the Arab-Israeli conflict. The Soviet Union is prepared, in active cooperation with all parties concerned, to make its own contribution in this regard.

The resolution adopted represents a major step towards a durable settlement in the Persian Gulf. Now that it is adopted, we should begin detailed work on those matters connected with the technical aspects and the financial implications of its implementation. Considerable work in preparing the necessary plans and recommendations will have to be done by the Secretary-General of the United Nations. The Security Council for its part should play a key role in keeping under constant supervision the entire process of implementing the resolution and take additional steps that may be required as its provisions are implemented.

This is the first time that the international community has demonstrated its united will in the face of one State occupying another. Possibly, this is not an ideal precedent in all respects, but we would like to believe that it may prevent such situations recurring in the future. The occurrence of such situations on the threshold of the twenty-first century is not in harmony with the new era in international politics, which may be difficult but is gradually emerging. If we all help those new trends to gain strength, then mankind will live in conditions of genuine security.

...

[104-105] **Mr. Ayala Lasso (Ecuador)** (interpretation from Spanish):

...

The resolution which the Council has just adopted is of vital importance, for two fundamental reasons: first, because it formally marks the end of the phase of hostilities in the Gulf conflict and seeks to establish the foundations for a stable, permanent peace in the region; and, secondly, because its provisions refer to matters of great gravity and importance which must, therefore, reflect a genuine advance towards consolidating the rule of law in international relations.

We must, therefore, be extremely careful to continue to seek to solve the Gulf conflict in strict conformity with the rules of international law enshrined in the Charter. For Ecuador, it is particularly significant that the two resolutions in the discussion of which we have taken part as a member of the Council - resolution 686 (1991) and the resolution the Council has just adopted - unequivocally confirm the nullity of territorial conquest by force. In that regard, my country stresses the relevance of resolutions 2625 (XXV) of 24 October 1970 and 42/22 of 18 November 1987, unanimously adopted by the General Assembly of our Organization, whose fundamental principles have been confirmed by the Council in this specific matter.

Lasting peace cannot be based otherwise than on justice and law. Victory should serve only to restore law when it has been broken, not to change it. If that were not so, peace would stand on shaky, weak ground, and, as history has taught us on more than one occasion, could sow the seeds of fresh conflicts in the future.

Ecuador believes that efforts have been made to ensure that the provisions of the resolution fall within the bounds of Chapter VII of the United Nations Charter. We consider it necessary that participation by the countries of the region in the diplomatic arrangements leading to the establishment of lasting international peace and security should be accorded all the importance it deserves.

It is also both positive and necessary that measures should be taken to put an end to the present arms race and prevent this tendency from emerging throughout the region. The presence of peace-keeping forces under United Nations authority will also be salutary; our Organization should be present and should cooperate in re-establishing and keeping the peace. Ecuador believes that any measures adopted to establish a nuclear-weapon free zone in the region deserve its support. It is also timely to insist on observance of the international agreements which prohibit the use of asphyxiating and toxic gases and bacterial warfare and which seek the universal elimination of chemical and biological weapons.

The measures adopted in the resolution in those respects are essentially constructive, and are a response to an objective reality in the area.

It is obvious that Kuwait has the right to live peacefully within its legitimately established borders, in accordance with the law. In taking a position on the territorial boundary between Iraq and Kuwait and in requesting the Secretary-General to make arrangements with both countries to demarcate the boundary, acting within the scope of Chapter VII of the Charter, the Council has made the interpretation that this case is one of the exceptions envisaged in Article 36, which says that the Security Council:

> "... should also take into consideration that legal disputes should as a general rule be referred by the parties to the International Court of Justice in accordance with the provisions of the Statute of the Court".

Ecuador does not share this interpretation of the Charter.

While Chapter VII of the Charter authorizes the use of all necessary means to implement the resolutions of the Council, it cannot confer on the Council more powers than those set forth in the Charter itself. A position of the Council in this matter, which is an extremely sensitive one, must fall unequivocally within the bounds of international law and of the United Nations Charter if it is not to become a fresh source of conflict.

For those reasons, if it had been possible to vote separately on the individual paragraphs of the draft resolution before us, Ecuador would have indicated its disagreement with those points which deal with the boundary between Iraq and Kuwait.

Ecuador has taken note with satisfaction of the statement by the representative of the United States to the effect that the present case of the boundary between Iraq and Kuwait cannot be considered in any way as an applicable precedent: its character as an exception is its particular distinguishing feature. The fact that several other delegations have concurred in expressing that view strengthens the validity of the principle Ecuador has stated.

Ecuador considers that the Council must also approve the lifting of the sanctions, which are affecting the civilian population of Iraq. The sanctions measures adopted in the Committee set up under resolution 661 (1990), positive and well-aimed though they may be, require action by the Council to lift them; this, indeed, is indicated in the report by the Secretary-General in document S/22409. My Government also considers that we must move towards taking the necessary action, as provided for by the resolution, so that the definitive withdrawal of the coalition forces can take place.

Ecuador is firm in its desire to strengthen the world Organization and the Council in their primary functions of preserving international peace and security, and it therefore believes that this process cannot be carried out unless there is strict obedience to the principles, ground rules and areas of competence set out in the Charter as the sole guarantee for maintaining the international legal order in full force and ensuring the integrity, sovereignty and peaceful coexistence of States. These considerations, which are of great general importance, are even more important for small countries which find their sole protection and refuge in their attachment to the law.

It is only on the basis of law and respect between States that the building of a stable peace can be guaranteed. We must come to a redefinition of collective security which incorporates all the new, positive elements originating in recent Security Council resolutions and in the developments in international society in the past few months, a redefinition which would, moreover, draw together the painful experiences of the Gulf crisis. It falls to the Arab nation to play an important role in solving all the problems of the region, just as all of us should take part in the task of building a more peaceful, more just world.

There are many provisions in the resolution we have adopted which, although they could have been improved upon, do constitute a suitable response by the international community, and the Security Council in particular, to the Gulf crisis which was created by the invasion, annexation and destruction of Kuwait by Iraq. My country wishes to place on record its agreements with those provisions. However, because of the misgivings I have expressed in respect of part A of the operative part of the resolution, concerning the boundary between Iraq and Kuwait, my country abstained in the vote.

...

[111] **Sir David Hannay (United Kingdom):**

...

The resolution we have just adopted marks an important milestone both in the crisis which began with Iraq's unprovoked and brutal invasion and annexation of Kuwait last August and in the overall development of the United Nations.

For more than five months the Security Council tried, by every means at its disposal short of the use of force, to bring about Iraq's withdrawal from Kuwait. During that period Iraq rejected every diplomatic approach made to it, systematically pillaged Kuwait and abused its population and, in the graphic words of the Secretary-General's recent report, pursued a deliberate attempt to extinguish that country. Faced by Iraq's refusal to withdraw peacefully, the coalition, specifically authorized to do so by the Council, had to use force to liberate Kuwait and to restore its sovereignty and its legitimate Government. My country is proud to have played its part in that just cause and to salute the courage and the professionalism of all those who fought so effectively to enable it to prevail.

But the expulsion of Iraq from Kuwait and the latter's liberation are of far greater and of far more positive significance for all countries in the world, and for this Organization as a whole, than the many regional conflicts with which we have tried to grapple over recent decades. They have marked a clear, firm and effective determination of the world community not to allow the law of the jungle to overcome the rule of law. They have shown that the Security Council, with not only the solidarity of its permanent members but with supporting votes from countries representing every region of the world, has been able to act to repel aggression in the way its founding fathers intended it to do. There are many small countries in each region of the world which have cause to worry about their larger, better-armed neighbours. They should be able to sleep more securely in their beds after this episode. Just think, on the contrary, how they would have felt if Saddam Hussein had been allowed by the United Nations to enjoy the fruits of his aggression.

Now the military action to liberate Kuwait is complete, and we face the far more difficult task of securing the peace - in the words of resolution 678 (1990), of restoring international peace and security in the area. Just as the Security Council had the primary responsibility to reverse the aggression, so it also has the responsibility to lay sound foundations for the future and to ensure that we are not again confronted with such a ruthless and comprehensive challenge to international law. That is the object of the resolution, and that is the yardstick by which it should be measured.

The resolution is a complex and detailed one, designed to cover the entire field traversed by the Council as it adopted the previous 13 resolutions. Only such a comprehensive approach has any hope of achieving the balance between firmness and fairness which is essential if lasting peace and stability are to be achieved. I have no intention of commenting on all its aspects, but I would like to concentrate on three crucial areas.

First, there is the question of the boundary between Iraq and Kuwait and of the future security of that small country, living always next door, as it is bound to do, to its larger and more powerful neighbour. The resolution is not attempting to settle the boundary between these two countries; that was done by the 1963 Agreement between them, which was registered with the United Nations. But the failure to demarcate that boundary and the determination of Iraq to raise territorial claims that are incompatible with the 1963 Agreement are at the roots of this dispute, and they must be addressed. Rapid demarcation of the boundary, the setting up of a United Nations unit to monitor a demilitarized zone along the frontier and a guarantee by the Security Council to step in if ever it is violated again are a carefully integrated package designed to ensure that there is no repetition of the events of last August. My Government is well aware of the great sensitivity to many Members of the Organization of the question of defining boundaries. We have no desire and no intention of overturning the principle that it is for the parties in question to negotiate and reach agreement, as was done in this case in 1932 and 1963. But, naturally, the Security Council has a duty to respond when disputes over boundaries arise and come to threaten international peace and security.

The second important issue I would mention is that of arms control and, in particular, the elimination of Iraqi weapons of mass destruction and of the missiles that can be used for their delivery. The resolution contains tough provisions for the destruction of Iraqi chemical and biological weapons and missiles and for ensuring that Iraq's attempts to evade its obligations under the Treaty on the Non-Proliferation of Nuclear Weapons and develop a nuclear-weapons programme are frustrated and never repeated. It is surely right to do so. For Iraq alone in the region has not only developed many of these weapons, it has actually used them both against a neighbouring State and against its own population, and it has made the threat of their use part of the daily discourse of its diplomacy as it has attempted to bully and to coerce its neighbours. That must be stopped if there is to be peace and security in the region. It is frankly a sick joke to argue that Iraq needs these weapons for its own security and defence. But action against Iraq's weapons of mass destruction must clearly not be the end of the affair, a one-off operation, and that is why the resolution so clearly situates this action within the wider framework of work towards a whole region free of weapons of mass destruction and, indeed, towards even wider actions - for example to outlaw chemical weapons worldwide. If the example of Iraq gives the impetus we would like to see given to such wider negotiations, then some good will have come out of the evil wrought by Saddam Hussein.

Similar considerations apply to the maintenance of a strict arms embargo on other weapons. It is Iraq's spending spree over recent years, linked to the aggressive policies of its ruler, which have so destabilized the security of the Gulf area. We hope the guidelines for the embargo which the Secretary-General has been asked to draw up will pay particular attention to the activities of countries engaged in the procurement of military equipment on behalf of Iraq.

Then, thirdly, there is the question of compensation for the appalling damage inflicted on Kuwait and many others by the Iraqi armed forces and their leadership. To take the two extremes to be avoided, it surely is quite unacceptable simply to overlook or to forget the need for compensation. Millions of dollars worth of Kuwait's irreplaceable natural resources are being destroyed every day, Kuwait's economy and infrastructure have been wantonly wrecked, dreadful environmental damage has been caused to the whole Gulf region and many companies and individuals have suffered appalling losses. On the other hand, it makes no sense at all so to cripple Iraq and its economy with the burden of paying for this damage that it is in fact unable to do so. The resolution seeks to tread a path between these two extremes by making financial provision for meeting claims out of a limited proportion of Iraq's future oil revenues. It is important to remember that what is really crippling the Iraqi economy already is the incredible burden of the military expenditure Saddam Hussein has loaded onto it - 28 per cent of Iraq's gross national product in 1988 was devoted to military expenditure. That is indeed a figure that gives pause for thought. Paying for two disastrous wars is what has brought the Iraqi economy to its knees. There is no reason at all why an Iraq, once rid of this terrible load of military expenditure and blessed as it is with the second-largest unused oil reserves in the world, should not be able both to assure a reasonable measure of economic development and prosperity to its people and to meet claims for compensation.

Iraq now has a clear choice. It can, by accepting this resolution and by implementing it rapidly and honestly, turn its back on the errors and crimes of the recent past; or it can perpetuate the suffering and damage for a further period until it becomes intolerable. If the rulers of Iraq opt for the second choice, they will once again have shown that they put personal ambition and the lust for domination at home and abroad above the welfare of their own people. It will be yet another tragic mistake in a long series of such mistakes.

My Government believes that it will in fact prove impossible for Iraq to rejoin the community of civilized nations while Saddam Hussein remains in power. Nothing illustrates this point better than the brutal repression that is taking place in Iraq now of all those, Kurds and others, who want a different sort of Iraq from the totalitarian tyranny of recent years. This Council must now urgently find an appropriate response to the human tragedy unfolding in the mountains of North Iraq and along the Turkish frontier. Our quarrel has always been and remains with Saddam Hussein and his cronies, not with the people of Iraq. We have recently been having contacts with many members of the Iraqi opposition, Sunni and Shia, Arab and Kurd. We have been impressed by their desire to cooperate together, to establish democracy and respect for human rights in Iraq, as well as to preserve its territorial integrity and its sovereignty. We share those goals. We too would be happy to see democracy and respect for human rights established in an Iraq whole within its present borders and free from tyranny.

...

[116] **Mr. Hohenfellner (Austria):**

...

Today the Security Council has taken another big step, in many ways an unprecedented one: on the one hand, this testifies to how far we, the Security Council, have come, and to what extent we are now able to cooperate, for such a resolution would previously have been impossible to achieve. On the other hand, the Council, by adopting such a comprehensive decision, also now assumes grave and unprecedented responsibilities.

I do not propose to comment on specific elements of the text. Suffice it to say that we are satisfied to see some of our ideas adequately reflected therein, in particular as far as humanitarian aspects are concerned. Instead, I should like to offer a few remarks of a more general and, indeed, forward-looking nature.

When I first addressed the Council on 14 February, I underlined the paradigmatic importance of the way we deal with, and finally resolve this conflict - not only for the future of the region, but also for the concept of collective security and the role of the United Nations as a whole. History will be the judge of whether we have chosen the right approach. Today, we can only say, in all honesty, we did what seemed best.

Power, as the old saying goes, grows out of the barrel of a gun. But peace does not: it grows out of human hearts and minds. The Security Council Committee established by resolution 661 (1990) acted, I believe, in this very spirit when it took, on 22 March, its decision on the determination of the humanitarian needs of the Iraqi people.

The resolution today also contains important provisions that should help to alleviate the grave situation the civilians in Iraq are facing. They can, however, only form the beginning of a larger process: a comprehensive, internationally concerted system of relief operations will be necessary in order to bring the fundamental basics of civilian life, like proper nutrition, waste disposal, health services, agriculture and related transport and communication facilities, back to normal. A number of States, from all regional groups. have sent, or are currently sending, relief goods to Iraq. Competent United Nations agencies and programmes, as well as the International Committee of the Red Cross, have already begun to help. But their resources are limited. It will be indispensable to raise funds by asking States and individuals for their generous support to assist the innocent civilian population. This could perhaps best be done in the form of an appeal by the Secretary-General. Aid for the vulnerable groups of the civilian population is not only needed desperately, it is also needed without delay.

Austria is also gravely concerned about reports of heavy fighting and bloodshed in Iraq with disastrous consequences for the civilian population, in particular in the area inhabited by Kurds and others. We hope, like the Secretary-General in his statement to the press of 2 April 1991, that maximum restraint will be exercised and urge that the present situation be resolved peacefully without further loss of life and suffering.

Yesterday Turkey informed you, Mr. President, about the plight of some 220,000 Iraqi citizens, many of them women and children, who are massed along the Turkish border. The world cannot idly stand by when international humanitarian and human rights norms are grossly violated. With a view to safeguarding the human rights of the Kurds and other persons threatened by the armed repression of the Iraqi Government forces, my Government therefore endorses both the request of Turkey that the Security Council urgently deal with that alarming situation and take effective measures and the position of France that the Security Council should pronounce itself on these pressing issues.

Every battle comes to an end. Fortunately, the end, in this instance, was timely. The task of now maintaining peace is endless, sometimes mundane, but ultimately even more challenging. Some elements of our decision today are of particular relevance in this respect. One is the deployment of United Nations observers. Austria has already declared its readiness to participate, at short notice, in such an operation. We look forward with interest to the Secretary-General's plan, in particular to the proposed duration of the operation. We see it as a provisional measure that should contribute to creating conditions conducive to negotiations. Another area to be covered in this plan will be the financing of this operation. I wonder whether this would not be the right moment to look into an idea put forward by other members of the Council some time ago, namely the provision of special contributions by those who benefit most by such an operation and are financially in a position to do so, be they States or private entities. This could possibly best be done by voluntary contributions to the working capital fund of the United Nations.

This resolution is rightly based on the premise that the relevant actions to be taken by Iraq represent only first steps towards the goal of establishing a zone free from weapons of mass destruction and all missiles for their delivery in the Middle East and towards the objective of a global ban on chemical weapons. It also highlights the objective of achieving a balanced and comprehensive control of armaments in the region. This will require a responsible approach on the part of the main suppliers of arms and of their buyers alike.

Austria does not believe that the role of the Security Council should end here. The security system that we are starting to establish today in the Gulf will need to be integrated into a broader regional approach, including a settlement of the Arab-Israeli conflict and the Palestinian problem. This obviously cannot be done overnight in one isolated act, but rather through a process which will require time to develop and to be carried out. Consequently, we need all the more to take the first steps as soon as possible. The elimination of economic tensions as a potential source of conflict is another task as well.

Let me conclude by offering a few more thoughts on what Sir Brian Urquhart has called "Learning from the Gulf" (*The New York Review of Books*, 7 March 1991). I have already mentioned the need for arms control, non-proliferation of weapons of mass destruction, restraint with regard to the flow of arms in sensitive regions, tackling economic disparities and the settlement of other conflicts. But there is more. One lesson from this crisis is, indubitably, that the preventive capacity of the United Nations has finally to be strengthened. There is already no shortage of ideas: closer monitoring of potentially dangerous situations both by the Security Council itself and the Secretary-General and the preventive deployment of United Nations personnel as a deterrent and as a trip-wire which could set in motion pre-planned enforcement action under Chapter VII of the Charter. Another lesson is to look more closely into United Nations enforcement action. As my colleague and friend, Ambassador Pickering, himself mentioned in a speech on 4 March, future Security Council recourse to authorizations to use force might well carry more "fine print" on how to apply and command that force. He went on to suggest that "we should begin now to look over the ground of possible United Nations enforcement arrangements as set forth in the Charter". Maybe we should indeed agree on discussing possible lessons from the Gulf crisis and the United Nations response in an appropriate framework.

...

[122] **Mr. Munteanu (Romania):**

...

We have adopted today the fourteenth resolution of the Security Council on the agenda item entitled, "The situation between Iraq and Kuwait". As a sponsor of this resolution, Romania attaches particular importance to all its provisions and believes that its implementation could indeed play a decisive role in the final settlement of the Persian Gulf crisis and in the restoration of peace and security in that area. My country's stand on this issue is well known to the members of the Security Council. We strongly defend the view that there is no justification for the use of force against a sovereign and independent State. That is why Romania condemned the annexation of Kuwait and demanded the unconditional and complete withdrawal of the Iraqi forces from the territory of Kuwait. Romania supported all the resolutions of the Security Council aimed at the liberation of Kuwait. This position is a clear reflection of Romania's strong and consistent commitment to morality and legality in all spheres of domestic and international life. Now we have the opportunity to see the concrete results of the actions taken by the Security Council, because Iraq has finally understood that there is no alternative to respecting the resolutions of the Security Council and the principles of international law as embodied in the Charter of the United Nations. In this context, the present meeting offers an appropriate occasion to welcome again the restoration to Kuwait of its sovereignty, independence and territorial integrity and the return of its legitimate Government, as well as the fact that Security Council resolution 686 (1991) marked the lifting of all the measures imposed under resolution 661 (1990) as they applied to Kuwait. From this point of view, the resolution we adopted a moment ago is of paramount importance. It proves that one of the basic objectives of the Security Council has been fully achieved. Kuwait now enjoys all the attributes of an independent and sovereign member of the international community. For my country, this is a source of particular satisfaction not only at the general political level but also with respect to specific diplomatic work. Romania very recently reopened its Embassy in Kuwait City and will continue to develop its relationship with Kuwait in various fields of cooperation, as well as in international organizations.

It is not the intention of my delegation to establish a hierarchy of the provisions of resolution 687 (1991), which should be considered and interpreted as a whole. Nevertheless, no one can ignore the political, legal and particular value of paragraph 33, by which the Security Council declares that, upon official notification by Iraq to the Secretary-General and to the Security Council of its acceptance of the provisions of the resolution adopted today, a formal cease-fire is effective between Iraq and Kuwait and the Member States cooperating with Kuwait in accordance with resolution 678 (1990). We expect that Iraq will soon make the required notification concerning the acceptance of resolution 687 (1991).

It has been rightly pointed out that the failure of attempts to achieve a peaceful solution to the Persian Gulf crisis has generated tremendous destruction and suffering for the people of Iraq, a part of the great Arab nation. We have deeply regretted the human losses and sufferings. They are indeed considerable. But no one should forget who bears the full responsibility for the invasion of Kuwait, the outbreak of war and its tragic consequences. Therefore, resolution 687 (1991) should be fully implemented by Iraq. It would help to put an end to the existing situation and enable the people of Iraq to regain a dignified place among the peace-loving peoples and nations and to work for the reconstruction of the economic infrastructure of the country and for the well-being of the entire Iraqi population. We are sure that the Iraq of tomorrow will enjoy the respect and sympathy of all the States of the international community.

My delegation notes with interest the provisions of resolution 687 (1991) concerning the creation of a fund to pay compensation for claims addressed to Iraq by foreign Governments, nationals and corporations as a result of Iraq's unlawful invasion and occupation of Kuwait. We understand that the implementation of those provisions will not affect the implementation of recommendations of the Security Council Committee established by resolution 661 (1990).

Requests for assistance made by Member States under the provisions of Article 50 of the Charter should be given the most serious attention by the Security Council. All the countries that have invoked Article 50 are confronted with special economic problems and difficulties arising from carrying out measures established by resolution 661 (1990). The Security Council knows very well the price of the implementation of sanctions against Iraq, and therefore we hope it will take appropriate action on the memorandum of 25 March 1991 (*S/22382*) addressed to it by 21 Member States. We also express the hope that the Security Council will make a valuable contribution to meeting the needs of the 31 States identified in the relevant recommendations made under resolution 669 (1990) of 24 September 1990.

At the same time, my delegation would like to emphasize the practical importance of paragraph 17 of resolution 687 (1991), by which the Security Council decides that all Iraqi statements made since 2 August 1990 repudiating its foreign debt are null and void and demands that Iraq scrupulously adhere to all its obligations concerning servicing and repayment of its foreign debt.

The Security Council has today adopted a resolution that is exceptional in all respects. We have in mind its far-reaching consequences for the Gulf area, world peace and security and the role of the United Nations in the peace-making process. Many new tasks are entrusted to the Secretary-General. Some, or even most, of them will be quite a novelty. The success of the resolution's implementation will depend on the degree of success of the Secretary-General in this endeavour. Therefore, my delegation would like to reiterate its full support for the Secretary-General in his noble mission during this very significant period in the whole history of this world Organization.

We are now facing a new chapter in the life of the United Nations. In matters of substance what counts now is to have solid guarantees that Iraq will commit no further violations of the Charter and the basic principles of international law.

Like other delegations, we are ready to pursue our efforts within the Security Council. Such efforts should lead to the strengthening of the solidarity of this body for the full implementation of all resolutions on the situation between Iraq and Kuwait and the restoration of peace and security in the area. The unique circumstances of the issue under consideration and the decisions taken on it by the Security Council should be a landmark in our common endeavours to promote the development of a new world order. That order should be a peaceful and rational one, and it should be based on the universal legal norms, principles and values cherished by the United Nations and the whole international community.

...

[127] **The President** (interpretation from French):

...

I should now like to make a statement in my capacity as representative of Belgium.

The resolution that the Council has just adopted represents a turning point in the crisis between Iraq and Kuwait. Indeed, provided Iraq accepts its provisions, it will establish a formal cease-fire and lay the foundation for a lasting normalization of relations between the two countries.

The members of an organization devoted to defending world peace and stability cannot but be overjoyed at that.

Belgium particularly welcomes the fact that this official cessation of hostilities is the culmination of a long process designed to restore the rule of law, in accordance with the means laid down in the Charter. This process will go down in the annals of the United Nations.

The actions of the Security Council over the past few months illustrate the fact that international relations can be governed by the essential principles of political cooperation through multilateral diplomacy. The confrontations that our Organization has sometimes witnessed should clearly now be a thing of the past. The energy and political will that have infused the Council in this period of trial should now be used tirelessly for the peaceful settlement of other conflicts as well as the fruitful consideration of other problems facing the international community.

While the resolution thus brings down the curtain on a painful episode, it opens a new chapter by defining for the Gulf region some of the principles that should henceforth govern relations between States. In this connection, my delegation is pleased to note that a number of matters to which it attaches great importance figure prominently in the resolution.

First, it was important to make the United Nations responsible for implementing the resolution. Our Organization authorized the re-establishment of the rule of law by the legitimate use of force, and it should maintain the rule of law in peacetime.

The Secretary-General has been entrusted with many difficult tasks. He may rest assured of my Government's full cooperation.

In this context, the dispatch of observers to monitor the border between Kuwait and Iraq is an important initial step.

The Security Council's guarantee of the inviolability of the international border already recognized by the two countries is an exceptional step. My delegation regards it as a reaffirmation, in a particular context, of a fundamental norm of international law whose flagrant violation obliged the international community to take unprecedented collective action.

Secondly, the resolution is seriously concerned with mitigating the impact of the war on the Iraqi population. Belgium welcomed the policy of extending a hand to the Iraqi population constituted by the provisional lifting of the food embargo by the Committee on sanctions. We can only express our pleasure that the embargo will soon be repealed once and for all.

We also note that while insisting that Iraq pay fair compensation, the resolution, particularly in paragraph 19, says nothing to prevent the creation of conditions for the reconstruction of the Iraqi economy.

Finally, the text indicates how Iraq will have to behave if henceforth it intends to abide by international law and the Charter. The essential measures that will allow Iraq to resume its place in the international community include repudiating resort to and encouragement of terrorism and eliminating weapons of mass destruction, in the context of regional arms control.

Over and above concepts to which my country is attached, such as respect for international law and the maintenance of a regional balance, there is the human dimension. Here I am thinking of respect for human rights and particularly those of ethnic and religious minorities. My delegation fully associates itself with the Secretary-General's appeal on 2 April on behalf of Kurdish and Shiite refugees.

My Government believes it to be essential that the Iraqi authorities grant international and private organizations now engaged in humanitarian activities in Iraq unrestricted access to populations in distress. The Iraqi Government should respect its commitment to ensure the equitable distribution of food and humanitarian aid to the Iraqi population as a whole - a commitment which the Under-Secretary-General, Mr. Ahtisaari, adverted to in the report he drew up immediately upon his return from his mission in Iraq.

Finally, may I say how pleased I am to see the Kuwaitis once again living in their country, with their sovereignty, integrity and independence restored, and free from the threats under which they had been living. They will doubtless still have to tackle the serious after-effects of a particularly brutal and destructive occupation, but they can now bend all their efforts to the reconstruction of their country. Belgium is prepared to help them to do so.

...

[131] **Mr. Abulhasan (Kuwait)** (interpretation from Arabic):

I am sorry to speak at this late hour, but I wish to make the following comments on some points raised by the representative of Iraq.

First, the representative of Iraq spoke at length about the destruction of Iraq - as if Iraq had been the victim. It seems that his memory failed him about the true nature of the aggression perpetrated by his country against Kuwait, the widescale destruction of the country, the fires which continue to blaze, the poisoning of the air not only of the people of Kuwait but also of all the peoples of the region. Indeed, the oil wells now on fire in Kuwait have caused great pollution, which will not be restricted to Kuwait but will extend to the entire Gulf region and even to India, and will affect public health, agriculture, soil.

It seems that the Iraqi representative found it convenient to overlook these acts perpetrated by his regime only hours before its defeat. But he did remember that some weapons had been used against Iraq which might give rise to some diseases among the Iraqi people.

Secondly, the representative of Iraq spoke about his country's right to reparations. In my view, the representative of Iraq should be the last person to speak about reparations, because Iraq and the Iraqi army looted, plundered and destroyed the entire economic infrastructure of Kuwait; and now they are showing reluctance to return the looted property despite their declaration that they were willing to do so.

Thirdly, the representative of Iraq said that the Security Council had never imposed boundaries before and that Iraq views the paragraphs of resolution 687 (1991) dealing with the question of boundaries as an infringement of the sovereignty and territorial integrity of Iraq. He said that Iraq would therefore reserve its legitimate rights. This is in contradiction with an unconditional acceptance of the Security Council resolution.

Indeed, there is no contradiction between the Security Council's request to demarcate the boundary and operative paragraph 3 of resolution 660 (1990). I wish to make two points in this regard.

The first point is this: The boundary provided for in the resolution was not imposed on Iraq or on Kuwait. Rather, it was agreed upon by the two countries on 4 October 1963. In fact, the boundary is not a question of any controversy or of any quarrel. This is clear from document S/22432, which illustrates the nature of the agreement between Iraq and Kuwait on the question of boundaries and on the agreement concluded between the two countries in this regard. All we are talking about here is the demarcation of the boundary; that is the thrust of this resolution.

My second point is this: We wonder what violation of the Iraqi border is constituted by the Security Council calling upon the Secretary-General to offer the necessary technical aid in order to demarcate the boundary. Through the demarcation of the boundary, the Security Council is testing Iraq's credibility in regard to its respect for legal documents and treaties. If Iraq had such credibility, the Security Council would not have to call upon the Secretary-General or to decide to guarantee the boundary between Iraq and Kuwait. The problem is Iraq's lack of credibility. As the Council is aware, Iraq invaded, occupied and annexed Kuwait. Therefore, the quarrel between Iraq and Kuwait following that aggression and annexation is no longer a quarrel over boundaries; rather, it has become a question of greed.

Our understanding - and I think this is the common understanding in the Security Council - is that Iraq's acceptance of the resolution adopted today should be an unconditional acceptance. The Iraqi representative said earlier that Iraq reserves its legitimate rights regarding boundaries. That must be regarded as a condition which violates, indeed undermines, any official acceptance of this resolution on the part of Iraq.

...

[133] Mr. Al-Anbari (Iraq):

I apologize for speaking at this late hour. I have not asked to be allowed to speak in order to reply to the obscene remarks made by an individual sitting on my right whom I have always called a man with no identity, personal or national: I am not going to give him the benefit of a reply from my side. However, I should like to make a few remarks concerning the references I have heard from some representatives to the Kurdish question in Iraq, to the human rights of Kurds in Iraq.

Prior to the aggression by the United-States-led coalition against Iraq, all the Iraqi people were in total solidarity, living in peace and defending their own country. This was true of all the Iraqi people, Arabs and Kurds, Christians and Muslims. I do not say "Shiites and Sunnis" because I believe that the dichotomization of Shiites and Sunnis is a very cynical means used in order to divide the Muslims in Iraq into two antagonistic segments.

However, following the bombardment of Iraq and the temporary cessation of hostilities at the end of February, quite a number of subversive elements, who had been hiding in some neighbouring countries, penetrated the international borders of Iraq and carried out some subversive acts - shooting and destroying buildings, hospitals and schools - taking advantage of the situation in which the Iraqi army found itself following the cessation of hostilities. As soon as the Iraqi army was in a position to root them out, they had to flee the country, avoiding any confrontation with the Iraqi army. So there was no shooting and no bloodshed, and they soon found themselves safe in their refuge in some foreign countries. While they were withdrawing, as always on many previous occasions, they managed by coercion or intimidation to force quite a number of farmers and innocent citizens to join them, fleeing what they were told were chemical weapons and slaughter - totally unfounded allegations.

As far as Iraq is concerned, we view those people not only as innocent but also as very precious parts of Iraqi society and the Iraqi population. I have to say, for the record as well as for the information of the rest of the world, that the Kurds in Iraq are among the noblest and the best people. I believe that the same description applies to those 12 million Kurds who live in Turkey and the approximately 8 million who live in Iran. However, as for the 2.5 or 3 million Kurds in Iraq, we are very proud of them and they are an integral part of Iraqi society, enjoying their autonomy and their citizenship and proud of being Iraqis.

As for any refugees - and there are many, unfortunately, whether in Turkey, Iran or anywhere else - the Iraqi Government has repeatedly made it clear and makes it clear now that they are most welcome to return in peace to their families, their land and their homes. We are ready in this respect to cooperate with our neighbouring countries in order to carry out the repatriation of those refugees in an orderly and peaceful manner and with the dignity they deserve.

It is cruel and cynical for any country, neighbouring or otherwise, to take advantage of the situation which Iraq and its Kurdish population are experiencing to interfere in Iraq's internal affairs and thereby attempt to avoid some domestic problems and make some political gains domestically; it is cruel and cynical to make some claims for international charity and donations while at the same time trying to hang some of these countries' dirty clothes on the shoulders of Iraq.

[137] The President (interpretation from French):

I must say that I regret the manner in which the representative of Iraq referred to his colleague from Kuwait.

...

L. S/PV.2982, 5 April 1991

...

[3] Mr. Aksin (Turkey):

...

Turkey has asked for this meeting of the Security Council in view of the grave threat to the peace and security of the region posed by the tragic events taking place in Iraq. I would like to thank you, Mr. President, for convening this meeting.

In their attempt to put down the various insurgencies in that country the Iraqi armed forces have attacked cities and other localities with helicopters, tanks and artillery. This indiscriminate use of deadly firepower has caused the inhabitants of the localities under attack to flee for their safety. Whole cities stand deserted as a consequence of these actions. The situation in the northern part of the country adjacent to the borders of Turkey and Iran is especially alarming.

When we wrote our letter asking for this meeting, three days ago, there were more than 200,000, and perhaps 300,000, people who had been driven to the Iraqi-Turkish border. Of these, over 100,000 have trekked across the border, and are now reported to be in Turkey. We have reports that perhaps 600,000 more people are on the move, heading for the Turkish border.

This is a remote, mountainous area. The cold is intense at this time of the year. These helpless people, who are exposed to the elements, are Kurds, Arabs and Turkomans. These displaced people are Sunni and Shiite Moslems, and also Christians. Many of them are women and children. All of them are in mortal danger. The groups at the border have come under intense mortar fire. Many of the mortar shells have actually landed on the Turkish side of the border.

My Government has summoned the Iraqi Ambassador to issue a serious warning against continuing these attacks on defenceless civilians, and to demand an immediate halt to this callous use of firepower.

There is no way in which what is going on in northern Iraq can be justified as an internal affair of that country. Given the scale of the human tragedy and its international implications, this Council cannot allow itself to be relegated to the role of a mere spectator as these calamitous events unfold.

The threat posed by these events to the security of the region needs no elaboration. In the chaotic conditions prevailing in northern Iraq, it is conceivable that a million people might be forced to move from that country to Turkey. No country can cope with such a massive influx of destitute people fleeing for their lives. Turkey will not allow its border provinces to be overwhelmed by such a flood of displaced persons.

We expect the Council to take urgent and forceful action to secure an immediate cessation of the repression of the inhabitants of this area. The Council must send a clear signal to Iraq demanding respect for international borders and respect for human rights. Only in this way can the terrible pressure of humanity pressing against Iraq's borders be alleviated. At the same time, we are duty bound to take whatever measures we deem necessary to prevent the anarchy and chaos reigning on the Iraqi side of the border from spilling over into our country.

This does not mean that we are insensitive to the tragedy taking place in Iraq next door. We have the greatest sympathy and compassion for the plight of the victims of this man-made disaster. It will be recalled that in the summer of 1988, Turkey admitted over 60,000 Iraqis in similar circumstances; however, the scale of this calamity bears no comparison with what occurred in 1988. Our efforts to render humanitarian assistance are being swamped by the magnitude of the needs of these uprooted people. We have been providing truckloads of food as well as medical services to the needy people at our border. Efforts are being made to provide temporary shelter for those who have already crossed into Turkey.

But, clearly, this is an operation which requires the full backing and generous support of the international community. The economic burden of caring for these victims of civil war is too great for any country to bear alone. The Secretary-General should be requested to send a humanitarian mission, urgently, to this region to assess the situation, to report on the magnitude of the requirements in terms of humanitarian assistance and to propose arrangements for distributing this assistance to the displaced persons.

Before concluding, I would like to make it very clear that in calling for a meeting of the Security Council it was not our intention to interfere in Iraq's internal affairs. We recognize Article 2, paragraph 7 of the Charter, and believe that it should be scrupulously observed. The steps we have taken have been taken because of the threat posed to the stability, security and peace of the region by Iraq's methods of repression. We firmly support the independence, sovereignty and integrity of Iraq. We feel that this independence, sovereignty and integrity should be protected without resort to methods that will directly affect the security of Iraq's neighbours. We welcome the news that Iraq has declared an amnesty, and hope that this will be backed by firm action which will inspire reconciliation and give confidence to the displaced persons that they can return in safety to their homes in Iraq.

...

[8] Mr. Marker (Pakistan):

...

We have just witnessed an unfortunate, tragic and bloody war in the Persian Gulf region. At a time when the region is still reeling under the effects of the war, and at a time when the devastated and shattered people of Iraq and Kuwait are struggling for existence under conditions where even the very basic amenities for living do not exist, we are confronted with a situation in which a large segment of the population of Iraq continues to suffer death and destruction.

My delegation would wish to emphasize, at the outset, that as a matter of principle Pakistan is opposed to any form of interference in the internal affairs of any country, and that this is especially so in the case of a brotherly, Muslim country, whose territorial integrity must be fully respected. At the same time, however, we cannot conceal our dismay at the infringement of human rights that is now taking place in Iraq, and at the continuing death and destruction in that devastated land.

At an earlier meeting of the Security Council during the recent conflict, my delegation expressed the anguish and concern of the people of Pakistan at the casualties suffered by innocent Iraqi civilians as a result of the bombing. The same sentiments of concern for the safety and welfare of the Iraqi people compels my delegation to appear once again before the Council and appeal for restraint.

Although the liberation of Kuwait is complete, peace has still not returned to a large number of people in Iraq who, for the past few weeks, have been the target of severe repression. The intensity of reprisals and military operations has forced a large number of the victims, many of them women and children, to abandon their homes and flee towards the borders of Iran and Turkey. Reportedly, approximately 220,000 Iraqi refugees are on the Turkish border alone, and a similarly massive number have sought refuge in Iran.

For Pakistan, which has provided refuge to more than 3 million Afghans over the past decade, the plight of Iraqis fleeing their own country is particularly poignant and distressing. Pakistan has consistently opposed violations of human rights in all parts of the world, and will continue to raise its voice against violence in any form. My country is thus deeply concerned at the current violation of the human rights of the Kurdish and other Iraqi citizens. We appeal for a stop to the military action and urge compassion and peaceful negotiation in the settlement of issues.

My delegation will support the Security Council in any action it may take to achieve these ends and prevent the further loss of precious, human lives.

...

[11] Mr. Kharrazi (Islamic Republic of Iran):

...

The Islamic Republic of Iran, sharing long borders as well as historical, religious and cultural ties with Iraq, has witnessed with deep concern and sadness the developments inside Iraq in the past few months. Throughout the crisis that began with Iraq's occupation of Kuwait, the Islamic Republic of Iran actively endeavoured to mitigate the suffering of the Iraqi people in both the diplomatic and the humanitarian fields. Our resolve to refrain from engagement in the hostilities in spite of all difficulties; our commitment to the territorial integrity and political independence of regional countries, including Kuwait and Iraq; our objection to the long-term presence of foreign forces in the region; our insistence on minimizing the hardship of the Kuwaiti and Iraqi people; our attempts to prevent and bring an early end to the bloodshed in the war between Iraq and coalition forces; our strong objection to the bombardment of civilian quarters inside Iraq; and our insistence on the necessity of maintaining the sanctity of holy cities inside Iraq were the major characteristics of our policy *vis-à-vis* the recent hostilities.

The very same principles govern our approach to the horrifying developments inside Iraq today. Again, in spite of all pressures and in the extremely difficult circumstances resulting from the unprecedented brutality exercised in crushing the uprising inside Iraq, we have refrained from interfering in the internal affairs of Iraq. But, as a neighbouring country with very strong bonds of religion and culture with the Iraqi people, the people and the Government of Iran cannot remain indifferent to the untold suffering of the Iraqi people and the indiscriminate measures taken by the Iraqi armed forces against innocent civilians, just as we did not remain silent when the suffering was inflicted by the allied forces.

Motivated by our strong desire to prevent the unfolding tragedy inside Iraq, the President of the Islamic Republic of Iran, in the very early stages of the uprising, called on the Iraqi Government to come to terms with its people, to submit to its will, and to adopt the approach of accommodation instead of confrontation and repression. We regret that this call to reason went unheeded inside the Iraqi leadership, as did our attempts in another context throughout the tragic military confrontation.

My country has had the humanitarian duty of providing refuge, as of noon yesterday, to more than 110,000 Iraqi civilians escaping their own Government's armed forces. Many more have been struggling to cross the borders into Iran. According to the latest information, the number of refugees has now exceeded 180,000, including about 120,000 in the north. This shows that the pace of the influx in the north is unbelievably rapid, while in the south it has subsided, but continues at a slower pace. The most conservative estimates put the number of Iraqi civilians who will take refuge in Iran within the next few days at half a million.

Other neighbouring countries are also faced with similar flows of civilians escaping the Iraqi army. This has added another international dimension to the crisis inside Iraq, threatening the security of the neighbouring countries and presenting the potential to further destabilize inter-State relations in our region. Furthermore, the magnitude of the problem of refugees in terms of numbers and the rate and speed of the influx, and in terms of the severity of the injuries and problems of some of the refugees, has made dealing effectively with this humanitarian problem beyond the capability of any one country of the region. Thus, there is a need for concerted international effort to deal both with the causes of the crisis and with its immediate symptoms.

In addition to the heavy task of sheltering the innocent victims of this tragedy, we have listened to gruesome details of horrifying accounts of the repression narrated by its victims. These accounts, as well as the available evidence, point towards the use of indiscriminate methods and unconventional weapons by the Iraqi armed forces against the people of the affected areas. These victims, whose accounts are not corroborated by televised pictures, talk also of unprecedented desecration of holy shrines inside Iraq.

It is evident that the situation inside Iraq, due to its gravity and implications for the neighbouring countries, has consequences that threaten regional and international peace and security. We believe that it is incumbent upon the Security Council to take immediate measures to put an early end to the suffering of the Iraqi people.

...

[16] **Mr. AL-ANBARI (Iraq)** (interpretation from Arabic):

Iraq has suffered since 6 August of last year - and continues to suffer - from an economic embargo by land, sea and air, during which the Iraqi people have been deprived of even food and medicine. And as the Council is aware, beginning on 16 January of this year, the United States and its allies waged round the clock air raids against all cities and villages in Iraq, laying waste urban and rural areas and killing civilians and military personnel alike.

The damages caused by such an unprecedented bombing campaign have been summarized by the United Nations mission which recently visited Iraq as having relegated it to a pre-industrial age, with its economy and basic infrastructure completely devastated, and all necessary means of daily modern life support for both civilians and military personnel destroyed.

That was the fruit of the aggression waged against Iraq, an aggression which led to the well-known consequences. The suffering of the Iraqi people in many cities and villages - whether because of starvation, the lack of any source of drinking water or electricity - led many Iraqis, following the destruction of their homes and their food sources, to seek food, shelter and medicine in the north.

Now we see the very perpetrators of these crimes, of this aggression against the Iraqi people, shedding crocodile tears for their plight and suffering.

I have had the opportunity, following instructions from my Government, to present documents condemning the acts of foreign intervention by some adjoining States - very regrettable acts - to try to sow dissent in the towns and villages of Iraq, in both the south and the north. We have firm evidence, either from those who have been imprisoned, or those who have confessed to acts of sabotage and destruction in many towns and villages in all parts of Iraq - north, south and in the middle of the country - proving the intervention of these neighbouring States in the internal affairs of Iraq, and their attempt to destabilize Iraq and perhaps even to partition Iraq into many mini-States.

Despite this, we continue to hear that this unjust war was not being waged against the Iraqi people. Nevertheless, we find, too, that all resolutions of the Security Council stress respect for the sovereignty and territorial integrity of Iraq and reject intervention in Iraq's internal affairs. But those very States continue to attempt to partition Iraq and to annihilate its people; and they continue to attempt to intervene in our internal affairs.

This draft resolution itself is a flagrant, illegitimate intervention in Iraq's internal affairs and a violation of Article 2 of the Charter of the United Nations which prohibits intervention in the internal affairs of other States.

I believe that, instead of shedding tears, instead of appealing to international humanitarian organizations to come to the assistance of the Iraqi people, the Security Council should have undertaken one essential act to lessen the pressure on and the plight of the Iraqi people: the lifting of the economic embargo, thus allowing the Iraqi people to buy food, medicine, and all the amenities to ensure a return to normal life in the country.

We have all seen on our television screens how some saboteurs who penetrated through the borders have wreaked destruction on many towns and villages in Iraq and how they have killed many innocent people. What reaction did the Security Council expect from the Iraqi Government and from the Iraqi army? Were we to let these saboteurs carry out their evil deeds, or were we to attempt to protect our civilians and to ensure law and order in the country? This is indeed what took place, God be thanked. Peace and stability have returned to all corners of our cherished Iraq. Yes, the saboteurs escaped before facing the Iraqi army. They went beyond the borders to safe haven, and through terror and intimidation on their way, convinced many innocent citizens, particularly in northern Iraq, to leave and go towards the northern and eastern international borders of the country.

We have declared that all Iraqi citizens may return at any time to their cities and homes. Furthermore, the Iraqi Government yesterday declared a general amnesty to all those who have contravened the laws, with the exception of those who have committed major crimes and murder, who will be prosecuted. All others have been forgiven all crimes and contraventions committed before leaving the country.

On the other hand, this morning, following instructions from my Government, I informed the President of the Security Council and the Secretary-General of the

Organization that the Iraqi Government welcomes an international mission to be formed by the Secretary-General or the Security Council in Iraq, with full guarantees for free movement and communications, so that its members may ascertain the facts and see things as they stand and then present their report to the Council or to the Secretary-General.

I had expected that the Security Council would wait and find out the true facts from such a mission before making haste - which has been its habit in the past months - and producing a draft resolution which, with all due respect to its sponsors, or those who would vote in its favour, offers no positive hope for the Iraqi people, with the exception of its first paragraph. With the exception of that paragraph, it seems to be a condemnation of the Iraqi Government. It does not represent a condemnation of the victim alone but, rather, is an attempt to claim innocence for the aggressors who have waged destruction against Iraq, as well as for those States which have attempted to foment dissent in Iraq and sent saboteurs to destroy towns and villages in my country.

Rather than condemning those parties, the sponsors of this draft resolution now call on the Security Council to condemn Iraq, instead of helping it.

I believe that it is the duty of everyone to assist Iraq in this critical period to stand on its feet again after the destruction wrought upon it - to do so, on the one hand, through lifting all economic sanctions and, on the other, through waiting for the return of the mission that may be sent by the Secretary-General or the Security Council to Iraq, in order to ascertain the real facts, without exaggeration and without the selfish objectives that some may have in mind.

...

[22] **Mr. Munteanu (Romania):**

...

At the very outset, my delegation would like to stress that the situation in Iraq is very serious, indeed alarming. It is quite understandable that the international community should be deeply concerned by the inhuman armed repression being carried out on a massive scale by the Iraqi authorities against their own population. The actions undertaken by Iraq against its population are correctly described as a violation of all norms of behaviour and of all Iraq's commitments arising from international legal instruments to respect and protect the fundamental human rights and freedoms of all its citizens.

As is emphasized in the draft resolution before the Council, this armed repression has led to a massive flow of refugees across Iraq's international frontiers. In fact, there is a mass exodus of a deeply disturbing magnitude. This massive flow of refugees is a source of tremendous human suffering. Romania's position on the general substantive aspect of the draft resolution was recently expressed by it through its participation in the General Assembly's adoption without a vote on 18 December 1990 of resolution 45/153, entitled "Human rights and mass exoduses".

We are indeed deeply disturbed by the continuing scale and magnitude of exoduses of refugees and displacements of population in many regions of the world and by the human suffering of millions of refugees and displaced persons. At the same time, we are aware of the increasingly heavy burden being imposed, particularly on poor neighbouring countries but also upon the international community as a whole, by these sudden mass exoduses and displacements of population. Like other countries, we express our concern at the serious and far-reaching consequences which the presence of massive numbers of refugees has on the security and stability of the neighbouring countries, and the overall negative impact on their basic infrastructure and social economic development.

We expect Iraq to guarantee respect for international standards applicable under international instruments in this field. In this regard, Iraq must put an immediate end to the atrocities against its population, resulting in the uprooting of a vast number of persons.

At the same time, the international community cannot remain passive in the face of such tremendous human suffering. Indeed, the international community is confronted with a great humanitarian problem, and the United Nations system should do its best to address urgently the critical needs of all the refugees and the displaced Iraqi population.

From that point of view, the delegation of Romania commends the delegation of France for its initiative in preparing the draft resolution before us, which deals with a real humanitarian issue of dramatic, indeed tragic, proportions. We are grateful also to you, Mr. President, for the great wisdom and patience you displayed in the process of negotiating the draft resolution.

Questions pertaining to the situation of various segments or components of populations from the ethnic, linguistic or religious points of view are matters of the national jurisdiction of States. In this respect, no one can disregard the imperative nature of Article 2, paragraph 7 of the Charter of the United Nations, which provides that

> "Nothing contained in the present Charter shall authorize the United Nations to intervene in matters which are essentially within the domestic jurisdiction of any State or shall require the Members to submit such matters to settlement under the present Charter ...".

We are indeed very happy to see this fundamental provision of the Charter well reflected in the draft resolution before us.

If we agree - and that is the case - that we should deal with an important humanitarian issue and a real threat to international peace and security, we have to take into account the fact that the cooperation of all States is needed in order to solve the issue. We welcome in this respect operative paragraph 6 of the draft resolution, which contains an appeal addressed to all States and to all humanitarian organizations to contribute to the humanitarian relief efforts. That is a very positive element of the draft. Indeed, it is generally recognized in the United Nations that humanitarian cooperation should make an effective and practical contribution to the task of preventing mass and flagrant violations of human rights.

We all agree that the armed repression of the Iraqi population can be a legitimate concern of the international community. Our action in this field should be guided by the principles of non-selectivity, by impartiality and objectivity. By the draft resolution under consideration we should not create a precedent that could be used - or, rather, misused - in the future for political purposes. If we want to prove that we have an unbiased and fair approach to the issue under consideration, we should emphasize its real humanitarian nature, addressing a special case in the aftermath of the Gulf war, and we should, with a feeling of responsibility, avoid any potential implications that could jeopardize the present and future actions of the Security Council.

Today, Romania is a democratic country carrying on the noble heritage of the revolution of December 1989. We know well the value of our freedom, and we are proud of it. We still have in our collective memory the true meaning of the repression to which the Romanian people were subjected during the old régime.

We are sensitive to the human sufferings of other peoples, and, in the case under consideration, we are aware of the alarming situation in Iraq and of the necessity to adopt appropriate measures to put an end to the inhuman repression being carried out on a massive scale against the Iraqi population. We fully support such measures.

But we also know that on such an issue the solidarity of the members of the Security Council is essential. As my delegation has stated on other occasions, that solidarity is a guarantee of the success of our actions. Therefore, it should be promoted and protected. No precedent which could erode such a solidarity should be established; on the contrary, all efforts should be deployed to strengthen our solidarity.

It is in this framework and in the light of these considerations that my delegation will vote on the draft resolution in document S/22448.

[26] **Mr. AL-ASHTAL (Yemen)** (interpretation from Arabic):

It is well known that wars harm civilian populations first. Indeed, civilian populations are the first victims of wars. Such is the case in Iraq today. The population of Iraq suffered for 8 months from the embargo imposed upon Iraq; then the Iraqi people suffered from the war. Now the Iraqi people are suffering from instability and turmoil and from the unrest inside the country.

From the outset the delegation of Yemen opposed the war, and we have expressed our support, sympathy and solidarity with the innocent civilian population of Iraq. We stated that yesterday, and we do so today. We declare our support and sympathy for the Iraqis who now find themselves prey to every form of suffering throughout the country, and we call upon the international community to contribute towards efforts to alleviate the suffering and pain of the Iraqi population. We would like to take this opportunity to express our thanks to the Secretary-General, who has mobilized all the energies of the United Nations system to reach out to the civilian population. We also welcome the offers made by many countries to provide aid to the Iraqi people, whether refugees or otherwise.

We would have supported the present draft resolution had it been confined to addressing humanitarian issues. There are many bodies within the United Nations system that are competent to address them. However, the draft resolution now before the Council, although dealing with the humanitarian issues that face the Iraqi people, focuses on only one area and one category of the Iraqi population. We object to the draft resolution because it attempts to politicize the humanitarian issue. Indeed, that, in our view, is the thrust of the draft resolution.

The draft resolution claims that there is a problem threatening international peace and security. We do not share that view. There is no conflict or war taking place across the borders of Iraq with its neighbours. The draft resolution also refers to political developments within Iraq, but according to Article 2 of the United Nations Charter it is not within the Council's purview to address internal issues in any country. Further, the draft resolution calls for internal dialogue, and that is obviously an attempt to intervene in the internal affairs of Iraq.

However, our position with regard to the draft resolution is based not only on certain provisions in its text but also on our objection to the fact that the whole issue is not within the competence of the Security Council. The Security Council is mandated only to safeguard international peace and security. In our view, the draft resolution sets a dangerous precedent that could open the way to diverting the Council away from its basic functions and responsibilities for safeguarding international peace and security and towards addressing the internal affairs of countries.

We wonder what State, big or small, has no internal problems; what State will not at some point in time encounter internal difficulties and experience transborder problems? In our opinion the text of the draft resolution is a first departure from the rule of maintaining a strict focus on the Council's responsibilities under the Charter. Over the past 40 years the Council has consistently refrained from intervention in the internal affairs of States.

On Wednesday of this week, when the Council voted on resolution 687 (1991), I mentioned in my statement what we view as a growing tendency on the part of the Security Council to circumvent the Charter of the United Nations. The draft resolution now before us is yet another example of such circumvention.

We have been told that one of the pillars of the new world order is respect for law and the rule of law. That statement has given us cause for hope. What we are witnessing, however, is in point of fact a gradual retreat from law and the rule of law and, in some cases, an attempt to circumvent the international rule of law for political ends.

We find this new world order ominous. We see a lack of balance. Indeed, there is an imbalance here. We see no firm application of law, and unless we are extremely careful this may lead to a change of the rules that have contributed to stability over the past four decades. It is indeed a strange world, and we may be in for many surprises.

[31] **Mr. ZENENGA (Zimbabwe):**

The draft resolution we are about to vote on addresses a very complex and delicate situation. Zimbabwe believes that a domestic political conflict lies at the core of the situation in the areas of Iraq referred to in the draft resolution.

We recognize that a serious humanitarian situation has arisen as a result of these developments. However, this is in our view essentially an internal matter, as defined in paragraph 7 of Article 2 of the Charter. It is our view that addressing this situation in the manner suggested by the draft resolution would be inconsistent with the clear parameters of the Council's competence as provided for in the Charter.

The draft resolution refers directly to the confrontation between the Government of Iraq and its population. It prescribes specific measures which it expects the Government of Iraq to take in resolving what is a domestic conflict. In our view, this would be inconsistent with the Charter. It also contradicts what the draft resolution states in its second preambular paragraph.

The humanitarian situation emanating from the present circumstances causes us great concern. We have taken note of the concerns expressed by the Governments of both Turkey and the Islamic Republic of Iran. However, we believe that the serious humanitarian situation and the question of refugees can be adequately addressed by the appropriate organs of the United Nations. The Secretary-General has on many occasions taken prompt and appropriate action to alleviate the suffering of refugees through the specialized agencies when similar situations have arisen. The present situation should be treated no differently.

While we realize that the humanitarian dimensions affect neighbouring States, we do not believe that this in any way makes the internal conflict in Iraq an issue that the Council should be seized of.

[32] **Mr. AYALA LASSO (Ecuador)** (interpretation from Spanish):

For several days the press has been bringing us tragic news of events affecting the Iraqi population. The tragedy that has been described to us is undoubtedly grave. It has shocked the entire civilized community of nations. There is no country in which comments have not been made about what has been happening in Iraq and in which peoples have not expressed their rejection of the situation and their demand that the international community act to remedy the situation. The acts of violence and cruelty that have occurred do violence to the spirit of the civilized community.

It is against this background that we are now considering the draft resolution that France has submitted to the Council for its consideration in document S/22448.

In order to take a position on the subject, Ecuador has most carefully studied two fundamental principles of the United Nations Charter. The first is that of unrestricted respect for human rights. In the Charter's preamble we see that the peoples of the United Nations are determined

> "to reaffirm faith in fundamental human rights, in the dignity and worth of the human person,"

and

> "to save succeeding generations from the scourge of war".

We see that we are determined to make a world in which the human race can live.

Any society - civilian or political, national or international - must be anthropocentric, in the sense that society is born for the human being and is for the good of the human being. Therefore, respect for the essence of the human being is a universal requirement which must be accepted and must be demanded.

Ecuador has accepted all commitments and subscribed to all agreements on human rights, and our record in this respect has never been questioned. I cannot tell the Council that there have been no shortcomings, because all human endeavours are subject to shortcomings, but there is no doubt that my country has always followed a policy of unconditional, unrestricted respect for human rights.

That is perhaps why over a decade ago Ecuador submitted an initiative to a number of Latin American countries that led to the signing of a document entitled "Charter of Conduct", the third paragraph of which states:

> "The Presidents of the countries subscribing to the document reiterate their solemn commitment to the fact that respect for human, political, economic and social rights constitutes a fundamental norm of the internal conduct of the countries of the Andean Group, that their defence is an international obligation to which States are committed, and that therefore joint action in defence of those rights does not violate the principle of non-intervention."

My country has regarded that doctrine as one of the pillars of its policy on human rights.

The second principle is that of non-intervention in the internal affairs of other States. The United Nations Charter considers that to be one of the main pillars of the community of nations and the ability of nations to work together effectively.

It is a principle which must be completely respected today, tomorrow and for ever. It is a principle which admits of no question, and must be given our complete support.

None the less, the application of this principle prompts us to think that the international community cannot remain indifferent to what is happening in Iraq. It might perhaps have been a question of internal jurisdiction in Iraq, if the situation had not gone beyond the borders of the country. The phenomenon which we are considering, in fact, has now reached the borders of neighbouring countries; the use of force has now been extended up to the borders of two of those neighbouring countries; the human pressures that the displaced communities of over 1 million people are exerting on those borders constitute, my delegation believes, a threat to international peace and security. In other words, this is a situation that goes beyond the sphere of the internal affairs of a State; it is a situation which is affecting international relations and may become a threat to peace. This has been the understanding of those countries which have sent communications to the Council condemning these events, communicating their concern and requesting action to prevent their being directly and immediately affected.

It might be said that, even assuming that the measures I have just set out are taken, the Security Council would not be the body competent to take them, given that Chapter IX of the Charter says that it is the General Assembly or the Economic and Social Council which would be the competent bodies in such situations.

This would be so - I repeat - if we were dealing solely with a case of violation of human rights by a country within its own frontiers; however, once again I say that this is a situation which affects international peace and security, and I therefore believe that the Council is competent to take a stand and to act by taking steps to put an end to this situation.

It is Ecuador's hope that Iraq will put an end to this persecution, that it will put an end to this indiscriminate violence against communities which are part of that nation, and that respect for the rights of those communities will be re-established.

I read just a short time ago that one of those communities had complained publicly of having had a shortage of friends throughout its history, and I think we, all the peoples of the world, should show that community that it does have friends and that we are concerned about its present and its future.

The statements we have just heard to the effect that the Government of Iraq has extended an amnesty are commendable; of course, we are not aware of the details of this amnesty, which will certainly have conditions attached, but it is something which may be a step in the right direction.

We also believe that it is encouraging that Iraq has expressed its readiness to accept a fact-finding mission; the Secretary-General will certainly have taken note of this offer, and will act under one of the provisions of the draft resolution now before us.

Taking into account that in the text of the resolution we see clear mention made of paragraph 7 of Article 2 of the Charter and also because of the fact that the situation under consideration is a threat to international peace and security, requiring us all to do everything in our power to see to it that this world is a better world for its inhabitants - the human beings whose future we are considering - Ecuador will vote in accordance with the above principles.

[37] **Mr. Kibidi Ngovuka (Zaire)** (interpretation from French):

...

We are called upon to vote upon a draft resolution submitted by France. Yesterday, in informal consultations, we stated clearly that the issue raised in that resolution was strictly humanitarian, since the repression of the Kurds and other Iraqis is forcing them to leave their homeland and seek refuge in neighbouring countries, especially Turkey and Iran.

We believe that this situation has to do with the internal policy of Iraq, but that it could have consequences which might result in a threat to international peace and security. In order to prevent any deterioration in the political and economic situation in the countries of a region which has been hard hit by two successive wars waged by Iraq against Iran and then by Iraq against Kuwait, my country will vote in favour of this resolution.

We are aware that, while the United Nations Charter cannot be tampered with, as to do so would weaken the Council's credibility, we must, however, in this particular case be far-sighted indeed if we are to avoid the occurrence of the worst in the Gulf region.

We are, therefore, pleased that the sponsors of the draft resolution have agreed to the inclusion in its preamble of a reference to Article 2, paragraph 7 of the Charter.

...

[38] **Mr. Bechio (Côte d'Ivoire)** (interpretation from French):

The Secretary-General, Mr. Perez de Cuellar, in his first report on the United Nations, in 1982, elaborated on the idea of enhancing the authority of the United Nations, stressing the fact that the United Nations might play a preventive role in helping maintain the peace. He indicated that Governments can, in many ways, help strengthen the system set forth in the Charter, and one of these ways is, he said, to appeal to the Security Council, and not to wait until the last minute to do so. If the Council were to monitor dangerous situations closely, and if it were to have discussions with the parties involved before reaching a critical threshold in a situation, perhaps we could often resolve disputes before they degenerated into conflicts.

The recent war in the Gulf, and the consequences thereof, which we have unceasingly deplored, shed new light on these wise words of the Secretary-General, and encourage the Security Council towards the preventive action it should take as part of its role in maintaining international peace and security.

It is a secret to no one that the massive exodus of the Kurdish population fleeing repression in Iraq threatens the stability of the host States. Furthermore, the countries concerned, and in particular Iraq's neighbours, have brought the situation before the Security Council. They have expressed their concern at this large influx of refugees and have also indicated that shots have been fired across the borders. Can the Council turn a deaf ear to their cry for help and take refuge behind the banner of non-interference in the internal affairs of another State?

We have before us a draft resolution which, we must say, is far from commanding the unanimous approval of the members. Reasoning has been put forward on all sides that can be defended from different standpoints. But my delegation feels that we should not focus on the points that divide us, but rather work in the quest for a consensus on the basis of elements and facts that are known to everyone. To this, we must add the pressing humanitarian problem posed by these refugees. Indeed, tens of thousands of men, women and children are subject to the elements, to hunger, to bombing. Can the Security Council be indifferent to so much human misery and suffering by invoking its incompetence to deal with humanitarian issues such as these, as some maintain?

Someone said yesterday that we should not lose sight of the fact that the longer we debate, the longer the list of victims will be. Neighbouring countries have drawn our attention to the possibility of a breach of international peace and security and to the danger that this massive exodus poses.

My delegation believes that if an end is not put to this brutal repression, if urgent humanitarian assistance is not deployed as soon as possible, we can expect developments that may come as a shocking surprise to us. The draft resolution before us, we believe, meets these concerns.

In any event, Côte d'Ivoire intends to support actions aimed at putting an end to this painful situation. I cannot conclude without reaffirming my country's respect for the principles of non-intervention in the internal affairs of other States and of the sovereignty, territorial integrity and political independence of States. Indeed, Côte d'Ivoire remains convinced that only respect by all States for those principles cherished by the United Nations and by the Non-Aligned Movement can make it possible for the United Nations to achieve the goal of universal peace and brotherhood.

[42] **Mr. Alarcon de Quesada (Cuba)** (interpretation from Spanish):

Throughout the consultations that we had yesterday, and during this meeting as well, reference has been made to the relationship that exists between the problem before us and certain principles and norms contained in the Charter of the United Nations. I believe that we all agree about the importance of Article 2, paragraph 7, of the Charter, which has been recalled in the preamble of the draft resolution before us.

In our view, the Security Council and all of the United Nations are duty bound to comply with that Article, whose text we need not reread. But they also have the duty to see to it that the fundamental principle is not violated.

We were struck by the fact that, thus far, no reference has been made in our deliberations to certain information which is in the public domain and which indicates how clearly at least one permanent member of the Council for some time now has been involved in activities that do intervene in Iraqi internal affairs and that are closely related to the issues now before the Council. I am certain that *The New York Times* is widely read among us and that some saw in yesterday's issue the few paragraphs that I shall now read out.

(*spoke in English*)

> "The Associated Press, quoting 'intelligence sources,' reported today that in January, around the time he was publicly exhorting the Iraqi people to overthrow Saddam Hussein, Mr. Bush signed secret orders authorizing the C.I.A. to aid rebel factions inside Iraq.
>
> "The orders were described as granting broad and general authority for clandestine activities to undermine Mr. Hussein and to support efforts by opposition forces inside Iraq.
>
> "The AP said it did not know to what extent the CIA authority might have been used.
>
> "Mr. Bush recently sidestepped reporters' questions about any contacts between the United States and Iraqi rebels. And, asked about such collaboration at a congressional hearing two weeks ago, Defense Secretary Dick Cheney said only, 'That's a subject I can't get into in open session'." (*New York Times, 4 April 1991, p. 10*)

(*continued in Spanish*)

Clearly, what Mr. Cheney could not discuss in public has quite a lot to do with a situation that is in violation of the principle of non-intervention, a principle with which the permanent members of the Security Council and the other members of the international community must comply.

Thus, if we are really going to express concern about the conflict which, we are informed, continues on Iraqi territory, we have no right to disregard the fact that, in an open way - in a way that has been very difficult to conceal - it has been revealed that a major Power is involved in efforts to overthrow the Government of Iraq and to intervene in the internal struggle which, it is reported, is occurring in that country.

This, in any event, is the issue on which, in accordance with the Charter, the Security Council would have power to decide. But to speak of the internal situation in Iraq, of the instability that may prevail throughout or in part of that country, to disregard the fact that a major Power has been overtly promoting and organizing such activity, is to say the least inconsistent.

The text of the draft resolution submitted to us glosses over that political aspect of the situation and in more than one paragraph refers to questions that are clearly part of the internal jurisdiction of the State of Iraq, contradicting the preambular paragraph in which the Council recalls paragraph 7 of Article 2 of the Charter.

It has also been said that, in any event, there are humanitarian concerns over the plight of civilians, of women, children and the elderly, to which the international community should devote its attention. We believe these are legitimate concerns but we feel that the members of the Council do not possess divine powers but, rather, have obligations that have been entrusted to them by all the Members of the United Nations and that are reflected in the Charter.

If it is felt that the international community should show concern for the humanitarian aspects of a question, then the Security Council simply has no right to do so in a way which the Charter specifically precludes. The Security Council has every right in the world to fulfil its role and to exercise its powers. In other words, it has every right in the world to act in accordance with Article 24, paragraph 2, which states that

> "the specific powers granted to the Security Council for the discharge of [its] duties are laid down in Chapters VI, VII, VIII and XII".

Those are the four Chapters under which the Security Council has specific powers granted to it by the entire membership of the United Nations. Those Chapters do not include the questions of a humanitarian nature about which concern has been expressed in this Chamber. The Charter devotes Chapter IX to those questions. The drafters of the Charter clearly established in Article 60 of Chapter IX that

> "Responsibility for the discharge of the functions of the Organization set forth in this Chapter shall be vested in the General Assembly".

The Security Council simply has no right to intervene unduly in the internal affairs of any State. It has no right to intervene unduly in matters within the competence of other organs of the Organization. If the Security Council considers that a subject is important and requires urgent action, the Charter provides the channels for that purpose.

I wonder why it has not been possible to follow the procedure laid down in the Charter in Article 20, which states:

> "The General Assembly shall meet in regular annual sessions and in such special sessions as occasion may require. Special sessions shall be convoked by the Secretary-General at the request of the Security Council or of a majority of the Members of the United Nations."

It would be extremely simple for the Council to combine the concern that has been expressed at this situation with respect for this little blue book, which has increasingly become a clandestine document of our Organization.

The General Assembly could easily be convened tomorrow by the Security Council, thereby enabling the item to be considered and decisions to be taken rapidly. It would not be the first time the General Assembly has been convened on an urgent basis. But what would the difference be? The difference would be that we would be respecting the Charter and would not be taking a course that allows this organ to assume powers that it does not possess, functions that no one has given it; a course of action that makes us depart from the letter and spirit of the Charter and that turns the Organization into a system dominated by an oligarchical group which attributes to itself powers that no one has given it and therefore imposes its will on the entire Organization.

I believe that if it is important and legitimate and appropriate for us to be concerned at the situation of the civilian population in Iraq and other parts of the world, it is equally important, legitimate and appropriate - and even more urgent - for the Members of the United Nations to show their concern about stemming the tendency to manipulate the Security Council and the Organization into conforming with the convenience and interests of just a few of the Members, because this is something that affects the entire world, the civilian populations of all countries, whether or not they are members of the Security Council, and the most cherished and legitimate interests of the entire international community.

It is also a bit surprising to see the Security Council dealing with humanitarian aspects or consequences affecting the civilian population in Iraq when, at the same time, the Council has been extremely reluctant to consider the situation on the basis of specific, objective, impartial reports submitted to it at its own request.

I have no doubt whatsoever that there are thousands of displaced persons in Iraq, thousands of refugees, thousands of persons seeking refuge and shelter and better living conditions. No one can have any doubt about that. We have received a report from the Secretary-General, prepared on the basis of Mr. Ahtisaari's mission. The Council expressed its satisfaction with the mission and indicated that immediate action would be taken in connection with it.

In this report Mr. Ahtisaari described the situation before the beginning of the bombing of Iraq. He said:

> "Sanctions decided upon by the Security Council had already adversely affected the country's ability to feed its people." (*S/22366, para. 11*)

This was the case before the destruction that we all know was launched against the country and that Mr. Ahtisaari describes in his report.

The draft resolution would establish that Iraq must allow immediate access by international humanitarian organizations to all those in need of assistance in all parts of Iraq, and must "make available all necessary facilities for their operations". In voting on this phrase shall we be acting seriously? Has not Mr. Ahtisaari told us on more than one occasion what the transportation situation is in Iraq, what the situation is in Iraq with regard to its destroyed infrastructure?

For example, did not Mr. Ahtisaari tell us the following in his report:

> "Underlying each analysis is the inexorable reality that, as a result of war, virtually all previously viable sources of fuel and power (apart from a limited number of mobile generators) and modern means of communication are now, essentially, defunct. The far-reaching implications of this energy and communications vacuum as regards urgent humanitarian support are of crucial significance for the nature and effectiveness of the international response"? (*S/22366, para. 9*)

Are we forgetting what Mr. Ahtisaari has said in his conclusions? This is what we read in the report:

> "... it will be difficult, if not impossible, to remedy these immediate humanitarian needs without dealing with the underlying need for energy, on an equally urgent basis. The need for energy means, initially, emergency oil imports and the rapid patching up of a limited refining and electricity production capacity, with essential supplies from other countries. Otherwise, food that is imported cannot be preserved and distributed; water cannot be purified; sewage cannot be pumped away and cleansed; crops cannot be irrigated; medicaments cannot be conveyed where they are required; needs cannot even be effectively assessed". (*ibid., para. 37*)

Mr. Ahtisaari recommended that the Security Council at least lift those sanctions that have a basic effect on the ability to feed the civilian population and to face the serious health situation in Iraq.

The very same Security Council that only recently decided to maintain strict control over Iraq and to maintain the sanctions is now supposedly expressing humanitarian concerns about the population of Iraq, while disregarding the realities and the fact that the political problems existing in Iraq itself are not unrelated to the actions of intervention by a major Power; what is worse, it is disregarding the very clear obligations that the members of the Council had before entering this Chamber, that they have during this meeting, that they will have at the time of voting, and that they will have in the future - that is, the obligations to act strictly in accordance with the functions granted to it by the Organization and not to think that the gods have given them permission to deal with various world problems in accordance with the interests of a transitory majority.

My delegation will vote on the draft resolution in accordance with those considerations.

[52] **The President** (interpretation from French):

I shall now put the draft resolution in document S/22448 to the vote.

A vote was taken by show of hands.

In favour:	Austria, Belgium, Côte d'Ivoire, Ecuador, France, Romania, Union of Soviet Socialist Republics, United Kingdom of Great Britain and Northern Ireland, United States of America, Zaire
Against:	Cuba, Yemen, Zimbabwe
Abstaining:	China, India

[52] **The President** (interpretation from French):

The result of the voting is as follows: 10 votes in favour, 3 against and 2 abstentions. The draft resolution has been adopted as resolution 688 (1991).

I shall now call on those members of the Security Council who wish to make statements following the voting.

[53] **Mr. Rochereau de la Sabliere (France)** (interpretation from French):

What does the Charter of the United Nations tell us? It opens with the following words:

> "We the peoples of the United Nations, determined to save succeeding generations from the scourge of war, ... to reaffirm faith in fundamental human rights, in the dignity and worth of the human person".

Those words announce an ambition. The League of Nations failed because it reflected only a dream. Faced with the reality - that is, the determination of certain States to exercise aggressive power - the dream was unable to resist the upheavals of history.

The United Nations has shown its effectiveness by putting an end to the aggression against one of its Members. The Security Council, which has adopted no fewer than 14 resolutions designed to restore peace and security in the region, would have been remiss in its task had it stood idly by, without reacting to the massacre of entire populations, the extermination of civilians, including women and children.

The civilian populations, Kurds in particular, already so sorely tried in the past, are once again the victims of armed violence. It is a matter of urgency that an end be put to the brutal repression of the Iraqi population and that all Iraqis be able to claim, within Iraq, respect for their rights and their identity.

Violations of human rights such as those now being observed become a matter of international interest when they take on such proportions that they assume the dimension of a crime against humanity. That is indeed what is happening in Iraq. The influx of refugees, the continued fighting in the border areas, the increasing number of massacres are arousing indignation and are threatening international peace and security in the region.

That is why France took the initiative of putting before the Security Council the text of the resolution we have just adopted. This text is at one and the same time a condemnation of the repression against Iraqi civilian populations in many parts of Iraq - particularly in the Kurdish area, but also in the South - an appeal for respect for the human and political rights of all Iraqi citizens, without discrimination, and a demand addressed to Iraq to allow immediate access by international humanitarian organizations to all those who need assistance in all parts of Iraq.

In our view, these demands are the minimum that the members of the international community must make in order to live up to the commitments they entered into when they adhered to the Charter of the United Nations. They are the minimum reflection of the faith they have expressed in the equality of rights of men and women in all nations; the most obvious expression of the guarantee they have given that no use will be made of the force of arms, except in the common interest.

Therefore, France hopes that the end of a painful conflict will be, for all those who have suffered from it on their own soil, the beginning of a genuine peace.

[54-55] **Mr. Li Daoyu (China)** (interpretation from Chinese):

We are concerned with the situation in Iraq and the huge influx of refugees into Turkey and Iran, as described in the letters from the Permanent Representatives of those two countries, and we wish to express sympathy for the difficulties confronting Turkey and Iran as a result of that influx. However, this is a question of great complexity, because the internal affairs of a country are also involved.

According to paragraph 7 of Article 2 of the Charter, the Security Council should not consider or take action on questions concerning the internal affairs of any State.

As for the international aspects involved in the question, we are of the view that they should be settled through the appropriate channels.

We support the Secretary-General in rendering humanitarian assistance to the refugees through the relevant organizations.

Based on the position I have just set out, we abstained in the vote on the resolution.

[56] **Mr. Hohenfellner (Austria):**

When I addressed the Council only two days ago, I expressed my country's grave concern about reports of heavy fighting and bloodshed in Iraq, with disastrous consequences for the civilian population, in particular in the area inhabited by Kurds and others. In the meantime, this situation has taken on an even more alarming dimension. Both Turkey and Iran have brought to the Council's urgent attention massive flows of Iraqi refugees towards and across their borders. Turkey has informed us about the plight of some 220,000 Iraqi citizens, many of them women and children, massed along the Turkish border; their number has since increased to some 500,000. Iran estimates that about an equal number of refugees will try to cross the border into Iran within the next few days. More than 110,000 Iraqi civilians have already done so, fleeing from repression by Iraqi Government forces.

This enormous flow of refugees constitutes an important factor of tension and potential destabilization in the countries neighbouring Iraq, thus posing a serious threat to peace and security in the region. With a view to safeguarding appropriate conditions for providing the civilian population with the necessary humanitarian assistance, Austria supported the French and Turkish initiatives to ensure that the Council fulfilled its duties and responsibilities under the Charter for the maintenance of international peace and security and urgently pronounced itself on this pressing issue.

The resolution just adopted addresses as a matter of urgency the issue of humanitarian relief to the refugees and the displaced Iraqi population. My country considers it of the utmost importance that immediate access to all Iraqi civilians in all part of Iraq be given to the international humanitarian organizations and that Iraq make available, to the extent feasible, all necessary facilities for their operation. The least the Council can do is to lend its full, strongest possible support for a massive humanitarian effort by the Secretary-General and the relevant United Nations agencies. Austria has already taken the first steps to provide humanitarian emergency aid to the refugee population concerned. In view of the exceptionally grave situation, Austria has asked the Government of Turkey to open its borders to the refugees.

[57] Mr. PICKERING (United States of America):

The United States warmly welcomes the adoption of resolution 688 (1991),

The United States is profoundly concerned about the plight of displaced civilians in Iraq, who are suffering because of the brutality of the Iraqi regime. This problem has tragic human consequences and presents serious implications for regional peace and security. We are gratified that the Security Council has addressed it on an urgent basis. This is, of course, a specific case which has arisen in the aftermath of the Gulf crisis.

President Bush has condemned the Iraqi Government's continued attacks against its own citizens - Kurds and Shiia and all the others, men, women and children, seeking to flee repression. We have called on Iraq's leaders to halt these attacks immediately and to allow international relief organizations to help these desperate people. We have demanded that Iraq facilitate the work of the appropriate international organizations to ensure that vital humanitarian aid reaches those in need throughout the country.

This resolution expresses the concern of the Council over the situation in Iraq, and the Council's condemnation of the Iraqi Government's continued violence towards its own people. The resolution insists that Iraq meet its humanitarian responsibilities. It is not the role or the intention of the Security Council to interfere in the internal affairs of any country. However, it is the Council's legitimate responsibility to respond to the concerns of Turkey and the Islamic Republic of Iran, concerns increasingly shared by other neighbours of Iraq, about the massive numbers of people fleeing, or disposed to flee, from Iraq across international frontiers because of the repression and brutality of Saddam Hussein. The transboundary impact of Iraq's treatment of its civilian population threatens regional stability. That is what the Council has addressed today.

The United States fully supports the resolution, and it urges all States to heed the Council's call to provide assistance to those in need. Throughout the crisis created by Iraq's invasion of Kuwait the United States has contributed generously to the care and maintenance of those displaced by the inhumane policies of the Iraqi Government. We will respond similarly to this latest example of inhumanity.

President Bush has just announced, this afternoon, his decision to undertake a major new effort by the United States, in light of the current tragedy, to assist Iraqi refugees and displaced persons. Beginning this Sunday, the United States Air Force will drop into northern Iraq food, blankets, clothing, tents and other relief-related items for suffering civilians. We expect the Government of Iraq to permit this effort to take place without interference.

We will also be consulting with the United Nations and coalition partners on how best to assist these people over the longer term. President Bush will shortly sign an order authorizing up to $10 million in additional aid for refugees in the region; we have already provided some $35 million in aid to refugees since the beginning of this crisis. Our military will continue to help displaced persons in southern Iraq, and we are willing to send a military medical unit to the Turkish border area to assist. We shall also be communicating to the Government of Iran our willingness to encourage and to contribute to relief efforts for refugees there. And we will be making additional contributions to the United Nations Children's Fund and the International Committee of the Red Cross for inoculation programmes to benefit children and civilians in Iraq.

President Bush has asked Secretary Baker to travel to Turkey, on his trip to the Middle East, to meet with President Ozal and to visit the border area in order to assess the situation personally and report back. It is our earnest hope that the resolution we have adopted today will send a clear message to Iraq and generate the desired response so that the suffering of its people can be alleviated and will stop.

[59-60] Mr. VORONTSOV (Union of Soviet Socialist Republics) (interpretation from Russian):

The Soviet Union reacted with understanding and concern to the appeal made to the Security Council by Turkey and Iran in connection with the extremely alarming situation that has come about on the borders with Iraq and the threat it has created to international peace and security in the region.

Hundreds of thousands of peaceful inhabitants, including women, the elderly and children, barefoot and hungry, are fleeing from Iraq along snow-covered mountain paths under artillery fire and bombardments, trying to save their lives. As we have seen from reports, the hostilities are already threatening to spill over into neighbouring countries. The continued worsening of the situation in the region, which is quite close to our own borders, cannot fail to arouse serious concern in the Soviet Union, and the situation is viewed with concern in many other countries. We agree with the view expressed by the Permanent Representative of Iran to the United Nations to the effect that the consequences that these events have for regional peace and security call for joint action by the Security Council from both the political and the humanitarian standpoint.

In its approach to the problems that are brought before the United Nations the Soviet Union firmly adheres to the principle of the inadmissibility of interference in the internal affairs of sovereign States, as set forth in the relevant provisions of the United Nations Charter. We therefore believe it important that reference is made in the very beginning of the resolution to Article 2, paragraph 7, of the Charter. Whatever conclusions are to be drawn from the Kuwait venture, this is a matter for the Iraqi people to solve. The sovereignty, territorial integrity and political independence of Iraq must be ensured. However, it is the duty of the Security Council and of the world community as a whole to put an end to the conditions that are forcing hundreds of thousands of peaceful inhabitants to leave their homeland and seek refuge in neighbouring countries; this is creating a destabilizing situation in the area and posing the threat of a new international conflict.

It is for that reason that the Security Council has drawn attention to the fact that the major cause of the massive transborder flow of refugees is the hostilities and repression being visited upon broad sectors of Iraq's civilian population. With other members of the Security Council, the Soviet Union cannot remain indifferent to the new sufferings of the Iraqi people, who have already been forced to bear an onerous burden and many privations. We therefore fully support the noble efforts of the United Nations Secretary-General, including his dispatch of a special mission to Iraq, as well as the efforts being made by the relevant United Nations specialized agencies and international and national humanitarian organizations, to do everything possible to alleviate the situation of the refugees and to solve the humanitarian problems of the entire Iraqi people.

Based on the foregoing considerations, the Soviet Union voted in favour of the draft resolution sponsored by the delegation of France and other countries, which has now become Security Council resolution 688 (1991).

[62] Mr. GHAREKHAN (India):

Throughout this tragic crisis my delegation has consistently made one point: its concern for the sufferings and loss of life of innocent people. My delegation is fully aware of the extremely unsettled conditions in Iraq and the horrendous toll they are taking on the people.

Only where such conditions, including indiscriminate use of force, result in a clear threat to international peace and security would it be within the competence of the Security Council to address the issue. My delegation is seriously concerned at the massive exodus of civilians from Iraq that has resulted from what is happening in that unfortunate land. The international community should be concerned enough to offer them succour and to demand that conditions be created to enable them to return to their homes in safety and in dignity. It should not prescribe what should be done, for that would impinge on the internal affairs of States.

In the situation as it prevails in the region my delegation urges restraint on all sides and expects them not to do anything that might further aggravate it. In our deliberations and decision-making within the Council, we should at all times keep in mind the need to respect the sovereignty and territorial integrity of States - including, in this case, of Iraq. This is a cardinal principle in international relations that deserves to be reiterated in the Council.

The Council, my delegation feels, should give serious consideration to the statement of the Permanent Representative of Iraq today inviting the Secretary-General or the Council to send a fact-finding mission to his country.

My delegation had the opportunity to consult closely with the sponsors of the resolution just adopted. Our endeavour was to focus the attention of the Council on the aspect of the threat or likely threat to peace and stability in the region rather than on the factors that have created the present situation. We believe that the Council should have concentrated on the aspect of peace and security, which is its proper mandate under the Charter, and left the other aspects to other, more appropriate organs of the United Nations. It was in that spirit that we had suggested to the sponsors some amendments to make the resolution more balanced and appropriate for this body. The response we received was serious, and we appreciate it. My delegation welcomes the inclusion of a reference to Article 2, paragraph 7, of the Charter, which is an element that improves the resolution.

However, the sponsors did not find it possible to accept the basic thrust of our amendments. This explains why we abstained in the voting.

[63] Sir David HANNAY (United Kingdom):

My delegation is delighted to see this resolution adopted and to have cosponsored it. Our only regret is that it should have taken so long for the Council to respond to the human tragedy which has been unfolding before our eyes in the mountains of northern Iraq during recent days. We have a way here of making even simple matters complicated, and I fear that the Council's recently acquired and well-justified reputation for decisiveness has taken a bit of dent in the last day or two.

But now we are moving ahead again, and we have adopted a resolution which accomplishes two crucial tasks. The first is, it sends a strong and clear message to the Government of Iraq that it must stop the repression, the harrying and the killing of innocent men, women and children which is at the root of this massive exodus into Turkey and Iran.

Secondly, it gives firm backing to the Secretary-General, to the United Nations specialized agencies and to all the governmental and non-governmental organizations whose efforts are now so urgently needed if even more lives are not to be lost. It has been argued in our debates that this action is in some way outside the scope of the Security Council, that it is an entirely internal matter. My delegation cannot accept that, and I am glad the resolution makes clear that it is not so. For one thing, Article 2, paragraph 7, an essential part of the Charter, does not apply to matters which, under the Charter, are not essentially domestic, and we have often seen human rights - for example in South Africa - defined in that category. In any case, the Turkish and Iranian letters to the Council make it clear that there is a very real threat here to international peace and security. The huge surge of refugees is destabilizing the whole region.

Thirdly, there are Iraq's international obligations, under Article 3 of the Geneva Conventions of 1949, to protect, in the case of internal armed conflicts, all innocent civilians from violence of all kinds to life and person. Now, all this fully justifies the action by the Security Council. The humanitarian problems are horrendous, and we therefore warmly welcome the intention of the Secretary-General to launch, on 8 April, an overall appeal for help, and we hope that, in his appeal, he will cover the activities of all the various United Nations specialized agencies. We need a massive aid effort, but we also need a well-focused and a well-coordinated one.

For our part, we have already announced that we will contribute £20 million, bilaterally and multilaterally, to this appeal for the relief of the Kurdish people and for other humanitarian needs of the Iraqi people. This is in addition to £1 million announced yesterday for an airlift of blankets and tents to Turkey and an earlier grant of £2.5 million to the International Committee of the Red Cross.

This huge international humanitarian effort is essential, but it must not conceal the basic responsibility for this human tragedy. That lies fair and square at the door of the Government of Iraq, whose brutality to its own population is matched only by its aggressive actions towards its neighbours, and by its disregard for international law and for all civilized standards of behaviour. Faced with a Government which ruthlessly gassed numbers of its compatriots a couple of years ago, no wonder the Kurds flee in terror in their hundreds and their thousands.

I said a few days ago that my Government found it hard to see how Iraq could hope to rejoin the civilized community of nations while Saddam Hussein and his acolytes remained in power. Nothing that has happened since then has encouraged us to change our mind.

[67] The PRESIDENT (interpretation from French):

I would now like to make a statement in my capacity as representative of Belgium.

My Government, at the very beginning of this week, expressed profound concern at the policy of blind and systematic repression of which the Iraqi civilian population has been the victim in some regions of Iraq, particularly in the Kurdish regions. Belgium condemns these acts in the strongest possible terms.

The policy of repression in some regions of Iraq has caused major displacements of populations towards the countries neighbouring Iraq. The scale of these exoduses, the destitution of the refugees and the enormity of their needs of all kinds have caused extremely critical situations to arise on the borders of these States. Furthermore, this policy of repression has already caused serious border incidents.

International peace and security are therefore threatened. The Council was therefore duty bound to respond to the initiative of the authors of the resolution which has just been put before it, which Belgium also sponsors. As far as Belgium is concerned, such support is in this case justified by the very specific considerations arising from an exceptionally serious situation which threatens peace and security in the region.

In joining in condemning the repression in Iraq, in the Kurdish regions most specifically, my country wishes, in addition, to ensure observance of the most basic principles of humanitarian law and of human rights. The relevant provisions of the Geneva Conventions, to which Iraq is party, oblige it, in the event of internal armed conflict, to show consideration for the civilian population and to treat it humanely. All the items of information we have in our possession prompt us to conclude that Iraq is deliberately refusing to comply with these essential, international legal obligations. My country fully supports the Council in its demand that Iraq put an immediate end to the current repression.

My delegation therefore reminds the Iraqi authorities of their international obligations and their previous undertakings, according to which they must afford the humanitarian organizations immediate, unrestricted access throughout Iraq to the populations in distress.

Furthermore, the Belgian Government urges the Iraqi leadership to establish without delay a political dialogue with all the components of the Iraqi people, especially the representatives of the Kurdish population of Iraq, with a view to ensuring that the Iraqi population in its entirety can exercise freely its civil and political rights and that human rights are observed, while at the same time reaffirming the principle of the territorial integrity of Iraq and of the other States in the region.

My country associates itself with the international community's effort to come to the aid of the victims of repression, and is taking the necessary steps to take part in it actively.

...

[68] Mr. SCIALOJA (Italy):

...

I am speaking to express the utmost concern of the Italian Government at the cruelty of the repression by the Baghdad Government of the civilian population in many parts of Iraq, including the Kurdish areas, where hundreds of thousands of refugees have gathered near the borders with Turkey and Iran. The European Community and its Member States have strongly condemned the brutal repression, which, by causing serious tensions along the borders, also threatens international peace and security.

The Italian Government fervently hopes that the Iraqi Government will promptly end this persecution and start a process of democratization by engaging in a constructive dialogue, with all the components of the Iraqi population, leading to the establishment of a just society based on full respect for human rights and civil and political freedoms.

For these reasons, Italy fully shares the concern expressed by members of the Security Council and other Members of the United Nations on the dreadful situation of the Kurdish refugees, and expresses its appreciation of the resolution just adopted by the Security Council. We expect that the Iraqi Government will immediately abide by the provisions of the resolution by bringing its illegal actions to an end. Moreover, we express our conviction that the Secretary-General will be able to address the critical needs of the refugees.

The Italian Government has, on a bilateral basis, decided to offer humanitarian assistance to the displaced populations and to supply emergency aid to help Turkey and Iran face the dramatic problems that would arise from the massive influx of several hundred thousand refugees into their countries. A technical mission to assess these needs is on its way.

We sincerely hope that concerted action on the part of the international community will convince the Iraqi Government of the necessity of solving any problem democratically, in order to eliminate tensions in a region of paramount importance for international peace and security. In this context, the Italian Government expresses its satisfaction at the decision of the Iraqi Government to receive the mission provided for in operative paragraph 4 of resolution 688 (1991).

...

[71] Mr. RANTZAU (Germany):

Germany is following the most recent developments in Iraq with the greatest concern. The brutal use of weapons and other agents of destruction against the Kurdish minority and other parts of the Iraqi population, and the mass exodus it has precipitated, harbour the danger of genocide. After the horrible crimes of 1988, human rights are again being flagrantly violated. International peace and security are in jeopardy. The United Nations, and in particular the Security Council, are called upon to take appropriate steps immediately.

In 1988, Germany cosponsored Security Council resolution 620 (1988), which condemned the use of chemical and biological weapons in the war between Iraq and Iran. It also requested the United Nations Secretary-General to launch an immediate investigation whenever the deployment of such weapons is suspected, even within a country's own borders. Already then, my Government was deeply concerned about the cruel treatment of the Kurdish minority in Iraq.

With resolution 687 (1991), the Security Council has set itself the goal of restoring peace and security in the region. The efforts undertaken to this end by the Security Council will only be successful if domestic peace in Iraq is also ensured.

It is the legitimate right of the international community to call for respect for human rights. This means that no ethnic or religious group may be persecuted or discriminated against. When a national minority keeps finding itself in a position where it is forced to fight for its rights, and when it therefore has to endure great sacrifices and human suffering, it proves that its legitimate claim is crudely violated by the leadership of the country. The repressive measures of the Iraqi army are of indescribable cruelty: villages are levelled, human beings are fired upon, and the civilian population is bombed.

The international community has to undertake all appropriate efforts to prevail upon the Iraqi Government to enter into negotiations with the representatives of the Kurdish minority and to concede to this brave and proud people a status commensurate with its hopes and aspirations. This should not infringe upon or jeopardize the integrity of the Iraqi State. My Government welcomes the fact that the Security Council has now followed up on its cease-fire resolution 687 (1991) by urgently calling upon Iraq to put an immediate end to the persecution of the Kurdish minority and other parts of the population. My Government also feels that their return to their settlements under the supervision of United Nations observers should be ensured.

The international community bears responsibility for ensuring that the human rights of all Iraqis, of all ethnic and religious communities, including the Kurds, be observed. The persecution of this ethnic group and the armed repression against it must be stopped. It must not be subjected to any punishment. The Kurds must be given the rights they were promised many years ago and that all Iraqis are entitled to. It is in the interest of the Iraqi Government, in the interest of stability and security in the region, and especially in the interest of those desperate human beings, that peace be restored within Iraq.

...

[73] **Mr. Feyder (Luxembourg)** (interpretation from French):

...

The Government of Luxembourg is alarmed and deeply concerned by current events in Iraq and on its borders. Hundreds of thousands of Iraqi citizens, especially Shiites and Kurds, are fleeing a bloody and pitiless repression visited upon them by the army of the Iraqi Government. What is absolutely shocking and contrary to the norms of international law is that soldiers are firing upon innocent and defenceless civilians, destroying homes and hospitals, and harassing and killing fleeing populations.

We believe that this is flagrant violation of the principles of humanitarian law as established by the Geneva Conventions. We are also witnessing massive and tragic violations of the human rights of all those men, women and children who have been forced to abandon their homes and flee towards an unknown fate.

The information we have been provided by the Governments concerned and by the media also clearly demonstrates that this problem has become international. The refugees, and especially the Kurds in the north of the country, wish to leave for the neighbouring countries, Turkey and Iran. Some have managed to do so, and others are hastening to reach the border. An enormous problem faces the Governments of those countries. An entire region is now threatened with destabilization, which affects peace and security. We are all called upon to show sensitivity towards and solidarity with those people now facing new trials following upon those imposed on them by Iraq's invasion of Kuwait.

Together with its partners in the European Community, my Government condemned the brutal repression against these civilian populations, especially the Kurds and Shiites, which gave rise to the flow of refugees I have just described. The Community and its 12 member States call upon the Iraqi authorities to put an end without delay to this repression which, in the past, already severely affected the Kurdish population. They believe that only the path of dialogue with all the parties concerned can lead to the restoration of a united and legitimate Iraqi State committed to respect the populations of which it is comprised.

That is why it was absolutely necessary for the Security Council to act and to take a clear-cut decision on the draft resolution submitted to it on the initiative of the French delegation. My Government welcomes its adoption a few moments ago. The Council thereby discharged its responsibilities in the face of the tragic situation in which the population of Iraq finds itself and in the face of the border problems which have arisen. I should like to thank all the delegations which so kindly extended me their cooperation in recent days.

My Government hopes that all national and international resources will be brought to bear in order to come to the assistance of the populations in distress. Special importance in this regard goes to the activities conducted by our Organization, its Secretary-General and specialized agencies. Emergency assistance will be undertaken by the European Community in the coming days.

Whatever the future of Iraq, the Luxembourg Government believes that the sovereignty, territorial integrity and political independence of Iraq and of all the other States of the area must be respected. We all agree, too, in emphasizing that it is up to the Iraqis alone to determine their future.

Last November some non-aligned members of the Council put before the Council a draft resolution in which they expressed the hope that the Governments of the region, especially that of Iraq, would take appropriate effective steps in order to strengthen their democratic institutions and practices. More and more Iraqis, both inside and outside Iraq, are now speaking out for the establishment of a pluralistic democratic system mindful of human rights.

We should ask ourselves whether this is not now the path to follow in order to enable the populations concerned to express their will, thus contributing to the establishment of a genuine peace in Iraq.

...

[77] **Mr. Mortensen (Denmark):**

...

Today, the world is once again witnessing human rights and fundamental freedoms being grossly violated.

The Danish Government has strongly condemned the brutal repression and suffering that has been imposed upon the civilian population in Iraq, notably the Kurds and the Shiites.

Iraq must immediately put an end to these atrocities and engage in an open dialogue to ensure that the human rights of all Iraqi citizens are fully respected. In this connection, we note the desire of the Kurdish leaders to preserve the territorial integrity and sovereignty of Iraq. The human tragedy unfolding in Iraq, as a consequence of the brutal and bloody actions against civilians, has brought about a flow of refugees towards Iraq's neighbouring countries.

The magnitude of the human suffering and the transboundary problems involved makes it natural for the international community to deal with the matter and for the Security Council to take the necessary measures. Denmark therefore welcomes the adoption of resolution 688 (1991).

The international community must render assistance to alleviate the plight and suffering of the Kurds and others fleeing the fighting and bloodshed in Iraq.

To that end, the Danish Government for its part has today decided to contribute, as an immediate step, 9 million Danish kroner, corresponding approximately to $1.5 million.

...

[78] **Mr. Hayes (Ireland):**

...

Ireland fully supports the resolution just adopted by the Security Council. The Government and the people of Ireland are deeply concerned at the situation of the civilian population in Iraq, notably the Kurds and the Shiites, and they firmly condemn the brutal repression being imposed on these population groups.

They call on the Iraqi authorities to put an end to this repression, which has already in the past severely affected the Kurdish people. The flow of refugees to neighbouring countries resulting from this repression is a cause of serious humanitarian concern. Ireland is ready to join with the rest of the international community to alleviate their plight. Iraq's neighbours must not be left to shoulder this burden alone.

The repression of the Kurds and Shiites must be condemned in the strongest terms. The Kurds have the right to live within Iraq, with full respect for their culture and language. We call on the Government of Iraq to follow the path of dialogue to ensure that the human and political rights of all Iraqi citizens are respected.

Any attempt to interfere with Iraq's sovereignty, territorial integrity, or political independence, would be unacceptable as well as detrimental to the prospects for peace and security in the region. The resolution just adopted makes this clear. At the same time, respect for the territorial integrity of Iraq does not take away from its obligations to engage in dialogue to ensure that the human and political rights of the Kurds and Shiites are respected within Iraq.

...

[81] **Mr. Viqueira (Spain)** (interpretation from Spanish):

...

Upon instructions from my Government, I have asked to be allowed to speak in order to express before the

Security Council Spain's complete support for resolution 688 (1991), which has just been adopted.

My country has been following with deep concern the brutal repression unleashed by the Iraqi authorities on its own civilian population, in particular the Kurds and the Shiites, and it fears the repercussions this may have on peace and security in the region.

In addition to the enormous magnitude of the suffering and the loss of human life, this repression has created a problem of displaced persons and refugees of epic proportions, has deeply moved the public opinion of the world, and of Spain in particular, and has inspired a number of States Members of the Organization to take an initiative whose result is the resolution just adopted.

Spain joins the rest of the international community in firm condemnation of the systematic violation of human rights committed by the Iraqi authorities against their own civilian population, and also demands an immediate end to these inhuman practices, as well as respect for the human and political rights of all Iraqi citizens.

In conclusion, my Government is prepared to cooperate with the Secretary-General and the United Nations in all efforts aimed at alleviating the suffering of the Iraqi civilian population.

...

[82] Mr. Eliasson (Sweden):

...

A great number of people in Sweden, many of them recent immigrants with their origin in the Middle East, view with sorrow and apprehension developments now unfolding in Iraq in the aftermath of the actions for the liberation of Kuwait. The credibility of the United Nations demands that the Organization shoulder its responsibility also for developments following measures authorized by the Security Council, especially as these developments entail the suffering of large numbers of innocent people.

The Iraqi leadership's violent suppression of opposition forces in various parts of Iraq - in the South and, most recently, in the Kurdish-populated areas - has brutally affected the civilian population. The desperate situation of thousands and thousands of civilians trying to take refuge in neighbouring countries is appalling. These people urgently need help from the international community as a whole.

The magnitude of the suffering of Iraqi refugees already has had international consequences across the borders of Iraq. Events in Iraq have a direct impact on the future peace and stability of the region as a whole. That peace and stability has been a stated objective of Security Council resolutions. Thus an international reaction through the Security Council is indeed legitimate and timely from both a political and a humanitarian perspective. This, in our view, in no way diminishes the validity and the importance of Article 2, paragraph 7 of the Charter.

Lasting regional peace and stability demand respect for human rights and decent treatment of minority groups. A solution to internal problems in Iraq can be achieved only by dialogue and a political process. Violence against a defenceless civilian population can never be excused. Instead of using what remains of its military machine against the opposition, the Iraqi Government should negotiate with the groups that oppose it.

The Kurds in Iraq must be put in a position of being able to enjoy their inalienable rights as a minority group. They should be given the possibility to express their identity freely within the State of Iraq and in accordance with their own aspirations.

Concerted action is needed to give humanitarian aid to the suffering civilian population in the Kurdish-populated and other areas of Iraq. We commend the Secretary-General for his efforts to prepare a coordinated programme of emergency relief for Iraq. Such an emergency programme should be based on established principles and criteria for humanitarian relief, designed to reach the affected populations in all areas of need, including the areas of the Kurdish population. We must also find ways of caring for the many displaced persons inside Iraq.

It is equally important for the United Nations to address the rapidly growing refugee problem in the border areas between Iraq and Turkey and between Iraq and Iran. The absorption capacity - long drawn upon - of those two neighbours of Iraq is obviously not adequate and must be strengthened by international assistance.

In line with its traditions, Sweden is ready to continue to make its contributions to the international efforts to alleviate the suffering of civilians in Iraq and the many refugees outside Iraq's borders.

Let me, in conclusion, say that we are today facing not only a pressing humanitarian problem but also a challenge for the United Nations and its standing as an organization that builds peace for the future and improves the condition of man.

...

[84-85] Mr. Van Schaik (Netherlands):

...

Like previous speakers, I wish to express my Government's grave concern about the repression of the Iraqi civilian population, including most recently in Kurdish populated areas. The fact that I have asked to speak about this very serious matter testifies to my Government's profound concern about the situation. The people of the Netherlands are deeply disturbed, for obvious humanitarian reasons. We are also preoccupied with the serious implications for international peace and security in the region. We insist that Iraq observe its commitments arising from international instruments to respect the fundamental rights and freedoms of its citizens.

We fully support this initiative, and my Government endorses the resolution that has just been adopted. The public at large would not have understood the dealings of this Council if after the 14 resolutions that have been adopted on the situation in the region the Council had remained silent on this matter.

The representative of Luxembourg, Ambassador Feyder, referred to the statement that the European Community and its member States have made, in which they have expressed their very deep concern over the situation of the civilian population of Iraq. We indeed firmly condemn the brutal repression being imposed upon these population groups.

We also wish to draw attention to the implications of the massive flow of refugees and displaced persons towards neighbouring countries. We look forward to any action the Secretary-General takes to pursue his humanitarian efforts in favour of the victims of repression. We trust that Member States will make a substantive contribution to humanitarian organizations to alleviate the plight of Iraqi people that find themselves in unbearable conditions as a result of these events. The Netherlands is prepared to shoulder responsibility with the international community in its humanitarian efforts to create conditions for a return to civilized life by the Iraqi people.

We urge Iraq to open a dialogue to ensure that the human and political rights of its people are fully respected.

...

[87] Mr. Da Costa Pereira (Portugal):

...

Portugal follows with great concern the grave situation on the borders of Iraq with Turkey and Iran. With the other members of the European Community, it firmly condemns the repression of the civilian population in many parts of Iraq, which constitutes brutal disrespect for basic human rights.

We believe that only dialogue with all the parties concerned would allow the shaping of a renewed Iraq, united and respectful of the legitimate rights and aspirations of the population groups of that country.

The Portuguese Government fully supports the resolution that the Council has just adopted and hopes that the current deterioration of the situation will soon come to an end in order to avoid further loss of life of innocent human beings.

We deeply hope that the humanitarian assistance efforts to take place under the auspices of the Secretary-General will alleviate the suffering and meet the critical needs of the refugees and displaced Iraqi population.

...

[88] Mr. HUSLID (Norway):

...

The behaviour and action of the Iraqi authorities, not least against their own population, have for an extended period of time given cause for grave concern. In this connection, we all remember with abhorrence the attack on Iran, the purges in Baghdad and in particular the shocking gassing of the civilian Kurdish population. Recently there was the unprovoked invasion and occupation of peaceful Kuwait, which the international community, under the Council's auspices, succeeded by a considerable joint effort in bringing to an end only a few weeks ago.

However, barely was that war over than we had to witness the destructive attacks against the people and the cities of the Shiite communities in the south of Iraq. Now the turn of the Kurds and other minorities in the East and the North has come.

The world cannot sit in silence and allow this to continue. The Iraqi regime must be brought to understand that its actions are totally unacceptable, reprehensible and, indeed, immoral.

For these reasons the Norwegian Government condemns the actions perpetrated against the Kurdish population and other groups, in contravention of internationally accepted human rights standards and norms of behaviour. We call on the Iraqi authorities to halt such actions immediately.

We join others in calling for concerted international humanitarian aid to Kurdish refugees and others suffering from the repression inflicted by the Iraqi authorities.

Finally, we express the hope that the international community as a whole will take joint responsibility in all these respects. On behalf of the Norwegian Government, I pledge our full support for all efforts to meet the needs of the refugees. Norway has already supported the international humanitarian actions in this respect, *inter alia*, by a recent cash contribution of 10 million Norwegian kroner - $1.5 million. We stand ready to offer further support in this hour of need.

On behalf of Norway, I wish to give our support to the resolution the Council has just adopted.

[91] The PRESIDENT (interpretation from French):

...

I should like to inform members of the Council that I have received letters from the representatives of Canada and Greece in which they request to be invited to participate in the discussion of the item on the Council's agenda. In conformity with the usual practice, I propose, with the consent of the Council, to invite those members to participate in the discussion, without the right to vote, in accordance with the relevant provisions of the Charter and rule 37 of the Council's provisional rules of procedure.

There being no objection, it is so decided.

At the invitation of the President, Mr. Fortier (Canada) and Mr. Exarchos (Greece) took the places reserved for them at the side of the Council Chamber.

...

[91] **Mr. FORTIER (Canada)** (interpretation from French):

...

(*continued in English*)

Canada continues to be deeply disturbed by the suffering of the Iraqi people as a result of the brutal repression by the Iraqi authorities of their civilian population. The Government of Canada has called upon Iraq to refrain from actions that would exacerbate the suffering of Iraqi civilians.

Regrettably, this suffering is continuing and growing. There has been a massive movement of civilians away from the areas of fighting and towards and across international borders. As the resolution just adopted by the Security Council makes abundantly clear, these movements, along with cross-border incursions, pose an undeniable threat to international peace and security in the region. That is why, in the opinion of my Government, it was proper and within the mandate of the Council to act as it has done on this matter.

Meanwhile, unfortunately, the suffering of the innocent civilians in Iraq continues. Canada remains in constant touch with the international humanitarian organizations such as the Red Cross and the United Nations Disaster Relief Organization. This afternoon in Ottawa Canada announced an initial contribution of $3.3 million to these and other organizations to help provide the basic needs of the displaced citizens of Iraq, both inside Iraq and in neighbouring countries.

But money alone will not end the suffering. The only way to do that is for Iraq to give the fullest cooperation to international humanitarian organizations, to facilitate their work and to respect fully the human and political rights of all Iraqi citizens without further delay.

...

[92] Mr. EXARCHOS (Greece):

...

On 28 March 1991 my Government expressed its grave concern and deep regret with regard to the recent developments in Iraq as well as the reported use of violence against its Kurdish-populated areas. That stand is consistent with Greece's firm opposition to the use of force, and particularly military methods, aimed at solving domestic problems.

Furthermore, Greece, along with its European Community partners, has condemned such practices and called upon the Iraqi authorities to put an end to the repression without delay and engage upon the path of dialogue. We firmly believe that these problems can be solved only through dialogue in full respect of the territorial integrity and unity of Iraq.

Finally, in order to alleviate the plight of the afflicted populations of Iraq, the Greek Government yesterday decided to dispatch immediately humanitarian assistance to the afflicted populations through the Hellenic Red Cross.

...

M. S/PV.2983, 9 April 1991

...

[3] The PRESIDENT (interpretation from French):

The Security Council will now begin its consideration of the item on the agenda.

The Security Council is meeting in accordance with the understanding reached in its prior consultations.

Members of the Council have before them the report (S/22454 and Add.1-3) of the Secretary-General on the implementation of paragraph 5 of Security Council resolution 687 (1991).

Members of the Council also have before them document S/22470, which contains the text of a draft resolution that has been prepared in the course of the Council's prior consultations. In this connection, I should like to draw attention to the fact that the following paragraph has been added to the draft resolution, as the second preambular paragraph: "Acting under Chapter VII of the Charter".

...

It is my understanding that the Council is ready to proceed to the vote on the draft resolution before it. Unless I hear any objection, I shall put the draft resolution to the vote now.

There being no objection, it is so decided.

I now put to the vote the draft resolution in document S/22470.

A vote was taken by show of hands.

In favour: Austria, Belgium, China, Côte d'Ivoire, Cuba, Ecuador, France, India, Romania, Union of Soviet Socialist Republics, United Kingdom of Great Britain and Northern Ireland, United States of America, Yemen, Zaire, Zimbabwe

[4] **The President** (interpretation from French): There were 15 votes in favour. The draft resolution has therefore been adopted unanimously as resolution 689 (1991).

The Security Council has thus concluded the present stage of its consideration of the item on the agenda. The Council will remain seized of the matter.

...

N. S/PV.2985, 29 April 1991

...

[2] **The President** (interpretation from French): The Security Council will now begin its consideration of the item on its agenda. The Council is meeting in accordance with an agreement reached in the course of its prior consultations.

As a result of consultations among members of the Security Council I have been authorized to make the following statement on behalf of the Council:

> "The members of the Security Council have considered the memorandum dated 22 March 1991 (S/22382) which was addressed to the President of the Security Council by the 21 States which have invoked Article 50 of the United Nations Charter owing to the special economic problems arising from the implementation of the sanctions imposed against Iraq and Kuwait under Council resolution 661 (1990).
>
> "The members of the Security Council have taken note of the Secretary-General's oral report to them on 11 April 1991, in which he supported the appeal launched by the 21 States that have invoked Article 50. The Secretary-General further informed the Council on 26 April 1991 of the conclusions reached by the Administrative Committee on Coordination (ACC) at the session it has just held in Paris, where members of ACC agreed to vigorously pursue their efforts to respond effectively to the needs of countries most affected by the implementation of resolution 661 (1990). The Secretary-General will coordinate through ACC, within the framework of this assistance, the activities of the organizations of the United Nations system.
>
> "The members of the Security Council have taken note of the replies from a number of States - Austria, Belgium, Denmark, France, Germany, Greece, Ireland, Italy, Japan, Liechtenstein, Luxembourg, Luxembourg on behalf of the European Community and its 12 member States, Netherlands, New Zealand, Norway, Portugal, Spain, Switzerland, the United Kingdom, the United States and the USSR - which have furnished specific information on the assistance they have provided to various affected countries; they have also taken note of the replies from officials of international financial institutions, such as those received from the President of the World Bank and the Managing Director of the International Monetary Fund (IMF). They invite other Member States and international financial institutions and organizations to inform the Secretary-General as soon as possible of the measures that they have taken on behalf of the States which have invoked Article 50.
>
> "The members of the Security Council make a solemn appeal to States, international financial institutions and United Nations bodies to respond positively and speedily to the recommendations of the Security Council Committee established under resolution 661 (1990) for assistance to countries which find themselves confronted with special economic problems arising from the carrying out of those measures imposed by resolution 661 (1990) and which have invoked Article 50.
>
> "The members of the Security Council note that the procedure established under Article 50 of the Charter remains in effect".

The Security Council has thus concluded the present stage of its consideration of the item on its agenda.

O. S/PV.2987, 20 May 1991

...

[2] **The President** (interpretation from Chinese): The Security Council will now begin its consideration of the item on its agenda. The Security Council is meeting in accordance with the understanding reached in its prior consultations. Members of the Council have before them the report of the Secretary-General pursuant to paragraph 19 of Security Council resolution 687 (1991), document S/22559. Members of the Council also have before them document S/22613, which contains the text of a draft resolution submitted by the United Kingdom of Great Britain and Northern Ireland and the United States of America. Belgium, France, Romania, the Union of Soviet Socialist Republics and Zaire have also become sponsors of the draft resolution.

I should like to draw attention to a technical change in paragraph 2 of the draft resolution. In the second line, the reference to "687" should read "resolution 687 (1991)".

It is my understanding that the Council is ready to proceed to the vote on the draft resolution before it. Unless I hear any objection, I shall put the draft resolution to the vote now.

A vote was taken by show of hands.

In favour: Austria, Belgium, China, Côte d'Ivoire, Ecuador, France, India, Romania, Union of Soviet Socialist Republics, United Kingdom of Great Britain and Northern Ireland, United States of America, Yemen, Zaire, Zimbabwe

Against: None

Abstaining: Cuba

[3] **The President** (interpretation from Chinese):
The result of the voting is as follows: 14 votes in favour, none against and one abstention. The draft resolution has been adopted as resolution 692 (1991).

The Security Council has thus concluded the present stage of its consideration of the item on its agenda. ...

P. S/PV.2994, 17 June 1991

...

[2] **The President** (interpretation from French):
The Security Council will now begin its consideration of the item on the agenda.

The Security Council is meeting in accordance with the understanding reached in its prior consultations.

Members of the Council have before them the following documents: report of the Secretary-General on the plan for the implementation of relevant parts of section C of Security Council resolution 687 (1991), document S/22614; note by the Secretary-General submitting to the members of the Council the text of a letter addressed to him under paragraph 13 of Security Council resolution 687 (1991) by the Director General of the International Atomic Energy Agency (IAEA), document S/22615; and report of the Secretary-General pursuant to paragraph 26 of Security Council resolution 687 (1991), document S/22660.

Members of the Council also have before them document S/22686, containing the text of a draft resolution submitted by France, the Union of Soviet Socialist Republics, the United Kingdom of Great Britain and Northern Ireland and the United States of America, and document S/22698, containing the text of a draft resolution submitted by Belgium, France, the Union of Soviet Socialist Republics, the United Kingdom of Great Britain and Northern Ireland and the United States of America.

I should like to draw the attention of members of the Council to document S/22682, which contains the text of a letter dated 9 June from the Chargé d'affaires a.i. of the Permanent Mission of Iraq to the United Nations addressed to the Secretary-General, and document S/22689, which contains the text of identical letters dated 11 June 1991 from the Chargé d'affaires, a.i. of the Permanent Mission of Iraq to the United Nations addressed respectively to the Secretary-General and the President of the Security Council.

The first speaker is the representative of Iraq, on whom I now call.

[3] **Mr. Al-Nima (Iraq)** (interpretation from Arabic):
...

My delegation has comments to make on the draft resolution in document S/22686. First I should like to give a comprehensive review clarifying the implementation of resolution 687 (1991) - the degree of Iraq's compliance and the fulfilment of its responsibilities under that resolution.

The Iraqi Government accepted resolution 687 (1991), expressing its formal acceptance on 6 April in a message to the President of the Security Council and the Secretary-General. I wish to state that the Iraqi Government both accepted the resolution and dealt with it positively.

Allow me, Sir, to review the measures taken by the Iraqi Government to implement the provisions of that resolution in fulfilment of its obligations under it.

First, as regards section A, on the demarcation of the boundary between Iraq and Kuwait, the Iraqi Government designated a representative to attend meetings of the demarcation Committee, which held its first meetings in New York on 23 and 24 May this year. The representative of Iraq participated effectively and constructively in the work of that session.

Secondly, as regards section B, concerning the deployment of observers in the area between Iraq and Kuwait, the Iraqi authorities on a number of occasions received in Baghdad the head of the observer team, Major-General Gunther Greindl, and his assistants following his appointment, and steps on the deployment of the team in the demilitarized zone were agreed in May.

There is constant cooperation between the competent Iraqi authorities and the observer team, through the proper channels, as well as between those authorities and the head of the team and the United Nations Secretariat.

Thirdly, as regards section C of the resolution, which called for the implementation of the obligation to destroy weapons of mass destruction and not to use, develop or possess such weapons, Iraq has deposited ratification documents in which it accepts the Convention on the Prohibition of the Development, Production and Stockpiling of Bacteriological (Biological) Weapons of 10 April 1972, as well as its unconditional obligations under the Geneva Protocol of 17 June 1925 for the Prohibition of the Use in War of Asphyxiating, Poisonous or Other Gases, and of Bacteriological Methods of Warfare. The Iraqi Government has presented information concerning the locations, quantities and types of chemical weapons and ballistic missiles and has agreed to submit to on-site inspection, in accordance with the resolution. Iraq has also undertaken the unconditional obligation not to use, develop, manufacture or acquire any of the material referred to in the resolution. It has confirmed the obligation it has assumed under the non-proliferation Treaty of 1968. Iraq has unconditionally agreed not to produce or possess nuclear weapons or any materials that could be used to manufacture such weapons. Iraq has also notified the International Atomic Energy Agency (IAEA) of the message by the Foreign Minister dated 27 April 1991 in which he expressed Iraq's willingness to cooperate in the implementation of the provisions of the resolution; annexed to the message were tables giving information on the nuclear facilities in Iraq. Detailed data on the situation regarding other weapons referred to in the resolution have been given to the Special Commission established in connection with the implementation of section C of the resolution.

In a letter to the Secretary-General in May 1991 Iraq expressed its agreement to the proposals concerning immunities and privileges for the Special Committee and its teams that would visit Iraq. The special inspection team on nuclear weapons visited Iraq between 14 and 22 May 1991. On 23 May 1991 the IAEA, in a statement, confirmed that the Iraqi side had cooperated fully with the inspection team and acceded to all its requests. The special inspection team on chemical weapons, accompanied by the Chairman of the Special Commission, started its mission with a visit to Iraq between 9 and 15 June. Iraq provided the inspection team with all the means necessary to ensure the success of its mission.

With regard to section D of the resolution, concerning the return of Kuwaiti property, Mr. Richard Foran, an Assistant Secretary-General, visited Iraq twice in May 1991. The Iraqi authorities expressed their willingness to return property about which it had notified the United Nations Secretariat. Actually, one civil aircraft belonging to Kuwait was handed over in Amman on 11 May 1991. Mr. Foran visited the sites and other locations and inspected the gold coins and banknotes, the antiquities and books, and the civil aircraft that were to be returned to Kuwait after agreement was reached on the place of delivery. Mr. Foran regarded the aforementioned items as having priority. There can be no doubt that the same treatment would apply to other Kuwaiti property.

Fifthly, as regards sections E and F of the resolution, concerning compensation and the lifting of sanctions, no measures are required by Iraq.

As for section G, measures continue to be taken by the Iraqi authorities in connection with the return of all Kuwaiti and third-country nationals to their countries of origin. Iraq has provided a list containing the names of such persons. A mission of the International Committee of the Red Cross was given access to the locations in Baghdad where these persons were being detained. It should be noted that 6,366 persons have been freed and repatriated. Among these, 6,289 were Kuwaitis, 36 Americans, 5 Italians, 13 Saudis, 17 French, 1 Spaniard, 2 Brazilians, 1 Norwegian, 1 Uruguayan and 1 Irish. The Iraqi authorities are still carrying out research to find the missing from among the Coalition countries so that they can be returned to their countries after registration by the mission of the International Committee of the Red Cross.

The competent Iraqi authorities have facilitated the task of the International Committee of the Red Cross in directly registering the Kuwaiti nationals in Iraq. More than 3,000 Kuwaitis have thus been registered. The remains of 15 persons have been returned to the Coalition countries.

As for section H of the resolution, concerning international terrorism, the following should be noted.

Iraq has participated with the international community in efforts to combat international terrorism. It should be noted that the draft resolution which was adopted by the General Assembly on 9 December 1985 as resolution 40/61 was adopted in the Sixth Committee under the chairmanship of Iraq during the fortieth session of the Assembly. The representatives of many countries expressed their appreciation of the efforts made by Iraq to that end. Moreover, Iraq is a party to some of the most important international conventions dealing with crimes of terrorism, such as the Convention on Offences and Certain Other Acts Committed on Board Aircraft, signed at Tokyo in 1963; the Convention on the prevention of hijacking, signed at The Hague in 1970; the Convention for the Suppression of Unlawful Acts against the Safety of Civil Aviation, signed in Montreal in 1971; and the Convention on the Prevention and Punishment of Crimes against Internationally Protected Persons, including Diplomatic Agents, signed in New York in 1973. Iraq also took part in the final stages of the drafting of the International Convention against the taking of Hostages, adopted in New York in 1979.

Moreover, Iraqi legislation approaches terrorist crimes from two angles: prevention and punishment. Iraq's penal code does not view terrorist crimes as political crimes.

The Government of the Republic of Iraq does not pursue any policy with respect to international terrorism that runs counter to international law. As stated previously, its position is consistent with that of most members of the international community. In his letter dated 11 June 1991 addressed to the Secretary-General in accordance with paragraph 32 of resolution 687 (1991), our Foreign Minister confirmed that Iraq would commit no act that could be considered international terrorism or permit any organization intending to commit such an act to operate within its territory, and that Iraq condemns unequivocally and renounces all acts, methods and practices of terrorism.

My country's Government wishes to affirm its absolute readiness to cooperate with respect to the implementation of section C of resolution 687 (1991) and its desire not to raise any obstacle to implementation of the resolution. Unfortunately, my Government notes that paragraph 4 of draft resolution S/22686, concerning adoption of the Secretary-General's plan for the implementation of section C of resolution 687 (1991), makes the Government of Iraq liable for all the costs of carrying out the tasks entrusted to the Secretary-General. My Government rejects liability for the cost of destroying the chemical weapons. On the other hand, it affirms its willingness to cooperate and by its own efforts voluntarily to destroy or render harmless the said weapons. It has at its disposal the necessary expertise and technical facilities to do so in a way that will achieve the desired objective under the supervision and to the satisfaction of United Nations experts. My Government is prepared to discuss this subject with United Nations experts in order to confirm the destruction plan formulated by its technicians and to establish the plan's exact details by carrying out practical tests and determining what additional measures the destruction will require, together with any additional input of resources, in accordance with internationally accepted procedures in this regard.

Participating in this way will reduce the cost of destruction and the period of time required for the implementation of the destruction plan and also reduce the dangers arising during the destruction process, especially at a time of extremely hot and dusty local weather conditions.

[12] **The President** (interpretation from French):

...

It is my understanding that the Council is now ready to proceed to the vote on the draft resolutions before it. Unless I hear any objections I shall put the draft resolutions to the vote in the order of their submission.

There being no objection, it is so decided.

I now put to the vote the draft resolution contained in document S/22686.

A vote was taken by show of hands.

In favour: Austria, Belgium, China, Côte d'Ivoire, Cuba, Ecuador, France, India, Romania, Union of Soviet Socialist Republics, United Kingdom of Great Britain and Northern Ireland, United States of America, Yemen, Zaire, Zimbabwe

[12] **The President** (interpretation from French):

There were 15 votes in favour. The draft resolution has thus been adopted unanimously as resolution 699 (1991).

I now put to the vote the draft resolution contained in document S/22698.

A vote was taken by show of hands.

In favour: Austria, Belgium, China, Côte d'Ivoire, Cuba, Ecuador, France, India, Romania, Union of Soviet Socialist Republics, United Kingdom of Great Britain and Northern Ireland, United States of America, Yemen, Zaire, Zimbabwe

[13] **The President** (interpretation from French):

There were 15 votes in favour. The draft resolution has thus been adopted unanimously as resolution 700 (1991).

I shall now call on members of the Council who wish to make statements following the voting.

[13] **Mr. Al-Ashtal (Yemen)** (interpretation from Arabic):

...

We listened to the statement by the representative of Iraq and have read his letter addressed to the Secretary-General (S/22682), and are thus aware that Iraq is prepared to cooperate in the implementation of section C of resolution 687 (1991) through the plan the Council has just approved in its resolution 699 (1991). This follows upon Iraq's acceptance on 6 April 1991 of resolution 687 (1991) and of its implementation.

It was natural for my delegation to vote in favour of resolution 699 (1991), but I should like to state the following. When the delegation of Yemen abstained in the vote on resolution 687 (1991), with particular concern about its section C relating to the destruction of weapons of mass destruction, we indicated that for the sake of maintaining international peace and security in the region we thought it essential to deal with the question of disarmament and the destruction of weapons of mass destruction on the basis of the entire region, not only for a single country.

It is well known that Israel possesses large quantities of chemical, bacteriological and nuclear weapons. Other countries in the area possess similar weapons. We believe that regional peace and security can be maintained only through a policy conducive to disarmament in the region as a whole. To deal with this problem by addressing one country exclusively, irrespective of the reasons for such an approach, would definitely lead to a military imbalance in the region, thus jeopardizing peace and security there. That is why we had hoped and wished that the question of disarmament would be considered in a broader perspective. We now hope that this is just the beginning and that similar measures will be taken regarding weapons of mass destruction in the Middle East.

Secondly, as regards paragraph 4 of the resolution, we believe that it is unjust to call upon Iraq to defray the costs of destroying these weapons, because the process of destruction itself has been imposed on Iraq and that country is currently experiencing a critical economic situation as a result of the embargo and the sanctions imposed on it since 6 August 1990. We have seen the reports prepared by such neutral circles as the United Nations Children's Fund (UNICEF) and the Harvard University mission, which show that the sanctions have led to serious difficulty for and harm to the Iraqi people, including the children. In addition to all the other victims of this destructive war, there are the Iraqi people, including the children. That is why we do not see any justification for calling on Iraq to bear the responsibility for paying for the destruction of these weapons.

...

[17] **Mr. ZAMORA RODRIGUEZ (Cuba)** (interpretation from Spanish):

...

I should like to comment on resolution 700 (1991), which we have just adopted. First, our delegation deems it a mistake to have decided to entrust to the Committee set up under resolution 661 (1991) the function of supervising compliance with the sanctions in the area of weapons laid down in paragraph 24 of resolution 687 (1991). In Cuba's opinion - and as we had occasion to express during the bilateral consultations held by the Secretariat with a view to preparing the report in document S/22660, and subsequently during the informal consultations held by members of the Council a few days ago - the task of supervising the arms embargo against Iraq should have been entrusted to an organ set up for that purpose, not to the body which already exists for supervising economic sanctions.

My delegation is convinced that the economic sanctions, which first and foremost have an intolerable effect on the civilian population of Iraq, and which may give rise to consequences of unforeseen magnitude and seriousness, as has been clearly indicated by university researchers and the expert missions of the Organization itself, should speedily be lifted - indeed they should have been lifted - whereas the military sanctions embodied in the arms embargo could last for quite a long time and will be characterized by a complex array of features. We believe that during the period in which the two types of sanctions are dealt with by the same body we will experience various technical difficulties which will bring excessive pressure to bear on the so-called Committee on Sanctions.

Furthermore, the fact that there is no list of the products and materials subject to the embargo could possibly lead to excessive flexibility. This will not only complicate the work of the organ which supervises the implementation of paragraph 24 of resolution 687 (1991), but may also lead to confusion, whether intended or not, with regard to so-called dual-purpose materials whose import into Iraq would be prohibited. While we are the first to understand that the drafting of a list would be a difficult and lengthy task, such a list would have the merit of allowing us clearly to differentiate between materials for military uses and those which are not. This would be particularly useful when the economic sanctions under resolution 661 (1990) are lifted.

There are some elements of the Secretary-General's report (S/22660) on which we would like to comment. First, in paragraph 6 of the guidelines proposed by the Secretary-General, one of the functions of the Committee is to provide guidance to States and to international organizations on matters concerning the implementation of paragraph 24 of resolution 687 (1991) through the elaboration, as necessary, of relevant criteria. It also makes clear that the Committee, when needed, will reach agreed interpretations of items falling within the specified categories of proscribed items and activities. It seems to us that these functions are legislative in nature and that they would fall more readily within the purview of the Security Council than of one of its subsidiary bodies.

In another respect, in paragraph 10 of the report, under the heading entitled "Principles of implementation", we read that:

> "Nothing in the present guidelines will preclude any State or group of States from adopting further measures aimed at achieving effective implementation of the arms and related sanctions against Iraq, in accordance with the relevant provisions of resolution 687 (1991)".

In our view, this paragraph should not be interpreted as an invitation to impose unilateral measures that could go beyond the resolution itself, the provisions of which are binding on all States. However, although Cuba has stated and continues to express its agreement on the arms embargo against Iraq, my delegation believes that we should not miss the opportunity offered by the post-war period to facilitate in the Middle East - where the ratio of weapons to inhabitants is one of the highest in the world - agreements on security, disarmament and arms control which include all countries of the region without exception and which could constitute a natural corollary to serious and equitable efforts aimed at a just and lasting solution to the Arab-Israeli conflict, and in particular the Palestinian question, which is at its core.

I should now like to refer to resolution 699 (1991), which we have just adopted, on the destruction of specific types of weapons in Iraq in accordance with the provisions of section C of resolution 687 (1991). Although in the course of consultations among members of the Council attempts were made to answer questions raised by some delegations - and I appreciate those efforts - some elements contained in the resolution continue to be of concern.

First, we are concerned about the fact that the Secretary-General's report and the plan presented to us in compliance with paragraph 9 (b) of resolution 687 (1991), contained in document S/22614, has not included a specific timetable for the destruction or removal of weapons and materials in Iraq referred to in section C of the resolution. We understand the technical complexities of such activities, but the fact of not having a provisional timetable for these activities runs the risk that the process will be continued and create additional difficulties for the Iraqi people to return to a normal life and for the country to recover its sovereignty.

Cuba is of the view - and it has so stated in the relevant bodies considering international agreements on the elimination of weapons of mass destruction - that each country should bear all the costs of destroying its own weapons. However, in the light of the request made to the Secretary-General in operative paragraph 4 of the resolution just adopted that he submit to the Council within 30 days for approval recommendations as to the most effective means by which Iraq's obligations in this respect may be fulfilled, we should not lose sight of that country's real capacity to pay, bearing in mind the sanctions regime still in place and the fact that once it is lifted Iraq will have to contribute to the compensation fund in accordance with amounts established by the Governing Council on the basis of the uppermost limits the Security Council may determine in due time.

Furthermore, we wish to state very clearly that, according to my delegation's interpretation, the assistance encouraged in operative paragraph 4 of the resolution is strictly voluntary in nature and in no way entails establishing any financing mechanism which would entail obligations for Member States in accordance with Article 17 of the Charter.

In connection with the item now under consideration, Sir, I recall the letter dated 19 April that I had the honour to address to the President for that month, the Permanent Representative of Belgium, reiterating the positions of my country at the time of the adoption of resolution 687 (1991), especially with regard to the selectivity in the area of the destruction and elimination of certain types of weapons.

It is well known that Cuba is in favour of the universal elimination of nuclear, chemical and biological weapons and all means of delivery, including ballistic missiles. In that context, it is our firmest belief that the elimination of these types of weapons and means of delivery, instead of having been imposed selectively on Iraq, should be imposed in a regional context without exception based on political or other considerations and should have included Israel, a country which not only possesses weapons of mass destruction but also maintains a policy of aggression in the Middle East in defiance of Security Council decisions.

We are pleased to see that other members of the Council concur with our views on the elimination of these types of weapons and military means, as can be seen in documents recently issued.

[24] **The PRESIDENT** (interpretation from French):

...

There are no further speakers on my list. The Security Council has thus concluded the present stage of its consideration of the item on its agenda. The Security Council will remain seized of the matter.

...

Q. S/PV.2995, 26 June 1991

...

[2-5] **The PRESIDENT** (interpretation from French):

The Security Council will now begin its consideration of the item on its agenda.

The Security Council is meeting in accordance with the understanding reached in its prior consultations.

Members of the Council have before them a letter dated 26 June 1991 from the Secretary-General addressed to the President of the Security Council (S/22739).

[6] **Mr. WATSON (United States of America):**

...

My delegation appreciates very much the Secretary-General's letter of this morning enclosing the shocking reports from Ambassador Rolf Ekeus, the Executive Chairman of the Special Commission, and Dr. Hans Blix, the Director General of the International Atomic Energy Agency (IAEA), concerning the treatment accorded to the IAEA and Special Commission nuclear inspection team by the Government of Iraq over the last five days. Those reports indicate incontrovertibly that the Government of Iraq has obstructed the work of the inspection team in carrying out the mandate to implement the destruction, removal or rendering useless of Iraq's weapons of mass destruction. The members of the Security Council have also seen other evidence that confirms fully the findings presented by Ambassador Ekeus and Dr. Blix.

It is patently clear that Iraq is engaged in nuclear deception. The United States is deeply dismayed by the Iraqi régime's unmistakable flouting of its obligations under United Nations Security Council resolution 687 (1991). This calls into serious question other commitments and reports the Government of Iraq has purportedly made in compliance with resolution 687 (1991). This incident, however, is only one example of Iraqi failure to abide by its obligations under United Nations Security Council resolution 687 (1991).

The specific case at hand involves Iraqi deception with regard to its nuclear-weapons-related activities. Paragraph 12 of resolution 687 (1991) obligates Iraq to cooperate with the Special Commission and the IAEA. Iraq is required to facilitate, and cooperate with any and all on-site inspections the Special Commission and the IAEA deem necessary. Resolution 687 (1991) also requires Iraq to declare all items related to the production of nuclear-weapons-usable material. Iraq accepted these obligations when it accepted resolution 687 (1991), thereby setting the stage for the Council to declare that a ceasefire had gone into effect. In addition, the Iraqi Government, in letters to the Secretary-General - most recently on 11 June - has pledged to cooperate with the Special Commission and the IAEA.

Despite its obligations and assurances, Iraq has acted to subvert the letter and the spirit of the provisions of resolution 687 (1991). There is ample evidence from multiple sources that Iraq has been conducting a covert nuclear programme that has included activities related to the production of nuclear-weapons-usable material. We know that Iraq was carrying out its nuclear programme at a series of sites. Prior to the IAEA/Special Commission inspections, Iraq began to dismantle its nuclear infrastructure. We know that some of this equipment was moved to the Abu Gharaib site. The Special Commission and IAEA have been fully briefed on this information and on our belief that the Abu Gharaib facility was being used as a temporary storage site for equipment from Iraq's undeclared uranium-enrichment programme.

As the briefing members of the Security Council received this morning made clear, equipment associated with an undeclared Iraqi uranium-enrichment programme was at that site prior to 22 June. Iraq is required under Security Council resolution 687 (1991) to declare and make such equipment available for inspection. Instead, that equipment has been removed. Even as Iraqi work crews were frantically removing the equipment, Iraqi officials were barring the Security Council-mandated inspection team access to that site. At one point the team had to move aside to allow the heavy moving equipment to proceed into the site. Only now, after it has spent several days removing equipment and material, has Iraq allowed the inspection team access to the site. This does not constitute compliance with resolution 687 (1991). This is obstructionism combined with an attempt to conceal equipment that Iraq is required to make available for inspection and appropriate treatment.

The episode at Abu Gharaib reveals a consistent pattern of Iraqi Government deceit and obfuscation on this issue. We have indisputable evidence, drawn from many sources, that Iraq has been seeking to produce unsafeguarded nuclear material and to acquire nuclear weapons, contrary to its obligations under the Non-Proliferation Treaty and its full-scope safeguards agreement with the IAEA. Our evidence includes - but is not limited to - statements from a former Iraqi nuclear official, the results of the IAEA/Special Commission inspection in May, the long record of Iraqi attempts illegally to acquire sensitive nuclear items from abroad, and photographs, some of which members of the Council have seen.

There are additional sites associated with Iraq's nuclear-weapons programme. Abu Gharaib was merely a storage site. We have confirmed the existence of an extensive nuclear infrastructure in Iraq, including a number of facilities intended for the production of weapons-grade nuclear material and for the development of nuclear weapons. While the war apparently interrupted operations at these sites, Iraq remains obliged under Security Council resolution 687 (1991) to provide a prompt and complete declaration of all such nuclear facilities and items to the IAEA and the Special Commission.

Instead, Iraq has tried to conceal as much of its nuclear-weapons programme as possible, moving key items away from nuclear sites into temporary storage at other locations. Clearly, if Security Council resolution 687 (1991) is to have any meaning, the Council must ensure that Iraq grants the IAEA and Special Commission inspection teams full and immediate access to designated sites. The Council must also ensure that Iraq provide a complete declaration of all of its nuclear-weapons-related items, including those items that were spirited away from Abu Gharaib.

This episode demonstrates that Iraq has been doing everything it can to conceal the full extent of its unsafeguarded nuclear-enrichment programme, which we believe is directed towards development of nuclear weapons. The Council needs to recognize that the stark nature of Iraqi deception in this area calls into serious question the accuracy of Iraqi declarations with respect to other items, facilities and materials proscribed under the provisions of resolution 687 (1991), as well as Iraq's intent to comply fully with the resolution's mandate.

Given the example in the nuclear field, are we to believe the Iraqi Government's outright denial of the existence of a biological weapons programme? We have reason to believe the contrary. Given the example in the nuclear field, are we to believe that the Iraqis have faithfully declared their holdings of long-range ballistic missiles and chemical munitions? We have reason to believe the contrary. In fact, Iraq has underreported its ballistic missile and chemical warfare stocks and it denies it has a biological capability. There is also strong evidence that the Iraqis have attempted to hide substantial portions of their missile and chemical munition infrastructure from access by the United Nations Special Commission.

The Council has recently completed a review of Iraq's policies and practices and its performance record regarding implementation of resolution 687 (1991). Wisely, the Security Council made no decision to lift the economic sanctions that remain in place against Iraq. So long as Iraq fails to comply fully and unequivocally with the requirements of resolution 687 (1991), the Council should not consider altering those sanctions.

Iraq must declare and make available for scrutiny any and all other nuclear-weapons-related equipment and material. Iraq must also made a full accounting of its ballistic-missile-and-other-weapons-of-mass-destruction capabilities. Iraq must provide full and complete access for the Security Council-mandated Inspection Teams to that material and to all sites associated with this programme. Anything less makes hollow Iraqi commitments to abide by all the provisions of the resolution.

Furthermore, the Security Council must reiterate its determination to ensure that Iraq complies with the Council's binding decisions. Let us be direct and clear: Iraq must comply fully with all the provisions of resolution 687 (1991), including its provisions on nuclear, chemical and biological weapons and ballistic missiles. In this regard, the equipment removed from the Abu Gharaib site must be declared and made available to the IAEA and the Special Commission for inspection.

...

[11] Mr. MERIMEE (France) (interpretation from French):

The French delegation most strongly deplores the fact that the Iraqi Government has hindered the proper functioning of the Nuclear Inspection Team now in Iraq, thus violating several provisions of resolutions 687 (1991) and 699 (1991), despite Iraq's undertakings in that respect.

Paragraphs 12 and 13 of resolution 687 (1991) are clear. Iraq is forbidden to acquire or develop nuclear weapons or nuclear-weapons-usable material or any subsystems or components or any research, development, support or manufacturing facilities related to the above.

To carry out his inspection mission in that connection, the Director-General of the International Atomic Energy Agency (IAEA), with the support and cooperation of the Special Commission, is entitled to carry out on-site inspections, even on sites not declared by Iraq. Such access, at any time and in any place, to sites declared by the Iraqi authorities or not, is the condition for the success of the verification mission under way in Iraq. Such access, free and unconditional, was therefore specified in the Secretary-General's plan for the implementation of section C of resolution 687 (1991), which the Council adopted in its resolution 699 (1991).

It is true that the Iraqi Government has permitted the Inspection Team to enter the site, but the fact remains that four days were lost, four days during which possible traces of impermissible activities could have been eliminated. That Iraqi violation of several provisions of resolutions 687 (1991) and 699 (1991) is extremely serious and must never be repeated.

If necessary, the Security Council would have to consider any further breach by the Iraqi Government and take the measures necessary to ensure close cooperation between Iraq and the Special Commission and the IAEA, whether their inspections are announced or unannounced.

[13] Mr. NOTERDAEME (Belgium) (interpretation from French):

...

This morning, like other members of the Council, I read the letters addressed to the Secretary-General by Ambassador Ekeus and the Director-General of the International Atomic Energy Agency (IAEA), Mr. Blix. They call attention to a most serious matter: the Special Commission established pursuant to section C of resolution 687 (1991) was prevented from inspecting an Iraqi site, in violation of the binding provisions of paragraph 12 of resolution 687 (1991).

This morning too members of the Council were informed about certain factors that establish the presumption that Iraq is attempting to conceal the existence of an ability to produce fissionable materials. That would be a blatant violation of the obligations set out in paragraph 12 of resolution 687 (1991).

We shall read with great interest the report to which Mr. Blix refers in his letter of 26 June. That additional report by Mr. Zifferero, Chief IAEA Inspector, who participated in the recent mission to Iraq, should enable us fully to assess Iraqi obstruction in this matter. We expect the Iraqi authorities speedily to make the necessary arrangements to inform the Special Commission about the site to which the equipment seen during the first attempt to inspect the Abu Gharaib Army Barracks has been transported.

We welcome the convening of this formal meeting of the Security Council to consider these events. This is a serious matter that should be brought to the attention of the international community and world public opinion.

We earnestly hope, Mr. President, that you will formally remind Iraq of its obligations under Security Council resolutions, and particularly under paragraph 12 of resolution 687 (1991), which obliges Iraq to submit to all inspections demanded by the Special Commission and the IAEA, and which reaffirms the prohibition of any nuclear production capacity for military purposes.

In our view, by shirking its responsibilities in this case Iraq has called into question its formal undertaking to respect all the provisions of resolution 687 (1991). We cannot fail to be deeply disturbed by this development.

...

[14-15] **Mr. Hohenfellner (Austria):**

Like previous speakers I cannot but voice the concern of my Government about what appears to have been an effort by Iraq to deny an International Atomic Energy Agency/Special Commission Inspection Team unhindered and immediate access to a designated site in Baghdad and to remove objects that had previously been seen there by the Team.

This is a grave violation of Iraq's obligations under resolution 687 (1991) which cannot be tolerated by this Council. We urge the Iraqi authorities not to repeat or continue their uncooperative attitude, but rather to comply fully with their obligations and to realize that anything less would entail unwelcome consequences.

[16] **Mr. Richardson (United Kingdom):**

We have before us the letters of Ambassador Ekeus and Dr. Blix of the International Atomic Energy Agency (IAEA). They are very clear. Indeed, they could not be clearer. They demonstrate that Iraq has violated paragraphs 12 and 13 of resolution 687 (1991). They demonstrate that Iraq has violated its own acceptance of that resolution, and they demonstrate also that Iraq has violated the exchange of letters which its Government signed with the Special Commission.

The letters also make clear that there has been some frenzied activity on the site in question during the last few days and that equipment has been hastily removed from that site, and although I take note of the fact that the inspection took place on a religious holiday, I am bound to say that that does not seem to have hindered the speed and promptness with which Iraqi personnel have acted during those days.

This Council created the Special Commission and this Council gave it a very specific mandate, which was to locate and destroy all Iraq's nuclear-capable material, as well as all its chemical and biological weapons and all ballistic missiles over a certain range.

The Council has to support the Special Commission in its work and to do so quickly. They will have many other inspections to carry out in the near future and they need to be assured of prompt access to designated sites wherever and whenever they want.

In my delegation's view therefore, the message from this Council must be twofold: first, that Iraq must never again obstruct the work of the Special Commission and of the IAEA, and, secondly, that the Iraqi authorities at the highest appropriate level must be called upon to reaffirm their commitment to cooperate fully with the Special Commission and the IAEA, not just in word but in deed.

[17] **Mr. Posso Serrano (Ecuador)** (interpretation from Spanish):

...

The inspection of Iraqi nuclear facilities is an inescapable prerequisite for the destruction, neutralization or removal of Iraq's nuclear arsenal. It is fundamental that the Government of Baghdad, in expressly accepting resolution 687 (1991) committed itself not only to allow but, what is more, to help in the collection of all information regarding the location of nuclear sites, their elements and components and to cooperate in the preparation of a plan that would be in keeping with Iraq's obligations under the provisions of the Treaty on the Non-Proliferation of Nuclear Weapons of 1968, and to allow permanent inspection and verification in the future.

The delegation of Ecuador does not want to venture any speculations regarding Iraq's failure to comply with these obligations. We do not want to infer any ulterior motive to interfere with the destruction, removal or neutralization of nuclear facilities that might be capable of producing weapons of this kind.

Ecuador would not like to conclude that Iraq's position regarding the Special Commission is a demonstration of the position the Iraqi Government will take on all the other obligations under resolution 687 (1991), nor do we wish to believe that the Government of Baghdad has any intention of trying to evade the nuclear embargo. Though as a matter of principle Ecuador can accept that Iraq's position in this matter is out of keeping with the circumstances and can be immediately rectified, we believe that Iraq must try to appreciate the risks involved in this position in the opinion of its neighbours.

Ecuador would therefore support an appeal to the Government of Baghdad that it fully comply with this and other obligations stemming from resolution 687 (1991). We believe that there is an overriding need for Iraq to spare its civilian population any further anguish and to realize the implications of resolution 687 (1991) for the strengthening of peace and stability in the region, which has been subjected to such great suffering because of the arms race and the constant threat of force.

...

[18] **Mr. Munteanu (Romania):**

...

My delegation supported the urgent convening of the Security Council in a formal meeting because of the serious nature of the information which has been brought to our attention in connection with Iraq's implementation of some specific provisions of resolution 687 (1991).

Since the very first days and weeks of the crisis in the Gulf, Romania has consistently advocated Iraq's full implementation of all resolutions adopted by the Security Council. In recent months we have had the occasion to reiterate our position in that respect while working with other members of the Security Council on various sections of resolution 687 (1991).

This time the Secretary-General submitted to the Council some documentation strengthened further by additional data on the difficulties which have emerged in the cooperation between Iraq and the International Atomic Energy Agency (IAEA), and the Special Commission nuclear inspection team appointed pursuant to part C of Security Council resolution 687 (1991). In fact, this international team was denied access to designated facilities which the Government of Iraq had been notified to submit to urgent on-site inspection in accordance with the terms of resolution 687 (1991).

From the documentation submitted by the Secretary-General we have learned that the Iraqi authorities have denied the international team access to the locations and facilities which the team wished to inspect. I will not go into additional detail, as other speakers have already provided clarification.

My delegation wishes to express its serious concern that in spite of their earlier promises the Iraqi authorities have not fulfilled their obligations in so important and sensitive a field as the nuclear one.

At a time when the question of the elimination of nuclear weapons is perhaps more topical than ever, the preoccupation of my Government with Iraq's fulfillment of its obligation not to possess or acquire nuclear weapons and to accept international inspections of all its nuclear facilities, is a legitimate one. Such concerns and apprehensions are indeed legitimate and well founded, as the area of the Persian Gulf is not so distant from our own geographic area, which we are making every effort to keep free from nuclear weapons.

To summarize, we fully share the grave concern expressed by the Secretary-General over the recent events in Iraq. We therefore support the appeal addressed to Iraq that it implement fully and in good faith the relevant provisions of resolution 687 (1991), and in particular those authorizing on-site international inspections.

The Iraqi Government should understand that it is in its own interest to make every effort to comply, without hesitation or reservations, with its international obligations. Iraq has to prove by its actual conduct that there is harmony between its deeds and its statements. It is only through honest behaviour, strictly consistent with the Security Council resolutions, that Iraq can illustrate its peaceful intentions and resume its place among peace-loving members of the international community.

It is in the light of those considerations that my delegation joins other delegations in asking Iraq to demonstrate its wisdom and sense of realism by respecting and implementing, beyond any shadow of a doubt, the relevant Security Council resolutions.

...

[21] **Mr. Al-Anbari (Iraq):**

...

Since the Security Council adopted its resolution 687 (1991) on 3 April, Iraq has accepted it and has done its best to implement all the requirements and obligations imposed on it by the resolution. We have cooperated with all United Nations agencies, commissions and missions, and we have evidence to prove this. We have done so particularly with the Commission entrusted with the task of destroying all the weapons of mass destruction and other weapons mentioned in the resolution - and this has been true from the very first day.

The IAEA mission had visited Iraq before and made it very clear to the public that it was very appreciative of the cooperation by the Iraqi authorities.

During the IAEA mission's second visit - the current one - Iraq has also extended full cooperation. The mission has visited a number of sites. It was only the last one that could not be made available to it - for one day, for practical reasons. May I remind the members of the Security Council that Iraq's entire communication system has been destroyed. The military base that the mission wanted to inspect is far from the centre of Baghdad and was not easy to reach by telephone or telex; there simply were no communications. I would also remind the members of the Council that the Commission insisted - and Iraq responded positively - that Iraq should put at its disposal all the facilities it required, including transportation and interpretation. So if we are asking the Commission to give us advance notice, it is because we need such notice simply to provide the facilities asked for by it.

I believe that no fair-minded person could draw the conclusion that the fact that the inspection was delayed for one day means that Iraq acted in bad faith or intended to remove certain prohibited materials. If Iraq had had such an intention, it would not have waited for more than 80 days since the adoption of the resolution on 3 April to take such action - and, after all, it knew that the Commission was in Baghdad to inspect various sites.

I fully understand the concern and interest of the members of the Council. Indeed, the issue is very sensitive and very critical. But I really feel that, given the lack of concrete evidence of the non-cooperation of the Iraqi authorities with the IAEA mission, we are faced with a non-issue. Iraq is fully cooperating and will continue to do so. We have made our commitment, and there is no way of going back on it.

That is why I am a bit perplexed about the motive behind this campaign. Is it to prepare world public opinion for another military attack against Iraq, like the one that took place in the past? Is it to perpetuate the economic sanctions imposed on the people of Iraq, including the children? Or is the campaign designed to justify the occupation of the northern part of Iraq? I hope that none of this will turn out to be true, but I have to wait and see.

Perhaps the best answer would be for Iraq's commitment to be confirmed at the highest level - and I remember that one representative made such a request. So, with your permission, Mr. President, I shall now read out parts of the statement issued this morning by our Foreign Minister in Baghdad. He said:

(spoke in Arabic)

> "Some diplomatic sources have claimed that Iraq has denied the Special Commission of the United Nations access to one of its nuclear facilities near Baghdad in order to inspect it, and that the United Nations was not officially informed of its existence. This is a fabrication, meant to put Iraq and its clear position of cooperation with the United Nations in ill repute on purpose.
>
> "The correct information is the following:
>
> "The inspection team requested to be allowed to visit Iraq and to inspect the nuclear material and facilities during the Holy Day of the Feast of the Sacrifice. We said that the Feast of the Sacrifice is an official holiday; indeed, it is one of the most important religious holidays for Muslims in Iraq and throughout the world. Therefore, we advised the inspection team to postpone the visit until after the holiday. Arabs and Muslims respect the holidays of others, and others should respect our holidays, including our religious holidays. However, the inspection team insisted on its position and said that it wanted to come to Baghdad to deliver a letter to the Iraqi Foreign Minister. When it reached Iraq, I interrupted my holiday and received the team in the evening of 22 June - the first day of the Feast of the Sacrifice. I received the letter.
>
> "During the meeting, the inspection team said that it wanted to visit a site near Baghdad. It turned out to be a military site within a military zone composed of this and other such sites coming under the Ministry of Defence and not the Ministry of Industry and Mineralogy.
>
> "Despite the difficulties - most of the officials in these places were enjoying the holiday - we did our best to obtain the agreement of the military authorities so that the inspection team could visit that site.
>
> "When the team reached the site, it wanted to visit other sites within the same military zone. We could not secure the approval of the officer-in-charge, because he had not received instructions to allow anyone to go to those sites. It is a well-known practice in all countries that military sites cannot be visited without approval being obtained through the normal procedures.
>
> "In his statement the Minister said that, when we heard from the Team that it could not visit the other sites it wanted to visit, we gave the reasons and we contacted the Iraqi authorities concerned and requested them to give instructions to the officer-in-charge in order to allow the Inspection Team to visit these sites.
>
> "The visit to the said sites was arranged as of 7 a.m. on 26 June, Baghdad time.
>
> "In his statement the Minister said that the Inspection Team of the United Nations visited on 23 June 1991 the sites belonging to the IAEA. The Team also requested, on 25 June, to visit two other sites belonging to the Ministry of Industry, and the Iraqi authorities agreed promptly and easily because the request of the Team was clear and definitive. This is the

clearest evidence of Iraqi cooperation with the United Nations; and it is proof which belies those who try to fish in troubled waters in order to serve their interests.

"The Minister also confirmed the established position of Iraq based on cooperation with the United Nations and the Secretary-General and he said that the United Nations Team confirmed in its press statement after its visit to the country from 9 to 14 June that it could not prove the existence of any undeclared activities relating to the biological and nuclear capacity of Iraq and missiles and the sites. The Team did not find any indication that Iraq is trying on purpose to mislead the Mission. The position of the Iraqi authorities was a position of cooperation."

R. S/PV.2996, 28 June 1991

...

[2-5] **The President** (interpretation from French): The Security Council will now resume consideration of the item on its agenda.

Members of the Council have before them document S/22743 containing the text of a letter dated 28 June 1991 from the Secretary-General addressed to the President of the Security Council.

Following consultations among the members of the Security Council, I have been authorized to make the following statement on behalf of the Council:

> "The members of the Security Council have learnt with grave concern of an incident which occurred today when the Iraqi military authorities denied a joint IAEA/Special Commission Nuclear Inspection Team immediate and unimpeded access to a site designed for inspection by the Special Commission under paragraphs 9 and 13 of Security Council resolution 687 (1991). In the course of this incident, the Iraqi military did not comply with a request by the Acting Chief Inspector that there should be no movement of transport or equipment pending inspection. The Iraqi military fired small arms into the air when members of the Team were endeavouring to photograph loaded vehicles leaving the site. This incident followed earlier incidents on 23 and 25 June 1991 when the Iraqi military authorities denied the Nuclear Inspection Team access to certain facilities at another designated site.
>
> "On 26 June 1991, the Security Council held a meeting to consider the incidents of 23 and 25 June at which time the Permanent Representative of Iraq confirmed that Iraq had accepted Security Council resolution 687 (1991) and was doing its best to implement all the requirements and obligations imposed on it by the resolution. He further asserted that Iraq was co-operating with all United Nations missions, including the Special Commission. The President subsequently conveyed the Council's serious concern regarding the incidents to the Government of Iraq.
>
> "The members of the Council strongly deplore the incidents of 23, 25 and 28 June, and in this connection condemn the conduct of the Iraqi authorities. All these incidents constitute flagrant violations of Security Council resolution 687 (1991) and of the undertakings contained in the exchange of letters between the Secretary-General of the United Nations and the Foreign Minister of Iraq governing the status, privileges and immunities of the Special Commission and of the Inspection Teams mandated under the Security Council resolution. Furthermore, these incidents demonstrate Iraq's failure to abide by its solemn undertakings to comply with all the provisions of Security Council resolution 687 (1991).
>
> "The members of the Security Council have decided to ask the Secretary-General to send a high-level mission to Baghdad immediately to meet with the highest levels of the Iraqi Government to convey the Council's urgent demand for unequivocal assurances that the Government will take all necessary measures to ensure that no hindrances are placed in the way of the discharge of the Special Commission's mandate and that it will accord full co-operation, including immediate and unimpeded access, to the inspection teams in compliance with Iraq's obligations and commitments *vis-à-vis* the United Nations and the IAEA. The members of the Council have also stressed that the Government must furnish the high-level mission with unconditional guarantees for the safety and security of all personnel engaged in the performance of functions in connection with Security Council resolution 687 (1991). The mission, composed of the Director-General of the International Atomic Energy Agency (IAEA), the Executive Chairman of the Special Commission and the Under-Secretary-General for Disarmament Affairs, will depart New York this evening, 28 June 1991.
>
> "At this time, the members of the Council call upon Iraq to grant the IAEA/Special Commission Nuclear Inspection Team currently in Iraq immediate and unimpeded access to the objects which the Team had endeavoured to inspect on 28 June 1991 and any other site deemed necessary.
>
> "The members of the Security Council request the high-level mission to report to it at the earliest opportunity, through the Secretary-General, on the results of its meetings with the highest levels of the Iraqi Government and, in particular, on such further undertakings by the Government to ensure compliance at all levels, including local military and civilian authorities, with Iraq's obligations under Security Council resolution 687 (1991).
>
> "The members of the Council wish to make it clear that the Council remains seized of this matter and that any recurrence of non-compliance would have serious consequences.
>
> "The members of the Council reiterate their views expressed in resolution 687 (1991) of the threat that all weapons of mass destruction pose to peace and security in the Middle East and of the need to work towards the establishment in the Middle East of a zone free of such weapons."

The Security Council has thus concluded the present stage of its consideration of the item on its agenda. The Council remains seized of the question.

...

S. S/PV.3004, 15 August 1991

...

[2] The PRESIDENT (interpretation from Spanish): The Security Council will now begin its consideration of the item on its agenda. The Security Council is meeting in accordance with the understanding reached in its prior consultations.

Members of the Council have before them the following documents: S/22559, which contains a report of the Secretary-General of 2 May 1991 pursuant to paragraph 19 of Security Council resolution 687 (1991); S/22661, which contains a letter dated 30 May 1991 from the Secretary-General addressed to the President of the Security Council; S/22792, which contains a report of the Secretary-General of 15 July 1991 pursuant to paragraph 4 of Security Council resolution 699 (1991); S/22799, which contains a letter dated 15 July 1991 from the Secretary-General addressed to the President of the Security Council transmitting a report by the Executive Delegate of the Secretary-General on humanitarian needs in Iraq; S/22761, which contains a letter dated 4 July 1991 from the Secretary-General addressed to the President of the Security Council; S/22871, which contains a report of the Secretary-General of 1 August 1991 transmitting a plan for future ongoing monitoring and verification of Iraq's compliance with relevant parts of section C of Security Council resolution 687 (1991); S/22872, which contains a note by the Secretary-General of 1 August 1991 transmitting a plan for future ongoing monitoring and verification of Iraq's compliance with paragraph 12 of Security Council resolution 687 (1991).

Members of the Council also have before them three draft resolutions contained in the following documents:

S/22940, containing the text of a draft resolution prepared in the course of consultations;

S/22941, containing the text of a draft resolution submitted by Belgium, France, the Union of Soviet Socialist Republics, the United Kingdom of Great Britain and Northern Ireland and the United States of America. On page 3 of the English version of this document, four lines from the bottom of paragraph 1 (c), a small correction has to be made. The line starts with the words:

(*spoke in English*)

> "regions of Iraq and to all categories of the Iraqi civilian population ...".

(*spoke in Spanish*)

A comma should appear after the word "population". The Secretary will make the appropriate correction in future editions of this text.

Lastly, we have document S/22942 containing the text of a draft resolution submitted by France, the Union of Soviet Socialist Republics, the United Kingdom of Great Britain and Northern Ireland and the United States of America.

...

[6] Mr. ABULHASAN (Kuwait) (interpretation from Arabic):

...

The Security Council is meeting today, one year after that sad day of 2 August 1990 and more than five months after the liberation of the sacred soil of Kuwait from the forces of aggression and oppression. Therefore, it would not be superfluous to recall the seriousness of Iraq's inhumane aggression against Kuwait and the tragic consequences of oppression, domination, violence and destruction, which are still visible today. The people of Kuwait are suffering from those consequences every day, as are people of other nationalities, who had made a good livelihood in Kuwait.

Iraq's aggression against Kuwait was not undertaken in order to settle any political, economic or border dispute, as the Iraqi regime claimed at the beginning. The aggression was an expansionist act. It was methodically planned, using every means of treachery. At the time of its crisis and difficulty, Kuwait, a justice- and peace-loving State, appealed to international legitimacy, represented by the Security Council to offer assistance and save it from the nightmare of occupation and its train of abominable crimes.

The Security Council responded effectively to the crisis and fulfilled its responsibility: it adopted resolutions to halt the aggression and mitigate the consequences of the crisis, to restore usurped rights and to ensure respect for existing conventions and boundaries. As a result, Kuwait is once again a free and independent State - an oasis of peace where justice reigns.

Kuwait has today begun its march towards the reconstruction of the fundamental infrastructure of its country, which was destroyed by the Iraqi aggression. As a country that adheres to universal values and principles, we are deeply appreciative of the preponderantly positive role played by the members of the Security Council. They have followed the path of righteousness and exemplified the international solidarity and support displayed by the entire international community in calling for an end to Iraqi aggression and to the seven-month occupation of Kuwait, which devastated my country.

The Security Council is meeting today to consider three draft resolutions that deal, in essence, with the results of Iraq's aggression against my country - aggression which the Council, by the adoption of its historic resolutions, notably resolution 687 (1991), has succeeded in arresting through the use of force within the framework of international legitimacy. Resolutions 686 (1991) and 687 (1991), both of which were adopted after the Iraqi defeat and its forced withdrawal from Kuwait, dealt with ending the consequences of the occupation of my country. The international community, as represented in this Council, has thus called upon Iraq to assume its responsibilities in order to put a complete and total end to its aggression and to safeguard the rights of the countries subjected to its aggression. The Council has called for a restoration of law based on justice and the tenets of the Charter - a system whereby countries would assume legal responsibility for all their actions.

The claims of Kuwait, of the Security Council and of the international community are the basis for lifting the sanctions against Iraq.

They will deal with the following:

First, the immediate and total return of all prisoners, Kuwaitis and Kuwait residents;

Secondly, all weapons of mass destruction must be eliminated. They must be destroyed, removed or made inoperable;

Thirdly, the boundary between Iraq and Kuwait should be determined in accordance with the 1932 Convention;

Fourthly, Iraq must return all assets stolen by the aggressor regime and its army from Kuwait;

Fifthly, compensation shall be paid for damages incurred by Kuwait and its residents.

The Iraqi regime agreed to those claims by accepting Security Council resolutions, especially resolutions 686 (1991) and 687 (1991). All of us have awaited the complete implementation of those resolutions. However, the Iraqi regime seems not to have learned from the lesson it was given. It has not appreciated the seriousness of the Security Council and that of the international community in the implementation of the Council's resolutions. This might create a dangerous precedent in international relations by allowing an aggressor, after his defeat, to enjoy the fruits of his aggression, or to allow that aggressor to get away without assuming responsibility for that aggression.

Despite everything that the Iraqi people and economy have undergone, the Iraqi regime has pursued a policy of deception and delay. It has refused to assume its obligations. It has used unacceptable pretexts and illegal grounds for its actions, the results of which are, of course, well known. Some of those results are as follows:

Two thousand four hundred and nine Kuwaiti and non-Kuwaiti prisoners, nationals of 13 countries, are still imprisoned in Iraqi prisons. They have been deprived of their fundamental rights affirmed by Security Council resolutions 686 (1991) and 687 (1991), which call for the immediate return of those people to Kuwait. The prisoners have been used by the Iraqi regime as a means of pressure in future. They have been used for blackmail purposes. One need not be clairvoyant to realize this: those are obvious consequences. The prisoners are innocent. The Iraqi regime must be held responsible for its future actions. The lifting of economic sanctions is closely linked to a number of commitments, in particular the return of prisoners to Kuwait in keeping with paragraphs 21 and 30 of resolution 687 (1991).

The Iraqi regime in its pursuit of its treacherous actions claims that Iraq would return those prisoners but that the Government of Kuwait does not want to accept them. That is a big lie. The Iraqi regime completely ignored the detailed lists of names of Kuwaiti and non-Kuwaiti prisoners when it was submitted to the International Red Cross, which has been trying in every way to learn about their situation. There was no positive response from the Iraqi regime. We transmitted to the International Red Cross information about the locations where those prisoners were being held that had been received from prisoners freed prior to the cease-fire. Iraq claims that there were Kuwaitis and others who were taken prisoner and who wish to be repatriated, but that Kuwait does not want to receive them. That is what the Iraqi regime says. In fact, the truth is as follows:

First, the Iraqi regime deliberately is not drawing a distinction between reunion and prisoners, that is, they are doing the same thing with prisoners as they are with those who were in Iraq when hostilities began on 17 January. Their repatriation has nothing whatever to do with those who were taken prisoner in Kuwaiti territory during the occupation and those who were prevented by hostilities from returning to Kuwait. Those people are not considered prisoners. All Kuwaitis wish to return to their country.

Secondly, the Iraqi regime wishes to send agents to Kuwait to implement its own plans under the pretext of repatriating prisoners.

Thirdly, a large number of Iraqis and others wish to flee that nefarious Iraqi regime. After throwing away their identity cards they have gone to the International Red Cross, saying that they were prisoners or people who wish to be repatriated.

Fourthly, the Government of Kuwait received from the International Red Cross the list that the Iraqi regime claims is the list of Kuwaiti and other prisoners who were imprisoned in Kuwait during Iraqi occupation and aggression. We looked at those lists and the names in them. We compared them with the Kuwaiti National Registry, a copy of which has been preserved in the United Nations in keeping with Security Council [*sic*] 679 (1990), which gives a census of all people in Kuwaiti territory up until 1 August 1990. We did not find among all those names what the Iraqi regime claims were Kuwaiti prisoners. We only found 252 names, which were immediately accepted for repatriation into Kuwait.

The clear truth is thus before you: the Iraqi regime is trampling upon human rights and dignity, even if the Iraqi people themselves are paying the price, in terms of their own health and of the famine existing in Iraq.

I urge the entire Council and the international community as a whole to exert pressure on the Iraqi regime to free those innocent people. The Council should tell that regime to free those innocent people, because that action would be in the interest of that regime. It would be in the interest of their credibility and of their people, and it would be in the interest of the cause of the lifting of sanctions.

There is another example of the deception practised by the Iraqi regime to avoid compliance with the Council's resolutions, namely, its possession of weapons of mass destruction - chemical, biological and nuclear. Only when threatened with the use of military force authorized by Security Council resolution 678 (1990) did the Iraqi regime disclose its capabilities.

We receive fresh information daily from the Special Commission on Iraqi practices and they are not those of complete cooperation. It reveals that Iraq has lost its credibility before the international community.

We ask: Is not the Iraqi regime aware of the fact that there is a link between the fulfilment of its obligations and the lifting of sanctions? Did not Iraq agree to those obligations as the basis for the implementation of a cease-fire, or is it just that the Iraqi regime has no respect for its people and its future and does not accept its obligations? Does it wish to maintain its aggression and expansion not only against its neighbours but also against its own people, who have no weapons with which to defend themselves?

In short, mere declarations by Iraq of its acceptance of Security Council resolutions must not make us complacent: we require a guarantee of the complete implementation of international legitimacy as embodied in those resolutions. If we follow the reports of the United Nations we will find wide discrepancies between what the regime says and what it does. In addition, experience teaches that this regime's practices show that it understands only the language of force in the monitoring and controlling of its irresponsible actions.

Despite the humanitarian and material disasters that have befallen Iraq, the policies of the Iraqi Government that led to the crisis are continuing. They are still at the basis of the tragedy of the Iraqi people, which today is still the object of aggression by the Iraqi regime, a regime that kills Iraqis both in the north and in the south.

But on the soil of Kuwait we find our oil wells ablaze, destroyed by the Iraqi forces before they retreated. These blazing oil wells are spewing poison and creating further problems. Those oil wells had been the very source of Kuwait's wealth and of the prosperity of other people living in Kuwait. The dimensions of the disaster are huge, and that is why Kuwaitis today feel that the Iraqi aggression against Kuwait, its people and residents of different nationalities, is a crime. Iraq's crime come within the terms of the Convention on the Non-Applicability of Statutory Limitations to War Crimes and Crimes against Humanity, adopted by the General Assembly on 26 November 1968. That Convention specifically stipulates that the effective punishment of such crimes is an important element in preventing their repetition, in the protection of human rights and fundamental freedoms, the furtherance of cooperation among peoples and the promotion of international peace and security.

It is our hope that the Security Council or an organ of its creation will undertake an inquiry regarding these crimes by the Iraqi regime during its occupation of Kuwait, when it oppressed the Kuwaiti people and wreaked destruction on the environment of the region. These war crimes against mankind are detrimental to peace and are among the worst crimes in international law. We must not forget them.

Today it is not a matter of reciting Iraq's crimes against Kuwait, its people and the people of the Gulf region, and consequently against millions in the world who have suffered great injury. We must unmask Iraq's position which is leading it away from its obligations and from international legitimacy. That is why we feel it is important for the Council to monitor closely the attitude of this outlaw regime. It is important that the Council keep Iraq's commitments under constant review in conformity with paragraph 21 of resolution 687 (1991), which states that the Security Council shall every 60 days review the policies and practices of the Government of Iraq, including the implementation of all relevant resolutions of the Security Council.

The sanctions imposed by the Security Council under its resolutions do not constitute war against Iraq nor do they arise out of a vacuum. They represent a legitimate collective action in keeping with the Charter. It has been implemented against a member of the international community whose regime is violating Security Council resolutions. For four months that regime has persisted in refusing to comply with legitimate international resolutions. Kuwait deems that it would be both useful and imperative for the Security Council to consider in detail any steps undertaken before the lifting of the embargo against the Iraqi regime, because we must be precise in the criteria that we have established for lifting the embargo. Iraq's commitment to respect and implement Security Council resolutions and the way in which it cooperates with the Secretary-General and the United Nations in establishing peace and security in the Gulf region on the basis of international legitimacy, as represented by the resolutions of the Security Council, must be scrutinized.

The Iraqi regime has exposed international peace and security in the Gulf and throughout the world to danger; that danger will continue, and the region will not recover its stability until the current regime is placed under effective international control and its vindictive spirit reined in. The sanctions that have been imposed must not be lifted until the Iraqi regime ceases its actions intended to deceive the international community and violate its resolutions.

Kuwait hopes that today's meeting and the resolutions to be adopted will provide a new glimmer of hope that the ordeal of Kuwaitis and others in detention will come to an end. We hope the resolutions will lead to positive action by consolidating the activities of the Secretary-General and the International Committee of the Red Cross (ICRC), especially since under modern standards the detention of innocent victims in unsafe conditions constitutes a crime against humanity. The vital question of those prisoners is not only of interest to Kuwait and Kuwaitis; it possesses dimensions related to civilization, morality and law, all of which are of concern to the international community as a whole. The families and friends of some 2,400 people today call on this Council to consider its commitment with respect to the Third and Fourth Geneva Conventions.

The Security Council is writing history. It is bringing about a new international order based on justice, law and a commitment to respect international legitimacy. We are seeing a start to the implementation of the Charter purpose "to save succeeding generations from the scourge of war".

God will help us. Together we ask God that all prisoners be freed.

...

[22] **Mr. AL-ANBARI (Iraq)** (interpretation from Arabic):

...

As usual, the representative of the Kuwaiti regime, who spoke before me, employed false and obscene words, but I shall not respond to him, first, because I refuse to stoop to his level and secondly because most of what he said in his boring statement had nothing to do with the item on the Council's agenda.

There are three draft resolutions before the Council today. I want to state the position of my Government on each of those draft resolutions, but to save time for the Council I shall be brief in stating my Government's position on two of those texts, draft resolutions S/22940 and S/22942. But I request that the complete reply of my Government be published in official documents of the Security Council.

My Government's position on draft resolution S/22940 is as follows: Iraq's foreign-currency revenue is almost totally dependent on its oil exports. On the basis of the production capacity of Iraqi oil fields, those exports over the next five years will not reach the level defined in July 1990 by the Organization of Petroleum Exporting Countries (OPEC). That is because of the destruction inflicted by aerial bombardment on our oil production and exporting facilities. It is thus anticipated that for the period 1991-1995 Iraq's oil revenues will be $64.2 billion. That projection is on the basis of 600,000 barrels exported in the remainder of 1991, owing to the grave damage inflicted on our oil facilities, and 2 million barrels a day in 1992. An optimistic estimate has it that this could rise to 2.85 million barrels a day in 1993 and 2.9 million in 1994. Those figures presuppose full lifting of the sanctions imposed on Iraq's oil exports and on its import of equipment and other necessities for the refinement, export and shipment of oil.

It is well known that our non-oil exports are extremely limited; in the five-year period 1991-1995 these are not expected to exceed $930.5 million.

A careful examination of the gap between those revenues and our foreign-currency requirements reveals a projected deficit over those five years of $149.2 billion, averaging $29.28 billion a year for that period - although the 1991 deficit is expected to reach $47.8 billion. The reason for the higher 1991 deficit compared with the average annual rate is the enormous cost of servicing the debts incurred this year and last: the installments include all payments due in 1991 and previous years, and no agreement has been reached on deferring these payments. The meagreness of the income Iraq estimates for the next five years will compel it to fall short of its financial obligations and its requirements for food and medicine - and that does not even take into account the deduction of 30 per cent of those revenues.

That is on the basis of these above-mentioned estimates, which clearly reflect the tremendous deficit and wide gap between Iraq's financial obligations relating to its foreign debt and its basic imports, on the one hand, and its limited revenues from its exports expected in 1991, and especially during subsequent years, and on the basis of Under-Secretary-General Ahtisaari's findings in Iraq, who stated in his report that the conflict had brought near-apocalyptic consequences on the basic economic infrastructure. The report goes on to say that most means of modern life have been destroyed or have become very weak and that Iraq has been returned to the pre-industrial age and will remain so for a period of time.

Hence, Iraq, with its current and expected financial resources during 1991 and subsequently, cannot on its own restore the social and economic life that prevailed before the events of January 1991. Intensive world efforts must be bent to compensate Iraq for the unjust damages inflicted by the aerial bombing of its civilian facilities and economic structure in order to help Iraq to accelerate the restoration of normal life.

My Government has therefore requested that it be given a grace period of five years. Such a period can be arrived at as necessary, on the basis of the statements in the Secretary-General's report which depended on the economic indicators expected for 1993, although the damages that will increase between now and 1993 because of the continued economic embargo will make such estimates much worse than what we have stated.

The premises of the Secretary-General's report before the Council make it necessary to defer the deductions until 1993 at the least, since Iraq's oil revenues during the balance of 1991 and in 1992 will be approximately $13 billion only. This means that the total Iraqi oil revenues during these two years are much less than what is required to fulfil the basic requirements estimated at $16 billion for the same two years, although there has been no opportunity until now for Iraq to export oil or oil products. Also, the extensive economic embargo is still being applied and Iraq's assets abroad are still frozen, despite the decision of the Sanctions Committee and the letter of the Chairman of that Committee which theoretically lifted the freezing of these assets but left the States where the Iraqi assets are to be found free to freeze these assets.

In the light of the above-mentioned facts, which any objective observer can ascertain, Iraq requests a grace period in order to allow it to face the major problems stifling its economy which are threatening to weaken the Iraqi people and its future generations. Iraq also requested a decrease in the ceiling of the deduction so as not to exceed 10 per cent of its total oil revenues.

I thank you, Mr. President, for your kind attention to the statement giving my Government's position regarding the first draft resolution on the compensation fund.

Allow me now to indicate in detail my Government's position on the second draft resolution, contained in document S/22941. Although this draft resolution alleges that it is designed to meet the humanitarian requirements of the Iraqi people, it is actually one of the most serious draft resolutions put before the Council since the outbreak of the so-called Gulf crisis. Therefore, allow me first to review the developments pertaining to meeting the humanitarian needs of the Iraqi people, after which I shall explain my Government's position regarding the grave political repercussions aimed at by this draft resolution. And then I shall make Iraq's technical comments on the various items in the draft resolution.

With regard to the humanitarian requirements of the Iraqi people, members will recall that the mission dispatched to Iraq by the Secretary-General during the period 10 to 17 March 1991, headed by Under-Secretary-General Martti Ahtisaari, which included representatives of the appropriate United Nations agencies and programmes, in its report of 20 March 1991, contained in document S/22366, affirmed the following:

> "there needs to be a major mobilization ... of resources to deal with aspects of this deep crisis in the fields of agriculture and food, water, sanitation and health." (*para. 37*)

The report concluded:

> "It is unmistakable that the Iraqi people may soon face a further imminent catastrophe, which could include epidemic and famine, if massive life-supporting needs are not rapidly met. The long summer, with its often 45 or even 50 degree temperatures (113-122 degrees Fahrenheit), is only weeks away. Time is short." (*ibid.*)

In spite of all those warnings, no humanitarian action has so far been taken. It is true that the Council adopted resolution 687 (1991) on 3 April 1991, taking into consideration the recommendations of the United Nations mission when, in paragraph 20 of the resolution, it exempted foodstuffs from the sanctions and provided for streamlining and accelerating the Committee's approval of the exception of basic civilian foodstuffs indicated in the United Nations mission's report.

Paragraph 23 of that resolution provides that the Sanctions Committee may approve exceptions from the ban on importing materials and products from Iraq in order to provide Iraq with sufficient financial resources to import those materials the importation of which into Iraq is approved by the Committee.[*sic*]

Yet it has been impossible for Iraq, as it has been for the Sanctions Committee, to exercise the powers provided for in paragraphs 20 and 23 of the resolution because of the arbitrary position insisted upon by a small minority of the members of the Sanctions Committee.

Paragraph 21 of resolution 687 (1991) also provided that the Council review the provisions of paragraph 20 of the resolution every 60 days for the purpose of determining whether to reduce or lift the prohibitions referred to in paragraph 21. In spite of the passage of more than 130 days since the adoption of resolution 687 (1991), the Council has not met to reconsider the prohibition measures and to provide the opportunity to the Council members and to Iraq to indicate the extent of its implementation of the Council's resolutions. Rather, the Council confined itself to informal consultations, after which the President issued a presidential statement indicating that the members had failed to agree on any resolution.

Here, I indicate once more that the failure of the Council to meet with the aim of reviewing the sanctions and adopting the necessary resolution is also due to the position of a small minority of its members. This minority is bent on not allowing Iraq to enjoy the exceptions provided for in paragraphs 20 and 23. This minority is also bent on not allowing other member States of the Council that support the lifting of the sanctions to express their views officially and to record their positions publicly.

Paragraph 22 of resolution 687 (1991) actually provides for the total lifting of the sanctions once the Council takes note of the report of the Secretary-General on the compensation fund - which has actually taken place - and once the Council acknowledges that Iraq has completed all the actions required of it in paragraphs 8 through 13 of the same resolution. That has actually happened, and this fact was communicated to the Council by Iraq.

Yet, the same small minority in the Council prevented the Council from deciding that the second condition - which is necessary for the lifting of all sanctions imposed on Iraq under resolution 661 (1990) of 6 August 1990 - had been met.

In the face of this situation, in a letter dated 7 June 1991, the Iraqi Mission submitted an application to the Sanctions Committee requesting a lifting of the freeze on the Iraqi funds deposited in British, American and other foreign banks - which, as of 31 March 1991, totalled $3,735 million - with a view to purchasing foodstuffs, medicines and basic civilian materials.

However, while the Committee acknowledged the admissibility of unfreezing those deposits, it affirmed that the States in which those Iraqi funds are deposited are not obligated to unfreeze these funds. This has led actually to continued freezing and to depriving Iraq from using its funds with a view to averting the dangers highlighted by the United Nations mission's report.

The States that have kept the Iraqi assets frozen are doing so for political considerations of their own that are irrelevant to Security Council resolutions.

In addition, on 14 March 1991, Iraq requested the Sanctions Committee to allow it to export such quantities of oil as to provide $1.2 billion on the basis of paragraph 23 of the resolution. However, the Committee did not take any action on the question. Then, on 9 July 1991, Iraq repeated its request to allow it to export oil to the tune of $1.5 billion for the same purpose. But once again the Committee failed to achieve consensus and the request was shelved.

Iraq once more requested the Committee to approve the export of quantities of oil, with a view to purchasing foodstuffs contracted for with foreign companies, while indicating the quantities and prices of such foodstuffs. Once again, however, the Committee failed to achieve consensus on the request and it was shelved.

The freezing referred to in paragraphs 20, 21, 22 and 23 of Security Council resolution 687 (1991) - each of which provides for exceptions to the sanctions, or for their total lifting - was due to the positions of a small minority which, in fact, does not exceed one State plus three. This minority is also credited with paralysing the work of the Sanctions Committee.

Moreover, that minority takes credit for preventing the Committee from adopting the necessary resolutions to implement the recommendations included in the report of the inter-agency mission, headed by the Executive Delegate of the Secretary-General, Prince Sadruddin Aga Khan, which are included in document S/22799 of 17 July 1991 which it drew up following its visit to Iraq during the period from 29 June until 13 July last.

The report is the most recent of the United Nations Inter-Agency Humanitarian Programme and contains the most accurate information and statistics in its 59 pages. Allow me to quote a number of paragraphs from the aforementioned document:

(*spoke in English*)

> "We saw with our own eyes the scenes already reported at length ... the children afflicted by malnutrition. Our report is inevitably but a photograph in time, fast obsolete, yet the urgency of relief from suffering remains. Further, the hard statistics speak for themselves. Conditions are already grave in all of the essential sectors assessed and can only worsen in the weeks ahead. We must achieve a breakthrough to avert the looming crisis" (*S/22799, para. 131*).

(*spoke in Arabic*)

The report of the mission goes on to say:

(*spoke in English*)

> "This mission has addressed the current humanitarian needs in Iraq and has concluded that their magnitude requires funding that exceeds international aid and short-term palliatives and can be met only from the country's own resources ... On the basis, however, of our deliberations and meetings with the authorities in Iraq, it would appear feasible to institute arrangements whereby Iraq's requests for imports to meet the needs outlined in this report would be submitted to the United Nations and subjected to appropriate monitoring. The precise mechanisms need not be specified here. The formula agreed upon would provide for clear records of all transactions to be furnished to the Organization." (*Ibid., para. 137*)

(*spoke in Arabic*)

Finally, I have to remind the Council of the contents of paragraph 138 of the report, because the draft resolution before the Council proceeds in the opposite direction from the one advocated in the report.

(*spoke in English*)

> "It remains a cardinal humanitarian principle that innocent civilians - and above all the most vulnerable - should not be held hostage to events beyond their control. Those already afflicted by war's devastation cannot continue to pay the price of a bitter peace. It is a peace that will also prove to be tenuous if unmet needs breed growing desperation. If new displacements of Iraq's population result from hunger and disease, if relief is again sought across national frontiers, the region's stability will once more be set at risk with unforeseeable consequences. Humanitarian and political interests converge in the aversion of catastrophe. It is clearly imperative that Iraq's 'essential civilian needs' be met urgently and that rapid agreement be secured on the mechanism whereby Iraq's own resources be used to fund them to the satisfaction of the international community" (*Ibid, para. 138*).

(*spoke in Arabic*)

But regrettably, this small minority in the Sanctions Committee succeeded in paralysing the work of the Committee and its ability to adopt a resolution. Hence, the Committee failed to achieve consensus on the recommendations of the mission headed by Prince Sadruddin Aga Khan, which prompted the Chairman of the Committee to refer the matter back to the Security Council for it to take whatever decision it deems appropriate, which was the aim of the small minority in the Sanctions Committee. Why? The secret lies in the provisions of the draft resolution before the Council, which are aimed not at fulfilling the humanitarian needs of the Iraqi people but at exploiting them and imposing on Iraq's economy new financial sanctions and restrictions which had not been mentioned before, and to breach its sovereignty contrary to the United Nations Charter and all norms of international law.

For all intents and purposes, the draft resolution is aimed at keeping the economic embargo in place indefinitely, regardless of the provisions of paragraph 22 of Security Council resolution 687 (1991), and confines itself to giving Iraq a minimum of first-aid so that the people will not starve to death, but without providing Iraq with the opportunity to reconstruct its economy, including its oil industry, its agriculture, its irrigation system, its roads, communications, bridges and health facilities.

The Sanctions Committee cannot violate Security Council resolution 687 (1991) or add new requests that were not included in the original resolution and impose them on Iraq. Hence, the Sanctions Committee referred the report of the Secretary-General's Executive Delegate to the Council and we have before us a draft resolution that actually leads to the catastrophe warned against in paragraph 138 of the report, which I quoted earlier.

The draft resolution before the Council will actually lead to keeping the Iraqi people hostage under the influence of the small minority that claims to defend human rights and democracy in the world but has had no qualms about besieging the entire Iraqi people for more than a year. It has refused to lift the siege unless Iraq agrees to pay the price: relinquish its oil revenues and place its economic requirements and monetary policy in the hands of one State, plus one which has appointed itself as trustee over the Iraqi people, as the European Powers did in the nineteenth century *vis-à-vis* the Ottoman Empire and with respect to Egypt under the Khedives. What is surprising is that, although the United States and its three allies have announced their rejection of using food as a political weapon, Iraqis, including children, the sick and the elderly continue to die every day as a result of malnutrition, the lack of medicine and the embargo on food, medicine, funds and oil. Every day thousands of people die because the same minority is determined that it, and not Iraq, through United Nations agencies, will market - if not distribute - foodstuffs and medicines and other basic requirements for civilian life in

Iraq, although such foodstuffs would be paid for by Iraqi funds and the Iraqi people itself, and not out of the generosity of those States.

In August 1990 the purpose of this inhumane embargo was supposedly to ensure Iraq's withdrawal from the territory of Kuwait, which actually took place last February. The continued embargo affirms what Iraq has always said: that this alliance had the sole aim of destroying Iraq as an effective Arab force influential in determining the fate of the region. Hence, the 30-State alliance did not stop at destroying the infrastructure and the basic civilian structures of Iraq, but persisted in attempting to destroy Iraq by continuing the economic embargo and adopting various resolutions, all of which are aimed at putting Iraq forever under the trusteeship of the United States and its allies, on behalf of the Security Council and the committees that it established, in order to administer the affairs of Iraq, control its exports and imports and its internal affairs.

I come now to the political aspects of the draft. Contrary to the United Nations Charter, the draft gravely impinges on Iraq's national sovereignty as a free country and Founding Member of the United Nations, and imposes a foreign guardianship on the free will of the Iraqi people. The draft also deprives the legitimate Government of Iraq of its powers and responsibilities with respect to its citizens and abolishes its role in caring for them and providing for their livelihood, their daily needs for foodstuffs and health and medical services.

On the other hand, the draft gives foreign Powers the right to control Iraq's natural resources and allows them to dispose of its wealth and oil revenues as they wish, without the Iraqi people and its Government having any right to invest those resources or funds or to define their own priorities in the elimination of the effects of the unjust aggression by the 30 States against them. The draft also subordinates the humanitarian objective of the report of Prince Sadruddin Aga Khan, to suspect political motives and creates further difficulties for Iraq, although the pretexts that were invoked to impose those sanctions have ceased to exist. The draft actually undermines the provisions of resolution 687 (1990) [*sic*] and converts the partial lifting of the sanctions into colonialist restrictions that would rob Iraq of its right to full sovereignty, interfere in its internal affairs, plunder its oil wealth and usurp its right to dispose of its own funds, even though resolution 687 (1990) [*sic*] allows Iraq to purchase civilian requirements, such as foodstuffs and medicine without any intervention or trusteeship.

The authors of the resolution have thus wanted to circumvent the report of the international humanitarian organization that undertook field trips throughout Iraq and implicitly uncovered the nature of the brutal crimes perpetrated against Iraq when its infrastructure and national economy were destroyed through a scheme that had nothing to do with the so-called Gulf crisis but was aimed at destroying the potential of Iraq and, isolating its people, overthrowing the symbols of its cultural renaissance and comprehensive progress as an expression of deep-rooted hatred, and to further the aims of world Zionism under the motto of "legitimacy" and a "new world order".

Here I should like to take up the negative aspects of the draft resolution. While the authors claim that their aim is to cope with the grave deterioration in the health and nutritional situation of the Iraqi people and the grim portrait contained in the report of the Executive Delegate, as provided for in preambular paragraphs B and C of the draft, the draft actually imposes conditions on Iraq which lead in the direction opposite to that of the alleged aim of its authors. When we consider the preambular paragraphs of the draft, we see that they shuffle the cards and blur the facts. We note the preambular paragraph that refers to the so-called Kuwaiti detainees in Iraq. That paragraph was superimposed on the draft and was formulated in such a way as to distort the truth.

Those who are impeding the return of Kuwaitis from Iraq are the Government of Kuwait itself. The Iraqi authorities, during the period from 4 March until 14 July 1991, returned 6,133 Kuwaiti captives to Kuwait under the supervision of the International Committee of the Red Cross. Also, that Committee recorded 3,400 Kuwaitis residing in Iraq who wished to return to their country, but the Kuwaiti side agreed to accept only 128 individuals and dragged its feet regarding the return of the others, under the pretext of wanting to ascertain their identification. With respect to those so-called missing, the Kuwaiti Government insists on providing lists of names of people whose existence in Iraq has not been borne out by the investigations undertaken by the Iraqi authorities. Perhaps some of them have died as a result of the allied bombardment. Also, the Kuwaiti Government did not bother to inquire about those people in other parts of the world. As is well known, it is not conceivable to expect Iraq to produce someone of whom there is no news. On the other hand, what does this have to do with a draft resolution allegedly dealing with the serious health and nutritional situation of the Iraqi people? The aim behind this artificial inclusion of the so-called Kuwaiti detainees is to create an additional pretext to keep the embargo against the Iraqi people.

Paragraph E of the draft refers to the conclusions of the report of Prince Sadruddin Aga Khan, in particular to the proposal to sell oil to finance urgent humanitarian relief. The draft resolution should have sought to achieve this accommodation, but it could not have been further from that recommendation in letter and spirit. The provisions of the draft do not allow Iraq to sell its oil, but rather allow other States through a slow and complicated mechanism to purchase limited amounts of Iraqi oil. In addition, no stress was laid on the humanitarian relief, but priority was given to the payment of sums to the Compensation Fund and to the expenses of the Commission dealing with the destruction of weapons, the Commission dealing with the restitution of Kuwaiti property, and the Iraq-Kuwait Border Demarcation Commission. These provisions include such conditions and costs as would undermine the recommendations of the report of Prince Sadruddin Aga Khan. Preambular paragraph G and operative paragraph (c) indicate the need for the United Nations to intervene in the distribution of foodstuffs, medicines and materials and supplies for essential civilian needs of all categories of the Iraqi people through providing for United Nations administration, monitoring and supervision.

This concept of the draft resolution runs completely counter to the concept of sovereignty assigned by the Charter of the United Nations. Moreover, it constitutes a grave precedent as regards the humanitarian role of the United Nations. There is in Iraq a just and comprehensive system for the distribution of foodstuffs, which includes all persons, Iraqis and foreigners, residing in Iraq, and allows everyone to obtain basic foodstuffs at subsidized prices. The process of sales is undertaken through an integrated mechanism through the State agents and commercial markets, not through random distribution of assistance. Hence, the attempt to impose a United Nations supervision system, which has no chance of succeeding anyway, is aimed solely at derogating from Iraq's sovereignty, disregarding its organizational, administrative and economic institutions, and adding to the administrative costs of the Iraqi citizen and those taken from Iraq's own resources.

In preambular paragraph H, the draft resolution recalls the importance which the Council attaches to Iraq allowing access by the humanitarian organizations to those in need of assistance in all parts of Iraq and affirms the important role played by the Memorandum of Understanding between the Government of Iraq and the

United Nations of 18 April 1991. The reference to this Memorandum in such a manner is invidious to Iraq and its rights. Iraq has been fulfilling its obligations under the Memorandum of Understanding and the United Nations humanitarian programme. Iraq is proceeding according to the agreement and there are no significant problems in this regard. On the other hand, the Memorandum of Understanding relates to a programme of voluntary assistance provided by foreign parties, whereas the draft resolution has to do with foodstuffs and medical supplies paid for and distributed exclusively with Iraqi funds.

Moreover, preambular paragraph J provides that the Council is acting in accordance with Chapter VII of the Charter. Invoking Chapter VII, regarding sanctions, in this draft resolution, which is alleged to be a humanitarian draft resolution, once again exposes the suspect intent of the authors. Furthermore, it reveals the inhumane and exploitive [*sic*] nature of the draft.

I now turn to the technical and practical aspects of the provisions of the draft resolution. Operative paragraph 1 subordinates the permission of States to import Iraqi oil to seven conditions, including a time condition - six months after the passage of the draft resolution. This condition does not take into consideration the procedure followed in the international oil trade, that is, annual contacting. Hence, the purpose behind the six-month period is to stymie the process of exporting Iraqi oil and to create impediments to the marketing of necessary amounts during the same period, which would definitely lead to a decrease in Iraqi oil. On the other hand, the draft resolution does not allow Iraq to export oil at its own responsibility and to sell it on the free market, as the exception was made exclusively for imports from Iraq and not for exports by the Government of Iraq. Hence, it is not possible for Iraq to sell its oil on the free market, and it allows States to buy oil in very limited quantities and at very low prices. There is a financial condition, which is that the imports from Iraq should not exceed the value of, as it is rumoured, $1.6 billion, which falls short of Iraq's needs to finance its imports. This is all the more serious when we see that the draft resolution gives priority in using the revenues from the imports of Iraqi oil to deducting 30 per cent for the Compensation Fund in addition to the costs of the various conditions established by the Council.

The third condition deals with approval by the Security Council Committee on Sanctions of every transaction, which is a waste of time and makes it difficult to pump Iraqi oil systematically because, as members know, the Committee usually meets once a week in a bureaucratic tradition and on a consensus basis so that any member of the Security Council in the Committee can obstruct any transaction for weeks by raising various questions which, whether they are prompted by good will or ill will, have the same effect: of obstructing the marketing of Iraqi oil and of wasting time.

The fourth condition involves placing the oil revenues directly in an escrow account in a bank chosen by the United Nations, to be administered by the Secretary-General. Naturally, the costs of such an account are to be deducted from its assets.

Operative paragraph 1 of the draft resolution provides that the materials needed by Iraq must be defined by the Secretary-General within 20 days after the adoption of the resolution, although the report of Aga Khan defines the type and amounts of the necessary materials to avert epidemics and famine in Iraq. Moreover, the draft makes it conditional that clear markings be placed to indicate that the imports are for humanitarian and civilian requirements, as if they were voluntary contributions by charitable organizations, and not imports financed by Iraqi funds.

Paragraph 1 also subjects the distribution of materials imported by Iraq to the monitoring and supervision of United Nations agencies to ensure their distribution throughout Iraq. This condition disregards the fact that Iraq is a country of 18 million people and that the materials will be distributed by means of ration cards, and not as voluntary grants. This also requires the presence of thousands of United Nations staff, the cost of which will be borne by Iraq indefinitely, which is contrary to the sovereignty of Iraq.

Finally, unfreezing the balance of the escrow account is also to be carried out through resolutions of the Committee on Sanctions in three equal stages, which would obstruct the import of humanitarian and civilian materials by Iraq. This is contrary to the conditions of paying these sums for imports.

Moreover, paragraph 1 (c) stipulates that the United Nations should provide administration, monitoring and supervision with a view to providing humanitarian assistance from other sources. This provision means that governmental and non-governmental humanitarian organizations and United Nations staff that provided assistance to the Iraqi people in coordination with the Government of Iraq will cease to provide assistance and will be transformed into a machinery of administration, supervision and monitoring, whose costs would be borne by the people of Iraq from their resources, without achieving any gains. Also, under this provision, the United Nations, if it so wishes, can provide more of these from other sources in the numbers it decides, and the people of Iraq have to bear the costs.

In operative paragraph 3 the draft also provides that a portion of the Iraqi oil sales be used to finance Iraq's contribution to the Compensation Fund because of the destruction of the weapons and the restitution of Kuwaiti property. Placing conditions on the export of oil to fill Iraqi humanitarian needs runs counter to resolution 687 (1991), particularly paragraph 19 thereof, which provides that the Iraqi people and their ability to pay must be taken into consideration. These provisions have not been included in the draft resolution. The deductions cannot begin with a partial and conditional lifting, because the limited amount of exported oil, if approved, would not be enough to finance the needs of the Iraqi people. How could it be sufficient after deducting the percentage for the Fund and other costs?

Fourthly, the draft resolution also breaches the sovereignty of Iraq when it calls upon it to submit monthly reports about its assets in foreign currency and wealth.

In brief, for its part Iraq has prepared and provided all forms of cooperation in seeking to fulfil its obligations under resolution 687 (1991) and has responded fully to the Special Commission and inspection teams in implementing section C of the resolution, the greater part of whose items have been complied with. In addition Iraq has facilitated the restitution of Kuwaiti properties. At present the gold is being returned and preparations are under way to return the museum items; and the Border Demarcation Commission is continuing its work in Geneva with Iraq's active participation. The Council should match responses by Iraq by the full lifting of sanctions. But the will of some of its members runs counter to that; for obvious political reasons not relevant to the Council's resolutions, to international law or to the Charter those States had no qualms about announcing their aims when they tied lifting the sanctions to changing the political regime in Iraq. On the other hand, Iraq is ready to ensure the necessary transparency and has proposed means necessary to inform international agencies of Iraqi imports. Iraq has also undertaken to provide immediately copies of all sales contracts and purchases of foodstuffs and has declared its readiness to sell oil to States permanent members of the Security Council and buy its medical, nutritional and other basic requirements from them so that they may be directly informed of all exports and imports.

The fact that this initiative by Iraq has not been taken into consideration, coupled with the insistence of the authors on their programme, reveals a deliberate attempt to obstruct the lifting of sanctions against Iraq. It also constitutes an attempt by some permanent members to evade their responsibility, starve the Iraqi people and blame it on the Iraqi Government by aborting the report of Sadruddin Aga Khan and proposing a complicated and impractical machinery - trusteeship over Iraq. The authors actually want to hold the Iraqi people hostage and to place before it two options: either to allow colonial and neocolonial States to plunder its oil wealth and control it indefinitely, or to keep the state of starvation and life on the brink of disaster. This will not be permitted by Iraq.

I shall now touch briefly on draft resolution S/22942. It should be noted that the draft resolution is based on two points, which are: the circumstances surrounding the second inspection team during its visit from 22 June to 3 July 1991, as indicated in preambular paragraphs c, d, e and f; and the resolution of the Board of Governors of the International Atomic Energy Agency (IAEA) of 18 July 1991.

Iraq has already clearly and unambiguously indicated on more than one occasion the circumstances surrounding the arrival of the second inspection team. The details of those circumstances were communicated to the high-level mission headed by Mr. Rolf Ekeus [*sic*] when that mission visited Iraq. The Iraqi Government provided assurances at the highest level that its authorities would open up all facilities to the inspection teams. The high-level mission mentioned these assurances in its report and indicated that the coming period would begin to show Iraq's fulfilment of those assurances. Since then, more than one team has visited Iraq and a nuclear inspection team and a biological team are still there.

Iraq has opened up all facilities to the third inspection team and provided it with immense quantities of information, as indicated by the Director of the IAEA in his press conference at United Nations Headquarters in New York on 30 July 1991. Also, the Chairman of the fourth team, Sir David Kay, [*sic*] stated before the news agency in Baghdad that his team was making progress and had obtained a great deal of information and that the Iraqis were cooperating with his team. As for the other teams that visited Iraq, they have not indicated the presence of any impediments or significant problems in their work.

Can one truly say, after the passage of more than one month since the circumstances surrounding the second team and after the experience of cooperating with all the teams, that Iraq is uncooperative and not fulfilling its obligations? We had hoped that the Security Council would express its satisfaction with the cooperation enjoyed by the international teams in Iraq, not that it would adopt a new resolution condemning Iraq for an isolated incident.

Most members of the second team are now in Iraq and enjoying unprecedented cooperation. Information is being supplied promptly, and the Council can be guided by the head of the team, who is now in Baghdad. Is this not further evidence of Iraq's abiding by the Council's resolution? This must be taken into consideration by the Security Council.

In spite of the aforementioned we find that the draft resolution does not include any legitimate provisions. Most of it is covered in the agreement on the privileges and immunities of the Special Commission, the IAEA and the inspection teams, which was accepted by Iraq. From our point of view, this agreement is appropriate to the circumstances for cooperation that may be available, and they have now become available as far as Iraq is concerned. Last month proved that they have improved.

Finally, we should like to inquire of the Special Commission, the teams and the Agency whether they were denied access to certain places or were prevented from inspecting any materials. As far as we know, there is not a single place, as indicated in the reports of the inspection teams, that has not been inspected by them. But, to be more accurate, there was a place over which a clamour was raised on 21 June. The Chairman of the third nuclear inspection team agreed to move the materials found there, and two members of his team supervised the process. The team recorded all the materials, which were photographed and unloaded from trucks under the team's supervision. The international team released the non-nuclear equipment for use in the reconstruction of Iraq. The trucks left there under the supervision and approval of the inspection team. All this is recorded in inventories and lists exchanged between the third inspection team and Iraq. The equipment was stored in warehouses, thus making it easier to be inspected by the team in future. This all took place quietly, so what can be the reason for the current draft resolution including operative paragraph 3? The Council should express its satisfaction with the practical measures taken in this regard instead of trying to condemn Iraq and impose new conditions on it.

I apologize for taking so long. Because of what happened for the first time in the Council, that is, taking up three draft resolutions consecutively for consideration, I was forced to speak at length.

[51] **The President** (interpretation from Spanish):

...

It is my understanding that the Council is ready to proceed to the vote on the draft resolutions before it. Unless there is any objection, I shall put the draft resolutions to the vote in the following order: S/22940, S/22941 and S/22942.

There being no objection, it is so decided.

I shall first call on members of the Council wishing to make statements before the voting.

[51] **Mr. Al-Ashtal (Yemen)** (interpretation from Arabic):

...

In my brief statement I shall comment on draft resolution S/22941.

A full year after the imposition of comprehensive sanctions against Iraq, and nearly six months after the end of the war that liberated Kuwait and enabled its legitimate Government to return, the Security Council is facing a humanitarian problem of tragic dimensions. Notwithstanding numerous and continuous reports depicting the suffering of the Iraqi people as a result of the ongoing of the embargo - whose dire consequences could include starvation and death for hundreds of thousands of the most vulnerable members of Iraqi society - the Security Council is still dragging its feet in dealing realistically with the tragedy of the Iraqi people, who were the first victims of the Gulf crisis, and with the resolution by which the Security Council imposed the embargo against Iraq following the war that destroyed Iraq's civilian infrastructure.

On 15 July 1991, Prince Sadruddin Aga Khan, the Secretary-General's Executive Delegate, who headed the inter-agency mission, submitted a comprehensive report on the sad human situation in Iraq. This was the second report, following the one submitted a few months ago by Mr. Martti Ahtisaari.

In its section II, "Summary of main findings and recommendations", the report says,

> "With respect to the possible sale of oil by the Iraqi Government to finance such imports, paragraph 23 of Security Council resolution 687 (1991) empowers the Security Council Committee established by resolution 661 (1990) to approve exceptions to the prohibition against the import of commodities and products originating in Iraq, with the explicit purpose of assuring 'adequate financial resources' on the

> part of the Iraqi Government to procure medicine and health supplies, foodstuffs and materials and supplies for 'essential civilian needs'". (*S/22799, annex, para. 32*)

Later in the same section, the report says that

> "If the Security Council Committee were to decide that Iraq should be allowed to use funds from oil sales or facilitate the use of blocked accounts in order to meet urgent humanitarian needs, the Government indicated that it would cooperate in making available documentation relating to sales of crude oil as well as purchases of the authorized imports. ... [A] suitable device for monitoring such credit balances could be established". (*Ibid., para. 34*)

It is regrettable that the Sanctions Committee, which heard an oral report from Prince Sadruddin and other members of his mission, was unable to take a decision on this matter, which falls within its mandate by the terms of paragraph 23 of resolution 687 (1991). A full month after the submission of Prince Sadruddin's report the Council is seized of draft resolution S/22941, which authorizes the exemption of the sale of some Iraqi oil for a limited period of six months and in the limited amount of $1.6 billion.

Although the draft resolution would ultimately enable needed medicine and food to reach Iraq, it raises many questions of principle. First, what is the justification for submitting a special draft resolution on the humanitarian aspects of the situation in Iraq when the Sanctions Committee possesses a mandate under paragraph 23 of resolution 687 (1991) to take decisions on this subject and to permit Iraq to export oil and petroleum products exclusively to meet humanitarian needs? In other words, why was the Sanctions Committee not permitted to take the necessary decision immediately after Prince Sadruddin Aga Khan's report was submitted? And why did the Committee and the Security Council not accept the well-considered and reasonable recommendations submitted by Prince Sadruddin in his report?

Second, would not these complicated conditions in the draft resolution lead to the creation of bureaucratic mechanisms and procedures which would delay the timely arrival of foodstuffs and medicines to Iraq? And why is the Secretariat involved in technical and commercial operations, something which would add to the burdens of this Organization?

Third, why is this humanitarian draft resolution based on Chapter VII of the Charter? True, the sanctions were imposed against Iraq on the basis of Chapter VII of the Charter; but we are not now dealing with the lifting of the sanctions. We are now dealing with the approval of some exceptions for purely humanitarian reasons. Was it not possible for the Sanctions Committee to allow the same exceptions that would lead to the importation of Iraqi oil for humanitarian needs without any reference to Chapter VII of the Charter? This question acquires a special significance in view of what might happen in the future and the position that the Security Council might take should Iraq reject the export of oil in accordance with the stipulated conditions. This is not a theoretical possibility, for the Prime Minister of Iraq has already rejected the draft resolution since it would not meet the humanitarian needs and would at the same time undermine Iraq's sovereignty.

Fourth, why does the draft resolution confuse the special humanitarian situation of millions of innocent Iraqis with financial matters related to the recovery of the cost of the Special Commission and the IAEA and the Iraq-Kuwait Boundary Demarcation Commission? Does the Security Council equate those Iraqi vulnerable people who could face famine and slow death should sanctions continue with the staff of the international organizations who would not be greatly hurt by the postponement of the receipt of their remunerations? Was it not possible for the Security Council to allow the sale of some shipments of Iraqi oil to meet the costs of international organizations in a specific manner, in addition to the financing of the Compensation Fund, which relates to many innocent people - Kuwaitis and non-Kuwaitis who lost their lives, positions or rights as a result of the war? How can we interpret this intentional confusion and in the same draft resolution accept that it represents the absence of interest and even the carelessness regarding the fate of millions of innocent Iraqis who are helpless both in war and in peace?

The people and the Government of Yemen are concerned about our brothers in Iraq, especially the vulnerable groups among them, those who would fall as a result of the miserable humanitarian situation in Iraq. United Nations experts have been issuing warnings for a long time and some of them announced that an imminent catastrophe was inevitable. For example, the report of the mission of Medicine for Peace declares, on page 17, that

> "Unless the sanctions are amended, it is probable that the public health system will collapse, which would lead to the death of many children without any justification whatsoever."

Moreover, press reports have indicated that Iraqi civilians with medium incomes have begun to sell their valuable possessions, and even household items, in order to buy the foodstuffs that are sold at astronomical prices. As for those with limited incomes in Iraq, they face want, poverty and famine.

It is expected that, given the Security Council's procrastination, the complications of the draft resolution submitted to us and Iraq's rejection, the blame for the starvation of the Iraqi people will be apportioned here and there. At that time, will it be possible for the Security Council to deny its share of responsibility? The famine that will afflict the children of the Iraqi people will not have been created by nature, and it will not be the result of the scarcity of resources; the continuation of the sanctions will be one of its main reasons.

The Security Council, which is mandated to serve peace and security the world over, should not allow the spread of famine which might lead to massive migrations across international borders, in addition to the possibility of instability and the break-down of internal security. This would ultimately lead to jeopardizing peace and security in the area. Furthermore, the Security Council is responsible for the preservation of the lives and safety of human beings. Everybody says that he is not against the Iraqi people. Why then do some insist on the continuation of its suffering? Why do these people not lift from its shoulders the embargo that is harming and weakening Iraqi society day by day?

It is known that there are political ends that are not declared in the Security Council. But would these ends justify inhuman means?

Each country has the right to impose an embargo against another country in implementation of its own policies and in defence of its interests. But the Security Council should not be used to achieve ends other than those which conform with the Charter and are based on the Charter in letter and in spirit.

...

[61] Mr. MUMBENGEGWI (Zimbabwe):

...

I shall confine my remarks to the draft resolution contained in document S/22941.

The critical humanitarian situation facing the people of Iraq following the end of the Gulf war has been a source of grave concern to Zimbabwe.

Zimbabwe was among the non-aligned members of the Council who submitted a draft resolution last March aimed at relieving the suffering of the civilian population of Iraq. In spite of the detailed report presented to Council members by Mr. Martti Ahtisaari, portraying the distressing humanitarian situation which had arisen in Iraq, the Council was not able to take action on that proposal from the non-aligned members of the Council.

The Executive Delegate of the Secretary-General on humanitarian issues in the Gulf area, Prince Sadruddin Aga Khan, submitted a detailed and comprehensive report last month that carried a timely warning that Iraq was on the brink of famine. He warned that any delay in the Council's taking action might result in a catastrophe in that country.

Zimbabwe had therefore expected the Council to respond swiftly through its Committee established by resolution 661 (1990), which, under paragraph 23 of resolution 687 (1991), is empowered to approve exceptions to the prohibition against the import of commodities and products originating from Iraq, when required, to ensure adequate financial resources for purchasing essential civilian needs. It is therefore to be regretted that the Council was not able to take advantage of this more expeditious procedure provided for in resolution 687 (1991).

In the view of my delegation, the principal merit of the draft resolution contained in document S/22941, on which we are about to vote, is that it creates an opportunity for the possibility of generating financial resources to meet the humanitarian requirements of the people of Iraq, as well as compensation for those who suffered loss and hardship as a result of the Gulf war. Zimbabwe therefore welcomes this step about to be taken by the Council to create a mechanism designed to address the needs of the victims of war, in both Iraq and Kuwait, as well as elsewhere.

While welcoming the fact that the Council is taking action to address the needs of the victims of the Gulf war, we cannot fail to register our reservations regarding those provisions of the draft resolution before us which encroach on national sovereignty.

Zimbabwe does recognize the need to ensure transparency in all the transactions to be carried out under the draft resolution before us. However, it is our view that monitoring arrangements could have been put in place that would have ensured transparency without encroaching on sovereignty.

In the final analysis, it is my delegation's view that no opportunity which offers the possibility of alleviating the suffering of innocent civilians should be allowed to slip through our fingers.

...

[63-65] **Mr. Alarcon de Quesada (Cuba)** (interpretation from Spanish):

...

I shall refer to the draft resolution contained in document S/22941. This draft resolution has been identified - and I do not quite know why - as the humanitarian resolution. It evidently has to do with situations with which the members of the Council are familiar, although the Council has not itself formally and expressly considered them.

Information has come to hand over the months reflecting the grave plight of the civilian population of Iraq as a result of the continuation of an ironclad economic sanctions regime. In the opinion of my delegation, the Council should have acted a long time ago in order to put an end completely to the economic sanctions, which cease to be justified at a time when the reasons which had justified them - which are set forth in Security Council resolution 661 (1990) - have been taken care of.

However, the draft resolution which is now before us, and which claims to be humanitarian in connection with the economic sanctions regime, in fact consolidates the sanctions. Indeed, it broadens them, as in the case of medicines and other supplies.

In resolution 661 (1990), adopted a year ago, before the military clashes took place on Iraqi territory, the Council decided to exclude supplies intended exclusively for medical purposes and, in humanitarian circumstances, foodstuffs. We have received much information, some of it through missions sent by the United Nations itself. From this information, we learned clearly of the existence of humanitarian circumstances. The Council is now invited to add medicine and medical supplies to the sanctions regime, plus foodstuffs, supposedly through an authorization which would be given subject to certain controls for the export of Iraqi oil and the acquisition of some of these supplies, but subject to what we regard as an unjustifiable and strict control system under the sanctions. The Council is considering this draft resolution and two others, one of which has been around for two months, namely, the one setting the ceiling for the Iraqi contribution to the Compensation Fund, and which everyone knows the Council has been unable to consider because one delegation had difficulties with the text. Apparently it has now overcome those difficulties, and again all that was done without debate.

This Council had the opportunity, indeed the mandate pursuant to its own resolutions, to address Iraq's humanitarian needs and to authorize supplies or to slacken the sanctions regime so that those needs could have been better met, thus satisfying the humanitarian concern by which the members of the Council claim to be motivated.

Security Council resolution 687 (1991), paragraph 21, provided that we were to review the provisions every 60 days for the purpose of determining whether to reduce or lift the prohibitions referred to therein. Two 60-day periods have elapsed since the adoption of that resolution and the Council has not strictly determined whether it is appropriate to reduce or lift the prohibitions, nor indeed has it been kind enough to meet to carry out such a review.

We are now meeting in certain circumstances, more or less agreed upon in the private consultations to which I referred earlier, in order to adopt, with whatever explanations anyone may wish to make, three draft resolutions. However, we should not suppose that, because in the Council we do not discuss openly the reasons or the non-reasons, as it were, for the continuation of a system that is having a severe impact on the civilian population, there is no such debate. There are public reports, public documents, reports of commissions that have been to Iraq and very interesting debates and discussions.

For example, I have here some documents that show how various committees of the United States Congress considered the same ideas more than a month ago. They considered the same points that we now see in the draft resolution in document S/22941. Indeed, one of those Congressional hearings was held just before the issuance of Prince Sadruddin Aga Khan's report. Obviously, that Congressional meeting took place before the Sanctions Committee's discussion of that report. In other words, the members of the United States Congress and people from the State Department who attended that meeting - the Permanent Representative of the United States, I understand, was among them - discussed with their parliamentary colleagues the ideas which one month later we, the members of the Security Council, are generously informed of and are convened this afternoon kindly to endorse.

So there has been discussion. A representative of UNICEF has drawn attention to a fact that should have prompted more diligent action from the Council a long time ago, action unlike the one that we are required to take now. He stated that he was aware that there were various political implications involved in this question, but he also pointed out that no matter what the political implications were, we should not forget that here we are confronting a human calamity whose consequences would rest on the conscience of mankind for a very long time. He emphasized that it was not a natural disaster but rather an entirely man-made disaster.

The representative of UNICEF stated that he personally wished to point out that children were dying every day and that he had to bury too many small children in Iraq to allow him to consider that the situation was acceptable.

This means that we are faced with a situation which clearly suggests the need for the international community to show sensitivity with respect to the various and repeated reports that emphasize the gravity of the humanitarian situation in Iraq. However, the draft resolution now before us, far from tackling the humanitarian issue, rather seeks to link it with other elements and to fit it into an overall context which we find unacceptable. It is quite unacceptable to try to use foodstuffs, medicines and medical supplies, which are vital to the health of human beings, as an instrument to attain certain political objectives. We believe that the sanctions against Iraq should have been eliminated at the moment when the causes which were argued in justification of it disappeared, and we feel that the sanctions regime should never have included elements which, from a moral point of view and from the point of view of civilization, cannot be imposed by anyone on anyone else.

My delegation does not believe that Chapter VII of the Charter, or indeed any other Chapter of the Charter, authorizes this Council to take upon itself certain functions and responsibilities, or to entrust them to the Secretary-General, which are clearly a breach of the principle of non-intervention in the internal affairs of States and of the principle of the sovereign equality of States. The establishment of the proposed mechanism would really mean appropriating elements of Iraqi sovereignty and would seek to apply to Iraq a type of trusteeship system, which is entirely contrary to the letter and spirit of the Charter.

I feel it appropriate to refer members to Article 78 of the Charter, which states:

> "The trusteeship system shall not apply to territories which have become members of the United Nations, relationship among which shall be based on respect for the principle of sovereign equality".

In actual fact, in practice, an attempt is being made to continue the war and the confrontation with Iraq after the end of the armed conflict and after the Council adopted various resolutions that claim to have put an end to it, making an improper use of the United Nations for these purposes. For these reasons, the Cuban delegation finds the draft resolution contained in document S/22941 to be unacceptable, and we will vote accordingly.

[71] **The President** (interpretation from Spanish):

...

I shall now put to the vote the draft resolution contained in document S/22940.

A vote was taken by show of hands.

In favour: Austria, Belgium, China, Côte d'Ivoire, Cuba, Ecuador, France, India, Romania, Union of Soviet Socialist Republics, United Kingdom of Great Britain and Northern Ireland, United States of America, Yemen, Zaire, Zimbabwe

[71] **The President** (interpretation from Spanish):

There were 15 votes in favour. The draft resolution has been adopted unanimously as resolution 705 (1991).

I shall now put to the vote the draft resolution contained in document S/22941.

A vote was taken by show of hands.

In favour: Austria, Belgium, China, Côte d'Ivoire, Ecuador, France, India, Romania, Union of Soviet Socialist Republics, United Kingdom of Great Britain and Northern Ireland, United States of America, Zaire, Zimbabwe

Against: Cuba

Abstaining: Yemen

[72] **The President** (interpretation from Spanish):

The result of the voting is as follows: 13 votes in favour, 1 against and 1 abstention. The draft resolution has been adopted as resolution 706 (1991).

I shall now put to the vote the draft resolution contained in document S/22942.

There being no objection, it is so decided.

A vote was taken by show of hands.

In favour: Austria, Belgium, China, Côte d'Ivoire, Cuba, Ecuador, France, India, Romania, Union of Soviet Socialist Republics, United Kingdom of Great Britain and Northern Ireland, United States of America, Yemen, Zaire, Zimbabwe

[72] **The President** (interpretation from Spanish):

There were 15 votes in favour. The draft resolution has been adopted unanimously as resolution 707 (1991).

I shall now call on those members of the Council who wish to make statements following the voting.

[72] **Mr. Rochereau de la Sabliere (France):** (interpretation from French):

...

The reasons we are once again meeting in this Chamber, a little more than one year after the invasion of Kuwait by Iraq, and five months after the liberation of Kuwait, are, first of all, to deal with a humanitarian problem; secondly, to respond to the repeated failures of the Iraqi authorities to comply with their obligations under an important section of resolution 687 (1991), calling for the elimination of weapons of mass destruction; and, finally, to complete arrangements for the operation of the Compensation Fund. We have just adopted three draft resolutions on these topics.

The situation created in Iraq, owing to the conduct of the Government of Baghdad, is being followed with great attention in France. Last March, in the light of Mr. Ahtisaari's report, the Sanctions Committee and the Security Council deemed it necessary to ease the embargo so as to allow the civilian population in Iraq easier access to essential materials and supplies. My delegation actively contributed to that effort. In April France alerted the international community to the tragic fate of the civilian populations, in particular the Kurds, who were fleeing from Iraq in the hope of escaping the intolerable oppression to which they had fallen victim. This action led to the adoption of resolution 688 (1991).

Less than one month ago, the report of Prince Sadruddin Aga Khan described to the Council in detail the humanitarian situation in Iraq. It made clear the need to take urgent measures to avoid a serious worsening of the living conditions of the Iraqi population, which could not be held responsible for the faults of a regime that it had not freely chosen. It was necessary to act rapidly on the basis of resolution 687 (1991), which provided that Iraq could be authorized from time to time to export oil to finance the purchase of essential goods. In fact, Iraq had presented several requests of this nature to the Sanctions Committee.

We took these elements as the basis for drafting the text that the Security Council has just adopted. It appeared indispensable to provide very specific modalities for the sale of Iraqi oil, for the use of the resources thus generated and for the distribution of essential goods that could thus be purchased, as it was necessary to have the assurance of achieving the priority goal pursued, namely, to meet the humanitarian needs of the Iraqi population as a whole.

Indeed, we could not trust a Government that attempts to get around Security Council resolutions, practises deception, still prohibits access to certain parts of its territory to United Nations representatives, detains by force Kuwaiti nationals and nationals of other countries and persists in refusing to allow Prince Sadruddin Aga Khan and the High Commissioner for Refugees to open humanitarian centres in those places where they are needed.

The text that has been adopted does not aim at establishing definitive rules. It was conceived as a response to an emergency situation for a period of six months. Hence, there was to be no prejudging of the future.

The authorized imports of Iraqi petroleum must produce a sum as determined on the basis of the evaluation of essential needs presented by Prince Sadruddin Aga Khan. One provision allows the Security Council to readjust that sum if it appears, in the light of a report requested of the Secretary-General or of information that might come later on, that that sum does not seem sufficient.

We felt that it was not up to the Security Council to specify either the details or the modalities for commercial and financial transactions authorized by the text nor the modalities for monitoring the distribution of food or medicine in order to ensure their availability to the Iraqi population. We are relying for all this on the Secretary-General, who will present us with his recommendations.

Finally, it was logical to provide, in implementation of prior resolutions, that income received from these exports by Iraq would also generate money for the Compensation Fund and make it possible to finance the operating costs of United Nations bodies set up within the framework of resolution 687 (1991), in particular the Special Commission for the elimination of weapons of mass destruction. The particular provision of the resolution regarding the amount to be levied for the Compensation Fund on the basis of approved authorizations reflects our concern over seeing the Fund built up rapidly. Thereafter the Fund will operate according to the modalities to be decided upon by its Governing Council.

The draft resolution on nuclear matters on which we have also just taken a decision is a response to the inadmissible behaviour of the Iraqi authorities. On several occasions, our Council expressed its concern over Iraq's repeated violations of its obligations, either those imposed upon it by resolution 687 (1991) or those deriving from its commitments to the IAEA. Non-compliance with those commitments has been established by the Board of Governors of that Agency. It has also indicated its deep concern over Iraq's attempts at deception. The information made available in recent weeks by the Chairman of the Special Commission for the Elimination of Weapons of Mass Destruction and by the Director General of the IAEA following on-site inspections goes overwhelmingly against the Iraqi Government. It clearly appears that Iraq was involved in a clandestine research programme intended to get nuclear weapons for Iraq, in flagrant violation of its international obligations.

The resolution therefore condemns the failures of Iraq and spells out certain provisions of resolution 687 (1991) regarding the activities of the Special Commission in order to help it carry out the important mission given it by the Security Council.

I shall complete my statement with the draft resolution regarding the percentage of the value of Iraqi petroleum exports within which the Governing Council of the Compensation Fund will have to set the actual amount of Iraq's contribution. The adoption of the proposal made to us by the Secretary-General in this regard, a proposal that takes into account both the needs of the Iraqi people and the need to ensure fair compensation, will complete the work of setting up the Compensation Fund established to compensate the victims of the invasion and occupation of Kuwait. Since the decision has already been taken in Geneva, the Fund will give priority consideration to small requests, essentially those which will be presented by persons who lived in Iraq or Kuwait and had to leave those countries and abandon their possessions.

...

[78] Mr. Pickering (United States of America):

...

Once again the Council has convened to take action on problems arising out of Iraq's aggression against Kuwait.

The resolution that we have just approved on compliance with part C of resolution 687 (1991) on inspection and destruction of weapons of mass destruction in Iraq draws the attention of the world to Iraq's failure to comply with resolution 687 (1991) and Iraq's repeated material breaches of its obligations under the nuclear non-proliferation Treaty. I will not detail the list of compliance failures and material breaches, which the International Atomic Energy Agency (IAEA) and the United Nations Special Commission have so well documented in recent weeks, but merely note that we have heard two further reports: the Special Commission's revelations of Iraq's biological [*sic*] weapons violations in its letter of 5 August and evidence of additional nuclear weapons violations contained in the International Atomic Energy Agency's letter to the Secretary-General of 6 August.

The primary purpose behind this resolution is to strengthen the role of the International Atomic Energy Agency and the Special Commission in performing their important task of eliminating Iraq's weapons of mass destruction capability and of assuring that such weapons are not reacquired.

On the one hand, this resolution provides the IAEA and the Special Commission with certain new tools to bolster the effectiveness of their work. On the other hand, the resolution sends a message to Iraq. What is expected, indeed demanded, is Iraq's full compliance with all its obligations under relevant Treaties and Security Council resolutions as well as its complete cooperation with the IAEA and the Special Commission.

The humanitarian resolution that we have just approved intends primarily to get humanitarian assistance to those in Iraq who need it the most. This is not a resolution lifting sanctions. In fact, it will strengthen the sanctions by preventing the Iraqi Government from seeking political and military gains through the misery of the Iraqi people which it has itself caused. Under the exceptions provision of paragraph 23 of resolution 687 (1991), we are making an exception for a special and limited purpose for a limited period of time. With its emphasis on equitable distribution and monitoring, the resolution seeks to ensure that food and other humanitarian assistance reaches those for whom it is most intended. The importance of vigilant monitoring of distribution of humanitarian assistance arising out of this resolution cannot be overemphasized. Careful monitoring is required to deter diversion of food and other humanitarian assistance to privileged sectors of Iraqi society or the misuse of this assistance at the expense of those most in need. Our sad experience has shown that this kind of diversion is a very real possibility unless we take strong steps to prevent it.

In adopting this resolution, the Council has put the Secretary-General and the Secretariat at the centre of the process of providing humanitarian assistance to Iraq. My Government recognizes that the resolution places a heavy burden on the Secretary-General in drawing up his report on a number of highly complex and technical issues never before tackled by the United Nations, but it also gives him the authority to propose whatever additional measures he deems necessary and appropriate to monitor, supervise and manage this operation. Subsequently we will be depending on the Secretary-General and the United Nations to ensure that the goals of the resolution are truly achieved. We stand ready, for our part, to help in any way we can. We appreciate the excellent work the Secretary-General has done throughout the Gulf crisis. We are confident that the United Nations will rise to this challenge once again. I should also note that we have agreed to support the 30-per-cent ceiling imposed by resolution 705 (1991) on the basis that it is fully and directly linked to resolution 706 (1991) and any subsequent Iraqi oil sales.

It is important to note that for the past 10 years Iraq itself has spent 28 per cent of its income on military equipment alone.

Finally, I want to mention the pressing and urgent need for Iraq to return all prisoners of war and all captives taken from Kuwait and from other States.

...

[81] **Mr. Li Daoyu (China)** (interpretation from Chinese):

...

The Chinese delegation wishes to state its position on resolution 706 (1991), which the Council has just adopted. The ever-deteriorating situation faced by the Iraqi people has for some time been a question of deep concern to the international community, including China. Sound recommendations were made in the report submitted by His Excellency Prince Sadruddin Aga Khan, Executive Delegate of the Secretary-General, but regrettably the Security Council has taken no action on those recommendations.

Resolution 706 (1991), just adopted, permits Iraq to export oil for a given period in order to finance the import of humanitarian goods. That will help alleviate to a certain extent the grave and deteriorating situation faced by the Iraqi people. It is with that in mind that the Chinese delegation voted in favour of resolution 706 (1991).

But we are of the view that the sovereignty of Iraq must be respected in the implementation of that resolution. Iraq is entitled to play its proper role in the purchase and distribution of the food, medicine and other materials required to meet essential civilian needs.

The designated sum from Iraq's oil income should be used principally for humanitarian relief work. The amount of oil the resolution permits Iraq to export seems insufficient to meet the humanitarian needs of the Iraqi people. For that reason, the Security Council should review this question again at an appropriate time to consider increasing the permitted amount of oil sales and extending the time limit for those sales.

Finally, I would note that it is within the terms of reference of the Governing Council of the United Nations Compensation Commission to decide the percentage of the value of Iraq's oil exports that should be paid into the Compensation Fund.

The Chinese delegation reserves its position on the questions to which I have alluded.

...

[82] **Mr. Richardson (United Kingdom):**

...

My Government welcomes the resolution the Security Council has just adopted setting a ceiling for the hypothecation of Iraq's oil revenues. That decision provides some assurance to the many individuals, companies and institutions which because of the Iraqi invasion and occupation of Kuwait lost their property and in some cases their lives that they will receive some recompense.

I noted sadly, but without surprise, that in the lengthy statement we heard earlier from the representative of Iraq there was not a word of regret for the suffering that Iraq had inflicted on so many innocent people. We tend sometimes to forget about them, and yet they are, of course, one of the main purposes and motivations behind this resolution.

We were pleased by the results of the first session of the Governing Council of the United Nations Compensation Commission, held in July and August, and, in the light of what I have just said, in particular the agreement to establish an expedited procedure for small claimants. We look forward to the continuation of the work of the Compensation Commission in September and October.

I turn now to the resolution we have just adopted on oil sales. As my delegation said in informal consultations among members of the Council on 5 August, when the last review of sanctions took place, my Government does not believe that the time has yet come to lift sanctions. The Iraqi Government has failed to live up to many of its obligations. It has failed, for example, to release Kuwaitis and other foreigners, including a British national, Mr. Ian Richter. There is still a great quantity of Kuwaiti property to return. And more generally, the policies and practices of Iraq have included the oppression of its own people in the north and the south of the country.

But it has never been the aim of my Government to harm the Iraqi people, who after all have no voice of their own in their own country. You cannot deal with the misdeeds of a country's Government without, regrettably, having some impact on the civilian population. But in view of the problems that have been highlighted in the reports by Mr. Ahtisaari and subsequently by Prince Sadruddin, my Government is ready to permit limited sales of Iraqi oil over a six-month period to fund the importation of food, medicine and other humanitarian supplies. A portion of the oil revenues must go to the Compensation Fund and to pay for the Special Commission, the costs of the Iraq-Kuwait Boundary Demarcation Commission and the arrangements for returning Kuwaiti property plundered by Iraq.

In view of the past record of the Iraqi Government, we need an effective United Nations system for monitoring oil sales and for the equitable distribution of humanitarian supplies. These monitoring arrangements, in our view, must ensure that supplies reach the vulnerable segments of the Iraqi population in all parts of Iraq, and we believe there should be provision for random sampling by United Nations officials to that end.

But that said, we shall look forward with keenness to seeing the Secretary-General's proposals in 20 days' time, and we shall take them fully into account in determining what practical steps are needed to fulfil the terms of this resolution.

I turn finally to the resolution we have adopted on the weapons of mass destruction, a resolution of great importance. We believe it is vital that the Special Commission and the International Atomic Energy Agency should have all the powers they need to carry out their duties under resolution 687 (1991); that, indeed, is one of the main purposes of this resolution.

I mentioned earlier the sad failure of Iraq to carry out all its obligations. and this applies with particular force to the question of weapons of mass destruction. More and more chilling details are being unearthed. We now have confirmation that there was indeed a super-gun project. We now have confirmation that Iraq did indeed have a biological-warfare research programme with an offensive capability. We have confirmation that Iraq held much greater stocks of chemical weapons than it had previously admitted. And finally, we have confirmation that it had separated plutonium from enriched uranium and was developing an industrial-scale facility for enriching its own uranium by using both centrifugal and electromagnetic isotopic separation processes - the latter, incidentally, in breach of the safeguards of the Treaty on the Non-Proliferation of Nuclear Weapons, of which Iraq is a signatory.

Only yesterday a spokesman of the Secretary-General issued a press release with further details of Iraq's biological weapons research programme.

I fear that this is further evidence that the declarations we received earlier fall far short of what is to be desired, and the resolution we have just adopted is wholly appropriate.

In this context, and to conclude, we do also welcome the publication of the plans produced by the Special Commission and the IAEA concerning future compliance. We are studying them carefully and we are sure that all members will be giving them close attention in the weeks to come.

...

[86] **Mr. Hajnoczi (Austria):**

...

Austria voted in favour of, *inter alia*, resolution 706 (1991), which contains a package of measures aimed at dealing with a number of questions, first and foremost measures to deal with the humanitarian situation in Iraq.

We are pleased to note that it has thus been finally possible to transform into a resolution the results of the consultations held by the Chairman of the Security Council Committee established by resolution 661 (1990) as reported by him to the members of the Security Council during informal consultations held on 25 July.

The action initiated today is indeed urgently needed. The latest report on the situation of the Iraqi civilian population, namely the report dated 15 July 1991 of the inter-agency mission headed by the Executive Delegate of the Secretary-General for the United Nations Inter-Agency Humanitarian Programme, presented an alarming picture of the serious nutritional and health situation of the civilian population and the risk of further deterioration.

We hope that the Iraqi Government will - previous statements to the contrary notwithstanding - take full advantage of the opportunity which will be provided to it to earn the necessary revenue for the purchase of foodstuffs, medicines and material and supplies for essential civilian needs of its population. Anything less could lead to serious consequences which should be avoided in the best interest of the Iraqi population.

In this connection the equitable distribution of imports for humanitarian purposes in all regions of Iraq and to all segments of the Iraqi civilian population is of course of paramount importance. We understand the relevant provisions in resolution 706 (1991) as inviting the Secretary-General to submit a plan for an effective United Nations role in this respect to be carried out, by and large, by the United Nations personnel currently in Iraq. Reports to the Security Council on the working of this scheme for ensuring an equitable distribution would enable us to monitor its implementation. Another important element of the report requested of the Secretary-General are [*sic*] the estimates of the humanitarian requirements of Iraq which will be the basis for our final decision.

While resolution 706 (1991) has at its origin our most serious concern regarding the humanitarian situation in Iraq, resolution 707 (1991), but also parts of resolution 706 (1991), address another fundamental problem: Iraq's failure to comply with or fully carry out its obligations under resolution 687 (1991). By voting in favour of resolution 707 (1991) Austria demonstrates the crucial importance it attaches to full compliance. In this context, I want to stress our support for the activities of the Special Commission and the IAEA with regard to Section C of resolution 687 (1991). The results of their missions undertaken hitherto have shown how significant their activities are. We view resolution 707 (1991) not only as sending a message to Iraq but also as strengthening the hand of the Special Commission and the IAEA.

...

[88] **Mr. Lozinsky (Union of Soviet Socialist Republics)** (interpretation from Russian):

...

The Soviet delegation is gratified that the Security Council has adopted three important resolutions - two of them unanimously and the other by an overwhelming majority. Their purpose is to secure the implementation of Security Council resolution 687 (1991), which defined the arrangements for eliminating the consequences of Iraq's aggression against Kuwait and restoring peace and security in that region. The resolutions that have been adopted make it possible for Iraq, in accordance with the arrangements set forth in resolution 687 (1991), to export a certain amount of oil in order to obtain sufficient financial resources with which to acquire foodstuffs, medicines and materials and supplies for basic civilian needs. In addition, the resolutions have triggered the functioning of previous decisions on the financing of the activities of the Compensation Fund, the Special Commission and the Boundary Demarcation Commission and various other relevant United Nations expenses. The Security Council has also emphasized the importance of the need to repatriate all citizens of Kuwait and other countries being held by force in Iraq and also compensation for plundered property - a point which Ambassador Abulhasan of Kuwait rightly emphasized in his important statement at the beginning of our meeting.

The ceiling established by the Council for deduction to be paid into the Compensation Fund, in our view, creates the necessary conditions for compensation for losses sustained by victims of aggression and also for the solution of the pressing humanitarian problems facing the population of Iraq, as well as enabling Iraq to make payments on its external debt. At the same time, the Security Council has condemned Iraq's grave breaches of its obligations as a party to the Treaty on the non-proliferation of nuclear weapons and of various obligations under Section C of resolution 687 (1991).

In this connection, the Security Council was obliged to stipulate the adoption of various concrete and effective measures to bring to an end Iraq's breaches of its international obligations. Clearly, many of the provisions of the resolutions we have just adopted would have been quite unnecessary had it not been for Baghdad's persistent attempts to deceive the international community about its military programmes, and in particular with regard to its activities in the nuclear sphere, in addition to the delays Iraq has incurred in the fulfilment of other obligations. We firmly expect Iraq henceforth strictly to fulfil its obligations under all relevant Security Council resolutions.

In the final analysis, that would be in the interests of Iraq itself. Only in this way can it turn a tragic page in its history and take a worthy place in the international community. The complete implementation of Security Council decisions would also bolster the ability of the United Nations to act as a guarantor of peace and security, based on the rule of law, and would help prevent such crises, both in that region and other regions of the world.

...

[91] **Mr. Van Daele (Belgium)** (interpretation from French):

...

We have just adopted a resolution enabling States to resume, for a period of six months and up to a fixed amount, oil imports from Iraq. That resolution meets the humanitarian concerns voiced on various occasions by my delegation in the Council and in the Sanctions Committee. That is why we decided to become one of the sponsors of the resolution.

The resolution enables Iraq to obtain revenues that will make it possible for it to finance its imports of foodstuffs and essential goods.

Since April my delegation has advocated this option, while making it clear - and this is an important point - that the international community had to make quite sure that the revenues in question were really being used for foodstuffs and essential imports, and that the distribution would be carried out equitably for the benefit of all segments of the population in all regions.

We are gratified that the resolution we have just adopted sets up a workable system that meets that two-fold requirement.

In this respect, the Belgian delegation is grateful to the Secretary-General for kindly agreeing to organizing this supervision and monitoring and making it possible also for the Council to assess Iraq's humanitarian needs, thanks to the excellent report of his special representative, Prince Sadruddin Aga Khan.

Resolution 706 (1991) before us creates the necessary conditions to generate additional revenues, which will make it possible to sustain the compensation fund and finance the cost of the elimination of Iraqi weapons of mass destruction. In this way, the compensation fund will quickly be equipped with funds to provide priority compensation for the individual human cases that its Governing Council, which met recently in Geneva, has rightly identified as being worthy of special attention.

Similarly, it was, in our opinion, very justifiable for the Council to reach a decision at the same meeting today on the two other resolutions we have just adopted. The compensation fund could not become operational, particularly in order to deal with individual cases until the ceiling for amounts to be withheld from Iraq's oil revenues had been set.

Lastly, I wish to conclude with these remarks: we felt it was necessary for the procedures for inspection of Iraqi weapons of mass destruction to be defined most meticulously at the same time as we were setting the modalities for the financing of the destruction of these weapons, and at the same time we were able to draw all necessary lessons from the reports of the special commission on its mission.

Those are the remarks of my delegation which were prompted by the adoption of these three draft resolutions.

...

[93] **Mr. Gharekhan (India):**

...

I shall confine my remarks to resolution 706 (1991). The events in the Gulf over the last year set in motion the circumstances that the Security Council has been addressing. In recent months, an issue of undoubted importance has been the international community's response to the humanitarian problems in the region. Kuwait's independence and sovereignty have been restored, and we rejoice with the people of Kuwait, but its ordeal is not yet over. Meanwhile, the civilian population in Iraq undergoes suffering and trauma. The latter is our concern here at the moment.

The question, I believe, is not just the need to deal with the humanitarian requirements of those who suffer for no fault of their own. Both the requirements and the need to address them are evident. What is at stake is the manner in which those needs can be met. Several reports, ranging from the former Under-Secretary-General, Martti Ahtisaari's, to various missions by United Nations bodies and non-governmental organizations, down to the latest report by the Secretary-General's Executive Delegate for the United Nations Inter-Agency Humanitarian Programme, Prince Sadruddin Aga Khan, have testified to the wretched conditions of the Iraqi civilian population affected by war and sanctions.

My delegation's anxiety to formulate urgent and effective action to alleviate the misery of civilians in Iraq dates back several months. India's view has always been that the Security Council has the obligation to redress the plight of the innocent, just as the international community, as a whole, has partially been doing.

In cooperation with other non-aligned members of the Security Council, my delegation has proposed a draft resolution on this issue right at the beginning, but the Council was not able to adopt it. In the event, the President of the Council drew attention in a statement to the importance of humanitarian relief for Iraq's civilian population.

In the Sanctions Committee, as well as during informal consultations, India has consistently and repeatedly advocated a generous and effective approach to tackling the humanitarian situation in Iraq. To our regret, our efforts did not receive the unanimous support of Council members. This concern of ours that I have just explained has motivated, and continues to motivate, our position in the Security Council's consideration of the matter.

Needless to say, the United Nations is not unaware of the need to respond. The Sanctions Committee, in particular, has paid considerable attention to the problem. Indeed, the Sanctions Committee devised procedures to expedite certain forms of relief assistance to Iraq.

As a result of the efforts of non-aligned countries, including my own, the Council recognized the need to address this issue in all seriousness and with urgency. My delegation's initial reservations at what we felt were inadequate measures to deal with a problem of considerable magnitude were none the less somewhat allayed by the purposeful manner in which the Sanctions Committee, under the able Chairmanship of Ambassador Hohenfellner of Austria, operated the simplified procedures to clear humanitarian assistance to Iraq. Security Council resolution 687 (1991) subsequently, among other things, defined the humanitarian context in the circumstances then prevailing.

The humanitarian situation in Iraq continues to be grim. The most recent proof of this was Prince Sadruddin Aga Khan's report following his inter-agency mission to Iraq last month. After describing the desperate plight of the Iraqi civilian population, the report concluded that more massive infusion of relief supplies into Iraq was needed than what voluntary international assistance could provide. And for this purpose, he advocated permitting Iraq to utilize some of its oil revenues. We all agree with him on this point.

Resolution 706 (1991), just adopted, tries to meet these concerns to some extent. My delegation supports the idea of permitting oil sales from Iraq to finance, in a certain measure, its humanitarian needs. Paragraph 23 of Council resolution 687 (1991) deserves to be recalled here. That resolution chartered post-war arrangements for Iraq, and paragraph 23 lays down the provisions that should enable a response to the humanitarian circumstances that currently exist and are so acknowledged.

My delegation would have preferred a clear and unambiguous approach to this issue. The simplest and most effective way would have been to take action under paragraph 23. That, however, was not to be. In the alternative, my delegation would have liked the resolution to deal with the humanitarian aspect on its own. I realize there are other important issues. In particular, the issue of the repatriation of Kuwaiti and third country nationals or their remains must be resolved without delay. But in view of the urgency of providing relief in Iraq, and realizing that this resolution was perhaps the only way of achieving it, my delegation decided to go along with it. I trust that the adoption of the resolution will indeed result in the quick and effective supply of humanitarian assistance to vulnerable sections of Iraqi society.

My delegation's view of the role of the United Nations in the provision of humanitarian relief to Iraq is clear. All would agree with the objective, as my delegation does, that the resources raised by Iraqi oil sales should be deployed for the purposes specified and that foodstuffs and other supplies should be provided equitably in all parts of Iraq and to all segments of the Iraqi civilian population. My delegation firmly believes that this should be sought to be achieved through means which are both consistent with the Charter, particularly the all-important principle of non-interference in the internal affairs of countries, and in as practical and simplified a form as possible. Of cardinal importance in any such exercise is the consent of the country concerned. Lack of consent, or the absence of a specific request that incorporates such consent, will only thwart the effort. My delegation considers it especially important that the measures adopted must not adversely affect or undermine Iraq's sovereignty. Prince Sadruddin Aga Khan himself observed in his report, in the context of equitable distribution, that a functioning food rationing system was already in place in Iraq. The Iraqi Government's willingness to accept suitable mechanisms for the monitoring of oil revenues as well as their utilization has also been indicated by the Prince. Prince Sadruddin's report in fact made useful suggestions regarding the United Nations monitoring system that could be instituted for the purpose essentially by further developing and strengthening the present monitoring arrangements in the context of the United Nations humanitarian presence in Iraq. It is, therefore, evident that the humanitarian objectives we aim at can be achieved with simple and yet effective arrangements for observation and regular reporting, combined with provisions for review, periodically and as necessary. None of this calls for extensive United Nations machinery for administration or management. Such a United Nations presence, superimposed as it were on Iraq, would be intrusive, cumbersome and expensive. In addition, problems would arise in regard to United Nations expertise and provision of personnel for such a massive operation.

My delegation is of the view that the provisions in the resolution do not call for arrangements of a tutelary kind that might have the effect of interfering in Iraq's internal affairs. The Secretary-General, who is requested to present his considered recommendations in the matter in 20 days' time, will no doubt keep these points in mind.

It is in the light of these considerations, and mindful of our concerns as I have tried to explain them, that we voted in favour of the resolution.

...

[99] Mr. FLOREAN (Romania):

...

The Council has just adopted three resolutions concerning the situation between Iraq and Kuwait, dealing with important aspects of the matter. The first resolution establishes the ceiling of the value of Iraq's petroleum exports to the Compensation Fund established under resolution 687 (1991). The second resolution concerns the plan for the ongoing monitoring and verification of Iraq's compliance with a number of its obligations under the relevant parts of section C of resolution 687 (1991). The third resolution authorizes, under special conditions, the import during a period of six months of petroleum and petroleum products originating in Iraq.

We see these resolutions as an important element in assisting in the normalization of the situation in the Gulf. Kuwait, which suffered so much during the six months of its occupation, and other affected countries and individuals, will start being compensated. The situation of the Iraqi civilian population in all its segments will be improved. We understand that the provisions of resolution 706 (1991), just adopted, are extraordinary ones and the Council was obliged to react in this manner in the light of the Iraqi Government's practices and policies. We should like to stress that the manner in which these resolutions will be implemented will be a test for the Iraqi authorities and will create the grounds for a more positive approach of the Council vis-à-vis the future requests of Iraq to ease the sanctions. In this spirit, the Romanian delegation voted in favour of all three resolutions. That is why we make a solemn appeal to the Iraqi Government to fulfil its international obligations and to act in good faith to implement the provisions of the resolutions just adopted.

[101] **The PRESIDENT** (interpretation from Spanish):

...

I shall now make a statement in my capacity as representative of Ecuador. ...

Ecuador voted in favour of the three draft resolutions adopted by the Council. As regards resolution 705 (1991), we did so because it incorporates a recommendation made by the Secretary-General about the percentage of Iraqi oil sales that should be paid into the Compensation Fund. Ecuador endorses the reasons set forth by the Secretary-General in his report for arriving at that recommendation.

With regard to resolution 706 (1991), Ecuador has always upheld the principle whereby the humanitarian needs of the people of Iraq deserve the most favourable and timely consideration. We were among the sponsors of a draft resolution to that end, and we have consistently advocated in the Council and in the Committee provided for in resolution 661 (1991) that the Council should heed the humanitarian needs of the Iraqi people. The measures contained in resolution 706 (1991) will no doubt contribute to the purpose of relieving suffering and meeting the essential needs of the civilian population of Iraq.

Ecuador, however, has previously expressed its doubt about the wisdom of considering the humanitarian situation in Iraq under Chapter VII of the Charter and in connection with various other subjects that have a bearing on obligations assumed by Iraq, which need to be fully discharged, but which have nothing to do with the humanitarian situation. Moreover, Ecuador considers that supervision and monitoring by the United Nations should not lead the Organization to engage in actions at variance with permanent respect for the principles of the Charter, particularly paragraphs 1 and 2 of Article II.

As to resolution 707 (1991), Ecuador considers that, in the light of recent experience, its adoption was entirely justified.

I shall now revert to my role as President of the Council.

The Security Council has thus concluded the present stage of its consideration of the item on its agenda. The Council will remain seized of the matter.

...

T. S/PV.3008, 19 September 1991

...

[2] **The PRESIDENT** (interpretation from French):

The Security Council will now begin its consideration of the item on its agenda. The Security Council is meeting in accordance with the understanding reached in its prior consultations.

Members of the Council have before them document S/23006 and Corr.2, which contains the report of the Secretary-General pursuant to paragraph 5 of Security Council resolution 706 (1991). Members of the Council also have before them the text of a draft resolution, contained in document S/23045, submitted by Belgium, France, Romania, the Union of Soviet Socialist

Republics, the United Kingdom of Great Britain and Northern Ireland and the United States of America.

The first speaker on my list is the representative of Iraq, on whom I now call.

[3-5] **Mr. AL-ANBARI (Iraq)** (interpretation from Arabic):

...

The Council is today considering a draft resolution calling for the implementation of resolution 706 (1991) of 15 August 1991 in the light of the report of the Secretary-General, which he prepared according to the provisions of paragraph 5 of that resolution, and which he presented to the Council on 4 September 1991. Therefore, the shortcomings and contradictions concerning resolution 706 (1991) that I underlined in my statement before the Security Council on 15 August 1991 apply automatically to the draft resolution that is before members inasmuch as the draft resolution aims at the implementation of a resolution that does not have the required elements for implementation. Thus I need not repeat the comments I have already made on resolution 706 (1991). I would merely remind the Council that this draft resolution, as was the case for resolution 706 (1991), [*sic*] while expressing the need to implement the recommendations of the Executive Delegate of the Secretary-General on the deteriorating economic situation in Iraq, and while expressing concern about the sanitary and living conditions of the Iraqi people, perpetuates the economic siege against Iraq, as well as the measures of the Sanctions Committee, which in many cases has proved unable to take the necessary decisions to agree to the import by Iraq of essential civilian commodities in accordance with paragraph 20 of resolution 687 (1991). In fact, one would fear lest resolution 706 (1991), as well as the draft resolution that is now before the Council, might indeed make the deterioration of the health and living conditions of the Iraqi people a political chip used to bring pressure to bear against Iraq and to make Iraq appear to be a State that pays no heed to the sufferings of its people, as if the inhuman siege against Iraq was imposed and maintained by the Government of Iraq, and not by the Security Council and the Committee established under resolution 661 (1990). That resolution and the draft resolution that is now before the Council aim, in contradiction with paragraph 20 of resolution 687 (1991), to provide moneys for the Compensation Fund and for the expenditures of the organs and experts, whose numbers are increasing daily. They are being appointed to strengthen the economic embargo against Iraq and to implement the other resolutions of the Council.

A careful reading of resolution 706 (1991) and of this draft resolution shows that under them Iraq has two choices, one more bitter than the other. The first choice involves the maintenance of the state of full siege with all the concomitant suffering and starvation of the Iraqi people. The second involves a limited exception to the siege, for which Iraq would in return concede its sovereignty over its oil resources, and acceptance of the hegemony of some Security Council members, through United Nations bodies, over Iraq's oil resources and prevention of Iraq from developing and manufacturing those resources. What is worse is that the second choice in practice implies maintaining the economic boycott, without limit in contradiction with resolutions 661 (1990) and 687 (1991), and merely allowing the Iraqi people to obtain the minimum essential commodities necessary to avoid starvation. However, the satisfaction of such requirements cannot provide a decent standard of living or development in Iraq. Even if Iraq were to choose the second option, the mechanisms of the resolutions, the conditions and limits therein concerning the import of Iraqi oil and essential civilian commodities would render that resolution unrealistic. Therefore, I believe that some members of the Security Council fully realize the difficulty of any practical implementation of the draft resolution. However, they are trying to escape their political, humanitarian and legal responsibilities through maintaining the siege against the Iraqi people. They are trying to escape the pressure of international public opinion and international humanitarian organizations and to place the blame on Iraq itself. If this was the position of some Council members, it would reflect political hypocrisy on the part of some States which, on the one hand, claim to defend human rights and the right to life while, on the other, they play with the lives of the Iraqi people in this distorted manner for political purposes.

While I have expressed Iraq's position of principle, allow me to mention some of the technical problems in the draft resolution that is before the Council. The draft resolution approves only some of the paragraphs in the Secretary-General's report. In doing so, it does not provide flexibility. Rather, it creates a vacuum and confusion for any import of Iraqi oil or the import by Iraq of essential civilian commodities. Entrusting the Secretary-General with all necessary measures to implement a draft resolution after its adoption will not eliminate these problems.

As for the operative paragraphs, we should like to make the following comments. Operative paragraph 1 confirms the figure of $1.6 billion, while totally ignoring the recommendation of the Executive Delegate of the Secretary-General, which requires, as a minimum, increasing that sum by $800 million. This observation reaffirms that some Council members, even in emergency conditions, wish to maintain a suffocating grip on Iraq, indeed to control its fate.

As to operative paragraph 2, it does not take into account the fact that oil marketing contracts usually provide the buyer with a payment period of from two to four months from the date the oil is shipped. Therefore, there will be no funds available to satisfy any of the purposes of resolution 706 (1991) during that period, even if all the paragraphs of that resolution are implemented. Moreover, the resolution and the draft resolution do not allow Iraq to export oil in the free market, which in practice leads to lowering the prices of oil and to instability in the oil market.

Regarding operative paragraph 3, which approves the recommendations in paragraphs 57 (d) and 58 of the Secretary-General's report, it allows illegitimate intervention in bilateral agreements between Iraq and Turkey on passage of Iraqi oil through Turkish territory. Indeed, it flouts the agreements between the two countries, as well as sums agreed between them and means of payment. That paragraph also ignores the expenses in respect of producing and transporting oil inside Iraqi territories, as well as the need to repair production and shipment facilities in Iraq. Paragraph 3, by agreeing to paragraph 58 of the report, represents an illegally unjustifiable intervention in the conditions of special contracts for the sale of oil. Furthermore, it specifies, without any practical purpose, the Turkish harbour as the only way through which Iraqi oil is to be exported.

Furthermore, paragraph 6, which gives all those who work in accordance with the paragraphs of the draft resolution the privileges and diplomatic immunities of the United Nations regardless of their position and responsibility, as well as full freedom to move inside Iraqi territory, reflects the way in which the Security Council is flouting Iraqi laws and international conventions on diplomatic privileges and immunities.

In conclusion, the draft resolution calls for continuing consultations between the Committee established by resolution 661 (1990) and Iraq in order to facilitate the export of Iraqi oil. However, it deliberately ignores the need for such consultations on the import by Iraq of goods to meet essential civilian needs, and would therefore leave to every member of that Committee the right to disagree with or to veto the import by Iraq of any essential supplies with the exception of food and medicines. Such discrimination between the measures concerning the export of Iraqi oil and the import by Iraq of goods to meet civilian needs reaffirms once again what I have already said in my statement and shows the truth behind resolution 706 (1991) as well as the objectives of the draft resolution now before the Council.

[11] **The PRESIDENT** (interpretation from French):

...

I understand that the Security Council is ready to vote on the draft resolution before it. If I hear no objection, I shall put it to the vote.

There being no objection, it is so decided.

I shall first call on those members of the Council who wish to make statements before the voting.

[11] **Mr. AL-ASHTAL (Yemen)** (interpretation from Arabic):

...

The draft resolution before the Council is an extension of resolution 706 (1991), adopted by the Council last month. Thus, the position of Yemen will be an extension of the position we had at that time. I have asked to speak at this time in order to explain briefly our great interest in the welfare of the innocent Iraqi people. We hope that they will not be adversely affected as a result of some parts of this draft resolution, which might not facilitate the arrival of foodstuffs and medical supplies at the right time and in the proper quantities. We agree to a great extent with the proposals of the Executive Delegate of the Secretary-General and we wish to state that this draft resolution should not be politicized, since it relates to humanitarian questions which transcend the differences that exist in the region. That is why my delegation will abstain in the vote on this draft resolution.

...

[12] **Mr. ALARCON de QUESADA (Cuba)** (interpretation from Spanish):

...

The draft resolution which has been submitted to us is inextricably related to resolution 706 (1991), which was adopted on 15 August by the Council. As stated by our colleague from Yemen, this draft is indeed an extension of that document. For obvious reasons, my delegation will not be able to vote in favour of it. I do not feel I need to elaborate on the reasons for this. We explained them at the time of the adoption of resolution 706 (1991) and they remain valid in connection with the draft now under consideration. In our opinion, the Council's approach involves a manipulation of humanitarian issues. It will mean a prolongation and strengthening of the sanctions imposed on Iraq in circumstances which, in our view, have long been unjustified. We also are witnessing an effort to disregard the principle of the sovereign equality of States and, in fact, the Council is acting in a way which goes beyond the attributes conferred upon it by the Charter.

My delegation, therefore, will vote on this draft in the same way as we voted on resolution 706 (1991).

[13] **The PRESIDENT** (interpretation from French):

...

We shall now vote on the draft resolution in document S/23045.

A vote was taken by show of hands.

In favour:	Austria, Belgium, China, Côte d'Ivoire, Ecuador, France, India, Romania, Union of Soviet Socialist Republics, United Kingdom of Great Britain and Northern Ireland, United States of America, Zaire, Zimbabwe
Against:	Cuba
Abstaining:	Yemen

[14-15] **The PRESIDENT** (interpretation from French):

The result of the voting is as follows: 13 votes in favour, 1 against and 1 abstention. The draft resolution has been adopted as resolution 712 (1991).

I shall now call on those members of the Council who wish to make statements after the vote.

[14-15] **Mr. PICKERING (United States of America):**

...

The United States is pleased to have been a sponsor of the Security Council resolution that has just been adopted, implementing the Council's earlier resolution, resolution 706 (1991) on humanitarian assistance to Iraq. Security Council resolution 706 (1991) provides a mechanism whereby some $1.6 billion-worth of Iraqi petroleum and petroleum products can be sold over a six-month period, primarily to finance Iraqi imports of food, medical supplies and other essential civilian needs. It also sets in train the process which will provide funds for an initial contribution from Iraq to the Compensation Fund, so that relief can also begin flowing at last to those outside Iraq who have suffered as a result of Iraq's unlawful invasion and occupation of Kuwait.

Resolution 706 (1991) will further generate funding for the work of the Special Commission and the Boundary Demarcation Commission, and for the return of Kuwaiti property still being held in Iraq. The Security Council has repeatedly stated its concern about Iraq's non-compliance with resolution 687 (1991), particularly with respect to the work of the Special Commission. This resolution will provide essential funding to help us ensure compliance, and it is entirely appropriate that the Iraqi Government should pay.

It is also important to emphasize that this limited authorization of the sale of Iraqi oil is being made within the existing sanctions regime, which remains firmly in place. It does not in any way represent a weakening of sanctions.

This implementing resolution is a key step towards bringing the Gulf crisis to a close and towards having Iraq meet its responsibilities.

My Government wishes to take this opportunity to compliment the Secretary-General and the Secretariat for their thorough, lucid and first-rate report on implementing resolution 706 (1991). The Secretary-General's report has made the Council's job much easier. In an unusually short time-frame the Secretariat produced a report which responded fully to the Council's needs and desires, spelling out the practical problems of implementation and making recommendations on overcoming such problems.

This implementing resolution responds closely to the Secretary-General's report. In drafting it, Council members also made a conscious effort throughout to take Iraq's legal standing into account. The implementing resolution sets up mechanisms to implement resolution 706 (1991), supports the Secretary-General in his implementation role and provides for ongoing review and assessment of the needs and requirements in Iraq.

I want to mention that the statement we have just heard from the representative of Iraq was somewhat unusual in that it had begun to address, perhaps for the first time, some important aspects of the draft resolution. The overall question of the sum, I think, accords very closely with the Secretary-General's recommendation to members of the Council in paragraph 57 (b) of his report, which is incorporated in paragraph 1 of the resolution we have just adopted, which not only permits the acceptance of the recommended sum from resolution 706 (1991) but also incorporates the essential principles of a continuing review mechanism, something the Secretary-General suggested that he himself would employ as the resolution moves towards full implementation.

With respect to privileges and immunities, I would mention only that they are strictly limited to the purposes of carrying out the resolution. Finally, there seemed to be something of a misreading of paragraph 4 of today's resolution, which talks about consultation to ensure the most effective implementation of the scheme approved in the resolution, which in the view of my Government touches upon not only the export of oil but also the import of food, medicine and other humanitarian items.

A crucial feature of the programme as mandated by resolution 706 (1991) and as detailed in the report and recommendations of the Secretary-General is that the sale of Iraqi oil and the procurement and distribution of relief supplies will be conducted, as I just noted, under the close supervision of the United Nations to ensure that the supplies reach those for whom they were intended.

Today's resolution will implement the international community's concern for providing Iraqi civilians humanitarian assistance. The way is now open for Iraqi authorities to allow that process to begin.

...

[18] **Mr. Lozinsky (Union of Soviet Socialist Republics)** (interpretation from Russian):

...

The Soviet delegation voted in favour of the resolution the Council has just adopted, and was among its sponsors, because we believe that its adoption opens the way to the early implementation of the plan proposed by the Secretary-General for the implementation of Security Council resolution 706 (1991).

As the policies and actions of the Government of Iraq have not yet provided the Council with a basis for reducing or removing the sanctions adopted against that Government, the resolution just adopted, in accordance with paragraph 23 of resolution 687 (1991), provides Iraq with financial resources adequate for the purchase of foodstuffs and medicine and for meeting the basic needs of the civilian population, with a view to easing the situation of the civilian population of Iraq, primarily its most deprived sectors. We expect that, in accordance with today's resolution, the Security Council Committee on Sanctions will immediately decide to release the first third of the sum established for those needs. We note that provision has been made for a procedure for possibly increasing that sum in accordance with future assessments of Iraq's needs.

Although the scheme for the implementation of resolution 706 (1991) is not simple, we draw attention to paragraph 4 of today's resolution, which encourages the Secretary-General and the Sanctions Committee to cooperate, in close consultation with the Government of Iraq, to ensure the most effective implementation of the scheme provided for in the resolution.

The Soviet Union believes that, in the light of the current humanitarian situation, the resolution adopted today fully responds to the vital interests of the Iraqi people and expects the Government of Iraq to comply with it scrupulously.

...

[20] Sir David Hannay (United Kingdom):

...

... I also begin by paying a tribute to the work of the Secretary-General and those who worked with him on the report which forms the basis for the resolution we have just adopted. We set him an extremely tough task in giving him only 20 days to produce a report on an extremely complex matter. I think he and his officials did a remarkable job. In the view of my delegation, they achieved the necessary balance between a rigorous scheme which would carry out the sense of the Council, as contained in Security Council resolution 706 (1991), to ensure that these exports of oil go to finance humanitarian supplies and other objectives of the United Nations, but in a sensitive way taking account of a number of the concerns expressed by members of the Council and by the Government of Iraq.

I should like to say that I agree wholeheartedly with what the representative of Iraq said when he suggested that it was incorrect to mix politics and humanitarian issues. I just wish he had not then gone on to do precisely that for the whole of his statement. This Council has never had any quarrel with the people of Iraq, who have suffered greatly from the misguided policies of their leaders and continue to suffer, and this present scheme that we are considering and have approved today is designed to relieve that suffering and to do so in a humanitarian way.

It is a pity that the views expressed from the Iraqi side should be such a caricature of what is in this resolution. For example, when criticism is levied at the figure of $1.6 billion, no account is taken of the fact that there is an explicit reference to the need to review this figure. The hard fact is that nobody can be precise today, in the middle of September, about the exact scope and scale of needs between now and the end of March, and we shall have to have ongoing reviews of this based, no doubt, on evaluations for which the Secretary-General and his Executive Delegate may be able to help us; and in the light of that we may have to take further decisions. All that is provided for in this resolution, and it is a great pity if that is not recognized.

Moreover, the representative of Iraq suggested that there is no way of realizing money from this scheme immediately because of the delay normally given for credit on oil sales. That is of course not the case for sales of oil on the spot market, and the way is therefore open to realize money much more quickly if the will is there. It is a pity to look always at the negative side when we are talking of human suffering and malnutrition and lack of medicine. With spot payments for oil it should be possible, if the Government of Iraq, in whose total control this is because it is its agency that will be conducting the sales, wishes it. My hope is that they will be so willing and that we will see money flowing into this account and being made available for all the purposes set out in the resolution.

Then it was also suggested that the cooperation between the Government of Iraq and the Committee would be limited to the sales of oil. As the representative of the United States has said, that is not the case. The reference is an encouragement to the Committee to cooperate on the effective implementation of the scheme approved in this resolution. This scheme relates to all aspects; in particular it relates to the purchasing by Iraq of humanitarian relief supplies for all segments of its population. So this cooperation is not simply limited. I hope this cooperation will be forthcoming; it will be very welcome to my delegation if it is. Meanwhile, I can merely say that I am glad to have been able to be a sponsor of this resolution, because I am convinced that it contains the potential to provide genuine relief to those in Iraq who need it. But whether or not it does so lies as much in the hands of the Government of Iraq as in anyone else's.

[22] **The President** (interpretation from French):

...

I shall now make a statement as representative of France.

The resolution which we have just adopted will make it possible to implement resolution 706 (1991), for which France had taken the initiative, in order to respond to the humanitarian needs of the entire Iraqi population. The Security Council, in resolution 706 (1991), established the general framework in which it will be possible for Iraq to sell petroleum and purchase goods to meet essential needs. But it conferred upon the Secretary-General the difficult task of submitting to it, in the brief period of twenty days, recommendations on the modalities and financing of these transactions and the equitable distribution of essential goods.

I thank the Secretary-General for his report and for his recommendations, which fully cover the many and often highly technical aspects of the implementation of resolution 706 (1991).

Since the issuance of Prince Sadruddin Aga Khan's report describing the nutritional and health situation in Iraq, France has expressed its support for urgent action on the part of the Security Council to avoid a deterioration of the living conditions in that country. The adoption of resolution 712 (1991) completes the establishment of the mechanisms that will make it possible to meet the essential needs of the Iraqi population. France hopes that these mechanisms will begin to operate as rapidly as possible in order to achieve, as soon as possible, the humanitarian objectives that we have consistently pursued in the Security Council and in the Committee on Sanctions.

I now resume my functions as President of the Security Council.

There being no further speakers on my list, the Council has thus concluded the present stage of its consideration of the item on its agenda.

...

U. S/PV.3012, 11 October 1991

...

[2] **The President:**

The Security Council will now begin its consideration of the item on its agenda.

Members of the Council have before them the report of the Secretary-General contained in document S/22871/Rev.1 and the note by the Secretary-General contained in documents S/22872/Rev.1 and Corr.1.

Members of the Council also have before them document S/23134, which contains the text of a draft resolution submitted by Belgium, France, Romania, the Union of Soviet Socialist Republics, the United Kingdom of Great Britain and Northern Ireland and the United States of America.

I call on the representative of Iraq.

[3] **Mr. Al-Anbari (Iraq)** (interpretation from Arabic):

...

The draft resolution seems at first sight to be a detailed procedural draft regarding the implementation of paragraph 10 of resolution 687 (1991) of 3 April 1991 in addition to paragraph 13 of that resolution. However, this is not the case. The draft resolution goes far beyond the horizons and objectives of that resolution and, contrary to the provisions of the Charter, aims to put Iraq under the permanent trusteeship of the Special Commission on armaments and to maintain the trade sanctions system indefinitely, contrary to the provisions of that resolution.

The draft resolution also seeks to establish permanent international mechanisms to tighten control on Iraq's future and prevent Iraq from carrying out economic and scientific development, at great cost to Iraq.

The draft resolution introduces very serious principles. However, the greatest danger is in the plan prepared by the Special Commission on armaments, contained in document S/22871/Rev.1 of 2 October 1991. The plan omits no detail affecting civil or military life. All those aspects, together with all Iraqi scientific institutions and educational institutes are placed under tight control and severe restrictions, in an absolutist and arbitrary fashion.

The plan has been drawn up in great detail with a great deal of complexity. Those details are scattered all over the text, but are intertwined with the threads of all the plan's provisions and those of the so-called four annexes that form an integral part of the plan. Therefore, it is no wonder that many of those concerned with the plan did not fully examine its details and accepted it in good faith as a technical plan to implement paragraph 10 of resolution 687 (1991), adopted six months ago, which has become a *fait accompli*. They think, therefore, that the plan does not warrant further examination and could not be more serious than resolution 687 (1991) itself.

I should like to cite first paragraph 13 of the plan, which reads:

> "In accepting unconditionally Security Council resolution 687 (1991) Iraq has undertaken"

to accept all the items mentioned in that paragraph. It is my duty, in deference to the behests of truth and history, to express the deep regret and disappointment of both the Government and people of Iraq that Iraq accepted resolution 687 (1991) without a guarantee in advance that the Council would lift the economic blockade against Iraq and refrain from adopting one resolution after another against Iraq and its people. Resolution 687 (1991) has become like a mythical tree which goes on sprouting branches that have no relationship with the resolution itself, and indeed are contrary to its provisions.

Iraq accepted resolution 687 (1991) and previous resolutions and implemented their provisions in good faith. Iraq did this, unfortunately, in the erroneous belief that the Council, in return, would look at the economic sanctions and other arbitrary measures adopted by the Council against the people and Government of Iraq. It is regrettable that Iraq has played its part but the Council has failed not only to fulfil its mandate but has tightened its sanctions against Iraq. In simple language, the Security Council has not adhered to its own resolutions as it has transformed the cease-fire resolution 687 (1991) into a document that makes the Iraqi Government and people hostage of one or two States with veto power in the Council.

I must also warn that if this plan is implemented against Iraq, many of the countries of the developing or the developed worlds which support its implementation either knowingly or out of ignorance, may well find that they will be next in line as potential victims of this plan which embodies, in practical terms, a new type of occupation that, through a system of remote control, dominates every aspect of life in the target country.

Paragraph 10 of resolution 687 (1991)

> "Decides that Iraq shall unconditionally undertake not to use, develop, construct or acquire any of the items specified in paragraphs 8 and 9 above and requests the Secretary-General, in consultation with the Special Commission, to develop a plan for the future ongoing monitoring and verification of Iraq's compliance with this paragraph, to be submitted to the Security Council for approval within one hundred and twenty days of the passage of this resolution".

The implementation of the first part of the aforementioned paragraph concerns Iraq. It was implemented, as Iraq, in a communication dated 18 April 1991 addressed to the Secretary-General from the Minister for Foreign Affairs, has undertaken, unconditionally, not to use, develop, construct, build or acquire any material specified in paragraphs 7 to 12 of resolution 687 (1991). The latter part of paragraph 10 calls for the formulation of a plan to monitor compliance by Iraq of its obligations under that paragraph and for ongoing verification in future.

The plan contained in the draft resolution, and its implementation, far exceeds that purview and gives the Special Commission and all those authorized by it, unrestricted, permanent and absolute police, political and executive powers. The plan is made up of 45 paragraphs and four annexes that form an integral part of the Plan. Strangely enough, while paragraph 26 stipulates that the Plan may be revised only by the Security Council, it gives the Special Commission the power of revising the annexes of the Plan and informing the Council, without prior Council approval. As the four annexes of the Plan contain detailed provisions that further elaborate the Plan, the Council, by approving the Plan, including paragraph 26, would be giving the Special Commission the authority to amend the Plan itself, which goes beyond the resolution itself.

My question is, does the Council have such authority under the Charter? The first deviation from resolution 687 (1991), especially operative paragraph 10, is what is stated in paragraph 3 of the Plan, which interpreted the future ongoing verification of weapons of mass destruction as inclusive not only of military installations, but also of civil installations and other materials that could be used or the activities that could be undertaken contrary to the obligations of Iraq under resolution 687 (1991).

Members may notice that that paragraph in expanding the scope of verification and monitoring to include civilian installations in addition to military installations also refers to everything that might be used contrary to the obligations of Iraq. The expansion of that Plan in such a fashion to include the military and the civilian both actual and potential leaves the door wide open in order to abuse the powers granted to the Special Commission and to all those delegated by the Special Commission.

The Plan calls for establishing an executive body under the authority of the Security Council, as provided for in paragraph 5, and in paragraph 7, establishes a compliance unit under the Special Commission to ensure that Iraq will not import any prohibited material. This is in addition to the roles of the IAEA and the Special Commission itself and the Sanctions Committee established under resolution 661 (1991). This in fact creates a new international organ with numerous offshoots in a manner unprecedented in history. The Plan, in seeking to tighten further the controls against Iraq, is not satisfied with one procedural control mechanism. For instance, paragraph 10 (b) provides that countries that supply Iraq with multipurpose materials - both military and civilian - will provide transparent information under a mechanism to be set up for this purpose. Yet, paragraph 9 of the Plan states that the monitoring and verification are required from within Iraq by the Special Commission and its personnel, who might stay in Iraq for a long time or even permanently. Therefore, in all humility, may I suggest that we confer upon the Head of the Special Commission the title of the political ruler or the High Commissioner as in the old days of colonial rule.

I have pointed out previously that giving any special commission or any body absolute powers in interpreting and implementing the provisions of the Plan, and even amending the Plan, would create the risk of abuse of power, whether intentionally or inadvertently. What might strengthen that possibility is the fact that the Plan puts more obligations on Iraq, and gives undefined and open-ended powers to the monitoring mechanism. For instance, under paragraph 16 (a), the Plan imposes on Iraq the obligation to provide the Commission on a regular basis, with full, complete, correct and timely information on activities, sites, facilities, material and other items that might be used for prohibited purposes. What are those other items, and how could we determine the purpose of using one material today or in future for a prohibited purpose? That same paragraph stipulates elsewhere, that Iraq should provide the Special Commission with similar information that I have just mentioned concerning any additional activities, sites, facilities, materials or other items that the Commission may designate. Paragraph 16 also stipulates that Iraq should fully, completely and promptly respond to any question or request that is made by the Special Commission. Is there any international organization or body that has such absolute power? Is it practicable for any country or any party to answer any question or request irrespective of whether or not it is arbitrary or irrelevant or unanswerable? The Plan makes all these obligations, some of which I have referred to, incumbent upon Iraq and gives the Special Commission and all those delegated by the Commission the right to enter Iraq and leave it without Iraq's approval, to use any sites and airports and to send any persons, irrespective of their nationality or identity or intentions, to enter Iraq and to engage in any activities with full diplomatic immunity and absolute freedom to move inside Iraq and to secure their safety and security, as provided for under paragraph 18 of the Plan.

Moreover, in paragraph 20, Iraq shall enact legislation and adopt all necessary measures to implement its obligations under resolution 687 (1991) and resolution 707 (1991) and other related resolutions before the passage of 30 days from the date of adoption of the Plan by the Security Council. This paragraph of the Plan, while it ignores all the legislative and executive measures adopted by Iraq to implement the Security Council's resolutions, comes up with general provisions that Iraq would be required to enforce within 30 days. It seems that the figure 30 has a very special significance in the Plan, given the fact that all the information and special statistics Iraq should provide the Commission with on chemical and biological materials as well as missiles should be submitted within 30 days.

The fact that the Plan far exceeds the Security Council resolutions and the provisions of the Charter becomes more evident in the four annexes to the Plan. For instance, annex I provides that the Special Commission has the right to secure any site and to inspect Iraq's exports and imports and any materials upon their arrival in Iraq or when they leave Iraq. Is the inspection of any material exported or imported by Iraq necessary to ensure compliance by Iraq of its obligations regarding weapons of mass destruction?

Moreover, the Special Commission gives itself, under the Plan, police powers. Under paragraph 9 of that annex, the Special Commission would make its own arrangements to ensure the safety and security of its personnel and property and to seize any material or other item.

Please note the general terms "any material or other item". We have the right to ask how the Special Commission could make such arrangements? Would the Special Commission come to Iraq on tanks? Does it have military forces to protect it or enable it to secure any site?

The same annex, in paragraph 10, imposes on Iraq the obligation to ensure the safety and security of the personnel and property of the Special Commission, and so on. The proposed Plan is unique in its deliberate complexity and scattering of intertwined provisions in a manner that would make it extremely difficult to implement, while it makes it easy to claim that its provisions are being contravened.

For example, paragraph 6 of annex II calls for the provision of information on sites or facilities, including the name of the site or facility and of the owner, company or enterprise operating the site or facility; the location of the site or facility; a general description of all types of activities at the site or facility; and the sources and amounts of the financing of the site or facility, and of its activities. Paragraph 8 calls for the provision of information in addition to that specified in paragraph 6. Paragraph 9 also calls for more information in addition to that specified in paragraph 6.

The four annexes of the Plan, in addition to the contents of the Plan itself, aim explicitly at denying Iraq the capacity to conduct scientific, biological and chemical research. Indeed, the Plan is so excessive that, in paragraph 38 (c), it prohibits Iraq's conducting activities on diseases other than those indigenous to or immediately expected to break out in Iraq. In paragraph 38 (d), Iraq is prohibited from conducting any breeding of vectors of human, animal or plant diseases. Should Iraq need to conduct any such activity, it has to submit a request to the Special Commission specifying all the information the Commission requires. The Commission will then accept or reject the request.

In other words, if Iraq is to abide by its commitment not to produce biological weapons, then it must desist from conducting medical research on diseases that are not expected to break out immediately in its environment. Iraq is also prevented from conducting research on the immunization and inoculation of children and others against infectious diseases. Is not the result of these restrictions the vulnerability of Iraq's people to disease and gradual extermination?

I may have spoken at length of the Plan, its annexes and details. But I do hope that I have been able to show that the Plan gives the Commission and its personnel absolute powers and imposes on Iraq obligations that gives the Special Commission absolute authority over the State and people of Iraq. It also imposes conditions that would make Iraq powerless to fulfil all the obligations imposed on it by the Plan. Furthermore, the Plan is arbitrary in its interpretation of the tasks outlined in resolution 687 (1991). While the provisions of that resolution focus on the weapons of mass destruction and ballistic missiles with a range greater than 150 kilometres, the Plan goes further and includes dual and multipurpose materials, scientific activities and medical activities. The Plan also introduces a mechanism that would monitor all Iraq's imports and subject all Iraq's requirements of multipurpose materials to the prior consent by the Commission established under resolution 661 (1990). Every member of that Commission has the right of veto regardless of the legitimacy of the requirements. Thus, this Plan would make the economic sanctions against Iraq - which are provisional pending the implementation of paragraph 22 of resolution 687 (1991) - permanent measures and would make the Sanctions Committee a permanent organ of the Security Council.

The main thrust of the Plan is not to destroy Iraq's weapons of mass destruction but to deprive Iraq of its industrial and scientific infrastructure and to project an image of Iraq as a State that does not cooperate with the United Nations or tries to exceed its international obligations in order to tighten further the economic, scientific and political siege imposed on Iraq's Government and its people.

If the Plan's aims are illegal and prohibited under the Geneva Conventions and the instruments of Human Rights and the United Nations Charter, then they and the draft resolution under consideration lack international legality and are not consonant with international law or the United Nations Charter.

...

[13] Mr. Pickering (United States of America):

I hope to be brief, but I feel I must comment on what we have just heard from the representative of Iraq. In contrast to what he has just said, I would like to extend the compliments of my delegation and my Government to the Special Commission and to the Director-General of the International Atomic Energy Agency (IAEA), who prepared excellent monitoring plans for dealing with a very serious and difficult situation.

We have seen Iraq's performance over the past months. It has continued to hide parts of its nuclear-weapons programme, its chemical-warfare programme, its biological programme and its missile programme. It has continued to try to block the cooperation that it is committed to give to the Special Commission and to IAEA. We have only to take note of the parking-lot incident and the difficulties which were put in the way of the Special Commission in actually operating the helicopters mandated by the Council.

There is, as we all know now, indisputable evidence that Iraq was seeking to build nuclear weapons and that it misused and abused its peaceful-nuclear facilities. Twice, the Governing Board of IAEA has found that Iraq was in violation of its safeguards agreements under the non-proliferation Treaty. One more such finding, we believe, is now pending on the basis of recent evidence. Several times, including as recently as in resolution 707 (1991), the Council has found Iraq in violation of its obligations under Security Council resolutions. This should all speak clearly for itself as to why this monitoring and verification Plan is required and why it has been so carefully prepared.

The bad news, unfortunately, is that, as we all know, in each of the resolutions relevant to the Iraq and Kuwait situations - between resolutions 661 (1990) and 712 (1991) - we have heard pretty much the same speech from the representative of Iraq. Perhaps the good news is that, at each turn, reluctantly, grudgingly and half-heartedly, Iraq has nevertheless complied with the general tenor of those resolutions as they have been applied by the Council. We hope and expect that Iraq will of course abide by the resolution which we hope the Council will move rapidly now to adopt.

[15] Sir David Hannay (United Kingdom of Great Britain and Northern Ireland):

I, too, feel that, after the statement made by the representative of Iraq, some points need to be made. I was struck, I must say, by the representative of Iraq's analogy, in which he describes resolution 687 (1991) as a tree. Having worked in gardens quite a long time myself, I have noticed that the branches of trees usually belong to the trees. This draft resolution belongs to this tree, which is resolution 687 (1991). It derives directly from it.

The draft resolution is stringent because of the long chapter of evasions, concealment and trickery that Iraq has employed to avoid revealing what it was required to reveal under resolution 687 (1991) and because of a long history of evasion that has demonstrated beyond any doubt Iraq's determination to preserve and continue the programmes for producing weapons of mass destruction which this Council has interdicted.

The representative of Iraq expressed surprise that there are parts of this continuing compliance programme that relate to dual-use items, civilian items. But he should hardly be surprised. After all, Iraq's nuclear-weapons programme was called by the Government of Iraq "Petrochemicals Project Number 3", and Iraq imported parts for a super-gun - which has now, fortunately, been destroyed - that were described as "pipes for petrochemical plant". So if there is a problem over dual use, there is nobody to blame but themselves.

The representative of Iraq expressed surprise that there should be references to the need to provide for the safety of the Special Commission. That is 10 days after armed Iraqi police detained the Special Commission inspectors for four days, against all of Iraq's international obligations and its agreement with the United Nations. It is surely hardly surprising that we have to guard against that.

Now, the representative of Iraq suggested that this draft resolution is designed to prevent Iraq from conducting research in the fields of health. Frankly, that is not true. Paragraph 38 (d) of the report makes it quite clear that projects for breeding vectors of human, animal or plant diseases will be permitted.

Therefore, I think it is a pity that this caricature should have been given to the Council when it is entirely contrary to the truth.

To conclude, the object of the draft resolution, I would say, is quite simply this: it is to prevent Iraq from breaking in the future the international obligations on weapons of mass destruction it so liberally broke in the past. One way or another, that objective will be achieved.

[17] The PRESIDENT:

It is my understanding that the Council is ready to proceed to the vote on the draft resolution (S/23134) before it. Unless I hear any objection, I shall put the draft resolution to the vote now. There being no objection, it is so decided.

A vote was taken by show of hands.

In favour: Austria, Belgium, China, Côte d'Ivoire, Cuba, Ecuador, France, India, Romania, Union of Soviet Socialist Republics, United Kingdom of Great Britain and Northern Ireland, United States of America, Yemen, Zaire, Zimbabwe

[17] The PRESIDENT:

There were 15 votes in favour. The draft resolution has therefore been adopted unanimously as resolution 715 (1991).

I shall now call upon those members of the Council who wish to make statements following the voting.

[17] Mr. MERIMEE (France): (interpretation from French):

In the view of my delegation the resolution we have just adopted is of great importance. We have approved the plan for future ongoing monitoring and verification, which is the only way to ensure that Iraq will no longer be able to pursue its plans, especially those to acquire nuclear armaments. The missions of the Special Commission and the International Atomic Energy Agency have furnished ample proof of those plans, and the international community is in duty bound to put an end to them.

This matter concerns the heart of the Security Council's responsibilities. My delegation welcomes the unanimity that has prevailed among Council members in this regard. We hope that, faced with this determination on the part of the international community, Iraq will understand that it is in its interests to comply without reservations with the obligations incumbent upon it under the plan and the resolution and cooperate with the Council and with the various bodies under its authority and responsibility.

[18] The PRESIDENT:

There are no further speakers inscribed on my list. The Security Council has thus concluded the present stage of its consideration of the item on its agenda. The Security Council will remain seized of the matter.

...

PART II

THE PRELUDE TO THE HOSTILITIES

Allegations concerning the practices of the Iraqi authorities in occupied Kuwait had been put forward in the Security Council and other UN organs since early August, 1990. (See *Chapters 3.4 and 6 of Volume I in this Series.) These allegations were formally considered in the General Assembly and the UN Commission on Human Rights shortly before and immediately after the initiation of hostilities by the coalition forces. The attempts to achieve a peaceful withdrawal of Iraqi forces from Kuwait before 15 January 1991, the deadline set in Security Council Resolution 678 (1990), were made against this background of alleged Iraqi atrocities. Materials on human rights in Iraq itself have been reprinted in Part V of this volume.*

3. HUMAN RIGHTS IN OCCUPIED KUWAIT

On 18 December 1990 the UN General Assembly adopted the following resolution, entitled "The Situation of Human Rights in Occupied Kuwait" *by 144 votes to 1 (Iraq). Afghanistan, Algeria, Cambodia, Jordan, Libya, Mauritania, Sudan, Tunisia, Viet Nam and Yemen did not participate in the voting.*

1. General Assembly Resolution 45/170

The General Assembly,

Guided by the principles embodied in the Charter of the United Nations, the Universal Declaration of Human Rights, the International Covenants on Human Rights and the Geneva Conventions of 12 August 1949,

Aware of its responsibility to promote and encourage respect for human rights and fundamental freedoms for all and resolved to remain vigilant with regard to violations of human rights wherever they occur,

Reaffirming that all Member States have an obligation to promote and protect human rights and fundamental freedoms and to fulfil obligations they have freely undertaken under the various international instruments,

Condemning the invasion of Kuwait on 2 August 1990 by the military forces of Iraq,

Noting with grave concern that the Iraqi forces in occupied Kuwait continue to commit acts of violence, leaving large numbers of victims and causing enormous human suffering to the civilian population,

Noting also with grave concern that the treatment of prisoners of war and detained civilians in occupied Kuwait does not conform to the internationally recognized principles of humanitarian law,

Expressing grave concern at the continued refusal of Iraq to receive representatives of humanitarian organizations, especially representatives of the International Committee of the Red Cross and a representative of the Secretary-General, to help in extending humanitarian assistance to the Kuwaiti people under occupation,

1. *Condemns* the Iraqi authorities and occupied forces for their serious violations of human rights against the Kuwaiti people and third-State nationals and in particular the continued and increasing acts of torture, arrests, summary executions, disappearances and abduction in violation of the Charter of the United Nations, the International Covenants on Human Rights, other relevant human rights instruments and the relevant instruments of humanitarian law;

2. *Affirms* that the Geneva Convention relative to the Protection of Civilian Persons in Time of War, of 12 August 1949, applies to Kuwait and that as a high contracting party to the Convention Iraq is bound to comply fully with all its terms and, in particular, is liable under the Convention in respect of the grave breaches committed by it, as are individuals who commit or order the commission of such breaches;

3. *Expresses its serious concern* about the systematic dismantling and pillaging of and attacks on the economic infrastructure of Kuwait, which seriously undermine the present and future enjoyment by the Kuwaiti people of their economic, social and cultural rights;

4. *Expresses its grave concern* at the living conditions in occupied Kuwait, especially those of women, children, elderly and third-State nationals, which are becoming increasingly difficult;

5. *Expects* Iraq to guarantee respect for international standards applicable under international law, in particular with reference to the protection of the civilian population and demands that Iraq co-operate fully with and give access to Kuwait to representatives of humanitarian organizations, especially the International Committee of the Red Cross, working to alleviate the suffering of the civilian population in occupied Kuwait;

6. *Expects* Iraq to comply with its obligations under the Charter and international law in respect of third-State nationals, and demands that Iraq release all nationals of third States;

7. *Urges* Iraq to treat all prisoners of war and detained civilians in accordance with the internationally recognized principles of humanitarian law and to protect them from all acts of violence, including ill-treatment, torture and summary execution;

8. *Condemns* the rejection by Iraq of the offer of the Government of Kuwait to send humanitarian assistance, especially medicine, to the Kuwaiti people under occupation;

9. *Requests* the Commission on Human Rights at its forty-seventh session to consider the situation of human rights in occupied Kuwait;

10. *Decides* to keep under consideration the situation of human rights in occupied Kuwait.

E/CN.4/1991/70, 7 February 1991

2. Letter from the Permanent Mission of Kuwait to the United Nations Office at Geneva addressed to the Under-Secretary-General for Human Rights

Please find enclosed the report of the situation of human rights in occupied Kuwait which we are submitting for consideration as an official document of the forty-seventh session of the Commission on Human Rights.

...

With the barbaric Iraqi invasion of Kuwait in the early hours of 2 August 1990, the stage was set for a many-faceted human tragedy. Both nationals and residents of Kuwait fell victim to criminal and inhumane acts committed by the Iraqi forces. From the very beginning of the invasion, the Iraqis committed the most heinous crimes, including murder, rape, arrests, threats and the destruction and looting of public and private property. It was clear that these barbaric and repressive practices were planned in advance by the Iraqi authorities as a means of achieving the primary objective of the invasion: to humiliate, demean and terrorize the Kuwaiti people and to obliterate the Kuwaiti national identity as a first step towards the achievement of their political plan of occupying Kuwait and annexing it to Iraq.

The barbaric practices of the Iraqi forces in Kuwait constitute a flagrant violation of the Geneva Conventions of 1949, which embody international human rights principles and are binding on all States Parties, including Iraq. The Arab Organization of Human Rights says in a report dated 16 October 1990 on the "Situation of Human Rights in Kuwait since the Iraqi Invasion" that "there has been a violation of almost every single paragraph of the body of international legislative instruments constituting international law and international human rights principles that have evolved as binding law for all parties, including Iraq".

Under an information black-out and with the refusal of Iraqi forces to allow humanitarian organizations to investigate violations of human rights in Kuwait, the Iraqi authorities committed daily the most outrageous mass and individual crimes against not only Kuwaitis, but also most Arab and non-Arab residents. Fearing these criminal acts, people stayed at home in terror and in fear, not knowing when Iraqi soldiers would break in to loot property, arrest a family member or sexually assault a woman.

People did not leave their homes because they wanted to spare themselves degrading and rough treatment at the hands of Iraqi soldiers at checkpoints. The soldiers normally harassed people and often stole their money, watches, pens, identification documents and even cars. People became more afraid to leave their homes when Iraqi soldiers used the checkpoints as stations for making arrests. While a driver sat behind the wheel, an Iraqi soldier would place a bullet or a leaflet in the trunk of the car, thus producing false evidence to warrant the arrest of the driver. Many people were thus arrested at these points. Movement, even for essential purposes, became difficult because of these checkpoints and the degrading treatment by Iraqi soldiers. To tighten their grip on Kuwait and their control over the population, moreover, the occupation forces imposed night-long curfews.

Iraqi soldiers resorted more frequently to mass punishment to induce fear in the population. They often arrested and tortured all members of the family in order to find one person, thus violating article 33 of the Geneva Convention Relative to the Protection of Civilian Persons in Time of War (1949). Iraqi soldiers would burn down several houses if the body of one Iraqi soldier was discovered or a shot was heard in the area. In this respect, attention is drawn to the Amnesty International report of 19 December 1990, which states that, on 7 September, after resistance in Kaifan, "Iraqi soldiers surrounded the area with their tanks and bombarded it with artillery fire, destroying a number of houses. In mid-September, Iraqi forces, upon discovering the bodies of four soldiers, surrounded the area, searched homes and burnt down 25 houses."

Iraqi soldiers also committed collective organized sabotage, looting and theft of Government offices, hospitals, schools, Kuwait University, research institutes and laboratories, companies, shops, private homes, stores, garages, etc.

Iraq stole 15 Kuwait Airways aircraft, as well as equipment and spare parts that were found in abundance in maintenance workshops and warehouses. They also stole equipment and medical supplies from hospitals and the Ministry of Health. They concentrated especially on dismantling and removing modern medical equipment from specialized medical centres, such as Hussein Makki Jomaa Hospital for the Treatment of Cancer and Hamed Al-Issa Centre for Kidney Treatment, Ibn Sina Hospital for Eye and Nerve Surgery [*sic*], Al-Razi Hospital for Bone Surgery and the Obstetrics Hospital, where they stole incubators, leaving 300 underdeveloped babies to die without any religious, human or ethical scruple ... .

From schools, Iraqis took away chairs, desks, blackboards and other educational equipment in addition to books. Kuwait University was not spared the looting, for Iraqis dismantled and removed research equipment and teaching aids from laboratories, as well as thousands of the latest computers and books, periodicals, documents and manuscripts from libraries, and destroyed remaining files and official [*sic*] papers. The Iraqis used schools and university buildings as centres of detention and torture and as barracks for soldiers and they set up anti-aircraft artillery on the roofs. Kuwait's Institute of Scientific Research, considered the most modern and most important scientific research centre in the Middle East, particularly in the areas of petroleum, agriculture, fisheries, energy and environmental research, was also ransacked. Iraqis stole scientific equipment and computers and took away books, periodicals and scientific reports from the Institute's specialized library.

Iraqis also stole Kuwait's reserves of gold ingots and cash from the Central Bank and the contents of the Treasury. They took away the assets of national banks and their looting spread to garages and car stores. According to car suppliers' estimates there were at least 10,000 new cars in the warehouses and stores at the time of the invasion and they were all stolen. The Iraqis also stole thousands of tons of foodstuffs from private dealers and food companies and the stores of co-operatives, thus producing a severe shortage of foodstuffs in Kuwait.

The Iraqis concentrated their efforts on confiscating the property and funds of senior Government officials and Kuwaiti families, destroying or burning houses and other property following looting. The Iraqis also removed the contents of the Kuwait National Museum which houses Kuwait's historical relics, some dating from 6600 B.C., as well as precious traditional Kuwaiti and rare Islamic pieces which were transported in a primitive way, that damaged many of them and made them worthless. These acts are contrary to article 53 of Additional Protocol I to the Geneva Conventions of 1949. There is no doubt that this criminal act harms not only Kuwait, but Islamic and world civilization as a whole, since these rare pieces form part of mankind's history and civilization.

The Iraqi authorities deprived Kuwaiti citizens of personal freedoms which they enjoyed before the invasion, such as freedom of movement, freedom of expression, freedom to work and freedom of education. The occupation forces set up checkpoints everywhere and controlled schools and the media, including radio, television and newspapers. They stole printing equipment from publishing houses and newspapers and published a daily newspaper containing military communiqués and decisions of the Iraqi leadership. A decision published by the Iraqi authorities threatened that Kuwaiti officials of higher grades who did not resume work as of 22 September 1990 would be liable to the death penalty.

As a result of these repressive and barbaric practices, hundreds of thousands of citizens and foreigners fled the country to save their lives and honour, leaving behind their property and relatives. One of the main reasons for the departure of Kuwaiti families from their country was the daily harassment by Iraqi forces and intelligence officers in search of military personalities and officials of the Ministry of the Interior, national guard and special forces officers, as well as members of the National Assembly and the National Council, other leading personalities and businessmen, any other persons who might be suspected of collaborating with the resistance and any personality that might play a leadership role in the country. Kuwaiti families were thus dispersed in various capitals of the world. In addition to nearly 300,000 citizens who left Kuwait after the invasion, there were over 100,000 Kuwaitis abroad for the summer holidays. Whether they are in Kuwait or outside the country, Kuwaitis have been living in despair since the invasion and in a disturbed psychological state owing to the breakdown of contacts between the members of families in Kuwait and those abroad.

What is happening in Kuwait has obviously drastically affected the psychological state of Kuwaiti children, especially those who live through the nightmare watching aircraft fly over their homes, hearing the deafening noise of guns and seeing their relatives arrested or shot. Thousands of children have fled the country with their families to escape the daily torture, leaving behind relatives, books, toys, playgrounds, friends and memories. Kuwaiti children have become refugees not knowing their own destiny.

The above are only a few examples of many inhumane and repressive practices by Iraqi authorities in occupied Kuwait. Such practices have no precedent in history and no explanation or justification, especially as there had never been any hostility between the two neighbouring Muslim peoples of Iraq and Kuwait. The only possible explanation is that these practices are simply a reflection of the greed of the Iraqi ruling authorities and their desire to plunder Kuwait. This is an aggressive scheme aiming at dispersing the people of Kuwait, obliterating the Kuwaiti national identity and removing the name of Kuwait from the world political map. The Kuwaiti citizen lost his right to self-determination when the Iraqi authorities, in violation of international law and custom, annexed a large part of Kuwaiti territory to the Basrah Governorate and called the remaining part of Kuwait the nineteenth Governorate of Iraq. The Iraqi authorities have also undertaken other measures to Iraqify Kuwait, such as:

> Forcing Kuwaitis to replace Kuwaiti identity cards by Iraqi cards;
>
> Changing names of districts, streets, hospitals and public buildings;
>
> Prohibiting the use of the Kuwaiti dinar after placing it on a par with the Iraqi dinar, which is worth 14 times less;
>
> Making Kuwaiti time the same as Iraqi time (there is a one-hour difference);
>
> Removing the picture of the Emir of the country and putting Saddam Hussein's picture up in establishments and public places;
>
> Replacing Kuwaiti car number plates by Iraqi plates; if plates were not changed, no petrol was allowed and the car would be confiscated;
>
> Setting up large portraits of Saddam Hussein in public squares and main streets;
>
> Installation of Iraqi families in Kuwait; and
>
> Taking away passports and other identity documents from Kuwaitis leaving Kuwait.

Arrests

Immediately after entering Kuwait, Iraqi forces started the implementation of their plan of aggression by arresting Kuwaiti citizens in the streets of Kuwait, especially at checkpoints set up at strategic points in the capital and other towns in contravention of the general provisions of the Geneva Convention Relative to the Protection of Civilian Persons in Time of War (1949). Iraqi army and intelligence officers arrested more than 1,000 Kuwaiti citizens, including businessmen, chairmen and members of the boards of banks and companies and senior officials in the Ministry of Finance and the General Authority for Investment. A large number of senior officials were arrested, particularly those working in the Ministries of Foreign Affairs, the Interior and Defence.

In each case, the Iraqis do not indicate either the reason for the arrest or the charges. Detainees are taken to detention centres which were set up in sports clubs and schools. Relatives of detainees are not allowed to visit them or even ask questions about them. It is known that some detainees were released after paying bribes to Iraqi officials, who are usually corrupt. Arrest is usually accompanied by violence and ill-treatment not only of the detainee, but also of all members of the family and any other person who may be involved in the matter, even by simply asking about the reason for the arrest.

Detention has increased sharply since mid-August, as Iraqi forces started to hold Kuwaiti youths to stop them from taking part in the resistance. One way or another, more than 100,000 persons were arrested at checkpoints and during the night. The Iraqi forces arrested many women and children, accusing them of writing statements of loyalty to their country and legitimate Government on the walls. In many cases, the person concerned is not arrested alone, but is taken along with all members of his family and all of them are subjected to torture. If Iraqi forces find themselves unable to arrest a certain person, they arrest all members of his family, as well as his neighbours and acquaintances, and subject them all to torture in order to force the person concerned to hand himself over to Iraqi authorities, in violation of article 53 of the Geneva Convention Relative to the Protection of Civilian Persons in Time of War (1949). According to official Kuwaiti statistics, there are some 8,170 military detainees in Baghdad and Mosul alone. There are 30 Kuwaiti women detained in Kuwait and 400 Kuwaiti women detained in Baghdad in addition to 50 Kuwaiti families detained in Basra. We do not yet have accurate statistics on the number and fate of other civilian detainees.

Detention may last for one day or several months; the fate of a large number of Kuwaiti citizens detained at the beginning of the invasion is still unknown. The Iraqi authorities do not permit visits to detainees, and on more than one occasion, any person who asked questions about the detainees was detained himself. It is also known that thousands of Kuwaiti detainees were removed to Basra, Baghdad and Mosul under very harsh and dangerous conditions. According to one detainee's account, during the first few days of the invasion, the Iraqi authorities tied detainees up hand and foot and left them in the desert without food or water. It should be noted that the temperature at that time was over 50° C in the shade. An official of the Kuwaiti Red Crescent Society says: "Daily aggressions and harassment of citizens have become a matter affecting people to a great extent; no man can move freely or without fear of detention, murder or kidnapping. Raids on houses became an ordinary event that was to be expected by any citizen at any time and arrest and torture became a danger threatening every person without exception. The Iraqi authorities do not bring detainees to trial; detention and investigation of individual cases under torture, punishment and even killing take place in the many detention camps in Kuwait depending on the mood of the intelligence and other occupation authorities".

There are many examples of arrests in official reports of the Government of Kuwait and the reports of international human rights organizations, such as Amnesty International, the Arab Organization for Human Rights and Middle East Watch, of which we quote some examples:

Iraqis arrested a number of former members of the National Assembly (Parliament) and the current members of the National Council and tortured them as a punishment for their refusal to co-operate with the occupation authorities. Reports mentioned the names of Mr. Mubarak Addoweileh, Mr. Khaled Sultan Al-Issa, Abdel-Kerim Aljoheidly and Jasser Aljasser.

Mr. Nihal Mokrad, former Secretary-General of Kuwait Labour Union, was arrested in the first days of the occupation and his whereabouts are still unknown.

Mr. Hamad Soyan, Chairman of the Union of Petroleum Workers, was detained more than once and his fate is still unknown.

A Kuwaiti citizen in his sixties (his family requested that his name should be withheld for his safety) who is a well-known businessman was arrested on the evening of 3 August at his home when soldiers came to inquire about one of his relatives who happened to be abroad at that time. This citizen was taken in place of the relative and, until now, no member of his family knows where he is being detained or how the state of his health is. He is known only to have been removed along with thousands of other detainees to Iraq.

In October, four young men were detained in Kaifan by Iraqi soldiers who saw them distributing frozen fish to citizens. These young men had already obtained a written authorization from the officer responsible for the district to do this job. Their fate is still unknown.

A 16-year-old Kuwaiti student at Farwanieh School was detained on 1 October for violation of the curfew and was taken to the police station of Rabia and placed in a cell with four other detainees. He was tortured and beaten every day and his body was burnt with a hot iron rod, which left a scar in the form of the letter H. He was released after being threatened that he would be murdered if he was arrested again.

On 10 November, an Iraqi officer went to Alfayhaa Co-operative and tried to enter the Co-operative, but officials of the Co-operative asked him to take his turn in the queue. The officer came back later in the evening with a number of soldiers and arrested the young men who work in the Co-operative and detained them in the Alfayhaa police station, accusing them of stealing municipality cars. A decision was made to detain them for 15 days prior to trial in Al Basra. However, after giving the officer a bribe of a television and a video cassette recorder and obtaining a letter from the municipality stating that the cars were given to the Co-operative as a gift, the five men were released.

Six doctors and officials of the Kuwaiti Red Crescent Society were arrested after being invited to a meeting with officials of the Iraqi Red Crescent Society; the meeting was never held. After being detained for 26 days, they were released and a decision was taken to dissolve the Kuwaiti Red Crescent. This decision had adverse effects on the health situation in Kuwait, as this Red Crescent Society was the only organization offering humanitarian services in the absence of the health system that had collapsed as a result of the invasion.

A 33-year-old Kuwaiti citizen who worked in the General Authority for Agriculture was detained on a charge of giving assistance to the resistance. His family, including his children, were cross-examined by the Iraqis, who threatened to detain them if they did not testify against him.

Iraqi forces raided the house of the noted Kuwaiti politician, Mr. Faisal Assanei, on 25 September and detained him with his 13-year-old son, Ziad, as well as 17 other persons who were visiting him. After detention and torture for three months, they were all released except for Mr. Assanei, whose whereabouts are still unknown.

A 22-year-old Kuwaiti, Abdullah Assalem, was arrested on 27 August upon leaving his house in the evening. He was detained for 17 days during which he was subjected to severe torture to make him give information on the resistance. Members of his family were harassed daily with telephone calls while he was in detention.

The Arab Organization for Human Rights states in its report on the "Situation of Human Rights in Kuwait Since the Iraqi Invasion" that reports received by the organization speak of the arrest of some elements of the Iraqi opposition who were living in Kuwait before the invasion and their deportation to Baghdad. The organization received the names of several of those opposition elements. Human rights circles are very concerned because some of those detainees are charged with membership of the prohibited Islamic Adda'awa (call) Party which is punishable by death in Iraq.

These are a few examples of detentions which have become a matter of routine in occupied Kuwait. The most striking examples of detentions are perhaps those of Western and Japanese nationals. The plight of those taken to Iraq to be used as human shields will be discussed below.

Acts of torture and violence

Immediately upon entering Kuwait, the forces of aggression started their practices of violence, intimidation and arrests in violation of international customs and the Geneva Conventions of 1949. The Iraqi authorities resorted to the most heinous methods and developed the most cruel ways of torturing innocent Kuwaiti citizens in violation of articles 27, 31 and 32 of the Geneva Convention Relative to the Protection of Civilians in

Time of War (1949). The above-mentioned Amnesty International report states that the Iraqi authorities used 38 different ways to torture detainees, the worst of which include plucking out the eyes, breaking bones, throwing the person from a rooftop, pulling out fingernails and toenails, drilling the hands and feet with an electric tool, cutting off tongues and ears, close-range shooting, rape and applying electric shocks to sensitive parts of the body.

Torture is used as a means of obtaining information on senior Government officials and the hiding places of members of the resistance, of army personnel and of foreigners, particularly Americans, British and French, and of forcing Kuwaiti citizens to co-operate with the Iraqis to abort resistance in all its forms and spread fear among the Kuwaitis.

Thousands of innocent Kuwaiti men, women and children have suffered from these terrorist acts and savage practices. No doubt the effects of most of these crimes will be permanent and will cause psychological disturbances for life. In this report, we record some cases of torture practised by the occupying Iraqi forces in Kuwait to illustrate the inhumane treatment of detainees.

Iraq is treating all detainees in a savage way; they are blindfolded, beaten, given electric shocks and crowded into very small rooms under very difficult conditions. The Iraqis starve detainees, throw garbage and rotten foodstuffs on them, allow them to go to the bathroom only once a day and give them contaminated drinking water which causes various intestinal diseases and diarrhoea. As part of the psychological torture of detainees and their families, Iraqi forces stage mock executions of detainees and contact their relatives in the middle of the night to give them terrifying accounts of what happened to their children.

In some cases, the torture of detainees continued for several days to force them to give false statements. Before a detainee was released, Iraqi authorities would force him to sign false statements, to undertake to carry out the instructions of the Iraqi forces and to co-operate with them at the risk of execution and killing his relatives if he did not obey those instructions.

An official of the Kuwaiti Red Crescent who was detained said that "Iraqi soldiers used to kick detainees in the stomach with their heavy army boots. I saw one of the detainees urinating blood, perhaps as a result of a haemorrhage in the kidney, his face showed signs that his hair had been pulled out by force and his nails had been pulled out; I also saw another detainee forced to walk after severe beatings on the soles of his feet; he was screaming and his face and clothes were blood-stained".

Following are examples of torture as described in official Kuwaiti reports and reports of human rights organizations.

A 32-year-old Kuwaiti was arrested on 3 August on his way home after buying some food from the co-operative. He was detained for five days in the Salibieh police station, where he was beaten, given electric shocks and shot in the foot at close range.

A man in his thirties was arrested in the third week of August and again on 20 September on charges of membership in the armed forces and the Kuwaiti resistance. He was detained in a school, from which he was moved to Jahra police station, where he was beaten, kicked, given electric shocks and had heavy objects placed all over his body.

A 22-year-old student was arrested on 24 August during house searches in Roda district. He was detained for eight days in Roda police station and removed to Farwanieh police station, where he was beaten, kicked and burnt with cigarette butts on various parts of his body; his thigh was gashed with a knife.

A Kuwaiti 17-year-old boy was arrested in early September on the charge of possession of a rifle and manuals on weapons. He was detained for 36 days in several camps in Kuwait and Basra where he was exposed to beatings, mock execution, beatings on the feet and electric shocks and was threatened with sexual assault.

A 38-year-old citizen was arrested on 5 September on the charge of membership of the Kuwaiti resistance. He was detained in Showeikh district before he was moved to Basra. He was exposed to beatings, mock execution, torture by exposure to extreme cold and hot temperatures, was burnt with electric shocks and was hanged from a ceiling fan.

A 31-year-old citizen was arrested on 14 September in Dewanieh at his home and detained for three weeks in Farwanieh and Jahra police stations and in a Kuwaiti house used as a detention centre. Later he was removed to Basra where he was exposed to beatings, electric shocks and mock execution; he was forced to watch his relatives under torture and he was tortured before their very eyes.

A Kuwaiti youth in his thirties was arrested on 22 September on a charge of possession of leaflets describing methods of protection from chemical weapons. He was tortured for a week by beatings, kicking and burns, as well as sexual assault, in Farwanieh police station.

A 27-year old student was arrested on 22 September after entering Kuwait to help his family leave the country. He was detained for 18 days in various detention camps in Kuwait City. Later he was removed to Basra and he was exposed to beatings, whipping, cold and hot temperatures for long periods and electric shocks.

An 18-year-old youth living in Sorra was detained in Farwanieh police station. When he returned to his family 10 days later he could neither walk nor talk normally. He was assaulted sexually and tortured with electric current on his genitals, ears and lips and was hanged by the feet.

A handicapped 24-year-old youth living in Do'ayah gives an account of his suffering with his handicapped colleagues: "They dragged me out of bed, I was taken to the police station, where I was beaten with a heavy stick on the first day; my body was black and blue with many bruises; I was threatened with execution and the aluminium bar I wore on my disabled leg was broken; after I was moved to the juvenile offenders' prison in Ferdaws district, I saw boys of 14-15 years and I heard their screams under torture. I shared the room with two others; one limped and was 16 years old; there [*sic*] were signs of torture and beating on his face. The other was 25 years old.

A 31-year-old Kuwaiti doctor specializing in vocational medicine who worked as a volunteer in Ahmadi and Al-Agdan hospitals during the months of August and September gave the following account of some aspects of Iraqi crimes:

Bodies were brought to the hospital at the rate of five or six a day. The dead were all males in their twenties with very clear signs of torture on their bodies. On the basis of my personal observation I could determine some of the methods of torture used on them. These included cigarette burns, burns caused by hot irons, electric shocks, cutting off tongues and ears, plucking out eyes and breaking of limbs, pulling out nails and beatings for a long time on the soles of the feet until pus formed. There were other clear signs that victims were left hanging by their feet for a long time. On other victims, there were signs that their beards were plucked out by force. Bullet shots were clear in the hand of one of the victims and in the thigh of another. In most cases, death was caused by one shot to the lower part of the back of the head.

Another doctor working in the Kuwaiti Crescent gives another account of dreadful torture before death:

> "I examined 60 bodies of persons who were killed by a shot to the lower part of the back of the head. Signs of torture were clear on 60

> bodies, including burning various parts of the body, breaking of limbs, beatings by sharp heavy objects, plucking out the hairs of the beard (in the case of one person), pulling nails off fingers and toes, electric shocks to the genitals (three cases) and cigarette burns in the eyes (three cases). It was clear that some victims died under torture and not by shooting."

Mohamed, a 20-year-old Kuwaiti youth who lived with his 80-year-old grandmother was detained and returned to the house with his eyes plucked out. Iraqi intelligence officers rang the bell and asked the grandmother to come and see him. She could not because of her old age and because she was blind. The Iraqis forced every person in the house to leave the house and to stand in one line in front of the house. They carried Mohamed from the car because he was unable to walk and shot him in the presence of his family and left his body on the street. They did not allow anyone to come near the body for 24 hours and prevented everyone from entering the house to console the grandmother.

A Kuwaiti youth of the Deshti family was arrested at his house in the middle of the night. Three days later, the Iraqis threw his body in a garbage sack. The body had no hands or ears and there were signs of torture on the other parts of his body.

Arbitrary killing

Iraqi invading forces and intelligence in the State of Kuwait since 2 August 1990 have practised the most heinous crimes of murder against innocent persons in occupied Kuwait. Hundreds of children, women and men, Kuwaitis and foreigners alike, were victims of these crimes which are violations of all international conventions and customs.

These crimes have shown the world the unspeakable truth of the intentions and methods of the Iraqi régime in dealing with innocent persons. Perhaps the most outrageous crime committed by the Iraqi authorities was the deliberate murder of 300 newborn babies who were taken out of their incubators in the Obstetrics Hospital (report of Amnesty International, December 1990, p. 56) for no other reason than to steal the incubators and ship them to Iraqi hospitals. The atrocity of murder is demonstrated by the manner of killing people, especially detainees. After being tortured until they are nearly dead, they are taken to their houses, where they are shot in the head or the chest in the presence of all members of the family, particularly the elderly, children and mothers who are forced to witness these crimes.

Random horrendous killings spread terror throughout the population and no citizen felt safe. Iraqi authorities carried out death penalties and killings for the slightest reason, without consideration for the elderly, children, men and women, in violation of article 168 of the Geneva Convention Relative to the Protection of Civilian Persons in Time of War. Many children and citizens were killed for merely carrying the flag of Kuwait or the portrait of the Emir of Kuwait or for writing national slogans on walls, distributing food, collecting garbage or participating in peaceful demonstrations. Iraqi authorities applied the death penalty to those who refused to put up the portrait of Saddam Hussein when asked to do so. They further extended the death penalty as of 25 August to any person who accommodated a foreigner, particularly a Westerner. Iraqi authorities also made another decision threatening senior Kuwaiti officials with the death penalty if they did not resume work as of 22 September 1990.

According to available estimates, more than 1,000 civilians have been killed at the hands of Iraqi authorities since the invasion of 2 August 1990. Until this very day, the Iraqi authorities continue their practice of killing without trial and murdering innocent Kuwaiti citizens in order to intimidate the Kuwaiti people and force it to submit to occupation.

Some examples are given below of the crimes of murder committed by Iraqi authorities, as reported by official sources and international humanitarian organizations.

The Kuwaiti Ambassador in London, Mr. Ghazi Arrayis, told a television audience how the Iraqis killed his brother in law (brother of his wife), Mr. Adel Al-Fallah: "While he was having lunch with his wife and three daughters (one, four and six years old), Iraqi soldiers came to the house and arrested him for investigation. After a while, they brought him home. He was on the point of death as a result of severe torture; the soldiers ordered the wife and the three daughters, as well as the neighbours, to assemble in front of the house where they shot Mr. Al-Fallah in their presence. His crime was providing food to Western residents."

Citizen Mubarak Fallah Annout, 44 years old, father of eight children, worked as a director of a co-operative and was a peaceful man who devoted himself to the service of citizens from the very first day of the occupation. A member of his family said that he was ordered by Iraqi authorities on 7 September to hang Saddam Hussein's portrait in the co-operative instead of the portrait of the Emir of Kuwait. When he refused, he was shot in front of the co-operative in the presence of all the employees of the co-operative as well as passers-by.

Citizen Mohammed Khalifa Al-Jassem, 32 years old, was the chairman of a youth fund in Salmiya and was a volunteer worker in a co-operative. He drafted and printed some leaflets urging citizens to conserve foodstuffs. The Iraqi authorities considered his leaflets a hostile act against the occupation and executed him in the presence of a crowd.

Dr. Balhan (Kuwaiti national), deputy director of the Cancer Centre at Sabbah Hospital, was executed by Iraqi authorities after being accused of concealing medical instruments and supplies in a hospital store.

Citizen Ali Mohammed Al-Ajami, member of the national Petroleum Trade Union, was executed in front of his house and nine children, some of whom are not even 10 years old.

Citizen Sanaa Annoury, a female student at the Kuwait University Faculty of Law, aged 25, was killed on 8 August when Iraqi authorities opened fire on a peaceful demonstration by a group of women in Jaberiya against the Iraqi occupation of Kuwait. In the same incident a girl in her twenties and two boys (aged 13 and 16) died as a result of head wounds. Iraqi authorities also opened fire on another peaceful demonstration in Ramithiya on 11 August and wounded several persons.

British businessman Douglas Croskery was killed when Iraqi soldiers shot him at the Kuwaiti-Saudi border on 11 August while he was trying to cross into Saudi Arabia.

Citizen Ahmed Qabazared, in his late thirties and employed by the Ministry of the Interior, was arrested for possession of leaflets. In the first week of September, he was returned home in Jaberiya, all members of his family were brought outside the house, the house was burned and he was shot in the presence of his entire family. Signs of severe torture were apparent on his hands, feet and the rest of his body. His left ear was cut, his right eye was plucked out and his fingernails and toenails were pulled out; cigarette burns were evident all over his body.

Citizen Saleh Hussein was arrested on 2 September at his home in Sabiya with some of his guests. He was executed on 8 September in front of his house in the presence of his mother, brothers and neighbours. According to the doctor who examined the body, there were clear signs of torture by electricity and burning by hot iron rods on his back, abdomen and hands. It was also clear that cigarettes were used to burn his entire body.

Citizen Badr Rajab, who was employed by Sabiya Co-operative and a father of eight children, was found dead in a garbage sack on 8 September in Sabiya. His hands were tied and his head was wrapped in the Kuwaiti flag. The cause of death was two blows on the head above the ear. It was said that he was planning with others to set up a bakery in his area.

Iraqis killed seven young Kuwaitis in September after detaining them for two weeks during which they were subject to severe torture. The seven were doing voluntary social work in Mubarak Hospital.

Eyewitnesses report that, on 9 September, a number of wounded Iraqi military men were brought to Al-Addan Hospital for treatment. An officer died on the same day and the Iraqis executed five employees of the hospital, including Citizen Adel Dashti, of the hospital public relations section, on the charge that they neglected to treat the Iraqi officer.

Kuwaiti doctor Hisham Al-Abeidan, in his thirties, was a member of the staff of the Obstetrics Hospital. He was arrested at his home on 1 October and accused of providing medical treatment to members of the resistance. He was executed in front of his house a few days later. According to the Egyptian doctor who examined the body, the deceased was tortured cruelly during his detention.

There is also the tragedy of a 19-year-old Kuwaiti student who was arrested on 11 September because he did not hand over his hunting rifles to the Iraqi authorities. He was detained for two weeks in a house in Jahra during which he was tortured. At 2.30 a.m. on 24 September, an officer told all detainees that they would be released upon instructions from the President of Iraq. The Kuwaiti youth was removed with 11 other detainees in a bus to the Dasman Palace where he was put on a bus with two others to take them home. The bus moved towards Al-Fayhaa district, where one of the detainees lived. In front of a house, the detainees were ordered to get out of the bus and stand in line in front of a house where they were blindfolded and shot. The three fell, two died, but the young man was wounded in the head. After Iraqi soldiers ascertained that the three had been shot in the head, they left the place, but the young man crawled to a neighbouring house, where he was treated.

Sexual Abuse and Rape

Iraqi soldiers committed the worst crimes against Kuwaiti citizens and residents of different nationalities in Kuwait. These include the sexual abuse and rape of women, as well as of men and children. In committing these abhorrent, immoral, irreligious and inhuman crimes, the Iraqis have added a black record to the history of mankind. They have violated article 27 of the 1949 Geneva Convention Relative to the Protection of Civilian Persons in Time of War and article 76 of Additional Protocol I.

We give here some examples of the brutal and shameful acts committed by Iraqi soldiers in occupied Kuwait. According to those who have left Kuwait, there are hundreds of cases of the sexual abuse of males and females, of Kuwaiti and other nationalities. However, in view of prevailing social traditions and customs and the implications of these shameful acts, the majority of cases of sexual abuse are, and will remain, under the seal of secrecy.

On the first day of the invasion, Iraqi soldiers sexually abused eight Philippine nurses in Al-Jahrah Hospital. In September, they sexually abused nurses of the same nationality in Al-Sabah Hospital. This brutal act terrified the rest of the nurses, especially the Philippine ones, who make up most of the medical staff in Kuwait, and they had to run away.

Dr. Fawziyah Al-Gattan, a gynaecologist, stated in her testimony to the House of Commons Foreign Affairs Committee that, during her work at the maternity hospital in Al-Sabah neighbourhood, she treated a large number of women of various nationalities who had been sexually and brutally abused by Iraqi soldiers. She described some cases as follows:

"I recall that, during the early days of the invasion, five Iraqi soldiers repeatedly sexually abused a Jordanian women in her 20s after having kidnapped her on the street. Seven Iraqi soldiers also sexually abused a Palestinian woman kidnapped on the street. I tried to treat the wounds of the victims but I was unable to relieve their psychological pain and suffering, which will undoubtedly be a nightmare for them for the rest of their lives."

Dr. Fawziyah went on to say: "I remember very well that, on 11 November, a Kuwaiti woman came to the hospital with her two daughters; she was trying to relieve them of the psychological shock they had had. She told me that Iraqi soldiers entered her house in the early morning hours and began beating the men and threatening them with guns. They took all the members of the family to the first floor, then they took the two girls one after the other to a separate room where they sexually abused them while the rest of the family listened to their cries without being able to do anything. The soldiers forced the mother to witness the sexual abuse of her single daughters".

A gynaecologist working at the maternity hospital during the early weeks of the invasion said: "Iraqi soldiers sexually abused a 20-year old Jordanian girl kidnapped on the street while she was going to the grocery store. Then she was thrown back on to the street once again. When I examined the victim, I found her vagina swollen as a result of violent rape. I also found traces of scratches and bruises on her face and hands. She was in a hysterical state".

The same doctor said in his report: "Iraqi policemen brought two girls to the hospital, one a 20-year-old of unknown nationality. She told me that, while she and her family were sleeping, Iraqi soldiers came to their house at about 6 a.m. and went up to the top floor, where they sodomized her several times". The doctor said: "When I examined her, I noticed a 4 cm fissure close to her vagina, which was treated with five stitches. In addition, I found signs of resistance on her body. The victim stated that the soldiers also raped her two older sisters". He also said that he knew of many such cases, but the victims did not want to reveal their identity.

Two Kuwaiti girls, 18 and 19 years of age, were taken from their house in Kuwait by occupation soldiers and sexually abused throughout the night. The aim was to force them to confess that their brother was a member of the Kuwaiti resistance. The next day, their brother went to the Iraqi authorities and lied to them, saying that he was a member of the resistance in order to save his sisters. He was punished by severe torture, including having his toe nails pulled out.

In September, a Western woman was sexually abused and soldiers forced her husband to witness the crime.

Iraqi soldiers at an inspection post forced Kuwaiti women to take off their clothes and walk back and forth while Iraqi soldiers cheered and laughed.

A report by Amnesty International (December 1990) states: "Since the beginning of September, Amnesty International has received increasing reports of sexual abuse of Kuwaiti and Arab women by Iraqi military men". An Egyptian diplomat states that, on 3 August, Iraqi soldiers sexually abused three Egyptian hostages staying at the Meridien Hotel. An Egyptian nurse working at Mubarak Hospital said that, in the hospital, she treated many cases of sexual abuse, including the case of a hysterical Kuwaiti woman from Al-Salimiyeah neighbourhood. A medical doctor of the Kuwaiti Red Crescent said that, according to their sources, Al-Jahrah Hospital received 15 cases of sexual abuse, Al-Rakah Hospital 15 cases and the maternity hospital 3 cases. An

Egyptian doctor working in Al-Sabah Hospital said that a Kuwaiti woman of a well-known family from Al-Jabiriyah neighbourhood came to the hospital with her 19-year-old daughter, saying that, at the end of August, while her daughter was returning home from the co-operative after having bought food, she was followed by three Iraqi soldiers and an officer. The mother knew what they were up to, so she pleaded with them not to abuse her virgin daughter sexually, and offered herself to them in order to spare her daughter. That is what actually happened.

The Amnesty International report also states: "A Kuwaiti woman left Kuwait on 27 November because she and her sister were threatened with sexual abuse in front of their brother, a journalist, who was arrested for his opposition to the Iraqi régime, in order to obtain information from him. This woman also described the tragedy of a Kuwaiti family living in the Al-Remethiyah neighbourhood, where Iraqi soldiers sexually abused four daughters in the presence of their father. She also told the story of a Kuwaiti girl whom she saw naked and sexually abused at Sabah Al-Salim police station".

Acts of sexual abuse by Iraqi soldiers and authorities are not limited to women, but extend to many men and children, especially those detained and tortured to make them provide information. There are many examples of threats against, and the sexual abuse of men, as indicated in the reports of humanitarian organizations.

A man in his thirties told an Amnesty International Official that he was arrested on 22 September. One of the acts of torture he was subjected to was that Iraqis spread his legs and introduced a bottle neck up his anus.

A 17-year-old student said that he had been detained for two months in Basra and subjected to various acts of torture, including sexual abuse by means of the neck of a whisky bottle.

Violation of the rights of non-Kuwaitis

The question of occupied Kuwait is a humanitarian issue with international dimensions. Suffering has not been limited to Kuwaitis, for war and repression by Iraqi authorities have affected nearly 1.5 million persons from more than 120 States who were making their living in Kuwait and contributing to the country's development and civilization.

The Iraqi invaders have made no distinction between Kuwaitis and other Arab citizens in denying them their basic human rights. Arabs working in Kuwait have been tragically affected, for many of them have been detained and subjected with their families to ill-treatment, including insults, beating, sexual abuse, confiscation of property, curfew, expulsion from their homes and confiscation of their cars.

The Palestinians are the most affected Arab community; nearly 400,000 of them lived in Kuwait before the invasion. Kuwait gave them a livelihood and shelter. They enjoyed a comfortable life and received free medical treatment and education in public hospitals and schools.

As a result of the Iraqi invasion of Kuwait and the repressive practices engaged in, more than 250,000 Palestinians left Kuwait for Jordan, leaving behind their livelihoods, including their shops, public and non-public posts, property, wealth and bank deposits. As for Palestinians who decided to stay in Kuwait, their actual material incomes have gone down because their monthly salaries are paid in Iraqi dinars, which have a low purchasing power after having been placed on a par with the Kuwaiti dinar. The Palestinians' salaries are therefore equivalent to 10 per cent of their value before the invasion. As a result, they lost their bank savings and became unable to send remittances to their relatives in Jordan and occupied territories or to their children studying abroad and to pay the liberation tax.

The Egyptians are the other Arab community which has also suffered a great deal. More than 200,000 Egyptians used to work in various fields such as medicine, teaching, law, nursing, secretarial work, industry, agriculture and construction. Some Egyptians had been living in Kuwait for more than 35 years and Kuwait was considered their second home. They lost the savings they had placed in Kuwaiti banks throughout their lives.

Egyptians in Kuwait suffered a great deal, for they were treated very badly by the invading Iraqi authorities, especially after Egypt made known its official position rejecting the Iraqi occupation of Kuwait. Most of them left Kuwait for Egypt via Iraq and Jordan under very harsh and dangerous conditions, which led in some cases to the death of many men, children and women in the desert because they were shot at by Iraqi soldiers or because of thirst and extreme heat.

Iraqi soldiers applied this cruel and brutal treatment to citizens of other Arab countries which rejected the Iraqi occupation of Kuwait, such as Syria and Lebanon. Reports received by humanitarian organizations dealing with human rights state that Iraqi soldiers sexually abused many Arab women, especially Egyptian, Jordanian and Palestinian women.

As for citizens of Western States and Japan, their suffering was different. They lived in a state of fear of being killed by Iraqis. This was after Iraq's decision of 25 August to require every Western and Japanese foreigner to give himself up to the Iraqi authorities (the decision also provided for the execution of anyone who gives shelter to a foreigner or helps him hide or run away). Thousands of foreigners were arrested, especially Americans, Canadians, English, French and citizens of other European countries, as well as Japanese, all of whom were taken to Baghdad. Iraq announced that they had been placed at military and industrial installations as human shields, thus violating international conventions, especially article 51, paragraph 7, of Additional Protocol I to the 1949 Geneva Conventions. These captives lived in a state of anxiety, terror and fear for their fate and that of their families. Even those who were not arrested did not dare leave their hiding places to meet their needs. They lived in a state of constant terror and were very afraid of being discovered or that the persons who gave them shelter and helped them obtain food would be arrested.

In addition to all this suffering, many foreign women were subjected to sexual abuse or the threat of sexual abuse and personal insults in the presence of their husbands and children.

Before the Iraqi invasion, there were about 450,000 Asians, most of whom were from India, Pakistan, Philippines and Bangladesh, who came to make their living in Kuwait. Their remittances to their countries, which amounted to millions of dollars annually, supported hundreds of thousands of families in those countries. These persons lived, and some still live, in a situation that is no less tragic than the situation of Kuwaitis themselves, for they were subjected to captivity, threats, torture, sexual abuse and killing. Many Asians have described their agony during their journeys back to their countries via Iraq and Jordan after having lost their savings and have told stories of hunger, pain, torture and insults. The Iraqi authorities also took away what was left of their savings and personal possessions.

Desecration of holy places and prevention of worship

Iraqi soldiers committed shameful acts contrary to the divine laws and teachings of various religions, including the desecration of mosques and churches in Kuwait. They not only bombarded these places with tank cannons, but also entered them with weapons and used them as headquarters for soldiers, in violation of article 53 of Additional Protocol I to the 1949 Geneva Conventions.

According to refugee witnesses from Kuwait, the Iraqis prevented worshippers from holding collective prayers and delivering speeches calling upon people to hold together and ask God to save Kuwait and citizens from the tyranny of the Iraqi invasion.

In addition, the Iraqi authorities insulted religious men and imams of mosques and desecrated the Holy Koran by throwing it on the ground and treading on it. On Friday, 3 August, Iraqi soldiers forced their way into a mosque in the Kefan neighbourhood where hundreds of Kuwaiti citizens had gathered for the Friday prayer. The soldiers ordered worshippers to leave the mosque and, when some of them refused to do so, a number of them were shot and killed. Several mosques were closed after their imams had been arrested for their opposition to the Iraqi invasion. The Iraqi authorities issued an order to have beards shaven, since they are a sign of religiosity; Iraqi soldiers plucked out hair from the face of anyone who resisted this order and, in some cases, they burnt the detainees' beards.

Iraqis denied worship on Sundays to about 300,000 or 400,000 Christians of Western, Asian and Arab communities, after having looted churches and destroyed places of prayer. Christians who have fled Kuwait have described their deep suffering as a result of the Iraqi soldiers' conduct and inhuman treatment.

The invasion of Kuwait on 2 August 1990 is the tragedy not only of Kuwait and the Kuwaitis, but also of the whole world. The events of Kuwait have adversely affected the States and peoples of the region and the States of the Arab and Islamic world. These events have especially affected the economies of countries that used to depend on the Gulf States for imported employment, trade, loans and foreign aid.

According to what has been said in the present report, there is no doubt that the Iraqi invading forces have committed, and continue to commit, the worst crimes against Kuwaitis and residents of Kuwait without any deterrent in terms of conscience, religion or law. They have added a black record to the history of Iraq and of mankind. If these acts suggest anything, it is the brutality of the Iraqi régime and Iraq's non-respect for human rights and non-compliance with international conventions, especially the 1949 Geneva Conventions and their Additional Protocols.

E/CN.4/1991/91, at 264

3. Report of the UN Commission on Human Rights, 1991

[*Extract.*]

...

Statements were made by the following members of the Commission: Austria (42nd), Brazil (41st), Burundi (34th), Canada (41st), China (40th), Cuba (40th), Gambia (43rd), India (40th), Iraq (36th), Japan (42nd), Mexico (39th), Peru (40th), Senegal (43rd), Sweden (42nd), Union of Soviet Socialist Republics (40th), United States of America (33rd), Zambia (36th).

477. The Commission also heard statements by the observers for: Bahrain (37th), Bolivia (41st), Egypt (40th), Finland (40th), Kuwait (40th), Luxembourg (on behalf of the European Community and its member States) (43rd), Norway (42nd), Oman (42nd), Poland (36th), Qatar (36th), Saudi Arabia (37th), Syrian Arab Republic (42nd), United Arab Emirates (37th), United Kingdom of Great Britain and Northern Ireland (40th).

478. A statement was also made by the representative of the International Labour Organization (37th).

479. The Commission also heard statements by the following non-governmental organizations: American Association of Jurists (40th), Arab Organization for Human Rights (34th), Christian Democratic International (40th), International Commission of Jurists (34th), International Council of Voluntary Agencies (35th), International Federation for the Protection of Rights of Ethnic, Religious, Linguistic and Other Minorities (40th), Liberal International (36th), World Federation of Trade Unions (35th), World Muslim Congress (34th), World Union for Progressive Judaism (39th).

480. Statements in exercise of the right of reply or its equivalent were made by the representatives of Iraq (39th and 41st) and the United States of America (39th) and the observers for Bahrain (39th), Egypt (42nd), Kuwait (37th and 39th) and Saudi Arabia (39th).

481. On 26 February 1991, a draft resolution (E/CN.4/1991/L.48) was submitted by Argentina, Australia, Austria, Bahrain, Brazil, Canada, Costa Rica, Cyprus, Czechoslovakia, Egypt, Finland, the Gambia, Hungary, Kenya, Lebanon, Luxembourg, Oman, the Philippines, Qatar, Saudi Arabia, Senegal, Somalia, Swaziland, Sweden, the Syrian Arab Republic, the Ukrainian Soviet Socialist Republic, the United Arab Emirates and Yugoslavia, reading as follows:

"*The Commission on Human Rights,*

Guided by the principles embodied in the Charter of the United Nations, the Universal Declaration of Human Rights, the International Covenant on Human Rights, the Geneva Conventions of 12 August 1949 and the First Additional Protocol of 1977 relating to the protection of victims of international armed conflicts and the Hague Convention IV of 1907,

Recalling General Assembly resolution 45/170 of 18 December 1990 concerning the situation of human rights in occupied Kuwait,

Also recalling Security Council resolutions 666 of 13 September 1990 and 661 of 6 August 1990 (paras. 3 (c) and 4),

Aware of its responsibility to promote and encourage respect for human rights and fundamental freedoms for all and resolved to remain vigilant with regard to violations of human rights wherever they occur,

Reaffirming that all Member States have an obligation to promote and protect human rights and fundamental freedoms and to fulfil their obligations under the relevant international instruments,

Condemning the invasion and occupation of Kuwait on 2 August 1990 by the military forces of Iraq,

Alarmed that the acts of the Iraqi forces in occupied Kuwait continue to cause enormous human suffering to the civilian population,

Noting with grave concern the information to the effect that the treatment of prisoners of war and detained civilians in occupied Kuwait does not conform to the internationally recognized principles of humanitarian law,

Expressing grave concern at the continued refusal of Iraq to receive representatives of humanitarian organizations, especially representatives of the International Committee of the Red Cross and a representative of the Secretary-General, to help in extending humanitarian assistance to the Kuwaiti people under occupation,

1. *Strongly condemns* the Iraqi authorities and occupying forces for their grave violations of human rights against the Kuwaiti people and nationals of other States and in particular the continued and increasing acts of torture, arbitrary arrests, summary executions and disappearances in violation of the Charter of the United Nations, the International Covenants on Human Rights, and other relevant legal instruments;

2. *Expresses its serious concern* about the systematic destruction, dismantling and pillaging of the economic infrastructure of Kuwait, which seriously undermine the present and future enjoyment by the Kuwaiti people of their economic, social and cultural rights;

3. *Demands* that Iraq comply with its obligations under the charter of the United Nations and the contemporary norms of international law in respect of nationals of other States, and demands that Iraq release all such nationals;

4. *Condemns* the rejection by Iraq of the offer of the Government of Kuwait and various humanitarian organizations to send humanitarian assistance, especially medicine, to the Kuwaiti people under occupation;

5. *Affirms* that the fourth Geneva Convention, of 12 August 1949, relative to the Protection of Civilian Persons in Time of War applies to Kuwait and that as a high contracting party to the Convention Iraq is bound to comply fully with all its provisions;

6. *Insists* that Iraq treat all prisoners of war and detained civilians in accordance with the internationally recognized principles of humanitarian law and that it refrain from subjecting them to all acts of violence, including ill-treatment, torture and summary execution;

7. *Demands* that Iraq guarantee respect for international standards applicable under international law, in particular with reference to the protection of the civilian population, and further demands that Iraq immediately cooperate fully with and give access to representatives of humanitarian organizations to Kuwait, especially the International Committee of the Red Cross, and to allow them to extend humanitarian assistance to the civilian population of Kuwait;

8. *Welcomes* the intention of the Government of Kuwait, immediately following its restoration, to provide access to the International Committee of the Red Cross and other humanitarian organizations in order to assist in caring for the civilian population of Kuwait;

9. *Decides* to appoint an individual of recognized international standing as special rapporteur with a mandate to examine the human rights violations committed in occupied Kuwait by the invading and occupying forces of Iraq and to report as soon as possible to the General Assembly and the Commission on Human Rights at its forty-eighth session;

10. *Requests* the Chairman of the forty-seventh session of the Commission on Human Rights, in consultation with the Bureau, to designate the special rapporteur;

11. *Authorizes* the special rapporteur to seek relevant information from the Government of Kuwait, specialized agencies and intergovernmental and non-governmental organizations;

12. *Requests* the special rapporteur to prepare a preliminary report as soon as possible and to transmit it to the Secretary-General for dissemination to all Member States of the United Nations;

13. *Requests* the Secretary-General to provide all necessary assistance to the special rapporteur to enable him to carry out his mandate in the best possible conditions;

14. *Decides* to consider the situation of human rights in occupied Kuwait at its forty-eighth session." [The text of the resolution, as revised and adopted, is reproduced below.]

482. At the 54th meeting, on 6 March 1991, the observer for Kuwait introduced a revised draft resolution (E/CN.4/1991/L.48/Rev.1), sponsored by Argentina, Australia, Austria, Bahrain, Brazil, Bulgaria, Canada, Costa Rica, Cyprus, Czechoslovakia, El Salvador, Egypt, Finland, the Gambia, Ghana, Hungary, Japan, Kenya, Kuwait, Lebanon, Luxembourg, Oman, Pakistan, the Philippines, Poland, Qatar, Saudi Arabia, Senegal, Somalia, Swaziland, Sweden, the Syrian Arab Republic, Turkey, Ukrainian Soviet Socialist Republic, the United Arab Emirates and Yugoslavia. Bangladesh and Liechtenstein subsequently joined the sponsors.

483. At the same meeting, the representative of Iraq proposed amendments (E/CN.4/1991/L.90) to draft resolution E/CN.4/1991/L.48/Rev.1 which read as follows:

(a) Add following new paragraph after the seventh preambular paragraph:

> "*Noting with grave concern* current reports from Kuwait about the subjection of Arab citizens, Palestinians, Egyptians, Sudanese, and Iraqis in particular, to acts of revenge by the Kuwaiti armed forces and by armed civilians,"

(b) Add a new paragraph 2, as follows:

> "2. *Strongly condemns* acts of revenge, killing, arbitrary arrest, torture, and other violations of human rights to which Palestinians, Sudanese, Egyptians, and Iraqis are now being subjected at the hands of the Kuwaiti military forces and the armed civilian forces currently controlling Kuwait City;"

Renumber subsequent paragraphs;

(c) In original paragraph 9 insert the words "and the acts of revenge currently being perpetrated by Kuwaiti forces against Arab citizens" between "Iraq" and "and to report".

484. Statements relating to the amendments proposed by Iraq were made by the representatives of Canada and France, and by the observer for Egypt.

485. The representative of France requested a vote on the amendments. The amendments were rejected by 33 votes to 2, with 5 abstentions.

486. The attention of the Commission was drawn to an estimate of administrative and programme budget implications ... .

487. A statement in explanation of vote before the vote on draft resolution E/CN.4/1991/L.48/Rev.1 was made by the representative of Iraq.

488. At the request of the representative of Iraq, a vote was taken on draft resolution E/CN.4/1991/L.48/Rev.1. The draft resolution was adopted by 41 votes to 1.

E/CN.4/1991/SR.35, 26 April 1991

4. Commission on Human Rights, Forty-seventh Session, Summary Record of the 35th Meeting, 1991

[*Extract.*]

...

67. **Mr. AL-MUTAWA (Minister of Planning of Kuwait)** said that the events that had occurred during the past few years in the world, particularly the destruction of the Berlin Wall, the unification of Germany and the independence of Namibia, had given rise to hope for the emergence of a better world where cooperation and democratic values and new relations between nations would triumph. That dream had unfortunately been shattered on 2 August 1990 when Iraqi forces had brutally invaded Kuwait, thus flagrantly violating the Charter of the United Nations, the Universal Declaration

of Human Rights and international law. The Iraqis had flouted all existing values, defied the international community as a whole and forced the world into war.

68. The Iraqi forces installed in Kuwait had murdered and tortured thousands of defenceless Kuwaiti citizens, destroyed and pillaged the country's industrial, economic and commercial facilities, expropriated public and private property and pillaged hospitals, even throwing patients out into the street. All schools had been closed and occupied by the military forces and the Iraqi secret police. Tens of thousands of Kuwaitis had been arrested and were still being held without trial. Rape, torture and summary executions had become daily events in Kuwait. In committing those criminal acts and atrocities, the Iraqi forces violated all the principles of international humanitarian law and made a mockery of the teachings of Islam. Defying religious laws and doctrines, they had profaned mosques and churches by transforming them into military quarters. They had also prevented the faithful from entering mosques to pray by shutting them down and arresting a large number of imams, some of whom had been summarily executed for refusing to obey their orders. The hundreds of thousands of non-Muslims living in Kuwait had also been prevented from practising their religion and had been subjected to all kinds of humiliations.

69. All members of the Kuwaiti armed forces who had surrendered to the Iraqi forces or had been captured by them since 2 August 1990 were prisoners of war under the Third Geneva Convention of 1949. However, there was nothing to show that they were treated as such since the Iraqis had given no information concerning their identity or their whereabouts as the Convention required. In addition, Iraq's announcement that it would use prisoners of war as human shields clearly illustrated the contempt in which it held international law.

70. The invasion of Kuwait had also had disastrous consequences for a large number of nationals of other countries who had found themselves without homes, without work and without resources or had been taken hostage. What had they done to deserve such cruel and inhuman treatment? In addition, the Iraqis were guilty of the unpardonable and inconceivable crime against nature of deliberately pouring millions of barrels of oil into the Gulf, thus destroying the life-source of all the States in the region.

71. The 300,000 Kuwaitis living under the yoke of the Iraqi occupation forces and the 450,000 Kuwaitis in exile were plunged in despair. No people had ever suffered so much in so short a time, and their tragedy had stirred the conscience of thousands of millions of persons enamoured of peace. The whole world had turned to the Commission in the hope that it would expressly condemn the inhuman crimes of Iraq in Kuwait and come to the help of the Kuwaitis who had become hostages and prisoners in their own country. Iraq also continued to refuse to allow the media, the humanitarian organizations and the International Committees of the Red Cross and the Red Crescent to enter Kuwait, thus depriving the Kuwaitis of the medicines and food they so badly needed during the present difficult period. Kuwait hoped that the Commission would require Iraq to allow such humanitarian organizations to enter Kuwait to enable them to do their work.

72. What was happening in Kuwait was a genuine tragedy not only for the people of Kuwait but also for all mankind. The perpetrators of the crimes committed in Kuwait should be judged and punished for violating international law and undermining world peace and security. Kuwait had always desired peaceful coexistence and aspired to peace, tranquillity and stability once it had regained its freedom. It had already taken steps to reconstruct the country and bind up the wounds of the Kuwaiti people and looked forward to taking an active part in future arrangements which, it was to be hoped, would bring peace and justice to the region and its inhabitants.

E/CN.4/1991/SR.36, 27 February 1991 [*sic.*]

5. Commission on Human Rights, Forty-seventh Session, Summary Record of the 36th Meeting, 1991

[*Extract.*]

...

140. Mr. MOHAMMED (Iraq) said that the turn of events in the Gulf had confirmed the falseness of the claims made by the United States of America and its allies about the protection of human rights in the region, and had confounded all the efforts they had made, using all the vast material and media sources at their disposal, to vilify someone else - as they had done at every session of the Commission, hitting out at the socialist countries of eastern Europe, afterwards at Cuba, and currently at Iraq. The aim of the United States imperialists, the Zionists and their allies was to extend their hegemony over the Gulf region; but having encountered one Muslim country whose will could not be destroyed, their full fury had been unleashed, venting itself first through economic warfare and then, when that had failed, through military force. The discredited Kuwaiti régime had played its part by manipulating oil prices to their lowest recorded level in an attempt to destroy Iraq's economy. The aggressive aims of the oil sheiks had been amply recorded, *inter alia*, in document E/CN.4/1991/74. The events of August 1990 were not as portrayed by the United States aggressors and their puppets; what had taken place was an Islamic uprising against imperialism and its alliance with zionism, whose ultimate aims, discernible from the outset, had led to one of the most pernicious campaigns in history, involving the full panoply of materials and methods at their disposal in furtherance of their hegemonistic aims, even including the use of pressure on the United Nations to adopt unrealistic and discreditable resolutions at variance with the justice of the Arab cause.

141. The fabricated claim that Iraq had violated human rights in Kuwait was part of a campaign on which the Kuwaiti régime had spent millions of dollars in order to injure Iraq's reputation and pave the way for the launching of military aggression against it. The false allegations made to the Commission by the representative of the Al-Sabah family had been made in the same context and designed to attract the Commission's sympathy. The actions falsely attributed to Iraq were practices to which Kuwaitis had been accustomed from their own sheikhs. The Al-Sabah family was being defended by the United States and Israel for the sake of its wealth, so long as that lasted. The former Kuwaiti régime would be willing to see a world conflagration if that would enable it to return to rule over the whole of Kuwait. Its so-called Minister for Foreign Affairs had said that the former régime would support the use of chemical and nuclear weapons against Iraq in order to implement the provisions of international law, and the Speaker of the former Kuwaiti National Assembly had told the press that Kuwaitis abroad would not care about the destruction of the region, including Kuwait itself, if that was the price that had to be paid for their return. That meant that 250,000 people could be expended to enable the Al-Sabah family to resume its rule.

142. Isolated events had taken place to force the military command in Iraq to adopt some necessary laws and regulations to ensure respect for the law in the former Kuwaiti territory by imposing capital punishment on anyone who violated lives or property. Such incidents had indeed occurred throughout the world.

143. It was strange to see the United States of America and the States of Western Europe defending the interests of the Kuwaiti sheikhs as if the world had forgotten the time when the Western media had been accustomed to reporting on the evils of those sheikhs and the backwardness of their régimes and when those States had considered the behaviour of the oil sheikhs detrimental to Arab citizens and to other Arab régimes. The Western press had made much of the fact that Jabar el Ahmed had married 78 women and was unable to recognize all his children and of the fact that the vast wealth expended by the sheikhs would have been sufficient to feed thousands of hungry people throughout the world. Iraq agreed with those comments but found it surprising that they could now be forgotten, that Western representatives could appear in the Commission in defence of such backward régimes and that the West could use the Kuwaiti cause in order to injure Iraq. That opportunistic attitude, based on a selective double standard and a distortion of the principles of human rights, would have the most harmful effects on human rights prospects throughout the world.

E/CN.4/1991/SR.37, 22 April 1991

6. Commission on Human Rights, Forty-seventh Session, Summary Record of the 37th Meeting, 1991

[*Extract.*]

...

61. **Mr. Al-Othman (Observer for Kuwait)**, speaking in exercise of the right of reply, denounced the allegations made by the representative of Iraq and said he had been surprised to hear him say that colonialism was responsible for the way the borders were drawn between Iraq and the neighbouring countries. Kuwait, for its part, adhered to the 1963 agreement which recognized its full sovereignty and independence.

62. How could Iraq say that the Kuwaiti régime had conspired against it to destroy the country economically when Kuwait had lent Iraq $14 billion during the war against Iran and opened its ports to Iraq.

63. On the question of oil, he pointed out that Iraq had increased its production without keeping to the established quotas. Kuwait had tried to find a solution to the problem and had taken part in the negotiations at Jeddah. Iraq had then decided to invade it.

64. He was surprised that the delegation of Iraq had forgotten the scenario of the annexation of Kuwait. The Iraqi régime had first claimed to have given birth to a revolution. It had subsequently tried to set up a mercenary government, then had declared Kuwait a republic, thereby recognizing that it was not part of Iraq, and had eventually tried to annex it outright. The delegation of Iraq was now describing the Members of the United Nations which had voted in favour of the Security Council resolutions as puppets. Would it also describe as puppets the 144 States which had supported General Assembly resolution 170/45 on the human rights situation in occupied Kuwait?

E/CN.4/1991/SR.39, 25 April 1991

7. Commission on Human Rights, Forty-seventh Session, Summary Record of the 39th Meeting, 1991

[*Extract.*]

...

65. **Mr. Al Nouri (Observer for Kuwait)**, speaking in exercise of the right of reply, said that all the allegations made by the representative of Iraq were false and that the sources he had cited were not verifiable. What was a fact, however, was that Iraq had used chemical weapons against Iran and the Kurdish people and had threatened to use them during the Gulf war in violation of international law. Furthermore, everyone knew that the National Council instituted in Kuwait since that country's independence worked with complete integrity and had certainly not accepted the destruction of the region as the price to pay for Kuwait's liberation. It should not be forgotten that 300,000 Kuwaitis were still in the country.

66. He would also like to point out that not only the Kuwaitis but also all foreigners working in Kuwait had enjoyed the country's wealth, and that in the past 20 years, Kuwait had devoted 7.8 per cent of its national income to assistance to third world countries. The economic situation in Iraq, however, had not improved, and the Iraqi people did not even earn a strict minimum, despite the fact that the country possessed very fertile land and had very substantial oil revenues. If the representative of Iraq took the trouble to compare the situation of the Iraqi people with that of the Kuwaiti people, he would reach more accurate conclusions.

E/CN.4/1991/SR.40, 4 March 1991

8. Commission on Human Rights, Forty-seventh Session, Summary Record of the 40th Meeting, 1991

[*Extract.*]

...

124. **Mr. Weston (Observer for the United Kingdom)** said that, as British Ambassador to Kuwait, he could speak from personal experience of the human rights situation in that country after the Iraqi invasion on 2 August 1990. From that day until the day he left, all supplies to his Embassy had been cut off by Iraqi troops, including tanks, and the staff had survived thanks to its own resourcefulness. After 24 August 1990, when he was able to move with reasonable freedom around Kuwait City, he had witnessed looting and wanton destruction on a massive scale by Iraqi soldiers and civilians. They stole everything that could possibly be carried away from shops and private homes and wantonly destroyed anything that was not worth stealing.

125. Many foreign nationals had lost everything they owned and roamed the streets searching for food. Thousands of the foreign residents in Kuwait from countries such as India, Pakistan, Sri Lanka, Egypt and the Philippines were to be seen begging for assistance from their embassies, which were completely overwhelmed. The plight of the Western nationals was, perhaps, less dramatic, though many of them had had their homes broken into and there had been several cases of rape. None of the Westerners had been allowed to leave the country and the policy of detaining them and transferring them to strategic sites as human shields had already started.

126. Because he had been confined to his Embassy from 24 August 1990, he had had no direct personal evidence of the atrocities carried out by Iraqi forces apart from looting and events he could witness from his windows. Open trucks piled with stolen goods of all kinds had constantly passed the Embassy and he had seen numbers of trailers heading north and carrying yachts and motorboats, as well as heavy equipment removed from factories and workshops. Many times daily he had received telephone calls from Kuwaitis, British citizens and others with appalling reports of suffering. The

persons to whom he had spoken had given eye-witness accounts of such incidents in sickening and convincing detail, some of which had been publicized the previous week at a press conference organized in London by the All-Party Parliamentary Committee on Human Rights.

127. He had finally left Kuwait on 16 December 1990, and on the journey to the airport he had seen further evidence of the destruction caused by the Iraqi invasion. Kuwait City had been a ghost town with signs of damage everywhere. On arrival at the airport, he had seen an enormous flight simulator being taken off by truck to Baghdad to join the works of art, furniture, electrical fittings, computers, machine tools and other equipment carried off to Iraq. The looting, which he had seen with his own eyes, paled into insignificance, however, compared with the more recent accounts of the activities of Iraqi troops in Kuwait City. He paid a tribute to the courage and endurance of Kuwaiti citizens who had remained behind and to the fortitude of members of foreign communities forced to stay with them, who had lived day by day like rats in the air conditioning ducts of their houses, coming out at night only to obtain supplies to enable them to endure another day. On that day - Kuwait's National Day - he hoped and prayed that an end to its people's suffering would not be long delayed.

...

133. **Mr. AL-SABAH (Observer for Kuwait)** recalled that, a day earlier, the coalition forces had begun the last phase in the liberation of Kuwait following Iraq's rejection of the last chance to implement the resolutions of the Security Council. Kuwait prayed that God would bring an early end to the war with minimum human casualties and material losses. During the past seven months, it had been subjected to much suffering, injustice, repressive practices, destruction and aggression as a result of Iraq's barbaric occupation. That aggression, and the subsequent dispersal of the Kuwaiti people, represented a clear violation of the Charter of the United Nations, the principles set forth in the Universal Declaration of Human Rights, and all international covenants and norms. Flagrant human rights violations had been committed against all sectors of the Kuwaiti people regardless of age or gender.

134. The noble principles set forth in the preamble to the Charter of the United Nations and in the Universal Declaration of Human Rights were aimed at preserving international peace and security, protecting human rights and the dignity of individuals and saving humanity from the miseries of war, injustice, repressive practices and destruction. Those principles had been adopted to be applied for the benefit of humanity, and were not to be disregarded.

135. The Iraqi aggression which, since 2 August 1990, had been directed against the Kuwaiti people, territory and Government, had been and continued to be the most outrageous aggression in modern history. Heavily armed with hundreds of thousands of soldiers, hundreds of fighter planes and thousands of tanks and items of artillery equipment, Iraq had occupied and annexed Kuwait by force, and the occupying forces had waged an organized campaign to terrorize and murder the defenceless people - a well-prepared campaign deliberately designed to obliterate a people's identity and eliminate it from the world map. Members of the Commission were aware of the suffering of the Kuwaiti people as a result of that barbaric aggression. From the first hours of the invasion, the Iraqis had committed the most heinous crimes against Kuwaiti and non-Kuwaiti residents and had caused massive destruction of property and of the country's infrastructure. They had looted public and private properties, terrorized Kuwaiti citizens and violated their privacy and destroyed the country's security system and socio-economic infrastructure with the aim of destroying the basic foundations of Kuwaiti society. Iraqi soldiers had crossed the dividing line between humanity and savagery and committed the most cruel crimes against the peaceful Kuwaiti people, some details of which were shown in document E/CN.4/1991/70. One example was the atrocity committed against Mr. Adel El-Falah, who had been arrested at his home and later taken back on the verge of death as a result of severe torture. His wife and three young daughters had then been forced to look on while he was shot. The reason for his execution was that he had been providing food to Western nationals hiding in Kuwait. Hundreds of Kuwaiti citizens had been executed in the streets in front of their relatives and thousands killed in detention centres following severe torture. A Kuwaiti physician had reported that five or six new bodies had been brought to his hospital daily. Many of the victims, mostly in their twenties, had borne marks of torture, which had included burning by cigarettes and heated metal rods, electric shock, cutting off of tongues or ears, gouging out of the eyes and the breaking of limbs. In most cases, the immediate cause of death appeared to have been a single shot in the back of the head or in the ear or mouth.

136. His delegation was deeply concerned about recent information received from occupied Kuwait which indicated that oppressive and inhuman practices by the occupying forces continued unabated and were of an intensity and cruelty hitherto unwitnessed. Since the beginning of the operations to liberate Kuwait, arbitrary arrests had escalated. When relatives inquired about detained persons, the Iraqis would reply that they had duties to perform and would return in a few days. Information had been received that the Iraqi forces had been ordered to arrest and detain 40,000 Kuwaitis indiscriminately, which meant that there was a deliberate plan to detain all Kuwaiti men remaining in the occupied country. They had already begun to be arrested in their homes and anyone refusing to give food and medical supplies to Iraqi soldiers who had forced their way into Kuwaiti homes was shot immediately. The unprecedented brutality of the Iraqi forces and their barbaric execution of Kuwaiti detainees was an affront to human feelings. Recent information indicated that they had begun to execute male and female Kuwaiti detainees and throw their naked and mutilated bodies into the streets. Moreover, in clear violation of international law, the Iraqi forces had greatly endangered the lives of civilians in Kuwait by concentrating their military personnel and equipment in residential areas and on rooftops. Recent crimes aimed at the destruction of the economic infrastructure of Kuwait included setting fire to more than 200 oil wells, oil storage tanks, refineries, petrochemical plants and water desalination and electricity production plants, thus not only crippling Kuwait's future economic welfare but also threatening the safety of people and the environment both inside and outside Kuwait.

137. It was shameful that the country committing those crimes, and notorious for its despicable violations of human rights and of the Third and Fourth Geneva Conventions, should continue to be a member of the Commission on Human Rights. The Iraqi delegation, which had uttered nothing but fallacies designed to divert the Commission from the true situation and to falsify Kuwait's history, should not be allowed to participate in further discussions of human rights issues. Kuwait called for the prosecution of Iraqi officials for their crimes against humanity and called upon all peace-loving nations which opposed aggression and upheld the principles of human rights strongly and decisively to condemn those atrocities. His delegation, which intended to submit a draft resolution for that purpose, requested that a special rapporteur should be appointed to examine and report on the human rights violations committed in Kuwait by the Iraqi invading and occupying forces. His country would be ready to welcome the special rapporteur, when appointed, and fully co-operate with him, and would also

welcome international humanitarian organizations, particularly the International Committee of the Red Cross, to help to lessen the suffering of the Kuwaiti people.

E/CN.4/1991/SR.43, 26 April 1991

9. Commission on Human Rights, Forty-seventh Session, Summary Record of the 43rd Meeting, 1991

[*Extract.*]

...

55. **Mr. AL-KADHI (Iraq)** said that he had at first hesitated to take the floor before a Power, the United States of America, which exercised hegemony over an entire region and which showed its complete disregard for human rights by attacking Iraq. He therefore preferred to address his remarks to the other forces present in the Commission which were genuinely striving to assert fundamental human rights. Human rights existed both nationally and internationally and no State could ignore them. Iraq was perfectly aware [*sic*] of its obligations and its rights in that area, which dated as far back as the Hammurabi Code and the age of Sumer and Babylon.

56. During the last decade, the country had experienced difficulty and eight years of war had sorely tried its land and its people. Since the war had completely mobilized attention, it was inevitable that respect for human rights should suffer. But when Iraq had entered the post-war period, it had deemed it necessary to review the entire political, economic, cultural and social organization of the country and reformulate certain laws, in particular those which had curtailed the exercise of rights and freedoms during the period of armed conflict. It was in that spirit that a bill on freedom of the press and another on the multi-party system, for example, had been drafted. Some had reacted to those measures with scepticism, but it should be recalled that on 11 February 1990, the National Iraqi Human Rights Committee had invited all the members of the Sub-Commission to visit the country to ascertain the real situation there regarding the exercise of human rights. Unfortunately, the Western countries had used flimsy pretexts to prevent that visit from taking place and had checkmated an initiative which could, however, have created a precedent in the area of human rights.

57. The situation of the Iraqi citizens of Kurdish origin in Iraq had been raised by many non-governmental organizations and recently by the Observer for Luxembourg, speaking on behalf of the member States of the European Community. However, it should be emphasized that the situation of those citizens was exemplary. In fact, a distinction should be made, on the one hand, between the recognition of the national rights of the Kurds and the rebellion fomented from abroad in order to destabilize the region of Kurdistan, on the other. In Iraq, there was no discrimination between communities and faiths, and the law governing the autonomy of Kurdistan was designed to promote the legitimate interests of the Kurdish population. In the political sphere, since 1974, Iraqi citizens of Kurdish origin had been able to elect members to the Legislative Council of the autonomous region of Kurdistan. Education at the primary and secondary levels was in the Kurdish language and there were publications, a television station and radio programmes in the Kurdish language. Iraq was in fact the only country that had recognized those rights for its Kurdish population. Nevertheless, some elements had made foreign contacts in an attempt to destabilize the Iraqi régime, which was striving to combat imperialism and zionism and to secure the well-being of the population. The former United States Secretary of State, Mr. Kissinger, had himself admitted in his memoirs that his country had cooperated with the Shah of Iran to incite the Kurdish population to revolt. A distinction should therefore be made between the legitimate recognition of the rights of the Kurdish population and the intolerable machinations of outlaws.

58. The high level of development that Iraq had attained in every area, development which was necessary for the establishment of democratic institutions and the exercise of human rights, had displeased the United States, the Western countries and their ally, Israel, which felt that Iraq had overstepped the bounds to which a developing country was restricted. Consequently an extensive, though unsuccessful media campaign had been waged against Iraq for two years and an economic blockade had been imposed on the country through cooperation between the United States and the Gulf kingdoms, in particular Kuwait.

59. In the same spirit of domination, the forces of the United States, in collaboration with other European countries, in particular France and the United Kingdom, had recently launched the most extensive aggression ever perpetrated against a third world country. The result was that Iraq's industrial and economic infrastructure had been destroyed, civilian areas and shelters had been bombed and prisoners of war humiliated. The resolutions adopted by the United Nations Security Council had been exceeded, and there had been no hesitation about carrying out napalm raids, although napalm was a substance whose use had been internationally banned. Those inhuman practices had revealed what the coalition countries really felt about human rights. Despite the fact that Iraq had agreed to withdraw from Kuwait, the coalition forces had launched their land offensive exactly when the Security Council had been meeting to consider the Soviet Union's proposal for a settlement obliging the Council to close the meeting! That defiant attitude towards the United Nations did not augur well for the future role of the Organization in the maintenance of international peace and security.

60. The aggression launched against Iraq by the United States of America and certain European countries, which claimed to be seeking a new international order, proved that they wished to establish a régime similar to the one which Hitler had wanted to establish in the 1940s. Furthermore, the United States was seeking to undermine the Commission by manipulating it on a daily basis and there was a huge gulf between the country's declarations of intent and its acts.

61. The observer for Luxembourg had just announced that a hostile decision against Iraq was being contemplated within the context of the Commission. He asked the delegations of the developing countries to cooperate with Iraq, because the problem facing his country was one which affected the whole third world. It was obvious, in fact, that the United States and the Western countries did not hesitate to use their economic and military might against any country which they felt had overstepped the limits which they had set for it, in order to keep it in a state of colonization. How could the European countries, which had opposed the adoption of so many resolutions concerning Palestine and South Africa still talk about respect for human rights? The question inevitably arose as to why human rights continued to be disregarded throughout the world. It was obvious that the cause of that situation was the political and economic hegemony exercised by the Western countries over the rest of the world in blocking the progress of the developing countries. But political democracy necessarily went hand in hand with economic development.

E/CN.4/1991/SR.54, 13 March 1991

10. Commission on Human Rights, Forty-seventh Session, Summary Record of the 54th Meeting, 1991

[*Extract.*]

...

Draft resolution E/CN.4/1991/L.48/Rev.1 and E/CN.4/1991/L.90

14. **Mr. Al-Sabah (Observer for Kuwait)**, introducing the draft resolution on behalf of its sponsors, said that he wished to reaffirm his Government's commitment to respect for human rights in accordance with the principles set forth in the Charter of the United Nations and the provisions of the International Covenants on Human Rights, the Geneva Conventions of 1949 and the First Additional Protocol of 1977 Relating to the Protection of Victims of International Armed Conflicts and Hague Convention IV of 1907. In addition, the Constitution of Kuwait stated that all persons were equal before the law, a provision which applied to both Kuwaiti citizens and foreigners.

15. The Government of Kuwait had returned to its homeland, following seven months of occupation, oppression and flagrant violations of human rights. It was struggling to guarantee the security of all persons there and to restore the rule of law and order in a land which had been subjected to lawless occupation.

16. The draft resolution, having referred to the principles embodied in the Charter of the United Nations, the Universal Declaration of Human Rights, the International Covenant on Human Rights, the Geneva Conventions of 1949 and the relevant General Assembly and Security Council resolutions, reaffirmed the obligation of all Member States to promote and protect human rights and fundamental freedoms. It condemned the invasion and occupation of Kuwait on 2 August 1990 by the military forces of Iraq and deplored the refusal of Iraq to receive representatives of humanitarian organizations and a representative of the Secretary-General to help in extending humanitarian assistance to the Kuwaiti people under occupation.

17. The operative part of the draft strongly condemned the Iraqi authorities and occupying forces for their grave violations of human rights and, in particular, the acts of torture, arbitrary arrests, summary executions and disappearances. It called for the immediate release of all prisoners of war and detained civilians. It also decided to appoint a special rapporteur to examine the human rights violations committed in occupied Kuwait by the forces of Iraq who would report as soon as possible to the General Assembly and to the Commission at its forty-eighth session.

18. **Mr. Al-Kadhi (Iraq)** said that his delegation had submitted some amendments to that draft resolution (E/CN.4/1991/L.90). Referring to a statement circulated the previous day by Amnesty International on acts of revenge currently being perpetrated by Kuwaiti forces and armed civilians against Palestinians and Iraqi civilians, he said that acts of violence, including collective massacres, arbitrary arrests and torture were being committed in Kuwait. That information was also to be found in reports in the various information media.

19. Those barbarous acts against innocent civilians must also be considered by the Commission, which had a historic responsibility with regard to the fate of those persons. It should not, therefore, consider draft resolution E/CN.4/1991/L.48/Rev.1 alone, without taking the other facts into account. To do so would be to fail in its duty to make an objective and balanced examination of the situation.

20. **Mr. Elaraby (Observer for Egypt)** said that the allegations contained in the amendments to the draft resolution (E/CN.4/1991/L.90) were based on hearsay and unconfirmed reports. The text referred to the ill-treatment of Egyptian citizens in Kuwait. He wished to point out that, historically speaking, Egyptians had always been well treated in Kuwait. It was true that, under the Iraqi occupation, those who had been unable to leave the country had encountered many hardships. That was why his delegation had become a sponsor of draft resolution E/CN.4/1991/L.41/Rev.1. He hoped that the Special Rapporteur would put the facts of the situation before the Commission in his report.

21. Kuwait had been liberated and its legitimate Government restored. All available information confirmed that law and order had been reintroduced. Moreover, the 40,000-strong Egyptian force that had participated in the liberation of Kuwait was still there. The Egyptian Embassy had been reopened and was functioning. It was therefore inconceivable that Egyptians were being subjected to any violations in those circumstances. Egyptians in Kuwait were enjoying the hospitality of that country and their safety and protection were not in doubt. Members had been assured by the representative of Kuwait that his Government would spare no effort to ensure that law and order prevailed in Kuwait with respect to all its inhabitants, citizens and non-citizens alike.

22. In his opinion, therefore, the amendments to the draft resolution contained in document E/CN.4/1991/L.90 should be rejected.

23. **Ms. Andreychuk (Canada)** said that draft resolution E/CN.4/1991/L.41/Rev.1 dealt with occupied Kuwait. It would not be in keeping with good order, therefore, if the Commission failed to reject the amendments in document E/CN.4/1991/L.90, which were not on the subject of the draft resolution.

24. **Mr. Hessel (France)** said that, for the reasons given by the representative of Canada, his delegation considered it essential that the amendments put forward by the representative of Iraq in document E/CN.4/1991/L.90 should be voted on and rejected without further delay. There was no point in continuing to discuss a text that did not refer to the problem of occupied Kuwait.

25. **Mr. Al-Kadhi (Iraq)** said that, in submitting its amendment, his delegation was put pursuing tactical aims or attempting to influence the fate of draft resolution E/CN.4/1991/L.48/Rev.1. While he certainly hoped that Egyptian citizens in Kuwait had not been subjected to violations of human rights, he wished to point out that the facts referred to came from neutral sources such as the international press and Amnesty International.

26. **Mr. Zamir (Bangladesh)** said that his delegation, which supported the proposal by the representative of France, wished to become a sponsor of draft resolution E/CN.4/1991/L.48/Rev.1.

27. **The Chairman** said that the observer for Liechtenstein should also be added to the list of sponsors of draft resolution E/CN.4/1991/L.48/Rev.1.

28. He invited the Commission to vote on draft resolution E/CN.4/1991/L.90.

29. *Draft resolution E/CN.4/1991/L.90 was rejected by 32 votes to 2, with 5 abstentions.*

30. **Mr. Pace (Secretary of the Commission)** said, with regard to the financial implications of draft resolution E/CN.4/1991/L.48/Rev.1, that the activities referred to in operative paragraph 12 would require the special rapporteur to undertake a trip to Geneva for a period of five working days in June/July 1991 for the purpose of holding consultations at the Centre for Human Rights. In July/August 1991, the special rapporteur would have to make a field trip to Kuwait for a period of

10 working days to collect information on the spot and then proceed to Geneva for five working days to prepare and finalize his report to the General Assembly. In October/December 1991, the special rapporteur would need to spend five working days in New York. In December 1991/January 1992, he would have to visit Geneva for a period of five working days to prepare his report for the Commission. In February/March 1992, the special rapporteur would again have to visit Geneva for a period of five working days to submit his report to the Commission at its forty-eighth session.

31. The relevant estimated costs would be $US 79,400 in 1991 and $US 14,200 in 1992. The costs of two interpreters to accompany the special rapporteur on his field mission would be $US 10,000. The cost of translating an estimated 100 pages from Arabic into English or another working language to facilitate information processing by the special rapporteur would be included in the regular budget. The draft resolution was considered to be within the scope of the Commission's perennial activities and resources would therefore be provided from the existing provision for the Economic and Social Council mandates under Section 23 and Section 28, respectively.

32. **Mr. AL-KADHI (Iraq),** speaking in explanation of vote before the vote, said that all the members of the Commission were aware that the aggression against Iraq had started not on 2 August 1990 but at the end of the Iran/Iraq War. That aggression had taken a number of forms aimed at destroying the military and economic structure of Iraq, after the United States and its Western allies had failed in their attack on Iraq using traditional and well-known methods. Iraq had acquired power that threatened their interests and designs in the area, which were concerned with the supply of natural resources, particularly oil.

33. Those circles had made use of the mass media to distort the international image of Iraq and to mislead world public opinion. The information media of those Powers were continuing to distort the facts and to cite false witnesses. A few days previously, for instance, television broadcasts had shown the bodies of Iraqi soldiers who had fallen victim to aggressive forces, alleging that they were the bodies of persons tortured by the Iraqi forces.

34. The draft resolution under consideration was yet another link in the chain of the campaign to tarnish Iraq's international image and he hoped that those delegations which really believed in human rights would understand the situation and adopt an appropriate position. Apart from any other consideration, the draft resolution had been overtaken by events. First of all, his Government had accepted the Security Council resolutions. Secondly, it had not rejected the humanitarian assistance offered by various humanitarian organizations, in particular medicine. Thirdly, with regard to the treatment of prisoners of war, members had heard the representative of the International Committee of the Red Cross state that all the prisoners were in good health. Furthermore, Iraq had freed all prisoners of war in accordance with the Geneva Conventions. Most of the provisions of the draft resolution were thus pointless and it was clearly being submitted for political reasons.

35. *At the request of the representative of Iraq, a vote was taken on draft resolution E/CN.4/1991/L.48/Rev.l.*

36. *Draft resolution E/CN.4/1991/L.48/Rev.1 was adopted by 41 votes to 1.*

E/CN.4/1991/91, at 167.

11. UN Commission on Human Rights, Resolution 1991/67, The Situation of Human Rights in Kuwait under Iraqi Occupation

The Commission on Human Rights,

Guided by the principles embodied in the Charter of the United Nations, the Universal Declaration of Human Rights, the International Covenant on Human Rights, the Geneva Conventions of 12 August 1949 and Additional Protocol I of 1977 thereto and The Hague Convention IV of 1907,

Recalling General Assembly resolution 45/170 of 18 December 1990 concerning the situation of human rights in occupied Kuwait,

Also recalling Security Council resolutions 661 (1990) of 6 August 1990, paragraphs 3 (c) and 4, 666 (1990) of 13 September 1990 and 686 (1991) of 2 March 1991,

Aware of its responsibility to promote and encourage respect for human rights and fundamental freedoms for all and resolved to remain vigilant with regard to violations of human rights wherever they occur,

Reaffirming that all Member States have an obligation to promote and protect human rights and fundamental freedoms and to fulfil their obligations under the relevant international instruments,

Condemning the invasion and occupation of Kuwait on 2 August 1990 by the military forces of Iraq,

Concerned that the acts of the Iraqi forces in occupied Kuwait have caused enormous human suffering to the civilian population,

Noting with grave concern the abduction from Kuwait and the continued detention of prisoners of war and civilians,

Noting also with grave concern the information to the effect that the treatment of prisoners of war and detained civilians does not conform to the internationally recognized principles of humanitarian law,

Deploring the refusal of Iraq to receive representatives of humanitarian organizations, especially representatives of the International Committee of the Red Cross, and a representative of the Secretary-General, to help in extending humanitarian assistance to the Kuwaiti people under occupation,

1. *Strongly condemns* the Iraqi authorities and occupying forces for their grave violations of human rights against the Kuwaiti people and nationals of other States and in particular the acts of torture, arbitrary arrests, summary executions and disappearances in violation of the Charter of the United Nations, the International Covenants on Human Rights, and other relevant legal instruments;

2. *Expresses its serious concern* about the systematic destruction, dismantling and pillaging of the economic infrastructure of Kuwait, which seriously undermined the present and future enjoyment by the Kuwaiti people of their economic, social and cultural rights;

3. *Demands* that Iraq comply with its obligations under the Charter of the United Nations and the contemporary norms of international law;

4. *Condemns* the rejection by Iraq of the offer of the Government of Kuwait and various humanitarian organizations to send humanitarian assistance, especially medicine, to the Kuwaiti people under occupation;

5. *Strongly condemns* the failure of Iraq to treat all prisoners of war and detained civilians in accordance with the internationally recognized principles of humanitarian law and insists that it refrain from subjecting them to acts of violence, including ill-treatment, torture and summary execution;

6. *Demands* that Iraq release immediately all prisoners of war and detained civilians;

7. *Condemns further* the failure of Iraq to ensure respect for international standards applicable under international law, in particular with reference to the protection of the civilian population, and its failure to cooperate fully with representatives of humanitarian organizations, especially the International Committee of the Red Cross, and give them access to Kuwait, and to allow them to extend humanitarian assistance to the civilian population of Kuwait;

8. *Welcomes* the intention of the Government of Kuwait to provide access to the International Committee of the Red Cross and other humanitarian organizations in order to assist in caring for the civilian population of Kuwait;

9. *Decides* to appoint an individual of recognized international standing as special rapporteur with a mandate to examine the human rights violations committed in occupied Kuwait by the invading and occupying forces of Iraq and to report as soon as possible to the General Assembly and to the Commission on Human Rights at its forty-eighth session;

10. *Requests* the Chairman of the Commission at its forty-seventh session, in consultation with the Bureau, to designate the special rapporteur;

11. *Authorizes* the Special Rapporteur to seek relevant information from the Government of Kuwait, the specialized agencies and intergovernmental and non-governmental organizations;

12. *Requests* the Special Rapporteur to prepare a preliminary report as soon as possible and to transmit it to the Secretary-General for dissemination to all Member States;

13. *Requests* the Secretary-General to provide all necessary assistance to the special rapporteur to enable him to carry out his mandate in the best possible conditions;

14. *Decides* to consider the situation of human rights in Kuwait under Iraqi occupation at its forty-eighth session.

BIO/2573, HR/CN/253, IK/22, 5 June 1991

12. Press Release: Walter Kalin Appointed Special Rapporteur on Human Rights in Kuwait under Iraqi Occupation, 4 June 1991

GENEVA, 4 June (UN Information Service) - The Chairman of the forty-seventh session of the Commission on Human Rights, Enrique Bernales Ballesteros, has appointed Walter Kalin, a professor of constitutional and international public law at the University of Berne, as Special Rapporteur on the human rights situation in Kuwait under Iraqi occupation. In accordance with the Commission's resolution 1991/67 of 6 March, the Special Rapporteur's mandate was to examine the reports of human rights violations committed in occupied Kuwait by the invading and occupying forces of Iraq and to report as soon as possible to the General Assembly and to the Commission on Human Rights. The resolution also authorizes the Special Rapporteur to seek relevant information from the Government of Kuwait, the specialized agencies and intergovernmental and non-governmental organizations.

Mr. Kalin, who was born in Zurich in 1951, is a member of several non-governmental organizations active in the field of development and human rights and has served on various occasions as a consultant for the Swiss Parliament and the Federal Administration on matters related to human rights. He is also the author of a number of books and articles on constitutional, refugee and human rights matters. He is married with two children.

E/CN.4/1992/84, at 140.

13. UN Commission on Human Rights, Resolution 1992/60, The Situation of Human Rights in Kuwait under Iraqi Occupation

The Commission on Human Rights,

Recalling its resolution 1991/67 of 6 March 1991,

Recalling also General Assembly resolution 46/135 of 17 December 1991,

Guided by the principles embodied in the Charter of the United Nations, the Universal Declaration of Human Rights, the International Covenants on Human Rights, the Geneva Conventions of 12 August 1949, The Hague Convention IV of 1907, and other internationally recognized principles of humanitarian law,

Aware of its responsibility to promote and encourage respect for human rights and fundamental freedoms for all and resolved to remain vigilant with regard to violations of human rights wherever they occur,

Reaffirming that all Member States have an obligation to promote and protect human rights and fundamental freedoms and to fulfil their obligations under the relevant international instruments,

Expressing its deep concern at the grave violation of human rights and fundamental freedoms during the occupation of Kuwait,

Noting with grave concern the continued detention of prisoners of war and civilians abducted from Kuwait and the refusal of Iraq to account for the whereabouts of these detainees,

Noting also with grave concern the information to the effect that the treatment of prisoners of war and detained civilians does not conform to the internationally recognized principles of humanitarian law,

1. *Expresses its appreciation* to the Special Rapporteur on the situation of human rights in Kuwait under Iraqi occupation for his report (E/CN.4/1992/26) [*not reproduced*];

2. *Expresses its deep concern* for Kuwaiti and third-country nationals detained and missing in Iraq;

3. *Strongly condemns* the failure of Iraq to treat all prisoners of war and detained civilians in accordance with the internationally recognized principles of humanitarian law and insists that it refrain from subjecting them to acts of violence, including ill-treatment, torture and summary execution;

4. *Requests* the Government of Iraq to provide full information on all Kuwaiti persons and third-country nationals abducted from Kuwait between 2 August 1990 and 26 February 1991 who may still be detained, and to free these persons without delay, in accordance with its obligations under article 118 of the Geneva Convention relative to Prisoners of War and article 134 of the Geneva Convention relative to the Protection of Civilian Persons in Time of War and its obligations under aplicable Security Council resolutions;

5. *Also requests* the Government of Iraq to provide, in accordance with its obligations under articles 120 and 121 of the Geneva Convention relative to Prisoners of War, and articles 129 and 130 of the Geneva Convention relative to the Protection of Civilian Persons in Time of War, detailed information on persons arrested in Kuwait between 2 August 1990 and 26 February 1991 who may have died during or after that period while in detention, as well as on the location of their graves;

6. *Further requests* the Government of Iraq to search for the persons still missing and to cooperate fully with international humanitarian organizations such as the International Committee of the Red Cross, in this regard;

7. *Demands* that the Government of Iraq cooperate with and facilitate the work of international humanitarian

organizations, notably the International Committee of the Red Cross, in their search for an eventual repatriation of Kuwaiti and third-country nationals detained and missing in Iraq.

E/CN.4/1992/84, at 296.

14. Report of the UN Commission on Human Rights, the Situation of Human Rights in Kuwait under Iraqi Occupation

...

509. In connection with agenda item 12 (b), the Commission had before it the following documents:

Note by the Secretary-General on the situation of human rights in Kuwait under Iraqi occupation (A/46/544 and Corr.1);

Report on the situation of human rights in Kuwait under Iraqi occupation, prepared by Mr. Walter Kalin, Special Rapporteur of the Commission, in accordance with Commission resolution 1991/67 (E/CN.4/1992/26);

Letter dated 2 January 1992 from the Permanent Mission of Iraq to the United Nations Office at Geneva addressed to the Centre for Human Rights (E/CN.4/1992/64).

510. At the 34th meeting, on 19 February 1992, the Special Rapporteur on the situation of human rights in Kuwait under Iraqi occupation, Mr Walter Kalin, introduced his report (E/CN.4/1992/26) to the Commission.

511. Statements 3/ were made by the following members of the Commission: Austria (41st), Canada (42nd), Portugal (on behalf of the European Community and its member States) (35th), Russian Federation (42nd).

512. The Commission also heard statements by the observers for: Bahrain (40th), Finland (43rd), Kuwait (34th), Oman (41st), Qatar (34th), Sweden (39th), United Arab Emirates (36th).

513. Statements were also made by the following non-governmental organizations: American Association of Jurists (40th), Arab Organization for Human Rights (34th), World Movement of Mothers (36th).

514. Statements in exercise of the right of reply or its equivalent were made by the representative of Iraq (34th) and the observer for Kuwait (34th).

515. At the 52nd meeting, on 3 March 1992, the representative of Kuwait introduced draft resolution E/CN.4/1992/L.46, sponsored by Argentina, Australia, Bahrain, Bhutan, Costa Rica, Egypt, the Gambia, Hungary, India, Kenya, Kuwait, Lebanon, Oman, Pakistan, Portugal, Qatar, Saudi Arabia, Senegal, Somalia, the Syrian Arab Republic, the United Arab Emirates, and the United States of America.

516. Statements relating to the draft resolution were made by the representative of Iraq and the observer for Kuwait.

517. At the same meeting, the representative of Iraq proposed amendments to draft resolution E/CN.4/1992/L.46, as follows:

(a) In operative paragraph 6, replace "the Government of Iraq" by "the Governments of Iraq, Kuwait and Saudi Arabia";

(b) In operative paragraph 7, replace "the Government of Iraq" by "the Governments of Iraq, Kuwait and Saudi Arabia" and replace "an eventual repatriation of Kuwaiti and third-country nationals detained and missing in Iraq" by "an eventual repatriation of Kuwaitis, Iraqis and third-country nationals detained and missing in Iraq, Kuwait and Saudi Arabia".

518. The representative of the United States of America requested a vote on the amendments proposed by the representative of Iraq. At the request of the representative of Iraq, a roll-call vote was taken. The amendments were rejected by 28 votes to 1, with 20 abstentions. The voting was as follows:

In favour: Iraq.

Against: Argentina, Australia, Austria, Bangladesh, Brazil, Bulgaria, Canada, Czech and Slovak Federal Republic, France, Gambia, Germany, Hungary, India, Indonesia, Italy, Japan, Kenya, Netherlands, Pakistan, Philippines, Portugal, Russian Federation, Senegal, Somalia, Syrian Arab Republic, United Kingdom of Great Britain and Northern Ireland, United States of America, Uruguay.

Abstaining: Angola, Burundi, Chile, China, Colombia, Costa Rica, Cuba, Cyprus, Gabon, Ghana, Iran (Islamic Republic of), Lesotho, Madagascar, Mexico, Nigeria, Peru, Sri Lanka, Venezuela, Yugoslavia, Zambia.

519. A statement in explanation of vote after the vote was made by the representative of Iraq.

520. At the request of the representative of Iraq, a roll-call vote was taken on draft resolution E/CN.4/1992/L.46. The draft resolution was adopted by 47 votes to 1, with 1 abstention. The voting was as follows:

In favour: Angola, Argentina, Australia, Austria, Bangladesh, Brazil, Bulgaria, Burundi, Canada, Chile, China, Colombia, Costa Rica, Cuba, Cyprus, Czech and Slovak Federal Republic, France, Gambia, Germany, Ghana, Hungary, India, Indonesia, Iran (Islamic Republic of), Italy, Japan, Kenya, Lesotho, Madagascar, Mexico, Netherlands, Nigeria, Pakistan, Peru, Philippines, Portugal, Russian Federation, Senegal, Somalia, Sri Lanka, Syrian Arab Republic, United Kingdom of Great Britain and Northern Ireland, United States of America, Uruguay, Venezuela, Yugoslavia, Zambia.

Against: Iraq.

Abstaining: Gabon.

...

4. PROPOSALS FOR A PEACEFUL TERMINATION OF THE OCCUPATION OF KUWAIT

The period of hectic negotiations and diplomatic initiatives from the adoption of Resolution 678 (1990) to the commencement of hostilities is detailed in the chronology at the beginning of this volume. This section reproduces a number communications to the Security Council in which member States set out conditions for a possible peaceful settlement. Earlier initiatives of this kind have been covered in chapter 6 of Volume I in this Series. While these initiatives were undertaken, the international coalition forces at the Gulf were being assembled, as is described in an unofficial Foreign and Commonwealth Office briefing note at the beginning of this section.

Foreign and Commonwealth Office
The Gulf Crisis: Briefing Note
[*Not an official document.*]
November 1990

1. FCO Briefing: The Multinational Force, November 1990

A unique coalition of forces from more than 25 countries has so far been established in the Gulf. They came in response to requests from Kuwait, Saudi Arabia and other Gulf States after Iraq's invasion of Kuwait on 2 August. This is the largest multinational force assembled since the emergency in Korea in 1950. It is an extremely potent reminder to President Saddam Hussein that if he does not comply with the Security Council Resolutions, other options exist to ensure his withdrawal from Kuwait.

International reaction to Iraq's invasion and destruction of Kuwait has been so strong that countries from all continents, even those without direct interests in the Middle East, are represented in the force. Senegal, Niger and Argentina are all despatching contingents. Many countries which have not been able to send ground troops are contributing to the naval and air capability of the international force. Canada has sent two destroyers and a squadron of fighter aeroplanes; Australia has deployed warships; Spain, Italy, Belgium, Denmark and the Netherlands have sent warships and aircraft, and other countries have offered to help with transport of men or equipment. Eastern Europe is playing a useful role with specialist contributions from Czechoslovakia and Poland.

The majority of the multinational force is deployed in Saudi Arabia, but elements are also based in other Gulf States. The USA, which has so far deployed over 200,000 troops and some 40 warships, has the largest presence in the area. But Muslim and Arab States from the region, like Saudi Arabia, Egypt, Syria and the countries of the Gulf Cooperation Council (Bahrain, Kuwait, Oman, Qatar and the United Arab Emirates) are also playing a very substantial part. In addition, Morocco, Bangladesh and Pakistan have sent significant contingents. Of the European nations who have sent forces, Britain's contribution is the most significant, with more than 16,000 troops deployed. France has sent strong naval and air forces, together with 4,000 ground troops, with more on the way.

The initial deployments to the Gulf were made by the United States and Britain to counter the threat that Iraq would extend its aggression to Saudi Arabia; this remains the force's prime aim. The other objective of the participating nations is to secure the removal of Iraqi forces from Kuwait and the restoration of the legitimate Kuwaiti Government, in accordance with United Nations Security Council Resolutions. To this end, a naval force of more than 100 ships from 12 countries is ensuring that the UN trade embargo is effectively implemented.

Unfounded anxieties

Religious groups in a number of countries have expressed concern at the presence of large numbers of armed forces, including non-Muslim troops, in Saudi Arabia, where Islam's two holiest places (Mecca and Medina) are situated. However, the main elements of the multinational force are deployed to the north of the country and are far away from the Holy Places. The areas around the Holy Places are forbidden to non-Muslims and the Saudis enforce this policy strictly. Many Islamic groups will have been reassured that the issue was considered by the Muslim World League at its Mecca Conference on 12 September, where it was concluded that Saudi Arabia's request for foreign military assistance was in accordance with Islamic law.

Some radical groups view the presence of European, and especially American, forces as evidence of their colonialist ambitions in the Middle East. Western leaders have made it clear that their forces will only remain in the area as long as the host countries believe that they have a job to do. President Bush said at the Helsinki Summit meeting in September: "The sooner our forces are out of the region the better. I have no intention of keeping them there a day longer than necessary" - a statement which precisely reflects British views on participation in the international force.

A/45/888, S/22018, 19 December 1990

2. Letter from the Permanent Representative of Italy to the United Nations addressed to the Secretary-General, 17 December 1990

I have the honour to transmit the texts, in English and French, of the Declarations on the Gulf Crisis ..., on the Middle East ..., issued by the Twelve States members of the European Community at the European Council held in Rome on 14 and 15 December 1990. ...

Declaration on the Gulf crisis

1. The European Community and its member States remain firmly committed to full implementation of the United Nations Security Council resolutions. Complete Iraqi withdrawal from Kuwait and the restoration of Kuwaiti sovereignty and of its legitimate Government remain the absolute conditions for a peaceful solution of the crisis.

2. Security Council resolution 678 (1990) sends the clearest possible signal to Iraq that the international community is determined to ensure full restoration of international legality. The responsibility lies on the Iraqi Government to ensure peace for its people by complying fully with the demands of the United Nations Security Council, in particular by a complete withdrawal from Kuwait by 15 January.

3. The European Community and its member States earnestly hope that implementation of the United Nations Security Council resolutions can be peacefully secured. To this end, they support a dialogue of the sort President Bush has offered. They also favour action by the Secretary-General of the United Nations and hope that the Security Council's permanent members will remain actively involved as well. They wish Arab countries to continue to play an important role in the efforts for a peaceful solution. The European Community and its member States underline the value of a contact between the Presidency and the Foreign Minister of Iraq, aimed at securing, in co-ordination with other members of the international community, full compliance with the Security Council resolutions.

4. The European Council expresses relief at Iraq's decision to release all foreign hostages, but underlines its deep concern at Iraq's failure to withdraw from Kuwait, at its oppressive and inhuman occupation of Kuwait and its attempt to destroy the fabric of the country.

S/22044, 3 January 1991

3. Letter from the Permanent Representative of Kuwait to the United Nations addressed to the Secretary-General, 2 January 1991

I have the honour to transmit to you herewith the text of a statement by the Kuwaiti Minister for Affairs relating to the Council of Ministers concerning international moves designed to put an end to the criminal occupation of Kuwait by Iraq.

...

Kuwait is following attentively international moves designed to put an end to the criminal occupation of Kuwait by Iraq, particularly the dispatch, several times, of the current President of the European Economic Community, the Minister for Foreign Affairs of Luxembourg, in order to reaffirm the Community's position on the question of the occupation of Kuwait.

Strongly convinced that the European Economic Community consistently represents an influential force capable of compelling the aggressor Iraqi régime to yield to the will of the international community, Kuwait wishes, in this critical situation, to stress the following points:

1. There is absolutely no way out of the grave situation into which the perfidious occupation of the State of Kuwait by Iraq has thrust the region other than to compel the Iraqi régime to implement fully and unconditionally all the decisions of the Security Council by the date set by the Council in its resolution 678.

2. Kuwait believes that the initiative of the European Economic Community reaffirming the Community's known, unified position and its commitment to full implementation of all the resolutions of the Security Council is designed to strengthen the international front against the aggressor Iraqi régime, with a view to compelling it to comply with the Council's resolutions on the occupation of the territory of the State of Kuwait.

3. The State of Kuwait, while appreciating all international efforts undertaken with a view to the implementation of the resolutions of the Security Council, reaffirms that the Iraqi régime seeks to exploit any form of intervention - whatever good intentions underlie the intervention - in order to accomplish its purpose, namely, to break out of the international isolation imposed on it and to consolidate its iniquitous occupation of Kuwait, by playing for time and prolonging the occupation and its violations of the resolutions of the Security Council, with the aim of weakening the position of the international community, which resolutely rejects the continuation of the Iraqi occupation, reaffirming the need to implement the will of the international community by liberating Kuwait and by ensuring unconditional withdrawal by Iraq from all Kuwaiti territory and the return of the legitimate Government of Kuwait, under the leadership of His Majesty the Amir of Kuwait, Sheikh Jaber Al-Ahmad Al-Jaber Al-Sabah.

We implore God to bring us a speedy victory and to liberate Kuwait from the horrors of the occupation.

UN Press Release, 4 January 1991

4. Comments made by the Secretary-General on the Gulf Crisis, 3 January 1991

Remarks made by the Secretary-General to the press at the Secretariat entrance on 3 January at approximately 9:30 a.m.

Q: Do you have any comments on the recently announced initiative by the United States for a meeting between Secretary of State Baker and Foreign Minister Tariq Aziz next week in Switzerland?

Secretary-General: I think any initiative in the sense of starting a dialogue between the Iraqis and the Western countries is something positive. In the 12 days that are left, I think that every effort should be made in order to find a solution to the present impasse. I myself am doing my best quietly and I hope that all those that have some influence could do something in the next 12 days.

Remarks made by the Secretary-General to the press at the Secretariat entrance on 3 January at approximately 1.10 p.m.

Q: What is your response to the dates that were chosen, the dates that the US is suggesting?

Secretary-General: I think that the American move has been the right move in the sense of presenting a new option to the Iraqis which I hope very much they will accept. My feeling is that in the next 12 days, we have all to be extremely active in order that military action does not take place.

Q: And how about you personally?

Secretary-General: Today is the first day that I have been in my office and I have been very active with the President of the Security Council and with the Ambassador of Luxembourg, since Luxembourg is now chairing the Twelve, and in my own quiet manner I am doing my best to be in touch with all parties concerned.

Q: Including Baghdad?

Secretary-General: I will go to Baghdad if they want me to be in touch with them. But I am as well in touch with the Iraqis and I hope that tomorrow I will see the Ambassador of Iraq - who I understand comes back today - in order to explore all possibilities to avoid a military conflagration.

Q: Is this a diplomatic initiative on your part or is that going too far to describe it that way?

Secretary-General: Well, I wouldn't say "initiative" in the sense that it is a proposed formula, because it is too early for that. What we need is to start a dialogue either directly between the Americans and their allies and the Iraqis, or through any third party, including the Secretary-General, among others. At the same time we have to be very careful not to duplicate efforts, not to give the impression that we are too many - as I used to say, "too many cooks in the kitchen" - in order not to create confusion. But I am persuaded by the initiative of the Americans and their allies that everyone wants to avoid a military conflagration.

Q: A lot of press people have wondered about the date of 15 January: is there a time limit, how do you read the resolution, when is this big deadline?

Secretary-General: I am afraid that there is a tremendous misunderstanding. People think that on the 15th of January they will start shooting, but that is not what the resolution says. Of course that is one option but there are other options, for instance to take other measures. Perhaps the Security Council could decide to apply other sanctions or to take another measure which is not a military action.

Q: Is it your understanding that it is at midnight on the 15 that authorises these other means?

Secretary-General: I think that it could be that the Security Council might perhaps meet before the 15th in order to see what would happen if the Iraqis don't withdraw on that very day. I think it is wrong to create this kind of "psychosis of war" on the 15 of January.

Q: When you say for the Security Council to get together before the 15th, it doesn't have to, I mean the way the resolution is, the authorization is already there?

Secretary-General: But if they know, for instance, that on the 15th at midnight nothing has happened, it is for the Security Council to see because it is their resolution and they may want to say, "What are we going to do because our resolution was not implemented?"

Remarks by the Secretary-General to the press at the Security Council Chamber entrance on 3 January at approximately 7.20 p.m.

Q: Can you tell us more about your proposal for a Security Council meeting?

Secretary-General: There has been a tremendous misunderstanding. First of all, it is not for me to make proposals to the Security Council. What I said is if on the 15th of January at midnight nothing happens, if the Iraqis do not withdraw, then it will be for the members of the Security Council to decide what to do in accordance with their own resolution.

Q: Does it mean that you would wish another resolution before the deadline of January 15?

Secretary-General: I don't think that before the deadline there is room for any resolution because the resolution is already there.

Q: Has anyone approached you among the members of the Council on an initiative on the Gulf crisis?

Secretary-General: All the members know that I am quietly in touch with all parties in order to see how I can contribute to a solution to the present crisis.

S/22050, 8 January 1991

5. Letter from the Permanent Representative of the Union of Soviet Socialist Republics to the United Nations addressed to the Secretary-General, 8 January 1991

I have the honour to transmit herewith the text of a statement issued on 4 January by the Ministry of Foreign Affairs of the Union of Soviet Socialist Republics.

...

The Soviet Union is consistently keeping to the objective of a peaceful political solution of the crisis in the Persian Gulf. In the course of recent days, the Soviet side has undertaken active efforts with a view to facilitating the arrangement of a direct dialogue between the United States and Iraq, without which it would be hard to imagine the possibility of any agreement on a peaceful outcome.

This particular endeavour constituted a major topic of the talks with Iraqi President S. Hussein and other Iraqi leaders which were conducted at the end of December 1990 in Baghdad by I.S. Byelousov, Deputy Chairman of the Council of Ministers of the USSR and leader of the interdepartmental working group set up by order of the President of the USSR. More specifically, this topic was discussed, on the instructions of the Soviet Minister for Foreign Affairs, with Iraq's Deputy Prime Minister and Minister for Foreign Affairs, T. Aziz, by the Head of the Middle East and North Africa Department of the Soviet Ministry of Foreign Affairs, V.I. Kolotusha, who was also in Baghdad.

Parallel contact was, of course, made with the representatives of the United States.

Opinions were also exchanged with other countries, particularly with Arab States, and with the Chairman of the Movement of Non-Aligned Countries. Consultations were held in Moscow on 3 December with Abu Mazen, Co-Chairman of the Soviet-Palestinian Committee on the Middle East and a member of the Executive Committee of the Palestine Liberation Organization.

The new initiative of United States President G. Bush, suggesting that a meeting be held between United States Secretary of State J. Baker and Iraq's Minister for Foreign Affairs in Switzerland on 7, 8 or 9 January, was welcomed in the Soviet Union. We hope that the United States President's proposal will meet with a positive response from the leadership of Iraq. Hopes for a breakthrough in the acutely critical situation in the Persian Gulf region, in accordance with the corresponding Security Council resolutions, are naturally focused on the conduct of a direct United States-Iraqi dialogue. The pause of goodwill must close with a victory for common sense and bring assurance that justice and stability will be restored in the Persian Gulf region.

S/22063, 11 January 1991

6. Letter from the Chargé d'affaires a.i. of the Permanent Mission of Pakistan to the United Nations addressed to the Secretary-General, 10 January 1991

I have the honour to attach herewith a message dated 10 January 1991 addressed to you by His Excellency Mr. Muhammad Nawaz Sharif, Prime Minister of the Islamic Republic of Pakistan.

...

The mounting crisis in the Gulf has brought the region close to catastrophe. It is evident that the situation in the Gulf is approaching the edge of a precipice, stepping beyond which can only lead to widespread devastation. It is in the shadow of this sombre reality that I address this letter to Your Excellency in the knowledge that you share with me the desire for a peaceful resolution of the crisis caused by the Iraqi occupation of Kuwait.

As Your Excellency is aware Pakistan has always opposed interference and intervention in the affairs of other States. We believe in the principle of non-use of force in international relations and the inadmissibility of the acquisition of territory by force. We believe that the maintenance of peaceful international order, in which small, weak and vulnerable States can continue to enjoy their independence, sovereignty and territorial integrity depends entirely on a firm adherence to these basic principles of international law. It is this fundamental belief that has led us to support all Security Council resolutions adopted on the crisis in the Gulf since the Iraqi invasion of Kuwait. We believe that the full implementation of these resolutions, including the immediate, unconditional and total withdrawal of Iraqi occupation forces from Kuwait and the restoration of the sovereignty, independence and territorial integrity of Kuwait and its legitimate Government forms the basis for a peaceful settlement.

It is my firm belief that a war in the Gulf will bring in its wake a major political, economic and ecological disaster for the countries directly involved in the conflict as well as for the entire region and indeed for the world. It is therefore essential for Iraq to withdraw unconditionally from Kuwait in order that such a cataclysm is averted. The international community must intensify its efforts to seek a peaceful way out of the present impasse, on the basis of respect of international law and norms of inter-State behaviour.

I was considerably encouraged to learn of your visit to Baghdad to engage in a dialogue with the Iraqi leadership. I would like to convey to you the full support of the Government and the people of Pakistan for your mission of peace and sincerely hope that it will contribute towards achieving a peaceful settlement of the crisis in the Gulf. I would also like to assure you of Pakistan's readiness to assist your Excellency in any appropriate manner, for safeguarding and preserving peace and security in the region.

S/22064, 11 January 1991

7. Letter from the Permanent Representative of the Ukrainian Soviet Socialist Republic to the United Nations addressed to the Secretary-General, 11 January 1991

I have the honour to transmit herewith the text of a statement issued on 11 January 1991 by the Ministry of Foreign Affairs of the Ukrainian Soviet Socialist Republic.

...

The course of events in the Persian Gulf region has reached a critical stage. The hopes which peoples had set on the meeting between United States Secretary of State James Baker and Iraqi Minister for Foreign Affairs Tariq Aziz were not, unfortunately, fulfilled. The collective will of the international community, which was demonstrated by the United Nations Security Council's resolutions in favour of a peaceful settlement of the crisis, are in essence being ignored by the leadership of Iraq.

All this gives rise to deep concern in the Ukraine. The Ukrainian SSR expressed its position *vis-à-vis* the Iraq-Kuwait conflict on the day it first erupted. In its statement on this subject, the Supreme Soviet of the Republic noted in particular that the Ukraine considers the use of force to settle any international conflicts not caused by acts of armed aggression to be unacceptable and stated that Iraqi forces must be withdrawn from the territory of Kuwait and the conflict solved by peaceful means.

In its address to the United Nations General Assembly at its forty-fifth session, the Ukrainian delegation called for the full restoration and safeguarding of the sovereignty, national independence and territorial integrity of occupied Kuwait and emphasized that this must be achieved by political means.

In these troubled times, the Ukrainian SSR would like to draw the attention of all parties, and particularly of the Iraqi leadership, to their major responsibility for any possible dangerous turn of events in the region. Obviously, a further exacerbation of the conflict would bring the threat of massive military action whose disastrous consequences are difficult to envisage.

The present situation in the Persian Gulf requires that everyone make the utmost effort to seek ways of solving the conflict peacefully. In this regard, the Ukrainian SSR sincerely wishes United Nations Secretary-General Javier Pérez de Cuéllar success in the complicated mission which he is undertaking to remove the threat of war.

All remaining possibilities for a peaceful settlement of the conflict must be explored.

S/22066, 11 January 1991

8. Letter from the Permanent Representatives of Egypt, Saudi Arabia and the Syrian Arab Republic to the United Nations addressed to the Secretary-General, 11 January 1991

We have the honour to transmit herewith a copy of the communiqué issued by the Ministers for Foreign Affairs of Egypt, Saudi Arabia and the Syrian Arab Republic following their fourth round of co-ordination and consultation, held at Riyadh on 5 and 6 January 1991.

...

Proceeding from their faith in the unity of the common Arab destiny and adherence to all Arab conventions and recognizing the importance of - and the need to continue - co-ordination and regular periodic consultation for the purpose of defending Arab and patriotic interests, the Ministers for Foreign Affairs of Egypt, Saudi Arabia and the Syrian Arab Republic held their fourth round of co-ordination and consultation at Riyadh from 19 to 20 Jumada II A.H. 1411, corresponding to 5 to 6 January A.D. 1991.

At the beginning of the session, His Royal Highness Prince Saud al-Faisal, Minister for Foreign Affairs of Saudi Arabia, informed His Excellency Dr. Esmat Abdel Meguid, Deputy Prime Minister and Minister for Foreign Affairs of Egypt, and His Excellency Mr. Farouk al-Shara', Minister for Foreign Affairs of the Syrian Arab Republic, of the results of meetings held by the Supreme Council of the Gulf Co-operation Council at Doha, as well as of the favourable and positive reaction of leaders of the Gulf Co-operation Council States to the evolution of co-operation and co-ordination with Egypt and the Syrian Arab Republic and their determination to make such co-operation a regular and established practice in all spheres.

The Ministers for Foreign Affairs then devoted their meetings to consideration of the critical situation resulting from Iraq's continued occupation of Kuwait. They reviewed the latest developments in the light of international contacts designed to ensure the full implementation of all Arab and Security Council resolutions relating to the Gulf crisis.

In this context, the Ministers for Foreign Affairs welcomed the international efforts and contacts designed to ensure the implementation of Arab and international resolutions calling for a complete and unconditional Iraqi withdrawal from Kuwait and the restoration of that country's legitimate authority.

They expressed the hope that these efforts would ensure that the Security Council resolutions were implemented and that the peoples of the region - and the Iraqi people in particular - were spared the dangers of the military option. They affirmed that the Iraqi leadership bore full responsibility if its forces did not respond to the resolutions of international legitimacy.

The Ministers for Foreign Affairs also reviewed the press communiqué issued by the European Community on 4 January 1991 concerning the Iraqi occupation of Kuwait.

The Ministers welcomed the imminent meeting between the Ministers for Foreign Affairs of Iraq and the United States at Geneva on 9 January 1991, representing as it did a last opportunity for a peaceful solution of the Gulf crisis in accordance with the resolutions of Arab and international legitimacy.

They extolled the European Community's affirmation of its resolute determination to ensure the full and unconditional implementation of all Security Council resolutions.

The Ministers for Foreign Affairs also affirmed the declared positions of their countries with respect to the rejection of any settlement based on the concept of partial withdrawal from Kuwait and rewarding of the aggressor.

The Ministers affirmed that the question of Palestine is an Arab issue and that responsibility for it is a patriotic matter for all Arabs.

They expressed their condemnation of the Iraqi régime's attempt to take advantage of the question of Palestine in order to justify its subjugation of Kuwait and expulsion of that country's people, together with hundreds of thousands of resident workers, including Palestinians.

The Ministers also stated their rejection of any attempt by the Iraqi régime to induce any party to negotiate over the problems of the region and its security. The régime is neither qualified nor trustworthy, given its policy of adventurism and subjugation of Kuwait, in violation of all international rules and conventions, as well as Arab and Islamic values.

The Ministers also affirmed their State's determination to solve the current crisis in the Gulf region as quickly as possible in order that all Arab efforts might be devoted to bringing about a just, comprehensive and lasting solution of the Arab-Israeli conflict and the question of Palestine, in accordance with United Nations resolutions calling for Israel's complete withdrawal from the occupied Arab territories and urging that the Palestinian people be enabled to exercise its inalienable legitimate rights, including the right to establish its own independent State on its national soil.

In the context of international efforts and contacts, the Ministers held a meeting with Mr. Loncar, Minister for Foreign Affairs of Yugoslavia, which currently chairs the Movement of Non-Aligned Countries. They discussed with him means of implementing United Nations resolutions relating to the Gulf crisis and the Movement's role in that connection.

The Ministers for Foreign Affairs agreed to hold their fifth round of meetings in the Syrian Arab Republic at a date to be agreed upon in due course.

S/22068, 14 January 1991

9. Letter from the Permanent Representative of Yemen to the United Nations addressed to the President of the Security Council, 14 January 1991

I have the honour to transmit herewith the text of the initiative announced by President Ali Abdullah Saleh, Chairman of the Command Council of the Republic of Yemen, at the meeting of the Council of Representatives held today, Monday, 14 January 1991, with a view to bringing about a peaceful settlement of the current crisis in the Gulf.

...

1. Withdrawal of Iraq from Kuwait.
2. Arab and international forces to take up position in the area of the dispute between Iraq and Kuwait, under League of Arab States and United Nations supervision.
3. Foreign forces in the region to withdraw immediately upon Iraq's agreement to withdraw from Kuwait.
4. Pledge by the Security Council to implement its resolutions concerning the Arab-Israeli conflict by hastening the convening of the International Peace Conference on the Middle East.
5. Pledge by those States which have forces in the Gulf and Arabian peninsula region not to use force against Iraq.
6. Cessation of the economic boycott against Iraq immediately after acceptance of these proposals by the parties to the dispute.

S/22069, 14 January 1991

10. Letter from the Permanent Representative of Tunisia to the United Nations addressed to the President of the Security Council, 14 January 1991

I have the honour to enclose a letter addressed to you by Mr. Habib Boularès, Minister for Foreign Affairs of the Republic of Tunisia ...

At a time when the world is facing the threat of imminent war, the Security Council remains the last recourse.

We note that, five months after it flared up, the Gulf crisis is on the point of degenerating into a devastating war which would be a disaster for the world, with absolutely unforeseeable consequences. This would also be the first instance of a war being waged on the responsibility of the Security Council.

The Middle East, which is at the heart of this conflict and which has already experienced six deadly wars since the establishment of the United Nations and is still suffering the consequences of a series of unresolved conflicts, would again pay the highest price for this new war.

The United Nations, and in particular the Security Council, have examined in turn the conflicts which have arisen in the region, and have on each occasion adopted substantive resolutions which have however for the most part remained a dead letter. The implementation of these resolutions would certainly have eased tensions and helped dissipate the antagonisms in order to bring about the necessary establishment in the region of a climate conducive to the development of trust, security and peace. It is the build-up of unresolved conflicts which lies at the root of the instability and the continuing violence.

A return to the international rule of law is not out of reach. The Security Council is in a position to ensure respect for its own resolutions, the essence of which is the obligation of all countries in the region to comply equally with the basic principles of:

- non-use of force;
- non-acquisition of territories by force;
- non-interference in internal affairs;
- and settlement of disputes by peaceful means.

Thus, right from the first days of the current crisis, Tunisia had called for the withdrawal of the Iraqi forces from Kuwait and the restoration of that country's sovereignty in line with international legality. Tunisia has also implemented the embargo decided upon by the Security Council, despite the heavy losses this has caused to its economy, quantified estimates of which have been communicated to the appropriate United Nations bodies.

Tunisia has, lastly, approached Iraq, Kuwait and the other parties concerned with a view to exploring ways of bringing about a peaceful solution which will safeguard the legitimate interests of all parties. The eight-point initiative of President Zine el Abidine Ben Ali, President of the Republic of Tunisia, his persistent efforts within the framework of the Arab Maghreb Union and the intense contacts he is maintaining with fraternal and friendly countries strengthen our conviction that a peaceful settlement without the use of force is possible within the framework of the international rule of law.

We consider that the opening of dialogue between Iraq and the United States of America, as well as the initiatives of the United Nations Secretary-General and those of the European Community, are only the beginning of a negotiating process which deserves to be maintained and strengthened with the support and involvement of the entire international community in order to ensure and hasten the chances of a peaceful settlement.

The commitment of the parties concerned to apply all the Security Council resolutions to the letter is a valuable asset for the United Nations; it is now up to the Security Council, under these circumstances, to examine ways and means of implementing its own resolutions while there is still time. The effort to design and structure this implementation, which it is the task of the Council itself to define, cannot be purely and simply set aside in favour of war. Quite the contrary, this effort is an earnest of the fact that war is not justified.

Should settlement of the Kuwaiti question through negotiation lead in tandem to the beginnings of a settlement of the other conflicts in the region, in respect for the international rule of law, this cumulative effect is certainly desirable, and deserves to be encouraged rather than rejected, particularly at the cost of war. On the other hand, encouraging the use of force as a means of solving the Gulf crisis alone will inevitably aggravate still further frustrations and destruction of a kind which would irreparably compromise the very purpose of the operation, as well as the conditions for settling other conflicts in the region.

The precedent of the use of force is a dangerous one, in that this practice might be extended to other situations, at the risk of engulfing the United Nations in a logic of war, contrary to its own vocation.

Lastly, the dispute between two fraternal and neighbouring countries, Iraq and Kuwait, calls rather for recourse to a peaceful solution as the only means of preserving the chances for reconciliation and concord and ensuring the future restoration of peaceful and lasting relations of trust between them.

The logic of peace is all the more essential in that the peoples of the region have, since the creation of the United Nations, experienced six deadly wars which have enabled them neither to settle the conflicts nor to attain peace. It is high time that we worked collectively to wrest the region from the infernal cycle of war by opting precisely for the peace that is the raison d'être of the Security Council.

Thus, while reiterating its support for the initiatives taken by the Secretary-General of the United Nations in his efforts to promote a dialogue between the parties concerned, Tunisia calls on the international community to help him in his task and to loyally assist his peace effort. The Security Council should thus be able to meet again in time to evaluate the results of the actions taken and to adopt the measures needed to secure the effective settlement of the present crisis while preserving the chances of peace for the benefit of the entire region.

Peace is indivisible. One of the lessons to be learnt from the history of this embattled Middle East region is that the legacy of past conflicts cannot be overcome either by further violence or by a selective approach whose future is uncertain.

The second lesson is that it is not enough to debate and adopt resolution after resolution; the Security Council must provide a framework for the application of its resolutions, including an appropriate timetable.

We formally invite the Security Council to assume its full responsibilities towards the region and to define such a framework for settling the main question, namely, the question of Palestine, for that is the basic problem whose outcome will determine the solution of all the other problems besetting the region. Only then will a way be found of settling such other related questions as collective security, supervised disarmament, the abolition of weapons of mass destruction and the creation of a denuclearized zone.

Thus, while commending the statement made by the President of the Security Council on 20 December 1990, Tunisia calls expressly on the Council to adopt a resolution deciding to convene an International Peace Conference on the Middle East at a definite date in 1991.

Such a contribution by the Security Council would not impede early settlement of the Kuwait crisis and would make it possible to set in motion, for the first time in the Middle East, a peace process that would guarantee a sustained and progressive settlement effort, putting an end to the cycle of violence and giving all parties a chance to contribute equally to establishing the peace that remains the legitimate concern of all the peoples of the Middle East and the fundamental vocation of the United Nations.

The Security Council must therefore choose in time between a negotiated settlement which will ensure a lasting peace beneficial to the entire region and the use of force, with disastrous and unforeseeable consequences. The Security Council, in short, holds the key to war and peace.

US Department of State Dispatch, January 14, 1991

11. US Secretary of State Baker, Press Statement of January 9, 1991

News conference following bilateral meeting with Iraqi Foreign Minister Tariq Aziz, Geneva, Switzerland

I have just given President Bush a full report of our meeting today. I told him that Minister Aziz and I had completed a serious and extended diplomatic conversation in an effort to find a political solution to the crisis in the Gulf.

I met with Minister Aziz today not to negotiate, as we have made clear we would not do - that is, negotiate backward from UN Security [Council] resolutions - but I met with him today to communicate. And communicate means listening as well as talking, and we did that - both of us.

The message that I conveyed from President Bush and our coalition partners was that Iraq must either comply with the will of the international community and withdraw peacefully from Kuwait or be expelled by force. Regrettably, ladies and gentlemen, I heard nothing today that - in over 6 hours, I heard nothing that suggested to me any Iraqi flexibility whatsoever on complying with the UN Security Council resolutions.

There have been too many Iraqi miscalculations. The Iraqi government miscalculated the international response to the invasion of Kuwait, expecting the world community to stand idly by while Iraqi forces systematically pillaged a peaceful neighbor.

It miscalculated the response, I think, to the barbaric policy of holding thousands of foreign hostages, thinking that somehow cynically doling them out a few at a time would somehow win political advantage. And it miscalculated that it could divide the international community and gain something thereby from its aggression. So let us hope that Iraq does not miscalculate again.

The Iraqi leadership must have no doubt that the 28 nations which have deployed forces to the Gulf in support of the United Nations have both the power and the will to evict Iraq from Kuwait. If it should choose - and the choice is Iraq's - if it should choose to continue its brutal occupation of Kuwait, Iraq will be choosing a military confrontation which it cannot win and which will have devastating consequences for Iraq.

I made these points with Minister Aziz not to threaten but to inform, and I did so with no sense of satisfaction, for we genuinely desire a peaceful outcome, and, as both President Bush and I have said on many occasions, the people of the United States have no quarrel with the people of Iraq.

I simply wanted to leave as little room as possible for yet another tragic miscalculation by the Iraqi leadership. And I would suggest to you, ladies and gentlemen, that this is still a confrontation that Iraq can avoid.

The path of peace remains open, and that path is laid out very clearly in 12 UN Security Council resolutions adopted over a period of over 5 months.

But now the choice lies with the Iraqi leadership. The choice really is theirs to make, and let us all hope that that leadership will have the wisdom to choose the path of peace.

Q: What do your allies plan to do next to bring this message home?

A: Well, you say, "What do the allies plan to do next?" and I think it's important for everyone to note that this is a coalition. This is not Iraq versus the United States. This is Iraq versus the international community. This happens to have been the first time that we've had an opportunity to find agreement on meeting - US and Iraq.

So I don't know what the next steps are. I do know this: that time is running on, as I said a day or so ago. After 5 months and 12 UN Security Council resolutions, it seems to me that it is almost evident that the time for talk is running out. It's time for Iraq to act and to act quickly by getting out of Kuwait.

But this is a coalition, and we are seeking to implement solemn resolutions of the United Nations. And so perhaps there may be a way that the Secretary General of the United Nations could use his good offices here in the remaining 6 or so days that we have left.

I will say that - I've already mentioned that I didn't hear anything that to me demonstrated flexibility, nor did I hear any new proposals. But I would like to take note of the fact that the minister did restate their proposal that the United States pick a day for him to come to the United States and Iraq pick a day for me to go to Baghdad.

Those of you who have been traveling with us know what our answer is to that. We've given it over the past 4 or 5 days, and I gave it to the minister tonight. We offered 15 separate days for a visit to Baghdad. The President of the United States made the proposal for face-to-face discussions. We're glad that Iraq accepted this one, because we did have 6 hours during which we could make our position known to them, they could make their position known to us.

But as far as next steps are concerned, it seems to me that because we are talking about a coalition and we are talking about implementing resolutions of the United Nations, that perhaps there could be - I don't know what the position of the government of Iraq would be on this - but perhaps there would be some room for us to seek the use of the good offices of the Secretary General of the United Nations.

Q: Did the Iraqi Foreign Minister reiterate his demands for what he calls "justice and fairness" for the Palestinians? I mean, was there any wavering in the US position, as you may have expressed it to him, that the two issues are not related, are not linked?

A: No. There was - he expressed his position. There was no change in our position, which is that the two issues are not linked. I did make the point that I don't think many people believe that Iraq invaded Kuwait in order to help the Palestinians, and, if they did, it was another miscalculation, because it hasn't helped the Palestinians.

I think most people believe that Iraq invaded Kuwait for Iraq's own aggrandizement, and I think most people realize that Iraq is trying to use the Palestinian issue to shield its aggression against Kuwait, which in my view at least remains an obstacle to broader peace in the region rather than a catalyst for achieving that broader peace.

And I made the point as well that rewarding Iraq's aggression with a link to the Arab-Israeli peace process would really send a terrible signal not only to genuine peacemakers in the region but also to other would-be aggressors at what we think is a defining moment in history.

Q: Are you willing - is the United States willing to talk again to Iraq before the January 15 deadline and did you discuss with the President the possibility that you may still go to Baghdad?

A: I had already discussed that with President Bush, and I had already told you what our view was. And the President himself, I think, said, "There will be no trip to Baghdad." The proposal which he originally made was in effect rejected by Iraq. We offered 15 separate days. They continued to insist upon only one - the 12th of January - which we think was and still is an obvious effort to avoid the deadline of January the 15th, and we're not interested in that.

We think this deadline is real, and our coalition partners think the deadline is real.

Q: Did you discuss this with the President today?

A: I reported fully to the President, of course.

Q: Could you run through for us - you spoke for 6 hours - could you give us a sense of how the discussions evolved over those 6 hours? What did you begin with? What did he counter with? Why did you feel it necessary after 2 hours to call the President?

A: Well, we broke for lunch. [Laughter] And I think this meeting is sufficiently important that I should call the President, and so I did, just as I did as soon as we were finished.

Q: Did you begin by reading your letter -

A: But I began by saying that I was here to - not to negotiate but to communicate, as I've just told you - that I was here for a serious dialogue in an effort to find a political and peaceful solution, but that they should not expect that we would be prepared to walk backward from UN Security Council resolutions, that the terms of those resolutions had already been set.

And I told the minister I wanted to handle the meeting in whatever way he wanted. And I gave him the choice, and he chose for me to go first, just as he - I gave him the choice as well as to how to report to you, and he suggested that I come down here first.

So that's how we got where we are here tonight. But let me say that I talked to him about how we saw the situation, about the history of the Security Council resolutions, about what I thought could happen in the event of observance of those resolutions, and what I feared would happen in the event of Iraq's non-observance of those resolutions.

He then presented the position of the government of Iraq, and he will be down here in a few moments, and he can - now, we can't run through 6 hours of dialogue here. Nobody else would get to ask any questions.

Q: One quick follow-up: How detailed were you about the extent of force that would be used against Iraq if it does not comply with the UN resolutions by January 15?

A: Well, I didn't get into things that would properly be in the realm of operational security matters. I hope I effectively made the case with respect to what at least our opinion was of the 28-nation multinational force that is there in the Gulf.

Q: Is the United States interested in any sort of phased withdrawal, be it one supervised by the United Nations? And if this withdrawal began by January 15, will the United States guarantee there will be no military attack on Iraq?

A: Let me say I should have said this in answer to Tom's question. I assured the minister that if they implement the UN resolutions, and if they withdraw from Iraq and permit the restoration - from Kuwait and permit the restoration of the legitimate government of Kuwait, that I could assure him that there would be no military action by the United States. And that I felt that there would, under those circumstances, be no military action by any other elements of the international coalition.

Q: (Inaudible).

A: On the first question, the UN resolutions speak for themselves. We are not here - after all, we are part of an international coalition. We are part of 28 countries. Even more countries that have been helping financially and economically. And it is not up to us to walk backward from solemn resolutions of the United Nations.

Q: You have said in the past that you would seek approval for the use of force at the highest levels. Are you now at that stage in the process in which you will be seeking the use of force from other governments?

A: No, but the clock is ticking on, and I made that point to the minister today. As far as we are concerned, we have not taken - the President of the United States who alone under - who alone in our executive branch under our system can make that decision has not taken that decision, and I'm not aware that any other governments have.

Q: In the remaining 6 days before the UN deadline, would you welcome an initiative by some other European allies or even Arab countries such as Algeria that would perhaps include sending a European foreign minister to Baghdad to seek a peaceful resolution?

A: Well, this is an international coalition - let me say it one more time - and, therefore, as I've just indicated to you, it's an international coalition seeking to implement solemn resolutions of the world's peacekeeping and security body. And, therefore, there might, it seems to me, be some useful purpose served by perhaps the Secretary General - Secretary General's good offices.

But I said last night, and I have said for months, we welcome any and all diplomatic efforts to solve this crisis peacefully and politically. We want it solved peacefully and politically. I'm disappointed, of course, that we did not receive any indications today whatsoever of any flexibility in the position of Iraq.

So we would welcome any and all diplomatic efforts. We do think if there are efforts by members of the international coalition, that the message should be uniform, as it has been for 5 months, and it should not be a mixed message. But we want a peaceful and political solution.

Q: Can you tell us - you keep saying you saw no indication of flexibility. Did the Foreign Minister actually tell you that Iraq intends to keep Kuwait and will not withdraw from Kuwait?

A: He did not make that statement, but he did not indicate that there was any chance that they would withdraw. But I did not see, frankly, any flexibility in their position. You can ask him questions when he gets down here.

Q: Did you discuss - in answer to any of the discussion about the problems raised elsewhere in the Middle East by the Iraqi Foreign Minister, did you discuss the efforts the United States has made in the past to seek Arab/Israeli peace -

A: Yes.

Q: - to persuade Iraq that the United States was serious, genuinely interested, in resolving those problems?

A: Yes. We went through a good bit of the history of the personal efforts that I made for 14 months to bring about a dialogue between Arab - between Palestinians and Israelis. We went through the experience of the United States in bringing about the Camp David accords and in bringing about peace between Israel and Egypt, and we had a full discussion of that issue - a complete discussion of it.

I want to make it clear that I made it very clear throughout that there would be no linkage here of that issue to Iraq's withdrawal from Kuwait. And we would not agree as a condition of their withdrawing to any subsequent specific steps to be taken with respect to that. But we did have - they brought it up, and we had a very full discussion.

Q: Well, what was their answer?

A: We disagree. We frankly disagree with respect to that, as I think you know. And I've already told you why I think linkage is a bad idea. I think that it would tend to be read as a reward for aggressors, and it would jeopardize future peace in the region.

Q: What did you tell the Foreign Minister about the willingness of the American people to go to war and the impact of political pressure on the President's decisionmaking?

A: I said, "Don't miscalculate the resolve of the American people, who are very slow to anger but who believe strongly in principle and who believe that we should not reward aggression and that big countries with powerful military machines should not be permitted to invade, occupy, and brutalize their peaceful neighbors."

Q: You've told us what you didn't hear. You didn't hear any flexibility, and you told us that there was quite a bit of discussion of history. Could you tell us what you did hear? Did you hear justifications from the Foreign Minister? Did you hear a repeat of what they've been saying in public for some time?

A: I heard some things that I quite frankly found very hard to believe, but I'll let him go into the detail here. I heard, for instance, that their action in invading Kuwait was defensive in nature; that they were being threatened by Kuwait. And I will tell you the same thing I told the minister, which is I found it very hard to believe that any nation in the world will believe that.

Q: Even though you did spend 6 hours here today talking to Foreign Minister Aziz, in the past 5½ months you haven't had much contact with Iraq. What's to prevent the historians of this conflict from concluding that there was a failure of diplomacy here, and we slid toward war without trying?

A: There's been a lot of conversations with the leadership of Iraq, all to no avail. The Secretary General has already had one failed mission. There have been any number of Arab efforts to solve this crisis, all to no avail. There have been efforts by other Western governments. The Soviet Union has tried very hard. They've had meetings. We have now had a meeting. So people can write whatever they decide they might want to write.

But the truth of the matter is, we have been very, I think - the international coalition - very responsible and measured in our approach to this. We have not, as some might suggest, gone off half-cocked. We have gone through the United Nations patiently, working for consensus within the Security Council. And it is only after 5½ months and the passage of 12 Security Council resolutions that we find ourselves at the point of use of force.

So I think that there's been more diplomacy exercised in this crisis than in almost any that I can think of. The one thing I would ask you all not to do is to equate diplomacy and appeasement. We made that mistake in the thirties, at least, for our part. We don't intend to make it again.

Q: In a sense, two questions: Did the Foreign Minister suggest Iraq might withdraw from Kuwait if there were linkage as, let us say, the French have suggested or others have suggested? And, if he did, is linkage - the principle of linkage - a reason for the loss of - and the insistence on that principle - a reason for the loss of lots of lives?

A: Well, I don't think he said that explicitly. I think perhaps it was implicit in his comments. But he'll be here, and you can ask him. It's more than just the principle of linkage, as I understand their position. There would have to be agreement to conferences and that sort of thing, that get you beyond just the simple fact of linkage.

Q: Did Minister Aziz make a specific proposal under which Iraq would get out of Kuwait, however unacceptable it was to you? Was there a specific proposal?

A: No. There was no specific proposal. He restated the positions that Iraq had stated publicly in the past. He defended their action in invading and occupying Kuwait. He explained how he feels that was justified. Again, he'll be down here and you can ask him yourselves.

Q: You made it clear that you were not going to Baghdad. But did you and the Foreign Minister talk about future diplomatic contacts at your level between the United States and Iraq? Or did this one 6½ hour meeting represent the conclusion of diplomatic initiatives by the United States?

A: We will maintain our diplomatic contacts through our chargé [d'affaires] in Baghdad until the 12th of January. I asked for and received the personal assurance of the minister that Joe Wilson and the four other Americans in our embassy there will be permitted to leave Baghdad on the 12th of January and will not be restrained from so doing.

Q: Your mood, if I may say, seems pretty somber at this point. Can you kind of describe your state of mind and your mood after what has occurred today?

A: Somber.

Q: Somber?

A: You got it.

Q: Are you advising an evacuation?

A: I'm not saying that. I'm telling you that we have asked for and received assurances for our remaining five diplomatic personnel to leave on the 12th of January, which is a date that you well know is very close to the January 15 deadline and happens to be the date that Iraq has been insisting on for 3 weeks for the meeting.

Q: What about other Americans?

A: I think most all Americans are out of Iraq. All that want to leave are gone, as far as I know.

Q: Can you tell us now about the letter from President Bush? Was it, in fact, in Arabic? What was the tone of it? Did it contain graphic military scenarios intended to intimidate?

A: I regret to inform you that the minister chose not to receive the letter from President Bush. He read it very slowly and very carefully, but he would not accept it nor would the Iraqi embassy in Washington accept an Arabic courtesy translation. You will have to ask the minister why he did not accept the letter.

My own opinion, for what it's worth - and it's only an opinion - was that he came here only authorized to accept a letter that walked away from the UN resolutions, which is something that we cannot and, of course, will not do.

Q: Have you discussed the possibility of convening the United Nations again to discuss the Gulf crisis? You know that [French] President Mitterrand - he has proposed that most probably a new discussion is possible; it might be helpful. Have you discussed this eventuality with the Iraqi minister?

A: No, it did not come up in my meeting today with the Iraqi minister. I did speak to that question and that issue a day or so ago, and I believe that President Bush has spoken to it as well.

I don't know what an additional Security Council meeting at this stage could do. Because what we are talking about here is faithful implementation of resolutions of the Council, the last one of which says that if Iraq does not withdraw by midnight on January 15, force can be used to effect that withdrawal.

We have had 12 resolutions of the UN Security Council.

Q: President Mitterrand is suggesting this.

A: I can't answer your question. I would refer you to President Mitterrand. But I have just said that perhaps there would be some utility in trying to use the good offices of the Secretary General.

Q: Do you have any reason to believe that there is any way to avoid a war as of right now?

A: Yes, I hope there is. There has been no decision taken for that eventuality. I would simply refer you to my opening statement where I made the point that I hope we do not have yet one more miscalculation by the government of Iraq.

I would also refer you to the statements which President Bush and I and other members of the coalition have made over the course of the last several days or weeks and which I repeated today to the minister, not in a threatening way but simply so that he would know where our head is and how we feel and what we think and that is that this January 15 deadline, in our minds, is real.

Iraq can choose to believe that or not, but it is real in our minds and in the minds of our coalition partners. We hope that they will believe that we think it's real and that they will act to implement the solemn resolutions of the United Nations.

Q: Do you regret that you would have still liked to go, even on the 12th, and meet - instead of Mr. Tariq - Saddam himself? It's still a difference of 3 days.

A: We've said for the last 3 weeks, the 12th of January was unacceptable to us because it is just an effort to avoid the deadline. It's obvious. That's why the 12th was originally suggested. We've said for a long time that date is unacceptable to us. It remains unacceptable to us.

Q: Did you spell out your vision of what the Gulf would look like if they withdrew peacefully? In other words, some of the restrictions that you have talked about that must be imposed upon Iraq even if they did withdraw? Did you lay that plan out for him in some way?

A: Yes, I did in my original presentation this morning. I don't have time to go through all of that with you now. But that falls right in the category of the assurance that there would not be military force used against Iraq by the United States if they withdrew from Kuwait and permitted the restoration of the legitimate government of Kuwait.

Q: Did you talk about the nuclear weapons, the chemical weapons, the size of the Iraqi military - things that are of concern to many in the Western coalition beyond the occupation of Kuwait?

A: We had a full discussion of the questions about weapons of mass destruction. I pointed out the interest of the United States, as we have expressed before in addressing that issue and addressing that subject. We talked about the multinational presence there and the fact that President Bush has said we do not desire nor want a permanent military ground presence in the Middle East - I mean in the Gulf. We want to see our troops come home just as fast as the security situation will allow. Those are the kinds of things that we discussed, as you might expect.

Q: Could you just please describe to us the point at which the meeting broke off? Why and how did it happen? Was it that you finished off? Did Mr. Aziz finish off? Or was there just nothing to talk about anymore? Please describe that.

A: It was simply a case, I think, that over 6 hours of discussion, we had both had pretty well made the points that we had come to make, and that was it. I don't believe that there was anything left unsaid. He said everything, I think, he came to say and I had said everything that I had come to say.

I think, frankly, it lasted longer than many of you might have anticipated at the beginning.

Q: You mentioned that you are going to call back the American diplomats. Are you also asking the Iraqi diplomats to leave the United States on January 12th?

A: No. We will ask the Iraqi government to draw down their diplomatic presence in the United States on the 12th. As I indicated to the minister, we would be willing to permit the presence of a small diplomatic contingent in Washington.

Q: Do you feel that if you would have accepted the fact of the linkage, there could have been a proposition of Iraq retiring from Kuwait?

A: I don't know. Why don't you ask the minister that? Because when you say "accepted linkage", I'm not entirely sure exactly what you mean. Do you mean if we had accepted - if we had indicated a willingness to go to an international conference to handle the question of the Middle East? Ask him the question. It would be very interesting.

You know what our position has been for a long time. It would set an extraordinarily unfortunate precedent, we think, and would not, in the long run, contribute to peace in the region but would contribute to instability because aggressors would be seen to be rewarded for their aggression. It's something we simply cannot consider.

Q: Was there any single issue on which the difference between the United States and Iraq was narrowed during this 6½ hours?

A: Well, let me say that I think that the discussions - I've already indicated it was a serious one. I think that the tone of it was good, as good as you could expect under the circumstances. We weren't pounding the table and shouting at each other. It was a very reasoned and, I think, responsible discussion by two diplomats who really would like to find a peaceful and political solution to this problem.

I've already said to you, I did not detect flexibility in the position of Iraq as they have stated it over the past several days.

Again, I invite you to my opening statement. We still have 6 days. I just hope that they will think about this meeting, that they will focus on it, that when Foreign Minister Aziz gets back and reports to his President, that perhaps there could be some change in their position.

There cannot be a negotiation here because the terms of the UN Security Council resolutions were worked out in the debate in the United Nations, and the international coalition is bound to those resolutions.

Q: Would you be willing to meet Saddam somewhere else, apart from Baghdad? And was that suggested?

A: That was not discussed. It has never been proposed by Iraq. The Iraqi proposal, as you know, for some weeks has been, we pick a date for Baker to come to Baghdad, you pick a date for Aziz to come to

Washington, and we'll work it that way. That's been out there for a long, long time. There's never been any suggestion of the other.

S/22070, 15 January 1991

12. Letter from the Permanent Representative of the Syrian Arab Republic to the United Nations addressed to the Secretary-General, 15 January 1991

I have the honour to transmit to you herewith the text of a message from President Hafez al-Assad of the Syrian Arab Republic addressed to President Saddam Hussein of the Republic of Iraq through the broadcast media on the afternoon of Saturday, 12 January 1991. ...

With unalloyed brotherly sentiments and sincere patriotic feeling, and with an understanding of the dangers encompassing the Arab world in general and fraternal Iraq in particular, I address you through the airwaves with this message in a desire for us to avert undesirable consequences for the nation and for Iraq. I am most hopeful that my message will meet with your understanding of the true nature of my motives and with the response that I would desire.

In the delicate circumstances through which the Arab world is passing, which are being monitored and whose developments are being followed with the greatest interests and concern, by the masses of our nation and the peoples and Governments of the world, I can find no better preface to my addressing you than that of affirming the ties of brotherhood which bind our two peoples in Syria and Iraq and of asserting my conviction that the constant concern of both fraternal countries should focus on addressing the challenges and dangers that confront the Arab nation.

I decided to address this message to you, despite the differences in viewpoint and the unfriendly relations that have separated us for many years, in the hope that such matters would become better and more useful for our two countries and for the nation. The matter with which we are concerned makes it necessary that we should be frank with each other and that we should exchange views, since any affront to Iraq is ultimately an affront, in one form or another, to Syria and to the Arab nation.

When we see that Iraq is confronting a grave danger, as is the case at the present time, the differences between the two fraternal countries diminish and disappear, because those things that bring us together are much greater and much more important than any differences or selfish gains that we may perceive, if, indeed, it is true to say that there are any such gains to be made.

A grasp of the seriousness of the danger posed impels one to speak with the frankness required of fraternal and patriotic ties. At the outset, I nevertheless hasten to express the hope that my words will not be understood as a wish to aggravate the situation but rather in the sense that it is my concern to speak to men's hearts. It is my goal that rationality and emotion should interact and that thought and action should rise to such a level as to realize the higher national interest and bring the enemies of our nation to miss an opportunity beyond anything that they could never dream, particularly since this opportunity comes to them by our own action and our own power of decision. Accordingly, we must eliminate it entirely by our own action and by virtue of our own decision, without being forced to do so by anyone and without fear of anyone but rather taking as our point of departure a belief in the need for such action and for such a decision. It is this that is the role of valiant Iraq at this time. Thus we will not allow the enemies of the nation to reap any benefit by exploiting this opportunity.

Although Arabs may undergo circumstances held to be sensitive, it does not prevent them from listening to the voices of their brothers who are concerned for them.

The Arab interest is of concern to us. And the interest of Iraq is of concern to us. We are both part of the Arab nation, and thence comes the commonality of outlook that stems from a common history, a common heritage, a common civilization, a common language, commonality of spiritual values, shared pains and hopes, a common destiny and a commonality in all that is implied by our affiliation with the Arab nation and from whose territory divine missions set forth and by whose philosophy, science and ideals the world was overwhelmed. Accordingly, the commonality in which we are involved in word and deed constitutes for us a right and a duty.

Hence, it is the duty of a brother that he should communicate what he has to say to his brother, whose duty it is, in turn, to listen to what his brother has to say with the greatest sensitivity and with an open mind, because they both share a common destiny. Whoever listens to what his brother has to say has suffered no loss and misses no new ideas.

While I would stress the grave danger confronting the Arab nation in general and Iraq in particular, and while I call for enemies to be deprived of opportunity, I am not concerned with discussing truth and falsehood with respect to Iraq's invasion of Kuwait, which is another matter and for the discussion of which this is neither the time nor the place. The important thing in present circumstances, however, is that we face a grave and dangerous situation threatening Iraq.

Our concern for Iraq, for its territory, its people and its army, is the same as our concern for ourselves, because Iraq is a dear and precious part of the land of the Arabs and of the Arab nation.

The beneficiary of the situation at the present moment is Israel, which is occupying Arab territory and plotting and striving for continued expansion on Arab land. It is profiting from the present inter-Arab situation and intra-Arab antagonism, while the Arabs, jointly and severally and headed by Iraq, are the losers. I do not see that any of the Arabs have an interest in what is happening now, and I do not see that Iraq has any interest in it either.

The fundamental interest of the Arab nation, particularly at the present stage of history, lies in coherence and genuine solidarity and in each Arab country ensuring the tranquillity of all other Arab countries, even if there are differences between them with respect to one or more inter-Arab issues.

I do not wish to believe that the Arabs' sense of a common destiny has lapsed or that solidarity among the Arabs has become impossible. I wish rather to stress that the grievous character of the danger is apt to strengthen the sense of a common destiny and to promote Arab solidarity and the solution of inter-Arab differences through dialogue rather than force.

I should like to stress in particular that the responsibility of Iraq, Syria and other Arab countries is to assist in ensuring the tranquillity and sense of security of neighbouring Arab countries, even if differences should emerge from time to time since such differences can be remedied by means of dialogue, and in such a manner as to build confidence and eliminate any Arab country's fear of another. This will help to promote a spirit of brotherliness and achieve effective Arab solidarity, and it will represent an important step on the way to a future Arab unity achieved through conviction and faith in the salvation of the nation through such unity.

The future before us is open to the unification of the entire nation, and our nation is a great nation in and of itself and by virtue of its mission, its heritage and the abundance of its capacities. It is capable of providing itself and the world with the same spiritual, intellectual and civilizing radiance with which it enriched mankind in the past.

The difficulty of the current situation in the Arab world and its complexity lie in the dangers entailed by Iraq's entry into Kuwait, its forcible annexation of that country and the elimination of Kuwait as an independent State member of the League of Arab States and of the United Nations. We do not believe that this is legitimate conduct, and Iraq has no right to engage in such conduct even from the point of view of unification since methods of force and violence are not proper and appropriate methods for the achievement of unity but are rather a factor impeding and precluding any endeavour for unity.

May Iraq's withdrawal from Kuwait then be the prelude to a new climate in which grave dangers can be averted and in which we may close ranks as a single force in the face of whoever threatens our territory, our interests, our dignity and our destiny.

Some may say that Iraq will be attacked even if it leaves Kuwait. In regard to this matter, I should like to affirm a brotherly covenant which is not open to doubt. If that were to happen after Iraq's departure from Kuwait, Syria, with all its material and moral capabilities, would stand by Iraq in one and the same trench and would fight alongside it with all its strength and all its valour until victory was achieved.

The interest of the nation is above all other interests. For its sake, every sacrifice is of slight importance and every danger is confronted with the appropriate decision and the appropriate stance, and this is what is expected of you yourself.

A decision now taken by you to defuse the crisis and to ward off from Iraq and from the Arab world the dangers of a devastating war will be recorded to your merit as a courageous act properly taken at a proper moment.

We beseech God that he will inspire us to righteousness and will guide us on the right path.

S/22071, 14 January 1991

13. Letter from the Permanent Representative of the Union of Soviet Socialist Republics to the United Nations addressed to the Secretary-General, 14 January 1991

I have the honour to transmit to you the text of the decision taken on 12 January 1991 by the Supreme Soviet of the Union of Soviet Socialist Republics concerning the situation in the Persian Gulf.

...

Having, at the request of the fourth session of the Congress of People's Deputies of the Union of Soviet Socialist Republics, reviewed the evolving crisis in the Persian Gulf and expressing its serious concern at the absence of any progress towards a peaceful settlement of the conflict and at the constantly rising tension prevailing in the region both militarily and politically, the Supreme Soviet of the USSR decides:

1. To support, because they correspond to the vital interests of the country, the many initiatives taken by the Government of the Soviet Union with a view to resolving the conflict in the Persian Gulf peacefully, in accordance with the rules of international law and with the requests made by the Security Council of the United Nations in its resolutions;

2. To invite all the parties to display a heightened sense of their responsibilities, to continue their efforts to find a political solution to this crisis, and not to accept a military confrontation which would have catastrophic consequences for the Middle East and the entire world. In this connection, the Supreme Soviet of the USSR hails and endorses the peace efforts being undertaken by the Secretary-General of the United Nations;

3. To instruct the Ministry of Foreign Affairs and the Ministry of Defence of the USSR to keep it regularly informed of any changes in the situation in the region of the Persian Gulf and the Middle East and to inform its international affairs, defence and national security committees of specific measures taken in accordance with this foreign policy of the Soviet Union.

The Supreme Soviet of the USSR affirms that decisions which, under the Constitution of the USSR, require the approval of the supreme legislative body cannot be taken without its agreement.

A/45/926, S/22074, 15 January 1991

14. Letter from the Permanent Representative of Luxembourg to the United Nations addressed to the Secretary-General, 14 January 1991

I have the honour to transmit herewith, in English and French, the text of the declaration on the Gulf question issued today by the European Community and its 12 member States.

..

Following a meeting between the President of the council and the Secretary-General of the United Nations, Ministers for Foreign Affairs of the European Community were informed of the substance of the conversations of Mr. Pérez de Cuéllar with the President and Foreign Minister of Iraq.

They note that the Secretary-General will this evening report on his mission to the Security Council of the United Nations, which will have the task of evaluating the results.

For their part, the Community and its member States have from the beginning of the Gulf crisis supported unreservedly the full and unconditional implementation of the relevant resolutions of the Security Council.

They have spared no effort in exploring all paths to a peaceful solution in conformity with these resolutions. In this spirit, the European Community had made known its readiness to meet at the level of the troika of Foreign Ministers the Iraqi Foreign Minister, Mr. Tariq Aziz, first in the Presidency capital and then in Algiers.

Through the Presidency statement of 4 January 1991, the Twelve had clearly indicated that if the resolutions of the Security Council were fully and unconditionally implemented, Iraq should receive the assurance that it would not be subject to a military intervention.

In the same statement, the Twelve had also clearly reaffirmed their commitment to contribute actively to the settlement of the other problems of the region and to establish a situation of security, stability and development, as soon as the Gulf crisis is resolved.

On the occasion of the Rome European Council on 15 December 1990, the European Community and its member States had indicated that they remained completely in favour of the convening of an international peace conference on the Middle East at the appropriate moment.

It is a fact that unfortunately must be acknowledged that the readiness thus displayed to contribute to a peaceful solution of the crisis opening the way to an equitable settlement of all the other problems of the region has not, up to this point, received a response from the Iraqi authorities.

In the face of the continued refusal of the Iraqi authorities to implement the resolutions of the Security Council and in the absence of any signal in this sense, the

European Community and its member States regret to have to conclude that the conditions for a new European initiative do not exist as at this moment.

Nevertheless, the invitation to Mr. Tariq Aziz to meet the ministerial troika remains on the table.

The European Community and its member States are conscious of having done everything that was possible to find a peaceful exit from the crisis. They remain determined to explore all possibilities for the preservation of peace in the respect of international legality. In this context, they request Arab countries and organizations to continue to devote every effort to bringing the Iraqi authorities to understand that it is in the interest of Iraq, as of the whole Arab world, that it should abide by the resolutions of the Security Council.

Ministers have asked the Presidency to stay in close contact with all parties concerned.

Ministers and their political directors will remain in permanent touch in the coming days to follow the course of the crisis and take any necessary decisions.

S/22077, 15 January 1991

15. Letter from the Permanent Representative of Sweden to the United Nations addressed to the President of the Security Council, 15 January 1991

I have the honour to enclose a statement today by Mr. Sten Andersson, Minister for Foreign Affairs of Sweden, on behalf of the Government of Sweden ...

Sweden regards the situation in the Gulf with deepest concern. Iraq's aggression against Kuwait can never be accepted. Iraq must withdraw immediately and unconditionally all its forces from Kuwait. It is the duty of the international community to ensure the compliance by Iraq with the relevant United Nations resolutions.

As a loyal member of the United Nations, Sweden supports the Security Council and its resolutions. Our support for the United Nations is based upon the fact that the ultimate goal of the Organization is to maintain international peace and security. The fulfilment of this objective may, in accordance with the Charter of the United Nations, ultimately require the use of force when other measures are inadequate.

In this extremely serious situation all peaceful means must be tried to their full extent. We urge maximum restraint until all such means have been exhausted.

Sweden directs an urgent appeal to the members of the Security Council to direct all their attention to the remaining possibilities to find a peaceful solution. Sweden expresses its support for the French efforts to this effect. We trust that the Council will remain actively seized with the matter until a peaceful solution will be found.

S/22083, 16 January 1991

16. Letter from the Representatives of Argentina, Bolivia, Brazil, Chile, Colombia, Costa Rica, Ecuador, Mexico, Paraguay, Peru, Uruguay and Venezuela addressed to the Secretary-General, 16 January 1991

The Governments of the Permanent Mechanism for Consultation and Concerted Political Action, Rio Group, deeply concerned that thus far it has not been possible to find a peaceful solution to the crisis in the Persian Gulf, reiterate their support for the purposes and principles of the Charter of the United Nations and their firm support for the resolutions of the Security Council and the efforts of the Secretary-General.

Given the imminence of actions in the region that will have serious repercussions on the rest of the world and will, in particular, aggravate the already serious economic and social consequences being endured by the developing countries, the Governments of the Rio Group, convinced that no effort must be spared to safeguard world peace, make an appeal for intensified diplomatic activity aimed at finding a just and stable solution to this dangerous situation.

...

S/22084, 17 January 1991

17, Letter from the Permanent Representative of the Union of Soviet Socialist Republics to the United Nations addressed to the Secretary-General, 11 January 1991

I have the honour to enclose the text of a statement issued by the Ministry of Foreign Affairs of the Union of Soviet Socialist Republics on 10 January 1991.

...

A meeting took place yesterday in Geneva between the Secretary of State of the United States of America, James Baker, and the Minister for Foreign Affairs of Iraq, Tariq Aziz. To judge from the reports that have been issued, it yielded no positive results.

This outcome of the meeting is profoundly regrettable, since the conduct of a direct United States-Iraqi dialogue offered some hope that the acute crisis in the Persian Gulf could be overcome on the basis of the Security Council resolutions and the clearly expressed will of the world community.

From the very outset of the crisis in the Gulf, the Soviet Union has sought to do everything possible to avoid the outbreak of large-scale armed conflict in the region and to channel the course of events towards a political settlement. Among the steps we have taken just recently were the talks in Baghdad with Saddam Hussein and other Iraqi leaders by the Deputy Chairman of the Council of Ministers of the USSR, Igor Belousov, and a group of people's deputies from the Soviet Union, and matching contacts with the United States side. On 8 January, the Soviet Ambassador in Baghdad transmitted to President Saddam Hussein a further appeal by the Soviet leadership, addressing the situation in the Persian Gulf region and the United States-Iraqi meeting, and aimed at facilitating the creation at the Geneva talks of an atmosphere of search for a political solution.

The "pause of goodwill" comes to an end on 15 January. The Soviet Union is convinced that the most energetic political and diplomatic efforts should be made to bring the Persian Gulf region back from the brink of an armed conflict which would have the most destructive consequences for the peoples living there, and in the first place for the people of Iraq.

We welcome the mission the Secretary-General, Mr. Javier Pérez de Cuéllar, intends to undertake to Baghdad, and we appeal to all parties, and especially to Iraq, to recognize the full seriousness of the moment and to demonstrate the sense of responsibility for the fate of the region and the fate of its peoples which is so vitally needed in this situation.

S/22087, 17 January 1991

18. Letter from the Permanent Representative of Yugoslavia to the United Nations addressed to the President of the Security Council, 16 January 1991

I have the honour to transmit herewith the text of the statement issued on 16 January 1991 by the Socialist Federal Republic of Yugoslavia, the current Chairman of the Movement of Non-Aligned Countries, regarding the situation in the Persian Gulf.

...

Yugoslavia, the current Chairman of the Movement of Non-Aligned Countries, believes that at this crucial juncture all the sides involved in the Gulf crisis should reflect once again upon the enormous dangers of a war conflict and its disastrous consequences. Therefore, at this dramatic moment, Yugoslavia appeals, first of all, to President Saddam Hussein and the Iraqi leadership to act in favour of peace, in the interest of Iraq and the Iraqi people, the security of the entire region and world stability. We make this appeal at a time when the Movement of Non-Aligned Countries, among the founding members of which is Iraq, faces the historical challenge to confirm stronger than ever the universal value of the principle of peace and the peaceful settlement of disputes.

We hope that it is still not too late for Iraq to comply with the principles of law and peace - which constitute the essence of the Charter of the United Nations and of the new international era, thus being imperative for each participant on the world scene - and to demonstrate its good will by taking the first step towards withdrawal from Kuwait, a State member of the Movement of Non-Aligned Countries. This could enable all the parties involved and the international community as a whole finally to assume their share of responsibility for the peace and security in the Gulf region and the Middle East, above all for resolving the Palestinian problem and for an early convening of an international conference on the Middle East.

In this spirit, Yugoslavia, as the Chairman of the Movement of Non-Aligned Countries, renders its full support to the latest statement by the Secretary-General of the United Nations, Mr. Javier Pérez de Cuéllar, and stands ready to continue its efforts so that reason may prevail and the way open for establishing a secure peace and stability to be shared by all the countries and nations of the region.

S/22091, 17 January 1991

19. Letter from the Secretary-General addressed to the President of the Security Council, 16 January 1991

I have the honour to transmit to you herewith the text, in French and English, of the statement which I made yesterday on the situation between Iraq and Kuwait.

...

As 15 January advances, and the world stands poised between peace and war, I most sincerely appeal to President Saddam Hussein to turn the course of events away from catastrophe and towards a new era of justice and harmony based on the principles of the Charter of the United Nations.

All our efforts in this direction will fail unless Iraq can signify its readiness to comply with the relevant resolutions of the Security Council, beginning with resolution 660 (1990).

If this commitment is made, and clear and substantial steps taken to implement these resolutions, a just peace, with all its benefits, will follow. I therefore urge President Saddam Hussein to commence, without delay, the total withdrawal of Iraqi forces from Kuwait.

Once this process is well under way, I wish to assure him, on the basis of understandings that I have received from Governments at the highest level, that neither Iraq nor its forces will be attacked by those arrayed in the international coalition against his country.

Further, with the commencement of withdrawal, as Secretary-General of the United Nations, I would, with the consent of the parties concerned, and the agreement of the Security Council, be prepared immediately to deploy United Nations observers and, if necessary, United Nations forces to certify the withdrawal and to ensure that hostilities do not erupt on the ground.

In addition, with compliance of the resolutions, I would urge the Security Council to review its decisions imposing sanctions against Iraq. I would also encourage a process whereby foreign forces deployed in the area would be phased out.

Peace in the region requires that all its problems be resolved justly and equitably, in accordance with the principles of the Charter of the United Nations.

I have every assurance, once again from the highest levels of government, that with the resolution of the present crisis, every effort will be made to address, in a comprehensive manner, the Arab-Israeli conflict, including the Palestinian question. I pledge my every effort to this end.

As I stated to the Council last night, all of us are aware of the extreme gravity of the decisions to be made in the period ahead. No one and no nation can - except with a heavy heart - resort to the other "necessary means" implied by resolution 678 (1990), knowing in advance that tragic and unpredictable consequences can follow.

I trust, in the circumstances, that wisdom and statesmanship will prevail in all quarters in order to move decisively away from conflict. In appealing to President Saddam Hussein today, I wish him to know that I will readily devote my every capacity to working with him, and with all others concerned, to this end.

In the tenth and final year of my tenure as Secretary-General of the United Nations, no cause would give me greater satisfaction than to set the Middle East as a whole on the road to just and lasting peace. And no disappointment would be greater and more tragic than to find the nations of the world engaging in a conflict that none of their peoples want.

PART III

THE APPLICATION OF MILITARY FORCE AGAINST IRAQ

5. THE OUTBREAK AND CONDUCT OF HOSTILITIES

This chapter details the responses of the UN membership to the outbreak of hostilities in the Gulf. It also contains reports on the conduct of hostilities made by the members of the international coalition to the UN Security Council and allegations concerning the violation of the laws of war put forward by the parties during and after the conflict. Extracts from United States and United Kingdom materials which were not submitted to the UN, such as reports of military authorities on the campaign made to Congress and Parliament respectively and documents relating to war powers, have been reprinted separately, in sections B and C. The chapter concludes with documents from the International Committee of the Red Cross dealing with the laws of war and with materials on the environmental consequences of the conflict.

A. UNITED NATIONS DOCUMENTS

S/22061, 10 January 1991

1. Letter from the Permanent Representative of Iraq to the United Nations addressed to the Secretary-General, 10 January 1991

On instructions from my Government, I have the honour to inform you of the violations of our international frontiers by enemy aircraft whose details appear below.

At 0954 hours on 9 January 1991, an enemy target consisting of one aircraft violated our international frontier in the area of 'Ar'ar, penetrating to a depth of between 1 and 2 kilometres while flying at an altitude of 12,000 metres and a speed of 850 kilometres per hour.

...

S/22080, 16 January 1991

2. Letter from the Permanent Representative of Kuwait to the United Nations addressed to the Secretary-General, 16 January 1991

I transmit herewith a statement issued from Taif on 16 January 1991 by a spokesman for the Government of the State of Kuwait.

...

A spokesman for the Government of the State of Kuwait has announced that Iraqi forces continue to occupy all territories of the State of Kuwait despite the expiration of the period specified by the Security Council in its resolution 678 (1990) for the completion by the end of 15 January 1991 of the immediate and unconditional withdrawal of Iraqi forces from all Kuwaiti territories to the borders behind which they were deployed before 2 August 1990.

The spokesman added that no action had been taken by the Iraqi régime that would signal its willingness to comply with the will of the international community, namely, by withdrawing from all Kuwaiti territories and implementing the relevant Security Council resolutions.

United Nations Press Release, 17 January 1991

3. Remarks of the UN Secretary-General at approximately 9.30 a.m. on Thursday, 17 January 1991

Q: Mr Secretary, your reactions, sir, to events overnight?

SG: In view of the failure of diplomacy we couldn'd expect anything different. And therefore, for the time being, I don't think that it is time for diplomacy at this very moment, which means that there's not much I can do. It would be, anyway, for the Security Council to act. As you know, yesterday there was a meeting of the Security Council at which three countries--the United States, France, and the United Kingdom, informed the members of the Council, but there was no decision of the Council. And no decision was expected, either.

Q: Have you had any contact with the US Government or the Government of Iraq?

SG: As you know President Bush called by one hour in advance (of hostilites).

Q: Sir, do you see any prosepect of peace any time soon?

SG: It depends on Iraq, whether Iraq capitulates.

S/22085, 17 January 1991

4. Letter from the Permanent Representative of Tunisia to the United Nations addressed to the President of the Security Council, 17 January 1991

I have the honour to transmit herewith the text of a communiqué issued by the Council of Ministers of the Republic of Tunisia on 17 January 1991.

...

The Tunisian Government has received the news of the outbreak of war in the Gulf region with serious concern and profound displeasure.

Tunisia, which upholds the values of dialogue and the principle of solving disputes by peaceful means, expresses its distress at the tragedy being undergone by the Arab community and its sorrow at the ordeal to which the two fraternal peoples of Iraq and Kuwait are subjected. It recalls its appeals and intensive endeavours since the outbreak of the crisis to secure the withdrawal of Iraqi forces, to solve the essence of the conflict by peaceful means in an Arab context and to avoid the internationalization and complication of the issue.

In conformity with these principles, to which it has always adhered, and in order to safeguard international peace and Arab capabilities, Tunisia addresses an appeal to the conscience of the world. It calls upon the Security Council to press ahead with the adoption of urgent decisive measures to put an end to the current fighting and to settle the conflict by peaceful means, in accordance with the requirements of international legitimacy.

S/22086, 17 January 1991

5. Letter dated 17 January from the Permanent Representative of India to the United Nations addressed to the President of the Security Council, 17 January 1991

I enclose herewith the text of a statement issued today by the Prime Minister of India. ...

I am deeply distressed that hostilities have broken out in the Gulf, in spite of all the efforts made to prevent them. The longer the war lasts, the higher will be the toll in terms of human life and suffering.

I would like to appeal to President Saddam Hussein to announce the commencement of immediate withdrawal from Kuwait, in accordance with the United Nations Security Council resolutions. This should be followed by a cessation of hostilities and the resumption of efforts to find a peaceful solution to the conflict. The modalities for it can be worked out by the United Nations Security Council.

I have a message from President Gorbachev about a Soviet initiative in this regard, and we will join them in a common endeavour for peace. We will co-operate actively within the Movement of Non-Aligned Countries and with all like-minded countries in these joint efforts.

S/22088, 17 January 1991

6. Letter from the Permanent Representative of Yugoslavia to the United Nations addressed to the President of the Security Council, 17 January 1991

I have the honour to transmit herewith the texts of the statements issued on 17 January 1991 by the President of the Presidency of the Socialist Federal Republic of Yugoslavia and by the Federal Executive Council of the Assembly of the Socialist Federal Republic of Yugoslavia regarding the outbreak of war in the Persian Gulf.

...

It is with great disappointment that we must recognize the failure of the efforts undertaken so far by the whole international community to attain a peaceful and political solution and to avoid the outbreak of war in the Persian Gulf, which unfortunately commenced last night.

Our country, as the current Chairman of the Movement of Non-Aligned Countries, did its utmost so that this conflict might be resolved by peaceful means. Until the last moment, we nurtured hope that reason would prevail and that the use of force could be avoided.

Yugoslavia has always founded its international activities on the unyielding position that interference in internal affairs, aggression and occupation cannot be a means of resolving international disputes. This is unacceptable, particularly at this time when the world is on the brink of a new era of peace and co-operation without confrontation, which in the decades behind us was a permanent threat to world peace and security.

Although the armed conflict that we all endeavoured to avoid is under way, it is still not too late to stop it so as to prevent further destruction and new casualties.

That is the reason that even in this hour of great danger we once again appeal to President Saddam Hussein and the Iraqi leadership to comply with the decisions of the United Nations and urgently to commence the withdrawal from Kuwait, the occupation and annexation of which brought about these tragic developments. At this juncture it is the only way of preventing the further escalation of this catastrophe which alas has begun.

The continuation of the war gravely affects all States of the world community in all economic, political and other aspects and therefore presents a real peril to democratic developments in international relations. It is indeed in the interest of all that this situation should be overcome as soon as possible.

...

As a country committed to peace and to the principles of humanity, democracy and international law of the Charter of the United Nations as well as to the policy of non-alignment, Yugoslavia is deeply saddened by the outbreak of war in the Gulf, with its threat of tragic losses of human life and grave consequences.

Yugoslavia, as the current Chairman of the Movement of Non-Aligned Countries, and in close co-operation with the non-aligned and other countries, has done its utmost to help bring about a political and peaceful resolution of the Gulf crisis.

Even after the deadline set by the Security Council in its resolution 678 (1990) has elapsed, exactly eight hours before the outbreak of war, we made yet another appeal for peace and reason.

To that effect we primarily urged President Saddam Hussein and the Iraqi leadership to act in concert with the principles of law and peace, to withdraw from Kuwait and thus to respond to the expectations of the entire international community and the Movement of Non-Aligned Countries in particular.

Now that the war has begun and the first casualties have been inflicted, we still believe that no efforts should be spared in order to restore peace as soon as possible. The Iraqi compliance with the Security Council resolution 660 (1990) - i.e., the withdrawal from Kuwait - would create conditions to bring the hostilities to conclusion, to avoid further losses and to address peacefully this crisis and the problems of the entire region, in accordance with the principles of the policy of non-alignment and the Charter.

Yugoslavia will continue to endeavour along these lines, in close co-operation with all international factors, the non-aligned countries, the permanent and other members of the Security Council and particularly with the Secretary-General of the United Nations.

S/22090, 17 January 1991

7. Letter from the Permanent Representative of the United States of America to the United Nations addressed to the President of the Security Council, 17 January 1991

In accordance with paragraph 4 of resolution 678 (1990), I wish, on behalf of my Government, to submit the following report on the actions undertaken pursuant to paragraphs 2 and 3 of that resolution.

On 10 August 1990, the United States reported to the President of the Council that, in the exercise of the inherent right of individual and collective self-defence, it had deployed military forces to the Persian Gulf region in response to requests from Governments in the region, including Kuwait and Saudi Arabia. Since that time, the military forces of the United States have joined with those of other States co-operating with the Government of Kuwait in accordance with resolution 665 for the purpose of implementing the sanctions imposed by resolution 661 (1990). On 29 November 1990, the Council adopted resolution 678 (1990), in which it decided to allow Iraq one final opportunity, as a pause of goodwill, until 15 January 1991 to resolve peacefully this crisis.

The United States strongly preferred a peaceful resolution of this crisis consistent with resolution 660 and the subsequent relevant resolutions. It has consistently supported diplomatic efforts since the outset of the crisis to achieve such a resolution. The United States, the European Community, the Arab League, the Non-Aligned Movement and numerous States and private individuals as well as the Secretary-General undertook extensive diplomatic efforts in order to reach such a solution.

President Saddam Hussein has rejected all of these efforts and has continued to defy the will of the Security Council and the community of nations. Economic sanctions have failed to force Iraq to comply with resolution 660 and the subsequent relevant resolutions. Iraq was continuing the destruction of Kuwait, its efforts to absorb Kuwait, and the strengthening of its military presence inside Kuwait. Further delay would only have prolonged the suffering of the Kuwaiti people and increased the risks to the military forces of the United States and other States co-operating with the Government of Kuwait.

Accordingly, pursuant to resolution 678, the military forces of the United States and other States co-operating with the Government of Kuwait initiated military action at 1900 (Eastern Standard Time) on 16 January 1991 to liberate Kuwait, restore the legitimate Government of Kuwait, and restore international peace and security in the area consistent with resolution 660 and the subsequent relevant resolutions.

The military actions initiated by the United States and other States co-operating with the Government of Kuwait are being carried out in full compliance with the applicable law of armed conflict. The purpose of these actions is the liberation of Kuwait, not the destruction, occupation or dismemberment of Iraq. They are directed strictly at military and strategic targets and every effort has been made to minimize civilian casualties. The United States hopes that these actions will be concluded as soon as possible consistent with the full implementation of resolution 660 and all subsequent relevant resolutions and the restoration of international peace and security in the area.

...

S/22092, 17 January 1991

8. Letter from the Chargé d'affaires a.i. of the Permanent Mission of Malaysia to the United Nations addressed to the Secretary-General, 17 January 1991

I have the honour to transmit to you herewith the text of a message from His Excellency Dato' Haji Abu Hassan Omar, Minister of Foreign Affairs, Malaysia on the outbreak of the Gulf war. ...

Malaysia is deeply saddened by the outbreak of hostilities in the Gulf. Since the beginning of the Gulf crisis in August, Malaysia has hoped that Iraq would have abided by all relevant United Nations Security Council resolutions and withdrawn from Kuwait by 15 January as required by United Nations Security Council resolution 678 to avoid the use of force.

The United Nations Security Council had from the beginning called for a negotiated settlement of the crisis and adopted a number of resolutions calling upon Iraq to withdraw unconditionally from Kuwait without risking war. As a small nation, Malaysia cannot prevent any action being taken against Iraq if it refuses to withdraw from Kuwait. Malaysia will not accept the invasion of a weak country by a stronger neighbour. Malaysia is especially distressed that the problems between the two Muslim countries could not be resolved in a spirit of brotherhood that should exist among Muslim nations.

As a member of the Security Council then, Malaysia together with other non-aligned countries had exerted every effort to bring about a peaceful resolution to the conflict without the use of force. Regrettably, Malaysia's initiatives were not accepted by the parties concerned.

Even though hostilities have broken out, Malaysia urges the United Nations Security Council to continue its effort in seeking a peaceful solution and bring the war to an immediate end.

Malaysia appeals to Iraq to withdraw from Kuwait to avoid further catastrophe which will not bring any benefits to itself, the Middle East and the world.

S/22093, 17 January 1991

9. Letter from the Permanent Representative of Kuwait to the United Nations addressed to the President of the Security Council, 17 January 1991

I transmit herewith a copy of the statement issued by the Council of Ministers at dawn today, Thursday, 2 Rajab A.H. 1411, corresponding to 17 January A.D. 1991 ...

...

> *"And say: 'The truth has come, and falsehood has vanished away; surely falsehood is ever certain to vanish.'"*

The Council of Ministers met at dawn today, Thursday, 2 Rajab A.H. 1411, corresponding to 17 January A.D. 1991, under the chairmanship of His Excellency the Deputy Prime Minister and Minister for Foreign Affairs, Sheikh Sabah Al-Ahmad Al-Sabah, following the beginning of military operations to liberate Kuwait, and issued the following statement:

The Council has followed the commencement of operations to liberate Kuwait from the defilement of iniquitous Iraqi aggression, as well as the statements relating to these operations. In expressing its appreciation and gratitude to all those fraternal and friendly States which took part and are taking part in the liberation operation, the Council affirms the legitimacy of this war and its necessity for the liberation of Kuwait. It underscores the principle of international legitimacy, as embodied in the implementation of Security Council resolutions and respect for the precepts of international law and customs, now that the entire world has exhausted all possible means to ensure the peaceful withdrawal of the Iraqi aggressor forces from Kuwait.

By virtue of its vanity and arrogance, the Iraqi régime deliberately closed the doors to all well-intentioned endeavours, the most recent of which was that undertaken by the Secretary-General of the United Nations. Over five months have passed since the beginning of the hated occupation, and the international community had to implement its resolutions to expel that régime by force from all Kuwaiti territories and to reinstate the legitimate authority by means of a decisive military operation designed to restore the rule of justice and to relieve the defiant Kuwaiti people - who have suffered and endured every form of brutality, killing and torture in a manner which contravenes all the precepts of international law, human rights and divine religions - from injustice and tyranny.

We cannot fail on this auspicious occasion to express our great appreciation for the historic address delivered this morning by the United States President, George Bush, which properly reflects the stand taken by him and the noble people of the United States in support of human justice and international legitimacy.

We are yet prouder because Kuwaitis took an active part in the liberation operations, with their hearts filled with faith in God, trust in His assistance, devotion to their dear country and readiness to expend what is most precious to them in order to defend its territory.

We pray that God will support the soldiers of justice and truth and grant them victory: He possesses that power.

S/22094, 17 January 1991

10. Letter from the Permanent Representative of Kuwait to the United Nations addressed to the President of the Security Council, 17 January 1991

On instructions from my Government, I hereby transmit the following information to you:

Following the expiry of the deadline set by the Security Council in its resolution 678 (1990) for the full implementation of its pertinent resolutions, Kuwait notified the Secretary-General of the United Nations that Iraqi forces continued to occupy all territories of the State of Kuwait. Accordingly, and pursuant to paragraph 4 of resolution 678 (1990), Kuwait wishes to inform you that it is exercising its right to self-defence and to the restoration of its rights, first and foremost among which is the recovery of its territories, occupied by Iraq since 2 August 1990. In doing so, the Kuwaiti forces are co-operating with the forces of fraternal and friendly States which are equally determined to end the obdurate Iraqi occupation.

We shall also transmit to you the statement issued by the Kuwaiti Council of Ministers concerning the beginning of the operation to liberate Kuwait.

...

S/22095, 17 January 1991

11. Letter from the Permanent Representative of the Ukrainian Soviet Socialist Republic to the United Nations addressed to the Secretary-General, 17 January 1991

I have the honour to transmit herewith the text of a statement issued on 17 January 1991 by His Excellency Mr. Leonid M. Kravchuk, Chairman of the Supreme Soviet (Parliament) of the Ukrainian Soviet Socialist Republic.

...

The events in the Persian Gulf have taken a tragic turn. These events are due to the refusal of the Iraqi Government to put an end to its occupation of Kuwait, as the United Nations demands.

It must be noted that the international community has spared no effort to ensure a peaceful settlement of the crisis that has arisen in the Persian Gulf following Iraq's aggression against a sovereign neighbouring State. That was precisely the purpose of the resolutions adopted by the Security Council.

Despite the many steps - diplomatic, economic and other - taken by the international community in connection with Iraq, and despite the attempts at mediation, particularly the efforts undertaken by the Secretary-General of the United Nations, to avert the threat of war, all has been in vain.

We wish to emphasize that by systematically pursuing a policy aimed at a peaceful settlement of the conflict and by appealing to all parties to do everything possible to that end, the Ukrainian Soviet Socialist Republic was hoping that the Iraqi Government would realize the enormity of the danger to which its policy was leading and would come to reason. That has unfortunately not been the case.

S/22096, 17 January 1991

12. Letter from the Permanent Representative of the Union of Soviet Socialist Republics to the United Nations addressed to the Secretary-General, 17 January 1991

I have the honour to transmit to you herewith the text of the statement made on national television, on 17 January 1991, by M. S. Gorbachev, President of the Union of Soviet Socialist Republics, on the situation in the Persian Gulf.

...

War has begun tonight in the Persian Gulf. The United States armed forces, in liaison with British, Saudi and other units, have struck at military targets and certain industrial targets in Iraq, and at positions of the Iraqi armed forces.

Events have taken this tragic turn as a result of the refusal of the Iraqi Government to respond to the demands of the world community and withdraw its troops from Kuwait.

From the start of the Iraqi aggression, the Soviet Union has done everything in its power to bring about a peaceful solution to this critical international conflict. Until the very last moment, we were working actively in the hope of averting war and restoring the independence of Kuwait by political means. When, one hour before the start of the military operations, I was informed by the United States Secretary of State, Mr. Baker, of the decision taken, I immediately proposed to President Bush that he take further action by contacting Saddam Hussein directly in order to secure a commitment from him that he would order the immediate withdrawal of Iraqi troops from Kuwait. At the same time, I instructed our ambassador to Baghdad to contact the Iraqi President and communicate to him the proposal I had made to George Bush. I emphasized the fact that it was necessary, in the interest of the Iraqi people itself and in order to preserve peace in the region, for the President of Iraq to state that he was ready to see to the evacuation of Kuwait. That would have made it possible to delay the onset of war and spare Iraq heavy losses and destruction. I expressed the hope that Saddam Hussein, guided by the higher interests of his people and of the world community, would take that path, the only way out.

This very evening, we have appealed to the Governments of a number of influential countries, among them France, China, the United Kingdom, Germany, Italy and India, and to the leaders of most of the Arab countries, to undertake joint and concomitant steps to limit the conflict and prevent it from taking on dangerous proportions.

Aware of the serious consequences that a war waged with immense military forces and the most modern technical capabilities can have for the Arab peoples and the people of the United States and for the state of the world, we express deep regret that it has not been possible to avoid a military conflict. I emphasize once again, however, that we have done everything conceivable to resolve the conflict by non-military means. I wish to state that none of the Soviet citizens currently in Iraq have as yet been victims of the conflict.

The Soviet people can rest assured that the government will take all the necessary steps to bring the war to an end and re-establish peace as soon as possible, in co-operation with other countries and with the United Nations.

S/22097, 17 January 1991

13. Letter from the Permanent Representative of the United Kingdom of Great Britain and Northern Ireland to the United Nations addressed to the President of the Security Council, 17 January 1991

I have the honour to inform you on behalf of my Government that the Armed Forces of the United Kingdom in association with those of other States co-operating with the Government of Kuwait commenced action on the evening of 16 January 1991 pursuant to operative paragraph 2 of resolution 678.

Military action initiated by the United States, United Kingdom, Saudi Arabia, Kuwait and France on 16 and 17 January is designed to achieve the liberation of Kuwait called for in the resolutions, and not the destruction, occupation or dismemberment of Iraq. The United Kingdom hopes these actions will be concluded as soon as possible consistent with the full implementation of resolution 660 and all subsequent relevant resolutions and with the restoration of international peace and security in the area.

...

S/22098, 17 January 1991

14. Letter from the Permanent Representative of Yemen to the United Nations addressed to the President of the Security Council, 17 January 1991

I have the honour to transmit to you herewith the text of the statement issued by the joint meeting of the Presidential Council and the Council of Ministers of the Republic of Yemen held on Thursday, 17 January 1991, which considered the recent developments in the region.

...

This morning, a joint meeting of the Presidential Council and the Council of Ministers was held under the chairmanship of Colonel Ali Abdullah Saleh, Chairman of the Presidential Council. It considered the recent developments in the region in the light of the attacks launched by the United States and its allies against the fraternal country of Iraq.

...

The Presidential Council and the Council of Ministers considered the painful developments in the present crisis in the region of the Gulf and the Arabian peninsula with the outbreak of armed conflict at 2.30 a.m. today, Thursday, 17 January 1991, under the leadership of the United States and the forces allied with it, in implementation of a military action that has the basic aim of destroying Iraq and inflicting heavy material and human losses on the people of Iraq, which is part of the Arab and Islamic nation, to say nothing of its consequences in terms of the dissipation of Arab capacities and resources. This represents a flagrant challenge to the declared will of the international community rejecting war and opposing the use of force, and it constitutes conduct that is unacceptable in an era of international reconciliation.

The Republic of Yemen, which has made an earnest and sincere effort to bring about peace, security and stability and to forestall foreign intervention, renews its commitment to this approach and to pursuing intensive efforts for a halt to military operations and for the parties concerned to sit down at the negotiating table in order to resolve all of the problems confronting the Arab region, including the issue of the Arab-Israeli conflict and all the various sources of tension arising therefrom, and to achieve peace and security in the entire Middle East region.

The Republic of Yemen calls upon the international community in general, and on the five States permanent members of the Security Council in particular, to bring an end to the bloodshed and aggression and to meet in full their responsibility for the establishment of a permanent and comprehensive peace in the Middle East region, given that the ongoing conflict represents one of the region's grievous manifestations resulting from double standards, negligence and procrastination in the application of international legitimacy as represented by binding resolutions adopted by the Security Council decades ago.

S/22099, 17 January 1991

15. Letter from the Permanent Representative of Jordan to the United Nations addressed to the Secretary-General, 17 January 1991

I have the honour to transmit to you herewith the text of a statement concerning ongoing events in the Gulf region, as issued on 17 January 1991 by the official Jordanian spokesman.

...

Since the outbreak of the Gulf crisis, Jordan has been doing its utmost to address its causes and its consequences within an Arab framework. In the first days of the crisis, its leadership was able to obtain an Iraqi commitment to withdraw from Kuwait, and a time was established for that withdrawal to begin. Jordan also obtained Iraq's agreement that it would attend a scaled-down summit meeting at Jeddah in order to address the underlying causes that had led to the eruption of the crisis. However, the insistance [*sic*] of the adoption of a resolution by the League of Arab States, as embodied in the Arab ministers for foreign affairs, as well as the emergence of extreme and inflexible positions among certain Arab parties, both facilitated the adoption by the Security Council of successive resolutions on the crisis.

There then ensued the arrival of foreign forces in the region, which made the withdrawal from Kuwait inoperative at its very outset and aborted the scaled-down summit meeting at Jeddah for which there had been hope.

Jordan continued to strive for peaceful action, but its repeated attempts encountered obstacles erected by a number of parties which were clearly resolved to choose war and playing for time in which to complete the mobilization of their forces and prepare for aggression against Iraq under the guise of implementing United Nations Security Council resolutions.

Jordan, which has always respected the resolutions of the Security Council and is constant in its commitment to their implementation, is grieved that an analogous crisis in the region was not met with speedy resolutions, economic boycott and the threat of hostile action despite its longstanding character and despite the fact that it gives rise to occupation and the expulsion of an Arab people from its land and the soil of its homeland.

The leadership, Government and people of Jordan condemn the brutal assault in the early hours of today on a peaceable Arab country and people - one that has always hastened to the assistance of its brother Arabs and unhesitatingly paid its due in terms of blood and sacrifice in all of the battles that have been imposed on the Arab nation - by an attack on its capital city in such great force and with the possibility of continued strikes against it. All of those who took part will bear responsibility for it, to God, to man and to history, for having set out to destroy an Arab military, intellectual and human power and a peaceable, proud and fraternal Arab people which is of and for the essence of this nation. God will watch over and safeguard our nation, and He will enable us to protect the integrity of its generations to come after us. It is from God that succour comes.

S/22100, 17 January 1991

16. Letter from the Permanent Representative of France to the United Nations addressed to the President of the Security Council, 17 January 1991

I have the honour to inform you, under paragraph 4 of Security Council resolution 678 (1990), of the action undertaken this day by France, in fulfilment of earlier commitments made within the framework of plans established jointly with its allies, with a view to securing the implementation of Security Council resolution 660 (1990) and of all pertinent subsequent resolutions of the Council.

The action by the French forces present in the region has no other objective than that of liberating Kuwait.

A first air strike was made by assault aircraft of the French Air Force on 17 January 1991 at the beginning of the morning, as part of a joint raid aimed at an Iraqi military target in Kuwait.

...

S/22102, 17 January 1991

17. Letter from the Permanent Representative of Bulgaria to the United Nations addressed to the Secretary-General, 17 January 1991

Upon instructions from my Government, I have the honour to forward to you the texts of a Declaration of the President of the Republic of Bulgaria ... and a Declaration of the Government of the Republic of Bulgaria ... in connection with the crisis in the Persian Gulf region. ...

The Republic of Bulgaria has learned with deep concern of the start of military action in the Persian Gulf region. Our anxiety is increased by the fact that this conflict is unfolding close to our country.

The responsibility for the outbreak of the conflict lies entirely with the Iraqi leadership, which, by occupying and annexing Kuwait, has flagrantly violated the basic principles and norms of international law, has refused to take into account the clearly expressed opinion of the international community to implement the respective resolutions of the Security Council of the United Nations, including resolution 678 (1990), and to respond constructively to the numerous peace initiatives.

All options for finding a peaceful outcome of the crisis in the Persian Gulf have been explored. Thus, the commencement of military action, despite the great risks involved, is a radical but necessary measure to guarantee international peace. It is envisaged in the Charter of the United Nations and is particularly appropriate when the security of small nations is at stake.

Throughout the time following Kuwait's illegal occupation by Iraq the Republic of Bulgaria has actively supported the efforts of the international community aimed at finding a political solution of the conflict. Bulgaria supported all resolutions of the Security Council on this matter by joining unconditionally in the international embargo against Iraq, despite the heavy price it has had to pay and the fact that this has made it even more difficult for the country to emerge from the severe economic crisis.

The Republic of Bulgaria is availing itself of this opportunity to yet again emphasize its consistent position that peace in the region cannot be achieved without a complete and unconditional Iraqi withdrawal from the State of Kuwait, without the restoration of its sovereignty, territorial integrity and legitimate Government in accordance with the resolutions of the Security Council of the United Nations.

The Republic of Bulgaria is thus supportive of the actions of the multinational forces for meeting those goals and is again reiterating its readiness, expressed on a number of occasions, to act with all means in implementation of the decision of the Grand National Assembly of Bulgaria.

At the same time it is our hope that the military action will be over soon, to be followed by steps for resolving the disputed issues between Iraq and Kuwait by diplomatic means.

The Republic of Bulgaria is and will continue to be a friend of the Arab peoples, including the people of Iraq. It will continue to work in the future for promoting mutually advantageous co-operation with all States in the region.

UN Press Release

18. Extract from Daily UN Press Briefing, 18 January 1991

Mr Giuliani [*the UN Spokesman*] went on to say that when he had arrived at his office this morning, the Secretary-General has telephoned the Permanent Representative of Israel to convey his deep regret about the Iraqi missile attack on his country last night. Correspondents would recall that the Secretary-General, on his arrival at the Secretariat entrance, had expressed regrets about the incident, firstly, because it could widen the conflict since Israel was not part of the coalition ranged against Iraq, and secondly, because the attack had been directed at civilian targets. Mr Giuliani said the Secretary General had also been asked what his message to the Government of Israel was, and how he expected Israel to respond. He had replied that he expected the Israeli Government to be as patient as possible. ...

S/22103, 18 January 1991

19. Letter from the Permanent Representative of Czechoslovakia to the United Nations addressed to the President of the Security Council, 18 January 1991

I have the honour to transmit to you herewith the text of the Declaration of the Government of the Czech and Slovak Federal Republic on the Outbreak of Hostilities against Iraq:

> "The Government of the Czech and Slovak Federal Republic considers the outbreak of hostilities against Iraq by the allied forces on 17 January 1991 to be a logical result of the present crisis in the Persian Gulf. This is a natural and legal consequence of the fact that Iraq has refused to comply with the United Nations Security Council resolution 678 (1990) demanding an immediate and unconditional withdrawal of the Iraqi troops from the illegally occupied territory of Kuwait.
>
> "The Government of the Czech and Slovak Federal Republic fully supports the adopted decision enforcing the will of the international community to free Kuwait by all possible means. At the same time, it appeals to the Government of the Republic of Iraq asking it to prevent further bloodshed and an increase in material damage in the whole region of the Persian Gulf - for which it is fully responsible - by expeditiously withdrawing its troops from Kuwait."

...

S/22104, 18 January 1991

20. Letter from the Chargé d'affaires a.i. of the Permanent Mission of Algeria to the United Nations addressed to the Secretary-General, 17 January 1991

I have the honour to transmit to you herewith the text of a statement issued on 17 January 1991 by the spokesman of the Ministry of Foreign Affairs of the People's Democratic Republic of Algeria. ...

Since 2 August 1990, the Arab nation has been confronted with a critical situation and one of the most dangerous in all its history. The tragedy reached its climax with the massive military intervention against fraternal Iraq carried out by an international alliance led by the greatest of the Western military powers. In order to carry out this operation against a third-world country, the greatest mobilization of means of destruction in the history of warfare was carried out in Arab territory over a period of only five months.

This war is an expression of intransigence, of a sense of power and of a desire for hegemony. True power, however, is that which is bestowed by God, and He requires of those upon whom he has conferred it that they should be wise and just. The conceit and sense of power of the parties concerned have left no room for flexibility and compromise. This is also true with respect to the righting of the greatest wrong committed in this century, namely that to which the heroic Palestinian people fell victim more than 40 years ago. This war which has been imposed on the fraternal Iraqi people has been forcefully rejected by Algeria in the past, and it condemns it today in the strongest possible terms.

The destiny of the Arab nation has never before been threatened in the tragic manner in which it is being threatened today.

Motivated by an awareness of the painful consequences that would stem from such a war and mindful of the great dangers that threaten the unity and destiny of the Arab nation, Algeria, together with those vital Arab forces that grasp the higher interest of the Arab nation in achieving a peaceful solution within an Arab framework, has striven for the full mobilization of the Arab nation's lively conscience and its deep awareness of its interests with a view to achieving an Arab solution within an Arab framework.

Algeria has spared no effort to appeal to all those States with which it has relations and to all men of good-will in the world to strive for more understanding and greater flexibility in the search for a solution that will ensure the higher interests of the Arab nation and, at the same time, achieve world peace. Such a solution would be based, on the one hand, on respect for the international rule of law and the restoration of the sovereignty of Kuwait and, on the other, on the preservation of Iraq, whose achievements and capabilities represent a precious acquisition for the Arabs as a whole.

Algeria has acted out of a conviction that this war, aimed as it is at the destruction of Iraq, will necessarily affect Kuwait and other Arab countries, that it will inevitably have an impact on the entire Arab world and that it will benefit only the enemies of the Arab nation, principally a Zionist entity that can only emerge from the war strengthened.

Since 2 August last, Algeria has constantly affirmed that the Gulf crisis, no matter how recondite and complex its underlying causes and regardless of its grave regional and international consequences, could have been resolved justly and honourably within an Arab framework by means of dialogue and negotiations.

However, the Cairo summit convened on 10 August 1990, at which the Arabs assembled in order to seek an Arab solution precluding direct or indirect foreign intervention, supplanted joint Arab action by resort to foreign forces and thus opened the way to intransigence, a hardening of positions and an irrational yielding to the logic of war.

Algeria has constantly rejected the logic of war. It has always been aware of the devastating impact of an armed conflict, of the instability and insecurity that the Arab world, and indeed the world as a whole, would undergo as a result of the political and economic upheavals that it would cause and of the sense of wrong and humiliation that it would produce in the Arab nation.

The Arab world, which will be afflicted with unprecedented destruction and division, will be the first victim of the end of the cold war and of the new international political order intended to be established on the woes of the Arab world.

The Palestinian cause, that sacred Arab cause which is present in the current conflict just as it is present in all crises which convulse the Middle East, is once more a victim of the interests of power and of a disregard of the international rule of law to which appeal is made by those who bear responsibility for the war.

Algeria has always been against the resort to violence and the forcible annexation of territory, and these are firmly established and deeply held principles that have constantly guided Algeria in its foreign policy.

Algeria further believes that international legitimacy is an indivisible whole, and this means that international legitimacy is to be applied to one and all, in all circumstances and in all places, beginning with the question of Palestine.

Algeria, which strove assiduously up to the last moment in order to avert a catastrophe, charges one and all with their responsibilities towards the Arab peoples and towards history.

The Arab nation is facing the gravest trial of its modern history, and the Algerian people must endure that trial with its well-known courage and determination and in the spirit of responsibility and solidarity with which it is graced.

Closer than ever to the fraternal Iraqi people, Algeria expresses its solidarity with that people in the ordeal that has been imposed upon it. It calls upon all peoples that cherish peace and justice to strive earnestly for an immediate halt to military operations, for the withdrawal of all foreign forces and fleets from Iraq, from Kuwait and from the entire region, and for an immediate start to be made on a process leading to the peaceful settlement of the Middle East issue through the convening of an international conference.

At this crucial stage in the history of the Arab nation, Algeria commits itself to exerting every effort for the mobilization and utilization of all such forces as may bring about a return to a state of lasting peace and stability in the region.

S/22105, 18 January 1991

21. Letter from the Permanent Representative of Saudi Arabia to the United Nations addressed to the President of the Security Council, 16 January 1991

On instructions from my Government, may I convey the following according to operative articles 2, 3 and 4 of Security Council resolution 678 (1990).

An official spokesman in Saudi Arabia has announced today that the operation for the liberation of the State of Kuwait commenced, with God's help and success, at dawn, at 2.50 a.m., the 17th of January 1991 Riyadh time (time difference, already 17th in Riyadh).

The official spokesman further added that in implementation of the Arab and Islamic resolutions as well as of the resolutions of the Security Council which stipulates the necessity for the unconditional withdrawal of the Iraqi invading forces from Kuwait territories and the restoration of legitimacy in the country; and whereas all efforts, initiatives and appeals that had been exerted and addressed to the ruler of Iraq up to the last minute of the deadline that has been set for the withdrawal of Iraqi forces from Kuwait, which is the 15th of January 1991, and what has followed from that up to this morning at dawn; and given that President Saddam Hussein had adamantly rejected all efforts, appeals and endeavours and has also rejected international legality, while it was possible for him to avoid the occurrence of these battles to prevent bloodshed; thus the military operations for the liberation of the State of Kuwait has commenced. Victory is bestowed by God.

...

S/22106, 18 January 1991

22. Letter from the Permanent Representative of Japan to the United Nations addressed to the Secretary-General, 17 January 1991

I have the honour to transmit herewith the text of a statement issued on 17 January 1991 by Prime Minister Toshiki Kaifu on actions in the Gulf taken in order to enforce the United Nations Security Council resolutions ...

...

I. Today a number of States Members of the United Nations, including the United States and European and Arab countries, resorted to the use of force in order to enforce United Nations Security Council resolutions which demand the total withdrawal of Iraq from Kuwait and the restoration of the legitimate Government of Kuwait.

Japan has insisted from the beginning that the Government of Iraq comply with the relevant United Nations Security Council resolutions without delay, and has made every possible effort until the very last moment to resolve the crisis peacefully. The Government of Iraq, however, has stubbornly ignored the Security Council resolutions and continued its invasion and annexation of Kuwait beyond the grace period that expired on 15 January. Japan strongly condemns this outrageous behaviour of Iraq, and deeply regrets that the efforts of the international community to find a peaceful solution to the crisis have achieved nothing.

Iraq's blatant invasion and annexation of its neighbour is a challenge to the authority of the United Nations which has a major responsibility for the maintenance of international peace and security. If condoned, such actions would jeopardize the just and stable international order that is so indispensable for the existence of every country, including Japan. Accordingly, Japan pledges its firm support for the use of force by the countries concerned, carried out in accordance with United Nations Security Council resolution 678, as the last resort in efforts to terminate the invasion and restore peace.

Japan is determined to extend maximum possible support, in accordance with the United Nations Security Council resolutions, to the actions taken by the countries concerned to restore international peace and stability. Furthermore, Japan will offer maximum possible assistance to evacuees and refugees in co-operation with relevant international organizations, and is already taking actions for its implementation.

Japan strongly calls upon the Government of Iraq to respect the united will of the international community and immediately accept all the relevant United Nations Security Council resolutions. It is our strong hope that hostilities in the Gulf region will promptly cease, and lasting peace and stability will prevail in the Middle East as soon as possible.

The Government of Japan has already taken necessary steps to ensure the safety of Japanese nationals remaining in and around the Gulf region. The Government will continue to make all possible efforts for the protection of those Japanese nationals, with a view to avoiding any unexpected adverse developments in the present situation. All necessary measures are also being taken to prevent hijackings and other emergency situations in Japan and overseas.

Likewise, the Government intends to work within a co-operative international framework to minimize the adverse impact on the Japanese economy and to ensure stability in the daily life of the people. At the same time, I would like to remind the Japanese people of the heightened need for energy conservation.

Japan has also established a Gulf crisis task force within the Cabinet and headed by myself as Prime Minister, and will respond vigorously to this emergency in a concerted, comprehensive and effective manner.

Confident that these policies are in Japan's own interests and are consistent with the desire for lasting peace through international harmony as expressed in our Constitution, the Government asks for the understanding and co-operation of all of the people.

II. Based on the position that I have just stated, the following concrete measures will be taken:

1. Assistance to the multinational forces.

The Government of Japan intends to extend, as assistance to the multinational forces, an additional contribution to the Gulf Peace Fund.

2. Assistance to evacuees.

(1) *Financial and in-kind co-operation*

To cope positively with the situation, the Government of Japan will disburse as soon as possible $ US 38 million, which is equivalent to the full amount which the Office of the United Nations Disaster Relief Co-ordinator (UNDRO) has requested from the International community to cover start-up costs for the relief of evacuees. Relief materials (including blankets) will also be provided to the countries around Iraq, as the need arises.

(2) *Transportation co-operation*

From a humanitarian viewpoint, the Government will ask civil airlines to transport evacuees, and under the assumption that conditions will vary from case to case, will consider the use of Self-defense Force transportation aircraft as necessary. I would like to request the understanding of the Japanese people in these actions.

S/22107, 18 January 1991

23. Letter from the Permanent Representative of Nicaragua to the United Nations addressed to the Secretary-General, 18 January 1991

I have the honour to transmit herewith the text of the communiqué issued by the Ministry of Foreign Affairs of the Republic of Nicaragua on 17 January 1991 concerning the situation in the Persian Gulf.

...

The Ministry of Foreign Affairs of the Republic of Nicaragua, in view of the grave crisis which has developed in the Persian Gulf, makes known to the people of Nicaragua and to the international community the following:

> In the spirit of respect for international law, the Charter of the United Nations and the principle of the sovereignty and territorial integrity of every nation, the Government of Nicaragua reiterates its support for the resolutions which the Security Council of the United Nations has adopted in relation to this conflict.
>
> The Government of Nicaragua deeply deplores the fact that the attempts at a peaceful settlement of the Gulf crisis by political and diplomatic means have been frustrated, and entertains the hope that the efforts which the Secretary-General of the United Nations and the international community have been making will result in the re-establishment of Kuwait as a sovereign and independent nation.
>
> The Government of Nicaragua likewise deeply regrets the suffering, the loss of lives and the devastating consequences inevitably occasioned by war. Nicaragua, having also suffered during its history the effects of armed confrontation, advocates a speedy solution to this conflict that will once again set humanity on the path of peace and reconciliation.

A/45/933, S/22109, 18 January 1991

24. Letter from the Permanent Representative of Hungary to the United Nations addressed to the Secretary-General, 18 January 1991

I have the honour to transmit to you herewith the text of a statement issued on 17 January 1991 by the Government of the Republic of Hungary regarding the developments in the Persian Gulf region ...

...

The Government of the Republic of Hungary, on the basis of Hungary's historical experience and as a matter of principle, does not accept actions in flagrant violation of the sovereignty of individual States, rejects all forms of aggression and firmly stands for the maintenance or, if necessary, the restoration of international legal order.

On the basis of these principles, Hungary has deeply condemned the aggression against the State of Kuwait in August 1990 and the annexation of that country. Hungary has been committed to and has fully implemented all United Nations Security Council resolutions regarding the Iraqi aggression against Kuwait in the sincere hope that the united stand of the international community will compel the Iraqi leadership to dismantle the consequences of aggression.

The Iraqi leadership, in defiance of the will of the international community, refused to adhere to the norms and stipulations of international law. Up until the final deadline set by the United Nations Security Council, Iraq had shown no readiness to withdraw its troops from Kuwait and had given no indication at all that it intended to seek a peaceful settlement of the conflict. Diplomatic endeavours had proved to be unsuccessful and all opportunities to find a negotiated settlement had been, in the general view, exhausted. Thus, the international - and, among them, Arab - forces deployed in the region have become compelled to make use of the authorization of the United Nations Security Council to uphold international law and employ all means at their disposal to enforce the mandatory resolutions of the world organizations.

The Hungarian people are aware that war and armed confrontation are an undesirable course of action, a necessary evil even in the most righteous cause. They are, however, also conscious of the lessons of history: aggression must be arrested, aggressors must be stopped even at the cost of sacrifices.

The Government of the Republic of Hungary sincerely hopes that the military operations aimed at the liberation of Kuwait will remain limited both in time and scope and will lead to the restoration of the sovereignty and territorial integrity of Kuwait and the security of all countries in the region with the least loss of life and damage. In keeping with its possibilities, Hungary is also contributing to these efforts and all the steps it has taken are aimed only at the elimination of aggression and its consequences and are in no way directed against the people of Iraq.

The Republic of Hungary is confident that, in the wake of an early and just solution to the crisis, new opportunities will open up to restore and enhance co-operation with Iraq and the other States in the region, as well as to create a security system encompassing the entire region and to solve decades-old conflicts.

S/22111, 18 January 1991

25. Letter from the Permanent Representative of the Union of Soviet Socialist Republics to the United Nations addressed to the Secretary-General, 18 January 1991

I have the honour to transmit to you herewith the text of the statement of the Ministry of Foreign Affairs of the USSR concerning the launching of missiles by Iraq against Israel, on 18 January.

...

During the night of 17 to 18 January, Iraq launched missiles on sections of Tel Aviv, Haifa and some other Israeli urban centres.

There is absolutely no doubt that the aim of this operation was to try to convert the problem of Kuwait into a regional conflict and to make the war spread like a conflagration to the Middle East as a whole.

The Soviet Union has always taken a firm and unambiguous stand against such a development, particularly in the course of its contacts with the Iraqi authorities. We are convinced that it is impossible to resolve one problem by creating another and that it would be dangerous, above all for the peoples of the region itself, if this conflict were to develop into another, even wider and more complex conflict.

At this critical juncture, we make another appeal to the Iraqi authorities to show that they are realistic and understand that their actions, beginning with the occupation of Kuwait, can bring only death and destruction to the Iraqi people and further misfortune to the region as a whole. The leaders of the Arab States cannot fail to understand this, responsible as they are for the well-being of their people. We hope that the Arabs will not let themselves be dominated by their emotions and will not take part in plans aimed at unleashing a new military confrontation with Israel.

In the Soviet Union, we also certainly hope that, for its part, the Israeli Government will show the necessary restraint and not embark on a path that would result in still greater tension in the Middle East.

Once again, the Soviet Union takes a firm stand in favour of a settlement of the problem of Kuwait on the basis of the resolutions of the United Nations Security Council and in favour of the earliest possible break in the stalemate in other situations of conflict in the Middle East. The peoples of the region must, finally, be able to enjoy peace and live in tranquillity.

S/22112, 18 January 1991

26. Note verbale from the Permanent Representative of Mongolia to the United Nations addressed to the Secretary-General, 18 January 1991

...

From the very start, the Government of the Mongolian People's Republic resolutely condemned Iraq's armed aggression against and violent annexation of neighbouring Kuwait on 2 August 1990 as an act that goes contrary to the Charter of the United Nations and basic principles of international law and inter-State relations.

All efforts made by States to attain complete withdrawal of Iraqi troops from Kuwait and restoration of its independence and sovereignty by political means, as well as the sanctions imposed in accordance with the United Nations resolutions had failed to achieve any results. Thus, owing to the position of Iraq's present leadership the deadline for peaceful settlement of the conflict set forth by Security Council resolution 678 (1990) had expired. In this condition, the multinational forces, under the provisions of the above-mentioned resolution of the Security Council, started today actions to free Kuwait.

The Government of the Mongolian People's Republic expresses its deep regret that the development of events has led up to an armed conflict, a serious exacerbation of the international situation, the imminent peril of human casualties and enormous material loss. The Mongolian People's Republic, while reaffirming its commitment to peaceful resolution of all disputes, once again voices its support to the United Nations resolutions regarding the settlement of the Persian Gulf crisis.

The Government of the Mongolian People's Republic expresses its hope that military actions aimed at reinstating the independence and sovereignty of Kuwait will not be further escalated, and peace and tranquillity be promptly restored in the Persian Gulf.

A/45/934, S/22113, 18 January 1991

27. Letter from the Permanent Representative of Egypt to the United Nations addressed to the Secretary-General, 17 January 1991

I have the honour to transmit to you herewith the text of the statement made by Mr. Esmat Abdel Meguid, Deputy Prime Minister and Minister for Foreign Affairs, to the Arab and Foreign Affairs and National Security Committee of the Shura Council on 17 January 1991. ...

As I speak to you, I address you in the midst of crucial and delicate circumstances in our region in which the eyes of the whole world are upon us and events are escalating and deteriorating with great rapidity. I have to inform you that, early this morning, I was in touch with a number of ministers for foreign affairs of friendly and brotherly countries so that we could exchange information, consult together and co-ordinate our positions on coping with the effects of this major occurrence.

It may be useful for me to present to you our analysis of the situation and our view of its various aspects and antecedents up to the stage to which matters had developed by the time the operation to liberate Kuwait began early today, 17 January 1991.

Iraq's invasion of Kuwait on 2 August 1990 was en event unprecedented in the history of the Arab nation and indeed in the contemporary era following the Second World War. For the first time, an Arab State was invading another Arab State, occupying its territory, removing its legitimate system of Government by force of arms and then announcing its annexation. In doing so, it established a dangerous international precedent violating inter-Arab and international covenants. Matters did not stop there, but a far-reaching disturbance was brought about in the balance of regional security in the strategically vital Middle East region.

This Committee has been in the forefront in monitoring events in the Gulf from the time the Iraqi invasion of Kuwait took place. It issued a statement on 4 August 1990 which truly captured the pulse of the masses in their condemnation of the Iraqi invasion of Kuwait and in their demand for an immediate and complete withdrawal of Iraqi forces. Then, on 22 August, a statement by the General Committee was issued supporting the historic and civilized position adopted by President Hosni Mubarak in addressing the crisis and calling upon Iraq to respond to appeals for peace out of a regard for higher Arab interests and in order to save the people of Iraq and the peoples of the region from the scourge of war.

The Iraqi invasion of Kuwait and Iraq's concentration of forces on the Kuwaiti-Saudi borders created a situation of concern and a sense of insecurity which impelled Saudi Arabia and some of the Gulf States, in exercise of their inherent right to legitimate self-defence, to request the aid and military assistance of their brothers and friends. That right is established as a principle by article 2 of the Joint Defence and Economic Co-operation Treaty between the States of the Arab League, by article 6 of the Pact of the League of Arab States in international law, and it was reaffirmed by the Arab Summit Conference resolution adopted by the meeting held at Cairo on 10 August 1990.

Egypt responded to the request made by Saudi Arabia and the United Arab Emirates in the light of its clear understanding of the challenges and dangers involved and in the context of the responsibility that it bears at the inter-Arab and international levels, given that the Egyptian forces in question provide a shield for the Arab nation as a whole, are helping a brother and are deterring an aggressor.

President Mubarak stressed the leading role being played by the valiant Egyptian armed forces when he said to the People's Assembly and the Shura Council on 15 December 1990: "It was natural for us to respond to the appeal of the fraternal Kingdom of Saudi Arabia ... to take part in the defence of this fellow Arab country ... and of all the Arab peoples of the Gulf region, regardless of the challenges, for this is our mission and our assignment, and we shall assist our brother and repel the deceit of the aggressors".

That courageous stance against aggression was accompanied by assiduous and intensive Egyptian diplomatic activity, particularly in the framework of the League of Arab States, the Organization of the Islamic Conference, the Movement of Non-Aligned Countries and the United Nations, in an endeavour to do the utmost to avert a devastating war.

In the context of intensive diplomatic efforts, many leaders and eminent personalities in Arab and foreign countries made visits to Baghdad in the attempt to persuade the Iraqi President to listen to the voice of reason and abandon inflexible positions that had no grounds in legitimacy or in law.

Most regrettably, all such efforts and meetings once again confirmed Iraq's position of rejecting the will of the international community.

Following the failure of the Geneva meeting between the United States Secretary of State and his Iraqi counterpart, the Secretary-General of the United Nations went to Baghdad with a mandate from the entire international community to transmit a clear message calling on the Iraqi President to make amends and to choose peace.

Although the Secretary-General announced that his mission had failed because of the intransigence of the Iraqi President, he nevertheless made one last appeal to the Iraqi President calling upon him to withdraw and to banish from the region the spectre of war.

Given Egypt's commitment to its deeply rooted positions of principle, the desire of the Egyptian leadership to preserve Arab solidarity and an appreciation of historical responsibility, President Mubarak spared no effort in striving to contain the tension and the escalation between Iraq and Kuwait. He addressed some 26 sincere and friendly appeals to the Iraqi President since tension began to mount, from the statement of the President of the Republic issued on 20 July 1990 up to that of 15 January 1991 in which he stated that we have no quarrel with the people of Iraq or with the Iraqi President and that the positions we have adopted stem from a profound faith in peace. He sincerely advised the Iraqi President to decide for peace in order to protect the people of Iraq, all the Arab peoples and all of those peoples which have become involved in the crisis from the disasters of war and from its devastating consequences. A statement concerning these appeals has been deposited with the Committee.

Following this detailed presentation of the efforts made by Egyptian, Arab and international diplomacy, which continued for some six months and which foundered on the rock of the Iraqi President's intransigence and his peremptory rejection of all initiatives and all appeals to restore peace and avert war, I have to tell you that early today the international community proceeded to implement the provisions of the Security Council resolutions relating to the use of force. That force was primarily directed against Iraqi military positions, and it does not have the purpose of destroying Iraq but of liberating Kuwait.

The information available indicates that there is yet time to avoid greater damage should Iraq proceed to a full and immediate withdrawal from Kuwait.

In these crucial moments, the Arab Republic of Egypt reaffirms the demand that it has made since the beginning of the crisis, namely that Iraq must comply immediately with Security Council resolutions reflecting the will of the international community.

Accordingly, Iraqi forces must withdraw from Kuwait fully and unconditionally, and Kuwait must be liberated and its legitimate authority restored, God willing, to the performance of its positive role in the Arab and international structure.

Our region has the greatest need for peace and for the allocation of its capacities to reconstruction and development for the sake of a better future for all our peoples.

In conclusion, I can only beseech the Most High, the Almighty, to safeguard and protect Egypt and to bestow upon it security and safety.

S/22114, 18 January 1991

28. Letter from the Permanent Representative of the Union of Soviet Socialist Republics to the United Nations addressed to the Secretary-General, 18 January 1991

I have the honour to transmit to you herewith the text of the decision of the Presidium of the Supreme Soviet of the Union of Soviet Socialist Republics entitled "Military operations in the Persian Gulf and action taken by the Soviet Government".

....

After having heard and reviewed the communication of Mr. A. A. Bessmertnykh, Minister for Foreign Affairs of the Union of Soviet Socialist Republics, on the situation in the Persian Gulf, and deeply regretting that the crisis has taken a tragic turn and is in fact becoming a conflict of vast proportions, the Presidium of the Supreme Soviet of the USSR decides:

1. To support the statement made by M. S. Gorbachev, President of the USSR, on the military operations in the Persian Gulf and the action taken in that regard by the Soviet Government.
2. To emphasize that it is necessary for the Government of the USSR, in keeping with the policy pursued by the Soviet Union in the Persian Gulf conflict, to keep the Supreme Soviet of the USSR regularly informed of developments in the Persian Gulf; and to communicate to the Cabinet the proposals and comments made by the people's deputies of the USSR during their consideration of the question.
3. To assign responsibility to the International Affairs Committee of the Supreme Soviet of the USSR for centralizing information on the question and communicating it to the people's deputies.

On behalf of the people's deputies of the USSR who represent the various parliamentary groups and associations, the Presidium of the Supreme Soviet of the USSR appeals to the parliamentarians of all countries to use their influence and do everything possible to obtain the immediate cessation of military operations.

The Presidium of the Supreme Soviet of the USSR urgently requests the United Nations and its Secretary-General to renew initiatives aimed at resolving the crisis in the Persian Gulf and preventing it from spreading further.

S/22115, 21 January 1991

29. Letter from the Permanent Representative of the United Kingdom of Great Britain and Northern Ireland to the United Nations addressed to the President of the Security Council, 21 January 1991

Further to my letter of 17 January (S/22097) and in accordance with paragraph 4 of resolution 678 (1990), I have the honour to inform you on behalf of my Government that the armed forces of the United Kingdom in association with those of other States co-operating with the Government of Kuwait have continued their military action pursuant to operative paragraph 2 of resolution 678 (1990).

The United Kingdom's objectives are as before to bring about Iraq's full and unconditional withdrawal from Kuwait and the restoration of the legitimate Government of Kuwait, and re-establish international peace and security in the area, and to uphold the authority of the United Nations.

Operations by United Kingdom forces have involved aerial attacks on Iraqi installations supporting Iraq's capacity to sustain its illegal occupation of Kuwait. The instructions issued to our pilots are to avoid causing civilian casualties so far as possible. British commanders have also been briefed on the locations and significance of sites of religious and cultural importance in Iraq, and operations will take account of this.

...

S/22116, 21 January 1991

30. Letter from the Permanent Representative of Mauritania to the United Nations addressed to the President of the Security Council, 21 January 1991

I have the honour to transmit to you below the text of the statement concerning the new developments in the Gulf region made at Nouakchott on 18 January 1991 by the Minister of Information, speaking on behalf of the Mauritanian Government:

> "The Gulf crisis has now entered a particularly dangerous phase.
>
> "Since Thursday, 17 January 1991, Iraq has been the target of serious aggression.
>
> "From the condemnation and embargo decided upon by the United Nations to the blockade and the deployment of a highly sophisticated and impressive military arsenal in the region, no means of demonstrating the firm resolve to destroy Iraq and its economic and military potential has been neglected. All of this has rapidly gone beyond the proclaimed objective of liberating Kuwait.
>
> "Under these exceptionally serious circumstances, the Islamic Republic of Mauritania, which has in the past expressed in connection with this crisis its rejection of the occupation of Kuwait as well as its condemnation of the presence of foreign forces in the region, cannot refrain from its duty of condemning this aggression and reaffirming its solidarity with the Iraqi people in this ordeal.
>
> "The Arab nation, the Islamic Ummah and all peace-loving peoples who espouse the cause of justice must without further delay acknowledge the extent of the risks and work actively for an immediate halt to the hostilities and the installation of a climate of peace and security which can guarantee the solution by peaceful means of all the region's problems."

...

S/22117, 21 January 1991

31. Letter from the Permanent Representative of the United Kingdom of Great Britain and Northern Ireland to the United Nations addressed to the President of the Security Council, 21 January 1991

Further to my earlier letter of 21 January (S/22115) I have the honour to inform you on behalf of my Government that the Government of the United Kingdom of Great Britain and Northern Ireland has been obliged to make clear to the Iraqi authorities its concern about Iraq's compliance with the Third and Fourth Geneva Conventions in its response to the military action undertaken by the United Kingdom and other States pursuant to SCR 678. Two separate demarches have been made to the Iraqi Ambassador in London on 19 January and 21 January.

On 19 January the Iraqi Ambassador was asked whether the Iraqi Government was holding any British prisoners of war and reminded of Iraq's obligations under the Third Geneva Convention to notify the names of any prisoners held and to arrange access by the ICRC. The Iraqi Ambassador gave an assurance that any British prisoners of war would be treated in accordance with the Geneva Conventions and that their names would be given to the ICRC. He drew attention to the first military communiqué of the Iraqi Government which contained such assurances and called on the civilian population to treat any servicemen humanely.

In the light of television and news agency reports on 21 January indicating that captured British airmen had been displayed on Iraqi television, the Iraqi Ambassador was summoned again. He was told of the British Government's acute concern. Article 13 of the Geneva Convention provides that "Prisoners of war must at all times be protected particularly against acts of violence or intimidation and against insults and public curiosity". There had also been news agency reports that the Iraqi authorities were considering sending the captured POWs to strategic sites in Iraq. This would be a serious breach of Iraq's obligations under the Conventions. We expected scrupulous compliance with the Conventions in respect of all British prisoners of war including British servicemen. The Iraqi Ambassador was reminded of the responsibility of his Government and of individual Iraqis for any grave breach of the Conventions.

The Iraqi Ambassador was also reminded on 21 January of Iraq's obligations under the 1925 Geneva Protocol in respect of chemical and biological weapons. The United Kingdom would take the severest view of any use of these weapons by Iraq. The United Kingdom sought an assurance that Iraq had no intention of using chemical or biological weapons. The Ambassador responded that he had no military authority to give such an assurance.

The British Government has made clear to the Iraqi Ambassador and to the International Committee of the Red Cross that for its part it will be complying scrupulously with its obligations under international humanitarian law, including the Third and Fourth Geneva Conventions. The British Government will be allowing full access by the ICRC both to Iraqi prisoners of war and to Iraqi citizens detained in the United Kingdom. The ICRC have already been provided with details of and access to all Iraqi nationals held in the United Kingdom.

...

A/45/936, S/22118, 21 January 1991

32. Letter from the Permanent Representative of the Sudan to the United Nations addressed to the Secretary-General, 21 January 1991

On instructions from my Government, I have the honour to convey the following:

1. The Government and people of the Republic of the Sudan are deeply shocked and concerned at the outbreak and continuation of a massive and destructive war between Iraq and the multinational forces in the Gulf area.

2. The Government of the Sudan condemns the resort to war as a means of settling disputes as this contravenes the Charter of the United Nations and exposes international peace and security to great dangers, especially in the volatile Middle East region.

3. The Government of the Sudan appeals to the international community to seek an immediate cease-fire in order to create the appropriate and suitable atmosphere to proceed with negotiations leading to a comprehensive peaceful settlement of all outstanding problems in accordance with the relevant United Nations resolutions.

4. The position of the Government of the Sudan with respect to the Gulf crisis has always been to seek a peaceful solution of the crisis within the Arab and Muslim framework without foreign intervention and resort to hostilities.

...

A/45/938, S/22119, 22 January 1991

33. Letter from the Permanent Representative of Ghana to the United Nations addressed to the Secretary-General, 18 January 1991

Upon instructions, I have the honour to transmit herewith the text of a statement issued on 17 January 1991 by the Government of Ghana on the outbreak of hostilities in the Gulf area.

...

The Government of Ghana wishes to express deep regret and sadness that developments in the Gulf area have resulted in the commencement of hostilities with the prospect of unprecedented loss of innocent lives and damage to property. This is a sad day for humanity. The hopes and aspirations of the international community for a new world order of peace, justice and equality are regrettably in jeopardy.

While the Government of Ghana appreciates the necessity to uphold international legality and respect for the principles of the Charter of the United Nations, it still believes that it is not too late for diplomacy to be given a chance to avert further disaster. More particularly, it is open to President Saddam Hussein of Iraq to save the people of Iraq from untold hardship and misery by agreeing to abide by United Nations Security Council resolutions. Meanwhile, the Government of Ghana calls upon Iraq and the allied forces to exercise restraint and, if possible, cease hostilities.

In terms of history, President Saddam Hussein must be seen as a product of frustration over centuries of marginalization of Arab interests. In the contemporary context, the problem of Palestine cries out for urgent solution. The Government of Ghana once again calls upon the international community, particularly the Western Powers, to do everything possible to convene as early as possible an international conference under United Nations auspices to resolve the outstanding problems of the Middle East. Only on such a foundation can peace return to the Middle East.

S/22121, 21 January 1991

34. Letter from the Permanent Representative of Pakistan to the United Nations addressed to the Secretary-General, 18 January 1991

I have the honour to enclose herewith text of the statement issued by the Government of Pakistan on the outbreak of hostilities in the Persian Gulf. ...

"The Government and the people of Pakistan have been deeply shocked and anguished at the outbreak of hostilities between Iraq and the multinational forces. Pakistan has consistently called for a peaceful resolution to the crisis and is profoundly concerned that the efforts for a peaceful solution have failed.

Pakistan's position and that of the international community to seek an Iraqi withdrawal from the brotherly Muslim country of Kuwait has been based on upholding fundamental principles of international law and inter-state conduct. International peace, security and sovereign independence of small and vulnerable states depend on the respect of these principles which were reflected in the resolutions of the United Nations Security Council, the OIC and the Arab League. It is regrettable that, in spite of the numerous appeals by world leaders, including the Prime Minister of Pakistan, Iraq could not be persuaded to agree to the withdrawal of its forces from Kuwait.

On its part, the Government of Pakistan has made a number of efforts to avert the conflict. In October, last year, Pakistan had joined five other Asian Islamic countries in calling upon President Saddam Hussein to withdraw Iraqi troops from Kuwait in the true Islamic spirit and for the unity and solidarity of the Ummah. The trilateral meeting of the Foreign Ministers of Iran, Pakistan and Turkey held on 3rd of January 1991, had appealed for a peaceful solution to the crisis through the implementation of the relevant resolutions of the UN Security Council. The meeting had also requested the Secretary-General of the OIC to exert all efforts for a peaceful solution including the possibility of the holding of an emergency meeting of the OIC. Pakistan had also endorsed the call by Iran for the holding of an emergency Summit meeting of the OIC. The Prime Minister addressed messages to fourteen Heads of State/Government directly involved, impressing upon them the need to find a peaceful solution to the problem. The Prime Minister had also sent a direct appeal to President Saddam Hussein to implement UN Security Council resolutions and withdraw from Kuwait in order to achieve a peaceful resolution of the crisis and save the Muslim people of the region from a major conflagration.

The Government and the people of Pakistan are deeply distressed at the failure of sustained peace efforts and the outbreak of war which could be disastrous for the region and particularly for the Islamic countries. It is our hope that statesmanship will prevail and the conflict will be brought to an end quickly to save human lives and suffering and to give peace another chance. Pakistan stands ready to support and undertake all efforts to restore peace on the basis of principles and resolutions of the UN Security Council."

S/22122, 21 January 1991

35. Letter from the Permanent Representative of the United States of America to the United Nations addressed to President of the Security Council, 21 January 1991

On behalf of my Government, I request that you distribute as documents of the Security Council the following diplomatic notes which have been given to the

Iraqi Chargé d'affaires in Washington. These notes concern the presence in the Persian Gulf of U.S. hospital ships, the Third Geneva Convention, and Iraqi treatment of prisoners of war.

The United States also protests the announcement of the intention of the government of Iraq to hold prisoners of war as hostages or to use them as human shields in flagrant violation of the Third Geneva Convention of 1949.

The Government of the United States calls upon the Government of Iraq to respect its obligations under the International Laws of armed conflict including the Geneva Conventions on the protection of the victims of war and The Hague Conventions on the conduct of hostilities on land and at sea. The Government of the United States expects the Government of Iraq to respect its obligations under the Geneva Protocol of 1925 not to use chemical or biological weapons.

Hostilities must be conducted in a manner so as to minimize injury to civilians. The civilian population, as such, as well as individual civilians, should not be the object of attack. Medical personnel, medical facilities and hospital ships must be respected and protected at all times. In resolutions 670 (1990) and 674 (1990), the United Nations Security Council specifically called upon Iraq to abide by its obligations under the Fourth Geneva Convention.

The Government advises the Government of Iraq that the United States intends to treat captured members of the armed forces of Iraq in accordance with the Geneva Convention relative to the protection of prisoners of war. Iraqi prisoners of war will not be mistreated and will be provided humane and safe detention and medical care. They will not be exposed to danger, insults or public curiosity. They will not be maltreated or misused to obtain military information or for propaganda purposes. They will not be denied food, water or medical treatment. They will be safeguarded against harm during combat operations.

The United States expects Iraq to provide the same treatment to members of the U.S. and other coalition armed forces captured by Iraq, in accordance with Iraq's obligations under the Geneva Conventions. We specifically expect the Government of Iraq to provide documentation on prisoners of war in accordance with the convention and to provide the International Committee of the Red Cross with access to prisoners of war as will be done by the United States.

The Government of the United States reminds the Government of Iraq that under International Law, violations of the Geneva Conventions, the Geneva Protocol of 1925, or related International Laws of armed conflict are war crimes, and individuals guilty of such violations may be subject to prosecution at any time, without any statute of limitations. This includes members of the Iraqi armed forces and civilian government officials.

The Government of the United States confirms to the Government of Iraq the earlier notification provided by circular note dated Washington, November 16, 1990, of the names and descriptions of the two United States military hospital ships present in the waters off the Arabian Peninsula, as well as their purpose and their markings.

The United States desires that all nations know of the presence of these hospital ships in the region and the expectation of the United States that those ships will be afforded the protections to which they are entitled under international law, including the Geneva Convention (II) of 12 August 1949 for the amelioration of the condition of wounded, sick and shipwrecked members of armed forces at sea, to which all parties to the conflict are party. As noted in the circular note:

- The two hospital ships are "USNS Mercy" (T-AH 19) and "USNS Comfort" (T-AH 20). These two converted San Clemente class tankers, ex-SS Worth ex-SS Rose City, have identical characteristics: tonnage 54,367, gross, 35,958 net; dimensions feet (meters) 894 length, 105.6 width 32.8 draft, i.e. depth, (272.6 x 32.2 x 10 meters); one mast forward, one funnel aft.
- Both ships are equipped specially and solely to assist, treat, and transport wounded, sick, and shipwrecked.
- The exterior surfaces of both ships are white, with dark red crosses painted on each side of the hulls and on the horizontal surfaces.

On January 19, 1991 the Government of the United States informed the Government of Iraq that it intends to treat captured members of the Iraqi armed forces fully in accordance with the Third Geneva Convention relative to the protection of prisoners of war and that the United States expects Iraq also to comply fully with this humanitarian convention.

The Government of the United States has heard audio recordings of Iraqi television broadcasts which purport to be interviews with captured American and coalition military personnel, and has heard other accounts of such broadcasts. The Government of Iraq appears to have subjected these men to unlawful treatment for propaganda purposes and coercion - both physical and mental - in order to secure information and statements from them. If these broadcasts are authentic, Iraq has committed serious violations of the Third Geneva Convention.

The Government of the United States protests the apparently unlawful coercion and misuse of prisoners of war for propaganda purposes, the failure to respect their honour and well-being, and the subjection of such individuals to public humiliation. All of these actions are in violation of the Convention.

The mistreatment of prisoners of war is a war crime, and the inhumane treatment of prisoners of war is a grave breach of the Convention. The United States demands that Iraq immediately desist from any further illegal action and that it respects its obligations under the Geneva Convention.

The Government of the United States again reminds the Government of Iraq that prisoners of war must at all times be humanely treated and must be afforded food, water, clothing and every guarantee of hygiene and healthfulness. It is requested that the International Committee of the Red Cross, which has representatives in Baghdad be provided immediate access to any prisoners of war.

A/45/937, S/22123, 21 January 1991

36. Letter addressed to the Secretary-General by the Permanent Representative of Luxembourg to the United Nations, 21 January 1991

I have the honour to enclose the text, in French and English, of the statement issued on 18 January 1991 by the European Community and its 12 member States following the Iraqi attack against Israel.

...

By launching a non-provoked and entirely unjustified missile attack on Israeli territory last night, Saddam Hussein is aiming, through a cynical and deliberate provocation, to draw Israel into the Gulf conflict.

The Community and its member States strongly condemn this attack, which represents a further violation of international law by the Iraqi authorities.

They express their sympathy to the Israeli people.

Recalling that Israel's right to security constitutes one of the fundamental principles of the policy of the Community and its member States in the Middle East, they do hope that Israel will not be drawn into the conflict.

Under the present circumstances, every restraint displayed by Israel must be interpreted as a sign of strength and not of weakness.

S/22124, 22 January 1991

37. Letter from the Permanent Representative of Cyprus to the United Nations addressed to the Secretary-General, 21 January 1991

I have the honour to transmit to you herewith the text of a message from the President of the Republic of Cyprus, His Excellency Mr. George Vassiliou, addressed to the people of Cyprus, on the commencement of military operations in the Gulf. ...

It is with mixed feelings of agony and hope that the whole world and the people of Cyprus are following the military operations that were launched a few hours ago with the aim of liberating Kuwait and restoring the lawful Government of the country. It is well known that since the Iraqi invasion on 2 August great efforts have been made by leading figures throughout the world to achieve a peaceful settlement of the problem. Mankind followed with anxiety all those efforts, which culminated in the last few days in the Geneva meeting and the subsequent visit of the United Nations Secretary-General, Mr. Pérez de Cuéllar, to Baghdad. Unfortunately, all these efforts failed because of the invader's intransigence. It emerged clearly that the only thing Saddam Hussein was interested in was to gain time in order to consolidate in this way the occupation of Kuwait. This is a tactic of which the Cypriot people are well aware and have bitter experience. It was therefore natural that since all efforts for a peaceful solution failed the only way out was the use of armed force.

At this moment we are turning our thoughts to the allied forces who are fighting for the implementation of the United Nations resolutions and decisions for the liberation of Kuwait and we express our full solidarity with them. We like to hope that hostilities will come to an end as soon as possible with the least possible loss of life.

Here in Cyprus, as you all very well know, there is absolutely no cause for concern. All our forces are in a state of alert. We are following the situation but, I repeat, there is no reason whatsoever for concern. Consequently, people should continue their life as usual.

It is natural that many innocent people will lose their lives as a result of the military operations. Loss of human life is always tragic. We like to hope and expect, however, that this sacrifice will not be in vain because, as President Bush said in his address to the entire world a few hours ago:

> "We have before us the opportunity to forge for ourselves and for future generations a new world order, a world where the rule of law, not the law of the jungle, governs the conduct of nations. When we are successful, and we will be, we have a real chance at this new world order, an order in which a credible United Nations can use its peace-keeping role to fulfil the promise and vision of the United Nations founders."

These principles, dear compatriots, are the principles in which we have always believed and in which the Cypriot people repose their hopes for a solution to the Cyprus problem. We are confident and expect that with the implementation of these principles the turn of the Cyprus problem will come and Cyprus will no longer be a victim of invasion and occupation and our island will be reunited peacefully.

S/22125, 22 January 1991

38. Letter from the Permanent Representative of Indonesia to the United Nations addressed to the Secretary-General, 21 January 1991

I have the honour to transmit to you herewith the statement by the President of the Republic of Indonesia and the text of press statement issued by the Ministry of Foreign Affairs of the Republic of Indonesia on 17 January 1991 regarding recent developments in the Gulf.

...

President Soeharto expressed his deep concern with the outbreak of hostilities in the Gulf and hoped that the war could end soon. The Head of State said that if the cessation of the conflict could be achieved at the earliest, new measures would be taken in order to bring about the settlement of the Middle East problems in general, and the Palestinian question in particular, through peaceful means.

He observed that the Indonesian position with regard to the Palestinian issue has been clear in the support extended to the struggle of the Palestinian people for independence and nationhood in their own sovereign State.

The Head of State reiterated that the termination of hostilities as soon as possible would be of great importance as it could prevent greater casualties and further destruction of economic infrastructures, which will have detrimental consequences on the Middle East region. Moreover, if the Gulf war is protracted, its impact on the world economy would also be felt.

The Government of Indonesia, which has since the very beginning of the Gulf crisis hoped for a peaceful settlement through negotiations, is very much saddened that all those endeavours could not bring about the desired results and in consequence the use of force is being resorted to.

Until the last moment various attempts were made by many parties, including the United Nations Secretary-General, asking Iraq to comply with the resolutions of the Security Council to withdraw from Kuwait, so that once the present crisis was resolved, efforts to settle the other big problems of the Middle East region which have caused so much turmoil and suffering could be initiated.

We express our deepest concern that the outbreak of the armed conflict will have far-reaching ramifications not only on the countries directly involved but also on world peace and stability, as well as the international economy.

We express our sincere hope and pray that the war may be ended soon so that the casualties and material damage could be limited.

S/22126, 22 January 1991

39. Letter from the Permanent Representative of Italy to the United Nations addressed to the President of the Security Council, 22 January 1991

Pursuant to paragraph 4 of Security Council resolution 678 (1990), I have the honour to inform you, on behalf of my Government, that Italy, consistent with its responsibilities under the Charter of the United Nations and in accordance with paragraph 2 of the above-mentioned resolution, is participating, together with other Member States co-operating with the Government of

Kuwait, in an action aimed at ensuring the implementation of resolution 660 (1990) and of all other relevant resolutions of the Security Council.

Italy's action, taken in close contact with the other States members of the European Community, is aimed at restoring international legality and respect of the Charter of the United Nations. This applies equally to the task of the military forces dispatched to the Gulf with the purpose of ensuring the implementation of resolution 678 (1990) in all its parts, as well as of all other relevant resolutions of the Security Council, acting in association with the other States that are co-operating with the Government of Kuwait in accordance with the Charter and resolutions of the United Nations.

Italy pledges to persevere in actions designed to restore peace, security and stability in the region, considering that the re-establishment of international legality in Kuwait is a prerequisite for the solution of all problems still pending in the Middle East.

...

S/22127, 22 January 1991

40. Letter from the Permanent Representative of Yemen to the United Nations addressed to the President of the Security Council, 22 January 1991

I have the honour to enclose the text of the Declaration regarding the tragic developments in the situation in the Arabian Gulf region issued on Monday, 21 January 1991 by the Presidential Council of the Republic of Yemen.

...

The Presidential Council of the Republic of Yemen is following with extreme grief the tragic developments in the situation created by the cruel and continuing aggression the United States and Allied forces are committing against the fraternal Iraqi people and against its scientific, industrial, economic and military potential and installations, which reveals the true dimensions of the sinister plan for aggression against the fraternal Arab and Muslim people of Iraq.

The Presidential Council considers that the cruel aggression the United States and Allied forces are perpetrating is not aimed at ensuring the implementation of the Security Council resolutions and liberating Kuwait - which continues to be an inter-Arab problem that can be settled only by Arabs, for Kuwait forms an integral part of the Arab Islamic nation and its people is our brother in Arabism and Islam - but has much broader objectives which comprise destroying the capabilities and potential of an Arab Muslim country and subjecting its population to genocide. This is apparent from the ongoing aggressive operations being conducted against civilians and civilian installations and against the economic and development infrastructures of fraternal Iraq. These operations reveal in fact the true scope of a dangerous plot directed not solely against fraternal Iraq, but against the entire Arab and Islamic nation, aimed at controlling its interests, potential and wealth and at endangering its security, independence and sovereignty.

The Presidential Council condemns the cruel aggression being perpetrated against Iraq, and appeals to all States of the world, and in the first place to the fraternal Arab and Islamic countries, to take the position that their national, religious and human obligations dictate towards the iniquitous aggression being perpetrated against the fraternal Arab and Muslim people of Iraq, and urges the international community to bring pressure to bear on the United States of America and its allies to put an end to this aggression without delay and thus give the parties the opportunity of engaging in peaceful dialogue to settle all pending problems so that a global, lasting and just peace can be achieved in the region which will guarantee peaceful coexistence among its peoples, safe from any foreign interference or from a military escalation which would drag the region as a whole towards a devastating conflagration and a terrifying catastrophe which would be difficult to control, and whose destructive effects would be difficult to foresee and would have dangerous repercussions for international peace and security.

In conformity with the firm position of principle of the Republic of Yemen and with the efforts it has made since the beginning of the crisis to ensure a peaceful settlement within the overall Arab context in order to spare the region catastrophic war and destruction, the Presidential Council affirms its intention to continue its efforts to put an end to the bloodshed and achieve peace in the region. At this crucial juncture and in these extremely serious circumstances the region and the world are experiencing, the Presidential Council urges the international community to take the following steps:

> 1. Adoption by the Security Council of a resolution calling for an immediate halt to all military operations;
> 2. Facilitation of Arab and Islamic efforts at peace and mediation designed to put an end to the causes of the dispute between Iraq and Kuwait;
> 3. Adoption by the Security Council of a resolution calling for the withdrawal of the foreign forces deployed in the region;
> 4. A commitment by the Security Council to implement immediately and without delay the resolutions of the United Nations relating to the Arab-Israeli conflict;
> 5. The adoption by the Security Council of a resolution rescinding its resolution 661 (1990) on the imposition of a total embargo against Iraq;
> 6. The conclusion of a general agreement aimed at eliminating all weapons of mass destruction in the possession of all States in the region and instituting a rigorous control system to ensure respect for this agreement. The conclusion of this agreement would take place after all forms of conflict in the region, including the Arab-Israeli conflict, have come to an end.

The Presidential Council urges the leaders and peoples of the Arab and Islamic nation to assume their historic responsibility in the face of this challenge with which their nation is confronted and to put an end to the aggression being perpetrated against a fraternal Arab and Muslim country, and reaffirms that it is motivated by the desire to halt the bloodshed, preserve the potential and capabilities of the Arab and Islamic nation and save it from the clutches of its enemies and those who have designs on it.

S/22128, 22 January 1991

41. Letter from the Permanent Representative of Kuwait to the United Nations addressed to the President of the Security Council, 22 January 1991

I have the honour to transmit to you the text of a statement made at Taef on 22 January 1991 by a spokesman for the Government of Kuwait.

...

An official spokesman of the Government of the State of Kuwait has stated that Kuwait is deeply concerned by the Iraqi régime's violations of international law and norms, and particularly by its recent announcement that prisoners of war are to be dispersed to various Iraqi economic and scientific installations to serve as human shields.

Kuwait holds the brutal Iraqi régime fully responsible for the safety of Kuwaiti and other prisoners of war and detainees. Kuwait condemns and brands as infamous the iniquitous Iraqi régime's persistent defiance of the will of the international community, as well as its inhumane practices which are in violation of the third and fourth Geneva Conventions relative to the treatment of prisoners of war and of civilian persons in time of war.

S/22130, 22 January 1991

42. Letter from the Permanent Representative of the United States of America to the United Nations addressed to the President of the Security Council, 22 January 1991

In accordance with paragraph 4 of resolution 678, I wish, on behalf of my Government, to submit the following report on actions undertaken pursuant to paragraphs 2 and 3 of that resolution, to follow the initial report submitted on 18 January.

Since that report, military forces of the coalition, including United States military forces, acting in accordance with UNSCR 678, have continued their air action against Iraq's military targets, including Iraqi biological and chemical warfare facilities, mobile and fixed surface-to-surface missile sites, and occupation forces in Kuwait and southern Iraq, as well as command and control centers, supply lines and the air defense networks that protect these facilities. Over 8,100 coalition air sorties have been carried out since hostilities began 16 January.

As of the morning of 21 January, United States forces have lost ten aircraft. Other coalition forces have also suffered losses. In addition, fifteen U.S. military personnel have been reported as missing.

The naval forces of the United States have also engaged Iraq's naval forces in the northern Gulf. These attacks have been on Iraqi units that are engaged in operations against coalition forces.

On 17 January, a brief episode of artillery fire was initiated by Iraqi forces, causing some damage to an oil installation in Northern Saudi Arabia. Coalition forces responded to this attack and suppressed any further action from those Iraqi artillery positions.

On 17 January, Iraq launched one surface-to-surface missile at Saudi Arabia. Coalition forces destroyed that missile in mid-air.

In the early evening of 17 January (Eastern Standard Time), Iraqi forces also launched a number of surface-to-surface missiles in an unprovoked attack on another UN Member, Israel. Another such unprovoked attack occurred against Israel the following day. This unlawful use of force against the territorial integrity of a UN Member State that is not a party to the conflict was obviously not directed at specific military targets, but rather at civilian targets resulting in civilian casualties.

Late 20 January and early on the morning of 21 January, the Iraqi forces launched ten surface-to-surface missiles against the Saudi Arabian cities of Dhahran and Riyadh. As of today, we have no reports of casualties resulting from these attacks.

On 19 January, the United States provided notification to the ICRC and the Government of Iraq of the presence of two U.S. military hospital ships in the waters off the Arabian peninsula, earlier notification of which had been provided to States party to the Geneva Conventions.

On 19 January, the Government of the United States in a diplomatic note informed the Government of Iraq that it intends to treat captured members of the Iraqi armed forces fully in accordance with the Third Geneva Convention Relative to the Protection of Prisoners of War, and that the United States expected Iraq also to comply fully with this humanitarian convention. United States forces have captured 23 members of the Iraqi armed forces and have told the ICRC we are prepared to facilitate access to those POWs.

Following Iraqi broadcasts 20 January of taped interviews with several coalition prisoners of war, the Department of State called in the Iraqi Chargé d'affaires in Washington to protest the apparent treatment of members of the United States armed forces and other coalition forces held by the Government of Iraq. In a diplomatic note, the United States protested Iraq's apparent treatment of U.S. prisoners of war as contrary to the Third Geneva Convention of 1949 Relative to the Protection of Prisoners of War. The U.S. Department of State reminded Iraq that the mistreatment of prisoners of war is a war crime, demanded full Iraqi compliance with the convention and requested immediate access for the ICRC to any prisoners of war held by Iraq.

Baghdad radio has subsequently reported that the Government of Iraq intends to locate United States and other coalition POWs at strategic sites that may be subject to attack. This is a violation of the Geneva Conventions for which the United States will also hold the Government of Iraq and individual Iraqi officers responsible. Under the Third Geneva Convention, POWs may not be unnecessarily exposed to danger, and must be evacuated to camps in safe areas as soon as possible after capture. The Department of State 21 January therefore called in the Iraqi Chargé d'affaires in Washington to protest strongly such action and to reiterate the protest delivered on 20 January regarding Iraqi treatment of United States and other coalition POWs. The Department of State reaffirmed the above in diplomatic notes to the Government of Iraq.

On 21 January the U.S., British and Kuwaiti Ambassadors in Geneva met with ICRC President Sommaruga to bring officially to his attention Iraqi violations of the Geneva Conventions and to request the ICRC to take appropriate action.

A copy of the 21 January diplomatic note to the Government of Iraq is attached. I have already requested that you distribute as documents of the Security Council the two preceding notes of 19 and 20 January, as well as a circular note dated 19 January 1991 to the States party to the Geneva Conventions on the presence of hospital ships (S/22122).

...

Baghdad radio has reported that the Government of Iraq intends to locate United States and other coalition POWs in Iraq at likely strategic targets of coalition forces. The United States strongly protests the Government of Iraq's threat to so endanger POWs.

Under Article 19 of the Third Geneva Convention, prisoners of war are to be evacuated as soon as possible after their capture to camps situated in an area away from the combat zone, so that they will be out of danger. Under Article 23 of the Third Geneva Convention, no prisoner of war may be sent to, or detained in, areas where he may be exposed to the fire of the combat zone, nor may his presence be used to render certain points or areas immune from military operations. Moreover, prisoners of war are to have shelters against air bombardment and other hazards of war to the same extent as the local civilian population. Iraqi POWs captured by the United States will be accorded these protections.

The United States and other coalition forces are only attacking targets of military value in Iraq; the civilian population, as such, is not the object of attack. Consequently the Government of Iraq is capable of placing coalition POWs in areas where military attacks will not occur.

If the Government of Iraq places coalition POWs at military targets in Iraq, then the Government of Iraq will be in violation of the Third Geneva Convention, and Iraqi officials - whether members of the Iraqi Armed Forces or civilian government personnel - will have committed a serious war crime. The Government of the United States reminds the Government of Iraq that Iraqi individuals who are guilty of such war crimes, as well as other war crimes such as the exposure of POWs to mistreatment, coerced statements, public curiosity and insult, are personally liable and subject to prosecution at any time.

S/22131, 22 January 1991

43. Letter from the Permanent Representative of France to the United Nations addressed to the President of the Security Council, 22 January 1991

Further to my letter (S/22100) of 17 January and pursuant to paragraph 4 of Security Council resolution 678 (1990), I have the honour to inform you of the action the French armed forces are continuing to take within the framework of the plans drawn up jointly with the allied forces with a view to securing the implementation of Security Council resolution 660 (1990) and of all pertinent subsequent resolutions of the Council.

The French air forces have engaged in further joint raids on Iraqi military targets in Kuwait. They have also continued their air defence mission in Saudi Arabia.

The French naval forces, for their part, are continuing their mission of monitoring logistics convoys in the inter-allied framework.

I wish also to inform you that France has decided to participate in the United Nations emergency plan on behalf of the displaced populations in the Gulf. The French contributions will be made to the Office of the United Nations High Commissioner for Refugees.

...

S/22132, 22 January 1991

44. Letter from the Permanent Representative of France to the United Nations addressed to the President of the Security Council, 22 January 1991

On instructions from my Government, I have the honour to inform you that on Monday, 21 January, the Ambassador of Iraq was called to the Ministry of Foreign Affairs to receive an official protest from the French Government following the decisions announced by Iraq with respect to prisoners of war.

The need for strict compliance by Iraq with the rules of humanitarian law, and in particular with the third Geneva Convention relative to the treatment of prisoners of war, which Iraq has signed and ratified, was firmly recalled on this occasion. The third Convention does not provide that, in order to benefit from its provisions, prisoners should be the subject of a public declaration by the forces of which they form a part.

France, for its part, will apply the Geneva Convention to all prisoners, whether or not declared. It will treat its prisoners humanely.

The blatant breach of the Geneva Conventions that the putting into effect the decisions announced by Iraq would constitute arouses the indignation of the international community. Persons guilty of such breaches will have to answer for them, whatever their level of responsibility.

...

S/22134, 22 January 1991

45. Letter from the Permanent Representative of Iraq to the United Nations addressed to the Secretary-General, 22 January 1991

The Permanent Mission of Iraq to the United Nations presents its compliments to the Secretary-General of the United Nations, and has the honour to inform him that the bombing raids and the pounding with missiles being conducted by the United States of America and their "allies" against urban concentrations in Iraq have resulted in the following losses of human life and material damage in many towns and urban concentrations:

1. Tamim province: 6 dead and 17 injured;
2. Ninawi province: destruction of a house at Mosul and other damage
3. Baghdad: 8 dead, 46 injured and several houses damaged
4. Al-Ambary province: 10 dead and 8 injured
5. Al-Qadissiah province: 4 dead and destruction of 4 private motor vehicles, several houses, shops and one ambulance
6. Najf province: 7 injured
7. Basra province: 5 dead, including 1 child, and 72 injured
8. Mathna province: 5 dead and 23 injured
9. Babel province: 2 dead and 7 injured.
10. Al-Houma region/Kuwait province: 1 dead and 11 injured (women and children).

...

S/22136, 23 January 1991

46. Letter from the Permanent Representative of Botswana to the United Nations addressed to the Secretary-General, 22 January 1991

I have the honour to enclose herewith text of the statement issued by the Government of the Republic of Botswana on the outbreak of hostilities in the Persian Gulf. ...

All Botswana must be aware by now of the crisis that has been looming in the Gulf since Iraq invaded the neighbouring State of Kuwait on 2 August 1990 and annexed it as part of its territory.

Since the invasion, the United Nations Security Council has adopted a number of resolutions aimed at forcing Iraq to withdraw from the Emirate. The last of these resolutions, resolution 678 (1990), gave Iraq a deadline of 15 January 1991 to withdraw peacefully without any pre-conditions or face the likelihood of forced withdrawal at the hands of countries co-operating with Kuwait.

Concomitant with the actions of the United Nations Security Council, efforts were made by some countries, organizations and individuals to try to resolve the crisis peacefully by diplomatic means. The latest of these efforts was the visit of the United Nations Secretary-General to Baghdad just two days ago.

Unfortunately, all these efforts seem to have failed to bring about a peaceful resolution of the problem. Although the very latest news on this subject is that the French Government is making yet another last-minute effort to seek a diplomatic solution to the problem, there is no guarantee that it will succeed.

The conclusion of the Department of External Affairs under the circumstances is that there is a high probability that war will break out in the Gulf on or after the deadline of 15 January set by the United Nations Security Council. In that event, Botswana and Batswana in general are likely to suffer direct and indirect harm as a result of the conflict. As a developing country dependent on imported oil, we can be certain that a sharp rise in the oil price will seriously affect the health of our economy, as indeed has already happened to some extent since the invasion.

For the general public, the Department would like to warn all Botswana to avoid travelling to the Gulf during this period if they can help it as there is nothing that Government can do to assist or protect them should they find themselves in difficulty while there.

This is an uncertain period in international relations. Botswana has condemned Iraq for its disregard of international law by invading a small and peaceful Member of the United Nations Organization. War always has terrible consequences and should be avoided at all costs. The Department deeply regrets the turn that events seem to be taking in regard to this crisis.

It is to be hoped that whatever difficulties there are for each of the directly concerned parties, reason will prevail in the end so that the people of the Middle East in particular and humanity in general could be spared the miseries of another war.

S/22137, 23 January 1991

47. Letter from the Permanent Representative of Italy to the United Nations addressed to the President of the Security Council, 23 January 1991

I have the honour to inform you that the Italian Government deemed it necessary to point out to the Iraqi authorities that, in the framework of the military action in which Italy is participating under the terms of Security Council resolution 678 (1990), it expects Iraq to comply strictly with the Third Geneva Convention.

Representations were made to the Embassy of Iraq in Rome on 20 and 22 January to remind Iraq of its obligations under the Third Geneva Convention.

Following the Iraqi television's broadcast displaying among others a captive Italian pilot, the Italian Government conveyed to the Ambassador of Iraq its strong condemnation of this action. Iraq was therefore enjoined to comply rigorously with article 13 of the Third Geneva Convention. Furthermore, Iraq was warned in the strongest terms, recalling article 23 of the same Convention, against carrying out its alleged intention to move prisoners of war to strategic sites in the country.

Italy also asked the International Committee of the Red Cross to play its institutional role concerning prisoners in Iraq.

At the same time, the Italian Government indicated that it will scrupulously comply with the Third and Fourth Geneva Conventions, as well as with all other relevant international agreements on human rights.

...

A/45/939, S/22139, 23 January 1991

48. Letter from the Permanent Representative of the Philippines to the United Nations addressed to the Secretary-General, 22 January 1991

I have the honour to bring to your attention certain events which occurred only days ago in the Philippines and which bear an unmistakable connection to the present conflict in the Middle East.

I regret to have to inform you that an Iraqi national was killed and another wounded in Makati, Metro Manila, last Saturday night (19 January 1991) when a bomb they intended to plant in the Thomas Jefferson Cultural Center exploded prematurely. The dead Iraqi was identified as a member of an international terrorist organization. The two were carrying 200 lbs. of explosives and were then 100 yards from their target.

In a related development, Philippine Secretary of Foreign Affairs, Raul S. Manglapus, announced that the Government of the Philippines had declared Mr. Muwafak A-Ani, First Secretary of the Iraqi Embassy in Manila, as *persona non-grata* in accordance with the 1961 Vienna Convention on Diplomatic Relations. He was given 72 hours from 21 January 1991 to leave the country. Philippine intelligence and security authorities asserted that they had unearthed strong evidence linking him to the failed bombing of the Cultural Center.

Secretary Manglapus said that the decision "should not be looked at as an action against the Government of Iraq and certainly not against the people of Iraq, but directed against the person for acts beyond his diplomatic functions and violation of local laws and regulations".

...

A/45/940, S/22140, 23 January 1991

49. Letter from the Permanent Representative of Luxembourg to the United Nations addressed to the Secretary-General, 23 January 1991

I have the honour to enclose the text, in French and English, of the statement on the situation of the prisoners of war detained by Iraq, issued by the European Community and its 12 member States on 22 January 1991 ...

...

The European Community and its member States express their deep concern at the unscrupulous use of prisoners of war and at the intention announced by Iraq to concentrate them near military bases and targets. They consider these actions particularly odious because they are contrary to elementary respect for international law and humanitarian principles. They condemn such actions unreservedly.

They request the Iraqi authorities rigorously to respect all the Geneva Conventions relating to the conduct of war and in particular the Convention of 12 August 1949 on the treatment of prisoners of war. This stipulated in particular in article 13 that "prisoners of war must at all times be protected, particularly against acts of violence or intimidation and against insults and public curiosity", and in article 23 that "No prisoner of war may at any time be sent to, or detained in areas where he may be exposed to the fire of the combat zone, nor may his presence be used to render certain points or areas immune from military operations".

In conformity with article 125 of this same Convention, the special position of the International Committee of the Red Cross in this field should be recognized and respected. The Community and its member States pay tribute to the work of the Red Cross and support all steps aimed at strengthening its role.

The Community and its member States hold the Iraqi authorities responsible in accordance with international law, including in their individual capacities, for all illegal acts endangering the physical integrity and the life of prisoners of war, which clearly constitute a war crime.

S/22141, 23 January 1991

50. Letter from the Permanent Representative of the Islamic Republic of Iran to the United Nations addressed to the Secretary-General, 23 January 1991

Upon instructions from my Government, and in light of grave and dangerous situation which has erupted in the Persian Gulf region as a consequence of Iraqi invasion and continued occupation of Kuwait and the ensuing forcible measures taken since 16 January 1991, I have the honour to bring the following to your attention.

The Islamic Republic of Iran, as Your Excellency is well aware, condemned Iraqi aggression against Kuwait, and called for immediate, unconditional and complete withdrawal of Iraqi forces to pre-invasion positions. My Government has also taken all necessary measures to comply, in line with its obligations under the United Nations Charter, with the relevant resolutions of the Security Council, in particular its resolutions 661 and 670. Your Excellency has already been informed of the measures taken by the Islamic Republic of Iran in this respect through letters contained in documents S/AC.25/1990/38 and S/22020.

Since the declaration of our rejection of Iraqi occupation of Kuwait early after the invasion, my Government endeavoured to bring this crisis to a peaceful end through realization of unconditional and complete withdrawal of Iraqi forces from Kuwait. This policy was pursued both in our bilateral contacts with Iraqi leadership and in our endeavours at regional, Islamic and international levels. Only days before 15 January 1991, during the visit of the Vice-Chairman of Iraq's Revolutionary Command Council, the authorities of the Islamic Republic of Iran emphasized the unavoidable necessity of Iraq's full compliance with Security Council resolutions in order to avert a catastrophic war. We also proposed the convening of an emergency extraordinary Summit of the Organization of Islamic Conference in an attempt to find a peaceful termination of the crisis in line with relevant Security Council resolutions. We regret that the collective efforts of the international community, including those of my country, to prevent the currently unfolding catastrophe failed.

The human loss and destruction inflicted upon the Muslim people of the region and their resources, the dangerous prospects for prolongation and spread of the conflict, and the evidence of violations of international humanitarian law and norms governing the conduct of armed hostilities are alarming. Under these grave circumstances, it is imperative that the Security Council - which was actively seized of this crisis prior to 15 January 1991 - assess the present situation in light of its resolutions and take a more active role in achieving, without further loss and destruction, the complete withdrawal of Iraq from Kuwait, termination of the present armed conflict and withdrawal of foreign forces from the region.

The Islamic Republic of Iran, for its part, is prepared to co-operate fully with Your Excellency and the Security Council in order to achieve the above-mentioned objectives as well as the long-term stability and security in the volatile and strategic Persian Gulf region which can only be realized through a regional security and co-operation mechanism within a United Nations framework and without intervention and presence of foreign forces - which has historically been misguided and destabilizing.

Furthermore, in line with its principles and requirements of its national security, the Islamic Republic of Iran considers it imperative to refrain from engagement in the present armed conflict. Needless to say, the Islamic Republic of Iran reserves the right to take all necessary measures, in exercise of its legitimate and inalienable right of self-defense recognized in Article 51 of the Charter, against any violation of its sovereignty or territorial integrity.

...

A/45/941, S/22143, 24 January 1991

51. Letter from the Permanent Representative of Egypt to the United Nations addressed to the Secretary-General, 23 January 1991

I have the honour to transmit to you herewith the text of the statement made on 22 January 1991 by Mr. Esmat Abdel Meguid, Deputy Prime Minister and Minister for Foreign Affairs, to the joint meeting of the Inter-Arab Affairs, Defence and National Security and Foreign Relations Committees of the People's Assembly.

...

The present delicate circumstances and the successive developments taking place in the region require that I should address you once again today in order to supplement and expand on the statement I made to you on 13 January, at which time I recalled the causes and background of the crisis and the Egyptian position with regard to it.

Events have evolved and succeeded each other with enormous speed since last we met. It may therefore be useful for me to review with you our analysis of the situation and our view of its dimensions and of the developments that it underwent between the time of our aforementioned meeting and the early morning of 17 January 1991, the day on which the operation for the liberation of Kuwait began.

In the days leading up to the expiry of the deadline established by the United Nations Security Council in its resolution 678 (1990), Egypt engaged in intense activity with the aim of thereby sparing the region a devastating and murderous war that would destroy everything root and branch.

In another respect, Egypt participated in the efforts made by a number of leaders and personalities of substance at the inter-Arab and international levels in order to prevent the outbreak of war. Those efforts were indeed gigantic and sustained, and they were made in an attempt to persuade the Iraqi President to give peace efforts a chance to bear fruit and the spectre of war a chance to vanish.

Most regrettably, all of those efforts and attempts foundered on the rock of Iraqi rejection, a rejection which forced the international community to resort to the use of armed force for the implementation of numerous Security Council resolutions, beginning with resolution 660 (1990) and ending with resolution 678 (1990) of 29 November 1990.

In the context of the efforts made with a view to preventing escalation and of the endeavour to contain the situation, I should like to note the sustained and sincere effort made by President Hosni Mubarak to spare the Iraqi people and the peoples of the region the hazards of war and the consequences of destruction.

In this perspective, before the expiry of the deadline on the evening of 15 January, President Mubarak addressed to the Iraqi President one last appeal, the twenty-sixth in the series of appeals that he had made to him since 20 July 1990. A detailed statement concerning these appeals has been deposited with your Committees.

I must not fail to refer to the statement of the joint committee formed by the Inter-Arab Affairs, Defence and National Security and Foreign Relations Committees issued on 13 January 1991, which referred to the negative consequences of the evolution of events in the Gulf crisis and which contained an appeal to the Iraqi President calling upon him to spare the people of Iraq and the Arab nation the horrors of a devastating war.

In these crucial moments, in which the fate of an entire people, namely the Iraqi people, is being decided, we find one individual gambling with the destiny of a whole people and controlling its fate in order to achieve ambitions for spurious power and ephemeral dominance.

In these critical times, when the fate of an entire nation is being determined, I can only reaffirm yet again that the Egyptian position, which is one that stems from commitment to the principles of truth and justice, urges the need for Iraq to comply with the resolutions of the Security Council, which are the result and the reflection of the will of the international community for the full and unconditional withdrawal of the Iraqi forces from Kuwaiti territory in order to allow the liberation of Kuwait and the restoration of the legitimate Kuwaiti authority, God willing, to the performance of its positive role in the inter-Arab and international arenas.

Our region, which has witnessed successive conflicts and the dissipation of capacities and efforts in marginal issues which are harmful and to no avail, is today, in light of its aspirations for a better future for its sons, more than ever in need of a peace that will allocate capacities to and focus efforts on development, that will build and not destroy and that will preserve and not squander, the very peace which is one of the glorious attributes of God.

In conclusion, I can only beseech the Lord Almighty to safeguard Egypt and the Arab nation and preserve them from all evil and all harm. He is the best guardian, and He is the most merciful of the merciful.

S/22145, 24 January 1991

52. Letter from the Permanent Representative of Singapore to the United Nations addressed to the Secretary-General, 24 January 1991

I have the honour to enclose herewith text of the press statement issued by the Ministry of Foreign Affairs of the Republic of Singapore on the implementation of United Nations Security Council resolutions on the situation in the Gulf, in particular resolution 678 (1990). ...

The Singapore Government supports the military actions taken by the multinational force in the Gulf to implement the United Nations Security Council resolutions, especially resolution 678.

The Singapore Government deeply regrets the failure of all the peace initiatives undertaken to implement the United Nations resolutions, including the mission undertaken personally by the United Nations Secretary-General. The international community could no longer do nothing given Iraq's continued defiance of the United Nations resolutions. Failure to implement the United Nations resolutions would have undermined respect for international law as well as the credibility of the United Nations. This would not be in the long-term interests of all nations, and especially small States like Singapore.

The Singapore Government hopes that the military actions taken in the Gulf will quickly end the unlawful Iraqi occupation of Kuwait with a minimal loss of life.

S/22146, 24 January 1991

53. Note verbale from the Permanent Mission of Iraq to the United Nations addressed to the Secretariat of the United Nations, 24 January 1991

The Permanent Mission of Iraq to the United Nations presents its compliments to the Secretariat of the United Nations and has the honour to enclose the text of the statement made on 22 January 1991 by the military spokesman for Iraq.

...

On Tuesday, 22 January 1991, at 1.41 p.m., United States aircraft bombed two Iraqi tankers, causing a vast oil slick in the waters of the Arabian Gulf which is bound to cause serious harm to the region's living marine resources and environment.

This is not the first time the United States has damaged the environment, and exposed man and fauna to serious danger, by undertaking nuclear tests and dumping nuclear wastes and other toxic chemicals.

Today, the United States is committing another offence by polluting the waters of the Arabian Gulf. Accordingly, Iraq appeals to world public opinion and to the organizations and individuals concerned, particularly to the "Greens", to denounce this criminal act and to do everything within their power to put an end to such acts.

For its part, Iraq, which respects the right to life of all human beings and which God has endowed with natural wealth, is prepared to co-operate with any party with a view to putting an end to these crimes.

S/22150, 25 January 1991

54. Letter from the Chargé d'affaires a.i. of the Permanent Mission of Bolivia to the United Nations addressed to the Secretary-General, 18 January 1991

I have the honour to transmit to you the text of the Statement by the Government of Bolivia on the conflict in the Persian Gulf issued on 17 January 1991.

...

Barely had the conflict in the Persian Gulf arisen when the Government of President Paz Zamora strongly condemned Iraq's invasion of Kuwait. The President of Bolivia has constantly expressed the dismay of the Bolivian people at the course of events and at the failure of the actions aimed at finding a peaceful solution to this conflict. Bolivia has been acting in close co-ordination with the fraternal countries of Latin America, particularly those making up the Rio Group, and within the framework of the initiatives taken by the international community and the United Nations.

Bolivia deeply regrets that all these efforts have proved fruitless in the face of immutable and irrational positions and that, following a process of various requests and initiatives for dialogue, no other course remained open than to implement the resolutions of the Security Council, under whose mandate the coalition forces have had to take action.

Likewise, the President stated that Bolivia is a country which lives in peace and is in favour of world peace, and will join in any effort by the international community to transform the process of violence that has been let loose into a process of peaceful solutions.

Despite these regrettable developments, the government of Bolivia considers that faith and confidence must not be lost that ultimately, and within the shortest possible time, peace will be restored in the affected region and mankind will enjoy again the right to develop free from the horrors of war.

S/22153, 25 January 1991

55. Letter from the Chargé d'affaires a.i. of the Permanent Mission of Canada to the United Nations addressed to the President of the Security Council, 21 January 1991

In accordance with paragraph 4 of resolution 678 (1990), the purpose of this letter is to inform the Security Council that, as of 16 January 1991, Canadian Armed Forces in the Persian Gulf region are participating with the Armed Forces of other Members of the United Nations in military action in accordance with that resolution to enforce Iraqi compliance with resolution 660 (1990).

Canadian Armed Forces naval vessels and aircraft will continue to enforce sanctions in accordance with resolutions 661 and 670 (1990) as the situation permits.

...

S/22154, 28 January 1991

56. Note verbale from the Permanent Mission of Iraq to the United Nations addressed to the Secretary-General, 25 January 1991

The Permanent Mission of the Republic of Iraq presents its compliments to the Secretariat of the United Nations and has the honour to transmit to it herewith the text of a letter from Mr. Tariq Aziz, Deputy Prime Minister and Minister for Foreign Affairs of the Republic of Iraq, addressed to the Secretary-General of the United Nations concerning the imperialist United States, NATO and Zionist aggression being waged against Iraq and the heinous and premeditated crimes thereby being committed against Iraqi citizens and against the economic, cultural, scientific and religious assets of our people.

...

Since the imperialist United States, NATO and Zionist aggression against our country began at 0230 hours on 17 January 1991, the attacking forces have been committing heinous premeditated crimes against Iraqi citizens and against the economic, cultural, scientific and religious assets of our great people, which is one that has made a centuries-old contribution to human civilization.

On all occasions - in the course of our meeting at Amman on 31 August 1990 and during your visit to Baghdad on 11 and 12 January 1991 - we have constantly indicated and have explained to you in a clear and detailed manner that the basic fact with regard to the events which preceded and followed 2 August 1990 is that the imperialist United States, NATO and Zionist alliance and its treacherous adherents among the régimes of the region have had the objective, as they continue to do, of destroying resurgent Iraq, which is pursuing a free and independent policy and which proudly rejects imperialist and Zionist hegemony over the region and over its resources. Everything that has happened has taken place within the framework of a conspiracy hostile to the hopes of peoples for freedom, sovereignty, independence and relations of equality, which are the very principles and objectives for the achievement and defence of which the United Nations is supposed to have been established.

The deliberate and brutal attacks launched on behalf of the United Nations by the forces of the criminal Zionist-imperialist alliance on civilian economic, humanitarian, medical, cultural and religious targets and on citizens and their families in all parts of Iraq - documented examples of which are provided to you in the present letter - give cogent proof of the fact that the Governments participating in this alliance have the sole objective of taking vengeance on the proud people of Iraq and its militant leadership because of their opposition to the imperialist goals of those Governments.

It is indeed shameful for the United Nations that these premeditated crimes should be committed under the cover provided by resolutions adopted by the Security Council. The most recent of these is Security Council resolution 678 (1990), which the United States of America succeeded in having adopted by means of pressure, blackmail and bribery. The facts with respect to the receipt of bribes by States members of the Council and by leaders in those States are common knowledge.

Hundreds of millions of people in the world, in Asia, Africa and Latin America, who have suffered from the oppression and the crimes of the former colonialists and the new imperialists, are today finding the so-called new international order of which the arrogant former colonialists and new imperialists are speaking to be a dark age of intimidation and threats against those peoples aspiring to freedom and independence and fighting for relations of equality. The removal of the balancing role formerly played by the Soviet Union opens wide the way for the arrogant former colonialists and new imperialists once again to impose hegemony and intimidation, not only by the use of new and innovative methods, as is well known, but also by the old methods, namely aggression and open military occupation. What is new is that the colonialist technique as witnessed in past centuries has this time been used under the cover provided by iniquitous resolutions fabricated in the name of the United Nations which the Governments of the imperialist colonialist alliance succeeded in having adopted by means of pressure, intimidation, blackmail and bribery.

The States that endorsed those resolutions for the motives indicated and you, personally, bear responsibility to history and to mankind for the heinous crimes being committed against the noble people of Iraq who are fighting for their freedom. Examples are given hereunder of the savage and premeditated acts of aggression committed by the aggressor forces between 17 and 21 January 1991.

Baghdad Governorate

I. *17 January 1991*

1. A pasteboard factory and a plastic foam factory in Za'faraniyah bombed.
2. Homes in the Urdunn, Bunuk and Wahdah quarters set on fire.
3. The Postal Department at Bab al-Mu'azzam set on fire and two citizens wounded.
4. A civilian vehicle set on fire near Al-Sha'b bridge.
5. The civil defence centre for the Abu Ghurayb area bombed.
6. Abu Nawwas Street bombed.

II. *18 January 1991*

1. A clinic bombed; one killed and 10 wounded and four ambulances damaged.
2. The 7 Nisan residential area bombed; seven killed.
3. The residential Kasrah area bombed.
4. The vegetable-oil factory bombed.
5. Al-Sha'b sports stadium bombed.

III. *19 January 1991*

1. The Iwadiyah area bombed, resulting in the wounding of one citizen, the collapse of a restaurant and damage to neighbouring shops.
2. The Ma'rifah residential district bombed; three wounded.
3. A building in the Kasrah area bombed; four civilians killed.
4. The Madinat Saddam residential area bombed; two homes damaged.
5. The Jazirat Baghdad tourist centre bombed; two killed and seven wounded; one home destroyed.
6. A building under construction for the Council of Ministers bombed.
7. The Al-Rashid Hotel area bombed; four homes damaged.
8. The Iraqi Museum bombed; six killed and 10 wounded; large-scale damage to the museum building.

IV. *21 January 1991*

1. Five killed and homes damaged in a residential neighbourhood in Baghdad.
2. The Civil Defence Directorate building in the Al-Sha'b area bombed; two of the staff killed and five wounded; five vehicles damaged.

V. *22 January 1991*

1. Homes in the 52 Street area bombed; two killed and three wounded.
2. Residential neighbourhoods bombed in Nuayrah, Kiyyarah, the Qadisiyah quarter and the Dur al-Shuhada' quarter.
3. Madinat Saddam bombed and homes set on fire.
4. The Karradat Maryam area bombed; two killed and four wounded; four homes destroyed; a number of neighbouring homes damaged.

VI. *23 January 1991*

Residential neighbourhoods in the Waziriyah area and the Amin II area bombed.

Salah al-Din Governorate

I. *17 January 1991*

One killed and nine wounded in the Khudayrah area of the Balad district as a result of the explosion of time-delay bombs dropped from aircraft.

II. *21 January 1991*

1. Air attack on the Biji - Qaryat al-Bujwari district, wounding six.
2. Attack on the Dur district, in the heavily populated southern region, killing 22 and wounding 33 and causing large-scale damage to 112 homes and 30 vehicles and damage to the Al-Abbasi Mosque.
3. Missile falling in a field in the Faris district, killing one woman and wounding two other citizens, one of them a woman.
4. The Tikrit district bombed with cluster-bombs dropped by two BRM-3A/As.

III. *22 January 1991*

Residential centres bombed in the town of Tikrit and the Samarra' and Biji districts.

Ninawa Governorate

19 January 1991

The historic St. Thomas's Church bombed and damaged.

Wasit Governorate

I. *17 January 1991*

Air attack on the provincial capital, killing nine and wounding nine others and damaging eight homes.

II. *18 January 1991*

Attack on residential neighbourhoods in the city of Kut, killing a woman and wounding 29 other citizens and damaging six homes and six civilian government offices.

Babil Governorate

I. *18 January 1991*

1. Residential areas bombed in the Latifiyah subdistrict; one woman wounded; a home damaged.
2. Attacks on the Musayyib district, damaging homes there.

II. *19 January 1991*

The provincial capital and the Musayyib, Mahmudiyah and Iskandariyah areas were subjected to air attacks in which the textile plant at Hillah was damaged and two of the workers were killed and 14 wounded and homes in Mahmudiyah were damaged.

III. *21 January 1991*

1. The health centre in the provincial capital bombed from the air; 24 wounded; extensive damage to the centre building, the Civil Defence Directorate building and neighbouring homes.
2. The Tall al-Dhahab area bombed; one wounded; homes damaged.

IV. *22 January 1991*

Residential areas bombed in the Mahmudiyah and Musayyib districts and the Iskandariyah subdistrict; four civilians wounded.

Anbar Governorate

19 January 1991

1. A food storage warehouse containing vegetable-oil and rice for the civilian inhabitants bombed in the Abu Ghurayb area.
2. Residential centres bombed in the Bubali area of the provincial capital; four children and two women killed; 16 other citizens wounded, including six women and five children; two homes destroyed; and a fire started.
3. The Nukhaym subdistrict bombed; 25 killed; nine wounded.

20 January 1991

1. Attack on the phosphate plant at Qa'im, killing three and wounding others.
2. A warehouse containing foodstuffs, meat and vegetable-oil bombed at Ramadi; two killed and seven wounded.

21 January 1991

1. The Hit district bombed; one killed and three wounded; homes damaged and destroyed; two civilian vehicles destroyed.
2. The Azrakiyah area in the Saqlawiyah subdistrict bombed; a woman killed and four other citizens wounded.
3. A home hit by a missile fired by an aircraft, killing three and wounding nine, all of them women and children.
4. A home hit by a missile fired by an aircraft, destroying the house and a civilian vehicle.
5. An infant formula factory bombed in the Abu Ghurayb area.
6. A poultry farm bombed in the provincial capital.

Qadisiyah Governorate

17 January 1991

1. Residential centres in the provincial capital bombed; four killed and 23 wounded.
2. A residential building bombed, the governorate office building, the civil defence building, a number of shops and houses and four civilian vehicles damaged and an ambulance set on fire.

Muthanna Governorate

18 January 1991
Air attack on a train travelling from Baghdad to Basra; three killed and 21 wounded.

Maysan Governorate

18 January 1991
1. Air attack on civilian areas in the Qal'at Salih and Kahla' districts, killing four in the Ka'bi area and wounding five others.
2. The sugar factory bombed.

Najaf Governorate

I. *18 January 1991*
Agglomerations of nomadic Bedouin bombed in the Huwaymal area near Umm Tayyarah; 20 killed, including 12 children and 5 women.

II. *21 January 1991*
1. The Kufa cement factory bombed.
2. The water purification plant for the civilian inhabitants bombed; five killed, including a woman, and 22 wounded.
3. Residential neighbourhoods in the cities of Najaf and Kufa bombed; 14 killed, including four children and three women; 24 wounded, including three children and 16 women; a number of homes destroyed and damaged in the Amir quarter of Najaf, where 130 citizens were killed, and in the Al-Mutanabbi quarter of Kufa.

Dhi Qar Governorate

I. *17 January 1991*
Air attacks, killing two and wounding five in the Batha' - Qaryat Al Budayr area and wounding two and damaging two homes and a vehicle in the provincial capital.

II. *18 January 1991*
Spherical bombs dropped on the Suq al-Shuyukh and Batha' areas, killing two and wounding two.

III. *19 January 1991*
One child killed in the Budur area in the course of an air attack.

Qadisiyah Governorate

19 January 1991
1. The State Vehicle Company complex bombed.
2. The food storage warehouse and flour factory bombed; damage caused; 10 killed and 22 wounded; two homes in the Mu'allimin quarter destroyed.

Karbala' Governorate

19 January 1991
1. Residential neighbourhoods bombed in the provincial capital.
2. The Karbala' cement factory bombed, causing large-scale damage.

22 January 1991
A residential neighbourhood bombed in the provincial capital.

Basra Governorate

17-19 January 1991
1. The provincial capital bombed, including areas of the city of Basra, Barjasiyah and Al-Asma'i and neighbouring residential apartments, and Atabat Bin Ghazwan; 28 wounded; 40 shops and some homes and civilian vehicles damaged.
2. The Harithah and Assafiyah areas bombed; six killed and 11 wounded, including a child aged three; six homes, an apartment and four shops destroyed; six shops and 15 vehicles damaged.
3. The Faw district bombed; one wounded; 40 homes damaged.
4. The Qurnah district bombed; two killed and six wounded; a number of homes damaged.
5. The Zubayr district bombed; 17 killed and another 17 wounded; 12 homes destroyed; six civilian vehicles damaged.

S/22155, 28 January 1991

57. Letter from the Permanent Representative of Tunisia to the United Nations addressed to the President of the Security Council, 26 January 1991

I have the honour to transmit herewith the text of the speech of H.E. Mr. Zine El Abidine Ben Ali, President of the Tunisian Republic, delivered on 26 January 1991.

...

The destruction and devastation which our brother Iraq is enduring are on the verge of becoming intolerable. Whatever my attitude may be as regards the heart of the problem - an attitude which, moreover, I clearly expressed on 11 August 1990 - I cannot, in any way, accept the turn of events. Actually, Iraq, in all its elements, has become threatened in its very existence.

I need hardly recall that, in my speech of 11 August, I affirmed my opposition to force being used by any party whatsoever to solve the problems. I also expressed the conviction, which is always my conviction, that every problem, however complex it may be, can be solved by peaceful means.

It was my conviction that wisdom, if lacking in one of the parties, cannot be lacking in the community of nations; that the problems of the region, although separated by their origin and their immediate causes, are closely linked by geography and their underlying reasons; and that genuine and lasting solutions are necessarily the fair and comprehensive solutions, even if they require a calendar to be established.

I have therefore spared no effort to avoid what is irreparable. That is why I asked Iraq to withdraw from Kuwait, stirred the international conscience and called upon the Security Council to announce the holding, this year, of the International Peace Conference. Iraq is not opposed thereto. This initiative, as any other, ought to have been sufficiently considered and ought to have benefited from the time required for it to be studied in greater depth.

While deploring the obstinacy of certain elements to let the chances for peace go by, I consider it my duty today, faced with the work of Iraq's destruction, to express my profound reprobation of the disastrous developments that conflict with the requirements of peace, human values and the principles on which the United Nations and the Security Council, reputed to be in the service of peace and security, were founded.

I believe that wishing to punish the Iraqi people is a political mistake, an error of judgement. The countries allied against Iraq have hastily applied the resolutions of the Security Council before even exhausting all the peaceful measures.

The date of 15 January, set by the Security Council as opening the way to a possible resort to force in order to induce Iraq to withdraw from Kuwait, has become the deadline.

The Security Council resolutions concerned the liberation of Kuwait and not the destruction of Iraq. That clearly shows that the battlefield - if battle it had to be - was not to extend beyond the boundaries of Kuwait. Most of the allied forces are in the process of unloading a deluge of fire and the sword on the whole territory of Iraq, on Basra, on Baghdad and on Mosul, thus targeting on the entire civil infrastructure and the entire material and human potential.

Through the non-stop destruction, of which our brother Iraq has been the victim since the dawn of 17 January, the true designs for which the Security Council resolutions were taken advantage of are becoming clear, just as in the same way it has been established since 2 August that international legality was not applied to all in accordance with the same standards and the same criteria.

More than 20 States have formed a coalition to strike Iraq. Is that international legality? That legality which no one has hastened to enforce, except when economic, political and strategic interests depend thereon.

The true aims, which have now become clear, consist in preventing the renaissance of the Arab nation, in prohibiting it from acquiring strength and invulnerability, from making progress and from mastering science and technology so that it will for ever remain condemned to dependence, having no place in this allegedly new world order.

It is distressing how these parties boast about unloading tens of thousands of bombs each day, using the most sophisticated engines of death on the Iraqi people, while the world echoes the cries of indignation when Israel finds itself the target of a resistance operation. But complete silence prevails when a people's potentials are wiped out and when this people is attacked even in its places of worship.

When we witness the ordeal endured by the Iraqi people and, through them, by each and every Arab citizen, we have a duty to ask ourselves: what about human rights and humanitarian law, what about the integrity of the human person and human dignity?

When we see the deceptions perpetrated by the mass media, the withholding and manipulation of information, we have a right to ask ourselves: what about the freedom and credibility of the press, what about these noble values, are they subject to limitations, do they apply to some and not to others, is this the new world order?

Citizens,

While there may be some justification for the way in which some countries use these values to serve their own interests, it is both surprising and repugnant to see Arabs and Muslims remain silent, each according to his own logic and for his own purposes, without a thought for the imperatives of the survival and dignity of the Arab nation as a whole.

Peoples always survive ordeals. We need look no further than the combatant Palestinian people, now stronger than ever despite the deportations, persecutions and genocide attempts that it has endured for half a century.

I appeal to all Arab and Muslim leaders, to all those the world over who love peace and believe in the right of peoples to peace and security, to call on the Security Council to end the war and apply the principles of international law without discrimination or restriction by convening the International Peace Conference in the course of this year with a view to ending the Gulf crisis and solving all the problems of the Middle East and, first and foremost, the problem of the struggling Palestinian people.

The Palestinian cause will remain a permanent source of instability for the entire region until a just and lasting solution is found which guarantees the right of the Palestinians to establish a state on their national soil.

I pledge our solidarity with the fraternal people of Iraq in their harsh ordeal. I am following developments in the situation constantly and am working tirelessly with our brothers in the Arab Maghreb Union, and with all peace- and justice-loving forces, to end this devastating war as soon as possible. In extending my gratitude and high regard to all Tunisians for the maturity and sense of civic duty they have shown in expressing their solidarity with the Iraqi people, I call on them to help me devote all my efforts to finding a solution to this problem, while exercising the utmost vigilance, acting calmly and responsibly, and, in keeping with the centuries-old tradition of hospitality for which we are famous, looking out for the safety and the interests of the foreign residents among us and of all those who are here to contribute to our country's development.

In view of our country's development situation and the adverse effects that this crisis is going to have, I again call on all Tunisians to commit themselves seriously to the task at hand and to redouble their efforts, now that it has become clear to all that the only path to salvation and dignity is self-reliance and that invulnerability and independence can be ensured only by our own efforts.

S/22156, 28 January 1991

58. Letter from the Permanent Representative of the United Kingdom of Great Britain and Northern Ireland to the United Nations addressed to the President of the Security Council, 28 January 1991

Further to my two letters of 21 January (S/22115 and S/22117), I have the honour to communicate to you a further report on operations in the Gulf pursuant to operative paragraph 2 of resolution 678 (1990).

Our overall aim throughout has been, in the words of the British Chief of Defence Staff, "to attack the Iraqi war machine so that it no longer casts its dark shadow over Kuwait and allows us to liberate Kuwait in accordance with the wishes of the United Nations". This has required detailed planning and meticulous execution, bearing in mind that Iraq has one of the largest armies in the world. The military objectives during the second week of operations have been to break down the intricate command network of the Iraqi armed forces, to disrupt and degrade their air defence system and thereby to gain air superiority. The attack has also concentrated on Iraq's unconventional weapons capabilities and against a whole spectrum of Iraqi military infrastructure targets which help sustain the occupation of Kuwait.

The results have been as follows. The SCUD threat has been reduced by attacks on Iraqi fixed and mobile launchers. Main Iraqi military airfields have been damaged and their capacity has been reduced. The Iraqi airforce has been so severely attacked that it has been unable to operate against allied air operations. Iraqi military command and control has been severely damaged and increasingly Iraq has moved to alternative, less effective means of communication. Iraq's ability to sustain a war has been steadily reduced. Oil refining capacity, which has been specifically targetted [*sic*] with the objective of reducing Iraq's military sustainability, has been reduced by 50 per cent. Operations continue against Iraq's chemical and biological warfare installations, production and storage capability. There has been disruption and harassment of Iraq's land army in the theatre of operations particularly orientated towards her command and control and logistical assets. The entire campaign has been conducted against military infrastructure with the express directions to avoid causing civilian casualties as far as possible, and with specific briefing to avoid sites of cultural and historic significance.

As the Secretary of State for Defence said in the House of Commons on 20 January, we have made the strongest representations again to the International Committee of the Red Cross, the representatives of which have been here seeking access to Iraqis who have been detained to ensure that they are receiving proper treatment. They were naturally granted access and we gave them every opportunity, to which they are entitled, to visit Iraqis to see whether they are receiving proper treatment. We have insisted that similar facilities must be available to representatives of the International Red Cross in Baghdad.

The ICRC team confirmed at the end of their visit that the United Kingdom in the UK was complying with the Geneva Conventions as regards Prisoners of War and civilian detainees.

There was also an ICRC visit to facilities for prisoners of war in Riyadh. They were able to see there the provisions made for the sick and wounded, and the arrangements to discharge our obligations under the Geneva Conventions.

...

S/22158, 28 January 1991

59. Note verbale from the Permanent Mission of Iraq to the United Nations addressed to the Secretary-General, 28 January 1991

The Permanent Mission of Iraq to the United Nations presents its compliments to the Secretary-General of the United Nations and has the honour to transmit herewith the text of a statement issued on 28 January 1991 by the spokesman for the Iraqi armed forces concerning the attack launched by aircraft of the United States-NATO-Zionist coalition against Iraqi oil installations in the province of Kuwait.

...

On the evening of 27 January 1991, at 2115 hours, aircraft of the United States-NATO-Zionist coalition launched an attack against oil installations in the province of Kuwait with a view to destroying oil distribution facilities. Enemy aircraft bombed oil pipelines and intake and regulatory valves at the port of Nida, starting a fire and causing oil to spill into the waters of the Arabian Gulf.

The United States of America and its allies are once again manifesting their insatiable desire to damage and annihilate Arab resources to prevent our people and our nation from enjoying them.

Despite our repeated warnings to the United States and its allies regarding the need to protect the environment of the region and to prevent it from becoming polluted, and although we mentioned the serious dangers arising from their acts, America and its allies persist in following the path of evil, scorning our national heritage and the quality of the environment in this part of the world, placing their limited interests, which lie in the damage they do to Iraq, above any humanitarian considerations. We appeal to world public opinion and to international organizations, particularly those working to preserve the environment, to raise their voices and take action in response to this crime.

Our forces, using all the technological tools at their disposal, are doing everything they can to put out these fires, stop the oil spills and mitigate the effects of the crime perpetrated by the United States.

S/22159, 28 January 1991

60. Letter from the Permanent Representative of Suriname to the United Nations addressed to the Secretary-General, 28 January 1991

I have the honour to enclose herewith the text of the statement by the Government of the Republic of Suriname on the situation in the Gulf.

...

The outbreak and continuation of war in the Gulf Region is of great concern for the Government of the Republic of Suriname.

Suriname has from the outset expressed its rejection of Iraq's invasion of Kuwait as an act that goes contrary to the fundamental principles of international law and the United Nations Charter. We once again appeal to the Government of Iraq to accept the relevant United Nations resolutions and commence its withdrawal from Kuwait.

The Government of Suriname deeply regrets the failure of sustained peace efforts to prevent the outbreak of war and the consequent human suffering and loss of lives and appeals to all parties concerned to undertake all steps necessary to still resolve the conflict by diplomatic means.

The Surinamese Government expresses its hope that a speedy diplomatic solution to this conflict will be found and that peace will be promptly restored in the Persian Gulf.

S/22160/Rev.1, 29 January 1991

61. Letter from the Permanent Representative of Israel to the United Nations addressed to the Secretary-General, 28 January 1991

Since Friday, 18 January 1991, Israel has been the target of a series of destructive and unprovoked attacks:

> On 18 January at 2.00 a.m., a salvo of Iraqi missiles was launched into Israel leading to the injury of 15 civilians and causing considerable property damage.
>
> On 19 January at 7.30 a.m., Iraq again launched a missile attack against Israel, injuring 10 civilians and causing considerable property damage.
>
> On 22 January at 8.37 p.m., missiles were fired by Iraq, which resulted in the death of 3 civilians and the injury of 95 others in the Tel-Aviv area.
>
> On 23 January shortly after 10.00 p.m., a missile was lunched [*sic*] by Iraq toward the northern region of Israel. Although there were no injuries, property damage was sustained.
>
> On 25 January at approximately 6.05 p.m., Iraq fired 7 missiles at the northern and central regions of Israel causing 1 fatality and 69 injuries.
>
> On 26 January at 10.03 p.m., missiles were fired by Iraq towards northern and central Israel. No injuries were sustained.
>
> Speaking to the Union of Arab Workers on 18 April 1990, Saddam Hussein said:

> "... Our planes and missiles will reach Israel ... Indeed we have positioned our missile launchers facing west, not east."
> (Iraqi News Agency)

On the eve of his invasion of Kuwait, Saddam Hussein threatened to destroy Israel, fully aware that Israel has no aggressive intentions against Iraq or any other Arab state. Later, on January 9th, during a press conference, Iraq's Foreign Minister went one step further. In response to the question: "If the war starts in the Middle East, in the Gulf, will you attack Israel?" - Tariq Aziz replied, "Yes, absolutely yes."

Saddam Hussein, who has used chemical weapons in his war with Iran, as well as having murdered thousands of his own citizens in this same horrible fashion, now threatens to use chemical weapons against Israel.

In a military ceremony on 1 April 1990, Saddam Hussein threatened to destroy Israel:

> "In the name of Allah, we shall light a fire that will engulf half of Israel should it take steps against Iraq ... we possess binary chemical weapons."
> (Iraqi Press Agency, April 2nd)

Iraqi's [*sic*] actions have already caused loss of life, scores of injuries and damage to homes and property. These repeated unprovoked acts of aggression by Iraq constitute an illegal use of force, in clear breach of the prohibition of threat and use of force in Article 2 (4) of the Charter of the United Nations.

The attacks were against civilians. The method of terror employed by Iraq against Israel, namely, intentional and unprovoked bombings is a flagrant breach of the norms of international law applicable between states.

Israel calls on all the members of the international community to condemn these deliberate attacks by Iraq on Israel's population and the resulting loss of life and suffering involved, and demands that such attacks cease immediately. Israel calls for appropriate and full reparations for Iraq's attacks.

Under these circumstances Israel reserves its right to call for a meeting of the Security Council as well as reserving its right to act in self-defense.

...

S/22162, 28 January 1991

62. Note verbale from the Permanent Mission of Paraguay to the United Nations addressed to the Secretary-General, 28 January 1991

The Permanent Mission of Paraguay to the United Nations presents its compliments to the Secretary-General of the United Nations and has the honour to transmit the communiqué of the Ministry of Foreign Affairs of Paraguay on the conflict in the Persian Gulf issued at Asuncion on 26 January 1991.

...

The Ministry of Foreign Affairs of Paraguay expresses the Paraguayan Government's repudiation of the attacks on the non-belligerent State of Israel by Iraq during the current war in the Persian Gulf and stands in solidarity with the Israeli people.

At the same time, as a member of the United Nations, Paraguay reiterates its support for the Security Council resolutions condemning the occupation of Kuwait by Iraq and aimed at restoring the situation obtaining prior to 2 August 1990

Paraguay laments the loss of human life and the adverse consequences of the conflict and hopes for the prompt restoration of peace.

S/22163, 28 January 1991

63. Letter from the Permanent Representative of the Islamic Republic of Iran to the United Nations addressed to the Secretary-General, 28 January 1991

Upon instructions from my Government, I have the honour to inform that a number of Iraqi military aircrafts have made emergency landing in the Islamic Republic of Iran.

The National Security Council of the Islamic Republic, reiterating the position of the Islamic Republic of Iran concerning non-engagement in present hostilities, warned the belligerent parties to refrain from any use of Iranian airspace. It further decided that in the event of emergency landing of any aircraft of either side in the territory of the Islamic Republic of Iran, the aircraft would be seized and held until the termination of hostilities.

In this connection, the Islamic Republic of Iran had registered to the government of Iraq its strong protest at the emergency landing of the above-mentioned aircrafts. Furthermore, reiterating the position of non-engagement of the Islamic Republic of Iran in the hostilities in the Persian Gulf and its commitment to resolutions of the Security Council, the Foreign Ministry of the Islamic Republic of Iran has informed the government of Iraq that, in line with relevant rules of international law, the Islamic Republic of Iran will not allow the use of military vessels and personnel who have entered the territory of the Islamic Republic of Iran to any of the belligerent parties until the termination of hostilities.

...

S/22164, 28 January 1991

64. Letter from the Permanent Representative of Kuwait to the United Nations addressed to the President of the Security Council, 28 January 1991

On instructions from my Government, in accordance with paragraph 4 of Security Council resolution 678 (1990) and pursuant to my letter of 17 January 1991 (S/22094), I have the honour to inform you of the following:

A unit of the Kuwaiti armed forces has, in conjunction with the armed forces of fraternal and friendly States, carried out military operations against Iraqi installations with a view to ensuring the complete and unconditional withdrawal of Iraq from Kuwait, in accordance with the relevant resolutions of the Security Council.

A unit of the Kuwait Navy took part in the attack against the oil rig occupied by Iraq.

Kuwait Air Force aircraft also took part in joint air operations directed primarily against ground-to-ground missile sites, missile launchers, artillery positions and concentrations of Iraqi mechanized units.

...

S/22165, 28 January 1991

65. Letter from the Permanent Representative of Kuwait to the United Nations addressed to the President of the Security Council, 28 January 1991

I have the honour to transmit herewith the text of a statement delivered on 26 January 1991 by the Minister of State for Cabinet Affairs and Executive Secretary General of the Regional Marine Environmental Protection

Organization concerning the recent spilling of oil in the Gulf by Iraq.

...

By polluting the environment and causing this disaster in the Gulf, the Iraqi régime once again demonstrates its contempt for marine, ecological and, indeed, human life. These events clearly show that this operation was undertaken for purposes of sabotage. This is also demonstrated by the concentration in the Gulf of Iraqi tankers carrying light petroleum which the Iraqis can easily set afire whenever they feel the time is right. The enormous oil slick created by the Iraqi régime imperils all forms of marine life and ichthyological resources and even poses a threat to the water used in desalinization plants.

The competent organizations and the international forces have been asked to contain this disaster as a matter of urgency, for the Gulf is threatened with a catastrophe on a massive scale, one even more serious than the disaster created by Nirouz oilfield during the war between Iran and Iraq. An operation of this type is difficult even in time of peace. One hardly dares think of the problems it would create in wartime.

A/45/942, S/22166, 29 January, 1991

66. Letter from the Permanent Representative of Bahrain to the United Nations addressed to the Secretary-General, 28 January 1991

I have the honour to transmit to you herewith the text of a statement issued by the Cabinet of the State of Bahrain on 20 January 1991 on the commencement of military operations for the liberation of Kuwait.

...

At its meeting held today, the Cabinet reviewed the evolution of events in the Gulf region, particularly with the commencement of military operations for the liberation of Kuwait in accordance with the resolutions of the Security Council and in keeping with international legitimacy. The Cabinet commends the positions adopted by Arab and Islamic States and other friendly States on this matter and, in particular, the major role being played by the Custodian of the Two Holy Mosques, King Fahd Bin Abdul-Aziz, and by the Kingdom of Saudi Arabia for the establishment of peace in the region and the elimination therefrom of resort to armed aggression and the violation of international covenants and international law and custom, as practised by the leaders of Iraq on 2 August 1990 in that country's occupation of the fraternal State of Kuwait. We call upon the leadership in Iraq to abandon its intransigent position and listen to the voice of reason and wisdom in order to spare Iraq further suffering and save the Arab nation from a possible catastrophe.

S/22168, 29 January 1991

67. Letter from the Permanent Representative of the United States of America to the United Nations addressed to the President of the Security Council, 25 January 1991

On behalf of my Government, I request that you distribute as documents of the Security Council the enclosed text of the briefing conducted by the Secretary of Defense and the Chairman of the Joint Chiefs of Staff of the United States on 23 January 1991 concerning the Crisis in the Gulf.

Following is the transcript of a news briefing conducted by Secretary of Defense Dick Cheney and General Colin Powell, Chairman of the Joint Chiefs of Staff, at the Pentagon on Wednesday, January 23, 1991 at 2 p.m.:

Mr. Pete Williams ASD (Public Affairs): Good afternoon, ladies and gentlemen, Secretary Cheney and General Powell are here to answer your questions. The Secretary will have a short statement, then General Powell will walk you through - we'll have some charts here. After the briefings are over the charts will remain here so that you can photograph them. We will try, this afternoon, to provide you smaller handouts of those. So let me, at this point, turn it over to the Secretary.

Secretary Cheney: Thank you very much, Pete.

Operation Desert Storm has now been underway for approximately one week, as of this evening. We believe that it's gone very well. We wanted to take this opportunity to try to put things in perspective, and then try to respond to some of your questions. Let me begin by expressing the pride that we all feel in the men and women of our armed forces who are carrying out these operations. It is an extremely complex and often dangerous undertaking, and they have our admiration and our gratitude. I also want to say to the families of those held prisoner or missing in action, that they are in the prayers of all Americans in these very difficult days.

I want to repeat what we told all of you last week at the beginning of this conflict. I urged caution in describing the events in the Persian Gulf, especially in claiming victory too soon. The next day, the President expressed his concern about what he called the initial euphoria and some of the early reactions and stories about the operation.

I also said that this operation was likely to run for a long period of time. Yesterday, with operation Desert Storm in its sixth day, I noticed a newspaper headline which said, "War drags on." Finally, this morning, I noticed that the style section in the Washington Post had three separate stories about the press covering the war in the Gulf. As an old Washington hand, I know that having the press reporting on the press reporting on a story is usually a sign that they've run out of things to say about this war. So Colin and I decided to spend a little time with you this afternoon to see if we could give you some new information. Some important qualifiers to keep in mind as we go through the briefing this afternoon, and many of these may be obvious, but I think need to be restated. The Iraqis and Saddam Hussein have a very large military force. Depending upon what criteria you use, certainly one of the largest in the world - some have said the fourth largest in the world. In the last decade he's spent over $50 billion on armaments. The force possesses thousands of tanks, hundreds of aircraft, over a million men in uniform, missiles, etcetera.

In the Kuwaiti theater of operations, in Kuwait and southern Iraq, there are over 120 brigades and some 30 plus divisions dug in in that area. I don't think anyone here expected that we would get rid of all that capability within the first week of the operation. Over 10,000 separate sorties have been flown on combat and support missions in just the past seven days. Our goal remains the same - to liberate Kuwait by forcing Saddam Hussein out. To do that, we have to weaken his military force, and to go after his offensive military capability. In pursuit of that objective, we began by concentrating on a carefully planned set of military targets that we will continue to hit over the course of the next several days and weeks. We've started with command and control, with his communications facilities, his air defense units and radars, his airfields, his scud missile launchers. We've gone after the factories where Iraq has produced chemical and biological weapons, and until recently, continued working on nuclear weapons. We've also gone after the mainstay of Saddam's command forces, the Republican Guard units located near the Iraqi/Kuwaiti border. All of these targets we chose in advance.

The pilots of the allied air forces have operated in accordance with clear instructions to launch weapons only when they are certain they've selected the right targets under correct conditions. Iraq, on the other hand, has chosen to launch a highly inaccurate weapon - the scud missile - at major population centers, with no certainty about where the scuds will land. In contrast, we have carefully chosen our targets and we've bombed them with precision.

Based on the reports we're getting from our pilots and the evidence of gun camera recordings, many of which you've seen, the bombing missions are going well. The missions are based on the target list drawn up before the operation started. At the same time, we've been eager to know about the kind of damage which we've been able to cause. That's why we do bomb damage assessment. These assessments are now coming in and will be used to make judgments about the success of our efforts to date, and to guide the planning of future operations.

I want to caution you, again, that a military operation of this intensity and complexity cannot be scored every evening like a college track meet or a basketball tournament. I know how hard it is for you to cover this kind of an operation when you cannot see what's going on inside Iraq or occupied Kuwait. Some of you have been critical of us for not putting information out more quickly - I understand your point, but we want to be certain that we don't rush down here with premature words of success. We are deliberately waiting until we have some confidence in the results of specific categories of targets. That may well not fit the 24-hour cycle that you're held to, but we want to have confidence in what we are saying before we say it.

Two final points: there may well be surprises ahead for us. No one should assume that Saddam Hussein does not have significant remaining military capability. We have to anticipate that he will try to use that against us and our allies. We have to assume that he may seek to launch air strikes and more scuds, or hit oil fields, or generate terrorist attacks. He is a man who will use any means at his disposal to break up the coalition and to avoid defeat, but he cannot change the basic course of the conflict. He will be defeated.

Our first obligation here in the Pentagon is to carry out the [*sic*] and to go after his offensive military capability, in pursuit of President's orders, and to win the war. We must also do everything possible to do it in a manner that holds American and allied casualties to an absolute minimum. We recognize that we also have an obligation to provide as much information as possible about the progress of our efforts to the press. We will do that. But you, the members of the press, have to understand that first and foremost we must safeguard the security of future operations, and to protect the lives of those who will be asked to carry them out.

With that, I'd like to turn the briefing over to my colleague, Colin Powell, the Chairman of the Joint Chiefs, with a general overview of the status of the operation to date.

General Powell: Thank you, Mr. Secretary. Let me also express my pride, and I expect it's the pride of all Americans, at the professionalism with which the men and women of the armed forces have carried out this operation so far; and of course, I share the Secretary's concern about our missing in action, and our prayers are with the families of those who have lost loved ones, and especially with the families of those who do have missing in action who may well be prisoners of war.

This is the end of the first week of operations. What I'd like to do is for a few moments take stock with you, and attempt to dampen out the oscillations between euphoria and distress that sometimes catches us up every hour on the hour. I'd like to do that by first reminding you of the military operational objective that we set out to accomplish, and that is simply to eject the Iraqi army from Kuwait. All of our activities must ultimately support this fundamental military objective. Of course when we achieve that objective, we then will be in a position to restore the legitimate Government of Kuwait and provide for the security of the region.

We also remind you once again, as we've said here previously, this is an air/land/sea campaign - not just an air campaign which at some point will end, and then something else starts. It is a single, coherent, integrated air/land/sea campaign. The campaign plan has executed, so far, pretty much as we have expected, with a few exceptions. The weather turned more severe after two and a half days of operation than we had expected. We knew we were going to have two and a half days, and then we thought we'd lose a day or two to weather conditions, but those weather conditions were more severe than we expected when they finally hit, when the front came in, and lasted a little bit longer than we expected. As a result, a number of our planned missions had to be aborted, the BDA process has been behind schedule because of cloud cover and other weather problems, and we have had to cancel some target coverage. All this means is that we have to make that up, over time, but we are still, essentially, on our original game plan.

The other point I might make is that we devoted more effort than we initially thought we might have to go after the scud targets that you have reported on so much in the last several days. Mobile scuds were the problem that we had anticipated they would be, and now that we are into it, and I'll say more about scuds later, we are finding that it's taking more of an effort on our part to go after those scuds than we had anticipated. But notwithstanding these sorts of problems, we're pleased with week one, and we are satisfied that the contribution that the strategic air campaign is making to our overall objective is a good contribution, and is about what we expected.

What I'd like to do is discuss certain parts of the air phase of the campaign and the results we've achieved in an effort to answer your questions with respect to how are we doing - how effective has the operation been so far. Let me first start talking about the air-to-air part of the campaign, how it's been going with respect to U.S. air forces engaged in aerial combat with Iraqi air forces.

Iraqi air-to-air interception, to date, has been, for the most part, totally ineffective. In air-to-air engagements, the results are 19 Iraqi interceptors destroyed in aerial combat; and we believe the most we might have lost is one. We were carrying it as zero until earlier today when we did some more analysis, talked with some pilots, and one of our planes may have been hit in air-to-air engagement. So at best, 19:0; at worst, at the moment, 19:1. Their losses, in the interceptor category, have all been F.1's and MIG.29's, their first line interceptor aircraft. Other losses that they have sustained raise their total combat aircraft losses to something in the neighbourhood of 41. But the real measure of effectiveness, the real way to look at this and make an assessment of how we're doing, is not by the number of aircraft downed or how many sorties we've flown or how many bunkers we've hit and how many bombs we've dropped. The real measure of effectiveness is what has the Iraqi air force been able to do to interfere with operation Desert Storm? The fact of the matter is that after a one week period of time, no Iraqi airplane has conducted a single ground attack against any coalition target; and with the one exception of perhaps the one airplane that may have gone down, the Iraqi air force has not been able to interfere with our air operation.

When you consider that the Iraqi air force had a massive amount of money and resources invested into it over the years, and has some 800 fighter bombers and interceptors, I think it's fair to say that this has not been, so far, a very good return on the investment that Saddam Hussein has put into the air force. Nevertheless, it is a large air force. It has a latent capability. It has the ability to conduct defensive operations and offensive operations if they can ever get their act together. But as you will see in the course of the briefing, their sortie rate is down, and their ability to operate has pretty much been constrained.

By way of illustration, this map - for those of you who wish to count the little dots, there are 66 little dots, and they reflect main operating bases in red, dispersal airfields in blue, and then the general scud launch areas from the west out to Israel and from the east down south into Riyadh, are shown by the black hatched marks.

This is a very extensive airfield system, hardened bunkers, you've seen pictures of them; underground command and control installations; hardened fuel facilities; hardened ammo facilities. But the fact of the matter is, that after one week of operation, we are not being challenged by this air force; and in fact, within the last 24 hours we have only seen activity at the air bases that you see being pointed out to you with a little yellow dot in the middle of the red. Those are the only ones that have shown any active work in the last 24 hours.

If I can turn to this chart, just to give you another illustration. This summarizes what I said earlier, 411 interceptors, 398 fighter bombers, 809 total; killed 19 in aerial combat, another 22 confirmed killed on the ground, for a total of 41 in this category. They have a lot of other kinds of aircraft that could run this total up to roughly 1400 if you add in transports and helicopters and things of that nature, but for the combat category, the thing that we worry about, this is the number. I'm not really concerned about this number for the moment. They are, for the most part, on the ground, in hardened shelters, trying to hide and survive. In due course, they may wish to come out and challenge us, or they just may try to ride it out for as long as possible. These numbers will rise over time as we continue the campaign to go after shelters, go after bunkers and essentially rip up the air force in its entirety.

Let me turn now to another part of the air battle, and that has to do with ground-to-surface air defense systems - the SAMS and anti-aircraft guns. This chart reflects, at a high level of aggregation because I don't want to give away too much information, but the main air defense SAM belts in red circles, and then the circles going all around the country reflect their early warning capability at the beginning of the operation. An extremely large, sophisticated air defense system, principally with Soviet equipment, Soviet missile equipment, some French, some U.S. that was captured, as well as a very comprehensive system of trying to integrate all of those missile systems and gun systems, hardened command and control centers around the country.

The fact of the matter is, that we were able to attack this air defense envelope with great success over the last week by first taking out the early warning capability, blinding them, and then going after the operating centers, the various sector operating centers that they used to wire this all together. For the most part, we have not been seriously affected by this very large air defense system. We have had a total of 10 aircraft lost, as you know. As we go through the analysis of how we lost those aircraft, at the moment it appears we lost two by SAM fire, surface-to-air missile fire, and three more by ground fire (AAA), and the other five we're still taking a look at. But when you take a look at our total losses of only ten U.S. aircraft, and I'll show you a chart there that, well this says SAM 1, AAA 3, I had it the other way around, but it's something close to that, and I apologize for the difference in numbers. When you take a look at the total of 16 aircraft losses for the coalition in its entirety, and you consider the number of combat sorties that have been flown, and the numbers of single aircraft that are involved in this operation - somewhere between 1,000 - 2,000 aircraft - this is a very low loss rate for an operation of this type.

Putting all that together, we can conclude that allied air forces have achieved air superiority over not only the Kuwaiti theater of operations, but throughout the entire theater, to include Iraq. We can debate whether it's air superiority as defined by American doctrine, or air supremacy as some of my British colleagues have alluded, or local air superiority as some of my friends in Riyadh say - I used to teach the subject, I own the JCS publication that has the definition in it, which I helped write when I was a captain - and I can assure you, that this qualifies for the definition of air superiority. When you can operate in an unhindered way, as we have been operating, over an area like this against an air force that size, and with an air defense system that sophisticated, we have achieved air superiority.

That is not to say that a young pilot who is taking off will say Powell says we have air superiority. I've got nothing to worry about. Not at all. We're dealing with an enemy that is resourceful, an enemy that knows how to work around problems, an enemy that is ingenious. You can be sure that while we're here today, they're in Baghdad trying to figure out work-arounds, trying to determine where their weaknesses are, and see if they have capability to fix those weaknesses. Every pilot that goes against this environment, still has to be concerned that he is going against an environment that has the potential of taking down his airplane, so we are not getting complacent, we are not writing this off, but in terms of how it looks at General Schwarzkopf's level and at my level, we have air superiority. With that air superiority, we can now begin to use our air forces to simply maintain this superiority and start to concentrate down closer to the Kuwaiti theater of operations, remembering once again, our military objective is the Iraqi army in Kuwait. We have free run of the area, as much as possible. There will still be losses, and I don't want to understate that, but in general, air superiority.

Any pilot will tell you, though, that the real danger is guns. As we get closer into the Kuwaiti theater of operations and our op tempo picks up, we will focus a great deal of our attention on knocking down the anti-aircraft gun threat to our pilots so they can get even lower and make their strikes more effective as we go after discreet units on the ground in due course.

Before turning to the Iraqi army, let me be totally joint and say a word about the Iraqi navy - a navy of almost no capability, of a limited number of patrol boats. We have destroyed several of those patrol boats. We have taken out a silkworm site they were manning. We have also sunk, or severely damaged - it isn't sunk, in fact it is floating - severely damaged a ship they have been using to lay mines. Also within the last week, we have destroyed a number of the mines, I think the count is 24 of the mines that have been floating free in the Persian Gulf. So I think we've dealt with the mine threat for the moment, and in due course, if the Iraqi navy in some way decides to come out any more and challenge us with these minor and insignificant patrol boats, it is, indeed, a manageable threat.

Let me turn now, to the Iraqi army in the Kuwaiti theater of operations. As the Secretary pointed out, this is a large combined arms army. It has tanks, it has personnel carriers, it has air defense guns, it has very redundant, resilient communications between the different operating echelons of the army. It has stockages of food, ammunition, and parts with the army in theater, and they have a very elaborate supply system coming down from the interior of the country to sustain that army.

Our strategy to go after this army is very, very simple. First, we're going to cut it off, and then we're going to kill it. To cut if off - that began last week when we started to go after the nerve center, the brains of the operation, the command and control of the operation, and the lines of communication that comes out of Baghdad and other places in the country, flowing down the Tigris and Euphrates valleys, down these lines of communication, to try to support somewhere in the neighborhood of a half a million men down here in the Kuwaiti theater of operations. All we have been doing to gain control over here, to begin severing this and try to deaden the nerve endings up here, all goes back to our original military objective - to get rid of the army that is in Kuwait.

Now that that has started, we will intensify this cutting-off process, go after the lines of communications as they enter the vicinity of Basrah, and as they come out of Basrah going down to the army. Going after the command control means, the means by which they exercise command and control over that force in the theater. Going after mobility, trucks that move supplies forward. Anything that allows that army to function, we will now go after. As we get into the process of cutting it off, we will also step up the process of killing it, by going after stockpiles, ammunition, food, stripping away their gun air defense, using air attacks, and if it becomes necessary, we are assembling a fairly sizeable ground force that could finish off the job, should that be necessary. I also want to emphasize that we have quite a capability at sea with naval gunfire, with naval aviation, as well as quite a formidable amphibious capability with our marine forces, and as some of you know, our two marine expeditionary brigades are conducting practice operations today. I'm not telegraphing anything, I just want everybody to know that we have a tool box that's full of lots of tools, and I brought them all to the party. General Schwarzkopf has them all at the party.

So how are we doing with respect to that major operational objective - the Iraqi army in Kuwait? We are really starting in earnest. I have to make a point to you, that assessing the damage on a deployed army in the field is quite a different proposition from assessing the damage on a building that you've just hit. You've seen some great film footage of a laser-guided bomb going down the vent shaft of a building, boom, it blows up, it burns down, there you have it. It doesn't work that way when you have a deployed armored brigade in the field. They're spread out, they're dug in, they're hiding - they're not standing out there like a building. They're avoiding air attack. They are going to put out dummies to try to deceive you as to their exact locations. They're going to put in primary positions and alternate positions and supplementary positions. They're going to dig in their lines of communication. They're going to put in overhead cover. Those tanks are designed not to be easily destroyed. So going after that kind of unit is a much more difficult proposition, but they are vulnerable, there's no question about it.

We are now turning our attention and selecting munitions, and selecting target packages to go after that army which, in effect, is sitting out there not doing anything. It has not moved since the operation began. There has been no major, in fact there has [*sic*] been no minor shifts of units around. It is, for the most part, sitting there, dug in, waiting to be attacked, and attacked it will be. But it is also sitting there without air support, without anything to keep the attack from being prosecuted against them, and with each passing day, with a reduced ability to bring in logistics down the lines of communication. There is no question that this large force will become weaker every day - that's absolutely mathematical. We're going to do everything we can to make sure that army cannot be reinforced with new troops, and over time, they will have increasing difficulty to resupply it. Yet that army has good soldiers. The units are of varying quality. The Republican Guard, as we've said many times, is quite good. Other parts of the force are not quite so good. We have anecdotal evidence of some low morale, and anecdotal evidence of some defections, but it is not a trend yet. We have started to get some bomb damage assessment on the Republican Guard units that we've been striking. In some cases, the analysts who look at these photos, and I look at them as well, tell me, you see that unit out there? It's taken about 40 percent damage. I can't tell that, you've got to be an expert. But there is damage taking place. Other units that we have hit, we've looked at the photographs and said we didn't get a good hit on that, they're just too dispersed, we've got to go back and do it again, very light damage against that unit. So you are not going to get, and we will be unable to give you, the kind of rapidly moving and adjusting score card on how we're doing against that army for some time.

You really don't know how you're doing against an army until that army tries to perform its function. If it's just sitting there taking the punishment, we know we're hurting it. We really don't know how badly we've hurt it until it starts to move, until it comes up on the radio so we can hear it talking to other units, until we can see defections come out of it, or if it's necessary to go in and fight it. So we are seeing some anecdotal evidence, but the BDA is still out on that, and we really have only begun to do the job on it.

I'd like to close by saying a few words about some of the strategic campaign targets we had up here. First, let me just make one point on this slide that I forgot earlier. As a measure of effectiveness of how we're doing in the air campaign, I just pull these two things out - I've laundered them so you can't really tell what I'm talking about because I don't want the Iraqis to know what I'm talking about, but trust me. (Laughter) This reflects an order of magnitude of electronic emissions out of the Iraqi radar system. It shows that early in December and through December they were operating about over here with SAM, AAA radars, and early warning radars. On the 17th of January, as you would expect, it peaked up to here. Over the last week, it has come down to here. This represents well over a 95 percent reduction. Now it's a combination of damage we have done, as well as, I suspect, clever operational security techniques on their part, to keep us from knowing exactly what's going on or how badly they have been damaged. I am also sure they are trying to work around and reconstitute capability so they can get back up. So I don't want to overstate it, just to give you a measure of effectiveness and let you know this is how we try to measure what's going on out there.

This also is, by another measure of effectiveness - and I'm sorry for this being so small, we just finished it - shows you their daily sortie rate. This was before the action began. On the 30th of December they were running about 235 sorties a day during that period. If weather was bad early in December, a little lower. But just as a benchmark, 235 sorties. The day of the war, they ran 115 sorties; and for the last couple of days they've been running 31-40 sorties. Once again, the kind of measure of effectiveness that is more useful to us than is how many sorties we flew or how many bombs we dropped, etcetera.

A couple of things about specific campaign targets that really go to the issue of how to make sure that when this is all over, the kind of threat that has existed in the region is quite different than the threat that existed before it began. First, with respect to nuclear weapons, we have targeted that nuclear facility they have very carefully. I have looked at the bomb damage assessment myself with trained analysts, and I think I can confirm for you that the two operating reactors they had are both gone. They're down, they're finished. The one that the Israelis took care of some years ago, remains down.

With respect to chemical facilities, the focus of our effort for the first week has been on their production capability and their ability to fill munitions. There are hundreds of bunkers out there, and it would have been a waste of our effort to keep chasing every single bunker which may or may not have chemical weapons stored in them, because they have dispersed a lot of that chemical weapon capability they have out to operating units. So we concentrated on production facilities and the facilities that they use to put the material into actual weapons to be delivered. We have had quite a bit of success, and without getting into specifics, I think I can say that we have done considerable damage to their ability to continue producing chemical weapons. But they still have a chemical weapons capability. Their artillery can fire chemical weapons, their multiple launch rocket system, their free rocket over ground systems, and their air force does have that capability, so it's still a threat to allied forces in the region.

With respect to their biological warfare facilities, we have gone after those and have created quite a problem for them, I think. We have seriously damaged those facilities. There was a story earlier today about the infant formula factory. It is not an infant formula factory. No more than the Rabta chemical plant in Libya made aspirin. It was a biological weapons facility, of that we are sure, and we have taken it out. We will continue to seek out any other facilities that we believe are involved in the production of biological weapons.

With respect to their national command authority and their command and control systems, they are very good at this. They have redundant systems, resilient systems, they have work-arounds, they have alternatives, and they are still able to command their forces. They have not lost command and control of their forces or of the country; but they are doing it without benefit of their Ministry of Defense, their Defense Intelligence Center, their main communications nodes, and they're doing it, for the mo link BLK: 965 part, on generator power, because we have taken care of the central power system within the city. He still does retain the ability to command and control.

We are also now turning our attention increasingly to military production facilities, how he makes bombs, how he makes weapons, how he makes repair parts. This is a target category that we will go after at our leisure over time. We're in no hurry. We don't want to waste sorties on things that are further down the priority list if we can get to them further down the priority list.

The most significant problem we have right now are the scuds - there's no doubt about it. When you think of what Saddam Hussein has done for the past week, he has not thrown a single military punch back at us. What he has done is used this weapon of terror, the scuds, as was mentioned earlier by the Secretary, to go after populations, to go after cities. Why? As a weapon of terror to try to expand the conflict, to try to draw in the Israelis - and I must say, I'm extremely pleased with the restraint that the Israeli Government has shown so far, but it is a vexing problem. They are mobile systems. Some of them are very sophisticated Soviet mobile systems - others are nothing more than a flat bed truck with a rail on it that they've locally fabricated. We only have estimates of how many of these weapons they have, but we have made it a high priority to locate these weapons and to go after them, and a significant part of our capability is directed toward that scud facility - those scud facilities and mobile scuds.

I know there's been a great deal of interest in bomb damage assessment. I wish I could show you the photographs that we have access to, but because of sources and methods, and because we are in an ongoing operation, and because we do not want an enemy to have knowledge of what our real capabilities are, we cannot show you those photographs. What I have done, instead, is I have made some line drawings, had some line drawings made. They're rather crude. They're kind of cartoonish, but I just want to give you a sense of what our analysts look at. I will assure you, that what I'm about to show you comes directly from the actual imagery, but we have, obviously, done it in a way that it does not give away any of our capability.

This was a large production facility, part of his military infrastructure. It was struck by precision weapons in the first couple of days of the operation. This is a very accurate reflection of what the thing looks like - total destruction. The point I want to make is, our analysts can see this to this level of detail and give us high assurance that this place has been destroyed.

Q: Were there weapons produced there at all?

A: It was an unconventional production facility. Here is an example of a bunker complex, and it's a case where we went after selected buildings. These two were revetted, they had barriers around them. We went after these with precision of weapons. I think this one was done over a period of a couple of days. You go strike it, you get an assessment back of the amount of damage you have inflicted on the facility, you go back and strike it again. This has received enough damage that I would suspect that the targeteers over in CENTAF are not going to waste a sortie at this time going back and taking care of this last remaining building. These were the key ones. These three fed into what was happening at these two facilities, so we have essentially destroyed this, even though there might still be a building standing. I'm just using it as illustrative of the process which our bomb damage assessment people go through. This next one is a case where initially we went in, destroyed - here's the bunker complex, destroyed this bunker. This one was hit once, and we had to go back and do it again to get the level of damage we needed. This one was also struck. As the analyst looks at it, part of it is still intact - the top. This part, the lower part has been blown through, but since the analyst can't see what happened under the part that still has a roof over it, he will not declare this destroyed. They tend to err on the conservative side. This one is completely undamaged, because there was no need to waste a sortie or risk a pilot going against that one. We knew what we were looking for in this complex, so we are satisfied with this target - even if somebody were to come along and say Aha, you only got 75 percent or 80 percent, because this one is still there. We didn't need to hit that one. It has no relevance to the rest of the facility.

This is an example which I'd like to put up, for my British colleagues. One of the things we did early on to deal with the airfields, and to keep the air force on the ground, was to essentially interdict the airfields so they couldn't be used. We could do that very quickly by trying to crater the runways. In this particular case, this shows a British weapon system, which I think was briefed earlier out of Riyadh, I believe, by a British officer, but it's a JP.233, which goes across the runway and is very effective at cutting concrete. It will cut up the concrete and break it up so that the airfield cannot be used for some period of hours, and I don't want to get into how long that might be - it depends on the airfield, depends on the kind of concrete, depends on the kind of cut that's made. You would use this weapon system and other weapon systems that we have, to try and cut this airfield in a number of places to keep it from being used for awhile. Then we can come back to it at our leisure and take care of what is on that airfield.

In this case, the pilot elected to cut these taxiways here so that the aircraft in these hardened aircraft shelters could not get out to the active runway to take off.

Let me conclude there by saying, as the Secretary said, I'm satisfied with the campaign. We have been trying to tell everybody in the beginning that we would do it in time, and do it as smartly as we can. We're in no hurry. We are not looking to have large numbers of casualties, but it is an integrated campaign - each part of the campaign bearing some relationship to the ultimate objective of ejecting the Iraqi army from Kuwait. Thank you.

Q: Mr. Secretary, given what you've told us today, can you tell us if you think that the scud search has had any effect on the campaign? And if you do believe what success rates you've had here, then does that mean you're able to go on a little bit more quickly to some of the phases earlier than you might have thought when this all started

Cheney: The scud search has been important because it has not only the problem of his being able to launch against Saudi Arabia or Israel, but obviously, there are major policy questions, major political questions involved in the issue of how you deal with the scud problem, because of course, as the Chairman mentioned, we've been pleased, as the President said, that the Israelis have restrained themselves up until now and not retaliated and gotten involved in the conflict, but that's a delicate proposition. Our ability to deal with the scud threat makes it easier for us to deal with the broader policy questions that are involved. It's a question of diverting resources and deciding how much you're going to put against the scud problems itself.

Q: Has that created a problem at all, for the rest of ...

Cheney: I wouldn't say it's created a problem in that sense. I think it would be fair to say that the systems that are focused on dealing with the scud threat are not available to deal with other threats, but we always knew we were going to have to deal with the scud threat, we always knew that was a potential problem. We've assumed he may have chemical warheads to go on the scuds, so until we've got a high degree of assurance that we've dealt with that problem, we will continue to devote resources to it.

Q: You said the campaign is going very well. The first thing you cited was the air superiority. Do you really feel that you were really challenged by the Iraqi army, number one? You said they really have been in the bunkers. Number two, you talked about command and control each day, but there are many reports saying that Saddam Hussein is four stories below, underneath the Presidential palace, and ferrying between the Defense Ministry. Number three, you talked about taking out the nuclear sites, but many people thought early on that this would not be a long-term threat. So do you feel that possibly you could be overly predicting a rosy type of outcome in light of this?

Cheney: I tried in my remarks towards the close to focus on the fact that we have to anticipate there will be additional surprises. You can by no means count him out yet, given the size force he has, that he could try to find some way to surge his air force all at once, or go after targets that he's not gone after yet. As the Chairman mentioned, we haven't really seen any aggressive military response by him to date. He's basically gone to ground and hunkered down. The only safe assumption for us to make, especially when we're talking to the press, is be cautious here. We're trying to be cautious, and no one wants to declare that he no longer constitutes a threat. That would be a very serious mistake.

Q: Do you think this could be a strategy, as many military analysts believe, to inflict maximum casualties?

Cheney: It could well be a strategy, and based in part upon the fact that he has not yet been able to find a way to deal with our capabilities.

Q: You mentioned, General Powell mentioned two times, Soviet air defenses, Soviet scud missiles. How much military cooperation are you getting from the Soviet Union in dealing with this?

Cheney: I had general discussions when I was in Moscow, in October, in a meeting with senior Soviet officials and Marshal Yazov, about the situation in the Gulf. I think it would be fair to say that it was their view that Saddam Hussein did not possess any significant capability that we were unaware of. They described the system that they had provided to him as systems that were generally available - like T.72 tanks, to their allies; specifically we talked about the scud. He made it clear then that there was no guidance system for the scud, it's just a ballistic missile that goes wherever it goes. It's not a highly accurate or very sophisticated system.

I think probably the greatest two contributions the Soviets have made to this venture - one has been their cooperation and support of the policy in the United Nations, which have been very significant; and the other is that they have shut off the flow of arms exports to Iraq. The situation we're faced with today would be far more difficult if Saddam Hussein were able to get resupplied in terms of the key pieces of military equipment that we've been working to destroy.

Q: Sir, how effective have the Iraqis been at repairing the damage to their airfields and other targets? And how effective have they been at fooling you with decoys in their scud missile department?

Powell: They use decoys, they're quite good at it. I'll let the chart I used earlier as to which airfields are active, speak for itself. They, obviously, are hard at work repairing some of the damage - we've seen it. We've also seen them paint damage on airfields to spoof us into thinking that it is still damaged, and therefore we don't have to worry about it. There are also reports that they are trying to put out dummy scud systems. This isn't a surprise to us, because they have a long history, and did it throughout the Iran-Iraq war, of using dummies in order to confuse their enemy. They probably are also making some efforts to take totally destroyed facilities and cover them over quickly, to make them appear as if they're not totally destroyed, to lure us into coming back. But I think our analysts and our targeteers are quite sophisticated - they're the best in the world - and they will be sensitive to the possibility of dummy installations and false repairs.

Q: On the air power question: you've indicated 19 killed in air combat maneuvers or, if you would, dog fights; another 22 on the ground - or at least that was the inference I got.

Powell: It's a number that changes every few hours as we get BDA assessment. We got three more just as we walked in, some badgers that had been destroyed on the ground.

Q: We're talking about roughly 50 aircraft gone, if we assume that. It still leaves roughly 750 left.

Powell: Correct.

Q: Do you have any indication the Iraqis are doing a move-and-hide strategy, perhaps in some of these dispersal fields that there was damage done, but they still have support facilities there to operate air power? Is that concerning you - especially since if they rebuild, they could put up a mass waive of 200, 300, 400 aircraft all of a sudden.

Powell: I attribute that capability to them. In addition to the facilities you saw on that map they are probably using highways and other things like that. So we assume they have that capability. They did not use it in the first seven days of the war; they did not challenge us with defensive air; they have not tried to attack us with offensive air - but that does not mean that we are not on the lookout for it, or we're not alert to it, or we are unmindful of the threat it represents. It does represent a threat, but it's a threat we understand. We believe we are quite able to deal with, and rather than spend air power now trying to run the body count up on airplanes that are not bothering us at the moment, I'd rather use that air power in more efficient ways against things that are of more immediate relevance to our battle plan.

Q: There have been reports that at least one other country in the area is providing a sanctuary for Iraqi aircraft or other equipment. Do you have any evidence at all to support or ...

Powell: I've seen those reports, and I can't confirm them.

Q: I'd like to ask you to expand a little bit on what you infer the Iraqi military strategy to be. You said their actions could be part of a strategy. Does the Iraqi military response to date, that is the absence of a response, surprise you? Were you surprised by that? Do you think it's an attempt to engage us in a costly land war? And a related question, General Powell implied that we hope not to have to use ground forces - at the same time, he said the Republican Guards will lie low, and that the only way we may determine if they survive attack is if they're forced to move. Does that mean we'll have to bring in our ground forces in order to determine whether we've knocked them out?

Powell: I don't know yet. The strategy right now, it seems to me, is they are hunkering down. It's obvious. They, I suspect, and not being an Iraqi General, I don't have complete insight into what they may be thinking, but I would suspect that right now they are hunkering down, and they probably are questioning whether we can keep this up for an extended period of time, and whether or not the political will and public support will be there to keep this up for an extended period of time, and I'm sure they're making an assessment day-by-day in what their losses are, and making their own judgment as to how long they can sustain this kind of punishment.

I would be the happiest guy in the world if one day one bomb goes in on a Republican Guard unit and they say that's it, we break. We can't take any more, we're heading home, and they leave - but I can't plan on that. So what I'm putting in place, what General Schwarzkopf is putting in place, I should say, and the campaign plan that General Schwarzkopf has worked out, is to anticipate that at the end of the day, when they are so weakened that we believe the time is right and air power alone won't do it, we're prepared to take this to a successful conclusion using other means of combat power besides air power. That's been a consistent ...

Q: ... anticipated in planning the air campaign by the Iraqi military, a lay-low strategy?

Powell: I'd rather not say what I anticipated, because it might give Mr. Hussein some insight on what I'm anticipating now.

Q: Mr. Secretary, you said a minute ago that Saddam Hussein cannot change the basic course of this conflict - he will be defeated. Is there any reason to believe that he and his circle of advisers believes that? And what are you doing to make him believe that? And if you're not doing anything, why not?

Cheney: I think if it was difficult before the conflict started to try to assess Saddam Hussein's mental attitude and his thinking about all these kinds of issues, it's probably even more difficult now. There's no press left in Baghdad, very little diplomatic communication through other countries. We know less today about what's going on inside Saddam Hussein's mind than we did then. So it would be risky business for us, I think, to make judgments about that.

It may well be that he does not have as much information as we do about the impact we've had on his forces; that having, in many cases, damaged his command and control system and had the impact that Colin shows with respect to his air capability, etc., that he simply doesn't know how badly he's been hit. I think ultimately, he'll get the message - I would hope that he will. And we are determined, in terms of the statement I made, to achieve our military objective, which is to do what the President has directed us to do, which is to get Saddam Hussein out of Kuwait.

Q: Is part of the plan that he should not know? Would you like to visit a minimum level of destruction, for instance, upon the Republican Guard, before he knows it?

Cheney: It's difficult to refine it that carefully. Once you start military action, you can go after those specific targets we've laid out there, but we believe the Republican Guard is at the heart of his military capability and his political power. But that's the unit that he used to take Kuwait, those are the units that he used in his war with Iran for offensive purposes - they are the heart of the regime. We're not really trying to fine tune it. We'll hit the Republican Guard just as hard as we have to until we've achieved our objectives.

Q: We know that he has, in the past several days, demonstrated a capability to put salvos of scuds over major cities from Tel Aviv across the area of the Persian Gulf. If he marries them now with chemical weapons, poison gas or other, are we prepared, and would we, respond in kind?

Cheney: We have to be concerned about the possibility that he may have chemical capability that he could marry up with his ballistic missiles. He's never previously used ballistic missiles with chemical warheads on them, but we have to assume he could. That's one of the reasons for the elaborate alarm systems we've worked out - both in Saudi Arabia and that the Israelis have worked out; the protective gear our troops are equipped with, etc.

In terms of how we might respond were he to use chemical weapons, I would simply reiterate what we've said previously, which is that the United States has a broad spectrum of capabilities available; that the President would make the decision about how we might respond to an unconventional attack by Saddam Hussein against U.S. or allied forces; and I wouldn't want to speculate further.

Q: Can I ask you a couple of questions, first of all, about the report of a coups attempt. Have you heard anything about this at all - within Iraq?

Cheney: Nothing that would give me any reason to believe it has credence.

Q: General Powell, I have another question about the exocets - we talked about the silkworms being taken out, but you didn't say anything about the exocets, and many people think that's one of the most effective weapon systems he has. It was very effective in the Falklands conflict. Have you done anything to take out the exocets?

Powell: The navy is working on it. They're of limited range and don't represent a very serious threat at the moment.

Q: You were saying before that the coalition would take as long as it had to, and yet you've outlined some goals that look like they might last long. [*sic*] You said you want to rip up the air force, yet they still have some 750 planes; and you said you wanted to shut up the army with cutting off its communications, which is still very resilient, a very large army; the chemical weapon threat is still a threat to the allies; and the scud is still a weapon of terror for the allies. Does that not sound like it's going to last some time?

Cheney: We've avoided consistently putting any artificial deadline out there by which this whole operation had to be completed. We do not know how long it will last. The kind of things you mentioned are specific objectives. We will operate until we've achieved those objectives, and I simply wouldn't want to put a time frame on it. I can't do that. I don't know how long it will take. Although I'm inclined to think given the size of the force we've deployed, and the success we've enjoyed to date, that it won't take that long.

Q: Is the allied force's patience going to outlast the patience of Saddam Hussein who is hunkering down? Which patience is going to outlast?

Cheney: There's no doubt in my mind but what the United States and our allies in this venture have the staying power to see to it that the job gets done - that he will quit long before we will.

Q: You're mentioning now that your main focus is the Republican Guards. Does that mean at this juncture in the air campaign you're pretty much sparing the troops right at the front line?

Powell: No, they are under attack as well. We're selectively probing against all of the forces in the Kuwaiti theater of operations, but because the Republican Guard is the Republican Guard, they get more attention than the rest.

Q: On the scud threat, what percentage of the scud launchers would you say - mobile and fixed - have been destroyed; and how well are the allies on their way toward destroying the full scud capability so that the Saudis and the Israelis won't have to worry about that?

Cheney: I don't think you can put a hard percentage on the amount of his capability that's been destroyed. We know he had a large number of missiles before this started. The missiles are important, but the launchers are even more important. We know we've been able to attack successfully many of the fixed sites. We continue to work on those fixed sites. We know he's got mobile capability, but we have some confidence we've destroyed some of that mobile capability. But it's a nebulous kind of thing. They're relatively small pieces of equipment; they can hide in the desert; they can come out at night and launch; it doesn't require any great degree of sophistication for them to be able to operate. It's one of those problems that may be with us for some period of time, and it's a matter of reducing the odds as much as possible, of going aggressively after his launch capability, but also defending the targets, which is why we've deployed patriot both in Saudi Arabia and in Israel.

Q: Who fired the patriot that apparently hit or didn't hit the scud that did the damage in Tel Aviv yesterday?

Powell: IDF. (Israeli Defense Force)

Q: Why did they do it instead of the U.S. crews?

Powell: Either one could have done it, whoever was in position. The U.S. crew was working with a power problem, a generator problem they had at the time, and IDF got acquisition and fired.

Q: Did that patriot hit the scud?

Powell: I really would prefer to defer to the IDF to comment on their actions. I'm just passing on a report I heard.

Q: Just going back to an earlier line of questioning, what is your view of the argument that in fact the Saddam Hussein strategy is simply to stretch this war out as long as possible, forcing the allied troops into a long, bloody ground war - he's enjoying some success in that. How do you view that; and is there anything you can really do if he continues to husband his resources as he's been doing?

Cheney: I'm not a military strategist to the extent that my colleague, General Powell, might be; but looking at it from the perspective of U.S. forces versus Iraqi forces, he really hasn't got much choice at this point. He is pursuing a strategy, perhaps of necessity. If he comes up with his air forces in significant numbers, I think we'll see the kind of ratio that Colin talked about in terms of 19:0 or 19:1 on his entire air force, and he would lose it and gain very little for it. He doesn't have any significant naval capability. He's really left with a very large army - that's always been the heart of his military strength, and his success in the Iran/Iraq war was to dig in and hunker down and defend against the human wave assaults by Iranian teenagers. That's not the kind of situation he's faced with today.

I think the reason he will not be successful with the wait-it-out strategy, is that as long as he is sitting there waiting, we are steadily and progressively destroying his unconventional warfare capability, finding and destroying his scuds, taking out his air force piece-by-piece, and now, as the Chairman pointed out, aggressively working over his ground forces in Kuwait. I think time is clearly on our side. And given our dominance in the air and our capability to do significant damage to his ground forces that each day, each week that goes by he gets weaker and we get stronger.

Q: You stated your goal, though, is to get his troops out of Kuwait - and in fact, while this pummeling continues, his troops remain still reasonably intact, which suggests that it's inevitable that he will draw the allies into a ground war.

Cheney: We may eventually, and I'll defer to General Powell and General Schwarzkopf, they'll have to come back and advise me and the President on when various pieces of the campaign kick in, but if we do have to go to using our ground forces to push him out of Kuwait, it will be after we've done enormous damage to his ground forces, after they've been significantly weakened. I think people have the same capability on the ground to display the kind of mastery over Iraqi forces that they've displayed in the air to date.

Q: The aircraft that you're showing us as destroyed on the ground, are those confirmed wreckages; or are you including in that any estimate of ...

Powell: The ones I'm showing you are confirmed. We had a couple more confirmed as we were walking down here. As the BDA gets better, and as the attack progresses, that number will grow. We're not doing estimates. We're trying to be as forthcoming as we can. I'm not down here to give you a happy talk - I'm trying to give you my best assessment as I know it now. I don't know how long the war will take. It's a war. I don't think we've done badly for seven days, and I think we're by no means bogged down, and we'll try to give you as much information as we can, and we'll give you that which we can confirm. What we can't do is try to keep up with the hourly news cycle. That's causing us a great deal of ...

Q: The map that you showed us, is that the radar coverage that they had on the first day of the war, or as of three hours ago?

Powell: It was not precise, obviously, I made it generic for security purposes - but it generally shows the scheme of coverage that they had on the first day.

Q: How about collateral damage?

Powell: I think we have been awfully good in avoiding collateral damage. An enormous amount of work went into the targeting for this operation. I can't say that there was no collateral damage, but some of the claims that have been out there that we have struck religious and cultural sites, I have seen no hard evidence to suggest we did that.

S/22169, 29 January 1991

68. Letter from the Permanent Representative of France to the United Nations addressed to the President of the Security Council, 29 January 1991

Further to my letter of 22 January 1991 (S/22131), I have the honour to inform you, pursuant to paragraph 4 of Security Council resolution 678 (1990), of the action taken by the French armed forces within the framework of the plans drawn up jointly with the members of the coalition of countries co-operating with Kuwait with a view to securing the implementation of resolution 660 (1990) and all pertinent subsequent resolutions of the Council.

Our air forces have participated in the attack on ground-to-air artillery sites in Kuwait and the attack on armoured units of the Republican Guard in Iraq; the two most recent raids on the Republican Guard were carried out this morning. Our aircraft also continue to help maintain allied air superiority.

Our naval forces, which are being deployed through the Western European Union, are operating in the Gulf, the Strait of Hormuz, the Bab al Mandab and the Red Sea. They continue to monitor the embargo and conduct escort and minesweeping missions.

Lastly, our ground forces are continuing their preparations. A number of additional logistical facilities have been installed.

...

S/22172, 30 January 1991

69. Letter from the Secretary-General addressed to the President of the Security Council, 30 January 1991

I would be grateful if you could bring to the attention of the members of the Security Council the letter I have sent today to His Excellency, Mr. Tariq Aziz. ...

I have read your letter of 24 January 1991 (S/22154) [*reprinted above*] with regret and cannot but reject its connotations.

When we met at Amman on 31 August 1990 and at Baghdad on 12 January 1991, and again when I met President Saddam Hussein on 13 January 1991, I stated that our efforts to avert the unfolding tragedy would fail unless Iraq could signify its readiness to comply with the relevant resolutions of the Security Council, beginning with resolution 660 (1990). On each occasion, after returning to New York, I reported the views of your Government to the Security Council.

As you know, on 15 January 1991 (see S/22091) [*reprinted in Chapter 4, document 19*], I appealed again to President Saddam Hussein to indicate his readiness to proceed in the manner I had suggested to him, so that the course of events could be turned away from catastrophe and towards a new era of justice and harmony, based on the principles of the Charter of the United Nations. I pledged, in such circumstances, to work with him, and with all others concerned, to bring just and lasting peace to the Middle East as a whole.

Today, I reiterate my 15 January appeal, as I did on 22 January 1991, when I also expressed my profound grief and anxiety at the increasing severity of the war, the widening of the area of hostilities and my fear that the toll in death and destruction would escalate unless my appeal received a positive response. I continue to believe that such a response is needed in order to find a peaceful solution to this grave and tragic conflict and to save human lives. In the mean time, in order to alleviate the present suffering which is causing me deep anguish, I have already asked the main humanitarian agencies of the United Nations system to co-ordinate their efforts with a view to ensuring that help is provided to those afflicted by the conflict as soon as circumstances permit.

You will recall, Mr. Minister, that when speaking in the formal meeting of the Security Council after the adoption of resolution 678 (1990), I stressed that, in requiring compliance with the resolutions of the Council, the United Nations sought not surrender but the most honourable way of resolving a crisis in a manner that respected all legitimate interests and was conducive to the wider peace and the rule of law. I also underlined that the actions of the United Nations in the present crisis must be perceived as part of the larger endeavour of the Organization to establish peace through justice, whenever the one was imperiled [*sic*] and the other denied.

That remains my view today and I would therefore urge your Government to make a serious effort to put this tragic situation on the road to a peaceful solution.

A/45/945, S/22174, 30 January 1991

70. Letter from the Permanent Representative of Haiti to the United Nations addressed to the Secretary-General, 17 January 1991

I have the honour to transmit to you herewith a statement issued on 17 January 1991 by the provisional Government of the Republic of Haiti concerning the events taking place in the Persian Gulf.

...

The provisional Government of the Republic of Haiti notes with regret that the obvious failure of the latest mediation efforts has left the international community no recourse other than the use of force to end the aggression perpetrated by Iraq against the sovereignty of the Kuwaiti people during the night of 1-2 August 1990.

The position of Haiti with regard to the Gulf crisis has been and continues to be based on respect for the principles of the Charter of the United Nations and on Security Council resolution 678 (1990).

By virtue of that resolution, the Republic of Haiti gives its total support to the friendly countries that have just made the difficult and courageous decision to intervene with a view to upholding international law and ensuring the restoration of Kuwait's sovereignty.

S/22177, 31 January 1991

71. Letter from the Permanent Representative of Venezuela to the United Nations addressed to the Secretary-General, 29 January 1991

I have the honour to transmit to you, ..., the text of the information note issued by the Ministers for Foreign Affairs of the Permanent Mechanism for Consultation and Concerted Political Action, Rio Group, on the conclusion of the meeting held at Caracas on 28 January 1991.

...

The Ministers for Foreign Affairs of the Permanent Mechanism for Consultation and Concerted Political Action, Rio Group, meeting at Caracas on 28 January 1991, informed the public that they had held a full discussion during which they had considered the possible effects of the Middle East crisis on Latin America and had exchanged views on the development of the events in that region, as well as on other matters of common interest.

They agreed to reiterate their support for the resolutions of the Security Council of the United Nations and to renew their backing of the role which the Secretary-General of the United Nations has to play in promoting a solution to the conflict whereby it would be possible to restore peace in accordance with international law, to initiate multilateral efforts towards a comprehensive, peaceful and definitive settlement of the problems of the region, and the submission of a report on the developments in implementation of the Security Council resolutions.

They jointly condemned expansion of the conflict in the form of attacks on non-belligerent countries of the zone, such as Israel. They were in agreement on the need to ensure that the Geneva Conventions on the treatment of prisoners of war are strictly adhered to, and that the parties to the conflict refrain from the use of chemical or biological weapons and from mass or indiscriminate destruction.

They jointly expressed their alarm at the damage being inflicted on the environment as a result of the conflict.

They decided to give thought to the system of international security embodied in the Charter of the United Nations and the possible changes which that system would require in order to reflect international reality, and to its relationship with Latin American security to which it must assign an economic priority which is lacking at present.

They agreed to retain the question of the Middle East on the agenda of its periodic consultations and to assign to a committee, consisting of Chile, Colombia and Ecuador, the task of following the Gulf crisis in all its aspects, including the study of proposals and mechanisms which would enable the Group to make an effective contribution to the establishment of a new order of peace in the region, based on the participation of all parties involved and on implementation of all the resolutions of the United Nations, including the solution of the Palestine problem.

The Ministers agreed to send a message to the Secretary-General of the United Nations in order to express their backing of the steps which he is taking to promote peace in El Salvador, and to urge the parties to the conflict and the Secretary-General to intensify their efforts towards achieving an early solution.

The Ministers received with concern the report of the Special Mission which recently visited Panama and reiterated the need for the Panamanian Government to comply, in all cases, with the provisions on diplomatic asylum set forth in the Caracas Convention, of which Panama is a party.

The Ministers considered the reports submitted by the Executive Secretary of the United Nations Economic Commission for Latin America and the Caribbean (ECLAC), the Permanent Secretary of the Latin American Economic System (SELA) and the Executive Secretary of the Latin American Energy Organization (OLADE) on the effects of the crisis in the region.

The Ministers expressed their deep concern at the consequences of the conflict in the Gulf for the world economy and especially for the economies of Latin America and the Caribbean.

New indications of instability and uncertainty in the world economy affect the principal economic variables, such as growth, interest rates, investment, inflation and trade, and threaten to create even greater disruptions in regional efforts to adjust economies and promote economic and social development.

Accordingly, the Ministers agreed as follows:

> To design and strengthen mechanisms to promote economic security in Latin America and the Caribbean in all areas where the region may be affected by the crisis and to undertake preparations in order to deal with unpredictable economic situations; they decided to request ECLAC and SELA to collaborate in assessing the possible economic consequences of the conflict in the Gulf.
>
> In the field of energy, they agreed to tackle problems of supply and pricing, without prejudice to existing commercial agreements in the oil sector and in respect of other sources of energy as well. In that connection, they agreed to request OLADE to look into storage capacities, oil trade flows, available refining capacities and transport more thoroughly.
>
> In the area of finance, they agreed to adopt financing mechanisms to soften the impact of energy price fluctuations on the economies of the region, as exemplified by the San José and Tuxtla agreements. They emphasized the need to accelerate the implementation of the commitment undertaken in the Caracas Declaration to establish a strategic investment fund for integration using resources obtained through increases in commodity price.

They agreed to hold an extraordinary meeting of Ministers of Energy to study the energy initiatives put forward at the present meeting. They also agreed to establish a standing evaluation committee to monitor external events that might affect the economies of Latin America and the Caribbean and the implementation of the measures adopted. They supported the holding of consultations among oil producers, consumers and operators, as proposed by the President of Venezuela at the United Nations.

S/22178, 31 January 1991

72. Letter from the Permanent Representative of Qatar to the United Nations addressed to the Secretary-General, 31 January 1991

On instructions from my Government, I have the honour to transmit to you herewith the text of the statement issued by the Ministry of Foreign Affairs of the State of Qatar on 17 January 1991. ...

With the exhaustion of all the efforts made and the frustration of the initiatives proposed and appeals launched to Iraqi President Saddam Hussein for his compliance with the inter-Arab and Islamic resolutions and the resolutions of the United Nations Security Council calling for the unconditional withdrawal of the Iraqi forces occupying the State of Kuwait and the restoration to Kuwait of its legitimate Government under the leadership of its Amir, His Highness Sheikh Jaber Al-Ahmad Al-Jaber Al-Sabah, and given that the Iraqi President has persisted in his intransigent stance of rejecting all such efforts, initiatives and appeals and that he rejected the international rule of law while it was yet in his power to avoid the worst and avert hostilities and bloodshed, military operations for the liberation of the State of Kuwait commenced early today in implementation of Security Council resolutions which are supported by the State of Qatar.

"If God helps you, none can overcome you."
"Help comes only from God, the All-mighty, the All-wise."

S/22179, 31 January 1991

73. Letter from the Permanent Representative of Guyana to the United Nations addressed to the Secretary-General, 30 January 1991

I have the honour to forward herewith the text of the statement by the Government of the Republic of Guyana on the conflict in the Persian Gulf.

...

The Gulf war has now entered its second week and, from statements being made by military experts, could be prolonged for months.

The Government of Guyana has regretted deeply the outbreak of the war which can only lead to massive destruction of property, tragic loss of human life and untold human suffering. The war, moreover, will have severe consequences for the world economy, with vulnerable developing countries, like Guyana, being the most seriously affected.

The Government recalls that, at the time of Iraq's invasion of Kuwait, leaders of the Caribbean Community (CARICOM), then meeting in Kingston, Jamaica, had issued a joint statement denouncing the invasion of Kuwait by the armed forces of Iraq and calling for their immediate and unconditional withdrawal.

The Government had hoped the crisis would have been settled by peaceful means. Unhappily this has not been so.

The Government has supported the various United Nations Security Council resolutions that have as their objective the removal of Iraq's presence from Kuwait. In this regard, Guyana notes with appreciation the untiring efforts of the Secretary-General of the United Nations to find a peaceful solution to the Gulf crisis. The Government reiterates its strong support for the set of resolutions the Security Council has adopted since the start of the crisis.

The Government of Guyana wishes also to reiterate its long-standing and uncompromising position on the inadmissibility of the acquisition of territory by force and to underscore the imperative of the peaceful settlement of disputes in accordance with the Charter of the United Nations.

As indicated earlier, the consequences of the war for developing countries are likely to be profound. In this regard Guyana faces the prospects of significantly increased acquisition costs for its oil prices. We will also have to contend with a range of consequential price increases. We will thus need to be more disciplined in the use of fuel products and in the management of all our resources.

The Government expresses the hope that, at this time of additional shocks to the domestic economy, arising from circumstances totally beyond its control, citizens would avoid any action that could disrupt production, undermine the export performance and retard the progress of our economic recovery programme.

In the mean time, the Government wishes to assure all citizens that it is taking all appropriate measures, including the making of arrangements with external friendly countries and international agencies to minimize the consequences of the war on our country's economy and the well-being of our citizens.

S/22180, 31 January 1991

74. Letter from the Permanent Representative of Saudi Arabia to the United Nations addressed to the President of the Security Council, 30 January 1991

I have the pleasure, pursuant to paragraphs 3 and 4 of Security Council resolution 678 (1990), to transmit herewith the report received from my Government on the progress of operations for the liberation of the State of Kuwait, until this day.

...

In accordance with the provisions of paragraphs 3 and 4 of Security Council resolution 678 (1990), I should like to inform you of the military operations currently under way for the liberation of Kuwait. These operations, at sea and in the air, are concentrated in particular on weakening the ability of the Iraqi forces to remain in Kuwait and weakening the capacity to support and assist them. Operations between 17 and 27 January 1991 have been as follows.

Military support:

1. The air forces of the Kingdom of Saudi Arabia have carried out 1,408 sorties against military targets in Iraq and Kuwait, while avoiding civilian targets.
2. The Kingdom of Saudi Arabia has participated in naval operations. There have been 177 naval sorties, and naval aircraft have carried out 158 sorties in support of naval operations.
3. The Kingdom of Saudi Arabia has provided five brigades, together with their command and combat support.
4. The air-defence forces of Saudi Arabia have provided two air-defence groups to provide cover to the theatre of operations.

Material support:

The Kingdom of Saudi Arabia is providing all elements of the armed forces located in the theatre of operations, estimated at 560,000, with food, water, fuel, communications, the buildings needed for accommodation and medical treatment and the facilities and services that they require, in addition to other material support already provided by the Kingdom of Saudi Arabia to the coalition forces.

Human losses:

The cities of the Kingdom of Saudi Arabia have been bombarded by 26 missiles, which have landed in purely civilian localities of no military value. Eight Saudis were wounded as a result of the explosion of missiles over Damman on 20 January 1991. Twelve persons, two Saudi civilians and the others of various nationalities, were wounded by the explosion of missiles launched against Riyadh on 20 January 1991. Four Saudis were killed and 30 persons wounded, including Saudi civilians and persons of different nationalities, as a result of the explosion of missiles over Riyadh on 25 January 1991.

Material damage:

Material damage resulted from the fall of an explosive device in the Sulaymaniyah quarter of Riyadh on 20 January 1991. Cracks appeared in nearby buildings, windows and doors were broken and damage was caused to a number of homes, buildings, shops and vehicles.

A missile warhead fell on the building of the Civil Status Directorate in Riyadh on 25 January 1991, destroying it, causing cracks to appear in adjacent buildings and destroying 12 vehicles belonging to inhabitants of the quarter.

We must stress that the Iraqi régime bears responsibility for all the suffering of the Iraqi people and the other peoples affected by this war, including the human and material losses, and for the destruction of Iraq's capacities, which it has misused for destruction and aggression instead of putting them to constructive use and promoting good-neighbourliness and which have become a danger to its neighbours instead of being a help and support to its own country and neighbouring countries.

The basic objective of the resort to force, to which there was no alternative for the implementation of the resolutions of the Security Council, continues to be the establishment of a peace that is not vitiated by aggressive intentions and acts of aggression.

I shall provide you with reports on ongoing operations in the war as long as they continue.

S/22181, 31 January 1991

75. Letter from the Permanent Representative of Senegal to the United Nations addressed to the Secretary-General, 29 January 1991

I have the honour to transmit to you herewith the text of the statement made in the Council of Ministers on 22 January 1991 by the President of the Republic of Senegal concerning the crisis in the Gulf.

...

The world entered into war on 16 January 1991 because of Iraq's flagrant violation of international law in invading and annexing Kuwait.

The Senegalese Government has unceasingly endeavoured to ensure respect for international law and to secure the withdrawal of Iraqi troops from Kuwait and the restoration of that country's legitimate Government.

Working in concert with the nations of the world, Senegal has sought to implement Security Council resolutions, particularly the resolution authorizing the use of force as of 15 January.

Senegal has always hoped that a decision by the Iraqi President to withdraw from Kuwait might preserve peace.

Unfortunately, the Iraqi President has persisted in his illegal acts. In the face of its failure to generalize the conflict, Iraq has, in the past 24 hours, used prisoners of war as human shields, in violation of the Geneva Convention on the treatment of prisoners of war.

Deeply shocked and angered, the Government of Senegal has condemned this inhumane policy which runs counter to law.

The Government of Senegal hopes that this war will come to an end as quickly as possible so that such major problems as Palestine, underdevelopment, and the search for a new, fairer international order can mobilize the energies of all the peoples of the world.

S/22183, 31 January 1991

76. Note verbale from the Permanent Mission of Belize to the United Nations addressed to the Secretary-General, 31 January 1991

The Permanent Mission of Belize to the United Nations presents its compliments to the Secretary-General of the United Nations and has the honour to transmit the text of the statement by the Government of Belize on the situation in the Gulf.

...

The Government of Belize laments the outbreak of hostilities in the Persian Gulf. Belize took the position throughout the crisis that a peaceful, diplomatic and political solution was the most desirable course of action.

We regard the decision taken by the coalition forces whose publicly stated goal is the liberation of Kuwait and not the destruction, occupation or dismemberment of Iraq, to be consistent and in compliance with the United Nations Security Council resolution 678.

It is our hope that the action taken can be concluded in the shortest possible time to avoid the loss of life, especially of innocent civilians.

Belize, a small nation itself, can never condone aggression and must at all times support the rule of international law, with particular regard for the sovereignty and territorial integrity of all States.

We are deeply concerned for the safety of all Belizeans and their relatives who may be in combat or residing in the area of conflict.

It remains our firm commitment to work within the United Nations system for a comprehensive peace settlement in order to secure to all peoples of the Middle East without exception, a future of peace, freedom and justice.

A/45/947, S/22187, 1 February 1991

77. Letter from the Permanent Representative of Qatar to the United Nations addressed to the Secretary-General, 1 February 1991

I have the honour to transmit to you herewith the text of the communiqué issued by the Ministerial Council of the Gulf Co-operation Council on 26 January 1991 concerning developments in the situation in the Gulf since the commencement of the operation to liberate Kuwait.

...

The Ministerial Council held its fourteenth extraordinary session on 26 January 1991 in the city of Riyadh.

The Council considered developments in the situation in the region since the commencement of the operation to liberate Kuwait carried out in implementation of Security Council resolution 678 (1990), which authorizes Member States to provide appropriate support to the Government of Kuwait and to use all necessary means to uphold and implement Security Council resolution 660 (1990) and all subsequent relevant resolutions concerning the aggression against Kuwait. The Council expressed its profound gratitude to the fraternal and friendly States which have placed themselves on the side of justice and supported lawfulness by taking a firm stand against the Iraqi aggression and taking part in the liberation of Kuwait.

The Council affirmed that the operation to liberate Kuwait was based on international lawfulness as reflected in the resolutions of the United Nations Security Council which that body had adopted in implementation of Chapter VII of the Charter of the United Nations.

Deeply convinced of the overwhelming need to liberate Kuwait and the merits of the position taken by the States of the Gulf Co-operation [*sic*] Council, and expressing its profound esteem for the entire international community, which has opposed the aggression and adopted historic measures to bring that aggression to an end, the Ministerial Council anxiously awaits the conclusion of the operation to liberate Kuwait, invoking God, may He be praised, exalted and glorified in order that He might protect the innocent, spare their lives and keep them far from the evil deeds of the Iraqi régime.

The Council endorsed in that connection the position taken by the Heads of State of the countries members of the council during their summit conference at Doha in December 1990, at which they had affirmed that Kuwait must be liberated at all costs, by peaceful means if possible or, failing that, by war.

The Council recalled the resolutions it had adopted on that same question at its preceding session, when it had announced that any effort that certain parties might make should be aimed at convincing the Iraqi régime to withdraw its forces from the State of Kuwait and restore the legitimate Government there, in accordance with the resolutions of the United Nations Security Council, and that all ideas and actions should be oriented towards that objective before any efforts were made to seek a cease-fire.

The Council reaffirmed its conviction that the operation to liberate Kuwait was taking place within the framework of Security Council resolution 678 (1990), which expressed the international community's determination to achieve the objectives set out in all Council resolutions concerning the invasion of Kuwait by Iraq and the terrible consequences thereof.

The Ministerial Council exhorted all Arab States, Muslim States and friendly States, as well as all other States of the world, to support the actions that reflected the will of the international community and to support all measures which the Security Council had adopted to liberate Kuwait and ensure the implementation of all the principles set out in its resolutions.

S/22188, 1 February 1991

78. Note verbale from the Permanent Mission of Iraq to the United Nations addressed to the Secretariat, 1 February 1991

The Permanent Mission of Iraq to the United Nations presents its compliments to the United Nations Secretariat and transmits herewith the interview of President Saddam Hussein, President of the Republic of Iraq, with the correspondent of CNN. ...

The American television station CNN has conducted an interview with President Saddam Hussein, lasting 90 minutes, in which various aspects of the American aggression against Iraq were discussed; the interview was broadcast yesterday.

The following is the full text of the interview.

Question: There are reports of Iraqi planes leaving Iraq for Iran; can you give any reasons for that?

Answer: Regardless of the figures which you have been hearing and of which we are unaware, the main thing is that Iraq and Iran are neighbouring Muslim countries. Regardless of the circumstances [*sic*] of the past, these considerations will remain paramount in the relationship between the two countries. Since the battle is now a battle between believers and unbelievers, between good and evil, between justice and fairness on the one hand and injustice, domination and aggression on the other hand, do not expect that a single Islamic country will not be part of such a battle. In this spirit and against this background, it is only natural, if some of Iraq's aircraft found themselves forced to land in one Islamic country or another, that they should do so.

Question: Will those aircraft be used in the present war? Will they return to Iraq?

Answer: Iraq respects under all circumstances the laws and will of the State of Iran.

The oil spill

Question: On the subject of the oil flowing into the Gulf, you say that the West and America are the cause of the oil spill. America says that it did not make any intentional strikes with that aim. It has also been said that you are the one who opened the pipelines. Is that what actually happened?

Answer: The American Administration cannot claim that it has been forced to do this, or that it has done this in exercise of the right of self-defence. Therefore, whenever military field commanders have used oil as a means of legitimate self-defence or defence of the country in one place or another, this has taken the form of filling trenches with oil which is then ignited, or through other means, and they have been justified in doing so, and this is the picture which obtains at present.

Question: Then you confirm that the oil was not spilled into the Gulf, but was leaked as a tactical move?

Answer: I did not say that. I said that America had used oil and that it had not admitted doing so, that the facts, which cannot be denied, are that America attacked oil tankers loaded with oil, that it knew they were loaded with oil, that when that oil flowed over the country it would cause the damage it did, that those tankers, when attacked, were in Iraqi territorial waters; I said that America had also attacked pipelines and that it had publicly announced its attacks against the oil terminals, which are in Iraqi territorial waters. The American specialists know that when they attack the oil terminals they destroy the pipelines to those terminals and that the oil spills into Iraqi territorial waters. They have not been forced to do this. If the Iraqis have used oil for defence purposes and even if we have used it for development, this is justifiable. Time will tell what America is responsible for and what Iraq is responsible for.

Oil as a weapon

Question: So you are saying that you have the right to use oil as a military weapon in the war?

Answer: I said what I said.

Question: Another matter on the minds of many is that you have stated that you have decided to use prisoners of war as shields against attacks. The West says that this is contrary to the Geneva Convention and international law. Will you continue to do so?

Answer: What we have stated is an official declaration. In any case, there are still those in the West who speak of violations of the law. Take this example which I shall give you: do you remember what happened when it was announced that Iraq would detain the foreigners in order to prevent war? Do you remember what was being said about our decision at that time? It was said that it was an immoral, illegal and inhuman decision. The West spoke of humanitarianism, and some of the Western leaders affected an idealistic attitude towards the people, who had not sufficiently perceived their true nature. Do you remember that?! Do you know what those very same people who criticized those decisions of ours are now doing?! Do you know that they are detaining Iraqis? They are even detaining students who have gone to study in the West, and have announced their detention publicly!! Do you know the restrictions that have been placed on Americans of Arab origin, and on Iraqis who have acquired Western nationalities, people of Iraqi and Arab origin?! In many Western countries there are a number of people who previously had Arab nationalities and who have acquired Western nationalities, and yet since the war, stringent measures have been applied to them in violation of the laws of their countries, including your country America. Is this not opportunistic?! Have you noticed how many lies have been exposed? Have you noticed how many of the shameful acts of the West we have exposed in the short space of the past 10 days? Rest assured, we feel that you in the West need to remain steadfast and to reject this arrogance which emanates from your leaders. We feel that the human being within you, your humanity as Americans and as citizens, your humanity as Frenchmen in the West, your humanity as Britons is in need of our stance in rejecting domination and opportunism more than it is in need of the decisions of dominance and double standards which are emanating from these and other centres. The world needs someone to tell the one who carries the biggest stick in the world that the stick which is in your hand cannot destroy the house of God, nor can it destroy the humanity of mankind. This is what you are now in need of. You do not need to know how many women and children in Iraq your planes can kill. You are people, and people do not need this. But Bush, or the devil within Bush, is in need of this.

Question: And yet you say that you are prepared to apply the Geneva Conventions to the prisoners?

Answer: Does the Geneva Convention stipulate that Iraqi students should be imprisoned?! Such are the double standards which obtain in the country which calls itself the number one country in the world. It urges the small countries, which it calls countries of the third world, to apply the law, while it considers itself to be above the law.

Bush a liar

Question: I believe you have visited the front. We have seen pictures of you there. Could you tell us your feeling about conditions on the front?

Answer: Men are believers, and they will stand firm. I think that Bush knows that, and this is shown by the fact that he did not move against those men. Rather, he came to kill women and children in Baghdad. Was not he the one who told you in America that he was going to get the Iraqi army out of Kuwait? Do you now see that he is a liar? Not to mention the other facts you have discovered about him?! I do not wish to direct criticism at anyone; I am merely using definitions which are found in the dictionary: he who is not truthful is called a liar. The Iraqi army is present in Kuwait. Certainly, you as Americans imagined that the attack would be launched against the army. The attack began on the night of 16-17 January. However, it did not begin against the armed forces in the nineteenth province. Rather, it began in Baghdad. It did not begin against the military forces. Rather, they launched it against scientific and economic sites. Surely, you as a journalist remember the announcement by the White House that nuclear power in Iraq had been destroyed. Did you not ask yourself why? Therefore, the battle was not for Kuwait. Rather, it was for other reasons, for the same reasons which the

American Administration used to induce the rulers of Kuwait to conspire against Iraq when they were still there. They are the same reasons which made the United States Administration decide to prevent grain and food from reaching Iraq five months before the events. They are the same reasons which led the United States Administration to call for a technical and scientific boycott of Iraq over five months before the events of 2 August. Unfortunately, the ordinary American citizen was unable to put together the whole series of measures adopted by the United States Administration against Iraq before the events of 2 August and draw the same conclusions which we had drawn before that date. Therefore, Bush was able to lie to American public opinion. However, we shall help you to unmask the liars with these truths which are now revealed. President Bush cannot deny that he launched the war against scientific and economic installations and not against the army in Kuwait. This mission has been confirmed by the pilots' logbooks. And you as media people were in Baghdad and know that.

Question: It seems that your eight-year-long war on the Iranian front has stood you in good stead and that this war has not affected you as much as was expected.
Answer: This is what we said and warned about before the war was launched. Surely you remember the length of time they were talking about. I heard it said on the radio that some were talking about 24 hours and that others were talking about 72 hours. Whether it is a matter of hours, days, months or years, blood is being shed. No matter whose blood it is, it is human blood. We were trying to spare mankind this bloodshed. Therefore, we stated the facts clearly and openly. Our people do not want war; they believe that dialogue is the way to save mankind from wars. But we have said that once war starts, you should not imagine that it will be a war of hours, days or weeks. In any case, when it starts, much blood will be shed. We have also said that we did not want this. It is not our purpose to drag any of the world leaders into war, because their calculations are bound to fail.

Question: Allied military experts say that you are able to withstand heavy bombing. How have your soldiers managed to survive this bombing?
Answer: Do you remember what the Western leaders, including President Bush, were saying? They were saying that they would enter the war without a single American being wounded! Has this been true? We are still at the beginning; there have only been 10 days. Has the American wish been fulfilled? How will it be when the all-out war starts?! Those who were wrong in their assessment of this war should reply to the questions of the peoples and public opinion. Whoever attacks the men in Kuwait will be beaten. And if you ask me how, you will get the same reply. I tell you the question now is not who has arms. The issue is who will be beaten. Whose side is the devil on and whose side is God on? Quite simply, who has come thousands of kilometres against whose homes? Who has come to occupy the land of the holy sites of the other? The answer is clear. Do you think the pilots who have come to bomb Baghdad from high altitudes, not knowing where the bombs will land, do you think they are happy? I have seen them on television. Of course, more have been killed than have appeared on television. That is only natural. You know that in such cases the proportion of survivors is roughly one fifth. When the time comes when you start receiving the bodies of your sons you will discover other facts. I have asked those who have seen them face-to-face, "Did you not ask them 'Do you not regret what you have done?'" They said they had. I asked them this question, and what was the answer? They said that some of them were crying. Some of them were in a bad way; I do not want to speak of the state they were in. If I were to go with you to see our anti-aircraft-gun crews you would see how proud each one is of what he is doing to defend Iraq and its values. Especially on the first, second, third and fourth days, bombs were raining down on them, but not a single Iraqi deserted the arms with which he was fighting the aircraft. You can be sure what the ground battle will be like if the enemy armies are thinking of attacking the men in the nineteenth province. It only remains to ask every honest Westerner one question. You must remember the background of events before 2 August, from 2 August to the night of 16-17 January and then after the outbreak of war on the night of 16-17 January. How is it possible for a people of 18 million to withstand all this evil aggressive might? You are bound to arrive at a simple answer, which is that if this people were not assured of the rightness of its stance it would not stand up to this tyrannical might. Does not such a phenomenon attract the attention of those who seek the truth? If it does, they will be guided to a solution through dialogue and not through war. And in doing so many truths will be revealed.

Question: What level of dialogue are you talking about?
Answer: I talk with peoples, not with the American President. I am talking to you as an ordinary citizen. I am talking about genuine dialogue with people, not with potent aggressors. Because we as a people shall remain. As for others, they must bear the burden of their evil. I am speaking about the humanitarian laws which must govern relations between peoples.

Question: What do you say to the leaders and peoples who want a peaceful solution? What about dialogue?
Answer: You should put that question to Bush yourself. Bush has used dialogue as a tactic. You know that we are the ones who proposed dialogue. He refused. Then he suddenly appeared on television and said that he wanted dialogue. It was immediately apparent to us that he had decided on war and that his new talk of dialogue was no more than a cover so that he could tell those who were saying "You have not exhausted the path of dialogue" that he had tried dialogue, that it had not led to any results, and that he had no choice but war. This is just as we said. Everything we have said since 2 August up to now has come true. When we said that keeping foreigners and preventing them from leaving would avert war, what were the Western political charlatans saying? They were saying that keeping the Westerners and preventing them from leaving would be a cause of war. If the Westerners left that would avert war. Now the matter is over and we do not regret any decision which we have taken, because we do not take any decision unless we are convinced. If the 5,000 Westerners and Japanese were still in Iraq, would Bush be striking Baghdad?! We were not afraid to take the decision to allow the Westerners to leave. Events have shown that we were not afraid; we took the decision out of respect for public opinion and simple, ordinary citizens, not for the politicians, because ordinary citizens do not confuse the issue. We allowed them all to leave so that our battle would be clean, and the issue would not be confused. I have disclosed this to you, and I shall also reveal to you that some politicians are playing a game of double standards and intelligence-gathering, rather than a statesmanlike role.

The land war

Question: What about the land war and when will it take place?
Answer: In any case, the war is already on. Why should we speak about the land war or other types of war? What has been achieved so far? Has Bush won? I say he hasn't. I say he lost from the very moment he took the decision to go to war. I see that you are embarrassed about this, and if I were in your place I would feel embarrassed too.

I am sure that every American is now embarrassed deep down, and as the war goes on this embarrassment will turn to pain and the pain will turn to revolt against the leaders who have deceived him. An American is a human being and he will ask himself a specific question: Are these the values of the great country that is America?! Are these the values of which Bush speaks and which he desires for the United States?! He is mobilizing and sending his army to attack a people of 18 million across the Atlantic, across the oceans. Are you still a great country? Do you feel that you are still a great country at a time when you are collecting money to support your army which you have sent to attack us?! Are you proud that the President of the greatest country is bragging that he has come to attack a people of 18 million?! These are the factors which now make the American Administration defeated from within. From the moment it decided to go to war, America was defeated, and these factors have made it fall from the status as a super-Power.

The length of the war

Question: How long do you expect the land war to last?
Answer: Only God knows how long it will last. But one thing of which we are convinced, as I have said, deep in our hearts and minds, is that the Iraqis will fight in a way that will win the admiration of the human being which is inside Americans. Much blood will be shed. Much blood has already been shed. But of course the officials who have decided on this aggression do not ask how many Iraqis will be martyred by it. I followed their statements before the military aggression, and not one of the top officials spoke of his desire not to spill Iraqi blood. They were trying to make their parliaments believe that there would be no American casualties, or if there were, that they would be very few, or that there would be no British casualties or no French casualties, and if there were, they would be very few, and so on.

Question: What blood are you talking of?
Answer: When we say that much blood will be shed we mean French blood, American blood, Saudi blood, the blood of all those taking part in the fighting, not just Iraqi blood.

Do not be fooled by the politicians

Question: The American leadership says that it has won the air phase of the war. What do you say?
Answer: Once again, do not be fooled by the politicians. They are dividing up the battle for you and speaking of the air battle and then they say wait until the land battle starts. War is war and it has begun and you must count the days, weeks and months and ask them: Did you not say that the war would be a matter of days? You have miscalculated just as you miscalculated before.

Chemical weapons

Question: Will you use chemical weapons in the war?
Answer: I have said that we will use weapons equivalent to the weapons used against us, and in any case it will be in defence of our country, Iraq, within all its borders from Zakho to the sea.

It is Israel which is attacking Baghdad!

Question: Were you disappointed that Israel did not respond to the missiles fired against it? Why did you fire Scud missiles at residential districts in Tel Aviv and Saudi Arabia?
Answer: The forces which are attacking Baghdad are those of Israel. If it weren't for zionism which has played its role in the corridors of the White House and goaded your army into such acts, you as an American would not have come here. Why would America take the decision to withhold food from the Iraqis five months before the events of August if it were not for zionism?! The enemy of Iraq? This battle is the battle of zionism, but zionism is fighting with American blood. And if it has not yet used arms it is because it wants to remain master of the situation after the war is over. But zionism is fighting us. If it weren't for zionism, you wouldn't have come to occupy the Kaaba and the tomb of the Prophet Muhammad and to come into confrontation with the Muslims as a whole and to attack Baghdad. We shall not be deceived by appearances. You may remember that we said if Baghdad were attacked we would attack Tel Aviv. Thus we say to the enemies in Tel Aviv that we know the whole game and we say to them: Leave the land of Palestine; stop slaughtering the Palestinians. Israel is occupying the land of us Arabs, it is occupying the land of Palestine, it is occupying the Golan, it is occupying a part of Lebanon. It is therefore an occupier and an aggressor against the Arabs. This is the message of the missiles, the reason for them and their meaning.

"Al-Hussein" and "Al-Abbas"

As we have said, why are you so sensitive about calling things by their names. The Russian Scud missile has a range of 270 kilometres. What we have is an Iraqi missile called "Al-Hussein". We also have its brother, "Al-Abbas", with a range of approximately 1,000 kilometres. It has been developed for use at distances which suit us. Some specialists are sensitive about this name. I do not mean ordinary Americans, but rather specialists who know that the name "Al-Hussein" reminds them of our ancestor who fought corruption and tyranny with only 70 men. How should we, who are now millions, not fight tyranny?! This sensitivity is because when you remember Al-Hussein you must remember the 70 men and you will certainly remember that the Iraqis are today 18 millions and they are capable of fighting endlessly until right triumphs over wrong.

Question: What weapons does the "Al-Hussein" missile carry?
Answer: It can carry nuclear, chemical or biological warheads.

Question: Will you use these weapons?
Answer: I have said that we will use weapons equivalent to those used against us. We are people who remember the values of our ancestors. This is an occasion on which to remember one's ancestral values. Despite all this air superiority, we have not been shaken and we have not departed in our behaviour from the "balanced course". I hope that not too much blood will be shed. We hope that we will not be forced into that.

Battle secrets

Question: Why do you have restrictions on publishing details of the battle?
Answer: The Americans are now imposing restrictions on you, on news about the troops in Saudi Arabia, and even simple details about the course of operations are being restricted. This is in a democratic country, as it is called in America! How do you expect that in a dictatorship (as you call us), we Iraqis should divulge such secrets? What is important to us is that, with every hour that the faith and self-confidence of individual Iraqis are put to the test, they become more and more convinced by additional factors that right is on their side. As long as the people have faith, they will give of their best. None of what has been destroyed or will be destroyed was donated to us by anyone. We built it through long hours of work, great patience and strong morals. When I say "we" I mean the Iraqis. We are one.

And when the Iraqis say "we" they mean ordinary citizens together with the leadership.

I have no doubt of victory

Question: Do you have any doubts about the outcome of the battle?

Answer: Not one in a million. I want to make one thing clear. When we called it "the mother of battles" we were not referring to the pages of military history, because they had not yet been written. It was called that because right is clearly distinguished from wrong and because we believe that God is with us. Is there any battle greater than one in which God Almighty is the leader on the one side, and where Satan is on the other side?! Please note - America, the super-Power, Great Britain (I am using the names which you yourselves constantly repeat), France, a great Power - who have the countries of massive weaponry, together with the countries of dirty money, ganged up against? Against Iraq!! After such a description can anyone believe that God is not with us?! Whoever has God on his side will not be vanquished. God, who brought the elephant into the Kaaba and then let it be vanquished, is capable of smashing all the armies of the invaders.

A word to the Americans

Question: What would you like to say to the Americans?

Answer: It suffices us to say that what has happened is what we believe in. I want you to tell the Americans that we wish them well, that we do not wish a single one of their sons to die. All Iraqis are grateful to the Americans of good will who have come out to demonstrate in America against the war and to the kind-hearted noble citizens of good will in France, Germany, Spain, Italy and everywhere, in Britain. We follow with interest this noble humanitarian movement which has sprung up against the aggressive policy being plotted in the corridors of power at the instigation of criminal zionism. All Iraqis, including the wounded children in the Iraqi hospitals which have been bombarded by the armies of the West, follow this with great interest. We will make a clear distinction between the evil decision of the administrations which have fallen under the influence of zionism and the attitude of the peoples. As we pledged to God, so we pledge to our people, to the sons of our nation, we pledge to people of good will in America, Europe, Japan and the Soviet Union, in the whole world, in the so-called advanced countries and in the so-called third world, we pledge that we shall not forget the noble souls who will discover day after day that they are right in rejecting the oppression that is falling on them, on our people and on our nation. I am happy to have met you and I thank you for listening to me with an open mind.

S/22189, 1 February 1991

79. Note verbale from the Permanent Mission of Iraq to the United Nations addressed to the Secretary-General, 1 February 1991

The Permanent Mission of the Republic of Iraq presents its compliments to the Secretary-General and has the honour to transmit herewith the text of communiqué No. 31, dated 31 January 1991, which was issued by the Iraqi Military Command … .

…

"Victory comes from God alone; our victory is nigh."
O great Iraqi people,
O Saudi people,
O people of the Nejd and the noble Hijaz,
Men of the land, wherever you may be,

We did not wish for this conflict, we swear to God, but Fahd the traitor, the American agent, wished it, and he made the Holy Places and the site of the revelation into a theatre of operations for the infidel despots. He has profaned the Holy Places, he has profaned the land and those who live on it and he has committed his perfidious crime, he and God's enemy, Bush, and both of them daily carry out aerial bombings to attack the faithful and steadfast people of Iraq. They kill not only the valiant and conscientious sons of Iraq but women and children as well. The aggressors have been amazed by the number of their own aircraft. They have so persisted in their crime that they have become drunk with perfidy and murder, and their madness has reached the same level as their aircraft. Their aggression has become obvious and their crime abominable in the eyes of all Muslims and the world, and we have had to call upon the faithful in order to face the most refined technologies. O Iraqis, your valiant ground forces have finally advanced. O Arabs, O Muslims, who believe in the truth, your valiant ground forces have advanced to teach the aggressors a lesson. Your forces have launched a stunning ground attack, glorifying God's name, and the infidel armies have been crushed. Your forces have advanced, provoking general flight amongst the enemy. God has put his curse on sin and the infidels, and our units have penetrated 20 kilometres into the territory of the Kingdom where the enemy dwells, into the iniquitous Saudi Kingdom: our forces have succeeded in penetrating the coastal town of Khafji during this night. By causing the infidel front to crumble on the land He has blessed, God has given the faithful a great victory so that they may continue to defend His faith and sing His praises.

O people of the Kingdom of Saudi Arabia, people of the Nejd and of the Hijaz, we have no designs on your land. We are your brothers and you are ours. We form a single army against the infidels, against crime and corruption, against the troops of Fahd and Bush and their treacherous agents. You must not view our arrival as an occupation. It is the fight against the infidel armies and against the aggression they have perpetrated from your land that has brought us to you.

The real nature of the enemy and of the aggression will not cause us to forget that we are your brothers and that you are ours. This relationship is permanent and transcends any ambition or gain. It will continue to transcend the material possessions of this life and all the ambitions to which the weak in intellect or spirit aspire. We are motivated by the same causes that inspire you: the desire to please the divine will, the right to self-defence and the noble principles which are shared by all Muslims, all believers and all noble Arabs, whom you are. Allah is great, Allah is great, He shall cast out the impure.

S/22190, 4 February 1991

80. Note verbale from the Permanent Mission of the Republic of Iraq to the United Nations addressed to the Secretariat, 2 February 1991

The Permanent Mission of the Republic of Iraq to the United Nations presents its compliments to the Secretariat of the United Nations and has the honour to transmit to it herewith a letter dated 1 February 1991 from Mr. Tariq Aziz, Deputy Prime Minister and Minister for Foreign Affairs of the Republic of Iraq, addressed to the Secretary-General of the United Nations, concerning the crimes that are being committed by the forces of the United States, NATO and Zionist alliance against the economic, cultural, scientific and religious institutions of the Iraqi people.

...

On 24 January 1991, I wrote you a letter to inform you that, since the commencement of their aggression at 2.30 p.m. on 17 January 1991, the forces of the United States, NATO and Zionist alliance have been committing heinous and premeditated crimes against Iraqi citizens and against the economic, cultural, scientific and religious institutions of the Iraqi people.

In that letter I presented a long list of tangible facts concerning such crimes committed in the period from 17 to 21 January. Those facts were subsequently confirmed and reported by neutral press agencies, and were widely discussed in political and media circles throughout the world.

We find it strange that the Secretary-General of the United Nations has not expressed his view in this regard, as expected not only by the Iraqi people but by all just and free persons throughout the world, who regard the United Nations as an institution whose purpose is to defend human values. Instead, you have remained silent concerning these crimes which, for the first time in history, are being committed in the name of the United Nations and under the cloak of groundless and unjust Security Council resolutions, the most recent of which is resolution 678 (1990). The whole world is aware that those resolutions were adopted as a result of pressure, blackmail and bribery by the United States and its allies, thereby bringing shame on the Security Council, the United Nations and the countries which received bribes and yielded to United States pressure and blackmail. Your silence in the face of these crimes will merely increase the shame of the United Nations, which is now being used by the imperialist Powers to subjugate peoples, muffle their free and independent voice, impose full control over oil and perpetuate Israeli hegemony over the region. Indeed, the very goals that the United Nations is supposed to embody are being violated before the eyes and with the knowledge of the Secretary-General of the United Nations, who utters not a word. Numerous free voices have denounced the crimes that are being committed against the people of Iraq, and officials of some countries participating in the aggression have protested against it and have declared that what is happening far exceeds the intended purpose of the resolutions adopted in the name of the United Nations, notwithstanding the fact that those resolutions are groundless and unjust. However, you still remain silent.

In this letter I am presenting further facts concerning the crimes that are being committed against the Iraqi people and which took place after the date of my first letter. It is a record for history, and the judgement of history is harsh and merciless.

Baghdad governorate

I. *26 January 1991.*

Air bombardment in which five citizens were wounded, one of whom subsequently died.

II. *28 January 1991.*

1. An air raid on residential areas in which 10 citizens were wounded.
2. Bombardment of the Radio and Television Building, in which two citizens were wounded.

III. *29 January 1991.*

Bombardment of Al-Jumhouriya Bridge in Baghdad.

IV. *30 January 1991.*

1. An air raid on the Central Bank, which suffered damage and in which two citizens were wounded.
2. Missile attack on the Ministry of Justice.

Salah al-Din governorate

I. *23 January 1991.*

Time-fuse bombs were dropped on agricultural areas in the district of Balad, as a result of which one citizen was killed and two others were wounded.

II. *25 January 1991.*

Air raid on residential areas on the Baghdad-Nineveh road and on Qadisiya quarter and the village of Arbida in the subdistrict of al-Alam, as a result of which five citizens were killed and nine others wounded.

Anbar governorate

I. *21 January 1991.*

Bombardment of a desert area in Kebisa district, as a result of which three citizens were killed and one wounded.

II. *23 January 1991.*

1. A missile fell on a house in the district of Abu Ghurayb.
2. A missile fell on al-Furat village in the district of Hit and another fell in the al-Boukamal area in the subdistrict of al-Karmah. Seven cluster bomb canisters were dropped in the district of al-Rutbah.

III. *26 January 1991.*

An air raid on al-Ramadi city and the districts of al-Qaim, al-Rutbah, Haditha and Hit killed eight citizens and wounded seven others.

IV. *22 January 1991.*

An air raid on al-Nakhib subdistrict killed four citizens and wounded one woman.

V. *26 January 1991.*

Bombardment of the Qadisiya Irrigation Dam, which was damaged.

VI. *27 January 1991.*

Air raids on al-Ramadi city including al-Ramadi city centre and the districts of al-Rutbah, al-Qaim, Haditha, Hit and the subdistrict of al-Ameriya, in which two citizens were killed and another wounded.

VII. *28-29 January 1991.*

1. Air raids on al-Ramadi city centre and the districts of al-Rutbah, al-Qaim, Haditha, Hit and the subdistricts of al-Ameriya and Kebisa.
2. Air raids on 28 January 1991 on the highway between al-Qaim and Akashat, in which four Jordanians were killed and seven persons wounded, including two Jordanians and one person from Thailand.

VIII. *30 January 1991.*

1. Bombardment of the al-Kindi Company for Medical Vaccines, the subdistricts of al-Nasr and al-Salam in Abu Ghurayb district and a Customs office, in which one citizen was wounded.

Dhi Qar governorate

22 January 1991.

Two citizens were wounded by a missile fired from an enemy aircraft.

Najaf governorate

23 January 1991.
Bombardment of residential areas at Najaf, Kufa and al-Manadhira.

Basra governorate

20 January 1991.
Bombardment of al-Najibiya residential area, in which 15 citizens were killed, 19 others wounded and 19 residential buildings destroyed. Four occupants of those buildings were wounded and two shops and a civilian vehicle were damaged.

Ta'mim governorate

20-25 January 1991.
An air raid on densely populated residential areas at Imam Qasim, al-Andalus, Azadi, Arafa and Bey Hasan quarters and al-Dibs district resulted in the death of 15 citizens, including 12 children and 2 women. Six citizens, including four children and a woman, were wounded.

Babil governorate

I. *23 January 1991.*
1. Four missiles fired at the residential areas of the modern village in the subdistrict of Iskandariya killed 20 citizens and wounded 25 others.
2. Bombardment of residential areas in the district of al-Mahmoudiya killed three citizens and wounded four others.

II. *24 January 1991.*
Two air raids on the Musayyib district, targeting residential areas at Jurf al-Sakhr, resulted in the death of two civilians.

III. *26-17 January 1991.*
An air raid on the principal city in the governorate and on the districts of Musayyib and Hashimiya and the subdistrict of Iskandariya killed eight citizens and wounded 36 others in the principal city of the governorate.

Karbala governorate

25 January 1991.
Bombardment of Karbala Cement Plant.

Arbil governorate

I. *24 January 1991.*
Bombardment of houses in the principal city of Arbil governorate killed two citizens and wounded 20 others, including seven women and four children.

II. *26 January 1991.*
Bombardment of residential areas in the Basterma area of Harir subdistrict resulting in the death of 13 citizens, including eight women, four children, and wounded 85 other citizens.

Wasit governorate

24-25 January 1991.
An air raid on the al-Badriya area in Wasit governorate killed two citizens and wounded another.

S/22192, 4 February 1991

81. Letter from the Permanent Representative of Canada to the United Nations addressed to the President of the Security Council, 1 February 1991

Further to our letter of 21 January 1991 (S/22153), and in accordance with paragraph 4 of resolution 678 (1990), Canadian Armed Forces in the Persian Gulf region continue to participate with other members of the United Nations in military action to enforce Iraqi compliance with resolution 660 (1990) and all subsequent relevant resolutions.

Military aircraft of the Canadian Forces continue to provide air defence of multinational shipping in the Persian Gulf and to support multinational air operations. Her Majesty's Canadian ships continue to operate in the Persian Gulf in support of multinational naval operations. A Canadian military hospital is in the process of deploying to the Kingdom of Saudi Arabia for the purpose of providing assistance to the armed forces of the United Kingdom in fulfilling its responsibilities under the Geneva Convention for the care and treatment of all casualties of war.

As you are aware, the world has recently witnessed a massive threat to the environment in the Gulf as a result of deliberate actions by Iraqi forces. Canada has despatched, at the request of Bahrain and Qatar, a team of experts to determine what assistance we might provide. Canada, working in cooperation with other countries and agencies, will do all in its power to minimize the impact of this disaster.

...

S/22194, 4 February 1991

82. Letter from the Permanent Representative of Italy to the United Nations addressed to the President of the Security Council, 4 February 1991

Further to the report submitted on 22 January (S/22126) and in accordance with paragraph 4 of Security Council resolution 678 (1990), I have the honour to inform you that since that day the Italian military forces have continued to participate in joint military actions together with the coalition forces in order to secure the implementation of resolution 660 and all pertinent subsequent resolutions of the Council.

While Italian air forces have been engaged in actions against military targets in the area, Italian naval forces, always in the framework of the coalition, have continued their mission of maritime interception, patrolling and escort in the Gulf waters.

I also wish to inform you that Italy has decided to participate in the various United Nations initiatives on behalf of the populations affected by the hostilities. Specific financial contributions have been made to that end to the Office of the United Nations Disaster Relief Co-ordinator and to the International Committee of the Red Cross.

...

S/22197, 4 February 1991

83. Note verbale from the Permanent Mission of Iraq to the United Nations addressed to the Secretariat, 4 February 1991

The Permanent Mission of the Republic of Iraq presents its compliments to the United Nations Secretariat and has the honour to transmit the text of the letter of resignation from the French Minister of Defence, Mr. Jean-Pierre Chevènement, as published by the French newspaper *Le Figaro* in issue No. 14443 of 30 January 1991 ...

Letter of Resignation

"Mr. President,

"A certain conception of the Republic has led me to request you to release me from the duties which I had the honour to be entrusted with by you.

"It seems to me that the basic reasons which I explained to you at the beginning of December have been borne out in all their force by events today. I would add that the logic of war may lead us every day farther from the objectives laid down by the United Nations.

"Kindly be assured, Mr. President, of my high esteem and loyal sentiments."

S/22199, 5 February 1991

84. Note verbale from the Permanent Representative of Turkey to the United Nations addressed to the Secretary-General, 4 February 1991

Pursuant to paragraph 4 of Security Council resolution 678 (1990), I have the honour to inform you on behalf of my Government that Turkey, consistent with its responsibilities under the Charter of the United Nations and in accordance with paragraph 3 of the above-mentioned resolution, has decided to extend, as of 17 January 1991, appropriate support to those nations that are undertaking a common effort aimed at ensuring the full implementation of resolution 678 (1990), as well as all other relevant resolutions of the Security Council.

...

S/22200, 6 February 1991

85. Letter from the Permanent Representative of Saudi Arabia to the United Nations addressed to the President of the Security Council, 6 February 1991

Pursuant to my letter dated 15 Rajab A.H. 1411 (31 January A.D. 1991) (S/22180) and in accordance with paragraph 4 of Security Council resolution 678 (1990) concerning military operations, I have the honour to inform you on behalf of my Government that the military forces of the Kingdom of Saudi Arabia, in co-operation with the forces of the other countries which are co-operating with the Government of Kuwait, have continued their military operations in accordance with paragraph 2 of resolution 678 (1990) to ensure the full and unconditional withdrawal of Iraq from Kuwait, the restoration of the legitimate Government of Kuwait, the restoration of international peace and security to the region, and the strengthening of the authority of the United Nations.

The military operations from 13 Rajab A.H. 1411 (28 January A.D. 1991) to 19 Rajab A.H. 1411 (2 February 1991) were as follows:

Military support

1. The Royal Saudi Air Force carried out 1,164 sorties against military targets in Iraq and Kuwait, while avoiding civilian targets.

2. The Kingdom of Saudi Arabia participated in the naval operations. There was a total of 24 naval attacks, while navy aircraft carried out 192 sorties with the purposes of patrolling and naval operations support.

3. The Kingdom of Saudi Arabia contributed five reinforced brigades and participated in battles on its borders, one of which was at Al-Khafji, in which the forces of the Kingdom of Saudi Arabia, with participation of units from the fraternal State of Qatar, inflicted heavy losses on the Iraqi aggressor forces.

Human casualties

Human casualties from Al-Khafji battle were as follows:

1. 18 martyrs killed
2. 35 wounded
3. 9 persons missing in action from the border forces and civil defence.

In addition, the Iraqi aggressor launched a Scud missile on Sunday 19 Rajab A.H. 1411 (3 February 1991) against Riyadh; it was intercepted and partially destroyed, and other parts fell on a residential area, causing light injuries to 29 persons, 14 of whom were Saudis and the rest of other nationalities. These figures include 3 Saudi children and 4 Jordanian children.

Material damage

Material damage included the destruction of some buildings and facilities in the town of Al-Khafji as a result of the Iraqi attack.

In addition, as a result of a Scud missile falling on the night of 19 Rajab A.H. 1411 (2 February A.D. 1991), on residential neighbourhoods, two houses were totally destroyed and neighbouring houses were slightly damaged.

Prisoners of war

An International Committee of the Red Cross team visited the prisoner-of-war facilities at Al-Nuairiya, Hafr al-Baten and Artawiya and met Iraqi prisoners of war. The competent Saudi authorities provided assistance in interviewing Iraqi prisoners of war to ensure that they were receiving proper treatment. The International Committee of the Red Cross expressed satisfaction with the Kingdom of Saudi Arabia's respect for its international obligations after ascertaining the arrangements that had been made for the treatment of the sick and the wounded, which were in keeping with the Geneva Convention relative to the Treatment of Prisoners of War. We insisted that the Iraqi authorities should provide the same facilities to representatives of the International Committee of the Red Cross in Baghdad, in accordance with the Geneva Convention, with respect to prisoners of war from the allied countries.

...

S/22203, 6 February 1991

86. Letter from the Permanent Representative of Iraq to the United Nations addressed to the Secretary-General, 6 February 1991

I have the honour to refer to the letter dated 24 January 1991 which Mr. Tariq Aziz, the Deputy Prime Minister and Minister for Foreign Affairs, sent to you, reporting the bombing, carried out on 21 January 1991 by aircraft from the coalition forces of aggression, of a factory that produces children's milk and is situated in the region of Abu Ghuraib.

You undoubtedly know that General Powell, the United States Chairman of the Joint Chiefs of Staff, claimed that this factory was manufacturing "bacteriological weapons".

In order to establish the truth and expose the empty allegations by the United States, which are designed to conceal the criminal nature of the aggression carried out by the United States-NATO-Zionist forces, I request you, on instructions from my Government, to send a fact-finding mission to investigate the type of factory involved so that the international community and world public opinion may learn the truth.

...

S/22204, 6 February 1991

87. Letter from the Permanent Representative of Iraq to the United Nations addressed to the Secretary-General, 6 February 1991

On instructions from my Government, I have the honour to inform you that the States which have been participating in the evil acts of aggression against Iraq since 16 January 1991 have concentrated their attacks on Iraqi civilian, economic, scientific, cultural and religious institutions and, in so doing, have attacked a large number of civilians, destroyed their property and seriously damaged the infrastructure of Iraq in order to lay waste to the country and deprive it of its achievements in the field of development. This aggression is part of the United States-NATO-Zionist plot aimed at establishing hegemony and a new imperialist order in the Middle East.

All the States which are collaborating in this concerted and deliberate campaign of aggression must compensate Iraq in full for all the damage caused to its enterprises and individual persons and their property. Iraq reserves the right to demand complete compensation for such damage from these States.

The creditor States to which Iraq is indebted and which are participating in this aggression will not be reimbursed the amounts corresponding to the compensation owed to Iraq for the damage inflicted on it.

...

S/22205, 7 February 1991

88. Letter from the Permanent Representative of Jordan to the United Nations addressed to the Secretary-General, 7 February 1991

On instructions from my Government, I wish to transmit to you the following information regarding human casualties and injuries and material damage resulting from the bombing by United States and allied aircraft of trucks and tankers belonging to Jordanian companies on the international Baghdad-Amman road inside the Iraqi borders during the period from 29 January 1991 to 5 February 1991.

1. The number of persons killed and wounded and the number of trucks and tankers damaged up to 4 February 1991 is as follows:

(a) Killed: 7 Jordanians and 1 Indian.

(b) Wounded: 14 Jordanians, 4 Indians, 2 Egyptians and 1 Thai.

(c) Motor vehicles: 42, many of which were completely destroyed.

2. The number of persons killed and wounded and the number of trucks and tankers damaged on 5 February 1991 is as follows:

(a) Killed: 6 persons.

(b) Wounded: 5 persons.

(c) Motor vehicles: 8.

...

S/22206, 8 February 1991

89. Letter from the Permanent Representative of Romania to the United Nations addressed to the Secretary-General, 8 February 1991

I have the honour to inform you that pursuant to paragraph 3 of the Security Council resolution 678 (1990) the Government of Romania has proposed and the Parliament of Romania has approved the sending to Saudi Arabia of a surgical hospital for medical assistance having a capacity of 200 beds and a staff of 360 persons. A similar approval has been given for sending to Saudi Arabia a unit of the Romanian Army of the strength of 180 persons, which can perform tasks of chemical decontamination.

The two units have been formed on a voluntary basis and will be stationed behind the operational area. They will perform a humanitarian mission.

The decision of Romania is based on the relevant resolutions of the Security Council and in particular on resolution 678 (1990), which requests all States to provide appropriate support for the actions undertaken to liberate Kuwait and to restore international peace and security in the area. It is consistent with the position of Romania, which has been committed to and has fully supported all resolutions of the Security Council on the situation between Iraq and Kuwait.

The decision of Romania to send the surgical hospital and the decontamination unit will become effective after the conclusion of the necessary agreements.

...

S/22210, 11 February 1991

90. Letter from the Permanent Representative of France to the United Nations addressed to the President of the Security Council, 8 February 1991

Pursuant to paragraph 4 of Security Council resolution 678 (1990), I have the honour to inform you of the actions which the French armed forces continue to take, in the context of plans drawn up jointly with the members of the coalition of countries that are cooperating with Kuwait, to secure the implementation of resolution 660 (1990) and all subsequent resolutions of the Council.

Members of the French land forces present in the field have continued their preparations in anticipation of a later engagement, in conjunction with other forces.

Our naval units continue to help protect allied maritime supply lines. The French vessels which are continuing, in the framework of the Western European Union, to monitor the embargo in the Straits of Tiran, Bab al Mandab and Hormuz, have identified over 6,520 vessels and searched nearly 125 of them.

Lastly, French fighter planes have flown more than 500 missions since 17 January, as part either of offensives against military targets in Kuwait and southern Iraq or of airspace monitoring operations.

...

S/22213, 11 February 1991

91. Letter from the Permanent Representative of Jordan to the United Nations addressed to the Secretary-General, 11 February 1991

I am transmitting to you herewith the text of the interview given by His Majesty King Hussein of Jordan to Mr. David Brinkley, which was broadcast by the United States television network ABC on Sunday, 10 February 1991.

...

Mr. Brinkley: Now, standing by to talk to us from Amman, Jordan is King Hussein, who just this week announced his support for Iraq and its war alongside the United States and other Western countries. Your Majesty, thank you for coming in and talking with us today. We're pleased to have you.

King Hussein: Thank you. It's a pleasure.

Mr. Brinkley: Now, you've just had a meeting with Deputy Prime Minister Hamadi of Iraq. What came out of the meeting? Can you tell us?

King Hussein: He visited Jordan from Iran and he is on his way to several Arab capitals. He gave us an impression of what is happening there and I was particularly struck by the news of the heavy civilian losses in Iraq and the destruction of the infrastructure there. He suggested that the losses could be in the thousands.

Mr. Brinkley: Now, Your Majesty, the President of the U.S., Secretary of State, the leadership of the U.S. Government were surprised and disappointed at your speech the other day supporting Iraq. Why did you do that?

King Hussein: I would like to seize this opportunity to point out something that's been repeated in the recent past by many American officials, in other words, their surprise that I didn't mention Kuwait or the invasion and annexation of Kuwait. I would like to make it very, very clear that I didn't do so, having done so zillions of times before and our position is very, very clear. On principle and in fact, we have always been against the occupation of territories by war and their annexation, regarding all the crises in this region and certainly, that applies to Kuwait and our position has not changed an iota in that particular regard.

What we were against and what I mentioned in my speech was my worry and concern as someone who has sought peace and a peaceful solution to this problem from the outset. My disappointment is great and that of the people of Jordan and the Arabs and many in the world over the fact that instead of peace, there is this terrible war with all the results that you could see in terms of the wounds it's going to open, the damage it's going to create and the ecological, economic - the turbulence, the instability that probably will grow from that point in circles that will become ever greater in the region. Ours was a commitment to peace, not to war and I was voicing concern for the Iraqi people in that speech and for their suffering, due to what we hear and what we receive in the way of information regarding their very, very heavy losses and the destruction of the infrastructure in Iraq, together with so many civilians.

Mr. Brinkley: Well, you oppose the occupation of Kuwait, but you still support the country that is occupying it. Americans find that a bit hard to understand. Could you explain that?

King Hussein: What do you mean by "support"? I would like to understand exactly what you meant by that.

Mr. Brinkley: No, I say you oppose it, oppose it.

King Hussein: I am supporting peace.

Mr. Brinkley: You oppose the occupation -

King Hussein: I have not - yes, I have opposed the occupation of Kuwait and I have sought a peaceful solution to the problem from the outset and I believe firmly that it was reachable within the first days of the conflict and I believe it was reachable throughout the months that have past.

And so I'm really concerned on a humanitarian level by all that this war is bringing about and nothing else. I am worried and I am Hashemite and I am an Arab and I belong to a people and I have a history and a people who feel very, very strongly that there are problems in this region that could be resolved peacefully, as we have been committed to the cause of peace for so many years, not only the Iraqi-Kuwaiti problem, but the Palestinian problem, the Cypriot problem, every other problem in this region.

Mr. Brinkley: Does the rising hostility among the Arab - Islamic population in your country and others toward America, does that help bring you to this decision?

King Hussein: No, sir. I have always echoed my own feelings against a background of who I am and to which family [*sic*] belong and with a background of the history that this family has had throughout the Arab struggle over the centuries. And also, I am proud to say that I feel very close to the people of Jordan who freely express themselves and their hopes. And therefore, I do not see why my statement, my appeal for peace has been so misunderstood and misinterpreted.

Mr. Brinkley: Well, many have appealed for peace, but there isn't any at the moment and when the American military tells us that they expect a victory over Iraq in a relative short time, there will be great destruction left behind, where will your country be then? What will happen then? How do you see it?

King Hussein: I can't honestly tell you what will happen because I believe that the entire region is liable to face instability and there will be turmoil in a very large area. This is what I've been trying to avert from the outset and rest assured that we are committed to the freedom of man, his human dignity, his rights and life, be he Arab or otherwise, and for peace in this entire region. This is our commitment in the past and this is our commitment now and will always be.

Mr. Brinkley: Here in Washington, we hear from people in our government that the embargo on shipments of arms and other material to Iraq is being violated by you. Is that true?

King Hussein: This is totally untrue, sir. Unfortunately, we don't have the luxury of having so many PR firms or any PR firms to put our case across in Washington or in the United [*sic*] States, but we believe that the American people will sooner or later find the truth.

Mr. Brinkley: Well, the PR firms apparently have not been effective because it is being said here and I am happy to hear your response to it. Now, you also said in your speech that this is a war for American dominance in the Middle East and a war against all Arabs. You believe that?

King Hussein: I don't understand what point you are at now. I would like to have a clear view of what many - and obviously, Arabs have a basic right to be a party to forming what is now referred to as a "new world order", but what is it? I was bringing in my speech the other day the comparison between what is happening to the Iraqi people on the one hand - the war that unfortunately all our best efforts could not avert - and on the other hand, the state of curfew that exists and has existed since the beginning of hostilities in the Occupied Territories and the West Bank and in Gaza, where people are not permitted to leave their homes, even to achieve or bring about what they need for their very survival; a problem of a few months' duration and a problem of 24 years; the problem of Cyprus. There are so many problems of a different context in terms of their location, but of a similar nature in terms of their having been there for so long.

What is a new world order? How are we going to put it together? How are [*sic*] going to insure peace and stability and progress and the rightful generations to come of all peoples in this region to live in peace and to enjoy what is their right? We are very confused about what we feel is special attention paid to one problem and the lack of it on another, not that we have any doubt that the Kuwaiti problem, the Iraq-Kuwait problem had precedence since it came about in the way it did, but we need a linkage with something else.

We need to know exactly where we are going. We need a commitment to resolve other problems. We need a dialogue, a dialogue that could have been there between Iraq and the United States, Iraq and its neighbours and maybe war could have been averted; a dialogue with the rest of the world to enable us to see what this future is and obviously, as Arabs and a people in this region, we are very concerned.

Mr. Brinkley: Your Majesty, what are your thoughts about Iraq firing Scud missiles at a country that is not in the war? Israel.

King Hussein: I am not an apologist for any, but in this regard, I believe that this whole war and everything that it has brought about is a tragedy and I really hope and pray that the worst nightmares that one has had over so many months will not come true of the effect it's going to have on so many. Iraq probably feels that it is being struck by the United States and it's striking at a strategic ally. As far as these missiles are concerned, once again, they are fired into outer space. They are missiles that we cannot detect nor intercept.

But we have not been a party to this conflict and we wish to emphasize that time and again. We are speaking out of concern for everybody in this region and of the United States and for its image and for the image of the President of the United States at a time of such change in the world in which we live. Well, people can hopefully interpret our position accurately in time.

Mr. Brinkley: Your Majesty, one last question. We have a little time left. I'm reasonably certain that the President, the Secretary of State and the other leaders of the U.S. Governments are listening to you now. What would you like to say to them?

King Hussein: I can only say one thing because it has hurt and hurt every Jordanian here, but our relationship was not based on material considerations. We are facing enormous difficulties, but we are not that cheap and believe me, we are proud to be friends of friends who treat us with mutual respect and who seek to be our friends and we will be theirs always. And I hope that all of this will be behind us someday and I hope for peace in this region and for stability in this region and for happiness for all concerned.

A/45/953, S/22214, 11 February 1991

92. Letter from the Permanent Representative of Kuwait to the United Nations addressed to the Secretary-General, 11 February 1991

On instructions from my Government, I am transmitting to you the text of the statement made by Dr. Beder Al-Yakoub, Minister of Information and Minister of State for National Council Affairs, by way of commentary on the address delivered by His Majesty King Hussein, ruler of Jordan, on 6 February 1991.

...

Commenting on the address delivered by His Majesty King Hussein on 6 February 1991, in which he referred to the ongoing military operations to liberate Kuwait, the Kuwaiti Minister of Information and Minister of State for National Council Affairs, Dr. Beder Jassim Al-Yakoub, declared:

"It is painful and distressing that this address came at a crucial stage in our history and that, instead of advising the Iraqi regime to do the right thing, to listen to the voice of reason and to abide by international law, it attempted to conceal the true reasons underlying the war of liberation: the Iraqi regime's occupation of the State of Kuwait and the agony and pain that the Iraqi occupation authorities are continuing to inflict on the Kuwaiti people.

The speech seems to have been an attempt to make the world believe, wrongly, that the goal of the military operations carried out by the multinational forces is the destruction of Iraq. It ignored the fact that these operations are entirely in accordance with international law and based on United Nations resolutions, particularly resolution 678 (1990). The goal of these military operations is the liberation of Kuwait. There is no other goal.

Moreover, these operations were undertaken only after the international community and all its bodies, institutions and officials had exhausted the peaceful methods to persuade the Iraqi regime to abide by international law and withdraw unconditionally from all Kuwaiti territory, so that legitimacy could be restored.

If truth be told, these legitimate military operations are a diligent attempt to put an end to the war launched against the State of Kuwait by the Iraqi regime on 2 August 1990. These operations constitute an endeavour to bring peace to our region of the world through the use of force, after the Iraqi regime turned down all other peaceful solutions.

Kuwait has the right to ask why His Majesty King Hussein remained silent when the Iraqi army displaced the people of Kuwait at dawn on 2 August; why did King Hussein remain silent in the face of the shameful acts of murder, torture and dishonour to which all sections of the Kuwaiti people were subjected, and are still being subjected; why did King Hussein remain silent when young children, fleeing from the brutality of the Iraqi army of occupation, breathed their last in the heat of the desert, after losing their way, on 2 August.

Nobody wants to hurt the Iraqi people or destroy Iraq, but justice and right must prevail. Those who decry the fate of Iraq should recall the ongoing bitter sufferings of the Kuwaiti people before and after 17 January and they should be calling on the Iraqi forces, with the utmost sincerity, to withdraw from Kuwait, so that legitimacy can be restored and so that there can be an end to this tragedy, which was brought about by the Iraqi regime.

History will have no mercy on those who try to conceal the truth and support those in the wrong, thereby helping to aggravate the situation and propel the destiny of this nation towards the brink of perdition."

S/22216, 13 February 1991

93. Letter from the Permanent Representative of the United States of America to the United Nations addressed to the President of the Security Council, 8 February 1991

In accordance with paragraph 4 of Security Council resolution 678 (1990), I wish, on behalf of my Government, to submit the following report on actions undertaken pursuant to paragraphs 2 and 3 of that resolution up to 7 February 1991, further to our report submitted on 30 January.

Since that report, the military forces of the coalition, including United States military forces, acting in accordance with resolution 678 (1990), have continued their air action against Iraq's military targets. Over 52,000 coalition air sorties have been carried out since hostilities began on 16 January. These sorties were not flown against any civilian or religious targets or against the Iraqi civilian population. Coalition forces have taken every precaution to minimize collateral damage to civilian facilities. Despite the destructive potential of modern warfare, collateral damage has been extremely limited.

In the third week of hostilities aimed at the withdrawal of Iraqi forces from Kuwait, the commander of the forces in the Gulf gave the following explanation of our objectives in the war. The first phase of allied attacks targeted command and control, air defence, combat aircraft in the air and on the ground, nuclear, biological and chemical storage facilities, and the Republican Guards.

Once the first phase was completed, coalition forces were to target air defence radars and missiles in Kuwait to achieve undisputed control of the air and to target the supply lines leading from Iraq into Kuwait. The third phase, in which we are now involved, includes extensive attacks on the Republican Guard and other ground troops in the Kuwaiti theater of operations. Despite a decrease in the priority given to most other targets in Iraq, surface-to-surface missile capabilities remain as high priority targets.

On 29 and 30 January, Iraqi forces supported by tanks and artillery invaded Saudi Arabia at four points. Coalition forces counter-attacked and, after heavy fighting, forced the Iraqi forces to withdraw after suffering heavy losses.

As of 7 February, United States forces have lost 16 aircraft in combat action. Other coalition forces have also suffered losses. In addition, 14 United States military personnel have been killed in action and 27 United States military personnel have been reported as missing in action, 8 of whom have been classified as prisoners of war.

The naval forces of the United States and the allied coalition have continued to engage Iraqi patrol and mine-laying craft in the Northern Arabian Gulf. Fifty-five Iraqi vessels have been confirmed to have been sunk or disabled since the opening of hostilities.

As of 7 February, Iraq has fired 57 surface-to-surface missiles - 29 at Saudi Arabia and 28 at Israel. However, the efforts of the coalition air forces, coupled with the success of the Patriot air defence system, have been effective in bringing about a dramatic decrease in the number of such missile attacks.

United States forces are currently holding 44 members of the Iraqi armed forces. One hundred and eighty-six Iraqi prisoners of war, who had been visited and registered by the International Committee of the Red Cross (ICRC), in accordance with the Third Geneva Convention Relative to the Protection of Prisoners of War, have been transferred to the Saudi authorities to be housed appropriately. More than 500 Iraqi soldiers have been captured by other members of the allied coalition, largely as a result of the Iraqi attack on Khafji. The coalition forces are granting ICRC timely access to all Iraqi prisoners of war.

Iraqi authorities have continued to ignore the standards of the Geneva conventions in blatant disregard for international law. They have denied access to coalition prisoners of war by ICRC, deliberately exposed them to combat danger, and otherwise abused them for propaganda purposes. They have targeted civilian areas for attack by surface-to-surface missiles, and have deliberately caused serious damage to the natural environment of the region. They have also continued to disregard their obligations towards the population of occupied Kuwait.

Iraqi aircraft continue to fly to airfields in Iran. As of 7 February over 130 aircraft are in Iran. The Government of Iran has given clear assurances that it will detain these aircraft until the conclusion of the current conflict.

We are pleased to be able to report that the flow of oil caused by Iraqi forces from the facilities at al-Ahmadi in Kuwait has been halted (at least temporarily). We continue to monitor other oil facilities that may be leaking into the waters of the Gulf and will take action if necessary to prevent further such damage to the region.

The United States has sent a supplemental advisory team to Saudi Arabia to help coordinate efforts to counteract the massive oil slick caused by the Iraqi forces. A key priority has been to protect desalinization and industrial plants that may be disrupted by the oil. The weather has been cooperative, allowing protective booms to be placed around these sites. The grave damage to the environment by this act has yet to be fully evaluated.

...

S/22217, 13 February 1991

94. Letter from the Permanent Representative of New Zealand to the United Nations addressed to the President of the Security Council, 13 February 1991

In accordance with paragraph 4 of Security Council resolution 678 (1990), I have the honour to inform you of the actions undertaken in pursuance of paragraph 2 of that resolution.

New Zealand has sent three military support units to act in conjunction with the forces of States cooperating with the Government of Kuwait. Two Royal New Zealand Air Force (RNZAF) C-130 Hercules aircraft, with about 60 personnel, are based in Saudi Arabia, under arrangements between the Government of New Zealand and the Governments of the Kingdom of Saudi Arabia and the United Kingdom of Great Britain and Northern Ireland. Two military medical teams, comprising about 50 personnel, are stationed in Bahrain, one working at a United States medical facility and the other at a British medical facility, under arrangements between the Government of New Zealand and the Governments of the State of Bahrain, the United Kingdom of Great Britain and Northern Ireland and the United States of America.

...

S/22218, 13 February 1991

95. Letter from the Permanent Representative of the United Kingdom of Great Britain and Northern Ireland to the United Nations addressed to the President of the Security Council, 13 February 1991

Further to my letter of 28 January (S/22156) I have the honour to communicate to you a further report on operations in the Gulf pursuant to paragraph 2 of resolution 678 (1990).

Air action has continued against military targets. Initially, British forces' air operations concentrated on attacks on airfields and on elements of the Iraqi air defence system. In the second phase, attacks were on bridges vital to the military supply effort to and from Kuwait. In the third phase, the Royal Air Force has attacked surface-to-air missile sites, artillery positions, ammunition storage and Silkworm surface-to-surface missile sites.

Attacks have been directed exclusively at military objectives, using precision weapons wherever possible, particularly in areas where there may be civilians near the targets. All targets are carefully selected because they pose a threat to coalition forces or because they support Iraq's illegal occupation of Kuwait. Pilots have clear instructions to minimize civilian casualties and to avoid damage to sites of religious and cultural significance. Indeed, on a number of occasions, attacks have not been pressed home because pilots were not completely satisfied they could meet these conditions. Latest reports suggest that the Government of Iraq is transferring military headquarters into buildings such as schools, precisely to take advantage of allied care and concern to avoid attacking areas housing civilians.

Indpendent [*sic*] reports from journalists coming from Iraq confirm that allied attacks in general have been remarkably accurate and have also confirmed that Iraqi propaganda is presenting military casualties as civilian. In the case of the attack on the An Nasiriyah bridge on 8 February, Baghdad Radio claimed 47 civilian casualties, but a Western journalist who was an eye witness reported that the bulk of the casualties were military.

The approach of the allies is in contrast to that adopted by the Government of Iraq, which has had no compunction about launching indiscriminate missile attacks directed at civilians and using environmental damage as a further weapon by deliberately releasing oil into the Gulf. In connection with the release of oil, the British Government has contributed to coping with the effects and helping to prevent an environmental disaster. We have airlifted ninety tons of pollution control equipment to Saudi Arabia and sent oil pollution experts from the Department of Transport to help with expert advice. The Natural Environment Research Council has produced an urgent report on wildlife biological impact which has been made available to the Saudi Arabian authorities. In addition, the Royal Society for the Protection of Animals, which has unique experience in coping with the impact of oil on wildlife, has sent a three-man team to instruct Saudi Arabian volunteers in the techniques of cleaning and rescuing oil-contaminated birds.

The British Government has taken up an offer from the Government of Kuwait to provide volunteer civilians to serve in the Gulf in support of British forces. Up to 70 personnel are to be employed as interpreters and liaison officers in hospitals and in prisoner-of-war (POW) camps. The deployed personnel will have the status of honorary officers in the Kuwaiti army, under the operational control of the Commander, British Forces Middle East. The first group of Kuwaiti personnel was deployed to the Gulf on 7 February.

The British Government has notified the International Committee of the Red Cross (ICRC) of 10 missing British airmen believed to be POWs in Iraqi hands. As yet, no notification as to their capture and whereabouts have been received by ICRC. As stated in my letter of 21 January, the British Government is complying scrupulously with its obligations under the Geneva Conventions and has given ICRC full and immediate access to Iraqi POWs and civilian detainees both in the United Kingdom and in the Gulf theatre. We look to see Iraq act similarly in keeping with its international humanitarian obligations.

We note statements made by the Iraqi Government as regards the conditions under which ICRC access would be granted to allied POWs. My authorities consider it a breach of Iraq's obligations under the Geneva Conventions that it is attempting to create extraneous linkages rather than simply comply with its legal obligations under the Conventions as the United Kingdom is doing.

...

S/22219, 13 February 1991

96. Letter from the Permanent Representative of Iraq to the United Nations addressed to the Secretary-General, 13 February 1991

On instructions from my Government, I have the honour to transmit to you herewith a letter dated 13 February 1991 from the Deputy Prime Minister and Minister for Foreign Affairs of the Republic of Iraq concerning the heinous crime committed by the United States when, early today, 13 February 1991, it deliberately bombed a shelter for civilian inhabitants of the Amiriyah area of Baghdad in which there were 400 civilians, most of them women, children and elderly persons.

...

I have the honour to inform you and all the Members of the United Nations that early today, 13 February 1991, the United States, NATO and Zionist forces of aggression that have been waging their squalid war against Iraq for four successive weeks committed a vile and heinous crime by deliberately bombing a shelter for civilians, located in the Amiriyah area of Baghdad, in which there were at the time about 400 civilians, most of them women, children and elderly persons.

Foreign networks and press correspondents present in Baghdad were witnesses to the crime. The heinous crime in question is to be added to the dismal criminal record of the United States, NATO and Zionist aggression against our steadfast and combatant people, a record that has come to be generally understood by all fair and honest men in the world despite all the frenzied efforts being made by the Governments of the States participating in the aggression to obscure the facts, to lie and to deceive. We call upon the United Nations and upon you personally to condemn this heinous crime and to take action to expose the true facts concerning the aggression launched against Iraq by the traditional axes of imperialism and colonialism under the leadership of the United States of America. The concealment of such crimes would be recorded against the United Nations as a mark of disgrace. In this connection, we must recall that those States which voted in the Security Council in favour of resolution 678 (1990) bear a particular legal, political and moral responsibility for such crimes, because they, in their submission to the will of the United States and in their consent to that disgraceful resolution, opened the way for the greater criminal, namely the United States, to commit them. They shall continue to bear this responsibility as long as they fail to adopt an honourable and resolute stance for a halt to the aggression and to the crimes against humanity being committed by the United States.

All of those contributing to such crimes, both those who gave permission for them and those who proceeded to perpetrate them, the Iraqi people holds fully responsible for them before history and humanity.

S/22222, 13 February 1991

97. Letter from the Permanent Representative of Tunisia to the United Nations addressed to the President of the Security Council, 13 February 1991

I have the honour to transmit herewith the text of a declaration made on 13 February 1991 by an authorized source in the Ministry of Foreign Affairs of the Republic of Tunisia.

...

The Tunisian Government was deeply disturbed and saddened to learn that hundreds of innocent Iraqi victims had perished as a result of an intensive aerial bombardment of a civilian shelter in a residential area of the Iraqi capital in the early hours of Wednesday, 13 February 1991.

On numerous occasions, Tunisia has emphasized its apprehensions concerning the continuation and escalation of the war, particularly after it became evident that Iraq's human resources and economic, scientific and cultural infrastructure was being targeted.

While strongly condemning this savage bombardment of civilians, which is incompatible with humanitarian values and international covenants, Tunisia expresses its solidarity with the fraternal Iraqi people in this severe ordeal and once again makes an urgent appeal to the conscience of the world to spare bloodshed, to put an end to the devastating war in the Gulf and to settle the dispute by peaceful means.

The Tunisian Government wishes to point out that this bombardment constitutes further evidence of the manner in which the Security Council resolutions on the Gulf, particularly resolution 678 (1990), are being flagrantly transcended and strongly urges this Council to assume its full responsibilities by imposing respect for the United Nations resolutions in order to preserve a minimum degree of credibility for the United Nations, in its capacity as the last resort for the maintenance of international peace and security.

S/22223, 14 February 1991

98. Letter from the Chargé d'affaires a.i. of the Permanent Mission of Algeria to the United Nations addressed to the Secretary-General, 14 February 1991

I have the honour to transmit to you herewith the text of the statement issued on 14 February 1991 by the Office of the President of the Republic. ...

"The savage bombing raids carried out daily by the coalition forces against Iraqi towns and cities yesterday hit with particular ferocity a shelter in which residents of the Amiriyah residential district of Baghdad had taken refuge as usual. This deliberate attack killed hundreds of people, most of them women and children.

Algeria indignantly censures and vigorously condemns this vile act, for which the coalition forces must take full responsibility.

This massacre reveals the true nature of the war being waged against the Iraqi people, which today has escalated from an operation designed to systematically destroy Iraq's economic and military potential to an actual war of extermination.

Algeria resolutely denounces the intentions of certain Powers to try to impose their new order by fire and bloodshed. It also denounces the complicity of certain Arab countries, who are thus lending support to a genocidal campaign against a fraternal people.

At this tragic time, Algeria shares the sorrow of the Iraqi people, bows to the memory of the many victims, salutes the determination and heroism of the Iraqi people in their resistance to aggression and pledges them its complete solidarity in this fight for honour and dignity.

Algeria wishes to recall that the intervention by the coalition forces, perpetrated under the cover of international law is, in reality, a campaign of all-out destruction which, through the massacre of innocents, is assuming the dimensions of a crime against humanity.

Far from contributing to the restoration of law and justice, such an excessive deployment and show of force simply reflects aggressive, hegemonistic intentions which totally contravene the purposes and principles of the United Nations.

Algeria wishes to emphasize that those who today claim to be acting in the name of international legality have even twisted the decisions of the Security Council relating to the Gulf crisis. The military adventure on which the coalition forces have embarked can in no circumstances be justified on the basis of either international law or humanitarian conventions, still less morality.

Algeria solemnly appeals to the Security Council to finally assume its responsibilities with regard to the serious deterioration of the situation in the Gulf and to call immediately for a cease-fire so that a process of dialogue and negotiations can begin, based on the relevant principles of the Charter of the United Nations.

It appeals to the Secretary-General to make full use of the prerogatives conferred on him by the Charter, with a view to hastening a cease-fire and making a decisive contribution to the restoration of peace.

Algeria is confident that all peace-loving peoples, in particular the Arab and Muslim peoples, will show a sense of responsibility and join together in an effort to end a conflict which is threatening international peace and security.

The Algerian people, who daily pledge their fraternal solidarity with Iraq, will be capable of mobilizing still further in a tangible demonstration of their support for the heroic struggle of the fraternal people of Iraq. In so doing, they will prove once again that they remain unswervingly committed to the noble values which guided them in their glorious liberation struggle and that they will not shrink from any sacrifice in providing support and assistance whenever a people is fighting for dignity, freedom and independence."

S/22224, 14 February 1991

99. Letter from the Permanent Representative of Iraq to the United Nations addressed to the Secretary-General, 14 February 1991

On instructions from my Government, I have the honour to transmit to you herewith a letter dated 11 February 1991 from Mr. Tariq Aziz, Deputy Prime Minister and Minister for Foreign Affairs of the Republic of Iraq, giving factual evidence of the savage crimes being committed by the United States, NATO and Zionist coalition forces against Iraqi citizens and against the economic and cultural assets of the Iraqi people.

...

I have already sent to you, on 24 January and 1 February 1991, two letters in which I provided you with factual evidence of the savage crimes being committed by the United States, NATO and Zionist coalition forces against Iraqi citizens and against the economic, cultural, scientific and religious assets of the Iraqi people. Those letters contained full details of the factual evidence of the said crimes and of the large-scale human and material losses to which they have given rise.

From the beginning of the aggression against Iraq on 17 January 1991 and up to today, numerous impartial sources have corroborated these crimes, and newspapers and television stations have disseminated information and unequivocal pictures which confirm their wide-scale occurrence in all parts of Iraq. In my two previous letters, I called upon you to adopt the stance required of you by your position as Secretary-General of the United Nations, particularly since the resolution in favour of aggression was adopted in the name of the United Nations and under its aegis. It is clear from the information that I shall provide in this letter that the bombing operations against various kinds of civilian targets and the slaughter of civilians have mounted as the days have passed since the beginning of the aggression and that they are, indeed, escalating daily in a vicious and savage manner. Despite that fact, your reaction to these crimes, including your statement at the meeting of the Security Council held on 8 February 1991, has been reticent and out of keeping with the enormity of the crimes being committed against the Iraqi people and with the responsibilities with which you are entrusted within the framework of the Organization. In the case of previous incidents, however, you have taken spirited action in accordance with your humanitarian responsibilities under the Charter of the United Nations with regard to acts and conduct that do not approach the degree of repulsiveness that characterizes the crimes to which our people has been subjected for four successive weeks or the vengeful and retaliatory character that has marked them.

World public opinion has begun to understand and to condemn the planned and deliberately vengeful, retaliatory and destructive character of the crimes committed by the United States, NATO and Zionist forces of evil and aggression against Iraq, despite all the frantic efforts being made by the leaders of the aggressor countries to obscure the truth. Such crimes have begun to be extended to hospitals, irrigation dams, civilian bridges and food and supply depots designated for civilians. The crimes of the ongoing aggression against Iraq, which have had the goal of cutting the vital arteries of the Iraqi people and of destroying Iraq's infrastructure and which have no relation whatsoever to the military effort, continue to be allowed to pass under the cover of United Nations resolutions. Here, we must recall the statements made by the American General Dugan before the aggression, when he said that the plan of attack was directed against all that was clear and precious to the Iraqi people. The factual evidence of the aggression has demonstrated that the plan of which the General spoke is indeed the very plan of aggression that was drawn up before the adoption of Security Council resolution 678 (1990), the execution of which in the name of the United Nations was sanctioned by that resolution.

The reticence that characterizes your reaction in the face of these crimes cannot be justified on any moral, humanitarian or legal grounds. If your motive in this has been political, then it constitutes a grave precedent for the first time in the history of the Organization and one for which history will hold the Secretariat responsible to all the peoples of the world as long as it fails to adopt a stance appropriate to the heinous character of the crimes being committed against Iraq.

So that the record of history may be clear to you and for the information of those fair-minded persons who believe in truth and justice, I communicate to you hereunder, further to my two previously mentioned letters, factual evidence of the fresh crimes that have been committed in the name of the United Nations Charter against the people of Iraq.

Baghdad Governorate

1. *30 January 1991*
Aerial bombardment of Dawrah and the residential Jihad quarter; two dead and two wounded.

2. *31 January 1991*
Aerial bombardment of New Baghdad and the residential Jihad quarter; two wounded.

3. *1 February 1991*
Aerial bombardment; 27 wounded.

4. *2 February 1991*
Aerial bombardment; one woman killed in the Karradah area.

5. *3 February 1991*
Air raids on residential areas; one infant girl killed and four children variously wounded.

6. *4 February 1991*
Two air raids; two killed.

7. *5 February 1991*
Aerial bombardment of residential areas; one child killed and four persons wounded, including two children.

8. *6 February 1991*
(a) Air raids on residential areas; one civilian wounded.
(b) Air raids on civilian areas; eight wounded.

9. *7 February 1991*
(a) Air raids targeted against residential neighbourhoods in the Sheikh Umar and A'zamiyah areas; 15 dead and 29 wounded.
(b) Air raids on residential neighbourhoods; five wounded.

Babil Governorate

1. *29 January 1991*
Air raids targeted against the Musayyib and Mahmoudiya districts and the Kifl subdistrict; five dead, including two women, and seven wounded, including one woman.

2. *1 February 1991*
Aerial bombardment of the Governorate centre and the Barkali centre; 11 dead and 11 wounded.

3. *3-5 February 1991*
Air raids on the centre of the city of Hillah, the Musayyib district and the Iskandariyah subdistrict; 17 dead and 89 wounded.

Wasit Governorate

1. *31 January 1991*
Air raids on the Governorate centre, the Kut irrigation barrage, the Kut bridge, the Electricity Department building and the village of Al-Diwaniyah al-Sharqiyah; damage to public buildings and dwelling houses.

2. *2 February 1991*
Air raids on residential neighbourhoods in the Burah area; five wounded.

3. *3-6 February 1991*
Air raids targeted against residential neighbourhoods in the Governorate centre; 59 dead and 70 wounded.

Muthanna Governorate

1. *1 February 1991*
Air raids on the old railway bridge, the main bridge in the city of Samawah, the circle line railway bridge, the Al Jurukhi bridge, the radio and television building and the main Khadar bridge; two killed.

2. *3 February 1991*
Bombing of the storage complex belonging to the State Central Marketing Company; destruction of warehouses and burning of stocks of infant formula, foodstuffs, other consumer goods and civilian vehicles. Five employees of the State Food Trade Company, two of them women, were killed by the bombing.

Najaf Governorate

30 January 1991
Bombing of residential neighbourhoods in the Governorate centre and the Munadharah district and of the Abbasiyah bridge in the Kufa district.

Qadisiyah Governorate

1. *20-30 January 1991*
Air raids on the Governorate centre, the Shamiyah district and the Shinafiyah and Ghammas subdistricts; 17 killed and 29 wounded.

2. *18 January 1991*
Bombing of the Qadisiyah flour mill, and its complete destruction.

3. *30 January 1991*
(a) Bombing of the Dunya flour mill building in the Qadisiyah Governorate and its complete destruction.
(b) Bombing of the storehouses of the State Vehicle Company in the Qadisiyah Governorate; damage to 153 new civilian vehicles.
(c) Bombing of consumer goods warehouses; damage to large quantities of sugar and other foodstuffs.

Irbil Governorate

26-30 January 1991
Air raids on the Governorate centre; one killed and eight wounded, including four women.

Ninawa Governorate

1. *29 January 1991*
Air raids on the Technical Institute in Salamiyah, the New Mosul area, the radio and television station, Shahid Adnan Street, the Danah district, Jabal Sanjar, the northwest power station, the Saddam dam and residential neighbourhoods in the Abdu Khawb area, and the Maydan area, the Wadi al-Ayn area, the Faysaliyah area, and the Qayyara district; 63 dead, including seven Sudanese citizens, and 147 wounded.

2. *30 January 1991*
Bombing of consumption goods warehouses in the Governorate centre; destruction of 332 sacks of beans, 97 sacks of sugar and 27 sacks of lentils and other foodstuffs.

Anbar Governorate

1. *30 January 1991*
Bombing of the expressway at Rutbah and of the State Vehicle Company.

2. *31 January 1991 to 2 February 1991*
(a) Air raids on the centre of the city of Ramadi and the Qa'im and Rutbah districts and bombing of six tents in the desert; one woman killed and seven persons wounded, all of them women and children.
(b) Bombing of storehouses of the State Vehicle Company in the Rutbah area; damage to 345 new civilian vehicles.

3. *3 February 1991*
Air raids on the Governorate centre and the Abu Eis area in the western desert belonging to the Rutbah district; seven dead and five wounded.

4. *6 February 1991*
Air raids targeted against residential neighbourhoods in the Governorate centre; 12 dead and one wounded.

Diyala Governorate

1.*February 1991*
Aerial bombardment of an agricultural area in the Governorate centre; some children killed.

Basra Governorate

1. *28 January 1991*
Air raids on the bridge connecting Basra and Maysan, the bridge connecting the Madina and Qurnah districts, the Zubayr district, Sha'biyah, Shush, Ma'qal, the Arabian Gulf Academy, Marid, Rafi'iyah, Mishraq, Atabat Bey Ghazwan, Karmat Ali, Junaynah, the Safwan district centre, Harithah, Abbasiyah, Tamimah, Ashshar, Jabaliyah, the Maftiyah area, Madinah district and Talhah sub-district; 38 dead and 201 wounded.

2. *30-31 January 1991*
Air raids on the radio and television complex, Sa'd Square, the site of the faculties of Basra University, the television building, Madinah district and Huwayr subdistrict; two dead and seven wounded.

3. *31 January to 4 February 1991*
Air raids extending to residential neighbourhoods in the Governorate centre, the Qurnah district, the Shatt al-Arab district, the Dayr subdistrict and the Haritha area; 22 killed and 91 wounded.

Ta'mim Governorate

26-30 January 1991
Air raids extending to the Kirkuk railway station, the Kirkuk-Baiji railway station in

Riyadh Square, residential neighbourhoods in the Andalus quarter, the Arama quarter and the Taza subdistrict; 31 killed and 48 wounded, including eight women and seven children.

Dhi Qar Governorate

1. *29 January 1991*
Air raids extending to the Governorate centre, the Uruba quarter, the Zu'ailat district and the Dhi Qar high-speed overpass; 2 killed and 13 wounded.

2. *3 February 1991*
Bombardment of the Qadisiya bridge; 100 killed and more than 200 wounded.

3. *4 February 1991*
Air raids on residential areas in the Governorate centre; 28 killed and 15 wounded.

Bombing of dams and other installations

1. *28 January 1991*
Air raid on the storage reservoir project adjacent to the Saddam dam in the Ninawa governorate, and on the Saddam dam itself, by means of cluster bombs; large-scale damage.

2. *29 January 1991*
Air raid on the Kut barrage; serious damage.

3. *29 January 1991*
Air raid on the Ramadi barrage; 40-metre-long gap in the surface of the bridge.

4. *30 January 1991*
Bombardment of the Dukan dam in the Sulaymaniyah governorate; large-scale damage.

5. *5 February 1991*
Bombing of the Kut barrage for the second time; additional serious damage.

S/22225, 14 February 1991

100. Letter from the Permanent Representative of Tunisia to the United Nations addressed to the President of the Security Council, 13 February 1991

Following the decision taken by the Security Council at its 2977th meeting on 13 February 1991 to meet in closed session, I have the honour to transmit to you herewith, on instructions from my Government, the text of the statement prepared by my delegation which was to have been delivered at the official, open meeting of the Security Council called for jointly by the five States members of the Arab Maghreb Union, including Tunisia, on 23 January 1991.

...

Since 23 January 1991, Tunisia, in association with the other member States of the Arab Maghreb Union, has been requesting the holding of this urgent meeting of the Security Council to consider the serious situation in the Gulf region. Other countries have also submitted similar requests.

...

By virtue of the responsibilities and powers vested in it under the Charter of the United Nations, the distinguished Security Council is the United Nations organ entrusted with the maintenance of international peace and security in order to save mankind from the scourge of war; this constitutes one of the most important purposes for which the United Nations was established, as indicated in the first paragraph of the Preamble to the Charter.

Accordingly, in view of the trust that has been placed in it, we expect the Security Council to meet spontaneously and without delay, as it did on 2 August in order to deal with the crisis that arose from the entry of Iraqi forces into the territory of Kuwait and their occupation of that country.

In fact, the Council adopted 12 resolutions between 2 August and 30 November 1990 and, under the terms of resolution 678 (1990), set 15 January as a deadline for the Iraqi withdrawal from Kuwait.

We can see no justification for the Council's failure to meet since 15 January, in spite of the outbreak of the war, nor for the attempts to prevent it from responding to the requests made by Member States of the United Nations, and even by members of the Security Council itself, in order to deliberate on the new situation arising from the commencement of large-scale hostilities, which have constantly escalated and have intensified the dangers threatening the region. Today, these dangers have extended to numerous countries and there is a risk that the scope of this disaster might have a baneful effect on international peace and security and might even lead to the use of weapons of mass destruction.

The Member States of the United Nations have an unquestionable right, as affirmed in the Charter and the provisional rules of procedure of the Council, to request that the Council be convened so that they can express their views on matters relating to international peace and security.

It has been said that the time is inappropriate for a favourable response to the Maghrebi request. However, we do not accept the logic that there are inappropriate times to work for peace, to put an end to war and to seek a peaceful solution to an international crisis, since this would run counter to the primary and most noble purpose specified in the Charter of the United Nations.

As far as we are aware, some members have proposed that the Council should hold a private meeting, as provided for in rule 48 of its provisional rules of procedure. However, we cannot see the justification for that proposal, since it fails to meet the request of the countries of the Arab Maghreb and, in particular, in our view, does not meet the requirements of the present situation. The Council has persistently remained silent on the serious events in the Gulf for almost two and a half months. We fear that, under the present circumstances, this proposal might constitute a dangerous precedent in regard to the Council's recognition of the right of Member States to express their views, freely and without restriction, before the Council on matters relating to international peace and security. It might also constitute a dangerous precedent in regard to the Council's assumption of its responsibilities in this connection and also *vis-à-vis* international public opinion since, for the first time, a general debate would be held before the Council at a closed meeting. For all these reasons, the delegations of the States of the Arab Maghreb Union have notified Your Excellency in advance that they would not participate in such a meeting.

...

Your distinguished Council has never ceded, and cannot cede, its responsibilities to any other body. In this connection, it should be noted that, in acknowledgement of those responsibilities, the distinguished Council did, in fact, decide to remain seized of the matter of the situation in the Gulf, as indicated in operative paragraph 5 of resolution 678 (1990).

In view of the serious situation arising from the outbreak of the war in the Gulf, the countries of the Arab Maghreb embarked on a peaceful initiative by calling for a meeting of the Security Council, not on the suggestion or at the request of any party nor as an expression of opposition to any party whatsoever, but merely with a view to sparing bloodshed, saving the region from further destruction and devastation and maintaining international peace and security.

In a statement issued on 17 January, the Tunisian Government appealed to your distinguished Council to endeavour to put an end to the war as soon as possible. On 31 January 1991, Mr. Zine al-Abidine ben Ali, President of the Republic of Tunisia, sent letters to the Heads of State of the member States of the Security Council, calling upon them to facilitate and support the Maghrebi initiative. On the same day, the Minister for Foreign Affairs sent a letter to the President of the Security Council, concerning the dangers threatening peace and security as a result of the Gulf war.

Tunisia was one of the first States to announce its rejection of the occupation and to call for withdrawal from Kuwait, initially in an official government statement and subsequently within the context of the resolution adopted by the Council of the League of Arab States on 3 August. Tunisia has also complied fully with all the resolutions adopted by the Security Council on the basis of Chapter VII of the Charter. Since 2 August 1990, President Zine al-Abidine ben Ali has done his utmost to promote a peaceful solution, particularly within the Arab context, and has made representations to all the influential Arab and international parties concerned, and also to the Secretary-General of the United Nations.

Although those endeavours proved fruitless - and there was a possibility that they and other peaceful initiatives might have borne fruit, as happened when the foreigners were enabled to leave Kuwait and Iraq - that did not deter Tunisia from continuing its peaceful representations. In this connection, Tunisia embarked on numerous initiatives, which continued until 14 January when, with the permission of the President of the Republic, it proposed that the Security Council should announce a date for the holding of an international peace conference on the Middle East during the present year in order to find a peaceful, just, comprehensive and lasting solution to the question of Palestine and the Arab-Israeli dispute on the basis of the Security Council's own resolutions, in the belief that such a step would enable the Security Council to shoulder its responsibilities in regard to the Middle East, which has been looking to it and to the international community for justice for more than 40 years. That would also undoubtedly pave the way for a peaceful solution to the Gulf crisis and for the restoration of Kuwait's freedom and sovereignty.

In this regard, I can only express my deep sorrow that the Council has not as yet responded to Tunisia's request for the consideration of its proposal. This is inconsistent with the principles and purposes of the United Nations, which are based on justice and equality in dealing with events and disputes, and not on discrimination and selectivity. Justice, peace and security are indivisible principles and Tunisia is therefore maintaining and reaffirming its request in the hope that the Council will respond to it without delay.

...

The numerous initiatives on which Tunisia has embarked since the outbreak of the Gulf crisis, on an individual basis and also in association with other countries of the Maghreb, have been motivated by its firm commitment to the principles of justice and peace and its consistent desire to settle disputes by peaceful means.

We believe that the international community did not exhaust all peaceful ways and means before resorting to war. We note that this devastating war, in spite of its ferocity and the sophisticated weapons that have been used to cause severe loss of life and damage to institutions in Iraq, has not led to the liberation of Kuwait; on the contrary, the war is escalating every day, with the consequent risk of the use of weapons of mass destruction and extension of the scope of the war in a manner that could trigger an explosion throughout the region.

History has shown that solutions imposed by force and resulting from wars engender hatred and resentment without eliminating the real causes of disputes; they also fail to create conditions conducive to the establishment of relations based on lasting peace and mutual confidence among peoples and States. The quest for peaceful and just solutions is the best guarantee of stability and security in the Middle East.

...

The 15th of January was the deadline set by the Council for the Iraqi withdrawal from Kuwait and not for the commencement of the war, as proved to be the case.

The events that we have witnessed since 16 January have created a new situation that necessitates a review and rapid action on the part of the Council; a devastating war is being waged against Iraq, the infrastructure and human and material resources of which are being targeted. The air raids have not spared any location in Iraq and are being continued relentlessly. In spite of the censorship and obscurantism which have recently characterized the international information media in an unprecedented manner, we have seen unbearable pictures of the civilian victims of war, including children and elderly persons, in Iraq, particularly at Basra, in addition to the damage and destruction suffered by residential areas and civil institutions such as schools and hospitals.

This indiscriminate devastation has even extended to civilian shelters, as we observed in this morning's tragedy in which the conscience of the world was shaken by the devastating raid on a shelter in a residential area of the Iraqi capital, in which hundreds of defenceless women, children and elderly persons lost their lives.

We also wonder, with great concern, about the possibility of the dissemination of gases and nuclear radiation as a result of the bombardment of chemical and nuclear installations in Iraq. Was this the purpose of the Security Council resolutions, including resolution 678 (1990)? We do not believe that it was. The Council's clearly-expressed purpose in adopting those resolutions was to liberate Kuwait.

The distinguished Council is an instrument for the maintenance of peace, the avoidance of war and the settlement of international disputes, primarily by peaceful means and negotiation. In fact, this has been the Council's customary practice, which was imposed on the conflicting parties in the case of the question of Namibia, Angola, racial discrimination in South Africa, the Iran-Iraq war, Afghanistan, Cambodia and Central America. However, that example has not yet been followed in the case of the question of Palestine and the Arab-Israeli dispute.

The bombardment of Iraq, with all the consequent damage and destruction, will lead to a serious imbalance that could give Israel an opportunity to embark on further expansion and aggression. The clearest evidence of this can be found in the statement made by the Israeli Prime Minister after the attack on the Iraqi nuclear research centre in 1981, in which he arrogated to himself the right to bomb any Arab country in order to prevent it from achieving scientific progress.

...

Resolution 678 (1990) made provision for the use of all necessary means. Those means, although unspecified, are undoubtedly numerous and varied and some of them are detailed in Article 41 of the Charter. However, no provision was made for resort to war. If that had been the intention, there would have been no delay in the adoption of the clearly-defined measures contained in Articles 39, 42, 43, 46 and 47 of the Charter of the United Nations.

Can it be said with certainty that the Council intended to exclude any means, including peaceful means, other than war, which is permitted neither by the Charter nor by the lofty purpose for which the Council was established.

An even more serious aspect can be found in the fact that the war that we have been witnessing since 16 January was launched against cities and installations in Iraqi territory, the very existence of which, as a country and a people, was targeted, although the Council's objective was to liberate Kuwait.

At the same time, we cannot disregard the fact that neither the Council nor its Military Staff Committee, nor the Secretary-General, had any hand in planning the use of force or leading or even supervising the military operations. The Council did not conclude agreements with any of the States members of the coalition, as provided for in Article 43 of the Charter. Under these circumstances, does the Council have any firm guarantee that some States might not participate in the coalition and in the ongoing military operations in order to further certain interests or serve particular purposes other than the liberation of Kuwait?

...

When the cold war ended, the world rejoiced and prepared to harvest the fruits of peace and enjoy the benefits of a new international order based on the rule of law, peace and security. However, the world is now being propelled into a war which could have the most baneful consequences.

We want the new international order to be based on real justice and peace, on the settlement of international disputes by peaceful means, and on equality rather than discrimination and selectivity. The Security Council has a historic responsibility to render international relations impervious to the logic of violence and force and to finally renounce such logic when dealing with problems and disputes between nations and peoples.

We expressed our optimism that the United Nations would recover its standing and its central role within the context of the new international order with a view to building a future based on cooperation for development, prosperity, peace and security among nations and peoples in an atmosphere in which the rule of law, mutual understanding, equality, democracy and respect for human rights would prevail. Today, we expect your distinguished Council to make every effort to ensure that those hopes are not disappointed and that the logic of force and the language of weapons do not prevail.

...

In an address to the Tunisian people on Saturday, 26 January, President Zine al-Abidine ben Ali appealed to all the Arab and Muslim leaders and all peace-loving persons throughout the world who believe in the right of peoples to peace and security to call upon the Security Council to put an end to the hostilities and apply international law without discrimination or remissness, through the holding of an international peace conference during the present year in order to put an end to the Gulf crisis and find a solution to all the Middle Eastern questions, particularly the question of the struggling Palestinian people, since this question will remain a constant source of dire instability in the region until it is solved in a just and lasting manner that guarantees the right of the Palestinians to the establishment of their State on their land.

In the same address, he also said: "In our address on 11 August, we made it clear that we are against the use of force, by any party whatsoever, for the purpose of imposing solutions. We expressed our belief, which we still hold, that all questions, however complex, can be solved by peaceful means. We also believe that a rational approach, although it might be abandoned by one party, must not be abandoned by the international community. Although the problems facing the region have separate histories and direct causes, they are interrelated in regard to their geographical location and indirect motives. Sound and lasting solutions must be just and comprehensive, even though based on a specified time schedule.

...

Tunisia appeals to the Council to adopt an early resolution calling for an end to this war, which has begun to threaten peace and security throughout the Middle East and has transcended the provisions of your distinguished Council's resolutions, in order to provide a proper opportunity for the achievement of a peaceful solution to the Gulf crisis. We appeal to the Council to renounce the logic of war, which is incompatible with the principles and purposes of the Charter, and to adopt the logic of peace and peaceful solutions.

We call upon the distinguished Security Council to announce an immediate cease-fire, even if only for a specified period of time, in order to provide an opportunity for peaceful endeavours and propitious attempts to find a peaceful solution to the conflict within the framework of international law and in accordance with the principles of the United Nations, with a view to the maintenance of international peace and security.

Thank you, Mr. President.

S/22227, 15 February 1991

101. Letter from the Permanent Representative of the United States of America to the United Nations addressed to the President of the Security Council, 14 February 1991

...

Statement by the White House Press Secretary on 13 February 1991

Mr. Fitzwater: Last night, coalition forces bombed a military command and control centre at Baghdad that, according to press reports, resulted in a number of civilian casualties.

The loss of civilian lives in time of war is a truly tragic consequence. It saddens everyone to know that innocent people may have died in the course of military conflict. America treats human life as our most precious value. That is why even during this military conflict in which the lives of our servicemen and women are at risk, we will not target civilian facilities. We will continue to hit only military targets. The bunker that was attacked last night was a military target, a command and control centre that fed instructions directly to the Iraqi war machine, painted and camouflaged to avoid detection, and well-documented as a military target. We have been systematically attacking these targets since the war began.

We don't know why civilians were at this location, but we do know that Saddam Hussein does not share our value in the sanctity of life. Indeed, he, time and again, has shown a willingness to sacrifice civilian lives and property that further his war aims.

Civilian hostages were moved in November and December to military sites for use as human shields. Prisoners of war reportedly have been placed at military sites. Roving bands of execution squads search out deserters among his own ranks of servicemen. Command and control centres in Iraq have been placed on top of schools and public buildings. Tanks and other artillery have been placed besides private homes and small villages. And only this morning we have documentation that two MiG 21s have been parked near the front door of a treasured archeologic site which dates back to the twenty-seventh century B.C.

His environmental terrorism spreads throughout the Persian Gulf, killing wildlife and threatening human water supplies. And, finally, Saddam Hussein aims his Scud missiles at innocent civilians in Israel and Saudi Arabia. He kills civilians intentionally and with purpose.

Saddam Hussein created this war. He created the military bunkers. And he can bring the war to an end. We urge him once again to save his people and to comply with the United Nations resolutions.

Excerpts from speech by the Secretary of Defense, Richard Cheney, in the United States Chamber of Commerce, 13 February 1991

We've gone back and checked very carefully on the facility that was struck yesterday. It was indeed a military facility, a hardened bunker, camouflage painted on top, plugged into his military communications system. There is no question in my mind or in the minds of key people that we hit a military target.

Some have suggested this morning that Saddam might now be resorting to a practice of deliberately putting civilians in harm's way, deliberately putting civilians on what he knows are military targets.

I have no way of knowing whether or not that was the case in this instance, but we do know that he had previously placed hundreds of foreign civilians held hostage all last fall at strategic sites throughout Iraq. We do know that he's threatened to place prisoners of war at strategic targets throughout Iraq. We do know that he is placing military equipment in civilian areas, especially in Kuwait, but also in Iraq.

And just this morning we received a new piece of intelligence that's interesting because of what it reveals about his practice with respect to his effort to try to blur the lines between military capabilities and civilian areas. There is, in Iraq, a city called Ur. Ur contains ruins that span history. Of particular interest are the remains of the famed Saqqara pyramid. Recent satellite imagery obtained just this morning indicates that there are now two MiG 21s, combat aircraft to the Iraqi air force, parked right next to the pyramid, obviously an effort to use the archeologically significant facility to protect his military capabilities. Clearly he's demonstrated repeatedly a willingness to use his population and cultural artifacts in an effort to shield and protect his military equipment.

Excerpts from a briefing by Lieutenant General Thomas Kelly and Captain David Herrington, the Pentagon, 13 February 1991

At the very beginning of the campaign we announced, since the first day, that we were targeting strategic command and control positions. Those targets in downtown Baghdad struck over a period of time were part of that targeting package. The net effect of that targeting was to force the Iraqi military away from these centralized command and control facilities to alternate command and control facilities. What you are seeing on television today is one of the alternate command and control facilities that we knew was active.

Why do we know this was a command and control facility? We know a great deal about this facility. For example we know that it was constructed in the early 1980s during the Iran/Iraq war and it was converted to a military command and control facility in the late 1980s. As a part of that conversion it was taken over by the military. The command and control equipment already there was hardened for protection from a conventional bombing attack, and with electromagnetic pulse protection to allow for continued communication despite a possible nuclear explosion in the area.

The building was not for free access. It had a camouflage roof and a security fence with barbed wire around it. Finally, there apparently was no air raid siren. You would not expect civilians to be fleeing into this facility.

Excerpts from a briefing by Assistant Secretary Margaret Tutwiler, United States Department of State, 13 February 1991

It is not the policy of the United States Government intentionally to target civilians. It is the policy of Saddam Hussein. For our part, we have gone to extreme length, often at the risk to our own pilots, not to target civilians or areas where they live. Indeed, any civilian casualties are a result of a war that Saddam Hussein imposed. Had he complied with the will of the international community, ended his aggression and withdrawn from Kuwait there would be no war. Unfortunately and tragically, the Iraqi people are paying the price for his aggression. The United States did not invade, annex or destroy Kuwait; Saddam Hussein did. It is Saddam, not the allied coalition, who continues to put his narrow ambitions above the well-being of his people and the welfare of his country. It is Saddam Hussein, not the allied coalition, who continues purposely to attack civilian targets in Israel and Saudi Arabia. It is Saddam Hussein, not the allied coalition, who abuses prisoners of war and destroys the ecology of the Gulf. It is Saddam Hussein, not the allied coalition, who continues to defy the will of the entire international community. And it is Saddam Hussein who has the ability to stop the violence by immediately withdrawing from Kuwait. But once again, his personal, ruthless ambitions makes him indifferent to the cost to his own people.

Excerpts from a briefing by Brigadier General Richard Neal, United States Central Command, 13 February 1991

I am here to tell you that it was a military bunker. It was a command and control facility. It is one of many that have been used by the Iraqi Government throughout this operation. We have been systematically attacking these bunkers since the beginning of the campaign.

Within the last two weeks, this particular bunker became even more active as a command and control facility. It is a hardened shelter. The roof was just recently painted with a camouflage patina to keep it out of aviation vision.

S/22235, 15 February 1992

102. Letter from the Permanent Representative of Colombia to the United Nations addressed to the President of the Security Council, 15 February 1991

I have the honour to transmit to you the following text of a letter from the Minister for Foreign Affairs of Colombia, Mr. Luis Fernando Jaramillo, addressed to the Minister for Foreign Affairs of Israel, Mr. David Levi:

> "Sir,
>
> "My Government is following developments in the crisis in the Persian Gulf particularly closely and hopes that the withdrawal of Saddam Hussein from Kuwait, as stipulated by the resolutions of the United Nations Security Council, will be secured shortly.
>
> "I wish to express to you my Government's firm condemnation of Iraq's successive attacks on the territory of Israel, which have caused suffering among the civilian population and considerable material damage. The Government of Colombia pledges its solidarity with the Israeli people and hopes that peace and tranquillity will soon be restored to Israel.
>
> "I take this opportunity to convey to you the renewed assurances of my highest consideration."

S/22239, 19 February 1991

103. Letter from the Permanent Representative of Australia to the United Nations addressed to the President of the Security Council, 17 February 1991

In accordance with paragraph 4 of United Nations Security Council resolution 678 (1990) I am writing to inform you of actions taken by the Australian Government, pursuant to paragraphs 2 and 3 of that resolution, to uphold and implement United Nations Security Council resolution 660 (1990) and subsequent resolutions.

On 17 January Australian armed forces in co-operation with those other States seeking to liberate Kuwait of occupying Iraqi forces and to restore the legitimate government of Kuwait were committed to participation in armed action necessary to implement resolution 660.

Any armed action by Australian forces seeks only to bring about the speedy withdrawal of Iraq's forces from Kuwait, restoration of the legitimate authorities in Kuwait and the restoration of international peace and security in the area.

...

S/22248, 20 February 1991

104. Letter from the Permanent Representative of Italy to the United Nations addressed to the President of the Security Council, 20 February 1991

Further to the report submitted on 4 February (S/22194) and in accordance with paragraph 4 of Security Council resolution 678 (1990), I have the honour to inform that since that day the Italian military forces have continued to participate in joint military actions together with the coalition forces in order to secure the implementation of resolution 660 and all pertinent subsequent resolutions of the Council.

Italian forces have continued to attack military targets in the area of deployment of Iraqi troops. Italian naval forces, always in the framework of the coalition, have continued their mission of maritime interception, patrolling and escort in the Gulf waters.

...

S/22251, 21 February 1991

105. Letter from the Permanent Representative of France to the United Nations addressed to the President of the Security Council, 20 February 1991

Pursuant to paragraph 4 of Security Council resolution 678 (1990), I have the honour to inform you of the actions which the French armed forces are continuing to undertake, within the framework of plans formulated together with the members of the coalition of countries cooperating with Kuwait, with a view to securing compliance with resolution 660 (1990) and all the subsequent resolutions of the Council.

The elements of the French ground forces in place - which include two motorized-infantry regiments, two armoured light-cavalry regiments, one tank regiment, one artillery regiment, one engineers regiment, and two combat-helicopter regiments, in other words, nearly 12,000 men - have continued their preparations in liaison with other forces.

Our naval units are continuing to help protect vessels of the allied navies. In addition, French vessels monitoring, within the framework of the Western European Union, the embargo in the Straits of Tiran, Bab al Mandab and Hormuz have identified more than 6,800 ships since the beginning of the conflict, and have inspected nearly 140.

Lastly, since 17 January, French combat aircraft have carried out more than 800 missions, participating in attacks in Kuwait and Iraq on Iraqi forces and their infrastructure. Also since that date, other French aircraft have conducted 950 airspace-control missions.

...

A/45/962, S/22252, 21 February 1991

106. Letter from the Permanent Representative of Kuwait to the United Nations addressed to the Secretary-General, 20 February 1991

I have the honour to refer to my letter of 25 January 1991 concerning the urgent appeal by my Government addressed through you to the international community and the relevant agencies and institutions for medical and food supplies to the Kuwaiti civilian population in occupied Kuwait.

Since my letter to you, the situation of the civilian population in occupied Kuwait has deteriorated to a point where mass starvation is a very possible reality, the health situation is more than non-existing, and the harsh circumstances under which the captive population and in particular the women and children live demands an immediate action.

I should like to draw your attention to the Declaration on the Protection of Women and Children in Emergency and Armed Conflict, which stipulates that:

> "Women and children belonging to the civilian population and finding themselves in circumstances of emergency and armed conflict in the struggle for peace, self-determination, national liberation and independence, or who live in occupied territories, shall not be deprived of shelter, food, medical aid or other inalienable rights, in accordance with the provisions of the Universal Declaration of Human Rights, the International Covenant on Civil and Political Rights, the International Covenant on Economic, Social and Cultural Rights, the Declaration of the Rights of the Child or other instruments of international law" (General Assembly resolution 3318 (XXIX)).

I have been instructed by my Government to request the immediate dispatch of a medical team to Kuwait to deliver emergency medical supplies and to identify health needs of the civilian population in occupied Kuwait.

...

A/45/963, S/22257, 22 February 1991

107. Letter from the Permanent Representative of Kuwait to the United Nations addressed to the Secretary-General, 22 February 1991

I should like to inform you that today, Friday, Iraqi occupation forces are rounding up any Kuwaiti man, woman or child on the streets, blindfolding them and transporting them in vehicles to Iraq. These vehicles were also parked outside mosques awaiting those attending Friday prayers.

Even at this stage of intense diplomatic activity concentrating on withdrawal by Iraq from Kuwait, the occupation forces are bent on their dastardly behaviour against the civilian population.

S/22258, 23 February 1991

108. Letter from the Permanent Representative of Saudi Arabia to the United Nations addressed to the President of the Security Council, 20 February 1991

In pursuance of the provisions of paragraph 4 of the Security Council resolution 678 (1990) concerning the military operations and in implementation of the second paragraph of the aforementioned resolution, I have the pleasure to transmit to you, on behalf of my Government, an additional report on the military operations for the liberation of the State of Kuwait during the period from 3 February to 9 February 1991.

...

The overall objective of the Royal Saudi Forces has always been to implement the Security Council resolutions concerning the liberation of fraternal Kuwait. Military objectives during the third week of operations were to destroy the Iraqi command structure and neutralize their air defence system, military machine and capability, while avoiding civilian targets and also sparing known air defence artillery positions in civilian populated areas. Such sites are left untouched, even if this means difficulties for Saudi pilots. Operations took place as follows:

1. *Military operations*

Air

The Royal Saudi Air Force carried out 1,290 sorties against targets inside Iraqi and Kuwaiti territory.

Sea

Saudi Arabian forces took part in naval operations, the total number of naval sorties involving its vessels amounting to 90. They also exploded a number of mines, and naval aircraft carried out 180 sorties on patrol, reconnaissance and combat missions.

Land

The Saudi Arabian ground forces are carrying out armed reconnaissance operations inside Kuwait and engaging in skirmishes with Iraqi forward elements, involving the use of artillery and rocket-launchers.

2. *Casualties*

The Iraqi aggressors fired one Scud missile at the city of Riyadh on the morning of Friday, 24 Rajab A.H. 1411 (8 February A.D. 1991), as a result of which one person was injured.

3. *Refugees and prisoners of war*

The total number of Iraqi refugees fleeing as a result of their dissatisfaction with the war of aggression launched by the Iraqi régime has risen to 17 officers and 291 others. Prisoners of war number 52 officers and 655 others, all of whom are receiving full care and attention and being treated in accordance with the precepts of Islamic law and the third Geneva Convention of 1949. This treatment has been commended by the International Committee of the Red Cross (ICRC) team. It is also a major item of concern for the commander of the joint forces and the operational theatre, His Royal Highness General Prince Khalid Bin Sultan Bin Abdul-Aziz, who has set up a committee to meet weekly under his chairmanship, with the participation of the regional representative of ICRC in the Arabian peninsula, to provide assurance that they are receiving proper care and attention.

S/22259, 23 February 1991

109. Letter from the Permanent Representative of Saudi Arabia to the United Nations addressed to the President of the Security Council, 21 February 1991

In pursuance of the provisions of paragraph 4 of the Security Council resolution 678 (1990) concerning the military operations and in implementation of the second paragraph of the aforementioned resolution, I have the pleasure to transmit to you, on behalf of my Government, an additional report on the military operations for the liberation of the State of Kuwait during the period from 10 February to 18 February 1991.

...

The objective of the Royal Saudi Forces has always been to implement the Security Council resolutions concerning the liberation of fraternal Kuwait. Military objectives during the fourth week of operations were to weaken the Iraqi military machine (air defence systems, airfields, ammunition depots, aircraft and other items used for military purposes). It was once again emphasized to Saudi pilots that they should avoid civilian targets and populated areas in order not to inflict harm on civilian installations.

1. *Military operations*

Air

The Royal Saudi Air Force carried out 1,209 sorties against targets inside Iraqi and Kuwaiti territory.

Sea

Saudi Arabian forces took part in naval operations, the total number of naval aircraft sorties from their vessels amounting to 61. They also exploded 11 mines.

Land

The Saudi Arabian ground forces carried out reconnaissance operations involving arms fire inside the Kuwaiti theatre. There were clashes with forward enemy units involving direct fire by artillery, rocket-launchers and other arms, while mopping-up operations continued in the town of Khafji.

The past week saw a major increase in clashes along the Saudi/Kuwaiti border and inside Kuwait itself, for the purpose of inflicting as much damage as possible on the Iraqi ground forces stationed in the territory, besides the continuation of aerial bombardment operations inside Iraq and Kuwait.

2. *Casualties*

The Iraqi aggressors fired four Scud missiles as follows: one missile at Riyadh on Monday, 27 Rajab A.H. 1411 (11 February A.D. 1991), one missile at Jubail on Thursday, 30 Rajab A.H. 1411 (14 February A.D. 1991), and two missiles at Hafr al-Batin on Friday, 1 Sha'ban A.H. 1411 (15 February A.D. 1991), as a result of which four people suffered various injuries. Casualties resulting from air operations amounted to 10 killed and 13 wounded in the mopping-up operation in Khafji.

3. *Material damage*

Three F-15 and F-5 aircraft were lost and one workshop annex building was destroyed in Hafr al-Batin.

4. *Refugees and prisoners of war*

The total number of Iraqi refugees fleeing as a result of their dissatisfaction with the war of aggression launched by the Iraqi regime has risen to 26 officers and 394 others. Prisoners of war number 61 officers and 782 others, all of whom are receiving full care and attention and being treated in accordance with the precepts of Islamic law and the third Geneva Convention of 1949. This treatment has been commended by the International Committee of the Red Cross (ICRC) team. It is also a major item of concern for the commander of the joint forces and the operational theatre, His Royal Highness General Prince Khalid Bin Sultan Bin Abdul-Aziz, who is monitoring their conditions weekly together with the regional representative of ICRC in the Arabian peninsula, to provide assurance that they are receiving proper care and attention.

5. *The latest Iraqi initiative*

In the course of the last week, Iraq announced an initiative comprising the implementation of Security Council resolution 660 (1990) and including - according to its claim - the subject of withdrawal. However, the Iraqis hedged the initiative with conditions, including compensation for their war losses and the solution of Middle East problems, particularly the Arab-Israeli dispute and the Syrian presence in Lebanon, etc. Since the statement by the Iraqi Revolution Command Council included conditions which were incompatible with the sense and content of Arab, Islamic and international resolutions, in addition to new conditions which did not demonstrate any serious and sincere desire on the part of Iraq to implement the resolutions adopted in that connection, the Government of Saudi Arabia has already stated its categorical rejection of each and every detail of the statement issued by the Iraqi Revolution Command Council.

A/45/964, S/22261, 24 February 1991

110. Letter from the Permanent Representative of Kuwait to the United Nations addressed to the Secretary-General, 23 February 1991

Further to our letter of 22 February 1991 (A/45/963-S/22257) [*reprinted above*], I should like to inform you that Iraqi occupation forces are stepping up their repressive acts against the people of Kuwait. These acts include the following:

> 1. Setting of fire and explosions in downtown Kuwait City, the commercial centre, the coastal area stretching from Al-Seif Palace, the headquarters of the Council of Ministers, the National Assembly all the way to Shuweikh industrial zone and the port area.
>
> 2. Arrest of people in the streets, particularly at Al-Amriya area, district no. 3 where civilian residents are being rounded-up and taken to unknown locations.
>
> 3. Murdering of youth and dumping their bodies in the streets, particularly in "Al-Bayan" area. Some disfigured corpses were found there.

...

S/22267, 25 February 1991

111. Letter from the Representative of Lesotho to the United Nations addressed to the President of the Security Council, 25 February 1991

I have the honour to transmit herewith the text of the press release issued by the Ministry of Foreign Affairs, Maseru, on 25 February 1991 regarding the Gulf crisis.

...

The Government of Lesotho is gravely concerned about the non-observance by Iraq of the deadline for unconditional and complete withdrawal from Kuwait, as set by the multilateral coalition, operating under the mandate of the United Nations Security Council. The Lesotho Government is equally concerned that the initiative by President Gorbachev to persuade Iraq to withdraw from Kuwait has not been crowned with success.

Since the beginning of the Gulf crisis, the Government of Lesotho has joined the peace-loving community of nations in repeatedly and consistently calling on Iraq to comply with the resolutions of the Security Council, to withdraw from Kuwait and to allow the long-suffering people of the country to regain their sovereign nationhood and to rebuild their country.

The Government of Lesotho now urges President Saddam Hussein to comply immediately with the Security Council resolutions in order to avert any more unnecessary suffering and hardship by the people of Iraq and Kuwait. Unconditional implementation of the Security Council resolutions is the only guaranteed means by which peace and security can be restored in the Gulf region.

S/22292, 1 March 1991

112. Letter from the Permanent Representative of Canada to the United Nations addressed to the President of the Security Council, 26 February 1991

Further to our letter of 1 February 1991 (S/22192), and in accordance with paragraph 4 of resolution 678 (1990), Canadian Armed Forces in the Persian Gulf region continue to participate with other members of the United Nations in military action to enforce Iraqi compliance with resolution 660 (1990) and all subsequent relevant resolutions.

Aircraft of the Canadian Forces continue to provide air defence of multinational shipping in the Persian Gulf. In addition, the aircraft are conducting air-to-ground missions against Iraqi military targets in Kuwait and southern Iraq in support of the multinational enforcement action.

Her Majesty's Canadian ships continue to support multinational naval operations in the central and southern Persian Gulf. In addition to escort and logistics support, the ships have conducted a total of 1,855 interceptions and 22 boardings of international shipping while enforcing the United Nations sanctions programme against Iraq.

The Canadian field hospital is in the final stages of its deployment to the Kingdom of Saudi Arabia and it is expected to be complete by 28 February. Two advanced surgical teams from the hospital are already in operation with British Forces medical units to assist in the care and treatment of all casualties of war in accordance with the Geneva Convention.

Canada has deployed an oil spill clean-up assessment team to Bahrain and Qatar and is responding to requests for material and technical expertise to assist those countries. Canadian Forces aircraft have assisted in the air movement of German clean-up material from Europe to the Gulf.

Canada has informed the Secretary-General of its preparedness and capabilities to assist the United Nations in the Gulf once Iraq has complied with the applicable United Nations Security Council resolutions.

...

S/22295, 1 March 1991

113. Letter from the Permanent Representative of Israel to the United Nations addressed to the Secretary-General, 1 March 1991

I wish to draw your attention to the role played by the Palestine Liberation Organization (PLO) in Iraq's unprovoked acts of aggression against various States in the Middle East, including Israel.

PLO officials have repeatedly backed Iraq's aggression and its defiance of binding Security Council resolutions, having hailed it as "the battle for Palestine". They have added their voice and arms to Iraqi efforts aimed at undermining other Arab States in the region, urging Iraq to cross the brink of war.

Casting itself as an unabashed supporter of Iraqi aggression, with renewed fervour since the start of the Gulf crisis, the PLO has exhorted Saddam Hussein to resort to the illegal use of force and to employ his arsenal of weapons of mass destruction against the civilian population of Israel.

Since 18 January 1991 Iraq has launched 39 Scud missiles at Israeli cities, causing scores of casualties and considerable damage to property.

While the international community has reacted with revulsion to these unprovoked acts of aggression against the civilian population of a country not involved in the hostilities, the PLO has responded with exuberance. This attitude, which applauds aggression, should be a cause of serious concern for States Members of the United Nations.

PLO verbal plaudits have been accompanied by action. Arafat has instructed his followers to support Saddam Hussein against the international coalition and has attempted to draw Israel into the war by calling for acts of terrorism both within Israel and throughout the world. As part of that effort, the PLO has fired scores of Katyusha rockets from Southern Lebanon and has attempted to infiltrate armed groups across Israel's boundaries. The PLO has sought to gather information on potential targets and on missile landing-sites for Iraqi intelligence. Moreover, it has contributed to the Iraqi disinformation campaign by alleging Israeli participation in the Gulf War.

The above constitutes clear evidence as to the true character of the PLO. It is time for Governments and international organizations to draw the inevitable conclusions regarding this organization. Attached is an annex containing a selection of statements by PLO officials supporting Iraq's aggression and terrorism on its behalf.

...

I. SUPPORT FOR IRAQI AGGRESSION

Arafat:

"We now ask this question to those who inquire about the Palestine position. We ask: Where does Israel stand in this confrontation? ... We can only be in the trench hostile to zionism and its imperialist allies." (*Sawt al-Sha'b*, 4 September 1990)

"I say welcome, welcome, welcome to war ... Iraq and Palestine represent a common will. We will be side by side and after the great battle, God willing, we will pray together in Jerusalem ... The Iraqi fighters and the Palestinian stone-throwers have an appointment with victory together." (The Associated Press, 7 January 1991)

Speaking of Saddam: "I am not his ally. He is my ally, he is the strongest ally to my people and their occupation." (Canadian Broadcasting Service, 7 January 1991)

"Yasir Arafat expressed the support of the Palestinian Arab people and their leadership in the face of the imperialist-Zionist aggression. He asserted that Palestine and Iraq are standing in the same trench to regain Arab rights." (Baghdad INA, 14 January 1991)

Speaking of Saddam: "Mountain, O mountain, the wind will not move you." (Monte Carlo, 30 January 1991)

"We stand alongside the Iraqi people since our struggle against the Americans and their allies is the Palestinian struggle." (Agence France Presse, 9 February 1991)

"These are fabulous days for our Arab nation, as we are witnessing the mythical steadfastness of the Iraqi people and its heroic army commanded by my knightly brother Saddam ... This is the mother of battles, waged for the mother of causes, our beloved Palestine." (Algiers, Voice of Palestine, 11 February 1991)

On 25 February Arafat sent a message of support to Saddam Hussein following the launching of the ground offensive against Iraq.

In it, Arafat pays tribute to "the fight of the people and the army of Iraq against American hegemony and dictatorship."

"In this historic and crucial moment for our nation," declared the chief of the PLO, "I pray for your victory and promise you the support of our people, who fight the same war to protect the honour, nobility, security and existence of our nation." (Agence France Presse, 25 February 1991)

Farouk Kaddoumi ("Foreign Minister"):

"We Palestinians are 100 per cent behind Iraq against the American aggression." (*Die Presse*, Vienna, 31 January 1991)

Hani al-Hassan (Arafat's chief political adviser):

"We have coordinated our plans to fight with Iraq in one trench." (The Associated Press, 12 December 1990)

Excerpts from PLO Executive Council statement:

"We call today for a firm stand ... on the side of the steadfast and combatant Iraq in the confrontation of the American-Zionist-Atlantic aggression ... The PLO calls on all the peoples of our nation and its dynamic forces to participate in the battle of confronting the American and allied aggression ... The PLO extends a salute of military brotherhood to the steadfast people of Iraq and its militant President Saddam Hussein and the valiant Iraqi army ..." (Algiers, Voice of Palestine, 29 January 1991)

II. SUPPORT FOR IRAQI MISSILE ATTACKS AGAINST ISRAEL

Arafat:

Addressing a public rally in Baghdad on 29 March 1990, while standing beside Saddam Hussein, Arafat declared that both leaders would enter Jerusalem victoriously, with Saddam mounted on a white horse, fighting Israel with stones, rifles and the "El-Abed" - Iraq's long-range missiles. (The Associated Press, 29 March 1990)

"The Iraqi military will resort to its chemical and biological weapons and the first missile will be directed at Israel." (Reuters, 5 November 1990)

"The Palestinian stone in Jerusalem has turned into that binary missile in Baghdad." (Algiers, Voice of Palestine, 31 December 1990)

"The Palestinian stones in Jerusalem would become chemical missiles from Baghdad." (Baghdad, Voice of Palestine, 31 December 1990)

"We will answer the Zionist enemy and say to him in 1991: a land without the Israeli or Zionist people. This land is Arab, Arab, Arab, Palestinian in her face and Arab in her heart ... The holy Palestinian stone in the hand of the Palestinian child will turn into the binary missile - this is a symphony." (Baghdad Television, 31 December 1990)

The Iraqi missiles "took the air out of the Israeli balloon." (*Al-Houriyyah*, Reuters, 23 January 1991)

Abu Iyad (Arafat's second in command):

"What they need is a missile that will put them in their place." (*Al-Dustur*, 2 January 1991)

Farouk Kaddoumi:

"Kaddoumi does not regret Iraqi missile attacks against Israel: 'When someone fights our enemy, we are pleased'" (Vienna Domestic Service, 31 January 1991)

Hawatimah (Democratic Front for the Liberation of Palestine (DFLP)):

"The Iraqi bombardment of Israel is a real wedding and the punishment for Zionist aggression." (Arab Voice of Lebanon, 20 January 1991)

"DFLP today hailed the Iraqi missile attack on Israel. *Hawatimah* said that this action calls for celebration by the Palestinians." (Radio Monte Carlo, 20 January 1991)

"*Hawatimah* described the launching of the Iraqi missiles at Tel Aviv as a cause of 'real rejoicing' for the Palestinians." (*Al-Ahali*, Egypt, 22 January 1991)

"When they say that the missiles that fall on Israeli towns fall on populated areas, we would say: it is a tit for tat ... We all must have seen ... how the Algerian youth called out in one voice: 'O beloved Iraq, strike, strike Tel Aviv'. In saying this, they speak for all peoples ..." (Algiers Radio, 29 January 1991)

Habash (Popular Front for the Liberation of Palestine (PFLP)):

"Iraq has restored its credibility by launching missiles against Israel, causing great satisfaction among the ranks of the Palestinian people." (Voice of the Mountain, 20 January 1991)

"PFLP said that by pounding Tel Aviv and other Zionist colonialist gatherings, Iraq has carried out the promises it issued before the war. This resulted in great relief among the Palestinian people's ranks." (Baghdad Domestic Service, 20 January 1991)

Abu al-Abbas (PFLP):

"Our masses in the occupied homeland have seen the enemy's forces trembling with fear and rushing to shelters to escape the Iraqi missiles, which crushed the heads of the Zionist occupiers ... Palestine will, God willing, be liberated. Today, the missiles of Iraq reached Tel Aviv. Tomorrow, the march of the believers will reach holy Jerusalem." (Baghdad Domestic Service, 19 January 1991)

Abbas Zaki Mazid (PLO Central Committee member):

"For the first time in history Tel Aviv has been bombarded and an Arab leadership has proven by a premeditated action that al-Hussein missiles reach Tel Aviv and all strategic targets in the Zionist entity. Shamir and all the arrogant forces were struck with fear and are totally impotent in the face of the fabulous steadfastness and tremendous combat capability of the secret Iraqi cavalry ... You have given the Palestinian people the most beautiful gifts ... The al-Hussein missiles constitute the most important gift in this dark era." (Baghdad Radio, 8 February 1991)

Muhammad Jihad (PLO official responsible for military affairs in Jordan):

"We are happy about the Scud missile attacks on Israel." (Berlin, *Der Morgen*, 30 January 1991)

Yasser Abd Rabbo (PLO Executive Committee member):

"... said Iraq has the right to attack Israel, as it is one of the parties in the confrontation. When asked about the firing of Iraqi missiles against Israel he praised the action." (French, British news agencies, 20 January 1991)

"The missiles have toppled the myth of the Israeli security barrier." (Baghdad Radio, 8 February 1991)

"Palestinian sources in South Lebanon said the purpose of the Katyusha attack was to do 'what the Iraqi Scuds had not yet succeeded in doing: to drag Israel into the Gulf war. When the Israelis react with fire, we shall turn this into an Israeli-Arab war'. The sources reported that Arafat has ordered the attack 'to defend innocent people in Iraq.'" (Agence France Presse, 29 January 1991)

III. FALSE ALLEGATIONS AS TO ISRAEL'S PARTICIPATION IN THE WAR

Arafat:

"I have information that Israel has been totally implicated in the war from the start ... Some of their planes participate in the attacks ... Moreover, there are missiles used by the Israeli Army from the Negev desert near Dimona against the western part of Iraq." (Paris Antenne-2 Television Network, 29 January 1991)

"Who said that Israel is not participating? Israel is taking part with its aircraft, its aircraft are deployed alongside United States aircraft at a number of bases ... there is now shelling from the Negev. The United States is covering this up and saying that submarines deployed in the Red Sea are doing the shelling. This is not correct. The shelling is originating from surface-to-surface missile launchers in the Negev." (Radio Monte Carlo, 30 January 1991)

Yasser Abd Rabbo:

Claimed that Israel, since the beginning of the war, has deployed aircraft in Turkish bases. (Agence France Presse, Reuters, 20 January 1991)

PLO representative in Mexico:

"Israel brought hundreds of Palestinians to the Israeli nuclear centre in the Negev so that they can serve as 'human shields' against a possible Iraqi missile attack." (*Uno más Uno*, 1 February 1991)

Bassam Abu-Sharif (adviser to Yasser Arafat):

"The B-52 bombers are being drawn from bases in Britain, Spain, Diego Garcia and Israel." (Reuters, 4 February)

"Abu-Sharif said the stationing of Patriot missiles in Israel was proof that Israel is now 'part of the war'." (Monte Carlo, 21 January 1991)

IV. TERRORISM IN SUPPORT OF IRAQ

Yasser Arafat is supplying the Iraqi intelligence services with hundreds of Tunisian, Algerian and Moroccan passports to assist the Iraqis in attacking American and other targets. (*Rhein-Pfalz*, 22 January 1991)

Hawatimah:

Each and every Arab people is called upon to besiege and strike at United States, British, and French interests wherever their hands can reach." (Algiers Radio, 29 January 1991)

George Habash:

"The Palestinian fedayeen will strike Western targets hostile to Iraq." (Radio Monte Carlo, 31 January 1991)

Muhammad Jihad:

"The PLO has stated that it will support Iraq all it can in order to face the United States-Israeli aggression. This means an armed fight against our enemy Israel, with guns, bombs and knives." (Berlin, *Der Morgen*, 30 January 1991)

Yasser Abd-Rabbo:

"The Palestinian fighters who launched an attack today against a convoy of the Israeli enemy in the heart of the Negev near the Dimona reactor are not only brothers-in-arms to the Iraqi fighters on the front, but share one destiny with her. Together, the Palestinian and Iraqi rifles are conducting the battle for the national destiny." (Baghdad Radio, 8 February 1991)

Abd al-Rahim Ahmad (PLO Executive Committee member):

"We urge the masses of our Arab nation and the Muslims to expand the theater of confrontations over the whole world. They must strike violently all United States interests and institutions everywhere." (INA, 22 January 1991)

Zayid Wahbah (PLO representative in Lebanon):

"When the shooting begins on Iraqi forces, the Palestinian forces will attack American interests in Palestine, outside Palestine and around the world." (Voice of the People, 14 January 1991)

"We'll act from Lebanon, Amman, Cairo and Damascus and orders have been given to fighters to prepare to attack United States and British interests around the world." (Agence France Presse, 16 January 1991)

"Zayid Wahbah called for attacking the interests of the coalition members and fighting the United States and Israel under the leadership of the president of Iraq." (Reuters, 27 January 1991)

V. THE PLO IN LEBANON: OPENING A SECOND MISSILE FRONT AGAINST ISRAEL

"Palestinian sources have said that Palestinian leader Yasir Arafat has called on the Palestinians in Lebanon to fight on the side of Iraq if a war breaks out in the Gulf. Palestinian sources also said that approximately 6,000 Palestinian fighters in the Sidon area have been placed on high alert." (Voice of Lebanon, 14 January 1991)

Arafat:

Concerning firing rockets at Israel, Arafat said, "It is our legal right" (Radio Monte Carlo, 30 January 1991)

Hawatimah:

"I call upon all PLO detachments to join the national Lebanese forces in the carrying out of fedayeen operations against the Zionist occupation forces in Southern Lebanon so that we can divert the largest possible power of the Israeli Army away from the battlefront with Iraq. I call on all PLO detachments ... to join in the fedayeen operations in Southern Lebanon and in the heart of Israel so that we prevent the Israeli forces from having a free hand ..." (Algiers Radio, 28 January 1991)

"DFLP ... called for clashing with and using arms against the Israeli enemy whenever possible and urged all the Palestinian fighters in Southern Lebanon to ... confront the Israeli enemy with arms and fire in order to open a new front with the enemy forces and zionism." (Amman, *Al-Ra'y*, 29 January 1991)

Zayid Wahbah:

"Zayid Wahbah has threatened that the PLO will shell deep inside Israel if the international alliance continues its raids on Iraqi civilians and installations. Wahbah said: Do not forget that we are struggling alongside Iraq, and that Southern Lebanon is an open front to contribute to the defence of Iraq." (Voice of Lebanon, 28 January 1991)

"Wahbah told AFP on 28 January that the PLO military forces are ready to launch attacks and bombardments deep inside Israel, if the bombardment of Iraqi civilians and institutions continues ... He added that one should not forget the PLO is fighting on the side of Iraq, and South Lebanon is an open front ... He called on the other Arab States bordering on Israel to fulfil their obligation and strike the Israeli enemy in order to thwart the destruction of Iraq ... these countries should enable Palestinian and Arab fighters to join in the battle from their own fronts." (Agence France Presse, 28 January 1991)

"We will respond to the attacks against Iraq by hitting targets inside Israel ... we view ourselves as part of the campaign in the Gulf." (Reuters, 29 and 30 January 1991)

Saher Habash (PLO Executive Committee member):

"The Fatah bases, the Palestinian resistance and the Lebanese national resistance front in Southern Lebanon have opened a front in South Lebanon against the Zionist enemy, in support of the just Arab front which Iraq is defending. This front will be an effective armed front in support of Iraq. He called for the opening of another front against the Zionist enemy from the Syrian-Palestinian border." (*Al-Jumhuriya*, Iraqi News Agency, 1 February 1991)

"In Sidon in Southern Lebanon, a PLO spokesman affirmed that Palestinian fighters shelled four settlements in northern Israel at dawn today. He indicated that 80 Grad projectiles were fired at the settlements of Metulla, Misgav Am, Kefar Gil'adi, and Nahariya." (Radio Monte Carlo, 29 January 1991)

"Palestinian sources in South Lebanon have announced the establishment of a unified military command embracing all Palestinian organizations to coordinate military action and open a front against Israel in South Lebanon to support Iraq." (Voice of Lebanon, 5 February 1991)

"A member of the PLO military leadership in Lebanon, Lt. Cl. Amran, said that Arafat and the PLO command gave instructions to increase the struggle against Israel in response to her military cooperation in the Gulf ... He said: 'The implementation of the instructions has already begun with the bombardment of a number of Zionist settlements in the Galilee ...'" (Agence France Presse, 29 January 1991)

"The PLO spokesman said the PLO has decided to carry out qualitative operations and escalate the armed struggle against Israel in solidarity with Iraq." (Free Lebanon Radio, 4 February 1991)

S/22341, 8 March 1991

114. Letter from the Permanent Representative of the United States of America to the United Nations addressed to the President of the Security Council, 5 March 1991

In accordance with paragraph 4 of resolution 678 (1990), I wish, on behalf of my Government, to submit the following report on actions undertaken pursuant to paragraphs 2 and 3 of that resolution up to the time of the suspension of offensive military operations against Iraq by coalition military forces at midnight (eastern standard time) on 27 February.

On the night of 23 February (eastern standard time), the military forces of the coalition, including United States' military forces, acting in accordance with Security Council resolution 678 (1990), launched ground operations to obtain full Iraqi compliance with all 12 relevant Security Council resolutions, and particularly to ensure the full withdrawal of Iraqi forces from Kuwait.

This move by the combined surface, naval and air units of the coalition forces came about following intensive diplomatic efforts aimed at achieving peaceful Iraqi withdrawal and after provocative actions by the Government of Iraq, including the continued indiscriminate launching of surface-to-surface missiles at civilian targets, commencement of a "scorched earth" policy, including large-scale destruction of oil facilities and public and private buildings in Kuwait, and evidence of increased atrocities against the Kuwaiti civilian population.

At least 600 oil installations were set on fire prior to 23 February. Coalition forces have physical evidence that these fires were deliberately set by Iraqi forces and have in their possession captured Iraqi documents giving orders to destroy oil installations. In the last few days of their occupation of Kuwait, Iraqi forces deliberately set about destroying major public buildings and hotels and some private residences.

Members of the Kuwaiti resistance report that in addition to cases of torture, rape and murder committed by the Iraqi forces during the period of control of Kuwait (currently being documented by the international media), large numbers of Kuwaiti civilians were rounded up and detained during the last days of Iraqi occupation. It is believed that these detainees were transferred to Iraq.

In response to these actions and in accordance with Security Council resolution 678 (1990), United States and other coalition ground forces attacked on several fronts on the night of 23 February. The operation included an outflanking movement to prevent the Iraqi forces in southern Iraq from moving into Kuwait. At no time did the coalition forces have any intention of destroying Iraq or of attacking Baghdad.

In a briefing on the last day of the military action, General Norman Schwarzkopf gave a description of the planning and execution of the ground campaign. He explained that a key purpose of the extensive coalition air campaign in the weeks leading up to 23 February was to isolate the Kuwaiti theatre of operations by destroying all the bridges and supply lines that ran between the northern and southern parts of Iraq. He said this action was taken to prevent the reinforcement and supply of forces in southern Iraq and Kuwait. Heavy bombing was necessary, he explained, to weaken Iraqi forces, particularly along the front line barrier that coalition forces would have to go through. He explained that once Iraqi air reconnaissance was deterred by coalition control of the air, in a massive move to the west, coalition personnel, equipment and supplies were positioned to outflank the Iraqi forces.

Coalition forces rapidly achieved their objectives of defeating the Iraqi forces that had carried out the invasion and occupation of Kuwait, and of permitting the return of the territory of Kuwait to its legitimate Government. This success constitutes a significant milestone towards the goal of restoring international peace and security to the area as set forth in Security Council resolution 678 (1990).

In the course of the engagement, coalition forces captured more than 50,000 Iraqi soldiers. These prisoners of war (POWs) have been treated in accordance with the Third Geneva Convention Relative to the Treatment of Prisoners of War, which has included the provision of medical care, shelter, food and water.

The Iraqi Government continues to hold United States POWs, other coalition POWs, an undetermined number of Kuwaiti civilians and military personnel, and other civilians of different nationalities. The Iraqi authorities have refused representatives of the International Committee of the Red Cross (ICRC) access to coalition POWs and have refused to enter into discussions with ICRC on those listed as missing in action.

The Iraqi forces continued to fire surface-to-surface missiles until the last days of the military engagement. The total number of such missiles fired since 16 January was 81 - 41 against Saudi Arabia, 38 against Israel, one against Bahrain and one against Qatar.

Coalition air attacks against military and strategic targets in Iraq and Kuwait continued until the suspension of military operations. Coalition forces took every precaution to minimize collateral damage to civilian facilities. The Iraqi Government, however, intentionally placed civilians at risk through its behaviour. Following are a few concrete examples of such behaviour:

(a) The Iraqi Government moved significant amounts of military weapons and equipment into civilian areas with the deliberate purpose of using innocent civilians and their homes as shields against attacks on legitimate military targets;

(b) Iraqi fighter and bomber aircraft were dispersed into villages near military airfields where they were parked between civilian houses and even placed immediately adjacent to important archaeological sites and historic treasures;

(c) Coalition aircraft were fired upon by anti-aircraft weapons in residential neighbourhoods in various cities. In Baghdad, anti-aircraft sites were located on hotel roofs;

(d) In one case, military engineering equipment used to traverse rivers, including mobile bridge sections, was located in several villages near an important crossing point. The Iraqis parked each vehicle adjacent to a civilian house.

Total casualties reported as of 1 March for United States forces participating in military actions in accordance with Security Council resolution 678 (1990) are 79 killed in action, 241 wounded in action and at least 44 missing or captured in action.

On 27 February, in an address to the nation, President Bush reported coalition action against Iraq had been successful and thus the coalition would suspend offensive combat operations as of midnight (eastern standard time) on that day.

In conclusion, I would like to quote from that address, in which President Bush said: "no one country can claim this victory as its own. It was not only a victory for Kuwait, but a victory for all the coalition partners. This is a victory for the United Nations, for all mankind, for the rule of law and for what is right."

...

S/22350, 14 March 1991

115. Letter from the Permanent Representative of Saudi Arabia to the United Nations addressed to the President of the Security Council, 14 March 1991

In accordance with paragraph 4 of Security Council resolution 678 (1990), and pursuant to paragraphs 2 and 3 of the said resolution, I have pleasure in transmitting to you herewith an additional report on the progress of the military operations undertaken by the armed forces operating under the command of General Khalid bin Sultan bin Abdul Aziz, commander of the joint forces and the theatre of operations, during the period 18-24 February 1991.

...

As you are aware, each of the States concerned has been notifying the Security Council, separately and consecutively, of the extent of the progress achieved in the measures that they are taking pursuant to paragraph 4 of Security Council resolution 678 (1990).

However, given the fact that the allied forces are stationed in the Kingdom of Saudi Arabia under our command, and in view of the joint endeavours that they are undertaking to liberate the sister State of Kuwait from Iraqi occupation and to restore international peace and security in the region, we have deemed it appropriate to save time and simplify the formalities, while achieving the same objective, by confining ourselves to a single joint report on all the collective measures and on the progress of the military operations of those forces, which I shall prepare and transmit to you, on behalf of those forces, in my capacity as commander of the joint forces and the theatre of operations.

Since the allied forces have a duty to implement the Security Council resolutions, during the fifth week of the operations the High Command diligently continued to weaken the Iraqi military machine and prepare the way for the ground campaign to recover the State of Kuwait while, at the same time, urging the pilots to avoid civilian targets and populated areas with a view to preventing civilian casualties or damage to civilian institutions.

I have pleasure in submitting the following first joint report:

The operations from 4 Sha'ban A.H. 1411 (18 February 1991) to 10 Sha'ban A.H. 1411 (24 February 1991) were conducted as follows:

1. Military operations

Air

The Royal Saudi Air Force flew 1,147 sorties against targets inside Iraq and Kuwait.

Sea

The Royal Saudi Navy took part in the naval operations. The total number of naval aircraft sorties on rescue missions and patrols amounted to 730.

Land

1. A mechanized infantry division, an armoured division and a commando brigade belonging to the Egyptian armed forces participated in the artillery bombardments of the enemy and also took part in the overall offensive.

2. A division and a commando brigade belonging to the Syrian armed forces participated in engagements with enemy patrols and also took part in the overall offensive.

3. Saudi ground forces carried out artillery bombardments, engaged a number of enemy patrols and opened several breaches in the enemy's positions. They joined in the overall offensive as part of the joint forces.

During the past week, there was a notable intensification of engagements on the Saudi-Kuwaiti border, and also inside Kuwait itself, with a view to inflicting maximum losses on the Iraqi ground forces stationed there. The aerial bombardments also continued inside Iraq and Kuwait, prior to the commencement of the ground campaign, with a view to minimizing human casualties.

2. Human casualties

These casualties were caused primarily by six Scud missiles which the Iraqi aggressor launched into the territory of the Kingdom of Saudi Arabia. The human casualties resulting from the battles that took place from the beginning of the offensive to the time of preparation of this report amounted to four killed, five wounded and four personnel carriers destroyed.

3. Material damage

This damage consisted mainly in the destruction of a school, as well as structural damage to neighbouring buildings in the city of Riyadh, caused by a Scud missile launched by the enemy at 4.45 a.m. on Sunday, 10 Sha'ban A.H. 1411 (24 February 1991).

4. Prisoners of war

The total number of Iraqi prisoners amounted to 141 officers and 1,899 other ranks, all of whom are receiving full care and attention and are being treated in accordance with the precepts of Islamic law and the provisions of the Third Geneva Convention of 1949. This treatment was commended by the team of the International Committee of the Red Cross.

Wishing to satisfy myself that the prisoners were being treated in a humanitarian and dignified manner in keeping with our Islamic ideals and principles, I paid an inspection visit to them during which I reassured myself in regard to their situation and proper treatment and issued the necessary directives in that connection to the responsible officials.

...

S/22358, 18 March 1991

116. Letter from the Permanent Representative of France to the United Nations addressed to the President of the Security Council, 15 March 1991

Pursuant to paragraph 4 of Security Council resolution 678 (1990), I have the honour to present to you a summary report on all the military operations carried out by the French armed forces with a view to the liberation of Kuwait, within the framework of the plans established jointly with the members of the coalition of countries cooperating with Kuwait.

Concerning ground forces, a division stationed in Saudi Arabia from the end of September 1990 to 23 February 1991 participated in the land offensive from 24 to 28 February, effecting a breakthrough and an encircling movement over a distance of 150 km. Two lives were lost, and 25 persons were wounded due to mine explosions.

Since 28 February, it has continued to ensure the safety of all the coalition forces facing the north-west.

Also since 28 February, a French detachment has been stationed in Kuwait City, in the compound of the French Embassy, which was able to reopen on the same day. Since that time, this detachment has responded to numerous requests from Kuwaiti and allied forces for assistance with mine-clearing operations, notably on the Kuwait City beach.

The Air Force deployed 48 combat aircraft and 22 support craft.

Until 17 January, our aircraft took part in missions for the air defence of the countries of the region.

From 17 January to 23 February, all our airborne forces were engaged in operations aimed at destroying hostile logistic installations and depots on the ground and weakening combat means to the greatest possible extent, with efforts also aimed at intelligence.

During the latter two phases, our Air Force carried out more than 2,700 sorties, including 826 ground attacks (bombing), 63 reconnaissance (intelligence) missions, 379 air defence missions and 1,460 support missions (in-flight refuelling, logistic transport, liaison).

As for naval forces, a regiment of combat helicopters embarked on an aircraft-carrier was put in place in the area on about 20 August 1990.

In addition, 12 vessels are taking part, either within a national framework or as part of EWU naval groups, in the monitoring of the Tiran, Bab al Mandab and Hormuz Straits: 7,612 vessels have been identified, 158 searched and 4 turned back.

Within the framework of the EWU naval groups, our vessels have also been engaged in escort, mine-clearing and straits surveillance operations.

French military operations ceased one hour before the announcement of the suspension of hostilities on 28 February, 0600, Paris time.

...

S/22413, 28 March 1991

117. Letter from Saudi Arabia transmitting a report on the progress of military operations, 28 March 1991

Further to our letter of 26 February 1991, which contained the joint report of the coalition forces on the military operations they had carried out on land, at sea and in the air during the period 18-26 February 1991 with a view to undermining the military strength of the Iraqi forces in preparation for the overall ground campaign for the liberation of the State of Kuwait, we should like to inform you that the ground campaign on all fronts began on Sunday, 24 February 1991, lasted a mere 100 hours and ended in the rout of the Iraqi forces and thence in the acceptance by the Iraqi Government of all 12 Security Council resolutions, as well as resolution 686 (1991).

...

I. *Military operations*

(a) *In the air*

1. The Air Force of the United Arab Emirates flew 91 sorties from the beginning of the air campaign.
2. The Bahraini Air Force flew 278 sorties from the beginning of the air campaign.
3. The Qatar Air Force flew 63 sorties from the beginning of the air campaign.
4. The Kuwaiti Air Force flew 792 sorties from the beginning of the air campaign.
5. The Royal Saudi Air Force flew 1,169 sorties against targets in Iraq and Kuwait.

(b) *At sea*

1. The Royal Saudi Naval Forces carried out naval operations, and there were 64 sea-borne missions in all.
2. Aircraft of the Royal Saudi Naval Forces completed 178 flight-hours carrying out patrols and rescue missions.

(c) *On land*

1. The United Arab Emirates contributed a unit estimated at brigade strength to the forces that entered Kuwait for its liberation and for mopping-up operations.
2. Bahrain contributed a unit estimated at company strength to the Saudi units that entered Kuwait for its liberation and for mopping-up operations.
3. The Syrian Arab Republic contributed an armoured division reinforced with an élite strike brigade to the overall assault operation for the liberation of Kuwait, and it is now in position and performing its functions for Kuwait's defence.
4. Oman contributed a force estimated at batallion strength to the forces that entered the City of Kuwait for its liberation and for mopping-up operations.
5. Qatar contributed a force estimated at brigade strength to the forces that entered Kuwait for its liberation and for mopping-up operations.
6. Kuwait contributed an estimated force of three brigades to the overall assault operation for the liberation of Kuwait.
7. The Arab Republic of Egypt contributed two divisions reinforced with an élite strike brigade to the overall assault operation for the liberation of Kuwait. They achieved their objectives and are participating in securing and defending the State of Kuwait.
8. The Kingdom of Morocco contributed a force estimated at regimental strength during the ground campaign to defending vulnerable locations within the Kingdom of Saudi Arabia.

9. Some 330 individuals belonging to the Afghan Mujahidin participated and defended vulnerable areas.

10. The Islamic Republic of Pakistan contributed a brigade to the defence of the Ar'ar area.

11. The People's Republic of Bangladesh contributed a force of one brigade, some of its units are defending vulnerable locations within the Kingdom of Saudi Arabia, and their medical units are carrying out duties in treating the war-wounded.

12. The Republic of Senegal contributed a force estimated at batallion strength to the defence of vulnerable and important locations within the Kingdom of Saudi Arabia.

13. The Republic of the Niger contributed a force estimated at batallion strength to the forces that entered the State of Kuwait for its liberation, and it is defending the headquarters and administrative support areas.

14. The Czech and Slovak Federal Republic contributed a chemical warfare unit estimated at company strength to the forces that entered the State of Kuwait for its liberation and for mopping-up operations.

15. The Saudi armed forces contributed five reinforced brigades in the overall assault operation that began on Sunday, 24 February 1991, with the goal of liberating the State of Kuwait. They achieved their objectives and are now mopping up in Kuwait City and other towns. They stand prepared to defend the State of Kuwait and the Kingdom of Saudi Arabia.

II. *Casualties*

Country	*Dead*	*Wounded*
United Arab Emirates	6	2
Bahrain	-	2
Syrian Arab Republic	-	1
Oman	-	1
Kuwait	1	3
Egypt	10	83
Senegal	- (by missile (fragments) fired at Saffaniyah)	8
Czechoslovakia	-	1
Saudi Arabia	33	123

III. *Prisoners of war*

The total number of prisoners of war, officers and men, held by the coalition forces is 50,568. All are receiving scrupulous care, and they are being treated in accordance with the precepts of Islamic law and the provisions of the third Geneva Convention of 1949. The joint command of the theatre of operations has endeavoured to ensure that Iraqi prisoners are treated in a humane and dignified manner, in keeping with our Islamic ideals and principles. Our forces have been instructed not to engage enemy elements who lay down their arms, to deal kindly with prisoners and to provide immediate attention to those wounded. Furthermore, I met this week with the delegate of the International Committee of the Red Cross, who has visited the Iraqi prisoner-of-war camp and the Saudi hospitals that have admitted enemy wounded for treatment. He expressed great admiration for the care that he saw being provided to prisoners and for the excellent treatment accorded to the Iraqi wounded in Saudi hospitals, which, given that the Kingdom of Saudi Arabia honours its international obligations, is the same as that received by the wounded from the coalition countries.

IV. *The Safwan meeting*

In an endeavour to attain the fulfilment of the conditions laid down by the Security Council for a declaration of an end to hostilities between the coalition forces and Iraqi forces preparatory to the establishment of a lasting peace in the Gulf region following the acceptance by the Iraqi Government of the resolutions adopted by the Security Council, a military delegation representing the coalition forces, under the leadership of General Norman Schwartzkopf, commander of Operation Desert Storm and Supreme Commander of the United States Central Command, and of myself in the capacity of commander of the joint forces and the theatre of operations, met at Safwan on Sunday, 3 March 1991, with an Iraqi military delegation consisting of the Deputy Chief of General Staff, a senior officer and an official of the Iraqi Ministry of the Interior so that the coalition countries could lay down the military conditions necessary for a cease-fire prior to reaching a cease-fire agreement at a subsequent stage.

The coalition delegation laid down the military conditions which, with the approval of the Iraqi side, might lead to agreement on a cease-fire. They were:

> (a) Immediate release of prisoners of war, with the establishment of a times [*sic*] and locations for their release, and release of civilian detainees, including Kuwaitis seized by the Iraqi forces in Kuwait.
>
> (b) Disclosure of all information relating to persons missing as a result of hostilities, and the return of the remains of those who have died in captivity or been killed in the course of military operations.
>
> (c) Provision of full information on all minefields, booby traps and weapons that might remain in the State of Kuwait.
>
> (d) Agreement on security and safety arrangements with a view to ensuring that there would be no accidental confrontations that might lead to a renewed outbreak of fighting. Such arrangements would guarantee the safety of all forces under the command of the Iraqi forces, including ships and aircraft.

The meeting had extremely positive results, in that the Iraqi side agreed to all the conditions laid down, bringing us to regard this as a historic meeting heralding an end to the war and the establishment of a lasting peace in the region under the new international order. I am optimistic that there will be no obstacle in the way of reaching a durable cease-fire agreement.

A/45/990, S/22444, 4 April 1991

118. Letter from the Permanent Representative of Kuwait to the United Nations addressed to the Secretary-General, 4 April 1991

On instructions from my Government, and in an attempt to assess the damages inflicted on the oil industry in Kuwait, I should like to inform you of the following preliminary assessment of damages to the oil wells:

> Out of the 1,080 producing wells in Kuwait, nearly 700 have been badly damaged.
>
> One of the problems is the large-scale danger of mines, unexploded bombs and boobytraps.
>
> With regard to specific fields, out of the 703 wells of the greater Burgan area fields, 365 are on fire. The Burgan area is very dangerous in terms of having unexploded mines and bombs. In the Menagish field, there are 22 wells that

are gushing with oil, but not burning. Again, the Menagish area is difficult to access because of the bombs and mines, but the real danger here is that the fields are emitting H2S gas in a very high concentration. To emphasize, 400 ppm is considered lethal but, in some areas, the concentration has been tested for as high as 20,000 ppm. There is a fear that, depending on the weather, there may be a development of large pockets of H2S in the air. Additionally, as water seeps into the field, more H2S is being produced.

In the Magwa field, the number of total wells burning is not yet identified, but there is a large oil spill of eight acres in size coming out from four wells, which is likely to close the main Ahmadi to Magwa Road. There is a concern that this oil seepage might catch fire.

Among the potential long-term damages to the wells are the serious water cuts in many of the wells. It is felt that, in six months, most of the wells would face water seepage. As an example, whereas the Burgan crude used to contain a maximum of 2 per cent of water, in some of the flank wells what was gushing out was 100 per cent water and, in other wells, water was coming through faster than oil. Additionally, there would be pressure loss in the reservoirs leading to a build-up of the deposits, which could close or kill some wells. The possibility of severe corrosion at the well tubing is a cause for concern as well.

As indicated, the above is a preliminary list of damages to the oil wells. As to the other sectors of the oil industry, the Kuwaiti Government is in the process of finalizing the assessment of the full extent of the damages to the refineries, tankage farms, loading terminals, pipelines and oil-gathering centres.

...

S/22438, 3 April 1991

119. Letter from the Permanent Representative of Iraq to the United Nations addressed to the Secretary-General, 3 March 1991

On instructions from my Government and further to the letter of the Deputy Prime Minister and Minister for Foreign Affairs of the Republic of Iraq addressed to you on 1 February 1991, I have the honour to transmit herewith a list of the civilian losses of Iraqi civilians and civilian property.

...

Baghdad governorate

I. 9 February 1991

Air raids aimed at the 14 July and Martyrs suspension bridges, which sustained large-scale damage. Two citizens were killed as a result of the raid and six wounded. Another citizen was drowned in the Tigris River.

II. 6 to 7 February 1991

Air raids resulting in the destruction of the Taji cold storage complex and damage to the stores of meat and foodstuffs.

III. 11 February 1991

Air raids over the building of the Ministry of Local Government resulting in the death of five citizens and the wounding of 17 others.

IV. 12 February 1991

Air raids aimed at residential areas and resulting in the wounding of two citizens.

V. 13 February 1991

Air raids aimed at the conference building, the Baghdad Razor Blade Manufacturing Company and the Basim Cosmetics Company in the Riyadh quarter area and shelter No. 25 in the Amiriyah area and resulting in the death of 319 citizens and the wounding of 38.

VI. 14 February 1991

Air raids over the residential areas in the Kifah Kulat area, Eastern Karradah and Kahramana Square resulting in the death of 11 citizens and the wounding of seven others.

VII. 19 February 1991

Air raids aimed at houses near Rashid Hotel and resulting in damage to two houses.

VIII. 11 February 1991

1. Air raids aimed at houses in the Palestine Street area and the Idrisi quarter and resulting in the wounding of seven citizens, including two women.

2. Air raids aimed at residential quarters and resulting in the wounding of 45 citizens.

IX. 23 February 1991

Air raids aimed at agricultural areas and residential quarters and resulting in the death of one citizen and the wounding of 11 others.

X. 24 February 1991

Air raids aimed at residential quarters and resulting in the death of one citizen and the wounding of 21 others.

XI. 25 February 1991

An air raid over a residential quarter.

Anbar governorate

I. 7 to 8 February 1991

Air raids aimed at the new bridge in the town of Fallujah and resulting in the deaths of two citizens and the wounding of eight others.

II. 10 February 1991

Air raids aimed at residential areas in the Albu Alwan area in Fallujah district and resulting in the wounding of 10 citizens.

III. 12 to 14 February 1991

Air raids aimed at residential areas, the new Fallujah bridge and the Albu Alwan railway bridge and resulting in the death of 27 citizens and the wounding of 71 others.

IV. 17 February 1991

Air raids aimed at residential quarters in the centre of the town of Fallujah and resulting in the death of 11 citizens.

V. 18 February 1991

1. Air raids aimed at the Sahidah area in the Qa'im District and resulting in the wounding of two citizens.

2. Air raids aimed at the international bridge and residential areas in the villages of Albu Dhiyah and Marqad al-Shaykh Hadid and resulting in damage to property.

VI. 19 to 20 February 1991

Air raids aimed at tents in the Jafayifah area and the Kabisah area and resulting in the death of three citizens and the wounding of two others.

VII. 22 to 23 February 1991

Bombardment of the Hadithah district, the railway bridge at Hadithah and the railway station at Qadisiyah, resulting in the death of 11 citizens and the wounding of 14 others.

VIII. 25 to 26 February 1991

Air raids aimed at the residential area of Al-Shaykh Hadid in Hadithah district and resulting in the wounding of one citizen.

Wasit governorate

I. 6 to 9 February 1991

Air raids aimed at residential quarters in the town of Kut and the Nu'maniyah bridge and resulting in the death of nine citizens and the wounding of nine others.

II. 17 to 20 February 1991

Air raids aimed at residential quarters in the Jamahir quarter of Kut and resulting in the demolition of a school in the town, the death of four citizens and the wounding of two others.

Dhi Qar governorate

I. 4 to 7 February 1991

Air raids aimed at the Nasr bridge, the horticultural station, the express railway bridge, the Islah bridge and tents in the Gharab subdistrict and resulting in the death of 51 citizens and the wounding of 157 others.

II. 7 to 11 February 1991

Air raids over the Rifa'i and Gharaf areas, the Nasr subdistrict bridge, the Suq al-Shuyukh bridge and the Saray and Bakr areas in the capital of the governorate, the township of Akikah in Suq al-Shuyukh, the Bakr express bridge, the Dutch iron bridge, the wooden pontoon bridge, the Fadliyah subdistrict bridge and the tents of Bedouin in the Batha' subdistrict, resulting in the death of 33 citizens and the wounding of 103 others.

III. 12 to 19 February 1991

Air raids over the wooden pontoon bridge in the capital of the governorate, the Batha' subdistrict bridge, the Ghalyun pontoon bridge, the Dhi Qar express bridge, the Fuhud subdistrict bridge and the Dutch bridge, resulting in the death of 42 citizens and the wounding of 76 others.

Arbil governorate

I. 16 February 1991

Air raids aimed at the centre of the town of Arbil and residential quarters in Altun Kubra and resulting in damage to houses.

II. 22 February 1991

Aerial bombardment aimed at the capital of the governorate and resulting in the death of one citizen and the wounding of three others, including a child.

Nineveh governorate

I. 8 February 1991

Air raids aimed at the residential complex in the Kindi installation, the wax factory in Hamidat subdistrict, the centre of the town of Mosul and the Husam al-Alil subdistrict and resulting in the death of one citizen and the wounding of three others.

II. 8 to 16 February 1991

Air raids aimed at the centre of the town of Mosul, the Husam al-Alil subdistrict, the household furniture company and the radio and television complex in the town of Mosul, the villages of Hanjiruk and Barazi belonging to the Skaykhan district, the Sukkar quarter and the municipalities and resulting in the death of five citizens and the wounding of 53 others.

III. 17 to 26 February 1991

Enemy air raids aimed at the Saddam dam, the residential and commercial quarters in the centre of the town of Mosul, the Tayran neighbourhood, the olympic pool and the Naft quarter and resulting in the death of 16 citizens and the wounding of 12 others.

Najaf governorate

I. 6 to 13 February 1991

Air raids over the Abbasiyah subdistrict, the Bahr area and Nazim al-Mishkhab, the Nafisha bridge in Qadisiyah subdistrict and the Khasaf bridge in Qadisiyah subdistrict, resulting in the death of two citizens and the wounding of one.

II. 14 February 1991

Air raids aimed at the Suq Sha'lan bridge, the Wafa' bridge in the Mishkhab subdistrict and resulting in the deaths of 19 citizens, the wounding of 25 others and the loss of four citizens in the river.

III. 18 to 20 February 1991

1. Air raids aimed at the village of Rahbah and its residential areas and resulting in the death of two women and one child and the wounding of six citizens, including three children and one woman.

2. Air raids aimed at Manadhirah main bridge and resulting in the wounding of three citizens, including one child.

3. Air raids aimed at the Qadisiyah bridge, as a result of which two civilian vehicles fell into the river and 20 citizens were wounded.

IV. 20 to 23 February 1991

Air raids aimed at the Wafa' bridge and residential tents and resulting in damage to the bridge and tents.

V. 23 February 1991

Air raids aimed at the Kufah bridge and resulting in the death of two citizens, the wounding of nine citizens, including one child and one woman, and the loss of four citizens in the river.

VI. 7 February 1991

An air raid aimed at the cement factory bridge.

Babylon governorate

I. 10 to 14 February 1991
Air raids aimed at the cold storage warehouses in the Yusufiyah subdistrict and residential quarters in the Akrad quarter in the capital of the governorate and resulting in the death of 32 citizens and the wounding of six others.

II. 16 to 18 February 1991
Air raids aimed at residential quarters in the Mahmudiyah district, residential quarters in the Iskandariyah subdistrict and the Khidr quarter in the Iskandariyah subdistrict and resulting in the death of 26 citizens and the wounding of three others.

III. 18 to 23 February 1991
Air raids aimed at charitable installations and residential areas in Iskandariyah and the Yusufiyah subdistrict and resulting in the death of one citizen and the wounding of eight others.

IV. 24 to 27 February 1991
Air raids aimed at the General Motors factory and resulting in the death of one citizen and the wounding of six others.

Muthanna governorate

I. 2 to 8 February 1991
Air raids over the foodstuffs complex, the Samawah railway station, the radio and television building, the Samawah bridge, the television station, residential areas near the sports stadium, the Hadar district bridge and the Saub al-Saghir area, resulting in the death of 58 citizens and the wounding of 134 others.

II. 10 to 12 February 1991
Air raids aimed at the Samawah railway station, Hadar, the Khayrat flour factory, the Khidr iron and wooden bridge, the Mahdi area bridge and the bridge of the al-Majd subdistrict and resulting in the wounding of three citizens.

III. 12 February 1991
Air raids aimed at the Samawah railway station, the wooden bridge in the town of Samawah and residential quarters in the capital of the governorate and resulting in the death of 47 citizens, including one child, and the wounding of 50 others and one child.

IV. 22-26 February 1991
Air raids aimed at the Mahdi wooden bridge, the main Samawah bridge, the Jarukhy bridge and orchards in the Mahdi area and resulting in the death of 12 citizens, including seven Bedouin and two children, and the wounding of nine citizens, including three migrant Bedouin, one woman and one child.

Dohuk governorate

I. 25 January to 8 February 1991
Air raids aimed at residential areas in the centre of the town of Dohuk, Jam'iyah quarter and Samil district and resulting in the death of 16 citizens, including two women and seven children, and the wounding of 75 citizens, including seven women and one child, the death of 120 head of small cattle and the burning of four tents.

Salah al-Din governorate

I. 5 to 7 February 1991
Air raids aimed at residential buildings in the residential complex of the Salah al-Din installation and the Mu'allimin residential quarter in Samara' district and resulting in the death of 14 citizens, including one woman, and the wounding of 56 citizens.

II. 20 to 21 February 1991
Air raids aimed at Khadraniyah in Sharqat district, the Asri quarter in the capital of the governorate and the Tikrit bridge and resulting in the wounding of eight citizens.

Diyala governorate

I. 24 February 1991
Aerial bombardment aimed at the Rashidiyah area and the village of Kazim al-Ilmi and resulting in the death of one citizen.

Maysan governorate

I. 16 February 1991
Air raids over residential areas, the Mijarr al-Kabir bridge, the Yugoslav bridge, the new children's hospital, the Saddam public hospital, the Amarah kindergarten and the Maysan television station building, the Hatin bridge and the Qal'at Salih district bridge, resulting in the death of 55 citizens and the wounding of 99 others.

II. 17 to 22 February 1991
Air raids over the Yugoslav bridge, the Mu'allimin quarter, the Sadr al-Mijarr bridge, Nazim Qal'at Salih, the Mijarriyah bridge and the Maysan and Intisar food warehouses complex, resulting in the death of 14 citizens and the wounding of six others.

Basrah governorate

I. 17 February 1991
Air raids which hit the Umm Qasr grain silo and caused great damage there.

II. 11 February 1991
Air raids resulting in:
1. The demolition of the General Grain Trading Company's building;
2. Damage to the stocks of the Basrah grain silo;
3. Destruction to three houses near the silo;
4. Great damage to the administration building of the Basrah grain silo;
5. The grave wounding of three employees.

III. 8 to 15 February 1991
1. Air raids aimed at the capital of the governorate, the Qadisiyah bridge, houses in the ports, Sa'd square, the Kifa'at quarter, Kut al-Hajjaj Buradi'iyah, Matimah, Ashshar, Karbat Ali bridge, the date warehouses, Ma'qil, the Andalus quarter, the Othman mosque and residential areas in the Majidiyah area in the Harithah area and residential quarters in the Kut al-Zaghir area in the Shatt al-Arab district and resulting in the death of 64 citizens, including eight women and eight children, and the wounding of 132 citizens, including 10 women and three children.

2. Air raids over the Harithah residential area, residential quarters in the Sharis and Nusayr areas and residential quarters in Mahallat Kut and Durayhimiyah in the Zubayr district and resulting in the death of 32 citizens, including nine women and one child, and the wounding of 170 citizens, including 10 women and 17 children.

3. Air raids resulting in the demolition of a girl's commercial preparatory school, the main building of a teacher's training institute, part of the Ashshar mosque and the Basrah industrial secondary school in the capital of the governorate.

4. Air raids aimed at residential quarters in the Atiriyah area, Shu'aybah, Ma'qil, the Shuhada' quarter and Aylah and resulting in the death of 110 citizens and the wounding of 60 others.

5. Damage to the Sayid Abd al-Hakim mosque.

6. Damage to the Basrah dairy plant.

Qadisiyah governorate

I. 7 February 1991

1. Air raids hitting the rice silo and causing great damage to it.

2. Air raids hitting the grain silo of the town of Diwaniyah and causing great damage to it.

II. 17 February 1991

Air raids aimed at the Hasaf bridge in the Shanafiyah subdistrict, the Shanafiyah iron bridge and the Salahiyah pontoon bridge in the township of Salahiyah and the grain mill and resulting in the death of 10 citizens.

III. 8 February 1991

Air raids aimed at residential quarters in the Qal'at Salih district, the Amarah-Basrah highway and the centre of the Mijarr al-Kabir district and resulting in the death of 21 citizens, including five women, and the wounding of 48 others, including four women and four children.

IV. 9 February 1991

Air raids aimed at residential quarters in the Hamzah district, the village of Ata' and the Diwaniyah silo and resulting in the death of four citizens and the wounding of seven others.

Ta'mim governorate

I. 16 to 17 February 1991

Air raids aimed at residential quarters in Wasiti quarter and 30 Tammuz quarter, residential areas in Dabs and the Kurdish radio station and resulting in the death of 10 citizens, including two children and the wounding of 39 others.

II. 24 February 1991

Air raids aimed at Kirkuk railway station, the Khadra' residential quarter and the Kurdish radio station and resulting in the death of three citizens, including one woman, and the wounding of one woman.

S/22522, 23 April 1991

120. Letter from the Permanent Representative of the United Kingdom of Great Britain and Northern Ireland to the United Nations addressed to the President of the Security Council, 23 April 1991

Further to my letter of 13 February 1991 (S/22218), I have the honour to communicate to you pursuant to paragraph 4 of resolution 678 (1990) a further report on operations in the Gulf.

British Armed Forces played a full part in the 100-hour ground campaign between 24 February and midnight (EST) on 27 February, which led to the liberation of Kuwait. The particular contribution of the British First Armoured Division to the coalition's ground campaign was to engage Iraqi forces to the west of Kuwait. At the end of their advance First Armoured Division troops had reached positions north and north-west of Kuwait City.

The Royal Air Force also continued to contribute to the coalition air campaign. Between 17 January and 27 February the Royal Air Force (RAF) flew over 6,500 sorties, including over 4,000 combat sorties.

The Royal Navy contributed to the maritime campaign and played a leading role in the coalition's mine counter-measures force. Since the end of the hostilities, Royal Navy mine counter-measure vessels have cleared channels into the ports of Ash Shu'aybah and Kuwait City.

The number of prisoners of war taken by British Forces during the ground campaign was some 8,000. All were treated in accordance with the United Kingdom's obligations under the Geneva conventions. Many of those captured had been poorly provided for by the Iraqi authorities, lacking adequate food and clothing. Arrangements were made to supply them with clothing and rations from British stocks before they were evacuated by helicopter from the combat zone for registration under International Committee of the Red Cross (ICRC) procedures. The most extensive medical facilities ever set up by the British Army in the field were used to ensure that the prisoners were properly looked after. They were subsequently passed to the Saudi Arabian authorities.

Just under 45,000 British service personnel were deployed to the Gulf in support of the operations. British casualties during the campaign were 25 killed in action and 43 wounded.

The United Kingdom has made a major contribution to the international response to the environmental threat posed by the oil released into the Gulf by Iraq, and by the oil well fires started by Iraq in the closing stages of the conflict. After the oil spills, the United Kingdom responded swiftly to requests for assistance from Gulf States. In particular, the United Kingdom helped with a military air lift of 90 tonnes of anti-pollution equipment, and donated six oil skimmers to Bahrain. It also provided expert advice on oil pollution response and the ecological aspects of the slick. It also offered help in training local volunteers in Saudi Arabia to clean oiled birds. The Royal Air Force and the British Army have helped to clean up debris from some of the offshore islands. On 6 March, the United Kingdom announced a contribution of £1 million to the trust fund established by the International Maritime Organization (IMO) for clean-up operations in the northern Gulf.

In response to the environmental damage caused by the burning oil wells, the United Kingdom has provided the affected States with an initial assessment of the nature and extent of the smoke plumes, their likely evolution, and their possible impact on the environment and human health. Preliminary analysis of data produced by a British research flight in March was incorporated into this report and further information will be provided to the affected States when it becomes available.

UN News Summary, 18-24 April
[published 25 April 1991]

121. UN Press Release: Secretary-General Says Gulf Conflict was not a UN War, April 1991

Secretary-General Javier Perez de Cuellar, in a statement to the European Parliament in Strassbourg on 18 April, referring to the Gulf conflict, said it was not a United Nations war. "General Schwarzkopf was not wearing a blue helmet." They only war which could nowadays be considered just, he said, was the sanctioned war provided for in the United Nations Charter as the last resort and decided upon by the international community, as represented in the Security Council. The establishment of a new world order would have to take place within the framework of the United Nations, but a United Nations which did not resort to the use of double standards and whose impartiality ensured its credibility.

122. Report of the Secretary-General on the Work of the Organization, September, 1991

[*Extract.*]

IV.

...

During the period under review, the Security Council took action of extraordinary consequence to reverse the invasion of Kuwait by Iraq and deter aggression in future.

...

Once the invasion occurred, the response of the Security Council was not only swift but systematic; in adopting 14 resolutions regarding the situation, the Council followed a step-by-step and considered approach to the use of its powers under Chapter VII of the Charter. Far from acting in haste, the Council afforded ample time--from 2 August 1990 to 15 January 1991--for the Government of Iraq to comply with the Council's demand. It was only when all warnings--including my own pleadings to Iraq to correct a manifest wrong--went unheeded and friendly advice was rejected that armed force was finally employed to restore the independence of Kuwait. This is the factual side of that fateful occurrence, which no balanced assessment, now or in the future, can ignore.

Another important aspect is that the enforcement action was not carried out exactly in the form foreseen by Articles 42 *et sequentia* of Chapter VII. Instead, the Council authorized the use of force on a national and coalition basis. In the circumstances and given the costs imposed and capabilities demanded by modern warfare, the arrangement seemed unavoidable. However, the experience of operations in the Gulf suggests the need for a collective reflection on questions relating to the future use of the powers vested in the Security Council under Chapter VII.

In order to preclude controversy, the question should include the mechanisms required for the Council to satisfy itself that the rule of proportionality in the employment of armed force is observed and the rules of humanitarian law applicable in armed conflicts are complied with. Moreover, careful thought will have to be given to ensuring that the application of Chapter VII measures is not perceived to be overextended. ...

B. UNITED STATES MATERIALS

101st Congress, 2d Session

1. H.J. Res. 658, 27 September 1990

To support actions the President has taken with respect to Iraqi aggression against Kuwait and to demonstrate United States resolve.

...

JOINT RESOLUTION

To support actions the President has taken with respect to Iraqi aggression against Kuwait and to demonstrate United States resolve.

Whereas the Government of Iraq without provocation invaded and occupied the territory of Kuwait on August 2, 1990, has brutalized the population of Kuwait, has taken large numbers of innocent hostages, and has disregarded the rights of diplomats, all in clear violation of international law and the norms of international conduct;

Whereas Iraq's actions have caused great suffering among the hundreds of thousands of innocent people who have been displaced by this crisis;

Whereas the President condemned Iraq's unprovoked and naked aggression and undertook a series of actions, including imposing comprehensive economic sanctions on Iraq and freezing Iraqi and Kuwaiti assets in the United States;

Whereas the United Nations Security Council in a series of resolutions condemned these actions as blatantly unlawful, imposed mandatory economic sanctions (including maritime and air embargoes) designed to compel Iraq to withdraw from Kuwait, called on all states to take appropriate measures to ensure that these sanctions are enforced, called for the immediate release of all hostages, strongly condemned aggressive acts perpetrated by Iraq against diplomatic premises and personnel in Kuwait, and reaffirmed the right of individual and collective self-defense in this situation;

Whereas the President, in response to requests from governments in the region and in exercise of the inherent right of individual and collective self-defense as specified in the Charter of the United Nations, has deployed United States Armed Forces into and around the Arabian Peninsula as part of a multinational force that includes Arab, Islamic, nonaligned, North Atlantic Treaty Organization members, and other states to deal with this armed aggression, to protect American lives, and to assist in enforcement of sanctions and the defense of friendly states in the region;

Whereas friends and allies have provided critical leadership in, and support for, the international efforts to impose sanctions on Iraq and otherwise oppose Iraqi aggression; and

Whereas these actions have thus far deterred Iraq from initiating hostilities against other friendly states in the region or against United States forces: Now, therefore, be it

Resolved by the Senate and House of Representatives of the United States of America in Congress assembled,

SECTION 1. SHORT TITLE.

This resolution may be cited as the "United States Policy on Iraqi Aggression Resolution".

SEC. 2. DECLARATION OF UNITED STATES OBJECTIVES AND POLICIES.

(a) UNITED STATES OBJECTIVES.

- United States policy in the Persian Gulf, as stated by the President and hereby affirmed by the Congress, is directed toward -

(1) the immediate, unconditional, and complete withdrawal of all Iraqi forces from Kuwait;

(2) the restoration of Kuwait's legitimate government;

(3) the security and stability of the Persian Gulf region;

(4) the protection of American citizens abroad, and the release of all those held hostage by Iraq; and

(5) the fostering of a new world order, freer from the threat of terror, stronger in the pursuit of justice, and more secure in the quest for peace.

(b) IMPORTANCE OF SECURITY AND STABILITY OF THE REGION. - The United States and the international community recognize the importance of the security and stability of the Persian Gulf region and adequate access to its energy resources. The United States and the international community must continue to oppose Iraq's armed aggression against Kuwait, a flagrant violation of international law which threatens global economic security and constitutes a serious challenge to international efforts to build a stable and peaceful environment in the post-Cold War era.

(c) CONDEMNATION OF IRAQ - THE UNITED STATES AND THE INTERNATIONAL COMMUNITY -

(1) should continue to condemn Iraq for its flagrant aggression, its abysmal human rights record, its support for international terrorism, its efforts to destabilize the region, its taking of civilian hostages, its terrorism of diplomats and violations of diplomatic premises, and its continuing efforts to develop and its demonstrated willingness to use weapons of mass destruction; and

(2) should hold Iraq and its leaders accountable for such actions.

(d) SUPPORT FOR DEPLOYMENT OF UNITED STATES ARMED FORCES. - The Congress -

(1) supports the deployment by the President of United States Armed Forces to the Persian Gulf region in response to Iraq's military aggression;

(2) expresses its appreciation to and support for the members of the Armed Forces who have been deployed to that region and to the members of the Ready Reserve and the National Guard who have been ordered to active duty; and

(3) declares its support for them as they perform their vital role in the achievement of United States objectives.

(e) UNITED STATES EFFORTS TO PROMOTE INTERNATIONAL COOPERATION.

- The Congress commends the President for his successful efforts to promote international consensus and cooperation in response to this crisis. The United States should continue its efforts to -

(1) strengthen the international consensus against Iraq's aggression, through broadening cooperation with the Soviet Union, other members of the international community, and the United Nations;

(2) obtain additional and substantial commitments of air, sea, and ground forces from other nations in support of the multinational forces deployed in the Persian Gulf region in response to Iraq's aggression;

(3) obtain increased financial assistance and other support from other nations for those multinational forces;

(4) obtain substantial tangible international assistance for those nations that have suffered financial losses as a result of their support for the United Nations trade embargo against Iraq; and

5) obtain adequate international humanitarian assistance for those foreign nationals who have fled Iraq and Kuwait.

(f) OTHER UNITED STATES ACTIONS.
- The United States should also -

(1) continue to seek international consensus -

(A) to contain Iraq's conventional, chemical, biological, and nuclear weapons and ballistic missile programs, and

(B) to stop the export to Iraq of dual use technology and military components, including technology and components of direct or indirect United States origin;

(2) continue to seek international consensus to address regional problems of arms proliferation, including conventional weapons, ballistic missiles, and weapons of mass destruction (chemical, biological, and nuclear weapons), and to seek to ensure that conventional weapons transfers to the region reflect legitimate security needs of the recipient nation;

(3) continue its stated policy to maintain Israel's economic well-being and qualitative military advantage in the Middle East (including through means such as technology transfers and defense cooperation), and continue its efforts to achieve an Arab-Israeli peace settlement; and

4) continue promoting respect for internationally recognized human rights and the rule of law, and support the development of democratic institutions, throughout the region.

(g) SUPPORT FOR ACTIONS OF THE UNITED NATIONS.

(1) COMMENDATION OF THE UNITED NATIONS. - The United Nations should be commended for its timely, unified, and strong response to Iraq's armed aggression against Kuwait.

(2) COMMENDATION OF SECURITY COUNCIL MEMBERS. - The member states of the United Nations Security Council who formulated a coordinated and unprecedented international policy response to Iraq's aggression through the adoption of Resolutions 660, 661, 662, 664, 665, 666, 667, and 668 should also be commended.

(3) AFFIRMATION OF RESOLUTIONS. - The Congress affirms its support for those Security Council resolutions.

(4) INTERNATIONAL IMPLEMENTATION OF RESOLUTIONS. - The Congress calls on all nations to fully support and comply with the resolutions adopted by the Security Council and to strengthen the enforcement of the sanctions imposed by the United Nations against Iraq.

(5) CONTINUATION OF DIPLOMATIC EFFORTS. - The United States and other members of the international community should continue efforts to achieve a diplomatic solution to the crisis in the Persian Gulf region through implementation of those resolutions.

SEC. 3. EFFORTS TO ACHIEVE UNITED STATES OBJECTIVES AND POLICIES.

The Congress supports the President's emphasis on diplomatic efforts, international sanctions, and negotiations under the auspices of the United Nations to achieve the United States objectives and policies set forth in section 2. The United States shall continue to emphasize the use of diplomatic and other nonmilitary means in order to achieve those objectives and policies, while maintaining credible United States and multinational deterrent military force.

SEC. 4. WAR POWERS FINDINGS.

The Congress finds that -

(1) on August 9, 1990, the President reported to the Congress that he had ordered the deployment of substantial elements of the United States Armed Forces into the Persian Gulf region in response to the threat posed by the actions of Iraq;

(2) in this report, the President stated that the report was being provided "consistent with the War Powers Resolution";

(3) the War Powers Resolution requires, in sections 4(a)(2) and 4(a)(3), that the President report to the Congress whenever, in the absence of a declaration of war, United States Armed Forces are introduced into the territory, airspace, or waters of a foreign nation while equipped for combat (except for deployments which relate solely to supply, replacement, repair, or training of such forces) or are introduced in numbers which substantially enlarge United States Armed Forces equipped for combat already located in a foreign nation;

(4) the War Powers Resolution also requires, in section 4(a)(1), that the President report to the Congress whenever, in the absence of a declaration of war, United States Armed Forces are introduced into hostilities or situations where imminent involvement in hostilities is clearly indicated by the circumstances;

(5) consistent with that requirement, the President declared in his August 9th report, "I do not believe involvement in hostilities is imminent"; and

(6) the President has consulted with the Congress and has kept the Congress informed with regard to the deployment of United States Armed Forces into the Persian Gulf region.

102nd Congress, 1st Session

2. H. Con. Res. 1, 3 January 1991

To express the sense of the Congress that Congress must approve any offensive military action against Iraq

Resolved by the House of Representatives (the Senate concurring),

SECTION 1. APPROVAL OF INITIAL RESPONSE TO THE INVASION OF KUWAIT.

The Congress supports the actions taken by the President of the United States to defend Saudi Arabia, demands that Iraq immediately withdraw from its illegal occupation of Kuwait, and supports the President's diplomatic and economic initiatives to resolve the Persian Gulf crisis.

SECTION 2. URGENCY OF CONGRESSIONAL AUTHORITY FOR OFFENSIVE OPERATIONS IN THE PERSIAN GULF.

The Congress finds that the Constitution of the United States vests all power to declare war in the Congress of the United States. Any offensive action taken against Iraq must be explicitly approved by the Congress of the United States before such action may be initiated.

3. Letter from President George Bush to Hon. Thomas S. Foley, Speaker of the House of Representatives, 8 January 1992

DEAR MR. SPEAKER: The current situation in the Persian Gulf, brought about by Iraq's unprovoked invasion and subsequent brutal occupation of Kuwait, threatens vital U.S. interests. The situation also threatens the peace. It would, however, greatly enhance the chances for peace if Congress were now to go on record supporting the position adopted by the UN Security Council on twelve separate occasions. Such an action would underline that the United States stands with the international community and on the side of law and decency; it also would help dispel any belief that may exist in the minds of Iraq's leaders that the United States lacks the necessary unity to act decisively in response to Iraq's continued aggression against Kuwait.

Secretary of State Baker is meeting with Iraq's Foreign Minister on January 9. It would have been most constructive if he could have presented the Iraqi government a Resolution passed by both houses of Congress supporting the UN position and in particular Security Council Resolution 678. As you know, I have frequently stated my desire for such a Resolution. Nevertheless, there is still opportunity for Congress to act to strengthen the prospects for peace and safeguard this country's vital interests.

I therefore request that the House of Representatives and the Senate adopt a Resolution stating that Congress supports the use of all necessary means to implement UN Security Council Resolution 678. Such action would send the clearest possible message to Saddam Hussein that he must withdraw without condition or delay from Kuwait. Anything less would only encourage Iraqi intransigence; anything less would risk detracting from the international coalition arrayed against Iraq's aggression.

Mr. Speaker, I am determined to do whatever is necessary to protect America's security. I ask Congress to join me in this task. I can think of no better way than for Congress to express its support for the President at this critical time. This truly is the last best chance for peace.

102d Congress, 1st Session

4. H.J. RES. 62, 10 January 1991

To authorize the use of United States Armed Forces pursuant to United Nations Security Council Resolution 678.

...

JOINT RESOLUTION

To authorize the use of United States Armed Forces pursuant to United Nations Security Council Resolution 678.

Whereas the Government of Iraq without provocation invaded and occupied the territory of Kuwait on August 2, 1990; and

Whereas both the House of Representatives (in H.J. Res. 658 of the 101st Congress) and the Senate (in S. Con. Res. 147 of the 101st Congress) have condemned Iraq's invasion of Kuwait and declared their support for international action to reverse Iraq's aggression; and

Whereas Iraq's conventional, chemical, biological, and nuclear weapons and ballistic missile programs and its demonstrated willingness to use weapons of mass destruction pose a grave threat to world peace; and

Whereas the international community has demanded that Iraq withdraw unconditionally and immediately from Kuwait and that Kuwait's independence and legitimate government be restored; and

Whereas the United Nations Security Council repeatedly affirmed the inherent right of individual or collective self-defense in response to the armed attack by Iraq against

Kuwait in accordance with Article 51 of the United Nations Charter; and

Whereas, in the absence of full compliance by Iraq with its resolutions, the United Nations Security Council in Resolution 678 has authorized member states of the United Nations to use all necessary means, after January 15, 1991, to uphold and implement all relevant Security Council resolutions and to restore international peace and security in the area; and

Whereas Iraq has persisted in its illegal occupation of, and brutal aggression against Kuwait: Now, therefore, be it

Resolved by the Senate and House of Representatives of the United States of America in Congress assembled,

SECTION 1. SHORT TITLE.

This joint resolution may be cited as the "Authorization for Use of Military Force Against Iraq Resolution".

SEC. 2. AUTHORIZATION FOR USE OF UNITED STATES ARMED FORCES.

(a) AUTHORIZATION. - The President is authorized, subject to subsection (b), to use United States Armed Forces pursuant to United Nations Security Council Resolution 678 (1990) in order to achieve implementation of Security Council Resolutions 660, 661, 662, 664, 665, 666, 667, 669, 670, 674, and 677.

(b) REQUIREMENT FOR DETERMINATION THAT USE OF MILITARY FORCE IS NECESSARY. - Before exercising the authority granted in subsection (a), the President shall make available to the Speaker of the House of Representatives and the President pro tempore of the Senate his determination -

(1) that the United States has used all appropriate diplomatic and other peaceful means to obtain compliance by Iraq with the United Nations Security Council resolutions cited in subsection (a); and

(2) that those efforts have not been and would not be successful in obtaining such compliance.

(c) WAR POWERS RESOLUTION REQUIREMENTS. -

(1) SPECIFIC STATUTORY AUTHORIZATION. -

Consistent with section 8(a)(1) of the War Powers Resolution, the Congress declares that this section is intended to constitute specific statutory authorization within the meaning of section 5(b) of the War Powers Resolution.

(2) APPLICABILITY OF OTHER REQUIREMENTS. - Nothing in this resolution supersedes any requirement of the War Powers Resolution.

SEC. 3. REPORTS TO CONGRESS.

At least once every 60 days, the President shall submit to the Congress a summary on the status of efforts to obtain compliance by Iraq with the resolutions adopted by the United Nations Security Council in response to Iraq's aggression.

Public Law 102-1, 102d Congress, 50 USC 1541

5. Joint Resolution 77, 14 January 1991

To authorize the use of United States Armed Forces pursuant to United Nations Security Council Resolution 678.

Whereas the Government of Iraq without provocation invaded and occupied the territory of Kuwait on August 2, 1990;

Whereas both the House of Representatives (in H.J. Res. 658 of the 101st Congress) and the Senate (in S. Con. Res. 147 of the 101st Congress) have condemned Iraq's invasion of Kuwait and declared their support for international action to reverse Iraq's aggression;

Whereas, Iraq's conventional, chemical, biological, and nuclear weapons and ballistic missile programs and its demonstrated willingness to use weapons of mass destruction pose a grave threat to world peace;

Whereas the international community has demanded that Iraq withdraw unconditionally and immediately from Kuwait and that Kuwait's independence and legitimate government be restored;

Whereas the United Nations Security Council repeatedly affirmed the inherent right of individual or collective self-defense in response to the armed attack by Iraq against Kuwait in accordance with Article 51 of the United Nations Charter;

Whereas, in the absence of full compliance by Iraq with its resolutions, the United Nations Security Council in Resolution 678 has authorized member states of the United Nations to use all necessary means, after January 15, 1991, to uphold and implement all relevant Security Council resolutions and to restore international peace and security in the area; and

Whereas Iraq has persisted in its illegal occupation of, and brutal aggression against Kuwait: Now, therefore, be it

Resolved by the Senate and House of Representatives of the United States of America in Congress assembled,

SECTION 1. SHORT TITLE.

This joint resolution may be cited as the "Authorization for Use of Military Force Against Iraq Resolution".

SEC. 2. AUTHORIZATION FOR USE OF UNITED STATES ARMED FORCES.

(a) AUTHORIZATION. - The President is authorized, subject to subsection (b), to use United States Armed Forces pursuant to United Nations Security Council Resolution 678 (1990) in order to achieve implementation of Security Council Resolutions 660, 661, 662, 664, 665, 666, 667, 669, 670, 674, and 677.

(b) REQUIREMENT FOR DETERMINATION THAT USE OF MILITARY FORCE IS NECESSARY.

- Before exercising the authority granted in subsection (a), the President shall make available to the Speaker of the House of Representatives and the President pro tempore of the Senate his determination that -

(1) the United States has used all appropriate diplomatic and other peaceful means to obtain compliance by Iraq with the United Nations Security Council resolutions cited in subsection (a); and

(2) that those efforts have not been and would not be successful in obtaining such compliance.

(c) WAR POWERS RESOLUTION REQUIREMENTS. -

(1) SPECIFIC STATUTORY AUTHORIZATION. - Consistent with section 8(a)(1) of the War Powers Resolution, the Congress declares that this section is intended to constitute specific statutory authorization within the meaning of section 5(b) of the War Powers Resolution.

(2) APPLICABILITY OF OTHER REQUIREMENTS. - Nothing in this resolution supersedes any requirement of the War Powers Resolution.

SEC. 3. REPORTS TO CONGRESS.

At least once every 60 days, the President shall submit to the Congress a summary on the status of efforts to obtain compliance by Iraq with the resolutions adopted by the United Nations Security Council in response to Iraq's aggression.

The Persian Gulf Crisis, Report Prepared by the Subcommittee on Arms Control and International Security and Science of the Committee on Foreign Affairs, US House of Represenatives, 102nd Congress, 1st Session, June 1991, at 124

6. Report for Use in Connection with Section 2(b) of the Joint Congressional Resolution Authorizing the Use of Military force against Iraq, 16 January 1991

[*Extract.*]

The report that follows is a summary of the diplomatic and other peaceful means used in an attempt to obtain compliance by Iraq with the twelve UN Security Council resolutions relating to its invasion and occupation of Kuwait.

...

In short international sanctions have not caused Iraq to comply with the January 15, 1991 deadline in UN Security Council Resolution 678, or to retreat from its insistence that its annexation of Kuwait is permanent. Even if the world community were able to maintain the current high level of success in sanctions enforcement, these economic results would not produce such compliance.

Further, the longer the sanctions continue, the more likely it is that leaks in the sanctions enforcement system will develop, that intermediaries will devise ways to circumvent sanctions, and that Iraq will find means of using its own resources to fill critical shortfalls. Even more important, if the coalition fails now to carry through on the UN Security Council's demands for immediate Iraqi withdrawal from Kuwait, there will be strong pressures and temptations on various countries to ease their enforcement of sanctions and to compromise on demands that Iraq meet existing objectives fully and unconditionally.

In summary, diplomatic and economic pressures have not diminished Iraq's intransigence despite five and one-half months of unparalleled international effort, and continued reliance upon them also could risk achieving the basic objective of bringing about Iraq's complete and unconditional withdrawal from Kuwait.

The Persian Gulf Crisis, Report Prepared by the Subcommittee on Arms Control and International Security and Science of the Committee on Foreign Affairs, US House of Represenatives, 102nd Congress, 1st Session, June 1991, at 129

7. Address by President Bush to the Nation, 16 January 1991

Just 2 hours ago, allied air forces began an attack on military targets in Iraq and Kuwait. These attacks continue as I speak. Ground forces are not engaged.

This conflict started August 2d when the dictator of Iraq invaded a small and helpless neighbor. Kuwait - a member of the Arab League and a member of the United Nations - was crushed; its people, brutalized. Five months ago, Saddam Hussein started this cruel war against Kuwait. Tonight, the battle has been joined.

This military action, taken in accord with United Nations resolutions and with the consent of the United States Congress, follows months of constant and virtually endless diplomatic activity on the part of the United Nations, the United States, and many, many other countries. Arab leaders sought what became known as an Arab solution, only to conclude that Saddam Hussein was unwilling to leave Kuwait. Others traveled to Baghdad in a variety of efforts to restore peace and justice. Our Secretary of State, James Baker, held an historic meeting in Geneva, only to be totally rebuffed. This past weekend, in a last-ditch effort, the Secretary-General of the United Nations went to the Middle East with peace in his heart - his second such mission. And he came back from Baghdad with no progress at all in getting Saddam Hussein to withdraw from Kuwait.

Now the 28 countries with forces in the Gulf area have exhausted all reasonable efforts to reach a peaceful resolution - have no choice but to drive Saddam from Kuwait by force. We will not fail.

As I report to you, air attacks are underway against military targets in Iraq. We are determined to knock out Saddam Hussein's nuclear bomb potential. We will also destroy his chemical weapons facilities. Much of Saddam's artillery and tanks will be destroyed. Our operations are designed to best protect the lives of all the coalition forces by targeting Saddam's vast military arsenal. Initial reports from General Schwarzkopf are that our operations are proceeding according to plan.

Our objectives are clear: Saddam Hussein's forces will leave Kuwait. The legitimate government of Kuwait will be restored to its rightful place, and Kuwait will once again be free. Iraq will eventually comply with all relevant United Nations resolutions, and then, when peace is restored, it is our hope that Iraq will live as a peaceful and cooperative member of the family of nations, thus enhancing the security and stability of the Gulf.

Some may ask: Why act now? Why not wait? The answer is clear: The world could wait no longer. Sanctions, though having some effect, showed no signs of accomplishing their objective. Sanctions were tried for well over 5 months, and we and our allies concluded that sanctions alone would not force Saddam from Kuwait.

While the world waited, Saddam Hussein systematically raped, pillaged, and plundered a tiny nation, no threat to his own. He subjected the people of Kuwait to unspeakable atrocities - and among those maimed and murdered, innocent children.

While the world waited, Saddam sought to add to the chemical weapons arsenal he now possesses, an infinitely more dangerous weapon of mass destruction - a nuclear weapon. And while the world waited, while the world talked peace and withdrawal, Saddam Hussein dug in and moved massive forces into Kuwait.

While the world waited, while Saddam stalled, more damage was being done to the fragile economies of the Third World, emerging democracies of Eastern Europe, to the entire world, including to our own economy.

The United States, together with the United Nations, exhausted every means at our disposal to bring this crisis to a peaceful end. However, Saddam clearly felt that by stalling and threatening and defying the United Nations, he could weaken the forces arrayed against him.

While the world waited, Saddam Hussein met every overture of peace with open contempt. While the world prayed for peace, Saddam prepared for war.

I had hoped that when the United States Congress, in historic debate, took its resolute action, Saddam would realize he could not prevail and would move out of Kuwait in accord with the United Nations resolutions. He did not do that. Instead, he remained intransigent, certain that time was on his side.

Saddam was warned over and over again to comply with the will of the United Nations: Leave Kuwait, or be driven out. Saddam has arrogantly rejected all warnings. Instead, he tried to make this a dispute between Iraq and the United States of America.

Well, he failed. Tonight, 28 nations - countries from 5 continents, Europe and Asia, Africa, and the Arab League - have forces in the Gulf area standing shoulder to shoulder against Saddam Hussein. These countries had hoped the use of force could be avoided. Regrettably, we now believe that only force will make him leave.

Prior to ordering our forces into battle, I instructed our military commanders to take every necessary step to prevail as quickly as possible, and with the greatest degree of protection possible for American and allied service men and women. I've told the American people before that this will not be another Vietnam, and I repeat this here tonight. Our troops will have the best possible support in the entire world, and they will not be asked to fight with one hand tied behind their back. I'm hopeful that this fighting will not go on for long and that casualties will be held to an absolute minimum.

This is an historic moment. We have in this past year made great progress in ending the long era of conflict and cold war. We have before us the opportunity to forge for ourselves and for future generations a new world order - a world where the rule of law, not the law of the jungle, governs the conduct of nations. When we are successful - and we will be - we have a real chance at this new world order, an order in which a credible United Nations can use its peacekeeping role to fulfill the promise and vision of the U.N.'s founders.

We have no argument with the people of Iraq. Indeed, for the innocents caught in this conflict, I pray for their safety. Our goal is not the conquest of Iraq. It is the liberation of Kuwait. It is my hope that somehow the Iraqi people can, even now, convince their dictator that he must lay down his arms, leave Kuwait and let Iraq itself rejoin the family of peace-loving nations.

Thomas Paine wrote many years ago: "These are the times that try men's souls." Those well-known words are so very true today. But even as planes of the multinational forces attack Iraq, I prefer to think of peace, not war. I am convinced not only that we will prevail but that out of the horror of combat will come the recognition that no nation can stand against a world united. No nation will be permitted to brutally assault its neighbor.

No president can easily commit our sons and daughters to war. They are the Nation's finest. Ours is an all-volunteer force, magnificently trained, highly motivated. The troops know why they're there. And listen to what they say, for they've said it better than any President or Prime Minister ever could.

Listen to Hollywood Huddleston, Marine lance corporal. He says, "Let's free these people, so we can go home and be free again." And he's right. The terrible crimes and tortures committed by Saddam's henchmen against the innocent people of Kuwait are an affront to mankind and a challenge to the freedom of all.

Listen to one of our great officers out there, Marine Lieutenant General Walter Boomer. He said: "There are things worth fighting for. A world in which brutality and lawlessness are allowed to go unchecked isn't the kind of world we're going to want to live in."

Listen to Master Sergeant J.P. Kendall of the 82d Airborne: "We're here for more than just the price of a gallon of gas. What we're doing is going to chart the future of the world for the next 100 years. It's better to deal with this guy now than 5 years from now."

And finally, we should all sit up and listen to Jackie Jones, an Army lieutenant, when she says, "If we let him get away with this, who knows what's going to be next?"

I have called upon Hollywood and Walter and J.P. and Jackie and all their courageous comrades-in-arms to do what must be done. Tonight, America and the world are deeply grateful to them and to their families. And let me say to everyone listening or watching tonight: When the troops we've sent in finish their work, I am determined to bring them home as soon as possible.

Tonight, as our forces fight, they and their families are in our prayers. May God bless each and every one of them, and the coalition forces at our side in the Gulf, and may He continue to bless our nation, the United States of America.

[President Bush spoke at 9.01 p.m. from the Oval Office at the White House.]

The Persian Gulf Crisis, Report Prepared by the Subcommittee on Arms Control and International Security and Science of the Committee on Foreign Affairs, US House of Represenatives, 102nd Congress, 1st Session, June 1991, at 132

8. Letter from President George Bush to Hon. Thomas S. Foley, Speaker of the House of Representatives, 18 January 1991

DEAR MR. SPEAKER: On January 16, 1991, I made available to you, consistent with section 2(b) of the Authorization for Use of Military Force Against Iraq Resolution (H.J. Res. 77, Public Law 102-1), my determination that appropriate diplomatic and other peaceful means had not and would not compel Iraq to withdraw unconditionally from Kuwait and meet the other requirements of the U.N. Security Council and the world community. With great reluctance, I concluded, as did the other coalition leaders, that only the use of armed force would achieve an Iraqi withdrawal together with the other U.N. goals of restoring Kuwait's legitimate government, protecting the lives of our citizens, and reestablishing security and stability in the Persian Gulf region. Consistent with the War Powers Resolution, I now inform you that pursuant to my authority as Commander in Chief, I directed U.S. Armed Forces to commence combat operations on January 16, 1991, against Iraqi forces and military targets in Iraq and Kuwait. The Armed Forces of Saudi Arabia, Kuwait, the United Kingdom, France, Italy, and Canada are participating as well.

Military actions are being conducted with great intensity. They have been carefully planned to accomplish our goals with the minimum loss of life among coalition military forces and the civilian inhabitants of the area. Initial reports indicate that our forces have performed magnificently. Nevertheless, it is impossible to know at this time either the duration of active combat operations or the scope or duration of the deployment of U.S. Armed Forces necessary fully to accomplish our goals.

The operations of U.S. and other coalition forces are contemplated by the resolutions of the U.N. Security Council, as well as H.J. Res. 77, adopted by Congress on January 12, 1991. They are designed to ensure that the mandates of the United Nations and the common goals of our coalition partners are achieved and the safety of our citizens and Forces is ensured.

As our united efforts in pursuit of peace, stability. and security in the Gulf region continue, I look forward to our continued consultation and cooperation.

102nd Congress, 1st Session, House Document 102-52

9. Message from the President of the United States to a Joint Session of Congress, 6 March 1991

Mr. Speaker, Members of Congress:

Five short weeks ago, I came to this House to speak to you about the State of the Union. We met then in time of war. Tonight, we meet in a world blessed by the promise of peace.

From the moment Operation Desert Storm commenced on January 16, until the time the guns fell silent at midnight one week ago, this Nation has watched its sons and daughters with pride - watched over them with prayer. As Commander-in-Chief, I can report to you: Our Armed Forces fought with honour and valor. As President, I can report to the Nation - aggression is defeated. The war is over.

This is a victory for every country in the coalition, and for the United Nations. A victory for unprecedented international cooperation and diplomacy, so well led by our Secretary of State James Baker. It is a victory for the rule of law and for what is right.

Desert Storm's success belongs to the team that so ably leads our Armed Forces - our Secretary of Defense and our Chairman of the Joint Chiefs: Dick Cheney and Colin Powell.

And of course, this military victory also belongs to the one the British call the "Man of the Match" - the tower of calm at the eye of Desert Storm - General Norman Schwarzkopf.

And let us not forget Saudi General Khalid, or Britain's General de la Billiere, or General Roquejoffre of France, and all the others whose leadership played such a vital role. And most importantly, all those who served in the field.

I thank the members of this Congress - support here for our troops in battle was overwhelming. And above all, I thank those whose unfailing love and support sustained our courageous men and women: I thank the American people.

Tonight, I come to this House to speak about the world - the world after war.

The recent challenge could not have been clearer. Saddam Hussein was the villain; Kuwait the victim. To the aid of this small country came nations from North America and Europe, from Asia and South America, from Africa and the Arab world - all united against aggression.

Our uncommon coalition must now work in common purpose to forge a future that should never again be held hostage to the darker side of human nature.

Tonight in Iraq, Saddam walks amidst ruin. His war machine is crushed. His ability to threaten mass destruction is itself destroyed. His people have been lied to - denied the truth. And when his defeated legions come home, all Iraqis will see and feel the havoc he has wrought. And this I promise you: For all that Saddam has done to his own people, to the Kuwaitis, and to the entire world - Saddam and those around him are accountable.

All of us grieve for the victims of war, for the people of Kuwait and the suffering that scars the soul of that proud nation. We grieve for all our fallen soldiers and their families, for all the innocents caught up in this conflict. And yes, we grieve for the people of Iraq - a people who have never been our enemy. My hope is that one day we will once again welcome them as friends into the community of nations.

Our commitment to peace in the Middle East does not end with the liberation of Kuwait. So tonight, let me outline four key challenges to be met:

First, we must work together to create shared security arrangements in the region. Our friends and allies in the Middle East recognize that they will bear the bulk of the responsibility for regional security. But we want them to know that just as we stood with them to repel aggression so now America stands ready to work with them to secure the peace.

This does not mean stationing U.S. ground forces on the Arabian Peninsula, but it does mean American participation in joint exercises involving both air and ground forces. And it means maintaining a capable U.S. naval presence in the region, just as we have for over 40 years. Let it be clear: Our vital national interests depend on a stable and secure gulf.

Second, we must act to control the proliferation of weapons of mass destruction and the missiles used to deliver them. It would be tragic if the nations of the Middle East and Persian Gulf were now, in the wake of war, to embark on a new arms race. Iraq requires special vigilance. Until Iraq convinces the world of its peaceful intentions - that its leaders will not use new revenues to rearm and rebuild its menacing war machine - Iraq must not have access to the instruments of war.

Third, we must work to create new opportunities for peace and stability in the Middle East. On the night I announced Operation Desert Storm, I expressed my hope that out of the horrors of war might come new momentum for peace. We have learned in the modern age, geography cannot guarantee security and security does not come from military power alone.

All of us know the depth of bitterness that has made the dispute between Israel and its neighbors so painful and intractable. Yet, in the conflict just concluded, Israel and many of the Arab states have for the first time found themselves confronting the same aggressor. By now, it should be plain to all parties that peacemaking in the Middle East requires compromise. At the same time, peace brings real benefits to everyone. We must do all that we can to close the gap between Israel and the Arab states - and between Israelis and Palestinians. The tactics of terror lead nowhere - there can be no substitute for diplomacy.

A comprehensive peace must be grounded in United Nations Security Council Resolution 242 and 338 and the principle of territory for peace. This principle must be elaborated to provide for Israel's security and recognition, and at the same time for legitimate Palestinian political rights. Anything else would fail the twin tests of fairness and security. The time has come to put an end to Arab-Israeli conflict.

The war with Iraq is over. The quest for solutions to the problems in Lebanon, in the Arab-Israeli dispute, and in the Gulf must go forward with new vigor and determination. I guarantee you: No one will work harder for a stable peace in the region than we will.

Fourth, we must foster economic development for the sake of peace and progress. The Persian Gulf and Middle East form a region rich in natural resources with a wealth of untapped human potential. Resources once squandered on military might must be re-directed to more peaceful ends. We are already addressing the immediate economic consequences of Iraq's aggression. Now, the challenge is to reach higher - to foster economic freedom and prosperity for all people of the region.

By meeting these four challenges we can build a framework for peace. I have asked Secretary of State Baker to go to the Middle East to begin this process. He will go to listen, to probe, to offer suggestions, and to advance the search for peace and stability. I have also asked him to raise the plight of the hostages held in Lebanon. We have not forgotten them. We will not forget them.

To all the challenges that confront this region of the world, there is no single solution, no solely American answer. But we can make a difference. America will work tirelessly as a catalyst for positive change.

But we cannot lead a new world abroad if, at home, our politics are as usual on American defense and diplomacy.

It's time to turn away from the temptation to protect unneeded weapons systems and obsolete bases. It's time to put an end to micro-management of foreign and security assistance programs, micro-management that humiliates our friends and allies and hamstrings our diplomacy. It's time to rise above the parochial and the pork barrel - to do what is necessary, what's right, and what will enable this Nation to play the leadership role required of us.

The consequences of the conflict in the Gulf reach far beyond the confines of the Middle East. Twice before in this century, an entire world was convulsed by war. Twice this century, out of the horrors of war hope emerged for enduring peace. Twice before, those hopes proved to be a distant dream, beyond the grasp of man.

Until now, the world we've known has been a world divided - a world of barbed wire and concrete block, conflict and Cold War.

Now, we can see a new world coming into view. A world in which there is the very real prospect of a new world order. In the words of Winston Churchill, a "world order" in which "the principles of justice and fair play ... protect the weak against the strong. ..." A World where the United Nations, freed from Cold War stalemate, is poised to fulfill the historic vision of its founders. A world in which freedom and respect for human rights find a home among all nations.

The Gulf war put this new world to its first test. And my fellow Americans: We passed that test.

For the sake of our principles - for the sake of the Kuwaiti people - we stood our ground. Because the world would not look the other way, Ambassador Al-Sabah, tonight, Kuwait is free.

Tonight, as our troops begin to come home, let us recognize that the hard work of freedom still calls us forward. We've learned the hard lessons of history. The victory over Iraq was not waged as "a war to end all wars." Even the new world order cannot guarantee an era of perpetual peace. But enduring peace must be our mission.

Our success in the Gulf will shape not only the new world order we seek but our mission here at home.

In the war just ended, there were clear-cut objectives, timetables and, above all, an overriding imperative to achieve results. We must bring that same sense of self-discipline, that same sense of urgency, to the way we meet challenges here at home.

In my state of the Union address and in my budget, I defined a comprehensive agenda to prepare for the next American Century.

Our first priority is to get this economy rolling again. The fear and uncertainty caused by the crisis in the Gulf were understandable. But now that the war is over, oil prices are down, interest rates are down, and confidence is rightly coming back. Americans can move forward to lend, spend and invest in this, the strongest economy on Earth.

We must also enact the legislation that is key to building a better America. For example: In 1990, we enacted an historic Clean Air Act. Now we've proposed a National Energy Strategy. We passed a Child Care Bill that put power in the hands of parents. Today, we're ready to do the same thing with our schools, and expand choice in education. We passed a Crime Bill that made a useful start in fighting crime and drugs. This year we're sending to Congress our comprehensive crime package to finish the job. We passed the landmark Americans With Disabilities Act. Now we've sent forward our Civil Rights Bill. We also passed the Aviation Bill. This year we've sent up our new Highway Bill.

And these are just a few of our pending proposals for reform and renewal.

Tonight, I call on Congress to move forward aggressively on our domestic front. Let's begin with two initiatives we should be able to agree on quickly: Transportation and crime. And then, let's build on success with those and enact the rest of our agenda. If our forces could win the ground war in 100 hours, then surely the Congress can pass this legislation in 100 days. Let that be a promise we make tonight to the American people.

When I spoke in this House about the state of our Union, I asked all of you: if we can selflessly confront evil for the sake of good in a land so far away, then surely we can make this land all that it should be. In the time since then, the brave men and women of Desert Storm accomplished more than even they may realize. They set out to confront an enemy abroad, and in the process, they transformed a nation at home.

Think of the way they went about their mission - with confidence and quiet pride. Think about their sense of duty, about all they taught us, about our values, about ourselves.

We hear so often about our young people in turmoil; how our children fall short; how our schools fail us; how American products and American workers are second class. Well, don't you believe it. The America we saw in Desert Storm was first-class talent.

And they did it using America's state-of-the-art technology. We saw the excellence embodied in the Patriot missile and the patriots who made it work.

And we saw soldiers who know about honour and bravery and duty and country and the world-shaking power of these simple words.

There is something noble and majestic about the pride, about the patriotism, that we feel tonight.

So, to everyone here, and everyone watching at home, think about the men and women of Desert Storm. Let us honour them with our gratitude. Let us comfort the families of the fallen and remember each precious life lost.

Let us learn from them as well. Let us honor those who have served us by serving others.

Let us honor them as individuals - men and women of every race, all creeds and colors - by setting the face of this Nation against discrimination, bigotry and hate.

I'm sure many of you saw on television the unforgettable scene of four terrified Iraqi soldiers surrendering. They emerged from their bunker - broken, tears streaming from their eyes, fearing the worst. And then there was the American soldier. Remember what he said? He said: "It's okay. You're all right now. You're all right now."

That scene says a lot about America, a lot about who we are. Americans are a caring people. We are a good people, a generous people. Let us always be caring and good and generous in all we do.

Soon, our troops will begin the march we've all been waiting for - their march home. I have directed Secretary Cheney to begin the immediate return of American combat units from the Gulf.

Less than two hours from now, the first planeload of American soldiers will lift off from Saudi Arabia headed for the U.S.A. It will carry men and women of the 24th Mechanized Infantry Division bound for Fort Stewart, Georgia. This is just the beginning of a steady flow of American troops coming home.

Let their return remind us that all those who have gone before are linked with us in the long line of freedom's march. Americans have always tried to serve, to sacrifice nobly for what we believe to be right.

Tonight, I ask every community in this country to make this coming 4th of July a day of special celebration for our returning troops. They may have missed Thanksgiving and Christmas, but I can tell you this: For them and for their families, we can make this a holiday they'll never forget.

In a very real sense, this victory belongs to them - to the privates and the pilots, to the sergeants and the supply officers, to the men and women in the machines, and the men and women who made them work. It belongs to the regulars, to the reserves, to the Guard. This victory belongs to the finest fighting force this Nation has ever known.

We went halfway around the world to do what is moral and just and right. We fought hard, and - with others - we won the war. We lifted the yoke of aggression and tyranny from a small country that many Americans had never even heard of, and we ask nothing in return.

We're coming home now - proud. Confident - heads high. There is much that we must do at home and abroad. And we will do it. We are Americans.

May God bless this great Nation - the United States of America.

[*The declaration of a cease-fire by President Bush is reprinted in Chapter 8.*]

The Persian Gulf Crisis, Report Prepared by the Subcommittee on Arms Control and International Security and Science of the Committee on Foreign Affairs, US House of Represenatives, 102nd Congress, 1st Session, June 1991, at 259

10. Letter from President George Bush to Hon. Thomas S. Foley, Speaker of the House of Representatives, pursuant to Public Law 102-1, 19 March 1991.

DEAR MR. SPEAKER: On January 18, 1991, I reported to you that I had directed U.S. Armed Forces to commence combat operations against Iraqi forces and military targets in Iraq and Kuwait. I am now writing to report to you, consistent with the Authorization for Use of Military Force Against Iraq Resolution (Public Law 102-1), that these operations have been successfully conducted, Kuwait is liberated, and its legitimate government has been restored. Iraq is not yet in full compliance with all pertinent U.N. Security Council resolutions, however, and I anticipate that all of our forces will not withdraw from Iraqi territory until the Security Council is satisfied that Iraq has complied with Security Council requirements, including a formal cease-fire.

On February 27, I ordered a suspension of offensive combat operations. On March 2, the Security Council adopted Resolution 686, which demanded compliance by Iraq with the 12 resolutions previously adopted by the Security Council. Diplomatic efforts continue to achieve such compliance. Although I do not anticipate resumption of hostilities between Iraqi and Coalition forces, our forces will continue to be prepared to defend themselves if that should be necessary. U.S. forces have already begun to withdraw from the region, and it is my hope that the great bulk of the forces committed to the region will soon return home. However, we will continue efforts to ensure peace and stability in the region as contemplated by Security Council Resolution 678.

I am grateful for the continuing support that the Congress has given to this effort, and I look forward to continued consultation and cooperation as we move forward toward attainment of our goals in this region.

11. Interim Report to Congress, Conduct of the Persian Gulf Conflict, Pursuant toTitle V Persian Gulf Conflict Supplemental Authorization and Personnel Benefits Act of 1991 (Public Law 102-25), July 1991

[*Extract.*]

QUESTION 4:

The conduct of military operations.

The success of combat operations during Operation Desert Storm directly flowed from the planning, deployment, and training operations mounted by US and Coalition forces during Operation Desert Shield. ...

Supporting Naval Operations - Maritime Interdiction, Protection of Shipping and Amphibious Presence

Some limited military options were available to the President immediately after the Iraqi invasion in the form of the forward deployed Middle East Naval Force, long range air strikes from carrier battle groups in the Indian Ocean and Mediterranean, and from long range Air-force land-based bombers around the world. However, the balance of forces in the region at the time was heavily in Saddam's favor. Executing the limited warfare options immediately available would have initiated action prior to the necessary military buildup and the critical political and Coalition building process that was needed to insure political and military victory.

The United States demonstrated its early resolve by emphasizing and in some instances moving forward its Naval forces already deployed in the region. The presence of these capable, sustainable, politically tenable Naval forces reduced the risk to the land-based fighter assets and facilitated the quick deployment of US Marine and Army light forces to the theater with the mission to deter and to defend airfields and ports for subsequent reinforcement. Early in August, US forces faced the possibility of combat operations against a numerically superior force.

While demonstrating this resolve, the US also had to broaden the international support for economic, political and potential military actions against Iraq. The Maritime Intercept Operations undertaken initially by the US as a unilateral action and eventually as a part of a multinational coalition allowed us to put teeth into its warnings and political statements. The multinational naval force grew to incorporate ships and aircraft from over 20 navies. Under the overall coordination of the Commander, Middle East Force, intercept operations implemented United Nations Security Council resolutions 661, 665, and 670 and the guidance of the UN Sanctions Committee. On 17 August 1990, warning shots were fired as US Navy forces moved to stop Iraqi shipping on the high seas. This predominance of seapower using forward deployed and surged forces from the United States imposed economic interdiction upon Iraq, frustrated some of its purpose in the conquest of Kuwait, and facilitated worldwide political and military participation in the actions against its aggression. The embargo enforced at sea and imposed upon all routes to and from Iraq and Kuwait, continued to deplete the civilian and military capabilities of the Iraqis. From the beginning of interdiction operations until 24 June 1991, Coalition vessels intercepted over 10,600 ships, boarded over 1,660, and diverted nearly 100 vessels. Interdiction operations continue as this interim report is submitted.

Amphibious forces provided a flexible deployment option in responding to the early developing situation. These units added security to vital areas during the buildup of forces. The 4th Marine Expeditionary Brigade (MEB), embarked aboard 13 amphibious ships, arrived in theater in mid September. The 13th Marine Expeditionary Unit (MEU) also arrived during the same time frame. The 5th MEB, embarked aboard 13 additional amphibious ships, joined Gulf operating units shortly after the first of the year. These forces presented a continuous threat to the lateral flank of an enemy that might have considered advancing south from Kuwait.

An additional facet of Operation Desert Shield was the naval escort of the many ships delivering forces and logistics into the theater. Iraq's lack of a significant open-ocean navy facilitated the movement of seaborne reinforcements. By December, 1990, however, the growing mine threat began to preclude easy transit of the Gulf. With all ships alert, explosive ordnance disposal (EOD) personnel assisted individual ships with the destruction of floating mines. During hostilities, EOD teams and arriving minesweeper helicopters and ships assured that channels to key ports remained open and began to clear mines from the approaches to some of the potential amphibious landing areas. Mine clearing operations also continue as this interim report is being submitted.

The naval operations built on the decades of "over the horizon" naval presence which had sustained an active US presence in the theater, reinforced the credibility of the US commitment to the region. ...

Operation Desert Storm

Air Campaign Overview

The Operation Desert Storm air campaign was designed to paralyze Iraq's ability to maintain its occupation of Kuwait. The air campaign strategy was to paralyze the Iraqis [*sic*] leadership's ability to operate offensively and defensively, destroy Iraqi capability to threaten the security and stability of the region, render Iraqi forces in the Kuwait Theater of Operations (KTO) ineffective as a fighting force, and minimize Coalition and Iraqi civilian casualties. In order to rapidly accomplish these ends, the Coalition directed numerous air strikes on the following 12 target sets in Iraq and Kuwait:

- Leadership command facilities.

- Electrical production facilities powering military systems.

- Command, control, and communication nodes.

- Strategic and tactical integrated air defense systems.

- Air forces and airfields.

- Known nuclear, chemical, and biological weapons research and production facilities.

- Scud production and storage facilities.

- Naval forces and port facilities.

- Oil refining and distribution facilities, as opposed to long-term oil production capability.

- Railroads and bridges connecting Iraqi military forces with logistical support centers.

- Iraqi military units to include Republican Guard Forces in the KTO.

- Military storage sites.

The initial strikes of the air campaign attacked the entire target base to achieve nearly simultaneous impact against all target sets as opposed to striking one target set at a time. In this way, visible pressure and destructive effects against key Iraqi centers of gravity would occur all at once. While attacking all target categories, focus was maintained within the target sets. The highest initial priorities were to establish air supremacy by eliminating the Iraqi integrated air defense system, render enemy air forces ineffective, and to prevent Iraqi use of chemical and biological weapons. Achieving air supremacy facilitated the conduct of continuous air attacks with non-stealth aircraft against the complete range of targets. Stealth aircraft and cruise missiles allowed the Coalition to keep continuous pressure on key leadership as well as command and control nodes. Follow on strikes were conducted against each target set until the desired objective for each was obtained. Prior to D-Day, 43 Iraqi Divisions were situated throughout Iraq and Kuwait (Map 1) [*The maps referred to in tis and subsequent reports are not reproduced in this volume.*]

Phase I - The Strategic Air Campaign

The Strategic Air Campaign used the combined air-power of the Coalition to attack carefully selected enemy centers of gravity deep inside Iraq. Among those targets singled out for destruction were the command and control centers vital to Saddam's ability to direct the war effort and key infrastructure targets, needed to sustain Saddam's war effort. During the first 24 hours, over 1,300 combat sorties were flown by US and Coalition air forces, including 812 strike sorties by fixed wing aircraft. Additionally, the US Navy launched 106 Tomahawk missiles. After disrupting the Iraqi regime's vital functions, strategic air attacks continued throughout the war to prevent reconstitution, to restrike targets not completely destroyed, and to destroy other, newly identified targets supporting Iraq's war effort. In the aggregate, over 18,000 attack sorties were flown against strategic targets.

Phase I of Operation Desert Storm attacks began well before sunrise on the morning of 17 January 1991 (Maps 2, 3). H-Hour was fixed at 0300 local time. Prior to H-Hour, US Army Apache helicopters of the 101st Airborne Division, led by US Air Force MH-53J Pave Low Helicopters from the US Special Operations Command, struck Iraqi early warning radar sites along the Iraqi border with Hellfire missiles. Minutes before H-hour, an Air Force F-117A Stealth fighter from the 37th Tactical Fighter Wing destroyed a hardened air defense operations control center in Southern Iraq. The Coalition achieved strategic, operational, and tactical surprise with these first attacks. Unrelenting strikes continued until the ceasefire was ordered 43 days later.

At H-Hour, other F-117A pilots, having passed undetected through Iraqi air defenses, struck selected targets in Baghdad. Precision guided 2,000 pound bombs were directed to specific aim points on communications buildings, command and control facilities, and the headquarters for the internal security and intelligence organizations (Maps 4, 5). These strikes began the systematic and progressive dissection of the most critical elements of the national-level Iraqi military and political command. Throughout the war, F-117A Stealth aircraft, attacking at night, were the only manned aircraft to attack targets in central Baghdad. Beginning a few minutes after H-Hour, US Navy TLAMS from the Red Sea and Persian Gulf repeatedly attacked military targets (military headquarters, communications links, and power distributions centers in Baghdad) to assure constant pressure on enemy decision makers.

Attacks continued across the theater (Map 6). Air Force F-15E Strike Eagles began attacks against Scud production and launch facilities in western Iraq. Simultaneously, large numbers of US Navy, Marine, Air Force, and Coalition attack and support aircraft closed on strategic targets throughout Iraq and Kuwait, focusing on the integrated air defense system and Iraq's command and control infrastructure, including its communications and electrical power distribution system which supported Iraqi military operations. The air defense system, partially blinded by the first attacks, was overwhelmed by the sheer number of attacking aircraft. Nothing approaching the depth, breadth, magnitude, and simultaneity of this coordinated air attack had been previously achieved. The Iraqi air defense system could not coordinate a defense.

The early impact of the strategic air campaign on Iraqi war supporting infrastructure was significant. Iraq's internal fuels refining and production capability (as opposed to its crude oil production system, which was not targeted) was shut down, thus limiting Iraq's ability to supply fuel to its tanks, planes, and war machine. Saddam Hussein's internal telecommunications capability was badly damaged so that, while he could broadcast televised propaganda to the world via satellite, he was limited in the use of telecommunications to influence the Iraqi populace (Map 7). NBC weapons research and production was hampered.

A wide variety of combat aircraft were involved throughout the campaign. Navy and Marine A-6s and F/A-18s, Marine AV-8s and Navy A-7s attacked and destroyed air defense radars, communications nodes, and military headquarters. US and Coalition aircraft, such as UK and Saudi Tornado fighter-bombers, attacked Iraqi airfields to destroy aircraft and bomb support facilities, and to suppress air defenses. Air Force F-15s, Navy F-14s and Marine F/A-18s provided combat air patrol and sweeps for attack packages and played an important role in quickly establishing air supremacy. Air Force F-111s during the day and F-15Es at night and Navy A-6s conducted "tank plinking" missions with precision guided bombs. F-16s bombed a full range of targets throughout the theater. B-52 bombers dropped their ordnance on logistics sites and other targets. Air Force A-10s performed Scud-hunter and tank-killer missions. Forward based Marine Corps AV-8B aircraft responded to calls for air support by attacking enemy artillery positions north of Khafji.

Critical to the success of the air campaign was the role played by support aircraft. Without airborne tankers from the Air Force, Marine Corps and Navy, many Coalition warplanes would not have been able to hit targets deep in Iraq. Many aspects of Coalition air operations, from the initial deployments to the Scud-hunting efforts later in the war, would have been nearly impossible without aerial refueling. It enabled full exploitation of air supremacy by allowing combat aircraft to extend operational missions in terms of both time on station and distance to targets.

Also crucial to success were electronic countermeasures (ECM) "jamming" or "defense suppression" provided by support aircraft. Air Force EF-111 Ravens and F-4G Wild Weasels, Marine and Navy EA-6B Prowlers and F/A-18 Hornets, and Air Force EC-130 Compass Call participated in actions which determined threat locations, jammed enemy radar installations and attacked them with high-speed anti-radiation missiles (HARM). Additionally, long range Army tactical missiles (ATACMS) were used to attack Iraqi air defense sites. The support aircraft benefited from the early attacks and the fragmentation of the Iraqi air defense system which enabled the destruction of individual nodes. The Coalition suppression of enemy air defenses (SEAD) effort was instrumental in limiting aircraft losses.

Air Force E-3 airborne warning and control aircraft (AWACS) and Navy E-2C early warning aircraft operated around-the-clock to guard against attacks by Iraq's remaining air force and to provide airborne command and control. The Joint Surveillance Target Attack Radar System (JSTARS) operated during hours of darkness to provide surveillance of battlefield ground movement, to include Scud activities.

Careful targeting and expert use of technological superiority - including precision guided munitions - throughout the strategic air campaign minimized collateral damage and casualties to the civilian population, reflecting US policy that Saddam Hussein and his military machine, not the Iraqi people, were the enemy. Regrettably, there were civilian casualties. The most notable incident of Iraqi civilian casualties occurred when a penetrating bomb destroyed a hardened shelter in Baghdad used for military command communications. Many civilians who had, unbeknownst to the Coalition, taken shelter inside, were killed or injured.

One target of the Coalition's initial air campaign was Iraq's strategic offensive capability, including Iraq's Scud capability from production, to assembly, to storage, to launch sites. The first anti-Scud missions were flown on D-Day against fixed launch complexes in western Iraq in an attempt to prevent launches against Israel. Chemical weapons filling capability was also attacked on the first day. By the third day of air operations, attacks had begun on ballistic missile production and storage capability.

However, as the Iraqis began launching Scuds from their mobile systems, the Coalition effort was shifted to finding and destroying the mobile launchers (Map 8). The equivalent of three squadrons of aircraft were eventually assigned this very difficult mission against targets which would emerge from hiding places, fire, and hide again. F-16s in the west and A-10s in the east were placed on constant airborne alert during daylight hours, with F-15Es, F-16s and A-6Es on constant airborne alert at night. RF-4C and F-14A reconnaissance aircraft flew daily flights against suspected Scud sites. However, once a suspected Scud site was found through intelligence or following a launch, aircraft would proceed to the target area to search for and destroy the launch complex. In the end, Scud launches were not stopped, but they were suppressed. Launches averaged five per day for the first 10 days; however, they averaged only one per day for the remainder of the war. Tragically, one struck an Army barracks in Dhahran, inflicting the greatest casualties of the war on US forces due to a single event.

Many of the Scuds that were successfully launched went astray or were engaged by US missile defenses. Sensors detected Scud launches and sent attack warning and assessment information to Patriot batteries. The Patriot air defense missile system intercepted a high percentage of the engageable Scud missiles, although the warheads were sometimes not destroyed and debris fell on civilians. Nonetheless, the Patriot system proved to be an effective counter to Iraqi Scud attacks on innocent civilians, boosting civilian morale and enhancing Coalition cohesion. Patriots countered a sense of helplessness that civilian populations would otherwise have encountered. Without them, and without close communications established between the US and Israel during the war, Israel might have retaliated against Iraq, stressing the Coalition's political unity. Analyses of the Patriot systems and engagements are continuing. (Patriot systems are also discussed in response to Question 6.).

Within the first three weeks of the air campaign, Naval air (A-6 and F/A-18) and surface ships with armed helicopters sank and disabled Iraq's missile gunboats, minesweepers, patrol craft, and armed hovercraft and also destroyed Silkworm anti-ship sites. By 2 February the Iraqi Naval force was considered combat ineffective.

Overall, with the growing success of the Strategic Air Campaign, the weight of operations shifted to the KTO.

Phase II - Air Superiority in the KTO

Phase II was envisioned as a short period of intensive, focused air attacks on Iraqi air defense capability in the KTO to establish air superiority. In reality it took place in conjunction with Phase I, and established air supremacy over both Kuwait and Iraq. Phase II was a combined operation involving the aircraft of a number of Coalition nations as well as Navy, Marine and Air Force assets. The effectiveness of the Coalition counter air effort can be seen in several ways. The air-to-air fixed-wing score was 35 to none; Coalition aircraft shot down 35 Iraqi fixed wing aircraft without a single loss of friendly aircraft. Six Iraqi helicopters also were destroyed. Other targets included surface-to-air missile sites, airfields and command and control systems in the KTO. When the Iraqi Air Force attempted to hide in hardened shelters,

Coalition air systematically began to destroy them, prompting the Iraqi Air Forces' "flight to Iran." The result was quick attainment of air supremacy over Iraq and the KTO, enabling use of the air for Coalition purposes while denying it to the enemy. The purpose was to prepare the way for Phase III of the air campaign by enabling the operation of fixed and rotary wing aircraft at the medium altitudes where Iraq's extensive network of anti-aircraft artillery (AAA) would be less effective and bombing accuracy would be improved. By the 10th day of the air campaign, air supremacy over Iraq and Kuwait was declared.

Phase III - Battlefield Preparation

Unrelenting Coalition airpower from Air Force, Navy, Marine, Army and Coalition air elements, naval gunfire from Navy units in the Gulf, and ground based artillery and rocket systems methodically reduced Iraqi armor, artillery, and infantry forces. Over 35,000 attack sorties were flown against targets in the KTO, including 5,600 against Republican Guard forces. Artillery, command posts, command and control facilities, armor, and logistics installations were hit daily. As the start of the ground war (G-day) approached, more sorties were allocated to pave the way for battlefield preparation and breaching operations. B-52s were used along enemy front lines in conjunction with aircraft delivering psychological warfare leaflets to warn Iraqi forces of what to expect if they did not leave Kuwait.

Other than Scud attacks on Saudi and Israeli cities, one of the only responses Iraq was able to mount was the attack on Khafji which occurred on 29 January. The attack achieved some tactical surprise. Saddam's exact purpose is not known for certain, although he may have sought to probe Coalition forces or provoke the ground battle he had repeatedly said he wanted. Although Iraqi forces were able to mount the probing attack, their effort said much about what they could not do and did much to bolster the confidence of Arab members of the Coalition and confirmed the difficulty and vulnerability for Iraqi forces of attempting to move under air attack. The inept way that the Iraqi forces handled the attack, their weakness in night operations, the failure to introduce follow-on forces to exploit the advantage gained initially, and the disorder and chaos that accompanied their withdrawal were strong indications that the capability and the will of Saddam's armed forces had been broken. In tactical terms what his forces had set out to do was not difficult. Yet they were unable to achieve these limited objectives and their efforts required the resources of several divisions where one should have sufficed. Two to three divisions of what should have been the main thrust were caught in marshaling areas and on the roads north of the border and attacked effectively by Coalition air in 10 hours of night air attacks. By morning these elite forces were retreating. Meanwhile, Saudi and other Gulf Cooperation Council (GCC) states, supported by Marine air and artillery assets, evicted those elements in Khafji after a short fight. Khafji was an early indicator of how the Iraqi ground forces might perform in a full ground campaign and instilled further confidence in Coalition ground forces.

Throughout the occupation of Kuwait, Iraqi forces had systematically committed atrocities against the Kuwaiti people that included acts of torture and rape, and the murder of men, women and children. The country was also being stripped of public and private property by indiscriminate looting. During Phase III, Iraqis intentionally spilled millions of barrels of crude oil into the Gulf and also set fire to Kuwaiti well heads - either as actions of wanton destruction or as futile defensive efforts. The Coalition reaction to these events is discussed in the answer to Question 13. Two Navy ships struck mines on 18 February and suffered damage in the Northern Persian Gulf.

Phases I through III sought to shift the correlation of forces more in favor of the Coalition: this goal was achieved. In all, approximately 112,000 total combat and support sorties were flown and 288 TLAMS launched during Phases I-III (Map 9). Of the total sorties flown, 60% were combat missions. Damage to Iraqi forces was extensive, and Iraqi command and control was radically disrupted. Saddam was unable to direct the operations of his fielded forces, and in many cases corps, division and brigade commanders lost touch with their commands. Large amounts of equipment were rendered useless. Vast stockpiles of supplies Iraq positioned to support the KTO were depleted or destroyed, and the road nets over which replenishment had to pass were degraded. The intensive interdiction operations against fielded forces during Phase III sapped the morale of Iraqi forces - according to Iraqi officers later captured, desertion rates were substantial. Finally, Phase III greatly reduced the ability of Saddam to bring the strength of his army to bear against the Coalition forces. At the end of over a month of bombardment Iraqi forces remained in Kuwait; however, they were in poor condition with heavy desertions, low morale and their capability to coordinate an effective defense severely degraded. At the time the ground war was launched, the Commander-in-Chief, Central Command (CINCCENT) had assessed that, largely through the results of the Coalition air campaign, the overall combat effectiveness of the opposing Iraqi forces had been degraded by about 50%.

Weather was a factor during all phases of the operation. Approximately 40% of all scheduled attack sorties during the first 10 days of the air war were cancelled due to poor visibility or low overcast sky conditions in the KTO. Ceilings of 5,000 to 7,000 feet were not uncommon, especially during the last few days of the ground war. Coalition planners assumed the customary 13% cloud cover, typical for the region at that time of year. In fact, the cloud cover measured 39%, the worst in 14 years and possibly longer.

Throughout the war, air supremacy attained by the Coalition air forces enabled the Coalition ground forces to move across the battlefield without fear of interdiction. Air supremacy also played a key role in keeping undetected and unopposed massive lateral movements by Coalition forces prior to conducting the sweep around the right of the Iraqi position. Additionally, air attacks, combined with the rapidity of the ground advance in phase IV, kept Saddam Hussein from mounting a successful counter offensive.

Phase IV - The Ground Campaign

Phase IV was a combined land-air-sea operation designed to cut the lines of communication in southeastern Iraq, liberate Kuwait, and destroy the Republican Guard formations in the KTO. In concept, it was a coordinated, multinational, air, naval, and ground attack along multiple routes into Iraq and Kuwait - highlighted by a massive left flank envelopment through the Iraqi desert. A violent, rapid combined arms main attack deep into the rear along the Euphrates River Valley avoided the strength of the enemy's prepared defensive positions, and enveloped the elite Republican Guard. The rest of the Iraqi Army, trapped in Kuwait by the envelopment to the north and west and pressed from the south, would be forced either to surrender or be destroyed.

The Coalition ground forces for Phase IV of Operation Desert Storm were arrayed from left to right (west to east) in five major formations (Map 10). On the left flank was the XVIII Airborne Corps consisting of the 82d Airborne Division, the 101st Airborne Division (Air Assault), the 24th Mechanized Division, the 6th French

Armored Division (light), the 3d Armored Cavalry Regiment (ACR), and the 12th and 18th Aviation Brigades. To the right of the XVIII Airborne Corps was the US VII Corps with the 1st Infantry Division, 1st Cavalry Division(-) (initially as theater reserve), the 1st and 3d Armored Divisions, the 1st British Armored Division, the 2d ACR, and the 11th Aviation Brigade. In the center was Joint Forces Command-North (JFC-N) which consisted of the 3d Egyptian Mechanized Division, the 4th Egyptian Armored Division, the 9th Syrian Armored Division, an Egyptian Ranger Regiment, the 45th Syrian Commando Regiment, the 20th Mechanized Brigade of the Royal Saudi Land Forces (RSLF), the Kuwaiti Shaheed and Al-Tahrir Brigades, the 4th Saudi Armored Brigade (RSLF). On the right of JFC-N was the I Marine Expeditionary Force (I MEF), composed of the 1st and 2d Marine Divisions and the attached 1st (Tiger) Brigade of the US Army's 2d Armored Division. On the right flank was Joint Forces Command-East (JFC-E), composed of three task forces. TF Omar was comprised of the 10th Infantry Brigade (RSLF). United Arab Emirates Motorized Infantry Battalion, and an Omani Motorized Infantry Battalion. The second Task Force, TF Othman, consisted of the 8th Mechanized Infantry Brigade (RSLF) Bahrain Infantry Company, and the Kuwaiti Al-Fatah Brigade. The final Brigade, Abu Bakr, had the 2d Saudi Arabian National Guard Motorized Infantry Brigade and a Mechanized Battalion from Qatar armed forces.

VII and XVIII Corps and a number of Coalition forces - over 65,000 armored and support vehicles - were moved to attack positions on Iraq's right flank (Map 11). (XVIII Corps moved approximately 250 miles; VII Corps moved 150 miles. The total amount of personnel and equipment moved exceeded that moved by General Patton during his Army's attack into the German flank during the Battle of the Bulge.) This movement, which continued 24 hours a day for more than three weeks prior to the start of the ground war, was one of the largest movements of combat power in the annals of warfare. Whole divisions and their extensive support structures moved hundreds of miles undetected by the Iraqis. The move was conducted over what were for the most part unimproved roads, hardly more than tracks in the desert. The paucity of the road network not only made movement difficult, but also complicated the management of the movement. In order to avoid massive traffic jams, movement schedules were worked out to the last detail - every 15 seconds a vehicle passed a checkpoint.

Vast quantities of supplies were also shifted to the west by the 22d Support Command. These supply bases contained enough materiel to support combat operations for up to 60 days. Some of them were moved several times, first to the west and then northward once the operation commenced. Several lessons emerged from the planning for this initial shift, including the fact that US forces lack sufficient heavy equipment transporters (HETs) and trucks with off-road capabilities. The necessary HETs and trucks were only obtained by seeking assistance from other Coalition countries. A more complete description of this issue is contained in the response to Question 7.

During the same period numerous active deception measures were carried out by Special Operations Forces, Marine, Navy and Army units to deceive Iraqi forces of the Coalition's true intent. These included aggressive patrolling by ground forces, artillery raids, amphibious feints and the movement of ships, as well as air operations. All were designed to distract Iraqi attention and fix its forces in place. Ground force units were also engaged in reconnaissance-counter-reconnaissance with Iraqi forces during this period to deny the Iraqis information about Coalition intentions. Coalition air superiority was one of the single most important factors in denying the Iraqis a grasp of Coalition actions and preventing them from responding if they had received better intelligence.

Efforts to prepare the battlefield included a number of innovative approaches. Iraqi artillery, modern by any standard, often outranged Coalition guns, and had acquitted itself well in the Iran-Iraq war. While the Coalition could fix Iraqi ground forces in position - and did so - Iraqi artillery, left unchecked, could disrupt Coalition ground assaults. It provided a degree of flexibility to the Iraqis. Properly employed, enemy artillery could have delayed bridging operations long enough for some Iraqi counter-attack units to be deployed against them. Additionally, at this juncture, the possibility that Iraqi commanders might employ artillery-delivered chemical weapons was still a real concern. Accordingly, artillery raids were conducted by US Army and US Marine indirect fire elements to destroy Iraqi artillery positions. The Marines employed attack aircraft to counterstrike Iraqi artillery responding to these raids.

Another innovative approach was the extensive use of helicopters to locate Iraqi observation and command posts. Flying at night, teams of observation and attack helicopters found and destroyed a number of these positions using Hellfire and laser designated rounds such as Copperhead. The same tactics proved effective for air defense sites, which improved access for fixed wing aircraft.

Deception and preparation operations continued through G-Day. At G-1 final preparations in the form of cross-border raids and artillery raids were conducted while units moved into their final assembly areas. I MEF, including 1st and 2d Marine Divisions, destroyed 18 tanks and took 143 enemy prisoners of war (EPWs) on G-1 and continued a series of deception operations. VII Corps, designed as the main effort and given the task of driving northeast to destroy the Republican Guard units in the KTO, continued reconnaissance, counter-reconnaissance, artillery raids, and heliborne raids. Some of its elements established screening positions as far as 15 miles into Iraq.

At 0400 hours local time, 24 February 1991, the ground assault to liberate Kuwait began (Map 12). Four supporting attacks were launched to fix Iraqi operational reserves and Republican Guard forces so that they could be destroyed by the main attack. I MEF began the assault at 0400 with the 1st Marine Division breaching the first and second obstacle belts quickly and continuing to attack toward Al Jaber airfield. The division defeated several armored counterattacks throughout the day. At 0530, the 2nd Marine Division conducted breaching operations and continued the attack on the left flank of 1st Marine Division. These breaching operations were conducted efficiently due to detailed preparation, including reconnaissance and mapping of obstacles, followed by extensive training and rehearsals. At the end of the day, I MEF had captured over 8,000 EPWs. In the east, JFC-E cut six lanes through the first obstacle belt and began moving at 0800. It secured its initial objectives and continued north, capturing large numbers of Iraqis as it went. In the Gulf, the battleship USS Wisconsin engaged targets in Kuwait in support of the ground forces. In the west, the 1st Cavalry Division, the theater reserve, continued to conduct a feint into Wadi Al-Batin, the dry ravine that separates Kuwait from Iraq, where the Iraqis believed a main attack would come.

XVIII Corps also swept forward through its sector, with the 101st Airborne Division leaping ahead by air assault to secure objectives half way to the Euphrates. The Corps attack carried it to the west of the Iraqi obstacle belt. Less than seven hours into the operation, the French 6th Light Armored Division, supported by the 82d Airborne, secured its objectives and continued the attack northward. The 24th Infantry Division and the 3d ACR, on the extreme right of XVIII Corps, crossed the line of departure abreast and pressed their attacks as well. In the first day, the XVIII Corps captured about 2,500 EPWs. The high rate of advance of the I MEF, JFC-E, and the XVIII Airborne Corps enabled the theater commander to accelerate the time table for the remainder of the force.

VII Corps, the European based corps whose training prior to the crisis had been focused on conducting operations in a completely different environment, was able to cross the line of departure almost 15 hours ahead of schedule as a result of the success of the supporting attacks. A total of 16 lanes were cut through a complex obstacle belt of wire and land mines against little resistance. With the 2d ACR leading, the 1st Infantry Division and 1st and 3d Armored Divisions crossed the line of departure and attacked north. Their zone of attack was well to the west of Wadi Al-Batin in Iraq proper.

The 3d Egyptian Mechanized Division of JFC-N, followed by Force Khalid, also attacked on 24 February and encountered fire trenches. The Egyptians, concerned about an Iraqi armored counterattack, established blocking positions in sector.

On the second day of the ground war (G+1, 25 February), Coalition forces continued to press the attack (Map 13). JFC-E secured its objectives against light resistance and with very few casualties; however, by this point, progress was slowed by the large number of Iraqis who had surrendered. The 1st Marine Division completed the consolidation of Al-Jaber airfield and penetrated to within 10 miles of Kuwait City. Both Marine Divisions, attacking on a battlefield obscured by fog and smoke from intense oil fires, repulsed repeated enemy armor counterattacks, destroying or capturing between 175 and 200 tanks. The 5th MEB began to offload from amphibious ships and assumed the mission of I MEF reserve.

In the center, JFC-N continued to attack in concert with VII Corps. The Egyptian Corps secured a 16 square kilometer bridgehead. The 3d Egyptian Division continued its attack to the north and captured 1,500 EPWs and two tanks. Other units, including the 9th Syrian Armored Division, prepared to follow.

In the VII Corps zone of attack, the 1st British Armored Division attacked through the breach expanded by the 1st Infantry Division and destroyed the Iraqi 12th Armor Division. The 1st and 3d Armored Division continued their drive north with the 2d ACR as the advance guard. Units of VII Corps continued to focus their efforts on destroying Republican Guard forces. XVIII Corps continued supporting attacks to isolate Iraqi forces and intersect lines of communication.

The 1st Cavalry Division, in the role of theater reserve, conducted feints into the tri-border area. Additionally, feints and demonstrations by Navy and Marine amphibious forces off the coast tied down up to 10 divisions along the coast. The Amphibious Task Force conducted strike missions against Faylaka and Bubiyan islands along with a simulated Marine helicopter assault against Kuwaiti beaches, added to the confusion paralyzing the Iraqi High Command.

During this period, the massive exodus of Iraqi forces from the eastern portion of the theater began. Elements of the Iraqi III Corps, commanded by one of the best Iraqi field commanders, were pushed back on Kuwait City by I MEF and JFC-E. Iraqi units became intermingled and disorder ensued. These forces were joined by occupation troops based in Kuwait City. During the early morning hours of 26 January, military and civilian vehicles of every description loaded with Iraqi soldiers and goods looted from Kuwait, clogged the main four-lane highway north from Kuwait City. To deny Iraqi commanders the opportunity to reorganize their forces and establish a cohesive defensive line, these forces were repeatedly struck by air attacks.

Coalition forces continued operations well ahead of schedule on G+2 (26 February), meeting generally light resistance, although there were several sharp engagements (Map 14). JFC-E was so successful that its boundary was changed twice, and it was given four additional objectives. By day's end, units of the JFC-E, which was composed of forces from each of the GCC states, were positioned to lead a drive into Kuwait City.

I MEF advanced against moderate resistance. The 1st Marine Division seized Kuwait International Airport. This engagement lasted until the airport was secured at 0330, 26 February. The 2d Marine Division secured key objectives and road intersections west and northwest of Kuwait City. By securing Al Jahrah and the Mutla Ridge above Kuwait City, movement was controlled into and out of the city.

The JFC-N continued to attack, seizing intermediate and final objectives before evening. The Egyptian Corps then turned east and drove 60 miles to seize Al-Salem airfield.

VII Corps penetrated deep into Iraq and attacked reserve formations composed of armored and mechanized units of the Iraqi army and Republican Guards. The Corps executed a right turn and changed its focus with 1st British Armored Division continuing its attack to the east along the Iraq-Kuwait border. This had the effect of trapping and leaving open to destruction large numbers of Republican Guard forces. The XVIII Corps secured objectives and, after driving more than 200 miles across inhospitable desert, the 24th Mechanized Infantry Division reached the Euphrates River ... to complete the envelopment of Saddam's forces in southern Iraq and Kuwait. Although many Iraqis surrendered, some did not and there were a number of engagements with those forces. Supported by air and artillery, elements of VII and XVIII Corps overwhelmed the Iraqis, took large numbers of prisoners, and destroyed their equipment. By sunset on G+2, Coalition forces had pushed hundreds of miles into Iraq; captured over 30,000 EPWs; destroyed or rendered combat ineffective 26 of 42 Iraqi divisions; overwhelmed the Iraqi decision making process, rendered its command and control ineffective; and forced the Iraqi Army into full retreat. The XVIII Airborne Corps had secured the Coalition's left flank, and elements of the 101st Airborne Division and the 24th Mechanized Division controlled Highway 8.

Coalition forces continued to advance on the night of 26 February. VII Corps made the main effort in a coordinated attack against the three mechanized Republican Guard Divisions - the Tawakalna, the Medina, and the Hammurabi. As this operation began, the 1st Infantry Division in the south of the Corps zone, conducted a night passage through the 2d ACR, a very difficult maneuver, and immediately engaged the Iraqi forces. To the north, the 1st and 3d Armored Divisions attacked to the east and the 1st Cavalry Regiment, now committed to the main effort, attacked on the northern flank to prevent an Iraqi breakout in that direction. These attacks - against pockets of sometimes stiff resistance - continued into the next day.

Coalition air forces provided deep and close air support under adverse weather and anti-air threats during the ground campaign. Air Force A-10s and F-16s were launched from bases in Saudi Arabia during the day while F-15Es provided coverage at night. Navy carriers in the Gulf provided A-6s, A-7s and F/A-18s to strike targets beyond the fire support coordination line. Marine F/A-18s and A-6s from Bahrain and forward based AV-8s attacked targets and responded to requests for close air support in Kuwait. Army AH-64 Apache and Marine AH-1W Cobra helicopters provided close-in fire support for ground forces. Some aircraft flying combat missions were damaged and lost to AAA and IR missiles made more formidable by those aircraft having to fly under deteriorating weather conditions.

Exploitation and pursuit continued through G+3 (27 February) against rapidly disintegrating resistance (Map 15). JFC-E consolidated its position in southern Kuwait City and coordinated a link-up with JFC-N forces which were preparing to enter Kuwait City from the west. I MEF completed its offensive operations by securing its last objectives; the international airport and the high ground west of the city ahead of schedule. VII and XVIII Corps continued their attacks at 0800 local time to complete the offensive against the Republican Guard forces.

On G+4 (28 February) offensive operations ceased (Map 16).

Military-to-Military Talks at Safwan, Iraq

After the US and Coalition decision to cease offensive operations on 28 February, the Iraqis agreed to attend military-to-military talks to discuss cessation of hostilities, implementation of a cease fire, return of prisoners of war, and accounting for those missing in action, among other matters. A meeting lasting about 90 minutes was held on 3 March at Safwan airfield in southern Iraq, immediately north of the Kuwaiti border. CENTCOM chose the location because it was inside Iraq and near an airfield.

CINCCENT, the senior US officer, was accompanied by the senior commander of each coalition contingent. On the Iraqi side was Lieutenant General Sultan Hashim Ahmad Al-Jabburi, the Iraqi Vice Chief of Staff, accompanied by a staff of 10 senior officers, including the commander of the Iraqi III Corps, Major General Al-Dughastani. After preliminary formalities, General Schwarzkopf stated that he assumed that Baghdad had agreed to all US conditions or the Iraqi delegation would not be there. The Iraqis indicated that they were there to cooperate, although their attitude appeared hostile.

Two points emerged during this meeting that underscore the breadth of the Iraqi defeat. Following the Iraqi accounting of Coalition prisoners of war in Iraqi hands, Lieutenant General Al-Jabburi asked that the Coalition reciprocate and provide an accounting of Iraqi prisoners of war being held by the Coalition. When told that the counting was still going on, but at that time the number was in excess of 58,000, Lieutenant General Al-Jabburi appeared stunned. In apparent disbelief he asked the Iraqi III Corps commander if that was a correct number. Major General Al-Dughastani replied that it was possible, but that he did not know.

General Schwarzkopf proposed that a line be drawn on a map from which all forces would withdraw at least one kilometer to prevent inadvertent contact between Iraqi and Coalition forces. Lieutenant General Al-Jabburi agreed. When shown the CENTCOM proposed line, the Iraqi asked why the line was drawn behind his troops. General Schwarzkopf said that the line was the forward line of the US advance. Lieutenant General Al-Jabburi again appeared stunned. Once again he queried his III Corps commander, who again said it was possible, but that he did not know. Following this, the Iraqi attitude was noticeably more subdued.

EMERGING OBSERVATIONS

Some Accomplishments

- Multinational air campaign isolated and incapacitated the Iraqi command structure and severely degraded and demoralized Iraqi forces.

- Multinational, multi-axis ground campaign succeeded in enveloping Iraqi forces, penetrating Iraqi lines to liberate Kuwait City, and destroying the remaining combat effectiveness of Iraqi units, including Republican Guard, in the KTO.

- Strategic deception was important to ground campaign success.

- Scud attacks failed to bring Israel into the war. With efforts, the number of Scud launches were reduced.

- Known Iraqi NBC production facilities were degraded.

- Coalition casualties were light by historical standards.

- US equipment previously untested in major combat engagements worked well.

Some Shortcomings

- Sea countermine and especially shallow water countermine capabilities need improvement.

- Continual expansion of the tactical missile threat, as illustrated by Iraqi Scud attacks, indicate that US anti-tactical ballistic missile (ATBM) capabilities must be improved.

- Many ground units lacked sufficient off-road mobility vehicles and heavy equipment transporters.

- The opportunity to place forces in theater with seven months to train aided in the effectiveness of the Coalition. In a faster paced situation, those opportunities may not be available. There needs to be continued emphasis on inter-Service training in combined and joint operations.

- Locating and destroying mobile missiles proved very difficult and diverted significant resources.

Some Selected Issues

- Available lift for a second large crisis would be severely constrained.

- The complexities of joint military contingency planning are compounded when forces of many nations respond together. Improved, flexible planning processes compatible with such improvised, quick response contingencies are needed.

- Strategic Air Command (SAC) combat wings in Southwest Asia were composed of people and equipment from more than one stateside wing in order to maintain Single Integrated Operations Plan (SIOP) capabilities.

- Maritime Intercept Operations were of enormous scope. They required that detailed guidance be issued to international merchantmen.

...

QUESTION 13:

The actions taken by the Coalition forces in anticipation of, and in response to, Iraqi acts of environmental terrorism.

During the Persian Gulf crisis, Iraq intentionally inflicted significant damage on the environment. It is estimated that 7-9 million barrels of oil were deliberately released into the Gulf and 590 oil wellheads were damaged (508 set on fire and 82 were free flowing). The long term effects of the deliberate and wanton assaults on the environment by Iraqi forces in Kuwait have not yet been determined, and may not be fully known for years to come.

While it was impossible to predict the scale of potential environmental damage, Coalition forces were aware relatively early on in the crisis that acts intentionally harmful to the environment were likely. Early efforts were made to formulate contingency responses and significant efforts were made during the war to minimize damage.

Pre-crisis contingency planning had identified the potential use of oil in attacks. Oil could be dumped into the Persian Gulf either from on-shore terminals or from tankers lying at anchor. This would foul the Gulf and might force states further south to shut down their desalinization plants with resulting shortages of potable water with severe military, as well as civilian and ecological consequences. In addition, dumping oil into the Gulf also might impact naval operations, including amphibious operations. This was based not so much on the fact that the oil might be ignited, as upon the fact that it might be drawn into the ships' cooling and evaporation systems.

Other contingencies included oil trench and well fires which could be ignited either as military obstacles or obscurants, or to damage Kuwait economically. Another oil-related danger was the creation of pools of oil high in hydrogen sulfide, creating potentially lethal pockets of gas.

A major concern during contingency planning was the protection of Saudi facilities. A threat to these facilities did not materialize. Nevertheless, countering it was part of the Coalition's planning.

Early recognition of the threat of inflicting environmental damage led to several interagency studies designed to assess the potential effects of what was essentially a new form of coercion. The Department collaborated closely with the intelligence community and the Department of Energy (DOE) in this effort. The intelligence community provided several assessments on Iraqi capabilities and probable intentions on the use of oil as a potential weapon. DOE sponsored a Sandia National Laboratories evaluation of the potential environmental impacts if oil were used against the Coalition. The problems that were faced were twofold: how to deter Iraqi use of oil, and, if it were used, how to minimize the effects.

Means to deter or restrict Saddam's capability to inflict environmental damage were limited. Assessments weighed whether aerial bombardment by the Coalition of key Kuwaiti facilities prior to Iraqi sabotage might cause more damage than it prevented or provoke the Iraqis to embark on an even more widespread campaign. As with other remaining uncertainties about Iraqi decision making, their motivation continues to be unclear.

When Saddam began the environmental sabotage, the Coalition responded with measured military force and technical assistance that achieved limited success. On 24 January, Iraq started releasing oil into the Gulf. US attempts to ignite floating oil slicks in the vicinity of the terminal to limit the spread of oil met with little success. On 25 January, DOD established a 24-hour oil spill task force. On 27 January, US air strikes against oil manifolds at the tank farms upstream from the Al-Ahmadi terminal stopped the flow of oil into the Gulf. DOD and intelligence community experts provided specific targeting information which was essential to mission success. At the request of the Saudi government, the US dispatched on 27 January an interagency team to provide advice and to train Saudi specialists on oil spill response techniques. The Saudi Arabian Ministry of Environmental Protection contracted for installation of additional deep and shallow water booming equipment and skimmers to mitigate the effects of oil spills on the coast line and to prevent leakage into ports, desalinization plants, and adjacent industrial areas. Some critical equipment was delivered by air. Action on the part of the Coalition, based upon prior consideration of the potential for environmental sabotage, did much to limit the damage.

The danger of oil slicks to ships' cooling and evaporation systems was avoided. Interagency assistance team members from the National Oceanic and Atmospheric Administration (NOAA), aided by US Coast Guard aircraft, closely tracked the oil slick. Based on accurate current reports, naval forces navigated around oil slicks or shut down vulnerable systems when needed to avoid damage.

The operational impact of oil fires and smoke on the Coalition forces attacking toward Kuwait City was mixed. Air support was severely hampered. As direction and strength shifted, surface winds initially complicated then ultimately favored Coalition forces by blowing from south to north during the ground offensive.

Oil fires continue as of this report; the environmental impact of the oil field fires and oil spills is massive and continuing. The environmental dimensions of such sabotage remains of great concern to the Department. Analysis of the effects of such environmental pollution on military operations remains an Administration priority.

EMERGING OBSERVATIONS

Some Accomplishments

- Early recognition of the threat of oil as a potential terrorist weapon resulted in study and planning to counter this threat to military operations, desalinization plants and the environment.

- US air strikes on 27 January 1991 on the oil manifolds at the tank farms upstream from the Al-Ahmadi terminal stopped the flow of oil into the Gulf. Cooperation of DOD and intelligence community experts resulted in mission success.

- Coalition bombing to destroy feeder lines and ignite fire trenches largely reduced this threat prior to the ground campaign.

- US and allied forces were strategically situated in Saudi Arabia to defend oil facilities within their zones.

- While preparations for a significant impact to Saudi Desalinization plants were made, the oil spilled had negligible impact on the fresh water supply. Rapid containment actions minimized the impact on water desalinization plants.

- Oil slicks did not have any significant impact on naval operations in the Gulf despite the earlier fears that oil might be drawn into ship evaporation systems and cooling lines.

- On 27 January 1991, a US Government Interagency Team was dispatched to Saudi Arabia, at the request of the Saudi Arabian Ministry of Environmental Protection to advise and train on oil spill response techniques.

Some Shortcomings

- Exercising physical control over Kuwait's oil fields and collection facilities, Iraq could not be stopped from detonating numerous oil wells. Iraq succeeded in releasing oil into the Persian Gulf.

- Significant environmental damage was done; its scope continues to be investigated.

A Selected Issue

- The deterrence of, and responses to, environmental attacks are new dimensions to national security challenges.

...

QUESTION 16:

The rules of engagement for Coalition forces.

In US use, Peacetime Rules of Engagement, or ROE, are formal guidelines approved by the National Command Authority (NCA) governing the employment of military weaponry in encounters with hostile or potentially hostile forces. Based on the principle of self-defense, the ROE are established through a process which is explicitly designed to support the needs of commanders in the field to tailor ROE to their specific circumstances and missions. Continued application and lessons learned over many years in many contingencies have led to the frequent refinement of both the ROE and the ROE-tailoring processes employed in this conflict.

The following sections briefly describe the management of formal US ROE, and then, going beyond the strict bounds of "ROE", the broader subject of the coordination achieved among the national forces of the different members of the Coalition.

US ROE Management

For Operation Desert Shield, standing Peacetime Rules of Engagement, supplemented with measures to enhance protection of US forces in light of demonstrated Iraqi aggressiveness, met the needs of the defensive mission. ROE were modified as the Iraqi threat evolved and as the mission expanded to include offensive tasks. In order to speed NCA approval, proposed changes were coordinated by a staff network which linked a Joint Staff planning cell and their Central Command (CENTCOM) counterparts with the office of the Under Secretary of Defense (Policy) and the office of the DOD General Counsel. This continuous process was judged to have provided timely, responsive ROE authorizations.

Coalition Coordination

As military command relationships developed among the Coalition, US ROE became effective for, or were consistent with, all Coalition combatant forces. This compatibility was ensured by coordination meetings between US and allied commanders. Additionally, US liaison teams linked US commanders with other forces to assure that US and many different Coalition forces acted in harmony and operated effectively together.

Guidance for the conduct of maritime intercept operations was derived from the principles established by United Nations Security Council resolutions and the UN Sanctions Committee. US Navy ships conducting the interdiction operations were augmented by US Coast Guard law enforcement detachments which provided training and technical expertise to Navy boarding teams and, where available, accompanied the ships' boarding parties. As with the operations ashore, meetings between the various national naval commanders and liaison teams ensured a notably effective degree of consistency and cooperation among the many different navies engaged in the sanctions-enforcing mission.

EMERGING OBSERVATIONS

Some Accomplishments

- The US ROE process proved effective in providing for timely NCA approval as the Commander-in-Chief, Central Command sought to tailor ROE to evolving circumstances and missions.

- The use of US liaison teams and coordination meetings provided for effective coordination among the multinational forces.

...

Number of military and civilian casualties sustained by Coalition forces. Estimates of military and civilian casualties sustained by Iraq and by nations not directly participating in the Gulf conflict.

All casualties, military or civilian, are significant. But in historical terms, Coalition casualties were relatively light in Operation Desert Storm. The effectiveness of the Coalition campaign took the initiative from Iraq and prevented Iraq from regaining its balance or inflicting significant casualties on Coalition forces. The precision of the Coalition attack minimized Iraqi civilian casualties. The humaneness of the Coalition spared many Iraqi military casualties. At the same time, Iraqi Scud attacks inflicted civilian casualties with no military purpose.

There is as yet no final total of US casualties. During Operation Desert Shield there were 84 US non-battle deaths. Non-battle deaths include personnel lost by reason of disease or injury not related to the enemy (such as vehicle accidents or heart attacks). US commanders are not required by established reporting procedures to report non-battle injuries to the National Command Authority during non-combat situations such as Operation Desert Shield. During Operation Desert Storm, non-battle injuries were required to be reported. The official US military casualty figures as of 24 June 1991 are as follows: killed in action - 148; wounded in action - 458; non-battle deaths - 138; non-battle injuries - 2,978. (Different organizations keep these figures on slightly different bases which accounts for slight discrepancies among different sources of data.) The vast majority of those receiving non-battle injuries have been returned to duty.

There were a number of Scud missile attacks on Coalition forces within the Kuwait Theater of Operations during Desert Storm. We do not know the number of casualties caused by particular weapon systems. However, the largest single cause of American losses was the 25 February Scud missile attack that hit a US barracks in Dhahran, Saudi Arabia, killing 28 US military personnel and injuring 97.

There is no formal system for reporting Coalition military casualty figures, much less Coalition civilian casualties. Estimates for non-US Coalition military casualties are: killed in action - 192; wounded in action - 318. Kuwaiti civilian casualties were undoubtedly substantial as a result of wanton acts of murder and torture on the part of Iraqi occupation forces. An accounting of these deaths continues.

Very limited information is available on which to base an assessment of Iraqi military casualties. Iraq probably cannot accurately account for its casualties given the destruction of administrative headquarters, the overrunning and scattering of entire divisions, the widespread desertions of officers and enlisted personnel, and the subsequent military actions against the Shi'ites in the south and the Kurds in the north.

In several ways, Coalition actions avoided unnecessary Iraqi military casualties. First, the Coalition Psychological Operations campaign induced Iraqi desertions and thereby lowered Iraqi and Coalition battle casualties. Coalition tactics also focused on targeting vehicles and equipment, not people. Coalition forces, on a number of occasions, held their fire to permit unarmed Iraqi soldiers to retreat, even though the rules of war would not have required this restraint.

The Department does not have accurate assessments of the collateral damage and casualties suffered as a result of Operation Desert Storm among the civilian population of Iraq. The accuracy of eventual estimates may be affected by the civilian deaths suffered when Saddam's regime crushed the Kurdish and Shi'ite uprisings following the war. The Coalition sought to minimize civilian losses through use of precision munitions and various restrictions on the employment of weapons during Desert Storm. For example, the Coalition restricted the use of weapons employed near civilian areas, permitting some attacks only during the night when most civilians would be home and not near the target area. Other restrictions included not allowing attacks if targets could not be positively identified and avoiding valid military targets in close proximity to civilian areas, including combat aircraft parked in civilian housing areas or near historic sites. In addition, as the ground war was prosecuted, the preparatory artillery fires and bombardment that would normally lead to further civilian casualties were obviated by the rapidity of the ground forces advance.

The Department has not developed an independent estimate of civilian casualties in Jordan, Iran, or Israel, although there were certainly Israeli civilian casualties from Scud missile attacks and, reportedly, Jordanian casualties along truck routes inside western Iraq. The Department knows of no military casualties sustained by countries not participating directly in the war.

EMERGING OBSERVATIONS

Some Accomplishments

- Although any losses are troubling, Coalition casualty figures were exceptionally light in historical terms.

- The precision and effectiveness of the Coalition campaign reduced Coalition casualties and Iraqi civilian casualties.

- The Coalition took several actions that reduced unnecessary Iraqi military casualties.

A Shortcoming

- There is limited information available to assess Iraqi military and civilian casualties.

12. Conduct of the Persian Gulf War, Final Report to Congress, Pursuant to Title V of The Persian Gulf Conflict Supplemental Authorization and Personnel Benefits Act of 1991 (Public Law 102-25), April 1992

[*Extract.*]

...

APPENDIX 0

THE ROLE OF THE LAW OF WAR

"Decisions were impacted by legal considerations at every level, [the law of war] proved invaluable in the decision-making process."

General Colin Powell,
Chairman, Joint Chiefs of Staff

BACKGROUND

The United States, its Coalition partners, and Iraq are parties to numerous law of war treaties intended to minimize unnecessary suffering by combatants and noncombatants during war. The US military's law of war program is one of the more comprehensive in the world. As indicated in this appendix, it is US policy that its forces will conduct military operations in a manner consistent with US law of war obligations. This appendix discusses the principal law of war issues that arose during Operation Desert Storm.

As defined in Joint Publication 1-02, Department of Defense (DOD) Dictionary of Military and Associated Terms (1 December 1989), the law of war is "That part of international law that regulates the conduct of armed hostilities. It is often termed the law of armed conflict." While the terms are synonymous, this appendix will use "law of war" for consistency. Both concepts of *jus ad bellum* and *jus in bello* are covered in this appendix.

In addition to the United Nations Charter, with its prohibition against the threat or use of force against the territorial integrity or political independence of any state, treaties applicable to the Persian Gulf War include:

- Hague Convention IV and its Annex Respecting the Laws and Customs of War on Land of 18 October 1907 ("Hague IV").

- Hague Convention V Respecting the Rights and Duties of Neutral Powers and Persons in Case of War on Land of 18 October 1907 ("Hague V").

- Hague Convention VIII Relative to the Laying of Automatic Submarine Contact Mines of 18 October 1907 ("Hague VIII").

- Hague Convention IX Concerning Bombardment by Naval Forces in Time of War of 18 October 1907 ("Hague IX").

- Geneva Protocol for the Prohibition of the Use of Asphyxiating, Poisonous or Other Gases, and of Bacteriological Methods of Warfare of 17 June 1925 ("1925 Geneva Protocol").

- Convention on the Prevention and Punishment of the Crime of Genocide of 9 December 1948 ("the Genocide Convention").

- The four Geneva Conventions for the Protection of War Victims of August 12, 1949:

  - Geneva Convention for the Amelioration of the Condition of Wounded and Sick in Armed Forces in the Field ("GWS").

  - Geneva Convention for the Amelioration of the Wounded, Sick and Shipwrecked Members of Armed Forces at Sea (hereinafter "GWS [Sea]").

  - Geneva Convention Relative to the Treatment of Prisoners of War ("GPW").

  - Geneva Convention Relative to the Protection of Civilian Persons in Time of War ("GC").

- Hague Convention for the Protection of Cultural Property in the Event of Armed Conflict of 14 May 1954 ("1954 Hague"). Since Iraq, Kuwait, France, Egypt, Saudi Arabia, and other Coalition members are parties to this treaty, the treaty was binding between Iraq and Kuwait, and between Iraq and those Coalition members in the Persian Gulf War. Canada, Great Britain, and the United States are not parties to this treaty. However, the armed forces of each receive training on its provisions, and the treaty was followed by all Coalition forces in the Persian Gulf War.

The United States is a party to all of these treaties, except the 1954 Hague Cultural Property Convention. While Iraq is not a party to Hague IV, the International Military Tribunal (Nuremberg, 1946) stated with regard to it that:

> The rules of land warfare expressed in ... [Hague IV] undoubtedly represented an advance over existing International Law at the time of their adoption ... but by 1939 these rules ... were recognized by all civilized nations and were regarded as being declaratory of the laws and customs of war.

As customary international law, its obligations are binding upon all nations. Neither is Iraq a party to Hague V, Hague VIII, or Hague IX. However, the provisions of each cited herein are regarded as a reflection of the customary practice of nations, and therefore binding upon all nations.

The United States, other Coalition members, and Iraq are parties to the 1925 Geneva Protocol which prohibits the use of chemical (CW) or bacteriological (biological) weapons (BW) in time of war. Both Iraq and the United States filed a reservation to this treaty at the time of their respective ratifications. Iraq's reservation accepted the 1925 Geneva Protocol as prohibiting first use of CW or BW weapons; the United States, having unilaterally renounced the use of BW in 1969, accepted without reservation the prohibition on BW and first use of CW. (The United States also is a party to the Convention on the Prohibition of Development, Production and Stockpiling of Bacteriological [Biological] and Toxin Weapons and on Their Destruction of 10 April 1972; Iraq is not.) All nations party to the Persian Gulf conflict, including Iraq, are parties to the four 1949 Geneva Conventions for the protection of war victims. The precise applicability of these treaties will be addressed in the discussion of each topic in this appendix.

Three other law of war treaties were not legally applicable in the Persian Gulf War, but nonetheless bear mention. They are:

- 1977 Convention on the Prohibition of Military or Any Other Hostile Use of Environmental Modification Techniques ("ENMOD Convention"). While the United States and many of its Coalition partners are parties to this treaty, Iraq has signed but not ratified the ENMOD Convention; therefore it was not legally applicable to Iraqi actions during the Persian Gulf War.

- 1977 Protocol I Additional to the Geneva Conventions of 12 August 1949 ("Protocol I"). From 1974 to 1977 the United States and more than 100 other nations participated in a Diplomatic Conference intended to supplement the 1949 Geneva Conventions and modernize the law of war. That conference produced two new law of war treaties: Protocol I deals with the law of war in international armed conflicts, while Protocol II addresses the law of war applicable to internal armed conflicts. Iraq and several Coalition members, including the United States, Great Britain, and France, are not parties to Protocol I; therefore it was not applicable during the Persian Gulf War. For humanitarian, military, and political reasons, the United States in 1987 declined to become a party to Protocol I; France reached a similar decision in 1984.

- 1980 Convention on Prohibitions or Restrictions on the Use of Certain Conventional Weapons. Iraq and most of the Coalition partners, including the United States, are not parties to this treaty; it had no applicability in the Persian Gulf War. However, US and Coalition actions were consistent with its language. Iraqi actions were consistent with the treaty except as to its provisions on land mines and booby traps.

ROLE OF LEGAL ADVISERS

The Office of General Counsel of the Department of Defense (DOD), as the chief DOD legal office, provided advice to the Secretary of Defense, the Deputy Secretary of Defense, the Under Secretary of Defense for Policy, other senior advisers to the Secretary and to the various components of the Defense legal community on all matters relating to Operations Desert Shield and Desert Storm, including the law of war. For example, the Secretary of Defense tasked the General Counsel to review and opine on such diverse issues as the means of collecting and obligating for defense purposes contributions from third countries; the Wars Powers Resolution; DOD targeting policies; the rules of engagement; the rules pertinent to maritime interception operations; issues relating to the treatment of prisoners of war; sensitive intelligence and special access matters; and similar matters of the highest priority to the Secretary and DOD. In addition, military judge advocates and civilian attorneys with international law expertise provided advice on the law of war and other legal issues at every level of command in all phases of Operations Desert Shield and Desert Storm. Particular attention was given to the review of target lists to ensure the consistency of targets selected for attack with United States law of war obligations.

TAKING OF HOSTAGES

Whatever the purpose, whether for intimidation, concessions, reprisal, or to render areas or legitimate military objects immune from military operations, the taking of hostages is unequivocally and expressly prohibited by Article 34, GC. [The United States is party to the International Convention Against Taking of Hostages of 17 December 1979, under which hostage taking is identified as an act of international terrorism.]

Applicability of the GC was triggered by Iraq's invasion of Kuwait on 2 August; thereafter Iraq was an Occupying Power in Kuwait, with express obligations. Under Articles 5, 42, and 78, GC, Iraq could intern foreign nationals only if internal security made it "absolutely necessary" (in Iraq) or "imperative" (in Kuwait). Iraq asserted no rights under any of these provisions in defense of its illegal taking of hostages in Iraq and Kuwait.

United Nations Security Council (UNSC) Resolution 664 (18 August) overrode authority inconsistent with its obligations under the GC that Iraq might have claimed to restrict the departure of US citizens and other third-country nationals in Kuwait or Iraq, and clarified the legal status of noncombatants.

Hostage taking by Iraq can be divided into four categories:

- The taking of Kuwaiti nationals as hostages and individual and mass forcible deportations to Iraq, in violation of Articles 34 and 49, GC;

- The taking of third-country nationals in Kuwait as hostages and individual and mass forcible deportations from Kuwait to Iraq, in violation of Articles 34 and 49, GC;

- The taking of foreign nationals within Iraq as hostages, with individual and mass forcible transfers, in violation of Articles 34 and 35, GC; and

- Compelling Kuwaiti and other foreign citizens to serve in the armed forces of Iraq, in violation of Article 51, GC.

The taking of hostages, their unlawful deportation, and compelling hostages to serve in the armed forces of Iraq constitute Grave Breaches (that is, major violations of the law of war) under Article 147, GC.

US and other hostages in Iraq, including civilians forcibly deported from Kuwait, were placed in or around military targets as "human shields", in violation of

Articles 28 and 38(4), GC. Use of Coalition prisoners of war (POWs) to shield military targets from attack will be considered in the section of this appendix on the treatment of POWs; other abuses of protected civilians will be addressed in the sections on Treatment of Civilians in Occupied Territory and War Crimes.

Iraq released US and other third-party hostages (i.e., other than Kuwaiti citizens) held in either Kuwait or Iraq in December. Because they were permitted to depart well before offensive combat operations began, Iraq's initial taking of hostages from such nations had no effect on US or Coalition force planning or execution of military operations.

Although it was known that some Kuwaiti nationals were being held in Iraq before offensive combat operations began, their presence did not appreciably affect Coalition force planning or execution of military operations. Thus, although the President had declared the United States would not be deterred from attacking legitimate targets because Iraq may have placed protected persons in their vicinity, it does not appear that any Kuwaiti nationals were placed at risk in that fashion after Iraqi release of its third party hostages. Iraq did use its own civilian population for this purpose, however, as will be explained in the section on targeting, collateral damage and collateral civilian casualties.

Kuwaiti nationals (and other residents of Kuwait) were taken hostage and forcibly deported from Kuwait to Iraq by retreating Iraqi troops as the Coalition forces' liberation of Kuwait reached its final phase. Although the plight of those hostages was a source of great concern to US and other Coalition forces, the fact of their seizure did not have a significant effect on the planning or execution of Coalition military operations.

TREATMENT OF CIVILIANS IN OCCUPIED TERRITORY

The GC governs the treatment of civilians in occupied territories. As previously indicated, all parties to the conflict, including Iraq, are parties to this convention. The treaty's application was triggered by the Iraqi invasion, and was specifically recognized in UNSC resolutions that addressed that crisis.

An earlier law of war treaty that remains relevant is Hague IV, which contains regulations relating to the protection of civilian property (public and private) in occupied territory; in contrast, the GC sets forth the obligations of an occupying power in providing protection for civilians in occupied territory. Cultural property in Kuwait also was protected by the 1954 Hague Cultural Property Convention.

Iraqi actions read like a very long list of violations of Hague IV, GC, and the 1954 Hague Cultural Property Convention. From the beginning of its invasion of Kuwait, Iraq exhibited an intent not only to refuse to conduct itself as an occupying power, but to deny that it was an occupying power. Its intention was to annex Kuwait as a part of Iraq, and remove any vestige of Kuwait's previous existence as an independent, sovereign nation. (Its transfer of a part of its own civilian population into Kuwait for the purpose of annexation and resettlement constitutes a violation of Article 49, GC.)

A case can be made that Iraqi actions may violate the Genocide Convention, which defines genocide as any of the following acts committed with the intent to destroy, in whole or in part, a national, ethnical, racial or religious group:

- Killing members of the group;

- Causing serious bodily or mental harm to members of the group;

- Deliberately inflicting on the group conditions of life calculated to bring about its physical destruction in whole or in part;

- Imposing measures intended to prevent births within the group; or

- Forcibly transferring children of the group to another group.

Iraq carried out every act of the types condemned by the Genocide Convention, except for forcibly transferring children. Many Kuwaiti citizens were deported forcibly to Iraq; many others were tortured and/or murdered. There were instances of Kuwaiti women of child-bearing age being brutally rendered incapable of having children. Collective executions of innocent Kuwaiti civilians took place routinely. Kuwaiti public records were removed or destroyed, apparently to prevent or impede the reconstitution of Kuwait if Kuwait were liberated. Kuwaiti identification cards and license plates were revoked and replaced with Iraqi credentials, identifying Kuwait as Iraq's 19th province.

In violation of Hague IV and the 1954 Hague Cultural Property Convention, cultural, private and public (municipal and national) property was confiscated; pillage was widespread. (Confiscation of private property is prohibited under any circumstance, as is the confiscation of municipal public property. Confiscation of movable national public property is prohibited without military need and cash compensation, while immovable national public property may be temporarily confiscated under the concept of usufruct - the right to use another's property so long as it is not damaged.)

Iraqi confiscation appears to have been primarily, if not entirely, part of a program:

- Of erasing any record of the sovereign state of Kuwait;

- Of looting directed by the Iraqi leadership to provide consumer goods for the Iraqi public; and

- Of looting by individual Iraqi soldiers, which was tolerated by Iraqi military commanders and higher civilian and military authorities.

Civilians who remained in Kuwait were denied the necessities for survival, such as food, water, and basic medical care, in violation of Articles 55 and 56, GC. Kuwaiti doctors were forcibly deported to Iraq; Filipino nurses working in the hospitals were raped repeatedly by Iraqi soldiers. Kuwaiti civilians were not permitted any medical care unless they presented Iraqi identification cards; presentation of an Iraqi identification card by a Kuwaiti citizen seldom resulted in any genuine medical care. Medical supplies and equipment in Kuwaiti hospitals necessary for the needs of the civilian population of Kuwait were illegally taken, in violation of Article 57, GC, in brutal disregard for Kuwaiti lives. For example, there are reports that infants died in Kuwaiti hospitals after Iraqis removed them from their incubators, which were shipped to Iraq.

The slightest perceived offense could lead to torture and execution of the purported offender, often in front of family members. Torture and murder of civilians is prohibited by Article 32, GC. Iraqi policy provided for the collective punishment of the family of any individual who served in or was suspected of assisting the Kuwaiti resistance. This punishment routinely took the form of destruction of the family home and execution of all family members. Collective punishment is prohibited expressly by Article 33, GC.

The Iraqi occupation remained brutal until the every end; civilians were murdered in the final days of that occupation to eliminate witnesses to Iraqi repression. The Government of Kuwait estimates that 1,082 civilians were murdered during the occupation. Many more were forcibly deported to Iraq; several thousand remain missing. On their departure, Iraqi forces set off previously placed explosive charges on Kuwait's oil wells, a vengeful act of wanton destruction.

Coalition forces acted briefly as an occupying power. When the Operation Desert Storm ground offensive began, Coalition forces moved into Iraq. Physical seizure and control of Iraqi territory triggered the application of Hague IV and the GC. Both treaties initially had little practical application, since Coalition forces occupied uninhabited desert. As hostilities diminished, the internal conflict that erupted in Iraq caused thousands of civilians to flee the fighting (such as in Al-Basrah, between Iraqi military units and Shi'ite forces) and to enter territory held by Coalition forces. Allied forces provided food, water and medical care to these refugees. As Coalition forces prepared to withdraw from Iraq, no international relief agency was ready to assume this relief effort. Consequently, refugees were offered the opportunity to move to the refugee camp at Rafha, Saudi Arabia. Approximately 20,000 refugees (including more than 8,000 from the Safwan area) accepted this offer.

In the conflict's latter phases, public and private international relief agency representatives entered the area of conflict, often without sufficient advance notification and coordination with Coalition authorities. While relief agencies undoubtedly were anxious to perform humanitarian missions, their entry onto the battlefield without the advance consent of the parties to the conflict is not consistent with Article 9, GWS (a provision common to all four 1949 Geneva Conventions), Article 125, GPW, and Article 63, GC. It impeded Coalition efforts to end hostilities as rapidly as possible, and placed these organizations' members at risk from the ongoing hostilities. Coalition aviation units searching for mobile Scud missile launchers in western Iraq were inhibited in their efforts to neutralize that threat by vehicles from those organizations moving through Scud missile operating areas that otherwise were devoid of civilians. The lack of timely, proper coordination by relief agencies with Coalition forces adversely affected air strikes against other Iraqi targets on other occasions. While well-intentioned, these intrusions required increased diligence by Coalition forces, placed Coalition forces at increased risk, and were factors in the failure to resolve the Scud threat.

Whether in territory Coalition forces occupied or in parts of Iraq still under Iraqi control, US and Coalition operations in Iraq were carefully attuned to the fact those operations were being conducted in an area encompassing "the cradle of civilization", near many archaeological sites of great cultural significance. Coalition operations were conducted in a way that balanced maximum possible protection for those cultural sites against protection of Coalition lives and accomplishment of the assigned mission.

While Article 4(1) of the 1954 Hague Convention provides specific protection for cultural property, Article 4(2) permits waiver of that protection where military necessity makes such a waiver imperative; such "imperative military necessity" can occur when an enemy uses cultural property and its immediate surroundings to protect legitimate military targets, in violation of Article 4(1). Coalition forces continued to respect Iraqi cultural property, even where Iraqi forces used such property to shield military targets from attack. However, some indirect damage may have occurred to some Iraqi cultural property due to the concussive effect of munitions directed against Iraqi targets some distance away from the cultural sites.

Since US military doctrine is prepared consistent with US law of war obligations and policies, the provisions of Hague IV, GC, and the 1954 Hague Convention did not have any significant adverse effect on planning or executing military operations.

TARGETING, COLLATERAL DAMAGE AND CIVILIAN CASUALTIES

The law of war with respect to targeting, collateral damage and collateral civilian casualties is derived from the principle of discrimination; that is, the necessity for distinguishing between combatants, who may be attacked, and noncombatants, against whom an intentional attack may not be directed, and between legitimate military targets and civilian objects. Although this is a major part of the foundation on which the law of war is built, it is one of the least codified portions of that law.

As a general principle, the law of war prohibits the intentional destruction of civilian objects not imperatively required by military necessity and the direct, intentional attack of civilians not taking part in hostilities. The United States takes these proscriptions into account in developing and acquiring weapons systems, and in using them in combat. Central Command (CENTCOM) forces adhered to these fundamental law of war proscriptions in conducting military operations during Operation Desert Storm through discriminating target selection and careful matching of available forces and weapons systems to selected targets and Iraqi defenses, without regard to Iraqi violations of its law of war obligations toward the civilian population and civilian objects.

Several treaty provisions specifically address the responsibility to minimize collateral damage to civilian objects and injury to civilians. Article 23(g) of the Annex to Hague IV prohibits destruction not "imperatively demanded by the necessities of war", while Article 27 of that same annex offers protection from intentional attack to "buildings dedicated to religion, art, science, or charitable purposes, historic monuments, hospitals, and places where the sick and wounded are collected, provided they are not being used at the time for military purposes." Similar language is contained in Article 5 of Hague IX, while the conditions for protection of cultural property in the 1954 Hague Cultural Property Convention were set forth in the preceding discussion on the treatment of civilians in occupied territory. In summary, cultural and civilian objects are protected from direct, intentional attack unless they are used for military purposes, such as shielding military objects from attack.

While the prohibition contained in Article 23(g) generally refers to intentional destruction or injury, it also precludes collateral damage of civilian objects or injury to noncombatant civilians that is clearly disproportionate to the military advantage gained in the attack of military objectives, as discussed below. As previously indicated, Hague IV was found to be part of customary international law in the course of war crimes trials following World War II, and continues to be so regarded.

An uncodified but similar provision is the principle of proportionality. It prohibits military action in which the negative effects (such as collateral civilian casualties) clearly outweigh the military gain. This balancing may be done on a target-by-target basis, as frequently was the case during Operation Desert Storm, but also may be weighed in overall terms against campaign objectives. CENTCOM conducted its campaign with a focus on minimizing collateral civilian casualties and damage to civilian objects. Some targets were specifically avoided because the value of destruction of each target was outweighed by the potential risk to nearby civilians or, as in the case of certain archaeological and religious sites, to civilian objects.

Coalition forces took several steps to minimize the risk of injury to noncombatants. To the degree possible and consistent with allowable risk to aircraft and aircrews, aircraft and munitions were selected so that attacks on targets within populated areas would provide the greatest possible accuracy and the least risk to civilian objects and the civilian population. Where required, attacking aircraft were accompanied by support mission aircraft to minimize attacking aircraft aircrew distraction from their assigned mission. Aircrews attacking targets in populated areas were directed not to expend their munitions if they lacked positive identification of their targets. When this occurred, aircrews dropped their bombs on alternate targets or returned to base with their weapons.

One reason for the maneuver plan adopted for the ground campaign was that it avoided populated areas, where Coalition and Iraqi civilian casualties and damage to civilian objects necessarily would have been high. This was a factor in deciding against an amphibious assault into Kuwait City.

The principle of proportionality acknowledges the unfortunate inevitability of collateral civilian casualties and collateral damage to civilian objects when noncombatants and civilian objects are mingled with combatants and targets, even with reasonable efforts by the parties to a conflict to minimize collateral injury and damage.

This proved to be the case in the air campaign. Despite conducting the most discriminate air campaign in history, including extraordinary measures by Coalition aircrews to minimize collateral civilian casualties, the Coalition could not avoid causing some collateral damage and injury.

There are several reasons for this. One is the fact that in any modern society, many objects intended for civilian use also may be used for military purposes. A bridge or highway vital to daily commuter and business traffic can be equally crucial to military traffic, or support for a nation's war effort. Railroads, airports, seaports, and the interstate highway system in the United States have been funded by the Congress in part because of US national security concerns, for example; each proved invaluable to the movement of US military units to various ports for deployment to Southwest Asia (SWA) for Operations Desert Shield and Desert Storm. Destruction of a bridge, airport, or port facility, or interdiction of a highway can be equally important in impeding an enemy's war effort.

The same is true with regard to major utilities; for example, microwave towers for everyday, peacetime civilian communications can constitute a vital part of a military command and control (C2) system, while electric power grids can be used simultaneously for military and civilian purposes. Some Iraqi military installations had separate electrical generators; others did not. Industries essential to the manufacturing of CW, BW and conventional weapons depended on the national electric power grid.

Experience in its 1980-1988 war with Iran caused the Government of Iraq to develop a substantial and comprehensive degree of redundancy in its normal, civilian utilities as back-up for its national defense. Much of this redundancy, by necessity, was in urban areas. Attack of these targets necessarily placed the civilian population at risk, unless civilians were evacuated from the surrounding area. Iraqi authorities elected not to move civilians away from objects they knew were legitimate military targets, thereby placing those civilians at risk of injury incidental to Coalition attacks against these targets, notwithstanding efforts by the Coalition to minimize risk to innocent civilians.

When objects are used concurrently for civilian and military purposes, they are liable to attack if there is a military advantage to be gained in their attack. ("Military advantage" is not restricted to tactical gains, but is linked to the full context of a war strategy, in this instance, the execution of the Coalition war plan for liberation of Kuwait.)

Attack of all segments of the Iraqi communications system was essential to destruction of Iraqi military C2. C2 was crucial to Iraq's integrated air defense system; it was of equal importance for Iraqi ground forces. Iraqi C2 was highly centralized. With Saddam Hussein's fear of internal threats to his rule, he has discouraged individual initiative while emphasizing positive control. Iraqi military commanders were authorized to do only that which was directed by highest authority. Destruction of its C2 capabilities would make Iraqi combat forces unable to respond quickly to Coalition initiatives.

Baghdad bridges crossing the Euphrates River contained the multiple fiber-optic links that provided Saddam Hussein with secure communications to his southern group of forces. Attack of these bridges severed those secure communication links, while restricting movement of Iraqi military forces and deployment of CW and BW warfare capabilities. Civilians using those bridges or near other targets at the time of their attack were at risk of injury incidental to the legitimate attack of those targets.

Another reason for collateral damage to civilian objects and injury to civilians during Operation Desert Storm lay in the policy of the Government of Iraq, which purposely used both Iraqi and Kuwaiti civilian populations and civilian objects as shields for military objects. Contrary to the admonishment against such conduct contained in Article 19, GWS, Articles 18 and 28, GC, Article 4(1), 1954 Hague, and certain principles of customary law codified in Protocol I (discussed below), the Government of Iraq placed military assets (personnel, weapons, and equipment) in civilian populated areas and next to protected objects (mosques, medical facilities, and cultural sites) in an effort to protect them from attack. For this purpose, Iraqi military helicopters were dispersed into residential areas; and military supplies were stored in mosques, schools, and hospitals in Iraq and Kuwait. Similarly, a cache of Iraqi Silkworm surface-to-surface missiles was found inside a school in a populated area in Kuwait City. UN inspectors uncovered chemical bomb production equipment while inspecting a sugar factory in Iraq. The equipment had been moved to the site to escape Coalition air strikes. This intentional mingling of military objects with civilian objects naturally placed the civilian population living nearby, working within, or using those civilian objects at risk from legitimate military attacks on those military objects.

The Coalition targeted specific military objects in populated areas, which the law of war permits; at no time were civilian areas as such attacked. Coalition forces also chose not to attack many military targets in populated areas or in or adjacent to cultural (archaeological) sites, even though attack of those military targets is authorized by the law of war. The attack of legitimate Iraqi military targets, notwithstanding the fact it resulted in collateral injury to civilians and damage to civilian objects, was consistent with the customary practice of nations and the law of war.

The Government of Iraq sought to convey a highly inaccurate image of indiscriminate bombing by the Coalition through a deliberate disinformation campaign. Iraq utilized any collateral damage that occurred - including damage or injury caused by Iraqi surface-to-air missiles and anti-aircraft munitions falling to earth in populated areas - in its campaign to convey the misimpression that the Coalition was targeting populated areas and civilian objects. This disinformation campaign was factually incorrect, and did not accurately reflect the high degree of care exercised by the Coalition in attack of Iraqi targets.

For example, on 11 February, a mosque at Al-Basrah was dismantled by Iraqi authorities to feign bomb damage; the dome was removed and the building dismantled. US authorities noted there was no damage to the minaret, courtyard building, or dome foundation which would have been present had the building been struck by Coalition munitions. The nearest bomb crater was outside the facility, the result of an air strike directed against a nearby military target on 30 January. Other examples include use of photographs of damage that occurred during Iraq's war with Iran, as well as of prewar earthquake damage, which were offered by Iraqi officials as proof of bomb damage caused by Coalition air raids.

Minimizing collateral damage and injury is a responsibility shared by attacker and defender. Article 48 of the 1977 Protocol I provides that:

> In order to ensure respect for and protection of the civilian population and civilian objects, the Parties to the conflict shall at all times distinguish between the civilian population and combatants and between civilian objects and military objectives and accordingly shall direct their operations only against military objectives.

Paragraph one of Article 49 of Protocol I states that "'Attacks' means acts of violence against the adversary, whether in offense or defense." Use of the word "attacks" in this manner is etymologically inconsistent with its customary use in any of the six official languages of Protocol I. Conversely, the word "attack" or "attacks" historically has referred to and today refers to offensive operations only. Article 49(1) otherwise reflects the applicability of the law of war to actions of both attacker and defender, including the obligation to take appropriate measures to minimize injury to civilians not participating in hostilities.

As previously indicated, the United States in 1987 declined to become a party to Protocol I; nor was Protocol I in effect during the Persian Gulf War, since Iraq is not a party to that treaty. However, the language of Articles 48 and 49(1) (except for the erroneous use of the word "attacks") is generally regarded as a codification of the customary practice of nations, and therefore binding on all.

In the effort to minimize collateral civilian casualties, a substantial responsibility for protection of the civilian population rests with the party controlling the civilian population. Historically, and from a common sense standpoint, the party controlling the civilian population has the opportunity and the responsibility to minimize the risk to the civilian population through the separation of military objects from the civilian population, evacuation of the civilian population from near immovable military objects, and development of air raid precautions. Throughout World War II, for example, both Axis and Allied nations took each of these steps to protect their respective civilian populations from the effects of military operations.

The Government of Iraq elected not to take routine air-raid precautions to protect its civilian population. Civilians were not evacuated in any significant numbers from Baghdad, nor were they removed from proximity to legitimate military targets. There were air raid shelters for less than 1 percent of the civilian population of Baghdad. The Government of Iraq chose instead to use its civilians to shield legitimate military targets from attack, exploiting collateral civilian casualties and damage to civilian objects in its disinformation campaign to erode international and US domestic support for the Coalition effort to liberate Kuwait.

The presence of civilians will not render a target immune from attack; legitimate targets may be attacked wherever located (outside neutral territory and waters). An attacker must exercise reasonable precautions to minimize incidental or collateral injury to the civilian population or damage to civilian objects, consistent with mission accomplishment and allowable risk to the attacking forces. The defending party must exercise reasonable precautions to separate the civilian population and civilian objects from military objectives, and avoid placing military objectives in the midst of the civilian population. As previously indicated, a defender is expressly prohibited from using the civilian population or civilian objects (including cultural property) to shield legitimate targets from attack.

The Government of Iraq was aware of its law of war obligations. In the month preceding the Coalition air campaign, for example, a civil defense exercise was conducted, during which more than one million civilians were evacuated from Baghdad. No government evacuation program was undertaken during the Coalition air campaign. As previously indicated, the Government of Iraq elected instead to mix military objects with the civilian population. Pronouncements that Coalition air forces would not attack populated areas increased Iraqi movement of military objects into populated areas in Iraq and Kuwait to shield them from attack, in callous disregard of its law of war obligations and the safety of its own civilians and Kuwaiti civilians.

Similar actions were taken by the Government of Iraq to use cultural property to protect legitimate targets from attack; a classic example was the positioning of two fighter aircraft adjacent to the ancient temple of Ur (as depicted in the photograph in Volume II, Chapter VI, "Off Limits Targets" section) on the theory that Coalition respect for the protection of cultural property would preclude the attack of those aircraft. While the law of war permits the attack of the two fighter aircraft, with Iraq bearing responsibility for any damage to the temple, Commander-in-Chief, Central Command (CINCCENT) elected not to attack the aircraft on the basis of respect for cultural property and the belief that positioning of the aircraft adjacent to Ur (without servicing equipment or a runway nearby) effectively had placed each out of action, thereby limiting the value of their destruction by Coalition air forces when weighed against the risk of damage to the temple. Other cultural property similarly remained on the Coalition no-attack list, despite Iraqi placement of valuable military equipment in or near those sites.

Undoubtedly, the most tragic result of this intentional commingling of military objects with the civilian population occurred in the 13 February attack on the Al-Firdus Bunker (also sometimes referred to as the Al-'Amariyah bunker) in Baghdad. Originally constructed during the Iran-Iraq War as an air raid shelter, it had been converted to a military C2 bunker in the middle of a populated area. While the entrance(s) to a bomb shelter permit easy and rapid entrance and exit, barbed wire had been placed around the Al-Firdus bunker, its entrances had been secured to prevent unauthorized access, and armed guards had been posted. It also had been camouflaged. Knowing Coalition air attacks on targets in Baghdad took advantage of the cover of darkness, Iraqi authorities permitted selected civilians - apparently the families of officer personnel working in the bunker - to enter the Al-'Amariyah Bunker at night to use the former air raid shelter part of the bunker, on a level above the C2 center. Coalition authorities were unaware of the presence of these civilians in the bunker complex. The 13 February attack of the Al-'Amariyah bunker - a legitimate military target - resulted in the unfortunate deaths of those Iraqi civilians who had taken refuge above the C2 center.

An attacker operating in the fog of war may make decisions that will lead to innocent civilians' deaths. The death of civilians always is regrettable, but inevitable when a defender fails to honour his own law of war obligations - or callously disregards them, as was the case with Saddam Hussein. In reviewing an incident such as the attack of the Al-'Amariyah bunker, the law of war recognizes the difficulty of decision making amid the confusion of war. Leaders and commanders necessarily have to make decisions on the basis of their assessment of the information reasonably available to them at the time, rather than what is determined in hindsight.

Protocol I establishes similar legal requirements. Articles 51(7) and 58 of the 1977 Protocol I expressly prohibit a defender from using the civilian population or individual civilians to render certain points or areas immune from military operations, in particular in an attempt to shield military objectives from attack or to shield, favor or impede military operations; obligate a defender to remove the civilian population, individual civilians and civilian objects under the defender's control from near military objectives; avoid locating military objectives within or near densely populated areas; and to take other necessary precautions to protect the civilian population, individual civilians and civilian objects under its control against the dangers resulting from military operations.

It is in this area that deficiencies of the 1977 Protocol I become apparent. As correctly stated in Article 51(8) of Protocol I, a nation confronted with callous actions by its opponent (such as the use of "human shields") is not released from its obligation to exercise reasonable precaution to minimize collateral injury to the civilian population or damage to civilian objects. This obligation was recognized by Coalition forces in the conduct of their operations. In practice, this concept tends to facilitate the disinformation campaign of a callous opponent by focusing international public opinion upon the obligation of the attacking force to minimize collateral civilian casualties and damage to civilian objects - a result fully consistent with Iraq's strategy in this regard. This inherent problem is worsened by the language of Article 52(3) of Protocol I, which states:

> In case of doubt whether an object which is normally dedicated to civilian purposes, such as a place of worship, a house or other dwelling or a school, is being used to make an effective contribution to military action, it shall be presumed not to be so used.

This language, which is not a codification of the customary practice of nations, causes several things to occur that are contrary to the traditional law of war. It shifts the burden for determining the precise use of an object from the party controlling that object (and therefore in possession of the facts as to its use) to the party lacking such control and facts, i.e., from defender to attacker. This imbalance ignores the realities of war in demanding a degree of certainty of an attacker that seldom exists in combat. It also encourages a defender to ignore its obligation to separate the civilian population, individual civilians and civilian objects from military objectives, as the Government of Iraq illustrated during the Persian Gulf War.

In the case of the Al-Firdus bunker, for example - repeatedly and incorrectly referred to by the Government of Iraq and some media representatives as a "civilian bomb shelter" - the Coalition forces had evidence the bunker was being used as an Iraqi command and control center and had no knowledge it was concurrently being used as a bomb shelter for civilians. Under the rule of international law known as military necessity, which permits the attack of structures used to further an enemy's prosecution of a war, this was a legitimate military target. Coalition forces had no obligation to refrain from attacking it. If Coalition forces had known that Iraqi civilians were occupying it as a shelter, they may have withheld an attack until the civilians had removed themselves (although the law of war does not require such restraint). Iraq had an obligation under the law of war to refrain from commingling its civilian population with what was an obviously military target. Alternatively, Iraq could have designated the location as a hospital, safety zone, or a neutral zone, as provided for in Articles 14 and 15, GC.

ENEMY PRISONER OF WAR PROGRAM

This section contains similar information to that contained in Appendix L, but is a more condensed version of that appendix, with emphasis on the legal aspects of the Enemy Prisoner of War (EPW) program. Appendix L used the same base information as Appendix O, but expands to include more operational issues.

Coalition care for EPWs was in strict compliance with the 1949 Geneva Convention relative to the treatment of Prisoners of War (hereafter "GPW"). Centralized management of EPW operations began during Operation Desert Shield and continued throughout Operation Desert Storm. The US National Prisoner of War Information Center (NPWIC) became operational before ground operations began and a new automated information program for preserving, cataloging, and accounting for captured personnel (as required by the GPW) was fielded in Operation Desert Shield. Trained Reserve Component (RC) EPW units were activated, and camp advisory teams were sent to Saudi Arabia to account for and to provide technical assistance on custody and treatment of US-transferred EPWs.

EPWs captured by Coalition forces during Operations Desert Shield and Desert Storm were maintained in either a US or Saudi EPW camp. The United States accepted EPWs captured by the United Kingdom (UK) and France, while Saudi Arabia managed a consolidated camp for those EPWs captured by the remaining Coalition forces.

The Army, as the DOD Executive Agent for EPW operations, processed 69,822 Iraqi EPWs captured by British, French, and US forces between 18 January, when the first EPW was captured, and 2 May, when the last EPW in US custody was transferred to Saudi Arabian control. In terms of campaign length vis-a-vis EPWs captured, this was the most extensive US EPW operation since World War II. US forces captured 62,456 EPWs during the conflict. Additionally, 1,492 displaced civilians were evacuated to Saudi Arabia through EPW channels. Some of these initially were believed to be EPWs; others were evacuated for their own safety. French and British forces captured an additional 5,874 EPWs and transferred them to US control. The Arab Command captured 16,921 EPWs. Always of international interest and concern, the humane treatment of and full accountability for EPWs and displaced civilians during this conflict received heightened attention because of religious and cultural sensitivities.

US and other Coalition forces treated EPWs and displaced civilians in accordance with the 1949 Geneva Conventions for the Protection of War Victims. The first three conventions mandate humane treatment and full accountability for all prisoners of war from the moment of capture until their repatriation, release, or death. The fourth convention (GC) requires humane treatment for displaced civilians. The International Committee of the Red Cross (ICRC) was provided access to Coalition EPW facilities and reviewed their findings with Coalition representatives in periodic meetings in Riyadh, Saudi Arabia. While US and Coalition forces worked closely with the ICRC on EPW matters throughout Operation Desert Storm, neither the ICRC nor any other human rights organization played any other role affecting the course of the war. The ICRC was ineffective in providing any protection for US and Coalition POWs in Iraq's custody.

NPWIC was established at the Pentagon during Operation Desert Shield using active duty personnel and became fully operational with Reserve staffing on 21 January. Its mission was to account for EPWs in US custody and to ensure compliance with the 1949 Geneva Conventions. Article 122, GPW requires a captor to establish a National Information Bureau within the shortest time possible after the onset of hostilities. The NPWIC, manned by Army Reserve Individual

Mobilization Augmentees, volunteer Reservists and retired personnel, served as a central repository for information relative to EPWs captured by or transferred to US forces, and coordinated information pertaining to EPWs and US POWs in Iraqi hands with the ICRC.

The US and Saudi governments concluded an agreement which allowed the US to transfer captured EPWs to Saudi control after processing by US EPW elements. This agreement was applicable to EPWs captured by the French and British, as those EPWs were processed and maintained in US EPW camps. The US provided camp advisory teams to work with the Government of Saudi Arabia to assist in compliance with the 1949 Geneva Conventions, to facilitate logistic and administrative cooperation, and to maintain accountability for US-transferred EPWs. The size of the host nation EPW camps limited the number of EPWs the United States could transfer, and required that EPWs remain longer in US EPW camps. After active hostilities ended, in order to transfer all EPWs still under US control, the Brooklyn (West) EPW camp, along with its EPWs, was transferred to the Saudi Arabian National Guard.

To help accomplish its multiple missions, the NPWIC and theater EPW units used the Prisoner of War Information System (PWIS-2), an automated system to speed processing and to provide a database of information on captured personnel. The development of PWIS-2 was accelerated during Operation Desert Shield to allow the US to process the massive numbers of EPWs projected from the Kuwaiti Theater of Operations. The system arrived in the field in November with the first EPW unit in SWA. Under the previous manual system, the average of eight EPW could be fully processed per hour per camp. With PWIS-2, EPW units were processing up to 1,500 EPWs per day per camp. Accuracy was at an unprecedented level of 99.9 percent.

Eight EPWs died while in US custody, all as a result of injuries or sickness contracted before capture. One died of malnutrition/dehydration, five as a result of injuries or wounds, and two from unknown causes. Three US-transferred EPWs died in Saudi Arabian camps from wounds received in the Saudi camp, either during an EPW riot or inflicted by another EPW. These deaths were investigated and reported to the ICRC, as required by Articles 120, 122, and 123, GPW.

When Operation Desert Storm began, psychological operations were undertaken to encourage maximum defection or surrender of Iraqi forces. Leaflets to be used as safe conduct passes were widely disseminated over and behind Iraqi lines with great success.

Photographs and videotapes of the first Iraqi EPWs captured were taken and shown by the public media. The capture or detention of EPWs is recognized as newsworthy events and, as such, photography of such events is not prohibited by the GPW. However, Article 13, GPW does prohibit photography that might humiliate or degrade any EPW. Media use of photographs of EPWs raised some apprehension in light of formal US condemnation of the forced videotapes of US and Coalition POWs being made and shown by Iraq. CENTCOM and other DOD officials also expressed concern for the safety of the family of any Iraqi defector who might be identified from media photographs by Iraqi officials. Because of these sensitivities, and consistent with Article 13, GPW, DOD developed guidelines for photographing EPWs. These guidelines limited both the opportunities for photography and the display of EPW photographs taken, while protecting Iraqi EPWs and their families from retribution by the Government of Iraq.

Operation Desert Storm netted a large number of persons thought to be EPWs who were actually displaced civilians. Subsequent interrogations determined that they were innocent civilians who had taken no hostile action against Coalition forces. In some cases, individuals had surrendered to Coalition forces to receive food, water, and lodging, while others were captured because they appeared to be part of hostile forces. Tribunals were conducted to verify the status of detainees. Upon determination of their status as innocent civilians, detainees were transferred from US custody to Safwan, a US-operated refugee camp, or to Rafha, a Saudi Arabian refugee camp.

In March, Coalition forces and Iraqi military representatives signed an agreement for the repatriation of prisoners of war, to be conducted under ICRC auspices. Repatriation of EPWs not in medical channels occurred at Judaydat 'Ar-'Ar, near the Jordanian border. Those in medical channels were flown directly to Baghdad on ICRC aircraft.

Treatment of Prisoners of War

US and Coalition personnel captured by Iraq were POWs protected by the GWS (if wounded, injured, or sick) and GPW. All US POWs captured during the Persian Gulf War were moved to Baghdad by land after their capture. With some exceptions, depending on their location at the time of capture, their route usually was through Kuwait City to Al-Basrah and then on to Baghdad. Those taken to Kuwait City and Al-Basrah usually were detained there for no more than a few hours or overnight. Limited interrogation of POWs occurred in these cities. Although some were physically abused during their transit to Baghdad, most were treated reasonably well.

On arrival in Baghdad, most Air Force, Navy, and Marine POWs were taken immediately to what the POWs referred to as "The Bunker" (most probably at the Directorate of Military Intelligence) for initial interrogation. They then were taken to what appeared to be the main long-term incarceration site, located in the Iraqi Intelligence Service Regional Headquarters (dubbed "The Biltmore" by the POWs). Since this building was a legitimate military target, the detention of POWs in it was a violation of Article 23, GPW; POWs thus were unnecessarily placed at risk when the facility was bombed on 23 February.

In contravention of Article 26, GPW, all US POWs incarcerated at the "Biltmore" experienced food deprivation. US POWs also were provided inadequate protection from the cold, in violation of Article 25, GPW.

After the 23 February bombing of the "Biltmore" by Coalition aircraft, the POWs were relocated to either Abu Abu Ghurayb Prison (dubbed "Joliet Prison") or Al-Rashid Military Prison ("The Half-Way House"), both near Baghdad. The Army POWs, on the other hand, were believed to have been sent directly to the Al-Rashid Military Prison, where they remained until their repatriation. All US POWs were repatriated from the Al-Rashid Military Prison. The detention of prisoners of war in a prison generally is prohibited by Article 22, GPW.

All US POWs suffered physical abuse at the hands of their Iraqi captors, in violation of Articles 13, 14, and 17, GPW. Most POWs were tortured, a grave breach, in violation of Article 130, GPW. Some POWs were forced to make public propaganda statements, in violation of Article 13. In addition, none was permitted the rights otherwise afforded them by the GPW, such as the right of correspondence authorized by Article 70. Although the ICRC had access to Iraqi EPWs captured by the Coalition, ICRC members did not see Coalition POWs until the day of their repatriation.

Lack of access to non-US Coalition POW debriefs precludes comments on their treatment. From US POW debriefings, it is known that several Coalition POWs, especially the Saudi and Kuwaiti pilots, were abused physically by their Iraqi captors, in violation of Articles 13 and 17, GPW.

Iraqi POW handling procedures and treatment of Coalition POWs were reasonably predictable, based on a study of Iraqi treatment of Iranians during the eight-year Iran-Iraq war. Iraqi mistreatment of Coalition POWs constituted a Grave Breach of the GPW, as set forth in Article 130 of that treaty.

REPATRIATION OF PRISONERS OF WAR

Article 118, GPW, establishes a POW's right to be repatriated. In conflicts since the GPW's adoption, this principle has become conditional: Each POW must consent to repatriation rather than being forced to return. This proved to be the case after hostilities in this war ended.

No EPW was forcibly repatriated. Coalition forces identified to the ICRC those Iraqi EPWs not desiring repatriation. Once an Iraqi EPW scheduled for repatriation reached the repatriation site, the ICRC reconfirmed his willingness to be repatriated. Those who indicated they no longer desired to return to Iraq were returned to the custody of the detaining power.

On 4 March, Iraq released the first group of 10 Coalition prisoners of war, six of whom were US personnel. The United States simultaneously released 294 Iraqi EPWs for repatriation to Iraq. Of the 294, 10 refused repatriation at the repatriation site and were returned to US custody.

Iraq and the Coalition forces continued repatriation actions through August 1991, at which time 13,318 Iraqi EPWs who refused repatriation remained under Saudi control. On 5 August 1991, Iraqi EPWs still refusing repatriation were reclassified as refugees by the United States (in coordination with Saudi Arabia and the ICRC), concluding application of the GPW.

When US custody of Iraqi EPWs ended, ICRC officials informed the 800th Military Police Brigade (PW) that the treatment of Iraqi EPWs by US forces was the best compliance with the GPW by any nation in any conflict in history. Coalition measures to comply with the GPW had no adverse effect on planning and executing military operations; if anything, by encouraging the surrender of Iraqi military personnel, they improved those operations.

USE OF RUSES AND ACTS OF PERFIDY

Under the law of war, deception includes those measures designed to mislead the enemy by manipulation, distortion, or falsification of evidence to induce him to react in a manner prejudicial to his interests. Ruses are deception of the enemy by legitimate means, and are specifically allowed by Article 24, Annex to Hague IV, and Protocol I. As correctly stated in Article 37(2) of Protocol I:

> Ruses of war are not prohibited. Such ruses are acts which are intended to mislead an adversary or to induce him to act recklessly but which ... no rule of [the law of war] and which are not perfidious because they do not invite the confidence of an adversary with respect to protection under that law. The following are examples of ruses: the use of camouflage, decoys, mock operations and misinformation.

Coalition actions that convinced Iraqi military leaders that the ground campaign to liberate Kuwait would be focused in eastern Kuwait, and would include an amphibious assault, are examples of legitimate ruses. These deception measures were crucial to the Coalition's goal of minimizing the number of Coalition casualties and, in all likelihood, resulted in fewer Iraqi casualties as well.

In contrast, perfidy is prohibited by the law of war. Perfidy is defined in Article 37(1) of Protocol I as:

> Acts inviting the confidence of an adversary to lead him to believe that he is entitled to, or is obliged to accord, protection under the [law of war], with intent to betray that confidence ...

Perfidious acts include the feigning of an intent to surrender or negotiate under a flag of truce, or the feigning of protected status through improper use of the Red Cross or Red Crescent distinctive emblem.

Perfidious acts are prohibited on the basis that perfidy may damage mutual respect for the law of war, may lead to unnecessary escalation of the conflict, may result in the injury or death of enemy forces legitimately attempting to surrender or discharging their humanitarian duties, or may impede the restoration of peace.

There were few examples of perfidious practices during the Persian Gulf War. The most publicized were those associated with the battle of Ras Al-Khafji, which began on 29 January. As that battle began, Iraqi tanks entered Ras Al-Khafji with their turrets reversed, turning their guns forward only at the moment action began between Iraqi and Coalition forces. While there was some media speculation that this was an act of perfidy, it was not; a reversed turret is not a recognized indication of surrender *per se*. Some tactical confusion may have occurred, since Coalition ground forces were operating under a defensive posture at that time, and were to engage Iraqi forces only upon clear indication of hostile intent, or some hostile act.

However, individual acts of perfidy did occur. On one occasion, Iraqi soldiers waved a white flag and laid down their weapons. When a Saudi Arabian patrol advanced to accept their surrender, it was fired upon by Iraqi forces hidden in buildings on either side of the street. During the same battle, an Iraqi officer approached Coalition forces with his hands in the air, indicating his intention to surrender. When near his would-be captors, he drew a concealed pistol from his boot, fired, and was killed during the combat that followed.

Necessarily, these incidents instilled in Coalition forces a greater sense of caution once the ground offensive began. However, there does not appear to have been any centrally directed Iraqi policy to carry out acts of perfidy. The fundamental principles of the law of war applied to Coalition and Iraqi forces throughout the war. The few incidents that did occur did not have a major effect on planning or executing Coalition military operations.

WAR CRIMES

Iraqi war crimes were widespread and premeditated. They included the taking of hostages, forcible deportation, torture and murder of civilians, in violation of the GC; looting of civilian property in violation of Hague IV; looting of cultural property, in violation of the 1954 Hague Cultural Property Convention; indiscriminate attacks in the launching of Scud missiles against cities rather than specific military objectives, in violation of customary international law; violation of Hague VIII in the method of using sea mines; and unnecessary destruction in violation of Article 23(g) of the Annex to Hague IV, as evidenced by the unlawful and wanton release of oil into the Persian Gulf and the unlawful and wanton sabotage of hundreds of Kuwaiti oil wells. The latter acts also constitute a violation of Article 53, GC and a Grave Breach under Article 147, GC.

As indicated earlier, the United States, Iraq, and the members of the Coalition that liberated Kuwait are parties to several law of war treaties. Each assumes good faith in its application and enforcement. Common Article 1 of the four 1949 Geneva Conventions for the Protection of War Victims requires that parties to those treaties "respect and ensure respect" for each of those treaties. The obligation to "respect and ensure respect" was binding upon all parties to the Persian Gulf War. It is an affirmative requirement to take all reasonable and necessary steps to bring individuals responsible for war crimes to justice. In a separate article common to the four 1949 Geneva Conventions, no nation has the authority to absolve itself or any other nation party to those treaties of any liability incurred by the commission of a Grave Breach (Article 50, GWS; Article 51, GWS (Sea); Article 130, GPW; and Article 147, GC).

The United States has one of the more comprehensive law of war programs in existence. DOD Directive 5100.77 is the foundation for the US military law of war program. It contains four policies:

- The law of war and obligations of the US Government under that law ... [will be] observed and enforced by the US Armed Forces.

- A program, designed to prevent violations of the law of war ... [will be] implemented by the US Armed Forces.

- Alleged violations of the law of war, whether committed by or against US or enemy personnel, ... [will be] promptly reported, thoroughly investigated, and, where appropriate, remedied by corrective action.

- Violations of the law of war alleged to have been committed by or against allied military or civilian personnel shall be reported through appropriate military command channels for ultimate transmission to appropriate agencies of allied governments.

The Joint Staff, each military department, the unified and specified commands, and subordinate commands have issued implementing directives. It is within this framework that war crimes investigations were conducted in the course of Operations Desert Shield and Desert Storm.

Each service has issued directives to implement DOD Directive 5100.77 with respect to the reporting and investigation of suspected violations of the law of war committed by or against its personnel. DOD Directive 5100.77 appoints the Army as the DOD Executive Agent for administering the DOD Law of War Program with respect to alleged violations of the law of war committed against US personnel. Army Chief of Staff Regulation 11-2 assigns to the Army Judge Advocate General (JAG) responsibility for investigating, collecting, collating, evaluating, and reporting in connection with war crimes alleged to have been committed against US personnel.

Collection of information of Iraqi war crimes began on 3 August, after media reports that US citizens in Kuwait had been taken hostage by Iraqi forces and forcibly deported to Iraq. As previously indicated, these acts constitute a Grave Breach of the GC. Collection of information continued as reports of other Iraqi war crimes were received.

Interagency meetings in late August established a process for informal coordination on war crimes issues, and ensured policy makers were kept informed. On 15 October, the President warned Iraq of its liability for war crimes. The United States was successful in incorporating into UNSC Resolution 674 (29 October) language regarding Iraq's accountability for its war crimes, in particular its potential liability for Grave Breaches of the GC, and inviting States to collect relevant information regarding Iraqi Grave Breaches and provide it to the Security Council.

Initial collection of information on Iraqi war crimes was carried out by the Army JAG's International Affairs Division and CENTCOM's Staff Judge Advocate in Riyadh. Although US hostages in Iraq were released in December, Iraqi abuses in Kuwait continued at such a pace that it became apparent a greater effort would be necessary with regard to collection of evidence and investigation of war crimes. The Army JAG accordingly recommended the mobilization of two Reserve Component Judge Advocate international law detachments. The 199th JAG Detachment was deployed to SWA, while the 208th JAG Detachment served within the Office of the JAG as the War Crimes Documentation Center. The former, in cooperation with the governments of Saudi Arabia and Kuwait, collected information on war crimes committed in Kuwait. The latter collected information from a variety of sources, including other agencies of the US Government, the media, and private sources.

Following Iraq's breach of international peace and security by its invasion of Kuwait, the UNSC, in Resolution 667, decided to take further concrete measures "in response to Iraq's continued violation of the [UN] Charter, of resolutions of the Council and of international law." Specific Iraqi war crimes include:

- The taking of Kuwaiti nationals as hostages, and their individual and mass forcible deportation to Iraq, in violation of Articles 34, 49 and 147, GC.

- The taking of third-country nationals in Kuwait as hostages, and their individual and mass forcible deportation to Iraq, in violation of Articles 34, 49, and 147, GC.

- The taking of third-country nationals in Iraq as hostages, and their individual and mass forcible transfer within Iraq, in violation of Articles 34, 35, and 147, GC.

- Compelling Kuwaiti and other foreign nationals to serve in the armed forces of Iraq, in violation of Articles 51 and 147, GC.

- Use of Kuwaiti and third country nationals as human shields in violation of Articles 28 and 38(4), GC.

- Inhumane treatment of Kuwaiti and third country civilians, to include rape and willful killing, in violation of Articles 27, 32 and 147, GC.

- As noted previously, possible violation of the Genocide Convention, through acts committed with the intent to destroy, in whole or in part, a national group (that is, the Kuwaiti people).

- The transfer of its own civilian population into occupied Kuwait, in violation of Article 49, GC.

- Torture and other inhumane treatment of POWs, in violation of Articles 13, 17, 22, 25, 26, 27, and 130, GPW.

- Using POWs as a shield to render certain points immune from military operations, in violation of Article 23, GPW.

- Unnecessary destruction of Kuwaiti private and public property, in violation of Article 23(g), Annex to Hague IV.

- Pillage, in violation of Article 47, Annex to Hague IV.

- Illegal confiscation/inadequate safeguarding of Kuwaiti public property, in violation of Article 55, Annex to Hague IV, and Article 147, GC.

- Pillage of Kuwaiti civilian hospitals, in violation of Articles 55, 56, 57, and 147, GC.

- In its indiscriminate Scud missile attacks, unnecessary destruction of Saudi Arabian and Israeli property, in violation of Article 23(g), Annex to Hague IV.

- In its intentional release of oil into the Persian Gulf and its sabotage of the Al-Burqan and Ar-Rumaylah oil fields in Kuwait, unnecessary destruction in violation of Articles 23(g) and 55, Annex to Hague IV, and Articles 53 and 147, GC.

- In its use of drifting naval contact mines and mines lacking devices for their self-neutralization in the event of their breaking loose from their moorings, in violation of Article 1, Hague VIII.

Iraq is a party to the 1925 Geneva Protocol, which prohibits use of CW/BW. Iraq, through its reservation at the time of ratification, pledged no first use of either CW or BW. Although Iraq did not use CW/BW in this war, it violated this treaty in its 1980-88 war against Iran. During the Persian Gulf War, Iraq threatened the use of CW/BW and deployed CW. Although prepared to do so, Iraqi forces did not use either of these weapons of mass destruction during this conflict, perhaps in part due to the success of Coalition efforts to destroy Iraqi CW/BW capabilities, Iraqi C2, and Iraq's inability to move its weapons to forward sites.

Article 29, GC, states that "The Party to the conflict in whose hands protected persons may be, is responsible for the treatment accorded to them by its agents, irrespective of any individual responsibility which may be incurred." Similarly, Article 12, GPW, declares that "Prisoners of war are in the hands of the enemy Power, but not of the individuals or military units who have captured them. Irrespective of the individual responsibilities that may exist, the Detaining Power is responsible for the treatment given them." Responsibility for the treatment (and mistreatment) of civilian detainees and POW in Iraqi hands, clearly lay with the Government of Iraq and its senior officials.

Criminal responsibility for violations of the law of war rests with a commander, including the national leadership, if he (or she):

- Orders or permits the offense to be committed, or

- Knew or should have known of the offense(s), had the means to prevent or halt them, and failed to do all which he was capable of doing to prevent the offenses or their recurrence.

In addition, the invasion of Kuwait was ordered by Saddam Hussein and is a crime against peace for which he, as well as the Ba'ath Party leadership and military high command, bear direct responsibility.

The crimes committed against Kuwaiti civilians and property, and against third party nationals, are offenses for which Saddam Hussein, officials of the Ba'ath Party, and his subordinates bear direct responsibility. However, the principal responsibility rests with Saddam Hussein. Saddam Hussein's C2 of Iraqi military and security forces appeared to be total and unequivocal. There is substantial evidence that each act alleged was taken as a result of his orders, or was taken with his knowledge and approval, or was an act of which he should have known.

It is important to note that, with the possible exception of the Coalition's need to direct considerable effort toward the hunt for Iraqi Scud missiles, no Iraqi action leading to or resulting in a violation of the law of war gained Iraq any military advantages. This "negative gain from negative actions" in essence reinforces the validity of the law of war.

ENVIRONMENTAL TERRORISM

Between seven and nine million barrels of oil were set free in the Gulf by Iraqi action. Five hundred ninety oil well heads were damaged or destroyed. 508 were set on fire, and 82 were damaged so that oil was flowing freely from them.

There has been international examination of these acts. From 9 to 12 July 1991, the Government of Canada, working with the UN Secretary-General, hosted a conference of international experts in Ottawa to consider Iraq's wanton acts of destruction and their law of war implications. There was general agreement the actions constituted violations of the law of war, namely:

- Article 23(g) of the Annex to Hague IV, which forbids the destruction of "enemy property, unless ... imperatively demanded by the necessities of war"; and

- Article 147 of the GC, which makes a Grave Breach the "extensive destruction ... of property, not justified by military necessity and carried out unlawfully and wantonly."

The Ottawa Conference of Experts also noted UNSC Resolution 687 (3 April 1991), which reaffirmed that Iraq was liable under international law to compensate any environmental damage and the depletion of natural resources.

Other treaties the Conference of Experts considered were the ENMOD Convention and the 1977 Protocol I, Articles 35 and 55 of which contain provisions for the protection of the environment. It was the general conclusion of the experts that the former did not apply to actions of the kinds perpetrated by Iraq, while the latter was not applicable during the Persian Gulf War for reasons previously stated.

Even had Protocol I been in force, there were questions as to whether the Iraqi actions would have violated its environmental provisions. During that treaty's negotiation, there was general agreement that one of its criteria for determining whether a violation had taken place ("long term") was measured in decades. It is not clear the damage Iraq caused, while severe in a layman's sense of the term, would meet the technical-legal use of that term in Protocol I. The prohibitions on damage to the environment contained in Protocol I were not intended to prohibit battlefield damage caused by conventional operations and, in all likelihood, would not apply to Iraq's actions in the Persian Gulf War.

The Ottawa Conference of Experts did not conclude that new laws or treaties were required; rather, it was the belief of those present that respect for an enforcement of the existing law of war was of greatest importance.

It is not clear why Iraq released oil into the Persian Gulf. Conceivably, Iraq had hoped to interfere with Coalition naval operations in the Gulf, perhaps to impede expected amphibious operations. By threatening desalinization plants, Iraq also may have hoped to disrupt Coalition military operations and Saudi civilian life dependent on a steady flow of fresh water. As it turned out, the cooperative efforts of the Coalition members, the US Coast Guard, and the US National Oceanic and Atmospheric Administration resulted in the oil slick's having a negligible effect on the operations of Coalition naval forces.

Perversely, Iraq's actions did necessitate responsive Coalition operations to protect the environment that inflicted further damage on Kuwaiti property. Specifically, the flow from the Al-Ahmadi terminal was stopped by aerial destruction of vital equipment near the terminal.

As the first Kuwaiti oil wells were ignited by Iraqi forces, there was public speculation the fires and smoke were intended to impair Coalition forces' ability to conduct both air and ground operations, primarily by obscuring visual and electro-optical sensing devices. Review of Iraqi actions makes it clear the oil well destruction had no military purpose, but was simply punitive destruction at its worst. For example, oil well fires to create obscurants could have been accomplished simply through the opening of valves; instead, Iraqi forces set explosive charges on many wells to ensure the greatest possible destruction and maximum difficulty in stopping each fire. Likewise, the Ar-Rumaylah oil field spreads across the Iraq-Kuwait border. Had the purpose of the fires been to create an obscurant, oil wells in that field on each side of the border undoubtedly would have been set ablaze; Iraqi destruction was limited to oil wells on the Kuwaiti side only. As with the release of oil into the Persian Gulf, this aspect of Iraq's wanton destruction of Kuwaiti property had little effect on Coalition offensive combat operations. In fact, the oil well fires had a greater adverse effect on Iraqi military forces.

Conduct of Neutral Nations

Neutrality normally is based on a nation's proclamation of neutrality or assumption of a neutral posture with respect to a particular conflict. Iran and Jordan each issued proclamations of neutrality during the Persian Gulf crisis and, as described, refrained from active participation in the war. Other nations, such as Austria and Switzerland, enjoy relative degrees of international guarantees of their neutrality.

Neutrality in the Persian Gulf War was controlled in part by the 1907 Hague V Convention; but traditional concepts of neutral rights and duties are substantially modified when, as in this case, the United Nations authorizes collective action against an aggressor nation.

It was the US position during the Persian Gulf crisis that, regardless of assertions of neutrality, all nations were obligated to avoid hindrance of Coalition operations undertaken pursuant to, or in conjunction with, UNSC decisions, and to provide whatever assistance possible. By virtue of UNSC Resolution 678 (29 November), members were requested "to provide appropriate support for the actions undertaken" by nations pursuant to its authorization of use of all necessary means to uphold and implement prior resolutions. The language of UNSC Resolution 678 is consistent with Articles 2(5), 2(6), 25, and 49 of the UN Charter. Article 2(5) states:

> All Members shall give the United Nations every assistance in any action it takes in accordance with the present Charter, and shall refrain from giving assistance to any state against which the United Nations is taking preventive or enforcement action.

Article 2(6) provides:

> The Organization shall ensure that states which are not Members of the United Nations act in accordance with these Principles so far as may be necessary for the maintenance of international peace and security.

Article 25 provides:

> The Members of the United Nations agree to accept and carry out the decisions of the Security Council in accordance with the present Charter.

Article 49 declares:

> The Members of the United Nations shall join in affording mutual assistance in carrying out the measures decided upon by the Security Council.

This section focuses on the conduct of Jordan, Iran, India and traditionally neutral European nations (primarily Austria and Switzerland) during the course of the hostilities, and the effect of Coalition maritime interceptions on neutral shipping.

UNSC Resolution 661, which called for an economic embargo of Iraq, pursuant to Article 41 of the UN Charter, obligated all member nations to refrain from aiding Iraq. The declarations of "neutrality" by Jordan and Iran were subordinate to their obligation as UN members to comply with UNSC resolutions. Although Jordan's attitude toward Iraq and the Coalition appeared inconsistent with its UN obligations, mere sympathy for one belligerent does not constitute a violation of traditional neutral duties, nor even a rejection of the obligations imposed by the UNSC resolutions cited. Conduct is the issue.

There were reports that Jordan supplied materials (including munitions) to Iraq during Operations Desert Shield and Desert Storm. Furnishing supplies and munitions to a belligerent traditionally has been regarded as a violation of a neutral's obligations. In this case, it would have been an even more palpable contravention of Jordan's obligations - both because of the request of UNSC Resolution 678 that all States support those seeking to uphold and implement the relevant resolutions, and because the sanctions Resolution 661 established expressly prohibited the supply of war materials to Iraq.

As the US became aware of specific allegations of Jordanian failure to comply with UNSC sanctions, they were raised with the Government of Jordan. Some were without foundation; some were substantiated. Regarding the latter, the Government of Jordan acted to stop the actions and reassured the United States those instances had been the result of individual initiative rather than as a result of government policy. Such logistical assistance as Jordan may have provided Iraq did not substantially improve Iraq's ability to conduct operations, nor did it have an appreciable effect on Coalition forces' operational capabilities.

During actual hostilities, Saudi Arabia stopped pumping oil to Jordan; Jordan obtained petroleum from Iraq, taking delivery by truck. Although not a violation of a neutral's duties under traditional principles of international law, such purchases were inconsistent with UNSC Resolutions 661 and 678.

While the Jordanian importation of oil products from Iraq did not substantially affect Coalition military operations, additional steps were required by Coalition forces to protect Iraqi and Jordanian civilians from the risks of military operations. Jordan imported Iraqi oil by truck across roads in western Iraq during the day and night. These oil trucks were commingled with military and civilian vehicles. At night, some oil trucks were mistaken for mobile Scud launchers or other military vehicles; other trucks and civilian vehicles were struck incidental to attack of legitimate military targets.

This collateral damage and injury, which occurred despite previously described Coalition efforts to minimize damage to civilian objects and injury to noncombatant civilians, is attributable to Jordan's failure to ensure adherence to UNSC sanctions and to warn its nationals of the perils of travel on main supply routes in a combat zone. It also is attributable to mixing of Iraqi military vehicles and convoys with Jordanian civilian traffic traveling in Iraq. Coalition forces continued to take reasonable precautions to minimize collateral damage to civilian vehicles and incidental injury to noncombatant civilians. As a result, the ability to target Iraqi military vehicles and convoys, including mobile Scud missile launchers and support equipment, was impeded.

Iran's conduct during Operations Desert Shield and Desert Storm essentially was consistent with that expected of a neutral under traditional principles of international law, including Hague V. Immediately after the Operation Desert Storm air campaign began, many Iraqi civil and military aircraft began fleeing to Iran, presumably to avoid damage or destruction by Coalition air forces. Under Article 11 of Hague V and traditional law of war principles regarding neutral rights and obligations, when belligerent military aircraft land in a nation not party to a conflict, the neutral must intern the aircraft, aircrew, and accompanying military personnel for the duration of the war. Both Switzerland and Sweden took such actions in the course of World War II, for example, with respect to Allied and German aircraft and aircrews. Some civil (and possibly some military) transport aircraft may have returned to Iraq. With respect to tactical aircraft, however, it appears Iran complied with the traditional obligations of a neutral. US forces nonetheless remained alert to the possibility of a flanking attack by Iraqi aircraft operating from Iran.

Although the situation never arose, the United States advised Iran that, in light of UNSC Resolution 678, Iran would be obligated to return downed Coalition aircraft and aircrew, rather than intern them. This illustrates the modified nature of neutrality in these circumstances. It also was the US position that entry into Iranian (or Jordanian) airspace to rescue downed aviators would be consistent with its international obligations as a belligerent, particularly in light of Resolution 678.

On several occasions, Iran protested alleged entry of its airspace by Coalition aircraft or missiles. The United States expressed regret for any damage that may have occurred within Iranian territory by virtue of inadvertent entry into Iranian airspace. The US replies did not, however, address whether Iranian expectations of airspace inviolability were affected by UNSC Resolution 678.

Although military aircraft must gain permission to enter another State's airspace (except in distress), both Switzerland and Austria routinely granted such clearance for US military transport aircraft prior to the Iraqi invasion of Kuwait. Early in the Persian Gulf crisis, the United States approached the Governments of Austria and Switzerland, seeking permission for overflight of US military transport aircraft carrying equipment and personnel to SWA. Despite initial misgivings, based upon their traditional neutrality, each nation assented. That there was a reluctance to grant permission early in the crisis - that is, when the United States was not involved in the hostilities, and thus not legally a belligerent - demonstrates that the view by these two States of neutrality may be more expansive than the traditional understanding of the role of neutrality in the law of war. At the same time, while Switzerland is not a UN member, its support for the US effort (through airspace clearances for US military aircraft) preceded UNSC Resolution 678.

Given their reluctance to permit pre-hostilities overflights, it was natural to expect that Switzerland and Austria would weigh very carefully any requests for overflights once offensive actions began, which each did. In light of the UNSC request that all States support the efforts of those acting to uphold and implement UNSC resolutions, each government decided that overflights by US military transport aircraft would not be inconsistent with its neutral obligations. Accordingly, permission for overflights was granted, easing logistical support for combat operations.

In contrast, overflight denial by the Government of India required Marine combat aviation assets in the Western Pacific to fly across the Pacific, the continental US, the Atlantic, and through Europe to reach SWA, substantially increasing the transit route. Air Force transport aircraft delivering ammunition to the theater of operations also were denied overflight permission.

UNSC Resolution 661 directed member states to prevent the import or transshipment of materials originating in Iraq or Kuwait, and further obligated member states to prevent imports to or exports from Iraq and Kuwait. In support of Resolution 661, on 16 August, the United States ordered its warships to intercept all ships believed to be proceeding to or from Iraq or Kuwait, and all vessels bound to or from ports of other nations carrying materials destined for or originating from Iraq or Kuwait. On 25 August, the Security Council adopted Resolution 665, which called upon UN members to enforce sanctions by means of a maritime interception operation. This contemplated intercepting so-called "neutral" shipping as well as that of non-neutral nations. These resolutions modified the obligation of neutral powers to remain impartial with regard to Coalition UN members.

The law of war regarding neutrality traditionally permits neutral nations to engage in non-war-related commerce with belligerent nations. During the Persian Gulf crisis, however, the Coalition Maritime Interception Force (MIF) was directed to prevent all goods (except medical supplies and humanitarian foodstuffs expressly authorized for Iraqi import by the UNSC Sanctions Committee) from leaving or entering Iraqi-controlled ports or Iraq, consistent with the relevant UNSC resolutions. The claim of neutral status by Iran and Jordan, or any of the traditional neutral nations, did not adversely affect the conduct of the Coalition's ability to carry out military operations against Iraq.

THE CONCEPT OF "SURRENDER" IN THE CONDUCT OF COMBAT OPERATIONS

The law of war obligates a party to a conflict to accept the surrender of enemy personnel and thereafter treat them in accordance with the provisions of the 1949 Geneva Conventions for the Protection of War Victims. Article 23(d) of Hague IV prohibits the denial of quarter, that is the refusal to accept an enemy's surrender, while other provisions in that treaty address the use of flags of truce and capitulation.

However, there is a gap in the law of war in defining precisely when surrender takes effect or how it may be accomplished in practical terms. Surrender involves an offer by the surrendering party (a unit or an individual soldier) and an ability to accept on the part of his opponent. The latter may not refuse an offer of surrender when communicated, but that communication must be made at a time when it can be received and properly acted upon - an attempt at surrender in the midst of a hard-fought battle is neither easily communicated nor received. The issue is one of reasonableness.

A combatant force involved in an armed conflict is not obligated to offer its opponent an opportunity to surrender before carrying out an attack. To minimize Iraqi and Coalition casualties, however, the Coalition engaged in a major psychological operations campaign to encourage Iraqi soldiers to surrender before the Coalition ground offensive. Once that offensive began, the Coalition effort was to defeat Iraqi forces as quickly as possible to minimize the loss of Coalition lives. In the process, Coalition forces continued to accept legitimate Iraqi offers of surrender in a manner consistent with the law of war. The large number of Iraqi prisoners of war is evidence of Coalition compliance with its law of war obligations with regard to surrendering forces.

Situations arose in the course of Operation Desert Storm that have been questioned by some in the post-conflict environment. Two specific cases involve the Coalition's breach of the Iraqi defensive line and attack of Iraqi military forces leaving Kuwait City. Neither situation involved an offer of surrender by Iraqi forces, but it is necessary to discuss each in the context of the law of war concept of surrender.

As explained in Chapter VIII, rapid breach of the Iraqi defense in depth was crucial to the success of the Coalition ground campaign. When the ground campaign began, Iraq had not yet used its air force or extensive helicopter fleet in combat operations, the Iraqi Scud capability had not been eliminated, and most importantly, chemical warfare by Iraq remained a distinct possibility.

It was uncertain whether the Coalition deception plan had worked or whether the Coalition effort had lost the element of surprise and there was also no definitive information about the strength and morale of the defending Iraqi soldiers. Because of these uncertainties, and the need to minimize loss of US and other Coalition lives, military necessity required that the assault through the forward Iraqi defensive line be conducted with maximum speed and violence.

The VII Corps main effort was the initial breaching operation through Iraqi defensive fortifications. This crucial mission was assigned to the 1st Infantry Division (Mechanized). The Division's mission was to conduct a deliberate breach of the Iraqi defensive positions as quickly as possible to expand and secure the breach site, and to pass the 1st UK Armoured Division through the lines to continue the attack against the Iraqi forces.

To accomplish the deliberate breaching operation, the 1st Infantry Division (Mechanized) moved forward and plowed through the berms and mine fields erected by the Iraqis. Many Iraqis surrendered during this phase of the attack and were taken prisoner. The division then assaulted the trenches containing other Iraqi soldiers. Once astride the trench lines, the division turned the plow blades of its tanks and combat earthmovers along the Iraqi defense line and, covered by fire from its M-2/-3 armored infantry fighting vehicles, began to fill in the trench line and its heavily bunkered, mutually supporting fighting positions.

In the process, many more Iraqi soldiers surrendered to division personnel; others died in the course of the attack and destruction or bulldozing of their defensive positions.

By nightfall, the division had breached the Iraqi defenses, consolidated its position, and prepared to pass the 1st UK Armoured Division through the lines. Hundreds of Iraqi soldiers had been taken prisoner; US casualties were extremely light.

The tactic used by the 1st Infantry Division (Mechanized) resulted in a number of Iraqi soldiers' dying in their defensive positions as those positions were bulldozed. Marine Corps breaching operations along its axis of attack into Kuwait used different, but also legally acceptable, techniques of assault by fire, bayonet, and the blasting of enemy defensive positions. Both tactics were entirely consistent with the law of war.

Tactics involving the use of armored vehicles against dug-in infantry forces have been common since the first use of armored vehicles in combat. The tactic of using armored vehicles to crush or bury enemy soldiers was briefly discussed in the course of the UN Conference on Certain Conventional Weapons, conducted in Geneva from 1978 to 1980 and attended by the United States and more than 100 other nations. It was left unregulated, however, as it was recognized by the participants to be a common long-standing tactic entirely consistent with the law of war.

In the case in point, military necessity required violent, rapid attack. Had the breaching operation stalled, the VII Corps main effort would have been delayed or, at worst, blunted. This would have had an adverse effect on the entire ground campaign, lengthening the time required to liberate Kuwait, and increasing overall Coalition casualties.

As first stated in US Army General Orders No. 100 (1863), otherwise known as the Lieber Code, military necessity "consists in the necessity of those measures which are indispensable for securing the ends of war, and which are lawful according to the modern law and usages of war ... [It] admits of all direct destruction of life or limb of armed enemies." As developed by the practice of nations since that time, the law of war has placed restrictions on the application of force against enemy combatants in very few circumstances (e.g., the first use of chemical or biological weapons). None of these restrictions were at issue during the breaching operations during Operation Desert Storm.

The law of war principle complementary to military necessity is that of unnecessary suffering (or superfluous injury). That principle does not preclude combat actions that otherwise are lawful, such as that used by the 1st Infantry Division (Mechanized).

In the course of the breaching operations, the Iraqi defenders were given the opportunity to surrender, as indicated by the large number of EPWs taken by the division. However, soldiers must make their intent to surrender clear and unequivocal, and do so rapidly. Fighting from fortified emplacement is not a manifestation of an intent to surrender, and a soldier who fights until the very last possible moment assumes certain risks. His opponent either may not see his surrender, may not recognize his actions as an attempt to surrender in the heat and confusion of battle, or may find it difficult (if not impossible) to halt an onrushing assault to accept a soldier's last-minute effort at surrender.

It was in this context that the breach of the Iraqi defense line occurred. The scenario Coalition forces faced and described herein illustrates the difficulty of defining or effecting "surrender". Nonetheless, the breaching tactics used by US Army and Marine Corps forces assigned this assault mission were entirely consistent with US law of war obligations.

In the early hours of 27 February, CENTCOM received a report that a concentration of vehicles was forming in Kuwait City. It was surmised that Iraqi forces were preparing to depart under the cover of darkness. CINCCENT was concerned about the redeployment of Iraqi forces in Kuwait City, fearing they could join with and provide reinforcements for Republican Guard units west of Kuwait City in an effort to stop the Coalition advance or otherwise endanger Coalition forces.

The concentration of Iraqi military personnel and vehicles, including tanks, invited attack. CINCCENT decided against attack of the Iraqi forces in Kuwait City, since it could lead to substantial collateral damage to Kuwaiti civilian property and could cause surviving Iraqi units to decide to mount a defense from Kuwait City rather than depart. Iraqi units remaining in Kuwait City would cause the Coalition to engage in military operations in urban terrain, a form of fighting that is costly to attacker, defender, innocent civilians, and civilian objects.

The decision was made to permit Iraqi forces to leave Kuwait City and engage them in the unpopulated area to the north. Once departed, the Iraqi force was stopped by barricades of mines deployed across the highway in front of and behind the column. Air attacks on the trapped vehicles began about 0200. The following morning, CENTCOM leadership viewed the resulting damage. More than two hundred Iraqi tanks had been trapped and destroyed in the ambush, along with hundreds of other military vehicles and various forms of civilian transportation confiscated or seized by Iraqi forces for the redeployment. The vehicles in turn were full of property pillaged from Kuwaiti civilians: appliances, clothing, jewelry, compact disc players, tape recorders, and money, the last step in the Iraqi looting of Kuwait.

Throughout the ground campaign Coalition leaflets had warned Iraqi soldiers that their tanks and other vehicles were subject to attack, but that Iraqi soldiers would not be attacked if they abandoned their vehicles - yet another way in which the Coalition endeavored to minimize Iraqi casualties while encouraging their defection and/or surrender. When the convoy was stopped by the mining operations that blocked the Iraqi axis of advance, most Iraqi soldiers in the vehicles immediately abandoned their vehicles and fled into the desert to avoid attack.

In the aftermath of Operation Desert Storm, some questions were raised regarding this attack, apparently on the supposition that the Iraqi force was retreating. The attack was entirely consistent with military doctrine and the law of war. The law of war permits the attack of enemy combatants and enemy equipment at any time, wherever located, whether advancing, retreating, or standing still. Retreat does not prevent further attack. At the small-unit level, for example, once an objective has been seized and the position consolidated, an attacking force is trained to fire upon the retreating enemy to discourage or prevent a counterattack.

Attacks on retreating enemy forces have been common throughout history. Napoleon suffered some of his worst losses in his retreat from Russia, as did the German Wermacht more than a century later. It is recognized by military professionals that a retreating force remains dangerous. The 1st Marine Division and its 4,000 attached US Army forces and British Royal Marines, in the famous 1950 march out of the Chosin Reservoir in North Korea, fighting outnumbered by a 4:1 margin, turned its "retreat" into a battle in which it defeated the 20th and 26th Chinese Armies trying to annihilate it, much as Xenophon and his "immortal 10,000" did as they fought their way through hostile Persian forces to the Black Sea in 401 BC.

In the case at hand, neither the composition, degree of unit cohesiveness, nor intent of the Iraqi military forces engaged was known at the time of the attack. At no time did any element within the formation offer to surrender. CENTCOM was under no law of war obligation to offer the Iraqi forces an opportunity to surrender before the attack.

OBSERVATIONS

Accomplishments

- DOD-mandated instruction and training in the law of war were reflected in US operations, which were in keeping with historic US adherence to the precepts of the law of war. Adherence to the law of war impeded neither Coalition planning nor execution; Iraqi violations of the law provided Iraq no advantage.

- CINCCENT conducted a theater campaign directed solely at military targets. As frequently noted during the conduct of the conflict, exceptional care was devoted to minimize collateral damage to civilian population and property.

- The special trust and confidence reposed in the professional capabilities of military commanders by the National Command Authorities permitted commanders at all levels to accomplish their respective missions in an unconstrained manner that simultaneously was consistent with the law of war.

- The willingness of commanders to seek legal advice at every stage of operational planning ensured US respect for the law of war throughout Operations Desert Shield and Desert Storm.

Issue

- A strategy should be developed to respond to Iraqi violations of the law of war, to make clear that a price will be paid for such violations, and to deter future violators.

C. UNITED KINGDOM DOCUMENTS

London Gazette, Second Supplement, No. 52589, 28 June 1991

1. Despatch by Air Chief Marshal Sir Patrick Hine, GCB ADC FRAES CBIM RAF, 29 June 1991

INTRODUCTION

Towards the end of July 1990, the warming of east-west relations had led to a marked reduction in international tension. The size and composition of the British armed forces were under scrutiny, and the initial conclusions of the Options for Change deliberations suggested significant restructuring of our defences in response to the clearly reducing threat from the Warsaw Pact. Within a week, there was a major change in the world order; the unprovoked Iraqi invasion of neighbouring Kuwait redirected the focus of our military attention from predominantly European issues to the Middle East. On 8 August, the Secretary of State for Defence, the Right Honourable Tom King PC MP, announced that British Forces were to prepare to deploy to the Gulf region. On 10 August, the Chief of the Defence Staff, Marshal of the Royal Air Force Sir David Craig GCB DSC MA FRAES, appointed me the Joint Commander of Operation GRANBY, on which some 45,000 servicemen and women were eventually deployed in theatre.

In this despatch I will describe the way the Operation developed over the ensuing eight months, looking briefly at the background and the military build-up, before covering in more detail the six week period of hostilities which began on 16 January, and drawing a line at the acceptance of the official ceasefire on 11 April 1991. I will often describe single-Service actions; I would, however, stress at the outset that this was a joint operation with each arm's activities frequently linked to the others'. Moreover, while I will detail the involvement of British forces, we must remember that this was an international operation fought by the largest military coalition since the Second World War, and we were but one nation among many. I list at the end of my despatch the senior commanders in Operation GRANBY. I also attach maps to represent the disposition of our forces in theatre.

A full length epic would be required to do justice to the endeavours, bravery and resolve of all those involved, military and civilian, at home and abroad. While, inevitably, it is impossible to refer to all of those whose contribution would otherwise merit it, the relative brevity of this despatch should not detract from the highest esteem in which we all should hold our participants in Operation GRANBY, whether those in the theatre of operations or those who supported them from bases in the United Kingdom, British Forces Germany and Cyprus.

BACKGROUND

The Iraqi dispute with Kuwait has its roots in the post colonial history of the Gulf region, but the catalyst for the recent invasion came in the middle of July 1990. The immediate source of conflict was the Rumaila oilfield which straddles the Iraq/Kuwait border; President Saddam Hussein of Iraq maintained that Kuwait had stolen £1.3 bn of Iraqi oil from this field and demanded compensation. Kuwait rejected the charges and, in response, Iraq cancelled £5.5 bn of loans which it had received from Kuwait during the Iran/Iraq war.

A week after these events, the two sides agreed to talks which were held in Jedda in Saudi Arabia; on the agenda were the disputed territory between the states, oil pricing and the cancelled Kuwaiti war loans to Iraq. On 1 August, in the middle of negotiations, Iraq pulled out of the talks; and the next morning, at 0200 hours local time, Iraqi troops crossed the Kuwaiti border. Iraq possessed the Arab World's most powerful military machine and, with a strength of over a million, the fourth largest permanent army in the World; facing them were the Kuwaiti defence forces, number a total of 20,300. In addition to his huge standing army, President Saddam Hussein had recalled the Popular Army, a militia of several hundred thousand men who had supported Iraqi frontline troops in the nine year war with Iran. He also issued orders to re-form fifteen infantry divisions and one armoured division which had been disbanded after the ceasefire in 1988.

Up to 100,000 Iraqi troops were massed on the border; the Republican Guard Force Command was chosen to lead the invasion. About 30,000 Iraqi troops, including armoured brigades equipped with modern T72 tanks, were used in the main attack across the desert towards Kuwait City, a distance of about 80 miles. Several Iraqi ships were off the Kuwaiti coast; some were used to mount a naval barrage on the capital while helicopters flew special forces from the ships into the city.

The troops crossed the border at three separate points in the north-west of the country and were met by artillery fire as they advanced rapidly towards the capital. The invading force had about 350 tanks, a mixture of T54s and T55s as well as the T72s. As the advance was taking place, some Iraqi units broke away and occupied a strip of Kuwaiti territory at Abdaly, 80 miles north of Kuwait City. Helicopters also landed troops on the two uninhabited Kuwaiti islands of Warbah and Bubiyan, strategically located at the head of the Gulf. Ports and military airfields were significantly damaged by continuous artillery bombardment and air attacks and, despite resistance from the Kuwaiti National Guard, key buildings and facilities in Kuwait City fell to the invaders, while Army bases at Al-Jahrah, west of the capital, were overwhelmed. This was the first time in modern history that an Arab nation had invaded and totally controlled another Arab state.

Furthermore, there were strong indications that President Saddam Hussein had further ambitions. He massed 100,000 troops on the border with Saudi Arabia and mobilized 140,000 volunteers in southern Iraq. The international community could not condone such overt aggression towards Kuwait and believed it had to act swiftly if it were to prevent Iraqi troops moving into Saudi Arabia. The United Nations Security Council adopted resolution 660 on 2 August, condemning the invasion and demanding Iraq's immediate and unconditional withdrawal. This was followed by resolution 661 on 6 August, calling for the restoration of the legitimate government of Kuwait and imposing mandatory economic sanctions on Iraq. The United States, on 7 August, was the first nation to send forces to the area. The following day, the United Kingdom announced that it too was sending forces to the Gulf. Thus began our military involvement under the title of Operation GRANBY.

OBJECTIVES

The initial objective of Operation GRANBY was to help deter any further aggression by Iraq in the Gulf and particularly against Saudi Arabia. The objectives were later expanded to: secure, together with our Coalition allies, a complete and unconditional Iraqi withdrawal from Kuwait; restore the legitimate government of that country; re-establish peace and security in the area; uphold the authority of the United Nations.

COMMAND AND CONTROL

As Joint Commander, I exercised overall command of the Operation from my Headquarters at Royal Air Force High Wycombe. On 11 August 1990, I appointed the Air Officer Commanding Number 1 Group, Air Vice-Marshal R A F WILSON CB AFC RAF, Air Commander British Forces Arabian Peninsula, and directed him to set up his Headquarters in Riyadh, Saudi Arabia. On the same day, Commodore P K Haddacks RN became the Senior Naval Officer Middle East (SNOME) but with the ships of the Royal Navy ARMILLA Patrol remaining at the time under the operational command of the Commander-in-Chief Fleet, Admiral Sir Benjamin Bathurst GCB. Commodore Haddacks embarked in HMS YORK on 19 August 1990 as Commander Task Group 321.1. On 1 October 1990, the title British Forces Arabian Peninsula was changed to British Forces Middle East (BFME), and Royal Navy forces came under my operational command. Lieutenant General Sir Peter de la Billière KCB CBE DSO MC was appointed commander in theatre; Air Vice-Marshal Wilson became the Deputy Commander and Air Commander. The United Kingdom Joint Force Headquarters in Riyadh, Saudi Arabia was located close to the United States CENTCOM Headquarters to allow our commanders to maintain a close liaison with their American counterparts. Air Vice-Marshal Wilson was succeeded on 17 November 1990 by Air Vice-Marshal W J Wratten CB CBE AFC RAF, Air Officer Commanding Number 11 Group. Commodore C J S Craig DSC RN relieved Commodore Haddacks as SNOME on 3 December 1990.

THE JOINT HEADQUARTERS

While Operation GRANBY was directed by Her Majesty's Government acting through the Ministry of Defence in Whitehall, the Operations Centre in the UK was established in the recently-completed Primary War Headquarters bunker at Royal Air Force High Wycombe. This Joint Headquarters had the great advantage of being largely self-contained with the battle staff, which numbered some 500 people per shift at the height of the conflict, working with the support of full administrative and catering facilities within the complex. I organized the staff into three tiers: functional cells, the Battle Management Group (BMG) and the Command Group. There were 32 functional cells, each responsible for a specific area of the Operation. They reported to ten Assistant Chiefs of Staff at the 1-star level who then met twice daily as the BMG, which was chaired by the 2-star Director of Operations (DOPS). I led the Command Group meetings, which followed on from the BMG meetings, when I was briefed by the DOPS and selected members of the BMG, was given advice from the senior representatives of each Service, and took decisions or gave direction. This structure proved to be resilient and efficient; and I knew that I was receiving the most timely, reliable and relevant information on which to plan the British contribution to the Coalition effort.

COMMUNICATIONS

The Headquarters was equipped with a comprehensive suite of sophisticated communications equipment which enabled us to maintain close contact with those issuing the political and military directives from London, as well as with the Joint Force Headquarters in Riyadh. The communications experts from all three Services worked unstintingly in the months following the Iraqi invasion and produced a network of satellite and land-based systems emanating from High Wycombe and the Naval Fleet Headquarters at Northwood which gave me and my staff at the Joint Headquarters reliable and totally secure links to the operational theatre by telephone, facsimile and signal. They also provided the facilities which allowed the Riyadh Headquarters to communicate easily and securely with front-line units, whether in established positions or on the move. Modern warfare demands extensive secure communications, and such provision played a significant part in our operations. We also, for the first time, made very substantial use of data systems in exercising command and control of all our deployed forces.

In addition to the almost global disapproval of Iraq's invasion of Kuwait, which was signalled by the strongest set of United Nations Security Council resolutions to have ever been agreed, the overriding aim in the early days was to deter and, if necessary, to check any Iraqi invasion of northern Saudi Arabia. Our intelligence assessment indicated that an invasion could be launched immediately and so it was crucial for the nations opposing Iraq to signal their resolve by rapid deployment of forces. From the British standpoint, the Royal Navy's ARMILLA patrol group WHISKY, consisting of HM Ships YORK, BATTLEAXE and JUPITER with RFA ORANGELEAF, was already available to respond. New directives were soon issued ordering the ships to provide protection for entitled merchant ships; to monitor shipping passing to, from and within the Gulf; to develop an assessment of ships, particularly tankers, breaking the sanctions imposed by the Security Council; to be prepared to support evacuation of British dependents from the Gulf states; and to support the activities of other British forces in the area.

Notwithstanding this naval presence, the first priority was rapidly to provide defense forces in Saudi Arabia, and to this end a squadron of Tornado F3 aircraft, on detachment at Akrotiri in Cyprus for armament practice, was deployed to the air base at Dhahran on the Gulf coast. These aircraft, armed with Sidewinder and Skyflash air-to-air missiles, are the most modern fighters in the Royal Air Force; they were supported by VC10K tanker aircraft. The Tornados landed at Dhahran early on 11 August, flew their first operational missions within two hours of arrival, and were soon mounting regular defensive Combat Air Patrols, an essential task that they undertook throughout the crisis. In parallel, the Air Headquarters was established at Riyadh, and the army deployed 70 men to provide satellite communications and postal and courier detachments to Saudi Arabia, Oman and Bahrain. Later this expanded to include also Royal Engineer and medical support to airfields, and Royal Artillery Javelin detachments aboard ships. As contingency planning progressed, we anticipated the possibility of a mine threat at sea by deploying, on 13 August, three Mine Counter Measures Vessels (MCMVs), HM Ships ATHERSTONE, CATTISTOCK and HURWORTH, from Rosyth to the eastern Mediterranean. By this date, HMS YORK had been joined by HMS JUPITER on station in the southern Gulf, and HMS BATTLEAXE had arrived at Fujairah in company with RFA ORANGELEAF. Augmented support for the increased naval activity was provided by deploying RFAs OLNA, FORT GRANGE and DILIGENCE. Royal Marines Air Defence detachments were quickly flown from Plymouth to provide additional close-range air defence.

Following the Government's announcement that both a Tornado F3 and a Jaguar squadron were to be sent to the Gulf, Jaguar ground attack and tactical reconnaissance aircraft from Royal Air Force Coltishall were deployed to Thumrait in Oman. The Sultan of Oman's Air Force also operates this aircraft and many of the RAF Jaguar pilots had flown from that airfield during bilateral exercises. In view of the distances involved, air-to-air refuelling support was necessary and two VC10K tankers were deployed with the Jaguars to Thumrait. Surface surveillance of the Gulf waters from the air was required and three Nimrod maritime patrol aircraft were deployed to Seeb airfield in Oman where they too had taken part in training exercises over recent years. By the middle of August, the Tornado F3, Jaguar, VC10K and Nimrod aircraft were all flying operational sorties from their detachment bases in the Arabian Peninsula.

The airfield at Akrotiri in Cyprus became an important staging base for transport flights, tanker support and transit sorties, and as a holding base for additional air assets. Phantom FGR2 aircraft from Royal Air Force Germany provided air defence against a possible Iraqi attack by medium bombers. This force was supplemented by the Rapier Blindfire surface to air missiles of 20 Squadron Royal Air Force Regiment. Three Royal Navy Attacker class patrol vessels were also deployed, becoming operational at the end of October, to counter the terrorist threat from seaward, while an RAF Regiment Light Armoured Squadron maintained protection on land. From the Army extra port operators were deployed to assist with the handling of ships destined for and returning from the Gulf which were routed via Cyprus. The heightened state of alert on the island meant considerable extra guarding commitments for the garrison troops and the deployment of extra soldiers from UK to assist with garrison security. In addition, Territorial Army composite transport squadron was deployed to replace the UN Force in Cyprus (UNFICYP) transport squadron as almost all Royal Corps of Transport (RCT) assets were deployed to the Gulf.

In Saddam Hussein we were facing an unpredictable opponent and we had to be prepared for a pre-emptive Iraqi attack including the use of Scud Short Range Ballistic Missiles and perhaps armed with chemical or biological warheads. Moreover, there was no sign that he intended to withdraw his troops from Kuwait. Indeed, his aggressive acts continued with the seizure of Western civilians as hostages and their movement to key military and strategic sites as human shields, with intense pressure put on western diplomatic staffs in Kuwait city, and with the occupying Iraqi soldiers looting shops and intimidating the civilian population. Consequently, economic and diplomatic pressure was increased with the United Nations playing the lead role. While we all hoped for a peaceful resolution, it became increasingly likely that allied offensive action would be required to drive Iraqi forces from Kuwait. Nevertheless, if we could rigorously enforce the UN sanctions, there was just a chance that war could be avoided: Royal Navy forces played a significant role in the embargo operations.

EMBARGO OPERATIONS

The imposition of a ban on the movement of commodities into or out of Iraq/Kuwait by United Nations Security Council resolution 665 shifted the objectives of the ARMILLA patrol ships from the protection of British entitled merchant shipping to the enforcement of the UN sanctions. The success of this endeavour depended upon the close co-operation of naval forces in the Multi-national Maritime Force, provided primarily by thirteen non Middle Eastern nations, namely Australia, Argentina, Belgium, Canada, Denmark, France, Greece, Italy, Netherlands, Norway, Spain, the United Kingdom and the United States, together with those of certain Gulf States. In addition, the United States and United Kingdom provided surface surveillance from maritime patrol aircraft. On 21 August Ministers of the Western European Union (WEU) countries agreed to co-ordinate enforcement activities; guidelines and a network of WEU naval points of contact were established. Representatives of the participating states attended a conference in Bahrain on 8 September to establish the basis of international co-operation, and the various naval commanders met the following week to develop the military *modus operandi* and to institute a series of patrol boxes throughout the Gulf and the Gulf of Oman.

Thereafter, a different country chaired respective monthly meetings to decide a schedule of nations to police the boxes.

A vital aspect of the embargo operations was the need to exchange information on the location, destination and cargo of all vessels within the region stretching from the Suez Canal to the Gulf. Well-founded arrangements for the monitoring of merchant shipping were extended to provide allied nations with a comprehensive appreciation of shipping movements, and a special cell was set up in London specifically to fuse data on Iraqi flagged vessels or other contacts of interest. Boardings themselves tended to be joint undertakings by warships of more than one nation, with one unit in contact designated the Scene of Action Commander (SAC). The Royal Navy made a considerable contribution to the enforcement effort, challenging a total of 3,171 merchant ships and participating in 36 boardings in the period up to the official ceasefire. In addition, RAF Nimrod aircraft flew 295 surveillance sorties from their base at Seeb in support of embargo operations. The professionalism and skill that our forces displayed in the conduct of boarding impressed other navies considerably; notably our use of high-powered Rigid Inflatable Boats (RIB) to enable boardings to take place while target vessels remained under significant headway, and the insertion of Royal Marine boarding parties and naval personnel using a method of abseiling from Lynx helicopters known as rapid roping.

The most effective allied action ensured, from the outset, that no merchant ship reached Iraq through the Gulf without being stopped and inspected, and it also demonstrated the unequivocal resolve of the world community. Iraq made little effort to break the embargo in this area and, despite a relatively high level of patrol activity, the Royal Navy was directly involved in only two such potential incidents. I will describe these, the successful interception and boarding of the Iraqi cargo vessel AL WASITTI and the diversion of the tanker MV TADMUR, to illustrate the complexities inherent in such operations.

On 7 October 1990, both vessels were located in the Gulf of Aden by HM Ships BATTLEAXE and BRAZEN who proceeded to shadow them, in company with ships from the United States Navy and Royal Australian Navy. The AL WASITTI was assessed to be empty but TADMUR was suspected of carrying a small cargo under a false bottom in her holds. Their interception was authorised and the United States Navy (USN) Task Group Commander promulgated a tri-national boarding plan; the two Royal Navy ships were designated as the SAC for their respective incidents.

The AL WASITTI boarding began with a conventional challenge on VHF radio channels by HMS BATTLEAXE but the freighter, rather than reply to repeated requests to stop, increased speed and ignored all communication attempts. This prompted the SAC, in close consultation with the Ministry of Defence, to implement the next level of the Rules of Engagement, which permitted the firing of shells across the bows of the vessel. Despite this measured escalation in the use of force, the AL WASITTI refused to co-operate and Royal Marine boarding teams from HM Ships BATTLEAXE and LONDON were inserted by helicopter before a United States search team boarded by RIB: the ship was then cleared to proceed. While this protracted episode was unfolding, HMS BRAZEN continued to shadow MV TADMUR before boarding her without undue difficulty. This incident, however, highlighted different aspects of international co-operation; after the vessel was discovered to be carrying excessive amounts of foodstuffs, it was decided to divert the TADMUR to a friendly port. The refusal of the vessel's master to divert voluntarily and the necessary diplomatic activity involved in establishing a suitable destination added to the complexities facing those responsible for embargo enforcement.

As the United Nations deadline of 15 January 1991 for Iraq to withdraw from Kuwait approached, attention turned to preparations for hostilities and embargo enforcement was then conducted from the operating areas allocated for transition to war. Routine boardings by Royal Navy ships continued at frequent intervals although, increasingly, the possibility that merchant ships might be used for covert military purposes had to be considered. On one occasion, our (MCMVs) were called in to check the Shar Allum Shoal in the central Gulf, which the United States Navy had declared a mine danger area after the Iraqi MV ZANOOBIA had been spotted lowering objects into the water. The interception of various merchant vessels, such as the Iraqi MV AIN ZALAH, re-emphasised the problematic nature of the boarding task itself. In the weeks before the United Nations deadline, and then once hostilities had started, the nations of the WEU assumed the lead in co-ordinating embargo operations in the Gulf, concentrating their patrols in the vicinity of the Straits of Hormuz, and I was pleased that HM Ships BRILLIANT and EXETER were able to participate in this operation for a short period as they entered the Gulf in early February 1991.

MILITARY BUILD-UP

Following our initial reaction to the Iraqi invasion, Her Majesty's Government assessed that we would have to consolidate our military stance to reinforce our political commitment for Iraq to withdraw from Kuwait, even as we waited to see what effect the economic embargo would have. While there were signs that sanctions were causing hardship within Iraq, there was no indication that it would force President Saddam Hussein to recall his troops. The military build-up therefore had to proceed in parallel.

In the latter part of August, the Secretary of State for Defence announced that our military contribution was to be increased. I deployed a composite squadron of Tornado GR1 aircraft from Royal Air Force Germany to Muharraq air base in Bahrain on the Gulf coast: the aircraft's capability to carry out offensive counter air operations and interdiction providing an additional deterrent to any further Iraqi aggression. The Secretary of State also announced that the naval force level in the Gulf was to be increased to four warships and authorised the deployment of the Type 42 air defence destroyer HMS GLOUCESTER. Furthermore, the three Royal Navy MCMVs already deployed to the Mediterranean were ordered to proceed through the Suez Canal to the Gulf on 6-7 September where the oceanographic survey vessel HMS HERALD sailed to join them to act as the MCM Command Ship. In September, HM Ships LONDON, BRAZEN and CARDIFF formed Group X-ray and sailed as planned to relieve the three escorts of Armilla Group Whisky which had been on station since July. The Royal Marines and Royal Artillery provided Javelin surface-to-air missile detachments in all the escorts, together with additional teams for port security duties and protection of the RFAs. During the campaign, for contingency purposes, we also assigned HMS OTUS and OPOSSUM, both conventionally powered diesel submarines. The Army had some 300 men deployed providing communications, medical and postal support throughout the theatre.

On 14 September, Her Majesty's Government gave a further clear indication that the United Kingdom was prepared to resist force by announcing that the 7 Armoured Brigade would deploy from BAOR to the Gulf. The Brigade, including War Maintenance Reserves, would comprise 9,500 men, 145 Challenger tanks, 110 Warrior infantry fighting vehicles and 28 M109 guns. Its support would include the provision of 2 engineer regiments, 2 transport regiments, 2 ordnance battalions, 2 armoured workshops and a host of other specialist units including an armoured field ambulance. A detailed reconnaissance was rapidly conducted, which laid the foundations for the start of a huge logistic operation soon afterwards; the Brigade was complete in theatre by 3 November and quickly started live firing and other work-up exercises. Fifteen Royal Air Force Puma helicopters were earmarked to support the ground forces and were flown direct to the Gulf in C5 aircraft of the United States Air Force.

On the same day that the deployment of 7 Armoured Brigade was announced, the Secretary of State also made public that a further 18 Tornados were to move to the Gulf: six fighter and 12 attack aircraft. The reinforcements arrived by mid-October - the fighters to increase the Dhahran force to 18 Tornado F3s, while the ground-attack aircraft deployed to a newly-activated airfield at Tabuk in north-western Saudi Arabia, quite close to the Iraqi border. The Tornado and Jaguar aircraft were supported in their training missions by VC10K tanker aircraft of 101 Squadron, operating from Muharraq and Seeb airfields; these aircraft subsequently moving to King Khalid International Airport near Riyadh.

The Royal Air Force Regiment was deployed in strength for 'Survival to Operate' (STO) duties, and two Rapier surface-to-air missile squadrons were detached to the air bases at Tabuk and Muharraq. STO tasks involved the defence, and if necessary recovery, of airfields from enemy air, ground and Nuclear, Biological and Chemical (NBC) attack. The Regiment provided STO command and control, as well as training elements, at Tabuk, Muharraq and Dhahran. These were established Host Nation Bases, but the prospect of air attack required the Royal Air Force Regiment and Royal Engineer units to enhance the facilities for collective protection. I also deployed two of the Regiment's Light Armoured Squadrons for ground defence and counter-terrorist operations at the airfields. Other teams guarded a US Patriot Battery, provided close protection for the Commander BFME, operated specialist chemical and biological defence vehicles, and secured our air-to-air refuelling aircraft at King Khalid International Airfield.

On 15 November, 7 Armoured Brigade was declared operationally ready south of the Kuwaiti/Saudi border and I transferred tactical control to the Commander of the United States 1st Marine Expeditionary Force. A week later, the Secretary of State decided to deploy the 4th Brigade and additional troops and so increase the United Kingdom ground forces to divisional strength. The plan was to have this division - 1 (British) Armoured Division - operational in theatre by 31 January. When complete the division would comprise, including War Maintenance Reserve, 28,000 men, 221 Challenger tanks, 327 Warrior infantry fighting vehicles and 79 M109 and M110 guns, 16 Multiple Launch Rocket Systems (MLRs) plus armoured reconnaissance and anti-tank helicopter regiments, 3 engineer regiments, a Rapier air defence regiment and 2 Javelin air defence batteries. Providing support would be 5 transport regiments, 2 ordnance battalions, 3 armoured workshops and other specialist sub units. Furthermore, the Army would provide 4 field hospitals, 1,600 beds in all, as the bulk of the medical support for our forces in the Gulf, and a further 5,000 soldiers would be deployed in all. Helicopter support for the Division was provided by the Royal Air Force with 12 Chinooks and 19 Pumas, and by the Royal Navy with 12 Sea Kings.

Our offensive air capability in theatre was also increased. The squadron of Jaguars moved forward from Thumrait to Muharraq which enabled them to carry out attack sorties into the Kuwaiti Theatre of Operations (KTO) without total dependence on air-to-air refuelling. Locating them closer to the KTO increased their daily sortie rate and, therefore, their overall warfighting capability and contribution to the Coalition's air effort. Following further reinforcement, there were, by mid-January, 45 RAF Tornado GR1s in theatre, six of which were the GR1A reconnaissance variant, with a further six being equipped to fire ALARM (Air-Launched Anti-Radiation Missiles). This weapon had been in the development stage but the manufacturer, British Aerospace, accelerated the clearance procedures to provide this vital defence suppression missile. The six Tornado GR1As at Dhahran represented the one type of allied aircraft which, flying at low level, would be able to provide day and night tactical reconnaissance of enemy positions. To support the defensive and offensive aircraft, I positioned 15 tanker aircraft at Muharraq and King Khalid International airfields, a mixed fleet of VC10Ks of 101 Squadron, Victors of 55 Squadron and a Tristar of 216 Squadron.

LOGISTICS

The distance from the United Kingdom to the Gulf is 3,000 miles by air of 6,300 miles by sea: the scale of moving such a large component of our fighting forces over such a distance was colossal. To give an indication of the size of the task, consider the deployment of 1 (BR) Armoured Division alone: 28,000 people, and up to 400,000 tonnes of freight, including ammunition, stores and 15,000 vehicles, were transported to theatre, and the Division was then sustained and committed to battle in inhospitable terrain some 200 miles from the port of entry at Al Jubayl.

The logistic outload required the use of an extensive sea tail, RAF air transport assets and chartered civilian air cargo aircraft. The first ship sailed on deployment for Operation GRANBY on 28 September and the last ship arrived on 15 February; at the height of the preparation phase, in late December, there were some 50 vessels loading or en route to the Gulf. A total of 114 different ships from 20 nations took part in the deployment; some made more than one return journey in accumulating the total number of 146 round trips. Unlike Operation CORPORATE, there was no need to requisition British flagged ships. Commercial merchant ships were chartered through representatives on the Baltic Exchange. There was competition for Roll On-Roll Off ferries, which were in heavy demand, but otherwise there was little difficulty in meeting our requirements. Most ships had armed military escorts aboard but the enemy did not seek to disrupt our extended sea lines of communication and every ship arrived safely; only a very small number were delayed by bad weather or mechanical problems. I count the sea tail, which was responsible for the delivery of the vast majority of all the necessary ammunition, equipment and stores to support our forces, as a most successful part of the Operation.

For the air outload, we relied heavily on the RAF Air Transport Force of Hercules, VC10 and Tristar aircraft and supplemented the fleet by chartering civilian cargo aircraft. Up to 500 tonnes of urgent freight was carried daily. The Force was mobilised to a high level of activity as soon as Operation GRANBY started and it operated over the whole eight months at between two and three times its normal peacetime rates, which themselves are demanding. On 30 October, an Air Transport Detachment was set up at King Khalid Air Base with 3 Hercules and supporting elements. As the demand for in-theatre airlift personnel increased, a further two Hercules were deployed in January 1991. I was very pleased when the New Zealand Government offered two Hercules to operate alongside those of the Royal Air Force. The New Zealanders made a significant contribution to our airlift and with my aircraft flew over 2,300 sorties in support of our forces operating from both normal and desert strips. Back in the United Kingdom, I had to deploy engineers from throughout the Royal Air Force to the transport bases to meet the increased routine maintenance and rectification tasks of the fleet. I also relied on the specialist movements teams to ensure maximum aircraft utilisation and that every load was safe. RAF Akrotiri in Cyprus, strategically located almost exactly half way between the United Kingdom and the Gulf, was a most important facility. This airfield was used as a staging base and its traffic increased tremendously. There were almost 14,000 Operation GRANBY movements at Akrotiri, and of these nearly 8,000 were dedicated freight moves by air transport aircraft. To place these figures in perspective, the number of Operation GRANBY movements corresponds to the total expected in almost 10 years at the normal peacetime rate. In addition, the Victor, VC10K and Tristar tanker aircraft were used extensively to deploy non-stop attack and air defence aircraft, including some from other Coalition air forces, to and from the theatre.

As for maritime and air forces, many new equipments were brought into service for the land forces. In some cases, such as MLRS and the rifle launched grenade, these were early purchases of equipment due to enter service in the future. However, there were new buys for which financial provision had not previously been available. Existing equipment was modified in view of the desert conditions and the Iraqi weapon systems. Night vision aids, computers and satellite communications equipment were made available on a much larger scale than had previously been envisaged. Both Challenger tanks and Warrior infantry fighting vehicles were uparmoured. These enhancements provided 1 (BR) Armoured Division with major improvements in its operational capability.

While the strategic deployment continued, the logistic units in Saudi Arabia were working intensively to receive and sort the supplies which were arriving, and then deliver them to the front-line units. To facilitate this process, a chain of logistic bases was established between Al Jubayl and the Forward Assembly Area from which 1 (BR) Armoured Division was to launch its offensive. Forward logistics bases had to cater for the anticipated daily consumption of up to 1,200 tonnes of ammunition, 500,000 litres of fuel, 400,000 litres of water and 30,000 individual rations. We positioned more than 120 replacement vehicles and some 1,600 tonnes of spare parts in the desert, and prepared to carry out running repairs in theatre. Moving all the troops with their vehicles, equipment and supplies was an enormous task. We used 800 vehicles ranging from tank transporters and fuel tankers to Landrovers, driving a total of over 14 million kilometres. The Royal Engineers produced over 12 million maps, moved 850,000 tonnes of soil and dug 160 kilometres of ditching. In a joint project with US forces, they designed, planned and built a fuel pipeline which eventually stretched some 290 kilometres across the desert.

The scale of the logistic operation was huge, as these figures demonstrate. To compare it with a previous, well-known operation, the daily needs of 1 (BR) Armoured Division were of the same order as those for the whole of 21 Army Group in the early part of Operation OVERLORD, the D-Day landings in 1944. I believe that 1 (BR) Armoured Division was probably the best prepared and supported force ever fielded by the British Army.

FINAL ALLIED PREPARATIONS

During the autumn of 1990, political pressure on Iraq continued. However, neither economic sanctions, diplomatic measures nor the threat of military action brought about any apparent softening of President Saddam Hussein's attitude. A crucial date for the Coalition was Thursday, 29 November, when the United Nations Security Council approved resolution 678 calling on Iraq to withdraw from Kuwait by 15 January and authorising the use of "all necessary means" to effect withdrawal if the deadline passed and Iraq had not acceded. Although our forces had to remain vigilant to react to any Iraqi provocation, this date now provided the focal point on which offensive operations by the Coalition could begin. However, we then had to consider other factors which would influence the timing of any allied attack. We realised that the high summer temperatures in the region would place our troops at a disadvantage compared with the indigenous armies, and this indicated that military action should be completed before April. Furthermore, the major Islamic religious festival of Ramadan would begin in mid-March and, with several Arab nations in the Coalition, it would have been inappropriate to be in the throes of war at that time. Finally, some allied forces had been in the area since August and we could not keep them at full war readiness indefinitely. Taking all these factors into consideration, Coalition leaders planned to begin an attack soon after the 15 January deadline if Iraqi forces were still occupying Kuwait. It was anticipated that the campaign would last about six weeks.

Early in December, President Saddam Hussein announced that all foreign hostages would be released. Barring this one concession, his intransigence remained absolute and hostilities seemed increasingly likely; so our soldiers, sailors and airmen reviewed their preparations for war. In addition to individual unit training, a series of large-scale exercises enabled ships, army formations and squadrons to practise their skills with their Coalition allies, with particular emphasis on operating under chemical and biological warfare conditions. The Christmas/New Year period saw a heightened alertness to guard against a pre-emptive Iraqi attack, followed by an increase in the intensity of work-up preparations as the United Nations deadline approached.

This preparation phase was not without cost. During the preparations for the land battle, nine soldiers of 1 (BR) Armoured Division died. Considering the intensity and hazardous nature of the training, the accidents which our land forces suffered were mercifully few. Similarly, there were two accidents to RAF aircraft: a Jaguar crashed while on a low flying sortie on 13 November, killing the pilot, and a Tornado GR1 flew into the ground in Oman on 13 January, killing both pilot and navigator. In addition, a Tornado GR1 was badly damaged in a night landing accident at Tabuk in November; both crew members ejected but were quite seriously injured. Tragic as these accidents were, the fact was that we had put a significant proportion of our armed Services on a war footing in a distant and environmentally demanding theatre in the space of only four months, and had trained and prepared them fully for combat. It reflects well on the professionalism of our forces and on the realism of our peacetime training that our fighting machine was mobilised so quickly and efficiently, and was at the highest state of readiness when the UN deadline expired.

IRAQI MILITARY STRENGTH

Despite the huge allied military build-up and our clearly stated intention to eject the Iraqi forces from Kuwait if Saddam Hussein refused to withdraw in compliance with UN Security Council resolution 660, President Saddam Hussein elected to reinforce his troops rather than withdraw them. Iraq mobilised its reserve forces and formed new divisions to protect Baghdad, while the majority of the army was deployed into Kuwait and south-eastern Iraq. The force in this area opposing the Coalition armies as the UN deadline approached was estimated as being over 600,000 men formed into over 40 divisions, with some 4,500 tanks and 3,250 artillery pieces. A substantial defensive barrier of minefields, sand walls, razor wire fences and oil-filled ditches was built along the border of Kuwait and southern Iraq with Saudi Arabia to obstruct our forces and attempt to channel them into areas favourable for Iraqi counter-attack. A further 20 divisions with 1,000 tanks and a similar number of artillery pieces were retained in central and northern Iraq, bringing the total number of Iraqi ground troops to an estimated 1.2 million. By comparison, the Iraqi Navy was less impressive, being equipped with only about 15 surface-to-surface missile armed fast attack craft, some 5 of which had been captured from the Kuwaiti navy, and a number of miscellaneous small craft many of which could be used for minelaying. The shore-based Silkworm anti-ship missile system also posed a significant threat.

The Iraqi Air Force fielded about 750 fixed-wing combat aircraft capable of operating in a variety of roles. Their inventory contained almost 50 MiG 29 Fulcrum air superiority fighters and 30 MiG 25 Foxbat interceptor/reconnaissance aircraft as well as 170 older generation air defence aircraft. Their 70 Mirage F1s could be used in the air defence or ground attack role with a diversity of weapons, and were supplemented in the attack role by a squadron of long-range SU-24 Fencers and 300 Flogger, Fitter and Frogfoot aircraft. Iraq had also recently acquired an air-to-air refuelling and airborne early warning capability and had a small air transport fleet. In addition, they had a diverse fleet of over 500 assault, attack and troop-lifting helicopters shared between the Air Force and Army Aviation. The Iraqi Air Force was deployed on more than 60 airfields, some of which were vast constructions with very considerable runway and taxiway redundancy. Over 600 hardened aircraft shelters had been built on the main operating bases. Defensively, Iraq had an extensive arsenal of surface-to-air missile and anti-aircraft artillery batteries. For command and control of its forces, a vast network of deep and hardened bunkers had been constructed throughout the country.

THE FREEING OF KUWAIT BEGINS

On the night of 16 January, at 2336 hours GMT, the Coalition forces began their attack against Iraq. The opening bombardment came from the air, with American F-117 stealth fighters and cruise missiles, fired from surface ships and submarines, being used to attack key command and control and air defence centres. They were followed shortly afterwards by formations of allied aircraft attacking a variety of targets from numerous directions. In addition to their significant contribution to air operations, naval forces began the task of gaining sea control of the Northern Gulf and thereby posing the threat of an amphibious landing. On land, half a million ground troops were poised along the 200 miles of Saudi border with Kuwait and Eastern Iraq. The objectives of the first phase of the campaign were to establish air superiority, to paralyse the enemy's command, control and communications system, to destroy his nuclear, chemical and biological warfare facilities, and then to begin the process of attrition of Iraqi ground forces from the air to prepare the way for the coalition armies to liberate Kuwait quickly and with minimum allied casualties.

This was a combined arms, multi-national assault with General Norman Schwarzkopf of the United States Army nominated as the overall commander. United Kingdom forces were involved in all aspects of the campaign and I will describe their activities under single-Service headings which, to maintain a logical sequence, will begin with air operations, then cover naval operations and finish with the land offensive. I reiterate that we were part of a large Coalition force and that the delineation by Service is for clarity only; for the operations of all three arms were independent throughout the hostilities. The total number of British servicemen and women in theatre was about 45,000 which made us the third largest contingent after the United States and Saudi Arabia. The Coalition force numbered over 700,000 men and women drawn from 30 nations. The United States provided the majority of the personnel - some 540,000 people - and consequently took the lead in formulating the operational plans.

AIR OPERATIONS

On that first night, as part of a complex, highly co-ordinated air campaign, twenty Royal Air Force Tornado GR1 aircraft, each armed with two JP233 airfield denial weapons, flew from the air bases at Muharraq, Tabuk and Dhahran to carry out attacks against Iraqi airfields. The aircraft refuelled in the air just south of the Iraqi border, in radio silence, from Victor and VC10K tankers. They then descended to very low level to delay detection by Iraqi radars and engagement by their surface-to-air missiles and guns. The crews were carrying out a role for which they have been well trained, both in Europe and in theatre. Although taken by surprise, the Iraqi ground defences soon recovered and began to engage our aircraft. However, the Tornados, flying low and fast in small packages in total darkness, and assisted by their electronic jamming pods, were able successfully to press home their attacks. Two additional Tornado GR1s, each armed with three ALARM, flew in support, firing their missiles just before the attacking aircraft dropped their JP233 weapons, which dispensed runway cratering bombs and anti-personnel minelets onto their targets. All of our aircraft returned safely. In the morning, a further wave of four Tornado GR1 aircraft from Muharraq, loaded with a total of 32 1,000lb bombs, carried out daylight attacks from low level against further Iraqi airfields; one aircraft failed to return from this raid. Later in the day (17 January) four Muharraq-based Jaguars flew successful attacks against a barracks in Kuwait with each aircraft delivering its load of 1,000lb bombs despite encountering severe enemy ground fire. And as darkness fell, Tornado GR1s took off on more airfield attack sorties. The Tornado F3s continued to mount defensive air patrols but were not put to the test by the Iraqi Air Force which failed to mount any offensive operations into Saudi air space. Our Nimrod aircraft from Seeb flew maritime surveillance sorties and contributed to the compilation of the surface picture in the Gulf. In the first 24 hours of the air campaign, Royal Air Force aircraft flew 58 offensive, 37 air defence, 19 air-to-air refuelling and 3 maritime surveillance sorties, which set a pattern and rate of flying for the whole campaign. I will now outline the contribution made by each RAF aircraft type to the air campaign.

For the next five days, the Tornado GR1s continued to carry out day and night attacks against Iraqi airfields using JP233, with each package being accompanied by further GR1s armed with 1,000lb bombs and ALARM missiles to suppress the enemy defences. However, the GR1's role changed significantly on 23 January. By then it had become apparent that the Iraqis were unlikely to commit their air force in any strength until the ground battle began. A few air defence aircraft had been launched to intercept allied raids but most had been destroyed by allied fighters. There was little point in continuing at that stage to attack airfield operating surfaces with JP233 which had to be delivered from low-level where the primary threat was coming from extensive enemy anti-aircraft gunfire. With the Iraqi surface-to-air missile threat largely negated by allied air action and electronic countermeasures, it was decided to switch the Tornado GR1s to medium level bombing where they could operate above the effective height of nearly all the Iraqi guns. Their targets included radar control centres, ammunition dumps, petroleum storage depots, power stations and Scud Short Range Ballistic Missile sites. To improve the accuracy of medium-level bombing, twelve Buccaneer aircraft from No's 12 and

208 Squadrons, both based at Lossiemouth in Scotland, were deployed to the Gulf to use their Pavespike laser designation equipment. The attack aircraft launched in mixed formation packages with the Buccaneer crews designating the target and the Tornado GR1 crews releasing the laser-guided bombs. The first such bombs were dropped on 3 February, initially against bridges being used for the resupply of Iraqi troops in the KTO and, later in the campaign, against petroleum storage sites, hardened aircraft shelters and aircraft operating surfaces. In all, the Buccaneers flew 214 sorties. On 10 February, the Tornado force obtained its own laser designation capability with the arrival at Tabuk of two pre-production TIALD (Thermal Imaging Airborne Laser Designation) pods. The TIALD system, unlike Pavespike, could be used at night as well as by day, and these pods - known affectionately by the crews as Sandra and Tracey - proved extremely successful. By 14 February, all three of our GR1 bases were conducting precision-guided bombing attacks, and these were sustained until hostilities ended. Throughout the air campaign, the Tornado GR1s flew over 1,500 offensive sorties, their crews displaying great skill and courage in pressing home their attacks. In addition to the aircraft shot down during the first daylight Tornado raid, another five Tornado GR1s were lost on operations, five aircrew were killed and seven became prisoners of war. One other Tornado developed serious mechanical problems shortly after take off and the crew ejected safely.

On the night of 18/19 January, the Tornado GRIA - the reconnaissance version of the aircraft - undertook its first operational mission. From then until hostilities ceased, the six Dhahran-based GR1As flew 123 night low-level sorties, often deep into Iraq, using their infra-red linescan equipment with considerable success. This Tornado variant provided the Coalition with much vitally important intelligence on the enemy's force dispositions, and it was also used in the hunt for Iraqi Scud missile launchers. The firing of Scuds posed little direct military threat but, by targeting them on Jerusalem, Haifa and Tel Aviv, Iraq sought to attempt to provoke Israel into military retaliation in the hope of turning the conflict into a holy war and thereby splitting the Coalition. This risk led the allied to divert considerable air effort onto attacking Scud launchers once they had been located.

From the outset of hostilities, the Jaguar Squadron at Muharraq was allocated a variety of targets in Kuwait including Iraqi barracks, coastal defence positions, surface-to-air missile batteries, supply depots and ammunition dumps. The Jaguars were also used to attack Iraqi naval vessels operating in the northern Gulf. The Jaguars were armed mainly with 1,000lb bombs and CRV7 rockets, they also dropped cluster bombs, from low and medium levels, on to concentrations of armour and artillery positions. On 29 January, a formation of Jaguars was returning from an attack on a Silkworm anti-ship missile site on the Kuwaiti coast when their pilots spotted some Iraqi fast patrol boats. Their location was passed to HMS GLOUCESTER, who instigated successful engagements on these and other enemy craft by naval forces and by further RAF Jaguars. The next day, two Jaguars used rockets and guns to disable a Polnochny class landing ship support vessel. In addition to its offensive role, the Jaguar was used for daylight tactical reconnaissance. Once the land offensive began on 24 February, the Jaguars were tasked on some longer-range interdiction missions into Iraq, which required them to flight refuel en route. Overall, although its attacks were limited to daylight bombing, our Jaguar force was most effective against a wide variety of targets, flying more than 600 operational sorties over enemy territory, often in the face of heavy fire, without loss.

Our Tornado F3 fighters, in common with other Coalition aircraft mounting defensive air patrols, were not involved in any engagement with Iraqi aircraft. The Royal Air Force had procured the F3 to defend the United Kingdom against attacks by long-range bombers. In this conflict, however, the threat was primarily from modern, agile fighter aircraft operating close to their home bases in Iraq, and the few that flew were engaged by American and Saudi F-15 air superiority fighters. However, the potential Iraqi air threat caused us early in the crisis to improve the survivability and performance of the Tornado F3. Modifications already in the pipeline were greatly accelerated as a result of excellent co-operation between the RAF and Industry. The F3's role was to mount combat air patrols by day and night, mainly over Saudi Arabia, but towards the end of the campaign some patrols were flown within Iraqi airspace. The aircraft proved extremely reliable and flew a total of 2,600 sorties during the 7 months deployment. However, while none of the RAF air defence forces - fighter aircraft or Rapier batteries - were involved in action, they nonetheless made a most valuable contribution to the overall air defence screen and undoubtedly helped to deter Iraqi air attacks against Coalition bases and forces.

Our Victor, VC10K and Tristar tankers played a vital role in support of the Coalition air forces, extending the range of offensive aircraft and the endurance of air defence fighters. In the six-week air war, these aircraft flew over 730 sorties and off-loaded 13,000 tonnes of fuel to almost 3,000 aircraft. While most recipients were our own Tornados, Jaguars and Buccaneers, RAF tankers also dispensed fuel to 800 other Coalition aircraft, including Saudi Arabian Tornado ADVs, Canadian CF-18s and USN F-14s and A-6s. Much of the refuelling was conducted at night, and usually in radio silence to deprive the enemy of warning of the timing and direction of attacks.

Just before the air campaign began, the nature of Nimrod operations changed from the search for vessels seeking to break the embargo to the direct support of allied warships operating at the northern end of the Gulf. Together with aircraft from the United States Navy, they provided constant surface surveillance of these waters, and whenever they located a potentially hostile vessel, passed its position so that naval fixed-wing aircraft or helicopters could investigate and, if confirmed hostile, engage. During hostilities, the Nimrods flew 112 sorties over the waters of the northern Gulf, contributing significantly to both offensive and defensive naval operations.

The heavy involvement of our Air Transport Force of Hercules, VC10s and Tristars throughout the build-up phase continued during hostilities. Indeed, the hours flown by the force rose as the urgency for resupply by air increased. By the end of the conflict, the transport fleet had logged over 50,000 flying hours on operation GRANBY, having flown at more than twice their normal peacetime rate. The aircraft had carried 30,000 tonnes of freight and 66,000 passengers, consuming 54 million gallons of fuel on over 12,500 sorties. By any standards, this was a most impressive performance.

When hostilities began, there were 43 support helicopters in theatre: 19 Puma and 12 Chinook aircraft from the Royal Air Force, together with 12 Royal Navy Sea King helicopters detached from duties with the Royal Marine Commando Brigade. The Support Helicopter (SH) Force was employed in direct support of 1 (BR) Armoured Division, their primary allocated task being casualty evacuation. However, in the event the force operated in a variety of support roles, including the ferrying of prisoners of war back to allied internment camps. Before the start of the land offensive, the SH Force was engaged in Divisional training exercises before moving, in mid-January, to its Forward Operating Bases to the south and east of Hafar al Batin. Once the land battle began, the force continued to support the Armoured Division into Iraq and then into Kuwait. When hostilities ended, the helicopters had flown a total of

2,358 sorties and carried more than 1,261 tonnes of equipment and stores, and 17,773 troops and prisoners of war. Fortunately, they were not required much for casualty evacuation. The SH Force overcame many unique engineering and operational challenges to become a most effective support element of the British land forces.

The Royal Air Force Regiment provided the SH Force with integral sections of Gunners and a Landrover-borne defensive element. As the land offensive approached, reinforcements were moved up from Muharraq and the majority of No. 1 Squadron (RAF Regiment)'s armour, consisting of Scorpion and Spartan vehicles, was flown from Germany into the desert strip of Al Qaysumah. The Squadron re-grouped quickly, crossed the breach into Iraq with 1 (BR) Armoured Division and ended the war astride the Kuwait-Basra highway. The Royal Air Force Regiment strength in theatre rose to 1,000, representing 20 per cent of the Royal Air Force's deployed manpower. As in previous conflicts, they responded rapidly to unforeseen circumstances and demonstrated a characteristic flexibility in performing a wide diversity of tasks.

In this section on the air campaign, I have dwelt, quite properly, on the operational aspects. However, I was also impressed by the achievements of logistics staffs in support of over 160 aircraft of 16 different types deployed in theatre. The establishment of large stockpiles of aircraft spares, weapons and fuel, and regular air resupply, ensured that there were no significant logistics constraints on our air operations. Moreover, the high availability and serviceability rates of our aircraft reflected the outstanding efforts of our ground crews and all those in a lengthy supply chain. In addition, I commend our engineering staffs for the extensive preparation work that they conducted in the early months of the Operation. As our aircraft had been optimised for war in the Central Region of Europe, they needed to be modified and enhanced to fit them for operations in the desert. A total of 242 different modifications were embodied in 303 aircraft, at a cost of over 300,000 service manhours.

NAVAL OPERATIONS

Once again, it is important to put the United Kingdom contribution into proper perspective. While we provided the second largest naval force after the United States, our ships represented less than 10 per cent of the total Coalition strength. Nevertheless, in some areas the Royal Navy played a proportionately much greater part than our numerical presence might imply; this necessitated full integration with the predominant USN and the transfer of tactical control of a number of our ships to USN Task Group Commanders. It is noteworthy that only the USN and Royal Navy took part in offensive maritime operations.

The overall plan envisaged that the Coalition naval force would move progressively further north to dominate the extreme northern Gulf, neutralise the Iraqi Navy, and conduct MCM operations and Naval Gunfire Support in preparation for the arrival of the main amphibious force off Kuwait. The Royal Navy's initial contribution was to provide two Type 42 destroyers, HM Ships GLOUCESTER and CARDIFF, which formed an important element of the forward air defence barrier protecting the three US Carrier Battle Groups, USS RANGER, ROOSEVELT and MIDWAY and their escorts, in the central Gulf. The Type 42s also supported surface surveillance operations in the north. The Iraqis had the capability to attack our ships with stand-off missiles launched from aircraft, ships and coastal batteries, which led SNOME to operate the remainder of his ships under the umbrella of the layered Coalition air defence established throughout the Gulf.

As the campaign progressed, the Primary Casualty Reception Ship, RFA ARGUS, was stationed close enough to the forwardmost ships to balance timely medical and airborne logistics support against acceptable risk, and was escorted by SNOME's Flagship, HMS LONDON, for added protection against air attack. It was from this position that RFA ARGUS was able to provide immediate medical assistance to the casualties sustained when USS TRIPOLI suffered mine damage. The rest of the British Underway Replenishment Group of RFAs ORANGELEAF, FORT GRANGE and OLNA, together with the Forward Repair Ship RFA DILIGENCE, remained further down threat in the Gulf in company with HMS BRAZEN, while RFA RESOURCE and three LSLs SIR PERCIVAL, SIR TRISTAM, and SIR BEDIVERE held the reserve ammunition stocks for 1 (BR) Armoured Division. The MCM Group consisting of the Hunt Class vessels ATHERSTONE, CATTISTOCK, HURWORTH, DULVERTON and LEDBURY, together with their command and engineering support ships, HMS HERALD and RFA SIR GALAHAD, were poised in the southern Gulf. Subsequently, these supporting echelons moved further north to maintain the cohesion of the force.

The non-appearance of the Iraqi Air Force was as apparent at sea as elsewhere, and the only airborne attack to be mounted in the direction of naval units was on 24 January when Saudi fighters successfully engaged two Floggers and one Mirage F1 before they could launch their missiles. Consequently, while HMS GLOUCESTER and HMS CARDIFF contributed fully to air defence in the front line, it was in the prosecution of anti-surface warfare that the Royal Navy made most impact in the early stages of the conflict. Although only a small element of the total Coalition surveillance effort, Lynx helicopters from Royal Navy escorts flew nearly 600 sorties in the northern Gulf on search and interdiction operations against Iraqi naval units.

The first anti-surface action occurred on 29 January when RAF Jaguars detected Iraqi fast patrol boats heading off the Kuwaiti coast as part of a combined operation to attack the port of Al Khafji. Lynx from HM ships GLOUCESTER, CARDIFF and BRAZEN were launched to locate and engage the enemy flotilla with Sea Skua missiles, leaving two sunk or damaged and scattering the remainder which were attacked by fixed-wing aircraft as they sought shelter along the coast. Over the next two days, our Lynx successfully pressed home further attacks against Exocet-armed patrol craft. These incidents, together with continued Coalition attacks on enemy units during the subsequent 'Battle of Bubiyan Channel', effectively broke the back of Iraqi naval resistance and led the allied Naval Commander to declare Coalition sea control of the Gulf on 8 February. Thereafter, Iraqi units made only isolated attempts to operate at sea, all of which drew attacks from the air, with more successful engagements by Royal Navy helicopters, including four by the Lynx embarked in HMS MANCHESTER which took our tally of sunk or disabled enemy ships to at least ten.

HMS MANCHESTER had arrived in the Gulf at the end of January with HM Ships BRILLIANT, EXETER and BRAVE as part of Group YANKEE to augment and subsequently relieve the ships of Group X-RAY. A minor but nonetheless notable aspect of HMS BRILLIANT's arrival was the inclusion in her complement of members of the Women's Royal Naval Service who were serving in combatant ships in a war zone for the first time.

The greatest threat to our ships was posed by mines. Evidence of the scale of Iraqi mine stocks was well known from our involvement in clearance operations after the Iran/Iraq war, and we fully expected a very large number of both moored and more sophisticated ground mines to be laid in preparation for this war. In the Gulf itself, the presence of this weapon, like the potential threat of chemical and biological munitions as well as the residual threat from air launched anti-ship missiles, had to be considered in every aspect of naval operations. Ships and aircraft frequently spotted free floating mines throughout the Gulf, some of which demanded ships to take swift avoiding action before specialist Explosive Ordnance Disposal teams could deal with them.

The primary role of the Coalition MCM Force was to conduct pre-cursor mine clearance operations off the Kuwaiti coastline so that the USN battleships MISSOURI and WISCONSIN could close to bombard shore defences in preparation for a possible amphibious landing by the US Marine Corps. The initial mine clearance operations were related to a raid on Faylakah Island east of Kuwait City, codenamed Operation DESERT SLASH, which represented an integral part of the overall campaign deception plan. Early on 14 February, HMS HERALD and the five Royal Navy Minehunters met up with the USN MCM Group north of Bahrain to transit towards the operation area. Based on available intelligence, the optimum route to the designated Battleship Fire Support Area (BBFSA) had been identified, but was necessarily close to enemy held territory and so put ships at risk not only from the mines themselves but also from shore missile sites. Meanwhile RFAs ARGUS, DILIGENCE, SIR GALAHAD and OLNA moved forward to provide close support for the Group. HM Ships LONDON, BRAVE and EXETER afforded air defence protection for these high value units, while HMS GLOUCESTER was assigned to escort USS MISSOURI. Clearance operations started on 15 February and were conducted without incident until the morning of 18 February when USS TRIPOLI, the USN MCM Command ship, and USS PRINCETON, a Ticonderoga Class cruiser, were each struck by a mine. The extent of resultant damage was a stark reminder of the danger posed by a weapon which is widely available and often extremely effective, and which can be laid from a variety of platforms by a relatively unsophisticated enemy. Nevertheless, after a brief pause to regroup, continued progress enabled USS MISSOURI to enter the BBFSA on 23 February and commence bombardment of Faylakah Island the next day.

As our ships approached within 10 miles of the coast, the threat from enemy shore defences was of increasing concern and early on 25 February HMS GLOUCESTER detected on radar a fast-moving contact leaving the coastline 21 miles to the west. In less than a minute, the ship's Operations Room team swiftly assessed the contact as a Silkworm missile, posing a direct threat to allied naval units including the US battleship nearby, and fired two Sea Dart surface-to-air missiles which destroyed the incoming Silkworm. Although this incident represented the final action at sea before the suspension of hostilities, allied naval units could not afford to relax as the task of clearing mines from the approaches to Kuwait was effectively only just beginning.

The logistic support provided by the Royal Fleet Auxiliary at sea and the naval stores organisation ashore was critically important. Unlike the other two Services, the presence of the ARMILLA Patrol had ensured that an existing structure of stores support was already available in theatre. Throughout the initial phase, our ships continued to use the port of Jebel Ali as the main base support facility, although augmentation with Royal Navy Supply and Transport Service personnel and expansion of its facilities was necessary. RFA DILIGENCE, the Forward Repair Ship, remained alongside to carry out more complex maintenance and the fitting of equipment enhancements; but following the outbreak of hostilities, she sailed to provide similar support and a Battle Damage Repair capability, the latter being effectively used to assist USS TRIPOLI and PRINCETON after their minestrikes. Similarly, RFA SIR GALAHAD accompanied the MCM force to meet their engineering support requirements. RFAs OLNA, ORANGELEAF and BAYLEAF took the lead in replenishing our ships with fuel, and by the end of the campaign had supplied over 40,000 tonnes of diesel and 2,000 tonnes of aviation fuel. Other Coalition tankers were used to fuel our escorts when the tactical situation demanded. RFA FORT GRANGE carried naval stores and ammunitions as well as six months supply of frozen and dry foodstuffs, while RFA RESOURCE, primarily tasked to hold the UK land forces war reserve of ammunition, carried 8,000 man months of frozen and dry provisions and NAAFI items. This balanced force of afloat support ships also exploited the utility of the LSLs as delivery vessels after they had off-loaded their ammunition at Al Jubayl. The contribution of the Sea King helicopters embarked in RFAs FORT GRANGE and ARGUS was vital in transporting high-priority items to front-line units as they advanced. In order to shorten what became a 500 mile supply chain, SNOME ordered the forward movement of the main support base from Jebel Ali to Bahrain. The availability and serviceability of Royal Navy ships and their equipment remained very high throughout the operation, and full credit must be given to the engineering and support staffs, predominantly civilian, who prepared and enhanced them.

SPECIAL FORCES OPERATIONS

United Kingdom Special Forces (SF), drawn from all three Services, were committed at an early stage in the campaign. This deployment developed into the largest and most significant UK SF operation since 1945. Operating in their classic strategic role they carried out long-range information reporting and offensive action missions in support of the overall allied campaign. Their area of responsibility included Western Iraq and the Kuwaiti theatre of operations (KTO). The forces deployed operated on foot, by vehicle and in helicopters in the worst weather conditions experienced in the area for 30 years. Troops had to endure climatic extremes which ranged from sandstorms through fog to nights where the cold was so intense that diesel fuel froze. In these arduous conditions re-supply was minimal due to enemy air defences and men were fighting in survival conditions. In this most testing environment it is a great tribute to the professionalism of all concerned that some patrols operated behind enemy lines for well over a month.

Their prime operational task was identified by General Schwarzkopf as countering the threat of Iraqi Scud missiles. This objective was achieved with outstanding success by the destruction of a number of fixed launcher sites, mobile launchers, command and control and air defence systems. This was done both by direct ground action and by the identification of targets for air attack. Quite apart from the damage wrought on Iraq's offensive ballistic missile capability, the psychological impact of these SF operations in Western Iraq, hundreds of miles behind the front line, cannot be over-estimated.

In course of the operation, the SF had to close with the enemy and there were many individual acts of outstanding bravery. Four men died in action and four men were wounded. The intensity of some of the combat and the courage displayed is rightly recognised by the high proportion of decorations awarded to the Special Forces.

The Royal Marines, Soldiers and Airmen of the Special Forces who rose to these high standards displayed qualities of fortitude, determination and courage which were in the highest traditions of our Services and of the special place which the SF hold in those Services. They earned my own highest regard and there is no doubt that the contributions the SF made to the Allied success was of an order out of all proportion to their numbers. To protect the security of their operational methods, and as requested by the SF themselves, it is not proposed to publish further details of their operations, which made an outstanding contribution to the overall campaign.

THE LAND CAMPAIGN

Between the arrival of 1 (BR) Armoured Division's advance party on 5 December and the air move being complete on 11 January, units married up with their equipment and started training; time was short for this since the main allied preoccupation was to plan and effect a discrete move of the bulk of coalition armoured forces from an area south of Kuwait to one south of eastern Iraq, in accordance with the overall offensive plan. This meant planning for 1 (BR) Armoured Division to be switched from the tactical control of the US Marines in the east to 7 (US) Corps which would move west, without making any public declarations to this effect.

As the land offensive approached, the final UK ground force order of battle consisted of 1 (BR) Armoured Division, comprising 4 Brigade, 7 Armoured Brigade and the Divisional troops; the Logistic Support Group; and the Prisoner of War Guard Force. Tanks and Warrior infantry fighting vehicles in 4 Brigade were manned by 14th/20th Kings Hussars, 1st Battalion The Royal Scots and 3rd Battalion The Royal Regiment of Fusiliers, with artillery and engineer support from 2nd Field Regiment and 23 Engineer Regiment. In 7 Armoured Brigade, the Royal Scots Dragoon Guards and Queen's Royal Irish Hussars provided the armour whilst 1st Battalion The Staffordshire Regiment manned Warrior, with support for the Brigade coming from 40th Field Regiment and 21 Engineer Regiment. Combat support for the Division - reconnaissance, artillery, engineers and anti-tank helicopters - was provided by 16th/5th The Queen's Royal Lancers, 26th Field Regiment, 32nd and 39th Heavy Regiments and 12th Air Defence Regiment, together with 32 Armoured Engineer Regiment and 4 Regiment Army Air Corps. The Prisoner of War Guard Force came from 1st Battalion Coldstream Guards, The Royal Highland Fusiliers and the King's Own Scottish Borderers. In-theatre Battle Casualty Replacements were drawn from across the Army. Excluding in-theatre war reserves, the fighting equipment of the Division was 180 Challenger Main Battle Tanks, 260 Warrior infantry fighting vehicles, 72 M109 and M110 guns, 16 MLRS, 24 Rapier and 72 Javelin air defence systems, and 18 Lynx anti-tank helicopters.

On 14 January, 1 (BR) Armoured Division began the planned move forward from its training areas north of Al Jubayl to the Divisional assembly area, codenamed KEYES, 35 kilometres east of Hafar Al Batin, which was in the 7 (US) Corps Assembly area JUNO. This in itself was a mammoth task. Successfully moving the Division, its Forward Maintenance Area and its armour on low loaders, on a single road used by all the other allies, over a distance of over 200 kilometres and under conditions of operational secrecy, was achieved by the outstanding efforts of the Royal Army Ordnance Corps, Royal Corps of Transport and Royal Military Police units involved, together with excellent staff planning. On 26 January, I formally transferred the tactical control of 1 (BR) Armoured Division to 7 (US) Corps, and the Division was declared ready for offensive operations on 31 January when it had completed its move forward. The Division continued its final preparations and work-up until 14 February when it started to advance to its final assembly area, codenamed RAY, north-west of Hafar Al Batin. This move was completed two days later and was carried out under conditions of tight operational security as part of a comprehensive deception plan. The move included a passage of lines exercise with 1 (US) Mechanised Infantry Division as a rehearsal for the forthcoming break-in battle. Rapiers from 12 Air Defence Regiment were deployed to cover the Forward Assembly Area, while 2 Squadron 14 Signal Regiment (Electronic Warfare) were busy contributing to the intelligence picture on the enemy facing us. The overall aim was to outflank the main Iraqi forces in Kuwait by pushing northwards into eastern Iraq before engaging the Republican Guard armoured and mechanised divisions located just to the north west and north of Kuwait, although we sought to deceive him into expecting our attack to be launched directly into southern Kuwait and by an amphibious landing from the sea.

We preceded offensive operations themselves by four days of extensive artillery strikes coupled with further deception tactics. The first British ground action of the war took place on 18 February when the Artillery Group of 32nd and 39th Heavy Regiments engaged enemy ground positions with M110 Self Propelled Guns and the new MLRs. On 23 February the Alternate Headquarters of 1 (BR) Armoured Division advanced to collocate with 1 (US) Mechanised Infantry Division's Tactical Headquarters. At this stage, 97 per cent of the Challenger main battle tanks, 98 per cent of our Warrior infantry fighting vehicles and M109 guns, and 90 per cent of our Lynx helicopters were serviceable and ready for action.

The ground offensive started at 0100 hours (GMT) on 24 February, deliberately in the way the Iraqi forces appeared to be expecting. Naval gunfire and amphibious feints from the Gulf, with frontal attacks through the defensive fortifications in southern Kuwait, were aimed at distracting Iraqi attention from the main thrust into eastern Iraq. The initial operations were by 18 (US) Airborne Corps on the left flank and MARCENT and the Joint Force Command (East) on the right; 1 (BR) Armoured Division Harbour Parties and Main Body began moving forward shortly afterwards. It was planned that the main armoured thrust from 7 (US) Corps, which included 1 (BR) Armoured Division, would begin its attack at least 24 hours after the ground operation began. However, because both 18 (US) Airborne Corps and MARCENT advanced much more quickly than was expected, 7 (US) Corps was ordered to attack on the afternoon of the first day. 1 (US) Mechanised Infantry Division conducted breach operations against the light enemy defensive positions throughout the remainder of 24 February, with 1 (BR) Armoured Division remaining at 2 hours notice to move once 16 lanes had been cleared through the enemy minefields facing their Forward Assembly Area.

The leading elements of 1 (BR) Armoured Division, 16/5 Lancers with 32nd and 39th Heavy Regiments providing fire support from the area of the breach, crossed into Iraq at 0200 hours on 25 February, followed at 1145 hours by 7 Armoured Brigade with the Queen's Royal Irish Hussars in the vanguard. The first contact with the enemy occurred at 1630 hours when the Brigade attacked and destroyed a major communication site, with 1st Battalion The Staffordshire Regiment fighting through this position and clearing enemy trenches and bunkers. An enemy armoured company counter-attacked and was defeated with the loss of all its tanks. 7 Armoured Brigade secured their initial objective (codenamed COPPER) by 2000 hours. 4 Brigade, with fire support from 2nd Field Regiment, then advanced towards its first objective (BRONZE) where it encountered pockets of enemy armour, artillery, infantry and logistic elements; the Brigade destroyed at least 12 tanks, 11 guns and 20 other vehicles and secured the position by 0200 hours on 26 February.

By daybreak on 26 February, 7 Armoured Brigade had destroyed 18 tanks, with anti-tank helicopters from 4 Regiment Army Air Corps taking their share, and defeated a weak enemy task force to secure objective ZINC, while 4 Brigade destroyed 50 more enemy vehicles and captured 2 Iraqi divisional commanders as it continued its advance to capture objective BRASS. The 1st Battalion The Royal Scots, supported by tanks from the 14/20 Hussars, destroyed numerous armoured personnel carriers as it overwhelmed enemy infantry emplacements in the position. During the afternoon, the Queen's Royal Irish Hussars Battle Group led the 7 Armoured Brigade attack on objective PLATINUM with the Royal Scots Dragoon Guards providing flank protection. Simultaneously, the 3rd Battalion The Royal Regiment of Fusiliers assailed 4 Brigade's next objective (STEEL), destroying three battalions of artillery.

As it became clear that the enemy was either retreating or surrendering in large numbers, the Division was ordered to swing east and continue the advance to capitalise on its early success. Both brigades encountered isolated groups of enemy tanks, infantry and supporting elements, but quickly destroyed them on their way to securing objectives VARSITY and TUNGSTEN by mid-morning on 27 February. 4 Brigade was subsequently inundated by thousands of Iraqi soldiers fleeing from abandoned positions in the south and seeking to surrender. That night 7 Armoured Brigade was tasked to race east towards what had been considered the vital ground for the defence of Kuwait, the Matla Ridge north of Kuwait City. The objective (COBALT) was seized by 0500 hours as planned and, in the process, 2 FROG missile launchers, a FROG missile and a command complex were captured.

By this time the lines of communication were extremely stretched. The Royal Highland Fusiliers and the King's Own Scottish Borderers, part of the Prisoner of War Guard Force following up behind the leading brigades, were awash with prisoners and busy supervising their move back to the divisional prisoner of war compound manned by the Coldstream Guards. Logistic resupply had been maintained despite a rapid advance across the desert over 200 kilometres from the initial breach. Moreover, communications were maintained throughout by the Royal Signals over the full length of the lines of communications, and the Royal Engineers and Royal Electrical and Mechanical Engineers had ensured that not only were all physical obstacles overcome but also that virtually the whole armoured vehicle fleet was still operational.

When hostilities were suspended at 0500 hours on 28 February, the Coalition commander ordered the land forces to remain in place and take up defensive positions, but to be prepared for further offensive operations should they prove necessary. Our troops were told to destroy all enemy military equipment within their areas of responsibility, while continuing the tasks of surveillance, reconnaissance and the collection and processing of Iraqi prisoners of war. Thereafter, both brigades moved to secure positions on the main road running from Kuwait City to Basra. The land campaign had lasted just short of 100 hours and in that time the Coalition force had routed an Iraqi army that originally had over half a million men. Mercifully, our own casualties were extraordinarily light, amounting to only 15 Army personnel killed and 43 wounded, although the tragedy of such small losses was magnified by the death on 26 February of nine soldiers from the 3rd Battalion, the Royal Regiment of Fusiliers, as a result of an air attack by friendly forces. Three of the soldiers were attached from the Queen's Own Highlanders, exemplifying how reinforcements were spread throughout the length and breadth of the Division.

MEDICAL SERVICES

One of the major concerns during the planning for Operation GRANBY was to seek to minimise the number of allied casualties. I was particularly conscious that Iraq possessed chemical weapons and had employed them against Iran and even against its own people. I therefore had to mobilise a significant medical presence in theatre and put in train a system for treatment of the injured back in the UK.

The medical plan ultimately resulted in the establishment of 1,800 UK hospital beds in Saudi Arabia, Bahrain and on board RFA ARGUS in the northern Gulf. The beds and their associated surgical facilities were formed as dressing stations and medical support troops, as well as general surgical and evacuation hospitals. We also developed a major aeromedical evacuation plan both within the theatre and from the theatre back to the UK, which involved the use of over 60 helicopters and fixed wing aircraft, some dedicated solely to aeromedical evacuation, together with arrangements to charter eight aircraft from civilian companies if the need arose. Regular medical personnel from all three Services staffed these facilities and were supplemented by the mobilisation of the Territorial Army (205 Scottish General Hospital RAMC(V)), Royal Auxiliary Air Force (4626 Aeromedical Evacuation Squadron) and other individual reservists with specialist skills.

In addition, we had to prepare to deal with the potentially large number of prisoner of war casualties. The Secretary of State for Defence invited other nations to assist in this task and Memoranda of Understanding were agreed with a number of countries. Canada, Norway, Romania and Sweden provided formed hospital units totalling 710 beds; and Denmark, the Netherlands, New Zealand and Singapore contributed surgical teams who worked in conjunction with UK and other national units. In addition a surgical team from Belgium worked in the RAF Hospital at Akrotiri in Cyprus.

Medical support was just one area where we received invaluable backing from the civilian community. Many of our medical personnel were reservists who readily volunteered. In addition, there was a considerable amount of preparatory work carried out at hospitals in the UK in anticipation of an influx of injured troops. Many people played a part, for example those who had retired from nursing and underwent refresher training to release specialist nurses for front-line duty, and those who freely offered transport and accommodation for relatives of injured servicemen returned to mainland hospitals. No-one was more relieved than I when the number of casualties was so low, but I take this opportunity to pay tribute to the dedication of the many who were instrumental in the establishment of comprehensive medical support facilities which, had the battle taken a different turn, would undoubtedly have saved many lives.

POST HOSTILITY EVENTS

After consultations with the British Government and other Coalition members, President Bush gave the order to suspend hostilities at 0500 hours GMT on 28 February. The limited resistance which the Iraqis mustered, almost certainly because of the constant air attacks and, later, the artillery barrages to which they had been subjected, resulted in fewer than 250 allied servicemen being killed. 47 British men gave their lives during the Operation, 9 in the pre-hostilities stage, 24 in action, 10 during hostilities (not in action) and 4 subsequent to hostilities.

There was much clearing up to be done. The extensive minefields laid by the Iraqis in the northern Gulf had to be cleared, with the immediate priority being to open up a deep-water channel into the port of Ash Shu'aybah for military and support shipping. In reflecting our pre-eminence in MCM operations, it was particularly fitting that Royal Navy mine clearance divers should confirm the safety of the harbour before HMS CATTISTOCK, the first vessel to enter, led a USN warship and a merchant ship towards their berths. Once plans of the Iraqi minefields had been handed over, our minehunters continued to clear the waters with MCM vessels from other nations joining the UK/US forces in this vital task. Further out to sea, the role of the frigates and destroyers reverted to that of enforcing sanctions under the United

Nations resolutions, and two Nimrods remained at Seeb to support these operations.

During hostilities, the Iraqis had deliberately pumped oil into the northern Gulf, creating the largest ever oil slick - 35 miles long and 10 miles wide. The flow had been stemmed by allied precision bombing of the pumping stations, and experts had already begun their efforts to contain the damage before the war ended. Their work is still ongoing. As the ground offensive started, we received reports that the occupying forces were setting fire to oil wells in Kuwait. Within a few days well over 500 oil heads were ablaze. The flames and plumes of smoke made an eerie backdrop to the ground operations in Kuwait, and thereafter remained a striking illustration of the vast amount of work which will be needed to restore the country to its pre-war state.

Our 12 prisoners of war were soon freed and quickly reunited with their families. The first British units returned to their home bases on 10 March but, in view of the continuing internal unrest in Iraq, an infantry battle group was retained in Kuwait and a squadron of Tornado GR1 aircraft held at Muharraq, together with two Victor tankers. Specialist teams from the Royal Engineers started to clear minefields and assisted in the recovery of essential services within Kuwait, while logistics personnel organised the return of the Division's equipment. On 3 April, the United Nations Security Council set out the terms for a formal ceasefire; Iraq indicated acceptance on 6 April and it came into force on 11 April. The focus of attention then turned away from the erstwhile battlefield towards the north and east of Iraq and in particular to the plight of the Kurdish refugees who were fleeing from the retribution being handed out by the Iraqi army. British forces soon became involved in providing humanitarian assistance and protection to the hundreds of thousands of Kurds who had fled to the mountains along the Turkish/Iraqi border. Operation HAVEN, spearheaded by 3 Commando Brigade Royal Marines, had begun.

PUBLIC INFORMATION AND MEDIA REPORTING

For me, one of the most enduring memories of the Gulf War was the television news film of a Tomahawk cruise missile flying towards its target in the centre of Baghdad. Throughout the preparation phase and during hostilities, media reporting of events was detailed and speedy, and we made a conscious decision early on to assist as best we could the many reporters and agencies. The Ministry of Defence negotiated with the Saudi Arabian authorities to obtain visas for some 170 British journalists, radio and television reporters and technicians so that they could cover British and allied military activities. A number of these people were formed into small Media Response Teams and were attached to major army formations in the field, went to sea in Royal Navy ships, or were based with Royal Air Force detachments. These teams were therefore able to report at first hand on the UK's participation in the conflict, and I compliment them for their generally accurate coverage. In addition to the specific information relayed by these teams, the broader picture was provided at daily press briefings in Riyadh and at other regular briefings notably in London.

The speed of modern satellite communications meant that the public sometimes received information on their television sets more quickly than I did through the military command chain. Media analysis of this information was extensive and provoked a lively debate on the war situation; however, there were occasions when media information from theatre was either inaccurate or incomplete; the resulting analysis was then at best speculative and at times misleading. It was vital to preserve the integrity of the Coalition deception plan, and thus a temporary news blackout was imposed when the land offensive began. The rationale for this was generally accepted by the media. Overall, Operation GRANBY was the most extensively reported campaign ever, and I was generally impressed by the quality of the reporting. It is clearly important that the public are kept informed of the progress of military operations, but there is a balance to be struck if operational security is not to be put at risk. While there was some frustration amongst journalists, I believe in the circumstances we got this balance about right.

CONCLUDING REMARKS

Since the formation of the North Atlantic Treaty Organization in 1949, most of our forces have been trained for war as part of a large international alliance. However, since the Korean War, actual hostilities involving British forces have all been outside the NATO area and, Suez apart, conducted either alone or with Commonwealth allies. Operation DESERT STORM/GRANBY has proved that disparate forces can fight together effectively under a coalition flag. I must mention also the leading role of the United Nations. All allied military action was in accordance with resolutions passed by the Security Council, and the highly successful interaction between political leaders and military commanders which led to such an efficient expulsion of Iraqi forces from Kuwait has provided an encouraging blueprint for the future. This crisis has shown that the United Nations can respond effectively in the face of unprovoked aggression, and it is to be hoped that this example of international resolve will deter other potential aggressors.

Operation GRANBY served as a timely reminder that our Services may be called upon to operate in distant theatres at short notice. In keeping with the campaigns that over the centuries have built up the history and traditions of the British Armed Forces, our servicemen and women acquitted themselves on Operation GRANBY with resolve, professionalism and courage, which rightly attracted the praise of the allies in theatre and the public at home. They did a marvellous job; I am very proud of them and greatly privileged to have commanded them during this operation.

P B HINE, Air Chief Marshal, Joint Commander,
Operation GRANBY

2. Preliminary Lessons of Operation Granby, Tenth Report, House of Commons, Defence Committee, Session 1990-91

Report, together with the Proceedings of the Committee relating to the Report, Minutes of Evidence and Memoranda

The Defence Committee has agreed to the following Report:

PRELIMINARY LESSONS OF OPERATION GRANBY

I. INTRODUCTION

Background

...

Operation Granby

2. The British deployment of forces to the Gulf area to deter further aggression, defend Saudi Arabia and enforce the United Nations embargo, and subsequently to liberate Kuwait, was known as Operation Granby. It was successful in every one of its objectives. Operation Granby was by any standards a remarkable achievement,

and one that deserves unstinting praise for the professionalism and valour of all those involved. 45,000 UK Service personnel, together with 15,000 vehicles and 400,000 tonnes of freight, were deployed several thousand miles to an unfamiliar and hostile terrain and climate: a signal victory was won; and most of those forces and their equipment have now been returned to the UK and Germany. The RAF flew over 4,000 combat sorties, dropping 3,000 tonnes of weapons; the Royal Navy sank or disabled 15 Iraqi patrol craft: the 1st (BR) Armoured Division mounted an armoured assault and advanced about 300 kilometres in under 70 hours, effectively destroying several divisions in the process. ... 47 Service personnel lost their lives during the operation as a whole, 24 of them in action. While we welcome General de la Billiere's commitment to as full a disclosure as possible of the report on the tragic incident in which nine British soldiers were killed in an attack by a USA-10 aircraft, ... we are concerned at the length of time taken to produce and publish this report.

...

Lessons

...

Exceptional factors

6. It must be remembered that there were a number of exceptional factors in Operation Granby, which lead us to counsel caution in attempting to draw specific lessons for general application: ...

- the predominant role of the United States, in an ad hoc coalition including non-NATO countries;

- the *exclusion* from the UK contribution of most of the forces designated for deployment out of area and *inclusion* of forces rarely contemplated in such a role;

- the geographical environment of generally featureless desert, exceptionally suited to the use of air power, the unusually cold and wet weather, and avoidance of the hottest season;

- the sophisticated and readily available in-place infrastructure, host nation support, including unlimited fuel and the availability of in-theatre support from equipment suppliers;

- the uninterrupted security of lengthy lines of supply;

- the exceptional length of time for which to deploy and prepare for war, to gather the intelligence necessary for the use of smart weapons, and to choose when and where to attack;

- the relatively slight resistance put up by Iraqi air, ground or naval forces, the early gaining of air supremacy, the freedom of manoeuvre enjoyed, on land, in the air and at sea, and the exceptionally low number of Allied casualties and of equipment losses; ...
- the nature of the land campaign, as an armoured assault on an aggressor's prepared positions, rather than the defensive campaign for which UK forces are in general prepared.

...

General lessons

8. The invasion of Kuwait, the random Scud ballistic missile attacks, and the threat of chemical or biological warfare has given new impetus to a range of on-going arms control initiatives, as well as prompting fresh ones. While the UK is not presently under direct threat of ballistic missile attack from outside Europe, recent events have also emphasised as never before the threat of modern ballistic missile warfare spilling over from a regional into international conflict, and so the requirement for some sort of anti-missile defence. We have recently been briefed in the US on the proposed transformation of the Strategic Defence Initiative (SDI) into the Global Protection against Limited Strikes (GPALS) programme, designed to protect US forces abroad, and their Allies. MoD will no doubt be reconsidering the UK requirement for limited anti-ballistic missile defence, as well as contributing to the formulation of HMG's arms control policy initiatives.

...

Resources

10. British forces were stretched in meeting this emergency commitment: ...

- The proportion of peacetime personnel strength deployed from British Forces in Germany (BFG) to the Gulf effectively destroyed BFG's operational capability, and its ability to meet peacetime commitments; the provision of the most up-to-date and best maintained equipment, ammunition and spares left BFG seriously depleted;

- the deployment of four of the five available landing ships logistic (LSLs) and 18 Sea King helicopters meant that a significant part of the UK's amphibious capability was in the Gulf area;

- 95 per cent of Royal Corps of Transport (RCT) personnel were deployed on operations in the Gulf or elsewhere, 51 per cent of them in the Gulf, meaning that it was at the limit of Regular availability; as a result, the UNFICYP transport squadron in Cyprus was largely replaced by TA personnel; Royal Electrical and Mechanical Engineer (REME) assets were also very stretched; ...
- all RAF Germany's support helicopters were committed to Granby, and a large proportion of the RAF's mobile support units;
- half of the Army's tanker trucks, over half of its stock of portable fuel tanks and all regular Royal Army Ordnance Corps (RAOC) Petroleum Platoons were deployed to provide for transport and storage of fuel; ...
- because of the deployment of Service medical personnel, bed availability in Service hospitals was reduced by 35 per cent, and several Service hospitals were temporarily closed.

11. MoD has told us that the effects on NATO commitments of deployments were notified "as and when they happened". We can only be thankful that NATO could, in the current situation, be confident enough to view with equanimity the stripping out of forces, US as well as UK, from the Central Region: and that there were sufficient UK forces available to make such a deployment possible.

12. It would only be possible for the UK to mount a similar operation drawing on the force levels proposed under Options for Change with considerably greater dependence on reserve forces, with significantly fewer forces left in Europe and with at least a comparable atmosphere of detente and general stability in Europe.

II. A MULTINATIONAL OPERATION

Allies

13. There is considerable room for useful debate as to the extent to which the United Kingdom should, by reorganisation or procurement, ensure that it could operate more independently of other countries and of the

commercial sector: for example, by procurement of further dedicated airlift, or of some equivalent to the US military sealift capability. Ten years ago, Operation Corporate seemed to demonstrate that, with technical assistance but without overt support from our principal allies, UK forces could still mount a major military operation out-of-area: that is, outside continental Europe. Given uncertainty as to the assumptions which can be made about which allies, and which alliance, will wish to participate on a given occasion, and in particular as to whether the US would lend active support, it is difficult to plan comprehensively for out-of-area contingencies. By and large, however, one lesson of Operation Granby must be to reinforce the existing planning assumption that the United Kingdom will not be involved in major hostilities without the support of allies, and that it is no longer realistic to plan for a major out-of-area operation without some support from Allies.

Host Nation support

14. Operation Granby was unusual in the degree of host nation support available, particularly:

- the availability of Jubayl, a vast, modern and little-used port, with full infrastructure, and other shore facilities at Mina Sultan and Jebel Ali;

- several modern military airfields, in some cases already used by Tornado aircraft of the Royal Saudi Air Force (RSAF);

- unlimited fuel at source;

- substantial provision of accommodation, food, water and transport.

Without these assets, the United Kingdom would have been stretched to provide logistic support; it would certainly have been a great deal more expensive. The scale of the deployment would have had to be reduced, and the time required to complete it greatly increased. It is questionable whether, without the host nation support and infrastructure available, the UK could have contemplated operations on anything like the same scale.

USA

15. At the peak of operations in the Gulf, the United States had over half a million personnel deployed. The United Kingdom, the second largest contributor besides the host nation of Saudi Arabia, had at its peak around 45,000. As General de la Billiere put it, speaking of command and control -

"inevitably, what the Americans did, everybody else really had to go along with". ...

The Joint Commander's Despatch notes that -

"The United States provided the majority of the personnel - some 540,000 people - and consequently took the lead in formulating the operational plans". ...

This dependence on the United States extended not only to overall strategic and tactical co-ordination, but also included a range of capabilities which were either unavailable to UK forces, or whose provision by each partner in the Alliance would have been a waste of resources. Capabilities not possessed by the UK, or not held in such effective form, included:

- M548 tracked supply vehicles; ...

- C-5A Galaxy aircraft: the US made 28 Galaxy sorties available to transport UK support helicopters; ...

- stealth ground attack aircraft;

- Patriot anti-missile defences;

- land attack cruise missiles;

- most satellite and airborne intelligence gathering and target acquisition;

- fixed wing anti-armour capability.

Capabilities which were provided primarily by the US, but which the UK could if necessary have provided, included -

- combat survival and rescue for downed pilots;

- close air support for ground forces; ...

- air cover for maritime forces; ...

- overall air traffic tasking and control.

Other nations

16. It should also be remembered that the UK benefited from assistance in kind of different sorts from many nations, as well as securing financial assistance. ... Nine nations provided medical assistance, to a total of around 1,700 personnel, to help the UK meet its obligations to provide medical care to injured Iraqis taken as prisoners of war. ... RN ships were supported by supply ships and oilers from several nations, including the Netherlands and Portugal, Australia and Kuwait. ... Portugal provided 34 Hercules sorties, Belgium 25 and Spain 2; New Zealand provided 2 Hercules aircraft for use in-theatre making a "significant contribution". ... Germany made available Fuchs NBC reconnaissance vehicles, Hummell armoured VHF Jammer vehicles and Skorpion vehicles with scatterable mine systems; it also filled in for UK medical personnel and aircraft needed elsewhere, and assisted with guard duties in Germany. ... Belgium loaned a bulk fuel installation for use by the RAF at Tabuk. ... Canadian rockets were procured for use against a variety of targets. ... Ships and aircraft were chartered commercially from a variety of nations, including a Romanian Boeing 707 and a Soviet registered Antonov AN124, ... The publicity given at the time to problems over, for example, the supply of ammunition, ... should not obscure the extent to which the deployment of British forces depended on assistance from many other countries.

UK

17. Although the UK contribution to the overall effort was dwarfed by that of the US, it was substantial enough to ensure that the British view on the overall pattern of operations, and in particular on the exact way in which UK forces were used, would be heard at the highest level of command. The UK was able to offer unusual and valuable capabilities: notably the JP233 airfield denial weapon, ... the RN's MCMV and area air defence capabilities, ... and heavy armour. This was reflected in the extent to which the UK was integrated into command structures, and able to influence deployments and operations.

- A senior British Officer was fully integrated into General Schwarzkopf's personal planning team of five US officers, thus enabling a British input into overall strategic planning at the conceptual stage: a parallel arrangement was made for an RAF officer on General

Horner's USAF planning staff and the RAF enjoyed a particular "rapport" with the USAF. ...

- General de la Billiere was able to see to the transfer of 1st (BR) Armoured Division from being "a rather over-generous part of a diversionary force" under US Marine command to US VII Corps. once it was fully deployed; the Division was a large enough unit to be able to operate with tactical freedom, its own logistic support, and with access to a high level of intelligence. ...

- Air Vice-Marshal Wratten had a power of veto over particular targets, a power used twice when selected targets were in locations where severe collateral damage would have resulted from any weapon system malfunction. ...

- Commodore Craig recounted the discussions at the highest levels on the way in which the RN would be deployed ... and in the event only the USN and the Royal Navy took a full part in offensive maritime operations. ...

18. While UK forces have long been subordinated to NATO commanders of various nationalities, the experience of Granby confirms that there is no alternative to making a substantial military commitment if it is desired to influence the way in which a military operation proceeds. The UK share of NATO commands must be expected to bear some relationship to the potential UK contribution of ships, aircraft and military units. The plain lesson in future arrangements for multinational forces is that the more a nation contributes, the greater the influence it can expect on the detailed conduct of operations, and on strategic planning.

NATO

19. Operation Granby demonstrated the full value of years of defence co-operation at every level within NATO, to the extent that it is difficult to imagine how operations could have proceeded at all without the existing common operating procedures and practices familiar to the forces of most of the participating nations. In his Introduction to SDE91, the Secretary of State referred to "habits of co-operation, procedures and standards honed over 40 years in NATO". ...

...

20. The above examples demonstrate that, whatever the optimal political framework under which multinational forces are organised for operations out-of-area, the common "military language" of European and North American forces is now, and is likely to remain, NATO. Other international organisations were of course involved. The United Nations played an essential political role. The Western European Union also played a part, politically in facilitating the participation of some European allies, and militarily in co-ordinating elements of embargo enforcement and general support operations before the outbreak of hostilities, and subsequently in co-ordination of MCMV, operations. ... In broad terms, however, the war was fought and won primarily on NATO principles, despite the involvement of non-NATO Arab allied forces. The forces were drawn at least as much from NATO's Central Region as from the United States or United Kingdom. NATO also committed air forces to the defence of Turkey, and extended a planned NAVOCFORMED exercise in the Eastern Mediterranean, ... This underlines the importance of persisting with the sometimes disheartening struggle to standardise procedures and equipment: Commodore Craig described incompatibility as "a running sore". ... rewards of greater interoperability have never been more clearly demonstrated. NATO practices and procedures enabled an ad hoc alliance of NATO national forces to fight together out-of-area as a coherent unit; those nations not participating as members of the Alliance cannot expect to be able to play a full part in future conflicts.

...

Versatility and flexibility

38. British forces were obliged to adapt to several fundamental changes of task in the course of the deployment and showed praiseworthy flexibility and versatility in so doing. The original deployments made in August and September 1990 were purely defensive, to defend Saudi Arabia against any further aggression by Iraq. ... That deployment then developed into "a defensive and potentially offensive operation", and finally into "an actually offensive operation". ...

- The original RN deployment was, as General de la Billiere told us, "based purely on a defensive concept", ... its primary task being enforcement of the UN embargo; following the outbreak of hostilities in January 1991, the RN force was involved in providing area air defence for US battle groups, in shipborne helicopter missile attacks on Iraqi shipping and in mine clearance to give substance to a threatened amphibious landing.

- 7th Armoured Brigade provided the necessary defensive armoured capability for the US Marine Division to deter and if necessary resist a ground attack by Iraqi forces into Saudi Arabia. ... Following the decision in November 1990 to bring these forces up to reinforced Divisional strength with the despatch of 1st (BR) Armoured Division, ... the land forces stance became potentially offensive. With the launching of the ground attack on 24 February, 1st (BR) Armoured Division was committed to an armoured attack against prepared positions.

- The RAF forces originally despatched were Jaguar ground attack aircraft intended to deter a further Iraqi attack, and Tornado F3 air defence fighters, together with Nimrods tasked to police the UN embargo. With the decision to send Tornado GR1 aircraft in greater numbers, the Tornado GR1/JP233 airfield denial weapon became the principal focus of attention, in the same defensive counter-air role for which the RAF is tasked in Europe. ... Within three or four days of intensive use of JP233, ... and a relatively high attrition rate, ... it was clear that, as Air Vice-Marshal Wratten told us,

"There was absolutely no point whatsoever in continuing to deploy JP233 against airfields which were not being used and at the same time flying through the only defence he exhibited". ...

Within five days of the decision to change tactics, Tornados were flying at medium rather than low level, and delivering laser-guided weapons first in conjunction with Buccaneers and subsequently also using two pre-production Thermal Imaging Airborne Laser Designation (TIALD) pods: over 1,000 laser-guided weapons were dropped. ...

39. Versatility and flexibility were also in evidence in the equipment field. The helicopter support ship RFA ARGUS, procured as an Aviation Training Ship to replace RFA ENGADINE, ... had one of her hangars fitted at Devonport with Portakabins, to enable her to operate as a primary casualty receiving ship, with the equivalent of an air-conditioned 100-bed hospital with an operating theatre. ... This designation enabled her to fulfil some military functions as well as medical ones, and to return recovered casualties to duty, neither of which are permitted to a dedicated hospital ship. MoD is studying whether it would be cost-effective to retain the

adaptations, and whether it can be done without prejudicing ARGUS' primary war and peace roles. ... This reverts to the pattern set by the roles given in 1956 to HMS OCEAN and HMS THESEUS.] The Landing Ships Logistic (LSLs) deployed to the Gulf to transport heavy equipment and ammunition fulfilled a variety of roles. SIR GALAHAD provided engineering support for the MCMV group, SIR PERCIVAL, SIR BEDIVERE and SIR TRISTAM [*sic*] held the reserve ammunition stocks for 1st (BR) Armoured Division, and required some on-site enhancements to enable them to be brought as far forward into the firing line as possible. ... In the absence of a command ship, SNOME commanded from a Type 22 frigate, despite the limited space and communications fit. ... The MCMV flotilla was commanded from a hydrographic survey vessel. ...

40. UK forces and their equipment are not wholly versatile and flexible. As the Director of Defence Logistics (NATO/UK) told us -

"all the British forces are optimised for operations in the European theatre and they were being employed in areas for which they were not optimised". ...

Tornado avionics are designed primarily with low-level attack in Central Europe in mind: so are the principal weapon systems deployed on RAF aircraft, including the BL755 cluster bomb. ... Air Vice-Marshal Wratten, while quite fairly observing that capability has to be related to the theatre of operations, and that the RAF's primary commitment was and remains to the European theatre, affirmed that he would have wished to have had available -

"a flexible weapon system, a system which is perhaps not as good at low level as one purely designed for that but which is good at all levels - flexibility". ...

41. It is greatly to the credit of all the forces that they were able to make radical changes to their expected patterns of operations so quickly and effectively.

- Tornado and Buccaneer crews were able to learn the difficult practice of co-ordination, at unfamiliar altitudes, practically on the job: some Tornado crews -

"flew their first live sortie with the TIALD pod over enemy terrain, so the learning curve was that steep". ...

- 1st BR Armoured Division were able to become skilled in a "totally new style of operational concept" within weeks, if not days. ...

- An example of the versatility built into the Services is the deployment in medical support roles of around 860 bandsmen from all Services, with varying degrees of preparedness, but all fulfilling a wartime role very different from their primary trade. ...

This versatility and flexibility can be attributed first and foremost to the high standards of training of Service personnel. As General de la Billiere put it, in referring to BAOR -

"They were working from a very sound base of knowledge and expertise in the first place ..." ...

This commendation applies to all Services. Versatility and flexibility must continue to be programmed into training and exercising of Service personnel, and into the procurement of equipment, from definition of the original requirement to purchase and maintenance of the finished product.

...

In-theatre mobility

43. In-theatre mobility has been recognised as an important quality, all the more so where the theatre is vast and the forces relatively small. 1st (BR) Armoured Division proved to be outstandingly mobile, in its ability first to move several hundred kilometres west from the coast to its assembly point west of the Iraqi-Kuwait border, and then in its intense 100 hour attack east to Kuwait. As the Secretary of State told us in March, it was the only Division at the imposition of the provisional ceasefire with its logistic support fully in place, and capable of further advance if required. ...

44. Not only was the high mobility of armoured formations validated, including the Warrior APCs and the accompanying tracked self-propelled elements of the Divisional Artillery Group, M109, M110 and MLRS, but even more significantly the ability of the divisional support elements to keep up with the first-line formations, to provide fuel, ammunition and supplies, to evacuate casualties, to manage prisoners of war &c. As General de la Billiere told us -

"you can only fight the battle which your logistic capability will let you fight". ...

The requirement for high mobility in logistic support was not met without difficulties -

- additional equipment to provide surface mobility in the desert terrain had to be procured, including 22 Bedford 8 x 8 Multidrive trucks, Supacat 6 x 6 light load carriers to carry and tow Rapier sets, and borrowed US M548 tracked supply vehicles; ...

- even with some host nation supply of trucks and drivers, it was necessary to deploy a substantial proportion of RCT drivers to the Gulf, producing a situation where any further demand would have had to be met by Reservists; ...

- support helicopter resources were stretched: 12 RAF Chinooks, 19 RAF Pumas and 12 RN Sea King IVs were deployed, and a further 6 RN Sea Kings used at sea for resupply, evacuation &c while commanders told us that they had had no difficulties over helicopter support, it seems to have been a scarce as well as a valued asset.

It is no use making front-line forces highly mobile if they outstrip their logistic support: this applies to air and naval as well as to ground forces. In considering the detailed lessons, MoD would do well to look again at some aspects of logistic support, with a view to increasing its in-theatre mobility.

Intelligence

45. Operation Granby provided a searching test of out-of-area intelligence capabilities, and pointed up several lessons.

- strategic and tactical aerial reconnaissance and early warning proved to be crucial, particularly given the obstacles to human intelligence; where it was not available ... or proved to be insufficient, as over mobile Scuds and Iraqi maritime minelaying, ... it was a capability sorely missed; and where available, from satellites, from the US JSTARS craft, from USAF and RSAF AWACS, from RAF Tornado GR1as and from remotely piloted vehicles operated by several of the Allied forces, it was highly valued;

- there were not unexpected shortcomings in the distillation and dissemination of intelligence,. ... in predictive intelligence, whether over Iraqi intentions and capabilities or the weather, and in all-weather surveillance: ... these applied in particular to the intelligence available to ground forces at divisional level and below;

- deception by both sides played an important part, showing that despite electronic intelligence gathering it is still possible to deceive an enemy, and necessary to have the means of identifying deception and disrupting counter-deception;

- that UK forces were able to deploy 93 Arabic speaking personnel to the Gulf, in addition to 78 Kuwaiti civilians deployed in mid-February to work in hospitals and prisoner of war camps is in marked contrast to experiences 10 years ago of a severe shortage of appropriate Spanish speakers in Operation Corporate, and emphasises the requirement for a range of language capabilities in out-of-area operations. ...

In our 1987 Report on Implementing the Lessons of the Falklands Campaign, we drew attention to the extent to which the Task Force had been "severely hampered" by the lack of tactical and satellite reconnaissance, and looked for progress on introduction of Tornado GR1as. ... While the quality of intelligence available to Allied forces in Granby was apparently higher, there are lessons to be learned which must be addressed in MoD's analysis.

...

Sophistication

47. While aspects of the performance of the military equipment deployed to the Gulf is being exhaustively analysed, and will be for some time to come, ... it is already clear that some of the massive investment in new technology which Western nations have made over the years of Cold War has been repaid:

- the ability of Allied forces at sea, on land and in the air to fight at night gave them "a tremendous tactical superiority, which in many ways made up for any imbalance in numbers": ... conversely, equipment only available for daytime use now looks increasingly limited in effectiveness;

- the performance of items of UK equipment brought forward for deployment in the Gulf: these included the anti-radar missile ALARM, TIALD, the Tornado GR1a reconnaissance aircraft, MLRS, NAVSTAR Global Positioning System and an improved performance APFSDS shot; ... we are also aware of some new equipments, and of some enhancements in train, which it did not prove possible to bring forward, and which might have made a small but significant difference;

- the use of stand-off and precision-guided munitions has revolutionised conventional warfare, providing greatly increased accuracy and lethality at greatly reduced risk: ... their use is however heavily dependent on full and accurate intelligence (see para 45 above); stealth and electronic counter-measures were also of critical importance;

- while modern weapon systems were validated in action, some relatively antique weapons platforms and systems were used, some of which proved effective: on the Allied side, naval gunfire from Second World War US battleships, and 1,000lb iron bombs, of which the RAF dropped around 4,500; and on the other side, Iraqi mines which, as Commodore Craig told us, and as was emphasised in the Joint Commander's Despatch, were the principal cause of anxiety to the RN Task Force; ... and dense concentrations of conventional anti-aircraft artillery (AAA) defences;

- the ever-present threat of chemical or biological attack ... showed the value of past investment in research into, and procurement of, protective clothing, detection, immunisation and decontamination equipment; the knowledge that UK equipment was the best available was a very important factor in maintaining morale; ... equipment procurement decisions will more than ever before have to address the issue of its resistance to NBC warfare. ...

The development and production of weapons at the leading edge of technology is essential if the UK wishes to retain a strong conventional capability.

...

V. CONCLUSION

49. This Report can only be at best a preliminary survey of some of the implications of Operation Granby for UK defence requirements, in advance of all but the most rudimentary published analyses by MoD. We look forward to continuing this task when we can review in full the studies currently in hand. We also reiterate our caution against drawing lessons too glibly or too freely from such an unusual course of events, in which the opposing forces rarely matched in ability the quality of the equipment they possessed. We have concentrated in this Report as much on perceived problems and weaknesses as on the far greater number of successes and strengths: that should not detract from the simple conclusion that, almost without exception, the operation went extremely well.

...

[*The following materials are included in the House of Commons Report.*]

MINUTES OF EVIDENCE
TAKEN BEFORE THE DEFENCE COMMITTEE

WEDNESDAY 6 MARCH 1991

Examination of Witnesses

THE RT. HON. TOM KING, a Member of the House, Secretary of State for Defence, examined.

...

... We have not yet moved on to an official ceasefire and it may interest the Committee to be reminded of what the conditions are for the ceasefire: that we must have immediate Red Cross access to all our prisoners-of-war and their release as soon as possible, information on those missing and the return of the remains of those who have died; that civilian detainees are to be treated exactly the same as prisoners-of-war; that information on all mines on land and at sea is to be made available; that information on the location of any nuclear, biological or chemical munitions within theatre is to be available as well; that there will be no further attacks by Iraq and that on that basis the multinational forces will withdraw from Iraq as soon as possible after a ceasefire. A number of measures have also been agreed to avoid clashes, including setting lines demarcating the positions of the troops. On prisoners-of-war, Mr Chairman, I can readily give to you the latest position as of now, which is that we have received the release of three British prisoners-of-war, who are now in Cyprus; we have now received a further nine, six RAF and three Army, who are now in Riyadh and are likely to be going forward to Cyprus quite shortly. That leaves us with five RAF and three Army still missing. Might I say, because you referred to concern and sadness over the losses that there are, that on this basis this means that in this whole campaign, as far as the UK forces are concerned, in which something just under 45,000 of our forces have been involved and which has involved conflict in the air, sea and land and very significant deployment of munitions and very significant conflict in certain areas, the casualties on our side are over the whole period since August to the present date, 36 killed, but in actual operations the total number of those who lost their lives is 17, there are eight missing and there are 43 injured, of whom very few were classified as very seriously or seriously injured. I think the Committee will share with me the feeling that whilst obviously every death is a tragedy which we all feel, that does, by any standards against the objective that we set ourselves of seeking to ensure that the casualties on our own side were minimised in that campaign represent a very remarkable achievement by our commanders in the organisation and the implementation of the campaign. The background to the overall campaign, if I could just give the Committee some very short basic facts, is this: the RAF flew over 4,000 combat sorties and the total number of sorties, including the supply side as well, was over 6,500, and that is 6,500 since 17 January; the RAF dropped some 3,000 tonnes of weapons, over 100 JP233 airfield denial weapons, some 6,000 bombs, of which over 1,000 were laser-guided, fired over 100 anti-radar missiles and nearly 700 air-to-ground rockets; no air-to-air weapons were used. On the Navy side, Royal Navy helicopters sank or disabled 15 Iraqi patrol craft. The mine counter-measures force, which is overwhelmingly British, but on the Coalition side has now located some 228 mines, of which 133 have been destroyed and, of course, the Royal Navy, as the Committee will remember, played a very active part in the embargo process in which the Navy challenged more than 3,000 ships during that time and took part in 36 boarding operations. On the Army side, the Committee are familiar with the success of the land campaign and its speed. The Committee will know that the 1st Armoured Division performed a feat of military skill and capability which must rank very high in any military achievement of the British Army. That Division moved fast and achieved its objectives in under 100 hours, in which time it travelled 350 kilometres - one could say from the Dutch border to Berlin - in the process destroying between 150 and 200 tanks in combat, 100 armoured vehicles and 100 artillery pieces. During that attack the Royal Artillery fired 2,500 MLRS rockets, over 2,500 rounds of 8" and 10,000 rounds of 155 mm. It completed that remarkable attack, which had the effect initially of destroying the Iraqi forces that were on the flank of the further thrust by the two heavy US Divisions and, of course, the 1st Armoured Division was part of the main thrust of the land campaign - destroyed that - and moved on and then unhinged the Iraqi defences on the Matla Ridge and then succeeded in capturing them in the Matla Ridge. Those interested in the logistics may like to know that when the 1st Armoured Division completed that - having incidentally installed behind it or made good the road over the whole of the distance that it travelled - it was in position when it reached its final objective, at the moment when finally hostilities ceased, with its full logistical chain up in position. It was the only Division at the time capable, if it had been required for any reason, to have further advanced on Basra. I think the Committee may like to study the details of this particular military operation. There is no secret that when the original plans were made the range of the deployment involved did raise concerns about the logistical capability of ensuring that over that massive distance we would be able to keep the full capability going and keep up the logistical support. It may also interest the Committee, who do take an interest in the reliability of our equipment, that at no stage during that 4 day campaign did availability of our equipment fall below 95 per cent of any of the equipment that was travelled and I think that is a great tribute to all the services involved and I think a great tribute, as I said earlier, to the backing we have had from British industry and the commitment of all the support arms in that achievement. In the process of the Allied campaign where the objective was not only the liberation of Kuwait, but also to deal as effectively as possible in the process that was necessary for the liberation campaign, with the scale of the Iraqi military machine, the latest assessment I have is that the Iraqis have lost either by destruction or by capture by the Allies 3,300 tanks, 2,100 armoured personnel carriers and 2,200 artillery pieces. If I can add two further points, Mr Chairman. I think that the lessons that we have learned in earlier campaigns, not least drawing on the Select Committee reports on, Operation Corporate as it was called, the Falklands. We were most anxious during this very complex international, political and military situation to do the best we could over the access for the media and over providing the fullest possible information that we could to the country, consistent with not putting at risk the security of our forces and not in any way releasing any information that might undermine the security and secrecy of the campaign plan. It was also decided, as things might have gone wrong, to try and be straight forward and clear about it and the Committee will recall that when it is possible that certain bombs did not guide at a place called Al-Fallujah, and it is possible that one of those bombs did fall way off target into the town and did cause civilian casualties, the RAF were very quick to explain the facts as they knew them and to the best of their ability. I think the media handling, particularly in theatre, which was one of the recommendations of the Select Committee after the Falklands, of the service of news in theatre was effective and it was only during the very beginning of the land campaign, when we had that short period of news blackout, otherwise we did seek to be as helpful as possible. I think it is interesting to think that when there were not far short of 1,000 journalists and correspondents in Saudi Arabia and adjoining areas, and with the daily briefings that were taking place, it is a remarkable achievement that it was still possible to have an element of surprise about the land attack and for the Iraqis not actually to be aware of where the main thrust of the land attack was coming from. The further points that I would like to make, Chairman, include our estimate of the cost so far which is £1.75 billion, which are the additional costs that we believe we have incurred so far, and that cost will certainly rise. We are giving consideration to how we should report to Parliament on the overall outcome of this campaign, the conclusions that we would draw from it. As you know, we had postponed in any case the Defence White Paper as it seemed inappropriate to publish it maybe in the middle of an on-going campaign and we are considering whether this might be the vehicle in which we would publish conclusions and a fuller report on the whole campaign. The next phase is the withdrawal as soon as we are satisfied that the ceasefire is established. On the first point we may make some initial moves before the ceasefire is established in respect of medical reservists. We had made very full provision to ensure that in the intensity of land conflict that we had absolute adequacy of medical provision there. We think the obvious thing is for medical reservists to return to their full-time work here in this country and it is possible that some of them will be returning in a very few days indeed. We shall then move on, as soon as the ceasefire is established, within a couple of weeks, I would hope to see the start after that of the return of our ground forces and indeed of all the services. ...

...

Mr Churchill: 3. Can you tell us, Secretary of State, how many Iraqi PoWs are in UK hands at the moment and whether it is the intention that they should remain in British custodianship until their hand-over or will they be handed over first to the Saudis or Kuwaitis, and are there any in British hospitals, either field hospitals, in Cyprus or the UK?

Mr King: The latest figure I have is something over 5,000 that we have in British custody. The figure is continually changing. We are processing them as fast as we can and we are then passing them on to the rear formation, which in our case, as we are part of the 7th US Corps. is actually on to US forces, and we are passing those on at a rate of some 500 a day at present. They do, of course, remain our responsibility as the capturing force but in the military structure that is the arrangement that we have made. There are, I believe, some 19 Iraqi prisoners-of-war that are in British medical facilities at the present time. Those are just two field hospitals that are in theatre. There are none in Cyprus and none in the UK.

Mr Churchill: 4. Can you tell us what is to happen to those Iraqi prisoners-of-war who on the media have made clear publicly that they denounce Saddam Hussein and have no wish to return while he is in power, and if press reports are to be believed, a high proportion of the 175,000 or so Iraqi prisoners-of-war have expressed a wish not to be forced to return until there is a change of regime?

(Mr King) I understand that is right about the number, that a very high proportion do not wish to return. The responsibility for them is, of course, under the Red Cross and the Red Cross will interview each prisoner and determine whether they do or do not wish to return. That is the position and the question then is about what will happen. It is very difficult: at one stage I was given a range of 75-175,000 as the bracket for the number of Iraqi prisoners-of-war. I think one has to understand this is a hugely confused situation. There are a number in transit and documentation finds is extremely difficult to keep up. I have to say that the question as to what may happen to them if a very considerable number of them do decline to return is going to be a very difficult problem indeed, on which we have not reached any conclusion yet. I think that I would have to say that the first stage will be to identify just what the scale of the problem is and then obviously it would be very much a matter for the host country where they will be as to what their future position may be.

...

(Mr Lee): 7. Secretary of State, moving on to the question of atrocities and the investigation of them. Could I ask one or two questions relating to that. First of all, is there a specialist Allied unit responsible for investigating atrocities and taking evidence and, if so, who is in charge of it? Secondly, can you give us a broad idea of how many Iraqis or any other nationalities have actually been detained and, thirdly, on the question of possible trials could you give us any indication at all of your thoughts on maybe the timing or the place of any trials?

(Mr King) Well, we have made clear all through, even back to the time when we had the British liaison team hiding in Kuwait before the conflict even started after the invasion when there were atrocities taking place at that time - we gave clear warning that any individual Iraqi could be held responsible under international law for his actions and we warned him of that circumstance. We took steps from then onwards to start recording any information that we had of any outrages or atrocities of that kind. We do have a unit now operating ourselves, who are coordinated although it is not under a single overall head, which is operating now in the Kuwaiti theatre based on the Royal Military Police, seeking to establish information on such matters and that is backed up by resources in this country as well. We have made clear that people will be liable, and some are already apprehended who have come from units that we believe may have been involved in some of the atrocities. The Kuwaitis themselves apprehended a number. We have been screening those moving north and we are separating out those who are - and this is being done principally by the Americans in this respect I think with Coalition help and, I believe, with the Saudis and Kuwaitis - going and identifying those units who were in Kuwait City rather than the ones who may have been out in the desert, as it were, where they did not come in conflict with the local population. I am seeking further information on how many of those there are. Of course, there is the situation which will arise where people who have committed crimes in Kuwait against the Kuwaiti people and others, who certainly will be liable to the due process of law in Kuwait.

...

(Mr McFall): 17. When the House met on September 7th last year it appeared that the UK and other forces in Saudi Arabia and her neighbours were there as a means of ensuring that there was no further aggression, and that Saudi Arabia was defended from attack. Indeed on that date you stated in Hansard, col 842, "We are not there to attack Kuwait or Iraq. We are there to defend Saudi Arabia and to ensure that the United Nations embargo is effectively implemented." And, "The purpose is to defend Saudi Arabia and to make the United Nations embargo work." And you underlined that. Can I ask when did deployment by the United Kingdom of the military resources necessary for the liberation of Kuwait, as opposed to the defence of Saudi Arabia begin? The Tornado GR1s on the 23rd August? When did we start sending out JP233s, for example? Or the necessary Armoured Engineering capability for breaching Iraqi defences? Was there a "step-change" from defensive to offensive capability?

(Mr King) We wanted until January 15th to see this settled by peaceful means. We went not just an extra mile but an extra two or three miles to achieve this. Mr McFall will remember the United Nations resolution that referred to the "pause for goodwill". I do not think it is a secret any longer that the date of January 15th was one that was encouraged by the Soviet Union to provide even longer time so that the Iraqis should have every chance to leave peacefully. I think there has been some earlier proposals that 1st January might have been a suitable day after which resolution 678 should come into effect and Member States were authorised to use all necessary means to achieve the United Nations resolutions. We made contingency plans that if the peaceful option failed that there was an offensive option. I repeated more times than I care to remember the fact that to make the peaceful option work it was necessary for Saddam Hussein to understand that there was no option that he could stay, that his choice was between a peaceful option or an option involving conflict. That is why we had to maintain the credibility of our military capability and we built it up over the period to reinforce the peaceful option to try and get the message through that one way or another he would lose. There were different dates and it was the beginning of November when President Bush decided significantly to increase his forces. I think it was on November 22nd that I made the announcement in the House of Commons that we would move from having the 7th Brigade to the 1st Armoured Division and increase our air assets in the area. There was really no magic moment, we had been building it up and it was a critical requirement for the achievement of the peaceful option.

(Mr McFall): 18. When you addressed the House on the 7th September and made that statement and with the Tornado GR1s that went out on the 21st August, is it true

that contingency plans for offensive action were being made before that date?

(Mr King) I think that is inferred from what I have said. I think you should understand exactly what I am saying, that we did want - everybody who had any sense wanted - to see this settled by peaceful means. The truth was when dealing with someone like Saddam Hussein - and the correctness of our judgment can hardly be challenged now - our only hope was that he actually believed that he was going to get hit and hit hard. The only mistake we made was that we thought he might actually care about the suffering of his people and the suffering they incurred. I think we have to question whether that judgment was actually right. What I said there was absolutely right, I said that we do not want to attack, the purpose is to defend and then to see the embargo work - that is the phrase that Mr McFall just read out - which is to see the achievement of the United Nations resolutions. Now it is true that in one sense we built on and the Coalition countries and the United Nations built on the situation in the face of the continuing intransigence of Iraq who refused and refused and refused. The question was did the United Nations just walk away and say, "We tried, did our best and that is it" or say, "Right, if he is not going to respond to this then we have to increase the pressures", and that is of course what the United Nations did.

...

(*Mr Home Robertson*): 27. Can we move on to the bombing campaign, Secretary of State. Can you give us some idea of the way in which the UK Government had any input into the establishment of a target list, not only for the RAF but also for the United States Air Force operating from Fairford and Diego Garcia?

(Mr King) It was a Coalition plan but we were involved in the preparation of the whole air campaign.

(*Mr Home Robertson*): 28. So you were directly involved in selecting the whole range of targets that were hit in Iraq?

(Mr King) The Air Commander, General Horner, and, indeed, the overall Commander-in-Chief, General Schwarzkopf had the ultimate decisions themselves but after consultation in any particular strategic decisions, but it was the air campaign plan that was made in which we played a full part in its preparation and it was agreed by us all, by our Joint Commander, Sir Patrick Hine, Air Vice Marshal Bill Wratten and our Commander of the British forces, Sir Peter de la Billiere.

(*Mr Home Robertson*): 29. Were there examples of targets that you were not prepared to go for either because of the risk of civilian casualties or because of the danger to our own air crew?

(Mr King) We agreed certain overall objectives between the governments concerned in the Coalition before the campaign started. We agreed on the importance, for example, of military objectives; we agreed on the need to minimise the risk of civilian casualties on the Iraqi side; we agreed on the importance, for example, of avoiding cultural or religious sites; we agreed that, for instance, we were not attacking water supplies or sewage installations; we agreed on what were military strategic targets and what were specific direct military targets and on the targets that we would seek to ensure were avoided, and I think anybody who saw the evidence which television provided of the incredible precision of the air campaign, the way in which life basically continued in Baghdad normally while key military installations were taken out, who has seen the care that went into the preparation of that air campaign ...

(*Mr Home Robertson*) 30. Are you telling us, for instance, that water pumping plants in Baghdad were not targets?

(Mr King) Yes. There was a problem, which I understood, about the power supplies and that was a problem, but, of course, the problem of power in the whole command control structure, the targeting of power supplies, is an important element in that.

(*Mr Home Robertson*): 31. Can you tell us something about the very disturbing events which had a lot of publicity right at the conclusion of the hostilities, that is to say, the bombardment or the attack on the retreating Iraqi forces on the road to Basra? Can you tell us anything about the decisions that were taken to attack these retreating people?

(Mr King) That was a military decision in which we fully agreed. I have flown up that road. I have seen the tanks, I have seen the APCs, I have seen the military lorries, I have seen elsewhere the pictures of the abandoned civilian vehicles that had been looted from the population of Kuwait which had been taken by Iraqi forces retreating, and a combination of them. I have seen pictures on television of their weapons, their ammunition, mixed up with a whole lot of loot and various items they had stolen from the Kuwaitis. There is no question that there was a late attempt by the Iraqi forces in Kuwait - and particularly including, I think, those from some of the units about which some of the greatest suspicion remains about their behaviour in Kuwait City, seeking to escape up the road to Basra and it was very important indeed that they did not succeed in escaping.

(*Mr Home Robertson*): 32. British forces were involved in that operation at the conclusion of hostilities?

(Mr King) That mainly involved US forces. We came through to the road I think a little further down.

(*Mr Home Robertson*): 33. You are satisfied everybody involved in the retreat at this stage was still a potential threat to coalition forces?

(Mr King) With the greatest respect, the conflict was engaged. There were significant amounts of Iraqi armour seeking to escape up that road. I have seen it for myself and you will no doubt have a chance to see it for yourselves as well. And that is exactly what, if it came to the allied land campaign, we needed to ensure did not happen.

(*Mr McFall*): 34. On the BBC last night it mentioned that 8,000 Kuwaitis had been seized in the last few days and they were amongst the people that were killed. Did your intelligence reports indicate that innocent Kuwaitis were there and therefore would that not have modified the approach? Would you not agree with the statement made in one of the Sunday newspapers that that was one of the most terrible harassments of a retreating army from the air in the history of warfare?

(Mr King) I think undoubtedly Allied air power did back a very significant punch and we know also - because you may be aware that there was a further later attempt, which is why the original ceasefire took place a day later than was originally expected - it is quite clear that the Republican Guard tried to do the same thing shortly afterwards on the day after we had announced the cessation of hostilities. A significant military force tried to break out of the encirclement they were in. I forget the exact figures but a significant amount of tanks, including a number of T72s, were knocked out in that engagement. The issue of whether there were Kuwaitis present in all that traffic and whether we should have allowed the Iraqi tanks and the other equipment through passage in case there were Kuwaitis involved as well was obviously a difficult judgment. It was, I think, recognised that once we had established the control by the advance of the Allied forces to the north and along that axis towards Basra north of Safwan, that President Bush announced, with our agreement, that there would be a cessation of hostilities. It was for precisely the sort of considerations that have been mentioned and the point had been reached where it was better to halt because we had then established the control that we needed.

...

MINUTES OF EVIDENCE
TAKEN BEFORE THE DEFENCE COMMITTEE

WEDNESDAY 8 MAY 1991

Examination of Witness

GENERAL SIR PETER DE LA BILLIERE, KCB, CBE, DSO, MC, examined

...

(*Chairman*): 62. If we can turn to operations, once you got out there what were the particularly difficult issues that confronted you before hostilities began as to the choices that were open to you, the priorities, the limitations because of getting stuff out there? Can you give us a general picture of how you saw it when you got there, not knowing if or when you were going to have to commit yourself to ground operations?

(Sir Peter de la Billiere) Yes. Of course, I think we need to remind ourselves - I certainly need to remind myself - that when I went out there we were not going out to take part in offensive operations, we were going out there to defend Saudi Arabia from any further aggression by Iraq, and therefore our deployment was on that basis and the whole conduct of our logistic support and our air manoeuvring and training was on that basis. Indeed, the Royal Navy was based purely on a defensive concept. Therefore, when I arrived, because the Air Force had already been there for some time, I saw my task as being, first of all, to ensure that the armoured brigade, which at that stage had been agreed should be committed, was properly, if I may use a very descriptive American phrase, bedded down and given a clear role within the American Marine Corps. I saw it as a major responsibility of mine to be in very close working harmony with both the Americans, in the form of General Norman Schwarzkopf and, of course, the Saudis - and the person I dealt with there was Lt. General Prince Khalid. I put a great deal of personal emphasis and importance on developing these relationships because I appreciated that, if I did not get that right, then nothing else was going to come right in terms of the way we were structured out there. My military responsibilities were much more of a co-ordinating and supervising role rather than the direct command role and I think this is perhaps a somewhat unique experience because we had agreed at a very early stage that the Army should be put under the tactical control of the American Forces when the Joint Commander and I considered the moment appropriate. The Royal Air Force was already *de facto* under American control, because you cannot run independent air operations on the scale that we were managing out there; they have to be co-ordinated by one organisation and that organisation inevitably was going to be the Americans. The Royal Navy did, in fact, maintain some considerable degree of independence at this stage and, indeed, throughout. They really came under tactical control of the Americans for specific minor and individual operations rather than for a whole phase of operations. So it was very important that I should make sure that the deployment of the British Forces was right in the planning stage because, once the planning stage was over and any operations took place, I knew my function as a commander would have been handed over to a local American commander and I would not be able to influence it very directly and, if I did start tinkering around with it, I was going to upset operational day-to-day planning. Therefore, it was of the greatest importance to me to see that the United Kingdom was represented throughout the Allied planning structure, from the very start and that it was able to influence the conceptual development of plans and not just comment on them as might normally have been expected to be what one would be authorised to do.

(*Chairman*): 63. How did you achieve that?

(Sir Peter de la Billiere) Well, the first thing was that I had to gain the confidence of General Norman Schwarzkopf and explain to him the importance that we, the British, attached to being able to influence the planning at the conceptual stage. I should say, first of all, that before I had arrived there my predecessor, Air Vice Marshal Wilson, had already been granted a place in General Schwarzkopf's component commanders' meeting each evening. That was a meeting he had with his main subordinate commanders. We were the only nation, apart from the Americans themselves, who had a seat at those component commanders' meetings. I had that access to General Norman Schwarzkopf every day. I wanted access at lower planning levels and so I asked him if he would agree to British officers being put into key places down the command chain so that they could influence the plan, and I have to say that he agreed to this readily. He saw the need for it. He greatly appreciated the commitment the British had made to support the whole operation out there. We must remember that we were the second largest commitment after the United States, apart from Saudi Arabia which was the host country. He recognised this by granting us privileges, and this was one of them. If I can perhaps just give you an example of how it worked in probably the most important area and that was on planning for the land battle. General Norman agreed that I should have an officer full-time on his own personal planning team. These were five specially selected United States officers who were responsible for producing a series of options and brain-storming through plans, and presenting them to him, of the various options that might be open to the ground forces. He agreed that we should put an officer there. He agreed that he should wear American uniform and he did. We got to the stage at one point where the only way you could tell whether an officer was American or British was by the length of his haircut. He was taken totally into the confidence of General Schwarzkopf, and this was at a stage when this planning was not available to anybody other than General Schwarzkopf, and of course to me. Now, because we had this officer there - and it was a very considerable concession by the Americans - so I was able to monitor the role the British would be playing in any forthcoming operations and, therefore, accept responsibility for what the British did, even if I did not command it in battle on the day.

(*Chairman*): 64. One last question because I think perhaps people are not as clear as they might be about the command structure and your relationship with Air Chief Marshal Hine, what aspects of joint command he exercised, and your relationship with General Schwarzkopf: could you just perhaps explain that in a rather more human way?

(Sir Peter de la Billiere) I was the senior British commander out there and I was never under American command or anybody else's command other than Air Chief Marshal Hine's command. He was my sole and only commander throughout the campaign. My relationship, therefore, with General Norman, and indeed with Prince Khalid, was very much one of being the leading national commander in theatre and thereby having a right of access and veto and a right to be considered that any other nation which was contributing to the Coalition should have. I did not have to take orders from anybody out there. I only took orders from Air Chief Marshal Hine.

(*Chairman*): 65. Was there any relationship between Air Chief Marshal Hine and General Schwarzkopf? Did they have a connection at all?

(Sir Peter de la Billiere) There was a very close working relationship in that they got on very well together and Air Chief Marshal Hine used to visit regularly, probably about once a fortnight, and on every visit he and General Norman would always have

discussions, lasting perhaps some two hours or more, and normally I would be at those discussions.

...

(*Chairman*): 68. One of the major problems you must have had, moving on in the operations side, was in the co-ordination of the land-air battle and the techniques that you used to manage that, particularly given the wide ranging nature of the coalition. Could you tell us about that? Could you tell us whether the old, tried and practised procedures were used, unchanged, or whether you had to make major changes in the way that you ran that co-ordination, given the Allies you were fighting with?

(Sir Peter de la Billiere) I think here we come back to our position there, which was that we were under the tactical control of the Americans. Can I just put this into perspective: the Americans, at their peak, had something in the region of 537,000 people out there, whereas our peak, remembering we were the second largest contributor, was something in the region of 45,000 people in theatre. So inevitably what the Americans did, everybody else really had to go along with; there was no choice if you wanted things to work, and work smoothly. Therefore the actual co-ordination between the three Services tactically, and once they had commenced fighting, lay in the Americans' hands and not our hands. This had an impact on the way my headquarters ran, because when I have been running joint service operations, either when I was commanding down in the Falklands or subsequent exercises, I have been involved in tri-service operations, in command of all three services. In Granby that was not the case, the three services were really working separately, as far as I was concerned and under American command, therefore it was up to the Americans to pull the whole thing together rather than the British. The result was my headquarters tended to have intelligence cells running the Army, Navy or Air Force, but all reporting to me, rather than me issuing orders to all three Services which co-ordinated their activities

...

(*Mr Home Robertson*): 86. Coming back to the theme of the tactics of pursuit in this operation, was there any flexibility built into the rules of engagement for the troops involved in this operation to cope with the fact they were dealing with an enemy in what turned into a rout frankly? It does appear at a certain stage in the operation, because we started taking prisoners, that we scaled down the offensive nature of the operation. Was that planned?

(Sir Peter de la Billiere) The rules of engagement, once we had deployed our land forces, were to destroy the enemy. Once the commanders realised that the enemy was largely seeking to surrender and there were only small pockets of resistance, they adjusted their plan in such a way as to encourage, put pressure on, these pockets of resistance to surrender rather than fight it out, when of course it was a simple matter for us to destroy them. It was very much in the commanders' minds to minimise casualties once they realised the Iraqi defence had collapsed.

(*Mr Home Robertson*): 87. Had you anticipated that was a possibility?

(Sir Peter de la Billiere) No, I think we expected, and I think this is a very important matter to understand, that until we were through that minefield gap and out the other side that the Iraqis were going to put up quite a fight, and we were going to suffer quite a lot of casualties, and in no way did those soldiers go into battle thinking it was going to be a walk-over.

...

(*Mr Home Robertson*): 95. A final question, I hope, on your role as Commander. Can you say something about your input into the framing of the terms of the ceasefire?

(Sir Peter de la Billiere) At Sathwan or the United Nations?

(*Mr Home Robertson*): 96. Obviously the point on which there is public attention in relation to the terms of the ceasefire is the fact that we apparently, sadly, were not in a position to restrict the ability of some Iraqi forces to go on doing terrible things in their own country. With the benefit of hindsight could more have been done? What was your role?

(Sir Peter de la Billiere) First of all, the Americans led. Let us talk about the Sathwan talks, because the United States' ceasefire was nothing to do with me; this was negotiated at a very high level at Washington, London and the United Nations. The Sathwan talks were run under the direction of General Norman. We really held a major position immediately subordinate to him, but were not directly involved in the talks. Before the talks took place he discussed the general nature and tenor of the discussions as he saw them going, and the main requirements of those discussions, and he also gave us an opportunity (by "us" I mean the French, myself and the Saudis - and the Saudis, incidentally, were also on a par with the Americans in these talks; Prince Khalid was there) to discuss the general tenor of the talks. But we must remember they were not ceasefire talks then, they were merely talks to agree not to take further offensive action. I suspect you are really alluding to the use of helicopters. What happened there was that the Iraqis, you will remember, had all their communications down, their bridges down, their telegraphic and radio communications pretty well written off; they had difficulties in controlling their own population, they had difficulties in providing medical support and all the administration necessary to try and bring some order into their country. They, quite reasonably, asked us if they could use helicopters to help them do this, and it was agreed. After it had been agreed that there should be no air movement they put in this request for helicopters to be allowed to help with administration. That, in a nutshell, was what was agreed, and then they abused that offer. Once the helicopters started flying it was very difficult to tell whether the thing was on an offensive mission or on a purely logistic or humanistic mission.

...

(*Mr Lee*): 110. Linked to that, did we actually ever discover any Iraqi chemical weapon stocks?

(Sir Peter de la Billiere) No. Did our Division discover any? The answer is, no.

(*Chairman*): 111. Does that mean the Americans did?

(Sir Peter de la Billiere) I do not think they did either. I hesitate slightly there because there may be things I do not know about. The only incident was when one American was clearing a weapon pit out and became contaminated with mustard gas, but there were no chemical weapons recovered to my knowledge, and I believe the reason for this is that they were not deployed.

...

(*Mr McFall*): 121. Sir Peter, I would like to take up some of the points following the Secretary of State's appearance before the Committee on Wednesday 6 March when I asked him about the bombing campaign. There were three issues: the power stations, the nuclear stations and the Mitla Ridge. On power stations, it is the case now that there is rampant disease and lack of sanitation in Iraq as a result of the bombing campaign. Can I ask you, was it necessary to bomb these power stations to the extent that they were?

(Sir Peter de la Billiere) The strategic air campaign was designed to destroy the Iraqi capability supporting his

forces in the field and delivering chemical weapons and generally giving any aid and succour to his military machine. An important aspect of this was, of course, to destroy his ability to produce power, which, in turn, supported a large area of strategic military support. In my view, I think to take out the power stations was essential. We do have to remind ourselves once again that although the war looked like being a bit of a walkover at the end of the day, we did not know that at the time. Indeed, it might not have been had we not taken action of this nature. If we had got it wrong the other way we would have paid for it with British lives.

(*Mr McFall*): 122. On the issue of nuclear power stations, if we were to believe the press, these two nuclear power stations were inactive. Had that been the case this would be the first occasion in war when nuclear power stations had been bombed and there are severe implications for the nuclear non-proliferation treaty. The Secretary of State, in answer to a question I put to him on Wednesday 6 March, said there was detailed planning to minimise the risk of contamination and radiation. I do not understand what the Secretary of State meant by that. Could you give us an insight into confining radiation contamination?

(Sir Peter de la Billiere) The strategic targeting was certainly discussed during the planning stage between London and Washington. I was not party to those discussions. However, there were several occasions when I was asked by my superiors to ascertain whether the Americans had taken into account, for example, all the possible side-effects of bombing the gas storage installations, gas production, chemical storage and chemical production installations. I know there was a great deal of care taken, by the British anyway, to make sure that whatever was planned strategically in the way of offensive operations had taken full account of what the by-product of those operations might be. So the feeling I get is that all these matters were considered carefully at a higher command level than mine.

(*Mr McFall*): 123. On the issue of Mitla Ridge and the public distaste at this distressing situation, was it possible to have a military campaign that encircled that area rather than going in and bombing it, considering that we did not know if there were Kuwaiti captives and, who knows, there possibly could have been some prisoners of war in that situation. Could I ask what position you played in halting the war when it was halted?

(Sir Peter de la Billiere) What role I had in halting the war?

(*Mr McFall*): 124. Yes.

(Sir Peter de la Billiere) Dealing with Mitla Ridge, that particular part of the air campaign was largely American, and so I am not totally privy to what the decision-making process was. All I would say is that at that stage the war was going full tilt, and you cannot run half a war, you are either out there to win or you have halted and peace arrangements are set in hand. At that stage we had been given a military objective and part of that objective was to destroy the Iraqi Army in Kuwait. There has been some criticism since the end of the war that we did not do this job thoroughly enough, and all I would say is that we were in a no-win situation. There was a vast amount of armoured and supporting equipment at Mitla Ridge, and a lot of Iraqis who had sequestered Kuwaiti vehicles and filled them with loot even, at that stage of the war. They were taking them across the border, and mixed up with that was military equipment, and at the height of battle you cannot start picking and choosing who you are going to attack. If you are going to mix up civilian vehicles with military vehicles, then I am afraid civilian vehicles will be taken out as well. As far as my part in bringing the war to a halt was concerned, I had no part in that, that was a high level political decision, and the instructions came, so far as I was concerned, to General Norman from Washington. Of course, once the Americans decided they were not going to go on fighting, there was no question of us going on on our own.

(*Mr McFall*): 125. Lastly, resolution 678 had us out in the Middle East to use all necessary means to uphold resolution 660 and all subsequent resolutions, to restore international peace and security in the area. Are you content you undertook that and discharged that well?

(Sir Peter de la Billiere) What aspect?

(*Mr McFall*): 126. To discharge resolution 678 in full. That was the rationale for going to war.

(Sir Peter de la Billiere) Yes, I think we did. Our commitment was to restore sovereignty to Kuwait, to destroy the Iraqi forces in Kuwait, so they could not initiate new, fresh operations, and we did that and no more. Indeed, the criticism is perhaps we ought to have done more, but had we done any more then we would have been stepping outside those limits, and it is my personal belief we should not have done any more.

...

MINUTES OF EVIDENCE
TAKEN BEFORE THE DEFENCE COMMITTEE

WEDNESDAY 22 MAY 1991

Examination of Witness

AIR VICE MARSHAL W J WRATTEN, CB, CBE, AFC, examined

...

(*Chairman*): 145. Can we turn now to the more detailed side of RAF operations. The principal Tornado ground attack concept was flying in very low under SAM defences and it seems that the American concept was more concentrated on defence suppression, and after we had carried out the runway denial tasks we seemed to turn more to the medium-level attack. How relevant in all that and the decisions you had to take about that were the tactics that you had trained for against Soviet and Soviet-style air defences, which were your *raison d'être?*

(Air Vice Marshal Wratten) We went into the Gulf, of course, with the GR1 JP233 combination expecting to be used in the airfield denial role as part of the offensive counter air campaign in exactly the same way as we had been training in the European theatre, and we expected, because of the size and potential capability of the Iraqi Air Force, to be committed to that role perhaps indefinitely. Now the fact that things worked in our favour ...

(*Chairman*): 146. Just before we go on, you expected, therefore, to have to use the same sort of tactics? You expected the Iraqi Air Force to employ the same sort of Soviet defence attacks?

(Air Vice Marshal Wratten) No, we expected the Iraqi Air Force to respond. We expected them to offer some opposition and, therefore, we expected to have to continue to attempt to close their airfields and, therefore, deny them their use, which would have implied the continual use of JP233s.

...

6. THE IMPLEMENTATION OF THE LAWS OF WAR

This section reproduces only materials emmanating from the International Committee of the Red Cross. Documents relating to comments and complaints concerning the implementation of the laws of war by individual governments are contained in the two preceeding sections of this chapter. Materials concerning the repatriation of prisoners of war at the conclusion of the hostilites are reprinted in Part IV of this volume.

1. Conflict in Kuwait: ICRC Stands Ready, ICRC Press Release No. 1640, 2 August 1990

Geneva (ICRC) - Following the outbreak of an armed conflict in Kuwait, the International Committee of the Red Cross (ICRC) today contacted the governments of both Iraq and Kuwait, through their Permanent Missions in Geneva, to remind them of their obligations under the four 1949 Geneva Conventions, to which both States are party.

The ICRC requested in particular that the parties comply with the Conventions' provisions relating to the protection of the sick and wounded, medical units and establishments, prisoners and civilians.

The ICRC is ready to dispatch a delegation to Kuwait to undertake humanitarian activities for people needing assistance or protection, in accordance with the mandate entrusted to it by the international community.

2. ICRC President to go to Baghdad, ICRC Communication to the Press No. 90/17, 29 August 1990

Geneva (ICRC) - Mr. Cornelio Sommaruga, President of the International Committee of the Red Cross (ICRC), will meet Mr. Tariq Aziz, Iraqi Minister of Foreign Affairs, in Baghdad on Sunday, 2 September 1990 to discuss all problems of humanitarian concern related to the Gulf crisis.

Since the crisis began, the ICRC has approached all parties concerned in order to bring help to the many people affected by the situation.

3. Communiqué Issued by the Standing Commission of the Red Cross and Red Crescent Societies, ICRC Press Release No. 1652, 23 October 1990

The Standing Commission of the Red Cross and Red Crescent, trustee of the International Conference of the Red Cross and Red Crescent, at its meeting in Geneva on October 22nd, 1990, expressed its deep concern about the consequences, in humanitarian terms, of the recent events in Kuwait, the massive deployment of military forces in the Gulf area and the possibility of the Middle East being drawn into an armed conflict that would cause innumerable victims among combatants and the civilian population. The Commission deplored the current difficulties encountered by the International Committee of the Red Cross (ICRC) in fulfilling its humanitarian mandate, difficulties which have left a countless number of people without protection, and the fact that disputes about the legal classifications of conflicts too often hinder the implementation of International Humanitarian Law.

Therefore, in conformity with Resolution I of the Twenty-fifth International Conference of the Red Cross (Geneva, 1986), the Commission solemnly appeals to the Parties involved to respect all their obligations under International Humanitarian Law so as to enable the ICRC to carry out its humanitarian activities.

The Standing Commission also appeals to all Parties concerned to do their utmost to find a peaceful solution to the present crisis in accordance with public international law.

4. *Note Verbale* from the ICRC to the Parties to the 1949 Geneva Conventions, 14 December 1990

The International Committee of the Red Cross (ICRC) presents its compliments to the Permanent Mission of ... and has the honour to request it to inform the Government of ... of the following:

After the Iraqi armed forces entered Kuwait on 2 August 1990, the ICRC offered its services and has since made repeated representations on the basis of the 1949 Geneva Conventions.

Regrettably, these representations have not proved successful so far. The ICRC therefore intends to pursue its efforts.

Without taking a stand on a matter that does not come within its competence, and expressing the hope that the present crisis will be resolved by peaceful means, the ICRC has taken note of the adoption by the United Nations Security Council of resolution 678 on 29 November 1990.

In view of the highly sensitive and tense situation in the Gulf, where large units of several States' armed forces are deployed, the ICRC deems it its duty to emphasize that the humanitarian consequences of military operations involving States party to the Geneva Conventions make it imperative for those States to respect all the provisions of the said Conventions and of other international treaties applicable in time of armed conflict.

The ICRC, in its capacity as a neutral, impartial and independent humanitarian institution and pursuant to its mandate to promote and ensure respect for international humanitarian law, is therefore sending the enclosed memorandum to all States party to the 1949 Geneva Conventions to remind them of their responsibilities and obligations under that law.

The International Committee of the Red Cross avails itself of this opportunity to convey to the Permanent Mission of ... the renewed assurances of its high consideration.

5. ICRC Memorandum on the applicability of international humanitarian law, 14 January 1991

I. Protection of persons not participating or no longer participating in hostilities

The four Geneva Conventions of 12 August 1949 are applicable as soon as armed hostilities break out between two or more parties to the Conventions.

Under the Conventions, the following principles in particular must be respected:

- persons not participating or no longer participating in the hostilities, such as the wounded, the sick, the shipwrecked, prisoners of war and civilians, must be respected and protected in all circumstances;

- the wounded, the sick and the shipwrecked must be collected and cared for regardless of the party to which they belong;

- civilians and all non-combatants must be respected and protected, and violence to life and person, the taking of hostages, deportations, outrages upon personal dignity, and the passing of sentences and carrying out of executions without fair trial are specifically prohibited.

II. Conduct of hostilities

The parties to an armed conflict must also observe a number of rules on the conduct of hostilities. These rules are, in particular, laid down in the Hague Conventions of 1899 and 1907, most of which have become part of customary law.

These rules have been reaffirmed, and in some cases supplemented, in 1977 Protocol I additional to the Geneva Conventions. The following general rules are recognized as binding on any party to an armed conflict:

- the parties to a conflict do not have an unlimited right to choose methods and means of injuring the enemy;

- a distinction must be made in all circumstances between combatants and military objectives on the one hand, and civilians and civilian objects on the other. It is forbidden to attack civilian persons or objects or to launch indiscriminate attacks;

- all feasible precautions must be taken to avoid loss of civilian life or damage to civilian objects, and attacks that would cause incidental loss of life or damage which would be excessive in relation to the direct military advantage anticipated are prohibited.

With regard to the use of certain weapons, the following rules are in particular applicable in an armed conflict:

- the use of chemical or bacteriological weapons is prohibited (1925 Geneva Protocol);

- the rules of the law of armed conflict also apply to weapons of mass destruction.

The ICRC invites States which are not party to 1977 Protocol I to respect, in the event of armed conflict, the following articles of the Protocol, which stem from the basic principle of civilian immunity from attack:

- Article 54: protection of objects indispensable to the survival of the civilian population;

- Article 55: protection of the natural environment;

- Article 56: protection of works and installations containing dangerous forces.

III. Respect for the emblem and medical activities

The red cross and red crescent emblems must be respected in all circumstances. Medical and religious personnel, ambulances, hospitals and other medical units and means of transport shall in particular be identified by one of the emblems and respected accordingly.

IV. Dissemination of international humanitarian law

It is extremely important for the members of armed forces stationed in the Gulf to be aware of their obligations under international humanitarian law. Proper instructions must be issued to this effect. The teaching of the law to the armed forces is, moreover, an obligation expressly stipulated by the Geneva Conventions and their Additional Protocols.

V. Role of the ICRC

The ICRC, whose primary function is to protect and assist the military and civilian victims of armed conflicts, is at the disposal of the States concerned to contribute, as far as its means allow, to the implementation of humanitarian rules and to perform the tasks entrusted to it by international humanitarian law.

6. ICRC Communication to the Press, No. 91/4, 13 January 1991

Geneva (ICRC) - The International Committee of the Red Cross (ICRC), while still hoping for a peaceful solution to the crisis in the Gulf, has recently increased the number of staff in all its delegations in the Middle East. It now has 77 delegates in the region, ready to take action from Saudi Arabia, Egypt, Iran, Iraq, Israel and the occupied territories, Jordan and Syria in the event of a conflict.

Fifty additional delegates are standing by in Geneva, ready to leave within 12 hours, and a third group of 50 can rapidly be mobilized.

Stocks of medical and other relief supplies have already been built up in the Middle East and Europe. Two ICRC aircraft are ready to leave and plans have been made to deploy nine mobile medical teams in a first phase.

Should an armed conflict break out and cause large-scale population movements, the ICRC envisages setting up reception camps with a total capacity of 300,000. The Jordan National Red Crescent, the League of Red Cross and Red Crescent Societies and the ICRC are already running three camps in Jordan which can accommodate 40,000 people. Three ICRC delegates are currently on the Iranian side of the Iran-Iraq border looking for suitable sites for similar facilities.

All these preparations are being made in close co-operation with the League and the National Red Cross and Red Crescent Societies.

At the same time the ICRC is stepping up its representations to the chiefs of staff of the armed forces present in the Gulf, reminding them of their obligations under international humanitarian law. Particular stress is laid on the need for measures ensuring the proper identification of prisoners of war and arrangements for the exchange of news with their families.

On 14 December last the ICRC reminded all 164 States party to the Geneva Conventions of their obligation to respect and ensure respect for international humanitarian law.

7. ICRC Appeal, Press Release No. 1658, 17 January 1991

"As fighting flares in the Gulf, the International Committee of the Red Cross solemnly reminds all the parties to the conflict of their commitments under the 1949 Geneva Conventions for the protection of the victims of war.

It is essential that the States involved honour those commitments in a situation where there is good reason to fear that the civilian population may suffer particular hardship. Indeed, the general context in which the hostilities are being conducted makes it extremely hazardous to provide effective protection for civilians exposed to the fighting.

In view of the circumstances, the ICRC, in a *note verbale* which will be handed over today to the States involved, insisted that all necessary precautions be taken by those conducting the hostilities to spare civilians. It also reminded them that wounded, sick or shipwrecked members of the armed forces must be cared for and that combatants placed hors de combat must be treated humanely. Medical personnel and establishments must be respected and protected at all times.

Moreover, the ICRC reminds the parties that the use of chemical and bacteriological weapons is prohibited under international humanitarian law and enjoins them not to have recourse to atomic weapons, the use of which is incompatible with the provisions of that law. Weapons of mass destruction having indiscriminate effects generally cause irreparable damage among the civilian population, which must be kept out of the fighting.

The ICRC confirms that it stands ready to fulfil the tasks entrusted to it by the Geneva Conventions and by the Statutes of the International Red Cross and Red Crescent Movement and reiterates that it is available to the parties as a neutral and independent intermediary. To this end it must be given access to victims of the conflict, such as prisoners of war and civilians, entitled to protection and assistance. It may also be called upon to fulfil any other task requiring the services of a neutral intermediary or which it might propose to undertake by virtue of its right of humanitarian initiative, recognized by the community of States.

Finally, the International Committee of the Red Cross appeals to all the parties involved to make sure that the conditions are created for the conflict to be resolved at the negotiating table rather than on the battlefield" .

ICRC Outline of Legal Aspects of the Conflict in the Middle East, 21 January 1991

This outline is only a provisional analysis of the legal aspects of the Middle East conflict and should not be considered as the official position of the International Committee of the Red Cross.

It was drawn up at the request of several national Red Cross and Red Crescent Societies at a meeting held on 21 January 1991 in Geneva.

1. Definition of the conflict

The Middle East conflict is beyond any doubt an international armed conflict as defined in Article 2 common to the Geneva Conventions of 12 August 1949.

The fact that military action has been authorized by security council resolution 678 does not affect this definition or the application of the laws of armed conflict.

The fact that there has been no formal declaration of war does not affect this definition either. In this respect, it may be pointed out that the Geneva Conventions "shall apply to all cases of declared war or of any other armed conflict which may arise between two or more of the High Contracting Parties, even if the state of war is not recognized by one of them" (Article 2).

The definition of the current hostilities as an international armed conflict has not been contested by any of the belligerents.

Therefore, the laws of international armed conflict apply in the present case.

2. Legal sources

The parties to the conflict are bound, *inter alia*, by the following sets of rules:

International customary law is binding on all parties; Hague Convention No. IV of 18 October 1907 concerning the laws and customs of war on land is binding on all parties, even though some of them have not acceded to it, since its customary character is universally accepted.

The Geneva Protocol of 17 June 1925 for the prohibition of the use in war of asphyxiating, poisonous or other gases and of bacteriological methods of warfare has been ratified by the parties to the conflict and is therefore binding on them.

The Geneva Conventions of 12 August 1949 have been ratified by all parties to the conflict and are likewise binding on them.

Iraq, the United States, the United Kingdom and France have not ratified Additional Protocol I to the Geneva Conventions of 12 August 1949; its provisions are therefore not binding unless they codify customary rules.

3. Fundamental Rules

A) Rules governing the conduct of hostilities

These are essentially governed by the following principles:

- the right of the parties to choose methods or means of warfare is not unlimited;

- it is prohibited to use methods or means of warfare of a nature to cause superfluous injury or unnecessary suffering;

- the civilian population must be protected against the dangers arising from military operations.

In practice, this means that a distinction should always be made between combatants and the civilian population, so as to spare the latter.

It is prohibited to direct attacks against the civilian population or to launch indiscriminate attacks that will affect the civilian population as well as military objectives. In any attacks, including bombardments, every precaution must be taken to spare civilians.

The use of indiscriminate weapons or weapons of mass destruction is prohibited. The use of chemical and bacteriological weapons is prohibited by the Geneva Convention of 17 June 1925 and the use of nuclear weapons is incompatible with the provisions of international humanitarian law.

B) Wounded and sick

The wounded and the sick must be collected and cared for, regardless of their nationality. Members of medical services as well as volunteers from National Red Cross or Red Crescent Societies, whose task it is to assist the victims of the conflict, must be respected and protected. The emblem of the Red Cross or Red Crescent must be respected in all circumstances.

C) Wounded, sick and shipwrecked

In case of naval operations or in case of attack against naval objectives, the shipwrecked must be collected and cared for; every precaution must be taken to spare hospital ships.

D) Prisoners of war and civilian internees

Soldiers who surrender or are captured in any other manner must be spared. Their lives and dignity must be respected and they must be treated humanely in all circumstances. They must be protected against any acts of violence, against insults and against public curiosity. They must be transferred from combat zones and their presence cannot be used to prevent attacks on military objectives or other installations.

The same principles apply to civilian internees or detainees.

E) Alien civilians on the territory of an adverse party

Alien civilians on the territory of an adverse party are protected by the Fourth Geneva Convention. In case measures of control, such as internment, are taken against them, they must benefit from all the guarantees set out in the Convention.

F) Population of occupied territories

The populations of occupied territories are protected by the Fourth Geneva Convention (Articles 13-34 and 47-149).

ICRC Appeal, ICRC Press Release No. 1659, 1 February 1991

"The conflict now raging in the Middle East will inevitably bring widespread destruction, perhaps on a scale unprecedented in this part of the world. Millions of civilians have been caught up in the violence, without shelter or protection against occupation and bombing. Growing numbers of combatants are falling into enemy hands. Hundreds of thousands of ground troops - most of them young men - are preparing to meet in a deadly confrontation. The determination of the parties in conflict and the build-up of awesome means of destruction are a presage of irreversible devastation. When the veil of censorship is lifted, the full horror of the suffering inflicted on the peoples of the region and on combatants and their families will be revealed for all to see.

One of the most disquieting aspects of this conflict is the possibility that the law of war, which is the expression of the most basic and universal principles of humanity and of the dictates of the public conscience, might be swept aside by the political, military or propaganda demands of the moment.

The right to choose methods or means of warfare is not unlimited. Weapons having indiscriminate effects and those likely to cause disproportionate suffering and damage to the environment are prohibited.

The wounded, whether civilian or military, and prisoners must receive special consideration and protection in compliance with specific rules which the entire international community has undertaken to respect.

The International Committee of the Red Cross therefore solemnly appeals today to all belligerents, in the name of all civilian and military victims, to have due regard for humanitarian considerations. To show respect for the victims and treat them humanely, in the spirit of the Geneva Conventions, is to recognize a heritage common to all mankind and thus pave the way to reconciliation. It is also the last chance of averting a tragedy even greater than the use of force"

7. ENVIRONMENTAL CONSEQUENCES OF THE CONFLICT

In the weeks preceding the outbreak of hostilities and during the conflict the environment was employed as a means of strategic warfare by the Iraqi government. Large-scale oil spillages into the Gulf and the incineration of oil fields in Kuwait resulted in considerable environmental damage, as is evidenced in the following reports. The Chapter opens with extracts from the 1978 Convention on the Protection of the Marine Environment *in the Gulf, to which both Iraq and Kuwait are parties.*

17 ILM 501, 511 [*Extracts*]

1. Kuwait Regional Convention for Co-operation on the Protection of the Marine Environment from Pollution, 24 April 1978

The Government of the STATE OF BAHRAIN,
The Imperial Government of IRAN,
The Government of the REPUBLIC OF IRAQ,
The Government of the STATE OF KUWAIT,
The Government of the SULTANATE OF OMAN,
The Government of the STATE OF QATAR,
The Government of the KINGDOM OF SAUDI ARABIA,
The Government of the UNITED ARAB EMIRATES,

REALIZING that pollution of the marine environment in the Region shared by Bahrain, Iran, Iraq, Kuwait, Oman, Qatar, Saudi Arabia and the United Arab Emirates, by oil and other harmful or noxious materials arising from human activities on land or at sea, especially through indiscriminate and uncontrolled discharge of these substances, presents a growing threat to marine life, fisheries, human health, recreational uses of beaches and other amenities,

MINDFUL of the special hydrographic and ecological characteristics of the marine environment of the Region and its particular vulnerability to pollution,

CONSCIOUS of the need to ensure that the processes of urban and rural development and resultant land use should be carried out in such a manner as to preserve, as far as possible, marine resources and coastal amenities, and that such development should not lead to deterioration of the marine environment,

CONVINCED of the need to ensure that the processes of industrial development should not, in any way, cause damage to the marine environment of the Region, jeopardize its living resources or create hazards to human health,

RECOGNIZING the need to develop an integrated management approach to the use of the marine environment and the coastal areas which will allow the achievement of environmental and development goals in a harmonious manner,

RECOGNIZING ALSO the need for a carefully planned research, monitoring and assessment programme in view of the scarcity of scientific information on marine pollution in the Region,

CONSIDERING that the States sharing the Region have a special responsibility to protect its marine environment,

AWARE of the importance of co-operation and co-ordination of action on a regional basis with the aim of protecting the marine environment of the Region for the benefit of all concerned, including future generations,

BEARING in mind the existing international conventions relevant to the present Convention,

HAVE AGREED as follows:

ARTICLE I

Definitions

For the purpose of the present Convention:

(a) marine pollution means the introduction by man, directly or indirectly, of substances or energy into the marine environment resulting or likely to result in such deleterious effects as harm to living resources, hazards to human health, hindrance to marine activities including fishing, impairment of quality for use of sea and reduction of amenities;

(b) "National Authority" means the authority designated by each Contracting States as responsible for the co-ordination of national efforts for implementing the Convention and its protocols;

(c) "Organization" means the organization established by the Contracting States in accordance with Article XVI;

(d) "secretariat" means the organ of the Organization established in accordance with Article XVI;

(e) "Action Plan" means the Action Plan for the Development and Protection of the Marine Environment and the Coastal Areas of Bahrain, Iran, Iraq, Kuwait, Oman, Qatar, Saudi Arabia and the United Arab Emirates adopted at the Kuwait Regional Conference of Plenipotentiaries on the Protection and Development of the Marine Environment and the Coastal Areas, convened from 15 to 23 April 1978.

ARTICLE II

Geographical coverage

(a) The present Convention shall apply to the sea area in the Region bounded in the south by the following rhumb lines: from Ras Dharbat Ali in (16° 39'N, 53° 3'30"E) then to a position in (16° 00'N, 53° 25'E) then to a position in (17° 00'N, 56° 30'E) then to a position in (20° 30'N, 60° 00'E) then to Ras Al-Fasteh in in (25° 04'N, 61° 25'E).

(Hereinafter referred to as the "Sea Area");

(b) The Sea Area shall not include internal waters of the Contracting States unless it is otherwise stated in the present Convention or in any of its protocols.

ARTICLE III

General obligations

(a) The Contracting States shall, individually and/or jointly, take all appropriate measures in accordance with the present Convention and those protocols in force to which they are party to prevent, abate and combat pollution of the marine environment in the Sea Area;

(b) In addition to the Protocol concerning Regional Co-operation in Combating Pollution by Oil and other Harmful Substances in Cases of Emergency opened for signature at the same time as the present Convention, the Contracting States shall co-operate in the formulation and adoption of other protocols prescribing agreed measures, procedures and standards for the implementation of the Convention;

(c) The Contracting States shall establish national standards, laws and regulations as required for the effective discharge of the obligation prescribed in paragraph (a) of this article, and shall endeavour to harmonise their national policies in this regard and for this purpose appoint the Appropriate Authority;

(d) The Contracting States shall co-operate with the competent international, regional and sub-regional organizations to establish and adopt regional standards, recommended practices and procedures to prevent, abate and combat pollution from all sources in conformity with the objectives of the present Convention, and to assist each other in fulfilling their obligations under the present Convention;

(e) The Contracting States shall use their best endeavour to ensure that the implementation of the present Convention shall not cause transformation of one type of pollution to another which could be more detrimental to the environment.

ARTICLE IV

Pollution from ships

The Contracting States shall take all appropriate measures in conformity with the present Convention and the applicable rules of international law to prevent, abate and combat pollution in the Sea Area caused by international or accidental discharges from ships, and shall ensure effective compliance in the Sea Area with applicable, international rules relating to the control of this type of pollution, including load-on-top, segregated ballast and crude oil washing procedures for tankers.

ARTICLE V

Pollution caused by dumping from ships and aircraft

The Contracting States shall take all appropriate measures to prevent, abate and combat pollution in the Sea Area caused by dumping of wastes and other matter from ships and aircraft, and shall ensure effective compliance in the Sea Area with applicable international rules relating to the control of this type of pollution as provided for in relevant international conventions.

ARTICLE VI

Pollution from land-based sources

The Contracting States shall take all appropriate measures to prevent, abate and combat pollution caused by discharges from land reaching the Sea Area whether water-borne, air-borne, or directly from the coast including outfalls and pipelines.

ARTICLE VII

Pollution resulting from exploration and exploitation of the bed of the territorial sea and its sub-soil and the continental shelf

The Contracting States shall take all appropriate measures to prevent, abate and combat pollution in the Sea Area resulting from exploration and exploitation of the bed of the territorial sea and its sub-soil and the continental shelf, including the prevention of accidents and the combating of pollution emergencies resulting in damage to the marine environment.

ARTICLE VIII

Pollution from other human activities

The Contracting States shall take all appropriate measures to prevent, abate and combat pollution of the Sea Area resulting from land reclamation and associated suction dredging and coastal dredging.

ARTICLE IX

Co-operation in dealing with pollution emergencies

(a) The Contracting States shall, individually and/or jointly, take all necessary measures, including those to ensure that adequate equipment and qualified personnel are readily available, to deal with pollution emergencies in the Sea Area, whatever the cause of such emergencies, and to reduce or eliminate damage resulting therefrom;

(b) Any Contracting State which becomes aware of any pollution emergency in the Sea Area shall, without delay, notify the Organization referred to under Article XVI and, through the secretariat, any Contracting State likely to be affected by such emergency.

ARTICLE X

Scientific and technological co-operation

(a) The Contracting States shall co-operate directly, or, where appropriate, through competent international and regional organizations, in the field of scientific research, monitoring and assessment concerning pollution in the Sea Area, and shall exchange data as well as other scientific information for the purpose of the present Convention and any of its protocols;

(b) The Contracting States shall co-operate further to develop and co-ordinate national research and monitoring programmes relating to all types of pollution in the Sea Area and to establish in co-operation with competent regional or international organizations, a regional network of such programmes to ensure compatible results. For this purpose, each Contracting State [*sic*] shall designate the National Authority responsible for pollution research and monitoring within the areas under its national jurisdiction. The Contracting States shall participate in international arrangements for pollution research and monitoring in areas beyond their national jurisdiction.

ARTICLE XI

Environmental assessment

(a) Each Contracting State shall endeavour to include an assessment of the potential environmental effects in any planning activity entailing projects within its territory, particularly in the coastal areas, which may cause significant risks of pollution in the Sea Area;

(b) The Contracting States may, in consultation with the secretariat, develop procedures for dissemination of information of the assessment of the activities referred to in paragraph (a) above;

(c) The Contracting States undertake to develop, individually or jointly, technical and other guidelines in accordance with standard scientific practice to assist the planning of their development projects in such a way as to minimize their harmful impact on the marine environment. In this regard international standards may be used where appropriate.

ARTICLE XII

Technical and other assistance

The Contracting States shall co-operate directly or through competent regional or international organizations in the development of programmes of technical and other assistance in fields relating to marine pollution in co-ordination with the Organization referred to in Article XVI.

ARTICLE XIII

Liability and compensation

The Contracting States undertake to co-operate in the formulation and adoption of appropriate rules and procedures for the determination of:

(a) civil liability and compensation for damage resulting from pollution of the marine environment, bearing in mind applicable international rules and procedures relating to those matters; and

(b) liability and compensation for damage resulting from violation of obligations under the present Convention and its protocols.

ARTICLE XIV

Sovereign immunity

Warships or other ships owned or operated by a State, and used only on Government non-commercial service, shall be exempted from the application of the provisions of the present convention. Each Contracting State shall, as far as possible, ensure that its warships or other ships owned or operated by that State, and used only on Government non-commercial service, shall comply with the present Convention in the prevention of pollution to the marine environment.

ARTICLE XV

Disclaimer

Nothing in the present Convention shall prejudice or affect the rights or claims of any Contracting State in regard to the nature or extent of its maritime jurisdictions which may be established in conformity with international law.

ARTICLE XVI

Regional Organization for the Protection of the Marine Environment

(a) The Contracting States hereby establish a Regional Organization for the Protection of the Marine Environment, the permanent headquarters of which shall be located in Kuwait.

(b) The Organization shall consist of the following organs:

(i) a Council which shall be comprised of the Contracting States and shall perform the functions set forth in paragraph (d) of Article XVII;

(ii) a secretariat which shall perform the functions set forth in paragraph (a) of Article XVIII; and

(iii) a Judicial Commission for the Settlement of Disputes whose composition, terms of reference and rules of procedure shall be established at the first meeting of the Council.

ARTICLE XVII

Council

(a) The meetings of the Council shall be convened in accordance with paragraph (a) of Article XVIII and paragraph (b) of Article XXX [omitted]. The Council shall hold ordinary meetings once a year. Extraordinary meetings of the Council shall be held upon the request of at least one Contracting State endorsed by at least one other Contracting State, or upon the request of the Executive Secretary endorsed by at least two Contracting States. Meetings of the Council shall be convened at the headquarters of the Organization or at any other place agreed upon by consultation amongst the Contracting States. Three-fourths of the Contracting States shall constitute a quorum.

(b) The Chairmanship of the Council shall be given to each Contracting State in turn in alphabetical order of the names of the States in the English language. The Chairman shall serve for a period of one year and cannot during the period of chairmanship serve as a representative of his State. Should the chairmanship fall vacant, the Contracting State chairing the Council shall designate a successor to remain in office until the term of chairmanship of that Contracting State expires.

(c) The voting procedure in the Council shall be as follows:

(i) each Contracting State shall have one vote;

(ii) decisions on substantive matters shall be taken by a unanimous vote of the Contracting States present and voting;

(iii) decisions on procedural matters shall be taken by three-fourths majority vote of the Contracting States present and voting.

(d) The functions of the Council shall be:

(i) to keep under review the implementation of the Convention and its protocols, and the Action Plan referred to in paragraph (e) of Article I;

(ii) to review and evaluate the state of marine pollution and its effects on the Sea Area on the basis of reports provided by the Contracting States and the competent international or regional organizations;

(iii) to adopt, review and amend as required in accordance with procedures established in Article XXI [omitted], the annexes to the Convention and to its protocols;

(iv) to receive and to consider reports submitted by the Contracting States under Articles IX and XXIII [omitted];

(v) to consider reports prepared by the secretariat on questions relating to the Convention and to matters relevant to the administration of the Organization;

(vi) to make recommendations regarding the adoption of any additional protocols or any amendments to the Convention or to its protocols in accordance with Articles XIX [omitted] and XX [omitted];

(vii) to establish subsidiary bodies and ad hoc working groups as required to consider any matters related to the Convention and its protocols and annexes to the Convention and its protocols;

(viii) to appoint an Executive Secretary and to make provision for the appointment by the Executive Secretary of such other personnel as may be necessary;

(ix) to review periodically the functions of the secretariat;

(x) to consider and to undertake any additional action that may be required for the achievement of the purposes of the Convention and its protocols.

ARTICLE XVIII

Secretariat

(a) The secretariat shall be comprised of an Executive Secretary and the personnel necessary to perform the following functions:

(i) to convene and to prepare the meetings of the Council and its subsidiary bodies and ad hoc working groups as referred to in Article XVII, and conferences as referred to in Articles XIX [omitted] and XX [omitted];

(ii) to transmit to the Contracting States notifications, reports and other information received in accordance with Articles IX and XXIII [omitted];

(iii) to consider enquiries by, and information from, the Contracting States and to consult with them on questions relating to the Convention and its protocols and annexes thereto;

(iv) to prepare reports on matters relating to the Convention and to the administration of the Organization;

(v) to establish, maintain and disseminate an up-to-date collection of national laws of all States concerned relevant to the protection of the marine environment;

(vi) to arrange, upon request, for the provision of technical assistance and advice for the drafting of appropriate national legislation for the effective implementation of the Convention and its protocols;

(vii) to arrange for training programmes in areas related to the implementation of the Convention and its protocols;

(viii) to carry out its assignments under the protocols to the Convention;

(ix) to perform such other functions as may be assigned to it by the Council for the implementation of the Convention and its protocols.

(b) The Executive Secretary shall be the chief administrative official of the Organization and shall perform the functions that are necessary for the administration of the present Convention, the work of the secretariat and other tasks entrusted to the Executive Secretary by the Council and as provided for in its rules of procedure and financial rules.

...

A/45/970, S/22327, 4 March 1991

2. Letter from the Permanent Representative of Saudi Arabia to the United Nations addressed to the Secretary-General, 4 March 1991

I have the honour to transmit to you the text of a letter from His Royal Highness Prince Saud Al-Faisal, the Foreign Minister, addressed to you.

...

As you are aware, the Iraqi régime has spilled more than 10 million barrels of crude oil into the waters of the Gulf, thus creating an environmental disaster that is considered the worst of its kind in history, and has waged an environmental war without regard for its neighbouring countries or for the lives of animals and plants in the region.

I do not need to mention to you that this oil pollution caused by the Iraqi régime is premeditated and intentional and is considered an irresponsible act of aggression against humans and natural resources with all the related living organisms and unique natural heritage; this, in addition to the great harm that befell many civilians who live on the coast of the Gulf, many of whom make their living from fishing or from the other resources of the sea.

This damage was reflected in particular in many human activities that are related to the waters of the Gulf, such as fisheries, desalination and other human activities, whose effect could extend to the next generation, as the Gulf is a shallow body of water and the rate of water renewal with the Indian Ocean is extremely slow because of the natural impediment presented by the Strait of Hormuz.

I would like to mention to you on this occasion some of the important natural resources that were actually exposed to danger as a result of the pollution that resulted from this environmental catastrophe and was caused by the Iraqi régime:

- Coral reefs;
- Sandy beaches;
- *Al-shora* plant (*manjaroof*);
- Seaweed;
- Lagoons;
- Tortoises and sea turtles;
- Sea and shore birds;
- The coastal environment;
- Fish and non-vertebrates.

Because the danger of crude oil leakage into the waters of the Gulf is continuing and its destructive effects have not become fully apparent, the Government of the Kingdom of Saudi Arabia will continue to monitor the environmental developments that will undoubtedly occur and keep you informed in this regard.

At the same time, I would like to communicate the Government of Saudi Arabia's willingness to receive technical assistance to face the expected dangers, whether from the Member States of the United Nations or from concerned specialized agencies.

...

Foreign and Commonwealth Office Briefing Note
(not an official document)

3. FCO Briefing Note: Oil Pollution in the Gulf, June 1991

Oil slicks and fires continue to pollute the atmosphere and waters of the Gulf - the result of sabotage, during the recent war, by Saddam Hussein's retreating armies. This was a deliberate crime against the planet, as the Iraqi President himself evidently recognised when, in an interview with Cable Network News transmitted on 28 January, he said that the Iraqi commanders had the right to use the oil weapon in self-defence. His threat was not entirely unexpected, since in October 1990 he had said that he would blow up Kuwaiti oil facilities if war broke out, that Iraqi engineers had attached explosives to one-third of Kuwait's 1,000 oil wells and that these would be detonated if the allied forces attacked.

Extent of the problem

Analysts now believe that predictions of ecological disaster on a global scale may have been exaggerated. The smoke cloud from burning oil wells is relatively low, with a ceiling of 3-4,500 metres - not high enough to affect stratospheric climate circulation, although some local convection may have caused unseasonal winds and rain. Nevertheless, the scale of the regional pollution from oil spillage (three times larger than that spilled during the Iran/Iraq war), and the smoke plumes and terrestrial damage from fired and leaking oil wells, is extremely serious. Its effects are most keenly felt in Kuwait and along the Saudi coastline.

Smoke from the burning oil wells was the subject of a study completed by the British Meteorological Office in March 1991 (a follow-up analysis is under way). Pollution haze, although often present, appears to be diminishing in intensity, helped by the prevailing winds, but under the plume it is dark and daytime surface temperatures can be reduced by as much as 10°-20°C. High sulphur levels in Kuwaiti crude make acid rain and photochemical smog particularly noxious (causing some respiratory problems in children, the sick and the elderly), comparable to the worst instances of industrial pollution. Soil contamination by heavy metals and other toxic materials has increased the acidity of soil and risks contaminating food and water.

Burning oil wells pose other problems. Of the approximately 650 said to be alight in March, about 150 which need pumping to bring oil to the surface will extinguish themselves when their fuel runs out. The rest must be capped before the fires are extinguished if oil is not to gush over the land, as has happened already. Large quantities of oil lying in lakes around the oilfields emit hydrogen sulphide into the air, and could begin to leak into the sea or to contaminate ground water. Such lakes are also dangerous because they impede access to the well heads and, in themselves a fire risk, mask the unexploded ordnance which still litters the desert.

Just how much oil was released into the waters of the Gulf is not known. It is thought to amount to around 300,000 tonnes. The oil is of two types: sheen and heavy oil. The latter, weathered to a thick emulsified mousse, very difficult to collect or remove, has formed against 460 Kms of Saudi coast from Khafji to Abu Ali Island, filling its sheltered bays and abutting on saltmarsh, mudflats and mangroves - important breeding and feeding grounds for wild-life. Perhaps as much as a third of the heavy oil, suspended beneath the surface of the water as tar balls and carried in plumes which bypass mechanical protections such as booms, could menace desalination plants before sinking to the sea floor or being washed ashore. The sheen covers thousands of square kilometres and is mixed with streamers and patches of oil mousse. It has struck some of the off-shore coral islands and the north-west coasts of Bahrain and Qatar. The areas of oil and sheen are moving slowly down the Gulf towards the Indian Ocean and further oiling in the lower reaches of the Gulf is likely. A slow discharge of oil from damaged installations and land drainage in the northern Gulf continues. With time, the oil should disintegrate and weather further; but in the Gulf, which is shallow, calm and semi-enclosed with little tidal action, this will take much longer than it would in deeper, rougher waters.

It is not yet known how great a threat is posed by oil pollution to the unique and fragile ecosystems of the Gulf. The coral reefs, sea grass, mangrove swamps and algal mudflats of the Gulf support a large population of mammals, birds, crustacea and fish, some of which, like the dugongs and turtles, are very rare. Worst affected are some 20,000 mainly off-shore sea birds, especially socotra and great cormorants, great crested and black-necked grebes. Many have died, and several hundred are being treated at a time in the Jubail Rescue Centre, Saudi Arabia. Numerous early spring migrants and passage migrants have also fallen victim to the oil. The local fishing industry is at risk, and shrimp farms have had to close along the Saudi coast.

A senior Saudi conservationist, Professor Abdul Aziz Abuzinada, has said that booms similar to those used to protect his country's desalination plants are helping to prevent oil from reaching some of the more important wildlife sites, such as the small islands where migrating birds and turtles breed. In conjunction with this work, the World Conservation Monitoring Centre (WCMC), Cambridge, England, has produced from the Centre's database, and from the regular reports reaching it, an assessment of the implications of the oil spillage for the Gulf's ecosystem. Its assessment concludes that recovery in the Gulf is ultimately possible and that the pollution damage is likely to be less serious than was at first predicted.

International response

In its initial response to requests for help from Saudi Arabia and other Gulf States, the international community acted quickly to minimise and contain the damage. An immediate need was to preserve desalination plants in the Gulf, which supply not only drinking water but also the water used as a coolant in the power supply and oil industries.

Some equipment was already held locally by oil companies and by the States whose coastlines are affected and who are directing clean-up operations. In Saudi Arabia, a United States Coastguard team helped the Saudi Meteorological and Environment Protection Agency (MEPA) to collect and remove oil, as did members of the British Department of Transport's Marine Pollution Control Unit. The London-based International Maritime Organisation (IMO) was asked by Saudi Arabia to co-ordinate offers of help. A fund was then set up to provide equipment and expertise to which Britain made the first and largest contribution - £1 million.

Part of Britain's contribution to the IMO fund was used to finance the clean-up of Karan Island, much of whose coastline was covered in thick oil. The island is the most important breeding site in the Gulf for green turtles, which come ashore in May to lay their eggs, and is also an important bird site. The Saudi Government gives this project a high priority. Other priorities for the fund include stopping the flow of oil from Kuwait and protecting the few remaining undamaged areas of saltmarsh.

In determining the effect of the oil spills on the environment and the means of promoting recovery in the long term, the UN Environmental Programme (UNEP) is taking the lead in co-ordinating the scientific expertise from different countries. The UNEP team is headed by Dr Michael Gwynne, British head of UNEP's Global Environment Monitoring System. UNEP has received contributions towards an inter-agency plan costing an estimated $3.2 million. The plan was first proposed on 9-16 March at an informal meeting in Nairobi to survey, assess and propose remedial action for the full range of environmental damage in the Gulf. Several States are offering help in kind through seconded experts and services, while the Japanese Government has contributed $1.25 million. The European Commission is also providing experts to advise on remedial action in the short term, and the industrialised countries of the Organisation for Economic Cooperation and Development (OECD) have pledged resources to help combat the disaster: the US has sent representatives of its Environmental Protection Agency; the Germans an oil pollution vessel, and the Norwegians a commercial oil-skimming vessel to recover oil at sea.

On 10 April, the European Commission announced a comprehensive aid package for the Gulf of $12 million, to be funded from the demonstration/research programme of the Commission's Energy Directorate. It intends to produce further research on the oil plume, give medical aid, fund a coastal nature reserve and contribute to oil slick cleaning.

Meanwhile, the British Government has provided expert advice from the Marine Pollution Control Unit (DTp) of the Department of Trade and transported 90 tonnes of specialist equipment, including booms and skimmers, which were flown to the Gulf region by Ministry of Defence aircraft at the end of January. The Natural Environment Research Council's (NERC) Proudman Oceanographic Laboratory adapted existing computer models to predict the behaviour of the oil slicks, and the Plymouth Marine Laboratory, also part of NERC, prepared an urgent assessment of the biological effects of the oil slicks. The results of both investigations were forwarded to the Gulf States, as was that of a Meteorological Office Research Flight C130 aircraft, sent to the Gulf to measure and analyse smoke plumes from the burning oil wells.

As part of Britain's efforts to make fire fighting and other assistance available to Kuwait, Ministers have made several visits to the Gulf. Mr Michael Heseltine, Secretary of State for the Environment, flew there to see for himself the environmental impact of the war and to make Gulf States aware of Britain's considerable scientific expertise in dealing with the environmental problems they currently face. Mr Tony Baldry (Environment) presented to the Bahraini Government a consignment of oil pollution equipment on 9 March. Mr Peter Lilley (Trade and Industry) went with a team of industrialists from 9-10 April to advise on fire-fighting, and Mr John Wakeham (Energy) led a delegation to Kuwait from 26-29 April. Mr Wakeham said on 24 April that "Saddam Hussein's callous destruction of much of Kuwait's oil-producing capacity highlighted not only the dependence of the industrial and developing world on a secure supply of oil and gas; but also the terrible impact the production - and in this case destruction - of energy can have on the environment".

4. United Nations Environment Programme, Report on the UN Inter-Agency Plan of Action for the ROPME region, 12 October 1991

1. INTRODUCTION

1.1. *Background*

The Second Special Session of the Governing Council of the United Nations Environment Programme (Nairobi, 1-3 August 1990) by its Decision SS 11/8 on the situation in the Middle East expressed its concern over the destruction of the environment and disruption of social and economic structures, resulting from the armed conflict over Kuwait. Pursuant to the above Decision, and with the breaking out of the hostilities in the region, the United Nations Environment Programme took the initiative to intensify co-operation within the UN system to optimize the diverse capabilities of the system to respond rapidly to the resulting environmental crisis and to the urgent requests from all Member States, both those who are or could become victims and those who wished to provide assistance.

To set this process in motion, UNEP immediately got in touch with all parties concerned as well as with other UN agencies, especially in the first instance with the International Maritime Organization (IMO), which had already initiated actions to assist the governments of the region in their response to the then reported massive release of oil into the marine environment of the Sea Area of ROPME, the Regional Organization for the Protection of the Marine Environment.

UNEP, cognizant of the immediate and long-term environmental threats to an ecologically fragile region that supports some ten million people, called for a concerted UN Inter-agency effort commensurate with the nature and magnitude of the crisis. To this effect, UNEP convened the first UN Inter-agency Consultation on the environmental consequences of the war in the ROPME region (Geneva, 5-6 February 1991). [UN Agencies and other bodies present at or invited to the Geneva UN Inter-agency Consultants were: WHO, WMO, FAO, IAEA, IMO, IOC/UNESCO, UNCED, UNDP, UNDRO, UNRWA, UNIDO, UNCHS, UNEP, IUCN, WWF, ROPME, GAOCMAO and IPIECA.] At the consultation, the need was recognized for a comprehensive and co-ordinated approach to deal with the potential local and regional environmental and socio-economic consequences of the war, affecting the marine, coastal and terrestrial environments, as well as the atmosphere and human health.

Considering the enclosed nature and the size of the ROPME Sea Area, and the vulnerability of the war-impacted environment, the questions asked by decision makers are as follows:

- What happens to the spilled oil and the smoke emitted from the burning oil wells and where do they go?

- What are the environmental and public health effects of the different polluting compounds, break-down products on the marine and terrestrial environment and their resources?

- What are the potential short- and long-term risks for the environmental damage caused by the recent pollution in the ROPME region, and outside the region?

- What control measures should be taken to minimize the adverse effects?

The above questions provided the main guidelines and framework for the international and regional communities in their response to the present environmental crisis.

1.2. *The UN Inter-agency Plan of Action*

Pursuant to the above UNEP initiatives, and to address the questions and concerns expressed above, a framework of action was developed by UNEP and presented to the ROPME meeting of technical experts on oil spill (Bahrain, 26-27 February). The meeting recommended that the UNEP framework, together with ROPME's proposal for joint action to combat the oil spill in the region, be the basis for a long-term plan of action for the mitigation of the adverse effects [*sic*] and rehabilitation of the environment in the ROPME region.

Subsequently, a UN Inter-agency Plan of Action was further developed by UNEP in co-operation with ROPME and a number of UN specialized agencies, and was adopted at the second UN Inter-agency Consultation (Geneva, 15 March 1991).

The Plan of Action consists of three distinct phases: the survey phase, the assessment phase and the plan design phase. Its focus is on four separate but interlinked areas: the marine and coastal environment, the atmosphere, inland terrestrial areas, and hazardous waste management … .

1.3 *Objectives of the Plan of Action*

The overall objectives of the UN Inter-agency Plan of Action for the ROPME region are as follows:

- to assess the environmental consequences of the war in the region, and

- to propose a programme for the mitigation of the adverse effects, rehabilitation and protection of the environment affected by the conflict.

The specific objectives of the first phase of the Plan of Action included:

- to conduct a multi-disciplinary initial survey and a preliminary assessment of the marine and coastal environment, the atmospheric environment, the inland terrestrial environment and the hazardous waste management in the war-impacted areas;

- to identify priority areas at risk and resources threatened in these areas;

- to formulate a proposal for the mitigation of the adverse effects, rehabilitation and protection of the environment in the area, to be submitted to the governments of the region through ROPME for the necessary follow-up;

- to develop, establish and operate a Computerized Data System (CDS) for storage/retrieval and processing of all data and information gathered through the Plan of Action, and

- to provide relevant training to ROPME experts on CDS operations and data management.

This will be followed by the implementation of the mitigation and rehabilitation measures during the second phase of the Plan of Action.

The present report summarizes the results obtained so far through the UN Inter-agency effort under the Plan of Action.

2. INITIAL SURVEYS

In the framework of the above Plan of Action, and under the overall co-ordination of UNEP and its Core Group stationed at ROPME Secretariat in Kuwait, initial surveys were carried out. The surveys covered the four areas of the Plan of Action. The survey activities dealt with a wide range of environmental aspects related to the aforementioned areas. Each of the co-operating agencies was responsible for the implementation of the component(s) of the Plan of Action relevant to its specific mandate … . However, all agencies have been working in concert in order to ensure the maximum coherence of results and recommendations. …

Activities supporting the Plan of Action, namely, satellite observations, remote-sensing flights and the establishment of the CDS were undertaken to complement the survey work carried out by the co-operating agencies. … .

It should be noted that the activities conducted during this phase were, due to certain constraints, necessarily limited to a few countries of the ROPME region, mostly Kuwait and Saudi Arabia. Activities are planned to be extended in the next phase, and recommendations to this effect are contained in the present report.

3. PRELIMINARY ASSESSMENT OF THE POST-WAR STATE OF THE ENVIRONMENT

3.1 *Identification of war-related pollutants*

Major sources of pollution

Impacts on the marine, atmospheric and terrestrial environments of the war-affected areas have originated from two principal sources: (1) spilled oil from well heads, platforms and tankers, and (2) smoke and other emissions from the damaged oil fields in Kuwait. In both cases the original pollutant is crude oil which is a complex mixture of compounds having different physical and chemical behaviours and biological effects.

Other significant pollutant inputs are chemicals and wastes from industry and other sources.

Main types of hazardous compounds/materials

i. Petroleum compounds:

Identification of the hazard depends on the chemical structure of the polluting compounds in the oil, which can be roughly extrapolated from the average chemical composition of the crude oil. The most hazardous components of the Kuwaiti crude oil are the Polycyclic Aromatic Hydrocarbons (PAHs) and some of the heteromolecules (e.g. thiophenes) which are present in relatively high concentration in this oil. In addition, heavy metals present in the crude oil also pose dangers to the environment under present circumstances.

ii. Compounds emitted from the burning oil wells:

Although the "fuel" of the burning oil wells is the same oil that spilled into the marine environment, it poses different environmental problems when burned. The composition of the smoke depends on the completeness of the burning, which controls the oxidation process and the alteration in the components of the crude oil. Accordingly, this can result in the presence of:

(a) completely oxidized gaseous end products (e.g., CO_2, SO_2, NOx, H_20, etc.),
(b) ashes containing heavy metals (Ni, V, Pb, etc.),
(c) soot,
(d) high-boiling, unburnt components,
(e) conversion products (e.g., pyrolytic, breakdown components),
(f) unchanged oil droplets, and
(g) dissolved salts after evaporation of the water from the subsurface water coming up together with the petroleum from the wells.

Transformation of the smoke components during their transport in the atmosphere, by chemical (photochemical) reactions may result in surface-active and toxic breakdown products (more toxic than the parent compounds). These compounds will influence the pathways of other pollutants (e.g. PAHs), present in the smoke particles, after deposition in the marine and terrestrial areas.

iii. Other hazardous compounds/materials:

In addition to the spilled oil and burning oil wells there are other sources which may emit hazardous compounds/materials into the environment or may danger human health. Such compounds/materials are:

- different kinds of industrial hazardous wastes, originating from war-damaged industries, hazardous waste disposal sites, commercial and residential facilities, etc.;
- pathological (hospital) wastes;
- uncontrolled incineration of municipal solid wastes which usually contains plastics and emits toxic chemicals, e.g., dioxins, etc.;
- chemical weapons, unexploded ordnance.

3.2. *Quantification of Hazardous Compounds in the Environment*

A. *Marine and Coastal Environment*

Pollution sources

i. Spilled oil:

There have been conflicting reports on the amount of oil spilled into the sea at Kuwait's Sea Island terminal and from other sources, as well as on the size of the spill and its movement.

The oil spill originated from different sources including: (a) oil loading terminals, Mina Al-Bakr (29°41'N, 48°48'E) and Mina Al-Ahmadi Sea Island (29°06'N, 48°18'E) which were battle-damaged, and (b) four sunken and leaking vessels: AMURIYA, Iraqi tankers, 155, 211 tonnes capacity, at East of Al-Bakr; AL FAO, AMPTC, 89, 180 tonnes capacity, at SE of Ash Shuaibah (29°03'N, 48°10'E); AIN Zalah, Iraqi tankers, 35,388 tonnes capacity, at Khawr Abdallah (29°59'N, 48°11'E); and an unknown tanker, about 40,000 tonnes capacity at Khawr Abdallah. The total capacity of the tankers was about 320,000 tonnes, or 2 million barrels. According to estimates, the amount of oil spilled from the terminals was approximately 4 million barrels. The total amount of the spilled oil is estimated to be 6 million barrels, based on loss from Kuwait sources. However, based on amounts recovered in Saudi Arabia from all possible sources in the northern ROPME region, the total amount of oil spilled is estimated between 6 - 8 million barrels.

[N.B. The yearly oil pollution input into the northern part of the ROPME Sea Area from oil production, transportation, etc., is about 2 million barrels and about the same amount was spilled during 8-10 months at the Nowruz oil field in 1983 as a result of the Iraq-Iran conflict. ... .]

ii. Airborne pollution:

In addition to the oil spilled into the marine environment, an unknown portion of the smoke generated from the burning of some 2 million barrels of crude oil daily, on average until capping the last burning wells, i.e., over 300-400 day period, is being deposited in the marine areas within and possibly outside the ROPME Sea Area.

Although the major part of the organic compounds in the crude oil is burnt and converted into gaseous oxidation products causing acid rain, the absolute amount of the heavy metals present in the petroleum is unchanged, and the most hazardous, high-boiling, aromatic compounds are enriched in the unburnt part of the crude oil, or produced by pyrolytic processes.

The quantification of the airborne input in the marine environment is difficult because the same polluting compounds originate also from other sources, such as natural seepage, frequent small spills in the area, etc., and have been accumulated in the marine ecosystem. An attempt to estimate the amount of this input can be done by collecting atmospheric particle fall-out in traps along the coastlines and on offshore islands, as recommended in the WMO's monitoring programme, or by conducting surface microlayer samplings from the sea water as initiated by IOC and IAEA.

Because airborne marine pollution will continue until the last burning oil well has been capped, a mass-balance calculation for estimating the total input could be performed on the basis of mathematical models for the atmospheric transport as well as on the measurement of the deposition in the terrestrial areas.

iii. Others:

- run-off, particularly in Shatt-al-Arab area.
- Hazardous materials from damaged industrial and disposal sites.

Pollution levels

The marine area and coastal zone of Kuwait have been restricted due to the heavy mining and the presence of unexploded ordnance. Therefore, sample collection from the water and sediment was impossible. Despite these restrictions, two groups of UN experts (IAEA/MEL and IUCN) were able to carry out surveys and limited sample collection on three offshore coral reef islands (Kubbar, Qaru and Umm Al-Maradem), approached by helicopter.

Quantities of fresh tar on Qaru island, in mid June, averaged 378 g per meter beach, but determining whether this oil originated from the conflict may prove difficult since Qaru is situated in an area of natural oil seepages ... . The one sediment and one fish sample collected in Kuwait showed higher concentration of hydrocarbons than those from Bahrain, the difference did not appear to be significant. If concentrations from Bahrain are considered during recent years then concentrations in post-war samples are less, which might result in part from the decreased traffic in marine exportation of oil products. Results of the analysis for heavy metals in the sediment and biota samples, for the elements for which comparison can be made, shows that the levels found are similar to those measures in previous surveys. Lead and vanadium levels in the single catfish sample from Kuwait also did not suggest any major input of oil-related contaminants.

A number of fish samples were analyzed by EPC Bahrain to assess the level of aliphatic and aromatic hydrocarbons. The results obtained for aliphatic hydrocarbons (F1) ranged from non-detectable to 49.06 ug/g dry weight. The higher levels were found in shark samples. The aromatic hydrocarbons' concentrations ranged from 0.35 to 3.7 ug/g dry weight.

Other countries such as Qatar, U.A.E., Oman and I.R. Iran are presently collecting and analyzing similar samples.

The survey of the three coral reef islands revealed that the reefs are perfectly healthy and there was nothing to indicate any general or specific ecological problem ... . There were no signs of oil pollution, nor macro algal cover. Indeed all the reefs were perhaps healthier in appearance than ever seen before. The fish populations appeared to be completely normal. From the limited evidence provided by studies on turns, whose breeding success depends on the richness of the surrounding waters, there is also no indication of a serious disruption in the food chain. The water temperatures appeared to be somewhat lower for the time of year. A survey in the late spring of 1992 will reveal whether the reef has survived the 1991/1992 winter.

During the August 1991 IUCN/IAEA/IOC/JICA/WWF mission to Saudi Arabia, samples of the sea surface microlayer and subsurface sea water were taken at three sites in the northern region. It is noteworthy that at the most northern site near Khafji which is subject to smoke from the Kuwaiti oil fires, levels of petroleum hydrocarbons quantified as the ROPME oil standard were as high as 18,000 $\mu g/l$ in the surface microlayer. These hydrocarbons were present as crude oil and the concentrations were one to two orders of magnitude higher than levels in the underlying seawater at that site. Further south at Tanajib and Manifa Bay, hydrocarbon concentrations in the surface microlayers were considerably lower ranging from 150-230 $\mu g/l$.

In addition to the surveys by UN experts, environmental scientists from the Kuwait Institute for Scientific Research (KISR) started with an oil pollution assessment in fishes and shrimp in Kuwait ... . 21 biota tissue samples, six fish species and one shrimp, all of them in triplicates, were collected from Kuwaiti marine waters and analyzed for heavy metals (nickel, vanadium, lead, cadmium and mercury), aliphatic hydrocarbons and PAHs. The concentrations of the heavy metals were similar to those obtained in previous studies, and were within the range of the world averages for unpolluted samples. In some samples low concentrations of aliphatic hydrocarbons were detected together with PAHs. Benzo(a)pyrene were identified in five samples within the range of 6 and 120 ng/g wet. In the other samples, the concentration was below detection limit, i.e., 2 ng/g. Present and future monitoring will need to gauge measured levels against food quality standards (e.g. 500 ng/g wet for benzo(a)pyrene).

Over 90 samples of fish and shrimp from Saudi Arabia were analyzed for several heavy metals, including nickel, vanadium, lead, cadmium and mercury. The results are still being interpreted by the Research Institute of King Fahd University of Petroleum and Minerals (KFUPM) ... . 23 fish tissue samples were analyzed for aliphatic and aromatic hydrocarbons, but in none of the samples were PAHs detected. In addition, the aliphatic hydrocarbon content was generally low.

Nevertheless, the existing data are sparse and far more measurements are needed before any conclusion can be made regarding current concentration trends on a regional basis. Furthermore, these sorts of measurements need to be carefully controlled for quality and comparability.

B. *Atmospheric Environment*

Pollution Sources

A recent report by the Kuwait Oil Company (KOC) places the original number of burning oil wells in Kuwait (including the Wafra area) at 613, with an additional 76 wells initially gushing oil but not on fire. The amount of oil originally being released has been estimated by KOC at 4 to 8 million barrels per day. Most of the burning wells, 449, were in the Greater Burgan field (Magwa, Ahmadi, and Burgan), located to the south of Kuwait City. Fifty-nine burning wells were located in the Minagish, Umm Gudair, and Wafra fields south of the Burgan area, and an additional 105 burning wells were located in the Raudhatain, Sabriyah, Bahra, and Ratya oil fields north of Kuwait City ... .

By 29 September 1991, 515 of the wells had been capped including all wells in the Ahmadi and Magwa fields bordering Kuwait City on the south.

Pollution Levels

Monitoring of the atmospheric pollution caused by the oil well fires in Kuwait was organized within the ROPME region under the co-ordination of WMO and WHO, and in collaboration with several institutes and organizations from different countries worldwide. It was carried out as a support to the national programmes conducted by governmental organizations in the countries affected, in particular the Environmental Protection Department (EPD) of the Ministry of Public Health in Kuwait, the Meteorology and Environmental Protection Administration (MEPA) and KFUPM in Saudi Arabia and the respective national meteorological services. This effort has involved: re-establishing the operational World Weather Watch observing system and telecommunications; implementing supplementary meteorological observations within Kuwait; real time production and distribution of forecasts of the behaviour of the plume over the ROPME region, and; a large variety of systematic surface and airborne air pollution measurements.

i. Characterization of source emissions

WMO recognized the need to obtain aircraft measurements close to the fires to characterize fully the chemical nature of the source. As part of the overall aircraft surveillance programme outlined during a special meeting held in Geneva, 27-30 April 1991, several missions were designed to obtain data of immediate importance to modelling and other assessment efforts being undertaken at several institutions throughout the world.

In June 1991, a University of Washington Convair flew through several individual plumes to characterize emissions from several wells of differing appearance. In early August 1991, investigators from the US, Saudi Arabia, and Kuwait flew through several plumes, as close to the flames as was possible, aboard a helicopter provided by the Royal Saudi Arabian Air Force.

Measurements taken aboard these aircrafts have indicated that the combustion process is relatively efficient. Ninety-five percent of the carbon emitted by the fires is in the form of carbon dioxide. University of Washington measurements of the plume in June 1991 suggest that about 1 to 2 million metric tons of carbon dioxide were being formed by the plume each day. The remaining carbon emissions were in the form of non-methane organic vapors (2.4%), carbon monoxide (1%), organic particles (0.65%), and soot (0.45%).

About 2% of the mass of the fuel burned is emitted as sulfur (mainly in the form of sulfur dioxide). Aircraft measurements indicated, however, that sulfur dioxide is rapidly lost in the plume (about 50% per hour for the first few hours of plume travel). Very little hydrogen sulfide was observed.

Oxides of nitrogen were similarly lost from the plume at a very rapid rate (up to 60% reduction in the first three or four hours of plume travel).

The smoke particles in the composite plumes are composed mainly of salt, soot, sulfate, and heavy hydrocarbons, in roughly equal amounts. The white plumes are composed largely of salt which probably originate from oil field brines expelled from the wells. Water vapor, if any, in the white plumes was below the detection limits of the aircraft instruments. The black plumes have a higher fraction of soot with a highly variable amount of salt.

ii. Aerial measurements downwind of Kuwait

To further characterize the plume at distances of up to 1,000 km from Kuwait, additional flights were undertaken by the University of Washington (U.S.A.), National Center for Atmospheric Research (NCAR), U.S.A., British Meteorological Service, U.K., Goeth University, Germany, and the US Department of Energy ... . These flights provided additional information for modelling efforts and indicated maximum values for various pollutants that might conceivably be experienced on the ground during adverse meteorological conditions.

The following typical values were reported for various chemical constituents observed at about 100 km downwind:

Sulfur dioxide (SO_2) 100 to 500 ppb
Carbon Monoxide (CO) 0.1 to 0.5 ppm
Ozone 20 to 45 ppb
Oxides of Nitrogen (NOx) 10 to 30 ppb
Carbon dioxide (CO_2) 400 to 460 ppm

Particulates were measured at values of 100,000 per cubic centimeter near the Kuwait border (University of Washington) and at 31,000 per cubic centimeter 100 downwind (British Meteorological Office).

The smoke was never detected above six kilometers and was generally below this level. The University of Washington aircraft detected smoke as far south as Sharjah, UAE, and the NCAR aircraft detected smoke over Oman, although at very low concentrations (several parts per billion sulfur dioxide, a few parts per million of excess carbon dioxide, and slightly above minimum detection limits of nitrogen dioxide). The US Department of Energy found similarly low levels of sulfur dioxide over Saudi Arabia's Empty Quarter in July 1991.

iii. Ground level measurements

Ground level measurements of air pollution from the Kuwait oil fires have been undertaken by many agencies and institutions throughout the ROPME Sea Area. Under the leadership of WHO and WMO, participation on the part of several national organizations outside the ROPME region has been effectively woven into the overall regional network of air monitoring capabilities.

While measurements of a variety of plume constituents have been undertaken, the following discussion is limited to those thought to pose the greatest risk.

Sulfur dioxide:

Initial measurements by the US Interagency Air Assessment Team in March 1991 found instantaneous values for sulfur dioxide as high as 0.68 ppm near the burning wells. Limited sampling in populated areas in the path of the oil plumes did not reveal concentrations of concern.

Measurements undertaken by France (AIRPARIF) from 27 March to 5 April 1991 reflected sulfur dioxide levels which were generally within accepted limits, except during adverse meteorological conditions when very high levels were observed (1.13 ppm). These levels were observed close to the oil fields.

Measurements made by the Japanese scientists at nine residential locations in Kuwait from 28 April to 5 May 1991 showed maximum concentrations of sulfur dioxide of 20 to 30 ppb.

Results obtained by Norway beginning in mid-May 1991 showed sulfur dioxide values of 14 ppb near the northern border of Kuwait and Iraq. A Saudi Arabian mobile van located near the Kuwait City airport measured hourly values of sulfur dioxide of 200 to 300 ppb on infrequent occasions throughout April, May, and June 1991.

The Kuwait Environmental Protection Department (EPD) has been continuously monitoring SO_2 at two sites in Kuwait City since early April 1991. Average levels of SO_2 during the April through July period was 1.8 ppb, slightly above average values for the preceding year. Peak 5 min value of 5.2 ppb occurred in April at Mansoria. The levels are much lower than those suggested for the Health Alert System. Higher levels were found at Al-Zoor to the south of Kuwait and in the town of Ahmadi during April before the fires were controlled.

Measurements by MEPA, KFUPM, and Saudi Aramco at several locations throughout Saudi Arabia have shown sulfur dioxide to be within acceptable limits. Similar results have been obtained in Bahrain.

Particulates:

Measurements of particulates have been especially difficult to interpret because of variable levels of sand mixed with smoke particles. Meteorological records and observations of the colour of various samples may ultimately lead to some subjective method of distinguishing the source of pollution.

The US Interagency Air Assessment Team measured levels of particulates between 200-300 $\mu g/m^3$ in populated areas of Kuwait and Saudi Arabia.

The Japanese measured total suspended particulates at maximum levels of 1014 $\mu g/m^3$ at nine locations in Kuwait at the end of April and early May 1991. Elemental carbon was measured to values of 445 $\mu g/m^3$ … .

Norway measured values approaching 300 $\mu g/m^3$ of soot along the northern border of Kuwait during May and June 1991 when winds were blowing from the south and southeast.

Monitoring for particulates in Kuwait has been undertaken since May 1991, Portable PM10 monitors have been used to collect daily samples from 5 sites covering the area in the vicinity of the Burgan oil field and Kuwait City. The overall mean in the period 1 May to 10 July was 287 $\mu g/m^3$ air. Higher levels were seen in Fahaheel (310 $\mu g/m^3$) and Ahmadi (338 $\mu g/m^3$). Much lower levels were found in the City of Kuwait (280 $\mu g/m^3$). Correlation between the daily values reported at the five sites was quite high. Higher levels were seen on certain days with a peak of 2009 $\mu g/m^3$ on 22 May 1991. The level was also high on 17 May 1991 (1329.7 $\mu g/m^3$) when full blown sand storms were reported.

Higher levels were observed in Kuwait at the sites to the south on the days when the wind was blowing from the direction of the Burgan field. The effect of the wind speed seems to be more critical. With calm winds, higher mean values (299 $\mu g/m^3$) were reported. A steep drop was seen with stronger winds; however, marked increase was reported by wind 5 m/s or more (367 $\mu g/m^3$) which are the days in which sand storms and rising sand were reported. More black filters were seen with calm winds denoting higher levels of soot. With strong winds, the colour of the filters was [*sic*] brown during sand storms.

France (AIRPARIF) recorded a "black smoke" level of 2030 $\mu g/m^3$ near Kuwait City during the period 27 March to 5 April 1991. During the period 28 April to 7 May 1991, the Harvard School of Public Health observed PM10 concentrations of between 50 and 800 $\mu g/m^3$ in residential areas near Kuwait City. Many of the samples were highly ensubed [*sic*] in carbon.

KFUPM in Saudi Arabia has measured total suspended particulates exceeding 350 $\mu g/m^3$ on a few occasions. High concentrations of particulates (PM10 levels above 1500 $\mu g/m^3$) were seen in Dhahran, Abquaik and Rahima in May 1991, especially on smoky days.

Polycyclic Aromatic Hydrocarbons (PAHs)

The US Interagency Air Assessment Team concluded that most of the PAHs in the air particulate samples in Kuwait and Saudi Arabia were below detectable levels, i.e., below 2.0-4.6 ppb. Out of 14 samples napthalene was quantified in four samples in the range of 0.09-0.31 ppb, 1-methylnaphthalene and 2-methylnaphthalene in one sample, 0.04 and 0.06 ppb, respectively. VOCs such as benzene, toluene, and aliphatic hydrocarbons were detected at 10-20 ppb level in the smoke plumes … .

The Research Institute at King Fahd University of Petroleum and Minerals (KFUPM), and the Meteorology and Environmental Protection Administration (MEPA) in Saudi Arabia detected up to 16 different PAHs in air particulate samples on three different days in March 1991. Low levels of PAHs have been reported without providing the actual concentration values … .

The French air pollution experts carried out air pollution monitoring with their mobile laboratory and collected air particulate samples from eight locations in Kuwait. The very high level of black smoke was associated with the highest concentration of PAHs at the Magwa oilfield. Fluoranthene (110 ng/m^3), benzo(c)pyrene (26 ng/m^3), benzo(a)pyrene (30 ng/m^3), benzo(ghi)perylene (26 ng/m^3) and indenopyrene (41 ng/m^3) were detected. Quantitative results are available for fluoranthene and indenopyrene in some other samples, but in the majority of the samples, PAHs were present below the detectable concentration … .

The Norwegian air pollution measurements in the northern part of Kuwait showed total PAH concentrations of between 207 and 412 ng/m^3. Naphthalene alone counted for 45-60 percent of the PAHs. Other PAHs included: phenanthrene 22-40 ng/m^3, fluorene 7-34 ng/m^3, fluoranthene 6-17 ng/m^3, pyrene 6-16 ng/m^3, benzo(a)pyrene 0.3-1.0 ng/m^3. It was concluded that the average total PAH concentration of 296 + 87 ng/m^3 is rather low, and much lower than the concentrations measured in some of the industrialized areas or in streets with high traffic … .

A Japanese team took air quality measurements at nine sites in Kuwait City including analysis of benzo(a)pyrene. The maximum concentration of the benzo(a)pyrene was 25.5 ng/m^3 and the mean of the nine samples was 9.2 ng/m^3 … .

C. *Terrestrial Environment*

Pollution Sources

It is evident that one of the major sources of pollution in the terrestrial environment is related to the burning and gushing oil wells in Kuwait. Information on the contaminant types and levels in the short-term can be obtained from surface soil analysis as well as from predictions from the atmospheric pollution.

In addition to the airborne pollution, which is a portion of the atmospheric deposition on the land surface (the other portion is being deposited on the marine areas), there are other sources of pollution in the terrestrial environment such as:

- oil spillage from the trenches in Kuwait, prepared for military purposes by the Iraqi army,

- damaged, burning oil wells spilling oil while on fire and during the firefighting activities creating stagnant oil pools in the vicinity of the oil wells,

- different kinds of hazardous wastes from damaged disposals e.g., damage of the drums containing used catalysts, and from damaged industries,

- solid wastes disposed from the municipal waste collection, including hospital wastes.

Pollutant levels in soils

Monitoring of surface soil layers in inland areas should be an important part of monitoring the airborne particle deposits. Preliminary results of analysis carried out by IAEA/MEL and VITUKI, Hungary of soil samples collected around oil wells on fire and areas impacted by the plume ... have shown that:

- lead isotopic ratios plotted against each other show that sample taken next to burning wells has a pattern similar to the ROPME Standard Oil (Kuwait crude oil) and the ratios are changing with distance. At present, the lead isotope ratios for the other samples are not available, therefore, no further conclusions could be drawn at this stage;

- regarding the "oil" characteristics of the soil samples the results indicate substantial contamination, and the concentrations recorded for the samples reflect their proximity and exposure to emissions from the burning wells. The surface of the desert soil contained about 1 cm thick oily layer, mainly crude oil at the Sampling site 11. A similarly thick, viscous layer was observed at Sampling sites 16, 17, 18, 22 and 23. It is noticeable, however, that the relative concentration of the PAHs were higher in the samples collected from Sampling sites 22 and 23 than that at 16, 17 and 18 which showed a similarity to the crude oil. The ratio between 4-6-ring aromatics (more carcinogenic) to the 1-3-ring aromatics (less carcinogenic), based on fluorescence spectra, were similar to the crude oil near the burning wells and significantly increased with distance;

- GC-MSD analysis revealed the presence of individual PAHs, particularly benzo(a)pyrene which showed correlation with the 4-6-ring aromatic content.

- levels of extractable organic matter (EOM) in the soil originating from burning wells were highly variable depending mainly on the proximity to the source and the prevailing wind direction. Levels from 1 to 7 ppm (dry wt) as chrysene equivalent in soils, and from 0.1 to 350 ppm (dry wt) as chrysene equivalent in the plant tissue were reported by the Environmental Protection Department (EPD) of Kuwait.

Some data on nickel and vanadium concentrations in the desert sand, surface and deeper layers, in Saudi Arabia were reported by KFUPM and MEPA ... . Their preliminary conclusion indicated decreasing concentration with increasing distance from the Kuwaiti border (the burning wells).

Effects of oil deposits on agriculture and surface water need to be studied.

D. *Hazardous wastes situation*

Before the invasion, the Kuwait Environmental Protection Department (EPD) did have a system for tracking chemicals imported into Kuwait. The disposal possibilities were: open-pit incineration, land disposal and storage. Records were kept on a dBase IV database. In practice, industries brought their waste, including liquids, sludge, etc. to the municipal dump without any restrictions or controls, although the Environmental Protection Department did have plans for an industrial wastewater treatment plant.

The present problem of the EPD includes identification and disposal of unknown chemicals left behind at abandoned or damaged industrial facilities. Furthermore, with the exception of an on-site dump at the Shuaiba complex, which has become an uncontrolled dump in the aftermath of hostilities, there are no special facilities in Kuwait to handle industrial wastes.

The following are some special observations on hazardous wastes in Kuwait as observed by a UNIDO mission:

- In the Shuaiba Industrial Area, the damage to the major industries, refineries and petrochemical industries is not significant. Units containing hazardous chemicals such as catalysts, acids, etc. are intact. The hazardous chemicals were properly stored and/or consumed by emergency operations during the invasion. Nevertheless, some oily materials were released from the broken pipes or tanks and through the industrial wastewater drainage systems into the inshore shallow sea water, but significant pollution was not observed.

- In contrast, however, the damage to the small- and medium-sized industries located in the Shuaiba Central and the Western Mina Abdullah Area are more significant. Several industries were looted and set alight, causing the release of potentially hazardous substances. Raw and auxiliary materials, and various chemicals could have been mishandled, poured from their containers and spread on the ground and yard. The liquid chemicals and solids dissolved or transported by liquids can penetrate into the soil contaminating it and/or the groundwater, and could possibly flow into the area drainage systems (industrial or municipal), thereby contaminating the inshore shallow sea water.

- It is also occurring that solid hazardous chemicals remaining on the surface are being collected and disposed of [*sic*] into pits intended for general waste landfill or into the desert, as their potentially dangerous qualities are unknown. This is important because the inadequate handling of such materials at this stage can cause latent pollution which will be realized as a multiplied contamination at a later time.

- Exact quantification and qualification of hazardous materials was not determined at this time and must await comprehensive investigation of each industry and plant. It is estimated that this is most urgent at the Shuaiba, Sabhan and Shuwaikh industrial areas of Kuwait.

As far as hydrocarbon pollution is concerned, the following types were identified in the oil fields:

- Large and small pools and spills of crude oil in various sites (in some cases 4-8 acres) accumulated around damaged oil wells.

- Contaminated bottom layers of the oil spills and pools. After pumping off the bulk of the oil, oily sludge and an oil contaminated soil layer remains in the area, to a depth of not more than 10-15 cm.

- The desert area is contaminated by airborne sooty ash and hydrocarbon droplets forming a sticky, continuous layer, less than 1 cm thick, which covers not only the soil but the desert plants as well.

3.3 *Fate of pollutants in the environment*

A. *Fate and transport of waterborne pollutants*

Processing of NOAA AVHRR Satellite images acquired between 15 January and 21 February 1991, provided information on the extent and movement of the major oil slick in the ROPME Sea Area (NRSC report, Christopher Legg, 1991). On 15 January 1991, the oil slick was not visible, however, on the next cloud-free day, 24 January 1991, an oil slick more than 50 km long and 5 km wide, covering about 200 square kilometres was visible. The slick became shorter between 24 January and 4 February and then lengthened by 9 February. This was mainly due to curvature and re-straightening of the oil slick. The slick moved a total of 173 km, between 24 January and 12 February, moving daily from less than five km to more than twenty. During the same period, the surface area of the oil slick decreased to 19 square kilometres. On 21 February, a partly cloudy day, the slick was invisible. The dissipation rates prior to 12 February suggested that the entire observable oil slick would have dispersed or been stranded on beaches by 16 February 1991.

Furthermore, the rapid dissipation of the slick suggested that it was unlikely that any portions of the slick would ever reach the major desalination plants further to the south. Observations suggested that a total of some 200 km of coastline, mainly in Saudi Arabia, had been polluted by this oil slick. The Abu Ali area was the most heavily oiled area on the Saudi Arabian coast.

In Saudi Arabia, researchers at the KFUPM/RI ... applied two mathematical models, GULFSLIK II and OILPOL, to simulate the fate and transport of oil spilled at the Sea Island terminal (Mina Ahmadi) off the Kuwaiti coast.

The oil spill trajectory model, GULFSLIK II, was used in a real time mode to predict the surface trajectory of oil spills at various locations, to support the tactical spill response. The oil spill fate and transport model, OILPOL, was applied to compute the surface and subsurface distribution of oil. Results were used to support damage assessment studies and environmental impact statements. Current information indicates that in Saudi Arabia, heavy beach impacts from latitude 28°44' to 27°10'N have actually occurred. After 80 days, results show that less than 8 percent of the initial volume remains on the sea surface, whereas, 15 percent is either suspended in the water column or settled on the sea bed. Approximately 45 percent of the initial volume has had an impact on the coastal region, and more than one third of the oil has evaporated. Sighting data from ground and aerial observation (SLAR), and satellite imagery showed excellent agreement with the model results in the case of prediction of the surface oil distribution. From the first reporting of the oil spills, the US deployed an Interagency Assistance Team to Saudi Arabia to provide advice on response and protection actions. As part of this effort, NOAA scientists provided daily model predictions of oil transport and evaluation of resources at risk. This information was faxed daily to ROPME. Similar model predictions were also provided to the region by CEDRE (France). However, a comprehensive trajectory Model is still needed for the ROPME Sea Area as a whole.

B. *Fate and transport of airborne pollutants*

The aircraft sampling missions provided much information on the plume's general characteristics from points close to the fire to those at a distance of over 1,000 km. The smoke was never detected above 6,000 m and was generally below this level.

The composition of the plume is modified during the transport. For instance a very rapid loss of SO_2 and NOx was observed in the first 3 or 4 hours of plume travel. Progressively, the large particles which make the plume visible are removed and only the chemical components remain. They will last several weeks in the atmosphere spreading around the world in the troposphere in a very dilute form. "Black rain" and "black snow", reported as far away as the Indian Continent, could be attributed to the plume. Even if the foreseen effects on the climate remain negligible and well within the natural variability, a very large quantity of greenhouse gases will have been produced. In particular the CO_2 released daily represents 3% of the daily production and offsets the present worldwide efforts to reduce such emissions.

C. *Fate and transport of pollutants in the terrestrial environment*

Preliminary experiments showed significant water solubility of the fluorescing compounds, e.g., PAHs, in the smoke deposits which may reflect the migratory capability of these compounds in the soil during rainy periods, and their possible infiltration into the ground water aquifer. This needs further investigation.

The crude oil in the soil may be mobilized, and its uptake into the roots of the vegetation might be of concern in agricultural areas.

Biological and chemical, particularly photo-chemical, fate processes will play a role during the rehabilitation of the desert environment, and they have to be considered during the selection of appropriate technology for remediation.

D. *Fate and transport of hazardous wastes*

There are two solid waste disposal sites in Kuwait: Jleeb Al-Shuyoukh (Abbasieh) and Sulaibiya. Both are managed by the Kuwait Municipality. The solid wastes are dumped onto the ground or in shallow pits with very little cover applied.

Since the invasion of Kuwait, there has been no overseeing of either of the above solid waste disposal facilities and no effort to manage the waste. In July, 1991, the disposal sites were receiving every kind of waste produced in Kuwait, including ashes from wastes burned in the city. Wastes were burning openly in a large number of these sites, contributing thick black smoke to that emitted from the burning oil wells.

None of the nine existing hospital waste incinerators were operating, so all hospital waste was being collected and disposed of with the regular municipal waste. High pressure water sprays are used to clean out the carts collecting the waste. The wash water drains into the storm sewers, from where it is discharged directly into the sea. Plastic syringes, medical vials and other debris is caught up in the grate over the catch basin.

3.4 *Impact and Risk Assessment*

A. *Marine and coastal environment*

Extent of Damage

There are conflicting reports on the level of oil contamination in the marine environment affected by the oil spill. However, these reports are based on subjective estimates and not actual measurement results. Unfortunately there are limited results available on pollution levels related to the war activities. However, quantitative signs of significant pollution may be restricted to certain parts of the ROPME Sea Area, particularly in Saudi Arabia north of Abu Ali. In some cases, concentrations are even lower in the post-war samples.

Preliminary results of the Coastal Zone Survey and Ecological Damage Assessment Investigation by KFUPM in Saudi Arabia indicated significant impacts from direct oiling on intertidal habitats: mangroves, sandy and rocky beaches and mudflats. However, benthic, pelagic and planktonic communities do not appear to have suffered significant damage, although oil has indeed sunk to the bottom and mixed with sediments. Nearshore seagrass beds in the Dafi Bay area were oiled. Nearshore reef corals, fishes, and macroinvertebrates were not affected; oil was not observed on the reefs, although some reefs are located near heavily oiled shores ... .

A joint IUCN/IAEA/IOC/JICA/WWF mission to the Saudi Arabian Coast, undertaken between 17 and 30 August 1991, carried out a rapid assessment of coastal resources, human uses and impacts at 35 sites ... previously examined by an IUCN/MEPA team in 1986 ... . Preliminary results indicate certain gross environmental changes since 1986, in particular heavy impact by oil along the northern sector of the Saudi Arabian coastline, especially on the intertidal zone. Some gross changes in the abundance of certain fauna and flora since 1986 are also evident. Generally, there do not appear to have been dramatic declines in abundance of major floral and faunal groups. In fact, abundances of several groups (algae, fish and birds) were significantly greater in 1991 than in 1986. However, detailed changes in community composition, biodiversity and productivity and possible sublethal effects on these from both oil and atmospheric emissions can only be determined by using more quantitative sampling methods. Such activities are being undertaken as part of an on-going detailed monitoring programme. Broadscale assessments and detailed monitoring are seen as complementary approaches.

Very heavy atmospheric pollution was encountered at Ras al Khafji in Saudi Arabia and further north ... . In these areas, in particular, marine pollution may originate as much or more from atmospheric sources (i.e. the burning oil wells), than from the actual oil slick. Analysis and fingerprinting of hydrocarbon fractions in the surface microlayer should confirm this observation. The possible threat to coral reefs and other photosynthetic communities from reduced solar radiation and temperatures next winter should be investigated.

A field mission to Saudi Arabia, Iraq, Iran, Qatar, Oman and U.A.E. was organized by IOC with a view to assessing the effects of the war on marine and coastal resources in the ROPME region. The mission concluded that because of the "background noise" created by spills in this oil-rich area, until all of the spills are fingerprinted, it will be impossible to tell with absolute certainty which effect is related to which sources ... .

Other zones of impact from the oil spill spread far south, from Jubail, [*sic*] Saudi Arabia to Bander Khomeynii, Iran. Long shore currents from Saudi Arabia and a mid-Gulf current account for this distribution ... . Oiled intertidal zones, tar balls and oiling by "sheens" have been observed to a greater or lesser extent. Impacted zones were: Bahrain, Northern Qatar, East Qatar, Middle and Eastern U.A.E., North Oman, East-West Coast of Iran at Quesh Island, and Bander Abbas, Iran. The extent of damage is assessed by the respective countries.

An FAO mission visited Iran, Saudi Arabia and Kuwait (1-13 Sept. 1991) in order to carry out a preliminary survey of the effects of war on the fishery resources and the fishing sector of the ROPME Sea Area, and to identify needs for the rehabilitation of the fishing sector as a whole in the ROPME region both at national and regional levels.

B. *Atmospheric environment*

Extent of Damage

On a regional scale, the extensive smoke coverage reduces the solar radiation which may cause temperatures to drop locally by 5 to 10 degrees Centigrade. This may affect the wind circulation within the region and in particular the sea breeze regime. The long-term effects on the atmosphere remain difficult to assess.

The human health consequences associated with exposure to the air pollutants from the fires cannot, at this time, be assessed with confidence. It is encouraging that, on the whole, the levels of irritant gases (e.g. SO_2, NOx, ...) in residential areas have been relatively low, almost always below both international ambient air quality guidelines and the US National Ambient Air Quality Standards. On the other hand, concentrations of inhalable particulate matter (and the associated organic compounds) have been relatively high (Advisory Committee Statement on Public Health).

Although the concentrations of inhalable particulate matter are of concern, it is difficult to assess the health impacts of the fires on the basis of the information collected to date. There are several reasons for this, including:

i) The particulate matter measurements from the ROPME region reflect a mixture of soot from the fires, crustal materials from wind erosion, and particles from other sources. The relative contributions of these sources, which vary from day-to-day and place to place, have not yet been well-characterized (Spingler, 1991). Until source apportionment studies (which have recently been initiated) are completed, health risk assessment will be hampered.

ii) Most of the measurements taken to date have characterized the concentrations of particulate matter outdoors. Proper assessment of human exposures to air pollution requires information about indoor concentrations and the impact of the smoke on "personal exposures". Until the upcoming WHO/HEAL/EPD (Kuwait) study of personal exposures to inhalable and fine particles is completed, risk assessment and epidemiology will be difficult (Wallace, et al, 1991).

iii) Although the smoke from the fire does not appear to be acidic, it may still be a pulmonary irritant. Preliminary results from animal bioassays support this interpretation. But these duties need to be expanded. (Brain, et al, 1991).

iv) The epidemiological studies that have been completed to date have been limited in scope, size and statistical power. Therefore, the generally "negative" findings (i.e., no excess effects observed) yielded by the studies to date provide only limited assurance. The health studies now underway (or under consideration) in Kuwait, Saudi Arabia and Bahrain may, in time, begin to provide more definitive evidence of effects (Etzel, 1991; and Advisory Committee Statement on Public Health).

v) In other severe air pollution episodes (e.g., London in 1952, 1962) daily mortality rates have been increased, particularly among the elderly and those with compromised cardiovascular and lung function. Direct extrapolation of these findings in Kuwait and the ROPME region is complicated by differences in the composition of the pollution and in the demographics (particularly age structures) of the populations (Thurston, 1991; Ozkaynak, 1991).

vi) The prevalence of asthmatics (a potentially sensitive group) is quite high in the Kuwaiti population and the levels of air pollution from the fires are well above those which have been associated with increased respiratory symptoms in asthmatic children. However, the population mix may be quite different in Kuwait than in the communities that have been previously studied (Etzel, 1991).

Despite these complexities, it would be premature to rule out significant public health impacts from the fires. If meteorological conditions this fall become less favourable for dispersion of pollutants, it is quite likely that acute respiratory impacts will occur. Even if this does not occur, there is a basis for concern. Risks, which from the perspective of an individual may be relatively small (e.g., in comparison with those associated with smoking cigarettes), may be substantial in the aggregate. Within the ROPME region, a large population has been exposed to pollutants which have the potential to elevate the prevalence and severity of both acute and chronic disease (Wilson 1991; and Advisory Committee Statement on Public Health).

C. *Terrestrial environment*

Destruction of terrestrial ecosystems

A UNEP (TEB(Soil)/ROWA) mission for rapid assessment of the impacts of the war on terrestrial ecosystems in the ROPME region visited the three most affected countries, Kuwait, Iraq and Saudi Arabia, between 1 August and 5 September 1991. On the basis of several field visits in the above countries, the mission made the following preliminary observations regarding the impact on the terrestrial ecosystem in the three countries.

i. Kuwait:

(a) The soot and oil mist coming out of the burning oil-wells has covered the soil surface and vegetation in large areas. The soot-affected areas were observed in the Burgan oil field and along the Ahmadi-Wafra road. The soot-affected area extends towards the south and into Saudi Arabia.

(b) Most of the native vegetation in the soot-affected areas has been adversely affected. The annual flora failed to set seeds. Only some perennial vegetation with food-reserve in the roots is alive but all other perennial vegetation has been either killed or severely damaged.

(c) Oil escaping from the damaged wells has accumulated in a number of oil lakes and has penetrated into the soil under it. The depth of oil penetration varies from a few centimeters to one meter, depending upon the nature of soil and depth of oil in the collection site.

(d) The sandy soil belt around the Kuwait Bay and along the coast has been disturbed by the military activities. The affected soils have been further exposed to wind erosion. Pulverization of the surface soil by off-road military vehicles in other areas has destabilised the soil increasing its vulnerability to wind erosion.

(e) Disruption of irrigation in afforested areas in the north of Kuwait City caused severe damage to young plants. Fences of the Jal Az-Zor national park and Sheikh Zayed park have fallen and stand in need of repair immediately.

(f) Al-Wafra and Abdali are the two main agricultural areas, which have been very adversely affected by the military activities. Buildings, irrigation systems, protected agriculture structures (green houses) and young date-farms were either destroyed or damaged.

(g) Explosive mines and live munitions, which threaten human as well as animal lives, were seen lying on the Al-Wafra road and in the Jal Az-Zor area as late as the second week of August.

(h) The vast lagoons of standing crude oil in the vicinity of the capped oil wells are an immediate threat to birds and the fragile desert ecology although they may not present an immediate threat to human health.

(i) There are three wastewater treatment plants in Kuwait: Ardiya, Jahra and Riqqa. In July none of them were working and all wastewater was being discharged into the sea. None of these plants sustained severe physical damage, but they were idle for 10 months during the occupation. As a result, much of the machinery and equipment was submerged in sewage and intruded groundwater. Work is underway to make the plants functional again.

ii. Iraq:

(a) Bombing, shelling and other military activities resulted in the complete destruction of the infrastructure, power stations, water installations, oil refineries and oil storage depots as well as 6 oil wells.

(b) The direct consequence of this was putting irrigation pumps, drainage water pumps and sewage pumps out of action for periods of 3-5 months which caused an accumulation of drainage water and sewage, a rise in the water table and an increase in the salinity in vast agricultural areas.

(c) Destruction of fertilizer plants and other factories left the country without these important agricultural inputs. These factories could not be restored to a functioning state due to a lack of spare parts under the circumstances.

(d) Mine fields in the Muthanna Directorate pose a grave danger to nomads.

(e) Some toxic chemicals were spilled into the soil and into running streams when several industrial factories were bombarded.

(f) Agricultural production. Both crops and livestock were very adversely affected. Wheat, the main crop, was attacked by pests which reduced its total production by about 40% as no pesticides were available. Livestock were devastated by serious epidemics e.g. rinderpest. Sheep herds were either subjected to over slaughtering or pasturalists fled with them to neighbouring countries for the sake of higher prices. The rangeland of Iraq, especially of the west desert, has been drastically affected and degraded.

(g) UNEP and UN Reports indicate that food production capability and agricultural infrastructure in Iraq have been adversely affected by war activities reducing food production capacity to about 40% of its pre-war level.

iii. Saudi Arabia:

(a) The demarcation of the area affected by soot falls south of the Saudi/Kuwaiti border and east of a line passing through Nairyah down to Al-Dammam and parallel to the ROPME Sea Area Coast. West of this line, the effect of soot decreases gradually.

(b) The limited oil spills on the land have influenced the halophytes growing in the Sebkhas.

(c) The sandy oil belt along the coast has been disturbed by military activities; it is subject to severe wind erosion and sand movement. Some soils affected by soot have been observed covered with moving sand sheets.

(d) Soils on the western sector of the region are shallow and loamy and underlain by hard pans. Scraping of these soils for building or road construction by military manoeuvers or for construction of earthen embankments have exposed the hard pans in many sites. Vehicle movement has pulverized the surface soil exposing it to severe erosion, both wind and water. In many sites the soils have been extensively compacted causing further deterioration.

(e) The adverse effects described earlier have reduced considerably areas of grazing, thus increasing the gravity of overgrazing which, in addition to severe soil disturbance, has caused the disappearance of perennial plants.

(f) Death of Hammada elegans and other species in the Al-Khafji area has occurred due to dense soot fall-out and possibly oil mist. The percentage of death in vegetation decreases as we proceed away (southward) from the source.

(g) Vegetation seed productivity has been reduced by the soot; this was quite evident in the case of Plantago boissieri. In severely affected areas the plants failed to produce seeds.

D. *Hazardous Wastes*

Three major industrial zones, Subhan, Shuaibah and Shuwaikh should be considered. The Subhan Industrial Area contains some 100 small and medium sized companies including paint manufacturers, plastic companies, box plants, pharmaceutical manufacturer, bakery, soda bottlers, soap and cleaner formulator, foam rubber manufacturer, etc. Most of the plants were shut down. There are tanks and drums in the area, a number of which have been overturned and broken open. This creates the risk of wind-blown hazardous substances endangering human and animal health in the dry season, and seepage of dangerous substances into the groundwater in the rainy season. This is the situation at the used catalyst storage area at another industrial zone, the new Mina Abdullah Industrial Area.

The Shuaiba Industrial area, located 15 miles south of Kuwait City, is home to a port, petroleum refiners and allied and other industries. The area suffered heavily from the war and only one refinery returned to partial operation. Other plants are: sulfur, chlorine, oxygen and nitrogen plants, plastics companies, cement plant, waste oil refiner, building materials, glass plant, power stations, desalination plants, etc. Prior to the war, there was a plan to construct secured waste disposal facilities to serve the industries in the Shuaiba Industrial Area only. It is unknown, however, when these facilities will be constructed.

The Abbasieh waste disposal site located west of the airport receives all kinds of municipal and industrial wastes as well as waste oil. Prior to the invasion, wastes were dumped onto the ground or in shallow pits, with no excavation and very little cover applied. It would appear that solid waste disposal in Kuwait would benefit from consolidated planning and management to accommodate future waste deposits. The dump at Abbasieh presents an immediate threat to public health (disease and exposure to toxic chemicals) and security (danger to commercial aircraft).

The risk to the environment and human health will remain fairly acute until plans are designed and implemented to assess and clean up the sites, each according to its particular characteristics.

3.5 *Identification of gaps and needs for further assessment and integration of results*

Marine Environment

Long lasting oil pollution related problems in the marine environment of the ROPME Sea Area might be observed as a result of falling out smoke residues, submerged oil, and oil on shorelines and intentional spillage by ships and platforms. The ROPME/IOC meeting of the Steering Committee on Oceanographic Co-operation in the ROPME Sea Area organized in co-operation with UNEP (Kuwait, 24-27 September 1991), identified the following objectives to address these problems:

a. Develop information required to support immediate clean up and public health decisions or to prevent further damage;

b. Determine damages to natural resources;

c. Identify restoration and mitigation opportunities to be undertaken;

d. Identify long-term monitoring requirements;

e. Develop institutional capacity in the region to respond to future spills; and

f. Add to the general scientific knowledge base for future spills.

Objective (b) above includes fisheries.

Further details on the specific projects to be carried out under these objectives were identified by the above Steering Committee in an Integrated Project Plan that included the following components:

i) Assessment of sources and transport of contaminants, including: a. sources of oil from the 1991 war; b. distribution and movement of oil and oil burn products; and c. observed movements of oil in water.

ii) Assessment of environmental damage, including: a. baseline (pre-spill) descriptions of resources at risk including data from remote sensing and maps; and b. exposure assessment.

iii) Restoration and rehabilitation, including: a. direct habitat restoration of impacted areas; and b. acquisition and protection of equivalent resources in impacted areas.

iv) Long-term monitoring and research requirements, including: a. oceanography and meteorology studies including particulate fall-out; and b. coastal studies.

v) Institutional development and capacity building, including: a. regional emergency response network; b. scientific infrastructure; c. public information; and d. living resources and coastal zone management.

Each ROPME Member State must identify the specific programme gaps relevant to their country within this framework. In addition, the programme will carry out fishery surveys and fish biological studies in order to assess the status of the major fish stocks and to identify the management measures for the rehabilitation of those affected by the crisis. Special attention should be paid to detailed surveys of ecosystems and associated species (e.g. birds) and other related studies.

Atmospheric environment

Based on limited sampling to date, the major hazard seems to be particulate matter emitted from the oil well fires, and further investigation is needed both to characterize more clearly the particulates and to assess their effects. Preliminary results indicate relatively low levels of metals and PAHs in the particulates. However, further analyses are needed to assess fully and understand the nature and magnitude of these pollutants. Such assessments should include careful evaluation of personal exposure to fine particulates from the smoke and both acute and chronic studies of the prevalence and severity of diseases in the exposed population, with particular attention to the impact on sensitive groups.

The WMO expert meeting on the Atmospheric part of the UN Interagency Plan of Action (Geneva, 27-30 April 1991) proposed the enhancement of the WMO/GAW network of air composition measuring stations within the ROPME region as well as in the Middle East and Asia. The following characteristics will be monitored: carbon soot, precipitation chemistry, atmospheric turbidity, solar radiation, greenhouse gases, surface ozone, sulfur dioxide, as well as meteorological parameters.

Terrestrial environment

In addition to the marine environment, the terrestrial areas are the final depositional sites of the airborne pollutants. It is important, therefore, that a sampling and analytical programme be developed for inland areas to assess qualitatively and quantitatively the atmospheric fall-out. Since the approaches for analyzing soil and surface water samples and those for marine sediment and water samples are similar, it is recommended that analysis for special pollutants relating to the burning oil be carried out in the same laboratory or with co-operation between laboratories carrying out the relevant analyses.

Initial sampling and analysis for the atmospheric fall-out pollutants, particularly those associated with the soot and smoke particulates as a result of the burning oil, in the desert sand in Kuwait by IAEA/VITUK (Hungary) and EPD (Kuwait) have been the only survey/monitoring element of the environmental assessment in the terrestrial areas, and this programme should be continued.

There is also a need to assess the impact of the war activities and oil well fires on food production in the region, particularly in Iraq and Kuwait.

Hazardous Wastes

Hazardous wastes at abandoned or damaged industrial and commercial sites need to be located, identified, and moved to safe interim storage or disposal facilities. A comprehensive waste management programme for Kuwait must be elaborated and include the following:

In the immediate term:

- development and inventory of sites
- prioritization of sites
- detailed survey of sites to collect information
- investigate temporary disposal sites
- select and prepare temporary sites
- move wastes to temporary site
- accept wastes from private companies

In the longer term:

- pursue and consolidate plans for treatment and storage of hazardous wastes, including previously mentioned common sites such as at Shuaiba Industrial Area.
- establish a comprehensive programme of environmental monitoring and analysis, including suitable framework for enforcement of ensuing legislation and regulation.
- investigate and implement suitable industrial safety measures.
- initiate training programmes on waste audits and waste minimization.

Quality Assurance/Quality Control

Quality Assurance/Quality Control (QA/QC) must be a major issue in the present and future monitoring programmes. It is relatively easy to ensure reliability and comparability of the results of some routine parameters, e.g. SO_2, NOx, but problems occur in the identification and quantification of some specific hazardous compounds such as PAHs, etc. Intercalibration among participating laboratories can be a solution.

Establishment of a sample bank, especially for particulate matter samples from the smoke plume, would ensure long-term availability of the samples and comparability of the results with the soil and marine sediments which are the final depositional sites of the atmospheric fall-out.

Surveys, Assessment and Data Integration in the future

It is essential that an integrated environment monitoring system be established in the ROPME region to develop the monitoring capability at national and regional levels covering the marine, atmospheric and terrestrial environments.

The main goal of this integrated monitoring will be to assess the environmental and public health risks, as well as the potential long-term consequences of the war.

Details of this approach should be worked out in a co-ordinated effort by organizations responsible for the relevant elements of the programme, i.e. UNESCO/IOC and IAEA for marine environment, WHO and WMO for atmosphere, IUCN and UNEP for coastal and terrestrial ecosystems. The overall co-ordination should be handled by ROPME including the implementation of the integrated monitoring system in co-operation with UNEP.

The future survey/assessment programme will be directly related to the mitigation/rehabilitation efforts and should monitor the effectiveness of the measures taken as well as the rate and level of recovery of the impacted environment. The survey and preliminary assessment should be extended to cover other ROPME Member States in order to provide for an integrated Regional Programme for the mitigation, rehabilitation and protection of the environment.

The assessment of the state of the environment of the ROPME region will be undertaken on the basis of the comprehensive data-base, collected under the integrated monitoring programme. This data-base is to be stored in the Computerized Data System established at ROPME Secretariat during the first phase of the UN Inter-agency Plan of Action.

4. Proposal for Mitigation of Adverse Effects, Rehabilitation and Protection of the Environment

In response to the environmental damage resulting from the war in the region, mitigative, rehabilitative and protective measures were initiated first in Saudi Arabia and then in Kuwait after its liberation. These two countries were directly affected and most seriously polluted by the oil spill and the burning of oil wells. Therefore, the first phase of the UN Inter-agency Plan of Action concentrated on initial surveys and a preliminary environmental assessment in these two countries, keeping in mind the regional and possibly global consequences of the massive atmospheric pollution. Environmental survey efforts are also being initiated in Iraq and other affected countries.

4.1 *Mitigation, Rehabilitation and Protection Strategies*

No clear regional/national strategies to define priorities among the options of mitigation, rehabilitation and protection were declared. Such regional/national strategies must be formulated, using cost benefit analysis. In addition, protection strategies should define priorities among areas to be protected and the best available means to deal with these priorities.

Mitigation strategies should include combating options, necessary legal framework, temporary and final waste disposal, etc.

Mitigation:

Mitigation efforts started with the oil spill operations in Saudi Arabia and have practically been completed by the removal of the last parts of the recoverable oil in June 1991.

Measures have been taken to mitigate effects of airborne pollution in Kuwait by Kuwaiti and foreign agencies. However, it is noticeable that during mitigation of the airborne pollution by extinguishing oil well fires, pollution occurs in the terrestrial environment by the spreading of gushed crude oil in the vicinity of the wells.

Mitigative measures through handling of the oil ponds in the desert will contribute significantly to the rehabilitation of the terrestrial environment.

Rehabilitation:

Rehabilitation options lie between the extremes: (a) wait and sea, the force of time and nature will solve the problem, and (b) rehabilitate and restore everything possible, including even the transporting of corals from other sea areas. It is inevitable that realistic rehabilitation programmes should be prepared in each affected country where the environmental damage caused by the war is significant and reversible.

Environmental rehabilitation measures will aim at the recovery of the normal, healthy life of the ecosystem affected by the pollution. Although nature will rehabilitate itself in many cases, feasibility studies, including effectiveness and cost-benefit studies, will help in the selection of the appropriate rehabilitation approaches and technology.

Protection:

Protective measures will include: (a) legislation, enforcement of environmental laws, and (b) application of appropriate technology to avoid pollution of the protected areas.

A brief account is given below on the mitigative and rehabilitative measures undertaken, planned or required for each of the environmental components.

4.2 *Marine and Coastal Environment*

(a) Mitigation

Oil spill combating activities were initiated immediately by MEPA, in co-operation with national and international agencies/organizations, such as IMO and Gulf Area Oil companies Mutual Aid Organization (GAOCMAO). Saudi Arabian spill response activities were conducted in five phases and managed by MEPA. These phases included:

- Phase I - Protection of desalination and industrial facilities;
- Phase II - recovery of oil from the water;
- Phase III - clean-up of environmentally sensitive areas;
- Phase IV - clean-up of other shoreline areas; and,
- Phase V - habit restoration actions.

During these phases activities included collection and recovery or disposal of oil, and disposal of oiled debris.

Phases I and II were completed by mid-June 1991 and produced significant results, including the recovery of 1.4 million barrels of oil, a record amount for an oil spill. Also, all water intake structures for desalination and industrial facilities were protected and remained operational for the entire oil spill period. The remaining Phases III, IV, and V and the recovery or disposal of oil, and the disposal of oil debris have not been implemented.

At the same time, the IMO clean-up operation included the following:

- Cleaning of oiled shorelines on Karan Island (over 14,000 cubic metres of oil removed) which is an important breeding location for endangered species of turtles and migrating birds; clean sand was used to re-establish the original contour of the beach,

- Flushing of over 35,000 barrels of oil from heavily affected area of mangroves and natural water inlets on Gurmah Island. A containment boom was also installed to prevent re-oiling of the flushed areas,

- Test programme for cleaning saltmarshes in Musallamiyah Bay which was heavily impacted by the oil spill; a number of techniques were tested and the best possible technologies were used in further clean-up,

- Provision of protective booming for unoiled salt water marshes in Saffaniyah Bay and Musharrabah Bay; the protected resources in these unoiled saltmarsh areas will be utilized for the future recolonization of other heavily contaminated saltmarshes, and

- Removal of standing oil, which has the potential to refloat during high tide and cause further pollution damage to the environment, from two sites in Dawhat Ad Dafi Bay.

- Cleaning oil/tar layers from shoreline of Jazirat al Maqta, a nesting and feeding habitat for birds and other fauna.

- Tests and evaluation of clean-up methods for sand beaches and intertidal areas near Jubal An Nuquiriyah to identify the most environmentally sensitive, effective and practical techniques.

In addition to the above mitigative efforts led by IMO, the Norwegian "Al Wassit", through bilateral arrangements, has recovered emulsified oil from Saudi Arabia and Kuwait.

Future efforts should be directed towards measuring the effectiveness of various mitigation procedures in order to improve actions in the future. In addition, reference sites, where no mitigation efforts have been made, should be set aside in order to compare action with no action.

(b) Rehabilitation

i. Rehabilitation of coasts and coastal waters:

After recovering nearly 2 million barrels of floating oil in Saudi Arabia, there are shoreline clean-up plans under consideration. This should be applied to all affected coastal areas in the region.

Mines and other unexploded ordnance pose serious and long-lasting threats to the marine environment of Kuwait. Minefields were spread along all the Kuwaiti coasts. Offshore areas, ports and harbours are facing extensive sea minefields. Clearance operations by the Explosive Ordnance Group may not always be totally successful, and a danger from missed items remains. This could be most serious in the coastal zone where areas of recreation attract large numbers of people.

ii. Rehabilitation of fisheries:

Effects on fishery resources and aquaculture are locally visible but lasting effects will be most evident in the medium term. FAO's views are that a field (short-term) project on a regional scale should be formulated to cover a period of at least two or three years and which would aim at assessing the effects of the oil spill on the major fish stocks and to recommend measures for the rehabilitation of those stocks that suffered most from the environmental changes ... .

A longer term regional project should be implemented for the development and management of the fisheries in the ROPME Sea Area. This project should aim, among other objectives at:

- making estimates of the major fisheries stocks, and
- assisting in the implementation of the rehabilitative measures as identified by the short-term project.

The rehabilitation efforts should be carried out through the existing regional co-ordination mechanism for fisheries, i.e., "The FAO/IOFC/Committee for the Development and Management of Fishery Resources of the Gulf"; considered by its members as the most suitable regional co-operation framework in fisheries development management.

iii. Rehabilitation of wildlife:

The Jubail Rescue Wildlife Center, in Saudi Arabia, was established to respond to the heavy oiling of seabirds, turtles, etc. Several hundreds of socotra cormorants and over 10 bird species and turtles have been treated at the facility and many of them have been successfully rehabilitated. Efforts in this direction should be continued.

(c) Protection

i. Rehabilitated areas:

After cleaning the oil-affected shorelines, etc. protective measures, such as the installation of containment booms, may be needed to prevent re-oiling of the cleaned areas.

ii. Sensitive areas:

To protect sensitive areas, critical habitats, living resources and fishery resources, the use of chemical dispersants in fish nursery grounds and coastal waters should be avoided as they may be more toxic than the oil itself.

iii. Water intakes (desalination plants, etc.):

Protective booms were deployed in some areas around the desalination plant intakes to protect them against oil spills. Preparedness for such protection should be enhanced.

Application of chemical oil dispersants near areas of desalination intake should be avoided and controlled by the concerned environmental protection authority in the country.

iv. Acquisition of equivalent resources:

An "Ecological Initiative" consisting of the establishment of a Marine Habitat and Wild Life Sanctuary in the ROPME Sea Area has been launched in co-operation with concerned authorities in Saudi Arabia in co-operation with the Commission of the European Communities (CEC); the Commission's contribution to this project will be 2 million ECU (about $2.3 million). This "Ecological Initiative" is considered by the Commission as particularly important, because it could become a model for similar initiatives to be implemented in other areas of the ROPME region.

4.3 *Atmospheric environment*

(a) Mitigation

By the end of September 1991, a total of 19 fire-fighting teams have been engaged with the oil well fires in the greater Burgan oilfield in Kuwait. As a result of the fire fighting activities, extinguishing and capping the wells progressed as follows:

- 53 wells extinguished and capped by 6 April 1991
- 79 wells by 3 May
- 114 wells by 17 May
- 137 wells by 31 May
- 159 wells by 14 June
- 184 wells by 28 June
- 216 wells by 12 July
- 230 wells by 19 July
- 256 wells by 29 August, and
- 515 wells by 29 September 1991 (This includes the 31 wells in the Kuwait/Saudi Arabia joint operation area).

More fire fighting teams are expected to join and a total of 28 teams will soon be involved in the firefighting effort.

Taking into account the total number of burning oil wells and the rate of capping them, it is expected that the last burning wells will be capped by the end of 1991. Capping the last burning well will be an important milestone in the environmental mitigation and rehabilitation programme.

(b) Protection

The air pollution in Kuwait has brought about major public health concerns. The comprehensive Emergency Health Plan of Action in Kuwait deals with human protection and should be implemented as proposed by WHO ...

Open burning of municipal solid wastes, which emit toxic compounds, e.g. dioxins, should be stopped in order to protect the population from the inhalation of these toxic chemicals.

4.4 *Terrestrial environment*

Mitigation

Kuwait

Mitigation measures proposed for immediate action for Kuwait's terrestrial environment include the following:

(i) clearing mines and live munitions;
(ii) capping burning oil wells;
(iii) draining oil lakes;
(iv) restoring irrigation of afforested areas and farms; and
(v) restoring and expanding meteorological facilities.

Further mitigative actions are needed with respect to Kuwait's populated areas and human settlements, particularly with respect to:

(i) Wastewater Treatment Systems: Although none of the treatment plants suffered physical damage during the occupation/war, they were unused over that period and the machinery and equipment were submerged in sewage and groundwater. The 17 major pumping stations and at least 50 smaller stations have to be pumped out, dismantled, rebuilt or replaced. The reconstruction work has [*sic*] already begun.

(ii) Solid Waste Disposal: Management of the solid waste disposal sites in Kuwait (Abbasieh and Sulaibiya) should be re-established and proper solid waste handling maintained. Open burning should be stopped, human scavenging limited, and rodents controlled.

(iii) Hospital Wastes: The existing hospital incinerators should be returned to service and the disposal of hospital waste at the municipal landfill should be stopped. On a long-term basis, the development of a single, central facility to handle pathological wastes should be considered, based on a feasibility study.

(iv) A significant percentage of the industrial, commercial and residential property in Kuwait is in need of extensive rehabilitation; this work has already begun by concerned national authorities.

(v) Enhancement of efforts for the rehabilitation of the country's human settlements with the related social services and recreational areas, e.g. along the water front, which was the main recreational outlet to the inhabitants ... .

(vi) Rehabilitation of the anti-desertification greenbelt plantation which suffered serious damage due to negligence during the occupation period. In addition, the smoke and soot coated the leaves depriving them of sunlight and causing them to wither ... .

Iraq

Some mitigation measures proposed for urgent action include:

(i) immediate removal of mines and unexploded ordnance;
(ii) initiation of long-term programme monitoring, assessing the effects of pollutants and toxic agents;
(iii) removal of litter;
(iv) restoration of essential services e.g. water treatment sewage treatment as an urgent need, and;
(v) repair or construction of structures required for water and sewage treatments.

Saudi Arabia

Considering the magnitude of the impacts of the war on the coastal plains and the desert plateaux in the eastern region of Saudi Arabia, the Kingdom initiated mitigation measures. The activities carried out so far were, however, limited to monitoring and combating the devastating effects on marine ecosystems. So far, little has been done on terrestrial ecosystems. The following additional mitigation measures are suggested:

(i) The establishment of 10 to 15 enclosures in the war-affected areas, one in each soil unit to improve the seed bank;

(ii) Encouragement of herders to transfer sizeable numbers of their animals to other areas or dispose of them to match the decreased biomass generation;

(iii) Monitoring the impact of soot and water activities on the desert ecosystems. Establishment of enclosures in the soot affected areas and in the areas where soils were drastically disturbed.

Rehabilitation and protection at regional level

The rehabilitation and protection of the fragile environment requires a strategy characterized by regional co-operation, simplicity and attraction to the public. The strategy should also be easy to execute and maintain, and it should have its built-in monitoring mechanisms. Several countries in the ROPME region have been hit hard during and after the war. To remove the damage and its primary and secondary impacts, a regional approach must be followed. The framework of such a rehabilitation plan for all affected countries in the region should take into consideration that the region possesses most of the potential capabilities required for a successful rehabilitation programme.

4.5 *Hazardous wastes*

Hazardous wastes in Kuwait and Iraq at abandoned or damaged industrial and commercial sites should be located, identified and moved to safe storage or disposal facilities. To this end, the following are needed:

- inventory and prioritization of sites,
- survey of sites (sweep for explosives),
- investigate possible sites to use for temporary storage of hazardous materials,
- select and prepare the temporary sites.

Based on survey and waste analysis data, clean-up teams should repack wastes (if necessary), load and transport to the storage site. As an example, there is an urgent need to carry out repacking of war-damaged drums containing used catalysts which have been stored at the hazardous waste disposal site of the Shuaiba Industrial Area in Kuwait.

Permanent hazardous waste disposal facilities should be established and be designed in such a way as to handle all hazardous wastes generated.

4.6 *Re-establishment of monitoring/research programmes*

Automatic air quality monitors, laboratories for routine monitoring and research, sampling vessels and equipment have to be re-established to enable the re-initiation of air quality monitoring and research activities at the pre-war level.

Sampling boats or research vessels should be acquired to enable the resumption of national monitoring programmes for off-shore sea water, sediment and biota sampling.

(a) Pollution monitoring

It is very important that Kuwait re-establishes an extensive environmental monitoring and analysis programme. In addition to the monitoring of air and marine pollution, the feed and finished waters should be monitored for contamination both at the desalination plant and in the distribution network; monitoring of leakage from storage tanks as well as of animal feed that is grown on land that may receive contamination is needed.

(b) Revitalization of environmental research

Despite the extensive physical damage of research facilities at the major research institutions in Kuwait, e.g., KISR and Kuwait University, the research work already started since April-May 1991 has been revitalized, particularly in the areas related to the assessment of the environmental and material damage in the country. Revitalization of the environmental research will require international assistance which could be provided by the relevant UN and non-UN agencies and organizations.

5. Conclusions and Recommendations

5.1 *Conclusions*

On the basis of the results of the initial surveys and preliminary assessment, the following conclusions could be drawn:

(i) General:

a) Available information clearly indicates that air pollution is the most crucial issue and has local/regional importance. Pollution from the spilled oil mainly affects the Kuwaiti and Saudi Arabian marine and coastal areas, with some indications that the Iraqi and Iranian waters were also affected. Atmospheric fall-out of the smoke particles might contribute to pollution in both marine and land areas. Damage to terrestrial ecosystems in Kuwait, Iraq and Saudi Arabia were extensive.

(ii) Marine and coastal environment

b) The recoverable portion of the spilled oil has been removed from the marine environment, and intensive mitigative measures for the burning oil wells may result in the capping of the last burning oil wells by the end of 1991. After that efforts should be concentrated on the rehabilitation of the desert from the massive pollution by atmospheric fall-out and crude oil. A feasibility study will be needed to select the appropriate technology.

c) Marine surveys are still preliminary and the extent of damage in the subtidal marine ecosystem is yet to be determined. Survey and assessment should be continued for a complete year to include seasonal effects.

d) The functions of critical habitats and special ecosystems in the ROPME Sea Area are poorly understood. Research programmes are needed to address the questions of: (a) the terrestrial interaction with nearshore ecosystems, the interaction of the intertidal/nearshore systems with the offshore areas, fisheries, fish/shrimp nurseries, etc.; (b) the biological and chemical breakdown processes acting on waterborne and airborne pollutants in the intertidal, nearshore and offshore areas, and; (c) the restoration of practices for selected ecosystem segments after the clean-up.

(iii) Atmospheric environment

(e) Concentrations of irritant gases (e.g., SO_2 and NOx) do not exceed international ambient air quality guidelines. However, the levels of particulate matter (and the associated organic compounds) may be of concern. The fires may contribute to acid rain.

(f) First priority should be given to more detailed characterization (identity, concentration and toxicological properties) of the hazardous compounds associated with the smoke particulates, taking into account the time-limitations. Most of the fires will be extinguished by the end of 1991 or early 1992. There is an urgent need, therefore, to collect suspended particulate samples from the smoke plume (1) near to the fires, within 100 km downwind, (2) 100-200 km downwind, and (3) 400-500 km downwind. If this approach fails, identification of the hazardous compounds could be attempted from soil surface samples.

(iv) Terrestrial ecosystem

(g) Pollutants emitted from burning oil wells (soot and oil mist) are accumulating in the top soil layer in the desert and may affect the vegetation (agriculture) as well as the groundwater aquifer by infiltration during the rainy season. Further investigation is needed in this respect.

(h) Movements of vehicles and heavy military equipment have pulverized the surface soil, particularly in the desert areas in Kuwait, Iraq and Saudi Arabia, exposing it to severe erosion and causing damage to the fauna and flora.

(v) Hazardous wastes

Serious problems related to hazardous wastes and waste disposal and management are evident. Almost every commercial or official-looking building sustained some damage, and a large percentage of commercial and residential property in Kuwait is in need of extensive rehabilitation. Much of the work has already begun. Proper care is needed in removing and handling lead-based paint and asbestos contained in construction materials. Inhalation of dust is hazardous to both workers and residents. Educational materials explaining the dangers and safety precautions should be prepared and distributed quickly, and other avenues of raising public awareness should be pursued.

5.2 *Recommendations*

The following are recommendations for action to be taken at different levels, i.e., national, regional and international, based on the findings of the first phase of the UN Inter-agency Plan of Action.

ROPME Member States

(a) Government organizations responsible for environmental protection in the ROPME Member States should co-ordinate their survey and assessment efforts and urgently initiate the implementation of mitigation and rehabilitation programmes in their respective countries.

(b) Monitoring and research activities to assess the quality and provide the scientific basis for rehabilitation of the different ecosystems, and to adopt appropriate rehabilitation techniques should be maintained and enhanced in the affected Member States.

(c) Member States of ROPME would benefit from greater access to up-to-date practical environmental information on pollution control practices through regional symposia, organized by ROPME in collaboration with relevant UN organizations, e.g. UNEP, WHO, WMO, IOC, IAEA and UNIDO.

(d) Epidemiological studies that have been initiated in Kuwait, Saudi Arabia and Bahrain should be continued and expanded. Depending upon the initial results from these studies, it may be appropriate to initiate similar studies in other countries in the ROPME region.

(e) The National Focal Point in each Member State should ensure the proper flow of environmental data and information to ROPME's Data-base.

ROPME as regional organization

(a) ROPME to revitalize and extend regional monitoring and research programme to include the atmospheric and terrestrial environment, ensuring the interlinkage of the pollution transports between, and the interactions among, the various environmental components.

(b) Intensive training programme should be promoted by ROPME in collaboration with relevant UN and non-UN agencies and organizations. The training should include pollution monitoring (sampling and analysis procedures), data handling, and interpretation, quality assurance and quality control, and environmental impact assessment as well as environmental mitigation, rehabilitation and protection practices.

(c) Building inter-governmental linkages and close liaison with governmental units responsible for the environment and with leading environmental institutions in the region are recommended so that ROPME may deal effectively with any future environmental crisis.

(d) ROPME to maintain and enhance its co-ordinating role among Member States concerning the implementation of the proposed surveys and assessment as well as the environmental mitigation, rehabilitation and protection programmes.

(e) ROPME to ensure free information/data exchange, through its Computerized Data System (CDS), established by UNEP for the UN Inter-agency Plan of Action, among institutions and organizations in the region.

(f) ROPME to publish and distribute information bulletins on the "Environmental Effects of the War", on the basis of information gathered in the CDS. These should contain information on monitoring data, operations underway, public health issues, etc. and be regularly disseminated to ministries and interested organizations in the ROPME Member States and other countries.

UNEP and co-operating agencies and organizations

(a) UN agencies and international organizations to continue the existing co-operation in the follow-up activities to the Plan of Action, keeping in mind that the environmental impacts of the hostilities in the ROPME region have long-term effects within and beyond this region. As it was agreed during the Third UN Inter-agency Consultancy (Geneva, 3-4 July 1991) UNEP is to continue to play its co-ordinating role in this respect.

(b) UNDP to intensify its effort in connection with the planned donors' meeting in autumn 1991, in order to secure appropriate funding for the proposed rehabilitation programme, taking into consideration the results of the UNEP co-ordinated UN Inter-agency Plan of Action.

(c) WHO to provide assistance to ROPME Member States in the design and implementation of public health related assessment and rehabilitation programmes.

(d) WMO in collaboration with WHO to co-ordinate and provide assistance to ROPME Member States in the implementation of the atmospheric pollution assessment programme to achieve the following objectives:

- provide a framework for an early warning advisory capability for areas expected to be adversely affected by emissions from Kuwait oil well fires;

- provide a cursory wide-area indication of the distribution and composition of the Kuwait oil well fire effluents;

- characterize the aerial smoke plume;

- develop a more complete profile of the smoke plume constituents;

- determine the need for expansion of the monitoring network to a wider regional coverage; and,

- provide a meteorological data stream to facilitate the modelling and prediction of areas expected to be impacted by emissions from Kuwait oil well fires.

(e) IOC/UNESCO and UNEP to provide assistance to ROPME and ROPME Member States through the Steering Committee for Oceanographic Co-operation in the ROPME region for the implementation of the Integrated Project Plan to achieve its short- and long-term objectives through (a) reconnaissance surveys; (b) assessment of marine ecological impacts, and (c) restoration planning.

(f) IAEA/MEL to continue its assistance to ROPME and ROPME Member States in the implementation of marine pollution surveys and assessment, as well as through providing reference sampling and analytical methodologies and training, and organizing inter-calibration exercises to ensure the data quality control and the comparability of analytical results. Assistance will also be required for the establishment of a sample bank which will store samples collected and make them available for later analysis by laboratories monitoring different environmental components.

(g) FAO to monitor closely the food production capabilities (fisheries and land crops) or the affected countries in the region and to assist whenever possible in alleviating difficulties in food production.

(h) UNIDO to continue to provide assistance on hazardous waste management, with particular regard to affected industrial operations. In this regard, close co-operation is expected with, among other agencies, WHO. Activities in the area of industrial safety should yield appropriate in-plant investigations and follow-up training, as well as assistance with preparation of relevant guidelines. UNIDO should also assist in identifying and applying the best technology to deal with oily waste in the desert environment.

(i) HABITAT to continue to provide its advice and assistance in rehabilitating the human settlements in the devastated countries in the region with the related social services and facilities, in close co-ordination with UNICEF, UNESCO and WHO. Plans for the restoration of existing social infrastructure should be formulated in conjunction with the projected population.

(j) Upon request from ROPME, or ROPME Member States, UN organizations (UNIDO, FAO, IMO, etc.) to provide assistance in the preparation of feasibility studies, development of abatement technologies and national contingency plans and in project implementation requested in any disciplines relevant to the recent environmental pollution.

In addition to the above recommendations at the ROPME/UNEP Meeting on the Evaluation of the UN Inter-agency Plan of Action for the ROPME region

(Kuwait, 28-30 September 1991), the following general recommendations were adopted:

- National institutions and agencies which represent the centre of excellence in the ROPME region in relation to certain components of the environmental programme should be identified as leading institutions to implement the components of the programme.

- The emergency fund already established by ROPME to be enhanced by the governments of the region and supplemented by international funds raised through the appropriate United Nations agencies.

PART IV

THE CEASE-FIRE AND ITS IMPLEMENTATION

8. THE ESTABLISHMENT OF THE CEASE-FIRE

Members of the United Nations proposed or demanded consideration of a UN-sponsored cease-fire almost from the beginning of the aerial offensive against Iraq. However, it was US President George Bush, rather than the UN Security Council, who declared a cease-fire effective midnight on 27/28 February 1991. This action was followed by the adoption of conditional cease-fire Resolution 686 (1991) of 2 March 1991, and the agreement to a military cease-fire between the coalition forces and Iraq a day later. The definite cease-fire came into force on 11 April 1991, when the President of the Council certified to Iraq that it had fulfilled certain conditions established in Resolution 687 (1991).

S/22135, 23 January 1991

1. Letter from the Representatives of Algeria, the Libyan Arab Jamahiriya, Mauritania, Morocco and Tunisia to the United Nations addressed to the President of the Security Council, 23 January 1991

On instructions from our respective Governments, we, the Representatives of the States members of the Arab Maghreb Union, have the honour to request you to convene an urgent meeting of the Security Council to consider the grave situation in the Gulf region.

...

S/22138, 23 January 1991

2. Letter from the Permanent Representative of the Sudan to the United Nations addressed to the President of the Security Council, 23 January 1991

Upon instructions from my Government, I have the honour to inform you that the Sudan supports the request made to you by the member States of the Arab Maghreb Union for the convening of an urgent meeting of the Security Council to consider the grave situation in the Gulf region.

...

S/22141, 23 January 1991

3. Letter from the Permanent Representative of the Islamic Republic of Iran to the United Nations addressed to the Secretary-General, 23 January 1991

...

The human loss and destruction inflicted upon the Muslim people of the region and their resources, the dangerous prospects for prolongation and spread of the conflict, and the evidence of violations of international humanitarian law and norms governing the conduct of armed hostilities are alarming. Under these grave circumstances, it is imperative that the Security Council - which was actively seized of this crisis prior to 15 January 1991 - assess the present situation in light of its resolutions and take a more active role in achieving, without further loss and destruction, the complete withdrawal of Iraq from Kuwait, termination of the present armed conflict and withdrawal of foreign forces from the region.

The Islamic Republic of Iran, for its part, is prepared to co-operate fully with Your Excellency and the Security Council in order to achieve the above-mentioned objectives as well as the long-term stability and security in the volatile and strategic Persian Gulf region which can only be realized through a regional security and co-operation mechanism within a United Nations framework and without intervention and presence of foreign forces - which has historically been misguided and destabilizing.

...

S/22144, 24 January 1991

4. Letter from the Permanent Representative of Yemen to the United Nations addressed to the President of the Security Council, 24 January 1991

I have the honour to request an immediate meeting of the Security Council to examine the grave situation in the Gulf region.

S/22147, 25 January 1991

5. Letter from the Permanent Representative of Jordan to the United Nations addressed to the President of the Security Council, 25 January 1991

On instructions from my Government, I have the honour to inform you that the Hashemite Kingdom of Jordan supports the request made to you by the Government of the Republic of Yemen and by the States members of the Arab Maghreb Union for the convening of an immediate meeting of the Security Council to examine the grave situation in the Gulf region.

...

S/22149, 25 January 1991

6. Letter from the Permanent Representative of Malaysia to the United Nations addressed to the Secretary-General, 25 January 1991

I have the honour to enclose herewith the text of the statement by the Government of Malaysia on the situation in the Gulf.

...

Malaysia is increasingly concerned over developments relating to the war being waged in the Gulf. All indications point to a protracted conflict and given the massive and incessant bombing that is being carried out there will be immense destruction, suffering and loss of lives in Iraq and in the areas involved.

Malaysia is troubled that the rapid escalation of the war will take it beyond the original objectives as contained in the relevant Security Council resolutions. Resolution 678 (1990) does not empower actions that would lead to the virtual destruction of Iraq. Malaysia is disturbed that the Security Council and the United Nations have been ignored ever since military action was initiated. Efforts to have the Council consider various aspects of the war are being blocked. It is to be underlined that Malaysia's support for resolution 678 (1990) and other relevant resolutions to bring about the withdrawal of Iraqi forces from Kuwait was in the context of a continuing central role of the United Nations. Countries concerned cannot assume to draw a blank cheque from the Security Council resolution to wage total war on Iraq. Malaysia would like to see greater accountability of the actions by participating forces, not only to the Council but also to the general membership of the United Nations. The concerns being expressed by many members of the United Nations, especially members of the Organization of the Islamic Conference and the Movement of Non-Aligned Countries, over the conduct of the war and fears of a widening of the conflict should be taken up immediately by the Council.

The possibility of an extended conflict raises the spectre of a general instability and turmoil internationally that will weaken important international structures and affect the role of the United Nations as a vehicle for conflict management and resolution. An extended conflict and a widening of the war may result in a continuing presence of outside military powers in the area. Additionally the conflict will also lead to depletion of resources and funds for much-needed development assistance.

Malaysia is further concerned that the war may lead to the neglect of other important issues, such as the Israeli occupation of Palestinian land and their oppression. This would be a grave injustice. The war must not in any way bring about the eclipse of the Palestinian issue. Israel can be expected to exploit the war situation to marginalize the Palestinian issue while extorting military and financial aid from countries sympathetic to it. The United States and the allied coalition would be committing a serious injustice if they allow themselves to be persuaded.

Malaysia calls for a reassertion of a United Nations central role in the crisis. Malaysia would support any move within the Security Council or any other forums such as the Organization of the Islamic Conference and the Movement of Non-Aligned Countries to employ initiatives to bring the war to the earliest possible peaceful conclusion and to have Iraq withdraw from Kuwait.

S/22151, 25 January 1991

7. Letter from the Permanent Representative of the United States of America to the United Nations addressed to the President of the Security Council, 24 January 1991

On behalf of my Government, I request that you distribute as a document of the Security Council the texts of the attached letters which were exchanged between President George Bush and the Chairman and the Secretary-General of the Organization of African Unity on the crisis in the Gulf:

> We, the current Chairman and the Secretary-General of the Organization of African Unity have the honour to inform you that we have today addressed an urgent and solemn appeal to President Saddam Hussein of Iraq on behalf of the people and countries of the African continent. We consider it our duty, at this rather late hour, to join our voice to those who have called for a cessation of hostilities in order to avoid further destruction and loss of human life and to allow for new efforts aiming at a peaceful solution of the crisis. We have therefore appealed to President Saddam Hussein to accept the withdrawal of Iraqi troops from Kuwait in accordance with the relevant resolutions of the Security Council.
>
> In deciding to do so, we are conscious of the devastating consequences of the prevailing war, particularly the loss of lives and the destruction of property. We are also aware of the gravity of the situation and its far-reaching implications for the stability and security of the region and the world.
>
> We sincerely believe that it is not too late to explore new avenues for peace and that every opportunity should be seized to achieve the objectives of the United Nations without further suffering and destruction. Our belief is based on the conviction that it is never too late to make an extra effort in the interest of peace.
>
> In making this appeal to President Saddam Hussein, we are mindful of the profound attachment of the African people and the countries of our continent to the principles of national sovereignty and territorial integrity and their commitment to international legality. It was indeed against this background that African countries took a clear and firm position against the invasion of Kuwait by Iraq and for the restoration of legality, sovereignty and territorial integrity of Kuwait.
>
> Your Excellency, we are aware of and encouraged by your personal commitment to the establishment of a new international order based on sovereign equality, peace and security. In this respect, we believe that you will do everything possible and spare no effort to ensure an end to further destruction and loss

of human life. We also make this appeal to Your Excellency as the leader of the international coalition with immense responsibility at this crucial hour.

We do understand the exceptional and difficult position your country has assumed in the present war. We are fully aware of all the efforts you and many others undertook to avoid the outbreak of the present war and to have the decision of the Security Council on the restoration of the sovereignty of Kuwait implemented by peaceful means. We are confident however that you will spare no effort at a slightest opportunity to give peace another chance.

...

Thank you for your letter of 21 January informing me of the appeal of the Organization of African Unity (OAU) to Saddam Hussein to withdraw Iraqi troops from Kuwait in accordance with the resolutions of the United Nations Security Council.

The United States appreciates the support it is receiving from OAU and the vast majority of its member States in the current crisis. We are encouraged by the fact that African countries have taken a clear and firm position against Iraqi aggression and for the restoration of the sovereignty and territorial integrity of Kuwait.

These are exactly the goals the United States and its coalition allies, including several African States, are pursuing through our combat operations. As is stated in my address to the American people on 16 January, the objectives of the United States and its allies are clear: "Saddam Hussein's forces will leave Kuwait. The legitimate Government of Kuwait will be restored to its rightful place and Kuwait will once again be free."

The United States and the entire world community had hoped that the Gulf crisis could be resolved peacefully. As you know, five and a half months of intensive diplomatic efforts failed to persuade Iraq to comply with the will of the United Nations. Iraq made it abundantly clear that it had no intention of obeying the resolutions of the Security Council.

In the face of Saddam Hussein's repeated rejection of all diplomatic and peaceful options to resolve the crisis, the United States and its allies in the coalition had no alternative but to initiate combat operations.

I sincerely hope that your appeal on behalf of the people and countries of Africa, together with the past appeals of so many others, succeeds in convincing Saddam to withdraw immediately and completely his troops from Kuwait. For when Iraq complies with all relevant United Nations resolutions, peace can be restored.

S/22157, 28 January 1991

8. Letter from the Permanent Representative of Cuba to the United Nations addressed to the President of the Security Council, 28 January 1991

On instructions from my Government, I have the honour to request you to call a formal meeting of the Security Council as soon as possible to review the situation in the Gulf.

The Government of the Republic of Cuba believes that the Council must assume its responsibilities under the Charter of the United Nations for the maintenance of international peace and security; in our view, the only legitimate way to do this is to hold a formal debate in the Security Council so that the Council can take appropriate steps to end the hostilities and bring the conflict now gripping this important part of the world towards a diplomatic and peaceful solution.

The request made to you by a number of delegations, including a member of the Security Council, to this end, a request in which my delegation joins, makes it necessary to implement the relevant regulatory measures immediately, particularly article 2 of the provisional rules of procedure of the Security Council, which stipulates that "The President shall call a meeting of the Security Council at the request of any member of the Security Council."

Under this rule, the Security Council is compelled to take action when requested to do so by a member State. It is also required to act under rule 3 of its provisional rules of procedure, which authorizes any State Member of the United Nations to request the Security Council to call a meeting in order to consider "a dispute or situation ... under Article 25" of the Charter.

In other words, the requests made by the countries of the Arab Maghreb, joined by the Sudan, Jordan and Yemen and now by Cuba, are covered by rules of the Council's provisional rules of procedure and by articles of the Charter, the clarity and relevance of which are beyond question.

In view of the foregoing, I should be grateful, Sir, if you would immediately call a formal meeting of the Security Council for the purposes set out in this letter.

...

S/22182, 31 January 1991

9. Letter from the Permanent Representative of Tunisia to the United Nations addressed to the President of the Security Council, 31 January 1991

I have the honour to transmit to you herewith a letter dated 31 January 1991 addressed to you by Mr Habib Boularès, Minister for Foreign Affairs of the Tunisian Republic ... .

The military operations in the Gulf which began in the early hours of 17 January 1991 have taken a dangerous turn today as the parties to the conflict threaten to use chemical, bacteriological and nuclear weapons. Indeed, the statements issued on Monday, 28 January 1991, raise the fear that the transition to non-conventional warfare is imminent.

Tunisia, which has always condemned the use of weapons of mass destruction, believes that this turn of events, which may occur at any moment, is not unstoppable. We do not accept the idea that the United Nations can do nothing about this situation, which will lead directly to the fateful deployment of the ultimate weapon. The Security Council still has time to call for a suspension of hostilities so that this fate can be avoided and preference can once again be given to the path of reason and negotiation over the vagaries of war.

While reiterating the demand it has made together with the countries of the Arab Maghreb Union, Tunisia calls upon the Security Council to take this decision to prevent a disaster which will have irreparable consequences and which we all will one day call unjustified and, above all, preventable. The peoples of the world would find it incomprehensible that the Security Council, which has the power to stop the war from escalating, did not do so at the appropriate time.

A United Nations victory ought not be identified with victory achieved by weapons; even less should it be achieved at the cost of destruction on a scale hitherto unseen in this part of the world, which has in fact been scarred by seven wars in less than 50 years. A United Nations victory lies only in peace: there is still time to give it every chance.

S/22185, 31 January 1991

10. Letter from the Permanent Representative of Yemen to the United Nations addressed to the President of the Security Council, 31 January 1991

In my letter addressed to you on 24 January 1991, I requested an immediate meeting of the Security Council to consider the grave situation in the Gulf region. In view of the fact that the Republic of Yemen is a member of the Security Council, to say nothing of the immediate character of the meeting it requested, we expected you to accede to our request on the basis of rule 2 of the provisional rules of procedure of the Security Council, which stipulates that "The President shall call a meeting of the Security Council at the request of any member of the Security Council".

Today, one full week having elapsed since the submission of our request for an immediate meeting of the Council, I am most distressed that you have not acceded to our request. This constitutes a dangerous precedent for the conduct of the work of the Council in accordance with its provisional rules of procedure, which remain in effect and which must be protected from becoming subject to personal whims or to the different official positions adopted.

Our concern is increased by the fact that our request for an immediate meeting has been made subject to procedures and conditions that have no relation to the provisional rules of procedure of the Council and the underlying objective of which is no more than to provide a means for procrastination, without any legal grounds, at a time when the situation in the Gulf region is becoming ever more serious owing to the fact that the scope of the military operations in the region has gone beyond that stipulated in Security Council resolution 678 (1990).

While recalling our request of 24 January 1991, we should like to state the following:

> 1. Rule 2 of the provisional rules of procedure of the Security Council is abundantly clear, and the request of any member of the Council for a meeting of the Council is not subject to or linked with any prior conditions. The grave precedent established by procrastination and delay in acceding to our request will give the opportunity for the Council to be accused of employing double standards in the positions that it adopts. This is particularly so given that there are clear and binding resolutions that the Council has adopted on the Middle East issue, on Lebanon and on the Golan which still await implementation despite the fact that some of them were adopted more than 20 years ago and despite the fact that Israel is continuing its occupation of Palestinian and other Arab territories, including Jerusalem, the Golan and southern Lebanon.
>
> 2. The procedure being followed by the Security Council can only undermine the confidence of those who regard the Council as a just and effective force for the resolution of disputes and conflicts in the world.
>
> 3. We believe that the Security Council must meet its responsibilities as stipulated in the Charter and that it should tirelessly pursue its efforts for an immediate halt to the military operations in the Gulf region and to the great bloodshed and destruction that they are causing to the region. Above all, the Council must pursue its efforts with a view to achieving a peaceful solution to the conflict in this vital area of the world and to all the hotbeds of tension from which the region and its people are suffering.

S/22186, 1 February 1991

11. Letter from the Permanent Representative of Mauritania to the United Nations addressed to the President of the Security Council, 31 January 1991

I have the honour to transmit to you the text of the statement made to the national and international press on 31 January 1991 by the Mauritanian Minister for Foreign Affairs and Co-operation.

> "I wanted to see you to share with you our feelings about what is happening in the Gulf two weeks after the outbreak of war.
>
> "We are now in the fourteenth day of continuous day and night attacks on Iraqi territory by all airborne means (aircraft and long-range missiles).
>
> "The media report, and eyewitnesses confirm, that these attacks have led in all regions of Iraq to the destruction of many scientific, cultural, social and economic infrastructural facilities, as well as to the deaths of a substantial number of civilians, including women, children and the elderly.
>
> "Throughout the world, including in countries which are permanent members of the Security Council, voices are being raised in denunciation of this departure from the objective initially defined by the Council itself.
>
> "The military operation has turned into an enterprise designed to break Iraq's human and material foundations.
>
> "The slaughter of women, children and the elderly as well as the destruction of the archaeological heritage and holy places are, to say the least, contrary to the principles of democracy, the international rule of law and respect for human rights.
>
> "I should like also to recall the sufferings experienced since 15 January by the citizens of Palestine, subjected to a continuous curfew in their occupied homeland.
>
> "In the face of this harrowing ordeal and the inherent risks of its extension, with the threat of further destruction and loss of human life, we draw the attention of all peace-loving peoples who espouse the cause of freedom to the seriousness of the present situation.
>
> "We further call on the Security Council to live up to its responsibilities so that it will remain a tool for peace and stability instead of serving as a means for legitimizing war and destruction.

"We also greatly appreciate the efforts being made by certain Islamic and non-aligned countries, as well as by men of good will throughout the world, to put an end to the war and find a peaceful settlement to the Gulf crisis and the whole range of problems in the Middle East, foremost among them the question of Palestine."

S/22201, 6 February 1991

12. Letter from the Permanent Representative of Jordan to the United Nations addressed to the Secretary-General, 6 February 1991

I have the honour to transmit to you the text of the speech of His Majesty King Hussein to the nation on Wednesday, 6 February 1991 concerning the war in the Gulf.

...

I choose to address you at this very difficult moment. Arab honour and religious duty move me to address you on the eve of the fourth week of this savage and large-scale war which has been imposed on brotherly Iraq, and which is aimed at Iraq's very existence, its role, its progress and its vitality. It is also aimed at Iraq's right to a life of freedom and dignity, and its determination to fulfil its historic, cultural and human role, which emanating from Babylon, Baghdad and Basra, has contributed to human civilization, scientific progress and culture.

Iraq, fellow Arabs and Muslims, is now paying the price in pure and noble blood of belonging to its nation. Iraq had always hastened, without hesitation, to pay the price of belonging, and to shed blood in all the battles which the Arabs have fought, or which have been forced upon them in defence of Arab land in Palestine, Syria, Egypt and Jordan. Arab blood has always been dear to Iraq; should not the blood of Iraqi men, women and children be dear to us?! How shamed will be the Arabs who allow Arab blood to be shed in this unjust war?!

The world has known cruel wars, but never one such as this which is being waged against Iraq, and the likes of which it may never know again. The armies of the largest and most powerful nations have gathered and unleashed their tremendous arsenals of the most modern and dangerous weapons on land, at sea, and in the air. These weapons had originally been arrayed by an international military alliance against an opposing alliance led by another super-Power. They are now all arrayed against the Baghdad of Haroun al-Rashid, the Basra of Islamic studies, poetry and date palms, the Kufa of Ali, may God honour Him, Holy Najaf, Kerbala, Diwaniyah, Mosul, Kirkuk, and every Iraqi city and village. Fire rains down upon Iraq from airplanes, battleships, submarines and missiles, destroying mosques, churches, schools, museums, hospitals, a children's milk factory, residential areas, Bedouin tents, electric power stations and water mains. This bombing has continued since the first hours of the war, which is aimed at obliterating all the achievements of Iraq and forcing it back to primitive life through the use of the most up-to-date forms of destructive technology. The first casualties of this war have been right, justice and peace. Its first victims have been the aspirations of humanity since the end of the Second World War, hoping that that war would be the last human tragedy, and that man would no longer be either killer or victim. All the hopes of our nation and the world community were thwarted the day the land of Iraq was turned into the arena of a third world war.

...

The irony of this war is that it is being waged under the cloak of international legitimacy; its crime is being committed in the name of the United Nations, which was established by humanity to preserve peace, security and justice, and to settle all disputes and conflicts through dialogue, negotiations and diplomacy. If this is an example of the role of the United Nations in the new world order, what an ominous future lies before all the peoples and nations! What international legitimacy will serve as a refuge for those whom the mighty seek to subjugate, humiliate, kill and whose God-granted rights they seek to usurp, along with all the principles, values and charters on which the United Nations was founded. We now realize fully the real reasons why we, the Arabs, have been deprived of our right to deal with our own problems, why the hegemony over the United Nations has prevented it from fulfilling its role, and why the doors have been shut against any sincere political attempt to end the Gulf crisis. It is now claimed that every possible effort had been made to solve the crisis during the five months before the war. This is not true. If the effort exerted in preparing for the war had been devoted towards a peaceful settlement, this disaster would not have occurred. Moreover, the current war, with all its destruction, is incompatible with the humanitarian objectives of the United Nations resolutions, which have been adopted to restore peace and security to the Gulf region.

In contrast, there has been no real honest attempt to seek a just solution to the Arab-Israeli conflict. The Palestinian Arab people and the Arab nation still await the implementation of a single United Nations resolution which rejects Israeli occupation and calls for an end to it. Twenty-four years have passed since the occupation of the West Bank, Gaza and the Golan Heights, and nine years have passed since the occupation of southern Lebanon, yet none of our hopes have been fulfilled. Nevertheless, we have not despaired of the United Nations. The major Powers continue to assure us that a peaceful solution is possible. As regards the Gulf crisis, the Arab parties concerned have chosen from the beginning to reject any Arab political dialogue with Iraq, and to block any attempt which might prevent the internationalization of the crisis and its resolution by dealing directly with all its causes and effects. All the good offices of Jordan and others who are concerned for the future of our nation have been thwarted. Why? Because the real purpose of this destructive war, as demonstrated by its scope and the declarations of the parties to it is to destroy Iraq, and rearrange the area in a manner far more dangerous to the present and future of our nation than the Sykes-Picot agreement. This arrangement would put the nation, its aspirations and its resources under direct foreign hegemony and would sever all links between its parts, thus further weakening, fragmenting and debasing it.

The talk about a new world order, whose features are the destruction of Iraq and its potential, and the persistence of this talk as the war continues, lead us to wonder about the essence of this order and to fill us with misgivings regarding its nature.

The new world order to which we aspire holds that all people are equal in their right to freedom, progress and prosperity. It deals with their causes by applying the same humanitarian standards and principles, regardless of any extraneous considerations or factors. The new world order which is needed would not mete out injustice to any one nation, nor would it discriminate between peoples or nations, but rather it would draw them together within the framework of mutual respect and fruitful co-operation for the benefit of our planet and all the people on it. It would be an order which believes in public freedoms and protects private freedoms, respects human rights and strengthens the foundations of democracy. It would not deny the Arab peoples their right to all this.

The nature of the military alliance against Iraq betrays its short- and long-term objectives. For when Israel supports this alliance, when two countries, one Arab, the other Islamic, both of which have normal political relations with Israel, whose leaders compete for prominence in this alliance and reiterate their desire and enthusiasm for the destruction of Iraq, it becomes easy to see that this is a war against all Arabs and Muslims, and not only against Iraq. When Arab and Islamic lands are offered as bases for the allied armies from which to launch attacks to destroy Arab Muslim Iraq, when Arab money is financing this war with such generosity as we and our Palestinian brothers have never known by reason of our national responsibilities and geographical position, when all this is happening I say that any Arab or Muslim can see the magnitude of this crime which is being committed against his religion and his nation.

...

From the very beginning we have shouldered our responsibilities to the Arab nation and Islam, as well as towards international peace and security. We have made every effort to fulfil these responsibilities. We are not hurt that our rewards have been successive punishments against our country and people. It has become clear to the whole world that these punishments are the price we must pay for having tried to avert the disaster which was planned and plotted in the dark. As a new form of punishment, there are now attempts to deprive us even of our oil needs, for no other reason than our stand of principle. It is because we are not a party to the conflict, nor part of the alliance, unwilling to dance to the tune others play, with no will of our own, no rights and no ability to express our own free opinion. We would not forsake this right because it is equal in importance to our human right to breathe the air, which is not yet rationed. Nevertheless, Jordan's leadership and people will remain firm in their position and believe that the opportunities for peace still exist. To return to these opportunities would be less costly and a truer expression of the commitment to principles and values than the continuation of this devastating war.

The voices of millions can be heard in every country, including those of the alliance. They all call for peace and an end to the killing of children, the destruction of homes, and the withholding of medicine from the sick. I know just as you do that against these voices stand political and military leaders, alas with Arabs in their forefront, calling for the continuation of this war. Which voices will prevail in the end? The voices of peace, love, reason and right, or the voices of war, hatred, insanity and wrong?

We and other brothers have made a resounding appeal to halt military action and open the way for diplomatic political action to deal with the problem, but no one has responded so far. How often before the war broke out did we not warn against its impact, the deep wounds which it would open, its ever-widening repercussions and its human, economic and ecological tragedies. We warned that war is a measure of the last resort, to be launched only after all efforts to avert it have been exhausted. Our calls and warnings were in vain.

Justice will be victorious, God willing, brothers, and our nation will prevail because through those victories humanity will prevail against its enemies. Life will prevail over death. Love among nations will prevail over the desire to sow and spread hatred. All those who had hoped that our nation would be divided, as are its leaders, and that it is a dead nation, will be proved wrong. Our nation will remain, God willing, a strong, proud and vibrant nation. "These, your people, are one people and I am your Lord, so worship Me" (Surat al-Anbiya', verse 92). Let us have fear of God and remember that if this situation continues it will only benefit those who covet our lands and resources, and first and foremost Israel. There are already signs that the spoils are being divided. We hear and read every day of plans to control our resources, limit our freedom of decision, stifle our aspirations and usurp our rights. There is talk of proposed military alliances and bases and foreign troops that will remain on Arab soil, of restrictions on our development and of a solution to the Palestinian problem which has been drawn up or which will be drawn up by others according to what they see, and according to the will of the powerful over the weak. We cannot imagine that such a solution will satisfy the legitimate national rights of the Palestinian people on its national soil.

This is a call from a Hashemite Arab to all honourable Arab and Muslim leaders. Let us join our efforts to stop this catastrophe and save the people of Iraq from the fate that is intended for them. Let us save our nation from the designs on it. Let us put an end to this war.

The starting-point for all this is immediate and serious efforts to have the alliance cease hostilities, in preparation for a responsible dialogue between the parties in conflict: an Iraqi-American dialogue and an Arab-Arab dialogue, both of which should appeal to reason, a balance of interests and international legitimacy, the legitimacy of peace and security, justice and equality.

By destroying Iraq, this war has exceeded the limits set by the United Nations in its resolutions. This is confirmed by the declarations of the alliance leaders. So where does the United Nations stand? The alternative to a cease-fire is the destruction of Arabs and Muslims, their humiliation, their degradation, their exploitation, the trampling on their honour, pride and legitimate hopes, the sowing of hatred and strife between nations. We in Jordan will remain the Arabs of all Arabs, the noblest of the noble, the men of all men. We shall always remain united, army and people, fully prepared to defend our country. If the battle is forced upon us we shall be equal to it and gain one of God's two favours (victory or martyrdom). ...

From Amman of the Arabs I convey to our people in Palestine our great pride in them, in their steadfastness, their resilience in their suffering. A whole nation is under house arrest, without work, without medicine, without a livelihood. But it is a people which believes in God and stands firm by the Al-Aqsa Mosque and the Church of the Holy Sepulchre.

As for our people in Iraq, what words can describe their great courage and pride, their tenacity and their unique ability to face 28 allied countries, 28 armies headed by the largest, most powerful and best-armed army of the world! To them we convey our love and our pride as they defend us all and raise the banner that says God is great, the banner of Arabs and Islam. We salute Iraq, its heroic army, its steadfast, courageous people, its glorious women, its brave children, and its aged who confront with the resolve of the faithful the bombers, the missiles and the tons of explosives.

We send special greetings of esteem and respect to His Holiness Pope John Paul II for his prayers and continuous calls for peace in the Middle East, and to the peoples and international figures everywhere who have come out against the war and who call for peace. We send greetings of pride to all our Arab and Muslim brothers and all those on the five continents who from the first moments of the war took a stand for life and peace against death, destruction and aggression.

I pay a special debt of thanks to all those who search for the truth and disseminate it because they respect and care for it, to all the newsmen, politicians and academics who live among us and do their duty with honesty and professionalism.

"Most of their conferrings together are devoid of good, except such as enjoin charity, or the promotion of public welfare or of public peace; and on him who strives after these, seeking the gratification of God, shall we soon bestow a great reward" (Surat al-Nisa', verse 114).

...

S/22215, 11 February 1991

13. Letter from the Permanent Representative of the Union of Soviet Socialist Republics to the United Nations addressed to the Secretary-General, 11 February 1991

I have the honour to transmit to you the text of the statement made by the President of the Union of Soviet Socialist Republics, M.S. Gorbachev, on 9 February 1991 concerning the development in the Persian Gulf.

...

Events in the Persian Gulf region are taking an increasingly disturbing and dramatic turn. The largest war in recent decades is gaining momentum. The number of casualties is increasing, *inter alia* among the peaceful population. The military actions have already caused enormous material damage. Entire countries - first Kuwait, then Iraq, and next, perhaps, others as well - are threatened with catastrophic destruction. The discharge of a vast quantity of oil into the Persian Gulf may develop into an extremely serious environmental disaster.

The Soviet leadership confirms once again its principled adherence to the Security Council resolutions which reflect the will of the majority of countries and the hopes of peoples for a new international order which will exclude aggression and encroachment upon other countries' territory and natural resources.

However, the logic of the military operations and the nature of the military actions create a risk that the mandate defined in these resolutions may be exceeded.

The provocative attempts to enlarge the scope of the war by involving Israel and other States in it, thus giving the armed conflict yet another destructive dimension, the Arab-Israeli one, are also extremely dangerous.

To judge from certain statements that have been made at a political level and by influential mass media, an attempt is under way to accustom people on both sides of the conflict to the idea that the use of weapons of mass destruction is possible, and permissible. If this happened, the whole of world politics and the entire world community would be shaken to their foundations.

The course this war has taken is a matter of great concern to the Soviet people and to the country's leadership, the more so in that it is raging close to the borders of the Soviet Union.

A sense of historical responsibility, common sense and humanity all lead to the same conclusion - that everything possible should be done to bring about a political settlement on the basis of the Security Council resolutions. At this critical juncture, I make a public and urgent appeal to the President of Iraq to weigh once again what is at stake for his country, and to demonstrate the realism which would make it possible to move towards a reliable and just peaceful settlement. I am sending my personal representative to Baghdad immediately for a meeting with President Hussein.

It is our hope that in this way we shall be able, together with the Arab and other Muslim States, with the countries of Europe and Asia, and above all with the United States of America and with all the permanent members of the Security Council, not only to help put an end to the state of war as soon as possible but also to pave the way for a strong and equitable system of security in this region that is so vital to the entire world, one which will of course include the settlement of the Arab-Israeli conflict and of the problem of Palestine - with the decisive role in the process being played primarily by the States of the region. A fitting place in the post-war order must be assigned to Iraq, whose people cannot be held responsible for what has happened, but rather deserve our sympathy, compassion and support.

I repeat: In order to effect a breakthrough to peace in the Near and Middle East, the flames of war in the Gulf must be extinguished as soon as possible. At the present juncture, that is what is most important.

S/22220, 13 February 1991

14. Letter from the Permanent Representative of Egypt to the United Nations addressed to the President of the Security Council, 13 February 1991

In my capacity as Chairman of the Islamic Group at the United Nations, I have the pleasure to request that His Excellency Ambassador A. Engin Ansay, Permanent Observer to the United Nations of the Organization of the Islamic Conference be invited to participate in the Security Council's meeting on the item entitled "Situation between Iraq and Kuwait" in accordance with rule 39 of the Council's provisional rules of procedure.

S/22222, 13 February 1991

15. Letter from the Permanent Representative of Tunisia to the United Nations addressed to the President of the Security Council, 13 February 1991

I have the honour to transmit herewith the text of a declaration made on 13 February 1991 by an authorized source in the Ministry of Foreign Affairs of the Republic of Tunisia.

...

The Tunisian Government was deeply disturbed and saddened to learn that hundreds of innocent Iraqi victims had perished as a result of an intensive aerial bombardment of a civilian shelter in a residential area of the Iraqi capital in the early hours of Wednesday, 13 February 1991.

On numerous occasions, Tunisia has emphasized its apprehensions concerning the continuation and escalation of the war, particularly after it became evident that Iraq's human resources and economic, scientific and cultural infrastructure was being targeted.

While strongly condemning this savage bombardment of civilians, which is incompatible with humanitarian values and international covenants, Tunisia expresses its solidarity with the fraternal Iraqi people in this severe ordeal and once again makes an urgent appeal to the conscience of the world to spare bloodshed, to put an end to the devastating war in the Gulf and to settle the dispute by peaceful means.

The Tunisian Government wishes to point out that this bombardment constitutes further evidence of the manner in which the Security Council resolutions on the Gulf, particularly resolution 678 (1990), are being flagrantly transcended and strongly urges this Council to assume its full responsibilities by imposing respect for the United Nations resolutions in order to preserve a minimum degree of credibility for the United Nations, in its capacity as the last resort for the maintenance of international peace and security.

S/22223, 14 February 1991

16. Letter from the Chargé d'affaires a.i. of the Permanent Mission of Algeria to the United Nations addressed to the Secretary-General, 14 February 1991

I have the honour to transmit to you herewith the text of the statement issued on 14 February 1991 by the Office of the President of the Republic. ...

"The savage bombing raids carried out daily by the coalition forces against Iraqi towns and cities yesterday hit with particular ferocity a shelter in which residents of the Amiriyah residential district of Baghdad had taken refuge as usual. This deliberate attack killed hundreds of people, most of them women and children.

Algeria indignantly censures and vigorously condemns this vile act, for which the coalition forces must take full responsibility.

This massacre reveals the true nature of the war being waged against the Iraqi people, which today has escalated from an operation designed to systematically destroy Iraq's economic and military potential to an actual war of extermination.

Algeria resolutely denounces the intentions of certain Powers to try to impose their new order by fire and bloodshed. It also denounces the complicity of certain Arab countries, who are thus lending support to a genocidal campaign against a fraternal people.

At this tragic time, Algeria shares the sorrow of the Iraqi people, bows to the memory of the many victims, salutes the determination and heroism of the Iraqi people in their resistance to aggression and pledges them its complete solidarity in this fight for honour and dignity.

Algeria wishes to recall that the intervention by the coalition forces, perpetrated under the cover of international law is, in reality, a campaign of all-out destruction which, through the massacre of innocents, is assuming the dimensions of a crime against humanity.

Far from contributing to the restoration of law and justice, such an excessive deployment and show of force simply reflects aggressive, hegemonistic intentions which totally contravene the purposes and principles of the United Nations.

Algeria wishes to emphasize that those who today claim to be acting in the name of international legality have even twisted the decisions of the Security Council relating to the Gulf crisis. The military adventure on which the coalition forces have embarked can in no circumstances be justified on the basis of either international law or humanitarian conventions, still less morality.

Algeria solemnly appeals to the Security Council to finally assume its responsibilities with regard to the serious deterioration of the situation in the Gulf and to call immediately for a cease-fire so that a process of dialogue and negotiations can begin, based on the relevant principles of the Charter of the United Nations.

It appeals to the Secretary-General to make full use of the prerogatives conferred on him by the Charter, with a view to hastening a cease-fire and making a decisive contribution to the restoration of peace.

Algeria is confident that all peace-loving peoples, in particular the Arab and Muslim peoples, will show a sense of responsibility and join together in an effort to end a conflict which is threatening international peace and security.

The Algerian people, who daily pledge their fraternal solidarity with Iraq, will be capable of mobilizing still further in a tangible demonstration of their support for the heroic struggle of the fraternal people of Iraq. In so doing, they will prove once again that they remain unswervingly committed to the noble values which guided them in their glorious liberation struggle and that they will not shrink from any sacrifice in providing support and assistance whenever a people is fighting for dignity, freedom and independence."

S/22225, 14 February 1991

17. Letter from the Permanent Representative of Tunisia to the United Nations addressed to the President of the Security Council, 13 February 1991

...

We call upon the distinguished Security Council to announce an immediate cease-fire, even if only for a specified period of time, in order to provide an opportunity for peaceful endeavours and propitious attempts to find a peaceful solution to the conflict within the framework of international law and in accordance with the principles of the United Nations, with a view to the maintenance of international peace and security.

... [*The full text of this document is reprinted in Chapter 5.A., document 100.*]

S/22228, 15 February 1991

18. Letter from the Permanent Representative of Jordan to the United Nations addressed to the President of the Security Council, 15 February 1991

With reference to the request submitted by a number of delegations in the latter part of last month, which my delegation supported, for the holding of a formal meeting of the Security Council to consider the situation in the Gulf, and in view of the Council's decision on 13 February 1991 to hold a closed meeting, I have the honour to transmit herewith the text of the statement that I would have delivered in the Council if the meeting had been public.

...

The Security Council is meeting today at a time when the momentous and devastating war that is being waged in the Middle East has entered its fourth week; a war which my country diligently endeavoured to avert, while warning of its disastrous consequences and repercussions not only for our region but for the entire world. Unfortunately, our endeavours were unsuccessful, since they were obstructed by a number of parties, and other peaceful initiatives that were made also failed for the same reason. While today expressing our anxiety concerning the outbreak of this war in the Gulf, which is a vital and sensitive region of the world, we also wish to express our regret that the Security Council failed to hold an early meeting immediately after the outbreak of this war in order to consider the action that is being undertaken, in its name, by a number of States, with a view to ascertaining whether those military operations have transcended the framework of its resolutions and whether there is still scope for an attempt to solve the problem peacefully. It was only natural that we should expect this from the Security Council in its capacity as the body that was established as an effective instrument for the maintenance of international peace and security. We believe that the most appropriate way to achieve that objective is to prevent the occurrence of wars and make every endeavour to avert them, instead of granting an open licence to wage them.

...

My country's position in regard to the Gulf crisis is clear and based on principle. We oppose the seizure of territory by force and we do not recognize the political and demographic changes resulting therefrom. We also believe in the peaceful settlement of conflicts and we regard peaceful, calm and constructive dialogue based on equality and mutual respect as the only appropriate method to settle disputes between States.

We were deeply grieved when the crisis erupted between two Arab countries on 2 August 1990 and His Majesty King Hussein made sincere and diligent endeavours to rapidly contain and overcome that crisis on the basis of international law, within the Arab context, which is the natural context for such endeavours. Although those endeavours almost achieved their aim, certain parties in and outside the region sought to expand the scope of that crisis by internationalizing it. The forceful intervention of external parties in that crisis, as well as the stubborn opposition to dialogue, the massive deployment of foreign forces in the Gulf region, the launching of organized and hostile information campaigns and the hasty adoption of resolutions, led to a dangerous escalation of that crisis by neutralizing the parties that could have acted as mediators and numerous opportunities for peace were therefore lost.

...

Our position on the Gulf crisis is in keeping with the views of the international community and our aim is to ensure the triumph of international law. However, we differ from some in regard to the means for the achievement of that aim. We have chosen to emphasize the preferability of a peaceful solution and we have stressed the need to make every possible effort to that end, with an open mind and in such a way as to take into account the background and interrelated aspects of the problem. In that regard, we feared the outbreak of a devastating war, the adverse consequences of which would outweigh its positive results, assuming that war can have any positive results. War is the worst option to which a party to a dispute can resort and it should not be regarded as a means to achieve a solution until all other means have been exhausted.

At the present time, now that the war has become a *fait accompli*, and considering the tremendous human suffering and large-scale devastation that it has caused, we feel impelled to make a strong appeal for the cessation of all the military operations in the Gulf region and for the parties concerned to return to the negotiating table, in order to avoid further human and material losses.

The United Nations was established to save succeeding generations from the scourge of war and to make every effort to maintain peace. Consequently, in accordance with the responsibilities vested in it under the Charter, the Security Council has an obligation to continue its endeavours to reach a peaceful solution to this conflict and also to solve the other outstanding problems in this vital region of the world, particularly the question of Palestine, the essence of the Arab-Israeli conflict, which is still awaiting a solution in accordance with international law. We fear that Israel might exploit the international preoccupation with the ongoing war in the Gulf in order to implement its well-known expansionist schemes and expel the Palestinian population from the occupied territories.

...

Any objective observer following the military operations that are being undertaken by the allied forces, under the leadership of the United States, against Iraq would inevitably reach the conclusion that the purpose of this large-scale and massive onslaught is not solely to liberate Kuwait, but also to destroy Iraq as a military and economic power. The devastation has extended to places of worship, schools, hospitals, residential areas, roads, bridges, electric power stations, water-supply networks and even a factory for the manufacture of infant formula. Large numbers of civilians, including women, children and elderly persons, have been killed or wounded in Iraq as a result of this widespread destruction. By now, the world should realize the dangerous and tragic nature of the situation following the bombardment by allied aircraft of a civilian shelter in which about 500 persons died. All this prompts us and others to wonder whether these military operations have not, in fact, transcended the aims of the Security Council resolutions.

It is also a source of concern and apprehension that some of the principal foreign parties participating in this campaign have begun to speak of restructuring the situation in the region, through the creation of military appliances and the establishment of a regional order, in a way that would serve their own ends but which would not be conducive to the interests and aspirations of the peoples of the region.

...

The recent international developments, culminating in the announcement of the termination of the cold war, gave mankind cause to hope for a better world in which mutual understanding and respect would prevail and in which the United Nations would play its role in the establishment and maintenance of peace. However, the outbreak of the Gulf crisis diminished that hope. We could have solved this problem in a peaceful and equitable manner, thereby setting an example to be followed under the so-called "new international order". However, in view of the deteriorating situation, we cannot but wonder about the nature of that new order in the name of which this war is being waged, with the destruction of Iraq as its primary "achievement", and also about the role of the United Nations in that order, given the fact that the Organization has been used to give this war the stamp of approval and to vest it with the cloak of international legitimacy, after which the Organization was expected to take a back seat and merely observe the acts that were being committed, in its name, as though the matter no longer concerned it.

Kuwait's resumption of its former status as a sovereign Member State of the United Nations cannot be achieved by destroying Iraq, which is also a Member State of this Organization, or by breaking its sovereign will and imposing hegemony on it. Our fears for Iraq and our commitment to the defence of its interests are as strong as our fears for Kuwait and our commitment to the defence of Kuwait's interests, since both are sister Arab countries with which we have links that are firmer and closer than any temporal interests. We must ask ourselves: In what situation will Iraq find itself if this war continues? In what situation will Kuwait find itself? Will this lead to the re-establishment of peace and security in the region, as indicated in Security Council resolution 678 (1990)? We have doubts in this regard. Moreover, we do not agree with the interpretation of the expression "use all necessary means", as contained in that resolution, as implying the use of force, to the exclusion of other means, on a historically unprecedented scale within 24 hours after the expiration of the deadline set by the Security Council for Iraq's withdrawal. Furthermore, the use of force, if indispensable, does not imply that it should continue to the bitter end without pausing to give peace a chance. Should the interpretation of the expression "use all necessary means" be left to the generals in the field?

...

Since human ingenuity has succeeded in manufacturing all these lethal weapons, should it not also be capable of finding a means, other than war, to solve a problem such as the occupation of Kuwait? If one State has used force to settle its dispute with another State, can this justify the use of the same means by a large number of States acting in association with each other? Although one State might be incapable of solving a particular problem without using force, the collective wisdom of the international community should certainly be capable of dealing with the problem in a different manner. If the time and efforts that were spent on establishing the coalition in the Gulf and on the preparations for the war had been devoted to the quest for a peaceful solution, this war would have been averted. We do not believe that a real peaceful endeavour was made in a manner commensurate with the capabilities of the principal parties to the alliance or with the seriousness of the problem. Moreover, when the problem became a matter of daily concern to the Security Council, the latter merely adopted one resolution after another, leaving States to embark on their own individual peaceful initiatives. The Council did not even request the Secretary-General to use his good offices and make diplomatic endeavours to reach a peaceful solution to the crisis.

...

At the present time, we feel obliged to warn, once again, of the dangers inherent in the continuation of this war, from the standpoint not only of the large numbers of human victims and the tremendous material destruction that would be caused in Iraq and Kuwait, but also of the probability of an extension of the scope of this war to include other parties in the region, or the probability of the use of non-conventional weapons, with all the devastating consequences that this would have for the future of the region as a whole, and possibly for the whole world. Has the time not come to halt this destructive war, to allow the voice of reason to prevail over the sound of bombs, and to provide scope for quiet diplomacy and constructive dialogue with a view to reaching the desired peaceful and equitable settlement?

I wish to conclude my statement by quoting a passage from the address delivered by His Majesty King Hussein on 6 February 1991, in which he said: "There are still opportunities for peace and the seizure of these opportunities would be less costly and more genuinely indicative of a commitment to values and principles than a continuation of this devastating war".

...

S/22229, 19 February 1991

19. Note verbale from the Permanent Mission of Iraq to the United Nations addressed to the President of the Security Council, 15 February 1991

The Permanent Mission of the Republic of Iraq to the United Nations presents its compliments to the President of the Security Council and has the honour to transmit to him herewith the text of the decision announced by the Revolution Command Council of the Republic of Iraq on 15 February 1991. ...

...

Ever since the United States, the Zionists and America's Western colonialist allies have realized that a Power was coming into being in an Arab Muslim country, Iraq, a Power capable of counterbalancing the Zionist hegemony supported by imperialism in the region, a free and noble Power, determined with sincerity and self-denial to confront the aggression and the Zionist ambitions and to reject imperialist domination of the region, the United States, the Zionists and all the colonialist forces full of hatred for the Arabs and the Muslims have begun to take measures and decisions and to launch campaigns of intrigue and incitement against Iraq in order to prevent the formation and growth of this Power, to isolate, contain and punish Iraq because it had, with faith, determination and competence, overstepped the bounds drawn by the United States, the Zionists and the colonialist forces for the countries of the region.

In 1988 and 1989 there were constant campaigns in the press and media, and on the part of officials in the United States and other colonialist countries, paving the way for the achievement of these wicked aims.

In 1990 these campaigns escalated at a feverish and accelerating pace and on an ever-widening scale. The aim was patently obvious to us and to all conscious Arabs and true Muslims, to all free and noble people who believe in freedom and justice in the world. The aim was to prepare for the destruction of this rising Power and to restore predominance in the region in favour of the United States, Zionists and the colonial Powers, this predominance which had for decades continued to prevent the Arabs from recovering their rights and their usurped and occupied territories in Palestine, the Golan and Lebanon, just as it had prevented the Arab nation from achieving its hopes of advancement, progress and justice in order that it might occupy the natural position it deserves in the world by reason of its glorious history and great contribution to human civilization.

During the first months of 1990 these campaigns intensified and broadened and acquired a hysterical character. They began to urge daily that Iraq should be attacked and its leadership liquidated, and that it should be deprived of the means of advancement and progress. The United States, together with other colonialist countries, adopted a series of unfair decisions and measures prohibiting the export of everything which might contribute to the development of Iraq, and to its scientific and industrial advancement. These decisions comprised an effective economic boycott, one of the effects of which was the cancellation of foodstuff contracts in March 1990. It was also clear that the United States was making preparations, in coordination with the Zionist entity, to strike at scientific and industrial facilities and sites and to liquidate the faithful national leadership of Iraq. When the United States discovered that this scheme, which depended to a large extent on the Zionist military capability, was insufficient to achieve its evil objectives, it recruited to the conspiracy its agents and protégés among the corrupt and imperious rulers in the region, the enemies of God.

The role of the latter was to weaken and exhaust the economy of Iraq, and bring it to the brink of economic collapse. At the same time the United States began to reinforce the network of the colonialist alliance in order to set up an American-NATO political and military coalition with the aim of attacking Iraq and gaining control of the region, since it had been afforded the opportunity to do so following the imbalance resulting from the preoccupation of the Soviet Union with its internal affairs.

...

The essence and purpose of the events of 2 August 1990 were not as portrayed by American and colonialist propaganda nor as recounted by the treacherous rulers and followers of America. They constituted a patriotic, national, Islamic uprising against the conspiracy and against the imperious, an uprising against oppression and decadence, against corruption and the imperialist, Zionist and colonialist hegemony over the region, against the imperious rulers, whose role had been revealed in the American Zionist conspiracy. This is why the imperialist Zionist NATO alliance revealed its true aims and intentions from the very first hours of those events. It massed its armies and forces and organized the most evil campaign of delusion, lying and deception the world has witnessed in recent times. This evil, tyrannical imperialist, Zionist, NATO alliance coerced the United Nations into issuing against Iraq, with unparalleled rapidity, a series of iniquitous and unprecedented resolutions. At the same time, this Organization has for decades been incapable of satisfying the simplest claims of the Arab nation and of preserving the simplest rights of the Arabs in Palestine, despite the clarity of the Arab right and the violence of the tragedy endured by the heroic people of Palestine and from which other Arabs suffer, including the oppressed people of Lebanon.

This iniquitous alliance imposed its will on the world, pursued methods of intimidation, blackmail and bribery and employed all the means of viciousness, falsehood and deception in the arsenal of the imperialists, Zionists and forces of colonialism in order to prepare the way for aggression against Iraq.

...

The aggression that has befallen the courageous, proud, combatant, believing and steadfast country of Iraq, has no counterpart in history. In the entire history of mankind, there is no record of the likes of such a coalition, in which there participated the United States, two major Powers and many other States, some 30 in number, against combatant, courageous, steadfast Iraq, whose population does not exceed 18 million. It is indeed an evil, iniquitous, malicious and disbelieving alliance against the stronghold of faith and principle, an alliance against the seat of freedom and the call for justice and fairness. For an entire month, the United States and its allies together with the Zionist entity, which has participated in the aggression from the outset, have been launching savage and devastating attacks against the people of Iraq, against its economic, scientific, cultural and services-related assets and its religious centres and against the country's sites of ancient civilization. History has not seen its like for intensity of fire nor means of slaughter and destruction, launched in the name of the United Nations, a fallacious international legitimacy and the new world order that they intend will be one of United States and NATO hegemony over the world.

The United States and the parties to the evil coalition have delivered, with aircraft that fire their missiles from afar and with long-range missiles, enormous quantities of bombs and explosives against women, children and elderly persons in all the towns and villages of Iraq and even the nomadic Bedouin of the desert. They have struck, in a premeditated manner, mosques, churches, schools, hospitals, civilian factories, bridges and major highways, telephone exchanges, electricity and water installations, irrigation dams, cultural centres and archaeological landmarks in the country. They have struck targets that have no connection of any kind whatever with the military effort or with the arena of the military clash of which they have spoken. The most recent such crime was that vile and heinous crime committed in the deliberate bombing of a civilian shelter, which killed and incinerated hundreds of women, children and elderly persons. The objective of this brutal act of aggression was abundantly clear, and it was to advance the process of destruction that was their intention, and to punish the proud, noble and combatant people of Iraq because it had chosen the way of freedom, independence and honour and rejected humiliation, degradation and subjection to the will of colonialism and zionism.

The United States and its allies have launched a vile and cowardly war against a courageous and believing people. The history and destiny of peoples and nations are not determined by the material possessions of States and ruling regimes. Throughout history, many a strong and wealthy empire has fallen because it adopted the way of shame, cowardice, oppression and dissoluteness. This is the destiny of iniquitous America and its decadent systems, and it is the destiny of zionism and all the forces of colonialism, God willing. Iraq has triumphed in this confrontation. It has triumphed because it has remained steadfast, courageous, believing, noble, and strong-willed. It has triumphed because it has maintained principles and spiritual values derived from its true religion and its centuries-old heritage. Its losses in terms of material assets in this battle, despite their enormity, are of slight importance when set against its preservation of its resolute spirit, its faith deeply rooted in principle and its strong determination to pursue the road of resurgence and progress.

...

On the basis of this strongly entrenched feeling and of this assessment of the character of the conflict, in order to deprive the vicious United States, Zionist and NATO alliance of the opportunity to achieve its planned destructive goals, in appreciation of the initiative of the Soviet Union conveyed by the envoy of the Soviet leadership, and in keeping with the principles set forth in the initiative of President Saddam Hussein, announced on 12 August 1990, the Revolution Command Council has decided to announce the following:

I. Iraq's readiness to deal on the basis of Security Council resolution 660 (1990) with a view to reaching an honourable and acceptable political solution, including withdrawal. The first step that must be taken, as a commitment on Iraq's part with regard to the matter of withdrawal, is linked with the following:

(a) A complete and comprehensive cease-fire on land, at sea and in the air;

(b) That the Security Council should decide to annul, with full retroactive effect, its resolutions 661, 662, 664, 665, 666, 667, 669, 670, 674, 677 and 678 and all the consequences to which they have given rise. Similarly, the annulment of all decisions and measures of boycott and embargo and the other detrimental decisions and measures adopted by certain States against Iraq, jointly and severally, prior to 2 August 1990, and which were the true cause of the Gulf crisis, so that the situation may be restored to normal, as if nothing had happened, and without any detrimental consequences for Iraq for any reason whatever;

(c) The United States, the other States participating in the aggression and all States that have dispatched forces to the region shall withdraw from the Middle East region and the Arabian Gulf region all the forces, armaments and matériel that they introduced before and after 2 August 1990, whether they are on land, at sea, in the oceans or in the gulfs, including the weapons and matériel provided by certain States to Israel on the pretext of the crisis in the Gulf, it being understood that the withdrawal of such forces, armaments and matériel shall take place within a period not to exceed one month from the date of the cease-fire;

(d) That Israel should withdraw from Palestine and from the Arab territories it is occupying in the Golan and in Lebanon, in implementation of the resolutions of the Security Council and the General Assembly of the United Nations. In the event that it should refuse to do so, the Security Council shall apply against Israel the same resolutions that it adopted against Iraq;

(e) The guarantee of Iraq's full and undiminished historical territorial and maritime rights in any political solution;

(f) The political arrangement to be agreed upon shall be based on the will of the people in accordance with genuine democratic practice and not on the acquired privileges of the House of Al Sabah. On this basis, national and Islamic forces must participate in a fundamental manner in the political arrangement to be agreed upon.

II. Those States that have participated in the aggression and in financing it shall undertake to rebuild that which the aggression has destroyed in Iraq, in accordance with the highest specifications for each of the activities, projects and installations targeted by the aggression, at their own expense and without Iraq's incurring any financial outlays.

III. Cancellation of all the debts incurred by Iraq, as well as by the States of the region damaged by the aggression which have not participated in it either directly or indirectly, to the Gulf States and those foreign States which participated in the aggression; the establishment of relations between the poor and wealthy States of the region and of the world based on justice and fairness so as to confront the wealthy countries with unequivocal obligations for the achievement of development in the poor countries and for the elimination of their economic sufferings, on the basis of the principle that the poor have a right to share in the resources of the wealthy; and a halt to the use of double standards in dealing with issues affecting peoples and nations, whether on the part of the Security Council or on the part of one State or another.

IV. The States of the Gulf, including Iran, shall be left free to undertake the task of devising security arrangements in the region and to regulate relations among themselves without any external interference.

V. The declaration of the Arabian Gulf region as a zone free of foreign military bases and of any form of foreign military presence; and commitment by all to that effect.

This is our clear and evident case, which we have brought against the perfidious traitors and their imperialist masters and which we have stated to the whole world. Our fundamental assurance, having placed our trust in the One and Only God, is in our mighty Iraqi people, in its combatant and valiant armed forces, and in those who believe in the road that we are taking in resisting oppression and the oppressors. In the coming days, victory over the oppressors shall be assured, just as it was assured in former days. God is most great. May the infamous be driven out.

S/22230, 15 February 1991

20. Letter from the Permanent Representative of Tunisia to the United Nations addressed to the President of the Security Council, 15 February 1991

I have the honour to transmit to you herewith the attached statement issued by the Ministry of Foreign Affairs of the Republic of Tunisia concerning today's announcement by Iraq that it intends to comply with Security Council resolution 660 (1990).

...

The Tunisian Government has learned with satisfaction that Iraq announced today that it was prepared to cooperate with a view to the implementation of Security Council resolution 660 (1990).

The Tunisian Government, which has worked ceaselessly for the application of international law and the peaceful settlement of the Gulf crisis, and which has called for Iraq's withdrawal and the preservation of the potential and achievements of the Iraqi people which are in danger of destruction and devastation, hopes that this positive initiative by Iraq will prompt a reaction which, by means of a halt to the fighting and a cessation of the conflict, will be able to put an end to this terrible tragedy and to arrive at a just and lasting settlement of all the region's problems, without which, it believes, the security and stability of the region cannot be assured.

The Tunisian Government strongly favours dialogue and peace and hopes sincerely that all the parties to the conflict will seize this opportunity to respond to the whole world's desire for security, stability and peace.

S/22231, 15 February 1991

21. Cuba: draft resolution

The Security Council,

Recalling its resolutions 660, (1990), 661 (1990), 662 (1990), 664 (1990), 665 (1990), 666 (1990), 667 (1990), 669 (1990), 670 (1990), 674 (1990), 677 (1990) and 678 (1990),

Guided by the purposes and principles of the United Nations, as set out in Chapter I of the Charter of the United Nations,

Mindful of the provisions of Article 29 of the Charter of the United Nations, which provides that "the Security Council may establish such subsidiary organs as it deems necessary for the performance of its functions",

Acting in accordance with Rule 28 of the Provisional Rules of Procedure of the Security Council, which states that "the Security Council may appoint a commission or committee or a rapporteur for a specified question",

Deeply concerned by the war situation existing in the Gulf region, which endangers international peace and security, and *determined* to put an end to the hostilities as soon as possible,

1. *Decides* to establish an Ad Hoc Committee, composed of all members of the Security Council, to examine the situation currently prevailing in the Gulf region and consider possible formulas for halting armed actions and achieving a peaceful settlement of the conflict on the basis of the above-mentioned resolutions of the Security Council, thus avoiding further loss of life and destruction;

2. *Decides also* that the Ad Hoc Committee referred to in paragraph 1 shall begin its work immediately after the adoption of the present resolution;

3. *Decides further* that the Ad Hoc Committee shall report back to the Security Council on its findings and on any specific proposals which may have been made not later than 28 February 1991.

S/22232, 15 February 1991

22. Cuba: draft resolution

The Security Council,

Deeply concerned by the state of war existing in the Gulf and, above all, by the losses of human life and the destruction of material property caused by the mass bombings suffered by the cities of Iraq,

Committed to restoring the independence, sovereignty and territorial integrity of Kuwait,

Considering its primary responsibility for the maintenance of international peace and security, as established in Article 24 of the Charter of the United Nations,

Convinced that it is its duty to use all peaceful means for the settlement of international conflicts and differences in order to maintain international peace and security and "save succeeding generations from the scourge of war", as proclaimed in the Preamble to the Charter of the United Nations,

1. *Demands* that the bombings of the cities of Iraq be immediately halted and *requests* that the negotiations for seeking a peaceful resolution of the conflict be immediately intensified without further resort to force;

2. *Decides* to remain seized of the matter.

S/22233, 15 February 1991

23. Cuba: draft resolution

The Security Council,

Reaffirming the need to take steps with a view to reaching a peaceful solution to the present situation in the Gulf,

Committed to restoring the independence, sovereignty and territorial integrity of Kuwait and to avoiding further losses of life and material property,

Considering the role which the Secretary-General has played in the elimination and avoidance of situations of conflict and the role he has to play in achieving a peaceful solution to the situation of war prevailing in the Gulf,

Considering also the efforts which the Secretary-General made to that end before hostilities erupted on 16 January 1991,

1. *Requests* the Secretary-General to renew his good offices and mediation efforts without delay, on the basis of his statement to the press of 15 January 1991, and to report back to the Council as soon as possible;

2. *Decides* to remain seized of the matter.

S/22236, 15 February 1991

24. Letter from the Permanent Representative of Mauritania to the United Nations addressed to the President of the Security Council, 14 February 1991

I have the honour to inform you that since our request submitted on 23 January 1991 in the framework of that made by the States members of the Arab Maghreb Union for an official, public meeting of the Security Council to consider the grave situation in the Arabian Gulf did not meet with a positive response from the Council, we should like to transmit to you the text of the statement that we would have made had the Council agreed to the holding of such a public meeting.

...

Notwithstanding the statement by previous speakers, and notwithstanding all that has been written about the new Gulf crisis since its outbreak on 2 August 1990, a great deal remains to be said and written about this tragedy, and above all about what has not been done in recent months to avoid it and to preserve peace. Nevertheless, in view of the seriousness of the present time, marked as we all know by the launching during the night of 16-17 January by a number of Member States of a war against the Iraqi people, and by the general eclipse of diplomacy since that date, a seriousness which leaves no room for speeches, my statement will be brief, all the more so, Mr. President, in that my country endorses the statement by the representative of the Libyan Arab Jamahiriya, who has spoken in this debate on behalf of the member States of the Arab Maghreb Union.

...

Despite the fact that the harmful impacts of the embargo on the economy and life of the Mauritanian people are various and substantial, and that the losses resulting from the Gulf crisis come at a time when my country is being subjected to an extremely unjust media campaign, the Islamic Republic of Mauritania has since the beginning of these painful events taken a position of sacrifice and of support for a peaceful settlement in conformity with the principles and rules of the organizations to which it belongs. It is in this spirit that it has, *inter alia*, advocated a negotiated Arab solution to this conflict, free from all outside interference, and likewise has rejected the occupation of Kuwait by Iraq and is implementing the provisions of Security Council resolution 661 (1990).

As soon as the conflict entered a particularly dangerous phase Mauritania expressed, through the spokesman for its Government, disapproval of the course of events, and called for a halt to hostilities with a view to the installation of a climate which could lead to the solution by peaceful means of all the region's problems. In a second appeal for a halt to the war, addressed to you on 31 January 1990, our Minister for Foreign Affairs stated that the military operations had turned into an enterprise designed to break Iraq's human and material foundations. Summarizing the consequences of that enterprise of mass destruction, he emphasized that the slaughter of civilian populations was, to say the least, contrary to the principles of democracy, the international rule of law and respect for human rights.

...

Iraq, a sovereign State and a member of our Organization, has for a month now been subjected to unceasing attacks by the coalition's air, sea and land forces. The military operations we are witnessing go, it is universally agreed, far beyond the objectives of the United Nations resolutions. They are apparently aimed at eliminating both Iraq's military capabilities and the human and economic potential of an entire people.

In any event, it cannot but be pointed out that the scope of these operations is unprecedented, as is the slaughter which, moreover, is contrary to all human principles and, naturally, to those of the United Nations Charter, and to the teachings of the Bible and the Koran, in particular. The deluge of bombs falling on the Iraqi people, whose capital has at times been pounded every two minutes, is simply unimaginable. The allied air forces are said to have flown more than 71,000 sorties in a single month. It is said that 40,000 tons of bombs were dropped on Iraq over a 48-hour period. On 17 January 1991, Baghdad is said to have received the equivalent of one Hiroshima, and since then an onslaught of this intensity has taken place against Iraq every day, in an unceasing bombardment. In our day and age, this is anachronistic and inadmissible.

The refusal of any Arab solution to the Gulf crisis and the rejection of a number of plans for peaceful settlement, followed by electronic military intervention against a developing country, give rise to serious concern for the nature of the post-Cold-War order, and equally for the future of the United Nations.

In this context, it is indeed regrettable to note that the Charter of the United Nations and the rules of procedure of the Council have been in abeyance since the outbreak of hostilities, despite a number of requests for an urgent meeting, made on 23, 24, 25 and 28 January by a group of Member States at a time when world peace and security are under serious threat. And who, today, given that this destructive war and this breach of the rules are taking place, is not surprised at the silence on the part of the international community? Do not these hostilities risk reviving, on the eve of the third millennium, the nightmares and frustrations built up in the course of previous wars?

Many new questions are arising and remaining unanswered, especially following the blind destruction which has spared neither holy places, nor historic monuments, nor archaeological sites, nor even shelters for the civilian population. The bombing of the shelter in the Amiriyah district of Baghdad, which claimed hundreds of victims, is a revolting crime which will unfortunately give rise to feelings of hatred and revenge.

I am thinking at this moment of the charter of another institution which declares that "since wars begin in the minds of men, it is in the minds of men that the defences of peace must be constructed".

We are convinced that not all opportunities of avoiding the war were exhausted, and we now hope that the resurgence of the United Nations, whose passive attitude since the outbreak of the war gives rise to many questions and much concern, will afford an opportunity for restricting the conflict to the limits set by the Council and overcoming the crisis in order to halt the tragedy to which a continuation of the confrontation would give rise.

Needless to recall, force has never been an appropriate, still less a civilized, means of settling disputes, and dialogue and diplomacy are the only means of resolving conflicts.

The Maghreb initiative follows this same logic. Its aim is to enable the Council to replace the military operations by diplomatic efforts and to prevent mankind from being engulfed in a devastating and reckless war.

It is certain ... that the vital interests of all States without exception and the ethics of the United Nations, which is the conscience of mankind and its essential forum, seeking to advance mutual understanding among States and to promote justice and peace, both call for the cessation of hostilities and for a return while there is still time to a climate conducive to dialogue and negotiations, which would be an honourable and responsible guarantee, in particular, of the future of the United Nations. Any other attitude would undoubtedly lead to a gloomy outcome for an era said to be one of progress, would do succeeding generations an injustice and would deserve to be condemned by history.

In any event, it would be highly regrettable and dangerous not to safeguard the future of multinational relations by refraining from any action that might accentuate the differences between North and South or lead to further humiliation for the Arab Muslim world.

In this connection, it would be a mistake to continue to disregard the civilization, the history, the faith and the sacred values of peaceful peoples for whom honour and dignity outweigh everything else.

...

In this exceptionally serious situation, the Islamic Republic of Mauritania, which rejected the occupation of Kuwait by Iraq and is an honourable and law-abiding country for which any war dishonours the human race, fully associates itself with all the appeals being made throughout the world for the Security Council to assume its full responsibilities and bring about the cessation of the armed conflict with a view to giving political solutions a chance. It considers that in the interests of the maintenance of international peace and security, everything must be done to effect an immediate halt to the hostilities initiated against Iraq on 16 January.

We call for the speediest possible end to be put to this horror, which has dramatic consequences on all levels and for all countries.

...

In these difficult days when valuable gains are everywhere threatened, it is highly appropriate that the Council should, before the conflict becomes unmanageable, make new efforts for a settlement of the crisis by peaceful means, and take effective measures to prevent a deterioration of the situation in the Middle East region, as well as in the rest of the world, where the atmosphere is everywhere tense.

It is important, at this crucial juncture when peace is threatened on all sides, that the United Nations, which is responsible for universal security, should play its role and work earnestly and without respite on those functions which are of the greatest importance to all peoples those which distinguish and do honour to the Charter of the United Nations, namely the maintenance of international peace and security.

With respect to the search for a political solution to the central problem, namely the Israeli-Arab conflict, and for ways of safeguarding the *détente* which emerged at the beginning of 1990, the Council has an obligation to take effective measures to put an end to the mass immigration of Soviet Jews into Palestine and to promote the earliest possible convening of the peace conference which the international community has for so many years so earnestly desired.

...

S/22237, 15 February 1991

25. Letter from the Representatives of Algeria, the Libyan Arab Jamahiriya, Mauritania, Morocco and Tunisia to the United Nations addressed to the President of the Security Council, 14 February 1991

We, the representatives of the countries members of the Arab Maghreb Union, regret that it took the Security Council three weeks to act on our request of 23 January 1991 for an urgent meeting of the Council. We also deeply regret the fact that the Council created a precedent by deciding that the general debate would be held in closed session.

We had already told you and the outgoing President that the delegations of the Arab Maghreb Union would not participate in debates held behind closed doors. We therefore wish to confirm that we will not participate in these closed meetings.

...

A/45/956, S/22238, 15 February 1991

26. Letter from the Permanent Representative of Kuwait to the United Nations addressed to the Secretary-General, 15 February 1991

I have the honour to transmit herewith the statement issued by the Government of Kuwait, concerning the report carried out by the information media on the declaration put out by the Iraqi regime today, containing its conditions for withdrawal from Kuwait.

...

Mr. Abd ar-Rahman Abdullah Al-Awadi, the Minister of State for Cabinet Affairs, said that the report carried by the information media, concerning the declaration put out by the Iraqi regime today and containing its conditions for withdrawal from Kuwait, added nothing new to Iraq's stubborn position and merely constituted a continuation of the policy of deception, duplicity and procrastination which the Iraqi regime had consistently pursued since its iniquitous invasion of Kuwait. It also constituted a further episode in that regime's desperate attempts and manoeuvres to circumvent the resolutions of the Security Council of the United Nations, with a view to breaking out of its present state of isolation and splitting the international consensus that rejected its ongoing tyrannical occupation of Kuwait.

The Minister of State for Cabinet Affairs emphasized Kuwait's clearly-defined and firm position, namely its insistence on full and unconditional compliance with all the Security Council resolutions relating to the question of Kuwait.

He said that world-wide attention should be drawn to the tragic situation that the steadfast Kuwaiti people had been experiencing in the territory of Kuwait since 2 August 1990, as well as the daily sufferings of our fellow citizens who were incarcerated in detention centres, where they were being murdered and subjected to various forms of torture and ill-treatment at the hands of the forces of the treacherous Iraqi regime.

Mr. Abd ar-Rahman Abdullah Al-Awadi went on to say that Kuwait was calling upon the international community to resolutely pursue its endeavours to put an end to the tragic situation in which the Kuwaiti people found itself, to intensify its diligent efforts to compel the Iraqi regime to comply fully and unconditionally with the relevant Security Council resolutions, and to restore justice in a manner conducive to the achievement of security and stability in the region and to the promotion of a new international order aimed at bringing about regard to a peaceful and secure world. At the same time, Kuwait was urging the fraternal Iraqi people to take a united stand in the face of injustice and tyranny and to rid Iraq of its despotic leadership whose perverse policy had brought about successive disasters, the main victims of which had been Iraq and its citizens. In particular, the grave consequences of that policy had led the Arab and Islamic nations into further disunion, fragmentation and destruction.

S/22232/Rev.1, 18 February 1991

27. Cuba: revised draft resolution, 18 February 1991

The Security Council,

Deeply concerned by the state of war existing in the Gulf and, above all, by the losses of human life and the destruction of material property caused by the mass bombings of the cities of Iraq and other military actions affecting the civilian populations in the countries of the region,

Committed to restoring the independence, sovereignty and territorial integrity of Kuwait,

Recalling the Geneva Conventions of 1949,

Considering its primary responsibility for the maintenance of international peace and security, as established in Article 24 of the Charter of the United Nations,

Convinced that it is its duty to use all peaceful means for the settlement of international conflicts and differences in order to maintain international peace and security and "save succeeding generations from the scourge of war", as proclaimed in the Preamble to the Charter of the United Nations,

1. *Demands* that the bombings of the cities of Iraq and all military actions against the civilian populations in the countries of the region be immediately halted;

2. *Decides* to remain seized of the matter.

S/22240, 19 February 1991

28. Letter from the Permanent Representative of Mauritania to the United Nations addressed to the President of the Security Council, 17 February 1991

I have the honour to transmit to you herewith the text of a statement issued on 15 February 1991 by the Mauritanian Ministry of Foreign Affairs and Cooperation concerning the situation in the Gulf region:

> "The Islamic Republic of Mauritania welcomes the initiative taken on 29 Rajab A.H. 1411, corresponding to 15 February 1991, by the Revolution Command Council of the Republic of Iraq. It believes that the initiative will contribute to the restoration of law and justice in the region.
>
> The Islamic Republic of Mauritania, which has constantly affirmed since the beginning of this crisis its commitment to the international rule of law and to peace and security for all the peoples of the region, has always rejected recourse to war.
>
> Through this initiative, Iraq has just offered the international community the means of averting a catastrophe.
>
> The Islamic Republic of Mauritania hopes that this opportunity will be seized by all the parties concerned, with a view to achieving a peaceful and lasting settlement of this crisis."

...

S/22241, 19 February 1991

29. Letter from the Permanent Representative of the Union of Soviet Socialist Republics to the United Nations addressed to the Secretary-General, 19 February 1991

...

"During the talks with the personal representative of the President of Iraq, the Soviet side proceeded from the assumption that the current spiralling crisis in the Persian Gulf called for immediate and resolute measures to avoid further escalation of the conflict, to save thousands of lives, and to prevent the threat of disruption of the ecological balance of the whole region.

In the course of a prolonged and substantive exchange of views on the situation in the military-operations theatre and on the whole range of issues that brought about those operations, President Gorbachev proposed a plan of specific measures.

This plan is predicated on the necessity of strictly abiding by the mandate set forth in the resolutions of the Security Council regarding the Gulf crisis. The key element of the plan consists in securing a rapid start of a withdrawal of the Iraqi forces from Kuwait, which would make it possible to put an immediate end to the bloodshed.

We hope that our proposals will be considered in a most serious manner. We are now awaiting a reaction from Baghdad, which we expect very soon. On the basis of that reaction, a substantive discussion of practical measures would be possible.

The current situation calls for a cautious, responsible approach. This is no time for loud and spectacular initiatives, but for a serious diplomatic process. The effectiveness of such a process will determine the prospects for a rapid movement towards political settlement on the basis of the decisions of the Security Council, with due regard for the important role of that body in maintaining international peace and security."

S/22242, 19 February 1991

30. Letter from the Permanent Representative of Egypt to the United Nations addressed to the Secretary-General, 19 February 1991

I have the honour to transmit to you herewith the text of a press statement, issued at Cairo on 15 February 1991 by a meeting of the Ministers for Foreign Affairs of the States members of the Gulf Cooperation Council, the Syrian Arab Republic and the Arab Republic of Egypt, with regard to the communiqué of the Iraqi Revolution Command Council concerning Iraq's readiness to deal with Security Council resolution 660 (1990).

...

Meeting at Cairo on Friday, 15 February 1991, the Ministers for Foreign Affairs of the States members of the Gulf Cooperation Council, the Syrian Arab Republic and the Arab Republic of Egypt considered the statement issued by the Iraqi Revolution Command Council, as broadcast by Radio Baghdad, concerning the readiness of the Iraqi regime to deal with Security Council resolution 660 (1990). As is common knowledge, in its resolution 660, the Council demands that Iraq withdraw immediately and unconditionally all its forces from the State of Kuwait to the positions in which they were located on 1 August 1990. The Ministers view the Iraqi proposal, which contains unacceptable conditions that are not in accord with the resolutions of the Security Council, as lacking in seriousness. The proposal further includes new conditions.

The Iraqi proposal hampers the implementation of the resolutions of the Security Council, which stipulate a complete and unconditional withdrawal from the State of Kuwait and the restoration of legitimacy thereto, and it is, accordingly, to be rejected as a whole and in its various aspects.

The Ministers meeting at Cairo call upon the Iraqi regime to withdraw its forces immediately from the State of Kuwait and to restore legitimacy thereto in implementation of the resolutions of the Arab Summit, the Organization of the Islamic Conference and the Security Council, in compliance with inter-Arab and international legitimacy and in accordance with the will of the international community.

A/45/957, S/22244, 19 February 1991

31. Letter from the Permanent Representative of Egypt to the United Nations addressed to the Secretary-General, 19 February 1991

I have the honour to transmit to you herewith the text of a press statement issued at Cairo on 16 February 1991 by a meeting of the Ministers for Foreign Affairs of the States members of the Gulf Cooperation Council, the Syrian Arab Republic and the Arab Republic of Egypt.

...

In the context of their national affiliation and their genuine commitment to the covenants governing joint Arab action, principally the Pact of the League of Arab States, the Joint Defence and Economic Co-operation Treaty between the States of the Arab League and the Arab Solidarity Pact of 15 September 1965,

Conscious of their national responsibility in the critical times through which the Arab world is passing,

In their desire to make all possible efforts to heal the rift in the Arab world arising out of the Iraqi occupation of the fraternal State of Kuwait,

The Minister for Foreign Affairs of the States members of the Gulf Cooperation Council, the Syrian Arab Republic and the Arab Republic of Egypt held a meeting at Cairo on 15 and 16 February 1991.

The Ministers reviewed all aspects of the operations for the liberation of the fraternal State of Kuwait, and they reaffirmed their adherence to the implementation of the resolutions of inter-Arab, Islamic and international legitimacy for the restoration of security and stability in the region, which require:

1. The withdrawal of Iraq without qualifications or conditions from all the territory of the fraternal State of Kuwait.

2. The restoration of legitimacy to Kuwait.

3. Commitment to the full implementation of the relevant Security Council resolutions.

4. Commitment to the principles of the peaceful settlement of disputes between States.

The Ministers expressed their deep pain and bitter sorrow at the sufferings of innocent members of the Kuwaiti and Iraqi peoples as a result of the continued Iraqi occupation of the State of Kuwait and of the intransigence of the Iraqi leadership and its refusal to comply with the resolutions of inter-Arab, Islamic and international legitimacy.

...

A/45/960, S/22247, 20 February 1991

32. Letter from the Permanent Representative of Luxembourg to the United Nations addressed to the Secretary-General, 20 February 1991

I have the honour to transmit to you herewith the English and French texts of the Declaration on the Gulf crisis issued on 19 February 1991 by the European Community and its 12 member States ... .

...

The Community and its member States have taken note with interest of the appeal of President Gorbachev to the Iraqi leadership and they welcome in particular its call for a full and unconditional withdrawal of the Iraqi troops from Kuwait and the re-establishment of the sovereignty and the legitimate government of that country in conformity with the relevant Security Council resolutions.

They renew their appeal to the Iraqi Government fully and unconditionally to implement all the relevant resolutions of the United Nations Security Council thus putting an end to the conflict and sparing new sufferings to their people and the people of Kuwait.

They reaffirm the commitment of the Community and its member States to contribute actively, once international legality is re-established, to security, stability and development for all the countries in the region, in an appropriate framework which also takes into account the need for a global, flexible and gradual approach to the various problems of the area. In this connection, they reaffirm their commitment to the sovereignty, unity, independence and territorial integrity of all the countries of the region. They will continue their consultations with the United States of America and other concerned countries, notably the Union of Soviet Socialist Republics.

They are fully committed to support the role of the United Nations in promoting security and international peace in the area. They believe that it is mainly for the States of the region to reach agreement on arrangements aimed at ensuring their future security both individually and collectively. The Community and its member States will be ready to play their full part in supporting the efforts of the States concerned, and to complement them with appropriate and convergent action. In this connection, the Community and its member States welcome the fact that, at their meeting held at Cairo on 15 and 16 February, the Foreign Ministers of Egypt, the Syrian Arab Republic and the Gulf Co-operation Council (GCC) agreed upon a framework for future co-operation. They will undertake the appropriate contacts with those countries. A meeting of the Troika will be held in the near future with Israel at Ministerial level. Other countries, notably the Islamic Republic of Iran, have also an important role to play for the future stability of the region.

The Community and its member States attach particular importance to their political dialogue with the GCC countries. They are looking forward to the early convening of the EC/GCC Co-operation Council.

The Community and its member States attach special importance to their co-operation and political dialogue with the countries of the Arab Maghreb Union. They will promote the pursuit of a meaningful and constructive dialogue at political level shortly, and will undertake the appropriate contact.

The Community and its member States believe that the Arab/Israeli conflict and the Palestinian question are fundamental sources of instability in the region. They consider that the international community should make renewed efforts urgently to achieve a comprehensive, just and lasting solution. They continue to believe that a properly structured international conference at an appropriate time will provide a suitable framework for negotiations. Such a conference will require serious preparation. They will actively promote the search for a peaceful settlement through dialogue with and between all concerned parties.

With regard to the situation in Lebanon, they express their strong support for the full implementation of the Taif agreement as the means to achieve national reconciliation in a Lebanon free of all foreign troops.

The Community and its member States endorse the view expressed at the Cairo meeting about the importance of efforts by the Arabs themselves to foster greater economic and social development, respecting the principle of sovereignty over economic resources. The Community and its member States share this perspective and stand ready, in full respect of this principle and in a spirit of mutual solidarity, to develop their co-operation with the countries of the region. Their immediate priorities are to ensure the early implementation of their new Mediterranean policy and the rapid disbursement of their aid for the three countries most directly affected by the economic consequences of the Gulf crisis.

The Community and its member States are aware of the need for a comprehensive approach to all the problems of the Mediterranean, Middle East and Gulf region. In this connection, they are willing to explore the modalities for launching a process aimed at establishing a set of rules and principles in the field of security, economic co-operation, human rights and cultural exchanges.

S/22254, 22 February 1991

33. Letter from the Permanent Representative of the Libyan Arab Jamahiriya to the United Nations addressed to the President of the Security Council, 22 February 1991

I have the honour to transmit herewith the statement issued after the meetings of the Council of Ministers of the Arab Maghreb Union, held in the city of Benghazi, Libya, on 20 February 1991.

...

The Council of Ministers for Foreign Affairs of the Arab Maghreb Union, during its emergency meeting in the city of Benghazi in the Socialist People's Libyan Arab Jamahiriya on 20 February 1991, after reviewing the serious situation resulting from the devastating war that is currently being waged in the Gulf region, and in continuation of its endeavours, including its request for a meeting of the Security Council in order to arrange a cease-fire and provide an opportunity to find a political solution to the Gulf crisis,

Expressing its deep regret at the Security Council's failure to respond by holding a public meeting to arrange a cease-fire,

Decides as follows:

1. The Council regards the Iraqi initiative, expressing willingness to deal on the basis of Security Council resolution 660 (1990), as a positive step towards the achievement of a political solution to the Gulf crisis, within the context of international legality, calls upon all the parties to respond to that initiative, and emphasizes the fact that Iraq's acceptance of the said resolution removes all justification for the continuation of this war.

2. The Council, recalling the position that it adopted on 3 September 1990 at Algiers, comprising a categorical rejection of the use of force to settle disputes, rejects the policy of starving, and impairing the capabilities of, the Iraqi people and condemns the brutal bombardment of innocent civilians in Iraq and Kuwait, as well as the deliberate and comprehensive destruction of Iraq's capabilities, including its infrastructure, with a view to the annihilation of its economic and scientific institutions and its cultural heritage, as flagrantly transcending the resolutions of the United Nations Security Council.

3. The Council draws attention to the real dangers arising from the showering of material, political and military aid on the Zionist entity, which has taken advantage of the war in the Gulf in order to strengthen its military and economic capabilities.

4. The Council affirms its ongoing support for the just struggle of the Palestinian people, under the leadership of the Palestine Liberation Organization, their sole legitimate representative, and for the Palestinian people's tempestuous uprising against the Zionist occupation and their resistance to the various methods of Zionist repression.

5. In view of the grave developments that the Arab nation is experiencing, the Council calls for an urgent meeting of the Ministers for Foreign Affairs of the Arab States, to be held in one of the Maghreb capitals, for the purpose of studying the Arab situation in such a way as to ensure the preservation of the higher interests and the capabilities of the Arab nation and the restoration of Arab solidarity.

6. The Council takes note of the appeal made to it by the European Economic Community, and the Council of Ministers will be contacting the Presidency of the EEC in this connection.

A/46/94, S/22256, 22 February 1991

34. Letter from the Permanent Representative of Egypt to the United Nations addressed to the Secretary-General, 21 February 1991

I have the honour to transmit herewith the text of the statement issued after the joint meeting of the Ministers for Foreign Affairs of the member States of the Bureaux of the Fifth Islamic Summit Conference and the Nineteenth Ministerial Conference and of the States chairing the standing committees of the Organization of the Islamic Conference, which was held at Cairo on 21 February 1991.

...

1. The joint meeting of the Ministers for Foreign Affairs of the member States of the Bureaux of the Fifth Islamic Summit Conference and the Nineteenth Conference of Islamic Foreign Ministers and of the member States chairing the standing committees of the Organization of the Islamic Conference was held at Cairo, in the Arab Republic of Egypt, on 6 Sha'ban, corresponding to 21 February 1991, to discuss the situation in the Gulf region and the role of the Organization of the Islamic Conference in settling the Iraqi-Kuwaiti dispute arising from the Iraqi occupation of Kuwait.

2. The meeting was attended by the Ministers for Foreign Affairs and the heads of the delegations of the following member States:
Egypt, Gabon, Kuwait, Maldives, Pakistan, Palestine, Kingdom of Saudi Arabia, Senegal and Turkey. This meeting was not attended by the Kingdom of Morocco.

3. The meeting took note of the contents of the report submitted by H.E. Dr. Hamid Algabid, Secretary-General of the Organization of the Islamic Conference, concerning the follow-up and implementation of the resolutions contained in the special declaration concerning the Iraqi occupation of Kuwait, which was issued by the Nineteenth Conference of Islamic Foreign Ministers, held at Cairo in the Arab Republic of Egypt from 9 to 14 Muharram 1411 A.H., corresponding to 31 July - 5 August 1990.

4. After an extensive study of the present situation prevailing in the Gulf region, particularly in the light of the events that are currently taking place, the meeting decided that the invasion, occupation and annexation of the State of Kuwait by the Republic of Iraq had thrust the region, the Islamic nation and the world as a whole into a serious crisis with immeasurable consequences.

5. The meeting noted, with great bitterness, that the crisis resulting from the invasion and occupation of Kuwait by Iraqi forces had led to a large-scale armed conflict with devastating and momentous consequences for mankind and the human environment. Moreover, the exile and cruel sufferings that had been imposed on the Kuwaiti people, as well as the mass emigration of hundreds of thousands of workers from Iraq and Kuwait, the loss of human life and the destruction of social and economic institutions in both Iraq and Kuwait, constituted far-reaching dimensions of the disaster that had been brought about by the presence of Iraqi armed forces in Kuwait.

6. The meeting strongly condemned the invasion and continued occupation of the State of Kuwait by the armed forces of the Republic of Iraq as an act incompatible with the principles of the Charter of the Organization of the Islamic Conference, Islamic values and the rules of international law. It emphasized the content of the declaration concerning the situation between Iraq and Kuwait, which was adopted by the Nineteenth Conference of Islamic Foreign Ministers, as well as the final declaration issued after the annual coordination meeting of the Ministers for Foreign Affairs of the member States of the Organization of the Islamic Conference, which was held at the United Nations in New York on 12 Rabi I 1411 A.H., corresponding to 1 October 1990, and the declaration issued after the joint meeting of senior representatives of the member States of the Bureaux of the Fifth Islamic Summit and the Nineteenth Conference of Islamic Foreign Ministers, which was held at Jedda on 22 Jumada II 1411 A.H., corresponding to 8 January 1991.

7. The meeting commended the numerous endeavours that had been made by the international community, jointly and severally, to contain the crisis since its outbreak and to help to find a peaceful solution thereto. It expressed its deep regret that Iraq had failed to respond to the appeals and entreaties which had been made to it by the Islamic nation and the world as a whole, and also that Iraq had chosen to defy them through its stubborn refusal to comply with Islamic and international law by withdrawing its forces from the State of Kuwait so that the latter country's legitimate Government could be restored.

8. With regard to the declaration issued by the Iraqi Government on 29 Rajab 1411 A.H., corresponding to 15 February 1991, the meeting once again stressed the fact that the immediate, full and unconditional withdrawal of the Iraqi forces from Kuwaiti territory, the restoration of the legitimate Government, headed by His Highness Sheikh Jaber Al-Jaber Al-Sabah, Amir of the State of Kuwait and current President of the Fifth Islamic Summit Conference, and a full commitment on the part of Iraq to respect the relevant resolutions of the Security Council and the Organization of the Islamic Conference, as well as the principle of good-neighbourliness, constituted a fundamental and imperative precondition for a political settlement of the crisis.

9. The meeting reaffirmed all the resolutions of the Islamic Summits and the Conferences of Islamic Foreign Ministers, concerning Palestine, and also re-emphasized the following facts:

Their States, which had made tremendous sacrifices and had provided ongoing moral, political and diplomatic support, in spite of all the challenges and obstacles, affirmed their continuing support for the heroic uprising of the Palestinian people living under occupation.

The member States affirmed their Islamic and historic commitment to the legitimate national rights of the Palestinian people, including the latter's inalienable right to exercise self-determination and to establish its State on its national soil.

Their commitment to the quest for a peaceful, just, comprehensive and lasting settlement of the question of Palestine outweighed any other consideration within the context of an international peace conference.

10. The meeting deplored Iraq's stubborn refusal to abide by Islamic and international law and denounced Iraq's attempts to link a solution to the crisis resulting from the occupation of Kuwait to other questions. The meeting stressed that the question of Palestine was a national responsibility of all Arabs and Muslims. Consequently, it deplored the Iraqi regime's attempts to exploit the question of Palestine in order to justify its invasion of Kuwait and its displacement of the latter's people, as well as hundreds of thousands of workers in that country, including Palestinians.

In the light of Iraqi practices, the meeting affirmed that regime's ineligibility to undertake any action to solve the region's problems and emphasized the spurious and invalid nature of its allegations concerning the role that it was playing as the defender of Arab and Islamic causes.

11. The meeting expressed its appreciation for the sacrifices that had been made by the countries and peoples of the region in order to counter the aggression and withstand its effects. In this connection, the meeting also stressed the solidarity of the member States of the Organization of the Islamic Conference with the Government and people of the State of Kuwait, the Kingdom of Saudi Arabia and the other States and peoples of the region in the face of the cruel and unjust ordeal with which they have been afflicted. The meeting affirmed the member States' commitment to the liberation of Kuwait, the restoration of its legitimate Government and support for the endeavours of the Gulf States to maintain and defend the security and stability of the region.

12. The meeting emphasized that stability in the Gulf region necessitated respect for the inviolable and universally recognized borders of all the States of the region, as they were before the beginning of the crisis.

13. The meeting took note of the apprehensions expressed by the international community and stressed the need to prohibit the use of chemical, biological and nuclear weapons. The meeting also emphasized the need for full respect for the rules of Islamic law, the provisions of the Geneva Conventions and the other principles of international humanitarian law.

14. The meeting called upon the international community as a whole to continue contributing to the achievement of these objectives in a manner consistent with the requirements of Islamic and international law.

15. In addition to the settlement of the present crisis in the Gulf, the meeting called upon the member States to begin the process of giving serious thought, within the context of joint Islamic action, to ways and means to promote security and cooperation in the Islamic world. This process must include the political, economic, social, cultural and other aspects and endeavours must be made to establish peace and security on a firm footing throughout the Islamic world. The objectives of cooperation and solidarity, which had been clearly defined in the historic Makkah Declaration, must also be put into practice in a tangible manner. In this connection, the meeting welcomed the endeavours that had been made by the member States of the Gulf Cooperation Council and other Islamic States.

16. The meeting declared that it shared the real distress felt by millions of Muslims throughout the world at the cruel ordeal that had been imposed on the peoples of the Gulf region, which contained their holiest places, due to Iraq's unjustifiable refusal to withdraw from Kuwaiti territory and respect the independence, sovereignty, security and territorial integrity of the other States of the region. The meeting expressed its hope that the day would come when Iraq would return to the ranks of the Islamic nation and act in concord with the peoples of the Gulf region and all other Islamic peoples in order to achieve the legitimate aspirations of the Muslims in regard to justice, freedom, peace and progress.

17. The meeting expressed its deep gratitude to the Arab Republic of Egypt for hosting this meeting and for the hospitable manner in which President Muhammad Hosni Mubarak, President of the Arab Republic of Egypt, had received the heads of delegations as a token of his desire to promote the spirit of Islamic solidarity at this crucial stage in the history of the Islamic world.

S/22260, 23 February 1991

35. Letter from the Permanent Representative of the Libyan Arab Jamahiriya to the United Nations addressed to the President of the Security Council, 23 February 1991

I have the honour to transmit herewith a letter from Colonel Muammar Qaddafi, Leader of the glorious Revolution of 1 September, addressed to Your Excellency.

...

Iraq has expressed its readiness to implement Security Council resolution 660 (1990). This means that Iraq has undertaken to comply with the decision of the international community, as represented by the United Nations.

In order to maintain the credibility of the Organization and ensure respect for its Charter, we are calling for the holding of an urgent meeting of the Security Council to make arrangements for the withdrawal. This matter should not be left to certain parties whose conduct might transcend the resolutions of the Security Council, thereby entailing disastrous consequences for peace and security in the region and the world as a whole.

Accordingly, we trust that this request will receive your support and attention and that you will immediately convene an urgent meeting of the Security Council before it is too late.

S/22262, 24 February 1991

36. .Letter from the Permanent Representative of Iraq to the United Nations addressed to the President of the Security Council, 24 February 1991

On instructions from my Government, I have the honour to inform you that the Government of the Republic of Iraq endorses the Soviet peace initiative.

...

S/22264, 25 February 1991

37. Letter from the Permanent Representative of the Libyan Arab Jamahiriya to the United Nations addressed to the President of the Security Council, 23 February 1991

I have the honour to transmit herewith a letter addressed to you by Colonel Muammar Qaddafi, Leader of the Great Revolution of 1 September.

...

Iraq is being subjected to a deliberate process of humiliation. It has become clear that the intention behind what is now taking place is not the recovery of Kuwait at all, nor is this operation being conducted in accordance with any of the Security Council resolutions.

What is occurring is an operation designed to debase the Arab community - through Iraq - in the eyes of the world. Iraq has decided to withdraw from Kuwait: whether within a week or two weeks, it is a matter of a few days. There can be no doubt that peace is more valuable than this.

We have patiently endured the occupation of Kuwait for months. Why should we not be patient for a few days in order to save peace and the future?

Even if the West does inflict its humiliation on the Arabs through Iraq, and even if Iraq is defeated, the result will be the collapse of the United Nations, just as the League of Nations collapsed. Bitter enmity will also be sown between West and East, and particularly Arabs and Muslims. The price will be a future loss greater than any temporary victory over Iraq and the Arab community.

There are historic moments in which we must exercise self-restraint in recognition of our responsibility to peoples and our responsibility to ensure a future free of revenge, hatred, the exchange of hostilities and their legacy.

Iraq will withdraw from Kuwait: this is an achievement for international legitimacy. Bloodshed can be prevented, and it is possible to maintain the prestige of the United Nations rather than to kill it off.

All that is lacking is self-restraint in these decisive moments.

We call upon the United Nations and the Security Council - and any civilized peoples - to allow a historic opportunity for reason and law to prevail and for the Security Council alone to determine the way in which steps may be taken to attain a solution which preserves the honour of all. The most important consideration is to preserve peace and to prevent bloodshed.

I am convinced that the problem of Kuwait is over, but Iraq has no choice other than to defend its dignity and the dignity of the Arab community, whatever the price. Libya places itself at the disposal of the United Nations to play the courageous role from which all others have shrunk.

S/22265, 25 February 1991

38. Letter from the Permanent Representative of the Union of Soviet Socialist Republics to the United Nations addressed to the Secretary-General, 25 February 1991

I have the honour to transmit to you the text of the statement by the Soviet Government concerning the start of ground operations in the Persian Gulf region.

...

United States President George Bush announced at dawn on 24 February that he had ordered the start of ground operations against Iraq.

The instinct to rely on a military solution prevailed, despite the fact that Iraq's agreement to withdraw its forces from Kuwait in keeping with United Nations Security Council resolution 660 (1990) had created a basically new situation, clearing the way to channelling the Gulf conflict towards a political settlement. As is known, Iraqi Foreign Minister Tariq Aziz told a news conference in Moscow on 23 February that the Iraqi leadership was prepared to withdraw all its forces immediately and unconditionally from Kuwait to the positions in which they were located on 1 August 1990.

The Soviet Union, which had done much to impel Iraq to take that step, urged the international community to take advantage of the opportunity to prevent the conflict from escalating into a still more acute and bloodier phase. In the course of 23 February, the Soviet President had telephone conversations with the leaders of the United States of America, the United Kingdom of Great Britain and Northern Ireland, France, Italy, Germany, Japan, Syria, Egypt and the Islamic Republic of Iran. Before that, the Soviet President had sent personal messages to the Heads of State and Government of all countries members of the Security Council, as well as to the Secretary-General of the United Nations, briefing them on the results of the latest round of talks with Tariq Aziz in Moscow, which produced qualitative shifts in Iraq's position. The Government of Arab States were informed of the steps we were taking. The Soviet representative to the United Nations took steps aimed at convening an emergency meeting of the Security Council to examine on an urgent basis the situation that had arisen, set the date for the start of the withdrawal of Iraqi troops from Kuwait, and resolve the issue of confirming, verifying and monitoring the cease-fire and the troop withdrawal.

The Soviet Union expresses regret that a very real chance of securing a peaceful outcome to the conflict and achieving the objectives set by the Security Council resolutions without further casualties and destruction has been missed.

The differences between the formulas accepted by Iraq and the proposals by a number of other countries were slight, and lent themselves to resolution in the Security Council framework within a day or two. It is still not too late to do this. The Security Council, which is now meeting, should get down to examining without delay the new situation that has taken shape.

S/22266, 25 February 1991

39. Letter from the Permanent Representative of Tunisia to the United Nations addressed to the President of the Security Council, 25 February 1991

I have the honour to transmit herewith the text of a Communiqué issued on 24 February 1991 by the Minister for Foreign Affairs of the Republic of Tunisia following the start of the ground offensive in the Gulf region.

...

The Tunisian Government has reacted with strong disapproval and great disappointment to the loss of the new opportunities for peace and the insistence on escalating the war against Iraq by launching a ground offensive despite that country's acceptance of the implementation of Security Council resolution 660 (1990).

It reaffirms Tunisia's total solidarity with and profound sympathy for the fraternal people of Iraq, who are being subjected to the ongoing and wholesale destruction of their human and material potential.

In the face of this serious deterioration in the situation, which is detrimental to the inviolability and destiny of the Arab nation and threatens world peace and security, Tunisia appeals to the conscience of the world and to all peace-loving forces to work to halt the hostilities and put an end to this terrible tragedy.

S/22271, 26 February 1991

40. Letter from the Permanent Representative of Yugoslavia to the United Nations addressed to the President of the Security Council, 26 February 1991

I have the honour to transmit the text of the statement by the Federal Secretariat for Foreign Affairs of the SFR of Yugoslavia dated 26 February 1991 on the war in the Persian Gulf.

...

Proceeding from the established positions of the Movement of Non-Aligned Countries concerning the war in the Persian Gulf and the latest developments in that region, Yugoslavia, also in its capacity as Chairman of the Movement of Non-Aligned Countries, considers that the United Nations Security Council should urgently review most recent situation. In Yugoslavia's assessment, the conditions have been created for the Security Council to take action so as to ensure the strict implementation of all relevant Security Council resolutions with a view to reestablishing peace in this area, restoring sovereignty and territorial integrity of Kuwait and to preventing further loss of life and destruction.

A/45/965, S/22272, 27 February 1991

41. Letter from the Permanent Representative of Luxembourg to the United Nations addressed to the Secretary-General, 26 February 1991

I have the honour to enclose the text, in French and English, of the statement of the Gulf crisis issued by the European Community and its 12 member States on 24 February 1991 ... .

...

The Community and its member States deeply regret that Iraq has failed to respond positively to the appeal of the international coalition to withdraw immediately and unconditionally from Kuwait in accordance with the United Nations Security Council resolutions. In this grave moment, the Community and its member States are at the side of the forces of the allied coalition.

The Community and its member States hope that the liberation of Kuwait can now intervene rapidly and with a minimum of loss in human lives on both sides.

S/22273, 27 February 1991

42. Letter from the Permanent Representative of Iraq to the United Nations addressed to the President of the Security Council, 27 February 1991

On instructions from my Government, I have the honour to transmit herewith a letter from Mr. Tariq Aziz, Deputy Prime Minister and Minister for Foreign Affairs of the Republic of Iraq, addressed to Your Excellency.

...

I have the honour to notify you that the Iraqi Government reaffirms its agreement to comply fully with Security Council resolution 660 (1990). The Iraqi armed forces have started to withdraw to the positions they were in prior to 1 August 1990. It is hoped that the withdrawal will be fully completed within the next few hours, notwithstanding the continued attacks by American and other forces on the Iraqi armed forces during the withdrawal process.

I should like to inform you further that the Iraqi Government agrees to comply with resolution 662 (1990) and 674 (1990) if the Security Council adopts a resolution providing for an immediate cease-fire and the cessation of all military operations on land, at sea and in the air and if it is deemed that the bases on which Security Council resolutions 661 (1990), 665 (1990) and 670 (1990) were adopted no longer exist and that those resolutions consequently are no longer in effect.

The Iraqi Government also affirms its full readiness to release all the prisoners of war immediately after the cease-fire and to return them to their home countries within a very short period of time in accordance with the Third Geneva Convention of 1949, under the auspices of the International Committee of the Red Cross.

...

S/22274, 27 February 1991

43. Letter from the Permanent Representative of Iraq to the United Nations addressed to the President of the Security Council, 27 February 1991

Upon instructions from my Government I have the honour to inform you that all Iraqi forces have withdrawn from Kuwait at dawn today 27 February 1991 local time. The American and other pro-aggressor forces continued to attack our forces during their withdrawal. ...

S/22275, 27 February 1991 [Reissued for technical reasons.]

44. Letter from the Permanent Representative of Iraq to the United Nations addressed to the President of the Security Council, 27 February 1991 [An identical letter addressed to the Secretary-General is contained in document S/22276.]

On instructions from my Government I have the honour to transmit herewith a letter addressed to you from Mr. Tariq Aziz, Deputy Prime Minister, Minister for Foreign Affairs of the Republic of Iraq.

...

I have the honour to inform you officially that the Government of Iraq agrees to comply fully with Security Council resolution 660 (1990) and all the other Security Council resolutions.

...

S/22277, 27 February 1991

45. Letter from the Permanent Representative of Cuba to the United Nations addressed to the President of the Security Council, 27 February 1991

I have the honour to transmit herewith the statement issued in Havana by the Ministry of Foreign Affairs of the Republic of Cuba concerning the situation in the Arabian-Persian Gulf.

...

After 37 days of savage air strikes against Iraq and Kuwait, the coalition of forces assembled from the war machine of the United States and its allies has initiated the ground offensive in Kuwait and parts of Iraq. As a result, the crisis in the Arabian-Persian Gulf is entering an increasingly tragic and bloody phase, with incalculable consequences for the fate of the region and international security.

Since 2 August 1990, the Government of Cuba, in addition to condemning the unacceptable invasion and annexation of Kuwait by Iraq and calling for the re-establishment of the sovereignty of that emirate, has been warning of the danger that the United States might take advantage of the occupation of Kuwait to achieve its ambition of destroying Iraq and solidifying its hegemonic presence in that strategic region.

An assessment of the events that have taken place since 16 January, after the Security Council, to the astonishment of the world, gave the United States a free hand to unleash a war of destruction that served its geopolitical interests, convincingly demonstrates the correctness and accuracy of Cuba's position and the warning it has been sounding.

Far from fulfilling the purposes for which it was created, the most important of which is the maintenance of peace, the Security Council has, by means of resolution 678 (1990), helped to thwart efforts to promote a just and peaceful settlement. With a zeal that it has not shown in the face of Israeli expansionism or the Yankee invasions of Grenada and Panama, the Council allowed the United States and its allies to turn Iraq and Kuwait into a testing ground for their most up-to-date weaponry, the use of which has already taken thousands of victims from among the civilian population and caused damage of unimaginable proportions to the economic and social infrastructure of both countries.

When Iraq announced its acceptance of the peace plan proposed by the USSR and its readiness to withdraw immediately and unconditionally from Kuwait in compliance with resolution 660 (1990), the opportunity was created for the crisis to enter a process that could lead to a definite solution. The reality that we are witnessing today has been dictated by Washington and the United States is seeking to impose its conditions. The United States is directing the war, deciding when and how it will end. All this from the country which scorns every peace initiative, which once again presumes to dictate standards to the international community.

What we are now witnessing is the first, bloody example of the unipolar world which the United States dreams of creating, the "new order" announced by President Bush as the future awaited by mankind.

The State which proclaims that it is destined by providence to establish and rule over this order has, by all appearances, the physical might to try to do it, but it is totally without any moral standing and historical authority. Its expansionist, interventionist and exploitative history would fill volumes. It is the very Power which had no scruples about using the atom bomb against a Japan that had already been defeated, the very Power which sowed death in Viet Nam, which subjected Nicaragua to a cruel and dirty war, and which continues to occupy Panama.

What is going on today in the Gulf is a vivid example of what could happen tomorrow anywhere in the world any time the United States should take on the role of supreme arbiter of peace and justice and decide with utter impunity how and where to act and what is right or wrong. Cuba calls upon the United Nations and the Security Council in particular to fulfil the function for which they were created and to make a genuine contribution to the maintenance of peace.

The war must be ended and there must be an end to the death of the thousands of men, women and children whose lives will be sacrificed for no other reason than the hegemonic interests of the United States.

Weekly Compilation of Presidential Documents, Vol. 27 No. 9

46. US Presidential Address to the Nation on the Suspension of Allied Offensive Combat Operations in the Persian Gulf, 27 February 1991

Kuwait is liberated. Iraq's army is defeated. Our military objectives are met. Kuwait is once more in the hands of Kuwaitis, in control of their own destiny. We share in their joy, a joy tempered only by our compassion for their ordeal.

Tonight the Kuwaiti flag once again flies above the capital of a free and sovereign nation. And the American flag flies above our Embassy.

Seven months ago, America and the world drew a line in the sand. We declared that the aggression against Kuwait would not stand. And tonight, America and the world have kept their word.

This is not a time of euphoria, certainly not a time to gloat. But it is a time of pride: pride in our troops; pride in the friends who stood with us in the crisis; pride in our nation and the people whose strength and resolve made victory quick, decisive, and just. And soon we will open wide our arms to welcome back home to America our magnificent fighting forces.

No one country can claim this victory as its own. It was not only a victory for Kuwait but a victory for all the coalition partners. This is a victory for the United Nations, for all mankind, for the rule of law, and for what is right.

After consulting with Secretary of Defense Cheney, the Chairman of the Joint Chiefs of Staff, General Powell, and our coalition partners, I am pleased to announce that at midnight tonight eastern standard time, exactly 100 hours since ground operations commenced and 6 weeks since the start of Desert Storm, all United States and coalition forces will suspend offensive combat operations. It is up to Iraq whether this suspension on the part of the coalition becomes a permanent cease-fire.

Coalition political and military terms for a formal cease-fire include the following requirements:

Iraq must release immediately all coalition prisoners of war, third country nationals, and the remains of all who have fallen. Iraq must release all Kuwaiti detainees. Iraq also must inform Kuwaiti authorities of the location and nature of all land and sea mines. Iraq must comply fully with all relevant United Nations Security Council resolutions. This includes a rescinding of Iraq's August decision to annex Kuwait, and acceptance in principle of Iraq's responsibility to pay compensation for the loss, damage, and injury its aggression has caused.

The coalition calls upon the Iraqi Government to designate military commanders to meet within 48 hours with their coalition counterparts at a place in the theater of operations to be specified, to arrange for military aspects of the cease-fire. Further, I have asked Secretary of State Baker to request that the United Nations Security Council meet to formulate the necessary arrangements for this war to be ended.

This suspension of offensive combat operations is contingent upon Iraq's not firing upon any coalition forces and not launching Scud missiles against any other country. If Iraq violates these terms, coalition forces will be free to resume military operations.

At every opportunity, I have said to the people of Iraq that our quarrel was not with them but instead with their leadership and, above all, with Saddam Hussein. This remains the case. You, the people of Iraq, are not our enemy. We do not seek your destruction. We have treated your POW's with kindness. Coalition forces fought this war only as a last resort and look forward to the day when Iraq is led by people prepared to live in peace with their neighbors.

We must now begin to look beyond victory and war. We must meet the challenge of securing the peace. In the future, as before, we will consult with our coalition partners. We've already done a good deal of thinking and planning for the postwar period, and Secretary Baker has already begin to consult with our coalition partners on the region's challenges. There can be, and will be, no solely American answer to all these challenges. But we can assist and support the countries of the region and be a catalyst for peace. In this spirit, Secretary Baker will go to the region next week to begin a new round of consultations.

This war is now behind us. Ahead of us is the difficult task of securing a potentially historic peace. Tonight though, let us be proud of what we have accomplished. Let us give thanks to those who risked their lives. Let us never forget those who gave their lives. May God bless our valiant military forces and their families, and let us all remember them in our prayers.

Good night, and may God bless the United States of America.

Note: President Bush spoke at 9.02 p.m. from the Oval Office at the White House. In his address, he referred to President Saddam Hussein of Iraq. The address was broadcast live on nationwide radio and television.

A/45/966, S/22278, 28 February 1991

47. Letter from the Permanent Representative of Kuwait to the United Nations addressed to the Secretary-General, 28 February 1991

I wish to refer to the recent developments in Iraq's position in regard to withdrawal from Kuwaiti territory and, in particular, the statement made by the Iraqi

President on 26 February, concerning Iraq's alleged historical claims to Kuwait, from which I quote:

> "Circumstances today have willed that Kuwait, which is part of your country and was carved from it in the past, shall remain in the state in which it will be after the withdrawal of our holy warriors from it. It hurts you that this should happen.
>
> We remember the day of the call, when it was decided that the gates of Kuwait should be one of the main gates to deter the conspiracy and defend Iraq as a whole from the conspirators. We say that we recalled Kuwait on the great day of the call, and on the days that followed it, in documents and events, some of which date back more than 70 years.
>
> The Iraqis will remember and will never forget that, on 8 August 1990, Kuwait became part of Iraq legally, constitutionally and in actual fact, and that it remained so throughout the period from 8 August 1990 until last night, when withdrawal began, and today we will complete the withdrawal of our forces, God willing.
>
> Today, special circumstances made the Iraqi army withdraw as a result of the developments which we mentioned, including the combined aggression by 30 countries and their odious embargo, in the evil and aggressive pursuit of which they were led by the machine and the criminal entity of America and its principal allies.
>
> Everyone will remember that the Gates of Constantinople did not open to the Muslims in the first tentative phase of their holy war."

At the very time when it is affirming its resolve to withdraw from Kuwait and to apply resolution 660 (1990), the Iraqi leadership is also reaffirming its alleged historical claims to Kuwait and, in actual fact, is merely seeking a cease-fire.

...

S/22282, 28 February 1991

48. Letter from the Permanent Representative of Malaysia to the United Nations addressed to the Secretary-General, 28 February 1991

I have the honour to transmit herewith the text of the statement by H.E. Dato' Haji Abu Hassan bin Haji Omar, Minister of Foreign Affairs of Malaysia dated 28 February 1991 on the situation in the Persian Gulf.

...

Malaysia shares in the happiness of the people of Kuwait over the liberation of their country and looks forward to the re-establishment of the legitimate Government of Kuwait. With the accomplishment of the task in fulfilment of resolution 678, all efforts must now be directed towards bringing an urgent cessation of hostilities to minimize further destruction and loss of lives.

Malaysia welcomes today's announcement by President Bush of the suspension of all offensive combat operations. Malaysia welcomes Iraq's declaration accepting all 12 Security Council resolutions on the Iraq-Kuwait situation and commends its earlier decision to withdraw from Kuwait in response to the Soviet Union's peace proposals. Given Iraq's acceptance, the Security Council should move immediately to arrange for a cease-fire and the cessation of hostilities. Governments of the allied forces must cooperate with the Security Council to bring about an immediate end to hostilities now that Kuwait has been liberated.

Malaysia calls upon the Arab States to begin the process of reconciliation amongst themselves and to agree on the necessary security arrangements to prevent the occurrence of a similar crisis in the future.

Malaysia believes it is now incumbent upon the Security Council to work towards a framework for a political settlement to the Gulf crisis and the broader issue of the Arab-Israeli conflict, including the Palestine problem. Malaysia strongly urges all parties concerned, including Iraq, to extend their fullest cooperation to the Security Council in this urgent task to restore international peace and security in the region.

S/22283, 28 February 1991

49. Letter from the Permanent Representative of Japan to the United Nations addressed to the Secretary-General, 28 February 1991

I have the honour to transmit herewith the text of the statement made by a spokesman of the Government of Japan on 28 February regarding the proposal for a cease-fire and the liberation of Kuwait.

...

1. The Government of Japan heartily welcomes the proposal for the cease-fire. It also expresses its heartfelt congratulations to the Government and the people of Kuwait on the liberation of their country. At the same time, Japan wishes to express its profound respect to the people of Kuwait, to the soldiers of the multinational forces and to all those who have made considerable sacrifice for the liberation of Kuwait.

2. The liberation of Kuwait has been achieved through the solidarity and cooperation of the international community, including, in particular, the countries participating in the multinational forces. The Government of Japan sincerely desires that true international peace and security in the Gulf region will now be achieved.

3. Japan strongly hopes that Iraq accepts the proposal for the cease-fire, which reflects the collective will of the international community, and to cooperate for the restoration of peace in the Gulf region.

4. Japan, which has actively supported the efforts of the international community for the restoration of peace and has also extended support to the Frontline countries, intends to continue to cooperate positively for the achievement of peace and security in the Gulf region, including the restoration and reconstruction of Kuwait.

S/22284, 28 February 1991

50. Letter from the Chargé d'affaires a.i. of the Permanent Mission of Algeria to the United Nations addressed to the Secretary-General, 28 February 1991

I have the honour to transmit herewith the text of the statement, dated 28 February 1991, by the spokesman for the Ministry of Foreign Affairs concerning the latest developments in the Gulf situation. ...

Following its withdrawal from Kuwait, Iraq informed the Security Council of its decision to comply with the resolutions of the United Nations. Since that time a suspension of hostilities has been observed.

The Security Council must consequently declare an immediate cease-fire and order the immediate withdrawal of all foreign forces from Iraqi territory.

It is also incumbent upon the Security Council to give the Secretary-General a mandate to act quickly to establish appropriate machinery with respect to peace-keeping operations for the consolidation of the cease-fire, the withdrawal of foreign forces from Iraqi territory and an exchange of prisoners.

It is Algeria's understanding that once the withdrawal of Iraq's forces from Kuwait has been completed, the rationale for some of the measures which the Council has taken against Iraq will no longer exist.

The lifting of these measures and the commitment on the part of the Security Council to guarantee respect for the sovereignty and territorial integrity of Iraq and Kuwait are needed to promote calm and a climate conducive to the reconstruction of Iraq and Kuwait.

Algeria maintains that future security concerns are the responsibility of the countries of the region alone.

It reminds the members of the Security Council and the entire international community of their commitment to seek an urgent and definitive solution to all the problems in the Middle East and to the Palestinian question in particular.

The promotion of stability that is lasting and genuine also requires that all nuclear weapons of mass destruction be eliminated from every part of the region.

Acting in the framework of the Arab Maghreb Union, Algeria calls for a rigorous and uncompromising appraisal of the consequences of the tragedy that has been thrust upon the Arab nation and expresses its readiness to unite its efforts with the efforts of those who are concerned with drawing the true lessons from this tragedy in order to find anew reasons for believing in their common destiny and in the abiding worth of the values embodied in their civilization.

S/22287, 1 March 1991

51. Letter from the Permanent Representative of Jordan to the United Nations addressed to the President of the Security Council, 1 March 1991

I have the honour to transmit to you the Arab and English texts of the speech His Royal Hashemite Highness, King Hussein Bin Talal addressed to the nation on Friday 1 March 1991 regarding the situation in the Gulf Region following the cease-fire in the war being waged there.

...

Brother citizens

Brother Arabs, in all parts of the Arab world,

Brother Muslims, in all parts of the world,

I send you greetings that spring from a pure Arab heart and conscience that believes in the will of God. On this historic moment I shall pause with you at two landmarks of Jordan's progress and that of the greater Arab nation.

The first is the thirty-fifth anniversary of the Arabization of the command of our Arab army, so that it may always remain a source of strength for our nation and people.

The second is the end of the Gulf crisis, which we sought from the outset to steer away from the dark tunnel it entered from the second of August until this day. This chapter ended at last, in one of the most cruel national disasters which our nation has ever endured. Now I address every one of you men and women, young and aged, Muslims and Christians, servicemen and civilians. I address every Arab and Muslim who lived the unfolding saga in his heart and mind, or who faced it as an inescapable reality. I address you, brother Jordanians, to tell you that we have every cause to hold our heads high. Never have we bowed them other than to Almighty God, nor will we now. Our vision was clear from the onset of the tragedy. We realized what the outcome would be if Iraq continued its occupation of Kuwait, and if we were not successful in solving the problem peacefully within the Arab framework. We tried our best to contain the problem in its early stages and at all subsequent stages before the outbreak of war. We sought to solve it and avert disaster through our concern for the greater national interest and our commitment to noble principles. We were not successful. I do not propose to go into the details of the sad drama because you know it well. You have lived it. I would like to say that the curtain has dropped on the final act, to herald a new dawn which beckons on the horizon. I realize that many of us in Jordan and in the Arab and Muslim world will carry with them as they look forward to a new tomorrow, painful memories which can be transformed into hatred and rancour if they are allowed to grow and fester. But vibrant peoples are those that can overcome their pain and grievance, and contribute lessons from which they themselves learn as they strive for their future, their hopes, and their aspirations. Dynamic nations do not allow bad memories to stall their progress or paralyse their ability to think. They emerge from the ashes and shake off the dust having drawn strength, confidence, and determination from their bitter ordeal, to resume normal life and to construct a brighter future.

You know that, after Iraq and Kuwait, Jordan suffered most from this crisis. We were isolated economically till our exports shrank. We were placed unwillingly in the war zone till our tourism ceased and our airspace was closed. We were obliged to shoulder over and above the responsibility of absorbing the Jordanian returnees who had worked in Kuwait. This entailed an additional burden to our financial and economic plight. Our standard of living was diminished, in the case of hundreds of thousands of our people, to below the poverty line. Unemployment soared to an unprecedented level. Our tankers were hit as they came from Iraq loaded with oil, without which, not only the wheels of the economy would grind to a halt, but so would our ability to provide drinking water, which requires energy to pump it from its various sources. Nevertheless, we did what we could to stay prepared to defend our country at all levels: we mobilized the armed forces, called up our reserves, equipped the People's Army, and provided basic food supplies for the country. We did not, however, bear a grudge towards anyone, nor did we place the blame on any. We realized that we would pay dearly for standing on principle, and maintaining our freedom of choice within a national context, and because of our geographical location.

Gloating and apportioning blame are not Arab traits, nor are they compatible with their spiritual values because they lead to enmity, hatred, and alienation. On the other hand, forgiveness and burying the past lead to healing the wounds and closing the ranks of the nation once again.

Let us place our trust in God and turn over a new leaf. Let everyone make an honest resolution to work for reconciliation and harmony, and to shun doubts, mistrust, and all causes of strife. Let us establish an inter-Arab relationship based on the fear of God, mutual trust, and faithfulness to the aspirations of our nation and its future generations to live in freedom, peace, security, and stability, so they can resume the quest for progress and fortitude, within its national character and Islamic values.

Let us turn over a new page, thanking God that the Gulf war has ended, that the bleeding has stopped, and that the people of Kuwait enjoy their independence once again. Let us pray to God that this be the last strife between Arabs, and that He may guide them to the true path, the path of righteousness, justice, fraternity, solidarity and affection.

As I say this a stream of images crowds my mind. Today our Kuwaiti brothers celebrate their return to their homes and the restoration of their independence. We share their happiness.

By contrast, our Iraqi brothers nurse their wounds and pain. We sympathize with them all, people and army, Arabs and Kurds, Sunnis and Shi'ites, in every city, village, and Bedouin camp. We all bear a responsibility towards Iraq, its heritage and history. We shall stand by the Iraqi people as they look forward to rebuilding their country and to healing their wounds. To all our brethren in Iraq we pledge that we shall neither forget them, nor the help they have given us in our moment of need.

On this day we see the beginning of a new Arab era, a new dawn between Iraq and Kuwait marked by reconciliation and reconstruction in both countries.

Today, pains and sorrows turn into hope and determination. Today is a day for reflection and self-appraisal, to heal the wounds, restore Arab unity, and lay solid foundations for a better future. The nation did not start with us that it should end with us.

This is the day when we should consider how to revive and develop the Arab regional order, to make it more capable of containing our problems and facing the challenges that face our nation.

It is a day of determination for us to build our national strength, to restore confidence in ourselves and to safeguard our values and beliefs.

It is a day when all should turn to solving their problems, the border issues being at the forefront, so that the nation will never again find itself in a situation of conflict that could lead to its ruin. It is the day when serious thinking ought to commence on how our abilities should complement construction and development in a context of cooperation, to safeguard our human and natural resources and to release the potential of our nation's youth.

It is the day on which we ought to bear witness to the interrelation of interests amongst the nations of the world, the interdependence amongst its peoples, the need to live in harmony with each other, to enjoy our resources in a framework of equality and by the grace of God to fulfil the trust of future generations. On this day we should also not be impervious to the anguish of the Palestinian Arab people, who look to the day of salvation when they too can rejoice as do the Kuwaiti people today. The Palestinian people look to a world that has applied international legality with the same vigour that it demonstrated over the question of the occupation of Kuwait, and await the same firmness and decisiveness in applying international legality to its humanitarian and national demands.

It has been said that Palestinians showed happiness when missiles hit Israel. If that is correct, should the world not analyse the cause for this happiness? I suggest to the Israeli leadership and people that they scrutinize this phenomenon closely for the Palestinians, like all living mortals, are also human, and it is humanity that constitutes their love for life, virtue and peace as it does for others. One cannot distinguish a line between this reaction to the attacks and the continued neglect by the international community of their suffering, a fact which can only have had a brutalizing effect. Such "happiness" is no more than a reflection of deep-seated and profound sorrow, coupled with despair of attaining international justice and of having waited so long for salvation in freedom and the right to a life with dignity.

On this day we urge the world again to address the question of Palestine by the same criteria that it has applied over the question of Kuwait. We should also like to renew our pledge to the world that we are committed to striving for the attainment of a just and durable peace that guarantees the national rights of the Palestinian people on their national soil. Foremost among these rights is their right to self-determination and to representation in a peace process aimed at resolving the Arab/Israeli conflict. These rights constitute the basis for the achievement of lasting peace and enduring stability in the region, a goal which we seek jointly with the international community, guided by the noblest of values and by a commitment to the application of all international principles with equal enthusiasm and dedication.

On this day we must also focus attention on the growing disparity between rich and poor nations in this region which predicates continuing social and political unrest if it is not addressed institutionally through planning in order to cope with the challenges to stability in this region and to world peace, and not just as an expression of charity. In our opinion this means a great deal for it addresses the core of international dealings with our region as an integrated region rather than a series of bilateralism.

On this occasion I should also like to thank all those who helped us during this crisis and who understood and appreciated our principled stand, our propensity for peace and our dedication to conflict resolution through peaceful means. We would like to assure the whole world that Jordan throws its arms open wide to all those who wish to establish friendly relations based on mutual respect and cooperation. Jordan extends its hand to all those who reciprocate with warmth and honour that we may work together in the knowledge that rhetoric will yield to meaningful deeds. Jordan will always belong to its nation, will always strive for international cooperation in achieving prosperity for all. This is Jordan's long-standing belief which, God willing, it will never abandon.

Here in Jordan we are proud of our democratic experiment which in this crisis has been a foundation stone of the edifice of our national unity. It has revealed the awareness of our people, their fears for the nation's welfare and their deep concern for regional developments in a context of responsible national and patriotic participation.

I congratulate you all in progressing on the path of democracy which we shall strive to consolidate and enhance. At the outset of this new phase, as we prepare ourselves to resume the process of reconstruction, we shall propose the national charter for national endorsement that we may, in the light of the charter, organize and, God willing, guide our participatory process with greater cooperation in the service of our country and our Arab nation equally. Our historic national responsibilities lie in providing the elements of success for our experiment which may offer a model for our Arab brethren, in their turn, to expand their participatory process in the service of their countries.

We in Jordan are confident that the Arab peoples have a greater sense of solidarity and harmony than the recent crisis suggests. They are capable of overcoming the causes of division and fragmentation which we have always cautioned against. Popular participation in the framework of democratic institutions is the guarantor of upholding that solidarity among peoples just as responsible freedom and respect for human rights and human dignity are the guarantors that prevent decision makers from following the paths of adventurism.

For it is through the widespread adoption of democracy in Arab countries that we can best save our nation from the pitfalls of armed conflict. We also see in democracy a sure way of preserving harmony in the Arab nation on an acceptable basis which would lead the nation to the realization of its hopes in interdependence, strength, progress and prosperity.

> *"It may be that you dislike a thing which is good for you and it may also be that you prefer a thing and it may be the worst for you. God knows all and you know not"* (Al Baqara 216).

...

S/22288, 28 February 1991. [*A similar letter addressed to the President of the Security Council is contained in document S/22274.*]

52. Letter from the Permanent Representative of Iraq to the United Nations addressed to the Secretary-General, 27 February 1991

Upon instructions from my Government I have the honour to inform you that all Iraqi forces have withdrawn from Kuwait the last unit of which left Kuwait at dawn today 27 February 1991 local time. The American and other pro-aggressor forces continued to attack our forces during their withdrawal.

...

A/45/967, S/22289, 1 March 1991

53. Letter from the Permanent Representative of Mongolia to the United Nations addressed to the Secretary-General, 1 March 1991

On instructions received from my Government, I have the honour to transmit herewith the statement made by the spokesman of the Ministry of Foreign Relations on the situation in the Persian Gulf ... .

...

As a result of the liberation by the multinational forces of the State of Kuwait pursuant to United Nations Security Council resolution 678 (1990), the independence and sovereignty of Kuwait have been restored and the combat operations in the Persian Gulf have been halted. The Government of the Mongolian People's Republic deems it as a triumph of justice and a victory of the United Nations and of the world community.

From the very beginning, the Mongolian People's Republic denounced firmly Iraqi annexation of the sovereign State of Kuwait by force. Mongolia's principled position was clearly set forth, *inter alia*, in the statement issued by the Government of the Mongolian People's Republic on 17 January 1991.* [* S/22112.]

Had the successive resolutions of the United Nations Security Council on the immediate and unconditional withdrawal of Iraqi troops from Kuwait and on restoration of this country's independence and sovereignty through political means, as well as the world community's legitimate demands, been implemented from the very beginning, the events would not have escalated into the armed conflict and would not have brought about numerous human casualties and extensive material losses. The Persian Gulf war has become a unique lesson in the history of mankind.

The Government of the Mongolian People's Republic considers that this event once again demonstrates the vital importance of the strict observance of the fundamental principles of international law and inter-State relations, and respect for sovereignty and independence of all States, large and small alike.

S/22290, 1 March 1991

54. Letter from the Chargé d'affaires a.i. of the Permanent Mission of Singapore to the United Nations addressed to the Secretary-General, 1 March 1991

I have the honour to enclose herewith [the] text of the statement made by the Minister for Foreign Affairs of the Republic of Singapore, H.E. Mr. Wong Kan Seng, regarding the proposal for a cease-fire and the liberation of Kuwait.

...

Singapore welcomes the announcement by President Bush that the United States and its coalition partners were suspending hostilities in the Gulf war. It hopes that the Iraqi Government will speedily accept all the resolutions of the United Nations Security Council, and end the sufferings of the Iraqi people.

Singapore shares the joy of the Kuwaiti people at the liberation of Kuwait. We have fully supported all international efforts to bring this about. We hope that the situation in Kuwait will soon return to normal so that the massive reconstruction task can begin.

The resolute and decisive actions of the multinational coalition to oppose aggression and enforce the decisions of the United Nations Security Council have strengthened the United Nations and made the world a better and a safer place. The international community has resoundingly reaffirmed its commitment to the principles of the United Nations Charter. The United Nations and the United States should now work to resolve the major outstanding issues in the Middle East, including the Palestinian problem to bring more durable peace and stability to the region.

S/22291, 1 March 1991

55. Letter from the Permanent Representative of Nepal to the United Nations addressed to the Secretary-General, 1 March 1991

I have the honour to enclose herewith a statement issued by His Majesty's Government of Nepal on the cessation of armed hostilities in the Persian Gulf region.

...

With the cessation of armed hostilities and the acceptance by Iraq of the resolutions of the Security Council, the war in the Persian Gulf has come to an end, which His Majesty's Government of Nepal heartily welcomes. We particularly welcome the withdrawal of Iraqi forces from Kuwait and the restoration of that small non-aligned country's independence and sovereignty. His Majesty's Government of Nepal supported the efforts of the United Nations and its Secretary-General as well as other nations whose moral and material contributions helped achieve these noble goals.

Now that the war has ended, His Majesty's Government of Nepal looks forward to the peaceful works of reconstruction in the Gulf and the political settlement of the entangled problems of the Middle East, including the Palestinian problem.

S/22293, 1 March 1991

56. Letter from the Permanent Representative of Yugoslavia to the United Nations addressed to the President of the Security Council, 1 March 1991

I have the honour to transmit the text of the statement by the Federal Secretariat for Foreign Affairs of the SFR of Yugoslavia dated 1 March 1991 concerning the ending of the hostilities in the Persian Gulf.

...

It was with greatest satisfaction and relief that Yugoslavia received news on the ending of the war in the Persian Gulf, on the liberation of Kuwait and the restoration of its sovereignty and legitimate Government. This historic moment for the Kuwaiti people represents at the same time the triumph of all the peoples and countries in the world in their quest for freedom and peace.

In times of building new and more just relations in the world, the international community through its decisive action, reaffirmed the unacceptability of the policy of aggression and *fait accompli*, which strengthened the possibilities and perspectives for achieving stable peace and security in the interest of all.

Ever since the outbreak of the crisis in the Persian Gulf, non-aligned countries and Yugoslavia, as the Chairman of the Movement, in a principled and decisive manner declared against the aggression, occupation and annexation of independent and non-aligned Kuwait and engaged themselves in seeking peaceful and just solution to the crisis on the basis of the Security Council resolutions and the basic principles of the policy of non-alignment. Such positions and activities were fully expressed at the Ministerial Meeting of Non-Aligned Countries, held in New York on 4 October 1990.

Acting within the mandate given to it at this meeting, Yugoslavia has made intensive and numerous contacts both with the parties directly involved in this conflict and with the major international factors, particularly with the permanent members of the Security Council, the European Community and the United Nations Secretary-General, putting forward the proposals and initiatives for the political solution of this dangerous crisis.

Regrettably, the efforts exerted by the Movement and the international community as a whole have not been met with favourable response and acceptance by the Iraqi leadership which resulted in unnecessary continuation of the war and further destruction, bloodshed and sufferings of the Kuwaiti and Iraqi people.

Yugoslavia particularly emphasizes the important and irreplaceable role of the United Nations in working out the uniform position of the entire international community in renouncing and condemning the policy of force and aggression and in seeking just solutions to the acute international problems, based on the United Nations Charter.

The countries of the region and the international community as a whole, and the Movement of Non-Aligned Countries accordingly, are now faced with a great responsibility and obligations to eliminate the grievous consequences of the war as soon as possible, and to consolidate peace, security and create durable stability in this area. This would provide the necessary conditions for the opening up of the process of speedy resolution of the Middle East crisis in its integrity, the Palestinian question in particular.

Yugoslavia will exert efforts to have non-aligned countries engage in rebuilding trust and cooperation among the peoples of non-aligned Kuwait and Iraq and all other countries of the region. Yugoslavia views this as a proper way for the realization of interests of the entire international community, as well as of the principles and goals of the United Nations Charter and the policy of non-alignment.

S/22299, 1 March 1991

57. Letter from the Chargé d'affaires a.i. of the Permanent Mission of Indonesia to the United Nations addressed to the Secretary-General, 1 March 1991

I have the honour to transmit herewith the text of the statement by H.E. Mr. Ali Alatas, Minister for Foreign Affairs of the Republic of Indonesia dated 28 February 1991 on the situation in the Persian Gulf.

...

The Government of Indonesia welcomes the announcement by the United States, on behalf of the Coalition Forces, of the suspension of offensive combat operations starting at noon of 28 February 1991. We are also pleased to learn that the Security Council will convene a meeting in which Iraq will convey its decision to comply fully with all the relevant resolutions of the United Nations Security Council.

We therefore fervently hope that steps will be taken towards a cease-fire and that a comprehensive cessation of hostilities will take place. Furthermore we would like to express our hope that the Council will immediately initiate the consideration of the political aspects of the settlement to the Gulf war and appropriate actions to be taken.

Finally, Indonesia shares in the happiness of the people of Kuwait as they regain their freedom and independence in conformity with the United Nations Security Council resolutions.

S/22320, 3 March 1991. [An identical letter addressed to the Secretary-General is contained in document S/22321.]

58. Letter from the Permanent Representative of Iraq to the United Nations addressed to the President of the Security Council, 3 March 1991

On instructions from my Government, I have the honour to transmit to you herewith a letter addressed to you by Mr. Tariq Aziz, Deputy Prime Minister and Minister for Foreign Affairs of the Republic of Iraq, dated 3 March 1991.

...

I have the honour to inform you that the Iraqi Government has taken note of the text of Security Council resolution 686 (1991) and that it has agreed to fulfil its obligations under the said resolution. We hope that the Council, in its turn, will interact in an objective and honourable manner, pursuant to the provisions of international law and the principles of equity and justice, with our faithful and - to the extent that we are able - speedy fulfilment of those obligations.

You and the members of the Security Council are well aware of the manner in which the American forces and their partners in the military operations against Iraq have implemented Security Council resolution 678 (1990), and of the major losses which Iraq has suffered to its infrastructure, economic, civilian, cultural and religious property, basic public services such as electricity, water, telephones, transport, fuel and other essential requirements of everyday life.

Despite these facts, resolution 686 (1991) has ignored the Iraqi people's suffering and the imposition on Iraq alone of a long series of obligations. A number of members of the Security Council referred to this fact, leading one of them (Cuba) to vote against the resolution, while three States - India, Yemen and China, the latter being a permanent member of the Council - abstained.

We record these facts for history and for the attention of those members of the Security Council and the international Organization - and those elements of international public opinion - who have a conscience. Our agreement to fulfil our obligations under this resolution stems from our determination to refute the pretexts which some may employ in order to persist in their aggression against Iraq and to inflict further harm on its people.

Iraq hopes that the Security Council will ensure the adoption of a resolution proclaiming an official cease-fire and the cessation of all military operations on land, at sea and in the air, as well as the immediate withdrawal of the foreign military forces stationed without any justification in various regions of Iraq. Iraq also hopes that the Security Council will proceed to declare, with all possible speed, the bases for its adoption of Security Council resolutions 661 (1990), 665 (1990) and 670 (1990) as having lapsed, with the result that the resolutions become null and void.

...

A/45/969, S/22323, 1 March 1991

59. Letter from the Permanent Representative of Luxembourg to the United Nations addressed to the Secretary-General, 1 March 1991

I have the honour to transmit herewith the French and English texts of the statement on the Gulf issues on 28 February 1991 by the European Community and its 12 member States.

...

The Community and its member States welcome the suspension of military operations in the Gulf.

The Community and its member States are greatly satisfied that Kuwait has recovered its freedom and that international legality has been restored. They express their gratitude to all States that committed forces to the cause of ensuring respect for the resolutions of the Security Council of the United Nations.

They pay their respects to all those who have lost their lives in this conflict.

They note Iraq's acceptance of the 12 resolutions of the Security Council of the United Nations and express the hope that its Government will rapidly accept the conditions put forth by the coalition.

It is now the task of the Security Council of the United Nations to define the necessary arrangements to put an end to the conflict.

As they stated on the day on which military operations began, the Community and its member States reaffirm their commitment to contribute to bringing about for all the peoples of the region, in dignity and security, a future of peace, stability and development in a context of social justice and regional economic solidarity.

To this end, they will make a major effort to develop an overall approach with regard to the region, bearing at one and the same time on security questions, political problems and economic cooperation.

S/22232/Rev.2, 2 March 1991

60. Cuba: revised draft resolution, 2 March 1991

The Security Council,

Deeply concerned at the loss of human life, the material destruction, the tension and the instability caused by the situation in the Gulf region,

Committed to restoring the independence, sovereignty and territorial integrity of Kuwait,

Recalling the Geneva Conventions of 1949,

Considering its primary responsibility for the maintenance of international peace and security, as established in Article 24 of the Charter of the United Nations,

Convinced that it is its duty to use all peaceful means for the settlement of international conflicts and differences in order to maintain international peace and security and "save succeeding generations from the scourge of war", as proclaimed in the Preamble to the Charter of the United Nations,

Noting the suspension of offensive combat operations in the Gulf region,

1. *Decides* to declare a cease-fire immediately;

2. *Requests* the Secretary-General to dispatch immediately a United Nations military observer mission to supervise the cease-fire declared in paragraph 1 above;

3. *Requests also* the Secretary-General to submit to it a plan for the urgent establishment of a United Nations peace-keeping force, in consultation with the countries where it would be deployed, for the purpose of re-establishing international peace and security in the Gulf region.

S/22232/Rev.3, 3 March 1991

61. Cuba: revised draft resolution

The Security Council,

Deeply concerned at the loss of human life, the material destruction, the tension and the instability caused by the situation in the Gulf region,

Committed to restoring the independence, sovereignty and territorial integrity of Kuwait,

Recalling the Geneva Conventions of 1949,

Considering its primary responsibility for the maintenance of international peace and security, as established in Article 24 of the Charter of the United Nations,

Convinced that it is its duty to use all peaceful means for the settlement of international conflicts and differences in order to maintain international peace and security and "save succeeding generations from the scourge of war", as proclaimed in the Preamble to the Charter of the United Nations,

Resolved to work assiduously in favour of the full restoration of peace in the Gulf region and of the role the United Nations should play in that process,

1. *Notes* the suspension of offensive combat operations in the Gulf region;

2. *Requests* the Secretary-General to dispatch immediately a United Nations military observer mission to supervise the suspension of offensive combat operations in the Gulf region and contribute to the speedy and effective conclusion of a definitive cease-fire;

3. *Requests also* the Secretary-General to submit to it a plan for the urgent establishment of a United Nations peace-keeping force, in consultation with the countries in which the peace-keeping force will be stationed, for the purpose of re-establishing international peace and security in the Gulf region.

S/22324, 4 March 1991

62. Identical letters from the Permanent Representative of Iraq to the United Nations addressed respectively to the Secretary-General and the President of the Security Council, 4 March 1991

On instructions from my Government, I have the honour to transmit a letter addressed to you from Mr. Tariq Aziz, Deputy Prime Minister and Minister for Foreign Affairs of the Republic of Iraq, dated 4 March 1991.

...

I have the honour to inform you that, between yesterday and the time of writing, American aircraft have deliberately broken the sound barrier over Baghdad four times. This has also been done in other Governorates. You are not unaware of the terror this causes to civilians, particularly children, as a result of the loud noise produced and the shaking of buildings and houses.

At 2155 hours (local time) yesterday, 2 March, the American forces discharged armed troops from six helicopters near kilometre 160 on the Baghdad-Amman road. This area is very distant from the theatre of operations.

These two acts are inconsistent with the bases and foundations of the agreement reached at the military meeting at Safwan on the afternoon of 2 March 1991.

These acts constitute flagrant and unjustified provocations. In expressing its condemnation of these acts, the Iraqi Government registers its vigorous protest against them and appeals to you to endeavour to halt them.

S/22325, 4 March 1991

63. Letter from the Permanent Representative of Czechoslovakia to the United Nations addressed to the President of the Security Council, 4 March 1991

I have the honour to transmit to you herewith the text of the Statement of the Federal Ministry of Foreign Affairs of the Czech and Slovak Federal Republic of 1 March 1991, on the suspension of military operations in the Persian Gulf.

...:

> "The Federal Ministry of Foreign Affairs of the Czech and Slovak Federal Republic was fully satisfied and pleased to receive reports on the suspension of military operations in the Persian Gulf and on the restoration of the independence and sovereignty of the State of Kuwait. Thus, the months-long unceasing efforts by the international community, expressed also in twelve United Nations Security Council resolutions, to eliminate the Iraqi aggression against and illegal annexation of the neighbouring Kuwait has been crowned with success. One can only regret that this outcome had to be achieved through the force of weapons and at the cost of human and material casualties due to the intransigence and stubbornness of the Iraqi leadership to comply with the relevant Security Council resolutions. The consequences of the military operations, that have affected so heavily Iraq itself and its people, fall solely and fully on the Iraqi leadership.
>
> The Federal Ministry of Foreign Affairs of the Czech and Slovak Federal Republic appreciates the unity, resolve and determination with which the international community has come forward to protect and liberate Kuwait, and with which it has adopted unambiguously the principle that the aggressor must not be allowed to benefit from its malevolent way of action. This is a result of the hopefully unfolding process of shaping the international relations on the principles of respect for national and human rights, friendship and cooperation.
>
> The crisis in the Persian Gulf has shown that the accumulation of unresolved problems between States, ethnic strife, and religious intolerance, combined with excessive armament and stockpiling of weaponry, are no guarantee for the security of nations and for the stability in the whole region. The Ministry expresses its conviction that the international community shall exert equal efforts not only to eliminate the political, economic and moral consequences of the Persian Gulf war but also to settle all long-standing and unresolved problems of the Middle East region. For its part, it is determined to contribute to such a settlement through a well-balanced policy and relations with all countries of the region, as well as through its diplomatic activities."

...

S/22326, 4 March 1991

64. Letter from the Chargé d'affaires a.i. of the Permanent Mission of Paraguay to the United Nations addressed to the Secretary-General, 4 March 1991

I have the honour to transmit herewith the communiqué dated 28 February 1991 from the Ministry of Foreign Affairs of Paraguay concerning the cease-fire in the Persian Gulf and the liberation of Kuwait.

...

The Ministry of Foreign Affairs of Paraguay expresses the satisfaction of that country's Government with respect to the cease-fire in the Persian Gulf and the liberation of Kuwait. It at the same time affirms its support for all the Security Council resolutions relating to that conflict which have made it possible to restore Kuwait's sovereignty and territorial integrity. It expresses its conviction that an effort must be made, in the framework of the United Nations and in accordance with the Charter and the principles of international law, to bring about a just and lasting peace in the region.

S/22329, 5 March 1991

65. Letter from the Permanent Representative of Guinea to the United Nations addressed to the Secretary-General, 4 March 1991

I have the honour to transmit herewith the French text of the communiqué concerning the Gulf crisis issued by the Government of the Republic of Guinea on 28 February 1991.

...

The Government of the Republic of Guinea is gladdened by the news of the suspension of hostilities following Iraq's withdrawal from Kuwait and unconditional acceptance of all the twelve (12) Security Council resolutions relating to the Gulf crisis.

The people of Guinea is deeply hopeful that all hotbeds of tension in that part of the world will be eliminated and is greatly heartened by the termination of this crisis, which has produced so many innocent victims and caused incalculable material losses.

With the help of courageous political will on the part of all the parties involved and with support from all countries which seek peace and social justice, everything must be done to facilitate the achievement of a permanent cease-fire, this being an essential precondition for the creation of an atmosphere of lasting and just peace in the region.

Such an attitude will then permit the peoples who have been reconciled to confront the many challenges facing them after this unfortunate crisis.

S/22332, 6 March 1991

66. Letter from the Permanent Representative of Iraq to the United Nations addressed to the Secretary-General, 5 March 1991

On instructions from my Government, I have the honour to transmit herewith letters dated 4 March 1991 from Mr. Tariq Aziz, Deputy Prime Minister and Minister for Foreign Affairs of the Republic of Iraq, addressed to the Ministers for Foreign Affairs of China, Cuba, India and Yemen.

...

The people and leadership of Iraq have followed the positions adopted by China in the Security Council during discussion of aspects relating to the Gulf crisis and, in particular, China's abstention from the vote on Security Council resolutions 678 (1990) and 686 (1991).

History will speak of a significant distinction whereby China abstained from the vote on the unjust resolution 686 (1991) at a time when Iraq agreed to fulfil its obligations under that resolution. History will provide the proper interpretation of that fact. We are pleased that China is able to speak the truth and to adopt the position which it deems fit in accordance with its assessments. Iraq, for its part, has acquiesced in its acceptance because of circumstances which are well known.

Another of the distinctions which history will record is that distortion of the truth has extended even to the formulation of resolutions by the highest international organization. Such resolutions are supposed to maintain at least a minimum level of credibility. The provisions of resolution 686 (1991) make frequent reference to "the forces of Kuwait and the Member States cooperating with Kuwait", implying that it is those forces which fought the war against Iraq. As everyone in the world is aware, the war plan is an American plan. It was the American President who declared war and it was he who announced the cessation of military operations. It was the American forces, together with much more limited forces from other Western countries, particularly Britain and France, which fought the war. As everyone in the world knows, it is the American political machine which dictates, directs and applies pressure in order to fashion the political position on this subject, and thus the resolutions of the Security Council.

These distinctions will not pass without being seen as signs of a dark age which the human race is now entering ... an age of domination by a brutal super-Power over the resources of the world and the international establishment, imposing its will on them with impunity ... distorting the truth as it distorts history. The free peoples of the world, their national Governments and all those with a clear conscience must draw the pertinent conclusions from these facts. They must also expose the premeditated designs against Iraq which lie behind everything that has happened in the past. The principal truth of the matter is that the fundamental issue, regardless of differences of opinion on one side or another, which are natural and legitimate, was not that of respect for international legitimacy and international law but the imposition of hegemony over the resources of the Gulf region and the Middle East and thereby over the world.

Events prove once again that peace, stability, security and justice cannot be secured in the Middle East region and that this region will not enjoy security and tranquillity until the question of the Palestinian Arab people is solved on a just basis which guarantees that people its legitimate rights to recover its territory and to establish its own free independent State in that territory, including its capital, Jerusalem.

S/22335, 6 March 1991

67. Letter from the Permanent Mission of Nigeria to the United Nations addressed to the Secretary-General, 6 March 1991

The Permanent Mission of the Federal Republic of Nigeria to the United Nations Organization presents its compliments to the Secretary-General of the United Nations and has the honour to forward herewith, the text of a statement, issued 1 March 1991 by the Federal Military Government of Nigeria on the Gulf crisis.

...

The Federal Government welcomes the announcement by President Bush of the suspension of fighting in the Gulf, following Iraq's unconditional acceptance of all the United Nations resolutions. Nigeria believes this will lead to a speedy arrangement of a permanent cease-fire and an end to the conflict.

Nigeria is further convinced that this offers opportunity for the international community to address itself to the issue of bringing a durable peace to the Middle East.

In the attainment of this objective, Nigeria stands ready to assist the United Nations in ensuring peace and security in that region.

A/46/111, S/22336, 6 March 1991

68. Letter from the Permanent Representative of Egypt to the United Nations addressed to the Secretary-General, 5 March 1991

I have the honour to transmit herewith the text of the statement made by President Muhammad Hosni Mubarak, President of the Arab Republic of Egypt, at the joint meeting of the People's Assembly and the Advisory Council on 3 March 1991.

...

In these historic days, in which a distinction is being drawn between light and darkness, between hopes and sufferings, and between the announcement of liberation and victory, on the one hand, and the horrors of war and the signs of devastation, on the other, ...

I have come to you mainly in order to present my second testimony, for the historical record, concerning all the circumstances surrounding the sanguinary disaster that has afflicted our Arab nation.

I have also come in order to launch a pan-Arab appeal, from the Egyptian people's Parliament, to all fraternal Arab peoples, calling upon them to strive towards a path of action and a new future; a future of peace and security, work and development.

I tell you frankly; in these last few weeks, I have faced my roughest and most difficult days in office and the most severe and overwhelming distress, in which my heart has been weighed down with anxiety and grief and I have asked myself in bewildered astonishment: Did we not caution the ruler of Iraq against all that has happened? Did we not give him sincere advice and tell him the truth from the very first day of his occupation of the State of Kuwait? Did we not diligently endeavour, by various means, to make him aware of the true situation, the real state of affairs and the proper course of action, since there was every indication that the international consensus would not condone that crime and would not permit it to continue? Did we not overlook all his insults, abuse and insolence? Did we not constantly warn him of his miscalculations and his erroneous assumptions, which inevitably led, as we had expected and warned, to ruin, destruction, death and collapse?

May God curse arrogance and self-delusion! May God curse the decision of an individual when that individual is deified!

Self-delusion, hypocrites, conspirators, self-interested persons and buffoons gave him the false impression that the world would be divided in the face of his arguments, his wisdom and his courage, that Kuwait would become an easy prey, and that its annexation to Iraq would be a fictitious crowning achievement of his misguided leadership.

However, it became clearly evident, from the outset, that his judgement was naive and capricious and that he had deluded himself, once again, into believing that, by maintaining his stubborn attitude and remaining entrenched in his fortified bunker, he would be able to bring down governments, overthrow systems and redraw the map of the world.

It then became unquestionably evident that his judgement was based on advice received from ignorant and dim-witted persons and adepts in the art of creating slogans and catchwords.

He subsequently deluded himself into thinking that the international community would not adopt a resolution calling for the use of armed force to ensure withdrawal. I warned him about this in a long letter - I repeat, I warned him about this in a long letter - in which I assured him that the resolution would be adopted in the very near future. He responded, as usual, with further abuse, vituperation and frivolity.

It then became increasingly evident that he had acted on blind impulse and that he was unaware of, or unable to understand, the most fundamental facts concerning the international community.

Yet again, he deluded himself into thinking that the Arab and friendly allied forces feared confrontation in a land battle and were terrified of his mythical overwhelming power capable of transforming vast territories into a huge cemetery and a sea of blood that would not be deep enough to cover the corpses of the tens of thousands of victims. He mistakenly believed that, if this happened, peoples would revolt against their leaders and governments, thrones would be toppled and presidents would be overthrown, leaving his misguided leadership to reign supreme and strut imperiously on the world stage.

Accordingly, he warned of ruin, death and calamity and announced, in an extremely confident, arrogant and boastful manner, that the odds against his overwhelming victory were less than one in a million!

He then announced that the damage suffered by military installations inside Iraq as a result of the air raids was much less than he had estimated on the basis of a careful calculation and that he would be able to wage a victorious war for a period of six years. He ridiculed those who had referred only to a period of three years!

There was also a constantly mounting deluge of statements, declarations and communiqués from four radio stations, concerning fabulous secret weapons that would cause the world to tremble, ingenious military strategies that would astound military leaders for all time, and frightful prospects of slaughter in which the combatants would be sent home in hundreds of thousands of shrouds.

The truth must be told! Whenever a head of State expressed a view contrary to his own, this man accused him of being ignorant, degenerate, contemptible, cowardly, irreligious, etc. All these shameful, vulgar and abusive epithets were heaped on a large number of world leaders, whom he expected to grovel at his feet pleading for mercy and forgiveness after the annihilation of their armies and the collapse of their regimes and governments!

He therefore believed that, when the leaders of the major Powers had been overthrown, his glorious historic victory would place the leadership of the world in his hands.

...

How could any intelligent, logical or perceptive student of military history imagine that he would be able to wage a battle, even on a very limited scale, when he did not possess a single aircraft, not even a single defensive missile, after the air war and before the air battle!

Even the aircraft that escaped destruction were surreptitiously flown to Iran.

Is this the heroic steadfastness of which he boasted and which was reiterated by some deceitful or gullible voices?

Does steadfastness imply that all military installations, armament factories and command and control centres in Iraqi territory should be left exposed to bombardment and destruction without the slightest resistance and without a single fighter aircraft capable of protecting a position?

Does steadfastness imply that civilian locations should be used as military centres or that military hardware should be placed in schools, in hospitals, in civilian shelters, in the vicinity of places of worship and in hotels, which would therefore be subject to bombardment, and that one should subsequently bewail the civilian victims?

There is a big difference between steadfastness and suicide ... a very big difference between steadfastness and suicide.

Steadfastness means that a person fights, while still in possession of his weapons, with the least possible losses.

Suicide means sacrificing thousands of men to fight for a lost cause. This is a decision to be taken by a leader.

A courageous leader is one who is the most steadfast of all and who assiduously protects the safety of his army and his people.

It is insanity and a betrayal of the honourable and responsible position of leadership for a leader to order his forces to commit suicide, while he himself remains safely in his bunker, out of a crazy desire to be hailed as a steadfast leader in mass demonstrations.

Gullible and other persons who took part in noisy demonstrations, raised banners and shouted slogans in a number of Arab countries sought to mislead the public and exploit the situation in order to achieve internal party political objectives designed to arouse and mislead the masses.

They tried to convince the world that he was the hero who would liberate Jerusalem.

They tried to convince the world that he would vanquish colonialism and smash imperialism.

They tried to convince the world that he was the audacious leader who would annihilate Israel.

They even tried to convince the world, as he tired to convince himself, that he was the messenger of divine providence who would raise the banner of Islam, propagate justice and rescue the poor. Of this and other things they tried to convince the world.

And while they tried to convince the world and he tried to convince himself of these things, he knew better than anyone that all these falsehoods and lies sprang from the trumpets of his own propaganda, on which billions had been spent in order to mask the crime of the occupation of an Arab country, a friendly and weak neighbour which had long given generously to him. He reckoned with his sick imagination and his even sicker calculations that these demonstrations were his path to the leadership of which he dreamt and that, since he had become a leader, any Arab force which liberated Kuwait was an infidel, treacherous force and that any international force which, with the Arab forces, implemented the Security Council resolution to liberate Kuwait were forces that had crossed the oceans to bring down his leadership, to destroy his military force and to obliterate Iraq from the map of the world.

Such is the game played by some who are still living with the mentality of the 1940s and 1950s, which sold out the cause of the Palestinian people and deceived the Arab masses with spurious slogans on the part of Israel and assertions that they would cast Israel into the sea.

In the meantime, it was Egypt that was fighting and Egypt that was sacrificing thousands of the lives of its purest sons and Egypt that was losing billions in its wars for the Palestinian cause and for the security of the Arab world.

Where is the Jerusalem which he has liberated?

Where is the Israel which he has annihilated and demolished>

Where is the Islam which this tyrant transformed into killing, plunder, rape and barbarous forms of torture where women are killed in front of their fathers and sons, eyes are gouged out with red-hot skewers and heads are cleft open with axes?

Where is justice for the poor in the destruction and burning of oil wells and the poisoning of the seas?

Who has brought the American, British, French and other allied forces to our land?

Who has sent the Iraqi army to its destruction and collapse?

Did not the ruler of Iraq have the opportunity over a long period of six months to accept the Security Council resolutions and withdraw within the period laid down by the Security Council, after which there would have been no war, no destruction or devastation?

Would it not have been nobler and more honourable for him to withdraw, as all the world's leaders were begging him and advising him to do, using every means to convince him and bring him to reason, rather than to be forced finally into a humiliating and ignominious withdrawal, with his forces surrendering, his military equipment destroyed and his army suffering tens of thousands of casualties?

Did we not warn him 30 times in letters and appeals on behalf of every man, woman and child, with the greatest respect and desire to see him save face; did we not warn him of the dreadful and terrifying consequences and did we not say at that time that those consequences would be humiliating and ignominious?

Even after the ground war began, which he in his innermost (if not inane) calculations had reckoned would not happen for fear of his false and empty threats, did we halt our efforts to advise him to announce a withdrawal and accept the Security Council resolutions? That is what we did. I say clearly that, even a few hours before the battle began, the international efforts from all capitals were not halted.

The Soviet Union intervened, advising him, indeed warning him, to weigh matters carefully and to accept the international resolutions. But he tried to prevaricate and accused the Soviet leader Gorbachev of being subservient! (He too was subservient - everyone is under some form of subservience nowadays.) Moscow did not succeed, after 10 days of efforts, in obtaining the necessary decision from him. He set impossible conditions, one of which was that he should be rewarded for what he had done and that Iraq should not forfeit its right to annex Kuwait.

Did he not propose, *inter alia*, that the withdrawal should take place within 21 days?

Did he not finally withdraw within hours?

Ladies and gentlemen, I tried my utmost, with all sincerity and perseverance, together with our brothers, the leaders of the Arab nation and our friends, the leaders of the major Powers of both West and East, I tried, they tried, we all tried together first to avoid this war, which was imposed by international legality, and then to avoid pursuing it. Yet we have found in this tyrant nothing but obstinacy, persistence, tortuous promises, deceitful undertakings and puerile manoeuvres which mock fate and destiny.

He says one thing and its opposite at the same time!

His promises carry within themselves confirmation of his clear intention not to carry them out.

And then there are vainglorious speeches, delivered in heroic tones, in which he deceives himself even more than he deceives the masses of the Arab nation with lies, delusions and distortions of the truth.

In the midst of all this, there is a sanguinary and evil insistence on the heedless sacrifice of thousands of innocent lives among the Iraqi army and the Iraqi people. There is an even more evil aberration in wanting to be surrounded by devastation and corpses, burning oil wells and a sea which is being poisoned. He destroyed Kuwait's facilities before withdrawing and plundered its coffers in the dark of night.

The future will soon reveal the hideous nature of these vile crimes, which are without historical precedent, even in the worst ages of oppression and tyranny; crimes committed and ordered by the ruler of Iraq.

In his first declarations, he was intent on laying down fanciful conditions, to which he added the guarantee that his rule should be safeguarded and that his life should not be endangered. He continued to equivocate with his conditions, hoping to gain time and prevent the continuation of the war, due to a change in the weather, which would give him an excuse not to withdraw. Then he became two-faced: one face announced that he would agree to withdraw, at the same time as the other face was destroying and burning the oil wells; one face was showing a desire for peace, while the other face was trying to avoid implementing the Security Council resolutions. It was therefore natural that the Soviet Union should declare its solidarity with the other countries of the coalition and the absolute necessity of unconditional withdrawal and compliance with all the Security Council resolutions, which the ruler of Iraq had lost four days in agreeing to one after the other!

...

The page has been turned and a new page has begun.

The days of darkness have passed and the dawn of a new day has broken.

The terrible tragedy has ended and Kuwait has been liberated. Our armed forces, in collaboration with the Arab and coalition forces, have played their heroic role in the battle for liberation. All the military leaders have praised the coalition. Through their military correspondents in the theatre of war, the greatest newspapers in the world have celebrated the valour of the Egyptian fighting man, his magnificent performance and the force of his onslaught. They have also commended the fact that the Egyptian armed forces completed all their combat missions in a shorter time than that envisaged in the planning of military operations.

It was another illustrious role performed, and one to be added to the distinctions achieved by our armed forces in protecting Arab security. They fought with faith and conviction. They attacked with courage, manliness and daring. They achieved their objectives with military expertise and superior execution. Each fighting man was an honour to Egypt and conferred honour and distinction on every family in Egypt.

Egypt will not forget, the people of Kuwait will not forget and free people everywhere will not forget our righteous martyrs who gave their lives in the most honourable of battles. I should like us, ladies and gentlemen, to stand for two minutes in salute to the departed spirits of our martyrs and of all the martyrs of the victory achieved in the liberation of Kuwait.

...

The flag of Kuwait has been raised over the land of Kuwait. The flag of Egypt has been raised over the Embassy of Egypt in the free, independent and sovereign State of Kuwait.

It is no secret that we had no desire that the obduracy, self-delusion and arrogance of the ruler of Iraq should lead to hostilities with the army of Arab Iraq. It is he who made the decision, it is he who sought the conflict, and it is he who insisted and acted with intransigence and contempt. It is he who declared, in the closed meeting of the Arab Summit Conference held at Casablanca and in a meeting with the Arab Lawyers Union, that the Arabs would be entitled to mobilize their armies against the army of Iraq if it were to violate the sovereignty of an Arab State.

From this podium, ladies and gentlemen, I address each individual member of our armed forces in the theatre of war, and I say to them with full pride: glory belongs to those who achieve glory; and honour is due to those who have fought with honour for their people and for their Arab nation. The banners of Egypt are deserving of manly arms.

From this podium, I also address the fraternal people of Iraq, the army of Iraq and all those on whom this war was forcibly imposed in the land of Kuwait and the land of Iraq. I say to them: the people of Egypt is a brother to the people of Iraq. The decision of a single individual cannot destroy this brotherliness. The people of Egypt will not stint in contributing to the reconstruction of Iraq. The people of Iraq is an inseparable part of the Arab nation, and it must play its own political, cultural and social role in days to come.

I say to Baghdad's broadcasting services: we have had enough of the ignominy of mendacity, deception and deceit. Do not make of noble, Arab Iraq, which has a civilization and a history, an object of ridicule to the people of the world with reports of fables about imaginary battles in which every day you exterminate thousands down to the last man! We have had enough of frustrating mockery, after you have done such things to Iraq, to the army of Iraq and to the people of Iraq as have filled the hearts of the Arab nation with sorrows that will not be effaced for decades to come and have done such things as relegate all of those responsible for this catastrophe to the darkest corner of our contemporary history. It saddens me, ladies and gentlemen, to have heard just recently one trying, with enviable boldness, to shed with honeyed words this grave responsibility, imagining to himself that history can be deceived by ignominious guises donned for every occasion without shame or embarrassment.

From this podium, I speak to the people of Kuwait in the land of Kuwait, a people that has borne the most heinous cruelties of a brutal occupation with forbearance and which has been subjected to the greatest crimes of repression, torture, plunder and looting. The most recent of these crimes have been the burning of the major hotels and the seizure of their stocks and the arrest of hundreds and their removal to Iraq, all in the last hours before the withdrawal. The forces of popular resistance, however, never hesitated in their defiance and opposition.

I also speak to those of the people of Kuwait in Egypt and in every Arab land. I say to all of them: warm congratulations on the liberation of your country, Kuwait, and it is a matter of pride and glory enough to you that there appeared among you none who broke faith and collaborated with usurpation, tyranny and aggression. ...

...

We do not gloat at the distress of others; rather do we commiserate with them. We do not rejoice at a shocking defeat and at abiding destruction. Rather do we hope for a speedy recovery and a wakeful vigilance that will draw all eyes and minds towards the future. We are not proponents of settling for the bloody present and dwelling on pains and sorrows; our call is for a forward-looking outlook that will address the inter-Arab situation seriously and realistically and for the building of the new international order so that we may salvage what has been lost in terms of lives, infrastructure and progress.

It would be wise to profit from the lessons of this ordeal and from all the bitter consequences that it has brought with it for the Arab world at a time when we had come close to interlinkage, solidarity and integrated planning for the present and the future and then calamity struck. If the catastrophe has set us back into remote and gloomy depths, the primary responsibility of the Arab leaders and of the Arab peoples is that they should, through remedial action, correct this grave situation. Then, all may lend a helping hand and work together to agree on a basis from which to set out towards a better future and a new life in which wounds are healed, mutual recriminations cease and new and rejuvenated blood is infused after the enormous bloodshed that has afflicted the Arab nation in battle.

The cruel experience that confronts us all in the entire Arab world is a moral lesson. The future will be harsher and more bitter if Arab forces, governmental or popular, proceed in the self same manner with regard to conflicts. Such conflicts may be compounded if we abandon our destiny to the rule of whims and exaggerations, factions may multiply, the trade in slogans and incantation may flourish, and policies for the deception of peoples may continue under clashing banners. The most pertinent example to that effect is the statement made only recently, as I have told you, in lofty contempt for the consciousness of the masses and their honour, by an Arab leader.

...

We do not intend to settle accounts or to exacerbate differences. The doors must be closed on all those who wish to augment the catastrophe: what we have undergone is already enough.

We are confronted with fundamental, topical and urgent issues. While the ruler of Iraq forced us to bring in foreign forces to help us defend the sovereignty of another Arab State, we should be aware that the vast expanses of the Arab nation have the political, economic and social capacities and resources to enable us alone to establish the new basis for progress towards a better future.

We must not squander these vast resources. It is already enough that we should have been afflicted by the greatest and most dangerous wastage of our material and spiritual resources ever to have been seen in the history of the Arab nation.

We do not seek a division between East and West. We do not look for a continuation of campaigns of resentment, deceptive allegations, slogans which take cheap advantage of events or the machinations of poisonous intrigues and multiple hypocrisies.

... We have no wish to see the Arab nation divided into two, and we do not want the single Arab people to be scattered as separate peoples and deceived by wicked objectives which drive them to internecine strife within a single country. It is neither the undercurrents nor the currents on the surface which dominate the consciousness of peoples, their true path, their just and legitimate right to a future of peace, safety, co-operation, solidarity and unity - with all honour and probity - in support of their principles.

The Arab world is confronted with crucial issues. Agreement must be reached on ways to address them in order to ensure that the correct path is followed.

We have before us the question of the Palestinian people. It is a question of a people and not a question of leaderships, exaggerations, intrigues and conspiracies.

The Palestinian people has the paramount right to self-determination after all these years of suffering, of the folly of slogans and of conflict between leaderships, the result being dissipation of the major issue and its conversion into a question of differences between individuals and the exchange of accusations.

No one will deny that the solution of the question of Palestine is the prime key to a just and lasting peace in the Arab region.

We do not treat this question as a commercial proposition. Sufficient offence has been dealt to our Arab history by this absurd and misleading assertion that the occupation of Kuwait represented the path to Jerusalem.

We must tear up all these rotten pages. We must tear them up in order to begin a clean and serious page which restored the freshness and integrity of this just and topical question, in order that banners of peace may be raised with faithful hearts, with open minds, with desires to attain solutions and without discourses of intrigue.

The Palestinian people represents a trust which is borne by all of us, and we shall not betray that trust. We have before us the question of the Golan and the question of the single united Arab people of Lebanon. All these questions are interrelated. The time has come for us to proceed, by solving them rapidly and decisively, towards stability and peace.

We have before us the question of Arab security.

This is an extremely important question. It warrants priority treatment following the exposure of the existence and destiny of the Arab nation to the most serious threat as a result of the Iraqi invasion of Kuwait and all the distresses and horrors which that has entailed.

Arab security shall be Arab and Arab alone, ensuring immunity and protection for this region of the world.

We have before us the questions of economic and social development and the integration required for planned comprehensive development such as will ensure social justice and draw upon the enormous Arab capacities in terms of resources, manpower and scientific evolution. In so doing, we shall construct a solid, strong, proud and upstanding Arab nation, which will have its eminent place in interaction with the new international order based on peace, technological and economic competition and consolidation of political democracy.

We have before us the questions of disputed boundaries with their long-standing conflicts.

We have before us the question of cooperation with the people of Iraq, which shall not be separated from the Arab nation. The people of Iraq is the master of its own fate and has the paramount right to determine its future. It is that people which is now experiencing the bloody tragedy brought upon it by the tyranny of falsehood over that which is right and the ambitions of one individual at the expense of the freedom of millions.

...

All these crucial and weighty issues require from us innovative thinking which relates to reality from a premise of strength and solidarity, as well as statements of fact from hearts which are free of caprice and arbitrary views.

My call is not one for Arab reconciliation by means of the declarations, statements and slogans which we have learned by heart. How easily those words flow in our political dictionary and in our Arab region.

My call is one for Arab candour, pledged to sincerity and to a deep conviction that the downfalls and collapses by which we have been beset can lead us only to a yet more severe and bitter fate, unless we all face up to the full dangers of the situation.

Candour which is constructive and not destructive.

Candour which brings protection and not disunity.

It is my belief that Egypt was the first to display such candour at the Arab Summit Conference held in Casablanca - the first summit meeting which it attended following the reconciliation between Egypt and the League of Arab States.

As you may remember, I raised some specific points at that Conference which I considered appropriate in order to enrich united progress as one nation. I wish to add the following points in the wake of the bloody events which began with the Iraqi invasion of Kuwait:

1. We must neither lose any time nor waste any effort in giving thought to reprisals, revenge or the settling of accounts. We must turn this sad page in our history and direct our hearts and eyes towards the future, with all the hope and aspiration which it bears for our peoples.

2. We must exert our utmost efforts to restore faith in the domain of the Arab family at the earliest opportunity, in order that doubts should not grow deeper and divisions spread in our ranks. No nation is capable of any joint action if doubt and suspicion hold sway over the minds of its members.

3. The events of the calamitous invasion and its aftermath make it necessary that every one of us should state his vision of objectives for both his nation and his country, as well as the means which he believes should be used in order to attain those objectives. In this way, each Arab country will have knowledge in advance of what the other countries intend to strive to implement and achieve.

4. We must also redouble our efforts in the months and years to come to settle the outstanding differences between all Arab countries, first and foremost among these being differences over boundaries, even if this means that new machinery must be invented in order to enhance our ability to overcome the difficulties and problems which cast gloom on Arab relations.

5. We must hasten to complete our concept of the situation in the region after the war, concentrating on two essential points - namely, security and development - which are complementary, interrelated and interdependent elements. They cannot be separated, nor can one be considered in isolation from the other. In order for this to come about, there must be collective thought and continuous consultation, because the future of all of us depends on our success in formulating a joint and integrated vision.

6. Events have proved how right we were to have urged, for more than two years, that the Middle East region - meaning the region as a whole, including Israel - should be kept free of weapons of mass destruction. When we urged that, the ruler of Iraq and the Iraqi leadership objected to making it free of nuclear, chemical and biological weapons of mass destruction. We should also consider other means of preventing the accumulation of weapons in the region and the race to acquire and make use of them.

7. If we are to bring about security and stability in the region, we must all devote our utmost efforts to settling the Arab-Israeli conflict, and particularly its Palestinian element, because this conflict is the principal source of anxiety and tension in the region and plunges it into a vicious circle of violence and counter-violence.

8. In order to consolidate comprehensive reconstruction in the phase to come, we must endeavour to extend opportunities for cooperation to every Arab citizen in public work and to strengthen the march of democracy in the manner which each Arab country determines in accordance with its circumstances and experiences.

9. We must become conscious of the falsehood of words spoken in the miasma of events over a period of seven sad months, which attempted to portray what happened as a battle between East and West, between Muslims and non-Muslims or as a return to the Crusades. All this was bogus, a sham. The battle was between legitimacy and anarchy, between right and wrong, between that which is lawful and that which is unlawful. We praise God that Arab legitimacy matched international legitimacy and that the victory - in the end - lay with the forces of right and good and not with the forces of aggression and injustice.

This, then, is my pan-Arab appeal, on your behalf and on behalf of the people of Egypt, which I direct to the Arab people at this decisive and crucial time when, if we are properly heedful, we may proceed to advance and to march upward and onward.

The downfalls of dispersal could sweep us away, and the exaggerations of slogans could lead us to a yet more wretched fate, a fate which we must not accept.

History will not forgive us ... nor will any generation forgive us ... nor will the blood of a free and noble life course once again through our Arab nation ... if we remain aloof and if we continue to chase our own tails in vicious circles which never end or fall still.

...

I know that you are expecting some words from me about our economic situation. We have been dealt major blows by the disaster of the invasion, over and above the crushing difficulties from which we already suffered, which have their obvious negative effects on our daily life. I know that you are waiting for me to speak on this subject, which is a matter of concern for every family in Egypt.

I shall say only this, on this vitally significant matter: our brothers in Saudi Arabia, Kuwait, the United Arab Emirates and the other Gulf States fully understand the realities of our economic situation and believe - with the best of possible intentions - that an Egypt with a strong foundation and economy means an Egypt committed to the principle and honour of its position and an Egypt which never abandons its pioneering role, whatever hardships that may entail. Important messages have been exchanged in this regard, and I hope that their effects will become apparent in the near future. In addition, steps were taken from the outset of the events of the invasion.

Egypt will play its constructive role in measures to rebuild Kuwait, and our brothers will welcome Egyptian workers in all matters relating to development. These workers will be treated with all due consideration and reverence: agreements to this effect ensure that the rights of every entitled person will be respected.

...

I am fully confident of my vision of the immediate and distant future. Our path stretches out, blazing and aglow, to horizons radiant with development and peace. This confidence is not unfounded.

It stems from the inspiration of the great and noble people of Egypt ... the great and noble people of Egypt which has stood as one man and whose heart has beat as one since the crime of the invasion began and which showed - as a matter of spontaneous civilized awareness - that the people knows how to make the right decision at the right time ...

The great and noble people of Egypt, which with all its vigour and strength brushed aside tendentious and arbitrary assertions that endeavoured to falsify the facts before its eyes, to distort the image in its mind or to stir up its feelings with superficial provocations and misleading appeals ...

The great and noble people of Egypt, which, massed in its millions, formed a mighty shield that swept aside spurious assertions and rose up in pride and glory above the provocations of those consumed by convulsions and the lies of those who deliberately incite trouble.

...

S/22338, 6 March 1991

69. Letter from the Chargé d'affaires a.i. of the Permanent Mission of Kuwait to the United Nations addressed to the Secretary-General, 6 March 1991

I have the honour to transmit herewith a message from His Excellency Sheikh Sabah Al-Ahmad Al-Jaber Al Sabah, Deputy Prime Minister and Minister of Foreign Affairs, addressed to Your Excellency.

...

I have the honour and pleasure to inform you that the Government of Kuwait is resuming the functions of the State and directing the affairs of the nation from Kuwait City.

I should like to seize this opportunity to express our gratitude and appreciation to you personally and to the United Nations system as a whole for the indispensable role played to reverse the Iraqi aggression and to end the occupation of Kuwait.

The contribution of the United Nations system to the restoration of Kuwait's territorial integrity, and the return of the legitimate government to the country has reconfirmed the purposes and objectives of the Charter and the importance of the Organization in maintaining international peace and security.

S/22339, 7 March 1991

70. Letter from the Permanent Representative of Thailand to the United Nations addressed to the President of the Security Council, 1 March 1991

I have the honour to transmit herewith the text of the statement by the Ministry of Foreign Affairs of Thailand issued on 1 March 1991 concerning the developments in the Persian Gulf.

...

1. Thailand warmly welcomes the agreement by Iraq to comply fully with Security Council resolution 660 (1990) and all the other Security Council resolutions on the Gulf crisis, as well as the agreement on the cease-fire of 28 February 1991.

2. Thailand has taken a firm position in opposing the invasion and occupation of Kuwait and has given its strong support to all the Security Council resolutions concerning the Gulf crisis. For these reasons, Thailand congratulates the coalition forces for their successful liberation of the State of Kuwait and the restoration of full independence and sovereignty of Kuwait to its nation and people.

3. In this connection, the spokesman of the Ministry of Foreign Affairs of Thailand also indicated that the maintenance of peace in the Gulf is a matter of great concern to Thailand. He said that if a United Nations peace-keeping operation should be required and should Thailand be requested to participate in it, Thailand would be willing to do so.

S/22340, 7 March 1991

71. Letter from the Chargé d'affaires a.i. of the Permanent Mission of Brunei Darussalam to the United Nations addressed to the Secretary-General, 7 March 1991

I have the honour to transmit herewith the text of the statement of the Government of Brunei Darussalam dated 1 March 1991 on the Liberation of Kuwait and the Suspension of War.

...

Brunei Darussalam joins the people of Kuwait in their happiness on the liberation of their country. Brunei Darussalam has consistently supported all the twelve United Nations Security Council resolutions towards the restoration of the sovereignty of Kuwait and the re-establishment of its legitimate Government.

Brunei Darussalam welcomes the announcement of President Bush in suspending all military operations against Iraq. Brunei Darussalam also welcomes Iraq's decision to accept all the twelve Security Council resolutions.

Brunei Darussalam urges the Security Council to arrange for an immediate cease-fire and cessation of hostilities. Brunei Darussalam also calls on the United Nations to address and resolve the many outstanding issues including the Palestinian problem to ensure lasting peace and stability in the region.

S/22342, 8 March 1991

72. Identical letter from the Permanent Representative of Iraq to the United Nations addressed respectively to the Secretary-General and the President of the Security Council, 8 March 1991

On instructions from my Government, and further to its acceptance of Security Council resolution 686 (1991), as indicated in the letter addressed to you by the Minister for Foreign Affairs of my Government, dated 3 March 1991, I have the honour to transmit to you a copy of Revolution Command Council decision No. 55 of 5 March 1991 concerning the application of paragraph 2 (a) of resolution 686 (1991).

...

In accordance with the acceptance by the Iraqi Government of Security Council resolution 686 (1991) and with its previous declarations regarding acceptance of the other Security Council resolutions, and pursuant to the provisions of article 42, paragraph (a) of the Constitution,

The Revolution Command Council has decided as follows:

> 1. All Revolution Command Council decisions subsequent to 2 August 1990 regarding Kuwait are null and void.
> 2. All laws, decisions, regulations, instructions, directives and measures issued by virtue of the decisions of the Council referred to in paragraph 1 above are abrogated and all the effects arising therefrom are nullified.
> 3. No text which is contradictory to the provisions of this decision shall have any effect.
> 4. This decision shall be published in the Official Gazette and shall take effect from 3 March 1991.
> 5. The competent ministries and authorities shall undertake the implementation of this decision.

S/22343, 8 March 1991

73. Letter from the Permanent Representative of Botswana to the United Nations addressed to the Secretary-General, 5 March 1991

I have the honour to transmit herewith a Press Release issued by the Government of Botswana on the liberation of Kuwait and the cessation of hostilities in the Gulf.

...

The Government of Botswana welcomes the liberation of Kuwait and shares in the happiness of its people as they celebrate the restoration of their country's sovereignty and freedom.

Botswana also welcomes the outcome of the meeting of the military commanders representing the allied forces and the Iraqi forces aimed at establishing the modalities for a permanent cease-fire so that the arduous task of building a durable peace in the Gulf area can begin in earnest.

Botswana urges all parties to the Gulf conflict and the international community as a whole to renew their efforts to address the broader problems of the Middle East, including, in particular, the Palestinian problem. A comprehensive process of reconciliation among the countries and peoples of the Middle East must begin if that vital area of the world is to be rid of the cycle of violence that has wreaked so much destruction and inflicted so much pain and sorrow on its peoples over the years.

S/22359, 18 March 1991

74. Letter from the Permanent Representative of Kuwait to the United Nations addressed to the Secretary-General, 18 March 1991

I have the honour to transmit herewith the letter from His Highness Sheikh Jaber Al-Ahmad Al-Sabah, Amir of the State of Kuwait, addressed to Your Excellency.

...

Thank you for the kind letter which you sent on the occasion of the end of the ordeal suffered by my country and my people and for the friendly feelings expressed in it towards Kuwait and its people. The people of Kuwait join me in expressing profound appreciation and immense gratitude towards the international community, represented by the United Nations, for its noble stand on the side of right and law, for its rejection of aggression, and for the collective resolutions adopted repeatedly by the Organization through the Security Council to restore justice and repel the aggressor. Moreover, I must praise your untiring personal efforts and the noble and scrupulous stand taken by you for the application of those resolutions.

You have earned our admiration and the admiration of the entire world for your tireless, persevering efforts to achieve a peaceful solution to this crisis from the outset. The important thing is that you made every effort in this respect with sincerity and integrity; yet you ran up against a frustrating, immovable wall of obstinacy. Without a doubt, the fact that your efforts to achieve a peaceful solution to the crisis met with failure is the sole responsibility of the aggressor, for he persisted in his aggression and his defiance of the will of the international community. Yet despite the overwhelming disaster that has befallen Kuwait, we now find some comfort in the fact that the international unity that came into being to repel the aggression has strengthened the position of the United Nations as an effective international Organization. The measures taken to restore justice now constitute an international precedent on which one can count and to which one will turn in future crises; what is more, they will be a powerful deterrent to any overbearing regime that feels tempted to swoop down upon a smaller State in order to engulf and control it.

Lastly, I thank you for the offer by the international Organization and your own personal offer of assistance. We shall turn to you for help whenever circumstances so require. I also assure you that the State of Kuwait will continue its commitment to the Charter of the United Nations and its strict compliance with it, as has always been the case in the past.

I extend my best wishes to you personally, and express my appreciation to the Organization for the work which it performed quietly yet untiringly throughout this crisis.

S/22370, 21 March 1991

75. Identical letters from the Permanent Representative of Iraq to the United Nations addressed respectively to the Secretary-General and the President of the Security Council, 21 March 1991

I wish to refer to my letter dated 8 March 1991 transmitting to you a copy of Revolution Command Council decision No. 55 of 5 March 1991 concerning the implementation of paragraph 2 (a) of resolution 686 (1991).

I have the honour to transmit herewith a copy of issue No. 3345 of *Al-Waqa'i'al-Iraqiyah*, the Official Gazette of the Republic of Iraq, issued on 18 March 1991, in which is published Revolution Command Council decision No. 55 of 5 March 1991 concerning the implementation of paragraph 2 (a) of the above-mentioned Security Council resolution.

...

Al-Waqa'i'al-Iraqiyah

Official Gazette of the Republic of Iraq

No. 3345, 2 Ramadan A.H. 1411, thirty-third year, 18 March A.D. 1991

Decision No.: 55

Date of decision: 17 Sha'ban A.H. 1411
5 March A.D. 1991

In accordance with the acceptance by the Iraqi Government of Security Council resolution 686 (1991) and with its previous declarations regarding acceptance of the other Security Council resolutions, and pursuant to the provisions of article 42, paragraph (a), of the Constitution,

The Revolution Command Council has decided as follows:

1. All Revolution Command Council decisions subsequent to 2 August 1990 regarding Kuwait are null and void.

2. All laws, decisions, regulations, instructions, directives and measures arising from the decisions of the Council referred to in paragraph 1 above are abrogated and all the effects arising therefrom are nullified.

3. No text which is contrary to the provisions of this decision shall be operative.

4. This decision shall be published in the official Gazette and shall take effect from 3 March 1991.

5. The competent ministries and authorities shall undertake the implementation of this decision.

A/46/120, S/22374, 21 March 1991

76. Letter from the Permanent Representative of the Syrian Arab Republic to the United Nations addressed to the Secretary-General, 20 March 1991

I have the honour to transmit herewith the text of the Damascus Declaration concerning coordination and cooperation between the Arab States, issued by the meeting of Ministers for Foreign Affairs of the States of the Gulf Cooperation Council and the Ministers for Foreign Affairs of the Arab Republic of Egypt and the Syrian Arab Republic, respectively, held at Damascus on 5 and 6 March 1991.

...

The Arab States members of the Gulf Cooperation Council and the Arab Republic of Egypt and the Syrian Arab Republic, participating in the Damascus meeting on 19 and 20 Sha'ban A.H. 1411 (5 and 6 March A.D. 1991),

Proceeding from the feelings of brotherhood and solidarity which link them and which have been enhanced by a deep-rooted heritage of mutual support, solidarity, joint struggle, a deep sentiment of common hopes and challenges, congruity of goals and unity of destiny,

Promoting their capacities to shoulder their national responsibilities for advancing the Arab nation, serving its causes, safeguarding its security and realizing its joint interests,

Within the framework of strong adherence to the goals and principles enshrined in the charters and the resolutions of the League of Arab States, the Organization of the Islamic Conference and the United Nations,

Aware of the profound transformations taking place on the international arena, which place before the Arab nation enormous challenges whose confrontation requires the highest degrees of coordination and cooperation between the Arab States,

Reaffirming their position rejecting the aggressive approach and partiality for it, such as was witnessed during the aggression against and occupation of the State of Kuwait by the forces of the Iraqi regime, which was a blatant violation of all established Arab, Islamic and international principles and customs and flouted the concepts and achievements of joint Arab action at a time when the Arab nation needs, more than at any time in the past, to reunite and mobilize its capabilities in order to repel many unprecedented dangers,

Declaring also that they welcome the liberation of the State of Kuwait and the return of legitimacy to it; expressing their deep pain and sorrow at the plight to which the fraternal Kuwaiti people has been exposed as a result of the aggression of the Iraqi regime against it; expressing also their profound regret at the most repugnant forms of suffering to which the Iraqi people is exposed as a result of the indifference of the Iraqi leadership to its interests; and affirming in this connection their support for the Iraqi people in its trial and their undivided concern for the territorial integrity of Arab lands,

Hereby affirm their resolve to endeavour to give a new spirit to joint Arab action and to place fraternal cooperation between the members of the Arab family on firm foundations based on the following:

I. *The principles of coordination and cooperation*

Coordination and cooperation rest on the following bases:

1. Action in accordance with the Pact of the League of Arab States, the Charter of the United Nations and other Arab and international constituent instruments; respect for and promotion of historic and fraternal links and relations of good-neighbourliness; adherence to respect for territorial integrity, equal sovereignty of States, the non-admissibility of the acquisition of territory by force and non-intervention in the internal affairs of States; and adherence to the settlement of disputes by peaceful means.

2. An endeavour to build a new Arab system for promoting joint Arab action, taking such arrangements as may be agreed on by the participants as the basis on which it is possible to build in order to achieve that end and leaving the field open to the other Arab States to associate themselves with this Declaration in the light of the agreement of interests and goals.

3. An endeavour to enable the Arab nation to channel all its potentials to meet the challenges to which stability and security in the region are exposed and to achieve a just and comprehensive solution to the Arab-Israel conflict and the question of Palestine on the basis of the Charter and relevant resolutions of the United Nations.

4. The promotion of economic cooperation between the participants as a means towards an economic grouping with the goal of achieving economic and social development.

5. Respect for the principle of the sovereignty of each Arab State over its natural and economic resources.

II. *The goals of coordination and cooperation*

1. *In the political and security fields*

(a) The participating parties consider that the current stage following the liberation of Kuwait from occupation by the forces of the Iraqi regime provides the best circumstances for confronting the other challenges and threats to which the region is exposed, first and foremost the challenges arising from the continuation of Israeli occupation of Arab territory and settlement of Jews there. The participating parties believe that the convening of an international peace conference under the auspices of the United Nations is the most appropriate framework for terminating Israeli occupation of Arab territory and guaranteeing the national rights of the Palestinian people on the basis of the relevant United Nations resolutions.

(b) The participants affirm their respect for the principles of the Pact of the League of Arab States, their commitment to the Joint Defence and Economic Cooperation Treaty between the States of the Arab League and their resolve to act together in order to guarantee the security and integrity of the Arab States. Recalling, in particular, article 9 of the Pact of the League of Arab States, they consider that the presence of Egyptian and Syrian forces in the territory of the Kingdom of Saudi Arabia and of other Arab States in the Gulf region, in response to the desire expressed by their Governments and for the purpose of defending their territory, represents a nucleus for an Arab peace-keeping force designed to ensure the security and integrity of the Arab States in the Gulf region and a model for ensuring the effectiveness of the overall Arab security and defence system. The participants further affirm that their coordination and cooperation shall not be directed against any other party but may rather constitute a prologue to the opening of a dialogue with those Islamic and international parties which respect the higher interests of the Arab nation and abide by the established principles of international legitimacy, in particular those relating to respect for the sovereignty of States, non-intervention in internal affairs and the peaceful settlement of disputes.

(c) The participants shall endeavour to make of the Middle East region a zone free of all weapons of mass destruction, particularly nuclear weapons, and shall strive to achieve that goal through the competent international organs.

2. *In the economic and cultural field*

In keeping with the Pact of the League of Arab States, the Joint Defence and Economic Cooperation Treaty between the States of the Arab League and the other agreements governing joint Arab action, the participants shall endeavour:

(a) To strengthen the foundations of economic cooperation among the founding parties as a first step which may be built upon, together with other Arab States, with a view to expanding the fields of cooperation and its scope;

(b) To adopt such economic policies as will achieve balanced economic and social development as a preliminary step towards the establishment of an Arab economic community in order to confront existing challenges and to keep pace with developments arising out of the establishment of large-scale economic groupings in the world at large;

(c) To encourage the private sector in the Arab countries to participate in the economic and social development process by, *inter alia*, promoting contacts among Arab chambers of commerce, industry and agriculture and providing small- and medium-scale establishments with the opportunity to profit from the fruits of joint cooperation in a convenient and tangible manner;

(d) To strengthen the role of scientific research centres and facilitate contacts among them with a view to enabling them to undertake joint studies to achieve integration in all fields;

(e) To make use of human expertise and human resources in the field of cultural and media exchange, subject to account being taken of respect for the values and traditions of participating States and non-interference in their internal affairs.

3. *Institutions of joint Arab action*

Support for the League of Arab States in resisting all attempts to weaken or dismember it, and reaffirmation of commitment and adherence to the purposes and principles enshrined in the Pact of the League, together with the possible further developments of the Pact by the addition thereto of annexes profiting from the results of the work of the Committee on the Amendment of the Pact, including the elaboration of a system for the settlement of disputes.

III. *Organizational framework for coordination and cooperation*

Coordination and cooperation among the founding parties for the achievement of the objectives indicated shall take place through meetings, to be hosted in rotation by each of the participants, at the level of ministers for foreign affairs and the utilization of experts and specialists to study the various aspects of cooperation with a view to reaching a new contractual modality for inter-Arab cooperation which will be open to all Arab States.

IV. *General provisions*

This Declaration was initialled at Damascus, in eight original copies in the Arab language, each copy being equally authentic, on 20 Sha'ban A.H. 1411, corresponding to 6 March A.D. 1991. This Declaration shall enter into force following acceptance by the principals, and the instruments indicating acceptance shall be deposited with the Ministry of Foreign Affairs of the Syrian Arab Republic.

S/22392, 21 March 1991

77. Letter from the Permanent Representative of the Union of Soviet Socialist Republics to the United Nations addressed to the Secretary-General, 21 March 1991

I have the honour to transmit herewith the text of some comments on a post-crisis settlement in the Persian Gulf area.

...

The Kuwaiti crisis and its solution have come as a test to see how strong the "new thinking" really is. By withstanding this test the world community has demonstrated that it has come a long way: from the cold war to a new system of international relations.

In order to build on this success in the post-crisis period, it is necessary to maintain a high degree of interaction and collaboration when addressing the problems the conflict has generated in the Persian Gulf area.

Sustained normalization in the Persian Gulf could be beneficial to the climate in the Middle East as a whole by promoting solutions to problems resulting from the long-standing Arab-Israeli conflict.

The Soviet Union is closely monitoring the current flow of ideas concerning the post-crisis settlement in the Gulf. Many of the initiatives in this regard contain approaches which are identical or similar to ours.

In our view, security in the post-crisis period could be achieved through a series of practical steps along the following lines:

1. The key role in determining the parameters of the post-crisis settlement in the Persian Gulf area belongs, of course, to the Gulf States themselves. It is for them, in the first place, to decide where the balance of their rights and interests lies because, for many years to come, that balance will form the basis of broad political and other cooperation among them. What is meant here is not the creation of closed, bloc-type groupings cut off from other countries, which would be a source of new antagonisms and would cause old ones to be revived. A post-crisis settlement should not be directed against anyone. On the contrary, it should promote interaction among all the interested States in the region and those which, though outside the region, are making an important contribution towards maintaining peace and stability there.

It is important that the fundamental principles of international law, such as, *inter alia*, non-interference in the internal affairs of other States, non-use or threat of force, settlement of disputes by peaceful means, acceptance of the right of every State in the region to sovereignty and territorial integrity within its existing internationally recognized borders, should serve as the basis for future agreements between the interested parties.

The best option would be a comprehensive multilateral treaty or bilateral treaties, in conformity with Chapter VIII of the Charter of the United Nations, supplemented by appropriate international guarantees on the part of the Security Council and its five permanent members.

2. The Kuwaiti crisis underlines the urgent need for consistent steps towards limitation of the arms race in the region. Notwithstanding all the complexities of this process, it is already feasible to put forward the goal of maintaining the balance of forces on ever-decreasing levels of armaments, until the lowest level compatible with defence requirements is reached.

The most critical issue is how to provide an effective shield against the proliferation of nuclear, chemical and other weapons of mass destruction in the region. Proposals on the establishment in the Middle East of a zone free of these types of weapons deserves serious attention. It is important that all the Middle East countries accede to the Treaty on the Non-Proliferation of Nuclear Weapons and to a convention on the prohibition of chemical weapons.

It is necessary to consider seriously the issue of the balanced reduction of arms supplies to the region. This matter requires a responsible approach on the part of the main suppliers of arms and of their buyers. It is of primary importance that the countries should demonstrate restraint as regards the supply and acquisition of offensive weapons, especially missiles and missile technology. For optimal solutions to this problem, appropriate collective agreements are required, including agreements on verification mechanisms.

It would be sensible to be guided by the experience of other regions in the matter of implementing confidence-building measures, such as notification of military manoeuvres, invitations to observers to attend them, establishment of demilitarized zones and zones with reduced concentrations of weapons.

3. Foreign military presence should not exceed the levels which existed in the region before 1 August 1990. If foreign military support is needed for a given period of time, United Nations peace-keeping forces or United Nations observers or both, together with the necessary contingents of Arab, Muslim and other countries, could play their role.

4. The task of developing the comprehensive economic cooperation of the countries of the region is in the first instance the task of effecting the post-war reconstruction of destroyed economies.

Coordinated international action must be taken to undo the damage caused to the environment by military operations.

Without calling into question the inviolability of the principle of States' sovereignty over their natural resources, a fresh look should be taken at the goal of ensuring greater social and economic stability of the region through a gradual levelling and harmonization of the economic development of its countries.

5. A broad consensus is emerging among countries, including the countries of the region, that an important role should be played by the United Nations in international support of the post-crisis settlement in the Persian Gulf. This is a logical consequence of the role which the Security Council played in organizing a collective rebuff to Iraqi aggression and also a corollary of Security Council resolution 598 (1987).

In the first place, the United Nations can act as an effective guarantor of compliance with agreements.

Our proposal to establish naval forces under the United Nations flag in case of any threats to shipping in the Persian Gulf remains relevant. A new level of confidence between the permanent members of the Security Council justifies the resumption of a detailed discussion of the question of the involvement of the United Nations Military Staff Committee in crisis situations.

6. The easing of military tension in the Persian Gulf subregion and in the Middle East as a whole requires purposeful efforts to eliminate political causes of instability and conflicts there.

Unanimous opinion on the part of the international community favouring a rapid and radical improvement of the situation in the region, where the interests of a large number of States are closely interwoven, provide a better environment for embarking on the settlement of the Arab-Israeli conflict without delay. Successful efforts in this respect would enable the security system which is in the process of being established in the Persian Gulf to be integrated into broader regional structures. This would undoubtedly enhance the security of the peoples in the Near and Middle East.

We believe that the establishment of a region-wide security system should not be an isolated act but should rather be a process which would require time to develop. There is therefore all the more need to undertake the first steps as soon as possible, in order to make progress in the areas where success is genuinely feasible.

In putting forward these ideas we are certainly not claiming to possess the ultimate answer. The introduction of new inter-State relations in the region will require active political and diplomatic efforts, with the participation of the largest number of interested countries. The Soviet Union is ready to contribute to the speedy solution of the problems related to the post-crisis settlement in the Persian Gulf, to discuss any constructive ideas and to collaborate actively with all the parties concerned: the Persian Gulf States, other Arab and Muslim States, the permanent members of the Security Council, and the Western European and non-aligned countries.

S/22395, 21 March 1991

78. Letter from the Permanent Representative of Kuwait to the United Nations addressed to the President of the Security Council, 14 March 1991

As you well know, Kuwait has welcomed the adoption by the Security Council of resolution 686 (1991). Indeed, His Excellency Sheikh Sabah Al Ahmad Al Sabah, the Deputy Prime Minister and Minister for Foreign Affairs, in a letter of 8 March to His Excellency, Mr. Javier Pérez de Cuéllar, declared Kuwait's commitment and readiness to implement all provisions of the resolution relevant to Kuwait.

Iraq's reluctance to abide by its own commitments to fulfil its obligations under resolution 686 (1991) is apparent in the letter addressed to the Foreign Ministers of China, Cuba, India and Yemen by Tariq Aziz (S/22332). In that letter, Iraq states its pleasure that these countries abstained by or voted against resolution 686 (1991), that these countries were able to speak the truth, and that Iraq "has acquiesced in its acceptance because of circumstances which are well known".

On their part, Kuwait and Member States cooperating with it, have duly registered Iraqi prisoners of war (POWs) and arranged for their orderly and prompt release to Iraq.

On the other hand, Iraq procrastinated, denying at times access to the International Committee of the Red Cross (ICRC). Iraq's lack of goodwill in abiding by the terms of paragraphs 2 (c), 3 (c) and 5 of resolution 686 (1991) is manifested in the disorderly release of 1,181 Kuwaiti detainees to ICRC on 8 March. Lack of access to these detainees and their sudden release precluded registration of their names, and the arrangement for their transport into Kuwait. Moreover, the argument advanced by Iraq that internal conditions made it difficult to register all detainees and POWs is unacceptable. Iraq had the opportunity since early August 1990 to proceed with all the necessary arrangements.

It is to be noted that on the question of rescinding its actions purporting to annex Kuwait, Iraq deliberately ignores the word "annexation". The decision by the Revolutionary Command Council (S/22342) refers merely to decisions "regarding Kuwait" as being null and void. Nor does the decision by the Revolutionary Command Council refer to paragraph 2 (a) as such, but to resolution 686 (1991) in general. Furthermore, the fact that the Iraqi National Assembly has not taken any action to endorse the decision is noteworthy. The National Assembly is the public forum where the Iraqi people had in August endorsed the annexation decision. In addition, Iraq is yet to publish the decision in its official *Gazette*. In short, Iraq seeks to satisfy its obligation under paragraph 2 (a), but reluctantly. By doing so, Iraq is inviting criticism that the Revolutionary Command Council decision addresses the sovereignty of Kuwait as if it were a local matter.

In regard to the return of Kuwaiti property seized by Iraq, paragraph 2 (d), we note the reluctant manner with which Iraq has responded so far. Even in the preliminary response, Iraq indicated its readiness to hand over partial quantities of four items rather than all the items (S/22330). Iraq's readiness to hand over Kuwaiti civilian aircraft is yet to be tested against their readiness to specify the locations of these aircraft so that Kuwait can make the necessary arrangements to retrieve them.

A further indication of Iraq's reluctance to implement fully resolution 686 (1991) is the absence of a commitment by Iraq to accept in principle its liability under international law in compliance with paragraph 2 (b). Iraq's acceptance should be unequivocally and officially stated to the Secretary-General.

...

S/22396, 22 March 1991

79. Identical letters from the Permanent Representative of Iraq to the United Nations addressed respectively to the Secretary-General and the President of the Security Council, 22 March 1991

I wish to refer to my letter to you dated 8 March 1991 in which I sent you a copy of Revolution Command Council decision No. 55 dated 5 March 1991 concerning the application of paragraph 2 (a) of Security Council resolution 686 (1991).

I have the honour to transmit to you herewith a copy of the decision of the Iraqi National Council of 20 March 1991 concerning the abrogation of its earlier decision regarding the annexation of Kuwait.

...

The National Council held a special meeting on Wednesday, 4 Ramadan A.H. 1411, corresponding to 20 March A.D. 1991, at which it discussed the current events which led to the issue of Revolution Command Council decision No. 55 on 17 Sha'ban A.H. 1411, corresponding to 5 March A.D. 1991, providing for the abrogation of all the decisions of the Revolution Command Council subsequent to 2 August 1991 relating to Kuwait.

Therefore, pursuant to the provision of article 47, paragraph 2, of National Council Act No. 55 of 1980, as amended,

The National Council decided as follows:

> The National Council abrogates its previous decision adopted at its meeting held on Tuesday, 16 Muharram A.H. 1411, corresponding to 7 August A.D. 1990, relating to the unification and merger with Kuwait, and also nullifies all the effects thereof.

S/22413, 28 March 1991

80. Letter from Saudi Arabia transmitting a report on the progress of military operations, 28 March 1991

...

IV. *The Safwan meeting*

In an endeavour to attain the fulfilment of the conditions laid down by the Security Council for a declaration of an end to hostilities between the coalition forces and Iraqi forces preparatory to the establishment of a lasting peace in the Gulf region following the acceptance by the Iraqi Government of the resolutions adopted by the Security Council, a military delegation representing the coalition forces, under the leadership of General Norman Schwartzkopf, commander of Operation Desert Storm and Supreme Commander of the United States Central Command, and of myself in the capacity of commander of the joint forces and the theatre of operations, met at Safwan on Sunday, 3 March 1991, with an Iraqi military delegation consisting of the Deputy Chief of General Staff, a senior officer and an official of the Iraqi Ministry of the Interior so that the coalition countries could lay down the military conditions necessary for a cease-fire prior to reaching a cease-fire agreement at a subsequent stage.

The coalition delegation laid down the military conditions which, with the approval of the Iraqi side, might lead to agreement on a cease-fire. They were:

(a) Immediate release of prisoners of war, with the establishment of a times [*sic*] and locations for their release, and release of civilian detainees, including Kuwaitis seized by the Iraqi forces in Kuwait.

(b) Disclosure of all information relating to persons missing as a result of hostilities, and the return of the remains of those who have died in captivity or been killed in the course of military operations.

(c) Provision of full information on all minefields, booby traps and weapons that might remain in the State of Kuwait.

(d) Agreement on security and safety arrangements with a view to ensuring that there would be no accidental confrontations that might lead to a renewed outbreak of fighting. Such arrangements would guarantee the safety of all forces under the command of the Iraqi forces, including ships and aircraft.

The meeting had extremely positive results, in that the Iraqi side agreed to all the conditions laid down, bringing us to regard this as a historic meeting heralding an end to the war and the establishment of a lasting peace in the region under the new international order. I am optimistic that there will be no obstacle in the way of reaching a durable cease-fire agreement.

S/22456, 6 April 1991

81. Identical letters from the Permanent Representative of Iraq to the United Nations addressed respectively to the Secretary-General and the President of the Security Council, 6 April 1991

On instructions from my Government, I have the honour to enclose the text of a letter dated 6 April 1991 addressed to you by the Minister for Foreign Affairs of the Republic of Iraq.

...

I have the honour to inform you that the Iraqi Government has taken note of the text of Security Council resolution 687 (1991), the authors of which are the first to recognize that it is unprecedented in the annals of the Organization, and wishes, before stating its official position, to make a number of fundamental comments regarding certain concepts and provisions contained therein:

I. While in its preamble the resolution reaffirms that Iraq is an independent sovereign State, the fact remains that a good number of its iniquitous provisions impair that sovereignty. In fact, the resolution constitutes an unprecedented assault on the sovereignty, and the rights that stem therefrom, embodied in the Charter and in international law and practice. For example, where the question of boundaries is concerned, the Security Council has determined in advance the boundary between Iraq and Kuwait. And yet it is well known, from the juridical and practical standpoint, that in international relations boundary issues must be the subject of an agreement between States, since this is the only basis capable of guaranteeing the stability of frontiers.

Moreover, the resolution fails to take into account Iraq's view, which is well known to the Council, that the provisions relating to the boundary between Iraq and Kuwait contained in the "Agreed Minutes Between the State of Kuwait and the Republic of Iraq Regarding the Restoration of Friendly Relations, Recognition and Related Matters" dated 4 October 1963 have not yet been subjected to the constitutional procedures required for ratification of the Agreed Minutes by the legislative branch and the President of Iraq, thus leaving the question of the boundary pending and unresolved. The Council has nevertheless imposed on Iraq the line of its boundary with Kuwait. By acting in this strange manner, the Council itself has also violated one of the provisions of resolution 660, which served as the basis for its subsequent resolutions. In its paragraph 3, resolution 660 calls upon Iraq and Kuwait to resolve their differences through negotiation, and the question of the boundary is well known to be one of the main differences. Iraq officially informed the Council that it accepted resolution 660 and was prepared to apply it, but the Council has gone beyond this legal position, contradicting its previous resolution, and adopted an iniquitous resolution which imposes on Iraq, an independent and sovereign State and a Member of the United Nations, new conditions and a boundary line which deprive it of its right to establish its territorial rights in accordance with the principles of international law. Thus the Council is also depriving Iraq of its right to exercise its free choice and to affirm that it accepts that boundary without reservation. Where the question of the boundary is concerned, the Council resolution is an iniquitous resolution which constitutes a dangerous precedent, a first in the annals of the international Organization and - as some impartial members of the Council indicated in their statements when the resolution was voted on - an assault on the sovereignty of States.

It is also to be noted that the United States of America, the author of the draft resolution on which resolution 687, which imposes a solution to the boundary-related and other differences between Iraq and Kuwait, was based, refuses to impose any solution whatsoever on its ally, Israel, in accordance with conventions, United Nations resolutions and international law.

Furthermore, the United States of America is preventing the Security Council from assuming the responsibilities incumbent upon it with respect to the Arab-Zionist conflict, the Israeli policy of annexation of the occupied Arab territories, the establishment of settlements, the displacement of populations and the disregard for the rights of the Palestinian people and the neighbouring Arab countries, by vetoing any draft resolution approved by the remaining members of the Council, for the simple reason that Israel does not want a resolution which favours a just settlement of the conflict.

II. Iraq's position with regard to the prohibition of chemical and bacteriological weapons is clear. It is indeed a party to the Protocol for the Prohibition of the Use in War of Asphyxiating, Poisonous or Other Gases, and of Bacteriological Methods of Warfare, signed at Geneva in 1925. In a statement issued in September 1988, Iraq reiterated its attachment and adherence to the provisions of that Protocol. It also participated in the Conference of States Parties to the 1925 Geneva Protocol and Other Interested States, held at Paris from 7 to 11 January 1989, and signed the Declaration issued by the participating States. On that occasion, Iraq took a position which was unanimously shared by all the Arab countries, namely that all weapons of mass destruction, including nuclear weapons, must be eliminated from the Middle East region.

Iraq is also a party to the Treaty on the Non-Proliferation of Nuclear Weapons, of 1 July 1968. As the many reports of the International Atomic Energy Agency confirm, it is applying all the provisions of the Treaty. The Security Council resolution obliges only Iraq, and it alone, to undertake the destruction of the non-conventional weapons left to it after the heavy destruction inflicted both on these weapons and on the related installations by the military operations launched against Iraq by the 30 countries of the coalition. It does not deprive the other countries of the region, particularly Israel, of the right to possess weapons of this type, including nuclear weapons. Moreover, the Council has ignored its resolution 487 (1981), which calls on Israel to place all its nuclear facilities under international safeguards, and has not sought to ensure the implementation of that resolution in the same way as it is now seeking to impose the position it has taken against Iraq. It is thus clear that a double standard is being applied with respect to the elimination of weapons of mass destruction in the region, and an attempt being made to disrupt the military balance there, and this is [sic] all the more apparent in that Iraq has not had recourse to weapons of this type.

The application of this provision of the resolution cannot but seriously endanger the regional balance, as indeed was confirmed by certain impartial members of the Security Council in their statements when the resolution was voted upon. There can be no doubt that Israel, an expansionist aggressor country which is occupying the territory of neighbouring countries, usurping the right of the Palestinian Arab people against which it daily commits the most horrible atrocities, and refusing to comply with the resolutions of the Security Council, which it holds in contempt, as well as all the resolutions of the international Organization, will be the first to benefit from this imbalance.

Whereas the resolution emphasizes the importance of all States adhering to the Convention on the Prohibition of the Development, Production and Stockpiling of Bacteriological (Biological) and Toxin Weapons, of a Convention on the Universal Prohibition of Chemical Weapons being drafted and of universal adherence thereto, it makes no mention whatsoever of the importance of universal adherence to the convention banning nuclear weapons or of the drafting of a convention on the universal prohibition of such weapons in the region. Instead, it emphasizes the importance of instituting a dialogue among the States of the region with a view to achieving a so-called balanced and comprehensive control of armaments in the region.

Proof of the resolution's biased and iniquitous nature is afforded by the Council's use of what it terms unprovoked attacks using ballistic missiles as grounds for calling for the destruction of all ballistic missiles with a range greater than 150 kilometres and of all repair and production facilities. The term unprovoked attacks is used of attacks against Israel, a country which itself launched an unprovoked attack in 1981, destroying Iraqi nuclear installations which were used for peaceful purposes and were under international safeguards. In this connection, the Security Council considered in its resolution 487 (1981), adopted unanimously, that the attack constituted a serious threat to the entire safeguards regime of the International Atomic Energy Agency, which is the foundation of the Treaty on the Non-Proliferation of Nuclear Weapons.

It should be pointed out as well that the Council has also considered in the same resolution that Iraq was entitled to appropriate redress for the destruction it had suffered. The Council has to date taken no steps for the implementation of that resolution, whereas it imposes particularly severe and iniquitous terms and mechanisms when it comes to the redress referred to in resolution 687 (1991), without taking into account even the basic humanitarian needs of the Iraqi people.

III. Furthermore, Iraq's internal and external security has been and remains seriously threatened, in that continuing efforts are being made to interfere, by force of arms, in the country's internal affairs. Thus the measures taken by the Council against Iraq to deprive it of its lawful right to acquire weapons and military *matériel* for defence directly contribute to the intensification of these threats and to the destabilization of Iraq, thus endangering the country's internal and external security and hence peace, security and stability throughout the region.

IV. Whereas the Council resolution provides for mechanisms for obtaining redress from Iraq, it makes no reference to Iraq's rights to claim redress for the considerable losses it sustained and the massive destruction inflicted on civilian installations and infrastructures as a result of the abusive implementation of resolution 678 (1990), which were testified to by the delegation sent by the Secretary-General which visited Iraq recently, and have been referred to by the President of a permanent member of the Security Council (Soviet President Mikhail Gorbachev) and by all impartial observers who have seen with their own eyes the consequences of the military operations launched against Iraq. The Council has not explained to world public opinion and the conscience of mankind what the relationship is between its resolution 678 and the deliberate destruction of Iraq's infrastructure - generating stations, water distribution networks, irrigation dams, civilian bridges, telephone exchanges, factories producing powdered milk for infants and medicines, shelters, mosques, churches, commercial centres, residential neighbourhoods, etc. Moreover, the resolution authorizes third parties to claim compensation from Iraq for damage that may have been caused to them, even when such damage resulted from unfulfilment of their commitments to Iraq immediately following the adoption of resolution 661.

Further evidence of the resolution's biased and iniquitous nature is that it holds Iraq liable for environmental damage and the depletion of natural resources, although this liability has not been established; on the other hand, it makes no mention of Iraq's own right to obtain compensation for the established facts of damage to its environment and depletion of its natural resources as a result of more than 88,000 tons of explosives, or from the destruction of water distribution networks, generating stations and the road network, which has spread disease and epidemics and caused serious harm to the environment.

These provisions partake of a desire to exact vengeance and cause harm, not to give effect to the relevant provisions of international law. The direct concrete consequences of their implementation will affect the potential and resources of millions of Iraqis, and deprive them of the right to live in dignity.

V. After imposing compulsory and universal sanctions against Iraq by adopting resolution 661 (1990) in consequence, according to it, of Iraq's refusal to comply with the provisions of resolution 660 (1990), the Council has maintained most of them in force despite Iraq's acceptance of all the Council's resolutions and the implementation of a good number of their provisions. The Council resolution provides for the progressive lifting of sanctions over an unspecified period, thus leaving broad discretionary authority to certain influential members of the Council which have drawn up the Council's resolutions in an arbitrary manner in order to impose them for political purposes which bear no relation to the Charter or to international law.

In essence, this procedure means that the Council has contradicted the initial resolution under which it imposed sanctions against Iraq, and moreover has not taken account of the offensive launched against Iraq, whereas the interests of the other parties have been taken into account, despite their wealth and their considerable resources.

VI. The Council does not deal clearly and directly with the question of withdrawal of the foreign forces occupying part of Iraqi territory, although the resolution declares a formal cease-fire.

The very conditions invoked in support of the declaration of a formal cease-fire also necessitate the withdrawal. The fact that the withdrawal is not explicitly mentioned is tantamount to authorizing the occupation of Iraqi territory for a period whose duration is at the discretion of the occupying countries, which make no secret of their intention to exploit the occupation for political purposes and to make use of it as a trump card in their hand. This position on the part of the Council constitutes a flagrant violation of Iraq's sovereignty, independence and territorial integrity, and cannot be justified by any provision of resolution 678 (1990). Under this same selective, premeditated and totally unjustifiable approach, the resolution stipulated that the observer forces will be deployed in Iraq to a distance of 10 kilometres from the boundary, and only five kilometres into the territory of the other party, despite the fact that the terrain in the region is flat everywhere, with no relief features that would justify this difference of treatment.

VII. Numerous mechanisms are envisaged which will necessitate consultation in the context of the implementation of the resolution's provisions, but the resolution is not at all clear about Iraq's participation in these consultations. The fact that Iraq is concerned to the highest degree in the application of the resolution makes its effective participation in all consultations bearing on the implementation of these provisions essential. However, the Council has once again opted for an arbitrary and inequitable method.

The questions raised in the resolution and discussed in the foregoing preliminary comments constitute, in substance, an injustice, a severe assault on the Iraqi people's right to life and a flagrant denial of its inalienable rights to sovereignty and independence and its right to exercise its free choice.

In practice, the provisions of the resolution embodying the criteria of duality in international relations and the application of a double standard to questions of the same kind hold Iraq and its population hostage to the designs harboured by certain Powers to take control of their resources, set quotas for their food and clothing needs, and deprive them of their right to live in dignity in the modern society to which they aspire.

Such injustices and such assaults on the rights of a member country of the United Nations and its people cannot under any circumstances be in conformity with the purposes and objectives of the Charter. The Council had a duty to discuss the issues before it with objectivity and in accordance with the provisions of international law and the principles of justice and equity.

By adopting this unjust resolution and by this selective treatment of the Iraqi people, the Council has merely confirmed the fact that we have never ceased to emphasize, namely that the Council has become a puppet which the United States of America is manipulating in order to achieve its political designs in the region, the prime objective being to perpetuate Israel's policy of aggression and expansion, despite the empty words about peace and justice in the Middle East uttered by one or another of the Council members which voted for this resolution.

It could not be more clear to all men of honour and justice that these iniquitous and vengeful measures against Iraq are not a consequence of the events of 2 August 1990 and the subsequent period, for the essential motive underlying these measures stems from Iraq's rejection of the unjust situation imposed on the Arab nation and the countries of the region for decades, a situation which has enabled Israel, a belligerent Power heavily armed with the most modern and fearsome conventional weapons and with weapons of mass destruction, including nuclear weapons, to exercise hegemony in the region. This reality confirms what Iraq had stated before the events of 2 August 1990, namely that it was the target of a plot aimed at destroying the potential it had deployed with a view to arriving at a just balance in the region which would pave the way for the institution of justice and of a lasting peace.

It is unfortunate that States whose intention was not in any way to help the United States of America and Israel attain their objectives should involuntarily have contributed to their attainment by voting for this iniquitous resolution.

As Iraq makes its preliminary comments on the juridical and legal aspects of this resolution, so as to encourage men of conscience in the countries members of the international community and world public opinion to make an effort to understand the truth as it is and the need to ensure the triumph of justice, it has no choice but to accept this resolution.

...

S/22457, 8 April 1991

82. Letter from the Permanent Representative of Kuwait to the United Nations addressed to the Secretary-General, 4 April 1991

I enclose the text of a letter from the Deputy Prime Minister and Minister for Foreign Affairs of Kuwait, Sheikh Sabah Al-Ahmad Al-Jaber Al Sabah, concerning Kuwait's acceptance of resolution 687 (1991), adopted by the Security Council on 3 April 1991.

...

I have the honour to refer to resolution 687 (1991) adopted by the Security Council on 3 April 1991, a copy of which you transmitted to me by your note dated 3 April 1991. We wish to inform you that we welcome the adoption of this resolution, which aims to eliminate the causes and effects of the occupation, and that we undertake, for our part, scrupulously to comply with all its provisions and to cooperate with you with a view to ensuring its implementation.

It is our hope that, in accordance with paragraph 33 of the resolution, Iraq will officially and unambiguously accept its provisions and make a sincere attempt to put them into practice.

S/22480, 11 April 1991

83. Letter from the Permanent Representative of Iraq to the United Nations addressed to the President of the Security Council, 10 April 1991

In accordance with your request, we transmit herewith the National Assembly decision adopted on 6 April 1991 concerning acceptance of Security Council resolution 687 (1991).

...

Decision

The National Assembly has decided at its session held on 6 April 1991 to agree to United Nations Security Council resolution 687 (1991).

S/22485, 11 April 1991

84. Letter from the President of the Security Council addressed to the Permanent Representative of Iraq to the United Nations, 11 April 1991

I have the honour to acknowledge receipt of your communication dated 6 April 1991 (S/22456).

You thereby transmit to me the letter addressed to me by the Minister for Foreign Affairs of Iraq, the penultimate paragraph of which contains official notification of the acceptance, irrevocable and without qualifying conditions, by Iraq of resolution 687 (1991), in accordance with paragraph 33 of that resolution.

You have subsequently confirmed to me on behalf of your Government, during our meeting on 8 April 1991, that the above-mentioned letter constitutes Iraq's irrevocable and unqualified acceptance of resolution 687 (1991) in accordance with paragraph 33 of that resolution. You have also transmitted to me the acceptance by Iraq's National Assembly on 6 April 1991 of the aforesaid resolution (S/22480), and confirmed to me, in the name of your Government, that the Revolution Command Council has used its constitutional powers to make this decision legally binding in the Republic of Iraq.

The members of the Security Council have, accordingly, asked me to note that the conditions established in paragraph 33 of resolution 687 (1991) have been met and that the formal cease-fire referred to in paragraph 33 of that resolution is therefore effective.

The members of the Council welcome this development as a positive step towards the full implementation of resolution 687 (1991).

S/22512, 19 April 1991

85. Letter from the Permanent Representative of Kuwait to the United Nations addressed to the President of the Security Council, 9 April 1991

On instructions from my Government, I should like to convey to you our position concerning the failure by Iraq to abide by the terms of relevant Security Council resolutions, which puts into question the credibility and motives of the Iraqi regime.

In the first instance, it should be indicated that a humanitarian but urgent concern is not being addressed by the Iraqi Government, specifically, the commitment by Iraq to abide by the terms of paragraphs 2 (c) and 3 (c) of resolution 686 (1991) and of paragraph 30 of resolution 687 (1991). Iraq is yet to repatriate the remaining Kuwaiti prisoners of war and detainees estimated at 5,433.

Second, Iraq has not to date declared its acceptance under the terms of paragraph 1 (b) of resolution 686 (1991) of its liability for any loss, damage or injury arising in regard to Kuwait and third States, and their nationals and corporations, as a result of the invasion and illegal occupation of Kuwait by Iraq.

Third, in spite of its declared readiness to return property seized in Kuwait, Iraq has not to date returned to Kuwait any of those items seized by it. Iraq has yet to implement faithfully the terms of paragraph 2 (d) of resolution 686 (1991) which demands that Iraq "immediately begins to return all Kuwaiti property seized by Iraq, to be completed in the shortest possible period".

...

86. Interim Report to Congress, Conduct of the Persian Gulf Conflict, Pursuant toTitle V Persian Gulf Conflict Supplemental Authorization and Personnel Benefits Act of 1991 (Public Law 102-25), July 1991

[*Extract.*]

Military-to-Military Talks at Safwan, Iraq

After the US and Coalition decision to cease offensive operations on 28 February, the Iraqis agreed to attend military-to-military talks to discuss cessation of hostilities, implementation of a cease fire, return of prisoners of war, and accounting for those missing in action, among other matters. A meeting lasting about 90 minutes was held on 3 March at Safwan airfield in southern Iraq, immediately north of the Kuwaiti border. CENTCOM chose the location because it was inside Iraq and near an airfield.

CINCCENT, the senior US officer, was accompanied by the senior commander of each coalition contingent. On the Iraqi side was Lieutenant General Sultan Hashim Ahmad Al-Jabburi, the Iraqi Vice Chief of Staff, accompanied by a staff of 10 senior officers, including the commander of the Iraqi III Corps, Major General Al-Dughastani. After preliminary formalities, General Schwarzkopf stated that he assumed that Baghdad had agreed to all US conditions or the Iraqi delegation would not be there. The Iraqis indicated that they were there to cooperate, although their attitude appeared hostile.

Two points emerged during this meeting that underscore the breadth of the Iraqi defeat. Following the Iraqi accounting of Coalition prisoners of war in Iraqi hands, Lieutenant General Al-Jabburi asked that the Coalition reciprocate and provide an accounting of Iraqi prisoners of war being held by the Coalition. When told that the counting was still going on, but at that time the number was in excess of 58,000, Lieutenant General Al-Jabburi appeared stunned. In apparent disbelief he asked the Iraqi III Corps commander if that was a correct number. Major General Al-Dughastani replied that it was possible, but that he did not know.

General Schwarzkopf proposed that a line be drawn on a map from which all forces would withdraw at least one kilometer to prevent inadvertent contact between Iraqi and Coalition forces. Lieutenant General Al-Jabburi agreed. When shown the CENTCOM proposed line, the Iraqi asked why the line was drawn behind his troops. General Schwarzkopf said that the line was the forward line of the US advance. Lieutenant General Al-Jabburi again appeared stunned. Once again he queried his III Corps commander, who again said it was possible, but that he did not know. Following this, the Iraqi attitude was noticeably more subdued.

9. GENERAL MATERIALS ON THE IMPLEMENTATION OF THE CEASE-FIRE

The documents reprinted in this chapter relate to more than one element of cease-fire resolution 687 (1991). Materials which concern individual issues only can be found in the respective chapters which follow.

S/23472, 24 January 1992

1. Letter from the Chargé d'affaires a.i. of the Permanent Mission of Iraq to the United Nations addressed to the President of the Security Council, 23 January 1992

I have the honour to transmit herewith a letter from the Minister for Foreign Affairs of the Republic of Iraq, Mr. Ahmad Hussein, dated 23 January 1992, to which is annexed a report containing a comprehensive review of the measures implemented by Iraq pursuant to Security Council resolution 687 (1991), with translations of both.

...

Annex

[Original: Arabic and English]

His Excellency
Sir David Hannay,
President of the Security Council
United Nations
New York

It is necessary to recall that the Security Council adopted resolution 661 (1990), imposing comprehensive and iniquitous economic sanctions against Iraq on the basis that Iraq had failed, at the time, to comply with resolution 660 (1990) connected with the events that had taken place since 2 August 1990.

However, in spite of Iraq's acceptance of the Council's resolutions, including resolution 660 (1990), the Security Council, by adopting resolution 687 (1991), not only maintained the economic sanctions, but also added new conditions, not contained in resolution 661 (1990), for the sanctions to be lifted. This was done under pressure from countries which had participated in the military aggression against Iraq, in order to achieve political objectives which bear no relation to the United Nations Charter, international law or the principle of fairness.

In a letter addressed to the President of the Security Council and the Secretary-General on 6 April 1991, the Minister for Foreign Affairs of the Republic of Iraq made clear the view held by Iraq regarding resolution 687 (1991). At the end of the letter the Minister pointed out that while wishing to go on historical record registering its principled and legitimate legal reservations before the conscience of the international community and international public opinion, Iraq finds itself left with no other alternative but to accept resolution 687 (1991).

During the period between the adoption of resolution 687 (1991) on 3 April and 31 December 1991, Iraq met a very large part of the conditions, restrictions and measures imposed upon it by resolution 687 (1991). The report enclosed herewith demonstrates through facts, figures and objective assessment what had been fulfilled in implementation of those conditions, restrictions and measures, which can be summed up as follows:

1. Elimination of weapons of mass destruction

The nuclear field

Iraq has taken a series of steps to implement the measures specified in resolution 687 (1991) in the nuclear field, and as follows:

(a) Iraq declared its commitment to, and implementation of, the requirements stated in paragraphs 11 and 12 of Security Council resolution 687 (1991), as follows:

First: Six letters from the Iraqi Minister for Foreign Affairs, reaffirming Iraq's commitment to its Non-Proliferation Treaty obligations;

Second: Sixteen letters and declarations issued by Iraqi official authorities stating Iraq's non-acquisition of nuclear weapons and non-production of such weapons or of any weapons-usable materials;

Third: Sixty-two letters containing Iraq's declaration of its nuclear sites and materials.

(b) By the end of 1991, the United Nations inspection teams made eight visits which altogether took 77 days, at an inspection rate of 2,120 man/days. The teams visited more than 50 sites, less than half of which were sites already declared by Iraq itself. The other sites were inspected by the teams on the basis of false intelligence information, and were then verified as non-nuclear sites after on-site inspection.

(c) Iraq declared all nuclear materials in its possession, which were:

First: 547,678 tons of natural uranium, in different forms;

Second: 50,066 kilograms of highly enriched fuel, of which the new type was removed from Iraq by the inspection teams;

Third: 1,850,629 kilograms of low enriched uranium;

Fourth: About 6 grams of plutonium removed from Iraq by the inspection teams;

Fifth: 6,004 tons of spent uranium.

The above-mentioned materials are all that Iraq has ever possessed. Iraq is in possession of no other nuclear materials whatsoever. The inspection teams have also verified that all Iraqi nuclear materials were made available to them and are now entirely in the possession of the International Atomic Energy Agency.

(d) Iraq has declared the stages in its nuclear programme, which include:

First: The extraction of uranium from its ores;

Second: The purification and conversion of uranium compounds;

Third: The methods of uranium enrichment (chemical, electromagnetic and centrifugal);

Fourth: Manufacturing nuclear fuel;

Fifth: Nuclear reactors;

Sixth: The Electronuclear Plant Project;

Seventh: The reprocessing of spent nuclear fuel;

Eighth: The processing of nuclear waste;

Ninth: Scientific research related to the programme;

Tenth: Agricultural and medical applications of isotopes;

Eleventh: Nuclear safety, engineering support and staff training;

Twelfth: Equipment/components related to the programme, their locations and quantities.

(e) Iraq presented to the inspection teams a lot of data and documents at their request. According to IAEA reports, the documents submitted were in excess of 60,000 pages.

(f) The inspection teams have destroyed, removed or rendered harmless all the equipment/components they deemed covered by their tasks.

(g) The Iraqi side extended all facilities requested by the different inspection teams, in addition to providing administrative and logistic services.

In view of the above, and as demonstrated in detail in the factual report attached hereto, [*not reproduced*] it becomes clear that Iraq has taken all practical steps to implement the measures imposed by Security Council resolution 687 (1991) in the nuclear field.

The field of ballistic missiles, chemical weapons and biological research activity

In implementation of paragraph 9, section C, of Security Council resolution 687 (1991), Iraq declared all its information and data concerning chemical weapons, ballistic missiles for defence purposes, and the biological research programme which had been totally abandoned since the autumn of 1990. The declarations were made by Iraq during the period from 18 April to 2 August 1991. The various inspection teams have verified on-site the credibility and factual nature of the Iraqi declarations. In their press statements, the heads of the various teams have themselves recognized the responsible manner in which Iraq provided the facilities required for the implementation of Security Council resolution 687 (1991).

(a) Ballistic missiles and their ranges

The inspection teams visited all various sites and verified the Iraqi declarations. They also supervised the destruction of the missiles, their mobile and stationary launchers, the support equipment and any significant parts related thereto.

(b) The field of chemical weapons

The Security Council Special Commission expressed understanding of, and support for, the Iraqi proposals to undertake the operation of destroying the agents and chemical weapons. As a first stage, the unfilled ammunition was destroyed. Work is in progress to prepare the requirements for the destruction operations under the supervision of the Special Commission. The inspection teams have verified the Iraqi declarations, on more than one occasion, and found nothing in them contrary to the above.

(c) The field of biological activity

The inspection teams have ascertained Iraq's total departure from and the fact that Iraq has no means of conducting any production, research or development activities in this field. The visits conducted by the teams in the three fields of inspection, took them to vast areas of Iraq, including military camps, production sites, warehouses, airbases and desert areas. The inspection teams conducted aerial inspection by using United Nations helicopters. Most of this was done in surprise visits without prior notice. Still, the teams found nothing contrary to Iraqi declarations, although their work was further assisted by satellite and U2 reconnaissance.

The Iraqi side answered all written and verbal questions put to it in relation to the allegations about ballistic missiles and submitted all clarifications required, especially details about the numbers of missiles.

As regards the ongoing monitoring, the Iraqi side has supplied all the information and data required by resolution 687 (1991), in connection with missiles, chemical weapons and biological research work. This was communicated in a letter sent to the Special Commission on 19 November 1991.

In the light of the above, it becomes apparent that Iraq has taken all the measures required for the implementation of section C of resolution 687 (1991), and has relinquished all ballistic missiles in its possession and abandoned its biological research activity. The destruction of chemical weapons is being carried out in accordance with such plans as jointly agreed between the Iraqi side and the Security Council Special Commission.

It is to be concluded that, following the implementation of measures imposed by resolution 687 (1991) in the nuclear, chemical and ballistic missiles fields, the fundamental objective of the resolution, which is to disarm Iraq of its weapons of mass destruction and of its capabilities to produce such weapons, has indeed been achieved.

Demarcation of boundaries with Kuwait

Paragraph 2 of Security Council resolution 687 (1991) imposed several measures for demarcation of the boundaries with Kuwait. Iraq has participated in all four sessions of the meetings held by the Iraq-Kuwait Boundary Demarcation Committee, which has discussed fundamental matters. In November 1991, the technical team visited all boundary areas it wished to see and surveyed and photographed those areas.

Iraq has not taken any action that would impede the measures of the United Nations, despite our clear position on this matter.

The United Nations Iraq-Kuwait Observation Mission (UNIKOM)

In implementation of paragraph 5 of resolution 687 (1991) and in observance of the United Nations Secretary-General's report on the establishment of a demilitarized zone and the immediate deployment of a United Nations Observation Mission (UNIKOM), Iraq has set up a Coordinating Committee with UNIKOM entrusted with the task of following up UNIKOM affairs in coordination with the Ministry of Foreign Affairs. A liaison body has also been established at Um Qasr for the same purpose. Prior to the deployment of UNIKOM forces, all military units had been withdrawn as deep inside Iraqi territory and as far from the demilitarized zone as is required. Assistance has been extended to facilitate the tasks of UNIKOM, which has also been supplied with all information related to the civil administration of the demilitarized zone under Iraq's responsibility. UNIKOM has also been granted full freedom of movement and communication, along with other rights, as well as the freedom of movement on land or in the air all over the said zone. The liaison body at Um Qasr notifies UNIKOM beforehand of any movement by Iraqi vessels in Khor Abdullah. An agreement has been reached between the Iraqi Government and the Secretary-General of the United Nations on the status, immunities and privileges of UNIKOM personnel, in accordance with the 1946 Convention on Privileges and Immunities. A UNIKOM headquarters has been established at Um Qasr, and a UNIKOM liaison bureau set up in Baghdad, all free of charge. A UNIKOM duty-free shop has also been opened at Um Qasr. At the request of UNIKOM, Iraq has agreed that UNIKOM may employ third-party international contractors to build surveillance points in the demilitarized zone, employ Iraqi technical staff and use Iraqi mechanical equipment free of charge. An agreement has been reached on a mechanism by which to notify UNIKOM of the violations committed by the Kuwaiti side and the coalition partners in the demilitarized zone. The number of such violations, during the period from 25 November to 22 December 1991, reached 226.

It is to be concluded from the above that Iraq has extended everything required to facilitate the work of UNIKOM and fully cooperated with the mission in order to ensure the success of its tasks and avoid any difficulties.

Return of Kuwaiti property

In implementation of section D, paragraph 15, of resolution 687 (1991), and in observance of the report of the Secretary-General, regarding the return of Kuwaiti property, and in accordance with the agreement reached with Mr. J. Richard Foran, the Assistant Secretary-General in charge of coordinating the return of Kuwaiti property, four priorities were determined for the return of Kuwaiti property and resources, all of which have been fully implemented, as follows:

May 1991	One civil aircraft delivered in Amman, Jordan.
31 July 1991	One civil aircraft delivered at Al-Muthenna airport in Baghdad.
5 August 1991	3,216 gold ingots and amounts of coins and banknotes delivered at Arar in Saudi Arabia.
10 Sept. 1991	Books belonging to the Central Library delivered at Arar.
16 Sept. 1991	Museum items delivered in Baghdad.
17 Sept. 1991	News Agency materials delivered at Arar.
20 Oct. 1991	Museum items delivered.
13 Nov. 1991	Nine large aircraft engines delivered through Habaniyah airport.
15 Dec. 1991	Four Hawk training military aircraft delivered.
15 Dec. 1991	Sixteen steel safes belonging to the Central Bank delivered.

In addition to the deliveries made, Iraq received a technical delegation, during December 1991, to examine the destroyed aircraft at Mosul and Muthenna airports. Iraq expressed its willingness to hand over Hawk missiles and equipment, along with other military equipment about which coordination was in process with Mr. Foran for delivery to be made in mid-January 1992.

It is to be concluded from the above that Iraq has returned the greater part of the property in question, expressed its willingness to return the remainder, and cooperated in earnest with the United Nations representative in order to accomplish this aspect. The delay and return of the remainder of the property has not been due to any reluctance on the part of Iraq but to United Nations measures and United Nations staff shortage. Iraq has in fact proposed that the delivery of returned property and equipment be done simultaneously at several points in order to expedite the return of the property.

Repatriation of Kuwaiti nationals

In implementation of section C, paragraph 30, of resolution 687 (1991), and in order to facilitate the repatriation of all Kuwaiti and third country nationals, the Government of Iraq has taken the following steps:

The Iraqi authorities concerned have, since 4 March 1991, and in cooperation with the mission of the International Committee of the Red Cross (ICRC) in Baghdad, repatriated 6,518 Kuwaiti and other nationals. There are at present 3,905 Kuwaitis; they are not living in detention, but live freely in the country and have full access to the ICRC mission in Baghdad, where they registered their names and submitted their requests to return to Kuwait. The ICRC has communicated their requests to the Kuwaiti authorities, which have so far agreed to the return of only 400 of the whole number. We are still awaiting Kuwaiti approval for the rest to be repatriated.

On 17 December 1991, the Iraqi Ministry of Foreign Affairs submitted a request to the ICRC mission in Baghdad in which the Ministry proposed that the ICRC prepare a complete implementation plan, to be agreed upon between Iraq and the coalition countries, for measures to be adopted in the search for Kuwaiti, Saudi, Iraqi and other nationals still missing, in accordance with the provisions of the Geneva Convention of 1949.

It is to be concluded from the above that Iraq has, for its part, implemented its commitments to facilitate the repatriation of all Kuwaiti and third country nationals carefully and in earnest, and has cooperated with the ICRC in this respect; but the Kuwaiti authorities still refuse to receive their nationals.

Excellency,

The campaign launched by certain States members of the Security Council, in relation to the extent to which the measures specified in resolution 687 (1991) have been implemented and to Iraq's intentions, is a biased campaign and at odds with the facts established in this report.

The United Nations missions dispatched to implement all the said measures have themselves acknowledged and stated in their reports that Iraq had cooperated with them in earnest and in a highly professional and practical manner. Except for the incidents deliberately created on two occasions by David Kay of the United States, a CIA man with political motives to justify aggression against Iraq and newfangled pretexts for the perpetuation of the iniquitous sanctions imposed against its people, the work of the United Nations missions bears no witness to any of the false claims made by those countries in their reports and statements against Iraq.

Those established facts and figures prove that the continued imposition of the sanctions against Iraq on the basis of resolution 687 (1991) does not have any legal or practical grounds. It is a purely political stand adopted by certain States members of the Security Council to achieve such ulterior political objectives as neither resolution 687 (1991) nor any of the other resolutions, however iniquitous, accommodated or provided for.

The Security Council is called upon to take, in accordance with the very resolutions it adopted and with the objectives set out in those resolutions, an unequivocal decision for a total lifting of the economic sanctions imposed upon Iraq. As for Iraq which has always cooperated in implementing the measures specified in resolution 687 (1991), it shall continue to honour its commitment towards those measures.

Refrainment by the Security Council from lifting the sanctions, at the instigation of certain countries, will undermine the resolutions themselves and render them meaningless; and the Council will have to draw the right conclusions from such an eventuality.

Iraq calls upon the Security Council to look deeply and objectively into this matter, away from the political objectives sought by certain countries. Iraq also invites the Security Council to appoint a mission consisting of members with no special political pretexts or objectives against Iraq, to examine these facts and present its conclusions to the Council. Iraq is ready to receive any such mission interested in conducting an on-the-spot investigation of the facts. Iraq is also prepared to dispatch a high-level delegation to New York to discuss these facts with the mission proposed herein, and submit Iraq's views and position before the Security Council.

...

[*An enclosed "factual report on the measures taken by Iraq in accordance with Security Council resolution 687 (1991)" has been omitted.*]

S/23514, 25 January 1992

2. Report of the Secretary-General on the status of compliance by Iraq with the obligations placed upon it under certain of the Security Council resolutions relating to the situation between Iraq and Kuwait

1. The present report is presented to the members of the Security Council pursuant to the request addressed to the Secretary-General in the statement issued by the President of the Council on 20 December 1991 (S/23305). By the President's statement, the Security Council, among other things, requested the Secretary-General "to prepare a factual report on Iraq's compliance with all the obligations placed upon it by resolution 687 (1991) and subsequent relevant resolutions", such a report to "be made available to the Security Council in good time before the Council undertakes its next review under paragraph 21 of resolution 687 (1991)".[1. The next review under paragraph 21 of resolution 687 (1991) falls due on 28 January 1992.]

2. The Secretary-General proceeded immediately to identify all the applicable obligations under the Security Council's request, and to determine Iraq's compliance with them, to date. While some of the obligations placed upon Iraq are of a rather general nature, many others were clearly specified in the resolutions imposing them. However, there are some obligations for which no monitoring body or mechanism under or outside the United Nations auspices could be readily identified and so approached for contributions in time for preparation of the present report.

3. For the purposes of the present report, the Secretary-General has focused his attention only on those provisions in the relevant resolutions that place mandatory obligations upon Iraq. The comments received from various sources relating to the observations and assessments of Iraq's compliance are reproduced in the annex to the present report.

A. Obligations of a general nature

4. There are two principal, general obligations upon which Iraq's compliance with all its obligations may be based and assessed.

1. *Acceptance by Iraq of the provisions of the entire resolution 687 (1991) (para. 33)*

5. Under paragraph 33 of resolution 687 (1991) Iraq was required to give official notification to the Secretary-General and to the Security Council of its acceptance of the provisions of the entire resolution, as a precondition for a formal cease-fire becoming effective between Iraq and Kuwait and the States cooperating with Kuwait.

6. By a letter dated 6 April 1991 addressed simultaneously to the Secretary-General and the President of the Security Council (S/22456), Iraq signified its unconditional acceptance of Security Council resolution 687 (1991). By a further letter dated 10 April (S/22480) Iraq transmitted the text of a decision adopted by the National Assembly of Iraq on 6 April 1991, accepting the resolution.

2. *Compliance by Iraq with all its international obligations (para. 5 of resolution 707 (1991))*

7. By paragraph 5 of resolution 707 (1991), Iraq is required to comply with all its international obligations, including those set out in resolutions 687 (1991) and 707 (1991), [2. For the purposes of the present report, the Secretary-General was guided by the President's statement of 20 December 1991 (S/23305) in so far as it referred to Iraq's compliance with the obligations set out only in the resolutions alluded to in that statement.] and in the Treaty on the Non-Proliferation of Nuclear Weapons of 1 July 1968, and Iraq's safeguards agreement with the International Atomic Energy Agency (IAEA). [3. For proper coverage of Iraq's compliance with the Treaty and the nuclear safeguards agreement, see paragraph 20, below.] No specific requirement was made of Iraq to confirm its compliance with the provisions of this paragraph.

B. Specific obligations

1. *Respect for the inviolability of the international border and allocation of islands between Iraq and Kuwait (para. 2 of resolution 687 (1991))*

8. Under paragraph 2 of resolution 687 (1991) it was demanded of Iraq to respect the inviolability of the previously agreed international border and the allocation of islands between Iraq and Kuwait (cf: document 7063, United Nations, *Treaty Series*, 1964). The comments on this item are contained in the annex to the present report (see annex, sect. A).

2 *Obligations relating to conventional, biological or chemical weapons and such materials for warfare (paras. 8, 9 (a) and 10 of resolution 687 (1991), para. 3 of resolution 707 (1991) and para. 5 of resolution 715 (1991))*

9. The monitoring of Iraq's compliance with, and the implementation of, the obligations as required under the relevant resolutions cited above was entrusted to the Special Commission established under paragraph 9 (b) (i) of Security Council resolution 687 (1991). The Special Commission's comments on this matter are contained in the annex to the present report (see annex, sect. B).

3. *Obligations relating to nuclear capability development programmes (paras. 10 and 12 of resolution 687 (1991), para. 3 of resolution 707 (1991) and para. 5 of resolution 715 (1991))*

10. The monitoring of Iraq's compliance with, and the implementation of, the obligations as required under the relevant resolutions cited above, was entrusted to IAEA. The comments of IAEA on this matter are contained in the annex to the present report (see annex, sect. C).

4. *Obligations relating to repatriation of and access to all Kuwaiti and third-country nationals in Iraq (para. 30 of resolution 687 (1991))*

11. Under the provisions of paragraph 30 of resolution 687 (1991) it was required of Iraq to extend all necessary cooperation to the International Committee of the Red Cross (ICRC) in all matters relating to the location of and access to all Kuwaiti and third-country nationals in Iraq for the purpose of their repatriation. [4. In paragraph 31 of the resolution, the Council invited ICRC to keep the Secretary-General apprised, as appropriate, of all the activities undertaken in pursuance of paragraph 30, as well as those relating to the return of the remains of Kuwaiti and third-country nationals present in Iraq on or after 2 August 1990.]

12. In his report to the Security Council dated 12 September 1991 (S/23012), the Secretary-General included information he had received from ICRC relating, among other things, to repatriation of former residents of Kuwait from Iraq, registration and repatriation of persons wishing to return to Kuwait, repatriation of third-country nationals, and details of a Kuwaiti list of civilians and military personnel missing since 2 August 1990. In response to the Secretary-General's request for information for the purposes of the present report, ICRC has submitted additional comments on the item, which are contained in the annex to the present report (see annex, sect. D).

5. *Iraq's liability under international law for loss or damage resulting from its unlawful invasion and occupation of Kuwait (para. 16 of resolution 687 (1991))*

13. Information received with regard to this item is contained in the annex to the present report (see annex, sect. E).

6. *Adherence to all obligations concerning the servicing and repayment of Iraq's foreign debt (para. 17 of resolution 687 (1991))*

14. The response from the International Monetary Fund (IMF) indicates that, as of 31 December 1991, Iraq was in arrears to the IMF in the sum of Special Drawing Rights (SDR) 7.3 million. Furthermore, the Chairman of the Paris Club of Creditor Countries has submitted a tabulation of Iraq's indebtedness to some of the Club members amounting to a total of some US $13,420 million due since 1 April 1991. The relevant communications concerning this item are contained in the annex to the present report (see annex, sect. F).

7. *Non-entitlement to claims deriving from the effects of the measures taken by the Security Council in resolution 661 (1990) and related resolutions (para. 29 of resolution 687 (1991))*

15. According to information received with regard to this item, Iraq attempted to enforce a claim under which it would have benefited from a contract frustrated by the coming into effect of the terms of resolution 661 (1990). Communications concerning this item are contained in the annex to the present report (see annex, sect. G).

8. *Liability by Iraq for the full cost of the tasks authorized under section C of resolution 687 (1991) (para. 4 of resolution 699 (1991))*

16. The comments received with regard to this item are contained in the annex to the present report (see annex, sect. H).

9. *Requirement to provide monthly statements of gold and foreign currency reserves holdings (para. 7 of resolution 706 (1991))*

17. To date, the Secretary-General has received no notification from Iraq of the amount of its holdings of gold and foreign currency reserves. Furthermore, IMF has reported that, since the adoption of resolution 706 (1991), it has not received from the Iraqi authorities any information concerning Iraq's holdings of gold and foreign currency reserves. (5. Subsequently, a representative of IMF amplified orally that disclosure of such information was obligatory to all signatory members to the Charter of that organization, of which Iraq was one.) The text of the letter on comments on this item from the Managing Director of IMF is reproduced in the annex to the present report (see annex, sect. F).

C. OTHER OBLIGATIONS

18. Two other types of obligations placed upon Iraq are drawn to the Council's attention, namely: obligations imposed upon Iraq under Chapter VII of the Charter (mandatory obligations) but for which no monitoring organ has been specifically designated.

1. *Undertaking required on not committing, supporting or abetting commission of any international terrorist acts (para. 32 of resolution 687 (1991))*

19. In the absence of any specifically designated organ for monitoring Iraq's compliance with the above-mentioned obligation, the Secretary-General is unable to offer any guiding information to the members of the Council. However, in a letter dated 11 June 1991 (S/22687) Iraq, with reference to paragraph 32 of resolution 687 (1991), stated that it was a party to the international conventions relating to this item, and affirmed that it had never pursued a policy favourable to international terrorism as defined by international law. In a further letter of the same date (S/22689) Iraq reaffirmed its position.

2. *Compliance with obligations in the Treaty on the Non-Proliferation of Nuclear Weapons of 1 July 1968 (para. 5 of resolution 707 (1991))*

20. In its letter of 6 April 1991 (S/22456), in which it signified its acceptance of resolution 687 (1991), Iraq also stated that it was a party to the Treaty on the Non-Proliferation of Nuclear Weapons of 1 July 1968, adding that many reports of IAEA confirmed that Iraq was applying all the provisions of the Treaty. IAEA for its part, in two letters dated 19 July (S/22812) and 27

September 1991 (S/23088) from the Director-General, informed the Security Council of the finding by the Board of Governors of IAEA that Iraq had not fully complied with its obligations under its safeguards agreements with the Agency. In a resolution adopted on 20 September 1991 (GC/(XXV)/RES/568) the General Conference of IAEA, taking note of Security Council resolution 687 (1991), had, among other provisions, strongly condemned "Iraq's non-compliance with its nuclear non-proliferation obligations", and demanded that Iraq "immediately and fully comply with all of its nuclear non-proliferation obligations".

Annex

Substantive texts of the communications received from various sources indicating their observations and assessments of Iraq's compliance

A. IRAQ'S COMPLIANCE WITH THE PROVISIONS OF PARAGRAPHS 2 AND 5 OF SECURITY COUNCIL RESOLUTION 687 (1991)

In view of the mandate of the United Nations Iraq-Kuwait Observation Mission (UNIKOM), the text below deals with both paragraphs 2 and 5 of resolution 687 (1991).

1. Paragraph 2 of Security Council resolution 687 (1991) requires Iraq and Kuwait to respect the inviolability of the international boundary and the allocation of islands as set out in the "Agreed Minutes" signed by them on 4 October 1963. Paragraph 5 of the same resolution requires the two States to respect a demilitarized zone (DMZ) established by the Security Council. The Council set up the United Nations Iraq-Kuwait Observation Mission (UNIKOM) to monitor the DMZ and the Khor Abdullah; to deter violations of the boundary through its presence in and surveillance of the DMZ; and to observe any hostile or potentially hostile action mounted from the territory of one State to the other.

2. Iraq has respected the DMZ.

3. With regard to respect for the international boundary it should be noted that, pending the boundary's demarcation on the ground, UNIKOM has not taken a position concerning its precise location. UNIKOM uses a British map, which it has given to both sides for reference; they have agreed to work with it as a practical arrangement to facilitate UNIKOM's task and without prejudice to their positions concerning the boundary. In order to avoid friction and incidents, UNIKOM has established the principle that the authorities on both sides should stay a reasonable distance of 1,000 metres from the boundary line shown on UNIKOM's map. However, five Iraqi police posts are on the Kuwaiti side of that line, and two are closer to it than 1,000 metres, on the Iraqi side. In response to repeated requests by UNIKOM to move these posts to positions at least 1,000 metres on the Iraqi side of the line, the Iraqi authorities have declined to do so on the grounds that this could prejudice their position relating to the border. They have said that Iraq will comply with the reasonable distance principle, once the border is demarcated.

4. In August and September 1991, there were a number of incursions from Iraqi into Kuwaiti territory by persons collecting weapons, ammunition and other battlefield items. The question was raised whether they were in fact military personnel but UNIKOM was not able to establish that this was so. The incursions ceased in October after the Iraqi authorities took effective measures to curb them. Since then, the Iraq-Kuwait border has been quiet.

B. EXTRACT FROM LETTER DATED 21 JANUARY 1992 FROM THE EXECUTIVE CHAIRMAN OF THE SPECIAL COMMISSION

As requested in the memorandum of 8 January 1992, I am sending herewith the contribution of the Special Commission to the Secretary-General's report. As you will see, the text submitted herewith provides for a part B of the chapter of the report involved in which the text on nuclear issues which you have received from the Director-General of IAEA can be inserted.

Attachment

Section C of Security Council resolution 687 (1991) and resolutions 707 (1991) and 715 (1991)

Introduction

1. The paragraphs which follow deal with the status of Iraq's compliance with the provisions of section C of Security Council resolution 687 (1991) of 3 April 1991 and resolutions 707 (1991) and 715 (1991) of 15 August and 11 October 1991 respectively. Section C of resolution 687 (1991) related to the elimination of Iraq's capabilities in regard to weapons of mass destruction and also to ensuring that the acquisition of such weapons is not resumed in the future. Resolutions 707 (1991) and 715 (1991) are concerned with matters directly related to implementation of section C of resolution 687 (1991), including ongoing monitoring and verification of Iraq's compliance with its obligations and the facilities, privileges and immunities of the Special Commission established under resolution 687 (1991) and of the International Atomic Energy Agency (IAEA).

2. The status of Iraq's compliance with the obligations arising from these particular provisions has been addressed in a number of previous reports, circulated by the Secretary-General to the Security Council, covering the period from the adoption of resolution 687 (1991) in April 1991 up to early December 1991. Two reports by the Executive Chairman of the Special Commission were circulated in documents S/23165 of 25 October 1991 and S/23268 of 4 December 1991. These reports cover all aspects encompassed by section C of resolution 687 (1991) and the subsequent related resolutions. At the request of the Director-General of IAEA, the Secretary-General issued, as documents of the Council, inspection reports prepared by eight of the nuclear inspection teams in Iraq led by the Agency (S/22788, S/22837, S/22986 and Corr.1, S/23112, S/23122, S/23215 and S/23283). A report from the ninth nuclear inspection team, which left Iraq on 14 January 1992, will be forthcoming in the near future. A further report by the Director-General, covering the Agency's operations under the relevant Council resolutions for the period April to December 1991, was circulated on 17 December 1991 in document S/23295.

3. Part A of the present chapter, based upon information provided by the Special Commission, updates the reports of the Executive Chairman listed above, in so far as they relate to paragraphs 8, 9 and 10 of resolution 687 (1991) and related provisions in resolutions 707 (1991) and 715 (1991). Part B is based upon information provided by the Director-General of IAEA, and is concerned with paragraphs 12 and 13 of resolution 687 (1991) and related provisions in resolutions 707 (1991) and 715 (1991).

Part A: Paragraphs 8, 9 and 10 of Security Council resolution 687 (1991) and related provisions in resolutions 707 (1991) and 715 (1991)

Chemical and biological weapons

4. Under paragraphs 8 and 9 of section C of resolution 687 (1991), Iraq is, *inter alia*, required to accept unconditionally the destruction, removal or rendering harmless, under international supervision, of all chemical and biological weapons and all stocks of agents and all related subsystems and components and all research, development, support and manufacturing facilities. It is further required to submit to the Secretary-General a declaration of the locations, amounts and types of the foregoing items and to permit urgent, ongoing inspection thereof by the Special Commission, both at sites declared by Iraq and at any additional locations designated by the Special Commission. Iraq is also required to yield possession of all the foregoing items, both at declared and designated sites to the Special Commission for destruction, removal or rendering harmless, taking into account requirements of public safety.

5. Iraq made declarations under the foregoing provisions of 23 locations. Twenty-three other sites were designated by the Special Commission. Inspections have been carried out by the Special Commission at 43 of these locations. Three sites declared by Iraq, but assessed by the Special Commission to be of low priority, will be visited shortly on future inspections.

6. Although the Iraqi authorities have been cooperative in efforts to destroy their declared chemical stockpile, they have as yet failed to disclose fully all the information required under resolution 687 (1991) on their chemical weapons programmes despite repeated requests from the Special Commission. Specifically, Iraq has not answered requests to identify the development, support and manufacturing components of those programmes. Such components clearly exist in view of the types of weapons which have been identified.

7. Ten types of weapons have been found in the Iraqi chemical weapons arsenal which, Iraq maintains, were manufactured locally or modified in Iraq for chemical weapons fill. The equipment so far found appears to have been involved in the manufacture of only two of these types, 250 and 500 gauge aerial bombs. Iraq has so far not accounted for the location of equipment for the fabrication of the remaining eight declared types of chemical weapons.

8. Furthermore, there is evidence that Iraq continues to attempt to retain machinery directly involved in the manufacture of chemical weapons by moving it away from its original location at the principal Iraqi chemical weapons facility, the Muthanna State Establishment. An example of this was encountered in December 1991 by the most recent chemical weapons team to visit Iraq (UNSCOM 21). Iraq had been directed by the Special Commission to return to Muthanna all the chemical bomb casing manufacturing equipment which had been removed from that site after the adoption of resolution 687 (1991), and Iraq claimed to have complied with this directive. However, during a short-notice inspection of a sugar factory in Mosul, Special Commission inspectors found almost 100 items of metal-working machinery originating from Muthanna. After attempting to argue that these items were of a general purpose nature for civil use, the Iraqi officials concerned admitted that the items had come from the chemical bomb casing and supporting general maintenance workshops at Muthanna. Iraq was again directed to return the equipment to Muthanna for disposal.

9. Iraq initially denied possession of biological weapons and related items. However, during the Special Commission's first biological weapons inspection of the site at Salman Pak, Iraqi officials admitted to having carried out a programme of biological research for both defensive and offensive purposes. Iraq has not to date disclosed a plan for a development and production component of its activities in this area. The Special Commission considers that such a plan is a logical part of the Iraqi programme and will continue to press for its disclosure.

10. In the absence of a full, complete and final disclosure by Iraq of its chemical and biological weapons programmes, the Special Commission will need to continue first phase inspections and to designate further suspected sites in order to uncover the full scope of those programmes before the Commission is able to conclude that in this area Iraq is meeting its obligations under paragraphs 8 and 9 of resolution 687 (1991).

Ballistic missiles and long-range guns

11. Under paragraphs 8 and 9 of section C of resolution 687 (1991), Iraq is, *inter alia*, required to accept unconditionally the destruction, removal or rendering harmless, under international supervision, of all ballistic missiles with a range greater than 150 kilometres and related major parts, and repair and production facilities. It is further required to submit to the Secretary-General a declaration of the locations, amounts and types of the foregoing items and to permit urgent, ongoing inspection thereof by the Special Commission, both at sites declared by Iraq and any additional locations designated by the Special Commission. Iraq is also required to destroy, under the supervision of the Special Commission, all its missile capabilities, including launchers, as specified in paragraph 8 of the resolution.

12. Iraq has declared under the foregoing provisions some 24 locations. An additional 47 locations were designated by the Special Commission. All these locations have been inspected.

13. Since the second report of the Executive Chairman of the Special Commission was submitted to the Security Council on 4 December 1991 (S/23268), a Special Commission ballistic missile inspection team, in inspecting components of the 1,000 mm "supergun", found that 22 barrel sections and some hydraulic buffers had not been adequately destroyed according to the specifications laid down by the previous inspection team. Iraqi personnel were requested to destroy the components as directed, which was done and subsequently verified. At another site the team found that two SCUD missile trailers that had been previously destroyed had been welded together and outfitted to carry shorter-range FROG-7 missiles. The team requested their complete destruction, together with six unaltered transporters and accepted an Iraqi proposal that they be blown up with explosives. The destruction of these eight trailers was verified by the team. Finally, with the destruction since the second report of the remaining fixed SCUD launchers, all declared missiles and their launchers and major parts have now been destroyed.

14. While the Special Commission is fully satisfied that all of Iraq's declared ballistic missiles have been destroyed, there remains substantial uncertainty whether all missiles subject to resolution 687 (1991), primarily SCUD or SCUD variants, have been declared as required. The Special Commission is endeavouring, by means of an exchange of information with Member States and by various interactions with Iraq, to attempt to resolve these uncertainties. Further, the Special Commission continues to receive information that various significant components intended for indigenously produced SCUDS were contracted for and received by Iraq. The Special Commission, with the cooperation of Member States, is seeking to confirm this information and to resolve the outstanding issues with the Iraqi authorities.

Ongoing monitoring and verification

15. Under paragraph 10 of section C of resolution 687 (1991), Iraq is, *inter alia*, required to undertake unconditionally not to use, construct or acquire any of the items proscribed in paragraphs 8 and 9 of the resolution relating to ballistic missiles and chemical and biological weapons. The Secretary-General is requested, in consultation with the Special Commission, to develop a plan for ongoing monitoring and verification of Iraq's compliance with that undertaking. Similar provisions in respect of Iraq's nuclear activities are laid down in paragraphs 12 and 13 of section C of the resolution, the plan for ongoing monitoring and verification in this regard to be prepared by the Director-General of the International Atomic Energy Agency, with the assistance and cooperation of the Special Commission.

16. On 11 October 1991, the Security Council adopted resolution 715 (1991), which approved the plans for future ongoing monitoring and verification of Iraq's compliance with relevant parts of section C of Security Council resolution 687 (1991) (S/22871/Rev.1 and S/22872/Rev.1 and Corr.1) submitted in accordance with resolution 687 (1991). Under paragraph 5 of resolution 715 (1991), Iraq is obliged to meet unconditionally all its obligations under the plans and to cooperate fully with the Special Commission and the Director-General of IAEA in carrying out the plans.

17. To ensure Iraq's full compliance, these plans - both in nuclear and non-nuclear areas - cover not only military but also those civilian facilities and items that could be used, or activities that could be involved, in contravention of the relevant Iraqi obligations. The plans provide for inspections, aerial overflights in Iraq and submission of information by Iraq so that the Special Commission, or in the nuclear area IAEA with the assistance and cooperation of the Commission, would be able to monitor and verify that no nuclear, chemical or biological weapons or ballistic missiles or other items prohibited under resolution 687 (1991) are acquired anew. The first step to be taken by Iraq under these plans was the submission, by 10 November 1991, of initial information on the specific dual-purpose activities, facilities and items outlined in the plans and their annexes.

18. Only in late November did the Special Commission receive from Iraq a document that was stated in the letter of transmission to be the information requested of Iraq in accordance with resolution 687 (1991). This document does not recognize that Iraq has any obligations under resolution 715 (1991) and the Special Commission's plan approved thereunder. Instead it arrogates to Iraq the right to decide what information it will provide to the Special Commission and, in this respect, does little more than repeat information already supplied. It thus falls well short of the information required under the Special Commission's plan adopted by resolution 715 (1991).

19. On 20 December 1991, the Chairman of the Special Commission sent a letter to the Permanent Representative of Iraq to the United Nations in which he stated that the present Iraqi attitude constituted a serious obstacle to the implementation of the monitoring and verification of Iraq's compliance with its obligations under resolution 687 (1991). He requested Iraq to rectify this situation immediately and fulfil its obligations under resolution 715 (1991) and the plan for ongoing monitoring and verification (S/22871/Rev.1). The Chairman requested Iraq to provide by 15 January 1992 all the information and data specified in that plan.

20. As of the time of the writing of this report no response has been received from Iraq to the Chairman's letter. Furthermore, Iraq has not provided its first semi-annual declaration which was due from it on 15 January under the Special Commission's plan approved by the Security Council.

21. The Special Commission is sending a special mission to Iraq scheduled for 27 to 29 January 1992. The mission will be led by two members of the Special Commission and its objectives will be twofold: first, to underline the most serious concern with Iraq's failure to provide required information under Security Council resolution 715 (1991) and, second, to urge Iraq, in accordance with resolution 707 (1991), to disclose, fully and completely, information on its programmes in areas related to chemical and biological weapons and ballistic missiles with a range greater than 150 kilometres.

Iraq's reporting obligations under Security Council resolution 707 (1991)

22. Under paragraph 3 (i) of Security Council resolution 707 (1991) Iraq is required to provide, without further delay, full, final and complete disclosure of all aspects of its programmes to develop weapons of mass destruction and ballistic missiles with a range greater than 150 kilometres, and of all holdings of such weapons, their components and production facilities and locations, as well as all other nuclear programmes, including any which it claims are for purposes not related to nuclear-weapons-usable material.

23. As will have been seen from the preceding sections, while Iraq has made a number of declarations relating to its weapons of mass destruction and the facilities for their production, these declarations have been far from complete. The Special Commission has found it necessary to make numerous designations of undeclared sites, and such designations are continuing in the absence of the full, final and complete disclosure called for by paragraph 3 (i) of resolution 707 (1991). Particularly in the nuclear field the Special Commission can have no confidence that Iraq has disclosed the full scope and nature of its programmes for fissile material production and of its research and development efforts in respect of nuclear weapons.

24. Since making its initial declarations, Iraq has consistently maintained that it has no further declarations to make except when confronted with evidence of the inadequacy of its prior declarations. At a meeting with the Minister of State for Foreign Affairs on 12 January 1992, in which the Deputy Executive Chairman of the Special Commission participated, the position was again taken by Iraq that it would not make any further declarations but would respond only to information, such as that reported above in part B of this chapter concerning its acquisition of large quantities of components for centrifuges for its gas centrifuge enrichment programme, when directly confronted with that information. This approach does not discharge Iraq's obligation to provide the full, final and complete disclosure called for in paragraph 3 (i) of resolution 707 (1991).

25. Under paragraph 3 (ix) of resolution 707 (1991), Iraq is required to respond fully, completely and promptly to any questions or requests from the Special Commission, IAEA and their inspection teams.

26. On a number of previous occasions, particularly as a result of inspection activities, specific questions on the relevant Iraqi capabilities have been put to the Iraqi authorities. Many of these questions remain unanswered, and thus Iraq is not meeting all its obligations to provide information to the Special Commission and IAEA at their request. Consequently, despite the inspection efforts undertaken by the Special Commission, some important lacunae remain which preclude full understanding of the Iraqi programmes concerned. There is therefore a need to seek from Iraq further information so that a more comprehensive understanding may be arrived at of the issues involved which would increase confidence in any assessments to be prepared for the Security Council.

Issues relating to the obligations of Iraq in connection with the facilities, privileges and immunities of the Special Commission and of IAEA

27. On 14 May 1991 an agreement between the United Nations and Iraq on the facilities, privileges and immunities of the Special Commission, contained in an exchange of notes between the Secretary-General and the Minister for Foreign Affairs of Iraq entered into force. This agreement spelled out the requirements for the Special Commission, IAEA and their inspection teams to discharge effectively the functions conferred on them in resolution 687 (1991). These requirements included unrestricted freedom of entry into and exit from Iraq for personnel, equipment and means of transport; unrestricted freedom of movement without advance notice in Iraq; unimpeded access to any declared or designated site; the right to request, receive and copy any record, data or other information; the right to take photographs from the ground or the air relevant to the Special Commission's activities; the right to operate the Special Commission's own means of transport, both on the ground and in the air and various other facilities, privileges and immunities, including ensuring the security and safety of inspectors and other personnel.

28. Difficulties encountered by the Special Commission and IAEA in the conduct of inspections, and the failure of Iraq on a number of occasions to abide by the terms of the agreement, have been reported in several documents submitted to the Security Council (see, for example, S/22739, S/22743, S/23165, para. 17 and appendix III, paras. 5 and 11, and S/23268, para. 3). These difficulties have included denial of access to certain sites; threats to the security of inspectors, on one occasion by means of rifle fire; detention of an inspection team in a parking lot for four days; destruction or movement for purposes of concealment of equipment and documentation from designated sites; forcible removal and refusal to return documentary evidence found by an inspection team and refusal for over three months to permit the Special Commission to introduce its own helicopters into Iraq for the transportation of inspection teams and for other official inspection activities.

29. Among the measures adopted by the Council in response to these violations are a number of provisions contained in paragraph 3 of resolution 707 (1991) confirming the facilities, privileges and immunities of the Special Commission and IAEA. These provisions demand, *inter alia*, that Iraq grant immediate, unconditional and unrestricted access to sites, facilities, equipment and records; cease attempts to conceal and to move or destroy any proscribed material or equipment without prior consent from the Special Commission; make immediately available items to which access was previously denied; and permit the operation of fixed-wing and helicopter flights in Special Commission or IAEA aircraft for all relevant purposes, including inspection, surveillance, aerial surveys, transportation and logistics. Resolution 707 (1991) further demands that Iraq ensure the complete implementation of the privileges, immunities and facilities of representatives of the Special Commission and IAEA and their complete safety and freedom of movement.

30. Since the second report of the Executive Chairman of the Special Commission was circulated to the Security Council on 4 December 1991, there have been no significant violations of the facilities, privileges and immunities of the Special Commission and of IAEA. Access has been granted to inspection teams at both declared and designated sites. There have been no threats to the security and safety of inspectors while engaged on official inspections, and the Special Commission has continued to operate its own fixed-wing and helicopter flights.

31. However, Iraq continues to protest, as a violation of its sovereignty, each aerial surveillance flight undertaken by the Special Commission despite the clearly established right of the Commission to undertake such flights. This right derives from resolution 687 (1991) and is expressly laid down in the agreement that entered into force on 14 May 1991 and in paragraph 3 of resolution 707 (1991). Moreover, the issue referred to in the Executive Chairman's report of 4 December 1991 regarding the possible application of control measures at Habbaniya airport which would interfere with the Commission's rights to unimpeded entry into and exit from Iraq of equipment, materials and other items has not been resolved definitively. Furthermore, Iraq has so far failed to deliver to IAEA documentation which was forcibly removed from a nuclear inspection team during the period of its detention in a parking lot in September 1991.

32. Resolution 707 (1991) also requires Iraq to provide or facilitate the provision of transportation, medical or logistical support requested by the Special Commission and IAEA. Iraq has responded readily to such requests.

33. The obligations of Iraq in respect of the facilities, privileges and immunities of the Special Commission and of IAEA are of a continuing nature. Those obligations are repeated and reinforced in the plans for ongoing monitoring and verification which were approved by the Security Council in its resolution 715 (1991), and their implementation in this context remains to be tested. Past experience has shown that the Special Commission and IAEA have to be vigilant and to take a strong stand in defence of the facilities, privileges and immunities to which they are entitled and this will continue to be the policy.

Summary

34. In the almost 10 months that have elapsed since the adoption of Security Council resolution 687 (1991), significant progress has been made in the implementation of section C of that resolution but much remains to be done.

35. In the first report of the Executive Chairman of the Special Commission (S/23165, para. 6) it was pointed out that this implementation involved a three-stage process - inspection and survey, disposal of weapons of mass destruction and the facilities for their production, and ongoing monitoring and verification of Iraq's compliance with its obligations under section C of resolution 687 (1991).

36. The inspection and survey phase has not yet been completed. It would have been completed by this time if Iraq had met in a comprehensive manner its obligations on reporting and had made the full, final and complete disclosure of all aspects of its programmes to develop weapons of mass destruction which is called for by resolution 707 (1991). Furthermore, the Special Commission has no confidence that such full, final and complete disclosure will be forthcoming in the immediate future as the Iraqi authorities have indicated very recently that they will respond only to specific items of evidence of undisclosed weapons, facilities and materials.

37. The disposal phase is being implemented with significant progress in the area of ballistic missiles where Iraq has, under Special Commission supervision, destroyed its declared missiles and launchers. Planning in relation to the destruction of chemical weapons is now in an advanced stage, with the active cooperation of Iraq under Special Commission supervision. In the nuclear area the fresh uranium fuel has been removed from Iraq, and arrangements are under negotiation for the removal of irradiated fuel and the long-term storage of nuclear wastes. Destruction, removal or rendering harmless of the facilities, materials and equipment involved in proscribed activities is now a matter of increasing urgency where difficult questions will arise in regard to

dual or multi-purpose items. This process may thus be protracted.

38. In respect of the third phase relating to ongoing monitoring and verification, while the Special Commission's and IAEA's plans have been approved by the Security Council in resolution 715 (1991), the Iraqi authorities have not made a clear acknowledgement of their obligations under these plans and resolution 715 (1991). Instead, they have adopted an approach which arrogates to themselves the determination of what they consider to be required of them under paragraphs 10, 12 and 13 of resolution 687 (1991). In the view of the Special Commission, Iraq is thus not in compliance with its obligations under resolution 715 (1991) and for this reason the Special Commission is dispatching a special mission to Iraq at the end of January to discuss the Commission's serious concern in this regard with the Iraqi Government. In the previous reports by the Executive Chairman of the Special Commission to the Security Council stress has been placed on the need for a change of policy on the part of Iraq to one of candour, transparency and cooperation at all levels. The experience of the Special Commission in the last two months has confirmed this need.

Part B: Paragraphs 12 and 13 of Security Council resolution 687 (1991) and related provisions in resolution 707 (1991) and 715 (1991)

(See sect. C of the present annex)

C. ATTACHMENT TO THE LETTER DATED 20 JANUARY 1992 FROM THE DIRECTOR-GENERAL OF THE INTERNATIONAL ATOMIC ENERGY AGENCY

Report of the Director General on Iraq's compliance with its obligations under Security Council resolutions as they relate to nuclear activities

I. *Introduction*

1. This report summarizes the compliance to date by Iraq with its obligations under Security Council resolutions 687 (1991), 707 (1991) and 715 (1991) as they relate to nuclear activities.

II. *Iraq's obligations related to nuclear activities*

2. Pursuant to paragraph 12 of Security Council resolution 687 (1991), Iraq is obliged not to acquire or develop nuclear weapons or nuclear-weapons-usable material or any related sub-systems, components or facilities, including research, development, support or manufacturing facilities. Iraq was required to submit by 18 April 1991 a declaration of the locations, amounts and types of all such items. Iraq is under a continuing obligation to accept urgent on-site inspections and to place all of its nuclear-weapons-usable material under the exclusive control of the International Atomic Energy Agency (IAEA) for custody and removal. Iraq is further obliged to accept the destruction, removal or rendering harmless, as appropriate, of all proscribed items and to accept the Agency's plan for the future ongoing monitoring and verification of its compliance with these undertakings.

3. Pursuant to its obligations under resolution 687 (1991), and in accordance with the 14 May 1991 exchange of letters between the Secretary-General and the Foreign Minister of Iraq, Iraq is obliged, *inter alia*, to extend to IAEA and personnel assigned to carry out inspections and other activities under resolution 687 (1991), the privileges and immunities necessary for the fulfilment of such functions, in particular, but not limited to those privileges and immunities identified in the exchange of letters. These included unrestricted freedom of entry, exit and movement without advance notice, unimpeded access to any site or facilities for on-site inspection and the right to request, receive, examine and copy records and examine, return, move or photocopy any relevant items.

4. Affirming Iraq's failure to act in strict conformity with its obligations under resolution 687 (1991), the Security Council on 15 August adopted resolution 707 (1991), which imposed additional obligations on Iraq. These include the requirement that Iraq make a declaration of all of its nuclear programmes, including any which it claims are for purposes not related to nuclear-weapons-usable material, and to halt all nuclear activities of any kind, except for the use of isotopes for medical, agricultural or industrial purposes. Iraq was specifically directed to cease immediately any attempt to conceal, and on its own initiative to move or destroy, any material or equipment relating to its nuclear programme. Resolution 707 (1991) reiterated Iraq's obligation to provide immediate, unconditional and unrestricted access to all items and locations the inspection teams wished to inspect, and to ensure the complete implementation of privileges and immunities of the representatives of IAEA and of the Special Commission. Resolution 707 (1991) further requires Iraq to comply fully with its obligations under the Treaty on the Non-Proliferation of Nuclear Weapons and its safeguards agreement with IAEA.

5. Pursuant to resolution 715 (1991), adopted on 11 October, by which the Security Council approved the Director General's plan for future ongoing monitoring and compliance with paragraph 12 of resolution 687 (1991) and paragraphs 3 and 5 of resolution 707 (1991), Iraq is required to meet unconditionally all of its obligations under the plan and to cooperate fully with the Director General in carrying out the plan. The plan itself calls for the submission by Iraq within 30 days of approval of the plan inventories of all nuclear material in Iraq; of all facilities, installations and sites in Iraq where nuclear activities have been, can be or are carried out; of material, equipment and items in Iraq required to be reported to the Agency; of all isotopes in Iraq used for medical, agricultural or industrial applications, of information on existing or proposed nuclear programmes; and of all facilities, installations and sites in Iraq which have electricity supplies greater than 10 mwe.

III. *Compliance*

A. *Declaration of a nuclear-weapons programme*

6. Iraq consistently denied the existence of any work related to nuclear-weapons development until 14 October, when, in the course of the seventh inspection it was acknowledged that research studies in weaponization had been under way. Inspection activities revealed that Iraq had gone to great lengths to conceal or destroy any evidence of such a programme, a fact later confirmed by Iraqi authorities. The inspection team had a strong component of nuclear-weapons experts who had become convinced as a result of a number of repeated visits that the Al Altheer site was involved in investigations related to nuclear-weapons design. Iraq maintained that this was a materials production development centre until, finally, on 21 October, it admitted that Al Altheer was also built to serve the weaponization programme.

B. *Declaration of nuclear-weapons-usable material*

7. In accordance with resolution 687 (1991), Iraq was to have submitted by 18 April a declaration of the locations, amounts and types of all nuclear-weapons-usable material. On 18 April 1991, Iraq submitted to IAEA a letter stating that there was no nuclear-weapons-usable material in Iraq. Based on information concerning

material under Agency safeguards, which included nuclear-weapons-usable material, clarification was requested by IAEA. A revised declaration was received by IAEA on 27 April reflecting only the safeguarded material.

8. Following the visit to Iraq in June of a high-level mission sent under the authority of the Security Council on account of the repeated failure of Iraq to fully reveal its nuclear programme and its denial of access to inspectors (see paras. 12-14 below), a new declaration giving details on different aspects of the Iraqi nuclear programme and a variety of nuclear material was submitted on 7 July. In response to follow-up questions, clarifications were provided on 14 July and on 27 July indicating, *inter alia*, the existence of additional nuclear material.

9. The July declaration and clarifications showed that Iraq had further processed material to chemical forms suitable for enrichment and for production of plutonium, material which Iraq was required to have declared to the Agency in accordance with the Safeguards Agreement between Iraq and IAEA and by resolution 687 (1991). Also revealed for the first time in the July communications was the existence of gram quantities of plutonium which had been clandestinely separated from irradiated fuel at the Tuwaltha nuclear centre. Associated with this was the clandestine production, irradiation and reprocessing of fuel assemblies fabricated from the previously undeclared uranium stocks.

C. *Declaration of facilities*

10. Prior to the first inspection, the only known nuclear facilities in Iraq were those in the Tuwaltha nuclear centre, where nuclear material was being safeguarded. No other facilities were declared in the initial Iraqi statements. As a result of the second inspection, the Tarmiya industrial centre was revealed as the site for the electromagnetic isotope separation process (EMIS), a facility capable of producing nuclear-weapons-usable material. This was a large site still in the installation stage, but with some production units having started operation and produced enriched uranium. It was declared to the first team as a plant for manufacturing transformers, an implausible claim. When its true nature was established, later inspections showed that extensive deception had taken place, including laying fresh concrete to hide evidence of the machinery that had been installed and to the painting of walls to impede the verification of the presence of uranium. Iraqi authorities also admitted that a facility at Ash Sharqat, which had initially been declared to be a non-nuclear plastic coating plant, was in reality, intended to be a duplicate of the plant at Tarmiya.

11. The Mosul chemical plant that produced the uranium oxide and tetrachloride material used as feed material in the enrichment programme was only declared on 7 July. Extensive subterfuge and deception had taken place to hide its true nature from inspectors.

D. *Declaration of equipment*

12. Most of the equipment for the EMIS process had been buried prior to the first inspection. It was then excavated and moved between various sites by convoy to hide it from detection. The second inspection team located the equipment, but was refused access a number of times to the military camps to which it had been moved. Photographs were eventually obtained as the convoy attempted to escape by a back entrance as inspectors were denied access at the front. In this incident warning shots were fired by Iraqi security personnel.

13. When this irrefutable evidence was obtained, and following the high-level mission, on 7 July the Iraqi authorities gave a detailed account of the EMIS programme, but denied any major progress in a centrifuge enrichment programme. As evidence accumulated, admissions were made of a small number of centrifuges and components as the first stages of a research and development programme, then of the intention to build a small (100 machine) cascade. A facility was located which was judged by the experts on the inspection team to be capable of producing a few thousand machines a year. Iraq denied such intentions.

14. Lately more openness has been shown by the Iraqi authorities in discussions held on this programme where some important inconsistencies remaining from previous inspections were resolved and important admissions were made as to the progress, objectives, and dimensions of the programme. These discussions took place in January 1992 when an inspection team visited Iraq to discuss evidence of the importation of key components sufficient for a few thousand centrifuges. This information was discussed at the Iraqi Ministry of State level in the presence of technical experts from both sides. As a result of this discussion, the Iraqi authorities acknowledged the procurement of these materials and components and explained that all these supplies had been destroyed or "rendered harmless" by melting and crushing prior to the beginning of nuclear inspections in Iraq under resolution 687 (1991). Iraqi authorities further acknowledged the procurement of 100 tons of the special high tensile strength steel (maraging steel) sufficient to produce a few thousand centrifuge rotors and rotor internal fittings and the procurement of several thousand aluminium forgings for the vacuum housing flanges. The Iraqi authorities stated that these materials had also been destroyed or rendered harmless by melting prior to the commencement of inspections.

E. *Access and inspection rights*

15. In addition to the denial of access and inspection rights referred to under paragraphs 12 to 14 above, a serious incident also occurred during the sixth inspection, when the inspection team attempted to remove documents relating to the nuclear programme from two sites at Baghdad. A confrontation took place resulting in the team being confined within a parking lot for four days. Some documents were forcibly removed from the team's vehicles. Most of the documents seized were returned, but some were not. Iraq claimed that these related to sensitive personnel matters such as salaries and health and were not relevant to the inspection work. Among the documents that were finally obtained by the team were two reporting progress on the Iraqi nuclear-weapon programme, making it clear that a large well-funded research programme had been under way to develop an implosion-type nuclear explosive.

F. *Removal and rendering harmless*

16. According to a number of statements made by Iraq, actions were taken prior to the beginning of inspections under resolution 687 (1991) to dismantle and/or destroy components, equipment and material related to the clandestine nuclear programmes. Components of the EMIS process together with centrifuges and related components have been destroyed by the Agency with the assistance of Iraqi personnel. The hot cells and glove boxes at the Tuwaltha nuclear centre have been rendered harmless by cutting the manipulator arms and pouring in cements or epoxy resin. The Iraqi authorities cooperated in the carrying out of this work.

17. Iraq has cooperated in the removal of the unirradiated high-enriched fuel for the IRT-5000 reactor. This was flown from Iraq on 15 and 17 November. The security and transport arrangements were undertaken by Iraq. Two streak video cameras and related equipment,

equipment suitable for nuclear-weapons development, were removed from Iraq.

IV. *Summary*

18. The response of Iraq to the inspection work of IAEA has largely followed a pattern of denial of clandestine activities until the evidence is overwhelming, followed by cooperation until the next case of concealment is revealed. As a consequence of this behaviour, it is not possible to be confident that the full extent of prohibited nuclear activities in Iraq has been disclosed. Continuation of the inspection activities, in parallel with the monitoring programme, is deemed necessary.

D. LETTER DATED 16 JANUARY 1992 FROM THE PRESIDENT OF THE INTERNATIONAL COMMITTEE OF THE RED CROSS

1. In his letter dated 8 January 1992, the Under-Secretary-General for Political and Security Council Affairs draws our attention to paragraphs 30 and 31 of United Nations Security Council resolution 687 (1991) and asks ICRC to inform your office accordingly, with a view to the preparation of your report in this connection to the Security Council.

2. In response to the Under-Secretary-General's request I have the honour to send you herewith an updated report covering activities related to the search for and repatriation of missing persons believed to be in Iraq. Earlier information on the subject was conveyed to your predecessor by ICRC in September 1991.

3. To summarize efforts to date, since the end of the war ICRC has invited representatives of Iraq, France, Kuwait, Saudi Arabia, the United Kingdom and the United States to six meetings, where pending issues related to the implementation of the Geneva Conventions of 1949 have been discussed, such as the repatriation of prisoners of war, civilian detainees and persons missing in action, and the return of mortal remains. Over the last 10 months ICRC has supervised the repatriation of thousands of military personnel and civilians captured or arrested by either side during the conflict.

4. Despite all these efforts, both during negotiations and in the field, there are still thousands of persons reported missing by the parties to the conflict.

5. I none the less remain confident that by pursuing our efforts as a neutral intermediary and implementing the provisions of the Geneva Conventions, methods and operational procedures will be found to achieve tangible results in the search for and repatriation of persons reported missing after the conflict.

Attachment

Report on activities related to the search for missing persons in Iraq and their repatriation

1. To date, the International Committee of the Red Cross (ICRC) has supervised the repatriation from Iraq of 4,299 prisoners of war, i.e. 4,233 Kuwaiti, 29 Saudi, 23 American, 12 British and 2 Italian nationals, including 2 Kuwaiti prisoners of war who were repatriated during the last three months.

2. It has furthermore supervised the return from Iraq of 1,436 civilians: 1,291 to Kuwait, 128 to Saudi Arabia, 11 to Egypt, 1 to the Syrian Arab Republic, 1 to the Philippines, 1 to Austria and 3 to the United States. These figures include the 112 civilians who have been returned over the last three months in eight separate operations to Kuwait (81), Saudi Arabia (26) or other countries (5). However, the 1,174 civilian internees who returned on 7 March 1991 to Kuwait via Safwan are not included in these statistics, since that repatriation did not take place under the auspices of ICRC.

3. Thus, a total of 6,909 persons (prisoners of war and civilians) have returned from Iraq to their home countries since the beginning of March 1991.

4. In the period from 13 March to 7 July 1991, three separate operations were carried out under ICRC supervision to repatriate the mortal remains of 8 British nationals, 7 Americans and 1 Kuwaiti.

5. In Iraq, ICRC has furthermore registered about 3,700 persons whose nationality could not be established with certainty. These persons claimed that they had been living in Kuwait and expressed their wish to return to their former place of residence. They are living in different locations and are free to move around within Iraqi territory. The large majority of them reported spontaneously to the ICRC office at Baghdad, where ICRC delegates recorded their personal data for transmission to the Kuwaiti authorities who, in turn, determine the applicants' eligibility for repatriation.

6. The Kuwaiti authorities have submitted a list of missing persons, the latest update of which contains 2,101 names (12 October 1991). The Kuwaiti authorities have repeatedly stressed that the names on that list are not identical with those mentioned under paragraph 5 above. They have also told ICRC that information from returning Kuwaiti prisoners has induced them to believe that many Kuwaiti nationals are still being held in Iraq.

7. The Saudi authorities have reported 17 Saudi nationals as missing in Iraq. Through ICRC, the Saudi military authorities have sent the Iraqi Government detailed testimonies by former Saudi prisoners, according to whom some of the missing Saudi nationals, including Colonel Nadira, a military pilot, had been seen in Iraqi captivity.

8. Pursuant to a decision taken by Iraq and the Coalition Forces, pending issues related to the implementation of the Geneva Conventions of 1949, such as the repatriation of prisoners of war, civilian detainees and persons missing in action and the return of mortal remains, are being dealt with by a special Commission made up of representatives of Iraq, France, Kuwait, Saudi Arabia, the United Kingdom and the United States. The Commission meets periodically under the auspices of ICRC.

9. At its last meeting, held at Geneva on 16 and 17 October 1991, the Commission discussed methods and operational procedures for achieving, in the shortest possible time, tangible results in the search for and repatriation of persons reported missing by both Saudi Arabia and Kuwait. Three different but complementary approaches were then considered and submitted as proposals to the Government of Iraq:

(a) Publishing of Saudi and Kuwaiti lists of missing persons in the Iraqi media;

(b) ICRC visits to places of detention in Iraq, in accordance with ICRC standard procedures, in order to assist the Iraqi authorities in the tracing of protected persons;

(c) Constitution of individual inquiry files by the Iraqi authorities in order to meet the request of the parties concerned for well-documented replies.

10. The Permanent Mission of Iraq to the United Nations at Geneva thereupon informed ICRC, in a diplomatic note dated 11 November 1991, of Iraq's position as regards the proposals mentioned under paragraph 9 above. It can be summarized as follows:

(a) The competent Iraqi authorities agreed to publish the names of the missing Kuwaiti and Saudi nationals in a newspaper in Iraq;

(b) Iraq is willing to provide ICRC with a list of prisons and places of detention in order to facilitate ICRC visits to these places. The visits will be restricted to one per site;

(c) The sole objective of these visits is to search for missing Saudi and Kuwaiti nationals;

(d) Iraq requests that the principle of reciprocity be applied, namely that the above-mentioned procedures in the search for missing persons be applied also in Kuwait and Saudi Arabia.

11. The representatives of the Coalition Forces responded officially to ICRC and Iraq on 21 November 1991 by expressing dissatisfaction with regard to three points in the Iraqi statement. First, they considered that publication in only one Iraqi newspaper was insufficient. Secondly, they objected to ICRC visits being limited to one per site. Thirdly, they objected to reciprocity being the basis for further action.

12. Five weeks after the October meeting, when no tangible results had been achieved in the search for and repatriation of missing Kuwaiti and Saudi military personnel and civilians, ICRC Delegate General for the Middle East and North Africa travelled to Baghdad for discussions with the Minister of Defence, Mr. Ali Hassan Al-Majid, the Minister of State for Foreign Affairs, Mr. Mohammad Sayed Al-Sahaf, and the Head of the Legal Department at the Ministry of Foreign Affairs, Dr. Akram Al-Witry. The discussions were inconclusive.

13. In a diplomatic note dated 17 December 1991, the Ministry of Foreign Affairs informed ICRC of its latest position. In addition to reiterating its previous position, outlined under paragraph 10 above, Iraq invited ICRC to prepare a plan containing methods and procedures for the tracing of missing Kuwaiti, Saudi, Iraqi or other nationals in accordance with the Geneva Conventions.

14. ICRC has not yet received any information as to the whereabouts of the persons reported missing in Iraq. Nor has it received detailed and documented information on the search conducted by the Iraqi authorities. Finally, it is also still awaiting information on persons who have died while in custody.

15. ICRC regrets that no substantive agreement could be reached between the Parties and that it has consequently not been possible hitherto to implement any of the proposals set out in Point 9 above.

16. This report is a specific response to the letter of the Under-Secretary-General for Political and Security Council Affairs, dated 8 January 1992, and is therefore confined to activities related to the search for and repatriation of persons protected by the Geneva Conventions in Iraq. Activities based on the Geneva Conventions and related to the search for and the repatriation of Iraqi prisoners of war and civilians in the Kingdom of Saudi Arabia and the State of Kuwait are consequently not covered by this report.

E. INFORMATION RECEIVED WITH REGARD TO IRAQ'S COMPLIANCE WITH THE PROVISIONS OF PARAGRAPH 16 OF RESOLUTION 687 (1991)

The text reproduced below includes a contribution received from the Secretariat of the Governing Council of the United Nations Compensation Commission.

1. In resolution 674 (1990) of 29 October 1990, the Security Council reminded Iraq "that under international law it is liable for any loss, damage or injury arising in regard to Kuwait and third States, and their nationals and corporations, as a result of the invasion and illegal occupation of Kuwait by Iraq". The liability of Iraq under international law was reaffirmed in paragraph 2 (b) of resolution 686 (1991), in which the Security Council demanded that Iraq, *inter alia*, "accept in principle its liability under international law for any loss, damage, or injury arising in regard to Kuwait and third States, and their nationals and corporations, as a result of the invasion and illegal occupation of Kuwait by Iraq". Paragraph 16 of resolution 687 (1991) again reaffirmed and further specified "... that Iraq ... is liable under international law for any direct loss, damage, including environmental damage and the depletion of natural resources, or injury to foreign Governments, nationals and corporations, as a result of Iraq's unlawful invasion and occupation of Kuwait".

2. In order to implement Iraq's obligation to compensate losses, damages and injuries arising out of Iraq's unlawful invasion and occupation of Kuwait, the Security Council decided in paragraph 18 of resolution 687 (1991) to create a Fund and to establish a Commission to administer the Fund. In paragraph 19 of the same resolution the Council provided, *inter alia*, that Iraq's contribution to the Fund would be based on a percentage of the value of the exports of petroleum and petroleum products from Iraq not to exceed a figure to be suggested to the Council by the Secretary-General.

3. Iraq communicated its acceptance of the provisions of resolution 687 (1991) with identical letters dated 6 April 1991 addressed to the Secretary-General and the President of the Security Council (S/22456). Iraq's unconditional acceptance also covered paragraphs 16 and 19 of the resolution, and in particular commits Iraq to accepting the decisions taken pursuant to paragraph 19 concerning the percentage of its exports of petroleum and petroleum products to be paid to the Fund. In paragraph 2 of resolution 705 (1991) the Security Council decided that in accordance with the suggestion made by the Secretary-General in paragraph 7 of his note of 30 May 1991 (S/22661), compensation to be paid by Iraq (as arising from section E of resolution 687 (1991)) should not exceed 30 per cent of the annual value of the exports of petroleum and petroleum products from Iraq.

4. The Compensation Fund and Compensation Commission referred to in paragraph 18 of resolution 687 (1991) were established by resolution 692 (1991) in accordance with part I of the report of the Secretary-General of 2 May 1991 (S/22559). Paragraph 5 of the resolution directed the Governing Council of the Commission to implement the relevant provisions of resolution 687 (1991), and paragraph 8 requested all States and international organizations to cooperate with the decisions of the Governing Council taken pursuant to paragraph 5. The Governing Council of the Compensation Commission has held three sessions to date and has adopted decisions, *inter alia*, on the expedited processing of claims by individuals, arrangements for ensuring payments to the Compensation Fund, and criteria for processing additional categories of claims. These decisions are not addressed directly to Iraq and do not impose new obligations upon it; they are rather intended to provide guidance to States and Commissioners. The decision concerning arrangements for ensuring payments to the Compensation Fund will only become binding upon Iraq after its approval by the Security Council pursuant to paragraph 7 of resolution 692 (1991). The delegation of Iraq has addressed the Governing Council on several occasions and has expressed Iraq's willingness to fully cooperate with its decisions. The comments and observations contained in those statements do not seem to qualify or contradict Iraq's pledge to cooperate with the Governing Council.

5. Iraq's compliance with its obligation under paragraph 16 of resolution 687 (1991) is dependent upon the resumption of its exports of petroleum and petroleum products. This has not yet taken place because the economic sanctions imposed by resolution 661 (1990) are still in force. In view of the persistence of the economic sanctions, albeit in the attenuated form provided for by

paragraph 20 of resolution 687 (1991), and in view of the serious nutritional and health situation of the Iraqi civilian population, the Security Council deemed it appropriate to partially lift the prohibitions against the import of commodities and products originating in Iraq and against financial transactions related thereto, in order to generate financial resources to meet such humanitarian requirements. This was achieved with resolution 706 (1991), which authorized all States to permit the import, during a period of six months, of petroleum and petroleum products originating in Iraq sufficient to produce a sum to be determined by the Council following receipt of a report of the Secretary-General, but not to exceed US $1.6 billion. Resolution 712 (1991) approved the recommendations contained in paragraph 57 (d) and 58 of the report of the Secretary-General of 4 September 1991 (S/23006) on the implementation of resolution 706 (1991), and confirmed the figure of $1.6 billion. The sum so produced would be destined to finance the purchase of the items referred to in paragraph 20 of resolution 687 (1991) as well as various activities undertaken by the United Nations in implementation of resolution 687 (1991), including appropriate payments to the United Nations Compensation Commission. Iraq has not yet agreed to sell petroleum and petroleum products under this regime. Iraq has objected to resolutions 706 (1991) and 712 (1991), stating that it had satisfied all conditions specified in paragraph 22 of resolution 687 (1991) and therefore sanctions should no longer be applied against Iraq.

F.(i) EXTRACT FROM LETTER DATED 16 JANUARY 1992 FROM THE MANAGING DIRECTOR OF THE INTERNATIONAL MONETARY FUND

With reference to paragraph 17 of resolution 687 (1991), Iraq is currently in arrears to IMF in the special drawing rights (SDR) department. As of 31 December 1991 the overdue obligations amounted to SDR 7.3 million. The Iraqi authorities have indicated to the Fund that although willing to meet their financial obligations to the Fund, their attempts to do so have failed because of the international sanctions in place. With reference to paragraph 7 of resolution 706 (1991), the Fund has not received since the adoption of the resolution any information from the Iraqi authorities concerning their holdings of gold and other foreign currency reserves.

(ii) LETTER FROM THE CHAIRMAN OF THE PARIS CLUB OF CREDITOR COUNTRIES

... In order to complete the United Nations information on Iraq's debt, please find enclosed some data that some creditor countries from the Paris Club asked me to convey to you.

The Paris Club Secretariat remains at the disposal of your services for any complementary information they would need.

Iraq's debt summary

Some of the creditor countries asked me to convey to you these figures
(outstanding amounts as of 1 April 1991):

(In millions of United States dollars)

Japan 3 482
France 2 327
Germany 1 914
Italy 1 433
United Kingdom 1 194
Austria 926
Australia 499
Spain 366
Canada 296
Belgium 276
Sweden 226
Finland 171
Netherlands 132
Switzerland 119
Ireland 41
Denmark 18

G. INFORMATION RECEIVED FROM THE SECURITY COUNCIL COMMITTEE ESTABLISHED BY RESOLUTION 661 (1990) CONCERNING THE SITUATION BETWEEN IRAQ AND KUWAIT

In connection with the Secretary-General's forthcoming report on Iraq's compliance with all of the obligations placed upon it by resolution 687 (1991) and subsequent relevant resolutions, the Security Council Committee established by resolution 661 (1990) concerning the situation between Iraq and Kuwait has no information to offer with respect to paragraphs 10 and 12 of resolution 687 (1991) at this stage. With respect to paragraph 29 of the same resolution, attention is drawn to the letter dated 30 September 1991 from the Permanent Representative of Denmark to the United Nations addressed to the Chairman, and the Chairman's reply thereto dated 23 October 1991, copies of which are attached hereto.

Attachments

1. *Letter dated 30 September 1991 from the Permanent Representative of Denmark to the United Nations addressed to the Chairman of the Security Council Committee established by resolution 661 (1990) concerning the situation between Iraq and Kuwait*

On instructions from my Government I have the honour to submit to the Committee the enclosed statement dated 24 September 1991 by the Danish shipping company A. P. Moller concerning a violation by Iraq of Security Council resolution 687 (1991), in particular its paragraph 29.

It appears from the statement that the company has been presented with a legal claim of approximately US $4 million by the "Agricultural Supplies Company of Baghdad", an Iraqi Government subsidiary. The claim has been raised in connection with a contract the performance of which was affected by reason of the measures taken by the Security Council in resolution 661 (1990) and related resolutions. In the opinion of the Danish company the claim represents a violation of Security Council resolution 687 (1991).

I should be grateful if you would have this question considered by the Committee, and I should appreciate to receive any views which the Committee might have on the matter.

Enclosure

Statement dated 24 September 1991 from A. P. Moller Company addressed to the Ministry of Foreign Affairs, Denmark

Applications to the European Community and to the Security Council of the United Nations for the violation by Iraq, *inter alia*, of resolution 687 (1991).

We refer to our meeting on 13 September 1991 and should like to submit the following matter to you.

1. On 9 July 1990, the vessel in question was time chartered to a company domiciled in Switzerland.

Pursuant to the time charterers' instructions and to the terms and conditions of the governing time charter party, the vessel loaded a cargo of 61,450 tons of corn in the port of Westwego, Louisiana. The loading was completed on 20 July 1990.

The bills of lading and the further shipping documents all provided for the discharge to be carried out in the port of Aqaba, Jordan, but expressly stated that the cargo was "in transit to Iraq" and was to be delivered to an Iraqi company. The time charterers consequently gave order for the vessel to proceed to Aqaba.

2. At the time when the Iraq/Kuwait war had started and the Embargo Rules of the United Nations and the EEC came into force (including resolution 661 (1990)) in the month of August 1990, the vessel was en route to the port of discharge.

The owners of the vessel and the Ministries and lawyers consulted all concluded that it would be a severe violation of the governing international Embargo Rules now in force to deliver the cargo as set out in the shipping documents. Consequently, the owners asked the time charterers and the Iraqi cargo interests for new but legitimate discharging orders, but in vain. Instead, the time charterers cancelled the time charter party.

3. In compliance with the Embargo Rules and in order to mitigate damages, the owners of the vessel applied to the Italian courts and were granted a legal order to discharge and to store the cargo in various Italian ports. The bill of lading holders were invited to be represented, but omitted to attend to their interests.

The Italian courts subsequently arranged for a local sale of the cargo and the proceeds were deposited with the courts. In the meantime, the owners of the vessel had unfortunately suffered considerable consequential losses.

4. In connection with the subsequent cease-fire, the Government of Iraq agreed, *inter alia*, to respect and acknowledge the international Embargo Rules and on 3 April 1991, the United Nations Security Council passed resolution 687 (1991), in which paragraph 29 provides:

> "that all States, including Iraq, shall take the necessary measures to ensure that no claim shall lie at the instance of the Government of Iraq, or of any person or body in Iraq, or of any person claiming through or for the benefit of any such person or body, in connection with any contract or other transaction where its performance was affected by reason of the measures taken by the Security Council in resolution 661 (1990) and related resolutions."

5. Nevertheless, the managers of the relevant vessel have received a writ apparently taken out by the alleged cargo owners, Agricultural Supplies Company of Baghdad, an Iraqi Government subsidiary. The plaintiffs seem to raise a claim of approximately US $4 million equal to the alleged cargo value less the proceeds deposited in Italy. The action seems to be based on the Iraqi resolution No. 377 dated 16 September 1990, according to which it is said to be a violation of Iraqi law to comply with the international Embargo Rules. In the aforesaid writ, the defendant carriers are apparently called upon to appear before the courts of Baghdad on 5 October 1991.

6. The defendant carriers have, however, returned the Iraqi writ as being incorrectly served, and according to advice given also by the Danish Ministry of Foreign Affairs the defendants will have to refrain from appearing in the action before the Iraqi courts.

7. It is our opinion that the aforesaid Iraqi claim and proceedings constitute a clear violation of the terms and conditions of the cease-fire and of resolution 687 (1991).

We are aware of the fact that the European Commission has recently put forward a proposal for an EEC regulation to implement paragraph 29 of United Nations Security Council resolution 687 (1991) addressing especially the problems of bonds and contracts whose performance have been affected by the Embargo.

With due respect, we find the draft EEC resolution somewhat insufficient and unclear to protect all parties, who have duly complied with the Embargo Rules such as the owners of the vessel in this particular matter. These owners are especially concerned that a judgement by default may be granted by the Iraqi courts, which judgement may be enforced by the Government of Iraq or by the courts in a country which is friendly towards Iraq. This may be done by way of arresting, detaining or perhaps of confiscating the relevant vessel, a sister vessel or other assets which are owned or managed by the same carriers.

While such enforcement procedure, if any, is being carried out, considerable losses may be suffered. It may even be regarded as a violation of the governing international rules if in such case the owners of their underwriters decide to honour the Iraqi claim to mitigate losses.

8. In consideration thereof, we call upon the Danish Government, as well as EEC, to see to it that the forthcoming Council regulations be drafted so properly and clearly as to protect and indemnify the law-abiding companies and individuals who have been put in situations like this.

We also request EEC to bring up this matter in the United Nations Security Council, in which France is a permanent member. The matter is of considerable importance and urgency.

We shall, of course, be ready to provide any supplementary information on the matter in question which you may require and we look forward to hearing from you.

2. *Letter dated 25 October 1991 from the Chairman of the Security Council Committee established by resolution 661 (1990) concerning the situation between Iraq and Kuwait addressed to the Permanent Representative of Denmark to the United Nations*

On behalf of the Security Council Committee established by resolution 661 (1990) concerning the situation between Iraq and Kuwait, I have the honour to acknowledge receipt of your letter dated 30 September 1991 concerning a legal claim against a Danish company by the Agricultural Supplies Company of Baghdad.

In that connection, pursuant to a decision of the Committee taken after considering this matter at its 52nd meeting, held on 18 October 1991, I have the honour to draw your attention to paragraph 29 of resolution 687 (1991).

H. SITUATION CONCERNING THE FINANCING OF OPERATIONAL COSTS

1. Security Council resolution 699 (1991) of 17 June 1991 established the principle that "... the Government of Iraq shall be liable for the full cost of carrying out the tasks authorized by section C [of resolution 687 (1991)] ...".

2. On the other hand, Security Council resolution 706 (1991) of 15 August 1991 covered in a comprehensive manner the question of Iraq's financial obligations, both in the military/political and the humanitarian fields. The former included:

(a) Appropriate payment to the United Nations Compensation Fund;

(b) The full costs of carrying out the destruction of Iraq's weapons of mass destruction (sect. C of Security Council resolution 687 (1991));

(c) The full costs incurred by the United Nations in facilitating the return of all Kuwaiti properties;

(d) Half the costs of the Boundary Commission.

3. The Council also required the Government of Iraq to provide the Secretary-General with a monthly statement of the gold and foreign currency reserves it holds in Iraq or elsewhere (para. 7 of resolution 706 (1991)).

4. In its resolution 706 (1991), the Council decided that the cost of the specific activities undertaken by the United Nations as a consequence of resolution 687 (1991) should be financed from the proceeds of the authorized sales of Iraqi petroleum and petroleum products.

5. However, the Government of Iraq has yet to signify its willingness to comply with the provisions of Security Council resolutions 706 (1991) and 712 (1991).

6. The Iraqi Government has indicated that it is not prepared to resume the production and export of petroleum and petroleum products on the basis of the procedures outlined in above-mentioned resolutions.

7. Notwithstanding the foregoing, the Secretary-General has authorized the appropriate departments and offices of the Secretariat to initiate the implementation of the tasks set forth in Security Council resolutions 706 (1991) and 712 (1991). As of 31 December 1991, financial commitments for the implementation of these four tasks amounted to $17.2 million. This amount was provided through a commitment authority of $10 million by the Advisory Committee on Administrative and Budgetary Questions under the provisions of General Assembly resolution 44/203 of 2 December 1989 on unforeseen and extraordinary expenses, as well as by contributions from certain Member States in the amount of $7.2 million.

8. These amounts, as well as all future amounts to be disbursed in connection with the implementation of the aforementioned Security Council resolutions, are to be reimbursed to the United Nations by Iraq from the proceeds of the authorized sales of Iraqi petroleum and petroleum products.

9. To this end, the Secretary-General has entered into discussions with the Iraqi authorities with a view to devising practical arrangements that would make it possible to achieve the objectives of Security Council resolutions 706 (1991) and 712 (1991). Two rounds of discussions have been held so far: in Baghdad, on 22 and 23 November 1991, and at the United Nations Office at Vienna, from 8 to 10 January 1992. While these discussions have been constructive, no concrete decision has been arrived at regarding the resumption of Iraqi oil production. A further round of discussions is due to be held in early February 1992.

S/23517 5 February 1992

3. Note By the President of the Security Council, 5 February 1992

On 5 February 1992, the President of the Security Council issued the following statement to the media on behalf of the members of the Council in connection with the item entitled "The situation between Iraq and Kuwait":

"The members of the Security Council held informal consultations on 28 January and 5 February 1992 pursuant to paragraph 21 of resolution 587 (1991). The members of the Council express their thanks to the Secretary-General for his factual report on Iraq's compliance with all the obligations placed upon it by resolution 687 (1991) and subsequent relevant resolutions (S/23514).

"After taking note of the Secretary-General's report and hearing all the opinions expressed in the course of the consultations, the President of the Council concluded that there was no agreement that the necessary conditions existed for a modification of the regime established in paragraph 20 of resolution 687 (1991), as referred to in paragraph 21 of that resolution.

"In the context of compliance, the Council members note with concern the recent incident at Baghdad, which demonstrates a lack of Iraqi cooperation in complying with the resolutions of the Council.

"In connection with the Secretary-General's factual report on Iraq's compliance with all the obligations placed upon it by resolution 687 (1991) and subsequent relevant resolutions, the members of the Security Council note that while much progress has been made, much remains to be done. There is serious evidence of Iraqi non-compliance over its programmes for weapons of mass destruction and the repatriation of Kuwaitis and other third-country nationals detained in Iraq. There is still much Kuwaiti property to be returned. The members of the Council are disturbed by the lack of Iraqi cooperation. Iraq must implement fully resolution 687 (1991) and subsequent relevant resolutions as was stated in the statement read out by the President of the Council on behalf of its members in the meeting held on 31 January 1992 with the participation of the heads of State and Government (S/23500).

"The members of the Security Council note that with a view to alleviating the humanitarian conditions of the civilian population of Iraq and facilitating the utilization of paragraph 20 of resolution 687 (1991), the Security Council Committee established by resolution 661 (1990) had been requested to prepare a study of those materials and supplies for essential civilian and humanitarian needs, other than medicines which have not been subject to sanctions and food shipments which have been permitted to move freely, that might be transferred from the "no objection" procedure to a simple notification procedure. The members of the Council also note the report of the Chairman of the Committee in this regard. They express their appreciation for the efforts the Chairman has made to reach a conclusion and encourage him to continue his consultations with the members of the Committee on the study and to report to the Council at an early date.

"The members of the Council strongly deplore that the Iraqi authorities have decided and communicated that decision to the Secretariat to discontinue contacts with the Secretariat regarding implementation of resolutions 706 (1991) and 712 (1991), which give to Iraq the possibility for oil sales to finance the purchase of foodstuffs, medicines and materials and supplies for essential civilian needs for the purpose of providing humanitarian relief. They underscore that the Government of Iraq, by acting in this way, is forgoing the possibility of meeting the essential needs of its civilian population and therefore bears the full responsibility for their humanitarian problems. They hope that a resumption of these contacts may lead to the early implementation of the scheme set out in those resolutions to enable humanitarian supplies to reach the Iraqi people."

S/23687, 7 March 1992

4. Further report of the Secretary-General on the status of compliance by Iraq with the obligations placed upon it under certain of the Security Council resolutions, 7 March 1992

1. The present report is submitted to the members of the Security Council in response to the request made to the Secretary-General by the members in the course of their informal consultations on 3 March 1992. By the terms of that request, the Secretary-General is providing herein an update, in so far as is available, of the information presented in his report of 25 January 1992 [1. S/23514.]

on Iraq's compliance with the obligations placed upon it by resolution 687 (1991) and subsequent relevant resolutions.

2. Under the same terms of the aforementioned request, the Secretary-General is also providing, in so far as is available, information on the status of Iraq's compliance with the provisions relating to the return of Kuwaiti property from Iraq to Kuwait (resolution 686 (1991), para. 2 (d)); information on the status of Iraq's compliance with the provisions relating to the demarcation of the international boundary between Iraq and Kuwait (resolution 687 (1991), para. 3); and information on Iraq's compliance with the relevant provisions of Security Council resolution 688 (1991) concerning the humanitarian situation of the Iraqi civilian population in many parts of Iraq, including in the Kurdish-populated areas. The requested information is presented in the four sections below.

I. UPDATE OF THE SECRETARY-GENERAL'S REPORT OF 25 JANUARY 1991

3. The update of the information in the Secretary-General's report of 25 January 1992,[1] in so far as is available, is presented herein in such a way as to follow the pattern of that report. Thus, any new or additional information received, or lack of any such information, from the original contributing sources is presented or entered under the corresponding headings and subheadings, as indicated below.

A. *Obligations of a general nature*

4. In his letter of 23 January 1992, [2. S/23472, annex.] the Minister for Foreign Affairs of Iraq reiterated the position of his Government, declared in his earlier letter of 6 April 1991, [3. S/22456, annex.] that Iraq had found itself left with no other alternative but to accept resolution 687 (1991). In the letter of 23 January 1992 the Minister further stated the following:

> "During the period between the adoption of resolution 687 (1991) on 3 April 1991 and 31 December 1991, Iraq met a very large part of the conditions, restrictions and measures imposed upon it by resolution 687 (1991). ..."

5. No other information has been received with regard to this item.

B. *Specific obligations*

1. *Respect for the inviolability of the international border and allocation of islands between Iraq and Kuwait (paras. 2 and 5 of resolution 687 (1991))*

6. In his letter of 23 January 1992, [2] the Minister for Foreign Affairs of Iraq specified the measures which he said the Government had undertaken in its dealings with the United Nations Iraq-Kuwait Observation Mission (UNIKOM), indicating that Iraq had "extended everything required to facilitate the work of UNIKOM and fully cooperated with the Mission in order to ensure the success of its tasks and avoid any difficulties".

7. Since the submission of the Secretary-General's report of 25 January 1992, [1] there has been no change with regard to Iraq's compliance with paragraphs 2 and 5 of resolution 687 (1991) in the context of UNIKOM's mandate.

2. *Obligations relating to conventional, biological or chemical weapons and such materials for warfare (paras. 8, 9 (a) and 10 of resolution 687 (1991), para. 3 of resolution 707 (1991) and para. 5 of resolution 715 (1991))*

8. In his letter dated 23 January 1992, the Minister for Foreign Affairs of Iraq gave an account of the measures taken by the Government of Iraq in implementation of section C of resolution 687 (1991). [4. S/23472, enclosure, sects. 3-23.]

9. In a communication dated 6 March 1992, the Executive Chairman of the Special Commission established under section C of resolution 687 (1991) submitted information bringing up to date the activities of the Commission that bear upon the status of Iraq's compliance with its obligations under the relevant Security Council resolutions. That information is reproduced in annex I to the present report.

3. *Obligations relating to nuclear capability development programmes (paras. 10 and 12 of resolution 687 (1991), para. 3 of resolution 707 (1991) and para. 5 of resolution 715 (1991))*

10. The comments in paragraph 8 above apply equally to this item.

11. In a communication dated 5 March 1992, the Director General of the International Atomic Energy Agency (IAEA) provided information on the developments that occurred in the course of the last two inspections carried out in Iraq (11-14 January and 5-13 February 1991). The text of the communication from the Director General of IAEA is reproduced in annex II to the present report.

4. *Obligations relating to repatriation of and access to all Kuwaiti and third-country nationals in Iraq (para. 30 of resolution 687 (1991))*

12. In his letter of 23 January 1992, the Minister for Foreign Affairs gave an account of the measures taken by Iraq with regard to the obligation under this item. [5. S/23472, enclosure, paras. 28 and 29.]

13. In a further letter dated 28 February 1992, [6. S/23661, annex.] the Minister for Foreign Affairs of Iraq specified the measures taken by Iraq in order to meet its obligations with regard to paragraph 30 of resolution 687 (1991). In that connection, he indicated that Iraq had extended all necessary cooperation to the International Committee of the Red Cross (ICRC) in implementation of the provisions of paragraph 30 of the resolution. The letter also mentioned the visit to Iraq, at Iraq's invitation, of a team from the League of Arab States (LAS), as well as contacts Iraq had made with the "Coalition States" under the auspices of ICRC. The attention of members of the Council is also drawn to the letter dated 6 March 1992, [7. S/23686.] addressed to the Secretary-General by the representatives of France, Kuwait, Saudi Arabia, the United Kingdom of Great Britain and Northern Ireland and the United States of America in response to the letter of 28 February 1992 from the Minister for Foreign Affairs of Iraq.

14. Additional information concerning this item has been received from ICRC in a letter dated 6 March 1992, the text of which is reproduced below:

> "The International Committee of the Red Cross (ICRC) is actively pursuing the matter of the above-mentioned resolution and relevant paragraph, along the lines discussed with all the parties concerned during a meeting held in Geneva on 16 and 17 October 1991 under the auspices of ICRC. The procedures laid out during that meeting are an ongoing process and the representatives of the coalition have regularly been kept informed of the results.

"Our Delegate General for the Middle East and Northern Africa is in Baghdad right now in an effort to negotiate further progress in the matter of concern to you. A new evaluation on the standing of the issue could therefore be made at a later and more appropriate stage."

5. *Iraq's liability under international law for loss or damage resulting from its unlawful invasion and occupation of Kuwait (para. 16 of resolution 687 (1991))*

15. The contribution from the United Nations Compensation Commission to the Secretary-General's report of 25 January 1992 [8. S/23514, annex, sect. H, para. 2.] was included in section E of the annex to that report.

16. Additional information has been received from the Commission in a letter dated 5 March 1992, the text of which is reproduced below:

"The only information that this office can add to our comments forwarded to you on 17 January 1992 is that at the end of the fourth session of the Governing Council held from 20 to 24 January 1992, the Council considered a request made by the Permanent Representative of Iraq asking for a five-year grace period for Iraq's contribution to the Compensation Fund in view of the country's financial obligations and its requirements in food and medicine.

"The Council decided that 'questions concerning compliance of Security Council resolutions are of the competence of the Security Council and should therefore be addressed to it through the appropriate channels'."

6. *Adherence to all obligations concerning the servicing and repayment of Iraq's foreign debt (para. 17 of resolution 687 (1991))*

17. Information received from the International Monetary Fund (IMF) in a letter dated 6 March 1992 indicates that as of 29 February 1992, Iraq's arrears to IMF had increased to 8.6 million special drawing rights (SDRs). In this connection, the letter again draws attention to the position of the Iraqi authorities that, although willing to meet their financial obligations to the Fund, their attempts to do so have failed because of the international sanctions in place. IMF has also stated that it still had not received any information from the Iraqi authorities concerning their holdings of gold and other foreign currency reserves.

18. The Office of the Paris Club has reported no changes in the figures of Iraq's indebtedness to the members of the Club published in section F (ii) of the annex to the Secretary-General's report of 25 January 1992.

7. *Non-entitlement to claims deriving from the effects of the measures taken by the Security Council in resolution 661 (1990) and related resolutions (para. 29 of resolution 687 (1991))*

19. No new information has been received with regard to this item.

8. *Liability by Iraq for the full cost of the tasks authorized under section C of resolution 687 (1991) (para. 4 of resolution 699 (1991))*

20. As of 29 February 1992, financial commitments for the implementation of the four tasks listed in the Secretary-General's report of 25 January 1992 amounted to $18.6 million. This amount was provided through a commitment authority of $10 million by the Advisory Committee on Administrative and Budgetary Questions under the provisions of General Assembly resolution 44/203 of 2 December 1989 on unforeseen and extraordinary expenses, as well as by contributions from certain Member States in the amount of $8.6 million.

9. *Requirement to provide monthly statements of gold and foreign currency reserves holdings (para. 7 of resolution 706 (1991))*

21. To date, the Secretary-General has received no notification from Iraq of the amount of its holdings of gold and foreign currency reserves. This has also been confirmed by IMF (see para. 17 above).

C. *Other obligations*

1. *Undertaking required on not committing, supporting or abetting commission of any international terrorist acts (para. 32 of resolution 687 (1991))*

22. In his letter of 23 January 1992, [9. S/23472, enclosure, para. 30.] the Minister for Foreign Affairs reiterated the position of the Government of Iraq regarding this item, as stated in the letters from Iraq mentioned in the Secretary-General's report of 25 January 1992. [10. S/23514, para. 19.]

23. No other information has been received with regard to this item.

2. *Compliance with obligations in the Treaty on the Non-Proliferation of Nuclear Weapons of 1 July 1968 (para. 5 of resolution 707 (1991))*

24. No new information has been received with regard to this item.

II. COMPLIANCE BY IRAQ REGARDING THE RETURN OF KUWAITI PROPERTY FROM IRAQ TO KUWAIT

(Resolution 686 (1991), para. 2 (d))

25. Pursuant to the adoption of Security Council resolution 686 (1991) of 2 March 1991 and an exchange of letters between the President of the Security Council and the Secretary-General, a Coordinator for the return of property was appointed by the Secretary-General on 26 March 1991. [11. S/22387.] Since that time a number of discussions and meetings have taken place with the responsible Iraqi and Kuwaiti officials. The return of the property has commenced and, to date, properties of the Central Bank of Kuwait, the Central Library of Kuwait, the National Museum of Kuwait, the Kuwait News Agency, Kuwait Airways Corporation and the Kuwait Air Force have been returned. A number of additional items are ready for return and the process is continuing. In addition, Kuwait has submitted lists of properties from other ministries, corporations and individuals that are being pursued. The Iraqi and Kuwaiti officials involved with the return of property have extended maximum cooperation to the United Nations to facilitate the return.

III. COMPLIANCE BY IRAQ UNDER THE MANDATE OF THE IRAQ-KUWAIT BOUNDARY DEMARCATION COMMISSION

26. The Iraq-Kuwait Boundary Demarcation Commission, which was established pursuant to the provisions of paragraph 3 of resolution 687 (1991), has provided information which states that Iraq has fully

participated in the work of the commission. The information further states as follows:

> "Iraq has attended all of the meetings, has participated in the voting procedures of the Commission and has taken an active role in the drafting of the Commission's report to the Secretary-General. The preliminary field work of the Commission, the first stage of surveying and mapping, was concluded in November 1991 without any hindrance on the part of Iraq.
>
> "It is expected that Iraq will fully participate in the next session of the Commission, which is scheduled for 8 to 16 April in New York."

IV. COMPLIANCE BY IRAQ UNDER SECURITY COUNCIL RESOLUTION 688 (1991)

27. In paragraphs 2, 3 and 7 thereof, Security Council resolution 688 (1991) of 5 April 1991 imposed obligations upon Iraq.

28. On 25 June 1991, the Chairman of the Commission on Human Rights, following decision 1991/256 of the Economic and Social Council, appointed a Special Rapporteur (Mr. Max van der Stoel, Minister of State of the Netherlands) for a fact-finding mission to Iraq, the Islamic Republic of Iran and Saudi Arabia. The Special Rapporteur, in accordance with the Commission's resolution 1991/74, prepared a report which was published on 18 February 1992 in document E/CN.4/1992/31. It is also to be circulated as document S/23685. Attention is drawn to the conclusions and recommendations contained in paragraphs 146 to 159 of that report.

29. Also, the Office of the Executive Delegate of the Secretary-General has forwarded observations on the issues identified as falling under its purview relating to paragraphs 2, 3 and 7 of resolution 688 (1991). Those comments are reproduced in annex III to the present report.

Annex I

Information received from the Special Commission

Section C of Security Council resolution 687 (1991) and resolutions 707 (1991) and 715 (1991)

Introduction

1. Since the circulation on 25 January 1992 of the report by the Secretary-General on the status of compliance by Iraq with the obligations placed upon it under certain of the Security Council resolutions relating to the situations between Iraq and Kuwait, [a. S/23514.] two notes by the Secretary-General dated 18 and 26 February 1992 respectively, [b. S/23606.] [c. S/23607.] have been issued which contain reports by the Executive Chairman of the Special Commission. These reports bring up to date the information contained in the report of 25 January regarding the status of Iraq's compliance with, in particular, Security Council resolutions 707 (1991) and 715 (1991).

2. The present document contains a brief account of the developments recorded in the reports just mentioned and the Council's actions on those reports. Thereafter it brings up to date the information contained in the report of 25 January 1992 in so far as it relates to the inspection activities undertaken under the aegis of the Special Commission in the discharge of its responsibilities under section C of Security Council resolution 687 (1991).

Security Council resolutions 707 (1991) and 715 (1991)

3. In the report of 18 February, [b] the Executive Chairman of the Special Commission indicated that, despite the Special Commission's best efforts, Iraq was continuing to refuse to make the full, final and complete disclosure called for under Council resolution 707 (1991) of all its programmes and capabilities relating to weapons of mass destruction and ballistic missiles with a range greater than 150 kilometres. While some additional information on Iraq's programmes for the production of weapons of mass destruction had been obtained since 25 January 1992, this had to be done through a procedure of question and answer. The Special Commission was convinced that such a procedure could not result in detection of as yet undeclared elements of the Iraqi programmes and that its usefulness had been exhausted. Information on such elements was essential for a full understanding of Iraq's programmes and could be obtained only if Iraq met its obligations under Council resolution 707 (1991) to provide a full, final and complete disclosure of its programmes (see para. 13 below). In respect of Council resolution 715 (1991), and the plans for ongoing monitoring and verification approved thereunder, Iraq was maintaining the position stated in a letter to the President of the Security Council of 19 November 1991 which constituted an apparent rejection of the plans and thus of the resolution.

4. Consultations held in the Council on 18 and 19 February 1992 on the Executive Chairman's report resulted in the issue by the President on 19 February of a statement on behalf of the members of the Council. [d. S/23609.] In this it was recorded, *inter alia*, that Iraq's failure to acknowledge its obligations under resolutions 707 (1991) and 715 (1991), its rejection of the two plans for ongoing monitoring and verification and its failure to provide the full, final and complete disclosure of its weapons capabilities constituted a continuing material breach of the relevant provisions of resolution 687 (1991). The statement further provided that unconditional agreement by Iraq to implement these obligations was one of the essential preconditions for any reconsideration by the Council under paragraphs 21 and 22 of resolution 687 (1991) of the prohibitions referred to in those paragraphs. In the statement the members of the Council welcomed the decision of the Secretary-General to dispatch a special mission headed by the Executive Chairman of the Special Commission to visit Iraq immediately to meet and discuss with the highest levels of the Iraqi Government for the purpose of securing the unconditional agreement by Iraq to implement all its relevant obligations under resolutions 687 (1991), 707 (1991) and 715 (1991).

5. The report by the Executive Chairman of the Special Commission of 26 February 1992 related to the outcome of the special mission's visit to Baghdad, which had taken place from 21 to 24 February 1992. In the course of the discussions held during that visit, the special mission and the Iraqi side had exchanged written statements of their positions. [e. S/23643, appendices I and II.] After a careful review of the statement of Iraq, and taking account of the discussions held, the Executive Chairman indicated that he had regretfully concluded that he had been unable to secure unconditional agreement by Iraq to implement all its relevant obligations under Security Council resolutions 687 (1991), 707 (1991) and 715 (1991). Iraq had indicated, instead, that its delegation to be dispatched to talk to the Security Council in the near future would convey Iraq's position on resolutions 707 (1991) and 715 (1991). In a letter of 24 February 1992 addressed to the Secretary-General, the Minister for Foreign Affairs of Iraq repeated essentially the points made in the written statement that had been given to the special mission. At the request of the Foreign Minister this letter was circulated to the Security Council. [f. S/23636.]

6. Consultations in the Council on this report of the Executive Chairman on 27 and 28 February 1992, during which the Council was also informed orally of Iraq's refusal to undertake as directed by the Special Commission destruction of certain of its ballistic missile capabilities (see document S/23673 and para. 12 below), resulted in the issue of a statement of 28 February 1992 by the President of the Council, on behalf of the Council, at its 3058th meeting on 28 February 1992. [g. S/23663.] In this statement the members of the Council approved in full the conclusions of the special mission. They also deplored and condemned the failure of Iraq to provide the special mission with the acknowledgements and undertakings which it had been sent by the Council to obtain and its failure to commence within the prescribed time destruction of ballistic missile-related equipment designated for destruction by the Special Commission. The statement records that this latter refusal constituted a further material breach of the relevant provisions of resolution 687 (1991). In the statement the members of the Council required Iraq to communicate directly to the Council without further delay an authoritative and unconditional acknowledgement of its agreement to accept and implement its obligations under the Council's resolutions.

Inspection activities and other issues arising under section C of Security Council resolution 687 (1991) and related resolutions

Chemical and biological weapons

7. From 27 January to 5 February 1992 the seventh chemical weapons inspection (UNSCOM 26) visited 10 sites, of which 5 were declared and 5 undeclared. The undeclared sites included a chemical-warfare training facility, an ammunition-storage depot, a fertilizer factory, a large military training complex and an ammunition repair facility. The declared sites visited included the Al-Qa'Qa phosgene plant and four commercial sites where fermentation equipment was either currently in use or had been in use at one time. Although there was no evidence of any proscribed items or activities the team determined that the phosgene plant, because of its chemical-warfare potential, required compliance monitoring. Additionally, the team observed a test run of a small-scale nerve agent hydrolysis operation as an ongoing evaluation of the Iraqi destruction proposals. Further test results are required before rendering a decision on the efficacy of the proposed process. The team also verified the return to the Muthanna State Establishment of all remaining chemical bomb-casing manufacturing equipment from a sugar factory in Mosul as directed by a previous inspection team.

8. A special mission headed by two members of the Special Commission was in Iraq at the same time as UNSCOM 26. That mission was able to obtain previously undisclosed information on the development, support and manufacturing components of the Iraqi chemical weapons programme. During question-and-answer sessions the Iraqi officials were asked to describe the function of each item of machinery at the Muthanna workshop to the UNSCOM 26 inspection team, allowing the inspectors to determine which of the chemical weapon systems had in fact been manufactured, modified or assembled at Muthanna.

9. During the special mission, Iraqi officials produced statistics for specific types of chemical munitions imported. However, many of these figures are contradictory or show a considerable increase from the previously declared numbers. Iraqi authorities have yet to provide consistent complete answers to fundamental weapon-stockpile issues as required under Council resolution 687 (1991). Without documentary evidence to validate constantly changing figures, the Special Commission cannot conclude that Iraq has complied with its responsibilities for full disclosure.

10. The first chemical destruction mission (UNSCOM 29) is currently in Iraq controlling the destruction of approximately 450 sarin-filled 122 mm rockets at Khamisiyah, which were judged by a previous inspection team (UNSCOM 20) to be too dangerous to move and thus to require destruction in place.

11. With respect to the biological warfare programme, Iraqi officials told the special mission that they had nothing further to add to what had already been provided to the two biological weapons inspection teams. They maintained that all documents and information related to the programme had either been handed over to the first biological inspection team or had been destroyed. The Special Commission remains convinced that this aspect will require watchful monitoring in the future.

Ballistic missiles

12. One ballistic missile inspection (UNSCOM 28) has been conducted since the last report. During the period 21 to 28 February a total of seven sites were inspected, three of which were on a short-notice basis. The team conducted an inventory at four of the sites, validated previous catalogued items and identified for destruction additional items that had been moved to the site or recovered from destroyed structures. The main focus of the inspection was to supervise the destruction of some of the missile repair and production facilities and equipment identified for destruction in a letter of the Special Commission to Iraq of 14 February 1992. [h. S/23673, annex I, enclosure I.] The date for destruction was set for 26 February. The Iraqi officials, however, refused to carry out the destruction, referring the issue to higher authority. On 27 February the Iraqi Government, through its Permanent Mission to the United Nations, requested from the Special Commission a delay of 24 hours for commencing destruction. The delay was granted. However after 24 hours the Iraqi authorities informed the Commission, in a letter of 28 February, [i. S/23673, annex III, enclosure.] and orally the inspection team, that it still refused to carry out the destruction required. The team was then withdrawn from Iraq and the matter referred to the Security Council (see para. 6 above).

13. At one location designated for a short-notice inspection, the team found equipment and machinery clearly designated for an Iraqi declared ballistic missile production activity at another location. This equipment had not been previously declared at any location. At the time this equipment was found the special mission headed by the Executive Chairman of the Special Commission was being informed that Iraq had already provided all necessary information. The concurrence of these two events underlines the importance of the full, final and complete disclosure called for by Council resolution 707 (1991).

14. The team also observed reconstruction of structures at sites declared by Iraq under the provisions of Council resolution 687 (1991).

15. The Special Commission can only conclude that Iraq has yet to provide full disclosure in the area of ballistic missile activity proscribed by Council resolution 687 (1991).

Additional inspections

16. In early February, a Special Commission inspection team (UNSCOM 30), augmented by inspectors from an IAEA inspection team, carried out an inspection at the Ministry of Industry and Minerals, a non-declared site. The purpose was to investigate a report that computers had been moved to that location which were suspected to have been used for activities prohibited by Council resolution 687 (1991). Four mainframe computers were

located at the site (referred to as the Al-Rafidien computer centre): three of them appeared non-operational and a random sampling of files present in the fourth revealed nothing related to Council resolution 687 (1991).

Issues relating to the obligations of Iraq in connection with the facilities, privileges and immunities of the Special Commission and IAEA

17. No progress has been made in respect of the issues raised in paragraphs 31 to 33 of the attachment to the Secretary-General's report of 25 January 1992. [a.] Regarding the Special Commission's aerial surveillance flights, Iraq continues to protest vigorously such flights despite the clear right of the Special Commission to undertake them. The problems at Habbaniyah airport, as the Executive Chairman reported to the Council on 18 February 1992 [b.] have led to an official approach to the Government, recalling the relevant provisions of resolution 707 (1991) on the Special Commission's landing rights and proposing that the Commission's incoming and outgoing flights use one of two now operational airports within the city limits of Baghdad. No reply has been received to date. During the visit of the most recent special mission to Baghdad the Executive Chairman of the Special Commission indicated, as he reported to the Council, [j. S/23643, enclosure, para. 9.] that he was prepared to discuss with the Government practical arrangements to take account of any legitimate concerns it might have regarding the use of airports. So far this offer has not been taken up.

18. Iraq has still not returned all the documents forcibly removed from a nuclear inspection team in Baghdad on 23 September 1991. [b.]

Summary

19. Since the Secretary-General's report of 25 January 1992 was issued, [a.] strenuous efforts have been made by the Security Council and by the Special Commission to obtain from Iraq acknowledgements of its obligations under Security Council resolutions 707 (1991) and 715 (1991) and its unconditional agreement to implement all of its obligations under resolutions 687 (1991), 707 (1991) and 715 (1991). So far, these acknowledgements and undertakings have not been obtained, much less tested in practice. If this situation persists, and if the high-level Iraqi delegation to meet with the Security Council in the immediate future does not provide the acknowledgements and undertakings demanded in the statements by the President of the Council of 19 and 28 February 1992, the Special Commission will be neither legally nor practicably able to initiate the programme for ongoing monitoring and verification of Iraq's compliance with its obligations under section C of Security Council resolution 687 (1991). This programme is an integral part of the cease-fire resolution. The solution to this matter, in accordance with the Security Council resolutions, now lies with Iraq.

20. Among the outstanding matters at this time, the following would appear to be the most important:

(a) Failure by Iraq to acknowledge its obligations under Council resolutions 707 (1991) and 715 (1991) and under the plans approved by resolution 715 (1991);

(b) Failure by Iraq to agree to implement unconditionally all its obligations under section C of Council resolution 687 (1991) and resolutions 707 (1991) and 715 (1991);

(c) Failure by Iraq to provide all the information required under resolutions 687 (1991) and 707 (1991) in order for the Special Commission and IAEA to have a full, final and complete picture of all aspects of Iraq's programmes for weapons of mass destruction and ballistic missiles with a range greater than 150 km; [k. Illustrative of the missing information is the list contained in the statement by the recent special mission delivered to the Government of Iraq on 22 February 1992 which is to be found in appendix I, part B, para. 2, of the special mission's report to the Secretary-General, *e.*]

(d) Failure by Iraq to provide the declarations required under the plans for ongoing monitoring and verification;

(e) Failure by Iraq to make arrangements necessary for the implementation, in the interests of efficient performance, of certain of the facilities, privileges and immunities of the Special Commission, such as airport landing rights;

(f) Failure by Iraq to comply with the Special Commission's instructions regarding the destruction of items and facilities used in its proscribed ballistic missile programmes.

Annex II

Information received from the International Atomic Energy Agency

Pages 16 to 20 of document S/23514 contain the report of the Director General of IAEA on Iraq's compliance with its obligations under United Nations Security Council resolutions as they relate to nuclear activities.

Some recent developments, occurring during the ninth (11-14 January 1992) and the tenth (5-13 February 1992) Agency inspections, may warrant an updating of document S/23514. We suggest the addition of the following paragraphs.

> "In the course of the two last inspections - IAEA/9 of 11 to 14 January 1992 and IAEA/10 of 5 to 13 February 1992 - the following developments occurred:
>
> (a) During the January inspection, the Iraqi technical team provided important information on the extent of procurement of stock materials needed for the manufacturing of several thousand ultracentrifuges intended for the production of enriched uranium. It stated that those stock materials had been rendered harmless or destroyed prior to the commencement of Agency inspections under resolution 687 (1991). Agency inspectors were taken to the sites where the remains of these materials were stored;
>
> (b) In the course of the February inspection, the Iraqi technical team repeatedly declared that it was anxious to close the present phase of inspection and to start implementing the plan for ongoing monitoring and verification. It proposed to clarify, once and for all, all the outstanding issues concerning past nuclear activities and that IAEA define what is still needed of it;
>
> (c) As to the position of the Iraqi authorities regarding the provision of information pursuant to Security Council resolution 715 (1991) and relevant to the plan for future ongoing monitoring and verification, [a. S/22872/Rev.1.] the Iraqi technical team conceded that the information transmitted so far

did not conform with the requirements under the plan, specifically:

(i) Annex II to document S/22872/Rev.1 requires that the initial information to be submitted by Iraq cover the period from 1 January 1989, whereas the information received from Iraq reflects the situation as of the date the information was prepared (November 1991), i.e. after the Persian Gulf War, during which certain facilities and equipment had been damaged, and subsequent to the destruction of items by the Iraqi side itself;

(ii) The list of items to be reported to IAEA, contained in annex III to document S/22872/Rev.1 should not have been limited to items in the possession of the Iraqi Atomic Energy Commission, but should have included all items of the kind in question existing in Iraq.

The Iraqi technical team advised the Agency team that, while modifications of the initial information could be made in order to reflect the situation as of 1 January 1989, it could not comply with the second requirement as it deemed it practically impossible to extend the list to cover all items of the kind in question existing in Iraq."

[Annex III, relating to the implementation of Resolution 688 (1991) has been reproduced below, in Part V.]

SC/5382, 11 March 1992
Security Council, 3059th meeting, AM Summary
[The substance of the Presidential statement reproduced in this summary is contained in document S/ 23699, 11 March 1992. The full text of the Council's deliberations can be found in S/PV.3059 of the same date.]

5. UN Press Release: Security Council Finds Iraq 'Not in Full Compliance' with Obligations Regarding Weapons Destruction, Property Restitution, Human Rights, 11 March 1992

Iraq was no longer in possession of any weapons or other systems prohibited by Security Council resolution 687 (1991), its Deputy Prime Minister told the Council this morning.

Tariq Aziz, who had been asked to address the Council regarding Iraq's compliance with its obligations under the various resolutions, said the equipment used in producing such items had either been frozen or turned to civilian use. That fact had been "deliberately hidden" from the Council, with a view to keeping it in a "climate of suspicion", he said.

The matter of the repatriation of Kuwaiti and third-country nationals had also been used, he said, as a "pretext to raise doubts and ill-intended allegations against Iraq".

Mr. Aziz spoke after the President of the Council, Diego Arria (Venezuela), made a statement on behalf of the members, in which he said the Council remained deeply concerned at the "grave human rights abuses" that the Government of Iraq continued to perpetrate against its population. The Council was particularly concerned at the reported restrictions on the supplies of essential commodities, in particular food and fuel, which had been imposed by the Government on the three northern governorates. Inasmuch as the repression of the population continued, the threat to international peace and security in the region remained, he said.

The President also said that despite Iraq's statements of unconditional acceptance of resolution 687 (1991), the Council had determined that Iraq was not in full compliance with all of its obligations. He cited its weapons-related obligations; its liability for the costs of destroying its weapons programmes; its cooperation with the repatriation of Kuwaiti and third-country nationals; its use of oil revenues to finance the Compensation Fund for claims against it; international debt payments; the return of property; and statements of gold and foreign currency reserves.

All 15 members of the Council made statements this morning, deploring Iraq's failure to comply fully with its obligations. Many of them stressed that it was for the Council, rather than Iraq, to determine what weapons Iraq should or should not destroy.

Particular concern was expressed about reports of Iraq's continued persecution of the Kurdish people and Shiite groups within its territory, and to the restricted access of the International Committee of the Red Cross (ICRC) to detention areas.

The representative of Cape Verde said that while his country sought Iraq's compliance with the resolutions, the sanctions imposed by the Council in response to Iraq's invasion of Kuwait must not unduly affect Iraq's economic development.

The meeting was suspended at 3 p.m. Following consultations scheduled to begin at 4:30 p.m. today, the meeting will resume. At that time, the Council is expected to hear statements by the representative of Kuwait, the Director-General of the International Atomic Energy Agency (IAEA) and the Executive Chairman of the Special Commission established under resolution 687 in connection with the disposal of Iraq's weapons of mass destruction.

The Security Council meets this morning to consider Iraq's compliance with its obligations under resolution 687 (1991) and subsequent relevant texts.

The Council has before it a further report of the Secretary-General, dated 7 March, on the status of compliance by Iraq with those obligations (document S/23687). In it, he provides information on the return of Kuwaiti property from Iraq to Kuwait; the demarcation of the international boundary between Iraq and Kuwait; and the humanitarian situation of the Iraqi civilian population, including in the Kurdish-populated areas. The report updates an earlier report of 25 January (document S/23514).

With regard to obligations of a general nature, the only information received is contained in a letter dated 23 January from the Foreign Minister of Iraq addressed to the Secretary-General (document S/23472), in which he states that during the period between 3 April and 31 December 1991, "Iraq met a very large part of the conditions, restrictions and measures imposed upon it by resolution 687".

As to specific obligations, the report states that there has been no change since the previous report with regard to respect for the inviolability of the international border and allocation of islands between the countries.

Regarding obligations relating to repatriation of, and access to, all Kuwaiti and third-country nationals in Iraq, the International Committee of the Red Cross (ICRC) reports that its representative is in Baghdad in an effort to negotiate further progress.

Also before the Council on the repatriation question is a letter dated 6 March (document S/23686) addressed to the Secretary-General by the representatives of France, Kuwait, Saudi Arabia, United Kingdom and United States in response to Iraq's letter of 28 February (document

S/23661). The letter from the five countries calls the Iraqi letter, on the issue of detained Kuwaiti and third-country-nationals, "an attempt by Iraq to delay fulfilling its commitments under the Geneva Conventions and the relevant Security Council resolutions".

The letter states that although Iraq's letter refers to its preparedness to take certain steps, Iraq has yet to comply. It has not published any names of the missing, has not allowed the ICRC access to prisons and places of detention, has not effectively responded to individual inquiry files submitted by Kuwait and Saudi Arabia, and has not responded to a request for information on persons who have died while in custody.

Elsewhere in the Secretary-General's report, he stated that the Governing Council of the United Nations Compensation Commission had considered Iraq's request for a five-year grace period for Iraq's contribution to the Compensation Fund established to compensate relevant claims. As to Iraq's foreign debt, the International Monetary Fund (IMF) had still not received any information from Iraqi authorities concerning their holdings of gold and other foreign currency reserves. The Office of the Paris Club also reported no changes in the figures of Iraq's indebtedness.

As of 29 February, the report states, financial commitments for implementing the tasks listed in the Secretary-General's report of 25 January amounted to $18.6 million.

The return of Kuwaiti property from Iraq to Kuwait has commenced, according to the report, which also states that Iraq has fully participated in the work of the Iraq-Kuwait Boundary Demarcation Commission. Regarding Iraq's compliance with resolution 688 (1991), a fact-finding mission was sent to Iraq, Iran and Saudi Arabia by the Commission on Human Rights. The Special Rapporteur's report on that mission is contained in document S/23685.

Annexed to the report is the text of information received from the Special Commission established under resolution 687 in connection with the disposal of Iraq's weapons of mass destruction. In it, the Commission summarizes its recent inspection activities. If the high-level Iraqi delegation meeting with the Council this morning does not provide the acknowledgements and undertakings demanded, the Commission says it will be neither legally nor practicably able to initiate the programme for ongoing monitoring and verification of Iraq's compliance with its obligations.

Other annexes contain information received from the International Atomic Energy Agency (IAEA) on developments that occurred in the course of its last two inspections in Iraq, and from the Office of the Executive Delegate of the Secretary-General.

The Council also has before it a letter dated 2 April 1991 from the Permanent Representative of Turkey, addressed to the Council President (document S/22935). In it, he requests an immediate meeting of the Council to consider the "alarming situation" posed by the 220,000 Iraqi citizens currently massed along the Turkish border. He calls on the Council to adopt the necessary measures to put an end to that "inhuman repression" being carried out by Iraqi Government forces.

A second letter before the Council, dated 4 April 1991, from the Chargé d'affaires a.i. of France addressed to the Council President (document S/22442), calls for an urgent meeting of the Council to discuss the "serious situation" resulting from the abuses being committed against the Iraqi population, which constituted a threat to international peace and security.

The Chargé d'affaires a.i. of Belgium has addressed another letter to the Council President, dated 5 March (document S/23685), in which he draws attention to the report on the human rights situation in Iraq, prepared by the Special Rapporteur of the Commission on Human Rights. That report will be issued as an addendum to the letter, and refers to Security Council resolution 688 (1991).

The President of the Council, Diego ARRIA (Venezuela), called the meeting to order at 10:54 a.m.

In accordance with the understanding reached in the Council's prior consultations, he invited the delegations of Iraq and Kuwait to participate in the consideration of the item on the Council's agenda and to take the seats reserved for them.

He then extended invitations, under rule 39 of the Council's provisional rules of procedure, to Hans Blix, Director-General of the International Atomic Energy Agency (IAEA), and Rolf Ekeus, Executive Chairman of the Special Commission.

The PRESIDENT said that, following consultations among members of the Council, he had been authorized to make the following statement on behalf of the Council.

I. GENERAL OBLIGATION

1. The resolutions concerning the situation between Iraq and Kuwait impose a number of general and specific obligations upon Iraq.

2. As regards the general obligation, Iraq is required, under paragraph 33 of Security Council resolution 687 (1991), to give official notification to the Secretary-General and to the Security Council of its acceptance of the provisions of that entire resolution.

3. Iraq signified its unconditional acceptance in letters dated 6 and 10 April 1991 (S/22456 and S/22480, respectively) and 23 January 1992 (S/23472).

4. When the Security Council met at the level of Heads of State and Government on 31 January 1992 the concluding statement made by the President of the Council, on behalf of its members (S/23500), contained the following passage:

> "Last year, under the authority of the United Nations, the international community succeeded in enabling Kuwait to regain its sovereignty and territorial integrity, which it had lost as a result of Iraqi aggression. The resolutions adopted by the Security Council remain essential to the restoration of peace and stability in the region and must be fully implemented. At the same time the members of the Council are concerned by the humanitarian situation of the innocent civilian population of Iraq."

5. On 5 February 1992, the President of the Security Council issued a statement on behalf of its members (S/23517) in which he stated, among other things:

> "In connection with the Secretary-General's factual report (S/23514) on Iraq's compliance with all the obligations placed upon it by resolution 687 (1991) and subsequent relevant resolutions, the members of the Security Council note that while much progress has been made, much remains to be done. ... The members of the Council are disturbed by the lack of Iraqi cooperation. Iraq must implement fully resolution 687 (1991) and subsequent relevant resolutions as was stated in the statement read out by the President of the Council on behalf of its members in the meeting held on 31 January 1992 with the participation of the Heads of State and Government (S/23500)."

6. In a statement made on behalf of the Council on 28 February 1992 (S/23663), the President said:

> "The members of the Council demand that Iraq immediately implement all its obligations under Council resolution 687 (1991) and subsequent resolutions on Iraq. The members of the Council require the Government of Iraq to communicate directly to the Council without further delay an authoritative and unconditional acknowledgement of its agreement to accept and implement the above noted obligations, including specifically to comply with the determination of the Special Commission requiring the destruction of ballistic missile-related equipment. The members of the Council emphasize that Iraq must be aware of the serious consequences of continued material breaches of resolution 687 (1991)."

7. I must also draw attention to the further report of the Secretary-General on the status of compliance by Iraq with the obligations placed upon it (S/23687).

8. From the aforementioned statements by the President and in view of the reports of the Secretary-General, it will be seen that, despite Iraq's statements of unconditional acceptance of Security Council resolution 687 (1991), the Security Council has determined that Iraq is not in full compliance with all of its obligations.

II. SPECIFIC OBLIGATIONS

9. In addition to the general obligation to accept the provisions of resolution 687 (1991) in their entirety, several Security Council resolutions impose specific obligations upon Iraq.

(a) Respect for the inviolability of the international boundary

10. By paragraph 2 of resolution 687 (1991) the Security Council demands that Iraq respect the inviolability of the international boundary and the allocation of islands previously agreed upon between Iraq and Kuwait. Pursuant to paragraph 3 of that resolution, the Secretary-General established a Boundary Demarcation Commission to demarcate the boundary between Iraq and Kuwait. Paragraph 5 of the same resolution requires Iraq and Kuwait to respect a demilitarized zone (DMZ) established by the Security Council. The Council has been informed that Iraq has respected the DMZ and that it has fully participated in the work of the Boundary Demarcation Commission. It has also been informed that Iraq refuses to withdraw a number of police posts that are not in line with UNIKOM's principle that both sides should stay 1,000 metres from the boundary line shown on UNIKOM's map.

(b) Weapons-related obligations

11. Section C of resolution 687 (1991) imposes certain specific obligations upon Iraq with respect to its chemical and biological weapons programmes, its ballistic missile programmes with a range greater than 150 kilometres and its nuclear programmes. These obligations are elaborated upon in resolutions 707 (1991) and 715 (1991). The obligations are defined in paragraphs 8, 9, 10, 11, 12 and 13 of resolution 687 (1991) and they are elaborated upon in paragraphs 3 and 5 of resolution 707 (1991) and paragraph 5 of resolution 715 (1991).

12. The information relevant to Iraq's compliance with the obligations laid down in the paragraphs of the Security Council's resolutions to which I have just referred is reproduced in annex I to the Secretary-General's report (S/23687).

13. By resolution 699 (1991), the Security Council decided that the Government of Iraq shall be liable for the full costs of carrying out the tasks authorized by section C of resolution 687 (1991). No funds have so far been received from Iraq to meet this liability.

14. The Council has noted that since the adoption of resolution 687 (1991) progress has been made in the implementation of section C of that resolution but that much remains to be done. There is serious non-compliance with the obligations concerning the programmes for weapons of mass destruction and ballistic missiles and the members of the Council have found this to be a continuing material breach of resolution 687 (1991).

15. The Special Commission has informed the Council about the outstanding matters that would at the present time appear to be the most important. The Council's attention is invited again to annex I of the Secretary-General's report, S/23687 of 7 March 1992.

16. The Council has also noted the statement by the International Atomic Energy Agency (IAEA) contained in the Secretary-General's report of 25 January 1992 (S/23514 section C of the annex). The attention of the Council is drawn to information annexed to the further report of the Secretary-General, S/23687 (annex II), of 7 March 1992, relative to the two last inspections by the IAEA, on Iraq's compliance with its obligations under United Nations Security Council resolutions as they relate to nuclear activities.

17. In a statement issued on behalf of the members of the Council (S/23609), the President stated on 19 February 1992 that:

> "Iraq's failure to acknowledge its obligations under resolutions 707 (1991) and 715 (1991), its rejection up until now of the two plans for ongoing monitoring and verification and its failure to provide the full, final and complete disclosure of its weapons capabilities constitute a continuing material breach of the relevant provisions of resolution 687 (1991)."

18. In a further statement made on 28 February 1992 on behalf of the Council (S/23663), the President said:

> "The members of the Council deplore and condemn the failure of the Government of Iraq to provide the Special Commission with full, final and complete disclosure, as required by resolution 707 (1991), of all aspects of its programmes to develop weapons of mass destruction and ballistic missiles with a range greater than 150 kilometres, including launchers, and of all holdings of such weapons, their components and production facilities and locations, as well as all other nuclear programmes; and the failure of Iraq to comply with the plans for ongoing monitoring and verification approved by resolution 715 (1991). ... Furthermore, the members of the Council equally deplore and condemn Iraq's failure, within the time prescribed by the Special Commission at the request of Iraq, to commence destruction of ballistic missile-related equipment designated for destruction by the Special Commission. The members of the Council reaffirm that it is for the Special Commission alone to determine which items must be destroyed under paragraph 9 of resolution 687 (1991)."

(c) Repatriation of and access to Kuwaiti and third country nationals in Iraq

19. As regards Kuwaiti and third-country nationals in Iraq, Security Council resolutions 664 (1990), 666 (1990), 667 (1990), 674 (1990), 686 (1991) and 687

(1991) impose an obligation on Iraq to release, facilitate repatriation of, and arrange for immediate access to them, as well as the return of the remains of any deceased personnel of the forces of Kuwait and of the Member States cooperating with Kuwait pursuant to resolution 678 (1990). Furthermore, paragraph 30 of resolution 687 (1991) requires Iraq to extend all necessary cooperation to the International Committee of the Red Cross (ICRC) in facilitating the search for Kuwaiti and third-country nationals still unaccounted for.

20. The Security Council was informed by the ICRC in January 1992 that almost 7,000 persons have returned from Iraq to their countries since the beginning of March 1991. The ICRC also stated that despite all its efforts, there are still thousands of persons reported missing by the parties to the conflict.

21. A special commission composed of the representatives of France, Iraq, Kuwait, Saudi Arabia, the United Kingdom and the United States has met under the auspices of the ICRC, to try to reach an agreement on, among other things, the implementation of paragraph 30 of resolution 687 (1991). However, the ICRC has informed the Council that it has not yet received any information as to the whereabouts of the persons reported missing in Iraq. Nor has it received detailed and documented information on the search conducted by the Iraqi authorities. Finally, it is also still awaiting information on persons who have died while in custody.

22. The attention of the Council is drawn to section 4, paragraphs 12 to 14, of the Secretary-General's report contained in document S/23687 of 7 March 1992.

(d) Iraq's liability under international law

23. Another obligation concerns Iraq's liability under international law. In resolution 674 (1990), the Security Council reminds Iraq "that under international law it is liable for any loss, damage or injury arising in regard to Kuwait and third States and their nationals and corporations, as a result of the invasion and illegal occupation of Kuwait by Iraq". Its liability under international law is reaffirmed in paragraph 2 (b) of resolution 686 (1991) and paragraph 16 of resolution 687 (1991). Resolution 687 (1991) further specifies that it "is liable under international law for any direct loss, damage, including environmental damage and the depletion of natural resources, or injury to foreign Governments, nationals and corporations, as a result of Iraq's unlawful invasion and occupation of Kuwait".

24. By paragraph 18 of the same resolution, the Security Council created a Fund to pay compensation for claims that fall within paragraph 16, to be financed by a percentage of the value of the exports of petroleum and petroleum products from Iraq. In view of the existing economic sanctions against Iraq under resolution 661 (1990), Iraq was permitted by the Security Council under resolutions 706 (1991) and 712 (1991) to sell a limited quantity of oil, as an exception, a portion of the proceeds from which would be used to provide financial resources for the Fund. To date, it has not availed itself of this possibility. The Council notes that this authorization is due to lapse on 18 March 1992. The members of the Council are aware of a request by Iraq for a five-year moratorium on meeting its financial obligations, including payments into the Compensation Fund.

(e) Repayment and servicing of Iraq's foreign debt

25. With regard to another obligation, the Security Council, in paragraph 17 of resolution 687 (1991), demands that Iraq scrupulously adhere to all of its obligations concerning servicing and repayment of its foreign debt.

26. The attention of the Council is drawn to paragraphs 17 and 18 of the Secretary-General's report (S/23687) of 7 March 1992.

(f) Return of property

27. I now turn to the question of return of property. The Security Council, in paragraph 2 (d) of resolution 686 (1991), demands that Iraq immediately begin to return all Kuwaiti property seized by it, to be completed in the shortest possible period. The members of the Council have noted with satisfaction that, as stated in the further report of the Secretary-General, Iraqi officials involved with the return of property have extended maximum cooperation to the United Nations to facilitate the return.

(g) Monthly statements of gold and foreign currency reserves

28. Another obligation is set out by paragraph 7 of resolution 706 (1991), under which the Government of Iraq is required to provide to the Secretary-General and appropriate international organizations monthly statements of its gold and foreign currency reserves. To date, no such statements have been provided to the Secretary-General or to the International Monetary Fund (IMF).

(h) Undertaking not to commit or support acts of international terrorism

29. By paragraph 32 of resolution 687 (1991), Iraq is required not to commit or support acts of international terrorism or allow any organization directed towards commission of such acts to operate within its territory and to condemn unequivocally and renounce all acts, methods, and practices of terrorism.

30. The Council notes Iraq's statements contained in letters dated 11 June 1991 (S/22687 and S/22689) and 23 January 1992 (S/23472) that it is a party to international conventions against terrorism and that it has never pursued a policy favourable to international terrorism as defined by international law.

(i) Security Council action with respect to the Iraqi civilian population

31. Resolutions 706 (1991) and 712 (1991) provide a means for Iraq to meet its obligations to supply its civilian population with needed humanitarian assistance, particularly food and medicine. To date, Iraq has refused to implement these resolutions. In fact after initiating discussions with Secretariat representatives on implementation, Iraq abruptly terminated the discussions.

III. SECURITY COUNCIL RESOLUTION 688 (1991)

32. I should now like to refer to the demands by the Security Council with respect to the Iraqi civilian population. In paragraph 2 of resolution 688 (1991), the Security Council demands that Iraq, as a contribution to removing the threat to international peace and security in the region, end the repression of its civilian population. In paragraphs 3 and 7, the Security Council insists that it allow immediate access by international humanitarian organizations to all those in need of assistance in all parts of Iraq, and demands its cooperation with the Secretary-General to these ends.

33. The Security Council remains deeply concerned at the grave human rights abuses that, despite the provisions of resolution 688 (1991), the Government of Iraq continues to perpetrate against its population, in particular in the northern region of Iraq, in southern Shi'a centres and in the southern marshes (Commission on Human Rights resolution 1992/71 of 5 March 1992). The

Security Council notes that this situation is confirmed by the report of the Special Rapporteur of the Commission on Human Rights (E/CN.4/1992/31, also to be circulated in document S/23685) and by the comments of the Office of the Executive Delegate of the Secretary-General contained in the further report of the Secretary-General.

34. The members of the Council are particularly concerned at the reported restrictions of the supplies of essential commodities, in particular food and fuel, which have been imposed by the Government of Iraq on the three northern governorates of Dohuk, Erbil and Suleimaniya. In this regard, as the Special Rapporteur has noted in his report, inasmuch as the repression of the population continues, the threat to international peace and security in the region mentioned in resolution 688 (1991) remains.

IV. CONCLUDING OBSERVATION

35. In view of the observations on the record of Iraq's performance, the Security Council has considered itself justified in concluding that Iraq has not fully complied with the obligations placed upon it by the Council. It is the Council's hope and expectation that this meeting will prove an invaluable opportunity to advance in the consideration of this issue as required in the interest of world peace and security, as well as that of the Iraqi people.

Peter HOHENFELLNER (Austria) stressed the importance of the Council's actions on the question before it, not only for the future of the region but also for the concept of collective security and the role of the United Nations as a whole. The decisions taken by the Council almost a year ago had laid down a number of obligations on Iraq, guided by the need to be assured of Iraq's peaceful intentions in light of its unlawful invasion and occupation of Kuwait.

Regarding the state of Iraqi compliance with relevant binding decisions of this Council, the picture before the Council was "to say the least, very disturbing".

He said that, although the Iraqi Government was protesting the embargo imposed by the international community, it had blocked the import of food, fuel and medicines to some areas of the country, in particular those inhabited by Kurds. Repressive measures continue to affect also the southern marshes. There was also additional evidence of massive human rights violations by the Iraqi Government. Resolutions 706 (1991) and 712 (1991) gave Iraq the possibility for oil sales to finance the purchase of foodstuffs, medicines and materials, and supplies for essential civilian needs. It was deplorable that the Government had not yet used that possibility to provide its population with access to adequate food and health care. He urged Iraq to resume the talks with the United Nations Secretariat on the implementation of that scheme immediately.

Regarding Iraq's obligations under section C of resolution 687 (1991) and resolutions 707 (1991) and 715 (1991), he said that while there had been signs of better cooperation with some inspections as referred to in the report of the tenth IAEA inspection (document S/23644), overall Iraqi cooperation and compliance continued to fall short. Iraq's failure to provide all information required under resolutions 687 and 707 and to acknowledge its obligations and provide the declarations required under the plans for ongoing monitoring and verification approved by resolution 715 was particularly worrying. Iraq's continuing material breach of its obligations placed it in a situation which might have serious consequences.

He said that the Council's decisions last year were part of a broader effort to establish peace and security in the area and in the region as a whole. They represented first steps towards the goal of establishing a zone free from weapons of mass destruction in the Middle East, a global ban on chemical weapons, and a balanced and comprehensive control of armaments in the region. Almost one year later that objective had not been achieved. "Indeed, if one believes recent reports, a new arms race in this volatile region is already well under way." Regarding the Council's role in the Gulf conflict, he said that, in many ways, a new beginning had been made and some important steps taken towards establishing a system of collective security. The Council should continue on that path in the future.

Sir David HANNAY (United Kingdom) said it was essential that the Iraqi leadership should hear directly from the Council the extent and nature of its concern about Iraq's non-compliance with Security Council resolution 687 and subsequent resolutions, and that they should get a clear, first-hand impression of the Council's determination that its resolutions should be fully implemented.

The discussion in the Council was about compliance or rather about the lack of it, he said. The key text must be the Presidential statement endorsed by the Council at its meeting at the level of Heads of State and Government on 31 January, that "The resolutions adopted by the Security Council remain essential to the restoration of peace and stability in the region and must be fully implemented."

The list of instances of non-compliance was long, he went on. They needed to be remedied urgently if there was to be any hope of restoring peace and stability in the Gulf region. The area of weapons of mass destruction was of very great concern, where the Iraqi performance had from the very beginning been one of evasion, dissimulation and often outright dishonesty.

He said that despite all the good work done by the Special Commission and the International Atomic Energy Agency (IAEA) to bring to light the matter concealed by Iraq, the international community was now confronted with three serious issues: there was not a full and complete disclosure of Iraq's programmes; Iraq had so far refused to acknowledge its obligations for long-term monitoring; and Iraq was resisting the implementation of the Special Commission's determinations on the material and installations that needed to be destroyed.

As a result of the present debate, he said, the Iraqi authorities should understand the absolute need for them to comply promptly on those three points. The full final and complete disclosure of Iraq's weapons of mass destruction capability demanded by the Council was essential to establishing a materials balance and to making any judgement as to whether Iraq had declared all relevant items.

As for the destruction issues, he continued, that was a further area in which there was no scope for negotiations. Nor was it acceptable that the Council should be drawn into a discussion of what it would or would not do if Iraq complied with its obligations. The obligation to comply was an absolute, not a conditional one.

He said it was a signal of the Iraqi Government's cynical disregard for the welfare of its own people that it had not cooperated with the implementation of resolutions 706 (1991) and 712 (1991), which provided for fair and equitable arrangements for the export of quantities of Iraqi oil to finance the import of food, medicine and other civilian supplies to meet the humanitarian needs in all regions of Iraq and of all categories of the Iraqi civilian population, and to finance the work of the Special Commission and the Compensation Fund. It was therefore the intransigence of the Iraqi Government and not the action of the Security Council that was the cause of the suffering of the Iraqi people.

Continuing, Sir David HANNAY (United Kingdom) said Iraq had also failed to comply with Security Council resolution 688 (1991), which was adopted in response to a threat to international peace and security arising from the brutal military action which Iraq took against its civilian population in the Kurdish and Shia areas of the country resulting in a massive flood of refugees across the frontiers of its neighbours. Far from engaging in the dialogue called for by that text, Iraq had now for several months operated an economic blockade against some of those areas, particularly the Kurdish areas. Until the last few days, it had frustrated the opening of United Nations humanitarian centres in some of the Shia areas and had in many other ways acted in a manner completely inconsistent with the resolution.

The recent report to the Commission on Human Rights by the Special Rapporteur on Iraq revealed very clearly that Iraq was in serious breach of its human rights obligations under the Charter, International Covenants on Human Rights and customary international law as embodied in the Universal Declaration of Human Rights.

The use of force had been required because Iraq had miscalculated and believed that the Council was bluffing, he said. There was an opportunity then for Iraq to comply, which that country failed to take. There was an opportunity again now for Iraq to comply; it should not again miscalculate.

Jean-Bernard MERIMEE (France) said that, following the liberation of Kuwait, the Council had imposed specific obligations on Iraq. Once Iraq complied with those obligations, the sanctions imposed on it could be lifted. The Council did not seek to punish the people of Iraq. He deplored the Iraqi authorities' refusal to sell oil for humanitarian purposes, as permitted by the Council. It was essential to ensure that Iraq's industrial capacity would not be used for military purposes.

Iraq had not supplied information required of it under resolution 687. "The situation cannot go on." It was not up to the Council or the Special Commission to ask questions of Iraq, from which it could choose what it could answer. Iraq would only resume its industrial civil production after it had complied with its international obligations.

He cited consistent reports of Iraqi oppression in Kirbuk and the region of the marshes. Large masses of Iraq's population were thus being deprived of their human rights. Iraq's numerous failures to abide by its obligations were abundantly evident. France, therefore, could not accept a lifting of the sanctions. As long as Iraq continued to hide documents and information, how could the arms of resolution 687 be ensured? Sanctions could not be lifted on a basis proportional to the degree of Iraq's compliance. They should remain fully in place until Iraq fulfilled its obligations.

Thomas PICKERING (United States) said from the first, Iraq had tried to obfuscate and evade its obligations. The record of its failure in regard to its weapons programmes was inescapable, clear and serious. An unfortunate pattern had developed: Iraq made declarations of minimal content, declarations which were clearly meant to misinform, misdirect and conceal. It repeatedly divulged information related to its weapons programmes only after being presented incontrovertible proof uncovered by the Special Commission and the IAEA in their inspections. That was not compliance, but "hide and seek, cat and mouse, cheat and retreat". That pattern of concealment had continued right down to the present day.

In its February discussions with the Special Commission, Iraq had stated it had already provided "all the necessary information" under resolution 687. Iraq's previous actions to the contrary made it impossible to believe now that such was true.

He said Iraq had claimed that it could render its ballistic missile production facilities and similar facilities for producing weapons of mass destruction harmless by converting them to civilian use. Given Iraq's clear record of non-compliance with United Nations efforts to identify Iraqi weapons of mass destruction, however, Iraq must not be allowed the option to return those facilities to use for production of those awful weapons. Those facilities must be destroyed rather than merely converted.

The critical point, he continued, was not whether facilities were capable of producing material for civilian use, but whether they were capable of being used for prohibited purposes. The Council continued to support the proposition that the Special Commission - and not Iraq - must and will determine which facilities were required under Security Council resolutions to be destroyed. That was not a matter for negotiations or haggling, but of a determination by the Special Commission.

On the repatriation of Kuwaiti, Saudi and other third-country detainees, he said once again Iraq had deliberately delayed any meaningful cooperation on that issue, displaying a totally callous and uncooperative attitude towards the plight of the missing and the suffering of their relatives.

Iraq, he went on, had repeatedly criticized the Council for causing shortages of food, medicines, and other essential civilian needs in Iraq - even though resolutions 706 and 712 provided the means for Iraq to assure the provision and equitable distribution of such goods to all the Iraqi civilian population.

Continuing, Mr. PICKERING (United States) said Baghdad also persisted in actions repressing its civilian population, particularly in the predominantly Kurdish-inhabited areas of the north and in the predominantly Shi'a-inhabited areas of the south.

The economic embargo instituted by the Government of Iraq in October 1991 on shipments of food, fuel, and other essential humanitarian supplies to northern Iraq was both impeding United Nations relief operations and inflicting severe hardship on Iraqi civilians as well as impeding their right to enter and leave the area, he said. It was ironic and truly tragic that the Government of Iraq should continue to issue distorted, fabricated and exaggerated claims about the alleged humanitarian impact of United Nations sanctions - which in no way restricted the flow of medicines, food and other essential humanitarian goods - while the Iraqi Government itself imposed an internal embargo consciously designed to deprive some selected Iraqi civilians of food, fuel, medicine and other essential supplies.

He said the Government of Iraq was apparently waging a concerted attack against the Shi'a clergy by arresting them, "disappearing" them, imprisoning them and torturing them. Iraq had yet to reply to an inquiry from the Special Rapporteur about the list of missing persons, including Shi'a clergy. More generally, Iraq's human rights records was abysmal. Much of the new evidence derived from the files, videotapes and documents of the Iraqi secret police and security forces themselves, who in particular carefully recorded the regime's brutality against the Kurdish people.

The Special Rapporteur, he went on, had already received more than 15,000 names of missing Kurds, which had led him to conclude that it would be difficult to dismiss the Kurdish claims of some 182,000 disappeared persons. Iraq's continuing repression of its civilian population had led the Special Rapporteur to conclude that the threat to international peace and security in reference to resolution 688 (1991) also continued.

Once again, he said, the Council stood at a critical juncture in its consideration of restoring and maintaining international peace and security in the Gulf region. His country and the Council would be watching closely Iraqi actions in the future. By distaining [*sic*] and failing to comply with the Council's resolutions, Iraq risked making, as it had in the past, yet another tragic miscalculation, the full consequences of which the Government of Iraq once again would have to bear.

Valetin V. LOZINSKIY (Russian Federation) said a year had passed since Iraq's aggression had been halted. The Council had then drawn up a series of measures to be followed by Iraq, which the Iraqi authorities had thus far failed to observe in full. Iraq had yet to demonstrate its unconditional agreement to abide by Council resolutions on the elimination of its weapons of mass destruction. Iraq had virtually refused to submit a comprehensive picture of its programmes for such weapons, compelling the Special Commission to seek out such information independently. He cited, in particular, Iraq's refusal to destroy certain ballistic missiles.

A great number of Kuwaiti citizens remained detained in Iraq, while access by the ICRC to detention areas was restricted, he said. The north of the country was receiving half the normal food supplies, resulting in serious deprivations. However, the Government had refused to use the limited sale of oil to meet humanitarian needs, as allowed by the Council.

Iraq, he said, had continued carrying out mass executions, torture and genocide. It seemed that there was no realization among the Iraqi authorities of the gravity of Iraq's actions. Iraq had invaded and occupied Kuwait and was engaged in developing a chemical, biological and nuclear weapons capacity.

Russia favoured the return of Iraq as a full-fledged member of the international community and the lifting of sanctions, he said. For that to happen, Iraq had to recognize and assume responsibility for its actions and to unconditionally implement all binding Council resolutions.

LI Daoyu (China) said it was necessary and useful for the Security Council to conduct dialogue today with the Iraqi delegation on implementation of Council resolutions and various post-war issues. China favoured dialogue instead of confrontation. He welcomed the Iraqi Government's decision to send its delegation to New York and hoped its dialogue with the Council would achieve positive results.

From the outset of the Gulf crisis, he said, China had resolutely opposed Iraq's armed invasion of Kuwait. In order to remove the consequences created by the invasion and ensure peace and security in the Gulf region, the international community had carried out fruitful cooperation, and significant progress had been made in the implementation of some of the important parts of the resolution. The Council's resolutions remained essential to the restoration of peace and stability in the Gulf region and must be fully implemented. "Since we still fall some distance short of this target", he expressed the hope that Iraq would cooperate with the parties concerned to fulfil its obligations under the relevant resolutions.

He said that, in the year since the ending of the Gulf war, the difficult situation confronting the Iraqi people had continued to deteriorate. The Iraqi people were innocent, and it was not fair to let them continue to suffer from hardships. China remained "in favour of an immediate abolition of restrictions on imports into Iraq of foodstuffs and other goods required for the restoration of people's normal life, and a timely and gradual lifting of other economic sanctions against Iraq in light of the development of the situation". He supported the proposal that the "no objection" procedure be changed to a "simple notification" procedure in allowing Iraq to import civilian products. Such a step would help alleviate the difficulties of the Iraqi people and would promote the economic recovery of the countries of that region.

Yoshio HATANO (Japan) said that in August 1990, Iraqi troops had invaded and occupied Kuwait, violating that country's sovereignty and contravening international law. The tragic consequences of Iraq's actions continued to be felt. More than a year since the ending of hostilities in the Gulf, the people of Kuwait continued to suffer in terms of human lives lost, material destruction and environmental degradation. As the Kuwaiti people, with the assistance of the international community, worked to rebuild [*sic*] their country, Iraq's leadership was held accountable. "Regrettably, I am not sure if the Iraqi leadership fully understands the gravity of the present situation."

He said that Iraq continued to persecute the Kurdish people and Shiite groups within its territory, to prevent the repatriation of large numbers of Kuwaiti nationals, and to refuse to return all Kuwaiti property. It had repeatedly blocked the efforts of the Special Commission established by the Council to oversee the destruction of Iraq's weapons of mass destruction and had submitted false reports to the Council. Through such actions the Iraqi Government was defying not only the Council, but the international community as a whole. "Iraq's leaders must realize that they are not in a position to interpret the Security Council's resolutions or to decide which provisions they will implement and which ones they will not. There is no room for negotiation."

He said that Japan was concerned about the innocent people of Iraq as they continued to face severe hardships. The Council had agreed to allow Iraq to sell oil to provide for the basic needs of its people. However, by refusing to export oil as laid out by the Council and by creating obstacles to the activities of various agencies, the Government of Iraq was denying its own people access to the humanitarian relief that has been made available. The Iraqi leadership had a moral obligation to alleviate the agony of its own people; it could do so by exporting oil.

He urged the Government of Iraq to agree once and for all to implement the provisions of all relevant Security Council resolutions. Continued material breaches by Iraq of its obligations would surely have serious consequences. He said he remembered how Japan had suffered after the Second World War. He also remembered how Japan had been helped by the international community. Iraq's return to the world community as a responsible member could only be achieved through its full and unconditional compliance with the relevant Security Council resolutions.

André ERDOS (Hungary) said the Council's resolutions were not subject to negotiations or bargaining. His country deeply deplored Iraq's failure to comply fully. Its attempts to reinterpret certain provisions of resolution 687 and subsequent texts dealing with Iraq's military potential reflected an attitude of which Hungary strongly disapproved.

While in recent weeks Iraqi authorities had demonstrated a greater willingness to cooperate with United Nations representatives, he went on, his country could not discern any real change in Iraq's behaviour. As to the information requested of it, Iraq insisted on a special interpretation, namely, it considered the information provided as sufficient. The facts continued to belie that assertion.

Iraq's attitude towards the destruction of materials and facilities was also not acceptable, he said; it constituted dilatory tactics. It was and would remain the competence of bodies authorized by the Council to determine what Iraq should or should not destroy.

He said Iraq's reference to "interference in its internal affairs" did not justify its refusal to sell oil. Hungary regretted that Iraq had seen fit to break off unilaterally the negotiations on that subject with representatives of the United Nations in Vienna. It was because of Iraq's total failure to cooperate that the question of compensations remained deadlocked.

Moreover, he went on, Iraq's failure to cooperate with the International Committee of the Red Cross (ICRC) was unacceptable. In view of the extraordinary seriousness of the human rights situation in that country, the competent United Nations bodies should consider sending a team of observers.

Paul NOTERDAEME (Belgium) said his country's position throughout the Gulf crisis had been based on respect for international law. Through the Council's actions, Kuwait was liberated and cease-fire conditions were adopted. The Council now had to ensure strict respect by Iraq for all of its international obligations. It must erase the effects caused by its aggression, which included pillage and destruction. The return of prisoners and stolen property was essential, as well as the employment of a Compensation Fund. Iraq must dismantle all its weapons of mass destruction.

Iraq's discriminatory actions against certain groups within the country were also a matter of continuing concern. So long as such human rights abuses continued, Iraq could not be said to be in compliance with its international obligations. He expressed concern for the suffering population of Iraq and had supported measures to enable Iraq to meet its humanitarian needs.

Continuing, Mr. NOTERDAEME (Belgium) urged the Iraqi Government to use the means available to it to meet the humanitarian needs of its population without any discrimination.

The Kurdish population was currently receiving only half of the food ration available to the rest of the country, he said. That situation had to stop. It was now up to the Iraqi Government to dispel the distrust which had been generated by its actions.

Jose AYALA LASSO (Ecuador) said Iraq must broaden its cooperation in all areas of its plans and programmes, as required by the Special Commission. Its compliance with the resolutions of the Council must be complete, without exception. It was up to the Council to evaluate the correct implementation of its resolutions, taking into account the good faith Iraq must demonstrate.

Ecuador was concerned, he said, by Iraq's lack of respect for human rights. The report of the Special Rapporteur on that subject should prompt Iraq to take immediate corrective measures, including repatriation of third-country nationals.

He said his country did not categorize Mr. Aziz's visit as a negotiation but rather as an opportunity for dialogue, which might help in finding specific solutions. The Minister should provide first-hand information and a satisfactory response to questions raised by the United Nations. The Iraqi Government should adopt measures enabling the Council to react by taking steps to restore normalcy.

Chinmaya Rajaninath GHAREKHAN (India) said that, during a series of meetings between August 1990 and mid-1991, the Council had created a framework of action in response to the Gulf crisis and its aftermath. Resolution 687 had been a landmark decision of the Council. Iraq, and the international community as a whole, had accepted that resolution and had to come together in an attempt to preserve and strengthen international peace and security.

He said there were areas in which Iraq's compliance with the obligations placed upon it by the relevant Council resolutions had either been achieved or actively pursued, and areas where compliance was yet to be achieved. The Council was aware of the incontestable hardships suffered by innocent civilians in Iraq. He expressed "deep disappointment" at the meagre progress achieved in addressing the humanitarian situation in the country. For instance, the Council had yet to formally accept the proposal of the non-aligned members to transfer items of undeniable humanitarian need from the "no objection" procedure to the "notification" category.

There was a need, he said, to strengthen the overall impact and influence of Council action by the activation, in concrete terms, of Article 50 of the United Nations Charter, enabling countries that faithfully implement Council resolutions to obtain redress wherever such implementation adversely affects them.

(Article 50 states: "If preventive or enforcement measures against any state are taken by the Security Council, any other state, whether a Member of the United Nations or not, which find itself confronted with special economic problems arising from the carrying out of those measures shall have the right to consult the Security Council with regard to a solution of those problems.")

He said his country's aim was to overcome divergences in views and misunderstanding, and to promote trust and cooperation. Today's opportunity of a dialogue with Iraq's Deputy Prime Minister should serve those purposes and open the doors to early, peaceful resolution of all outstanding problems in the Gulf.

Jose Eduardo BARBOSA (Cape Verde) said his country appealed to the Government of Iraq to be more forthcoming in its acceptance of, and compliance with, the relevant Council decisions. Iraq should be more cooperative in order to obtain the release of Kuwaiti prisoners and third-country nationals and facilitate access to them.

Complete and full compliance with the resolutions would very much facilitate the lifting of sanctions and would re-establish peace and cooperation in the area, he went on. The Council should continue to be sensitive to the humanitarian needs of the Iraqi population. His country was not and would never be against the people of Iraq but was in favour, and very much so, of strict observance of the Charter provisions.

While Cape Verde supported Iraq's compliance with the resolutions, he continued, it was also sensitive to the legitimate needs of its people. The economic development of Iraq should not be unduly affected. The purpose of the sanctions was to restore the situation as it existed before the invasion of Kuwait, to repair the damages and losses suffered and to create a situation that would guarantee peace and security in the area, and should not affect unnecessarily the economic structure and future well-being of the Iraqi people.

Simbarashe S. MUMBENGEGWI (Zimbabwe) said that recent history had shown the Council's determination to enforce compliance with its resolutions and to assert the collective will of the international community to right wrongs and protect the vulnerable. The Council's authority and credibility could only be enhanced through the uniform and consistent enforcement of its resolutions, regardless of who the offender might be.

He expressed great concern about the humanitarian situation in the region. Nearly a year after the end of the war, the serious humanitarian situation in the region showed no signs of diminishing. The Council had a moral obligation to do all in its power to ease the suffering of the civilian population in the region, as did the Iraqi authorities.

Regarding the unresolved question of missing Kuwaiti nationals, he said that the Geneva Convention's provisions, as well as resolution 687, clearly imposed upon Iraq an obligation to release all Kuwaiti nationals in its custody and to do so expeditiously in cooperation with the ICRC. He called on Iraq to cooperate fully, to provide the ICRC with information on the missing persons, to facilitate searches by the ICRC, and to accede to its requests to undertake searches for the missing persons.

Ahmed SNOUSSI (Morocco) said his country deplored the cataclysm that had affected the Gulf region. The Council wished to express, not only its vigilance, but its willingness to listen. The Council did not wish to disregard the human effects of the war.

It was now up to the Iraqi authorities to demonstrate their willingness to comply with Iraq's obligations, he said. The Council must also have concern for the humanitarian needs of the region.

Mr. ARRIA, speaking in his capacity as the representative of Venezuela, said it was of the highest significance that Tariq Aziz had come before the Council. The international community could and must make use of all forums to resolve the situation. He welcomed Iraq's initiative to establish dialogue with the Council.

The sole, entire responsibility lay with the Government of Iraq for its violation of international law, he went on. It had invaded and devastated Kuwait. At its present meeting, the Council was beginning an exhaustive consideration of the matter, which should provide an opportunity for constructive progress. The Iraqi Government should meet the obligations imposed on it by the Council which it had unconditionally agreed to respect.

Iraq had not used the mechanisms set up for the sale of its oil, which was contrary to the interests of its people, he said. It should meet all its international obligations so that its people could fulfil economic and social aspirations, a fulfilment to which they were entitled.

He said Iraq should also fulfil all its obligations to third-country nationals and ensure the human rights of its own citizens. Iraq had in its hands the ability to normalize its relations with the international community.

Tariq AZIZ, Deputy Prime Minister of Iraq, said the whole world knew the way in which resolution 678 (1990) had been implemented to inflict, in a deliberate manner, a total destruction of the whole civilian infrastructure in Iraq. In addition, there was the damage and destruction inflicted on the civilian population. Not only his country, but also members of the Security Council, including permanent Members, had said the operations of destruction carried out had gone beyond the framework of resolution 678, which "became a political tool used to destroy a free, independent country", he said.

However, he continued, Iraq had informed the Security Council on 28 February 1991 of its acceptance to comply fully with resolution 660 and all other Council resolutions.

Mr. AZIZ, Deputy Prime Minister of Iraq, went on to say resolution 687 had come up with such measures and conditions that were unprecedented in the whole history of the United Nations; they transcended the initial limits and declared objectives of the Council's previous resolutions. As an independent sovereign State, Iraq had stated its views about the resolution on the basis of the Charter, international law and the principles of fairness and justice. His Government had, however, accepted the resolution in order to ward off the dangers threatening the people of Iraq.

More than 11 months had now elapsed since resolution 687 was adopted, during which Iraq had seriously endeavoured to implement its provisions, he went on. The contents of the letter sent by the Iraqi Foreign Minister on 23 January made clear that the fundamental contents of the resolution had already been implemented.

Turning to aspects that had, since last summer, often become a cause for problems and allegations thrown at Iraq without careful examination, he said the weapons which Iraq was prohibited from possessing had been totally destroyed. Whatever remained, especially in the missiles and chemical ammunition fields, was being successively destroyed under the supervision of the inspection teams and according to a plan about which there was no argument between the Iraqi authorities concerned and those teams. As to the equipment used, or allegedly used, in producing those weapons, they had all been identified.

The items already destroyed under the supervision of the inspection teams had reached a total of 14,000, he went on. In addition, the Iraqi side had destroyed more than 270,000 items and more than 1,500 tons of raw materials.

The clear conclusion, Mr. AZIZ, Deputy Prime Minister of Iraq, continued, was that Iraq was no longer in possession of any weapons, munitions or major or minor systems prohibited by resolution 687. The equipment used, or allegedly used, in producing such items had been identified, and their use had either been frozen or turned to civilian industries or to industries not prohibited by the resolution. All that was taking place under the supervision of the inspection teams. That fundamental fact had been deliberately hidden from the Council with a view to keeping it in a climate of suspicion as to the position of Iraq.

He said a second matter had also been used as a pretext to raise doubts and ill-intended allegations against Iraq. Since March 1991, the Iraqi authorities concerned had repatriated, in cooperation with the ICRC, 6,520 Kuwaiti and third-country nationals. There were now in Iraq 3,594 Kuwaitis who were not detainees there, but lived in freedom. But the Kuwaiti authorities had agreed to the return of only 468 of them.

While the Kuwaiti authorities had submitted a list of 2,242 persons claimed to be in Iraq, 233 of them were proved to have returned to Kuwait through the ICRC, he said, and 59 of them remained in Iraq awaiting approval from the Kuwaiti authorities for their return. The false allegation, however, that Iraq was holding Kuwaiti individuals as detainees continued to be thrown about by certain Governments, without bothering to ask themselves the obvious question: Why should Iraq do this thing? What benefit could it expect to gain from detaining one or two thousand Kuwaiti citizens when Iraq had already repatriated high-ranking Kuwaiti officers and other high officials, including 20 members of the ruling family in Kuwait? Iraq had requested on 20 February that the whole matter be entrusted to the ICRC.

Mr. AZIZ, Deputy Prime Minister of Iraq, went on to state that the same thing applied to the subject of properties. Iraq had submitted inventories, expressed willingness to return the items, and had indeed returned great numbers and huge quantities of them. That there were other items to be returned was not an Iraqi responsibility but the responsibility of the Secretary-General's delegate entrusted to take the measures required for the properties to be received from Iraq. Iraq had indeed fulfilled the greatest and most fundamental part of the provisions of resolution 687 in relation to the other matters addressed in sections A, B, D and H of the resolution. Implementation of the remaining provisions, which by their nature required a period of time to be fully implemented, was being carried out in the proper manner, and Iraq was extending serious and professional cooperation in order to achieve such implementation.

All Iraq's efforts to explain the extent of its compliance with resolution 687, he said, had been ignored under pressure from a small, but influential and perhaps even tyrannical number of members of the Council. The Council was repeatedly put in an atmosphere of distortion aimed to suggest non-compliance by Iraq with the provisions of the resolution. "Some members of the inspection teams visiting Iraq had been selected from people linked to the intelligence services of certain countries in order to create problems and hence keep the Council in this atmosphere of distortion", he said.

He went on to say that none of the parties adopting the resolution had attempted to show any understanding of, or sympathy with, the terrible tragic situation forced upon Iraq. A series of demands and decisions on the implementation of this or that paragraph of the resolution was taken in rapid succession and came hammering down, regardless of the facts of the situation suffered by Iraq.

The countries to which he referred did not stop at Iraq's compliance with the provisions of resolution 687 as a condition for lifting the economic sanctions, he said. Weeks after the resolution had been adopted and Iraq had begun implementing its provisions, those countries announced that they would not be prepared to lift the economic embargo until the political leadership of Iraq was replaced. Those countries continued reiterating that precondition despite its flagrant contradiction of Charter principles and the resolutions issued by the Council itself.

Continuing, Mr. AZIZ, Deputy Prime Minister of Iraq, said those States had exploited resolution 687 to achieve political objectives not accommodated for in the resolution, just as they had earlier exploited resolution

678. The objective, he said, was to blackmail Iraq, keep the finger of accusation pointed at it, use that false and distorted climate to maintain the iniquitous economic embargo imposed upon the people of Iraq, and ultimately exploit the situation in a manner that would enable those countries to issue, whenever they chose to, threats of the use of force against Iraq in order to complete the fulfilment of the dream to destroy Iraq.

Why, despite Iraq's cooperation with the inspection teams, were people still resorting to provocation and accusation? he asked. The reasons were [sic] clearly political, completely ill-intended and had nothing to do with the process of fulfilling the provisions of resolution 687.

He said his Government had come to the meeting in good faith and with a true desire to make the facts clear and reach an understanding with the Council on the matters relevant to implementing resolution 687. Iraq was ready to continue cooperating with the Special Commission and the IAEA in order to accomplish the tasks stipulated in that resolution. Having submitted huge amounts of data, information and documents and answered thousands of questions put by inspection teams, Iraq was ready to continue cooperation in order to complete the picture.

His country, he went on, was ready to reach a practical solution to the question of the Council's verification of Iraq's capabilities to produce the weapons prohibited by resolution 687. It was ready to reach a practical mechanism for rendering the relevant equipment harmless. Iraq was willing to do that on the basis of respect of its sovereignty and dignity and of non-infringement on its national security; and on that basis not allowing the objectives stipulated in resolution 687 to be turned into means of preventing people and the country of Iraq from living a free, normal life like all other free people in the world.

Continuing, Mr. AZIZ, Deputy Prime Minister of Iraq, proposed that a technical meeting be held, at the earliest time convenient to the Council, between Iraqi representatives and representatives from the Special Commission, and attended by representatives from all member States of the Security Council. The Special Commission would submit at that meeting all its demands for data and information and put to the Iraqi representatives all questions connected with resolution 687. A comprehensive review would be made of all data, information and documentation presented by Iraq at the request of the Special Commission. Following that, a comprehensive report on the situation would be presented to the Council.

Regarding the operations of verifying Iraq's capabilities to produce prohibited weapons in the future, he said the Special Commission had chosen to use U2 aircraft to conduct flights over Iraqi territory. That aircraft belonged to the United States, whose administration had daily been announcing its intention to strike at and destroy the political leadership of Iraq. Was Iraq to accept that that aircraft was used solely for the tasks of the Special Commission, or was it being used for intelligence purposes? he asked. Did not the basic principle of respect for Iraq's sovereignty and security call for a reasonable period to be determined for those suspect reconnaissance operations to be brought to an end? he asked. He also proposed a discussion of the plans for determining the issue of ongoing monitoring in a final and constructive manner.

He asked what the real objective of resolution 687 was in regard to the equipment which could be modified for non-prohibited use. Was it to prevent Iraq from becoming an industrialized country and to destroy all its industries and all the advanced industrial property in its possession? Or was it to verify the non-production of weapons prohibited under resolution 687? If the objective was the latter, Iraq was ready to cooperate in that regard.

The current resolutions and plans, with their general language, were capable of being used in this or that direction, he continued. What Iraq asked for was that the language be carefully selected in the light of the objective set; and for methods of implementation and conduct to be determined for the Special Commission and IAEA to follow, again in the light of the objective set.

Mr. AZIZ, Deputy Prime Minister of Iraq, went on to say there was an extremist approach in determining specific provisions. That approach called only for destruction, whereas the original paragraph allowed such equipment to be rendered harmless.

In order to solve all those matters, he said, Iraq proposed that the Special Commission prepare a complete and final list of all the machines and equipment concerned, which the Commission proposed for destruction or for being rendered harmless. The list would be submitted to the Security Council with representatives from Iraq attending to convey their view on whether it was possible to use the equipment for prohibited purposes.

The Security Council, he continued, had entrusted to the Special Commission certain tasks. But those tasks should remain technical in nature, and the Council should not relinquish its authority in taking the final decision on matters of a political and legal nature relating to the destiny of a free people.

What was the position of the Security Council on the subject of the economic embargo? he asked. In spite of everything that had been fulfilled in the context of implementing the provisions of resolution 687, the Council had not budged an inch in its position on the embargo.

Thirteen months had gone by since the economic embargo was imposed, and the people of Iraq remained deprived of their right to normal life. In theory, Iraq had been allowed to import medicines and foodstuffs, but Iraqi assets in other countries continued to be frozen. Nor was Iraq allowed to export any commodities or goods whatsoever, which would enable it to use the revenues to purchase food, medicine and other humanitarian needs.

He said Iraq had made an outstanding contribution to the establishment of human civilization. It was from among the people of Iraq that Abraham, the father of all prophets, had emerged to the world; and it was the Iraqi people that had established the world's first legal code determining the rights and obligations of man. That people was subjected today to such injustice and such iniquity.

The Iraqi people, he went on, was prohibited from importing the chlorine it needed to sterilize its drinking water. And now demands were made that the factory producing chlorine be destroyed. Iraq was further prevented from importing or producing the materials it needed to combat such plant diseases as may claim a major share of its agricultural produce, under the pretexts that those are chemical materials which can be used in weapons production.

Continuing, Mr. AZIZ, Deputy Prime Minister of Iraq, said Prince Sadruddin Aga Khan, the former Executive Delegate of the Secretary-General, had said it would be difficult to deny the fact that the Iraqi people were being punished through the economic sanctions, although that had not been the objective sought by the resolutions of the Security Council. The question constantly asked by 18 million Iraqis, he said, was how long that iniquitous siege would continue to be imposed on Iraq. For how long would the Sanctions Committee continue to hold the absolute and arbitrary powers to determine the needs of Iraqi people?

What obligations had the Council, for its part, fulfilled towards the people of Iraq? he asked. The answer was: Nothing whatsoever. Even when the Council adopted a resolution theoretically allowing Iraq to export limited quantities of oil in order to be able to pay for food and medical purchases, the Council included both in the resolution itself and in its implementation plan, an endless list of preconditions, all of which infringed on Iraq's sovereignty and security; preconditions which constituted flagrant interference in Iraq's internal affairs and which stemmed from ill-intended political objectives.

Iraq, he said, demonstrated, in good faith, its readiness to cooperate. The Security Council ought, for its part, to show willingness to fulfil its obligations towards the people of Iraq and proceed from good faith in dealing with Iraq.

The meeting was suspended at 3 p.m. It is scheduled to resume following consultations at 4:30 p.m. today.

S/23709, 12 March 1992

6. Note by the President of the Security Council, 12 March 1992

Following consultations among members of the Security Council, the President of the Council made the following statement, on behalf of the Council, at its 3059th meeting (resumed), on 12 March 1992, in connection with the Council's consideration of the item entitled:

"(a) The situation between Iraq and Kuwait

"(b) Letter dated 2 April 1991 from the Permanent Representative of Turkey to the United Nations addressed to the President of the Security Council (S/22435)

Letter dated 4 April 1991 from the Chargé d'affaires a.i. of the Permanent Mission of France to the United Nations addressed to the President of the Security Council (S/22442)

Letter dated 5 March 1992 from the Chargé d'affaires a.i. of the Permanent Mission of Belgium to the United Nations addressed to the President of the Security Council (S/23685)".

"In concluding the present stage of the consideration of the item on the agenda, I have been authorized, following consultations among members of the Security Council, to make the following statement on behalf of the Council:

'The views of the Security Council having been expressed through its President and by the statements of its members on the extent of compliance by the Government of Iraq with its obligations under the relevant Security Council resolutions, the Security Council has listened with close attention to the statement by the Deputy Prime Minister of Iraq and his responses to the questions posed by Council members.

'The members of the Security Council wish to reiterate their full support for the statement made by the President of the Council on their behalf at the opening of the 3059th meeting (S/23699).

'In the view of the Security Council, the Government of Iraq has not yet complied fully and unconditionally with those obligations, must do so and must immediately take the appropriate actions in this regard. It hopes that the goodwill expressed by the Deputy Prime Minister of Iraq will be matched by deeds.'"

10. BOUNDARY DEMARCATION

In Resolution 687 (1991), the Security Council had demanded that Iraq and Kuwait respect the inviolability of the international boundary and the allocation of islands set out in the Agreed Minutes Between the State of Kuwait and the Republic of Iraq, *signed on 4 October 1963 (Document 2). The Council called on the Secretary-General to lend his assistance to make arrangements with Iraq and Kuwait to demarcate the boundary between Iraq and Kuwait, drawing on appropriate material including a map transmitted by the United Kingdom to the Security Council.*

The following section details the work of the Demarcation Commission and the responses of Iraq, Kuwait and the Security Council to its activities. The maps relevant to this chapter have been reproduced in the Annex.

S/22412, 28 March 1991

1. Letter from the Permanent Representative of the United Kingdom of Great Britain and Northern Ireland to the United Nations addressed to the Secretary-General, 28 March 1991

I am sending you with this letter a set of 10 sheets in the K7611 Series of topographic maps of Kuwait produced, on a scale of 1:50,000, by the United Kingdom Director General of Military Survey. The numbers of the sheets are:

5348 - I Edition 2
5348 - III 3
5349 - II 3
5449 - I 3
5449 - III 1
5449 - IV 3
5449 - I 2
5549 - IV 2
5649 - I 4
5649 - IV 3

The maps have been produced on the basis of the letter of the Prime Minister of Iraq of 21 July 1932 and the letter of the Ruler of Kuwait of 10 August 1932.

As you know those letters do not offer a precise description of the boundary on the ground. You will also notice that the maps carry the standard Director General of Military Survey note as follows:

> "Maps produced under the direction of the Director General of Military Survey are not to be taken as necessarily representing the view of the UK Government on boundaries or political status."

Nevertheless, I hope they will be of use in connection with any demarcation of the Kuwait-Iraq boundary.

[*These maps are reproduced in the Annex.*]

S/22432, 2 April 1991

2. Letter from the Permanent Representative of Kuwait to the United Nations addressed to the Secretary-General, 2 April 1991

I should like to refer to the United Nations Treaty Series No. 7063 which contains the text of the agreed minutes between the State of Kuwait and the Republic of Iraq regarding the restoration of friendly relations, recognition and related matters. ...

NO. 7063. AGREED MINUTES BETWEEN THE STATE OF KUWAIT AND THE REPUBLIC OF IRAQ REGARDING THE RESTORATION OF FRIENDLY RELATIONS, RECOGNITION AND RELATED MATTERS. SIGNED AT BAGHDAD, ON 4 OCTOBER, 1963

In response to the desire felt by both parties to eliminate all that blemishes the relations between both countries, the official Kuwaiti Delegation visiting the Republic of Iraq on an invitation from the Iraqi Prime Minister, held a meeting with the Iraqi Delegation in Baghdad on 4th October, 1963.

The Kuwaiti Delegation was constituted as follows:

H.H. Shaikh Sabah Al-Salim Al-Sabah, Heir Apparent and Prime Minister;
H.E. Shaikh Saad Al-Abdullah Al-Salim Al--Sabah, Minister of the Interior and Acting Minister of Foreign Affairs;
H.E. Khalifa Khalid Al-Ghunaim, Minister of Commerce;
H.E. Ambassador Abdulrahman Ateeqi, Under-Secretary of the Ministry of Foreign Affairs.

The Iraqi Delegation was constituted as follows:

Major-General Ahmad Hassan Al-Bakre, Prime Minister;
First General Salch Mahdi Ammash, Minister of Defence and Acting Minister of Foreign Affairs;
Dr. Mahmoud Mohammad Al-Homsi, Minister of Commerce;

Mr. Mohammad Kayyara, Acting Under-Secretary of Foreign Affairs.

The talks between the two delegations were conducted in an atmosphere rich in fraternal amity, tenacity to the Arab bond and consciousness of the close ties of neighbourliness and mutual interests.

Both sides affirming their deep-rooted desire in reinforcing their relations for the welfare of both countries, inspired by the high Arab aims; and

Believing in the need to rectify all that blemished the Iraqi-Kuwaiti relations as a result of the attitude of the past Kassim regime towards Kuwait before the dawn of the blessed revolution of the 14th of Ramadhan;

Convinced with the national duty dictating the inauguration of a new page consistent with the bonds and relations between the two Arab countries which are free from the artificial gap created by the past regime in Iraq;

Spurred by the belief of the two Governments in the entity of the Arab Nation and the inevitability of its Unity;

And after the Iraqi side having seen the statement delivered by the Government of Kuwait at the Kuwaiti National Assembly on the 9th of April, 1963, embodying the desire of Kuwait to work for the termination, in due time, of the Agreement concluded with the United Kingdom;

The two delegations have agreed to the following:

1. The Republic of Iraq recognized the independence and complete sovereignty of the State of Kuwait with its boundaries as specified in the letter of the Prime Minister of Iraq dated 21.7.1932 and which was accepted by the ruler of Kuwait in his letter dated 10.8.1932;

2. The two Governments shall work towards reinforcing the fraternal relations subsisting between the two sister countries, inspired by their national duty, common interest and aspiration to a complete Arab Unity;

3. The two Governments shall work towards establishing cultural, commercial and economical co-operation between the two countries and the exchange of technical information.

In order to realize all the foregoing objectives, they shall immediately establish diplomatic relations between them at the level of ambassadors.

IN WITNESS WHEREOF the heads of the two delegations have appended their signatures unto these minutes.

Sabah Al-Salim AL-SABAH	Ahmad Hassan AL-BAKRE
Head of Kuwaiti Delegation	Head of Iraqi Delegation

S/22453, 5 April 1991

3. Letter from the Permanent Representative of Kuwait to the United Nations addressed to the Secretary-General, 5 April 1991

I have the honour to enclose a copy of the letter from Sheikh Sabah Al Ahmad Al Jaber Al Sabah, Deputy Prime Minister and Minister for Foreign Affairs, concerning the demarcation of the boundary between the State of Kuwait and the Republic of Iraq.

...

Further to my letter dated 4 April 1991, in which Kuwait welcomed the adoption by the Security Council of resolution 687 (1991), and with a view to facilitating your mission with regard to the demarcation of the boundary between Iraq and Kuwait, I have the honour to inform you that Kuwait confirms its approval of the sheets in the K7611 Series of topographic maps of Kuwait on the scale 1:50,000 referred to in document S/22412. These maps indicate the official land and sea boundaries between Kuwait and the Republic of Iraq and served as a basis for, among other matters relating to bilateral relations, the signature of the "Agreed Minutes between the State of Kuwait and the Republic of Iraq" on 4 October 1963.

...

S/22558, 2 May 1991

4. Report of the Secretary-General regarding paragraph 3 of Security Council Resolution 687 (1991)

1. The present report is submitted pursuant to Security Council resolution 687 (1991) of 3 April 1991. In paragraph 3 of the resolution, the Security Council called upon me to lend assistance to make arrangements with Iraq and Kuwait to demarcate the boundary between Iraq and Kuwait, drawing on appropriate material, including the map transmitted by Security Council document S/22412, and to report back to the Security Council within one month.

2. In lending my assistance to Iraq and Kuwait with a view to making the arrangements to demarcate the boundary between them, I have borne in mind that, in paragraph 2 of Security Council resolution 687 (1991), the Council demanded "that Iraq and Kuwait respect the inviolability of the international boundary and the allocation of islands set out in the 'Agreed Minutes between the State of Kuwait and the Republic of Iraq regarding the Restoration of Friendly Relations, Recognition and Related Matters', signed by them in the exercise of their sovereignty at Baghdad on 4 October 1963 and registered with the United Nations and published by the United Nations in document 7063, United Nations, *Treaty Series*, 1964". I have also taken into account that, in a letter dated 4 April 1991 addressed to me by the Deputy Prime Minister and Minister for Foreign Affairs of Kuwait, Kuwait has expressed its intention to scrupulously comply with all the provisions of resolution 687 (1991) and to cooperate with me with a view to ensuring its implementation (S/22457, annex) and that, in accordance with paragraph 33 of Security Council resolution 687 (1991), the Minister for Foreign Affairs of Iraq in the penultimate paragraph of a letter dated 6 April 1991 (S/22456) has notified the Security Council and the Secretary-General of Iraq's acceptance of the provisions of that resolution. The text of the Agreed Minutes referred to in paragraph 2 of Security Council resolution 687 (1991) is contained in Security Council document S/22432.

3. After consultations with the Governments of Iraq and Kuwait, I will now establish an Iraq-Kuwait Boundary Demarcation Commission, to be composed of one representative each of Iraq and Kuwait and three independent experts who will be appointed by me, one of whom will serve as the Chairman. The Council will be informed as soon as the Commission is established. The terms of reference of the Commission will be to demarcate in geographical coordinates of latitude and longitude the international boundary set out in the Agreed Minutes between Kuwait and Iraq referred to above. In view of the fact that one of the main purposes of the demarcation of the boundary between Kuwait and Iraq is to promote stability and peace and security along the border, the Commission will also make arrangements for

the physical representation of the boundary. The coordinates established by the Commission will constitute the final demarcation of the international boundary between Iraq and Kuwait in accordance with the Agreed Minutes of 4 October 1963. They will be lodged in the archives of both Governments and a certified copy will also be submitted to me, which I will communicate to the Security Council and will retain for safe-keeping in the archives of the United Nations.

4. The demarcation of the boundary between Iraq and Kuwait will be accomplished by drawing upon appropriate material, including the map transmitted by Security Council document S/22412, and by utilizing appropriate technology. The physical representation of the boundary will be carried out through the erection of an appropriate number and type of boundary pillars or monuments. The Commission will provide for arrangements for maintenance on a continuing basis and locational accuracy (including repositioning, if necessary) of the surficial boundary representation.

5. As soon as the Commission is constituted and after an initial assessment of the resources required for the demarcation of the boundary has been made, the Commission will transmit to me an estimate of costs, which I will communicate to the Security Council; simultaneously, I will make a proposal that all costs, including the initial costs of the Commission, should be shared between the two interested parties.

6. The Commission will be assisted by a small staff that will adopt its own rules of procedure and working methods and make the necessary arrangements for the identification and examination of appropriate material relevant to the demarcation of the boundary. The Commission will be responsible to me in the conduct of its work and will report regularly to me on the progress of its work with a view to the earliest possible finalization of the demarcation of the boundary. The Commission will take its decisions by majority. Its decisions regarding the demarcation of the boundary will be final.

7. The Commission shall enjoy unimpeded freedom of movement in the area of the demarcation of the international boundary as well as all necessary privileges and immunities for the fulfilment of its task. The three independent experts shall enjoy the status of experts on missions within the meaning of article VI of the Convention on Privileges and Immunities of the United Nations of 1946.[1] [1. General Assembly resolution 22 A (I).]

8. In the exercise of its task of demarcating the boundary, with respect to physical security and clearance of mines the Commission will rely on the relevant arrangements made for the United Nations Iraq-Kuwait Observer Mission (UNIKOM).

Annex I:

Letter from the Permanent Representative of Kuwait to the United Nations addressed to the Secretary-General, 19 April 1991

I should like to refer to the report regarding paragraph 3 of Security Council resolution 687 (1991) and to convey the acceptance by the Government of Kuwait of the terms set out in the report and its readiness to cooperate with the United Nations in implementing those terms.

Annex II:

Letter from the Permanent Representative of Iraq to the United Nations addressed to the Secretary-General, 23 April 1991

On instructions from my Government and with reference to the meeting that we held with the Legal Counsel of the United Nations, Mr. Fleischhauer, on 17 April 1991, I have the honour to transmit herewith a letter addressed to you by Mr. Ahmed Hussein, Minister for Foreign Affairs of the Republic of Iraq, dated 23 April 1991 concerning the Iraq-Kuwait Boundary Demarcation Commission.

Enclosure:

Letter from the Minister for Foreign Affairs of Iraq addressed to the Secretary-General, 23 April 1991

[Original: Arabic]

With reference to the meeting held between our Permanent Representative and the Legal Counsel of the United Nations on 17 April 1991 and your draft report which you intend to submit to the Security Council concerning paragraph 3 of Security Council resolution 687 (1991) and regarding which you asked for the view of my Government, I have the honour to state the following.

Part I of the letter that I addressed to you on 6 April 1991 explained that, although in its preamble Security Council resolution 687 (1991) affirms that Iraq is an independent sovereign State, many of its iniquitous provisions do not respect this sovereignty but constitute an unprecedented assault on it and on the rights that stem therefrom, embodied in the Charter and in international law and custom. With regard to the question of the boundary, the Security Council has imposed a specific position with regard to the Iraqi-Kuwaiti boundary, whereas the custom in law and in practice in international relations is that boundary questions are left to an agreement between States, because this is the sole basis that can guarantee the principle of the stability of boundaries.

Furthermore, the Council resolution does not take into account the viewpoint of Iraq, namely, that the "Agreed Minutes between the State of Kuwait and the Republic of Iraq regarding the Restoration of Friendly Relations, Recognition and Related Matters" of 4 October 1963 have not yet been subjected to the constitutional procedures required for their ratification by the legislative authority and the President of Iraq, thus leaving the question of the boundary pending and unresolved. The Council has nevertheless imposed on Iraq the line of its boundary with Kuwait. By acting in this strange manner, the Council itself has also violated one of the provisions of resolution 660 (1990), which was the basis for the subsequent resolution adopted by the Council. In its paragraph 3, resolution 660 (1990) called upon Iraq and Kuwait to resolve their differences through negotiations, and the question of the boundary is well known to be one of the main differences. Iraq officially informed the Council that it accepted resolution 660 (1990) and was prepared to implement it, but the Council has disregarded this legal position, contradicting its previous resolutions, and adopted an iniquitous resolution that imposes new conditions on Iraq. It has imposed a border situation on Iraq, an independent sovereign State and Member of the United Nations, and has deprived it of its right to establish its territorial rights in accordance with the principles of international law. Thus the Council would also deprive Iraq of the right to exercise its free choice and to affirm that it accepts that boundary without reservation. Where the question of the boundary is concerned, the Council resolution is an iniquitous resolution, which constitutes a dangerous precedent, a first in the annals of the international Organization and - as some impartial members of the Council indicated in their statements when the resolution was voted on - an assault on the sovereignty of States.

The Iraqi Government remains convinced of the legitimate character of the position reflected in the above observations. This legitimate character is especially borne out by the mission entrusted to you by virtue of paragraph 3 of resolution 687 (1991). The above-mentioned paragraph calls upon you to lend your assistance to make arrangements with Iraq and Kuwait to demarcate the boundary between Iraq and Kuwait, drawing on appropriate material, including the map transmitted by Security Council document S/22412.

Accordingly, my Government wishes to make the comments set forth below concerning your draft report to which I referred above.

1. My Government wonders on what legal foundation the Council based its resolution 687 (1991) and you your draft report in considering the map that was transmitted by Security Council document S/22412, dated 28 March 1991, at the request of the Permanent Mission of the United Kingdom and which your Legal Counsel described to our Permanent Representative as a United Kingdom map mentioned in the Agreed Minutes of 1963. The Agreed Minutes did not refer to any map, as is clear from the text published in the United Nations *Treaty Series*, vol. 485, No. 7063. It is blatantly true also that the sole mention of the map in question in paragraph 3 of Council resolution 687 (1991) was introduced without any legal grounds.

The Government of my country was not a party to the drawing of that map. It did not recognize the map, nor is there any proof of its having extended such recognition. Accordingly, the fact that you and the Council consider the map to be a part of the material to be drawn upon for the demarcation process constitutes an iniquitous and unilateral imposition against the will of Iraq, a sovereign State Member of the United Nations, and a prejudgement of the course of the land boundary before any commission embarks on the process of demarcating that boundary.

2. In addition, the assistance that you have offered in making arrangements for the demarcation of the boundary between Iraq and Kuwait must ensure a perfect balance between the positions that either side may adopt with regard to the demarcation process, together with a just and equitable approach to the settlement of any differences that might arise between them concerning technical matters. The Iraqi Government therefore believes that, if the Commission entrusted with the demarcation process is constituted in accordance with your proposal, the result cannot be just and equitable, particularly in view of our comments in paragraph 1 above. You have suggested that the Commission consist of five members, of whom two would represent Iraq and Kuwait respectively, together with three independent experts to be chosen by you, one of whom would be appointed as the Chairman. You have also suggested that the Commission's decisions should be taken by a majority vote. Although it has no doubts as to your credibility with respect to the selection of the three independent experts, my country's Government nevertheless believes that, since it will play no part in the selection of the three experts, it will have no way of ensuring in advance that they are truly independent. Its views with regard to the demarcation process will thus be represented only by one of the five members.

3. You mention in the draft report that the demarcation of the boundary will be accomplished by drawing upon appropriate material, including the map transmitted by Security Council document S/22412, as referred to in paragraph 3 of resolution 687 (1991). However, you add that the Commission may "utilize appropriate technology" (para. 4 of the draft report) and that it will "make the necessary arrangements for the identification and examination of appropriate material relevant to the demarcation of the boundary" (para. 6 of the draft report). The Government of Iraq believes that the terms "appropriate material", "appropriate technology" and "identification and examination of appropriate material relevant to the demarcation of the boundary" must be explained. This explanation will permit my Government to express its views, if such views are welcome, on a solid basis. The requested explanation will also help to reduce the possibilities of disagreement in the future when the Commission begins its work.

4. You propose in paragraph 5 of the draft report that the costs of the demarcation process should be shared between the two parties. The Government of Iraq fails to understand the basis for this proposal, since the overall thrust of the proposals contained in the draft report amounts - in the opinion of my Government - to a virtual "act of capitulation" in which Iraq is denied any freedom to join in the harmonious agreement of its contents. Accordingly, and in the light of my comments at the beginning of this letter, the suggestion seems to be that Iraq should bear half the costs of the demarcation process without any account being taken of its views on the boundary question as a whole, with respect to either demarcation or delimitation. The Iraqi Government cannot therefore see any justification, based on principles of justice or equity, for bearing any costs relating to a process which is imposed upon it.

I should like, in conclusion, to assure you that the Iraqi Government is fully prepared to consult with you concerning the comments contained in this letter, either in New York or elsewhere. In this connection, I also wish to note that, just as we accepted resolution 687 (1991) despite our objections to any criticism of its provisions, we will cooperate with you and will nominate a representative of our Government to participate in the Demarcation Commission, even if you take no account of the views and comments we have expressed above. We do this because the circumstances forcing our acceptance persist.

Annex III

Letter from the Secretary-General addressed to the Minister for Foreign Affairs of Iraq, 30 April 1991

I have the honour to refer to your letter dated 23 April 1991, which was transmitted to me by a letter of the same date from the Permanent Representative of Iraq to the United Nations and which contained comments on the proposals made with regard to the implementation of paragraph 3 of Security Council resolution 687 (1991) and on which I must report to the Security Council no later than 2 May 1991. In informing me of your Government's readiness to cooperate with me and to nominate a representative of Iraq to participate in the proposed Boundary Demarcation Commission, a decision which I welcome, the letter nevertheless contains a number of comments to which I would like to respond.

The first comment of your Government is that, in international law, a boundary demarcation between two States can be carried out only by agreement between the parties and that the Security Council has no competence to impose such a demarcation. In this connection, I would like to recall that, in paragraph 2 of resolution 687 (1991) the Security Council, acting under Chapter VII of the Charter of the United Nations demanded that Iraq and Kuwait respect the inviolability of their international boundary and the allocation of islands "set out in the 'Agreed Minutes between the State of Kuwait and the Republic of Iraq regarding the Restoration of Friendly Relations, Recognition and Related Matters', signed by them in the exercise of their sovereignty at Baghdad on 4 October 1963". In paragraph 3 of that resolution the Council called upon me to lend my "assistance to make arrangements with Iraq and Kuwait to demarcate the boundary between Iraq and Kuwait". In identical letters dated 6 April 1991 addressed to me and to the President of the Security Council (S/22456), your Government formally notified its acceptance of the provisions of that resolution. You further reconfirmed your Government's acceptance of paragraph 3 of resolution 687 (1991) at the end of your letter of 23 April 1991 ... Therefore, the element of agreement as far as Iraq is concerned, is provided by your Government's official notifications of acceptance. Since the Government of Kuwait has also expressed to me its willingness scrupulously to comply with all provisions of the resolution and to cooperate with me to ensure its implementation (S/22457), the necessary element of consent has been provided by the two parties.

Secondly, your Government states that the proposed demarcation would be prejudged by a specific reference to a map made available by the United Kingdom and which, according to the letter, the Legal Counsel described as "a United Kingdom map mentioned in the agreed minutes of 1963". On a purely factual point, I wish to state that the Legal Counsel of the United Nations did not describe the map as having been mentioned in the 1963 agreed minutes. In response to a question as to which map was referred to in document S/22412, your Permanent Representative was informed that the map in question was "a United Kingdom map". On a substantive level, however, I am obliged to point out that the resolution provides that the demarcation of the boundary should be based on "appropriate material, *including* the map transmitted by Security Council document S/22412" [emphasis added]. In the light of this wording, I have proposed that the Commission will have to make "necessary arrangements for the identification and examination of appropriate material relevant to the demarcation of the boundary".

Thirdly, your Government queries the independence of the experts to be appointed by me to serve on the Boundary Commission and comments on the proposed decision-making by majority. I would like to assure you that, in appointing the independent experts of the Commission, I shall, as always, base my decisions on the need to ensure independence, competence and integrity. Furthermore, to ensure an equitable approach and the effective functioning of the Commission, I have proposed that neither Government should be able to frustrate the work of the Commission.

Fourthly, your Government has requested me to explain such terms as "appropriate material", "appropriate technology" and "identification and examination of appropriate material relevant to the demarcation of the boundary". It is up to the Commission to examine and identify the relevant documentation and to determine which technology or combination of methods can best be used for the fulfilment of its mandate. In my view it would prejudice the work of the Commission, and even hinder its independence, if at this stage I were to go beyond the level of detail concerning the working methods of the Boundary Commission set out in my draft report.

Finally, your Government objects to paying half of the costs of the demarcation on the ground that its views on the boundary question are not fully being taken into account. However, through your Government's participation in the work of the Boundary Commission its views will find such expression. Together with your Government's acceptance of paragraph 3 of resolution 687 (1991), both in its letter of 6 April 1991 (S/22456) as well as in the letter of 23 April 1991, I can see no basis for objections to the paying of its share of the costs, which will be determined by the Commission.

In the light of your Government's expressed readiness to cooperate with me, I intend to proceed immediately with the establishment of the Commission and will accordingly convey my proposals, together with this exchange of correspondence, to the Security Council.

5. Press Release by the Iraq-Kuwait Boundary Demarcation Commission, 24 May 1991

The Iraq-Kuwait Boundary Demarcation Commission held its first meeting on 23-24 May 1991 at the United Nations Headquarters in New York.

The exchange of views and discussions were held in a cordial atmosphere with a spirit of cooperation. The Commission considered the task at hand which is to demarcate the Iraq-Kuwait Boundary. Organization of the work and a tentative schedule were drawn up. The Commission had decided to undertake an on-site visit in June. Substantive discussions on the actual plan of work will start on the 2nd of July at the United Nations Headquarters in Geneva.

6. Press Release by the Iraq-Kuwait Boundary Demarcation Commission, 19 June 1991

The Iraq-Kuwait Boundary Demarcation Commission completed an on-site visit from the 16th to the 18th of June 1991.

The independent experts of the Commission, appointed by the Secretary-General, held fruitful discussions with the Kuwaiti representative and Kuwaiti experts in Kuwait City as well as with the Iraqi representative and Iraqi experts in Baghdad. On the 18th of June, the entire Commission, accompanied by experts from Iraq and Kuwait inspected the entire length of the border area. The flight over the border area was facilitated by UNIKOM officers and helicopters. Commission members will review the findings of the on-site visit and commence substantive discussions on the 2nd of July at United Nations Headquarters in Geneva.

7. Press Release by the Iraq-Kuwait Boundary Demarcation Commission, 15 July 1991

The Iraq-Kuwait Boundary Demarcation Commission has just concluded its second round of talks held in Geneva on 2-12 July 1991.

Decisions were reached on the methodology to be applied in demarcating the western portion, on the approximate location of the boundary in the vicinity of Safwan in the northern section, and on the need to undertake new survey and mapping to facilitate final demarcation. Surveying on a wide zone around the boundary will be undertaken by the national survey departments of New Zealand and Sweden in a joint venture. The next round of talks is scheduled for 12 August 1991 in Geneva.

8. Press Release by the Iraq-Kuwait Boundary Demarcation Commission, 16 August 1991

The Iraq-Kuwait Boundary Demarcation Commission held its third session at the United Nations Office in Geneva on 12-16 August 1991.

The Commission completed consideration of material available for the demarcation of the eastern portion of the boundary. It authorized its independent experts to undertake a survey and mapping of the entire border and to prepare material on various technical questions and report on that to the Commission. The Commission plans to meet again in mid-October to consider the experts' work and its own report. The results and the products of the mapping will be available in February 1992.

9. Press Release by the Iraq-Kuwait Boundary Demarcation Commission, 15 October 1991

The Iraq-Kuwait Boundary Demarcation Commission held its fourth session at United Nations Headquarters in New York from 7 to 15 October 1991.

The Commission reviewed and approved the final work plan for the surveying and mapping of the border area and received a report on the installation of a 10-man ground survey team. The first stage of control surveying began on 1 October 1991 with the assistance of UNIKOM. A specially outfitted aircraft for aerial photography has also arrived in Kuwait from Sweden and will shortly commence this stage of the operation.

At the current session, the Commission also prepared its first report on its work, together with an estimated budget. This report shall be submitted to the Secretary-General in due time.

During the first week of November, the two independent experts will visit the border area to review the progress of the field work. It is experted that the maps for the actual demarcation of the boundary will be ready at the end of February 1992.

10. Press Release by the Iraq-Kuwait Boundary Demarcation Commission, 5 March 1992

The joint team from the National Survey Offices of New Zealand and Sweden completed its work in the border area. In November 1991, the two independent experts of the Commission travelled to the region and reviewed the conclusion of the field survey. They visited a number of survey stations along the demilitarized zone as well as certain specific locations, such as the village of Safwan, with respect to the demarcation of the boundary.

At the present time, data gathered in the field is being analyzed for the purposes of producing a set of large-scale orthophoto maps, covering the entire length of the boundary, and a series of cross-sectional profiles of the Wadi Al-Batin. Digital terrain mapping will also be done. This new, highly accurate survey, along with earlier maps, charts, aerial photographs and other documents, will be used to determine the precise boundary for demarcation purposes as mandated by Security Council resolution 687 and set out in the 1963 agreed minutes between Kuwait and Iraq.

Contrary to recent reports in the media, no recommendations or decisions on the boundary have yet been made. The Commission will next meet in New York from 8 to 16 April 1992. At that time, it will review the results of the surveying and mapping and address the actual demarcation of the boundary.

11. Press Release by the Iraq-Kuwait Boundary Demarcation Commission, 16 April 1992

The Iraq-Kuwait Boundary Demarcation Commission held its fifth session at United Nations Headquarters in New York from 8 to 16 April 1992.

The Commission reviewed the field work of the Joint New Zealand-Swedish Survey Team which provided the basis of the orthophoto mapping of the Iraq-Kuwait border area. For the control survey 4 datum stations and 25 primary control stations were established at approximately 15 to 25 kilometre intervals along the boundary and were observed with Doppler and GPS equipment. Aerial photography was carried out by the Swedish team in a specially outfitted Rockwell turbo commander aircraft from two main altitudes, at 5,500 metres and at 3,000 metres, producing images with respective scales of 1:36,000 and 1:19,600. Photo control consisted of a network of over 200, pre-signalized control stations.

From the control survey and aerial photography the National Survey offices of New Zealand and Sweden produced a set of 29 orthophoto maps at the scale of 1:25,000 with elevation contours at 5 metre intervals. The map projection used for orthophoto mapping is the Universal Transverse Mercator (UTM) projection, Zone 38 extended eastward to cover the entire boundary area.

Additional detailed mapping was undertaken for the western part of the boundary defined by Wadi Al-Batin. Approximately 1,420, three and a half kilometre long, transverse, photogrammetric profiles were created at 100 metre intervals for the length of the Wadi. These were used to determine the lowest point line in the Wadi. Digital terrain models were also created to generate 2-metre elevation contours. Computer generated three-dimensional presentations were used as well to interpret the data.

Pursuant to earlier decisions, the independent experts of the Commission requested the representatives of Iraq and Kuwait to provide them with any and all relevant information. The independent experts presented to the Commission exhaustive analyses in detailed documentations of all available data for the determination of the location of the boundary at key points: south of Safwan, northern end of Wadi Al-Batin, Umm Qasr on the western shore of Khowr Zhobeir and the junction of Khowr Zhobeir and Khowr Abd Allah.

At Safwan, the independent experts were able to identify the old customs post and the old road from aerial photographs and by positioning techniques. Accordingly the independent experts were able to reestablish the position of the noticeboard south of Safwan as close as possible to its original location marking the boundary during the period of 1923-1939. The boundary due west of this point is in terms with all previous boundary depictions in direction and it originates from the reestablished position of the noticeboard. The boundary at Umm Qasr is in terms of the early map depictions and the map in Security Council document S/22412.

These results were compared with and transferred to the new, highly precise, orthophoto maps and were fully discussed by the Commission at the present session.

Adhering to the delimitation formula, and based on the findings of the independent experts and the deliberations of the Commission, the Commission has reached the following decisions on the boundary by voting with Iraq not participating in the vote:

1. That the boundary monument on the Iraq-Saudi Arabian border, Pillar No. 1, shall be the starting point for the boundary along the Thalweg of Wadi Al-Batin, and therefore, the tripoint of Iraq, Kuwait and Saudi Arabia;

2. That the boundary south of Safwan shall be located at the distance of 1,430 metres from the south-west extremity of the compound wall of the old customs post along the old road from Safwan to Kuwait;

3. That the boundary at the northern end of Wadi Al-Batin shall be the intersection of the Thalweg of the Wadi and the latitude of the point south of Safwan;

4. That the boundary south of Umm Qasr shall coincide with the location at which the boundary line on map sheet 5549-I of Series K7611, Edition 2 (1990), produced by the Military Survey of the United Kingdom, crosses the western shore of Khowr Zhobeir; and

5. That the junction of Khowr Zhobeir and Khowr Abd Allah shall be the one best identified for the epoch 1932 and transposed onto modern orthophoto maps produced by the Commission.

The Commission has further decided that,

(A) The boundary line in the Wadi Al-Batin shall be a series of straight line segments of about 2 kilometres length best approximating to the lowest point line in the Wadi;

(B) The boundary line from the point at the northern end of the Wadi Al-Batin to the point south of Safwan shall be a line running along the common latitude of the points;

(C) The boundary line from the point south of Safwan to the point south of Umm Qasr shall be the shortest line between the points; and that

(D) The boundary line from the point south of Umm Qasr on the shore shall follow the low water line up to the location of directly opposite the junction of Khowr Zhobeir and Khowr Abd Allah.

Immediately following the present session, the Commission will mark each of the three key points along the boundary with a temporary pillar. Physical representation of the boundary on the ground is expected to take place in the latter part of 1992.

The Commission also gave further consideration to the boundary in the Khowr Abd Allah. This matter, as well as the consideration of the Commission's report to the Secretary-General on the present session, will be taken up at the next session of the Commission scheduled for July 1992.

The Commission has thus been able to draw the line of the boundary to the best of its ability and in light of all available information.

S/24044, 1 June 1992

12. Letter from the Permanent Representative of Iraq to the United Nations addressed to the Secretary-General, 21 May 1992

On instructions from my Government I wish to transmit herewith a letter dated 21 May 1992 from Mr. Ahmad Hussein, Minister for Foreign Affairs of the Republic of Iraq, concerning the decisions to demarcate the land boundary between Iraq and Kuwait adopted by the Commission you appointed in connection with that boundary.

...

Letter from the Minister for Foreign Affairs of Iraq addressed to the Secretary-General, 21 May 1992

You are, no doubt, aware of the decisions of your appointed Commission on the subject of the Iraq-Kuwait boundary-line, which were adopted on 14 April 1992, during the Commission's fifth session in New York, and upon which the boundary demarcation is to be based.

On this occasion I would like to elucidate to you the viewpoint of the Government of Iraq regarding this matter which, in view of its vital importance, is serious not only to Iraq's interests, but also to the common interests, be it in our Arab region or the other regions in the world that witness international disputes regarding boundaries.

First, before anything else, I would like to refer to my letter to Your Excellency of 6 April 1991, regarding the Government of Iraq's position on Security Council resolution 687 (1991), adopted by the Council on 4 April 1991 (S/22456). I dealt in the first section of my letter with what was specified in the aforementioned resolution with regard to the subject of the boundary between Iraq and Kuwait. In this respect I stated in my letter the following:

> "While in its preamble, the resolution reaffirms that Iraq is an independent sovereign State, the fact remains that a good number of its iniquitous provisions impair that sovereignty. In fact, the resolution constitutes an unprecedented assault on the sovereignty, and the rights that stem therefrom, embodied in the Charter and in international law and practice. For example, where the question of boundaries is concerned, the Security Council has determined in advance the boundary between Iraq and Kuwait. And yet it is well known, from the juridical and practical standpoint, that in international relations boundary issues must be the subject of an agreement between States, since this is the only basis capable of guaranteeing the stability of frontiers.
>
> "Moreover, the resolution fails to take into account Iraq's view, which is well known to the Council, that the provisions relating to the boundary between Iraq and Kuwait contained in the "Agreed Minutes between the State of Kuwait and the Republic of Iraq regarding the Restoration of Friendly Relations, Recognition and Related Matters" dated 4 October 1963 have not yet been subjected to the constitutional procedures required for ratification of the Agreed Minutes by the legislative branch and the President of Iraq, thus leaving the question of the boundary pending and unresolved. The Council has nevertheless imposed on Iraq a boundary with Kuwait. By acting in this strange manner, the Council itself has also violated one of the provisions of resolution 660, which served as the basis for its subsequent resolutions. In its paragraph 3, resolution 660 calls upon Iraq and Kuwait to resolve their differences through negotiation, and the question of the boundary is well known to be one of the main differences. Iraq officially informed the Council that it accepted resolution 660 and was prepared to apply it, but the Council has gone beyond this legal position, contradicting its previous resolutions, and adopted an iniquitous resolution which imposes on Iraq, an independent and sovereign State and a Member of the United Nations, new conditions and a situation which deprives it of its right to establish its territorial rights in accordance with the principles of international law. Thus the Council is also depriving Iraq of its right to exercise its free choice and to affirm that it accepts the boundary without reservation. Where the question of the boundary is concerned, the Council resolution is an iniquitous resolution which constitutes a dangerous precedent, a first in the annals of the international Organization and - as some impartial members of the Council indicated in their Statements when the resolution was voted on - an assault on the sovereignty of States.
>
> "It is also to be noted that the United States of America, the author of the original draft resolution on which resolution 687, which imposes a solution to the boundary and other differences between Iraq and Kuwait, was based, refused to impose any solution whatsoever on its ally, Israel, in accordance with conventions, United Nations resolutions and international law.

> "Furthermore, the United States of America is preventing the Security Council from assuming the responsibilities incumbent upon it with respect to the Arab-Zionist conflict, the Israeli policy of annexation of the occupied Arab territories, the establishment of settlements, the displacement of populations and the disregard for the rights of the Palestinian people and the neighbouring Arab countries, by vetoing any draft resolution approved by the remaining members of the Council, for the simple reason that Israel does not want a resolution which favours a just settlement of the conflict."

Second, in paragraph 3 of resolution 687 (1991), the Security Council called upon the Secretary-General "to lend his assistance to make arrangements with Iraq and Kuwait to demarcate the boundary between Iraq and Kuwait, drawing on appropriate material, including the map transmitted by Security Council document S/22412 and to report back to the Security Council within one month;". In accordance with this, the Secretary-General prepared a draft report which was presented by the Legal Counsel of the United Nations Secretariat to Iraq's Permanent Representative to the United Nations in New York during a meeting that was held between them on 17 April 1991, asking him to present the Iraqi Government's opinion. We have presented our remarks in my letter dated 23 April 1991 (S/22558, annex II, enclosure), and which can be summed up in the following points:

1. The unavailability of any legal basis for the Security Council's consideration of the map attached to document S/22412 dated 28 March 1991 upon a request from the Permanent Mission of the United Kingdom of Great Britain and Northern Ireland amongst the appropriate material which the process of demarcation depends upon. The Iraqi Government has not been a party in the drawing of the said map; also, it has not recognized it and there is no evidence of such recognition. On this basis, the consideration of this map amongst the materials upon which the process of the demarcation depends is tantamount to an arbitrary imposition from a single party on the will of Iraq, which is a sovereign State and a Member of the United Nations. It is also a preconceived judgement on the course of the border line on the ground before any commission has embarked on the process of boundary demarcation.

2. Lending assistance from the Secretary-General for laying down measures to demarcate the boundary between Iraq and Kuwait must offer complete balance between the extremes any of the two parties might go to in the course of implementing the demarcation process, and provide for the solution of disputes that might arise between them in their technical positions, a method which ensures justice and fairness. From this standpoint, we observed that the composition of the Commission that was proposed by the Secretary-General for implementing the process of demarcation could not render justice and fairness and in particular, in the light of what is explained in section 1 above. The Secretary-General had proposed that the Commission be composed of five members, two representing Iraq and Kuwait and three independent experts chosen by the Secretary-General who appoints one of them as Chairman of the Commission. The Secretary-General also suggested that the Commission's decisions be taken by a majority vote. Nevertheless, the Government of Iraq expressed at the same time its belief that, as long as it would not have any role in the choice of the said experts, then it would not be able to confirm in advance the fact of their independence; hence its opinion in the course of the demarcation process would be represented by a single member only, out of five members.

3. In addition to what was provided in resolution 687 (1991) about the basis upon which the process of demarcation depends, the Secretary-General's draft report provided other bases that were expressed in a vague and undetermined manner. The draft report mentioned that the Commission could utilize "appropriate technology" and that the Commission would "make the necessary arrangements for the identification and examination of appropriate material relevant to the demarcation of the boundary". It is for this reason that Iraq had requested the elucidation of these concepts because it would help to minimize the possibilities of dispute in the future when the Commission embarked on its work.

4. The Secretary-General's draft report imposed upon Iraq half the expenses of the demarcation process. This prompted the Government of Iraq to question the basis of this opinion as long as the overall content of the suggestions, provided in the draft report, seemed to be almost a "contract of adhesion" in which Iraq had no free will to agree consensually on its content. It was proposed that Iraq bear half the expenses of the demarcation process without having any consideration for its opinion in the overall boundary process, whether in its delimitation or in its demarcation. From this standpoint the Iraqi Government did not find any justification on the basis of the rules of justice and fairness to bear any expenses of a process which was imposed upon it.

It is worth mentioning that the Government of Iraq had assured the Secretary-General of its full readiness for consultations regarding its stated remarks, whether it be in New York or any other place. It had also been indicated that, like Iraq's acceptance of resolution 687 (1991), in spite of its objections to it and its criticism of its contents, the Iraqi Government would cooperate with the Secretary-General and would nominate its representative in the Demarcation Commission even if the Secretary-General did not take into consideration the remarks and views of the Iraqi Government owing to the continuation of the same circumstances which imposed acceptance upon Iraq.

The Secretary-General replied in his letter, dated 30 April 1991 (S/22558, annex III), to the remarks and views of Iraq. He relied in his reply on the text of resolution 687 (1991) regarding the basis of demarcation as if they were unknown to Iraq, and he expressed to Iraq his assurances that he would be keen to guarantee the independence of the experts. He referred to the Demarcation Commission the task of interpreting some of the vague concepts of the demarcation bases on the pretext that his interpretation would affect the independence of the Commission's work. He stated that Iraq's participation in the Commission would enable the Iraqi Government to express its views, hence it had to bear half the expenses of the demarcation process. The Secretary-General did not target, with such replies, the substantive issue of Iraq's remarks and views, the point of which had been to hope that the Secretary-General would seek, in the light of the imposition by the Security Council resolution of a boundary delimitation formula between Iraq and Kuwait and the basis of the boundary demarcation process, to ensure justice and fairness throughout by the achievement of balance and equality between the positions of the two parties in some very vital aspects, namely, the method of the Commission's composition, the manner of carrying out its technical task, the method of taking its decisions, the nature of the said decisions and their characteristics, and other important matters. For that matter the Iraqi Government had called for consultations, a call which was totally ignored by the Secretary-General after he had submitted his draft report, without any alterations, to the Security Council in document S/22558 dated 2 May 1991. Yet, in spite of all this Iraq participated in the Commission's work.

Third, as you know, the Commission held its first session in New York on 23 and 24 May 1991. During that session, which dealt with organizational matters, the Commission decided that its work was "technical and not political" and that the nature of the task entrusted to it related solely to "the demarcation of the boundary". It requested the two independent experts Mr. Ian Brook (Sweden) and Mr. William Robertson (New Zealand) to present a plan of work during the next session.

The second session was held in Geneva from 2 to 12 July 1991. The two independent experts presented in that session a "discussion paper", which contained, as they put it, background information on the interpretation of the boundary demarcation which could be considered as the starting-point in the discussions of the Commission.

As you are aware, the Commission adopted during that session a number of crucial decisions, both substantive and technical, by which it settled the fundamental bases of what was to be the course of the land boundary. This was done in an atmosphere distinguished by a number of characteristics that cannot be overlooked by any fair and objective observer. Permit me to take one example of the manner in which the Commission reached one of its major decisions on substance, namely the one relating to the creation of a turning-point at Safwan, a point which controlled the overall course of what was called the northern frontier in the direction towards the east. The two independent experts relied in their interpretation of the said direction on cartographic considerations based fundamentally on British correspondence and maps going back to the period when Britain was the dominating colonial Power in the region. In their attempt to substantiate their viewpoint, the two experts referred to some Iraqi maps in order to prove the existence of Iraqi concepts of the boundary despite the fact that the maps presented contained explicitly a disclaimer which has the effect of negating any recognition, implied acceptance or acquiescence in regard to demarcation. The two experts also sought to substantiate their viewpoint on the Iraqi concept of demarcation by relying on an Iraqi diplomatic note going back to June 1940, which related to the position of the noticeboard placed by the British south of Safwan, and on an Iraqi proposal relating to the demarcation of the boundary between Safwan and the sea which entailed an amendment of a formula called the delimitation formula of 1932. This was done, although everybody knows that Iraq has never accepted any formula relating to demarcation, whether British or otherwise, and that Britain had rejected the Iraqi note of 1940, and that it had marred the Iraqi proposal of 1955, which Kuwait rejected. In response to the views of the experts in this connection, the representative of Iraq, for example, pointed out that in the creation of a turning-point on the course of the so-called boundary at Safwan the two experts failed to look precisely at the formula in the 1932 document; they simply concentrated their attention on maps. It is clear from the said formula that Safwan was mentioned twice: once as "south of the latitude of Safwan" to describe the terminal point of the boundary line in the western area in Wadi al-Batin only and for no other purpose, and the second as "passing south of the Safwan Wells" to describe the course of the boundary line eastward from the point at al-Batin to the point of intersection between Khowr Abd Allah and Khowr Zhobeir. It is very clear, therefore, that the turning-point at Safwan was created without any justification. The representative of Iraq also pointed out in this regard that depending purely on a cartographic point of view on the question would present an incomplete picture of the appropriate material. To substantiate this point, the representative of Iraq requested the Commission to look into the factual phenomena of territorial encroachment by the Kuwaiti authorities in a northward direction after 1963. This was achieved by moving border posts, border police and oil excavation sites and the establishment of agricultural plantations. All these acts were protested by Iraqi notes presented through official channels. All those notes referred to the "area of the border" and not to a specific line. The representative of Iraq showed the Commission a compilation of documents which represented photocopies of passports that used to be stamped at a site fixed by the Kuwaiti authorities at "al-Mitla'a" in the 1960s, and which moved to the north more than 70 kilometres. The representative of Iraq stated that a translation of those documents and notes would be made in order to present them to the Commission. He noted that Iraq had not presented them at that session of the Commission as it was not possible to know what needed to be presented before looking at the report of the two experts; and so he requested the Commission to make the time available for that. In this connection, the representative of Iraq recalled that, during the visit carried out by the Commission to the area separating Iraq and Kuwait in June 1991, he had pointed out that the Commission should grant its members ample opportunity to carry out precise research in archives and libraries in order to do a clean and honest job.

I have referred above in a concentrated fashion to the manner in which the Commission has dealt with one fundamental point among those relating to the course of the border as an example in order to clarify the picture of how the material known as "appropriate material" was handled. Actually, what I stated in regard to this point applies also to all others. The fact is that the Commission, instead of being patient in deciding upon matters and waiting for the presentation of the documents and notes referred to by the representative of Iraq, prevented all that by adopting in clear haste substantial technical decisions in regard to the demarcation of the so-called land boundary. This was done under the influence of clear pressure from the representative of the rulers of Kuwait. The decisions came successively one after another through a steam-rolling process led by the representative of Kuwait in full harmony with the two experts. The said representative addressed leading questions which ended with proposals for a vote, some of which were formulated in consultations between him and the two experts. Hence, the Commission did not pay attention to the correct application of the rules of procedure, neither did it pay any attention to the interrelated nature of the substance of the questions to be decided upon, with the result that the one decision negatively affected the substance of the following decision. In addition, the decisions of the Commission far exceeded the bounds of the recommendations presented by the two experts.

Moreover, the decisions were adopted in full contradiction with the delimitation formula. The haste in the adoption of the substantive and technical decisions during the second session was justified by the pretext that the report of the Secretary-General had stated that the demarcation should be achieved as soon as possible in order to promote stability and peace and security along the border (S/22558, para. 4). But in fact the Commission had ended up with one-sided decisions both in source and in substance. Here again emerges another fundamental fact, which cannot be overlooked. The question of the boundary between Iraq and Kuwait was thought of, initiated and set in motion along preconceived lines in order to end with options imposed upon Iraq whether in regard to delimitation or demarcation of the boundary without any regard to Iraq's interests and all the historical facts which support them. In doing so, no room was left for rendering justice and equity to Iraq's territorial interests. Security Council resolution 687 (1991) imposed the delimitation formula and the pursuit in a preconceived manner of demarcation by interposing the concept of the appropriate material and the consideration of a British map as included in such material. Then came the report of the Secretary-General to complete the preconceived imposition through the manner chosen for the composition of the Commission, the method of adopting its decisions and the addition of further points for the demarcation process when the Commission was constrained to demarcate the international boundary in geographical coordinates of latitude and longitude. All this led *a priori* to the adoption of pure cartographic evidence without leaving any possibility for the presentation of any other evidence drawn from other appropriate material.

It is worth noting that the Commission could not consider for lack of time the question of intersection of Khowr Abd Allah with Khowr Zhobeir, which represents the eastern point of the boundary line. This question was taken up by the Commission during its third session held in Geneva from 12 to 16 August 1991. In this connection, the two independent experts opted for the view that the determination of the position of the intersection should be made in the epoch of 1932 as that was the period in which the exchange of letters had taken place. This view was supported by the Chairman.

What should not be overlooked is that the Commission has reached that conclusion after prolonged discussions, which seem to have been prompted by the desire to placate, and show courtesy to, the representative of Kuwait at the expense of full adherence to the rules of procedure. The said representative sought to achieve two objectives. The first was to determine the position of the point in question as it is today in order to deprive Iraq of its historic rights in the waters of the intersection of the Khowrs. The second objective was to push the Commission into demarcating the maritime boundary in Khowr Abd Allah despite the fact that the mandate of the Commission did not include that. At any rate, this second objective still stands, for the Commission granted the representative of the Kuwaiti authorities the opportunity to present the subject again in its fifth session held in New York from 8 to 16 April 1992 and decided to continue with its consideration at its next session.

After the Commission had adopted its decisions in regard to the fundamental points of demarcation of the land boundary, the technical criteria for the operation of demarcation and the technical measures to be carried out in the field, the experts went on to implement those decisions during the period falling between the third and fifth sessions of the Commission. As you know, the Commission decided upon the land boundary line at its fifth session held in New York recently. In this connection, it is necessary to record some essential facts.

In implementing a technical decision adopted by the Commission at its second session, the two independent experts investigated the position of a turning-point of what was called the boundary at Safwan in a manner that flatly contradicted the substance of the said decision. The decision of the Commission, which was adopted on 11 July 1991, authorized the experts to conduct investigations and collect information necessary to enable the Commission to decide upon the northern boundary precisely. It emerged during the fifth session of the Commission that the representative of Kuwait and his experts had accompanied the independent experts in their investigations in the area of Safwan contrary to the decision of the Commission. As is clear from the discussion raised by the representative of Iraq on the question at the 33rd meeting of the Commission, the representative of Iraq was informed of this after the investigation had been carried out, and he had in fact objected to the idea on the basis of the decision of the Commission as soon as he was informed of it.

It is also clear that the experts did not only accompany the representative of the authorities in Kuwait and his experts to witness the determination of the position of the turning-point at Safwan but also they had relied on the opinion of the Kuwaiti experts in addition to the British sources. Accordingly, the representative of the Kuwaiti authorities participated in the determination of the position of the point at Safwan in the field despite the fact that he is a party with a direct interest in the question and that the decision of the Commission did not authorize anyone to proceed along those lines, in which the representative of Iraq was tricked contrary to the principles of ethics and good faith.

The turning-point for the land boundary at Safwan was created contrary to what was stated in the text of the delimitation formula in the 1932 document as we explained simply because the British officials had decided during the period of their colonial authority in the area to demarcate that point. The experts had taken an Iraqi note of 1941 as a starting-point in the creation of the point in question despite the fact that the successive Iraqi Governments have not agreed at all to any formula to demarcate the boundary as we explained.

It is worth noting that the experts of the Commission were not content to rely only on the British sources in demarcating the boundary from that point to the west and east, on the basis that the said demarcation is dictated by the cartographic and the technical nature of the task entrusted to the Commission, as the Commission itself had emphasized on many occasions since its first session. This is because the state of the deliberations of the Commission clearly indicates the contrary, as, at the 34th meeting, the experts expressed their opinion on the necessary force to be given to evidence relating to occupation when they carried out the demarcation. The Commission approved what the experts opted for, which resulted in seizing very large areas of Iraqi territory fully acknowledged to be so before with all that it contains of the oil resources which were not unknown to the British colonialists who used to control the region. Iraqi citizens were deprived of their homes and plantations, which constitute their source of income and which they have inherited from generation to generation throughout history. This is in addition to depriving Iraq of numerous installations and of any meaningful access to the sea. As for the position of the oil wells, the Kuwaiti authorities themselves acknowledged their trespass thereon through Saad al Abdullah during the meeting with the Deputy Chairman of the Revolution Command Council of Iraq held in Jeddah on 30 July 1990.

There is yet another fundamental fact which should be recorded for history. The work of the Commission, and the speed with which it adopted its decisions in regard to demarcation, was not immune from interference by the Secretariat. All the members of the Commission are fully aware of the fact that the Senior Political Adviser to the Secretary-General, Mr. Alvaro de Soto, called in the Chairman of the Commission, its two experts and its Secretary in the morning of 13 April 1992 and pressed them to complete the work speedily and without hesitation. This uncalled-for interference was prompted by a request from the Permanent Representative of Kuwait to the United Nations. Some quarters may imagine that this intervention was in harmony with what was stated in the report of the Secretary-General that the Commission was responsible in the conduct of its work to the Secretary-General (S/22558, para. 6). If this is so, such an imagination is not well-founded, because the Commission is not only composed of the Chairman and the two independent experts but also includes in addition a representative of each of the parties.

One of the striking facts relating to the results of the work of the Commission is that the United Nations Commission came out with a boundary line on the basis of British sources and interpretations which is worse for Iraq's interests than the British line drawn on the basis of the same sources and interpretations on the British map (S/22412) referred to in Security Council resolution 687 (1991) and which successive Iraqi Governments did not recognize.

Fourth, the results which the Commission reached contradict the facts of history and geography.

Iraq is known to have always been a political entity and the seat of more than one civilization throughout history. It is a fact known for millenia. Throughout its long history, Iraq has always been a coastal State and a major trading centre. The small village established some two centuries ago on the banks of the Arabian Gulf under the name of "Kuwait", an Iraqi term for "a small settlement of people", remained throughout the nineteenth century and up to the First World War an Iraqi Qadhaa' (district) belonging to the Province of Basrah. Under Ottoman administrative law, Kuwait was an integral part of Iraq, subject to the Province of Basrah.

In 1897, the Governor of Basrah, Muhsin Pasha, informed the Sheikh of Kuwait, Mubarak al-Sabah, of the Sultan's decree appointing him as Qa'im-Maqam (District Administrator) of the Qadhaa' of Kuwait, a district of the Province of Basrah. By then, Mubarak had been instigated by the British to kill his two older brothers, Muhammad and Jarrah, who had opposed the British plan to turn Kuwait into an entity under British dominance.

In 1899, Britain goaded Mubarak al-Sabah into signing a secret agreement under which the British were to provide him with protection even though he was a vassal of the Ottoman Empire and, accordingly, had no authority to sign any international accord. The agreement was therefore strongly rejected by the Ottoman Sultan, who forced Mubarak to retreat and declare his allegiance and subordination to the Ottoman State in 1901.

Britain never ceased these attempts, but continued to establish bases in various parts of the Arabian Gulf in order to consolidate its colonial grip over this region, the strategic importance of which had increased both militarily and politically, within the framework of the competition with the Ottoman Empire, and economically as it constituted an important trade route and was known by the British to contain vast oil reserves. In order to secure the interests of the British Empire by weakening all major States in the region, Britain focused its influence on Kuwait and drew artificial boundaries as they did later, together with their French ally, in the Sykes-Picot Agreement of 1916. By so doing Britain perniciously severed a part of Iraq in a manner that deprived a country, ancient in its civilization and great in its land and population, of its natural access to the waters of the Arabian Gulf, the access which it had possessed throughout history.

Since its establishment in 1921, the State of Iraq has refused to recognize what had emanated from this British colonial deed. All successive Iraqi Governments continued to demand the return of this severed part of Iraq and that historical and geographical justice be done to Iraq to guarantee its commercial and economic interests and provide it with the requirements necessary for the defence of its national security. This was the position adopted by successive Iraqi Governments, despite the fact that the Iraqi regime at the time was closely linked to Britain.

Then Britain consistently pressurized Iraq into accepting the *fait accompli*. When the British Government forced the Prime Minister of Iraq in 1932 to exchange letters with the British Commissioner in Baghdad regarding the demarcation of the boundaries on the basis of the draft agreement proposed between the Ottoman and the British Governments, which had remained unratified because of the outbreak of war, the Iraqi House of Representatives refused, in its capacity as the country's legislative authority in accordance with the Constitution, to ratify the said letters.

During the 1930s, popular demand in Iraq and Kuwait for the return of Kuwait to Iraq increased. The national press adopted those demands and supported them with articles and historical documents affirming this call. The British Political Agent in Kuwait, Colonel Dickson, warned, in his letters to the British Political Resident in the Gulf, in 1933, against *rapprochement* and called for the separation of the people of Kuwait from the people of Iraq.

In 1940, the ruler of Kuwait replaced the Iraqi administration of the post office in Kuwait with British staff. In 1945, the Iraqi school curricula applied in Kuwaiti schools were replaced by Egyptian curricula.

King Ghazi, the second monarch of Iraq, supported enthusiastically the necessity of the unification of Kuwait with Iraq. He expressed his desire to visit Kuwait. Britain, however, did not encourage the visit and endeavoured to prevent Iraq and Kuwait from reaching any agreement.

In April 1938, Mr. Tawfiq al-Suwaidi, Iraq's then Foreign Minister, informed the British Ambassador in Baghdad, Mr. Peterson, that:

> "The Anglo-Ottoman Agreement of 1913 had recognized Kuwait as a district belonging to the Province of Basrah, and since sovereignty over Basrah had been transferred from the Ottomans to the State of Iraq, then that sovereignty should include Kuwait as provided for in the agreement of 1913. Iraq, therefore, does not recognize any change in the status of Kuwait".

In Kuwait the Kuwaiti youth took an active part in the call for Kuwait's return to Iraq.

In May 1938, a group of "free Kuwaitis" submitted a petition to the Iraqi Government inviting Iraq to help them to achieve their aspirations regarding the return of Kuwait to Iraq. To this end, a "national coalition" was established to call upon Ahmed al-Sabah, the then Sheikh of Kuwait, to set up a legislative Council representing the free people of Kuwait. He was forced to agree to this demand. During the first session of the said Council in 1938, the members expressed their demand for the return of Kuwait to Iraq. The Council's demand displeased the ruler of Kuwait and he dissolved the Council on 21 December 1938, and waged a campaign of arrests and oppression against its members.

Nevertheless, the free people of Kuwait continued to demand the return of Kuwait to Iraq. They sent many telegrams to petition King Ghazi. One of those telegrams, which was broadcast on Baghdad radio on 7 March 1939, called upon King Ghazi to intervene, saying:

> "Our history confirms the integration of Kuwait with Iraq. We shall live and die under the Iraqi flag. Ghazi! Help your brothers in Kuwait!".

The situation escalated into a sweeping uprising led by the youth of Kuwait against the authorities on 10 March 1939. The ruler of Kuwait had to resort to armed force to disperse the youth, a great number of whom he then arrested and imprisoned.

King Ghazi tried to intervene to secure the release of the prisoners. He warned the Sheikh of Kuwait against the continued harassment of the free Kuwaitis.

King Ghazi and the then Iraqi Government were subjected to intense British pressure to desist from Iraqi demands for the return of Kuwait. To this end, the British Ambassador in Baghdad, Mr. Peterson, had several secret meetings with King Ghazi before the latter's death, in an attempt to press him to give up the claims to Kuwait. A short while afterwards King Ghazi was killed in a mysterious accident on the night of 5 April 1939, giving every reason to believe that Britain was actually behind his death because of his strong advocacy for the return of Kuwait to Iraq.

Following the assassination of King Ghazi, Britain's collaborators seized power in the country. With the outbreak of the Second World War and the following years, Iraq and the region witnessed a series of successive events and changes, among which the creation of Israel, the Arab-Israeli war and the revolution in

Egypt. This gave the British colonialists the pretext to concentrate their influence in Kuwait, severing its political and human links with Iraq.

On 9 March 1956, while Selwyn Lloyd, the British Foreign Secretary, was on a visit to Baghdad attending a consultative meeting of the Permanent Council of the Baghdad Pact, Prime Minister Nouri al-Said of Iraq raised the subject of accession of Kuwait to the Arab Union which was intended to be formed between Iraq and Jordan. Lloyd promised to put the matter before the British Cabinet. Britain's reply, which was delivered through the British Ambassador in Baghdad, Michael Wright, was that Britain was prepared to grant Kuwait independence and Kuwait would have the freedom to decide the question of joining the Union. In order to present Britain with a *fait accompli*, Iraq dispatched the then Deputy Prime Minister Tawfiq al-Suwaidi in April 1957 to Shtoora in Lebanon, where Sheikh Abdullah al-Salim al-Sabah was staying, in order to negotiate with him about the necessity of Kuwait's accession to the expected Union. That effort, however, did not produce any positive result.

Early in 1958, Prime Minister Nouri al-Said of Iraq submitted to the Baghdad Pact the necessity of the integration of Kuwait with Iraq, at a meeting attended by the representatives of Turkey, Iran, Pakistan and Britain along with United States Secretary of State, John Foster Dulles, who attended the meeting as an observer. No success was achieved at that meeting owing to the British opposing position.

Following the establishment of the Arab Union between Iraq and Jordan on 14 February 1958, King Faisal II, joined by Prime Minister Nouri al-Said and the Foreign Minister of the Union, Tawfiq al-Suwaidi, raised the issue of Kuwait's accession to the Arab Union with the British Foreign Secretary, Mr. Selwyn Lloyd. The British, however, also rejected that.

When Abdullah al-Salim al-Sabah, Sheikh of Kuwait, visited Baghdad on 10 May 1958, King Faisal II and Prime Minister Nouri al-Said, raised with him the issue of Kuwait's accession to the Arab Union. The Sheikh of Kuwait responded by saying that he had to consult the British and seek their advice on the matter.

On 5 June 1958 the Government of the Union presented a confidential note to the British Embassy in Baghdad in which it presented the international status of Kuwait before the First World War by stating:

> "The land of Kuwait had, from the point of view of international law, been under the sovereignty of the Ottoman State, as a qadhaa' (district) belonging to the province of Basrah. This sovereignty had never been subject to doubt or dispute from the point of view of either the local authorities in Kuwait or the British Government. Indeed, the latter had implicitly recognized this fact in the Anglo-Turkish Agreement signed in London on 29 July 1913 which stated, in article 6, the right of the Sheikh of Kuwait to exercise the administrative authority invested in him as an Ottoman district administrator subordinate to the Province of Basrah."

The note also presented Kuwait's international status after the war by stating:

> "As a consequence of the settlements that were concluded after World War I, Turkey relinquished all the Arab provinces that were subordinated to the Ottoman State, amongst them the three provinces from which the Kingdom of Iraq was formulated, including the Basrah Province which Kuwait was one of its districts. But the international status of Kuwait remained vague during the period of British occupation of Iraq and Britain's assumption of Mandate on it and its practice of actual authority in the country.
>
> "It is only natural in such circumstances that Iraq, who was not free to run its foreign affairs, be obliged to accept any arrangements or settlements decided by the British authority regarding Kuwait, in particular what concerns depriving Iraq from the territorial waters that belonged to the Province of Basrah during the Ottoman era. Before Iraq's accession to the membership of the League of Nations, the Iraqi Government raised with the British authorities the matter of boundaries between Iraq and Kuwait, demanding the return of the islands situated in the said territorial waters and the delimitation of the land boundary in a manner that is righteous and justifiable. Yet, it did not attain the achievement of its justifiable demands because the British Government had presented the text of an agreement signed between it and the Ottoman Government in 1913 which includes, among other things, articles concerning the protection of the Sheikh of Kuwait and the designation of Kuwait's current boundaries. Later on, it was found that this agreement had not been ratified and did not attain the legal status.
>
> "Iraqi Government's last attempt to restore the islands situated in Iraq's territorial waters and the designation of land boundaries came when it approached the British Government during the Baghdad Pact negotiations and the termination of the Anglo-Iraqi Treaty when the matter of boundaries was discussed but they did not reach any result".

The note mentioned the importance of Kuwait for Iraq and Iraq's interest in putting an end to the widespread smuggling operations via Kuwait, and

> "the addressing of the big trouble in securing peace in the southern regions bordering Kuwait because Kuwait had become a haven for escaped criminals not only from Iraq but from different nearby countries."

It also mentioned the necessity of finding a naval outlet for Iraq on the Arabian Gulf in order to avoid the economic damages that had been inflicted on Iraq. Finally, it mentioned the treatment of counter-Iraq activity after Kuwait became a centre for adverse propaganda aiming at the destabilization of Iraq's security. The note offered two suggestions: the first being the achievement of Kuwait's accession to the Arab Union established between Iraq and the Hashemite Kingdom of Jordan. The second was:

> "If the British Government saw that accession cannot be achieved for the time being, then the Government of the Arab Union finds itself compelled to announce that all the islands existing in the territorial waters are within the boundaries of the Arab Union, and that the land border line between the Arab Union and Kuwait starts from the meeting point of al-Oja valley with al-Batin valley and heads eastwards in a direct line until it reaches al-Jahra on the sea of Kuwait's Gulf provided it would be understood that the Government of the Arab Union recognizes all the existing oil concessions on their current terms. As regards the region being invested by the oil companies and what financial arrangements have ensued between

different parties it would remain as it is except for the necessary financial needs of the Union Government."

The note expressed the hope that the British Government would be able to advise the Sheikh of Kuwait on choosing what is best for him of the two solutions and with all possible speed. If he chooses the first solution, then there remains a necessity for discussing the boundary matter, and if he chooses the second solution, which deals with boundaries, then the Government of the Arab Union would be prepared to sign a treaty of friendship and good-neighbourliness with him.

The note represented the last position of the monarchy regime that ruled Iraq after the establishment of the modern State of Iraq until the 14 July 1958 revolution took place. That regime was known to be one among the staunchest allies of the West. The Iraqi Government and the Government of the Arab Union became firmly convinced that Britain was behind the obstacles preventing the achievement of this objective. This generated tension in Iraqi-British relations and led Iraq to intensify its efforts and pressure upon Britain. The Iraqi Government prepared an official note bolstered by documented evidence which supports the necessity of Kuwait's entry into the Arab Union. It was decided to publish this note on 12 July 1958, but the British Ambassador requested the postponement of the publication and conveyed to the Arab Union's Foreign Minister, Tawfiq al-Suwaidi, Britain's initial acceptance of the idea of Kuwait's accession to the Arab Union provided that the details of the matter be discussed at a meeting which was set to be held on 24 July 1958 in London between the Prime Minister and the Foreign Minister of the Arab Union on the one side, and their British counterparts on the other. However, the 14 July 1958 revolution in Iraq prevented such a meeting.

In 1961, Britain decided to grant Kuwait "independence", a decision which prompted the then Prime Minister of Iraq to declare, in a press conference on 25 June 1961, that Iraq considered Kuwait an integral part of its territory and that Iraq did not recognize the special relationship agreement between Britain and Kuwait which the Sheikh of Kuwait, Abdullah al-Salim al-Sabah, had signed with Colonel M. J. Meade, the British Political Resident in the Gulf, on 19 June 1961. Following that declaration, Britain deployed its armed forces to confront Iraq.

Because of the mistake made by Iraq's Foreign Minister at the time, Hashim Jawad, when he withdrew, in angry protest, from the meeting of the Arab League Council, the chance arose to make Kuwait a member of the League, because the decision to admit a new member to the Arab League must win the unanimous approval of the members.

The Iraqi Foreign Ministry issued a statement on 21 July 1961, declaring that the Arab League's decision No. 35-1777, accepting Kuwait as a member of the League of Arab States, to be a flagrant "violation" of the League's Charter, which stipulated unanimity. Iraq also declared the said decision to be null and void and its belief that Kuwait would remain an integral part of its territory and that Iraq would seek to restore this part by all legitimate means.

The Government of the Kuwaiti regime failed in more than one attempt to join the United Nations between 1961 and late 1963.

Following the downfall of the political regime which ruled Iraq between July 1958 and February 1963, the Prime Minister of the Government of Kuwait, in late 1963, visited Baghdad in circumstances of political confusion and instability in Iraq. A joint communiqué was issued referring to the correspondence of 1932. However, the National Revolution Command Council, the highest Iraqi legislative authority according to the interim constitution of 1963, did not ratify the said communiqué.

This historical review shows that all the successive Governments of Iraq were never convinced of severing any part from the land of Iraq and had not signed a border treaty. No constitutional law in Iraq describing this border has ever been promulgated.

Such was the situation prevailing by the time of the Revolution of 17 to 30 July 1968. The revolutionary Government has been keen, under instruction from President Saddam Hussein, to settle this problem in a manner that would secure for Iraq a reasonable measure of its historical rights and remove at least a limited part of the injustice done to it since the beginning of this century.

During the 1970s, Iraq was the party that took the initiative in approaching the rulers of Kuwait to find such a settlement. But those rulers, encouraged by their foreign allies, insisted that Iraq accept the measures imposed by the British colonialists. The Foreign Minister of Iraq visited Kuwait City in 1972 and 1973 to discuss this issue. The Interior Minster, too, visited Kuwait City for the same purpose on 16 May 1978. Several committees were formed without achieving any result.

This chapter on the discussions of this issue was put aside following the outbreak of the Iran-Iraq war. Immediately after the liberation of Fao, and while attending the Algiers Summit, the Iraqi Foreign Minister took the initiative in informing the Foreign Minister of Kuwait of Iraq's genuine desire to settle this issue. What raised astonishment was that the regime in Kuwait did not respond promptly to this desire and did not reply to the offer of Iraq until the beginning of July 1988, when the Foreign Minister of Kuwait visited Iraq and it was agreed that the subject be discussed by the two Foreign Ministers.

The talks between the two Ministers were delayed owing to the start of the Iraqi-Iranian negotiations and the preoccupation of Iraq's Foreign Minister with them. It was decided to send the Vice-Chairman of the Revolution Command Council to Kuwait City on 6 December 1988 to urge the authority there to resume discussing the matter. It was agreed that the Vice-Chairman of the Revolution Command Council from the Iraqi side and the Crown Prince from their side would discuss the subject.

The visit of the Vice-Chairman of the Revolution Command Council was returned by Saad al-Abdullah's visit to Baghdad on 6 February 1989. It was clear that he was not prepared to consider even the simple and minimum of Iraq's legitimate demands.

On 27 March 1989, Minister Saud al-Usaimi made a visit to Baghdad, during which he officially asked that the talks on this issue be postponed. During the visit made by the Sheikh of Kuwait to Baghdad in September 1989, President Saddam Hussein proposed to him once again the resumption of talks on the issue. It was agreed to pursue the matter between Deputy Prime Minister Dr. Saadoun Hammadi on the Iraqi side and their Foreign Minister on the Kuwaiti side. Dr. Saadoun Hammadi did actually visit Kuwait City on 19 November 1989 to discuss the matter. Their former Foreign Minister did not return that visit until February 1990.

It ought to be mentioned here that the former Sheikhs of Kuwait took advantage of the situation during the entire period while the settlement of this issue remained pending. They also exploited Iraq's internal and regional preoccupations, the last of which being the Iran-Iraq war, which lasted eight years. They exploited it to consolidate their territorial encroachment northwards by the establishment of police posts, military installations, farms and oil installations. In 1963, for instance, the checkpoint for crossing from Kuwait to Basrah was at al-Mitla'a, where passports were stamped for departure. We enclose some photocopies of them. But this checkpoint was moved more than 70 kilometres to the north in order to press a *fait accompli* upon Iraq which was preoccupied during the said period with its internal affairs and the region's problems.

The historical and geographical facts which I have elucidated above indicate in an irrefutable manner that Iraq did not accept, at any past time, any formula for the delimitation of the boundary and did not agree to any interpretation of it or any manner of its demarcation. This position was not spontaneous because it rests upon a factual reality which states that the boundary delimitation formula and its British interpretations and the British endeavours aiming at the demarcation of the boundaries as based upon them usurp Iraq's territorial rights and its legitimate interests, such rights and interests that are in perfect harmony with the facts of history and geography. This factual reality explains the uniformity of the Iraqi position throughout the different political regimes in Iraq and all of the successive Governments, a position which had stayed as it is without change. Thus, the Commission decisions that came in the course of imposing the boundary issue upon Iraq from the beginning in a predetermined course are baseless and bear no evidence.

Following this review of the facts of history and geography, it becomes unequivocally clear to every impartial observer that the decisions adopted by the Commission during its New York session from 8 to 16 April 1992 represent a purely political decision imposed by the Powers dominating the Security Council at present, particularly the Government of the United States and the United Kingdom.

The political objective of this decision is clearly not only to deny Iraq its historical territorial rights and undermine its vital interests, but also deliberately to create an illegal and illogical situation which arouses the indignation, and threatens the interests, of an ancient people whose predicament has been imposed upon it by armed force and political blackmail. The objective is also to create a climate of dissatisfaction, dissent and instability in the whole region.

It is this kind of climate which the decision makers (the United States and the United Kingdom), want to preserve in the region as a whole, in order to justify the perpetuation of their military bases and of the presence of their armed forces in a state of occupation which will enable them to continue extorting the ruling regimes in Kuwait and the region and pillaging the oil wealth of the area.

Any ratification by the Security Council of this unjust decision, which has been deliberately directed by two of its permanent members, will constitute a very dangerous precedent, contrary in substance and consequences to the duties and responsibilities entrusted to the Council by the Charter of the United Nations. Once the Security Council has ratified this decision, it will not have contributed to the preservation of security and stability in the region but will rather have consciously created a continuous hotbed of tension as well as deliberately violated the legitimate and vital interests of a State Member of the United Nations. If there were compelling circumstances which force the Iraqi authorities to take certain positions regarding this decision, the people of Iraq could never be convinced that its historical rights had been respected and its vital interests safeguarded by the Security Council in a manner compatible with the rules of international law and the criteria of justice and fairness. The Arab Nation will continue to view this decision as one link in the chain of Western imperialist games which began after the First World War and which have always been the subject of indignation and rejection on the part of the Arab Nation, and which have caused many of the disturbances and changes witnessed in the Arab Nation. The situation which we witness today is not new to the world, and the world knows the outcome resulting from such instances.

In bringing this letter to an end, I would like to recall that this conclusion is not ours alone, but it is also shared by many fair-minded people in the region and the world at large.

Allow me at this point to draw your attention to some of the views on the subject published in the Arab and foreign press:

In an article by Caryle Murphy published by *The Washington Post* on 5 May 1992, one official was reported to have said:

> "I think that's something Kuwait should consider if it wants a boundary for keeps. Both parties can still agree on another line for other reasons."

The writer quotes Mr. Fred Halliday, an expert in international relations at the London School of Economics, as saying in regard to the situation as it now stands:

> "We have the seeds of another war. I can't see any way that any Iraqi Government would support this demarcation."

The article quotes also Mr. Mochtar Kusuma-Atmadja, the Chairman of the Commission, as saying:

> "The task given to us, according to the resolution, says demarcation, not delimitation ... only countries can delimit boundaries."

The article noted that:

> "Even early documents show that this border has never been a pacific one."

It reported Mr. Ian Brook a member of the Commission to have said:

> "Some of the most acrimonious discussions have been between British and British", referring to letters exchanged when Kuwait was administered from Britain's India Office and Iraq was under the Colonial Office."

In an article entitled "The Umm Qasr time bomb", written by G. H. Jansen in *Middle East International* and published on 6 March 1992, the following was stated:

> "The UN Commission's giving Umm Qasr to Kuwait can only be explained as a further example of America's punitive campaign against Iraq and already US officials are reported as saying that they will insist that the new boundary be respected as Iraq's southern border."

The writer adds:

> "The UN has produced a time bomb which only the Security Council can defuse, by basing itself on natural justice and rejecting the Commission's findings when they are submitted in April."

In an article published by the *Wall Street Journal* on 5 December 1991, entitled "The UN hires a sleuth to find border between Iraq and Kuwait", which presented a somewhat detailed account on the role of the British expert and of the representative of Kuwait investigating the point at Safwan, the following was said:

> "But some experts warn that such an adjustment - which Iraq, with only one vote on the Commission, can't prevent - could sow the seeds for future conflict."

The article quoted Mr. Richard Schofield, Deputy Director of the Geopolitics and International Boundaries Research Centre in London as saying:

> "The age-old problem of Iraqi access to the Gulf remains. Iraq never felt able to live with this, and may not in the future."

The Financial Times concluded an article published on 19 February 1992 as follows:

> "Common borders are finally a matter of bilateral consent between neighbouring countries but US officials say they will insist the new boundary be respected as Iraq's southern border."

Under the title "The new outline of the frontier between Iraq and Kuwait raises serious problems" *Le Monde* on 21 April 1992 stated that:

> "Situated at the mouth of Khowr Zhobeir at the north-west extremity of the Gulf, the Umm Qasr port and naval base, today threatened, are only part of the gigantic complex built 20 years ago by Iraq in this area vital for its development: petrochemical, steel, gas liquefaction and fertilizer plants, and dry docks for the repair of vessels. The water channels leading to the Gulf were dredged in 1990 in order to permit the entry of larger tankers. All this area has become a priority after the cease-fire with Iran because it constitutes an alternative to Basrah on the Shatt al-Arab, which is filled with wreckage and falls within the range of Iranian fire. The new line of the frontier is in danger of reducing these enormous investments to nothing."

The newspaper adds:

> "But voices are being raised to the effect that, apart from the technical work of the Commission, political considerations and commonsense should be taken into account so as to ensure respect for the interests of the two countries and to avoid future conflicts."

In an article published in the Jordanian daily *Al-Ra'i* on 19 April 1992, Mr. Tariq Msarwa wrote the following:

> "During the recent meeting of the Committee for the demarcation of the Iraq-Kuwait boundary line the Commission "discovered" that parts of the land of the Iraqi side (the whole of the Rumaila oilfield and three quarters of the port of Umm Qasr, Iraq's single port on the Gulf which was developed at huge cost) belong to Kuwait!!! The objective of the Commission is no different from the objective the British assigned to themselves - the task of speaking for all concerned at al-Eqair negotiations and "agreed with themselves" to isolate Iraq. Otherwise, why was the uninhabited island of Bubiyan given to Kuwait at a time when the whole population of Kuwait was less than 10,000? What is important now is that the boundary line between Iraq and Kuwait is being determined by a United Nations Commission which knows that both the scope and outcome of its work are predetermined by the United States and Britain. If the objective of the Eqair negotiations in the 1920s was to isolate Iraq from the world, what is being done now is to plant the seeds of ongoing Iraqi-Kuwaiti enmity regardless of whether the political system on either side remains or changes!!!"

In an article published on 19 April 1992, in the Jordanian daily *Al-Distour*, Mr. Mohammed Daoudiyah stated that:

> "Encroaching upon the territory of Iraq means very simply planting highly volatile explosives in inter-Arab relations and closing the door before all reason and wisdom."

Mr. Dawoodiyah wonders: [sic]

> "How can any Iraqi overlook this flagrant violation of his or her country's territory, or remain indifferent while Iraqi life is being denied all access to the Arabian Gulf?"

In an article entitled: "Beware the seditious work of the Iraq-Kuwait Boundary Demarcation Commission", the Jordanian daily *Sawt al-Shaab* wrote on 19 April 1992 the following:

> "It seems that the United States of America and its allies are bent on planting inter-Arab division and conflict, and remain determined to create pretexts, motives and justifications for the eruption of self-destructive regional wars which will render all parties involved military and economically worn-out and politically vulnerable, a state of affairs ripe at all times for American and Western intervention to settle the disputes at hand. Otherwise, what is the meaning of the decision taken by the Iraq-Kuwait Boundary Demarcation Commission to bestow upon Kuwait part of the Iraqi port city of Umm Qasr and push about 200 kilometres of the boundary line 600 metres inside Iraq to the benefit of Kuwait?"

The article goes on to say that:

> "To take advantage of Iraq's difficult circumstances in order to violate its right to sovereignty and territorial integrity or usurp part of its land with the help of the enemies of Iraq and the Arab nation is like playing with fire, and may be even far more dangerous than that. So, beware the sedition planted by the enemies of our nation in order to stir wars amongst brothers."

In a news analysis by Dr. Saad Aboudiyah published in *Al-Shaab* of Jordan on 21 April 1992, the writer wrote:

> "In my view, as long as these allocations remain unacceptable to either party, they will continue to constitute the time bomb they have always been."

Dr. Aboudiyah also said:

> "In brief, the Commission, by taking the decision it has taken, has in fact contributed to rekindling the flames of conflict anew. The people of Iraq will continue to feel the grave injustice done to them in the boundary demarcation issue."

In an article entitled "Inter-Arab boundaries set ablaze ... Why now?", published in the *Al-Distour* daily of Jordan, Dr. Nabeel Al-Shareef wrote, on 21 April 1992:

"Let's begin with the Iraq-Kuwait boundary demarcation question which has been determined in a manner which makes it ready to explode at any time in the future. It is illogical to bestow Iraqi territory upon Kuwait and deny Iraq all access to the sea; and those who have accepted this iniquitous demarcation of the boundary line have in fact done nothing to help in any way to resolve the boundary issue between the two countries. Indeed, all they have done is to leave this issue unresolved, fraught with bitterness and ready to explode and unleash its bloody outcome. They would have much better evinced the far-sightedness which would assure the coming Arab generations the right climate of security, brotherliness and good-neighbourliness. Iraq, whose name runs back to the deep roots of human history and which has stamped its mark on geography, will never disappear from the map. The presence of foreign forces in this region cannot be eternal, in spite of the success achieved in this particular instance by the tendency to enflame inter-Arab boundary disputes."

The writer sums up by saying:

"The Arab borders have not blazed suddenly with no reasons behind it, but rather to perpetuate the frazzled Arab state of affairs and augment the already existing atmosphere of panic to impel others to stick the American Grand Protector, especially that those borders that were set ablaze exist in the Gulf and Jazirah area, an oil region which the United States of America needs today and will continue to need tomorrow."

In a report published in the *Al-Quds Al-Arabi* newspaper on 21 April 1992, a diplomat is quoted as saying:

"There is nothing the Iraqis can do in the short term other than complain. But this will pose a permanent danger, a time bomb, to the long-term relations between the two countries, a danger that will persist."

In *Al-Ahram al-Dawli* of 22 April 1992, Mr. Mohammed Othman started his daily column, entitled "Hatha-assabah (This morning)", by saying:

"The new borders between Iraq and Kuwait that have been demarcated lately can be nothing other than a time bomb waiting to be exploded at any moment, sooner or later."

The Jordanian *Akhbar al-Asbou'* daily of 23 April 1992 addressed the border dispute in the Arab Jazirah and the Arabian Gulf, referring to it as:

"A tribunal inheritance nourished by the oil boom and petro-dollar wealth, perpetuated by the foreign companies which were backed by the British colonial occupations that were imposed throughout the Jazirah and the coastal strip along both sides of the Gulf reaching Iraq following its occupation in early twentieth century."

The newspaper added:

"Britain, as protector country, felt that it would be difficult to bring those tribes under control. Therefore it resorted to the scheme of containing those tribes within entities among which it sowed the seeds of fear with a view to facilitating their control. In addition, it made open maps available to those tribes to serve as an element of demolition of any future national unity."

The paper concluded by saying:

"This agonizing state of affairs is being experienced in the Arab Jazirah. The most prominent event of it is perhaps what is being done on the Iraq-Kuwait boundary question, in which the United Nations intervened to usurp Iraq's Rumaila oil field and the port of Umm Qasr according to British maps, in a move to further debilitate Iraq and consequently ignite further eruptions in the area."

In a piece entitled: "By relying on British maps, the United Nations Commission adopts a resolution to divide the Arabian Gulf", *Al-Ra'i* newspaper of Jordan wrote on 24 April 1992:

"This is not the first time for the United Nations to use British maps to destroy existing political entities and divide the people who have struggled to maintain their national unity and preserve their pan-Arab character."

Having touched on the issue of Palestine, the paper went on to write the following on the issue of the Iraq-Kuwait borders:

"The decision adopted by the United Nations Commission on the demarcation of the boundary line between Iraq and Kuwait will leave both sides for many generations to come, and with the blessings of the United Nations, engaged in an endless fight and in a state of permanent enmity, especially in view of the fact that Umm Qasr and the Rumaila oilfield have both always been part of Iraq since the day it bore its name and long before the arrival of any British colonialist in the Gulf region. The British policy of "divide and rule" is not new to Britain and its maps. For this policy has been implemented for dozens of years in our Arab land. But when such a policy marches to the United Nations and finds its way to UN practice, then we begin to realize the potential dangers of this international Organization which has actually become the "Organization of the American nations".

Mr. Abdul Latif Al-Furati, Editor-in-Chief of the Tunisian *Al-Sabah* daily, wrote in an editorial article on 26 April 1992:

"It is imperative that a stand of rejection emerge on the Iraq-Kuwait border demarcation issue, since boundary lines cannot be forcefully imposed upon one party or the other without the consent of the two sides concerned. Otherwise, any boundary delimitation carried out against the will of any of the two countries will become a time bomb which may explode at any moment. Furthermore, any agreement reached must be based on justice and on the history of the situation."

(*Signed*) Ahmad HUSSEIN
Minister for Foreign Affairs

[*An enclosure reproducing photocopies of passports stamped for departure at al-Mitla'a has been omitted.*]

S/24060, 9 June 1992

13. Letter from the Chargé d'affaires a.i. of the Permanent Mission of Kuwait to the United Nations addressed to the Secretary-General, 9 June 1992

I have the pleasure to transmit to you herewith the text of a letter dated 9 June 1992 addressed to you by the Deputy Prime Minister and Minister for Foreign Affairs of the State of Kuwait, Sheikh Salem Sabah al-Salem al-Sabah, in which he responds to the Iraqi allegations contained in document S/24044 of 1 June 1992.

...

Kuwait has taken note of the letter dated 21 May 1992 addressed to you by the Minister for Foreign Affairs of Iraq concerning the decisions of the Iraq-Kuwait Boundary Demarcation Commission appointed by the Security Council.

The majority of countries in the world were surprised by that letter and by its contents. Kuwait, however, was not surprised, since the contents of the letter are in the long tradition of the practices of the Iraqi regime, which consists in challenging international legitimacy, persisting in its aggressive intentions, proclaiming its refusal and rejecting all agreements and conventions ratified by Iraq.

The letter from Iraq can be summed up in one sentence: Iraq refuses to recognize the catastrophe with all its consequences and all the misery which it has caused and the tragedy and damage which it has inflicted on Kuwait, on Iraq, on the Arab nation and on the whole world.

After the crime of the invasion, the adventure of the war, the crushing defeat, the sacrifices and loss of human life and the hostility of the whole world, Iraq brings us back to the starting-point. In its letter, it closes its eyes and stops its ears to the reality which has been recognized by all the States of the world and all international institutions and which it has endeavoured to disregard by resorting to invasion, violence and the law of the jungle and by trying to impose its point of view by force of arms.

This reality is based on the fact that Kuwait is an independent sovereign State, a Member of the United Nations and a member of the League of Arab States and of other international, regional and Arab organizations, that it has its own historical and legal existence, that it does not depend on any State or part of a State, and that it has diplomatic representation to various States throughout the world, including Iraq.

Kuwait's boundaries are described in the agreements which Iraq signed and recognized and which it deposited with the League of Nations with a view to confirming that those boundaries were settled and agreed. That was, moreover, a precondition for its membership in that organization, which refused to admit to membership States which disputed their boundaries with their neighbours. The course of the boundary was reaffirmed in the Agreed Minutes signed in 1963 by the two parties, Kuwait and Iraq. In that text it is stated that Iraq recognizes the independence and boundaries of Kuwait. This instrument was deposited with the United Nations, and Iraq accepted it once again in a letter dated 11 April 1991 (S/22480) in which the Iraqi National Assembly announced that it accepted Security Council resolution 687 (1991).

The boundaries between Kuwait and Iraq are delimited precisely. The problem arises from the fact that Iraq has constantly delayed the demarcation of the boundary and the installation of frontier posts, indulging in provocatory and aggressive manoeuvres and thereby going back on its promises.

Iraq has taken no account of the agreements reached and of this reality and has committed a treacherous act of aggression against Kuwait, its peaceful neighbour. It has invoked pretexts which the world deems futile and grasped at illusions, challenging the international community and rejecting the appeals to withdraw and to respect international legitimacy. This refusal has cost Iraq a crushing defeat and enormous losses in terms of property and human life and forced it to accept unconditionally the Security Council resolutions which have restored legitimacy and reminded Iraq of its obligation to respect the instruments which it signed on 4 October 1963 when it freely and of its own will recognized Kuwait, its independence and its boundaries as specified in the instrument deposited with the United Nations as Treaty No. 7063. What is more, Iraq has accepted all the Security Council resolutions and the Iraqi National Assembly has ratified them, a step which the world had hoped would mark the end of the tragedy and the beginning of a new era of peace and cooperation in the region.

The letter from the Minister for Foreign Affairs of Iraq, which would appear to express Iraq's objection to the decisions of the Boundary Demarcation Commission, in reality, in the light of both the wording and the content, constitutes a further blatant proclamation of Iraq's refusal to accept international legitimacy and decisions and its rejection of all previous agreements, as well as the reaffirmation of the claims which served as a pretext for the invasion. In this letter, Iraq repeats and implicitly reiterates its threats when it states that the decision of the Boundary Demarcation Commission is a time bomb which may explode at any moment.

Although the letter from Iraq is nothing but a repetition of claims which consist in denying facts which are as clear as daylight, we will endeavour below to deal, in all objectivity and simplicity, with some of the points which the Minister for Foreign Affairs of Iraq touched upon in his letter in order to show that Kuwait is constantly guided by reason and justice, that it can draw a lesson from the catastrophe and from the past in order to turn a new page and restore peace and security in the world and unity of direction to the region and that it rejects any claim to domination and aggression in a world which can find salvation only through fraternity, cooperation and joint action in mutual respect and in relations governed by legitimacy and principles.

I. In his letter, the Minister for Foreign Affairs starts by stating that the fact that, in delimiting the boundary between Iraq and Kuwait, the Boundary Demarcation Commission established by the Security Council had to take as a basis the agreement signed between the two countries on 4 October 1963 prejudged the demarcation of the boundary with Kuwait instead of leaving the two countries to settle their differences through negotiations. In so doing, he ignores the long history of persistent attempts and efforts by Kuwait, using all means, to persuade Iraq to delimit the boundary (attempts which were met with repeated delays, provocations and acts of aggression at the frontier until the very day before Iraq's treacherous act of aggression). In order to settle this dispute, Kuwait had proposed recourse to arbitration by a neutral commission of the League of Arab States. Iraq reacted the following day by its infamous invasion.

Has Iraq forgotten that it was its treacherous act of aggression and its disregard of international legitimacy which placed this problem outside the regional context, thus moving its obligation to respect such legitimacy to an international context? Iraq having rejected all acceptable means of resolving the boundary dispute thus created, it was essential that the United Nations should intervene and take charge.

Iraq proclaimed its opposition at the time of the adoption of Security Council resolution 687 (1991) by pointing out that questions relating to boundaries between States, including their delimitation and demarcation, were not within the competence of the Security Council. In view of the invasion of Kuwait by Iraq and the effects of that invasion on the security and stability of the region -

questions which are within the competence of the Security Council, which is responsible for monitoring and eliminating hotbeds of tension in the world and for taking the necessary measures to avert them - the Council, which, in paragraph 4 of resolution 687 (1991), had decided to guarantee the inviolability of the international boundary between Kuwait and Iraq, nevertheless felt that it should intervene to delimit the boundary in order to settle the problem once and for all.

Iraq accepted Security Council resolution 687 (1991), which was ratified by its legislative and executive authorities, as evidenced in United Nations documents. By rejecting the foundation which served as a basis for the work of the Boundary Demarcation Commission, Iraq has gone back on its unconditional acceptance of the aforementioned Security Council resolution.

It should be pointed out that resolution 687 (1991), which, *inter alia*, provided for the establishment of the Boundary Demarcation Commission, has priority over all other relevant resolutions since in paragraph 1 it confirms the provisions of all other previous resolutions "except as expressly changed below to achieve the goals of this resolution".

II. Iraq has attempted to justify its opposition to and its rejection of international intervention in the demarcation of the boundary by referring in the note to its supposed attempts to convince Kuwait to delimit the boundary and its "sincere" desire to find a solution to the problem. According to Iraq, Kuwait "did not respond".

The time has come to shed full light on the historical events so that future generations will know what this "sincere desire" to resolve the boundary question really was.

At the end of 1971, Saddam Hussein declared that, if Kuwait wanted to put an end to the boundary problem, it should take initiatives, both at the national level and at the level of the Arab nation. The Minister for Foreign Affairs of Iraq, Murtada Sa'id Abd al-Baqi, explained, during a visit to Kuwait at the beginning of May 1972, what form those initiatives by the Government of Kuwait should take. They can be summarized as follows:

(a) Complete political coordination between Kuwait and Iraq;
(b) Investment of Kuwaiti capital in Iraq specifically;
(c) Authorization for the entry of Iraqi workers into Kuwait;
(d) Association of Kuwait with Iraqi defence planning;
(e) Creation in Kuwait of strategic zones reserved for Iraq, including the necessary access to the sea for the latter.

Earlier, Taha al-Jazrawi, Minister of Industry and member of the Revolution Command Council, had informed Sheikh Sabah al-Ahmed al-Sabah, Minister for Foreign Affairs of Kuwait, during talks which they held at Baghdad to study the boundary question, that the two Kuwaiti islands of Warbah and Bubiyan were of particular importance to Iraq, as a Gulf country. He had asked Kuwait to renounce them.

During that same visit, the Kuwaiti delegation, headed by Sheikh Sabah al-Ahmed, met with Saddam Hussein, at that time Vice-President of the Republic, who reiterated that demand.

Kuwait's reply was categorical: it was out of the question that it should renounce any part of its territory; that was inconceivable for any Kuwaiti.

That was the kind of initiative at the national level and at the level of the Arab nation which Iraq took to convince Kuwait to delimit the boundary and which affected Kuwait's homeland, sovereignty, will, territory and freedom and the management of its resources.

III. Once again, the Iraqi regime reiterates its repeated attempts, in the aforementioned note, and endeavours by all means to obstruct the delimitation of the boundary. It began by refusing to allow the Security Council to intervene in the delimitation, as we have indicated. It cast suspicion on the Commission and the choice of its members, asking to be allowed to have a role in that choice. But it is not for Iraq alone, but for Kuwait also to have such a role, since, under the mandate assigned to it, the Commission is a technical commission not an arbitration commission, nor a political commission called upon to decide on the course of the boundary or to make any modifications thereto. This is not within its competence since the Security Council, in defining the boundary between Kuwait and Iraq, has taken as a basis the text of the 1963 Agreed Minutes signed between the two countries. In accordance with the functions entrusted to it, the Commission is confined to delimiting on the ground the boundaries specified in the said Agreed Minutes and to placing the border posts required for that purpose. Similarly, the choice of independent technical experts is the responsibility of the Secretary-General of the United Nations, who is responsible for carrying out the mission entrusted to him.

IV. The letter states that the Security Council resolution on the Boundary Demarcation Commission is unprecedented in the international Organization. That allegation is totally inaccurate and contrary to common knowledge, inasmuch as the League of Nations established similar commissions to demarcate the boundaries under its supervision in order to resolve the border conflict issues in certain parts of the world, and they arrived at the Treaties of Versailles (demarcation of the boundary between Poland and Czechoslovakia), Saint-Germain (between Austria and Hungary), Neuilly (between Bulgaria and Yugoslavia) and Trianon (between Hungary and Romania).

The casting of doubts in the letter on the Commission and its members is the procedure and fashion of this regime. It has cast doubts on the United Nations and the Security Council and has described them as tools in the hands of others seeking to injure it. That is an extension of its position of hostility to the world and its States whenever they stand in the way of its ambitions and its will to impose wrong by force and falsification. In particular, during the work of the Commission, Iraq has not registered one single objection against any of the independent experts there or cited a single fact indicating bias on the part of any of them.

V. By way of seeking flimsy justifications, the letter objects to what was contained in the draft report of the Secretary-General of the United Nations, to the effect that the Commission could utilize appropriate technology relevant to the demarcation of the boundary and considers that vague, undetermined and requiring elucidation. The technology used in boundary demarcation consists of technical operations with well-known methods known to all specialists in this field, so that the Secretary-General's reference to it is surprising. The Commission has utilized this technology within sight of the Iraqi side and without any objection from it. The New Zealand/Swedish survey team carried out field work that laid the foundation for the vertical photographic maps of the Iraq-Kuwait border area. Four stations were established to supply data for survey control, as well as 25 major control stations at intervals of approximately 15 to 25 kilometres along the border. Its observation activity was conducted with Doppler and GPS equipment. The Swedish team carried out aerial photography operations using a commando jet aircraft specially equipped for this purpose from two main altitudes. Photographs were taken from each altitude, and picture control consisted of a network comprising more than 200 control stations with pre-processing of signals.

As a result of these operations, 29 vertical photographic maps were produced on the 1:25000 scale with elevation contours at 5-metre intervals. The map projection used in the preparation of the vertical photographic maps was the Universal Transverse Mercator (UTM) Projection, with an extension of 38 to the East to cover the boundary area fully.

Work was begun on the preparation of additional separate maps for the western part of the boundary known as Wadi al-Batin, and approximately 1,430 survey photographs were taken over a distance of 3.5 kilometres at intervals of 100 metres along the wadi. These pictures were used to determine the nearest line of a point in the wadi. Numerical ground samples were also established to plot the contours at 2 metres' elevation. In addition, three-dimensional pictures were used with the help of computers to interpret the data.

We should ask ourselves questions about the nature of the details and explanations sought by Iraq following this detailed exposition on the technology used in the Commission's work that we have summarized briefly here and which have been published at greater length by the Commission.

It is amazing that Iraq did not respond to the Commission's request to supply any information available to it relating to its mission and contented itself with promises. It promised to furnish documents and admits in its letter that it was unable to furnish them during the Commission's meetings. It blames the Commission and the United Nations for not waiting until Iraq had done so. Of course, it did not do so in spite of the lapse of more than a year between the first and the fifth meetings of the Commission, in which it announced that it had demarcated the land boundary.

Nevertheless, Iraq describes the work of the Commission as, in its opinion, unacceptably hasty, although until the last meeting of the Commission it was unable to give a firm deadline for the handing over of what it claimed it had. How much time was Iraq proposing that the United Nations, the Security Council and the issue of establishing security in this part of the world should wait until Iraq was ready to furnish its documents, which, it knows very well, as everyone knows, do not exist and are merely, as we have said, an extension of attempts in past decades to prevaricate in the demarcation of the boundary so that it should become a point of dissension to be exploited for obtaining gains and obfuscating the situation and the facts?

VI. The note reproaches the representative of Kuwait with having put leading questions to the independent experts. We do not understand what prevented the representative of Iraq from putting questions since he is a member of the Commission and has every right to ask for explanations and to state his views.

VII. The note of the Iraqi regime rejects what the Commission took as a basis in its interpretation of the course of the boundary south of Safwan, on the grounds that the Commission relied on cartographic considerations (although that was the very nature of the Commission's work), on documents and letters which had been exchanged between Britain and Iraq and on Iraqi maps! We do not understand why the Boundary Demarcation Commission is reproached for that.

The note justifies this objection by arguing that at that time Britain was the dominant colonial Power in the region and that the Iraqi maps on which the Commission had relied had not at the time they were drawn up been intended to demarcate the frontier.

These are objections which any fair and impartial person would reject. In the Agreed Minutes signed in 1963, after the end of British domination and Britain's withdrawal, at a time when Iraqi national rule had been established, Iraq explicitly declared, in appending its signature to paragraph 1, that "the Republic of Iraq recognized the independence and complete sovereignty of the State of Kuwait with its boundaries as specified in the letter of the Prime Minister of Iraq dated 21 July 1932 which was accepted by the ruler of Kuwait in his letter dated 10 August 1932".

Where then are the British pressure and the imperialist and hegemonistic force which would justify a disavowal of this recognition of the boundary line by Iraq? In reality, it is nothing but the greed of the current Iraqi regime, which has been confirmed by its treacherous invasion and its designs on the territory, population and existence of Kuwait!

The Iraqi regime's objection to the Commission's reliance on Iraqi maps is surprising. Its allegation that they are maps not drawn up for demarcation purposes is even more surprising. Surely the boundary entered on maps issued by a State are a decisive proof of its borders with its neighbours, whether they be utilized for demarcation or for other purposes.

VIII. The letter mentions that Kuwait moved the boundary more than 70 kilometres, with military forces and oil installations, basing its allegation on the fact that Kuwaiti passports had been stamped at the Mitla' checkpoint but were later stamped at Safwan, at a distance of 70 kilometres. We know of no relation between a passport checkpoint and the choice of its location as an international boundary.

In this context of falsification of the facts, Kuwait has travel documents that register the checkpoint as the town of Zubayr. Does that mean that Kuwait claims the extension of its frontier to Zubayr?

It is known in all States of the world that the checkpoint for departure may be at an airport located in the area of the city rather than at the frontier point.

The purpose of the Iraqi letter is clearly renunciation of the boundary-line indicated in the agreements signed by Iraq and a shift to other evidence that is totally unreasonable.

IX. The letter objects to two things on which the work of the Boundary Demarcation Commission is based. The first is its reliance on survey evidence alone and adoption of the geographical coordinates of longitude and latitude, without leaving scope for the furnishing of other evidence derived from appropriate materials (although Iraq does not specify the nature of these appropriate materials). The Boundary Demarcation Commission, in ensuring that the boundary corresponds to reality, must rely essentially on survey evidence, provided that the boundary is agreed previously, because the basis of the operation is congruence, not adjustment.

However, it is clear that the Iraqi letter wishes to distance the Commission from the task of demarcation in order to enter into the labyrinth of demarcating the boundary on the basis of the Iraqi regime's rejection of the boundary contained in the agreements, to embark on the seas of disputation where all parties will founder and to make a fresh start on the course towards a boundary demarcation agreement that will, of course, be rejected by the Security Council, the United Nations and the Commission, which proceed from international legitimacy and the binding agreements concluded.

The second thing to which the letter objects is that the Commission adopted the British map from the appropriate materials that it took as the basis for its work of demarcation. The letter proceeds to reject any boundary demarcation carried out by the British, even though Iraq is the one that officially endorsed it with the signatures of its presidents and ministers in the exchange of letters of 1932 and the Agreed Minutes of 1963, as we have explained. Nevertheless, the British map was not regarded as the basis for the Commission's work but as one of the appropriate materials, to be necessarily supported by other materials and was accordingly not used for some purposes.

We do not know why the Iraqi regime rejected the Iraqi maps issued by its Government, the boundary demarcation recognized by Iraq's agreements and the maps that were available at the time of the boundary demarcation and, rather than submit fresh documents or proofs, produced promises and prevarications about submitting them. On what can any agency undertaking the demarcation of the boundary rely, unless all that was deliberate hamstringing designed to place the international effort aimed at ending the problem in a vacuum, leaving the question of stability, security and peace in the region dependent on whoever possesses weapons and a will to aggression.

X. The letter objects to the fact that the representative of Kuwait accompanied the two independent experts on their investigations of the Safwan area, even though the representative of Kuwait accompanied them in accordance with the decision of the Commission, of which he is a member, and he only entered the border area under the auspices of the United Nations, within the framework of which the Commission operates.

In this context, the letter accuses Commission members of lack of neutrality, an accusation not based on any evidence. On the contrary, it is a random judgement intended to prejudice the Commission's work. In such matters, judgements should be based on firm evidence stemming from reason and credibility.

The Commission's decisions were not biased in favour of Kuwait as the Iraqi letter claims. The Commission decided to deprive Kuwait of its territorial waters in Khawr al-Zubayr, which means Iraq's full utilization of that channel. The Commission's decision in this matter is a clear response to the accusation of lack of neutrality launched against it.

The Iraqi letter seeks a way to nullify the agreement of its representative on the Commission to the demarcation of the Safwan point. The letter justifies that by saying that the representative of Iraq was "tricked contrary to the principles of ethics and good faith". We do not know what good faith or bad faith has to do with the facts, the boundary and the survey lines or how a representative of a State can be tricked in such a situation.

Although the agreement of the representative of Iraq and the Commission was based on the Iraqi letter presented to the British ambassador on 25 June 1940, wherein the Iraqi Government stated that the boundary line lay south of Safwan 1,250 metres from the old customs post, the Iraqi regime tried to renege on the Iraqi letter and the indicators marking the Safwan line contained in it.

This is a blatant contradiction. A letter of a State demarcates the beginning of a boundary line in an official letter in 1940 and now the Minister for Foreign Affairs of the State proceeds to reject and deny that, because any specification regarding boundary demarcation that does not suit the Iraqi regime, whether it be past or present, is rejected by it.

The letter continues its objections to the Commission's decisions and states that these decisions have led to the appropriation of large areas of Iraq's territory uncontested before this date, including its oil resources and the installations established by Iraq in that territory.

The letter deliberately omits any mention of the fact that was demonstrated beyond doubt or dispute by the technical survey operations of the Boundary Demarcation Commission. It was established that over the years Iraq had gone beyond the boundary lines accepted by it in the exchange of letters of 1922, and the Agreed Minutes of 1963 and had violated the border areas by force, encroachment and military aggression, as in the case of its armed attack and encirclement of the Kuwaiti Al-Samitah guardpost in 1973 and the other attacks launched by it on the border areas. Kuwait registered its objection at the time by successive official notes dating back to 1934 and set up those installations to serve as justification in the future for its claim to ownership of that territory.

International legitimacy does not bow to the *fait accompli* imposed by force. It calls upon the parties to show respect for the treaties they have signed and imposes on the encroaching party the obligation to return to his legitimate boundaries.

XII. The Iraqi letter regards the resolution admitting the State of Kuwait to the League of Arab States as null and void because the Minister for Foreign Affairs of Iraq was absent from the meeting of the Council. The letter claims that a decision admitting a new member to the League of Arab States must be supported unanimously by all members.

Iraq admits in its letter that Kuwait became a member of the League of Arab States and that that was due to a mistake made by Iraq's Minister for Foreign Affairs. How can this be expressly admitted together with a statement that the League decision is null and void?

However, the subsequent conduct of Iraq towards Kuwait confirms that, for approximately three decades, it has been dealing with Iraq as an independent State, on the one hand, and as a State member of the League of Arab States, on the other. This conduct is represented in the various aspects of diplomatic, political, economic, social and cultural interaction.

XIII. The Iraqi letter alleged that "the Kuwaiti authorities themselves acknowledged their trespass" on Iraqi oil wells through His Highness Sheikh Saad al-Abdullah al-Sabah, the Crown Prince and Prime Minister, during a meeting with the Deputy Chairman of the Iraqi Revolution Command Council at Jeddah on 30 July 1990. No such statement was made either at the talks conducted during that meeting or on any other occasion. Kuwait held to the view expressed in the two official letters submitted by the Deputy Prime Minister and Minister for Foreign Affairs to the Secretary-General of the League of Arab States on 18 and 21 July 1990, in reply to the Iraqi letters of 15 and 21 July 1990.

Kuwait affirmed, in front of the Iraqi delegation at the Jeddah meeting, that it was prepared to set up neutral commissions to examine all issues arising between the two parties, including the question of the oil wells. However, the Iraqi side did not reply to the proposal, preferring instead to launch its treacherous surprise attack against Kuwait only hours after the meeting ended.

XIV. In its challenge to the decisions of the Boundary Demarcation Commission, Iraq's letter resorts to that country's consistent practice of reneging on every agreement or commitment into which it has entered and imposing instead its viewpoints and ambitions as facts which must be accepted and complied with by all. Accordingly, it has interpreted the decisions of the Boundary Demarcation Commission, and indeed anything which conflicts with its wishes, as an act of colonialism and an international conspiracy.

By way of example, it rests its claim to Kuwaiti territory and islands in the Gulf not on any agreements which it has concluded or on historically documented boundaries but on its status as a coastal State which must have an outlet to the Gulf. It chooses that this outlet should be located in the territory of its neighbour, Kuwait, and insists that its demand must be translated into reality, regardless of whether that claim is justified or not. It is deliberately ignoring the well-known facts that it already has a 40-kilometre coastline at Al-Faw and that it controls the entire northern shore of Khawr Abdullah (35 kilometres) and Mina al-Bakr, which, following expansion, can now accommodate supertankers.

All nations have aspirations, with some seeking warm-water ports and others desiring areas rich in minerals or other resources. If such aspirations were allowed to become reality through imposition by force, the map of the world would be altered and further successive wars would consume human lives and deprive mankind of the benefits of progress in ensuring increased respect for the rule of law, good-neighbourliness and legitimacy.

Iraq's letter, inspired as it is by covetous fancy, states that its chosen maritime outlet lies in what it refers to as a "small village established some two centuries ago on the banks of the Arabian Gulf under the name of 'Kuwait'". When it refers to Kuwait in this way, it appears to deny the State's existence because of its small population and surface area. If the world were to adopt that approach, many effectively existing nations would disappear from the map. Countries should be measured by their performance and vitality rather than by their size or population.

XV. Iraq claims that it is not bound by the Agreed Minutes of 1963 because its legislative authority did not ratify them. Our answer to this assertion is as follows:

1. The question of whether an agreement is subject to ratification or not depends on the intentions of the parties concerned, which in turn depend on the circumstances, context and subject of the agreement.

Benheim (an expert on international law) says that, in the case of a protocol, a statement or an exchange of letters, there is no requirement for ratification - unless specifically stated otherwise - if any of the aforementioned agreements represents no more than the addition of a point of minor significance or the registration of an agreement between the two parties concerning the interpretation of an item in the original treaty.

As is well known, the Agreed Minutes do not abolish any boundaries or establish others in their place. With respect to the boundary issue, they simply record an acknowledgement of boundaries on which agreement had already been reached.

If we suppose for the sake of argument that ratification of the agreement was required, then the responsibility for failure to comply with the conditions for ratification rests with the defaulting State rather than with the other party to the agreement. It is the defaulting State which must bear the consequences of the unratified agreement. To claim otherwise would have the effect of entitling other States to interfere in the internal affairs of nations on the grounds that they were testing the agreement and verifying the soundness of ratification procedures. This is not acceptable in international practice.

2. It was the intention of the two contracting parties, Iraq and Kuwait, that the Minutes should be implemented immediately following their signature. This is indicated by the fact that most items of the Minutes were indeed implemented, such as recognition, the exchange of diplomatic representation, the establishment of a commercial and economic agreement, etc. The Kuwaiti side provided financial assistance amounting to 30 million dinars in accordance with the agreement.

3. Other agreements with Iraq (meaning those on matters other than the boundary) specifically stated that ratification was required, including, for example, the protocol on bilateral cooperation between Iraq and Kuwait. This shows that the practice established between the two countries requires the incorporation of a specific provision concerning ratification if the intentions of the two parties so require. The failure to incorporate such a provision into the documents concerning the boundary is a strong indication that such ratification was not required.

4. The Minutes were registered with the Secretariat of the United Nations on 10 January 1964 without any objection from either of the two States to the Minutes' coming into force on the grounds of non-ratification.

5. The Iraqi regime's objection to and constant violations of this agreement are nothing new. The regime has been in the habit of breaking all international agreements and treaties which are incompatible with its expansionist designs. Before the beginning of its war with Iran, it repudiated the Algiers Agreement of 1975 with Iran concerning the Shatt al-Arab and then announced its recognition of the Agreement once again after its invasion of Kuwait. The very fact of its invasion of Kuwait, thereby breaking and violating related Arab and international pacts, is in itself irrefutable evidence of the regime's inclinations and behaviour, namely, a failure to respect any law or regional or international treaty. Accordingly, and particularly with regard to this issue, Kuwait is firmly convinced that the will of the international community is the only appropriate instrument which must be applied to such a regime to enforce its respect for international laws and treaties.

XVI. The Iraqi letter attempted to draw the United Nations and the Security Council into labyrinths of allegations about Kuwait's historical existence which have already been answered and investigated from documented scholarly sources and in respect of which evidence, maps and studies showing the pursuit of this historical illusion to be a waste of time have already been published. Kuwait is a land, a people and a real historical State which is not susceptible to denial. This practice of alleging historical rights is entirely incompatible with the fundamental principles established under international law whereby the boundaries between neighbouring States which define the territory of each individual State in accordance with the boundaries drawn prior to their independence are considered to be binding. This principle was applied between Latin American States and was confirmed by the leaders of the African continent at the African summit meeting in 1964 for the purpose of settling border issues and disputes.

The Security Council adopted these principles when it endorsed the boundary agreed to by Kuwait and Iraq in 1932 and 1963, in conformity with studies on international law which rule out any repudiation of boundary agreements on the grounds that they have not been ratified.

Meanwhile, an objective scholarly study of the question of the boundary between Kuwait and Iraq always reaches the same conclusions, namely, those on the basis of which the world decided to support Kuwait and its cause.

The reason for this support is clear. The boundaries claimed by Kuwait are recorded in documents, maps and well-known internationally documented agreements which are not denied or contested by anyone other than those who espouse contrariness and falsify attested facts.

The history of these documents goes back to the time before Iraq's emergence as an independent State. They are not fabricated for the purpose either of inventing evidence or of claiming spurious rights raised when the border dispute erupted; they are firm, documented historical facts.

Any neutral historian will recognize that for almost three centuries (1709-1922) Kuwait - this land overlooking the north shore of the Arabian Gulf - has continued to exist as a distinct entity, maintaining its independence under all circumstances and despite all changes. The relationship of this distinct entity to the Ottoman State, whose influence extended throughout Iraqi territory, was clear: it was confined to the general

Islamic ties which linked Islamic lands under the Ottoman caliphate. There was no Ottoman presence in any part of Kuwait's territory, neither was there any form of political subordination. The relationship was a religious one, did not affect independence and did not detract from the Kuwaiti people's sovereignty over their territory.

This distinct and independent nature was demonstrated by the Kuwaiti people's self-reliance in defending themselves against tribal attacks and raids on Kuwait without assistance from the Ottoman authorities in Basra or Baghdad. They themselves - without help from anyone - built the walls of Kuwait in 1760 to protect their city.

Further evidence may be seen in the fact that Kuwait served as a refuge for rebels against the Ottoman authorities in Baghdad. Both Sheikh Thuwayni, the Sheikh of Muntafaq, and Mustafa Agha, the Governor of Basra, took refuge with Sheikh Abdullah al-Sabah, the Ruler of Kuwait (1762-1815) after rebelling against Suleiman Pasha, the Vali of Baghdad. Sheikh Abdullah refused to surrender them, despite a threat to attack Kuwait and force it to do so.

Kuwait's lack of subordination to the Ottomans is demonstrated by the fact that the Ruler of Kuwait permitted the British Agency of the British East India Company to be transferred from Basra to Kuwait (1793-1795) following a dispute with the Ottoman authorities. This could not have happened if Kuwait had owed allegiance or been subordinate to the Ottoman State.

If we set aside the evidence, testimonies and reports of travellers and politicians to consider instead the position of Kuwait in atlases, we find even stronger evidence of Kuwait as a distinct entity, particularly in two nineteenth-century maps, as follows:

1. The map of Carl Ritter, a German scholar and one of the founders of modern geography. Kuwait is included on the German-language map of the Arabian peninsula published in 1867 on the authority of his book *Erdkunde* (Geography), which appeared in several dozen volumes from 1818 onwards.

Kuwait is referred to as "Kueit or Korein" within a district encompassing its present location and including Warbah, Bubiyan and parts of southern Iraq. The map was printed in Berlin and is kept at the Cambridge University Library (Map No. C.336.58.1).

2. The map of the Arabian peninsular is contained in the journal of Arabian travel compiled by W. G. Palgrave in 1862-1863. This shows Kuwait in a colour marking it as completely independent from the other political entities in the region, meaning the Ottoman State to the north and Najd in the south. It is to be noted that the northern boundaries of Kuwait include Warbah and Bubiyan, as well as the west bank of the southern part of the Shatt al-Arab, including Umm Qasr and most of Al-Faw.

The agreement of 1913 between the Ottoman State and Britain contains no ruling whatsoever that Kuwait should be subordinate to the province of Basra, as repeatedly asserted in the Iraqi letter. Article 2 of the agreement specifies that the Sheikh of Kuwait shall exercise independent authority in his territory and that the Ottoman Government shall refrain from interfering in Kuwait's affairs, including the issue of inheritance, as well as from any other administrative activity and from any occupation or military action in the districts belonging to Kuwait.

Nevertheless, the agreement detached various parts of Kuwait's territory in Iraq's favour, in accordance with a request made by Sheikh Mubarak al-Sabah on the basis of documents and historical facts.

Iraq itself recognized these established facts and affirmed them on two occasions when it clearly recognized the State of Kuwait and its boundaries, in 1962 and 1963 respectively. The Annual Report of the Republic of Iraq for 1988 bears witness to this fact by way both of the information it includes on Kuwait as a neighbouring fraternal State and of the map accompanying that information, which locates the Kuwait-Iraq boundary very close to where it was eventually placed by the United Nations Boundary Demarcation Commission.

It is to be hoped that this review will serve to disperse all fancy and delusion and to establish the foundation of the truth, namely, that the administrative entity and political borders of Kuwait are a historical fact the features of which were clear over half a century before Iraq's independence.

XVII. Despite the lesson received by the Iraqi regime when it asserted that it was undertaking an invasion in response to appeals on the part of the Kuwaiti people, inasmuch as what it found was a people united behind its leadership, opposing the aggressive regime in a resistance, witnessed by the entire world, that came into being with considerable self-sacrifice - for indeed, the documents left behind by the invading forces at liberation showed the extent of the terror and consternation from which those invading Iraqi forces suffered on experiencing the resistance of the Kuwaitis - despite all that, this Iraqi letter goes back half a century, in the illusion that one can distort history and twist the facts in order to challenge Kuwaiti national unity by asserting that at the time of the first Legislative Council, during the reign of Sheikh Ahmad al-Jaber, the Council members called for the unification of Kuwait with Iraq! It also asserts that the free youth of Kuwait asked the Iraqi Government for assistance for that purpose - it is the same theme, being repeated half a century later.

It will suffice, in order for us to refute these claims, to go back to the letter presented by those youths, who met with the Amir of Kuwait, calling for a number of reforms and the constitution of a Legislative Council:

> "The course of events and the present conditions of the country have encouraged the sincere among your subjects to turn to you with earnest advice in their desire to come to an understanding with you concerning what may be a beneficial approach and a proper manning of warding off adversities from themselves and from you, preserving the existence of our country and safeguarding our independence, their sole aim being to remove the causes of complaint and to effect reforms."

This letter bespeaks only love and affection and the exchange of sincere advice between the shepherd and his flock, stressing the independence of Kuwait and the preservation of its existence.

At the close of this review of the statements made by the Iraqi Minister for Foreign Affairs in his letter concerning the conclusions of the Boundary Demarcation Commission, we are firmly convinced that his letter is nothing other than a link in an endless chain of attempts to create obstacles to a definitive conclusion of the boundary issue between Iraq and Kuwait.

Iraq is seeking to remove the problem from its present sphere, governed by international legitimacy, to the sphere of bilateral relations, in which Kuwait has, throughout its life, held out its hand with love and cooperation, offering dialogue and assistance in an absolute commitment to brotherliness, neighbourly rights, historical ties and shared destiny to its neighbour and brother; yet the reply was a hostile bullet pointed at its heart and aggression aimed at its existence and its land and the taking of lives and property.

The Iraqi regime believes that by once again raising a clamour in the news it can hamper the legal process and thwart the countries of the world in their insistence on restoring to the region security, stability and secure boundaries which the Security Council believes to protect; but it is time for the Iraqi regime to give up this belief, to face reality and to cooperate with its neighbours on a principled basis in a meeting between equals.

It would have sufficed, in order to refute this letter with all its particulars, to call attention to the clear statement which, after all the disastrous events for which it was to blame, it made in its letter, concerning its refusal to accept peaceful coexistence with its neighbours to the effect that under no circumstances would Iraq accept any formula relating to demarcation, British or otherwise.

Yet, in deference to Arab and world public opinion, against which the letter of the Iraqi regime has been published, we considered it our duty to provide the facts together with the documents presenting the correct information concerning them, hoping for a return to reason and truth and placing our trust in God.

...

S/24113, 17 June 1992

14. Note by the President of the Security Council, 17 June 1992

Following consultations of the Security Council held on 17 June 1992, the President of the Council issued the following statement on behalf of the members of the Council in connection with the item entitled "The situation between Iraq and Kuwait":

> "The members of the Security Council have noted the letter of 17 April 1992 from the Chairman of the Iraq-Kuwait Boundary Demarcation Commission to the Secretary-General and express their complete support for the work of the Secretary-General and the Boundary Demarcation Commission in implementing paragraph 3 of resolution 687 (1991). They recall in this connection that through the demarcation process the Boundary Demarcation Commission is not reallocating territory between Kuwait and Iraq, but is simply carrying out the technical task necessary to demarcate the precise coordinates of the boundary between Kuwait and Iraq for the first time. This task is being carried out in the special circumstances following Iraq's invasion of Kuwait and pursuant to resolution 687 and the Secretary-General's report (S/22558) for implementing paragraph 3 of that resolution. They look forward to the completion of the work of the Commission.
>
> "The members of the Council have noted with particular concern the letter of 21 May 1992 from the Minister of Foreign Affairs of the Republic of Iraq to the Secretary-General (S/24044) concerning the work of the Boundary Demarcation Commission, which appears to call into question Iraq's adherence to Security Council resolution 687 (1991). The members of the Council are concerned in particular that the letter from Iraq of 21 May 1992 may be interpreted as rejecting the finality of the Boundary Demarcation Commission's decisions notwithstanding the terms of resolution 687 and the Secretary-General's report for implementing paragraph 3 of that resolution, both of which were formally accepted by Iraq.
>
> "They note with dismay that the letter recalls past Iraqi claims to Kuwait without also recalling Iraq's subsequent repudiations of these claims, *inter alia* through its acceptance of resolution 687 (1991). The members of the Council firmly reject any suggestion that tends to dispute the very existence of Kuwait, a member State of the United Nations.
>
> "The members of the Council remind Iraq of its obligations under resolution 687 (1991), and in particular paragraph 2 thereof, and under other relevant resolutions of the Council.
>
> "The members of the Council also remind Iraq of its acceptance of the resolutions of the Council adopted pursuant to Chapter VII of the United Nations Charter, which forms the basis for the cease-fire. The members of the Council wish to stress to Iraq the inviolability of the international boundary between Iraq and Kuwait being demarcated by the Commission and guaranteed by the Council pursuant to resolution 687 (1991), and the grave consequences that would ensue from any breach thereof."

United Nations Press Release, IK/114, 27 July 1992

15. Iraq-Kuwait Boundary Demarcation Commission completes sixth session, New York, 15-24 July

Declares Northern Section of Boundary Demarcated

The Iraq-Kuwait Boundary Demarcation Commission held its sixth session in New York from 15-24 July, during which it completed a further report covering the land boundary and agreed on arrangements for the physical representation of this boundary.

The Commission stated that the land boundary was demarcated after a detailed analysis of evidence assembled by the Commission over a period of a year. Both Iraq and Kuwait had every opportunity to provide the Commission with all relevant material and evidence.

To demarcate the northern section of the boundary, the Commission investigated the position of the noticeboard which was accepted by both countries as demarcating the boundary to the south of Safwan between 1923 and 1939. This noticeboard determined the latitude of the line between the western boundary in the Batin and Safwan as well as the point at Safwan. This is a point which is fundamental to the definition of the northern boundary and which has never been accurately depicted on any map prior to the maps produced for the Commission.

In determining the position where the northern boundary would fall, the Commission had to assess conflicting claims ranging from 1,000 metres south of the old Customs post in the centre of Safwan, as claimed by Kuwait, 1,250 metres as asserted by an Iraqi diplomatic note in 1940, and rough descriptions of one mile south of various points in Safwan used in historical records. The Commission, after detailed studies, decided on a distance of 1,430 metres south of the Customs post, that is, 180 metres farther south than the distance specified in the Iraqi note.

It should be noted that the oil wells in the fields between Safwan and the Batin exploited in the past by Iraq fell already in Kuwait according to the boundary shown on the British map referred to in Security Council resolution 687 (1991).

The Commission's demarcation leaves Umm Qasr port complex, including all the warehouses, crane installations, deep-water anchorage and two wide berths, as well as the whole of Umm Qasr village, the Navy hospital and the sulphur works within Iraqi territory. With the port and the Khowr Zhobeir in Iraq, the Commission's decisions on this section of the land boundary affirm Iraq's access to the sea.

The Boundary Demarcation Commission is not reallocating territory between Kuwait and Iraq, but is simply carrying out the technical task necessary to demarcate the precise coordinates of the international boundary between Kuwait and Iraq for the first time. It unequivocally rejects any allegations of partiality.

The demarcation of the land boundary with permanent markers is in progress, and will be completed by the end of 1992.

The Commission agreed to investigate the Khowr Abd Allah section further and to discuss it at a meeting to be held for that purpose in October.

[*At the time of going to press this document had not been issued under an official Security Council reference number.*]

16. Letter from the UN Secretary-General to the President of the Security Council, 12 August 1992

Dear Mr. President

I have the honour to transmit to you the "Further Report of the United Nations Iraq-Kuwait Boundary Demarcation Commission" of 24 July 1992, together with a transmittal letter dated 28 July 1992 from the Chairman of the Commission addressed to me. I should be grateful if you would bring this report to the attention of the members of the Council.

I.

The present report is called "Further Report" because it continues and complements an interim report submitted to my predecessor by the Commission after its fourth session, and before decisions on the actual demarcation of the boundary were taken by the Commission. It contains and explains comprehensively the substantive decisions taken by the Commission at its fifth session on the land boundary as well as its future plans as to a renewed consideration of the offshore boundary in October 1992 and the physical representation of the land boundary. It also covers the Commission's field work in the border area from September to December 1991 and the subsequent cartographic production, research and analysis of all available material.

In order to carry out the demarcation of the boundary the Commission decided at its third session that a new and independent mapping was essential and requested a survey of the whole boundary area. The purpose of the survey was to establish an accurate survey network to provide coordinate points relevant to the definition of the boundary, to produce orthophoto maps and profiles along the Wadi al Batin, and to leave a primary control survey network in place which could be used to set out the boundary pillars. The survey produced a cartographic base consisting of 31 orthophoto maps covering the entire length of the border area.

Having examined the new survey and the cross-sectional profiles the independent experts were able to determine the thalweg of Wadi al Batin which forms the western section of the boundary. Based on a site visit and exhaustive research and analysis of all available documentation the independent experts were able to identify the old customs post in the center of Safwan and the old road leading south from it along which a noticeboard marking the boundary once stood until 1939. With the use of early charts and aerial photographs the independent experts were also able to establish the most probable position of the junction of Khowr Zhobeir and Khowr Abd Allah at epoch 1932. The independent experts also performed comparisons of boundary representations on earlier maps. Thus, the Commission had before it identification of key locations, south of Safwan, at the shore south of Umm Qasr and the junction of the Khowrs, for the determination of the northern section of the land boundary.

The Commission has reached the following findings on the land boundary by voting, with Iraq not participating in the vote: (1) the boundary monument on the Iraq-Saudi Arabian border, pillar no. 1, is the starting point for the boundary along the thalweg of Wadi al Batin, and therefore, the tripoint of Iraq, Kuwait and Saudi Arabia; (2) the boundary south of Safwan is located at the distance of 1,430 meters from the south-west extremity of the compound wall of the old customs post along the old road from Safwan to Kuwait; (3) the boundary at the northern end of Wadi al Batin is the intersection of the thalweg of the Wadi and the latitude of the point south of Safwan; (4) the boundary south of Umm Qasr coincides with the location at which the boundary line on the map circulated in Security Council document S/22412 crosses the western shore of Khowr Zhobeir; and (5) the junction of Khowr Zhobeir and Khowr Abd Allah is the one best identified for the epoch 1932 and transposed onto modern orthophoto maps produced by the Commission.

The Commission has further decided: (1) that the boundary line in the Wadi al Batin shall be demarcated as a series of straight line segments of about 2 kilometers length best approximating to the lowest point line in the Wadi; (2) that the boundary line from the point at the northern end of the Wadi al Batin to the point south of Safwan shall be demarcated as a line running along the common latitude of the points; (3) that the boundary line from the point south of Safwan to the point south of Umm Qasr shall be demarcated as the shortest line between the points; and (4) that the boundary line from the point south of Umm Qasr on the shore shall be demarcated following the low-water line up to the location directly opposite the junction of Khowr Zhobeir and Khowr Abd Allah.

In connection with the Commission's further consideration of the eastern section of the boundary, which includes the offshore boundary, the representative of Kuwait at the fifth session expressed his view, citing historical evidence and the language of the 1932/1963 frontier agreement, that the Commission's mandate extended to demarcation of the boundary to the east of the junction of the Khowrs. The Commission decided to consider this part of the boundary in October 1992.

At the end of April 1992, according to the decisions reached by the Commission, temporary pillars marking three key locations were emplaced at the north end of the Wadi, south of Safwan and on the shore south of Umm Qasr. Preparations are currently under way to identify a suitable contractor to manufacture and construct the necessary number of pillars to demarcate the land boundary on the ground. The setting out of the pillars by the Commission's survey team will begin at the end of September and is scheduled to be completed by the middle of December 1992.

II.

As far as the land boundary is concerned, the Council might wish to express, in the form considered most appropriate by its members, its appreciation of, and gratitude for, the work accomplished by the Commission. As far as the offshore boundary is concerned, the Council might wish to encourage the Commission to demarcate that part of the boundary as soon as possible, and thus to complete its work.

I also wish to draw the attention of the members of the Council to the fact that the decision taken by the Commission on the land boundary raises the question of whether and when the demilitarized zone monitored by UNIKOM should be brought into line with the boundary as demarcated by the Commission. The re-alignment, which I would like to carry out with the concurrence of the Council, could be effected either immediately or after all the boundary markers have been erected. While the Government of Kuwait has informed me of its strong interest in the earliest possible completion of the re-alignment, the Under-Secretary-General for Peace-Keeping, Mr. Goulding, as well as the Chief Military Observer of UNIKOM, Major General Dibuama, have informed me that, for practical reasons, they would favour that the re-alignment be carried out after the boundary markers have been put into place. The re-alignment would not necessitate moving any of UNIKOM's fixed installations. I believe that it will be sufficient to redraw the lines of the demilitarized zone on the maps which UNIKOM uses for operational purposes, and to move the notice boards which have been established on the main routes and tracks to indicate to travellers that they are entering the demilitarized zone.

The demarcation of the border will also have consequences for the Iraqi police posts which lie on the Kuwaiti side of the boundary as demarcated or within 1,000 meters from it on the Iraqi side. It will be recalled from my report of 31 March 1992 on the United Nations Iraq-Kuwait Observation Mission (S/23766, paragraph 19), that the Iraqi authorities have maintained that the posts concerned must remain in their present location until the border between Iraq and Kuwait has been demarcated.

Finally, while Iraq was represented at all previous sessions of the Commission, it was not represented at the last session at which the attached report was adopted. The Council might thus wish to urge the Government of Iraq to be represented at the future sessions of the Commission.

...

FURTHER REPORT OF THE UNITED NATIONS IRAQ-KUWAIT BOUNDARY DEMARCATION COMMISSION, 28 JULY 1992

...

I. INTRODUCTION

1. The present report of the Iraq-Kuwait Boundary Demarcation Commission covers the Commission's field work conducted in the border area from September to December 1991, the subsequent cartographic production, the work of its fifth session, which was held at United Nations Headquarters from 8 to 16 April 1992, and the execution of the decisions reached by the Commission at that session.[1] [1. For a report on the previous work of the Commission see the "Interim Report of the Iraq-Kuwait Boundary Demarcation Commission" (IKBDC/Rep.2, 31 October 1992).]

2. The terms of reference, mandate and composition of the Commission remain as described in paragraphs 1 to 5 of the Commission's interim report (IKBDC/Rep.2).

3. The Commission was provided with, and approved, minutes of all its meetings (IKBDC/Min.29-39), which were then authenticated by the Chairman. It also issued a press release at the end of its deliberations (IKBDC/Press.7) describing the work accomplished since the fourth session and the final decisions concerning the land boundary adopted by the Commission at its fifth session and its future work programme.

4. The present report is submitted pursuant to paragraph 6 of the Secretary-General's report of 2 May 1991 (S/22558).

II. FIELD WORK OF THE COMMISSION

5. As indicated in the first report of the Commission to the Secretary-General (IKBDC/Rep.2, annex I), the surveying and mapping work of the Iraq-Kuwait border area was to be undertaken in two stages; (a) geodetic control, aerial photography and mapping and (b) boundary demarcation. The present report describes the first stage.

6. The national survey departments of New Zealand and Sweden were mobilized to form survey and aerial photography teams and to undertake the final map preparation. Work in the field began with the replacement of photo control marks by the United Nations Iraq-Kuwait Observation Mission (UNIKOM) at the beginning of September 1991. At the end of that month, the ground survey team arrived, followed shortly after by the air crew. The field survey was completed by the end of November 1991 with some additional work in the spring of 1992. Orthophoto map production was completed in March 1992 and the results of the work along with complete sets of maps were reviewed by the Commission at its fifth session.

A. Datum survey

1. Monumentation

7. One existing and three new datum stations were occupied. Two of the new stations are concrete pillars established inside UNIKOM observation posts. These are provided with four buried witness marks each to allow reinstatement if necessary.

8. A third new station was established on the roof of a concrete building at UNIKOM headquarters at Umm Qasr. This has been provided with three witness marks, which are away from the building to allow reinstatement of the datum station in the event of the building being demolished.

9. An existing datum station (concrete pillar) was chosen, which is already provided with witness marks.

2. Network geometry

10. The three new stations are located near the south-west, north-west and north-east extent of the Iraq-Kuwait land boundary. The fourth datum station is located near Kuwait City to provide good overall network geometry. This station has existing Doppler coordinates.

11. Two stations are in Kuwait: one near Kuwait City, as noted above, and one on the eastern side of Wadi al Batin.

12. One station is in Iraq on the western side of Wadi al Batin. The remaining station is at Umm Qasr.

3. Accuracy

13. The four datum stations were observed with Doppler and Global Positioning System (GPS) instruments over a period of approximately 68 hours. The Doppler observations in a network adjustment were consistent with an accuracy of ± 0.75 metres in each coordinate. The new datum is based on the data at all four stations and therefore has a standard deviation of approximately half this value.

14. The relative positions of the stations were determined from five or six GPS observation sessions. These repeated measurements gave horizontal coordinate accuracy better than ± 0.010m + 1 part per million

(ppm) of the interstation distance. The relative ellipsoidal height accuracy is better than ±0.020m + 2 ppm of the interstation distance.

B. Primary control survey

1. Monumentation

15. In addition to the datum stations, 14 existing and 11 new primary control stations were occupied. Ten of these new primary control stations are concrete pillars and one is a mark set in concrete at ground level.

2. Network geometry

16. Of the 14 existing primary control stations, 13 are in Kuwait and one (P-6) is located close to the Iraq-Kuwait-Saudi Arabian boundary junction (trijunction point). All of the 11 new primary control stations are in Iraq. No existing stations in Iraq could be occupied as no information was made available on the location or coordinates of Iraqi control stations.

17. Of the datum and primary control stations, 15 stations are in Kuwait, 12 are in Iraq, 1 is at Umm Qasr and 1 is near the trijunction point at the south end of Wadi al Batin.

18. The primary control stations (including datum stations along the boundary) are at approximately 15 to 25 kilometre intervals along the boundary. Some variation was required to make use of existing stations and to meet the requirements of the photo control.

3. Accuracy

19. The relative positions of the primary control stations were determined by GPS observations. Repeated measurements, loop closures and the network adjustment indicate horizontal coordinate accuracy better than ±0.020m + 2 parts per million (ppm) of the interstation distance. The relative ellipsoidal height accuracy is better than ±0.030m + 3 ppm of the interstation distance.

4. Equipment

20. *Hardware*:
Four JMR 1A Doppler receivers
Six Ashtec L-XII dual frequency GPS receivers

21. *Software*:
Various commercial and NLS (National Land Survey of Sweden) and DOSLI (Department of Survey and Land Information, New Zealand) utilities programmes. (IKBDC/Doc.15).

C. Aerial photography

1. The programme

22. The main aerial photography programme was carried out during the period October-December 1991. Some additional photography was also done during March 1992.

23. The photography was carried out from two main altitudes: 14 strips from 5,500m, with a negative scale of 1:36,000, were flown for the orthophoto mapping and one strip, in 4 segments, was flown from 3,000m, negative scale 1:19,600, for the profiling. The longitudinal and lateral overlap for the high level photography was 62 per cent and 25 per cent respectively; the longitudinal overlap for the 3,000m photography was 60 per cent. In March 1992 an additional strip of photography was flown from 3,000m with a longitudinal overlap of 60 per cent and a lateral overlap 30 per cent. A number of strips at a negative scale of 1:36,000 were flown along the Khowrs at low water. All of the signalized points in this photography were also photographed in colour from an altitude of 1,100m.

24. The towns of Safwan and Umm Qasr were photographed at a scale of 1:6,500.

2. Aircraft and equipment

25. *Aircraft*: Rockwell Turbo Commander, model 690A.

26. *Camera*: Zeiss Jena LMK 500 FMC camera with forward motion compensation and 15 cm optics, mounted on an SM 2000 gyro ring mount.

27. *Lens cone and lens*: lens cone 265014A and lens 738310C. The calibrated focal length of the lens is 152.44 mm.

28. *Navigational equipment*: Ashtec, 12 channel, L1 GPS receiver with an air photo module for navigation and steering of exposures at predetermined points. The PC-based software permits continuous logging of data.

29. *Film*: Kodak Panatomic X and Agfa Avicolor N200.

30. *Products*: all films were developed at the National Land Survey of Sweden where all contact prints and diapositives were also produced. The numbering of the negatives and the production of the flight plans were also done in Sweden.

D. Photo control survey

1. Monumentation

31. One existing Kuwaiti survey station was used for photo control but not as a primary control station. The remaining 136 stations, set out for photo control only, consisted of metal stakes driven into the ground. All of these points were signalized. The photo-control signals consisted of four arms made up of filled sandbags.

2. Network geometry

32. The network geometry was as dictated by the orthophoto and profiling flight plans.

33. The high-level photo control was set out in north-south and east-west lines at approximately 6.25 to 12.5km intervals. The photo-control marks for the profiling of Wadi al Batin were at approximately 3 to 3.5km intervals across the Wadi and 5 to 5.5km intervals along the Wadi.

34. Several primary or datum stations served as photo control also.

3. Accuracy

35. The accuracy requirement for orthophoto control was ±0.20m for the horizontal coordinates and ±0.50m in height. The requirement for the profiling was ±0.10m relative accuracy between adjacent stations in each coordinate.

36. The height accuracy requirements apply to the orthometric height of the ground at the station. Orthometric heights are derived from the GPS ellipsoidal height by the application of geoid heights from a global geopotential model and measurements of the height of the

station mark above ground level. These accuracy specifications were met for the photo control survey.

E. Coordinate systems

1. Datum

37. A new three dimensional datum was determined and called the Iraq-Kuwait Boundary Datum 1992 (IKBD-92). It is based on GPS and Doppler observations. Within the accuracy of these observations, it is equal to the World Geodetic System 1984 (WGS-84). The ellipsoid which was used for the IKBD-92 datum is the WGS-84 ellipsoid.

38. A new orthometric height datum has been defined and called the Iraq-Kuwait Boundary Height Datum 1992 (IKBHD-92). Heights in this datum are based on:

(a) IKBD-92 ellipsoidal heights;

(b) A global geopotential model, OSU-86E, developed at Ohio State University.

Kuwaiti survey records were used to modify the origin of the height datum to ensure that the contours depicted on the orthophotos are approximately in terms of mean sea level.

2. Projection

39. The map projection used for orthophoto mapping is the Universal Transverse Mercator (UTM) projection, Zone 38, extended eastward to cover the entire boundary area.

F. Orthophoto mapping

40. As described above, the aerial photography for the mapping was flown at a height of 5,500m, approximate negative scale 1:36,000: 10 strips along the western boundary and 4 along the northern boundary. The scale of the orthophoto map is 1:25,000 with contour intervals of 5 metres. The exposure points were preplanned so that one full sheet could be assembled from four negatives. All ground control points were pre-signalized.

41. Two blocks of map sheets were produced: a western block of 18 sheets and a northern block of 11 sheets. The sheet layout was designed and submitted to the Secretary for approval. The format sheets, in Arabic and English, were produced using an Intergraph CAD system.

1. Equipment

42. Mapping:

Analytical plotters: Zeiss Planicomp C110 & C120 and Wild BC2 & BC3 Aviolyt
Projector: Wild 0.R1 Avioplan
Plotters: Hewlett Packard HP7585B and Wild TA2 and TA10
Software: PAT-MR and PAT-M-43, SCOP and DOSLI programmes

43. Profiling:

Analytical plotters: Wild BC2 and BC3 Aviolyt
Computers: Intergraph Workstation
Plotters: Wild TA2 & TA10
Software: INSITE/ONSITE and DOSLI programmes

2. Western block

44. The aerial triangulation of the 137 models was done using Zeiss Planicomp C110 and C120 analytical plotters. The adjustment of the measurements was done using the PAT-MR software package. The standard error of unit weight of the adjustment is ± 0.28m in planimetry and ± 0.41m in height.

45. Digital terrain models (DTMs) were created on Planicomp analytical instruments by measuring a regular 100x100m grid and breaklines. The number of points measured per sheet was of the order of 15,500.

46. The data from the block adjustment and the DTMs were used to generate the steering information for the projection of the orthophotos. The orthophoto diapositives were first reversed to produce negatives and then projected in a Wild Avioplan OR 1 orthophoto projector. Four continuous tone positives at a scale of 1:25,000 were produced for each sheet.

47. The four positives for each sheet were assembled using pass points obtained from the aerial triangulation. Nine passpoints were used per negative.

48. Contours, with a 5-metre vertical interval were, thereafter, generated from the terrain models using the SCOP software package and then plotted using a Hewlett Packard plotter. The contour manuscripts were edited and then used for the manual scribing.

3. The northern block

49. The measurements for the aerial triangulation of the 66 models were done in Wild BC3 Aviolyt analytical plotters. The adjustment of the measurements was done using the PAT-M-43 software package. The standard errors of unit weight of the results is ± 0.25m in planimetry and ± 0.47m in height.

50. Terrain data was captured in the form of a 100x100m grid with breaklines using Wild BC2 and BC3 Aviolyt analytical plotters (approximately 15,500 points per sheet). These data were used as the source information for generating the steering data for the Wild OR1 Avioplan orthophoto projector. Four continuous tone negatives at a scale of 1:25,000 were produced for each sheet.

51. The four negatives for each sheet were assembled using passpoints obtained from the aerial triangulation. Nine passpoints were used per image.

52. The feature separations with contours with a 5m vertical interval were automatically plotted.

4. Final sheets

50.[sic] The 31 sheet-size orthophoto negatives were registered with the contour separations and format sheets and produced as positive halftone transparencies from which bromide and ozalid prints were made. (IKBDC/Doc.6).

III. RESEARCH AND ANALYSIS OF DOCUMENTATION, EVIDENCE AND MAPPING OF THE BORDER AREA

53. Since the first session of the Commission in May 1991, the independent experts have been gathering any material that might have relevance to the determination of the precise demarcation of the Iraq-Kuwait boundary. In their work they have been guided by Security Council resolution 687 (1991), and in particular, by paragraph 2 of that resolution which refers to the 1963 Agreed

Minutes between Iraq and Kuwait (United Nations *Treaty Series*, vol. 485, No. 7063) incorporating the following description of the "existing frontier" as contained in the 1932 Exchange of Letters, hereinafter referred to as the delimitation formula:

> "From the intersection of the Wadi-el-Audja with the Batin and thence northwards along the Batin to a point just south of the latitude of Safwan; thence eastwards passing south of Safwan wells, Jebel Sanam and Um Qasr leaving them to Iraq and so on to the junction of the Khor Zobeir with the Khor Abdullah. The islands of Warbah, Bubiyan, Maskan (or Mashjan), Failakah, Auhah, Kubbar, Qaru and Umm-el-Maradim appertain to Kuwait."

54. The independent experts have been further guided by the terms of reference provided by the Secretary-General (Document S/22558) which specifically referred to the use of appropriate material and technology, *inter alia*.

55. In order to provide a mapping base for objective reference of appropriate material and subsequent demarcation the independent experts have also conducted highly detailed and accurate survey and mapping of the border area. They have requested the representatives of both Governments to submit to them all documents and other material and information deemed important to their work. The results of the research and analysis of all the available documentation by the independent experts is described below.

A. Western section

56. The western section of the Iraq-Kuwait boundary has been defined in the delimitation formula as that formed by Wadi Al Batin. The Commission at its second session decided that the boundary in the Wadi would be determined by the thalweg. The task of the independent experts was, therefore, to determine the lowest point line in the Wadi.

1. Profiling

57. The determination of the lowest point line was carried out by examining the elevation contours and by measuring transverse, photogrammetric profiles across the Wadi Al Batin. For the purposes of generating the profiles, four additional strips of aerial photography were taken at the scale of 1:19,600. Furthermore, in an area where the Wadi broadened beyond the limits predetermined for profiling, and where the determination of the lowest point was very difficult, additional aerial photography was carried out at a subsequent stage.

58. Approximately 1,420 profiles were produced along the line of the Wadi at 100m intervals with the use of Wild BC2 and BC3 Aviolyt analytical plotters. The length of each profile is approximately 3,500m. Measurements were made along the profiles at 50m intervals; measurements were also made at change of grade. The data for the individual profiles were stored in D-Map files. After the completion of a profile a verification plot was made on Wild TA 2 or Wild TA 10 plotting tables. The horizontal scale of the profiles is 1:25,000 and the vertical scale is 1:1,000. The standard error of unit weight for a height measured in a profile is between ± 0.2 and ± 0.3m. A complete set of these profiles were [sic] distributed to the members of the Commission. (IKBDC/Doc.9, annex I).

59. A program package, written at the Department of Survey and Land Information of New Zealand, was then used to determine the X, Y and Z coordinates for the lowest point on every profile.

60. The final data were reformatted to the Intergraph computer system and the InSite/InRoad software package was used for on-screen viewing on an Intergraph workstation. In addition to viewing the position of the profile in the terrain, the Intergraph system was used to generate a digital terrain data model from which 2m supplementary contours were derived. The recommended location of the lowest point on a longitudinal profile was produced by working interactively with the computer system.

61. On a separate set of orthophoto maps the 2m contours were plotted in addition to the 5m ones. The alignments of the cross-sectional profiles and a recommended line of lowest points were indicated on these maps. (IKBDC/Doc.9, annex II).

62. At the fifth session of the Commission, an Intergraph workstation was set up and the three-dimensional profiling was demonstrated to the members of the Commission for the entire length of the Wadi.

B. Northern section

63. The northern section of the Iraq-Kuwait boundary is defined as that segment which runs from the northern end of Wadi Al Batin, from "a point just south of the latitude of Safwan", to the shore of Khowr Zhobeir at Umm Qasr.

64. The Commission at its second session reached an agreement that the boundary south of Safwan lay between approximately 900 and 1,900 yards south of the old (Iraqi) customs post and requested the independent experts to collect any material necessary for the determination of the precise location of the northern boundary. The independent experts needed to locate the old customs post at Safwan, to narrow down as far as possible the distance of the boundary south of the old customs post, to determine the position of the boundary at the northern end of the Batin, and to determine the position of the boundary at Umm Qasr.

1. Orthophoto mapping

65. Separate orthophoto maps at the scale of 1:7,500 were prepared, one for the Safwan and three for the Umm Qasr areas.

2. Safwan village and the old Iraqi customs post

66. The old customs post has been used as an important the reference point [sic] for several boundary interpretations. In order to determine and plot the boundary on the orthophoto maps of the Commission it was necessary that the identity and location of the customs post be established as closely as possible. To facilitate this task written and oral records were considered, aerial photographs were examined and a site visit was conducted.

a. Written and oral records

67. Several descriptions of Safwan and the customs post are available. In 1907, J.G. Lorimer described the village of Safwan as, "consisting of two or three small enclosures containing a few houses and of a date grove, surrounded by a wall belonging to the Naqib of Basra ... To the east of the date grove is a post garrisoned by a detachment of 40 regular Turkish infantry, and one mile to the west is a Bedouin halting place with wells of

passable water 12 feet deep: between the halting place and the village is a ruined enclosure".

68. In 1949, the Political Agent in Kuwait, Galloway, defined Safwan as consisting of a well, a palm grove, the Security Police Post and, 100 yards south of the that [sic] Post, the customs post enclosed by a compound wall.

69. The Commission also had before it a recent description of the customs post at Safwan. (IKBDC/Doc.8).

b. Site visit

70. From 3 to 10 November 1991, the independent experts conducted a site visit to the village of Safwan in order to locate the customs post. Representatives of both Government were invited to participate. The representative of Kuwait and four of his experts joined the independent experts. The representative of Iraq did not participate and left the work in the hands of the independent experts.

71. Aided by a position finding instrument (GPS) and using the astronomical coordinates for a concrete pillar, erected in 1942 by a team from the Indian Army, the general locality of the customs post was established. With the guidance of one of the Kuwaiti experts, the independent experts were able to locate the villas immediately north of the customs post on the ground.

72. The additional oblique aerial photographs taken immediately after the site visit gave further verification of the locality of the customs post.

c. Aerial photographs

73. The independent experts obtained and reviewed vertical aerial photographs from 1945, 1954, 1958 and 1991 and oblique aerial photographs from 1965, 1966 and 1991 to identify the customs post at Safwan. (IKBDC/Doc.8, annexes I and II).

Aerial photography-analysis

1945 The customs post (fort) can be clearly identified with its walls, buildings, compound and the large lthl [sic] tree. Palm groves can be seen to the south and south west of the fort. A large walled compound with distinctive features is visible about 300m south-east of the fort. There are very few other buildings in Safwan.

1954 Safwan village has developed south of the customs post. The palm groves to the south west of the post is still there. The post appears not to have changed significantly since 1945 although the trees in the compound are larger. The walled compound to the south-east is unchanged. North of the post a row of four houses has been built. The size of the buildings comprising the fort have been measured on the photograph and they agree well with the measurements made of the buildings on the 1945 photograph. The outer wall is still clearly visible although it is difficult to identify an inner wall. This wall may have been the same as the wall of the buildings that faced the inner compound. A distance has been measured on the photograph from the south-west corner of the outer wall - the southernmost extremity - to the intersection of the frontages of the two nearest buildings which line the inner court. Taking into account uncertainties in the scale of the photograph, the distance of approximately 40m agrees reasonably well with Jackson's (the Political Agent, Kuwait) paced distance of 40 paces. The position of the palm grove agrees reasonably well with Jackson's paced distance.

1958 Safwan continues to develop, mainly to the south. A large building in the shape of an inverted T has been erected to the north-west of the post. Further to the north-west there is a large square building with an inner compound. The distinctive trees in the compound of the post are clearly visible but the walls of the compound are now partly demolished.

1965 and 1966 The trees in the compound of the post are very distinctive. There are now six houses in the row of houses north of the post. The two buildings to the north-west are clearly identifiable.

1991 On the large-scale, vertical photograph, Safwan is a small town with a well-developed infrastructure with a wide road running through the town from north to south. The post can still be clearly identified: the trees are still in the area which was the compound, the large building to the west of the post can be seen as can the row of six buildings to the north of the post. Measurements on the photograph would seem to indicate that the original buildings along the northern side of the compound and along the eastern side of the compound are still in existence. A street running in a west-south-westerly direction cuts through what was the southern part of the compound close to the southern wall of the building which stood on the eastern side of the compound.

3. Location of the boundary at Safwan

a. Definitions

74. In order to determine the location of the boundary it was necessary to examine the definitions of the boundary that have been used in draft conventions and agreements, notes and official documents.

Those which are most frequently cited are the following:

Year-description

1912 "So as to pass immediately south of Umm Qasr and Safwan to Jebel Sanam".

1913 "Up to and past the walls of the fort of Safwan" was proposed on 26 February 1913, and was modified on 26 March to read "up to and past but not including the walls of the fort at Safwan". This modification was made to clarify the British Government's position, namely, that it did not accept the claim of the Ruler of Kuwait to Safwan.

1913 In the Anglo-Ottoman Convention of July 1913 the boundary delimitation formula reads: "The demarcation line departs from the coast at the mouth of the Khor Zobeir estuary towards the north-west and passes immediately south of Umm Qasr, Safwan and Jebel Sanam, in a manner so as to leave these places and their wells to the Vilayet of Basra ...". The line, which was marked in green on the map annexed to the Convention, almost touched the circles depicting Safwan and Umm Qasr and the hatching of Jebel Sanam. The unreliability of the map which accompanied the Convention was later highlighted. The Convention was never ratified.

1923 "Just south of the latitude of Safwan: thence eastward and south of Safwan wells". This is the position of the noticeboard marked "Iraq-Kuwait Boundary" which was erected by the Political Agent in Kuwait, Major John More and Shaikh Ahmed of Kuwait. According to Schofield (p. 62) "it was established that More had decided on the site of the noticeboard by marching out paces from the most southerly date palms at Safwan". The distance which was paced is not stated.

According to Colonel Dickson, the noticeboard was believed to lie just inside Kuwaiti territory.

1932 The noticeboard was removed on 5 June 1932, allegedly on the orders of the Mutasarrif in Basra for refurbishing, and had been replaced by 13 July 1932 by the Iraqis. In a letter dated 21 July 1932, from the Prime Minister of Iraq to the High Commissioner for Iraq the frontier is described as running "along the Batin to a point just south of the latitude of Safwan; thence eastward passing south of Safwan Wells, Jebel Sanam and Umm Qasr leaving them to Iraq ...".

1935 Colonel Dickson, the Political Agent in Kuwait, recognized the shortcomings and lack of precision in the definitions of the boundary and, in connection with discussions as to how the boundary should be depicted on the new Survey of India map, wrote to the Political Resident stating that, "we have always understood the northern boundary of the frontier to run in a due east-west line, from the Batin (centre line) to a point one mile south of Safwan Wells (where a large noticeboard exists on the side of the road which today marks the actual boundary)". Some years later, Dickson recollected that the noticeboard had been erected on a slight rise.

1936 A new British map (GSGS No. 3954) at a scale of 1:500,000 showed a turning point about one and a half miles south of Safwan.

1937 The Adviser to the Iraqi Minister of the Interior, Major Edmonds, proposed that demarcation of the frontier should be done and suggested that the boundary should be "through a point one mile south of the Safwan date palms".

1939 A temporary Kuwaiti post was established 1.6km (1 mile) south of the palms at Safwan at "a very short distance south of the long established noticeboard", which was removed by the Iraqi authorities on 28 March 1939.

1940 Galloway, the Political Agent in Kuwait, replaced the noticeboard close to the tenth telegraph pole counted south from Safwan. This was done after consultation with Colonel Dickson, although Dickson had said that the board had originally been located between the tenth and eleventh poles. Afterwards, Galloway wrote to Prior, the Political Resident, saying, "I did my best to check by the poles but I discovered that Dickson's spot did not bring me to a mile away from Safwan. I did not know then that there were 17 or 18 poles to the mile ...". This latter statement gives the distance between the poles as between 95 and 101m, i.e. a mean of 98m, which is closer to 100m than 100 yards.

1940 The Iraqi Ministry of Foreign Affairs protested (note 2635/2635/7/12364, dated 25 June 1940) that the new noticeboard had been erected by people who had "crossed the Iraqi frontier to a depth of 1,000m from Safwan post" and placed it "far from the site of the old one ... at a distance of 250m within the Iraqi frontier".

1940 The allegation was rejected by a British note (note verbale No.355 of 3 August 1940). Two months earlier Dickson had been of the opinion that the noticeboard was somewhat less than a mile south of Safwan.

1940 Daubeny, with the assistance of Dickson, ascertained that the noticeboard was located about 1,050 yards south of the most southerly palm at Safwan.

1940 The British ambassador in Baghdad sent a note to the Foreign Minister of Iraq, Nuri al-Said, proposing demarcation of the boundary. The point south of Safwan was defined as "The point a little to the south of Safwan at which the noticeboard marking the frontier stood until March 1939".

1942 Surveyors from the Indian Army erected two concrete pillars: according to the survey records one was in Safwan village, amongst the palm trees, and a second pillar half a mile to the south of the first pillar. The surveyors determined co-ordinates, by astronomic observations, for the pillars and also for a point on the north-west corner of the customs post wall. Documentation of the results of the survey observations is available. There are a number of ambiguities in this material: the computed distance between the pillars is approximately 1,006m and not 800m as stated in the documents. Also, a telegram from the Political Agent in Kuwait, dated 19 March 1942, reported that the first pillar was at the most southerly palm tree and the second one exactly one kilometre south of it.

1942 An official of the British Foreign Office wrote that, "it has always been argued that the point just south of Safwan should be defined as one mile south of the most southerly palm, if definition by reference to the site of the former noticeboard, which is apparently rather less than one mile south of Safwan, proves impossible".

1949 The positions of some of the reference points in and near Safwan were checked by Jackson of the Political Agency in Kuwait who found that:

(a) The most southerly palm was 160 paces from the outer wall of the customs post and 200 paces from the inner wall.

A study of the aerial photographs from 1945 and 1954 indicates that the distance of 40 paces between the outer compound wall and the inner wall could only have been paced between the southern extremity of the outer compound wall and the line of buildings surrounding the (inner) compound which may have been part of an inner wall. Nowhere else is the distance between inner and outer walls 40 paces. During the 1940s additional date palms had been planted south of Safwan;

(b) The sweet-water well was approximately 50 yards south-west of the customs post.

1950 On 21 June 1950, Dickson wrote a note to Jakins, the Political Agent in Kuwait, and enclosed a sketch showing that the noticeboard was placed at the thirteenth telegraph pole. Dickson stated that "the first of the telegraph posts should be the one closest to the masonry covered-in well, not the one next to it ...".

1950 Shaikh Abdullah III of Kuwait accepted the boundary shown to him on a map by the Political Agent, J.A. Gethin. He was of the opinion that it should be located at a point no further than one mile south of the oasis. The Political Agent was sceptical about the information provided by Dickson concerning the position of the boundary relative to the telegraph poles since Dickson had first related it to the tenth and then changed to the thirteen pole. The poles were said to be 100m apart.

Dickson attempted to relate the position of the boundary to the line of telegraph poles running south from Safwan. At different times he used a point between the 10th and 11th poles (1940) and at the 13th poles (in a note dated 21 June 1950 with a sketch) as reference points. Interpolation of Dickson's notes presents difficulty and the independent experts do not consider that the distances derived from his notes should be used in fixing the position of the boundary.

Jakins, the Political Agent in Kuwait, with the help of Dickson attempted to relate the position of the boundary to the line of telegraph poles. By 1951 the original line of poles had been changed and the distances between them was measured as 100 yards. Jakins identified slight rises at the 12th and 15th poles and Dickson considered that either of those rises could have been the site of the noticeboard. Jakins wrote, "the fifteenth pole seemed as far as I could judge at the time about a mile from the customs post."

1951 Sir Rupert Hay, the Political Resident in Bahrain, based on Dickson's statement that the noticeboard stood near to the thirteenth telegraph pole, placed the border 1,300m south of the southern wall of the customs post.

b. Reference points

75. It is impossible to re-establish the exact position of "the most southerly palm" south of Safwan. But, by using Jackson's placed distances it is possible, within reasonable limits, to relate the positions of the palm trees and the sweet-water well to the customs post. The point at the customs post to which the distances to these two points are related is defined in the various documents as "the southern wall", as "the southern extremity (south-west corner) of the compound", and as "the outer wall".

76. From evidence available it can be assumed that the most likely and best defined point to refer a paced distance to is the southernmost corner of the compound.

77. In a telegram dated 22 March 1949, Galloway made a similar suggestion writing, "I suggest that a closer definition of Safwan is necessary due to the fact that the term itself leads to ambiguity. Safwan consists of a well, a palm grove, the Security Police Post, and 100 yards south of the that [sic] Post the customs post enclosed by a compound wall. I suggest that the definition might read "x yards south of the southern extremity of the outer compound wall of the Safwan customs Post".

78. Based on the paced distances by the Kuwaiti Political Agent, Jackson, from the customs post - assumed to be the southern extremity of the outer compound wall - to the most southerly palm and to the sweet water well, and on the positions of the telegraph poles as defined by Dickson, the following calculations have been made to relate the various definitions of the position of the boundary to the customs post.

79. The most southerly palm is taken to be 160 paces south of the southern extremity of the outer compound wall of the customs post. One pace has been assumed to be just under one yard which gives a distance of approximately 150 yards (c. 137m).

80. The IKBD 1992 UTM grid coordinates of the concrete pillar which was built beside the palm by the team of Indian surveyors in 1942 are 3334405 N, 761774 E. The coordinates of the second pillar south of Safwan are 3333398 N, 761800 E. The coordinates of the north-west corner of the customs post are 3334561 N, 761826 E.

81. The computed distance between the pillar at the southern palm and the second pillar is 1,006m. The distance between the north-west corner of the customs post and the pillar at the southern palm is 164m which gives a distance of approximately 125m from the south-west corner of the post to the palm.

82. A further reference point is "one mile south of the wells". Assuming that the wells to which reference is made lie near to, or include, the well that is described as being 50 yards (or 43m) south-west of the southern extremity of the outer compound wall of the customs post, the distance to the border is approximately 1,652m.

c. The noticeboard

83. The noticeboard that was erected by Major More in 1923 was the first and longest-standing demarcation of the point south of Safwan. For many years it was recognized as a boundary point by the local population, by the British authorities who erected it and by the Iraqi authorities.

84. In a note written on 6 June 1932, Dickson described the location of the noticeboard erected by More in 1923 as follows: "Near Safwan and, as near as one can judge, on the Kuwait side of the frontier line between Iraq and Kuwait my predecessor Colonel More on behalf of the Shaikh erected a large 'noticeboard' marked Iraq-Kuwait Boundary ... The noticeboard I understand from the Shaikh was originally erected in consultation with the Iraqi authorities". It would appear, therefore, from Dickson's statement that both parties thereby recognized the establishment of a boundary point south of Safwan.

85. On 5 June 1932, Dickson recorded having seen the noticeboard at the Iraqi frontier post at Safwan. He was told that it had been removed on the immediate orders of the Commandant of Police at Basra. A week later Dickson was informed by the Administrative Inspector in Basra, Jardine, that the order to repaint the board had been given without knowing that the board was the property of Kuwait. The Mutasarrif of Basra was requested by Jardine (administrative inspector, Basrah) to have the board replaced and to have it recorded that it belonged to Kuwait to prevent any recurrence of the incident. Jardine wrote to Dickson on 10 July 1932, enclosing a translation of a letter from the Mutasarrif in which the latter apologized to Dickson and the Shaikh. Three days later Dickson wrote to the Shaikh stating that, "... from the Mutasarrif's letter it is clear that the board has been replaced in its original state and I would strongly urge Your Excellency to send a party of men to have it repainted at the first opportunity ...". The board was not removed again until March 1939.

86. When More erected the noticeboard, he is believed to have paced out the distance without leaving any written record; Dickson states the distance as one mile without there being evidence of how he came to that conclusion. However, as an experienced traveller in a desert environment, Dickson would certainly have been used to estimating distances. But an estimated mile in an area with very few reference points could certainly be a mile plus or minus some hundred metres. He later introduced the telegraph poles as reference marks, presumably to improve his determination of the distance from Safwan. Here again, however, Dickson was imprecise and uncertain of which telegraph pole was the critical one. Most importantly, there are difficulties in ascertaining where the first pole stood relative to the masonry-covered well. A further complication is the confusion regarding the distance between the poles. Was it 100m as Gethin stated or 100 yards as paced out by Jakins?

87. In 1940, Galloway, advised by Dickson and accompanied by Shaikh Ali al Khalifa, replaced the noticeboard which had been removed by the Iraqi authorities. According to Galloway the position chosen "as far as (he) could tell ... was at the tenth pole". This is the point which is also called the Ali al Khalifa pillar. Galloway's action led to a protest by the Iraqi Government and the exchange of notes.

88. In its note verbale to the British Embassy in Baghdad (2635/2635/7/12364 of 25 June 1940) the Iraqi Government protested that the party which erected the noticeboard had "crossed the Iraqi frontier to a depth of 1,000m from the Safwan Post ... at a distance of 250m within the Iraqi frontier". This gives a distance of 1,250m from the customs post to the boundary.

89. In a letter dated February 1951, Jakins at the Political Agency in Kuwait wrote to the Political Resident in Bahrain, after a visit to the frontier with Dickson and the chauffeur who had accompanied Shaikh Ali al Khalifa in 1940 when he erected the pillar, giving distances between the poles in yards, and the distance to the boundary measured by the Iraqis in 1940 as 1,250m as 1,250 yards.

90. The distance given in the Iraqi protest note of 1940 should be given considerable credence as it is reasonable to assume that the distances, so precisely stated in a protest note, were measured. It is unlikely that a protest would be based on estimated distances.

91. When Galloway replaced the noticeboard - which led to the Iraqi protest note - the telegraph poles were used as reference points.

92. Jakins' attempt to clarify the situation contains several assumptions, he did not go up to the customs post and his determination would seem to be based on estimations, both by him and his companions. But he does indicate that Dickson believed the noticeboard to have been on a rise.

d. The road south of Safwan

93. The present tar-sealed road which runs southwards from Safwan, as shown on the 1991 orthophoto map, did not exist at the end of the 1950s and is not aligned with the old road on which the noticeboard once stood. With the help of aerial photographs from 1945, 1954 and 1958, the independent experts were able to establish the alignment of the old road and plotted it on a separate orthophoto map at the scale of 1:7,500. (IKBDC/Doc.8, annex III).

e. Conclusions

94. Written documents, oral testimony, coordinates established by early surveyors, and an analysis of the aerial photographs taken over a considerable span of time, have narrowed the differences and led to the identification and location of the customs post. The independent experts were able to identify its location on early aerial photographs. They were able to plot the southwest extremity of the post and the alignment of the old road south to Kuwait, to a standard permitted by the material available. They were able to determine that the boundary lies between a minimum of 1,250m and a maximum of 1,609m, which gives a mean distance of 1,430m, from the south-west extremity of the old customs post compound at Safwan.

C. Eastern section

95. The delimitation formula calls for the boundary to lead to the junction of the Khowr Zhobeir with the Khowr Abd Allah, after passing south of the Safwan wells, Jebel Sanam and Umm Qasr. The eastern section of the boundary is defined as that segment which runs (eastwards) from the shore of Khowr Zhobeir at Umm Qasr.

96. In order to locate the junction of the Khowrs in the epoch of 1932, the task of the independent experts was to study all available documents and to identify and evaluate whether significant erosion and accretion had occurred that might affect its probable location.

1. Evidence of erosion and accretion

a. Comparison of aerial photographs

97. As a first step to study the evidence of erosion and accretion earlier aerial photographs, taken on 21 April 1951, 5 January 1953, 17 August 1965, 5 November 1966 and 12 November 1991, were obtained and analyzed. Since the scale of the prints varied between 1:15,750 and 1:25,000, enlargements were made and transparencies were produced at a common scale of 1:25,000. The 1991 photograph was intentionally taken at low-water level, whereas the others were taken at varying tidal stages. (IKBDC/Doc.7, annex II).

The following is a comparison of these photographs with the 1991 orthophoto map of the Commission:

Year Description

1951 Good fit between the photograph and the map.

1953 A very good fit between the photograph and the map.

1961 A good fit between the photograph and the map. The water level is higher on the photograph.

1965 An acceptably good fit despite the higher water level at the time of photography in 1965.

1991 The fit is good although the water level is lower on the photograph that was taken at low water.

98. The comparisons clearly show that no significant change occurred in the shoreline over a period of 40 years apart from those that were man-made on the southern side of the Fao peninsula and along the waterfront at Umm Qasr. Many common shapes and other features such as channels through the offshore mud can be clearly identified throughout the period of comparison. No evidence of significant erosion or accretion on the banks and mud flats have been detected over this period.

b. Comparison of nautical charts

99. Several nautical charts were obtained dating from 1907 to 1991. They were examined and compared to assist in the location of the junction of the thalwegs of the Khowrs. Appropriate portions of each chart were enlarged to a common scale of 1:25,000. (IKBDC/Doc. 7, annex III).

1907 Persian Gulf. A Sketch survey of the Khor-Zobeir. By the Marine Survey of India, scale 1:74,000.

1926-1930 Persian Gulf. Approach to the Shatt Al Arab, Khor Musa and Kuwait Harbour. By the Port Directorate of Basra, scale 1:316,000.

1939 Persian Gulf. Khor Abdullah. Um Qasr to Warbah Spit. By the Basra Port Directorate, scale 1:24,250.

1948 Persian Gulf. Mouth of the Euphrates. Shatt Al Arab and Khor Abdullah. By the Port Directorate Basra, scale 1:100,000.

1964 Persian Gulf. Approaches to Shatt Al 'Arab and Khor 'Abdullah. By the Port Directorate Basra, scale 1:100,000.

1971 Persian Gulf. Khawr Abd Allah and Approaches to Shatt Al 'Arab. By the Iraqi Ports Administration, scale 1:100,000.

1991 Iraq and Kuwait. Khawr Az Zubayr. By the Hydrographer of the Navy, United Kingdom, scale 1:50,000.

100. Overall the charts compared reasonably well, with the accuracy of the detailed survey of the 1939 chart making it the best basis for comparisons.

c. Comparison of topographic maps

101. Sheets 5549-1 and 5649-IV of the K7611 Series, Edition 2-GSGS, produced under the direction of the Director General of Military Survey, Ministry of Defence, United Kingdom, at the scale of 1:50,000 and partially revised in 1990, were used for the study. These comparisons have not shown any significant changes of the coastlines apart from those which are man-made on the southern side of the Fao peninsula and along the waterfront at Umm Qasr.

2. The junction point

102. Six junction points were plotted on a semi-transparent overlay by transferring the shorelines and other significant features, such as the limits of drying mud, channels through the mud and rivers from the 1:25,000 scale orthophoto map.

103. The individual junction points were plotted by obtaining the best possible fit between the overlay and the 1:25,000 scale copies of the nautical charts using common outlines and features. Although the cartographic quality of the charts varies greatly, the relative positions of the low water line south-east of Bahrah Point, the mouth of the Khowr Sabiyah and the junction of the thalwegs of the Khowr Abd Allah and the Khowr Zhobeir are very similar. For this reason it is considered that the use of physical reference points will give a better comparison between charts than the use of graticules in different and uncertain coordinate systems and origins.

104. The most reliable chart for determining the junction of the Khowrs at epoch 1932 is chart 3. To improve its readability, the chart has been coloured according to the soundings. The junction point derived from chart 2 cannot be given the same weight in view of the qualifications outlined above. The junction points derived from the remaining charts fall within a circle of very small radius around the point from chart 3. (IKBDC/Doc.7, annex I).

105. Production of the 1988 map revealed serious distortions in the depiction of the Khowrs on the 1936 map. This has been confirmed by a comparison with the orthophoto maps produced for the Commission. The reason for these distortions are errors in the mapping east of Umm Qasr. This area was mapped in 1917, and the quality is significantly lower than the main part of the map. The 1936 map is based on plane table surveys except that it has used 1917 triangulation surveys for the area east of Umm Qasr. This 1917 version was used and has influenced charts and maps up until more accurate mapping became available in 1988.

106. The effect of these distortions has been to displace the intersection of the Khowrs south and west on the 1936 map and on the charts of 1907 and 1932. The result for the boundary has been that the earlier exchange of correspondence and related diagrams of the boundary from Safwan have shown the boundary to be further south at Umm Qasr than it would have been if the true position of the intersection had been used. This is the reason why the line from the new position at Safwan now plots significantly above the position on the map circulated in document S/22412.

107. The independent experts concluded that the most probable position of the junction of the khowr at epoch 1932 should be primarily based on the position derived from the 1939 chart with a slight southward shift to take some account of the 1926-1930 chart.

D. Consideration of the boundaries

108. The independent experts were requested to present the land boundary in its totality and to give a comparison with boundaries on existing maps. They made a presentation which showed a comparison of the boundaries on the map in document S/22412, the 1936 map and its revisions, the new line of the Wadi Al-Batin taken from the orthophoto maps and the position of the point south of Safwan. Also, lines were shown east to the old and new depictions of the intersections of the Khowrs and west on a parallel from the point south of Safwan and one to meet the boundary shown on S/22412.

1. Line of demarcation along the Wadi

109. The line of demarcation along the Wadi Al-Batin recommended by the experts was plotted on the accompanying map. The line follows as closely as possible the low point line which was determined photogrammetrically (see Section A.1 above).

110. Boundary segments of approximately 2 km in length have been plotted on the orthophoto maps so that the low points generally follow the segments or fall equally on both sides of the boundary. The boundary, as shown, has ben graphically estimated, but the final delineation will be based on calculations of equivalence of areas on both sides between the low points and the boundary segments. The Iraq-Saudi Arabia boundary pillar No. 1 falls on the thalweg and has been adopted as the tripoint, that is, the beginning of the boundary down the Wadi.

111. The boundary in Wadi Al-Batin compares reasonably closely with the map circulated in document S/22412. It falls alternately slightly east and slightly west of the boundary depicted on that map. The differences between the identifications of the thalweg are due to the higher accuracy and quality of the latest mapping undertaken for the Commission. The differences are small.

112. The thalweg identified from this latest mapping represents its most accurate determination. The Hulaiba Wells fall in Iraq, as required by British assurances to the Iraqi Prime Minister in 1932. All the Iraqi and Kuwaiti police posts are located on their respective sides of the boundary down the Wadi.

2. Line of demarcation along the northern boundary

113. At Safwan, the position of the boundary is taken as 1,430 metres south of the south-western extremity of the compound of the customs post which is judged to be the southernmost position that the noticeboard could have been positioned. It has been set on the most likely line of the road at the time the noticeboard was in place. The noticeboard is the earliest point of demarcation, and thus its likely position is crucial to any present-day demarcation.

114. Maps done prior to the mapping done for the Commission have depicted the position of the northern boundary on east-west lines which are not related to any

of the positions which have been previously identified for the noticeboard. All of the depictions of the boundary are at significantly greater distances south of Safwan than the mile or lesser distances invariably given for the noticeboard. The investigation of the basis for the position of the northern boundary in these maps revealed that there was no foundation for the position of the boundary and that no map used the old position of the noticeboard to plot that boundary.

115. The boundary between Iraq and Kuwait on the 1:50,000 scale British K7611 map series is plotted approximately 2,200 metres south of the customs post. It has not been possible to find the rationale behind the position. In a letter dated 10 January 1991 from the Ministry of Defence, United Kingdom, it is stated, "it has not been possible to identify the origin of this turning point on series K7611. For practical purposes K7611 has been accepted by Mil Svy, but doubt must remain as to its precise position".

116. The independent experts believed that the position of the noticeboard is the primary position for the demarcation at the parallel on the northern boundary.

117. The independent experts recommended that the boundary from the point south of Umm Qasr should follow the low water line to the junction of the Khowrs.

3. Comparison of boundary lines

118. The Security Council resolution refers specifically to the map circulated in document S/22412. There are, in addition, two other maps of interest - the 1936 United Kingdom map and its revised versions, and the Iraqi 1:1,000,000 maps, sheets H-38-L-SE (1987) and H-38-R-NW (1989).

119. The first significant representation to scale of the boundary was that depicted on the 1936 British map serial No. 3954, scale 1:500,000, produced by the Geographical Section, General Staff, United Kingdom.

120. The 1936 map, and the revisions in 1942 and 1955, are in close agreement for the boundary of the Batin.

121. The position of the line from Safwan to the west depends solely on the identification of the point at Safwan. An examination of the boundary to the west shows a commonality of shape for all maps. The northern boundary represented on the 1936 and 1942 revisions of the British map, serial No. 3954, are the same. The boundary between Safwan and the Batin represented by the map circulated in document S/22412 is approximately 1,500 metres north of the same boundary shown on the 1936 map. On the 1955 revision, the boundary has been moved northwards to a position approximately 2,200 metres south of the customs post in Safwan and appears to conform with the boundary as shown on the map circulated in document S/22412.

122. The old British maps were used as a basis for diagrams representing the boundary, including the diagram sent by the Prime Minister of Iraq in 1955. It is only with the production of the map circulated in document S/22412 in 1988 that new and more accurate maps were available. Thus, the representation of the boundary on the old British maps served as a reference for over 50 years, as a source of graphical information relevant to the delimitation formula and correspondence.

123. A comparison of the 1936 map and the map circulated in document S/22412 indicates that the same boundary alignment has been used between Umm Qasr and a point on a minor road south-east of the boundary turning-point plotted on the latter map. The boundary shown on the 1955 revision of the 1936 map is, on the other hand, in conformity with the boundary shown on the map circulated in document S/22412.

124. The boundaries shown on the Iraqi map agree in general with the boundaries shown on the 1936 map.

125. The only significant development along the boundary between the Batin and Safwan is the oil well complexes at Ratga and Rumaila. The independent experts requested information from both the Iraqi and the Kuwaiti representatives as to whether this development had any relevance to the demarcation of the boundary. No such evidence was provided.

IV. SUMMARY OF THE DELIBERATIONS OF THE COMMISSION

A. Western section

126. With regard to the western section, one of the independent experts described a representation of the Batin on a computer display that members had attended following the formal presentation on the research and analysis of documentation and mapping. The three-dimensional representation along the western border had included identification of the lowest point of the Batin and an area that was at a 0.5m vertical distance from the floor of the Batin. Various features had been illustrated. An example had been given of a boundary made up of 2km segments being produced interactively on the computer to give a best fit along the lowest point on the Batin to indicate how the setting of a boundary could be demarcated.

127. The experts requested from the representatives of Iraq and Kuwait their ideas about the criteria for the boundary so as to run them through the computer and plot them on the maps. For example, the independent experts suggested that they could run 2km segments along the low line of the Batin, reduced in some cases to 1km. Another criterion might be one of balance: there should be as much area on the Kuwaiti side as on the Iraqi side of the low point. Cartographers might have a tendency to go into great detail in the interest of accuracy. The question was one of marking and of future administration of an international boundary. The experts would carry out the technical work but there were other practical considerations.

128. The representative of Kuwait recalled that a decision had already been taken. It was up to the experts to execute that decision in a practical way. There should be no new decisions on the methods to be applied. The experts had been asked to map the thalweg and to give a well-defined proposal for acceptance by the Commission, but in one area the line split due to a deep isolated depression. He left it in the Chairman's hands to solve that problem.

129. The Chairman declined to do so. He said he could not take the decision for the Commission: that would be too heavy a responsibility. He said that the boundary line should be correct from the cartographic point of view and from the point of view of the decision taken by the Commission. It should also be practical from an administrative standpoint.

130. The representative of Iraq recalled that, when the Commission had adopted its decisions on the Batin during the second session (see IKBDC/Min.13, pp. 18 and 19), his position had been non-participation in part of the vote, and on another part of the decision he had voted against. His position remained exactly the same now: on the part that related to procedure, his vote was still negative and

on the part that related to substance, his position remained non-participation.

131. The Commission agreed that the independent experts should develop a boundary line in the Wadi al Batin consisting of a series of straight line segments of about 2km length best approximating to the thalweg along the Wadi. The final location of the end points of the segments were to be determined after the area between the low points on the profiles on both sides of the boundary line had been mathematically balanced.

B. Northern section

132. One of the independent experts emphasized the significance of the point south of Safwan. When, in 1923, More had put the marker up, that had been an act of demarcation by a person actually involved in the 1923 Agreement. The marker had remained there until 1939; in other words, it had been there when Iraq joined the League of Nations. Since the emplacement of the noticeboard had been an act of demarcation, the Commission needed to identify its probable location. The differences in distance could be narrowed down from the 1940 Iraqi protest note and the frequent references to one mile. The other independent expert said that there was no substantive evidence for the location of the point south of Safwan on the British map circulated in document S/22412. Moreover, that map carried the disclaimer "approximate alignment" and what the Commission needed was a final alignment.

133. The representative of Iraq, referring to document IKBDC/Rep.3, said that it had been a somewhat irregular procedure for a visit to be effected to Safwan contrary, in his opinion, to the decision adopted by the Commission. The Commission had decided on 11 July to authorize the experts to conduct an on-site visit and to conduct investigations with a view to locating the point south of Safwan (see IKBDC/Min.14). He did not believe that the Commission had authorized anyone else to decide who should accompany the experts. It seemed, however, that a decision had been taken by a person or persons unknown to take a Kuwaiti party into Iraq's sovereign territory to go and roam around to investigate the point at Safwan. Moreover, he himself had been informed of the visit only after the fact and through a source not authorized for the work of the Commission. The totality of the episode had been highly irregular and he wished his strongest protest to be recorded.

134. The Secretary said that he had been advised that it would be appropriate for the party to make the visit on the basis of the decision that had been reached. He had consulted with everyone he could on the matter, both at United Nations Headquarters and in the field, and, based on advice received in the field, every effort had been made to inform the representative of Iraq prior to the visit.

135. The representative of Iraq stressed that the incident had been highly irregular and wondered why, as a member of the Commission, he had not been informed before a decision had been taken, or before it had been put into effect.

136. The Chairman said it was his understanding that the work of the independent experts, starting with their meeting at Gävle in August 1991, had been open to participation by other parties who were members of the Commission.

137. The representative of Kuwait said that from the outset Kuwait and Iraq had been asked to assist the Commission and the members thereof to reach a conclusion. The Commission had seen that Iraq's refusal to do so went back to the beginning of the Commission's work and had been constant. Iraq had refused to take part in the Gävle meeting as it had refused to take part elsewhere.

138. The representative of Iraq said that he had stated Iraq's position in formal session and on the record. That position had been that Iraq was leaving the technical work to the Commission. Iraq had indicated that it was not going to be present at the Gävle meeting.

139. At the 39th meeting, the representative of Iraq complained that the statement made by one of the independent experts in exercise of the right of reply had not been reproduced in the manner in which it had been delivered, particularly in the portion that related to the Safwan visit and the presence of a Kuwaiti expert. In his view, the record had been tampered with.

140. One of the independent experts said there was a simple explanation and explained, with the Secretary's confirmation, that when the statement had been made the name of the Kuwaiti expert participating in the Safwan visit was not at hand, and he had said in an aside that he would provide that later. It was in the report (IKBDC/Rep.3) and they wished to record it properly.

141. In response to a query by the representative of Iraq, one of the independent experts further explained that they interviewed no one in Safwan. The location of the old customs post had been ascertained by a careful comparison of earlier aerial photographs dating back to 1945, new vertical and oblique aerial photographs, coordinates, by the use of position-finding instruments and the assistance of a Kuwaiti expert who identified the villas.

C. Eastern section

142. The representative of Kuwait asked for clarification concerning which of the three points in the circle was the recommended point for the intersection of the Khowr Zhobeir and the Khowr Abd Allah. The independent experts concluded that the most probable position of the junction of the khowrs at epoch 1932 should be primarily based on the position derived from the 1939 chart with a slight southward shift to take into account of [sic] the 1926-1930 chart.

D. The boundary in its totality

143. In reply to a question raised by the representative of Iraq, one of the independent experts confirmed that the line on the 1936 map was in conformity with the delimitation formula in that it descended straight down to the junction of the Khowrs. The point where it crossed the shore should be the accepted point taking into account the small scale of the map.

144. The representative of Iraq asked for clarification of the last sentence of the third paragraph on page 3 of document IKBDC/Doc.12/Rev.1:

> "The map in document S/22412 shows the boundary in relation to the Kuwait and Iraqi oil wells",

and of how it should be interpreted in conjunction with the first sentence of the last paragraph of the document:

> "The only significant development along the boundary between the Wadi and Safwan are the oil well complexes at Ratga and Rumaila."

What was the force of the phrase "in relation to"? Was its significance cartographic or otherwise? Had the boundary line been drawn with the oil wells as a basis or criterion?

145. One of the independent experts replied that the meaning was that the map simply showed a boundary labelled as "approximate boundary", and some oil wells.

146. An adviser to the representative of Kuwait summarized the historical evidence concerning the point at the northern end of the Batin (Mufrash) from 1910 onwards, including the 1913 Anglo-Turkish Convention, the 1932 Exchange of Letters, the October 1940 British clarification and the December 1951 British clarification. All official maps from the 1922 British map onwards, whether [sic] British, Iraqi or United States maps, seemed to portray a boundary from the Batin to Safwan [sic] as a straight parallel of latitude at the latitude of the Safwan point. The adviser made a statement with regard to the frontier point at Umm Qasr; referring to the draft agreement between the United Kingdom Ambassador in Baghdad and the Iraqi Foreign Minister concerning the draft treaty of 1955 [sic] said that he now realized that the measurements given in the draft agreement did not make sense in terms of the map circulated in document S/22412 but related rather to the 1936 map.

V. STATEMENTS OF POSITIONS

A. Position of the representative of Kuwait

147. At the 33rd meeting (10 April 1992), referring to the location of the point at Safwan, the representative of Kuwait stated his position, as follows:

148. His country had sought for 30 years to demarcate its boundary with Iraq. His countrymen, who had recently suffered greatly, believed that the earliest possible finalization of the work of the Commission was of great importance for stability and peace along the border, as had been stated so well in the Secretary-General's report (S/22558) setting out the detailed mandate of the Commission.

149. He was therefore, in the interest of peace, stability and the expeditious work of the Commission, prepared to support the conclusion of the independent experts on the location of the boundary south of Safwan; specifically, he was prepared to accept the conclusion of the independent experts that "the point south of Safwan was most probably a mean point located 1,430m from the south-west extremity of the old customs compound at Safwan" (IKBDC/Doc.8, para. 19), provided that the boundary demarcation work of the Commission as a whole was otherwise satisfactory.

150. He believed that the boundary south of Safwan should lie between approximately 1,250 and 1,000m south of the old customs post, i.e., the boundary should lie between the figure of 1,250m given officially by Iraq in its protest note of 25 June 1940 and the figure of 1,000m given in the official British reply of 3 August 1940. The latter figure had also been reflected in the important British note verbale of December 1951. No other indications in the historical record achieved the degree of authority of those official positions.

151. He would be remiss if he let the opportunity pass to thank the independent members of the Commission, the secretariat of the Commission and all those who worked with them; they had performed an inestimable service in their superb surveying, mapping and other work in connection with the work of the Commission. Their work had in every respect met the highest standard of professionalism. The Commission as a whole, and the generations of people who would benefit from their work, owed the experts a debt of lasting gratitude. It was, in no small measure, his great respect for that work that had induced him to accept the conclusion of the experts on the location of the Safwan boundary.

152. At the 35th meeting (14 April 1992), the representative of Kuwait made the following statement on the totality of the boundary:

153. Much hard work had gone into the compilation of lines which had been shared with Commission members at the 34th meeting. In particular, he was pleased to see that the independent experts had produced a line (designated A on the western boundary on the Batin and C otherwise) that reflected the discussion within the Commission. The agreed boundary was represented by the line drawn by the experts for the demarcation of the western boundary to implement the Commission's decision in adopting the thalweg as the principle to be used for that section of the boundary. From there the boundary ran to a point at Safwan located 1,430m from the south-west extremity of the compound of the old Safwan customs post along the line of latitude at that point. It then ran from that point at Safwan along the shortest possible line towards the point identified by the experts as the junction of the Khowr Zhobeir with the Khowr Abd Allah, with possible minor modifications to reflect the point discussed at the 33rd meeting represented by a tangent on the circle, to the low-water mark on the west bank of the Khowr Zhobeir. The line, which followed the Commission's consistent discussions as to the demarcation of the agreed boundary from the thalweg in the Batin to the point at Safwan, towards a point at the junction of the Khowrs, reflected the work of the Commission as to the location of the agreed boundary. While he had reservations about some elements in the line, and particularly whether the point at Safwan was too far south, in the interest of facilitating the Commission's work, he was prepared to accept the line as the line of the land boundary, provided, as he had indicated earlier, that the demarcation work as a whole, including the boundary to the east of the point where the land boundary met the shore in the region of Umm Qasr was otherwise satisfactory.

154. While he was pleased that the Commission had produced a line reflecting its work to date based on a careful review of the historical record, he viewed with concern other lines drawn apparently for "comparison" purposes. He appreciated the position taken by the experts that those lines should not be taken as a proposal from the experts, but, because they reflected an abrupt shift in the Commission's work and thus could be easily misinterpreted, it was important to put the Commission's work in an overall context. He thus wished to make the following general points with respect to those other lines that did not reflect the discussions of the Commission.

155. The mandate of the Commission was, in the language of the Secretary-General's report of 2 May 1991 (S/22558), "... to demarcate in geographical coordinates of latitude and longitude the international boundary set out in the Agreed Minutes between Kuwait and Iraq". According to paragraph 10 of the Commission's interim report to the Secretary-General (IKBDC/Rep.2), "it was generally agreed that the work of the Commission was technical and not political and that the nature of the task was demarcation". The Commission's mandate did not include redrawing the agreed boundary that was being demarcated, whether such a redrawing was based on the United Kingdom map circulated in document S/22412 or some other source, when the evidence before the Commission as to the agreed boundary and as consistently discussed in the

Commission would produce a different line. To assist the Commission in its work, he was circulating a short paper entitled "The map transmitted by Security Council document S/22412 and the work of the Commission". Nothing in the Commission's mandate gave it power to deviate from the overall best available evidence as to the agreed boundary.

156. While it might be interesting to have other lines for comparison purposes, none of the bases for those other lines had been discussed in the Commission and, in so far as they were inconsistent with the best available evidence as to the location of the agreed boundary, they were not useful to the Commission. The record as compiled in the Commission's interim report was clear that the line marked A in the Batin and C elsewhere reflected the best evidence from the careful historical review conducted by the Commission over five full sessions, constituting almost a full year's work. Nothing in the summary of the debate in the interim report suggested that the Commission had felt that the point of intersection of the Khowrs could be used to set aside the preponderance of the record and the work of the Commission to the effect that the line from the point at Safwan to the low-water mark on the west bank of the Khowr Zhobeir ran along the shortest possible line towards the junction of the Khowrs. Indeed, that point had been reaffirmed in the Commission only the previous meeting.

157. The Commission should be cautious about giving too much weight to maps where such maps were isolated and not confirmed by other evidence. A single map did not in itself provide a standard for demarcation.

158. In line with the experts' request, he wished to offer observations and additional evidence with respect to two points in the Commission's work. The first was the nature of the line between the point at Safwan and the western boundary and the second was the point used as a point of direction for the line between the point at Safwan and the low-water mark on the west bank of the Khowr Zhobeir.

159. There was overwhelming evidence that the line between Safwan and the western boundary was regarded as running either on a parallel of latitude of the point at Safwan or, in the period prior to 1932, even north of that latitude. There was virtually no evidence that the line should run south of the parallel of latitude of the point at Safwan. Thus the line offered under the designation A was entirely novel and not consistent with the overwhelming evidence. Moreover, the line would not seem consistent with the language in the 1932 Exchange of Letters: "along the Batin to a point just south of the latitude of Safwan; thence eastward passing south of Safwan Wells ...". He wished to request that one of his experts be allowed to develop that evidence further immediately after his statement.

160. With regard to the point of direction for the line between the point at Safwan and the low-water mark on the Khowr Zhobeir, it was astonishing to see, in representations A and B, the point of intersection of the British map with the Khowr used as opposed to the apparent view of the Commission to the contrary. Members of the Commission seemed to have consistently taken the view that the point of intersection of the land boundary with the low-water mark on the west bank of the Khowr Zhobeir was governed by a point of intersection on the shortest possible line running from the point at Safwan towards the junction of the Khowrs. The record of the Commission's discussion in its interim report suggested that members had regarded that as the decisive factor in locating the point south of Umm Qasr. The record showed that, when he had sought to offer other historical evidence as to the location of the point south of Umm Qasr, there had been little discussion of that evidence. If any lines drawn even for comparison purposes departed from the junction-of-the-Khowrs method of determining that method, the Commission should review the additional evidence that he had suggested at that time. He therefore would also request that one of his assistants be allowed to develop further the historical evidence from the period 1932 to 1963 as to the location of the point south of Umm Qasr. The evidence showed that, if the Commission sought to locate the point of intersection of the northern boundary with the Khowr Zhobeir by locating an independent point south of Safwan, then the preponderance of the evidence would suggest a point north of line C, which used the intersection-of-the-Khowrs method. It was of great importance to note that any method of locating the point south of Umm Qasr by ignoring the junction of the Khowrs, as was apparently represented by lines A and B, did violence to the plain language of the 1932 Exchange of Letters which stated "... and so on to the junction of the Khowr Zhobeir with the Khowr Abd Allah". Simply to ignore that language, so that the clause would have no meaning for the direction of the boundary, would signal a departure from the formula that governed the demarcation mandate of the Commission.

161. He then reviewed the work of the Commission concerning the point determining the direction of the line running from the point at Safwan to the low-water mark on the Khowr Zhobeir. When the Commission had begun to examine the eastern section of the boundary during its second session in July 1991, the important question of the precise location of the point south of Umm Qasr had arisen. It had been clearly stated by the experts that the location of that specific point of the boundary was tied to the definition both of the turning-point south of Safwan and of the intersection of the Khowrs. One of the independent experts had said:

> "As far as the delimitation was concerned, the point south of Umm Qasr appeared to be defined by two points, one north-west of it and one south-east of it, the one south-east being the intersection of the Khowrs". (IKBDC/Min.12, pp. 3 and 4)

162. The other expert had concurred in that opinion and observed that "there was no point south of Umm Qasr" but there was a line running south of it. He had added:

> "There was a relationship between the location of the line south of Umm Qasr and the point at the junction of the Khowrs". (ibid., p. 4)

163. Later, the expert had explained that:

> "The border was defined as a straight line between a point south of Safwan and the junction ... a point would of course be created on the ground ... by a line going through it but that line must be defined relative to the straight line starting at Safwan". (ibid., p. 13)

164. He had asked the experts whether there was a turning-point to the Khowr or a straight line from south of Safwan. The answer that had been given was derived from the wording in the delimitation formula, which did not speak of the line by saying "to a point south of Umm Qasr", but rather "south of Umm Qasr". That was why one of the experts had stated that:

> "The distance to Umm Qasr would be defined relative to a line which in itself was defined by

> joining together two points: one at the junction of the Khowrs and one south of Safwan". (ibid.)

165. At its third session, the Commission had reverted to the issue. When he had expressed the opinion that there was more than one piece of evidence that a point existed on the coast south of Umm Qasr, one of the experts had said:

> "... the experts considered that there was a point on the coast, the location of which was a consequence of two other decisions ... the experts needed more research into the question of the junction of the Khowrs and to look more closely into the point south of Safwan. Once established, drawing a line between those points would give the point on the coast". (IKBDC/Min.19, pp. 7 and 8)

166. The expert had repeated that:

> "The shortest line between the point south of Safwan and the junction point, once established, would automatically establish the point south of Umm Qasr. In other words, that point was dependent on the other two". (ibid., p. 7)

167. That view had been confirmed by the other expert, who had called attention to the fact that:

> "The experts had seen no evidence as to where the point south of Umm Qasr was located, but it could be determined from the other two". (ibid.)

168. Replying to a question by the representative of Iraq, the expert had repeated that:

> "... a straight line from the point south of Safwan to the intersection would give the third point, which would be on the waterline". (ibid., p. 8)

169. The situation had been clarified by the other expert, who had stated:

> "... the point of Umm Qasr depended on the other two. The location of the point south of Safwan was known within a certain circle of error. There was a degree of uncertainty regarding the location of the junction of the Khowrs. A straight line between the two, once they had been established, would give the third". (ibid.)

170. When he had pointed out the usefulness of considering the historical evidence, because as far back as 1913 there had been references to the walls of the fort, such references had been set aside. In particular, the expert had said:

> "... He had studied the history and was cognizant of the references to the walls of the fort. However, he was also aware of later interpretations, which had developed into a more geometric formula with parallels, intersection points, turning-point and straight lines. In other words, history had evolved. The Commission had discussed the turning-point at Safwan and the straight line to the intersection, thereby moving from the historical formula to the later interpretation of delimitation". (ibid., p. 9)

171. The Commission's interim report reflected the views exchanged on that question and the position taken by the experts.

> "The representative of Kuwait said that it was his understanding that the point south of Umm Qasr would then be fixed at 1932.
>
> "The understanding of the independent experts was that the point appeared to be defined by two points: one north-west of it, i.e. the point at Safwan, and the other south-east of it, i.e. the junction of the Khowrs". (IKBDC/Rep.2, paras. 80 and 81).

172. The discussion that had taken place at the third session of the Commission was summarized in paragraphs 95 to 101 of the interim report.

173. The record reflected a consistent use of the location of the intersection of the Khowrs as the method for determining the direction of the line running from the point at Safwan to the low-water mark on the Khowr Zhobeir. In the absence of any serious evidence to the contrary, it would seem that the point used in representations A and B was simply not supported by the work of the Commission.

174. He wished to remind the Commission that, when he had said that he was prepared to support the conclusion of the independent experts on the location of the boundary south of Safwan and had subsequently extended that support to their conclusion as to the location of the point at the junction of the Khowrs, he had made it clear that he was doing so provided that the boundary demarcation work of the Commission as a whole was otherwise satisfactory. It would not be satisfactory for the Commission to set aside the evidence it had carefully developed. He wished to assure the members of the Commission, however, that he stood ready to work for broad agreement on those issues with a view to facilitating "the earliest possible finalization" of the Commission's work.

B. Position of the representative of Iraq

175. At the 37th meeting (15 April 1992), the representative of Iraq, upon instructions, made a general statement to explain his position of non-participation in the voting taken on the demarcation of the totality of the boundary.

176. Firstly, he recalled that Iraq had left the technical work in its entirety to the Commission, as recorded on page 4 of document IKBDC/Min.24. That had been Iraq's position then, it remained Iraq's position now, and would continue thus in the future.

177. Secondly, with respect to the line decided by the Commission in the western section of the boundary, namely Wadi Al Batin, the Commission had purported to give effect to the two decisions of 11 July 1991, as contained in document IKBDC/Min.13. He recalled that he had not participated in the vote on one decision, had voted against the other decision, and had explained his position fully, as recorded on page 19 of document IKBDC/Min.13. He reaffirmed that explanation of vote: those decisions had been adopted hastily, under the steam-rolling efforts of the representative of Kuwait, and had resulted in having a prejudicial effect on a crucial aspect of the boundary relating to its northern section.

178. Looking at the decision adopted by the Commission at its current session, it was clear that the criterion adopted by the Commission in its earlier decisions on the

demarcation of the western section of the boundary. namely, the thalweg, had not been strictly followed.

179. Thirdly, with regard to the northern section of the boundary, he recalled the circumstances surrounding the adoption of the decision of the Commission, on 11 July 1991, on the creation of a turning-point south of Safwan, and the procedure to be followed in the process of that creation, which were fully recorded in document IKBDC/Min.14. The Commission would recall that he had voted against the Commission's decision for the reasons he had advanced at the time, as recorded on pages 6 and 7 of document IKBDC/Min.14.

180. In Iraq's view, the substance of those reasons still applied to the decisions adopted by the Commission at the current session. Those decisions flatly contradicted the delimitation formula. The formula made a reference to "south of the latitude of Safwan" for one function only, that of determining the terminal point at the Batin. The decision of the Commission had created a point at Safwan not mentioned in the delimitation formula.

181. The procedure that had been followed in disposing of that crucial question for the whole demarcation operation had been the result, again, of a steam-rolling process and pressure. The material depended upon had been limited to a single source, namely, British colonial and British-controlled sources, at the expense of other material which had not been looked into.

182. He could not fail to add that, as the process of implementing the earlier decisions of the Commission had been carried out, it had not been done in conformity with the Commission's instructions. As he had protested at an earlier meeting - which the records fully showed (see IKBDC/Min.33) - the representative of Kuwait and his experts, an obvious interested party in the creation of the turning-point at Safwan, had been taken to Safwan to construct the creation of a turning-point there, contrary to the clear terms of a decision of the Commission.

183. On top of that violation, he pointed out that he had noted to the Commission the irregularity of relying on the memory of Mr. Julian Walker, who was an expert of the representative of Kuwait in the Commission, as one of the sources in point in document IKBDC/Doc.8, which had been presented to the Commission by the two independent experts, and in which his title had been designated as of the Middle East Section Research and Analysis Department of the Foreign and Commonwealth Office of the United Kingdom.

184. Not only that: Mr. Walker had taken the liberty of speaking to the press on the affair. Writing from Umm Qasr for the *Wall Street Journal*, in its issue dated 5 December 1991, the reporter had described Mr. Walker as:

> "A British official and renowned border sleuth, who is advising the United Nations team",

and Mr. Walker was reported to have said:

> "Memories fade, scenery changes, and people who could answer certain questions are dead. One can't say with certainty where the line is".

185. There was another interesting passage in the report of the *Wall Street Journal* about the expertise of Mr. Walker. He assured Mr. Walker that there was nothing personal in what he (the representative of Iraq) was saying; he was repeating what the newspaper had said, which was as follows:

> "Mr. Walker, the British border expert, is one man the Boundary Commission has called on for answers. As a diplomat in the 1960s, he helped map the United Arab Emirates, a crazy-quilt confederation of seven sheikhdoms, some of which own pockets wholly inside another's borders. Now, at 62, Mr. Walker has returned from the field. 'One must try', he says, 'to imagine what the old world looked like'.
>
> "To do this, he visited Safwan and sought elderly guides who could describe the town's layout when it was just a few huts and trees. Their stories, and records from Indian surveyors in the 1930s, led to the remains of a customs building often referred to in earlier records. This could provide a reference point to roughly ascertain where the missing signpost stood.
>
> "But the surveyors won't try to locate the spot on foot. 'One doesn't want to scramble around in the open,' Mr. Walker explains. 'Too many explosives.' The surveyors have already survived one close call, when their helicopter touched down beside a land mine."

186. He said that the Commission would note that, when the two distinguished experts had explained to it the outcome of that investigation, they had not told the Commission how they had carried it out. The Commission was, he added, entitled in his view to have some documentation as to how the investigation had been conducted. Had people been asked, as the *Wall Street Journal* report claimed?

187. He noted that, strangely enough, when the experts had come to fix the turning-point at Safwan created by the British colonial administrators, they had given considerable weight to a document described as an Iraqi protest note dated 25 June 1940. That note had been taken by the experts of the Commission to calculate a minimum figure of a distance compared with a maximum figure of another distance overwhelmingly emphasized by the British sources, as produced to the Commission, and so had recommended the location of the mean point between the two distances to arrive at the figure approved by the Commission. One was left to wonder why the British evidence there had not been sufficient, as it had in other places.

188. Fourthly, as regards the point of the intersection of the Khowr Abd Allah with Khowr Zhobeir, the Commission had decided to locate the point between the two points of the intersection as they appeared on charts presented for the years 1932 and 1939. That fixation was incorrect.

189. He recalled that, in his presentation on 10 July 1991 one of the experts had indicated that:

> "The Commission had before it a chart that was significant because it was from the time of the 1932 Exchange of Letters and which clearly indicated where the intersection of the Khowrs was" (IKBDC/Min.11, p. 1).

The expert had gone on to say:

> "On the chart the intersection of the thalwegs in 1932 could be determined as the place of the deepest soundings in both Khowrs" (ibid.).

At that juncture, the minutes indicated that:

> "He demonstrated where that point was" (ibid., p. 2).

A little further on in the minutes, the expert was reported to have said:

> "He believed that point to be reasonably accurately represented on the chart" (ibid.).

190. Later on in the deliberations of the Commission, the notions of an epoch, the effects of accretion, erosion or difference of datum on the point of the intersection and of a circle of error had been introduced. Then there had been the conclusion that there had been no shift as a result of accretion or erosion, but the circle-of-error notion seemed to have been maintained, probably as a result of differences in datum, or so it had been said.

191. There again, as had been done in respect of the point at Safwan, a so-called Iraqi 1939 chart had been heavily relied upon, and the 1932 chart had been strongly criticized, to produce the tangent between the 1932 and 1939 points as being the point of intersection, which the Commission had approved. That result flatly contradicted the decisive opinions that had been expressed earlier on the quality and the clarity of the point on the 1939 chart.

192. In that connection, he recalled that during the 19th meeting of the Commission, held on 13 August 1991, an adviser to the representative of Kuwait had indicated that:

> "His research group had inquired of the keepers of the charts, namely the United Kingdom Admiralty Hydrographic Office, particularly about the 1932 chart. It appeared that it was based on a 1923 survey and was not considered accurate. There was no information on the datum used in its compilation, which meant that it might be more difficult to ascertain the 1932 point of intersection than Mr. Robertson envisaged" (IKBDC/Min.19, p. 13).

Noting the conclusions reached by the experts and the decision adopted by the Commission, it was not difficult to comprehend how those conclusions and decisions had been arrived at. He left it to the impartial and objective observer to understand.

193. There were numerous intimations in the records of the Commission that its work was technical and had proceeded on the basis of cartographic considerations. He had, he said, already touched upon that matter the previous day, and the records would show what had transpired from Monday morning on to have the Commission reach the result it had.

194. He added that those intimations had been completely cancelled by the opinion expressed regarding the nature and qualification of the decisions adopted by the Commission. Indeed, two days previously, one of the experts had said:

> "The experts had chosen the expression 'evidence of demarcation' carefully: highly disputed occupancy probably did not constitute such evidence; accepted occupancy might well do so" (IKBDC/Min.34, pp. 5-6).

195. All Kuwait had wanted, Kuwait had got, thanks to its friends in the Security Council. The Commission had produced a boundary line, contrary to the delimitation formula and in the absence of any true, independent and impartial demarcation efforts in which Iraq had participated, which ignored completely Iraq's rightful ownership of vital oil fields and structures, Iraq's rightful ownership of civilian and military installations, and rightful ownership by Iraqis of farms and houses; those were facts that had developed on the ground throughout decades.

196. He said that, as a matter of fact, the impartial observers and Iraqis, now and in the future, would not fail to note that, on the basis of British material, a United Nations Commission had produced a line of a border between Iraq and Kuwait which was worse for Iraq's interests than the line depicted on a British map referred to in a Security Council resolution adopted under Chapter VII of the Charter of the United Nations.

197. The Chairman would, he said, recall that on 16 August 1991, he (the representative of Iraq) had made a general statement on the Commission's work as it stood at that time. The results reached by the Commission at the current session more than confirmed what he had stated, upon instruction, at that time. He reiterated that, looking on the whole process of the Commission's work, one could not escape the feeling, if not the conviction, that the work entrusted to the Commission had been preconceived, initiated unprecedentedly, and pursued along predetermined lines, reaching the extent of a logic of conspiracy. His reasons for so saying were the self-same ones he had set out in that previous statement (IKBDC/Min.23, pp. 9-11), and he would spare the Commission a reiteration of them.

198. He reminded the representative of Kuwait that, in his statement of 7 October 1991, as reported on pages 2 to 7 of document IKBDC/Min.24, all the examples he had quoted to prove the existence of a precedent to the Commission did not apply to the manner in which the mandate, the composition and the accountability of the Commission had been imposed.

199. He (the representative of Iraq) noted that the Kuwaiti examples had been extracted from First and Second World War experience. The implications were therefore clear, and he wondered whether the Commission was the equivalent of a punitive action. If so, had the Commission gone back to the notion that, as a result of war, countries should pay in land? Or was it, as the representative of Kuwait had tried to argue, a consequence of the general powers of the Security Council, which powers were absolute - as the International Court of Justice was alleged, quite wrongly, to have ruled? It would seem, he said, that the former notion was entertained not only by the Kuwaitis, but by others as well.

200. He quoted an extract on the question from the *Middle East International*, issue of 6 March 1992, as follows:

> "Apart from its old suspicion that it had been 'squeezed out of the Gulf', Iraq has more recent reasons for not accepting the UN ruling on Umm Qasr. During and since the Iran-Iraq war, Iraq, basing itself on the fact that since 1950 Kuwait had accepted the de facto international border which gave Umm Qasr to Iraq, went ahead not only to build a naval base at Umm Qasr, but also on the coast of Khor Zubair undertook a major construction programme costing billions of dollars and comprising a petrochemical plant, an iron and steel plant, a fertilizer complex, a liquid gas plant, a dry cargo port and facilities for the export of petroleum products. The channels of the khors were dredged during 1990 and 1991 from a

> depth of 8 metres to 13.5 metres to allow 35,000-tonne tankers to sail through. Under the UN plan, Kuwait would be given control over the entrance to the whole of this vast complex and to Iraq's only outlet to the Gulf.
>
> "For a country with a single outlet to the sea, control of that outlet is of crucial strategic importance. After all, one of the main reasons for the eight-year Iran-Iraq war was Iraq's maritime access to the Shatt al-Arab. No Iraqi Government could ever accept Kuwaiti control of Umm Qasr.
>
> "The UN Commission's giving Umm Qasr to Kuwait can only be explained as a further example of America's punitive campaign against Iraq, and already US officials are reported as saying that they will insist that the new boundary be respected as Iraq's southern border. The Kuwaiti Ambassador to the United Nations, Muhammad Abu Hassan, certainly seems to subscribe to the punishment thesis, for he has said that 'if Iraq does not accept the results of the Commission, that in itself is an invitation not only to maintain economic sanctions against Iraq but to use all necessary means to make Iraq accept, even by force'. The United Nations has produced a time bomb which only the Security Council can defuse, by basing itself on natural justice and rejecting the Commission's findings when they are submitted to it in April".

201. He recalled that when he had spoken of inequitous [sic] results to Iraq in his general statement on 11 July 1991 in Geneva (IKBDC/Min.14, p. 16), the Chairman had stated that:

> "to say that the result was inequitous [sic] to Iraq was premature when the material on which results would be based had not even been considered by the Commission" (ibid.).

The results were now in, and he had indicated the consequences; what he had said had been borne out by the facts.

202. He had not, he said, been the only one who had anticipated those results with certainty. Others also had, as was amply shown in numerous press reports going back long before the previous day. Some of those reports could be seen in the *Wall Street Journal* of 5 December 1991; *The Economist* of 29 February to 16 March 1992; and the *Middle East International* of 6 March 1992. The latest report in his possession was that of the *Financial Times* of 8 April 1992.

203. Surprisingly, those reports also included statements made by various participants in the work of the Commission. He has even witnessed a statement by the Secretary of the Commission in the *Financial Times*. Another was attributed to the representative of Kuwait.

204. The *Financial Times* report of 19 February 1992 stated that "a fact" - that was, the fact of so much being given to Kuwait -

> "which this month prompted Mr. Tarek Razzouki, Kuwait's representative on the Commission, to declare that the new border will entrench the emirate's historic rights. But more pertinently to the question of future political peace in the region, it will also deny Iraqi claims".

That report was by Mark Nicholson in Kuwait City.

205. There was a reference in the *Wall Street Journal* article of Thursday, 5 December 1991 to a statement reported to have been made by the Secretary of the Commission, which read as follows:

> "We have to take a general description and make it specific. What does the term 'just south of Safwan' mean, or 'along the Batin'?"

206. If those reports, which had evidently prompted a press release on the part of the Commission saying that the Commission had not done that, had not yet got that far - at least until the previous day - were compared, one could see that they were exactly the same in respect of the common denominator of the consensus that the work of the Commission was ill-conceived, to put it mildly. Some had even gone further in describing the outcome of the work of the Commission.

207. He said that he did not know how the information had got out to the press. Iraq had certainly not revealed it, and could not be presumed to have done, because it had not participated in the technical work of the Commission.

208. The statement that had concluded the article in the *Financial Times* of 19 February 1992 had been very revealing; he attributed significance to it because it was correct, not only in terms of international practice, but also in terms of what was fair. It said:

> "Common borders are, finally, a matter of bilateral consent between neighbouring countries, but US officials say they will insist the new boundary be respected as Iraq's southern border".

That sentence explained it all, as it explained much about the work of the Commission.

C. Response by the independent experts

209. At the 38th meeting (16 April 1992), one of the independent experts, speaking also on behalf of the other expert, made a statement in exercise of the right of reply to the statement made by the representative of Iraq at the 37th meeting.

210. At the second session of the Commission in July 1991 the experts had been fully satisfied that they had sufficient evidence to take the decisions adopted at that time. That had been confirmed by the results, namely, that the decisions taken at the current session were fully in line with the earlier decisions. The boundary along the western section had strictly followed the thalweg to the agreed resolution on the ground.

211. For the northern section of the boundary, the evidence of an earlier demarcation and observance of a point at Safwan had been, quite frankly, overwhelming. That boundary position had been referred to in the delimitation formula. It had been signposted in 1932, the year of the Exchange of Letters, and had been consistently recognized over the years. The suggestion of a boundary line from the Batin direct to the intersection of the Khowrs was a diversion that had been introduced by the representative of Iraq at the second session. After a very thorough examination of the evidence, the experts had concluded that that interpretation had no basis on which to contribute to the demarcation.

212. The source of information used by the experts had included all available material relevant to the demarcation of the boundary. Indeed, the Commission had approved its own mapping and surveying to ensure that an independent basis was available for demarcation. On frequent occasions from the very first meeting onwards, the experts had asked to be provided with appropriate information.

213. The representative of Iraq had referred to the most recent of a continued series of requests. Again, the experts had asked for evidence of demarcation. The qualifying comments about what might or might not constitute such evidence could not be construed as anything but a sincere attempt to explore all possibilities for appropriate information in order to achieve proper demarcation.

214. Much of the information had been provided from United Kingdom archives and some from Kuwait. That appeared to be because those were the only sources in possession of appropriate material. However, the recommendations of the experts had depended only on factual considerations and had not been subject to distortion because of the place from which the information was obtained.

215. With regard to the customs post at Safwan, the position had been established by surveying techniques and a comparison of aerial photographs taken in 1945, 1954, 1958 and 1965-1966 and the vertical and oblique aerial photographs taken in 1991. During the on-site visit, the approximate location of the post had first been found by using the Magellan GPS receiver to locate the coordinates determined from the Indian surveyors' astronomical fix in 1942. Once the general location had been found, the villas had been identified by a Kuwaiti adviser.[2] [2. The independent expert subsequently informed the secretariat that the name of the adviser had been Mr. Abd Al-Lateef Al-Thowaini.]

216. Based on a study and comparison of aerial photographs, the customs post and associated reference points, e.g. the fort, the palm trees, etc., had been identified and traced from aerial photograph to aerial photograph and onto the current orthophoto maps. In the same way, the position of the road had been traced through old photography and plotted for position on the current orthophoto maps. The estimated distance from the old customs post along the old road had then given the experts a position judged to be the most southerly position of the noticeboard. Although the term "mile" had been used for distance, there was no evidence that that distance had ever been measured while the noticeboard had been standing. Indeed, there was considerable evidence to indicate that the distance was somewhat less than a mile. In taking the mean from the documented Iraqi protest note, the experts considered that they were also recognizing the likely distance that the term "mile" actually represented on the ground. The boundary west to the Batin had then followed from the identification of that point. All graphic representations available to the Commission had shown the line to be a parallel. The position of the point in the Batin had varied according to the distance below Safwan used for the change in direction. However, that position was determined by the position of the old noticeboard. None of the maps appeared to have a rationale for any graphic depiction of the position for the change of boundary direction south of Safwan.

217. Mr. Walker had attended the visit to Safwan but he had not contributed to the identification of the customs post. His (Mr. Walker's) recollection, along with other descriptive material about the building, had been added for completeness. It had not been contributory to the experts' identification of the customs post.

218. With regard to the position of the point of intersection of the Khowr Abd Allah with Khowr Zhobeir, the point taken for the boundary was that of the 1932 chart for the boundary position on the waterline at Umm Qasr. Thus the 1932 chart had been used to determine the land boundary at Umm Qasr. The alignments of the boundaries represented on the 1936 map, derived diagrams and the map circulated in document S/22412 were all consistent. The identification of the intersection in the water had been influenced by the very detailed bottom information of the 1939 chart in order to fix the 1932 position on the orthophoto maps. That was a notional position and had not determined the land boundary from Umm Qasr to Safwan.

219. The decision to use the 1936 mapped position and earlier mapped positions of the intersection had resulted in the rejection of a straight-line boundary from Safwan to the actual 1932 intersection position. That decision avoided having a boundary through Umm Qasr north of the boundary recommended by the Commission.

220. The Commission had been directed to demarcate the boundary. The experts had sought throughout to obtain sufficient appropriate material to enable the Commission to undertake that task. With the demarcation evidence generated through mapping and through other material, the experts were satisfied that they had had the necessary evidence to take the decisions that had been adopted during the current session. Those decisions had been taken only on the evidence and without any pressure. Indeed, after all the investigation and work done over the past year, the experts felt that the decisions were fully warranted and timely. Further delay would not in their opinion have provided significant further evidence for demarcation.

221. Neither of the experts had been responsible for the newspaper articles. The information in them appeared speculative. Despite finding the general location of the customs post in Safwan in early December 1991, no analysis had been done at that time. The experts had had to wait for the orthophoto maps. It was only at the meeting in Wellington that the photo comparison of the location of the customs post had been undertaken and the possible boundary positions identified. Only with the production of the orthophoto maps in late March 1992 could any impact of the visit to Safwan be reasonably estimated.

222. In conclusion, the experts believed that the mapping and surveying work had been of the highest standard. That, together with the appropriate material, had satisfied them that the decisions taken were sound and fair. They unequivocally rejected any suggestion of outside pressure or undue haste.

D. Response by the representative of Kuwait

223. Also at the 38th meeting (16 April 1992), the representative of Kuwait, speaking in exercise of the right of reply, said that once again the representative of Iraq, after participating in the work of the Commission, had presented a statement attacking that work. The purpose of that and similar statements seemed to be to build a record seeking to discredit the Commission.

224. The Commission, however, had undertaken its mandate with care, accuracy and fairness. In particular, the representative of Iraq had received every opportunity to present relevant materials and to comment on documents and other materials before the Commission.

Unfortunately, recent events in Kuwait had understandably hampered Kuwait's ability to produce documents and other evidence. Despite that, however, he (the representative of Kuwait) had been able to produce more Iraqi material than had the representative of Iraq himself. The Commission had been blessed with three independent experts of great ability and technical knowledge in boundary demarcation. Those experts, appointed by the Secretary-General, in his view had been scrupulously impartial. To accuse the Commission of a "logic of conspiracy" was an injustice to the high standards of its work.

225. If he should express some disappointment, he would only remark that, although the representative of Iraq had initially promised "... to cooperate fully in the work of the Commission ..." and later said "... he was not playing procedural games ...", he (the representative of Iraq) had not always entirely fulfilled the expectations aroused by his statements. He had explained his position on substantive votes as "non-participation". In reality, he had actively presented his views to the Commission, including interpretation of the delimitation formula and of criteria for its application; he had given the Commission the unstinting benefit of his knowledge of procedural matters with marked effect on the expedition of its work. He (the representative of Kuwait) also noted the attention the representative of Iraq paid to the outpourings of a free press.

226. He had shown flexibility in order to ensure the rapid and effective functioning of the Commission, but it was certainly not true that "... all what Kuwait had wanted Kuwait had got ..." (IKBDC/Min.37, p. 15). He had wanted a point at Safwan between 1,000 and 1,250m south of the customs post. He had wanted a point at Umm Qasr further north than the one decided on to reflect the position of the junction of the Khowrs as had been previously discussed by the Commission. He had wanted a full opportunity for the Commission to discuss and consider all the evidence on the Khowr Zhobeir before recommendations were brought forward.

227. The Commission did not need to worry about the judgement of history. The substantial work it had so far accomplished was a major contribution to the restoration of international peace and security in the area.

E. Response by the representative of Iraq

228. The representative of Iraq, responding to the statement made by the independent expert, said that he wished to seek information from the expert on whether or not interviews had been conducted in the Safwan area. He noted that, at the beginning of his statement, the expert had indicated quite clearly that it had been a Kuwaiti adviser who had helped the experts to identify the location of the old customs house. However, the latter portion of the expert's statement appeared to cast doubt on whether the experts had relied on the memory of Julian Walker and he had then named him by name. The experts had clearly stated that the experts had not relied on Julian Walker. The net effect of what he had said was true: the Kuwaiti representative and his advisers had sneaked into Safwan and relied on the memory of Julian Walker. He wanted the record to be straight from the outset.

229. One of the independent experts had concluded his statement by rejecting any inference that he (the representative of Iraq) had evidently made that pressure might have been employed. Again, he was forced to say what he had to say, even though he did not like it. So he wished to put it very mildly. Everyone around the table knew what had transpired the previous Monday on the thirty-eighth floor of the United Nations Secretariat, information which he had happened to get hold of purely accidentally.

230. He wished to respond to only two of the points raised by the representative of Kuwait. The latter had cast doubts as to his (the representative of Iraq's) contribution to and cooperation with the Commission. When the record was evaluated, it would show that on several occasions he had helped the Commission out of certain sticky spots. If it was the representative of Kuwait's view, and that of his Government, that he (the representative of Iraq) had not cooperated, in no uncertain terms could the representative of Kuwait, his Government or its supporters on the Security Council claim that the representative of Iraq had rejected the work of the Commission, so that sanctions against Iraq could be perpetuated. If they meant that the Iraqi representative on the Commission had to say yes all along or else he would be rejecting the work of the Commission, he would refer them to the rules of procedure of the Commission, the mandate of the Commission and the way in which it had been composed and set up by the Secretary-General. The Commission was to take its decisions by vote and he could vote in favour, against, abstain or not participate. Such a characterization by the representative of Kuwait, his Government and its supporters was a political ploy. Everybody knew that.

231. The second point he wished to make related to the representative of Kuwait's reference to "the restoration of international peace and security in the area". It should be left to history to see if the Commission had made a contribution to international peace and security. He himself had quoted certain newspaper articles. In his statement the previous day, he had not offered any characterization of those articles. He had just read out what people were already saying. He had quoted from American and British publications. If he had quoted from the Arabic press, it would have been seen that far-reaching conclusions were already being drawn on the basis of the work of the Commission, but he had not read from the Arabic press. He would leave it for history to judge if the Commission had contributed to the restoration of international peace and security. No one at the table would be convincing if he said that, at the end of the day a pillar was put in the house of an Iraqi citizen who had lived there for decades or if an Iraqi citizen was deprived of his means of livelihood - a farm, an orchard, which had been handed down from father to son, who had tilled the soil for decades - that would be a contribution to international peace and security in the area.

232. Everyone was aware that, at the second session, the representative of Kuwait had bulldozered the Commission into adopting decisions. Kuwait had been impatient and the representative of Kuwait had got his decisions. Now, however, he wanted to move at a mellower pace. He would leave it to those who had incisive judgement to conclude for themselves why the representative of Kuwait had wanted haste then and wanted a mellower pace now.

233. Like it or not, no one could escape the judgement of history. The Commission was involved in historic work of the highest order. Frequent reference had been made to Dickson, to More and to others, who were long gone. If anyone thought that the Commission was making a contribution to history by the results it had achieved in terms of the boundary, they should realize that people would not stop there. They would evaluate the results the Commission had reached all over the globe wherever there was a territorial dispute and would think hard about the manner in which the question had been handled by the Security Council, the Secretary-General and the

Commission. People had rushed in without giving sufficient thought to the adverse implications of their actions. Members of the Commission thought of themselves as technicians, diplomats, politicians, but the newspapers were calling the situation a time-bomb. History would plead not guilty: let the Commission not plead innocence.

F. Further response by the independent experts

234. At the 39th meeting (16 April 1992), one of the independent experts said that he wished, once and for all, to clear up the misunderstandings concerning what information had been obtained from whom during the visit to Safwan. He said that he had not spoken on the matter at the 38th meeting because the representative of Iraq had made a long statement on a rather sombre note, after which he had felt that it would be out of place to begin once again to talk about the point at Safwan.

235. The independent expert said that he had done the greater part of the research on the point at Safwan and assured the Commission that the description of the customs post provided by Mr. Julian Walker had very little significance although it did confirm evidence obtained by other technical methods. In document IKBDC/Doc.8, he had mentioned Lorimer's Gazetteer, which went a long way back in time, Galloway's later description of old Safwan, and had wanted to include an even later eyewitness description of Safwan. The basic evidence had been obtained from the interpretation of aerial photographs.

236. If the representative of Iraq gave particular attention to the aerial photographs in the document, he would find that it was relatively easy to go from photograph to photograph over the years: the first showed the fort and the compound. The fort and the compound were present in the next photograph, and could therefore be identified as the same building. Four houses had been built to the north of the fort. In the next photograph, six houses had been built, the earlier four remaining exactly the same. The development of the fort could be followed solely from the aerial photographs. The final evidence had been the coordinates for the north-west tower of the fort, which had been observed in 1942 and fell into place on the photograph.

237. The verbal description of the fort had had little or no significance in the research. He added that there must be many people living in Safwan who knew that the building was the old fort, so, had the experts been provided with that information, they would have solved the problem in 10 minutes; however, they had never been provided with that information. He assured the Commission that he had carried out the research, and that it had been based purely on documentation, aerial photographs and coordinates.

238. Responding to a question by the representative of Iraq, the independent expert further added that no interviews had been conducted: the experts did not speak Arabic. The experts had had at their disposal coordinates and a Magellan Global Positioning System receiver built into their vehicle. They had attempted to locate points, for which they had coordinates, in Safwan. They had a good idea what they were looking for: they had also had at their disposal oblique photographs confirming that the tree pattern and other features in the courtyard of the compound in 1991 could be related to patterns visible in the aerial photographs from 1965, 1958, 1954 and 1945.

239. The experts' determination had been based on image interpretation and coordinates. They guaranteed that they had interviewed no one.

G. Concluding statement by the Chairman

240. At the 39th meeting the Chairman said that he wished to express his appreciation to all members of the Commission for their participation and the contributions they had made to the work of the Commission, which had enabled the Commission to achieve what it had.

241. He thanked the secretariat and the staff, and said that, if he thanked the members of the Commission for their participation, he did so without any exception: he had heard various comments on the participation of the representative of Iraq, whom he was singling out for no other reason but to say that, in his view, the representative had participated fully in the work of the Commission. Any allusion to the effect that the representative of Iraq had not participated or had not supported the work of the Commission was incorrect.

242. There might be confusion between not participating in the vote and not participating in the work of the Commission. In the Chairman's view, not participating in the vote could not be construed as not participating in the work of the Commission or not cooperating with the Commission; it was a consequence of an inherent contradiction, if it might be so called, in the membership of the Commission. Some of the members were experts, but were also representatives of their Governments; the member from Iraq, in his personal capacity as an expert, had participated fully; indeed, he had been very active.

243. As the representative of Kuwait had stated at the previous meeting, the Commission had benefited from the representative of Iraq's participation, particularly on matters of procedure. Where voting was concerned, however, the representative of Iraq had not participated, as was his right, because he was then acting as the representative of the Government of Iraq. To deny the representative of Iraq the right not to participate in the vote would not be consistent with recognizing him as a representative of that Government. That fact was an instance of the uniqueness of the Commission.

244. Speaking as a technical expert, an impartial observer and also as Chairman, he took the view that, despite the representative of Iraq's non-participation in the vote, the Commission had been able to carry out its work; that it had been able to do so proved that there had been participation in the work of the Commission by all its members.

245. From its very first meeting, the Commission had determined that it would limit its work to demarcation. The Commission had, in his view, been consistent in that respect; he confessed that he had perhaps caused some confusion at some meetings by saying that there were some cases where the borderline between demarcation and delimitation would be difficult to draw, but, based on the excellent work of the experts and because all members had been consistent in their adherence to what they had decided at the 1st meeting, the Commission had been true to its intent to carry out the demarcation of the boundary.

246. It was important, in his view, to make the above point because the Commission had included in its deliberations a discussion of the offshore part of the eastern section. Discussion of the problem was not precluded in carrying out the task of demarcation, but he recalled that the independent experts had at an earlier session responded to a request to demarcate the offshore section by stating that in their view they could not do so.

247. There was thus a difference of opinion, which was, of course, quite possible between experts, and should not be construed as a lack of cooperation on the part of members. The Commission had allowed the representative of Kuwait to give another presentation on the offshore section, in which the representative had tried to prove that there was a case for demarcation. The issue of demarcation as against delimitation was thus a difficult one.

248. The Commission was adhering strictly to demarcation because it was a technical commission. In his view, the Commission should indeed restrict itself to demarcation, which was technical in nature, the setting of boundaries, including other considerations, especially political matters, being the province and task of the Governments as an attribute of their sovereignty. By no stretch of the imagination could that task be entrusted to the Commission, which, he recalled, would at its next session embark on the question of the offshore section.

249. As far as the Commission was concerned, it had done its part in respect of the land boundary, and had, in his view, carried out the task of assisting the Secretary-General to the best of its ability and with the support of its members. He emphasized that the Commission had had the support of all its members. He emphasized that the Commission had had the support of all its members without exception. It was the Commission's job to report what it had done to the Secretary-General, and what the Secretary-General did with that report was up to the Secretary-General.

250. He thanked all the members of the Commission, their staff and their advisers for their contributions, which had benefited the Commission as a whole. The discussions had been heated, but they should leave no aftertaste; all members had done the jobs given to them, and past heat should not hinder the Commission's future work.

VI. FURTHER CONSIDERATION OF THE EASTERN SECTION

251. In accordance with the request made at the fourth session (IKBDC/Rep.2, para. 106) and the discussion at the 29th meeting of the Commission on 8 April 1992 (IKBDC/Min.29), the representative of Kuwait made a statement in connection with the Commission's further consideration of the eastern section.

252. He recalled that, on 8 April 1992, he had introduced a working paper entitled "Demarcation of the offshore section of the Iraq-Kuwait boundary". The paper was presented not as a formal brief but rather as a working paper, which it was hoped would assist the Commission in its work. He was pleased to begin a Commission review of questions discussed in the paper that had been raised concerning demarcation of the offshore section of the boundary and particularly whether the mandate of the Commission extended to demarcation of the boundary to the east of the junction of the Khowrs. The issue in the working paper and review was a narrow one related solely to the Commission's mandate and its work in demarcating the agreed boundary in accordance with the directions of the Security Council and the report of the Secretary-General (S/22558). By the "offshore" section, he now meant the sections of the boundary beyond the low-water mark on the shore opposite the junction of the Khowrs and he was addressing demarcation of the boundary as specified in the Commission's mandate. He was not discussing ocean issues in general or the area beyond territorial waters.

253. He wished to address two important implications for this subject further to the Commission's decision to demarcate the boundary in the Khowr-Zhobeir by the use of the low-water line to a point opposite the junction of the Khowrs. To his knowledge the only sources in the record suggesting such a use of the low-water mark for that area to the junction of the Khowrs were the 1940 and 1951 British diplomatic notes interpreting the 1932 frontier. Both of those notes did not stop at the junction of the Khowrs but specifically extended "to the open sea". The 1940 note stated that from the junction of the Khowrs "... to the open sea the boundary shall follow the thalweg of the Khowr Abd Allah". The 1951 note stated that from that junction "... to the open sea the frontier shall follow first, the thalweg of the north-westerly arm of the Khowr Abd Allah known as the Khowr Shetana and then the thalweg of the Khowr Abd Allah proper". It would be anomalous for the Commission to use those notes to adopt the low-water line within the Khowr Zhobeir in a setting in which much contrary evidence in the record relied on a middle or centre line to mark the area, yet to fail to use the reference in the same notes to the open sea beyond the junction, when that feature of the notes was overwhelmingly supported by the record and confirmed by document S/22412. The difference certainly did not lie in the language of the 1932 delimitation formula, since nothing in that language remotely suggested the use of the low-water line in the Khowr Zhobeir.

254. A second implication of the decision was that the Commission had not yet demarcated the offshore section from the low-water mark of the shore of the Khowr Zhobeir opposite the junction of the Khowrs to the point identified by the Commission as that junction. That section of the boundary was also implicitly dealt with in the 1940 note and further explicitly described in the 1951 note as "the shortest line which can be drawn". Were the Commission to fail to deal with that offshore section, it would also be failing to give effect to the language in the 1932 Exchange of Letters which provided "... and so on to the junction of the Khowr Zhobeir with the Khowr Abd Allah".

255. The mandate of the Commission required complete demarcation of the 1932/1963 agreed boundary. Nothing in that mandate from the Security Council or the Secretary-General suggested that the Commission was empowered to demarcate only a portion of the boundary or was only limited to onshore sections of the boundary. If the 1932/1963 agreed boundary included an offshore section east of the junction of the Khowrs, as well as the short section from the low-water mark to the junction of the Khowrs, the Commission had also to demarcate that section of the boundary. Failure to demarcate the full 1932/1963 frontier agreement, including the offshore section, would be inconsistent with the Commission's mandate.

256. As the working paper showed in great detail, the agreed boundary did indeed include an offshore section. Failure to demarcate that offshore section would harm important goals expressed in Security Council resolution 687 (1991), including maintenance of the "territorial integrity" of Kuwait and respect for "the allocation of islands set out in the 'Agreed Minutes' ...". It could also harm the work of the United Nations Iraq-Kuwait Observation Mission in accordance with paragraph 5 of resolution 687 (1991). The UNIKOM area of deployment included a northern sector between Safwan and the entrance of the Khowr Abd Allah. Moreover, the language of that paragraph indicated that the Security Council clearly had in mind the importance to international peace and security of the Khowr Abd Allah. Most importantly, to fail to demarcate the complete boundary, and particularly to leave out the sensitive Khowr Abd Allah, would not serve the important purpose

expressed by the Secretary-General in his mandate to the Commission in that "one of the main purposes of the demarcation of the boundary between Kuwait and Iraq is to promote stability and peace and security along the border ...". It was well known that access through the Khowr was an essential requirement for stability along the border. The map transmitted by document S/22412, "appropriate material" specifically mentioned by the Council and referred to in the Secretary-General's mandate, confirmed the existence of a boundary through the Khowrs Shetana and Abd Allah.

257. There was no ambiguity about the scope of the 1932/1963 agreement when all its language was interpreted in the light of its object and purpose, precisely as was required by the most authoritative rules of interpretation. It should be noted that the final sentence of the specific boundary description in the 1932 Exchange of Letters read that "the islands of Warbah and Bubiyan ... [and others listed] appertain to Kuwait". There was thus an inescapable task before the Commission to ascertain the extent to which waters adjacent to those islands were part of the "existing frontier" necessarily running between those islands and mainland Iraq.

258. The language of the 1932 Exchange of Letters suggested in yet another way that the "existing frontier" being described included an offshore section: the concluding phrase in the preceding sentence provided "... and so on to the junction of the Khowr Zhobeir with the Khowr Abd Allah". That was a reference to the junction of two important navigable bodies offshore from the land boundary. Such a reference strongly implied a purpose to ensure navigation rights to both parties up to the point of intersection of the land boundary. On that basis, as well as the history, practice, object and purpose of the agreement, the Commission had had no difficulty in accepting that that section of the boundary was within its mandate. The Commission had already before decided on the low-water line as the boundary within that area, despite the lack of any language suggesting it in the 1932 delimitation formula. It was equally implicit, if not even clearer, from the last sentence of the 1932 boundary description concerning the offshore islands that the Khowr Shetana and the Khowr Abd Allah formed the boundary with respect to the continuation of the offshore section.

259. Most importantly, the language of the 1932/1963 agreement had to be taken as a whole and all its relevant language considered. During the exchange of letters in 1932, both parties had specifically reiterated the important language explaining the object and purpose of the exchange; "to reaffirm the existing frontier between Iraq and Kuwait ...". A review of the record in the light of those factors was compelling in showing that the "existing frontier" that the parties were reaffirming in 1932 and 1963 included a division of the Khowr Shetana and the Khowr Abd Allah down the "middle" or "centre" to the open sea. The 1932/1963 agreement delimited the frontier along the middle or centre of the Khowr Shetana and the Khowr Abd Allah to the open sea, thereby ensuring critical navigational access to both parties. Language used throughout the development of the frontier to describe the offshore section included "middle", "centre", "mid-channel", "thalweg" and "median line". All those phrases implied a delimitation of the offshore section intended to ensure navigational access for both parties through the Khowr Abd Allah to the open sea.

260. The historical record was as follows. From 1910 until the conclusion of the 1963 Agreed Minutes, the boundary was thought of as traversing the middle or the centre of the Khowr Abd Allah so that both parties could enjoy navigational access through the area. Such a boundary through the Khowr Shetana and the Khowr Abd Allah was explicitly incorporated in the unratified 1913 Anglo-Ottoman Convention as part of the "red line" denoting "the limits of Kuwait and adjacent country". The boundary, which was authoritatively referred to in the period before the 1932 Exchange of Letters as "not open to dispute" was identical with the "existing frontier" reaffirmed in the 1932 Exchange of Letters. Moreover, the 1932 boundary agreement had been confirmed by the Prime Minister of Iraq in contemporaneous statements made to facilitate Iraq's admission to the League of Nations and those statements left no doubt that all frontier areas between Iraq and Kuwait were "well defined". The record then contained numerous indications from the conclusion of the 1932 Exchange of Letters, which reaffirmed "... the existing frontier between Iraq and Kuwait ..." to the conclusions of the 1963 Agreed Minutes, that clearly indicated that some variant of a middle or centre line was regarded as delimiting the existing boundary down the Khowr Shetana and the Khowr Abd Allah to the open sea. As had been noted, both the 1940 and 1951 British interpretations of the 1932 frontier, apparently relied on by the Commission previously for its decision on the low-water line of the Khowr Zhobeir to the junction of the Khowrs, included a line following the thalweg of the Khowr Abd Allah "... to the open sea ...". There was no record that Iraq had objected to the boundary specified in those interpretations as not accurately describing the existing frontier. Particularly important was a 1955 proposal by the Iraqi Prime Minister to the British Ambassador to alter the existing boundary as part of a project to develop the port of Umm Qasr, illustrated by a map clearly showing that the "present Iraqi-Kuwaiti frontier" extended down the centre or middle of the Khowr Zhobeir, the Khowr Shetana and the Khowr Abd Allah from the point of intersection of the land boundary with the Khowr Zhobeir to the sea. The map was clear in differentiating what the Iraqi Prime Minister regarded as the existing boundary and the proposed change since the map used the labels "boundary line" and "proposed boundary" (with arrows pointing to the respective lines). Also in 1955 a map which was apparently approved by the Iraqi Foreign Minister identified the "present Iraq-Kuwait frontier" by a line continuing from the onshore section of the frontier down the middle of the Khowr Shetana and the Khowr Abd Allah. Those 1955 indications as to where the boundary was delimited were highly authoritative with respect to the position of Iraq since they had been made or approved by the Prime Minister and Foreign Minister of Iraq during official diplomatic exchanges.

261. Following an international trend towards the median line as the preferred mode for delimiting overlapping territorial sea boundaries and its adoption as the basic rule in article 12 of the 1958 Geneva Convention on the Territorial Sea, a report prepared for Iraq by Capt. W. Coucheron, who had participated in the 1958 United Nations Law of the Sea Conference, clearly showed that the median line was regarded as the boundary of Iraq within the Khowr Abd Allah to the seaward point of intersection of the territorial seas of Iraq and Kuwait. The report was almost contemporaneous with the 1963 Agreed Minutes and was thus of particular significance as to the expectations of Iraq at that time. Subsequently, an official Iraqi map, bearing the seal of the Iraqi Ministry of Petroleum, attached as annex IV to the Coucheron report, which was sent on 22 August 1960 to the Danish Embassy in Baghdad by the Iraqi Foreign Ministry and subsequently published in the official records of the International Court of Justice, also used the median line through the Khowrs Zhobeir, Shetana and Abd Allah to the open sea.

262. The full historical record, which included the above examples among at least 22 indicators or groupings of indicators, consistently showed that the "existing frontier" agreed in 1932 incorporated a middle or centre line down the Khowr Shetana and the Khowr Abd Allah to the open sea, that that was an integral part of the "existing frontier" as reaffirmed by the parties pursuant to the 1932/1963 agreement and that accordingly the line down the Khowrs was a delimited part of the 1932/1963 agreement. Modes by which the middle or centre line had been described more precisely included "mid-channel" (a form of thalweg), "thalweg" and "median line". Of those, the "median line" best reflected the agreed boundary. It bore emphasis that the median line was recommended as the best mode of demarcation of the 1932/1963 agreement because it best carried out that agreement and not simply because it reflected maritime law. The most authoritative, precise description of the offshore boundary of Iraq was that of the median line as incorporated in the Coucheron report and Iraq's transmission in 1960 of the map to the Danish Embassy. That was the most contemporaneous indication with respect to the conclusion of the 1963 Agreed Minutes of a demarcation of the middle or centre line down the Khowr Abd Allah to the open sea. Significantly, the "median line" mode of demarcation also conformed with the law of the sea, both at the time of the 1963 agreement (thus reflecting within the law of treaty interpretation the "relevant rules of international law applicable in the relations between the parties" as clearly acknowledged in the Coucheron report and the Coucheron map) and today as incorporated in article 12 of the 1958 Geneva Convention on the Territorial Sea (which was widely regarded as customary international law) and article 15 of the 1982 Law of the Sea Convention (which was not yet in force, but which both Iraq and Kuwait had ratified).

263. There was also a series of practical reasons why a median line would better reflect the agreed boundary than a thalweg. A thalweg might change more rapidly and it would be difficult to locate a thalweg free of the influence of past dredging or to deal with the possible impact of future dredging. Soundings would be required to locate the changing boundary accurately, and as the boundary continued seaward a thalweg might be difficult to ascertain and even functionally unnecessary in providing navigational access if the general area was sufficiently deep.

VII. DECISIONS

264. At the 36th meeting, the independent experts suggested the following recommendations concerning the various locations on the boundary.

265. The Chairman put to the vote the motion for division of the recommendations. The result of the voting was as follows: the representative of Kuwait and the independent experts voted in favour, the representative of Iraq voted against, and the Chairman abstained.

266. The Chairman put to the vote recommendation 1, which read as follows:

> "*Trijunction point*. The independent experts recommend that the existing boundary monument on the Iraq-Saudi Arabian border, pillar No. 1, be adopted as the starting point for the boundary along the thalweg of Wadi Al Batin, and therefore, the tripoint of Iraq, Kuwait and Saudi Arabia."

The result of the voting was as follows: the representative of Kuwait, the independent experts and the Chairman voted in favour, and the representative of Iraq announced that he was not participating in the vote.

267. The Chairman put to the vote recommendation 2, which read as follows:

> "*Point at the northern end of Wadi Al Batin*. The independent experts recommend that the point at the northern end of Wadi Al Batin be located at the intersection of the thalweg of the Wadi and the latitude of the point south of Safwan."

The result of the voting was as follows: the representative of Kuwait, the independent experts and the Chairman voted in favour, and the representative of Iraq announced that he was not participating in the vote.

268. The Chairman put to the vote recommendation 3, which read as follows:

> "*Point south of Safwan*. The independent experts recommend that the point south of Safwan be located at the mean distance between 1,609 metres (one mile) and 1,250 metres from the south-west extremity of the compound wall of the old customs post along the old line of the road from Safwan to Kuwait."

The result of the voting was as follows: the representative of Kuwait and the independent experts voted in favour, the Chairman abstained and the representative of Iraq announced that he was not participating in the vote.

269. The Chairman put to the vote recommendation 4, which read as follows:

> "*Point south of Umm Qasr*. The experts recommend that the point south of Umm Qasr coincide with the location at which the line on map sheet Umm Niqa (Series K7611, sheet 5549-I, Edition 2 (1990), produced under the direction of the Director General of Military Survey, Ministry of Defence, United Kingdom) crosses the western shore of Khowr Zhobeir."

The result of the voting was as follows: the representative of Kuwait, the independent experts and the Chairman voted in favour, and the representative of Iraq announced that he was not participating in the vote.

270. The Chairman put to the vote recommendation 5, which read as follows:

> "*Junction of the Khowr Zhobeir and Khowr Abd Allah*. The independent experts recommend that the coordinates of Khowr Zhobeir and Khowr Abd Allah be the one best identified for the epoch of 1932 and transposed onto modern orthophoto maps produced by the Commission."

The result of the voting was as follows: the representative of Kuwait, the independent experts and the Chairman voted in favour; and the representative of Iraq announced that he was not participating in the vote.

271. The Chairman put to the vote the motion made by the representative of Kuwait for separate votes on the four subparagraphs of recommendation 6. The result of the voting was as follows: the representative of Kuwait and the independent experts voted in favour, the representative of Iraq voted against and the Chairman abstained.

272. The Chairman put to the vote recommendation 6(a), which read as follows:

> "(a) The boundary line in the Wadi Al Batin should be a series of straight-line segments of about 2 kilometres in length best approximating to the lowest-point line in the Wadi;

The result of the voting was as follows: the representative of Kuwait, the independent experts and the Chairman voted in favour; and the representative of Iraq announced that he was not participating in the vote.

273. The Chairman put to the vote recommendation 6(b), which read as follows:

> "(b) The boundary line from the point at the northern end of Wadi Al Batin to the point south of Safwan should be a line running along the common latitude of the points;

The result of the voting was as follows: the representative of Kuwait, the independent experts and the Chairman voted in favour; and the representative of Iraq announced that he was not participating in the vote.

274. The Chairman put to the vote recommendation 6(c), which read as follows:

> "(c) The boundary line from the point south of Safwan to the point south of Umm Qasr should be the shortest line between the points;

The result of the voting was as follows: the representative of Kuwait, the independent experts and the Chairman voted in favour; and the representative of Iraq announced that he was not participating in the vote.

275. The Chairman put to the vote recommendation 6(d), which read as follows:

> "(d) The boundary line from the point south of Umm Qasr on the shore should follow the low-water line up to the location directly opposite the junction of Khowr Zhobeir and Khowr Abd Allah;

The result of the voting was as follows: the independent experts and the Chairman voted in favour, the representative of Kuwait voted against, and the representative of Iraq announced that he was not participating in the vote.

276. The representative of Kuwait, speaking in explanation of vote, said that he had taken note of the additional information the independent experts had provided at the 35th meeting concerning the point on the western shore of the Khowr Zhobeir in relation to the junction of the Khowrs. With regard to his negative vote on subparagraph 6(d), he considered that the question of the offshore section had not been adequately discussed.

277. The representative of Iraq reserved the right to make a statement in explanation of his position at a later stage and asked whether the decisions just taken were final. The Chairman said that as far as the Commission was concerned, its decisions were final.

278. At the 37th meeting, upon the proposal of the independent experts, the Chairman put to the vote a motion to adopt document IKBDC/Doc.14, "Determination of Primary Boundary Points" which includes a list of coordinates for the points. The result of the voting was as follows: the representative of Kuwait, the independent experts and the Chairman voted in favour, and the representative of Iraq announced that he was not participating in the vote.

279. The representative of Kuwait said that the reservations he had expressed at the previous meeting concerning the recommendation contained in subparagraph 6(d) should be maintained in relation to document IKBDC/Doc.14.

280. At the 38th meeting, on the proposal of the independent experts, the Chairman put to the vote the future work plan of the Commission contained in document IKBDC/Doc.10, "Proposed work plan for the establishment of three key demarcation points". The result of the voting was as follows: the representative of Kuwait, the independent experts and the Chairman voted in favour, and the representative of Iraq announced that he was not participating in the vote.

281. On the proposal of the Secretary, the Chairman put to the vote the presentation of the boundary pillars contained in document IKBDC/Doc.11, "Proposed work plan for stage 2B of the surveying and mapping programme of the Iraq-Kuwait Boundary Demarcation Commission". The result of the voting was as follows: the representative of Kuwait, the independent experts and the Chairman voted in favour, and the representative of Iraq announced that he was not participating in the vote.

282. The representative of Iraq, speaking in explanation of position, said that the reasons for his non-participation were the same as he had confirmed earlier. Iraq would leave the technical work in the hands of the Commission.

A. Execution of the decisions

283. As decided by the Commission at its 38th meeting, the Commission's survey team was mobilized immediately following the fifth session to emplace temporary boundary pillars at three key demarcation points (IKBDC/Doc.17).

284. At the end of April 1992, the survey team and the Secretary assembled at the Commission's field office in Umm Qasr. With the assistance of UNIKOM, temporary pillars were constructed at Umm Qasr, at Safwan and at the northern end of Wadi Al Batin.

285. At Umm Qasr and at Safwan each demarcation point consists of a 15cm diameter, approximately 2m long metal tube set in concrete. Four buried witness marks were emplaced around each pillar. The metal tubes were filled with concrete and brass boundary markers were imbedded on the top of each. The pillars were surrounded with sand-filled bags in a cross-shape and were painted white for better visibility. At the northern end of Wadi Al Batin a similar demarcation point on the parallel in the Wadi was set up with a metal tube of approximately 3.5m in length and with only two buried witness marks.

286. Each pillar and witness mark was surveyed relative to the primary control network established in stage 1 of the Commission's survey project. In addition, the Iraq-Saudi Arabia boundary pillar No. 1 at the southern end of Wadi Al Batin was also surveyed relative to the primary control network.

287. The boundary in the Wadi was calculated in terms of the requirement of the Commission as detailed in IKBDC/Doc.16.

B. Preparations for boundary demarcation on the ground

288. A set of specifications for the boundary pillars, witness marks and pointer pillars has been prepared prior to the fifth session of the Commission. These specifications have been circulated to all members for their review. Incorporating all comments received, the final design of the markers was presented to the Commission (IKBDC/Doc.11) and was adopted at its 38th meeting.

289. At that meeting, the Secretary reported that, at the suggestion of the Procurement Office of the United Nations Secretariat, UNIKOM was contacted to assist the Commission in identifying an appropriate firm to undertake the construction of the pillars.

290. The Secretariat further reported that UNIKOM, in carrying out the Commission's request, has contacted 10 companies to obtain estimates for budgetary purposes. The estimates received varied considerably from $300,000 to $1.5 million and were found unreliable for contract awarding. It was felt that perhaps the specifications were not detailed enough for obtaining proper tenders. UNIKOM recommended that in the absence of appropriate expertise within the Organization, an outside technical consultant be hired.

291. Following consultations, UNIKOM hired Commercial Contracting Establishment (CCE) on behalf of the Commission. CCE was contracted to undertake the following tasks, if and when requested:

a) to review and make recommendations to the existing specifications package,
b) to assist with the identification and evaluation of bidders,
c) to serve the Commission as quality assurance representative for both in-plant manufacturing and for on-site construction.

292. CCE prepared a new set of drawings and manufacturing specifications based on the requirements adopted by the Commission. The technical consultants, assisted by leader of the Commission's survey team, conducted a field visit to the border area during the last week of June. They have also discussed and reviewed the working methods and established a full schedule for demarcation. Following that, a tender package was prepared by UNIKOM and requests for quotations were issued on 26 June 1992 to eight companies. Six quotations were received, two firms declined to participate. UNIKOM conducted a bid opening session on 8 July and prepared an abstract of the bids.

293. Company profiles of the two lowest bidders ($725,000 and $1,058,666) were reviewed and evaluated. Visits to these bidders will be made to interview key personnel. Following the interviews UNIKOM's local committee on contracts will review all bids and submit its formal recommendation to the Commission.

294. The Commission took note of the fact that the boundary demarcation exercise requires careful planning. Logistically it is extremely important that all elements of pillar manufacturing, construction and emplacement be carried out as planned and as scheduled. Hence, the Commission called upon the cooperation of everyone including all local authorities.

VIII. FURTHER WORK OF THE COMMISSION

295. The future programme of the Commission includes the finalization of the demarcation of the land boundary on the ground and a review of the eastern section of the boundary, east of the junction of Khowr Zhobeir and Khowr Abd Allah and a proposal to hold a further meeting on this subject.

296. Arrangements are being made to demarcate the entire length of the land boundary by the manufacture and emplacement of concrete pillars as was decided upon (IKBDC/Doc.11). It is planned that this work will commence with the manufacturing of the pillars at the end of August 1992. The setting out of the pillars by the Commission's survey team will begin at the end of September 1992 and will be followed shortly by the emplacement of all boundary markers by a construction firm. The demarcation exercise is scheduled to be completed by the middle of December 1992. The Commission will then conduct a site visit of the border area to confirm the surveyed and demarcated boundary. Final documentation will be prepared by March 1993 and a concluding meeting of this stage of the Commission's work will be held in April 1993. Detailed and certified documentation on the demarcated boundary will be presented to the Secretary-General at that time. As requested, the Commission will also make arrangements to provide for maintenance of the boundary pillars on a continuing basis.

297. The Commission also decided to consider at its sixth session the boundary in the Khowr Abd Allah section. In this regard, the independent experts will further investigate and present appropriate material on the Khowr Zhobeir and the Khowr Abd Allah for the use of the Commission. A meeting of the Commission to discuss this matter will be held in October.

...

S/RES/773 (1992), 26 August 1992

17. SC Resolution 773 (1992)

Adopted by the Security Council at its 3108th meeting, on 26 August 1992

The Security Council,

Reaffirming its resolution 687 (1991) of 3 April 1991, and in particular paragraphs 2, 3 and 4 thereof, and its resolution 689 (1991) of 9 April 1991,

Recalling the report of the Secretary-General dated 2 May 1991 concerning the establishment of the United Nations Iraq-Kuwait Boundary Demarcation Commission (the Commission) and the subsequent exchange of letters of 6 and 13 May 1991 (S/22558, S/22592 and S/22593),

Having considered the Secretary-General's letter of 12 August 1992 to the President of the Security Council transmitting the further report of the Commission,

Recalling in this connection that through the demarcation process the Commission is not reallocating territory between Kuwait and Iraq, but it is simply carrying out the technical task necessary to demarcate for the first time the precise coordinates of the boundary set out in the Agreed Minutes between the State of Kuwait and the Republic of Iraq regarding the restoration of Friendly Relations, Recognition and Related Matters signed by them on 4 October 1963, and that this task is being carried out in the special circumstances following Iraq's invasion of Kuwait and pursuant to resolution 687 (1991) and the Secretary-General's report for implementing paragraph 3 of that resolution (S/22558),

1. *Welcomes* the Secretary-General's letter of 12 August to the President of the Council and the further report of the Commission enclosed therewith;

2. *Expresses its appreciation* to the Commission for its work on the demarcation of the land boundary, and welcomes its demarcation decisions;

3. *Welcomes* also the decision of the Commission to consider the Eastern section of the boundary, which includes the offshore boundary, at its next session and *urges* the Commission to demarcate this part of the boundary as soon as possible and thus complete its work;

4. *Underlines* its guarantee of the inviolability of the above-mentioned international boundary and its decision to take as appropriate all necessary measures to that end in accordance with the Charter, as provided for in paragraph 4 of resolution 687 (1991);

5. *Welcomes further* the Secretary-General's intention to carry out at the earliest practicable time the realignment of the demilitarized zone referred to in paragraph 5 of resolution 687 (1991) to correspond to the international boundary demarcated by the Commission, with the consequent removal of the Iraqi police posts;

6. *Urges* the two States concerned to cooperate fully with the work of the Commission;

7. *Decides* to remain seized of the matter.

11. THE IRAQ-KUWAIT OBSERVER MISSION

In Resolution 687 (1991) the Security Council provided for the creation of a UN observer unit to monitor the Khor Abdullah and a demilitarized zone extending 10 kilometres into Iraq and 5 kilometres into Kuwait from the boundary established in the 1963 Iraq-Kuwait Agreed Minutes reproduced in the previous chapter. Its mandate is to deter violations of the boundary through its presence in and surveillance of the demilitarized zone and to observe any hostile or potentially hostile action mounted from the territory of one State to the other. The Council, in Resolution 689 (1991), affirmed that the Observer Mission was not a peace-keeping operation in the traditional sense, as "it can only be terminated by a decision of the Council", i.e., its existence is not exclusively dependent on the consent of the host States. In the context of the guarantee of the inviolability of the boundary given in operative paragraph 4 of Resolution 687 (1991), the Security Council substantially increased the Observer Mission, both in terms of manpower and function, in February of 1993 (Resolution 806 (1993), Document 17).

S/22454, 5 April 1991

1. Report of the Secretary-General on the implementation of paragraph 5 of Security Council resolution 687 (1991)

1. The present report is submitted in pursuance of Security Council resolution 687 (1991) of 3 April 1991. In paragraph 5 of that resolution, the Council established a demilitarized zone along the boundary between Iraq and Kuwait and requested the Secretary-General to submit to the Council, within three days, for approval a plan for the immediate deployment of a United Nations observer unit.

Terms of reference

2. In accordance with paragraph 5 of resolution 687 (1991), the terms of reference of the unit, which I propose should be called the "United Nations Iraq-Kuwait Observation Mission" (UNIKOM), would be:

> (a) To monitor the Khor Abdullah and a demilitarized zone extending 10 kilometres into Iraq and 5 km into Kuwait from the boundary referred to in the Agreed Minutes between the State of Kuwait and the Republic of Iraq regarding the Restoration of Friendly Relations, Recognition and Related Matters of 4 October 1963; [1] [1. United Nations *Treaty Series*, vol. 485, No. 7063.]
>
> (b) To deter violations of the boundary through its presence in and surveillance of the demilitarized zone;
>
> (c) To observe any hostile or potentially hostile action mounted from the territory of one State to the other.

General principles

3. Four essential conditions would have to be met for UNIKOM to be effective: first, it would need to have at all times the confidence and backing of the Security Council. Second, it would have to be given the necessary cooperation of the parties. Third, it would have to function as an integrated and efficient military unit. Fourth, adequate financial arrangements would have to be made to cover its costs.

4. In accordance with established principles,

(a) UNIKOM would be under the command of the United Nations, vested in the Secretary-General, under the authority of the Security Council. Command in the field would be exercised by a Chief Military Observer appointed by the Secretary-General with the consent of the Security Council. The Chief Military Observer would be responsible to the Secretary-General. The Secretary-General would report regularly to the Security Council on the operations of UNIKOM and immediately if there were serious violations of the demilitarized zone or potential threats to peace. All matters that might affect the nature or the continued effective functioning of UNIKOM would be referred to the Council for its decision;

(b) UNIKOM would be composed of military contingents provided by Member States at the request of the Secretary-General. The military contingents would be selected in consultation with the parties and with the concurrence of the Security Council, bearing in mind the accepted principle of equitable geographic representation;

(c) As recommended below, the contingents would comprise armed and unarmed military personnel. UNIKOM and its personnel would be authorized to use force only in self-defence;

(d) UNIKOM would proceed on the assumption that the parties would take all the necessary steps to comply with the decisions of the Security Council. It would have to have the freedom of movement and communication and other rights and facilities that would be necessary for the performance of its tasks. UNIKOM and its personnel would also have to be granted all relevant privileges and immunities provided for by the Convention on the Privileges and Immunities of the United Nations; agreements with the host Governments concerning the status of UNIKOM would have to be concluded without delay. The Governments of Iraq and Kuwait would be expected to provide, free of charge, the land and premises required by UNIKOM.

Considerations relevant to the discharge of the mandate

5. As an observation mission, UNIKOM would be required to monitor and observe and would not be expected and, indeed, would not be authorized to take physical action to prevent the entry of military personnel or equipment into the demilitarized zone. Further, it is my understanding that the clause requiring UNIKOM to "observe any hostile or potentially hostile action mounted from the territory of one State to the other" refers to activities that can be observed in or from the Khor Abdullah and the demilitarized zone.

6. UNIKOM would not assume responsibilities that fall within the competence of the host Governments and would avoid unnecessary interference in the normal civilian life of the area. It is assumed that the Governments of Iraq and Kuwait would each carry out all aspects of civilian administration in their respective part of the demilitarized zone, including the maintenance of law and order. At the same time, if UNIKOM is to be effective, it would need to have certain powers and facilities. In this connection, the two Governments would be expected to extend to UNIKOM full freedom of movement, on land and through the air, across the border and throughout the demilitarized zone; to control movement into and out of the demilitarized zone by requiring all traffic to be routed past United Nations observation posts; to notify UNIKOM in advance of sea and air traffic in the demilitarized zone and the Khor Abdullah; and to establish limitations on the right of their citizens to bear arms in the demilitarized zone. Further details regarding the regulation of activities in the demilitarized zone and the Khor Abdullah would be worked out in consultation with the two Governments, including the number and armament of police deployed in the area.

Area of operation

7. The demilitarized zone is about 200 km long, the Khor Abdullah about 40 km. For the most part, the zone is barren and almost uninhabited, except for the oilfields and two towns, Umm Qasr and Safwan. A small airfield is at Safwan. A port and airfield are at Umm Qasr, which became Iraq's only outlet to the sea after the Shatt al-Arab was blocked. A number of roads cross the demilitarized zone, most of them in the eastern part, but the terrain makes cross-country travel easy, and the inhabitants, particularly the bedouins, are accustomed to moving freely throughout the area and across the border.

Concept of operation

8. In order to carry out the mandate defined by the Security Council, UNIKOM would monitor the situation (on a continuing basis) to ensure that no military personnel and equipment were within the demilitarized zone and that no military fortifications and installations were maintained in it. To this end, it would:

(a) Monitor the withdrawal of any armed forces now in the zone which is to be demilitarized;

(b) Operate observation posts on the main roads to monitor traffic into and out of the demilitarized zone;

(c) Operate observation posts at selected locations in the demilitarized zone;

(d) Conduct patrols throughout the demilitarized zone by land and by air;

(e) Monitor the Khor Abdullah from observation posts set up on its shores and from the air;

(f) Carry out investigations.

Requirements

9. The tasks defined above are essentially tasks for military observers. However, in the circumstances obtaining in the UNIKOM area of operations, they could not be carried out by military observers alone. This is for three main reasons.

10. First, the area of operations, apart from Umm Qasr and territory to the east of it, is currently controlled by the forces of Member States cooperating with Kuwait. As those forces bring their military presence in Iraq to an end, in accordance with paragraph 6 of resolution 687 (1991), there is a risk that disorder would ensue, at least for a period of time. In particular, the forces of Member States cooperating with Kuwait are at present providing humanitarian assistance to some tens of thousands of refugees and displaced persons, many of them in what will become the UNIKOM area of operations. I am taking urgent steps to arrange for the United Nations system to provide such humanitarian support as may be needed by these people. It is also hoped that the host Governments' police forces would soon be in a position to maintain law and order in their respective parts of the demilitarized zone. Nevertheless, during this delicate transitional phase there might well be a threat to the security of UNIKOM personnel, equipment and supplies. My plan therefore includes the provision of an infantry element to ensure UNIKOM's security at that stage.

11. Second, I have been informed by Member States cooperating with Kuwait that mines and unexplored ordnance are a serious hazard in the area. Considerable effort would be required to clear areas required for UNIKOM observation posts and other installations, to make existing roads and tracks safe for patrolling and to establish additional tracks to enable UNIKOM to patrol the length and breadth of the demilitarized zone. Unless satisfactory arrangements can be made to complete this work before UNIKOM is deployed, the mission would have to include a field engineer unit.

12. Third, the demilitarized zone is barren and sparsely populated, the climate is harsh and the infrastructure in the area has suffered greatly. The military observers would therefore need a greater degree of logistic support than is the case in areas that are more settled and have less severe climates. There would thus be a continuing need for a logistic unit.

13. To carry out the tasks described in paragraph 8 above, a group of 300 military observers would be required initially, although this number would be reviewed as the mission gained experience and refined its methods. As regards support for the observers, my plan would be to assign temporarily to UNIKOM five infantry companies drawn from existing peace-keeping operations in the region, with the agreement of the troop-contributing Governments concerned. These units would provide essential security for UNIKOM during the setting-up phase. The Chief Military Observer would be instructed to advise me, approximately four weeks after the beginning of the operation, whether he foresaw a continuing need for an infantry element. If he did, I would seek the Council's authority to replace the units temporarily assigned to UNIKOM with one or more battalions on a more permanent basis. As indicated in paragraph 11 above, a field engineer unit would also be required if the necessary clearance of mines and unexploded ordnance had not been completed by the time UNIKOM was deployed. In addition, UNIKOM would have an air unit with fixed-wing aircraft and light helicopters, a logistic unit responsible primarily for medical care, supply and transport, and a headquarters unit. The maximum initial strength of UNIKOM would be approximately 1,440 all ranks, of which the infantry temporarily attached to it from already established

missions would be approximately 680, and the field engineer unit, if it is deployed, approximately 300.

14. UNIKOM's headquarters would need to be within the demilitarized zone, where Umm Qasr would seem to be the most suitable location. A logistic base would be established in Kuwait. The military observers and the infantry units would be deployed throughout the demilitarized zone. Liaison offices would be maintained at Baghdad and Kuwait City. At the start of the mission, liaison would also need to be maintained with the forces of the Member States cooperating with Kuwait, whose withdrawal through the demilitarized zone would need to be coordinated with UNIKOM.

15. A preliminary estimate of the cost of UNIKOM and my observations on its financing will be circulated in an addendum to the present report.

Consultations with the parties

16. As already stated, UNIKOM would be able to function effectively only with the full cooperation of the parties. In accordance with resolution 687 (1991), I have informed the Permanent Representatives of Iraq and Kuwait of the plan contained in the present report and requested their urgent confirmation that their respective Governments would cooperate with the United Nations on this basis. I will report further to the Security Council as soon as this has been received.

S/22454/Add.1, 5 April 1991

2. Report of the Secretary-General on the implementation of paragraph 5 of Security Council Resolution 687 (1991)

Estimated cost and method of financing

1. Should the Security Council establish the United Nations Iraq-Kuwait Observation Mission (UNIKOM) on the basis set out in the main part of the present report, it is estimated that the cost of the Mission for the first six months would be approximately $83 million. The costs of continuing UNIKOM for the following six months would be approximately $40 million. These estimates do not include additional costs that would be incurred if the infantry units temporarily assigned to UNIKOM are replaced with infantry battalions on a more permanent basis; nor do they include the costs that would be incurred if the engineer unit had to be continued beyond six months. These are preliminary estimates, which might be subject to revision as further details are clarified and/or as a result of decisions taken by the Security Council.

2. It would be my recommendation that the costs of the Mission be considered an expense of the Organization to be borne by Member States in accordance with Article 17, paragraph 2, of the Charter. I would recommend to the General Assembly that the assessments to be levied on Member States be credited to a special account that would be established for this purpose.

3. The capacity of the United Nations to deploy UNIKOM would depend in large measure on the availability of the financial resources necessary to meet the start-up costs of the operation. This in turn would depend not only on the appropriation of the necessary funds by the Assembly but, equally importantly, on payment of assessed contributions for peace-keeping contributions. As is known, the payment of assessed contributions for peace-keeping operations established by the Security Council has been at rates far lower than were necessary to meet cash-flow requirements. In order to meet the start-up costs of UNIKOM, I would therefore appeal to Member States to make voluntary payments, which would be repaid as soon as sufficient assessed contributions have been received. I would also appeal to Member States to make voluntary contributions in cash and in kind for setting up and maintaining the Mission.

4. I take this opportunity to point out that the above cost estimate covers only paragraph 5 of resolution 687 (1991). The financial implications of the resolution's other provisions will become clearer after the necessary detailed examination of the manner in which these provisions may be implemented by the Secretary-General and of the various commissions to be established under the resolution. It is already apparent, however, that the aggregate financial implications of the resolution are likely to be quite substantial.

[*A map provided in Adendum 2 to Document S/22454 has been reprinted in the map section at the end of this volume.*]

S/22454/Add.3, 9 April 1991

3. Report of the Secretary-General on the implementation of paragraph 5 of Security Council Resolution 687 (1991)

1. In reference to paragraph 16 of my report of 5 April 1991 (S/22454), the Permanent Representative of Iraq informed me on 8 April 1991 that his Government accepted the plan contained in my report and would cooperate with the United Nations on that basis.

2. On 9 April 1991, the representative of Kuwait conveyed to me his Government's acceptance of the plan and its undertaking to cooperate with the United Nations on its implementation.

S/22477, 10 April 1991

4. Letter from the Chargé d'affaires a.i. of the Permanent Mission of Kuwait to the United Nations addressed to the Secretary-General, 10 April 1991

Upon instructions from my Government, I should like to inform you that the State of Kuwait will fully cooperate with the United Nations towards successfully accomplishing the tasks that the United Nations Iraq-Kuwait Observation Mission shall undertake in accordance with Your Excellency's report (S/22454 and Add.1-3) dated 5 and 9 April 1991 on the implementation of paragraph (5) of Security Council resolution 687 (1991), which was endorsed by the Council in resolution 689 (1991) of 9 April 1991.

...

S/22478, 10 April 1991

5. Letter from the Secretary-General addressed to the President of the Security Council, 9 April 1991

I have the honour to refer to my report dated 5 April 1991 concerning proposed arrangements for the establishment of the United Nations Iraq/Kuwait Observation Mission (UNIKOM) (S/22454 and Add.1-3), which was approved by the Security Council in its resolution 689 (1991) of 9 April 1991. In paragraph 4 (a) of my report (S/22454), I stated that the command of UNIKOM would be exercised by a Chief Military Observer appointed by the Secretary-General with the consent of the Security Council.

I now wish to inform you that it is my intention, with the consent of the Council, to appoint Major-General Günther Greindl of Austria as Chief Military Observer of UNIKOM.

...

S/22479, 10 April 1991

6. Letter from the President of the Security Council addressed to the Secretary-General, 10 April 1991

I have the honour to inform you that your letter dated 9 April 1991 (S/22478) concerning your proposal to appoint Major-General Günther Greindl of Austria as Chief Military Observer of the United Nations Iraq/Kuwait Observation Mission (UNIKOM) has been brought to the attention of the members of the Security Council. They considered the matter on 10 April 1991 and agreed with the proposal contained in your letter.

S/22488, 12 April 1991

7. Letter from the Secretary-General addressed to the President of the Security Council, 11 April 1991

I have the honour to refer to Security Council resolutions 687 (1991) of 3 April 1991 and 689 (1991) of 9 April 1991, in which the Council decided to set up the United Nations Iraq-Kuwait Observation Mission (UNIKOM).

I intend to proceed without delay with the deployment of UNIKOM.

Having consulted the parties, I propose that UNIKOM be composed of contingents from the following Member States, all of whom have expressed their readiness in principle to make the necessary personnel available: Argentina, Austria, Bangladesh, Canada, Chile, China, Denmark, Fiji, Finland, France, Ghana, Greece, Hungary, India, Indonesia, Ireland, Italy, Kenya, Malaysia, Nepal, Nigeria, Norway, Pakistan, Poland, Romania, Senegal, Singapore, Sweden, Thailand, Turkey, Union of Soviet Socialist Republics, United Kingdom of Great Britain and Northern Ireland, United States of America, Uruguay and Venezuela. The Government of Switzerland has also informed me of its readiness to contribute to UNIKOM.

...

S/22489, 12 April 1991

8. Letter from the President of the Security Council addressed to the Secretary-General, 12 April 1991

I have the honour to inform you that your letter dated 11 April 1991 (S/22488) concerning the proposed composition of the United Nations Iraq-Kuwait Observation Mission (UNIKOM) has been brought to the attention of the members of the Security Council. They considered the matter on 12 April 1991 and agreed with the proposal contained in your letter.

9. United Nations Iraq-Kuwait Observation Mission (UNIKOM), Notes for the Guidance of Military Observers on Assignment (Version II), 23 April 1991

Field Operations Division
United Nations, New York

I. Purpose

1. These notes provide basic information for military observers to acquaint them with the United Nations Iraq-Kuwait Observation Mission (UNIKOM) and to enable them to make the necessary arrangements prior to their departure for the mission area. Observers will receive more detailed information upon arrival at UNIKOM headquarters.

2. The notes were prepared by the Office for Special Political Affairs in conjunction with Field Operations Division, Office of General Services, United Nations Secretariat.

II. General Background

A. *Functions*

3. UNIKOM's mandate in accordance with operative paragraph 5 of Security Council resolution 687 will be:

a. To monitor the Khor Abdullah and a demilitarized zone (DMZ) extending 10 kilometres into Iraq and 5 km into Kuwait from the boundary referred to in the Agreed Minutes between the State of Kuwait and the Republic of Iraq regarding the Restoration of Friendly Relations, Recognition and Related Matters of 4 October 1963;

b. To deter violations of the boundary through its presence in and surveillance of the DMZ;

c. To observe any hostile or potentially hostile action mounted from the territory of one State to the other.

4. In accordance with this mandate, UNIKOM's terms of reference will be:

a. To monitor the withdrawal of any armed forces now in the zone which is to be demilitarized;

b. To operate observation posts (OPs) on the main roads to monitor traffic into and out of the DMZ;

c. To operate OPs at selected locations in the DMZ;

d. To conduct patrols throughout the DMZ by land and by air;

e. To monitor the Khor Abdullah from OPs set up on its shores and from the air;

f. To carry out investigations.

B. *Authority and Duration of Mandate*

5. The authority for the mission is Security Council resolution 689 (1991) of 9 April 1991. The initial duration of the mandate will be six months.

C. *Location*

6. The demilitarized zone is about 200 km long, the Khor Abdullah about 40 km. For the most part, the zone is barren and almost uninhabited, except for the oil fields and two towns, Umm Qasr and Safwan. A small airfield is at Safwan. A port and airfield are at Umm Qasr, which became Iraq's only outlet to the sea after the Shatt al-Arab was blocked.

[*A geographical description of the region has be omitted.*]

...

E. *Organization*

10. UNIKOM will consist of 300 military observers from 33 Member States - Argentina, Austria, Bangladesh, Canada, China, Denmark, Fiji, Finland, France, Ghana, Greece, Hungary, India, Indonesia, Ireland, Italy, Kenya, Malaysia, Nigeria, Norway, Pakistan, Poland, Romania, Senegal, Singapore, Sweden, Thailand, Turkey, Uruguay, UK, USSR, USA and Venezuela. UNIKOM will be organized on the following lines:

(a) Commanded by a Chief Military Observer (CMO) of the rank of Major-General;

(b) Likely location of headquarters (HQ UNIKOM) is Umm Qasr, Iraq;

(c) DMZ will be divided into three sectors: Northern, Central and Southern. Suitably composed teams of international military observers will carry out the assigned tasks in the sectors;

(d) UNIKOM will also have:
(1) an Engineer (EOD) mine clearance unit; and
(2) an air wing of six helicopters and two STOL aircraft;

(e) In the initial stages, five infantry companies pooled from the existing peace-keeping missions, will be provided to UNIKOM for a period of four to six weeks. The requirement of infantry will then be reviewed by the CMO. Based on his recommendations, provision of infantry may be made on a permanent basis.

(f) There will also be two Liaison Offices (LO's) - one in Baghdad and one in Kuwait City.

F. *Civilian Personnel*

11.a Professional staff are assigned to UNIKOM to carry out political, legal, public information and administrative functions.

b. A civilian administrative element headquartered in Umm Qasr and headed by the Chief Administrative Officer (CAO) is responsible for the necessary administrative and logistical support to the mission, including the provision of communications, vehicle and aircraft transport, supply, contractual services and finance. The staffing comprises Professional and General Service staff assigned from other United Nations Offices, Field Service Officers and staff recruited locally in the mission area.

G. *Duty Stations*

12. UNIKOM will operate a number of observation posts in Kuwait and Iraq. In the course of a tour of duty, observers may be required to serve in any one of these places as well as in the towns and cities.

III. MILITARY OBSERVERS

A. *Definition*

13. Observers are military officers assigned to serve with the United Nations on a loan basis by Governments of Member States at the request of the Secretary-General.

B. *Conduct and performance*

14. While in the mission area, observers are under the command of the CMO and are directly answerable to him for their conduct and the performance of their duties. The CMO is authorized to accord official recognition of service merits of the observer, as well as to enforce military discipline.

15. Observers shall, during the term of their appointment, discharge their functions and regulate their conduct solely within the interests of the United Nations and shall not seek or accept instructions in respect of the performance of their duties from their own Government or from any other authority external to the United Nations.

16. Military observers must always be completely impartial and objective, and should avoid any action that might give rise to doubts about their ability to remain so. For this reason, military observers should have neither family ties nor other close ties with individuals or organizations in Kuwait and Iraq.

17. Observers must exercise the utmost discretion in respect of all matters of official business. They must not communicate to any person any information known to them by reason of their official position that has not been made public, except in the course of their duties or with the authorization of the CMO. In addition, they must not use such information to private advantage. These obligations should not cease after the term of their appointment with UNIKOM, and on taking up their assignment, observers are required to sign an undertaking, the text of which is reproduced in annex I to the present notes.

18. Observers are not permitted to carry arms, and therefore are not to bring them into the mission area. All photography, both while on leave or on duty, is prohibited anywhere in the mission area, as is taking cameras into and out of the country. In the mission area, observers are not authorized to carry cameras while on duty, and on arrival must acquaint themselves with the directives concerning the off-duty use of cameras in the mission area.

19. Observers are assigned to UNIKOM headquarters or duty stations as decided by the CMO.

C. *Privileges and immunities*

20. The privileges and immunities of observers are defined under article VI, "Experts on missions for the United Nations" of the Convention on the Privileges and Immunities of the United Nations, (General Assembly resolution 22 A (I)), which must be adhered to by all Governments in the mission areas. The text of article VI is reproduced in annex II to the present notes.

21. These privileges and immunities are granted in the interests of the United Nations and not for the personal benefit of individuals. Additionally, a national authority can take whatever legal or disciplinary action may be warranted against an observer, in accordance with his country's laws and regulations. The Secretary-General has the right and the duty to waive the immunity of an observer in any case where, in his opinion, the immunity would impede the course of justice. Such a waiver should be without prejudice to the interests of the United Nations.

D. *Financial liabilities*

22. Observers may be required to reimburse the United Nations either partially or in full for any financial loss suffered by the United Nations as a result of their negligence or of their having violated any regulation, rule or administrative instruction. This may be done by withholding the mission subsistence allowance (see para. 72).

IV. QUALIFICATIONS

23. The following qualifications are considered essential for military observers assigned to UNIKOM.

A. *Professional*

24. Military observers must have the following qualifications:

(a) A minimum of six years of regular, active military service experience;

(b) The rank of the observers should be that requested by the United Nations. If observers arrive in the mission area with a higher rank than requested or are promoted during their tour of duty, UNIKOM will not be obliged to take those ranks into consideration in determining the observers' assignments;

(c) Proficiency in map reading, a working knowledge of infantry operations at the company level, experience or training in ground-weapon identification and the rapid identification of aircraft deployed in the area;

(d) The ability to speak English fluently and to read and write English, the working language of UNIKOM. Observers are required to write or type their own reports and to communicate in clear English on voice radio sets;

(e) Be experienced vehicle drivers and capable of supervising the daily maintenance of light military vehicles. Observers should have at least two years recent experience in driving standard shift motor vehicles and be in possession of valid national and international drivers licences. Many of the observers duties will involve driving four-wheel drive vehicles in rough terrain. Driving in the mission area is on the right hand side of the road.

B. *Physical*

25. Military observers must be in first-class physical condition. Observers may have to live and work in conditions of hardship and, sometimes, physical danger. It may be necessary to investigate on foot in rugged terrain with no roads.

C. *Other Requirements*

26. Additional qualifications considered desirable are as follows:

(a) A knowledge of Arabic;

(b) Combat experience or combat troop-training experience, in order to properly evaluate or analyse situations that observers may be called upon to investigate;

(c) Staff training or staff experience.

...

S/22515, 22 April 1991

10. Letter from the Permanent Representative of Iraq to the United Nations addressed to the Secretary-General, 21 April 1991

On instructions from my Government, I have the honour to inform you that United States forces stationed in the northern part of the Rumaila oilfield have prevented the Iraqi personnel who work there from taking the minimum measures to protect property of the Southern Oil Company from sabotage and theft. The United States forces have allowed saboteurs to commit premeditated acts of plunder and destruction, the latter having loaded dozens of large hauling vehicles without licence plates with cement, stocks, supplies and equipment belonging to the above-mentioned company; the vehicles then set out for an unknown destination, apparently Kuwait. Our belief that Kuwait is their destination is reinforced by the fact that the Americans have claimed that the property that was plundered before the eyes of the United States forces belongs to Kuwait. Preliminary estimates place the losses at around 18 million dinars.

These acts, which constitute a flagrant violation of Iraq's sovereignty, were committed with the premeditated aim of plundering Iraqi property. In bringing these acts to your attention, we lodge a most vehement protest against them. We await action on your part to put an end to such acts as required by the principles and provisions of the Charter of the United Nations.

...

S/22519, 23 April 1991

11. Letter from the Permanent Representative of Iraq to the United Nations addressed to the Secretary-General, 21 April 1991

On instructions from my Government, I have the honour to inform you that United States military forces are continuing their encroachments on Iraqi territory and their support of saboteur elements in the areas occupied by them, inasmuch as there are United States military forces, consisting of tank units, on both sides of the Safwan-Basra highway, on the earth road through the agricultural area and on the clover-leaf intersection. These forces are offering assistance to saboteur elements and providing them with a refuge, which has encouraged them to carry out acts of theft and plunder in respect of buildings, property and government and private premises. In addition, the United States military presence has enabled the Kuwaitis to circulate in the town of Safwan and seize motor vehicles there on the pretext that the vehicles are Kuwaiti.

The continuation of these acts constitutes a breach of Iraq's sovereignty, an infamous intervention in its internal affairs and an incitement to elements beyond the law to disrupt internal security and stability.

In informing you of these violations, I request you to adopt such measures to put a halt to them as are dictated by the purposes and principles of the Charter of the United Nations.

...

S/22692, 12 June 1991

12. Report of the Secretary General on the United Nations Iraq-Kuwait Observation Mission, 12 June 1991

1. This is a further progress report on the United Nations Iraq-Kuwait Observation Mission (UNIKOM); it follows my report of 9 May 1991 (S/22580).

Organizational aspects

2. Following the arrival of seven observers each from Senegal and Turkey, UNIKOM now has its full complement of military observers, as follows:

Argentina	7
Nigeria	7
Austria	7
Norway	8
Bangladesh	7
Pakistan	9
Canada	1
Poland	7
China	20
Romania	7
Denmark	7
Senegal	7
Fiji	7
Singapore	7
Finland	7
Sweden	7
France	20
Thailand	7
Ghana	8
Turkey	7
Greece	7
Union of Soviet Socialist Republics	20
Hungary	7
India	8
United Kingdom of Great Britain and Northern Ireland	20
Indonesia	7
Ireland	8
Italy	7
United States of America	20
Kenya	8
Uruguay	8
Malaysia	8
Venezuela	7
Total	299

3. Administrative and logistic support is provided by the following units:

Engineers (Canada)	293
Logistics (Sweden)	31
Movement control/postal (Denmark)	23
Helicopters (Chile)	50
Medical (Norway)	50
Total	447

Two fixed-wing aircraft from Switzerland are operated by civilians. In addition, UNIKOM has had the use of chartered aircraft for the movement of troops and equipment and for communications between Baghdad and Kuwait. The Government of Sweden provided free airlift at the beginning of the Mission.

4. Two infantry companies (Fijian, Nepalese) and one logistic company (Swedish) temporarily assigned from the United Nations Interim Force in Lebanon (UNIFIL) and one infantry company (Danish) from the United Nations Peace-keeping Force in Cyprus (UNFICYP) have returned to their parent missions. Two infantry companies, one from UNFICYP (Austrian) and one from UNIFIL (Ghanaian), remain with UNIKOM; their combined strength is 217 all ranks. As a result, the overall strength of the Mission has been reduced to 963 all ranks.

5. Logistic support for the Mission is still difficult, given the lack of normal infrastructure in the area. However, thanks to assistance from the United States Army and forces of other Member States cooperating with the Government of Kuwait, UNIKOM is now able to meet its requirements as regards rations, vehicles and accommodation. Conditions in the field, however, remain austere, with all personnel living under canvas and subsisting largely on field rations. The situation is expected to improve gradually, with the provision of fresh rations and prefabricated accommodation.

6. UNIKOM headquarters has remained in a hotel annex south of Kuwait City, which was made available by the Government of Kuwait. By 15 June, the headquarters will be moved, as an interim measure, to the logistic base at Doha, pending completion of the necessary refurbishment of the premises at Umm Qasr, which still lack basic facilities such as electricity, water and sewerage.

7. UNIKOM has maintained contact with and provided logistic support to other United Nations missions working in Iraq and Kuwait.

Demilitarized zone

8. The situation in the demilitarized zone (DMZ) has been calm. It is sparsely populated; the main population centres are the towns of Umm Qasr and Safwan, both on the Iraqi side. South of Safwan, on Kuwaiti territory, some 5,000 displaced persons still live in the Abdali camp. They are being assisted by the International Committee of the Red Cross (ICRC) and the League of Red Cross Societies. The camp is guarded by Kuwaiti police.

9. The Governments of Iraq and Kuwait, which are responsible for civil administration on their respective sides of the DMZ, have deployed border police to maintain law and order. Iraq currently has some 250 police in the DMZ. Kuwait is in the process of restoring its police presence and plans to rebuild and man some 30 police stations along the border. Both Governments have agreed to limit the armament of their police to sidearms.

10. Much of the DMZ is littered with unexploded ordnance and mines, particularly in the south. UNIKOM maintains maps delineating cleared routes; only on these routes is movement authorized.

Deployment and concept of operations

11. For operational purposes, UNIKOM has divided the DMZ into three sectors. Each sector has a headquarters and six observation posts, of which one in the southern sector has not yet been established. The Austrian security company has platoons in the central and northern sectors and at Umm Qasr; the Ghanaian security company has platoons in the southern sector, the Doha Logistic Base and at the temporary UNIKOM headquarters. The deployment of UNIKOM is shown on the attached map.

12. In addition to its fixed observation posts, UNIKOM deploys temporary observation points, mobile patrols (on land and in the air) and investigation teams. The temporary observation points are established from the fixed observation posts, either in areas of particular activity or where roads and tracks enter the DMZ. They are augmented by mobile ground patrols and by aerial reconnaissance. The latter is the only means of maintaining adequate observation of the Khor Abdullah waterway and the southern sector of the DMZ, where mines and unexploded ordnance severely limit UNIKOM's ability to carry out ground patrols. The security companies serve as a quick reaction force and maintain a high state of readiness in order to provide protection to the military observers.

13. UNIKOM maintains close liaison with the Governments of Iraq and Kuwait. Both have given the Mission all the support and cooperation necessary for it to carry out its mandate.

Violations and complaints

14. Since the DMZ was established on 9 May, there have been a number of instances in which personnel of the armed forces of both Iraq and Kuwait and personnel of the Saudi Arabian forces stationed in Kuwait were observed in the DMZ. These observations have been brought to the attention of the parties concerned, which have explained that the majority were due to errors of navigation or misunderstandings over the boundaries of the DMZ. UNIKOM has posted signs on all major access roads and tracks leading into the DMZ and it is hoped that this will help to prevent future incursions.

15. UNIKOM has also observed a number of overflights of the DMZ by military aircraft. Most of them have been by F-15 and F-16 type aircraft flying along the Iraq-Kuwait border. UNIKOM has brought these overflights to the attention of the Government of Kuwait.

16. Since 9 May, UNIKOM has received two complaints from the Kuwaiti authorities and three from the Iraqi authorities. The complaints of Kuwait arose from reports of Iraqi policemen carrying rifles in the DMZ and of the massing of Iraqi military formations south of Basra. After investigation by UNIKOM both were considered unfounded. Of the Iraqi complaints, one concerned an air violation that could not be substantiated. Another concerned the alleged establishment of a Kuwaiti military checkpoint within the DMZ south of Safwan; this was in fact a police post. The last complaint was that weapons were being kept at the Abdali camp and flags were being flown in a provocative manner. This complaint has been brought to the attention of the Kuwaiti authorities for appropriate action.

Infantry companies

17. The task of the infantry companies temporarily assigned from UNIFIL and UNFICYP was to provide essential security for UNIKOM during the setting-up phase, in view of the uncertainties at that time and the potential risks that might arise (see S/22454, paras. 10 and 13). After 30 days in the Mission, these companies were reduced from 5 to 2. Major General Greindl, the Chief Military Observer, has now recommended that 1 company of some 150 all ranks continue to be assigned to provide security for the Mission; 1 platoon would be deployed to each of the 3 sectors, and 1 at the headquarters in Umm Qasr. This company would also provide the basis for expansion should this be required for security reasons. General Greindl has based his recommendation on his assessment that the area is still in transition and there remains, for the time being, a risk to UNIKOM personnel.

18. I have weighed the above recommendation most carefully. In addition to General Greindl's military assessment, I have taken into consideration the excellent cooperation received from all concerned in the area and the fact that the perceived threats to the security of UNIKOM personnel during the setting-up phase did not in practice materialize. I have also borne in mind the financial implications and the growing financial burden on Member States as a result of the expansion of peace-keeping activities. In the light of these considerations, I have decided not to recommend, in the present circumstances, that UNIKOM be provided with an infantry element on a permanent basis. I intend, however, to explore with Member States the possibilities of rapid reinforcement of UNIKOM in case of emergency. I will monitor developments carefully and revert to the Security Council on this matter, should it become necessary.

Observations

19. As will be apparent from the above report, UNIKOM is now established and fully able to carry out the tasks assigned to it by the Security Council. It only remains for it to occupy its headquarters at Umm Qasr, which will be done as soon as possible. The mission area has now entered the season of great heat and this will be a testing period for UNIKOM's personnel and equipment. In the light of its experience during the remaining months of the current mandate period, I will, in October, undertake a further review of its strength and make appropriate recommendations to the Security Council. Meanwhile I take this opportunity to pay tribute to the determination and professionalism which General Greindl and all under his command have shown in setting up UNIKOM in difficult circumstances.

[*For the statement of the UN Security Council of 8 January 1993 relating to the free access of members of the UN Special Commission and of UNIKOM* see *Chapter 12.*]

10 January 1993

13. Special report by the Secretary-General on the United Nations Iraq-Kuwait Observation Mission, 10 January 1993

1. I wish to report to the Security Council a number of serious developments concerning the United Nations Iraq-Kuwait Observation Mission (UNIKOM).

2. Firstly, this morning at about 0700 hours local time, a party of some 200 Iraqis with trucks and heavy loading equipment forced entry into the six ammunition bunkers located in a former Iraqi naval base at Umm Qasr, on Kuwaiti territory, and took away most of their contents, including four "HY-2G" anti-ship missiles.

3. UNIKOM, which had maintained a 24-hour guard over the bunkers, made an effort to prevent access to them but was unable to do so. UNIKOM then attempted to prevent the Iraqi trucks loaded with items from the bunkers from leaving the scene by placing United Nations vehicles in their path. After some manoeuvring, the Iraqis surrounded the United Nations vehicles, preventing them from moving without seriously injuring or killing Iraqi personnel. The Iraqis then breached the fence and left.

4. At the first news of this incident, UNIKOM's Chief Military Observer, Major-General Timothy K. Dibuama, summoned the Senior Iraqi Liaison Officer at Umm Qasr and protested to him this serious violation. He also instructed UNIKOM's Chief Liaison Officer in Baghdad to lodge a formal protest with the Iraqi Ministry of Foreign Affairs. In their contacts with the Iraqi authorities, General Dibuama and his representatives pointed out that the Iraqi personnel, without prior clearance, had entered an area which is now known to be Kuwaiti territory and had contravened the Security Council's decision, laid down in the President's letter of 3 November 1992, that the contents of the bunkers should be destroyed by UNIKOM or by a specialized firm acting at UNIKOM's request and under its supervision.

5. Secondly, General Dibuama has reported that up to 500 Iraqi personnel continued today to dismantle prefabricated buildings in the former naval base, also on Kuwaiti territory, and to remove the parts and other items. This activity is in violation of the procedure established by the Security Council and conveyed to me in the President's letter of 8 January 1993. A copy of this letter was sent to the Permanent Representative of Iraq to the United Nations the same day and General Dibuama informed the Senior Iraqi Liaison Officer in Umm Qasr one day later, that is yesterday.

6. General Dibuama has kept the Kuwaiti authorities informed of the above developments. He has stationed

observers at the crossing points along the border in the Umm Qasr area with instructions to stop approaching Iraqis, to warn them that they are about to enter Kuwaiti territory, and to describe to them the procedure established by the Security Council for the removal of Iraqi property and assets.

7. Thirdly, I wish to report that in a meeting at Umm Qasr on 4 January 1993, Major-General Abdallah Firas, the Chairman of Iraq's Higher Committee for Coordination which is responsible for liaison with UNIKOM, raised with General Dibuama the question of the retrieval by Iraq of the prefabricated buildings which Iraq had made available to UNIKOM in a part of the former naval base (Camp Khor). General Dibuama referred this question to United Nations Headquarters and my colleagues have raised it with the Permanent Representative of Iraq, asking that his Government stop the workers. They have suggested that the matter be discussed, with a view to finding an agreed solution which would preserve UNIKOM's ability to carry out the mandate entrusted to it by the Security Council. The Permanent Representative had not yet responded when, on 9 January, General Firas informed General Dibuama that on 11 January the dismantling of prefabricated buildings in the former naval base would be extended to include the buildings used by UNIKOM. General Firas suggested that UNIKOM evacuate these premises.

8. The premises in question consist of 19 buildings, which house such elements as the UNIKOM's northern sector headquarters, helicopter support, and transport workshops. Others are used for the accommodation of personnel. Additional prefabricated buildings have been added by UNIKOM. I should like to point out that, by an exchange of letters, respectively dated 15 April and 21 June 1992, the Government of Iraq has agreed that the land and premises it has made available to UNIKOM shall be inviolate and subject to the exclusive control and authority of the United Nations.

9. The above developments are taking place at a time when the Security Council is already actively seized of other aspects of the situation, such as Iraq's ban against United Nations aircraft. They cast doubt on Iraq's continued willingness to cooperate with UNIKOM and to abide by the commitments it has undertaken in this respect. As the Security Council is aware, Iraq's cooperation is essential for UNIKOM to perform its tasks effectively. It is for this reason that I am bringing these matters to the Council's attention.

Annex I

Letter dated 8 January 1993 from the President of the Security Council addressed to the Secretary-General

On behalf of the members of the Security Council, I have the honour to refer to your letter dated 23 December 1992, in which you brought to the Council's attention some issues arising from the demarcation of the boundary between Iraq and Kuwait. The members of the Council considered this matter in the course of consultations of the whole on 5 January 1993 and asked me to convey to you the following:

The members of the Council concur with the general approach outlined in your letter. They are particularly concerned at the continued presence of six Iraqi police posts on Kuwaiti territory and insist on their speedy removal, by 15 January at the latest. They also note the unsafe proximity of the boundary of three other Iraqi posts and two Kuwaiti police posts.

The members have also before them a letter dated 4 January 1993 from the Charge d'affaires a.i. of the Permanent Mission of Kuwait to the United Nations and they have since taken note of UNIKOM's weekly report for the period 28 December 1992-3 January 1993. They believe the presence of Iraqi military personnel in the demilitarized zone was a serious violation of resolution 687 (1991). They also consider that the removal of the Iraqi property and assets from Kuwaiti territory should be undertaken only after prior clearance by UNIKOM and by the Kuwaiti authorities through UNIKOM and should be completed by 15 January 1993. The members of the Council would be obliged if you would keep them informed of development in these matters.

(Signed) Yoshio HATANO
President of the Security Council

Annex II

Letter dated 23 December 1992 from the Secretary-General addressed to the President of the Security Council

I have the honour to refer to the situation in the area of operation of the United Nations Iraq-Kuwait Observation Mission (UNIKOM), following the placement of the border pillars along the land boundary between Iraq and Kuwait by the United Nations Iraq-Kuwait Boundary Demarcation Commission. The demarcation of the land boundary is thus nearly complete, except for minor technical matters.

I consider it timely, therefore, to bring to the Council's attention some issues arising from the demarcation of the boundary. These concern six Iraqi police posts, part of the Iraqi town of Umm Qasr, several Iraqi farms along the eastern part of the boundary and some well heads of the Ratqah oil field, all of which have been shown to be on Kuwaiti territory.

The issue of the Iraqi police posts on Kuwaiti territory was first raised with the Iraqi authorities more than one year ago. At that time, the boundary had not yet been demarcated and the Iraqi authorities maintained that they could not withdraw the posts as this might prejudice their position regarding the boundary. They stated, however, that they would abide by the decision of the Boundary Demarcation Commission. This assurance has recently been repeated. I have requested the Iraqi authorities to withdraw the six police posts from Kuwaiti territory as soon as possible and I have instructed Major-General Dibuama, the Chief Military observer of UNIKOM, to be in touch with those authorities regarding the necessary arrangements.

Three Iraqi police posts and two Kuwaiti police posts are now closer to the boundary than 1,000 metres, which UNIKOM, with the concurrence of both sides, has established as a reasonable distance to prevent incidents. Persistent complaints about shooting incidents involving police posts underline the continuing validity of this rule. I have accordingly instructed Major-General Dibuama to arrange with the authorities concerned that the police posts in question be moved further away from the boudary at an early date.

The issue of the Iraqi citizens and their assets which remain on Kuwaiti territory is potentially volatile and apt to give rise to increased tension and friction unless resolved soon. At the same time, it is clearly in the interest of all involved that this issue be settled in a reasonable way. I am in touch with the Governments of Iraq and Kuwait in order to promote such a settlement and to determine how the United Nations may help to bring it about. I trust that the Security Council concurs with this approach and shall keep it informed of the results of my contacts.

I should be grateful if you would bring the contents of this letter to the attention of the members of the Security Council.

(Signed) Boutros BOUTROS-GHALI

Annex III

Letter dated 3 November 1992 from the President of the Security Council addressed to the Secretary-General

The members of the Security Council have examined the question you brought to the attention of the President through your letter dated 23 September 1992. They fully share the concerns expressed by the UNIKOM Commander related to the threats to security linked to the presence of Iraqi and Kuwaiti military equipment in six bunkers within the demilitarized zone, near the headquarters of the Observation Mission. The members of the Security Council deem it necessary, as recommended by the Commander of the Observation Mission, for the bunkers to be emptied of their contents.

The members of the Security Council have noted that UNIKOM has carried out, within the demilitarized zone where it is deployed, destruction of mines and ammunition that might be harmful to the observers (your reports S/22454, approved by resolution 689 (1991), S/23106, S/23766 and S/24615). They are of the opinion that the military equipment referred to in your letter dated 23 September 1992, which also represents a threat to the security of the members of the Observation Mission, should similarly be destroyed by UNIKOM or by a specialized company acting upon the request of the Mission and under its supervision.

In the event of UNIKOM entrusting a specific company with the destruction of the military equipment contained in the six bunkers, the cost of this operation should not be covered by the regular budget of UNIKOM but by Iraq and Kuwait. Each of these two States should support the financial burden related to the destruction of the contents of the bunkers located on its territory, i.e. on its side of the border as demarcated by the Boundary Demarcation Commission.

The members of the Security Council are of the opinion that it would be useful for UNIKOM to consult the Special Commission to enable the latter to check whether any of the military equipment contained in the six bunkers fall into the category mentioned in paragraph 8 of resolution 687. In this case, this equipment should be destroyed by the Special Commission, in coordination with UNIKOM.

(Signed) Andre ERDOS
President of the Security Council

SC/5536, 11 January 1993

14. UN Press Release: Security Council Condemns Iraqi Incursions Into Demilitarized Zone, 11 January 1993

The full text of the Council's statement reads as follows:

"The Security Council notes that there have been a number of recent actions by Iraq as part of its pattern of flouting relevant Security Council resolutions. One was the series of border incidents involving the United Nations Iraq-Kuwait Observation Mission (UNIKOM); another was the incident concerning the United Nations Special Commission (UNSCOM) and UNIKOM flights.

"The Security Council is deeply concerned at the incidents reported in the Secretary-General's special report of 10 January 1993 on UNIKOM (document S/25085). The Security Council recalls the provisions of resolution 687 (1991) that established the Demilitarized Zone between Iraq and Kuwait and demanded that both countries respect the inviolability of the international boundary between them. It reaffirms that the boundary was at the very core of the conflict and that, in resolutions 687 (1991) and 773 (1992), it guaranteed the inviolability of the boundary and undertook to take as appropriate all necessary measures to that end in accordance with the Charter of the United Nations.

"The Council condemns that action taken by Iraq on 10 January 1993 to remove equipment by force from the Kuwaiti side of the demilitarized zone without prior consultation with UNIKOM, and through UNIKOM with the Kuwaiti authorities, as set out in the letter of 8 January 1993 from the President of the Security Council to the Secretary-General. In particular, the Council draws attention to the removal by Iraq of four HY-2G anti-ship missiles and other military equipment from the six bunkers in the former Iraqi naval base at Umm Qasr on Kuwaiti territory, in spite of the objections of UNIKOM and their efforts to prevent this. This action is a direct challenge to the authority of UNIKOM and amounts to clear-cut defiance by Iraq of the Council, which stipulated in the letter of 3 November 1992 from the President of the Council to the Secretary-General that the military equipment in the six bunkers should be destroyed by or under the supervision of UNIKOM. The Council demands that the anti-ship missiles and other military equipment removed by force from the six bunkers at Umm Qasr in Kuwaiti territory be returned immediately to the custody of UNIKOM for destruction, as previously decided.

"The Council also condemns further Iraqi intrusions into the Kuwaiti side of the demilitarized zone on 11 January 1993. It demands that any future retrieval mission be in accordance with the terms set out in the letter of 8 January 1993 from the President of the Council to the Secretary-General. On the UNIKOM facilities at Camp Khor, the Council stresses that the land and premises occupied by UNIKOM shall be inviolate and subject to the exclusive control and authority of the United Nations.

"The Council invites the Secretary-General, as a first step, to explore on an urgent basis the possibilities for restoring UNIKOM to its full strength and to consider the need for rapid reinforcement as set out in paragraph 18 of his report of 12 June 1991 (document S/22692), as well as any other suggestion that he might have to enhance the effectiveness of UNIKOM, and to report back to the Council.

"The Council is also alarmed by Iraq's refusal to allow the United Nations to transport its UNSCOM and UNIKOM personnel into Iraqi territory using its own aircraft. In this connection the Council reiterates the demand in its statement of 8 January 1993 that Iraq permit UNSCOM to use their own aircraft to transport their personnel into Iraq. It rejects the arguments contained in the letter of 9 January 1993 from the Minister of Foreign Affairs of Iraq to the President of the Security Council (document S/25086).

"These latest developments concerning the activities of UNIKOM and UNSCOM constitute further material breaches of resolution 687 (1991), which established the cease-fire and provided the conditions essential for the restoration of peace and security in the region, as well as other relevant resolutions and agreements. The Council demands that Iraq cooperate fully with UNIKOM, UNSCOM and other United Nations agencies in carrying out their mandates, and again warns Iraq of the serious consequences that will flow from such continued defiance. The Council will remain actively seized of the matter."

S/25085/Add.1, 19 January 1993

15. Special report of the Secretary-General on the United Nations Iraq-Kuwait Observation Mission, 19 January 1993

1. The Chief Military Observer of the United Nations Iraq-Kuwait Observation Mission (UNIKOM) has reported that the Iraqi authorities have withdrawn the six police posts that were located on Kuwaiti territory.

2. The withdrawal was announced to UNIKOM in the afternoon of 17 January. The Iraqi police personnel withdrew with their equipment that evening and dismantled and removed three of the posts. The next morning, they returned and removed the other three posts. This happened under UNIKOM's supervision and with the agreement of the Kuwaiti authorities, which UNIKOM had consulted. UNIKOM has inspected the six sites and has reported that everything has been removed.

3. As of midday on Wednesday, 13 January 1993, the retrieval of Iraqi assets from Kuwaiti territory has ceased.

4. In my letter of 23 December 1992 (see S/25085, annex II), I mentioned that three Iraqi police posts, as well as two Kuwaiti police posts, were closer to the boundary than 1,000 metres, which has been established as a reasonable distance to prevent incidents. Through an oversight, these figures did not include two Iraqi police posts that were set up in the central sector in early December 1992. UNIKOM had asked that these posts also should be moved further from the boundary. In Umm Qasr, where the boundary runs through a built-up area, three police check-points and a border post are also within the 1,000-metre range.

16. UN Press Release on Reinforcement of UNIKOM, 19 January 1993

Secretary-General Boutros Boutros-Ghali has recommended, in a further special report to the Security Council, dated 18 January, to reinforce the United Nations Iraq-Kuwait Observation Mission (UNIKOM) with three infantry battalions, together with an increase in headquarters and support elements, comprising a total deployment of 3645 personnel in the area. According to the proposal, this military personnel would replace the current UNIKOM's unarmed observers in order to enable the Mission to rapidly respond to violations of the border between Iraq and Kuwait.

The Secretary-General's recommendation follows Security Council's request of 11 January that Mr. Boutros-Ghali explore urgently "the possibilities for restoring" UNIKOM to its full strength in order to enhance its effectiveness in cases of emergency.

In its "restructured" format, UNIKOM would undertake to prevent or redress small scale violations of the demilitarized zone or the boundary between Iraq and Kuwait. It would also try to prevent or redress "problems that might arise from the presence of Iraqi installations and Iraqi civilians and their assets in the demilitarized zone on the Kuwaiti side of the newly demarcated boundary", suggests the report.

Arguing that the proposed task "could not be performed by unarmed observers", the report says that, should the Council vote in favour of the recommendations and decide that UNIKOM's present mandate does not permit an adequate response to violations "as have occurred", then UNIKOM would require a capacity to take "physical action".

The current mandate of UNIKOM observers is to observe any hostile or potentially hostile action mounting from the territory of one State to the other. In case of violations, the unarmed observers report and make representations. With regard to the incidents occurred since the beginning of the month, stresses the report, protests and representations were for the most part ineffective because UNIKOM's interlocutors were powerless to influence a course of events which had been set in motion at the highest levels of the Iraqi Government.

The Secretary-General also emphasizes that his proposal is based on the assumption that the Government of Iraq as well as the Government of Kuwait would undertake to cooperate with the restructured Mission. In the absence of such cooperation, the report says, "it would become impossible for UNIKOM to carry out its functions, in which case the Security Council would need to consider alternative measures".

17. Security Council Resolution 806, 5 February 1993

The Security Council,

Reaffirming its resolution 687 (1991) of 3 April 1991, and in particular paragraphs 2, 3, 4 and 5 thereof, and its resolutions 689 (1991) of 9 April 1991 and 773 (1992) of 26 August 1992, and its other resolutions on this matter,

Having considered the report of the Secretary-General of 18 January 1993 (S/25123),

Noting with approval that work is being completed on the realignment of the demilitarized zone referred to in paragraph 5 of resolution 687 (1991) to correspond to the international boundary demarcated by the United Nations Iraq-Kuwait Boundary Demarcation Commission,

Deeply concerned at recent actions by Iraq in violation of relevant Security Council resolutions, including the series of border incidents involving the United Nations Iraq-Kuwait Observation Mission (UNIKOM),

Recalling the statements made by the President on behalf of the Council on 8 January (S/25081) and on 11 January 1993 (S/25091),

Acting under Chapter VII of the Charter of the United Nations,

1. *Underlines* once again its guarantee of the inviolability of the international boundary between the State of Kuwait and the Republic of Iraq and its decision to take as appropriate all necessary measures to that end in accordance with the Charter, as provided for in paragraph 4 of resolution 687 (1991);

2. *Approves* the report, and decides to extend the terms of reference of UNIKOM to include the functions contained in paragraph 5 of the report;

3. *Requests* the Secretary-General to plan and execute a phased deployment of the strengthening of UNIKOM taking into account the need for economy and other relevant factors and to report to the Council on any step he intends to take following an initial deployment;

4. *Reaffirms* that the question of termination or continuation of UNIKOM and the modalities of UNIKOM will continue to be reviewed every six months pursuant to paragraphs 2 and 3 of resolution 689 (1991), the next review to take place in April 1993;

5. *Decides* to remain seized of the matter.

12. THE DETECTION, CONTROL OR DESTRUCTION OF CERTAIN IRAQI ARMAMENTS AND FACILITIES

According to Section C of Resolution 687 (1991) Iraq was to accept unconditionally the destruction, removal or rendering harmless, under international supervision, of all chemical and biological weapons and all stocks of agents and all related subsystems and components and all research, development, support and manufacturing facilities and of all ballistic missiles with a range greater than 150 kilometres. Iraq also was obliged to undertake not to use, develop, construct or acquire any of these items. A UN Special Commission was created to facilitate implementation of that section of Resolution 687 (1991). In addition, Iraq was obliged to reaffirm unconditionally its adherence to the Nuclear Non-Proliferation Treaty and to collaborate with the International Atomic Energy Agency in the destruction of nuclear weapons-related facilities or items and in the long-term monitoring of its nuclear programme. The obligations incumbent upon Iraq under Section C have been confirmed and amplified in Security Council Resolutions 699 (1991), 707 (1991) and 715 (1991) and in a number of statements by the President of the Security Council.

The implementation of Section C of Resolution 687 (1991) has already generated a vast amount of material. All relevant documents, including reports from the International Atomic Energy Agency concerning detailed findings of inspection missions to Iraq, will be reproduced in a separate volume in this series. The materials which follow have been selected to give a brief overview of the subject. Documents concerning the continued imposition of an arms embargo against Iraq, as demanded in paragraphs 24-29 of Resolution 687 (1991) and Resolution 700 (1991), have been included in this Chapter, rather than in the one which follows.

S/22508, 18 April 1991

1. Report of the Secretary-General, 18 April 1991

Implementation of paragraph 9 (b) (i) of Security Council resolution 687 (1991)

1. The present report is submitted in pursuance of Security Council resolution 687 (1991) of 3 April 1991. In paragraph 9 (b) (i) of that resolution the Council decided that the Secretary-General should submit to it for approval a plan calling *inter alia* for the forming of a Special Commission to carry out the tasks enumerated in paragraphs 9 (b) (i-iii), 10 and 13.

2. To enable the Special Commission to play its proper part in assessing information and preparing and planning the activities envisaged in Section C of the resolution, including assisting the Director-General of the International Atomic Energy Agency to present a plan within his designated area, there is an urgent need for the Special Commission to be established. The implementation, within or near the time-frames indicated by the resolution, of all the mandates in Section C will in fact depend on the existence of the Commission, and its advice in the early stages would be essential.

3. Subject to the approval of the Security Council, it is my intention to set up the Special Commission as described below and to make all necessary arrangements for it to begin implementation of its tasks.

4. In setting up the structure for the Special Commission I wish to emphasize the need for an efficient and effective executive body. I propose that it should have an Executive Chairman with a Deputy Executive Chairman to assist the Chairman in carrying out his functions. Following the appointment of these two individuals the remainder of the Special Commission would be established on an expanding basis as appropriate individuals are found to fill the positions. Under the Executive Chairman and Deputy Executive Chairman, the planning and operational direction of the functions of the Commission should be carried out by five groups, each under a head of group with appropriate executive experience in the assigned field and each consisting of a small number of experts. The major areas of responsibility would be: biological and chemical weapons; ballistic missiles; nuclear-weapons capabilities; future compliance and operations support. Thus the formal membership of the Special Commission would be of the order of 20 to 25 persons.

5. Although the specific timing of the Special Commission's activities have yet to be determined, under the provisions of Section C of the resolution, most of the Commission's functions are time-limited. With the accomplishment of the tasks entrusted to four of the five groups, the major active phases would be completed and those four groups would cease to exist. The fifth group would continue in order to implement the activities relating to future compliance.

6. In carrying out its various tasks the Special Commission would be assisted by a number of technical experts serving as inspectors, disposal teams and field support officers. These experts would be either specially engaged for this purpose or made available to the Commission by Member States. Their total number

would have to be determined in relationship to the size of the task to be carried out. This can be fully assessed only after the baseline field inspections have been completed by the Special Commission, but it is likely that the personnel involved will number in the several hundreds.

7. As soon as the baseline field assignments of the Special Commission and of the International Atomic Energy Agency have been completed, I intend to work out, in consultation with the Commission, a detailed plan for the implementation of the various tasks entrusted to it, and to submit it to the Security Council for its approval.

8. Following the acceptance by the Government of Iraq of Security Council resolution 687 (1991), expressed in the penultimate provision of the letters addressed respectively to me and to the President of the Security Council on 6 April 1991 by the Minister for Foreign Affairs of the Republic of Iraq, the execution of the baseline field inspections and the subsequent implementation plan is predicated on the assumption of full cooperation by the Iraqi authorities. The Special Commission would enjoy the relevant privileges and immunities provided for in the Convention on the Privileges and Immunities of the United Nations. Members of the Special Commission, experts attached to it and other specialists assigned to assist it in the implementation of Section C of Security Council resolution 687 (1991), would be regarded as experts on mission within the meaning of Article VI of the Convention on the Privileges and Immunities of the United Nations, relevant Annexes to the Convention on the Privileges and Immunities of the Specialized Agencies and Article VII of the Agreement on the Privileges and Immunities of the IAEA, respectively. Taking into account the tasks to be performed by the Special Commission, it may be necessary to conclude special agreements covering the status, facilities, privileges and immunities of the Commission and its personnel. The existing agreements mentioned above would equally apply to tasks to be performed in Iraq by the IAEA and could be supplemented by special agreements, should the need arise.

9. While the financial implications relating to the establishment and functioning of the Special Commission cannot at this stage be assessed with accuracy, it is anticipated that certain start-up funds will be required. This sum will defray the initial costs of establishing the Headquarters of the Special Commission in New York as well as a field office in the region and the early deployment of advanced elements of the operation in the field. This sum will also defray some of the initial costs to be borne by the IAEA in carrying out the assignments entrusted to it under Section C of the resolution. Comprehensive cost estimates will, of course, be provided to the Security Council as soon as possible. It is my intention, however, to proceed in this regard on the basis of the following principles: (a) that Member States whose nationals will serve on the Commission or assist it in the discharge of its responsibilities should be responsible for their salaries, while the United Nations will bear the costs of travel and daily subsistence, and (b) that the whole exercise will be carried out in the shortest possible time, with a progressive decrease in the number of technical experts and of members of the Special Commission as various operations are completed.

S/22509, 19 April 1991

2. Letter from the President of the Security Council addressed to the Secretary-General, 19 April 1991

I have the honour to inform you that your report of 18 April 1991 on the implementation of paragraph 9 (b) (i) of Security Council resolution 687 (1991) has been brought to the attention of the members of the Council. They agree to the proposals contained in the report.

S/22510, 19 April 1991

3. Letter from the Chargé d'affaires a.i. of the Permanent Mission of Cuba to the United Nations addressed to the President of the Security Council, 19 April 1991

I have the honour to refer to your note of 18 April transmitting to the members of the Council the preliminary version of the report of the Secretary-General on the implementation of paragraph 9 (b) (i) of Security Council resolution 687 (1991).

As you will recall, Cuba voted against Security Council resolution 687 (1991) and, at the Council's 2981st meeting, Ambassador Ricardo Alarcón de Quesada, Permanent Representative of Cuba to the United Nations, made a statement which made perfectly clear Cuba's position and the reasons for its vote, which included the text's selectiveness on the issue of disarmament when such a measure should have been regional in scope.

Accordingly, while the Republic of Cuba will not obstruct the adoption of the report of the Secretary-General which you have brought to our attention, nor the letter which you propose to send to the Secretary-General, since they derive from a resolution which the Security Council adopted without Cuba's supporting vote, we none the less wish to reaffirm all the elements of our 3 April 1991 statement and to inform you that the Government of the Republic of Cuba does not associate itself with the implications which implementation of this measure could have for the peace, stability and security of the Middle East.

...

S/22614, 17 May 1991

4. Report of the Secretary-General, 17 May 1991

Plan for the implementation of relevant parts of section C of Security Council resolution 687 (1991)

Introduction

1. The present report is submitted in pursuance of Security Council resolution 687 (1991) of 3 April 1991. In paragraph 9 (b) of that resolution, the Council decided that the Secretary-General, within 45 days of the adoption of the resolution, should develop and submit to it for approval a plan calling for the completion of the tasks enumerated in paragraphs 9 (b) (i to iii) and 10.

2. For the purpose of developing this plan, consultations were held with appropriate Governments, as called for in paragraphs 9 (b) and 13 of the resolution, and, where appropriate, with the Director General of the International Atomic Energy Agency (IAEA) and the Director-General of the World Health Organization (WHO). Furthermore, in order to assess the information submitted by the Government of Iraq and to assist me in developing the plan for the implementation of the tasks enumerated in section C of the resolution, I set up a Special Commission as described in my report of 18 April 1991 to the Security Council (S/22508), which the Council accepted on 19 April.

3. I appointed 21 experts as members of the Special Commission. I have requested Ambassador Rolf Ekeus (Sweden) to serve as its Executive Chairman and Dr. Robert Gallucci (United States of America) to serve as its

Deputy Executive Chairman. The other members of the Special Commission are as follows: Dr Paal Aas (Norway), Lieutenant General (ret.) Ken Adachi (Japan), Professor B.N.C. Agu (Nigeria), Lieutenant-Colonel Andrzej Badek (Poland), Professor Bryan C. Barrass (United Kingdom of Great Britain and Northern Ireland), Mr. Peter von Butler (Germany), Colonel Armando Caputo (Italy), Mr. Ronald Cleminson (Canada), Dr. John Gee (Australia), Professor Helmut Hönig (Austria), Mr. B.A. Kuvshinnikov (Union of Soviet Socialist Republics), Dr. A.J.J. Ooms (Netherlands), Dr. Marjatta Rautio (Finland), Mr. Michel Saint Mleux (France), Mr. Roberto Sanchez (Venezuela), Lieutenant Colonel B. Simandjuntak (Indonesia), Dr. Miroslav Splino (Czechoslovakia), Mr. Emile Vanden Bemden (Belgium), Dr. Yuan Renfeng (China).

4. In order to enable the Special Commission as well as IAEA to discharge their responsibilities properly, a number of technical arrangements are being made to facilitate their work. They include the establishment of a field operations office and a support office. After consultations with the Governments concerned, the Field Operations Office is being set up in Bahrain. The Office will become fully operational by the end of May 1991. The Support Office is being established at Baghdad, Iraq.

I. The Plan

5. The provisions of section C of resolution 687 (1991) lend themselves to a three-stage implementation procedure: gathering and assessment of information; disposal of weapons and facilities and all other items specified in paragraphs 8 and 12 of resolution 687 (1991); and monitoring and verification of Iraq's compliance in the future.

A. *Gathering and assessment of information*

6. The first stage of the plan is of crucial importance for the success of the entire operation. It requires input from both the Iraqi Government and the special Commission. Pursuant to paragraphs 9 (a) and 12, Iraq is responsible for the submission, within fifteen days of the adoption of the resolution, of information on the locations, amounts and types of all items specified in paragraphs 8 and 12, which are to be destroyed, removed or rendered harmless. The Special Commission, pursuant to paragraphs 9 (b) (i) and 13, is responsible for designating any additional locations of these items in Iraq. In carrying out the immediate on-site inspections envisaged in paragraphs 9 (b) (i) and 13 of the resolution, the Special Commission and IAEA respectively must retain the right to choose the timing and locations of the inspection.

7. On 18 and 28 April and 4 May 1991, the Government of Iraq forwarded to the Secretary-General information relating to its chemical and biological weapons and ballistic missiles. On 18 April, the Government of Iraq also forwarded to the Director General of IAEA information of relevance to the responsibilities entrusted to the Agency as stated in paragraphs 12 and 13 of resolution 687 (1991). Further information was communicated to the Agency on 27 April. In communications both to the Secretary-General and the Director General, the Government of Iraq also conveyed its acceptance of on-site inspections as called for in paragraphs 9 (a) and 12. There has also been a continued exchange of communications between the Special Commission and the Government of Iraq with a view to obtaining additional information and clarifications.

8. Based on the information received so far from the Iraqi authorities, as well as taking into account additional locations designated by the Special Commission, the process of on-site inspections by the Special Commission and IAEA has been initiated. In the course of the inspections, the special Commission will check the information that has been gathered earlier against the actual situation in the field (i.e. establishing a database); assess the magnitude of the task of disposal of weapons and facilities that it will perform in the second stage of the plan; and determine, with the advice of WHO, the requirements and modalities for carrying it out. The Special Commission is also rendering assistance and cooperation to the Director General of IAEA in connection with on-site inspections for which the Agency is responsible.

9. The on-site inspections to be carried out by both the Special Commission and IAEA cover a large number of sites with different numbers of facilities at each site. For the purpose of ensuring safe access to sites subject to the measures specified in paragraphs 9 (b), 12 and 13 of resolution 687 (1991), teams of explosive ordnance disposal (EOD) experts, construction engineers and security personnel have been engaged to assist the Special Commission and IAEA in the process of carrying out the on-site inspections. The safety of all such personnel is a major consideration. Detailed arrangements covering these and related aspects and governing the precise modalities for carrying out the inspections are embodied in an agreement between the United Nations and the Government of Iraq. The volume of work as well as the physical state of the various objects, installations and facilities subject to inspection, and the paramount concern regarding the safety of the inspection teams and the local population, make it difficult to establish, at the present stage, the exact time-frame within which the first stage can be concluded. Early assessments of the tasks involved make it possible, nevertheless, to outline the general framework of the second stage of the plan, which is described below.

B. *Disposal of weapons and facilities*

10. The main purpose of the second stage of the plan, as specified in paragraphs 8, 9 and 13 of resolution 687 (1991), is to dispose of weapons, facilities and all other items specified in paragraphs 8 and 12 of the resolution. Owing to the highly different nature of the weapons, material and facilities involved, separate procedures are envisaged for their actual disposal, with different teams of experts carrying them out.

11. Regarding chemical weapons and biological weapons-related items and facilities, technical modalities are being worked out with a view to ensuring the complete and safe yielding of possession by Iraq of all items referred to in paragraph 8 (a) of the resolution, for their subsequent destruction, removal or rendering them harmless. Regarding ballistic missiles, procedures for the identification and securing of all items referred to in paragraph 8 (b) of the resolution are being developed with a view to ensuring the supervision of their complete destruction by Iraq. The Special Commission will further assist and cooperate with IAEA in carrying out inspections and in the destruction, removal or rendering harmless of all items referred to in paragraph 12 of the resolution.

12. As far as the disposal process itself is concerned, Iraq will destroy, under the supervision of the Special Commission, all its missile capabilities, including launchers, as specified under paragraph 8 (b) of resolution 687 (1991). The Special Commission and IAEA respectively, with appropriate Iraqi assistance, will dispose of all other items specified under paragraphs 8 (a) and 12 of the same resolution, including missile warheads fitted with chemical warfare agents. It should be noted that under the resolution the Special Commission has the authority to conduct activities related to inspection, yielding and disposal of the items specified in paragraph 8 (a) of the resolution and the inspection and disposal of the items specified in paragraph 8 (b) of the resolution

after the expiration of the 45-day period that follows the approval of this plan, if such activities have not been completed.

1. *Ballistic missiles*

13. The disposal of ballistic missiles and related items and facilities raises a relatively smaller number of problems as compared to other types of weapons and facilities. In principle, their disposal should not pose any danger to public safety as it involves a largely mechanical operation. Consequently, the disposal of missiles and related major parts including launchers will be carried out *in situ* and, if possible, it will be done concomitantly with the initial on-site inspection process. Those items not disposed of immediately will be secured, sealed and appropriately documented for later disposal. Furthermore, items such as warheads and fuel might be moved to a special destruction location or facility and disposed of there.

14. As regards repair and production facilities, many of them appear no longer operational as a result of the hostilities. The Special Commission will ascertain the extent to which these facilities are permanently affected, with a view to determining what other steps, if any, are necessary to comply with paragraph 9 (b) (ii) of the resolution.

15. In order to carry out the responsibilities regarding this category of weapons and related facilities, the Special Commission will require individuals with expertise in such fields as launching and guidance systems, propellants and warheads. Teams of experts will be needed to conduct both the on-site inspections and the supervision of the disposal process. The number of teams and their exact composition is currently under study.

2. *Chemical weapons*

16. As regards chemical weapons, in view of the practical problems inherent in their destruction, including possible safety and environmental hazards, the Special Commission, in consultation with WHO, has focused its attention on determining the best methods for their disposal. Taking into account the paramount importance of maintaining acceptable safety standards for the disposal teams and for the local population, the Special Commission will identify and evaluate safe destruction techniques that could be made operable within stringent time-frames.

17. Given the danger chemical weapons represent, their disposal will be initiated only after thorough on-site inspection and assessment of the conditions of stocks and facilities. In this connection, the Special Commission has requested the inspection teams to mark munitions and relevant facilities, to the extent possible, with tamper-indicating devices. In addition, the special Commission foresees monitoring, between the time of the inspections and the disposal process, by inspectors at relevant locations.

18. The disposal methods will involve neutralization and/or incineration. Movement of chemical weapons and agents will be minimized. In this connection the Special Commission is investigating the use of transportable or mobile destruction equipment. The Special Commission may also consider the possibility of the construction of a destructive facility which would have greater capacity than that offered by transportable or mobile equipment. In this and other options the question of costs will need to be kept under review.

19. As regards research, development, support and manufacturing facilities in connection with chemical weapons, information available to the Special Commission at present suggests that a number of them may have been destroyed as a result of the hostilities. Upon establishing firm data the Special Commission will determine its requirements, both in terms of equipment and human resources, for complying with provisions of paragraph 9 (b) of resolution 687 (1991).

3. *Biological weapons*

20. In the area of biological weapons, it is noted that, in accordance with paragraph 7 of Security Council resolution 687 (1991), Iraq has become a party to the Convention on the Prohibition of the Development, Production and Stockpiling of Bacteriological (Biological) and Toxin Weapons and on Their Destruction.[1] [1. General Assembly resolution 2826 (XXVI).] The Government of Iraq deposited, on 8 April, its instrument of ratification in Moscow.

21. However, as required by the Security Council in its resolution 687 (1991), the Special Commission is seeking to determine whether Iraq possesses any biological weapons-related items that should be disposed of pursuant to the resolution and whether there remains in Iraq a capability to produce such weapons that would also be subject to disposal. In this context, the Special Commission has brought to the attention of the Government of Iraq the report of the Ad Hoc Meeting of Scientific and Technical Experts from States Parties to the Biological Weapons Convention held at Geneva from 31 March to 15 April 1987 and contained in document BWC/CONF.II/EX/2 of 21 April 1987 and has requested the information called for in section II of that report.

22. Biological warfare agents can be destroyed through either standard laboratory equipment or special mobile units.

4. *Nuclear weapons-related items*

23. In the area of nuclear-weapons-usable material and related items and facilities, the Special Commission will assist IAEA in the removal of weapons-usable material from Iraq and in the disposal of all other relevant items and facilities covered by resolution 687 (1991), by removal or destruction as appropriate.

24. An inspection team, composed of experts from IAEA and the Special Commission, is currently in Iraq to carry out a first inspection based on declarations by the Government of Iraq and the designation by the Special Commission of additional locations. Further inspections will follow prior to the disposal of weapons-usable-material and other items subject to paragraph 12 of resolution 687 (1991).

C. *Monitoring and verification of compliance*

25. The third stage of the plan represents a long-term operation. Its main purpose is to ensure ongoing monitoring and verification of Iraq's compliance with paragraphs 8, 9, 10 and 12 of resolution 687 (1991). A detailed plan as called for in paragraph 10 of resolution 687 (1991), will be submitted to the Security Council for its approval, subsequent to the establishment of a complete database. In developing the plan, the Special Commission will also take into account the provisions for permitted activities in the framework of the Biological Weapons Convention and by the monitoring/verification methods under discussion in the context of a future Convention on the Prohibition of Chemical Weapons. With the eventual entry into force of such a Convention, the inspectorate envisaged in it should at an appropriate time take over the function of monitoring and verification of compliance in the area of chemical weapons.

26. The verification will be conducted through full and effective on-site inspections including those on short notice. The inspections will cover, as appropriate, military bases, production facilities and storage, as well as research facilities and laboratories. The frequency of on-site inspections will vary considerably for each

category of weapons, facilities and activities in question. It will be contingent on previous findings and also on Iraq's clear and continuous demonstration of compliance with resolution 687 (1991).

II. GENERAL CONCEPT OF OPERATIONS

27. The Special Commission, under the guidance of its Executive Chairman, will use a small staff at United Nations Headquarters in New York to prepare detailed plans for field operations in Iraq with regard to all items related to chemical and biological weapons and to ballistic missiles, and together with IAEA with regard to items related to nuclear weapons and nuclear-weapons-usable materials. The plans will describe the composition of teams of experts, drawn from a number of countries, and their movements and activities in Iraq - whether survey, inspection or disposal. The teams will assemble for briefing at the field office in Bahrain and move by dedicated aircraft to Baghdad or some other point-of-entry in Iraq. Vehicles or rotary-winged aircraft will be used to move the teams within Iraq to the sites concerned. Teams will leave the area via Bahrain following debriefing and initial analysis of any samples or data collected in Iraq.

International Atomic Energy Agency,GOV/INF/614, 29 May 1991

5. Letter from the IAEA Director General to the Secretary-General of the United Nations, 16 May 1991

The Director General is herewith circulating to Member States a copy of a letter which he addressed to the Secretary-General of the United Nations on 16 May 1991, with an enclosure containing a plan for the destruction, removal and rendering harmless of items specified in paragraph 12 of Security Council resolution 687.

Letter from the Director General of the International Atomic Energy Agency (IAEA) addressed to the Secretary-General, 16 May 1991

Under paragraph 13 of Security Council resolution 687 (1991), the Director General of the IAEA is requested, through the Secretary-General of the United Nations, to develop within forty-five days of the adoption of the resolution a plan for the destruction, removal and rendering harmless of the items specified in paragraph 12 of the resolution.

...

Plan for the destruction, removal and rendering harmless of the items specified in paragraph 12 of Security Council resolution 687 (1991)

Introduction

1. Paragraph 13 of Security Council resolution 687 (1991) *inter alia* requests the Director General of IAEA through the Secretary-General, with the assistance and cooperation of the Special Commission ... to develop a plan for submission to the Security Council within 45 days calling for the destruction, removing or rendering harmless of all items listed in paragraph 12 of the resolution.

2. In order to implement the actions required of the Agency pursuant to paragraphs 12 and 13 of the resolution, the Director General of IAEA established on 15 April 1991 an action team placed under the direction of an Agency Deputy Director General and composed of a Deputy Director for Administration and Management and a Deputy Director for Operations.

3. The Agency established contact with the Special Commission set up by the Secretary-General following the approval by the Security Council on 19 April 1991 of the Secretary-General's report submitted to it in document S/22508. Assistance and cooperation is being rendered by the Special Commission and certain modalities for this cooperation have been agreed upon.

Immediate on-site inspection

4. On 18 April 1991, the Government of Iraq submitted to the Director General of IAEA a declaration required by paragraph 12 of resolution 687 (1991). Further information was provided on 27 April 1991.

5. The first on-site inspection, based on the Iraqi declaration to IAEA and additional designations by the Special Commission, started on 15 May 1991. The inspection team on this occasion was headed by a Chief Inspector appointed by IAEA and consisted of 34 persons, including Agency officials and experts as well as representatives and other personnel of the Special Commission. The team's expertise covers all areas of nuclear technology as well as supporting specialties such as radiation protection, explosive ordnance disposal, communications and field security.

THE PLAN

Nuclear-weapons-usable material

6. Nuclear-weapons-usable material or, as it is referred to in Agency practice, "direct-use material" [a]
[a. Direct-use material is nuclear material that can be converted into nuclear explosives components without transmutation or further enrichment, as for instance plutonium containing less than 80 per cent plutonium-238, high-enriched uranium (HEU) (uranium enriched to 20 per cent uranium-235 or more) and uranium-233.]
cannot be destroyed or rendered harmless in Iraq. The Agency will have to take exclusive control of this material for custody and removal from Iraq pursuant to paragraph 12. This is considered to be the foremost task to be undertaken. Known amounts of direct-use material, located in the Tuwaltha [*sic*] area and listed in the Iraqi statement of 27 April 1991, are contained in fresh or irradiated fuel assemblies. Part of this material appears to be stored in accessible conditions. The on-site inspection, which is now under way, is verifying declared quantities and conditions of this material. Further direct-use material, according to the Iraqi declaration, consisting of irradiated fuel assemblies for the IRT 5000 nuclear research reactor, is buried under the rubble of the reactor building. In all probability, a complex and costly decommissioning operation will be needed to render this material accessible for removal and disposal.

7. Following the preliminary on-site verification now under way of the existence of irradiated direct-use material in the damaged reactor building, it is intended to begin the early removal of easily accessible direct-use material, the decommissioning of the building and the removal of the irradiated fuel assemblies, once their accessibility is achieved.

8. In the event that any additional sites are designated by the Special Commission under paragraphs 9 (b) (ii) and 13 of resolution 687 (1991) further inspections will be carried out.

9. The Agency will take custody, through the application of Agency verification, containment and surveillance methods, of the direct-use material in Iraq. Agency safeguards will be applied to all direct-use material removed from Iraq.

10. Negotiations with countries possessing the technology for the transportation and storage of direct-use material to ascertain their willingness to receive this material are under way. Consideration is being given to various options for the long-term disposal or rendering harmless of this material.

Other items subject to paragraph 12 of resolution 687 (1991)

11. The declaration of Iraq listed only direct-use material and a yellow-cake production unit. Inspection of sites for other items subject to paragraph 12 of resolution 687 (1991) that may be designated by the Special Commission will aim to determine if such items exist and, if so, to remove, destroy or render them harmless.

12. Identification of research, development, support or manufacturing facilities and materials relevant or connected to reprocessing of irradiated fuel and isotopic enrichment of uranium will be given priority as they are capable of producing additional direct-use material.

S/22660, 2 June 1991

6. Report of the Secretary-General pursuant to paragraph 26 of Security Council resolution 687 (1991), 2 June 1991

1. The Security Council, acting under Chapter VII of the Charter of the United Nations, adopted on 3 April 1991 resolution 687 (1991), paragraph 1 of which affirmed all 13 resolutions (660 (1990) of 2 August 1990, 661 (1990) of 6 August 1990, 662 (1990) of 9 August 1990, 664 (1990) of 18 August 1990, 665 (1990) of 25 August 1990, 666 (1990) of 13 September 1990, 667 (1990) of 16 September 1990, 669 (1990) of 24 September 1990, 670 (1990) of 25 September 1990, 674 (1990) of 29 October 1990, 677 (1990) of 28 November 1990, 678 (1990) of 29 November 1990 and 686 (1991) of 2 March 1991) concerning the situation between Iraq and Kuwait, except as expressly changed by resolution 687 (1991). By paragraph 26 of resolution 687 (1991) the Security Council requested the Secretary-General, in consultation with appropriate Governments, to develop within 60 days, for its approval, guidelines to facilitate full international implementation of paragraphs 24, 25 and 27 of resolution 687 (1991), and to make them available to all States and to establish a procedure for updating those guidelines periodically.

2. Paragraphs 24, 25 and 27 of resolution 687 (1991) read as follows:

> "*The Security Council,*
>
> "...
>
> "24. *Decides* that, in accordance with resolution 661 (1990) and subsequent related resolutions and until a further decision is taken by the Security Council, all States shall continue to prevent the sale or supply, or the promotion or facilitation of such sale or supply, to Iraq by their nationals, or from their territories or using their flag vessels or aircraft, of:
>
> "(a) Arms and related *matériel* of all types, specifically including the sale or transfer through other means of all forms of conventional military equipment, including for paramilitary forces, and spare parts and components and their means of production, for such equipment;
>
> "(b) Items specified and defined in paragraphs 8 and 12 above not otherwise covered above;
>
> "(c) Technology under licensing or other transfer arrangements used in the production, utilization or stockpiling of items specified in subparagraphs (a) and (b) above;
>
> "(d) Personnel or materials for training or technical support services relating to the design, development, manufacture, use, maintenance or support of items specified in subparagraphs (a) and (b) above;
>
> "25. *Calls upon* all States and international organizations to act strictly in accordance with paragraph 24 above, notwithstanding the existence of any contracts, agreements, licences or any other arrangements;
>
> "...
>
> "27. *Calls upon* all States to maintain such national controls and procedures and to take such other actions consistent with the guidelines to be established by the Security Council under paragraph 26 above as may be necessary to ensure compliance with the terms of paragraph 24 above, and calls upon international organizations to take all appropriate steps to assist in ensuring such full compliance".

3. Implementation of paragraph 24 of resolution 687 (1991) is to be effected in accordance with resolution 661 (1990) and subsequent related resolutions. Resolution 661 (1990) established a comprehensive set of sanctions to be implemented by all States against Iraq and occupied Kuwait, including the sale or supply or weapons or any other military equipment, whether or not originating in their territories, and any activities that promoted or were calculated to promote such sale or supply of such items. Under paragraph 3 of resolution 661 (1990), the Security Council established a committee consisting of all the members of the Council to undertake the tasks set out in that paragraph. By resolution 665 (1990), the Council called upon those Member States cooperating with the Government of Kuwait and deploying maritime forces to the area to use such measures commensurate to the specific circumstances as might be necessary under the authority of the Security Council to halt all inward and outward maritime shipping in order to inspect and verify their cargoes and destinations and to ensure strict implementation of the provisions related to such shipping laid down in resolution 661 (1990). By resolution 670 (1990) the Council confirmed that resolution 661 (1990) applied to all means of transport, including aircraft. With the specific purpose of preventing the carriage of any commodities or products prohibited under resolution 661 (1990) to or from Iraq or occupied Kuwait, resolution 670 (1990) established mandatory provisions concerning flights. Under those provisions the Council required all States, *inter alia*, to deny any aircraft permission to take off from or overfly their territory if such aircraft was destined to land in Iraq or occupied Kuwait, unless certain conditions were met, as specified in paragraphs 3 and 4 of the resolution. The Committee established by resolution 661 (1990) concerning the situation between Iraq and Kuwait was vested with specific responsibilities, including notification or approval procedures for such flights.

4. On the basis of the above observations, the Secretary-General undertook consultations with

appropriate Governments, in accordance with paragraph 26 of resolution 687 (1991). The input from those consultations has been taken into particular account by the Secretary-General in the preparation of the draft guidelines called for by paragraph 26 of that resolution. The draft guidelines are herewith transmitted for the consideration of the Security Council (see annex).

ANNEX

Draft guidelines to facilitate full international implementation of paragraphs 24, 25 and 27 of Security Council resolution 687 (1991)

INTRODUCTION

1. The present guidelines have been developed in accordance with paragraph 26 of Security Council resolution 687 (1991), to facilitate full international implementation of paragraphs 24, 25 and 27 of that resolution.

I. CATEGORIES OF PROHIBITED ITEMS AND ACTIVITIES

2. For the purpose of the present guidelines, the items and activities proscribed are those referred to in paragraph 24, in conjunction with paragraphs 8 and 12, of resolution 687 (1991) and are the following:

(a) Arms and related *matériel* of all types, specifically including the sale or transfer through other means of:

(i) All forms of conventional weapons and military equipment, including for paramilitary forces, and spare parts and components and their means of production, for such equipment;

(ii) All chemical and biological weapons and all stocks or agents and all related subsystems and components;

(iii) All ballistic missiles with a range greater than 150 kilometres and related major parts;

(iv) Nuclear weapons or nuclear-weapons-usable material or any subsystems or components;

(b) All research, development, support and manufacturing facilities for the items as specified and defined in paragraphs 8 (a) and 12 of resolution 687 (1991);

(c) Repair and production facilities for all ballistic missiles with a range greater than 150 kilometres and related major parts;

(d) Technology under licensing or other transfer arrangements used in the production, utilization or stockpiling of items as specified in paragraphs 24 (a), 8 and 12 of resolution 687 (1991);

(e) Personnel or materials for training or technical support services relating to the design, development, manufacture, use, maintenance or support of items as specified in paragraphs 24 (a), 8 and 12 of resolution 687 (1991).

II. UNITED NATIONS MECHANISM FOR MONITORING THE ARMS AND RELATED SANCTIONS

3. The Committee established by resolution 661 (1990) concerning the situation between Iraq and Kuwait (hereinafter referred to as "the Committee") will be the organ of the Security Council responsible for monitoring the prohibitions against the sale or supply of arms to Iraq and related sanctions established in paragraph 24 of resolution 687 (1991) (hereinafter referred to as "arms and related sanctions"). The Committee will carry out its functions in accordance with the mandate provided in resolutions 661 (1990), 665 (1990) and 670 (1990) in so far as it relates to the items proscribed under paragraph 24 of resolution 687 (1991).

4. The Committee will closely cooperate and coordinate its activities with any present and future bodies that will, pursuant to paragraphs 10 and 13 of resolution 687 (1991), be responsible for the monitoring and verification of Iraq's compliance with the obligations set forth in paragraphs 10 and 12 of that resolution, in so far as they concern the acquisition of the items referred to in those paragraphs. The bodies referred to above will therefore have access to the committee and will draw its attention to any problems that they may encounter in pursuing their mandate.

5. In discharging its tasks as regards the items referred to in paragraphs 8 (a) and 12 of resolution 687 (1991), the Committee will work in close cooperation with the Special commission established under paragraph 9 of the resolution and with the International Atomic Energy Agency. In carrying out its work, the Committee will also be able to make use of any expertise or information relevant to its functions available elsewhere within the United Nations system.

6. For the purposes of the present guidelines, the functions of the Committee will be the following:

(a) To meet at regular intervals to examine reports submitted by the Secretary-General on the implementation of the relevant resolutions;

(b) To provide guidance to States and to international organizations, either upon their request or at its own initiative, on matters concerning the implementation of paragraph 24 of resolution 687 (1991), *inter alia*, through the elaboration, as necessary, of relevant criteria;

(c) To reach, in connection with subparagraph (b) above, when needed, agreed interpretations of items falling within the specified categories of proscribed items and activities;

(d) To seek information and maintain contact with States, international organizations and those non-governmental organizations whose activities and/or expertise are likely to promote strict implementation of the arms and related sanctions against Iraq;

(e) To bring to the attention of the States and international organizations concerned information reported to it of alleged violations of the arms and related sanctions against Iraq for appropriate action by those States and international organizations;

(f) To report at 90-day intervals to the Security Council on the implementation of the arms and related sanctions against Iraq contained in the relevant resolutions.

III. PRINCIPLES OF IMPLEMENTATION

7. The actual implementation of the arms and related sanctions against Iraq will be effected at three levels: by all States, by international organizations and through

intergovernmental cooperation. States and international organizations are called upon to act strictly in accordance with the arms and related sanctions, notwithstanding the existence of any contracts, agreements, licences or any other arrangements.

A. *States*

8. All States should report to the Secretary-General within 45 days of the approval by the Security Council of the present guidelines on the measures they have instituted for meeting the obligations set out in paragraph 24 of resolution 687 (1991).

9. All States should ensure the institution or maintenance of national controls, procedures and other measures consistent with the present guidelines as may be necessary to ensure compliance with the terms of paragraph 24 of resolution 687 (1991). On that basis, States should ensure that these measures:

(a) Prevent any circumvention of the arms and related sanctions against Iraq, including but not limited to direct circumvention, indirect or clandestine circumvention, and circumvention through subcontracts to companies within the State itself or in other States;

(b) Prohibit the export to Iraq of those dual-purpose or multi-purpose items that States may have reason to believe will be used for military purposes;

(c) Ensure against the provision of any technology, research, personnel or materials for training or technical support services relating to the production, utilization, stockpiling, design, development, manufacture, use, maintenance or support for any of the items as described in paragraph 2 of the present guidelines;

(d) Require that the sale, licensing or other contracts with States or foreign companies contain end-user transfer assurances that ensure no transfer, retransfer, transshipment or servicing to Iraq or to individuals or bodies inside Iraq or to individuals or bodies outside Iraq acting for the benefit of Iraq or of individuals or bodies inside Iraq of any of the items described in paragraph 2 of the present guidelines;

(e) Require from exporters and other commercial intermediaries a declaration that the items for export described in paragraph 2 of the present guidelines are not destined for Iraq directly or through third-party arrangements;

(f) Provide for legal powers to inspect documents and goods and to detain and seize goods where appropriate;

(g) Impose appropriate penalties for non-compliance in their territories and by their nationals elsewhere, and to notify the Committee of all incidents of such non-compliance.

10. Nothing in the present guidelines will preclude any State or group of States from adopting further measures aimed at achieving effective implementation of the arms and related sanctions against Iraq, in accordance with the relevant provisions of resolution 687 (1991).

11. States should ensure that the provisions of the national measures instituted by them are adequately publicized and disseminated within their territories and among their nationals elsewhere, particularly to arms technology developers, producers, traders and exporters and to the transport sector. In implementing the present guidelines, States should pay particular attention to companies known to have been involved in illegal arms procurement activities on behalf of Iraq.

12. States are requested to report to the Committee any information that may come to their attention relating to possible violations of the arms and related sanctions against Iraq committed by other States or foreign nationals. In this regard, States are reminded of their duties under paragraph 7 of resolution 661 (1990) to cooperate fully with the Committee in the fulfilment of its task, including supplying such information as may be sought by the Committee.

13. States ought to consult the Committee on the question whether certain items fall within the provisions of paragraph 24 of resolution 687 (1991) as well as in cases relating to dual-use or multiple-use items, that is to say, items meant for civilian use but with potential for diversion or conversion to military use.

B. *International organizations*

14. In accordance with paragraphs 25 and 27 of resolution 687 (1991) international organizations should take all appropriate steps to assist in ensuring full compliance with the arms and related sanctions against Iraq, including providing to the Committee any relevant information that may come to their attention.

15. International organizations having any dealings with, or activities in, Iraq should carefully review their programmes to make sure that they do not facilitate any of the activities prohibited under paragraph 24 of resolution 687 (1991). Paragraph 13 above shall also apply to international organizations.

C. *Intergovernmental cooperation*

16. States are encouraged to cooperate with each other bilaterally or within the framework of existing regional or other appropriate intergovernmental organizations or through other appropriate intergovernmental arrangements in the implementation of the arms and related sanctions against Iraq. Such cooperation would be particularly useful in matters, among others, of verification of the origin and destination of the items specified in paragraph 24 of resolution 687 (1991), as well as in the exchange of documentary evidence relating thereto.

IV. REVIEW OF THE GUIDELINES

17. Taking into account Iraq's compliance with resolution 687 (1991), the general progress towards the control of armaments in the region, information received from States and international organizations and from the Committee, the Security Council may wish to review the guidelines at the same time as its regular reviews of paragraphs 22, 23, 24 and 25 of resolution 687 (1991) as set out in paragraph 28 of the same resolution, that is to say, with the first review being undertaken 120 days after the adoption of that resolution.

18. The Security Council may also wish to consider, in the light of any comments or reports that the committee may make to it, what further action may be necessary to ensure the implementation of the arms and related sanctions against Iraq.

[On the episode described below see *S/PV.2992 & S/PV.2996, reprinted at pp. 142-6, and the statement of the Council President contained in the latter document.*]

S/22761, 5 July 1991

7. Letter from the Secretary-General addressed to the President of the Security Council, 4 July 1991

I have the honour to transmit to you herewith the report of the high-level mission, composed of Mr. Hans Blix, Director-General of the International Atomic Energy Agency, Mr. Rolf Ekéus, Executive Chairman of the Special Commission established under Security Council resolution 687 (1991), and Mr. Yasushi Akashi, Under-Secretary-General for Disarmament Affairs, which I sent to Iraq at the request of the members of the Security Council, as noted in the statement by the President of the Council of 28 June 1991 (S/22746).

...

Report of the high-level mission to Iraq

A. *Introduction*

1. The report of the high-level mission is submitted to the Security Council, through the Secretary-General, within the context and the framework of the statement by the President of the Council of 28 June 1991 (S/22746), pursuant to which the mission was constituted. Furthermore, the mission has understood that it was to proceed against the background of the three incidents of 23, 25 and 28 June 1991 covered in the President's statement. The report, therefore, does not deal with the experience of three other teams dispatched to Iraq under the provisions of section C of Security Council resolution 687 (1991). The cooperation extended by the Iraqi authorities to these inspection and disposal teams was found to be satisfactory and gave rise to no complaints in respect of the granting of immediate and unimpeded access or of other rights of the Special Commission established under Security Council resolution 687 (1991) and the International Atomic Energy Agency (IAEA) under the resolution.

B. *Composition of the high-level mission*

2. The high-level mission was composed of Mr. Hans Blix, Director-General of IAEA, Mr. Rolf Ekéus, Executive Chairman of the Special Commission and Mr. Yasushi Akashi, United Nations Under-Secretary-General for Disarmament Affairs. The Secretary-General requested Mr. Ekéus to lead the mission.

3. The mission was assisted by a team of experts: Mr. M. El Baradei (IAEA); and Mr. Johan Molander and Mr. John Scott (Office of the Special Commission).

C. *Itinerary of the high-level mission*

4. The mission assembled in Bahrain on 29 June 1991. On 30 June, the mission proceeded to Baghdad, where it remained until 3 July. On 3 July, the mission travelled to Geneva, reported orally to the Secretary-General on 4 July on the outcome of its work and adopted its report.

... 6. At the final meeting with the Foreign Minister, the mission presented in broad outline the findings it intended to present to the Secretary-General and to the Security Council. On the request of the Foreign Minister for another meeting the following day, the mission stated that at that point no new developments of significance to its tasks could be expected. The mission recalled that it had already extended its visit by one day and that the Security Council had requested the mission to report to it at the earliest opportunity. If, however, further developments from the Iraqi side were to be forthcoming, they could be communicated to and presented in New York or Vienna.

2. *Presentation of the demands of the Security Council*

7. During its meetings, the mission emphasized that it had been sent to Iraq in order to convey the urgent demand of the Security Council for unequivocal assurances that the Government of Iraq would take all the necessary measures to ensure that no hindrances were placed in the way of the discharge by the Special Commission of its mandate under Security Council resolution 687 (1991) and would accord, in compliance with Iraq's obligations and commitments *vis-à-vis* the United Nations and IAEA, full cooperation, including immediate and unimpeded access to sites declared or designated under paragraphs 9 and 13 of Security Council resolution 687 (1991), to the inspection teams sent to Iraq by the Special Commission and IAEA. The mission further emphasized that it was under instructions from the Council to obtain unconditional guarantees for the safety and security of all personnel engaged in the performance of functions in connection with Security Council resolution 687 (1991). It was also under instructions to seek detailed information on undertakings and measures by the Government to ensure compliance at all levels, including local military and civilian authorities, with Iraq's obligations under Security Council resolution 687 (1991).

8. In transmitting the Security Council's demands, the mission stressed the Council's grave concern over the incident of 28 June, in particular the use of firearms by Iraqi personnel, and drew attention to the fact that the members of the Council had strongly deplored the incidents of 23, 25 and 28 June 1991 and had condemned the conduct of the Iraqi authorities in this connection. It also underlined that the President's statement recorded the unanimous view of the members of the Council.

9. The mission drew attention to the fact that the Security Council remained seized of the matter. The mission underlined the importance of full compliance by Iraq so as to enable the United Nations to continue to carry out resolution 687 (1991) and that any non-compliance by Iraq would have serious consequences. The mission reiterated the view of the Security Council on the threat that weapons of mass destruction pose to peace and security in the Middle East and on the need to work towards the establishment in the Middle East of a zone free of such weapons.

3. *Assurances given by the Government of Iraq*

10. The mission received from the Ministers with whom it met the various assurances indicated below:

> (a) A decision by the President of Iraq, which had been conveyed to the Security Council in New York by the Permanent Representative of Iraq to the United Nations (S/22749), to the effect that the President had ordered all the Iraqi authorities concerned to extend full cooperation to the United Nations representatives and to facilitate their tasks in line with the obligations undertaken by Iraq. The President had also instructed that all bureaucratic problems arising in the cooperation process should be overcome and had authorized the Minister for Foreign Affairs to issue immediate instructions to all authorities and departments which the United Nations representatives desired to visit and inspect to give access without hesitation;
>
> (b) A further statement by the President of Iraq which, *inter alia*, contained the assurance that Iraq had abandoned all activities that might be in contravention of Security Council resolution 687 (1991);

(c) An assurance that Iraq would take all necessary measures to ensure that no hindrances were placed in the way of the inspection activities of the Special Commission and IAEA and that it would accord full cooperation to the inspection teams, including immediate and unimpeded access, and the right to stop and inspect vehicles in movement;

(d) The information that, in order to implement the assurances of cooperation at all levels, orders had been issued to all Iraqi military and civilian personnel to that effect "and so as to ensure the safety and security of all personnel engaged in the performance of functions in connection with Security Council resolution 687 (1991);"

(e) The information that full authority had been given to the Minister for Foreign Affairs to issue directives relating to compliance with Special Commission and IAEA requests under resolution 687 (1991), and that a high-level military liaison officer was, as of that point, placed in the Ministry of Foreign Affairs with authority to grant immediate access to any military site or installation.

4. *Access to the objects observed by the nuclear inspection team*

11. The mission insisted throughout on the call by the members of the Security Council that Iraq grant the nuclear inspection team, present in Iraq, immediate and unimpeded access to the objects which the team had endeavoured to inspect on 23, 25 and 28 June 1991. The mission reiterated this call when it was reported to it that materials which the team was invited to inspect at Fallujah on 1 July and on 2 July 1991 did not comprise objects which the team had observed on 28 June.

12. The Iraqi side explained that some equipment and material belonging to the Atomic Energy Commission of Iraq had been transferred to the Ministry of Defence for purposes of destruction of items that might be in contravention of Security Council resolution 687 (1991) and of redistribution of other items which could be used for the civilian reconstruction programme in Iraq. It was further stated that some of this equipment and material had been present at the Fallujah site. No specification of these items was given, but the Chairman of the Atomic Energy Commission of Iraq promised to provide, in the near future, a list of all items that had been destroyed. Following these explanations, in the afternoon of 2 July the inspection team, accompanied by the Director-General of IAEA, was taken to a destruction site and was shown certain destroyed equipment. The large pieces of equipment which were thus inspected were related to nuclear research and could not have had relevance for the production of weapons-usable material. No meaningful explanation was given why they had been destroyed.

13. The mission stated that if Iraq had interpreted Security Council resolution 687 (1991) in such a way as not to cover research or other facilities, or equipment for the enrichment of uranium or the separation of plutonium, an additional declaration would be needed to include such items as centrifuges, calutrons, facilities for production of uranium tetrachloride or uranium hexafluoride. The Chairman of the Atomic Energy Commission of Iraq stated categorically that there had not been and there was currently no programme under the Commission for the enrichment of uranium in Iraq. The Deputy Prime Minister added that there was only one nuclear programme in Iraq.

5. *Observation by the Government of Iraq*

14. The Iraqi side, while reiterating the Government's acceptance of the Security Council's resolutions, none the less considered the resolutions to be harsh and unjust. In this connection, reference was made in particular to Security Council resolution 699 (1991), regarding the liability of Iraq for the costs incurred under section C of Security Council resolution 687 (1991) and their offer to undertake the destruction of chemical weapons. The mission stated that this offer was under serious consideration in the Special Commission.

15. The Iraqi side, when referring to the incidents of 23, 25 and 28 June 1991, complained that insufficient notice of inspection had been given. Furthermore, insistence on undertaking the inspections during the Muslim religious holiday of Eid, when the civilian or military officers concerned could not be easily contacted, was inappropriate. Iraq's industrial base had been badly damaged during the conflict and serious communications and logistical problems existed. All these factors had contributed to the incidents. The mission stated that appropriate notice would always be given, but that the Special Commission and IAEA had the right to inspect mobile objects with short or no notice. The inspection teams had no intention to disregard the religious feelings of the people of Iraq. However, it was now a common feature of verification under modern arms control agreements that inspections might take place at any time when there were reasons for believing that otherwise the purposes of the inspection might be frustrated. Furthermore, on 23 June, it was noticed that considerable Iraqi activity was under way at the inspection site, despite the religious holiday.

16. The Iraqi side referred to its reservations concerning the composition of certain inspection teams and expressed the hope that in the future they would be more widely drawn. The mission stated that, in composing the teams, primary emphasis had to be put on technical competence. Most teams were composed of personnel of many nationalities. A restricting factor existed in the nuclear weapons and related fields, where the available expertise was largely limited to the five nuclear-weapons States. It was agreed that the selection of the members of the inspection teams was the sole prerogative of the special Commission and of IAEA.

E. *Findings of the high-level mission*

17. In spite of their unambiguous character, the general assurances given and the specific measures promised can only be evaluated in the light of present and future implementation by the Iraqi authorities. As described in the present report, the Iraqi response to the request for access to the objects which the inspection team had endeavoured to inspect on 28 June falls short of what has been called for by the Security Council.

S/22762, 5 July 1991

8. Letter from the Secretary-General addressed to the President of the Security Council, 5 July 1991

Further to my letter of yesterday's date (S/22761), I wish to inform you that, while in Geneva on 4 July 1991 and having received the report of the high-level mission which I had earlier dispatched to Iraq at the request of the members of the Security Council, I asked the Permanent Representative of Iraq to the United Nations Office at Geneva to see me.

In our meeting, at which I was accompanied by the members of the high-level mission, I asked the Permanent Representative to convey an informal paper to H.E. Mr.

Saddam Hussein, President of the Republic of Iraq. The Permanent Representative undertook to do so immediately. The text of the paper is attached ...

I have today received in response a communication from His Excellency the President of Iraq, under cover of a transmittal note signed by the Permanent Representative of Iraq to the United Nations in New York. The texts of both the transmittal note and the President's communication are attached hereto ...

Paper handed by the Secretary-General to the Permanent Representative of Iraq to the United Nations Office at Geneva on 4 July 1991

The high-level mission was given unambiguous assurances as regards full cooperation and specific measures to ensure compliance by Iraq with its obligations under Security Council resolution 687 (1991).

However, the response by Iraq to the request for access to the objects, which the nuclear inspection team had observed on a long convoy of trucks and had endeavoured to inspect on 28 June, was deemed not satisfactory by the mission. Only a full demonstration of what all these objects were and inspection of them by a nuclear inspection team would be satisfactory.

The high-level mission noted information given to it that a decision had been taken by Iraq not to retain any items that might be in contravention with Security Council resolution 687 (1991), nuclear or other, and that equipment of the Atomic Energy Commission of Iraq had been transferred to the army, some for destruction and the other for use in the reconstruction work. Explanations were not given on what nuclear items Iraq had considered to be in contravention with Security Council resolution 687 (1991).

Full explanations about nuclear activities and equipment that had been deemed by Iraq to be in contravention of the resolution and inspection of this equipment and facilities related to them - destroyed or not - are imperative.

Letter from the Permanent Representative of Iraq to the United Nations addressed to the Secretary-General

On instructions from my Government, I have the pleasure of enclosing herewith a facsimile message in Arabic from H.E. President Saddam Hussein dated 5 July 1991 (Baghdad time) in reply to Your Excellency's message handed to the Permanent Representative of Iraq to the United Nations Office at Geneva, Ambassador Barzan Al-Tikriti.

Letter from President Saddam Hussein addressed to the Secretary-General dated 5 July 1991 (Baghdad time)

We highly appreciate the initiative of the Secretary-General of the United Nations and affirm the guarantees, given to the high-level mission during its visit to Baghdad, whereby prompt and unimpeded access will be ensured to the locations and items designated for inspection in accordance with Security Council resolution 687 (1991), in addition to guaranteeing the security and safety of members of the inspection team. We also affirm that Iraq is committed to the fulfilment of its obligations under the aforesaid resolution.

With respect to the concerns of the mission, it has been arranged that the mission should be provided with a list of the items about which it sought information. This list will be ready on the evening of Sunday, 7 July, or the morning of Monday, 8 July 1991, at which time it may be studied by the inspection team.

S/22792, 15 July 1991

9. Report of the Secretary-General pursuant to paragraph 4 of Security Council resolution 699 (1991), 15 July 1991

1. The present report is submitted pursuant to paragraph 4 of Security Council resolution 699 (1991), of 17 June 1991, which reads as follows:

> "*Decides* to encourage the maximum assistance, in cash and in kind, from all Member States to ensure that activities under section C of resolution 687 (1991) are undertaken effectively and expeditiously; further decides, however, that the Government of Iraq shall be liable for the full costs of carrying out the tasks authorized by section C; and requests the Secretary-General to submit to the Council within 30 days for approval recommendations as to the most effective means by which Iraq's obligations in this respect may be fulfilled".

I

2. The fulfillment by the Government of Iraq of the obligations set out in paragraph 4 quoted above is contingent upon both the availability of funds to meet the financial requirements, as well as concrete arrangements to ensure that the necessary resources are channelled to the United Nations.

3. It will be recalled that the Security Council, in deciding upon the financing of the Compensation Fund, did not envisage the use of "frozen assets" of Iraq held in third countries (see paragraph 16 of the Secretary-General's report dated 2 May 1991 pursuant to paragraph 19 of Security Council resolution 687 (1991), document S/22559). It is therefore assumed that the Council would not wish these assets to be used to meet Iraq's obligations in connection with the fulfillment of paragraph 4 of this resolution.

4. The Secretary-General considers that the most obvious way of obtaining financial resources for this purpose would be the sale of some Iraqi petroleum and petroleum products. The net proceeds of such sales would be deposited in a United Nations account to be used to reimburse the costs of carrying out the tasks authorized under section C of Security Council resolution 687 (1991). The quantities to be sold would therefore have to be established in the light of these costs.

5. While the approach outlined above might ensure that Iraq can meet these financial obligations, it would, at the same time, reduce the resources available for the Compensation Fund and/or those remaining for the Government of Iraq. In this connection, the Secretary-General, in determining the appropriate level of Iraq's contribution to the Compensation Fund, had taken account of: (a) the requirements of the people of Iraq; (b) Iraq's payment capacity, taking into consideration external debt servicing; and (c) the needs of the Iraqi economy.

6. The approach proposed in paragraph 5 above would also necessitate that the sanctions imposed on Iraq under Security Council resolution 661 (1990) be lifted, for a limited period and under clearly defined conditions. It may be necessary to repeat this process in the light of the ultimate costs to be reimbursed.

7. This arrangement presupposes cooperation by Iraq as well as strict supervision of the sale of petroleum and petroleum products from Iraq. To this end, appropriate monitoring would have to be ensured. Should Iraq fail to meet its payment obligations, the Secretary-General would need to report the matter to the Security Council.

II

8. Following the adoption of Security Council resolution 699 (1991), the Secretary-General requested the Permanent Representative of Iraq to inform him by 10 July 1991 of the manner in which the Government planned to meet its obligations under paragraph 4 of that resolution. The reply of the Government of Iraq, dated 7 July 1991, reads as follows:

> "With reference to your letter dated 26 June 1991 I have the honour to inform you that my Government still believes that its offer to take an initiative and destroy the weapon systems would have reduced the costs of destroying the weapons and reduced the related risks and time and would have been the safest solution, but the Security Council did not favour this offer and issued its rash and unfair resolution 699 (1991). Nevertheless, Iraq has recently received encouraging signals from the Special Commission concerning this offer to destroy the chemical weapons, and this offer is still valid and it together with Iraq's experience in this area should help in carrying out the tasks assigned to the Special Commission and the IAEA under part C of resolution 687 (1991)."

9. It should be noted in this connection that the Special Commission is considering the Iraqi offer and no decision has yet been taken on this matter.

10. As far as assistance in cash and in kind is concerned, it may be of interest to the Security Council to note that as of 15 July 1991, voluntary contributions in the amount of $US 2 million have been received from Member States in response to paragraph 4 of Security Council resolution 699 (1991).

International Atomic Energy Agency, GOV/2530, 16 July 1991

10. A report by the IAEA Director-General on Non-Compliance by Iraq with its Obligations under the Safeguards Agreement Concluded with the Agency, 16 July 1991

1. By Security Council resolution 687, the Agency was entrusted, *inter alia*, with the task of carrying out immediate on-site inspections of Iraq's nuclear capabilities based on Iraq's declarations and on the designation of additional locations by the Special Commission established pursuant to para. 9(b) of that resolution. Pursuant to the resolution, Iraq was to submit to the Secretary-General of the United Nations and to the Director General of the IAEA within 15 days of adoption of the resolution [1] [1. Security Council resolution 687 was adopted on 3 April 1991.] a declaration of the locations, amounts and types of nuclear weapons, nuclear weapons-usable material and any subsystems or components and any research, development, support or manufacturing facilities related to nuclear weapons or nuclear weapons-usable material.

2. By letters of 18 and 27 April, Iraq submitted to the Secretary-General of the United Nations and to the Director General of the IAEA a list that included all material previously declared to the IAEA under the Safeguards Agreement between Iraq and the Agency for the Application of Safeguards in Connection with the Treaty on the Non-Proliferation of Nuclear Weapons (INFCIRC/172). Iraq also reported a uranium concentrate production plant.

3. The first Agency inspection under resolution 687 took place from 14 to 22 May. The second inspection mission arrived in Iraq on 22 June. During the course of that inspection, the inspection team was denied access on 23, 25 and 28 June to sites designated by the Special Commission.

4. At the request of the Security Council, a high-level mission composed of the Director General, the Chairman of the Special Commission and the Under Secretary-General for Disarmament Affairs went to Iraq on 30 June to secure immediate and unimpeded access to all sites and objects which the team had endeavored to inspect. Pursuant to the mission's visit, Iraq indicated its intention to submit an additional list of nuclear items relevant to Security Council resolution 687.

5. By a letter dated 7 July 1991 from the Foreign Minister of Iraq to the Secretary-General and copied to the Director General (Annex 1), Iraq submitted an additional list of nuclear equipment and material in its possession.

6. A review of the 7 July letter suggested that Iraq had been in non-compliance with its obligations under its Safeguards Agreement with the Agency, in particular with regard to Article 34(c), which requires nuclear material of a composition and purity suitable for fuel fabrication or isotopic enrichment, and any nuclear material produced at a later stage in the nuclear fuel cycle, to be subject to all of the safeguards procedures provided for in the Agreement; with regard to Article 34(b), which requires notification to the Agency of imports of material containing uranium or thorium which has not reached the stage provided for in Article 34(c), unless the material is imported for specifically non-nuclear purposes; and with regard to the requirements set forth in Article 42 of the Agreement and Code 3.1.2 of the Subsidiary Arrangements General Part concerning submission of design information in respect of facilities. On 9 and 11 July, the Director General wrote to the Foreign Minister of Iraq requesting urgent comments on the matter (Annexes 2 and 3).

7. On 12 July 1991, the Director General received from the Iraqi Resident Representative a letter from the Foreign Minister responding to the 9 July letter of the Director General, and providing observations and clarifications with regard to the enrichment activities in this context (Annex 4). In that letter the Foreign Minister stated that the enrichment activities were not subject to safeguards because they were still in the early stage of research and development, because there was no facility for isotope separation as defined in Article 98 of the Safeguards Agreement, and because the amount of material produced was less than a significant quantity. He further stated that in the interpretation of Iraq, Article 34(c) referred only to imports of nuclear material of a composition and purity suitable for fuel fabrication, and that as the material in question (a half kilogramme of uranium enriched to 4% U235) had been produced domestically, Article 34(c) was not applicable. Alternatively, it was maintained, as the material had not been produced in a "facility" as defined under the Agreement, Article 34(c) was not applicable.

8. On 13 July 1991, the IAEA received a further communication from the Foreign Minister responding to the Director General's letter of 11 July (Annex 5). In that communication, it was stated that, as regards the yellowcake and uranium dioxide referred to in Table 9 of the Iraqi declaration of 7 July, the material was meant for non-nuclear use, and accordingly, the Agency had not been notified of such material in accordance with Article 34(b) of the Safeguards Agreement. With respect to the uranium hexafluoride, Iraq's view was that the quantity was insignificant and, hence, was not required to be notified or inspected. With regard to the uranium tetrachloride, it was maintained that the amount was the normal amount required for feeding experimental separators using the electromagnetic enrichment process and did not require notification. Finally, it was noted that

the Government of Iraq considered its letter of 7 July 1991 a "corrective" measure meeting the requirements of Article 19 of the Safeguards Agreement.

9. The Safeguards Agreement between Iraq and the Agency, a standard INFCIRC/153-type agreement, requires the application of safeguards to all nuclear material in all peaceful nuclear activities in the State. Pursuant to Article 34(b), when any material containing uranium or thorium which has not reached the stage of the nuclear fuel cycle described in Article 34(c) is imported, the State is required to inform the Agency of the quantity and composition of such material, unless the material is imported for specifically non-nuclear material purposes. Article 34(b) applies, *inter alia*, to imports of yellowcake. Pursuant to Article 34(c) of the Agreement, when any nuclear material of a composition and purity suitable for fuel fabrication or for isotopic enrichment leaves the plant or processing stage in which it has been produced, the nuclear material becomes subject to the other safeguards procedures specified in the Agreement. In addition, Article 34(c) requires the application of such other safeguards procedures to nuclear material of the composition and purity suitable for fuel fabrication or for isotopic enrichment, or any other nuclear material produced at a later stage in the nuclear fuel cycle, which is imported into the State. Article 34(c) would include, therefore, any domestically produced or imported uranium dioxide of a purity suitable for fuel fabrication, uranium tetrachloride, uranium hexafluoride and enriched uranium, as well as any nuclear material produced therefrom.

10. Peaceful nuclear activities include research and development activities in the nuclear field. The Safeguards Agreement provides no automatic exemption from the application of safeguards to nuclear material which is used or intended for use in such activities. Although the Agreement provides a mechanism for exempting nuclear material of certain quantities (Article 36) and for certain uses (Article 37), both mechanisms require the material to have been subject to safeguards and then, upon request by the State, to be exempted therefrom by the Agency.

11. The production of nuclear material in a location which is not a "facility" as defined in Article 98(I) of the Safeguards Agreement does not exempt the State from reporting such material to the IAEA. Article 49 of the Agreement requires that when nuclear material is customarily used outside facilities, the State must provide the Agency with, *inter alia*, a general description of the use of such material, its geographic location and the user's name and address for routine business purposes. The State is also obliged to provide a general description of the existing and proposed procedures for nuclear accountancy and control.

12. The technical objective of the safeguards procedures set forth in the Agreement, as described in Article 28, which relates to the timely detection of diversion of significant quantities of nuclear material, and deterrence of such diversion by the risk of early detection, does not imply that any minimum quantity of nuclear material is required for the application of safeguards.

13. On the basis of the information and comments provided to the Agency by the letters of 7, 10 and 12 of July, and on the basis of reports by the Agency Chief Inspector currently in Iraq, it is concluded that Iraq failed to report to the Agency the existence in Iraq of nuclear material of the composition and purity provided for in Article 34(c), including the uranium dioxide, the uranium tetrachloride and the uranium hexafluoride identified in Table 9 of the annexes to the 7 July letter. In addition, it is concluded that Iraq failed to report the half kilogramme of enriched uranium as nuclear material past the stage provided for in Article 34(c). It is concluded, therefore, that Iraq has not been in compliance with its obligations under the Safeguards Agreement with the IAEA, in particular with respect to the obligation to accept safeguards on all nuclear material in all peaceful nuclear activities in Iraq.

14. It is not yet possible to reach a conclusion as to whether Iraq has failed to comply with its obligation to provide information with respect to facilities. Results of current inspection activities may provide additional data on which to base such an assessment. This, however, will not change the conclusion regarding non-compliance that has already occurred.

ANNEX

Letter from the Minister for Foreign Affairs of Iraq to the Secretary-General of the United Nations, 7 July 1991

...

I wish to refer to the visit of the high-level mission, under instructions from the Security Council, to Baghdad from 30 June to 3 July 1991, and to its encounters and discussions with Iraqi officials.

We have reflected for some time following the useful meetings with the mission. Given the impressions which it voiced after viewing some of the parts destroyed, and in the light of whatever opinions that may emerge after consideration of the lists of equipment destroyed, we have decided that it would be appropriate to give an account of our peaceful nuclear programme in order to provide a more comprehensive picture of the real situation both before and after the aggression, and to permit a better assessment of the future of such a programme.

By careful examination of the attached details, you will be able to conclude that the programme does not entail any departure from, or violation of, the Treaty of the Non-Proliferation of Nuclear Weapons and the IAEA safeguards agreement. Indeed, I wish to affirm that both the Treaty and the agreement have been constantly observed by the programme initiators and those responsible for any progress made therein. However, Iraq had sound reasons related to its national security which induced it to refrain from declaring some of the stages of the programme though this was not in any way inconsistent with either the Treaty or the agreement.

The most important of these reasons, which we still believe to be valid, was a fear of exaggeration, abuse and aggression. Iraq was hoping that the international political situation in the region would so develop as to ensure security and stability and bring about a just peace, with the use of nuclear technology serving even as a stabilizing factor. It was hence believed best to abstain from overt reference to nuclear technology so that such reference might not be taken as a threat to the security of States or be used to hinder the propagation of the peaceful uses of such technology.

The current situation, as will be clear from a detailed consideration of the documents attached to this letter, and perhaps from the field inspection which may follow, is the result of two factors: first, the comprehensive destruction to which the programme was subjected as a result of the aggression; second, Iraq's decision to destroy anything which might possibly be interpreted as incompatible with Security Council resolution 687(1991) which was accepted by Iraq. You have chosen to consider the destruction carried out by Iraq, without prior notification and without your participation, as inconsistent with the requirements for the implementation of the Security Council resolution. I wish to reaffirm the interpretation which we expressed to you, namely, a fear of exaggeration and deliberate alarmism in various fields, particularly the nuclear field. That was precisely what caused the President of the United States to declare in November 1990 that Iraq would produce a nuclear weapon within two months and that he was accordingly obliged to expedite launching the war and destroying

Iraq's nuclear capabilities before Iraq could take advantage of that opportunity.

In our view, this alone was sufficient reason for a decision to proceed with destruction. The second reason, as you may be well aware, is that Iraq is now a poor country with extremely limited financial resources as a result of the economic sanctions which have continued for almost a whole year now. Moreover, according to Security Council resolution 700(1991), it was decided to make Iraq bear the financial costs arising from measures to implement Security Council resolution 687(1991), and it was for that reason that Iraq hastened its decision on destruction before receiving interminable lists of equipment to be destroyed.

In conclusion, I would like to reiterate Iraq's continued commitment to the Treaty on the Non-Proliferation of Nuclear Weapons and the IAEA safeguards system. At the same time, I wish to express my deep sorrow that the Treaty is unable to preserve the rights and material achievements attained by Iraq up to this time, though I hope that this can be achieved in the future. I am entirely optimistic that the Agency will continue to help Iraq to exercise its rights with respect to the peaceful use of atomic energy, in accordance with the Treaty.

Please find enclosed an overview of Iraq's nuclear programme, together with details of all its components, as shown in the relevant tables. [Tables omitted] Enclosed are also the tables of nuclear equipment and materials which we pledged to draw up by the evening of Sunday, 7 July or the morning of Monday, 8 July 1991. The equipment in question is ready and may be viewed by the inspection team.

...

Enclosures:

1. Overview of the Iraqi nuclear programme;
2. Nine tables of nuclear equipment and materials. These include materials and equipment which have already been checked by the inspection team and are still on their respective sites. [*Tables omitted.*]

Overview of the Iraqi nuclear programme

Iraq initiated nuclear activities in 1956, after President Eisenhower's announcement that the United States was launching a peaceful nuclear programme in exercise of the fundamental right of all societies to promote scientific and technological progress, and as one of the pillars of its new civilization. The Iraqi programme was implemented in the following three stages:

First stage

The first stage of the programme was initially carried out through collaboration with some Western countries and later, in the 1960s, with the Soviet Union. Its objective was to build a research reactor and laboratories for producing radioactive isotopes for medical and industrial applications.

Second stage

The second stage began with Iraq's accession to the Treaty on the Non-Proliferation of Nuclear Weapons and to the system of safeguards relating thereto. In this way Iraq wished to express its sincere peaceful intentions and to facilitate its access to nuclear technology through the help of those States which had it, in accordance with the provisions of the Treaty. In fact, Iraq concluded agreements with France, Italy and other countries and thus achieved the following stages of the fuel cycle:

1. Experimental laboratories producing nuclear fuel for nuclear power plants;

2. Research laboratories for processing spent nuclear fuel;

3. The nuclear power plant programme;

4. Uranium extraction from phosphate ores;

5. The establishment of the Tammuz 1 reactor with its related facilities and equipment.

Although the activities of this stage were publicly disclosed, and despite their transparent nature, Israel aborted these endeavours when it destroyed the Tammuz 1 reactor and all its facilities and equipment on 7 June 1981. That operation had been preceded by an assassination campaign directed against several leading experts of the Iraqi atomic energy sector.

Third stage

It was evident that all the international guarantees and bilateral agreements have been unable to protect the facilities and their personnel against aggression. Hence, it was necessary to adopt new formulas in order to acquire the relevant nuclear know-how for the important and sensitive phases of the nuclear fuel cycle, through self-reliance and the non-disclosure of information. These phases included the following:

1. Uranium extraction from carbonate ores;

2. Purification and conversion of uranium-bearing compounds;

3. Enriching uranium isotopes using the electromagnetic method;

4. Enriching uranium isotopes using the centrifugal method;

5. Enriching isotopes by chemical methods.

United States aircraft bombed the nuclear reactors while they were in operation, as well as the nuclear fuel stockpiles, without prior warning and without concern for the danger of a serious nuclear accident which could cause extensive harm to the population and the environment of the region. Such an act is contrary to civilized human behaviour and to the international resolutions which have been adopted on the subject and hence cannot be justified under any circumstance. This attack on declared nuclear facilities devoted to peaceful purposes is equivalent to a nuclear attack carried out by a major power which has committed itself to respecting the Treaty on the Non-Proliferation of Nuclear Weapons against a State which is a signatory to that Treaty.

It clearly follows from the foregoing, in particular from the reasons which led to the non-disclosure of some phases of the programme and its real state of progress, and from the nature of the aggression against it, that the purpose of such aggression was to cut short Iraq's scientific progress which belongs to its people and which is a basic factor in its development. Truly, the bringing of scientific activity to this sudden halt was one of the main objectives of the aggression, whereby the aggressor wished to ensure that Iraq and the Arab Nation would continue to lag far behind in terms of human progress.

It was therefore necessary to issue this clarification in response to ill-intentioned interpretations and exaggerations concerning the objectives and goals of Iraq's nuclear programme. ...

...

Annex 2

Letter from the Director General to the Minister for Foreign Affairs of Iraq, 9 July 1991

...

I refer to your letter dated July 7, 1991, to the Secretary-General of the United Nations, a copy of which was transmitted to me by the Iraqi Resident Representative in Vienna.

The Agency is examining in detail your Excellency's letter to the Secretary-General and its annexes. I note, however, with concern the reference in your letter to the existence in Iraq of a programme for enrichment of uranium that was not submitted to Agency safeguards in accordance with the Safeguards Agreement between your Government and the Agency in connection with the Treaty on the Non-Proliferation of Nuclear Weapons (INFCIRC/172).

Annex 3 to your letter states that half a kilogram of uranium enriched to 4% U_{235} has been produced during experiment through an electromagnetic process. The same annex also refers to the production of an "unappreciable" quantity of uranium enriched through an ultracentrifuge process.

Article 34(c) of the Safeguards Agreement provides that:

> When any nuclear material of a composition and purity suitable for fuel fabrication or for isotopic enrichment leaves the plant or the process stage in which it has been produced, or when such nuclear material, or any other nuclear material produced at a later stage in the nuclear fuel cycle, is imported into Iraq, the nuclear material shall become subject to the other safeguards procedures specified in this Agreement.

In addition, Article 42 of the Agreement provides that:

> Pursuant to Article 8, design information in respect of existing facilities shall be provided to the Agency during the discussion of the Subsidiary arrangements. The time limits for the provision of design information in respect of the new facilities shall be specified in the Subsidiary Arrangements and such information shall be provided as early as possible before nuclear material is introduced into a new facility.

Code 3.1.2 of the Subsidiary Arrangements General Part specifies that completed Agency information questionnaires for new facilities are to be submitted to the Agency "normally not later than 180 days before the facility is scheduled to receive nuclear material for the first time".

It appears from the above that certain activities by the Iraqi Government with respect to the enrichment programme have not been carried out in accordance with Iraq's obligations under the Safeguards Agreement. In view of Article XII.C of the Statute, which requires the Director General to report non-compliance with safeguards obligations to the Board, I would appreciate if Your Excellency would provide me with urgent comments on the above.

...

Annex 3

Letter from the Director General to the Minister for Foreign Affairs of Iraq, 11 July 1991

...

I refer to your letter dated July 7, 1991, to the Secretary-General of the United Nations and to my letter of July 9, 1991, in which, as a result of a preliminary examination of the annexes to your letter, I expressed concern with respect to the reported enrichment programme.

Upon further examination of the annexes, I note that large quantities of nuclear material identified in Table 9 has not previously been reported to the Agency pursuant to Article 34(c) of the Safeguards Agreement between Iraq and the Agency (INFCIRC/172), which provides, *inter alia*, that when nuclear material of a composition and purity suitable for fuel fabrication or for isotopic enrichment leaves the plant or process stage at which it has been produced, or is imported, it shall become subject to the full range of safeguards procedures provided for in the Agreement. Furthermore, Article 34(b) of the Agreement requires that imports of material which has not reached that stage, including yellow cake, be reported to the Agency unless it is imported for specifically non-nuclear purposes.

As with the activities referred to in my letter to you of 9 July, the non-reporting of the material in Table 9 appears not to have been in compliance with Iraq's obligations under the Safeguards Agreement. Keeping in mind Article XII.C of the Statute, I would appreciate if Your Excellency would provide me urgently with comments on the above.

...

Annex 4

Letter from the Minister for Foreign Affairs of Iraq to the Director General, 10 July 1991

...

I received, through the Iraqi Resident Representative to the IAEA, your letter addressed to me dated 9 July 1991.

In response to your request for our comments on the contents of your letter, I wish to make the following observations and clarifications.

You have mentioned in your letter that Iraq has a programme for enrichment of uranium that was not submitted to Agency safeguards, in accordance with the Safeguards Agreement between the Iraqi Government and the Agency (INFCIRC/172). I would like to refer here to the fact that the Safeguards Agreement, which is based on the Treaty on the Non-Proliferation of Nuclear Weapons (NPT), does not bar any Member State of the Treaty from carrying out research and development in the field of uranium enrichment, without notifying the Agency, provided that this research did not reach the stage that necessitates such notification and its submission to the safeguards system. Table 3 attached to my letter dated 7 July 1991 [table omitted] refers to this fact: the three processes are still in the early stage of research and development; there is no laboratory for isotope enrichment according to the definition of Article 98 of the Safeguards Agreement. Article 28 of the Safeguards Agreement, as you understand, refers to significant quantities of nuclear material. We would like to refer, in this connection, to the definition of the significant quantity of nuclear material, as specified in paragraph 89 of document IAEA/SG/INF/1, which amounts to 75 kg of enriched uranium at less than 20% ^{235}U. Therefore, half a kilogramme is far less than the significant quantity.

We would like to refer you to the findings of the Zangger Committee, which approved the control standards for the exportation of sensitive technologies, whose work was a main source for the material of the safeguards system. This Committee pointed out that the least amount of enriched uranium that could be submitted to safeguards is one effective kilogramme. We wish to refer you in this connection to paragraph 300 of document IAEA/SG/INF/1/Rev.1 issued in 1987.

All the above-mentioned facts confirm that the amount in question cannot be covered by the safeguards system.

With regard to your reference to the uranium enriched through an ultracentrifuge process, we have revised the English translation prepared by the Agency of our letter and the attached tables in the light of what you have mentioned in your letter, and we found a discrepancy between that translation and what you have referred to on the one hand, and between the Arabic text of our letter on the other hand. Therefore, we find it imperative to provide an accurate technical interpretation of this point.

A single centrifuge prototype, and not a successive chain, has been experimented on. The aim of the single prototype experiment was to determine the separation performance of the centrifuge. Therefore, the material was recycled in the centrifuge, where the enriched product was mixed with depleted products, and the mixture was used to feed the centrifuge. Since the experiment adopted the recycling principle, no enriched material was obtained. This is the accurate scientific interpretation of the reference in the table to the fact that no significant quantities were produced during the experiment, since the resulting enrichment effort was offset during the mixing process previously mentioned.

It is quite evident from the above that the enrichment process by the centrifuge method is still in the early stages of scientific research.

You have established a sort of relationship between the production of half a kilogramme of uranium enriched to 4% ^{235}U and Article 34(c) of the safeguards agreement. The three paragraphs of Article 34, as we understand, deal with the importation and exportation of nuclear material to and from Iraq and with Iraq's obligations thereupon to notify the Agency of such nuclear material. Article 34(c) refers to the importation into Iraq of nuclear material of any composition and purity at any stage in the nuclear fuel cycle. Since the amount of half a kilogramme of uranium enriched to 4% ^{235}U in question was not imported by Iraq but locally produced through R&D experiments, our interpretation of Article 34 is that it does not apply to this case. Even if we suppose that the provisions of Article 34(c) go beyond the subject of importation, we believe that our comments on Article 42, especially the definition of the technical terms therein, make us stick to our belief that Article 34(c) does not apply to the case of the half kilogramme of uranium enriched to 4% ^{235}U.

With regard to Article 42, to which you referred in your letter, the information referred to in Table 3 concerning the three enrichment methods does not mean in any way the existence of an installation, but simply technological compounds which are still in the early stages of development, whose technical specifications were not finally and comprehensively established. The comprehension of some technical and physical aspects is still incomplete and requires further research and development in order to reach technical and industrial design specifications that will be adopted for the construction of an integrated installation whose design capacity, operation and other technical details are known in such a way to provide the Agency with final design information.

The establishment of such specifications is not possible before carrying out real experiments using uranium. Therefore, our interpretation of Article 42 is that it does not apply to the present situation of the enrichment processes mentioned in Table 3 which was attached to my letter dated 7 July 1991.

As you may notice, we were keen to clarify in our message the scientific and technical facts in an accurate way and to explain our committed attitude with regard to the Safeguards Agreement. However, we are willing to send a specialized technical delegation, if you so wish, to provide answers and clarification for any enquiries you may have.

...

Annex 5

Letter from the Minister for Foreign Affairs of Iraq to the Director General, 12 July 1991

...

Further to our letter dated 10 July 1991, and with reference to your letter of 11 July 1991 pointing out that there were large quantities of unreported nuclear material under Articles 34(c) and 34(b) of the Safeguards Agreement, we wish to clarify the following.

1. As regards the amount of yellow cake and uranium dioxide, the Ministry of Defence earlier requested the Iraqi Atomic Energy Commission (IAEC) to conduct research and experiments on the uses of ceramic and metallic uranium for non-nuclear purposes, which included, among other things, reinforcing anti-tank warheads.

The said research has made good progress but has not yet been completed, particularly as far as technological and manufacturing aspects are concerned.

The programme in question requires large quantities of uranium, but as these quantities were needed for non-nuclear purposes, the IAEA was not informed thereof under Article 34(b) of the Safeguards Agreement.

In this connection we wish to recall that the IAEC, as a gesture of good will, has in fact always taken the initiative in giving Agency inspectors access to stores of nuclear material not included among the items subject to inspection whenever such material was present in the stores with other nuclear material which the inspectors were verifying; the inspectors had themselves pointed out that yellow cake was not subject to inspection, and on no occasion did they ever demand that the issue of notification be brought up.

2. As for uranium hexafluoride, the quantity of this material - containing only 465g of natural uranium - is very small, yet it is essential for any nuclear laboratory working with such materials: we believe it is not a quantity that calls for either reporting or control.

3. With regard to the uranium tetrachloride, these quantities are intended as feed material for the experimental systems required in connection with the electromagnetic enrichment process.

As you are aware, the ratio of the [flow of] material produced within the enrichment chamber to the feed material inserted into it is normally very low. This is a common feature of all enrichment processes. In electromagnetic enrichment in particular, cycling of the material within the separator is not automatic since the amount of feed material required depends on several factors: the vaporization rate of the material inside the chamber, the ionization efficiency, the ratio of positive uranium ions produced from the source to other ions, the fraction of produced material reaching the collector, the collection efficiency, the weight of uranium-235 in the collector and the rate of enrichment achieved.

Indeed, the production of half a kilogramme of 4%-enriched uranium requires about half a tonne of uranium tetrachloride. It is clear from the above that the amount of 2.5 tonnes mentioned in the table is the normal amount required as feed material for the experimental separators and does not, in our view, call for notification.

In conclusion, and in the light of the above clarifications, we feel that our reporting of this material (with our letter of 7 July 1991), pursuant to UN Security Council resolution 687 (1991), constitutes a corrective step which in our view means that we have adequately met the provisions of Article 19 of the Safeguards Agreement.

...

International Atomic Energy Agency, GOV/2532, 18 July 1991

11. International Atomic Energy Agency: Iraq's Non-Compliance with its Safeguards Obligations, Resolution adopted by the Board of Governors, 18 July 1991

The Board of Governors,

(a) *Stressing* the importance of non-proliferation of nuclear weapons to international and regional peace and security,

(b) *Expressing* grave concern about the conclusion of the report of the Director General (GOV/2530) that the Government of Iraq has failed to comply with its obligations under its safeguards agreement with the IAEA (INFCIRC/172),

(c) *Recalling* United Nations Security Council resolution 687 which, *inter alia*, called upon Iraq to declare all its nuclear activities to the International Atomic Energy Agency,

(d) *Noting* with appreciation the efforts of the Director General and his staff to implement the tasks assigned to the Agency by that resolution, and the diligent and effective conduct of the Agency's inspections of Iraqi nuclear activities, and

(e) *Expressing* grave concern about the evident deception and obstruction of IAEA inspectors in their efforts to carry out the Security Council's mandate in resolution 687, in violation of that resolution and the undertakings by Iraq governing the status, privileges and immunities of the IAEA and the inspection teams mandated under Security Council resolution 687,

1. *Finds*, on the basis of the report of the Director General in GOV/2530, that the Government of Iraq has not complied with its obligations under its safeguards agreement with the Agency (INFCIRC/172);

2. *Condemns* this non-compliance by the Government of Iraq with its safeguards agreement;

3. *Calls upon* the Government of Iraq to remedy this non-compliance forthwith, including placing any and all additional source and special fissionable material within Iraq's territory, under its jurisdiction or its control, regardless of quantity or location under Agency safeguards in accordance with the relevant provisions of INFCIRC/172 and in accordance with relevant technical determinations of the Agency;

4. *Decides*, in accordance with Article XII.C of the Statute, to report this non-compliance to all members of the Agency and to the Security Council and General Assembly of the United Nations;

5. *Calls upon* Iraq to cease all obstruction or interference with the IAEA inspection teams in their efforts to implement Security Council resolution 687;

6. *Requests* the Director General to keep the Board and the General Conference informed of progress in the implementation of this resolution so that they may consider appropriate action in accordance with Article XII.C and XIX.B of the Statute in the event of the Government of Iraq's failing to take fully corrective action; and

7. *Decides* to inscribe an item entitled "Iraq's non-compliance with its safeguards obligations" on the agenda of the September Board of Governors and requests the Director General to include such an item in the provisional agenda for the thirty-fifth regular session of the General Conference.

S/22871, 1 August 1991

12. Report of the Secretary-General, Plan for future ongoing monitoring and verification of Iraq's compliance with relevant parts of section C of Security Council resolution 687 (1991), 1 August 1991

I. GENERAL

A. *Introduction*

1. The present report is submitted in pursuance of Security Council resolution 687 (1991). In paragraph 10 of section C of that resolution, the Security Council requested the Secretary-General, in consultation with the Special Commission, to develop and submit for approval a plan for the ongoing monitoring and verification of Iraq's compliance with its obligations under that paragraph. The Plan is contained in section II of the present report.

2. As outlined in my report to the Security Council of 17 May 1991 (S/22614), the provisions of section C of resolution 687 (1991) lend themselves to a three-stage implementation procedure: gathering and assessment of information; disposal of weapons and facilities and all other items specified in paragraphs 8 and 12 of resolution 687 (1991); and ongoing monitoring and verification of Iraq's compliance. The first two stages are currently being implemented and will continue until their objectives are fully achieved.

3. The Plan submitted in the present report addresses the third stage, i.e. ongoing monitoring and verification of Iraq's compliance with its unconditional obligation not to use, retain, possess, develop, construct or otherwise acquire any weapons or related items prohibited under paragraphs 8 and 9 of resolution 687 (1991). Thus, monitoring and verification will need to cover not only military but also civilian sites, facilities, material and other items that could be used or activities that could be involved in contravention of Iraq's obligations under resolution 687 (1991).

4. The Plan should enter into force directly upon its approval by the Security Council, which means that the early stages of its implementation and the later stages of the disposal of existing prohibited weapons, facilities and related items would take place simultaneously. This would, at an early stage, prevent Iraq from developing new capabilities regarding the relevant weapons categories, thus already closing a potential loophole during the first stages of the implementation of section C of resolution 687 (1991). Carefully managed use of available resources would make it possible to carry out the dual tasks in parallel, to great effect. With the gradual completion of the disposal of Iraq's present weapons capabilities, resources can gradually be transformed and streamlined without therefore, at any stage, compromising the efficiency of the verification of Iraq's compliance with its obligations under resolution 687 (1991).

B. *Institutional and organizational aspects*

5. Bearing in mind that resolution 687 (1991) was adopted by the Security Council acting under Chapter VII of the Charter of the United Nations, it is assumed that the task of carrying out the monitoring and verification provided for under the Plan should be entrusted to an executive body under the authority of the Security Council. This is particularly important should any situation arise of non-compliance by Iraq with its obligations under section C of resolution 687 (1991).

6. The intrinsic interrelationship between paragraphs 8, 9 and 10 of resolution 687 (1991) requires that this body make direct use of the expertise, the information gathered and assessed and the experience gained by the Special Commission established pursuant to paragraph 9 of resolution 687 (1991).

7. In view of these considerations, it would appear most practical and efficient that a compliance unit be organized under the Special Commission in order to carry out the monitoring and verification tasks provided for under the Plan. The present arrangements for staffing would continue on a revised scale, with appropriate support from the Department for Disarmament Affairs. The financing of the Plan would have to be determined by the competent United Nations organs, possibly in the same way as the arrangements agreed upon for the present phase of the Special Commission's work.

8. The operational requirements will be similar to those now in place for the Special Commission. These include a staff at the United Nations Headquarters in New York to compile and analyse information, organize inspections and aerial overflights, prepare other field operations and provide general administrative support. A staff will be needed in the region to provide logistic, administrative and other support for field operations in Iraq.

C. *Cooperation with the Security Council Committee established by resolution 661 (1990) concerning the situation between Iraq and Kuwait*

9. Through resolution 661 (1990) and subsequent related resolutions, including resolution 687 (1991), a comprehensive set of sanctions was established to be implemented by all States against Iraq. The prohibition of the acquisition by Iraq of any weapons and related items specified in paragraphs 8 and 12 of resolution 687 (1991) and of the sale or supply to Iraq by other States of these items is of unlimited duration. However, it cannot be excluded that the Security Council, at a future date, may wish to review the present sanctions regarding items with dual use, i.e. items that could be used for prohibited as well as non-prohibited purposes. In order to ensure that such items are not used for prohibited purposes, the Plan submitted in the present report includes specific provisions for the monitoring and verification, from within Iraq, of any eventual import by Iraq of relevant items with dual use.

10. The efficacy of these provisions would be enhanced if they were complemented by transparency and timely information as regards any future sale or supply by other States to Iraq of relevant items with dual use. Such a comprehensive approach would call for the development of a mechanism that:

(a) Upholds the prohibition on the sale and supply to Iraq by other States of any weapons or related items prohibited under section C of resolution 687 (1991);

(b) Provides for timely information about any sale or supply to Iraq by other States of items that could be used not only for permitted purposes but also for purposes prohibited under resolution 687 (1991).

11. The Plan submitted in the present report contains in its annexes lists of items relevant to the monitoring and verification, from within Iraq, of prohibited items as well as of items with dual use. These should be taken into account in the development of a mechanism related to the sale or supply of items to Iraq by other countries.

12. Such a mechanism should be developed with the cooperation of the Special Commission and the Committee established by resolution 661 (1990) at the earliest possible date, and not later than before the lifting of sanctions covering relevant items.

II. THE PLAN

A. *Scope*

13. In accepting unconditionally Security Council resolution 687 (1991), Iraq has undertaken not to use, retain, possess, develop, construct or otherwise acquire:

(a) Any chemical or biological weapons or any stocks of agents or any related subsystems or components or any research, development, support or manufacturing facilities;

(b) Any ballistic missiles with a range greater than 150 kilometres or any related major parts, including launchers, or any repair or production facilities.

14. In order to ensure Iraq's compliance with these undertakings, the Special Commission shall, through inspections and through aerial overflights, as well as through the provision of information by Iraq, monitor and verify that activities, sites, facilities, material and other items, both military and civilian, are not used by Iraq in contravention of its obligations under Security Council resolution 687 (1991).

15. To this end, the provisions set forth in the Plan and its annexes, which constitute an integral part of the Plan, shall apply.

B. *General provisions*

1. *Information*

16. Iraq shall:

(a) Provide to the Special Commission, on a regular basis, full, correct and timely information on activities, sites, facilities, material and other items, both military and civilian, that might be used for purposes prohibited under paragraph 10 of resolution 687 (1991);

(b) Provide to the Special Commission full, correct and timely information on any additional activities, sites, facilities, material or other items that the Commission may designate for provision of information on a regular basis;

(c) Provide to the Special Commission, promptly and fully, any additional information or clarification that the Commission may request.

Further provisions related to the submission of information are set forth in sections C, D and E and in annexes II, III and IV of the Plan.

2. *Inspections and aerial overflights*

17. The Special Commission shall have the right:

(a) To designate for inspection any site, facility, activity, material or other item in Iraq;

(b) To inspect, at any time and without hindrance, any site or facility declared by Iraq or designated by the Special Commission;

(c) To inspect, at any time and without hindrance, any activity, material or other item at any site or facility, including any material or other item in movement;

(d) To inspect any number of declared or designated sites or facilities simultaneously or sequentially;

(e) To designate for aerial overflight any area, location, site or facility in Iraq;

(f) To carry out, at any time and without hindrance, aerial overflight by fixed- or rotary-wing aircraft with appropriate sensors as necessary, of any area, location, site or facility designated by the Special Commission;

(g) To carry out, at any time and without hindrance, all such other flights, by fixed-or rotary-wing aircraft, as it deems necessary.

18. Iraq shall:

(a) Accept unconditionally the inspection of any site, facility, activity, material or other item declared by Iraq or designated by the Special Commission;

(b) Accept unconditionally aerial overflight of any area, location, site or facility designated by the Special Commission or any other flight, by fixed- or rotary-wing aircraft used by the Special Commission;

(c) Provide immediate and unimpeded access to any site, facility, activity, material or other item to be inspected;

(d) Not obstruct aerial overflights or take concealment measures at any area, location, site or facility designated by the Special Commission for overflight;

(e) Accept unconditionally the inspectors and all other personnel designated by the Special Commission;

(f) Cooperate fully with the Special Commission and facilitate its inspections and overflights;

(g) Designate its inspection representative for each inspection to accompany the inspection team in Iraq.

19. Further provisions related to inspections and aerial overflights are set forth in annex I.

3. *National implementation measures*

20. Iraq shall adopt the necessary measures to implement its obligations under section C of resolution 687 (1991) and the present Plan, in particular:

(a) To prohibit all natural and legal persons under Iraq's jurisdiction or control from undertaking anywhere any activity that is prohibited for Iraq by resolution 687 (1991), by subsequent related Security Council resolutions or by the present Plan;

(b) To enact penal legislation which, in conformity with international law, shall extend to the activities referred to under subparagraph (a) above undertaken anywhere by any natural or legal persons under Iraq's jurisdiction or control.

21. Iraq shall inform the special Commission of legislative and administrative measures taken to implement resolution 687 (1991), not later than 30 days after the approval by the Security Council of the Plan and thereafter as determined by the Special Commission.

4. *Non-compliance*

22. In case the Special Commission discovers any item that Iraq, under resolution 687 (1991), is obliged to destroy or to yield to the Special Commission for destruction, removal or rendering harmless, the Special Commission shall have the right to take it into custody and shall provide for its disposal, as appropriate.

23. In case the Special Commission discovers any activity taking place in contravention of resolution 687 (1991), it shall have the right to call upon Iraq to halt the activity and to prevent its recurrence. The Special Commission shall also have the right to take any prohibited item involved into custody and shall provide for its disposal, as appropriate.

24. Findings by the Special Commission that indicate that Iraq is not in compliance with its obligations under resolution 687 (1991) shall be brought to the attention of the Security Council.

5. *Reports*

25. The Special Commission shall, through the Secretary-General, report to the Security Council every six months on the implementation of the Plan and at any other time the Security Council may request.

6. *Revisions*

26. The Special Commission may, after informing the Security Council, revise the technical and procedural provisions in annexes II, III and IV, including the lists of material, equipment and other items, in the light of information and experience gained in the course of the implementation of resolution 687 (1991) and the Plan. The Special Commission shall inform Iraq of any such change.

27. The present Plan shall enter into force immediately upon its approval by the Security Council. The duration of the Plan shall be determined by the Security Council.

C. *Provisions related to chemical items*

28. Chemicals, equipment and facilities set forth herein and in annex II could be used for purposes related to chemical weapons. They shall therefore be subject to monitoring and verification in accordance with the following additional provisions in order to ensure that Iraq does not use, develop, produce or otherwise acquire chemical weapons or related items prohibited under resolution 687 (1991).

29. Chemicals that could be used for the development, production or acquisition of chemical weapons but which also have significant uses for purposes not prohibited by

resolution 687 (1991) are set forth in list A in annex II. These chemicals may be used, developed, produced, stored or acquired solely for purposes not prohibited by resolution 687 (1991), subject to the provisions under paragraphs 30 and 31 below, and annex II.

30. Iraq shall, not later than 30 days after the adoption of the Plan by the Security Council, and on a regular basis thereafter, provide to the Special Commission information in accordance with annex II regarding:

(a) The total national quantity of the production, processing or consumption of any chemical specified in list A of annex II and of the import and export of any of these chemicals specifying the countries involved;

(b) Any site or facility that is involved in production, processing, consumption, storage, import or export of one tonne or more per year of any chemical specified in list A of annex II or which at any time has been involved in activities with any of these chemicals for chemical weapons purposes;

(c) Any site or facility that is involved in production or processing of organophosphorus chemicals or which is involved in production of organic chemicals by chlorination;

(d) Any site or facility where production, processing, consumption, storage, import or export of one tonne or more per year of any chemical specified in list A of annex II, or where production or processing of organophosphorus chemicals or where production of organic chemicals by chlorination is planned;

(e) Any import or any other acquisition of equipment or technologies intended for production and processing of any chemical specified in list A of annex II, of any organophosphorus chemical or for production of organic chemicals by chlorination.

31. Should Iraq plan any production, processing, consumption, storage, import or export not notified under paragraph 18 (d) above, it may begin such an activity only after providing to the Special Commission a special notification not later than one month in advance.

32. Chemicals that have little or no use except as chemical warfare agents or for the development, production or acquisition of chemical weapons or which have been used by Iraq as essential precursors for chemical weapons are set forth in list B of annex II. Iraq shall not retain, use, transfer, develop, produce, store, import or otherwise acquire these chemicals. Should Iraq require any chemical specified in list B of annex II, it shall submit a request to the Special Commission specifying precisely the chemical and the quantities required, the facility where it is to be used and the purpose of its use. The Special Commission will examine and decide on the request and establish the special arrangements it considers consistent with resolution 687 (1991).

33. Further provisions related to chemical items are set forth in annex II.

D. *Provisions related to biological items*

34. Micro-organisms and toxins, equipment and facilities set forth herein and in annex III could be used for purposes related to biological and toxin weapons affecting humans, animals or plants. They shall therefore be subject to monitoring and verification in accordance with the following additional provisions in order to ensure that Iraq does not use, develop, produce or otherwise acquire biological and toxin weapons or related items prohibited under resolution 687 (1991).

35. Iraq shall, not later than 30 days after the adoption of the present Plan by the Security Council, and on a regular basis thereafter, provide to the Special Commission information in accordance with annex III regarding:

(a) Any site or facility, except purely diagnostic facilities, at which work with toxins or with micro-organisms meeting the criteria for risk groups IV, III or II according to the classification in the 1983 World Health Organization (WHO) *Laboratory Biosafety Manual* is carried out, or any facilities at which work with genetic material coding for toxins or genes derived from the aforementioned micro-organisms is carried out;

(b) Any site or facility having a laboratory meeting the criteria for a "maximum containment laboratory" or "containment laboratory" as specified in the 1983 WHO *Laboratory Biosafety Manual*, such as those designated as biosafety level 4 (BL4) or P4, biosafety level 3 (BL3) or P3 or equivalent standards;

(c) Any site or facility at which fermentation or other means for the production of micro-organisms or toxins using vessels larger than 50 litres individually or 200 litres in the aggregate is carried out;

(d) Any site or facility for the bulk storage of toxins or of micro-organisms meeting the criteria for risk groups IV, III or II;

(e) Any site or facility for the production of vaccines;

(f) Any research, development, testing or other support or manufacturing facility for items and equipment specified in paragraph 1 of annex III;

(g) Any imports, other acquisition or exports of micro-organisms meeting the criteria for risk groups IV, III and II, toxins and vaccines, as well as related equipment and facilities.

36. Iraq shall, no later than 30 days after the adoption of the present Plan by the Security Council, and on a regular basis thereafter, provide to the Special Commission:

(a) A list of all documents of a scientific and technical nature published or prepared by any site or facility engaged in work relating to toxins or micro-organisms meeting the criteria for risk groups IV, III and II, including those of a theoretical nature. Documents of a purely diagnostic nature relating to risk group II micro-organisms are excepted;

(b) A description of any kind of work being conducted on the dissemination of micro-organisms or toxins into the environment or on processes that would lead to such dissemination, specifying the site or facility involved.

37. Iraq shall provide to the Special Commission information on all cases of infectious diseases affecting humans, animals or plants, that deviate, or seem to deviate, from the normal pattern or are caused by any micro-organism meeting the criteria for risk groups IV and III and on all cases of similar occurrences caused by toxins. The information shall be provided within one week of the occurrence and the standardized form contained in document BWC/CONF.II/EX/2 should be utilized as appropriate.

38. Iraq shall not:

(a) Import items referred to in paragraph 23 (g) above without giving prior notice to the Special Commission not later than 30 days in advance in accordance with annex III. As an exception, the emergency import of vaccines may take place with simultaneous notification to the Special Commission;

(b) Conduct any activities in the field of micro-organisms and toxins except by civilian personnel not in the employ of any military organization. Such activities shall be conducted openly; no classified or secret programmes or activities shall be permitted. The facilities engaged in such activities shall not be under the control of, or owned by, any military organization. Should any military organization need to be involved in such activities for prophylactic or therapeutic purposes, Iraq shall submit a request to the Special Commission specifying precisely the toxins, micro-organisms and the quantities required, the facility where they are to be used and the purpose of their use. The Special Commission will examine and decide on the request and establish the special arrangements it considers consistent with resolution 687 (1991);

(c) Conduct activities on diseases other than those indigenous to or immediately expected to break out in its environment;

(d) Conduct any breeding of vectors of human, animal or plant diseases. Should Iraq need to conduct any such activity, Iraq shall submit a request to the Special Commission specifying precisely its requirements, the facility where the activity is to take place and the purpose of the activity. The Special Commission will examine and decide on the request and establish the special arrangements it considers consistent with resolution 687 (1991);

(e) Possess at any one time more than one facility having a laboratory meeting the criteria for a "maximum containment laboratory" as specified in the 1983 WHO *Laboratory Biosafety Manual*, such as those designated as biosafety level 4 (BL4) or P4 or equivalent standard. Iraq shall not possess at any one time more than two facilities having a laboratory meeting the criteria for a "containment laboratory", such as those designated as BL3 or P3 or equivalent standard. Should Iraq require any additional such facilities, Iraq shall submit a request to the Special Commission specifying the precise requirement. The Special Commission will examine and decide on the request and establish the special arrangements it considers consistent with resolution 687 (1991).

39. Further provisions related to biological items are set forth in annex III.

E. *Provisions related to missiles*

40. Facilities, equipment, other items and technologies set forth herein and in annex IV could be used for the development, construction or acquisition of ballistic missiles with a range greater than 150 kilometres. They shall therefore be subject to monitoring and verification in accordance with the following additional provisions in order to ensure that Iraq does not use, develop, construct or acquire any ballistic missiles with a range greater than 150 kilometres or related items prohibited under resolution 687 (1991).

41. The range of missiles that are prohibited for Iraq shall be determined on the basis of the maximum distance that a missile is capable of flying over a ballistic trajectory with a zero delivery payload. The prohibition applies to any missiles, whether or not flying a ballistic trajectory, or delivery system, capable of such a range and to any related major parts of such missiles, which include missile/rocket stages, re-entry vehicles, solid- or liquid-fuel motors, guidance sets, thrust vector controls, warheads and fusing systems, launchers capable of launching ballistic missiles with a range greater than 150 kilometres and related principal launch equipment and transporters for such missiles. The prohibition also applies to any missiles not in themselves capable of such a range, but which are capable of such a range in combination with technologies such as tube- or gun-type launchers.

42. Iraq shall, not later than 30 days after the adoption of the present Plan by the Security Council and on a regular basis thereafter, provide to the Special Commission the following

(a) A list of all its missiles designed for use, or capable of being modified for use, in a surface-to-surface role with a range greater than 75 kilometres, specifying their name and type, type of propulsion, number of stages and/or boosters, guidance systems, warhead and re-entry vehicle types, launcher types, airframe and warhead transporters and the sites or facilities where these items or equipment are located;

(b) Information on any site or facility for such missiles, including sites or facilities for production, assembly, repair and maintenance, storage and operational bases, specifying their locations;

(c) Information on any site or facility for missile research, development and testing, specifying their locations;

(d) Information on the development, production or acquisition of the items, equipment and technologies listed in annex IV, specifying sites or facilities where such items, equipment and technologies are located, and the purposes for which they are being used.

43. Iraq shall notify the Special Commission of the developmental or test launch of any missiles not later than 14 days prior to the date of launch, specifying where and when the launch is to take place.

44. Iraq shall not construct, otherwise acquire or operate facilities for the use, development and production of ballistic missiles capable of a range greater than 150 kilometres, including facilities for research, development, manufacture, assembly, testing, storage, repair, training, flight simulating and operational use of such missiles, nor acquire related major parts specified in paragraph 29 and the items listed in annex IV for such missiles.

45. Further provisions related to missiles are set forth in annex IV.

Annex I

Detailed provisions related to inspections, aerial overflights, privileges and immunities

1. In addition to the basic rights and obligations set forth in paragraphs 5 and 6 of the Plan, the provisions set out in this annex shall apply.

Scope

2. The Special Commission shall have the right:

(a) To secure any site to be inspected and prevent any material or other item from being taken to or from the site until the inspection is concluded;

(b) To stop and inspect vehicles, ships, aircraft or any other means of transportation within Iraq;

(c) To inspect imports or exports of material and other items upon arrival or departure;

(d) To establish special modes of monitoring and inspection, including prolonged or continuous presence of inspectors or use of instruments.

Notification

3. The Special Commission shall, at a time it considers appropriate, notify Iraq of:

(a) The site, facility, activity, material or other item to be inspected;

(b) The name of the head of the inspection team (the Chief Inspector) and the estimated number of personnel who will take part in the inspection;

(c) The estimated time of departure and arrival of any flight from, to or within Iraq, and other appropriate details, by any aircraft of the Special Commission.

4. Iraq shall, upon receipt of the name of the Chief Inspector for an inspection, immediately inform the Special Commission of the name of the individual who will be the Iraqi Inspection Representative for the inspection.

Conduct of inspections or aerial overflights

5. The Special Commission shall have the right:

(a) To request, receive, examine and copy any record, data or information;

(b) To examine, retain, move or photograph, including by videotaping, any material or other item under inspection;

(c) To conduct interviews with any personnel at a site or facility under inspection, or with any Iraqi official;

(d) To install equipment or construct facilities for inspection, testing or monitoring activities;

(e) To take samples of any kind and perform on-site analyses of the samples using its own equipment;

(f) To remove and transfer samples outside Iraq for analysis off-site at laboratories designated by the Special Commission;

(g) To mark, tag or otherwise identify any material or other item;

(h) To use its own instrumentation to collect data during aerial overflights, including photographic, video, infrared and radar data.

6. Iraq shall:

(a) Provide clarification of any ambiguity that might arise during an inspection;

(b) Perform, upon request by the Special Commission, analysis of samples in the presence of inspectors, including on-site;

(c) Perform, upon request by the Special Commission, any additional task.

Travel, transport and communications

7. The Special Commission shall have the right:

(a) To unrestricted freedom of entry into and exit from Iraq, without delay or hindrance, for all its personnel, property, supplies, equipment, spare parts, material and other items, including means of transport;

(b) To unrestricted freedom of movement within Iraq, without advance notice, delay or hindrance, for all its personnel, property, supplies, equipment, spare parts, material, means of transport and other items;

(c) To fly the United Nations flag on the Special Commission's premises and its means of transport;

(d) To use its own means of transport, including fixed- and rotary-wing aircraft;

(e) To communicate from any place within Iraq, and without any hindrance, by radio, satellite or other forms of communication, and to connect with the United Nations by its radio and satellite network, as well as by telephone, telegraph and other means;

(f) To use codes and receive papers, correspondence and other items by courier or sealed bags.

8. Iraq shall:

(a) Permit, without delay or hindrance, the Special Commission's personnel, property, supplies, equipment, spare parts, material, means of transport and other items, to enter or leave Iraq, promptly issuing entry and exit visas if required and accepting United Nations laissez-passers or United Nations certificates as valid travel documents;

(b) Accept United Nations registration of means of transport on land, sea and in the air and United Nations licensing of the operators thereof;

(c) Provide priority clearance processing for aircraft used by the Special Commission;

(d) Provide, upon the request of the Special Commission, the means of transport, maps or other information needed;

(e) Take every necessary measure to ensure that the inspection team arrives at the site or facility to be inspected by the time notified by the Special Commission;

(f) Provide, upon the request of the Special Commission, appropriate means of communication;

(g) Provide, upon request by the Special Commission, appropriate escort and/or support personnel;

(h) Not interfere with or censor any communication to or from the Special Commission or its personnel.

Security, privileges and immunities

9. The Special Commission shall have the right to make its own arrangements to ensure the safety and security of its personnel and property and to provide custody of any material or item.

10. Iraq shall ensure the safety and security of the personnel and property of the Special Commission and shall provide the arrangements to this end when so requested by the Special Commission.

11. In addition and without prejudice to the foregoing provision, the Special Commission and any agency of the United Nations system participating in the carrying out of the Plan, its property, funds, assets and personnel shall enjoy the facilities, privileges and immunities provided for in the applicable convention or agreement, namely the Convention on the Privileges and Immunities of the United Nations, the Agreement on the Privileges and Immunities of the International Atomic Energy Agency (IAEA) and the Convention on the Privileges and Immunities of the Specialized Agencies.

12. Iraq shall extend to:

(a) The officers and other members of the Special Commission, whose names shall be communicated to the Government, the privileges and immunities, exemptions and facilities that are enjoyed by diplomatic envoys in accordance with international law;

(b) The officials of the United Nations, of IAEA and any of the specialized agencies of the United Nations, performing functions in connection with the implementation of the Plan, the privileges and immunities applicable to them under articles V and VII of the Convention on the Privileges and Immunities of the United Nations; or articles VI and IX of the Agreement on the Privileges and Immunities of the International Atomic Energy Agency; or articles VI and VIII of the Convention on the Privileges and Immunities of the Specialized Agencies;

(c) The technical experts and other specialists performing functions in connection with the implementation of the Plan, whose names shall be communicated to the Government upon arrival in Iraq, the privileges and immunities accorded to experts performing missions for the United Nations, for IAEA or for the specialized agencies of the United Nations under article VI of the Convention on the Privileges and Immunities of the United Nations, article VII of the Agreement on the Privileges and Immunities of the International Atomic Energy Agency, and the relevant annexes to the Convention on the Privileges and Immunities of the Specialized Agencies, respectively.

Other provisions

13. Iraq shall designate the Ministry responsible for liaison with the Special Commission and shall inform the Special Commission of the name or names of the liaison officers within that Ministry who shall have the full authority to secure for the Special Commission the effective implementation of the rights laid down in the Plan.

14. The official points of contact between Iraq and the Special Commission during the course of an inspection shall be the Chief Inspector designated by the Special Commission and the Inspection Representative designated by Iraq.

15. Iraq shall provide, at no cost to the Special Commission, in agreement with the Special Commission, all such premises as may be necessary for the accommodation and fulfilment of the functions of the Special Commission in Iraq. All such premises shall be inviolable and subject to the exclusive control and authority of the Special Commission.

16. For the purposes of the performance of the functions of the Special Commission in implementation of the Plan under paragraph 10 of Security Council resolution 687 (1991), the rights, facilities, privileges and immunities conferred in this annex where necessary supplement and elaborate upon the rights, facilities, privileges and immunities provided for in the exchange of notes between the Secretary-General of the United Nations and the Minister for Foreign Affairs of Iraq, which entered into force on 14 May 1991, regarding the status, privileges and immunities of the Special Commission as originally established pursuant to paragraph 9 of Security Council resolution 687 (1991). To the extent of any incompatibility, the provisions of this annex shall prevail.

Annex II

Provisions related to chemical items

[*A detailed list of compounds has been omitted.*]

...

3. The initial information under paragraph 18 of the Plan to be submitted not later than 30 days after the adoption of the Plan by the Security Council shall cover the period from 1 January 1989. Subsequent information shall be provided each 15 January and 15 July and shall

cover the six-month period prior to the provision of the information. The advance notification under paragraph 30(d) of the Plan shall cover the subsequent six months.

4. Whenever the information that Iraq is required to provide under section C of the Plan and this annex is equal to nil, Iraq shall provide nil returns.

5. The information on chemicals to be provided under section C of the Plan shall for each chemical include:

(a) The chemical name, common or trade name used by the site or the facility, structural formula and Chemical Abstracts Service registry number (if assigned);

(b) The purposes for which the chemical is produced, processed, consumed, stored, imported or exported;

(c) The total amount produced, processed, consumed, stored, imported or exported.

6. The information on sites or facilities to be provided under section C of the Plan shall for each site or facility include:

(a) The name of the site or facility and of the owner, company or enterprise operating the site or facility;

(b) The location of the site or facility;

(c) A general description of all types of activities at the site or facility;

(d) The source(s) of the financing of the site or facility, and of its activities.

7. The location of a site or facility shall be specified by means of the address and a site diagram. Each diagram shall be drawn to scale and shall indicate the boundaries of the site or facility, all road and rail entrances and exits and all structures on the site or facility, indicating their purpose. If the site or facility is located within a larger complex, the diagram shall specify the exact location of the site or facility within the complex. On each diagram, the geographic coordinates of a point within the site or facility shall be specified to the nearest second.

8. In addition to information specified in paragraph 6 of this annex, the following information shall be provided for each facility that is or will be involved in production, processing, consumption, storage, import or export of chemicals specified in list A of this annex:

(a) A detailed description of activities related to the chemical(s) specified in list A of this annex, including, as applicable, material-flow and process-flow diagrams, chemical reactions and end-use;

(b) A list of equipment used in activities related to chemical(s) specified in list A of this annex;

(c) The production capacity for the chemical(s) specified in list A of this annex.

9. In addition to information specified in paragraph 6 of this annex, the following information shall be provided for each site or facility that is or will be involved in production or processing of organophosphorus chemicals or involved in production of organic chemicals by chlorination:

(a) A detailed description of activities related to the relevant chemical(s), and the end-use(s) for which the chemicals are produced or processed;

(b) A detailed description of the processes used in the production or processing of organophosphorus chemicals or in the production of organic chemicals by chlorination, including material-flow and process-flow diagrams, chemical reactions and list of equipment involved.

10. The information on each import to be provided under section C of the Plan shall include:

(a) Specification of each item and the quantity imported and the purpose of its use in Iraq;

(b) Country from which the item is imported and the specific exporters;

(c) Point and time of entry of the item into Iraq;

(d) Site or facility where it is to be used.

Annex III

Provisions related to biological items

1. The following list contains items and equipment relevant to the acquisition of biological weapons or biological weapons capability:

(a) Detection or assay systems for micro-organisms and toxins;

(b) Biohazard containment equipment;

(c) Equipment for the encapsulation of live micro-organisms;

(d) Complex media for the growth of micro-organisms;

(e) Bio-reactors and fermentation vessels;

(f) Recombinant deoxyribonucleic acid (DNA), equipment for its isolation or production and equipment for the construction of synthetic genes;

(g) Equipment for the release into the environment of biological material;

(h) Equipment for studying the aerobiological characteristics of micro-organisms or toxins;

(i) Equipment for breeding of vectors of human, animal or plant diseases.

2. The initial information under paragraphs 35 and 36 of the Plan to be submitted not later than 30 days after the adoption of the Plan by the Security Council shall cover the period from 1 January 1989. Subsequent information shall be provided each 15 January and 15 July and shall cover the six-month period prior to the provision of the information.

3. Whenever the information that Iraq is required to provide under section D and this annex is equal to nil, Iraq shall provide nil returns.

4. The information on each site or facility to be provided under section D of the Plan shall include the following:

(a) The name of the site or facility and of the owner, company, or enterprise operating the facility;

(b) The location of the site or facility (including the address, geographic coordinates to the nearest second, location of the facility within any larger complex, including the specific building and any structure number);

(c) The source(s) of financing of the site or facility and of its activities;

(d) The main purpose of the site or facility;

(e) The level of protection, including, as applicable, the number and size of maximum containment or containment laboratories;

[*sic*] (f) is missing from list

(g) Scope and description of activities, including, as applicable, a list of types and quantities of micro-organisms, toxins or vaccines and equipment specified in paragraph 1 of this annex;

(h) A list of micro-organisms and toxins, equipment and vaccines imported for the use of the site or facility, or exported, indicating the countries involved.

5. The information on import to be provided under paragraphs 35(g) and 38(a) of the Plan shall cover:

(a) Toxins and micro-organisms meeting the criteria for risk groups IV, III, and II according to the classification in the 1983 WHO *Laboratory Biosafety Manual* and genetic material coding for toxins or genes derived from the aforementioned micro-organisms;

(b) Equipment and facilities for the production, utilization or storage of micro-organisms, toxins or vaccines;

(c) Personnel or material for training or technical support services related to the design, development, use, manufacture or support of items specified in paragraph 35(a) of the Plan and paragraphs 1 and 5 (a) of this annex;

and shall for each import into Iraq specify:

(a) Types and quantities of micro-organisms, toxins or vaccines;

(b) Quantities of any items listed under paragraph 1 of this annex;

(c) Country from which the micro-organisms, toxins, vaccines or items are imported and the specific exporter;

(d) Point and time of entry into Iraq;

(e) Site or facility where it is to be used and purpose of its use.

Annex IV

Provisions related to missiles

1. The following list contains items, equipment and technologies relevant to the development and manufacture of missiles that could be used in the development and manufacture of ballistic missiles capable of a range greater than 150 kilometres:

(a) Subsystems usable in missile systems:

(i) Individual rocket stages;

(ii) Re-entry vehicles, and specially designed equipment therefor;

(iii) Solid- or liquid-fuel rocket engines;

(iv) Guidance sets;

(v) Thrust vector controls;

(vi) Warhead safing, arming, fuzing and firing mechanisms;

(b) Propulsion components and equipment:

(i) Lightweight turbojet and turbofan engines;

(ii) Ramjet/Scramjet engines and production equipment therefor;

(iii) Rocket-motor cases and production equipment therefor;

(iv) Staging mechanisms and production equipment therefor;

(v) Liquid-fuel control systems and components therefor, specially designed to operate in vibrating environments of more than 12g rms between 20 Hz and 2,000 Hz;

(vi) Propellants and constituent chemicals for propellants;

(vii) Production technology or production equipment for the production, handling, mixing, curing, casting, pressing, machining and acceptance testing of the liquid- or solid-missile propellants and propellent constituents;

(c) Guidance and control equipment:

(i) Gyroscopes, accelerometers and inertial equipment and software therefor;

(ii) Flight control systems usable in missile systems;

(iii) Avionics equipment specially designed or modified for use in unmanned air vehicles or rocket systems and software and components therefor usable in missile systems;

(d) Equipment and technical data for the production of structural composites usable in missiles and components, accessories and software therefor;

(e) Pyrolytic deposition and densification equipment and technology;

(f) Launch and ground support equipment and facilities usable for missile systems;

(g) Analog computers, digital computers or digital differential analysers usable in air vehicles, rocket systems or missile systems;

(h) Test facilities and equipment usable for missile systems, to include vibration test equipment unsung digital control techniques, wind tunnels and test benches for solid or liquid fuel rockets;

(i) Specially designed software or components for missile design, production or operation;

(j) Materials and devices for reduced observables in missile systems;

(k) Material and devices for protecting missile systems against nuclear effects.

2. The initial information under paragraph 30 to be submitted not later than 30 days after the adoption of the Plan by the Security Council shall cover the period from 1 January 1989. Subsequent information shall be provided each 15 January and 15 July and shall cover the six-month period prior to the provision of the information.

3. Whenever the information which Iraq is required to provide under section E of the Plan and this annex is equal to nil, Iraq shall provide nil returns.

S/22884, 1 August 1991

13. Report of the Secretary-General on the implementation of paragraph 4 of Security Council resolution 700 (1991)

1. On 17 June 1991, the Security Council adopted resolution 700 (1991) in connection with its consideration of the item entitled "The situation between Iraq and Kuwait". By that resolution the Security Council approved the Guidelines for facilitating full international implementation of paragraphs 24, 25 and 27 of resolution 687 (1991), which had been developed by the Secretary-General pursuant to paragraph 26 of the same resolution.

2. Paragraph 4 of resolution 700 (1991) reads as follows:

> "*The Security Council*,
>
> ...
>
> "4. *Requests* all States, in accordance with paragraph 8 of the Guidelines, to report to the Secretary-General within 45 days on the measures they have instituted for meeting the obligations set out in paragraph 24 of resolution 687 (1991);".

3. Immediately following the adoption of resolution 700 (1991) on 17 June 1991, the Secretary-General transmitted the text of the resolution by telegram to the Minister for Foreign Affairs of Iraq.

4. By a note verbale dated 3 July 1991 the Secretary-General transmitted the text of resolution 700 (1991) as well as the text of his report (S/22660) to all other States, drawing their particular attention, *inter alia*, to paragraph 4 of the resolution and requesting them to submit by 1 August 1991 at the latest information on the measures instituted by their Governments for meeting the obligations set out in paragraph 24 of resolution 687 (1991). On the same day the Secretary-General also transmitted copies of resolution 700 (1991) and of his report (S/22660) to all international organizations.

5. As of 1 August 1991, replies have been received from 32 States, pursuant to paragraph 4 of resolution 700 (1991). Each of the replies has been issued as a document of the Security Council in the chronological order of receipt, as indicated below:

Norway, 8 July, (S/22783)
Israel, 9 July, (S/22784)
The Holy See, 9 July, (S/22802)
Hungary, 12 July, (S/22801)
France, 16 July, (S/22800)
Turkey, 18 July, (S/22815)
Ecuador, 23 July, (S/22851)
Japan, 24 July, (S/22835)
Belgium, 25 July, (S/22840)
United Kingdom, 25 July, (S/22841)
Spain, 25 July, (S/22842)
Malta, 26 July, (S/22852)
Greece, 26 July, (S/22858)
Sri Lanka, 29 July, (S/22848)
Singapore, 29 July, (S/22849)
Chile, 29 July, (S/22859)
Finland, 29 July, (S/22860)
China, 29 July, (S/22866)
Myanmar, 30 July, (S/22861)
Australia, 30 July, (S/22867)
Austria, 30 July, (S/22868)
Czechoslovakia, 31 July, (S/22869)
New Zealand, 31 July, (S/22874)
Italy, 31 July, (S/22880)
Thailand, 31 July, (S/22882)
Brazil, 1 August, (S/22875)
Ireland, 1 August, (S/22876)
Liechtenstein, 1 August, (S/22877)
Netherlands, 1 August, (S/22878)
Yugoslavia, 1 August, (S/22879)
Argentina, 1 August, (S/22881)
Sweden, 1 August, (S/22883)

International Atomic Energy Agency, GOV/INF/622, 5 August 1991

14. Plan Submitted by the IAEA for Future Ongoing Monitoring and Verification of Iraq's Compliance with its Undertaking under Paragraph 12 of Security Council resolution 687 (1991), 5 August 1991

As provided for in paragraph 13 of Security Council resolution 687, adopted on 3 April 1991, the Agency submits to the Security Council for its approval this plan for future ongoing monitoring and verification of Iraq's compliance with its undertaking under paragraph 12 of resolution 687.

In accordance with paragraph 12 of the resolution, Iraq is obliged:

- not to acquire or develop nuclear weapons or nuclear-weapons-usable material or any subsystems or components or any research, development, support or manufacturing facilities related to the above;

- to submit to the Secretary-General and the Director General of the IAEA within 15 days of adoption of the resolution a declaration of the locations, amounts and types of items specified above;

- to place all of its nuclear-weapons-usable materials under the exclusive control, for custody and removal, of the IAEA, with the assistance and cooperation of the Special Commission appointed by the Secretary-General in accordance with paragraph 9(b) of the resolution;

- to accept, in accordance with the arrangements provided for in paragraph 13 of the resolution, urgent on-site inspection and the destruction, removal or rendering harmless, as appropriate, of such items; and

- to accept the plan referred to in paragraph 13 for the future ongoing monitoring and verification of its compliance with these undertakings.

Pursuant to paragraph 13 of the resolution 687, the Director General of the International Atomic Energy Agency was requested, with the assistance and cooperation of the Special Commission:

- to carry out immediate on-site inspection of Iraq's nuclear capabilities based on Iraq's declarations and the designation of any additional locations by the Special Commission;

- to develop a plan for submission to the Security Council within forty-five days following adoption of the resolution calling for the destruction, removal, or rendering harmless as appropriate of the items proscribed under in paragraph 12 of the resolution;

- to carry out the plan within forty-five days following its approval by the Security Council; and

- to develop a plan, taking into account the rights and obligations of Iraq under the Treaty on the Non-Proliferation of Nuclear Weapons of 1 July 1968, for the future ongoing monitoring and verification of Iraq's compliance with paragraph 12 of the resolution, including an inventory of all nuclear material in Iraq subject to the Agency's verification and inspections to confirm that Agency safeguards cover all relevant nuclear activities in Iraq, to be submitted to the Security Council for approval within 120 days of adoption of the resolution.

The plan for future ongoing monitoring and verification has had to be developed while the immediate on-site inspection is still ongoing, and while the plan for the destruction, removal or rendering harmless of proscribed items is still in an early stage of implementation. Despite nearly 1,000 inspection days and an extensive mapping of nuclear activities in Iraq, the Agency has not yet been in a position to come to a conclusion on a complete inventory of activities and items in Iraq relevant to the resolution. In view of this, the present plan is, of necessity, provisional in nature, and may need to be supplemented in the light of results of the current ongoing activities undertaken by the IAEA in Iraq. The plan consists of two phases as described below. The role of the Agency in both phases will be to monitor and verify Iraq's compliance with its obligations under resolution 687, and any other relevant obligations determined by the Security Council.

I. *Current and Near-Term Monitoring and Verification*

The first phase is characterized by monitoring and verification activities related to the identification of all items proscribed under the resolution and to the removal, destruction or rendering harmless of all such items. This phase continues to be governed for the purpose of monitoring and verification by the existing arrangements reflected in the exchange of letters between the Secretary-General and the Foreign Minister of Iraq dated 6 May 1991 and 17 May 1991 concerning the privileges and immunities relevant to the conduct of activities pursuant to Security Council resolution 687. It is expected that during this phase, the sanctions currently imposed on Iraq by the Security Council will continue to apply and that the Security Council will continue to closely monitor the situation. As a practical matter, Iraq's nuclear activities during this period will be limited in nature. At this time, it is not possible to determine the duration of the first phase.

II. *Future Long-term Monitoring and Verification*

The second phase of this plan will be put into operation by decision of the Security Council upon completion of all the activities contemplated in the first phase. In accepting unconditionally Security Council resolution 687, as indicated above, the Government of Iraq undertook inter alia not to acquire or develop nuclear weapons or nuclear-weapons-usable material or any subsystems or components or any research, development, support or manufacturing facilities related to the above. During this phase, it is proposed, the IAEA will monitor and verify Iraq's compliance with these obligations.

The undertakings by Iraq under the resolution necessarily limit the nuclear activities otherwise open to Iraq under the Treaty on the Non-Proliferation of Nuclear Weapons (NPT). In particular, reprocessing, enrichment and the possession of nuclear weapons-usable material, and all related activities, are proscribed under the terms of Security Council resolution 687. The permissibility of Iraq's carrying out other nuclear activities is to a large measure dependent upon the position of the Security Council with regard to the continuation of sanctions.

The resolution does not define the term "nuclear-weapons-usable material". Nuclear-weapons-usable material or, as it is referred to in the practice of the Agency, direct-use material, is understood for the purposes of this plan to mean nuclear material which can be used for the manufacture of nuclear explosive components without transmutation or further enrichment. This includes plutonium containing less than 80% plutonium-238, uranium enriched to 20% or more U-235 (high enriched uranium) and uranium-233. Chemical compounds, mixtures of direct-use materials (e.g. mixed oxide) and plutonium contained in spent nuclear fuel also fall in this category. For the purposes of the plan, and in view of the fact that Iraq will be prohibited from having reprocessing capability, the proscription against the possession of nuclear-weapons-usable material would not be interpreted as precluding the possession of plutonium in spent fuel resulting from the use of low enriched uranium as fuel in a research or power reactor. To include such material in the proscription would necessitate the removal from Iraq of irradiated uranium enriched to 10 per cent which, in light of the small quantities of plutonium in the spent fuel, may not be cost effective in relationship to the non-proliferation benefit.

The obligation not to acquire or develop any subsystems or components or any research, development, support or manufacturing facilities related to nuclear-weapons-usable material would preclude all activities relevant to or connected with reprocessing of irradiated fuel and isotopic enrichment of uranium. This proscription would extend to any research and development activities directed at reprocessing and isotopic enrichment technologies, as well as laboratory-, pilot- and industrial-scale facilities. This would also preclude conversion preparatory for reprocessing or for enrichment.

The undertaking not to acquire or develop nuclear weapons or any subsystems or components or any research, development, support or manufacturing facilities related to nuclear weapons would include items or components that could significantly contribute to or that are intended for use in the development or production of nuclear weapons. Certain dual-use items may be necessary for the conduct of permitted nuclear activities in Iraq in the future. The Agency's activities under the plan will include identification of such dual-use items and monitoring or verification of the use of such items.

General provisions

Under Article II of the NPT, Iraq has an obligation not to acquire nuclear weapons or other nuclear explosive devices. The safeguards agreement with the Agency is designed to verify that nuclear material in peaceful nuclear activities is not diverted to such use. Iraq's undertakings under paragraph 12 of Security Council resolution 687 are broader in scope than any non-proliferation undertaking previously verified by the International Atomic Energy Agency. The plan for monitoring and verifying Iraq's compliance with those obligations will have to be commensurate with the scope of the undertakings and be so designed as to create confidence that the restrictions accepted by Iraq are actually complied with. This requires a more comprehensive approach than heretofore applied by the Agency.

Resolution 687 notes that the actions required of Iraq, including those relevant to nuclear weapons and nuclear-weapons-usable material, represent steps toward the goal of establishing in the Middle East a zone free from weapons of mass destruction. The terms of any such zone would have to be negotiated between the parties to such an arrangement. Nevertheless, verification features envisaged in the present plan may be found of interest in future discussions about verification in such a zone.

The plan is based on the following premises:

(a) The verification and monitoring activities contemplated in the plan will be carried out by the IAEA in accordance with detailed modalities to be developed by the Agency.

(b) All nuclear material, facilities and installations, as well as equipment and non-nuclear material which, in the judgment of the IAEA, is relevant to Iraq's undertaking under the resolution, shall be subject to monitoring and verification. The items subject to monitoring and verification will be identified to Iraq by the IAEA. This list of items may be added to or modified from time to time by the IAEA.

(c) While the approaches and techniques to be used under the plan draw upon the Agency's safeguards experience, the scope and intensity of the verification and monitoring under this plan are much greater in order to satisfy the requirements of Security Council resolution 687. These measures may be administered and operated by a special Secretariat unit.

(d) The safeguards agreement concluded with Iraq pursuant to the NPT shall continue to be in force. The verification activities pursuant to this plan will be carried out in a manner that takes into account the safeguards activities required under the safeguards agreement.

(e) In accordance with Articles IX and VII of the Agreement Governing the Relationship between the United Nations and the International Atomic Energy Agency,[*] [* Article IX provides that the Agency "shall co-operate with the Security Council by furnishing to it at its request such information and assistance as may be required in the exercise of its responsibility for the maintenance or restoration of international peace and security."

Article VII provides *inter alia* that, "At the invitation of the Security Council, the Director General may attend its meetings to supply it with information or give it other assistance within the competence of the Agency."] the Agency will report on the implementation of the plan to the Security Council at its request, and to any subsidiary organ that the Council may designate (i.e., the Special Commission or its successor).

(f) The activities under the plan for the future ongoing monitoring and verification of Iraq's compliance with paragraph 12 of the resolution (nuclear) will be closely coordinated with the monitoring and verification activities relevant to Iraq's compliance with paragraph 10 of the resolution (chemical, biological and missile), and with the body designated by the Security Council to carry out these activities (i.e., the Special Commission or its successor).

(g) Financing of the verification and monitoring activities by the Agency in Iraq under the present plan will be secured by the United Nations.

Obligations of Iraq

Iraq shall provide to the Agency, and maintain current, the following:

(a) An inventory of all nuclear material in Iraq, including nuclear material containing uranium or thorium which has not reached the composition and purity suitable for fuel fabrication or for being isotopically enriched, and notification to the Agency one month in advance of any change in the inventory; the inventory and any changes thereto shall include quantity, form, composition, location and use of such material.

(b) An inventory of all facilities and installations, as well as equipment and non-nuclear material relevant to Iraq's undertaking, and notification one month in advance of any change in the inventory; the inventory and any changes thereto shall include quantity, form and composition of such items, where applicable, as well as the location and use of all items on the inventory.

(c) Complete design information for any planned nuclear facility or installation 180 days before the start of construction of any such facility or installation.

(d) Information on Iraq's nuclear programme one year in advance and any changes to that programme before they are made.

(e) Other information or data which the Agency requires to enable it to monitor Iraq's compliance with resolution 687 and any other relevant Security Council resolutions.

Obligations of other States

Paragraphs 24, 25 and 27 of Security Council resolution 687, *inter alia*, direct States not to provide to Iraq any of the items proscribed in paragraph 12 of that resolution. In addition to that proscription, all States should be required by the Security Council to provide the Agency, one month in advance, with full and complete reporting of intended exports to Iraq of nuclear material, facilities, equipment, technological information, including training, and any other relevant items, including non-nuclear materials which could be used in proscribed activities. The IAEA will submit to the Security Council a list of items the export of which should be subject to advance reporting.

Rights of the IAEA

Without prejudice to the rights which the Agency has under the safeguards agreement with Iraq and under the Agreement on the Privileges and Immunities of the IAEA, the Agency should have the following rights to the extent deemed necessary by the Agency to enable it to carry out its verification and monitoring activities under the resolution. These rights are similar to those contained in the exchange of letters between the Secretary-General of the United Nations and the Government of Iraq dated 6 May 1991 and 17 May 1991 concerning privileges and immunities relevant to the conduct of activities pursuant to Security Council resolution 687.

(a) The right, on its own initiative or at the request of the Security Council or any body established or designated by it (i.e., the Special Commission or its successor), to carry out inspections of any locations or facilities in Iraq.

(b) The right to full and free access at any time to all locations, all persons and all information which, in the Agency's judgment, may be necessary for the verification of Iraq's undertaking. This includes unimpeded access to all nuclear material, facilities and installations, as well as equipment and non-nuclear material relevant to Iraq's undertaking, and the right to conduct unannounced inspections and inspections upon short notice. This also includes the right of the Agency to restrict and/or stop movement of suspected material and equipment.

(c) Freedom of entry and exit to and from Iraq without delay of Agency personnel and experts, supplies and equipment. No visas shall be required of such personnel travelling on a UN laissez-passer and possessing an inspection assignment document.

(d) Freedom of movement within Iraq of Agency personnel and experts, supplies and equipment.

(e) The right to request, receive, examine and copy any record, data or information and examine, retain, move or photograph, including videotape, any item relevant to the Agency's monitoring and verification activities.

(f) The right to install equipment and construct facilities for observation, testing, verification or monitoring activities.

(g) The right to take and analyse samples relevant to the Agency's monitoring and verification activities, as well as to remove and export samples for off-site analysis.

(h) The right to have its own means of transport and communication and the right to unrestricted communication by telephone, telegraph, radio or other means.

(i) The right to use fixed wing and helicopter overflights throughout Iraq for the purpose of inspection, surveillance, transportation and logistics.

Duration

The duration of the verification and monitoring plan established under Security Council resolution 687 shall be decided by the Security Council.

[*A more detailed Plan for Future Ongoing Monitoring and Verification contained in IAEA document GOV/INF/631 of 18 October 1991 will be reprinted in the next Volume in this Series, concering specifically the issues covered in this Chapter.*]

International Atomic Energy Agency, GOV/2530/Add.1, 9 August 1991

15. A Report by the IAEA Director General on Non-Compliance by Iraq with its Obligations under the Safeguards Agreement Concluded with the Agency, 9 August 1991

1. In document GOV/2530 the Director General reported to the Board on non-compliance by Iraq with its obligations under the safeguards agreement concluded by Iraq with the Agency, and on 18 July 1991 the Board adopted a resolution (contained in document GOV/2532) in which it - *inter alia* - found, on the basis of the Director General's report, that Iraq had not complied with those obligations. The Board requested him to keep it and the General Conference informed of progress in the implementation of that resolution.

2. Since that time it has become clear, as a result of inspections and from information obtained from the Iraqi authorities in the course of the inspections, that Iraq's non-compliance included the undeclared production and separation of plutonium in safeguarded facilities. The Annex to this document sets out the findings on the basis of which the Director General is bringing the matter to the attention of the Board in accordance with the resolution contained in document GOV/2532 and with the Agency's Statute.

Annex 1

1. In the course of the fourth inspection conducted by the IAEA pursuant to UN Security Council resolution 687 (1991), the inspection team obtained additional information in response to requests made by the IAEA during the third inspection. This information included a "List of Nuclear Material" dated 28 July 1991 [*not reproduced*]. An introductory note at the top of the list stated that "the table of nuclear material previously mentioned in the letter of the Iraqi Foreign Minister dated 7 July 1991 was rearranged in fulfilment of the promise of the Vice-President of the Iraqi Atomic Energy Commission ...". However, the "List of Nuclear Material" dated 28 July 1991 included approximately three grams of plutonium, whereas "Nuclear Material Table No. 9" enclosed with the Iraqi Foreign Minister's letter of 7 July 1991 did not mention plutonium (see

Annex 1 to GOV/2530). Another table enclosed with the letter of 7 July 1991 ("Table 7 Processing of spent nuclear fuel", also in Annex 1 to GOV/2530) provided a short description of laboratory activities, but it did not indicate the quantities of plutonium or uranium in the spent nuclear fuel which had been processed.

2. The Chief Inspector for the fourth inspection submitted a set of written questions (see Attachment 2) [*not reproduced*]. Replies by Iraq to questions 2.A, 5.A and C, and 10.B and C (see Attachment 3) [not reproduced] show the following:
   a. Approximately 3 g of plutonium in PuO_2 and solutions as a result of unreported irradiation of 46 UO_2 ceramic fuel rods (about 11 kg of uranium) in the IRT-5000 research reactor with subsequent reprocessing;
   b. Approximately 8 kg of natural uranium in the form of UO_2 pellets in two fuel elements which had been subjected to unreported irradiation;
   c. Approximately 11 kg of natural uranium in the form of UO_2 pellets in 60 cm long fuel assemblies prepared for irradiation in the IRT-5000 research reactor and subsequent reprocessing.

3. In the replies, it is stated that these materials were used for the purpose of carrying out "research and development (R&D) in the field of plutonium extraction from spent nuclear fuel" and "assessment processes of ceramic fuel manufactured in the ERLFF (Experimental Research Laboratory for Fuel Fabrication)" with a view to determining "operational conditions for the manufacture of ceramic nuclear fuel which can be used in nuclear power plants".

4. Although the IRT-5000 research reactor has a low potential as a producer of plutonium, any production and recovery of plutonium by Iraq without due notifications to the Agency is a non-compliance with the provisions of INFCIRC/172, the general part of the subsidiary arrangements, and the facility attachments for the IRT-5000 research reactor and the Experimental Research Laboratory for Fuel Fabrication. In particular, the modifications to the design information should have been provided to the Agency not later than 60 days before each modification was scheduled to be completed.

5. These research and development activities in plutonium production and separation are not comparable in terms of significance to Iraq's industrial-scale efforts to produce enriched uranium as identified in GOV/2530. However, the fact that the activities with respect to plutonium occurred in safeguarded facilities is of special concern.

International Atomic Energy Agency, GOV/INF/625, 6 September 1991

16. Letter from the Resident Representative of Iraq to the IAEA Director General, 3 September 1991

The attached communication of 3 September 1991 addressed to the Director General and setting forth the views of Iraq on "A report by the Director General on non-compliance by Iraq with its obligations under the safeguards agreement concluded with the Agency" contained in document GOV/2530/Add.1 is being circulated at the request of the Resident Representative of Iraq.

Attachment

1. In his letter of 7 July 1991 to the Secretary-General of the United Nations the Foreign Minister of Iraq referred to certain laboratory activities relating to ceramic fuel and its irradiation in the IRT-5000 research reactor. Although the inspection team and the Secretariat could have sought further clarifications on the subject and could have included it in the agenda of the special meeting of the Board of Governors held on 18 July 1991, they did not do so. Only part of the matter was dealt with at that meeting, the other part being left for discussion at the following meeting. This was an attempt to persist in accusing Iraq of non-compliance with the Safeguards Agreement.

2. The Agency and its Department of Safeguards are fully aware of the IRT-5000 reactor's specifications which were provided by Iraq in accordance with its obligations under the Safeguards Agreement. The reactor contains vertical channels which have been used for over 20 years to irradiate various materials for the production of radioisotopes employed in medical diagnosis and therapy. For a number of years uranium has been one of the materials irradiated in this reactor. The researchers published their work in scientific journals and in the annual reports of the Iraqi Atomic Energy Commission (IAEC), copies of which were sent to the Agency's Library.

The Department of Safeguards never requested the reactor personnel or any other Iraqi authority to enter the data on irradiation in the operating records. Nor did it consider this a violation of the Safeguards Agreement. Why should this issue be raised now, especially as, during the first inspection mission, Iraq did declare its activities relating to fuel fabrication, processing of irradiated fuel pins and separation of uranium and plutonium therefrom?

3. The Agency's insistence that it should be provided with full information at once completely ignores the reality of what has happened in Iraq as a result of the aggression which it suffered. The bombs which were dropped on Iraq and its installations, factories and towns weighed more than all the bombs used during World War II. The Atomic Energy Commission's installations bore the brunt of the American bombing, which totally destroyed these installations and as a result of which most material, equipment and documents of importance were lost. Logistics were also seriously affected. We see that, instead of raising their voice against and condemning the American-led 30-nation aggression against safeguarded installations, the Agency and its Board of Governors are demanding that Iraq take meaningless measures as though the conditions in Iraq were normal. That the inspectors persisted during each of their visits in demanding, in an unprogrammed manner and sometimes even on the spot, detailed information which is very difficult to obtain under such conditions indicates deliberate intention to show that Iraq is not co-operating with the International Inspection Teams and, consequently, not complying with the Board's resolution.

4. The Iraqi authorities have made extraordinary efforts to retrieve and collect material buried under debris and to make it available to the inspection teams. Any objective observer will recognize that an operation of such magnitude and difficulty takes time and can only yield results little by little. The inspectors should have appreciated the work done by the Iraqi team, which was able to complete this huge task in record time. It must also be pointed out that no one could have found all this material buried under debris but for Iraq's sincere desire

and its honest decision to declare fully all it had in the nuclear field and to leave no part of it undeclared.

5. The small quantity of plutonium produced is insignificant from the scientific and practical standpoints and indeed similar quantities are produced in scores of laboratory experiments all over the world without arousing the Agency's interest. Why should some wish to portray such a trivial matter as a serious problem, making the IAEA mobilize legal, technical and administrative brains (putting in long hours of work and incurring enormous costs) for this purpose? The Director General has emphasized that such a quantity of plutonium is not significant from the practical point of view.

6. The fuel bundles mentioned in paragraph 2(c) of document GOV/2530/Add.1 are not bundles, nor are they intended for irradiation purposes. They are fuel pins used under the programme of the regular fuel laboratory, whose specifications and activities are known to the Agency as they are subject to safeguards. These fuel pins were fabricated for experimental purposes and are not suitable for making bundles since they are of various types. The fuel laboratory's programme of work involves fabrication of fuel of various forms and types, which are then dismantled and refabricated for experiments related to fuel fabrication. Hence the quantity of 11 kg of natural uranium mentioned in paragraph 2(c) was not at any time intended for irradiation purposes.

7. In compliance with the resolution adopted by the Board of Governors at its meeting held on 18 July 1991, Iraq provided, in addition to the information contained in the Foreign Minister's letters, lists of fuel found under debris and supplied without delay data and explanations to the third and fourth inspection teams, held several meetings with them and replied to all their queries. As a result, the material was collected in its entirety, the Agency's seal was affixed to it and it is ready for any further action that may be decided on.

8. The measures taken by Iraq clearly reflect its desire to comply with the resolution of the Board of Governors and to co-operate fully with the inspection teams. Why then should such issues be raised against Iraq despite its commitment to implement the Board's resolution? Would it have been better, then, for Iraq to conceal this material and information in order to appear in a blameless light?

S/22998, 1 September 1991; GOV/INF/626, 9 September 1991

17. Letter from the Minister for Foreign Affairs of Iraq to the Secretary-General of the United Nations, 28 August 1991

The attached text of a letter addressed to the Secretary-General of the United Nations by the Minister for Foreign Affairs of the Republic of Iraq is being circulated at the request of the Resident Representative of Iraq to the Agency.

...

I have the honour to refer to Security Council resolution 707 (1991).

The Government of Iraq considers that this resolution is unwarranted and that, like many of the other resolutions of the Council, it was adopted for motives based on the desire of a number of influential parties in the Security Council to harm Iraq and to contrive yet more pretexts for the non-implementation of the particular provisions of the Security Council resolutions from which Iraq may benefit by a lifting or mitigation of the unjust economic embargo imposed upon it. Iraq has fulfilled all of its obligations under the terms of resolution 687 (1991) in the manner requested by the inspection teams in general and the nuclear inspection teams in particular. It has done so by declaring all aspects of the Iraqi nuclear programme, whether in letters addressed to you or in those exchanged by the Chief of the Iraqi team and the Chiefs of the inspection teams that have visited Iraq. This has also been done in the seminars held, by answering all questions asked, and in the direct meetings held with those responsible for the nuclear programme and with research workers. This demonstrates the full cooperation that has been shown by the Iraqi authorities concerned.

For greater precision, we should like to state our view with regard to the provisions of the operative paragraphs of the Security Council resolution in question.

1. With regard to paragraphs 1 and 2, in which Iraq is condemned twice in the same resolution, it must be said that Iraq has adhered to all of its undertakings under the terms of Security Council resolution 687 (1991). It has, moreover, complied with the safeguards agreement concluded with the International Atomic Energy Agency (IAEA). It has done so by means of the full disclosure of all aspects of the Iraqi nuclear programme and the measures it has taken on remedial action in implementation of the resolution adopted by the IAEA Board of Governors on 18 July 1991. We should like once more to ask the question we have addressed to IAEA on more than one occasion: what more is now required of us, after all the measures we have taken and all the information we have provided, so that Iraq may meet all of its obligations under the terms of the resolution?

2. With regard to paragraph 3 (i) of resolution 707 (1991), Iraq has already provided full, final and complete disclosure, as required by resolution 687 (1991), of all aspects of its programmes. There are no programmes of this type, of any kind whatever, that Iraq has not declared.

3. Since 28 June 1991, the inspection teams have noted no obstacle to their work in gaining access to any and all areas, facilities, equipment, records and means of transportation which they wish to inspect, as demanded in paragraph 3 (ii). We should like, in this connection, to refer to the recent reports of the inspection teams, including that of the third nuclear inspection team contained in document GOV/INF/621 of 2 August 1991, in which reference is made to the full cooperation provided by the Iraqi side. We should like to ask once again: what site is there that a team has not been permitted to enter and inspect?

4. With regard to paragraph 3 (iii), the Government of Iraq took the decision, as of 28 June 1991, to cease any movement or destruction of any material or equipment relating to Security Council resolution 687 (1991). With the arrival of the third nuclear inspection team, agreement was reached by the Chief of the team and his Iraqi counterpart on the movement of certain equipment, after it had been seen by the team, to an appropriate location so as to facilitate future monitoring and inspection by the inspection teams. Certain of these measures were taken under the supervision of members of the third team, and the fourth team once again verified them. Agreement was also reached with the Chief of the fourth team on the continued movement and assembly of those materials and equipment that the team had seen and recorded to the collection sites on which the two parties had agreed for the purpose of facilitating future inspections.

5. Paragraph 3 (iv) refers to the concomitants of an issue which has become part of the past and which was over and done with even before the arrival of the third nuclear inspection team in the first week of July 1991. The third team examined all items and, together with the Iraqi side, undertook its removal to the locations agreed on. We therefore wish to ask what items are still outside the supervision of the inspection teams and to what were they denied access.

We should be very grateful if you or the Special Committee would kindly inform us about such items as are referred to in paragraph 3 (iv). Since there were no such items, we wonder what were the grounds for including this paragraph in the resolution.

6. With regard to paragraph 3 (v), Iraq has already given its opinion concerning aircraft flights. Although Iraq has no objections to that in principle, all that Iraq wishes to make clear, for its part, is that there are issues relating to administration, communications and logistics that must be taken into consideration in order to guarantee the safety of the aircraft and their crews and passengers and that Iraq is most concerned about that and hopes that the issue will be resolved by agreement and cooperation with the competent Iraqi authorities, in order to safeguard the security and safety of all.

7. With regard to the halting of all nuclear activities of any kind, as referred to in paragraph 3 (vi), although this goes beyond the measures set forth in resolution 687 (1991), from the scientific and the practical viewpoints there is no longer any nuclear activity, even in the most elementary sense, following the comprehensive destruction of Iraqi nuclear locations - reactors, laboratories, materials and other. This is referred to also in the report of the Director-General of the International Atomic Energy Agency.

I wish to point out that all the requirements of privileges and immunities and travel facilities of the inspection teams and medical care for them, referred to in paragraphs 3 (vii) and 3 (viii), have been made available in full and to the furthest extent possible in the light of the economic embargo imposed on Iraq. The recent reports of the inspection teams are the best testimony to that.

8. With regard to paragraph 5, Iraq reaffirms its full commitment to its international undertakings, including the Non-Proliferation Treaty and the Safeguards Agreement with the International Atomic Energy Agency.

The preambular and operative paragraphs of resolution 707 (1991) are based on the provisions of resolution 687 (1991), but it deliberately overlooks the rights of Iraq set forth in resolution 687 (1991). In this connection, we wish to inquire what is requested of Iraq, in order that it may show even greater good will in demonstrating its compliance with Security Council resolutions.

We wish also to ask how long the Security Council will disregard the rights of Iraq laid down in Security Council resolutions and when the iniquitous economic embargo imposed on its people will be lifted.

...

International Atomic Energy Agency, GC(XXXV)/RES/568, September 1991

18. Resolution adopted during the 341st plenary meeting of the IAEA General Conference, 20 September 1991

The General Conference,

(a) *Noting* United Nations Security Council resolutions 687 and 707,

(b) *Deploring* Iraq's non-compliance with its safeguards obligations with the IAEA and violation of its obligations under the Treaty on the Non-Proliferation of Nuclear Weapons and Security Council resolution 687,

(c) *Recalling* with approval the statements and actions of the Director General and the Board of Governors concerning Iraq's non-compliance with its nuclear non-proliferation obligations, including the Board resolution of 18 July 1991 and the report by the Board to the General Conference dated 13 September 1991, and

(d) *Deeply concerned* by continuing Iraqi efforts to obstruct implementation of Security Council resolutions 687 and 707,

1. *Supports* the above mentioned actions taken by the Board of Governors;

2. *Strongly condemns* Iraq's non-compliance with its nuclear non-proliferation obligations, including its safeguards agreements with the IAEA;

3. *Demands* that Iraq immediately and fully comply with all of its nuclear non-proliferation obligations;

4. *Commends* the Director General and his staff for their strenuous efforts in the implementation of Security Council resolutions 687 and 707, in particular the detection and destruction or otherwise rendering inoffensive equipment and material which could be used for nuclear weapons; and

5. *Requests* the Director General to report the views of the General Conference to the Secretary-General, and to report to the Board of Governors and to the thirty-sixth General Conference on his efforts to implement Security Council resolutions 687 and 707, and decides to remain seized of this issue.

International Atomic Energy Agency, GOV/INF/627, 26 September 1991

19. Statement issued by the Ministry of Foreign Affairs of Iraq, 23 September 1991

1. The Director General has received from the Resident Representative of Iraq a letter under cover of which the Resident Representative has forwarded a copy of a statement issued by the Iraqi Ministry of Foreign Affairs. The letter and the statement are being circulated at the request of the Resident Representative. They are contained in Attachments 1 and 2 to this document.

2. Attachments 3-8 contain letters dated 23 and 24 September 1991 from the Director General to the Iraqi Minister for Foreign Affairs and communications dated 23 and 24 September 1991 from the Director General to the United Nations Secretary-General.

Attachment 1

Letter to the Director General from the Resident Representative of Iraq, 24 September

I have the honour to forward to you a copy of the statement issued by the Ministry of Foreign Affairs of the Republic of Iraq in connection with the reported dispute between the Iraqi authorities and the inspection team headed by Mr. David Kay over certain documents.

Contrary to Mr. Kay's claims, the statement shows that the Iraqi authorities have indeed allowed the team to take custody of these documents provided that the transfer is done in a proper manner. The team was asked to make a listing of the documents wanted and acknowledge their receipt in writing. Such a procedure was necessary to ensure that no document is lost and no non-authentic document is added. The team is still in a position to acquire the documents they sought.

Taking these explanations into account, it appears that actions taken by the IAEA on 23 September 1991 which were based on Mr. Kay's report - i.e. informing the UN Secretary-General and sending a letter to the Minister of Foreign Affairs of Iraq - were done in haste and without due verification of Mr. Kay's report.

I have the honour to request your Excellency to bring this note and the statement of the Foreign Ministry to the attention of the Chairman of the Special Commission and all States members of the Board of Governors of the IAEA.

Attachment 2

24 September 1991

Text of a statement issued by the Foreign Ministry spokesman concerning a news item carried by foreign media on 23 September 1991

Today 23.9.1991 foreign media carried a distorted news item claiming that the Iraqi authorities had prevented the sixth nuclear inspection team currently in Baghdad from taking possession of certain documents and that Iraq had thus violated its commitments under resolution 687.

In clarifying the facts, we should like to state the following: In the early morning of Monday 23.9.1991, the sixth nuclear inspection team, accompanied by the competent Iraqi team, visited one of the buildings in Baghdad for inspection purposes. Upon entering the building and checking some of the documents there, the inspection team wished to take possession of a part of those documents. The competent Iraqi authorities agreed to this request, subject to the preparation of a record of handing over and receipt of the documents which the team wanted to take possession of. The Foreign Ministry spokesman went on to say:

It is clear from the above that the competent Iraqi authorities did not prevent the inspection team from taking possession of the documents requested; they had only asked for a record to be prepared for handing over and receipt of the documents which Iraq had the right to do, lest some fake documents or papers should be slipped among these documents and then be attributed to Iraq as being among the documents taken by the inspection team, giving a pretext to some ill-intentioned quarters to direct baseless accusations against Iraq. This is all that the Iraqi side had asked for; however, the inspection team did not accept the Iraqi request which involved no more than the exercise of a right agreed upon with all inspection teams, a right which has been effectively observed in dealings with other inspection teams when they wished to take possession of documents or equipment.

The Foreign Ministry spokesman concluded: Iraq stresses that the documents requested by the inspection team are available in the building, and the team can take whatever it wishes from among these documents after preparing a record of handing over and receipt, to be signed by both the inspection team and the competent Iraqi side.

Attachment 3

23 September 1991

Your Excellency,

On 23 September 1991, the sixth IAEA inspection team was prevented by Iraqi authorities from carrying out the activities entrusted to the Agency under Security Council resolution 687 (1991).

A convoy of Agency vehicles into which documents were loaded by inspectors were refused exit from the premises. The documents were then forcibly removed from the vehicles by the Iraqi authorities.

I have reported this obstruction met by our inspectors to the Security Council through the Secretary-General.

I hereby strongly protest the obstruction of the work of the inspectors. They have every right under Security Council resolutions 687 (1991) and 707 (1991) to take into custody documents relevant to nuclear activities in Iraq. The action by the Iraqi authorities is in clear violation of the obligations of Iraq under these resolutions and of the exchange of letters between the Secretary-General and you. In particular, I refer to the right of the Agency "to request, receive, examine and copy any record, data or information or examine, retain, move or photograph, including videotape" any item relevant to its activities.

I demand that the documents taken from the inspectors be immediately returned undamaged and unaltered in any form, and that there be no repetition of any obstruction of the teams carrying out inspections pursuant to Security Council resolution 687.

(Signed) Hans Blix

Attachment 4

24 September 1991

Your Excellency,

In my letter of 23 September 1991, I registered my protest to the actions taken that day by the Iraqi authorities in the course of an inspection being carried out by the sixth IAEA nuclear inspection team.

At 06:00 hours Baghdad time today, another inspection was begun by the Agency team at a building in Baghdad where administrative records of the Iraqi Atomic Energy Commission are stored. The inspection was undertaken in accordance with agreed procedures and continued until approximately 11:00 hours Baghdad time. At that time, the Iraqi authorities, contrary to the agreed procedures, prevented the team from copying the remaining documents being reviewed. The inspection was terminated and the team boarded the UN vehicle awaiting them, carrying the copies which they had been able to make.

The team's exit was then blocked by Iraqi security. The team was advised that they would be unable to leave the premises unless they submitted to personal search and surrendered all photographs, films and videotapes and all copies of Iraqi documents. As of our last communication from Baghdad, the inspectors have been detained for over six hours.

I must further protest these actions by the Iraqi authorities and I insist that measures be taken immediately to secure the unconditional and immediate exit of the inspection team from the premises.

I have informed the Secretary-General of this matter and requested that it be brought to the urgent attention of the Security Council.

(Signed) Hans Blix

Attachment 5

23 September 1991

To: UN Secretary-General, United Nations, New York
From: Hans Blix, Director General, IAEA, Vienna

Subject: *Nuclear Weapons Development Program*

This morning at 06:45 a.m. Vienna time, the Chief Inspector of the IAEA team now operating in Iraq under resolution 687 reported that inspectors had found documentary evidence that Iraq was engaged in a substantial nuclear weapons development program.

In the course of a short-notice inspection in an office building in Baghdad, the inspectors found that several rooms had been emptied of all documents. Other rooms, however, contained drawings and other documents showing work unequivocally relating to nuclear weaponization activities.

You may wish to bring this information to the attention of the Security Council.

The inspection will be continuing this week, after which the Chief Inspector and I myself will be available for reporting to you and to the Security Council if this is considered desirable.

Attachment 6

23 September 1991

To: UN Secretary-General, United Nations, New York
From: Hans Blix, Director General, IAEA, Vienna

Subject: ***Resolution 687 - Field activity of the IAEA 6th inspection - 23 September 1991***

Following my earlier fax on the subject matter, I am now (12 noon Vienna time) informed by the Chief Inspector in Baghdad that he is facing refusal by the Iraqi authorities to allow the IAEA team to take custody of the documents found.

It is the judgement of the Agency that these documents fall into the category of those items which eventually will have to be removed, destroyed or rendered harmless under resolution 687 (1991) of the UN Security Council.

While efforts are being made by the Chief Inspector to have the Iraqis respect the right of the Agency to take evidence into custody and at the same time to preclude that the documents are again made use of for weapon development purposes, I thought you may wish to bring this development to the attention of the Security Council.

Mr. Nelson Sievering, who has been introduced to you as my personal representative for Agency contacts with the UN in matters regarding resolution 687 is in New York and is authorised by us to represent the Agency and to present information on our behalf.

Attachment 7

23 September 1991

To: UN Secretary-General, United Nations, New York
From: Hans Blix, Director General, IAEA, Vienna

Subject: *6th IAEA inspection in Iraq pursuant to resolution 687*

The radio operator at UNSCOM-Baghdad relayed the following message from IAEA Chief Inspector David Kay at 17:45 hours Vienna time:

> "Documents being forcibly removed from vehicles in convoy".

This message followed a previous one transmitted at 17:00 hours, which read:

> "Convoy stopped from exiting the facility".

The attempts made by the Chief Inspector to have the Iraqis respect the right of the Agency "to request, receive, examine and copy any record, data or information or examine, retain, move or photograph, including videotape any item relevant to the Special Commission activities ..." have failed and this is a clear violation of the Iraqi acceptance of the terms contained in your letter of 6 May 1991 to the Iraqi Minister of Foreign Affairs.

I am consulting with the Special Commission for the course of action which must now be taken with regard to the continuation of the inspection.

Attachment 8

24 September 1991

Dear Secretary-General,

At 06:00 hours Baghdad time on Tuesday, 24 September, an inspection was begun by the sixth IAEA nuclear inspection team at a building in Baghdad where administrative records of the Iraqi Atomic Energy Commission are stored. The building contained documents related to foreign procurement relevant to the Iraqi nuclear programme, as well as information concerning high-level personnel engaged in different aspects of the Iraqi nuclear programme.

The inspection initially proceeded without incident until approximately 11:00 Baghdad time, when the Iraqi authorities prevented the inspection team, over the strong protest of the Chief Inspector, from copying the documents which the team was reviewing. Iraqi security surrounded the premises and blocked the exits. The inspection was terminated and the team left the building with the copies they had been able to make, and entered the UN vehicle awaiting them. The inspection team was then told that they would not be allowed to leave the premises unless they underwent personal search and surrendered all photographs, films and video tapes and all copies of Iraqi documents. At 13:30 Baghdad time, we received a new communication informing us that the inspection team was still being detained, but that the team was prepared to remain in the bus until further instructions are provided.

To carry out its activities in Iraq pursuant to Security Council resolution 687, the IAEA must have access to all documents relevant to Iraq's nuclear capabilities, and the authority to determine the relevance of any such documents, data and information. Of equal importance is the immunity of the inspection officials from detention and their right to unrestricted freedom of movement within Iraq

From the above, it is clear that as a result of Iraq's breach of its obligations under resolutions 687 (1991) and 707 (1991), and the exchange of letters between the Foreign Minister of Iraq and you on privileges and immunities, which entered into force on 14 May 1991, the inspection team is prevented from carrying out its activities in Iraq.

May I request that this matter be brought to the urgent attention of the Security Council.

(Signed) Hans Blix

20. UN Press Release, 27 September 1991

The Security Council, in a statement issued on 25 September, demanded that the UN inspection team held by Iraqi authorities be immediately allowed to leave the site and to take the document "they deem appropriate" with them. the sixth International Atomic Energy Agency nuclear inspection team was detained by Iraqi authorities on 24 September on premises where administrate records of the Iraqi Atomic Energy Commission are stored. ...

21. UN Press Release, 12 December 1991

UN TEAM FINDS CHEMICAL BOMB-MAKING EQUIPMENT AT SUGAR FACTORY IN IRAQ

The first combined chemical and biological weapons inspection team to Iraq has reported the discovery of chemical bomb-making equipment at a sugar factory in Mosul. The Special Commission announced on 11 December that the United Nations team had inspected 16 sites throughout Iraq. The mission was unique in that all designations were undeclared sites, and concentrated on possible weapons storage sites, such as airfield bunkers and ammunition depots. All inspections were carried out without advance notice to the Iraqi side. The mission used UN helicopters for transport and for conducting aerial reconnaissance.

In his second report to the Security Council, dated 4 December, covering the period since 15 October, the Chairman of the Special Commission in Iraqi Disarmament, Rolf Ekeus, said there was "no change of policy on the part of Iraq [*sic*] to "one of candour, transparency and cooperation at all levels". He said resolute stands must be taken in response to challenges by Iraq to the implementation of the mandate of the Special Commission. Such stands should be based on the full support of the United Nations Member States which was crucial to the Commission's effectiveness. He referred to the "difficult issues" that would arise regarding the Special Commission's future monitoring of the destruction and removal of Iraq's weapons of mass destruction.

...

S/23643, 26 February 1992

22. Note by the Secretary-General, 26 February 1992

The Secretary-General has the honour to refer to the statement issued by the President of the Security Council on 19 February 1992 (S/23609) concerning the dispatch to Iraq of a special mission headed by the Executive Chairman of the Special Commission established under Security Council resolution 687 (1991), "to meet and discuss with the highest levels of the Iraqi Government for the purpose of securing the unconditional agreement by Iraq to implement all its relevant obligations under resolutions 687 (1991), 707 (1991) and 715 (1991)".

In this context, the Secretary-General wishes to transmit herewith the attached letter and its enclosure dated 25 February 1992, addressed to him by Ambassador Rolf Ekeus, Executive Chairman of the Special Commission, upon the completion of the latter's mission to Iraq.

Annex

Letter from the Executive Chairman of the Special Commission addressed to the Secretary-General, 25 February 1992

I have the honour to refer to the statement issued by the President of the Security Council on 19 February 1992 (S/23609), in which the Council supported your decision to send a special mission headed by me to meet with the highest levels of the Iraqi Government for the purpose of securing the unconditional agreement by Iraq to implement all its relevant obligations under Council resolutions 687 (1991), 707 (1991) and 715 (1991). I am submitting herewith my report on the proceedings and outcome of the special mission's visit to Baghdad in view of the Council's request that you report to it on the results of the mission.

(Signed) Rolf EKEUS, Executive Chairman, Office of the Special Commission Enclosure

Report to the Secretary-General by the Executive Chairman of the Special Commission established pursuant to paragraph 9 (b) (i) of Security Council resolution 687 (1991)

A. Introduction

1. After the consideration by the Security Council of a report by the Secretary-General (S/23606), the President of the Council issued an agreed statement (S/23609) on 19 February 1992 regarding the item before the Council on the situation between Iraq and Kuwait. In that statement, the members of the Council recorded their support for the decision of the Secretary-General to dispatch a special mission headed by the Executive Chairman of the Special Commission to visit Iraq immediately to meet and discuss with the highest levels of the Iraqi Government for the purpose of securing the unconditional agreement by Iraq to implement all its relevant obligations under Security Council resolutions 687 (1991), 707 (1991) and 715 (1991).

2. On 19 February 1992, immediately after the issue of the statement by the President of the Security Council, the Executive Chairman left United Nations Headquarters for Baghdad. The Executive Chairman was accompanied by the following members of the staff of the Office of the Special Commission: Mr. John F. Scott, Mr. Stefan Nore, Mr. Martin Trevan and Ms. Olivia Platon.

3. The special mission arrived at Baghdad on 21 February 1992. Over the course of its stay in Baghdad from 21 to 24 February, the Executive Chairman and the members of his staff held the following four meetings with the highest levels of the Government of Iraq.

...

[*List of meetings omitted.*]

4. At the meeting with the Deputy Prime Minister on 22 February it was agreed that, in order to clarify their respective positions, both sides would prepare and exchange written statements. The statement by the Executive Chairman was delivered to the Iraqi delegation at the second meeting held the same day. The Executive Chairman received the statement by Iraq the following afternoon. The text of the Executive Chairman's statement appears in appendix I and that of the Government of Iraq in appendix II.

5. On 24 February 1992, the special mission left Baghdad for Bahrain, where the Executive Chairman prepared the present report for submission to the Secretary-General on the outcome of his discussions with the highest levels of the Government of Iraq.

B. Points presented in the discussion

1. Special mission

Mandate and aims

6. The Executive Chairman explained to the Iraqi side the background to the special mission and its mandate. He drew on the following:

(a) The statement made by the President of the Security Council at the conclusion of the meeting held at the level of heads of State and Government on 31 January 1992, which stated that all relevant Security Council resolutions on Iraq should be fully implemented;

(b) The report of 18 February 1992 of the Secretary-General to the Security Council, which was written in response to the foregoing statement. This concluded that the Special Commission was unable to carry out the plans for ongoing monitoring and verification without Iraqi recognition of its obligations and without full, final and complete disclosure of its programmes for weapons of mass destruction under Security Council resolution 707 (1991). That report also pointed out the problems that the Special Commission faced over air transport within Iraq;

(c) The statement of 19 February 1992 issued by the President of the Security Council.

7. The Executive Chairman raised, in particular, the following points:

(a) Recognition that progress had been made but that much still remained to be done to implement the Council's resolutions;

(b) The Council's grave concern at the continued Iraqi failure to acknowledge its obligations under resolutions 707 (1991) and 715 (1991) and rejection of the ongoing monitoring and verification plans and the Council's view that that constitutes a continuing material breach of the relevant provisions of resolution 687 (1991);

(c) That full disclosure of the weapons programmes, together with supporting documentary and physical evidence, was required under resolution 707 (1991) to enable progress on implementation of resolution 715 (1991);

(d) That monitoring and verification of Iraq's obligations was an integral part of resolution 687 (1991);

(e) That such monitoring and verification was of the utmost importance in achieving the goal of a zone in the Middle East free of weapons of mass destruction and all missiles for their delivery;

(f) That unconditional agreement of Iraq to implement its obligations under all the relevant resolutions of the Council was one of the essential preconditions for any reconsideration by the Council of the sanctions;

(g) That the purpose of the special mission was to obtain Iraq's unconditional agreement to implement all its relevant obligations under Security Council resolutions 687 (1991), 707 (1991) and 715 (1991) and to stress the serious consequences if such an agreement was not forthcoming. These included delaying the lifting of sanctions. Furthermore, the destruction of more of Iraq's dual-capable production facilities would be required than might otherwise be the case;

(h) That the special mission was to report to the Council through the Secretary-General upon its return.

Security Council resolutions 687 and 707 (1991)

8. The Executive Chairman stated that the Special Commission needed full, final and complete disclosure by Iraq of its weapons programmes because it had to be convinced that Iraq had declared all of these programmes before it could make any statement for any determinations by the Security Council under paragraph 22 of resolution 687 (1991); only on the basis of such disclosure would dialogue on Iraq's compliance be meaningful. Given that understanding, the Executive Chairman said that the Special Commission was prepared to pursue Iraqi suggestions to clarify the big picture for the weapons programmes.

9. The Executive Chairman drew attention to the rights of the Special Commission in respect of the operation of its own aircraft and use of airfields of its choice which were elaborated upon in Security Council resolution 707 (1991) and in the plans for ongoing monitoring and verification. He emphasized that the Special Commission had made proposals to the Iraqi Government regarding the use of newly operational airport facilities within the city of Baghdad which would greatly expedite the Commission's flights into and out of Iraq from abroad. The Special Commission was prepared to discuss with the Government practical arrangements to take account of any of its legitimate concerns regarding the use of airports. The Executive Chairman also drew attention to a request by a chemical weapons destruction team then in Iraq to land one of the Commission's C-160 fixed-wing aircraft at Al-Tallil airfield at Nasiriyah to be available for medical evacuation purposes should any emergencies arise in the course of destroying a considerable number of rockets equipped with chemical weapons at Khamisiyah.

Security Council resolution 715 (1991)

10. The Executive Chairman pointed out that if Iraq were planning to declare acceptance of resolutions 707 (1991) and 715 (1991), it would benefit more by announcing its acceptance now rather than during the Iraqi visit to the Security Council, which was expected to take place in March 1992.

11. The Executive Chairman explained in depth the background of the ongoing monitoring and verification plans and drew a sharp distinction between the destruction of items identified as being linked with programmes related to section C of Security Council resolution 687 (1991) and the monitoring of industry, which, if confined to permitted purposes, would not involve destruction. He continued that, with full cooperation and full declarations, implementation could be relatively painless and easy. Initial visits would draw up facility attachments for each site which would then govern the conduct of future monitoring inspections of declared facilities. There would be random on-site inspections of non-declared facilities but if declarations were full, this should pose only limited problems. However, without Iraqi cooperation it would be difficult, if not impossible, for the Special Commission to fulfil the monitoring task. Identifying by U-2 and on-site inspection all the sites to be monitored would not be sufficient.

Compliance

12. The Executive Chairman stated that conditions for the Special Commission to report to the Security Council that Iraq was in substantial compliance would require implementation of all Iraq's obligations, including ongoing monitoring and verification and destruction of all items. The Security Council would be informed accordingly once it was evident to the Special Commission and the International Atomic Energy Agency (IAEA) that everything was on the right track and that the ongoing monitoring and verification was functioning smoothly and on a routine basis.

2. Iraq

Security Council resolutions 687 and 707 (1991)

13. The Iraqi side stated that it considered that it had provided all the necessary information under Security Council resolution 687 (1991). It recognized that Iraq may not have presented its declarations in a coherent manner and suggested that it present them a second time in a consolidated format so that the Commission could get a better idea of the overall programmes. If the Special Commission and IAEA continued not to be satisfied with the completeness of the information provided, they should then address specific questions to Iraqi experts.

14. In order to achieve this, the Iraqi side proposed a procedure culminating in a "seminar" of Iraqi, Special Commission and IAEA experts. This procedure should take place within a set timetable and should deal "once and for all" with the overall consolidated picture of Iraq's weapons programmes. It should, they insisted, result in a joint statement, signed by both sides, to the end of which a definitive list of outstanding issues could be appended. Iraq, however, would need to have guarantees that this was "once and for all". The Iraqi side further insisted that this procedure should result in a report to the Security Council stating that Iraq was in compliance with its obligations under stage 1 of the Special Commission's work (see para. 19 below).

15. The Iraqi side further suggested that, in order to facilitate the completion of stage 1 of the Special Commission's work, the Commission should draw up a final list of exactly what equipment needed to be destroyed.

16. The Iraqi side did not respond to the Special Commission's questions about its rights to operate its own aircraft and use airfields in Iraq of its own choice. However, in the general discussion it became apparent that Iraq's concerns in this regard were linked to general concerns relating to its sovereignty, territorial integrity and national security. Upon leaving Baghdad, the special mission learnt that the Iraqi side had agreed to emergency landings of a fixed-wing aircraft for medical evacuation purposes at the Al-Tallil airfield for the duration of the programme to destroy chemical-filled rockets at Khamisiyah. On its way out of Iraq, the C-160 fixed-wing aircraft carrying the special mission landed at Al-Tallil as a test run.

Security Council resolution 715 (1991)

17. The Iraqi side admitted that Iraq had obligations under Security Council resolution 687 (1991) to permit ongoing monitoring of its obligations not to reacquire the weapons systems destroyed under section C of that resolution. It had not rejected the two plans for ongoing monitoring and verification approved under Security Council resolution 715 (1991). It had merely expressed its position on resolution 715 (1991). Iraq had likewise earlier expressed its objections to Security Council resolution 687 (1991) but had nevertheless accepted it. The main problem with the plans, from Iraq's standpoint, lay in the general provisions, continuing into the indefinite future the privileges, immunities and facilities for the Special Commission and IAEA, agreed as part of the cease-fire arrangements, which infringed Iraq's sovereignty, territorial integrity, national security and industrial capabilities.

18. To assist Iraq in identifying how the plans for ongoing monitoring and verification could be implemented in a practical manner acceptable to both sides, the Iraqi side proposed that the Special Commission provide a detailed description of how the ongoing monitoring and verification plans would be implemented.

Sanctions and compliance

19. The Iraqi side insisted that there should be linkage between Iraqi cooperation with the Special Commission and the easing or lifting of sanctions. In addition, a clear distinction should be made between stage 1 of the Special Commission's work - the identification and destruction of weapons systems under section C of Security Council resolution 687 (1991) and the identification of production equipment from those programmes for future monitoring - and stage 2, the long-term monitoring plans under Security Council resolution 715 (1991). Sanctions, according to the Iraqi side, should be progressively eased as implementation progressed of stage 1. Stage 2, they insisted, should not be used as a mandate in perpetuity for those with the veto to keep sanctions in place. To the Iraqi side it appeared that, no matter what Iraq did, sanctions remained in place. In such circumstances it was difficult for them to see what incentive there was for Iraq to be cooperative.

C. Conclusions

20. After a careful review of the written statement by the Government of Iraq (hereafter referred to as "the statement"), and taking account of the discussions which were held, the Executive Chairman has regretfully concluded that, at this stage, he is not able to report to the Council that he has secured from the highest levels of the Government of Iraq unconditional agreement by Iraq to implement all its relevant obligations under Security Council resolutions 687 (1991), 707 (1991) and 715 (1991).

21. Security Council resolution 707 (1991) demands that, without further delay, Iraq provide full, final and complete disclosure, as required by resolution 687 (1991), of all aspects of its programmes to develop weapons of mass destruction and ballistic missiles with a range greater than 150 kilometres, including launchers, and of all holdings of such weapons, their components and production facilities and locations, as well as all other nuclear programmes. In its statement, Iraq gives no undertaking to provide such a full, final and complete disclosure. Instead, it expresses the opinion that it has provided all the necessary information required of it.

22. Iraq indicates, however, that it is ready to cooperate in the provision of any additional information still deemed necessary, and proposes that this should be done by an expert level dialogue with the Special Commission to clarify the overall picture of each of the programmes concerned. It proposes that, for the purposes of such a dialogue, Iraq should prepare "in a consolidated format, the information required of Iraq". In the discussions, this was indicated to be the information already provided. While the Executive Chairman welcomes this offer to consolidate prior information, he is of the view that it would not constitute the full, final and complete disclosure called for by resolution 707 (1991), which would provide the Special Commission and IAEA with a complete picture and understanding of all Iraq's prohibited weapons programmes.

23. For instance, while the discussions between the special mission and the Iraqi representatives were in progress, a ballistic missile inspection team found at two sites prohibited items that had not previously been declared. Furthermore, major aspects on which Iraq has not yet provided any or sufficient information are outlined in the Executive Chairman's written statement provided to the Government of Iraq. In its statement, the Government indicates it is willing to provide some, but not all of this information. If Iraq were to provide declarations containing full, final and complete disclosure on all the proscribed programmes, supported by documentary and physical evidence, this could serve as a useful basis for dialogue in order to clarify points of

detail and to seek to close any gaps that might appear to exist.

24. While the Executive Chairman welcomes the decision by Iraq to permit the landing of the Special Commission's C-160 fixed-wing aircraft at Al-Tallil airfield for medical evacuation purposes during the operations at Khamisiyah of a chemical weapons destruction team, he notes that no progress was made during the special mission's visit on the use of an operational airfield for the Special Commission's fixed-wing aircraft within the limits of the city of Baghdad. The Iraqi authorities did not immediately take up the Executive Chairman's offer to explore practical arrangements that could accommodate legitimate government concerns in this regard. Given the rights of the Special Commission, both under Council resolution 707 (1991) and under the plans on ongoing monitoring and verification, to use airfields of its own choice, the Executive Chairman will continue to press for an affirmative response from the Iraqi Government for landing rights at Rasheed airport. This would consolidate both fixed-wing and helicopter operations by the Commission's aircraft at one place, thus greatly facilitating its tasks at an airfield not far removed from the Commission's field office in Baghdad. If an affirmative response is not shortly obtained, the Executive Chairman reserves the right to raise this matter again with the Council.

25. In the statement by Iraq, it is indicated that Iraq does not reject the plans for ongoing monitoring and verification approved under Security Council resolution 715 (1991). In elaborating on this statement, Iraq indicates that it has accepted only the principle of ongoing monitoring and verification, and this is subject to considerations of sovereignty, territorial integrity, national security and non-infringement on Iraq's industrial capabilities. The Executive Chairman cannot conclude that such a statement constitutes unconditional agreement by Iraq to implement its obligations under the plans for ongoing monitoring and verification.

26. In its statement, Iraq further indicates that "the Iraqi delegation to be dispatched to talk to the Security Council will convey Iraq's position on resolutions 707 (1991) and 715 (1991)". Unconditional agreement by Iraq to implement its obligations under these resolutions is not therefore provided to the Executive Chairman, and it is not in fact clear that it will be provided to the Security Council.

27. If unconditional agreement is not provided, the initiation and practical implementation of resolution 715 (1991) and the plans approved thereunder cannot be undertaken in a credible manner. However, should Iraq provide, in a form acceptable to the Council, the acknowledgement and the unconditional guarantee called for in the statement by the President of the Council, a possibility for the implementation of the resolution and the plans will have been opened up.

28. Nevertheless, much will remain to be done. For example, particularly in the chemical, biological and ballistic missile fields, declarations complying with the requirements of the Special Commission's plan on ongoing monitoring and verification will have to be received and verified. Thereafter, successful initiation and conduct of ongoing monitoring and verification will require the full cooperation and goodwill of the Government of Iraq. Only through successful implementation in the field, on the basis of adequate declarations and periodic reporting by Iraq, can progress be made in carrying out the Security Council's resolutions to the point where the Special Commission and IAEA would be in a position to report to the Council that, in their view, Iraq was in substantial compliance with its obligations under section C of Security Council resolution 687 (1991).

Appendix I

STATEMENT BY THE SPECIAL MISSION

(Delivered to the Government of Iraq at Baghdad on 22 February 1992)

A. General purpose

The Executive Chairman has been dispatched by the Secretary-General and the Security Council to secure unconditional agreement by Iraq to implement all its relevant obligations under Security Council resolution 687 (1991), 707 (1991) and 715 (1991). The Council acted on the basis of a report (S/23606) indicating that the most serious difficulty currently confronting the Special Commission and IAEA was Iraq's rejection of the plans for ongoing monitoring and verification approved by the Council under Chapter VII of the Charter in its resolution 715 (1991).

In order to achieve its objectives the mission requires:

(a) An acknowledgement by Iraq of its obligations under resolution 715 (1991) and the plans approved under it;

(b) An undertaking by Iraq to provide all the remaining information required under resolutions 687 (1991) and 707 (1991) in order for the Special Commission and IAEA to be able to report to the Security Council that, in their view, Iraq is in substantial compliance with its obligations under section C of resolution 687 (1991);

(c) An undertaking by Iraq to implement the other obligations imposed under resolution 707 (1991).

B. Action required

In addition to the general acknowledgements and undertakings referred to above, the following is an indicative list of specific steps required of Iraq in implementation of its obligations under the Security Council resolutions.

1. Resolution 715 (1991) and the plans approved thereunder:

- Declarations required under the plans;
- An undertaking that Iraq will cooperate to ensure implementation of the plans;

2. Resolutions 707 (1991) and 687 (1991):

- All information required to provide a clear overall picture of each of the weapons programmes concerned, including the evolution of the programmes and the links between all the elements;
- Information on procurement to support the programmes, including detailed year-by-year breakdown of production and imports, and their sources;
- Full records of the use of all relevant weapons and components thereof to enable adequate material balances to be established;
- Credible detailed information on items destroyed unilaterally by Iraq;

- Sufficient supporting documentation and/or physical evidence for all declarations made by Iraq to establish their credibility;

- Practical arrangements permitting use by the Special Commission of facilities, including those relating to the operating and landing of United Nations aircraft, which best facilitate the performance of the Commission's tasks.

Appendix II

STATEMENT BY THE GOVERNMENT OF IRAQ

(Received by the Special Mission at Baghdad on 23 February 1992)

General position

1. Iraq reaffirms its willingness to cooperate and deal constructively with the mission headed by H.E. Ambassador Ekeus, and points out the following grounds:

(a) Iraq is of the opinion that it has provided all the necessary information required of it;

(b) Iraq is ready to cooperate in the provision of any additional information still deemed necessary;

(c) The best modality for implementing what is mentioned in (b) above is to have the opportunity to conduct an expert level dialogue with the Special Commission to clarify the overall picture of each of the programmes concerned, and reach specific conclusions, specially in respect of the modification of equipment for non-prohibited purposes within a specific period of time.

2. Once this has been accomplished within a specified period of time, the Special Commission and IAEA should then report to the Security Council that, in their view, Iraq is in substantial compliance with its obligations under Security Council resolution 687 (1991), and that Iraq requests the Security Council to draw a fair balance between the level of progress achieved at this stage and the position on the sanctions with a view to lifting them.

3. Iraq insists that the Special Commission take a clear position as to the first stage (the destruction of weapons and the identification of the equipment which produce them), in view of the link between this position and the position on the sanctions. Iraq also insists that the Special Commission present to the Security Council a fair and accurate factual report on this subject.

Proposed action

1. Iraq proposes that Iraqi experts be invited to present, in a consolidated form, the information required from Iraq, and to respond to the questions relating thereto.

2. To respond to any questions that may be raised by the Special Commission in this regard.

3. To enable adequate material balances to be established for all weapons and their components.

4. To provide credible detailed information on items destroyed unilaterally by Iraq.

5. To provide, upon specific requests, any available evidence relating to Iraq's declarations.

6. To discuss the scope of destruction proposed by the Special Commission, so as to ensure the specific non-prohibited use of the facilities, equipment, materials and components in an irreversible manner.

Plans for monitoring and verification

1. Iraq does not reject the plans for ongoing monitoring and verification. By recognizing resolution 687 (1991), Iraq has accepted the principle that the Security Council should ascertain and verify that industry in Iraq is not directed in a manner which does not satisfy the Security Council as to the non-production of prohibited weapons. In this regard, Iraq can deal with the Security Council and the Special Commission on the basis of respect to sovereignty and the requirements of national security, and of refrainment from the methods of provocation and infringement upon Iraq's industrial capabilities which will be devoted to peaceful purposes or to military purposes not prohibited by Security Council resolution 687 (1991).

2. The Iraqi delegation to be dispatched to talk to the Security Council will convey Iraq's position on resolutions 707 (1991) and 715 (1991).

S/23663 28 February 1992

23. Note by the President of the Security Council, 28 February 1992

Following consultations among members of the Security Council, the President of the Council made the following statement, on behalf of the Council, at its 3058th meeting, on 28 February 1992, in connection with the Council's consideration of the item entitled "The situation between Iraq and Kuwait":

"The members of the Security Council express their gratitude to the Secretary-General for the report submitted to the Council on 27 February 1992 (S/23643), transmitting the results of the special mission dispatched to Iraq by the Secretary-General pursuant to the statement of the President of the Council of 19 February 1992 (S/23609). The members of the Council approve in full the conclusions of the special mission as contained in the report and in particular its finding that Iraq is not prepared to give its unconditional agreement to implement all of its obligations under resolutions 687 (1991), 707 (1991) and 715 (1991).

"The members of the Council deplore and condemn the failure of the Government of Iraq to provide the special mission with full, final and complete disclosure, as required by resolution 707 (1991), of all aspects of its programmes to develop weapons of mass destruction and ballistic missiles with a range greater than 150 kilometres, including launchers, and of all holdings of such weapons, their components and production facilities and locations, as well as all other nuclear programmes; and the failure of Iraq to comply with the plans for ongoing monitoring and verification (S/22871/Rev.1 and S/22872/Rev.1 and Corr.1) approved by resolution 715 (1991). In the statement made on 19 February 1992 (S/23609) prior to the dispatch of the special mission to Iraq the Council noted that Iraq's behaviour constituted a material breach of resolution 687 (1991). Regrettably this continues to be the case.

"Furthermore, the members of the Council equally deplore and condemn Iraq's failure, within the time prescribed by the Special Commission at the request of Iraq, to commence destruction of ballistic missile-related equipment designated for destruction by the Special Commission. The members of the Council reaffirm that it is for the Special Commission alone to determine which items must be destroyed under paragraph 9 of resolution 687 (1991). Therefore, the Government of Iraq's letter of 18 February 1992 to the Executive Chairman of the Special Commission is unacceptable. Iraq's refusal to implement the determinations of the Special Commission constitutes a further material breach of the relevant provisions of resolution 687 (1991).

"The members of the Council demand that Iraq immediately implement all its obligations under Council resolution 687 (1991) and subsequent resolutions on Iraq. The members of the Council require the Government of Iraq to communicate directly to the Council without further delay an authoritative and unconditional acknowledgement of its agreement to accept and implement the above noted obligations, including specifically to comply with the determination of the Special Commission requiring the destruction of ballistic missile-related equipment. The members of the Council emphasize that Iraq must be aware of the serious consequences of continued material breaches of resolution 687 (1991).

"The members of the Council note that an Iraqi delegation is prepared to come to New York as soon as it is invited to do so. The members of the Council have asked its President to extend such an invitation to the delegation to come to New York without further delay. The members of the Council intend in any event to continue their consideration of this question no later than the week beginning 9 March 1992."

S/23803, 10 April 1992

24. Note by the President of the Security Council, 10 April 1992

After the consultations held on 10 April 1992, the President of the Security Council issued the following statement on behalf of the members of the Council in connection with the item entitled "The situation between Iraq and Kuwait":

> "The members of the Security Council have learnt with grave concern from the Executive Chairman of the Special Commission of recent developments which appear to call for a halt in and constitute a threat to the safety and security of the Special Commission's aerial surveillance flights over Iraq. The members of the Council wish to point out that the surveillance flights are carried out under the authority of Security Council resolutions 687, 707 and 715 (1991). Reaffirming the right of the Special Commission to conduct such aerial surveillance flights, the members of the Council call upon the Government of Iraq to take all the necessary steps to ensure that the Iraqi military forces will not interfere with or threaten the security of the flights concerned and to comply with its responsibilities to secure the safety of the Special Commission's aircraft and personnel while flying over Iraq. The members of the Council warn the Government of Iraq of the serious consequences which would ensue from any failure to comply with these obligations."

S/24036, 29 May 1992

25. Note by the Secretary-General, 29 May 1992

The Secretary-General has the honour to transmit to the members of the Security Council the attached communication that he has received from the Director General of the International Atomic Energy Agency (IAEA).

...

Letter from the Director General of the International Atomic Energy Agency addressed to the Secretary-General, 26 May 1992

As requested by the President of the Security Council, I am submitting herewith a report on the status of compliance by Iraq with the obligations placed upon it under section C of Security Council resolution 687 (1991) and Council resolutions 707 (1991) and 715 (1991) for use in the Council's 60-day review of the sanctions imposed upon Iraq.

...

Appendix

Report on the status of compliance by Iraq with the obligations placed upon it under section C of Security Council resolution 687 (1991) and resolutions 707 (1991) and 715 (1991)

1. Since the 7 March 1992 report by the Secretary-General on the status of compliance by Iraq with its obligations under Security Council resolutions relating to the situation between Iraq and Kuwait, some developments have occurred which the Secretary-General might wish to bring to the attention of the Security Council.

2. Following the appearance before the Security Council (on 11 and 12 March) of the high-level Iraqi delegation headed by the Deputy Prime Minister, an Iraqi team drawn from members of the Iraqi delegation and headed by the Chairman of the Iraqi Atomic Energy Commission have met (on 12 and 13 March) the Director General of IAEA and members of the IAEA's Action Team. In the course of the discussions, which touched upon a number of outstanding issues, the Director General referred to several matters in which better cooperation and full compliance of the Iraqi Government were still needed. Such matters included the centrifuge uranium enrichment programme, the nuclear weapon development effort and the provision of full information on the procurement of critical equipment, materials and technical advice. The Director General also underlined that a formal and explicit acceptance by Iraq of Security Council resolutions 707 (1991) and 715 (1991) was essential for starting the implementation of the long-term ongoing monitoring plan.

3. A series of meetings was held in Vienna from 20 to 24 March between Agency officials and an Iraqi technical delegation consisting of representatives of the Iraqi Atomic Energy Commission and the Al Atheer Centre. The meetings had been requested by the Iraqi authorities in order to clarify the role and functions of the Al Atheer Centre before a decision was finalized by the Agency as to the destruction of the Al Atheer nuclear-weapons-related capabilities.

4. In spite of lengthy and detailed explanations by the Iraqi team regarding the peaceful nature and functions of the Al Atheer Centre, the Agency remained convinced that the technical core of this facility had been designed to accommodate special processes needed for nuclear weapon development and manufacture, including uranium metallurgy. This conclusion was based on the results of inspections, on the detailed examination of documents taken in Iraq and on admissions - previously made by Iraqi experts and confirmed during the meetings - that certain buildings at Al Atheer had been designed to accommodate activities related to nuclear-weapon development.

5. On 25 March IAEA transmitted to Iraq its decision about the destruction of the relevant facilities and equipment at the Al Atheer-Al Hatteen site in conjunction with the eleventh inspection mission and under the supervision of IAEA inspectors.

6. The eleventh inspection mission took place from 7 to 15 April. The detailed report on this mission has been circulated by the Secretary-General to the members of the Security Council in document S/23947. The Iraqi team cooperated actively in the destruction operation, but little or no progress was made as regards procurement, sources of technical advice, centrifuge enrichment and nuclear-weapon studies. Promises were made, however, to provide information by the time of the next inspection mission.

7. In conclusion, although much has been achieved in uncovering the nature and objectives of Iraq's clandestine nuclear programme, a number of actions remain to be taken before IAEA can report to the Security Council that Iraq is in substantial compliance with its obligations.

8. In particular,

(a) Iraq has to accept its obligations under Security Council resolutions 707 (1991) and 715 (1991);

(b) Pursuant to resolution 707 (1991), Iraq has to make a full, final and complete disclosure of all aspects of its nuclear programme, including procurement details, and IAEA has to verify the correctness of the submitted data;

(c) Iraq has to provide, under the plan adopted through resolution 715 (1991), a complete list of equipment and materials used for prohibited purposes and of equipment and materials having dual-use capability;

(d) The operations of removal, destruction and rendering harmless called for in resolution 687 (1991) have to be completed to the full satisfaction of IAEA (however, the delay in the removal of irradiated nuclear fuel from Iraq cannot be attributed to lack of cooperation from the Iraqi side);

(e) Monitoring and verification activities designed to ensure that Iraq does not reacquire capabilities prohibited under resolution 687 (1991) must be initiated and must proceed smoothly.

S/24110, 17 June 1992

26. Note by the Secretary-General, 17 June 1991

The Secretary-General has the honour to transmit to the Security Council, pursuant to paragraph 3 of Security Council resolution 699 (1991), the attached second semi-annual report on the implementation by the IAEA of the plan for the destruction, removal or rendering harmless of items listed in paragraph 12 of United Nations Security Council resolution 687 (1991).

...

Second semi-annual report (covering the period 17 December 1991 - 17 June 1992) on the implementation by the IAEA of the plan for the destruction, removal or rendering harmless of items listed in paragraph 12 of UN Security Council resolution 687 (1991).

Introduction

By resolution 699 of 17 June 1991, the Security Council approved the plan submitted by the IAEA through the Secretary-General for the destruction, removal or rendering harmless of all items listed in paragraph 12 of Security Council resolution 687. Resolution 699 also called for the Secretary-General to submit every six months a progress report on the implementation of the plan.

The first of these reports was circulated by the Secretary-General to the members of the Security Council in document S/23295 dated 17 December 1991. The Secretary-General also circulated on 29 May 1992 a report (S/24036) submitted by the Director General of the IAEA on the status of Iraq's compliance with its obligations under Security Council resolutions 687 (1991), 707 (1991) and 705 (1991). In this report, the Director General provided information related to destruction activities carried out in Iraq during the 11th inspection mission.

This is the second semi-annual report on the implementation by the IAEA of the plan for destruction, removal or rendering harmless covering the period from 17 December 1991 to 17 June 1992. Its content has been structured in such a way as to facilitate comparison with the previous report and evaluation of progress.

PRESENT SITUATION

Direct-Use Material

Fresh fuel

After the removal of all the fresh fuel for the IRT 5000 reactor, which was accomplished in November 1991, in conjunction with the 8th IAEA inspection, the 12.24 kg of U235 contained in the fuel was processed in a Russian facility and transformed through isotopic dilution into approximately 61 kg of uranium enriched to slightly less than 20% in U235. Once the product specifications have been verified by the Agency, this material will be transferred from the processing plant to an agreed facility for storage in Russia. Agency safeguards will continue to be applied during storage.

The French-origin MTR type plates containing a total of 372 grams of U235, and the Russian-origin pins, containing a total of 116.1 grams of U235, were removed from Iraq in June 1992 by the inspectors of the 12th team and are now temporarily stored at laboratory of the IAEA in Seibersdorf, Austria.

Irradiated fuel

As referred to in the first report (S/23295), other irradiated enriched research reactor fuel containing a total of 35.58 kg of U235 is held in storage in two locations, one within Tuwaitha in the Russian reactor building, the second, at a site identified as Location B, a few kilometers north of Tuwaitha in farm land area.

Inadequate storage conditions at Location B led to serious corrosion problems. New containers were brought to this site and filled with demineralized water, into which all of the fuel elements in Location B were transferred with the exception of 6 control rods. The situation is now stable and the corrosion rate should decrease.

Negotiations with the consortium of commercial companies from France and the UK for the removal and reprocessing of this fuel have met with difficulties of a legal, technical and financial nature. Efforts are being made to overcome these difficulties.

Plutonium and Other Nuclear Material

There is nothing further to report on plutonium. As to other nuclear material, the material balance is still not satisfactory. The IAEA is continuing efforts to reconcile discrepancies in the declarations.

Installations, equipment and other materials relevant to enriched uranium production

Information received from Governments of other States and, in particular, from the Government of Germany about the procurement by Iraq of large quantities of special materials and components needed in the manufacturing of gas centrifuges for the production of enriched uranium, was used in the course of the 9th IAEA inspection mission. The Iraqi authorities acknowledged the procurement of these materials and components, but stated that all of them had been destroyed or "rendered harmless" before the start of inspection activities under UN Security Council resolution 687 (1991). In the course of the same mission, the Iraqi side acknowledged the procurement of additional special material and components not included in the information previously received by the Agency from Iraq or other States. The Iraqi authorities stated that destruction of these materials and components had also occurred prior to commencement of the inspection activities. A detailed description of the material and components in question is contained in document S/23505. The extent and effectiveness of the destruction carried out by the Iraqi authorities of these items is now under assessment by the Agency. Additional measures will be necessary, in some cases, to rule out any possibility of recovery.

The destruction of components specific to the Electromagnetic Isotope Separation (EMIS) program, begun in the previous six month reporting period, continues. The destruction activities have included the removal to a nearby storage area of 51 return irons (30 tons each) from the alpha calutron pier at Tarmiya.

A plan for the dismantling of EMIS uranium enrichment production capabilities at the Tarmiya and Ash Sharqat sites was prepared and communicated to the Iraqi side on 15 May 1992. The plan included reduction of the electrical power delivery to both sites, removal of general utilities from buildings and destruction of eight key technical buildings. Implementation of this plan was begun, with full co-operation of the Iraqi Atomic Energy Commission, in the course of the 12th IAEA inspection (26 May - 4 June 1992) and is presently more than 50% complete. Dismantling operations at Tarmiya and Ash Sharqat will be completed by the time of the next inspection, scheduled to take place in July 1992, in the course of which the destruction of relevant buildings at these sites will also be completed.

Installations and equipment relevant to the weaponization activities

On 25 March 1992, following a series of meetings in Vienna between IAEA officials and an Iraqi technical delegation, a formal communication containing a list of buildings and equipment to be destroyed at the Al Atheer-Al Hatteen site was transmitted to the Iraqi authorities. The Al Atheer-Al Hatteen site had been identified by the IAEA as the main research centre where the IAEC intended to pursue its program for developing nuclear weapons. Eight buildings covering a surface of approximately 35,000 square meters, and 26 major equipment items, some consisting of several components, were destroyed under the supervision of Agency inspectors in the course of the 11th and 12th IAEA inspection missions. In the case of one additional item on the equipment list, essential components were removed to IAEA, Vienna.

The techniques employed for destruction included the use of explosive charges. A total of more than 6 tons of explosives were used. The large bunker at the Al Hatteen site was filled with concrete and scrap iron to prevent its further use (350 cubic meters of concrete were poured), as the use of explosives in this case was judged to be impractical. The bunker's high protective berm was levelled. Cutting torches were used to destroy the steel liner shell of the internal explosion test chamber and to cut off reinforcing bars of the internal explosive test chamber and of the contained firing facility that was part of the physics building. The Iraqi side provided all the equipment, materials and manpower necessary for fulfilling the destruction plan under the supervision of the IAEA teams. Details of the buildings and equipment destroyed at the Al Atheer-Al Hatteen site are given in the inspection reports of IAEA-11 (doc S/23947) and IAEA-12 (in preparation).

FUTURE ACTIVITIES

The removal from Iraq of the remaining 35 kilograms of U235 contained in the irradiated fuel elements of the Tamuz 2 and IRT 5000 research reactors is one of the major tasks still pending. It is hoped that negotiations with the contractors can be brought to a successful conclusion and that the financial resources necessary for removal and processing of the irradiated fuel will be found.

The destruction of key buildings and installations at Tarmiya and Ash Sharqat will be completed in the course of the next IAEA inspection in Iraq. Once this operation is finished, Tarmiya, Ash Sharqat, Tuwaitha and Al Atheer-Al Hatteen will not be equipped for undertaking activities proscribed under United Nations Security Council resolution 687 (1991). The verification of compliance by Iraq with the requirements of the resolution at these sites will rest on the IAEA plan for future ongoing monitoring and verification.

Additional destruction, removal or rendering harmless may be necessary in the near term pending the result of ongoing sample analysis. In the long-term, as provided for in paragraph 31 of the IAEA plan for future ongoing monitoring and verification, the inspection of any sites designated by the Special Commission or the IAEA in the course of implementation of that Plan may also give rise to the need for destruction, removal or rendering harmless not foreseen at this time.

S/24240, 6 July 1992

27. Note by the President of the Security Council, 6 July 1992

Following consultations of the Security Council, held on 6 July 1992, the President of the Council issued the following statement on behalf of the members of the Council in connection with the item entitled "The situation between Iraq and Kuwait":

> "The members of the Security Council have learnt with concern of the refusal of the Government of Iraq to permit a team of inspectors sent to Iraq by the Special Commission to enter certain premises designated by the Special Commission for inspection."
>
> "The members of the Council recall that, under paragraph 9 (b) (i) of section C of Security Council resolution 687 (1991), Iraq is required to permit the Special Commission to undertake immediate on-site inspection of any locations designated by the Commission. This obligation is imposed as a result of a decision of the Council, taken under Chapter VII of the Charter. Furthermore, Iraq has agreed to such inspections as a condition precedent to the establishment of a formal cease-fire between Iraq and Kuwait and the Member States

cooperating with Kuwait in accordance with Security Council resolution 678 (1990). The members of the Council further recall that by paragraph 2 (ii) of resolution 707 (1991) the Council has reaffirmed the relevant provision of resolution 687 (1991) and expressly demanded that Iraq "allow the Special Commission ... and their Inspection Teams immediate, unconditional, and unrestricted access to any and all areas, facilities, equipment, records, and means of transportation which they wish to inspect."

"Iraq's present refusal to permit access to the Inspection Team currently in Iraq to the premises designated by the Special Commission constitutes a material and unacceptable breach by Iraq of a provision of resolution 687 which established the cease-fire and provided the conditions essential to the restoration of peace and security in the region. The members of the Council demand that the Government of Iraq immediately agree to the admission to the premises concerned of the inspectors of the Special Commission as required by the Chairman of the Special Commission, so that the Special Commission may establish whether or not any documents, records, materials, or equipment relevant to the responsibilities of the Commission are located therein."

SC/5534, 8 January 1993

28. UN Press Release: Security Council Demands That Iraq Not Interfere With UN Flights Transporting Personnel Into Iraqi Territory, 8 January 1993

The Security Council this evening demanded that the Government of Iraq should not interfere with the currently envisaged flights of United Nations personnel into the country, and warned it of the serious consequences which would ensue from failure to comply with its obligations.

The Council, in a statement read out by its President, Yoshio Hatano (Japan), said it was deeply disturbed by the Iraqi Government's recent Notes to the Office of the Special Commission in Baghdad and to the headquarters of the United Nations Iraq-Kuwait Observation Mission (UNIKOM) that it would not allow the United Nations to transport its personnel into Iraqi territory using its own aircraft.

According to the Council statement, the restrictions set out in the recent Iraqi communications would seriously impede the activities of the Special Commission, the International Atomic Energy Agency (IAEA) and UNIKOM, and constituted an unacceptable and material breach of the relevant provisions of resolution 687 (1991), which established the cease-fire and provided the conditions essential to the restoration of peace and security in the region, as well as relevant resolutions and agreements.

The statement referred to a number of resolutions and an agreement by which Iraq was obliged to permit the Special Commission and IAEA to undertake on-site inspection of locations designated by the Commission, among them, resolutions 687 (1991), 707 (1991) and 715 (1991), which elaborated on Iraq's obligations by demanding, among other things, that the Special Commission and IAEA be allowed to use their own aircraft throughout Iraq and any airfield in the country without interference or hindrance of any kind. The statement also referred to the agreement on facilities, privileges and immunities between the Iraqi Government and the United Nations.

With regard to UNIKOM, the Council said Iraq was obligated by resolution 687 (1991) and committed by an exchange of letters dated 15 April 1992 and 21 June 1992, respectively, to the unrestricted freedom of entry and exit without delay or hindrance of its personnel, property, supplies, equipment, spare parts and means of transport.

The Security Council meets this evening on the situation between Iraq and Kuwait. The President of the Council, Yoshio Hatano (Japan), called the meeting to order at 9:30 p.m.

The President said the Council was meeting in accordance with the understanding reached in its prior consultations and that, following consultations, he had been authorized to make the following statement on behalf of the Council:

"The Security Council is deeply disturbed by the Government of Iraq's recent Notes to the Office of the Special Commission in Baghdad and to the headquarters of the United Nations Iraq-Kuwait Observation Mission (UNIKOM) that it will not allow the United Nations to transport its personnel into Iraqi territory using its own aircraft.

"The Security Council refers to resolution 687 (1991) requiring Iraq to permit the Special Commission and the IAEA to undertake immediate on-site inspection of any locations designated by the Commission. The agreement on facilities, privileges and immunities between the Government of Iraq and the United Nations, and resolutions 707 (1991) and 715 (1991) elaborated on Iraq's obligations by demanding, inter alia, that the Special Commission and the IAEA be allowed, as they determined necessary, to use their own aircraft throughout Iraq and any airfield in Iraq without interference or hindrance of any kind. Concerning UNIKOM, Iraq is obligated by resolution 687 (1991) and committed by an exchange of letters dated 15 April 1992 and 21 June 1992 respectively to the unrestricted freedom of entry and exit without delay or hindrance of its personnel, property, supplies, equipment, spare parts and means of transport.

"The implementation of the measures set out in the recent communications of the Iraqi Government would seriously impede the activities of the Special Commission, the IAEA and UNIKOM. Such restrictions constitute an unacceptable and material breach of the relevant provisions of resolution 687 (1991), which established the cease-fire and provided the conditions essential to the restoration of peace and security in the region, as well as other relevant resolutions and agreements.

"The Council demands that the Government of Iraq abide by its obligations under all relevant Security Council resolutions and cooperate fully with the activities of the Special Commission, the IAEA and UNIKOM. In particular, it demands that the Government of Iraq not interfere with the currently envisaged United Nations flights. The Security Council warns the Government of Iraq, as it has done in this connection in the past, of the serious consequences which would ensue from the failure to comply with its obligations."

The meeting was adjourned at 9:35 p.m.

[*For the statement of the UN Security Council President of 11 January 1993, see the preceding Chapter, Document 14.*]

13. CLAIMS, SANCTIONS AND OTHER FINANCIAL MATTERS

In Section E of Resolution 687 (1991) the Security Council reaffirmed that Iraq is liable for any direct loss, damage, including environmental damage and the depletion of natural resources, or injury to foreign Governments, nationals and corporations, as the result of Iraq's unlawful invasion and occupation of Kuwait. The Council decided to establish a Compensation Fund to meet claims arising from this circumstance and to establish a Commission to adminster the Fund. It was envisaged that Iraq would finance the Fund by making available to the United Nations up to 30 per cent of the annual value of its exports of petroleum and petroleum products (Resolutions 692 (1991) and 705 (1992)). It was also envisaged that proceeds from the sale of Iraqi oil and oil products would be used to cover the full costs of the tasks authorized by Section C of Resolution 687 (1991) (see the preceding Chapter), the full costs incurred by the United Nations in facilitating the return of all Kuwaiti property seized by Iraq and half the costs of the Boundary Commission. In addition, the Security Council provided for the payment of humanitarian relief operations within Iraq from these proceeds. (Resolutions 706 (1991) and 712 (1991)). When Iraq failed to sell petroleum or petroleum products and, as a consequence, no funds were raised, the Security Council adopted Resolution 778 (1992), which is reprinted below.

With the exception of provisions concerning the sale of Iraqi petroleum and petroleum products and medicine, foodstuffs and materials and supplies for essential civilian needs, the Council has kept in place comprehensive economic sanctions against Iraq. Documents concerning the export to Iraq of armaments and other strategic products, materials, technologies and related services have been reprinted in the preceeding Chapter. Materials on the provision of humanitarian aid can be found in Part V of this volume.

Section D of Resolution 687 (1991) provides for the return of all Kuwaiti property seized by Iraq. Information on compliance with that obligation can be found in the general materials on the implementation of Resolution 687 (1991) reprinted in Chapter 9.

S/22559, 2 May 1991

1. Report of the Secretary-General pursuant to paragraph 19 of Security Council Resolution 687 (1991)

Introduction

1. The present report is submitted pursuant to paragraph 19 of Security Council resolution 687 (1991) of 3 April 1991. In paragraph 16 of that resolution, the Council reaffirmed that Iraq "is liable, under international law, for any direct loss, damage, including environmental damage and the depletion of natural resources, or injury to foreign Governments, nationals and corporations, as a result of Iraq's unlawful invasion and occupation of Kuwait". In paragraph 17 of the resolution, the Council decided "that all Iraqi statements made since 2 August 1990 repudiating its foreign debt are null and void", and demanded that "Iraq adhere scrupulously to all of its obligations concerning servicing and repayment of its foreign debt". The Council also decided, in paragraph 18 of the resolution, "to create a fund to pay compensation for claims that fall within the scope of paragraph 16 ... and to establish a Commission that will administer the fund".

2. In paragraph 19 of the resolution, the Security Council directed the Secretary-General "to develop and present to the Security Council for decision, no later than 30 days following the adoption of the present resolution, recommendations for the fund to meet the requirement for the payment of claims established in accordance with paragraph 18 ..., and for a programme to implement the decisions in paragraphs 16, 17 and 18 ..., including: administration of the fund; mechanisms for determining the appropriate level of Iraq's contribution to the fund based on a percentage of the value of the exports of petroleum and petroleum products from Iraq not to exceed a figure to be suggested to the Council by the Secretary-General, taking into account the requirements of the people of Iraq, Iraq's payment capacity as assessed in conjunction with the international financial institutions taking into consideration external debt service, and the needs of the Iraqi economy; arrangements for ensuring that payments are made to the fund; the process by which funds will be allocated and claims paid; appropriate procedures for evaluating losses, listing claims and verifying their validity and resolving disputed claims in respect of Iraq's liability as specified in paragraph 16 ...; and the composition of the Commission designated [in paragraph 18]". In making the following recommendations, I have borne in mind the need for maximum transparency, efficiency, flexibility and economy in the institutional framework that will be required for the implementation of the decisions contained in paragraphs 16, 17 and 18 of the resolution.

I. Institutional Framework

A. *The Fund*

3. The Fund created by paragraph 18 of Security Council resolution 687 (1991) will be established by the Secretary-General as a special account of the United Nations. The Fund will be known as the United Nations Compensation Fund (hereinafter referred to as "the Fund"). The Fund will be operated in accordance with the United Nations Financial Regulations and Rules. As a special account of the United Nations, the Fund, therefore, will enjoy, in accordance with Article 105 of the Charter and the Convention on the Privileges and Immunities of the United Nations of 13 February 1946, [1] [1. General Assembly resolution 22 A (I).] the status, facilities, privileges and immunities accorded to the United Nations. The Fund will be used to pay compensation for "any direct loss, damage, including environmental damage and the depletion of natural resources, or injury to foreign Governments, nationals and corporations, as a result of Iraq's unlawful invasion and occupation of Kuwait" as provided for in paragraph 16 of resolution 687 (1991).

B. *The Commission*

4. The Fund is to be administered by the Commission established by the Security Council in paragraph 18 of resolution 687 (1991). The Commission, which is to be known as the United Nations Compensation Commission (hereinafter referred to as "the Commission"), will function under the authority of the Security Council and be a subsidiary organ thereof. In accordance with the terms of paragraph 19 of resolution 687 (1991), in carrying out its functions, the Commission will be required to address a variety of complex administrative, financial, legal and policy issues, including the mechanism for determining the level of contribution to the Fund; the allocation of funds and payments of claims; the procedures for evaluating losses, listing claims and verifying their validity; and resolving disputed claims. In the light of the multifarious nature of the tasks to be performed by the Commission, it will, in my view, be necessary to distinguish between questions of policy and the functional aspects of the Commission's work. The Commission should, therefore, operate at a policy-making level and a functional level. A secretariat will be necessary for servicing the work of the Commission at both the policy-making and the functional levels.

C. *Structure and composition of the Commission*

5. The principal organ of the Commission will be a 15-member Governing Council composed of the representatives of the current members of the Security Council at any given time. The Governing Council will be assisted by a number of commissioners who will perform the tasks assigned to them by the Governing Council. The precise number of commissioners will be determined by the Governing Council in the light of the tasks to be performed. The commissioners will be experts in fields such as finance, law, accountancy, insurance and environmental damage assessment, who will act in their personal capacity. They will be nominated by the Secretary-General and appointed by the Governing Council for specific tasks and terms. In nominating the commissioners, the Secretary-General will pay due regard to the need for geographical representation, professional qualifications, experience and integrity. The Secretary-General will establish a register of experts which might be drawn upon when commissioners are to be appointed.

6. A secretariat, composed of an Executive Secretary and the necessary staff, will be established to service the Commission. The Executive Secretary's primary responsibility will be the technical administration of the Fund and the servicing of the Commission. He will be appointed by the Secretary-General after consultation with the Governing Council. The staff of the secretariat will be appointed by the Secretary-General. The Executive Secretary and staff will serve under the United Nations Staff Regulations and Rules.

D. *Status, privileges and immunities of the Commission*

7. The Convention on the Privileges and Immunities of the United Nations of 13 February 1946 [1] [1. General Assembly resolution 22 A (I).] will apply to the Commission and its secretariat. The members of the Governing Council will have the status of representatives of States, the commissioners will have the status of experts on missions within the meaning of article VI of the Convention and the Executive Secretary and the staff of the secretariat will have the status of officials within the meaning of articles V and VII of the Convention.

E. *Expenses of the Commission*

8. The expenses of the Commission will be borne by the Fund. More detailed recommendations regarding the budgetary administration of the Commission are set out in paragraph 29 below.

F. *Headquarters of the Commission*

9. For reasons of economy and practicality, particularly in the secretariat servicing of the Governing Council and the commissioners, the headquarters of the Commission should be in New York. Alternatively, it might be located at the site of one of the two Offices of the United Nations in Europe, i.e. Geneva or Vienna. The Governing Council may decide whether some of the activities of the Commission should be carried out elsewhere.

G. *Functions of the Commission*

1. *The Governing Council*

10. As the policy-making organ of the Commission, the Governing Council will have the responsibility for establishing guidelines on all policy matters, in particular, those relating to the administration and financing of the Fund, the organization of the work of the Commission and the procedures to be applied to the processing of claims and to the settlement of disputed claims, as well as to the payments to be made from the Fund. In addition to its policy-making role, the Governing Council will perform important functional tasks with respect to claims presented to the Commission. Except with regard to the method of ensuring that payments are made to the Fund, which should be decided upon by consensus, the decisions of the Governing Council should be taken by a majority of at least nine of its members. No veto will apply in the Governing Council. If consensus is not achieved on any matter for which it is required, the question will be referred to the Security Council on the request of any member of the Governing Council. The Governing Council may invite States that it considers to have particular interest in its work to participate without a vote in its discussions. It may also invite members of the United Nations Secretariat or other persons to supply it with information or to give other assistance in examining matters within its competence. The Governing Council will, on behalf of the Commission, report periodically to the Security Council.

2. *The commissioners*

11. The commissioners will, under the guidelines established by the Governing Council, carry out such tasks and responsibilities as may be assigned to them by the Governing Council.

3. *The secretariat*

12. Under the direction of the Executive Secretary, the secretariat will carry out such tasks as may be assigned to it by the Governing Council and the commissioners, in particular the technical administration of the Fund, and the provision of secretariat services to the Governing Council and the commissioners.

II. THE IMPLEMENTATION OF THE DECISIONS CONTAINED IN PARAGRAPHS 16, 17 AND 18 OF RESOLUTION 687 (1991)

A. *Mechanisms for determining the appropriate level of Iraq's contribution to the Fund*

13. In accordance with the institutional framework outlined in section I above, it would be for the Governing Council to establish the mechanisms for determining the appropriate level of Iraq's contribution to the Fund in accordance with the criteria laid down in paragraph 19 of Security Council resolution 687 (1991). In carrying out this task, the Governing Council should consider the probable levels of future oil export revenues of Iraq, the amounts of military spending and arms imports in the past, the service of Iraq's foreign debt and the needs for reconstruction and development in the country. The objective should be to settle compensation claims within a reasonable period of time. The Governing Council will, of course, be free to draw upon expert advice as it sees fit. It might wish to be assisted by one or more commissioners who, under the guidance of and within the terms of reference provided by the Governing Council, might give advice with regard to the appropriate level of Iraq's contribution to the Fund as well as to the periodic monitoring of that level of contribution. Simultaneously with the establishment of the Governing Council, I will undertake the appropriate consultations as required by paragraph 19 of resolution 687 (1991) so that, as soon as possible, I will be in a position to suggest the figure not to be exceeded by the Iraqi contribution.

B. *Arrangements for ensuring that payments are made to the Fund*

14. The arrangements for ensuring payments to the Fund are among the most technical and difficult of the tasks that have been entrusted to the Commission. The decisions taken in this regard will determine, *inter alia*, the financial viability of the Fund and its capacity to meet the compensation claims decided upon by the Commission as well as the size and organization of the secretariat.

15. In addressing the question of the possible arrangements for ensuring payments to the Fund, there is an obvious necessity for securing constant and reliable financing of the Fund, without which the essential purpose of the Fund will be defeated. It is also desirable to seek modalities for the financing of the Fund that avoid the necessity of legal and other proceedings in a multiplicity of third countries and jurisdictions.

16. The legal basis for the payments by Iraq to the Fund is to be found in paragraph 19 of resolution 687 (1991). Iraq has officially notified the United Nations of its acceptance of the provisions of the resolution, including paragraph 19, in accordance with paragraph 33 of the resolution. It follows from paragraph 19 of resolution 687 (1991) that the method envisaged by the Security Council for the financing of the Fund is a contribution by Iraq based on a percentage of the value of its exports determined in accordance with the mechanism referred to in paragraph 13 above. It also follows from the resolution that the Security Council did not envisage using "frozen assets" of Iraq held in third countries for the financing of the Fund.

17. Under these circumstances, there are several options for ensuring that Iraq makes payments to the Fund. These options include the following:

(a) Iraq would pay to the Fund the established percentage of the market value of its exports of petroleum and petroleum products; the market value to be calculated on the day of the export. The payment would be effected in United States dollars and made within 30 days of the export from Iraq;

(b) An escrow account would be opened into which Iraq would deposit advance payments of lump sums equivalent to the estimated quarterly or semi-annual contribution required of it. These lump-sum payments would be re-evaluated periodically;

(c) A physical share of the exports would be taken and sold on the market on behalf of the Fund;

(d) The Fund would be designated as either the sole or co-beneficiary on the bill of lading or other title document and any letter of credit issued. The Fund, in turn, would retain its share and remit the remainder to Iraq;

(e) An escrow account provided with the appropriate privileges and immunities (e.g. at a central bank or an appropriate international institution) would be designated as beneficiary on the bill of lading or other title document and any letter of credit issued. The escrow agent would remit to the Fund the sum designated to be used to satisfy claims and the remainder to Iraq.

It would be for the Governing Council to decide among these various options.

18. All of these methods presuppose cooperation by Iraq and strict supervision of the exports of petroleum and petroleum products from Iraq. To this end, the Commission should arrange for appropriate monitoring. Whatever approach is adopted, should Iraq fail to meet its payment obligation, the Governing Council would report the matter to the Security Council.

19. It must be recognized that, in all probability, it may be some time before Iraq is able to resume oil exports. In the short term, the Fund is therefore unlikely to receive revenues, and some consideration will have to be given to the financing of the work of the Commission, a problem which is addressed in paragraph 29 below, but more particularly to the financing of the Fund in the near term from assets other than resumed oil exports by Iraq.

C. *Claims procedure*

20. The process by which funds will be allocated and claims paid, the appropriate procedures for evaluating losses, the listing of claims and the verification of their validity and the resolution of disputed claims as set out in paragraph 19 of resolution 687 (1991) - the claims procedure - is the central purpose and object of paragraphs 16 to 19 of resolution 687 (1991). It is in this area of the Commission's work that the distinction between policy-making and function is most important. The Commission is not a court or an arbitral tribunal before which the parties appear; it is a political organ that performs an essentially fact-finding function of examining claims, verifying their validity, evaluating losses, assessing payments and resolving disputed claims. It is only in this last respect that a quasi-judicial function may be involved. Given the nature of the Commission, it is all the more important that some element of due process be built into the procedure. It will be the function of the commissioners to provide this element. As the policy-making organ of the Commission, it will fall to the

Governing Council to establish the guidelines regarding the claims procedure. The commissioners will implement the guidelines in respect of claims that are presented and in resolving disputed claims. They will make the appropriate recommendations to the Governing Council, which in turn will make the final determination. The recommendations that follow have been divided for the sake of convenience under three main headings: the filing of claims; the processing of claims; and the payments of claims.

1. *Filing of claims*

21. With regard to the filing of claims, the Governing Council must first decide in what manner the claims of foreign Governments, nationals and corporations are to be filed with the Commission. It is recommended that the Commission should entertain, as a general rule, only consolidated claims filed by individual Governments on their own behalf or on behalf of their nationals and corporations. The filing of individual claims would entail tens of thousands of claims to be processed by the Commission, a task which could take a decade or more and could lead to inequalities in the filing of claims disadvantaging small claimants. It will be for each individual Government to decide on the procedures to be followed internally in respect of the consolidation of the claim having regard to its own legal system, practice and procedures. The Governing Council may, in addition, consider whether, in exceptional circumstances involving very large and complex claims, a somewhat different procedure could apply. The question might be considered whether such claims, the character of which, of course, would have to be defined by the Governing Council, could be filed individually with the Commission by Governments, nationals or corporations and whether the individual Government, national or corporation could be authorized to present these claims.

22. In this context, there is another matter that requires consideration by the Commission and regarding which the Governing Council should establish guidelines, namely the question of the exclusivity or non-exclusivity of the claims procedure foreseen in paragraph 19 of the resolution. It is clear from paragraph 16 of the resolution that the debts and obligations of Iraq arising prior to 2 August 1990 are an entirely separate issue and will be addressed "through the normal mechanisms". It is also clear from paragraph 16 that the resolution and the procedure foreseen in paragraph 19 relate to liability under international law. Resolution 687 (1991) could not, and does not, establish the Commission as an organ with exclusive competence to consider claims arising from Iraq's unlawful invasion and occupation of Kuwait. In other words, it is entirely possible, indeed probable, that individual claimants will proceed with claims against Iraq in their domestic legal systems. The likelihood of parallel actions taking place on the international level in the Commission and on the domestic level in national courts cannot be ignored. It is, therefore, recommended that the Governing Council establish guidelines regarding the non-exclusivity of claims and the appropriate mechanisms for coordination of actions at the international and domestic levels in order to ensure that the aggregate of compensation awarded by the Commission and a national court or commission does not exceed the amount of the loss. A particular problem might arise in this regard concerning default judgements obtained in national courts.

23. In addition to deciding on the consolidation of claims, the Governing Council may also wish to establish a categorization of claims according to both type and size. The categorization of claims according to type might, for example, distinguish between claims for loss of life or personal injury and property damage, environmental damage or damage due to the depletion of natural resources. The categorization of claims by size might for example, differentiate between small-, medium- and large-sized claims. A further categorization might be to distinguish between losses incurred by Governments, on the one hand, and losses incurred by nationals and corporations, on the other hand.

24. Governments could be requested by the Governing Council to use these categorizations when filing their consolidated claims. The Governing Council should also establish guidelines regarding the formal requirements for the presentation of claims such as the type of documentation to be presented in support of the claim and the time-delays for the filing of claims. The time-delays should be of sufficient length to permit Governments to establish and implement an internal procedure for the assembling and consolidation of claims. It is recommended that a fixed time period be established for the filing of all claims. A period of two years from the adoption of the filing guidelines would appear to be adequate. Alternatively, the Governing Council could set different filing periods for different types of claims in order to ensure that priority is given to certain claims, for example, loss of life or personal injury. In this respect, I am of the opinion that there would be some merit in providing for a priority consideration of small claims relating to losses by individuals so that these are disposed of before the consideration of claims relating to losses by foreign Governments and by corporations.

2. *Processing of claims*

25. The processing of claims will entail the verification of claims and evaluation of losses and the resolution of any disputed claims. The major part of this task is not of a judicial nature; the resolution of disputed claims would, however, be quasi-judicial. It is envisaged that the processing of claims would be carried out principally by the commissioners. Before proceeding to the verification of claims and evaluation of losses, however, a determination will have to be made as to whether the losses for which claims are presented fall within the meaning of paragraph 16 of resolution 687 (1991), that is to say, whether the loss, damage or injury is direct and as a result of Iraq's unlawful invasion and occupation of Kuwait. It is recommended that the Governing Council establish detailed guidelines regarding what constitutes such direct loss for the guidance of all claimants as well as the commissioners.

26. Claims will be addressed to the Commission. The Commission will make a preliminary assessment of the claims, which will be carried out by the Secretariat, to determine whether they meet the formal requirements established by the Governing Council. The claims would then be submitted to verification and evaluation by panels normally comprised of three commissioners for this purpose. In carrying out these tasks, it is recommended that the commissioners be given the necessary powers to request additional evidence, to hold hearings in which individual Governments, nationals and corporations can present their views and to hear expert testimony. The Governing Council might wish to address the question of possible assistance to ensure the adequacy of the representation of countries of limited financial means. Iraq will be informed of all claims and will have the right to present its comments to the commissioners within time-delays to be fixed by the Governing Council or the Panel dealing with the individual claim. Recommendations of the commissioners regarding the verification and evaluation of claims will be final and subject only to the approval of the Governing Council, which shall make the final determination. The Governing Council should have the power to return claims to the commissioners for further revision if it so decides.

27. Where a dispute arises out of the allegation made by a claimant that the Panel of Commissioners, in dealing

with its claims, has made an error, whether on a point of law and procedure or on a point of fact, such disputes will be dealt with by a board of commissioners who for this purpose should be guided by such guidelines as have been established by the Governing Council and the Arbitration Rules of the United Nations Commission on International Trade Law (UNCITRAL). The UNCITRAL Arbitration Rules will be modified as necessary. The final decision will be made by the Governing Council.

3. *Payment of claims*

28. It is to be anticipated that the value of claims approved by the Commission will at any given time far exceed the resources of the Fund. It will, therefore, be incumbent upon the Commission to decide on an allocation of funds and a procedure for the payment of claims. It is recommended that the Governing Council establish criteria for the allocation of funds, taking into account the size of claims, the scope of the losses sustained by the country concerned and any other relevant factors. In this connection, it might be necessary to distinguish between Kuwait, on the one hand, and other countries on the other hand. As far as the payment of claims is concerned, it follows from the consolidation of the claims and their filing by individual Governments that payments will be made exclusively to Governments. Individual Governments will be responsible for the appropriate distribution to individual claimants. The Governing Council should establish further guidelines regarding the payment of claims, for example, whether claims should be paid in full or whether percentages should be paid. In the latter case, the unsatisfied portions of the claims will remain as outstanding obligations.

D. *Expenses of the Commission*

29. The expenses of the Commission, including those of the Governing Council, the commissioners and the secretariat, should in principle be paid from the Fund. However, as some time will elapse before the Fund is adequately financed, consideration must be given to the financial implications of the programme outlined. It is recommended that urgent consideration be given to the means by which the initial costs of the Commission will be met.

S/22885, 2 August 1991

2. Letter from the President of the Governing Council of the United Nations Compensation Commission to the President of the Security Council, 2 August 1991

In accordance with a decision taken by the Governing Council of the United Nations Compensation Commission, at its tenth meeting, held on 2 August 1991, I have the honour to transmit the following for the information of the members of the Security Council.

The Governing Council of the United Nations Compensation Commission established by Security Council resolution 692 (1991), of 20 May 1991, held its first session at Geneva from 23 July to 2 August 1991.

At its fourth meeting, held on 25 July 1991, the Governing Council approved Guidelines for the conduct of its work, a copy of which is attached. In accordance with paragraph 5 of its Guidelines, the Governing Council invited the representatives of Bangladesh, Iraq, Kuwait, Pakistan, the Philippines and Sri Lanka to address the Council and reply to questions put to them by the members.

At its ninth meeting, held on 1 August 1991, the Governing Council decided to hold informal consultations the week beginning 16 September 1991 and to convene its second session the week beginning 14 October 1991.

At its tenth meeting, held today, 2 August 1991, the Governing Council adopted the attached criteria for expedited processing of urgent claims, a copy of which is attached. The criteria will be issued as a document of the Governing Council for general distribution (S/AC.26/1991/1).

At the same meeting, the Governing Council approved the proposals contained in a working paper submitted by the United States of America on arrangements for ensuring payments to the Compensation Fund (S/AC.26/1991/WP.4/Rev.1), as originally revised. The text of that decision is contained in document S/AC.26/1991/2 of the Governing Council, which is being given general distribution [*reproduced below*].

...

Guidelines for the conduct of the work of the Governing Council of the United Nations Compensation Commission

(Approved at the 4th meeting, held on 25 July 1991)

1. The mandate of the Governing Council is defined in the report of the Secretary-General pursuant to paragraph 19 of Security Council resolution 687 (1991) (S/22559). By paragraphs 3 and 5 of its resolution 692 (1991) the Security Council decided to establish the Fund and the Commission referred to in paragraph 18 of resolution 687 (1991) in accordance with section I of the Secretary-General's report, and directed the Governing Council to implement the provisions of section E of resolution 687 (1991), taking into account the recommendations in section II of the Secretary-General's report.

2. The Governing Council will hold its meetings in private but will open them to the public as and when it deems it necessary for the enhancement of the effectiveness of the Governing Council.

3. As provided for in paragraph 10 of the Secretary-General's report, decisions of the Governing Council on the method of ensuring that payments are made to the Fund should be taken by consensus. Other decisions will be taken by a majority of at least nine of its members. No veto will apply in the Governing Council.

4. As provided for in paragraph 10 of the Secretary-General's report, if consensus is not achieved on any matter for which it is required, the question will be referred to the Security Council on the request of any member of the Governing Council.

5. The Governing Council may invite States that it considers to have particular interest in its work to participate without a vote in its discussions. It may also invite members of the United Nations Secretariat or other persons to supply it with information or to give other assistance in examining matters within its competence.

6. Information on the work of the Governing Council will be made publicly available by the President when so decided in consultation with the members of the Governing Council.

7. The Governing Council will be provided with summary records of all its meetings in all official languages.

8. The success of the work of the Governing Council depends upon the cooperation of all States.

9. Prior to the close of each session, the Governing Council will decide on the dates and duration of its next session. In between sessions, if any member of the Governing Council or the Executive Secretary raises a matter that requires prompt consideration by the Governing Council, the President will hold consultations with the members of the Governing Council and could decide to convene it. Members will be informed of the opening date of the session as well as the provisional agenda at least five days in advance.

10. The Governing Council will, on behalf of the Commission, report periodically to the Security Council.

...

[*Also issued as document S/AC/26/1991/1*]

Criteria for expedited processing of urgent claims

1. The following criteria will govern the submission of the most urgent claims pursuant to resolution 687 (1991) for the first categories to be considered by the Commission. It provides for simple and expedited procedures by which Governments may submit consolidated claims and receive payments on behalf of the many individuals who suffered personal losses as a result of the invasion and occupation of Kuwait. For a great many persons these procedures would provide prompt compensation in full; for others they will provide substantial interim relief while their larger or more complex claims are being processed, including those suffering business losses.

2. These criteria are without prejudice to future Council decisions with respect to criteria for other categories of claims, which will be approved separately as promptly as possible, with expert advice from Commissioners as may be required.

3. The following criteria are not intended to resolve every issue that may arise with respect to these claims. Rather, they are intended to provide sufficient guidance to enable Governments to prepare consolidated claims submissions. It will probably be necessary for the Council to make further decisions on the processing of claims after receiving expert advice where needed.

4. Each Government may submit one or more consolidated claims for each category established by the Council. Thus, each Government may make separate consolidated submissions covering claims in each of the categories set forth below; and it may later submit separate consolidated claims for each additional category to be established by the Council.

5. The Council will promptly establish criteria for additional categories of claims, to permit consolidated submissions by Governments for all losses covered by paragraph 16 of resolution 687 (1991). Business losses of individuals may be part of consolidated claims under the expedited procedures set forth below. The Council will provide further advice on an urgent basis as to the types of business losses eligible for consideration under the expedited procedures. Business losses of corporations and other legal entities will be covered in other criteria to be established. The Council will also consider separately claims on behalf of third parties, such as Governments, insurance companies, relief agencies and employers, which have made payments or provided relief to persons suffering compensable losses.

6. The Council will consider promptly, after receiving expert advice, the circumstances in which claims for mental pain and anguish may be admitted, the amounts to be awarded, and the limits to be imposed thereon.

7. The Council will separately examine the question of the eligibility or otherwise of claims by or in respect of members of the allied coalition armed forces of the Member States that cooperated with the Government of Kuwait; the Executive Secretary will have available, *inter alia*, the provisions of the relevant national legislation of the Governments concerned.

8. The Commission will process the claims in the initial categories in paragraphs 10 to 16 on an expedited basis. While decisions on the precise method of processing these claims will be made at a later stage, the following steps are contemplated. As the claims are received they would be submitted to a panel of Commissioners for review within a set time-limit. If, as expected, the volume of claims in these categories is large, the Commissioners would be instructed to adopt expedited procedures to process them, such as checking individual claims on a sample basis, with further verification only if circumstances warranted. The Commissioners would be asked to report to the Council on the claims received and the amount recommended for the claims submitted by each Government. The Council would then decide on the total amount to be allocated to each Government. To the extent necessary, the Council would seek expert advice (for example, on what constitutes serious personal injury) at any stage of the process.

9. As contributions are made to the Fund, the Council will allocate those funds among the various categories of claims. If resources of the Fund are insufficient with respect to all claims processed to date, *pro rata* payments would be made to Governments periodically as funds become available. The Council will decide on the priority for payment of various categories of claims.

PAYMENT OF FIXED AMOUNTS

10. These payments are available with respect to any person who, as a result of Iraq's unlawful invasion and occupation of Kuwait: (a) departed from Iraq or Kuwait during the period of 2 August 1990 to 2 March 1991; (b) suffered serious personal injury; or (c) whose spouse, child or parent died.

11. In the case of departures, $2,500 will be provided where there is simple documentation of the fact and date of departure from Iraq or Kuwait. Documentation of the actual amount of loss will not be required. Claims submitted under this procedure for departure from Iraq or Kuwait cannot be resubmitted for a greater amount in any other category. If the loss in question was greater than $2,500 and can be documented, it may instead be submitted under paragraph 14 and in other appropriate categories.

12. In addition, in the case of serious personal injury not resulting in death, $2,500 will be provided where there is simple documentation of the fact and date of the injury; and in the case of death, $2,500 will be provided where there is simple documentation of the death and family relationship. Documentation of the actual amount of loss resulting from the death or injury will not be required. If the actual loss in question was greater than $2,500, these payments will be treated as interim relief, and claims for additional amounts may also be submitted under paragraph 14 and in other appropriate categories.

13. These amounts are payable cumulatively where more than one situation applies with respect to a particular person. However, no more than $10,000 will be paid for death, and no more than $5,000 for departure, with respect to any one family (consisting of any person and his or her spouse, children and parents).

CONSIDERATION OF CLAIMS FOR UP TO $100,000 OF ACTUAL LOSSES PER PERSON

14. These payments are available with respect to death or personal injury, or losses of income, support, housing or personal property, or medical expenses or costs of departure, as a result of Iraq's unlawful invasion and occupation of Kuwait. The Commission will give expedited priority consideration to claims for such losses up to $100,000 per person.

15. (a) Such claims must be documented by appropriate evidence of the circumstances and the amount of the claimed loss. The evidence required will be the reasonable minimum that is appropriate under the circumstances involved, and a lesser degree of documentary evidence would ordinarily be required for smaller claims, such as those below $20,000.

(b) If the loss in question was greater than $100,000, claims for additional amounts may also be submitted in other appropriate categories. Criteria for the submission of claims in excess of $100,000 will be approved separately. Claims larger than $100,000 may be submitted in their entirety at a later date under those separate procedures, or the first $100,000 may be submitted at this time and the remainder separately.

16. Compensation will not be provided for losses suffered as a result of the trade embargo and related measures, nor will costs of attorneys' fees or other expenses for claims preparation be compensated under this category. Any compensation, whether in funds or in kind, already received from any source will be deducted from the total amount of losses suffered.

REQUIREMENTS APPLICABLE UNDER BOTH CATEGORIES

17. Claims will not be considered on behalf of Iraqi nationals who do not have bona fide nationality of any other State.

18. Claims must be for death, personal injury or other direct loss to individuals as a result of Iraq's unlawful invasion and occupation of Kuwait. This will include any loss suffered as a result of:

(a) Military operations or threat of military action by either side during the period 2 August 1990 to 2 March 1991;

(b) Departure from or inability to leave Iraq or Kuwait (or a decision not to return) during that period;

(c) Actions by officials, employees or agents of the Government of Iraq or its controlled entities during that period in connection with the invasion or occupation;

(d) The breakdown of civil order in Kuwait or Iraq during that period; or

(e) Hostage-taking or other illegal detention.

19. Claims will be submitted by Governments. Each Government will normally submit claims on behalf of its nationals; each Government may, in its discretion, also submit the claims of other persons resident in its territory. In addition, the Council may request an appropriate person, authority or body to submit claims on behalf of persons who are not in a position to have their claims submitted by a Government. Each Government shall make one or more consolidated submissions of all such claims for each category. The Council encourages the submission of such claims within six months from the date on which the Executive Secretary circulates to Governments the claims forms described below; and the Commission will thereupon give consideration to such claims as provided herein. The Council will consider at a later time the period within which all such claims must be submitted.

20. Each consolidated claim must include:

(a) A signed statement by each individual covered containing:

(i) His or her name and address, and any passport number or other identifying national number;

(ii) For claims under paragraph 14, the amount, type, and reason for each element of the loss, and any compensation, whether in funds or in kind already received from any source for the claim asserted;

(iii) Any documents evidencing the matters set forth in the definition of each category, as well as the items set forth in the preceding subparagraph; and

(iv) His or her affirmation that the foregoing information is correct, and that no other claim for the same loss has been submitted to the Commission;

(b) The affirmation of the Government submitting the claim that, to the best of the information available to it, the individuals in question are its nationals or residents, and the affirmation of the Government or of the person, authority or body as referred to in paragraph 19 that it has no reason to believe that the information stated is incorrect.

21. The Executive Secretary (or a Commissioner) will prepare and the Executive Secretary will distribute a standard form for submission of claims within each category, incorporating the above elements in a clear and concise manner. Except as may otherwise be agreed between the Executive Secretary and the Government in question, claims will be submitted to the Executive Secretary by Governments or by persons, authorities or bodies as referred to in paragraph 19 on the standard form and must include the information in an official language of the United Nations. Each Government may adopt such procedures as it finds appropriate in preparing its consolidated claim. The Executive Secretary (or a Commissioner) will be available to answer questions or provide assistance to any Governments which may request it.

...

[*Also issued as document S/AC.26/1991/2*]

Decision taken by the Governing Council of the United Nations Compensation Commission, at its 10th meeting, held on 2 August 1991

Arrangements for ensuring payments to the Compensation Fund

The elaboration of a system for ensuring payments to the Fund with respect to future Iraqi oil exports is too complex for adoption at the first session of the Governing Council. It is clear that the Governing Council will require adequate factual information to understand the pre-invasion and current oil situation and on options for holding revenues from Iraqi exports of petroleum and petroleum products. The Governing Council taking into account the decision of the Security Council, decides:

(a) To request the Executive Secretary, with the assistance of an expert in the oil trade, to report to the Governing Council by early September on the following: the legal, financial, market and other technical aspects of Iraq's pre-invasion oil trade; the quantity, quality and value of oil subject to paragraph 6 of Security Council resolution 692 (1991); the capacity of Iraq to resume oil exports, in what quantities, quality and time-frame, and the estimated value of resumed oil exports under various possible scenarios; the technical possibilities for monitoring Iraq's oil exports, including oil pipeline flows, metering, measurements at terminals (tank and/or flange), and the resources needed to implement various options;

(b) To request the Executive Secretary, with the assistance of an expert or experts in international financial transactions, and after contacting appropriate institutions, to report to the Governing Council by early September on options for holding and managing revenues from Iraqi exports of petroleum and petroleum products;

(c) To request a Working Group of Governing Council members, after consultation with an expert or experts in the oil trade and in related financial transactions, to meet in September to develop a proposal for a mechanism for ensuring payments to the Fund for presentation to the second session of the Governing Council in October. The Working Group would take into account the reports of the Executive Secretary and the experts' advice, as well as paragraph 19 of Security Council resolution 687 (1991) and the Secretary-General's report.

S/AC.26/1991/3, 23 October 1991

3. Decision taken by the Governing Council of the United Nations Compensation Commission during its second session, at the 15th meeting, held on 18 October 1991

PERSONAL INJURY AND MENTAL PAIN AND ANGUISH

The Council has adopted the following formulations on serious personal injury and on mental pain and anguish, for the purpose of application of the Criteria adopted on 2 August 1991, for expedited processing of urgent claims. These formulations draw heavily upon the excellent work of the Commission secretariat in preparing studies on these matters.

The Council shared certain common understandings with respect to the interpretation and application of these formulations.

First, all references to detention and hiding are understood to mean detention and hiding within Iraq or Kuwait.

Second, the terms "detention" and "detained" are to be interpreted in a restrictive manner with respect to these criteria. Specifically, they are used in this context to mean the holding of persons by force in a particular location by Iraqi authorities.

Third, the phrase "manifestly well-founded fear" is likewise to be interpreted in a restrictive manner with respect to these criteria. Specifically, this phrase is used in this context to mean a fear based upon clear indications that Iraqi authorities were seeking to kill or detain the individual in question or some group of which he or she was a member.

Fourth, the Council has taken no action at this time on the question of possible ceilings or fixed amounts for compensation for mental pain and anguish.

The Council requests the Commission secretariat to prepare a study on these matters on an urgent basis, so that the Council may take a decision at its next meeting in November. The Council also notes that its reference to recovery of pecuniary losses resulting from mental pain and anguish is simply an application of the general principle that there will be recovery for pecuniary losses falling within the Criteria; as such, there is no intention to provide duplicative recovery for pecuniary losses.

Serious personal injury

1. "Serious personal injury" means:

(a) Dismemberment;

(b) Permanent or temporary significant disfigurement, such as substantial change in one's outward appearance;

(c) Permanent or temporary significant loss of use or limitation of use of a body organ, member, function or system;

(d) Any injury which, if left untreated, is unlikely to result in the full recovery of the injured body area, or is likely to prolong such full recovery.

2. For purposes of recovery before the Compensation Commission, "serious personal injury" also includes instances of physical or mental injury arising from sexual assault, torture, aggravated physical assault, hostage-taking or illegal detention for more than three days or being forced to hide for more than three days on account of a manifestly well-founded fear for one's life or of being taken hostage or illegally detained.

3. "Serious personal injury" does not include the following: bruises, simple strains and sprains, minor burns, cuts and wounds; or other irritations *not requiring a course of medical treatment.*

Mental pain and anguish

Compensation will be provided for pecuniary losses (including losses of income and medical expenses) resulting from mental pain and anguish. In addition, compensation will be provided for non-pecuniary injuries resulting from such mental pain and anguish as follows:

(a) A spouse, child or parent of the individual suffered death;

(b) The individual suffered serious personal injury involving dismemberment, permanent or temporary significant disfigurement, or permanent or temporary significant loss of use or limitation of use of a body organ, member, function or system;

(c) The individual suffered a sexual assault or aggravated assault or torture;

(d) The individual witnessed the intentional infliction of events described in subparagraphs (a), (b) or (c) on his or her spouse, child or parent;

(e) The individual was taken hostage or illegally detained for more than three days, or for a shorter period in circumstances indicating an imminent threat to his or her life;

(f) On account on a manifestly well-founded fear for one's life or of being taken hostage or illegally detained, the individual was forced to hide for more than three days; or

(g) The individual was deprived of all economic resources, such as to threaten seriously his or her survival and that of his or her spouse, children or parents, in cases where assistance from his or her Government or other sources has not been provided.

S/AC.26/1991/4, 23 October 1991

4. Decision taken by the Governing Council of the United Nations Compensation Commission during its second session, at the 15th meeting, 18 October 1991

BUSINESS LOSSES OF INDIVIDUALS ELIGIBLE FOR CONSIDERATION UNDER THE EXPEDITED PROCEDURES

The Council has adopted the following conclusions with regard to business losses of individuals eligible for consideration under the expedited procedures, subject to the reservation made by the Government of India regarding the eligibility of claimants who were engaged in business in Kuwait on a "rent-a-permit" basis, and with the exception of paragraph (f) part of which is in square brackets.

(a) The owner of a single proprietorship may claim for his business losses.

(b) Losses suffered by a business entity that has separate legal personality must, in principle, be claimed by that entity - on another claim form.

(c) Losses suffered by a partnership which has no separate legal personality must, in principle, be claimed jointly by all partners.

(d) In the event that a partnership which has separate legal personality is, because of its nationality, not eligible to claim for its losses, each of the eligible partners may claim *pro rata* for his proportionate interest.

(e) In the event that, because of his nationality, a partner of a partnership which has no separate legal personality is not eligible to join in a claim for losses suffered by the partnership, each of the eligible partners may claim *pro rata* for his proportionate interest.

(f) Shareholders of a corporation which [is not able] [because of its nationality, is not eligible] to claim for its losses, may claim for losses with respect to that corporation. The same applies, *mutatis mutandis*, to members/shareholders of other business entities akin to shareholdings.

(g) Preventing access, removal, looting and destruction are examples of circumstances under which business losses may have occurred.

(h) Premises, equipment and stock are examples of business property whose loss may be claimed.

(i) Damage to intangible assets, lost business revenues and losses in connection with contracts may only be claimed if they are a direct loss resulting from Iraq's invasion and occupation of Kuwait.

S/AC.26/1991/5, 23 October 1991

5. Decision taken by the Governing Council of the United Nations Compensation Commission during its second session, at the 15th meeting, 18 October 1991

Guidelines Relating to Paragraph 19 of the Criteria for Expedited Processing of Urgent Claims

1. These guidelines are made in pursuance of the third sentence of paragraph 19 of the Criteria for Expedited Processing of Urgent Claims contained in document S/AC.26/1991/1 of 2 August 1991.

2. The third sentence of paragraph 19 provides that, in addition to Governments as subjects submitting claims, the Council may request an appropriate person, authority or body to submit claims on behalf of individuals who are not in a position to have their claims submitted by a Government.

3. A high number of individuals will most likely not be in a position to have their claims submitted by a Government. Among these individuals Palestinians represent the most numerous groups. Furthermore, stateless persons and other individuals in the same position who still remain in Kuwait or who are situated on border lines are to be included in this category.

4. The international community, represented by the UNCC, bears the overall responsibility for protecting the interests of the above-mentioned individuals. It will be necessary, however, that an appropriate person be entrusted with various aspects of the implementation of this task which shall include, *inter alia*, providing information to future claimants, distributing and collecting forms, submitting claims and, finally, executing payments.

5. To engage in this task in a comprehensive manner would, however, go beyond the administrative and personnel capacities of the Commission. Therefore, the person to be appointed in order to submit claims on behalf of individuals who are not in a position to have their claims submitted by a Government should, prior to and throughout the execution of his work, seek advice and any appropriate cooperation from established and experienced international bodies, such as UNRWA, UNHCR and the ICRC. Cooperation would appear especially appropriate with international bodies having a network of regional offices at their disposal.

6. If one of the above-mentioned organizations should take part in any operation in cooperation with the UNCC, this organization and the UNCC may discuss the financial implications.

7. The Governing Council therefore requests that the Executive Secretary obtain all information necessary to appoint an appropriate person, authority or body to submit claims on behalf of individuals who are not in a position to have their claims submitted by a Government and to make a recommendation to the Governing Council at its next session regarding the appropriate person, authority or body, to be appointed.

S/AC.26/1991/6, 23 October 1991

6. Decision taken by the Governing Council of the United Nations Compensation Commission during its second session, at the 15th meeting, 18 October 1991

Arrangements for Ensuring Payments to the Compensation Fund

1. Paragraph 7 of Security Council resolution 692 (1991) requested the Governing Council to report as soon as possible on the actions it has taken with regard to the arrangements for ensuring that payments are made to the Fund, so that the Security Council could give its approval in accordance with paragraph 22 of resolution 687 (1991).

2. The arrangements in the following paragraphs will be revised when circumstances warrant.

3. These arrangements will come into operation only when sanctions are removed pursuant to paragraph 22 of resolution 687 (1991) and are consistent with the approach adopted in resolutions 706 (1991) and 712 (1991) and with the reports of the Secretary-General dated 2 May 1991 (S/22559), and 4 September 1991 (S/23006). The Governing Council will oversee the implementation of these arrangements.

Payment mechanism

4. Purchasers of Iraqi petroleum and petroleum products will continue to be required to make all payments to an escrow account established by the Secretary-General as a special account of the United Nations. This Escrow Account will replace the escrow account established pursuant to resolutions 706 (1991) and 712 (1991). The Executive Secretary and the Secretary-General will consult to establish the appropriate arrangements for the administration of this Escrow Account and on the question of which person or institution should be the Escrow Agent. Use of an escrow account will ensure continuity and predictability for those involved in transactions involving Iraqi petroleum and petroleum products.

5. The Compensation Fund will be a separate account administered by the Executive Secretary under the policy guidance of the Governing Council. The Executive Secretary will report periodically to the Governing Council on the administration of the Fund. The Escrow Agent will transfer from the Escrow Account to the Compensation Fund the percentage due it and remit the remainder to Iraq, without any further deduction except as specifically provided in this paper. The Compensation Fund will bear interest. The Executive Secretary will be authorized to enter into any agreements or arrangements necessary to implement this paragraph and will report to

the Governing Council on these agreements or arrangements.

6. Contracts for the sale and purchase of Iraqi petroleum and petroleum products will be made directly by Iraq (SOMO) with purchasers. They must provide that payment will be transferred directly to the Escrow Account. To ensure payment occurs, purchasers will be required to open a confirmed irrevocable letter of credit for each transaction providing that the proceeds will be paid to the Escrow Account, except where the Executive Secretary determines that there is an alternative equivalent guarantee of payment. A letter of credit form will be established. The issuing or confirming bank for each transaction will be required to be a reputable commercial bank notified by the parties to the transaction and acceptable to the Executive Secretary. The amount and timing of payments will be in accordance with normal commercial practice (for crude oil shipments, market price, with payment 10-60 days after loading in Iraq or in a contiguous State). The Escrow Agent will notify the Executive Secretary of each payment into the Escrow Account. In cases where payment to the Escrow Account is not made by documentary letter of credit and is not made within the time period specified in the contract, the Executive Secretary will arrange for the stand-by letter of credit (or alternative equivalent guarantee) to be called.

7. With regard only to exports by truck of Iraqi petroleum and petroleum products, a special system will apply. Iraq's neighbouring States will be required, within five days, to provide the Executive Secretary with copies of the customs documents specifying the volume and value of such shipment. If the petroleum or petroleum products are bought for use in a neighbouring State or for re-export, the purchaser will be required to pay the percentage to the Escrow Account within 30 days after petroleum or petroleum products are exported from Iraq. The Escrow Agent will transfer this full amount to the Compensation Fund. Instead of a letter of credit, if payment is not made within 30 days, the Executive Secretary will notify the Escrow Agent of the additional amount to be provided on account of the shipment. The Escrow Agent will then transfer such additional amount to the Compensation Fund out of other funds passing through the Escrow Account. Truck shipments for direct sales by Iraq from terminals in neighbouring States will be handled in the same manner as shipments from pipeline terminals, i.e., the requirements for payment of the full purchase price into the Escrow Account, backed up by a letter of credit, will apply.

8. With respect to barter transactions, Iraq will be required to choose either of the following two options for each shipment: (a) arrange another cash sale from which such additional funds will be deducted as are required to make payment for the barter transaction, with these funds being remitted to the Escrow Account in advance of transfer of title of the petroleum or petroleum product, or (b) pay the required percentage from other sources in advance of the transfer of title. Agreements for such barter transactions must indicate a market contract price for the petroleum or petroleum products. The amount of the required percentage under either of the preceding alternatives will be fixed by reference to this price. If a barter, or other transaction mentioned above occurs without the required payment being made to the Escrow Account, the Executive Secretary will notify the Escrow Agent of the amount to be provided on account of the shipment, and the Escrow Agent will transfer such additional amount to the Compensation Fund out of other funds passing through the Escrow Account.

9. The question of exports of petroleum and petroleum products for debt repayment will be addressed by the Governing Council at a later stage, noting Security Council resolutions 687 (1991) and 692 (1991).

10. The Executive Secretary will report on the status, location and value of the Iraqi petroleum and petroleum products previously exported and subject to the percentage deduction under paragraph 6 of resolution 692 (1991) and, taking into account the results of payments under resolutions 706 (1991) and 712 (1991), will develop, for the consideration of the Governing Council, proposals for assuring that contributions are made to the Compensation Fund with respect to such previous exports.

11. The Escrow Account and Compensation Fund will be special funds of the United Nations with appropriate privileges and immunities. The Compensation Commission will ask the Security Council to reaffirm that the Escrow Account and Compensation Fund enjoy the privileges and immunities of the United Nations. Before the Escrow Account or Compensation Fund are established, a satisfactory legal opinion will be obtained from the institution or institutions in which they are to be held attesting that they will be immune from suit or other form of judicial process, including attachment, garnishment and offsets.

12. The Compensation Commission will ask the Security Council to decide under Chapter VII that exports of Iraqi petroleum and petroleum products, while in transit, are immune from attachment or other legal action. Before Iraqi petroleum or petroleum products transit any State other than Iraq, the Executive Secretary will obtain a satisfactory legal opinion attesting to such immunity from that State or, if he deems it appropriate, may enter into any agreement with that State providing for such immunity. Upon transfer of title to the purchaser, the petroleum and petroleum products will not be subject to garnishment by Iraq's creditors.

13. These arrangements are designed to permit normal commercial marketing of Iraqi petroleum and petroleum products once sanctions are lifted, while both ensuring that the Compensation Fund receives all the payments it is due and protecting the petroleum and petroleum products and the sales proceeds from garnishment by Iraq's creditors. The Escrow Account and Compensation Fund will be immune from garnishment. Payments that purchasers owe the Escrow Account will not be subject to garnishment since the payment will be owed to the account and not to Iraq.

Monitoring

14. The monitoring system is to be implemented with the greatest possible use of existing commercial mechanisms and with a view to imposing the minimum burden on normal commercial activity that is consistent with ensuring payments to the Compensation Fund.

15. The Executive Secretary is requested to hire Commission agents to monitor the flow of petroleum and petroleum products at appropriate points, including any functioning loading terminals and at meters situated at the Iraqi border in any functioning pipeline running into a neighbouring State. Before any loading, Commission agents will check that the contract or barter transaction agreement has the approved content, that the letter of credit has the approved form and content, and that the transaction contains no indication of fraud. This paragraph would not apply to truck shipments; the Commission would essentially rely on the assistance of the Customs authorities in Iraq's neighbouring States to assist in the monitoring, but would have the authority to make spot checks.

16. Commission agents will also check that the pricing is within an acceptable range of the market price as determined by the Executive Secretary, with expert assistance, taking into account other relevant transactions, the commercial usages of the parties to the particular transaction, and other relevant circumstances. If the Commission agents determine that the contract

price is below the acceptable range for petroleum or petroleum products that have been loaded and shipped, the Executive Secretary will notify the Escrow Agent of the additional amount needed to cover the resulting shortfall in contributions to the Compensation Fund. The Escrow Agent will transfer such additional amount to the Compensation Fund out of other funds passing through the Escrow Account. Commission agents will have authority to prevent loading and shipment if these matters are not in order. In accordance with standard practice in the industry, the parties to the transaction will be required to provide a report from a recognized independent petroleum inspector of international reputation attesting to quality and quantity. The Commission agents will provide copies of the contracts, letters of credit and the independent inspectors' reports to the Executive Secretary, who will maintain a register of all transactions and of related payments into the Escrow Account and Compensation Fund.

17. Where the loading terminal is outside Iraq, the Executive Secretary is requested to obtain the assistance of the State where it is located in conducting the monitoring and otherwise assisting in the implementation of the decisions of the Governing Council. (Resolution 692 (1991) requested all States and international organizations to cooperate fully with such decisions.) When Iraq's offshore terminal again becomes operational, the Executive Secretary will make arrangements for monitoring exports from it.

18. The Executive Secretary will consult with the Secretary-General to draw on the relevant experience and staff used by the Secretary-General, to avoid duplication of efforts.

Governing Council and Security Council action

19. The Governing Council requests that the Executive Secretary make all the arrangements, consulting with the Secretary-General as necessary, so that this system can be implemented immediately when the Security Council takes action pursuant to paragraph 22 of resolution 687 (1991). The Governing Council should, when it reports to the Security Council pursuant to paragraph 7 of resolution 692 (1991), request that in the resolution of approval pursuant to paragraph 22 the Security Council include the provisions necessary for the effective implementation of these arrangements, including provisions (a) reaffirming the immunity of the Escrow Account and Compensation Fund, (b) establishing the immunity of the Iraqi petroleum and petroleum products while in transit, until title is transferred to a purchase, and (c) requiring that all States take any necessary domestic measures to implement the arrangements decided upon by the Governing Council for ensuring payments to the Compensation Fund.

S/AC.26/1991/7/Rev.1, 17 March 1992

7. Decision taken by the Governing Council of the United Nations Compensation Commission during its third session, at the 18th meeting, 28 November 1991, [as revised at the 24th meeting, 16 March 1992]

CRITERIA FOR ADDITIONAL CATEGORIES OF CLAIMS

I. Criteria for processing of claims of individuals not otherwise covered

1. The following criteria will govern the submission of all claims of individuals not filed under the criteria adopted by the Governing Council on 2 August 1991, pursuant to resolution 687 (1991).

2. The following criteria are not intended to resolve every issue that may arise with respect to these claims. Rather, they are intended to provide sufficient guidance to enable Governments to prepare consolidated claims submissions.

3. The Commission will process the claims as expeditiously as possible. While decisions on the precise method of processing these claims will be made at a later stage the following steps are contemplated. The Secretariat will make a preliminary assessment of the claims to determine whether they meet the formal requirements established by the Governing Council. The claims would then be submitted to a panel or panels of Commissioners for review within a set time-limit. The Commissioners would be instructed to utilize different procedures appropriate to the character, amount and subject-matter of particular types of claims. In so far as possible, claims with significant common legal or factual issues should be processed together. The Commissioners would be asked to report to the Council on the claims received and the amount recommended for the claims submitted by each Government. The Council would then decide on the total amount to be allocated to each Government. The Council may decide to refer unusually large or complex claims to panels of Commissioners for detailed review, possibly involving additional written submissions and oral proceedings. In such a case, the individual would be allowed to present his or her case directly to the panel.

4. As contributions are made to the Fund, the Council will allocate those funds among the various categories of claims. If resources of the Fund are insufficient with respect to all claims processed to date, *pro rata* payments would be made to Governments periodically as funds become available. The Council will decide on the priority for payment of various categories of claims.

5. Claims may be submitted under this category for the loss of earnings or profits; the Commission will consider at a later time the circumstances in which such claims may be admitted, the amounts to be awarded, and the limits to be imposed thereon.

Claims covered

6. These payments are available with respect to any direct loss, damage, or injury (including death) to individuals as a result of Iraq's unlawful invasion and occupation of Kuwait. This will include any loss suffered as a result of:

(a) Military operations or threat of military action by either side during the period 2 August 1990 to 2 March 1991;

(b) Departure from or inability to leave Iraq or Kuwait (or a decision not to return) during that period;

(c) Actions by officials, employees or agents of the Government of Iraq or its controlled entities during that period in connection with the invasion or occupation;

(d) The breakdown of civil order in Kuwait or Iraq during that period; or

(e) Hostage-taking or other illegal detention.

7. These payments are available with respect to individuals who claim losses in excess of those compensable under claim forms B or C. These payments are also available with respect to individuals who have chosen not to file under claim form A, B, or C because their losses exceed $100,000. In addition, these payments

are available to reimburse payments made or relief provided by individuals to others - for example, to employees or to others pursuant to contractual obligations - for losses covered by any of the criteria adopted by the Council.

8. Since these claims may be for substantial amounts, they must be supported by documentary and other appropriate evidence sufficient to demonstrate the circumstances and the amount of the claimed loss.

9. Direct losses as a result of Iraq's unlawful invasion and occupation of Kuwait are eligible for compensation. Compensation will not be provided for losses suffered as a result of the trade embargo and related measures. Further guidance will be provided on the interpretation and application of this paragraph.

10. Any compensation, whether in funds or in kind, already received from any source will be deducted from the total amount of losses suffered.

Submission of claims

11. Claims will not be considered on behalf of Iraqi nationals who do not have bona fide nationality of any other State.

12. Claims will be submitted by Governments. Each Government may submit claims on behalf of its nationals, and may in its discretion also submit the claims of other persons resident in its territory. In addition, the Council may request an appropriate person, authority, or body to submit claims on behalf of persons who are not in a position to have their claims submitted by a Government.

13. Each consolidated claim must include:

(a) For each separate claim, a signed statement by each individual covered containing:

(i) his or her name and address, and any passport number or other identifying national number;
(ii) a description of and documents evidencing the amount, type, and reason for each element of the loss;
(iii) identification of any compensation, whether in funds or in kind, already received from any source for the claim asserted;
(iv) his or her affirmation that the foregoing information is correct, and that no other claim for the same loss has been submitted to the Commission;
(v) a copy of any previously submitted individual claim; and

(b) The affirmation of the Government submitting the claim that, to the best of the information available to it, the individuals in question are its nationals or residents, and the affirmation of the Government or of the person, authority, or body as referred to in paragraph 12 that it has no reason to believe that the information stated is incorrect.

14. The Executive Secretary (or a Commissioner) will prepare and the Executive Secretary will distribute a standard form for submission of these claims, incorporating the above elements in a clear and concise manner. Except as may otherwise be agreed between the Executive Secretary and the Government in question, claims will be submitted to the Executive Secretary by Governments or by persons, authorities, or bodies as referred to in paragraph 12 on the standard form and must include the information in an official language of the United Nations. Each Government may adopt such procedures as it finds appropriate in preparing its claims. The Executive Secretary (or a Commissioner) will be available to answer questions or provide assistance to any Governments which may request it.

15. Governments must submit all claims on behalf of individuals within one year of the date on which the Executive Secretary circulates these claims forms. The Council encourages the submission of such claims within six months from the date on which the Executive Secretary circulates to Governments the claims forms; and the Commission will thereupon give consideration to such claims as provided herein.

II. Criteria for processing claims of corporations and other entities

16. The following criteria will govern the submission of claims of corporations, other private legal entities and public-sector enterprises (hereinafter referred to as "corporations and other entities") pursuant to resolution 687 (1991).

17. The following criteria are not intended to resolve every issue that may arise with respect to these claims. Rather, they are intended to provide sufficient guidance to enable Governments to prepare consolidated claims submissions.

18. The Commission will process the claims as expeditiously as possible. While decisions on the precise method of processing these claims will be made at a later stage the following steps are contemplated. The Secretariat will make a preliminary assessment of the claims to determine whether they meet the formal requirements established by the Governing Council. The claims would then be submitted to a panel or panels of Commissioners for review within a set time-limit. The Commissioners would be instructed to utilize different procedures appropriate to the character, amount and subject-matter of particular types of claims. In so far as possible, claims with significant common legal or factual issues should be processed together. The Commissioners would be asked to report to the Council on the claims received and the amount recommended for the claims submitted by each Government. The Council would then decide on the total amount to be allocated to each Government. The Council may decide to refer unusually large or complex claims to panels of Commissioners for detailed review, possibly involving additional written submissions and oral proceedings. In such a case, the entity would be allowed to present its case directly to the panel.

19. As contributions are made to the Fund, the Council will allocate those funds among the various categories of claims. If resources of the Fund are insufficient with respect to all claims processed to date, *pro rata* payments would be made to Governments periodically as funds become available. The Council will decide on the priority for payment of various categories of claims.

20. Claims may be submitted under this category for the loss of earnings or profits; the Commission will consider at a later time the circumstances under which such claims may be admitted, the amounts to be awarded, and the limits to be imposed thereon.

Claims covered

21. These payments are available with respect to any direct loss, damage, or injury to corporations and other

entities as a result of Iraq's unlawful invasion and occupation of Kuwait. This will include any loss suffered as a result of:

(a) Military operations or threat of military action by either side during the period 2 August 1990 to 2 March 1991;

(b) Departure of persons from or their inability to leave Iraq or Kuwait (or a decision not to return) during that period;

(c) Actions by officials, employees or agents of the Government of Iraq or its controlled entities during that period in connection with the invasion or occupation;

(d) The breakdown of civil order in Kuwait or Iraq during that period; or

(e) Hostage-taking or other illegal detention.

22. These payments are available to reimburse payments made or relief provided by corporations or other entities to others - for example, to employees, or to others pursuant to contractual obligations - for losses covered by any of the criteria adopted by the Council.

23. Since these claims may be for substantial amounts, they must be supported by documentary and other appropriate evidence sufficient to demonstrate the circumstances and the amount of the claimed loss.

24. Direct losses as a result of Iraq's unlawful invasion and occupation of Kuwait are eligible for compensation. Compensation will not be provided for losses suffered as a result of the trade embargo and related measures. Further guidance will be provided on the interpretation and application of this paragraph.

25. Any compensation, whether in funds or in kind, already received from any source will be deducted from the total amount of losses suffered.

Submission of claims

26. Each Government may submit claims on behalf of corporations or other entities that, on the date on which the claim arose, were incorporated or organized under its law. Claims may be submitted on behalf of a corporation or other entity by only one Government. A corporation or other entity would be required to request the State of its incorporation or organization to submit its claim to the Commission. In the case of a corporation or other private legal entity whose State of incorporation or organization fails to submit, within the deadline established in paragraph 29, such claims falling within the applicable criteria, the corporation or other private legal entity may itself make a claim to the Commission within three months thereafter. It must submit at the same time an explanation as to why its claim is not being submitted by a Government, together with the relevant information specified in paragraph 27. In such a case, any award of the Commission will be paid directly to the corporation or other private legal entity.

27. Each consolidated claim must include:

(a) For each separate claim, a signed statement by an authorized official of each corporation or other entity covered containing:

(i) documents evidencing the name, address and place of incorporation or organization of the entity;

(ii) a general description of the legal structure of the entity;

(iii) a description of and documents evidencing the amount, type, and reason for each element of the loss;

(iv) identification of any compensation, whether in funds or in kind, already received from any source for the claim asserted;

(v) his or her name and address and affirmation that the foregoing information is correct, and that no other claim for the same loss has been submitted to the Commission;

(b) The affirmation of the Government submitting the claim that, to the best of the information available to it, the entities in question are incorporated or organized under its law and the affirmation of the Government that it has no reason to believe that the information stated is incorrect.

28. The Executive Secretary (or a Commissioner) will prepare and the Executive Secretary will distribute a standard form for submission of these claims, incorporating the above elements in a clear and concise manner. Except as may otherwise be agreed between the Executive Secretary and the Government in question, claims will be submitted to the Executive Secretary by Governments on the standard form and must include the information in an official language of the United Nations.Each Government may adopt such procedures as it finds appropriate in preparing its claims. The Executive Secretary (or a Commissioner) will be available to answer questions or provide assistance to any Governments which may request it.

29. Governments must submit all claims on behalf of corporations or other entities within one year of the date the Executive Secretary circulates the claims forms. The Council encourages the submission of such claims within six months from the date on which the Executive Secretary circulates to Governments the claims forms; and the Commission will thereupon give consideration to such claims as provided herein.

III. Criteria for processing claims of governments and international organizations

30. The following criteria will govern the submission of claims of Governments and international organizations pursuant to resolution 687 (1991). Each Government will submit claims of its own and those of its political subdivisions, or any agency, ministry, instrumentality, or entity controlled by it.

31. The following criteria are not intended to resolve every issue that may arise with respect to these claims. Rather, they are intended to provide sufficient guidance to enable Governments and international organizations to prepare consolidated claims submissions.

32. The Commission will process the claims as expeditiously as possible. While decisions on the precise method of processing these claims will be made at a later stage the following steps are contemplated. The Secretariat will make a preliminary assessment of the claims to determine whether they meet the formal requirements established by the Governing Council. The claims would then be submitted to a panel or panels of Commissioners for review within a set time-limit. The Commissioners would be instructed to utilize different procedures appropriate to the character, amount and subject-matter of particular types of claims. In so far as possible, claims with significant common legal or factual

issues should be processed together. The Commissioners would be asked to report to the Council on the claims received and the amount recommended for the claims submitted by each Government. The Council would then decide on the total amount to be allocated to each Government. The Council may decide to refer unusually large or complex claims to panels of Commissioners for detailed review, possibly involving additional written submissions and oral proceedings. In such a case, when an international organization is involved, it would be allowed to present its case directly to the panel.

33. As contributions are made to the Fund, the Council will allocate those funds among the various categories of claims. If resources of the Fund are insufficient with respect to all claims processed to date, *pro rata* payments would be made to Governments periodically as funds become available. The Council will decide on the priority for payment of various categories of claims.

Claims covered

34. These payments are available with respect to any direct loss, damage, or injury to Governments or international organizations as a result of Iraq's unlawful invasion and occupation of Kuwait. This will include any loss suffered as a result of:

(a) Military operations or threat of military action by either side during the period 2 August 1990 to 2 March 1991;

(b) Departure of persons from or their inability to leave Iraq or Kuwait (or a decision not to return) during that period;

(c) Actions by officials, employees or agents of the Government of Iraq or its controlled entities during that period in connection with the invasion or occupation;

(d) The breakdown of civil order in Kuwait or Iraq during that period; or

(e) Hostage-taking or other illegal detention.

35. These payments are available with respect to direct environmental damage and the depletion of natural resources as a result of Iraq's unlawful invasion and occupation of Kuwait. This will include losses or expenses resulting from:

(a) Abatement and prevention of environmental damage, including expenses directly relating to fighting oil fires and stemming the flow of oil in coastal and international waters;

(b) Reasonable measures already taken to clean and restore the environment or future measures which can be documented as reasonably necessary to clean and restore the environment;

(c) Reasonable monitoring and assessment of the environmental damage for the purposes of evaluating and abating the harm and restoring the environment;

(d) Reasonable monitoring of public health and performing medical screenings for the purposes of investigation and combating increased health risks as a result of the environmental damage; and

(e) Depletion of or damage to natural resources.

36. These payments will include loss of or damage to property of a Government, as well as loses and costs incurred by a Government in evacuating its nationals from Iraq or Kuwait. These payments are also available to reimburse payments made or relief provided by Governments or international organizations to others - for example to nationals, residents or employees or to others pursuant to contractual obligations - for losses covered by any of the criteria adopted by the Council.

37. Since these claims will be for substantial amounts, they must be supported by documentary and other appropriate evidence sufficient to demonstrate the circumstances and the amount of the claimed loss.

38. Direct losses as a result of Iraq's unlawful invasion and occupation of Kuwait are eligible for compensation. Compensation will not be provided for losses suffered as a result of the trade embargo and related measures. Further guidance will be provided on the interpretation and application of this paragraph.

39. Any compensation, whether in funds or in kind, already received from any source will be deducted from the total amount of losses suffered.

Submission of claims

40. Each consolidated claim must include:

(a) For each separate claim, a signed statement by an authorized official of the Government or international organization containing:

(i) his or her name and address, and government agency instrumentality, or ministry or controlled entity, or the international organization, with which associated;

(ii) a description of and documents evidencing the amount, type, and reason for each element of the loss;

(iii) identification of any compensation, whether in funds or in kind, already received from any source for the claim asserted;

(iv) his or her affirmation that the foregoing information is correct, and that no other claim for the same loss has been submitted to the Commission;

(b) The affirmation of the Government or international organization submitting the consolidated claim that to the best of the information available to it, it has no reason to believe that the information stated is incorrect.

41. The Executive Secretary (or a Commissioner) will prepare and the Executive Secretary will distribute a standard form for submission of claims, incorporating the above elements in a clear and concise manner. Except as may otherwise be agreed between the Executive Secretary and the Government or international organization in question, claims will be submitted to the Executive Secretary on the standard form and must include the information in an official language of the United Nations. The Executive Secretary (or a Commissioner) will be available to answer questions or provide assistance to any Governments or international organizations which may request it.

42. Governments and international organizations must submit all claims within one year of the date on which the Executive Secretary circulates the standard form. The Council encourages the submission of such claims within six months from the date on which the Executive Secretary circulates to Governments and international organizations the claims forms; and the Commission will

thereupon give consideration to such claims as provided herein.

S/AC.26/1992/8, 27 January 1992

8. Decision taken by the Governing Council of the United Nations Compensation Commission during its fourth session, at the 22nd meeting, 24 January 1992

DETERMINATION OF CEILINGS FOR COMPENSATION FOR MENTAL PAIN AND ANGUISH

At its third session, the Governing Council examined the question of possible ceilings or fixed amounts for compensation for mental pain and anguish on the basis of a study prepared by the Secretariat (S/AC.26/1991/WP.18).

After having discussed the issue, the Governing Council decided to adopt ceilings rather than fixed amounts for compensation for mental pain and anguish, but postponed the actual determination of the amounts for the Governing Council's fourth session. In order to assist the Governing Council in its discussion of applicable ceiling amounts, the Secretariat prepared an information sheet on the number of potential claimants eligible for compensation for mental pain and anguish (S/AC.26/1992/CRP.5).

Following extensive exchanges on the subject, a consensus of opinion was reached resulting in the following formulations on ceiling amounts for compensation for mental pain and anguish:

CATEGORY A: A spouse, child or parent of the individual suffered death.

US $15,000

US $30,000 ceiling per family unit.

CATEGORY B: The individual suffered serious personal injury involving dismemberment, permanent or temporary significant disfigurement, or permanent or temporary significant loss of use or limitation of use of a body organ, member, function or system.

US $15.000 ceiling for dismemberment, permanent significant disfigurement, or permanent loss of use or permanent limitation of use of a body organ, member, function or system;

US $5,000 ceiling for temporary significant disfigurement or temporary significant loss of use or limitation of use of a body organ, member, function or system.

CATEGORY C: The individual suffered sexual assault or aggravated assault or torture.

US $5,000 ceiling per incident.

CATEGORY D: The individual witnessed the intentional infliction of events described in Categories A, B or C on his or her spouse, child or parent.

US $2,500 ceiling per claimant;

US $5,000 ceiling per family unit.

CATEGORY E: The individual was taken hostage or illegally detained for more than three days, or for a shorter period in circumstances indicating an imminent threat to his or her life.

US $1,500 per claimant for being taken hostage or illegally detained for more than three days, or for a shorter period in circumstances indicating an imminent threat to life;

US $100 per day for each day detained in Iraq or Kuwait beyond three;

Ceiling of US $10,000 per claimant.

CATEGORY F: On account of a manifestly well-founded fear for one's life or of being taken hostage or illegally detained, the individual was forced to hide for more than three days.

US $1,500 per claimant for being forced to hide for three days;

US $50 per day for each day forced to hide in Iraq or Kuwait beyond three;

Ceiling of US $5,000 per claimant.

CATEGORY G: The individual was deprived of all economic resources, such as to threaten seriously his or her survival and that of his or her spouse, children or parents, in cases where assistance from his or her Government or other sources has not been provided.

US $2,500 ceiling per claimant;

US $5,000 ceiling per family unit.

These amounts are payable cumulatively where more than one situation applies with respect to particular claimants. However, the following overall ceilings will apply to total cumulative amounts available to claimants for payments for mental pain and anguish:

US $30,000 ceiling per claimant;

US $60,000 ceiling per family unit.

S/AC.26/1992/9, 6 March 1992

9. Decision taken by the Governing Council of the United Nations Compensation Commission during its resumed fourth session, at the 23rd meeting, 6th March 1992

PROPOSITIONS AND CONCLUSIONS ON COMPENSATION FOR BUSINESS LOSSES: TYPES OF DAMAGES AND THEIR VALUATION

1. The propositions and conclusions contained in this Decision shall apply to compensation for the loss of earnings or profits and other business losses covered by Security Council resolution 687 (1991).

2. The basic premise underlying all of the findings concerning business losses is that, pursuant to paragraph

16 of Security Council resolution 687 (1991), Iraq "is liable under international law for any direct loss, damage, including environmental damage and the depletion of natural resources, or injury to foreign Governments, nationals and corporations as a result of Iraq's unlawful invasion and occupation of Kuwait".

3. This Decision does not attempt to describe all of the conceivable factual and legal situations result from Iraq's invasion and occupation of Kuwait. Bearing in mind Security Council resolution 687 (1991), other types of losses may have been suffered, and they are eligible for compensation if they result from Iraq's invasion and occupation of Kuwait. Ultimately, it will be up to the Commissioners to identify the applicable principles and apply them to the circumstances of particular cases.

4. The propositions and conclusions contained in this Decision are not intended to be a comprehensive statement of relevant principles. The Governing Council will review the matter and will provide further guidance concerning business losses as required in the future. In particular, the Governing Council will request the Secretariat to consider the question of steps which might be taken to protect against multiple recovery of compensation by claimants, or to confirm that claimants have attempted to avail themselves of particular possible sources of recovery, as a prerequisite to relief from the Commission.

5. When reference is made herein to corporations and other legal entities, it is understood that such corporations or other legal entities may be either publicly or privately owned enterprises.

6. The trade embargo and related measures*,[*. The trade embargo and related measures refers to the prohibitions in United Nations Security Council Resolution 661 (1990) and relevant subsequent resolutions and the measures taken by states pursuant thereto.] and the economic situation caused thereby, will not be accepted as the basis for compensation. Compensation will be provided to the extent that Iraq's unlawful invasion and occupation of Kuwait constituted a cause of direct loss, damage or injury which is separate and distinct from the trade embargo and related measures. (Where, for example, the full extent of the loss, damage or injury arose as a direct result of Iraq's unlawful invasion and occupation of Kuwait, it should be compensated notwithstanding the fact that it may also be attributable to the trade embargo and related measures). The total amount of compensable losses will be reduced to the extent that those losses could reasonably have been avoided. Further guidance on the matters dealt with in this paragraph will be provided by the Governing Council for the use of the Commissioners when assessing claims.

I. LOSSES IN CONNECTION WITH CONTRACTS OR PAST BUSINESS PRACTICE

A) Contracts

7. The following general conclusions apply with regard to Iraq's liability for contract losses.

Contracts with Iraq

8. Where Iraq itself was a contracting party and breached its contractual obligations, Iraq is liable under general contract law to compensate for all actual losses suffered by the other contracting party, including, inter alia, losses relating to specially manufactured goods. Future lost profits may be compensable in such a case if they can be calculated under the contract with reasonable certainty. An alternative measure of damages may apply where a governing contract specifically provides for a particular measure, except that the amount of compensation provided should not exceed the loss actually suffered. Breaches of contract not resulting from the invasion and occupation of Kuwait are not within the jurisdiction of the Commission.

9. Where Iraq did not breach a contract to which it was a party, but continuation of the contract became impossible for the other party as a result of Iraq's invasion and occupation of Kuwait, Iraq is liable for any direct loss the other party suffered as a result, including lost profits. In such a situation, Iraq should not be allowed to invoke *force majeure* or similar contract provisions, or general principles of contract excuse, to avoid its liability.

Contracts where Iraq is not a party

10. Where losses have been suffered in connection with contracts to which Iraq was not a party, the following conclusions apply. Iraq is responsible for the losses that have resulted from the invasion and occupation of Kuwait. A relevant consideration may be whether the contracting parties could resume the contract after the lifting of the embargo against Kuwait, and whether they have in fact resumed the contract. Iraq principally cannot be relieved from its responsibility by *force majeure* provisions of contracts to which it is not a party or contract excuse rules of other applicable laws.

B) Past business practice

11. Where a loss has been suffered relating to a transaction that has been part of a business practice or course of dealing, Iraq is liable according to the principles that apply to contract losses. No liability exists for losses related to transactions that were only expected to take place based on a previous course of dealing.

II. LOSSES RELATING TO TANGIBLE ASSETS

12. Where direct losses were suffered as a result of Iraq's invasion and occupation of Kuwait with respect to tangible assets, Iraq is liable for compensation. Typical actions of this kind would have been expropriation, removal, theft or destruction of particular items of property by Iraqi authorities. Whether the taking of property was lawful or not is not relevant for Iraq's liability if it did not provide for compensation.

13. In a case where business property had been lost because it had been left unguarded by company personnel departing due to the situation in Iraq and Kuwait, such loss may be considered as resulting directly from the invasion and occupation.

14. On the other hand, losses that occurred because company personnel was detained by Iraqi authorities, must clearly be considered a direct result. In this context. it is relevant to note the Hague Regulations on Land Warfare annexed to Conventions II of 1899 and IV of 1907 respecting the Laws and Customs of War on Land, which require that an occupying power has to restore and to ensure public order and safety as far as possible (Hague Regulations, Article 43).

15. Depending on the type of asset and the circumstances of the case, one of several valuation methods may be used. Methods typically used to value tangible assets are book value and replacement value. *Book value* is considered to mean value at which an asset is carried on a balance sheet. Book value at any time is cost of an item minus accumulated depreciation. *Replacement value* is considered to mean the amount required to obtain an asset of the same kind and status as the asset damaged or

lost. Replacement value would not normally allow for replacement of an old item with a new one.

III. LOSSES RELATING TO INCOME-PRODUCING PROPERTIES

16. The following general conclusions apply with regard to losses suffered as a result of Iraq's invasion and occupation of Kuwait in connection with income-producing properties. These include various kinds of businesses whose value is determined not only by the value of their individual assets but also by the greater value they possess due to their capacity to generate income. The conclusions are based on the premise that the business affected was a going concern, i.e. it has the capacity to continue to operate and generate income in the future.

17. In principle, Iraq is liable to compensate for the loss of a business or commercial entity as a whole resulting from Iraq's invasion and occupation of Kuwait. In the event that the business has been rebuilt and resumed, or that it could reasonably have been expected that the business could have been rebuilt and resumed, compensation may only be claimed for the loss suffered during the relevant period.

18. For the valuation of income-producing properties there are several alternative concepts. One is to measure by reference to costs, which leads to the determination of book value. Another is to determine the value of the property as a going concern. This is often done by reference to the market value of similar properties. Where such market value cannot be ascertained, the economic or current value of that asset can be ascertained by the *discounted cash flow (DCF)* method or by the *price/earnings (P/E)* method. The DCF method calculates the value at one specified time of cash flows that are to be received at a different time by discounting the yearly net cash flows to present value, with the discount rate including cost of capital and risk components. The price/earnings method takes as a basis past periods' business results and then capitalises them by the application of a multiple (P/E ratio) which reflects expectations about future performance and growth, or lack of it.

19. In principle, the economic value of a business may include loss of future earnings and profits where they can be ascertained with reasonable certainty. In the case of the loss of businesses and their earning capacity resulting from the invasion and occupation of Kuwait, it can be expected that a number of such businesses can be or could have been rebuilt and resumed. The method of a valuation should therefore be one that focuses on past performance rather than on forecasts and projections into the future. Compensation should be provided if the loss can be ascertained with reasonable certainty based on prior earnings or profits. For example, the loss of any earnings or profits during the relevant time period could be calculated by a multiple of past earnings and profits corresponding to that time period.

10. UN Press Release, 7 February 1992

Talks between the United Nations on the subject of oil sales have been cancelled, according to a message delivered by the Permanent Representative of Iraq to the United Nations, Abdul Amir A. Al-Anbari. The Security Council, which met on 5 February pursuant to paragraph 21 of Resolution 687 (1991) which requests the Council to review the sanctions regime against Iraq every sixty days, strongly deplored the Iraqi decision to discontinue contacts with the United Nations regarding oil sales to finance the purchase of humanitarian relief. ...

S/23732, 19 March 1992

11. Note by the President of the Security Council, 19 March 1992

Following consultations among members of the Security Council, the President of the Council made the following statement, on behalf of the Council, at its 3061st meeting, on 19 March 1992, in connection with the Council's consideration of the item entitled "The situation between Iraq and Kuwait":

> "The Security Council welcomes the announcement of the Iraqi authorities that they will resume discussions with the United Nations Secretariat concerning implementation of the scheme of sales of Iraqi petroleum and petroleum products, as provided for in Security Council resolutions 706 (1991) and 712 (1991), and for the use of the proceeds of such sales in accordance with the Secretary-General's report of 4 September 1991 (S/23006) and the above-mentioned resolutions.
>
> "The Council also welcomes the Secretary-General's intention that these discussions be organized without delay.
>
> "The Council is prepared to authorize the regime for the sale of Iraqi petroleum and petroleum products on the above basis for a like period of time as that specified in these resolutions as soon as the Secretary-General indicates that the Iraqi authorities are prepared to proceed on a date certain with the export of petroleum and petroleum products in accordance with the scheme.
>
> "The members of the Council are prepared at an appropriate time to consider possible further extensions of time based upon Iraq's cooperation with the above and the Council's ongoing assessment of the needs and requirements in accordance with paragraph 1 (d) of Security Council resolution 706 (1991)."

S/AC.26/1992/10, 26 June 1992

12. Decision taken by the Governing Council of the United Nations Compensation Commission at the 27th meeting, sixth session, 26 June 1992

The Governing Council decides:

To approve the Provisional Rules for Claims Procedure the text of which is annexed to the present decision.

ANNEX

PROVISIONAL RULES FOR CLAIMS PROCEDURE

I) GENERAL PROVISIONS

Article 1. Use of Terms

The following definitions apply for the purpose of these Rules:

(1) "Commission" means the United Nations Compensation Commission.

(2) "Compensation Fund" or "Fund" means the United Nations Compensation Fund, created by paragraph 18 of Security Council resolution 687 (1991) and established by paragraph 3 of Security Council resolution 692 (1991) in accordance with section I of the Secretary-General's Report (S/22559) dated 2 May 1991.

(3) "Secretary-General" means the Secretary-General of the United Nations.

(4) "Governing Council" or "Council" means the Governing Council of the Commission.

(5) "Commissioners" means experts appointed by the Governing Council for the verification and evaluation of claims.

(6) "Executive Secretary" means the Executive Secretary of the Commission and includes any Deputy of, or other person, authorized by the Executive Secretary.

(7) "Secretariat" means the Secretariat of the Commission.

(8) "Standard Forms" means claim forms prepared and distributed to Governments by the Executive Secretary for claims under claims criteria adopted by the Governing Council.

(9) "Claim Forms" means standard forms and any other form agreed between the Executive Secretary and the Government or international organization in question for filing claims.

(10) "Rules" means the Commission's Provisional Rules for Claims Procedure.

(11) "Criteria" means Criteria for Expedited Processing of Urgent Claims (Governing Council's decision No. S/AC.26/1991/1 dated 2 August 1991), and Criteria for Additional Categories of Claims (Governing Council's decision No. S/AC.26/1991/7 dated 4 December 1991) as well as any other criteria that the Governing Council may adopt.

(12) "Claimant" means any individual, corporation or other private legal entity, public sector entity, Government or international organization that files a claim with the Commission.

(13) "Person or Body" means an individual, corporation or other private legal entity, public sector entity, Government, or international organization.

(14) "International Organization" means an international organization of States.

(15) "Documents" means all submissions and evidence presented by a claimant in support of a claim, in whatever form, including Statements of Claim in categories E and F.

(16) "Database" means computerized information, pertaining to individual claimants and claims, kept by the Commission to assist in the processing of claims.

Article 2. Scope of the Rules

These Rules apply to processing of claims submitted to the Commission under the criteria adopted by the Governing Council.

Article 3. Calculation of Periods of Time

For the purposes of calculating a period of time under these Rules, such period shall begin to run on the day following the day when the document is received or a notification is made. If the last day of such period is an official holiday or a non-business day at the headquarters of the Commission, the period is extended until the first business day that follows. Official holidays and non-business days occurring during the running of the period of time are included in calculating the period. The Executive Secretary will issue a list of such days.

II) SUBMISSION AND FILING OF CLAIMS

Article 4. Submission of Claims

1) Claim forms and documents are to be submitted to the Commission at the Secretariat's headquarters (Palais des Nations, Villa La Pelouse, Geneva, Switzerland).

2) Claim forms shall be deemed to have been submitted when they are physically delivered to and received by the Secretariat.

Article 5. Who May Submit Claims

1) Governments and international organizations are entitled to submit claims to the Commission.

a) A Government may submit claims on behalf of its nationals and, at its discretion, of other persons resident in its territory. In the case of Governments existing in the territory of a former federal state, one such Government may submit claims on behalf of nationals, corporations or other entities of another such Government, if both Governments agree.

b) A Government may submit claims on behalf of corporations or other entities that, on the date on which the claim arose, were incorporated or organized under the law of that State. If the Governments concerned agree, one Government may submit claims in respect of joint ventures on behalf of the nationals, corporations or other entities of other Governments.

c) Claims may be submitted on behalf of an individual, corporation or other entity by only one Government.

d) International organizations may submit claims only on their own behalf.

2) An appropriate person, authority, or body appointed by the Governing Council may submit claims on behalf of persons who are not in a position to have their claims submitted by a Government.

3) A corporation or other private legal entity is required to request the State of its incorporation or organization to submit its claim to the Commission. In the case of a corporation or other private legal entity whose State of incorporation or organization fails to submit, within the time-limit established by the Governing Council, such claims falling within the applicable criteria, the corporation or other private legal entity may itself make a claim to the Commission within three months thereafter. It must provide at the same time an explanation as to why its claim is not being submitted by a Government.

Article 6. Claim Forms and Language

1) Except as may otherwise be agreed between the Executive Secretary and the Government or international organization in question, claims must be submitted on the standard forms prepared and distributed by the Secretariat.

2) Due to the fact that the Commission's computerized software and database system, which is technically required for the processing of a large number of claims, has been designed in English, the working language of the claims procedure before the Commission will be English.

3) Claim forms can be submitted in any of the official languages of the United Nations. However, since English is the working language of the claims procedure and of the Commission's computerized database, in cases where claim forms are not submitted in English, an English translation of the form must be provided. The translation as submitted, will serve as the basis for the evaluation of the claim.

4) With respect to claims in categories A, B and C, the documents supporting the claims are not required to be translated into English at the stage of the submission of the claims. The Secretariat, on the basis of methods adopted for processing and evaluation of claims, will notify each Government as to the extent of the translation required and the time-limit for providing it.

5) With respect to claims in categories D, E and F, all documents supporting the claims must also be submitted in English or be accompanied by an English translation.

6) In the case of oral proceedings, the Executive Secretary shall arrange for interpretation as necessary into and from other official languages of the United Nations.

Article 7. Format of Claims

1) Claim forms in category A must be submitted only in the computer format distributed by the Secretariat. Governments will maintain custody of the original paper copies of Form A and supporting documents and will make them available to the Commission upon request.

2) Claim forms and documents in all other categories must be submitted on paper. In addition to filing claims in these categories on paper, Governments may also submit them in a computer format.

3) All claim forms and documents filed with the Commission on paper are to be submitted on paper 8½ inches x 11 inches or on A-4 size paper (21 cm x 29.5 cm) or on paper no larger than A-4. If a document cannot conveniently be reproduced on paper no larger than A-4, it is to be folded to A-4 size, unless the Executive Secretary agrees otherwise in special circumstances.

4) Claims and documents filed with the Commission in a computer format are to be submitted on MS/DOS or UNIX compatible formats, or in such other format as may be agreed to by the Executive Secretary.

Article 8. Copies

1) Except as otherwise agreed to by the Executive Secretary, claim forms and documents must be submitted with the following number of copies:

For category A: 3 copies of micro floppy disk

For categories B & C: 1 original and 2 copies

For D & other categories: 1 original and 8 copies

2) The Secretariat, or the Commissioners, may request additional copies or accept a smaller number in exceptional circumstances.

Article 9. Representatives

For the purpose of these Rules, all communications between the Commission's Secretariat and a Government concerning claims shall take place through its Permanent Mission in Geneva. Further, except in cases where a specially authorized representative is designated by a Government and notified to the Executive Secretary, the head of the Permanent Mission of a Government shall be considered as its representative before the Commission. Governments that do not maintain Permanent Missions in Geneva and international organizations shall notify the name of their duly authorized representatives to the Executive Secretary.

Article 10. The Registry

A registry will be set up within the Secretariat. A member of the Secretariat will be designated by the Executive Secretary as Registry Officer. The Registry Officer will receive the claims and register them.

Article 11. Receipt of Claims

1) Upon the submission of a claim, the Registry Officer will issue a delivery receipt identifying the parcel received and confirming the date it was received and the person who presented it.

2) The Registry Officer will in due course verify:

a) that the claim has been submitted by a person or body who, in accordance with the decisions of the Governing Council, has a right to file claims with the Commission;

b) that the claim has been submitted within the relevant time-limit established by the Governing Council;

c) that, in the case of a corporation or other private legal entity making a claim directly to the Commission in accordance with Article 5, paragraph 3, above:

i) evidence is attached indicating that a request was made by the entity concerned to the State of its incorporation or organization to submit its claim to the Commission;

ii) explanation is provided as to why the claim was not submitted by a Government.

Article 12. Unauthorized or Late Submissions

1) In the case of claims submitted by an unauthorized person or entity, including claims presented by a corporation or other private legal entity without showing that a previous request has been made to the State of its incorporation or organization, the Executive Secretary will return the documents received, and inform the

person or entity concerned of the reasons why the claim cannot be registered.

2) In the case of claims submitted by an authorized person or body after the expiration of the time-limit set by the Governing Council for a given category of claims, the Executive Secretary will report to the Governing Council. The Governing Council will decide whether to accept the late-filed claims or not.

Article 13. Filing Receipt

If the claim is submitted by an authorized person or body within the established time-limit, the Registry Officer will register the claim and issue a filing receipt indicating:

a) the claim and its category;
b) the party who presented the claim;
c) the number of claims contained in a consolidated claim;
d) the number assigned to the claim for identification.

Article 14. Preliminary Assessment

1) The Secretariat will make a preliminary assessment of the claims received in order to determine whether they meet the formal requirements established by the Governing Council. To this end the Secretariat will verify:

a) that the claims have been submitted on the appropriate claim forms with the required number of copies, and in English or with an English translation;

b) that the claims contain the names and addresses of the claimants and, where applicable, evidence of the amount, type and causes of losses;

c) that the affirmation by the Government has been included in respect of each consolidated claim stating that, to the best of the information available to it, the claimants are its nationals or residents, and that it has no reason to believe that the information stated in the claims is incorrect;

d) that all required affirmations have been given by each claimant.

2) In the case of claims of corporations and other legal entities the Secretariat will also verify that each separate claim contains:

a) documents evidencing the name, address and place of incorporation or organization of the entity;

b) evidence that the corporation or the legal entity was, on the date on which the claim arose, incorporated or organized under the law of the State the Government of which has submitted the claim;

c) a general description of the legal structure of the entity;

d) an affirmation by the authorized official for each corporation or other entity that the information contained in the claim is correct.

Article 15. Claims Not Meeting the Formal Requirements

If it is found that the claim does not meet the formal requirements established by the Governing Council, the Secretariat will notify the person or body that submitted the claim about that circumstance and will give it 60 days from the date of that notification to remedy the defect. If the formal requirements are not met within this period, the claim shall not be considered as filed.

Article 16. Reports and Views on Claims

1) The Executive Secretary will make periodic reports to the Governing Council concerning claims received. These reports shall be made as frequently as required to inform the Council of the Commission's case load but not less than quarterly. The reports shall indicate:

a) Governments, international organizations or other eligible parties that have submitted claims;

b) the categories of claims submitted;

c) the number of claimants in each consolidated claim;

d) the total amount of compensation sought in each consolidated claim;

In addition, each report may indicate significant legal and factual issues raised by the claims, if any.

2) The Executive Secretary's report will be promptly circulated to the Government of Iraq as well as to all Governments and international organizations that have submitted claims.

3) Within 30 days in case of claims in Categories A, B and C, and 90 days in case of claims in other categories, of the date of the circulation of the Executive Secretary's report, the Government of Iraq as well as Governments and international organizations that have submitted claims, may present their additional information and views concerning the report to the Executive Secretary for transmission to panels of Commissioners in accordance with Article 32. There shall be no extensions of the time-limits specified in this paragraph.

4) Requirements set forth in Articles 3, 4, 6 (3), 7, 8 and 11 (1) shall apply to such additional information and views.

Article 17. Categorization of Claims

In order to facilitate the work of Commissioners and to ensure uniformity in the treatment of similar claims, the Secretariat will proceed to categorize claims according to, *inter alia*, the type or size of the claims and the similarity of legal and factual issue.

III) COMMISSIONERS

Article 18. Appointment

1) Commissioners shall be appointed for specific tasks and terms by the Governing Council upon nomination by the Secretary-General on the basis of recommendations of the Executive Secretary.

2) The Secretary-General has established a Register of Experts which, as stated in his 12 June 1991 invitation

for the submission of names of experts, while not limiting his selection, might be drawn upon when Commissioners are nominated for appointment. The Executive Secretary will keep and up-date the register.

Article 19. Qualifications

1) In nominating and appointing the Commissioners, due regard shall be paid to the need for geographical representation, professional qualifications, experience and integrity.

2) Commissioners will be experts in fields such as finance, law, accounting, insurance, environmental damage assessment, oil, trade and engineering.

3) Nominations and appointments of Commissioners shall be made paying due regard to the nature of the claims and categories of claims to be assigned to them.

Article 20. Procedure for Appointment

1) The Executive Secretary will transmit to the Governing Council the nominations for Commissioners proposed by the Secretary-General, indicating which Commissioners are to serve on each panel and who, within each panel, will act as a Chairman.

2) The Executive Secretary will recommend to the Secretary-General for nomination as many panels of Commissioners as necessary to process claims in an expeditious manner.

3) When transmitting to the Governing Council the nominations for Commissioners, the Executive Secretary will specify the claims or categories of claims to be assigned to each panel, indicating the expertise and the number of Commissioners required.

4) If the Governing Council does not agree on the appointment of a nominee for a panel, it will request the Secretary-General, through the Executive Secretary, to submit a new nomination.

5) If, at the time the Executive Secretary transmits the new nomination, the Governing Council is not in session, the new nomination will be communicated to the members of the Governing Council. The Governing Council may approve replacement Commissioners at intersessional meetings.

6) The same procedure will apply whenever a new Commissioner must be nominated.

Article 21. Requirements

1) Commissioners will act in their personal capacity. Commissioners shall not have financial interests in any of the claims submitted to them or to the panel to which they belong. They may not be associated with or have financial interests in any corporations whose claims have been submitted to them or to the panel to which they belong.

2) Commissioners shall not represent or advise any party or claimant concerning the preparation or presentation of their claims to the Commission during their service as Commissioner or for two years thereafter.

Article 22. Disclosure

1) All prospective Commissioners shall file a statement that shall disclose to the Executive Secretary any prior or actual relationship with Governments, corporations or individuals, or any other circumstances, that are likely to give rise to justifiable doubts as to his impartiality or independence with respect to his prospective tasks. This information will be provided to the Governing Council at the time the nomination of the prospective Commissioner is transmitted.

2) A Commissioner, once appointed, shall disclose to the Executive Secretary any new circumstances likely to give rise to justifiable doubts as to his impartiality or independence.

3) When any Commissioner obtains knowledge that any particular claim before his panel involves circumstances likely to give rise to justifiable doubts as to his impartiality or independence with respect to that claim or group of claims, he shall disclose such circumstances to the Executive Secretary and, if appropriate, shall disqualify himself as to that case.

4) If any Government, international organization, individual claimant, or Commissioner becomes aware of circumstances that give rise to justifiable doubts as to a Commissioner's impartiality or independence, such circumstances must be communicated to the Executive Secretary not later than fifteen days after they became known.

5) The Executive Secretary will inform the Governing Council about the circumstances brought to his attention or of which he learns that are likely to give rise to justifiable doubts as to the impartiality or independence of a Commissioner, transmitting a statement of the Commissioner concerned.

6) In any case in which such circumstances are disclosed to the Governing Council, it may determine whether the Commissioner should cease to act, either generally or with respect to a particular claim or claims. Pending such a determination by the Governing Council, the Commissioner concerned will continue to perform his tasks.

Article 23. Resignation

1) A Commissioner who intends to resign from his office shall communicate his decision, through the Executive Secretary, to the Governing Council.

2) A Commissioner who has submitted his resignation shall continue to perform his functions until such time as his resignation is accepted by the Governing Council.

Article 24. Completion of Work

If a Commissioner resigns during the course of consideration of any particular claim or groups of claims, the Commissioner will continue to serve for the limited purpose of completing work on that particular claim or group of claims, unless excused by the Governing Council.

Article 25. Failure to Act

In the event that a Commissioner fails to act or in the event of *de jure* or *de facto* impossibility of his performing his functions, the Executive Secretary shall inform the Governing Council, which may decide to replace the Commissioner in accordance with the procedures set forth in Article 20 (6).

Article 26. Privileges and Immunities

Commissioners, when performing functions for the Commission, will have the status of experts on mission within the meaning of Article VI of the Convention on the

Privileges and Immunities of the United Nations of February 13, 1946.

Article 27. Declaration

Every Commissioner shall, before taking up his duties, make the following declaration:

> "I solemnly declare that I will perform my duties and exercise my position as Commissioner honourably, faithfully, independently, impartially and conscientiously."

This declaration shall be signed and delivered to the Executive Secretary, and attached to the documents pertaining to the Commissioner's appointment.

IV) PROCEDURES GOVERNING THE WORK OF THE PANELS

Article 28. Constitution of Panels

1) Unless otherwise decided by the Governing Council, Commissioners will work in panels of three members. Each of the members of a panel shall be of different nationality.

2) Priority is to be given to the establishment of panels of Commissioners to deal with claims in categories A, B and C.

Article 29. Organization of Work

Chairmen of the panels will organize the work of their respective panels so as to ensure the expeditious processing of the claims and the consistent application of the relevant criteria and these Rules.

Article 30. Confidentiality

1) Unless otherwise provided in these procedures or decided by the Governing Council, all records received or developed by the Commission will be confidential, but the Secretariat may provide status reports to Governments, international organizations or corporations making claims directly to the Commission in accordance with Article 5, paragraph 3, regarding claims that they have submitted.

2) Panels will conduct their work in private.

3) Commissioners shall not disclose, even after the termination of their functions, any information not in the public domain that has come to their knowledge by reason of their working for the Commission.

Article 31. Applicable Law

In considering the claims, Commissioners will apply Security Council resolution 687 (1991) and other relevant Security Council resolutions, the criteria established by the Governing Council for particular categories of claims, and any pertinent decisions of the Governing Council. In addition, where necessary, Commissioners shall apply other relevant rules of international law.

Article 32. Submission of Claims to Panels

1) Following the appointment of Commissioners by the Governing Council, the Executive Secretary will submit to panels of Commissioners the single claims or categories of claims assigned to each of them together with the related documentation, containing the results of the preliminary assessment made by the Secretariat and any other information deemed to be useful for the work of the Commissioners, as well as the additional information and views submitted in accordance with Article 16.

2) Any information received by the Secretariat after the expiration of the time-limits as established in Article 16 will be submitted when received, but the work of the panel will not be delayed pending receipt or consideration of such information.

3) The Executive Secretary may, after consulting the relevant panel chairmen, reallocate a claim or claims from one panel to another in order to ensure the efficient processing of claims.

Article 33. Work of the Panels

1) After receiving claims from the Executive Secretary, Commissioners will examine them and meet to deliberate and prepare their recommendations to the Governing Council.

2) Panels of Commissioners will normally meet at the headquarters of the Secretariat. Meetings will be held to the extent deemed necessary by the Chairman of each panel. Commissioners will continue their work on the claims while away from the headquarters of the Secretariat, conducting the necessary communications among themselves and with the Secretariat.

3) Any recommendation or other decision of the panel shall be made by a majority of the Commissioners.

Article 34. Assistance by the Executive Secretary

1) The Executive Secretary and the staff of the Secretariat will provide administrative, technical and legal support to the Commissioners, including the development and maintenance of a computerized database for claims and assistance in obtaining additional information.

2) In considering the claims, the Commissioners will take into account the results of the preliminary assessment of claims made by the Secretariat in accordance with Article 14, as well as other information and views that the Executive Secretary may provide in accordance with Article 32.

3) A member of the Secretariat may attend sessions of the panel and may, if required, provide information to the Commissioners.

Article 35. Evidence

1) Each claimant is responsible for submitting documents and other evidence which demonstrate satisfactorily that a particular claim or group of claims is eligible for compensation pursuant to Security Council resolution 687 (1991). Each panel will determine the admissibility, relevance, materiality and weight of any documents andV other evidence submitted.

2) With respect to claims received under the Criteria for Expedited Processing of Urgent Claims (S/AC.26/1991/1), the following guidelines will apply:

> a) For the payment of fixed amounts in the case of departures, claimants are required to provide simple documentation of the fact and date of departure from Iraq or Kuwait. Documentation of the actual amount of loss will not be required.
>
> b) For the payment of fixed amounts in the case of serious personal injury not resulting in death, claimants are required to provide simple

documentation of the fact and date of the injury; in the case of death, claimants are required to provide simple documentation of the death and family relationship. Documentation of the actual amount of loss will not be required.

c) For consideration of claims up to US $100,000 of actual losses, such claims must be documented by appropriate evidence of the circumstances and amount of the claimed loss. Documents and other evidence required will be the reasonable minimum that is appropriate under the particular circumstances of the case. A lesser degree of documentary evidence ordinarily will be sufficient for smaller claims such as those below US $20,000.

3) With respect to claims received under the Criteria for Processing Claims of Individuals not Otherwise Covered, Claims of Corporations and Other Entities, and Claims of Governments and International Organizations (S/AC.26/1991/7/Rev.1), such claims must be supported by documentary and other appropriate evidence sufficient to demonstrate the circumstances and amount of the claimed loss.

4) A panel of Commissioners may request evidence required under this Article.

Article 36. Additional Information

A panel of Commissioners may:

a) in unusually large or complex cases, request further written submissions and invite individuals, corporations or other entities, Governments or international organizations to present their views in oral proceedings;

b) request additional information from any other source, including expert advice, as necessary.

Article 37. Review by Commissioners of Urgent Claims

With respect to claims received under the Criteria for Expedited Processing of Urgent Claims (S/AC.26/1991/1), the following expedited procedures may be used:

a) The Secretariat will proceed to check individual claims by matching them, insofar as possible, against the information in its computerized database. The results of the database analysis may be cross checked by the panel.

b) With respect to claims that cannot be completely verified through the computerized database, if the volume of claims is large, the panel may check individual claims on the basis of a sampling with further verification only as circumstances warrant.

c) Each panel will make its recommendations on the basis of the documents submitted, taking into account the preliminary assessment conducted in accordance with Article 14, any other information and views submitted in accordance with Article 32 and any information submitted in accordance with Article 34. Each panel will normally make its recommendations without holding an oral proceeding. The panel may determine that special circumstances warrant holding an oral proceeding concerning a particular claim or claims.

d) Each panel will complete its review of the claims assigned to it and issue its report as soon as possible but no later than 120 days from the date the claims in question are submitted to the panel.

e) Each panel will report in writing through the Executive Secretary to the Governing Council on the claims received and the amount recommended to be allocated to each Government or other entity for each consolidated claim. Each report will briefly explain the reasons for the recommendations and, to the extent practicable within the time-limit, contain a breakdown of the recommendations in respect of individual claims within each consolidated claim.

Article 38. Review by Commissioners of Other Claims

With respect to claims received under the Criteria for Processing of Claims of Individuals not Otherwise Covered; Claims of Corporations and Other Entities; and Claims of Governments and International Organizations (S/AC.26/1991/7/Rev.1), the following procedures will be used:

a) In so far as possible, claims with significant common legal and factual issues will be processed together.

b) Panels may adopt special procedures appropriate to the character, amount and subject-matter of the particular types of claims under consideration.

c) Each panel will complete its review of any claim or group of claims and report in writing through the Executive Secretary to the Governing Council within 180 days of the date the claims in question are submitted to the panel, except for any unusually large or complex claims referred for detailed review, as described below. Each panel will make its recommendations on the basis of the documents submitted, taking into account the preliminary assessment conducted in accordance with Article 14, any other information and views submitted in accordance with Article 32 and any information submitted in accordance with Article 34.

d) Unusually large or complex claims may receive detailed review, as appropriate. If so, the panel considering such a claim may, in its discretion, ask for additional written submissions and hold oral proceedings. In such a case, the individual, corporation, Government, international organization or other entity making the claim may present the case directly to the panel, and may be assisted by an attorney or other representative of choice. The panel will complete its review of the case and report in writing through the Executive Secretary its recommendations to the Governing Council within twelve months of the date the claim was submitted to the panel.

e) Each panel will report in writing through the Executive Secretary to the Governing Council on the claims received and the amount recommended to be awarded for each claimant. Each report will briefly explain the reasons for the recommendations.

Article 39. Additional Time

If a panel considering a claim or group of claims cannot complete its work within the allotted time, the panel will notify the Governing Council through the Executive Secretary of the estimated additional time required. The Governing Council will decide whether the panel should continue its work on the claims or groups of claims, with a time-limit to be decided by the Council, or should be discharged of the claim or group of claims, which would be given to another panel.

Article 40. Decisions

1) The amounts recommended by the panels of Commissioners will be subject to approval by the Governing Council. The Governing Council may review the amounts recommended and, where it determines circumstances require, increase or reduce them.

2) The Governing Council may, in its discretion, return a particular claim or group of claims for further review by the Commissioners.

3) The Governing Council will make its decisions on amounts to be awarded at each session with respect to claims covered in any reports of Commissioners circulated to members of the Governing Council at least 30 days in advance of the session.

4) Decisions of the Governing Council will be final and are not subject to appeal or review on procedural, substantive or other grounds.

5) Decisions of the Governing Council and, after the relevant decision is made, the associated report of the panel of Commissioners, will be made public, except the Executive Secretary will delete from the reports of panels of Commissioners the identities of individual claimants and other information determined by the panels to be confidential or privileged.

Article 41. Correction of Decisions

1) Computational, clerical, typographical or other errors brought to the attention of the Executive Secretary within 60 days from the publication of the decisions and reports, will be reported by the Executive Secretary to the Governing Council.

2) The Governing Council will decide whether any action is necessary. If it is determined that a correction must be made, the Governing Council will direct the Executive Secretary as to the proper method of correction.

Article 42. Withdrawal of Claims

A claim pending before the Commission may be withdrawn at any time by the Government or entity that submitted the claim to the Commission. In any case where the claim has been paid, settled or otherwise resolved, it shall be withdrawn.

Article 43. Additional Procedural Rulings

Subject to the provisions of these procedures, Commissioners may make such additional procedural rulings as may be necessary to complete work on particular cases or categories of cases. In so doing, the Commissioners may rely on the relevant UNCITRAL Rules for guidance. Commissioners may request the Governing Council to provide further guidance with respect to these procedures at any time. The Governing Council may adopt further procedures or revise these Rules when circumstances warrant.

S/AC.26/1992/11, 26 June 1992

13. Decision taken by the Governing Council of the United Nations Compensation Commission at its sixth session, 27th meeting, 26 June 1992

ELIGIBILITY FOR COMPENSATION OF MEMBERS OF THE ALLIED COALITION ARMED FORCES

The Governing Council decides that members of the Allied Coalition Armed Forces are not eligible for compensation for loss or injury arising as a consequence of their involvement in Coalition military operations against Iraq, except if the following three conditions are met:

(a) the compensation is awarded in accordance with the general criteria already adopted; and

(b) they were prisoners of war as a consequence of their involvement in Coalition military operations against Iraq in response to its unlawful invasion and occupation of Kuwait; and

(c) the loss or injury resulted from mistreatment in violation of international humanitarian law (including the Geneva Conventions of 1949).

S/24352, 27 July 1992

14. Note by the President of the Security Council, 27 July 1992

After the consultations held on 27 July 1992, the President of the Security Council issued the following statement on behalf of the members of the Council in connection with the item entitled "The situation between Iraq and Kuwait":

"The members of the Security Council held informal consultations on 27 July 1992 pursuant to paragraphs 21 and 28 of resolution 687 (1991) and paragraph 6 of resolution 700 (1991).

"After hearing all the opinions expressed in the course of the consultations, the President of the Council concluded that there was no agreement that the necessary conditions existed for a modification of the regimes established in paragraph 20 of resolution 687 (1991), as referred to in paragraph 21 of that resolution; in paragraphs 22, 23, 24 and 25 of resolution 687 (1991), as referred to in paragraph 28 of that resolution; and in paragraph 6 of resolution 700 (1991)."

S/AC.26/1992/12.

15. Decision adopted by the Governing Council of the United Nations Compensation Commission during its seventh session, at its 29th meeting, 24 September 1992

CLAIMS FOR WHICH ESTABLISHED FILING DEADLINES ARE EXTENDED

1. The established filing deadlines are extended for the following claims

(a) Claims of individuals under the criteria for expedited processing of urgent claims (see S/22885, annex II), and the criteria for processing claims of individuals not otherwise covered (see S/23765, annex) for losses and personal injuries resulting from public health and safety risks that occur after or within one year prior to the expiration of the established filing deadlines: these claims should be submitted to the Commission within one year of the date of such loss or injury, but no later than the time-limit to be established pursuant to paragraph 2 of this decision.

(b) Claims of individuals under the criteria for expedited processing of urgent claims (see S/22885, annex II), and the criteria for processing of claims of individuals not otherwise covered (see S/23765, annex) who have been detained in Iraq until after or within one year prior to the expiration of the established filing deadlines: these claims, including claims for losses and personal injuries resulting from detention in Iraq, should be submitted to the Commission within one year of the detainee's release or of the death of the detainee, as legally determined by the detainee's Government, but not later than the time-limit to be established pursuant to paragraph 2 of this decision;

(c) Claims under the criteria for processing claims of Governments and international organizations (see S/23765, annex) for losses resulting from environmental damage: these claims should be submitted to the Commission no later than 1 February 1997.

2. When the Executive Secretary determines that the processing of all remaining claims before the panels of Commissioners is likely to take no more than one year to complete, he should so notify the Governing Council. The Governing Council should thereupon establish the final time-limit for the submission of claims covered by paragraphs 1(a) and 1(b) of this decision.The Governing Council should establish the final time-limit at its next meeting after receiving such notification and should allow at least three additional months from the date of its decision for the filing of the claims.

3. In submitting claims pursuant to this decision, Governments must include in their affirmation pursuant to paragraph 14 (1) (c) of the Provisional Rules for Claims Procedure (see S/24363, annex I, enclosure) that such claims are the ones for which an extended deadline has been granted. In addition, individual claimants filing claims in these categories must include with their claim forms statements explaining the circumstances as to why they were unable to file their claims within the previously established deadlines.

4. Claims covered by this decision should be submitted at the earliest possible time within the time-limits established by the Governing Council. The Commission should thereupon give consideration to such claims as provided for in the applicable criteria.

5. The Governing Council may consider the extension of established filing deadlines for other categories of claims if, in the future, additional situations are identified.

S/AC.26.1992/13

16. Decision adopted by the Governing Council of the United Nations Compensation Commission during its seventh session, at its 29th meeting, held on 24 September 1992

FURTHER MEASURES TO AVOID MULTIPLE RECOVERY OF COMPENSATION BY CLAIMANTS

With a view to avoiding multiple recovery of compensation by claimants for the same losses, the Governing Council, in addition to measures already taken:

1. Decides to request the Government of Iraq to provide the Commission with information about claims against Iraq in national courts or other forums for losses that would also be eligible for compensation by the Commission and about compensation awarded for such losses.

2. Decides to invite Governments to seek to obtain and to provide the Commission with any information regarding:

(a) Any lawsuit pending in the courts for their jurisdiction against Iraq, or any compensation granted by those courts, for losses resulting from Iraq's invasion and occupation of Kuwait;

(b) Recipients of payments made or relief provided by the respective Government, including, where available, their names, civil I.D. or residency permit numbers, passport numbers, dates of birth, types of losses and amounts paid; and

(c) Recipients of payments made or relief provided by employers known to have operated in Iraq or Kuwait, for losses incurred by their employees as a result of Iraq's invasion and occupation of Kuwait, including, where available, their names, civil I.D. or residency permit numbers, passport numbers, dates of birth, types of losses and amounts paid.

3. Noting that, in light of decision 1 (see S/22885, annex II), the questions of multiple recovery and deductions from payments made in respect of claims in categories A and B do not arise, decides to adopt the following guidelines for the payment of compensation in cases where multiple recovery for the same loss may occur:

(a) Governments or employers that seek reimbursment under category E or F claims of amounts paid for losses that had already been paid from the Fund to individual claimants under categories C and D claims, will not be eligible for compensation. If a request for reimbursment from the Fund is submitted to the Commission to the Government or the employer while the C or D claim of the individual concerned is being processed before the Commission, the amount of compensation already received by the individual (as shown by the Government or employer) will have to be deducted from his or her claim;

(b) When the Commission learns, either through the information provided by the claimant or through other means, and before compensation from the Fund, that a claimant in categories C,D, E and F has received compensation elsewhere for the same loss, the amount already received will be deducted from the compensation to be paid from the Fund to that claimant for the same loss.

17. Security Council Resolution 778 (1992), 2 October 1992

The Security Council,

Recalling its previous relevant resolutions and in particular resolutions 706 (1991) and 712 (1991),

Taking note of the letter of 15 July 1992 from the Secretary-General to the President of the Security Council on Iraq's compliance with the obligations placed on it by resolution 687 (1991) and subsequent resolutions,

Condemning Iraq's continued failure to comply with its obligations under relevant resolutions,

Reaffirming its concern about the nutritional and health situation of the Iraqi civilian population, and the risk of a further deterioration of this situation, and *recalling* in this regard its resolution 706 (1991) and 712 (1991), which provide a mechanism for providing humanitarian relief to the Iraqi population, and resolution 688 (1991), which provides a basis for humanitarian relief efforts in Iraq,

Having regard to the fact that the period of six months referred to in resolutions 706 (1991) and 712 (1991) expired on 18 March 1992,

Deploring Iraq's refusal to cooperate in the implementation of resolutions 706 (1991) and 712 (1991), which puts its civilian population at risk, and which results in the failure by Iraq to meet its obligations under relevant Security Council resolutions,

Recalling that the escrow account provided for in resolutions 706 (1991) and 712 (1991) will consist of Iraqi funds administered by the Secretary-General which will be used to pay contributions to the Compensation Fund, the full costs of carrying out the tasks authorized by section C of resolution 687 (1991), the full costs incurred by the United Nations in facilitating the return of all Kuwaiti property seized by Iraq, half the costs of the Boundary Commission, and the cost to the United Nations of implementing resolution 706 (1991) and of other necessary humanitarian activities in Iraq,

Recalling that Iraq, as stated in paragraph 16 of resolution 687 (1991), is liable for all direct damages resulting from its invasion and occupation of Kuwait, without prejudice to its debts and obligations arising prior to 2 August 1990, which will be addressed through the normal mechanisms,

Recalling its decision in resolution 692 (1991) that the requirement for Iraqi contributions to the Compensation Fund applies to certain Iraqi petroleum and petroleum products exported from Iraq before 2 April 1991, as well as to all Iraqi petroleum and petroleum products exported from Iraq after 2 April 1991,

Acting under Chapter VII of the Charter of the United Nations,

1. *Decides* that all States in which there are funds of the Government of Iraq, or its State bodies, corporations, or agencies, that represent the proceeds of sale of Iraqi petroleum or petroleum products, paid for by or on behalf of the purchaser on or after 6 August 1990, shall cause the transfer of those funds (or equivalent amounts) as soon as possible to the escrow accound provided for in resolutions 706 (1991) and 712 (1991); provided that this paragraph shall not require any State to cause the transfer of such funds in excess of 200 million dollars or to cause the transfer of more than fifty per cent of the total funds transferred or contributed pursuant to paragraphs 1, 2 and 3 of this resolution; and further provided that States may exclude from the operation of this paragraph any funds which have already been released to a claimant or supplier prior to the adoption of this resolution, or any other funds subject to or required to satisfy the rights of third parties, at the time of the adoption of this resolution;

2. *Decides* that all States in which there are petroleum or petrolwum products owned by the Government of Iraq, or its State bodies, corporations, or agencies, shall take all feasible steps to purchase or arrange for the sale of such petroleum or petroleum products at fair market value, and thereupon to transfer the proceeds as soon as possible to the escrow account provided for in resolution 706 (1991) and 712 (1991);

3. *Urges* all States to contribute funds from other sources to the escrow account as soon as possible;

4. *Decides* that all States shall provide the Secretary-General with any information needed for the effective implementation of this resolution and that they shall take the necessary measures to ensure that banks and other bodies and persons provide all relevant information necessary to identify the funds referred to in paragraphs 1 and 2 above and details of any transactions relating thereto, or the said petroleum or petroleum products, with a view to such information being utilized by all States and by the Secretary-General in the effective implementation of this resolution;

5. *Requests* the Secretary-General:

(a) To ascertain the whereabouts and amounts of the said petroleum and petroleum products and the proceeds of sale referred to in paragraphs 1 and 2 of this resolution, drawing on the work already done under the auspices of the Compensation Commission, and report the results to the Security Council as soon as possible;

(b) To ascertain the costs of United Nations activities concerning the elimination of weapons of mass destruction, the provision of humanitarian relief in Iraq, and the other United Nations operations specified in paragraphs 2 and 3 of resolution 706 (1991); and

(c) to take the following actions:

(i) transfer to the Compensation Fund, from the funds referred to in paragraphs 1 and 2 of this resolution, the percentage referred to in paragraph 10 of this resolution; and

(ii) use of the remainder of funds referred to in paragraphs 1, 2 and 3 of this resolution for the costs of United Nations activities concerning the elimination of weapons of mass destruction, the provision of humanitarian relief in Iraq, and the other United Nations operations specified in paragraphs 2 and 3 of resolution 706 (1991), taking into account any preference expressed by States transferring or contributing funds as to the allocation of such funds among these purposes;

6. *Decides* that for so long as oil exports take place pursuant to the system provided in resolutions 706 (1991) and 712 (1991) or to the eventual lifting of sanctions pursuant to paragraph 22 of resolution 687 (1991), implementation of paragraphs 1 to 5 of this resolution shall be suspended and all proceeds of those oil exports shall immediately be transferred by the Secretary-General in the currency in which the transfer to the escrow account had been made, to the accounts or States from which funds had been provided under paragraphs 1, 2 and 3 of this resolution, to the extent required to replace in full the amounts so provided (together with applicable interest); and that, if necessary for this purpose, any other funds remaining in the escrow account shall similarly be transferred to those accounts or States; provided, however, that the Secretary-General may retain and use any funds urgently needed for the purposes specified in paragraph 5 (c) (ii) of this resolution;

7. *Decides* that the operation of this resolution shall have no effect on rights, debts and claims existing with respect to funds prior to their transfer to the escrow account; and that the accounts from which such funds were transferred shall be kept open for retransfer of the funds in question;

8. *Reaffirms* that the escrow account referred to in this resolution, like the Compensation Fund, enjoys the privileges and immunities of the United Nations, including immunity from legal proceedings, or any forms of attachment, garnishment or execution; and that no claim shall lie at the instance of any person or body in

connection with any action taken in compliance with or implementation of this resolution;

9. *Requests* the Secretary-General to repay, from any available funds in the escrow account, any sum transferred under this resolution to the account or State from which it was transferred, if the transfer is found at any time by him not to have been of funds subject to this resolution; a request for such a finding could be made by the State from which the funds were transferred;

10. *Confirms* that the percentage of the value of exports of petroleum and petroleum products from Iraq for payment to the Compensation Fund shall, for the purpose of this resolution and exports of petroleum or petroleum products subject to paragraph 6 of resolution 692 (1991), be the same as the percentage decided by the Security Council in paragraph 2 of resolution 705 (1991), until such time as the Governing Council of the Compensation Fund may decide otherwise;

11. *Decides* that no further Iraqi assets shall be released for purposes set forth in paragraph 20 of resolution 687 (1991) except to the sub-account of the escrow account, established pursuant to paragraph 8 of resolution 712 (1991), or directly to the United Nations for humanitarian activities in Iraq;

12. *Decides* that, for the purposes of this resolution and other relevant resolutions, the term "petroleum products" does not include petrochemical derivatives;

13. *Calls upon* all States to cooperate fully in the implementation of this resolution;

14. *Decides* to remain seized of this matter.

18. European Political Cooperation Press Release, 9 December 1992

STATEMENT ON IRAQ

On 7 December, the Foreign Affairs Council approved a Council Regulation prohibiting the satisfying of Iraqi claims with regard to contracts and transactions whose performance was affected by United Nations Security Council Resolution 661 (1990) and related Resolutions.

The Community and its member States note with concern Iraq's persistent failure to comply with its obligations under SCR 687 and other relevant Resolutions of the UN Security Council. The Community and its member States underline the importance of paragraph 29 of SCR 687 and agree that Iraq must comply in full with the provisions of operative paragraph 29 of SCR 687, whether by legislation, renouncing claims, returning bonds cancelled to their originators or otherwise releasing parties to contracts and transactions from obligations under them. The Community and its member States consider that, in deciding whether to reduce or lift measures taken against Iraq, pursuant to paragraph 21 of SCR 687, particular account must be taken of any failure by Iraq to comply with paragraph 29 of the same Resolution. Iraq should not expect such measures to be reduced or lifted in the absence of full compliance with paragraph 29.

14. ASSISTANCE TO THIRD STATES

The economic implications of the Kuwait crisis for third states have been fully covered in Volume II of this Series. This section merely adds the text of a consolidated request of 21 states for action under Article 50 of the UN Charter and the response given by the UN Security Council. Communications to the Council, listing the amount of assistance given by individual states have not been reproduced.

S/22382, 25 March 1991

1. Letter from the Representatives of Bangladesh, Bulgaria, Czechoslovakia, Djibouti, India, Jordan, Lebanon, Poland, Romania, Seychelles, Sri Lanka, the Sudan, the Syrian Arab Republic, Tunisia, Mauritania, Pakistan, the Philippines, Uruguay, Viet Nam, Yemen and Yugoslavia to the United Nations addressed to the President of the Security Council, 22 March 1991

We have the honour to submit herewith a memorandum of 21 Member States confronted with special economic problems arising from the application of sanctions against Iraq pursuant to Security Council resolution 661 (1990) which addressed the Security Council under Article 50 of the Charter of the United Nations and on which the Security Council Committee established by resolution 661 (1990) concerning the situation between Iraq and Kuwait made recommendations for appropriate action.

...

1. By resolution 669 (1990), the Security Council entrusted its Committee established by resolution 661 (1990) with the task of examining requests for assistance under the provisions of Article 50 of the Charter of the United Nations. It was the first time that a large number of States addressed the Security Council on the basis of this Article.

2. All the 21 States addressing the Security Council under Article 50 of the Charter emphasized their full adherence to the relevant Security Council resolutions relating to the Gulf crisis and their solidarity with the international community. They expressed their firm determination to continue to comply fully with the provisions of resolution 661 (1990), in spite of the grave economic, financial and commercial losses incurred as a result of implementation of sanctions, which are estimated at more than $US 30 billion.

3. The Security Council Committee considered the cases referred to it and by the recommendations adopted, launched individual appeals to all States and specialized agencies of the United Nations and international financial institutions to provide urgent assistance to the affected States in order to mitigate the adverse economic and social problems confronted by them.

4. The problems affecting these countries persist, and in certain respects have been aggravated, while the appeals launched pursuant to the recommendations of the Security Council Committee and addressed to all concerned by the Secretary-General, have not evoked responses commensurate with the urgent needs of the affected countries.

5. Assistance to the affected countries in accordance with Article 50 of the Charter would reaffirm international solidarity and unity.

6. The 21 States launch a collective appeal, particularly to all donor States, to respond urgently and effectively in providing assistance to the affected countries by allocating additional financial resources both through bilateral channels and by supporting the actions of the competent organs and specialized agencies of the United Nations system.

7. The 21 States most seriously affected believe that it is essential that all Member States, as well as the United Nations, the specialized agencies and other international organizations of the United Nations system, take all appropriate action to cooperate with them in the fields of trade, employment, economic assistance and other areas, in order to alleviate the difficult economic problems facing them.

8. The affected countries believe that, given the magnitude of the difficulties they face, the Security Council should give renewed attention to these problems with a view to finding quick and effective solutions.

S/22548, 29 April 1991

2. Note by the President of the Security Council, 29 April 1991

Following consultations with the members of the Security Council, the President of the Council made the following statement, on behalf of the Council, at its 2985th meeting on 29 April 1991, in connection with the Council's consideration of the item entitled "The situation between Iraq and Kuwait":

> "The members of the Security Council have considered the memorandum dated 22 March 1991 (S/22382) which was addressed to the President of the Security Council by the 21 States which have invoked Article 50 of the United Nations Charter owing to the special economic problems arising from the implementation of the sanctions imposed against Iraq and Kuwait under Council resolution 661 (1990).
>
> "The members of the Security Council have taken note of the Secretary-General's oral report to them on 11 April 1991, in which he supported the appeal launched by the 21 States that have invoked Article 50. The Secretary-General further informed the Council on 26 April 1991 of the conclusions reached by the Administrative Committee on Coordination (ACC) at the session it has just held in Paris, where members of ACC agreed to vigorously pursue their efforts to respond effectively to the needs of countries most affected by the implementation of resolution 661. The Secretary-General will coordinate through ACC, within the framework of this assistance, the activities of organizations of the United Nations system.
>
> "The members of the Security Council have taken note of the replies from a number of States (Austria, Belgium, Denmark, France, Germany, Greece, Ireland, Italy, Japan, Liechtenstein, Luxembourg, Luxembourg on behalf of the European Community and its 12 member States, Netherlands, New Zealand, Norway, Portugal, Spain, Switzerland, United Kingdom, United States and the USSR) which have furnished specific information on the assistance they have provided to various affected countries; they have also taken note of the replies from officials of international financial institutions, such as those received from the President of the World Bank and the Managing Director of IMF. They invite other Member States and international financial institutions and organizations to inform the Secretary-General as soon as possible of the measures that they have taken on behalf of the States which have invoked Article 50.
>
> "The members of the Security Council make a solemn appeal to States, international financial institutions and United Nations bodies to respond positively and speedily to the recommendations of the Security Council Committee, established under resolution 661, for assistance to countries which find themselves confronted with special economic problems arising from the carrying out of those measures imposed by resolution 661 and which have invoked Article 50.
>
> "The members of the Security Council note that the procedure established under Article 50 of the Charter remains in effect."

PART V

HUMANITARIAN AND HUMAN RIGHTS ISSUES

The Iraq-Kuwait crisis brought in its wake a tremendous amount of human suffering. Although international attention focussed mainly on the persecution of northern Iraq's Kurdish population following upon the cease-fire with the coalition forces, human suffering was intense in all parts of the region. In the southern areas of Iraq, Shiah minorities were persecuted as vigorously as the Kurds were in the north. Throughout Iraq, the economic embargo and the destruction brought about by the conflict led to considerable hardship, as is evident from the reports of UN missions to the area which are reproduced in Chapter 16. This emergency was answered by the United Nations with a partial lifting of sanctions and with the implementation of an overall humanitarian action plan (Chapter 17).

The misery within Iraq was also due to the policy of the Government of that State. Chapter 18 reproduces extensive reports on the human rights situation in Iraq. The developments relating to the situation in northern Iraq and the establishment of "safe havens", mostly for Kurdish displaced persons, and the establishment of the aerial exclusion zone in southern Iraq are covered in Chapter 19.

The situation in Kuwait following upon the restoration of its lawful government is addressed in Chapter 20. In addition to the report of the UN mission to that state, the chapter includes materials relating to the charge of mistreatment of Palestinians in Kuwait, brought by the Palestinian oberserver delegation to the UN.

This Part opens with a brief historical section to provide the particular background to the Kurdish issue.

15. BACKGROUND TO THE KURDISH ISSUE

The situation in Kurdish populated areas of Iraq has commanded considerable international attention in the aftermath of the conflict. For a better understanding of that situation a number of documents tracing the development of the Kurdish issue as it relates to Iraq have been reproduced. Although most documents reprinted in this series emanate from governments or international governmental organizations, several memoranda published by the Kurdish Democratic Party have been included in this Chapter. That party is referred to in the proposed constitutional arrangements for an autonomous Kurdistan within Iraq and its views are therefore of relevance.

Background Brief, United Kingdom Foreign & Commonwealth Office, May 1992 [not an official publication].

1. FCO Background Brief: The Kurdish Problem in Iraq

The Kurds, who number more than 15 million, have existed as a tribal people with their own cultural tradition and language for at least 3000 years; but despite their strong desire for independence from external authority, they have never been united under one ruler. They live mainly in the mountainous areas of northern Iraq, north-western Iran and south-eastern Turkey. Smaller numbers are to be found in Syria, the Transcaucasian States of the former Soviet Union and Lebanon. The majority are Sunni Muslims although in Iran, and to a lesser extent Iraq, some are Shia. Tribal divisions have always been deep, and central governments have been able to exploit these as well as political differences between conservative feudal leaders and left-wing radicals. Other obstacles to unity have been the high rate of illiteracy among Kurds and dialectal differences within their language.

Hopes of autonomy

From the 17th to 20th centuries, the majority of Kurds came under the Ottoman Empire, though there was a sizeable group in Persia. During the disintegration of that Empire following the First World War, the unratified Treaty of Sevres between the Allies and the Ottoman Sultan envisaged local autonomy for the predominantly Kurdish areas, with the possibility of the creation of the independent Kurdish State. However the Treaty was rejected by the new Turkey of Kemal Ataturk, and replaced by a Treaty of Peace with the Allies at Lausanne on 4 July 1923 which made no mention of Kurdistan. Thereafter the Kurds were divided between Turkey, Persia (Iran), and the newly created States of Syria and Iraq. But it was not until the signing of the Anglo/Turkish/Iraqi Treaty of 5 June 1926, after a League of Nations Commission had decided the Vilayet of Mosul, with its large Kurdish population, should be included in Iraq, that the frontier between Turkey and Iraq was settled.

In the 1960s and 1970s the Kurdish Democratic Party (KDP), led by Mulla Mustapha Barzani, conducted a campaign against the Government in Baghdad aimed at securing local autonomy for Iraqi Kurds. The Kurdish rebellion broke out in 1961 and fierce fighting continued throughout the 1960s, despite the recognition of Kurdish nationality in the Iraqi provisional Constitution of 1968. The Iraqi authorities feared that Kurdish successes might lead to the secession of the oil-producing region around Kirkuk in the north. In March 1970, a 15-point peace plan was agreed between Kurdish leaders and the Revolutionary Command Council (RCC). (Saddam Hussein was then only Vice-President, but already the real power in the Ba'ath Arab Socialist Party. He became President in 1979). According to the plan, which was to be implemented within four years,

- Kurds would participate fully in the government and the army, and one national Vice-President would be a Kurd;
- Kurdish officials would administer areas populated by a Kurdish majority;
- Kurdish areas would receive a fair share of economic resources;
- Kurdish nationality would be recognised and Kurdish designated an official language in Kurdish areas (as well as in Arabic);
- a census would take place to determine those areas with a Kurdish majority.

There also appears to have been a secret protocol to the March 1970 agreement, dealing with the position of the Kurdish fighters (Peshmerga) and the disbanding of the local forces opposed to them, the rights of the KDP to operate in the Kurdish region and the holding of the census within one year. Little progress was made towards the implementation of the agreement, and relations between the Kurds and the Government steadily deteriorated. Four years after the signing of the agreement, the Government unilaterally promulgated an autonomy law purporting to implement the agreement of 1970 but in fact falling to do so.

A Kurdish Legislative Council opened in Arbil in October 1974, but this and other concessions were rejected by the Kurds as falling short of their demands, particularly on representation in government. (A Kurd was appointed Vice-President, but he had little authority and was not regarded as a true representative by the Kurds). There was no progress on the census to show Kurdish majority areas. Fresh fighting broke out and Iran, taking advantage of the opportunity to destabilise Saddam Hussein's regime, provided the Kurds with material support. The Iraqi Government began deporting tens of thousands of Kurds, mainly to parts of southern Iraq. Hundreds of villages are believed to have been razed at this time, in a scorched earth policy to prevent the return of the former inhabitants. The regime hoped to weaken the power-base of the Kurdish Peshmerga, and to dissipate any feeling of Kurdish national identity, to allow the growth of Iraqi nationalism.

When, in 1975, as part of the Algiers Agreement, the Shah withdrew his support for the Iraqi Kurds partly in return for Iraq's acceptance of Iranian frontier claims, the rebellion collapsed. The Iraqi Government subsequently implemented a construction programme in Kurdish areas, redistributing land and allowing the return of some of the

40,000 Kurds who had been forcibly resettled in the south. In September 1980, elections were held for a new 50-member Legislative Council of the Kurdish Autonomous Region.

The other main Kurdish opposition party, the Patriotic Union of Kurdistan (PUK), was created in 1975 by a breakaway faction of the KDP and led by Jalal Talabani. The PUK saw themselves as leftist, urban and modernising against the tribalised and more traditional KDP. The PUK inclined towards the Baghdad Government in the late 1970s but then took up arms against it, with the KDP, when Iraq's preoccupation with fighting in Iran caused the Kurds to believe that they had an opportunity to assert their own autonomy. In July 1983 the KDP, supported by Iranian troops and Iraqi Shi'ite dissidents, and using weapons supplied by Iran, retook the mountain stronghold of Hajj Omran six kilometres inside Iraq, which they had lost eight years previously. During the summer and autumn of 1983, Iranian forces made further incursions into Iraq's and Kurdish areas.

Saddam's tactics

At times of difficulty, Saddam Hussein has tried to pacify the Kurds by negotiations, which have broken down when it no longer suited one side or the other. Talks with the PUK, one of the two largest Kurdish political groupings, which began in December 1983 (when Iraq was having particular difficulty in finding military and financial resources for the war with Iran), broke down after a few months, although they were resumed sporadically until January 1985. The PUK had demanded the return of 8,000 families deported to the south, the release of political prisoners, control of the security forces in their autonomous region, the inclusion within this region of oil reserves around Kirkuk, and a fixed percentage of oil revenues. Also required was the dissolution of the "Jash" - those irregular troops formed into "Light Brigades" serving the Baghdad Government. The Jash kept many of the tribes of northern Iraq official supporters of the regime during the Iran/Iraq war.

The year 1987 saw the progressive gathering of Kurdish political and military strength, though the rapprochement of the KDP and PUK, and the subsequent formation of the Iraqi Kurdistan Front, a coalition of five main Kurdish parties. As the Iranian military threat in the south diminished in 1987, Saddam Hussein's regime turned to the north to punish the Kurds for their collaboration with Iran. Saddam's cousin Ali Hassan al-Majid, now Minister of Defence, supervised its repressive policies. By 1988, it is estimated that 3,000 Kurdish villages had been destroyed. A third of the Kurdish area had become uninhabited. Many Kurds considered disloyal, including a large number of the male members of the Barzani tribe, were apparently eliminated; others were deported to camps in southern Iraq. Later most Kurds from the destroyed villages were settled in camps in northern Iraq, where they could be more easily controlled than in their mountain villages. Over 60,000 troops were sent into an offensive against rebel fighters and civilians. Chemical weapons were used, and in the most widely publicised case of the town of Halabja, perhaps as may as 5,000 people, many of them women and children, were killed by poison gases. According to some reports, scores of other villages suffered gas attacks with thousands more casualties.

In September 1988 the "resettlement" campaign intensified. Iraqi forces created a 30-kilometre wide, uninhabited "security zone" along the borders with Turkey and Iran. Some 300,000 people were moved from these areas in the next year; the Government claimed they were being provided with better facilities.

Over the last decade, many thousands of Kurds have "disappeared". A report published by Amnesty International, the independent human rights group, in June 1990, indicated that the number of disappearances and executions of Kurds had increased since 1988. Some of the victims were those who returned from exile in response to a series of amnesties granted by the Government.

Even when it is not being actively persecuted, the Kurdish population of Iraq is deprived of basic political and economic rights. Candidates for election to the Kurdish Legislative Council are vetted in advance by the Government, and the Council is widely viewed as a puppet of Saddam's regime. Until the discovery of oil in southern Iraq in 1969, the Kurdish north, with its oil and agricultural produce, supplied most of Iraq's wealth; it still produces a substantial proportion of Iraqi oil. The regime has tried to make the Kurdish regions economically dependent on Baghdad and undermined local economic activity. It was reluctant to carry out the census because it feared that it might have shown a Kurdish (and Turcoman) majority in the oil-producing Kirkuk area, strengthening the arguments for its incorporation in the Kurdish Autonomous Region. The Government has brought numerous Arab Iraqi families (and other nationals) from the south to Kirkuk, to dilute the population of kurds and Turcomans (a regional minority which moved into the area some centuries ago).

Recent developments

Following Iraq's invasion of Kuwait in August 1990, and subsequent defeat by the multinational coalition forces, large areas of Shia southern Iraq, particularly around Basra, and the largely Shia areas between Basra and Baghdad, rose in revolt against the central authorities in late February 1991. Saddam Hussein moved the remains of his army to deal with the situation there, withdrawing fresh forces from their bases in the north. The Kurdish opposition groups used this opportunity to rise in revolt. Much of the population in the region supported them, and the Jash and their leaders decided to turn against the Baghdad regime.

With the regime distracted elsewhere, the Kurds made significant advances, capturing much of north-eastern Iraq, including the major towns of Arbil, Sulaymaniya, Dohuk and, briefly Kirkuk by 25 March. However, once the revolt in the south had been crushed, the Government moved its forces north. The lightly armed resistance had little chance, and by 3 April the Government had regained control of much of the north. Large sections of the local population began to flee from their homes in the face of the Government counter-offensive involving helicopter gunships, tanks, multiple rocket launchers and heavy artillery.

About 1.5 million Kurds and other Iraqis left home to take refuge in the mountains of Iraq, Turkey and Iran, where they were forced to live in appalling conditions with many dying every day from cold, hunger, exposure and injuries. Their suffering was portrayed nightly on the world's television screens. The international community moved swiftly to address the situation. At the initiative of the British Prime Minister the "safe havens" where refugees, particularly Kurds, would be safe from attack. The UN set up a major relief operation in northern Iraq with some 900 personnel involved in food distribution, rehabilitation of water supplies, health and sanitation projects. Many thousands of lives were saved.

The security of these temporary sites was provided by British, Dutch, US Turkish and French air and ground forces. This deployment was short-term to meet the immediate needs of the refugees. The objective was to give them sufficient assurance of their future security to enable them to come down from the mountains and, later, return to their homes. The Iraqis signed a memorandum with the UN, allowing the establishment of a comprehensive relief operation. This Memorandum of

Understanding was renewed in December 1991 for a further six months.

In March 1991, the Iraqi regime took the initiative to resume talks with the Kurdish Front, offering autonomy on the basis of an improved 1970 agreement. Saddam Hussein realised in his weakened position that he had to come to terms with the Kurds. The opprobrium he faced for the plight of the Kurdish refugees was hindering his efforts to persuade the UN to lift sanctions against Iraq; and he hoped to accelerate the departure of the multinational forces protecting relief operations in the north. But he remained determined to achieve an agreement on his terms.

The Kurdish leaders accepted the offer of talks, which took place in Baghdad. The KDP were more enthusiastic than the PUK. Saddam's tactics were to maintain military and economic pressures on the Kurds while continuing to negotiate on an autonomy agreement with Kurdish political leaders, no doubt hoping to force them to accept either the return of Government authority or a much less favourable form of autonomy than originally envisaged.

Barzani suspended talks in autumn 1991, when Baghdad imposed a partial economic blockade on Kurdish areas. But the KDP made clear that they were ready to resume talks when the blockade was lifted. The majority of public servants in the north (ethnic Kurds) are no longer in receipt of Government salaries. The senior, Baghdad based, civil servants such as governors (as well as the remaining units of the Iraqi armed forces), were removed from the Kurdish areas after the imposition of the blockade. Pensions have been stopped, as has all Government funding for public sector projects. Baghdad has significantly reduced the supply to the north of food and fuel from Government stocks for sale at officially-controlled prices. Iraqi army check points were set up on all the roads leading north; vehicles were searched; and food, fuel and consumer goods were confiscated. Kurdish leaders responded by asserting a measure of economic independence; tolls were collected from Turkish truck drivers crossing into Iraq and the Kurdish Front reportedly began distributing its own ration cards. The Iraqis are acting contrary to the terms of the UN Security Council Resolution 688, which demands an end to repression in Iraq and Iraqi cooperation with the humanitarian effort. Iraqi policies against Shia refugees in the south have been even more repressive.

Regional elections in northern Iraq are taking place during May to elect a single Kurdish leader and an Iraqi-Kurdish regional assembly, to take charge of the civil administration and to place the Peshmerga under unified command. The KDP have emphasised that the elections are consistent with the 1970 agreement establishing a Kurdish autonomous area, and are not intended to create an alternative government.

Saddam Hussein hopes to bring the Kurds of northern Iraq back under central government control without provoking intervention by the international community. The coalition maintains aircraft in southern Turkey, which continue to deter renewed repression of the people of northern Iraq. The UN continues to undertake a major relief operation in Iraq.

2. The [unratified] Treaty of Sèvres, Annex, Section III, 10 August 1920

KURDISTAN

Article 62. A Commission sitting at Constantinople and composed of three members appointed by the British, French and Italian Governments respectively shall draft within six months from the coming into force of the present Treaty a scheme of local autonomy for the predominantly Kurdish areas lying east of the Euphrates, south of the southern boundary of Armenia as it may be hereafter determined, and north of the frontier of Turkey with Syria and Mesopotamia, as defined in Article 27 II (2) and (3) [*Relating to the "Frontiers of Turkey"*]. If unanimity cannot be secured on any question, it will be referred by the members of the Commission to their respective Governments. The scheme shall contain full safeguards of the protection of the Assyro-Chaldeans and other racial or religious minorities within these areas, and with this object a Commission composed of British, French, Italian, Persian and Kurdish representatives shall visit the spot to examine and decide what rectifications, if any, should be made in the Turkish frontier where, under the provisions of the present Treaty, that frontier coincides with that of Persia.

Article 63. The Turkish Government hereby agrees to accept and execute the decisions of both the Commissions mentioned in Article 62 within three months from their communication to the said Government.

Article 64. If within one year from the coming into force of the present Treaty the Kurdish peoples within the areas defined in Article 62 shall address themselves to the Council of the League of Nations is such a manner as to show that the majority of the population of these areas desire independence from turkey, and if the Council then considers that these peoples are capable of such independence and recommends that it should be granted to them, Turkey hereby agrees to execute such a recommendation, and to renounce all rights and title over these areas.

The detailed provisions for such renunciation will form the subject of a separate agreement between the Principal Allied Powers and Turkey.

If an when such renunciation takes place, no objection will be raised by the Principal Allied Powers to the voluntary adhesion to such an independent Kurdish State of the Kurds inhabiting that part of Kurdistan which has hitherto been included in the Mosul vilayet.

1926 LNOJ 190; Cmd. 2565, 1925

3. League of Nations Report by M Unden on the Question of the Turco-Irak Frontier, Geneva, 16 December 1925

FRONTIER BETWEEN TURKEY AND IRAK

At the moment when the Council is about to take its decision on the question of the frontier between Turkey and Irak which was submitted to it in accordance with Article 3 of the Treaty of Lausanne, it seems necessary to give in a few words an account of the question and of the procedure followed since the moment when the matter was laid before the Council.

I.

The discussions at Lausanne regarding the frontier between Turkey and Irak did not result in the determination of a frontier line, and the following provisions were therefore inserted in Article 3 of the Treaty of Peace with Turkey:-

> "The frontier between Turkey and Irak shall be laid down in friendly arrangement to be concluded between Turkey and Great Britain within nine months.
>
> "In the event of no agreement being reached between the two Governments within the time

> mentioned, the dispute shall be referred to the Council of the League of Nations.
>
> "The Turkish and British Governments reciprocally undertake that, pending the decision to be reached on the subject of the frontier, no military or other movement shall take place which might modify in any way the present state of the territories of which the final fate will depend upon that decision."

The negotiations between the two Governments which took place at Constantinople from the 19th May to the 9th June, 1924, were not successful, and the British Government, by a letter dated the 6th August, 1924, then asked that, in accordance with the provisions of the Treaty, the question should be placed on the agenda of the Council.

At its thirtieth session, the Council took cognisance of the documents setting forth the respective cases of the two Governments, and heard their representatives in regard to the position and scope of the question, and also in regard to the main point at issue. With a view to obtaining the data of various kinds which it thought essential before it could come to any conclusions with full knowledge of the facts, the Council, on the 30th September, 1924, decided, by the following resolution, to institute an enquiry:-

> "The Council, having had the question of the delimitation of the frontier between Turkey and Irak referred to it under Article 3, paragraph 2, of the Treaty of Lausanne;
>
> "Having heard the statements of the representatives of the British and Turkish Governments, who undertook on behalf of their respective Governments to accept in advance the decision of the Council on the question referred to it;
>
> "With a view to collecting the facts and data which it requires to fulfil the mission entrusted to it under Article 3, paragraph 2, of the Treaty of Lausanne:
>
> "Decides to set up a special Committee of three members. This Committee shall lay before the Council all information and all suggestions which may be of a nature to assist it in reaching a decision. It shall give due consideration to the existing documents and to the views expressed by the interested parties both as regards the procedure and as regards the substance of the question. It shall receive all communications which the parties may wish to transmit to it. It may proceed to investigate on the spot, and in that case may avail itself of the services of advisers appointed respectively by each of the two Governments concerned."

As a result of complaints received from the British Government with regard to certain incidents which had taken place on the borders of the territories occupied by the two parties, and with a view to assuring a more satisfactory fulfilment of the mutual undertaking contained in the concluding lines of Article 3, paragraph 2, of the Treaty of Lausanne with regard to the maintenance of the *status quo* pending a decision as to the frontier, the Council, on the 29th October, 1924, during its 31st session, held at Brussels, decided, with the agreement of the two parties, upon a provisional line.

The Commission set up under the resolution of the 30th September, 1924, was composed of MM. de Wirsen (Swede), Count Teleki (Hungarian) and Colonel Paulis (Belgian). After an enquiry on the spot conducted with the assistance of assessors appointed by the British and Turkish Governments, the Commission submitted a report, of which the Council took note at its meeting on the 3rd September, 1925.

After carefully studying all the documents and visiting the two Governments concerned, the Commission proceeded to the disputed territory and remained there from the middle of January to the middle of March 1924. It visited the principal localities, interrogating not only the leading inhabitants but representatives of all classes and creeds, with the assistance of the British and Turkish assessors. Its report begins with an account of the Commission's work and a careful analysis of the arguments of the two sides. It includes a profound study of the geography of the district, the frontiers proposed and the means of communication; the various races, the statistics regarding them, their distribution, their character and affinities; an examination of the arguments advanced - historical, economic, strategical and political - on both sides; and, lastly, all the information it was possible to collect concerning the inclinations of the peoples themselves.

After this comprehensive survey come a number of conclusions on all the points examined, and these themselves are summarised in a set of final conclusions.

The Commission unanimously recognised the practical impossibility of holding the plebiscite suggested by the Turkish Government for ascertaining the wishes of the population, and came to the conclusion that the best method of preparing the way for a solution would be to make its own enquiries, and endeavour to find suggestions which it could lay before the Council.

The work of the Commission therefore led up to a series of reasoned proposals to assist the Council in discovering a solution. The Council heard the observations of both parties on the contents of the report, and appointed from among its members a Committee of the Council, consisting of the Spanish, Swedish and Uruguayan representatives. This Committee was instructed to examine the documents and to conduct, with the assistance of the parties, any enquiries it considered necessary in order to reach a just and peaceful solution.

In the course of conversations between the Committee of the Council and the representatives of the two Governments concerned, disagreement arose as to the precise force and character of the decision to be taken by the Council under Article 3 of the Treaty of Lausanne.

According to the representative of the British Empire, Article 3 of the Treaty of Lausanne empowered the Council to fix the frontier by a final decision, which should be binding on both parties, and not by a recommendation which would only take effect if both parties agreed.

The Turkish representative, on the other hand, maintained that the Council's decision could be nothing more than a recommendation made within the limits of the competence of the League of Nations as defined by the Covenant, and therefore subject to the consent of the parties concerned. Consequently, the Council decided, on the 19th September, 1925, that it would be desirable to request the Permanent Court of International Justice to give an advisory opinion on the following questions:-

> 1. What is the character of the decision to be taken by the Council in virtue of Article 3, paragraph 2, of the Treaty of Lausanne - is it an arbitral award, a recommendation or a simple mediation?
>
> 2. Must the decision be unanimous or may it be taken by a majority vote? May the representatives of the interested parties take part in the vote?

The two interested Governments were invited by the Council to hold themselves at the disposal of the Court to furnish any documents or explanations that might be required.

The representative of Great Britain agreed to this procedure. The Turkish representative stated that the opinion of the Court could not in any circumstances affect the rights which the Turkish Government held itself to possess under the Treaty of Lausanne. The Turkish Government having received the notification of the Court, informed the Registrar of the Court in a telegram dated the 8th October "that there was no need for it to be represented at the extraordinary session of the Court." It nevertheless forwarded to the Court certain documents and written replies to certain questions which the Court had already seen fit to put to it before the hearings. The Court found in its advisory opinion, given on the 21st November, 1925, that "the decision to be taken by the Council will be binding on the parties and will constitute a definitive determination of the frontier between Turkey and Irak." The Court held that the decision "must be unanimous, the representatives of the parties taking part in the voting, but their votes not being counted in ascertaining whether there is unanimity."

At its meeting on the 8th December, 1925, the Council took note of this opinion and heard the observations of the two Governments concerned. The representative of Great Britain pointed out that the British Government had always regarded itself, under the terms of the Treaty, as bound in advance by the decision of the Council. The Turkish representative said that he could not accept any interpretation of article 3, paragraph 2, of the Treaty of Lausanne other than that which had been given by the Great National Assembly of Turkey when the latter had ratified the Treaty. According to him the Council could only adopt the opinion of the Court by a unanimous decision of its members, including the representatives of the parties.

The Council refused to accept this argument and decided unanimously, the votes of the two parties not being counted, to adopt the opinion of the Court. The Turkish representative who had voted against this resolution, then stated that the powers of his delegation, according to the instructions which he had received, would come to an end in the face of an arbitral procedure.

The Court itself had pointed out in its advisory opinion that "the powers of mediation and conciliation of the Council form an essential part of the functions of that body. If such procedure fails the Council will make use of its power of decision." The Council has continued to carry on its work of conciliation in accordance with the spirit of the Covenant. At every stage of the procedure described above it has given both parties an opportunity to make suggestions or proposals which could be used as a basis for negotiation and agreement. After receiving and adopting the opinion of the Court and before reaching its decision, it felt bound to do so once again. None of the suggestions offered by either side to the Committee seemed to it to constitute a starting point for further mediation with a view to a friendly settlement.

The Council has never lost sight of the possibility of reaching an equitable agreement between the parties; it has accordingly listened on many occasions to the arguments of the representatives and instructed the Commission of Enquiry to furnish it with all useful information and suggestions. The Council has not thought fit itself to formulate proposals; such proposals should have been made by the parties themselves with a view to a compromise, and even so, the Council could not act as mediator if the divergence between the proposals were so wide as to exclude all hopes of conciliation.

Moreover, the Council was bound to maintain its absolute right to take a decision - a right of which it would avail itself if necessary. In the absence, therefore, of conditions making it possible to reach a friendly solution, the Council finds itself obliged to use the power conferred on it by the Treaty.

The decision of the Council will, in accordance with the findings of the Court in its advisory opinion, be binding on both parties, and will constitute a final determination of the frontier between Turkey and Irak.

It is important to point out that the provisions of article 16 of the Treaty of Lausanne, under which "Turkey hereby renounces all rights and title whatsoever over or respecting the territories situated outside the frontiers laid down in the present Treaty and the islands other than those over which her sovereignty is recognised by the said Treaty, the future of these territories and islands being settled or to be settled by the parties concerned."

In view of these provisions, Turkey has, since ratifying the Treaty, renounced her claim to the territories beyond the frontier line to be fixed either by agreement between the parties or by a decision of the Council. As it has been impossible to bring about an agreement between the two parties, the decision of the Council must determine the territorial limit of the respective sovereignties of the Turkish Republic and the Kingdom of Irak. As the Court has clearly stated in its advisory opinion, "this renunciation is suspended until the frontier has been determined, but it will become effective, in the absence of some other solution, in virtue of the binding decision."

II.

This decision of the Council cannot be based on a more solid foundation than that provided by the Report of the Commission of Enquiry, whose exhaustive investigations were conducted with a conscientiousness to which both parties paid a tribute.

The final conclusions of the Commission are worded as follows:

> "Looking at the question entirely from the point of view of the interests of the populations concerned, the Commission considers that it would be to some advantage that the disputed area should not be partitioned.
>
> "On the basis of this consideration the Commission, having assigned a relative value to each of the facts which it has established, is of opinion that important arguments, particularly of an economic and geographic nature, and the sentiments (with all the reservations stated) of the majority of the inhabitants of the territory taken as a whole, operate in favour of the union with Irak of the whole territory south of the 'Brussels line,' subject to the following conditions:-
>
> > "1. The territory must remain under the effective mandate of the League of Nations for a period which may be put at twenty-five years.
> >
> > "2. Regard must be paid to the desires expressed by the Kurds that officials of Kurdish race should be appointed for the administration of their country, the dispensation of justice, and teaching in the schools, and that Kurdish should be the official language of all these services.
>
> "The Commission is convinced that if the League of Nations' control were to terminate on the expiry of the four-year Treaty now in force between Great Britain and Irak, and if certain guarantees of local administration were not to be given to the Kurds, the majority of the

people would have preferred Turkish to Arab sovereignty.

"The Commission is also convinced that the advantages of the union of the disputed territory with Irak would in that case be exchanged for very serious political difficulties, and considers that, under those circumstances, it would be more advantageous for the territory to remain under the sovereignty of Turkey, whose internal conditions and external political situation are incomparably more stable than those of Irak. Whatever decision may be taken, it is essential, however, that Irak should retain the Diala region, which is necessary for the solution of the irrigation problem.

"The Commission feels bound to leave it to the Council of the League of Nations to appraise the legal and other political arguments stated in its report, and to decide what relative weight should be given to them as compared with the other arguments. Should the Council, as the outcome of its examination, consider it equitable to partition the disputed territory, the Commission would suggest that the best line would be that approximately following the Lesser Zab. This line is described in greater detail elsewhere in the present report."

The Committee of the Council recognised that an equitable solution of the dispute could only be found in following the main lines of the final conclusions of the Commission of Enquiry.

The advantages and disadvantages of each of the solutions indicated were carefully weighed together with all the considerations raised by the Commission of Enquiry, the other information collected and all the legal and political data left by the Commission of Enquiry for the appreciation of the Council.

As a result of this examination the members of the Committee arrived at the conclusion that two solutions were possible:-

1. The allocation to Irak of all the territory south of the so-called Brussels line;

2. The partition of the disputed territory by a line for the most part following the course of the Lesser Zab.

In view of the great complexity of the problem and the special responsibilities of the Council of the League of Nations, which was called upon to take a decision in so important a matter, the members of the Committee thought that they would benefit by consulting the opinion of their colleagues. After all the arguments and factors mentioned above had been taken into consideration the first of the solutions mentioned above in fact appeared the best adapted to solve the problem submitted to the Council under article 3 of the Treaty of Lausanne.

If this is the opinion of the Council, the final frontier between Irak and Turkey would be fixed on the line of demarcation established for the purpose of maintaining the *status quo*, by the Council's resolution adopted at Brussels on the 29th October, 1924, and described in that resolution.

The Council, on the basis of the recommendation of the Commission of Enquiry, subject, however, to the eventual admission of Irak to the League of Nations in accordance with the provisions of article 1 of the Covenant, will no doubt consider that during 25 years' of the régime laid down by the Treaty of Alliance between Great Britain and Irak, and by the undertaking entered into by the British Government and approved by the Council on the 27th September, 1924, is an essential condition, and that if that condition be not executed the decision would not become definitive. Article 7 of this undertaking reads as follows:-

"On the conclusion of the period for which the Treaty of Alliance has been concluded, the Council of the League of Nations shall, if Irak has not been admitted to the League, be invited to decide what further measures are required to give effect to article 22 of the Covenant."

In approving this clause the Council took the view that the continuation of this régime should at once be assured by the conclusion of a new Treaty between the British Government and Irak; it therefore thought that it should enquire from the British representative what period of time would be required for submitting to the Council a new Treaty for a period of twenty-five years between the British Government and Irak.

The representative of Great Britain replied:-

"In answer to the question put to me by the Council, I see no difficulty in submitting, within six months from the present date, a new Treaty with Irak, which will continue the Mandatory responsibility towards the League which is embodied in the current Treaty and in the League decision of the 27th September, 1924, for twenty-five years or until such earlier date as Irak is, in the opinion of the Council, qualified for admission to membership of the League.

L. AMERY."

Furthermore, the Commission of Enquiry thought it necessary to grant the Kurds certain guarantees of local administration, as contemplated in the conclusions quoted above. If the Council adopts this recommendation it will no doubt ask the Mandatory Power to acquaint it with the measures which will be taken to give effect thereto.

The Council will also wish to ask the Mandatory Power to follow as faithfully as possible the Commission of Enquiry's other suggestions concerning measures to secure pacification and to afford equal protection to all the elements of the population and also concerning the commercial measures indicated in the special recommendations.

The Committee therefore proposes to the Council that it adopt the following resolution:-

[*Here follows resolution contained in "Miscellaneous No. 17 (1925)," Cmd. 2562*, reprinted immediately below.]

1926 LNOJ 500; Cmd. 2562, 1925

4. League of Nations Council Decision Relating to the Turco-Iraq Frontier, Geneva, 16 December 1925

TURCO-IRAK FRONTIER

The following decision relating to the Turco-Irak frontier was unanimously adopted by the Council of the League of Nations on the 16th December, 1925:-

"The Council,

"Having regard to Articles 3 and 16 of the Treaty of Peace signed at Lausanne on the 24th July, 1923,

"In view of the conclusions of the report of the Commission of Enquiry,

"Adopting the reasons and proposals contained in the report of the Committee of the Council,

"Decides:

"1. The frontier between Turkey and Irak shall be fixed as follows:

"From the junction of the River Tigris and the River Khabur, along the river Khabur in mid-stream, up to its junction with the river Hazil; in mid-stream, along the river Hazil to a point three kilometres upstream of the junction of that river with the side-stream which passes by Sirnez. From this point in a direct line eastwards to the northern crest of the valley of the side-stream which passes by Sirnez. The northern crest bordering this valley up to Mount Bilakish, and in a straight line from this point to the source of the tributary of the Baijo at Robozak. Along this tributary to its junction south of Robozak with a river coming down from point 6834 east-south-east of Robozak, then following a straight line to the hill north-north-east of point 6834. Along the small river in mid-stream which comes down in an easterly direction from this hill to its junction with the river Khabur. The river Khabur downstream for about a kilometre and a half to its junction with the river coming from the Arush and Geramus district. Along this river (leaving to the north the river coming from Qashura) to the junction of its two large branches, the first coming from Geramus and the second from Arush. From this junction along the bottom of a valley eastwards to point 6571 on the watershed between the two tributaries mentioned above. Following this watershed to point 9063 east of point 6571, then along the crest bordering the valley of the tributary, which passes by Geramus up to its junction with the crest on the south side of the valley of Lizan. From the latter crest along the crest on the north side of the valley of the tributary of the river Zab which comes down from Ora, then up to a point west-north-west of Duskia and about two-and-a-half kilometres from that place. A straight line from this point to the source of this tributary of the river Zab - downstream along the river Zab to a point one kilometre south of Baishuka - a straight line eastwards up to the southern crest of the river valley which runs south of Bayhi and north of Chal - along the southern crest of the valley of the tributary of the Zab which passes by Borijan, up to the point nearest to the source of the Ave Marek west-south-west of Shiluk - a straight line of this course - the western arm of the Ave Marek from this source to the junction of the small river which comes down from the pass between Quasrik and Nervek - along this small river up to its source - following a straight line between this source and the tributary of the eastern arm of the Ave Marek which flows into the Ave Marek north of Nervek - along this tributary to its junction - following a straight line from this junction to the watershed between the Ave Marek and the Rudbar i Shin - along this watershed to the nearest point to the source of that river - following this tributary and down that [*sic*] river just north of Shaikh Momar - in a straight line up to the source of that river - following this tributary and down the Rudbar i Shin to the mouth of the river which flows just south of Deh - along this river to its source - in a straight line from the source of that river to the watershed between the Rudbar i Shin and the tributary of the Shemsdinan Su which flows just east of Herki - in a straight line thence to the side-stream nearest to this tributary - along this side-stream and then along the tributary to the Shemsdinan Su - in a direct line from the junction of these two streams to the southern crest of the valley of the Shemsdinan Su - along this crest to the point where it meets the watershed between the River Haji Beg and its tributary which runs just east of Upah along the line of this watershed direct to the River Haji Beg - up the River Haji Beg to the Persian frontier.

...

"2. The British Government is invited to submit to the Council a new Treaty with Irak, ensuring the continuance for twenty-five years of the mandatory régime defined by the Treaty of Alliance between Great Britain and Irak and by the British Government's undertaking approved by the Council on the 27th September, 1924, unless Irak is, in conformity with Article 1 of the Covenant, admitted as a Member of the League before the expiration of this period.

"As soon as, within a period of six months from the present date, the execution of this stipulation has been brought to the knowledge of the Council, the Council shall declare that the present decision has become definitive and shall indicate the measures required to insure the delimitation on the ground of the frontier line.

"3. The British Government, as Mandatory Power, is invited to lay before the Council the administrative measures which will be taken with a view to securing for the Kurdish populations mentioned in the report of the Commission of Enquiry the guarantees regarding local administration recommended by the Commission in its final conclusions.

"4. The British Government, as Mandatory Power, is invited to act, as far as possible, in accordance with the other suggestions of the Commission of Enquiry as regards measures likely to ensure pacification and to afford equal protection to all the elements of the population, and also as regards the commercial measures indicated in the special recommendations of the Commission's report."

Subsequently Mr. AMERY said:-

"I should like in the first instance to express the thanks of His Majesty's Government to the Council of the League, to the Commission of the League upon whose report the decision of the Council has been based, and to General Laidoner and the members of his commission whose investigations have elicited facts relevant to the main issue, for all the care which they have given to the consideration of the important and difficult problem before them. I trust it is not presumption on my part to express the belief that a decision based on methods so scrupulous and so impartial will have contributed, in no small measure, to building up the jurisprudence of peaceful settlement in the world, and to strengthening the authority of the League. His Majesty's Government regret that the Council has not been able to accept their proposals for a rectification of the present frontier, which would have been preferable on strategic and administrative grounds, and which would have given security in their own homes to the refugee Assyrians as well as to the Goyan Chaldeans whose unhappy fate has been set forth in the reports of General Laidoner's

Commission. But His Majesty's Government, on their own behalf and on that of Irak, accept the decision of the Council and will loyally conform to it.

"I hope to submit at a very early date the new treaty whose execution will give final effect to the decision announced by the Council to-day, as well as to lay before the Council proposals for giving effect to the recommendations of the Commission of Enquiry as regards local administration in the Kurdish districts of Irak, the pacification and protection of all the elements in the population, and the establishment of a liberal system of commercial intercourse between Irak and its neighbours, with whom the one desire of the British and Irak Governments is to live on terms of goodwill and mutual assistance.

"I observe that the decision of the Council contains no reference to the maintenance of the *status quo* pending final effect being given to the decision of the Council. I presume that in the meantime the provisions of the last paragraph of article 3 of the Treaty of Lausanne binding each of the parties to observe the *status quo* remain of full effect."

Sir AUSTEN CHAMBERLAIN spoke as follows:-

"Mr. President, as His Britannic Majesty's Principal Secretary of State for Foreign Affairs, I desire to thank you and the other members of the Council for the statement you have just made in their name, and to ask your permission to read a statement on behalf of His Britannic Majesty's Government.

"The British Government have no wish to take up a rigid or uncompromising attitude towards Turkey. If they have pressed for a decision by the Council, it is only because they believed that until the Council had pronounced upon the question submitted to it by the Treaty of Lausanne, it was impossible to find a common basis on which to found the discussion of an agreement with the Turkish Government. The British Government most earnestly desire to live on terms of peace and amity with the Turkish Government. The Council having given its decision, His Majesty's Government will gladly lend itself to conversations with the Government of the Republic of Turkey in order to see whether, while taking due account of the Council's decision, it may not be possible to render the relations between our two countries easier and safer. With this object in view the British Government is ready to take into consideration any proposal made by the Turkish Government which is compatible with their duty as mandatory to protect the interests of the people of Irak."

Hudson, 1 *International Legislation* 39 (1937) [Text from *League of Nations Document*, A. 17. 1932.VII. Entered into force 29 June 1932.]

5. Declaration by the Kingdom of Iraq, Baghdad, 30 May 1932

CHAPTER I

Protection of Minorities

Article 1. The stipulations contained in the present chapter are recognised as fundamental laws of Iraq, and no law, regulation or official action shall conflict or interfere with these stipulations, nor shall any law, regulation or official action now or in the future prevail over them.

Art. 2. - 1. Full and complete protection of life and liberty will be assured to all inhabitants of Iraq without distinction of birth, nationality, language, race or religion.

2. All inhabitants of Iraq will be entitled to the free exercise, whether public or private, of any creed, religion or belief, whose practices are not inconsistent with public order or public morals.

Art. 3. Ottoman subjects habitually resident in the territory of Iraq on August 6th, 1924, shall be deemed to have acquired on that date Iraqi nationality to the exclusion of Ottoman nationality in accordance with Article 30 of the Lausanne Peace Treaty [28 *League of Nations Treaty Series*, p. 11.] and under the conditions laid down in the Iraqi Nationality Law of October 9th, 1924.[Flournoy and Hudson, *Nationality Laws*, p. 348.]

Art. 4. - 1. All Iraqi nationals shall be equal before the law and shall enjoy the same civil and political rights without distinction as to race, language or religion.

2. The electoral system shall guarantee equitable representation to racial, religious and linguistic minorities in Iraq.

3. Differences of race, language or religion shall not prejudice any Iraqi national in matters relating to the enjoyment of civil or political rights, as, for instance, admission to public employments, functions and honours, or the exercise of professions or industries.

4. No restriction will be imposed on the free use by any Iraqi national of any language, in private intercourse, in commerce, in religion, in the Press or in publications of any kind, or at public meetings.

5. Notwithstanding the establishment by the Iraqi Government of Arabic as the official language, and notwithstanding the special arrangements to be made by the Iraqi Government, under Article 9 of the present Declaration, regarding the use of the Kurdish and Turkish languages, adequate facilities will be given to all Iraqi nationals whose mother tongue is not the official language, for the use of their language, either orally or in writing, before the courts.

Art. 5. Iraqi nationals who belong to racial, religious or linguistic minorities will enjoy the same treatment and security in law and in fact as other Iraqi nationals. In particular, they shall have an equal right to maintain, manage and control at their own expense, or to establish in the future, charitable, religious and social institutions, schools and other educational establishments, with the right to use their own language and to exercise their religion freely therein.

Art. 6. The Iraqi Government undertakes to take, as regards non-Moslem minorities, in so far as concerns their family law and personal status, measures permitting the settlement of these questions in accordance with the customs and usage of the communities to which those minorities belong.

The Iraqi Government will communicate to the Council of the League of Nations information regarding the manner in which these measures have been executed.

Art. 7. - 1. The Iraqi Government undertakes to grant full protection, facilities and authorisation to the churches, synagogues, cemeteries and other religious establishments, charitable works and pious foundations of minority religious communities existing in Iraq.

2. Each of these communities shall have the right of establishing councils, in important administrative districts, competent to administer pious foundations and charitable bequests. These councils shall be competent to deal with the collection of income derived therefrom, and the expenditure thereof in accordance with the wishes of the donor or with the custom in use among the community. These communities shall also undertake the supervision of the property of orphans, in accordance with law. The councils referred to above shall be under the supervision of the Government.

3. The Iraqi Government will not refuse, for the formation of new religious or charitable institutions, any of the necessary facilities which may be guaranteed to existing institutions of that nature.

Art. 8. - 1. In the public educational system in towns and districts in which are resident a considerable proportion of Iraqi nationals whose mother tongue is not the official language, the Iraqi Government will make provision for adequate facilities for ensuring that in the primary schools instruction shall be given to the children of such nationals through the medium of their own language; it being understood that this provision does not prevent the Iraqi Government from making the teaching of Arabic obligatory in the said schools.

2. In towns and districts where there is a considerable proportion of Iraqi nationals belonging to racial, religious or linguistic minorities, these minorities will be assured an equitable share in the enjoyment and application of sums which may be provided out of public funds under the State, municipal or other budgets for educational, religious or charitable purposes.

Art. 9. - 1. Iraq undertakes that in the liwas of Mosul, Arbil, Kirkuk and Sulaimaniya, the official language, side by side with Arabic, shall be Kurdish in the qadhas in which the population is predominantly of Kurdish race.

In the qadhas of Kifri and Kirkuk, however, in the liwa of Kirkuk, where a considerable part of the population is of Turcoman race, the official language, side by side with Arabic, shall be either Kurdish or Turkish.

2. Iraq undertakes that in the said qadhas the officials shall, subject to justifiable exceptions, have a competent knowledge of Kurdish or Turkish as the case may be.

3. Although in the qadhas the criterion for the choice of officials will be, as in the rest of Iraq, efficiency and knowledge of the language, rather than race, Iraq undertakes that the officials shall, as hitherto, be selected, so far as possible, from among Iraqis from one or other of these qadhas.

Art. 10. The stipulations of the foregoing articles of this Declaration, so far as they affect persons belonging to racial, religious or linguistic minorities, are declared to constitute obligations of international concern and will be placed under the guarantee of the League of Nations. No modification will be made in them without the assent of a majority of the Council of the League of Nations.

Any Member of the League represented on the Council shall have the right to bring to the attention of the Council any infraction or danger of infraction of any of these stipulations, and the Council may thereupon take such measures and give such directions as it may deem proper and effective in the circumstances.

Any difference of opinion as to questions of law or fact arising out of these articles between Iraq and any Member of the League represented on the Council shall be held to be a dispute of an international character under Article 14 of the Covenant of the League of Nations. Any such dispute shall, if the other party thereto demands, be referred to the Permanent Court of International Justice. The decision of the Permanent Court shall be final and shall have the same force and effect as an award under Article 13 of the Covenant.

CHAPTER II

Most-favoured nation Clause

Article 2. - 1. Subject to reciprocity, Iraq undertakes to grant to Members of the League most-favoured-nation treatment for a period of ten years from the date of its admission to membership of the League of Nations.

Nevertheless, should measures taken by any Member of the League of Nations, whether such measures are in force at the above-mentioned date or are taken during the period contemplated in the preceding paragraph, be of such a nature as to disturb to the detriment of Iraq the balance of trade between Iraq and the Member of the League of Nations in question, by seriously affecting the chief exports of Iraq, the latter, in view of its special situation, reserves to itself the right to request the Member of the League of Nations concerned to open negotiations immediately for the purpose of restoring the balance.

Should an agreement not be reached by negotiation within three months from its request, Iraq declares that it will consider itself as freed, *vis-à-vis* of the Member of the League in question, from the obligation laid down in the first sub-paragraph above.

2. The undertaking contained in paragraph 1 above shall not apply to any advantages which are, or may in the future be, accorded by Iraq to any adjacent country in order to facilitate frontier traffic, or to those resulting from a Customs union concluded by Iraq. Nor shall the undertaking apply to any special advantages in Customs matters which Iraq may grant to goods the produce or manufacture of Turkey or of any country whose territory was in 1914 wholly included in the Ottoman Empire in Asia.

Judicial Organisation

Art. 12. A uniform system of justice shall be applicable to all, Iraqis and foreigners alike. It shall be such as effectively to ensure the protection and full exercise of their rights both to foreigners and to nationals.

The judicial system at present in force, and based on Articles 2, 3 and 4 of the Agreement between the Mandatory Power and Iraq,[123 *League of Nations Treaty Series*, p. 77.] signed on March 4th, 1931, shall be maintained for a period of 10 years from the date of the admission of Iraq to membership of the League of Nations.

Appointments to the posts reserved for foreign jurists by Article 2 of the said Agreement shall be made by the Iraqi Government. Their holders shall be foreigners, but selected without distinction of nationality; they must be fully qualified.[On June 15, 1936, the Iraqi Government, acting under Article 16 of this declaration, requested the Council of the League of Nations to agree to a modification of this provision so as to allow the appointment of eight foreign jurists, instead of nine as required by the Anglo-Iraq Agreement. The Council gave its consent, September 25, 1936. *League of Nations Official Journal*, 1936, pp. 1161, 1321.]

International Conventions

Art. 13. Iraq considers itself bound by all the international agreements and conventions, both general and special, to which it has become a party, whether by its own action or by that of the Mandatory Power acting on its behalf. Subject to any right of denunciation provided for therein, such agreements and conventions shall be respected by Iraq throughout the period for which they were concluded.

Acquired Rights and Financial Obligations

Art. 14. Iraq, taking note of the resolution of the Council of the League of Nations of September 15th, 1925: [*League of Nations Official Journal*, 1925, p. 1511.]

1. Declares that all rights of whatever nature acquired before the termination of the mandatory régime by individuals, associations or juridical persons shall be respected.

2. Undertakes to respect and fulfil all financial obligations of whatever nature assumed on Iraq's behalf by the Mandatory Power during the period of the Mandate.

Freedom of Conscience

Art. 15. Subject to such measures as may be essential for the maintenance of public order and morality, Iraq undertakes to ensure and guarantee throughout its territory freedom of conscience and worship and the free exercise of the religious, educational and medical activities of religious missions of all denominations, whatever the nationality of those missions or of their members.

Final Clause

Art. 16. The provisions of the present chapter constitute obligations of international concern. Any Member of the League of Nations may call the attention of the Council to any infraction of these provisions. They may not be modified except by agreement between Iraq and the Council of the League of Nations acting by a majority vote.

Any difference of opinion which may arise between Iraq and any Member of the League of Nations represented on the Council, with regard to the interpretation or the execution of the said provisions, shall, by an application by such Member, be submitted for decision to the Permanent Court of International Justice.

The undersigned, duly authorised, accepts on behalf of Iraq, subject to ratification, the above provisions, being the declaration provided for by the resolution of the Council of the League of Nations of May 19th, 1932.

DONE at Baghdad on this thirtieth day of May 1932 in a single copy which shall be deposited in the archives of the Secretariat of the League of Nations.

NOURY SA'ID, Prime Minister of Iraq

Ministry of Information, Baghdad 1974, Documentary Series (31).

6. March 11 Manifesto on the Peaceful Settlement of the Kurdish Issue in Iraq, 11 March 1970

MARCH 11 MANIFESTO:

... The Revolution, sincere to the principles and resolutions of the Party, has recognised for the Kurdish citizens their entitlement to their national rights and to developing their national characteristics within the framework of the unity of the people and the homeland and the country's constitutional system.

As the Arab nation is engaged in a large-scale conflict with imperialism, Zionism and local reaction - a conflict placing it in the frontline of the struggle of the peoples of the Middle East, (it being understood that the struggle of the people of Iraq is closely linked with the struggle of the Arab nation for democracy and for combating the forces of reaction on both world-wide and local levels) - the Revolution considers that the first prop of the Arab-Kurdish national unity in Iraq lies in the fact that the Kurdish national unity, like its Arab counterpart, is a democratic movement directed against the same forces of reaction. In Iraq, it is tied up to the Arab liberation movement by the unity of struggle against imperialism and its reactionary allied forces. It is also tied up to the struggle of the Arab people by the traditions of historic fraternity, the unity of economic interests and the concerted evolution of the Arab and Kurdish nationalities. Any breach of this harmony will, of necessity, inflict immense damage on the common struggle and on the progressive national resurgence in general.

Imperialism has long realised that the unity of Arab-Kurdish struggle has the effect of reinforcing the Arab-Kurdish liberation movement and enabling it to occupy important positions in the face of the imperialistic-Zionist-Israeli aggressive schemings in the region, particularly in regard to the national battle of destiny currently raging in Palestine and the surrounding Arab countries. As such, the imperialistic and hireling quarters have been trying madly to break cohesion and fraternity between the Arab and Kurdish masses with the purpose of undermining the front of the revolutionary national struggle of Iraq.

The Revolution, understanding the national issue as an integral part of the revolution struggling against imperialism, Zionism and reaction, will necessarily abide, in every step taken towards settling [*sic*] the Kurdish national issue, by the measures conducive to cementing and consolidating national and nationalist struggles against those inhuman forces combined.

From this it follows that the exercising by the Kurdish masses of their national rights and the achievement of equal opportunities for free development, constitute the two paths leading to the unification and cementation of Iraq's national struggle against the enemies of the people and the enemies of the Arab nation and of the people of Iraq, namely imperialism, Zionism and reaction.

It was by no means a coincidence that the imperialistic-Zionist-reactionary conspiracies on the Republic of Iraq occurred at a time when signs of peace began looming large on the horizon of our beloved North, thanks to the meaningful endeavours exerted by the Revolutionary Government and sincere response on the part of the leadership of Sd. Mustafa Al-Barazani.

It is public knowledge that the Revolution had taken all necessary measures for the re-establishment of calm and peace throughout northern Iraq. The following steps have been taken:

> A) Recognition has been given to the legitimacy of the Kurdish nationality, this being in accordance with the Resolutions of the Seventh Regional Conference of the Arab Baath Socialist Party, and the official and press statements issued by the revolutionary authority. This fact shall be enshrined in a lasting manner in the Interim Constitution and the Permanent Constitution.
>
> B) The Revolutionary Command Council has approved the establishment of a university in Sulaimaniyah and the establishment of Kurdish academy of letters. It has also recognized all cultural and linguistic rights of the Kurdish nationality, prescribing that the Kurdish language be taught in all schools, institutes and universities, teachers training institutes, the Military College and the Police College. The Revolutionary Command Council further prescribed the wide dissemination of Kurdish literature - scientific, literary and political - expressive of the national and nationalist ambitions of the Kurdish people. It ordered measures to be taken to help Kurdish authors, poets and writers to form a federation of their

own, get their works printed and afford them all opportunities and possibilities for developing their scientific and artistic talents. The Revolutionary Command Council also ordered arrangements to be made for founding a Kurdish publishing and printing house and a directorate general of Kurdish culture, the publishing of a weekly newspaper and a monthly magazine in Kurdish and expanding Kurdish programmes on the Kirkuk TV Station, pending the construction of a TV station broadcasting exclusively in Kurdish.

C) In recognition of the rights of the Kurds to revive their traditions and national days and to make it possible for the whole of the people to join in the observance of national days, the Revolutionary Command Council has decreed Nawrooz Day as a National Day in the Republic of Iraq.

D) The Revolutionary Command Council has promulgated the Governorates Law which provides for the decentralisation of the local administration and for the creation of the Governorate of Dohuk.

E) The Revolutionary Command Council has issued a general amnesty for all civilian and military personnel who had joined in acts of violence in the North so as to do away with all vestiges of former negative and exceptional conditions and lay the new national life on solid foundations of pervasive security and national fraternity.

The Arab Kurdish masses of Iraq received with acclamation and welcome the acts and measures of the Revolutionary Command Council, thereby setting the stage for proceeding with the realisation of the aims which have become the object of popular consensus and on which the will and unity of word of the people came to be centered.

In view of the above, the Revolutionary Command Council established contacts with the leadership of Sd. Mustafa Al-Barazani, Chairman of the Kurdistan Democratic Party and viewpoints were subsequently exchanged. All were convinced of the necessity of accepting and implementing the contents of this Manifesto. The Revolutionary Command Council reiterates its determination to deepen and broaden the effective measures made with the object of achieving the means of the cultural and economic uplift and the general development of the Kurdish area, aiming in the first place, at enabling the Kurdish masses to exercise their legitimate rights and secure their actual participation in the national build-up and the struggle for the realisation of the great nationalist objectives of the homeland.

The Revolutionary Command Council has thus decreed the following:

1) The Kurdish language shall, side by side with the Arabic language, be an official language in the areas populated by a majority of Kurds. The Kurdish language shall be the language of instruction in these areas. The Arabic language shall be taught in all schools where teaching is conducted in Kurdish. The Kurdish language shall be taught elsewhere in Iraq as second language within the limits prescribed by the law.

2) It has been one of the main concerns of the revolutionary government to secure participation by our Kurdish brothers in Government and eliminate any discrimination between Kurds and other nationals in regard to holding public offices including sensitive and important ones as cabinet ministries, army commands, etc. While endorsing this principle, the revolutionary government stresses the need of endeavouring to have the principle achieved in fair proportions with due care to considerations of merits, the population ratio and the deprivations experienced by our Kurdish brothers in the past.

3) In view of the backwardness experienced in the past by the Kurdish nationality in the cultural and educational domains, a plan should be worked out for the treatment of this backwardness. This is to be achieved through:

(a) Implementing expeditiously the resolutions of the Revolutionary Command Council in regard to the language and cultural rights of the Kurdish people and tying up the preparation and direction of special programmes on Kurdish national affairs in the radio and TV network to the Directorate General of Kurdish Culture and Information.

(b) Reinstating students who were dismissed or had to leave school because of former conditions of violence in the area. These students should be allowed to return to their respective schools regardless of age limits or else have a convenient remedy suggested for their problem.

(c) Building more schools in the Kurdish area, elevating the standards of education and admitting, at a fair rate, Kurdish students to universities and military colleges and grant them scholarships.

4) In the administrative units populated by a Kurdish majority, government officials shall be appointed from among Kurds or persons well versed in the Kurdish language as long as these are available. The principal Government functionaries - governor, district officer (Qaimuqam), director of police, director of security, etc. - shall be drawn from among the Kurds. Steps shall immediately be taken to develop state organs in the area in consultation within the framework of the High Committee supervising the implementation of this Manifesto in a manner insuring its proper enforcement and consolidating national unity and stability in the area.

5) The Government recognises the right of the Kurdish people to set up student, youth, women and teachers organisations of their own. These organisations shall be affiliated in the national counterparts in Iraq.

(6) (a) The validity of paras (1) and (2) of the Revolutionary Command Council's Decree No. 59 dated August 5, 1968, shall be extended to the date of the issuance of this Manifesto. This shall cover all of those who took part in hostilities in the Kurdish area.

(b) Workers, government functionaries and employees, both civilian and military, shall go back to service without this being subject to cadre considerations. The civilian personnel shall be posted to the Kurdish area within the limits of its requirements.

7) (a) A committee of specialists shall be formed to speed up the uplift of the Kurdish area in all respects and provide indemnities for the affliction of the past number of years, side by side with drawing up an adequate budget for all of this. The committee in question shall be attached to the Ministry of Northern Affairs.

(b) The economic plan shall be drawn up in such a way as to ensure equal development for various parts of Iraq, with due attention to the backward conditions of the Kurdish area.

(c) Pension salaries shall be made available to the families of members of the Kurdish armed movement who met with martyrdom in the regrettable hostilities as well as to those rendered incapacitated or disfigured. This shall be regulated in a special legislation patterned on the existing laws of the land.

(d) Speedy action shall be taken to bring relief to aggrieved and needy persons by means of building housing units and other projects ensuring work to the unemployed, offering appropriate aid both in kind and in cash and granting reasonable indemnities to aggrieved persons who stand in need for help. This shall be the responsibility of the High Committee, with the exception of those specified in the above paras.

8) The inhabitants of Arab and Kurdish villages shall be repatriated to their places of habitation. As to villagers whose villages lie in areas requisitioned by the Government for public utility purposes in accordance with the provisions of the law, they shall be settled in neighbouring districts and shall be compensated for whatever loss they might have incurred as a result.

9) Steps shall be taken to speed up the implementation of the Agrarian Reform Law in the Kurdish area and have the Law amended in such a way as to ensure the liquidation of all feudalistic relationships, handing out appropriate plots of land to all peasants and waiving for them agricultural tax arrears for the duration of the regrettable hostilities.

10) It has been agreed to amend the Interim Constitution as follows:

(a) The people of Iraq are composed of two principal nationalities: the Arab nationality and the Kurdish nationality. This Constitution recognises the national rights of the Kurdish people and the rights of all nationalities within the framework of the Iraqi unity.

(b) The following paragraph shall be added to Article (4) of the Constitution: "The Kurdish language shall be, beside the Arabic language, an official language in the Kurdish area.

(c) This all shall be confirmed in the Permanent Constitution.

11) The broadcasting station and heavy arms shall be given back to the Government - this being tied up to the implementation of the final stages of the agreement.

12) One of the vice-presidents of the Republic shall be a Kurd.

13) The Governorates Law shall be amended in a way conforming with the contents of this Manifesto.

14) Following the issuance of the Manifesto, necessary steps shall be taken in consultation with the High Committee supervising its enforcement, to unify the governorates and administrative units populated by a Kurdish majority as shown by the official census to be carried out. The State shall endeavour to develop this administrative unity and deepen and broaden the Kurdish people's process of exercising their national rights as a measure of ensuring self-rule. Pending the realisation of administrative unity Kurdish national affairs shall be coordinated by means of periodical meetings between the High Committee and the governors of the northern area. As self-rule is to be established within the framework of the Republic of Iraq, the exploitation of the natural riches in the area shall obviously be the prerogative of the authorities of the Republic.

15) The Kurdish people shall contribute to the legislative branch in proportion to the ratio they have to the population of Iraq.

Kurdish Countrymen!

These accomplishments achieved by the Revolution are nothing more than a step up the ladder of attaining to your national objectives in the shade of this beloved homeland and the unity of its great people. History will bear witness that you never had and never will have as dependable brothers and allies as the Arab people.

...

It is your will in national unity which will triumph in the end. All attempts made to undermine your militant cohesion shall get smashed up on the rock of your maturity and your determination to live up to your historic responsibilities. Your struggling masses are today shedding off the dust of the intrigues spun by the enemies and greedy elements and are proceeding hand in hand vigorously and resolutely for backing up the major cause of the Arab nation, namely Palestine, and realise your sublime objective in respect to unity, liberty and socialism.

...

A page of the history of this struggling country is thus folded out and a new bright one is opened by the Revolution and by all free militant strugglers of this homeland. On this beloved soil, the bonds of affection, peace and fraternity are rejuvenated between two nationalities that are held together by a long record of common struggle across history. Today, tomorrow and for ever, they shall have endless honour across history. Today, tomorrow and for ever, they shall have the honour of reviving common struggle for vanquishing the enemies of the two nationalities and the enemies of peoples and humanity in its entirety, namely Zionism, imperialism and backwardness. They shall have the honour of joint contribution to backing up man's struggle for liberation and progress and for consolidating the civilisation of the age on foundations of right, equality and justice among all peoples.

Forward for common struggle, common hopes and common nationalist and human victories!

Ministry of Information, Directorate General, Baghdad 1972, Information Series 31

7. Revolutionary Command Council Statement, 11 March 1970

The Implementation of March 11 Manifesto

...

The National Action Charter and the Kurdish Issue

The National Action Charter has devoted one of its clauses to discussing the Kurdish issue. It said:

"For many years, the Kurdish national issue remained in the forefront of the major national problems awaiting settlement. Because that problem remained in a state of suspense, our people had to suffer enormous losses, bear great pains and have their unity and the unity of the homeland jeopardized.

"The July 17 Revolution, by virtue of its reflection of the democratic and humane doctrines of the Arab Baath Socialist Party, opened broad vistas for giving this problem a final peaceful and democratic settlement. Through cooperation between the Arab Baath Socialist Party and the Kurdistan Democratic Party, its endeavours were capped with the issuance of the March 11 historic Manifesto.

"The March 11 Manifesto provides the sound framework of ensuring the rights and legitimate national aspirations of our Kurdish people, self-rule included, and guaranteeing the unity of the homeland and the people and the unity of progressive national and nationalist forces in the struggle against imperialism, Zionism and reaction.

"So as to press on with the accomplishment of the assignments of the peaceful and democratic settlement of the Kurdish issue in conformity with the letter and spirit of the Manifesto and within the framework of common national efforts to build a unitary revolutionary democratic society, the Charter proclaims the following:

> "1 - Alliance between the Arab Baath Socialist Party and the Kurdistan Democratic Party, forming as it does the cornerstone of national coalition, is based on the historic and revolutionary alliance of destiny between the Arab and Kurdish peoples and between the Arab and Kurdish toiling masses in particular. This alliance rests on these masses, represents their interests and reflects their legitimate aspirations and ambitions.
>
> "2 - The exercising by the Kurdish masses of their legitimate national rights, including self-rule takes effect within its natural framework fully illustrated by the unity of national sovereignty, the unity of land and the unity of the political system in the Republic of Iraq. It also takes effect on the basis of recognising and believing that Iraq is an integral part of the Arab homeland and that the possibilities and energies of the Arab nation, along with its legitimate and just struggle for full liberation from the imperialistic control and Zionist invasion and for the achievement of unity and socialism, are all historic guarantees for the freedom and legitimate rights of all nationalities and minorities.
>
> "3 - The implementation of all clauses of the March 11 Manifesto and the accomplishment of all links in the peaceful and democratic settlement of the Kurdish national issue are inseparably tied up to the preservation of the existing revolutionary regime and contributing to its constant evolution and the consolidation of its position in the face of the conspiracies and sabotage perpetrated by the imperialistic and Zionist quarters, and local and neighbouring reaction. Likewise, they are tied up to the struggle for the liquidation of all suspect forces and elements and adventures set in motion by those quarters.
>
> Relationship between the people's democratic and national revolution heading for the accomplishment of unity and socialism and reinforced by the alliance of the Arab Baath Socialist Party and the Kurdistan Democratic Party on the one hand and all progressive national and nationalist forces and elements on the other, is a dialectical and unbreakable relationship. Any factional view must, in the end, play into the hands of imperialism, Zionism and local and neighbouring reaction thereby striking at the Revolution and curbing the aspirations of our Kurdish people to exercise their legitimate national rights.
>
> "4 - The revolutionary transformations unfolding in all political, economic, social and cultural fields proceeding in the direction of achieving the tasks of the popular democracy stage in the transition to socialism, side by side with securing the interests of the peasants, workers and the rest of the toiling masses, are all objective guarantees for the democratic and peaceful settlement of the Kurdish issue and the consolidation of its progressive substance.
>
> "5 - Responsibility for the implementation of the March 11 Manifesto and the realisation of the peaceful and democratic settlement of the Kurdish issue rests not on the shoulder of one single party to the issue, but is rather a joint national responsibility from which none of the national parties to the issue can be absolved.
>
> "6 - Incessant ideological and political struggle against chauvinistic, isolationist, supremacist and separatist elements and currents is a prerequisite for safeguarding the peaceful and democratic settlement of the Kurdish issue, guaranteeing its development and preserving national unity and the revolutionary transformations that seek the achievement of all national and nationalists assignments."

THE INTERIM CONSTITUTION AND THE KURDISH ISSUE

The Interim Constitution, promulgated by an edict of the Revolutionary Command Council on July 16, 1970, laid stress on the legitimate rights of the Kurdish people. Para (b), Article (5) of the Interim Constitution reads as follows:

> "The people of Iraq are composed of two main nationalities: the Arab nationality and the Kurdish nationality. This Constitution accedes the national rights of the Kurdish people and the legitimate rights of all other minorities within the framework of the Iraqi unity."

Para (b), Article (7), reads as follows:

> "The Kurdish language shall be an official language, side by side with the Arabic language, in the Kurdish area."

Article (19) of the Constitution provided that "all citizens are equal before the law without any discrimination on account of sex, race, language, social origin or religion", and that "equal opportunities are guaranteed to all countrymen within the limits of the law".

To accentuate the cultural and linguistic rights of the Kurdish nationality, the Revolutionary Command Council approved the creation of a university in Sulaimaniyah. The establishment of that university was a very important step that went beyond the limit of founding the nucleus for developing Kurdish culture into founding scientific and technical cadres among the Kurdish people to undertake the tasks of subsequent development in the area.

On October 10, 1969, the Revolutionary Command Council issued an edict prescribing the Kurdish language to be taught in all secondary schools, institutes, universities, teachers training institutes, the military college and the police college. The Revolutionary Command Council's edict further prescribed that Kurdish scientific, literary and political books and other publications expressive of the national and nationalist aspirations of the Kurdish people should be widely popularised. Kurdish writers and poets should be helped to form a federation of their own, have their works printed and be afforded all opportunities for developing their abilities and scientific and technical talents. A printing and publishing house in the Kurdish language shall be set up. The edict also provided for the creation of a directorate general of a Kurdish culture, the publishing of a weekly newspaper and a monthly magazine in Kurdish, and augmenting Kurdish programmes in the Kirkuk-T.V. Station, pending the building of a T.V. station broadcasting exclusively in Kurdish.

Following are the texts of the edicts issued by the Revolutionary Command Council in this respect:

The Revolutionary Command Council's edict No. 288 of March 11, 1970, in its initial clauses, laid stress on cultural matters related to our Kurdish brothers. It provided as follows:

> 1) The Kurdish language shall, side by side with the Arabic language, be an official language in the areas populated by a majority of Kurds. The Kurdish language shall be the language of instruction in these areas. The Arabic language shall be taught in all schools where teaching is conducted in Kurdish. The Kurdish language shall be taught elsewhere in Iraq as a second language within the limits prescribed by law.
>
> 2) It has been one of the main concerns of the revolutionary government to secure participation by our Kurdish brothers in Government and eliminate any discrimination between Kurds and other nationals in regard to holding public offices including sensitive and important ones as cabinet ministries, army commands, etc. While endorsing this principle, the revolutionary government stresses the need of endeavouring to have the principle achieved in fair proportions with due care to considerations of merits, the population ratio and the deprivations experienced by our Kurdish brothers in the past.
>
> 3) In view of the backwardness experienced in the past by the Kurdish nationality in the cultural and educational domains, a plan should be worked out for the treatment of this backwardness. This is to be achieved through:
>
> (a) Implementing expeditiously the resolutions of the Revolutionary Command Council with regard to the language and cultural rights of the Kurdish people and tying up the preparation and direction of special programmes on Kurdish national affairs in the radio and TV network to the Directorate General of Kurdish Culture and Information.
>
> (b) Reinstating all students who were dismissed or had to leave school because of former conditions of violence in the area. These students should be allowed to return to their respective schools regardless of age limits or else have a convenient remedy suggested for their problem.
>
> (c) Building more schools in the Kurdish area, elevating the standards of education and admitting, at a fair rate, Kurdish students to universities, military colleges and scholarships.
>
> 4) In the administrative units populated by a Kurdish majority, government officials shall be appointed from among Kurds or persons well-versed in the Kurdish language as long as these are available. The principal Government functionaries - governor, district officer (Qaimuqam), director of police, director of security, etc. - shall be drawn from among the Kurds. Steps shall immediately be taken to develop state organs in the area in consultation within the framework of the High Committee supervising the implementation of this Manifesto and in a manner ensuring its proper enforcement and consolidating national unity and stability in the area.

The Revolutionary Command Council, in its sitting on September 14, 1970, resolved to set up a directorate general of Kurdish Culture and Information at the Ministry of Information comprising the following directorates:

> 1. The directorate of Culture. This shall be composed of:
>
> (a) The Authorship and Publication Division, whose task shall be to encourage and publish all forms of literature related to the objectives of the Directorate and provide stimuli to Kurdish authors in various spheres. It shall also be the duty of the Directorate to revive the Kurdish cultural heritage and have it disseminated in every conceivable way.
>
> (b) The Translations Division, whose task shall be to translate all publications and other official papers into and from Kurdish.
>
> (c) The Arts Division, whose task shall be to encourage and back up the Kurdish art movement in all domains.
>
> 2. The Directorate of Information, combining:
>
> (a) The Guidance Division, whose task shall be to organise cultural activities in the Kurdish area and work for enlightening the masses by various information media including the distribution of printed matter, organising film shows, holding exhibitions and arranging for group discussions, lectures, etc. ...
>
> (b) The Press Division, whose task shall be to supervise the affairs of Kurdish-language press, work out plans for elevating its standard and organise archives for its own use and for the use of Kurdish journalists, in addition to various other forms of journalistic activities.
>
> (c) The Programme Division, which will be responsible for drawing up and steering the programmes related to Kurdish national affairs in the broadcasting and T.V. stations.
>
> 3. The Directorate of Administration, combining:
>
> (a) The Filing, Coordination and Follow-up Division, whose task shall be to coordinate correspondence with other quarters.
>
> (b) The Personnel Division.
>
> (c) The Typing Division.
>
> (d) The Distribution and Stores Division.
>
> (e) The Accounts Division.
>
> 4. This edict shall be considered as amending the Ministry of Information Ordinance.

Signed: AHMED HASSAN AL-BAKR
Chairman: The Revolutionary Command Council

Ath-thawra Publications
[Central organ of the Ba'ath Socialist Party (ABSP), 30 October 1972.]

8. Settlement of the Kurdish Problem in Iraq, 30 October 1972

...

5. DELINEATION OF THE SELF-RULE ZONE

One of the basic points of the March Manifesto and the peaceful and democratic solution to the Kurdish problem is the delimitation of the Zone covered by self-rule.

The ABSP and the revolutionary government recognized the right of the Kurdish people to enjoy self-rule - within the framework of the Iraqi Republic, the unity of both the political system and national sovereignty and the unity of the interests and aspirations of the Arab and Kurdish peoples.

This was confirmed in the Manifesto. But the Manifesto did not define the geographical zone to be covered by self-rule.

Nevertheless, the Manifesto did contain distinct bases in this respect. Article 14 says:

> "After the proclamation of this Manifesto, necessary measures shall be taken, in consultation with the High Committee entrusted with its enforcement, to unify the governorates and administrative units populated with a Kurdish majority, as shown by an official population census to be carried out later on. The state shall endeavour to develop this new administrative unit and expand the exercising, therein, by the Kurdish people of all their national rights as a surety for enjoying full self-rule. Pending the realization of this administrative unity, co-ordination of Kurdish national affairs should be undertaken through periodical meetings between the High Committee and the governors of the northern area."

From the above article of the March Manifesto, which the KDP endorsed and recognized as a sound basis for the settlement of the Kurdish question, it is evident that the road to the delimitation of the Self-rule Zone passes through "unifying the governorates and administrative units populated with a Kurdish majority - as shown by an official population census to be carried out in due course".

As to the question of the census, we should like to point out some facts. During the talks that preceded the Manifesto, the representatives of the KDP declared that they did not recognize the legality of the 1965 census, conducted under the Arifite dictatorial regime, pointing out that that census had been guided by racism. We agreed with them upon ruling out that census as a basis for finding out the areas populated with a Kurdish majority. Instead, we proposed depending upon the 1957 census as a basis for the new census scheduled to be carried out after the declaration of the Manifesto.

This meant conducting a new population census in the areas whose Kurdish majority is disputed, provided that any population presence that took place in any of these areas after the 1957 census is not recognized.

After the announcement of the Manifesto, and in the course of the action taken to translate it into a reality, the question of commencing practical measures to delimit the areas populated by Kurdish majority was discussed.

Mr. Murtada Saeed Abdul Baqi, in his capacity as Chairman of the Peace Committee entrusted with the implementation of the Manifesto, conferred with Mr. Mustafa al-Barzani over the question of census. The latter told Mr. Abdul Baqi that he was not prepared to recognize the results of the proposed census if they indicated that the areas which he took for granted to be Kurdish were not so. He said literally: "Kirkuk is part of Kurdistan. If the population census shows that the majority of its inhabitants are not Kurds, I will not recognize this. I will not bear, before the Kurds, the responsibility for relinquishing Kirkuk. May be this can take place after me"!!

This being the situation, the census became meaningless. Commencing it rather meant the resumption of fighting. Therefore, the Revolutionary Command Council preferred to defer the census and Mr. Al-Barzani endorsed the postponement.

In the course of the current talks between the ABSP and the KDP, we presented the following other proposals:

> "In view of the obstacles hindering the conduction of a population census, and because of the desire to speed up granting self-rule to the Kurdish-populated areas, we propose the re-arrangement of the administrative partition in the light of national reality as follows:
>
> > a. Creation of national administrative units in the areas populated by Kurds.
> > b. Amalgamation of the administrative units populated exclusively by Kurds (governorates, districts and sub-districts) into one administrative area; and this area shall be considered the zone covered by self-rule.
> > c. As to Kurdish nationals living in the mixed areas outside the Self-rule Zone, their cultural and administrative rights, within the areas where they live, shall be guaranteed on a par with the other ethnic groups living in the same units".

This is our stance towards the question of the delimitation of the Self-rule Zone. It originates from the following principles:

> 1. Belief in the legitimate rights of the Kurdish people.
> 2. Assuring the pre-requisites for exercising these rights.
> 3. Recognizing that the practising of these rights takes place only within the framework of one united homeland, namely, Iraq.

However, we have to state quite frankly that we do not feel that brothers in the leadership of the KDP and the Kurdish Movement view the matter from the same angle. This is no illusion. On the contrary; this is the result of many actual practices and real conditions. It is also proved by the internal publications of the KDP. These publications themselves are a very dangerous aspect, because internal indoctrination expresses opinions and attitudes of political parties more openly than does their public information media which are governed by many circumstances and considerations that prevent the surfacing of all harboured positions.

To clarify our opinion on this matter more precisely, we quote below this excerpt from an article entitled "What is Self-rule?" carried by "al-Kadir" (the internal theoretical magazine of the KDP), issue No. 14/15 for July/August, 1972:

> "The central objective of our KDP and the Liberation Movement of our Kurdish people, at the present phase, is the realization and practising of self-rule. The March Agreement specified certain measures and steps to draw the

landmarks of the road leading to self-rule. But neither the substance nor the general guidelines of self-rule were spelled out in the agreement".

In the same article, we continue to read this passage:

> "Self-rule is not a substitute for the Kurdish people's right to self-determination. But the objective realities of the development of the Kurdish Liberation Movement, together with the circumstances and conditions surrounding the Movement, necessitate raising the self-rule slogan, so as to enforce the common struggle against the enemies of the two nationalities".

Now, what are we to make of this preaching?

We believe, one does not need thoughtful analysis and lengthy scrutiny to arrive at this obvious conclusion:

"Self-rule is a central objective in this phase", [*sic*] "Self-rule is not a substitute for self-determination", "The objective realities and the surrounding circumstances and conditions necessitate raising the slogan of self-rule" ... These are indeed the essence of the Kurdish attitude; the rest of the phrases and words are secondary indications, meaning nothing stable and profound.

We wish to ask brothers in the KDP: What is the right for self-determination in your opinion?

As is well known, the right for self-determination is two-sided:

a. Voluntary union.
b. Separation.

To our mind, the KDP identified itself with the first side, namely voluntary union, by endorsing the March Manifesto. In our opinion, too, this is what is desired by the Kurdish masses.

Now, are we to understand from the sentence "self-rule is no substitute for the right to self-determination" that such a right is to be achieved in phases - the first being self-rule as implied by the sentence reading "The central objective of our KDP and the liberation movement of our Kurdish people, at the present phase, is the realization and practising of self-rule" and by the other sentence saying "The objective realities of the development of the Kurdish liberation movement, together with the circumstances and conditions surrounding the movement, necessitate raising the slogan of self-rule to enforce the common struggle against the enemies of the two peoples"?

The above quotations from the literature used by the KDP for indoctrinating its members is, on the one hand, more important than anything published by "al-Taakhi" in this respect for the reasons stated earlier. On the other hand, they shed sufficient light on the whole incidents, attitudes and points of view presented by the KDP ever since the proclamation of the March Manifesto. They also illuminate the source of this leadership's concept of the March Manifesto and the ways and means for implementing it as well as its attitude towards its own commitments regarding the implementation of all the clauses of the Manifesto and the restoration of normal life in both the northern area and the entire Iraq and regarding the establishment of self-rule and all its essential local and national institutions. (We will deal with these matters in detail later on).

In addition to all we have said, we reproduce here, by way of example, a large portion of an article published by "al-Kadir" magazine, in the same issue referred to above, under the title: "The Kurds and Kurdistan, Between the Arab Nation and the Arab Countries". This article sheds more light on the perspective of the leadership of the KDP of the subjects under discussion.

Know the Kurds Series No. 1, The Information Department of The Kurdistan Democratic Party, published June 1973

9. Kurdish Democratic Party: On the Kurdish Movement in Iraq, June 1973

THE KURDS AND THEIR HOMELAND

Although Kurdistan is seen today as only parts of the territories of many states in the Middle East where international frontiers cut across the land and the people, geographically and ethnically these parts of Kurdistan continue to form one homogeneous and contiguous unit where the Kurds form the great majority of the population.

Kurdistan has undergone two major fragmentations, once during the 17th century when it was divided into areas of influence between the Ottoman and the Persian Empires and more recently after World War I when various parts of Kurdistan were added to the territories of the modern states of Iraq, Syria and Turkey. At present therefore, Kurdistan can be said to form the northwestern part of Iran, east and southeastern part of Turkey, northeastern part of Syria, a sliver of Soviet Armenia in the U.S.S.R. and north and northeastern part of Iraq.

The pattern of life within the Kurdish society has slowly but steadily changed from one of nomadism to one of settled communities that pursue a basically agricultural way of life supplemented by the raising of livestock, limited amount of trade, and small locally established handicrafts and industries. Like the rest of the Middle East, Kurdistan is also divided into rural and urban communities where the people live in villages, towns and urban centers. However, in general Kurdistan is the least economically developed areas of the countries among which it is divided.

The Kurds are an Indo-European people and they speak Kurdish which, as an Indo-European language constitutes one of the major languages of the Iranian groups such as Persian, Tajik, Pashtu and others. Perhaps some of the most obvious national characteristics which form a distinct badge of identity for the Kurds are their language, their colorful national costume which distinguishes both Kurdish men and women, and their land of Kurdistan where the Kurds have lived for many centuries.

Although thus far no definitive effort has been made to define the origin of the Kurds, more and more authorities on the subject seem to agree that, based on linguistic arguments and the pattern of movement of the peoples from Central Asia, the Medes can be considered as the ancestors of the present-day Kurd.

A Kurd may be best characterized as a mountaineer well adapted to the terrain and climate of his homeland. He is considered by many to be a brave, gay and sincere person. He is hospitable and makes a good family man and a loving father. Kurdish women are normally considered more free than those among the neighboring peoples. As a religious community the Kurds are faithful and liberal practitioners of Islam, and the Muslim religion is the faith of the great majority of the Kurds. Although statistics vary as to the number of the Kurds, one may estimate the population of Kurdistan to be between 18-20 million divided among Turkey, Iran, Iraq, Syria and a small number in the Soviet Union.

Judging from their rich folklore, the Kurds are a people very fond of music, dancing and poetry. Names such as Ahmed i Khane, Haji Qadir Koyi, Piramerd, Mawlawi Goran, Hajar and Bekas are only a few among many poets and literary figures. By the same token Jam'iyati Taali u Taraqi of 1908, the Kurdistan newspaper which was first published in Cairo in 1882 and the organizations of Hoybun of 1927 and Hiwa of 1938 are only a few landmarks in a long series of literary and political efforts made by the Kurds during the 19th and the 20th centuries.

EVOLUTION OF POLITICAL ORGANIZATIONS IN KURDISTAN

The many nationalist efforts that have been spent by various Kurdish nationalist groups both in Kurdistan and abroad are the result and reflection of the long and difficult struggle of the Kurdish people in self-defense and against efforts made to deny his existence and to ignore his legitimate nationalist demands.

During and after World War I the Kurdish people struggled for the principle of self-determination and for this the Kurds achieved recognition as a nation within the framework of the Treaty of Sevres of 1920 which specifically provided for the establishment of an independent Kurdistan.

The guiding principle for the nationalist Kurds during and after World War II was the desire for the creation of more widely-based and better organized political efforts which could gather within one body and under one leadership all existing Kurdistani groups and therefore the natural outcome was the birth of the Kurdistan Democratic Party on August 16, 1946 under the guidance and initiative of its president Mustafa Barzani. A remarkable feature of our present Kurdish nationalist movement is the fact that for almost three decades this movement has grown and matured under the leadership of an increasingly popular man like Barzani and has been served by a constantly growing and well-organized political party such as the KDP.

The Kurdistan Democratic Party is a nationalist progressive party which endeavors to serve the people of Kurdistan by initiating and leading lasting social and economic changes within the Kurdish society. It is a party which believes in both principles of democracy and social justice, principles that are reflected in the Party's program and internal regulations which in turn are formulated on the basis of the concept of democratic centralism. The following are a few of KDP's principles as they are stated in its program:

> *Article 3*. "We struggle for freedom and for the implementation of the March 11 Agreement in both letter and spirit and to enable the people of Kurdistan to achieve autonomy and to protect, consolidate and develop that autonomy in Kurdistan and within the Iraqi Republic."
>
> *Article 6*. "We struggle for the sake of establishing a popularly elected, revolutionary and democratic form of government. We also struggle to achieve far-reaching social and economic changes within all aspects of the society and to guarantee for all the citizens the freedoms of worship, belief, press, and political association."
>
> *Article 7*. "We struggle: a) for the strengthening of brotherly relations between the Arab and Kurdish nations, b) for the consolidation of brotherhood among the Arabs, the Kurds and the minorities within Iraq and for the strengthening of national unity, c) for the strengthening of bonds of friendship between our Kurdish people and all peoples of the world."
>
> *Article 8*. "a) We struggle for peace in the world and for the lessening of international tensions and we are guided by the principles of the United Nations, the Bandong Conference resolutions, the principles of peaceful co-existence, peaceful solution of international disputes, the banning of nuclear weapons and tests on them, b) We pursue a nationalist anti-imperialist policy and we strive to strengthen friendly relations with all peoples of the world based upon the principle of mutual benefit and the support of national liberation movements waged by people for the sake of independence and the right of self-determination."
>
> *Article 9*. "We endeavor to strengthen bonds of friendship and cooperation between our party and all other Iraqi parties and organizations which believe in the justice of the Kurdish question and which support the common struggle of our party and the other democratic organizations in all parts of Kurdistan. We also endeavor to strengthen ties of friendship with the democratic parties and organizations throughout the world."
>
> *Article 12*. "We struggle to develop our national economy and to raise the standard of living of the people by following the principle of comprehensive economic and social planning, taking into consideration the human and natural resources of the land and hoping to make available the basic needs for development and encouraging both the public and private sectors of the economy while insuring the leading role of the former."
>
> *Article 16*. "We support the new Land Reform Law No. 37 of 1970 in the hope that all farmers of Kurdistan will be able to own some land and so that feudalism in Kurdistan will be uprooted ..."
>
> *Article 17*. "We believe in the regulating of domestic and foreign trade while assisting and stimulating the business community, all this while taking into consideration the interests of both the public and private sectors based upon the national interest of the country and on the principle of combating monopoly and price speculation. We also believe in establishing commercial ties with other countries based upon the principle of reciprocity and the encouragement of exports and the limiting of imports to the basic and necessary commodities."
>
> *Article 22*. "We support women's political, economic, social and cultural rights and we work to see the necessary laws passed which will guarantee all rights of women prior, during and after childbirth as well as the rights of mothers and children."
>
> *Article 23*. "We struggle to a) guarantee the rights of the Kurdish student and in order to wipe out illiteracy and to give education a nationalist and democratic content while fighting reactionary, fascist and racist tendencies; b) revitalize Kurdish history, literature and art and to enrich them with the humanist elements from other cultures and to protect and preserve historic sites in Kurdistan and to build museums for them; c) to develop the University of Sulaimaniya, protect its independence and to turn it into a center for academic research and for the revitalization of the Kurdish national culture; d) emphasize the teaching of Kurdish language, history and culture during all stages of education, promote the teaching of Kurdish throughout Iraq, establish a Kurdish academy of science, a press and publishing house, and a separate radio and television station in Kurdistan; e) make primary school education compulsory for both sexes, open night schools for workers, farmers and others, and to increase the number of libraries, laboratories and literary clubs in order to raise the cultural and educational standards of the people; f) promote Kurdish art and culture and

to use their potentials to serve humanity in general and the objectives and interests of the Kurdish people in particular, and to encourage the literary and artistic movement by increasing the number of assistantships and scholarships, the building of theaters and opening of clubs, g) guarantee the rights of teachers in Kurdistan and to raise their standard in various aspects of their profession."

THE KURDISH REVOLUTION AND ITS OBJECTIVES

The Kurdish revolution which began in September 1961 was a natural reaction to the oppressive and discriminating policies which the Iraqi government was carrying out against the Kurdish people. In the face of constant harassment and in order to defend their national existence and right, the Kurdish people were forced to pick up arms. It is during the last several years of struggle that the Kurdish Revolution has evolved into a definite political movement the objectives of which have crystalized into the demand of Kurdish autonomy within Iraq.

Since the Kurds constitute one of the two major nationalities within Iraq, they have as a people, put forth the legitimate demand of having their separate and distinct national identity both recognized and respected. Through the many years of association with the Iraqi Arabs and the bitter struggle which they have had to undertake in the face of various Iraqi regimes - particularly since 1961 - the Kurds have come to the conclusion that the only guarantee which will safeguard and promote their nationalist development is through enjoying autonomy within Iraq.

Since the concept and application of Kurdish autonomy is conceived of within the larger framework of the Iraqi state, it is important that there should be no contradictions between the proposed regional (Kurdish) administration and the larger national (Iraqi) form of government. Thus another objective of the Kurdish Revolution is democracy for all of Iraq and this is based on the belief that the best atmosphere within which Kurdish autonomy can flourish is the general framework of a democratic system of government for Iraq as a whole.

The Kurdish Revolution is led by the Kurdistan Democratic Party under the leadership of Barzani who in addition to being the President of KDP and the leader of the Kurdish people and his revolution, is the only man that has successfully led the Kurdish nationalist movement in Iraq and whose leadership is widely believed in and accepted by the Kurdish people.

The political state of affairs in Iraq has been such that while the Kurdish Revolution has continuously grown in its organization and in its positive response to the principle of a peaceful solution for the Kurdish problem within Iraq, various Iraqi regimes have persisted in their insensitive and hostile policies toward the Kurdish people and their movement. However, the failure of racist and aggressive policies on the one hand and the resolution of the Kurdish people for their legitimate demands on the other hand, have finally and after long years of dampened hopes and broken promises brought the Ba'th Arab Socialist Party and the present Iraqi Government to a better and more responsive understanding of the nature of the Kurdish question and it was this understanding which resulted in the conclusion of the March Agreement.

Thus on March 11, 1970 the long and difficult struggle of the Kurdish people ended by the victory of the will of the people of Kurdistan, a victory that produced the March Agreement which recognizes and provides for autonomy for Kurdistan. The cornerstone of the ensuing alliance between the KDP and the Ba'th Arab Socialist Party is nothing other than the latter's recognition and acceptance of the national rights of the Kurdish people, a recognition which will seem genuine only when the provisions of the Agreement are implemented fully and in good faith.

The March Agreement has established a principle which requires a constitutional, administrative and economic framework within which the concept as well as the practice of Kurdish autonomy must be consolidated. Thus [*sic*] the ruling Ba'th Arab Socialist Party and the Iraqi Government have failed to produce even after three and a half years of hopeful anticipation by the Kurdish people. This is not an attempt to deny the implementation of minor provisions of the Agreement during this period, but the fact remains that the provisions which have a direct bearing on the preservation and consolidation of the Kurdish national identity and the existence of the Kurdish people in his homeland of Kurdistan, have not only been ignored, but feverish and systematic efforts are being made to blur the reality of Kurdish existence in Southern Kurdistan and to disrupt and distort the geographic and ethnic homogeneity of Kurdistan.

The present policy of Arabization which is being diligently pursued inside Kurdistan is a perfect example of how sincere efforts for the implementation and practice of Kurdish autonomy have been replaced by sinister and systematic plans to arbitrarily detach parts from the area of the proposed Kurdish autonomy and to cut up and divide the area and population of Kurdistan. One has only to follow the progress of this hateful policy in the areas of Kirkuk, Khanaqin, Sinjar and parts of the provinces of Nineveh and Duhok to see in use such measures as the bringing of Arab tribes from outside to settle them in Kurdistan; the deliberate creation of antagonism between the Kurds and the ethnic and religious minorities living in Kurdistan; the resort to terror and the arming and financing of suspicious and pro-government elements; the mass deportation of Kurdish families and clans; and the pursuit of a definite policy of discrimination against the Kurds of these areas by refusing them government jobs and by arbitrarily transferring Kurdish civilian and military officials to the southern part of Iraq. All this is done to make life miserable for the original Kurdish population of these parts and consequently to force them out. One can only wonder whether such treatment by a government of its citizens can ever produce any sense of loyalty and belonging to a system which is so discriminating and which is that hostile. All this is in addition to the plots that are organized against the life of Barzani and the local military attacks which have been carried out against such areas of Kurdistan as 'Aqra, Barzan and others.

No doubt that the accumulative effect of all this has made the implementation of the provisions of the March Agreement more complicated, although the Kurdish Revolution and the Kurdish people on their part continue to try and overlook the negative aspects of the present policy and to find points of agreement with the government in order to salvage a deteriorating situation and to spare the Iraqi people the recurrence of the sad and regretful events of the past. The Kurdish Revolution's policy of constantly asking the government to put an end to certain undesirable and unworkable policies and to instead cooperate towards a genuine implementation of the March Agreement is based on the belief that this type of cooperation is the only foundation upon which the sovereignty and independence of Iraq can be consolidated and by which peace and stability of not only Iraq but perhaps of the whole area of the Middle East can be affected. On the other hand if our call to reason fails and it is instead met with indifference and hostility, then the Kurdish people will no doubt practice the legitimate right of self defense whenever and wherever that becomes necessary.

The sense of fairness and responsibility that characterizes the leadership of the Kurdish Revolution, and the general feeling that cooperation and friendship with the Christian community is not only necessary but desirable have all caused the Kurdish Revolution to pay particular attention to solving the problems and insuring the well-being of this community in Kurdistan. As a practical application of these principles the Kurdish Revolution and the Kurdistan Democratic Party have established joint committees with the representatives of the Christian community to work with and help the religious leaders particularly in repairing, and preserving their places of worship; to keep contact with the Assyrian speaking community and to focus on their problems by publicising them in the KDP Publications; to ask the Christian community to present its own list of names of people who could be appointed as officials in their own areas; and in general to try and explain to them the rights and privileges which they will enjoy within the framework of an autonomous Kurdistan.

The Kurdish Revolution is also a social movement and as such it both depends on the support of the Kurdish people and strives to translate its own achievements into tangible services for the people of Kurdistan. Having suffered many years of official neglect and lack of development, the Kurdish community has remained plagued with many social and economic ills which require immediate and full attention. More than 75% of the people of Kurdistan remain illiterate, a situation which was aggravated by the constant disruption of education due to the general lack of peace and the lack of educational facilities within the liberated Kurdish areas. All this has led to the growth of a whole generation of Kurdish children without any education. To say that tuberculosis, kidney disease, rickets and numerous contagious diseases are rampart throughout Kurdistan is to demonstrate in only few examples the constantly deteriorating health condition of the people of Kurdistan. The picture grows gloomier when we realize that health and sanitation facilities practically do not exist in the area and that facilities for the treatment and prevention of various diseases exist on a very limited scale. To effectively demonstrate this lack of medical care, one has only to state the fact that there is only one doctor for every 250,000 of the inhabitants and there is only a very small supporting group of dressers and male nurses.

The Kurdish Revolution therefore must broaden its social content and it intends to do this by focusing on community development in areas where the people need most help. In areas where the community needs direct assistance, such as in health and education, the Kurdish Revolution tries to help by operating the existing schools and hospitals, by opening new ones whenever possible, by attracting doctors and teachers and providing medical care when possible and available.

The Kurdish Revolution's concept of community development is also based on the principle of helping the people to help themselves. The thousands of village communities throughout liberated Kurdistan are not only deprived of basic tools of development, but they often are not even aware of how they can improve their own social and economic conditions with relatively little cost and effort. With all this in mind, the Kurdistan Democratic Party has recently created a Department for Community Development which will try to tackle the problems of rural Kurdistan, specifically those of health and education.

Needless to say that the ambitions and aspirations of this department by far exceed its means, for it is the organ of a movement which in turn is the product of a society that has remained poor and underdeveloped for too long. The fact that Arabization disperses and dislocates our population, and the fact that our political question remains unsolved, and that for more than a decade we have had to put everything else aside and to pick up arms in order to defend ourselves, all these are factors which have prevented the Kurdish Revolution and its various organs from keeping the economic and social conditions of Kurdistan from further deterioration, let alone trying to keep pace with the basic and increasing needs of our community.

While we confirm our belief in the fact that the peaceful solution of the Kurdish question in Iraq, based on the full implementation of the March Agreement and the consolidation of autonomy for Kurdistan, is the most correct and practical way of consolidating peace and national unity, we call upon all concerned and peace-loving individuals to carry the peaceful message of our Kurdish people home to their peoples and governments. We also ask you to encourage the various humanitarian organizations in your countries to heed the call of the needy people of Kurdistan and to offer their help in the form of food, clothes, medical care and other basic needs. We finally invite the delegates of all friendly nations to come and visit Kurdistan in order to witness the difficult struggle which our people put up for their national existence and their dire need for help to lead a simple and peaceful life.

Published by The Information Department of The Kurdistan Democratic Party, December 1973

10. Kurdistan Democratic Party: Arabization of Kurdistan [and] Racialist Designs of the Ba'thist Regime in Iraq, December 1973

Our national question is the question of a people inhabiting his own homeland and bent upon determining his own destiny. It was this determination which enabled our people to stand bravely and endure all the tragedies which befell him since the beginning of this century and up to the time of the March Agreement. The latest in this series of tragedies was the military campaign which was waged in its most savage form against Kurdistan during the last ten years by successive Iraqi governments and which was intended to destroy our national movement and thereby eliminate our national existence. However, at the end the campaign failed and the will of the Iraqi people won and produced the historic March Agreement.

The March 11, 1970 Agreement was a harbinger of good will and optimism, especially since it could pave the way for the spread of a democratic atmosphere and the development of the country through diligent and persistent efforts. The Agreement can therefore be considered a victory for the Iraqi people in general and for the Kurdish people in particular. Immediately after the announcement of the Agreement, we began strengthening our relations with the Ba'th Arab Socialist Party, guided by our belief that our sincerity in working for the implementation of autonomy for Kurdistan and democratic rule for Iraq could best be demonstrated through efforts spent to consolidate the alliance between our two parties, something which could serve as a basis for the creation of a united national front that will stand up to and thwart all internal and external plots against the country.

However, all hopes were dampened when signs of a negative attitude emerged immediately after the announcement of the Agreement until this attitude warned of a possible explosion and indicated a return to the days which preceded the March Agreement. The most dangerous sign of this negative attitude was the Ba'th Party's persistent pursuit of a policy of Arabization of Iraqi Kurdistan which continues up to the present. Specifically, this policy aims at a reduction of the territory of Kurdistan by detaching important parts from it. For the execution of this policy, they have concentrated their efforts on the areas of Kirkuk, Khanaqeen, Sinjar and various districts within the provinces of Nineveh and Dihok, areas of Kurdistan which they consider of mixed population due to the presence of Turkman, Assyrian and Arab minorities.

Facts of history and geography prove that these areas have always been and will continue to be integral parts of Southern Kurdistan, parts of Kurdistan which were appended to the territory of the Iraqi State when the latter was created. The Ba'th Party and the present government knew these facts well but they intentionally try through intrigues and illegal measures to change the true ethnic composition of these areas by deporting the Kurds and replacing them with Arabs. The following plans are used to achieve this end:

1. The bringing of Arab tribes in large numbers for the purpose of settling them in Kurdistan.

2. The creation of animosity and hatred between the Kurdish people and the ethnic and religious minorities inside Kurdistan.

3. Resort to terror and other inhumane means against the Kurds of these areas; liberal distribution of money and weapons among certain Kurdish elements; mass deportation of Kurdish families and clans as it happened to our Faily brethren and was attempted against the tribes of Goyan and Omiryan in the province of Nineveh.

4. The constant pursuit of policy of open discrimination against the Kurds of these areas through the rejection of their just demands by government authorities; refusal to appoint them to government jobs; and arbitrary transfer of Kurdish officials both civilian and military, to the southern part of Iraq.

5. The purchase of land and property from Kurdish landlords with the intention of forcing the immigration of Kurdish farmers from these areas and replacing them with Arabs.

One of the simplest rights of a citizen is that of having one's national identity and one's desire to remain attached to one's homeland and people both recognized and respected. Furthermore it is the duty of a national government to deepen the citizen's sense of belonging to his land and people. Yet the prevailing conditions in these areas indicate something contrary to this sound logic and to the proper treatment of the citizens. Naturally under such conditions our Kurdish people and our Kurdistan Democratic Party will be forced to take a strong defensive stand and no doubt the true status of our relations with the government and the Ba'th Party will come into the open and may even take the form of regrettable bloody confrontations. Under persistent pressure the branches and committees of our Party may have to leave their headquarters and head for rural Kurdistan.

If we were to look for the real reasons of our problems with the government and the Ba'th Party, we will find that 75% of the unfortunate incidents which occur in Kurdistan are due to justified and understandable reaction to the policy of Arabization. This Arabization plan is not only one of the points of contention between us and the government, but it is also the greatest danger to our Kurdish people and to the cause of peace and stability in Iraq.

The basis of this policy may be found in the interim constitution which was promulgated, without the knowledge of our party and of the other patriotic forces in the country, by the Ba'th Party after July 17, 1968. One of the articles of this constitution states that "the Iraqi people is an integral inseparable part of the Arab nation ..." A statement to the same effect was further strengthened and repeated in the National Pact where it says that "Iraq is a part of the Arab homeland ..." All this is in addition to the statements of government officials which further support and elaborate on these racist techniques and which deny the existence of the Kurdish people who has lived for centuries in his homeland of Kurdistan.

We often wonder for whose benefit does the government resort to these measures that are contrary to a genuine desire for peace and the consolidation of national unity. While we see the common national interest threatened by the policies of Arabization and Ba'thization, and as we can predict the dire consequences of these acts, we condemn them and we warn against their continuation. We also call upon the patriotic forces to reveal the facts so that we may be able to put an end to these inhumane policies of Arabization and Ba'thization in these areas. We call for this so that in the future we will not be forced to stand in defense of our Kurdish people's rights and the rights of the Iraqi people to enjoy a democratic way of life; we call for this now so that there will not be a recurrence of the sad and bloody events of the past which occur as the result of chauvinistic policies which are void of any true nationalist sentiment.

In spite of the fact that on many occasions we have, through the representatives of our Party in the Peace Committee, warned against the dangers of these policies, we have not only found no response, but the situation has deteriorated and the danger has increased. Here at the end of this article we are referring to some examples of this racist policy so that both Iraqi and world public opinion and others who support peace, democracy in Iraq and freedom throughout the world, will be fully aware of the conditions in those areas, areas of Kurdistan where an honest census will easily prove their true ethnic identity.

Once again we condemn these racist policies and we ask the government to put an end to them. We also call upon the Iraqi, Arab, and world public opinion to seek out the truth in this matter by coming to Kurdistan. We turn to all Arab and international humanitarian and political organizations to extend a helping hand to the victims of this Arabization policy and particularly those who have been forced out of their land such as thousands of refugees in Sinjar, an area where drought has caused famine and where this policy of Arabization has been brutally carried out. Our Kurdish people will forever defend his existence on his land and all fait accompli policies which antagonize the people of these areas and stand in contradiction to facts of history and geography shall never find success in Kurdistan.

Nineveh Province - Sinjar District:

The number of villages that have been hit by artillery under instructions given by the Iraqi authorities in the above area since the signing of the March 1970 Agreement, has reached 24 villages. All this has been carried out with the intention of forcing out the Kurds who live in these villages: ...

The number of people affiliated with our party and whose land has been expropriated in the area of Sinjar, has reached 366 who live in 30 villages and the area of this land that has been taken over is 36955 Donums. This land has been taken over by the Iraqi authorities and part of it has already been marked for the building of a camp for the 29th Brigade. The rest of the land thus expropriated from the Kurds has been distributed among the landlords and other pro-government elements in the area. ...

Shaikhan District:

On February 5th 1973, and under orders from the Government, the village of Qani Qone was shelled by artillery.

Zimar District:

On March 25th 1973, the Iraqi army surrounded the village of Chifri; however, the population sensed the coming danger and fled. The Iraqi soldiers began by looting the properties of peasants, then they shelled the village. Some people were killed, and others were wounded during the attack.

Mosul Centre:

On March 12, 1973 and at the time when the Kurds were preparing to celebrate NEW-ROZ, the national Kurdish holiday, certain elements, helped by official police and security men, began surrounding the headquarters of our Kurdistani organizations and fired on them.

Kirkuk Province:

1. Kirkuk is a Kurdish city in which live some minorities. There has been agreement between us and the Ba'th Party to run the city jointly; however, in reality it is being ruled by a purely Arab Ba'thist administration.
2. 6 new quarters have been built in Kirkuk under the names of:
El Karama, El Huriya, 14 Ramadan, El Wahda, Yarmouk and El Andulus. All this for the purpose of bringing Arabs from outside and settling them in these parts.
3. The use of the Kurdish language within the government offices is banned and its use in schools is being fought.

Dibis District:

... 24 villages in this area have been evacuated, and there was agreement that the original population should be returned to them; however Government authorities have prevented the carrying out of this step and refused to allow the population to return to their villages ...

Kifri, Tuz and El Dawida Districts:

...
2. The land in these areas is taken away from their owners either by temptation or intimidation and such land is then given to members of Arab tribes.
3. The land reform office refuses to give the Kurdish farmers the right to use these lands in order to force them to leave the area.
4. There are efforts to mobilize mercenaries in the area of Tuz in order to assault the Kurdish farmers in this area and the neighbouring villages in order to force them to leave.
5. In the area of Siqizli, which is located on the cross roads to Kirkuk and Koi Sanjaq, the Government has taken over big stretches of land and under the pretext of wanting to build a new military camp there, although the real intention is to Arabize the area and its population.

Khaniqin and Mendeli areas:

1. Although the area is Kurdish, it is being administrated by an Arab Ba'thist administration.
2. The land reform office refuses to hand over land ownership certificates to the Kurds while generously distributing them among Arabs who are strangers to the area.
3. The use of Kurdish language in schools and the Government offices is banned.
4. The population of these areas have been deported in large numbers to Iran, and others have been forced to flee to the liberated Kurdish zone. All this is being done under the pretext that such people do not possess citizenship certificates.

The following text was transmitted to the Research Centre by the Iraqi Embassy in London, in May 1974

11. Statement made by the President Ahmed Hassan Al-Bakr, Chairman of the Revolutionary Command Council, together with the Revolutionary Command Council Decisions No. 247 and 248 on the Occasion of the Application of Autonomy in the Kurdistan Area, 11 March 1974

"...

In confirmation of citizenship ties and historic brotherhood among the sons of Iraq, Arabs, Kurds and fraternal minorities, and in compliance with the democratic principles of the July 17 Revolution, and in meeting its pledge, and in application of the March 11, 1970 Manifesto and the contents of the National Action Charter and in consolidation of the common struggle and interests of all people's sons and the aims for which they struggle and called for by all progressive national and nationalist forces, the Revolutionary Command Council decided to apply autonomy in Kurdistan area. The application of autonomy in Kurdistan area which have a majority of Kurdish population and on democratic basis, will provide necessary means for our Kurdish people to exercise their full national rights within the boundary of one homeland and under ties of brotherhood, equality and common responsibility among its sons, consolidate the national unity and the gains made in various fields by the revolution for the masses and will avert the intrigues of imperialism and reactionary forces. The exercise of full rights by the sons of our Kurdish people in the national bodies and the guarantee of cultural rights to fraternal minorities in accordance with the laws promulgated by the 17th July revolution, under its democratic principles and institutions and within the context of the joint national action of the National and Nationalist Front, is bound also to alleviate the injustice caused to the sons of our Kurdish people and the fraternal minorities during the dictatorial and reactionary regimes and under the chauvinistic and tyrant policies. It will also cause an extensive economic, social and cultural rights in Kurdistan area and will open wide horizons to all sons of the people to march forward with a firm confidence and a spirit of security and constructive work on the path of democratic transformation for building socialism."

REVOLUTIONARY COMMAND COUNCIL DECISION NO. 247

Pursuant to the provisions of Paragraph B of Article 63 of the Interim Constitution, the Revolutionary Command Council decided in the name of the people at their meeting held on March 11, 1974, to amend the Interim Constitution promulgated on July 16, 1970, as follows:

"Article One - the following phrase shall be added to Article 80".

"The area the majority of its population are Kurds shall enjoy autonomy in accordance with stipulations of the law."

"Article Two - This constitutional amendment shall come into force from the date it is published in the Official Gazette".

"Taken in Baghdad on this 17th day of Safar 1394 hijira, the 11th day of March 1974."

signed: AHMED HASSAN AL-BAKR

Chairman of the Revolutionary Command Council.

REVOLUTIONARY COMMAND COUNCIL DECISION NO. 248

Pursuant to Para (a), Article 42 of the Interim Constitution, the Revolutionary Command Council decided in the name of the people at their session on March 11, 1974, the promulgation of the following Law No. 33 of 1974.

LAW FOR AUTONOMY IN THE AREA OF KURDISTAN
PART ONE: FOUNDATION OF AUTONOMY
CHAPTER ONE: GENERAL PRINCIPLES

ARTICLE ONE

A) The area of Kurdistan shall enjoy autonomy and be called the area whenever it is mentioned hereinafter.

B) The area shall be so defined as to be populated by a majority of Kurds and the general census shall specify the demarcation of the area in accordance with the provisions of March 11 Manifesto and the general census records of 1957 shall be the foundation for defining the national nature of the absolute population majority in the places where general census is to be conducted.

C) The area shall be considered an integral administrative unit, enjoying a juridical personality and autonomy within the framework of the legal, political and economic integrity of the Republic of Iraq, and the administrative divisions therein shall be conducted in accordance with the provisions of the governorates' law, with due consideration to the provisions of this law.

D) The area is an integral part of the Iraqi territory and its people an integral part of the Iraqi people.

E) The city of Arbil shall be the metropolitan centre for the administration of autonomy.

F) The administrative bodies of autonomy shall be part of the administrative bodies in the Republic of Iraq.

ARTICLE TWO

A) The Kurdish language shall be the official language, besides the Arabic language in the area.

B) The Kurdish language shall be the language of education for Kurds in the area, and the teaching of Arabic shall be compulsory in all stages and institutions of education.

C) Educational institutions shall be established in the area for members of the Arab nationality, wherein education shall be in Arabic and the Kurdish language shall be taught in a compulsory manner.

D) All citizens in the area shall enjoy the option to join the schools for their education, regardless of their mother tongue.

E) Education shall be subject, in all stages in the area, to the general educational policy of the state.

ARTICLE THREE

A) The rights and liberties of members of the Arab nationality and minorities in the area shall be guaranteed in accordance with the provisions of the Constitution, laws and resolutions promulgated in that connection, and the autonomous administration shall be bound to guarantee their exercise.

B) Members of the Arab nationality and minorities in the area shall be represented on all autonomous bodies, in proportion of their ratio to the population of the area, and shall participate in assuming public civil service posts, in accordance with laws and regulations governing them.

ARTICLE FOUR

Legislature shall be independent and void of any other control than the law, and the legal formations in the area shall constitute an integral part of their legal system in the Republic of Iraq.

CHAPTER TWO: FINANCIAL PROVISIONS

ARTICLE FIVE

The area shall constitute an autonomous financial unit, within the financial integrity of the state.

ARTICLE SIX

A) The area shall have a special budget within the consolidated budget of the state.

B) For the preparation and compilation of the budget of the area the same rules and principles of compiling the consolidated budget of the state shall be adopted.

ARTICLE SEVEN

The budget of the area shall consist of the following components:

1 - The ordinary budget.
2 - The annual investment budget of the area.
3 - The budgets of productive institutions and administrations of a local character established in the area.
4 - The budgets of local administrations and municipalities in the area.

ARTICLE EIGHT

The budgetary resources of the area shall consist of the following components:

A) Self resources comprising:

1 - Revenues from taxes and duties specified for municipalities and local administrations under relevant laws.
2 - Values of sales and charges of services.
3 - The share appropriated from the profits of administrations and institutions covered by the budget of the area.
4 - Basic and additional real estate tax within the area.
5 - The agricultural land tax and share of agrarian reform from proceeds.
6 - Government (dead-land) land tax.
7 - Estate tax.
8 - Estate registration duties.
9 - Charges and fines imposed by courts of justice.
10 - Revenue stamp duties.
11 - Car registration and title-deed transfer charges.

B) Appropriations from the ordinary budget of the state, the annual investment programme and the national development plan, to cover the expenditures of the budget of the area, so as to guarantee its balanced growth and development, in consistency with other parts of the Republic of Iraq.

ARTICLE NINE

Accounts of the area shall be the supervision of the Board of the Supreme Auditing and financial inspection.

PART TWO: AUTONOMOUS BODIES
CHAPTER ONE: LEGISLATIVE COUNCIL

ARTICLE TEN

The Legislative Council is the legislative body elected for the area, and its formation, organisation and progress of work therein shall be defined by law.

ARTICLE ELEVEN

A) The Legislative Council shall elect a chairman, vice-chairman and secretary from amongst its members.

B) Meetings of the Legislative Council shall be convened by the presence of the majority of its members, and its decisions shall be adopted by the majority of the present members, unless otherwise provided for in this law or the law for the Legislative Council.

ARTICLE TWELVE

The Legislative Council shall exercise, within the definition of the Constitution and laws, the following powers:

A) The formulation of its articles of association.

B) The adoption of legislative decision required for the development of the area and promotion of its social, cultural constructional and economic aspects of local character within the framework of the general policy of the state.

C) The adoption of legislative decision connected with the development of culture and the nationalist characteristics and traditions of citizens in the area.

D) The adoption of legislative decisions related to semi-official departments, institutions and administrations of local character after consultation with the competent central authorities.

E) The ratification of projects covered by detailed plans drawn up by the Executive Council on the economic, social and developmental affairs, as well as the educational and health affairs, and the discharge of activity in accordance with the requirements of the general central planning of the state and prerequisites of its implementation.

F) The proposition of the special budget of the area.

G) The adoption of final statements of accounts, following their auditing by the Board of the Supreme Auditing and submitting them to the legislative power for ratification.

H) The introduction of amendments to the special budget of the area after their ratification, within the scope of amounts allotted thereto and purposes allotted therefor, provided that such measures shall not contravene with the laws and development plans of the state.

I) Discussion with and questioning of the Executive Council members on the affairs covered by their fields of competence.

J) Withdrawal of confidence from the Executive Council, or one or more of its members, and from whom confidence is withdrawn shall be relieved. The confidence withdrawal decision shall be adopted by the majority number of the Legislative Council's members.

CHAPTER TWO: EXECUTIVE COUNCIL

ARTICLE THIRTEEN

A) The Executive Council is the executive body for the administration of autonomy in the area.

B) The Executive Council shall consist of the chairman, vice-chairman and a number of administrations referred to in Article (14), or two members more.

C) The President of the Republic shall entrust one of the Legislative Council's members to preside over it and form the Executive Council.

D) The chairman-designate shall select the vice-chairman and the Executive Council's members from among the members of the Legislative Council or from among those who enjoy the qualifications of membership therein, and shall submit to the Legislative Council, for confidence. Upon realisation of confidence by the majority of the Council's members, a Republican ordinance shall be promulgated to the effect of calling the Executive Council.

E) The chairman and members of the Executive Council shall hold a grade of minister.

F) The President of the Republic may dismiss the chairman of the Executive Council from his position, in which case the Council shall be considered as dissolved.

G) In the case of dissolving the Executive Council, or withdrawing confidence therefrom, the Council shall carry on with the discharge of current affairs only, pending the formation of a new council provided that this shall take place within a maximum period of fifteen days.

ARTICLE FOURTEEN

A) The governorates of the area shall be annexed to the chairman of the Executive Council.

B) The Executive Council shall seek, in the exercise of its powers, the assistance of following bureaus:

1 - The Executive Council Bureau.
2 - The follow-up and Inspection Bureau.
3 - The Statistical and Planning Bureau.
4 -

I - The following administrations shall be affiliated with the Executive Council:

1 - The Education and Higher Education Administration.
2 - The Works and Housing Administration.
3 - The Agricultural and Agrarian Reform Administration.
4 - The Internal Affairs Administration.
5 - The Transport and Communications Administration.
6 - The Culture and Youth Administration.
7 - The Municipalities and Summer Resorts Administration.
8 - The Social Affairs Administration.

9 - The Economic and Financial Affairs Administration.
10 - The State Property Affairs Administration.

II - The powers of the following administrations shall be defined in the following manner:

1 - The Internal Affairs Administration: police, civil defence and civil affairs.
2 - The Social Affairs Administration: health, labour and social affairs.
3 - The Economic and Financial Affairs Administration: financial departments and local, trade and industrial facilities.

C) Responsibilities in the administrations provided for in the Para above shall be undertaken by Executive Council members, called "the secretaries-General" each of whom shall have a deputy appointed to a special grade.

ARTICLE FIFTEEN

The Executive Council shall exercise the following powers.

A) Securing the implementation of laws and regulations.

B) Abiding by the provisions of legislature.

C) Realisation of justice, security and public order, and protection of national and local public amenities and the public and private properties.

D) Promulgating decisions on all that is required for the implementation of provisions of the resolutions adopted by the local Legislative Council.

E) Drawing up projects under the detailed plans for the economic, social and developmental affairs, as well as the educational, health and labour affairs, in accordance with the requirements of the general central planning of the state and prerequisites of its implementation, and submitting the same to the Legislative Council for ratification.

F) Supervising the local public amenities and institutions in the area.

G) Appointing officials for the autonomous administration whose appointment does not require the promulgation of a Republican ordinance or approval of the President of the Republic, in accordance with the service and personnel laws on whom shall apply provisions of the laws applied to the civil servants in the administrative formations where a Kurdish resides shall be Kurds or those who are well-versed in the Kurdish language, with due consideration to Article (3) hereof.

H) Implementing the budget of the area in accordance with the laws and principles adopted in the accounting system of the state.

I) Preparing an annual report on the conditions of the area, to be submitted to the President of the Republic and Legislative Council.

PART THREE: RELATIONSHIP BETWEEN THE CENTRAL AUTHORITY AND THE AUTONOMOUS ADMINISTRATION

ARTICLE SIXTEEN

With the exception of the powers exercised by the autonomous bodies in accordance with the provisions of this law, the exercise of authority in the entire part of the Republic of Iraq shall revert to the central bodies or their representatives.

ARTICLE SEVENTEEN

A) Police, security and nationality formations in the area shall be attached to their directorates general at the Ministry of Interior and their staff shall be subject to the provisions of the laws, regulations and instructions applied in the Republic of Iraq.

B) The head of the Executive Council or his authorised representatives from [*sic*] among the Council members, may assign to the formations mentioned under Para Eight of this Article duties within the area, within the scope of their duties and within the framework of the general policy of the state.

C) The directors of the formations mentioned under Para Eight of this Article shall be appointed and transferred by order of the Minister of Interior after consultation with the head of the Executive Council.

D) The ranks of police shall be transferred within the area by the order of the secretary of the interior affairs administration or his authorised representatives, with due compliance of the provisions of Para (C) of this Article.

E) The ranks of the formations mentioned under Para Eight of this Article shall be appointed and transferred according to the rules and instructions valid in the Republic of Iraq with due compliance with the provisions of the previous paragraphs.

ARTICLE EIGHTEEN

A) The offices of the central authority in the area shall fall under the ministries they are attached to and shall discharge their duties within their jurisdictions, the autonomous bodies may submit reports on them to the respective ministries they are attached to.

B) The central authority may within the scope of their jurisdiction make general guidance to the local administrations mentioned under Article 14 of this law.

C) The central authority shall appoint a minister of state who will coordinate between the activity and the autonomous bodies. He may attend all meetings of such bodies. The central authority may delegate any other minister to carry out such a mission.

D) The decisions of the autonomous bodies shall be conveyed to the minister of state as soon as they are taken.

E) The head of the Executive Council shall attend the cabinet meeting.

ARTICLE NINETEEN

A) Supervision over the legality of the decisions of the autonomous bodies shall be exercised by the Cassation Court of Iraq through a special committee made of the chief judge of the court and four other [*sic*] members selected by the members of the cassation court from [*sic*] among themselves for a period of three years renewable for one time only.

B) The Minister of Justice or the Minister of State may object to the decision of the autonomous bodies before the supervisory committee mentioned under the previous paragraph in case they violate the Constitution, laws or regulations within 30 days from the date the Minister of State is notified of them.

C) Objections to the decisions of the autonomous bodies before the supervisory committee shall suspend their implementation pending the result of the settlement.

D) The supervisory committee shall give a ruling on the objection within a maximum period of 30 days from the date such objection is submitted to it and its decisions shall be final.

E) The decisions of the autonomous bodies which the supervisory committee rules as non-legal, shall be considered as wholly or partly abrogated from the date of their issue and all legal consequences resulting therefrom shall be null [*sic*] and void.

F) The supervisory committee shall submit its decisions to the objection authority and to the head of the Legislative Council and shall be published in the Official Gazette.

ARTICLE TWENTY

A) The President may dissolve the Legislative Council in case it is not possible for the Council to exercise its authority due to the resignation of half of its members or due to failure of securing the legal quorum within 30 days from the date it is called for a session or due to failure in getting the confidence stipulated under Para (D) of Article 13 of this law for two successive times or due to its failure to comply with the decisions of the supervision committee stipulated under Article Nineteen of this law.

B) In case the Legislative Council is dissolved, the Executive Council shall continue exercising its authority until the elections of a new Legislative Council in a maximum period of 19 days from the date the Republican ordinance has been issued to dissolve it.

ARTICLE TWENTY ONE

This law shall come into force from the date it is published in the Official Gazette.

Taken in Baghdad this day the 17th of Safar 1394 the 11th day of March 1974.

Text supplied by the Ministry of Information of the Government of Iraq.

12. Saddam Hussein: Statement on Current Events in Iraq, 11 March 1974

Brothers,

We are meeting today to give you a direct explanation of the developments of the dialogue conducted by the High Committee of the Progressive Pan-Arab National Front with the Kurdish Democratic Party and those concerned in its leadership. The text of the Autonomy Law for our Kurdish people in the area of Kurdistan will be broadcast in a few hours' time.

This is not meant to reduce the importance of the direct dialogue with you. However, a number of meetings have been held to discuss a draft proposal for the autonomy of the area of Kurdistan. In the copies distributed to you, you will find clear evidence of the opinions which you kindly offered at the time.

Before talking about the dialogue, it is necessary to say a few words, if only in haste, about the birth of the 11th of March Proclamation itself. After four years of work on drafting the Autonomy Law which is the basic essence of the 11th of March Proclamation, it is imperative that we get to know how the Proclamation was born.

You are all aware of the state of Iraqi society as it existed in 1970: the political currents and the negative inheritance of the past with regard to relationships between the political and national movements and also the relationship between the Ba'th Arab Socialist Party and the Kurdish Democratic Party, with all its negative aspects. You will know that the leading party, the Ba'th Arab Socialist Party, was not fully capable in 1970 of playing its leading role in the armed forces. There were elements at the level of command in the armed forces who did not believe in the essence of the Proclamation made on 11th of March 1970. Those elements - and they were not few in number - considered that the issue of such a proclamation amounted to putting them under pressure and depriving them of any means of self-defence on account of the circumstances which had prevailed prior to 11th of March in current relationships and Iraqi society as a whole. Iraqi society itself did not entirely believe in the Proclamation of 11th of March. Therefore the leading Ba'th Party undertook at that time a different struggle within itself and within our society in order to bring the Proclamation of 11th of March 1970 to birth.

In relation to the consolidation of the position of the leading Party at that time, the issue of the Proclamation was considered an extraordinary adventure by conventional calculations and in view of the connection between such matters and the circumstances we have just mentioned.

Prior to this, contacts had been made with the Kurdish Democratic Party, and the representative of the Party at that time had made certain suggestions for the end of the armed conflict. The essence of his suggestions was that the economic blockage imposed on the Kurdish fighters at that time should be lifted. He was Mr Dara Tawfiq, and we told him in explicit terms that those were not the aims for which the Kurds were fighting. If there was a genuine desire to build up a new democratic relationship within Iraqi society and repair the damage which affected this society, we should have had before us the proposals related to the final destination of the aspirations for which you were struggling.

The same words were also exchanged with Mr Aziz Sharif during the first journey which he made to the northern area. The dialogue was then developed to make the Proclamation of 11th of March the essential expression of the good intentions of the Iraqi people and their national and political forces.

As we meet in this hall today, four years have passed since the issue of the Proclamation of 11th of March 1970. The last four years, full of the achievements which are known to you, have had a passage strewn with thorns, particularly in regard to the relationship with the Kurdish Democratic Party and the unusual circumstances, indeed the exceptional circumstances, which have prevailed over the northern area of our dear homeland.

There are many parts in the northern area where neither the authority of the state nor its laws played any fundamental role in shaping the social relationships. I don't think that there is anyone in the Iraqi society who is not aware of this fact.

On the basis of the rationale which I have briefly outlined, we refused then to make the Proclamation of 11th of March anything more than a developed sequel to the Proclamation of 29th of June which was made during the government of Bazzaz and brought the fighting to an end at that time. In our judgement we relied on our view of future events, the ideas which we believe in and the principles which we consider suitable in building the Iraqi society for which we are struggling.

It is natural, therefore, to consider the Proclamation of 11th of March as marking the end of all the negative and exceptional features which had prevailed to that date.

Yet the Proclamation of 11th of March was and will remain adequate for building the national relationships which the Iraqis deem conducive to their ultimate interests, and in which we and all the political forces believe.

You know that in previous discussion in the National Assembly, we rejected the idea of debating the 11th of March Proclamation, that is discussing its principles, when it was suggested by one of our brothers. Is the 11th of March Proclamation necessary, he asked? Is it necessary to set up an autonomous area or should we allow the opportunities to materialise on the basis of Iraqi laws and the principles upheld by the system or the National Front, within the framework of a single Iraqi Society? An answer was given to this brother in the following words: We have come here to discuss this matter on the basis of a belief in the realisation and implementation of autonomy for our Kurdish people.

In the light of the same concepts we meet in this hall as representatives of the High Committee of the Progressive Pan-Arab National Front so that we may explain to you the developments of the dialogue about the Autonomy Law Draft. These began with a working paper proposed by the Regional Command of the Arab Ba'th Socialist Party and ended in the form of a law approved today, 11th of March 1974. An opportunity was given to all the political forces and individual citizens who are not affiliated to any party to discuss the working paper. The opinions expressed at that time were discussed with all objectivity because of the good intentions we feel towards the ideas and opinions expressed by all the patriots of Iraq, whether members of the political parties or citizens who are unaffiliated to any political party.

Various ideas were put forward during the dialogue with the Kurdish Democratic Party. When embarrassed about their opinions, our brothers used sometimes to say that the 11th of March Proclamation was issued on 11th of March 1970 and that there had been a long interval between 11th of March 1970 and the discussions which we were holding then on the Autonomy Draft. Society evolves and ideas evolve.

The last point is correct. Ideas evolve and society evolves, but does the first of what was said imply that evolution means abandonment of true obligations? This was the question with which the responsible leaders of the Kurdish Democratic Party were confronted during our discussions with them.

We appreciate that evolution takes place and we believe in any evolution which moves us forward. But we cannot in any circumstances consider or believe in making the word "evolution" and the concept of evolution a cover for shirking true obligations, especially when we are concerned with the relationship within one people and in matters of destiny such as the question we are discussing now.

In harmony with the concept of evolution, we ask our brothers in the Kurdish Democratic Party: "Can we allow an element, individual or persons in Iraqi society to put to us the following questions: 'Why the proclamation of 11th March and why autonomy?' In other words, can we allow, along with this attitude, a trend to emerge in Iraq which leads to asking for the abrogation of the Proclamation of 11th March and the cancellation of the Autonomy Draft?"

This does not imply that we believe in the emergence of such a trend or will allow it to emerge. We do not intend by these words to suppress unjustifiably the ideas which contradict our own, but we believe that the will of the Iraqis has approved this Draft Law since 11th March 1970. The Iraqi people implicitly expressed their opinion of the Proclamation in the form of celebrations and demonstrations of joy at that time. We consider any opinion outside the framework of the concepts of the 11th of March Proclamation as dangerous to Iraqi society and the future of Iraq.

For this reason we do not accept or allow the contrary opinions which argue that there is no need for the 11th March Proclamation and no need to implement the Autonomy Law in regard to our Kurdish people in the area of Kurdistan.

The dialogue was long and practical. It started on 16th January 1974, but this was not the real beginning of the dialogue. The dialogue about the 11th March Proclamation, the implementation of the Proclamation and the essence of the Proclamation - autonomy - has been a continuous process since 11th March 1970 until this morning. As we shall explain, the essence of the dialogue concentrated on the basic principles which govern the concept of autonomy. Although the dialogue has not been as explicit and direct as the question of the form which I have just given it, the essence of the dialogue was, in fact, based on this form during the submission of proposals and counter-proposals.

To explain some of the differences in opinion we give you samples of that dialogue. I have just mentioned that this dialogue was held with some of our brothers in the Kurdish Democratic Party. To put it on record, the speaker was Muhammad Mahmud Abd al-Rahman and the meeting was held at the National Assembly on the date mentioned before. Those present included Mr Habib Muhammad Karim, Secretary General of the Kurdish Democratic Party, together with other representatives from the same party. For the National Front there were myself and the brothers Mr Mukarram al-Talabani, Mr Ghanim Abd al-Jalil and a number of other brothers from the Ba'th Arab Socialist Party and the Iraqi Communist Party. There were also some patriots, nationalists and progressive people including Mr Hisham al-Shawi and Mr Abd al-Latif al-Shawwaf. Independent Kurds included Mr Ihsan Shirzad, Mr Fuad Arif and others.

One of the points put forward for discussion was that the circumstances had changed and a long time had passed between the issue of the Proclamation of 11th March 1970 and the discussions of the Autonomy Law. It was said that if any ideas were submitted by the Kurdish Democratic Party and found incompatible with the terms and provisions of the 11th March Proclamation such ideas should be treated in this context. Our brothers in the Kurdish Democratic Party were answered by the assertion that we were debating matters submitted in accordance with the terms and concepts of the 11th March Proclamation and that the discussions thereon should be confined to these concepts. The terms of the Proclamation were not open to any individual interpretation.

In the opening remarks which Mr Habib Muhammad Karim delivered to the meeting, he said that many people had found their way into the United Nations Organisation. He was told that we were debating the fate of one people and not other peoples represented in the United Nations. We were debating a draft for autonomy and not a draft for a new state in Iraq. He apologised and explained that he did not mean such ideas. Yet, according to our own belief, he did have something of such ideas in his mind at that time.

The Draft of the National Front was delivered to the Kurdish Democratic Party on 12th December 1973 and the first meeting between the representatives of the National Front and the representatives of the Kurdish Democratic Party was held on 16th January 1974. The discussions continued up to the last meeting, which was an extended meeting including all representatives. This extended meeting was scheduled for 2nd March 1974 but we were surprised by the absence of the representatives of the Kurdish Democratic Party. The National Front decided to issue the Autonomy Law at the appointed time despite the disagreement with the Kurdish Democratic Party and this party's lack of any desire to make its will part of the collective will of the national parties and national forces in declaring the Autonomy Draft as a law issued at the appointed time.

Every one of you now has a copy of this Law and you must have already acquainted yourself with it. In our judgement, and according to our interpretation, this is the basic essence of the 11th March Proclamation issued in 1970. It is the embodiment of self-rule as we see it and understand it, bearing in mind the particular attributes of our people and their special circumstances and, at the same time, the immense benefits gained from the experiences of other peoples.

The discussion then moved to the demarcation of the administrative borders of the autonomy region. We told them that we understand that the demarcation of the administrative borders of the autonomy region must be carried out according to the following principles. The fundamental principles in the delineation of the region is that its administrative borders should be fixed on the basis of national entity and the population density of the nationality granted the right of autonomy, provided that the area remains part of the state and the territory of the country and subject to the state's full sovereignty. We also understand that the demarcation of the administrative borders must not be based on an absolute separation, in the sense of segregation, that is segregating all Kurds, removing them from the society of Iraq, putting them on a certain piece of land, surrounding them with a fence and prohibiting them from moving outside this area. We cannot accept an autonomy which means segregating non-Kurdish Iraqis from the region of autonomy in an absolute manner and in accordance with the concepts I have just mentioned. Our understanding of autonomy is on the basis of free mixing of people and of specifying an area where national rights may be exercised within Iraq and the sovereignty of Iraq in present and future terms. In addition, and in accordance with the foregoing principle, we understand that it is impossible to follow up the shadow of every citizen belong to the nationality covered by autonomy so that we may trace this shadow and treat it as a fixed spot of land belonging to the autonomy region. In order to appreciate this concept clearly, we consider the facts of our existence as we are discussing it in this hall: the Iraqis are composed of two main nationalities and some minorities.

This is the society of Iraq. The Iraqi Arab citizen is to be found in Kerbala, and in Erbil; there is a Kurdish Iraqi citizen in Kirkuk, and a Kurdish Iraqi citizen in Basrah. Perhaps the total number of Kurdish citizens spread all over Iraq outside the autonomy region is more than the total of Kurdish citizens living in any other mixed area. Is it possible to understand autonomy in the sense of following up the shadow of every citizen belonging to the nationality covered by the autonomy measures and demarcating the administrative areas on that basis? If we adopted this concept it would be impossible for us to delineate the administrative borders of the autonomy region at all.

Such was the main point on which we based our concepts when discussing the subject of the demarcation of the administrative borders for the autonomy region. Whenever our brothers found themselves in difficulties they invoked history. They said that historically there were Kurds in such and such area, and in this and that area the Kurds were living. We argued against such reasoning and said that it was possible to refer to history but not for the purpose of the demarcation of the autonomy region. In one society and one state the weight of the population density of the nationality receiving autonomy should be the guiding rule even if this nationality did not exist previously where it does now, but was known to exist in some other places where it doesn't exist today.

Based on the considerations of history, ancient history, and international axioms, the logic of following up a citizen with his shadow for the purpose of the demarcation of the political frontiers of any state has been discounted by international conventions. For example, the Arabs cannot ask for Spain just because they were there some time in the past nor can they ask for any other area outside the frontiers of the Arab homeland.

More important than all this, we have to discuss the matter fundamentally within a logical framework which preserves our unity, protects our future, spreads love among the people, cultivates confidence and unites our hopes, not on the basis of present-day calculations only but also on the basis of calculations for the future.

Our brothers then submitted a proposal providing for a division of the revenue of Iraq according to the ratio of population, and the allocation of the autonomy budget on that basis. In reply our brothers, the representatives of the Kurdish Democratic Party, were told quietly and with ample affection that this logic raised the following objections.

This is not the logic of autonomy nor is it the logic of one people. It would be conceivable in the case of confederation, for example, but is not suitable for autonomy. Leaving the issue of autonomy aside, this kind of logic is also unsuitable for a unified people.

If you accept the fact of one people, is it possible to give the Governorate of Imara a share of the revenue of Iraq in proportion to the ratio of the population in Imara? How can we build up a well-balanced economy based on centralised indicators and present and future calculations if we act on this basis?

We are concerned with the phenomenon of backwardness within Iraqi society wherever it may be and whatever area it may affect, and give it exceptional attention, but we cannot distribute the revenue of the country on the basis of population ratios. In truth, it is known that there is a budget for the state and an investment programme. At the same time there are special allocations to deal with backwardness in the region of Kurdistan. This is legitimate and we believe in it as our duty towards the Iraqi people and with a high sense of responsibility towards our people in the region of Kurdistan. We are introducing a special chapter in the next five-year plan. This chapter will deal with backwardness in the region of Kurdistan. This is right and we shall work towards this end.

These discussions were interrupted on 2nd March 1974 as mentioned. Efforts continued, the efforts of people of good will, until they led to the visit of Mr Idris Barzani to Baghdad. Last Friday we had a meeting with our brother Idris which was brief in view of the limited time available. We had less than four days only left at our disposal. We were determined to proclaim the Autonomy Draft at its appointed time, that is today. Our determination was in accordance with the resolutions of the Regional Congress of the Arab Ba'th Socialist Party and the decisions of the Progressive Pan-Arab National Front. As we are dealing with this subject there may be somebody who will put the following question: Why all this determination and what happens if autonomy is proclaimed after two months, for example.

We deal with this question also in this way: the determination to implement the Autonomy Law by the latest date, which is 11th March 1974, is not a matter of formality. It is an essential matter according to our calculations. This people (the Kurdish) has become accustomed to many negative features in its relationship with the regimes which preceded us over a long period of time. For a long time this people has become accustomed to hear from the rulers promises which were never fulfilled. The precise fulfilment of promises has therefore become one of the most important requirements for the restoration of self-confidence and mutual trust between the leader or ruler and the people.

...

16. THE HUMANITARIAN SITUATION IN IRAQ UPON THE CONCLUSION OF HOSTILITIES

The reports which follow detail the situation within Iraq immediately before and after the hostilities.

S/22328, 4 March 1991

1. Note by the Secretary-General, enclosing a Report of the WHO/UNICEF Special Mission to Iraq, 4 March 1991

At the request of the Chairman of the Security Council Committee established by resolution 661 (1990) concerning the situation between Iraq and Kuwait, I have the honour to bring to the attention of all States the attached report of the WHO/UNICEF Special Mission to Iraq.

...

Iraq Mission Team Members

Dr. Ali Khogali, WHO/EMRO, co-leader.
Mr. Richard Reid, UNICEF/MENA, co-leader.
Dr. Abdullah Dirya, WHO/EMRO
Dr. El-Fateh El-Samani, UNICEF/MENA
Dr. Gianni Murzi, UNICEF/MENA
Mr. Raymond Naimy, UNICEF/MENA
Dr. Annette Verster, WHO/EMRO

I. BACKGROUND & OVERVIEW

On Saturday morning, 16 Feb 1991, a seven-person joint WHO/UNICEF mission to Iraq crossed the border at Khosravi/Munzaria by road from Tehran, bringing with it a 12-truck convoy carrying 54 tons of basic medical and health supplies.

The mission's broad mandate, set out by the UN Secretary General in his press statement Feb. 6, was "to deliver a shipment of emergency medical supplies to assist in the care of children and mothers, and to ascertain essential health needs". Under this mandate, the joint mission was to look at immediate needs for further medical supplies; for protection against communicable diseases; at the status of supplies and sanitation; and at other health needs for children and mothers. The team's conclusions and recommendations were to be delivered, respectively, to the Director General of WHO and the Executive Director of UNICEF.

Prior to the mission, the Secretary-General had informed the Security Council Committee Established by Resolution 661 (1990), which took note of his intention to send the team without objection. The mission's mandate fell within the spirit of the provision of the Geneva Convention of 1949, the UN Convention on the Rights of the Child and the World Summit for Children.

This report emerges from that mandate, and is the joint product of the mission's four UNICEF and three WHO team members. It covers the five days that the team spent in Iraq, and summarizes the observations and recommendations of its members.

...

The mission found in Baghdad that normal life had come almost to a halt. The city's citizens now spend much of their time in family support preoccupations, searching for food, trying to find water, and improvising cooking and heating amidst an acute shortage of all kinds of fuel. Baghdad has no public electricity, no telephones, no gasoline for civilian vehicles, and less than 5% of its normal water supply. None of its water treatment plants are functioning. Toilets go unflushed, and unpumped raw sewage is backing up and overflowing in residential areas. Basic food items are scarce; rice and sugar are increasingly difficult to find. Most basic food items that are available are expensive. Meat is $ 36 per kilo - this in a society where $ 300 is an average monthly urban wage. Homes have no refrigeration for the preservation of food. Bottled gas for cooking and heating is so hard to come by that sales of it set off near stampedes.

A lack of heating fuel has left homes and public buildings so cold that the writers of this report have worn overcoats, sweaters, and scarves to all visits and meetings. Conditions in rural areas and other cities -- where electricity, water and fuel are also absent -- are said to be equally bad, and Basra is reported to be worse.

These conditions appear to have had a heavy impact on public health and the quality of life of children and mothers in Baghdad, whose population is a quarter of that of all of Iraq, and in which a single large popular quarter, Saddam City, has 40,000 inhabitants per square kilometer.

At this writing, the single most urgent health threat, to Baghdad and the country, is that of waterborne epidemics that could soon result from increasingly widespread public use of the Tigris river and other heavily polluted bodies of water for drinking. Free-lance tank trunks are already selling water taken straight from the Tigris in urban neighborhoods. Radio warnings to boil water (there is no television) are largely unheeded, since the hard-pressed population is using scarce fuel for other purposes.

A main concern of the team was the need to assure that the supplies it delivered would be distributed evenly, and according to need, to all civilian populations under Iraqi Government administration -- including Kuwait. A plan to guide this distribution was agreed upon with the MOH, and is being monitored on the ground by UNICEF team members who remained in Baghdad after the mission completed its stay.

In another distribution-related context, the team was aware that the timing of shipment of a number of the supply items recommended in this report may need to be delayed until the overall situation permits.

The drinking water and sanitation threat spelled out above is one of several central problems that the remainder of this report will take up. The following sections will address 1) The Situation of Women & Children in Baghdad, 2) The Situation of the Health Services, 3) Communicable Diseases, 4) Essential Drug and Vaccine Needs, and 5) Water & Sanitation. Each section will present a summary sectoral picture, outline problems and needs, and suggest actions to be taken.

II. The Situation of Women and Children in Baghdad

The situation of women and children is severely affected by the general conditions described above. The lack of fuel and electricity at the household level has caused great strains, especially on food preparation. The team visited families at home, observed the improvised stoves, and saw firewood collected on the streets of Baghdad. Bread is baked at home on improvised ovens. Food preparation is much more time-consuming than before the crisis, and food preservation is impossible due to lack of electricity for refrigeration.

Sufficient water for basic needs is not available in most homes, and when available it is in short supply. The collection of water from rivers and the search for fuel put a great strain on women.

All children are at home, as schools have been closed since the start of the bombardment. The team was repeatedly informed about, and observed, children's fear of being left alone. Women bear the burden of these additional care needs.

Essential commodities are rationed. An official ration of rice, flour, sugar, cooking oil, tea and soap is provided at low cost. The present ration provides an estimated 750 to 1000 calories per day, irrespective of age. Children under one year of age receive, in addition, two tins of 450 grams of powdered milk per month. This is 30 grams per day.

It was noted that due to limited supplies of infant formula, the milk ration consists often of full cream milk powder, which is unsuitable for babies. Diarrhoea in small children was reported as a consequence.

The ration of 750-1,000 calories available at present is less than half the daily requirements of a five-year old child, or less than one-third of the requirement of a pregnant woman. This is obviously not enough for subsistence. The diet must be supplemented by purchases from the market.

The team visited local markets and shops to ascertain what kinds of food are available and at which cost. Families were interviewed about their food intake, both from rations and purchases. At present, fruits, vegetables, potatoes, dates, dried beans and meat are available. Families report that they rely heavily on potatoes and such vegetables as tomatoes to supplement their rations. Prices are, however, prohibitive.

The only high-energy food source is dates. Cooking oil is unavailable on the open market. The official ration contains 7-10 grams of cooking fat per person per day.

The quality of the foods now available on the market is low and deteriorating. Transport problems limit availability. In the near future the season for vegetables will be over. Storage is not possible.

At present, it appears that the amount of food the average family is able to purchase, combined with the government's ration, may give each person something close to the daily minimum calorie requirement.

The team is convinced that in the near future, that is a month or less from now, the gap will widen as purchasable goods will rapidly become unavailable. The team saw strong indications of this decrease in availability during the five days it was in Baghdad.

Nutrition of Children

The general food situation has particularly severe consequences in the case of children. Children are at present receiving a diet that is very different from what they are used to, both in quality and in quantity. The available rations are bulky staples such as rice and wheat, as are the foods available on the market, such as potatoes. Energy-dense foods like oil and sugar are scarce. Iraqi infants are traditionally kept on a milk diet for several months, with the introduction of solid foods late in the first year.

Reports from before the war give evidence that most Iraqi mothers have customarily breastfed for a very short time. Artificial feeding is introduced right from the start. The team was repeatedly told that small babies are now given rice and water and orange juice when milk is unavailable. Mothers do not have the knowledge to prepare the necessary and proper diet with the ration and other foods available. Breastfeeding failure was reported by many health staff interviewed, due to the stress and anxiety caused by the bombing.

The current high incidence of diarrhoea and upper respiratory trace infections result in an increased need for food. At the same time, the child's appetite is reduced by these illnesses, and depressed further by the anxiety and fear noticeable in many children. Bed-wetting and sleeplessness were reported. All these mechanisms together lay the foundation for malnutrition, sooner rather than later.

Iraq has no evidence of malnutrition from past records, although accurate data is scarce. The team did not yet see malnutrition, but prodromal symptoms like listless behaviour was observed in some children seen by the team, suggesting conservation of energy. Weight-loss was reported by health staff interviewed and by mothers. This could not be substantiated by records, as no growth monitoring is carried out at present. The increased incidence of diarrhoea, coupled with food shortages, will certainly result in outright malnutrition, specially among one-to-three-year-olds, in the near future.

Given the difficulty of assessing present food intake or supplies, it is not easy to make a reliable estimate of additional needs for young children and pregnant women. A very rough estimate on the immediate needs was made by the team on the basis of the following assumptions:

- The present population of Iraq is 18 million. Of these 4%, (770,000) are children below one year of age. Infant formula will be needed for the children under 4-6 months only.
- Pregnant women will also number an estimated 770,000.
- Children aged 0-5 years will be an estimated 20% of total population, and of those the 1-3 year age group can be estimated to number 2,500,000.
- A period of 30 days is arbitrarily chosen for the first phase. Within this period it will be necessary to undertake a more detailed assessment of the situation in the country.
- Quantities are expressed for infant formula and in rations for other supplements. The kind of supplements available will determine costs.

The mission recommends that an appropriate high energy/protein food ration be provided to these vulnerable groups for an initial period of 30 days. During this time it will be necessary to reassess the situation in order to determine any changes in the food availability and the nutritional status of the population.

Growing from these needs, the recommended short term programmatic actions are:

(1) A resumed supply of infant formula for children under four months, as detailed above.
(2) The promotion of breastfeeding.
(3) The development and promotion of a weaning food, based on the commodities presently available. A cereal-legume mixture mixed with dates could be envisaged.

(4) Social mobilization of all population groups and religious and political leaders, to support the promotion of breastfeeding and appropriate weaning foods.

(5) Resumed growth and monitoring of all children visiting health facilities, so as to monitor the nutrition situation.

III. THE SITUATION OF THE HEALTH SERVICES

Disruption of routine health services was observed by the team at all levels. A main cause of this is the lack of private or public transport, tied to the non-availability of vehicle fuel; professional and para-medical staff regularly fail to come to work because there is no way to get there. Those who do come often arrive by foot or bicycle. On average, the health centers visited by the team operate at a third of their total manpower, with each doctor coming to the center once every three days.

As a result, several of the usual services have been stopped or severely curtailed. Primary care and preventive activities have suffered the most. Antenatal care, MCH [*sic*] clinics, and growth monitoring have ceased. Laboratory services in Baghdad health centers are closed, including those for pregnant women such as blood sugar and albumine, as well as haemoglobin tests. The team was told that the same conditions obtained throughout the country.

Before the war, the majority of urban women delivered in hospitals. In today's war circumstances, hospital deliveries are growing more and more improbable, especially at night. The great majority of deliveries now take place at home, aided by traditional birth attendants wherever possible. In a visit to a rural health center catering to 65,000 people, the team learned that more than 70 per cent of deliveries now take place at home, compared to 47 per cent before the war.

At the center of the health system, further disarray has come from the dispersal of all staff, including the Minister, from the Health Ministry after the building was put out of operation. Staff from the Ministry have now been reassigned to several improvised locations in Baghdad. This has cut contact among Ministry departments and services to a minimum, and has created constant difficulties in communication and coordination.

The immunization of children stopped completely at the start of the war when electricity was cut. All vaccines were sent back to generator-operated central stores and hospitals. Only in the few days prior to the mission's visit had some centers resumed immunization one day per week, using cold boxes and vaccine carriers. However, not enough vaccines are available. The team observed up to 20 children in one health center who were sent away for lack of vaccines. Booster doses and the third shots of DPT and polio have been stopped in order to conserve supplies.

The team observed a serious shortage of syringes. It was reported that syringes were being reused after boiling, if fuel was available, or were cleaned with spirit, introducing a new dimension of risk of hepatitis B and other infections.

The team looked into prescription practices, and observed that only a day's dose of the doctor's prescription is issued at a time. Many women and children are not able to come back every day to complete the treatment. The danger of introducing resistance to antibiotics due to this non-compliance cannot be over emphasized. Treatment cannot be effective under these circumstances.

The shortage of medical staff and medicine, the lack of continuity of care, and the fear of going outside all combined to reduce attendance and render the primary health care system ineffectual.

IV. COMMUNICABLE DISEASES

All the technical services of the Ministry of Health have been disrupted, but none more severely than epidemiological surveillance and the reporting of communicable diseases. These have practically ceased. Laboratory services in Baghdad have been cut back almost to zero. No information has been available since September, 1990 on communicable diseases that were routinely reported by the health services up to that date.

However, as the team reviewed the registers of health facilities visited during the mission, it became clear that the incidence of diarrhoeal diseases reported in these centres had increased fourfold over expected levels since the war began, and that the incidence of acute respiratory infections has shown a very similar upward trend.

Since such communicable diseases as typhoid, meningitis, measles, poliomyelitis, hepatitis A, and malaria are endemic in Iraq, the present conditions of contaminated main water supply and untreated, back-up sewage have set the stage for the onset of some of these diseases in epidemic proportions. No cases of cholera, typhoid, or meningitis have bene officially reported to date, but the danger is real and increasingly present. This situation is compounded by the fact that the MOH is not at present in a position to respond to any epidemic.

The team urged the Ministry to resume immediately some form of monitoring, sentinel on [*sic*] otherwise, of the more serious communicable diseases, and accepted a list of laboratory reagents submitted by the Ministry.

It is recommended that supplies for the control of cholera and meningococcal meningitis be procured and prepositioned in Iran for immediate shipment to Iraq.

V. ESSENTIAL DRUGS AND VACCINE NEEDS

Essential Drugs

Iraq's health situation has been exacerbated by a critical shortage of essential drugs and medical supplies. The stoppage of industrial production, the absence of raw materials, and the lack of electricity have also knocked out the 25 per cent of national drug and medical needs that were met by local production before the crisis. A further loss has been the cutting off of the five per cent of national needs that were met by imports from Jordan.

Visits by the team to the national drug and medical warehouses in Baghdad, along with reports and statistics provided by procurement officials of the Ministry of Health, show that Iraq's civilian reserves have been reduced to one-sixth their normal level -- that is, to a point at which an unevenly depleted three-month supply of basic drugs exists at this writing.

During its mission, the team visited a number of health centers whose pharmacies lacked virtually all essential drugs, including antibiotics.

The production of disposable plastic bags for intravenous infusions, as well as disposable syringes, has been brought to a halt. These are even more needed at a time when sterilization cannot be done for lack of fuel and electricity.

Recommendation for proposed supplies of essential drugs have been prepared by the team and will be reviewed at their respective headquarters.

Vaccines (EPI)

The Iraqi national vaccination programme has been essentially stopped by the lack of electricity needed to protect vaccines, and the inability to import them.

Added to this, the lack of fuel for transportation greatly limits the possibility of carrying vaccines from the central vaccine store to the peripheral health centres, while the production of ice appears to be limited and does not suffice.

Due to the pre-crisis success of the Iraqi EPI, there is still a great demand for vaccination, But the number of vaccination days has been reduced from a daily schedule to one day a week, due to shortages.

A new vaccine supply system was discussed by the team and MOH officials. Under this radical alternative plan, vaccines would be flown to Tehran and transported to Baghdad by road, possibly using UNICEF drivers and some of the seven refrigerated trucks ordered last year by UNICEF for the MOH, but held back by the embargo.

The new plan would see three or four new vehicles supplementing the present available MOH vehicles, to take vaccines in cold boxes from the Baquba stores to outlying governorates and districts. There, cold storage facilities, based on small generator-powered ice-lining refrigerators and freezers, would hold the vaccines for administration in carefully-monitored batches.

UNICEF Baghdad has on order 250 cold boxes that could not be delivered due to the situation. These cold boxes would be most useful in the new system, and it is suggested they be shipped to Baghdad to be used under UNICEF supervision. Ice making capacity has to be evaluated. At this stage it is estimated that at least 18-20 ice making freezers should be supplied for running the cold chain.

VI. Water and Sanitation

The mission gave high priority to its inspection of Baghdad's water and sanitation situation, and saw a grim picture. If quick intervention does not take place, the Iraqi population faces the prospect of epidemics. Diarrhoeal rates are already four times their normal level.

An in-depth assessment was carried out for Baghdad city. Interviews and discussion took place at the MOH Department of Communicable Diseases, from which two doctors and two engineers accompanied us to the Water Authority Directorate. Here the team discussed with the Director the obstacles now confronting water supply and sanitation. Field trips took place to the April 7 water treatment station, where the full current process of treatment was followed and observed. There was then a tour with network maintenance engineers to observe damages to pipes. Further visits took place to the banks of the Tigris river, to see and discuss with people their own water supply improvisations.

For the affected parts of the country, outside Baghdad, information is not yet fully available. Time did not permit visits to those areas. But all reports indicate that the situation faced by Baghdad is similar in other areas, with the most severe conditions in Basra. Wherever the team went, in meetings with the Director of the Baghdad Water Authority, the Directorate of the Ministry of Local Government, and otherwise, there were detailed reports that the whole of the Iraqi drinking water system is in or near collapse.

General Situation

Most of Iraq's population of 18 million enjoyed, before the crisis, an average of over 250 litres per head daily. Baghdad city, with 4.5 million, received up to 500 litres per head. Over 95 percent of this water was the product of river water treatment provided by seven electro mechanical plants, all of which operated with electric power and required chemicals for treatment.

All significant electrical power generating plants in Iraq have now been destroyed, and similarly the refineries and main fuel storage facilities, leaving water treatment plants dead for all but six hours per day of operation on stand-by diesel generators. This necessitates a careful rationing of the systems remaining fuel supply, which will not last more than five more weeks.

The chemical plants which used to supply the main treatment elements, aluminium sulphate (alum) and chlorine, have been destroyed by bombing. Small quantities of alum and chlorine are still stored at treatment plants, and minimal amounts of these dwindling supplies are used for treating the water that is still sent out. On February 21, the chlorine residue in the water was measured at the plant in the team's presence. The level was found to be only 0.75 mg/litres. Double this figure should have been expected even at the end of the water network, where chlorine levels should be diffused to their lowest strength.

Water quality tests, which are usually carried out at the treatment plant laboratories, are much less frequent than before the crisis. There are shortages of the reagents used to carry out chemical tests. Bacteriological tests are not being carried out at all, because the available equipment that performs these tests requires 24 hours of electricity. Hence the water is distributed without knowing its bacteriological characteristics, at a time when treatment levels are markedly sub-standard.

Baghdad City

The city of Baghdad is served by the seven treatment stations mentioned above, each pumping directly into a network of over 6,000 kilometers of pipes. At present, the water supply to the inhabitants is between zero and 15 litres per person daily, with minimum treatment specifications at the stations and insufficient disinfection. The distribution is rationed in an uneven manner, since the rationing operation requires the manual maneuvering of over 20,000 valves. This cannot be performed adequately by the available personnel, who have no fuel to travel about in their few vehicles.

In no sector of the city can water reach higher than the ground level of buildings, due to the weak pressure in the pipes. Some districts of the city receive 3-4 hours of water every three to four days, other districts 3-4 hours every two weeks. During the team's presence at the Water Authority Director's office, people came complaining that they had not received water for 20 days. About one million people receive almost nothing, since their main water feeder pipes have been severely damaged and cannot be repaired for lack of parts. These areas are fed from other ends of the system, with pressure which is barely enough to drive water.

Interrupted pumping inevitably leaves stagnant water in the pipes. This causes further degradation of the originally poor quality of the water.

Intervention

In order to limit the on-going health threats and prevent epidemics, it is proposed to supply the city with 40 liters of water per head per day. In order to achieve that, the following intervention is urgently recommended for Baghdad city. It must be understood that some of the supply items listed below can be provided only when circumstances permit.

...

Considering the situation of the whole country, an additional budget of US $ 4,000,000 should be kept in mind as an initial step for three months, until more accurate figures are obtained.

Sanitation

During our five days' stay in Baghdad, members of the team saw that the sanitation status of the city is critically deteriorating. The three main sectors of concern are the following:

- Shortage of water;
- Stoppage of the sewer system;
- Acute decrease of garbage disposal.

The water shortage has been discussed earlier. The garbage disposal system, which depends on a large equipment fleet and labour force, is not addressed in this report. The proposed focus of sanitary intervention at this stage is the sewerage system. Baghdad is a flat city. The sewerage system cannot operate by gravity; therefore sewerage is passed through to the treatment plants by pumping stations (lifting stations) at intervals. There are 252 of these stations, which are electrically operated, about 192 of which have stand-by generators.

If those lifting stations do not operate, the sewage pipes fill up and houses flood with sewage. This is occurring in Baghdad now. Additionally, large pools of sewage are forming due to the overflow of sewage at the pumping pits, creating other health hazards.

Three main problems face the sewerage system.

1. Lack of fuel to operate the stand-by generators.
2. Stoppage of generators due to lack of spare parts.
3. Absence of stand-by generators in 60 stations, meaning that half a million homes cannot flush out their sewage.

The above matter was discussed with the directors of both the Baghdad Water Authority and the Baghdad Sewerage Authority. Visits took place to sites. The team observed the manual operation of the lifting pumps, which requires the constant presence of staff at a time when they are frequently unavailable and have very little transport.

In order to partially contain this problem and keep up operation at a minimum safety level, the following are required:

- Enough diesel fuel to operate the lifting pumps, generator, and sewage treatment stations for three months.

Quantity required for three months: 900 m. tons
Estimated cost of diesel for 3 months: US $ 270,000.

- A supply of essential spare parts sufficient to repair stopped generators. The list is being prepared and will be ready within a week of this writing.

Estimated figure for this activity: US $ 100,000.

- The supply of four 110 kva generators for mobile use, in order to supply power to the 60 lift pumps which have no stand-by power.

Estimated cost for 4 generators: US $ 150,000.

- Estimated total budget for sanitation for three months: US $ 520,000.

In short, the children and mothers of Iraq are living in a very acute water supply situation and in dangerous sanitation conditions, in weather which is now favourably cold, but which will warm to more than 40 degrees in another five or six weeks. Few public services whatsoever are available. Fuel is not existent. Transport services do not function. If nothing is done to remedy water supply and improve sanitation, a catastrophe could beset Iraq.

S/22366, 20 March 1991

2. Letter from the Secretary-General addressed to the President of the Security Council, 20 March 1991

Further to my decision to dispatch a mission in order to assess the humanitarian needs arising in Iraq and in Kuwait in the immediate post-crisis environment, I have the honour to inform you that the mission, led by Under-Secretary-General Martti Ahtisaari and comprising representatives of appropriate United Nations agencies and programmes, visited Iraq in the period from 10 to 17 March 1991.

In the light of the wish of the members of the Security Council to be kept informed of the progress of the mission (S/22322), I have the honour to transmit herewith, for their consideration, the report prepared by Mr. Ahtisaari concerning his visit to Iraq.

The Mission will commence its visit to Kuwait on 22 March 1991. I shall of course convey to you as soon as possible the report on that visit. ...

INTRODUCTION

1. You asked me to travel, as a matter of urgency, to Kuwait and Iraq to assess humanitarian needs there in the immediate post-crisis environment, and to bring with me a team comprising representatives of the appropriate United Nations agencies and programmes. Your decision was announced in a press statement of 1 March 1991.

2. On 3 March 1991, the President of the Security Council made a statement on behalf of the Council, in which it welcomed your announcement and invited you to keep it informed in the shortest possible time of the progress of this mission, in respect of which it pledged to take immediate action (S/22322).

...

I. MODUS OPERANDI IN IRAQ

5. The mission began its work immediately upon arrival at Baghdad on 10 March, first linking up with local UNDP and UNICEF representatives and, later that day, meeting with His Excellency Mr. Mohamed Sa'eed Al-Sahaf, Minister of State for Foreign Affairs, and senior officials of the relevant government departments and of local authorities. Joint working groups were established with the various United Nations specialist members of the mission. These held their first meetings that same evening to establish work programmes. Field work was undertaken from 11 to 16 March at various locations in and around Baghdad. A longer field trip was made by a group from the mission, led by myself, to Mosul, 400 kilometres north-west of Baghdad, and I myself also inspected numerous locations in Greater Baghdad. I and members of the mission held meetings with representatives of foreign diplomatic missions at Baghdad and with senior representatives of ICRC. Members of the mission also met with representatives of several non-governmental organizations (NGOs) who had made their way to Iraq to see the situation for themselves. I held final meetings in respect of the specialist teams' work with the Foreign Minister, His Excellency Mr. Tariq Aziz, and with the Minister of State and the participating senior officials, on the evening of 16 March.

6. The Iraqi authorities were fully cooperative in regard to the activities of the five specialist working groups. These dealt with: food and agriculture; water, sanitation and health; transportation and communications; energy; and refugees and other vulnerable groups. Members were able to inspect all locations and facilities that they had requested to see in the Baghdad area and in several other governorates, and could also engage in independent field research in wholesale and retail markets and undertake household surveys. However, the Government was

unable to accede to my request that we visit Souera, Moussayeb, Basrah, Nasiriyah and Kirkuk. In respect of some, the problems were said to be logistical; in regard to others, concern for security was conveyed. I expressed regret at our inability to cover the whole country, because it was important that the United Nations should be able to assess the humanitarian needs of the entire population of Iraq in all regions. The authorities also expressed their regret on this subject, and we agreed that locally based United Nations staff would travel to these areas as soon as conditions permitted. It has, however, been possible to infer from information available from various other sources that needs are unlikely to vary greatly from what we ourselves observed, but it is reported that conditions may be substantially worse in certain locations.

II. SUMMARY OF FINDINGS AND RECOMMENDATIONS IN REGARD TO IRAQ

7. A summary of the mission's findings and conclusions is set out below. It is based upon a number of internal working papers, technical annexes, visits to sites and oral reports by mission specialists.

A. *General remarks*

8. I and the members of my mission were fully conversant with media reports regarding the situation in Iraq and, of course, with the recent WHO/UNICEF report on water, sanitary and health conditions in the Greater Baghdad area. It should, however, be said at once that nothing that we had seen or read had quite prepared us for the particular form of devastation which has now befallen the country. The recent conflict has wrought near-apocalyptic results upon the economic infrastructure of what had been, until January 1991, a rather highly urbanized and mechanized society. Now, most means of modern life support have been destroyed or rendered tenuous. Iraq has, for some time to come, been relegated to a pre-industrial age, but with all the disabilities of post-industrial dependency on an intensive use of energy and technology.

9. My mandate was limited to assessing the need for urgent humanitarian assistance. It did not extend to the huge task of assessing the requirements for reconstructing Iraq's destroyed infrastructure, much less, to developmental matters. Accordingly, my report to you, in its several technical sections, seeks with as much exactitude as possible to convey the extent of needs in the primary areas of humanitarian concern: for safe water and sanitation, basic health and medical support; for food; for shelter; and for the logistical means to make such support actually available. Underlying each analysis is the inexorable reality that, as a result of war, virtually all previously viable sources of fuel and power (apart from a limited number of mobile generators) and modern means of communication are now, essentially, defunct. The far-reaching implications of this energy and communications' vacuum as regards urgent humanitarian support are of crucial significance for the nature and effectiveness of the international response.

10. These conditions, together with recent civil unrest in some parts of the country, mean that the authorities are as yet scarcely able even to measure the dimensions of the calamity, much less respond to its consequences, because they cannot obtain full and accurate data. Additionally, there is much less than the minimum fuel required to provide the energy needed for movement or transportation, irrigation or generators for power to pump water and sewage. For instance, emergency medical supplies can be moved to health centres only with extreme difficulty and, usually, major delay. Information regarding local needs is slow and sparse. Most employees are simply unable to come to work. Both the authorities and the trade unions estimate that approximately 90 per cent of industrial workers have been reduced to inactivity and will be deprived of income as of the end of March. Government departments have at present only marginal attendance. Prior to recent events, Iraq was importing about 70 per cent of its food needs. Now, owing to the fuel shortage, the inability to import and the virtual breakdown of the distribution system, the flow of food through the private sector has been reduced to a trickle, with costs accelerating upwards. Many food prices are already beyond the purchasing reach of most Iraqi families. Agricultural production is highly mechanized, and much land depends on pumped-water irrigation. Should the main harvest in June 1991 be seriously affected by a lack of energy to drive machines and pump water, then an already grave situation will be further aggravated. As shown below, prospects for the 1992 harvest could, for combined reasons, be in at least as much jeopardy. Having regard to the nature of Iraq's society and economy, the energy vacuum is an omnipresent obstacle to the success of even a short-term, massive effort to maintain life-sustaining conditions in each area of humanitarian need.

B. *Food and agriculture*

11. Mission members held working sessions with counterparts from the relevant ministries, visited social centres where various vulnerable groups are cared for, agricultural production areas, a seed production centre, a veterinary health centre and a dairy production unit. The mission noted that Iraq has been heavily dependent on food imports which have amounted to at least 70 per cent of consumption needs. Seed was also imported. Sanctions decided upon by the Security Council had already adversely affected the country's ability to feed its people. New measures relating to rationing and enhanced production were introduced in September 1990. These were, however, in turn, negatively affected by the hostilities which impacted upon most areas of agricultural production and distribution.

12. Food is currently made available to the population both through government allocation and rations, and through the market. The Ministry of Trade's monthly allocation to the population of staple food items fell from 343,000 tons in September 1990 to 182,000 tons, when rationing was introduced, and was further reduced to 135,000 tons in January 1991 (39 per cent of the pre-sanctions level). While the mission was unable to gauge the precise quantities still held in government warehouses, all evidence indicates that flour is now at a critically low level, and that supplies of sugar, rice, tea, vegetable oil, powdered milk and pulses are currently at critically low levels or have been exhausted. Distribution of powdered milk, for instance, is now reserved exclusively for sick children on medical prescription.

13. Livestock farming has been seriously affected by sanctions because many feed products were imported. The sole laboratory producing veterinary vaccines was destroyed during the conflict, as inspected by the mission. The authorities are no longer able to support livestock farmers in the combat of disease, as all stocks of vaccine were stated to have been destroyed in the same sequence of bombardments on this centre, which was an FAO regional project.

14. The country has had a particular dependence upon foreign vegetable seeds, and the mission was able to inspect destroyed seed warehouses. The relevant agricultural authorities informed the mission that all stocks of potatoes and vegetable seeds had been exhausted. Next season's planting will be jeopardized if seeds are not provided before October 1991.

15. This year's grain harvest in June is seriously compromised for a number of reasons, including failure of irrigation/drainage (no power for pumps, lack of spare

parts); lack of pesticides and fertilizers (previously imported); and lack of fuel and spare parts for the highly-mechanized and fuel-dependent harvesting machines. Should this harvest fail, or be far below average, as is very likely barring a rapid change in the situation, widespread starvation conditions become a real possibility.

16. The official programme for the support of socially dependent groups of the population (the elderly, disabled, mothers and children, hospital patients, orphans, refugees, etc.) is affected by the overall grave deficiencies in the food situation.

17. The mission had the opportunity to conduct independent research relating to household costs and living standards in Baghdad. Such standards have declined rapidly in the last months, while food and fuel prices have climbed dramatically. Price increases in the August to January period reflected shortages of supply, but since January there has been a further acceleration of price increases reflecting both supply shortages and the breakdown of the transport system. Interviews with private wholesale food distributors revealed that their stocks are near depletion and they no longer have an organized private transport capacity, owing to fuel shortages. The government-initiated rationing system was designed to provide families with a fraction of their basic necessities at prices comparable to those prevailing before August. The system allows families either 5 kilograms per person, per month, of flour or 3 loaves of baked bread; 10 kilograms per family, per month, of liquid cooking gas; 1 bar of soap per person, per month, etc. However, independent surveys conducted by the mission in several diverse areas of Baghdad showed that many families cannot draw their full rations, since the distribution centres are often depleted and they have great difficulty in travelling to other centres. The quality of food distributed has itself deteriorated to the point of causing health problems. Most families also reported that they could not meet their needs through the private markets. Despite official price controls, the independent market surveys conducted by the mission showed hyperinflation since August. The price of most basic necessities has increased by 1,000 per cent or more. For example, flour is now 5-6 dinars per kilogram (and seemingly still rising); rice has risen to 6 dinars per kilogram; sugar to 5 dinars per kilogram; lentils to 4 dinars per kilogram; and whole milk to 10 dinars. In contrast to this hyperinflation, many incomes have collapsed. Many employees cannot draw salaries, the banking system has in large measure closed down and withdrawals are limited to 100 dinars per month. The minimum monthly wage was 54 dinars and the average monthly salary of a civil servant was 70 dinars. In short, most families lack access to adequate rations or the purchasing power to meet normal minimal standards.

18. The mission recommends that, in these circumstances of present severe hardship and in view of the bleak prognosis, sanctions in respect of food supplies should be immediately removed, as should those relating to the import of agricultural equipment and supplies. The urgent supply of basic commodities to safeguard vulnerable groups is strongly recommended, and the provision of major quantities of the following staples for the general population: milk, wheat flour, rice, sugar, vegetable oil and tea. These are required to meet minimum general requirements until the next harvest. Safeguarding the harvest means the urgent importation of fertilizers, pesticides, spare parts, veterinary drugs, agricultural machinery and equipment, etc. The mission was able to quantify many of these needs. The disappearance of vegetables from the country's markets also appears likely by the summer, and seed importation is crucial.

19. The mission observes that, without a restoration of energy supplies to the agricultural production and distribution sectors, implementation of many of the above recommendations would be to little effect. Drastic international measures across the whole agricultural spectrum are most urgent.

C. *Water, sanitation and health*

20. As regards water, prior to the crisis Baghdad received about 450 litres per person supplied by several treatment stations purifying water from the Tigris river. The rest of the country had about 200-250 litres per person per day, purified and supplied by 238 central water-treatment stations and 1,134 smaller water projects. All stations operated on electric power; about 75 per cent had standby diesel-powered generators. Sewage was treated to an acceptable standard before being returned to the rivers.

21. With the destruction of power plants, oil refineries, main oil storage facilities and water-related chemical plants, all electrically operated installations have ceased to function. Diesel-operated generators were reduced to operating on a limited basis, their functioning affected by lack of fuel, lack of maintenance, lack of spare parts and non-attendance of workers. The supply of water in Baghdad dropped to less than 10 litres per day but has now recovered to approximately 30-40 litres in about 70 per cent of the area (less than 10 per cent of the overall previous use). Standby generating capacity is out of order in several pumping stations and cessation of supplies will therefore ensue if current machinery goes out of order for any reason (spare parts are not available owing to sanctions). As regards the quality of water in Baghdad, untreated sewage has now to be dumped directly into the river - which is the source of the water supply - and all drinking-water plants there and throughout the rest of the country are using river water with high sewage contamination. Recently, the water authority has begun to be able to improve the quality of drinking water by adding more of the remaining stock of alum and chlorine after assurances from UNICEF and ICRC that emergency aid would be provided. Chemical tests are now being conducted at the stations but no bacteriological testing and control is possible because of the lack of electricity necessary for the functioning of laboratories, the shortage of necessary chemicals and reagents and the lack of fuel for the collection of samples. No chlorine tests are being conducted because of the lack of fuel for sampling. While the water authority has warned that water must be boiled, there is little fuel to do this, and what exists is diminishing. Cool winter conditions have prevailed until recently.

22. Only limited information is available to authorities regarding the situation in the remainder of the country because all modern communications systems have been destroyed and information is now transmitted and received (in this sector as in all others) by person-to-person contact. In those areas where there are no generators, or generators have broken down, or the fuel supply is exhausted, the population draws its water directly from polluted rivers and trenches. This is widely apparent in rural areas, where women and children can be seem washing and filling water receptacles. The quantity and quality of water produced by treatment centres is very variable and in many locations there are no chemicals available for purification. No quality control - chlorine testing, chemical testing or bacteriological testing - is being conducted.

23. The mission identified the various problems mentioned above: heavy sewage-pollution of water intakes; absence or acute shortage of water-treatment chemicals, especially aluminium sulphate (alum) and chlorine; lack of power to operate equipment; lack or shortage of diesel to run generators; inability to repair generators because of lack of spare parts; in some instances a total absence of generators; the destruction of

some stations; absence of water-testing; lack of health surveillance system in respect of communicable, and, especially, water-borne diseases. A further major problem, now imminent, is the climate. Iraq has long and extremely hot summers, the temperature often reaching 50 degrees Celsius. This has two main implications: (a) the quantity of water must be increased, and a minimum target of 50 litres per person per day has to be attained (this entails a gross output of 65 litres per person at the source); and (b) the heat will accelerate the incubation of bacteria, and thus the health risks ascribable to the water quality (already at an unacceptable level) will be further exacerbated - especially viewed in the overall sanitary circumstances which have already led to a fourfold increase in diarrhoeal disease incidence among children under five years of age, and the impact of this on their precarious nutritional status.

24. As regards sanitation, the two main concerns relate to garbage disposal and sewage treatment. In both cases, rapidly rising temperatures will soon accentuate an existing crisis. Heaps of garbage are spread in the urban areas and collection is poor to non-existent. The work of collection vehicles is hampered by lack of fuel, lack of maintenance and spare parts and lack of labour, because workers are unable to come to work. Incinerators are in general not working, for these same reasons, and for lack of electric power. Insecticides, much needed as the weather becomes more torrid, are virtually out of stock because of sanctions and a lack of chemical supplies. As previously stated, Iraqi rivers are heavily polluted by raw sewage, and water levels are unusually low. All sewage treatment and pumping plants have been brought to a virtual standstill by the lack of power supply and the lack of spare parts. Pools of sewage lie in the streets and villages. Health hazards will build in the weeks to come.

25. As regards health conditions, the mission reviewed the situation since the special joint WHO-UNICEF mission in February 1991. It found that the recommendations made in that report (S/22328), subsequently approved by the Security Council Committee established by resolution 661 (1990) concerning the situation between Iraq and Kuwait, were well-founded. The mission also identified any further immediate health problems that needed to be addressed over the next three to six months. It also identified constraints that hamper the implementation of the already-agreed recommendations of the joint mission. It found that health conditions in Baghdad and throughout the country remain precarious. A major factor is the water and sanitation situation described above. Additionally, the total lack of telephone communication and drastically reduced transport capability pose other problems to the health system since basic information on communicable diseases cannot be collected and disseminated, and essential drugs, vaccines and medical supplies cannot be distributed efficiently to the country. Mission health experts therefore focused especially on control and prevention of communicable diseases; water quality control; and logistics support for an effective distribution system from Baghdad to outlying regions of vaccines, drugs and medical supplies, as well as infant formula.

26. There is an urgent need to establish a national surveillance and reporting capacity for communicable diseases. This would require the establishment of sentinel sites that can test for the major communicable diseases, as well as the capacity to collate and analyse resulting data on a national scale in a timely manner. Communications, functional laboratories, including necessary chemicals and reagents, and transport and power resources are essential to provide for this emergency humanitarian need. The question of water quality control has already been described. The fourfold increase in incidence of diarrhoeal diseases amongst young children reported by the WHO/UNICEF mission has been reconfirmed by findings recently obtained in 11 sentinel sites in Baghdad. The water and sanitation situation contributes to this problem which must be expected to increase as the summer approaches. The mission concluded that a catastrophe could be faced at any time if conditions do not change. It assessed the detailed requirements for water quality control. As for logistics, this sector is at present especially affected by the same problems that exist in the rest of society.

27. The mission's recommendations regarding water, sanitation and health, on an urgent humanitarian basis, are as follows:

(a) For water, needs have to be calculated in such a way as to permit a minimum quantity of safe water through the hot season from April to September. Assistance, similar to that approved earlier, should be provided to cities outside Baghdad, including the necessary quantities of fuel for generators and transport; lubricants for engines; aluminium sulphate; chlorine; generators for water stations; skid-mounted river water treatment units; chemical dosing pumps; gas chlorinators; pump sets; spare parts; collars for water pipes; and reagents for chemical tests;

(b) For sanitation needs, these include: fuel and spare parts for garbage collection trucks, as well as insecticides; fuel and spare parts for the sewage disposal system (all of which is mechanical and imported); and hoses for drawing water with tanker-trucks;

(c) As regards medical needs, the mission concluded that a number of items were essential to deal with urgent humanitarian needs and established requirements. They include the provision of essential drugs and vaccines, as approved earlier, on a more extended scale, chemicals and reagents, generators, battery-operated incubators, means of alternative communication, requirements for the reinstitution of the cold chain for vaccines, and some vehicles;

(d) Without fuel, power and communications, the needed measures indicated above could, however, prove more or less ineffectual. Estimates of related fuel requirements have been made by the mission.

D. *Refugees and other vulnerable groups*

28. Conditions described above affect the whole population of Iraq and, most especially, low-income groups. The mission paid particular attention to the plight of especially vulnerable groups, whether Iraqi or non-Iraqi. Thus, it found that care for orphans, the elderly and the handicapped had been in many instances disrupted, with residents of institutions having had to be moved and regrouped at various locations. It recommends the urgent implementation of a humanitarian programme aimed at enabling some 25 orphanages and 71 other social welfare centres to resume their normal activities and at providing their beneficiaries with essential relief supplies, and specifies essential inputs for this purpose.

29. As regards the displaced and the homeless, the authorities themselves have not yet been able fully to assess the impact of the recent hostilities. They have, however, calculated that approximately 9,000 homes were destroyed or damaged beyond repair during the hostilities, of which 2,500 were in Baghdad and 1,900 were in Basrah. This has created a new homeless potential total of 72,000 persons. Official help is now hampered by the conditions described throughout this report and, especially, a virtual halt in the production of

local building materials and the impossibility to import. The input of essential materials should be permitted.

30. The mission was unable, in the time available and having regard to the incomplete data in the hands of the authorities, to ascertain the number of foreign workers of Arab and other nationalities still resident in Iraq. It has been estimated that approximately 750,000 were still present in January 1991. It can at this stage be no more than a matter of surmise whether a number of those remaining may be in need of support to return to their countries of origin.

31. Some 64,000 Iranian nationals, protected under either the Fourth Geneva Convention relative to the Protection of Civilian Persons in Time of War of 14 August 1949, or the 1951 Convention relating to the Status of Refugees, had previously resided in three camps in Iraq. There has been substantial dislocation of some of these persons. Others have indicated their desire for repatriation. Limited relief assistance is urgently needed for some of those who have been obliged to leave one of the camps. Additionally, some 80,000 Palestinians are resident in Iraq, including a group of 35,000 considered as refugees benefiting from the protection of the Iraqi Government. It has been reported that several hundred Palestinians have recently come to Baghdad from Kuwait and are now in need of emergency assistance. Certain measures have been developed to provide urgent assistance to those most in need.

E. *Logistics: transportation, communications and energy*

32. The mission examined transportation, communications and energy facilities, as it increasingly emerged that adequate logistics and energy would be essential to support and make effective emergency humanitarian assistance.

33. As regards transportation, the fact that the country has been on a war footing almost continuously since 1980 has undermined its capacity. At present, Iraq's sole available surface transport link with the outside world is via Amman to Aqaba. (It has been reported that a bridge has recently been destroyed on the Iskenderun/Mersin road to Iraq from Turkey; and the ports of Basrah and Umm Qasr are currently out of use; nor has there for some years been any direct cargo traffic to Iraq via the Syrian Arab Republic.) Internal transportation by road is now severely affected by a lack of spare parts and tyres and, above all, by a lack of fuel. Some internal railway capability still exists on the Baghdad-Mosul line. The mission was informed that a total of 83 road bridges had been destroyed and a number were inspected.

34. As regards communications, the mission was informed that all internal and external telephone systems had been destroyed, with the exception of a limited local exchange in one town. It had the opportunity to inspect a number of war-damaged or destroyed facilities and experienced for itself the situation in the Greater Baghdad and other urban areas. Communication in Iraq is now on a person-to-person basis, as mail services have also disintegrated.

35. The role of energy in Iraq is especially important because of the level of its urbanization (approximately 72 per cent of the population lives in towns), its industrialization, and its prolonged, very hot, summers. Pre-war energy consumption consisted of oil and refined products (85 per cent), electricity (14.8 per cent) and other sources (0.2 per cent). About 30 per cent of electric power generation was hydro-power. Bombardment has paralysed oil and electricity sectors almost entirely. Power output and refineries' production is negligible and will not be resumed until the first repair phase is complete. The limited and sporadic power supply in some residential areas and for health facilities is provided by mobile generators. There have, officially, been virtually no sales of gasoline to private users since February. The mission was told that the only petrol, oil and lubricants (POL) products now available are heating oil (rationed to 60 litres per month, per family) and liquefied petroleum gas (LPG), which is rationed to one cylinder per month, per family. The authorities stated that stocks of these two products are close to exhaustion and that their distribution is expected to cease within the next 2-4 weeks. While work is under way to clear sites and assess damages, lack of communications and transport is retarding this activity. Initial inspections are said to show that necessary repairs to begin power generation and oil refining at minimal levels may take anywhere from 4 to 13 months. Minimal survival level to undertake humanitarian activities would require approximately 25 per cent of pre-war civilian domestic fuel consumption. Its absence, given the proximate onset of hot weather conditions, may have calamitous consequences for food, water supply and for sanitation; and therefore for health conditions. It seems inescapable that these fuel imports must take place urgently, and units and spare parts will also be required to enable Iraq to meet its own humanitarian needs as soon as possible. Under optimal circumstances it would be difficult or impossible for such needs to be provided from other sources given all the circumstances of that country's economy and social conditions, and bearing also in mind the limited bulk transportation possibilities that are likely to exist for the foreseeable future.

36. During my final meetings in Baghdad on 16 March I made reference to the need to be able to assess the effective utilization of all inputs that might in future be established under the responsibility of the United Nations. The Government assured the mission that it would accept a system of monitoring of imports and their utilization.

F. *Observations*

37. The account given above describes as accurately as the mission has been able, using all sources, including much independent observation, to ascertain the situation, which, within the time available and the travel limitations referred to earlier, was perceived to exist in regard to urgent humanitarian needs in Iraq during the week of 10-17 March. I, together with all my colleagues, am convinced that there needs to be a major mobilization and movement of resources to deal with aspects of this deep crisis in the fields of agriculture and food, water, sanitation and health. Yet the situation raises, in acute form, other questions. For it will be difficult, if not impossible, to remedy these immediate humanitarian needs without dealing with the underlying need for energy, on an equally urgent basis. The need for energy means, initially, emergency oil imports and the rapid patching up of a limited refining and electricity production capacity, with essential supplies from other countries. Otherwise, food that is imported cannot be preserved and distributed; water cannot be purified; sewage cannot be pumped away and cleansed; crops cannot be irrigated; medicaments cannot be conveyed where they are required; needs cannot even be effectively assessed. It is unmistakable that the Iraqi people may soon face a further imminent catastrophe, which could include epidemic and famine, if massive life-supporting needs are not rapidly met. The long summer, with its often 45 or even 50 degree temperatures (113-122 degrees Fahrenheit), is only weeks away. Time is short.

17. THE PARTIAL LIFTING OF SANCTIONS AGAINST IRAQ AND HUMANITARIAN ASSISTANCE RENDERED BY INTERNATIONAL AID AGENCIES

Resolution 661 (1990) on economic sanctions against Iraq and occupied Kuwait prohibited the importation into Iraq of all commodities, except for medical supplies and, in humanitarian circumstances, foodstuffs and relief supplies. Even before hostilities broke out, disagreement arose in the UN Security Council about whether or not humanitarian circumstances prevailed within Iraq. On 22 March 1991, after having considered the reports reproduced in the preceding chapter, the Council determined that humanitarian circumstances prevailed within Iraq and, while leaving sanctions in place generally, approved the supply of foodstuffs to Iraq. This procedure was endorsed in Resolution 687 (1991) and subsequently attempts were made to obtain funding for humanitarian deliveries from the proposed sale of Iraqi petroleum and petroleum products (see *Chapter 13).*

Although hostilities between Iraqi armed forces and the forces of the coalition ceased on 28 February 1991, remnants of the Iraqi army continued to engage groups of Shiites and Kurds in the border regions with Iran and in northern Iraq respectively. As a result, large numbers of refugees poured into Iran and Turkey. The Security Council responded by adopting, on 5 April, Resolution 688 (1991) which has been reprinted in Chapter 1 of this volume. That resolution expressed grave concern about the repression of the Iraqi civilian population in many parts of Iraq, including in Kurdish populated areas, and demanded that Iraq immediately end this repression. It insisted that Iraq allow immediate access by international humanitarian organizations to all those in need of assistance in all parts of Iraq.

The vast scale of the international humanitarian effort to ameliorate the consequences of the turmoil that ensued within Iraq is documented in the pages which follow.

S/22322, 3 March 1991

1. Note by the President of the Security Council, 3 March 1991

Following consultations of the Security Council, the President made the following statement, on behalf of the council, at its 2979th meeting on 3 March 1991, in connection with the Council's consideration of the item entitled "The situation between Iraq and Kuwait":

> "The Council welcomes the decisions taken to date relating to food and medical needs by the Committee established under resolution 661 including those just taken to facilitate the provision of humanitarian assistance including infant formula and water purification material.
>
> "It calls upon the Committee to continue to act promptly on requests submitted to it for humanitarian assistance.
>
> "It urges the Committee to pay particular attention to the findings and recommendations on critical medical/public health and nutritional conditions in Iraq which have been and will continue to be submitted to it by the World Health Organization, UNICEF, the International Committee of the Red Cross and other relevant organizations, consistent with the relevant resolutions, and urges these humanitarian agencies to play an active role in this process and co-operate closely with the Committee in its work.
>
> "The Council welcomes the Secretary-General's announcement that he plans to send urgently a mission led by Under-Secretary-General Martti Ahtisaari comprising representatives of the appropriate United Nations agencies to Iraq and Kuwait to assess the humanitarian needs arising in the immediate post crisis environment. The Council invites the Secretary-General to keep it informed in the shortest possible time on the progress of his mission on which it pledges to take immediate action."

S/22364, 20 March 1991

2. Identical letters from the Permanent Representative of Iraq to the United Nations addressed respectively to the Secretary-General and the President of the Security Council, 20 March 1991

On instructions from my Government, I have the honour to inform you that, as a result of acts of sabotage carried out by bands which infiltrated from a neighbouring State, the contents of the people's food warehouses were plundered in the cities and villages of the governorates of Basra, Wasit, Maysan, Dhi Qar, Al-Qadisiyah, Al-Muthanna, Najaf, Karbala and Babil.

Similar acts were perpetrated in the governorates of Sulaymaniyah, Arbil and Dahuk by other bands which entered from the same neighbouring State.

The plundering of basic foodstuffs and the destruction of public and private warehouses by these bands has resulted in a severe food crisis that has the most dire consequences for these 12 governorates, which account for the majority of the population of Iraq.

This extremely grave crisis necessitates the adoption of immediate measures by the Security Council to remove any form of embargo on the import of foodstuffs and supplies to Iraq.

It is clear that measures taken by the Sanctions Committee cannot, owing to their slowness, provide an adequate solution to this grave problem affecting the humanitarian needs of the citizens.

I request you to take urgent measures with a view to the consideration of this question by the members of the Council.

...

S/22400, 22 March 1991

3. Note by the Secretary-General, 22 March 1991

The Secretary-General has received the attached letter from the President of the Security Council. In light of its final paragraph, he is circulating the letter herewith as a document of the Security Council for the attention of all States.

I have the honour to inform you that the members of the Security Council, in consultations of the whole, held on 22 March 1991, took note of the following decision of the Security Council Committee established by resolution 661 (1990) concerning the situation between Iraq and Kuwait, adopted at its 36th meeting, on 22 March 1991, with regard to the determination of humanitarian needs in Iraq:

> "1. The Security Council Committee established by resolution 661 (1990) concerning the situation between Iraq and Kuwait has carefully considered Under-Secretary-General Ahtisaari's report of 20 March 1991 on his recent visit to Iraq (S/22366), as well as the report of the ICRC of 19 March 1991 (S/AC.25/1991/COMM.102) summarizing the conclusions of its own delegation in Iraq.
>
> "2. Under paragraph 5 of resolution 666 (1990), the Committee has the power to determine, after receiving all relevant reports and information, that circumstances have arisen in which there is an urgent humanitarian need to supply foodstuffs to Iraq in order to relieve human suffering; and in that event the Committee will report promptly to the Council its decision as to how such needs will be met.
>
> "3. In the light of the new information available to it, the Committee has decided to make, with immediate effect, a general determination that humanitarian circumstances apply with respect to the entire civilian population of Iraq in all parts of Iraq's national territory. The Committee has also concluded that civilian and humanitarian imports to Iraq as identified in Mr. Ahtisaari's report are integrally related to the supply of foodstuffs and supplies intended strictly for medical purposes (which are exempt from sanctions under the provisions of resolution 661 (1990)) and that such imports should also be allowed with immediate effect.
>
> "4. The Committee decides upon a simple notification procedure for foodstuffs supplied to Iraq and a no-objection procedure for those civilian and humanitarian imports (other than supplies intended strictly for medical purposes) described in the preceding paragraph.
>
> "5. Subject to prior notification to the Committee of the flight and its contents, the Committee hereby gives general approval under paragraph 4 (b) of resolution 670 (1990) for all flights which carry only foodstuffs or supplies intended strictly for medical purposes. This procedure applies equally to the civilian and humanitarian imports referred to in paragraph 3 above, the supply of which is subject to the no-objection procedure laid down in paragraph 4.
>
> "6. It notes with satisfaction that the Government of Iraq has assured Mr. Ahtisaari's mission that it would accept a system of monitoring of imports and their utilization. The Secretary-General is requested, in consultation with the Government of Iraq and the ICRC, to arrange for such a system of on the spot monitoring to proceed in conjunction with the despatch of United Nations personnel to Iraq to supervise the effective utilization, for the benefit of the civilian population in all areas, of all imports to be established under the responsibility of the United Nations."

...

S/22371, 21 March 1991

4. Identical letters from the Permanent Representative of Iraq to the United Nations addressed respectively to the Secretary-General and the President of the Security Council, 20 March 1991

On instructions from my Government, I have the honour to transmit herewith a letter dated 20 March 1991 from Mr. Tariq Aziz, Deputy Prime Minister and Minister for Foreign Affairs of the Republic of Iraq, concerning the infiltration of large numbers of armed groups into Iraq from a neighbouring State and their engagement in acts of widespread subversion, murder, destruction, arson and pillage in a number of Iraqi governorates.

...

I have the honour to draw your attention and the attention of the members of the international community to the fact that, immediately after the announcement of the cessation of military operations by the armed forces of the United States and its allies, large numbers of armed and organized groups infiltrated into the country from a neighbouring state, as already indicated in the address by the President of the Republic of 16 March 1991. These groups engaged in widespread acts of subversion, murder, destruction, arson and pillage in the governorates of Basra, Meisan, Dhi Qar, Qadisiya, Karbala, Najaf, Muthanna and Babil and the same thing happened a few days later in the governorates of Sulaimaniya, Irbil and Dohuk.

It is noteworthy that the neighbouring State from the territory of which these groups came has not concealed its sympathy, as expressed in statements by its officials, with the acts committed by these groups. These armed groups have engaged in widespread sabotage operations, including the destruction and pillage of hospitals, universities, schools, court-houses, food warehouses, official government offices, public utilities such as electricity and water supply and fire-fighting facilities and other public service institutions, as well as the large-scale destruction and pillage of houses, commercial establishments, vehicles and other private property.

The losses suffered by State institutions and citizens as a result of these deliberate criminal acts are estimated at very large amounts. Moreover, these criminal acts have created an extremely serious situation from the standpoint of the living conditions, health and welfare of several million Iraqi citizens who have already suffered greatly from the damage caused by the military operations, as indicated in the letter which I sent to you on 3 March 1991.

The purpose of this letter is to give you a general idea of the nature of the losses suffered by Iraq as a result of these deliberate acts of sabotage. We will subsequently be providing you with detailed information concerning these losses.

...

S/22379, 23 March 1991

5. Letter from the Permanent Representative of the Islamic Republic of Iran to the United Nations addressed to the Secretary-General, 22 March 1991

Upon instructions from my Government, and with reference to public statements made by a number of Iraqi officials and insinuations made in the letters addressed to Your Excellency from the Foreign Minister and Permanent Representative of Iraq, contained in Security Council documents S/22371 and S/22364, respectively, I have the honour to bring the following to your attention.

The Islamic Republic of Iran pursued vigorously an active policy of neutrality in the tragic conflict in the Persian Gulf, while taking every possible measure in order to bring the bloodshed and destruction of Iraq and the region to a speedy end and mitigate the suffering of the innocent people of Iraq. In this context, in addition to its intense diplomatic efforts, my Government, in coordination with the Security Council Sanctions Committee, has dispatched several shipments of humanitarian assistance including medicine and foodstuff to Iraq.

The Government of the Islamic Republic of Iran, in response to allegations of dubious character, has declared at the highest level that, in line with its Constitution, it does not seek to interfere in the internal affairs of Iraq, and has categorically rejected all such irresponsible allegations. Furthermore, in accordance with the same principles governing its foreign policy and consistent with the very strong and clear position it adopted against bombardment of civilian areas in Iraq by allied forces, the Islamic Republic of Iran cannot remain but alarmed at numerous reports of horrifying attacks by government forces against innocent civilians as well as reported desecration of holy shrines and prominent religious personalities. Such concerns are shared by Muslims all over the world, and by the international community in general.

...

S/22419, 28 March 1991

6. Note by the Secretary-General, 28 March 1991

At the request of the Chairman of the Security Council Committee established by resolution 661 (1990) concerning the situation between Iraq and Kuwait, I have the honour to bring to the attention of all States the attached decision of the Committee with regard to the procedure to be followed by non-governmental organizations wishing to provide humanitarian assistance to the civilian population of Iraq.

> In the case of non-governmental organizations (NGOs) wishing to ship to Iraq any of the items indicated in paragraph 3 of the decision adopted by the Security Council Committee established by resolution 661 (1990) concerning the situation between Iraq and Kuwait on 22 March 1991 (S/22400), the notifications on requests for authorization mentioned in paragraphs 4 and 5 of the same decision should be communicated to the Committee by the governments of the States in which the NGOs in question have their headquarters. It will be the responsibility of those Governments to bring this procedure to the attention of the relevant NGOs headquartered in their territories, as well as to ensure that the contents of the specific consignments are in conformity with Security Council resolutions 661 (1990) and 666 (1990) and with the decision adopted by the Committee on 22 March 1991.

S/22435, 3 April 1991

7. Letter from the Permanent Representative of Turkey to the United Nations addressed to the President of the Security Council, 2 April 1991

Upon instructions from my Government, I have the honour to inform you that owing to the action taken by the Iraqi army against the local population in Northern Iraq, approximately 220,000 Iraqi citizens, many of them women and children, are currently massed along the Turkish border.

It is apparent that the Iraqi Government forces are deliberately pressing these people towards the Turkish border in order to drive them out of their country. These actions violate all norms of behaviour towards civilian populations and constitute an excessive use of force and a threat to the region's peace and security. In the course of the Iraqi operations, which are being carried out with the support of helicopters and artillery, many mortar shells have actually landed on Turkish territory.

Turkey is taking appropriate action to bring urgent humanitarian assistance to the affected Iraqi civilians. It is expected that the heavy burden of caring for these victims of repression will be shared by international organizations as well as by those countries in a position to assist.

I request that a meeting of the Security Council be convened immediately to consider this alarming situation and to adopt the necessary measures to put an end to this inhuman repression being carried out on a massive scale.

S/22439, 3 April 1991

8. Letter from the Permanent Representative of Iraq to the United Nations addressed to the Secretary-General, 3 April 1991

On instructions from my Government, and with reference to the letter dated 1 April 1991 addressed to you by the Permanent Representative of the Islamic Republic of Iran to the United Nations, I have the honour to inform you as follows:

1. Fifty Iranian elements who were among those who participated in subversive operations during the month of March have been taken prisoner in Iraqi territory. They are currently being held by the Iraqi authorities.

2. For the most part, these subversive actions were carried out by members of the "Badr" ninth company, including Iraqi prisoners of war held by Iran and Iranian elements who had fled Iraq and been welcomed and trained by the Government of Iran and sent into Iraqi

territory. Moreover, identity papers were found on the body of one of the volunteers indicating that he was a member of the "Badr" ninth company - an Iraqi combatant.

3. The Iranian prisoners have confirmed that they took part in the subversive actions at the instigation of the Iranian authorities, which had:

(a) Made available to them transport vehicles belonging to the Revolutionary Guard to drive them into Iraqi territory (in the Tannuma, Basra and Amara regions), where they infiltrated a number of Koranic schools and charitable institutions, and to supply them with rations;

(b) Cared for the wounded and evacuated the dead from Shalamjah and Tannuma (Basra) to hospitals located at Abadan;

(c) Assigned groups of the Revolutionary Guard to evacuate to Iran vehicles, weapons and *matériel* abandoned in Iraq;

(d) Established at Khoramshahr a committee for aid to the Iraqi people, forming part of the Iranian Red Crescent and supervised by the Iranian armed forces, whose task is to provide food aid;

(e) Provided these troops with information obtained by forward reconnaissance groups which had infiltrated into Iraqi territory.

4. On 1 April 1991, five Iranian elements belonging to the 32nd, "Partisans of Hussein", company were taken prisoner in the Khalifa Murad region in Iraqi territory, between 8 and 10 kilometres from Khanaqin/Klar.

5. Identity papers were found on the body of an Iranian national named Hassan Bakhtiari, found in the region of Jabal Marorid, in Iraqi territory, between 10 and 12 kilometres from Khanaqin, which establish his membership in the Bakhtaran Guard.

This information, backed by documents and irrefutable pieces of evidence which are in the hands of the Iraqi authorities, show that the Iranian Government has "flagrantly" violated the provisions of the cease-fire and withdrawal agreed upon by the two parties under the auspices of the United Nations. In this connection, my Government will make public in due course, with supporting evidence, further information which proves beyond dispute that the Government of Iran was involved in the preparations for these subversive activities, and that it is inciting them and participating in them directly, in violation of the engagements it has entered into to respect the Iraqi peace initiatives aimed at settling the disputes between the two countries in accordance with Security Council resolution 598 (1987), under the auspices of the United Nations.

My country's Government holds the Iranian Government fully responsible for these acts of subversion and for the ensuing destruction which has resulted from its "direct" and "active" participation in these operations.

...

S/22440, 3 April 1991

9. Letter from the Permanent Representative of Iraq to the United Nations addressed to the Secretary-General, 3 April 1991

On instructions from my Government, I have the honour to draw attention to the actions of certain circles within the Security Council aimed at disrupting the internal security of my country, and to clarify that groups of saboteurs have taken advantage of the situation created by the military operations conducted against Iraq with the authorization of the Security Council to infiltrate, with outside support and following plans drawn up abroad, into towns in the south and the north of Iraq. These groups have committed abominable criminal acts directed against the life and security of the inhabitants, their property and their honour, and State property and officials.

Since the State is called upon to assume the obligations and responsibility incumbent on it of restoring public order throughout the country and putting an end to the sabotage and the criminal acts perpetrated against the population by armed groups, it had to take the necessary measures to restore public order in the southern and northern provinces. Now that the authority of the State and of the law has been restored in the south and the north, the security measures that had to be taken to suppress the rebellion and the sabotage operations have achieved their objective.

My country's Government reiterates that the vast majority of inhabitants of Iraq's towns and villages have not collaborated with the groups of saboteurs. Some of them may however have been victims of the campaign of terror and lies disseminated by the saboteurs or have been compelled by armed force to leave the country - as has happened on other occasions - serving as a shield for the above-mentioned groups or a means of facilitating their escape abroad.

The Iraqi Government is in a position to affirm that the inhabitants of the towns and provinces where public order has been restored have nothing to fear in terms of their personal safety, their property or their legal rights, whether or not they remained in the towns and villages in question. The authorities will bring to book and prosecute only those who have been responsible for murders, fires, rapes or theft, or have taken up arms against the State and the law.

My country's Government invites all those of its citizens who have had to leave their homes or their places of residence to return to their town or village in Iraq in full security and full dignity. In this connection, the Iraqi authorities are prepared to cooperate with any third party.

The Iraqi Government also appeals to the Governments of neighbouring countries to cooperate with it in restoring the situation and reinstating public order so as to avoid the relations they maintain with Iraq being affected. It also calls on the foreign circles which have discovered their humanitarian vocation to stop exploiting the sufferings of the Iraqi population for political and basely self-interested purposes.

...

S/22442, 4 April 1991

10. Letter from the Chargé d'affaires a.i. of the Permanent Mission of France to the United Nations addressed to the President of the Security Council, 4 April 1991

On instructions from my Government, I have the honour to request you to convene an urgent meeting of the Security Council to discuss the serious situation resulting from the abuses being committed against the Iraqi population in several parts of Iraq, and more particularly in the Kurdish-inhabited areas. By virtue of its repercussions in the region, this situation constitutes a threat to international peace and security.

A/45/989, S/22443, 4 April 1991

11. Letter from the Permanent Representative of Luxembourg to the United Nations addressed to the Secretary-General, 4 April 1991

I have the honour to enclose the text, in French and English, of the statement on the situation in Iraq issued by the European Community and its 12 member States on 2 April 1991 ...

...

The Community and its member States are very deeply concerned at the situation of the civilian population in Iraq, notably the Kurds and the Shiites.

They firmly condemn the brutal repression being imposed upon these population groups, bringing about a flow of refugees towards the neighbouring countries.

They call upon the Iraqi authorities to put an end without delay to this repression, which has already, in the past, severely afflicted the Kurdish people. Only the path of dialogue with all the parties concerned will allow the shaping of a renewed Iraq, united and respectful of the legitimate aspirations of the population groups of which the country is made up.

S/22447, 4 April 1991

12. Letter from the Permanent Representative of the Islamic Republic of Iran to the United Nations addressed to the Secretary-General, 4 April 1991

Upon instructions from my Government, I have the honour to bring to your urgent attention the desperate situation of Iraqi civilians who are crossing all along the border into the Islamic Republic of Iran.

Events in Iraq and the method by which Iraqi military has dealt with the uprising of Iraqi population has lead to uprooting and driving of hundreds of thousands of them towards the neighbouring countries. It is estimated that about 500,000 Iraqi civilians will try to cross the borders into Iran within a very short period of time of the next few days.

Up until noon today, more than 110,000 Iraqi civilians have already crossed the border into Iran along the border including more than 45,000 in the North. Hundreds of thousands of Iraqi people and their vehicles, forming a line of more than 60 kilometres, are crossing into Iran at the only paved road at Haji Omran border post. Thousands of other Iraqi people including elderly and children, many on bare foot in mountainous areas in the north and under heart-breaking circumstances are trying to escape the military attacks and find refuge in the Islamic Republic of Iran. The influx of refugees is also continuing in the South, albeit at a slower pace.

The Islamic Republic of Iran - in line with its long standing policy and in spite of the hardships it is facing - has kept its borders open to Iraqi people escaping repression so as to decrease the pressure upon them. The influx of refugees in addition to its obvious economic and social problems has caused tension and chaos at the borders of the Islamic Republic of Iran.

The prolongation of the situation, with its implications for Iraq's neighbours, will have consequences that in fact threaten regional peace and security. The magnitude of the suffering of Iraqi refugees, its international character and its consequences for regional peace and security make a concerted international reaction by the Security Council of the United Nations a political and humanitarian imperative.

...

S/22452, 5 April 1991

13. Letter from the Permanent Representative of Iraq to the United Nations addressed to the Secretary-General, 5 April 1991

On instructions from my Government, I have the honour to transmit herewith the text of the statement issued by the Revolution Command Council of the Republic of Iraq on 5 April 1991.

...

We praise God Almighty in this pre-eminent month as we announce to the mighty people of Iraq the news that a complete end has been put to acts of sedition, sabotage and strife in all the towns of Iraq. The latest achievement was the putting of an end to the state of rebellion and sabotage in the beloved town of Sulaymaniyah. The rule of law and order has returned, and security and stability have been restored to all the towns of Iraq. The spirits, honour and property of Iraqis have been rescued from the violation, pillaging, burning and destruction unprecedented in our history that befell them during the black and gloomy days of dissension.

The President and leader Saddam Hussein announced on 16 March the end of the criminal dissension in the towns of the south. With God's help and success from him, the State has now put a final end to the last page of the dissension in the beloved north of Iraq.

The malicious enemies depicted the acts of slaughter, violation of honour, sabotage, plundering, burning and destruction that took place in the towns of the south and the north as a [*sic*] "uprising" and ascribed to it spurious characteristics, but the aware people of Iraq, which had experience of life and men and had lived through the experience of true and authentic revolutions, first and foremost being the great revolution of 17 to 30 July, exposed the spuriousness and exposed the criminal conspiracies, just as it exposed and knew the truth about the perpetrators and the treacherous foreign enemy forces behind them. It was no coincidence that these disgraceful acts, which are not consonant with the ethics of Iraqis or the traditions of their national struggle, should occur during the United States-NATO-Zionist aggression against Iraq. All estimates and information confirm that the planning took place at the same time as the preparation for this treacherous aggression and in coordination with its foreign elements and with a number of the regimes in the region. As the President and leader said in his historic speech on 16 March 1991:

> "At the time when the country from the extreme north to the extreme south and from the extreme east to the extreme west was exposed to the 30-State aggression and while all our towns and villages were bleeding as a result of the brutal aggression aimed at the whole of Iraq and all its citizens and aimed at the life and property of all Iraqis and what they had built over tens of years with effort, sweat and creativity, at this very time, there infiltrated into the country from outside hordes of malicious traitors holding forged Iranian identity cards to spread bloodshed, terror, sabotage and plundering in a number of towns and villages of southern Iraq, assisted by rebels who had strayed from the right path in Basra, Amarah, Nasiriyah, Karbala, Najaf and Hillah. These renegade traitors attacked some isolated army units and barracks that were withdrawing under enemy fire and seized weapons and equipment and burned the property of the people. They pillaged government premises, schools, hospitals and citizens' houses and violated

> honour. They even burned civil registers, property registers, and records of marriage and inheritance in State departments. Through dastardly, treacherous methods they killed some State and party officials and some officers and citizens in those towns. Our country, which was subjected to imperialist NATO-Zionist aggression, was subjected to an attack like that of Hulagu on Baghdad in 1258."

His Excellency said in the same speech:

> "At the same time when the troops of dissension were entering from the other side of the frontiers into our towns in the south, armed elements entered from the same place into a number of villages and towns in the north. The malicious elements raised slogans of factional schism in the towns of the south. The elements that entered the towns of the north raised, for the same base purpose, slogans of national schism and acted accordingly, engaging in terrorism, sabotage, schism, murder, plunder and incendiarism. It became quite clear that the lines of infiltration into some of the southern regions and some of the northern regions had a single source and identical ends, namely, the destruction and division of Iraq, the spread of disorder, destruction and desolation in Iraq and the subjection of Iraq to a foreign will. May their efforts be frustrated."

...

The achievement of crushing the dissension and the traitors coming from over the borders emphasizes the noble steadfastness of Iraq and the Iraqis and the capacity of Iraq and the Iraqis to face trials and confront conspiracies. Iraq survives and is sound, with God's help. This achievement also emphasizes the crushing of the spinal column of the most significant part of the conspiracy aimed at Iraq. After the United States -NATO aggression against our dear country and its affliction at the hands of the aggressors, the enemies of God and enemies of Iraq sought to turn this united, peaceable and proud country into another Lebanon divided and crushed by factional, confessional and racial struggles. However, in spite of the trial afflicted on it by the enemy coalition, Iraq proved that it was stronger than the conspiracy and the conspirators, in spite of the capacities they marshalled, the schemes they devised and the propaganda campaigns, unprecedented in the world, with which they surrounded the conspiracy.

Beloved Iraqis,

We should therefore feel joy and pride that our country is sound and has emerged from this dissension united and secure, with the gates of the future, God willing, open before it.

Most illustrious Iraqis,

The President and leader said in his speech on 16 March:

> "Today, after the crushing of the sedition and rebelliousness and the restoration of security, stability and State authority, the time has come to start building the pillars of the new stage, which is not without difficulties and which calls for enormous sacrifice. However, our people, whose present is rooted in the history and heritage of 6,000 years, is capable, after passing through the trial, of opening up the horizons of the radiant future, with its mighty potentials, by the power of the Iraqis, which is unlimited when they bare their forearms and apply their intelligence to kindling the brand of building and reconstruction. The steadfast Iraqis, loyal to their country and concerned about Iraq's independence, greatness, construction and prosperity will find in the institutions and formulas of this new stage free and constructive scope for participation in everything that ensures the greatness of Iraq and the Iraqis, their interests, security and stability and the building of a democratic society based on the Constitution, law, the institutions and a multi-party system."

Beloved Iraqis,

This is the future programme. In spite of the treacherous conspiratorial schemes that have been and are being concocted against us and the schemes that have been hatched and are being hatched in the Council of Iniquity and the Iniquitous, which is wrongly and spuriously called "the Security Council", we are confident that the future will be like most of the pages of our country's centuries-old history, bright, radiant and strong, with God's permission.

Greetings to all men in all institutions of State, in the armed forces and in the security, police and administration organs, and to all men of good faith, Kurdish and Arab citizens of mighty Iraq who have participated with bravery and dedication to the crushing of the dissension and the restoration of security, stability and the rule of law throughout the country.

Beloved Iraqis,

Kurdish Iraqi citizens,

Since the Kurdish question, with all its well-known complexities, has interposed itself in our Iraqi life, with a view to preserving the continuity of the differentiation of colours, positions and personalities that serves great Iraq and strengthens the national humanitarian path of our victorious progress, we have decided to pardon the Iraqi Kurds for any conduct punishable by law except the crimes of murder, rape and theft, occurring in the circumstances of discord and treachery. The pardon covers Kurds generally in the Autonomous Region and also the members and advisers of the national defence detachments, the members of the special troops and the members of internal security and the armed forces. When any of them returns to the national ranks, he will be secure in all his rights and will perform his duties in accordance with the law. All organs of State, including the armed forces are called upon to adhere to this decision and to provide the necessary facilities for it. This decision shall be in effect for a period of a week in respect of those covered by it inside Iraq and for a period of two weeks in respect of those covered by it outside Iraq.

S/22460, 8 April 1991

14. Identical letters from the Permanent Representative of Iraq to the United Nations addressed respectively to the Secretary-General and the President of the Security Council, 8 April 1991

On instructions from my Government I have the honour to inform you of the following:

Once again, and in the course of a mere 48 hours, the Security Council has seen fit to adopt another tendentious and biased resolution against Iraq. The character of resolution 688 (1991) is clear, in particular, from the fact that it was adopted despite the Council's being informed of Iraq's readiness to receive a fact-finding mission from the United Nations.

Such a disregard for the readiness expressed by Iraq constitutes yet another precedent in the Security Council's treatment of Iraq that has no counterpart in the history of the Council.

Once again, the Council in this resolution perpetuates the use of double standards in its treatment of Iraq, if we take as an example the way in which it dealt with the massacre perpetrated by the Israeli occupation authorities against Palestinians at the Haram al-Sharif in Jerusalem on 8 October 1990. Now, however, while Iraq is expressing its readiness to receive an international commission of inquiry, the Council ignores that fact and adopts its condemnatory resolution.

Furthermore, in its resolution the Council refers to what it calls "cross border incursions", and this is a calumny for which it does not provide any evidence. In its resolution, the Council further requests that Iraq should allow international humanitarian organizations to function for the purpose of providing relief. A text containing such a request is meaningless, because these organizations are now, already, operating in Iraq and the Iraqi authorities are cooperating fully with them, as the organizations themselves acknowledge.

It is extremely paradoxical that the Council should show interest in letters from Iran and Turkey concerning the situation of the Kurds despite the fact that the world knows full well that these States do not by any means recognize any of the rights of the Kurds (such as distinct nationality) in their countries, where the majority of Kurds are to be found. The allegations made in these letters are no more than an exercise in hypocrisy, blackmail and tendentious propaganda against Iraq, which has been, and which continues to be, in the vanguard of the countries of the region in dealing with the Kurdish issue in a humane and democratic manner. The legal, political and actual facts in this regard are well-established.

It is also paradoxical in the extreme that such countries as Iran, Syria and the United States should incite agents and subversives against authority in Iraq or infiltrate their lackeys across international boundaries and provide them with weapons and *matériel* and, when the government authorities undertake to perform their duties for the restoration of security and stability to their country and for the protection of civilians against intimidation, murder, plunder, sabotage and the other criminal acts being committed by these agents, that these very countries should stir up campaigns of defamation against Iraq and should condemn it.

The great majority of so-called refugees are peaceable inhabitants who have been deceived by agents. They have intimidated them with false allegations in order to induce them to flee from their homes, and they have obliged them to do so by force of arms when the hope of the subversives to impose their domination over the areas in which they have wreaked havoc was thwarted.

...

S/22463, 8 April 1991

15. Letter from the Permanent Representative of the Islamic Republic of Iran to the United Nations addressed to the Secretary-General, 8 April 1991

Upon instructions from my Government, I have the honour to bring to the attention of the international community through Your Excellency the tragic news that as of 1200 GMT Monday 8 April, 771,850 Iraqi refugees have escaped their country and entered Iran through the western borders. The numbers are steadily increasing. The situation at the borders is desperate.

The Government of the Islamic Republic of Iran has taken the following steps to alleviate the sufferings of thousands of refugees including the elderly and the children.

- Keeping the borders continuously open to the flow of human beings seeking refuge in Iran.
- Increasing the emergency budget to deal with this crisis from 1 billion rials ($US 14,285,714) to 4 billion rials ($US 57,142,856).
- Appealing to people and national organizations to mobilize their resources to assist the Iraqi refugees.
- Calling upon international agencies and all States to take speedy measures to fulfil their international responsibility and to provide relief assistance to Iraqi refugees.
- The Islamic Republic of Iran is determined to embark on a soul searching national mobilization to provide emergency shelter, food and clothing for the massive number of refugees who are expected to rise beyond 1 million by the end of this week. The problem is, however, so tremendous that the host country alone will not be able to cope with the speed of the influx and provision of a decent emergency living condition for so huge a number of refugees. The international community is expected to shoulder its humanitarian responsibility to a defenceless and innocent people who are leaving their homes and fleeing from the armed forces of their own Government.

The Government of the Islamic Republic of Iran trusts that under the guidance of Your Excellency, the United Nations machinery and its agencies will be fully mobilized to provide relief assistance to Iraqi refugees.

...

S/22465, 9 April 1991

16. Letter from the Permanent Representative of Iraq to the United Nations addressed to the Secretary-General, 8 April 1991

On instructions from my Government, I have the honour to submit to you new proof of the grave violations by Iran of the cease-fire agreement between Iraq and Iran and the barefaced interference of Iran in the internal affairs of Iraq, namely the following:

1. Iraq is in possession of documents indicating that the Iranian regime has undertaken to provide facilities to what is referred to as the Iraqi opposition movement and to facilitate the sending of assistance and forces into Iraq.

2. A number of casualties among the Iranians who clashed with our forces in the governorate of Diyala were found to be in possession of documents confirming the participation of the Khomeini Guard in that clash; in addition, the code used by a commander of the Khomeini Guard was accidentally discovered.

3. Six members of the Khomeini Guard belonging to Company 32 ("Ansar Al-Husayn"), the Guard that had infiltrated the governorate of Diyala, were taken prisoner.

4. In the governorate of Diyala, following a clash with groups of infiltrators coming from Iran, canned goods, a water flask and a transmitter were found, all of which were produced by the factories of the Ministry of the Khomeini Guard. In another clash between the Khomeini Guard and our forces in the governorate of Diyala, a quantity of ammunition for the RPG 7 launcher and portable radio communications equipment were seized, on which were written the words "made in the factories of the Ministry of the Iranian Guard".

5. It has been confirmed by the competent Iraqi authorities, with evidence and proof, that the elements which seized the Iraqi border complex "Al-Mundhiriya" in early March 1991 were Iranian.

6. Information has been obtained concerning the entry of an armed group belonging to the 9th Company ("Badr") on 3 March 1991, heading in the direction of the

cities of Basra, Nasiriyah and Amarah for the purpose of holding demonstrations and stirring up riots in those cities.

7. The competent Iraqi authorities are in possession of information concerning the formation of committees which have among their members representatives of the Iranian intelligence service, the Al-Da'wah party and the Supreme Council of what is known as the Islamic Revolution in Iraq, whose mission is to enlist fleeing Iraqis and Iraqi refugees and to provide them with military uniforms, weapons and identity cards and introduce them into Iraq via Ahvaz-Basra.

8. On 6 March 1991 an armed Iranian group occupied the region of Hayy Al-Shurtah, at the entrance to the district of Khanaqin, and clashed with the Iraqi police forces, resulting in the killing of two members of the Iranian group, who were bearing their personal identification papers confirming that they were members of the Khomeini Guard.

9. It was ascertained from the confessions of one infiltrator that he had been instructed by the Iranian officers in charge to proceed to the area of Tanumah in Basra as part of a convoy including two lorries, one for weapons and the other for ammunition, and five other lorries for the transport of 300 armed persons belonging to what are known as the "Tawwabin", who were brought to the area of Tanumah.

10. It was ascertained from the confessions of another infiltrator who was arrested during the riotous events that he had been instructed by his superiors in the Guard command to accompany armed elements from inside Iran and take them to the governorate of Basra, district of Tanumah, and that he had also taken other armed elements from Iran to the governorate of Maysan via Halfayah.

11. The competent Iraqi authorities are in possession of information concerning Iran's intention to occupy the town of Kut and cut off the Baghdad-Kut-Basra road by means of a thrust by members of Company 9 ("Badr") together with Company 11 ("Amir Al-Mu'minin").

12. Information has been obtained concerning the participation of three battalions of the "Al-Nabiy Al-Akram" brigade in Mehran-Kut operations.

13. Information has been obtained concerning an agreement entered into between Iran and the saboteurs in northern Iraq on the opening of all roads to Iran in the event of a retreat by the saboteurs.

14. Information has been obtained concerning the leadership of agitation activities in the cities of Kut and Badrah by a leader of the Khomeini Guard known as Mortaza Qorba'i.

The above evidence and the documents which confirm it are in the possession of the competent Iraqi authorities, who are willing to present them to such authority as is authorized by the Secretary-General with a view to proving the barefaced interference of Iran in the internal affairs of Iraq, and Iran's violations of the cease-fire agreement between the two countries and the principles of good-neighbourliness.

On this occasion we appeal to the peoples and organizations of the world to intervene in order to put a stop to these Iranian practices and ward off further harm to the people of Iraq and the peoples of the region.

...

International Committee of the Red Cross, Bulletin, April 1991 - No. 183

17. ICRC, Assistance Given in the Middle East Conflict, April 1991

ICRC trucks and aircraft leave for Baghdad

From 30 January to 16 March, ten ICRC convoys made their way overland to Baghdad, with more than 166 tonnes of medical supplies, 144 tonnes of sanitation equipment, 876 tonnes of food and 253 tonnes of fuel on board.

The tenth convoy of 29 vehicles which left Amman on 15 March was also carrying all the equipment needed to set up a transit camp for 5,000 people.

That same day, a cargo plane chartered by the ICRC and containing 23 tonnes of relief supplies, including kitchen utensils and five electric generators, arrived in Baghdad via Luxembourg and Larnaca. Within the context of the Middle East conflict this was the 32nd flight made by an ICRC aircraft since 19 January.

The plane was also carrying two mobile water purification and packaging units and various supplies needed to repair the city's sewerage and water supply system.

Ninety-four doctors from the Algerian Red Crescent who had arrived in Baghdad aboard an ICRC convoy from Amman began working in the city's hospitals on 4 March.

A transit camp for 1,000 people was recently set up in Khorramshahr, in the Iranian province of Khuzistan, near the border with southern Iraq. A second camp now under construction will be able to accommodate some 5,000 people for longer periods. There are presently 4,000 displaced persons, mainly women and children, in the area.

One of the ICRC's primary objectives in Iraq is to expand its activities in Baghdad and other parts of the country, in close cooperation with the Iraqi Red Crescent and with the agreement of the Iraqi authorities. The top priority is to cover the medical and sanitation requirements of the civilian population, focussing on the most vulnerable groups, such as the wounded, the sick, children and the elderly.

18. Appeal by the UN Secretary-General, The Humanitarian Emergency in Iraq, 8 April 1991

INTRODUCTION AND SUMMARY

1. The aftermath of war in the Gulf will afflict the peoples of the region for years to come. Such has been the devastation in human, economic and environmental terms, that children yet unborn will also inherit its fruits. Much developmental progress, painstakingly achieved over several decades, lies in ruins; and none can yet say how much time reconstruction will take, nor calculate its price in billions of dollars. The peoples who underwent these traumas must now also begin to measure the realities of their future in the knowledge that they themselves will have to bear most of its costs.

2. Dismayed by reports of the extent of human suffering, I last month asked Under-Secretary-General Martti Ahtisaari to lead a mission to assess the need for urgent humanitarian assistance on the part of the peoples of Iraq and Kuwait. Earlier, indeed, I had asked UNDRO, in conjunction with my Personal Representative for Humanitarian Assistance related to the crisis between Iraq and Kuwait, Sadruddin Aga Khan, to coordinate assistance to third country nationals in the framework of a regional plan of action for countries neighbouring Iraq,

and had dispatched to Baghdad, in February 1991, a WHO/UNICEF mission to assess the impact of war on the women and children of that city. The Ahtisaari mission was in Iraq from 10 to 17 March, and in Kuwait from 23 to 27 March. I presented Mr. Ahtisaari's reports to the Security Council on 20 and 28 March (S/22366 and S/22409). They described deeply disturbing situations in each country. My present appeal relates to Iraq, and was prepared with the close collaboration of UNDP, UNICEF, UNHCR, WFP, UNDRO, FAO and WHO, mindful of the need to maintain a unitary approach to a problem of this dimension. A second appeal, in respect of Kuwait as well as the continuing needs of refugees in neighbouring countries, will follow immediately upon finalization of their assessment of needs by certain agencies and programmes whose visiting experts were still in transit when this appeal was finalized.

3. In Iraq, the mission reported grim and ominous conditions regarding food, water, sanitation, health, communications, energy and logistics, and as to the plight of the most vulnerable members of society. It also noted that it had been unable, for security reasons, to travel to areas in both the north and south of the country. Mr. Ahtisaari had expressed regret to the Iraqi authorities at this, because it was important that the United Nations should be able to assess the humanitarian needs of the entire population in all regions. The report stated that needs were unlikely to vary greatly from what had been observed by the mission, except that "conditions may be substantially worse in certain locations". At that time and thereafter, as has now clearly emerged, insurrection against the Government, and major civil strife, had broken out in certain parts of the country. A UNICEF mission has recently examined the resulting situation in southern cities. It has confirmed that circumstances are even more bleak and life-threatening than had been depicted in the original report (S/22366). In the last few days, UNDP's Resident Representative has come to headquarters and told of a deteriorating situation, and diminishing hope, among the people in the nation's capital.

4. The Ahtisaari mission, during its visit to Kuwait, witnessed the beginning of a major movement of Iraqi people to the Kuwait border (S/22409, paragraphs 32-33), and media reports from this area have since described the parlous state of many seeking refuge from conditions in southern Iraq, in need of shelter, food, water and medical help. But even this calamity has been overshadowed by the mass flight of Kurdish people from their homes in north-eastern Iraq towards Iran and Turkey, with many thousands crossing the borders. These refugees and displaced persons, victims first of war, then of civil conflict, had already been debilitated by post-war conditions in Iraq. On 5 April, the Security Council adopted its resolution 688 (1991) regarding this new and grievous situation. Reports show the often desperate circumstances of those fleeing.

5. The misery of the people of Iraq is beyond the present capacity of their authorities, or those of adjoining States, to assuage. The plight of many who remain is not greatly less than those who have fled. I am appalled by unanimous, consistent reports of deteriorating conditions and a growing hopelessness among the people. And I am convinced that the international community will wish to show its compassion, and every support, for a population few of whom bear any responsibility for the series of calamities which have befallen them.

6. As, however, the Ahtisaari report showed, it is also clear beyond any doubt that the present needs of the population of Iraq are so great that they far exceed the capabilities of the donor community. Only through the regeneration of the Iraqi economy can these basic requirements be met on a secure and continuing basis. The key is oil-based energy production, permitting Iraq to fund imports that its people must have, and to drive machinery upon which their lives depend. My present appeal includes some limited temporary fuel provision to enable Iraq to evolve from its present condition of almost total civilian disablement.

7. Accordingly, this Emergency Humanitarian Appeal for Iraq for US$ 178 million addresses only some of the minimal, most immediate, needs of the population during the forthcoming period of six months. It also takes into consideration such limiting factors as existing logistic capabilities, accessibility, and capacity to deliver the assistance required to the intended beneficiaries. The requirements that it presents cover only a portion of their emergency needs, and focuses especially upon those of the most vulnerable groups - mothers and children, the elderly, the handicapped, orphans, the sick, the homeless, the refugees and the displaced. My appeal is intended to minimize suffering by meeting food needs, by providing clean water, and by reinstating primary health standards and support. It is addressed only to staving off yet another catastrophe.

8. This prioritization in favour of those who are most at risk represents the barest minimum that must be achieved if such imminent disaster is to be avoided. The substantive chapters which follow show that even the resources which are immediately needed dwarf the capacity of the international system to mobilize. Such needs, beyond the small fraction identified in this appeal, must be referred to the Security Council for its consideration under the procedures established by its resolution 687 (1991), paragraph 23. It is clear that a mechanism must be worked out quickly to allow the use of some of Iraq's assets to procure these urgent requirements, else the international community will certainly be asked soon to meet them as part of a further emergency response on a much larger scale. Such requirements are particularly critical in the agricultural, health, logistical and physical infrastructural sectors. It is also an immediate priority to help reestablish a basic communication system so that not only an emergency programme, but the rehabilitation activities that must invariably follow in its wake, can be implemented in an effective and coordinated manner. As the Ahtisaari report pointed out, such has been the destruction that communication in Iraq has been reduced to a person-to-person basis. The appeal figure of US$ 178 million will have to be kept under continuous review, and I will consider this to be an important part of the work of the Executive Delegate whom I have appointed in the context of a United Nations Inter-Agency Humanitarian Programme for Iraq, Kuwait and the Iraq/Turkey and the Iraq/Iran border areas. In his tasks, he will be assisted by a coordinator resident in Iraq.

9. Each of the constituent parts of the United Nations system which has contributed its expertise to its appeal stands ready to provide further descriptions and greater detail of its proposed activities. Such organizations have had lengthy experience in relating to the donor community and in seeking its support for their field activities. Experience has shown that direct links between donors and operational organizations play an essential part in a successful resource mobilization operation.

...

19. United Nations Regional Humanitarian Plan of Action Relating to the Crisis between Iraq and Kuwait, Second Update, 9 April 1991

Introduction and Background

1. This is the second update of the Regional Humanitarian Plan of Action relating to the crisis between Iraq and Kuwait.

2. Iraq's invasion of Kuwait on 2 August 1990, precipitated an exodus of more than one million people into neighboring countries, mainly Jordan. The great majority of evacuees were "third country nationals" from various Arab and Asian countries who were forced by events to return to their home countries.

3. To deliver assistance to these people and facilitate their repatriation a Regional Humanitarian Plan of Action was first issued by UNDRO on 19 October 1990 and then updated on 11 January 1991, few days prior to the dead line set by the Security Council and outbreak of hostilities. The plan and its first update assumed that 400,000 people would need assistance for 3 months in each transit country, and Iran, Jordan, Syria and Turkey, were indicated as the main routes of escape. At that time an appeal was made for funding of start-up costs in the order of one fourth of the plan, i.e. USD 38 million.

4. When hostilities began on 17 January, the Humanitarian Plan of Action became operational. However, due to the military operations and logistic constraints the outflow of evacuees, mainly third country nationals, of whom 36,368 were repatriated by IOM.

5. After the cessation of hostilities between the Coalition and Iraqi forces a wave of unrest and turmoil struck Iraq with widespread fighting in the country.

6. As a result, hundreds of thousands of Iraqi nationals, mainly of Kurdish origin, crossed the borders into Turkey and Iran. In a few days some 800,000 Iraqis sought refuge and protection in the Islamic Republic of Iran, while about 300,000 crossed into Turkey.

7. On 5 April 1991, UNDRO on behalf of the participating agencies appealed for USD 137 million together with the start-up costs representing the full funding of the Regional Humanitarian Plan of action. Today, only a few days later, the number of refugees in the region has almost tripled. Due to the fluidity of the present situation, the indication of more people heading for the borders and, at the same time, taking into consideration the diplomatic efforts to ease conditions in Iraq, the number of 1.5 million refugees in the region has been fixed as a planning figure. In particular, the target refugee population have [*sic*] been estimated at 1 million for Iran and 500,000 for Turkey. Nevertheless, until further notice, the contingency measures for Syria and Jordan remain in force due to the unpredictability of further movements into these countries, although number [*sic*] of beneficiaries will be adapted to the number of arrivals of refugees and evacuees.

8. In order to assist 1.5 million refugees in Turkey and Iran, the financial inputs required, for a period of 90 days, are estimated at USD 400.2 million, which includes the USD 137 million in the appeal of 5 April. In view of the presence of 1.1 million Iraqi nationals in Iran and on the Turkish border region, donors are requested to give urgent priority to immediate contributions for at least 75 per cent of the total appeal.

Co-ordination Mechanism

At this stage of the crisis, to guarantee the prompt and adequate assistance to the affected population, it is essential to ensure the cohesion and co-ordination of the joint efforts of the international community, the U.N. system, other international organizations and Ngos.

Due to the change in the nature of the ongoing emergency, the U.N. Inter-Agency Working Group and IOM met in Geneva on 8 April 1991 to revise the division of responsibilities among the concerned technical agencies according to specific mandates and fields of expertise.

The situation has become a "refugee" emergency. Therefore, UNHCR is to undertake full operational responsibility, with the other organizations of the U.N. system and IOM playing a supportive role.

The needs are extremely urgent and demand immediate action.

Full co-ordination among the U.N. agencies and IOM will continue to take place at Headquarters and field levels.

In addition, the U.N.-IOM Inter-Agency Working Group in Geneva will also co-ordinate with the newly appointed Secretary-General's Executive Delegate for the U.N. Humanitarian Programme for Iraq, Kuwait and border areas with Turkey and Iran, to facilitate activities in fields of common interest.

In this context, at the Headquarters level UNDRO will continue to provide the framework for overall co-ordination, in full co-operation with UNHCR and the other participants in the Inter-Agency Working Group.

At field level, in close association with the U.N. Resident Co-ordinator, UNHCR is responsible for all relevant negotiations with host governments, implementing partners and donor countries.

In particular, the responsibility of each agency can be summarized as follows:

- UNICEF: Emergency assistance to vulnerable groups (children under 15 and mothers), particularly responsible for immunization, control of diarrhoeal diseases, safe motherhood, supply of high energy food and clothes for children. In addition, UNICEF will provide technical assistance and procure appropriate equipment to support UNHCR in water supply and sanitation in the camps.

- UNDP: The UNDP Resident Representatives in the field, who act also as U.N. Resident Co-ordinators and UNDRO Representatives, will continue to place a major role in the co-ordination effort by facilitating, when required, contacts at all levels with governments, donors and NGOs. The U.N. Resident Co-ordinator will also continue to lead the local inter-agency emergency groups.

- UNHCR: overall operational co-ordination and direct responsibility for protection and assistance, camp management, provision of camp infrastructure, including water and sanitation, transport of non-food and complimentary and supplementary food items.

- WFP: Technical and operational assistance for mobilization, procurement and transportation of food requirements. In addition, WFP will assist in updating records of food pledges/contributions for this crisis.

- WHO: Technical assistance for design and implementation of public health services for refugees with emphasis on norms and standards, epidemiological surveillance, staff training and supply of drugs and medical equipment.

- IOM: Will continue to be responsible for operational assistance in all programmes concerning internal transportation of refugees and displaced persons, and for the repatriation of third country nationals as required.

Further UNESCO stands ready to provide its contribution to UNHCR-assistance programmes for activities of its concern in the refugee camps.

Proposed Plan for the Islamic Republic of Iran

1. At the time of drafting this update, over 700,000 Iraqi refugees have already arrived in Iran. They are presently located in five western provinces, namely: Khuzistan (68,150), Ilam (2,500), Bakletaran (426,500), Kurdistan (31,500) and West Azerbaijan (243,200).

2. The Iranian authorities are providing emergency assistance to this population, mainly from local resources, with the support of the International Community which has already provided, through the implementation of the U.N. Regional Humanitarian Plan of Action, relief items and camp equipment and material for 35,000 people. Since the beginning of the present influx, the United

Nations is delivering additional assistance to Iran, particularly through either the redeployment of stocks held by UNICEF, WHO, WFP and UNHCR in places such as Denmark, Holland, Bulgaria, Germany, Cyprus, Pakistan, etc. or the provision of financial support.

3. However, this effort is almost insignificant compared to the magnitude of the human tragedy which is unfolding in western Iran. Therefore, the burden of the humanitarian response at present lies with the government and people of Iran.

4. In this connection, the Iranian spiritual leader, Ayatollah Khomenei has appealed to the government and nation to extend whatever assistance necessary to the Iraqi refugees. A special bank account has been established to receive cash contributions from the public, while the Iranian Red Crescent Society and the Imam Relief Committees are utilizing and channelling public donations to the affected areas. Similarly, a presidential decree, issued on 7 April, is requesting all government organizations and companies to put at the disposal of the Ministry of Interior financial and in kind resources.

5. Therefore, in order to provide meaningful support to existing relief efforts in Iran, the United Nations is endeavouring to urgently channel substantial additional relief to Iran in order to assist up to 800,000 people, bearing in mind that there are clear indications that the pace of increase would be maintained or even enhanced. To meet this target, financial and in kind support of an exceptional magnitude is urgently required from the international community.

6. As mentioned in the update of 11 January, the Iranian authorities are providing the focal point for emergency relief operations, while the United Nations and IOM focus on supporting the government action and assist in mobilizing requested financial support, monitoring the activities, procuring relief supplies and co-ordinating the international response.

Proposed Plan of Action for Jordan

1. As mentioned in the up-date of the Humanitarian Regional Plan of Action of 11 January 1991 Jordan had already a reliable basic infrastructure for about 60,000 to 70,000 persons through a network which included camps managed by ICRC and the Jordanian Red Crescent Society. This capacity was further strengthened through the United Nations input during the first quarter of 1991, which brought the potential reception capacity of the country to almost 100,000 persons.

2. During this period, contrary to several expectations, less than 50,000 third country nationals came to Jordan (only a handful of Iraqi nationals arrived) and most of them were rapidly transferred to their home countries. Presently, there are less than 1,000 persons in the country, and daily arrivals have come down to less than one hundred, while IOM endeavours to transfer them to either their countries of origin or to countries where they are granted residency.

3. In this connection, third country nationals, especially Egyptians, constitute the majority of the current new inflow. While in Jordan, they are assisted by UNHCR and then receive repatriation assistance from IOM through now well established mechanisms. Most of them are repatriated within a matter of days.

4. Since 17 January, and as of 8 April, 28,257 persons had been repatriated. Others returned to their home countries by their own means or through arrangements made by their own governments.

5. Some five hundred persons of concern to UNHCR (mainly Somalis) have not been able to leave the country yet. At their request, IOM and UNHCR are endeavouring to organize the voluntary repatriation of the vast majority, in spite of numerous difficulties to find reliable routes and transportation facilities.

6. Therefore, considering the fact that part of the objectives of the Plan of Action are already met, but also that arrivals are still taking place and that the evolving situation in Iraq may still originate further departures to or via Jordan, a certain level of preparedness should be maintained and the situation closely monitored.

Proposed Plan of Action for Syria

1. During the first months of 1991, only several hundred of Iraqi and third country nationals arrived in Syria, where over 1,000 Iraqis had already arrived during the second semester of 1990.

2. Through the United Nations Regional Humanitarian Plan of Action, camps and stockpiling for 25,000 people were set up and stored. This has been achieved with the full co-operation of the Syrian authorities who, noting the reduced number of arrivals but still concerned by the possibility of large influxes, should the situation in Iraq prevail, have agreed to release part of the relief items provided by the United Nations for redeployment to more severely affected countries. This has been agreed in the understanding that part of the stockpiling will remain in the country, until the situation returns to normal in Iraq. Besides, should large movements to Syria take place, the United Nations will, again, strengthen the reception and assistance capacity of the government of Syria.

3. In Syria, as in Iran and Turkey, those now entering the country are mainly Iraqis, with approximately 1,500 persons having arrived in the last few weeks, bringing the total to some 4,500 people. An additional 330 evacuees have been repatriated by IOM.

4. Considering the relatively small number of arrivals, and the adequacy of resources previously established in the country, UNHCR will maintain stockpiles for some 15,000 persons in Syria and transfer remaining items (for a total of 10,000 people) to Turkey.

5. Moreover, in order to keep an adequate level of preparedness, and considering that the majority of the caseload is made up of refugees, the UNHCR Emergency team will remain in the country until further notice, while the camps established in El Hol (capacity: 10,000 people) and Tartous (capacity: 2,500) will remain operational. Other camp sites are kept on hold, but can be completed at any given time, should new and massive arrivals take place.

6. Therefore, although no additional financial or in kind support is required for the time being, except for ongoing transportation requirements of IOM, preparedness levels for at least 10,000 remain in force.

Proposed Plan of Action for the Republic of Turkey

1. Events have confirmed the pattern of movements of displaced persons from Iraq that was described in the update of the Regional Humanitarian Plan of Action of 11 January 1991. At the beginning of March about 5,000 people had reached the Turkish territory.

2. However, during March, despite the still hard weather conditions, far over a hundred thousand Iraqi nationals have left their home areas and headed towards the border between Iraq and Turkey. At the time of the drafting of the present document, according to the Turkish authorities, over 250,000 Iraqi nationals have reached the border area after a dramatic exodus.

3. The number of Iraqi nationals presently within the Turkish boundaries is still unknown, as large numbers are stranded at the border in the Iraqi territory. The government of Turkey has expressed its willingness to assist them, in particular numerous children, women and elderly, who urgently need shelter, medical care, food and other basic assistance. In spite of the deployment of relief items to the border by the Turkish authorities, the needs are such that national resources are insufficient to cope with the emergency.

4. To help a population whose health and living conditions have reached an almost unbearable dimension and hoping to prevent further suffering which might lead to the death of the weakest among the vulnerable groups (mainly children, women and elderly), the governments of several countries, as well as some non-governmental organizations, are air dropping, or sending through Ankara, into the border area planeloads of relief goods.

5. All United Nations Agencies present in the country and IOM have offered their assistance to the government. Stocks of relief goods available in Turkey or abroad have been released and sent to the reception areas. Several interagency missions have proceeded to the border in order to assess the situation. Their preliminary reports confirm the urgent need for humanitarian assistance.

6. Nevertheless, in spite of the fact that the border has not been officially opened, it seems that a large proportion of the reported 250,000 people who have reached it, has managed to enter the Turkish territory.

7. In these circumstances, financial and in kind support should be put at the disposal of the United Nations for them to provide the Turkish authorities with sufficient relief equipment and material in order to reinforce the existing infrastructure set up during the last phase of the Regional Humanitarian Plan of Action.

8. According to several sources, further movements of thousands of Iraqi nationals towards the Turkish border are still taking place. Hence, the already dramatic situation prevailing in the border area, may still worsen to unprecedented levels of hardship.

9. Therefore, while requesting donors' immediate support on behalf of 300,000 people presently located in or heading towards the border area between Turkey and Iraq, preparedness measures for an eventual further arrival of at least 200,000 additional people should be taken into consideration.

Resource Mobilization

Financial contributions for which the United Nations and IOM are now appealing amount to USD 400.2 million and represents an urgent imperative requirement. This amount is to cover the needs of 1.5 million refugees for three months in Iran and Turkey (one million and 500,000 beneficiaries respectively). Due to the uncertainty of the present conditions in Iraq, this will need to be revised as the situation requires.

However, considering the presence of 1.1 million Iraqi nationals in Iran (800,000) and along the Turkish border with Iraq (300,000), donors are requested to give urgent priority to immediate contributions for at least 75 per cent of the total appeal.

Agencies' financial requirements for emergency programmes for refugees in Iran and Turkey can be summarized as follows:

UNHCR: 238,521,000
WFP: 47,500,000
WHO: 31,500,000
UNICEF: 23,700,000
IOM: 57,040,000
UNDRO: 2,000,000
TOTAL: 400,261,000

This budget has been established keeping in mind that numerous governments have, or will, offer direct assistance to both countries through bilateral action. Therefore, to prevent duplications and keep track of the overall international effort, donors providing bilateral support to the governments of Iran and Turkey, or through other humanitarian organizations, are requested to announce their contributions to UNDRO. These contributions, to the extent they address the requirements of the U.N. Plan of Action, will be considered as part of the international response.

Details on financial requirements can be obtained directly from concerned agencies, which will be available to provide donors with the elements of organization/country programmes.

As for the past, all agencies will continue to directly seek support from donors with specific fund-raising follow-up actions placed within the context of this Plan of Action.

The present appeal includes the USD 137 million requested on 5 April to activate the full original Plan of Action.

S/22482, 11 April 1991

20. Letter from the Permanent Representative of the Islamic Republic of Iran to the United Nations addressed to the Secretary-General, 11 April 1991

Upon instructions from my Government, and pursuant to my letter of 4 April 1991 (S/22447), I have the honour to enclose herewith the text of a letter by His Excellency Dr. Ali-Akbar Velayati, Minister for Foreign Affairs of the Islamic Republic of Iran addressed to Your Excellency.

...

The influx of Iraqi refugees into the Islamic Republic of Iran and other neighbouring countries has surpassed all estimates and preparations, and has reached and indeed passed dangerous levels, jeopardizing the lives of tens of thousands of innocent human beings. In addition to the unprecedented human suffering, this massive influx directly or by consequence is threatening peace and security of the recipient countries and indeed of the whole region.

Even our own estimates transmitted to Your Excellency on 4 April have now been proven by far lower than the actual number of civilians who have up to now sought refuge in Iran. According to the latest information, about 900,000 Iraqis have crossed our borders in the south, centre and the north. Such massive flow of refugees - whose most common characteristic is not ethnicity but fear of repression, hunger, dehydration, and exhaustion of a tedious journey of several days of escaping bullets and freezing cold is bound to lead to nothing but disaster and human tragedy of unprecedented dimensions.

Even if the up-to-now negligible international assistance were to gain some badly needed momentum and substance, it is highly unlikely that any degree of local effort and international relief aid could meet the most primary requirements of the mass of wounded, sick, hungry and cold-stricken refugees and prevent the unfolding tragedy.

It is, therefore, the strong conviction of my Government, that, without prejudice to the sovereignty and territorial integrity of Iraq, the necessary arrangements should be made for the safe and dignified repatriation of these refugees to their homeland. In order to provide a credible alternative to exodus and create the necessary atmosphere of confidence for voluntary return of the refugees, the process should be carried out under active and effective United Nations supervision and with United Nations guarantees for the safety and honour of the affected population, with the necessary safeguards to preclude any hampering - however temporary - of Iraq's territorial integrity.

The magnitude of the disaster requires immediate action by the United Nations without further delay both in order to address the basic needs of the refugees and also to arrange for their repatriation. The Islamic Republic of Iran is prepared to extend its full cooperation to the United Nations and Your Excellency in these efforts.

S/22486, 11 April 1991

21. Letter from the Permanent Representative of Luxembourg to the United Nations addressed to the Secretary-General, 11 April 1991

I have the honour to inform you that, following the extraordinary European Council held on 8 April 1991 in Luxembourg, the European Community and its 12 member States have decided to grant special assistance in the amount of 150 million ECUs - equivalent to 185 million dollars - for refugees and displaced Iraqis, particularly Kurds.

In view of the urgency and magnitude of the problem, this programme of assistance was launched on Tuesday, 9 April 1991 in close cooperation with the competent international humanitarian organizations, including UNHCR and ICRC.

This assistance is complemented by the assistance which member States are providing on a bilateral basis.

...

S/22502, 16 April 1991

22. Letter from the Permanent Representative of Iraq to the United Nations addressed to the Secretary-General, 16 April 1991

On instructions from my Government, I have the honour to inform you that Mr. Ali Khamenei, the spiritual leader of the Islamic Republic of Iran, made a provocative speech against Iraq during the Friday prayer on 5 April 1991. In his speech he asked the Iraqi army and its leaders to rise up against the regime and he incited the Iraqi people to engage in acts of sabotage, describing them as "hostile" acts. This provocative act, constituting as it does blatant interference in the internal affairs of Iraq, clearly reveals the involvement of the Iranian leaders in encouraging and aiding the saboteurs and riff-raff who have destroyed civilian property and been bent on killing innocent people, committing their criminal acts of plunder and pillage, burning the property of the Iraqi people and sowing civil strife, as has been their wont since 1980.

We enclose below several passages from that sermon, in which Mr. Khamenei said, "I wish to impress upon the leaders of the regime that it cannot possibly achieve victory through such acts over its people in opposition, for whenever there is a clash between the regime and opponents of the regime, the victor is bound to be the people, and the vanquished, the regime against the people. Similarly, all the leaders of the Iraqi army must know that whenever they go against the Iraqi people a very dire fate shall be theirs, and that the army which joins the people shall be beloved of the people; the army which stands against the people shall be beaten; whenever the people does not wish these officials to be in power, they must not be so. There is no other solution for the leaders of Iraq, from Saddam Hussein to those around him.

"I appeal unambiguously to the Iraqi people. The Iraqi people must realize fully that this is a crucial moment. If they resist, their fate shall be resplendent. Indeed, this path may be difficult and require struggle and self-sacrifice. Without struggle, no goal can be attained. They must assume these difficulties, which will be of short duration. On the other hand, if they back down and submit to this regime, woe betide them from punishment by the regime, for it shall visit upon them incomparably greater cruelty than that experienced hitherto. Should this regime reassert its control over the people (God forbid), it will take a great revenge on the Iraqi people, who will be forced to continue along the same path, relying on God and asking God for help and making the sacrifices of freedom fighters - then God shall make them victorious."

Mr. Khamenei added, "Here I should like to say one word to you, the Iranian people. Note the arrogance, note his anger at and aversion towards the uprising of the vigilant Muslims and the Islamic resurgence. This is what we are witnessing in the events of Iraq. Saddam today, confronting his people in this barbarous fashion, is the same Saddam as two months ago, about whom all the Western newspapers wrote, painting such a cruel picture of him. If this person is really so, why did you deal with him in previous years? And now when the day has come when Saddam is confronting his people, everyone has fallen silent and all this talk which was being heard against Saddam has ceased. All these newspapers, international propaganda services and all these reports have fallen under the arrogant sway of America and Britain. Now, all the propaganda services are working against the cause of Iraq and the Iraqi people, which is fighting for its rights. They turned a blind eye to the murder committed against the Iraqi people at Najaf and Kerbala and Basra and other cities. All of the northern cities have been placed under an umbrella of silence and this cruel figure has ceased to be. Now, when one looks at international newspapers one sees that what these newspapers are writing against the Baathist regime is the same as what they wrote during the imposed war and that the arrogant propaganda is on the side of Iraq ..."

On this occasion I should like to point out that while Mr. Ali Khamenei is the spiritual leader of the Islamic Republic of Iran, he is also its highest official, by virtue of the Iranian Constitution. Therefore my Government interprets his words as constituting an official incitement to the Iraqi army and people to rise up against the regime. It considers this to be blatant interference in the internal affairs of Iraq and incitement to civil strife, on which the leaders of the Iranian regime have been intent ever since 1980.

...

S/22500, 15 April 1991

23. Letter from the Permanent Representative of the Islamic Republic of Iran to the United Nations addressed to the Secretary-General, 15 April 1991

Upon instructions from my Government and further to my letter of 12 April 1991 (S/22490), I have the honour to inform that Iraqi violations of the terms of cease-fire and agreements between the two countries are becoming increasingly more serious and in fact quite dangerous. Shelling the territory of the Islamic Republic of Iran, concentration of military personnel at the international borders, and extending support and encouragement to certain elements to launch military operations against the Islamic Republic of Iran from Iraqi territory were among provocative acts the Iraqi military committed during the past three weeks. Such violations have now turned to downright aggression and occupation of the territory of the Islamic Republic of Iran in northern Ghasr-e-Shirin.

Yesterday, 14 April 1991, one Iraqi brigade crossed the international border and made an incursion into the territory of the Islamic Republic of Iran in northern Ghasr-e-Shirin, at Tang Havan (Sutak post) across from Tazeh Abad. The Iraqi brigade occupied an area 3 kilometres deep inside the territory of the Islamic Republic of Iran.

The Foreign Ministry of the Islamic Republic of Iran has strongly protested to the Government of Iraq for this dangerous violation. Note No. 598/4216 dated 15 April 1991 to that effect, addressed to the Embassy of the Republic of Iraq is herewith annexed.

The Government of the Islamic Republic of Iran calls for an immediate withdrawal of all Iraqi forces from the territory of the Islamic Republic of Iran and it cannot but hold the Government of Iraq solely responsible for both losses of life, material damages and all repercussions of this aggressive act. Under the current circumstances, the Iraqi Government is best advised to find a solution other than creation of an external enemy to face up with her internal turmoil.

The Ministry of Foreign Affairs of the Islamic Republic of Iran presenting its compliments herewith informs:

Following the numerous violations of the terms of the cease-fire and bilateral agreements between the two countries by Iraqi forces during past three weeks, including shelling parts of territory of the Islamic Republic of Iran, concentration of Iraqi military forces behind the international boundaries, embarking on hit and run operations as well as military actions by elements supported by Iraqi Government - some of whose details have been transmitted to that Embassy in previous notes of this Ministry - giving rise to the prediction that these measures were a prelude to another aggression against the territory of the Islamic Republic of Iran, on 14 April 1991, a brigade of Iraqi forces crossing over the international borders of the two countries in the region of north of Ghasr-e-Shirin in Tang Havan (Sutak border post) across Tazeh Abad embarked on a new military aggression against the Islamic Republic of Iran, occupying an area of 3 kilometres deep inside Iranian territory.

The Islamic Republic of Iran strongly protesting this hostile act of the Government of the Republic of Iraq calls for the immediate and unconditional withdrawal of all Iraqi forces from the territory of the Islamic Republic of Iran and holds the Government of Iraq fully responsible for all casualties and damages as well as the grave consequences of this aggression.

The Ministry of Foreign Affairs of the Islamic Republic of Iran avails itself of this opportunity to renew its highest consideration.

Hoping for the victory of the oppressed over the oppressors.

S/22513, 21 April 1991

24. Letter from the Minister for Foreign Affairs of Iraq addressed to the Secretary-General, 21 April 1991

As you are certainly aware, United States armed forces and the forces of other foreign countries cooperating with them have entered the Zakhou region in northern Iraq. The objective of this operation has been stated to be the establishment in Iraqi territory of centres for assisting displaced Iraqi citizens in Turkey. You are also aware that the Government of Iraq is opposed to this measure, since it would constitute a serious, unjustifiable and unfounded attack on the sovereignty and territorial integrity of Iraq.

This measure was announced at a time when the Iraqi Government had made significant progress in its negotiations with Prince Sadruddin Aga Khan, the representative to whom you have entrusted responsibility for relief operations. Steps to carry out the above-mentioned measure were taken on 20 April 1991, even though the Government of Iraq had signed a comprehensive agreement with your representative on 18 April, which provided for the establishment of humanitarian centres throughout Iraq, and in particular in the northern part of the country, with a view to undertaking the assistance operations necessary to induce Iraqi citizens displaced outside Iraq's frontiers to return in complete security to their places of residence in Iraq. It should be pointed out that the Government of Iraq, while opposing the steps taken by United States forces and the foreign forces cooperating with them for the reasons stated above, has not hindered these operations because it is not opposed to the provision of humanitarian assistance to Iraqi citizens who are in need of it and because it wishes to avoid any complication that may prevent the return of all Iraqi citizens in security to their places of residence.

Because the measures taken by the United States forces and the forces cooperating with them constitute a flagrant violation of Iraq's sovereignty and territorial integrity, and bearing in mind our opposition to the creation of centres under United States control inside Iraqi territory and our belief that the agreement which our Government concluded with your representative on 18 April 1991 has made it possible to define all relief operations in Iraq in an integrated and balanced manner, particularly those targeted to Kurds who are Iraqi citizens in such a way as to avoid the realization of the alleged objectives of the United States centres and to remove any justification for the establishment of such centres, which would in one way or another impair Iraq's sovereignty, the Government of Iraq, in pursuance of the above-mentioned agreement, is approaching you to request the United Nations to assume responsibility for the centres referred to above and to have the coordinator appointed by your representative, who is at the present time in Baghdad, immediately to take the measures necessary for the achievement of the purpose which we have described above. I can assure you that my Government will provide you with all necessary assistance in accordance with the above-mentioned agreement. Please find enclosed the memorandum of understanding signed with your representative on 18 April 1991.

...

MEMORANDUM OF UNDERSTANDING SIGNED ON 18 APRIL 1991

This memorandum summarizes the results of discussions held in Baghdad between the Government of the Republic of Iraq, in the context of its request to the Secretary-General of the United Nations in relation to the suffering of the Iraqi population affected by recent events and Security Council resolution 688 of 5 April 1991, which has not been accepted by the Government of Iraq, and:

(a) From 13 to 18 April 1991, the United Nations Mission led by Mr. Eric Suy, Personal Representative of the United Nations Secretary-General, and

(b) From 16 to 18 April, the United Nations Inter-Agency Mission led by Prince Sadruddin Aga Khan, Executive Delegate of the United Nations Secretary-General for the United Nations Humanitarian Programme for Iraq, Kuwait and the Iraq/Iran and Iraq/Turkey Border Areas.

Both Missions have been welcomed by the Government of Iraq.

1. Both sides recognize the importance and urgency of adequate measures, including the provision of humanitarian assistance, to alleviate the suffering of the affected Iraqi civilian population.

2. The Government of the Republic of Iraq welcomes the United Nations efforts to promote the voluntary return home of Iraqi displaced persons and to take humanitarian measures to avert new flows of refugees and displaced persons from Iraq. It pledges its full support to and cooperation with the United Nations and its specialized agencies and programmes in this regard.

3. Both sides agree that the measures to be taken for the benefit of the displaced persons should be based primarily on their personal safety and the provision of humanitarian assistance and relief for their return and normalization of their lives in their places of origin.

4. For this purpose, the Government of the Republic of Iraq agrees to cooperate with the United Nations to have a humanitarian presence in Iraq, wherever such presence may be needed, and to facilitate it through the adoption of all necessary measures. This shall be ensured through the establishment of United Nations sub-offices and Humanitarian Centres (UNHUCs), in agreement and cooperation with the Government of Iraq.

5. Each Centre will be staffed by United Nations civilian personnel which, in addition to the regular staff members of the relevant United Nations agencies, may also include staff co-opted from the non-governmental organizations, the International Committee of the Red Cross and the League of Red Cross and Red Crescent Societies. The Red Crescent Society of Iraq shall be called upon to play a role in the implementation of humanitarian assistance and relief projects.

6. UNHUCs shall facilitate the provision of humanitarian assistance to the needy and would include, *inter alia*, food aid, medical care, agricultural rehabilitation, shelter and any other humanitarian and relief measures geared to the speedy normalization of life, in conformity with the principles of this memorandum. UNHUCs shall also monitor the overall situation in this regard to advise the Iraqi authorities regarding measures needed to enhance their work.

7. Routes of return, with relay stations along the way as well as logistic back-up capabilities, will be set up urgently in cooperation with the Iraqi authorities to provide to civilians, particularly the women and children as well as the aged and the sick going back to their home areas, the food aid, shelter and basic health care they will need along the way. United Nations staff will accompany such groups, as required.

8. The United Nations shall take urgent measures, in cooperation with the Government of Iraq, for the early stationing of staff as well as the provision of assistance and relief in all designated centres and, as a matter of priority, those close to the Iraqi borders with its neighbouring countries. For this purpose, the United Nations may, in agreement and cooperation with the Government of Iraq, organize air lifts to the areas concerned, as required, as well as transportation by road of humanitarian assistance and relief goods from and through the neighbouring countries under United Nations or other humanitarian auspices. The Government of the Republic of Iraq shall adopt the necessary measures in order to render such aid in a speedy and effective manner.

9. United Nations humanitarian assistance and relief shall be provided simultaneously to the displaced persons, returnees as well as all other populations covered by the relief Programme in order to encourage a speedy normalization of life.

10. The basic framework for United Nations humanitarian action outlined above is intended to facilitate the task of coordination, effective implementation and monitoring of humanitarian assistance and relief operations. Further specifications are contained in the paragraphs which follow.

11. It is agreed that humanitarian assistance is impartial and that all civilians in need, wherever they are located, are entitled to receive it.

12. All Iraqi officials concerned, including the military, will facilitate the safe passage of emergency relief commodities throughout the country.

13. The Government will establish forthwith, together with the United Nations, a relief distribution and monitoring structure to permit access to all civilians covered by the relief Programme, as soon as possible.

14. A Coordinator, at the Assistant Secretary-General level, has been assigned to Baghdad to coordinate, under the Executive Delegate's direction, the implementation of the Humanitarian Relief Programme. He will have permanent access to a high-level government official responsible for emergency activities in the country, to discuss and resolve policy and operational issues that may arise during the implementation of the Programme.

15. The Government of Iraq shall cooperate in granting United Nations field staff access to the parts of the country requiring relief, by air or road as needed, to facilitate the implementation and monitoring of the Programme.

16. Intergovernmental organizations, NGOs and other relief agencies will be encouraged to participate in the implementation of the Programme, in close cooperation with the United Nations and under clearly defined terms of association agreed with the Government.

17. The Government of Iraq will help in the prompt establishment of United Nations sub-offices in support of UNHUCs and other programmes in towns. These will be selected so as to facilitate the relief Programme when required, to encourage the voluntary return of, and to provide essential assistance to, internally and externally displaced, as well as to local populations covered by the Programme.

18. A United Nations radio communication system which is an indispensable instrument for the success of relief and rehabilitation activities will be set up. The system will cover communications requirements within Baghdad and other cities covered by the relief Programme and within and outside the country, as appropriate.

19. In order to facilitate implementation of, and resource mobilization for, the relief Programme, the Government will make available cash contributions in local currency to help cover in-country operational costs while pursuing discussions regarding the establishment of a special exchange rate for relief operations carried out by the agencies and organizations participating in the Programme.

20. The implementation of the above-mentioned principles shall be without prejudice to the sovereignty, territorial integrity, political independence, security and non-interference in the internal affairs of the Republic of Iraq.

21. The above-mentioned principles shall apply for a period ending on 31 December 1991. Two weeks before the expiration of the said period, the principles and their operational modalities shall be reviewed with a view to assessing any further need for their operation.

...

ICRC Bulletin, May 1991, No 184

25. ICRC Activities Relating to the Middle East Conflict

Relief for displaced persons in Iran

In conjunction with the Iranian Red Crescent, the ICRC has been distributing medicines, blankets, tents and 130 tons of food per day since mid-April to several hundred thousand Iraqi Kurds who have taken refuge in the Iranian provinces of Kurdistan, West Azerbaijan and Bakhtaran.

The ICRC's goal is to provide reception facilities for some 200,000 refugees. Camps already set up or under construction in Khorramshahr, Sanandaj, Gilan-e-Gharb, Ravansar and Oshnovieh will have an initial capacity of 100,000 people.

United Nations High Commissioner for Refugees,
Information Service

26. Statement of the High Commissioner for Refugees at the Donor Information Meeting, Geneva, 15 May 1991

Exactly one month ago today, I visited Iran. A human tragedy was unfolding right in front of my eyes, In the course of 7 days, the number of refugees had gone from 50,000 to more than 1 million. At the time of my visit, thousands of Iraqis were still waiting to cross the border. The following day, I visited Turkey and met the first group of Iraqis who had been brought down from the mountain. Today, the exodus may have stopped, the plight of the refugees may have somewhat stabilised and the first return movements begun. As of today, UNHCR Field Officers in Turkey estimate that 200,000 people have begun the trek home. An estimated 80,000 of the 1.3 million Iraqi refugees who found sanctuary in Iran have also started for home.

Massive bilateral assistance has been mobilized, notably to the Iraqis amassed on the Iraqi/Turkish border. Significant local efforts have also been deployed. Iran alone is spending some US$ 10 million a day. UNHCR's resources, in comparison, are limited but our efforts - I believe - not insignificant. Over the last few weeks, UNHCR has arranged some 240 relief flights carrying some 9,000 metric tons of cargo. Among other things, UNHCR has brought into the region 1,100,000 blankets and 82,000 tents. We have more than 200 UNHCR field personnel deployed in the region to deal with a situation in constant flux and we are in the process of getting more staff on the ground. To perform this job of providing relief and ensuring a degree of protection, we appealed on 12 April for US$ 238 million. To date, we have committed US$ 82 million and more is rapidly being obligated following recent contributions bringing our income to US$ 130.5 million. I am grateful to those governments and private organizations who have provided us with the resources to do our job.

A few weeks ago, we were thus faced with the fastest growing refugee crisis in memory. We now have to be prepared for an equally rapid return movement in case conditions allow for that to happen.

The appeal we are presenting to you today clearly defines UNHCR's responsibilities and needs. It takes into account the considerable assistance being provided by the various United Nations agencies, the IOM, the Red Cross Movement as well as by governments and NGOs. My Office will continue being responsible for the refugees in Iran and those in need on the Iraqi/Turkey border. In accordance with our mandate, we are also assuming responsibility for the return of the Iraqis - by following them back, by being present in the transit centres/and relay-stations and by providing the returnees with initial relief assistance in their homes, villages and towns. UNHCR's actions will stop short of rehabilitation of infrastructure.

Voluntary repatriation in safety and dignity is an important function for my Office. There is wide agreement among all parties that in the present situation, it provides the best solution to an operation that should not be allowed to perpetuate. It is, however, obvious that only the security conditions inside Iraq will determine the response by the refugees themselves. In order to promote and pursue this solution, my Office has taken control of a transit centre in Zakho. Six UNHCR field officers moved into the camp last Monday assuming full responsibility for camp management. UNHCR will also coordinate the relief activities of non-governmental organizations and monitor the assistance which will continue to be provided by the various coalition forces in the sectors of water, food and sanitation facilities. UNHCR currently mans three sub-offices in the northern Iraq towns of Arbil, Dohuk and Suleimaniya. In addition, we are opening eight field offices in the region to distribute relief supplies and are in the process of deploying 20 mobile units to monitor the well-being of the returnees. One of the features of this important mobilization of human resources is that due to its own shortage of staff UNHCR is relying heavily on staff seconded by various Government and NGOs. Requests have already been sent for 150 such emergency secondments.

Our duty is to provide relief to those who have sought sanctuary outside Iraq while at the same time being prepared to seize all opportunities for voluntary return. I am convinced that if we are given the required resources - and if necessary conditions of security prevail - we can take a major step towards a solution to this problem. Your immediate response to the appeal for which UNHCR still needs US$ 135 million will be an important contribution.

As yet, the full legacy of the Persian Gulf War can hardly be ascertained. But at least one lesson is clear. *Now* is the time to join forces and give the United Nations the capacity and resources it needs to cope with future disasters. I look forward to further discussions with you on these vital issues of concern to all of us.

Thank you.

27. United Nations High Commissioner for Refugees Information Bulletin No. 3 on Operations in the Persian Gulf Region, 21 May 1991

- The repatriation movement to Iraq gains momentum. Over 200,000 persons have returned from the Turkish/Iraqi border and 80,000 from Iran.
- The new UNHCR Plan of Action foresees the presence of over 540 staff members in Iran, Iraq and Turkey, in co-operation with NGOs and Governments.
- Financial requirements have been established at US$ 267 million. To date, some US$ 140 million have been received.

INTRODUCTION

The voluntary return of Iraqi refugees to their homes has now started, only six weeks after one of the largest and most sudden refugee exodus of our times.

UNHCR estimates that close to 300,000 Iraqis previously in emergency sites along the Iraq/Turkey border or admitted in the Islamic Republic of Iran have started their trek back home. Unfortunately, not all of them have managed to reach their destination as groups totalling up to 150,000 are reportedly stranded around the city of Sulaimaniyah, while another 100,000 are delaying their return to Dohuk and other cities. It is hoped that discussions now under way in Baghdad will rapidly lead to the return to their homes, in safety and dignity, of these returnees and of other groups still waiting in emergency camps.

As intensive deployment of human and material resources takes place to support voluntary repatriation in Northern and Eastern Iraq, humanitarian assistance must continue to respond to the basic needs of refugees on sites of the Iraq/Turkey border and in the 77 camps established in Iran. Whatever the magnitude of voluntary repatriation over the summer months, urgent steps must be taken now to consolidate the infrastructure of certain camps in preparation for the harsh winter.

Plan of Action, May-August 1991

The developments mentioned above and the wish of many to see the United Nations come out with a single consolidated appeal have resulted in the issuance on 15 May 1991 of a revised Plan of Action incorporating activities undertaken between January and April 1991 ... [*reproduced above*]. Despite a longer time-frame and the introduction of substantial activities in support of voluntary repatriation in Iraq itself, the revised UNHCR budget for the region is thus of US$ 267,6 million, an increase of only US$ 29,1 million as compared to the estimate of US$ 238 million given on 9 April 1991. This is due - to a very large extent - to the full credit given throughout our planning exercise to the important inputs made available directly by Governments, Inter Governmental Organisations (EEC), the Movement of the Red Cross/Red Crescent and NGOs.

Deployment of Staff

The sheer magnitude of the emergency and the particular conditions in which the movement of voluntary repatriation is taking place call for the rapid deployment of a large contingent of UNHCR emergency staff. ...

One of the major features of the staff deployment programme proposed by UNHCR is its reliance on the cooperation of several NGOs and the support of Governments to mobilize these human resources in a timely and effective manner. Indeed, over half of the 286 international officers needed by UNHCR for this operation will be seconded to the Office as contributions from various Governments and NGOs. They will be fully integrated in the UNHCR field structure for the duration of the operation and will bring with them much needed logistical support.

In Iraq, the role of these UNHCR teams will be to support voluntary repatriation and to constitute a network of humanitarian workers having constant access to major returnee areas, in accordance with the terms of the Memorandum of Understanding signed in Baghdad between the Government of Iraq and the Executive Delegate of the Secretary-General. As the lead agency for matters relating to refugees and returnees, UNHCR will concentrate its activities in the Northern and Eastern parts of Iraq and play a co-ordination role in relation to emergency programmes for these categories of persons.

Financial information

By 20 May 1991, a total of US$ 140 million had been contributed to UNHCR against revised requirements of US$ 267,6 million, leaving a funding shortfall of US$ 127,6 million.

Given the rapidly changing situation and the need to re-deploy resources rapidly as the pace of voluntary repatriation accelerates, donors are urged to avoid geographical earmarkings.

SUMMARY PLAN OF ACTION

On 15 May, the UN Agencies involved in the humanitarian relief effort in the Persian Gulf region and IOM made an appeal indicating their needs and programmes to be implemented between now and August. UNHCR's assumptions and plan of action for the period are summarised below.

Assistance to refugees in Iran

A total of 1,3 million refugees from Iraq have been given asylum in five provinces of the Islamic Republic of Iran. Up to 30 April 1991, UNHCR expenditure for this group amounted to some US$ 43,5 million, mainly to purchase and transport much needed emergency shelter material, domestic items such as blankets, medicine, high protein food and emergency sanitation and water distribution equipment.

Activities foreseen during the period from May to August are based on the assumption that trends recently noted regarding voluntary repatriation will gain significant momentum and that over 50 percent of the refugee population would trek back to their places of origin, mainly in North-Eastern Iraq, leaving a refugee population of some 600,000 persons in need of international assistance. The continued care of such a large number of persons will require some investments in more permanent camp infrastructure - in preparation for the winter season - as well as uninterrupted supplies of basic relief items meant to complement what is already being provided through bilateral efforts or by the Government of the Islamic Republic of Iran.

UNHCR requirements for refugees in Iran for the four-month period from May to August 1991 amount to US$ 102,4 million as shown on the attached summary budget.

Assistance to refugees in camps at the Turkey/Iraq border

The rapidly decreasing population in camps at the Turkish border coupled with the massive relief assistance already mobilised by Turkish authorities and the international community substantially reduces the requirements for basic supplies over the coming months. Current trends indicate that by the end of June, the population remaining in emergency encampments on the Iraq/Turkey border could be in the range of 20,000 to 50,000 only. These persons will need temporary care and shelter in sites best suited for that purpose until such a time as they opt for repatriation. This implies continued care and maintenance and a number of technical studies, as well as investment in essential infrastructure. Estimated costs total US$ 11,4 million as shown in the attached summary budget.

Support to voluntary repatriation in Northern and Eastern Iraq

Given the rapid pace of spontaneous movements back to the valleys, cities and villages of Northern Iraq and to a more limited extent [*sic*] towards North-Eastern Iraq, UNHCR's strategy of support to voluntary repatriation now requires a major deployment of human and logistics resources to help create a United Nations network that can complement and gradually replace services provided through various military efforts and generally provide active support to the return movement. As part of this strategy, monitoring of the voluntary character of repatriation, as well as occasional material support will be required.

To carry this out, international staff will be temporarily deployed for up to one month in the camps on the Iraq/Turkey border, for the purpose of monitoring voluntary repatriation and putting into place an accelerated registration mechanism for refugees wishing to avail themselves of this service. Assistance to refugees who are without transport to return to their homes will be implemented by IOM in cooperation with UNHCR. It is expected, however, that a large number of refugees will continue to receive transport assistance from military forces and that up to 50 percent of the refugees in Iran will use their own vehicles to return.

Basic emergency relief items, such as tents, blankets, jerrycans, soap, clothing, high protein food, etc., will be distributed to up to 500,000 returnees through UNHCR mobile teams and relay stations. A small reserve fund for emergency projects, transport and storage costs of relief items has also been included. Costs relating to the rehabilitation of infrastructure and services are excluded.

To facilitate its repatriation programme, UNHCR will assume management and running of three transit centres for 20,000 persons each, in the areas of Zakho and Suriya. Once these centres have been fully handed over to UNHCR, management and running costs for a 90-day period are calculated at US$ 30 million. This cost takes into account the high turnover of population expected in the transit centres during the next three months. In addition, relay stations will be set up by UNHCR at strategic locations corresponding to the exit points from Iran. These relay stations will be managed by UNHCR and will have sufficient food and non-food items, stocks and facilities (water, fuel, health) to assist returnees on their way back. Assistance to some 40,000 Irania [*sic*] at Al Tash is also foreseen, including the voluntary repatriation of up to 10,000 of them at the estimated cost of US$ 3 million.

Staff Deployment

To effectively implement the above activities in Iran, Iraq, and Turkey, and provide an international presence commensurate with the tasks of promoting the safety and well-being of returnees and refugees, UNHCR will be deploying in the three countries a total of over 540 staff members. Of these, 91 will be assigned to the Islamic Republic of Iran and 176 to Southern Turkey. In Iraq, a network of three sub-offices, nine field offices and twenty mobile teams is needed. These will provide an outreach capacity to support spontaneous returns, to assess the well-being of returnees in their places of origin and to provide material assistance. Altogether a total of 163 international officers and up to 112 local support staff will be assigned to Iraq and must be provided with full logistics support, including telecommunications. More than half of the international staff requirements will be provided to UNHCR by NGOs and Governments as contributions in kind; the balance will be met through redeployment of UNHCR's own resources. A number of UNHCR regular staff members are thus being deployed from Turkey, in parallel with the movements of refugees.

...

CO-OPERATION WITH NON-GOVERNMENTAL ORGANISATIONS

From the outset of the Gulf emergency in January 1991, UNHCR has recognised the vital importance of effective coordination and information links with non-governmental organizations. On Jan 20, the Office organized the first of what became regular, weekly NGO/UNHCR coordination meetings to inform voluntary agencies of our plans and activities and to request that they in turn examine their own resources and operation plans in order to avoid duplication of efforts and to make optimal use of emerging logistics and transport networks. The regular participants to these meetings are Geneva-based NGOs and umbrella agencies on whose capacity to disseminate information UNHCR traditionally depends. NGO field staff passing through Geneva are also encouraged to attend these meetings and brief both UNHCR and their sister-NGO staff on events and developments in their area of operations.

Information on NGO activities and cooperation in the Gulf was also recognised as a necessary component of UNHCR's Information Bulletins. While systematic and thematic information structures are being developed, it was decided that this first NGO chapter of Bulletin No. 3 should provide concrete examples of NGO/UNHCR cooperation for the benefit of refugees. The stories hereafter are unfolding as these lines are read and the staff of the NGOs mentioned, as well as many others, are in the field ensuring the survival and wellbeing of Iraqi refugees and returnees.

The Lausanne Switzerland Branch of Terre des Hommes and the considerable umbrella structures of the Norwegian and Danish Refugee Councils may be considered at opposite ends of the northern NGO spectrum, having nonetheless in common prosperous, industrialized European societies and humanitarian-oriented governmental bodies as a source of support and funding. They also share that most precious of resources, a wealth of human energy and vision directed to those less fortunate than themselves.

Their respective [*sic*] approaches to the Middle East refugee emergency have been fundamentally different but have led them to a common ground, coordinating in concrete terms through the secondment of their staff to UNHCR assistance projects for Iraqi refugees and returnees.

In the words of Jeremy Condor, Coordinator for Middle-East Programmes, Terre des Hommes could offer but "a drop of help in an ocean of suffering" generated by the enormous exodus of Iraqis forced to flee their homes. In April, Jeremy made a discreet and solitary assessment journey through the refugee-hosting areas of Iran. His conclusion was that Terre des Hommes staff could most effectively operate within UNHCR's assistance structure rather than in administrative uncertainty as an independent NGO. He and several colleagues contacted our Chargé de Mission in Teheran and the Gulf Task Force at headquarters. A refugee camp with medical needs corresponding to his agency's response capacity was identified. Terre des Hommes went into fund raising and recruiting action. With a focus on services to children in tune with local realities, Terre des Hommes is also operating in harmony with UNHCR's policy that children cannot be assisted in isolation, but rather in the context of their families and communities.

The Nordic Refugee Councils have long been among UNHCR's most valuable partners in fund raising, advocacy, public information and education. When advised of the Office's urgent need for staff in the repatriation coordination operation underway in southern Turkey, the Danish and Norwegian Refugee Councils, funded from their Governments' contributions to UNHCR, responded with speed and efficiency. UNHCR needed field officers and Kurdish-speaking interpreters seconded to the Office. Within 24 hours, 20 qualified staff, equipped with personal survival kits and collective enthusiasm, were on a flight to Ankara. Thereafter, they were deployed to southern Turkey with the responsibility to shift with the refugee population into northern Iraq if necessary.

UNHCR is cooperating with the above NGOs, with the Lutheran World Federation, the World Council of Churches, Pharmaciens sans Frontières, Rädda Barnen of Sweden, Redd Barna of Norway and with numerous other NGOs to identify up to 150 additional staff members who will be incorporated into UNHCR teams in Iran, Iraq and Turkey. Some 40 officers will thus be leaving for Northern and Northeastern Iraq on 23 May 1991.

An NGO Liaison Officer has been assigned to the Gulf Emergency Task Force at UNHCR headquarters whose responsibilities include coordinating operational links between NGOs and the Office, expanding and improving information exchange, developing contacts and a data network to permit rapid secondment of NGO staff to UNHCR field posts, and assisting in the production of this bulletin. ...

ISLAMIC REPUBLIC OF IRAN

Location and Estimated Returnee/Refugee Population (15/5/91)

...

Repatriation: An estimated 80,000 refugees have returned to Iraq from Iran. For planning purposes it is assumed that some 800,000 will repatriate over the next few months while an estimated 600,000 will require winter shelter in Iran.

UNHCR Operations and Activities

The UNHCR assistance programme for Iraqi refugees in Iran is based on support to the government at the central and provincial levels. UNHCR has a field presence in four out of the five border provinces which are hosting refugees (Ilam is currently supported out of Bakhtaran).

Among the sectors covered by UNHCR operations and activities are food, health, water/sanitation, and non-food relief items. UNHCR has provided 750 MT of dates and 650 MT of high-protein biscuits, for instance, to complement the basic food basket provided by WFP.

In cooperation with the Ministry of Health, a UNHCR mission has assessed the health situation in West Azerbaijan and Kurdistan and is currently visiting Khuzistan). As a result, most of the drugs and medical supplies needed by the Ministry of Health as well as a buffer stock against the spread of communicable diseases have been airlifted to Iran. The medical supplies include cold chains and vehicles for an Expanded Poli-Immunization campaign that is already being undertaken by the Ministry of Health provincial structure.

Insufficient potable water and limited sanitation facilities are among the major causes of death among the refugee population and the onset of the warm season increases the risk of disease outbreaks. In order to meet the water/sanitation requirements, THW - a German technical agency - has started a project in Bakhtaran province which supplies water to 100,000 refugees in its first phase and in the very near future will cover the needs of 200,000 additional persons.

Similar arrangements are being sought for West Azerbaijan and Kurdistan. Negotiations are ongoing with a Swedish firm in order to drill urgently 40 bore holes.

A UNHCR water/sanitation mission has finalized assessments in all three northern provinces (it is currently in Khuzistan) and their recommendations are being implemented: 230 fixed water tanks have been procured by UNHCR and an additional 1,000 are needed. Sixty water trucks and 60 sewage trucks to service the systems being implemented are also needed.

As reported previously, limited tent availability in the international market has been hampering delivery. Thus far UNHCR has delivered 46,000 family tents (an additional 25,000 were supplied by non-UNHCR sources). Tarpaulins and plastic sheetings have also been delivered as shelter materials, but it is estimated that more than 50 percent of the refugees are still in need of shelter.

Coordination

UNHCR has daily meetings with the Ministries of Interior and of Health. At the provincial level there are meetings with the respective offices of the governors and deputy-governors. In Tehran [*sic*] representatives of donor missions are invited for briefings or meetings as needed. These representatives, notably the EEC group, hold weekly meetings among themselves and UNHCR, IOM and the Red Crescent are invited to participate.

Coordination of arrival and distribution of relief supplies has been very difficult due to the quantities involved (UNHCR alone, for example, was sending an average of 10 flights a day to provincial and national airports), but in a meeting held on 12 May the representatives of EEC member countries, Scandinavian countries, Australia, New Zealand, Canada and Japan in Tehran decided to recommend more coordination through UNHCR, which has logistics officers posted in those airports.

Priorities

The water/sanitation and the shelter sectors are the priorities in Iran. Providing refugees with appropriate water and sanitary services is of fundamental importance to improve the health conditions of the group. Some 189,000 family tents are still needed to cover the shelter needs of the Iraqi refugee population currently in Iran.

It is estimated that a sizeable portion of the Iraqi refugees might not repatriate as fast as others and that will mean the need for shelter facilities capable of protecting people from harsh winter conditions. The current planning figure for winterized shelter is for some 600,000 persons.

REPUBLIC OF IRAQ

Estimated Returnee/Refugee Population and their location (15.05.91)

A. Returnees

Returnees in transit centres

Zakho One: UN transit centre since 13 May 18,000
Zakho Two: still under US Armed Forces management 19,000
Zakho Three: being set up by US Armed Forces 11,000
Kani Masi: relay station 15,000
Sub-total: 63,000

Returnees elsewhere (estimate)

Northern Region (Zakho Valley, Al Amadiah, Dohuk) 140,000
Sulaimanyah Region (including displaced persons returning from Iranian border) 50,000

Erbil Region 30,000
Sub-total 220,000

Total 283,000

B: Refugees

Iranian nationals at Al Tash camp (near Ramadi) 40,000
Iranian nationals in districts of Nisan and Wasit 8,000

Total 48,000

UNHCR Operations and Activities

Presently there are 23 International UNHCR officers in Iraq (including four redeployed from Turkey presently in Zakho) and 22 local staff members. Twelve of the former are located in the Northern provinces together with four IOM experts. Between forty and fifty additional UNHCR field officers and experts will arrive in Baghdad on 23 May together with vehicles and operational equipment including radio communication, survival emergency kits, generators etc. Most of the staff and the equipment will come from European Nordic countries, particularly Sweden, Denmark and Norway.

Northern and North Eastern Provinces

From 24 to 26 April and 30 April to 8 May, survey missions were undertaken from Baghdad to Dohuk, Erbil and Suleimanyah. Since then, UNHCR sub-offices were established in the three provincial capitals, and in Zakho. Exploratory work has been done to establish additional offices in Al Amadiah, Rawandez, Shaklawa, Chuarta, Halabja and Khanaqin. However, locations of some of these field offices may change when the situation has been fully assessed. Out of these field offices, twenty mobile teams (five international officers each) will be created to undertake surveys, monitor returns and provide assistance in the areas of refugee return. As required, they will establish relay stations along return routes.

South Eastern Provinces

In addition to the sub-office established in Mosul, UNICEF has opened a second one in the city of Basrah where UNHCR staff members are being assigned in order to cover the South Eastern borders of Iraq.

Assistance to refugees in Al Tash

In Al Tash, near Ramadi, three UNHCR staff members assist an estimated 40,000 Iranian refugees. Activities in Al Tash include registration for voluntary repatriation (3,250 families registered as of 13 May).

Return movements

A great proportion of the 200,000 people remaining at the Turkish border do not wish to move either to existing transit centres or to their home regions until further guarantees of security and protection can be granted or until an agreement is reached between the Government of Iraq and their leaders. UNHCR is therefore focussing on the setting up of an assistance network on their behalf.

The estimated 80,000 returnees from Iran together with several tens of thousands displaced persons returning from the border with Iran are stranded in the region of Suleimanyah and are in urgent need of the most basic assistance, particularly shelter, health and food. Hence, UNHCR Baghdad is concentrating efforts on the procurement of food, tents and other relief items, while ICRC, MSF, MDM and PSF (Pharmaciens sans Frontières) are operating, supporting or establishing some fifteen health centres in the area concerned. UNICEF is strengthening its presence in Basrah and operates with the support of UNHCR and other UN Agencies concerned.

Co-ordination

Interagency meetings are held daily in Baghdad under the chairmanship of the Representative of the Secretary General's Executive Delegate. Interagency missions have visited the North, East and South. This latter region included the provinces of Basrah, Nisan and Wasit where the major problems identified are water, health, food supply and a displaced population currently estimated at 150,000.

IOM, UNICEF, WHO and WFP are reinforcing their presence alongside UNHCR, while ICRC is providing most valuable support to the UN and partnership or ad hoc arrangements are being worked out with NGOs active or due to arrive in Iraq.

Priorities

To reach an effective level of operationality, UNHCR as well as other UN Agencies have to dramatically increase their presence (UNHCR has established a staffing table of 163 international and 112 local staff members), their operational capacity, (UNHCR has nine vehicles and thirty are expected before 23 May) and their communication network.

The urgent need for the strengthening of this operational capacity is obvious when almost everything is urgently required: medical care, shelter, potable water, food, sanitation and, particularly for returnees, the international monitoring foreseen in the Memorandum of Understanding signed by the Executive Delegate of the Secretary General.

REPUBLIC OF TURKEY

...

UNHCR Operations and Activities

The emergency situation in Turkey continues to evolve at an extraordinary pace. Six weeks from the start of the massive influx from Iraq, voluntary repatriation has become a major feature of the emergency.

On 6 May UNHCR began to register refugees for voluntary repatriation and to monitor return movements. Since then, the pace of repatriation movements has become such that the registration process is presently overcome by direct assistance and monitoring activities. Camp management is increasingly difficult, especially when refugee leaders leave the camps. However, with the decreased population, health, water and sanitation problems are easier to resolve. Food supplies (particularly thanks to the Turkish Red Crescent and coalition armed forces) remain satisfactory but logistic operations are hampered by mass movements along poor quality roads.

UNHCR has 65 staff members (international and local) present in Ankara, Incirlik, Diyarbakir, Adana, Van and all refugee sites. Additional experts and field staff should arrive in the coming days as redeployment to Northern Iraq is already underway. UNHCR staff includes regular staff members as well as UNVs, NGOs and government seconded or released personnel (particularly from the Danish and Norwegian Refugee Councils and Radda Barnen (Sweden), with the support of their governments).

In addition to relief activities in the camps and overall co-ordination, UNHCR, together with IOM, is directing increasing efforts towards the organization of transportation of refugees (particularly vulnerable groups) wishing to return. With regard to the eventual residual caseload not wishing to repatriate discussions are taking place with the Turkish authorities to ensure their stay in consolidated sites to be identified (Silopi and Yekmal have already been mentioned but assessment of the situation continues). This residual caseload seems to concern mainly: Christians (although some repatriation has been reported); military deserters; persons from areas located outside the allied security zone and persons with third country links.

Co-ordination

UNHCR co-ordination efforts are made at the camp level as well as in the main operational bases (Diyarbakir, Silopi, Adana, Van). This effort concerns the local authorities as well as the foreign military forces, other UN Agencies and the NGOs.

In this context UNICEF has strengthened its presence (it has deployed a team of 20 medical doctors) and focus, *inter alia*, on services to children and mothers including a measles vaccination campaign in the camps. WFP, as agreed with the Turkish Government, will provide food for 500,000 people along the border for a period of ninety days. A WHO team, in close co-operation with UNHCR, has assessed the situation in the camps, distributed 100,000 doses of measles vaccine and began a crash course in disaster management for Turkish health officials assigned to refugee camps.

Priorities

Priorities are: to improve camp conditions in consolidated refugee sites (this includes shelter and basic care, i.e. food, health, water and sanitation); to deploy additional human resources and to ensure rapid and secure transportation for refugees, particularly vulnerable groups, wishing to repatriate.

INTERNATIONAL PROCUREMENT AND LOGISTICS

As in previous weeks, UNHCR has continued to identify, purchase and transport priority relief supplies for Iran, Turkey and Iraq. To date, 235 flights (of which 138 funded by the E.E.C.), carrying 7,270 MT of relief supplies have been arranged by SFAS, in addition to quantities moved by ship and overland.

During the first four and half months of 1991, total international purchases by UNHCR, for all programmes, amounts to slightly over US$ 65,300,000. As a comparison, in 1990 the total purchases amounted to some US$ 43,000,000 for the entire year. This increased activity and the complicated logistics arrangements involved have put considerable strain on staff since the beginning of the emergency operations in the Persian Gulf region.

The table below provides further details about main items and quantities delivered and en route to Iran and Turkey. It is worth noting in particular that some 1,600,000 blankets and 82,000 tents have been purchased and are being delivered to the respective locations.

The two major constraints have been the shortage of competitively priced tents on the world market and the unexpected temporary closure of provincial airports in Iran for a variety of reasons which included fuel shortage, slow clearance of cargo and repair works on runways.

Procurement and delivery have already started for Iraq, where UNHCR presence is being dramatically increased to assist returnees. Urgent relief items are being delivered by air and road. 91,000 blankets have already been sent to Cyprus for onforwarding to Iraq.

International Organization for Migration, Press release No. 686, 31 May 1991

28. International Organization for Migration: Iraqi Kurds-Return Movements from Turkey Pass the 200,000 Mark, 31 May 1991

Amid growing confidence in the safety of returning home, as of 31 May 1991, over 205,000 Iraqi Kurds have moved to their home villages in the Zakho/Dohuk area with IOM assistance. Responsibility for the operation of movements has increasingly been taken over by IOM from the military.

The rotation of trucks arranged by IOM carries up to 20,000 persons per day, and it is expected that the general camp clearing process will be completed within a matter of days.

IOM's involvement will now focus increasingly on assisting in the return from the Zakho valley of 40,000 Iraqi Kurds now in camps and a substantially larger number in the surrounding area. Future movements will depend on the assessment of Kurdish elders as to the security situation in their home regions.

29. United Nations High Commissioner for Refugees Information Bulletin No. 4 on Operations in the Persian Gulf Region, 11 June 1991

- Some one million Iraqis have left Turkey and Iran. Many have gone back to their villages and towns of origin, but approximately 500,000, still in an unsettled situation, need continued UN support inside Iraq.

- UNHCR has now deployed 169 staff in Iraq and assistance programmes to returnees cover all North and Northeastern borders of the country. Field offices and mobile teams monitor repatriation movements.

- WFP food supplies, distributed by ICRC in Northern Iraq, will be exhausted in the next few days if new donations are not made immediately. Situation particularly serious for protein-rich food.

- Over half a million Iraqi refugees from the recent influx remain in Iran. Water and sanitation still top priority, but shelter for the winter season under discussion with the Iranian Government.

- UNHCR has received contributions totalling US$ 166,5 million towards an estimated budget (January - August 1991) of US$ 267,6 million.

INTRODUCTION

Close to one million refugees have now returned to Iraq. While about half of them are back in their previous places of residence, an estimated 500,000 persons are still in an unsettled situation and need continued UN support inside Iraq. This group is composed of people not able, or not allowed, to return to their home towns and villages as well as families attempting to resettle in those Kurdish villages which had been evacuated and destroyed over the years.

Only 13,400 refugees are now left in the two remaining Turkish camps of Semdinli and Silopi, where those who felt they could not return to Iraq are being given temporary sanctuary by the authorities. UNHCR has also requested access to some 26,000 refugees from the 1988 influx, to offer them assistance with voluntary repatriation, should they want it.

As many as 500,000 of the refugees registered in camps in Iran have now crossed back to Iraq. Discussions are under way between UNHCR and the Government of the Islamic Republic of Iran on ways of helping those who want to return, but needing vehicles and material assistance. As a priority, UNHCR and the Government of the Islamic Republic of Iran are also identifying sites that can be improved in preparation for the winter for refugees who remain.

Since 7 June, UNHCR has assumed full responsibility co-ordinating humanitarian activities in Northern Iraq, centred on its office in Dohuk. The process of handing over humanitarian activities carried out by members of the coalition forces in parts of Northern Iraq is now well under way. For this purpose, UNHCR is in close liaison with the local authorities, representatives of the allied forces, other U.N. agencies primarily involved such as UNICEF, WHO and WFP (who are all represented in the field), and NGOs active in the area.

The rapid repatriation and the resultant closing down of most camps on the Iraq/Turkey border, as well as the process of camp consolidation and family re-grouping currently going on in Iran, demonstrate UNHCR's need to review constantly its programme priorities and shift human and budgetary resources.

The series of violent incidents that swept major cities of Northern Iraq between 30 May and 2 June 1991, resulting in scores of deaths, illustrate the fragility of recent return movements. Following these events, UNHCR field officers in Iraq have reported a sharp drop in the rate of returns. However, the resumption of talks between the Government of Iraq and the Kurdish leadership has revived hopes for a negotiated settlement which most observers consider as the only credible basis for restoring internal stability and security.

Deployment of staff

A number of staff members previously assigned to Turkey under emergency procedures have now been redeployed to Iraq. UNHCR has also implemented a successful scheme of secondment of NGO staff, mainly with the support of Denmark, Norway and Sweden.

...

Financial information

The United Nations appeal of 15 May 1991 identified UNHCR requirements for the period May - August 1991 as US$ 194,7 million. Total UNHCR requirements since the launching of the Regional Humanitarian Plan of Action on 15 January 1991 thus amounted to US$ 267,6. On 10 June, the funding shortfall was US$ 101,1 million, as shown by the table below.

ISLAMIC REPUBLIC OF IRAN

Location and estimated returnee/refugee population (30 May 1991)

Province	Refugees/Returnees
West Azerbaijan (16 sites)	188,766/199,282
Bakhtaran (27 sites)	230,500/220,200
Kurdestan (27 sites)	57,297/85,950
Kuzestan (10 sites)	65,000/-
Ilam	2,689/-
Total	544,252/505,432

The above numbers are UNHCR estimates based on recent information provided by the Iranian Government and on the earlier figure of 1,049,486 (Information Bulletin No. 3) which corresponded to the number of refugees registered at camp sites by mid-May. UNHCR estimates that there would be an additional 100,000 to 150,000 refugees not registered in camps.

UNHCR operations and activities

The repatriation movement is coordinated between UNHCR and the Iranian provincial authorities who have been providing free transportation to the border, supplying fuel free of charge and sometimes distributing food baskets. UNHCR also provides support to those returning (transport, food and non-food items).

Many of the returnees have not yet returned to their places of origin in Iraq. Due to a perceived lack of stability in the area, many have chosen to temporarily camp near the Iranian border in Iraq. Some 170,000 persons (returnees and internally displaced), for instance, are currently at the Savoje enclave bordering Iranian Kurdestan. As a result of the various incidents that took place in Northern and Eastern Iraq recently, the pace of return has considerably decreased (for more details, see section on Iraq).

UNHCR presence in Iran continued to be built up during the month of May. Field presence in the four provinces hosting the largest number of refugees has been achieved although more expertise at field level is still required and will be met during the month of June.

There are currently 90 UNHCR staff in Iran. As a result of an agreement signed with the Government, a UNHCR presence has been established in Orumieh, Sanandaj, Bakhtaram and Ahwaz.

The main areas of assistance covered by UNHCR continue to be food (to complement WFP's programme), water, sanitation and health (in cooperation with UNICEF and WHO) as well as supply of shelter equipment.

UNHCR is also focussing on sectors which will meet the needs of those refugees who might remain in Iran during the next winter season. Heavy equipment is being procured to accelerate the upgrading and consolidation of the refugee sites which will remain open to that caseload. Winter shelter continues to be actively pursued, as indicated in Information Bulletin No. 3.

While temporary solutions are being implemented to cover the refugees' immediate needs, current UNHCR plans are for their short and medium-term basic needs to be met during the months of June and July, according to the recommendations and results of a recently concluded UNHCR multi-sectoral, technical mission which re-assessed the health, water and sanitation sectors.

The mission confirmed that health requirements (medicines and equipment) have generally been met.

Water supply remains problematic both in terms of quantity as well as quality although the situation is gradually improving with the assistance of technical agencies working in close cooperation with the Government. The 60 water tankers identified as a need in Information Bulletin No. 3 have already been purchased.

Efforts must also be concentrated on improving the sanitary conditions of the refugee sites. Government, NGOs and technical agencies are working in a coordinated fashion to achieve that. The 60 sewage tankers previously identified as a priority need have also been procured by UNHCR and other heavy equipment (front loaders, tip-up trucks, etc) are also in the pipeline.

Coordination

During May there was a substantial improvement in the coordination of all relief activities for refugees in the country. The Government as well as the international community and the non-governmental organizations have recognised the need for closer coordination to improve the efficiency and effectiveness of the operation.

This new understanding has made it possible for UNHCR to improve its coordinating role in the country. An improved monitoring system is being set up while the assistance efforts of the international community are more efficiently organized.

A number of NGOs are planning to leave Iran, which will certainly have an impact on the timely implementation of the sectoral activities at the provincial level (for more details see section on NGOs).

Priorities

All outstanding items in the water, sanitation and health sectors need to be urgently procured. The water, sanitation, drainage and health systems/facilities must be set up in the sites chosen by the Government to host any possible residual refugee population during the next winter season. Contractors have been identified for the construction of winter shelter as a result of the repatriation movement. A winterized shelter pilot project is to be tested in the very near future.

Closer coordination of activities between Iran and Iraq must be achieved to improve assistance to returnees.

Though the requirements for non-food items have been partially met by UNHCR in cooperation with the international community, contingency stocks must be prepositioned in the southern part of the country for a possible influx into Khuzistan province from people in Southern Iraq.

Republic of Iraq

UNHCR operations and activities

The last month has been characterized by a very fast repatriation from Turkey and Iran into areas in Northern and North-Eastern Iraq. UNHCR has responded by mounting an emergency operation through rapid deployment of staff and equipment, international procurement of relief items and the putting in place of implementation arrangements with NGOs to provide life saving services to the returnees. These efforts are now somewhat threatened by the eruption of violence in several of the major towns in Iraqi Kurdistan. Serious incidents leading to loss of lives have occurred in Suleimania, Erbil and Dohuk.

UNHCR has now deployed 32 local and more than 137 international staff members in Iraq of whom 72 are seconded by Nordic governments/NGOs. The sub-offices in Dohuk, Suleimania and Erbil are now fully operational. In addition to the large field office in Zakho, UNHCR has established field offices in Amadia, Sadik, Ranya, Penjwin and Sayed Sadeq.

Radio communication equipment has been installed in all these offices (for more details please see Logistics section). Thirty 4WD vehicles have been sent to Baghdad and after installation of radios these vehicles have been deployed to the sub/field offices and the mobile teams. UNHCR is now able to monitor developments at the North-Eastern border from the Iraqi side.

Subject to prevailing security conditions, UNHCR is planning to deploy additional staff, vehicles and equipment to increase the number of mobile teams. At least 50 more staff members will be sent to Iraq as soon as more vehicles/radio equipment become available.

UNHCR is in the process of procuring/delivering shelter materials such as tents (12,000) and plastic sheeting (20,000), as well as blankets (150,000) and stoves (150). The first batch of family tents (2,000) has already been delivered.

Northern Iraq/Allied Security Zone

About 400,000 refugees have now returned to Northern Iraq from Turkey. Both organized and spontaneous returns have taken place to the provincial capital Dohuk, which is technically outside the allied security zone. The majority have returned to their homes.

The population remaining in transit centres and relay stations has been decreasing as people have been able to return to their places of origin. The population in the remaining two Zakho transit centres is approximately 10,000, while only a few thousand are staying in relay stations.

UNHCR and the Combined Task Force Provide Comfort have agreed to a transition plan which transferred [*sic*] overall responsibility for humanitarian relief operations in the allied security zone to UNHCR from 7 June 1991. However, security in the zone will continue to be dealt [*sic*] with separately under the responsibility of the allied forces until the situation is stabilized.

UNHCR, in close coordination with other UN agencies, is making appropriate arrangements with NGOs and other operational partners present in the area to provide health, sanitation, water and social services as well as logistical support. The allied forces will continue to support the humanitarian operation while UNHCR is making arrangements for a phased takeover of actual implementation of these activities.

North-Eastern Provinces

The Iranian Government has reported that some 500,000 refugees have returned to Iraq from camps in Iran. UNHCR's staff in the North-Eastern provinces and organizations like ICRC have come across many returnees/displaced persons in the area between Suleimania/Erbil and the Iran/Iraq border. However, it has not yet been possible to verify their numbers and identify all the various groups that have returned. Many of these persons are now displaced on Iraqi territory while they are waiting for the situation to improve to enable them to return home.

Both sub-offices in Erbil and Suleimania as well as their field offices and mobile teams operate in areas which are controlled by either the Iraqi Government or the opposition. Full cooperation from both sides has been established which makes it possible for UNHCR and other UN staff to circulate freely, for relief items to be distributed and for returnees to be transported all the way to their villages of origin.

The transportation of returnees is done in coordination with IOM. In the Erbil area, the first such operation took place on 31 May. Thirty IOM trucks are based in Suleimania to help returnees who are settling back in that area.

The four field offices and their mobile teams in the North/Eastern parts of Iraq provide assistance to returnees and monitor seven cross border points which are the main repatriation routes for those leaving Iran from the provinces of West Azerbaijan, Kurdistan and Bakhtaran.

The Sadik field office monitors the Haj Umram crossing point, the Raniah field office monitors Siyagowez, the Panjwin field office monitors the Seyran Bent, Gohlan, Khanakan and Bashmak crossing points, and the Saidi Sadik field office monitors the Nosoud/Paven cross border point.

With the arrival of more vehicles and equipment, more mobile teams and relay stations are being deployed, but all field offices have already begun emergency operations. Saidi Sadik, for instance, is clearing an area in the destroyed city of Saidi Sadik which has made it possible for MSF to move its tent hospital to the bulldozed site.

The Panjwin field office is finalizing this week road repairs and diversions in order to facilitate the repatriation movement from the Iranian province of Kurdistan and practically eliminate the possibility of road congestion.

UNICEF has finalized an assessment of water needs in the region, UNHCR, as a result, immediately supplied five Oxfam type water tanks which were installed by UNICEF by the end of last week. ICRC is distributing WFP food for 300,000 persons in the next two months and is expecting EEC food supplies soon while UNHCR is procuring 128 MT of high protein biscuits.

Co-ordination

Since mid-May a series of formal co-ordinating mechanisms for NGOs and UN agencies has been established in Baghdad. Co-ordination meetings in food, water, sanitation and health are now held on a weekly basis, while United Nations inter-agency meetings continue to take place each fortnight. The main objective of such meetings is to avoid duplication of effort, time and resources, including funds, and to ensure that priority needs are met timely.

In the Erbil area, NGOs, ICRC and UNHCR meet weekly with local authorities. Responding to the co-ordination requirements in that region, UNHCR has now appointed a medical co-ordinator from within its ranks for Erbil. For the north there is agreement that health co-ordination should be done by the sub-offices in association with UNICEF and WHO, NGOs covering all sectors (health, water, sanitation and food) and UNHCR meet regularly at the UNHCR Zakho field office.

Priorities

Completion of transition from Combined Task Force to UNHCR through appropriate implementation arrangements with NGOs and other non-military partners present in Northern Iraq.

Provision of emergency assistance to returnees/displaced persons in Northeastern Iraq. UNHCR will focus on supply of shelter materials and other non-food items. WFP and ICRC will supply food, while UNICEF, ICRC and NGOs will provide medical assistance. WFP has informed that its food supplies for Northern Iraq will be exhausted by mid-June, i.e., in a few days. The situation is particularly serious for protein-rich food, commodities (canned fish/meat/cheese). Donations are needed immediately and details can be obtained directly from WFP/Rome.

Establishment of more relay stations along major return routes from Iraq where health, sanitation and water services can be provided.

REPUBLIC OF TURKEY

Location and Estimated Refugee Population (1 May to 6 June 1991)

01 May/12 May/20 May/06 June

Isikveren 80,000/1,000/closed/closed
(including Kayadibi)
Yekmal 80,000/60,000/12,000/closed
Uzumlu 50,000/28,000/6,600/closed
Asma Kopru 30,000/5,000/(none)/closed
Cukurca 115,000/100,000/78,600/closed
Narli Bridge 19,500/19,750/closed
Pirinceken 8,000/3,500/900/closed
Semdinli 22,500/15,000/6,500/5,200 (including Yesilova)
Silopi 21,500/21,500/16,000/8,200

Total 413,500/252,000/140,350/13,400

(In addition, there are 5,000 Iraqis who arrived January to March 1991 located in six small camps at some distance from the border. Similarly, there are some 26,500 refugees in three temporary accommodation centres in Diyarbakir, Mardin and Mus. These refugees arrived in 1988)

UNHCR operations and activities

The voluntary repatriation movement from Turkey, either spontaneous or organized, has almost been completed. Remaining refugees, approximately 13,400 (excluding pre-March 1991 caseload), have been regrouped in two remaining camps, Silopi and Semdinli. The remaining population in Cukurca, approximately 1,000, were airlifted by US forces to Silopi on 6 June. Care and maintenance assistance will be continued in Silopi and Semdinli until a durable solution can be identified for this residual caseload.

UNHCR continues to have a field office in Silopi, a sub-office in Diyarbakir and a liaison officer in Incirlik (Adana). After numerous redeployments of staff to Northern Iraq, only 21 international staff members are still in Turkey under the emergency programme partly to provide logistical/communication support to the operation in Northern Iraq and to maintain a presence in case of any new influx of refugees.

UNHCR has proposed a project to the Turkish Government to clean up the closed camps in view of the need to close the open latrines, remove refuse and garbage.

CO-OPERATION WITH NON-GOVERNMENTAL ORGANIZATIONS

UNHCR continues to promote effective coordination and information links with non-governmental organizations in the face of the rapidly evolving situation in Iran, Iraq and Turkey.

Turkey-Iraq

With the major shift of refugees from Southern Turkey into Northern Iraq, many NGOs shifted their assistance programmes accordingly. While cross-border operations have indeed been effective, they cannot be considered a long-term arrangement. Thus, NGOs implementing Iraqi-based assistance programmes need official recognition by the Government of Iraq in order to operate from within the country.

As regards NGOs cooperating with UNHCR, an administrative process has been instituted through the UNHCR sub-office in Dohuk to have that recognition granted. All the necessary paper work including the remittance of passports to the Ministry of Foreign Affairs and their delivery back to NGO staff with the required official Iraqi visa will be done through the Dohuk office.

Once the Iraqi Government clearance is obtained, those NGOs currently operating only in the security zone will be in a position to extend their operations well into Northeastern and Eastern Iraq.

Many NGOs are currently working outside the allied controlled-area, around Erbil and Suleimania, and have already obtained Government clearance. They have been collaborating with UNHCR sub-offices, field offices and mobile units, particularly for medical and material assistance along return routes and at relay points.

Iran and the Iran/Iraq border

NGO operations in Iran started in different ways. Some agencies have become operational as a result of direct cooperation with UNHCR both in Tehran as well as in the five western provinces hosting Iraqi refugees. UNHCR has provided guidance in the definition of the scope and nature of assistance activities, selection of sites, facilitating clearance of goods and equipment, logistics services and liaison with local authorities.

For NGOs with no direct operational links with UNHCR, there is a regular exchange of information and UNHCR (Tehran and field) facilitates contacts with local authorities.

As a result of the ongoing repatriation, some NGOs are getting ready to leave the country while some others have indicated they will remain in Iran and will focus on services to the sites designed to accommodate [*sic*] any remaining caseload over the coming winter. Assistance activities in the water, health and sanitation sectors are also being planned by NGOs in cooperation with UNHCR for Southern Iran.

...

SG/SM/4574, IK/24, 13 June 1991

30. Statement by the Secretary-General, 12 June 1991

Following is the text of the statement (translated from French) by Secretary-General Javier Pérez de Cuéllar, delivered yesterday, 12 June, in Geneva at the pledging conference for the United Nations Humanitarian Programme for Iraq, Kuwait and the Iraq/Turkey and Iraq/Iran Border Areas:

I wish first of all to thank you for having responded to my invitation.

The time chosen for this meeting and the nature of the challenges that it addresses give it special importance: these challenges require, on the part of the international community as a whole, a major effort, an expression of its will to act efficiently and speedily to come to the aid of hundreds of thousands of families in need, within the framework of the Humanitarian Programme for Iraq, Kuwait and the Iraq/Turkey and Iraq/Iran Border Areas.

On 15 May, in view of the inadequacy of the funds contributed so far by States, a revised and restructured appeal was launched, which, on the basis of the development of the situation and the assessment of needs, called upon the international community once again in order to obtain the necessary financial support.

This appeal stated that, at the beginning of May, some 415,000 refugees had been at the Iraq/Turkey border and that, two weeks later, that number had fallen to 208,000. It is today around 13,000. Furthermore, 539,000 refugees are currently still in Iranian territory, as against 1,402,000 as of 1 May. The same appeal of 15 May stressed that, in the course of the two preceding weeks, some 106,000 refugees from seven localities in the north of Iraq had been able to receive food aid and that United Nations Humanitarian Centres had been established at Zakho, Mosul, Basra, Arbil, Sulaymaniyah and Dohuk.

Today, in this same region, various population groups, among the most vulnerable, still lack shelter, food and care.

This fact cannot but prompt the entire international community to mobilize with all due dispatch and to demonstrate its generosity by coming to the aid of these people who are in such a sorry situation.

An important aspect of this Programme, having to do with the security of operations, has been the subject of new negotiations in recent weeks. These negotiations have produced an agreement which can be described as extremely innovative, an agreement which deals with the deployment in the region in question of a United Nations Guard Contingent - a contingent of veritable "humanitarian witnesses" whose task will be to ensure the smooth conduct of operations and the security of the field personnel who are to carry them out and, as necessary, to prepare reports on any incidents affecting the beneficiaries of United Nations programmes.

This agreement, which is essential to the success of the Humanitarian Programme and which has been made a part of the Memorandum of Understanding signed in Baghdad on 18 April, calls for the community of States to make available for the Programme both personnel and equipment, and the money needed to fund the Contingent.

We have a responsibility vis-à-vis both the beneficiaries of the Programme and donors to it to ensure that operations proceed without incident. We therefore hope to be in a position before long to complete the deployment of the Contingent, which is to be placed under the command of a commander stationed in Baghdad and under the authority of the Coordinator and Special Representative of the Executive Delegate.

...

.. Indeed, the United Nations guards will constitute an important element in the overall plan for dealing with the problem of the security of operations. As Secretary-General, I consider it essential today that the necessary attention be given to the different elements of this comprehensive plan, which should, in time, allow for calm to be restored in the region.

Needless to say, the United Nations operation in Iraq cannot succeed unless it has the support of the parties concerned. I therefore wish to appeal once again for moderation so that the spirit, if not the letter, that must characterize the demilitarization which is an integral part of any peace agreement may prevail and so that the civilian authorities may be genuinely respected by all.

If I have dwelled on thus Guard Contingent, it is because the success of the Humanitarian Programme which we have developed depends in large measure on it. We must not, moreover, lose sight of the fact that this Programme is targeted to all vulnerable groups wherever they may be. Thus, we are not talking just about the Kurds but also about the Shi'ites in the southern part of the country, of whom there are many, and about quite a few other minorities who, unfortunately, tend to be neglected. Public attention, as you all know, is focusing above all on the plight of the Kurds. Unfortunately, they are not the only ones who need our help. Consequently, all the vulnerable groups must be brought within the scope of our Humanitarian Programme.

As for the funding of the Programme, the overall budget of the action stemming from the appeal of 15 May, including establishment of the Guard Contingent, is estimated at $448.9 million. This figure covers needs relating to United Nations programmes of emergency humanitarian assistance until 31 August 1991. As of this time, we have an overall deficit of $340.3 million and we must make good this deficit as a matter of urgency so that we can respond to the needs and established priorities, inter alia, food aid to refugees and repatriated persons in Iraq, refugee repatriation projects undertaken under the auspices of the United Nations High Commissioner for Refugees (UNHCR), the International Organization for Migration, the United Nations Children's Fund (UNICEF) and the World Health Organization (WHO), and the projects of emergency assistance to the most vulnerable groups in Iraq, under the supervision of such organizations as UNICEF, WHO and UNHCR. We are still far short of the $35 million needed to finance the Guard Contingent; as yet, we have less than $25 million. As you see, a substantial effort is still needed in order for us to achieve our objective.

However, I will not dwell further on the details regarding the funding of these projects. Clearly, this Humanitarian Programme is a major operation, an exceptionally big challenge for the United Nations. The presence of the United Nations in this region has already made it possible to help several hundreds of thousands of refugees and to repatriate them to their places of origin. It has made it possible to provide food aid to more than

100,000 people and to vaccinate more than 100,000 children against measles.

However, that is only a beginning. The international community must now help us to take up this challenge. It must also realize that Iraq must embark on its reconstruction on a stable basis, or else the world community will be responsible for the fate of 18 million people, and it will be unable to do this on a long-term basis.

It is true that the Security Council has imposed sanctions on Iraq. However, we must reconcile those sanctions with the humanitarian assistance which is essential to the needs of the population and particularly those of the most vulnerable groups. It is therefore vital that States come to our assistance in these troubled times and give us this support without which our action cannot be completed. Recent history has demonstrated that, despite limited means, our interventions have been able to achieve their objectives.

I know that, once again, the United Nations can count on your generosity.

I thank you.

IHA/407, IK/25, 14 June 1991

31. UN Press Release: International Donor Community Pleges, 12 June 1991

GENEVA, 12 June (UN Information Service) - Emergency humanitarian assistance totalling about $85 million, in cash or in kind, was pledged today, by representatives of the international donor community in support of the United Nations inter-agency programme for Iraq, Kuwait and the Iraq/Turkey and Iraq/Iran border areas. This amount does not include the total costs involved in providing personnel for the United Nations guards contingent or other activities, as was pledged by several delegations.

The pledges were announced at a one-day conference organized in Geneva by the Office of the United Nations Disaster Relief Coordinator (UNDRO), with the Office of the Executive Delegate of the Secretary-General. The Secretary-General, representatives of Governments and heads of United Nations and other agencies carrying out the Plan of Action participated in the meeting. The Resident Coordinators of Turkey, Kuwait and Iran also attended, as did the Coordinator for United Nations operations in Iraq.

Representatives of the following States made new pledges, in cash or in kind, or in human resources: United States, $63.1 million; Czechoslovakia (amount to be specified); Romania, 14 million ley in materials; Sweden, $4.9 million; Finland, $4 million plus 50 guards; Norway, $1 million; Italy (amount to be specified); Denmark, 50 guards; Austria, 20 guards; Spain, $100,000; Greece, 30 guards; and Belgium, $12.5 million. These figures are subject to revision following confirmation and additions.

In making their pledges, many delegates remarked on the imaginative and resourceful use of the United Nations guards contingent, for which they expressed particular support. It was pointed out, however, that the ultimate responsibility for the safety of the returning refugees lay with the Iraqi Government. Several delegates also called for a more equitable sharing of burdens in the donor community.

The consolidated report on the current status of the United Nations Administration Plan of Action states that although conditions have improved in refugee camps, additional shelter, safe water supplies and sanitation services were still required in Iran, as well as supplementary foods to address the poor nutritional conditions of many mothers and children.

Due to the large numbers of refugees returning to Iraq, and the worsening conditions in some parts of the country, the report says emergency assistance must be expanded to meet the needs of returning refugees and to stave off new calamities. Cholera outbreaks were continuing in some areas.

The total budget for humanitarian relief activities is $414,050,737 to cover a four-month period until the end of August. Of this total, $64,970,099 are required for food supplies. Assistance to refugees and returnees amounts to $235,478,158. To provide the full complement of United Nations guards (60 guards are presently in Iraq), an additional $34,865,000 is required. To date, only $7.5 million have been pledged.

32. Office of the Executive Delegate of the Secretary-General for a United Nations Inter-Agency Humanitarian Programme for Iraq, Kuwait and the Iraq/Turkey and Iraq/Iran border areas, 15 May 1991, Updated Appeal, 12 June 1991

In the month since the 15 May 1991 Appeal refugees have returned to Iraq in large numbers from the Iraq/Turkey border, Turkey and also from Iran - where, however, many are still in transit in the border areas. Many have been assisted to go back to their homes by the provision of transport, food and essential supplies made available through the United Nations Inter-Agency Humanitarian Programme and other ongoing relief efforts. The return to Iraq of so many of those displaced is an achievement in which we can take great satisfaction. But hard challenges lie ahead.

During the course of the month, many initiatives have continued to be taken by the United Nations to facilitate the repatriation of Iraqi refugees and ensure their well-being. The chief amongst these have included extensive use of the "blue routes", which were established by the Office of the Executive Delegate working with Non-Governmental organisations and concerned member states; the opening of additional United Nations Humanitarian Centres (UNHUCs), sub-offices and relay stations in key locations and the posting of the first contingent of 60 United Nations Guards. The blue routes have guided many thousands of those coming back from Iskiveren to Zakho and from Uzumlu/Cukura through Kani Masi to Zakho and Dohuk, while the relay stations have been, and continue to be, instrumental in assisting returnees.

As of 4 June, only 13,000 refugees remained in camps on the Iraq/Turkey border. All but two camps, including Iskiveren, which has been used by the world media as a symbol of the tragic exodus of Iraqis who fled, have been emptied of their populations and are now closed. A key to the voluntary return home of refugees in Turkey and those who have been displaced near Zakho has been the creation of confidence in the greater Dohuk area. Here we sent, as a first step, a United Nations convoy to Dohuk, carrying 117 mts of food for the 20,000 people remaining out of a pre-war population of 250,000. A sub-office was established to distribute essential supplies and to maintain the United Nations presence. Thereafter, the first contingent of United Nations Guards was posted to Dohuk, becoming fully operational on 19 May. By 1 June the population of Dohuk had increased to 120,000 and today is estimated at 216,000.

In Iran, out of an original estimated total of 1.3 million Iraqi refugees, 539,252 people now remain in camps, mostly in West Azerbaijan and Bakhtaran - a reduction of 250,000 from 30 May. As yet, unfortunately, many of those who have returned from Iran remain displaced around towns and cities or close to border areas largely due to a sense of unease regarding their safety and assured provision of adequate supplies.

There must be no delay in the rapid deployment of the additional United Nations Guards. While their assignment can be considered only as a part of a wider package, it constitutes - and has already proven to be - a significant contribution to the successful implementation of the humanitarian programme as a whole.

The needs of the vulnerable groups in Iraq, as well as preventative measures for health and nutrition, cannot be forgotten. If unmet, they too could well lead to a further mass population exodus. In Kuwait, the plight of displaced persons and the health sector must also be addressed with the utmost urgency. The ecological damage caused by the oil fires and oil slicks in the Persian Gulf will spill over far beyond the borders of the region and calls for immediate international response.

I have mentioned earlier some of the successes during the past month. I am sorry to say that international response to the 15 May Appeal cannot be counted amongst them. While it is clear that at this critical time the initial momentum achieved by the United Nations Inter-Agency Humanitarian Programme must be sustained and expanded, to date funds contributed to the Appeal have been extremely limited and have not matched the magnitude of the crisis. Of the total amount requested in the Appeal, less than a quarter has yet been received. On the food aid side, extremely poor support is already seriously jeopardising the ability of the United Nations to meet the needs of returnees, displaced and vulnerable groups. Their needs are urgent and must be satisfied in full and without delay, but unless substantial assistance is forthcoming immediately, new orders for food cannot be made.

In view of the task which lies ahead and the need to continue and expand the crucial work started by the United Nations, I urge you once more to respond generously and rapidly to this Appeal.

(Signed) Sadruddin Aga Khan

INTRODUCTION

On 15 May 1991 a revised Appeal was made by the United Nations for refugees on the borders of Iraq/Turkey and inside Iran; for emergency humanitarian assistance for returnees and vulnerable groups inside Iraq and for health and environment projects in Kuwait. The Appeal, totalling US$ 414,050,737 for the period 1 May 1991 to the end of August 1991 was presented by the Secretary-General's Executive Delegate.

The 15 May appeal consolidated two earlier United Nations Appeals made in April, which together totalled US$ 578.2 million. Of this, US$ 178 million covered initial emergency needs in Iraq and US$ 400.2 million was for the estimated 1.8 million people refugees on the borders of Iraq and Turkey and in Iran. In response to these two earlier Appeals, by the end of April 1991 approximately US$ 208 million had been received, leaving an unmet balance of US$ 370.2 million. The revised Appeal of 15 May thus carried forward the unmet portion and included additional funding needed up to the end of August 1991 for requirements not previously covered.

Since the 15 May Appeal, additional initiatives to facilitate repatriation have continued to be taken by the United Nations. A major initiative has been the agreement of the Government of Iraq for the posting of 500 United Nations Guards inside Iraq. The United Nations Guards, operating within the provisions of the Memorandum of Understanding of 18 April 1991 between the Government of Iraq and the Executive Delegate, have the mandate to protect United Nations personnel, assets and operations. While the Guards will not intervene in law enforcement issues that do not involve United Nations resources, any security or safety related incident will be reported on rapidly and communicated through United Nations channels.

With the deployment of United Nations Guards and the opening of additional UNHUCs, sub-offices, relay stations and extended delivery points, the earlier spontaneous repatriation of refugees from the border of Iraq and Turkey and from Iran substantially gained in momentum. Since 1 May over one million of the original 1.8 million who fled their homes have voluntarily returned to Iraq.

This present document is a first revision of the 15 May Appeal. It has been undertaken to reflect the current situation and to once more remind the international community of the magnitude of the crisis and the urgency of ensuring needs are met. The revision provides up-to-date information on returnee movements and the situation inside Iraq. It details once more the urgent actions identified in the 15 May Appeal to ensure the well-being of the people who have returned, or are returning to Iraq, as well as refugees who remain on the Iraq-Turkey border and in Iran. The document re-emphasises the urgent need for emergency humanitarian assistance in Iraq to avert fresh calamities and further displacements of people. A number of urgent health and environmental-related projects to alleviate the suffering of the people of Kuwait, upon which appalling damage has been inflicted, are also included.

The budget for this revised Appeal is US$ 448,915,737. This figure includes the US$ 414,050,737 portion of the 15 May appeal and an additional US$ 34,865,000 for deployment of the United Nations Guards inside Iraq, which was not included in the May Appeal. To date, of the total US$ 414,050,737 requested in the 15 May appeal, only US$ 134 million has yet been pledged or received. Out of the required US$ 34,865,000 for 500 United Nations Guards, US$ 27,365,000 is still unfunded. Contributions in kind to ensure mobility of Guards, such as vehicles, trucks and helicopters, are also urgently required.

In view of the recent growing unease of refugees, returnees and displaced persons alike as regards to both security issues and assurances of continued assistance upon their return to Iraq, it is imperative that the needs of these people are met in full as quickly as possible.

In reviewing this appeal, several factors must be considered. Firstly, the document reflects a scenario which is based on assumptions that arrangements will be put into place in regard to safety and security in areas of return. In this regard it should again be noted that the representatives of the United Nations and other humanitarian organisations can not by themselves provide the same type of guarantees as those provided by concerned member states in regard to the safety of returning nationals. Secondly, actions proposed in the document rely on the full co-operation of the Governments of Iraq, the Islamic Republic of Iran and Turkey, as well as on continued mobilisation of substantial resources by concerned countries.

...

EXECUTIVE SUMMARY

1. In spite of the massive financial, logistic and human resources which have been mobilised since early April, largely on a bi-lateral basis, the misery of the peoples of Iraq and Kuwait continues. In human, economic and social terms, the devastation resulting from the war and the displacement of large numbers of people in the civil conflict which followed is incalculable.

2. Of the 1.8 million people, mostly of Kurdish origin, who left their homes in Iraq, thousands have died during the long arduous trek to the inhospitable border areas of Iraq and Turkey and into Iran. In some areas, deaths due to malnutrition and disease were as high as 800 a day. In

some camps in Iran, where women and children continue to comprise 80% of the refugee populations, until recently only a third had access to shelter.

3. Inside Iraq, food rationing for those who have remained in their homes continues at a level well below the minimum required to sustain normal life. This has resulted in a steady increase in malnutrition and a growing concern that without urgent assistance further massive displacements of people into Iran may occur. Reconstruction is taking place in the larger towns and cities, but in many parts of the country the war has robbed civilians of basic health and sanitation services and clean water supplies. Coupled with poor nutrition, the lack of such services threatens the lives of the most vulnerable groups.

4. In good years, harvests inside Iraq account for 30% of the total food requirements, the remainder being covered by food imports, costing approximately US$ 2 billion. With the disruption of this year's harvests because of war and displacements of populations, substantial additional amounts of food from the international community are required. Without agricultural assistance, such as seeds and machinery to replace lost assets, the harvest of 1992 will also be disrupted. If Government financial assets for such imports can not be used, massive international assistance totalling billions of dollars may well be required in order to avert a major famine.

5. Since April 1991, a number of major initiatives have been taken which have resulted in an initial spontaneous repatriation of some 200,000 refugees followed by a rapid mass return to Iraq of an additional 800,000 people.

6. Among the first initiatives to be taken in April, several nations joined together to create a security zone in Northern Iraq, mounting massive logistics operations through rapid mobilisation of financial and human resources. This was followed on 18 April 1991 by the signing of the Memorandum of Understanding by the Executive Delegate of the Secretary-General, Prince Sadruddin Aga Khan, and the Minister of Foreign Affairs of the Republic of Iraq. The MOU aimed at facilitating urgent humanitarian assistance and the voluntary return home of those who wish to go back to their places of origin. The United Nations was requested both by the Iraqi authorities and concerned member states to take over refugee camps, including those set up bilaterally. Parallel to these events, negotiations took place in Baghdad between the President of Iraq and the Kurdish leadership.

7. Other major initiatives which have continued to be taken by the United Nations include the establishment of UNHUCs, sub-offices and relay stations in key locations along the border areas and inside Iraq. By 10 June, in addition to the UNHUCs established in May at Dohuk and Zakho, United Nations sub-offices had been established in Erbil, Suleimaniya, Mosul and Basrah, each sub-office serving as a logistics hub for 5-7 UNHUCs and relay stations, some of which are mobile. Currently there are 22 active permanent and mobile centres. In addition to this WFP has established 18 extended delivery points to facilitate both repatriation and delivery of food supplies for refugees and vulnerable groups.

8. Further to this, within the framework of the MOU, a subsequent agreement on arrangements for the posting of United Nations Guards inside Iraq was also signed in Baghdad. As of 19 May 1991, the first United Nations Guards contingent was fully operational in Dohuk. Today, there are 60 United Nations Guards inside Iraq, with the remaining 440 to be posted by the end of June.

9. Coupled with the continued reassurance provided by the presence of concerned member states and the perceived progress of the ongoing political discussions between the Government and the Kurdish leadership, these measures have encouraged the return to Iraq of all but 13,000 refugees from camps on the Iraq/Turkey border. All but two camps at the Turkish border have been emptied of their populations and are now closed. Between 4 May and 10 June, the International Organisation for Migration (IOM) working closely with UNHCR, reports some 262,539 people have been assisted to return from Turkey to Iraq, from the mountains of Zakho and from Zakho to other towns of origin. Most of these people were escorted by United Nations Guards through established blue routes, or were met at United Nations Guards welcome points at the entrance to the town of Dohuk and near-by villages.

10. An estimated 500,000 refugees have also returned to Iraq. Of the original estimated 1.3 million Iraqi refugees in Iran, as of 30 May population in refugee camps was 505,432, mainly located in West Azerbaijan and Bakhtaran. In addition, it is estimated that a further 150,000 refugees who have not yet registered in camps also remain in Iran. Many of those who have returned from Iran to Iraq have not gone back to their places of origin. Large numbers of people have gathered at Savojoe Enclave bordering Iranian Kurdestan and a further massive concentration of people is reported on the Iraqi side of the border near Piranshahr exit point.

11. The great reluctance on the part of large numbers of people to return to their places of origin underlines the growing sense of unease with which displaced Iraqis, refugees and returnees alike have greeted the announcement of the imminent withdrawal of concerned member states. In addition to this, the political talks between the Government and the Kurdish leadership has been more protracted than expected, following initial optimistic pronouncements of progress. Doubts about the outcome of these talks, as well as recent disturbances in Suleimaniya, Erbil and Dohuk, have had the effect of slowing down returnee movements and the resettlement of displaced in their home areas. The amnesty deadline of 26 May announced by the Government for return of refugees has also passed without a Government statement on whether it will be extended.

12. A third factor which has led to unease, concerns the disappointing response of the international community to the 15 May Appeal. The shortfall in the amount of food required and what has so far been received or pledged is 118,225 mts, of which 83,989 mts is urgently needed in Iraq. Unless adequate food supplies can be assured for those in transit or settling back into their homes and some means of reassurance about security can be provided, major reverse movements could well be triggered. In addition to food shortages, deployment of the full contingent of United Nations Guards by the end of June is also jeopardised by the limited response from the international community.

13. In regard to refugee and returnee matters, UNHCR continues to have the lead operational role and is concentrating its activities in the northern and eastern parts of Iraq from which most of the refugees originate. As originally agreed, UNHCR and UNICEF have divided the organisational responsibility for setting up the various sub-offices and reception stations with other participating agencies using them as a base for their operations. NGOs have been and continue to be encouraged to make use of the logistic facilities that such centres can provide, either as associated institutions or as sub-contractors. Some 20 NGOs are operating in Iraq, many of them having entered Iraq from Turkey, along with the returning populations. As of 10 June, their combined strength in terms of staffing was in the region of 270, most of them working loosely under the United Nations umbrella or closely liaising with the United Nations agencies in the areas.

14. In order for the United Nations to carry out the huge task ahead, an inter-agency task-force has been established. As of 10 June, the inter-agency team of United Nations personnel, including a significant number

of UNVs, as well as seconded NGO staff and personnel secured through bi-lateral assistance, stood at 324. Additional staff are still required and further bi-lateral support is requested, both in the identification and equipping of additional relief workers. Bi-lateral assistance is also required in the secondment of personnel to the United Nations Guards Contingent. While the United Nations has already identified many candidates, it is envisaged that the bulk of these Guards will be secured on an individual basis through bi-lateral assistance. Such contributions will be fully reflected against the proposed budget.

15. To ensure the safety and well-being of refugees who are unwilling to repatriate, at least immediately, new refugee camp sites must be established or existing camps significantly upgraded to provide better conditions for temporary asylum. Some work on this has already been undertaken by Iranian provincial authorities and the Iranian Red Crescent. To prevent further health hazards, UNHCR has also presented to the Turkish Government a proposal aimed at clearing up closed refugee sites.

16. In Iran, although conditions have improved in refugee camps, additional shelter, safe water supplies and sanitation services are still required, as are supplementary foods to address the poor nutritional condition of many mothers and children. Accelerated immunisation programmes must also be carried out to protect women and children from common, killer diseases. The Government of Iran has also requested UNHCR to preposition relief items in south Khuzestan to meet a possible influx of Iraqi Shi'a reported to have remained in the marshes. UNHCR has also been requested by the Iranian Authorities to undertake responsibility for the transport requirements of Iraqis who return from Iran in coming months. Although repatriation from Iran has been co-ordinated with UNHCR, until recently provincial authorities have provided free transport to the border and in some cases a two-day supply of food. To facilitate further returns from Iran, similar blue routes to those of Iraq/Turkey will be established with IOM assistance.

17. Due to the large numbers of refugees returning to Iraq, and the worsening conditions in some parts of the country, emergency assistance must be expanded to meet the needs of returning refugees, and to stave off new calamities. Cholera outbreaks are continuing to occur in some areas. In the south, which is of particular concern, severe food rationing and lack of health and sanitation services have led to increased malnutrition and the continued likelihood of major epidemics. The plight of women and the newborn is particularly serious. If the situation is allowed to deteriorate, it is feared that further migration from the south will be inevitable. Emergency interventions needed for vulnerable groups are provision of health, water, medical and sanitation services and high protein foods for infants and mothers, many so poorly nourished they have stopped lactating.

18. In respect of the emergency humanitarian needs and provision of emergency short-term material assistance which is so urgently required by large numbers of the Iraqi people, overall responsibility for the co-ordination of efforts continues to lie with the Executive Delegate who has been appointed by the Secretary-General as his representative to oversee the implementation of a United Nations Inter-Agency Humanitarian Programme for Iraq, Kuwait and the Iraq/Turkey and Iraq/Iran border areas, and his Co-ordinator in Baghdad.

19. Operational activities have been undertaken by UNICEF, UNHCR, WHO, WFP, FAO, and the International Organisation for Migration (IOM). UNDP is assisting the Executive Delegate and his Co-ordinator with the provision of professional staff in Baghdad, Geneva and New York. Following upon the work done in the earlier phase of the Gulf emergency, UNDRO continues to provide substantial co-ordination support at Headquarters level. ITU is currently preparing requirements for a basic communication system in Iraq. This will depend partly on information obtained from Iraqi authorities as to what equipment remains effective and a mission has now been sent to Iraq for this purpose. UNV also continues to assist overall relief efforts through the secondment of relief personnel.

20. In Kuwait, the health care system, which prior to August 1990 compared very favourably with those of industrialised countries, still lies in disarray. The departure of large numbers of health professionals, following the invasion of the country, has created major difficulties in managing curative and preventive health services. In addition, large quantities of medical equipment have been damaged or removed. The unprecedented situation caused by the burning of oil wells and the uncontrolled spilling of oil over large areas are also matters of grave environment concern. Vast resources have been made available by Kuwait itself but funds are required to begin tackling some of the urgent health-related problems, without delay.

21. The cost of carrying out the tasks detailed in this document is considerable. The total budget for humanitarian relief activities is US$ 414,050,737 to cover a four month period until the end of August 1991. Of this total, US$ 64,970,099 is required for food supplies. Assistance to refugees and returnees amounts to US$ 235,478,158.

22. For vulnerable groups in Iraq, US$ 43,032,480 is required. This will provide foodstuffs, such as high protein biscuits, immunisation, health and sanitation services and installation of clean water supplies. Also included is US$ 64 million for short-term material assistance, such as seeds, protection of livestock and agricultural machinery and re-establishment of a basic communication system. An additional US$ 7.6 million is required for environment and health-related programmes in Kuwait. To provide the full complement of United Nations Guards, an additional US$ 34,865,000 is required. Of this, to date only US$ 7.5 million has been pledged.

23. The activities and budgets proposed are the minimum basic requirements for the months ahead. To ensure that efforts are not duplicated and to complement the activities of other agencies, interventions proposed have been co-ordinated with the International Committee of the Red Cross and the League of Red Cross and Red Crescent Societies. Regular meetings will be held with ICRC/LRCRCS to further enhance efforts in the field.

...

PART ONE: OPERATIONAL DETAILS

Responsibilities

24. In view of the exceptional dimensions of the human tragedy which has affected the region, on 8 April 1991 the Secretary-General of the United Nations appointed Prince Sadruddin Aga Khan as his Executive Delegate in the context of a United Nations Inter-Agency Humanitarian Programme for Iraq, Kuwait and the Iraq/Turkey and Iraq/Iran border areas. The responsibilities of the Executive Delegate are as follows:

> Facilitate identification of needs, future problems and operational gaps in the UN system at work in the Persian Gulf and recommend appropriate measures;
>
> Prepare, together with relevant components of the UN system, timely consolidated appeals and regular updating;
>
> Act as a catalyst to highlight humanitarian needs and stimulate a generous response from the international community, as required;

Keep the Secretary-General informed about humanitarian issues relating to the Gulf crisis by constant monitoring and reporting;

Provide a means of bringing urgent matters to the attention of the Secretary General, donors, appropriate government authorities and UN agencies at the request of affected countries and other UN agencies;

Represent the Secretary-General at Inter-Agency and other meetings and to ensure that his overall policy guidelines are adhered to;

Maintain contacts at a high level with all Governments particularly those directly concerned both in Geneva and in the field.

25. Operational activities are being carried out by individual United Nations agencies, according to their areas of expertise. On refugee and returnee matters, UNHCR is the designated lead agency, in line with its international mandate. UNHCR is being supported by UNICEF, WHO, WFP, FAO and IOM in the provision of assistance to returnees or refugees who continue to seek asylum. IOM is also providing transport for returning refugees as needed both in the return to Iraq from Turkey and Iran and their travel back to their homes from the border.

26. Regarding emergency humanitarian assistance in Iraq, overall co-ordination lies with the Executive Delegate and his Co-ordinator. UNICEF is responsible for emergency assistance to vulnerable groups i.e. children under five and mothers, particularly in the areas of immunisation, control of diarrhoeal diseases, safe motherhood, supply of high energy food and children's clothing.

27. WHO continues to provide technical assistance for design and implementation of public health services with emphasis on the production, dissemination and verification of norms and standards, as applied to the health sector. It will establish and maintain epidemiological surveillance and disease prevention and control measures, deploy international and locally recruited personnel and carry out in-service training. WHO will also continue to provide drugs, food supplements for specific groups and medical equipment as part of its operations within the broad spectrum of inter-agency activities.

28. WFP will continue its primary responsibility for provision of adequate food supplies for returnees; those who remain in camps and for vulnerable groups in Iraq. It will provide technical and operational assistance for mobilisation, procurement and transport of such food requirements. WFP has already supplied through the UNHUC established by the Executive Delegate in Zakho, food aid to 106,000 beneficiaries in northern Iraq, most of these newly returned home.

29. UNDRO will continue to work closely with the Executive Delegate in providing co-ordination and information support. It will report on contributions received and will keep donors informed of activities and new needs which emerge through the production of regular situation reports. UNDRO is also responsible for notifying military authorities of United Nations relief flights into Iraq. Individual agencies, such as FAO and ITU, will assist in the provision of specific projects which will include provision of seeds, farm machinery, livestock protection and re-establishment of basic communications systems.

30. The fullest possible use is being made of United Nations volunteers, many of whom have already been fielded by individual United Nations agencies. In Kuwait, environmental programmes will be co-ordinated by UNEP. Health rehabilitation will be supported and monitored by WHO. Both agencies will report directly to the Executive Delegate's office.

31. In view of the massive task which lies ahead, an inter-agency task force has been mobilised to ensure adequate and effective provision of emergency humanitarian assistance as outlined in this appeal. To cope with the emergency, individual United Nations agencies have already substantially increased their staff in the border areas and further increases are continuing to take place inside Iraq.

32. The magnitude and scope of humanitarian relief efforts in Iraq requires considerable numbers of personnel (preliminary estimates of between one and two thousand), working directly or indirectly under United Nations responsibility, as well as significant quantities of material. In addition to relief personnel provided by the United Nations and other international agencies, non-governmental organisations have also substantially increased staffing with some already seconded or sub-contracted to the United Nations.

33. Material investments, in the form of installations, vehicles, medical and food supplies, etc., represent many millions of dollars and must be protected against pilferage, looting or misuse. The United Nations has a responsibility to donors and beneficiaries alike to protect these valuable human and material assets and has accordingly begun to deploy a United Nations Guards Contingent to do so. This Guards Contingent will operate within the provisions of the MOU of 18 April 1991, and within the subsequent agreement on arrangements for the assignment of Guards, signed in Baghdad on 24 May 1991. The Contingent's mandate is to protect United Nations personnel, assets and operations.

34. The 60 Guards have already been deployed in the Dohuk/Zakho area and at transit centres/zones established along blue routes. Up to 440 others will be posted wherever there is a United Nations presence (transit camps, UNHUCs, relay stations, transit centres, as well as the Co-ordinator's office in Baghdad and sub-offices in the governorate), by the end of June, 1991.

35. The United Nations Guards Contingent is not mandated to intervene in law enforcement issues which do not involve United Nations resources. However, any security/safety related incidents, of any nature, will be reported on rapidly and communicated through United Nations channels. Reports will accordingly be submitted on any unusual activities, including incidents which do not have a direct bearing on United Nations resources, given their possible impact on the overall security situation which affects the safety of United Nations relief personnel and material, as well as the implementation of the ongoing relief operation. Reports will be communicated through the established chain of command for the Contingent, headed by its Chief who is located in Baghdad and acts under the direct responsibility of the Co-ordinator and Special Representative of the Executive Delegate.

36. As always, NGOs continue to play a major and vital role in the provision of urgent relief assistance. In all areas covered by the appeal, individual United Nations agencies will provide support to NGOs to facilitate their work and help them expand activities where possible.

37. In order to ensure that sufficient relief personnel, United Nations staff and Guards are available, substantial bi-lateral support is still urgently required to locate, fund and equip teams of relief workers and in secondment of appropriate personnel for the United Nations Guard Contingent.

38. In regard to foreign relief personnel, including United Nations guards, agreement has been reached under the Memorandum of Understanding of 18 April between the Executive Delegate of the Secretary-General and the Government of Iraq for free and safe passage for all relief workers working under the United Nations umbrella.

Operational Modalities

39. As part of the agreement with the Government of Iraq to facilitate the provision of urgent humanitarian assistance to returnees, displaced and vulnerable groups, a network of United Nations offices and mobile teams (UNHUCs) have been established. Up to 20 mobile teams based in eight field offices reporting to sub-offices are being deployed to facilitate voluntary repatriation and provide material support to returnees. Relay stations have been established since early May along the main blue routes (1. Iskenderen-Quasroq-Zakho, and 2. Uzumlu-Kaminasi-Dohuk) identified by the Executive Delegate.

40. These blue routes have been instrumental in facilitating the return of refugees and provision of supplies, such as food, clothing, domestic items and emergency shelter material. Health services have been made available at the relay stations and, where possible, mothers and children have been vaccinated against common diseases. IOM has also been responsible for assisting refugees without transport to travel to Iraq and for onward journeys to their homes. So far, 262,534 refugees have been assisted by IOM under United Nations co-ordination. The government of Iran has also recently requested UNHCR to assist in the transport back to Iraq of refugees inside Iran and on border areas. It is thus planned to establish similar blue routes on the Iranian border as soon as possible.

41. In order to enable the work to be carried out effectively in the field, telecommunications will need to be established in all key locations. Mobile radios will also be necessary. To support logistics operations, maintenance units will be required to service the deployed mobile teams. Transport in North and Eastern Iraq is still problematic. Lack of transport, in particular aircraft, has forced UNHCR and other United Nations operational agencies to depend upon scarce local services or on donor support.

Co-ordination, Monitoring and Reporting

42. Effective co-ordination, both at headquarters and at country level, is an integral part of this humanitarian effort. This involves close collaboration among United Nations agencies, operational partners and with ICRC/LRCRCS. Within the United Nations system, the close co-operation which has already evolved out of previous humanitarian efforts and which draws on the skills and experience of individual United Nations agencies has been maintained and will be further strengthened.

43. At provincial and camp level in Iran and Turkey, UNHCR has set up committees where local authorities, bi-lateral donors, NGOs and UN agencies co-ordinate their efforts. Similar mechanisms are being established in Northern and Eastern Iraq. The Inter-Agency Working Group set up in Geneva with the participation of all concerned agencies, the Red Cross Movement, IOM and NGO representatives will continue to meet weekly.

44. In Iraq, the Co-ordinator and Special Representative in Baghdad has established the Iraq Relief Coordination Unit (IRCU), a small-size office of four professional staff, in addition to the Co-ordinator and Deputy Co-ordinator. The Chief of the Guard Contingent, who reports to the Co-ordinator, is setting up a central office with three professional assistants. The Deputy Co-ordinator has been nominated by UNHCR as the designated lead operational agency with a view to harmonizing policy and approach. With Baghdad deprived of telephones, daily meetings with the heads of all Iraq-based agencies have proved essential for information exchange and consultation on operational issues of common interest. A formal weekly meeting, the Inter-agency Relief Committee, is held to review policy-related matters and questions of longer term concern. A bi-weekly meeting is held with NGO's working out of Baghdad, again to exchange information and to coordinate relief work.

45. Priority attention has been given to establishing an effective and agreed system of monitoring of all activities under the responsibility of the United Nations. United Nations sub-offices now opened will greatly facilitate the distribution and tracking of relief goods and collection of data to ensure that new and unmet needs are regularly and effectively assessed. As necessary and appropriate, NGOs will also be enlisted in regard to monitoring of food distribution to target groups.

46. In Iraq, UNDP, UNICEF, WFP, and UNHCR have offices in Baghdad and this presence has already been strengthened by additional international and local staff to facilitate monitoring. The Office of the Executive Delegate is identifying key indicators and field reporting formats to facilitate situation evaluation and higher level reporting. Reporting and evaluation will be further enhanced through a computerized data base of field information, which is now being developed. In addition to tracking numbers of refugees, displaced, and vulnerable persons, and United Nations field staff in the area, food, water and sanitation services provided, camp sanitary conditions, shelter, health services, transport, disease incidence, and other indicators will be tracked. The current conditions will be evaluated against identified needs, to determine needs currently met and unmet needs. The information will also be used to identify gaps in the assistance so that adjustments may be made as required.

47. To enable effective United Nations responses and resource mobilisation, regular reports covering all activities under United Nations supervision will be produced and distributed through UNDRO. Copies of the situation report will be circulated to the international community, relevant governments, the United Nations system, NGOs and ICRC and LRCRCS. Individual United Nations agencies will continue to handle their own press and public relations activities. Press materials required by the Executive Delegate will be produced through the United Nations Department of Information.

Finance Mobilisation

48. The executive Delegate will keep the international community continually informed of new needs and priorities. This will involve regular donor briefings and, as deemed appropriate, visits to the capitals of donor countries. In order to foster and permit donors to channel contributions to individual priority sectors, this appeal has been separated into chapters representing consolidated updates of requirements for refugees, returnees, the vulnerable groups in Iraq, short-time material assistance for populations in Iraq and health and environmental assistance to Kuwait. Contributions can thus be directed to individual chapters or specific projects being implemented by agencies within the frame-work of the appeal.

49. Donors are encouraged to make their contributions directly and preferably without any earmarking to individual United Nations agencies and IOM. Those who wish to contribute to the programme as a whole may make contributions to UNDRO. UNDRO will organise allocations of such contributions in consultation with the United Nations Inter-Agency Working Group. To facilitate the work of the Executive Delegate, UNDRO is producing a weekly update of funding received, with regular reporting to the Executive Delegate's office. Individual United Nations agencies will continue to report directly to their respective donors.

PART TWO: CURRENT SITUATION AND REQUIRED RESPONSES

Situation on the Iraq/Turkish border

50. In the aftermath of civil conflict that shook most of the cities and towns in Northern Iraq, more than 500,000 persons, mostly of Kurdish origin, fled from their homes towards the Turkish border. As of the beginning of May 1991, an estimated 415,000 of them were living in nine different sites along the Iraq/Turkey border. An additional 100,000 or so were located in the mountains of northern Iraq. Many of those who fled were without food or clothing and relief efforts to meet the needs of these people were severely hindered by the mountainous terrain and poor quality access roads.

51. As detailed in the Introduction and Executive Summary, various initiatives taken during the last month have resulted in the initial trickle of spontaneous repatriation gaining significant momentum. From 14 May 1991, the estimated 230,000 refugees left in camps at the Iraq/Turkey border had been reduced by 4 June to just over 13,000.

52. Although many of the earlier returnees have moved back to Iraq by their own means, walking back through mountain passes that they had crossed just a few weeks earlier, many have received transport assistance from IOM through the established blue routes. From 4 May to 10 June, IOM has assisted in the transport of some 262,534 Iraqis from the mountains to Zakho, from Zakho to towns of origin and from Turkey to Iraq.

53. On 7 June UNHCR also assumed full responsibility for the Zakho transit centres in Northern Iraq. As of that date, the transit centres at Zakho held less than 30,000 people. UNHCR and the concerned member states have now agreed a transition to United Nations management of all humanitarian activities in the security zone, effective by mid-June. A transition schedule for services to be provided by various NGOs has been agreed. In order to assume this role, UNHCR has substantially increased its staff in Northern Iraq. Some 70 staff have been seconded from Nordic NGOs and Governments.

54. Given the rapid pace of movements back to the valleys, cities and villages of northern Iraq, UNHCR's strategy of support to voluntary repatriation has involved a major deployment of human and logistics resources to the areas of origin of the refugees. This has created a United Nations humanitarian network to complement and gradually replace services now provided by member states. To the extent possible, material assistance provided by UNHCR has been limited to immediate relief and transport in co-operation with IOM. Activities related to emergency rehabilitation of community services will continue to form part of more extensive emergency assistance provided by the United Nations system as a whole.

55. WFP reports that for Turkey and cross-border to Zakho a balance of 2,260 mts of cereals is in Iskenderum for delivery to Northern Iraq. From local purchases in Turkey a balance of 270 mts of oil and 33 mts of feta cheese are ready to be transported to Zakho. 680 mts of rice and 210 mts of oil arrived in Iskenderum 30 May and were directly delivered on 31 May to Zakho. Next shipment of some 900 mts wheat flour is expected in Iskenderum on 1 July.

56. Basic emergency relief such as cooking utensils, stoves, blankets, jerrycans, soap and clothing, as well as fuel for returnees travelling with their own vehicles, have been given by the United Nations, the various NGO and concerned member states to refugees already returned. These will continue to be distributed through UNHCR's mobile teams.

57. In view of the coming summer season and possible other movements of refugees, mobile water tanks are still required at the relay stations along return routes. ICRC and NGOs have already established health facilities in areas where return routes are located. However, health provision has to be extended to relay stations where there is no other international presence. Stocks of emergency shelter materials continue to be required for vulnerable groups pending reconstruction of their homes. Tents, tarpaulins and floor mats are also needed.

58. The Turkish authorities have recently moved the remaining population from Cukurca to Silopi and this, coupled with the rapidly decreased population in camps at the Turkish border and the massive relief assistance already mobilised by the Turkish authorities and international community, substantially reduces the requirements for basic supplies for those who choose to stay in camps. These persons will, however, need continued temporary care and shelter in sites best suited for that purpose.

59. Using the planning figure of 500,000 for the period until the end of June and 50,000 from 1 July to 31 August 1991 to cover refugees who remain in camps and those who continue to need assistance in North Iraq, WFP calculates that 8,071 mts of food, in addition to what has been pledged so far, will be required. This total amount includes wheat flour, rice, oil, pulses, canned fish or meat, cheese and sugar. Given the immense difficulties of deliveries to the mountainous border areas, this food, as well as other basic relief items, such as water and water systems, shelter, sanitation equipment and household supplies, will need to be pre-positioned as quickly as possible.

60. UNHCR and WFP are actively collaborating in the logistics programme of the Turkish Red Crescent aimed at channelling all supplies entering Turkey to border sites and to Northern Iraq. UNHCR's collaboration with the Red Crescent, through the services of several UNHCR logistics experts and the hiring of additional transport, will continue.

61. Total United Nations staff in Turkey as of 5 June were 201, of whom 83 were international and 118 local. In addition to the large numbers of UNHCR staff members working in assistance and protection related issues, the Turkish Red Crescent Society has deployed some 300 relief and medical personnel who are engaged in relief logistics, camp management and provision of health services. With the continuation of the active involvement of the Red Crescent - supported by a team of 30 from the League of the Red Cross Society - it is envisaged that a large portion of UNHCR staff and some equipment can be transferred to Iraq.

62. In order to address the urgent needs of refugees in relation to water, health and sanitation services, 17 UNICEF staff were at the border during May. As repatriation gained momentum, this has been reduced to nine, with further reductions anticipated following the closure of many border camps and consolidation of co-ordinating offices. WHO will further support UNHCR on the Iraq/Turkey border by establishing a health monitoring team covering the two refugee camps anticipated to remain inside Turkey.

63. To support health interventions, UNICEF and WHO have delivered emergency health kits. Medicines now in stock, including measles vaccine, are sufficient for 400,000 persons for two months. Since reported cases of measles have increased, measles vaccination programmes are now underway.

64. Under UNHCR operational co-ordination, UNICEF will continue to focus its attention in coming months on the needs of women and children, monitoring and assessment, immunisation (EPI) and diarrhoeal control, safe motherhood, nutritional supplements and provision of children's clothing. Technical advice will continue to be provided to UNHCR's water and sanitation teams.

65. The travel through snow and rugged mountains and further difficulties in finding sufficient food has resulted in malnutrition amongst children and pregnant women. A

recent survey in one camp indicated that approximately 30 per cent of children were malnourished. Some supplementary foods are being delivered but wider distribution of foods, such as high protein biscuits, is still urgently needed.

Situation in Iran

66. In April 1991, the United Nations faced one of the largest influx rate of refugees in its entire history. From the end of March 1991, the total number of refugees was 47,000, mostly arriving in Khuzestan. By 26 April, this had increased to 1.3 million, 1 million of them registered by the Government of Iran. Although much planning had been done for anticipated influxes by the Government of Iran, the magnitude and rate of influx overwhelmed the material, financial and human resources of the provincial and central authorities.

67. On 5 May 1991, UNHCR emergency teams reported spontaneous repatriation estimated to be in the region of 5,000 per province a day. While it is thought that assumptions about security arrangements may have influenced the decision of these refugees to return home, agricultural and economic factors have also acted as strong incentives. The spring harvest in Iraq is from mid-May to July, with winter crops planted September to November for harvesting in the spring of 1992.

68. By 30 May 1991, 505,432 of the registered Iraqi refugees are reported to have left Iran. Many of these, however, have not as yet returned to their places of origin. Large numbers have gathered around towns and cities in the North of Iraq, with some 170,000 returnees and internally displaced currently at Savoje Enclave bordering Iranian Kurdestan. There is also a massive concentration of persons on the Iraqi side of the border near Piranshahr Exit point, camping on the side of the road, and at the town of Rawanduz. Recent disturbances in North Iraq and concerns about the continued provision of adequate food supplies are believed to have contributed to the hesitation amongst these groups to commit themselves fully to return to their homes.

69. Of the 539,252 refugees remaining in camps in Iran, populations are distributed as follows:

West Azerbaijan 188,766
Bakhtaran 230,500
Kurdestan 57,297
Khuzestan 60,000
Ilam 2,689
Total 539,252*

* An additional 150,000 refugees who have not yet registered in camps are also in Iran.

70. Although repatriation is co-ordinated between UNHCR and the Iranian Provincial Government, local authorities have until recently been providing free transportation to refugees to the border and sometimes two-day food supplies. The Iranian Government has now, however, requested UNHCR to provide this assistance in collaboration with IOM.

71. Inside Iran, refugee movements are still occurring from cities and villages or temporary sites to more permanent camps. The Government of Iran anticipates more influxes to its southern provinces and has requested UNHCR to pre-position supplies in south Khuzestan.

72 Although food distribution is still problematic, especially in West Azerbaijan and Bakhtaran, water and sanitation sectors are being strengthened following recommendations of a UNHCR technical mission. ICRC reports that the work of the Iranian Authorities, Iranian Red Crescent, UNHCR and NGOs have greatly improved conditions in refugee camps for those who remain. At least one new camp has been constructed and several have been upgraded.

73. As part of its continued support to UNHCR, UNICEF reports that up to 4 June it air-freighted 14.5 mts of additional emergency supplies including hospital equipment, 25 Mother and Child Health centre (MCH) kits and 25 midwifery kits for MCH centres in refugee camps.

74. The refugees in Iran continue to be made up of two distinct groups. The Iraqi Kurds, who arrived in Iran through seven main entry points, comprise 50% children, 30% women and 20% men. Around 50% of this group arrived with vehicles, including a substantial percentage of Northern Iraq's farm mechanical power. Between 55-60% of these refugees are urban populations with a substantial number of urban professionals and businessmen who have capital assets invested in the Iraqi economy.

75. The second group of Iraqis to flee into Iran are the Arab Shi'a of South Iraq, who have settled mainly at six camps in Khuzestan and at one site in Ilam. Some southern Iraqis are also being sheltered in Bakhtaran province. The profile of this second group is similar to that described above.

76. Most of the refugees with vehicles who have returned to Iraq used Piranshar, Sarasht (West Azerbaijan) Baneh and Marivan (Kurdistan) and Pevh/Nosoud (Bakhtaran) as entry points. As in the case of returnees from the Iraq/Turkey border, fuel and basic repatriation kits will need to be pre-positioned at relay stations established on return routes. To assist those who do not have vehicles, further buffer stocks of food, water and medical supplies will also be pre-positioned at strategic relay stations and other UNHUCs. In collaboration with UNHCR, IOM will arrange for their transport from the border back to their home regions.

77. Since April, most refugees have been supplied with blankets, high protein food, as well as other relief items, with support from the Iranian authorities and the Iranian Red Crescent. To alleviate the earlier serious problem with shelter, 50,000 tents have been airlifted. Basic food stocks, mostly air-freighted due to the urgency, are being drawn from the Government of Iran reserves on a replenishment basis by WFP.

78. For the large number of people who may wish to remain in camps in Iran, the problem of water borne communicable diseases, although much improved, continues to be serious. To further improve the situation and avoid epidemics, potable water, sanitation and health screening are being provided. Through May and June, urgent procurement of water tanks of 10,000 lt capacity, additional buffer stocks of medicines and other health precautions are being undertaken.

79. Several bilateral and NGOs have also been co-opted to assist in provision of water and sanitation. One of these is covering water and sanitation needs of up to 300,000 refugees in Bakhtaran province with funds provided by the Government of Germany. The Governments of Sweden and Switzerland have been approached to field similar fully equipped water/sanitation implementing agencies for Kurdistan and West Azerbaijan provinces. Water tankers and sewage tanks are also still required to complement the efforts of the teams and provide sound hygienic conditions.

80. As in the Iraq/Turkey border, UNICEF is supporting UNHCR in activities to address the special needs of women and children. Of special concern in some camps is the increased number of women no longer able to breast-feed their children due to poor nutrition. This will be addressed through the provision of high protein supplements.

81. Since the majority of children in camps have not been vaccinated in the past eight months, accelerated immunisation programmes are being undertaken. Communal life and lack of hygienic conditions, coupled with acute respiratory problems and lack of shelter and appropriate clothing, have already resulted in many

deaths. Proposed UNICEF activities in the camps in Iraq/Iran include the establishment of MCH centres, through which children can be treated with Oral Rehydration Solution (ORS). These centres will also distribute supplementary foods to malnourished children and provide health education services for pregnant and lactating mothers.

82. Pregnant mothers continue to constitute a high percentage of the Iraqi refugee population and given the level of suffering they have already faced, UNICEF activities include provision of special care during pregnancy and delivery in hygienic environments and by trained personnel, as well as post natal care.

83. To support these efforts and reduce the incidence of deaths due to disease and malnutrition, WHO will continue to support UNHCR with technical assistance in the design and implementation of public health services with emphasis on the dissemination and verification of norms and standards as applied to the health sector. WHO is also providing a health monitoring team. Four doctors will be attached to UNHCR field teams to co-ordinate the planning, implementation and evaluation of health sector activities.

84. In order to feed those remaining in camps in Iran and those who have now returned to Iraq, it is calculated by WFP that some 27,465 mts of food, such as wheat flour, rice, pulses, oil and canned fish or meat, in addition to what has already been pledged will be required until the end of August. WFP reports that from local purchases in Turkey, the balance to be shipped to Iran is 10,222 mts of wheat flour and 484 mts of oil. 675 mts of feta cheese from Denmark will also have to be delivered.

85. In view of the amount of aid which has already been received and the reduced populations through repatriation, UNHCR will undertake to co-ordinate other basic supplies required, taking into account known bilateral/NGO contributions and limit further provision of aid to filling gaps in existing efforts.

Situation in Iraq

86. As the hot summer months approach, the situation of children and women in Iraq grows more critical by the day. The slow and partial rehabilitation of infrastructure is gradually increasing the availability of electrical power but limited access to safe water and sanitation services and disrupted health services continue to increase the risk of epidemics in some areas. Food rationing is at levels well below the minimum required for a healthy diet. As a result, malnutrition is increasing.

87. The destruction of Iraq's power plants, oil refineries and oil storage facilities brought the country to a standstill on 16 January 1991. Despite the slow and partial restoration of these facilities, water plants are still operating at less than 40% capacity due to lack of electricity and generators. Water obtainable from taps is untreated due to lack of chemicals. In some areas, drinking water is obtained from rivers choked by raw sewage.

88. Sanitation services are in disarray and cities like Samawa and Amara are plagued by lakes of sewage and dirty water. Entire streets are blocked by rubbish. Diarrhoea, typhoid, cholera, hepatitis and dehydration have all become common place. Acute shortages exist in essential drugs, vaccines, ORS and epidemic containment equipment. This has come as a result of looting, burning and destruction of medical stores. In Basrah, only five out of 20 health centres are still functioning.

89. Basic health services continue to suffer from shortages of essential drugs, vaccines, syringes and oral rehydration salts. UNICEF and WHO have distributed quantities of these items throughout the country but the availability of transport for drugs and medical supplies is limited. More supplies are still needed but all available funds have been spent or committed.

90. Food rationing is at 1,000 calories a day per person and most food items are beyond the means of the average person. Because of poor diet, many mothers are unable to breast-feed their infants and since powdered milk and baby formula is unavailable, this has led to increasing severe malnutrition. Both marasmus and Kwashiorkor cases are reported amongst children under five. In the north, although many refugees are now returning to their homes, large numbers of people have become displaced as a result of the war and civil conflict. These people are living in make-shift lodgings which ribbon the valleys by the sides of rivers. Food availability varies from place to place, depending upon the presence of markets on the Iranian side of the border. Reports from the north indicate the health of the displaced is deteriorating and diarrhoeal diseases, acute respiratory infections, scorpion and snake bites are common.

91. Prior to the war, the country depended upon 70% of its food from outside imports. Agriculture has been adversely affected by disrupted irrigation systems, broken farm machinery and lack of spare parts. It is estimated that the cost of restoration of seed stocks, warehouses and seed cleaning lines alone is 29.8 million Iraqi dinar. Livestock numbers, sheep, cattle and buffaloes are decreasing due to the combined shortages of feed and lack of vaccines and veterinary services. Poultry has been similarly affected.

92. Crops are also threatened by insects due to the Government's inability to carry out annual spraying. To prevent further crop losses, FAO has assisted the Government through the provision of helicopter pilots who have carried out crop dusting under FAO supervision. This intervention is estimated to avert potential crop losses of US$ 300 million. Without other urgent interventions in agriculture, such as provision of agricultural combines and spare parts, considerable constraints have already been imposed on June harvesting and could lead to a further deterioration in food supplies in 1991/1992.

93. Given the current precarious food situation in Iraq it is essential that some agricultural inputs are provided in time for the next planting season. The outcome of the 1991 cereal harvest and food imports and distributions must also be closely monitored. In this connection, in addition to its regular monitoring through Global information and early warning systems, FAO stands ready to undertake ad hoc crop and food needs assessments if and when necessary. FAO also plans to field periodic teams to evaluate progress within the implementation of the agricultural rehabilitation programme, identify problems and further measures which are required.

94. War devastation has severely reduced the supply of fuel for essential services including agriculture. Power output and refineries production will not be restored until the first phase of repairs is completed. Modern communications systems in Iraq are now virtually defunct and limit the capacity to collate essential health information. Materials to perform laboratory tests for the control of water-related and communicable diseases remain in short supply. This, coupled with a severe lack of transport which inhibits transport of even most urgent medical supplies, means that the spread of communicable diseases throughout the country will be difficult if not impossible to contain. It is thus increasingly essential that a basic means of communication to collect data from different parts of the country is quickly restored. A mission to examine what is required has now been sent to Iraq by ITU.

95. The thrust of this appeal for Iraqi civilians is two-fold. The first is to provide assistance to vulnerable groups, including returnees and displaced persons. The suffering of these people has already been so great that

urgent actions must now be taken to ensure their earlier anguish is not prolonged.

96. The second objective is to provide some basic assistance for the people of Iraq whose lives have been devastated by the war and who continue to suffer in its aftermath.

97. Due to serious problems in transport and to facilitate the work of relief workers in Iraq, it has become evident that air transport will be the key to effective implementation of assistance to returning refugees. It is thus envisaged that aircraft, particularly helicopters, should be hired. UNHCR is also keeping in close contact with the Co-ordinator in Baghdad to advise him and other agencies of areas to which large numbers of refugees have returned and where necessary, emergency assistance such as water, health and sanitation provision is being provided through inter-agency co-operation.

98. In the provision of emergency assistance to vulnerable groups, UNICEF has taken the major responsibility, along with WHO, for provision of assistance to mothers and children. Co-ordinating its efforts closely with those of ICRC and the Iraqi Red Crescent Society, UNICEF and WHO will establish supplementary feeding centres in key locations.

99. Interventions will continue to be made in water and sanitation sectors to provide people with the minimal requirement for safe drinking water and sanitation services. Repairs to water networks are urgently required to prevent further contamination of the water supply. Generators are needed for rural areas without electricity.

100. UNICEF, together with WHO, will continue to assist in the reactivation of health care services to reduce disease incidence and outbreak of epidemics. Children will be protected from diarrhoeal disease through diarrhoeal disease control measures. Crash courses in training for health staff will also be undertaken to enable these staff to adapt to equipment of a lower technology than they have been used to. Vaccination programmes will be reactivated in at least 60% of health facilities and cold chain equipment supplied.

101. To prevent further serious deterioration in the nutritional status, particularly of vulnerable groups, it is planned that the WFP feeding programme for vulnerable groups, will continue until 30 September 1991. The feeding of displaced persons must also be expanded to provide for the estimated 500,000 returnees who may need support between 1 July and 30 August. In addition to food needs for returnees, an additional 85,061 mts of basic food supplies is required to supplement what has already been pledged. In spite of WFP efforts to mobilise these resources, food aid inside Iraq remains in short supply and large quantities of especially pulses, cheese and sugar are urgently required.

102. The activities proposed for funding in the appeal represent the barest minimum requirements for the various vulnerable groups identified above. It is presumed that the importation of food and other essential needs for the bulk of Iraqi's population will be negotiated within the framework of existing Security Council resolutions. ...

UN Guards Contingent

Introduction

The magnitude and scope of humanitarian relief efforts in Iraq will require considerable numbers of personnel (preliminary estimates of between one and two thousand), working directly or indirectly under UN responsibility, as well as significant quantities of material. Relief personnel will be provided by the UN and other international agencies, as well as non-governmental organizations, and may include sub-contracted staff. Material investments, in the form of installations, vehicles, medical and food supplies, etc., will represent many millions of dollars which must be protected against pilferage, looting or misuse. The UN has a responsibility to donors and beneficiaries alike to protect these precious human and material assets and will accordingly deploy a UN Guards Contingent to do so.

The UN Guards Contingent will be formed and operate within the provisions of the MOU of 18 April 1991, and within the subsequent agreement on arrangements for the assignment of Guards, signed in Baghdad on 24 May 1991.

The Contingent's mandate will be to protect UN personnel, assets and operations. The Guards will thus be deployed wherever there is a UN presence (transit camps, UNHUCS, relay stations, transit centres, as well as the Co-ordinator's office in Baghdad and sub-offices in the governorate): they will accordingly be assigned on a priority basis in the Dohuk/Zakho area and thereafter at transit centres/zones established along communications routes in other areas. Their mobility between the various UN relief installations will be assured.

The UN Guards Contingent is not mandated to intervene in law enforcement issues which do not involve UN resources. However, any security/safety related incidents, of any nature, will be reported on rapidly and communicated through United Nations channels. Reports will accordingly be submitted on any unusual activities, including incidents which do not have a direct bearing on UN resources, given their possible impact on the overall security situation which affects the safety of UN relief personnel and the protection of material, as well as the implementation of the ongoing UN relief operation. Reports will be communicated through the established chain of command for the Contingent, headed by its Chief, located in Baghdad, who acts under the direct authority of the Coordinator and Special Representative of the Executive Delegate.

The Contingent will be properly formed, managed, administered, equipped and oriented on its mission to ensure the effective implementation of its mandate. It is expected rapidly to reach a strength of some 500 guards.

Logistical resources, including ground and air transportation, communications, barracks and administrative facilities, rations and other supplies, as well as related services, will be required to support the Contingent. Transportation and Communications are particularly vital, and related contributions in kind are urgently needed. Specifically, at least 100 vehicles of a suitable type (20 equipped with transceivers to communicate with hf radios at base stations and walkie-talkies), fifteen large (5 ton) trucks, one 30-passenger bus, five observation and two utility helicopters with crews, six long distance high frequency radio sets, six satellite link stations, and two hundred walkie-talkie transceivers are required.

Personnel familiar with security operations in the region are required to conduct initial and ongoing orientation and training of the Guards Contingent.

Operations

1. *Organization*

A. The Guards Contingent will be headed by the *Chief, Guards Contingent*, who will be located in Baghdad, Iraq, and will report directly to the Coordinator and Special representative in Iraq. He will be supported by a small administrative unit. The responsibilities of the Chief will be to:

- interface directly with the Coordinator of the Executive Delegate, keeping him informed of all ongoing activities;
- prepare security assessments and project resource requirements;

- submit requests for required resources, and to monitor the utilization of those resources when they become available;
- establish boundaries for and allocate resources to geographic sectors;
- communicate with appropriate Iraqi security officials, as directed by the Coordinator of the Executive Delegate;
- ensure the initial orientation and equipment for newly assigned personnel;
- ensure all appropriate records and reports are properly prepared and maintained.

The Chief, Guards Contingent, will be assisted by a Deputy.

B. There will be five Sector Guard Offices, each supervised by a Sector Commander. Each Sector Guard Office will be supported by an administrative officer/assistant. The responsibilities of the *Sector Commander* will be similar to those of the Chief, but for a smaller geographic area. Coordination upward will always be through the Chief, Guards Contingent's office. In addition, the Sector Commander will:

- deploy assigned guards so as to ensure the protection of UN resources;
- conduct ongoing training of all assigned personnel, as needed;
- submit regular status reports, morning and evening, as well as immediate reports of any unusual activities, including incidents which do not directly impact UN resources but which could indirectly increase risk of unrest, and thus have impact upon the ongoing UN relief operation.

C. There will be approximately ten Guard Teams per Sector Guard Office. Each team will consist of approximately 8 guards, depending on local circumstances. Teams will generally be assigned to specific locations such as towns or areas, or to "blue routes". *Team Leaders* will:

- ensure that guards perform all assigned responsibilities;
- personally monitor any unusual incidents, to include communications with higher elements.

D. The UN Guards Contingent in Iraq will report operationally to the Executive Delegate's Office, through the Coordinator in Baghdad. For the recruitment and administration of the Contingent, the UN Field Operations Division in New York will lend its support directly as well as through the administrative services of the UN Office in Geneva.

A minimal increase of staff in New York and in Geneva is foreseen for this purpose.

...

UN GUARDS CONTINGENT

1. *Conduct of Activities*

General: The United Nations Guards Contingent is assigned the responsibility of protecting all persons and material committed to Humanitarian relief under the auspices of the Office of the Executive Delegate. The safety and protection of these assets will best be assured via a highly visible, mobile, well trained, effectively coordinated, professional guard contingent.

Personal Conduct: All members of the Contingent will conduct themselves at all times so as best to represent the mission of the United Nations and the Guards Contingent. In effect, members of the Contingent are "on duty" at all times.

Dress and Appearance: Members of the Guards Contingent will, at all times, wear issued uniforms bearing the distinctive emblems of the United Nations.

Priorities of Responsibility: As a first priority, guards will protect personnel assigned under the auspices of the United Nations. Although the use of force is authorized to protect the lives of UN personnel, guards should act with restraint whenever possible. All efforts should be made to avoid the use of physical force.

As a second priority, guards will protect the property of UN and the associated relief agencies.

As a third priority, it is essential that operational and situation status be reported frequently by subordinate echelons. Similarly, it is important that such information not be extended outside of UN channels.

Other tasks may be assigned by the Chief of the Guards Contingent as situations warrant.

2. *Recruitment*

UN Contingent guards will be recruited from existing UN resources in so far as possible. This will assure clear understanding of UN operating principles. Secondarily, non-UN seconded persons familiar with such operations (through previous UN assignments or other suitable background) will become available.

The Office of the Executive Delegate will ensure that the Chief of the Guards Contingent, his deputy, Sector Commanders, Team Leaders, and key members of administrative support elements are drawn from UN resources.

Personnel will be recruited for a period of up to seven months, extending from 1 June 1991 through 31 December 1991. However, some individuals will arrive earlier than others.

...

Personnel will be encouraged to remain in assignment for the entire period of operations.

...

S/22799, 17 July 1991

33. Letter addressed to the President of the Security Council, 15 July 1991

I have the honour to transmit herewith for the attention of the members of the Council the report of the inter-agency mission headed by my Executive Delegate for the United Nations Inter-Agency Humanitarian Programme for Iraq, Kuwait and the Iraq/Turkey and Iraq/Iran border areas, Sadruddin Aga Khan.

The task entrusted to the mission, which visited Iraq from 29 June to 13 July 1991, was to assess current needs for humanitarian assistance and recommend measures for meeting those needs.

...

II. SUMMARY OF MAIN FINDINGS AND RECOMMENDATIONS

13. The mission members concluded that the scale of damage and decline in Iraq in the past year had indeed been dramatic. Eight years of war with the Islamic Republic of Iran had taken their toll even before the destruction of the Persian Gulf war. In significant parts of the country, the destruction caused by the internal civil conflicts that followed the war was comparable or even greater. A final factor had been the consequence of economic and financial sanctions imposed on Iraq, including the freezing of its foreign assets and a ban on the international sale of its oil. It was clear to the mission that the impact of the sanctions had been, and remains,

very substantial on the economy and living conditions of its civilian population. The mission was informed that the last reserves of food commodities that are included in the ration basket are in the process of being exhausted.

14. During the past several months major efforts have been made by the Government of Iraq to restore the country to some semblance of its pre-war situation. These efforts have been only partially successful. For example, a number of bridges have been repaired, and with the limited pumping of oil for local consumption, internal transport capabilities have in large part been restored.

15. However, the mission found that in the sectors of concern to it, the process of restoration had in many crucial respects reached its limit. Indeed, there are a number of problem areas that are likely to worsen in the foreseeable future. A review of several of the main findings within each of the sectors, which are discussed in more detail in the later sections of this report, gives reason for alarm.

16. As far as water is concerned, damage to water-treatment plants and the inability to obtain needed spare parts have cut off an estimated 2.5 million Iraqis from the government system they relied upon before the war. The perhaps 14.5 million Iraqis who continue to receive their water through this system are now provided on average with one quarter the pre-war amount per day. Much of this water is of doubtful quality, owing to such problems as defective treatment and lack of sufficient hours of electric power. Major damage was also suffered by the national sewerage system owing to the loss of electric power during the war. Most of this damage has not been repaired, with raw sewage now flowing in some city streets and into the rivers. Diarrhoeal diseases, thought to be mainly caused by water and sewage problems, are now at four times the level of a year ago. The country is already experiencing outbreaks of typhoid and cholera.

17. The health of the population in Iraq is now challenged by growing environmental hazards, insufficient access to quality medical care and inadequate nutrition. Public health programmes have reduced their activities for lack of supplies. Hospitals and public health centres are severely affected by lack of electricity, water and medicines. Medical, surgical, dental and laboratory equipment suffer from the lack of spare parts, reagents and maintenance. The fleet of vehicles that once assured the effectiveness of the health services has been reduced to a few units. Iraq used to import annually approximately $US 360 million worth of drugs and medical appliances alone. It is highly improbable that international humanitarian aid will be able to meet this demand. Mechanisms need to be established urgently for the country to procure its own medical supplies and to maintain its equipment in operation. Failing this, the health situation will further worsen. Vulnerable groups, each day more numerous, will be the first victims.

18. As for the food supply, the position is deteriorating rapidly in virtually all parts of the country. Preliminary forecasts for the current main harvest indicate that this year's aggregate cereal production will be around one third of last year's. This will further increase the country's dependence on imports, which even in good years has meant that approximately 70 per cent of its food needs must be imported. Data collected on prices throughout the country show tremendous levels of inflation. For example, current retail prices for wheat and rice - the two normal staple food items - remain 45 and 22 times their corresponding price levels of last year, while average incomes have shown only moderate gains. The government rationing system, even if basically equitable in its distribution, can provide only about one third of the typical family's food needs, resulting in a strikingly low level of dietary intake. The situation is particularly alarming with respect to the nutritional status of children, pregnant and lactating mothers as well as households headed by widows. Several independent studies and direct observation by the mission confirmed the high prevalence of malnutrition among children. There are numerous, reliable reports of families resorting to sales of personal and household items to meet their immediate needs. Taken collectively, this information clearly demonstrates a widespread and acute food supply crisis which, if not averted through timely intervention, will gradually but inexorably cause massive starvation throughout the country.

19. The current emergency feeding programmes, such as those being implemented by WFP for vulnerable groups, refugees, returnees and internally displaced persons accordingly acquire special significance and need to be maintained for at least the next few months. The process of repatriation must be encouraged by the continued provision of timely and adequate amounts of relief aid, not least to ensure that the situation in the areas to which the refugees are returning reverts to normal as quickly as possible. It should be noted that the economic sanctions also lessen the ability of the returning refugees to resume their ordinary lives and traditional economic activities. Indeed, the mission was informed by the Kurdish leadership that the sanctions were taking an unfortunately harmful toll upon the living conditions of the Kurdish population.

20. In terms of power generation, Iraq's capacity had been reduced to a negligible level by the end of February 1991. At present, the power generating capacity has been restored to 25 per cent of the pre-war level. As it is operating continuously, electricity production is about 40 per cent of the 1990 level. However, this restoration process has been accomplished through such methods as cannibalizing parts from damaged units, making risky makeshift repairs and operating the remaining plants without the normal breaks for maintenance and repairs. At this point, little more can be done to increase power generation further unless major imports of new parts are allowed. Barring this, power output can be expected to decline from now on. The mission has also assessed the situation of the oil sectors. The requirements of the internal market can essentially be met with the current production and refining capacity, although with repairs needed soon for some refineries that are in precarious condition. The main concern is the oil export capacity, which is now only one third of the pre-war level.

21. As for telecommunications, the ITU team noted that at least 400,000 of the original 900,000 telephone lines were damaged beyond repair, while additional ones were partly damaged. The main microwave links connecting most of the cities were also damaged. This has had an obvious negative impact on the operation of health and social services as well as on humanitarian assistance programmes. All international telecommunications were put out of service. Even after restoration work, the system can still handle only 30 per cent of its pre-war internal service, while international telecommunications remain out of service.

22. Clearly, the situation described above is one that deserves urgent attention and immediate response. In considering what actions to recommend, the mission came to a series of additional conclusions.

23. As spelled out in the specific sector reports, the primary action that is needed to address these needs is the import of material goods. This includes such items as drugs, vaccines, medical equipment, ambulances, spare parts and replacements for water and sewerage equipment, food and agricultural inputs and equipment and parts for power generation plants and the oil sector, as well as for the telecommunications network.

24. A review of the relevant Security Council resolutions and decisions by the Security Council Committee established by resolution 661 (1990) concerning the situation between Iraq and Kuwait indicates that the sale or supply to Iraq of most of these items is not restricted, although for most items

notification to or prior approval by the Sanctions Committee would be required. Many fall under the clauses exempting "medicine and health supplies" and "foodstuffs" from the sanctions (see resolutions 661 (1990), 666 (1990) and 687 (1991)). Others fall under the category of materials and supplies for "essential civilian needs" as exempted in resolution 687 (1991), as well as the clause contained in the 20 March 1991 Sanctions Committee decision. The latter provides that civilian and humanitarian imports to Iraq, as identified in the report of that date to the Secretary-General, are integrally related to the supply of foodstuffs and supplies intended strictly for medical purposes ... and that such imports should also be allowed ..., subject to approval by the Sanctions Committee under its no-objection procedure. So far, the relevance to the humanitarian programme of the import of spare parts and equipment for the restoration of electric power plants and for the telecommunications network has not been recognized.

25. In this context, the mission observed that, in most of the cases that came to its attention, problems to date with importing the above items had more to do with the financing of such imports than actual prohibitions. The question of financing becomes even more crucial in relation to future importations that need to be made.

26. The mission members utilized the best information available to them to estimate the costs of returning the systems in each of the four sector areas to their pre-war condition. This proved possible for most sectors, with the estimates being $US 12 billion for the power-generating capacity, $US 6 billion for the oil sector, $US 450 million for the water and sanitation systems, $US 2.64 billion for food imports and $US 500 million for agricultural imports. While these calculations were not possible for health, an indicative figure would be the typical level of international imports for the health sector for one year, which has been approximately $US 500 million.

27. The principal criterion adopted by the mission in evaluating these needs has been that it is concerned not only with addressing immediate requirements of humanitarian scope and nature, but also with averting a crisis in the next 6 to 12 months. To illustrate this point, urgent measures must be taken now to ensure that the next agricultural planting season can be completed under reasonably normal conditions.

28. Consequently, the mission attempted to determine the costs for some lower level of actions, over a one-year time-frame. Figures were calculated for providing approximately two fifths of the pre-war per capita levels of clean drinking water and putting a corresponding proportion of the damaged sewage-treatment capacity back in operation. Expenditures for imports for health services were calculated at the pre-war level. Food import calculations were based on the ration level that WFP provides to sustain disaster-stricken populations. Special supplemental feeding programmes to support the nutritional needs of malnourished children and pregnant and lactating mothers for one year were calculated. Power generation estimates were based on restoring approximately one half of the pre-war capacity of the country. For the oil sector, the mission worked out a cost based on the consolidation of existing refineries, the restoration of lubrication units, the repair of the Iraq-Turkey pipelines, and of the oil facilities in the Kirkuk areas. This would not include repair of the southern oil fields.

29. The total estimated costs for this greatly reduced level of services came to approximately $US 6.8 billion over a one-year period. This includes $US 180 million for water and sanitation, $US 500 million for health services, $US 53 million for supplemental feeding, $US 1.62 billion for general food imports, $US 300 million for essential agricultural needs, $US 2 billion for the oil sector and $US 2.2 billion for power generation. If this analysis is supplied to a four-month time-frame, the requirements would come to $US 60 million for water and sanitation, $US 167 million for health services, $US 18 million for supplemental feeding, $US 540 million for food imports, $US 100 million for essential agricultural imports, $US 667 million for the oil sector, and $US 1.1 billion for power generation. The power and oil sectors include allowances for the front-end costs occurring in these sectors. Thus, the total for an initial four-month period would be $US 2.63 billion.

30. The massive financial requirements to establish even this reduced level of service are of a scale far beyond what is, or is likely to be, available under any United Nations-sponsored programme. The current United Nations appeal for humanitarian assistance for Iraq, Kuwait and the border areas with the Islamic Republic of Iran and Turkey has received only some $US 210 million to date. Most of these funds are pledged for the needs of refugees and returnees. Further, any additional requests for aid to Iraq must compete with a continually lengthening list of other emergency situations around the world with very compelling needs.

31. It is evident that the Iraqi Government itself will have to revise its priorities and mobilize all internal resources. It will also have to finance the import of the type of materials under discussion, for which it has already requested approval from the Security Council Committee established by resolution 661 (1990). It certainly appeared that the Iraqi Government has the potential itself to generate the funds required to cover the needs identified by the team. This could be done either by the unfreezing of substantial amounts of Iraqi assets now held abroad or through the pumping and subsequent international sale of oil. The mission was informed that foreign exchange reserves of only $US 14.75 million were on hand in the central bank and that the government's holding of gold bullion in support of the national currency had remained constant for the last 20 years.

32. With respect to the possible sale of oil by the Iraqi Government to finance such imports, paragraph 23 of Security Council resolution 687 (1991) empowers the Security Council Committee established by resolution 661 (1990) to approve exceptions to the prohibition against the import of commodities and products originating in Iraq, with the explicit purpose of assuring "adequate financial resources" on the part of the Iraqi Government to procure medicine and health supplies, foodstuffs and materials and supplies for "essential civilian needs".

33. According to the Government, the current oil-production capacity of the country is 1,455 million barrels per day. Taking into account internal consumption requirements, the production available for export could be about 1 million barrels per day. This would mean a potential net revenue of $US 5.5 billion over one year. Furthermore, in order to increase the production to the pre-war level, extensive repairs and rebuilding would have to take place, particularly in the Basra area. The mission therefore recommends that Iraq be allowed to import over a four-month period $US 1 billion worth of equipment, spare parts and consumable materials to start restoration of the oil sector.

34. If the Security Council Committee were to decide that Iraq should be allowed to use funds from oil sales or facilitate the use of blocked accounts in order to meet urgent humanitarian needs, the Government indicated that it would cooperate in making available documentation relating to sales of crude oil as well as purchases of the authorized imports. It noted that all revenues accruing from oil sales were normally held in United States banks and that a suitable device for monitoring such credit balances could be established. This procedure could include information on the use of unfrozen accounts. In addition, the staff of the United Nations and other humanitarian agencies present in Iraq, as well as special

missions designated by the Secretary-General as required, might for instance submit periodic assessments and in particular report on the changes in the composition of the rations of foodstuffs and the provision of health and social services brought about by increased imports. The staff concerned would also obtain up-to-date information on the repair and improvement of power-generating capacity, the operation of water and sewerage plants and the like. The envisaged procedure would thus help to ensure the actual receipt of the civilian and humanitarian goods in Iraq and their utilization by the intended beneficiaries.

35. In summary, the mission recommends that:

(a) Immediate steps be taken to alleviate the priority needs identified by the mission in the areas of food supply, health services, water and sanitation, power generation, the oil sector and telecommunications;

(b) To meet these needs, essential goods and materials should be imported, including:

(i) Food to meet the minimum consumption requirements, in part to reduce and shorten the emergency relief operation now in operation at donors' expense;

(ii) Agricultural inputs, including fertilizers, pesticides, animal feed and drugs, machinery and spare parts needed to repair the damaged irrigation and drainage system;

(iii) Drugs, including raw materials needed for local pharmaceutical production, vaccines, medical supplies and medical, surgical, dental and diagnostic equipment for the health system;

(iv) Vehicles (and spare parts for them) needed by the health system, including ambulances;

(v) Spare parts, supplies and equipment and replacement pumps and other heavy equipment needed by water-treatment and pumping facilities and by the sewage treatment system;

(vi) Equipment, materials and spare parts for the electric power system, the oil sector and for the telecommunication sector;

(c) A monitoring system should be instituted for this purpose. The relevant commercial transactions relating to the export of oil and the import of the above-mentioned goods and services could be made sufficiently transparent at the international level to allow adequate controls with respect to their shipment and entry into Iraq. The monitoring arrangements in the context of the United Nations humanitarian presence in Iraq, as outlined in paragraph 13 of the Memorandum of Understanding of 18 April 1991, could be further developed and strengthened so as to provide adequate information on the destination and use of the goods in question.

[Individual sector reports on the issues raised in this Summary have been omitted.]

34. Updated Plan of Action for the [UN] Inter-Agency Humanitarian Programme, 1 September-31 December 1991

To respond to enormous humanitarian needs in Iraq and the surrounding region in the wake of the Persian Gulf war, the United Nations launched a consolidated Appeal for urgent humanitarian action on 15 May 1991. A variety of actions were proposed for the period up to 31 August, *inter alia*, food aid requirements, repatriation efforts, provision of emergency humanitarian assistance to vulnerable groups in Iraq, environmental and health related assistance to Kuwait, and the deployment of UN Guards.

Of the US$ 460,320,000 requested, US$ 261,452,000 was received. Despite such a serious shortfall in financial resources, a number of important successes were achieved. Most importantly, through the system of blue routes and humanitarian centres established under this program, virtually all of the refugees have returned from Turkey and Iran. Credit here is due largely to the exceptional effort and devotion of United Nations agencies and NGOs, both in the field and in their respective headquarters.

The humanitarian program inside Iraq has been effective in protecting and caring for the returnees and other vulnerable groups. Some 470 UN Guards have been deployed and are serving throughout Iraq, acting primarily to protect UN personnel and property, but serving further as a symbol of international attention and concern that eventual violations of fundamental human rights will not be ignored by the international community. United Nations agencies described in this report, assisted by private organizations, have provided basic humanitarian services, including provision of food, clean water, basic health and sanitation programs, to at least two million refugees and returnees and millions of other vulnerable people in Iraq.

These results, impressive as they have been, fall far short of meeting the enormity of humanitarian needs that continue to exist in Iraq. This updated action plan addresses some of those needs, but by no means all. It became obvious in mid-July that the scope of the problem surpassed the assistance that could be expected from voluntary contributions by the international community. With this in mind, the Executive Delegate proposed a complex programme of action which resulted in the 15 August adoption of Security Council Resolution 706. When put into motion, it will resolve at least for the time being many of the humanitarian problems confronting the population of Iraq.

...

WHAT HAS BEEN ACHIEVED

The launching of the 15 May Appeal activated a broad range of activities throughout the UN, its specialised agencies, and related NGOs in response to the many crises then confronting the population of Iraq and its border areas. On behalf of the United Nations, the Office of the Executive Delegate (OED) has co-ordinated an inter-agency humanitarian programme in which many UN organs have played an important part, UNHCR, UNICEF, WFP and WHO primary among them. Beyond this, eighteen NGOs have utilized 192 international staff and considerable local manpower to implement a wide range of complementary projects and programmes.

Together, they achieved the following during the period covered by the appeal:

FOOD REQUIREMENTS

WFP:

Assistance to vulnerable groups in Iraq:

As of April 1991, emergency food allocations were made available through ICRC (from stocks in Jordan) to war-affected vulnerable groups in Iraq. This programme provided food to vulnerable populations through Iraqi institutions - orphanages, kindergartens. old age homes, health care centres - as well as to Iranian refugees in one refugee camp. In addition, WFP provided food to those beneficiaries of the Iraqi social welfare system who were destitute and to displaced people in northern and southern Iraq.

...

Assistance to vulnerable groups in Iran:

WFP's ongoing emergency food assistance programme (EMOP 4715), in place since last April, initially targeted 1 million people in Iran's five border provinces, later reducing its caseload as refugees returned. WFP provided transport to extended delivery points in the provinces involved.

Assistance to refugees in Turkey:

A WFP emergency operation for up to half a million Kurdish refugees was carried out from May onward. The operation became cross-border as the refugees involved returned to Iraq.

FAO:

In May 1991, FAO arranged to have the wheat crop in northern Iraq sprayed against sunn pest. According to reports available from the Iraqi Ministry of Agriculture, spraying destroyed between 90 and 95 per cent of the sunn in treated areas. In numerical terms, the area covered by six helicopters in ten days of FAO-monitored operations was some 90,000 hectares.

Assistance provided by the Kingdom of the Netherlands has allowed FAO/OSRO to formulate and implement emergency relief assistance aimed at the urgent provision of staple vegetable seeds, veterinary drugs and vaccines, and plastic sheeting for greenhouse covers. Tenders have been issued, and the required inputs should reach Iraqi farmers in time for the September/October vegetable planting season.

REFUGEES AND REPATRIATION

UNHCR:

Assistance to refugees in Iran

Some 1.4 million refugees fled from Iraq in April-May 1991, to be given asylum in five provinces of the Islamic Republic of Iran. From the onset of the emergency, the main objective was to keep people alive until they could return home. This was achieved by supplying food, blankets, tents, high protein food, and other material relief supplies, and by providing basic services (clean water, sanitation and health care).

The voluntary return of Iraqis to their homes, which had already been noted in the mid-May Appeal, increased dramatically during the implementation period. Today approximately 120,000 refugees remain. This massive return was assisted by the UNHCR and private organisations. UNHCR also started a winterisation programme for the 75,000 who are expected to remain in camps.

Assistance to refugees in Turkey

The number of Iraqis who fled their homes with the intention of seeking asylum in Turkey is estimated to be 450,000. Most of these returned home during the appeal period. Only 4,300 remain today, mostly at the Haj camp near Silopi.

An enormous effort was launched by the United Nations, by coalition military forces, by the Turkish Government and by private organizations to save the lives of the refugees who fled. The U.S. Centres for Disease Control estimates that fewer than 5,000 people lost their lives.

UNHCR activities in the Haj Camp since June were devoted primarily to repatriation (approximately 10,000 voluntarily returned to Iraq), protection, and implementation of short-term sanitation and water projects. Additionally, supplementary food and clothing distributions were provided. Projects begun during the Appeal period and continuing today include primary education for young children and organizing basic sanitation and hygiene instruction for refugee women.

Another 23,000 refugees who remain in Turkey arrived in August 1988. They were provided basic protection and life-sustaining necessities during the Appeal period.

WHO dispatched technical missions to supervise assistance given to the approximately 500,000 Kurdish refugees who flooded the border region and to assess the health needs of the refugees in Turkey. The team operated along the Iraqi-Turkish border. It organized training courses in emergency relief operations for local staff and coordinated the health component of the United Nations operational measures.

With the closing of most of the camps in the Turkish territory, work shifted to areas within Iraq.

Support for Voluntary Repatriation in North and Eastern Iraq

In Northwestern Iraq, the UNHCR assumed responsibility for all assistance activities from the departing coalition armed forces on 7 June. Working in close cooperation with other United Nations agencies, most notably the Office of the Executive Delegate, WFP, WHO, and UNICEF, as well as IOM and other NGOs, UNHCR worked to ensure the reintegration of the returnee population. Key electrical and water services were successfully re-established. The process of re-introducing basic public services formerly provided by governmental entities, e.g., health, food distribution, was begun in co-operation with relevant national institutions.

The return movement to north-eastern Iraq of an estimated 1.3 million Iraqi refugees occurred during the Appeal period. About 50% have either returned or are in the process of returning to the homes from which they fled. They were assisted in all aspects of re-integration by the United Nations.

An estimated 250,000 are attempting to return to their ancestral villages along the border in Kurdish-controlled areas. Many are simply living in temporary arrangements because they hesitate to return to government controlled population centres. UNHCR, together with other United Nations and private agencies, provided basic life sustaining assistance to these people during the appeal period. In addition, UNHCR began a winterisation programme which will be the centrepiece of their proposed activity in the updated action plan.

Transport and Storage

The United Nations agencies combined established a network of 34 warehouses, permanent and portable, in thirteen different locations in Iraq, for the storage and distribution of emergency and relief material. This network was supplied by air shipments transitting through

Baghdad and by over-land shipments from or through Turkey and Jordan.

Distribution within Iraq was accomplished using the services of trucking agencies contracted directly by UNHCR or the International Organisation for Migration (IOM). Special arrangements were made for the transport and distribution of medical supplies.

Domestic Needs

To meet the most immediate domestic necessities of nearly 50% of the estimated 1.8 million people who returned to Iraq from Iran and Turkey, the UNHCR developed and distributed a basic relief "package" consisting of jerry cans, cooking sets, water buckets, and soap. Tents, blankets and plastic sheeting were distributed early in July to those returnees who possessed no shelter whatsoever.

UNHCR planned for and ordered other basic domestic supplies necessary for survival during the winter months. These supplies, including kerosene stoves and storage containers, will be distributed during the next several months, with priority being given to those in mountainous, severe-weather regions.

Water and Sanitation

In order to ensure the quality of water in areas where the returnees settled, an extensive programme was initiated to prepare the ground for the rehabilitating water systems. Planning for the purchase and installation of generators, pumps, and pipes, sufficient for at least 50 villages and town delivery systems, was completed. Water testing kits were also provided to water engineers working on the rehabilitation project.

UNHCR water activities have been predicated on the need to link reconstruction and re-integration of national systems with the systems in areas not under governmental control. The plan was developed to strengthen the entire system by purchasing essential spare parts for water transport and delivery equipment which has fallen into disrepair. Plans were also developed to procure insulating material for water delivery during winter and chlorine to treat water delivered to larger population concentrations.

Sanitation planning was predicated on the requirement of meeting immediate public health needs of returnees and displaced persons, but also of strengthening the national sanitation system. Latrines were constructed, and garbage systems set up for those who needed them. Spare parts were purchased to make minor repairs on urban sanitation systems.

In the Dohuk valley, the coalition armed forces together with NGOs provided water tanks which were centrally placed to provide potable water immediately to areas where large groups of returnees first gathered. These stationary tanks were supplemented by the rental for local circulation of 25 mobile water-tankers.

Health

In addition to supplies provided by UNICEF and WHO, UNHCR conducted nutritional surveys and provided basic and emergency health kits to clinics established to render immediate medical care to returnees. It also conducted nutritional surveys. Sera for the treatment of snake bites, scorpion stings and tetanus - endemic to the northern regions - were purchased jointly by WHO and UNHCR for distribution through local clinics. A non-governmental agency was engaged by UNHCR to distribute pharmaceuticals through established clinics and other NGOs in the regions.

UNHCR, UNICEF, and WHO worked in close co-operation with the Ministry of Health to strengthen and extend the health care systems in the governorates of Dohuk, Erbil and Sulaymaniyah. Medicines and medical equipment were distributed through clinics in communities where the returnees settled.

Renovations in preparation for winter were begun in at least 20 health facilities. Spare parts were purchased for distribution to these facilities.

As in the case of water and sanitation, many of the health-related projects were collaborative efforts with both Kurdish and national organizations.

IOM:

The International Organization for Migration (IOM), in line with its responsibilities within the U.N. inter-agency programme, continued to assist in the repatriation of displaced Iraqis from Turkey and Iran, to meet transportation needs within Iraq from border areas to individuals' home areas, and to repatriate third-country nationals from various countries in the region.

To cover its operational requirements, IOM expanded its existing structure in the region and opened additional bureaus; within Iraq, IOM is now present in Baghdad, Basrah, Dohuk, Erbil, and Sulaymaniyah. IOM hired a fleet of over 200 trucks and buses and dispatched them to areas where displaced persons were concentrated. This transport capacity was also utilized to assist various UN organizations in the shipment of relief supplies. In addition to ground transportation, movements by air were arranged for the repatriation of third-country nationals.

During the period between January and August 1991, a total of 447,185 movements were effected by the Organization. Of these, 402,477 involved international repatriation and domestic return of Iraqi nationals, while 44,708 were repatriation movements of third-country nationals from Jordan, Kuwait, Saudi Arabia, Syria, and other countries. When added to the 162,600 movements that IOM had already effected in the first phase of the Gulf Emergency Programme (September - December 1990), this brings the total number of those assisted by IOM to date to 609,785.

Emergency Humanitarian Assistance in Iraq

UNICEF:

Water and Sanitation

The general approach adopted by UNICEF in the water and sanitation sector was to channel international contributions to assist Iraq in the rehabilitation of its existing water and sanitation networks. This approach has proven to be effective.

UNICEF responded early to address critical water and sanitation problems besetting Iraq in the aftermath of the war. The initial response, commencing immediately after the cease-fire, centred on Baghdad. UNICEF provided water purification reagents, spare parts and fuel for generators, and collars to repair broken water pipes. UNICEF also played an important role in the prompt restoration of minimal water supplies to the city.

At the same time, UNICEF water and sanitation specialists were dispatched to various regions of the country to perform related needs assessments, identify areas of potential UNICEF assistance, provide technical advice and assistance to Iraqi water department engineers in regional centres, and monitor the restoration progress of water and sanitation systems.

To date, the following supplies have been received and put into use: 2,849 tonnes of water purification reagents, 7 incubators, 1,797 collars for repairing pipes, 80,000 litres of diesel, 4 generators, and 28 water tanks.

Basic Health

In an effort to control diarrhoeal diseases, UNICEF supplied over 8 million sachets of oral rehydration salts to health centres and hospitals throughout the country. In addition, workshops and orientation sessions were conducted in various governorates for those involved in diarrhoeal disease control programmes. A trainers' training course on control of diarrhoeal diseases covering thirty trainers has also been concluded. Oral rehydration therapy/nutrition corners were established in many health centres.

During the Appeal period, the emergency provision of essential drugs was a top UNICEF and WHO priority. After finalizing distribution plans, drug shipments were promptly dispatched to Baghdad and other governorates. To date, UNICEF has provided essential drugs, as well as some 275 basic emergency health kits sufficient for 10,000 people for 3 months. Total medical supplies distributed amounted to more than 1,000 tonnes.

As a means to control communicable diseases, UNICEF provided technical assistance in disease surveillance to local health officials. Programme interventions such as sentinel site surveillance and laboratory testing were introduced as means of providing early warning and control of communicable diseases. As a result, surveillance systems were established in 11 Baghdad health centres. Programme interventions in other parts of the country were planned.

UNICEF also provided the necessary resources and technical assistance to upgrade primary health-worker technical skills and logistical support to the health programme.

WHO helped in the introduction of the epidemiological surveillance of infectious diseases, including control measures for diagnosing and treating diarrhoeal diseases and monitoring cholera, typhoid fever, and malaria.

Immunization

Perhaps the most important UNICEF health sector contribution was its central role in re-instituting Iraq's Expanded Programme for Immunization (EPI). UNICEF launched a massive supply and logistics effort, acquiring and transporting large quantities of vaccines and cold chain equipment, supplies, and manpower development, while WHO provided technical assistance. Training of key trainers on cold chain maintenance has been concluded in all eighteen governorates by a UNICEF consultant.

In March 1991, EPI activities recommenced in 81 centres in Baghdad; in the following weeks, the programme quickly expanded nationwide. UNICEF provided over 2.5 million doses of DPT, BCG, polio, measles and tetanus vaccines, as well as supplies and equipment. Approximately 850 health centres across the country are now being equipped to provide immunization services for a special drive beginning in October 1991.

Nutrition

UNICEF fielded a mission to assess the nutritional status of malnourished vulnerable populations; plans were developed to implement the mission findings. A pilot therapeutic feeding and supplementary nutrition programme was started in Basrah with plans to expand to other areas of demonstrated need. High energy biscuits (over 100 tonnes) and special weaning foods were provided. A breast-feeding promotion campaign was also launched.

UNV:

A total of 81 UNVs were in various stages of recruitment and deployment during the appeal period. UNV was particularly effective in the rapid fielding of crucially needed manpower in the initial stages of the UN humanitarian emergency programme in Iraq. The bulk of the UNVs have served in Iraq itself, and, to a lesser degree, in Turkey, Iran, Syria, and Jordan, working with WFP, UNICEF, UNHCR, IRCU, IOM, and WHO.

The UNVs have played key roles within each agency's field operation and management of field offices. They have provided technical assistance as repatriation and relocation officers, logisticians, water and civil engineers, physical planners, food aid monitors, and public health co-ordinators.

KUWAIT

WHO:

Accomplishments in Kuwait have been limited. WHO established a Country Liaison Office in Kuwait on 15 May 1991 with the aim of implementing the Emergency Health Plan. Activities covered during the Appeal period include:

- assignment of a short term consultant epidemiologist who worked with the Environment Protection Council (EPC),
- assignment of a WHO Headquarters air pollution specialist to develop project proposals for the protection of human health and the environment,
- supply of two fixed monitoring stations,
- provision for data collection and management of aerometric data to initiate real-time model forecasts of air pollution,
- provision of spare parts for monitoring systems,
- provision of consultative services,
- provision of modems and data transmission equipment.

...

UN GUARDS CONTINGENT

Project 6.1: UN Guards Contingent

Implementing: Office of the Executive Delegate (OED)
Agency: UN Field Operations Division (UNFOD)

Revised Funding: US$ 46,269,000

Revised Project Implementation:

As of 1 September 1991, the total number of Guards deployed in Iraq was 420. The contingent is expected to reach 470 by September 20, with the deployment of 50 additional donor sponsored Guards. In order to reach the target of 500 Guards, as set out in the Memorandum of Understanding of 18 April 1991, the Office of the Executive Delegate is presently seeking to fill the remaining thirty posts with personnel from other donors.

In view of the UN Guards mandate to protect UN personnel, assets and operations linked to the humanitarian programme, the Contingent will continue operations in the areas of Dohuk, Sulamaniyah, Erbil and Basrah, with the central command in Baghdad.

Administration of Guards. As of 1 September, the United Nations Field Operations Division in New York will manage administrative, financial and personnel functions related to the Guards. OED will maintain overall responsibility for the operation as well as for the co-ordination of operational and activity reporting functions.

The Guards are expected to continue playing a vital role in maintaining a climate of security in the region where they are present thereby also facilitating the return and resettlement of displaced persons.

OED:

The agreement to deploy 500 United Nations Guards was signed in Baghdad on 24 May 1991 under the provisions of the Memorandum of Understanding with the Iraqi government. This agreement was crucial to the successful turnover of humanitarian operations from the coalition forces in the Dohuk area to the United Nations. As of 17 September, 1991, 470 Guards will have been deployed in the region.

The guards have been successful in protecting UN personnel, assets, and operations, including sub-offices in the governorates, United Nations Humanitarian Centres (UNHUCS), and the Coordinator's office in Baghdad. By their presence, the Guards have also performed a humanitarian protection role.

As of August 31, the UN Guards have provided 311 escorts to convoys of UN organizations. Patrols totalling 233,921 kilometres have been conducted in areas of operation.

UNHCR Information Bulletin No. 6, 3 October 1991

34. UNHCR, Operations in the Persian Gulf Region, October 1991

Of the 1.4 million Iraqis who had taken refuge in Iran in early May, and the 400,000 who had fled to Turkey and its border regions, all but some 60,000 in Iran and some 5,000 in Turkey have returned.

On 24 September, 2,500 trucks began to ship winter building materials from Turkey to northern Iraq for UNHCR's comprehensive winter preparation programmes for the most vulnerable Iraqi returnees.

The updated United Nations Plan of Action issued in Geneva on 1 September foresees the revised 1991 requirements of UNHCR at US$ 220 million.

In Saudi Arabia and Kuwait, UNHCR is increasing its presence in order to find durable solutions for refugees and stateless persons stranded after the Persian Gulf war.

The Persian Gulf crisis has proved to be an unprecedented example of UN-NGO collaboration. UNHCR works in partnership with over 30 NGOs in Turkey, Iran and Iraq.

INTRODUCTION

The Emergency Shelter Programmes

As a harsh winter approaches in Northern Iraq and Iran, UNHCR has launched one of the most ambitious emergency shelter programmes ever undertaken by the Office. In Iraq, the aim is to provide up to 62,000 displaced returnee families - close to 400,000 people - in the Governorates of Dohuk, Erbil and Suleimaniyah with temporary shelter and the basics to survive freezing winter temperatures. For this purpose 22,000 cubic meters of timber, 5,400 MT of corrugated iron sheets, tools, heaters, stoves, blankets, quilts and sleeping bags will be transported and distributed using a logistics chain comprising some 2,500 trucks, and a network of some forty warehouses. The massive operation will be coordinated through UNHCR's 12 Field Offices by 150 international staff. UNHCR will also count on the precious support of local authorities and numerous NGOs. For the 40,000 Iraqi refugees threatened by a cold winter in the north-western Provinces of Iran, UNHCR is delivering and setting up 3,300 pre-fabricated dwellings that can withstand temperatures of minus 26 degrees centigrade.

Recent Unrest

Recent unrest compelled UNHCR to change its initial planning assumptions. When the Iraq winter programme was planned in early July, it was assumed that the majority of the 650,000 displaced returnees would return to their previous homes in lower altitude areas. The target population for the winter programme, those who would remain in the mountains, was estimated at 40,000 families. Renewed violence at the beginning of September in some of the major cities in northern Iraq compelled a revision of the initial planning figures as the flow of the displaced down from the mountains slowed down and in some cases, was even reversed. The target beneficiary figure, as a result, was revised to 62,000 families in need of winter shelter by mid-November. The return of the displaced to their habitual homes has not been encouraged by the absence of a UN office in Kirkuk for which a number of requests have been made to the authorities.

Case by Case Review

In Turkey, UNHCR has initiated a case by case review of the remaining Iraqi refugees, both those who fled in 1988 and in 1991, in order to ascertain their status and eventual eligibility for resettlement. UNHCR is also assisting with on-going repatriation. To counter environmental hazards, a cleaning campaign has been started in ex-camps. Turkey is furthermore the major staging post for UNHCR's winter programmes in Iraq and Iran.

Stranded Refugees

In Kuwait, a high level UNHCR mission at the beginning of August, reached an agreement with the authorities for sending staff to address the pressing needs of refugees and stateless persons stranded in the Abdali camp and in Kuwait city. As a result of close cooperation developed with the Kuwaiti authorities, durable solutions have been found for most of the people in Abdali and it should be possible to close the camp shortly. Similarly in Saudi Arabia, UNHCR is addressing the individual needs of stranded refugees and asylum seekers. In Jordan and Syria, UNHCR offices established at the height of the Persian Gulf crisis, continue to assist refugees displaced as a result of the war.

Financial Update

An up-dated United Nations Plan of Action covering the period until 31 December was issued on September 1. UNHCR activities for 1991 are budgeted at US$ 220 million. Contributions recorded by 30 September amount to US$ 206 million leaving a shortfall of US$ 14 million.

...

IRAQ

Over half a million not back home

Internal conflict in Northern Iraq in March compelled some 1.8 million Iraqis to flee to the border regions of Turkey and Iran. By the end of September the majority had returned to Iraq. Some moved back to their previous homes, but at least 650,000 remained away from their homes in border areas of the Sulaimanyia, Erbil and Dohuk Governorates. Of this group, some decided to settle in the ruins of their original villages, while others are awaiting the outcome of negotiations between the Government of Iraq and the Kurdish leadership in temporary shelters in the mountains. As winter approaches, many of the latter group are expected to move down to the valleys where permanent shelter is available in towns or collective villages. UNHCR has made special arrangements for those who will not move.

Preparing for a winter in the cold

In one of its largest logistics operations ever, UNHCR on 25 September, began to move 2,500 trucks with construction materials from Turkey to the Suleimaniyah, Erbil and Dohuk provinces in Iraq. This operation is part of UNHCR's preparations for up to 62,000 families (372,000 people) who may remain in exposed areas where temperatures drop to well below freezing. Many have already started to insulate their makeshift dwellings with mud bricks and stone from destroyed villages. UNHCR's shelter programme will supplement their efforts by providing them with a full winter kit: roofing materials, tools (pickaxes, shovels, nails ...) blankets, kerosene stoves, heaters, kerosene, jerry cans, mattresses and winter clothing. Some 15,000 winter tents will also be kept in reserve. The programme is being implemented by local committees and NGOs, some of whom are contributing their own funds to the winter shelter construction programme. It will be completed by the end of November.

A fully integrated programme

Under the same programme, health services and water supply systems are being restored in valley towns and villages to allow the displaced in the mountains to return. Sufficient generators, pumps and piping will be installed to repair at least 50 village and town water systems. At least twenty health centres, hospitals and clinics are to be renovated and provided with sufficient medical supplies for the winter. Winter preparations are being undertaken in both Government and non-Government controlled areas. With UNHCR, WFP will continue to provide food during the winter for some 390,000 returnees. IOM in coordination with UNHCR will provide transport to those displaced who wish to return to the towns or Government resettlement villages.

Repatriation to Iran

UNHCR has now initiated organized repatriation of Iranian refugees from Al Tash camp, west of Baghdad. The first convoy of 400 returnees has left on 28 September. Regular convoys will follow with some 500 repatriants [*sic*] each. The truck convoys are accompanied by UNHCR staff members from Iraq and from the Islamic Republic of Iran.

...

ISLAMIC REPUBLIC OF IRAN

...

Reduced repatriation flow

In only a few months, the Islamic Republic of Iran witnessed one of the most dramatic rates of influx as well as one of the largest repatriation movements ever. In late April there were some 1.4 million refugees in 98 camps. Now only 30 camps remain. Since mid-August the number of refugees returning to Iraq has decreased. Regular cross border meetings between UNHCR and IOM officers ensure the coordination of the steady, but reduced flow of repatriants.

Winter preparations

The Iranian winter is harshest in the three northern border Provinces of West Azerbaijan, Kurdistan and Bakhtaran. UNHCR is preparing six winter camps in these provinces. 3,300 prefabricated shelter units that can withstand temperatures of minus 26 centigrade are being installed to provide, housing, health posts and administrative centres for a population of 40,000.

The first units will be in place by early November. Should repatriation lead to an affected Iraqi refugee population of less than 40,000, the winter shelter units will be put at the disposal of Iranian returnees from Al Tash camp in Iraq, whose homes were destroyed in prior conflict.

...

REPUBLIC OF TURKEY

Repatriation down to a trickle

The refugee population in Turkey has remained broadly stable after the massive return movement of some 400,000 Iraqi refugees in May and June. Small groups continue to repatriate from the Haj camp at Silopi, where there are now 5,000 refugees. UNHCR is also facilitating voluntary repatriation from the camps in Turkey hosting the 25,000 Iraqi refugees who fled in 1988. In September, a total of 2,000 Iraqi refugees returned home from Turkey with UNHCR assistance.

Upgrading camp facilities

Parallel to the repatriation programme, UNHCR is upgrading camp facilities. Major upgrading will occur of sanitation and water facilities at Silopi and the 1988 camps. To avoid pollution of neighbouring village water sources, a clean up campaign is being planned at the Cukurca mountain camp.

Logistic support

UNHCR has remained in Diyarbarkir and Silopi in eastern Turkey to support the enormous logistics effort required for UNHCR's winter programme in the Kurdish area of Iraq. The assembly of convoys and the cross-border movement of some 2,500 trucks bringing building materials to Iraq is being coordinated by UNHCR from Silopi. Purchase of some winter materials is also being undertaken in Turkey.

KINGDOM OF SAUDI ARABIA

Durable solutions sought

At the end of the Gulf war, Saudi Arabia like other countries in the region, was faced with an influx of refugees. The country now accommodates 35,000 Iraqis in two camps, Artawiyeh and Rafha. The Saudi Government has informed UNHCR that it has spent over US$ 220 million on food, medical and relief supplies for the refugees and prisoners of war.

The ICRC is assisting the Iraqi prisoners of war and helping those who want to return to Iraq. In early September, the Saudi authorities made an official request to UNHCR to assist in finding a durable solution for those Iraqis who could not return home. A survey of the refugee population is planned to facilitate status determination on a case by case basis. For this purpose, UNHCR is discussing the strengthening of its presence with the Saudi authorities.

KUWAIT

Increased UNHCR presence

As a result of a high level UNHCR mission at the beginning of August, UNHCR has increased its presence in Kuwait, where there are an estimated 800 refugees and stateless persons stranded in the desert camp of Abdali near the Iraqi border and some 60 persons, of concern to UNHCR, detained in centres in Kuwait city. As a result of intensive work by UNHCR technical teams and close cooperation with the Kuwaiti authorities, a range of durable solutions are now being implemented. These include repatriation, resettlement to a third country and admission to Kuwait. The implementation of durable solutions will enable the Kuwaiti authorities to close the Abdali camp, where living conditions were not satisfactory. UNHCR is discussing with the Kuwaiti authorities the future prospects of other persons, whose status requires determination.

Cooperation with NGOs

UNHCR works with NGOs in Iran, Iraq and Turkey. Collaboration occurs through formal operational agreements, letters of association and informal cooperative measures. In numerous recent international conferences, the Gulf emergency has been cited as a comprehensive living case study in partnership between voluntary agencies and operational UN organizations. The winter preparation programme became the basis of an effective coordinated approach comprising three basic components: Joint needs assessment and project planning, decentralization of operational decision-making and the secondment of NGO staff. The use of specialized, technical NGO staff from SCF/USA and LWF and personnel from the Danish and Norwegian refugee councils, funded by their Governments, has recently proved particularly invaluable.

In Turkey NGOs cooperate with UNHCR in the traditional assistance programmes, in camp clean up activities and as a support structure for the Iraq programme. In Iran, NGOs operate with UNHCR in the health, water, sanitation, food and non-food relief sectors.

The winter shelter programme is an example of close cooperation in Iraq. It was brought to life as follows. A water/sanitation/site planning specialist seconded to UNHCR by the Lutheran World Federation with HCR and other NGO technical staff drafted a winter shelter programme for north and north-eastern Iraq taking various population movement scenarios into account. The plan was shared with NGOs operating in Iraq and, through meetings in Geneva and missions in Europe, with other interested NGOs. Having studied the plan, numerous NGOs sent missions to the area and in consultation with UNHCR, geographical and technical areas of operation were established. International NGOs assisting in the implementation of the project are: Architectes Ingenieurs du Monde, the International Rescue Committee, Shelter Now International, Caritas Switzerland, Inter Church Aid Switzerland in Dohuk Governorate, Action Nord-Sud, Save the Children Fund UK in Erbil Governorate and Christian Outreach, Danish Church Aid, Equilibre, and IRC in Suleimaniyah Governorate.

...

International Committee of the Red Cross, Press release No. 1685, 9 October 1991

36. Northern Iraq - Appeal by the ICRC

Geneva (ICRC) - The International Committee of the Red Cross (ICRC) is deeply concerned about the consequences in human terms of the heavy fighting taking place in Iraqi Kurdistan.

Alarmed by reports that residential areas have been shelled and that captured soldiers have been executed, the ICRC urgently calls on all the parties involved to care for the wounded, to respect the lives and the physical and mental integrity of captured persons and to spare and protect the civilian population.

International Committee of the Red Cross, Press Release, Geneva, 15 November 1991

37. Review of ICRC Relief Operations in Iraq, November 1991

INTRODUCTION

The International Committee of the Red Cross (ICRC) is the only foreign organisation to have remained in Iraq throughout the duration of the Middle East conflict, and to have seen from the start the breakdown of essential services as a result of the conflict itself, internal disturbances in the south and north of Iraq, and the continuing sanctions against the country.

A situation that rapidly became dramatic in terms of water purification and sewage treatment, transport and energy, medicines and medical supplies, food and nutrition, forces the ICRC to launch major relief operations in Iraq. These operations have had to continue well beyond the end of active hostilities as the sanctions have prolonged and exacerbated the already serious effects of the Gulf crisis.

The ICRC has approached the members of the United Nations Security Council and of the Sanctions Committee, as well as the UN Secretary General, on several occasions, so as to allow Iraq to assume its responsibility for the Iraqi population's medical, food and other basic needs. The ICRC requests the political authorities of the States members of the United Nations Security Council and of Iraq to renew their efforts to break the present deadlock and to find solutions to the humanitarian needs of the Iraqi population.

The following is a summary of the ICRC's main relief activities in Iraq since 17 January this year.

MEDICAL

The ICRC sent a first convoy of medical and surgical supplies to Baghdad from Iran on 31 January, in the midst of the conflict between coalition and Iraqi forces. This was just the beginning of a medical operation which has led to the distribution to date of over 800 tonnes of medical supplies to hospitals and medical facilities around the country, for a value of around 15 million Swiss francs.

This operation has aimed as much to treat war wounded, as to combat diseases related to unsafe drinking water and to provide treatment for illnesses which were becoming fatal as a result of diminished medical stocks. The ICRC has also taken care to adapt its aid, as other humanitarian organisations have become operational, concentrating on areas with less access to assistance.

Currently, a three-month supply of antibiotics and surgical disposable material is being distributed to some

140 hospitals nationwide, under a programme launched in mid-October.

In northern Iraq, ICRC medical teams are concentrating on emergency medical aid to hospitals and dispensaries affected by continuing clashes. A 40-bed ICRC field hospital at Naopares, south of Penjwin, was forced to open ahead of schedule in early October, to treat war wounded following fighting in the region. A week later, a temporary extension was set up to increase the hospital's capacity, as it already had to cope with 75 in-patients.

WATER AND SANITATION

By early February, the ICRC was concerned about the shortage and quality of drinking water. The war had damaged major power stations, affecting the supply of potable water and sewage treatment stations. This situation was responsible for a dramatic increase in cases of diarrhoea among children in particular. Assessments carried out by ICRC medical staff indicated that the incidence of water-born diseases and death related to these diseases had risen rapidly.

The ICRC immediately sent in sanitation equipment and engineers to help municipal water and sewage authorities to purify and distribute water in Baghdad and other cities. Mobile water purification units were set up as from mid-March producing hundreds of thousands of litres of potable water per day, while water trucks carried [*sic*] the supplies to storage tanks which served as distribution points.

By October, almost 250 million litres of potable water had been distributed from the north to the south of the country, taking care to reach hospitals and dispensaries, and the most vulnerable groups of the population. Thanks in part to these efforts, combined with the provision of medicines to treat water-born diseases, the number of diarrhoea cases, which accounted for 60% of patients attending dispensaries in April, fell to 10 - 20% in July.

As from July, the ICRC has been able to give priority to improving the output of existing water systems, providing technical assistance to water boards and chemicals and spare parts for water treatment plants.

Over 6 million Swiss francs have been spent on water and sanitation programmes in Iraq, since the beginning of the conflict.

FOOD AND OTHER RELIEF SUPPLIES

The ICRC was rapidly authorized by the Iraqi authorities to assist civilians affected by the conflict in all areas of the country. It quickly deployed additional staff (four at the outbreak of the conflict, 128 by mid-April) and increased its logistics to a fleet of over 200 trucks.

Distributions of food and non-food aid began in Baghdad for vulnerable groups, including people in hospitals, orphanages and other social welfare institutions. In early April, assistance was extended to the north and south of the country.

In northern Iraq, the first round of major distributions of food, blankets, tents, kitchen sets and stoves had taken place by the first week in June. While awaiting the start of UN assistance programmes, and in view of the events in the north and the predicted scarcity of food in winter months, two more rounds of food distributions, covering more than 300,000 people, were carried out. The Office of the United Nations High Commissioner for Refugees (UNHCR) took over food aid in the Penjwin area in September.

The ICRC's relief programme provided over 10,600 tonnes of food (800,000 monthly food rations) and more than 560 tonnes of other relief supplies to the displaced population and vulnerable groups of civilians in Iraq.

LOGISTICS

The ICRC organized 126 road convoys carrying 28,000 tonnes of relief, sanitation, medical and operational material from Jordan and Iran to Iraq up to the end of October. At the beginning of operations, 36 flights also took place transporting 776 tonnes of goods into Iraq.

[*Text supplied by the UN Secretariat*]

38. UN-Irak Memorandum of Understanding, 24 November 1991

The present Memorandum of Understanding summarizes the results of the discussions held in Baghdad on 20-23 November 1991 with the Government of the Republic of Iraq during the mission of the Executive Delegate of the Secretary-General for the UN humanitarian programme for Iraq, Kuwait and the Iraq/Iran and Iraq/Turkey Border Areas, pursuant to paragraph 21 of the Memorandum of Understanding signed on 18 April 1991 [*reproduced above*] by H.E. the Minister of Foreign Affairs of the Government of Iraq and the Executive Delegate.

The parties conducted a thorough joint review of the humanitarian operations carried out under the auspices of the office of the Executive Delegate in cooperation with the Government of Iraq over the past seven months. They noted that the overall context in which these activities were taking place has undergone significant changes. They further concluded that the Programme, carried out with the full support of the Iraqi authorities, has substantial achievements to its credit. This includes assisting the repatriation of large numbers of refugees from neighbouring countries, the majority of them to their homes and places of origin. Tangible results have also been attained in providing help to the most vulnerable groups throughout Iraq, thanks to resources donated by the international community in response to the successive appeals that have been issued by the Executive Delegate. These contributions have amounted to more than 290 million dollars, of which 249 million are either spent or obligated. The present Memorandum of Understanding shall constitute a self-contained agreement, and its implementation shall not be construed as having any relation with other measures not envisaged therein.

The parties have agreed as follows:

1. Both sides affirm the importance of the need to continue to provide humanitarian assistance to Iraq to alleviate the suffering of the affected Iraqi civilian population.

2. The Government of Iraq welcomes the efforts of the United Nations and its specialized agencies in providing humanitarian assistance and relief to the civilian population and undertakes to support and cooperate in those endeavours on the basis of this Memorandum of Understanding.

3. For this purpose, the Government of Iraq agrees to cooperate with the United Nations to continue its humanitarian presence in Iraq, wherever such presence may be needed, and to facilitate it through the adoption of all necessary measures. This shall be ensured through the establishment of UN sub-offices and Humanitarian Centres (UNHUCs), in agreement and cooperation with the Government of Iraq.

4. Each Centre will be staffed by United Nations personnel which, in addition to the regular staff members of the relevant UN agencies, may also include staff co-

opted from the non-governmental organizations. The parties are mindful of the special contribution provided by other organizations, such as the International Committee of the Red Cross, the League of Red Cross and Red Crescent Societies and the International Organization for Migration. The Red Crescent Society of Iraq shall be called upon to play an effective role in the implementation of humanitarian assistance and relief projects.

5. UNHUCs shall facilitate the provision of humanitarian assistance to the needy and would include, inter alia, food aid, medical care, agricultural rehabilitation, shelter and any other humanitarian and relief measures in conformity with the principles of this memorandum.

6. Both sides agree that measures continue to be needed for the benefit of the persons who are still displaced and that such measures should be based primarily on their safe return and the provision of humanitarian assistance to facilitate their return and normalization of their lives in their places of origin.

7. The United Nations Guards Contingent as an integral part of the United Nations humanitarian programme will continue to perform its functions in protecting UN personnel, assets and operations linked with the UN humanitarian programme. The UN Guards will continue to be assigned as needed to any sub-offices and UNHUCs which are or may be established by the United Nations in Iraq.

8. The number of UN Guards will continue to be kept under review, and will not exceed a total strength of 500. The number of UN Guards assigned to the various Governorates will be decided in consultation with the Government authorities concerned, but would not exceed 150 in any Governorate.

9. The UN Guards will continue to be allowed to move freely, as their duties require in accordance with this Memorandum of Understanding, between all places where United Nations humanitarian assistance activities take place.

10. United Nations Guards are authorized to carry side-arms (pistols/revolvers) provided by the Iraqi authorities with the approval of the United Nations.

11. The Iraqi authorities will maintain the Chief Liaison Officer appointed to facilitate the Contingent's operations and the liaison officer at each centre to facilitate their work with the Iraqi authorities. The Iraqi authorities will continue to make available the facilities in Baghdad and elsewhere, including office space, maintenance and repair support, maps, etc.

12. It is agreed that humanitarian assistance is impartial and that all civilians in need, wherever they are located, are entitled to receive it without discrimination.

13. In order to encourage the normalization of life where required, the United Nations will take all necessary measures, in cooperation with the Government of Iraq, for making the relief items available in all designated Humanitarian Centres, by road or by air as required, including from and through the neighbouring countries. The Government of Iraq will take all required measures on its side to facilitate the safe passage and delivery of emergency relief commodities throughout the country in a speedy and effective manner.

14. The Government of Iraq has established together with the United Nations a relief distribution monitoring structure to permit access to all civilians covered by the relief programme. An appropriate coordinating mechanism will be established between the two parties to meet regularly in order to monitor, review and plan future activities, as well as address any difficulties that may arise in the implementation for the current humanitarian assistance programme.

15. The implementation of the humanitarian assistance programme will continue to be coordinated by a senior UN official assigned to Baghdad, under the Executive Delegate's direction. He will have permanent access to high level government officials responsible for relief activities in the country to discuss policy and operational issues that may arise during the implementation of the programme.

16. Inter-governmental organizations, NGOs and other relief agencies will continue to be encouraged to participate in the implementation of the programme in close cooperation with the United Nations and under clearly defined terms of association agreed upon with the Government of Iraq.

17. The Government of Iraq will help in the prompt establishment in appropriate locations of United Nations sub-offices in support of humanitarian programmes for the civilian population including the returnees where necessary.

18. The Government of Iraq shall continue to cooperate in granting United Nations field staff access to the parts of the country requiring relief, by air or road as needed, to facilitate the implementation and monitoring of the Programme. United Nations staff will be allowed, in coordination with the Government of Iraq, to accompany the returnees to their home areas as required.

19. A United Nations radio communication system, which is an indispensable instrument for the success of relief and rehabilitation activities, will be maintained. The system will cover communications requirements within Baghdad and other cities covered by the relief Programme and within and outside the country, as appropriate.

20. In order to make optimal use of programme resources, the Government of Iraq will consider the establishment of a special exchange rate for relief operations carried out by agencies and organizations participating in the programme. Pending a decision in this regard the Government of Iraq undertakes to make available cash contributions in local currency in the amount of ID 1,000,000 at the beginning of each month, or in accordance with the estimates provided by the United Nations Coordinator, if less. Any unused balances remaining at the conclusion of the programme will be refunded to the Government of Iraq.

21. The basic framework for United Nations humanitarian action outlined above is intended to facilitate the task of coordination, effective implementation and monitoring of humanitarian assistance and relief operations.

22. The implementation of the above-mentioned principles shall be without prejudice to the sovereignty, territorial integrity, political independence, security and non-interference in the internal affairs of the Republic of Iraq.

23. This Memorandum of Understanding shall apply for a period of six months beginning on 1 January 1992 and ending on 30 June 1992. Six weeks before the expiration of the said period, the principles of the Memorandum and

their operational modalities shall be reviewed with a view to assessing any further need for their operation.

Done at Baghdad on 18 Jamada al-Oula 1412 Hijrah corresponding to 24 November 1991 AD.

...

[*After difficult negotiations, and a period of several months of humanitarian operations without a memorandum of understanding being in force, another agreement was concluded in October 1992. That memorandum was due to expire on 31 March 1993.*]

39. UNHCR Update on Operations Within the Regional Humanitarian Plan of Action, 5 December 1991

More than 200,000 people have been driven from their homes in northern Iraq since the beginning of October bringing the number of internally displaced to more than 700,000 and seriously straining UNHCR's resources.

"We are extremely worried about the situation," said Carrol Faubert, UNHCR's Persian Gulf Emergency Coordinator. "We see the possibility of hundreds of thousands of newly displaced under the snow.

"The situation in northern Iraq responds to the worst case scenario of our contingency planning," Faubert added.

Shelling of areas around Kelar, Kifri and Chamchamal in Sulemaniya Province has driven 140,884 into the Said Sadik area since early October. Another 60,000 people were displaced in Erbil Province after the inhabitants of villages southwest of Erbil were ordered to evacuate their homes.

UNHCR was already caring for some 500,000 people who remained displaced after the war, either because their homes were destroyed or because they were afraid to return to their home towns. A winterization project to provide shelter during the freezing months was completed just last month for these people.

UNHCR field officers said stockpiles of food, blankets and tents were barely sufficient for the original caseload and fuel shortages made transport of food to the newly displaced difficult.

"We only have contingency stocks for half a million people," said one field worker, adding that there were fears hungry people would be drawn to border areas where UNHCR distribution centers had been set up but where shelter was in short supply.

"I hope reason will prevail and the Iraqi Kurds will not have to face the freezing months without shelter for a second time," said High Commissioner Sadako Ogata. "It is both their survival and our capacity to deliver which is at stake."

International Committee of the Red Cross, Summary Review, 13 December 1991

40. Current Activities for the Kurdish Population in Northern Iraq, December 1991

In the coming months the ICRC will maintain its presence in northern Iraq with a sub-delegation in Suleymaniyah and offices in Penjwin, Shaklawah and Dohuk. The ICRC surgical hospital in Naopares was opened on 9 October 1991 and treated over a hundred people wounded during the clashes in Suleymaniyah in the early October. Since then, it has been fully operational and receives three to five patients with mine-blast injuries per day; it will be run for a further period of six months by ICRC expatriate (Finnish Red Cross) staff, seconded by Kurdish doctors and nurses. The ICRC has some twenty expatriate staff in northern Iraq.

The main task of these delegates consists in protection-related and medical activities, understood in the broad sense of the words.

The continuous capture during clashes and the maintenance in detention of Iraqi military personnel has created a need for protection and assistance work, which has been carried out by ICRC delegates. During emergencies, delegates organized medical evacuations and supplied health facilities with emergency medical material.

In accordance with the division of labour with UNHCR, the ICRC is standing by to supply, displaced people, especially in north-eastern Iraq, with food, blankets, cooking facilities and emergency shelter if the need arises.

It is currently starting to distribute disposable surgical equipment and basic medicines used in surgery to all hospitals in Iraq with surgical facilities. Activities related to sanitation and water treatment also remain a priority with the ICRC supplying technical know-how and spare parts.

With regard to the after-effects of the Gulf war, the ICRC is continuing its efforts to trace persons reported missing in action, to reunite families and to resolve the continuing problems of prisoners of war and civilian internees.

S/24309, 17 July 1992

41. Note by the President of the Security Council, 17 July 1992

Following consultations with the members of the Security Council, the President of the Council made the following statement, on behalf of the Council, at its 3098th meeting, on 17 July 1992, in connection with the Council's consideration of the item entitled "The situation between Iraq and Kuwait":

> "The Security Council deeply deplores the murder of a member of the United Nations Guards Contingent in Iraq on 16 July 1992 in the Governorate of Dohuk. It supports the Secretary-General's decision to order an immediate and thorough investigation of this appalling crime. Members of the Council wish to express their sincere condolences to the family of the victim, Mr. Ravuama Dakia, and to the Government of Fiji.
>
> "The Security Council wishes to register its profound concern at the deteriorating security conditions affecting the safety and well-being of United Nations personnel in Iraq. The Council demands that attacks perpetrated against the United Nations Guards Contingent and other humanitarian personnel deployed in Iraq cease immediately and that maximum cooperation be extended by the authorities in the investigation of this crime, as well as in the protection of United Nations personnel."

18. HUMAN RIGHTS IN IRAQ

The human rights situation within Iraq in the aftermath of the armed action gave rise to increased international concern. Indeed, the coalition powers invoked Iraqi human rights performance as a justification for the imposition of aerial exclusion zones and their forcible maintenance.

1. Amnesty International, Annual Report 1989, pp. 257-260

IRAQ

Large numbers of Kurds and other government opponents were extrajudicially killed by Iraqi Government forces. Among the victims were whole families, including children. Thousands of political prisoners, among them prisoners of conscience, continued to be arbitrarily arrested and detained. Many were held for long periods without trial or following summary trials. Torture of political prisoners remained widespread, as did the "disappearance" of large numbers of people, many of whom, it was feared, had been killed. Hundreds of people were reportedly executed; in most cases it was difficult to ascertain whether they had been tried and sentenced to death or extrajudicially executed.

In July the Iran-Iraq war came to an end. In the months before the ceasefire Iraqi Government forces had carried out a series of attacks on Kurdish civilians, including in areas in which the Kurdish armed opposition was active. In the weeks following the ceasefire there were similar sustained attacks on Kurdish civilians, thousands of whom fled Iraq to neighbouring countries.

In January an amnesty was declared for army deserters and for those who failed to report for military service, and in April there was a further amnesty for detainees convicted of certain economic and political offences and, under certain circumstances, of robbery and desertion from the army. Three amnesties were declared in September for detainees convicted of certain criminal and political offences, for all Iraqi Kurds sought for crimes committed before 6 September 1988, and for Egyptian nationals convicted of criminal offences excluding drug-trafficking and premeditated murder. In November a general amnesty was declared for those wanted for or convicted of political offences. It was not known how many people benefited from these amnesties.

Over 6,000 people, the majority unarmed civilians, were reported to have been deliberately killed by government forces and information was received about the deliberate killing of hundreds of others in 1987. Many were victims of extrajudicial execution; the great majority were Kurdish civilians, including whole families, killed as a result of large-scale military attacks on civilian targets. Amnesty International believed these killings were part of a systematic and deliberate policy on the part of the Iraqi Government to eliminate large numbers of Kurdish civilians, both as punishment for their imputed political sympathies and in retaliation for the activities of Kurdish opposition forces, which have included armed attacks on Iraqi Government targets.

Some 400 Kurdish civilians, among them women and children, were reported to have been executed on 2 April at Tanjaro Military Garrison, Sulaimaniya province. The victims were said to have been wounded as a result of chemical weapon attacks on villages in the Qaradagh region in March, and to have been apprehended as they made their way to the city of Sulaimaniya to seek medical treatment. Information was also received that in April 1987 some 360 people from the village of Shaikh Wasanan, Arbil province, had been detained, reportedly after seeking medical treatment in hospitals in the city of Arbil for wounds inflicted as a result of chemical weapon attacks in the Balisan Valley in mid-April 1987. The majority were civilians said to have "disappeared" after being moved to an unknown destination outside the city. There were allegations, which Amnesty International was unable to confirm, that they had been executed.

On 16 and 17 March an estimated 5,000 people were deliberately killed and thousands wounded as a result of chemical weapon attacks by Iraqi forces on the town of Halabja, Sulaimaniya province, reportedly after Kurdish opposition forces had entered the town. Most of the victims were civilians, many of them women and children. The government denied responsibility for the incident and stated that Iranian forces had carried out the killings. In August hundreds of unarmed Kurdish civilians were deliberately killed and thousands wounded when Iraqi Government forces attacked Kurdish villages in the north. Thousands of Iraqi troops were reported to have launched attacks using tanks, helicopter gunships, artillery and chemical weapons on hundreds of villages in the provinces of Duhok, Mosul and Arbil. The offensive came in the wake of the Iranian Government's acceptance of a ceasefire in its conflict with Iraq. On 28 August Iraqi Government forces reportedly entered several villages near the town of Duhok and arrested over 1,000 people, some of whom were suffering from wounds sustained in chemical weapon attacks. Those detained were allegedly summarily executed and then buried in mass graves nearby.

In late August and early September tens of thousands of villagers fled the affected areas to seek refuge in Turkey and Iran. On 1 September the Turkish Government announced that it would grant temporary refuge on humanitarian grounds to some 57,000 Kurdish civilians. The Iraqi Government denied that chemical weapons had been used against Kurdish civilians and refused a United Nations team permission to travel to Iraq to investigate reports that such weapons had been deployed.

In January the Shi'a opposition leader Sayyid Mahdi al-Hakim was assassinated by a gunman in the lobby of the Khartoum Hilton Hotel, Sudan. The Sudanese authorities began an investigation into the killing amid allegations that Sayyid Mahdi al-Hakim was killed by an agent working for the Iraqi Government. According to a Sudan News Agency (SUNA) dispatch of 22 July, the investigation revealed that the escape car used by the gunman belonged to the Iraqi Embassy in Khartoum, and that eye-witness descriptions of the suspect implicated a diplomat at the embassy. The SUNA dispatch went on: "In view of this suspicion, the Public Prosecutor addressed a letter to the Iraqi Minister of Justice on 13th January 1988 requesting him to lift the immunity on the diplomat concerned so he could be interrogated." In February this request was refused and Iraq later recalled its Ambassador to Sudan in protest at the allegations.

As in previous years hundreds of executions were reported but it was not possible to ascertain the precise number. Those executed were said to have included members of banned political parties, other suspected government opponents, and army deserters. Many were reported to have been executed without charge or trial, among them five members of the Kurdistan Socialist Party-Iraq (KSP-I) executed in Arbil between November 1987 and January 1988. The bodies of four of them were returned to their families bearing marks of torture. The body of the fifth was allegedly buried secretly in a cemetery in Arbil. In December some 80 people were reported to have been executed in the Koi Sanjaq region of Arbil province. The majority of the victims were said to be army deserters arrested in mid-1988. It was not known whether they were brought to trial before execution.

Thousands of political prisoners, including possible prisoners of conscience, continued to be detained without charge or trial, or after summary trials. They included actual or suspected members of prohibited political parties such as *al-Da'wa al-Islamiyya*, Islamic Call; the Iraqi Communist Party (ICP); the Kurdistan Democratic Party (KDP); the Patriotic Union of Kurdistan (PUK); the Kurdistan Socialist Party-Iraq (KSP-I); and the Kurdistan Popular Democratic Party (KPDP). Others included army deserters and draft resisters. Relatives of such people were arrested as hostages in lieu of suspects being sought by the authorities. The children of political opponents were also arbitrarily arrested and detained as hostages in order to compel their parents or relatives to "confess" to alleged political offences.

Mirza and Mardan Rasho, two brothers arrested in July 1985 in al-Shaikhan when they were aged six and 13 respectively, were believed still to be in detention at the end of the year. They were reportedly arrested because of their father's suspected membership of the *Pesh Merga* forces (armed Kurdish units). In mid-December some 200 military personnel and Ba'th Party officials were reportedly arrested, most in Baghdad and Mosul, on suspicion of plotting a coup. They included two brigadier generals - 'Abd al-Ghani Shahin and Taleb 'Ali al-Sa'dun. At the end of the year their fate was unknown.

Routine torture and ill-treatment of prisoners continued to be widely reported. The victims included political prisoners tortured in order to force them to sign "confessions" or to renounce their political affiliations. Some political prisoners were reported to have been tortured shortly before being executed. The victims included detainees below the age of 18, who were said to have been beaten, whipped, sexually abused, given electric shocks and deprived of food. According to the testimony of a former prisoner released from Abu Ghraib Prison in 1988, female prisoners have also been hung upside-down by the feet during menstruation. Objects have been inserted into the vaginas of young women, breaking the hymen. Another detainee released from Abu Ghraib in September testified that he was tortured during 14 months spent in detention. Arrested on suspicion of working with the KSP-I *Pesh Merga*, he was allegedly beaten, given electric shocks and made to face a mock execution.

The fate of some 178 people who "disappeared" while they were in detention between 1980 and 1985 was still unknown at the end of the year (see *Amnesty International Report 1988*). Among them were 17 children aged between 12 and 17. Most belonged to Shi'a families from regions such as Baghdad, Karbala' and Najaf who were declared by the authorities to be of Iranian descent. The fate of some 8,000 Kurds, among them 315 children, who "disappeared" following their arrest in August 1983, was still unknown. All were male members of the Barzani clan, arrested in Arbil and sent to unknown destinations. It was believed that the arrests had been carried out in retaliation for the KDP's military activities: the detainees included close relatives of Mas'ud Barzani, leader of the KDP. It was feared that many had been executed.

Amnesty International repeatedly appealed to the government for an end to the deliberate killing of unarmed Kurdish civilians. It also expressed concern about the imposition of the death penalty and about allegations that some of those executed had been tortured before their death. In January Amnesty International urged the government to investigate reports of the security forces' use of thallium poison against political opponents (see *Amnesty International Report 1988*). There was no response from the government on the poisonings but in press reports Iraq's Ambassador to the United Kingdom described the allegations as "false" and "bizarre". In August, the government replied to appeals by Amnesty International regarding the reported execution and deliberate killing of some 360 people - including 17 children - in November and December 1987 (see *Amnesty International Report 1988*). The government confirmed the execution of 12 people among the 116 victims whose names were submitted by Amnesty International. One of the 12 was 16-year old Ribwar Muhammad Karim 'Aziz, a Kurd from Sulaimaniya who had been arrested when he was 13. He had been sentenced to death by a special court and executed in Abu Ghraib Prison in December 1987.

In an oral statement delivered to the United Nations Commission on Human Rights in March, Amnesty International drew attention to reports of the execution and deliberate killing by Iraqi forces of some 360 people in November and December 1987. In another oral statement delivered in August to the United Nations Sub-Commission on Prevention of Discrimination and Protection of Minorities, Amnesty International explained its concern about the deliberate and systematic killing of unarmed Kurdish civilians by government forces. An Iraqi Government representative responded: "with respect to the town of Halabja, my delegation makes clear that this town was the site of military operations, and that it was occupied during these operations by Iranian troops which used various weapons, including chemical weapons, against its Iraqi civilian inhabitants".

In September Amnesty International appealed to the UN Security Council to act immediately to stop the massacre of Kurdish civilians by Iraqi forces. The appeal was issued following the reported killing of hundreds of unarmed civilians in Kurdish villages at the end of August. In October Amnesty International called on the Turkish Government to allow international protection for thousands of Iraqi Kurdish refugees in Turkey who had fled the August offensive. The call followed an Amnesty International fact-finding visit to refugee camps in southeastern Turkey in early October and reports that some refugees had been threatened with forced repatriation to Iraq. Some 1,900 Kurds were reported to have returned from Turkey to Iraq after the Iraq Government's announcement of an amnesty for Kurds on 6 September. At the end of the year their fate was unknown.

In May Amnesty International submitted information about its concerns in Iraq to the United Nations procedure (under Economic and Social Council Resolutions 728F/1503) for confidentially reviewing communications about human rights violations. A copy of the communication was also sent to the Iraqi authorities with an invitation to comment. At the end of the year no response had been received from the Iraqi Government.

E/CN.4/1989/86, at 244.

2. UN Commission on Human Rights, Report on Draft Resolution E/CN.4/1989/L.82

...

"*Concerned* by reliable reports of mass extrajudicial executions, enforced or involuntary disappearances and arbitrary detention in Iraq, as reflected in the report of the Special Rapporteur on summary or arbitrary executions (E/CN.4/1989/25, paras. 149-164), the report of the Working Group on Enforced or Involuntary Disappearances (E/CN.4/1989/18, paras. 177-189) and specific and detailed reports of non-governmental organizations,

"*Recalling* Security Council resolution 620 (1988) of 26 August 1988 [*condemning resolutely the use of chemical weapons in the conflict between Iran and Iraq (also Resolution 612 (1988) and the report of the Secretary-General's mission to investigate alleged uses of chemical weapons in that conflict, S/19823 of 25 April 1988).*],

"1. *Expresses concern* at the situation of human rights and fundamental freedoms in Iraq;

"2. *Expresses grave concern* about reports of the killing of unarmed Kurdish civilians, in particular by military attacks during 1988 using, *inter alia*, chemical weapons and causing a mass exodus to neighbouring countries;

"3. *Urges* the Government of Iraq to ensure full respect for human rights and fundamental freedoms;

"4. *Requests* the Chairman, after consultation within the Bureau, to appoint a special rapporteur of the Commission whose mandate will be to make a thorough study of the human rights situation in Iraq, based on all information which he may deem relevant, including any comments and material provided by the Government of Iraq, and to report thereon to the Commission at its forty-sixth session;

"5. *Requests* the Secretary-General to give all necessary assistance to the Special Rapporteur of the Commission;

"6. *Decides* to continue its consideration of human rights and fundamental freedoms in Iraq at its forty-sixth session."

379. At the 55th meeting, on 8 March 1989, the representative of Iraq moved, under rule 65, paragraph 2, of the rules of procedure of the functional commissions of the Economic and Social Council, that the Commission take no decision on draft resolution E/CN.4/1989/L.82.

380. Statements relating to the motion were made by the representatives of Bangladesh, Belgium, the Federal Republic of Germany, Morocco and Sweden.

381. The representative of Iraq requested a roll-call vote on the motion, which was adopted by 17 votes to 13, with 9 abstentions. The voting was as follows:

> *In favour*: Bangladesh, Botswana, Brazil, China, Cuba, Cyprus, Ethiopia, India, Iraq, Morocco, Pakistan, Philippines, Sao Tome and Principe, Senegal, Somalia, Sri Lanka, Yugoslavia.
>
> *Against*: Belgium, Canada, France, Germany, Federal Republic of, Italy, Japan, Peru, Portugal, Spain, Sweden, Togo, United Kingdom of Great Britain and Northern Ireland, United States of America.
>
> *Abstaining*: Argentina, Colombia, Gambia, Mexico, Nigeria, Panama, Rwanda, Swaziland, Venezuela.

The representative of Bulgaria, the German Democratic Republic, the Ukrainian Soviet Socialist Republic and the Union of Soviet Socialist Republics stated that their delegations were not participating in the vote [Decision 1989/111, *Situation of Human Rights in Iraq.*].

E/CN.4/1991/91, at 167.

3. UN Commission on Human Rights, Resolution 1991/74. Situation of Human Rights in Iraq, 6 March 1991

The Commission on Human Rights,

Guided by the principles embodied in the Charter of the United Nations, the Universal Declaration of Human Rights and the International Covenants on Human Rights,

Reaffirming that all Member States have an obligation to promote and protect human rights and fundamental freedoms and to fulfil the obligations they have undertaken under the various international instruments in this field,

Mindful that Iraq is a party to the International Covenants on Human Rights,

Concerned by reliable reports of enforced or involuntary disappearances, mass extrajudicial executions, torture and arbitrary detention by the Government of Iraq, especially as reflected in the report of the Working Group on Enforced or Involuntary Disappearances (E/CN.4/1991/20, paras. 217-236) and the report of the Special Rapporteur on summary or arbitrary executions (E/CN.4/1991/36, paras. 269-289),

Concerned especially by the fact that chemical weapons have been used on the Kurdish civilian population, by the forced displacement of hundreds of thousands of Kurds and the destruction of Kurdish towns and villages, as well as by the situation of tens of thousands of displaced Kurds living in camps in the north of Iraq, and by the deportation of thousands of Kurdish families,

Concerned moreover by the denial of human rights and fundamental freedoms, including freedom of expression and of the press, by the Government of Iraq,

Considering Sub-Commission on Prevention of Discrimination and Protection of Minorities resolution 1990/13 of 30 August 1990, in which the Sub-Commission recommended that the Commission appoint a special rapporteur with the mandate to examine the human rights situation in Iraq,

1. *Expresses grave concern* at the flagrant violations of human rights by the Government of Iraq;

2. *Urges* the Government of Iraq to ensure full respect for human rights and fundamental freedoms and, in particular:

(a) To halt the arbitrary and summary executions as well as the arbitrary detention of political and religious opponents;

(b) To put an end to the practices of enforced or involuntary disappearances and the practice of torture;

(c) To guarantee full respect for human rights of all persons in Iraq irrespective of their origin, halt deportation of Iraqi citizens and allow the deported persons to return to their villages of origin and receive reparation for the damage suffered as a result of their forced displacement;

3. *Calls upon* the Government of Iraq to abide by its obligations under the International Covenants on Human Rights;

4. *Urges* the Government of Iraq to cooperate with the Commission on Human Rights and, in particular, to help clarify the pending cases of enforced or involuntary disappearances noted in the report of the Working Group on Enforced or Involuntary Disappearances and to communicate to the Commission any new measures the Government of Iraq may take in the field of human rights;

5. *Requests* its Chairman, after consultation with the Bureau, to appoint an individual of recognized international standing in the field of human rights as special rapporteur of the Commission whose mandate will be to make a thorough study of the violations of human rights by the Government of Iraq, based on all information the special rapporteur may deem relevant, including information provided by intergovernmental and non-governmental organizations and any comments and material provided by the Government of Iraq, and submit an interim report thereon to the General Assembly at its forty-sixth session and a report to the Commission at its forty-eighth session;

6. *Urges* the Government of Iraq to afford all necessary cooperation to the Special Rapporteur of the Commission;

7. *Requests* the Secretary-General to give all necessary assistance to the Special Rapporteur of the Commission;

8. *Decides* to continue its consideration of the situation of human rights in Iraq under the present agenda item at its forty-eighth session.

E/CN.4/1991/91, at 260

4. Report of the UN Commission on Human Rights, the Situation of Human Rights in Iraq, 1991

...

438. At the 54th meeting, on 6 March 1991, the representative of Belgium introduced draft resolution E/CN.4/1991/L.68, sponsored by Australia, Austria, Belgium, Canada, Costa Rica, Czechoslovakia, Denmark, Finland, France, Gambia, Germany, Greece, Hungary, Ireland, Italy, Japan, Luxembourg, Netherlands, Norway, Portugal, Rwanda, Spain, Sweden, Togo, United Kingdom of Great Britain and Northern Ireland and United States of America. Kuwait and Liechtenstein subsequently joined the sponsors. Gambia subsequently requested to be deleted from the list of sponsors.

439. The representative of Belgium orally revised the draft resolution by adding the following text at the end of operative paragraph 4: "and to communicate to the Commission any new measures the Government of Iraq may take in the field of human rights".

440. The attention of the Commission was drawn to an estimate of the administrative and programme budget implications (E/CN.4/1991/) of draft resolution E/CN.4/1991/L.68 in a statement by the Secretary of the Commission.

441. A statement relating to the draft resolution was made by the representative of Oraq.

442. Statements in explanation of the vote before the vote were made by the representatives of Canada and Cuba.

443. At the request of the representative of Iraq, a roll-call vote was taken on draft resolution E/CN.4/1991/L.68. The draft resolution was adopted by 30 votes to 1, with 10 abstentions. The voting was as follows:

In favour: Argentina, Australia, Austria, Belgium, Brazil, Burundi, Canada, Colombia, Cyprus, Czechoslovakia, Ethiopia, France, Gambia, Germany, Hungary, Italy, Japan, Mexico, Panama, Peru, Philippines, Portugal, Senegal, Swaziland, Sweden, Ukrainian Soviet Socialist Republic, Union of Soviet Socialist Republics, United States of America, Venezuela, Yugoslavia.

Against: Iraq

Abstaining: Bangladesh, China, Cuba, Ghana, India, Indonesia, Madagascar, Pakistan, Somalia, Zambia.

84. The representative of Morocco stated that his delegation was not participating in the vote.

...

A/46/647, 13 November 1991

5. Interim Report by the Special Rapporteur on Human Rights in Iraq, 13 November 1991

HUMAN RIGHTS QUESTIONS: HUMAN RIGHTS SITUATIONS AND REPORTS OF SPECIAL RAPPORTEURS AND REPRESENTATIVES

Situation of human rights in Iraq

Note by the Secretary-General

The Secretary-General has the honour to transmit to the members of the General Assembly the interim report on the situation of human rights in Iraq prepared by Mr. Max van der Stoel, Special Rapporteur of the Commission on Human Rights, in accordance with Commission resolution 1991/74 of 6 March 1991 and Economic and Social Council decision 1991/256 of 31 May 1991 (see annex).

I. INTRODUCTION

1. At its forty-seventh session, the Commission on Human Rights adopted on 6 March 1991 resolution 1991/74 entitled "Situation of human rights in Iraq". Resolution 1991/74 referred to reports of various serious human rights violations, viz. "enforced or involuntary disappearances, mass extrajudicial executions, torture and arbitrary detention", in addition to the use of chemical weapons "on the Kurdish civilian population, ... the forced displacement of hundreds of thousands of Kurds and the destruction of Kurdish towns and villages ... and ... the deportation of thousands of Kurdish families". Further specific reference was made to the denial of "freedom of expression and of the press".

2. Taking note of the report of the Commission's Working Group on Enforced or Involuntary Disappearances (E/CN.4/1991/20, paras. 217 to 236), the report of the Commission's Special Rapporteur on summary or arbitrary executions (E/CN.4/1991/36, paras. 269 to 289) and resolution 1990/13 of the

Subcommission on Prevention of Discrimination and Protection of Minorities of 30 August 1990, the Commission expressed its "grave concern at the flagrant violations of human rights by the Government of Iraq". The said resolution additionally urged the Government of Iraq "to ensure full respect for human rights and fundamental freedoms", calling in particular for the halt of "arbitrary and summary executions as well as the arbitrary detention of political and religious opponents" and for putting to an end "the practices of enforced or involuntary disappearances and the practice of torture". The Government of Iraq was further urged to "guarantee full respect for human rights of all persons in Iraq irrespective of their origin, halt deportation of Iraqi citizens and allow the deported persons to return to their villages of origin and receive reparation for the damage suffered as a result of their forced displacement".

3. By resolution 1991/74, the Commission requested its Chairman to appoint a special rapporteur to make "a thorough study of the violations of human rights by the Government of Iraq". In so doing, the Special Rapporteur was more specifically directed by the Commission to consider "all information the special rapporteur may deem relevant, including information provided by intergovernmental and non-governmental organizations and any comments and material provided by the Government of Iraq". The said resolution further urged the Government of Iraq to cooperate with the Commission and "to afford all necessary assistance to the Special Rapporteur".

4. With respect to the procedural terms of the Special Rapporteur's mandate, the Commission required that a report be submitted to the Commission at its forty-eighth session and that an interim report be submitted to the General Assembly at its forty-sixth session.

5. On 31 May 1991, the Economic and Social Council adopted decision 1991/256 approving Commission resolution 1991/74.

6. Pursuant to Commission resolution 1991/74 and Economic and Social Council decision 1991/256, the Chairman of the Commission appointed, on 25 June 1991, Mr. Max van der Stoel as Special Rapporteur.

7. Following the terms and references contained in Commission resolution 1991/74, the Special Rapporteur on the situation of human rights in Iraq therefore submits this interim report, outlining the course of study undertaken and providing information on the nature and content of the discourse thus far established with the Government of Iraq.

8. Given the evident breadth and complexity of the matters being studied, matters further compounded and clearly exacerbated by a continuing state of war in Iraq through much of the past decade and states of civil unrest in certain parts of Iraq at various times in Iraq's recent history, the Special Rapporteur points out that the approach taken has necessarily been one of careful consideration of all the relevant factors affecting the situation of human rights in Iraq. Moreover, the volume and extent of allegations of human rights violations by the Government of Iraq so far received by the Special Rapporteur (whether in concern of civil and political rights or economic, social and cultural rights), and each day increasing, are such as to necessitate considerable and detailed examination. Respecting the propriety and necessity of seeking the Government's response to this volume of allegations, the process of study has further dictated a programme of exchanges of information and views as detailed below.

9. In the conduct of his study, the Special Rapporteur has sought and received information on the situation of human rights from numerous individuals and organizations. This information continues to be sought and received on a daily basis.

10. On 22 July 1991, the Special Rapporteur addressed a letter to the Minister for Foreign Affairs of the Republic of Iraq in which he expressed his interest in establishing direct contacts with relevant authorities of the Government of Iraq on all matters pertaining to his mandate. Subsequently, a meeting took place on 27 August 1991 between the Special Rapporteur and the Counsellor of the Permanent Mission of the Republic of Iraq to the Office of the United Nations at Geneva. At the meeting, the Counsellor conveyed the message that the Government of Iraq intended to cooperate fully with the Special Rapporteur, with such cooperation including acceptance of a visit to Iraq. In reply, it was suggested by the Special Rapporteur, and thereupon agreed, that the best course of action would be to initiate the study by a written exchange which could be followed by a visit to Iraq. The agreed time-frame required the submission of a memorandum by the Special Rapporteur to the Government of Iraq by mid-September, allowing the Government of Iraq one month to reply; further exchanges and study could be accommodated through the end of the calender year with the visit to take place around the New Year. It is the opinion of the Special Rapporteur that in this way he shall be able to collect as much information as possible prior to visiting Iraq, thus making a visit more meaningful and productive. Further, the Special Rapporteur hopes that this programme shall place him in a position to report in a comprehensive manner, presenting the most up-to-date information available, to the Commission on Human Rights at its next session.

11. Following the above programme, an initial memorandum summarizing various allegations of human rights violations, and seeking information thereon, was sent by the Special Rapporteur to the Minister for Foreign Affairs of Iraq on 16 September 1991 (see para. 12). A reply from the Government of Iraq was received on 25 October 1991. The texts of the memorandum and of the reply are reproduced below in sections II and III, respectively.

II. MEMORANDUM OF THE SPECIAL RAPPORTEUR

12. By the following letter, addressed to the Minister for Foreign Affairs of the Republic of Iraq and dated 16 September 1991, the Special Rapporteur communicated a memorandum concerning allegations which he had received:

> "Excellency,
>
> "With reference to Commission on Human Rights resolution 1991/74, by virtue of which I was appointed Special Rapporteur on the situation of human rights in Iraq, I have the honour to refer to my recent meeting of 27 August 1991 with Dr. Al-Kadhi, Counsellor at the Permanent Mission of the Republic of Iraq to the Office of the United Nations at Geneva.
>
> "Let me first express my sincere appreciation for your Government's offer, communicated through Dr. Al-Kadhi, of full cooperation with my mandate, including an offer to entertain a visit by me to Iraq.
>
> "In the course of the aforementioned meeting of 27 August 1991, a general programme of cooperation was discussed. To recapitulate, it was agreed that a written exchange would take place prior to the submission of my interim report to the forty-sixth session of the General Assembly under the terms of resolution 1991/74. It was also agreed that I would submit a memorandum to your Government in mid-September, to which your Government would reply before mid-October so as to enable me to present the position of your Government to the General Assembly.
>
> "With the intention of visiting Iraq as close as possible to the date of submission of my report to the Commission on Human Rights at its forty-eighth session in February 1992, it was agreed that I would visit Iraq in early January 1992. In terms of the programme of my visit, I would like to reiterate my requests for the honour of audiences with the President of the Revolutionary Command Council, the Foreign Minister, and such other Ministers of

Government as may be appropriate, along with unrestricted access to all parts of the country and to such establishments, centres, compounds, buildings, documents, persons, etc., as may be deemed necessary for me to carry out my mandate, accompanied by such United Nations personnel and necessary advisers as would be required for the fulfilment of my tasks. Having been advised that the Ministry of Foreign Affairs would be the coordinating office for my visit, I shall submit to you the full details of my anticipated visit in due course.

"With the above in mind, I submit to you herewith my memorandum to which I shall await the receipt of your reply. I consider it of the greatest importance in the conduct of my work to have access to first-hand information and to be fully aware of the views of the Government of Iraq at all times in order that I may properly inform the General Assembly and the Commission on Human Rights on the situation of human rights in your country. To this end, and while I fully appreciate the technical constraints affecting communications at this time, I must stress the importance of receiving your reply to the enclosed memorandum by 15 October 1991. Of course, should you have something to add after that date, I shall always be available to receive any such supplementary information thereafter.

"Accept, Excellency, the assurances of my highest consideration.

Max van der Stoel
Special Rapporteur of the Commission on Human Rights on the situation of human rights in Iraq."

13. The following paragraphs reproduce the memorandum which was attached to the above letter.

A. Arbitrary detention

14. Notwithstanding constitutional guarantees against arbitrary arrest and detention, allegations have been made that thousands of persons have been arrested and detained by government forces without ever being informed of charges against them, without access to legal counsel or due process of law, and often without the opportunity to contact their relatives or anyone else. It has been further alleged that such practices of arrest and detention extend to women, children and the elderly. Please comment on these general allegations.

15. As a general matter relating to the detention of persons, please indicate whether or not an equivalent to a writ of *habeas corpus* is available to detainees, or, in any event, the maximum duration of time a person may be lawfully held in detention without being informed of the charges underlying his detention and without being brought before a court or judge. If an equivalent to a writ of *habeas corpus* does exist, please indicate the number of applications received and granted in this regard over the last year. Where lawful exceptions to the application of the rule exist, please indicate the number of persons taken into custody in the last year without the possibility of recourse to *habeas corpus* or an equivalent safeguard.

B. Disappearances

16. With reports of disappearances dating back many years, and 3,562 cases under consideration by the United Nations Working Group on Enforced or Involuntary Disappearances still unresolved, it has been alleged that this practice has been employed systematically throughout the country as part of a general programme aimed at quelling opposition. A particularly significant incident reported among these allegations concerns the disappearance of some 8,000 Kurdish Barzani tribesmen (including more than 300 children) taken from camps at Qushtapa and Diyana in Arbil on 30 July 1983, the names and particulars of 2,280 of whom appear on a list transmitted by the United Nations Working Group on Enforced or Involuntary Disappearances to the Government of Iraq on 29 July 1988. With reports of widespread disappearances still being made in connection with, *inter alia*, the March 1991 uprisings, the 20 March 1991 arrest of the Grand Ayatollah Sayyid Abul Qasim al-Khoei along with many of his family and associates (see paras. 38 to 40), the April and July 1991 amnesties (see paras. 43 to 46), and recent and continuing disturbances in the Kurdish Autonomous Region, please comment on these allegations, indicating the procedural recourses available for the investigation of such reports, and whether or not there has been established an independent national commission of inquiry into the problem. In particular, please provide detailed information on the whereabouts of those persons named in appendix 1 hereto who reportedly disappeared in southern Iraq in March 1991.

C. Torture, inhuman or degrading practices

17. Numerous allegations have been received that torture and other cruel, inhuman or degrading practices are widely used by national security forces (whether military or police forces) throughout the country, that such practices constitute regular techniques for the extraction of confessions from persons held in detention and are, in fact, part of a structured programme of repression aimed against opposition groups. Specifically, it has been alleged that various types of torture and physical abuse (including beatings, burnings, extraction of finger-nails, sexual assaults, electric shocks, acid baths, and deprivation of food, water, sleep or rest) and psychological abuse (such as subjection to mock executions) are regularly suffered by those in detention, particularly those detained or imprisoned for political offences. Moreover, in the course of alleged extrajudicial killings such as those reported in the north and south in March and April 1991, it has been alleged that persons suffered violations of the body including mutilation prior to actual death. Further, reports have been received, accompanied with photographic evidence, that women and children were strapped to tanks during the March uprisings in order to keep insurgent forces from attacking the tanks.

18. In the light of these very serious and continuing allegations, please comment, detailing available recourses for complainants, available procedures for investigation, and the means of disciplining violative security personnel, specifying the number of complaints received, investigations conducted, and security personnel disciplined in each of the last four years. In this connection, please also indicate those measures which have been taken to implement the Body of Principles for the Protection of All Persons under Any Form of Detention or Imprisonment (General Assembly resolution 43/173 of 9 December 1988) and the Declaration on the Protection of All Persons from Being Subjected to Torture and Other Cruel, Inhuman or Degrading Treatment or Punishment (General Assembly resolution 3452 (XXX) of 9 December 1975).

D. Extrajudicial killings

Political killings

19. It has been alleged that political killings commonly occur in (and outside) Iraq in order to maintain political power within the country. From the murder of village mayors to Ministers of State and from high-street assassinations to elaborate extraterritorial thallium poisonings, reports suggest that such political killings are carried out by government agents. In addition to evident assassinations are the largely unexplained helicopter accidents that took the lives of General Abdul Rashid in August 1988, General Salman Shuja in September 1988, and Minister for Defence Adnan Khairallah Talfah in June 1989. In commenting on these serious allegations, please indicate those *post mortem* procedures which are available and have been used in investigations of such incidents.

Summary or arbitrary executions

20. Reports of arbitrary or summary executions have been constant since the summer of 1979, affecting both members of the Government and civilians. In particular, arbitrary or summary executions are said to have become more and more frequently carried out as a general form of terror suppressing opposition sentiments, or as reprisals against specific groups or persons such as in relation to Kurdish guerrilla attacks during the mid-1980s to the late 1980s, and in the course and aftermath of the March 1991 uprisings in the north and south. In terms of these latest events, information has been received alleging: the summary execution of some 150 men and boys taken to the Al-Mahawil Garrison near Al-Hilla on 16 March 1991; the summary execution of another 70 civilians in Al-Hilla on 19 March 1991; the summary execution of scores of persons during house-to-house searches for insurgents in Al-Samawa between 20 and 29 March 1991; the arbitrary execution (e.g. through injuries sustained when thrown out of windows) of some 70 patients and medical personnel in Al-Hilla hospital on 9 March 1991; the summary execution of hundreds of civilians in Qara Hanjir between 27 and 29 March 1991; the summary execution (by burning) of 40 persons in Arbat on 3 April 1991; the summary execution (by firing squad) of 17 persons in Arbil on 17 April 1991; and the massive and indiscriminate bombings and machine-gunnings cited in paragraphs 22 and 23. It is further alleged that such executions are continuing to take place throughout the country, particularly in the northern Kurdish Autonomous Region, in southern Shiah centres, and in the southern marshes.

21. In view of the seriousness of the many allegations referred to above, please comment, indicating whether or not any government inquiry has been constituted to consider these

allegations. In so doing, please specify such civilian and military laws as may exist which may permit the prosecution of those responsible for such crimes, citing the number of such prosecutions that have been made in each of the last four years. In addition, please indicate the legal recourses available to the relatives of the victims, citing the number of times such procedures have been resorted to in each of the last four years.

E. Control of civil disturbances

22. In reaction to various public demonstrations and civil disturbances aimed against the Government, it has been reported that the Government has employed extreme and indiscriminate measures resulting in the injury, maiming and death of thousands of persons, including women, children and the elderly. Of note in this connection is the use of chemical weapons on the town of Halabja in March 1988 in which an estimated 5,000 unarmed civilians died, followed by the reported use of chemical weapons on various other villages in northern Iraq during August 1988. More recently, it has been reported that indiscriminate bombardment of residential areas of Basra, Najaf and other southern cities during the March 1991 uprisings included the use of phosphorous bombs and napalm. During the uprisings in northern Iraq, indiscriminate bombardment of residential areas of Chamchamal (1 to 8 April 1991), Altin Kopri and Zakho (30 March 1991) reportedly killed hundreds of civilians, while numerous refugees on the Arbil-Salahuddin and Rawanduz-Haj 'Omran roads were reportedly attacked by helicopter gunships on 31 March 1991 and 1 to 8 April 1991, respectively. Concerning this same period, several reports have been received alleging instructions by Iraqi military and security forces for immediate civilian evacuation of whole towns and larger population centres under threat of the use of chemical weapons and gases.

23. In view of the serious nature of these widespread and continuing allegations (and notwithstanding the equally serious issues raised by these same incidents in the context of paragraphs 19 to 21, please comment on their substance, specifying government policies dealing with control of civil disturbances, existing controls and prohibitions on the use of weapons of indiscriminate destruction, and the available legal recourses against those responsible for employing such measures in violation of controls and prohibitions. Please also indicate the steps which have been taken to implement the Basic Principles on the Use of Force and Firearms by Law Enforcement Officials (adopted by the Eighth United Nations Congress on the Prevention of Crime and the Treatment of Offenders, held in Havana from 27 August to 7 September 1990), and whether or not any government inquiry has been established to consider the above allegations.

F. Hostage-taking and the use of persons as "human shields" during hostilities

24. In connection with the detention in 1990 of several thousand foreign civilians within Iraq, and their acknowledged distribution around the country as "human shields" designed to dissuade attacks on potential targets of war within Iraq, together with the subsequently similar treatment of prisoners of war captured in early 1991, please provide the legal basis of these detentions and treatment, citing the relevant orders, and noting those measures which have been taken to afford compensation to the victims.

G. Laws in force

Political organization

25. It has been widely alleged that the present Constitution and composition of the Government of Iraq does not represent the freely expressed will of the people of Iraq, and that divergencies from the democratic principles of the Charter of the United Nations, the Universal Declaration of Human Rights and the International Covenant on Civil and Political Rights are manifest in an unaccountable executive power that routinely bypasses even the ostensible institutions of democratic government. In view of these allegations, please provide the following information requested.

26. With respect to the legal status of the Revolutionary Command Council, please explain its constitutional relationship with the National Assembly. Please also indicate: the constitutional powers of the President of the Revolutionary Command Council; the nature of the Revolutionary Command Council's accountability to the general population; the number of times in the last two years that the National Assembly has rejected bills originating from the Revolutionary Command Council, and the number of bills it has approved; and the number of decrees promulgated by the Revolutionary Command Council in the last two years. In relation to decrees of the Revolutionary Command Council in general, please specify whether or not they supersede normal laws or whether they must be subsequently endorsed by the National Assembly. In addition, please indicate the date of the last general national elections (including a copy of the pertinent elections laws) together with the anticipated date(s) of the next general national elections. With regard to regional and local government, please indicate the immediately previous occupations and basis of authority (i.e. whether they were appointed or elected, by whom, when and for how long) of the governors of all regions and the mayors of all cities with populations exceeding 250,000.

Functioning of the judiciary

27. According to various reports, there is considerable doubt concerning the independence of the judiciary from the powers of the executive. These doubts surrounding the administration of justice in general are compounded by additional allegations that many appointed members of the judiciary are not properly qualified and that, in any event, a large part of the administration of criminal justice and laws entailing serious penalties against the person are administered outside the normal judicial system. With regard to these allegations, please provide the following information requested.

28. Please indicate the method of appointment of members of the judiciary (both regular and special courts), detailing such professional requirements as are necessary for appointment to the judiciary. In this connection, please indicate the names and immediately previous occupations of all higher court justices (of both regular and special courts).

29. With reference to Law No. 180 of 1968, amended by Laws Nos. 1, 85 and 120 of 1969, please explain the constitution of the Revolutionary Court established in Baghdad under this Law. In the functioning of this Court, please indicate the percentage of cases resulting in findings of guilt, and describe the process of appeal permissible from the Revolutionary Court noting the percentage of successful appeals from the findings of this Court.

30. As regards the composition, constitution and functioning of the numerous special and temporary courts (including the Revolutionary Court) variously established throughout the country, please provide details of the scope of judicial functions assumed by these courts. In so doing, please indicate the number of death sentences and sentences of lengthy incarceration declared by these courts in each year since 1987, noting the total number of such sentences declared by all civilian courts in these same years.

31. In the practices of the Revolutionary Court and other special and temporary courts, please indicate the percentage of trials conducted *in camera*, the percentage of defendants represented by lawyers of their own choosing, and the percentage of convictions reviewed on appeal.

Offences

32. In view of the continuing force of various broadly applicable and imprecise laws (carrying extreme penalties for violators) prohibiting such things as "insults against the President", it has been repeatedly alleged that freedom of speech and other liberties guaranteed by those human rights instruments to which Iraq is a party are severely curtailed if not fully undermined. Indeed, it has been further alleged that the existence of such laws, broadly interpreted and widely employed, is at the foundation of a system of repression that permeates the general population. On the basis of these allegations, please provide the following information requested.

33. Under the terms of Revolutionary Command Council Decree No. 840 of 4 November 1986 (appearing in the Iraqi *Official Gazette* of 17 November 1986) which prescribes severe penalties including death for, *inter alia*, anyone directing slanders or insults against the President of the Revolutionary Command Council or anyone representing him, the Revolutionary Command Council, the Al-Baath Party, the National Assembly or the Government, please indicate the number of people prosecuted and found guilty under this law in each year since its promulgation, specifying the actual sentences declared in each case.

34. In relation to article 164 of the Penal Code, under which "any person who, in time of war, attempts to jeopardize the military, political or economic situation of Iraq" may incur the death penalty, please indicate the number of death sentences declared under this law in the course of the last year.

35. As regards Revolutionary Command Council Resolution No. 461 of 31 March 1980, retroactively applying the death penalty to persons having been members of the Shiah fundamentalist Da'wa Party, please specify the number of persons charged under this Resolution, noting the names of those sentenced to death.

36. With respect to the rules and regulations applying to membership in the Al-Baath Party, please indicate the number of persons who have been charged under: article 200 of the Penal Code (making it a capital offence for an Al-Baath Party member

to conceal his previous party affiliations); Law No. 107 of 1974 (making it a capital offence for an Al-Baath Party member to maintain links with any other political party or organization); Law No. 145 of 1976 (making it a capital offence for a former Al-Baath Party member to have any connection with any other political party or grouping); and Law No. 111 of 1978 (making it a capital offence to recruit into another political party or grouping anyone who has or has had any organizational relationship with the Al-Baath Party). In relation to each of these laws, please also provide the names of all persons sentenced to death under these laws.

37. As concerns political offences in general, please provide a list of all such offences carrying penalties of incarceration or death, indicating the number of persons arrested under these laws in each year since 1 January 1988, and detailing the names and specific offences of all persons sentenced to death for such crimes over this same period.

H. Individual cases

Situation of the Grand Ayatollah Sayyid Abul Qasim al-Khoei

38. According to information received, the Grand Ayatollah Sayyid Abul Qasim al-Khoei was arrested in Najaf on 20 March 1991 along with members of his family and associated scholars, was taken in custody to Baghdad, and has since been returned to Najaf where he remains under continuous surveillance, restricting his personal liberty.

39. With respect to this case, please provide the following information requested:

(a) A detailed account of the legal basis of the Grand Ayatollah's detention and that of those taken into custody with him, including copies of the laws sanctioning the arrests and detentions;

(b) A detailed description of the terms of the Grand Ayatollah's detention, including whether or not he is permitted to receive visitors of his own choosing and at his discretion or on any other terms;

(c) An account of the whereabouts of those persons reportedly arrested with the Grand Ayatollah, as named in appendix 2. In this connection, please specify the whereabouts of those subsequently released and/or the date(s) of their release from custody, or the places and terms of detention of those persons named in appendix 2 who continue to be held in custody.

40. As regards the general health and well-being of the Grand Ayatollah, assurances are requested that proper and necessary health care be provided including those medicines and treatments required for his heart ailment.

Situation of Mr. Ian Richter

41. According to information received, Mr. Ian Richter, a British national, was arrested on 17 June 1986 at Baghdad International Airport, was subsequently tried for offences of bribery and corruption under the Iraqi Criminal Code, and has since been imprisoned in Iraq serving a sentence of life imprisonment.

42. With respect to this case, please provide the following information requested:

(a) A summary account of the process of law against Mr. Richter from the date of his arrest through to his present incarceration, including account of all places of his detention before, during and after his trial;

(b) A detailed description of the charges brought against Mr. Richter, the constitution of the court before which he was tried, and the evidence upon which he was found guilty. In this connection, please specify the date on which Mr. Richter was informed of the charges against him, the names of witnesses brought by Mr. Richter in his defence, the number of times and the length of each time Mr. Richter was allowed to consult with a lawyer, and whether the defence lawyer was appointed by the Government or was freely chosen by Mr. Richter;

(c) A detailed description of the appeal process granted to Mr. Richter, together with the results of such appeals.

I. Effects of recent amnesties

43. In keeping with practices dating at least from 1988, the declaration of amnesties has been reported from Iraq during 1991. According to information received, there were a series of amnesties declared in April subsequent to the internal uprisings in the north and south of Iraq, and another amnesty recently declared in July. While the declaration of recent amnesties has been generally applauded in several quarters, allegations remain that the amnesties are also used as a means of rounding up members of opposition groups, and that the terms of the amnesties are frequently violated by government agents who arrest certain persons returning out of places of hiding (within Iraq or beyond) in order to take advantage of these declarations. Several reports allege that persons already detained, as with several of those arrested during (and in violation of) the amnesties, rather than being released have actually "disappeared" in the custody of the Government. In this connection, please respond to the following requests.

44. With respect to the April amnesties (beginning with the initial announcement of the Revolutionary Command Council on 5 April and subsequently extended in scope and time), please forward copies of all relevant decrees and indicate the number of persons who may be said to have taken advantage of the amnesties together with the number and names of those released from detention under them. Please also indicate whether any foreigners were permitted to benefit from these amnesties, whether in fact any did, or, if not so permitted, the number of foreigners (citing names and nationalities) held as a result of their participation in the activities for which the amnesties were accorded to Iraqi nationals. In relation to this last matter, please also indicate the number of foreigners (citing names and nationalities) killed during the insurgencies.

45. In the light of significant and repeated allegations that certain persons taking advantage of the April amnesties, particularly Kurds in the city of Arbil, were detained upon their return, taken to the city stadium, subjected to punishments or executed, or have subsequently disappeared, please comment on these allegations.

46. With regard to Decisions Nos. 241 and 242 of 21 July 1991, issued by the Revolutionary Command Council, granting general and comprehensive amnesties to "fugitives for political reasons", Iraqi prisoners and detainees convicted of political offences, and military service deserters, please indicate the number and names of persons who have taken advantage of these amnesties, especially those released from prisons or centres of detention.

J. Treatment of ethnic groups

The Kurdish minority

47. The Special Rapporteur has noted the 1991 reports submitted and representations made by the Government of Iraq before the United Nations Committee on Human Rights and the United Nations Committee on the Elimination of Racial Discrimination, referring to the extensive legal provisions securing the rights of the Kurdish minority in Iraq, particularly in the Kurdish Autonomous Region. Nevertheless, evidence of the implementation of these guarantees is lacking and the effectiveness of these laws is uncertain in the face of considerable allegations of oppression. In addition, the massive flight of people from Kurdish regions (essentially unaffected by the Gulf war) after the March 1991 disturbances is alleged to be evidence of the extensive fear instilled in the population after many years of general oppression. In the light of the related allegations of the use of extreme measures, including the aforesaid use of weapons of indiscriminate destruction, against the Kurdish population on many occasions over several years, and in view of the reports of regular expulsions of Kurds to Iran of their forced resettlement in newly established villages and city suburbs, please comment on the massive exodus of Kurds in April 1991. In so doing, please indicate the percentage of ethnic Kurds in the National Assembly, the method of appointment of the Executive Officers of the Kurdish Autonomous Region, and explain the June 1986 law requiring candidates for the Kurdish Legislative Council to have a well-established record of fulfilling Al-Baath Party objectives. In addition, please indicate those measures which are presently being taken to guarantee the health, lives and property of the Kurds, noting the degree of active participation of Kurdish representatives in the administration of these programmes.

The Turkoman minority

48. With respect to the Turkoman population centred in and around Mosul and Kirkuk provinces, please describe those measures which have been taken to assure Turkoman participation in the government of these regions. In so doing, please respond to allegations that the limitation on the sale of Turkoman-held real estate only to Arab Iraqis (effected through the requirement of special licences), in conjunction with the practice of granting confiscated Turkoman properties to resettling Arab Iraqis, is part of a structured programme to alter the ethnic ratios of the populations of these regions. Further, please specify the extent to which the Turkoman language may be used in public institutions in those regions with large Turkoman populations.

The practice of expulsion

49. According to information received, large groups of persons who have been resident in Iraq for generations before Iraqi independence have been expelled from Iraq in recent years on the basis of the argument that they are not Iraqi nationals due to their ethnic lineage. It has been further reported that there exist, in fact, various types of Iraqi "nationality" such that millions of people live in constant fear of being deported. In this connection, please comment on these allegations and reports, providing copies of Iraqi laws pertaining to nationality and deportation.

K. Religious practices and cultural properties

50. In the light of considerable reports of widespread harassment of religious leaders, scholars and students, the closing of their centres of learning and worship and/or the destruction of such schools, mosques and monuments, please provide the following information requested:

(a) The number of religious centres of learning, mosques, shrines and major monuments in each of Najaf, Karbala, Basra, Kirkuk, Arbil, Mosul, Dihuk, and Sulaimaniya as of 1 January 1988, and in those same cities as of 1 September 1991;

(b) The number of religious scholars and students (distinguishing Iraqi nationals from foreigners) resident in Najaf and Karbala as of 1 January 1991, and in those same cities as of 1 September 1991;

(c) The current conditions of Darul Hikma school, Qazwini school, Sheikh Tusi mosque and Al-Khoei Hussainiya in Karbala, together with the present conditions of the Wadi Al-Salem cemetery in Najaf.

51. In addition to the information requested, comments and responses are invited on the following allegations communicated to the Special Rapporteur:

(a) Recent reports allege that there are no functioning religious centres of learning in Najaf and Karbala, including the ancient universities, at this time, and that the Al-Khoei school has been razed to the ground. Please comment on these allegations;

(b) Recent reports allege that the traditional call to prayer and pilgrimage in the holy shrines of Najaf and Karbala has been banned along with public prayers in these holy cities. In addition, it has been reported that many Shiah clergymen are banned from wearing their traditional uniforms and from performing their religious duties. Please comment;

(c) As a part of a general policy aimed against organized religion in general and the Shiah religious community in particular, it has been reported that more than 1,000 religious books have been banned by the Ministry of Information, and that various religious practices (such as Shiah traditional rituals about Imam Hussein) are prohibited both in public and in private places. Please comment;

(d) Recent reports allege that the holy shrines of Shiah Islam (especially in Najaf and Karbala) have been desecrated by government forces, have incurred severe damages, and have been sealed off from worshippers. Further, religious manuscripts and books in a number of libraries are said to have been either burnt or otherwise purposefully destroyed. Please comment, explaining government actions if true;

(e) Recent reports allege that reparations to the damaged shrines of Najaf and Karbala, including their ancient perimeter walls, are being carried out in such a way as to deface the religious art and to damage these cultural properties permanently. It is also alleged that these reparations are being conducted without consultations with the members of the local religious communities. Please comment, explaining government actions if true.

L. Access to food and health care

52. Information has been received that stores of food and medicaments are held by government authorities in secure facilities out of reach of the general public, and that access to these stores is available only to certain persons and organizations close to the Government. Moreover, and despite the severe conditions and shortages affecting the great majority of the population, it has been reported that military personnel and government officials enjoy ready access to these stores and have, in fact, received increases in their pay and benefits in recent months. Please comment on these reports.

53. In view of the severe post-war conditions affecting large parts of the population through the destruction of various parts of the health-care infrastructure, food-producing and food-distributing systems, please indicate those measures being taken to ensure sufficient allocations of available resources to meet the requirements of the population, particularly those most in need. In this connection, please indicate measures being taken to ensure fair and sufficient access to foodstuffs and medicines in the least-serviced areas, including rural areas, the regions of the north and south that suffered insurgencies in March 1991, and in the region of the southern marshes. With particular concern for those in the southern marshes, please also indicate measures being taken to provide clean drinking water for the residents and refugees situated there.

54. With regard to fair access to such supplies as exist, please indicate such guarantees as may exist which ensure priority access for the most vulnerable, for infant children, lactating mothers, the elderly and the ill. In addition, please also indicate such measures which guarantee equal access to basic necessities for all without distinction.

III. REPLY OF THE GOVERNMENT OF IRAQ

55. The following text constitutes the reply of the Government of Iraq to the memorandum of the Special Rapporteur which was received on 25 October 1991; some 120 pages of annexes submitted together with the reply are not reproduced. (For the titles of the annexes, see appendix below.)

Introduction

In our view, the question of human rights in any country, including Iraq, cannot be discussed without taking into consideration the economic, political and social background and the evident manner in which the situation is influenced by the factors of time and place. Under wartime conditions, human rights cannot be discussed in the same spirit and with the same degree of objectivity as in times of peace. A country with a long-standing democratic tradition cannot be compared with a developing country that is making diligent efforts to attain both democracy and economic prosperity. Every country has its own particularities and indigenous values which cannot be set aside in any discussion on human rights, especially in the light of the intensive dialogue which has given rise to controversy on this subject in various countries with different cultural or religious affiliations.

We have drawn attention to the above in the introduction to our reply to your questions because we wish to highlight the fact that the humanitarian, ethical and universal aspects of human rights are not doubted or questioned by us, since Iraq firmly believes in these rights. Moreover, it is an indisputable fact that human rights should be respected and promoted as a humanitarian facet of present-day life. They also constitute the basis for social development and they have a positive impact on the achievement of peace and justice at the international level.

Being motivated by this belief and perception, Iraq has already ratified a number of international human rights instruments and is carefully examining those which it has not ratified in order to adopt a clear, objective position thereon. Iraq has participated, and will continue to participate, in conferences, symposia and committees seeking to promote human rights at the national, regional and international levels. Our country is also faithfully fulfilling its obligations in regard to the submission of periodic reports on the evolution of the human rights situation in Iraq. It replies to the questions raised by the international bodies and non-governmental organizations concerned. Iraq has never defaulted in this regard, except on rare occasions and by reason of *force majeure*. Even the advent of the Iraq-Iran war, which was an exceptional period in Iraq's modern history, had little effect on Iraq's fulfilment of its obligations in this regard.

The sufferings of the Iraqi people throughout the period of foreign occupation, in which their individual and collective rights and their legitimate aspirations for dignity, freedom and sovereignty were disregarded, and the deliberate neglect or indifference shown by the previous political regimes in Iraq for the question of human rights, were among the reasons which prompted the present political regime in Iraq to pursue a diligent policy reflecting the people's desire to strengthen and promote human rights. This popular desire was expressed in numerous resolutions and official documents, particularly the present Constitution, and was reflected in several legislative enactments affirming the need to respect the people's will, as well as their right to a decent life and their right to exercise their fundamental freedoms in a democratic environment conducive to the growth and development of their individual and collective personality.

The fact that Iraq is a relatively recently established developing country means that there are a number of constraints relating to the degree of development attained in the cultural, economic and social fields. Hence, recognition of, and belief in, human rights does not imply that they are put into practice, since major efforts are needed to resolve various practical problems.

Positive changes had been made since 1968. From that time until the start of the Iraq-Iran war in 1980, no serious violations of human rights were reported in Iraq. However, the Iraq-Iran war, the economic embargo which began in August 1990 and the Gulf war in 1991 inevitably had an impact on the human rights situation in the country.

Human rights cannot flourish in time of war, although respect for these rights increases when peace and tranquillity prevail. This was exactly what we began to witness after the cessation of military operations in August 1988 and until August 1990. During this short period, the current Constitution was reviewed and a new draft constitution was discussed. Several emergency laws and decrees that had been issued during the war were also re-examined and many of them were abrogated. The beginning of a new era was proclaimed in which citizens were allowed to travel without restrictions and freedom of the press was respected. This new era was also characterized by political pluralism and abrogation of the emergency laws and regulations which had restricted the freedom of citizens.

This new era soon started to wane as a result of the Gulf war and the economic embargo on Iraq.

This unjust economic embargo is still having an extremely adverse impact on the life and dignity of the Iraqi people and, consequently, on human rights in the economic, social, cultural, civil and political spheres. We are all aware that the insecurity, price rises and scarcity of basic foodstuffs and medicines resulting from the abnormal circumstances experienced by Iraq have all had a direct impact on the enjoyment of human rights by Iraqi citizens and on the State's ability to promote them.

The situation was aggravated by the total destruction of the country's infrastructure in the agricultural, educational, health, industrial and communication sectors. It is well known that the United States/European bombing destroyed bridges, fields, schools, streets, civilian houses, hospitals and electricity and water supplies. Fear and chaos increased as gangs of ruffians, outlaws and military deserters, together with groups who had crossed the border from Iran, committed barbaric acts which were totally alien to the time-honoured values of Iraqi society. These barbaric acts included the murder, mutilation and rape of thousands of innocent civilians, and the pillaging and theft of public funds and private property in the areas where the disturbances took place. Hospitals, schools, universities and courts of law were destroyed and these outlaws even went so far as to set up "special courts" in which many innocent citizens were killed, including children, women and elderly persons, in addition to the physical liquidation of a large number of civil servants.

These criminal acts appear to have been planned in advance by foreign bodies; yet another page in the history of military aggression against Iraq for the achievement of well-known political ends.

Accordingly, these events can under no circumstances be regarded as an "*intifada*". It was an exceptional state of chaos, disorder and armed rebellion which soon ended, after only a few days, when order and authority were restored in the areas afflicted with this abnormal situation.

While the government troops were regaining control of these areas, the armed conflicts which occurred between the troops and those subversive groups inevitably led to loss of life among citizens, the security forces and those groups, some of which fled the country.

Finally, a general amnesty was granted to the persons involved in the disturbances, except those who had committed acts of murder or rape.

The re-establishment of order and tranquillity in these areas during a very short period of time highlights the fact that these disturbances characterized by chaos and lawlessness were provoked by the circumstances of the military aggression against Iraq and by foreign intervention.

However, in spite of the major tragedy experienced by Iraq, there are still some bright spots on which we would like to focus. The Government and people of Iraq have spared no effort to diminish the extent of the material and moral damage suffered by Iraqi society and its citizens, since the crisis and the continuing embargo are still having an adverse impact on the human rights situation.

In this connection, we wish to refer to the numerous amnesty decrees that were promulgated, the abolition of the Revolutionary Court and the abrogation or amendment of several laws and decisions issued during the war. Travel restrictions were lifted, the Political Parties Act was promulgated and a new constitution and press law for the country are also under preparation.

The criticisms levied against Iraq during the two wars, regardless of their validity, came as no surprise to us. We have already replied to these criticisms on the basis of the available information, although it was impossible for us to reply in some cases due to the lack of reliable information, particularly in regard to the disappearance of many persons who have not yet been traced and some of whom are included in the lists of "enforced disappearances".

How can a country, having fought a ferocious war like the one with Iran, an eight-year military conflict entailing human and material disasters, ascertain the fate of citizens missing in border areas which were the theatre of military operations from which people fled seeking safe refuge or which they were forced to leave due to the threat from armed bands? How can we imagine the possibility of promoting human rights, democracy and freedom under conditions of foreign occupation and intervention?

The State is faced with a difficult choice between defending the country's territorial integrity and national unity and ensuring the rule of law through the adoption of emergency measures to attain these objectives in a manner which might temporarily or marginally infringe some individual rights, or sacrificing everything.

We cannot therefore claim, in the light of this difficult situation, that human rights in our country are not beset by any problems or obstacles. However, the Iraqi Government has the resolute political will to overcome these obstacles so that human rights and fundamental freedoms can be better exercised in Iraq.

Finally, although the Special Rapporteur has not inquired about the impact on human rights in Iraq of the unjust economic embargo to which the Iraqi people have been subjected since August 1990, any talk of human rights in any country must necessarily touch upon the fundamental issue of whether its citizens have sufficient food and medicines, since this relates to the right to life, especially in the case of the most vulnerable categories of the population such as children, infants, pregnant women and the elderly. How could such a sensitive issue be disregarded by the Special Rapporteur and, in turn, by the United Nations Commission on Human Rights, by non-governmental organizations and especially by the members of the international community which show concern for the question of human rights.

We hope that the Special Rapporteur will give due attention to this sensitive issue, particularly in view of the fact that the scarcity or lack of basic foodstuffs and medicines has had a direct impact on the enjoyment of most human rights in Iraq, especially the right to life as exemplified by the loss of thousands of human lives.

In this connection, we wish to refer to the close interrelationship between economic, social and cultural rights, on the one hand, and civil and political rights, on the other, as affirmed in numerous resolutions adopted by the United Nations and human rights bodies, the most recent of which was United Nations General Assembly resolution 45/96 of 14 December 1990.

Replies to the Special Rapporteur's questions

Arbitrary detention

The questions concerning arbitrary detention were very general and abstract. To enable the competent authorities to answer them, they must refer to specific incidents and contain detailed information that can be verified. Accordingly, we will confine our reply to the legal framework of judicial and administrative detention and cases of such detention.

Detention by court order

Articles 20 and 22 of the Constitution guarantee the right to liberty. The provisions of articles 421-429 of the Penal Code prescribe very severe penalties for acts prejudicial to personal liberty and the inviolability of homes. These provisions apply to all persons, without any discrimination, and the penalty is increased if the offence is committed by a public official. The right of defence through the appointment of a lawyer is fully guaranteed by the explicit text of article 20, paragraphs (b) and (c), of the Constitution and article 144 of the Code of Criminal Procedure stipulates that the court must appoint a lawyer to defend a person accused in a criminal case. Article 92 of the Code of Criminal Procedure (Act No. 23 of 1972) stipulates as follows: "No one may be arrested or detained without a warrant issued by a magistrate or a court of law, except in circumstances in which such is permitted by law." Article 93 of the Code of Criminal Procedure further stipulates that: "The arrest warrant must contain the name, surname, identity and description, if known, of the person to be arrested, as well as his place of residence, his occupation, the type of offence with which he is to be charged, and the section of the law applicable thereto. The order must be dated, signed by the person who issues it, and stamped by the court." Under the terms of article 94, paragraph (b), of the Code of Criminal Procedure: "The person to be arrested must be shown the arrest warrant and, after his arrest, must be brought before the authority by which it was issued."

If the investigating officer exceeds his authority and contravenes the provisions of the law by subjecting persons to arrest or detention without a court order, the victim is entitled to lodge a complaint in person. A complaint can also be lodged by the Department of Public Prosecutions, by virtue of its authority to monitor investigation procedures as an impartial body in criminal cases, unlike the public prosecutors who conduct the investigation. Under article 1 (a) of the Code of Criminal Procedure, any person who is aware of the commission of such an offence, including the relatives of a person who has been unlawfully arrested or detained, has the right to file an application demanding that the arrested person be brought before the judiciary to make a statement in that regard. The perpetrators of the offence are liable to the legally prescribed penalty if the person concerned was detained arbitrarily. The system constitutes an application of the principle of *habeas corpus*.

The accused must be informed of the charges against him and must be brought before an examining magistrate within 24 hours from the time of his arrest (article 123 of the Code of Criminal Procedure) so that the competent examining magistrate can take a legal decision based on the facts presented to him.

Cases of administrative detention in 1990

The legal derogations from the principle that no one can be detained without a court order were confined to the power vested in the Minister of the Interior, under the terms of Revolution Command Council Decision No. 26 of 1971, to detain non-political persons suspected of criminal conduct. In 1990, 1,610 persons were detained for breaches of public order and morality. It should be noted that their detention orders were of an administrative nature and, consequently, were subject to appeal to the Administrative Court which was established under the terms of the State Advisory Council Act, as amended by Act No. 106 of 2 December 1989.

Cases of disappearance

Although the competent authorities are investigating the cases of disappearance mentioned in the report of the Working Group on Enforced or Involuntary Disappearances, reference must be made to the difficulties that the authorities are facing in their attempts to ascertain the fate of those persons, particularly since most of the cases of disappearance occurred during the Iraq-Iran war. Moreover, they occurred in remote and rugged border regions which were the scene of ferocious military operations that induced the local population to leave those regions. We believe that a large number of them fled to neighbouring States. It should be borne in mind that extensive areas of the border regions were subjected to Iranian military occupation for long periods. With regard to the figure of 8,000 unnamed missing persons that has now been submitted to us, this is something new that has not previously appeared in the report of the Working Group on Enforced or Involuntary Disappearances. This figure cannot be verified until detailed information has been received concerning all the individual cases concerned. With regard to the Barzani clan, we wish to refer to the two notes which our Mission sent to the Centre for Human Rights on 10 May 1990 and 20 June 1990, which read as follows:

> "The areas of Iraq which are inhabited by the Barzani clan were the scene of a number of military operations during the Iraq-Iran war when Iranian forces attacked the areas of Haj Umran, Banjwin, Choarta and Sidikan in northern Iraq in 1982, 1983 and 1984. That clan collaborated with the invading forces and facilitated their entry into those areas after providing them with all the reconnaissance information that they required. The clan also actually participated in the attacks which the Iranian forces launched against Iraqi military units, as a result of which many of its members were killed.
>
> "When Iraqi forces recovered control over those areas and forced the Iranian forces to retreat across the Iraqi frontier into Iran, many members of that clan fled with the retreating hostile forces. In view of these events, during which many of them were killed during the battles and some of them fled to Iran, it is difficult for the Iraqi authorities to investigate the truth of the allegations contained in the note received from the Centre for Human Rights and, at the present time, it is impossible to ascertain the whereabouts of the persons who allegedly disappeared."

His Eminence Grand Ayatollah Sayyid Abul Qasim al-Khoei

His Eminence Grand Ayatollah Sayyid Abul Qasim al-Khoei was never detained. In this connection, it is sufficient to refer to the visit which Prince Sadruddin Aga Khan, the Executive Delegate of the Secretary-General of the United Nations, paid to Ayatollah al-Khoei at his residence on 12 July 1991. He can be visited at any time and no restrictions are placed on his personal freedom, since he receives Arab and foreign visitors and is carrying out his religious functions in a normal manner. With regard to the names contained in annex I,[sic] we wish to state the following:

After a careful investigation, the competent authorities have ascertained that the persons named in the above-mentioned annex are not currently in Iraq and were probably either killed during the disturbances or fled to Iran, Saudi Arabia or other States with those who participated in the disturbances, particularly since, at that time, the State was unable to exercise full control over the border regions.

The disturbances

The persons who participated in the disturbances committed crimes punishable under Iraqi law, particularly murder, rape and other offences to which reference has already been made. When the State recovered its sovereignty and authority in the governorates in which those disturbances occurred, the persons who had participated in those disturbances and who had not fled across the borders into neighbouring States were taken into custody for questioning in the manner prescribed by law. On 5 April 1991, it was officially announced that the disturbances had been suppressed in all parts of Iraq. Revolution Command Council Decision No. 103 of 10 April 1991 granted a general and comprehensive amnesty to Iraqi Kurds in the Autonomous Region in respect of all the consequences of, and prosecution for, any act punishable by law which was committed during the disturbances. However, acts of murder, rape and theft were excluded from that amnesty.

The amnesty covered the advisers and members of the national defence regiments and members of the special detachments, special forces and internal security forces. The provisions of the decision applied to the persons covered thereby with effect from 5 April 1991 and for one week if they were inside Iraq and for two weeks if they were abroad. The time-limit was subsequently extended by one week under the terms of Revolution Command Council Decision No. 104 of 11 April 1991, and by a further week under the terms of Revolution Command Council Decision No. 105 of 17 April 1991. The Council then promulgated Decision No. 109 of 20 April 1991, extending the general and comprehensive amnesty granted in Decision No. 103 of 10 April 1991 to all Iraqis in northern, southern and central Iraq in respect of the consequences of, and prosecution for, any act punishable by law and which was committed during the disturbances and incidents involving treason. That amnesty did not apply to acts of murder, rape or theft. The decision ordered all the governmental agencies and armed forces to duly facilitate its implementation. On 29 April 1991, the Revolution Command Council promulgated Decision No. 121 granting Iraqi Kurds a general and comprehensive amnesty and exempting them from all consequences of, and prosecution for, any act punishable by law which was committed during the disturbances and the sabotage. The amnesty did not apply to acts of murder or rape. The provisions of the decision entered into force on 26 April 1991 for a period of one month. Decision No. 126 of 8 May 1991 granted a general and comprehensive amnesty to all Iraqi fugitives, wherever they might be, in respect of all consequences of, and prosecution for, any act punishable by law which was committed during the disturbances and the sabotage. Only acts of murder and rape were excluded from the amnesty. The provisions of this decision entered into force on 26 April 1991 for a period of one month. The Revolution Command council also promulgated Decision No. 53 of 4 March 1991 granting an amnesty to fugitives, absentees and absconders guilty of evading military service, desertion or failing to report for duty. Decision No. 98 of 7 April 1991 covered fugitives, absentees and persons who had failed to register for military service but who had subsequently repented and joined their units before 4 March 1991. The time-limit specified in Decision No. 53 of 1991 was subsequently extended by Decision No. 60 of 1991 and Decision No. 73 of 1991, under the terms of which an amnesty was granted to persons who had participated in the disturbances but who had not committed acts of murder and rape. Persons not covered by those amnesties were arrested, questioned by the competent authorities and prosecuted for the offences they had committed.

Torture and inhuman or degrading treatment

Like many of the allegations against Iraq, the statements made in this connection were of a general nature and, as already indicated, cannot be answered unless the names, dates and details pertaining to specific cases are provided so that the competent authorities can conduct an investigation. We are willing to look into any specific allegations and to cooperate with a view to clarifying those cases.

The prohibition of torture under Iraqi law and the prosecution of persons guilty of torture

Iraqi law prescribes extremely severe penalties for the practice of torture during the detention and examination of accused persons. Torture is prohibited by article 22 (a) of the Constitution and articles 332 and 333 of the Penal Code designate the practice of torture as a punishable offence and, in certain circumstances, as a felony. Article 137 of the Code of

Criminal Procedure regards a confession made by an accused person under physical or psychological duress as legally invalid. In actual fact, the criminal courts have convicted and sentenced a number of persons guilty of this offence. As stipulated in Directive No. 4 of 1988, one of the most important duties of members of the Department of Public Prosecutions is to monitor investigation procedures and inspect prisons and places of detention in order to ensure that the law is respected and that detainees are being well treated and not subjected to violations. The Ministry of Justice, in collaboration with the Ministry of the Interior, is constantly monitoring the proper application of the provisions of the law, regulations and directives concerning places of detention through joint committees consisting of senior officials of these two ministries.

Although we cannot categorically deny that some practices of this nature have occurred, whenever they come to the notice of the competent authorities their perpetrators are called to account in accordance with the law. In this connection, it should be noted that a number of investigating officers have been referred to the competent courts and sentenced in accordance with the law. The following court judgements have been handed down in this regard:

(a) Judgement No. 334/M/1983 of the Misdemeanours Court at Saddam City;
(b) Judgement No. 397 of 25 July 1987 of the Court of Cassation;
(c) Judgement No. 1590 of 13 June 1988 of the Court of Cassation;
(d) Judgement No. 256 of 19 July 1989 of the Criminal Court in the governorate of Qadisiya.

(Annex I contains copies of the above-mentioned judgements.)

Allegations concerning assassination and summary execution

(a) Acts of political assassination

The allegations concerning widespread political assassinations in and outside Iraq are questionable, since they do not make detailed reference to specific incidents and names. With regard to the military leaders mentioned, we wish to point out that they were senior commanders who died in the line of duty and of whom the Government and people of Iraq are proud due to the major role that they played in defending their homeland. The information media published details of the incidents in which they lost their lives. Details of the helicopter incidents in which these military leaders died are given below:

(i) Staff Brigadier General Tahir Abdul Rashid

On 23 July 1988, the helicopter in which Staff Brigadier General Tahir Abdul Rashid was conducting a reconnaissance operation on the battlefront came under enemy fire and was forced to make an emergency landing. On alighting from the helicopter, he failed to observe the safety instructions and received a severe blow on the head from the main rotor blade, as a result of which he died. The helicopter pilot is still living. A commission of inquiry was established to determine the extent to which his death could be regarded as in the line of duty in order to safeguard his rights and entitlements. Details of the incident were included in the daily operations report that was submitted to the higher authorities.

(ii) Staff Major General Salman Shuja'

On 31 July 1988, the helicopter in which Staff Major General Salman Shuja' was conducting a reconnaissance and command operation on the battlefront came under direct enemy fire, as a result of which it crashed, killing him and one of the pilots. The other pilot survived and remains in the service. A commission of inquiry was established to determine the extent to which his death could be regarded as in the line of duty in order to safeguard his rights and entitlements. Details of the incident were included in the daily operations report that was submitted to the higher authorities.

(iii) Staff General Adnan Khairallah Talfah

On 5 May 1988, the helicopter in which Staff General Adnan Khairallah Talfah was returning from Mosul to Baghdad found itself in an abnormal situation due to bad weather conditions, reduced visibility and dust-storms, as a result of which the crew lost control of the machine, which crashed and was totally destroyed, killing all its passengers. A commission of inquiry was established to determine the extent to which his death could be regarded as in the line of duty in order to safeguard his rights and entitlements. Details of the incident were included in the daily operations report that was submitted to the higher authorities. A technical air safety commission was also established and published its report in the *Qadisiya* newspaper on 7 May and 11 June 1989 (annex II).

(b) Summary or arbitrary executions

The references to summary executions in March and April 1991 are astonishing, since it was the insurgents who carried out summary executions of many innocent persons, including patients who were disconnected from medical apparatus and thrown out of hospitals. Many of the witnesses who are still alive have confirmed the atrocious acts of murder committed by the subversives. In this connection, we wish to point out that the number of persons whom they executed amounted to more than 2,500. The following have also been discovered:

(i) A mass grave in the city of Sulaimaniya, in which 370 citizens were buried;
(ii) A mass grave in the Kut Sawadi area on the Iraqi-Iranian border, containing the bodies of 150 persons who had been killed by the groups participating in the disturbances;
(iii) Another mass grave containing 50 bodies in the Kushk al-Basri area of the governorate of Basra.

Many persons also disappeared during those disturbances and, up to the time of preparation of this report, the governmental authorities had been unable to trace them. The military operations conducted by the Iraqi armed forces to restore security and stability in the governorates in which the disturbances occurred obviously led to the deaths of many of the persons participating in those disturbances, in addition to members of the Iraqi armed forces, during the exchanges of fire between the two sides. Such consequences cannot be avoided in situations of that type.

Suppression of the civil disturbances

Iraq has already replied, on many occasions, to the allegations concerning the use of chemical weapons in Halabja and other towns. It has pointed out that it was the Iranian forces who used chemical weapons, since it was they who were occupying the town of Halabja. This was confirmed by the analytical study prepared by the United States Department of Defense and published in the *Washington Post* on 3 May 1990. That study concluded that it was Iran which used chemical weapons, by firing artillery shells filled with cyanide gas at Halabja when the Iranian commanders mistakenly believed that the Iraqi forces were occupying the town, which had a population of 75,000 persons before the war. Moreover, Iran's affirmation, on 20 March 1988, that many of the victims at Halabja had been killed by cyanide gas was an important indication of the fact that Iran had been covering up its use of that gas.

A Pentagon official said: "We know that Iraq has not used cyanide gas. We have a very good idea of the nature of the chemical agents which Iraq is developing, manufacturing and using." He went on to say: "We know that Iraq has not used any types of such agents and we are convinced that Iran has used cyanide gas."

Iranian Revolutionary Guards fought beside the Kurdish militias in the battle in which the Iraqi forces overran the area to the east of Halabja and captured the neighbouring town of Khormal. The Kurdish militias had infiltrated on 16 March 1988 and had prepared the way for their Iranian allies to enter the town on the following day. Whereas the Iranian leaders claim that the Iraqis used chemical weapons against the town, the leaders of the Kurdish militias at Halabja affirm that the town had been bombarded with chemical weapons from Iranian positions to the east and from Iraqi positions to the west (annex III).

With regard to the disturbances and their consequences, we wish to point out that, following the cease-fire after the aggression by the coalition forces led by the United States of America, some Iraqi towns were the scene of disturbances caused by groups of outlaws who attacked persons and official as well as religious, social and educational institutions and places of worship, which they converted into bases and command posts in which they committed the most abominable acts of torture, murder and rape of innocent citizens who refused to collaborate with them. They also burnt and destroyed the contents of those institutions. These acts of widespread sabotage and the forms of pillage, murder and sexual assault to which innocent civilians were subjected led to a complete breakdown of public order and security and endangered the lives and property of citizens. The competent authorities therefore fulfilled their customary duty by opposing those acts of anarchy, sabotage and subversion in order to restore order and security, enforce the rule of law and prevent any violations.

The acts of sabotage and aggression continued for several days before the official authorities were able to exert their authority and restore order and security in all spheres of daily life in the places in which those criminal acts occurred. The subversives used various types of heavy weapons which they had seized in the military barracks that they captured and, consequently, the governmental authorities were forced to take appropriate measures to confront them. These confrontations inevitably led to loss of life not only among innocent civilians, regardless of their religious beliefs and their confessional and ethnic affiliations, but also among the police and security forces and the subversives and infiltrators themselves.

With regard to the allegations concerning the use of phosphorus and napalm bombs, it is sufficient to note that the fighter aircraft belonging to our air force were forbidden to fly. The helicopters supported our military units in their operations to rid the northern region of saboteurs and did not use such weapons; they merely fulfilled their duty by opposing the armed saboteurs and returning their fire. The Iraqi armed forces did not use any chemical weapons.

The taking of hostages and the use of persons as human shields during the acts of aggression

The refusal to allow foreigners to leave Iraq after August 1990 was a preventive measure designed to avert military aggression against Iraq. However, in response to the appeals of humanitarian organizations, and in order to protect their lives, they were all allowed to depart before the outbreak of the war. It should be noted that they were provided with every facility for their comfort and health care during their stay in Iraq.

In this connection, we wish to point out that some of the coalition States detained Iraqis residing in their territory, particularly military and civilian students, whom they held until the cease-fire. It is noteworthy that the question of the refusal to allow foreigners to leave Iraq was dealt with in the Security Council resolutions that were accepted by Iraq. It should also be borne in mind that article 12, paragraph 3, of the International Covenant on Civil and Political Rights permits restrictions of the right of residents to leave a country if such restriction is necessary to protect national security.

Laws in force

A. Political organization

The allegation that the Constitution and the composition of the Iraqi Government do not represent the free will of the Iraqi people totally disregards the true manner in which the political regime in Iraq represents the will of the people. Since the changes that were brought about between 17 and 30 July 1968 embodied the will of the people, the Revolution Command Council is considered to be the true representative of the Iraqi people's will. Indeed, article 1 of the current Iraqi Constitution indicates that Iraq is a sovereign people's democratic republic and article 2 stipulates that the people are the source of legitimate authority.

As for the Revolution Command Council itself, article 37 (a) stipulates that the Revolution Command Council is the supreme body in the State which, on 17 July 1968, assumed responsibility for the realization of the collective will of the people by wresting authority from the corrupt, individualistic and reactionary regime and returning it to the people.

The allegation that the executive authority routinely encroaches on other authorities is untrue and contrary to the Constitution. In this connection, we wish to refer to the powers exercised by the Revolution Command council under the terms of article 42, paragraphs (a) and (b) of the Constitution. According to this article, the Revolution Command Council is empowered to promulgate laws and decrees having the force of law, in addition to decisions concerning the requirements for the implementation of provisions already in force.

The relationship between the Revolution Command Council and the National Assembly is defined in articles 52 and 53 of the Constitution, which read as follows:

Article 52: The National Assembly must examine bills of law proposed by the Revolution Command Council within 15 days from the date on which they reach the office of the President of the National Assembly. If the Assembly approves the bill, it is referred to the President of the Republic for promulgation. However, if it is rejected or amended by the National Assembly, it is sent back to the Revolution Command council. If the latter accepts the amendment, the bill is then referred to the President of the Republic for promulgation. If, on the other hand, the Revolution Command council persists in its opinion at the second reading, the bill is again brought before the National Assembly for discussion at a joint session of the Revolution Command Council and the National Assembly and the decision reached by a two-thirds majority is regarded as final.

Article 53: The National Assembly must examine, within 15 days, any bill of law submitted to it by the President of the Republic. If the National Assembly rejects it, it is referred back to the President of the Republic, with a statement of the reasons for its rejection. If the National Assembly makes any amendments, the amended bill is referred to the Revolution Command Council. If the latter approves the amendments, the bill can be promulgated. However, if the Revolution Command Council refuses to amend the bill or makes a counter-amendment, it is referred back to the National Assembly within seven days. If the National Assembly adopts the opinion of the Revolution Command Council, the bill is then referred to the President of the Republic for promulgation. If, on the other hand, the National Assembly persists in its opinion at the second reading, a joint session of the Revolution Command Council and the National Assembly is held and the decision reached by a two-thirds majority is regarded as final, after which the bill is referred to the President of the Republic for promulgation.

Article 4 of the Council of Ministers Act No. 20 of 1991 stipulates that the Council of Ministers exercises the following powers:

1. Drafting of bills of law for submission to the President of the Republic for promulgation in accordance with the provisions of the Constitution.
2. Drafting and promulgation of regulations, with the exception of the special regulations applicable to the Ministry of Defence and the bodies and departments responsible for security which must be promulgated by the President of the Republic.
3. Monitoring the application of legislation and promulgation of the decisions needed for its enforcement.
4. Supervision of the legality of instructions issued by the competent ministers to facilitate the application of laws and regulations.

During the last two years, the total number of bills of law submitted to the National Assembly amounted to 105, of which 60 were adopted without amendment, 41 were amended and 4 were rejected. During the same period, the Revolution Command Council promulgated 262 decisions.

The constitutional powers vested in the Chairman of the Revolution Command Council are defined in article 44 of the Constitution, as amended by Decision No. 680 of 1987, which reads as follows:

> "The Chairman of the Revolution Command Council exercises the following functions:
>
> "(1) Presiding over the Council's meetings, representing the Council, directing its sessions and administering its financial affairs;
> "(2) Signing any laws promulgated by the Council;
> "(3) Signing the Council's decisions which have the force of law. He can also delegate this function to any other person of his choice;
> "(4) Supervising the work of ministries and other government departments, consulting with ministers on the affairs of their respective ministries, calling them to account if necessary, and keeping the Revolution Command Council informed of the outcome."

The accountability of the Chairman of the Revolution Command Council

Article 45 of the Constitution stipulates that the Chairman, Vice-Chairman and members of the Revolution Command Council are held accountable for any breach of the Constitution.

Elections

Elections to the National Assembly have been held on three occasions, in 1980, 1984 and 1989. In view of the promulgation of the Political Parties Act and the expected adoption of the new draft constitution in the near future, early elections to the National Assembly will probably be held to take into account the requirements of the new era characterized by greater democratization and a multi-party system. It is noteworthy that the new draft constitution makes no reference to a Revolution Command Council; it provides for the establishment of an Advisory Council working with the National Assembly. The principle of election of the President of the Republic is reinforced by direct and secret public ballot. (See the National Assembly Act and its Rules of Procedure in annex IV.)

Appointment of governors and mayors

Governors and mayors are appointed on the basis of their attested competence and integrity either in accordance with the Governorates Act of 1969, under which governors are appointed by presidential decree on the recommendation of the Minister of the Interior and with the approval of the Council of Ministers, or in accordance with a decision of the Revolution Command Council. Mayors are appointed by the Minister of the Interior in accordance with the Administration of Municipalities Act No. 165 of 1964, as amended.

B. The functions of the judicial authority

Chapter 5, section 4, articles 63 and 64, of the Constitution contain specific provisions concerning the judiciary. Article 63, paragraph (a), stipulates that the judiciary is independent and subject to no authority other than the law and that the right of legal redress is guaranteed to all citizens. The law defines the manner in which the courts should be constituted, as well as their jurisdictional hierarchy and the conditions for the appointment of judges. The Judicial Organization Act No. 160 of 1979 embodied these constitutional principles, thereby affirming the judiciary's total independence of the executive authority. The long-established independence and integrity of the Iraqi judiciary cannot be impeached by biased and unfounded allegations. Judges are carefully selected from amongst the most highly qualified jurists and lawyers and the rules governing their eligibility and selection are based on clearly defined, meticulous, scientific principles.

(a) With regard to the questions raised in this connection:

All Iraqi judges must be graduates of the Law Academy and every candidate for admission to the Academy must be a graduate of a faculty of law and must have worked in legal institutions or as a lawyer for not less than three years before entering the Academy. He has to pass an examination, set by the Academy, in various branches of law for the final selection of the most qualified candidates. Studies at the Law Academy cover two academic years. The first year is devoted to various branches of law, such as criminal law and procedure, civil law and procedure, the law of evidence, family law, Islamic law, methods of investigation, the Arabic language and either the English or French languages. A rigorous written and oral examination is set at the end of the first year and the student then has to undergo practical legal training in the mornings during the second term of the first year and throughout the second year and is required to attend evening lectures on legal theory. During the second year, he continues his practical training in the mornings and attends evening lectures on criminal investigation, forensic medicine, criminal psychology, the conflict of laws, the theory of public prosecution, administrative law and other subjects. The student is also required to prepare a legal thesis, under the supervision of the most eminent judges and university professors, which is then discussed by the Council of the Law Academy, consisting of the President of the Court of Cassation, the President of the State Advisory Council, the Director of Public Prosecutions, the Chairman of the Judicial Supervisory Board, the President of the Baghdad District Appeal Courts and the Director-General of the Law Academy. On passing the examinations, the graduate is appointed as a judge or as a member of the Department of Public Prosecutions by presidential decree.

The judges of the Court of Cassation are senior members of the judiciary who must have had at least 22 years' experience in the legal profession. They must also be graduates of a faculty of law who have worked in courts from the time of their graduation until their appointment to the Supreme Court. The judges of the Court of Cassation are appointed in accordance with article 47, paragraphs 3, 4 and 5, of the Judicial Organization Act No. 160 of 1979, paragraph 3 of which stipulates as follows:

> "Judges of the Court of Cassation are appointed by Presidential decree on the basis of a recommendation by the Minister of Justice. They are selected from amongst the highest ranking judges who have held one of the following posts for at least two years:
>
> "(a) President of the Court of Appeal;
> "(b) Vice-President of the Court of Appeal;
> "(c) Judge of the Court of Appeal;
> "(d) Chairman of the Judicial Supervisory Board and Legal Controller;
> "(e) President, Vice-President or Counsellor of the State Advisory Council;
> "(f) Director or Deputy Director of Public Prosecutions or Attorney General;
> "(g) Director-general of a central department in the Ministry of Justice or one of its branches."

Paragraph 4 of the same article stipulates that the Vice-President of the Court of Cassation must be appointed by presidential decree, on the basis of a recommendation by the Minister of Justice, from amongst the judges who have served on the Court for at least three years.

Paragraph 5 stipulates that the President of the Court of Cassation must be appointed by presidential decree, on the basis of a recommendation by the Minister of Justice, from amongst the Vice-Presidents of the Court. At the present time, the Court of Cassation comprises 26 judges. (See annex V.);

(b) The Revolutionary Court, which has now been abolished, was composed of three judges with a juristic background and the Department of Public Prosecutions was represented therein by a public prosecutor with a similar juristic background. The right of defence was guaranteed and the Court applied the provisions of the Penal Code and the other laws in force. It followed the Code of Criminal Procedure and its decisions were final. The confidentiality of its proceedings was a matter regulated by law in specific cases; that applied not only to this Court but also to the ordinary courts if publicity would prejudice the reputation of an individual, public order or public morality. Revolution Command Council Decision No. 140 of 19 May 1991 abolished this court;

(c) From 1987 to 1991, the ordinary courts and the former Revolutionary Court passed 1,714 death sentences for offences prejudicial to internal and external security and also for other offences. It should be noted that, under the Penal Code, political offences are not punishable by death. The number of long-term prison sentences amounted to 7,790, although the vast majority of these were covered by the amnesty decrees.

Offences

With regard to the allegations made in this connection, we wish to provide the following information:

1. In accordance with Revolution Command Council Decision No. 840 of 4 November 1986, 463 convicted persons were sentenced to various penalties involving deprivation of liberty. They were released under the terms of the general amnesty decrees;

2. Only six convicted persons have been sentenced under the terms of article 164 of the Penal Code from 1988 to date;

3. No one has been tried in accordance with Revolution Command Council Decision No. 461 of 31 March 1985; i.e. this decision has never been put into practical effect;

4. Only three persons have been prosecuted under the terms of article 200 of the Penal Code, as amended by Act No. 107 of 1974, Act No. 145 of 1976 and Act No. 111 of 1978. The case against one of them was closed on 6 October 1987 and the other two were released on 13 September 1989 and 16 May 1990 respectively.

Individual cases

(a) The case of His Eminence Grand Ayatollah Sayyid Abul Qasim al-Khoei

Reference has already been made to this subject earlier in our report, in which we stated that he had not been detained and was carrying out his daily activities in a normal manner. With regard to Ayatollah al-Khoei's state of health, he is receiving constant medical attention and he has a physician who has been supervising his treatment, as and when required, for a long time. Doctor Jaafar al-Kuwaiti, a well-known cardiologist, and other physicians from the Saddam General Hospital at Najaf are also tending him.

With regard to the persons named in annex 2,[sic] we wish to state that those listed under Nos. 35, 36, 39 and 41 are alive and enjoying full freedom. The competent authorities have no information concerning the others, bearing in mind the fact that Nos. 12, 18, 19, 27, 42, 56, 57 and 59 are names that also appear in annex 1.[sic]

(b) The case of Mr. Ian Richter

On 7 February 1987, the Revolutionary Court (which has since been abolished) sentenced Mr. Ian Richter to life imprisonment and a fine of 10,000 dinars in accordance with articles 167/2/b and 289 of the Penal Code. He had been arrested for questioning under the terms of a court order that had been duly issued in accordance with articles 167 and 298 of the Penal Code. When the examining magistrate ordered his detention, he was confined in a detention room equipped with all the necessary facilities during the period of the examination. He received proper health care and food, in addition to the newspapers, letters, books and food that were sent to him by the British Embassy and his wife. He was also permitted to write letters to his family and to receive visits from representatives of his Embassy and his wife during and after the trial.

The charges brought against him and the principal proceedings and circumstances of the case were as follows:

1. Falsification of an import permit in respect of material destined for the Karkh water project and the Qalaat Sukkar water project, which were implemented by the British company Patterson Candy, following the expiration of the import permit for the latter project;

2. Falsification of a letter addressed to the Customs Authority, concerning the cession of a vehicle by the company's first manager to its second manager. The letter was signed in the name of the first manager in an illegal manner;

3. His bribery of a group of persons, including Abdul Wahhab al-Mufti, the convicted former mayor of Baghdad, who were paid 2.5-3 per cent of the value of the contract with a view to ensuring its award to his company. As a result of collusion between him and the accused, he was able to commit fraudulent acts in the implementation of projects, thereby damaging the country's interests in a manner that constituted economic sabotage;

4. The convicted person Abdul Wahhab al-Mufti advised him to leave the country and be on his guard. He also told him to make a false statement to the effect that the fugitive Akram Shammas was the company's legal adviser;

5. He transmitted a forged passport to the accused fugitive Akram Shammas, together with three letters that al-Mufti sent to him in London. He had also been passing bribes between al-Mufti and Akram Shammas;

6. He was convicted on the basis of his full confession to all the charges brought against him, which were substantiated by evidence and by the damaging statements made by Abdul Wahhab al-Mufti. He concluded his confession with the words: "But for Mr. al-Mufti's cooperation and the credit agreements that had been signed by the British and Iraqi sides, it would have been very difficult, if not impossible, to win the contract.";

7. Mr. Richter was informed of the charges brought against him on 17 June 1986;

8. There were no witnesses for the defence in his case, since he had not requested such witnesses;

9. He was visited by the British ambassador and consul and his lawyer on 22 November 1986. They were shown the examination reports, which had been translated from Arabic into English, as well as the statements that he had made during the examination. They held a discussion with him and none of them made any protest concerning his confessions. They discussed this matter with him and he confirmed their truth and accuracy, as well as the correctness of the legal proceedings. The British ambassador and consul both expressed their satisfaction and gratitude when the accused told them that the examination had been fair and that he was being treated in a humane manner. They lodged no protest or objection against the examination proceedings and their representatives and defence counsel attended the subsequent court hearings.

Effect of the recent general amnesty decrees

Following the cessation of military operations by the coalition forces against Iraq, disturbances were instigated from outside Iraq with the participation of groups which crossed the border. These disturbances completed the destruction of what had not already been destroyed by the coalition forces. The persons who participated in the disturbances committed acts of mass murder, rape and pillage. They also burnt and destroyed schools, hospitals, warehouses, government offices, banks and courts of law and stole public and private property, in addition to fomenting ethnic and intercommunal strife among citizens. All these acts are punishable by law. In the face of these acts, the State reimposed its authority and put an end to the disturbances, finally restoring public security and stability on 5 April 1991. When the State reimposed its authority in the governorates in which the disturbances had occurred, many persons who had participated in the disturbances fled the country and induced some population groups to seek refuge in neighbouring countries, particularly Turkey and Iran, by spreading false rumours concerning the measures which the authorities might take against them. In some cases, such groups were used as human shields and the refugees wishing the return to their homeland were prevented from doing so by the subversives holding out in the areas occupied by foreign forces.

The Iraqi Government took steps, both internally and internationally, to repatriate the refugees. At the international level, on 18 April 1991 Iraq signed a memorandum of understanding with Prince Sadruddin Aga Khan, the Executive Delegate of the Secretary-General for the United Nations humanitarian programme for Iraq, Kuwait and the Iraq/Iran and Iraq/Turkey border areas, in which Iraq welcomed the endeavours of the United Nations to repatriate the refugees. In fact, by the month of August 1991, more than half a million persons from the areas that had suffered during the disturbances had returned home.

At the internal level, the Revolution Command Council promulgated a number of amnesty decrees, inviting the refugees to return to Iraq and facilitating their repatriation. In this connection, it should be noted that the number of participants in the disturbances who were arrested and detained by the competent authorities during the course of their operations to restore the rule of law amounted to 15,105, of whom 14,005 were released under the terms of the amnesty decrees due to the lack of proof of their involvement in acts of murder and rape. The number of persons whose involvement in such acts was proved amounted to 1,100. (Their names are listed in annex VI.) The investigation procedures have been completed so that they can be brought before the courts. (Annex VII contains the amnesty decrees promulgated by the Revolution Command Council.)

The number of foreigners arrested and detained on the charge of participating in the disturbances amounted to 62. They were all Iranians and were visited and registered by the delegation of the International Red Cross. They are being detained at camp No. 9 at Ramadi and the Iranian authorities have been duly informed. (Annex VIII contains the names of the Iranians who participated in the disturbances.)

The repeated allegations concerning the detention or execution of refugees, and particularly Kurds, who returned home on the strength of the general amnesty decrees are totally unfounded. These allegations were made by certain parties seeking to discredit those decrees and discourage potential beneficiaries from returning home with a view to maintaining the pressure on Iraq and bringing the country into disrepute in a manner consistent with the international campaign which the coalition States are conducting to the detriment of Iraq's independence and sovereignty, so that this can be used as a pretext for intervening in its internal affairs. These allegations are of an extremely general nature and we hope to be supplied with precise details so that the competent authorities can give specific replies.

The beneficiaries of the amnesty decrees promulgated by the Revolution Command Council

The number of persons who have benefited from those decrees amounts to 24,981. (Annex IX lists those decrees and gives the number of persons who benefited therefrom.)

Treatment of ethnic groups

(a) The Kurdish minority

The reports that Iraq has submitted to the Committee on the Elimination of Racial Discrimination (the eighth, ninth and tenth reports) and to the Commission on Human Rights (the second and third reports) contain an objective review of Iraqi legislation concerning the Kurdish citizens of Iraq, who have been granted autonomy and rights that are not enjoyed by the Kurds in neighbouring countries.

Before replying to the Special Rapporteur's questions concerning the application of this legislation, we feel that we should give a brief summary of this legislation and the obstacles impeding its application.

The legal framework of autonomy in Iraqi Kurdistan

It should be noted that the Kurdish question in Iraq is not new, since it predates the establishment of the Iraqi State. However, the autonomy enjoyed by Iraqi Kurdistan within the legal framework described in this summary was achieved only with effect from the Declaration of March 1970, which constituted an important step forward in regard to the enjoying of Kurdish rights within the framework of Iraqi national unity.

In Iraq, the requirements for the prevention of racial discrimination in the Autonomous Region are firmly based on the provisions of the Constitution, since Iraq has recognized the ethnic rights of the Kurdish people, together with the legitimate rights of all minorities, within the framework of Iraqi unity.

Article 5 (b) of the Iraqi Constitution stipulates that:

> "The Iraqi people consists of two main ethnic groups: Arabs and Kurds. This Constitution recognizes the ethnic rights of the Kurdish people, as well as the legitimate rights of all minorities, within the framework of Iraqi unity."

Article 8 (c) of the Constitution further stipulates that:

> "The region in which the majority of the population are Kurds shall enjoy autonomy in accordance with the provisions of the law."

Revolution Command Council Decision 288 of 11 March 1970, which has the force of law, contained the following general guidelines for autonomy:

(a) One of the vice-presidents of the Republic must be a Kurd;
(b) In administrative units where the majority of the population is Kurdish, civil servants must be Kurds or proficient in the Kurdish language;
(c) There must be no discrimination between Kurds and others in regard to access to public office, including key positions in the State such as ministries and army commands, subject to the requirements of competence.

Act No. 33 of 11 March 1974, concerning autonomy for the region of Kurdistan, was promulgated to that end and subsequently modified by Revolution Command Council Decision 28 of 20 September 1978. The following is a review of the principles on which autonomy is based under the terms of that Act.

A. The legal status of the Autonomous Region

Article 1 of Act No. 33 of 1974 stipulates that:

> "The region of Kurdistan shall enjoy autonomy and shall be regarded as a separate administrative unit endowed with distinct personality within the framework of the legal, political and economic unity of the Republic of Iraq. The region shall be an inseparable part of the territory of Iraq and its people shall constitute an integral part of the Iraqi people. The city of Arbil shall be the headquarters of the autonomous administration and the autonomous institutions shall form part of the institutions of the Republic of Iraq."

Under the terms of Revolution Command Council Decision 119 of 4 August 1981, the autonomous institutions referred to in the autonomy Act report directly to the Council of Ministers. This is a clear indication of the legal importance attached to those autonomous institutions.

B. The official language and the language of education in the Autonomous Region

Article 2 of the above-mentioned Act stipulates that:

(a) In addition to Arabic, Kurdish shall be an official language in the region;
(b) Arabic and Kurdish shall be the languages of education, at all stages and in all establishments, for Kurds in the region, in accordance with paragraph (e) of this article;
(c) Educational facilities for members of the Arab ethnic group shall be established in the region. In such facilities, instruction shall be in Arabic and the Kurdish language shall be taught as a compulsory subject;
(d) All residents of the region, regardless of their mother tongue, shall have the right to choose the schools in which they wish to be taught;
(e) All stages of education in the region shall be governed by the general education policy of the State.

Act No. 28 of 1983 stipulated that Arabic and Kurdish would be the languages of instruction for Kurds in the region and that the Arabic language would be taught from the fourth primary grade and at all subsequent stages of education.

C. The rights of citizens, whether Arabs or members of minority groups

Article 3 of the Act stipulates that:

(a) The rights and freedoms of Arabs and members of minority groups in the region shall be safeguarded in accordance with the provisions of the Constitution, the law and the decisions promulgated in connection therewith. The autonomous administration shall be under an obligation to guarantee the exercise of the said rights and freedoms;
(b) Arabs and members of minority groups in the region shall be represented in all the autonomous institutions on the basis of their number in proportion to the total population of the region and they shall have access to public office in accordance with the regulations and decisions pertaining thereto.

D. Basic financial structure and budget of the Autonomous Region

Article 5 of the Act stipulates that the region shall be an independent financial unit within the overall financial unity of the State. Article 6 stipulates that the region shall have its own budget which shall be prepared, drafted and approved in accordance with the principles and guidelines laid down in the regulations in force.

Article 8 defines the budgetary resources of the Autonomous Region as follows:

(a) Locally generated resources, consisting of:

(i) The stipulated income of municipalities;
(ii) The proceeds from sales and services accruing to the autonomous administrative departments;
(iii) The stipulated share of the profits of governmental agencies and institutions included in the region's budget;
(iv) The tax on real estate in the region;
(v) The tax on agricultural land and the proportion of crop yields allocated to agrarian reform in the region;
(vi) The tax on unbuilt landed property in the region;
(vii) The tax on legacies;
(viii) The fees prescribed under the legislative act governing real estate registration fees;
(ix) Court fees and charges in respect of court orders;
(x) Fiscal stamp duty;
(xi) Fees in respect of the registration and change of ownership of vehicles.

(b) Amounts allocated in the regular budget of the State and in the annual investment programme of the national development plan to cover the region's budgetary expenditure with a view to ensuring its development in a manner commensurate with that of all other regions of the Republic of Iraq.

Autonomous institutions

1. The Legislative Council

(a) Terms of reference

The Legislative Council of the Autonomous Region has the following terms of reference, as set forth in Act No. 33 of 1974:

(i) Adoption of the legislative measures needed to develop the region and to improve its local social, cultural and economic facilities within the limits of the general policy of the State;
(ii) Adoption of legislative measures relating to the cultural development and ethnic traditions of the citizens of the region;
(iii) Adoption of legislative measures concerning semi-official departments and institutions and agencies of a local nature;
(iv) Approval of detailed planning proposals prepared by the Executive council in connection with socio-economic affairs, development projects, education, health and employment in accordance with the State's general central planning requirements;
(v) Ratification of the region's regular budgets after they have been approved by the Executive Council;
(vi) Amendment of the region's regular budget after its approval. Such amendments must remain within the limits of the appropriations made and of the purposes for which they have been allocated and must not conflict with the regulations in force;
(vii) Holding discussions with the Executive Council, and calling the latter to account, on matters falling within its responsibility and terms of reference;
(viii) Establishment of the Council's rules of procedure.

(b) Composition of the Legislative Council

In accordance with Act No. 56 of 15 March 1980, the Legislative Council consists of not less than 50 members chosen by secret ballot in free and direct public elections.

Each member of the Legislative Council represents the entire population of the Autonomous Region. It is not permitted to combine membership of the Legislative Council with membership of the National Assembly. (The purpose of this is to enable the maximum number of Kurdish citizens to participate democratically in the two Councils.) Any citizen meeting the legal requirements may stand as a candidate for membership of the Legislative Council.

(c) Procedures and decision-making of the Legislative Council

The Legislative Council meets at Arbil. At its first meeting, it elects a president and a vice-president, who acts as secretary of the Council. The term of office of the Legislative Council is three years beginning on the date of its first meeting and ending on the conclusion of its final meeting at the end of the third year.

The Legislative Council holds two annual sessions. The duration of each session may be prolonged for a period of one month by decision of the President of the Republic or if so decided by a majority of members of the Legislative Council. Legislative measures may be proposed by the Executive Council or by 10 members of the Legislative Council.

The Executive Council must promulgate bills of law within 10 days from the date of their submission. During the said period, it may request reconsideration of all or part of a draft bill. However, if the Legislative Council persists in its opinion, the bill is regarded as final and must be promulgated.

Any member of the Council may put questions to, and seek clarification from, members of the Executive council on matters falling within their respective spheres of competence.

One quarter of the members of the Legislative Council may introduce a substantiated motion for the withdrawal of confidence in the Executive Council or in any of its members. The said motion cannot be discussed by the Council before the expiration of seven days from the date of its introduction and a vote thereon is taken two days after the conclusion of the discussion.

2. The Executive Council

The Executive Council is the executive body responsible for the administration of autonomy in the region. It consists of a President, a Vice-President and a number of members corresponding to the number of autonomous departments.

The President of the Republic appoints a member of the Legislative Council to form and preside over the Executive Council. The names of the President and members are submitted to the Legislative Council for a vote of confidence.

The President and members of the Executive Council hold the rank of minister.

If the President of the Executive council fails to win the confidence of the Legislative Council, his nomination is withdrawn and another candidate is nominated.

3. Powers of the Executive Council

The Executive Council exercises the following powers:

(a) Enforcement of laws and regulations;
(b) Enforcement of court orders;
(c) Administration of justice and preservation of order and security;
(d) Promulgation of local bills of law approved by the Legislative Council;
(e) Preparation of draft plans for the comprehensive development of the Autonomous Region;
(f) Supervision of local public facilities and institutions in the region;
(g) Appointment of civil servants in the Autonomous Region in cases in which such appointment does not require a presidential decree;
(h) Administration of the region's regular budget;
(i) Preparation of the region's draft regular budgetary estimates for submission to the Legislative Council;
(j) Preparation of an annual report on the situation in the region, for submission to the President of the Republic and the Legislative Council.

4. The relationship between the central authority and the autonomous administration

The relationship between the central authority and the autonomous administration can be defined along the following lines:

(a) With the exception of the powers legally vested in the autonomous institutions, authority in all parts of the Republic of Iraq is exercised by the central institutions;
(b) Departments of the central authority in the region discharge their functions within the limits of their terms of reference and are subject to the jurisdiction of the ministries to which they belong. The autonomous institutions are entitled to submit reports on such departments to their respective ministries;
(c) The President of the Executive Council attends meetings of the Council of Ministers. Secretaries-general of branches of the autonomous administration enjoy membership of the councils of the ministries with which their respective branches have a functional relationship;
(d) The legal validity of decisions taken by the autonomous institutions is monitored by a special body established at the Iraqi Court of Cassation and consisting of the President of the Court and four members chosen by the Court of Cassation from among its own members for a renewable period of three years. Decisions taken by the autonomous institutions are communicated to the Minister of Justice who may contest their validity by lodging an appeal with the special body at the Court of Cassation within 30 days from the date on which they are communicated to him.

In the event of such appeal, implementation of the contested decision taken by an autonomous institution is suspended until a judgement is delivered concerning its validity. Such judgement must be delivered by the special body within 30 days from the date on which the appeal is lodged. Judgements delivered by the special body are final.

Decisions taken by autonomous institutions and which the monitoring body finds to be legally invalid are regarded as null and void, in whole or in part, from the date of their promulgation.

5. Elections to the Legislative Council of the Autonomous Region

In accordance with the Autonomy Act and Act No. 56 of 1980, establishing the Legislative Council, as amended, three elections have been held. In the most recent election, held on 10 September 1989, votes were cast by 784,338 electors, who chose 50 members of the Legislative Council from a total of 174 candidates standing for election in 211 constituencies distributed among the governorates of the Autonomous Region (101 constituencies in the governorate of Arbil, 80 in Sulaimaniya and 30 in Dohuk).

Of the elected candidates, 21 represent the governorate of Arbil, 22 the governorate of Sulaimaniya and 7 the governorate of Dohuk.

It is noteworthy that the citizens of the Autonomous Region have participated with other Iraqi citizens in the election of their representatives to the National Assembly on three occasions, the last such election being held in April 1989. This means that the citizens of the Autonomous Region exercise their political rights at two levels: in elections to the central National Assembly and in elections to the Legislative Council of the Autonomous Region.

6. Obstacles to the optimum application of the Autonomy Act

The difficulties and obstacles with which autonomy in Iraqi Kurdistan has been faced should not be viewed in isolation from the political, geographical, internal, regional and international circumstances and the conflicts that have arisen in the region.

Since the promulgation of the Autonomy Act in 1974, groups of foreign interventionists have endeavoured to obstruct the autonomy plan and the region has been subjected to a series of incidents involving acts of violence and infiltration from the other side of the border. That phase ended in 1975 with the Algiers Agreement between Iran and Iraq and reconstruction work began in the region in order to enable the citizens who had returned to their villages and homes to lead a normal life.

When the armed conflict broke out between Iran and Iraq in 1980, Iraq continued to diligently implement the Autonomy Act, although outside intervention once again impeded it. As a border region characterized by its mountainous and rugged terrain, Iraqi Kurdistan was used for the commission of acts prejudicial to Iraq's national security and some parts of Iraqi territory, including the border town of Halabja, were occupied by hostile forces in March 1988 with the help of some local groups. When Iraqi forces succeeded in liberating that territory, those groups which had collaborated with the hostile forces were frustrated and attempted to incite the local population to leave Iraq by spreading false rumours to the effect that they would probably be endangered as a result of the Iraqi forces' resumption of control over the region.

After the cease-fire between Iraq and Iran on 8 August 1988, Iraq promulgated several amnesty decrees for the benefit of Kurds living in and outside Iraq, with the exception of persons who had committed acts of murder and theft. Most of the refugees returned after the promulgation of those amnesty decrees. However, the situation had barely stabilized when the coalition States hostile to Iraq began the war which lasted from 17 January to 27 February 1991 and was followed by disturbances in northern Iraq, the purpose of which was to destroy the economic infrastructure, loot public and private property and murder citizens. The coalition forces then entered Iraqi Kurdistan, as a result of which the government authorities lost control over the northern part of the country.

When government forces began to restore order in the region, many of its residents were once again induced to seek refuge in mountainous areas in and outside Iraq by false information and rumours which were circulated by various bodies. Iraq cooperated with the United Nations to facilitate the return of those refugees by signing a memorandum of understanding on 18 April 1991. A number of amnesty decrees, to which reference has already been made, were also promulgated for the benefit of the Iraqi Kurds.

In the light of the above, it is evident that the autonomy plan for the region of Iraqi Kurdistan was not given a fair opportunity to achieve the objective for which the Autonomy Act was promulgated. Several negative factors, and primarily external intervention, combined to thwart the plan, the legal framework of which could have been developed through serious dialogue free of external influences. However, during the last few months a series of discussions have been held between the political leadership in Iraq and representatives of Kurdish political parties with a view to devising a better formula for autonomy.

Reply to the questions concerning the Kurdish minority

1. The Kurdish exodus in April 1991

We have already explained the reasons for the Kurdish exodus in April 1991 when the State was re-establishing security and stability in the region after the suppression of the disturbances. The loss of life that occurred while the Iraqi armed forces were recovering their control over the region was a natural consequence that could not be avoided.

It must be emphasized, however, that the purpose of those military operations was not to prosecute the Kurds; it was merely to enable the State to restore security and the rule of law. No operations were conducted with a view to driving out the Kurds; on the contrary, we note that their departure was influenced by the external intervention. The serious intention of the Iraqi Government to encourage those citizens to return is evident from the signing of the memorandum of understanding with the United Nations and the promulgation of the above-mentioned general amnesty decrees.

2. Concerning the percentage of Kurdish citizens in the National Assembly

The number of seats in the National Assembly held by representatives of the population of the Autonomous Region amounts to 36 out of a total of 250, i.e. 14.4 per cent of the total number of seats.

3. Concerning the procedure for the appointment of executive civil servants in the Autonomous Region

Civil servants in the Autonomous Region are appointed by the Executive Council, as explained during our review of the powers of that Council within the legal framework of autonomy, except in the case of persons whose appointment requires a presidential decree.

4. Concerning the Act promulgated in June 1986 regulating eligibility for membership of the Legislative Council

The provision of article 2 of Act No. 56 of 12 June 1986, amending article 15 of Legislative Council Act No. 56 of 1980 and stipulating that candidates for membership of the Legislative Council must believe in the leading role of the Arab Baath Socialist Party, does not mean that a candidate must necessarily belong to that Party. The reference to the "leading role of the Party" merely reflects the actual state of affairs in so far as the Party has been the leading authority in Iraq since the revolution of 17-30 July 1968. Following the promulgation of the Political Parties Act No. 30 of 1 September 1991, the previous legislation, including the provision contained in the amended article 15 of the Legislative Council Act, will be modified in a manner consistent with the multi-party system.

5. Concerning the evacuation of the border strip

When the border villages were subjected to Iranian artillery bombardment and the border areas were used for infiltration operations, thereby threatening the security of the local population, Iraq took a preventive measure to safeguard the security of the local population by establishing a 30 km-deep security zone, from which all residents would be evacuated, within Iraq territory along the country's 1,200 km borders with Iraq and Turkey. That measure was not confined to the region of Kurdistan, since it also applied to the Iraqi governorates in the central and southern parts of the country. The residents of that zone were transferred to newly constructed residential settlements in which all the requisite services, including electricity, water, schools, clinics and roads, were provided. Evacuated farmers were given agricultural land, together with a financial indemnity, and every family was paid adequate compensation to enable it to build a new house.

It should be noted that this decision was of a provisional nature and was to be reviewed as soon as the reasons that had led to its promulgation were no longer regarded as valid. On 14 January 1991, instructions were issued for the decision to be reviewed periodically at intervals ranging from six months to two years, as a result of which the restrictions have been lifted in some parts of the border strip in the interests of the population. The freedom of citizens to use areas within that strip for agricultural, grazing and other purposes was never restricted at any stage of the evacuation.

(b) The Turkoman minority

In accordance with article 19 of the Constitution, all Iraqi citizens are equal before the law, without any discrimination on grounds of their ethnic, religious or confessional affiliations. Persons belonging to the Turkoman minority enjoy their cultural rights and are entitled to develop their culture through the publication of books and magazines. With regard to the allegations concerning restrictions on property ownership, there is no legal provision applicable to the land registration departments under which a Turkoman Iraqi is obliged to sell his real estate property to an Arab Iraqi. On the contrary, all Iraqis are subject to the same legal regulations concerning the disposal of real estate. However, administrative procedures must be complied with before real estate can be registered in the name of a purchaser. In the governorate of Baghdad, for example, under the terms of Revolution Command Council Decision No. 1562 of 1982, only Iraqis registered as residents of the governorate in the 1977 census are entitled to purchase such property therein. The purpose of this is to halt the increasing migration from rural areas and other governorates to the capital. Many developing countries which are suffering from this adverse phenomenon have been forced to formulate plans and adopt measures to curb it. There are no restrictions on residence in the other governorates, including Kirkuk and Mosul to which the question referred. Ownership of real estate in those governorates is not subject to any restrictions based on ethnic affiliation; there are merely administrative and organizational procedures for town planning purposes.

(c) Expulsion and deportation measures

Large numbers of Iranians were living in Iraq before the Iraq-Iran war. After the Shah's regime was overthrown in Iran, those Iranians living in Iraq began to collaborate with the new Iranian regime against Iraq by engaging in attempts to assassinate Iraqi officials and acts of terrorism directed against such officials and Iraqi institutions. On the outbreak of the Iraq-Iran war, the presence of those Iranians posed a threat to Iraq's security and territorial integrity due to their collaboration with Iran, their terrorist activities and the atmosphere of fear and instability that they were provoking among citizens. Consequently, their deportation was a legitimate right which any State can exercise against persons who engage in acts of terrorism prejudicial to its security and stability and the safety of its citizens.

On the outbreak of the Iraq-Iran war, the defence and security interests of the Iraqi State necessitated the application of the principles of international law that are invoked in time of war. Foreigners holding Iranian nationality or regarded as being Iranians by virtue of their origin and allegiance, were detained and subsequently deported from Iraq. The allegation that Iraq deported them on grounds of their ethnic affiliation is untrue.

What Iraq did was consistent with the Fourth Geneva Convention of 2 August 1949, relative to the Protection of Civilian Persons in Time of War, article 5 of which stipulates as follows:

> "Where in the territory of a Party to the conflict, the latter is satisfied that an individual protected person is definitely suspected of or engaged in activities hostile to the security of the State, such individual person shall not be entitled to claim such rights and privileges under the present Convention as would, if exercised in the favour of such individual person, be prejudicial to the security of such State.
>
> "Where in occupied territory an individual protected person is detained as a spy or saboteur, or as a person under definite suspicion of activity hostile to the security of the Occupying Power, such person shall, in those cases where absolute military security so requires, be regarded as having forfeited rights of communication under the present Convention.
>
> "In each case, such persons shall nevertheless be treated with humanity and, in case of trial, shall not be deprived of the rights of fair and regular trial prescribed by the present Convention. They shall also

be granted the full rights and privileges of a protected person under the present Convention at the earliest date consistent with the security of the State or Occupying Power, as the case may be."

With regard to the position of Iraqi legislation, the Iraqi Nationality Act No. 43 of 1963 did not adopt the principle of ethnic origin as a basis for the granting of Iraqi nationality. Article 3 of that Act stipulated that all adult persons normally resident in Iraq and who held Ottoman nationality prior to the entry into force of the Treaty of Lausanne of 6 August 1924, which recognized the establishment and independence of the Iraqi State, lost their Ottoman nationality and were regarded as Iraqis with effect from the said date.

The Act also contained naturalization provisions under which Iraqi nationality could be granted to foreigners. Although some foreigners acquired Iraqi nationality, others who were living in Iraq did not apply for it at the time of Iraq's independence and have still not done so, in spite of the promulgation of numerous legislative acts facilitating their acquisition of Iraqi nationality, since they preferred to retain their foreign nationality with a view to benefiting from the rights and privileges enjoyed by Iraqis while, at the same time, avoiding the duties and obligations which the latter assume. Accordingly, they are subject to the Residence of Foreigners Act and the residence permits of those who do not meet the residence requirements can be withdrawn. The only Iraqi citizens against whom deportation orders are issued are foreigners who acquired Iraqi nationality in accordance with the naturalization provisions of the Act, and only after their acquired nationality has been withdrawn from them under the terms of article 19 of the Iraqi Nationality Act No. 43 of 1963 if they have engaged, or attempted to engage, in an activity that endangers the security or integrity of the State. This is because the naturalization of a foreigner is conditional; if he commits an act that endangers the security of the State which granted him this honour, it can be withdrawn from him since he is no longer worthy thereof. With regard to the allegations concerning the deportation of Iraqis and the permanent fear of deportation in which millions of persons are allegedly living, we deny the existence of organized campaigns to deport Iraqis and would like to know the source of the information to the effect that millions of persons are living in permanent fear of deportation. There is no justification for raising a question of such a general nature. The persons who were deported were foreigners residing in Iraq and they were expelled in accordance with the laws in force.

Religious practices and cultural institutions

Over the ages, Iraq has been known as a country of many religions and religious tolerance in which various religious groups and communities have lived in a spirit of fraternal harmony that was an attested source of humanitarian enrichment.

However, in some periods of Iraq's history, this pluralism has been exploited with a view to prejudicing national unity and social harmony by instigating religious intolerance and odious sectarianism. The Iraqi Government, which is aware of the dangers that are threatening society, is diligently endeavouring, in a responsible manner, to promote a spirit of fraternity and tolerance among the people, without any discrimination whatsoever.

Contrary to the allegations made in the reports which affirm that religious leaders are subjected to constant harassment, the State is catering for their welfare, in addition to that of the theologians, students, theological colleges, mosques and holy shrines.

The holy shrines at Najaf and Karbala, like the other religious, historical and cultural institutions in Iraq, are a matter of great and direct concern to the Iraqi Government in view of the high esteem in which they are held by Iraqis and Muslims as part of their glorious historical and cultural heritage. The Ministry of Awqaf and Religious Affairs is taking full and proper care of those institutions by maintaining, restoring, rebuilding and expanding them. Many of their buildings have been renovated and embellished in such a way as to preserve their architectural style and display them in a manner befitting their spiritual and historical status.

Immediately after the direct military aspect of the aggression ended with the cease-fire on 28 February 1991, groups of Iranians and others who had been trained in Iran infiltrated into Iraq where, with logistical support from the coalition forces, they helped to instigate widespread sabotage and anarchy in the southern and central governorates, including the cities of Karbala and Najaf, which contain holy shrines. The saboteurs occupied those shrines, in which they erected gallows and which they converted into centres for the murder, torture and rape of innocent persons. When they realized that their occupation would be short-lived, they wrecked the premises and plundered the contents of those shrines. In this connection, it is noteworthy that preliminary estimates of the damage caused by those saboteurs amount to 20 million Iraqi dinars, quite apart from other damage which cannot be estimated due to the historical and artistic importance and value of the items concerned. Not content with this, they also stole many valuable objects and extremely important historical manuscripts forming part of the cultural heritage. They burnt the library at the Husseini Shrine, which contained rare religious and cultural books, reference material and manuscripts and plundered all the equipment and objects of value that they found in those mausoleums and shrines.

When the State re-established law and order in those two cities, the Iraqi authorities began to make urgent and comprehensive plans for the repair and reconstruction of those holy places. In fact, the State allocated an amount of 35 million Iraqi dinars (equivalent to $US 105 million), as well as 100 kg of pure gold and 200 kg of silver, for the reconstruction, development, repair and restoration of those holy places.

With regard to the specific information requested, we wish to state as follows:

1. The nature of the numerous religious educational centres ranges from small houses supervised by religious groups to classrooms and colleges of various sizes, some of which are independent while others are attached to mosques. These centres can be found in numerous governorates. The city of Najaf contains 24 colleges that were abandoned due to their dilapidated state, and two colleges that are still operating. Karbala has 10 colleges and Arbil, Kirkuk, Dohuk and Sulaimaniya have two each. Mosul, Aqrah and Tall'Afar each have one college.

2. *Mosques*

With regard to the number of mosques, congregational mosques and Husseiniyas, Najaf has 69 mosques, a congregational mosque and a Husseiniya; Karbala has 126; Basra 138; Kirkuk 116; Arbil 259; Sulaimaniya 275; Dohuk 109; and Mosul 465. The mausoleums are distributed as follows: 11 at Najaf, 7 at Karbala, 3 at Basra, 3 at Kirkuk, one at Arbil and Sulaimaniya and 18 at Mosul, which also has 2 Yezidi mausoleums and 5 Christian mausoleums. There are 124 theologians in the governorate of Najaf, 49 of whom are affiliated to religious endowments (awqaf), and 33 at Karbala, 3 of whom are foreigners. There are 15 non-Iraqi theologians and 135 foreign students of various nationalities, including Iranians, Afghans, Indians, Pakistanis, Saudis and Lebanese. The present situation in regard to the Dar al-Hikma and Qazwini theological colleges and the Wadi al-Salam cemetery at Najaf is as follows:

1. The Dar al-Hikma theological college: This was an ancient college belonging to Sayyid al-Khoei in which the majority of the students were foreigners. The saboteurs used it as a base in which they stored various types of weapons and executed many citizens. It was destroyed during the armed clashes that took place between those saboteurs and the Iraqi army.

2. The Qazwini theological college: This was an ancient college, run by Sayyid al-Khoei, at which 50 Iranian students were studying. The saboteurs used it as a base and it was destroyed by fire during the clashes between the armed forces and the saboteurs.

3. The Sheikh al-Tusi Mosque at Najaf is run by Sayyid Hussein Bahr ul-Ulum, a well-known Shi'ite theologian. About 15-20 Iraqi students are still studying there.

4. The Al-Khoei Husseiniya at Karbala: This was destroyed during the clashes between the armed forces and the saboteurs, who had converted it into a base for their operations.

5. The Wadi al-Salam cemetery at Najaf: This is an ancient cemetery on the outskirts of the city of Najaf. The saboteurs took over its buildings and used it as a base for their operations. As a result of the clashes which occurred between the armed forces and the saboteurs, burials therein were suspended for one month but are now proceeding normally.

Access to food and health care requirements

As a party to the International Covenant on Economic, Social and Cultural Rights, Iraq is committed to the provisions thereof and is endeavouring to enable its citizens to exercise their rights more fully, without any discrimination. This has already been stated in Iraq's periodic reports, particularly its report on the application of articles 11 and 12 of the Covenant, as published in document E/1986/4/Add.3 which indicates that Iraqis are exercising the right to an adequate standard of living, as required under the terms of article 11 of the Covenant, as well as the right to the enjoyment of the highest attainable standard of physical and mental health, as required under the terms of article 12 thereof. It is noteworthy that the first and second paragraphs of article 11 refer to the importance of international cooperation, in addition to the national endeavours of States, to ensure enjoyment of the right to an adequate standard of living.

Iraq is among the States which attach special importance to the use of resources in order to ensure an adequate standard of living for its citizens, provide them with health services, subsidize basic foodstuffs to a large extent, supply medicines free of charge to patients in government hospitals and also subsidize the medicines which are sold at pharmacies.

The adoption of Security Council resolution 661 (1990) of 6 August 1990, calling for the imposition of a comprehensive economic embargo on Iraq, dealt a severe blow to the enjoyment by its citizens of their economic, social, health and cultural rights.

The effects of that set-back were aggravated by the war launched by the coalition forces hostile to Iraq, which led to the destruction of the country's economic infrastructure, and the situation became even more serious as a result of the continuation of the economic embargo on Iraq in spite of the fact that it was no longer justifiable after Iraq had accepted the Security Council resolutions adopted after 2 August 1990.

Although article 11 of the International Covenant on Economic, Social and Cultural Rights emphasizes the importance of international cooperation to ensure enjoyment of the right to an adequate standard of living, we believe that international cooperation is taking place in a negative sense with a view to impeding the effective exercise of the Iraqi people's right to an adequate standard of living in regard to food, clothing and housing. This has been confirmed in all the international reports concerning the effects of the economic embargo and the war on the lives of the Iraqi people (such as Mr. Marti Ahtisaari's report contained in document S/22366 of 20 February 1991 and Sadruddin Aga Khan's report contained in document S/22799 of 17 July 1991). In fact, the Security Council has not taken positive and practical steps to exempt food and medicine from the embargo imposed on Iraq.

In the face of this tragic situation, the Government of Iraq has taken every possible measure to enable its people to exercise their right to an adequate standard of living, without any discrimination and with due regard for the circumstances of the economic embargo, and is continuing to provide health services.

We wish to reply as follows to the questions raised concerning food and health care:

1. Access to food warehouses and stocks of medicines

The food warehouses and stocks of medicines in all Iraqi cities are intended for all citizens, without any discrimination. However, these stocks of food and medicines are not distributed to citizens directly. Foodstuffs are distributed through agents who supply citizens with their quotas, on the basis of ration cards, in the light of the number of members in their families. Medicines are distributed to private pharmacies and are dispensed to sick persons on the basis of medical prescriptions. The government hospitals also distribute medicines free of charge to their patients. In this connection, we wish to point out that there are State-operated warehouses, known as "central markets", at which consumer goods other than those distributed through the ration card system are sold to civil servants and military personnel. These markets were established to help civil servants on low incomes. Other citizens who are not employed by the State can obtain these consumer goods from the consumer cooperative associations, membership of which is restricted to persons unable to benefit from the central markets.

2. Increases in the salaries of government employees

It is a well-known fact that the economic embargo on Iraq and the adverse economic effects of the subsequent war led to a substantial rise in the prices of basic necessities, as confirmed in all the international reports describing the situation in Iraq. The State therefore had to deal with this problem, the consequences of which were being felt primarily by citizens in low-income categories, i.e. government employees and military personnel.

Accordingly, the State decided to increase the salaries of government employees by 30-55 per cent and the pensions of retired government employees by 15-20 per cent. This measure did not involve any discrimination among citizens, since its purpose was to deal with the economic effects of the war on a broad section of the population, namely government employees.

Self-employed persons, such as those exercising liberal professions, were less affected by the rise in the prices of basic necessities, since their incomes usually rise in proportion to the cost of living.

3. Measures taken to ensure adequate allocations for the population

Since the adoption of Security Council resolution 661 (1990), the State has been applying a comprehensive and exemplary system to ensure that its citizens received a minimum allocation of basic foodstuffs, such as flour, rice, sugar, cooking oil, detergents, soap and tea. The monthly per capita allocation amounts to 8 kg of flour, 1 kg of rice, 1.5 kg of sugar, 50 gm of tea, 1 kg of legumes and 50 gm of oil. The cost of these items, which are distributed on a monthly basis, amounts to the equivalent of $US 6 per month, since their prices are subsidized by the State. On the open market, their cost would be 20-30 times higher. However, since this monthly ration does not fully meet the needs of citizens in the quantities that they require under normal circumstances, the State has permitted the private sector to import foodstuffs by its own means. It has been emphasized that these items must be essential commodities listed in the supply schedule and must not involve transfers in hard currency, which cannot be obtained due to the economic embargo.

The monthly allocation of foodstuffs is distributed on the basis of ration cards, which have been supplied to all Iraqi families in all parts of the country and also to Arab and foreign residents of Iraq. These ration cards, which are issued by officials of the Ministry of Trade with assistance from the district and village people's councils, are periodically inspected and verified.

The rationed items are handed to citizens by the 48,823 agents of the State Enterprise for Trade in Foodstuffs. Foodstuffs are distributed without any discrimination among citizens or residents of Iraq, since their distribution is effected on the basis of ration cards.

The widespread destruction of roads, bridges, railways, petroleum installations and food warehouses as a result of the bombing raids carried out by the coalition forces hostile to Iraq caused numerous problems in rural and remote areas during the post-war period. The State-owned food warehouses in a number of governorates were also looted and burnt by groups participating in the disturbances and this led to an acute shortage of stocks of food and medical supplies. At the present time, however, the distribution operations have improved considerably, particularly after the repair of some of the damage caused to the roads and fuel supply routes.

With regard to the measures taken to supply food to the rural areas which suffered greatly as a result of the disturbances, we wish to point out that the distribution system was planned in accordance with the approved system of supply in such a way as to ensure that foodstuffs reach all geographical areas of the country, even the most remote, through an extensive and comprehensive network of private sector trading and transport agents, in addition to the transport fleet belonging to the Ministry of Trade. The supply, distribution and transport systems which are being applied ensure that food reaches all citizens, even those living in the most remote areas, regardless of their ethnic origin and place of residence.

With regard to the measures taken to ensure the supply of pure drinking water, we wish to refer to the report of Sadruddin Aga Khan, which stated that, before the Gulf war, more than 90 per cent of the population of Iraq were supplied with drinking water from a network of about 1,500 water treatment plants and the remainder of the population depended on untreated water from the rivers and springs. However, the water treatment plants and distribution networks were destroyed or damaged during the hostile air raids and about 300 wells, together with their protective installations and pipelines, were also extensively damaged. In this connection we also wish to point out that the damage caused to the bridges destroyed the supply and distribution networks, including the principal pipelines that had been laid from those bridges, quite apart from the severe shortage of aluminium sulphate and chlorine due to the ongoing economic embargo. This situation obviously led to a severe shortage of drinking water in all parts of the country and particularly in the southern marshes and other outlying areas.

The effects of the economic embargo on the health and environmental situation

The economic embargo and the war had serious adverse effects on the environmental and health situation, increasing the incidence of diseases resulting from the lack of medicines and insecticides, in addition to the bombing of drinking water projects, water purification plants and sewage systems. These effects are summarized below:

(a) There was a five to sixfold increase in the annual incidence of typhoid, paratyphoid and amoebic and bacillic dysentery;

(b) The annual incidence of viral hepatitis (types A and B) increased more than eightfold as a result of the bad environmental situation (in the case of type A) and the shortage of laboratory equipment to detect the virus before carrying out blood transfusions (in the case of type B);

(c) There was a cholera epidemic in Iran after the war and the number of registered cases amounted to 1,217, of whom dozens died. The epidemic would have assumed alarming proportions but for the intervention of international health organizations;

(d) During the period from August 1990 to August 1991, a total of 14,232 persons died under five years of age, i.e. 21 per 1,000 live births, whereas the corresponding number of deaths from August 1989 to August 1990 had amounted to 3,188, i.e. only 5 per 1,000. In other words, there was a fourfold increase. The causes of death were septicemia, emaciation, malnutrition, diarrhoea, acute enteritis, pneumonia and bronchitis.

The number of deaths among persons over five years of age amounted to 36,968, i.e. 2.5 per thousand, whereas the number recorded from August 1989 to August 1990 had amounted to only 13,921, i.e. 0.96 per thousand. It should be noted that the diseases which led to most of these deaths among adults were diabetes, hypertension, cardiac disorders and cancerous tumours.

The State has done its utmost to overcome the serious effects of the environmental and health situation resulting from the economic embargo, the war and the disturbances. However, the State cannot provide the same health services which its citizens were enjoying before the imposition of the embargo until such time as that embargo is lifted, thereby enabling the health institutions to assume their responsibilities without any restrictions.

Finally, the following is a summary of the findings of a survey which was conducted by United States humanitarian organizations, under the auspices of the United Nations, and published at Washington on 22 October 1991: "The infant mortality rate in Iraq has increased fourfold since the end of the Gulf War due to the lack of food and medicine, water pollution and the collapse of the health system."

A survey published at London on Tuesday, 22 October 1991, indicated that the infant mortality rate had increased from 28 per 1,000 before the war to 104 per 1,000 and that 29 per cent of Iraqi children under five years of age, i.e. 900,000 children, were suffering from malnutrition.

Psychiatrists have observed unprecedented levels of anxiety, tension and abnormal behaviour among children of primary school age. They also reported that about two thirds of the children whom they interviewed believed that they would not live to the age of maturity.

A number of physicians have referred to the spread of typhoid fever and cholera in the country and have noted that children afflicted with diabetes or leukaemia are condemned to death due to the total lack of medicine.

In conclusion, the survey warned that thousands of children in Iraq would die unless they were rapidly provided with food and medicine and the lives of dozens of other children were also at risk.

Conclusion

After completing the preparation of this report, reference must be made to the fact that the authorities concerned made diligent and tireless endeavours to complete it on time, although they were faced with considerable difficulties in gathering and coordinating the requisite information due to the consequences of the recent aggression against Iraq, which led to the destruction of the State's institutions and communications, in addition to the acts of sabotage which made it difficult to obtain many of the official documents from the government offices affected, including the courts of law.

But for the tight deadline, the authorities had hoped to prepare a more detailed report in a manner consistent with Iraq's desire to cooperate closely with the Special Rapporteur so that he can fulfil his task in the most satisfactory way. In spite of those problems, however, the authorities are continuing to follow up on the questions that have not been covered in a detailed and specific manner in this report and they hope to deal with them in the near future with a view to preparing their replies, as far as possible, before the Special Rapporteur's visit at the beginning of next year. They will also keep him informed of all new measures, developments and additional information in the field of human rights within the context of the State's review of all the legislation necessitated by the circumstances, as well as its examination of the questions raised, in such a way as to promote human rights and overcome the difficulties and obstacles impeding the achievement of that objective.

Iraq is looking forward to further cooperation with the Special Rapporteur and hopes that the information contained in this report will be considered in an objective manner, taking into account the circumstances with which the country has been faced, and is still being faced, as a result of the ongoing economic embargo which disregards the most fundamental rights that should be enjoyed by human beings, namely the right to life and to an adequate standard of living.

In conclusion, Iraq will do its utmost to further the Special Rapporteur's task in a manner conducive to the promotion of human rights and hopes that his forthcoming visit to Iraq will provide an opportunity for closer cooperation so that he can fulfil his task in the most satisfactory way. ...

...

6. General Assembly Resolution 46/134, 17 December 1991

The General Assembly,

Guided by the principles embodied in the Charter of the United Nations, the Universal Declaration of Human Rights and the International Covenants on Human Rights,

Reaffirming that all Members States have an obligation to promote and protect human rights and fundamental freedoms and to fulfil the obligations they have undertaken under the various international instruments in this field,

Mindful that Iraq is a party to the International Covenants on Human Rights,

Recalling Security Council resolution 688 (1991) of 5 April 1991, in which the Council demanded an end to the repression of the Iraqi civilian population and insisted that Iraq cooperate with humanitarian organizations and ensure that the human and political rights of all Iraqi citizens are respected,

Recalling also the pertinent resolutions of the Commission on Human Rights and the Subcommission on Prevention of Discrimination and Protection of Minorities, which expressed grave concern at the flagrant violations of human rights by the Government of Iraq,

Recalling in particular Commission on Human Rights resolution 1991/74 of 6 March 1991, by which the Commission requested its Chairman to appoint a Special Rapporteur to make a thorough study of the violations of human rights by the Government of Iraq, based on all information the Special Rapporteur may deem relevant, including information provided by intergovernmental and non-governmental organizations and any comments and material provided by the Government of Iraq, and to submit an interim report thereon to the General Assembly at its forty-sixth session and a report to the Commission at its forty-eighth session,

Deeply concerned by the volume and extent of allegations of human rights violations by the Government of Iraq, such as arbitrary arrests and detentions, enforced or involuntary disappearances, torture, inhuman or degrading practices, extrajudicial killings, summary or arbitrary executions, hostage-taking and use of persons as "human shields", lack of freedom of expression and of an independent judiciary,

Noting the Special Rapporteur's view that these allegations are each day increasing and necessitate considerable and detailed examination,

Deeply concerned by the fact that chemical weapons have been used on the Kurdish civilian population, by the forced displacement of hundreds of thousands of Kurds and the destruction of Kurdish towns and villages, as well as by the situation of tens of thousands of displaced Kurds living in camps in the north of Iraq, and by the deportation of thousands of Kurdish families,

Also deeply concerned by the repressive measures taken by the Government of Iraq against the Shiah communities in the south of Iraq,

Concerned especially by the alleged use of excessive force by the Government of Iraq against Iraqi civilians, in particular the Kurds and the Shi'ites,

Taking note with interest of the message conveyed to the Special Rapporteur by the Government of Iraq of its intention fully to cooperate with him, with such cooperation including acceptance of a visit to Iraq to investigate the allegations of violations of human rights in that country,

Regretting, however, that the Government of Iraq has failed to answer a considerable number of specific questions asked by the Special Rapporteur on acts being committed by the Government of Iraq that are incompatible with international human rights instruments that are binding on that Government,

1. *Takes note with appreciation* of the interim report of the Special Rapporteur and the considerations and the observations contained therein;

2. *Expresses its deep concern* about the numerous and detailed allegations of grave human rights violations by the Government of Iraq to which the Special Rapporteur has referred in his report, in particular:

(a) Arbitrary detention, including women, children and the elderly, as well as the systematic practice of torture and other cruel, inhuman or degrading practices, and of enforced or involuntary disappearances as a part of a general structured programme of repression aimed at quelling opposition;

(b) Extrajudicial killings, including political killings and summary or arbitrary executions throughout the country, particularly in the northern Kurdish autonomous region, in southern Shiah centres and in the southern marshes;

(c) Hostage-taking and the use of persons as "human shields", a most grave and blatant violation of Iraq's obligations under international law;

3. *Calls upon* the Government of Iraq to release all persons arrested and detained without ever being informed of charges against them, and without access to legal counsel or due process of law;

4. *Calls furthermore upon* the Government of Iraq, as a State party to the International Covenant on Civil and Political Rights, to abide by its obligations under this Covenant and under other international instruments on human rights, and particularly to respect and ensure these rights to all individuals irrespective of their origin within its territory and subject to its jurisdiction, including Kurds and Shi'ites;

5. *Regrets* the failure of the Government of Iraq to provide satisfactory replies to all the allegations of violations of human rights, and calls upon the Government of Iraq to reply quickly in a comprehensive and detailed manner to these allegations so as to enable the Special Rapporteur to form an accurate assessment as a basis for his recommendations to the Commission on Human rights;

6. *Urges*, therefore, the Government of Iraq to accord its full cooperation to the Special Rapporteur of the Commission on Human Rights during his forthcoming visit to Iraq to investigate the allegations of violations of human rights;

7. *Requests* the Secretary-General to give all necessary assistance to the Special Rapporteur of the Commission to fulfil his mandate;

8. *Decides* to continue the examination of the situation of human rights in Iraq during its forty-seventh session under the item entitled "Human rights questions", in the light of additional elements provided by the Commission on Human Rights and the Economic and Social Council.

[*Adopted by a vote of 129 to 1, with 17 abstentions.*]

E/CN.4/1992/31, 18 February 1992

7. Report on the situation of human rights in Iraq, prepared by Mr. Max van der Stoel, Special Rapporteur of the Commission on Human Rights, in accordance with Commission resolution 1991/74, 18 February 1992

...

8. In determining the parameters of his mandate, the Special Rapporteur was limited by resolution 1991/74 to consideration of "violations by the Government of Iraq". There has therefore been no consideration of violations of human rights committed by other parties, though it is clear from the information available to the Special Rapporteur that such violations have occurred.

9. As concerns the absence of express limitations relating to both the period of time during which violations of concern to the Special Rapporteur may have occurred and the territory upon which they may have occurred, the Special Rapporteur has found it necessary to focus on violations having occurred in recent years and in the territory of Iraq. The focus on recent years is explained mostly by the quality of information available. However, in as much as recent and continuing violations may be directly related to past violations and to a continuing system, the Special Rapporteur has examined issues and reports concerning events which occurred even earlier. With respect to territory, and in view of the fact that the Commission on Human Rights has also appointed a Special Rapporteur to study the "situation of human rights in occupied Kuwait", it was thought appropriate to concentrate on violations having occurred in the territory of Iraq, although the Special Rapporteur is cognizant of allegations of violations having occurred in the territory of the Islamic Republic of Iran during the Iran-Iraq war and allegations of violations, including political killings, having affected persons on the territories of other States.

10. Subsequent to the Special Rapporteur's submission of his interim report, his presentation to the Third Committee of the General Assembly on 19 November 1991, and the subsequent debate in that forum, the General Assembly adopted resolution 46/134 on 17 December 1991, by a vote of 129 to 1, with 17 abstentions.

B. Activities of the Special Rapporteur

11. The Special Rapporteur was assisted in his task by Mr. John Packer, Associate Human Rights Officer in the Centre for Human Rights. In performing his task, Mr. Packer showed great skill, and, moreover, a willingness to work harder than could reasonably be demanded for many months on end. The Special Rapporteur also expresses his gratitude to Mr. Georg Mautner-Markhof, Chief of the Special Procedures Section of the Centre for Human Rights, who was always prepared to help and to provide advice. Lastly, he expresses his thanks for the valuable assistance provided by Mr. Gudmundur Alfredsson, Human Rights Officer in the Centre for Human Rights, and to United Nations interpreters Ms. Leila Dimitry and Ms. Nadia Abu-Rida, who accompanied him during his journey to Iraq, Iran and Saudi Arabia.

12. In taking up his responsibilities to study the situation of human rights in Iraq, the Special Rapporteur sought information from various sources and made himself available to any and all who cared to submit information in person or by other means. On this basis, information was received from a wide variety of non-governmental organizations (see annex I) and individuals. However, in the process of information collection, it immediately became clear that testimony from victims and eye-witnesses would not be readily forthcoming (even outside Iraq) owing to an overwhelming fear of reprisals against these individuals or their families, a fear which became the subject of the Special Rapporteur's concern. The Special Rapporteur therefore found it necessary to travel to London on three occasions to meet with persons in conditions that they felt provided them with sufficient security. The Special Rapporteur also received testimony in Geneva and The Hague.

13. With the agreement of the Government of Iraq, the Special Rapporteur undertook a visit to Iraq from 3 to 9 January 1992. In the course of this visit, and in accordance with his own wishes, the Special Rapporteur spent two and a half days in Baghdad, one day in the

southern cities of Najaf and Karbala, two days in the Autonomous Region of Kurdistan, and one morning in Abu Graib prison west of Baghdad. During this visit, he was received by the Minister for Foreign Affairs, the Minister of the Interior, the Minister of Labour and Social Affairs, the Minister of Awqaf and Religious Affairs, the Minister of Justice, and the Deputy Prime Minister. Other government interlocutors included members of the Consultative Committee on Human Rights to the Ministry of Foreign Affairs, the Governors of Najaf and Karbala, the President of the Court of Cassation and the Director of Abu Graib prison. The Special Rapporteur also met with the Acting Governor of Arbil. Non-governmental interlocutors included: the members of the Board of Directors of the Human Rights society in Iraq, the Secretary General of the Union of Arab Jurists' Iraqi Branch, the Grand Ayatollah Sayyid Abul Qasim Al-Khoie together with his son Mohammed Taqi Al-Khoie, the leaders of three Christian communities in Iraq (said to be representing all Christians in Iraq), representatives of the Arbil and Sulaimaniya Branches of the Organisation of Human Rights in Kurdistan, representatives of the Arbil and Sulaimaniya Committees for Investigation of Disappeared Kurdish Citizens, Mr. Massoud Barzani (leader of the Kurdistan Democratic Party) and Mr. Jalal Talabani (leader of the Patriotic Union of Kurdistan). In addition, the Special Rapporteur received oral testimony in the Autonomous Region of Kurdistan from numerous victims and eye-witnesses of alleged human rights violations, and was also presented with significant quantities of written allegations and documentary evidence. In Abu Graib prison, the Special Rapporteur was able to review some records in the "heavy section" and to speak with a few prisoners in both the "heavy" and "special" sections. Throughout the course of his visit, the Special Rapporteur also visited various sites of relevance to his mandate and took note of the general conditions affecting the economic rights of the people.

14. Following his visit to the Republic of Iraq, the Special Rapporteur travelled to the Islamic Republic of Iran and then to the Kingdom of Saudi Arabia in order to hear testimony from Iraqi refugees who claim to be victims and eye-witnesses of human rights violations committed by the Government of Iraq. In the Islamic Republic of Iran, the Special Rapporteur visited the refugee camps of Kangavar and Sefid Chegha in Bakhtaran province on 13 and 14 January 1992, and Ashrafi Isfahani and Ansar camps in Khouzestan province on 15 January 1992. While in Ahwaz on the evening of 15 January 1992, the Special Rapporteur also heard testimony from Iraqi refugees living outside the camps and from persons who had previously been expelled from Iraq. In Saudi Arabia, the Special Rapporteur visited the refugee camps of Artawiya and Rafha on 17 and 19 January 1992, respectively. Like the testimony received some days earlier in the Autonomous Region of Kurdistan, the testimony received in the refugee camps of Iran and Saudi Arabia proved to be most valuable.

15. In connection with his mandate, the Special Rapporteur took note of the last two periodic reports submitted by the Government of Iraq to the Human Rights Committee (the second periodic report dated 21 April 1986, contained in document CCPR/C/37/Add.3, and the third periodic report dated 5 June 1991, contained in document CCPR/C/64/Add.6) and the last two periodic reports submitted to the Committee on the Elimination of Racial Discrimination (the ninth periodic report dated 7 December 1987, contained in document CERD/C/159/Add.2, and the tenth periodic report dated 9 October 1989, contained in document CERD/C/185/Add.2). The Special Rapporteur also consulted the summary records of the meetings at which those reports were addressed (the 744th to 748th and 1080th to 1082nd meetings of the Human Rights Committee, and the 917th and 920th to 922nd meetings of the Committee on the Elimination of Racial Discrimination). Further, the Special Rapporteur took note of the relevant parts of the report of the Committee on the Elimination of Racial Discrimination to the General Assembly (A/46/18, paras. 248-258) and the report of the Human Rights Committee to the General Assembly (A/46/40, paras. 618-656).

16. In addition to these primary sources of information, the Special Rapporteur received significant documentary material in the form of written documents, photographs, video-cassettes and audio-cassettes. Portions of this material are said to be official records of the Government of Iraq which were found in government security centres during the uprisings of March 1991.

17. The Government of Iraq cooperated with the Special Rapporteur by arranging his meetings with a number of Ministers. However, his requests for meetings with the President and the Minister of Defence remained unanswered. The Government did, however, facilitate his visits to the Grand Ayatollah Al-Khoie and to Abu Graib prison. The cooperation of the Governments of Iraq and of Saudi Arabia in facilitating the Special Rapporteur's travel to the refugee camps mentioned above is to be noted.

I. OBLIGATIONS UNDERTAKEN BY IRAQ

A. Applicable instruments

18. Mr. Tariq Aziz, the Deputy Prime Minister of Iraq, urged the Special Rapporteur during his visit to show "at any rate some degree of objectivity". The Special Rapporteur replied that he was neither applying the standards of others nor his own subjective standards; the only yardstick he intended to use was the treaties in the field of human rights to which Iraq had become a party.

19. The applicable standards of international law reside primarily in the obligations freely undertaken by Iraq as a result of its accession to the following instruments: the Charter of the United Nations; the International Covenant on Economic, Social and Cultural Rights; the International Covenant on Civil and Political Rights; the International Convention on the Elimination of All Forms of Racial Discrimination; the Convention on the Elimination of All Forms of Discrimination against Women; and the Convention on the Prevention and Punishment of the Crime of Genocide. Other significant conventions that Iraq has freely accepted include the four Geneva Conventions of 12 August 1949.

20. In addition to conventional instruments of international law, applicable standards also reside in obligations arising under customary international law. In this connection, the basic tenets of the Universal Declaration of Human Rights and the Declaration on the Protection of All Persons from Being Subjected to Torture and Other Cruel, Inhuman or Degrading Treatment or Punishment, to name two other significant instruments, are relevant.

21. With regard to the origin of these obligations, the Special Rapporteur categorically rejects the arguments advanced by Deputy Prime Minister Tariq Aziz, during their meeting of 8 January 1992, to the effect that "standards of Europe and the West" have been thrust upon Iraq and are simply impossible to meet. Such an argument is patently false in so far as the standards of each convention mentioned above were freely accepted by the Government of Iraq upon its accession to the

instruments. Moreover, it must be noted that Iraq voted in favour of the General Assembly resolution 1948 (resolution 217 A (III), adopted by a vote of 48 in favour with 8 abstentions and none against), while the Declaration on Torture of 9 December 1975 (resolution 3452 (XXX)) was unanimously adopted. Consequently, these standards apply not as those of "Europe and the West" but as conventional obligations of Iraq or as universal norms of international law.

B. The relevance of special circumstances

1. Introduction

22. The notion of "special" or "exceptional circumstances" is known to international law as such circumstances as may require the application of special standards or permit derogation from the application of normal standards. Such a notion is specifically foreseen by and accommodated in international human rights instruments.

23. In as much as the issue of special circumstances was raised by the Government of Iraq in its first reply to the memorandum of the Special Rapporteur (see A/46/647, pages 18-21 and 57), and was subsequently repeated at each meeting between the Special Rapporteur and a minister of the Government of Iraq, at the meetings of the Special Rapporteur with the Governors of Najaf and Karbala, at the meetings of the Special Rapporteur with the Consultative Committee on Human Rights of the Foreign Ministry, and again in the Government of Iraq's second reply (dated 23 January 1992) to the Special Rapporteur's inquiries, it is evident that the relevance of special circumstances to the situation of human rights in Iraq must here be addressed. Specifically, it is necessary to reply to the Government of Iraq's various invocations of: "abnormal circumstances", "this difficult situation", "wartime conditions", "*force majeure*", "the Iraq-Iran war", "conditions of foreign occupation and intervention", "the Gulf war in 1991", "the disturbances", "chaos, disorder and armed rebellion", "the circumstances with which the country has been faced, and is still being faced, as a result of the on-going economic embargo", the situation of "a developing country", and the situation of a country with "its own particularities and indigenous values". Indeed, the clearest and most sweeping reference, aside from those offered in person to the Special Rapporteur by various representatives of the Government, is to be found in the second reply of the Government in the section headed "Paragraph 60": "the abnormal circumstances with which the country was faced had adverse effects on human rights, for reasons beyond our control." As such, it is evident that the Government of Iraq contends that "abnormal circumstances" caused human rights violations to occur for which the Government is not to be held responsible - either because the violations are not imputable to the Government or because the violations are imputable to the Government but are somehow to be excused by the circumstances.

2. The relevance of war to human rights

(a) In general

24. Regardless of who may be responsible for the initiation of a war, and faced with the reality that war or armed conflicts short of war continue to inflict their pain on humanity, international human rights law requires that its norms continue to be respected. These norms admit, however, to a sub-order which accords with the special laws that may be permissible under the derogation clauses of international human rights law. The law of derogation is considered in greater detail below. Nonetheless, it is worth mentioning at this point that should the Government of Iraq have chosen to invoke the law of derogation, such measures as it might have sought so to justify would have to have accorded with the strict requirements of the exigencies of the situation and could not have been inconsistent with other obligations under international law. Moreover, there is a long list of human rights standards (including what some call the "fundamental rights" to life, freedom from torture, freedom of thought, etc.) that simply must be respected fully at all times and in every circumstance.

(b) The Iran-Iraq war

25. With respect to the Government of Iraq's references to the period of the Iran-Iraq war as a period of abnormal circumstances somehow mitigating the Government's responsibility for human rights violations, the Special Rapporteur finds this argument untenable primarily because there is no relation in law or in logic between the existence of a state of emergency like a war and the commission of the various egregious acts of which the Government has been accused, such as widespread and systematic torture and arbitrary or summary execution of civilians or combatants. In this last respect, it must be noted that even the tenets of international humanitarian law (which may be said to be largely embodied in the four Geneva Conventions of 1949, to which Iraq is a party) prohibit such acts as are attributed to the Government. Moreover, the Special Rapporteur observes that many of the allegations of violations by the Government of Iraq relate to events that took place well outside the actual war zone, while many other allegations relate to events before or after the period of the war which began with Iraq's attack on Iran in September 1980 (see Security Council document S/23273) and continued to the ceasefire of July 1988.

(c) The Gulf War of 1991

26. For the same reasons as expressed in paragraph 25, the Special Rapporteur cannot accept the argument of the Government of Iraq that its responsibility is mitigated or removed by the events of the war that it initiated with the invasion of the sovereign State of Kuwait on 2 August 1990 and that concluded with its withdrawal from Kuwait on 26 February 1991. The waging of aggressive war, most clearly demonstrated by the armed invasion and occupation of another sovereign State, not only is not an excuse for human rights violations, but is absolutely incompatible with the notion of respect for human rights. In any event, the events of the Gulf crisis were also limited in time and space: the great majority of allegations refer to events before and after the period of the crisis, while many others refer to events well beyond the theatres of armed conflict.

3. The relevance of civil disturbances

27. Subsequent to the withdrawal of Iraq from the territory of Kuwait, popular uprisings were initiated in the essentially Shi'a southern cities and the essentially Kurdish northern cities of the country. These uprisings, which the Government of Iraq has characterized as "armed rebellion" and has said could "under no circumstances be regarded as an 'intifada'" (A/46/647, p. 20), were of such a nature as to have rendered several of the cities in question under the control of the insurgent forces for some days, while large parts of the Autonomous Region of Kurdistan remain today essentially in the hands of the insurgents. Under these circumstances, and notwithstanding the continuing validity of human rights standards throughout the duration of the conflicts, it is evident that the conflicts were of such a nature as to have reached the threshold of

applicability of Article 3 common to the four Geneva Conventions of 1949. In addition to these standards, and though Iraq is not a party to the 1977 Protocol II Additional to the Geneva Conventions of 12 August 1949, and relating to the Protection of Victims of Non-International Armed Conflicts, there are standards expressed in this Protocol which are essentially the same as those expressed in the instruments of international human rights law (to which the Protocol explicitly refers in its preamble), namely: protection of the right to life, protection from torture and mutilation, protection against arbitrary punishments, protection against outrages upon personal dignity, protection against pillage, protection against threats of any of the afore-mentioned, respect for the rights of those in detention and against whom penal prosecutions have been initiated, protection of the wounded and of medical personnel, and protection of the civilian population in general, including protection of objects indispensable for their survival and cultural objects and places of worship. Indeed, it should be observed that many of these most fundamental protections may be said to be part of the customary law of human rights.

28. Irrespective of the exact "level" of the rebellion, i.e. whether or not the conflicts rose to the level of those considered under Article 3 common to the four Geneva Conventions of 1949 or whether they remained at the level of a large-scale and coordinated criminal disturbance (which the Special Rapporteur is persuaded was not the case), it must be stressed that the response of the Government must be relevant and proportionate, such that the standards of human rights may be respected for every individual in every case; the existence of such internal disturbances, no matter what their "level", does not permit a *carte blanche* response. Certainly, international law can never accept a return to the justice of "an eye for an eye": any violations on the part of the insurgents (which the Special Rapporteur acknowledges are most likely to have occurred) cannot be used as an excuse for violations by the Government, either during the uprisings or thereafter. In any event, and as in the cases of war discussed above, it must be observed that the events in question affected only certain parts of the country and only during a very limited time almost one year ago. Hence, the invocation of the excuse of the March 1991 uprisings cannot generally be accepted even for the limited period of its conflicts.

4. The relevance of economic sanctions

29. It has not escaped the attention of the Special Rapporteur that the central argument advanced by the Government of Iraq in reply to allegations of violations revolves around the existence of the economic sanctions levied against Iraq for its previous and continuing violations of general international law. In fact, in his conversation with the Special Rapporteur of 8 January 1992, Deputy Prime Minister Tariq Aziz argued that Iraq's respect for human rights would improve if the sanctions were to be lifted - suggesting that the existence of the sanctions causes Iraq to violate human rights. However, here again it must be noted that such an argument is fallacious since there is no relation in law or logic between the existence of economic sanctions and compliance with obligations of international human rights law. This is certainly so for violations of the rights to life, torture, due process and, indeed, virtually all other human rights: simply put, shortages of spare parts for car engines cannot be said to cause government forces to carry out acts of torture.

5. The relevance of other circumstances

30. Aside from the major arguments of "special circumstances" advanced by the Government and considered above, the Government has at various times and to a lesser degree attempted to invoke the relevance of certain other "circumstances" as bearing on the content of its obligations under international human rights law. These may be said to fall into three categories: the circumstance of a "developing country", the circumstance of a country in the process of "revolution", and the circumstance of a country with "its own particularities and indigenous values". As with the other arguments discussed above, these demand some response.

31. With regard to the "circumstance" of a "developing country", it is first to be observed that international human rights law does not provide for varying regimes dependent upon the level of a State's development. It has long been established that the norms of international human rights law are indivisible and complementary; that there is no hierarchy such that one "category" of human rights may be said to prevail over another. Respect for human rights is not an "either/or" proposition: it is both possible and necessary to respect all rights at the same time. Even the standards of respect for economic rights may be said to be universal in so far as there are generally standards of reasonableness which expressly take into account "available resources" (article 2, paragraph 1 of the Covenant on Economic, Social and Cultural Rights). Moreover, respect for fundamental human rights such as freedom from torture and the right to life in no way may be said to depend on the circumstances of a State's "development". In any event, Iraq cannot be said to be a poor or underdeveloped country. On the contrary, Iraq's natural wealth and gross national product through much of the last generation has propelled the country along the road of development.

32. The notion of the "circumstance" of a country in the process of "revolution" was raised by Deputy Prime Minister Tariq Aziz in conversation with the Special Rapporteur when Mr. Aziz explained why movement from the Provisional Constitution of 1970 had not been possible. According to the argument, the process of the revolution had been delayed for the last 22 years by other special circumstances of war, uprisings and now the embargo. As a consequence, the regime of "revolutionary legality" had had to be extended under the guardianship of the "vanguard of the people". However, such a notion of "circumstance" is simply not provided for under the terms of any instruments of international human rights law, and the nature and duration of this "revolution" would exclude it from being considered as a "public emergency" in the sense of article 4 of the Covenant on Civil and Political Rights. Moreover, the Special Rapporteur notes that Iraq did not consider this "circumstance" as interfering with its ability to accede to the two Covenants of 1966, as it did in 1971. Consequently, the "revolution" referred to by Mr. Aziz must be deemed irrelevant to the application of international human rights law in and by Iraq.

33. The concept of a country with "its own particularities and indigenous values" undoubtedly applies for each and every State in the world. To say that it somehow has a bearing on the standards applicable in each State is to ignore the universality of international human rights law. Though the question of "universal values" may be the subject of considerable debate in academic circles, as a matter of positive international law the standards do not vary by country and are not amenable to unilateral interpretation. Again, the Special Rapporteur must repeat that the standards in question have been freely accepted by Iraq after due consideration, or are universal

standards arising under customary international law. National "particularities and indigenous values" cannot be said to vary these standards or serve as excuses for violations: otherwise the standards would soon be meaningless.

6. The relevance of derogation clauses

34. Although the Government of Iraq has at different times alleged that examination of its human rights record has been a politicized exercise, the Special Rapporteur has steadfastly analysed the situation of human rights in Iraq according only to the norms of the applicable international law. In the case of so-called "special circumstances", such an analysis leads directly to a consideration of the purposes and procedures of the relevant derogation clauses.

35. As a matter of law, there is really only one relevant article: article 4 of the Covenant on Civil and Political Rights. It reads as follows:

> "1. In time of public emergency which threatens the life of the nation and the existence of which is officially proclaimed, the States Parties to the present Covenant may take measures derogating from their obligations under the present Covenant to the extent strictly required by the exigencies of the situation, provided that such measures are not inconsistent with their other obligations under international law and do not involve discrimination solely on the ground of race, colour, sex, language, religion or social origin.
>
> "2. No derogation from articles 6, 7, 8 (paragraphs 1 and 2), 11, 15, 16 and 18 may be made under this provision.
>
> "3. Any State Party to the present Covenant availing itself of the right of derogation shall immediately inform the other States Parties to the present Covenant, through the intermediary of the Secretary-General of the United Nations, of the provisions from which it has derogated and of the reasons by which it was actuated. A further communication shall be made, through the same intermediary, on the date on which it terminates such derogation."

Although the Convention on the Elimination of All Forms of Racial Discrimination and the Convention on the Elimination of All Forms of Discrimination against Women do not refer to derogations, it is clear both from the absence of such a reference and from the prohibition in the last part of article 4, paragraph 1, quoted above that no derogation from these obligations is permissible. In a similar vein, derogation cannot be permissible under the Convention on the Prevention and Punishment of the Crime of Genocide, for obvious reasons. For its part, the Covenant on Economic, Social and Cultural Rights does not speak to the issue of derogations (suggesting none are permissible), but refers instead in its article 4 to "such limitations as are determined by law only in so far as this may be compatible with the nature of these rights and solely for the purpose of promoting the general welfare in a democratic society".

36. Article 4 of the Covenant on Civil and Political Rights may be said to have both procedural and substantive aspects. As far as procedure is concerned, paragraph 1 makes clear that any public emergency invoked as justification for derogations must be "officially proclaimed" within the State, while paragraph 3 requires the State party to "immediately inform the other States Parties to the present Covenant, through the intermediary of the Secretary-General of the United Nations, of the provisions from which it has derogated and of the reasons by which it was actuated"; similar notification is required upon termination of such derogation. These procedures are necessary both for the purposes of other States (so that, *inter alia*, they may be aware of the protections that may or may not be available to their nationals), and for the determination of the substance of the derogations; only by complying with the procedure of article 4 can it be possible to know whether or not the derogations sought are inconsistent with other obligations under international law and do not otherwise conflict with the limitations established in the article.

37. Assuming that the procedural aspect of article 4 is respected, the substance of any derogations invoked will comprise only such measures as are "strictly required by the exigencies of the situation", "are not inconsistent with ... other obligations under international law" and do not impinge upon the non-derogable rights specified in paragraphs 1 and 2.

38. From the clear wording of article 4 of the Covenant on Civil and Political Rights, as read in the light of the whole Covenant and in the spirit of international human rights law in general, it is apparent that derogations are to be strictly limited and can never be implied. For if the procedure of notification and justification were not to be respected, then it would not be possible to determine the substance or legitimacy of derogations, and potentially arbitrary and abusive measures could undermine respect for human rights in general. Moreover, it is equally apparent that the notion of derogation is linked to exceptional circumstances, which in turn implies the temporary nature of any derogations; an order of derogations cannot be permitted to become the normal state of affairs. On this last matter, the Human Rights Committee has observed the following in its General Comment 5 (13):

> "The Committee holds the view that measures taken under article 4 are of an exceptional and temporary nature and may only last as long as the life of the nation concerned is threatened and that, in times of emergency, the protection of human rights becomes all the more important, particularly those rights from which no derogations can be made. The Committee also considers that it is equally important for States parties, in times of public emergency, to inform other States parties of the nature and extent of the derogations they have made and of the reasons therefore" (CCPR/C/21/Rev.1).

39. As far as the Special Rapporteur has been able to determine, the Government of Iraq has neither officially declared a state of emergency nor otherwise proceeded under article 4 of the Covenant on Civil and Political Rights to effect permissible derogations from its human rights obligations. While this fact alone may perhaps be telling, the Special Rapporteur refers to his remarks in paragraph 60 of his interim report in rejecting the above arguments of "special circumstances" and concluding again that all normal standards apply.

II. ALLEGED HUMAN RIGHTS VIOLATIONS

A. Issues affecting the population as a whole

1. Summary or arbitrary execution

40. Regular and consistent reports of executions have reached the Special Rapporteur throughout the period of his mandate. Allegations have ranged from inadequate

judicial review to orchestrated mass executions and burials. With respect to this last issue, the use of weapons of mass destruction and the issue of mass graves will be discussed. However, the problem of "normal" summary or arbitrary executions will first be addressed here.

41. Executions continue to be routinely carried out. This conclusion is fully justified in the light of the Special Rapporteur's visit in January 1992 to Abu Graib prison where, in one wing of the "heavy" section 96, he found prisoners awaiting execution. This figure (from just one prison) is to be compared with the figure given by the Government in its reply of 23 January 1992, in which it is stated that there were only 24 death sentences proclaimed for the whole of 1978.

42. While it is apparent that the death penalty is regularly administered, this fact is all the more disconcerting in view of the failings of the due process of law described below. Moreover, information and testimony received by the Special Rapporteur make it clear that executions have routinely been carried out without judicial review. In fact, according to the documents reproduced in annex II and said to have been found in the Security Department offices of Arbil, Sulaimaniya and various other offices now under Kurdish control, the security service reporting to the President and other officers of the State (or simply to the Baath Party) has carried out executions on executive or party authority without judicial review. Most significantly, arbitrary executions were carried out on thousands of families of those thought to have been "saboteurs".

43. Information and testimony received by the Special Rapporteur affirm that there have been practices of mass execution. A report of a recent medical fact-finding mission, sent by Middle East Watch and Physicians for Human Rights, provides further evidence of the practices of the Iraqi security forces. Of particular interest is the following statement attributed to a grave digger from Arbil:

> "It was in the autumn of 1986. I was called to the morgue soon after the attempted assassination of the governor of Arbil, Ibrahim Z'angang. In fact, it was the fourth attempt. An Iraqi officer met me at the morgue entrance and took me to a security police vehicle. Inside were the corpses of about 19 young men. Their bodies were riddled with bullets, their hands were tied behind their backs, and they were blindfolded. The officer said I was to bury these 'dogs'. Later, the morgue workers told me that these young men were students who had been randomly rounded up and shot by a firing squad only a few hours earlier. It was nothing more than retaliation for the botched execution attempt, a way of warning the Kurds ... So I went with the officer and the bodies to the cemetery. Traditionally, we wash the dead before burial and then wrap them in a white cloth. But the officer wouldn't allow it. He said it had to be done quickly. So I buried them with their clothes on. However, I did manage to place stones around the bodies and to turn their heads toward Mecca."

Exhumation of one of the graves indicated by the grave digger provided corroborative[sic] evidence of the story's accuracy.

44. In Sulaimaniya, a grave digger made the following statement to the same fact-finding mission:

> "I must have buried 600 or maybe up to 1,000 people - all killed by the secret police between 1985 and 1989. Sometimes they were *peshmerga*, sometimes women, sometimes children. Sometimes they'd been tortured. There were other grave diggers but I'm sure I buried most of them."

Exhumation of unmarked graves indicated by the grave digger again provided corroborative evidence of the truth of this story.

45. Testimony received by the Special Rapporteur also confirmed that arbitrary or summary executions were common during and after the March 1991 uprisings. House-to-house searches by Government forces were said to have regularly resulted in executions, including of women and children.

46. One particularly disturbing piece of evidence viewed by the Special Rapporteur was a video-taped official and public execution of five men. Blindfolded and tied to poles, the men were placed before a large crowd, including various military officers and public officials. After some statements had been read out, the men were repeatedly shot. With the bodies crumpled to the bottom of the poles, an apparent security officer walked past the corpses placing a bullet from his pistol to each one's head; maintaining his stride, he delivered the five shots in a few seconds. Young children observed these executions from the front rows of the public assembly.

47. With regard to mass killings as a result of the use of chemical weapons and other weapons of mass destruction, the Special Rapporteur refers to paragraphs 22, 23, 74 and 75 of his interim report (A/46/647). After further study including consideration of eye-witness testimony received by the Special Rapporteur, there can be no doubt that Iraq has used excessive force, including chemical weapons, on several occasions during the past few years.

48. With regard to the use of chemical weapons in particular, Mr. Tariq Aziz, then Foreign Minister, stated during a press conference in Bonn on 1 July 1988 that both sides in the Iran-Iraq war had used chemical weapons. It has been established, however, that Iraq also used chemical weapons against civilians. In a report of 19 August 1988 to the Security Council (S/20134, annex), the Secretary-General of the United Nations noted with deep regret the conclusion of an expert group, which had been sent to investigate the matter, that chemical weapons had been used against Iranian civilians in an area adjacent to an urban centre lacking any protection against that kind of attack.

49. But there is also abundant evidence that Iraq used chemical weapons against its own civilians. For instance, a report of a medical mission to Turkish Kurdistan by Physicians for Human Rights dated February 1989 concluded that Iraqi aircraft attacked Kurdish villages in northern Iraq with bombs containing lethal poison on 12 August 1988. This conclusion was based on responses to a systematically administered questionnaire, videotaped eyewitness accounts, and the physical examination of people residing in refugee camps in south-eastern Turkey at the time of the mission.

50. The Special Rapporteur has himself spoken with several people in the Kurdish part of Iraq who claimed that members of their families were either killed or severely injured as a consequence of chemical attacks by Iraqi aircraft, or that they had themselves been victims of such attacks. A list of 103 people who were killed during the chemical bombardment of the village of Sheekwassan

in the governorate of Arbil on 16 April 1987 was submitted to the Special Rapporteur in this connection. In addition, he received another list with the names of 45 inhabitants of the same village. These people, it was claimed, had been transferred to a hospital after having been injured during the chemical attack. They were subsequently killed by the secret police and buried in mass graves near Arbil.

2. *Torture and other cruel, inhuman or degrading treatment*

51. Throughout the decade of the 1980s, Amnesty International denounced, in several reports, the widespread, systematic torture of detainees by Iraqi Government security forces (both police and military).

52. The use of torture in order to compel political prisoners, and also detainees held for any security-related offence, to sign "confessions", to give information regarding themselves as well as other persons, and to force them to renounce their political affiliations, was said to be routine practice. Victims were reportedly most often subjected to torture immediately after their arrest and during interrogation under pre-trial detention, when they were held incommunicado. In many cases, they were suspected of being members of prohibited political parties such as the Kurdistan Popular Democratic Party (KPDP), the Kurdistan Democratic Party (KDP), the Patriotic Union of Kurdistan (PUK), the Kurdistan Socialist Party-Iraq (KSP-I), the Iraqi Communist Party (ICP) and *al-Da'wa al-Islamiya*. It has further been alleged that the relatives of such suspects, including children, were held in lieu of such suspects sought by the authorities and were also tortured in the process.

53. Interrogation practices have been described as brutal and have, in some cases, resulted in permanent physical or mental damage to the victims. In its report "Torture in Iraq 1982-1984" of 15 April 1985, Amnesty International provides a list of 30 different methods of torture allegedly used by members of the Iraqi security forces. They include both physical and psychological torture, such as beatings, burnings, extraction of finger-nails, sexual assault including rape, electric shocks, acid baths, deprivation of food, water, sleep or rest, as well as subjection to mock executions. Several of the victims were said to have died as a result of torture, which would explain why government documents brought to the attention of the Special Rapporteur frequently speak of "criminals" having "died during interrogation" (see, for example, document No. 5 in annex II). Moreover, it was reported that in several cases of alleged extrajudicial execution the victims were subjected to torture before being killed.

54. In particular, Amnesty International reports that brutal treatment of children has become routine practice in Iraqi prisons. Young people have reportedly often been tortured to force them to reveal information about their relatives. Allegedly, even infants have been ill-treated to compel members of their families to "confess" to alleged political offences. According to these reports, some of the 300 children and youths arrested in Sulaimaniya in September and October 1985 had been tortured, and three of them died in custody as a result. Their bodies were said to have been found in the streets on the outskirts of the town, bearing marks of torture. The bodies of 29 others of these children and youths, reportedly executed in January 1987, were returned to their families. They also showed marks of torture.

55. Quoting its Constitution and several other laws prohibiting torture, the Government of Iraq has repeatedly denied that torture frequently occurs in the country. Allegations submitted to it by Amnesty International have been qualified as "bizarre", "false" and "without foundation" since torture is prohibited by the nation's Constitution and laws. These allegations were denied even when they had been presented with consistent evidence in the form of detailed medical examination results and other material findings. According to the Government's response to Amnesty International, occasional cases of torture had been investigated and those responsible had been dealt with. The Special Rapporteur has received similar assurances. However, as torturers remain anonymous, and only very few (former) prisoners will take the risk of severe retaliation, it must be assumed that the torturers can continue their practices in the knowledge that the chances are extremely small that they will ever be punished for their crimes.

56. The Special Rapporteur has received considerable testimony from victims of and eye-witnesses to torture; testimony from victims was frequently corroborated by scars remaining on their bodies. The testimony received recounts a wide variety of methods of torture, although certain practices appear to be routine given the frequency of references and consistency of accounts given by the witnesses. The testimony of victims was also corroborated by that of former security officers, who were able to provide specific information concerning the security apparatus in general and its use of torture in particular.

57. The findings of the Special Rapporteur confirm that torture, including in its most cruel forms, has been used on a large scale as a method of extracting confessions and terrorizing the population throughout the 1980s and to the present day. The summaries of a small number of testimonies are provided below:

(a) In early 1982, the witness' son was taken from the University in Baasra, and for 6 months the witness sought his whereabouts. Finally deciding to ask the officer in charge of the security centre in Baasra about the fate of his son, the witness was taken blindfolded to the General Security Centre in Baghdad in November 1982. There he was interrogated, being told that his son was a "criminal". In an attempt to get him to "confess" his son's criminal activity, the witness was tortured during seven months, having his legs and back burnt and being hit on the back of the head (from which he still bears a scar). Finally, he was brought before a court and released in July 1983. His son was tortured and released in November 1983.

(b) In early March 1991, before the uprisings began, the witness was arrested by the intelligence services in Baasra. He was blindfolded and taken to the city's security centre, where he remained for one month. During his detention, he was beaten and subjected to electric shocks. In April 1991, he was transferred to Radwaniya prison in Baghdad where his interrogation began; he was subjected to more electric shocks, suffered burns and was hanged by his hands tied behind his back. He was released some two months later because of lack of evidence. The witness suffers from a weak left leg as a consequence of his tortures.

(c) On 28 December 1985, the security forces and intelligence services stormed the witness' home at 3.00 a.m. He was taken to the General Security Centre in Baghdad and placed in its "Third Section". He subsequently remained in prison for three and a half years, being transferred to many different prisons in the country, including that of Tikrit. During his detention, he was badly tortured, being subjected to beatings, the dripping of acid on his skin, the use of electric shocks, and beatings with cables. He had been charged with slandering Saddam Hussein and with being a member of the al-Da'wa Party, but he was released in 1988 when the Revolution Court could find no evidence against him.

(d) The witness was arrested in 1990 and imprisoned for having deserted from the army. While in prison, he was severely beaten and kicked, was subjected to electric shocks and was burnt with a hot iron.

(e) On 17 July 1988, the witness deserted from the army. He was caught and taken to the Security Centre in Baasra where, from 20 July 1988, he was subjected to various forms of torture, including hangings, electric shocks, sexual assaults, the extraction of his right eye and the removal of his fingernails by pliers[sic]; he suffered damage to his left eye as the result of a kick.

(f) The witness was arrested at the University of Mosul in 1985. During his detention, his arm was broken in the course of beatings. Upon an escape attempt, he was shot in the left hand. The witness also suffers stiffness in his fingers which he attributes to electric shocks administered during his detention.

(g) In September 1984, the witness was arrested by the security forces and taken to Najaf Security Centre where, in the course of interrogation, he was hung from a ceiling fan, subjected to electric shocks and beatings to all parts of his body including his genitals, and had hot water poured over him. He also suffered psychological torture as he was placed in solitary confinement, hearing screams and cries. After 11 months, he promised to give names and collaborate with the security forces, whereupon he was released. He fled the city.

(h) In 1985, the witness was arrested with her family and taken to the Karbala Security Centre. She was separated from her family and placed in solitary confinement. During her interrogation, she had her clothes torn off and was sexually assaulted.

(i) The witness had been arrested several times by the Security Forces, beginning in 1979. During his fourth arrest, in 1988, he was severely tortured by the use of electric shocks and sexual assaults. He was witness to other persons having their eyes pulled out and being dragged over broken glass.

(j) On 19 April 1990, the witness was arrested for the second time, having previously been taken to the Security Centre in al-Shanafiya. During his second detention, he was subjected to electric shock and was threatened with the rape of his wife before his eyes in order to extract a confession. Having fainted from torture, he was taken to Saddam Hospital, but the witness refused a suggested injection because his friend had previously been poisoned. On 22 November 1990, the witness was released, but he suffers from a paralysed left hand as a result of his torture.

(k) On 29 May 1984, the witness was arrested and taken blindfolded to the Baasra Security Centre where he remained for 13 months. During his detention, he had his teeth pulled out and lost his hair as a result of scaldings with boiling water.

(l) The witness was arrested for having refused to join the army. During his imprisonment, he suffered from various forms of torture (beatings, cablings, electric shocks, being hung from the ceiling) along with 30 other persons who had refused to join the army. The witness reports that some of those 30 persons had teeth and nails pulled out, while others had their tongues cut.

(m) In April 1986, the witness was taken from his house for having refused to join the army. Being told that he must either join the army or be executed, he was tortured by electric shocks and had his nails pulled out. During his detention, the witness also saw a girl being raped.

(n) During the March 1991 uprisings, the witness was arrested with his brother. He and his brother were both subjected to severe beatings, electric shocks, and the removal of their fingernails. As a result, his brother (who was badly tortured) is now emotionally disturbed.

(o) The witness was arrested in 1989 and suffered injuries during interrogation. As a result, he was taken to a military hospital where he was subjected to further torture, having some of his flesh scraped off. He was subsequently transferred to a prison where toxic materials were put on his wounds.

(p) During a military action against "communists" in the governorate of Sulaimaniya in September 1988, the witness (then an army medic) covered a body in the street with a cloth, whereupon he was arrested for sympathizing with the saboteurs. He was next charged with being a communist. Taken to the "Fifth Section" of the General Security Centre in Baghdad, he was handcuffed and blindfolded and was then forced to sign various documents. In an effort to extract his confession, he was told that his two sisters would be brought before him and raped. When the sisters were brought before him, he confessed and was thereupon imprisoned.

58. The use of torture by Iraqi security forces violates both national and international law. Torture is prohibited by article 22(a) of the Iraqi Constitution and by article 127 of the Iraqi Code of Criminal Procedure No. 23 of 1971. However, it is reported that no safeguarding mechanisms and procedures have been established to ensure respect for the prohibition of torture by security and police forces. Indeed, it would appear that torture is a systematic practice conforming to government directives.

59. The use of torture is a serious violation of several international human rights standards, such as those embodied in: article 5 of the Universal Declaration of Human Rights; article 7 of the Covenant on Civil and Political Rights; and the Declaration on the Protection of All Persons from Being Subjected to Torture and Other Cruel, Inhuman or Degrading Treatment or Punishment. With respect to this last instrument in particular, the Iraqi Government stated officially on 3 September 1979 that it intended to comply with the Declaration and "to continue the implementation, through its national legislation and other effective measures, of the provisions of the said Declaration."

3. Enforced or involuntary disappearances

60. The Commission on Human Rights has been confronted with the phenomenon of disappearance for well over a decade and in that time the phenomenon has come to be considered as one of the most heinous of crimes. Disappearance presents a complex of violations against the individual, the family, and the community in general. The wives and children of disappeared husbands and fathers are particularly hard hit. Often, families are left without support, and in a state of limbo, without being able to take over property rights or have the peace of mind of knowing the fate of their loved ones, and with wives being unable to remarry.

61. From the information received, it is beyond doubt that the problem of disappearances is enormous in Iraq. In receiving testimony from witnesses, the Special

Rapporteur was several times reminded that there is hardly a family in Iraq that has not been touched by the phenomenon. Indeed, both the Minister of Interior and the Deputy Prime Minister agreed with the Special Rapporteur that the problem is widespread and complex, while Professor al-Duri of the Consultative Committee on Human Rights of the Ministry for Foreign Affairs offered the information that he had two nephews who had gone missing. While these admissions relate primarily to war losses, it would seem most appropriate and long overdue for the Government to establish an independent body of enquiry and record keeping.

62. In connection with his mandate, the Special Rapporteur takes note of the valuable work of the Working Group on Enforced or Involuntary Disappearances. Specifically, it is interesting to note that of the 3,874 detailed and individual cases transmitted to the Government, the Government has only ever seen fit to respond to a mere 206, clarifying just 70 of these. Such a response does not bode well for the Special Rapporteur, who is at present in possession of over 17,000 names of persons who have allegedly disappeared, of which an estimated 12,000 cases contain sufficient detail to be taken up by the Working Group. In fact, since the submission of the Special Rapporteur's interim report, a steady flow of cases has been received, often accompanied by identity documents and photographs. This has presented logistical problems in so far as most are received in Arabic and Kurdish; the great majority of these cases are still being translated and analysed, and so the Government of Iraq has yet to receive many of these lists. In any event, and judging from the volume of cases already received by the Special Rapporteur, it is within the realm of possibility if not probability that Kurdish estimates of up to 182,000 disappeared are realistic.

63. Many examples of cases of disappearance could be cited. But one case is perhaps revealing; that of a Mr. al-Subeiti who was sentenced to death *in absentia* for being a member of the al-Da'wa al-Islamiya Party. While working some time later in Jordan in 1981, he was arrested and imprisoned by the local authorities. In 1981, Mr. Barzan al-Tikriti came to obtain him on an extradition order that stipulated that he would not be executed. His children received two personal letters from him thereafter: one in 1982 and the other in 1983. There has been no news from him or of him since then. The terror an event like this transmits, even across borders, is considerable.

64. Annex III contains only a sample of cases of disappearance received by the Special Rapporteur. This list of 238 names and particulars has been compiled from seven collective case files received by the Special Rapporteur during his recent visit to Iraqi Kurdistan. In each case detailed information is provided. Viewed together with the thousands of cases submitted to the Working Group on Disappearances in the early 1980s and the large numbers being submitted as a result of the Anfal Operations and in relation to the March 1991 uprisings, the Special Rapporteur can only conclude that there has been and continues to be a systematic policy of enforced disappearance.

4. Arbitrary arrest and detention

65. Testimony received by the Special Rapporteur continues to affirm that arbitrary arrest and detention are routinely practised in Iraq and remain a major contributing factor to the general climate of fear. In the context of other violations, such as torture, enforced disappearance and summary or arbitrary execution, victims are almost always arbitrarily arrested and detained. In fact, arbitrary arrest and detention is often the precursor to such greater violations. With respect to this subject, the Special Rapporteur refers to his remarks in his interim report (see A/46/647, paras. 14, 15 and 63-65) and to the related matters discussed above.

66. With regard to places of detention, the Special Rapporteur notes that information and testimonies received reveal the use of all sorts of centres of detention, with over 100 places having been identified by witnesses. This information stands in stark contrast to the Government's contention that there are at present only four functioning prisons in Iraq.

5. Due process and the rule of law

67. The notions of "due process of law" and "rule of law" are integrally linked: the rule of law is poorly served and undermined if the requisites of due process are not respected, and the notion of due process becomes meaningless if the rule of law is not secure. As matters of international human rights law, these two notions are defined particularly in terms of articles 10 and 11 of the Universal Declaration of Human Rights and articles 9 and 14 of the Covenant on Civil and Political Rights. However, the rule of law requires more than respect of procedural rights; it requires respect for most if not all rights and a concerted effort to eradicate the scourge of arbitrariness.

68. In Iraq, neither is the due process of law generally respected nor is the rule of law upheld. On the contrary, information and testimony received reveals a consistent if not routine failure to respect due process. At the same time, and perhaps partly because of it, the rule of law has been completely undermined.

69. While numerous testimonies alleged the absence of counsel during trial, the absence of time and support to prepare a defence, and all other such attendant guarantees (assuming any trial in the first place), perhaps examination of an individual case will help demonstrate where the problems lie. In this connection, the case of Mr. Ian Richter, raised in the interim report (paras. 41, 42 and 84, 85), is a useful example, regardless of the fact that he was released some months ago.

70. According to Mr. Richter's own testimony, and contrary to the obligations of Iraq under article 9 (2) of the Covenant, Mr. Richter was never informed of the charges against him. Under the terms of article 14 of the Covenant, Mr. Richter was not given adequate time or facilities to prepare his defence, he was brought before a Revolution Court without benefit of legal representation, he was not permitted to examine any witnesses against him, he was forced to sign documents in Arabic which he did not understand, and he was not allowed the right of appeal. In Mr. Richter's case, however, the arbitrariness may be said to have come full circle as his release has not been explained in law and it is not certain whether or not he is entitled to any compensation for the five and a half years he spent in prison. Virtually all testimony received by the Special Rapporteur cites the same violations.

71. Turning to the rule of law, the Provisional Constitution of July 1970, which is still essentially in force, speaks neither of "government" nor of "executive power" but refers only to the "Council of Ministers" - an organ "comprised of ministers and presided over by the President of the Republic" (article 61). However, the real power in the country resides (apart from in the Office of the President) in the Revolution Command Council, which is the "State's supreme organ" (article 37). The membership of the Revolution Command Council is constituted by nine persons whose names, including that

of Saddam Hussein, are listed in Revolution Command Council Decree No. 836 of 12 July 1982; the said Decree, which is an amendment to article 37 of the Constitution, also appoints the President of the Revolution Command Council who, ipso facto, is the President of the Republic. Any modification of the composition of the Revolution Command Council would thus require a modification of the Constitution.

72. The Revolution Command Council holds extensive legislative and executive powers at one and the same time. Significantly, it may establish laws and make decisions that have the force of law (article 42). It supervises the laws voted upon by the National Assembly, which it may dissolve, and pronounces the decisions necessary to bring ordinary laws into force. The Revolution Command Council has exclusive competence to adopt laws and make decisions relating to the Ministry of Defence and to the State Security, particularly those relating to their powers, organization and budgets (article 43 of the Constitution and article 105 of Law No. 55 of 1980, Law on the National Assembly). Moreover, the Revolution Command Council is the only authority that may, by a two-thirds majority decision, modify the Constitution (article 66). Further, without the approval of the Revolution Command Council (which meets *in camera*), no steps can be taken against the President, the Vice-President or any other members of the Revolution Command Council. In sum, the Revolution Command Council and its members are subject to no legislative or judicial constraints: they are accountable to no one.

73. Without being elected, either directly or indirectly, by the people, the President of the Republic holds, at the same time, the offices of: Head of State, President of the Revolution Command Council, President of the Council of Ministers, Commander-in-Chief of the Armed Forces, and Secretary General of the Baath Party. Perhaps most importantly, he is also de facto chief of State Security in as much as it reports directly to him and to no other minister. The length of the President's mandate is not specified in the Constitution, although it is presumably for life since all other members of the Government are required to believe in the "Qadissiyah of Saddam" (see, for example, article 14 of Law No. 55 of 1980). The Vice-President and Ministers are appointed by the President and are responsible to him. He can dismiss them at will. He is the head of the executive, has wide-ranging diplomatic powers, presides over the meetings of the Revolution Command Council, promulgates the laws passed by the National Assembly, commands the armed forces, decides on national defence policies and conducts military operations in time of war. To carry out his duties, he has full and sole constitutional authority to decree whatever measures he deems appropriate, for which he alone is responsible.

74. Until very recently, there was a "Revolution Court" which decided all cases of crimes against the State's domestic[sic] and foreign security as well as a wide variety of other offences (Revolution Command Council Decree No. 1016 of 1978); there was no possibility to appeal decisions of the Revolution Court. While this Court was eliminated by Revolution Command Council Decree No. 140 of 1991, it is interesting to note that in 1985 the Revolution Command Council had given the President of the Republic the right to annul any decision taken by the Revolution Court and to refer cases back to the Court for reconsideration.

75. In view of the vast constitutional and de facto powers of the President, it is clear that there are at least two systems of law operating within Iraq: a "normal" system of ordinary laws that addresses the typical affairs of daily life, such as highway traffic ordinances, and a parallel system of Revolution Command Council and Presidential decrees that addresses all matters of internal and external security together with whatever other matters the Revolution Command Council and President care to address. In fact, the power lies essentially in this second system of what may be called "extra-judicial legality" (or what Mr. Tariq Aziz has characterized as "Revolutionary legality"). However, beyond these two systems provided for within the Constitution, there may be said to be yet another order of rule - an order that might be called "extra-legal" in as much as it is not provided for in any texts of Iraqi law. This is the order of rule that proceeds from the personal whims and wishes of a few individuals who hold positions in the inner circle of the President. Irrespective of the extent of their legal authority, these persons have a de facto power to instruct the agents and organs of the State. An example of such power may be seen in the words of Mr. Ali Hassan al-Majid (then Secretary General of the Office for the Organization of the North and now Minister of Defence) when he asserted that he "went beyond the instructions of the leadership" in carrying out his tasks in the north - for which he was subsequently decorated by the President (the quoted words were expressed in a taped conversation, in the possession of the Special Rapporteur, involving a person the Special Rapporteur is confident is Mr. al-Majid). In fact, therefore, one is confronted in Iraq with a totalitarian system which does not take into account the rights of the individual. In such a system, human rights violations are inevitable.

6. The freedoms of thought, expression and association

76. The freedoms of thought, expression and association are guaranteed, respectively, by articles 18, 19 and 20 of the Universal Declaration of Human Rights and articles 18, 19 and 22 of the Covenant on Civil and Political Rights. Their proximity in these instruments is no accident in as much as these freedoms are so closely related that restrictions on one of these freedoms almost always has an impact on the others. In Iraq, the relationship is clear in so far as it would appear that the Government will not permit any thought, expression or association that significantly conflicts with the ideology of Arab Baath Socialism as interpreted by the party leadership, led by General Secretary Saddam Hussein.[sic]

77. While several Ministers maintained before the Special Rapporteur that Iraq is an open and pluralistic society that tolerates all varieties of beliefs in private and in public, the Special Rapporteur cannot ignore the longstanding government policies aimed against members of the al-Da'wa al-Islamiya Party (which follows Shi'a Islamic teachings), the Communist Party and members of all manner of other political parties and religious or philosophical groupings that do not accord with Baath Party ideology.

78. Perhaps the simplest evidence of the holding of a belief is one's private and public statements and affiliations. Here, thought is clearly linked with expression and association. In Iraq, it has been alleged that personal convictions have been captured by a web of government infiltrators and informants present throughout Iraqi society. Other evidence of convictions is given by confessions which, it is alleged, are frequently extracted under torture. But, the clearest evidence of violation of the freedom of expression continues to be found in Iraqi law which, for example, prescribes severe penalties including death for, *inter alia*, anyone slandering or insulting the President or anyone representing him, the Revolution Command Council, the Baath Party, the National Assembly or the Government (see the Special

Rapporteur's interim report, A/46/647, paras. 33 and 80, and page 34 for the Government's response, all referring to Revolution Command Council Decree No. 840 of 4 November 1986). Irrespective of the number of prosecutions under this law, its very existence clearly inhibits freedom of expression in violation of Iraq's obligations.

79. Turning to the issue of freedom of association, violations come in two principal forms: restrictions on associations of a political nature, and restrictions on the right to form and join independent trade unions. As far as associations of a political nature are concerned, several are specifically outlawed, such as the al-Da'wa al-Islamiya Party and the Communist Party. According to the relevant laws, membership in or association with these groups could carry the death penalty. While the Government denies that the law related to al-Da'wa al-Islamiya Party affiliation has ever "been put into practical effect" (A/46/647, page 35), the very existence of such laws has a far-reaching effect and is a violation of obligations under international human rights law. Moreover, information and testimony received by the Special Rapporteur indicates that this law has been regularly used not only against actual Party affiliates but also against anyone that might be considered an "enemy of the State" as determined by any number of security officers. Indeed, information from one source gave the particulars (including personal photographs) of over 50 individuals who had been allegedly executed for being members of the Party.

80. With respect to the right to form and join trade unions, and notwithstanding the fact that Iraq is a Party to International Labour Organisation Convention No. 98 of 1948 concerning Freedom of Association and the Right to Organise (to which article 22, paragraph 3, of the Covenant on Civil and Political Rights specifically refers), Iraq's Trade Union Organisation Law of 2 June 1987 establishes a trade union structure that places all trade unions within the Government's control. Thus, no independent trade union associations may be formed.

7. Access to food and health care

81. Access to food and health care continues to be a problem for a large part of the population. But, while it is clear that the economic sanctions imposed by the United Nations have had a significant impact on the economy as a whole, the Special Rapporteur repeats the note in his interim report (A/46/647, para. 96) that the sanctions specifically exempt "supplies intended strictly for medical purposes, and, in humanitarian circumstances, foodstuffs". It is the Government of Iraq's obligation, therefore, to adjust its food rations and social welfare to address the specific needs of all its people, and to help international relief agencies serving the most vulnerable.

82. Iraq is not a poor country, and so the Security Council has devised the formula of "oil for food" (and medicine) to allow Iraq to utilize its natural wealth to satisfy the minimum needs of the people. While the formula may be somewhat cumbersome, and perhaps not economically advantageous to the Government of Iraq, the issue at hand does not concern economic advantage and the Special Rapporteur remains convinced that an appropriate formula could have been worked out had there been sufficient political will on the part of the Government. Having recently chosen to break off negotiations to find an appropriate formula, and thereby having dismissed an opportunity to enlarge the available resources of food and medicine at a time when the people are in dire need (according to the Government's own argument), the leadership of Iraq has evidently made a political determination that its notions of "sovereignty" are more important than its obligations to respect human rights.

83. Considering the fact that the Government has itself imposed an economic embargo (specifically including medicaments, foodstuffs, gasoline and heating oil) against the portions of its population essentially living in the Autonomous Region of Kurdistan, and so far as it fails to distribute adequately such goods in the southern marshes, the Government cannot reasonably complain about the embargo instituted under the supervision of the United Nations Security Council. According to information received by the Special Rapporteur and confirmed by his own observations on 6 and 7 January 1992, the Government of Iraq has reduced the flow of rations to those in the Autonomous Region of Kurdistan to only 10 per cent of those given to other citizens. Similar controls on distribution are said to be affecting the southern marshes where great numbers of people are reportedly in need of humanitarian relief. In this connection, it has been reported that the use of health clinics, churches and mosques as centres for food distribution has been prohibited, while the issuance of visas for humanitarian aid personnel has been delayed or they have not been extended. Consequently, while the Government's rationing system and social welfare (together with the efforts of international relief agencies, including specialized United Nations bodies) appears to be functioning relatively satisfactorily through most of the country, its internal embargos and reported interference with the work of certain relief agencies in selected areas is evidence of a policy of discrimination in violation of articles 2, 11 and 12 of the Covenant on Economic, Social and Cultural Rights. The violations against those living in the Autonomous Region of Kurdistan are all the more objectionable because they appear to be directly linked to the Government's political goals of exacting concessions in any future autonomy negotiations.

8. The situation of women and children

84. Women and children are protected in general by the two Covenants of 1966 and in particular by articles 2 and 24 of the Covenant on Civil and Political Rights. In addition to the provisions of the Covenants,[sic] Iraq is obliged to respect the provisions of the Convention on the Elimination of All Forms of Discrimination against Women. As is often the case, however, women and children suffer both violations against themselves as individuals and hardships resulting from the violations committed against their husbands and fathers. Such violations as summary or arbitrary executions and disappearances have had a harsh impact on the lives of Iraqi women and children, if not as the victims, then as the survivors of victims. As the families of alleged "saboteurs", they have suffered the severest penalties; several of the cases of execution and disappearance that have been brought to the attention of the Special Rapporteur involve women and children, including infants.

85. One of the most serious allegations affecting women is that of systematic rape. According to information and testimony received by the Special Rapporteur, security personnel would sometimes rape a young women in order to later use her as an informant under the threat that her non-compliance would result in the revelation of her rape, thus subjecting her to public disgrace and ostracism. It has been alleged that some of these rapes were recorded on video-cassettes to be given to the victim's family in the event of non-compliance. Other women were reportedly raped simply as an act of insult or vengeance[sic] directed against their families. Testimony received from former Iraqi security officers corroborates these allegations.

86. Another unconfirmed allegation of discrimination against women is the allegation that women between the ages of 15 and 45 are still required to obtain an exit visa to leave the country, in contrast to men who are not. It has been explained that the purpose of this particular discrimination is to restrict women and their children from leaving the country to reunite with their husbands and relatives abroad or to otherwise escape the order of repression. Such a restriction would constitute violations of article[sic] 2 and article 12, paragraph 2, of the Covenant on Civil and Political Rights and article 2 of the Convention on the Elimination of All Forms of Discrimination against Women.

9. Property rights

87. Information received by the Special Rapporteur points to numerous violations of property rights under the terms of article 17 of the Universal Declaration of Human Rights (refers to the right of everyone "to own property alone as well as in association with others" and the right not to be "arbitrarily deprived" of property). In addition, property rights must be respected in so far as they relate to articles 17, 18 and 27 of the Covenant on Civil and Political Rights and article 15, paragraph 1 (a), of the Covenant on Economic, Social and Cultural Rights.

88. Allegations received by the Special Rapporteur focus on the conduct of the Government in four specific areas: action against alleged criminals; expulsion of those said to be of "Persian ancestry"; discrimination against the Turkoman population; and matters relating to religious and cultural property.

89. With respect to Iraqi action against alleged criminals, it appears to be a routine practice to confiscate both the movable and immovable property of persons accused of criminal activity. Whether or not such accusations have been proved in a court of law, and whether or not there have been convictions and sentences in this regard, seems to be irrelevant to the process of confiscation. As evidence of this apparently widespread practice, the Special Rapporteur heard considerable testimony and is in possession of numerous allegedly official government documents which attest to the practice. In this connection, document 6 in annex II to the present report specifically states that "criminals' movable and immovable property was confiscated because of their association with pro-Iranian subversive groups", while documents 3 and 6 specifically refer to the demolition of the houses of the families of criminals. On this last point, it is evident that the property rights of the said families have clearly been violated in an arbitrary fashion. The heavy impact that such confiscations and demolitions would have on the family members is evident.

90. The practice of confiscation attains an entirely different dimension in the context of the long-established practice of expulsion of those said to be of "Persian ancestry". Information and testimony received by the Special Rapporteur alleges that the process of expulsion was normally accompanied by the confiscation of all movable and immovable property belonging to those expelled. Aside from all types of personal property, confiscation extended to houses, real estate, and commercial property, including businesses. Having been stripped of their possessions and livelihood, these persons were then expelled from the country without any form of compensation.

91. The issue of discrimination against the Turkoman population in relation to property was raised by the Special Rapporteur in his interim report (A/46/647, paras. 48 and 89). While the Government of Iraq initially denied the existence of any such discrimination, responding that "all Iraqis are subject to the same legal regulations concerning the disposal of real estate" and justifying certain "administrative procedures" by the argument of halting the "increasing migration from rural areas" (see page 48 of the interim report), the Special Rapporteur observes in the Government's reply of 23 January 1992 that such "administrative procedures governing the ownership of land in the Iraqi governorates, including the governorate of Ta'mim, have been abolished and any citizen living in the latter governorate, regardless of his ethnic affiliation, is now entitled to acquire ownership in real estate without being obliged to follow any of the administrative procedures that were formerly in force". Acknowledging this admission of discrimination having taken place, the Special Rapporteur wonders what steps are being taken by way of restitution or at least compensation for those discriminated against.

92. As regards matters relating to religious and cultural properties, the Special Rapporteur is especially disturbed by reliable reports of expropriation, confiscation and destruction of properties belonging to religious and cultural communities, specifically with regard to the destruction of churches and mosques, the destruction of religious schools, the confiscation of books and artifacts, and the expropriation of titles to real estate and corporate entities. However, in so far as these matters are directly related to other violations affecting these communities, they will be addressed below.

93. While the violations referred to above are serious in their own right, the Special Rapporteur is even more concerned about the reported abuses that their lawful sanction has permitted. Specifically, it has been reported that the large amount of wealth often involved in such violations has caused various authorities to invoke spurious allegations as a means of obtaining desired property or injuring personal enemies. Such abuses appear to have occurred on a large scale, owing largely to the absence of the rule of law, as discussed above.

B. Violations affecting ethnic and religious communities

General observations

94. It should be noted that the observations made elsewhere in this report also cover cases involving the ethnic and religious communities of Iraq, as well as all other parts of the state population. In this chapter, attention is drawn to situations which particularly affect these communities.

95. As noted above, Iraq is a party to the International Convention on the Elimination of All Forms of Racial Discrimination. Paragraph 4 of article 1, paragraph 2 of article 2, and article 5 of this Convention lay down certain duties of States Parties with regard to the undertaking of special measures for the purposes of establishing and maintaining equality between racial and ethnic groups within a country. In this relation, it would seem that the internal blockade against the Kurds and actions taken by the Government of Iraq to enforce many of the other official activities described in this chapter are contrary to the obligations the Government has accepted under this Convention.

1. Violations affecting the Kurds

96. The Kurdish population in Iraq numbers between 3.5 and 4 million. With its own language, history and cultural identity, the Kurdish population is territorily identified with the north-eastern part of Iraq running from the plains of Kirkuk to the mountainous borders of Turkey and

Iran. While clearly identifiable as a cultural and linguistic minority in Iraq, Kurdish identity is not determined by any particular religious beliefs, although they are generally Sunni Moslems. Especially important, however, is the role of tribe or clan and its identity with traditional lands which have been cultivated for centuries.

(a) Genocidal practices

97. When large-scale violations of human rights are inflicted on one or more communities of a State population, in addition to those violations which have been directed against the population of the country as a whole, the question inevitably arises whether a government has engaged in genocidal practices as defined in article II of the 1948 Convention on the Prevention and Punishment of the Crime of Genocide to which Iraq is a State Party. In this instance, the inquiry must address allegations brought against the Government of Iraq relating to the mass murder and execution of Kurds, the destruction of Kurdish towns and villages, forced urbanization and internal deportation, limits on ownership of private property by Kurds in areas designated by the authorities for inhabitance by the majority population, restrictions on agricultural activities, and the use of excessive force, including chemical weapons, against the Kurds in times of conflict.

98. The Special Rapporteur has heard in person and received in writing several testimonies about mass executions and murder of Kurdish civilians. A particularly gruesome account describes in detail the mass murder of Kurdish men, women and children during the "Anfal Operations" (see para. 103 below) of the Iraqi armed forces in 1988. An eye-witness, who had served as a governmental employee assisting with the many trucks used to bring victims numbering in the thousands to the execution sites, outlined an operation and identified the location of the resulting mass graves. It is worth noting that this account coincides with the horrifying story told by a young boy who survived a very similar massacre.

99. Several other accounts detail alleged mass executions and other atrocities committed by the Government against the Kurds which go beyond the cruelty and brutality directed against the population at large.

100. It is clear that deliberate actions of the Iraqi Government have caused refugee flows, forced urbanization and internal deportation affecting hundreds of thousands of Kurds. Detailed reports allege the destruction of some four thousand villages affecting well over a million people. One such report running into hundreds of pages details with charts and maps the destruction of 3,839 villages, hamlets and towns, 1,757 schools, 2,457 mosques and places of worship and 271 hospitals and clinics, along with the deportation of 219,828 families. However, according to Mr. Jalal Talabani of the Patriotic Union of Kurdistan, 1,732 villages have been rebuilt to some degree during the past year.

101. Another alleged method employed by the Iraqi authorities and leading to Kurdish displacement has been the denial of or placing of limits on the ownership or use of private property by Kurdish civilians, including private homes and farmland, in areas which the authorities have designated for inhabitance by the majority population or have designated "prohibited security zones". The Special Rapporteur has thus received recent reports of houses having been demolished in Kirkuk and of the Government preventing sowing in nearby and other farming districts. A concerted programme of urbanization or "village amalgamization" as the Iraqi authorities called it (see document 2 in annex II) has consequently changed the lifestyles and threatened the culture of the hundreds of thousands of persons affected. Information and testimony received allege a policy aimed at ending the traditional agricultural practices of a large part of the Kurdish population; sowing and cultivation has frequently been forbidden in large areas said to cover up to 75 per cent of the arable land, seeds have been stolen, hundreds of poultry farms closed and explosive mines laid over large parts of traditional farmland. These practices (especially the laying of explosive mines which have caused and continue to cause terrible injuries and loss of life) have been instituted in particular in areas under dispute with regard to the delimitation of the proposed autonomous zone.

102. The use of excessive force, including chemical weapons, against the Kurds is an established pattern. The Special Rapporteur heard several eye-witness accounts by survivors of various attacks by the Iraqi armed forces using bombardments from the air and chemical weapons against the unprotected civilian populations, resulting in large numbers of deaths and injuries. Specific attacks have been well-documented (as discussed above). In addition, the Special Rapporteur has heard a number of other accounts concerning indiscriminate shelling and the use of other heavy weaponry against unarmed or lightly armed Kurds during the various stages of the March 1991 uprisings.

103. Perhaps the most heinous violations against the Kurds involve the systematic execution of the families of so-called "saboteurs". Documents said to be from Security offices in Kurdish cities corroborate the existence of a series of "Anfal" operations administered under the Office for the Organisation of the North between the autumn of 1987 and mid-1989. A great many of these documents would appear to refer only to confiscation of property, control of cattle movement and the closure of poultry farms, or the relocation of people into "amalgamated villages". However, when read as a whole and with the interspersed records of mass executions of "saboteurs" and their families, the scope of these operations becomes more and more apparent. Moreover, in as much as certain documents specify huge numbers of people (such as document 6, para. 5, in annex II) and other documents describe "saboteurs" as including the "Barzani group" (referring to the clan of that name), and in so far as none of the actions under these operations were subject to judicial review, it is evident that the scale of the operations was massive. Further, the previously referred to audio-taped conversation of the then Secretary General of the Office for the Organisation of the North (and present Minister of Defence) Mr. Ali Hassan al-Majid, confirms that these operations were indiscriminately aimed against Kurds as such. Hence, and in the light of the already over 15,000 names of disappeared Kurds that have been brought to the attention of the Special Rapporteur, Kurdish claims of some 182,000 disappeared persons cannot easily be dismissed. Thus, it would seem beyond doubt that these policies, and the "Anfal" operations in particular, bear the marks of a genocide-type design.

(b) The internal blockade

104. It is noteworthy that, at a time when the Iraqi Government is adamantly protesting against the embargo imposed by the international community, the same Government has put up an internal blockade on the import of food, fuel and medicines to the Kurdish areas of the country. Referred to by one Kurdish leader as "a siege within the siege", there can be no doubt that the internal blockade has resulted in more hardship for the most vulnerable in this part of the country. Particular

hardship has been endured by the Kurdish community during this cold winter as the Government instituted the blockade, including of paraffin for heating, on 23 October 1991, just as the winter started setting in. Implemented through a series of armed checkpoints on every route in and out of that part of the Autonomous Region which is under Kurdish control, scrupulous sentries confiscate the smallest quantities of food and fuel, leaving half a tank of gas in cars and burning the rest.

105. Apart from imports of basic goods, the blockage involves the wholesale withdrawal of civil services from Kurdish areas, either by removing centrally based civil servants or by withholding the salaries of local civil servants. Obviously, this practice has resulted in the denial or reduction of social and other services which a government is expected to render. Remuneration for pensioners is also being withheld.

(c) Autonomy

106. International human rights law provides for equality for individuals and groups of different national, ethnic, linguistic and religious origins within one and the same State. As a means of achieving this objective, the relevant international instruments prohibit discrimination and lay down rules concerning special measures and special rights for the benefit of those disadvantaged. In certain spheres of national life, such as in the fields of education, language, culture and religion, these rules are quite specific in nature and content, while States, still under the same obligation of guaranteeing and maintaining equality and non-discrimination, have so far enjoyed greater discretion in the regulation of other national sectors, such as those affecting their political and economic order.

107. The Government of Iraq has repeatedly emphasized the fact that it has chosen the path of suggesting autonomy for the Kurds. In itself, such a choice deserves praise because, although practised by many countries, it is not part of international human rights standards. However, in the light of the history and fate of these autonomy regulations and negotiations, not least in the light of recent and indeed current developments, serious doubts arise as to the significance of the autonomy which the Iraqi Government is willing to grant to the Kurds. The peaceful resolution of the conflict and harmonious relations appear low on the agenda of the Government. Its insistence on placing officials from security agencies within the autonomous zone, the arbitrary and unilateral delimitation of the Region's borders, and the ongoing internal blockade of food and fuel defeat the very purpose of the exercise.

108. At present, the negotiations on autonomy seem to have reached a complete impasse. In this context, it is worth repeating the clear and unambiguous statement of Deputy Prime Minister Tariq Aziz in conversation with the Special Rapporteur on 8 January 1992: discussing the issue of the negotiations on autonomy, Mr. Aziz asserted that "Iraq would be the first to recognize Kurdish independence". However, the Special Rapporteur equally notes the expressed will of the Kurdish representatives to resolve their disputes with the central authority within the framework of an autonomy agreement.

2. Violations affecting the Assyrians

109. According to information and testimony received by the Special Rapporteur, the Assyrians (a community primarily located in northern Iraq) have reportedly suffered continuous persecution since the coming to power of the Baath Party. The majority of the Assyrian population in Iraq belongs to the Christian faiths of Chaldae and Nestor, and, to a lesser extent, the Syrian-Orthodox Jacobites. Their total number is estimated at about one million, though some estimates are considerably higher.

110. Information received alleges that the Iraqi military destroyed large numbers of Assyrian villages throughout the past two decades, killing many of the inhabitants and forcing others to flee. The Assyrian community was also affected by mass internal deportations away from the northern border region. Further, it was reported that, in the course of air raids on Assyrian villages, after massacres, and after forced relocations, but also because of administrative regulations of the Baath party, numerous Assyrian churches and monasteries (some of them over one thousand years old) were destroyed. In 1987, for example, a total of 85 Chaldean and Nestorian monasteries and churches were reportedly destroyed.

111. In an appeal made to humanitarian and international organizations on 19 September 1988, Bishop Zia Bobo Doubatou, the leader of the Assyrian Eastern Church in northern Iraq, denounced the continuing oppression and persecution of both Kurds and Assyrians in the northern Iraqi governorates of Heenoy, Dohuk, Arbil, Kirkuk and Sulaimaniya. Bishop Doubatou asserted violations ranging from executions, imprisonment for political reasons and destruction of churches and monasteries to the razing of villages. In particular, the Bishop alleged the use of chemical weapons, poisonous gases, and phosphorous and napalm bombs in the regions of Berwari, Afra and Al-Sheikhan, causing the death and injury of thousands of people as well as the loss of their homes of more than 150,000 people who fled to Turkey or Iran. Although the Bishop's letter was written some two months after the ceasefire between Iraq and Iran, he also alleged that a border strip 50 kilometres deep had been evacuated by the military after the destruction of the villages.

112. Other information received by the Special Rapporteur includes lists of allegations concerning the destruction of villages and the deportation of people from the regions of Berwari Balla, Nahla ('Oqra), Zakho, Dohuk and Neeroy Reekan between 1969 and 1987. Among these, the case of Soureya village stands out: it is alleged that the villagers - numbering 700, including children, women and elderly persons - were killed and burnt at the hands of Lieutenant Colonel Abd al-Karim al-Jouhaifi.

113. Notwithstanding the testimony to the contrary of three Christian leaders received by the Special Rapporteur in the al-Rashid Hotel in Baghdad on the evening of 8 January 1992, reports of the violations referred to above were corroborated by official documents said to have been found in Iraqi security offices and by testimony received from victims and eye-witnesses. One such testimony was received from a former Iraqi soldier who claimed to have taken part in the destruction of several Assyrian villages in 1988.

3. Violations affecting the Turkomans

114. The Turkoman minority is considered to be the third largest ethnic group in Iraq. Originally from Central Asia, they began settling in Iraq one thousand years ago and still inhabit the north and middle of Iraq, concentrated mainly in the provinces of Mosul, Arbil, Kirkuk and Diyala. At present, it is said, they number some two million people.

115. According to information received, a declaration on the rights of ethnic minorities, dated 24 January 1970, originally permitted the use of the Turkoman language in

primary education and in newspapers and magazines. The Turkoman community was also granted permission for the broadcasting of radio and television programmes. However, according to reports, all of these rights were withdrawn a year later and the Turkoman population was subjected to systematic discrimination and abuse.

116. Alleged oppression and persecution includes arrest without charge, torture, internal deportation and exile, confiscation of personal and community properties, and execution. Such oppression and persecution is said to originate in a government policy to replace the Turkomans with Arabs in Kirkuk and other cities and towns where the Turkomans are particularly represented. In particular, Turkoman citizens of the Kirkuk and Ta'mim governorates are reported to have been subjected to restrictions on the purchase and sale of real estate (as discussed above); they have been allowed to sell only to Arabs.

117. Other communications addressed to the Special Rapporteur similarly denounce the discrimination suffered by the Turkoman minority, particularly the fact that they have been forced to leave their lands in the regions they have been inhabiting for centuries. It has further been alleged that, contrary to official statements according to which the Turkomans are considered a minority and thus granted the right to exercise all their cultural rights, the Iraqi Government obliged them to be registered either as Kurds or as Arabs. As such, the people are denied their rights as a Turkoman community.

4. Violations affecting the Shi'as

118. The Special Rapporteur has received considerable and significant information concerning the destruction, especially after the March 1991 uprisings, of the traditional culture of the Shi'as who constitute a large part of the population of Iraq. The Shi'a of southern Iraq are the descendants of the original population of Mesopotamia. Their culture, especially in their holy cities, has been described as extraordinarily rich.

119. With respect to violations affecting the community as a whole, certain events are relevant. For example, on 23 March 1991, the shrine of Immam Ali at Najaf was sacked and desecrated. This shrine is as sacred to the Shi'a as Mecca, since it contains the tomb of the Immam. All treasures stored in two large rooms of the shrine (jewels, gold and manuscripts) were said to have been taken by the Iraqi army. When the Special Rapporteur visited the vast Wadi al-Salaam cemetery, where Shi'a pilgrims from as far away as India and Afghanistan have been buried for over one thousand years, he noticed that a highway is being constructed over the graves in what is alleged to be an act of deliberate desecration; leaders of the religious community have not been consulted. In addition, the thousand-year-old Houza, the Shi'a university, was closed along with many other schools, private as well as religious, at Najaf, while libraries with manuscripts that constituted part of the Islamic tradition were destroyed.

120. The Government has also been waging a concerted attack against the Shi'a clergy. The number of clergy at Najaf had been reduced from eight or nine thousand twenty years ago to two thousand 10 years later and 800[sic] before the uprisings of 1991. It is alleged that virtually all of them are now under arrest or disappeared, as the Baath regime is seeking to destroy Shi'a culture by wiping out its traditional leaders of the *ulema* class. Several of them have allegedly been executed. Among those tortured and murdered was Ayatollah Bakr al-Sadr, a noted poet and author of famous works of Islamic philosophy. Among those who are still under constant surveillance is the 95-year-old Grand Ayatollah Abul Qasim al-Musawi al-Khoei, together with members of his family and staff, as well as teaching clergymen. Thousands of other Iraqis in the south are said to have suffered the same fate as the clergymen: arrests, imprisonment, torture and execution. It has been estimated that 150,000 people have been arrested in southern Iraq, 15,000 people from Najaf alone.

121. In the aftermath of the uprisings in March 1991, the shrine of Immam Hussain in Karbala was shelled, badly damaged and desecrated. The Baathists later claimed that this was the work of the rebels, but it seems inconceivable that the Shi'a would defile their holiest shrine in such a manner.

122. In Samarra, the third among the sacred cities of the Shi'a, the Special Rapporteur was able to establish that the only Shi'a *madrasi* (school) was destroyed and levelled. According to information received, this happened some weeks after the uprisings. In addition to this destruction, all the Shi'a clergy of Samarra, numbering some 48, have reportedly been arrested. Further, the Shi'a call to prayer, reinstated in a limited fashion in Najaf and Karbala, is said to be still prohibited in Samarra, as has been the Muharram mourning for Immam Hussain (the central religious ritual for all Shi'a Muslims) for the last five years.

123. In addition to the aforementioned, the Government's measures to suppress Shi'a religious and cultural rights have allegedly included:

(a) Restrictions on the public practice of Shi'a rites as prescribed by their religious notables;

(b) Seizure from the Shi'a *ulema* of the administration of the Holy Shrines;

(c) Surveillance and intimidation of worshippers in Shi'a mosques and halls;

(d) Closure of Shi'a religious colleges and universities and prohibition of religious seminars except under official sanction;

(e) Restriction on the movements of religious leaders and scholars, both within the country and in terms of travel abroad;

(f) The launching of frequent "informational" campaigns against Shi'aism, accusing it of deviationism and heresy;

(g) Prohibition or strict censorship in the publication of many Shi'a books, magazines and pamphlets, while the Government's own religious affairs units refuse to countenance the publishing of any Shi'a works, contemporary or traditional;

(h) Prohibition of the broadcasting of any radio or television programme with Shi'a content;

(i) The launching of a campaign to prohibit the application of Shi'a law on personal and family matters, such as in the rites of marriage, inheritance, etc.;

(j) Prohibition of communication between Shi'as outside Iraq and the Supreme body on religious authority in the city of Najaf al-Ashraf;

(k) Special restrictions affecting the religious students and scholars who remain.

124. Several other measures have been said to have been undertaken by the Iraqi Government in its policy against the Shi'a cultural heritage. These are said to include the following forms of educational repression:

(a) Closure of all Shi'a parochial schools;

(b) Prohibition of the teaching of the Shi'a creed in any form in the State school system which, in its official curriculum, teaches only a variant of the Sunnite creed, despite the fact that the largest number of school children are Shi'a;

(c) Nationalization, expropriation and closure of al-Fiqh College in Najaf (officially part of the state sponsored University of Kufa); reports indicate that this was the only remaining Shi'a academic religious college in Iraq teaching Shi'a theology and religious studies. According to these reports, its buildings have been converted into a commercial market and all of its students were transferred to the College of Shari'a (teaching Sunni theology) in Samarra, which is registered as part of the state-sponsored University al-Mustansariya;

(d) Nationalization, expropriation and closure of the Faculty of Islamic Jurisprudence and Literature at Baghdad, Department of Religion, which is attached to the Faculty of Shari'a at Baghdad University;

(e) Nationalization of the Faculty of Jurisprudence in order to attach it to the Ministry of Higher Education;

(f) Refusal of visas to foreign Muslim students in order to keep them from contributing to Shi'a religious scientific studies in Iraq, while other students and lecturers have been forced to leave the country under different pretexts, such as violation of the laws of residency.

125. The Special Rapporteur has received several lists containing the names of a large number of people detained by the Government, among them numerous people from the Grand Ayatollah's[sic] family, staff, and their relatives, and various Iranian, Lebanese, Indian, Bahraini, Afghani and Pakistani nationals (see, for example, appendix 2 to the interim report) as well as a list of religious scholars killed between 1974 and 1987. He has also received lists of large numbers of holy shrines, mosques, husainiyas and other religious institutions and schools, Muslim cemeteries[sic] and public libraries destroyed by the Government forces. Evidently, the situation of the Shi'a religious community is extremely serious. However, the situation of the Shi'a community in the southern marshes appears to be more urgent and so warrants particular attention.

126. In connection with the so-called "Marsh Arabs" (an ancient people living in the southern marshes), it is worth noting a series of articles published in *Al-Thawra* (the Baath Party newspaper) in April 1991, in which it was said that the Marsh Arabs are a "monkey-faced" people who are not "real Iraqis" but are rather the descendents of black slaves brought to the south in the Middle Ages. The articles condemn the Marsh Arabs' culture as "primitive, debased and un-Iraqi". Their habits of personal hygiene and their intellects are said to be inferior.

127. According to information received by the Special Rapporteur, the Iraqi army is said to encircle the region of the marshes at the present time. The army is said to dispose of several helicopter airports within the region. Recent and continuing measures instituted by the Iraqi military forces against the population of the marshes (including Marsh Arabs, internally displaced persons and refugees, and army deserters) are said to include the tightening of control over food destined for the area, the confiscation of boats, and the evacuation of all areas within three kilometres of the marshlands. Further reports indicate that military attacks have been launched against the Marsh Arabs between 4 December 1991 and 18 January 1992, resulting in hundreds of deaths. Animal and bird life have also been said to have been killed in large numbers, while the marsh waters themselves have allegedly been filled with toxic chemicals. The apparent recent and continuing nature of the policy aimed against this particular part of the Shi'a community is most disturbing.

C. Hostage taking and the use of persons as "human shields"

128. Iraqi acts of hostage-taking and the use of persons as "human shields" are two of the most conspicuous violations and are alarming in the complex of violations they reveal: the taking of hostages is contrary to the terms of article 13 of the Universal Declaration of Human Rights and article 12 of the Covenant on Civil and Political Rights, and it is strictly prohibited by article 34 of the Fourth[sic] Geneva Convention of 1949. While the Special Rapporteur has already addressed the issue in relation to the events leading up to the recent Gulf war (A/46/647, paras. 24 and 76), subsequent allegations indicate that these events were not unique, but rather reflect a pattern of behaviour going back to the beginning of the Iran-Iraq war. Specifically, testimony received in refugee camps in southern Iran concerned Iranian civilians who had been taken hostage by attacking Iraqi forces in the southern Iranian border regions as long ago as the early part of the Iran-Iraq war. This testimony asserts that many Iranian civilians were rounded up by occupying Iraqi forces and transported back to Iraqi camps where they were generally mistreated and tortured, if not arbitrarily executed. Witnesses claim that many Iranians[sic] were forcibly conscripted into the Iraqi army to return and fight the Iranian army, which would be a "grave breach" under the terms of article 147 of the Fourth[sic] Geneva Convention of 1949. Those who refused were subjected[sic] to summary execution, which would be a "war crime" under the terms of article 6 of the Charter of Nuremberg. Several of those so brought out of Iran remain missing, while others stripped of their identity documents appear stateless.

129. The story of hostage-taking involving Iranian civilians during the Iran-Iraq war parallels strongly the proven cases of hostage-taking during the occupation of Kuwait. The Government of Iraq originally took some several thousand non-Kuwaiti foreigners hostage in Iraq and Kuwait. The release of these persons before the start of the coalition's attacks was off-set by the taking of Kuwaiti and other civilian hostages (including, among others, Egyptians and Saudis). Although many of these persons escaped during the March 1991 uprisings in southern Iraq, and many others were released by the Government of Iraq as part of the ceasefire agreement, allegations remain to the effect that Iraq continues to hold 2,101 Kuwaitis along with small numbers of nationals of other States. For its part, the Kuwaiti Association to Defend War Victims (a non-governmental organization) has a list of 1,053 persons of various nationalities who are allegedly still being held hostage in Iraq; 546 of these cases reportedly involve persons who have either been seen in detention in Iraq or were seen being abducted during the occupation of Kuwait. In reply to these allegations of the continuing detention of hostages in Iraq, the Government has acknowledged that there remain a significant number of Kuwaitis in Iraq, but asserts that they are all at liberty to return and have simply chosen not to do so (E/CN.4/1992/64, para. 1).

130. According to reports from former hostages and according to testimonies received, those detained were subject to various forms and degrees of mistreatment. Allegations include: detention in inhumane conditions, lack of access to food and clean water, lack of medical treatment, the cutting of women's hair, beatings, rapes, and mental and physical torture. According to the testimonies of those formerly taken as hostages during the Iran-Iraq war, many were also forced to do labour while many others were arbitrarily or summarily executed. Aside from the clear breaches of human rights law that these allegations entail, such acts as are alleged are violations of article 27 of the Fourth[sic] Geneva Convention of 1949 and constitute "grave breaches" under article 147 of that same Convention. It is further to be noted that the killing of hostages constitutes a "war crime" in accordance with article 6 of the Charter of Nuremberg.

131. In as much as certain of those taken hostage were used as "human shields" to protect potential military targets, Iraq committed outrageous acts in violation of a host of human rights norms and in violation of article 28 of the Fourth[sic] Geneva Convention of 1949, which reads as follows: "The presence of a protected person may not be used to render certain points or areas immune from military operations". Article 23 of the Third Geneva Convention of 1949 similarly prohibits the use of prisoners of war as "human shields".

132. Given that many of the above allegations have been definitely proven, and given that Iraq has in fact admitted to the taking of hostages and the use of certain of them as "human shields", and given further that there can be no excuse for such grave breaches of the norms of international human rights and humanitarian law, the Special Rapporteur expresses the hope that appropriate compensation will be paid to the victims of these violations.

D. The plight of refugees

133. Undoubtedly the most striking testament to the situation of human rights in Iraq in recent years has been the decision of millions of Iraqi citizens to flee their homes in search of refuge. Perhaps this fact alone speaks volumes about the order of repression suffered for so long by so many. There can be no doubt that these people gave testimony with their feet to the extent of violations of human rights in Iraq.

134. During his January visits to Iraq and certain of its neighbouring countries, the Special Rapporteur saw with his own eyes the conditions these people had chosen to endure as refugees and heard with his own ears their stories of the outrages and indignities many of them had experienced and virtually all had witnessed. Of the over two million people who fled to the Kurdish hills and southern deserts to escape the indiscriminate attacks in March 1991 and the subsequent repression in April 1991, several hundreds of thousands of whom found temporary refuge in neighbouring countries, some 83,000 persons in Iran and another 33,000 in Saudi Arabia still remained in refugee camps at the time of the Special Rapporteur's visits in mid-January 1992. In the course of their flight, many became separated from their families or saw their very young, elderly and sick perish in the escape. Having left their homes and belongings behind them, these people now have to spend their lives as refugees. Many display the physical scars of their tortures, while all carry the deep emotional burden of their experience. Against this background, the Special Rapporteur cannot doubt that these refugees remain outside Iraq owing to a well-founded fear of persecution.

135. In assessing the causes of this flight of refugees, the Special Rapporteur observes that the arrival of refugees across frontiers corresponds directly with expulsions (forced eviction, confiscation of properties and the stripping of all rights and legal status), the use of chemical weapons against Kurds in 1987 and 1988, and the use of weapons of indiscriminate and mass destruction during the March 1991 uprisings.

136. It is clear that the Government of Iraq is responsible for the causes of this flight of millions of refugees and remains responsible for the continued suffering of these people, in addition to that of the hundreds of thousands of persons expelled in previous years.

III. GOVERNMENT CORRESPONDENCE

A. Replies to the Special Rapporteur's inquiries

137. The following texts constitute additional replies of the Government of Iraq to the memorandum of the Special Rapporteur which was addressed to the Minister for Foreign Affairs on 16 September 1991, together with some replies to questions put by the Special Rapporteur to various authorities during his visit to Iraq from 3 to 9 January 1992. These texts are reproduced in their entirety, including all annexes.

138. By a letter from the Permanent Mission of the Republic of Iraq to the United Nations Office at Geneva, Ref. 7/4/Special/589, dated 11 December 1991, the Government of Iraq communicated the following:

> "The Permanent Mission of the Republic of Iraq to the United Nations Office at Geneva presents its compliments to the Centre for Human Rights[sic] and has the honour to request it to transmit the following information to the Special Rapporteur of the Commission on Human Rights on Iraq:
>
> "1. During an investigation in due and proper form which was supervised by an examining magistrate, it was decided to release seven accused persons (see Annex I) in view of the lack of adequate evidence to convict them on the charges brought against them.
>
> "2. Four accused persons (named in Annex II) were arrested in accordance with a written order issued by the competent examining magistrate when it was established that they were involved in criminal acts of murder and rape during the disturbances. They confessed to the charges brought against them and they were duly indicted under the supervision of the examining magistrate so that they could be brought before the courts.
>
> "The Mission takes this opportunity to convey to the Centre for Human Rights the assurances of its highest consideration.
>
> Annex I
>
> 1. Karim Sami Farhan
> 2. Abbas Abdul Hussein Jasim
> 3. Muhammad Dhia' Abdul Amir
> 4. Haider Darib Muhsin
> 5. Jadir Abed Ni'ma
> 6. Ali Jallab Tahir
> 7. Haidar Kadhim Sa'id
>
> Annex II
>
> 1. Haidar Abbas Hussein
> 2. Abbas Jasim Muhammad
> 3. Ali Muslim Musa
> 4. Haidar Mahdi Ubaid"

139. By a letter dated 18 December 1991, ref. 7/4/Special/599, the Permanent Mission of the Republic of Iraq to the United Nations Office at Geneva communicated the following:

> "The Permanent Mission of the Republic of Iraq to the United Nations Office at Geneva presents its compliments to the Centre for Human Rights and has the honour to request the Centre to transmit the following to the Special Rapporteur of the Commission on Human Rights on Iraq:
>
> "With reference to paragraph 88 of the report prepared by the Special Rapporteur of the Commission on Human Rights on Iraq for the Third Committee of the United Nations General Assembly, contained in document A/46/647, the Iraqi authorities wish to state that, as already mentioned in their report submitted to the Special Rapporteur, which was annexed to the note dated 24 October 1991 from the Mission of Iraq at Geneva, the previous legislation shall be amended in a manner consistent[sic] with the multi-party system provided for in the Political Parties Act No. 30, which was promulgated on 1 September 1991. This legislation includes article 15, as amended, of Legislative Council (Autonomous

Region of Kurdistan) Act No. 56 of 1980. To this end, the Revolution Command Council promulgated Act No. 37 of 10 December 1991, amending the afore-mentioned Act No. 56. The text of the amendment reads as follows:

"Article 1

"Paragraph 1(c) of article 15 of the Legislative Council (Autonomous Region of Kurdistan) Act No. 56 of 1980 is hereby abrogated and replaced by the following text:

"(c): Believing in the independence, territorial integrity, sovereignty and national unity of Iraq; cherishing and taking pride in Iraq's heritage and glorious history and the achievements made during the national struggle, particularly the revolutions of 14 July 1958 and the glorious revolution of 17-30 July 1968; and undertaking not to adopt a hostile attitude towards the legitimate aspirations of the Arab nation to complete its liberation and achieve Arab solidarity and unity.

"Article 2

"This Act shall be published in the Official Gazette."

"The Mission takes this opportunity to convey to the Centre for Human Rights the assurances of its highest consideration."

140. By letter ref. 7/4/Special/43 dated 23 January 1992, the Permanent Mission of the Republic of Iraq to the United Nations at Geneva communicated the following:

"The Permanent Mission of the Republic of Iraq to the United Nations Office at Geneva presents its compliments to the Centre for Human Rights and requests that the following documents attached herewith be forwarded to the Special Rapporteur on human rights in Iraq:

"1. The replies of the Iraqi authorities to the Special Rapporteur's report contained in document (A/46/674) dated 13 November 1991.

"2. The replies of the competent Iraqi authorities to several questions raised by the Special Rapporteur during his visit to Iraq of 3 to 9 January 1992, which include the following:

"a. Table issued by the Department of Juvenile Reformatories indicating the numbers of youths detained.

"b. Table issued by the Department of Adult Reform Centres, indicating the names of the social reform centres in Iraq and the numbers of their inmates.

"c. Table indicating the number of persons sentenced to life imprisonment in accordance with article 1/225 of the amended Penal Code.

"3. Several decisions which had been annulled in accordance with the recommendations made by the Committees dealing with the review of exceptional laws and decisions, though the Special Rapporteur had previously been informed of the repealed Decree No. 140 of 1990 on the annulment of the Revolution Court and also Decree No. 460 of 1985 which stipulated the punishment of persons who are members of the Da'wa Party.

"4. As for the other questions raised by the Special Rapporteur, the Iraqi authorities are currently studying them so as to reply to the Special Rapporteur in due course.

"The Permanent Mission takes this opportunity to convey to the Centre for Human Rights the assurances of its highest consideration."

141. The following texts were appended to the letter of 23 January 1992:

"Paragraph 60

"We wish to state that Iraq was not forced to engage in acts likely to restrict human rights. However, the abnormal circumstances with which the country was faced had adverse effects on human rights, for reasons beyond our control.

"Paragraphs 63 and 64 (arbitrary detention)

"With regard to paragraph 63 of the report, we wish to draw attention to a typographic error in the text of article 92 of the Code of Criminal Procedure, in which the word "law" was omitted between two words at the end of the article[*][*. Translator's note: This error appears only in the Arabic version of document A/46/647 (the omission of "by law").] The true text of the article reads as follows: "No one may be arrested or detained without a warrant issued by a magistrate or a court of law, except in circumstances in which such is permitted by law". Accordingly, the conclusions drawn from that erroneous text should be rectified in the light of its correct wording. There can be no arrest or detention without a warrant from a magistrate or a court of law, except in circumstances in which such is permitted by law. There are no exceptions to those circumstances and no persons are detained on the basis thereof.

"With regard to habeas corpus, we have already pointed out that the provisions of article 1 (a) of the Code of Criminal Procedure cover this principle, which is therefore applicable since, under the terms of that article, any person who comes to know of the commission of an offence has the right to institute proceedings against the offender. The persons vested with this right obviously include the victim himself, his relatives or representative, or any other person.

"With regard to paragraph 64 of the report, we have already stated in our reply to the remarks contained in paragraph 63 that there are no exceptions to the rule set forth in article 92 of the Code of Criminal Procedure that would permit arrest or detention in circumstances other than those provided for by law. Concerning the allegations that "thousands of persons have been arrested and detained by government forces without ever being informed of charges against them, without access to legal counsel or due process of law, and without the opportunity to contact their relatives", we wish to reaffirm our previous reply to the effect that these allegations are of a general nature and are not based on specific cases that can be verified. In this connection, it should be noted that these allegations are politically motivated and intended to besmirch the Government's reputation.

"With regard to the need for clarifications concerning the reference in Revolution Command Council Decision No. 26 of 1971 to "non-political persons", and "breaches of public order and morality", the mention of "non-political persons" is clearly intended to restrict the Administration's authority so that politicians can under no circumstances be liable to detention; i.e. the objective is to protect politicians from the possibility of a broader interpretation or abusive application of this text, thereby averting any possibility of its application to politicians. The expression "public order and public morality" means the elements of social discipline and the need for the individual to observe the social conventions that might have a religious, ethical or social basis. These elements differ from one society to another and from one period of time to another. The important point is that there are patterns of individual behaviour which might lead to an infringement of the social rights of others or the moral values of society and preventive measures must therefore be taken against such individuals. This forms part of the concept that we have already explained in our reply. At all events, such measures are of an exceptional nature and are subject to appeal before the administrative courts.

"Paragraph 66

"While expressing its concern at the allegations made in regard to the cases of disappearance referred to in paragraph 66, the Government of Iraq reaffirms its desire to ascertain the fate of the persons who are alleged to have disappeared. The Government makes inquiries and carefully examines all the names received from the Working Group on Disappearances, the Special Rapporteur or any other body. However, it should be borne in mind that some major and disturbing obstacles still exist, such as the lack of State control in some border regions since the beginning of the Iraq-Iran war, particularly in the Autonomous Region in the north and in some parts of the Marshes in the south. This situation was aggravated by the Gulf war and the subsequent disturbances, which led to illegal movements by individuals over whom the State had no control. Many of them are undoubtedly living in special camps on Iraq's borders with Iran, Saudi Arabia and Turkey and this is creating further difficulties for the Government of Iraq in its endeavours to ascertain the fate of those missing persons, some of whom may be living in those camps. The emphasis that is being placed on this question is politically motivated and designed to besmirch Iraq's reputation. However, in spite of this situation and notwithstanding the Iraqi Government's awareness that this matter is being used to achieve well-known political aims to its detriment, the Government reaffirms its desire to cooperate with the United Nations with a view to reaching a final solution in this regard.

"Paragraphs 68, 69 and 70 (torture and inhuman or degrading practices)

"Paragraph 68 of the report states that the Government of Iraq chose to refrain from answering the questions concerning the allegations "of a general nature". We had replied that the statements made in that connection were of such a general nature that the Government of Iraq could not answer them unless details were provided concerning the incidents and persons concerned. Therefore, Iraq did not refrain from replying; it merely indicated that a reply was impossible for the above-mentioned reasons.

"With regard to paragraph 69 of the report, requesting details of acts of torture and inhuman or degrading practices during investigations and the actual extent of those practices in so far as they relate to the general allegations made to the effect that women and children were strapped to tanks during the disturbances, we wish to reaffirm that Iraq did not refrain from replying to those questions; in accordance with the requirements of accuracy and objectivity, it merely requested details concerning those incidents and the persons who were allegedly victims of that course of conduct so that the matter could be investigated and a reply given. We therefore once again stress the need for details concerning the incidents and the persons involved in those practices so that a legal investigation can be conducted. We deny that these alleged acts were committed by the armed forces.

"With regard to the reference to a number of Iraqi court judgements imposing penalties on some persons who ill-treated and tortured suspects under investigation, the judgements sent were those that had become final. We wish to emphasize, once again, that the courts are never indulgent towards persons guilty of these violations, who are punished severely in accordance with articles 332 and 333 of the Penal Code. The victims are also awarded compensation for the material and moral damage that they have suffered.

"With regard to paragraph 70 of the report, we reaffirm that the measures taken to implement the principles concerning the protection of persons from arbitrary detention, torture and other cruel treatment are indicative of Iraq's constant desire not only to respect those principles in its legislation but also to put them into actual practice, as explained in detail in our reply to the questions. With regard to the comment concerning the widespread nature of such practices, as alleged in the reports received by the Special Rapporteur, we wish to reply that, as stated in the comment itself, this information was received in the form of unspecified allegations. If the Special Rapporteur could provide us with details of specific incidents and persons, on the basis of the information received by him, we would be able to take the requisite legal measures against the offenders.

"Paragraph 78

"However, it is a well-known fact that the aggression against Iraq following the Gulf crisis, together with the change in Iraq's overall political circumstances, the delay in the promulgation of the Political Parties' Act and the unstable situation in the region of Kurdistan, led to the postponement of the promulgation of the Permanent Constitution.

"With regard to section K, concerning religious practices, cultural properties and the destruction of some holy places and centres of religious studies, in our reply to the Special Rapporteur we did not say that "local Shiahs, assisted by Iranian Shiahs, were committing outrageous acts of desecration and destruction against their own most holy sites". We say that gangs of subversives and perfidious traitors, instigated by hostile political bodies which took their orders from leaders outside the country, turned religious centres into bases for resistance against the government authorities. These bases were also used for purposes of torture, trials and executions by those same gangs. The Government has all the evidence needed to prove this.

"With regard to the practice of religious observances in Iraq, as referred to in paragraph 94 of the report, there are no restrictions except in the case of those which are incompatible with public order and which might have adverse consequences for society, in so far as some of them reflect reprehensible customs that are detrimental to the individual and the community.

"The damage caused to religious sites is currently being repaired by joint committees consisting of representatives of the Ministry of Awqaf (Religious Endowments), ministers of religion and local officials. This matter was clarified by the Minister of Awqaf and Religious Affairs during his meeting with the Special Rapporteur on 4 January 1992. With regard to banned religious books, a number of books have been banned due to the inter-communal bigotry that they promote, which poses a threat to the unity and future of society and is incompatible with the Islamic religion, the values and aims of society, and the laws in force.

"Paragraphs 79, 80 and 81, concerning the laws in force

"With regard to paragraph 79 of the report, we wish to reaffirm our reply to the effect that, from the time of its establishment, the Revolutionary Court was composed of three judges with a juristic background and the Department of Public Prosecutions was represented therein by a public prosecutor with a similar juristic background. The right of defence was guaranteed and the Court applied the provisions of the Penal Code. It followed the Code of Criminal Procedure, as applied in the ordinary courts. We also clearly indicated that this Court was abolished under the terms of Revolution Command Council Decision No. 140 of 1991 within the context of the abrogation of the laws, decisions and procedures of an exceptional nature which were necessitated by the abnormal circumstances with which the country was faced in past years.

"Only a few judgements were handed down by the Revolutionary Court pursuant to Decision No. 461 of 1985, Decision No. 840 of 1986 and article 200 of the Penal Code, as amended by Act No. 107 of 1974, Act No. 145 of 1976 and Act No. 111 of 1978. We wish to emphasize the fact that those decisions were originally promulgated solely in order to act as a deterrent and were not intended to be put into actual practice. This is a well-known practice in penal policy, particularly in exceptional circumstances, and is known as "promulgation of a text solely as a deterrent". We also wish to draw attention to two points that were emphasized in the general considerations: (i) the date of entry into force of Decision No. 840 was 4 November 1986, since it was promulgated on that date and not in 1980 as stated in the considerations;[*][*. Translator's note: This is a typographic error in the Arabic version of document A/46/647.] (ii) we wish to reaffirm our reply to the questions, in which we pointed out that the State, through its competent committees, is diligently reviewing all the exceptional laws, decisions and procedures, including the decisions referred to in the considerations. This is confirmed, inter alia, by the abolition of the Revolutionary Court and the abrogation of Decision No. 461 of 1985, etc. The measures that have recently been taken include prohibition of the televised broadcasting of pictures of accused persons unless a final judgement has been handed down or in very exceptional cases in which such is required in order to promote a feeling of social stability and security in the face of crimes against society. This applies to the comments made in the first sentence of paragraph 81 of the report. With regard to the second sentence of that paragraph, we wish to emphasize that political offences, as defined in article 21 of the Penal Code, are offences which are politically motivated or detrimental to public or individual political rights. However, under the terms of that article, an offence is not deemed to be political if it constitutes: (i) an offence committed for a base and selfish motive; (ii) an offence prejudicial to the external security of the State; (iii) an act of murder or attempted murder; (iv) an attempt on the life of the President of the Republic, or an act of terrorism; (v) an offence against morality and decency, such as theft, embezzlement, forgery, breach of trust, fraud, bribery and rape. This yardstick, which Iraqi law has adopted to define political freedom, is the same as that adopted in many other countries.

"Treatment of ethnic groups

"Legislative developments concerning the region of Iraqi Kurdistan since the publication of the interim report

"Further to the statements made in paragraph 88 of the interim report, concerning the requirements to be met by candidates seeking election to the Legislative Council of the Autonomous Region:

"In its reply to the Special Rapporteur's questions, Iraq referred to the amendment of its legislation in a manner consistent with the Political Parties Act No. 30 of 1991, which provided for political pluralism. The legislative provisions that have been amended include article 15, paragraph 1 (c), of Legislative Council Act No. 56 of 1980, as amended by Act No. 56 of 12 June 1986.

"Act No. 37 of 1991, which was promulgated on 10 December 1991 and published in the Official Gazette No. 3385 on 23 December 1991, amended article 15, paragraph 1 (c), of the Legislative Council Act to read as follows:

"(c) Believing in the independence, territorial integrity, sovereignty and national unity of Iraq; cherishing and taking pride in Iraq's heritage and glorious history and the achievements made during the national struggle, particularly the revolution of 14 July 1958 and the glorious revolution of 17-30 July; and undertaking not to adopt a hostile attitude towards the legitimate aspiration of the Arab nation to complete its liberation and achieve Arab solidarity and unity.

"The Special Rapporteur was duly informed of the above through the Iraqi Mission at Geneva. This text, which is consistent with the Political Parties Act No. 30 of 1991, will lead to the establishment of a country-wide multi-party political system.

"Concerning the power of the President of the Republic to nominate the President of the Executive Council

"Paragraph 88 of the interim report states that only the President of the Republic may nominate the President of the Executive Council who, in turn, controls the membership of that Council.

"The same paragraph goes on to say that: "... it would appear that the wishes of the President of the Republic are to be served rather than those of the Kurdish people themselves. This would seem all the more true in view of the quoted legislation that requires candidates for the Legislative Council (from which candidates for the Executive Council may subsequently be nominated) to 'believe in the leading role of the Arab Baath Socialist Party' ...".

"This paragraph does not distinguish between "nomination as a candidate" and "appointment". In fact, the power of the President of the Republic in this regard is confined to the nomination of a candidate to serve as President of the Executive Council; it does not extend to his actual appointment. This candidature is subject to a vote of confidence by the Legislative Council and, if the candidate fails to win the latter's confidence, the President of the Republic must withdraw his nomination and nominate someone else. Accordingly, the power of the President of the Republic in regard to this nomination is subject to the approval of the Legislative Council itself.

"The amendment of Legislative Council Act No. 37 of 1991, regulating the conditions for the nomination of candidates to serve on this Council, also applies to candidates for the presidency of the Executive Council and will therefore contribute to the achievement of political pluralism.

"Difficulties and obstacles impeding the optimum application of the Autonomy Act

"We believe that the visit which the Special Rapporteur paid to the region of Iraqi Kurdistan on 6 and 7 January 1992 in an atmosphere characterized by the absence of official (central and autonomous) authority there, as well as his meeting with Mr. Tariq Aziz, the Deputy Prime Minister, on his return from the Autonomous Region, helped to clarify the background underlying the external political interference which had made it impossible to surmount the obstacles impeding the establishment of a better formula for autonomy. Although the serious dialogue between the Government and the Kurdish parties has produced sophisticated formulas for autonomy, the continuation of this dialogue is being threatened by multilateral external interference in spite of the affirmation by the political leadership of its earnest desire to promote more extensive autonomy within the framework of Iraq's territorial unity and integrity and the principle of non-discrimination among its citizens. For this reason, in our first reply, we stated that the autonomy plan for Iraqi Kurdistan was not given a fair opportunity to achieve the objective for which the Autonomy Act was promulgated, since a combination of several negative factors had thwarted the plan, the legal framework of which could have been developed through serious dialogue free of external influences.

"We believe that the developments that have taken place in recent months, including the Special Rapporteur's visit to Iraq, have lent added weight to this point of view. The Government of Iraq emphasizes its desire and insistence that this dialogue should continue in an atmosphere far removed from external interference.

"The Turkoman minority

"We wish to point out that the administrative procedures governing the ownership of land in the Iraqi governorates, including the governorate of Ta'mim, have been abolished and any citizen living in the latter governorate, regardless of his ethnic or national affiliation, is now entitled to acquire ownership of real estate without being obliged to follow any of the administrative procedures that were formerly in force.

"Access to food and health-care requirements

"With regard to paragraph 95 of the interim report, we agree with the Special Rapporteur that obligations of non-discrimination arising under article 3[*][*. Translator's note: In this connection, the Special Rapporteur refers to article 2.] of the International Covenant on Economic, Social and Cultural Rights, do not depend on the degree of availability of the goods.

"Iraq has scrupulously respected the principle of non-discrimination in the distribution of basic foodstuffs, which are rationed. All the international organizations that have visited Iraq have testified to the equitable distribution of these goods in accordance with their availability, which is unquestionably insufficient by the international standards that have been adopted by the Food and Agriculture Organization of the United Nations. This equitable distribution is based on non-discrimination between citizens and residents and also among citizens themselves, regardless of their ethnic, religious or linguistic affiliation or the region in which they are living.

"With regard to paragraph 96, concerning the effect of the resolutions concerning the economic embargo on foodstuffs, a review of the series of Security Council resolutions shows that, although resolution 661 exempted foodstuffs in principle, resolution 666 vested the Security Council with the sole authority to assess the humanitarian circumstances that necessitates the import of foodstuffs. Moreover, the manner in which the Security Council has treated the question of the food security of the Iraqi people has been characterized by a politicization of this question since, although resolution 687 permitted the import of foodstuffs subject to prior notification, resolutions 706 and 712 subsequently made them subject to prior approval by the Sanctions Committee. Furthermore, without the provision of the resources needed to cover the cost of imports, the permission granted to import foodstuffs remains theoretical without any possibility of being put into practical effect.

"With regard to paragraph 97, in which the Special Rapporteur expresses concern that the Government of Iraq has not cooperated with the United Nations in the sale of oil for humanitarian purposes, we believe that Iraq's position on this question, and more specifically on Security Council resolutions 706 and 712, was explained to the Special Rapporteur during his meeting with the Deputy Prime Minister and the Minister for Foreign Affairs at Baghdad on 8 January 1992 and his meeting with Dr. Abdul Amir al-Anbari, Iraq's Permanent Representative at New York.

"Iraq has also submitted a document to the forty-eighth session of the Commission on Human Rights, under agenda item 7, concerning the effects of the economic embargo on the enjoyment of economic, social and cultural rights and Iraq's position in regard to Security Council resolutions 706 and 712.

"Through its dialogue with the United Nations, which began at Vienna on 7 January 1992 and is still continuing, Iraq is endeavouring to reach a positive solution on the question of the sale of petroleum.

"With regard to paragraph 98 of the report, concerning the government warehouses that are open only to State employees, we explained the reasons for this in our reply. These warehouses do not involve any discrimination among citizens, since their purpose is to help persons with limited incomes. Persons who are not State employees are able to join consumer cooperative associations. With regard to the increase in salaries, we explained that persons not employed by the State, i.e. those working in the private sector, were less affected by rising prices because their income increased in proportion to inflation.

"In reply to the Special Rapporteur's question concerning special measures taken to satisfy the needs of the most vulnerable sections of the population, such as infant children, lactating mothers, the elderly, the wounded and the sick, the State is endeavouring to satisfy their needs, within the limits of its available resources, since they are undoubtedly the most adversely affected by the economic embargo.

..."

B. Considerations of the Special Rapporteur

1. Information yet to be received from the Government

143. Before commenting on the substance of the replies the Special Rapporteur has so far received from the Government of Iraq, it is perhaps necessary to summarize those matters on which he has yet to receive any reply whatsoever. While the following list is not exhaustive, it reflects those matters to which the Special Rapporteur attaches considerable significance.

(a) The Special Rapporteur has yet to receive information on the number of applications for the equivalent of a writ of habeas corpus received and granted by the Government in the past year.

(b) The Special Rapporteur has yet to receive information on the number of persons taken into custody in the past year without the legal possibility of the equivalent right of habeas corpus.

(c) Notwithstanding the Government's oft repeated desire to cooperate, it has yet to indicate what procedural recourses are available for the investigation of reports of disappearances.

(d) The Special Rapporteur has yet to receive detailed replies to the specific individual cases of disappearance brought to the Government's attention in the memorandum of 16 September 1991.

(e) The Special Rapporteur has yet to receive information on the number of complaints of torture received, the number of investigations conducted, or the number of security personnel disciplined for each of the last four years.

(f) The Special Rapporteur has yet to receive information on the actual measures that have been taken to implement the Body of Principles for the Protection of All Persons under Any Form of Detention or Imprisonment and the Declaration on the Protection of All Persons from Being Subjected to Torture and Other Cruel, Inhuman or Degrading Treatment or Punishment.

(g) In addition to failing to respond to specific cases of allegations of extrajudicial killings (as noted in para. 73 of the interim report), the Government has failed to indicate whether or not a government inquiry has been established to look into the various allegations.

(h) The Special Rapporteur has yet to receive specific details of the civilian and military laws permitting prosecution of those responsible for orchestrating and carrying out extrajudicial killings.

(i) The Special Rapporteur has yet to receive information on the number of persons prosecuted in each of the last four years for extrajudicial killings.

(j) The Special Rapporteur has yet to receive an indication of the recourse procedures available to the relatives of victims of extrajudicial killings.

(k) The Special Rapporteur has yet to receive a response to the allegation of the Government's indiscriminate bombardment of residential areas during the March 1991 uprisings.

(l) The Special Rapporteur has yet to receive a response to the allegation that the Government gave instructions (during the March 1991 uprisings) to civilians to evacuate whole towns and larger centres, under threat of the use of chemical weapons and gases.

(m) The Special Rapporteur has yet to receive information concerning the percentage of cases heard by the Revolutionary Court that resulted in findings of guilt.

(n) The Special Rapporteur has yet to receive information on the percentage of trials by the Revolutionary Court and other special and temporary courts that were conducted *in camera*, or information on the percentage of defendants represented by lawyers of their own choosing.

(o) The Special Rapporteur has yet to receive information concerning the number of persons arrested for political offences each year since 1 January 1988.

(p) Irrespective of the fact that Mr. Ian Richter has since been released by the Government of Iraq, the Special Rapporteur remains interested in, but has yet to receive, most of the information requested in paragraph 42 of his interim report, especially a detailed description of the evidence upon which Mr. Richter was found guilty and spent five and a half years in prison.

(q) The Special Rapporteur has yet to receive information concerning the extent to which the Turkoman language may be used in public institutions in those regions with large Turkoman populations.

(r) The Special Rapporteur has yet to receive copies of the Iraqi laws pertaining to nationality and deportation, as requested in his memorandum of 16 September 1991 and reiterated in paragraph 90 of his interim report. Likewise, he has yet to receive information on the definitions of the terms "Iranians" and "foreigners" as found in the Iraqi laws in question.

(s) The Special Rapporteur has yet to receive information on the numbers of religious institutions and theologians as of 1 January 1988 in the cities mentioned in paragraph 51 (a) of the interim report.

(t) The Special Rapporteur has yet to receive information on the consultations held between the Minister of Awqaf and Religious Affairs and representatives of the relevant religious communities concerning reparations to the damaged religious institutions and properties.

(u) The Special Rapporteur has yet to receive replies to the allegations relating to various prohibitions and restrictions on religious practices ranging from traditional dress to the performance of rites.

(v) The Special Rapporteur has yet to receive a reply to the allegation that more than 1,000 religious books have been banned by the Ministry[sic] of Information.

(w) The Special Rapporteur has yet to receive information detailing the exact special measures the Government claims to have taken to respond to the needs of the most vulnerable, such as infant children, nursing mothers, the elderly, the wounded and the ill.

144. In addition to the information noted above, the Special Rapporteur awaits the reply of the Government of Iraq to his specific requests for information about the fate of those persons named on the following three lists handed to Mr. Tariq Aziz on 8 January 1992:

(a) 104 Shi'a clerics said to have been arrested in Najaf during the period 20-23 March 1991;

(b) 6 Shi'a clerics said to have been taken to Najaf with the Grand Ayatollah[sic] Al-Khoie on 20 March 1991, and never seen again;

(c) 238 persons said to have been recently executed in Kirkuk, according to a letter from Iraqi Intelligence dated 16 September 1991.

2. Observations on information received

145. With respect to the substance of the replies from the Government of Iraq replies to the inquiries of the Special Rapporteur, there are several points worth mentioning. In general, the replies of the Government are simply inadequate in the face of the extremely serious violations that have been alleged. However, on the basis of the information that the Special Rapporteur has so far received from the Government, the following observations are called for:

(a) With regard to the Government's reference to "abnormal circumstances" appearing under the heading "Paragraph 60", it is sufficient to refer to the comments made in chapter II.B above.

(b) With respect to the second paragraph under "Paragraphs 63 and 64 (arbitrary detention)", it has already been pointed out that mere legal provisions, such as "the right to institute proceedings", do not satisfy the requirements of international obligations unless there is an appropriate order through which such a right may be secured. For this reason, it is important to know how often such a right has actually been invoked.

(c) The third paragraph, under the heading "Paragraphs 63 and 64 (arbitrary detention) seems clearly to miss the point in stating that "there are no exceptions to the rule ... other than those provided for by law"; it is precisely these exceptions to the rule ("provided for by law" or not) that interest the Special Rapporteur. To put the question more directly: Exactly what exceptions are provided for by law? In this respect, it is of course also relevant that Decrees of the Revolution Command Council have the force of law.

(d) With regard to the "breaches of public order and morality" referred to in the last paragraph under "Paragraphs 63 and 64 (arbitrary detention)", the Special Rapporteur does not doubt the legitimacy of the notion, but is only concerned to know the substance of these prohibitions, the method of their determination and the way in which these prohibitions are implemented.

(e) Turning to the comments under "Paragraph 66", it cannot escape the attention[sic] of the Government that many of the cases submitted relate to events outside of war zones or areas of limited Government control. While it may be true that some of the "disappeared" may be displaced in various camps, such an argument does not explain many other cases. Indeed, given the scale and seriousness of the issue of disappearances, as discussed above, the reply of the Government that "emphasis ... on this question is politically motivated and designed to besmirch Iraq's reputation" shows insensitivity and disrespect for the families of those who continue to suffer the consequences, several of whom the Special Rapporteur has met.

(f) On the issue of torture, the Special Rapporteur insists that the matter is of such a grave nature and that the testimonies received from all parts so consistently indicate the same extreme practices that some reply is necessary beyond dismissal of the subject on the ground of its "general nature". At the very least, the Government should indicate the content of the specific measures it claims to have taken, indicating any preventive mechanisms it may be putting in place.

(g) In view of the Government's claim (at the end of the third paragraph under "Paragraph 78") that it has "all the evidence needed to prove" that others were responsible during the March 1991 uprisings for the desecration and destruction of various holy places, the Special Rapporteur would very much welcome such evidence being brought to his attention.

(h) Regarding the fifth paragraph under "Paragraph 78", the Special Rapporteur does not agree that the matter of consultations for reparations of religious sites was "clarified by the Minister of Awqaf and Religious Affairs during his meeting with the Special Rapporteur on 4 January 1992." Without doubting the existence of the "joint committees", the Special Rapporteur remains sceptical about the role of these committees and remains to be convinced of the existence of any genuine consultations in the absence of specific information from the Government about the composition and functioning of the committees and in the face of wholly contradictory information coming to the Special Rapporteur from reliable sources. As to the Government's admission of the banning of "a number of books ... due to the intercommunal bigotry they promote", the Special Rapporteur would appreciate a detailed and exhaustive list of these books, together with information on the exact terms by which they have been judged as promoting "intercommunal bigotry".

(i) With regard to the first paragraph under "Paragraphs 79, 80 and 81, concerning laws in force", the Special Rapporteur would appreciate precise information on the procedures by which the "right of defence was guaranteed" under the Revolutionary Court. Moreover, and regardless of the fact that the Revolutionary Court was abolished in 1991, the Special Rapporteur would like to know what steps have been taken to address the problem of persons still serving sentences handed down by that Court and to compensate those having improperly served penalties under judgement of that Court.

(j) In response to the Government's argument in the next paragraph that the cited Decisions were promulgated "solely as a deterrent", and that "only a few judgements were handed down by the Revolutionary Court" pursuant to them, it is to be observed that the mere promulgation of such a law as Decision No. 840 of 1986 (which, *inter alia*, subjects slanderers of the President, and others, to the death penalty) constitutes a violation of Iraq's obligations under international human rights law. Clearly, the effect, through fear, of this Decision would be to silence critics of the Government, thereby infringing upon the freedom of expression. Such fear and such an infringement would no doubt have been all the more pervasive and far-reaching given the fact that there actually were judgements rendered against "delinquents". On this point, it should be added that it is alleged that the actual use of these Decisions by security forces went far beyond "a few judgements".

(k) Near the end of the paragraph just referred to in the reply of the Government of Iraq, it is observed that what the Government contends is "not deemed to be political" under the terms of article 21 of the Penal Code includes "an offence prejudicial to the external security of the State", which seems to the Special Rapporteur to be a very broad notion and one perhaps even more broadly applied in Iraq during the conflicts that have run throughout most of the last decade. This is evidently the case in as much as the Special Rapporteur is in receipt of hundreds of official documents relating to arrest, detention and execution and referring very generally to "saboteurs".

(l) With respect to the third paragraph under the section on "the President of the Executive Council" of the Kurdish Autonomous Region, it is to be observed as a matter of logic that it would not be possible for the President of the Executive Council ever to be someone the President of the Republic did not approve owing to his prior control over all nominations. Hence, by controlling the process of nomination, the President of the Republic controls the process in general; any President of the Executive Council would be forever beholden for his nomination. So, there cannot be any apparent or real independence.

(m) In relation to the application of the Autonomy Act, and as already noted above, representatives of the Kurdistan Front made it clear to the Special Rapporteur that the real stumbling block in the negotiations concerned the insistence[sic] of the central authorities on the reintroduction of the security apparatus in the Autonomous Region.

(n) As concerns the Turkoman minority, it needs to be pointed out that while the removal of administrative procedures impacting upon their ability to acquire real estate is welcome, the effect of those previous procedures may well have been to alter the demographic make-up of certain specific localities. Consequently, the real issue is now one of reparation or compensation. To this end, the Special Rapporteur would be interested to know what measures have been taken.

(o) In reply to the Government's contention at the end of the second paragraph under "Access to food and health-care requirements" that "the permission granted to import foodstuffs remains theoretical without any possibility of being put into practical effect", the Special Rapporteur notes that the application of this formula would necessitate the solution of a number of technical problems. However, the Special Rapporteur finds it difficult to believe that it would have been impossible to find a solution for them. In any event, it comes as a surprise to read in the communication of the Iraqi Government of 23 January 1992 that "Iraq is endeavouring to reach a positive solution on the question of the sale of petroleum", only to be informed on 4 February 1992 that Iraq has decided to break off the negotiations on this subject. As a consequence of this action of the Government of Iraq, an opportunity to purchase food and medical supplies in the sum of some 900 million dollars has been lost. As a result, the poorest and most vulnerable of the population will suffer.

(p) The Special Rapporteur finds the assertion that those in the private sector are less affected by inflation because their incomes increase "in proportion to inflation" to be an interesting explanation for the large pay increases in Government salaries. In fact, in most societies, it is often the civil service that belongs to the best protected from inflation because of their indexed incomes and because of the Government's power to print money. Usually, it is the low end of the private sector and those on fixed incomes (pensioners and persons supported by the State) who are in the greatest need. In this connection, the Special Rapporteur continues to be interested to know precisely how the Government is "endeavouring to satisfy" the needs of the most vulnerable.

IV. CONCLUSIONS AND RECOMMENDATIONS

146. Since he was appointed in June 1991, the Special Rapporteur has received a constantly growing stream of information concerning human rights violations by the Government of Iraq, in the form of testimonies, written documents, photographs, videotapes and audiocassettes. It is to be expected that even more information will reach the United Nations Centre for Human Rights in the months to come. The evidence at present available might have been even greater if some people who were in a position to provide valuable evidence had not refused to do so because they were afraid, even after having been promised anonymity, that their relatives living in Iraq might suffer reprisals as a consequence.

147. The Special Rapporteur has carefully examined the evidence provided to him. He has been especially at pains to find out whether there might be any element in any information brought to his attention which would make it unreliable. As a consequence of this sifting process he has rejected some of the evidence.

148. The Special Rapporteur recognizes that the evidence he has received during the two months preceding the writing of this report, and especially the evidence he has received during his journeys to Iraq, Iran and Saudi Arabia, could not yet be submitted for comment to the Government of Iraq. On the other hand, he has to conclude that for many of the questions on which he did submit evidence to the Government of Iraq concerning human rights violations he either did not get a reply at all or received an unsatisfactory response. In any case, the evidence not yet submitted to the Government merely adds additional allegations to those which have already been submitted.

149. The Special Rapporteur does not discount the risk that, notwithstanding his considerable precautions, some exaggerations, mistakes or even falsehoods may have slipped through. But he also stresses the fact that the evidence he has collected shows remarkable consistency, even though it has come from a great number of different sources. Each testimony he received confirms the allegations that the State security services can deal with any Iraqi citizen as they see fit, without due process of law. Testimonies and documents received corroborate each other. For instance, it cannot possibly be maintained that the accusations concerning mass executions are just stories concocted by some exiles bearing a grudge against the Government of Iraq. As this report shows, there is a great deal of evidence supporting this allegation. Equally, the large number of people who complained to the Special Rapporteur about having been submitted to torture, and showed him the lasting effects on their bodies, provided irrefutable evidence of torture, often in its gravest forms, being practised on a very large scale. Also, it is not possible to explain away the long lists of people having disappeared by arguing that they might have been killed during the war or during the uprisings, or that they might have left for another country. Quite often, family members, neighbours or friends actually saw these people being arrested; afterwards, no more was heard from them. Finally, the Special Rapporteur feels obliged to point out that even persons who currently hold ministerial rank in Iraq apparently consider the execution of people suspected of being political opponents an acceptable practice. For example, Deputy Prime Minister Tariq Aziz stated during a discussion with the Special Rapporteur concerning the disappearance of a considerable number of Shi'a clerics: "If they have been executed, I am not going to apologize for this". For his part, the present Minister of Defence, Ali Hassan al-Majid, did not hesitate to state some years ago (in the recorded conversation referred to above), when he was Secretary-General of the Office for the Organization of the North, that his way of looking after the families of Kurdish "saboteurs" was "to bury them".

150. Weighing all the evidence he has assembled, the Special Rapporteur has no hesitation in concluding that there have been massive violations of human rights of the gravest nature for which the Government of Iraq may be held responsible. Nor is there any reliable indication that the Government of Iraq has taken steps to ensure that there will be no further violations of human rights.

151. With respect to the many violations which have occurred, the Special Rapporteur concludes that any special circumstances which may currently prevail in Iraqi society cannot be employed to justify exceptions from the applicable international human rights standards beyond what is allowed in the relevant derogation clauses, that is to say those of article 4 of the Covenant on Civil and Political Rights.

152. The volume of accumulated evidence described above, much of which the Special Rapporteur collected himself, leads to the firm conclusion that the Government of Iraq has systematically violated and continues to violate the international human rights obligations it has undertaken. The number of victims suffering from these violations is certainly in the hundreds of thousands, if not much higher. In the light of the above, meaningful improvement in the human rights situation in Iraq requires drastic changes in the conduct of government, including the review and revision of national legislation to make it consistent with the applicable international human rights instruments, the extension of the rule of law to all branches and levels of governmental activity, and guarantees for the independence and impartiality of a judiciary with jurisdiction over all these branches and levels of activity. Such changes have to be complemented by unambiguous measures aimed at securing the confidence of the population in the institutions.

153. With respect to the Kurdish minority, there is reason for special alarm because there have been human rights violations directed against the Kurdish people *as such*. Specifically, there have been violations of the Convention on the Elimination of All Forms of Racial Discrimination and of article 27 of the International Covenant on Civil and Political Rights. Moreover, whether or not the design and implementation of the Anfal Operations may actually constitute breaches of the Convention on the Prevention and Punishment of the Crime of Genocide, it is clear that the Anfal Operations constituted genocide-type activities which did in fact result in the extermination of a part of this population and which continue to have an impact on the lives of the people as a whole. Further, and in relation to the Anfal Operations specifically, there can be no doubt that particular individuals bear the burden of a large part of the responsibility.

154. Having studied the situation of human rights in Iraq, after having been to Iraq and after having met numerous persons inside and outside the country (at least such persons as would dare to speak), the Special Rapporteur concludes that the violations of human rights which have occurred are so grave and are of such a massive nature that since the Second World War few parallels can be found. Nor is it likely that these violations will come to an end as long as the security forces have the power to decide over the freedom or imprisonment, or even life or death, of any Iraqi citizen. With every day that passes, new names will be added to those of the thousands of Iraqi citizens who have been victims of human rights violations.

155. Given the legal and political order that characterizes the Government of Iraq, the Special Rapporteur concludes that the present order precludes full respect of human rights obligations. Specifically, so long as the rule of law remains undermined by the parallel orders of extra-judicial and even extra-legal rule, administered essentially by a security apparatus only accountable to the inner circle of the Presidency, there cannot be any meaningful enjoyment of human rights or any genuine respect for the dignity of the individual. Further, because it is clear that power over all three parallel orders of rule - "normal", "extra-judicial" and "extra-legal" - is concentrated in the persons of the President and a few senior members of the Government, special responsibility must accrue to these persons.

156. In the light of all of the above, therefore, the Special Rapporteur recommends that the Commission on Human Rights, confronted with such an intolerable situation, does not confine itself to condemnation alone. In his view, this exceptionally grave situation demands an exceptional response - a response that would have to be considered as disproportionate in most other cases of human rights violations. Specifically, the Special

Rapporteur recommends the sending to Iraq of a team of human rights monitors who would remain in Iraq until the human rights situation had drastically improved and who should be able to: (i) move freely in any part of Iraq; (ii) investigate information concerning alleged violations of human rights; (iii) visit, without prior notification and at the time of their choosing, places where persons are deprived of their liberty; and (iv) observe trials and court proceedings.

157. Considering the fact that thousands of persons are in danger of arbitrary detention, torture or execution, the Special Rapporteur urges that no effort be spared to ensure that the monitoring system comes into being as soon as possible. If the Iraqi Government could be persuaded to accept the monitors, this could be a highly significant step towards improvement of the human rights situation.

158. Irrespective of the reaction of the Government of Iraq to the formula of a human rights monitoring system, there are some other important steps which it ought to take in order to ensure that it respects the obligations which it has undertaken in accepting a number of human rights conventions. The Special Rapporteur therefore recommends that the Government of Iraq be urged:

1. To ensure that the activities of the security services are submitted to completely transparent legal constraints so that the arbitrary arrest, torture or extrajudicial execution of Iraqi citizens no longer occurs;

2. To set up a commission of enquiry into the fate of tens of thousands of disappeared persons. Such a commission should be able to work independently and without governmental guidance. Considering the atmosphere of fear prevailing in Iraq, the Government ought also to give a public promise, guaranteed by appropriate legal mechanisms, that no retaliatory action would be taken against citizens who ask the commission for information about the fate of family members who have disappeared. The commission of enquiry ought to have free access to any data the security and police services might possess about the fate of persons they have arrested since the present regime came to power. It should also be enabled to make its findings public at regular intervals and to make recommendations concerning the release of disappeared persons who might still be found alive;

3. To take measures to end the widespread practice of torture. The assurances of Ministers that those found guilty of practising torture will not escape punishment are clearly insufficient for the simple reason that, as long as torturers enjoy any degree of impunity and, indeed, protection from the government apparatus, scarcely any (former) prisoner or any of his relatives will dare to complain;

4. To renew the negotiations on a "food for oil" formula, which, once agreement has been reached, could enable the Government of Iraq to buy food and medical supplies with a total value of over 900 million dollars;

5. To end the blockade of the Kurdish controlled area of Iraq;

6. To restore full religious freedom to the Shi'a community, including control of their religious properties.

159. Finally, the Special Rapporteur notes Security Council resolution 688 of 5 April 1991 in which Iraq was called upon to "immediately end this repression" as "a contribution to remove the threat to international peace and security in the region". In as much as the repression continues, the Special Rapporteur can only conclude that the threat remains and thus extraordinary measures, such as the recommended broad-based human rights monitoring operation, are warranted.

E/CN.4/1992/84, at 166.

8. UN Commission on Human Rights, Resolution 1992/71, Situation of human rights in Iraq, 1992

The Commission on Human Rights,

Guided by the principles embodied in the Charter of the United Nations, the Universal Declaration of Human Rights and the International Covenants on Human Rights,

Reaffirming that all Member States have an obligation to promote and protect human rights and fundamental freedoms and to fulfil the obligations they have undertaken under the various international instruments in this field,

Mindful that Iraq is a party to the International Covenants on Human Rights and to other human rights instruments,

Recalling Security Council resolution 688 (1991) of 5 April 1991, in which the Council demanded an end to the repression of the Iraqi civilian population and insisted that Iraq cooperate with humanitarian organizations to ensure that the human and political rights of all Iraqi citizens were respected,.

Recalling also Security Council resolutions 706 (1991) of 15 August 1991 and 712 (1991) of 19 September 1991,

Recalling further its resolution 1991/74 of 6 March 1991, in which it requested its Chairman to appoint a special rapporteur to make a thorough study of the violations of human rights by the Government of Iraq, based on all information the Special Rapporteur might deem relevant, including information provided by intergovernmental and non-governmental organizations and any comments and material provided by the Government of Iraq, and to submit an interim report thereon to the General Assembly at its forty-sixth session and a report to the Commission at its forty-eighth session,

Recalling General Assembly resolution 46/134 of 17 December 1991, in which the Assembly expressed its deep concern at the flagrant violations of human rights by the government of Iraq and decided to continue the examination of the situation of human rights in Iraq at its forty-seventh session in the light of additional elements provided by the Commission on Human Rights and the Economic and Social Council,

Deeply concerned at the massive and grave violations of human rights by the Government of Iraq, such as summary and arbitrary executions, torture and other cruel, inhuman or degrading treatment, enforced or involuntary disappearances, arbitrary arrest and detention, lack of due process and the rule of law and of freedom of thought, of expression, of association and of access to food and health care, hostage-taking and the use of persons as "human shields",

Deeply concerned also at the fact that chemical weapons have been used on the Iraqi civilian population, at the forced displacement of hundreds of thousands of Kurds and at the destruction of Iraqi towns and villages, as well as at the fact that tens of thousands of displaced Kurds have to take refuge in camps and shelters in the north of Iraq and at the deportation of thousands of Kurdish families,

Deeply concerned further at the repressive measures taken by the Government of Iraq against the Shiah communities in Iraq, in particular those in the southern marshes,

Noting that, despite the formal cooperation extended to the Special Rapporteur by the Government of Iraq, this cooperation needs to be improved, in particular by giving full replies to the Special Rapporteur's inquiries about acts being committed by the Government of Iraq that are incompatible with international human rights instruments that are binding on that country,

1. *Takes note with appreciation* of the report on the situation of human rights in Iraq submitted by the Special Rapporteur (E/CN.4/1992/31) and the conclusions and recommendations contained therein;

2. *Expresses its strong condemnation* of the massive violations of human rights, of the gravest nature, for which the Government of Iraq is responsible, in particular:

(a) Summary and arbitrary executions, orchestrated mass executions and burials, extrajudicial killings, including political killings, in particular in the northern region of Iraq, in southern Shiah centres and in the southern marshes;

(b) Widespread routine practice of systematic torture in its most cruel forms, including the torture of children;

(c) Enforced or involuntary disappearances, routinely practised arbitrary arrest and detention, including of women and children, consistent and routine failure to respect due process and the rule of law;

(d) Hostage-taking and the use of persons as "human shields", a most grave and blatant violation of Iraq's obligations under international law;

(e) Suppression of freedom of thought, expression and association, violations of property rights;

3. *Deplores* the fact that the Government of Iraq has failed to comply with the terms of Security Council resolutions 706 (1991) and 712 (1991), and has thereby failed to provide the Iraqi population with access to adequate food and health care;

4. *Calls upon* the Government of Iraq to release immediately all persons arbitrarily arrested and detained, including Kuwaitis and nationals of other States;

5. *Expresses its particular concern* at the fact that the Special Rapporteur could find no reliable indication that the Government of Iraq has taken steps to ensure that there will be no further violations of human rights and concluded furthermore that meaningful improvement in the human rights situation in Iraq requires drastic changes in the conduct of government;

6. *Calls once again upon* the Government of Iraq, as a State party to the International Covenant on Economic, Social and Cultural Rights, as well as to the International Covenant on Civil and Political Rights, to abide by its freely undertaken obligations under these Covenants and under other international instruments on human rights, and particularly to respect and ensure the rights of all individuals irrespective of their origin within its territory and subject to its jurisdiction;

7. *Expresses its special alarm* at the repressive policies and practices directed against the Kurds which resulted in the extermination of a part of this population and which continue to have an impact on the lives of the Iraqi people as a whole;

8. *Expresses its deep concern* at the repressive measures taken by the Government of Iraq against the Shiah communities, in particular the suppression of Shiah religious and cultural rights;

9. *Strongly deplores* the exceptionally grave human rights violations by the Government of Iraq in recent years, which in the Special Rapporteur's view demand an exceptional response in the form of sending to Iraq a team of human rights monitors;

10. *Requests*, therefore, the Special Rapporteur, in consultation with the Secretary-General, to develop further his recommendation for an exceptional response and to report thereon to the General Assembly at its forty-seventh session;

11. *Urges* the Government of Iraq to set up an independent commission of inquiry to look into the fate of tens of thousands of disappeared persons;

12. *Regrets* the failure of the Government of Iraq to provide satisfactory replies concerning the violations of human rights brought to the attention of the Special Rapporteur, and calls upon the Government to reply without delay in a comprehensive and detailed manner so as to enable the Special Rapporteur to formulate the appropriate recommendations to improve the human rights situation in Iraq;

13. *Decides* to extend the mandate of the Special Rapporteur for a further year as contained in Commission resolution 1991/74 and requests the Special Rapporteur in pursuing his mandate to visit again the northern area of Iraq, in particular;

14. *Urges*, therefore, the Government of Iraq to accord its full cooperation to the Special Rapporteur of the Commission on Human Rights, notably during his next visit to Iraq;

15. *Requests* the Special Rapporteur to submit an interim report on the human rights situation in Iraq to the General Assembly at its forty-seventh session and a final report to the Commission at its forty-ninth session;

16. *Requests* the Secretary-General to provide the Special Rapporteur with all the necessary assistance in performing his task;

17. *Decides* to continue its consideration of the situation of human rights in Iraq, under the present agenda item, at its forty-ninth session.

E/CN.4/1992/84, at 293

9. Report of the UN Commission on Human Rights, the Situation of Human Rights in Iraq, 1992

...

487. At the 55th meeting, on 5 March 1992, the representative of Portugal introduced draft resolution E/CN.4/1992/L.76, sponsored by Argentina, Australia, Austria, Belgium, Canada, the Czech and Slovak Federal Republic, Denmark, Finland, France, Germany, Greece, Hungary, Iceland, Ireland, Italy, Japan, Kuwait, Liechtenstein, Luxembourg, the Netherlands, Norway, Portugal, Rwanda, Spain, Sweden, Switzerland and the United Kingdom of Great Britain and Northern Ireland. Lithuania and the United States of America subsequently joined the sponsors.

488. In introducing the draft resolution, the representative of Portugal orally revised it as follows:

(a) In the ninth preambular paragraph, the word "Kurdish" was replaced by the word "Iraqi" between the words "used on the" and "civilian population" and also between the words "destruction of" and "towns and villages";

(b) In operative paragraph 2(a), the words "the northern Kurdish region" were replaced by the words "northern region of Iraq";

(c) In operative paragraph 6, the words "including Kurds and Shi'ites" were deleted;

(d) In operative paragraph 7, the word "Kurds" after the words "lives of the" was replaced by the words "Iraqi people";

(e) In operative paragraph 13, the word "Kurdish" before the words "northern area of Iraq" was deleted.

489. In accordance with rule 28 of the rules of procedures of the functional commissions of the Economic and Social Council, the attention of the Commission was drawn to an estimate of the administrative and programme budget implications 1/ of draft resolution E/CN.4/1992L.76.

490. A statement relating to the draft resolution was made by the representative of Iraq.

491. A statement in explanation of vote before the vote was made by the representative of the Islamic Republic of Iran.

492. At the request of the representative of Iraq, a vote was taken on draft resolution E/CN.4/1992/L.76. The draft resolution was adopted by 35 votes to 1, with 16 abstentions.

S/23687, 7 March 1992

10. Further report of the Secretary-General on the status of compliance by Iraq with the obligations placed upon it under certain of the Security Council resolutions, 7 March 1992

[Extract]

...

Annex III

Comments from the Office of the Executive Delegate of the Secretary-General

Paragraph 2 of Security Council resolution 688 (1991) demands that Iraq end the repression (of the Iraqi civilian population in Iraq, including in Kurdish-populated areas).

Since late October 1991, serious restrictions on the supplies of essential commodities, in particular food and fuel, have been imposed by the Government on the three northern Governorates of Dohuk, Erbil and Suleimaniya. While these restrictions have not affected the three Governorates in a uniform manner, the population has experienced considerable hardship as a result: less than half of the regular food rations were distributed to the northern region during December. At the same time, the salaries of civil servants in the three Governorates have not been paid since November 1991.

On 9 December 1991, the executive heads (the Executive Delegate, the United Nations High Commissioner for Refugees, the Executive Directors of the United Nations Children's Fund and the World Food Programme and the Director General of the World Health Organization) expressed their concern in this respect to the Government of Iraq, noting that United Nations humanitarian agencies were not in a position to replace essential services and assure the provision of goods denied to the Kurdish population at large. The Government's position, as conveyed to the Coordinator and Special Representative in Baghdad, is that the restrictions have been imposed in view of the inability of the Kurdish leadership to maintain security and protect Government personnel and resources. To date, the series of discussions between the Government and representatives of the Kurdish leadership have not succeeded in putting an end to the supply restrictions.

By paragraph 3 of the same resolution, the Council "insists that Iraq allow immediate access by international humanitarian organizations to all those in need of assistance in all parts of Iraq and to make available all necessary facilities for their operations" ... and, by paragraph 7, it "demands that Iraq cooperate with the Secretary-General to these ends".

The Executive Delegate negotiated with the Government of Iraq and signed with the Minister for Foreign Affairs on 18 April 1991 a Memorandum of Understanding for the implementation of the United Nations inter-agency humanitarian programme in Iraq.

Paragraph 15 of the Memorandum provides that the Government of Iraq shall cooperate in granting international humanitarian organizations access to the parts of the country requiring relief, by air or road as needed, to facilitate the implementation and monitoring of the programme. Paragraphs 4 and 8 also provide for the Government's cooperation for the establishment of United Nations sub-offices and relief centres as required for humanitarian assistance.

On 24 November 1991, the Foreign Minister and the Executive Delegate agreed to renew and extend the Memorandum of Understanding up to the end of June 1992. In the new Memorandum of Understanding (paras. 3, 13, 14, 17 and 18), the Government commits itself to the extension of further cooperation for United Nations relief activities in facilitating access to those in need.

On the basis of this Memorandum, the Government has extended its cooperation in facilitating the access of United Nations agencies and other international organizations where necessary in most parts of Iraq. Repeated endeavours by the Executive Delegate, however, for the establishment of humanitarian centres at Kirkuk, in the north, and at Nasariya and Hammar, in the south, have not yet met with the approval of the Government. The Executive Delegate notified the Government that its refusal failed to comply with the letter and the spirit of the Memorandum of Understanding concluded with the United Nations for the implementation of the inter-agency humanitarian programme.

The Government's position in this respect, as conveyed to the Executive Delegate, is that, according to the Memorandum of Understanding, the establishment of United Nations humanitarian centres and the determination of humanitarian needs is to be undertaken "in agreement and cooperation with the Government of Iraq" and with due respect for the latter's independence, sovereignty and territorial integrity; given the need for agreement, the Government's refusal is not to be construed as a unilateral act.

Under the original Memorandum of Understanding, the Government committed itself to make available cash contributions in local currency to help to cover in-country operational costs while pursuing discussions regarding the establishment of a special exchange rate for relief operations carried out by the agencies and organizations participating in the programme. During 1991 Iraq accordingly contributed 1.5 million Iraqi dinar. Under the new Memorandum of Understanding, the Government undertook to make available cash contributions in local currency in the amount of 1 million Iraqi dinar at the beginning of each month. As of 17 January 1992, however, no such contribution had yet been received by the inter-agency programme despite repeated requests to this effect with the respective authorities.

S/23699, 11 March 1992

11. Note by the President of the Security Council, 11 March 1992

[Extract]

III. SECURITY COUNCIL RESOLUTION 688 (1991)

32. I should now like to refer to the demands by the Security Council with respect to the Iraqi civilian population. In paragraph 2 of resolution 688 (1991), the Security Council demands that Iraq, as a contribution to removing the threat to international peace and security in the region, end the repression of its civilian population. In paragraphs 3 and 7, the Security Council insists that it allow immediate access by international humanitarian organizations to all those in need of assistance in all parts of Iraq, and demands its cooperation with the Secretary-General to these ends.

33. The Security Council remains deeply concerned at the grave human rights abuses that, despite the provisions of resolution 688 (1991), the Government of Iraq continues to perpetrate against its population, in particular in the northern region of Iraq, in southern Shi'a centres and in the southern marshes (Commission on Human Rights resolution 1992/71 of 5 March 1992). The Security Council notes that this situation is confirmed by the report of the Special Rapporteur of the Commission on Human Rights (E/CN.4/1992/31, also to be circulated in document S/23685) and by the comments of the Office of the Executive Delegate of the Secretary-General contained in the further report of the Secretary-General.

34. The members of the Council are particularly concerned at the reported restrictions of the supplies of essential commodities, in particular food and fuel, which have been imposed by the Government of Iraq on the three northern governorates of Dohuk, Erbil and Suleimaniya. In this regard, as the Special Rapporteur has noted in his report, inasmuch as the repression of the population continues, the threat to international peace and security in the region mentioned in resolution 688 (1991) remains.

[Also submitted to the Council as Annex to S/24386, 5 August 1992.]

12. Letter from the UN Special Rapporteur on the situation of human rights in Iraq to the President of the UN Security Council, 30 July 1992

Excellency,

I have the honour to enclose herewith for your consideration an advance copy of the first part of my interim report to the General Assembly on the situation of human rights in Iraq. Please note that the enclosed is an unedited version; the final version will be edited and translated by the services prior to publication in two or three weeks.

By way of explanation, you may be interested to know that I was appointed by the Commission on Human Rights in 1991 to study the situation of human rights in Iraq and to report to the General Assembly and the Commission. Since my appointment, I have presented reports to each of these bodies. However, in view of the fact that the situation of human rights in Iraq is so grave, such as to have been the subject of Security Council resolution 688 of 5 April 1991 in as much as the internal repression is seen to be the direct cause of instability in the region, I believe it is important for the Security Council to be fully informed of the current situation of human rights in Iraq.

As President of the Security Council, I trust you will appreciate the relevancy of my report for the Security Council. In this connection, perhaps you will see fit to circulate copies of the enclosed report to the members.

...

Introduction

Subsequent to Commission on Human Rights resolution 1991/74 of 6 March 1991, entitled "Situation of human rights in Iraq", Mr. Max van der Stoel was appointed by the Chairman of the Commission to serve as Special Rapporteur of the Commission on Human Rights on the situation of human rights in Iraq. Pursuant to the terms of resolution 1991/74, as approved by decision 1991/256 of 31 March 1991 of the Economic and Social Council, Mr. van der Stoel took up his duties in an individual capacity and subsequently delivered an interim report (A/46/647) to the General Assembly on 13 November 1991, following with his full report (E/CN.4/1992/31) to the Commission on Human Rights on 18 February 1992.

On the basis of the Special Rapporteur's reports to the General Assembly and Commission on Human Rights, his mandate was extended for a second year by Commission resolution 1992/71 of 5 March 1992. Resolution 1992/71 received the approval of the Economic and Social Council in decision 1992/241 on 20 July 1992. Accordingly, Mr. van der Stoel was requested to submit an interim report to the forty-seventh session of the General Assembly and a final report to the forty-ninth session of the Commission on Human Rights.

In the light of the considerable number of serious allegations of human rights violations especially occurring[sic] in the southern marsh area of Iraq, several of which emanate from reliable sources and certain of which the Special Rapporteur has been able to independently confirm, the Special Rapporteur feels that the urgency of the situation is such as to require the division of his report into two parts. While Part One of the Special Rapporteur's interim report concerns itself with the current situation in the southern marshes, and elaborates to some degree the previous recommendation for the sending of human rights monitors to Iraq as part of an exceptional response to this exceptional situation, the Special Rapporteur must emphasise the fact that he is actively studying the situation in the rest of the country and will be submitting Part Two of his interim report in due course. In this regard, the Part Two shall appear as an addendum to the present report.

The special alarm that strikes the Special Rapporteur at this time relates to the reliable and disconcerting information that Iraqi military forces have launched a series of attacks against the civilian population in the marsh area which borders the Islamic Republic of Iran. As international humanitarian agencies have been withdrawing, there remains little or no source of protection or support for the victims. Thus, the Special Rapporteur is of the opinion that immediate steps must be taken in response to what appears to be a deteriorating situation, before too much irreparable damage is done and too many individuals are victimized.

Although the situation in the southern marshes warrants special and immediate attention, it would be wrong to neglect the human rights situation elsewhere in the country. In fact, there is unfortunately no reason to assume that the situation of human rights has improved since the Special Rapporteur concluded in his report of 18 February 1992 (E/CN.4/1992/31) that it was so exceptionally grave as to require exceptional steps aimed at curbing the repression. Indeed, there are even more reasons to take steps insofar as the present situation of human rights in Iraq continues to constitute a violation of mandatory Security Council resolution 688 of 5 April 1991 which demanded that Iraq immediately end its policy of repression in order to contribute to peace and security in the region.

The exceptional step that the Special Rapporteur continues to have in mind is the sending of teams of human rights monitors to all parts of Iraq (including that part of Iraqi Kurdistan from which the Iraqi authorities have withdrawn, but which is affected by the internal blockade and where it is alleged that Iraqi Government actions constituting human rights violations frequently take place). In this relation, the Human Rights Commission decided to extend the mandate of the Special Rapporteur with the specific instruction that, with reference to his proposal to send human rights monitors to Iraq, the Special Rapporteur "develop further his recommendation for an exceptional response" in consultation with the Secretary-General (resolution 1991/71, operative paragraph 10). Subsequently, the Special Rapporteur had consultations on the subject with, inter alia, the Secretary-General and Members of the Security Council. The elaboration of the Special Rapporteur's original proposal is therefore contained within this first part of his interim report.

I. The situation in the southern marshes

The southern marsh area of Iraq is a vast maze of lakes and waterways, clotted with reedbeds and islands, which is inhabited by a unique people who trace their origins back to before 3,000 BC. The exact number of people who live in the marshes is unknown, but several hundreds of thousands live in small towns and villages on the edges of the area. Millions more populate the cities of Baasra, Nassiriya and Amara which are located near the marsh area.

According to a variety of reports brought to the attention of the Special Rapporteur, there appears to be a resurgence of grave violations of human rights by the Government of Iraq against the population in the area in various ways. Viewed together, the Special Rapporteur has considerable cause for concern that there is in fact a specific policy aimed at the Marsh Arabs in particular. In this connection, the Special Rapporteur is especially cognizant of a video-tape in his possession wherein the present Prime Minister is heard to instruct late last year several Iraqi Army Generals to "wipe-out" three specified Marsh Arab tribes. The same video-tape, portions of which have been broadcast on various national television networks, shows Iraqi Army personnel apparently training to carry out assaults on the population, with some portions of the video-tape appearing to show actual interrogations and raids in progress. In this context, then, the many recent reports of full-scale military attacks on southern marsh villages are extremely disturbing and may be seen as the manifestation of a preconceived policy.

Certain of the recent reports of military attacks on the civilian population were taken up by the Special Rapporteur on extrajudicial, summary or arbitrary executions in an urgent appeal to the Government of Iraq. Expressing the same and many other concerns, the Special Rapporteur on human rights in Iraq has also addressed a letter to the Government of Iraq, a copy of which is annexed to this report. Clearly, the greatest immediate concern is for the lives of the people. Military attacks on civilians, whether on the basis of orders against particular individuals or as part of indiscriminate mass bombardments, clearly violate the rights to life, personal integrity, and due process of law. Indeed, such attacks constitute assaults against the essential principles of any rule of law compatible with the very notion of human rights.

In the Special Rapporteur's report of 18 February 1992 (E/CN.4/1992/31) to the Commission on Human Rights, certain concerns were raised in relation to the Marsh Arabs who are also Shi'a Muslims. At that time, the Special Rapporteur considered the policies affecting them as partly related to their religious beliefs. However, it is here worth recalling that the Special Rapporteur also cited a series of articles in *Al-Thawra* (the Baath Party newspaper) which characterized the Marsh Arabs as an inferior and "un-Iraqi" people. These sinister and ominous references may now be viewed in relation to the current wave of repression.

The most blatant violations of human rights being perpetrated by the Government are constituted by the military attacks against the civilian population. In the past, small military operations have been explained by the need to seek out so-called criminal elements who had sought refuge in the marshes. These persons were generally said to be either military deserters or participants in the March 1991 up-risings and who were accused of murder or rape. However, the Special Rapporteur cannot understand how indiscriminate bombardments of civilian settlements could possibly be justified by police actions directed against a small number of individuals. As pointed out by the Special Rapporteur on extrajudicial, summary or arbitrary executions in his recent urgent appeal concerning these attacks, the Government of Iraq must respect the rights to life and physical integrity included in the Universal Declaration of Human Rights and the International Covenant on Civil and Political Rights. Further, the tactics employed by the Government in using military attacks are completely incompatible with their obligations to provide for due process of law such that innocent persons are not wrongly penalized and such that guilty persons are nevertheless dealt with according to a rule of law including a fair and public trial. In the face of confirmed reports of artillery bombardments and reliable reports of considerable troop movements and fixed-wing aircraft flights in the region, it would seem clear that the level and nature of force being employed in the region for whatever purpose exceeds by far the standards detailed in the Basic Principles on the Use of Force and Firearms by Law Enforcement Officials and the Code of Conduct for Law Enforcement Officials (General Assembly resolution 34/169 of 17 December 1979).

According to information received by the Special Rapporteur, a series of military attacks are alleged to have commenced as of early July 1992. Initial artillery attacks are said to have been aimed at certain tribes concentrated in the villages named in the letter to the Iraqi Foreign Minister which is annexed to this report. The main activities appear to have focused on villages southwest of the city of Amara. In the villages of Adil, al-Salaam, Maimona and al-Majar, curfews were in effect prior to the commencement of bombardments. Following the bombardments, reliable reports indicated that local hospitals and medical clinics showed significant increases in patients being treated for related injuries. As a result of the continuing military operations, there have also been reports of disappearances.

At the same time as the local population has been suffering stepped-up military attacks, the Government of Iraq has apparently also been proceeding with the forced relocation of Marsh Arabs and inhabitants of the neighbouring villages. According to certain reports, the programme of village amalgamization is justified by the Government by the necessity to bring these people closer to better medical and other services. Some Marsh Arabs are said to have been given new homes closer to places of fixed employment. The precise "necessity" of these relocations has still to be sufficiently explained, but it is clear that many of the persons affected were unwillingly moved in violation of their human right to freedom of movement. On this point, the Special Rapporteur cannot help but to recall the programme of forced relocations, village amalgamization and internal expulsion that constituted part of the "Anfal Operations" waged by the Government of Iraq against the Kurdish population in the late 1980s.

In addition to the programme of forced relocations of the local population, the Government of Iraq has held the marsh area subject to an internal economic blockade for some time. By restricting the inflow of basic foodstuffs and medicaments needed by the inhabitants, it is alleged that the Government is trying to draw people out of the relative protection of the marshes in order to control the population and arrest those labelled "criminals". In this connection, it has also come to the attention of the Special Rapporteur that the Government of Iraq has acted to cause the international non-governmental humanitarian agencies previously working in the area to withdraw, thus leaving the local population with even fewer sources of assistance. As the United Nations family of humanitarian agencies also scales down its presence, concern for the well-being of the people increases.

Perhaps the greatest threat to the inhabitants of the southern marshes is posed by the enormous water diversion programme which is proceeding at a rapid pace. Known as the "Third River Project", the Government programme to create another central waterway in the region for the purpose of irrigating salted flats will clearly result in the draining of much of the marsh area of its watercover, surrendering the silty soils to the dry air. As the reedbeds become exposed, they die, further contributing to the deterioration of the environment; this process is said to have been sped up by the occasional burning of reeds. Insofar as the Marsh Arabs are integrally linked to this special natural environment, they are threatened both in terms of their daily needs (which are largely met through fishing) and in terms of the survival of their ancient culture. Quite apart from potentially serious environmental effects, the programme may also be seen as a method to facilitate Government control over the population in the area. In the opinion of the Special Rapporteur, the Government's programme of the "Third River Project" should be immediately brought to a halt pending a comprehensive environmental assessment and consultations with the affected population.

Considering the developments recounted above, the Special Rapporteur is of the opinion that, irrespective of the reply the Iraqi Government may send to his appeal of 29 July 1992, there is an urgent need to send a team of human rights monitors to the specific region of the southern marshes. These monitors would constitute an independent source of reliable information following the course of events in the marsh area.

II. A system of human rights monitoring

A. Introduction

While the notion of a body of a human rights monitors serving a Commission on Human Rights appointed Special Rapporteur would definitely be an innovation, it is to be observed that the basic idea of human rights monitoring is neither new to international relations in general nor to United Nations practice in this field in particular. Indeed, it is rather clear from the important existence of a human rights dimension in many recent peace-keeping and peace-making operations (e.g. El Salvador and Cambodia) that monitoring of the human rights situation at the least, often accompanied by active encouragement of specific improvement, has become a normal element of an adequate response to such situations. Incorporating a monitoring operation into the service of the Special Rapporteur would thus seem a natural and logical development appropriate to the local situation. Indeed, given the terms of Security Council resolution 688, in relation to which the Special Rapporteur has commented on the obvious link between the human rights situation in Iraq and the interest of maintaining peace and security in the region, it would seem almost imperative that some kind of instrument be developed to assess compliance by Iraq, just as mechanisms have been developed to assess Iraq's compliance with other terms of the same and other resolutions which concern, e.g., weapons of mass destruction. Simply, an occasional visit by the Special Rapporteur is not enough. Through a monitoring mechanism providing a continuous flow of reliable information, the Special Rapporteur could better assess the continuing situation of human rights in Iraq and contribute constructive criticisms and comments.

B. The operation

Based on his own experience, consideration of the specific situation in Iraq, and informed by examination of other monitoring operations, the Special Rapporteur recommends that a relatively small operation of some number of mobile teams of monitors be sent to Iraq. Obviously, such a complex human rights situation as that in Iraq could well warrant a more comprehensive system of monitoring. Nevertheless, the Special Rapporteur believes that the placement of a limited number of mobile teams would prove very helpful and be appropriate to the need. The precise number and placement of teams would be determined with due account to logistical factors and prevailing conditions in the various parts of the country.

...

...

ANNEX

The following is the text of a letter, dated 29 July 1992, from the Special Rapporteur addressed to the Minister for Foreign Affairs of the Republic of Iraq.

"Excellency,

As Special Rapporteur of the Commission on Human Rights on the situation of human rights in Iraq, I find myself in receipt of a considerable number of reports of serious human rights violations said to have been committed by your Government in recent weeks in the area of the southern marshes. The sudden increase in the number of these reports, emanating from a wide variety of sources, together with the breadth of specific allegations that they caste, is particularly alarming. Moreover, insofar as reliable information received appears to demonstrate a policy of aggression directed by Government authorities against the population inhabiting the southern marshes, i.e. principally the so-called Marsh Arabs, I find myself bound to appeal to your Government to cease any and all activities as may constitute violations of its obligations under international law.

In terms of general allegations, it has come to my attention that the Government of Iraq is moving rapidly ahead with the so-called "Third River Project" in the south, in the framework of which large parts of the marsh area are being drained ostensibly to irrigate salted flats. Coupled with the alleged use of defoliants and the reported burning of reedbeds, the essential environment intrinsically linked with the lifestyle and ancient culture of the Marsh Arabs is being threatened, without the affected population ever having been consulted. The population inhabiting the marshes is itself being forcibly relocated into population centres in the region, as was apparently recently admitted by Assembly Speaker Saadi Mehdi Salleh. At the same time, there are reliable reports of artillery fire being directed against purely civilian targets in and around the marshes, including entire villages, causing growing numbers of deaths and injuries while many others are said to have lost their homes and been forced to flee. Of general effect is also the economic situation which has been exacerbated by a continuing internal blockade against the region and its population.

By way of referring to specific cases, it has, for example, been reliably reported that the villages of Adil and Al-Salam, some 30 kms south-west of Amarah, were evacuated and burnt earlier this month. Heavy artillery, fire bombs and even strafing have been reportedly used against the local population in recent weeks. Mounting casualties have been observed in the local medical centres.

Certainly, I am also aware of the urgent appeal that the Special Rapporteur on extrajudicial, summary or arbitrary executions recently addressed to you subsequent to most disconcerting reports of widespread deaths, arrests and disappearances resulting from attacks on 9 and 10 July 1992 on the villages of Shumbaara, al-Awaili, al-Kabab, al-Mouzar, Abu Saboor and Um al-Hosh, and attacks on 15 July on the villages of al-Wadia, Um al-Hosh, al-Mouzar and al-Hajia. Of course, I share the concern that civilian protections and human rights, especially effective protection of the rights to life and physical integrity, do not appear at all to be respected. In relation to these concerns, I urge your Government to bring an immediate halt to what appear to constitute repressive activities in the region and to respect the rights of the unique minority population located therein. In this connection, I would like to draw your Government's particular attention to Security Council resolution 688 of 5 April 1991, which calls upon the Government of Iraq to end its repressive policies which constitute a threat to international peace and security in the region. I would also urge your Government to consult the local population about such major projects as appear to be constituting a threat to their immediate livelihood and the survival of their culture.

Accept, Excellency, the assurances of my highest consideration.

...

13. S/PV.3105, 11 August 1992

The PRESIDENT (interpretation from Chinese): I should like to inform the Council that I have received a letter from the representative of Iraq, in which he requests to be invited to participate in the discussion of the item on the Council's agenda. In conformity with the usual practice, I propose, with the consent of the Council, to invite that representative to participate in the discussion without the right to vote, in accordance with the relevant provisions of the Charter and rule 37 of the Council's provisional rules of procedure.

There being no objection, it is so decided.

At the invitation of the President, Mr. Al-Anbari (Iraq) took a place at the Council table.

[3-5] **The PRESIDENT** (interpretation from Chinese): In letters dated 7 August 1992 addressed to the President of the Security Council from the Chargé d'affaires *ad interim* of the Permanent Mission of Belgium to the United Nations, the Chargé d'affaires *ad interim* of the Permanent Mission of France to the United Nations, the Permanent Representative of the United Kingdom of Great Britain and Northern Ireland to the United Nations, and the Chargé d'affaires *ad interim* of the United States Mission to the United Nations, documents S/24393, S/24394, S/24395 and S/24396, respectively, it is requested that the Security Council extend an invitation to Mr. Van der Stoel under rule 39 of the provisional rules of procedure of the Council.

The question to be decided by the Council is an invitation under rule 39 of the Council's provisional rules of procedure to Mr. Van der Stoel in his personal capacity.

[6] **Mr. GHAREKHAN** (India): It is the consistent position of the Indian delegation that the various organs and bodies of the United Nations should restrict their deliberations and actions within their respective spheres of competence as defined under the Charter. Deviation from the Charter, in which the nations of the world have reposed their faith and support, could erode that confidence and have grave consequences for the future of the Organization as a whole.

We recognize that matters relating to the situation in Iraq come up before the Security Council on account of Iraq's illegal occupation of Kuwait in 1990. The Security Council has dealt effectively with that situation and remains vigilant against any breach of international peace and security. The Council can focus its legitimate attention on the threat or likely threat to peace and stability in the region but it cannot discuss human-rights situations *per se* or make recommendations on matters outside its competence.

It is in this context that my delegation has reservations about the appropriateness of the Security Council's inviting Mr. van der Stoel. Matters pertaining to human rights should appropriately be discussed by the Commission on Human Rights or the General Assembly, which are the organs competent to do so. In the present case, the requests before us from some members of the Council to invite Mr. van der Stoel to assist in its deliberations, under rule 39 of the provisional rules of procedure, would appear to impinge directly on this consistent position of my delegation.

We note that the requests made for inviting Mr. van der Stoel contain references to Security Council resolution 688 (1991). My delegation abstained on that resolution for reasons mentioned in the explanation of vote at the time of adoption of that resolution. At the same time, my delegation has noted the explanations given by the sponsors of this request, as well as the [7] statement just made by you, Mr. President, to the effect that Mr. van der Stoel is being invited strictly in his personal capacity and not in any representative capacity.

Mr. AYALA LASSO (Ecuador) (interpretation from Spanish): Permit me to express Ecuador's view in connection with the request made by the representatives of Belgium, France, the United Kingdom and the United States to have the Council meet on an urgent basis in order to hear Mr. Max van der Stoel speak in his personal capacity.

Three of the four petitioners declare that the repression of the civilian population in Iraq constitutes a threat to international peace and security. All four recall resolution 688 (1991), in which the Security Council decided, among other things, to keep the question under consideration. The four also request that the Council invite Mr. Max van der Stoel in accordance with rule 39 of the Council's provisional rules of procedure.

According to rule 39 of the provisional rules of procedure of the Council,

> "The Security Council may invite members of the Secretariat or other persons, whom it considers competent for the purpose, to supply it with information or to give other assistance in examining matters within its competence."

Mr. Max van der Stoel, in his capacity as Special Rapporteur of the Commission on Human Rights on Iraq, has submitted a report distributed as an official document of the Security Council, as was the case with the report submitted to the Commission on Human Rights on 18 February 1992. The Security Council does not intend to examine the report of Mr. van der Stoel or to take a stand on it. If it were to do so, it would be disregarding the competence of the General Assembly and of the Economic and Social Council, and would be [8] attributing to itself authority that it does not have.

Indeed, Articles 10 through 17 of the Charter reflect the responsibilities of the General Assembly and Article 13 specifically refers to its competence as regards human rights and fundamental freedoms. Chapter IX of the Charter refers to international cooperation in connection with economic and social matters, and Article 55 refers to fundamental freedoms and respect for human rights. Article 60 says that responsibility in this respect shall fall to the General Assembly and, under its authority, to the

Economic and Social Council, whose powers are described in Chapter X. Among the powers and functions of the Economic and Social Council, according to Article 62, are those having to do with the promotion of and respect for human rights and fundamental freedoms.

The Economic and Social Council established the Commission on Human Rights in 1946 and that Commission appointed Mr. Max van der Stoel Special Rapporteur on the Human Rights situation in Iraq. Mr. van der Stoel, in that capacity, has submitted his reports to the Commission on Human Rights and to the General Assembly. The Economic and Social Council, acting within its lawful competence, has expressed itself in this connection. Therefore, since the Security Council does not have competence in matters relating to human rights, it would not be possible for it either to examine the report of Mr. van der Stoel or to take a stand on it. Furthermore, it must be recalled that the Security Council, on 5 April 1991, adopted resolution 688 (1991), in which it condemned the acts of repression committed by Iraq against the Iraqi civilian population in many parts of the country,

> "including most recently in Kurdish populated areas, the consequences of which endanger peace and security in the region" (*resolution 688 (1991), para. 1*).

[9] The Security Council adopted that resolution because it felt that the mass violations of human rights and the resulting flow of refugees to international borders endangered international peace and security in the region. In other words, the Council decided to act on this matter, which is not normally part of its competence, because a phenomenon had come about that could affect international peace and security, the maintenance of which is the primary responsibility of the Security Council.

In addition, the Council considered it necessary to reaffirm the principle of

> "commitment of all Member States to the sovereignty, territorial integrity and political independence of Iraq and of all States in the area" (*resolution 688 (1991), seventh preambular para.*)

It also recalled the provisions of "Article 2, paragraph 7, of the Charter of the United Nations" (*resolution 688 (1991), preambular para. 2*). In other words, the Security Council felt that resolution 688 (1991) did not affect those basic principles because a situation had come about in connection with the maintenance of international peace and security, which was the reason why it was possible for the Security Council to act.

The delegation of Ecuador voted in favour of resolution 688 (1991) and thus agreed with the Council's assessment, although it made it clear that matters relating to human rights *per se* do not fall within the competence of the Security Council. It is important to point out that the four countries that have requested this meeting of the Council invoke resolution 688 (1991), pursuant to which Mr. van der Stoel, in his personal capacity, would be invited to provide information on matters that are within the purview of the Security Council. Ecuador therefore understands that the invitation to [10] Mr. van der Stoel does not in any way affect or increase the normal authority of the Council, because this invitation falls within the scope of a resolution already adopted, and should be understood to reflect all the limitations inherent in that resolution itself.

[11] **Mr. Mumbengegwi** (Zimbabwe): Zimbabwe fully subscribes to the principles enshrined in the Universal Declaration of Human Rights and is a firm believer in the principle that abuses of human rights, where they are alleged, should be open to scrutiny in accordance with the obligations of Member States by the appropriate organs of the United Nations and as provided in existing regional and international conventions relating to human rights.

However, we are all aware that there is a division of responsibility among the various organs of the United Nations. Such a division of responsibility is not by accident and therefore needs to be taken very seriously. The Security Council has the primary responsibility for the maintenance of international peace and security. Not too long ago, in this very Chamber, my delegation expressed in the need for caution in the manner the Council interprets its mandate. Indeed, it can be argued that everything that happens has a bearing on international peace and security. This kind of approach would clearly render other organs of the Organization redundant.

Under the present circumstances, it is clear to my delegation that the issue of human rights belongs to the Commission on Human Rights and the General Assembly. The Commission on Human Rights, in the exercise of its mandate, appointed Mr. van der Stoel as its Rapporteur on Iraq. His report has been circulated to all members of the Security Council. We have all read it and are all aware of its contents.

As far as my delegation is aware, Mr. van der Stoel's report has not yet been considered by the United Nations organ that commissioned it. My delegation has taken note of the explanations given by the co-sponsors that the Security Council is not meeting to receive Mr. van der Stoel as the Rapporteur on Iraq appointed by the Commission on Human Rights but that the [12] Council was receiving him purely in his personal capacity. Let me state here that Zimbabwe believes that all information that can help the Security Council execute its mandate more effectively should be brought to the attention of Council members. In this context, my delegation welcomed the circulation of Mr. van der Stoel's report to Council members for their information.

What is of concern to my delegation is the tendency of the Security Council to encroach on the mandates of other organs of the United Nations Organization. If this trend continues, there is bound to arise a serious institutional crisis which can only be to the detriment of this world body.

The President (interpretation from Chinese): I will now speak in my capacity as representative of China.

The Chinese delegation is of the view that the competence of the Security Council is to deal with matters bearing upon international peace and security. Questions of human rights ought to be dealt with by the Commission on Human Rights. These questions have never been within the scope of the Council's mandate. Mr. van der Stoel is the Rapporteur appointed by the Commission on Human Rights. It is natural and right that he should be accountable to the Commission and that he should report to it on his work.

In our view, inviting Mr. van der Stoel to participate in the meetings of the Council is inappropriate. The Chinese delegation therefore expresses its reservations in this regard.

I now resume my capacity as President of the Security Council. The observations made will be reflected in the records of the Security Council.

If I hear no objection, may I take it that the Council agrees to extend an invitation under rule 39 of the provisional rules of procedure to Mr. van der Stoel?

There being no objection, it is so decided.

[13] The Security Council will now begin its consideration of the item on its agenda.

The Security Council is meeting in response to the requests contained in letters dated 7 August 1992 addressed to the President of the Security Council from the Chargé d'affaires, a.i. of the Permanent Mission of Belgium to the United Nations, the Chargé d'affaires, a.i. of the Permanent Mission of France to the United Nations, the Permanent Representative of the United

Kingdom of Great Britain and Northern Ireland to the United Nations, and the Chargé d'affaires, a.i. of the United States Mission to the United Nations, in documents S/24393, S/24394, S/24395, and S/24396, respectively.

I should like to draw the attention of members of the Council to document S/24386, letter dated 3 August 1992 from the Chargé d'affaires, a.i. of the Permanent Mission of Belgium to the United Nations addressed to the President of the Security Council, and document S/24388, letter dated 6 August 1992 from the Permanent Representative of Iraq to the United Nations addressed to the Secretary-General.

Members of the Council have received photocopies of a letter dated 10 August 1992 from the Chargé d'affaires, a.i. of the Permanent Mission of the Islamic Republic of Iran to the United Nations, which will be issued as document S/24414.

The first speaker is Mr. Max van der Stoel, to whom the Council has extended an invitation under rule 39 of its provisional rules of procedure. I invite him to take a place at the Council table and to make his statement.

[14-15] **Mr. VAN DER STOEL**: On 17 June, the Ministry of Health of Iraq provided me with information about the health situation of the Iraqi people. It is a shocking report. For instance, it says that the number of deaths caused by various types of dysentery is now five to six times higher than in preceding years. A cholera epidemic has broken out and 1,270 cases requiring treatment have been reported. Dozens have died. The report claims that respiratory diseases are 7 to 8 times higher than in the past. Infant mortality has also risen sharply.

I have not yet been able to check the accuracy of this data, but in my opinion there is little doubt that the poorer sections of the population in particular are suffering. The Government food-rationing programme, with its low prices, provides the population with only 1,400 calories per person per day, while large parts of the population cannot afford the high prices for additional food on the free market.

All this underlines the need for a quick breakthrough in the endless negotiations on the implementation, on the basis of Security Council resolutions 706 (1991) and 712 (1991), of the so-called "food for oil" formula. In this way, a rapid improvement of the nutritional situation could be achieved.

[16] It is also obvious that if the health of the population is deteriorating as rapidly as these data suggest, there is an even increased need for uninterrupted international humanitarian assistance.

Against that background, I can only express my alarm at the fact that the humanitarian aid programme in Iraq is at present inexorably grinding to a halt. The Government of Iraq has refused new visas for eight workers who were due to come into the country under rotation schemes. It has refused to renew the visas of those who were staying. They are, moreover, subjected to various forms of harassment.

Even more dangerous incidents are reported from the Kurdistan area in the north of the country. Restrictions on the supply of fuel for humanitarian agencies add to their difficulties.

While complaining about the effect of the embargo against Iraq, the Government of Iraq has not hesitated to impose an even stricter embargo against the population of the marshes in the south and against the population of the governorates in the north which are no longer under Government control. The embargo against the population in the north has even tightened in recent weeks. Virtually no food supplies are coming in. The supply of petroleum products has been cut. As reserve stocks dwindle, prices increase rapidly in the north. A constantly increasing number of Kurds are discovering that their income is no longer sufficient to provide for their most basic needs. They are forced to sell their possessions in order to stay alive. As petroleum products get more and more scarce, people start to cut wood; if this continues, the danger of deforestation will become very real.

As it is summer now, the situation is at present alleviated to some extent by the fact that there is a supply of local products like vegetables [17] and fruit. But with the coming of winter the situation would worsen dramatically.

In the eighties, tens of thousands of Kurds were killed as a consequence of the repressive policies of the Government of Iraq. Now a new danger is threatening the Kurds: hunger. If the Government of Iraq continues its present policy of tightening the embargo against the Kurds, there will be only one method to avoid a new human tragedy - that is, a massive humanitarian aid programme for the north.

In this respect, I must recall resolution 688 (1991), which the Security Council adopted in April last year. In operative paragraph 3 of that resolution the Council

> "Insists that Iraq allow immediate access by international humanitarian organizations to all those in need of assistance in all parts of Iraq and to make available all necessary facilities for their operations". (*resolution 688 (1991), para. 3*)

Clearly, the present policy of the Government of Iraq, which makes it virtually impossible for international humanitarian organizations to continue their work, constitutes a clear violation of this resolution.

In this respect, I must also make a comment about the hit-and-run raids that have occurred in the north in recent months. The Government of Iraq denies any responsibility for them. But, on the other hand, it is difficult to imagine that such acts would be committed by Kurds, who, whatever their differences, all have a clear interest in the continuation of the humanitarian work in their area.

The rapidly deteriorating food situation in the north has so far attracted little international attention. Human tragedies elsewhere in the [18] world may provide an explanation for this. But, in my view, we cannot afford to forget that in the Kurdish area of Iraq, too, thousands of human lives are at stake. It is essential that steps be taken right now to avoid a catastrophe in the coming winter. First and foremost, it is necessary that the international humanitarian organizations be enabled to resume their work in the north without being endangered or hindered in any way.

If, as I fervently hope, current negotiations with the Government of Iraq lead to agreement on unimpeded continuation of the work of international humanitarian organizations in Iraq, the United Nations, in my view, cannot afford to forget the situation in the marshes in the south. The population of the marshes is also subjected to a food embargo, even though such a policy of discrimination by a State against a part of its own population constitutes a clear violation of articles 2, 11 and 12 of the Covenant of Economic, Social and Cultural Rights, to which Iraq is a party.

The population of the marshes is in urgent need of humanitarian relief. But the Government of Iraq has never allowed international humanitarian organizations to establish a presence there. This, again, constitutes a violation of paragraph 3 of resolution 688 (1991), which speaks of immediate access to all those in need of assistance in all parts of Iraq.

The Government of Iraq, while condemning the United Nations embargo as inhuman and endangering the health situation of the country, does not hesitate to pursue a food blockade against parts of its own populations - which constitutes a threat to the most basic human right: the right to life.

The life of the population of the north and of the population in the marshes in the south is also threatened in a more direct way. In the north there is intermittent shelling by Government forces of parts of the Kurdish [19-20] area. Even more critical is the situation in the marshes. Since early June there has been an alarming increase of military activity. There have been artillery bombardments of parts of the marsh areas. There are reports of fixed-wing aircraft carrying out attacks. And, even though there are days when no attacks take place, there are reports of heavy casualties among the civilian population. Moreover, people are forced to leave their villages and to accept relocation in new settlements - an ominous development because in the late eighties, during the so-called Anfal operations against the Kurds, similar measures were used to subdue them. And then, finally, causeways are being built to dry sections of the marshes. These works, carried out without any consultation with the local population, constitute a threat both to their daily needs, which are largely met through fishing, and in terms of the survival of their ancient culture.

[21] All these developments serve to point to the same conclusion: The Government of Iraq is now in the process of undertaking a major operation to subdue the population of the marshes. The "Anfal operations" in the north against the Kurds in the 1980s have shown how ruthless such a campaign can be. There is no evidence at all that might lead to the conclusion that this time a more humane approach will be followed. The Government of Iraq claims that criminals are hiding in the marshes. But how can this justify air attacks and artillery bombardments, which clearly affect an innocent civilian population?

Security Council resolution 688 (1991) demands, in paragraph 2, that Iraq, as a contribution to removing the threat to international peace and security in the region, should immediately end this repression. What has been happening in the southern marshes in recent weeks constitutes a flagrant violation of that paragraph. Nor are there any signs that the policy of repression in other parts of Iraq has been discontinued.

Permit me to summarize my main conclusions concerning the present human-rights situation in Iraq.

The first is that while it is even more urgent than immediately after the end of the Gulf war that international humanitarian organizations should be able to perform their task to the full, continuous harassment, travel restrictions and refusals to grant visas rapidly make continuation of their work virtually impossible.

The second is that the food blockade against the Kurds in the north and the Shiites in the southern marshes can rapidly lead to a situation in which famine can be avoided only by a major international relief operation.

[22] The third is that recent artillery bombardments and attacks by fixed-wing aircraft in the area of the southern marshes point to the start of a major military effort by the Government of Iraq to restore its control over that region, whatever the cost in human lives.

In the late 1980s the world looked on passively as the Government of Iraq conducted operations against the Kurds that resulted in the extermination of a part of the population. I hope that members of the Council will agree that everything possible ought to be done to avoid a repetition of that tragedy.

Iraq has a totalitarian regime, which uses totalitarian methods to crush any opposition or even any dissenting opinion. As I have demonstrated in the report for the Commission on Human Rights which I published last January, many thousands of people have disappeared in Iraq after being arrested by the security services. It is likely that many of them have been liquidated. Several witnesses have testified that summary executions have often taken place. I have spoken with many people who have been subjected to the gravest forms of torture. Iraq has in the past not refrained even from using chemical weapons against the Kurdish population.

I must also express great concern over the treatment of the Shia clergy. After the uprising in the north in the spring of last year, many have been arrested. Efforts on my part to obtain information about their fate from the Government of Iraq have remained fruitless. The attitude of the Government of Iraq towards the Shia faith was again demonstrated after the death last Saturday of the Grand Ayatollah Abul Qasim al Musawi al Khoei. In normal circumstances thousands of Shias would have attended the burial of their religious leader. But the Government did not allow this. According to a report I received, only six aides and one family member were permitted to [23] attend the burial, which took place at dawn. The report also states that the authorities even denied the al Khoei family the right to perform al-fatehah, the reciting of traditional Koranic verses. Also, I have to express my particular concern about the fate of the Grand Ayatollah's son, Sayed Mohammed Taki al Khoei, who stayed with the Grand Ayatollah during the last years of his life.

I have spoken repeatedly about violations of Security Council resolution 688 (1991). Violations because the Government of Iraq refuses to end its policy of repression, as has been demanded in this resolution. Violations because the Government of Iraq does not respect the obligation to allow international humanitarian organizations access in all parts of Iraq. I have emphasized this not because I enjoy making legal points. I have done so because I am convinced that if a full implementation of resolution 688 (1991) cannot be ensured, many thousands of innocent people are in danger of losing their lives. I express the hope that the members of the Council will keep this in mind in their consideration of this matter.

Mr. AL-ANBARI (Iraq): When I read the letters addressed to you, Mr. President, by representatives of the United Kingdom, Belgium and France, suggesting that Mr. van der Stoel should be invited in a personal capacity rather than as Special Rapporteur, I thought that the Special Rapporteur must have resigned his job and that he was invited to tell us about something else, about the new world disorder, the history of Iraq or other things. And then, when I saw the letter addressed to you by the representative of the United States yesterday, emphasizing that Mr. van der Stoel is to be invited as Special Rapporteur, I thought that the Council would refuse to do that because it would violate its mandate, since the report that he presented a few days [24-25] ago to the Council should have been presented first and discussed by the Commission on Human Rights rather than by the Security Council, which has no mandate in matters of human rights. Then today, we used a new sort of device, saying that we are inviting him as a person, that perhaps he will talk not about the report or about human rights, but about something else. He did speak about something else, I have to admit: he spoke about oil, he spoke about Memorandums of Understanding, he spoke about all sorts of subjects. Unfortunately, he did not inform himself well about these subjects.

[26] I know that more than anyone else here, as I chaired my delegation during the oil negotiations and while the memorandum of understanding was being negotiated, and I know the gentleman does not really know all the realities of these issues.

Then, after his brief introduction, full of half truths, he came to his report, presenting it paragraph by paragraph, except when he realized the fiasco he had made in devoting so many pages in his paper to the "Third River" in Iraq. I believe he avoided mentioning this after he had heard my explanation and after he had read the letter from our Minister for Foreign Affairs addressed to the Secretary-General (S/24388) explaining what the Third River really is.

Permit me, Mr. President, to come first to the letter addressed by the Special Rapporteur to the Foreign Minister of Iraq (*S/24386 p. 12, Appendix*). This letter reveals a lot about the motives and the tactics followed in the preparation of this report: it is referred to prominently in the report and is annexed thereto. The letter presumes that the reported allegations of a military offensive against the Marsh Arabs, the indiscriminate killings and the deliberate starvation of the civilian population in the south of Iraq and so on are established facts and require no proof whatsoever.

Hence, the letter appeals to the Foreign Minister to have such acts stopped immediately. Given the gravity of the allegations, one wonders why the Special Rapporteur did not first seek clarification from the Government of Iraq about the alleged violation of human rights. Should not the Government of Iraq be given a chance to reveal the dark motives and the unethical tactics of those who do not hesitate to abuse the noble cause of human rights by fabricating non-existent offensives and fictitious indiscriminate murders?

[27] I fully appreciate the heavy responsibility the Special Rapporteur agreed to shoulder by accepting the assignment to be a Special Rapporteur on the human rights situation in Iraq. However, having accepted the assignment, should he not have taken the necessary precautions against becoming a conduit for those who do not hesitate to abuse the cause of human rights and, indeed, do not hesitate to commit the most draconian crimes against the Iraqi people yet shed buckets of crocodile tears about their plight? I have every reason to trust and respect the judgement and discretion of the Special Rapporteur, but surely he should have known, as someone from Human Rights Watch recently said, that

> "Human rights have always been a political tool: When it is useful to them, they talk about it. When it is not useful, they go completely deaf."

That was quoted in the *Daily News* of 7 August.

One wonders, therefore, why the Special Rapporteur did not seek to conduct a field survey inside Iraq, not only to satisfy himself but to convince others of his objectivity, his seriousness and his independence. Why did he not bother to take such elementary measures? I hope that, after I conclude my speech, he might answer this question.

I do not want to make any speculation of my own, but the letter (S/24386, p. 12, Appendix) itself reveals that it was not meant to be a serious appeal to the Government of Iraq. The letter is dated 29 July 1992; instead of waiting for the letter to arrive on the desk of the Minister for Foreign Affairs, the Special Rapporteur presented his report to the President of the Council the very next day, on 30 July 1992, not forgetting to annex his letter of 29 July to his report. Is it too far-fetched to conclude that the main reason for writing the letter was to prepare an annex to the report, thereby giving it [28] the appearance of a well-documented, highly accurate report, even though it is totally innocent of any technical, historical or factual evidence or, for that matter - despite what we have just heard from him - of any legal foundation? So much for the credibility and bona fide character of the annexed letter.

Let me turn to some of the main points that were emphasized in the report. The Special Rapporteur made four assertions: firstly, concerning indiscriminate military attacks against the civilian population in the marshes; secondly, concerning forced relocation of the Marsh Arabs in the south; thirdly, concerning an internal economic blockade; and, fourthly, the so-called Third River Project.

The report describes the aforementioned Project as

> "Perhaps the greatest threat to the inhabitants of the southern marshes ..." (*S/24386, para. 15*).

It goes on to conclude that the project will

> "... clearly result in the draining of much of the marsh area of its watercover, surrendering the silty soils to the dry air. As the reed beds become exposed, they die, further contributing to the deterioration of the environment ..." (*ibid.*).

Given these dire consequences of the Third River Project, the report recommends that it

> "... should be immediately brought to a halt ..." (*ibid*).

Because of the exceptional importance that the Special Rapporteur gives to this project in his report, I shall take up this point before the other three he raised.

One must assume that the Special Rapporteur, although he does not say so, must have had the benefit of engineering, irrigation, environmental and even anthropological specialists; otherwise, he would not make such dire [29] predictions. However, given the irrefutable data detailed in the letter of the Foreign Minister of Iraq dated 6 August 1992 addressed to the Secretary-General (S/24388) about the said project, the Special Rapporteur could not have had the benefit of bona fide experts.

Whom he consulted and how he arrived at such a dire conclusion I do not know, nor does the Special Rapporteur let us know. The only thing that really puzzles me is why the esteemed Rapporteur did not bother to consult genuine experts or ask the Iraqi Government about the project, or at least read a book about the irrigation system in Iraq. I should greatly appreciate it if the Special Rapporteur would explain to us why he chose not to follow any of those courses before committing himself to the recommendation he made.

The so-called Third River Project, known in technical parlance as the Main Outfall Drain (MOD), is 566 kilometres long. It is one of the largest and oldest irrigation projects in Iraq. It was started more than 40 years ago to collect high-salinity drainage water from agricultural enterprises in central and southern Iraq into one main drain and to channel it into the Arabian Gulf without - and I emphasize the word "without" - intermixture with any of Iraq's rivers or marshlands. Thus, contrary to what the Rapporteur claims, the Third River is not a new project, it is not limited to the southern part of Iraq and it is not intended to drain the waters of the marshes nor will it do so.

For those who are interested in the engineering history of this project, I can refer them to the feasibility study carried out way back in 1952 by the American consulting firm Tippet, Appett, McCarthy. It was this company that recommended that a network of main drains should be built, of which the Main Outfall Drain, i.e., the Third River, is the backbone. The work on the MOD has gone through several phases since 1952, until 6 August 1990, when the [30] Brazilian company Mandes Junior, which was working on the project, had to stop because of Security Council resolution 661 (1990). Because of the sanctions imposed by that resolution, which has cynically and inhumanely been interpreted by a small minority of the members of the Council to include even irrigation equipment and drainage operations, Iraq decided to complete the project using Iraqi engineers and workers.

I do not want to burden the Council with additional technical and historical data, as they are fully detailed in the letter from the Foreign Minister (S/24388). However, one [sic] crucial point must be made clear. The Third River does not mix with any of the marsh waters or with any fresh water in Iraqi rivers, for it is to

> "run inside a strictly separate dyke, built parallel to the southern edges of the marshland and from there to the Arabian Gulf through the Shatt al-Basrah canal" (*S/24388, p. 4*).

[31] The report also refers to the lowering of the water level of the marshes. Here I have to agree with the report, although the report was again mistaken as to the causes of the paucity of the marshlands water. Contrary to what the report suggests, this paucity is not related to the Third River Project. It is caused by the reduction of the Euphrates water, which is the main source of the

marshlands water. Some of our neighbouring countries, sensing the prevalence of lawlessness in international relations, built a large number of big dams on the Euphrates, such as the Kayban and Karakayan dams in Turkey, the Tabgah dam in Syria and the filling since 1990 of the giant Ataturk dam in Turkey. I feel compelled to appeal once again to the Special Rapporteur on human rights in Iraq to seek solid and objective information from the Iraqi Government or, for that matter, from any other bona fide source before making his condemnations and recommendations for the improvement of human rights in Iraq.

I do hope that when preparing his revised version of this report, the Special Rapporteur will correct his data and reconsider his recommendation concerning the Third River Project. But if the report in its present form is so oblivious of such basic, elementary and unclassified technical and economic data concerning the Third River, what credence can a fair-minded person give to the other subjective, secretive and vague allegations regarding indiscriminate killing, internal economic blockade and forced relocation? The Special Rapporteur keeps us in total darkness as to the evidence he possessed and the sources, countries, intelligence organizations and other outlaws that provided him with the secret evidence that convinced him that he must make sweeping claims and recommendations about killing, shelling and starving, as sweeping as the ones he made about the Third River.

[32] Anyone familiar with the marshes in Iraq - and for those who may be interested, let me refer them to the books written by Wilfred Thesiger and Gavin Young - knows that, given the difficulty of gaining access to some parts of the marshes, where reeds could be as high as several metres, they become safe havens - yes, such safe havens are not new - for many deserters, murderers and smugglers, as well as agent-infiltrators from neighbouring countries. On many occasions Government forces do carry out raids to arrest such elements and to collect material evidence, such as communications equipment, grenades and other spying and subversive articles brought into the country by foreign agents. It is those elements, not the Government forces, that steal, kill and destroy the houses and property of the marsh Arabs, particularly in areas where Government authority cannot always function effectively to provide safety and protection to innocent civilians. Are we to accept the idea that only the deserters, murderers, smugglers and foreign infiltrators have human rights to be protected and that if a sovereign State wants to free the innocent citizens from the terror those criminals inflict on them, it must be condemned? But the report asserts that the Government's main objective in carrying out aerial surveys, or sending police patrols, or attacking the hideouts of foreign agents and other criminals, is actually to carry out indiscriminate murders, on a massive scale, of the innocent inhabitants of the marshlands. Here I must quote an Iraqi proverb. We have a saying: "Tell any person something unreasonable, and if he believes it, he is not a reasonable person." Is it reasonable that the Government would intentionally attempt to kill the Iraqi citizens living in the marshes? Those people have been living in the marshes for thousands of years. All Iraqis are proud of their heritage and their contribution to Iraq's [33] agriculture, fisheries and civilization. They live under such difficult conditions in small and isolated villages that they can hardly afford to do anything except manage their daily life. True, their conditions have improved recently, but life there is still difficult. They can hardly organize themselves, let alone carry out any political actions against the Government. Why should they? And why should the Government attempt to alienate them, let alone destroy them? Without our people in the marshes, the marshes would have become a colony of criminals, subversives and foreign agents. As to the video cassette which the Special Rapporteur says he possesses, I have not seen it, though I very much doubt its authenticity. The claim on the video cassette that the Prime Minister ordered tribes to be wiped out is such an ignorant and naive claim as to prove its lack of authenticity. I say "ignorant claim" because those tribes do not live only in the marshes - some members do, but the majority of members live in major towns, such as Basra, Omara and others throughout the country, partly to escape the harsh conditions of the marshes or for other social and economic reasons.

It is in this context that the Government offered voluntary - yes, voluntary - relocation to the marsh people, giving them free housing and free agricultural land in nearby villages. The report made reference to the speaker of the National Assembly, asserting that he confirmed the compulsory nature of the relocation programme. That assertion is simply untrue. The fact that no source, written or otherwise, was cited indicates how flimsy the assertion is.

The most ironic, albeit tragic, allegation in the report is the one to the effect that the Government has imposed an internal economic blockade on the marshlands. How could the Government do that? Such assertions reveal [34] once more the lack of knowledge or even familiarity with the living conditions in the marshlands, in view of their relative inaccessibility and the nature of the rationing system which the Government adopted to help the Iraqi people withstand the inhumane embargo imposed against them. Nor do such assertions show any understanding of the nature and structure of the Iraqi rationing system. It is the embargo, covering everything except air and water, that violates every Iraqi citizen's right to life, be he or she an Arab, a Kurd, a Sunni, a Shiite or a marshland inhabitant. To divert the attention of the Council and world public opinion to the so-called internal economic blockade is a cruel and inhumane act, to say the least, on the part of the Special Rapporteur.

In conclusion, I would like to make it clear that my intervention in this discussion is not made because of the contents or recommendations of a report which my Government considers as irrelevant as it is insignificant. The reason for any intervention, or for my intervention, is that regardless of the merits or demerits of the report, it is an illegal attempt to help accomplish an illegal aim, namely, to dismember my country by calling for the so-called permanent human-rights observers, then eventually to establish another so-called safe haven in the south. We know the countries, be they big ones or small ones in the region, which aim at destroying Iraq and the Iraqi people through a perpetual embargo, through the establishment of safe havens in the north and the south and eventually through dismemberment. Iraq and the Iraqi people recognize those countries, but we do regret that the Special Rapporteur, knowingly or not, should lend his name and position to such a scheme.

[35] **Mr. Perkins** (United States of America): It is evident from the statement we have just heard from Mr. van der Stoel that Iraq is in clear and direct violation of Security Council resolution 688 (1991), which requires Iraq to end repression of its citizens and allow humanitarian organizations access to all those in need.

Saddam Hussein has long relied on fear and repression to govern Iraq, maintaining what can truly be described as a reign of terror. The full scope of these brutalities, it seems to us, is yet to be revealed, but what is known provides a clear indictment of his practices.

[36] He is guilty of human rights abuses throughout the country involving every ethnic and religious group. We believe it appropriate for the Security Council to address these wider issues as well as the violations cited by Mr. van der Stoel in his report to the Council, We urge Mr. van der Stoel to issue his report on conditions in north Iraq as soon as possible.

Saddam Hussein is also obstructing the work of those who seek to help the people of Iraq. His Government has refused to issue visas to replacements for United Nations guards who have rotated out of the country. Those who remain are being harassed constantly. These guards perform an essential job. Besides providing a measure of protection for United Nations personnel and equipment, they are an important symbol of the United Nations humanitarian commitment in Iraq. If we accept that Iraq can control the entry of United Nations personnel by denying visas, Iraqi intransigence could reduce the number to 127 United Nations guards of a needed contingent of 500 one week from today. With a reduced number of United Nations guards, and with United Nations personnel unable to travel between Baghdad and the north, the Iraqi Government could increase its harassment of groups throughout the country that rely on the United Nations presence to care for their humanitarian needs.

In recent months we have witnessed a resurgence of the Iraqi regime's cruel treatment of its citizens in the north. Last week three key checkpoints into Kurdistan were closed to humanitarian aid, petroleum products, or people, including United Nations personnel. In addition, Iraq is refusing to sell fuel to humanitarian organizations. The blockade and inadequate fuel supplies are seriously hampering relief operations. Saddam Hussein has not paid Government workers in the north since last October.

[37] On the eve of local elections in north Iraq, three bombs were discovered in Zakho, including a car bomb in front of a hotel housing Western journalists and election observers. On 30 June Iraq refused to renew the Memorandum of Understanding on United Nations activities in Iraq. In early July there were grenade and bomb attacks against United Nations offices in northern Iraq, including against United Nations guard headquarters.

Events in southern Iraq show an equally heinous disregard for the human rights of the Iraqi people. In southern Iraq last year, observers reported that Government troops indiscriminately fired on civilians and hanged some from the barrels of tanks. Government forces damaged mosques and desecrated tombs, razed residential areas around the mosques to create free-fire zones for security units, and banned access to cemeteries.

Recently the Government intensified its attacks against Shia civilians, possibly to compensate for its inability to eliminate insurgent groups based in the southern marshes. Iraqi commanders recently were ordered to destroy Shia villages and kill their occupants. A videotape shows Iraq's Prime Minister ordering Government commanders to "wipe out" three marsh Arab tribes. Rural Shia villages are often shelled, as are residential areas near Shia cities such as Nasiriayah. Numerous settlements have been abandoned as villagers either flee the fighting or are forcibly relocated. During a recent offensive, Government forces destroyed more than 45 dwellings in settlements such as Saiqal and Wadiyah.

Reports coming from southern Iraq say that a Government offensive in April produced more than 1,000 casualties, and hundreds of families reportedly fled into the marshes after their homes were set on fire. Fixed-wing [38] aircraft, including sophisticated fighter-bombers and helicopter gunships, were used to strafe villages and other portions of the marshes. The Government has begun executing civilians accused of supporting the rebels. Baghdad has severely limited the number of relief workers in the south because they could monitor the regime's abuses. Baghdad has refused to renew visas for relief officers.

In April the Government authorized the removal of Shia villagers living in or near the southern marshes. This operation is reminiscent of the "Anfal operations" - Iraq's forced relocation of thousands of Kurds in the 1980s.

Since the uprising, Saddam Hussein also has increased the level of economic pressure on the south. The Government maintains a virtual economic embargo against the Shias by diverting most goods and services to Iraq's Sunni community. Saddam Hussein has refused to reconstruct water and sewage treatment facilities in the south, even though such facilities have been repaired elsewhere in Iraq.

Nor have the Iraqi citizens of Baghdad and other areas in central Iraq escaped the repression of the Saddam Hussein regime. Government manipulation and control of incoming food and medical supplies plus unrestrained printing of currency by the Iraq Central Bank have contributed to escalating prices for basic commodities. The response of the Baghdad regime was to execute merchants, more often than not Sunni Arabs, who have been loyal supporters. Obviously, the regime represses ruthlessly any sign of dissent.

In his most cruel hoax, Saddam Hussein has blamed the number of malnourished Iraqis on the United Nations sanctions rather than the Iraqi military and his own policies of repression.

[39] Mr. van der Stoel has dramatically highlighted the plight of the Iraqi people. One of the most serious new developments is the use of fixed-wing aircraft, including jet fighters, for the first time in bombing Shia villages in the southern marshes.

Unfortunately, we have no reason to hope for amelioration of the situation under the cruel regime of Saddam Hussein. Instead, we have reason to believe that additional villages will be attacked, bombed and destroyed, and civilian casualties will rise. Baghdad's opposition to relief efforts throughout the country, moreover, will deny the means to care for the wounded and the displaced.

In 1991 the Council condemned the repression of the Iraqi civilian population in many parts of Iraq, including in the Kurdish populated areas, finding it a threat to international peace and security. At that time, the United States Government and other Governments concluded that the situation was so serious and Iraqi intransigence so manifest that additional measures had to be taken to help prevent further Iraqi repression of the civilian population. Now, not only in the north but also in the south of Iraq the situation exists.

It is imperative that Iraq, without further delay and deception, abide by all relevant Security Council resolutions, including resolution 688 (1991), and its economic blockade of the north and south, renew the United Nations humanitarian programme in Iraq, and cease its repression in the southern marshes.

[40] **Mr. van Daele** (Belgium) (interpretation from French): ...

The presentation just made to us by Mr. van der Stoel demonstrates - if need be - that it was useful and important for that observer who is monitoring events in Iraq to be heard by the Council, as requested by the Belgian delegation, among others. Our most sincere and heartfelt thanks go to Mr. van der Stoel for his statement.

[41] The distressing information that he has provided us confirms and indeed worsens the data that my delegation has on the deplorable human-rights situation in Iraq.

In the southern marshes the Shi'a civilians, victims of ruthless repression, are being subjected to an economic blockade which deprives them of food and all humanitarian assistance. Subjected to measures that amount to a veritable deportation policy, they are the victims of indiscriminate bombings and massive military attacks.

The plight of other populations, and in particular that of the Kurds, is, unfortunately, equally pitiful. Many witnesses, including Mr. van der Stoel, have alerted public opinion to this situation, and it seems that since then the situation has not evolved favourably - quite the contrary. The difficulties faced by the United Nations staff in charge of structuring humanitarian assistance operations add to our concern.

Furthermore, our information indicates that the harsh repressive measures used by the Iraqi regime now extend to the population of Baghdad itself. My delegation is concerned at this development, which, in addition to inflicting immense suffering on a large portion of the Iraqi population, shows continuing disdain for the goals and principles of the United Nations Charter and constitutes a violation by Iraq of various international human-rights instruments.

In this respect, the Security Council has imposed specific obligations on Iraq. Need I recall that resolution 687 (1991) provides in paragraph 21 that the Security Council shall review the embargo imposed on Iraq in the light of the policy and practices followed by its Government, and that resolution 688 (1991) in paragraph 2 demands that Iraq immediately end its repression of the civilian population?

[42] More than a year has passed since the adoption of those two resolutions. On 11 March 1992 the President of the Security Council made a statement which included the following passage:

> "The Security Council remains profoundly concerned by the grave human rights abuses that, despite the provisions of resolution 688 (1991), the Iraqi Government continues to perpetrate against its population" (*S/PV.3059, p. 18*).

To our profound regret, nothing in that text is any less true today.

The repression that is being inflicted on the Iraqi people is not only a massive and flagrant violation of human rights, but, in addition, could once again gravely jeopardize the peace and security of the entire region. Therefore it is important, in this sphere as well, for the Council to follow with extreme watchfulness the behaviour of the Iraqi Government. The repression committed by the Baghdad authorities, like its attitude towards other matters covered by resolution 687 (1991), prevents Iraq from reassuming its place in the international community.

Mr. Vorontsov (Russian Federation) (interpretation from Russian): The Russian Federation attaches great importance to the full and consistent implementation of the resolutions of the Security Council which are intended to eliminate the consequences of the Iraqi aggression against Kuwait and to establish a lasting peace and security in that region. Accordingly, we, like other Council members, are very seriously alarmed by reports of a continuing policy of repression against the civilian population in various parts of Iraq, which constitutes a direct violation of the demand, contained in resolution 688 (1991), that Iraq, as a contribution to the removing of the threat to [43] international peace and security in the region, should end the repression against its own civilian population.

We are receiving reports concerning increasing military attacks against the civilian population in the marshlands of southern Iraq, concerning actions by the Government for the forcible resettlement of people who are living there, concerning measures intended to force international non-governmental humanitarian organizations previously active in that region to leave the region. A very serious situation with regard to the observance, or I should rather say the violation, of human rights has been created in northern Iraq, where there is a continued blockade against the Kurdish population, and in other regions as well.

Useful information on the tragic situation of many population groups in Iraq as a result of the policy of their own Government has just been given to the Council by Mr. Max van der Stoel, a man of great and well-deserved international prestige. The delegation of the Russian Federation expresses its gratitude to him for that information.

The Russian delegation received with particular alarm the information provided by the Secretary-General at our informal consultation on 7 August 1992 about the worsening situation with regard to the safety of our Organization's personnel in Iraq. We consider totally inadmissible the increasing frequent attempts to intimidate United Nations personnel and the instances of attempts on their lives, one of which ended tragically.

These and other facts are evidence of the obvious unwillingness of the Iraqi authorities to have witnesses to their repressive actions against the civilian population and of their efforts to interfere with the activities of representatives of the international community in Iraq. That is [44-45] also what we conclude from the fact that Baghdad has avoided extending the memorandum of understanding with the United Nations.

The deep concern of members of the Security Council at the failure to comply with resolution 688 (1991) has been indicated on a number of occasions, including the Council meeting in March 1992 in which a high-level Iraqi delegation participated. The members emphasized that Iraq must allow international humanitarian organizations access to all those in need in all parts of Iraq and must conscientiously cooperate with the Secretary-General in carrying out humanitarian efforts.

However, there has not yet been any adequate response by Baghdad to these demands. The letter dated 6 August 1992 from the Minister for Foreign Affairs of Iraq to the President of the Security Council (S/24388) and the statement made today by the Permanent Representative of Iraq to the United Nations are further convincing evidence of that fact.

The delegation of the Russian Federation wishes to emphasize the groundlessness and uselessness of any attempt by Iraq to test the firmness of the Security Council's determination to obtain Iraq's full and unconditional compliance with all Council decisions, including resolution 688 (1991). The Iraqi authorities must understand at last that the world community will not stand for any further delay, much less Iraq's refusal to heed the demands of the Council. Only by constructive cooperation with the international community can Iraq avoid the serious consequences it will face if it continues on its course of confrontation with the Security Council, especially since such cooperation would, first and foremost, be in the national interest of Iraq itself.

[46] **Mr. Hatano** (Japan): As we all know, information is scarce on the southern marsh area of Iraq owing to restrictions on access imposed by the Iraqi Government. But Japan, too, has received some reports that the Iraqi Government was violating human rights in the area.

In his briefing today, Mr. van der Stoel seems to have confirmed many of these reports. The story of the burial ceremony of Grand Ayatollah Khoei, which I heard for the first time today, adds to the sadness of the situation. Last year, with resolution 688 (1991) the Security Council condemned the repressive practices of the Iraqi Government against the civilian population in many parts of the country. We deplore that such practices still continue. We consider that the repression of its people and the denial of their human rights is a matter for the international community's concern and constitutes a threat to the peace and security of the region.

In this connection, the plight of the Kurdish people in the northern part of Iraq also requires our continued attention. Japan urges Iraq to accept the extension of the Memorandum of Understanding to insure that their safety is guaranteed. Nor must we forget the Kuwaiti nationals who are missing or detained in Iraq, and Japan urges that Iraq grant the International Committee of the Red Cross free access to all areas so that it can gain information on these people.

In short, the Government of Iraq should stop the repression of its people and its confrontational attitude with respect to the implementation of all the relevant Security Council resolutions.

Mr. Hajnoczi (Austria): ...

I want to express our gratitude to Mr. van der Stoel for his briefing on the manifold - in particular, human rights - aspects of the situation in the southern marshlands of Iraq, in the northern Kurdish-populated sectors, and other regions of that country. Mr. van der Stoel's presentation was extremely interesting and at the same time worrying.

In this context, I should like to recall what Austria's Federal Chancellor Vranitzky said in the Council meeting of 31 January 1992:

> "The protection of human rights and, in particular, of the rights of ethnic minorities too, has had an important impact on the development of peaceful relations between States. There is a direct connection between democratic processes within countries and the evolution of a political culture which is conducive to the peaceful settlement of disputes. From our own history, we know that peace was most threatened when human rights were abolished and minorities persecuted and when democratic processes gave way to totalitarian practices. Human rights, minority rights and democracy are, therefore, important cornerstones in our common endeavour" (*S/PV.3046, p. 66*).

The briefing given by Mr. van der Stoel is indeed alarming not only with regard to the human rights situation but also in relation to international peace and security in the area, which are threatened, as emphasized in paragraph 1 of Security Council resolution 688 (1991), by the repression of the Iraqi civilian population.

[48] Paragraph 2 of resolution 688 (1991) demands that Iraq, as a contribution to removing the threat to international peace and security in the region, immediately end this repression. After today's presentation, my delegation cannot but call upon Iraq with utmost sincerity to take all measures possible in order to alleviate the suffering of its civilian population in the southern marshes as well as in other parts of Iraq, among these the Kurdish areas.

Both the southern marshlands and the northern, Kurdish-populated parts of Iraq are extremely sensitive areas as regards regional security and stability. We are therefore all the more concerned by the information on restrictions to the activities and programmes of humanitarian agencies there. Austria is proud to be a contributor to the United Nations guards contingent in Iraq because we consider the work done by this contingent to be of great importance, in the humanitarian field as well as in the security area. We have therefore registered with great dismay the recent deterioration of the security conditions of those guards and other humanitarian personnel.

In a hand-grenade attack on 8 July 1992, two Austrian members of the guards contingent were severely wounded. On 16 July, another United Nations guard, a Fiji national, was killed by a gunshot. Other members of the guards contingent have been injured since. Austria therefore reiterates its call upon Iraq to ensure to the extent feasible the safety of all international personnel within its territory and to make available all the facilities and cooperation necessary for the continued and safe implementation of all humanitarian programmes of the United Nations, the International Committee of the Red Cross, and non-governmental organizations, as well as to give them access to all Iraqi civilians in all parts of the country, as also insisted upon in paragraph 3 of resolution 688 (1991). In particular, we expect that the Memorandum of Understanding will be renewed quickly.

[49-50] Paragraph 21 of Security Council resolution 687 (1991) stipulates that the sanctions against Iraq have to be reviewed in the light of the policies and practices of the Government of Iraq. Austria hopes that Iraq, by heeding these calls and cooperating fully, will contribute to the creation of conditions under which the sanctions soon can be lifted.

The information provided by Mr. van der Stoel, as well as by Ambassador Al-Anbari, on the so-called Third River Project or Main Outfall Drain Project demonstrates clearly the impact of ecological questions on a wide range of issues, among them a country's relationship with its immediate and mediate neighbours and hence on international peace and security. The ecological impacts of actions and projects affecting neighbouring States must therefore always be taken duly into account.

[51] In conclusion, let me make one thing absolutely clear: Austria's aim in participating in this debate is of a principled nature, not confined to matters related merely to Iraq. Humanitarian and human rights questions are important for peace and stability equally in all parts of the world. We therefore hope and expect that the international community will devote the same degree of attention and determination to threats to the peace by violations of human rights and humanitarian law in other regions as it is currently devoting to the very tragic cases of Bosnia and Herzegovina or Somalia.

...

Mr. Rochereau de la Sabliere (France) (interpretation from French): Last year, during the tragic exodus of Kurds caused by terrible repression, the Security Council undertook an examination of the humanitarian situation in Iraq. At that time, on the initiative of my country, it adopted resolution 688 (1991).

In the same context, we have just listened to a presentation by Mr. van der Stoel of the results - damning for the Government of Iraq - of the very serious, detailed work he has been doing for several months with a view to establishing the truth about the situation of the civilian populations in Iraq.

Mr. van der Stoel's testimony, which supplements the information available to us from other sources, is extremely disquieting. It confirms that on the whole of Iraqi territory elementary human rights are being trampled upon and that repression against the civilian population is [52] continuing, in the north and in the south. It confirms, also, that resolution 688 (1991) is disregarded by the Baghdad Government.

While the United Nations, the specialized agencies and the Non-Governmental Organizations are exerting remarkable efforts to bring relief to the civilian population, the Iraqi Government is placing ever-greater obstacles in the way of humanitarian action. In fact, it is seeking to put an end to that action. The Secretary-General submitted to us last Friday a report in this regard which causes us great concern. Indeed, the Baghdad authorities are refusing to grant the necessary visas to make it possible to relieve personnel involved in the implementation of the humanitarian programme. They refuse also to authorize these persons to move about freely. At the same time, we note a worsening of the security conditions of the United Nations guards, international staff and persons serving with Non-Governmental Organizations. The latter are, indeed, subjected to hostile acts, going so far as assassination. Unfortunately, we have an example of this, which prompted our Council to react on 17 July last.

We learned yesterday that the Iraqi authorities had, after weeks of procrastination, decided to invite Mr. Eliasson to go to Baghdad to continue the discussion on the Memorandum of Understanding signed between Iraq and the United Nations on 18 April 1991. Better late than never: for it is essential that this Memorandum of Understanding be renewed.

My delegation attaches particular importance to the presence of the contingent of United Nations guards. It must be enabled to carry out the task given it by the Secretary-General. Hence, we shall be very vigilant and shall follow very closely the negotiation on the Memorandum of Understanding as well as its results.

[53] In the field - as Mr. van der Stoel emphasized - the Baghdad authorities continue to impose the blockade of Kurdistan by force. The principal access roads to that region are cut and, therefore, the shortages are worsening. Thus, for lack of fuel, the harvested wheat could not be sent to silos and the harvest is being lost. The Kurdish population, which has suffered so much, continues to live a life of anguish.

In the south, the repression continues. Mr. van der Stoel has given us crushing examples of this. The Shiite population is subjected to unacceptable treatment. The marsh area is encircled by the army. Villages located there are bombarded by aircraft. But the Iraqi regime does not confine its abuses to this tragic manhunt going on in the marshes. We know that it is also doing irreparable damage to the cultural and religious heritage of the southern cities. Places of worship, religious schools, libraries have been sacked.

The Iraqi authorities must allow the United Nations guards to be deployed in the south, in particular in the area of the marshes, and must give unrestricted access to the humanitarian organizations so that they can carry out their elementary tasks of assistance and protection.

Last year the Security Council found that the repression by the Baghdad authorities constituted a threat to international peace and security. My Government, along with others, took measures to protect the population in the north, which at that time was particularly affected. We note today that a situation just as serious as the one I have just recalled exists now in the south. The international community cannot remain indifferent to the fate of the population in the south. It must do everything possible to prevent massive violations of human rights from continuing, and to prevent an exodus.

[54] **Sir David Hannay** (United Kingdom): This afternoon, at the opening of our debate, we heard two contributions, the first of which I found horrific and the second, disturbing.

The report to the Security Council by Mr. van der Stoel, for which I greatly thank him and which related principally to resolution 688 (1991) and is therefore very much a matter for the Council, is deeply disturbing. But I am afraid I found the comment by the Iraqi Permanent Representative on that report - no doubt on instructions from his Government - if anything, even more disturbing. For all that could be found to be said in the face of these horrific facts were some rather cynical and legalistic arguments and a long analysis about whether or not Mr. van der Stoel's engineering experience was sufficient to analyse the Third River Project. Well, I have always based myself on the assumption that the Dutch know rather a lot about large water projects, and I am not inclined to follow the Iraqi representative's line of argument. But, in any case, it is irrelevant to the business of the Security Council. The Ambassador of Iraq asked us: is it reasonable for a Government to wish to kill large numbers of its population? I shall reply straightaway: no, it is not reasonable. But by that criterion the Government of Iraq must be the most unreasonable Government in the world.

Now, Mr. van der Stoel spoke to us first about the state of health in Iraq and about the failure of the Iraqi Government to implement the scheme under resolutions 706 (1991) and 712 (1991). I think that the Ambassador of Iraq suggested that this was irrelevant. I do not myself believe it is irrelevant at all. The reality is that if that scheme had been implemented, a billion dollars - one billion dollars - of value and money could have been used for buying foodstuffs and medicine for the people of Iraq. And that is [55] not the limit of it: for the Security Council said when it adopted the scheme that it would review the figure if that proved to be necessary. We have never had to do that, alas, because we have never been able to implement the scheme, thanks to the obstruction and, finally, the rejection of the Iraqi Government. That in itself is a tragedy which contributes to the repression by the Iraqi Government of its population - which is so greatly in contravention of resolution 688 (1991).

Mr. van der Stoel also spoke to us about the humanitarian work of the United Nations and the way this was being hampered. We already had the Secretary-General's report of 7 August to Council members about the negotiations on the Memorandum of Understanding, and we had heard from the Secretary-General that Iraq was trying to force United Nations humanitarian agencies and Non-Governmental Organizations to leave and was bringing pressure to bear to reduce the number of United Nations guards and, if possible, get them all out of Iraq by a process of attrition.

I entirely agree with Mr. van der Stoel's statement that the humanitarian programme is desperately needed in Iraq - and that includes the work of the United Nations guards, which is vital for the well-being of the Iraqi people in all parts of the country. So to my Government it is very welcome news that Under-Secretary-General Eliasson has now been invited to visit Baghdad. I hope this is a sign that the Iraqi Government will see the light and will renew the Memorandum of Understanding without more ado. Failing to do that will certainly be another step down the road towards the repression and the inhumane treatment of its own population.

[56] What Mr. van der Stoel told the Council is enough to indicate to us, together with reports that we receive in the press and elsewhere, that Iraq is engaged in a full-scale repression of the Shia population in the southern marshes. There is no way in which this can be other than a straightforward defiance of this Council and of Security Council resolution 688 (1991), which expressly asked Iraq to end the repression of its civilian population.

It is also clear from both Mr. van der Stoel's account and other accounts that the situation in other parts of Iraq, notably in the north of the country, is very nearly as bad. Not quite as bad, because there is not, at the moment, actual military force being used, but very bad nevertheless, because the maintenance of an economic blockade against the north is bringing great privation and suffering to the people who live there, and that too is inconsistent with resolution 688 (1991). In the south, Iraq has begun to use fixed-wing aircraft for the first time in the recent period to bomb Shia villages and to destroy human habitations and human beings throughout the marshes. That action is not tolerable.

Last year, 15 months ago, this Council concluded that the repression of the Iraqi civilian population in many parts of Iraq, including the Kurdish-populated areas but also in the south, which led to a massive exodus of refugees to Turkey and Iran, itself threatened international peace and security. My Government and a number of others felt that the situation was so serious and Iraqi intransigence so evident that measures had to be taken to help prevent the population from being further repressed. That situation now appears to exist in the south of Iraq, as it did last year in the north.

[57] From what we have heard, Iraqi actions appear, in fact, to be threatening the very existence of large sections of the civilian population. So I should like to conclude by saying that if the Government of Iraq wishes this Council to accept the claim that its intentions are good, then there are three things that need to be done immediately. One is to end the economic blockade of the north of Iraq; the second is to stop the forceful repression in the south of Iraq; and the third is to renew the Memorandum of Understanding.

Mr. Budai (Hungary): The delegation of Hungary remains deeply concerned about the systematic, massive and grave violations of human rights in Iraq, the consequences of which have a direct bearing on international peace and security in the region. The statement made by Mr. van der Stoel before this Council, for which we thank him, provides us with new and shocking information about the humanitarian and human-rights situation of the Iraqi civilian population.

Our delegation considers the participation of Mr. van der Stoel in this meeting of the Council as an important contribution towards enhancing the awareness of the link that exists between the way a Government treats its own citizens and the way it acts in the international arena, as well as the link between enforcing respect for human rights and maintaining international peace and security. Resolution 688 (1991) of the Council and the Presidential statement of 11 March 1992 have clearly recognized this relationship by keeping the question of repression in Iraq under review by the Security Council.

[58] This disregard for international standards, including the provisions of treaties in the field of human rights to which Iraq has become a party, is indeed alarming. The practices of mass execution, the extensive use of torture by security forces, enforced disappearances, violations affecting ethnic and religious communities, in particular the massive repression of the Kurds and now the resurgence of grave violations of the population's human rights in the area of the southern marshes cannot but be condemned by the international community.

Earlier last year, in launching a large-scale humanitarian operation to save the Kurds of Iraq, the Security Council acted in an exemplary manner. Those steps were directed towards peace-building, towards the safeguarding of human rights and the rights of minorities. Therefore reports about the lack of cooperation on the part of the Iraqi Government regarding the United Nations humanitarian operation should not escape the attention of the Council either. We urge Iraq to cooperate with the United Nations for the early finalization of the negotiations on the renewal of the Memorandum of Understanding covering the humanitarian programme.

The Iraqi authorities should put an end to the repression of the civilian population throughout the country. Humanitarian relief efforts should continue unhindered. The Government of Iraq bears full responsibility for the deterioration of the humanitarian situation in its country. Early implementation of the relevant Security Council resolutions, including resolution 688 (1991), as well as resolutions 706 (1991) and 712 (1991), would contribute to the improvement of the human-rights situation and the living conditions of the suffering civilian population of Iraq.

As was stressed in the statement of the head of the Hungarian delegation to the summit meeting of Security Council members in January, for the [59] Republic of Hungary respect for human rights and the rights of national minorities is not merely a legal or humanitarian question. It is also an integral part of international collective security, as exemplified during and after the Gulf crisis, and also more recently in the conflict among the southern Slav peoples. Therefore it is indispensable for the Security Council, in the context of its peace-building efforts, to take an unambiguous and clear-cut stand for the protection of those rights whenever and wherever they are flagrantly violated.

Mr. Arria (Venezuela) (interpretation from Spanish): ...

Mr. van der Stoel's appearance before the Council today was not in his capacity as Special Rapporteur of the Commission on Human Rights. Nonetheless, Mr. van der Stoel is no ordinary person. He has twice been Minister for Foreign Affairs of his country, the Netherlands, a prestigious distinguished and democratic nation, and today he is also a member of his country's Council of State. His credibility and prestige are backed by a distinguished public career. We feel that his good faith is beyond question. For that reason, my country attaches particular value and importance to his statement before the Council.

Mr. van der Stoel's first report before the Council in March of this year caused Council members deep concern and serious alarm - as did today's report - in the light of resolution 688 (1991). On 11 March, exactly five months ago, the Council held its 3059th meeting, at which the Deputy Prime Minister of Iraq, Mr. Tariq Aziz, was invited to speak. On behalf of the Council, in my capacity as President, I referred on that occasion to [60] paragraph 2 of resolution 688 (1991), which indicated that in order to remove the threat to international peace and security in the region, an end had to be put to the repression of the civilian population.

[61] It also mentioned operative paragraphs 3 to 7 of Security Council resolution 688 (1991), in which it was agreed that immediate access by international humanitarian organizations must be allowed to all those in need of their assistance. The resolution also required the full cooperation of the Government of Iraq in this respect.

Lastly, in this connection, in my capacity as President of the Council I said that as long as the repression continued, there would be a threat to international peace and security. The fact that the Memorandum of Understanding has not been extended implies *de facto* the withdrawal of the Non-Governmental Organizations, bodies whose presence enhanced the credibility of the international humanitarian action, and it is of course regrettable that this should be so. Preventing access by the international humanitarian organizations - the Non-Governmental Organizations - is clearly a violation of resolution 688 (1991), but it also lends credibility to the condemnations heard today in the Council.

I do not think that the letter dated 10 August from the Deputy Permanent Representative of the Islamic Republic of Iran - which was circulated today as Security Council document S/24414 - can go unnoticed at this meeting, because it states that:

> "The annihilation of large numbers of people in the south of Iraq, mainly Shiites, may lead to a situation like the one which obtained in the spring of 1991 and so threatens peace and security in the region".

I shall repeat here what I said, as representative of Venezuela, during the meting on 11 March this year:

> [62] "We are ... confident that the Government of Iraq will understand its humanitarian responsibilities to ensure the national reconciliation of its people with full respect for the human rights of all its citizens, many of whom are now subjected to untold and unjustifiable violations of such rights". (*S/PV.3059, p. 89*).

The final responsibility for normalizing its relations with the international community, symbolized here by the Security Council, and for not jeopardizing international peace and security in the region yet again, lies in the hands of Iraq.

In conclusion, I think it is important to highlight the fact that the concern of my country in this debate is founded on its unswerving solidarity and concern in respect of a subject of primary importance for humankind, namely, the defence of human rights wherever they are violated or trampled underfoot, and on its aspiration to see peace and harmony restored in a region whose people are traditionally friends of Venezuela.

The President (interpretation from Chinese): ...

The Security Council has thus concluded the present stage of its consideration of the item on its agenda.

The Security Council will remain seized of the matter.

The meeting rose at 6.05 p.m.

14. UN General Assembly Resolution 47/145, Situation of Human Rights in Iraq, 18 December 1992

The General Assembly,

Guided by the principles embodied in the Charter of the United Nations, the Universal Declaration of Human Rights and the International Covenants on Human Rights,

Reaffirming that all Member States have an obligation to promote and protect human rights and fundamental freedoms and to fulfil the obligations they have undertaken under the various international instruments in this field,

Mindful that Iraq is a party to the International Covenants on Human Rights and to other human rights instruments,

Recalling its resolution 46/134 of 17 December 1991, in which it expressed its deep concern at the flagrant violations of human rights by the Government of Iraq,

Recalling also Security Council resolution 688 (1991) of 5 April 1991, in which the Council demanded an end to the repression of the Iraqi civilian population and insisted that Iraq should cooperate with humanitarian organizations and ensure that the human and political rights of all Iraqi citizens were respected,

Recalling in particular Commission on Human Rights resolution 1991/74 of 6 March 1991, in which the Commission requested its Chairman to appoint a special rapporteur to make a thorough study of the violations of human rights by the Government of Iraq, based on all information the special rapporteur might deem relevant, including information provided by intergovernmental and non-governmental organizations and any comments and material provided by the Government of Iraq,

Recalling the pertinent resolutions of the Commission on Human Rights condemning the flagrant violations of human rights by the Government of Iraq, including its most recent, resolution 1992/71 of 5 March 1992, by which the Commission extended the mandate of the Special Rapporteur for a further year and requested him in pursuing his mandate to visit again the northern area of Iraq, in particular, and to submit an interim report to the General Assembly at its forty-seventh session and a final report to the Commission at its forty-ninth session,

Recalling also Security Council resolution 706 (1991) of 15 August 1991, 712 (1991) of 19 September 1991 and 778 (1992) of 2 October 1992,

Deeply concerned by the massive and grave violations of human rights by the Government of Iraq, such as summary and arbitrary executions, torture and other cruel, inhuman or degrading treatment, enforced or involuntary disappearances, arbitrary arrests and detentions, lack of due process and the rule of law and of freedom of thought, of expression, of association and of access to food and health care,

Deeply concerned also by the fact that chemical weapons have been used on the Iraqi civilian population, by the forced displacement of hundreds of thousands of Iraqi civilians and by the destruction of Iraqi towns and villages, as well as by the fact that tens of thousands of displaced Kurds had to take refuge in camps and shelters in the north of Iraq,

Deeply concerned further by the current severe and grave violations of human rights by the Government of Iraq against the civilian population in southern Iraq, in particular the Shiah communities in the southern marshes,

Expressing concern in particular that there has been no improvement in the human rights situation in Iraq, and, therefore, welcoming the Special Rapporteur's proposal for the deployment of a team of human rights monitors in Iraq,

Noting that, despite the formal cooperation extended to the Special Rapporteur by the Government of Iraq, that cooperation needs to be improved, in particular by giving full replies to the Special Rapporteur's inquiries about acts being committed by the Government of Iraq that are incompatible with the international human rights instruments that are binding on that country,

1. *Takes note with appreciation* of the interim report on the situation of human rights in Iraq submitted by the Special Rapporteur of the Commission on Human Rights and the observations, conclusions and recommendations contained therein;

2. *Expresses its strong condemnation* of the massive violations of human rights, of the gravest nature, for which the Government of Iraq is responsible and to which the Special Rapporteur has referred in his recent reports, in particular:

(a) Summary and arbitrary executions, orchestrated mass executions and burials, extrajudicial killings, including political killings, in particular in the northern region of Iraq, in southern Shiah centres and in the southern marshes;

(b) The widespread routine practice of systematic torture in its most cruel forms, including the torture of children;

(c) Enforced or involuntary disappearances, routinely practised arbitrary arrest and detention, including of women and children and consistent and routine failure to respect due process and the rule of law;

(d) Suppression of freedom of thought, expression and association, and violations of property rights;

3. *Deplores* Iraq's refusal to cooperate in the implementation of Security Council resolutions 706 (1991) and 712 (1991), and its failure to provide the Iraqi population with access to adequate food and health care;

4. *Calls upon* the Government of Iraq to release immediately all persons arbitrarily arrested and detained, including Kuwaitis and nationals of other States;

5. *Calls once again upon* Iraq, as a State party to the International Covenant on Economic, Social and Cultural Rights as well as to the International Covenant on Civil and Political Rights, to abide by its freely undertaken obligations under the Covenants and under other international instruments on human rights, and particularly to respect and ensure the rights of all individuals irrespective of their origin within its territory and subject to its jurisdiction;

6. *Recognizes* the importance of the work of the United Nations in providing humanitarian relief to the people of Iraq, and calls upon Iraq immediately and fully to implement the Memorandum of Understanding between the United Nations and the Government of Iraq and to cooperate with the United Nations programmes, including ensuring the safety and security of United Nations personnel and humanitarian workers;

7. *Expresses special alarm* at the repressive policies and practices directed against the Kurds, which continue to have an impact on the lives of the Iraqi people as a whole;

8. *Also expresses special alarm* at the resurgence of grave violations of human rights against Shiah communities, especially in southern Iraq, which is the result of a preconceived policy against the marsh Arabs in particular;

9. *Further expresses its special alarm* at all internal embargoes, which prevent the equitable enjoyment of basic foodstuffs and medical supplies, and calls upon Iraq, which has sole responsibility in this regard, to remove them;

10. *Welcomes* the Special Rapporteur's proposal for a system of human rights monitors which would constitute an independent and reliable source of information, and invites the Commission on Human Rights to follow up this proposal at its forty-ninth session;

11. *Urges once more* the Government of Iraq to set up an independent commission of inquiry to look into the fate of tens of thousands of disappeared persons;

12. *Regrets* the failure of the Government of Iraq to provide satisfactory and convincing replies concerning the violations of human rights brought to the attention of

the Special Rapporteur, and calls upon it to reply without delay in a comprehensive and detailed manner;

13. *Urges*, therefore, the Government of Iraq to accord its full cooperation to the Special Rapporteur of the Commission on Human Rights to enable him to make the appropriate recommendations to improve the human rights situation in Iraq;

14. *Requests* the Secretary-General to provide the Special Rapporteur with all the necessary assistance in carrying out his mandate;

15. *Decides* to continue its consideration of the situation of human rights in Iraq during its forty-eighth session under the item entitled "Human rights questions" in the light of additional elements provided by the Commission on Human Rights and the Economic and Social Council.

[*Adopted by 126 votes to 2, 26 abstentions.*]

19. THE RESPONSE OF MEMBERS OF THE INTERNATIONAL COALITION: SAFE-HAVENS AND AERIAL EXCLUSION ZONES

By the second week of April 1991 forces of the coalition states commenced supplying displaced persons in northern Iraq with food, clothing and tents, using air drops from military aircraft. Subsequently coalition ground forces entered northern Iraq in support of a large-scale humanitarian relief effort. As is evidenced in Chapter 17, the operation was later taken over by UN and other relief agencies who were present in Iraq in accordance with a memorandum of understanding concluded with the government in Baghdad on 18 April. A limited number of UN guards were later deployed in northern Iraq to foster the climate of trust necessary for the return of refugees and displaced persons to their homes.

The coalition operation in northern Iraq was supported by an aerial exclusion zone covering Iraqi airspace north of the 36th parallel. In August 1992, coalition powers also declared an aerial exclusion zone covering Iraqi territory south of the 32nd parallel. The justification for the latter operation heavily relied on the allegations concerning Iraqi human rights performance detailed in the preceding chapter.

United Kingdom Foreign and Commonwealth Office Press Office, 8 April 1991.

1. Statement by the UK Prime Minister: A Safe Haven for the Kurds, 8 April 1991

Following is transcript of a press conference given by the Prime Minister Mr John Major in Luxembourg [*after having attended a meeting of the European Council*]:

PRIME MINISTER: This meeting of the European Council was planned some time ago at the request of President Mitterrand. What has become apparent in the last week or so has been that the need it has become urgent as the events have unfolded in Iraq in front of all of us on television and elsewhere. I wrote last week to Prime Minister Santer asking him to put the plight of the refugees in Iraq at the top of our agenda for today's meeting. He did so and I would like to record my gratitude to him for his action in that respect.

This afternoon we have seen a meeting that has been characterised amongst all those who spoke at it by real anger at what has been happening in Iraq in recent days, not only real anger but an agreement on practical action to relieve the suffering of the refugees and a determination to stop the blood-letting that has been going on.

At Prime Minister Santer's invitation I spoke at the beginning of the meeting at which point I put forward an action plan of four main points that are intended to build on Security Council Resolutions 687 and 688. The first of those was that we should agree today a generous Community contribution to the international appeal which has also been launched today by the Secretary General of the United Nations. Britain had taken the lead last week in pledging 20 million pounds sterling to the relief fund. The Community today as a whole will now contribute on a level which matches that sum, a total of 150 million ECU. I urged in discussion this afternoon that the money should be disbursed as quickly as possible. It is needed now and we should not get bogged down in budgetary procedures. I am confident in the light of discussion that the money will be made available speedily and will get where it is most needed within a matter of days.

The Royal Air Force have been dropping supplies into Iraq today. That air drop will continue for as long as is necessary. But although that is valuable and worthwhile it is not in itself a substitute for organised relief on the ground.

The second suggestion was to propose the establishment of a safe haven in northern Iraq under United Nations control where refugees, particularly Kurds, although there would be some of course who would not necessarily be Kurds, would be safe from attack and able to receive relief supplies in a regular and in an ordered way.

Thirdly, I said that sanctions must remain in force until Saddam Hussein's offer of an amnesty is made permanent and the persecution of the Iraqi Kurds ceases.

Fourthly, I proposed to colleagues a total arms embargo must be maintained on Saddam Hussein's Iraq for as long as he remains in power. One of the most frightening things about Iraq under his leadership has been the ability of a tin pot dictator to acquire high technology weapons as well as conventional weapons on a truly massive scale. As a result of this I proposed a register of arms sales at the United Nations to monitor and control the scale of arms build-up in any one country. This is a vexed and a difficult issue and it is one in the past where honest feeling has not always applied, but with all the means open to us I believe it would be possible to get an early warning of a country that was building up an offensive rather than a defensive capacity in military weapons and then put ourselves in a position where the international community could do something about it.

I wanted to put those ideas to our Community partners this afternoon and we put them in parallel to our American partners as well also this afternoon. At the same time I instructed our Ambassadors in the capitals of the five Permanent Members of the Security Council to discuss them with those governments. I also instructed our Ambassador at the United Nations to put my proposals to the Secretary General and to discuss them with the Permanent Five in New York. This action is under way as we speak.

I am glad to say that in this afternoon's meeting all of those four points were agreed. We then went on to discuss other issues including longer term support for stability in the Middle East and the lessons for European policy that we need to learn from the Gulf war. We have shown that we have learned one lesson very clearly. When faced with a human tragedy of appalling dimensions we need a response that is swift, generous and determined. I believe the Community have agreed precisely that this afternoon.

(QUESTIONS AND ANSWERS)

QUESTION: What kind of scale of enclave are you envisaging? Secondly, we understand that if this proposal were to be rejected by Baghdad you would nonetheless wish to see it implemented even if this involved the use of force to defend the enclave. Thirdly, that the enclave should remain in being for as long as Saddam Hussein is in power.

PRIME MINISTER: In terms of the size of the safe haven, which I think is perhaps a way I would prefer to put it rather than an enclave, I see it as a two stage process and it will certainly be progressive. The immediate aim will be to get the Kurds and the other refugees actually down from the mountains and into a safe area, that is the first stage. The second is to get them back home. So it is a progressive concept and we will have to discuss the precise size. The question lurking perhaps at the back of your mind is would that include some of the large towns and I would not rule out that, though I think that would be the second stage of the progressive van [*sic*] that I have in mind.

I would be surprised if it was rejected by Baghdad in the light of the wording of UN Security Council resolution 688, I would also be surprised in view of the amnesty that has been offered, but I certainly would not be deterred in proceeding with this in the event that Baghdad did deny ready and willing access to the United Nations to establish this particular safe haven, I think it is necessary for us to go ahead with it.

The third point as to whether it was necessary for it to stay there for so long as Saddam Hussein is in power is impossible to answer at this moment. I do not necessarily envisage it as a short term option. It may continue for some time and we would have to see how events unfolded, but the key question would be that it would need to be there for so long as it was necessary to ensure that the Kurds and the other refugees were safe.

QUESTION: How would this actually work in practice? Would the Iraqis have any presence in such an area. Who would patrol it? Who would administer it? Who would pay for it and presumably you would need a Security Council resolution to set it up? Secondly, how was the idea received here and what assurances have you been given by the meeting that this idea is something which people believe is a practical one?

PRIME MINISTER: The idea was received here with I think universal support. There was no opposition and there was very generous support for it from a number of colleagues. The French and the Germans spoke very warmly of these proposals, and I think there is no doubt that they have European Community support. Insofar as controlling and patrolling is concerned, that will be a matter for the United Nations and it will be funded in the usual way through the United Nations. As to whether we will need a new Security Council resolution, we do not believe so. We believe the rubric exists within 688 to avoid the need for a separate resolution but clearly we will need to discuss that in New York.

QUESTION: What would be the nature of any military force that was necessary to protect this safe haven and would it involve British forces?

PRIME MINISTER: That may depend upon the negotiations that are actually yet to proceed and the discussion that there is to be in the United Nations. It may be that there would be a need for a military presence on the borders to ensure that it remained a safe haven. But predominantly it would be civilian since the conflict with the Western powers has ended and we would certainly hope that under the proposal that I have in mind the Kurds and other refugees would be in a safe haven and that Iraq would not be in a mood to attack that safe haven. That is clearly one of the matters that we would wish to discuss with our United Nations partners before we can be definitive about that. One thing is clear, there is a need for such a safe haven and we will press the case for it very hard indeed in the United Nations.

QUESTION: Have you discussed this idea with Washington before presenting it to your Community partners tonight?

PRIME MINISTER: No I did not discuss it with Washington prior to that. I put it to the Community this afternoon having asked for the Kurds to be the first item on the agenda today and in parallel we put it to the United States this afternoon.

QUESTION: What makes you think that a tin pot dictator, as you described him, would respect a United Nations presence in Kurdistan, especially if it is only a civilian presence?

PRIME MINISTER: The Iraqis have offered an amnesty. We expect them to keep to that amnesty, despite his actions in the past in attacking Kuwait I think he would be very ill advised to attack a safe haven that was under United Nations control.

QUESTION: What was the reaction from Washington?

PRIME MINISTER: I have not yet spoken to President Bush personally but I understand the reaction from Washington was supportive. ...

QUESTION: How confident are you of getting the full support of all five Permanent Members of the Security Council and in particular the Chinese and Soviets?

PRIME MINISTER: I do not know whether we will achieve that but whether we can achieve it easily or not I do know that it is right to try and achieve it and that is what we have put in train today. Clearly France will support us for she has already done so. There is every indication that the United States will support us, we will press the case, indeed our Ambassadors even as we speak will be doing so, in Peking and in Moscow, so I hope very much we will be able to get an agreement. One of the reasons for launching it today was that on this occasion we have managed to get the agreement of all the members of the European Community. That is a very substantial and worthwhile beginning to getting any approval from the United Nations and I think that was the right way to proceed.

QUESTION: You expressed your uncertainty as to whether the Soviet Union and China would go along with this. If they do not could this project be carried out outside the United Nations? Are you willing to pursue it say with European and American forces?

PRIME MINISTER: I do not at this stage accept that we will not be able to get agreement and I think that would be the best way to proceed. I would prefer not to speculate beyond that.

QUESTION: For as long as this safe haven lasts, is it not the reality that Iraq is being partitioned; and secondly is it your understanding or desire that within the safe area all Iraqi forces would have to withdraw?

PRIME MINISTER: No I do not accept that it would be partitioning. What we are actually seeking to do is to provide what is a safe haven. We are not dividing the country in the sense that one talks of it as a partition into two particular halves. That is not what we are seeking to do. The moment that it is clear that the Iraqis are no longer going to persecute the Kurds and the other refugees and that we are absolutely clear beyond a doubt that that is the case then there would be no more need for a safe haven. But clearly for a while we will need it and we will wish to judge the Iraqis by their actions rather than necessarily by their words. I think the world has learned to its distress over the last year or so that you cannot necessarily take the present Iraqi government's word at face value so it would be there for some time but I do not think we are in the business of partitioning the country. I made it clear and so did other people throughout the whole of the Gulf conflict that we were not in the business of altering the borders of Iraq. We are still not in the business of doing that. What we are seeking to do is to provide protection for Kurdish and other refugees within Iraq from the treatment that they have faced in the last few weeks.

S/22459, 8 April 1991

2. Identical letters from the Permanent Representative of Iraq to the United Nations addressed respectively to the Secretary-General and the President of the Security Council, 8 April 1991

On instructions from my Government, I have the honour to transmit to you herewith a letter dated 7 April 1991 from Mr. Ahmed Hussein, Minister for Foreign Affairs of the Republic of Iraq.

...

The President of the United States of America, George Bush, announced on 5 April 1991 that United States aircraft belonging to the United States Air Force would begin on Sunday, 7 April 1991, to conduct flights in Iraqi airspace, over northern Iraq, in order to drop what he referred to as relief supplies for the refugees and other civilians suffering hardship owing to the conditions prevailing there. The American President maintained that these operations were based on humanitarian considerations. On the following day the British Government hastened to join its major ally the United States, announcing that it would conduct a similar operation on 8 April.

Iraq was informed of these initiatives through the Permanent Missions of the United States of America and the United Kingdom to the United Nations in an insolent manner constituting an insult to the people and sovereignty of Iraq.

The affliction suffered by the Iraqi people is due to the destruction of the amenities of daily life as part of the savage annihilation wrought by the forces of the United States and its allies; what this people now needs is the immediate removal of the economic embargo imposed on it, not the dropping of crumbs of food and blankets in an ostentatious operation that has nothing humanitarian about it.

Iraq strongly protests against this American and British action which infringes the sovereignty of Iraq in a shameful violation of the principles of international law and constitutes direct interference in the internal affairs of Iraq, inasmuch as this is not taking place through the Iraqi authorities and the Iraqi Red Crescent Society.

The entire operation reveals and confirms the ill will of the United States and the United Kingdom towards Iraq and further corroborates the propagandistic aims of the operation, which purports to show the concern of those two imperialist Governments with humanitarian issues. If the offer of aid genuinely stemmed from good intentions and humanitarian goals, it would have been possible to deliver the alleged relief supplies to Iraq directly or through Jordan or Turkey, rather than by violating Iraq's sovereignty.

...

S/22499, 15 April 1991

3. Letter from the Permanent Representative of Japan to the United Nations addressed to the Secretary-General, 12 April 1991

I have the honour to transmit herewith the text of a statement issued on 12 April 1991 by the Press Secretary for Public Information and Cultural Affairs of the Ministry of Foreign Affairs regarding the air drop of relief materials to evacuees stranded in Iraq.

...

1. On 10 April, the Government of Japan, in response to requests from Iran and Turkey, with which it enjoys friendly relations, and out of humanitarian concern, decided to dispatch a Japanese disaster relief team to Iran and to send emergency relief materials to Iran and Turkey, where a large number of evacuees, most of whom are Kurdish, are entering from Iraq. This is in addition to the financial aid of 10 million dollars it is extending to international organizations concerned through the United Nations Disaster Relief Coordinator's Office (UNDRO).

2. There are still also a large number of evacuees stranded in Iraqi territory. The situation of these evacuees is even more severe than that of the evacuees who have fled to Iran and Turkey, because it is more difficult to get assistance to them. Despite United Nations Security Council resolution 688, which "insists that Iraq allow immediate access by international humanitarian organizations to all those in need of assistance in all parts of Iraq", international humanitarian organizations have thus far been unable to get adequate assistance to the evacuees in Iraq. Several countries, including the United States, the United Kingdom, and France have therefore been airdropping relief materials for them. The actions of these countries will help to alleviate the suffering of the evacuees in Iraq, and the Government of Japan appreciates and firmly supports their humanitarian activities.

4. UK House of Commons Parliamentary Debate, 15 April 1991

The Secretary of State for Foreign and Commonwealth Affairs (Mr. Douglas Hurd):

With permission, Mr. Speaker, I wish to make a statement about the relief of suffering in Iraq. We are faced with suffering and fear on a huge scale - inside Iraq, on both sides of the border with Turkey, on both sides of the border with Iran, and in the demilitarised zone bordering Kuwait. Each of these areas has its difficult problems and in all of them the needs are formidable.

Our response has two elements: first, to keep the refugees alive; and, second, to create conditions in which they can return home in safety.

We have given prompt humanitarian help. We airlifted relief supplies to the Turkish and to the Iranian Red Crescent Societies. With the United States and France, Royal Air Force aircraft have been airdropping supplies into northern Iraq. With the Americans and Germans we are now engaged in a helicopter airbridge. My right hon. Friend the Secretary of State for Defence has arranged for six more Chinook helicopters to deploy to Turkey from the middle of this week, bringing to nine the British helicopters joining in this effort. We are contributing over £20 million to appeals by the United Nations and other international agencies. This includes the International Committee of the Red Cross, which is at present providing the most effective help inside Iraq. Part of this money will go to our own non-governmental organisations whom I met this morning.

We helped bring about Security Council resolution 688 which requires Iraq to co-operate with the United Nations and other international humanitarian organisations and to stop repression. The Iraqis are receiving UN missions led by the Secretary-General's representative, Mr. Suy, and by the UN co-ordinator, Prince Sadruddin.

At the special European Council at Luxembourg on 8 April, my right hon. Friend the Prime Minister put forward a four-point plan to build on the resolutions of the Security Council. First, he proposed the establishment of temporary safe havens in Iraq, in which UN officials can provide for the basic needs of refugees and monitor their security until they can return to their homes in safety. Secondly, he proposed a generous contribution by the European Community to the UN and other appeals for funds for humanitarian relief. The Community immediately contributed 150 million ecu.

Thirdly, apart from food and humanitarian supplies, he proposed that economic and financial sanctions against Iraq should remain in force until Saddam Hussein's offer of an amnesty is made permanent and the international community is satisfied that persecution of minorities in Iraq had ceased. Fourthly, he proposed a strict arms embargo against Iraq to remain in force as long as Saddam Hussein is in power.

We are vigorously pursuing this proposal for safe havens. Our aim is to create places and conditions in which the refugees can feel secure. We are not talking of a territorial enclave, a separate Kurdistan or a permanent UN presence. We support the territorial integrity of Iraq.

But we have to get the refugees off the mountains. That is the unanimous view of those who have visited the area on behalf of the ODA and the British NGOs with whom I talked this morning. Some refugees are now being admitted to places in Turkey and Iran where they can be better cared for. That is welcome, but it is not the right answer except temporarily. We should not aim to add a new permanent refugee problem to the others that already disfigure the world.

The Kurds should be enabled and encouraged to return to their homes, where effective help can be given, but they will not do that unless they feel secure. Undertakings such as those made yesterday by the Iraqi Government will not suffice for that purpose. The United Nations presence in Iraq must build up fast and solidly to monitor and to ensure the safety of those whom the Security Council has resolved to help. We share the view of President Bush when he said yesterday:

> "We will not tolerate any interference in this massive international relief effort".

To help to carry the British relief effort forward, my right hon. Friend the Minister for Overseas Development will visit Turkey and Iran, including the frontier areas, later this week.

...

Weekly Compilation of Presidential Documents
Vol. 27. No. 16.

5. US The President's News Conference, April 16, 1991

The President. I have a brief statement here, and then I'll be glad to take a few questions.

Eleven days ago, on April 5th, I announced that the United States would initiate what soon became the largest U.S. relief effort mounted in modern military history. Such an undertaking was made necessary by the terrible human tragedy unfolding in and around Iraq as a result of Saddam Hussein's brutal treatment of Iraqi citizens.

Within 48 hours, our operation was providing scores of tons of food, water, coats, tents, blankets, and medicines to the Iraqi Kurds in northern Iraq and southern Turkey. The scale of this effort is truly unprecedented. Yet the fact remains that the scale of the problem is even greater. Hundreds of thousands of Iraqi Kurds are in difficult-to-reach mountain areas in southern Turkey and along the Turkish-Iraq border.

The Government of Turkey, along with U.S., British, and French military units, and numerous international organizations, have launched a massive relief operation. But despite these efforts, hunger, malnutrition, disease, and exposure are taking their grim toll. No one can see the pictures or hear the accounts of this human suffering - men, women, and most painfully of all, innocent children - and not be deeply moved.

It is for this reason that this afternoon, following consultations with Prime Minister Major, President Mitterrand, President Özal of Turkey, Chancellor Kohl this morning, U.N. Secretary-General Perez de Cuellar, I'm announcing a greatly expanded and more ambitious relief effort. The approach is quite simple: If we cannot get adequate food, medicine, clothing, and shelter to the Kurds living in the mountains along the Turkish-Iraq border, we must encourage the Kurds to move to areas in northern Iraq where the geography facilitates rather than frustrates such a large-scale relief effort.

Consistent with United Nations Security Council Resolution 688 and working closely with the United Nations and other international relief organizations and our European partners, I have directed the U.S. military to begin immediately to establish several encampments in northern Iraq where relief supplies for these refugees will be made available in large quantities and distributed in an orderly way.

I can well appreciate that many Kurds have good reason to fear for their safety if they return to Iraq. And let me reassure them that adequate security will be provided at these temporary sites by U.S., British, and French air and ground forces, again consistent with United Nations Security Council Resolution 688. We are hopeful that others in the coalition will join this effort.

I want to underscore that all that we are doing is motivated by humanitarian concerns. We continue to expect the Government of Iraq not to interfere in any way with this latest relief effort. The prohibition against Iraqi fixed- or rotary-wing aircraft flying north of the 36th parallel thus remains in effect.

And I want to stress that this new effort, despite its scale and scope, is not intended as a permanent solution to the plight of the Iraqi Kurds. To the contrary, it is an interim measure designed to meet an immediate, penetrating humanitarian need. Our long-term objective remains the same: for Iraqi Kurds and, indeed, for all Iraqi refugees, wherever they are, to return home and to live in peace, free from repression, free to live their lives.

I also want to point out that we're acutely concerned about the problem of the Iraqi refugees now along the Iran-Iraq border and in Iran. I commend the members of the European Community for their efforts to alleviate hardship in this area. We, ourselves, have offered to contribute to international efforts designed to meet this humanitarian challenge.

As I stated earlier, the relief effort being announced here today constitutes an undertaking different in scale and approach. What is not different is basic policy. All along, I have said that the United States is not going to intervene militarily in Iraq's internal affairs and risk being drawn into a Vietnam-style quagmire. This remains the case. Nor will we become an occupying power with U.S. troops patrolling the streets of Baghdad.

We intend to turn over the administration of and security for these sites as soon as possible to the United Nations, just as we are fulfilling our commitment to withdraw our troops and hand over responsibility to U.N. forces along Iraq's southern border, the border with Kuwait.

But we must do everything in our power to save innocent life. This is the American tradition, and we will continue to live up to that tradition.

Assistance for Iraqi Refugees

Q. Mr. President, your administration estimates that up to 1,000 Kurds are dying each day. How do you respond to critics who say that you've acted too little, too late, and that you've turned your backs on the very people that you inspired to rise up against Saddam Hussein?

The President. I don't think we have responded too little, too late. It is an extraordinarily difficult logistical problem. And we have been, as I said in my statement, sending lots of humanitarian relief in there - not just the United States, incidentally, other countries as well, a lot of private relief organizations helping out. So, this has been our policy. But I think we have a better chance to facilitate the relief and to get the Kurds in more sanitary conditions by this new program I've announced here today. There's been an awful lot of consultation with the Turks and others going into this. And in terms of the other, I simply don't accept that.

Q. How long do you think that it will be before the United Nations forces can take over from the U.S. and other allies?

The President. You mean in this new operation? We don't know that. We don't know that, but clearly the sooner the better. The United Nations forces will be coming down into the south - the Blue Helmets. And we hope and expect that to be accomplished in a very few days. But this one we're just starting, but we'll have to see what we do. And it may require for a U.N. peacekeeping force in there - or U.N. Blue Helmets - a new resolution from the Security Council. And that's a complicated problem, given the fact that some of the members who were steadfastly with us in the coalition might have problems with something of this nature.

Q. Mr. President, you keep absolving yourself of any responsibility, and yet time after time you are on the record of calling on the Iraqis to take the matter in their own hands, and you never said, not you the Kurds, not you the Shiites. So, how can you really continue to justify that in your own mind when the world's conscience - go ahead.

The President. No, go ahead, finish your question.

Q. Well, the world's conscience has been aroused by this, and we are seeing pictures of this terrible suffering.

The President. Well, I think all Americans - yes -

Q. Obviously, you were taken by surprise, and you have no long-term policy for what is going to happen eventually. Will they be refugees for the rest of their lives?

The President. I hope not. We've got enough - what looks like permanent refugees, and we're trying to do something about that in various areas. The objectives were set out very early on. And the objectives never included going into Baghdad, never included the demise and destruction of Saddam personally. You had many people that were telling me early on, let sanctions work. Let sanctions work. Don't do anything about the aggression at all. We led an international coalition of unprecedented, historic proportions and achieved objectives.

And you're asking me if I foresaw the size of the Kurdish refugee problem? The answer is: No, I did not. But do I think that the United States should bear guilt because of suggesting that the Iraqi people take matters into their own hands, with the implication being given by some that the United States would be there to support them militarily? That was not true. We never implied that. Do I think the answer is now for Saddam Hussein to be kicked out? Absolutely. Because there will not be -

Q. Is he -

The President. May I finish, please? There will not be normalized relations with the United States - and I think this is true for most coalition partners - until Saddam Hussein is out of there. And we will continue the economic sanctions.

Q. Do you concede you encouraged the revolt and the exodus?

The President. I don't concede encouraging an exodus. I did suggest - and it's well documented - what I thought would be good is if the Iraqi people would take matters into their own hands and kick Saddam Hussein out. I still feel that way, and I still hope they do.

Q. You have hundreds of thousands of refugees which will require a large number of forces. How many allied and U.S. forces will be involved inside northern Iraq?

The President. I think rather small numbers because I don't think Saddam Hussein, given the assurances he made today to the United Nations in Iraq - they had some representatives there - would venture to use force. But the problem isn't what we think about it; the problem is what do these Kurdish refugees who have been brutalized by this man think. And what they think is, look, we don't want to take his word. We need some security.

Q. Mr. President, have you actually formally notified Iraq that this is what you're going to do - set up encampments?

The President. No.

Q. Well, I mean, so this is the first word they've received of it?

The President. Well, I think they're talking with the United Nations people about encampments being set up. But this is the first word they know as to what the United States is going to do about it - authoritative word.

Q. Are you sure that they're not going to respond militarily to seeing force come in?

The President. They should not respond militarily. And they underestimated the United States once before on that, and they shouldn't do it again. And I don't think they will. And the United Nations people who have been talking to them in Baghdad don't think that there will be a military response. And since we said no action north of the 36th parallel, in fairness, there hasn't been any military action north of the 36th parallel.

Q. You said before that you didn't like the idea of a protected enclave within Iraq itself. But doesn't this, in effect, establish for months and the foreseeable future the United States military protecting Kurdish refugees in that area? And do you want to continue to leave it ambiguous what the U.S. would do in case there is any effort by the Iraqis against the Kurdish refugees?

The President. I hope we're not talking about a long-term effort. We're working with the French, who've taken a leadership role in a policy to encourage the Kurds to return to the cities. There's some talk about trying to get a U.N. presence along these various way stations as they go back. That would be a very useful idea, and I told Mr. Mitterrand I supported him strongly on that.

But in this one, I don't think it has to be long-term. The main thing, long-term or short-term, from the very beginning we've been trying to save the lives of these women and children and men, and now this is a logical next step to get it done much more sanitarily - get it done in a safe and sensible way.

And some might argue that this is an intervention into the internal affairs of Iraq. But I think the humanitarian concern, the refugee concern is so overwhelming that there will be a lot of understanding about this.

Q. Will the American military be militarily protecting these areas? And what will they do if there is any attack on the refugees?

The President. Well, that was the question I used to get before the war started against - what are you going to do; how are you going to respond to this? And I won't give you any details, but I will simply suggest that these people will be protected. We are not going to say to them, "Come down from the mountains; you will be protected", and then not protect them.

Q. Mr. President, given the condition of many of these refugees, how are you going to get them to these new camps? How far away or how far distance are we talking about moving them, and what role might the U.S. or the allies play in getting them there?

The President. We're going to have what you call a supply train. There will be strong - I mean, not train in the sense of railroad train, but a supply train - and there will be a lot of international support for that. The Turks will facilitate this. I can't give you - there will be maybe five or six camps in these so-called - what Özal calls "flat areas" - but I can't give you an exact estimate on the mileage.

It's not too far in terms of long distances. But what we've got to do now is get in there and build these camps and keep our commitment to be sure that they are safe, and I think they will be. And then you ask a very good question, because how you talk these scared people into coming down, that's another question. But we will be doing our level-best, and we have very good people on the ground there now.

Q. Mr. President, how many troops do you envision being involved in this, and how certain are you of their safety?

The President. Relatively small numbers, and I'm very confident of their safety. We'll have air power around there if needed. We'll be able to protect not only our own people but we'll be able to protect the people that we're setting out to protect, which is these refugees.

Q. May I follow up on that sir? You feel certain enough of their safety that you feel this is not inconsistent with your earlier statements about not putting one U.S. soldier's life on the line?

The President. Yes, I do. I think this is entirely different, and I just feel it's what's needed in terms of helping these people. Some may interpret it that way; I don't. I think it's purely humanitarian. And I think representations have been made as recently as today that these people would be safe, so I hope it proves that way.

Q. Mr. President, you haven't mentioned anything about the situation in the south where there are thousands of Shiites who are equally concerned about what happens when Americans withdraw.

The President. Exactly.

Q. Can we offer the same kind of assurances that they won't be attacked?

The President. The United Nations will be in there soon, and we think that will be very good assurance that they will not be attacked. People forget that the United States has been doing a wonderful job for those refugees for a long time. I've seen no credit given to our troops that are handling that with great concern and compassion. They have done a superb job.

So, what we want to do is see - in that neutral zone - see the Blue Helmets come in there, and then I will continue to keep moving our people out as rapidly as possible. I want to bring them home.

Q. But if the U.N. forces aren't enough to deter Iraqi problems down there, is there some kind of an allied coalition commitment to those people as well?

The President. I think there will be enough. I think that we're operating on the assumption that they will not be attacked with the United Nations in there. I think that would be a serious problem for Saddam Hussein if he took on the entire United Nations, having agreed to these cease-fire conditions. So, I would just stand with that.

President Saddam Hussein of Iraq

Q. Mr. President, your wife suggested yesterday - Mrs. Bush suggested that Saddam Hussein be tried for war crimes and hanged. Do you agree?

The President. I seldom differ with my wife, and I don't know that I would differ with her here. I'll tell you what's the most important thing, however, and that is to get Saddam Hussein out of there. So, if you came to me as a broker and you said, I can get him out of there, but he'd have to be able to live a happy life forevermore in some third country with all kinds of conditions never to go back and brutalize his people again, I'd have to think about it, but I might be willing to say, well, as far as our pressing charges, we'd be willing to get him out. We want him out of there so badly, and I think it's so important to the tranquillity of Iraq that under that condition we might.

But his crimes - do I think he's guilty of war crimes? The environmental terror, the rape and pillage of Kuwait, what he's done to his own people? I would think there would be plenty of grounds under which he would be prosecuted for war crimes.

Q. Former President Nixon suggested a little bit earlier that maybe you should put out a contract and have Saddam Hussein assassinated. What about that?

The President. I think that's unacceptable. I'm not sure that's exactly what President Nixon said, either.

Situation in Iraq

Q. Mr. President, here you are, talking about getting rid of Saddam Hussein, putting additional U.S. forces back into Iraq. How can you be sure that the U.S. is not going to get entangled in that internal situation there, that civil war that you so much want to avoid.

The President. Well, I'm positive in my own mind - put it this way - in my own mind, my judgment is - and I think it's the collective judgment of the people that figured the war out pretty well - is that he won't risk this. And Saddam Hussein is not going to want to reengage in that nature. So, we'll have to see. But certainly, any U.S. forces - and we're not talking about large numbers, I don't know exactly what the numbers are - will be protected. And they will be protected vigorously. But I don't anticipate that. I don't expect, and I don't think the French President expects that; I don't think the British Prime Minister expects it; I don't think the United Nations Secretary-General expects it; the President of Turkey - and we've got a lot of people working this problem.

It is the collective judgment - and they've been right far more than wrong on these matters - that this will not take place. But we're prepared if any force should be used against these helpless people in the refugee camps.

Q. And, Mr. President, some in Congress who voted against the war resolution to begin with now say that you didn't complete the job and have, in fact, created another Vietnam. What's your reaction on that?

The President. I've got to be careful about my reaction to some of that because - maybe you could help me by explaining which people - from what view? The ones that wanted sanctions to work, or ones that didn't want use of military force ever under any condition? Which ones are you talking about?

Q. There were some in Congress who had - well, Senator Kennedy, for example, yesterday in a public statement said that you didn't go far enough to complete the job.

The President. Well, he's entitled to his opinion. I think we completed the objectives that we spelled out; they were fulfilled. And I think the whole world knows that. Now we have another problem, a problem that's a recurring problem. This man has brutalized these people before, and now he's doing it again.

I think I would call to the attention of the critics what the objectives were, what the United Nations resolutions called for. And I think that they were admirably completed. And I am surprised at some who strongly oppose the use of force now sound to me, from some of their clarion calls, that they want to use force to solve the matters in Baghdad, and that is not what we are going to do. And if you did do it, you'd certainly want to go back through the diplomatic approach, and certainly I would not want to do that without having a lot of these people on the record in terms of support.

But I don't think that's needed. I don't believe that's what we ought to be doing. I think the American people want their sons and daughters to come home, and they're going to come home. And the only little difficulty now in terms of coming home is that we have a responsibility to do what we can to help these refugees. We've been doing it from day one. And now, as the problem gets worse and as we see the fear in these people's hearts about coming down out of the mountains, we're taking this next step.

But the fundamental policy is to bring our men and women home, and that's exactly what we're going in the south. Gerry [Gerald Seib, Wall Street Journal] asked the right question: What guarantee? The guarantee is the agreement itself that was enacted by the United Nations and agreed to by Iraq, and the presence of Blue Helmets of the United Nations peacekeeping force.

Q. In all fairness to Senator Kennedy, his reference was to the use of helicopter gunships against the rebels after they had apparently felt that they were encouraged by your remarks to rebel against Saddam.

The President. So, what does he want us to do? I just haven't followed what he's been saying on this subject.

Q. His criticism was that you didn't go ahead and shoot down those helicopter gunships.

The President. You know, I can understand people thinking that. I can understand their criticism. And then, how do you take care of the tanks and the riflemen and the other parts of the divisions that remained in northern Iraq? Helicopters is but a part of it.

You can say, well, if you'd have done that, maybe he'd have stopped. I don't believe that, but I don't fault him for that, if that's what his position was.

Q. Mr. President, the Kurds say that they want an independent Kurdistan. They were promised one after World War II. Why shouldn't they have that?

The President. I said early on that it was not an objective of the United States to see a fractured, destabilized Iraq. And that is the position of our Government, the position of our coalition forces. That's the answer.

Q. I'm sorry, that was after World War I they were promised one. Doesn't that bear any weight with you?

The President. A promise from World War I?

Q. Yes.

The President. No. I say, no, I believe Iraq ought to live in peace and reconciliation with the various factions in Iraq. You've got the Shiites in the south, you've got the center - the Sunis and the Baathists and whoever in the center, and you have the Kurds in the north. They should reconcile their differences and keep that country, with its proud traditions, intact.

But that's a matter that we are not going to try to suggest that it be divided up, if that's what your question is. And I hope I've made that clear from the very beginning.

Q. But can they ever go back to their homes as long as Saddam Hussein is in power?

The President. Yes, I hope they can. Well, good question. They're scared to death to come down out of the mountains. But that's a very good question. But they've got to figure that out. And I think one of the things we're - I'm most hopeful about is that this plan by François Mitterrand bears some fruit - this way station approach so people can come back.

Now, Saddam Hussein has said for them to come back; they don't believe him. They've been betrayed by him. So, I would hope, yes, that someday they would be able to go back. A lot of them aren't country people. I've heard yesterday on some of the news of city people who were lawyers and doctors and have fled from their rather pleasant lives.

So, I would hope that there could be a reconciliation. And the easiest way for the country to be reconciled is to have a new leader. There's no question about that.

6. UK House of Commons Parliamentary Debates, 17 April 1991

The Secretary of State for Foreign and Commonwealth Affairs (Mr. Douglas Hurd):

With permission, Mr. Speaker, I should like to make a further statement about the relief of the suffering in Iraq.

On Monday I reported to the House on the plan put forward by my right hon. Friend the Prime Minister to establish temporary safe havens in Iraq for the refugees until they can return to their homes in safety. I said that we were pressing the plan vigorously. I can now report good progress.

Following my right hon. Friend's initiative, we continued intense discussions with our close allies, particularly the French and United States Governments, our partners in the European Community and the Secretary-General of the United Nations. We warmly welcome the decision announced by President Bush late yesterday to establish, in conjunction with ourselves and the French, several encampments in northern Iraq where relief supplies for the refugees will be made available in large quantities and distributed in an orderly way. This is essential for the survival of the refugees. Security will be provided at these temporary sites by United States, British and French forces. The details are now, today, being worked out in close consultation with our allies and with the United Nations Secretary-General.

These proposals are to help provide emergency aid, as authorised by Security Council resolution 688. We regard these camps as temporary. They will provide first the emergency supplies and shelter needed to keep the refugees alive and, secondly, over time, the reassurance they need to move on in safety to their homes. This is an immediate measure designed to save lives. We shall be working closely with the United Nations. UN resolution 688 requires the Iraqi Government to co-operate, both with measures undertaken to ensure the implementation of that resolution and generally with the Secretary-General's efforts for the refugees.

Meanwhile we shall continue our own additional relief effort. My right hon. Friend the Minister for Overseas Development gave evidence on this to the Select Committee on Foreign Affairs this morning. In addition to our contribution to the air aid bridge, we have contributed over £20 million to appeals by the United Nations and other agencies. We are supporting the efforts of our own non-governmental organisations, and our efforts are not confined to Turkey. My right hon. Friend will leave for Turkey and Iran tomorrow to help to ensure that the relief effort is being properly co-ordinated. Last week we sent 80 tonnes of relief supplies to Iran, and two additional flights, carrying a similar amount, will leave for Iran this week and more will follow.

The Iranian authorities and their Red Crescent are making strenuous efforts, but it is clear to me that a substantial build-up of the international effort to help the Kurds in Iran is essential and urgent.

...

S/22513, 21 April 1991

7. Letter from the Minister for Foreign Affairs of Iraq addressed to the Secretary-General, 21 April 1991

As you are certainly aware, United States armed forces and the forces of other foreign countries cooperating with them have entered the Zakhou region in northern Iraq. The objective of this operation has been stated to be the establishment in Iraqi territory of centres for assisting displaced Iraqi citizens in Turkey. You are also aware that the Government of Iraq is opposed to this measure, since it would constitute a serious, unjustifiable and unfounded attack on the sovereignty and territorial integrity of Iraq.

This measure was announced at a time when the Iraqi Government had made significant progress in its negotiations with Prince Sadruddin Aga Khan, the representative to whom you have entrusted responsibility for relief operations. Steps to carry out the above-mentioned measure were taken on 20 April 1991, even though the Government of Iraq had signed a comprehensive agreement with your representative on 18 April, which provided for the establishment of humanitarian centres throughout Iraq, and in particular in the northern part of the country, with a view to undertaking the assistance operations necessary to induce Iraqi citizens displaced outside Iraq's frontiers to return in complete security to their places of residence in Iraq. It should be pointed out that the Government of Iraq, while opposing the steps taken by United States forces and the foreign forces cooperating with them for the reasons stated above, has not hindered these operations because it is not opposed to the provision of humanitarian assistance to Iraqi citizens who are in need of it and because it wishes to avoid any complication that may prevent the return of all Iraqi citizens in security to their places of residence.

Because the measures taken by the United States forces and the forces cooperating with them constitute a flagrant violation of Iraq's sovereignty and territorial integrity, and bearing in mind our opposition to the creation of centres under United States control inside Iraqi territory and our belief that the agreement which our Government concluded with your representative on 18 April 1991 has made it possible to define all relief operations in Iraq in an integrated and balanced manner, particularly those targeted to Kurds who are Iraqi citizens in such a way as to avoid the realization of the alleged objectives of the United States centres and to remove any justification for the establishment of such centres, which would in one way or another impair Iraq's sovereignty, the Government of Iraq, in pursuance of the above-mentioned agreement, is approaching you to request the United Nations to assume responsibility for the centres referred to above and to have the coordinator appointed by your representative, who is at the present time in Baghdad, immediately to take the measures necessary for the achievement of the purpose which we have described above. I can assure you that my Government will provide you with all necessary assistance in accordance with the above-mentioned agreement. Please find enclosed the memorandum of understanding signed with your representative on 18 April 1991.

...

S/22531, 24 April 1991

8. Letter from the Permanent Representative of Iraq to the United Nations addressed to the Secretary-General, 24 April 1991

On instructions from my Government, I have the honour to transmit herewith a letter dated 24 April 1991 from Mr. Ahmed Hussein, Minister for Foreign Affairs of the Republic of Iraq, requesting that you take immediate action to assume your functions with respect to the provision of relief at the American camps established by force inside Iraq.

...

At 1840 hours (local time) on 22 April 1991, the American liaison officer notified our military representative in the town of Zakho that the American forces were to conduct a relief operation and to use helicopters to land military forces in the town of Amadiyah and neighbouring areas on 23 April. The American liaison officer requested that military forces in the area be notified of the action to be carried out there by the American armed forces, in order to avoid any confrontation or friction.

This American measure comes five days after the agreement which I concluded on 18 April 1991, on behalf of the Iraqi Government, with Prince Sadruddin Aga Khan, your Executive Delegate for relief operations. We have already begun, together with the Coordinator appointed by the Executive Delegate, to take immediate practical steps to implement that agreement. This American action constitutes the second precedent set since 20 April as regards persistent flagrant violations of Iraq's sovereignty and territorial integrity.

In protesting this measure, the Government of Iraq once again requests you to ensure that the United Nations takes immediate action to assume its functions of providing relief at the American camps established by force inside Iraq, in accordance with the agreement of 18 April. That agreement covers the relief operations in Iraq, particularly those on behalf of Kurdish Iraqi citizens, in a comprehensive, integrated and balanced manner, ensuring that each and every purported objective of the American measures will be fulfilled. We submit this request at a time when the Coordinator of relief operations appointed by your Executive Delegate is visiting the northern region in order to establish the United Nations Humanitarian Centres, with our full cooperation.

S/22545, 27 April 1991

9. Letter from the Permanent Representative of Iraq to the United Nations addressed to the Secretary-General, 27 April 1991

On instructions from my Government, I have the honour to inform you that American forces are persisting in their violations of Iraqi territory and their gross encroachments on the sovereignty and security of Iraq. At 1410 hours on 20 April 1991, 11 Chinook aircraft landed foreign forces estimated at one infantry battalion, with complete arms and equipment and supported by four helicopters, in the restricted area between the Iraqi districts of Tall Akbar and Dar Hawzan. At 1630 hours on the same day, four large transporter vehicles carrying American soldiers entered Iraqi territory from Turkey along the road from Ibrahim al-Khalil to Zakho, driving up to the Ibrahim al-Khalil checkpoint and then entering Iraqi territory.

These operations constitute a flagrant violation of Iraq's sovereignty and an act of overt intervention in its internal affairs, for the purpose of undermining its security and internal stability. In informing you of these violations, I request that you take whatever measures are required to halt them in accordance with the purposes and principles of the Charter of the United Nations.

...

S/22550, 29 April 1991

10. Letter from the Permanent Representative of Iraq to the United Nations addressed to the Secretary-General, 29 April 1991

On instructions from my Government, I have the honour to provide you with some evidence and information available to us concerning serious breaches and unprecedented violations of the sovereignty, independence and territorial integrity of Iraq by the United States of America and its allies, as follows:

1. American helicopters and fighter aircraft transported units in the northern Iraqi area of Zakho throughout the day on 22 April 1991. They also carried out low-altitude reconnaissance and provocation missions, particularly in the direction of the Iraqi units stationed to either side of the Zakho mountain pass.

2. Seventy-eight American vehicles crossed from Turkey on 22 April 1991, across the Ibrahim al-Khalil bridge.

3. As of 2400 hours on 22 April 1991, American units were located at the following positions:
(a) One infantry battalion plus in the restricted area between Tall Akbar and Kirin;
(b) One infantry battalion minus on the two sides of the Zakho pass.

4. At 0115 hours on 24 April 1991, four American fighter aircraft flew low over the area of Zakho. One of them dropped flares between the Ibrahim al-Khalil bridge and the town of Zakho.

5. A number of saboteurs were sighted on 24 April 1991 in a Coaster bus near the fuel station set up by the Americans at Tall Akbar.

6. A number of foreign correspondents in Zakho are conducting unauthorized interviews with Iraqi citizens.

7. On 26 April 1991, Netherlands patrols guided by a number of saboteurs told security authorities in the Zakho municipal area that they must leave the town. They also prevented the local police from performing their duties at the town's water supply department.

This evidence proves that the United States of America is persisting in its violation of the sovereignty, security and independence of Iraq and overtly intervening in its internal affairs. In placing these facts before you, my country's Government hopes that you will take appropriate measures to halt such action in accordance with the Charter of the United Nations.
...

US Department of State Dispatch, Vol. 3, No. 26, 29 June 1991

11. Edward P. Djerejian, Assistant Secretary for Near Eastern and South Asian Affairs, Statement before the Subcommittee on Europe and the Middle East of the House Foreign Affairs Committee, Washington, DC, 24 June, 1992

In Iraq, we continue our leading role in the international effort to maintain sanctions and pressure on Saddam Hussein. Iraq has failed to comply with Security Council requirements in many areas. In light of this clear record of non-compliance, we joined in the Security Council vote last month to maintain economic sanctions against Iraq. As President Bush has made clear, we favor the continuation of sanctions as long as Saddam Hussein continues to hold on to power.

Because of the Iraqi Government's threats to its own people, we have asked Turkey for further extension of Operation Provide Comfort. This presence, particularly low-level aircraft flights, was significant in keeping recent Kurdish elections free of Iraqi interference. We welcomed those elections in the context of Kurdish statements that they did not challenge Iraqi territorial unity. Let me make it clear that Iraq's territorial integrity remains an important part of US policy and a vital element of regional stability. We look forward one day to elections throughout Iraq so that the Iraqi people can freely choose their representatives and a government that reflects the pluralistic nature of Iraqi society. Currently, we are closely monitoring Saddam Hussein's actions throughout the country and will not tolerate violations of the UN resolutions, including UN Council Resolution 688, which demands an end to acts of repression.

... Hundreds of international relief workers are acting to meet the humanitarian needs of the Iraqi people.

Clearly, Saddam hopes to frustrate and outlast the will of the Security Council. However, he should have no illusion that the international community will forget his record of lawless brutality or accept anything less than full compliance with the UN Security Council resolutions. He is simply, in our view, unredeemable. We will enforce the UN sanctions fully.

The Iraqi people deserve new leadership which will not only be representative of the pluralistic nature of Iraqi society but ready to live a[t] [sic] peace with Iraq's neighbors. To that end, we applaud the Iraqi opposition for their courage in standing up to a ruthless regime by meeting last week in Vienna. We hope this is a step toward greater unity under freely chosen leaders and toward a future in which all Iraqis can enjoy the freedoms so long denied them by Saddam Hussein.

US Department of State Dispatch, Vol. 3, No. 26, 29 June 1991

12. Assistant Secretary of State Edward Djerejian's testimony before the US House Foreign Affairs Subcommittee on Europe and the Middle East, 30 June 1992.

REP. HAMILTON: Now the - and I know I'm jumping around quite a bit, but there - a lot has happened in the few days since you were here.

The Turkish government has renewed the mandate for the forces related to Operation Provide Comfort, and I guess - where are we now in obtaining a renewal for the 1100 UN personnel presence in Iraq?

MR. DJEREJIAN: Well, we're - the UN is negotiating this with the regime in Baghdad, and I think we're coming to the close of those discussions with the Iraqi regime.

REP. HAMILTON: Iraq is balking at their presence, are they?

MR. DJEREJIAN: Yes, sir. Saddam Hussein has been balking at the presence of the UN in Iraq. He wants to, obviously, mitigate their effectiveness, he's disturbed by the numbers, he certainly is trying to counter the thrust of the UN resolutions which call for a - the activities of the UN Special Commission, the Humanitarian Commission, the activities directed against his weapons of mass destruction, but quite frankly, the pulse we get from the UN, Mr. Chairman, is that regardless of his attitude, the international community and the UN is intent on maintaining the UN presence in Iraq, and to continue with the various inspection regimes we have, and monitoring regimes we have in Iraq.

REP. HAMILTON: So our position is that the 1100 shall stay, and the 500 armed UN guards among them shall remain.

MR. DJEREJIAN: Yes, sir.

REP. HAMILTON: And do we have the solid backing of the Security Council with respect to that?

MR. DJEREJIAN: I believe we do, sir, yes.

REP. HAMILTON: Do you expect this to be resolved soon?

MR. DJEREJIAN: I do, sir.

...

13. Transcript of interview given by the UK Prime Minister, Mr John Major, in London, on Tuesday, 18 August 1992

INTERVIEWER: Prime Minister, have you in effect issued an ultimatum to Iraq?
PRIME MINISTER: What we have said to the Iraqi authorities is that we are now perfectly clear that they are engaged in systematic repression of the Shias in the south of Iraq but that is not acceptable and that it has got to stop. What we propose to do, therefore, is to monitor the whole area from the air and whilst we are doing that to ensure the security both of the Shias and of their aircraft we will instruct the Iraqis not to fly in that area.
INTERVIEWER: And if they do?
PRIME MINISTER: If they do they will be perfectly well aware that we are likely to attack them.
INTERVIEWER: So they will be attacked?
PRIME MINISTER: They will be attacked if they fly in the area that is proscribed, yes.
INTERVIEWER: What happens if they fight back?
PRIME MINISTER: I think we have seen that in the past they would lose, but I hope that that would not be the case, I hope they would accept the fact that the coalition, particularly the Americans, the French and the British, will be there in force monitoring what happens from the air and I hope and believe that they will accept the edict that will be laid before them and not fly in that area.
INTERVIEWER: The fact is that this could conceivably lead to an escalation, you fire on them, they respond and there could be an escalating situation once again in Iraq?
PRIME MINISTER: I think you have to realise why we are doing it. We are not doing it for no good reason, it is happening because there is clear evidence now of the systematic murder, genocide, of the Shias, bombing by Saddam from the air on the Shias, reports not yet confirmed but fairly good reports of napalm being used. This has been going on for some time, increasing evidence of this is coming to light and it is no longer tolerable. In northern Iraq sometime ago we established safe havens in order to protect the Kurds from Saddam Hussein, now it is the Shias who need protection and the international coalition have decided that that is necessary.
INTERVIEWER: You talk about this now but there is a smell about this, certainly when one hears news about it from the United States, that here is an American President in trouble, going into his Republican Party convention and desperate to do something to be seen as very strong and decisive in foreign policy, does that worry you?
PRIME MINISTER: I am not just going into an election and President Mitterrand is not going into an election and we both feel very strongly about this particular issue. What has happened in the last few days is increasing evidence of what is happening to the Shias in the marshlands around the Tigris and the Ufreitis, it is not at all attractive what is happening there. There has also recently within the last few days been a report from the special United Nations Commissioner detailing the atrocities in that area. It is that issue, not an electoral issue, it is that issue that has brought this matter to the forefront of concern.
INTERVIEWER: Although everything that you say about what Saddam Hussein has been doing has been going on for some time?
PRIME MINISTER: The details of what has been happening have not been clear for some time, they are now becoming increasingly clear, monitoring from the air will make it increasingly clear in the future what else is happening and prevent further attacks from the air, that is the purpose of this proscription.

14. Douglas Hurd, Secretary of State, UK, interview with "Today" programme: 19 August 1992
...

Q: Well, let us turn if we may to Iraq. The New York Times this morning says shooting them down, this is if we have planes over there, would put the US in the position of breaking an accord it had pledged to uphold and it says the whole policy is legally untenable and politically unwise and apparently there's nothing in the UN resolution that specifically says you can have an exclusion zone.
A: But we operate under international law. We don't have to do everything. Not every action that a British Government or an American Government or a French Government takes has to be underwritten by a specific provision in a UN resolution provided we comply with international law. International law recognises extreme humanitarian need. No-one has looked at the report which the UN, not President Bush, received the other day from Mr Van der Stoel, its representative can doubt extreme humanitarian need. In support of the UN resolution, it happens to be 688, which ... Saddam Hussein not to commit these acts of aggression against his own people. We're clear, the French are clear, the Americans are clear on a strong legal as well as humanitarian ground in setting up this no-fly zone.
Q: But is this again strictly a UN operation or US/France/UK operation?
A: US/France/UK.
Q: Good. Now our ... I gather our great skill is that we're the ones who can look from above and see what's happening?
A: The RAF lads do that, don't they? They do that and we're keen to take part alongside the Americans and I hope the French. This is a no-fly zone, it's designed to do two things. To prevent Saddam Hussein's helicopters and fixed wing aircraft from zapping his own people, the Shias and the ... and to make sure that we know what is happening and this has provided a deterrent in the north, I mean there hasn't been ground action on any scale against the Kurds, partly because there is the no-fly zone there and our patrols are there in the air knowing what happens.

15. UK Secretary of State's interview on the BBC World Service, 20 August 1992

Foreign Secretary, what is really the main aim of the allies in Iraq, what is the real purpose of the exclusion zone?
A: To try to protect those who are being oppressed in the south, in the same sort of way as we've been protecting those who were oppressed in the north of Iraq.
Q: But it has been suggested of course that there is another agenda, that in fact the *dismemberment* of Iraq is planned and the establishment of a southern Shia state.
A: I think we've always been clear about that. We believe in the integrity of Iraq. Iraq is one country but within that country its rulers have obligations towards their subjects, which is laid down in Security Council resolution 688. We believe in the integrity of Iraq, in one Iraq, decently governed, respecting its obligations to the United Nations.
Q: Now you're taking action under resolution 688 as you've mentioned, which doesn't actually mention the use of force but you see an overwhelming humanitarian need but what about the action you will in fact take if Iraqi aeroplanes appear over the territory. Will you shoot them down, will you attack artillery on the ground?
A: We believe that the no-fly zone should include, well it's a ban obviously on Iraqi helicopters or fixed wing planes and so they will be deterred from flying but they would be excluded if they did fly. I think ground

operations are different now. We have to take this one stage at a time. Obviously one advantage of monitoring a patrol is that you see clearly without any contradiction what is happening on the ground. We would therefore be in a strong position to go back to the Security Council and say, look, despite your resolution 688, this is clearly happening and further steps need to be taken.
Q: But when you deliver the ultimatum to President Saddam Hussein, will he be told that there is the possibility of the use of force if he failed to conform to your wishes?
A: Well, I think that is implicit in the whole exercise. It's implicit in what happens in the north. What happens in the north is interesting. There are these patrols. They haven't given rise to attacks and to combat, they have achieved their purpose and it is because of the success of that operation in giving some protection to people in the north of Iraq and because of the new evidence, the van der Stoel report, about the wholesale breaches of human rights to put it mildly in the south, that we believe the time has come to extend the same principle which has worked in the north.
Q: But there must be contingency plans if things should go wrong?
A: Let us take one step at a time. I have set out the position as it is at the moment and as we plan it at the moment.
Q: Now we have had indications from the United States, in particular from the White House press spokesman in Houston, that there are differences among the allies on the details of this operation. What are these differences?
A: I think what Mr Fitzwater said was that the details have not all been worked out. It's rather a different proposition. I don't think there's any difference between the allies. We've been working very closely indeed. This is a concept which has emerged from all three of us and been agreed by all three of us but as Mr Fitzwater said there are details which remain to be worked out.
Q: Would they in fact influence the timing of the delivery of the ultimatum? Are there in fact such complications that would mean that we would have to wait a while until the ultimatum is prepared?
A: No, I don't think so. But one of the points that needs to be decided is the exact timing.

FCO Press Release 1

16. UK FCO spokesman: Thursday, 20 August 1992

IRAQ

In answer to questions, Spokesman said that there was absolutely no difference between the positions of the Governments of UK, France and the United States on the measures to be taken to protect the Shia' in southern Iraq. Detailed discussions continued between allies and partners.

In answer to further questions, Spokesman stated that the measures proposed were justified under international law in response to a situation where there was demonstrably overwhelming humanitarian need. This action was in support of UN SCR 688 which demanded that the Iraqi Government ceased its repression of the civilian population and demanded that it cooperate with the United Nations humanitarian relief programmes.

S/24475, 21 August 1992

17. Letter from the Permanent Representative of Iraq to the United Nations addressed to the Secretary-General, 21 August 1992

On instructions from my Government, I have the honour to transmit to you herewith a letter dated 21 August 1992 from Mr. Muhammed Said al-Sabaf, Minister for Foreign Affairs of the Republic of Iraq, concerning the very dangerous decision of the United Kingdom, the United States and France to prevent Iraqi aircraft from flying in southern Iraq below the 32nd parallel.

...

I have the honour to refer to the decision - fraught with consequences - of the United Kingdom, the United States of America and France to prevent Iraqi aircraft from flying in southern Iraq below the 32nd parallel on the pretext of protecting the Shiite population from Iraqi air attacks. International press agencies have disseminated the statements made by the highest officials of those three States, which contain a warning of the imminent use of brute force against Iraq.

At its meeting on 18 August 1992, the British Cabinet decided to dispatch Tornado fighter aircraft to take part in that operation. Mr. Douglas Hurd, the British Foreign Minister, stated on 19 August that the decision taken by the United States of America, the United Kingdom and France to prevent Iraqi aircraft from flying over southern Iraq in order to protect the Shiite population was, as he claimed, an operation that the three countries could undertake without any need for authorization from the Security Council.

Such a belligerent and dangerous attitude on the part of the United States, the United Kingdom and France - permanent members of the Security Council - is a prelude to the use of armed force for military aggression against Iraq's independence, territorial integrity and national unity. This represents a grave threat to international peace and security in the region. The true objective of this operation is to divide Iraq on an ethnic and confessional basis in order to control it, plunder its wealth and enslave its people. Iraq will never accept this, as an official Iraqi spokesman stated on 20 August 1992.

The three States in question have assumed the authority to interpret international law and international humanitarian law, as well as to interpret Security Council resolutions without reference to the Council itself, in order to be able to use force to achieve their colonialist goals. Such a step, based on flimsy and mendacious pretexts, is fraught with consequences for the independence and sovereignty of all independent and sovereign States.

In drawing your attention to the extreme gravity of the position adopted by the United States, the United Kingdom and France, we call upon you to assume your responsibilities and prevent the occurrence of this new act of aggression against the Republic of Iraq, a sovereign and independent State, and a founding Member of the United Nations.

18. US Press Release: Coalition to impose "no-fly" zone in southern Iraq, 26 August 1992

Washington - Coalition aircraft will begin flying surveillance missions in southern Iraq August 27, President Bush says, and the coalition "is establishing a no-fly zone for all Iraqi fixed and rotary-winged aircraft.

Bush announced August 26 that the surveillance will "provide coverage of the areas where a majority of the most significant recent violations" by Iraq of UN resolution 688 have taken place.

He said the no-fly zone will be similar to the one the coalition imposed on northern Iraq more than a year ago.

Following is the text of Bush's announcement:

In recent weeks and months we have heard and seen new evidence of harsh repression by the government of Saddam Hussein against the men, women and children of Iraq. What emerges from eyewitness accounts, as well as from the detailed August 11 testimony before the UN Security Council of UN Human Rights Envoy, Max van der Stoel, is further graphic proof of Saddam's brutality.

We now know of Saddam's use of helicopters and beginning this spring, fixed wing-aircraft to bomb and strafe civilians and villages there in the south, his execution last month of merchants in Baghdad and his gradual tightening of the economic blockade against the people of the north. These reports are further confirmation that the government of Iraq is failing to meet its obligations under UN Security Council resolution 688.

This resolution, passed in April of 1991, demands that Saddam Hussein end repression of the Iraqi people.

By denying access to human rights monitors and other observers, Saddam has sought to prevent the world from learning of his brutality. It is time to ensure the world does know.

And therefore, the United States and its coalition partners have today informed the Iraqi government that 24 hours from now coalition aircraft, including those of the United States, will begin flying surveillance missions in southern Iraq, south of the 32 degrees North latitude to monitor the situation there. This will provide coverage of the areas where a majority of the most significant recent violations of resolution 688 have taken place.

The coalition is also informing Iraq's government that in order to facilitate these monitoring efforts, it is establishing a no-fly zone for all Iraqi fixed and rotary-wing aircraft. This new prohibition will also go into effect in 24 hours over this same area. It will remain in effect until a coalition determines that it is no longer required.

It will be similar to the no-fly zone the coalition imposed on northern Iraq more than a year ago. I want to emphasize that these actions are designed to enhance our ability to monitor developments in southern Iraq. These actions are consistent with longstanding US policy toward Iraq. We seek Iraq's compliance, not its partition.

The United States continues to support Iraq's territorial unity and bears no ill will towards its people. We continue to look forward to working with a new leadership in Baghdad, one that does not brutally suppress its own people and violate the most basic norms of humanity. Until that day, no one should doubt our readiness to respond decisively to Iraq's failure to respect the no-fly zone.

Moreover, the United States and our coalition partners are prepared to consider additional steps should Saddam continue to violate this or other UN resolutions.

19. Statement issued by the Members of the Coalition at New York, 26 August 1992, 10 a.m. (New York time)

Through repeated attacks on civilian population centers in southern Iraq, its continuing harassment and economic blockade of minorities in northern Iraq, and its harassment of UN personnel and non-governmental humanitarian workers, the Iraqi Government has continued to demonstrate its unwillingness to comply with the terms of UNSCR 688.

We have previously made clear to you on many occasions that continued repression of the Iraqi population in contravention of UNSCR 688 could not be tolerated.

The debate in the Security Council on 11 August provided alarming new evidence of increased military activity against the civilian population in the south of Iraq, in particular in the southern marshes. This amounts to clear defiance of the Council's resolutions. The use of fixed wing aircraft for the first time in the bombardment of Shi'a villages in particular is a very serious development. The survival of large sections of the population is now at risk.

At the same time the Iraqi Foreign Minister has written to the President of the Security Council rejecting any monitoring by the United Nations of the human rights situation in Iraq.

In view of these failures to comply with UNSCR 688, the coalition has concluded that it must itself monitor Iraqi compliance with UNSCR 688 in the south. Coalition aircraft will therefore begin flying surveillance missions over Iraqi territory south of 32 degrees north to monitor and report on the state of Iraqi compliance with the provisions of the resolution.

In support of this monitoring effort a no-fly zone for all Iraqi fixed and rotary wing aircraft - military and civilian - will be established south of 32 degrees north. This no-fly zone will go into effect twenty-four hours from now and will remain in effect until further notice.

To be clear:

-- Iraq may not fly military or civilian aircraft, whether fixed or rotary wing, south of the 32nd parallel. We will respond appropriately and decisively to any Iraqi failure to comply with this requirement.

-- No threat to coalition operations over southern Iraq will be tolerated. The Iraqi Government should know that coalition aircraft will use appropriate force in response to any indication of hostile intent as defined in previous diplomatic demarches. Inter alia, illumination and/or tracking of aircraft with fire control radars and any other action deemed threatening to coalition aircraft, such as the intrusion of Iraqi aircraft into the no-fly zone, would be an indication of hostile intent.

We remind the Government of Iraq of its obligations under UNSCR 688 and call upon it to end armed repression of the civilian population in the south, end the economic blockade of the north, and end the harassment of UN and other personnel providing humanitarian relief to the Iraqi people.

20. THE SITUATION WITHIN KUWAIT

The extent of damage in Kuwait and the humanitarian situation in that state were assessed by a UN mission shortly after the conclusion of hostilities. This section reproduces the report of that mission along with materials relating to the allegations of mistreatment of Palestinians residing in Kuwait.

S/22333, 6 March 1991

1. Letter from the Secretary-General addressed to the President of the Security Council, 1 March 1991

I have the honour to inform you that the Permanent Representative of Kuwait addressed a letter to me on 27 February 1991, in which, on behalf of his Government, he requested that I authorize the immediate dispatch of a mission to Kuwait. A copy of the letter is attached.

In view of the fact that this request has direct bearing on Security Council resolution 674 (1990), I would appreciate it if you would bring this letter to the attention of the members of the Council so that I may receive their guidance on how to respond.

...

> Upon the instructions from my Government, I should like to request that a mission, authorized by Your Excellency, be immediately dispatched to Kuwait to assess the losses in life incurred during the Iraqi occupation of Kuwait, and to examine the practices by the Iraqi occupation forces against the civilian population in Kuwait. It is requested that the team assesses, as well, the damages inflicted on the general infrastructures in Kuwait. In this regard we propose that the team includes representatives from UNEP, UNESCO, UNICEF and WHO. A report by such a team shall, among other things, guide us in drawing up the requirements for the reconstruction of the country.

S/22334, 6 March 1991

2. Letter from the President of the Security Council addressed to the Secretary-General, 6 March 1991

I have the honour to inform you that I have brought your letter dated 1 March 1991 and its enclosure to the attention of the Council members (S/22333). They have considered the matter and they would welcome your responding positively to the request contained in the letter dated 27 February from the Permanent Representative of Kuwait to send a mission to Kuwait, recognizing the importance of taking all actions possible to facilitate Kuwait's reconstruction and re-integration into the international economic system.

S/22331, 5 March 1991

3. Letter from the Permanent Representative of Kuwait to the United Nations addressed to the Secretary-General, 5 March 1991

I have the honour to forward herewith the text of the statement made today by His Excellency Sheikh Sabah Al Ahmad Al Jaber Al Sabah, Deputy Prime Minister and Minister for Foreign Affairs of the State of Kuwait ...

...

Some irresponsible parties in Palestinian circles have been deliberately circulating false allegations and slanders to the effect that the official authorities in Kuwait have initiated certain practices against the Palestinian community residing in Kuwait. In doing so, those parties aim only to spread a spirit of resentment and disunity in a blatant attempt to cast themselves as the defenders of the fraternal Palestinian people.

As all are aware, the State of Kuwait has embraced expatriates from all parts of the world, including the fraternal Palestinian community, and provided them with the means to make a decent and comfortable living. It has done so on the basis of its belief in its Arab, Islamic and humanitarian obligations and its constant keen commitment to noble Arab values and principles.

Following the wicked occupation of Kuwait's land and people by the Iraqi forces for more than six months, the Kuwaiti authorities resumed - immediately the hated Iraqi occupation was ended - their normal duties of maintaining security in Kuwait. The criminal Iraqi occupiers had destroyed all the country's assets and set up a gang of conspirators and collaborators with a view to achieving their aim of perpetuating the occupation. In order to perform their duty of establishing security and stability in the country, the Kuwaiti authorities are obliged relentlessly to pursue any criminal elements, from whatever community they may come, and to show them no leniency, because those elements have not treated Kuwait and the security of its people in a manner consistent with the dictates of their position as expatriates and guests.

In categorically rejecting these allegations, Kuwait draws attention to its honourable record in its dealings with all those living in its territory and affirms that allegations by diseased minds such as these are false and utterly untruthful. The right of Kuwait to ensure and enhance its security can in no way be interpreted as being directed against any honourable person in the territory of Kuwait - the land of love and peace and the community of building and giving.

S/22337, 6 March 1991

4. Letter from the Chargé d'affaires a.i. of the Permanent Observer Mission of Palestine to the United Nations addressed to the Secretary-General, 6 March 1991

I am instructed by the Executive Committee of the Palestine Liberation Organization, which has the powers and responsibilities of the Provisional Government of Palestine, to bring the following to your immediate attention.

The violent and hostile actions against the Palestinian people living in Kuwait continues at the hands of the armed vigilantes and some elements from the Kuwaiti army in an illegal manner. This includes terror and harassment campaigns launched in the regions of Al Noukra, Hawali, Khitan and Al Salmieh in Kuwait City, resulting in the arrests of great numbers of Palestinians; many of these actions have been covered by several media networks and news agencies. Noting further that the issue of the safety and security of the Palestinians living in Kuwait has been raised on my part with the President of the Security Council, who in turn informed the members of the Council, during the informal consultation of 3 March 1991, of my grave concern expressed to him in this regard.

The Palestine Liberation Organization believes that the Kuwaiti Government and the Arab forces, as well as the foreign forces present in Kuwait, are responsible for the safety and security of our people. At the same time, and as a result of the special existing situation, the international community and the Security Council, in particular, cannot be exempted from this responsibility.

The Palestine Liberation Organization would like to recall that the majority of Palestinians living in Kuwait are long-time residents of the country, and expresses its hope that the Kuwaiti Government will take the initiative in presenting a clear-cut position on this situation, as well as taking action towards a concrete and immediate solution to the problem.

...

S/22391, 21 March 1991

5. Letter from the Chargé d'affaires a.i. of the Permanent Observer Mission of Palestine to the United Nations addressed to the Secretary-General, 21 March 1991

I am instructed by the Executive Committee of the Palestine Liberation Organization, which has the powers and responsibilities of the Provisional Government of the State of Palestine, to bring the following to your immediate attention:

> Violent and criminal actions are being continuously committed against the Palestinians still living in Kuwait who number around 150,000.
>
> Examples of such actions are beating, torturing to death, detaining and kidnapping of thousands, imposing a siege on areas where Palestinians live and excluding them from getting available essentials of life, including food, thus, creating an unbearable situation of suffering and fear. Here I would like to draw your attention to the wide coverage by the media of this situation.
>
> The Palestine Liberation Organization has made unlimited efforts and contacts with Arab and friendly Governments in order to bring this tragedy to an immediate end. It once more calls upon all to do everything they can in this respect.
>
> While I recall my letter of 6 March 1991 on the very same situation (A/45/972-S/22337), I reiterate the responsibility of the international community, particularly the United Nations Security Council, for the safety and well-being of Palestinian civilians in Kuwait under the present prevailing circumstances.

...

A/45/979, S/22372, 21 March 1991

6. Letter from the Permanent Representative of the Sudan to the United Nations addressed to the Secretary-General, 20 March 1991

Upon instructions from my Government I have the honour to convey, with deep regret, that some Sudanese nationals resident in Kuwait are being subjected, among nationals of other countries, to atrocities, humiliation and inhuman harassment by irresponsible elements among the Kuwaiti people. The incidents reported showed that at least one Sudanese national was murdered in cold blood in one of the streets of Kuwait City before the eyes of his wife, who was later subjected to the most indecent and inhuman treatment. This incident was reported by the British paper *The Independent*, on Sunday, 3 March 1991, as well as by other Arab and international mass media. Worse, a number of other similar incidents of killing and maltreatment of Sudanese in Kuwait were also reported to have occurred.

The Government of the Sudan hereby requests the Secretary-General and all relevant United Nations bodies to intervene with the Kuwaiti authorities in order to investigate and put an end to such heinous atrocities, which are now taking place in liberated Kuwait.

The will and determination the United Nations and its organs have exhibited in the process of liberating Kuwait should now continue and persist in order to protect, maintain and safeguard the human rights of each and every individual in that country, in conformity with the norms of international law and human rights.

Furthermore, the Sudan strongly hopes that the legitimate authorities of the State of Kuwait will expeditiously enforce law and order and assume their responsibilities as regards the protection of Sudanese and other foreign nationals living in Kuwait and bring to justice those responsible for the said atrocities.

Prompt action by the Kuwaiti authorities in this direction will definitely improve the existing situation of inter-Arab relations and enhance the spirit of understanding, co-operation and mutual respect.

...

S/22406, 27 March 1991

7. Letter from the Permanent Representative of Kuwait to the United Nations addressed to the President of the Security Council, 26 March 1991

I have the honour to enclose herewith a statement made by H.E. Dr. Badr Jassem Al-Yaqoub, Minister of Information and Minister of State for National Assembly Affairs, on behalf of the Government of Kuwait.

...

Dr. Badr Jassem Al-Yaqoub, ... has made the following statement concerning the rumours that are circulating in some political and media circles to the effect that Kuwait is mistreating its Palestinian brothers residing in Kuwait:

> "1. These strategems, lies and allegations which are being circulated to the detriment of Kuwait under the present circumstances are merely a continuation of the hostile policy that has been pursued by well-known parties since the beginning of the criminal Iraqi invasion of Kuwait's territory. We are fully confident that world public opinion will not be deceived by these strategems, that it will realize their underlying aims and objectives and that it will be able to separate the wheat from the chaff.
>
> 2. Kuwait has always diligently endeavoured to apply the law fully to all Kuwaiti and non-Kuwaiti residents alike, without discrimination among them on grounds of race, origin or affiliation. Anyone who infringes or violates the sacrosanct provisions of the law is subject to its penalties in keeping with the principle of the

rule of law and public order in the State, as is the practice throughout the world.

3. If certain acts have been committed against Kuwaiti or other residents in the circumstances that Kuwait has been experiencing, these matters will be referred to the judicial authorities for judgement in accordance with the law and Kuwait's consistent practice.

Kuwait wishes to assure world public opinion, at all levels from leaders to Governments, peoples and organizations, that it will maintain its tradition as a land of security, justice and peace and that, even under the present circumstances that it is experiencing in the aftermath of the criminal aggression against its territory, Kuwait is perfectly willing to receive all petitions and claims concerning any allegedly unlawful practices against residents of Kuwait, so that appropriate measures can be taken in this regard in accordance with the provisions of the law. Kuwait also affirms its full willingness to receive representatives of international humanitarian bodies and organizations in order to examine this question."

S/22409, 28 March 1991

8. Letter from the Secretary-General addressed to the President of the Security Council, 28 March 1991

Further to my letter to you dated 20 March 1991 (S/22366), I have the honour to inform you that the mission led by Under-Secretary-General Martti Ahtisaari to assess the humanitarian needs arising in the immediate post-crisis environment in Iraq and Kuwait visited Kuwait from 23 to 27 March 1991.

...

Introduction

...

5. In Kuwait, the Mission comprised representatives of the Secretariat, the United Nations Development Programme (UNDP), the Office of the United Nations Disaster Relief Coordinator (UNDRO), the Office of the United Nations High Commissioner for Refugees (UNHCR), the World Food Programme (WFP) and the Food and Agriculture Organization of the United Nations (FAO). It received substantial assistance from Mr. Abdulrahim Abby Farah and members of his mission who were at the time in Kuwait looking into the subject of damages sustained by Kuwait during events subsequent to 2 August 1990 and, in particular, from the technical knowledge and experience of members of Mr. Farah's mission from the United Nations Environment Programme (UNEP). It was also materially assisted by representatives of the United Nations Children's Fund (UNICEF) office in the Arab Gulf States, and by a World Health Organization (WHO) mission that was also in the country at that time. The mission completed its work in Kuwait on 27 March and departed on that date. I returned to New York today, 28 March 1991.

I. *Modus operandi in Kuwait*

6. In close consultation with myself, members of the mission who had remained in Bahrain while I was undertaking consultations in New York began their work immediately upon arrival in Kuwait on 23 March 1991. Teams began to meet with Kuwaiti officials in the fields of food, agriculture, water, sanitation, health, transportation, communications, energy and environmental matters, and to visit various sites and locations throughout Kuwait. Upon my arrival on 25 March 1991 I was briefed by senior members of the mission and immediately met for a working session with Mr. Suleiman Abdul-Razaq Al-Mutawa, Minister of Planning in the Government of Kuwait. With him, I was then briefed at Camp Freedom by Brigadier-General Mooney, United States army, and members of the Kuwaiti Joint Task Force. I met that evening with Mr. Sheikh Nasser As-Sabah, Minister of State in the Kuwaiti Foreign Ministry, and other Ministers. On 26 March I was received by His Highness, Sheikh Saad Al-Abdullah As-Salim As-Sabah, Crown Prince and Prime Minister of Kuwait. I also met with Mr. Abdul-Wahab Al-Fozan, Minister of Health, and with representatives of the diplomatic community. I toured the city of Kuwait and by helicopter, many parts of the country and saw conditions there. Members of the mission accompanied me on these visits and inspections and continued and completed their technical work in the country. With the excellent cooperation of Mr. Farah and his team I and my mission had access to relevant aspects of its technical findings, upon which certain parts of this report also draw. I was briefed by Dr. Daniel Tarantola of a WHO mission that had been invited to the country by the Government of Kuwait for an assessment of health conditions and needs.

7. The Kuwaiti authorities afforded the mission their fullest cooperation.

II. *Summary of findings and recommendations in regard to Kuwait*

8. A summary of the mission's findings and conclusions is set out below. It is based upon a number of internal working papers, technical annexes, visits to sites and oral reports by members of the mission and by other United Nations specialists present at the time in Kuwait.

A. *General remarks*

9. Kuwait is scarred by the ravages of illegal occupation and, subsidiarily, of war. At least two thirds of the population present on 2 August 1990 are now scattered throughout the world. Those who remained have fresh memory of a brutal occupation and the sacking and pillaging of their homes, their resources and their environment. Many vividly recount inhuman or degrading treatment undergone by themselves or family members. I and my mission saw for ourselves prolific evidence of arson, looting, malicious destruction of homes, businesses, markets, museums, libraries and all that a nation cherishes. Kuwait's coast is disfigured by broken buildings and rolls of barbed wire; its beaches made lethal by hundreds of thousands of mines. Above it hangs a thick cloud of oil dark smoke that, on some days, brings a chilly twilight at noon, as well as still-uncharted perils to health. No one knows exactly how many of its oil wells are on fire; but at least half, perhaps 600 to 700, are belching flames and smoke. From the air, the horizon sometimes comprises only black clouds and pillars of fire, torched in a final deliberate onslaught by retreating troops. The environmental havoc still cannot be authoritatively assessed, but its consequences are already felt by neighbouring countries, and may affect yet others still more distant. Rivers, ponds and even lakes of spilling oil lie on the sand and edge towards the wadis, the roads and the sea. Power stations, oil refineries, communications facilities and water-desalination plants have been destroyed by war or vandalized so that they are irreparable. Harbours are blocked, ships sunk, cranes toppled. Life-preserving medical equipment, even ambulances, have been removed; mainframe computers

have been ripped out of government offices and carried off.

10. This scene of devastation, some being calculated, much wanton, was, I learned, even worse four weeks ago, when Kuwaitis began to return to their liberated country. For much has already been done, as the following paragraphs will show, to put Kuwait back on the road to reconstruction. Food supplies are being brought in and distributed, although both officials and observers say that such distribution has at times been somewhat uneven. Some water and power have been restored. Petrol is being made available, free of charge, even for private vehicles. Telephone communications have been partly re-established, and international traffic will soon follow. An assessment of damages to homes, businesses and economic facilities and resources is under way, and much contracting for reconstruction has already been completed. Means of internal and external transportation are starting to function, in a limited fashion, even though there may still be limited air- and seaport capability and many vehicles were stolen or destroyed. Teams of specialists are beginning to assess and remedy the oilfield disasters. A Kuwaiti Government is in place (at this time, on a caretaker basis) and, despite vast logistical and all other species of practical problems, is drawing up plans for reconstruction. It is working closely with a joint Kuwaiti task force, comprising elements of the armed forces allied with Kuwait in the recent conflict, which was established in December 1990 to plan for the time when liberation should have taken place. The allied element of the Joint Task Force comprises civil affairs elements of the United States, United Kingdom, French, Canadian and Saudi Arabian armed forces, with medical, communications, police, transportation, intelligence, aviation, finance, engineering and sanitation specialists and teams from those Governments. At a briefing on 25 March 1991 General Mooney of the United States Army and some of his senior staff described the work of the Joint Task Force in regard to water, food and medical supplies, sanitation, power, telecommunications and transportation, as well as in regard to damage assessment and surveys during the period from December 1990 to date. He said that contracts worth more than $US 550 million had already been signed for work in these various areas. The Joint Task Force said that it believed that the country had now largely overcome the emergency phase and that it anticipated that power and communications would be effectively restored by mid-April in Kuwait City and that most services would be functioning throughout the country in between three and six months. The oil industry would take the longest to restore. The Minister of Planning called the burning of the oil wells "the crime of all centuries", because of its multifarious short- and long-term negative consequences - health, environmental, economic - for Kuwait and other countries as well. General Mooney said that the amount of unexploded mines and other ordnance was colossal. There was, he added, a good military programme for clearance, but he said that he had never seen so much of that hazard before. Many members of the mission saw unexploded weaponry during their work in Kuwait. The Task Force said that clearance of the quantities left behind exceeded the capabilities of the allied forces.

11. Kuwaiti government ministers told me that they were taking the opportunity to review questions of population composition and the future of the workforce. Prior to 2 August 1990 the population was about 2.3 million, of whom about 700,000 were Kuwaiti nationals (about 30 per cent). Most of the population had left the country during the period of occupation and conflict. At the time of my mission to Kuwait, estimates of the remaining population varied between 600,000 and 700,000, of whom perhaps one third were Kuwaitis. The authorities have recommended that their exiled countrymen not return to Kuwait for three months to allow essential services to be rehabilitated, and spoke of the possibility that the future permanent population should be limited, with others being in the country on a more or less short-term basis. They planned that return from exile should keep pace with the gradual resumption of economic activity, the re-establishment of basic social amenities and the reduction of environmental health hazards. While the mission was in Kuwait this policy had not yet been finalized.

12. As during the previous mission to Iraq, we focused our initial attention upon the basic areas of humanitarian concern: the need for shelter, food supplies, clean water, sanitation and adequate health support, as well as on the logistical capability to make these effective for the people as a whole. Particular local conditions may create additional hazards. The account which follows regarding the situation in these various areas of basic concern is affected in one form or another by the general factors that I have sketched above. Kuwait, with the assistance of the Governments cooperating with it in the Joint Task Force, is steadily assessing its needs and seeking to overcome them within the parameters which it is establishing. My recommendations are formulated in the spirit of cooperation with which my mission was received and welcomed, and in the context of the assistance of which the international community is, I believe, capable.

B. *Food and agriculture*

13. Prior to August 1990, Kuwait imported approximately 95 per cent of its food needs, with local agriculture and fisheries playing only a minor role in the national economy (0.7 per cent of gross domestic product (GDP) in 1989). The country had established a six months' strategic food reserve, which was substantially looted during the occupation. Despite this, a sufficient quantity remained to sustain the population until liberation.

14. Emergency food plans for the next three months are hypothesized upon a population of 800,000. The country is organized into 40 consumer cooperatives, each having a food distribution centre. The State-run Kuwait Supply Company has, since liberation, imported large amounts of food. These staples are distributed directly to the cooperatives and then made available, free of charge, to their members. Apart from this, items such as meat, fruits, vegetables and eggs are sold at subsidized prices, and in some instances made available free of charge, to cooperative members. Private retail facilities are now also beginning to open. Some shortages, apparently due to delivery delays, have been noted in respect of baby products and, on the whole, only logistical and administration bottlenecks at frontiers have hampered the general reinstitution of supplies.

15. However, the overall situation has not as yet permitted the reinstatement of the domestic agricultural and fisheries industries whose expansion had been encouraged in recent years. The spread of oil across the land towards the sea and the heavily mined coastal areas have bleak implications for the future of this sector.

16. The mission concluded that the Kuwaiti Government has already established an effective food system aimed at ensuring proper standards of nourishment and preventing suffering amongst the whole population of Kuwait, although it heard a number of complaints that there had been discrimination against certain groups, especially in the days immediately following liberation. It does not appear that any further external food aid is required by Kuwait.

C. *Water, sanitation and health*

17. Kuwait's water supply depends largely on desalination and partly on artesian reservoirs, Moderate

damage was done to the infrastructure by events subsequent to 2 August 1990, and the mission saw one desalination plant which appeared to have been wrecked by the departing forces and was said to be irreparable. Water has, however, been available in limited quantities and areas since liberation. The Joint Task Force informed the mission that it had distributed 11.75 million litres since that time in bulk or bottles. As power was restored, supplies were slowly returning to normal and reaching more neighbourhoods. The authorities believed that the situation would return to normal in a matter of weeks. It remains necessary, however, to monitor the quality of water being supplied, having regard to all the circumstances, including the various current environmental problems.

18. As regards sanitation, the country's three major plants suffered no structural damage and only superficial repairs are required. The Joint Task Force estimated that the system would be fully operational, having been thoroughly tested, by the end of March. A contract for the collection of garbage has been concluded and this is being undertaken.

19. Prior to 2 August 1990 the standard of health care in Kuwait was one of the highest in the world. The national health services had gradually expanded their scope by creating diagnostic and treatment facilities for non-communicable diseases, which required a constantly increasing level of technical sophistication and amount of resources. This was reflected by the number and quality of health facilities, the efficiency of the emergency care service and the creation of centres specializing in a wide range of advanced medical techniques. Six regional and 9 specialized hospitals, 72 health centres and several medico-social institutions in the country were providing medical care and rehabilitation services to the entire population, free of charge. Over 3,200 doctors and 9,900 nurses - the great majority being foreign - were providing such services, with a ratio to the population of around 2.3 million that compared favourably with most countries in the world. Many of the medical technicians whose skilled work helped to make this advanced system work were also from overseas.

20. The immediate consequence of the invasion was the departure from Kuwait of a very large number of medical personnel. The situation is now critical as regards, especially, nursing and technical staff, and the mission was told that the authorities were seeking to recruit several hundred nurses from abroad. The environment is also medically challenging, having special regard to pollution and widely prevalent explosives. Many hospitals, specialists [*sic*] clinics and health centres are either closed down or are operating at reduced capacity. There was little structural damage to the health facilities, which were also used by the occupying forces, but advanced equipment was removed and some destruction was carried out by departing troops. Despite these major difficulties, existing medical, surgical and dental facilities are able to deal with the most urgent needs of a population, which is temporarily reduced in size.

21. A WHO team, together with the Ministry of Public Health, has developed a plan of action for an emergency response period covering the next three months. During this time the situation would be reassessed and further plans formulated. The plan deals with reconstruction of the health care infrastructure (both human and material); the development of surveillance centres during a critical period for the appearance of health hazards; environmental health systems; disease prevention and control, particular vigilance being required during the current period; the establishment of a post-war programme to deal with post-war trauma of various kinds; and the provision of essential drugs. As to this last, while large quantities have been received from various sources, some are at or beyond expiration date, thus requiring careful inventory and verification of shipments. Other short-term needs include the resumption of diagnostic facilities and a blood bank; meeting the high demand from the population for health information and education; the restoration of emergency medical care, including intensive care units; and the reinstatement of managerial, coordinating and technical skills to rehabilitate and reconstruct the health infrastructure. In this regard, the secondment of staff on a multilateral or bilateral basis to the Ministry of Public Health, and the creation of coordinating committees are urgently required.

22. A UNICEF mission arrived in Kuwait on 1 March to provide emergency relief assistance to children. The outcome of its work was a decision to mount an airlift of urgently needed vaccines and cold-chain equipment, and the fielding of a team to assist the Government of Kuwait in dealing with the psychological trauma effects of war on children. Members of the UNICEF team briefed me and the members of my mission on 25 March 1991.

D. *Environmental questions*

23. Kuwait has between 1,200 and 1,400 oil wells (estimates vary). According to local sources, between 500 and 800 were premeditatedly set on fire in the last days of February by the retreating forces. They pour huge clouds of dark oily smoke into the skies, and their flames can be seen for many miles. Damaged wells are also pouring crude oil onto the desert and rivers or lakes of oil are moving forward towards roads, towns and the sea. Several, which have gone out, have had to be set on fire again in order to reduce the flow of oil onto the land. The smoke from the fires forms a dense cloud ceiling at various heights up to about 12,000 feet. Depending upon weather conditions, the smoke is visible in a number of other Persian Gulf littoral States, and I am informed that its impact could spread beyond the Gulf area. The authorities have sought international help in bringing the situation under control and a number of firms, representing 80 per cent or more of the world's present oil-well firefighting capacity, are at present in Kuwait. Work has begun on dealing with the fires, and new equipment is in some instances being built for this purpose. It is, however, made more difficult by land mines and unexploded ordnance in the surrounding areas. No authoritative estimate can as yet be given of the time that will be needed to restore the situation. It is possible that some wells could self-extinguish as water begins to be drawn into them from surrounding strata. It is estimated that about 4 to 6 million barrels of oil are burning each day.

24. Environmental protection agencies of the allied Governments have inspected the situation but there is as yet no certainty regarding the hazards to the atmosphere, to the adjacent territories or to health. The presence of smoke clouds has appeared to lower temperatures locally. They move according to climatic conditions, especially the wind, and have been reported from several other Gulf States. Depending upon atmospheric conditions, environmentalists believe that these clouds could spread further afield.

25. While the mission was unable to make or find any scientific assessment of the impact on health of these emissions, local anecdotal evidence relates to skin, eye and lung ailments, and the situation is being actively studied. It seems clear that monitoring, on a regional basis, is urgently required of the environmental, including health, aspects of the oil-well fires, and that a national infrastructure should be created in Kuwait to assess and communicate related data.

26. Urgent steps are being taken in Kuwait to prevent unignited oil from reaching the sea, thereby creating a further potential marine disaster.

27. As regards mines and other unexploded ordnance, the situation is extremely grave. A number of deaths and

injuries have already been reported both among private persons and among military engineers seeking to neutralize mines. Some maps showing the location of minefields have been handed over to the Kuwaiti authorities. However, both urban and outlying areas are reported to have a plethora of live bombs, rockets, grenades and other unexploded devices. The authorities also stated that explosive booby-traps had been scattered. As regards mines, many thousands have been laid on and around beaches, along the border between Kuwait and Saudi Arabia and in other areas. It appears that they are of a non-ferrous composition, thus being especially difficult to locate using orthodox mine-detecting equipment. They are, moreover, reported to be at least semi-buoyant. If this be so, the future location of at least some may be anticipated to depend upon tides and currents, and to present a threat to the coasts of other Gulf States. My mission was told that engineering detachments of the allied Governments were currently engaged in dealing with the threat from mines and other unexploded ordnance, and members indeed saw military personnel remove some from the area of mission headquarters. However, the onerous task was stated to be too great for the combined resources of the allied Governments, and other engineering concerns were being contacted.

28. I believe that the threat to the civilian population of Kuwait (and possibly of other nearby States), as well as to livestock, requires urgent coordinated action in support of the endeavours of the Government, which is clearly deeply concerned over the situation. Already, a public education programme has been instituted to warn of the dangers, and many areas, including the intensively mined region on the Saudi Arabian border, may need permanent fencing with crossing points. It may also be necessary to develop medical resources for those unfortunate occasions when prevention has failed. This could include the creation of specialist units to deal with injuries and an immediate rescue operation capability.

29. I believe that the ordnance problem is of such gravity that every possible assistance, both through the United Nations and on a bilateral basis, should be extended to assist the Kuwaiti authorities with this programme on an emergency basis. Without it, an acute danger could remain for years to come. In my opinion, this may be one of the most urgent humanitarian needs, as summer begins and the population, adults and children, begins to return to their country from exile.

E. *Refugees and other vulnerable groups*

30. The mission was informed that the Government is in the process of formulating a policy with regard to its human resources requirements with a view to reducing Kuwait's overall dependence on foreign labour. Such review of policies and practices had not been completed at the time of the mission's departure. Depending on its outcome, a revision might affect some categories of workers and, perhaps, some national groups, who might either wish to be re-admitted or whose residence could be discontinued as a result of loss of employment.

31. During a meeting with His Highness the Crown Prince and Prime Minister Sheikh Saad Al-Abdullah As-Salim As-Sabah on 26 March 1991, I alluded to reports emanating from Kuwait, especially in the days immediately following liberation, containing allegations affecting non-Kuwaitis, including Palestinians. The Joint Task Force had also mentioned these matters in the briefing given to me, and representatives of the authorities had emphasized steps being taken to ensure non-discriminatory treatment for the whole population. These included strengthening the police presence and deploying officials of the Ministry of Justice to each police station. His Highness assured me that many fabrications had been circulated on this subject and said that he was himself meeting that evening with a large Palestinian delegation to hear their concerns and provide every possible reassurance. In a statement issued shortly before my departure, the Minister of Information and Minister of State for Kuwaiti National Council Affairs, Mr. Badr Jassem Ya'coub, emphasized that Kuwait would apply its laws equally and without discrimination on grounds of race, origin or descent. The rule of law would be upheld, and whoever infringed it would be punished in accordance with its provisions. The statement concluded that:

> "Even in the current circumstances which it is experiencing as a result of the evil aggression against its territory, Kuwait is fully prepared to receive all requests and claims regarding any practice believed to be illegal to which residents in Kuwait may have been subjected, in order that the appropriate measures regarding such practices may be taken in accordance with the precepts of the law. Kuwait also reaffirms that it is fully prepared to receive representatives from competent international bodies and organizations in order to examine this matter".

32. The mission looked into reports of numbers of displaced persons at the Kuwait-Iraq border and held discussions with the Kuwait authorities, with representatives of the International Committee of the Red Cross (ICRC), the Kuwaiti Red Crescent, the International Organization for Migration, and with the civil administration of the United States Army concerning these persons and others without documentation. It visited a temporary camp at Abdili in northern Kuwait and the border post of Safwan.

33. The Abdili camp accommodated approximately 1,000 persons at the time of the visit, some in tents provided through the Kuwaiti Red Crescent and some in makeshift shelters. Food and medical assistance is also provided by the Kuwaiti Red Crescent. The camp population was composed of some 450 Egyptian nationals who were in the process of being registered for repatriation, 50 persons of various other nationalities and up to 500 Iraqis who arrived prior to a decision by the Kuwaiti authorities to admit only third-country nationals at the border checkpoint. Several thousand Iraqis are also reported displaced to the Iraqi border town of Safwan, fleeing areas of civil unrest in major cities of southern Iraq, in search of security and shelter. Most of them are accommodated in vacated premises within the city and benefit from food and medical assistance dispensed by military forces. A temporary tented camp located on the outskirts of Safwan had already received 200 newcomers only 24 hours after it had been established. This may be indicative of a reported sizeable movement of displaced persons towards the southern tip of Iraq. The mission was also informed of the presence on Kuwaiti territory and at the border with Iraq of several thousand undocumented persons, known as "bedoons", who had previously been working in Kuwait and would now wish to regain either Kuwaiti citizenship or residence.

34. In the circumstances described above and having regard to the type of humanitarian problem observed developing at the border, the mission believes that urgent action may be required including consideration by UNHCR of the establishment of an office in Kuwait. In this connection, the mission is also mindful of a possible need for rapid repatriation, assistance or protection and of the status of the Iraqi territory adjacent to Kuwait in relation to the Geneva Conventions. It would also be desirable, in my opinion, for UNHCR to initiate consultations, along with the International Committee of the Red Cross and the International Organization for Migration, with the Kuwaiti authorities and, as appropriate, the civil administration of the occupying forces, in order to define the most appropriate assistance

or protection measures for all categories of person who may be in need.

F. *Logistics: transportation, communications and energy*

35. According to surveys undertaken by the United States Army's Corps of Engineers, Kuwait's roads underwent moderate damage during the events from August 1990 to February 1991 with bomb craters, surface damage by tracked vehicles and damage to three bridges. As regards Kuwait International Airport, runways and taxiways are only slightly damaged, if at all. However, the landing system, terminals and the other buildings have undergone serious damage and the control tower has been destroyed. Kuwait's two commercial ports of Shuwaikh and Shuaiba are currently being assessed. There are sunken ships and mines, and dock facilities have been seriously affected. The mission was informed that repairs to these various facilities were anticipated to be complete before the end of 1991 at a total cost of around $US 13 million. All the work is expected to be covered by bilateral agreements between Kuwait and the United States, and by commercial subcontracting.

36. The Kuwaiti vehicle fleet suffered major losses during the period. It is estimated that there were around 800,000 motor vehicles in the country in 1990, of which about 85 per cent were private cars. Approximately two thirds of this asset was reported stolen, looted or vandalized. The loss of public and private vehicles is very apparent. For instance, all Kuwait City's fire-engines and the Government's stock of ambulances were removed from the country. The mission was also informed that the authorities are organizing large-scale procurement of replacement vehicles.

37. As regards communications, major damage was caused by war, vandalism and looting to most forms of telecommunications. The Joint Task Force's surveys showed that about one third of the facilities were moderately to severely damaged. Contracts for repair and replacement have already been signed to a total value of $US 23.7 million, with leading international private companies. As of 15 March, 57 per cent of the capacity of the telecommunication facilities had been restored. There is now also a limited international service with the possibility for the whole population of free calling, within certain criteria.

38. Prior to August 1990, Kuwaiti oil production was at the rate of approximately 2 million barrels per day. Currently, at least half its oil wells are on fire; many others are severely damaged. It is estimated that between 4 and 6 million barrels per day are currently being lost and there was, at the time of the mission's presence in the country, no production of crude oil or refined products. However, certain reserves are in storage and are being replenished by imports. Repairs to certain facilities are under way and, it is anticipated, production may be resumed by the end of April to a sufficient degree to sustain adequate supplies of electricity and other services to the population. The timing of a return to previous levels of production is problematical.

39. Electrical supplies have already been restored to most of Kuwait. Its previous power system was regarded as one of the most advanced in the world, with a highly developed grid system. All four of its power stations were damaged during the events. Repairs are under way, as well as to more than 40 substations that incurred varying degrees of damage.

40. My mission has concluded that, despite severe damage done to the nation's transportation, communications' and energy resource base, the process of repair and replacement has already proceeded to such a degree that the systems are fully capable of providing adequate support for humanitarian needs.

G. *Observations*

41. There can be no doubt that a deliberate attempt was made to extinguish Kuwait, its national identity, the pride of its people in their history and achievements. The manner of destruction, with its coordinated vandalism and massive looting, leaves an indelible image. It was a privilege for me and the members of my team to witness the rebirth of a nation, however painful the circumstances. Already, with the cooperation of its friends and allies, the country has made remarkable progress in dealing with immediate humanitarian needs. It is now moving swiftly towards meeting the major tasks of reconstruction. Therefore, little in the way of traditional humanitarian aid is immediately required of the international community at large. Certain vital assistance, as described above, is, however, urgently necessary so that the suffering of the population of Kuwait is not further prolonged, and so that it and its neighbours can again live in good health and peace.

42. Finally, I should like to place on record my appreciation to the executive heads of UNDP, UNICEF, UNHCR, UNDRO, UNEP, WFP, FAO and WHO for the cooperation which permitted a mission of so wide a range of specializations and experience to work with me in Iraq and Kuwait. I believe it most important that the United Nations family of organizations establish ever-closer coordination, and matters of emergency humanitarian assistance provide an excellent area in which this can be developed further. I was especially fortunate in the members assigned to this mission. Their objectivity, expertise and professionalism, often under trying circumstances, and the excellent spirit of cooperation, reminded me once again of the great reservoir of experience and dedication available to the United Nations.

9. ICRC Statement, The Middle East Conflict, May 1991

In Kuwait, since 23 March the ICRC has been visiting persons detained in police stations and the Kuwait City military prison.

10. ICRC Statement, The Middle East Conflict, July 1991

In early June ICRC Director of Operations Jean de Courten went to Kuwait, where he discussed with the authorities various problems relating to people who have been arrested.

The ICRC has been present in Kuwait since 2 March last and its team of over 20 delegates is continuing its activities to protect vulnerable groups among the population. Delegates visit people held in places of detention and regularly attend, as observers, the trials of civilians arrested after the end of hostilities.

Four ICRC offices have been opened in several districts of Kuwait City to register tracing requests concerning missing persons or people presumed to have been arrested. The delegates are also keeping a close watch on the situation of the civilians stranded in El Abdali camp on the country's northern border.

PART VI

FURTHER HOSTILITIES INVOLVING IRAQ

The aerial operations of the United States, the United Kingdom and France against Iraq of January 1993 have been justified both with reference to humanitarian motives and to the need to ensure compliance with the cease-fire terms accepted by Iraq. Rather than prejudicing the issue of the possible justification for these armed actions by reprinting the materials they have generated either in Part IV or Part V of this volume, it has been found more convenient to add this further section to the book. The materials, mostly press releases, were obtained immediately before going to press and it has generally not been possible to await their official publication. Unfortunately, the military operations did not engender a public debate in the UN Security Council.

21. FURTHER HOSTILITIES INVOLVING IRAQ

1. US Press Release: Iraq Warned to Stop Harassment of U.N. Operations, 28 December 1992

Washington - The United States has warned the Baghdad regime to stop harassing U.N. activities in Iraq or face further military action following the December 27 downing of an Iraqi fighter jet that disregarded a verbal warning after entering a "no-fly" zone imposed over southern Iraq.

Joseph Snyder, the State Department's acting spokesman, described the flight of the Iraqi plane into the no-fly zone imposed by the United States, Britain and France last August "as part of an Iraqi challenge to the United States and the U.N."

The Defense Department said a U.S. Air Force F-16, assigned to the Southwest Asia Joint Task Force (JTF), shot down an Iraqi fighter aircraft on December 27 inside the no-fly zone, about 30 kilometers south of the 32nd parallel.

"At approximately 10:20 a.m. (Iraqi time, 0820 GMT), a flight of two Iraqi aircraft crossed the no-fly line," the Pentagon statement said. "Two F-15 aircraft attempted identification, but the Iraqi aircraft flew back north out of the no-fly zone. Approximately 20 minutes later, coalition forces identified another flight of Iraqi aircraft approximately 20 miles (30 kilometers) inside the no-fly zone.

"Two U.S. F-16 aircraft were vectored toward the Iraqi aircraft. The hostile aircraft were issued a verbal warning. The Iraqis turned to confront the U.S. aircraft. One Iraqi aircraft was destroyed. The other escaped back north out of the no-fly zone."

An Iraqi search-and-rescue helicopter from an air base north of the no-fly zone was permitted to fly to the crash site and then return to base, the Pentagon said, adding that the fate of the pilot is unknown.

As President Bush arrived in Texas for a two-day hunting vacation December 27, he said Iraqi President Saddam Hussein had made a "big mistake" by sending aircraft into the no-fly zone.

"I've heard that it might be some test of our will near the end of my presidency," Bush said, "but those F-16s sent the message to him pretty clearly."

President-elect Clinton voiced support for the downing of the Iraqi jet. "This is part of a series of tests of international resolve to bring Iraq into compliance with United Nations resolutions," Clinton said in a statement issued in Little Rock, Arkansas. "Saddam Hussein is mistaken if he believes the United States or the United Nations lacks that resolve. I support efforts to bring Iraq into compliance."

Responding to questions at a December 28 news briefing, Snyder said he was not aware of any further sorties by Iraqi jets or other specific Iraqi actions during the past 24 hours.

"Iraq has continued to engage in a pattern of harassment against various U.N. operations in Iraq," including against U.N. Special Commission (UNSCOM) inspectors in the south and against humanitarian operations in the north, he said.

"These actions appear aimed at testing the resolve of U.N. officials as well as the U.S. and coalition allies in enforcing U.N. Security Council resolutions on Iraq," Snyder said. "This testing continued yesterday with their deliberate intrusion into the no-fly zone established by coalition forces to facilitate monitoring of Iraqi compliance with U.N. Security Council Resolution 688.

"U.S. and allied forces remain on alert and capable of enforcing relevant U.N. resolutions. We are closely monitoring the situation and are prepared to respond as necessary to further harassments of U.N. operations."

State Department officials met December 27 with the chief of the Iraqi interest section in Washington, and Ambassador Edward Perkins, the U.S. permanent representative to the United Nations, raised the incident with his Iraqi counterpart at the United Nations as well.

"We are warning the Iraqis against a repetition of this or other acts which interfere with U.N.-authorized operations, including humanitarian operations and the efforts of coalition forces in support of those operations," a State Department press officer explained.

Snyder said it was his understanding that the United Nations was trying to organize a relief convoy to bring humanitarian assistance to northern Iraq on December 28.

Humanitarian relief convoys have been suspended in the north since December 16, when at least 15 trucks were damaged or destroyed by bombs planted by Iraq, putting the vehicles' Turkish drivers at mortal risk.

"There are continuing concerns on the part of Turkish truck drivers regarding security for these convoys," Snyder said, "so we'll have to see what happens."

A Memorandum of Understanding, signed by Iraq and the United Nations in October establishes a framework for humanitarian relief efforts inside Iraq. Although Iraq agreed to facilitate the safe and rapid passage of relief supplies, it has systematically frustrated relief operations, prompting the United States to deplore Iraq's continued refusal to comply with U.N. Security Council Resolution 688, which requires Iraq to cooperate with U.N. humanitarian efforts.

2. Statement issued on behalf of Tariq Aziz, Deputy Prime Minster of Iraq, 6 January 1993

Iraqi Deputy Prime Minister Tariq Aziz has deplored the manufactured noise whipped-up in United States circles about the deployment of anti-air weapons in the south of the country.

Deputy Prime Minister Aziz said that US circles persist in their campaign of distortion by trying to depict the decision of the Bush administration to impose a no-fly zone on the southern part of Iraq as a UN decision. This decision is, as we have already stressed, a decision taken by the United States, with British and French participation, during the circumstances of the Bush election campaign in order to achieve personal objectives.

Deputy Prime Minister Aziz reiterated the fact that Iraq does not recognize this embargo, that Iraq has the right to deploy its air defences all over the country, and that Iraqi pilots are not prohibited from flying within their country's airspace on training and patrol missions. He reaffirmed that all Iraqi military activities are limited to purely defensive duties.

Mr. Aziz said that Iraq rejects the American threats and that any new hostilities against Iraq will constitute another aggression perpetrated against an independent state in violation of international law, and will have to be met with condemnation and denunciation in the Arab nation and in the world at large.

Mr. Aziz said: "we have already made clear our position on the comments linking Iraq's defensive activities with the position of President-elect Clinton. We said that Iraq has no intention whatsoever to test President Clinton's position, as is claimed. Iraq hopes to see the United States government adopt an objective and non-aggressive policy, regardless of who occupies the White House. Iraq's keenness to preserve its sovereignty, independence and legitimate rights is a matter in no way related to the change of the President of the United States of America".

3. US Press Release: Iraq Warned Move Missiles-- Keep Out of No-Fly Zone, 7 January 1993

Washington - Iraq has been told to stop threatening allied aircraft and to remove its surface-to-air missiles from the no-fly zone south of the 32nd parallel, State Department spokesman Richard Boucher said January 7.

The demand was delivered late January 6 to Nizar Hamdoon, the Iraqi permanent representative to the United Nations, by Ambassador Edward Perkins, the U.S. permanent representative to the U.N. and his French, British and Russian counterparts, Boucher told a news briefing.

All four are permanent members of the United Nations Security Council. The other permanent member of the Security Council, China, was not associated with the diplomatic demarche.

"There was no immediate" or "substantive response" from the Iraqi official, Boucher told questioners, although he noted that Hamdoon did make some comments to television reporters later.

David Mack, deputy assistant secretary of state for Near Eastern and South Asian affairs, also gave the same warning to the head of the Iraqi interest section in Washington.

"It was a clear warning that told them to cease their threats to our pilots and our air activity, that told them to stop violating the no-fly zone," Boucher said. "It asked them for specific actions and it asked them to comply right away."

Boucher would not provide "too much detail on the exact nature" of the warning, but he left little doubt about U.S. impatience with Iraq's continuing violations of the no-fly zone and the U.N. Security Council resolutions that provide its underpinning.

The threat to U.S. and allied forces will remain "as long as Iraq maintains its aggressive posture," the spokesman said. "They have repeatedly violated the no-fly zone. They've augmented their surface-to-air assets - their missiles - in the no-fly zone. Those actions are violations and are coupled with other actions that suggest an aggressive intent," he said.

"That circumstance has made it necessary for the coalition to take measures to ensure the safety of its air crews and to discourage further Iraqi attempts to evade the no-fly regime in both the north and the south," he said. "Until Iraq changes its attitude, basically, that sort of aggressive posture and intent will not have dissipated."

Boucher refused to confirm reports the Iraqis had been given 48 hours to remove their missiles from the territory covered by the no-fly zone imposed last August by the U.S., France and Britain in an effort to protect Iraqi civilians there from repression by the Baghdad regime. He did point out that While House Press Secretary Marlin Fitzwater said January 6 the Iraqis had been told to "remove the missiles beyond the 32nd parallel."

Asked about reports from Baghdad that the Iraqi regime had rejected the demand to withdraw the missiles, Boucher replied: "We saw those reports. We would judge Iraqi policy by its actions, not by the various and often contradictory statements that they make."

While the exact contents of the message has not been made public, diplomats at the United Nations said January 6 that Iraq has been given 48 hours to remove the missiles from the area along the no-fly zone. The countdown began when the message was delivered at about 5:30 p.m. New York time (2230 GMT), they said.

French Ambassador Jean-Bernard Merimee said that "the essence" of the message the ambassadors delivered was "the final warning to the Iraqi authorities to the effect that we have to see (the missile batteries as) hostile acts and they have to remove their missile batteries."

"The language was the language of an ultimatum. We gave them a certain delay," Merimee said, refusing to divulge the details of the message.

At the Pentagon, spokesman Pete Hall said the United States is "monitoring" the location of the "handful" of Iraqi missiles moved into the area "very closely" and will not "tolerate" any "interference with our enforcement of the no-fly zone." He added there should be no "question in their minds about what we expect ... We are not going to put our pilots at risk."

Hall emphasized: "We certainly hope that they will respond to the contents of the demarche" (the deadline for moving the missiles) and that the United States is "certainly ready, capable, of doing what is necessary to enforce" the U.N. mandated no-fly zone."

4. US Press Release: Iraq Ignores Allied Warning, 7 January 1993

Iraq January 7 has indicated it will ignore an allied ultimatum to move its missiles from the no-fly zone in southern Iraq.

Iraqi Ambassador Nizar Hamdoon said that "Iraq does not recognize the no-fly zone because it is not a U.N. job. It was imposed by the three Western powers and, based on that, Iraq reserves its right to move whatever it wants at the time it deems necessary." (U.N. Security Council resolutions provide underpinning for the zone which was imposed in an effort to protect Iraqi civilians there from repression by the Baghdad regime.)

Hamdoon refused to characterize the response as final, saying, "There is no last word," but he said that the response "focused on the Iraqi right of sovereignty ... and Iraq has decided not to give up that right."

The United States, France, Great Britain and Russia told Iraq January 6 to remove the surface-to-air missiles deployed along the 32nd parallel in southern Iraq within 48 hours or face serious consequences.

The response was a four-page communique from Baghdad delivered to the U.S., French, British and Russian envoys at the United Nations by Hamdoon 24 hours after he received the ultimatum from the same group.

U.S. Ambassador Edward Perkins said afterwards that the four decided "to refer the answer to our governments ... I would hesitate to put any value judgment on it. We all agreed to leave it to our capitals to make that decision" on how to interpret the response.

Hamdoon said he hoped the crisis was defused, but acknowledged that the outcome is "dependent on the attitude of the four."

He also said that Iraq "is interested in receiving an American delegation in Baghdad mainly from the American Congress."

The Iraqi envoy emphasized Iraq's desire for a "dialogue" with the United States. "We think in Iraq the time has come to put all the complexities of the past behind us and try to work out normal relations ... It reflects our desire for better relations," he said.

5. United Kingdom Foreign and Commonwealth Office, Spokesman's Statement, 7 January 1993

...

Spokesman said that following the demarche made by the allies to Iraq in New York on 6 January we had today summoned the Head of the Iraqi Interests Section in London to the FCO. The meeting lasted 10 minutes and was conducted in a business-like atmosphere. We emphasised to Mr Ibrahim that we regarded this as a very serious matter. He undertook to report back to the Iraqi authorities.

6. Interview with Malcolm Rifkind, UK Secretary of State for Defence, BBC Radio 4, on 8 January 1993

Chris Lowe: Presenter--Saddam Hussein is keeping the allies guessing - he's good at that. The deadline for Iraq to remove its anti-aircraft missiles from the no-fly zone in the south of the country runs out at 10:30 tonight, our time.

Well, we know that some missiles are on the move, but we still don't know for certain where they're going. So, let's assume that Saddam will not back down. Does that mean the West will inevitably use force? A little earlier I put that question to the Defence Secretary, Malcolm Rifkind, who's on an official visit to Hong Kong.

Malcolm Rifkind MP: Defence Secretary--It is very important that Iraq fully complies with its obligations and it's been made clear to Iraq, with all the authority of the United Nations Security Council, that it is necessary for them to guarantee that there should be no further incursions of the no-fly zone. We've had a number of items of provocative action by Iraqi aircraft over the last week or so. These must not be allowed to continue.

Chris Lowe: And if they do?

Malcolm Rifkind MP: We are determined to ensure, and when I say we I mean the United Nations is determined to ensure, that Iraq does not flout the United Nations authority. And of course this is something which has the support not simply of the United Kingdom and the United States - Russia and France and of course the Security Council as a whole have made clear what is required and it's very important indeed that the Iraqi government realise that the United Nations is completely serious about this matter.

Chris Lowe: Would you be prepared to increase Britain's military presence in the area?

Malcolm Rifkind MP: The precise level of our presence in the area will depend on the judgment that is made as to what is required to carry out our obligations. We, as you know, have at the moment a number of Tornado aircraft in the area and they have been very effective in policing the no-fly zone. Clearly, it's not simply a British operation; a number of countries are involved and we discuss, with those who are involved, what is required to meet our overall obligations.

Chris Lowe: And you would be prepared, if that was decided, you would be prepared to increase our presence there, if necessary?

Malcolm Rifkind MP: Clearly, if it was necessary, then it's for the international community as a whole, obviously, to come to a judgment as to what is required, and for those who are making the specific contribution to meet that requirement that of course would be done.

Chris Lowe: Mr Rifkind, isn't there a sense of unfinished business about all this? With President Bush determined to finish a job he didn't complete in the Gulf War and Britain loyally following suit?

Malcolm Rifkind MP: No, it's not worked out like that. In fact, it's the other way 'round. What has happened in the last week or so is that the Iraqi government, Saddam Hussein and his colleagues, have clearly followed a quite deliberate and conscious policy of sending in their fighter aircraft into the no-fly zone in clear breach of the United Nations Resolution. This was not a particular matter that was precipitated either by the United States, or by any country, other than Iraq itself. And therefore Iraq must cease its activities in order to ensure that the United Nations authority is upheld.

Chris Lowe: What's the difference, Mr Rifkind, between military action against Iraq and military action in Bosnia? Is it simply a question that one works and one doesn't?

Malcolm Rifkind MP: Well, the no-fly zone of course is relevant in both territories. The situation in Iraq is certainly more serious in that there have been incursions by fighter aircraft, by fixed-wing fighter aircraft, in Iraq. That is fortunately not a situation that has been the case in former Yugoslavia since the introduction of the United Nations Resolution.

Chris Lowe: It's just that one gets the impression that we take action against evil where we can win and we don't take action against where we can't win - that mortality no longer has anything to do with it. It's all a question of whether we can win or not.

Malcolm Rifkind MP: On the contrary. I think that is not a fair assessment at all. Of course you have to take into account what is subject to military policy, whether there is a military solution available, but in the case of both Iraq and in the case of former Yugoslavia, the United Nations has introduced a no-fly zone; in the case of former Yugoslavia, there have been breaches with regard to helicopters, fortunately there have not been any with regard to fixed-wing fighter aircraft. In the case of Iraq, the events that we are discussing today are a direct consequence of the Iraqi government sending in a number of Iraqi fixed-wing aircraft; they clearly had hostile intent.

...

7. White House Statement on Iraq, 8 January 1993

We continue to keep the situation in Iraq under close scrutiny. We have observed no penetrations by Iraqi aircraft of the no-fly zone below 32 degrees north latitude since Wednesday's coalition warning. The disposition of surface-to-air missiles specified in the January 6 demarche is less clear. There has been a good deal of movement involving these missiles, but we are still in the process of determining whether Iraq is in compliance with the terms of the coalition demarche.

8. European Political Cooperation Press Release, 8 January 1993

The European Community and its member States remain deeply concerned about Iraq's repeated violations of relevant UN Security Council Resolutions.

Iraq has continued its deliberate policy of hindering UN inspection teams in performing their responsibilities in accordance with SCR 687 and subsequent resolution. Harassment and intimidation of humanitarian relief convoys and personnel are part of the overall pattern.

the Community and its member States strongly condemn this Iraqi pattern of non-compliance with its obligations under international law.

The repeated Iraqi incursions into the no-fly zone south of the 32nd parallel and the deployment of surface-to-air missiles into the zone pose an imminent threat to the international community's efforts to see that all relevant UN Security Council resolutions are implemented by Iraq, and cannot be accepted.

The Government of Iraq bears the full responsibility for the present unacceptable situation. the Community and its member States demand that Iraqi evasion of the no-fly zone is brought to an end immediately.

SC/5534, 8 January 1993

9. UN Press Release: Security Council Demands That Iraq Not Interfere With UN Flights Transporting Personnel Into Iraqi Territory, 8 January 1993

The Security Council is deeply disturbed by the Government of Iraq's recent Notes to the Office of the Special Commission in Baghdad and to the headquarters of the United Nations Iraq-Kuwait Observation Mission (UNIKOM) that it will not allow the United Nations to transport its personnel into Iraqi territory using its own aircraft.

The Security Council refers to resolution 687 (1991) requiring Iraq to permit the Special Commission and the IAEA to undertake immediate on-site inspection of any locations designated by the Commission. The agreement on facilities, privileges and immunities between the Government of Iraq and the United Nations, and resolutions 707 (1991) and 715 (1991) elaborated on Iraq's obligations by demanding, inter alia, that the Special Commission and the IAEA be allowed, as they determined necessary, to use their own aircraft throughout Iraq and any airfield in Iraq without interference or hindrance of any kind. Concerning UNIKOM, Iraq is obligated by resolution 687 (1991) and committed by an exchange of letters dated 15 April 1992 and 21 June 1992 respectively to the unrestricted freedom of entry and exit without delay or hindrance of its personnel, property, supplies, equipment, spare parts and means of transport.

The implementation of the measures set out in the recent communications of the Iraqi Government would seriously impede the activities of the Special Commission, the IAEA and UNIKOM. Such restrictions constitute an unacceptable and material breach of the relevant provisions of resolution 687 (1991), which established the cease-fire and provided the conditions essential to the restoration of peace and security in the region, as well as other relevant resolutions and agreements.

The Council demands that the Government of Iraq abide by its obligations under all relevant Security Council resolutions and cooperate fully with the activities of the Special Commission, the IAEA and UNIKOM. In particular, it demands that the Government of Iraq not interfere with the currently envisaged United Nations flights. The Security Council warns the Government of Iraq, as it has done in this connection in the past, of the serious consequences which would ensue from the failure to comply with its obligations.

10. White House Statement on Iraq, 9 January 1993

All available evidence indicates that Iraq is acceding to the requirements of the coalition's January 6, 1993 demarche. No Iraqi aircraft have entered the no fly zone south of the 32nd parallel and the Iraqi surface-to-air missiles have been dispersed and are no longer threatening coalition flight operations.

3. Once again Saddam Hussein has backed down in the face of coalition solidarity. Iraq remains isolated and a pariah among nations due to its flagrant attempts to violate the cease fire regime.

4. The coalition's January 6 demarche remains in effect. We will continue to scrutinize Iraqi activity. No further warning will be issued if Iraq violates the requirements of the January 6 demarche.

5. This episode should make clear to Iraq that interference with United Nations and coalition operations, including humanitarian relief operations, Operation Provide Comfort, United Nations Special Commission (UNSCOM) and International Atomic Energy Agency (IAEA) inspections of Iraq's weapons of mass destruction, and the United Nations Iraq-Kuwait Observer Mission (UNIKOM) force on the Iraq-Kuwait border, will not be tolerated. In this regard, we fully support the United Nations Security Council presidential statement of January 8 that demanded that Iraq comply with its obligations. We underscore the Security Council's warning of serious consequences if Iraq fails to do so.

SC/5536, 11 January 1993

11. UN Press Release: Security Council Condemns Iraqi Incursions Into Demilitarized Zone, 11 January 1993

The Security Council notes that there have been a number of recent actions by Iraq as part of its pattern of flouting relevant Security Council resolutions. One was the series of border incidents involving the United Nations Iraq-Kuwait Observation Mission (UNIKOM); another was the incident concerning the United Nations Special Commission (UNSCOM) and UNIKOM flights.

The Security Council is deeply concerned at the incidents reported in the Secretary-General's special report of 10 January 1993 on UNIKOM (document S/25085). The Security Council recalls the provisions of resolution 687 (1991) that established the Demilitarized Zone between Iraq and Kuwait and demanded that both countries respect the inviolability of the international boundary between them. It reaffirms that the boundary was at the very core of the conflict and that, in resolutions 687 (1991) and 773 (1992), it guaranteed the inviolability of the boundary and undertook to take as appropriate all necessary measures to that end in accordance with the Charter of the United Nations.

The Council condemns that action taken by Iraq on 10 January 1993 to remove equipment by force from the Kuwaiti side of the demilitarized zone without prior consultation with UNIKOM, and through UNIKOM with the Kuwaiti authorities, as set out in the letter of 8 January 1993 from the President of the Security Council to the Secretary-General. In particular, the Council draws attention to the removal by Iraq of four HY-2G anti-ship missiles and other military equipment from the six bunkers in the former Iraqi naval base at Umm Qasr on Kuwaiti territory, in spite of the objections of UNIKOM and their efforts to prevent this. This action is a direct challenge to the authority of UNIKOM and amounts to clear-cut defiance by Iraq of the Council, which stipulated in the letter of 3 November 1992 from the President of the Council to the Secretary-General that the military equipment in the six bunkers should be destroyed by or under the supervision of UNIKOM. The Council demands that the anti-ship missiles and other military equipment removed by force from the six bunkers at Umm Qasr in Kuwaiti territory be returned immediately to the custody of UNIKOM for destruction, as previously decided.

The Council also condemns further Iraqi intrusions into the Kuwaiti side of the demilitarized zone on 11 January 1993. It demands that any future retrieval mission be in accordance with the terms set out in the letter of 8 January 1993 from the President of the Council to the Secretary-General. On the UNIKOM facilities at Camp Khor, the Council stresses that the land and premises occupied by UNIKOM shall be inviolate and subject to the exclusive control and authority of the United Nations.

The Council invites the Secretary-General, as a first step, to explore on an urgent basis the possibilities for restoring UNIKOM to its full strength and to consider the need for rapid reinforcement as set out in paragraph 18 of his report of 12 June 1991 (document S/22692), as well as any other suggestion that he might have to enhance the effectiveness of UNIKOM, and to report back to the Council.

The Council is also alarmed by Iraq's refusal to allow the United Nations to transport its UNSCOM and UNIKOM personnel into Iraqi territory using its own aircraft. In this connection the Council reiterates the demand in its statement of 8 January 1993 that Iraq permit UNSCOM to use their own aircraft to transport their personnel into Iraq. It rejects the arguments contained in the letter of 9 January 1993 from the Minister of Foreign Affairs of Iraq to the President of the Security Council (document S/25086).

These latest developments concerning the activities of UNIKOM and UNSCOM constitute further material breaches of resolution 687 (1991), which established the cease-fire and provided the conditions essential for the restoration of peace and security in the region, as well as other relevant resolutions and agreements. The Council demands that Iraq cooperate fully with UNIKOM, UNSCOM and other United Nations agencies in carrying out their mandates, and again warns Iraq of the serious consequences that will flow from such continued defiance. The Council will remain actively seized of the matter.

[*For further materials on this series of incidents* see *Chapters 11 and 12.*]

12. Transcript of Statement by the Prime Minister, Mr John Major in Downing Street on Wednesday, 13 January 1993

Prime Minister:

As you know, Royal Air Force Tornadoes and tankers have today taken part in a limited Coalition attack on surface-to-air missiles and their associated command and control facilities in southern Iraq. There have been no Allied casualties. All our aircraft have returned safely to base and preliminary information - and I emphasise that, preliminary information - indicates that the aircraft accomplished their mission satisfactorily.

Let me say that we did not take this action lightly. Last year, we established a no-fly zone over southern Iraq and the purpose of that was quite clear - it was to stop Saddam Hussein from the repression of his own people. Over the last few weeks, our aircraft in that no-fly zone have come under increasing threat, threat from Iraqi aircraft themselves entering the no-fly zone and from missile batteries installed in southern Iraq.

Over recent days, the Iraqis have been given ample warning. The action that we have taken tonight has deliberately been both limited and proportionate but we believe it will be effective in establishing the conditions which will enable our aircraft to operate in the no-fly zone with safety.

The Iraqi regime are in breach of Security Council requirements on a number of fronts. They pose a threat to aircraft protecting the Kurds in northern Iraq, they are impeding the actions of the UN inspection teams, they are illegally entering Kuwaiti territory. Each and every one of those breaches needs to stop. If they don't, we shall have no hesitation - again with our Allies - in taking the necessary action to enforce Security Council Resolutions.

The Secretary of State for Defence will be making a statement to the House at 10 o'clock.

I will take one or two questions:

Question: Prime Minister, have you spoken to President Bush about your next action?

Prime Minister: I shall be speaking to President Bush again within a few minutes.

Question: Do you have any idea of the level of Iraqi casualties that might have come from such missions?

Prime Minister: Not at this stage.

Michael Brunson (ITV): How long can this cat-and-mouse game with Saddam go on? People are saying he should be taken out once and for all.

Prime Minister: I think he has had a very clear indication today of the fact that people are growing increasingly intolerant of his defiance of the Security Council Resolutions. I hope that he will learn from the lesson.

Robin Oakley (BBC TV): Do you expect this action to put an end to violations by Saddam Hussein and are the Allies prepared to step up action if he continues to defy UN Resolutions?

Prime Minister: We are prepared to make sure that the Security Council Resolutions are enforced. I hope this will put an end to the infringements. We have hoped that before and it has not. If he infringes again, he must expect us to retaliate again and we have made it entirely clear to him that we will certainly do that.

Question: Do you regret not dealing with Saddam Hussein tougher two years ago?

Prime Minister: No. I think the decision that was taken to stop the fighting at the time we did was the right decision at the time. One has to recall we were operating under a UN mandate; that mandate had been enforced; we had no legal authority to do more and I believe it was right to stop when we did.

Question: Are you prepared to take the same tough action against the Serbs since many Muslims may feel that Christians in Europe are applying double standards?

Prime Minister: I think people know the action that we have already taken in humanitarian aid in Bosnia and we have a substantial number of troops on the ground and you will know the very sad news indeed that one of them was killed this morning.

Thank you very much indeed.

13. Statement from 10 Downing Street released to press, 13 January 1991

RAF tornadoes and an RAF tanker have today taken part in a coalition attack on surface-to-air missiles and their associated command and control facilities in Southern Iraq. Preliminary information indicates that the coalition aircraft accomplished their mission.

This action was taken in self-defence to ensure the safety of coalition aircraft patrolling the No-Fly Zone and following the demarche made by the coalition on 6 January 1993. In that demarche we demanded that Iraq take steps within 48 hours to ensure that its aircraft and surface-to-air missiles did not pose a threat to coalition aircraft operating south of the 32nd Parallel. Those aircraft are there to monitor Iraqi compliance with UN Security Council Resolution 688 which demanded that Iraq end the repression against her civilian population.

The Iraqis initially appeared to comply with the terms of the demarche but subsequently violated it by putting in place missile batteries which threatened allied aircraft. The coalition have tonight acted to restore conditions which do not pose a threat to our aircraft.

All the requirements of the 6 January demarche regarding potential threats to the air operations of the coalition south of 32 degrees remain in effect. We will continue to scrutinize Iraqi activity. No further warning will be issued if Iraq again violates the requirements of the 6 January demarche.

The Government of Iraq should also understand that continued defiance of other UN Security Council Resolutions and related coalition demarches will not be tolerated. The British Government fully associates itself with the statements made by the President of the UN Security Council on 8 and 11 January which declared Iraq in material breach of UN Security Council Resolution 687 and the associated ceasefire. We stand ready to take part in further coalition action if Iraq continues to flout the will of the international community and to disregard its international obligations.

14. Statement by the UK Secretary of State for Defence, 13 January 1993

At 1815 hrs GMT tonight, 4 RAF Tornado GR1 aircraft and 2 Victor tankers took part in a coalition operation, involving some 114 US, British and French aircraft, against Iraqi military targets in southern Iraq. This action was taken to ensure the safety of coalition aircraft patrolling the no-fly zone below the 32nd parallel in support of UNSCR 688. Early indications are that serious damage was inflicted and assessment of the results is continuing. No losses were sustained by coalition forces.

This coalition action was taken in self defence under international law and is both a necessary and proportionate response to the serious threat posed to the safety of coalition aircraft. The coalition action took the form of air strikes against air defence facilities and command and control facilities. Attacks were also carried out to suppress air defence installations which threatened the security of coalition aircraft participating in the operation. UK forces participated in attacks against command and control facilities at Al Amarah, with RAF Tornado GR1 aircraft using 1,000lb laser guided bombs against targets designated by the thermal imaging airborne laser designator, known as TIALD, carried by two of the four aircraft.

This action is to be seen against the background of recent Iraqi violations of the no-fly zone and their deployment of SA-2 and SA-3 missiles in a threatening posture below the 32nd parallel, south of the airfield used by Iraqi aircraft which were violating the no-fly zone. These posed a new and unacceptable threat to the security of coalition aircraft. A strongly worded demarche was issued to Iraq in New York on 6 January by the US, UK, France and Russia, which demanded that the SAM systems recently established south of the 32nd parallel be returned to their previous locations and configurations and that violations of the no-fly zone should cease. The demarche went on to say that, should Iraq fail to comply, the coalition would respond appropriately and decisively, without further warning.

This demarche elaborated on an earlier one on 26 August 1992, which announced the creation of the no-fly zone south of the 32nd parallel. The no-fly zone was necessitated by a situation of severe humanitarian need in southern Iraq arising from Iraq's failure to comply with the terms of UNSCR 688 which calls upon Iraq to refrain from further repression of its civilian population. Iraq largely respected the no-fly zone until late December 1992 when Iraqi military aircraft began deliberate and systematic violations. This resulted in an Iraqi fighter aircraft being shot down on 27 December 1992 by coalition aircraft.

Following the demarche there were indications that Saddam Hussein was backing down. There were no fresh violations of the no-fly zone and the missiles were dispersing. However, despite the clear warning issued on 6 January, Iraq moved SA-3 missiles, which were the subject of the demarche, to new locations south of the 32nd parallel where they posed a significant threat to coalition aircraft. Other missile systems in the south were placed on an operational footing also threatening the safety of coalition aircraft. The coalition action was in direct response to this threat.

The Baghdad regime can now be in no doubt about our determination to maintain the no-fly zone south of the 32nd parallel, in support of UNSCR 688. Should the need arise the Government will consider the need for further action in consultation with coalition partners.

The House will also be aware of the deep concern expressed by the UN Security Council following Iraqi incursions into the demilitarised zone on the border with Kuwait and Iraq's violation of land and premises occupied by UNIKOM. The Security Council has also expressed alarm at Iraq's refusal to allow UNIKOM and UNSCOM flights into Iraq using UN aircraft. The Government will continue to participate fully in consideration of these matters within the Security Council and report developments to this House.

I am sure the House will wish to join me in expressing admiration for the bravery and professionalism of the personnel of all the coalition forces who participated in this operation and in particular to the men and women of Her Majesty's Armed Forces serving in the Gulf. They have once again demonstrated the high degree of dedication and ability we have learned to expect from them and have contributed immeasurably to the success of this operation.

15. U.S. Press Statement: Coalition Planes Attack Iraqi Missile Sites, 13 January 1993

Washington - The United States and its coalition partners have taken "forceful actions against Iraq" for violating requirements set forth by U.N. Security Council resolutions, White House spokesman Marlin Fitzwater said January 13.

Briefing reporters on coalition aircraft attacks against Iraqi surface-to-air missiles and associated infrastructure, Fitzwater said "we will continue to scrutinize Iraqi activity."

He also said President Bush "has directed the deployment of a battalion task force to Kuwait to underline our continuing commitment to Kuwait's security and independence."

Following is a transcript of Fitzwater's briefing:

Fitzwater: The United States and its coalition partners today took forceful actions against Iraq. Coalition aircraft, at approximately 1:15 p.m. Eastern Standard Time this afternoon, attacked surface-to-air missiles and associated infrastructure in southern Iraq. Preliminary information indicates that the mission was accomplished.

This action was taken pursuant to the coalition's warning of January 6, 1993. This communication demanded that Iraq take steps within 48 hours to ensure that its aircraft and surface-to-air missiles did not pose a threat to coalition aircraft operating south of the 32nd parallel in attempting to monitor Iraqi compliance with U.N. Security Council resolutions.

After initially responding to the terms of the January 6 warning, Iraq violated its requirements, and the coalition is acting to restore an environment that poses no threat to coalition aircraft. All requirements of the January 6 demarche, regarding potential threats to coalition air operations south of 32 degrees remain in effect. We will continue to scrutinize Iraqi activity. No further warning will be issued if Iraq again violates the requirements of the January 6 warning.

Similarly, the government of Iraq should understand that continued defiance of U.N. Security Council resolutions and related coalition demarches will not be tolerated. The U.S. government fully associates itself with the January 8 and January 11 statements by the president of the U.N. Security Council that declared Iraq in material breach of U.N. Security Council Resolution 687 and the cease-fire regime, and also that warned of the serious consequences of Iraq's actions. We stand ready to take additional forceful actions with our coalition partners if Iraq continues to flout the will of the international community and if it continues to disregard its international obligations. Consistent with the above, the president has directed the deployment of a battalion task force to Kuwait to underline our continuing commitment to Kuwait's security and independence.

In terms of Kuwait's future actions, we ask that they comply with all the U.N. resolutions. In particular we have in mind the UNSCOM right and authority to operate U.N. aircraft within that country.

QUESTION: Does it appear now that Iraq has said it will no longer make these raids into the Kuwaiti territory and that it will now allow U.N. flights into the area?

ANSWER: I don't think we have definitive information now on Iraq's response. There were some reports, as I was walking down here, of statements being made in New York, but I do not have access to those.

Q: When did the president make the decision? Is he going to go on the air to the American people at any point? And who did he consult with before he made the decision?

A: The president made this decision in a meeting with his national security advisers Monday afternoon. The original timetable called for this action to occur yesterday, but it had to be put off until today because of weather conditions in Iraq.

I might add that this is in response to a series of violations of the U.N. resolutions over the last several months, precipitated most recently, of course, by the moving of the missiles below the 32nd parallel. But it's also the case that the president has considered over the last many weeks a number of options at a number of different times in response to the cheat-and-retreat pattern that Saddam Hussein has established over the last many months. And so these options were ones that had been considered for some time. And it was on Monday, as he analyzed the recent series of violations, that he gave the execute order to go ahead with this mission.

Q: Did he talk to Clinton about it?

A: Let me just answer that question. President Bush called President-elect Clinton at noon today and discussed the mission with him. The president-elect indicated his support. And I would leave it to them for any further response.

In addition, General Scowcroft met with Sandy Berger and Anthony Lake of the president-elect's national security staff on Monday, and he spoke to them by telephone again yesterday. So they were fully briefed on the operation.

Q: What is the mission of the battalion that is being dispatched, and where is that battalion coming from?

A: The battalion is going into Kuwait. I don't have the base. I'll leave that to military briefers. I would note that General Hoar will give a briefing this afternoon in Tampa - he's the Commander of the Southern Command - and he will fill you in on the military aspects in terms of planes involved and the basings and so forth. But those soldiers will go into Kuwait to help us in the sense of any preparations that might be necessary there in terms of follow-on activities.

Q: Did Kuwait ask for these troops?

A: No.

Q: Could you give us an idea of just how many targets were involved? And were there any allied casualties?

A: I can't give you specific numbers, but I can say there were several. They were missile sites in the south. And all of our planes have returned to their bases. We have some preliminary information based upon pilot reports, but we do not have damage assessments at this time.

Q: You talked in the original warning about planes and missiles, but you only took out missiles. Why didn't you go after planes as well? Why didn't you go after air bases?

A: The missile sites were determined to be, first of all, a direct threat to coalition aircraft that are overflying the country, and therefore of more direct military threat that needed to be dealt with. Secondly, they provided a very strong warning and message to Saddam Hussein that we are prepared to enforce the resolutions, that we have the capability to do that again if necessary. And it was felt that this was adequate.

Q: Were you attempting to minimize civilian losses in Iraq?

A: Yes, of course. We're not interesting in causing any more civilian losses than are absolutely necessary. Our purpose is to send the appropriate message to Saddam Hussein and his government: that they should comply with the U.N. resolutions; that the coalition partners are strong in their belief that those resolutions must be enforced.

Q: But these weren't population centers you struck?

A: No, I think most of the missile sites were in nonpopulated areas.

Q: Will this battalion-sized unit be told to prevent the incursion of Iraqis dressed in civilian clothes coming over to take weapons in Kuwait and take them back to Iraq?

A: I just don't have any rules of engagement for the battalion of troops that's going in.

Q: Well, we consider that a violation, don't we, as part of the reason we took this action?

A: On that cross-border violation, absolutely. They did not seek permission from the United Nations, and they took Silkworm missiles and other kinds of weapons that they were not allowed to take, which we want back. And the communication from the United Nations on January 11 makes that very clear.
Q: Does the United States believe that Saddam Hussein is acting now because he thinks it's a time of weakness for the United States, since we're in a transition of power? And do you think that it is a miscalculation on his part that Clinton may be less willing to take action against him than Bush has been?
A: It's difficult to judge his motives. And Saddam Hussein has acted in what we consider to be irrational ways throughout this two-year period that we have been involved. And it's just very difficult to say. However, that certainly is a fair speculation and a wrong one. I think it is definitely a miscalculation on his part. Both President Bush and President-elect Clinton have been quite specific in their support of the United Nations. President-elect Clinton has been very precise in terms of making sure that there could be no miscalculation. And I think he makes a great mistake if that's indeed what he's trying to do.
Q: In the course of weighing all of our options, did the administration ever consider trying to go after Saddam Hussein himself? And if not, why not? And does that still remain an option?
A: That has not been considered, and for the same reasons it has never been considered, that it has not been authorized by the U.N. resolutions that are, after all, the legal and driving force behind these actions.
Q: Your statement made specific reference to the southern missile situation that started this whole round, or at least publicly started it. Over the weekend, you had said and others had said it appeared as if they moved those missiles out of the danger zone. Did they, in fact, move them back that prompted this, or what missiles are we now talking about that pose a danger that prompted this?
A: Our judgment that the crisis had ended in terms of those missiles being moved was based upon their being moved either back north or back to bases where they had been originally located and replaced in essentially in inert status, or they had been moved out of configurations that posed a direct threat to our aircraft. But it is true that not all of them were moved back north of the 32nd parallel. Some were kept on the move, some were parked in various locations around the south. But from a military threat standpoint, it was determined that they had complied in the sense of the movement that took place.

However, it has become equally clear that those missiles have continued to be moved and could have very easily been placed back in a threatening position.
Q: But were they?
A: I don't know that they were in the last day or two. I would have to refer you to the military.
Q: Were the northern missiles, the northern zone missiles that we began to hear about yesterday, did that play a role in this - you mentioned those not at all along the northern -
A: It played a role in the sense of emphasizing the apparent fact that Saddam Hussein was willing to tempt the coalition in every way possible and willing to try it on a number of fronts.

I might just briefly note that in November and December, he placed bombs on relief trucks in the northern zone where Operation Provide Comfort was under way: in late December, their Iraqi aircraft penetrations of the southern no-fly zone. On December 27, there is evidence that indicates an Iraqi missile was fired from an Iraqi aircraft at a U.S. plane. In the first week of January, surface-to-air missiles were moved into threatening positions. In the northern no-fly zone, Iraq has moved surface-to-air missiles into threatening positions only this week. And Saddam Hussein announced a ban on all U.N. flights in Iraq. And then over the last four days, we've seen a number of these incursions across the Iraqi-Kuwait border. So, yes, those missiles in the north are a clear part of the pattern.
Q: Could I follow up on a question - if the missiles in the north were part of the pattern, why were they also not targets in this instance? And was that perhaps because you didn't have compliance of the Turks, whom you might have needed to base the operation from there?
A: It was because we felt that this was an appropriate response to force action on the part of Saddam and his government on the broad range of U.N. resolutions. And because they are varied, as I indicated by this list, the issue was to seek a military action that would have the desired diplomatic and political ramifications.
Q: Well, if I can follow, were the British and the French then the only partners that you had in this and the only ones perhaps that you sought, or were the Turks reluctant to get engaged?
A: I don't have a list of all the countries that were involved, but there were other countries that were partners in this coalition.
Q: What about Turkey?
A: I don't know on specific countries.
Q: You said that President Bush called President-elect Clinton at noon. Was the mission underway at that point, and did he just call him to tell him that? And had they had conversations between Monday or at any time leading up to this decision?
A: They had not had conversations, but as I said, General Scowcroft talked to Sandy Berger and Tony Lake at least twice, once on Monday and once on Tuesday. Presumably, they had briefed the president-elect. And they, of course, were fully briefed on the mission itself, which was decided on Monday. And the phone call at noon today was to inform the president-elect that we were going ahead with it.
Q: A follow-up on that?
A: Yes.
Q: Were they only briefed, or was there any advice sought on whether Clinton would stand by this next week?
A: Our purpose was in briefing them on what our plans were and our intentions and purposes and reasons. I'd leave it to them to describe their reactions. But obviously, this was the decision of this administration and of President Bush and was based upon our knowledge and information. I don't think it's reasonable to expect them to be involved in that kind of planning. But I would leave it to them to characterize their attitudes.
Q: Following up on that, this is a fairly extraordinary, maybe even unprecedented military action for a president so close to the end of his term. Given the fact that - if I understand you correctly - the missiles on the southern border did not pose any imminent military threat, was there any consideration given to leaving this action for the Clinton administration to take?
A: Well, first of all, we believe that the missiles do pose a threat. U.N. aircraft are flying over this region continually on observer missions and for other purposes, and these missiles do represent a military threat. Secondly, again, it was our calculation that this was the best way to make the point, to inflict damage that was strategically valuable, and to do so with the least amount of risk to our own forces.
Q: Why now rather than say waiting a week or eight days?
A: Well, that was certainly considered, and it is a unique circumstance to have this come up in the waning days of the administration. But on the other hand, the president's commitment to the United Nations and our support and involvement with the coalition demands that action be taken now because the problem is now and it must be dealt with now. And we also think it's important that

Saddam understand that the United States government, whether this administration or the next, is firmly committed to the U.N. resolutions. And the president simply felt it couldn't wait.
Q: What was the final straw that prompted this action and the decision on Monday? And does the threat of further military action by the allies stand if Saddam continues these games?
A: Well, the final straw in this case was the movement of the missiles south of the 32nd parallel, the activities of last weekend when we warned them that they should be moved back and their failure to fully comply in a permanent sense. However, there have been other violations even since then, in the last two or three days. So, it clearly is a continuing problem. And, yes, as my opening statement made clear, we are prepared to follow up as necessary.
Q: In these final days of the presidency, how does he feel about making such a move? And did he consult with the congressional leaders?
A: Yes, we notified congressional leaders this morning of the imminent status of the action. They have been briefed over the last several days on a more informal basis. We also had contacts with all the members of the coalition, many of the other allied powers who may not be directly involved but who have interests as well as countries in the Middle East.

So there was an extensive notification and consultation process that took place this morning and yesterday.
Q: How about his mood?
A: The president's mood is that he's very concerned about this problem and is managing it on a full-time basis. As you know, we've had a couple of other events here during the day, including the Medal of Freedom for former President Reagan. But the president is on top of this matter and will see it through until noon of the 20th.
Q: Will he address the nation on this at any point?
A: I don't know. We don't have anything planned at the moment.
Q: If I can follow on that. He had planned to spend - he's only got seven days left. He'd planned to spend four of them at Camp David. Will that change at all with this crisis?
A: I don't think that will change. Certainly the communications system is adequate to manage this matter and any other problems that may come up.
Q: You're talking about many different kinds of violations here. Your terms for - on which you might strike again - is that if there's a violation of any of these different kinds, or is it just missiles in the no-fly zone?
A: As we have said before, without warning.

16. US Press Release: Allies determined Iraq will comply with U.N. measures, 13 January 1993

Washington - Lauding the successful strike by the allied coalition's military forces in Iraq January 13, President Bush said, "We are determined that Saddam Hussein will abide by the United Nations resolutions."

Speaking to reporters in the Oval Office, the president said the operation against targets in Iraq was launched because of the Iraqi leader's failure to comply with U.N. Security Council resolutions and because Saddam Hussein had been moving Iraqi missiles around in an unacceptable manner.

Following is a transcript of Bush's remarks:

You wanted to ask a question on the military action. Let me simply say that once again the American military in coalition, with strong allies, has performed in a superb fashion. Our planes are all accounted for. I've not yet seen a damage assessment or results of the strike. But they did the right thing, and the coalition did the right thing. And I have said before that we are determined that Saddam Hussein will abide by the United Nations resolutions. And we're very serious about that.

And I can say with confidence here, and I think it's important, that I'm confident Governor Clinton, the president-elect of the United States, feels that way, too. And I have talked to him before these strikes hit, and he as much as told me that. And then I've statements out of Little Rock. But I think that's a very important message to go, not just to our coalition forces, that we have every intention of working together in the future as we have in the past, but to Saddam Hussein, who has violated the resolutions.
Q: Do you think it will work?
THE PRESIDENT: Well - know what work means, but I am confident that when I - I will continue to insist that he abide by these resolutions. We've taken action, and I hope that will convince his [sic] he must do that. And I'm as confident that President Clinton will do this and feel the same way after the 20th.
Q: You have any reservations, sir, doing it so close to the end of your term in office?
THE PRESIDENT: No, absolutely not. I'm president until the 20th, and I will run foreign policy and conduct these - make these kinds of decisions as long as I'm president. We will keep the new team fully informed. And I believe they've been very generous and gracious in saying that we have done that. General Scowcroft is in almost daily contact with the transition people from the national security field; and then I know Dick Cheney's had good visits with, as has Larry Eagleburger, with the people coming in. So we'll just keep it closely informed.

But I have no reservations at all. You've got to do what you have to do. And there should be no question about that. What triggered the question, sir, was there any particular action by Saddam that -
THE PRESIDENT: Just his failure to live up to the resolutions and then his moving around of these missiles in a way that was unacceptable to the coalition of the United Nations.
Q: Are you prepared to order additional sites to be -
THE PRESIDENT: I will conduct myself until the 20th just as I have in the almost four years gone by; and that is, I don't say what we might or might not do, but I would think that soon Saddam Hussein would understand that we mean what we say and that we back it up. And I have no intention of changing that approach to life in the last six or seven days of my presidency.

Thank you very much. I'm very proud - I should say I'm very proud of the pilots and those who supported the pilots. Once again, we see what superb training we have and what dedicated young people are out there. I must say I worried when I heard premature stories of this because I - I hesitate ever, and I would never put a young flyer in harm's way because of leaked information. And fortunately the leaks that occurred on this did not result in the lose [sic] of life for any of our pilots. But I will always - I would just urge everybody - in whatever administration is here, now or in the future.
Q: Did they encounter - resistance?
THE PRESIDENT: We'll have more to say about that when we do a fuller briefing on the mission itself. But any time you divulge plans when somebody's life is at stake, it is not a good thing to do. I just never understood it. I don't like it. I saw it happen today. But that's history now. But we ought to have more responsibility, when you risk the life of a single U.S. pilot.

17. UN Press Release: Statement made by the Secretary-General of the United Nations in Paris, 14 January 1993

The raid yesterday, and the forces that carried out the raid, have received a mandate from the Security Council, according to Resolution 678 and the cause of the raid was the violation by Iraq of Resolution 687 concerning the cease-fire.

So, as the Secretary-General of the UN, I can say that this action was taken and conforms to the Resolutions and of the Security Council and conforms to the Charter of the United Nations.

[Mr Sills, UN Press Spokesman, speaking in New York, added] that a "no fly zone" in Iraq was not specifically authorized by a United Nations resolution, but he understood that the Member States involved felt that there was authorization within the overall framework of the relevant resolutions, specifically resolution 688 (1991), which dealt with humanitarian aid. He added that questions about how member States interpreted resolutions should be directed to member States.]

18. UK House of Commons Parliamentary Debate, Kuwait Border (Iraqi Violations), 13 January 1993

Mr. George Robertson (Hamilton) (*by private notice*): To ask the Secretary of State for Foreign and Commonwealth Affairs whether he will make a statement on the situation on the Iraq-Kuwait border.

The Minister of State, Foreign and Commonwealth Office (Mr. Douglas Hogg): Over the past few weeks, there have been a number of violations by the Iraqis of the border with Kuwait. The United Nations Secretary-General reported on 10 January that, on that morning, a party of some 200 Iraqis with trucks and heavy loading equipment forced entry into six ammunition bunkers in a former Iraqi naval base at Umm Qasr on Kuwaiti territory and took away most of their contents, including four anti-ship Silkworm missiles. Later that day, 500 Iraqis continued to dismantle prefabricated buildings in the former naval base. Similar violations have continued until today.

The Secretary-General reported to the Security Council that these activities were in violation of the procedures established by the Security Council. The Security Council responded on 11 January with a statement condemning the action taken by Iraq which constituted further material breaches of Security Council resolution 687, which established the formal ceasefire at the end of the Gulf war.

The Council demanded that Iraq co-operate fully with the United Nations Iraq-Kuwait Observer Mission - UNIKOM - and warned Iraq of the serious consequences that would flow from continued defiance. We hope that Iraq will not miscalculate, that the violations of the border will cease immediately, as will other Iraqi provocations, and that Iraq will comply with all United Nations resolutions.

Mr. Robertson: We fully understand why the Foreign Secretary cannot be here but has to be in Brussels this evening.

Is the Minister aware that there is wide international agreement that the conduct of President Saddam Hussein in the last few days has been designed as a deliberate and calculated provocation by a despicable regime, which calls in one breath for constructive dialogue and with the next says that it will recover Kuwait again? Is he further aware that there is no question but that Saddam Hussein must comply with the provisions of the United Nations Security Council resolutions that formed the basis for the ceasefire at the end of the Gulf war?

I assure the Minister that the good reasons for implementing the two air exclusion zones over northern and southern Iraq - protection from Saddam's genocidal attacks on the Kurds in the north and the Shi'ite Muslims in the south - remain as valid as they ever were. The imposition of the two air exclusion zones was supported by the Opposition in order to save many lives which were and are still in danger, and for that same reason we shall continue to support the air exclusion zones and their enforcement.

I welcome the assurance that the Foreign Secretary gave the House earlier today - that whatever necessary military action is taken will be taken in accordance with international law. I also strongly welcome the Foreign Secretary's assurance that he will keep the House fully informed of all developments, because that is an assurance which is of extreme importance to hon. Members from both sides.

Mr. Hogg: I am grateful to the hon. Gentleman for what he has said. He is right: Saddam Hussein must comply with the Security Council resolutions. I am grateful to the hon. Gentleman for his support for the no-fly zones. He is right to say that Iraq must not infringe the zones.

I can give the assurance once again that any action that may be contemplated at any stage by any party would proceed in accordance with international law. I can also assure the House once again that any material acts of any kind will be reported to the House.

Mr. Matthew Carrington (Fulham): Everybody supports action against Saddam Hussein to make sure that he complies with United Nations resolutions, but will my right hon. and learned Friend ensure that any action is taken with the agreement and support of our Arab allies in the Gulf war?

Mr. Hogg: It is very important that our Arab allies should support any action that the international community might deem appropriate: that is why it is important that any appropriate action should proceed in accordance with international law.

Sir David Steel (Tweeddale, Ettrick and Lauderdale): Does the Minister agree that it is not just border incursions but the deployment of anti-aircraft missiles in southern Iraq and the interference with the United Nations arms inspection teams' rights to fly into Baghdad which mount up to a worrying picture? Is it not necessary to remind Saddam Hussein that he finds himself in the position that he does today only because of his invasion of a neighbouring member state of the United Nations?

In view of the disturbing report this morning by Saddam Hussein's press officer in an Iraqi newspaper that Iraq intends to "retake Kuwait", is it not important that the Government enjoy cross-party support in the House for whatever action they take in an international context against Saddam Hussein?

Mr. Hogg: I am grateful to the right hon. Gentleman and to the hon. Member for Hamilton (Mr. Robertson) for the remarks that have already been made this afternoon. I agree with the great importance of proceeding in accordance with international law and maintaining cross-House agreement. It also needs to be said that the violations that the right hon. Gentleman has described amount to a pattern of conduct which must be deeply deplored.

Miss Emma Nicholson (Torridge and Devon, West): Does my right hon. and learned Friend agree that no United Nations aid has reached the south of Iraq for many months, nor are there any plans for it to be sent, and that the recent meagre aid flows to the Kurds in the north were fire-bombed and have now ceased completely? Therefore, does he agree that the memorandum of understanding and the United Nations' plans to send food to the south and the north are in rags and tatters and that nothing save intervention on the ground will save millions of people in the north and hundreds of thousands in the south from death by starvation this winter?

Mr. Hogg: As the House is well aware, my hon. Friend has been deeply involved in trying to take assistance to the people of south Iraq. She deserves all our praise.

The suffering in south Iraq, especially among the Shia people, is one of the reasons why it was thought right to impose a no-fly zone south of parallel 32.

Mr. David Winnick (Walsall, North): Has not the ceasefire agreement been systematically broken over the past two years, ever since it was signed by Iraq's criminal regime? Saddam Hussein has taken every possible opportunity to test and tease the allies.

I understand the difficulties that arose when the war of aggression against Kuwait was decisively defeated; but does not the Minister appreciate that many people - probably not least those in Iraq - are asking why the allies did not take the opportunity of ending once and for all the bloodstained tyranny that has been responsible for so many deaths and tortures in Iraq, and for all that has occurred since the invasion of Kuwait?

Mr. Hogg: I well understand why people ask on occasion why Saddam Hussein was not removed at the end of the Gulf war. The hon. Gentleman should bear in mind, however, that we were part of a coalition acting under the authority of the United Nations, for the purposes authorised by the Security Council and none other. Had we tried to go beyond the scope of those authorised purposes, the coalition would have fallen apart - and, incidentally, Ministers would have betrayed the word that they gave hon. Members in the House.

Mr. James Hill (Southampton, Test): Does my right hon. Friend agree that Saddam Hussein has won every move on the board? He is still in power, and he is still mocking all the western countries and treating them as a laughing stock.

What worries me particularly is the fact that, for some years, one of my constituents has been waiting for compensation for the death of her husband in Baghdad. There has been no movement whatever. The United Nations compensation committee has agreed that she should receive compensation, but Saddam Hussein simply refuses to sell oil for that purpose. Is it not time that he was taught a fundamental lesson in keeping his word? Should we not go in and do exactly what the United Nations has recommended, instead of playing what amounts to a game of draughts with him? Is it not time for firm action?

Mr. Hogg: I do not agree with my hon. Friend's observation that Saddam Hussein has won every game on the board. He has not. He invaded Iran; he lost that war, and tens of thousands of his people were killed. He invaded Kuwait; he lost that war too, and again tens of thousands of his people were killed. His country is now in a state of ruin. That is not winning every game on the board.

Mr. John McWilliam (Blaydon): The Minister's reply to my hon. Friend the Member for Walsall, North (Mr. Winnick) was disingenuous, to say the least. Hostilities ceased because of American domestic political opinion, not because our forces would have been acting beyond the constraint of the United Nations resolution; and the Republican Guard army units just north of our forces should have been taken out.

Will the Minister tell us which idiot left those Silkworms where they are? They pose a real threat?

Mr. Hogg: I was responding to a specific question from the hon. Member for Walsall, North (Mr. Winnick) - whether we should in some way have deprived Saddam Hussein of the leadership of Iraq. My point was that we were acting within the authority given to us by the Security Council: we could not go outside that authority without the coalition falling apart, and without Ministers having misled the House in previous statements.

Sir George Gardiner (Reigate): I refer to my right hon. and learned Friend's comment about the need to maintain coalition at the end of the Gulf war. Will he give a further assurance that, if counter-action against Saddam Hussein is authorised, at least he will do his level best to ensure that, this time, the effort does not fall short of the objectives to be achieved?

Mr. Hogg: We shall proceed, in anything we do, in accordance with the principles of international law.

Mr. D.N. Campbell-Savours (Workington): Why does not the Government more strenuously support the Iraqi opposition abroad, and in particular the Iraqi National Congress? Should not moneys owned by the Iraqi Government in the form of assets abroad be defrozen in part and handed to the INC to promote its internal campaigning in Iraq and to give it credibility in Baghdad?

Mr. Hogg: We have done various things to encourage the Iraqi opposition. We welcome the fact that a broad-based opposition is developing because that provides the people of Iraq with an alternative. As to compensation and assets, the hon. Gentleman makes an interesting proposal that has not yet been advanced. I can see two obvious difficulties. It would be a clear breach of the Security Council resolution freezing those assets, and there is a whole range of other claims on them. However I shall reflect on the hon. Gentleman's point, as I do on all his points.

Lady Olga Maitland (Sutton and Cheam): Has my right hon. and learned Friend held any discussions with the Kuwaiti Government, and will he confirm that it is no use the international community extending threats to Saddam Hussein, but that it must publicly be seen to be prepared to act?

Mr. Hogg: Discussions with the Kuwaiti Government have continued over many months, and will naturally continue. As to Iraq's violations of Kuwait, it is important for us to say that Iraq must comply with the Security Council resolutions and cease its violations of the no-fly zone - otherwise it will be exposed to great risk.

Mr. Tam Dalyell (Linlithgow): Count some of us out of the so-called all-party, cross-party agreement. Why is it that *Al Ahram* and the rest of the authoritative Egyptian press are against military action? Was not the Foreign Secretary's candid answer - which the right hon. and learned Gentleman knows very well - to my question on Egyptian and Bahraini support a blunt "No"? They do not support us in military action in the circumstances.

Mr. Hogg: One interesting aspect of the Security Council discussion and of the debate about Iraq generally is the broad consensus in support of the proposition that Saddam Hussein must comply with Security Council resolutions and cease to infringe the no-fly zones. There is very broad agreement for the proposition that, if Iraq does not do those things, it faces serious consequences.

Mr. Michael Colvin (Romsey and Waterside): I agree with my right hon. and learned Friend's answer to my hon. Friend the Member for Southampton, Test (Mr. Hill) - that Saddam Hussein has twice been severely defeated in the battlefield recently, but why do we continue to permit him to turn military defeat into propaganda victory? What steps are the Government taking in the Security Council to obtain its authority to take action to stop once and for all Saddam Hussein's retreat and cheap tactics?

Mr. Hogg: The best thing we can do to deflate Saddam Hussein's reputation is to explain the facts. They point to continued and dramatic failure - loss of the war against Iran, loss of the war in Kuwait, and a total destruction of Iraq's economy. That pattern of failure has seldom been surpassed.

Mr. George Galloway (Glasgow, Hillhead) *rose* -

Madam Speaker: Mr. George Gardiner - I mean Mr. George Galloway.

Mr. Tony Banks (Newham, North-West): My hon. Friend is much better looking.

Madam Speaker: My apologies all round.

Mr. Galloway: Notwithstanding the consensus that exists across the Front Benches, I must say - like my hon. Friend the Member for Linlithgow (Mr. Dalyell) - that, whatever bloody act has been planned, it will not be done in my name, in the name of many people in this country or in the name of many members of the coalition that fought the Gulf war only a couple of years ago. Does not the Minister understand that, in the Islamic world and elsewhere, the new coalition is regarded as a bunch of bloody hypocrites? They are ready to pulverise Iraq for its transgressions against international agreements, yet stand by and watch while Israel - which for nearly 40 years has been breaking every international law in the book - expels, imprisons, tortures and kills people in occupied territories every day of the week: and they do absolutely nothing while Bosnian Muslims are massacred in the centre of Europe. They will be seen as a bunch of hypocrites and will receive the response from the international community that they deserve.

Mr. Hogg: The hon. Gentleman's threat that he will be unable to support any action that we may have in mind is a threat that can be borne with equanimity.

Mr. John Wilkinson (Ruislip-Northwood): Given that, sadly, my right hon. Friend has unfinished business still to be accomplished, will he ensure that, rather than concentrating on the no-fly zone over southern Iraq, Her Majesty's Government and their western allies will concentrate on creating an effective no-go zone for Iraqi troops on the ground in neighbouring Kuwait? Will he also ensure that any further incursions into Kuwait by Iraqi forces or civilians will not go unpunished - because, if they do, Saddam Hussein will be further emboldened to defy international opinion and international law and to commit further acts of aggression?

Mr. Hogg: My hon. Friend will have heard me say in answer to the private notice question that the Secretary-General is of the opinion that what has happened in Kuwait constitutes a serious breach of the relevant procedures. In answer to his question, let me make it plain that Iraq must comply with the resolutions of the Security Council and must cease to infringe the no-fly zone. If she does not, she faces very serious consequences.

Mr. Donald Anderson (Swansea, East): As some sort of military response on the part of the Gulf war coalition seems more and more probable, can the Minister comment on reports that, this time round, the use of airfields in Turkey will be denied to the coalition forces?

Mr. Hogg: I do not wish to speculate about matters of that kind.

19. Press statement issued by the Ministry of Foreign Affairs of France, 14 January 1993

The spokesperson of the Ministry made the following statement in the course of today's press conference.

The Defence Minister indicated this morning the manner in which the operation which was led yesterday in the south of Iraq unfolded on the military level.

From the political point of view, it is fitting to recall that the action of France, since the beginning of the conflict, takes place in the context of the continuation [*of the conflict*], in the unstinting solidarity with the coalition states and finally within the limits of the strict application of the resolutions of the United Nations. We have always placed ourselves within the limits of the decisions of the United Nations.

After the end of the Gulf conflict, a certain number of resolutions of the UN Security Council were adopted. These resolutions, which have not been adhered to by Iraq, began with 687, which fixed, as you know, the terms of the cease-fire.

For several months, and in particular since last July, Iraq has deliberately refused to submit to the demands of the UN and it has manifestly placed itself in violation of international law.

At the time, warnings were addressed to Iraq. On several occasions, we expressed our concerns with the behaviour of that state.

At the end of the month of August, France, together with the United States and Great Britain, decided to put in place a no-fly zone south of the 32nd parallel in a manner symmetrical to the one which was put in place north of the 36th parallel, in order to assure the protection of the civilian population of Iraqi Shiites in the south and Kurds in the north, victims of the armed actions of Iraq.

Since then, last week in particular, the violations of the resolutions perpetrated by Iraq once again have brought, I emphasize, the Security Council, through the voice of its President, to issue a declaration, adopted unanimously as is the attribute of all declarations of this type. This declaration was destined to send a warning to Iraq and to warn Iraq against the grave consequences which might follow its manoeuvres. It was aimed at two precise violations: on the one hand the incursions made by Iraq across the Kuwait border in the zones where one UNIKOM is located - there have been at least 4; on the other hand, the refusal to allow the UN inspection mission, despatched by the resolutions with the mandate to inspect the elimination of arms of mass destruction, to use their aircraft.

The refusal of Iraq, in spite of the warnings, to comply with our demands has brought the allies to intervene, as they did yesterday, founding their actions on the resolutions authorizing the use of force, in particular resolution 678.

After the aerial operation of yesterday, the Ambassadors to the UN of France, Great Britain, the United States and Russia approached the Iraqi Ambassador to emphasize the previous warnings and the necessity incumbent on Iraq to comply with the whole of its obligations under international law and the UN.

[Answers of the spokesperson to press questions:]

- On the absence of prior investigation of the United Nations - There was the declaration of the President of the Security Council of 11 January. It spoke of grave consequences. That declaration was a warning in itself. The decision has been taken to carry out that operation in conformity with the law.
- On the sending by France as by the United States, of ground troops to Kuwait - I am not informed of that possibility.
- On the use of the term coalition, even though only three states participated in the operation - I would point out to you that the aircraft which were engaged were stationed in Saudi Arabia.
- On the possibility of new actions against Iraq and on the absence of action vis-à-vis Israel - There are a certain number of decisions of the United Nations. We consider that they ought to be put in practice. Those who do not respect them incur the consequences of their actions. We have given the necessary warnings to the Iraqis.

Concerning the second part of the question, when the problem is raised in the Security Council we will examine it.

- On the reservations expressed by certain states, such as Egypt - I have nothing to say on the Egyptian declarations. I believe that no one can contest the necessity to see to it that when there is a violation of commitments, one reaps the consequences.

20. Press Release: Statement by the Russian Foreign Ministry, 14 January 1993

The following statement was released in Moscow today:

The blow dealt on January 13 by the coalition air force of the United States, Britain and France at Iraqi ground-to-air missile complexes was provoked by the latest Iraqi violations of the UN Security Council resolutions on a post-crisis settlement in the region. These violations include the deployment of Iraqi missiles in areas south of the 32nd parallel, the seizure of military hardware slated for destruction, and the blocking of UN humanitarian actions.

Russia had repeatedly, i.a. through her Embassy in Baghdad, urged the Iraqi side to display wisdom and readiness to cooperate with the UN Security Council, to refrain from steps leading to escalation of tension in the region. The Security Council President's statement on Iraq, dated January 11, and the demarche of four Permanent Members of the UN Security Council to Iraq on January 9 were clear-cut signals to stop disregarding the decisions taken by the United Nations. A clear warning was given that such obstructionist policy would lead to the execution of all measures which would be deemed necessary.

We hoped that Iraq would obey the will of the international community and a military action would thereby be avoided. However, unfortunately, that never happened.

The action of the coalition forces in Iraq was taken in the context of the international community's efforts to ensure the observance of a decision jointly adopted under UN aegis to alleviate the consequences of Iraqi aggression.

We hope that this time the Iraqi leadership will heed the voice of reason and will strictly abide by the provisions of all resolutions of the UN Security Council. The tough statements still heard from Baghdad do not testify to the latter's realistic assessment of the current situation.

21. US Press Release: U.S. will "Deal Forcefully" with Iraqi Provocations, 17 January 1993

Washington - The United States and other members of the Persian Gulf are determined "to deal forcefully" with any threats to their aircraft by Iraqi forces, the White House warned Saddam Hussein January 17.

Speaking hours after U.S. planes had shot down a threatening Iraqi MiG-29 aircraft in the "no-fly" zone in northern Iraq, and just hours before U.S. missiles attacked an Iraqi nuclear weapons plant outside Baghdad, White House spokesman Marlin Fitzwater explained the no-fly zone incident and declared:

"We are prepared to defend ourselves and to take action where necessary ... We have said before that we won't give any further warnings of our actions to enforce the resolutions, and that remains in effect.

Following is a transcript of the Fitzwater briefing:

Fitzwater: Iraqi aircraft and air defense systems today attacked coalition aircraft over northern Iraq. In response to the hostile Iraqi actions, United States and coalition aircraft took defensive measures to retaliate. Coalition forces attacked in their air defense site and shot down an Iraqi aircraft. The coalition aircraft were monitoring the no-fly zone north of the 36th parallel in that country.

These actions underscore the coalition's determination to deal forcefully with any threats to its aircraft operating in the two no-fly zones. These zones were created to monitor compliance with U.N. Security Council Resolution 688 which demands the Iraqi leadership cease repressing its own people.

For almost two years, the no-fly zone in northern Iraq has effectively ensured Saddam Hussein does not take large-scale military actions against the people of northern Iraq. Saddam has now openly proclaimed his intent to challenge these zones.

As we noted on January 13, we will not tolerate challenges to the U.N. Security Council resolutions and the measures enacted by the coalition to monitor and enforce those resolutions.

This morning at about 2:00 a.m. (0700 GMT), Iraqi anti-aircraft guns fired at two United States F-16 aircraft patrolling in northern Iraq. Later, Iraqi MiG-23s violated the northern no-fly zone. And shortly after 3:00 a.m., Iraqi SA-6 missiles were fired at coalition aircraft also in the north. At 4:38 this morning, a United States F-16 encountered a threatening MiG-29 in the northern no-fly zone and shot it down. We will continue to take active defensive action in the north.

President Bush this morning discussed this matter with Prime Minister Major, President Mitterrand, and, of course, Prime Minister Mulroney, who is at Camp David with the President. The President's National Security Advisor, General Brent Scowcroft, is at the camp and his deputy, Admiral John Howe, is here in the White House. There have been numerous consultations this morning with General Powell, Secretary Cheney and Secretary Eagleburger. Sandy Berger of the Clinton transition team has been fully briefed.

The no-fly zones were designed to protect Iraqi citizens in the north and south who had come under attack by the Iraqi government. Endorsed by the U.N., these zones also provide safety and freedom of movement for U.N. inspectors. The United States supports the United Nations' conclusion last night that Iraq has not complied with its requests for uninterrupted and safe access by its inspection flights. The United Nations inspections are designed to detect and eliminate the nuclear, chemical and biological weapons capability of Iraq. This process must continue.

With that, I'll try to take your questions.

Question: What is the President going to do? Has he ordered any renewed bombing of Iraq? Or what is it? Is there a new military intent here?

Answer: The situation remains ongoing in terms of the Iraqi government's challenge to the U.N. resolutions and to the no-fly zones. There was a lengthy statement this morning by Saddam Hussein which once again stated their intentions with regard to Kuwait and the no-fly zones, all of which we find unacceptable. We continue to consider all options. And as we obviously demonstrated last night, we are prepared to defend ourselves and to take action where necessary.

Q: The President on Friday laid down an ultimatum and then seemed to back away from it. Was that at all due to objections from British Prime Minister Major?

A: No, it was not. Those stories were wrong. There have been continuous consultations. Prime Minister Major has been extraordinarily strong and supportive of all the actions, but there are other reasons and other kinds of considerations that have been taken into effect concerning the timing of our actions. And again, I would repeat that this is an ongoing process.

Q: The President yesterday saying he wasn't trying to be belligerent. He seemed more amenable to a prolonged discussion for this. Is he still consulting with allies, or is there now a new deadline laid out?

A: We have said before that we won't give any further warnings of our actions to enforce the resolutions, and that remains in effect. There are continuing consultations going on. This latest provocation certainly ratchets up the concern of the United States about the intentions of Iraq, and we are considering it in a most urgent fashion.

Q: Marlin, doesn't your appearance, though, out here on a Sunday morning, and use of the words "deal forcefully," signal that the United States is, in these last few days of the Bush administration, fully willing to launch a strong attack on Iraq?

A: Well, we want to signal that this is a very serious matter. Certainly any time we shoot down an aircraft of another country, that's a serious matter and provocation. And so we want to make it clear what our reasons are and what the stakes are.

I think it's important to point out here again that the United Nations resolutions were established for a purpose, and a big part of that purpose is to eliminate the nuclear and biological and chemical weapons threat of Saddam Hussein. And that threat faces all the countries of the world and one which was clearly recognized by the U.N. resolutions.

The U.N. inspectors have had considerable success in the last many months at eliminating great quantities of chemical weapons delivery systems and nuclear weapons capability, and that must be continued. And the United Nations and the United States and other countries remain firm that we will demand compliance. And so I want to emphasize that we have a continuing threat to that compliance and one which the coalition takes very seriously.

Q: Do you think Saddam Hussein misreads the transition of power in Washington and is being bellicose now and then may step back to try to win favor with the Clinton administration?

A: Well, if he's reacting on that basis, then I think he does misread it. We don't have any question about President-elect Clinton's support and his intentions. He's been quite specific. And if that is his thinking, then we believe he is wrong.

But on the other hand, our experience with Saddam is such that it's always difficult to ascertain his motives. He may be doing this for other reasons: his own people, his own country, et cetera. We see statements like the one by Mr. Aziz yesterday that apparently now is an empty statement with regard to - after what they did last night. And so actions have always been the only way we can gauge Saddam's thinking.

Q: Is there any diplomacy going on now? And does the U.S. now feel that it has a free hand from the U.N. to act militarily as it did in the previous raid?

A: No, we continue to work with the United Nations and with the coalition. We consult with them very closely. There have been a number of discussions in the last couple of days with Mr. Ekeus about the work of his inspection teams and what their plans are. And we take any actions within the directives and the confines of the U.N. resolutions.

Q: Marlin, can you take us back to Friday? Planes were in the air Friday evening and they did not go ahead and make strikes. What happened? We understood - it wasn't Prime Minister Major - that it was somewhere within the United Nations Security Council, somebody objected to this.

A: Well, I just can't discuss targets or timing. Someday that will all come out. But I would try to emphasize again that we are in the midst of a serious situation, and those kinds of questions simply can't be answered at this point.

Q: But wasn't there disagreement within the coalition on this, not saying who it was?

A: No, there's not. The coalition has been together on this; there have been discussions back and forth. We've had to go through a lot of very tactical kinds of discussions, and we are proceeding through it. But there's not been any basic disagreements at all.

Q: Marlin, there are new reports now that the Iraqis are saying that they might allow flights from Bahrain. Are you aware of that? Does the White House have any reaction? And does that show any indication that they may be trying to come around?

A: Well, I am not aware of that. I don't have any specific response. But once again, I would go back to the U.N. mandate, which calls for uninterrupted travel and total freedom of movement.

Q: Marlin, who, beyond Prime Minister Major, has the administration talked to? And has the President talked to President-elect Clinton personally about this?

A: He talked to Prime Minister Major, President Mitterrand and Prime Minister Mulroney, and of course, France, Great Britain and the United States, all three countries, have planes in the air over the no-fly zone and did last night. We're also having consultations with members of Congress and certainly with the Transition Team. Sandy Berger has been fully briefed as well as Tony Lake has too. And the President is certainly prepared to discuss it with President-elect Clinton at any time.

Q: Marlin, you said that at 2:00, F-16s were fired at by anti-aircraft weaponry. Were they in the no-fly zone?

A: Yes. They were.

Q: So that the anti-aircraft, too, was in the no-fly zone?

A: Yes, that's right.

Q: Marlin, is there a feeling now that Wednesday's results - Wednesday's raid - produced few results, that you missed most of the targets there?

A: No, it's a feeling that we're in a ongoing process. We are - we are facing a continuing challenge to the U.N. resolutions. It is premature at this point to judge the outcome, but it would be clear that Saddam Hussein has started an intensive challenge about that point and it continues to this time.

Q: You mentioned at 3:00 a.m., that an SA-6 fired at coalition aircraft. Were those American aircraft? And if so, identify them. If not, identify them.

A: American, British, and French. All three were up there. I don't know the exact specifics, but the Pentagon will have all those details later this morning.

22. US Press Release: Attack Shows U.S. Fully Backs U.N. Iraq Mandate, 17 January 1993

Washington - The U.S. missile strike against a nuclear facility near Baghdad January 13 [17] reflects coalition resolve to back-up U.N. Security Council resolutions against Iraq developing weapons of mass destruction, says White House Press Secretary Marlin Fitzwater.

"The strike was designed to help ... ensure that Iraq never again acquires weapons of mass destruction," the press secretary told reporters after Tomahawk Cruise missiles hit a plant that produces nuclear explosives.

"It also demonstrates the United States' and the coalition's determination to demand Iraq's compliance with all U.N. resolutions," he said.

Following is the transcript of the Fitzwater briefing:

Fitzwater: United States Tomahawk cruise missiles today attacked a nuclear fabricating plant near Baghdad, Iraq, which is part of its weapons-of-mass-destruction program. This plant made components for Iraq's nuclear enrichment program, including parts for its electromagnetic isotope separators, which Iraq has used in its program to create nuclear weapons.

This strike was designed to help achieve the goals of United Nations Security Council Resolutions 687, 707, and 715, namely to ensure that Iraq never again acquires weapons of mass destruction: nuclear, chemical, and biological, as well as ballistic missiles. It also demonstrates the United States' and the coalition's determination to demand Iraq's compliance with all U.N. resolutions.

It is important to remember that Operation Desert Storm and over 40 subsequent United Nations inspections revealed Iraq's aggressive program to build a nuclear bomb and other weapons of mass destruction. The United Nations has demanded the freedom to inspect and eliminate these weapons.

Since the war, the U.N. has supervised the destruction of dozens of missiles and their launchers, hundreds of tons of chemical munitions, chemical Scud warheads, and numerous nuclear installations. This process must not be stopped. Iraq's weapons of mass destruction must be destroyed.

Iraq has again today refused to allow inspections without interference of any kind and with complete safety and freedom of movement, as is required by the United Nations resolutions.

It is the Iraqi leadership that bears full responsibility for today's events.

On January 7, 1993, Iraq informed the U.N. that it would no longer grant flight clearances for U.N. aircraft. The Security Council, on both January 8 and January 11, warned Iraq that its refusal to allow inspectors unhindered freedom to enter the country constituted a material breach of the U.N. Security Council resolutions. The Council also warned Iraq of the serious consequences that would stem from such refusal. On January 13, we underscored our full support for the Council's statements. On January 15, the U.N. concluded that Iraq had refused to guarantee the safety of flights and personnel. On January 16, the U.N. found that Iraq's decision to ensure the safety of flights only if they entered via Jordanian airspace to be an unacceptable attempt to prevent the inspectors from carrying out their mission.

Today's action is designed to make clear to Iraq that non-compliance with U.N. Security Council resolutions will not be tolerated.

Question: What role did the President play in this? Does this mean you're going to continue these attacks as long as there is defiance?

Answer: Well, the President, of course, has been involved in the decisionmaking since early this morning, of course, when he was notified of the United States aircraft that shot down a MiG last night in northern Iraq. There have been a series of consultations and meetings during the day. The President held a conference call around 6:30 this morning with his national security advisers. He talked with Prime Minister Major, with President Mitterrand, and with the Prime Minister of Turkey during the course of the day today. So, there have been a lot of consultations to go forward.

Q: Was the facility destroyed?

A: The facility that was attacked by the missiles is in Zafraniyah which is a suburb of Baghdad approximately 13 miles from the center of the city. We don't have a damage assessment at this point.

Q: Marlin will there be any other attacks at this point as part of this operation or are you going to take a wait and see attitude at this juncture?

A: Well, I would say that, of course, we don't comment on specific targets or what might be under consideration for attack or - or that we wouldn't. I would say that the purpose, the goals of this operation is to seek compliance with the U.N. resolutions. We do not have that yet. And I don't believe you can assume that these kinds of episodes are over until we get compliance.

Q: Marlin, these were U.S. Cruise missiles. Did we act unilaterally or in concert with our allies?

A: We acted in concert with our allies. They were all the Tomahawk Cruise missiles. There were no airplanes involved.

Q: Marlin, with the inauguration coming so close, what role has President-elect Clinton been playing in this? He has described it, and I think you have described it as he's being briefed and informed. Has he been asked to write - to sign off on this, to give his approval?

A: He's not been asked for his approval, but we have tried to keep he or his national security staff informed at every step of the way. There were discussions early this morning about the incident last night with Sandy Berger and Tony Lake. There have been discussions again this morning with Sandy Berger concerning this action. And President-elect Clinton has been - has had the benefit of all the details. I've just talked to Dee Dee Myers a few minutes ago, and she is aware of our public statements.

Q: Marlin, did the decision to use Tomahawk missiles instead of command aircraft have anything to do with the Turkish refusal to let us use our planes from Incirlik?

A: The main reason is that we wanted to use the missiles because it did not put U.S. Personnel in jeopardy. It did not - we did not have to use aircraft. We did not have to suffer the risk of having personnel go down.

Q: Marlin, is this target considered appropriate, being an alleged nuclear research site because the inspectors you feel are not being given freedom of movement, therefore because the inspectors, one of their jobs is to look for nuclear and chemical sites so that you felt a nuclear site would be an appropriate target?

A: Yes. The nuclear site has several advantages. One is that it is near Baghdad and makes the point to the people of the country as well as to the government that we are demanding compliance and that we are willing to enforce the resolutions; another is that it can be attacked with the TLAM missiles; another is that it also helps in the process of eliminating nuclear weapons in the sense of the destructive act itself. There are separators and processors and other equipment there that have been used in the past, and that use has been verified by U.N. inspectors.

U.N. inspectors have been there. They know that what this equipment is and so there was a relatively high degree of assurance about what we were going after.

Q: Marlin, what is the next step - that the U.N. file yet another flight plan and then if that is not approved, then we have another deadline and another strike?

A: The U.N. will continue to attempt to receive permission to inspect on an uninterrupted basis and with safety.

Q: We could be hitting them literally daily, every day until they finally come around to allowing unfettered inspection flights?

A: We will continue to seek compliance with the resolutions.

Q: Marlin, is this part of continuing operation Southern Watch, or is this a new operation that we're doing now that we're going into attack them maybe daily?

A: Well, I would say that there have been a series of actions over the last several days designed to get compliance. And those are all related in the sense of the single objective of allowing the inspectors to carry out their work. And so in that sense it is a continuing process. And we'll have to wait and see what the future brings.

Q: Does it continue Southern Watch - which was the name of the monitoring actions?

A: Well, I don't know the exact name for all these specific operations.

Q: The wires are saying a hotel in central Baghdad has been hit. Do you know anything about that?

A: I don't. I saw the television film of it, the speculation there that it was fragments of anti-aircraft weaponry which sounds more logical. But I don't really know.

Q: Where did the missiles come from, Marlin?

A: We don't want to designate exactly where those came from. As you all know, they're primarily launched from ships. But we don't want to say exactly where or how many?

Q: Marlin, I'd like to ask two questions about the action. First of all, you describe it as basically in retaliation for their inability to send in the - allow the U.N. inspectors to move freely.

A: And in furtherance of our objectives to eliminate the nuclear weapons program.

Q: First, is this pursuant to some proposal by the U.N.? The U.N. has given a blanket authority, but what is the relationship here between the U.N. and the United States as the single power that has carried out the attack? And, secondly, the broader challenge by the Iraqi government seems to be to the no-fly zones, which they now are rejecting. How are you going to deal with that?

A: First of all, the United States and its coalition partners have been working together in their consultations and they have been working with the U.N. very closely. We have been in contact with Ralph Ekeus several times today and yesterday and the day before, and all of our

actions have been in concert with the U.N. authorities. Certainly from a legal standpoint and from the standpoint of authorization, they are all derivative of the U.N. resolutions. And I would say that there has been no action taken that has not been the result of consultations between all of these parties involved.
Q: And what about the no-fly zone problem?
A: And the no-fly zone is similarly important, and I go to some pains here to make that point, that from our perspective, the no-fly zones, which have been endorsed by the U.N., are essential to the safety of patrolling the areas and particularly to the safety of the people who live there. Those no-fly zones were established, you'll recall, because Iraq was bombing its own citizens, both in the north and in the south. But it's also true that our inspectors used the entry through the no-fly zone, certainly in the southern part of the country below the 32nd parallel, as well as many of the inspections that they carried out north of that.

And so, we believe that the no-fly zones are an integral part of the entire inspection regime, as well as the authority of all the other resolutions.
Q: Marlin, back to an earlier question, did Turkey or Saudi Arabia or any other coalition partner in the region object to the use of their facilities to launch an air raid today?
A: I'm not aware of any objections on any part of this. But there again, let me emphasize this was entirely by missiles and not by aircraft.
Q: Marlin, could you clarify one thing on the question of inspections? You say they refused inspections, but that we had been inside this specific plant that was hit. Was this plant involved with any refusal of inspection?
A: No. The refusal is to allow United Nations inspectors to fly United Nations aircraft within the country, involving all their inspections activities. Over the last couple of days, you're aware of all the requests that have been made by Mr. Ekeus in the U.N. inspections for the right to fly their aircraft with assurances of safety wherever they want to inspect, whatever site it is, whether it's chemical, nuclear, biological, or whatever. And it is that principle that we are there to uphold. This facility had been used in the past for nuclear weapons fabricating; the equipment and buildings and other material are there, and it has been inspected in the past, so we knew that it had a direct relevance.
Q: Given the previous record of Iraqi harassment of U.N. inspection teams, that means not just one time - a one-time incident would be refusal to give them access. Why was only one target selected?
A: It was our feeling that this was an appropriate target for the reasons I stated earlier in terms of making the political and diplomatic point that we wanted to make and in terms of its relevance to the direct objectives to eliminate their nuclear weapons program.
Q: Marlin, was this in a civilian population area? And if it was, wouldn't you then be contradicting what you said on Wednesday that we're not interested in targeting civilian population centers?
A: We're not targeting civilian populations. It is 13 miles from Baghdad, and we have used the missiles, which we believe are very accurate.

23. Doorstep Interview with the UK Prime Minister, 17 January 1993, 21.20 hours

Q: Is this a punishment that fits the crime of Saddam Hussein?
A: The action that was taken this evening was taken after a great deal of consideration, after a great deal of consultation and after giving Iraq every opportunity to comply with the Security Council resolutions. They were aware that they were breaking them. They were blatantly breaking them and they were aware that they were at risk of a response. And after very careful consultation between the allies there was a response.
Q: Did you counsel caution on President Bush?
A: No, there was complete agreement between the allies about the nature and timing of the response this evening. It has been discussed for two or three days. I have had a number of discussions over the weekend with President Bush and the outcome of those discussions and with President Mitterrand and others was the action taken this evening.
Q: [Will you take further] action if necessary?
A: I am not going to anticipate what may happen now. We have said repeatedly that there are Security Council resolutions that we require Iraq to comply with. They know that. It could not possibly be clearer to them. They have been told time and time and time again. They have now had illustrations that if they will not comply with the Security Council resolutions then there will be a response. I hope they will comply.
Q: Do you regret the civilian casualties?
A: We do not yet know any details about that. The military advice I have is that it is very unlikely, that those casualties, if you mean the Rashid Hotel, that the casualties were caused by the action of the United States. We do not know that. There was a great deal of random and haphazard fire from within Baghdad and it may well be that that was self inflicted but at this moment we do not know.
Q: What about British military involvement, do you expect any of that?
A: I am not going to anticipate what may happen in the future. On this occasion it was considered operationally the right way to deal with the problem was to use the Tomahawk cruise missiles and that was what happened.
Q: What about those who say that this was reckless and will escalate problems in the Gulf?
A: I disagree with them. The problem, originally the invasion of Kuwait came from Iraq. The disobedience of the Security Council resolutions is by Iraq. It is not just the occasional disobedience, it's wilfully disobeying the requirements of the international community time and time again. He has been courting trouble, he has had trouble. He knew what was likely to happen. It has happened.
Q: Will you be making a statement Prime Minister to the House of Commons tomorrow?
A: The Defence Secretary will make a statement tomorrow afternoon.

24. Statement in the House of Commons by the UK Secretary of State for Defence, 18 January 1993

With your permission Madam Speaker I wish to make a further statement on coalition military action against Iraq.

Yesterday and earlier today the coalition took further military action against Iraq. There were a number of separate operations.

At 0845 hrs GMT today, 4 RAF Tornado GR1 aircraft and 2 Victor tankers took part in a further coalition operation, involving over 40 US, British and French aircraft, against Iraqi air defence facilities and command and control facilities in southern Iraq, which had continued to pose a threat to coalition aircraft in the no fly zone. Attacks were also carried out to suppress air defence installations which threatened the security of coalition aircraft participating in the operation. All coalition aircraft and aircrew returned safely.

Four RAF aircraft participated in the attack against an air defence operations centre at Al Najaf. Two Tornado GR1 aircraft were to use 1,000lb laser guided bombs against targets designated by the TIALD pods, carried by the other two aircraft. One of the Tornados was unable to clearly identify the target and did not release its weapons in order to avoid the possibility of causing civilian casualties or damage to other buildings in the area. However, the other Tornado successfully completed the attack.

Like the operation on 13 January, this action was taken in self defence to ensure the safety of coalition aircraft patrolling the no fly zone below the 32nd parallel in support of UNSCR 688. This was a follow-up to the action taken on 13 January. Early indications are that further significant damage has been inflicted on Iraq's residual air defences in the southern no fly zone. Assessment of the results is continuing. This followed action in the latter part of yesterday when cruise missiles, launched from the US Navy ships in the region, attacked a facility connected with the Iraqi weapons of mass destruction programme. The early indications are that the facility was extensively damaged. This action was taken to ensure that Iraq complies with its mandatory obligations under UNSCR 687 and related resolutions. Iraq has committed a number of material breaches of UNSCR 687 and wilfully ignored the warnings given by the Security Council and the US, UK, France and Russia on 11 and 14 January respectively.

There has also been a number of incidents in the northern no fly zone. On 17 January, an Iraqi fighter aircraft violated the no fly zone in the north of Iraq. The Iraqi aircraft was engaged and shot down by coalition aircraft. In addition, coalition aircraft were illuminated by Iraqi air defence radars on a number of occasions in the last few days, including an RAF Jaguar on 16 January. This was in violation of the coalition demarche of 14 April 1992, which warned Iraq against a number of specific actions which would be taken as indicators of hostile intent. Following one such incident an SA-6 Battery was attacked on 17 January by coalition aircraft armed with the high speed anti radiation missile (HARM). Initial damage assessments indicate that the SAM system was put out of action. Iraqi air defence radars were again attacked using HARM on 18 January.

These coalition actions have clearly demonstrated to the Iraqis the seriousness of our demand that Iraq should comply with UN resolutions and our continuing determination to maintain the no fly zones in the north and south of Iraq. If the Iraqis still refuse to comply with United Nations resolutions the Government will not shirk from considering the need for further action in consultation with coalition partners.

The House would not wish me to conclude without expressing again our appreciation of the continuing efforts of our servicemen and women serving in the Gulf. They can be assured that they enjoy the whole hearted support of the vast majority in this House and of the British public at large.

25. Russian Foreign Ministry Statement on the situation around Iraq, 18 January 1993

The situation around Iraq has once again crossed the critical line, there have been casualties among civilian population, which is a cause for particular remorse. The keys to normalizing the situation are in the hands of Baghdad, which simply would not listen to multiple warnings. It must be clear that a solution lies in fully implementing the decisions of the Security Council. This will allow relieve the situation in the Persian Gulf, provide Iraq's neighbours and itself with security and territorial integrity guarantees.

We proceed from the fact that reaction to Iraq's actions must be adequate and follow only agreed decisions. It looks as if it is once again necessary to review the situation in the UN Security Council.

For us the security of the Russian community in Baghdad is of paramount importance. We have informed the Americans of our anxieties. We want this to be known in Iraq.

26. Reply by Chinese Foreign Ministry Spokesman, 18 January 1993

Question: What is China's reaction on recent attack of cruise missile against Iraq?

Answer: We do not wish to see further deterioration of situation in the Gulf region. Our consistent position is to peacefully settle international disputes.

27. US Press Release: Strikes in Iraq Continue in Support of U.N. Mandate, 19 January 1993

Washington - U.S. forces continue to strike back at Iraqi forces defying U.N. Security Council resolutions, says Defense Department spokesman Pete Williams.

Williams said during his last regularly scheduled briefing as the Bush administration's defense spokesman January 19 that the resolve of the United States and the Gulf coalition remains unchanged in the face of Iraqi President Saddam Hussein's continuing defiance of lawful U.N. orders.

"The coalition remains united on two issues," Williams told reporters. "The most important one is that Saddam Hussein must comply with the U.N. Security Council resolutions. There's absolutely no daylight between any members of the coalition on that issue.

"And secondly, they remain united that Iraq must not interfere with flights of coalition aircraft in the southern and northern no-fly zones. On that there is no disagreement.

"There's been absolutely no change in the administration's posture on its willingness to continue to ... use force to force Saddam Hussein to comply with the U.N. Security Council resolutions. So there's been no change in our position. And, of course, Governor Clinton's (spokespersons) have said that they fully support the administration's approach."

Williams pointed out that the end of the Bush administration and the start of the Clinton administration January 20 will not impact the readiness of U.S. military forces. "There's an enormous amount of continuity here from a military perspective," he declared. In particular, he told reporters, the U.S. commands in the Persian Gulf region do not change and forces in the region continue with their missions.

Williams summarized the results of ongoing coalition air strikes.

"Since the coalition attacks began, in northern Iraq we are now in a position where we're hitting back at their air defense and anti-aircraft artillery sites that are shooting at coalition aircraft. In southern Iraq, we have functionally disabled ... their air defense system, and we have their surface-to-air missiles on the run. And in the attack on Baghdad, we have destroyed key parts of the facilities that the Iraqis use to develop nuclear weapons," he said.

"And why are we continuing these attacks? Because there continue to be threats against coalition aircraft in the south and in the north (no-fly zones), and because Saddam Hussein hasn't fully complied with the resolutions," the defense spokesman asserted.

Williams described three incidents January 19 in which Baghdad violated the no-fly zones and to which U.S. forces responded:

- An Iraqi surface-to-air missile radar facility targeted a U.S. F-4G aircraft that was on routine patrol just east of

Mosul. In response, the U.S. plane fired one missile, which the pilot said probably hit the radar site.

- An Iraqi anti-aircraft installation near Saddam hydroelectric dam fired at and missed a U.S. F-16 fighter plane.
- Iraqi anti-aircraft artillery just north of Mosul fired on and missed two F-16s on routine patrol. Both aircraft then dropped cluster bombs on the site but could not confirm that the ensuing explosions were on target.

"We will strike back" when fired upon or tracked by radar, Williams told reporters.

Williams said that Iraqi aircraft sometimes fly over missile sites in order to lure coalition aircraft into especially dangerous zones. "I think our pilots are wisely not being drawn into that trap," he said.

Williams provided further information on a coalition air raid in the southern no-fly zone January 18. "The Iraqi air defense system has been functionally neutralized - no one part of the system can communicate with any other part. Many parts have been destroyed. There are a few radars still left, but the system doesn't function anymore as an air defense network," he said.

Regarding the January 17 U.S. Cruise Missile attack on the Zaafaraniyah nuclear facility, Williams said that the missile that struck the Al-Rashid hotel was probably shot down by Iraqi anti-aircraft fire and hit the ground near the building without exploding.

"And I think it's safe to say that ... the warhead ... did not explode. That was a crater caused by the ... impact of ... the weight. A cruise missile weighs about 2,000 pounds, nearly a (short) ton. And then, of course, there's some unspent fuel, and that's what caused the fireball. But it doesn't look like the warhead blew up," he said.

"In terms of the situation on the border between Iraq and Kuwait, I would say that that has improved substantially over the last ... two weeks. The Iraqis are in the process of withdrawing their police posts from the demilitarized zone," Williams said.

"Some Kuwaiti oil well heads that were in the disputed area that are now in the Kuwaiti side of the border, are now in Kuwaiti hands. The Iraqis are no longer there, and the Kuwaitis say that there is no damage to those oil well facilities. We haven't seen any more of the raids at Umm Qasr. So the situation on the border there has considerably improved," he said.

28. US Press Release: U.S., Coalition Agree on Need for Use of Force in Iraq, 19 January 1993

Washington - The United States sees "no disagreement" between itself and its coalition partners on the necessity for and appropriateness of the recent U.S. air strikes in Iraq aimed at forcing Saddam Hussein to comply with United Nations resolutions.

State Department spokesman Joseph Snyder, speaking at the department's daily news briefing January 19, noted that "There's no disagreement between the United States and our coalition partners, including the Russians and those in the Arab world, on the fundamental objective of assuring Iraq's full compliance on all U.N. Security Council resolutions."

Snyder also warned that if Iraq continues to flout the U.N. resolutions, the United States feels that it has full authority to attack again.

Snyder spoke in the wake of press reports that Arab nations and the Russians do not fully support the recent military actions against Iraq. However, he emphasized that "These (recent military) actions were taken in consultation with other coalition members in and outside the region, including the Russians, the Turks, and Arab states." In addition, he noted, "There's no disagreement on the fundamental objective of assuring Iraq's full compliance with all U.N. Security Council resolutions."

Asked whether the United States agrees with what the questioner described as "the Russian contention that there has to be another meeting and another action by the U.N. Security Council before further attacks ... against Iraq", Snyder replied "No, we don't." He added, however, that he is "not sure that the Russians said that is absolutely their position."

The spokesman warned: "Further coalition action will depend on the Iraqi regime's behaviour. If Baghdad continues to disobey the requirements of U.N. resolutions, we will act."

Snyder emphasized that "We have consulted closely with the Russians, and we will continue to have close consultations with the Russians and other key allies, including more discussions in the United Nations on the problems of Iraqi intransigence, and what actions we could take to ensure compliance."

However, he added, "We're very clear on the legal basis. We think that there's sufficient authority for what we've done and for what we might have to do in the future."

Snyder noted that the U.S. government shares "the frustrations expressed from various quarters over the Iraqi regime's continued belligerence and aggression ... Our forceful action against Iraqi military and weapons-of-mass-destruction targets over the past week followed weeks of increasingly provocative behavior by the Iraqi regime and repeated warnings by the Security Council and coalition members."

Snyder recalled that, starting in mid-November, the Iraqis used "terrorist bombings and bureaucratic interference to sabotage U.N. humanitarian relief convoys" and that "with increasing frequency in December, Iraq repeatedly put at risk coalition aircraft monitoring Iraqi compliance with U.N. Security Council Resolution 688 and its demand that Baghdad cease repression of the Iraqi people."

In January, Snyder noted, "Baghdad placed unacceptable conditions on the U.N. Special Commission, UNSCOM, which is charged with overseeing the destruction of Iraq's ambitious program of weapons of mass destruction."

He recalled that "the Iraqis also violated agreements with the U.N. Iraq-Kuwait border commission by failing to abandon police posts determined to be in Kuwait by the January 15th deadline" and that "on January 8th and again on January 11, the U.N. Security Council declared Iraq's interference (in United Nations operations) to be 'unacceptable and material violations' of Security Council Resolution 687" and "warned of 'serious consequences' which would flow from Iraq's failure to meet its obligations."

Snyder noted that Iraq also "ignored repeated clearcut warnings by the United States, the United Kingdom, France and Russia that provocative actions would not be tolerated" and concluded that "against this backdrop, the coalition's limited military actions of the past week were appropriate responses."

29. Statement issued by The Revolution Command Council of the Republic of Iraq, 19 January 1993

In view of the advent of new American Presidency, and as a gesture of goodwill from Iraq to Mr. Bill Clinton, the new President of the United States of America, and through him to the people of the United States and all peace-lovers in the world, and as an expression of the will of our Great People which has confirmed its love for peace and conviction in the high values of humanity, the Revolution Command Council has decided:

To begin a ceasefire at 800 hrs. in the morning of the 20th of January 1993 (Baghdad local time), unless the other side begins firing, so that the new US Administration may have the opportunity to study the question of the ban imposed on Iraqi flights in areas in the north and south of Iraq, and be sure, in a circumstance of calmness uninfluenced by the considerations of the conditions of military engagement, that the decision to impose this ban was an unjustifiable measure unilaterally taken by the last US Administration and the parties collaborating with it, with the objective of achieving special political ends entirely unrelated to the resolutions of the United Nations; and with a view to creating the climate for the new US Administration to establish constructive dialogue.

We believe that the months ahead will be sufficient for the new US Administration to study this question and understand the other outstanding issues, particularly that of lifting the iniquitous blockade imposed on the people of Iraq despite the fact that Iraq has implemented the unjust obligations imposed upon it by Security Council Resolution 687.

30. Press briefing held by M. Roland Dumas, Minister of State for Foreign Affairs of France, following his appearance before the National Assembly Foreign Affairs Committee, Paris, 20 January 1993

Question: On Iraq, can you confirm that the United States have exceeded the UN mandate in bombing Baghdad?
Minister: I confirm that France did not participate in that operation against Baghdad and its suburbs. That decision was taken in the exercise of sovereignty and freedom of judgment by the President of the Republic after having taken all the appropriate advice. And France did not participate for the reasons we have indicated.
Question: As you have said at the Council of Ministers, the United States have, in some way, exceeded the mandate which was accorded to them?
The Minister: I have given the reasons which have determined the decision of France. This evening I shall be seeing Mr. Douglas Hurd [*United Kingdom Secretary of State for Foreign Affairs*] over dinner in London. I recall in this context that the United Kingdom has adopted the same attitude. Therefore, I recognize the reasons that have led them also to take this decision.
Question: Did France not have the military means to intervene?
The Minister: Also, France did not have the military means to intervene since the weapons were launched from ships in the Gulf, in particular from American ships.

31. Comment attributed to Mr Roland Dumas, French Foreign Minster, speaking before the French Council of Ministers, 20 January 1993

[*Note: The following comment has not been officially released by the French Foreign Ministry. It was made available in agency reports of remarks made by Government Spokesman Lois Mermaz during a press conference.*]

The Minister of Foreign Affairs, Roland Duams, explained on Wednesday before the Council of Ministers that the non-participation of France in Sunday's US military operation against a suburb of Baghdad was deemed to have overstepped the resolutions of the UN Security Council. ... Mr Dumas also voiced the opinion that the arrival of a new President in the White House would bring with it a new phase in this crisis involving Iraq. This new phase could involve a lessening of tension, provided Saddam Hussein undetakes to execute, without reserve, the Security Council resolutons and that he ceases the aerial provocations against the coalition powers.

32. Doorstep Interview with the UK Prime Minister, Wednesday, 20 January 1993

Question: Will you be taking seriously Saddam Hussein's offer of a ceasefire?
Prime Minister: We will have to wait and see what actually he means by it, we have seen offers from him before, we have also seen the outcome of it before, let us see whether there is any practical action, in particular let us see whether he is going to obey the Security Council resolutions without let, without hindrance and without frustration, that would be a great move forward if he would do that.
Question: The French Government has criticised the bombing raid on the Baghdad nuclear plant as a step too far, do you share that concern?
Prime Minister: No I do not share that concern at all, this was a raid made by the United States rather than the allies because they had the equipment in site to do it, but there was discussion between the allies, including the French, the legal position is quite clear, this was within international law and I think the United States were wholly justified, I have no reservations about it.

33. Statement from the Pakistan Mission to the United Nations, 21 January 1993

The Foreign Office Spokesman expressed the Government of Pakistan's deep concern at events that have led to the Allied raid into Iraq. In calling for the scrupulous adherence to UN Security Council Resolutions the Spokesman stated that the Government of Pakistan urged that the use of force may be avoided and all differences relating to the interpretation of the resolutions should be resolved through discussions.

The Spokesman underlined Pakistan's unequivocal support for the sovereignty and territorial integrity of Kuwait and of Iraq. He deplored the official pronouncements emanating from Iraq which claimed Kuwait as part of its territory.

34. US Press Release: Clinton Backs Force to Compel Iraq's Compliance, 21 January 1991

Washington - President Clinton backed the use of force to compel Iraq's compliance with United Nations resolutions January 21.

Questioned about the attack on an Iraqi air defense installation in the northern "no-fly" zone, Clinton said he did not want to comment, except to say that he intended to follow his predecessor's policy of backing the United Nations.

"We're going to adhere to our policy," Clinton told reporters during a photo session with his senior White House staff. "We're going to stay with our policy. It's the American policy."

Two U.S. aircraft, while escorting a French reconnaissance plane 13 kilometers southwest of Mosul, attacked the anti-aircraft site after the battery's radar locked onto the French aircraft. A U.S. F-4G fired a HARM missile, which hones in on radar signals, and a second U.S. plane, an F-16 fighter-bomber, dropped two cluster bombs on the site. The extent of damage was not immediately known. Pilots consider it a hostile act if radar "paints" their aircraft with its beam, or locks-on to the plane. "Painting" and "locking-on" are preliminaries to firing anti-aircraft missiles.

In his inaugural address, Clinton promised the United States "would not shrink from challenges" abroad during his tenure. "When our vital interests are challenged," he said, "or the will and conscience of the international community is defied, we will act - with peaceful diplomacy whenever possible, with force when necessary."

Clinton's spokesman, George Stephanopoulos, pointed out that the attack "was consistent with previous practice, and President Clinton supports it."

Stephanopoulos, Clinton's director of communications, avoided characterizing Iraq's motives in turning on the radar set, but he added, "We continue to hold the position that they must comply with all U.N. resolutions." Stephanopoulos said Clinton had approved "past practices" in reacting to Iraq's activity, rather than approving specific acts; "We expect to continue that," he added.

The U.S. position, he said, is the same as stated "many, many times: We expect full compliance with U.N. Security Council resolutions. As far as the military situation goes, we will continue the past practices."

Asked if the Russian demand that the United States seek specific Security Council approval for military action compromises the international consensus on Iraq, Stephanopoulos replied, "We think the coalition is strong."

He said the President is "encouraged" that U.N. monitors had been able "to return to Iraq and to continue their work" of discovering and dismantling Baghdad's weapons of mass destruction.

At the State Department, spokesman Richard Boucher told reporters that President Clinton and Secretary of State Christopher have both made clear "their full determination to see that Iraq complies with U.N. resolutions" and that U.S. pilots, when threatened by Iraq over the no-fly zones, "will respond as necessary."

Christopher told reporters earlier in the day that "the United States intends to protect our pilots in the no-fly zone."

"The Iraqis know perfectly well what it takes to comply with U.N. resolutions and the establishment of the no-fly zones," he said before a meeting with African National Congress leader Nelson Mandela.

"I think what happened today (January 21) is a reflection of the determination that the Clinton administration will have in that area," he added. When Iraqi radar "illuminates our pilots, we are going to protect our pilots."

Boucher emphasized that the United States consulted with France before launching the January 17 cruise missile attack against an Iraqi nuclear fabrication plant. The attack was in response to continued Iraqi violations of the U.N. resolutions on the no-fly zones.

He made the comments when asked about French criticism of the U.S. attack.

The spokesman noted that the White House, in announcing the attack, said that President Bush had consulted in advance of the U.S. action, with a number of leaders including British Prime Minister Major, French President Mitterrand and Turkish Prime Minister Demirel.

He said Bush told them that the United States would act in concert with its allies.

"We had consulted with them (the French). We felt this strike was necessary to demonstrate to Iraq that it had to pay a price for failing to meet the requirements of the U.N. Security Council resolutions," the spokesman said.

He noted that there have been "very consistent statements" by the coalition partners that Iraq's compliance with the resolutions is a "necessity."

35. Official Declaration issued by the Ministry for Foreign Affairs of France, 21 January 1993

On the legal basis of the aerial exclusion zones: Two points must be made clear. On the one hand there is resolution 687 which establishes the modalities of the cease-fire. On the other hand there is Resolution 688 which establishes the limits of action of the international community as it concerns assistance given to populations placed in danger by the policy of the Iraqi government.

I note, as far as the rules applicable to the implementation of the Special Mission--founded on Resolution 687 and in charge of identifying the presence of weapons of mass destruction in Iraq--is concerned, that mission has now finally been able to resume its activities without preconditions or restrictions.

Besides, as far as the areas north of the 36th parallel and south of the 32nd parallel are concerned, one always has to remember that the decisions have been taken in light of the judicial opinions of the United Nations in the spirit of the idea of affording protection to the populations which are particularly affected by the policy of the Government of Iraq and its approach to its Kurdish people in the north and Shiites in the south. It is by virtue of this desire to assure the protection of these populations which have been endangered that our measures were taken.

...

On the "definite position" of France on Sunday's US operation: "I have already had the occasion to state that there exists amongst the coalition powers a global political agreement on the attitude of the Iraqi Government which does not respect its obligations and the authority of the United Nations.

I have equally pointed out as far as the use of French forces is concerned, that their utilization is determined in the exercise of the sovereign right of decision-making by the French government, or rather its head of states who is also the commander in chief. In that sense, France has participated on two occasions, within the framework of global agreement, in aerial raids over the past week against military targets south of the 32nd parallel. Those targets constituted a threat to the freedom of overflight of coalition aircraft in the exclusion zone.

As I have already indicated, as far as Sunday's raid is concerned, that was undertaken by the US only and I remind you again that the Americans alone have the ships and missiles necessary for the conduct of such operations.

Finally, I repeat that in all instances involving France, her action in this respect has been strictly confined by the texts of the United Nations and we do not operate outside of the framework of the United Nations.

MAP SECTION

Diyarbakir
TURKEY
Tabriz
Orumiyeh
Silopi
Amadia
Zakho
Sheladiza
Dohuk
SYRIA
Choman
Mosul
Rawanduz
Khalifan
Erbil
Ranya
Qala Diza
Choman
ISLAMIC REPUBLIC OF IRAN
Sulaimania
Panjwin
Kirkuk
Sayid Sadiq
Halabja
Tawila
Tigris
Euphrates
Tikrit
Musa al Kadhin
Bakhtaran
Ba'quba
Ramadi (Al Tash)
Baghdad
IRAQ
Karbala
Hillah
Al Kut
Tigris
Najaf
Diwaniyeh
Al Amarah
Euphrates
Samawa
Nasiriyah
Basrah
Al Salman
Safwan
KUWAIT
Kuwait City
SAUDI ARABIA
IRAQ
International Boundary
Main Road
River
Railway
UNGCI Center
WFP Extended Delivery Points
Major City
UNHUC Field Office
UN Sub-Office
UN Relay Station
The designations employed and the presentation of material on this map do not imply the expression of any opinion whatsoever on the part of the United Nations Secretariat/OED concerning the legal status of any country, territory, city or area or of its authorities, or concerning the delimitation of its frontiers or boundaries.
Subject to revision according to priority.

TURKEY
4,300
450,000
Zakho
Amadia
Dohuk
Erbil
ISLAMIC
REPUBLIC OF
IRAN
Ranya
Kalaf
Sadiq
SYRIA
Sulaymanyah
Sayid
Sediq
Tigris
Euphrates
1,280,000
120,000
Baghdad
IRAQ
Tigris
Euphrates
Basrah
KUWAIT
Kuwait City
SAUDI ARABIA
IRAQ
International Boundary
Main Road
River
Railway
UNGCI Guard Stations
UNGCI Sectoral Command Offices
UNGCI Headquarters
Arrows indicate number of refugees who have returned to date, out of those who fled after 2 August 1990. Boxes indicate the number remaining.
The designations employed and the presentation of material on this map do not imply the expression of any opinion whatsoever on the part of the United Nations Secretariat/OED concerning the legal status of any country, territory, city or area or of its authorities, or concerning the delimitation of its frontiers or boundaries.
Subject to revision according to priority.

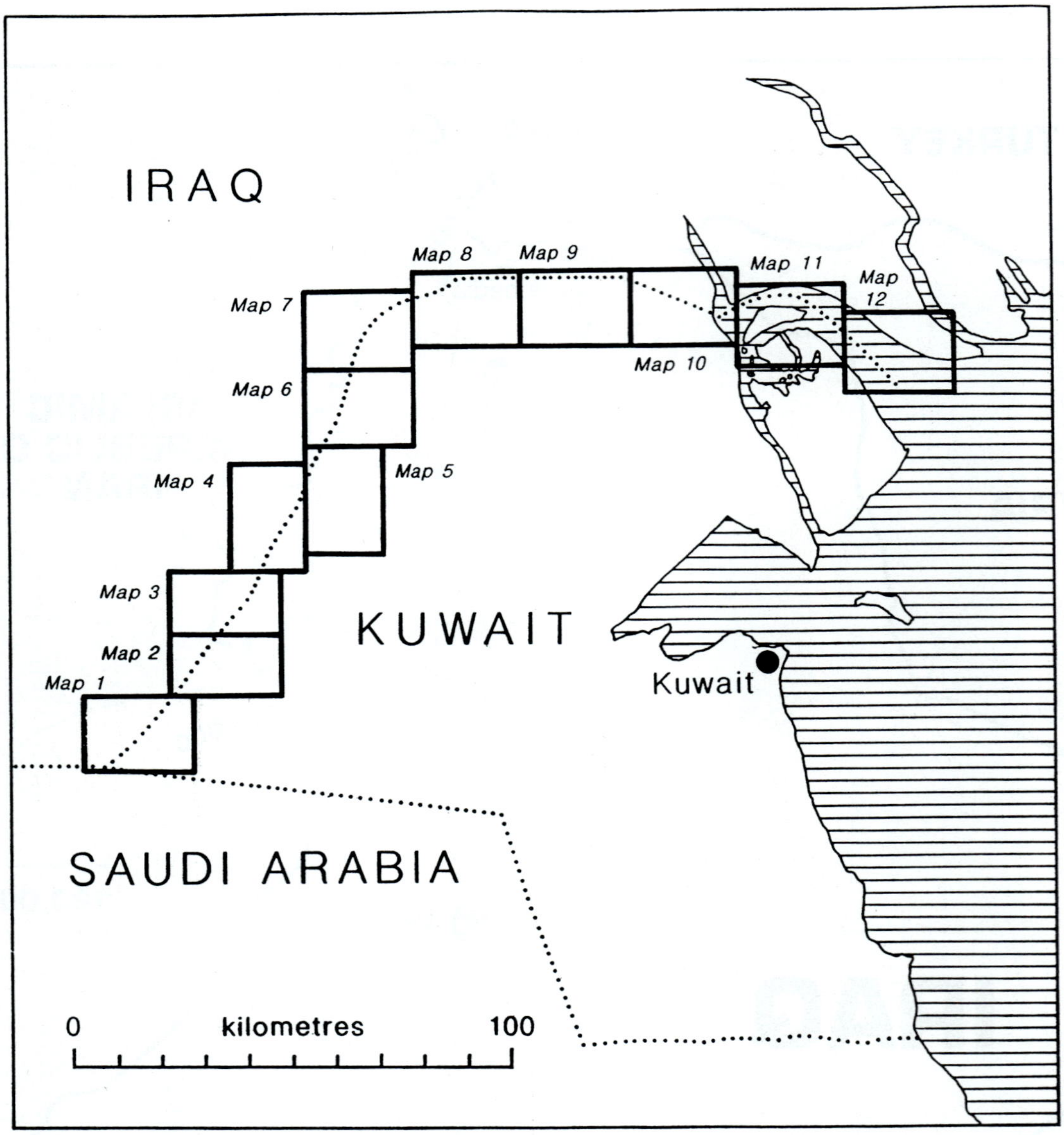

The following 12 maps were placed before the Security Council in a letter from the Permanent Representative of the United Kingdom, 28 March 1991. This letter is reprinted in Chapter 10, Document 1, page 433. The maps are referred to in Resolution 687 (1991).

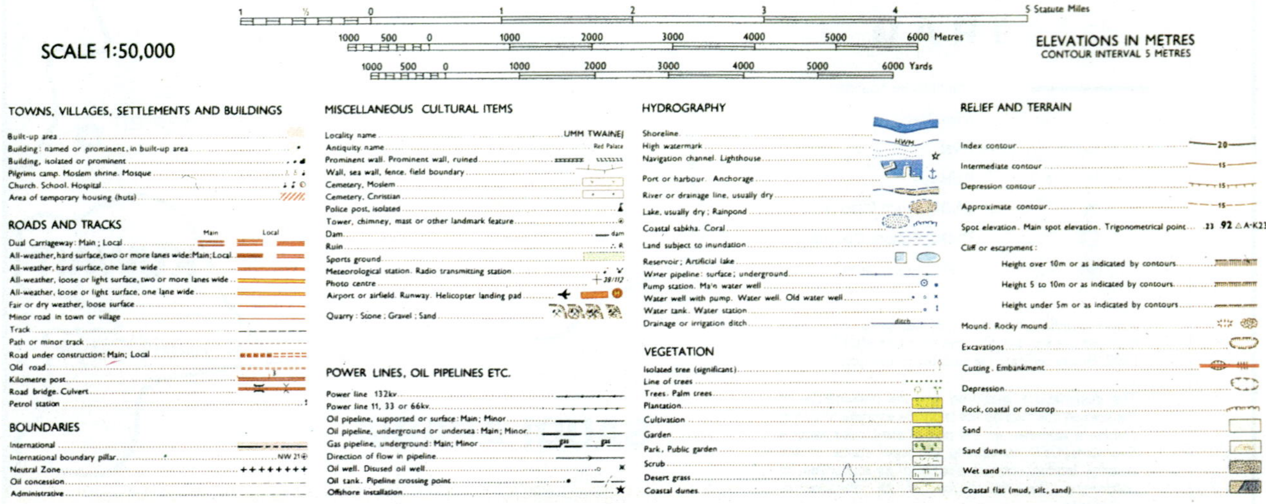

[Slight colour variation occurs in the original maps in this section.]

MAP 1 – ASH-SHIQĀYĀ – K7611 5348-III

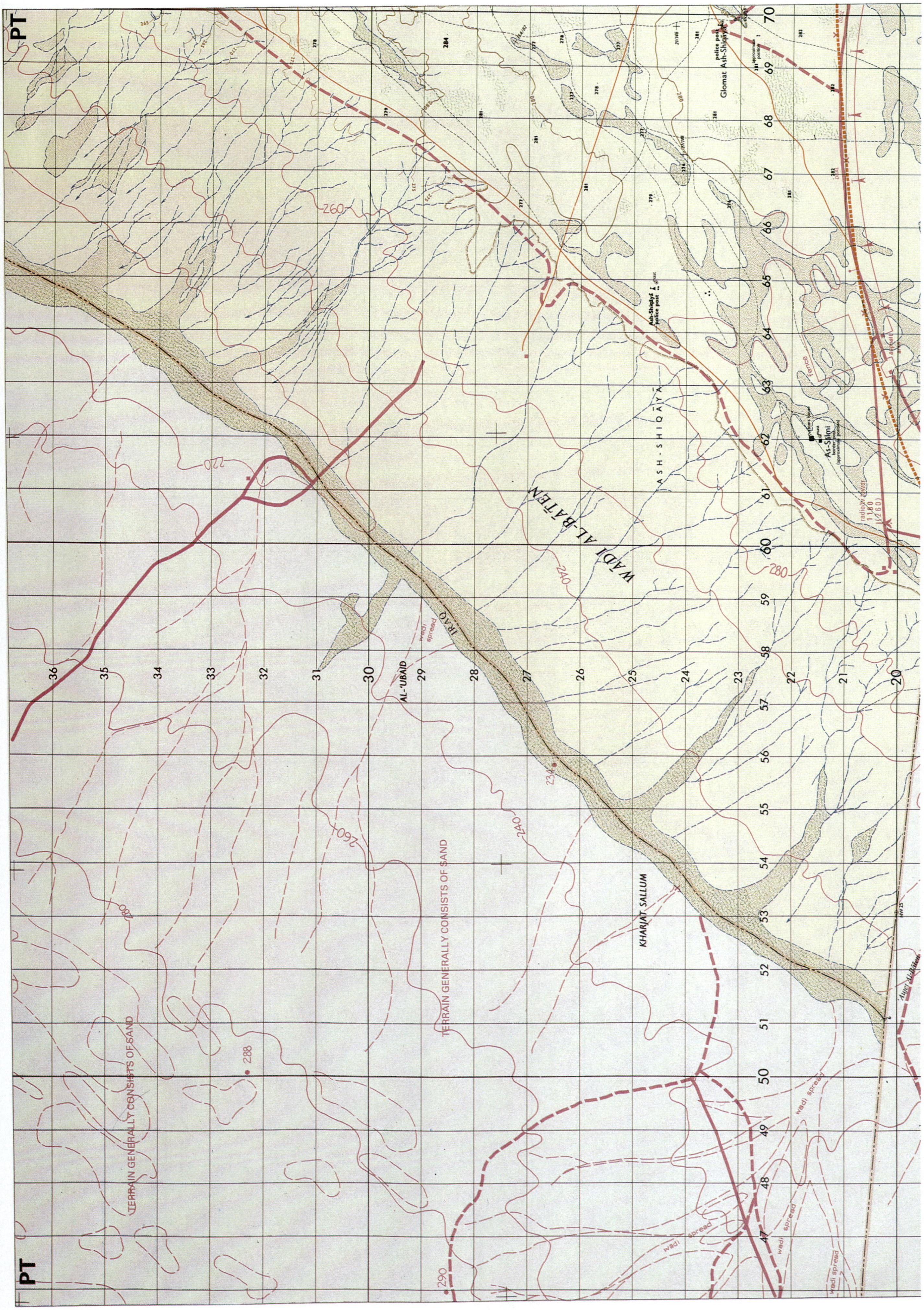

MAP 2 – AL-ABRAQ – K7611 5348-I

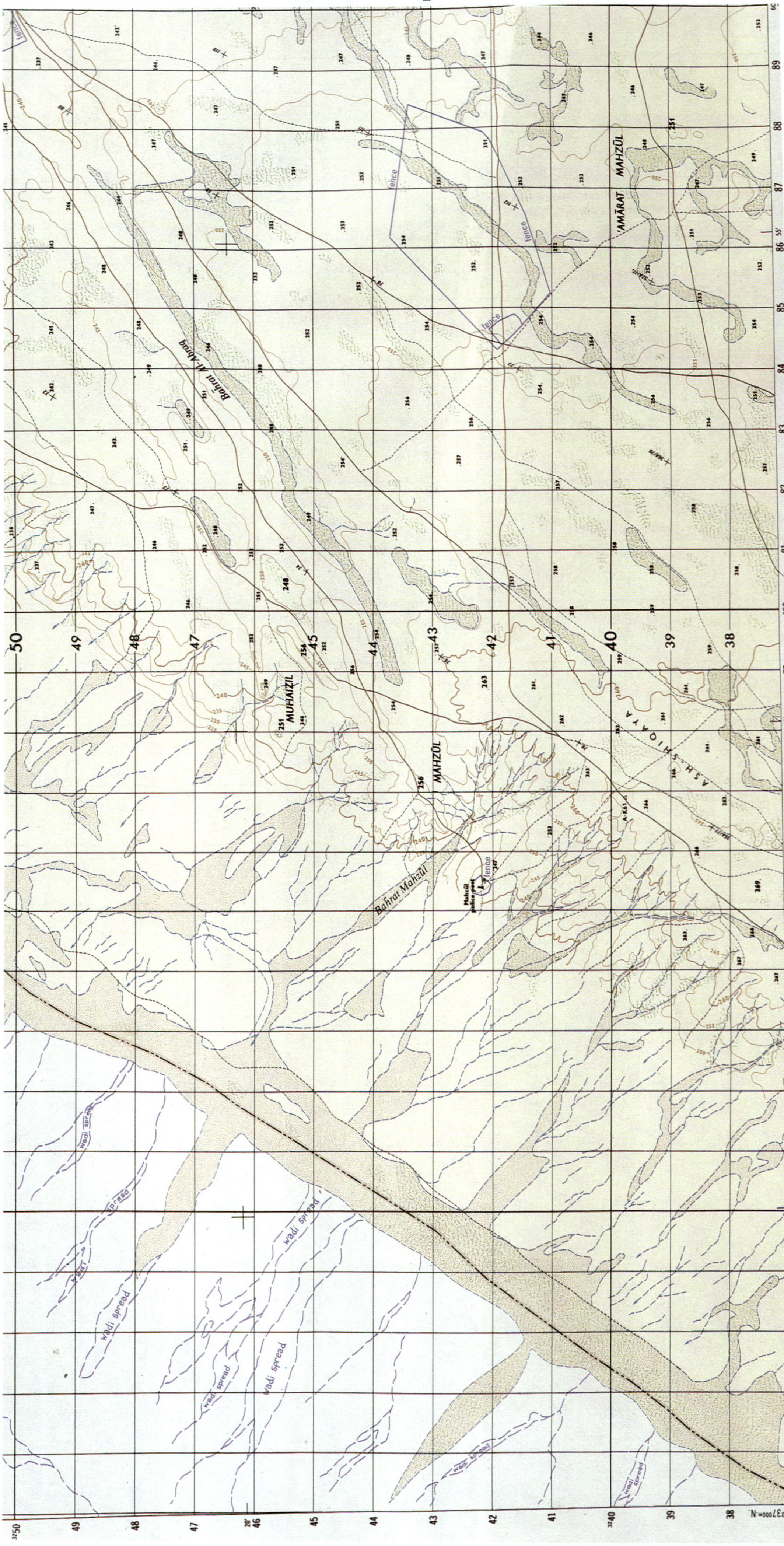

MAP 3 – AL-ABRAQ – K7611 5348-I

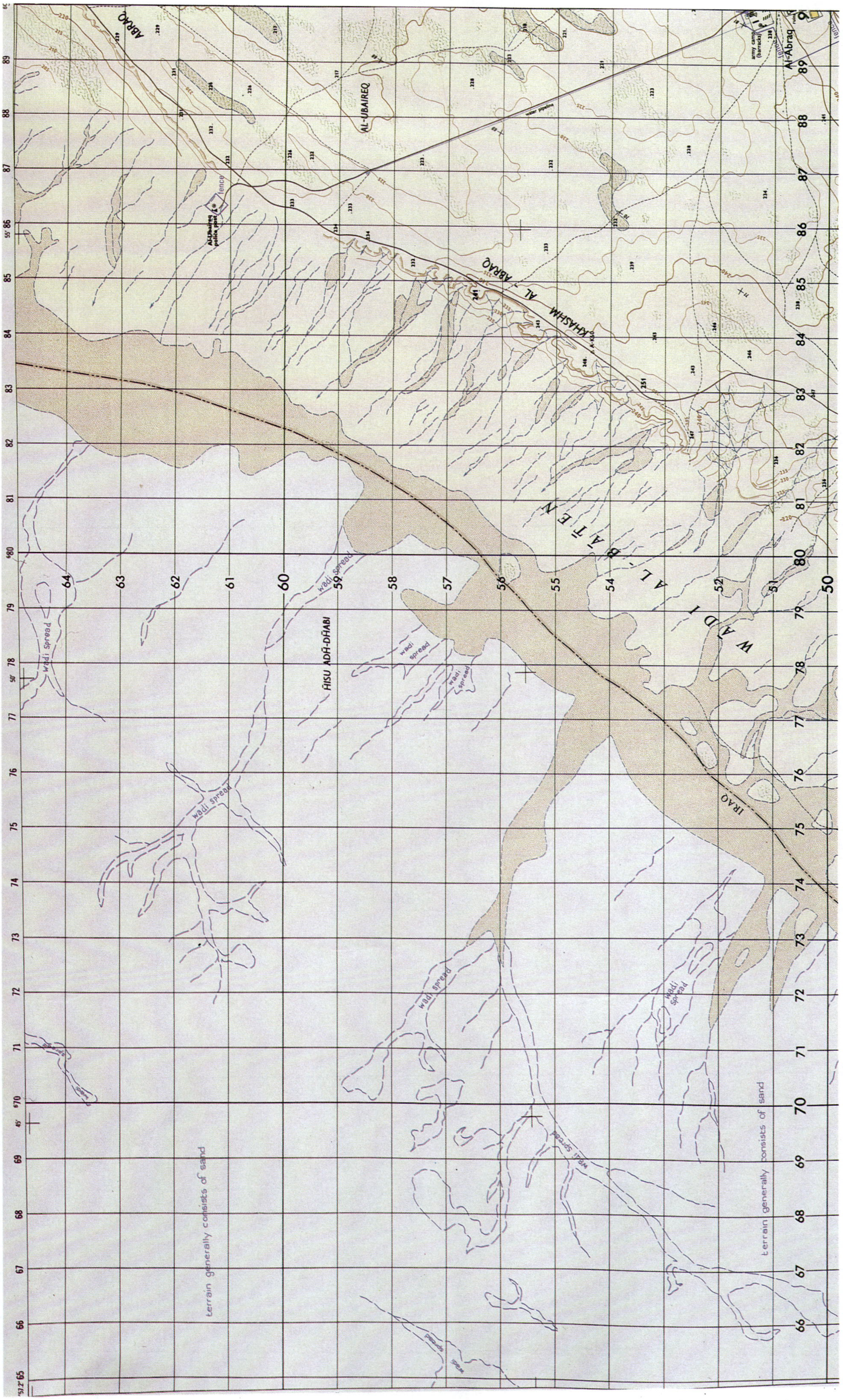

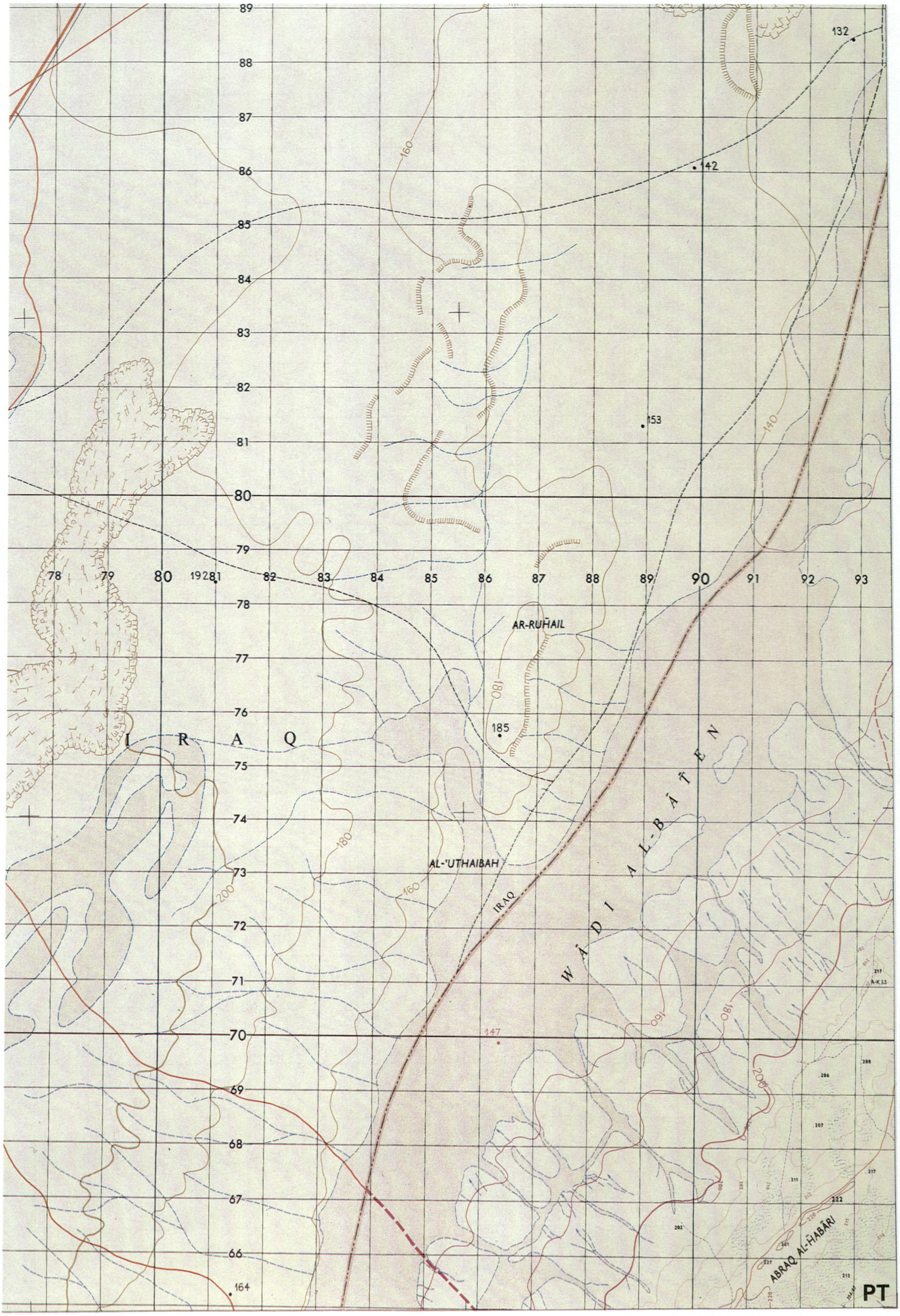
I R A Q
AR-RUHAIL
AL-'UTHAIBAH
WĀDI AL-BĀTEN
IRAQ
ABRAQ AL-HABARI
PT

MAP 5 – H̄OUMAH – K7611 5449-III

MAP 6 – AL-HUWAIMLIYAH – K7611 5449-IV

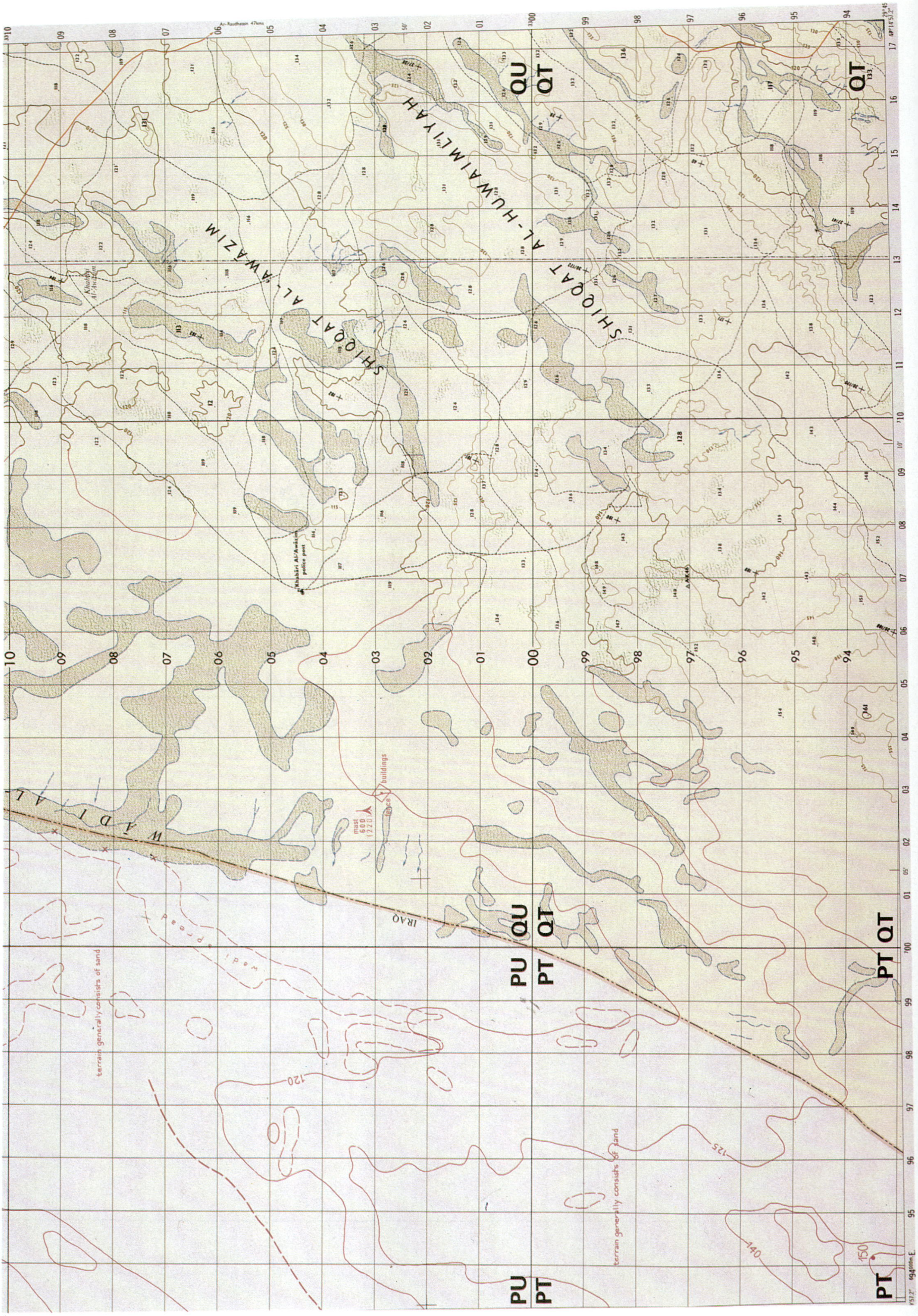

MAP 7 – AL-HUWAIMLIYAH – K7611 5449-IV

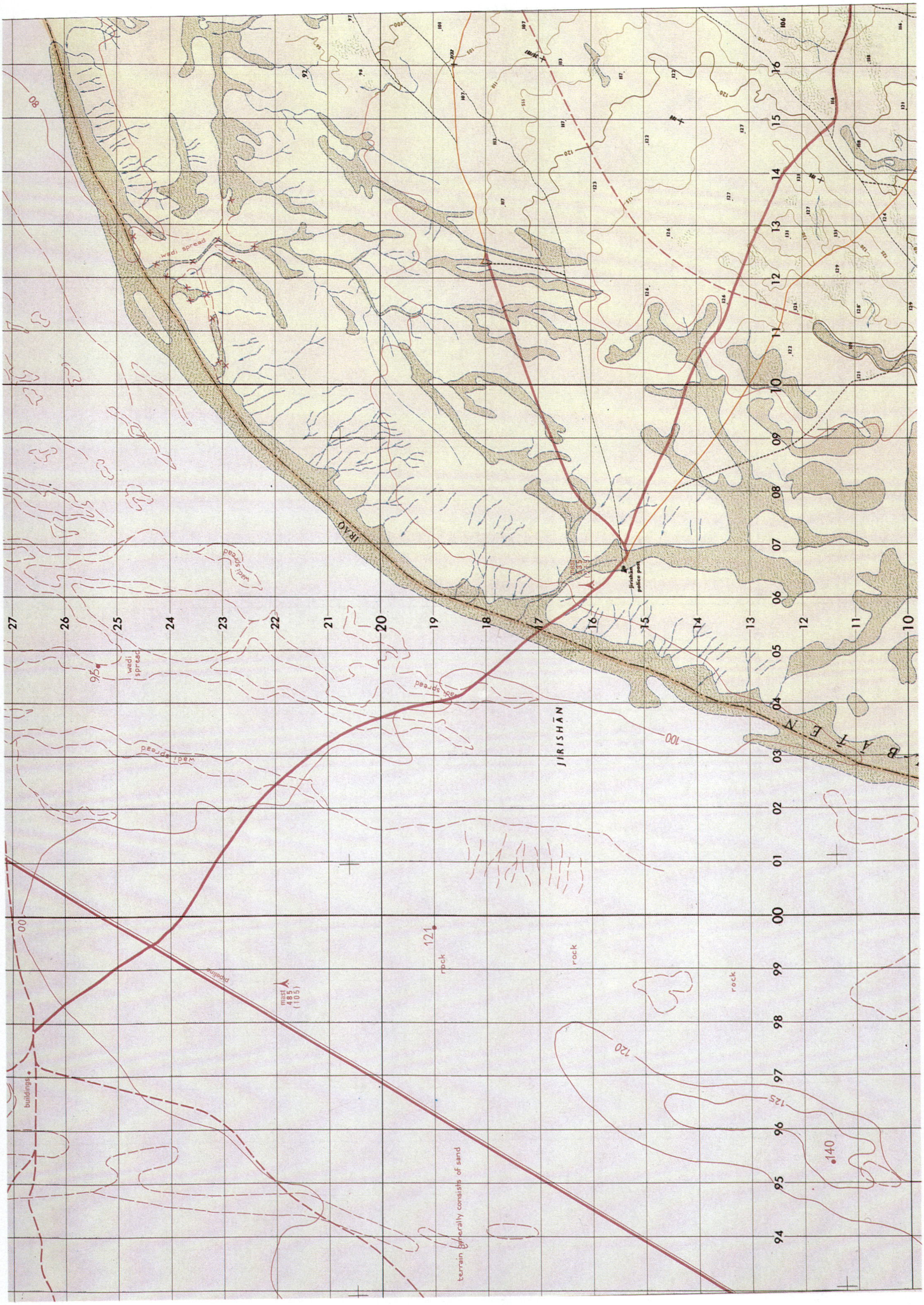

MAP 8 – UMM AL-MADĀFAI' – K7611 5449-I

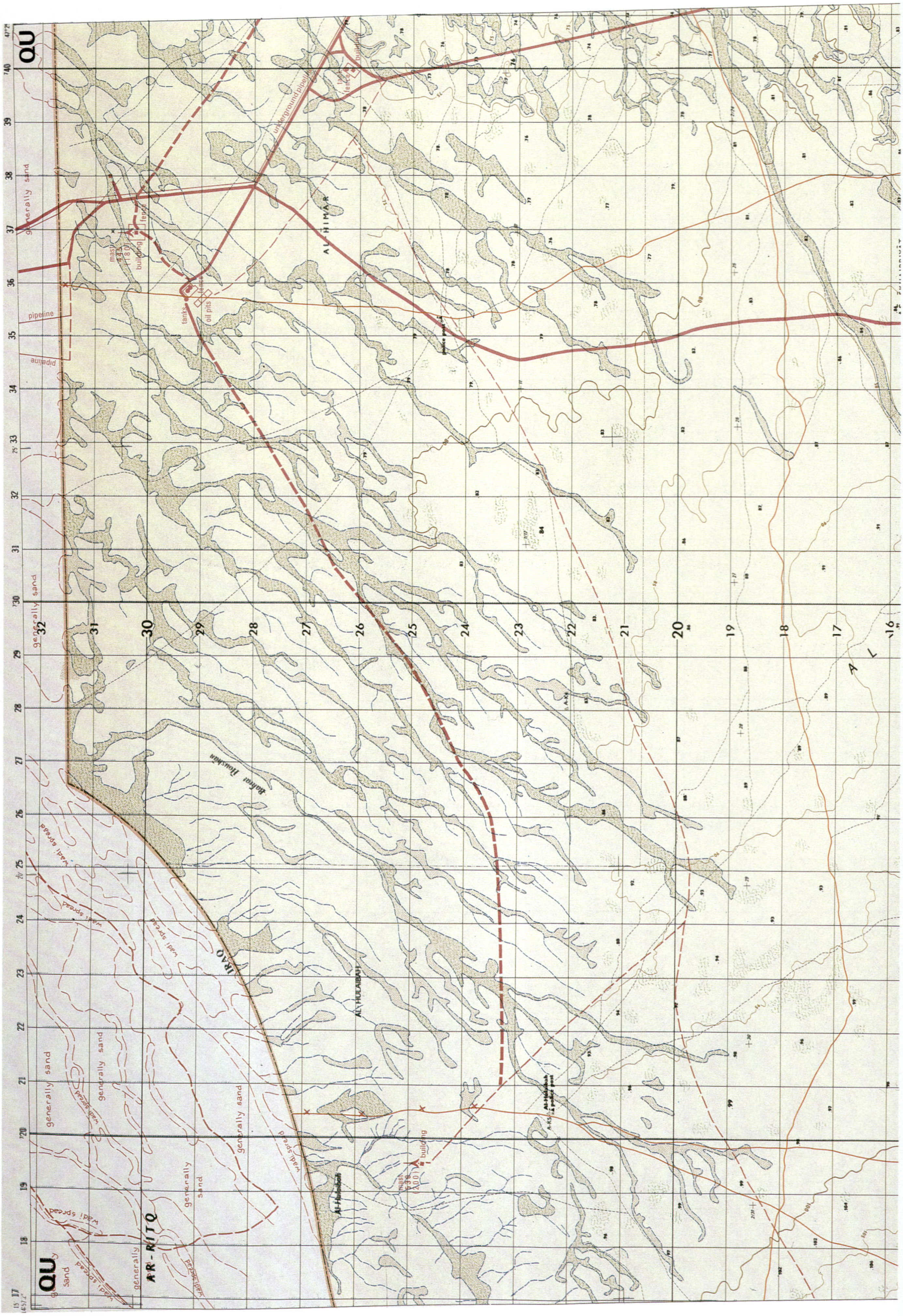

MAP 9 - AR-RAUDHATAIN – K7611 5549-IV

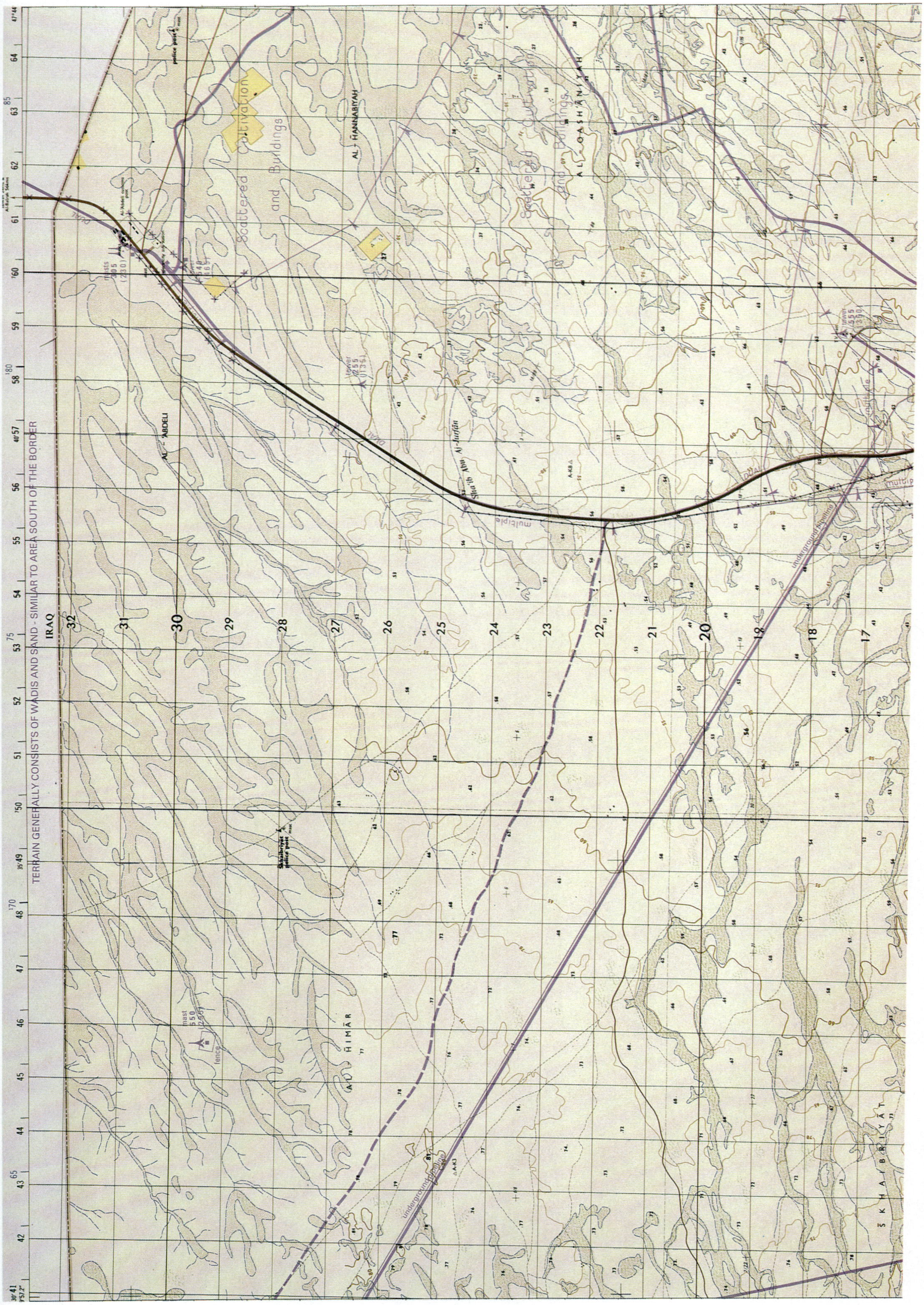

MAP 10 – UMM NIQA – K7611 5549-I

MAP 11 – JAZIRAT WARBAH – K7611 5649-IV

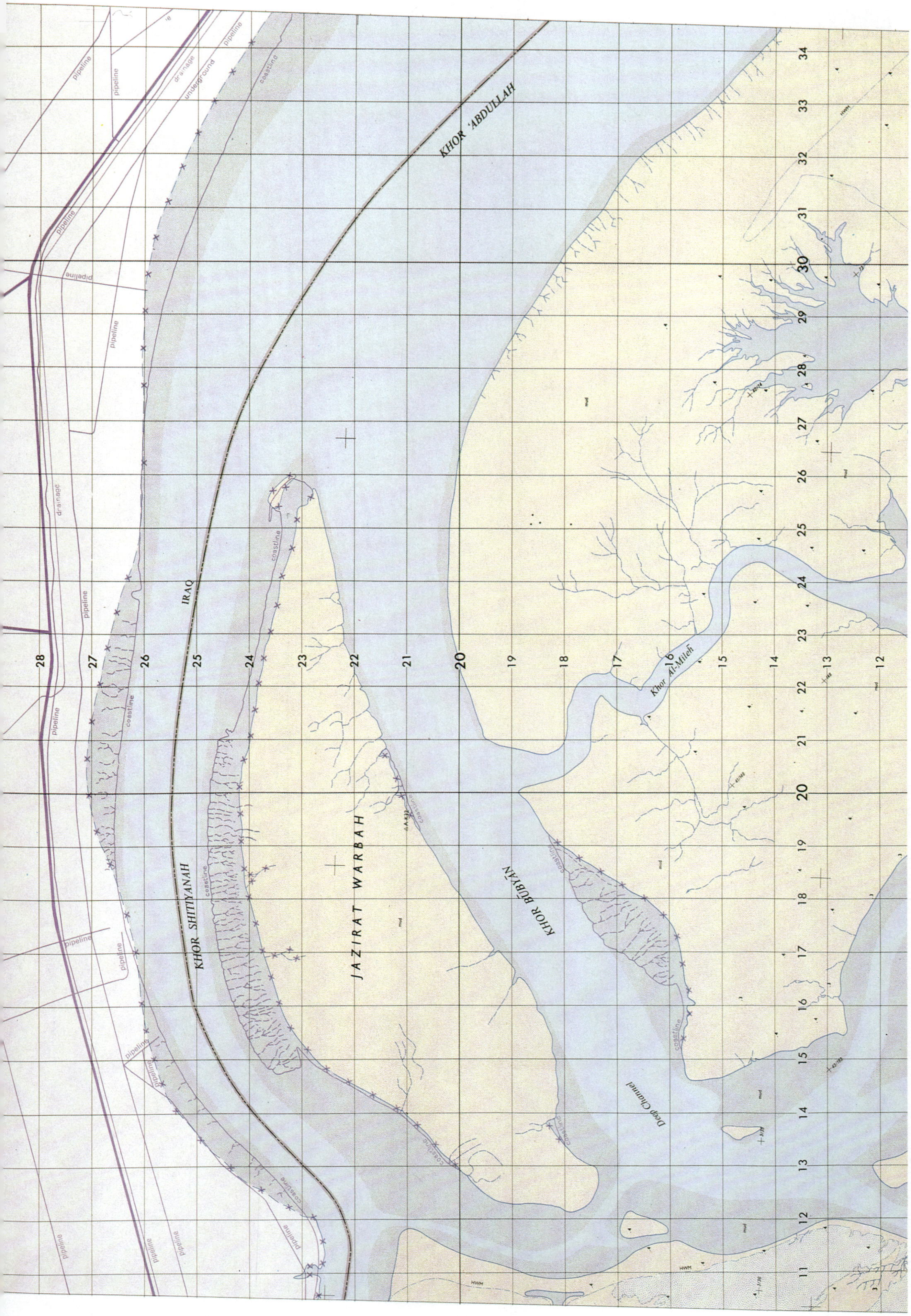

MAP 12 – BŪBYĀN (N) – K7611 5649-I

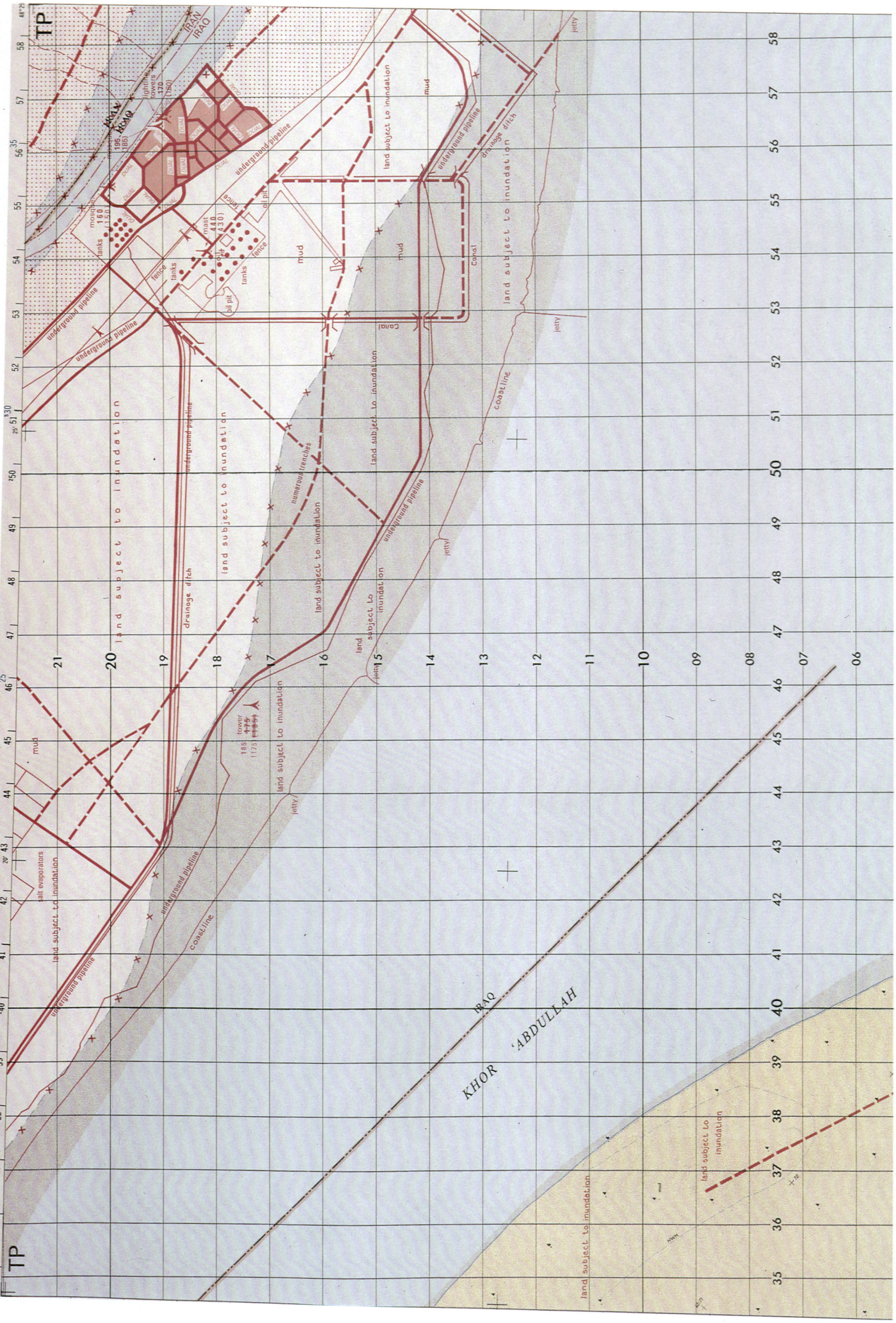

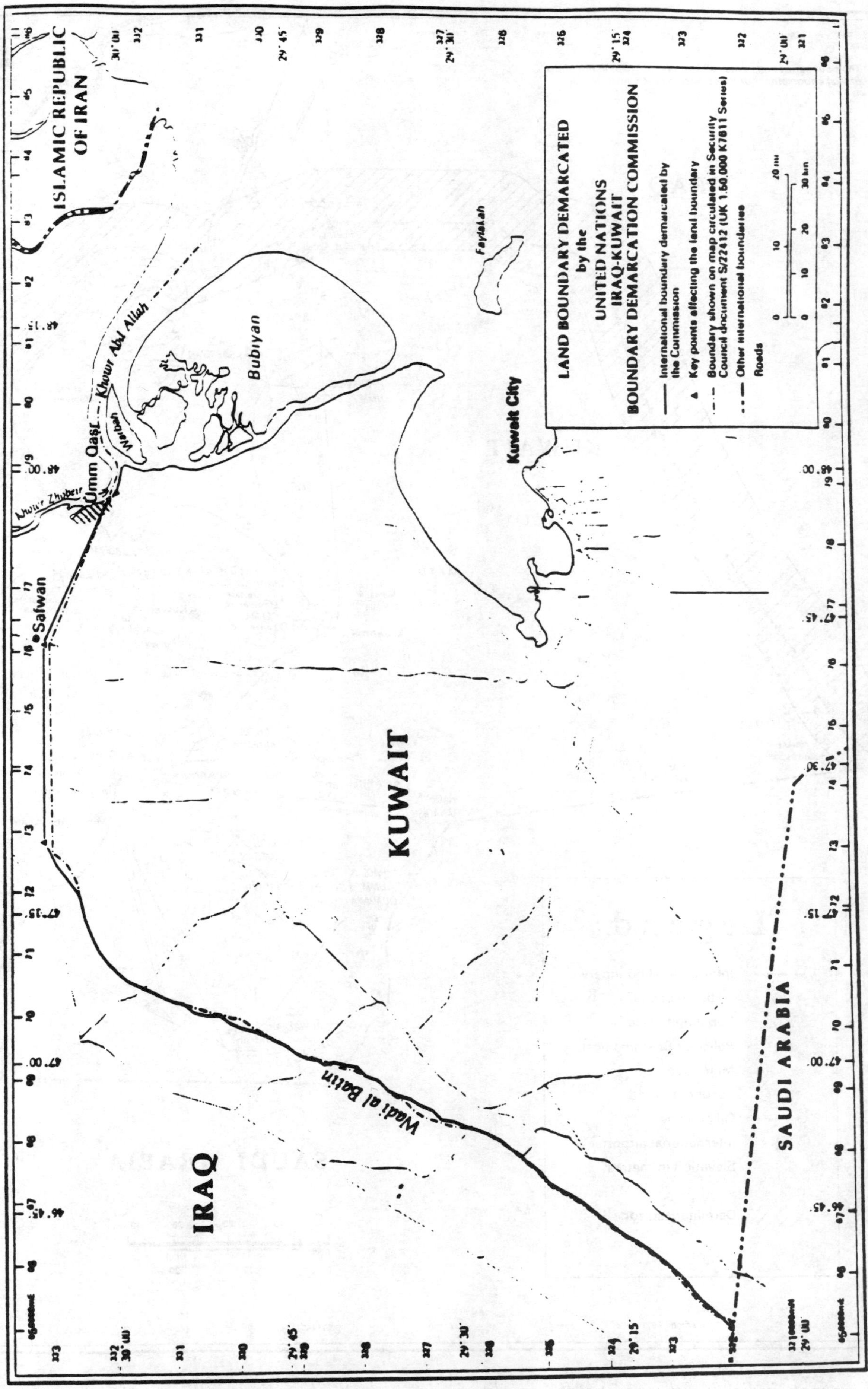

The above map is reproduced from the Further Report of the Iraq-Kuwait Boundary Demarcation Commission, contained in the Letter from the UN Secretary-General to the President of the Security Council, 12 August 1992, reprinted in Chapter 10, Document 16, p. 456.

U.N. MAP No. 3632, S/22454/Add. 2

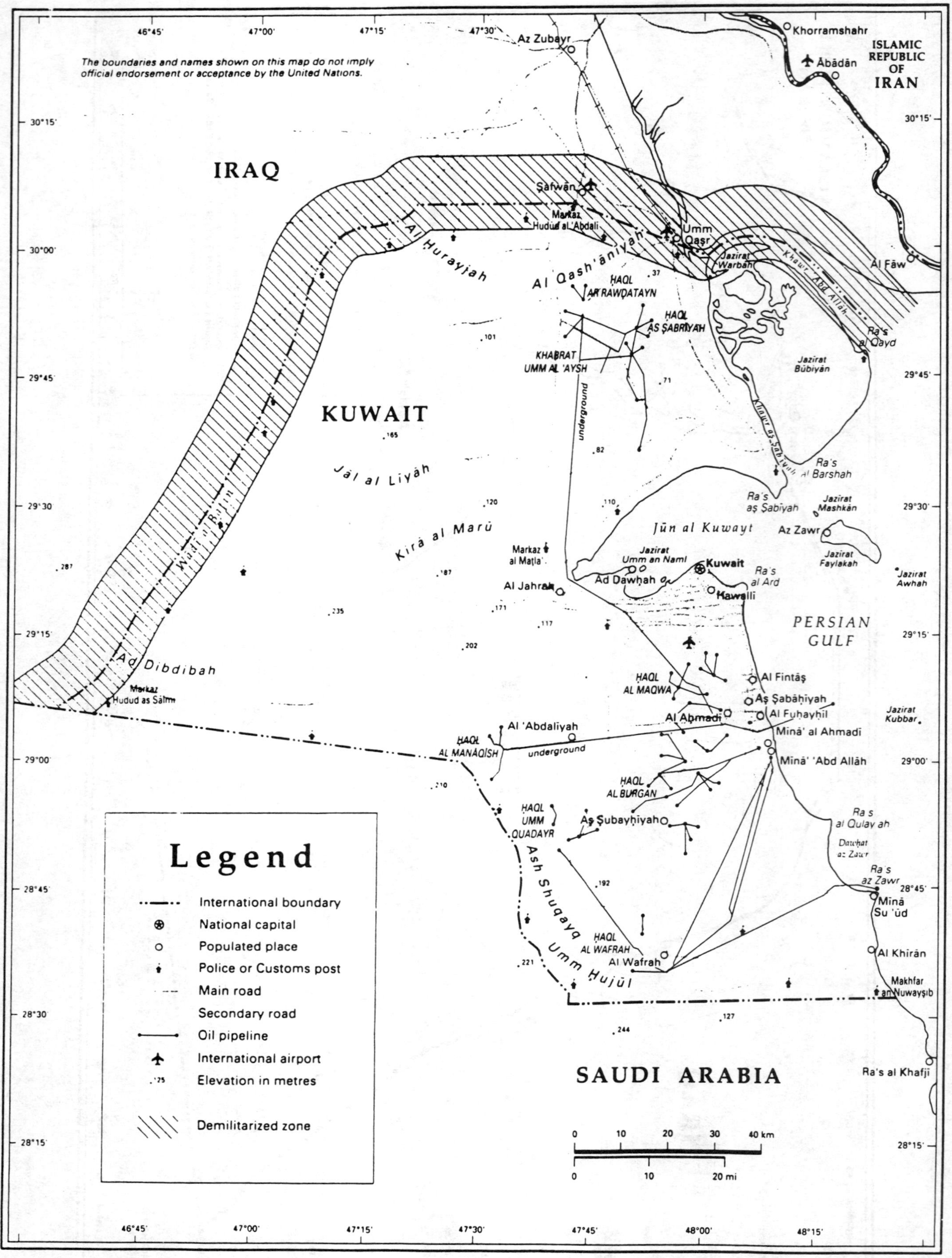

The above map, indicating the extent of the demilitarized zone on the Iraq/Kuwait border, was transmitted by the UN Secretary-General in his Addendum to the Report on the Implementation of Paragraph 5 of Security Council Resolution 687 (1991), 5 April 1991, S/2245/Add.2. The zone, and the deployment of the United Nation Iraq-Kuwait Observation Mission forces within it, has been modified in accordance with the changes indicated on the map reproduced on the preceding page.

U.N. DOCUMENT INDEX

Security Council Resolutions:

Security Council Meetings:

Communications of and to the Security Council:

Decisions taken by the Governing Council of the United Nations Compensation Commission:

Resolutions of the General Assembly:

Documents of the UN Commission on Human Rights:

Documents of the International Atomic Energy Agency:

SUMMARY INDEX